MARANATHA!

THE NIV WORSHIP BIBLE

NEW INTERNATIONAL VERSION

P.O.Box 1077, Dana Point, CA 92629-5077
www.maranathamusic.com

Library of Congress Catalog Card Number 99-071064
Published by Zondervan Publishing House
Grand Rapids, Michigan 49530, U.S.A.
http://www.zondervan.com

Printed in the United States of America

00 01 02 03 04 05 8 7 6 5 4 3 2 1

RRD-C

You will be pleased to know that a portion of the purchase price of your new NIV Bible has been provided to International Bible Society to help spread the Gospel of Jesus Christ to the world!

Table of Contents

The Old Testament

The New Testament

ALPHABETICAL ORDER *of the Books of the Bible*

The books of the New Testament are in *italic*.

CONTRIBUTORS

Contributors

General Editor
Buddy Owens
Vice President, *Maranatha! Book Publishing*

Contributing editors and writers

Robert O. Bakke, M.Div., D.Min.
Director of The National Prayer Advance, *Evangelical Free Church of America*

Rev. James Bradford, Ph.D.
Sr. Pastor, *Newport Mesa Christian Center*, Costa Mesa, CA.

Dirk Buursma, M.Div.
Sr. Theological editor, *Zondervan Publishing House*

Michael Cassidy, M.A., D.H.L.
Founder and President, *African Enterprise*, an interdenominational, interracial, and international mission team in Africa.

Claire Cloninger, M.Ed.
Author, Songwriter, Speaker, Retreat leader.

Jacquelyn Coffey, M.S.
Writer; Founder, *Creative Christian Resources;*
Teacher of arts in worship

Jamie Owens-Collins
Songwriter, Recording artist, Worship leader,
Bible teacher

Nancy Leigh DeMoss
Director of Publications and Women's Ministries,
Life Action Ministries

Charles E. Fromm, Ph.D. Candidate, Cross-cultural Communication
Founder, *Worship Leader Magazine*

Steve Fry
Author, Songwriter, Recording artist

Lela Gilbert
Author, lyricist

John Goldingay, Ph.D., D.D.
Professor of Old Testament, *Fuller Theological Seminary*

Rev. Guy Gray, M.A., Exegetical Theology
Sr. Pastor, *River West Christian Church*, Portland, OR

Walt Harrah, B.A.,Church Music, M.Div.
Songwriter, Bible teacher

Donna Huisjen
Assistant Bible Editor, *Zondervan Publishing House*

Rev. Dr. Bruce Larson
Author, Pastor Emeritus, *University Presbyterian Church*, Seattle, WA

Robin Lopez
Freelance writer

Grace Marestaing, M.A.
Musician, Professor, Writer, Teacher of arts in worship

Hughes Oliphant Old, D.Th
Author, Member of *The Center For Theological Inquiry*, Princeton, NJ; Teacher of Worship at *Princeton Theological Seminary*

Rose Ottosen, M.A., Biblical Studies

Carol Owens
Author, Songwriter, International teacher of worship, intercession and spiritual warfare.

Melinda Joy Price

Robert Redman, Jr. , D.Th
Author, Teacher, Consultant

Pete Richardson, M.Div.
Vice President of Creative Services, *Promise Keepers*

Rev. Mark D. Roberts, Ph.D.
Sr. Pastor, *Irvine Presbyterian Church*, Irvine CA
Adjunct Professor, *Fuller Theological Seminary*

Rev. Randy L. Rowland, D.Min.
Sr. Pastor, *Church at the Center*, Seattle, WA
Adjunct Professor, *Fuller Theological Seminary*

Pastor James Ryle
President of *TruthWorks Ministries*

Lin Sexton
Lyricist, Playwright,
Director of Drama, *First Baptist Church*, Modesto, CA

Daniel Sharp, D.M.A.
Minister of Worship and Music, *University Presbyterian Church*, Seattle, WA

Andrew Sloan, M.Div.
Freelance writer and editor in Christian publishing

Rev. Scotty Smith, M. Arts & Religion
Sr. Pastor, *Christ Community Church*, Franklin, TN
Adjunct Professor, *Covenant Theological Seminary*

Bishop Kenneth C. Ulmer, M.A., D.Min, Ph.D., D.D.
Sr. Pastor, *Faithful Central Missionary Baptist Church*, Inglewood, CA
Board of Trustees, *The King's College and Seminary*

Michael A. Vander Klipp, M.A.
Sr. Bible Editor, *Zondervan Publishing House*

Thomas D. Vegh, M.B.A.
Chief Executive Officer, *The Corinthian Group*

Bruce H. Wilkinson, Th.M., D.D.
Founder and President, *Walk Thru The Bible Ministries*

Connie Witter
Devotional author

Editorial assistance: **Jo Bonilla**, Vice President of Music Publishing, *Maranatha! Music;* **Alexis Bonilla; Y Bui; Susan Goetz**

Graphic designers: **Kathy Camarillo; Russell Heistuman**

We give special thanks to **God** for the inspiration and theological insight of **Matthew Henry, Charles Spurgeon, William Lasor, David Hubbard, Frederic Bush, Jack Hayford,** and **Mark Roberts.**

To **God** be the glory! *Luke 17:10*

Introduction

An Introduction to The NIV Worship Bible

WORSHIP *101*

Welcome to *The NIV Worship Bible*, a new and exciting resource for personal and corporate worship. This Bible is designed to help you recognize the voice, the heart and the hand of God through Scripture, and to assist you in responding Biblically to God in worship.

All of the notes within the Bible are intended to be starting points for your own personal worship experience. As your personal worship life becomes deeper and more intimate, the corporate worship in your church community will also be enriched.

"What Is the Main Idea behind The NIV Worship Bible?"

St. Ambrose said, "As in Paradise, God walks in the Holy Scriptures, seeking man." This profound insight leads us to the question: When God finds me in the Holy Scriptures, what will I say to Him?

This is the question we tried to address in crafting the notes for this project. As the authors and editors took on this challenge, the very task of producing a worship Bible became an act of worship in itself.

We believe that worship is one of those things that are better "caught" than "taught." As C.S. Lewis said, "Worship is like dancing. You're not doing it until you stop counting the steps." Our purpose in *The NIV Worship Bible* is to model worship, and thereby to assist you in learning to express your personal worship response to your encounters with God in Scripture.

"What Is Unique About The NIV Worship Bible?"

Study Bibles, such as *The NIV Study Bible*, focus on what we can learn about God, His people, and the Scriptures themselves. They do this by delving into the text and revealing nuances of meaning implied by the original languages, or by adding notes that clarify and amplify the text itself. Devotional Bibles focus on the application of Biblical concepts and precepts to our daily life. Devotional notes use story, analogy and questions to shed new light on various passages of Scripture. Study and devotional Bibles are important tools for spiritual growth, and we encourage the use of them.

But *The NIV Worship Bible* is neither a study Bible, nor is it a devotional Bible. The unique aspect of this Bible is that the notes do not interact with you, the reader. Instead, they interact with God.

The NIV Worship Bible is neither a study Bible, nor is it a devotional Bible. The unique aspect of this Bible is that the notes do not interact with you, the reader. Instead, they interact with God.

For *The NIV Worship Bible*, the editors' underlying premise was that the Bible is the starting place of your conversation with God. It is a personal letter that reveals the deepest thoughts and feelings of its Author toward you, the one to whom it was written.

The Scriptures tell us not just what God did, but what God does and how He does it. Yes, they document God's historical dealings with His people, but they also reveal to us His unchanging nature and character. As A.W. Tozer said, we should "approach our Bible with the idea that it is not only a book which was once spoken, but a book which is now speaking ...God's speaking is in the continuous present."

God has given us the Bible as a means of knowing Him and enjoying His presence. It is a catalyst for worship. As Peter Kreeft so aptly stated, "Reading and praying [the Bible] is putting yourself in the way, standing in God's great waterfall of 'living water.' If you stand in the street, you'll get hit by a truck. If you stand in [the Bible], you'll get kissed by God. It is God's mistletoe."

The notes we created for this Bible are our efforts to respond to God's letter. They are the results of our encounters with Him as we "stood under His mistletoe." We have prayed through every page of the Bible, and we are sharing our prayers with you in the hope that they will become launching points for your own personal worship.

Features of The NIV Worship Bible

The NIV Worship Bible has worship-related elements on every single page to assist you in your worship response. As you page through the Bible, you will notice the different typefaces and colors we used to identify these features.

The features are the NIV Scripture text, Book Introductions, Hear My Prayer, Quotations, Song Texts, White Space, My Beloved and Reference Materials. As we explain these features, it is important to remember that personal worship needs to be developed in dialogue, not only with God through the Bible, but also with the broader Christian community. The Hear My Prayer features, song texts and quotations on these pages will help to connect your personal worship to the worship of others.

Pastors, Worship Leaders and small group leaders will find the prayers, quotes and song texts to be helpful materials in planning worship services. You might even wish to use the Hear My Prayer features as congregational responsive readings.

Scripture Text

First, and most important, is the text of Scripture itself. Scripture is central to all authentic worship. The Holy Scriptures are the Word of God—they are your primary means of hearing His voice and learning His will for your life. In reading the Word, you encounter God, the Object of your worship, and you discover the language of worship. Jesus said that the Father is looking for worshipers who will worship Him in Spirit and in truth (Jn 4:23). Therefore, everything we do or say in worship must line up with the truth of Scripture.

It stands to reason that if worship is our response to God, we would do well to discover first what God is saying to us through His Word. Let Him begin the conversation.

Book Introductions

The NIV Worship Bible book introductions prepare you for your encounter with God in each book. They point out unique aspects of God's character as revealed in the book; and they help to direct your worship expression. You will notice that we grouped a few of the books together for reasons of historic or literary continuity.

We approached the book introductions with the following questions in mind: "What does God uniquely reveal about His nature and character in this book?" "How is Christ foreshadowed or revealed, and what sort of worship does this revelation evoke?" "What does this book teach us about worship practices?" "How is God worshiped by the people we meet in this book?" "How are Old and New Testament worship connected, and how are they distinct?"

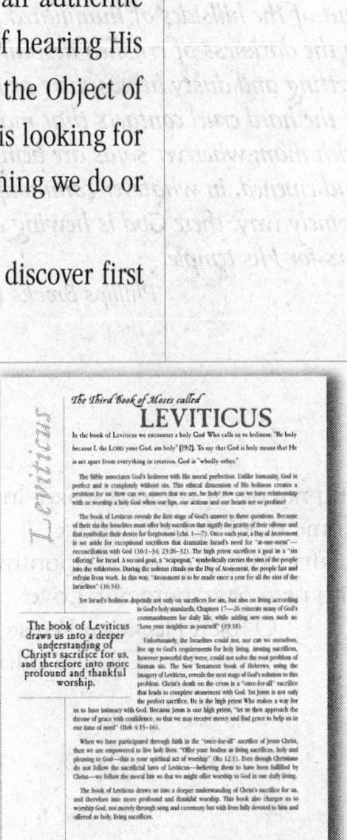
Leviticus

The Third Book of Moses called
LEVITICUS

In the book of Leviticus we encounter a holy God Who calls us to holiness: "Be holy because I, the LORD your God, am holy" (19:2). To say that God is holy means that He is set apart from everything in creation. God is "wholly other."

The Bible associates God's holiness with His moral perfection. Unlike humanity, God is perfect and is completely without sin. This ethical dimension of His holiness creates a problem for us: How can we, sinners that we are, be holy? How can we have relationship with or worship a holy God when our lips, our actions and our hearts are so profane?

The book of Leviticus reveals the first stage of God's answer to these questions. Because of their sin the Israelites must offer holy sacrifices that signify the gravity of their offense and that symbolize their desire for forgiveness (chs. 1—7). Once each year, a Day of Atonement is set aside for exceptional sacrifices that dramatize Israel's need for "at-one-ment"—reconciliation with God (16:1–34; 23:26–32). The high priest sacrifices a goat as a "sin offering" for Israel. A second goat, a "scapegoat," symbolically carries the sins of the people into the wilderness. During the solemn rituals on the Day of Atonement, the people fast and refrain from work. In this way, "Atonement is to be made once a year for all the sins of the Israelites" (16:34).

Yet Israel's holiness depends not only on sacrifices for sin, but also on living according to God's holy standards. Chapters 17—26 reiterate many of God's commandments for daily life, while adding new ones such as: "Love your neighbor as yourself" (19:18).

The book of Leviticus draws us into a deeper understanding of Christ's sacrifice for us, and therefore into more profound and thankful worship.

Unfortunately, the Israelites could not, nor can we ourselves, live up to God's requirements for holy living. Atoning sacrifices, however powerful they were, could not solve the root problem of human sin. The New Testament book of Hebrews, using the imagery of Leviticus, reveals the next stage of God's solution to this problem. Christ's death on the cross is a "once-for-all" sacrifice that leads to complete atonement with God. Yet Jesus is not only the perfect sacrifice, He is the high priest Who makes a way for us to have intimacy with God. Because Jesus is our high priest, "let us then approach the throne of grace with confidence, so that we may receive mercy and find grace to help us in our time of need" (Heb 4:15–16).

When we have participated through faith in the "once-for-all" sacrifice of Jesus Christ, then we are empowered to live holy lives: "Offer your bodies as living sacrifices, holy and pleasing to God—this is your spiritual act of worship" (Ro 12:1). Even though Christians do not follow the sacrificial laws of Leviticus—believing them to have been fulfilled by Christ—we follow the moral law so that we might offer worship to God in our daily living.

The book of Leviticus draws us into a deeper understanding of Christ's sacrifice for us, and therefore into more profound and thankful worship. This book also charges us to worship God, not merely through song and ceremony but with lives fully devoted to him and offered as holy, living sacrifices.

REVELATION 3-4

(3:11–12) O Lord, what joy there will be when all things become new in You! There will be a new heaven and a new earth, and upon each of us who remain faithful to You, You will write Your own name as an author signs his name to a finished work. Lord, You are aware of my struggles and see my limitations, but You know my potential. So strengthen my grip of faith. Renew my hope of eternal life. Grow me into the identity that yet awaits me; transform me into the person You always knew I would become. And help me to remember, in this present time, that all earthly titles, labels, degrees and honors are worth less than the dust of the earth compared to the glory that awaits Your people. (Isa 62:12; 2Co 3:18; 1Jn 3:2; Rev 21:1–5).

In what strange quarries and stoneyards the stones for the celestial wall are being hewn! Out of the hillsides of humiliated pride; deep in the darkness of crushed despair; in the fretting and dusty atmosphere of little cares; in the hard cruel contacts that man has with man; wherever souls are being tried and ripened, in whatever commonplace and homely way, there God is hewing out the pillars for His temple.

Phillips Brooks (1835-1893)

Thy nature, gracious Lord, impart;
Come quickly from above;
Write Thy new name upon my heart,
Thy new best name of Love.

"O for a Heart to Praise My God"
Charles Wesley (1742)

Hear My Prayer

Along the outside margin of each page you will find Hear My Prayer features that respond to a specific passage of Scripture. As we approached the text, we asked ourselves, "What is God revealing about Himself in this passage; and how should we respond to Him?" Admittedly, our sight is blurry and none of us has the complete picture—after all, "we see but a poor reflection as in a mirror" (1Co 13:12). But as we meditated on each passage, we began to see more of the nature and character of God. We wrote our worship responses in the form of prayers.

This is a process that you can follow in your devotions. Let the Bible feed your thoughts and then let your thoughts flow into prayer. Begin by selecting a passage of Scripture. Read slowly, read deeply, read prayerfully, read aloud. Read for depth, not for distance. Read "with your ears"—hear the Word of the Lord.

After reading the passage, stop and think long and deeply about it. As you think about what God is saying, put your thoughts into words and speak them to God or write them down. Say back to God what you hear His Word saying to you. In this way, you are praying God's thoughts—you are agreeing with God in prayer. Your worship will then take on a variety of forms, including thanksgiving, praise, adoration, confession, repentance, intercession, supplication, lamentation, and others.

Quotations

To inspire your worship, we have drawn deeply from the treasury of great worshipers and thought-leaders from church history. You will see how these men and women of faith encountered God and responded to Him. At times your worship may be led by St. Augustine, Catherine of Siena, Martin Luther, Matthew Henry, Charles Spurgeon, C. S. Lewis, A.W. Tozer, Corrie ten Boom, Jack Hayford, Max Lucado, or some 400 other great men and women of faith.

Song Lyrics

The familiar hymns and worship songs quoted throughout each book of the Bible relate directly to the Scripture text and the Hear My Prayer feature on the page. You will be amazed at how often the truth of Scripture comes alive through the majestic poetry of the past and the personal praise of today.

Over the centuries and still today, great songs of worship have been written and passed down from one generation to the next. They are reminders of the awesome things God has done. They are altars along the way of the cross—memorials to human encounters with a loving, forgiving, delivering God. Through these musical expressions, you may find your own voice in the song of worship.

White Space

The white space you will find on most of the pages is also a feature in this Bible. We deliberately left this space on the page for you to write your own thoughts and prayers—you might even want to date your entries. By doing this, your prayers will serve as testimonials to your devotional journey. The next time you read the passage, you will have a permanent reminder of when and how God met you there, and how you responded to Him in worship.

A special note about the Psalms: Because the Psalms are already responsive writings, we decided to leave the entire margin available for your personal use. Rather than fill the pages with our prayers, we encourage you to fill them with yours—in a sense, to make the Book of Psalms your own personal Psalter.

My Beloved

In these 36 full-page features, we have taken favorite Scripture passages and paraphrased them into the form of personal letters from God to you. They help give fresh perspective to the timeless truths of God's love and faithfulness.

MY BELOVED

If you live according to My word, then I will guide you always. I will satisfy all your needs and will make you strong. You will be like a well-watered garden, like a spring whose waters never fail. So trust Me with all your heart and lean not on your own understanding. Acknowledge Me in everything you do, and I will make your journey easier.

I will guide you in the way of wisdom and lead you along straight paths. When you walk, your steps will not be hampered; when you run, you will not stumble.

I am your Rock and your Fortress; because I am your God, I will lead and guide you. If you will listen, I will instruct you and teach you the way you should go. I will counsel you and watch over you. I am your God forever and ever, and I promise I will be your guide—even to the end of time.

When you cannot see the way, I will lead you through unfamiliar territory; I will turn the darkness into light before you and make the rough places smooth. These things I will do. I will not forsake you. Once again, I am the Lord your God, who teaches you what is best for you, who directs you in the way you should go. You are not alone.

These features are not meant to take the place of the Scriptures, nor are they an attempt to somehow improve on the Word of God. Our desire in these paraphrases is to help you discover God's heart toward you—to see just how much He loves you and cares for you—to see how very much God desires to have a personal relationship with you. At the end of each feature we have included a list of the Scriptures that inspired the feature.

Reference Materials

The NIV Worship Bible offers an Index of Quotations, a Bibliography of Quotations, an Index of Lyrics, a Directory of Song Publishers, and an NIV Concordance to complement your worship and study experience.

"Where Do I Start?"

From cover to cover, the Bible is filled with worship opportunities. You can start at the very beginning, or choose a specific book. Or you can just "dive in" anywhere, on any page, because God has promised to meet you through His Word. After you have read your selected passage, take time to reflect on what God has said to you personally. Read the prayer aloud, along with the additional quotations and song lyrics in the margin. They will help to guide your conversation with God. Then offer prayers in your own words.

May you enjoy God's presence and grow in His image as you read *The NIV Worship Bible*.

Thomas D. Vegh

President, Maranatha! Music

PREFACE TO
The New International Version

THE NEW INTERNATIONAL VERSION is a completely new translation of the Holy Bible made by over a hundred scholars working directly from the best available Hebrew, Aramaic and Greek texts. It had its beginning in 1965 when, after several years of exploratory study by committees from the Christian Reformed Church and the National Association of Evangelicals, a group of scholars met at Palos Heights, Illinois, and concurred in the need for a new translation of the Bible in contemporary English. This group, though not made up of official church representatives, was transdenominational. Its conclusion was endorsed by a large number of leaders from many denominations who met in Chicago in 1966.

Responsibility for the new version was delegated by the Palos Heights group to a self-governing body of fifteen, the Committee on Bible Translation, composed for the most part of biblical scholars from colleges, universities and seminaries. In 1967 the New York Bible Society (now the International Bible Society) generously undertook the financial sponsorship of the project—a sponsorship that made it possible to enlist the help of many distinguished scholars. The fact that participants from the United States, Great Britain, Canada, Australia and New Zealand worked together gave the project its international scope. That they were from many denominations—including Anglican, Assemblies of God, Baptist, Brethren, Christian Reformed, Church of Christ, Evangelical Free, Lutheran, Mennonite, Methodist, Nazarene, Presbyterian, Wesleyan and other churches—helped to safeguard the translation from sectarian bias.

How it was made helps to give the New International Version its distinctiveness. The translation of each book was assigned to a team of scholars. Next, one of the Intermediate Editorial Committees revised the initial translation, with constant reference to the Hebrew, Aramaic or Greek. Their work then went to one of the General Editorial Committees, which checked it in detail and made another thorough revision. This revision in turn was carefully reviewed by the Committee on Bible Translation, which made further changes and then released the final version for publication. In this way the entire Bible underwent three revisions, during each of which the translation was examined for its faithfulness to the original languages and for its English style.

All this involved many thousands of hours of research and discussion regarding the meaning of the texts and the precise way of putting them into English. It may well be that no other translation has been made by a more thorough process of review and revision from committee to committee than this one.

From the beginning of the project, the Committee on Bible Translation held to certain goals for the New International Version: that it would be an accurate translation and one that would have clarity and literary quality and so prove suitable for public and private reading, teaching, preaching, memorizing and liturgical use. The Committee also sought to preserve some measure of continuity with the long tradition of translating the Scriptures into English.

In working toward these goals, the translators were united in their commitment to the authority and infallibility of the Bible as God's Word in written form. They believe that it contains the divine answer to the deepest needs of humanity, that it sheds unique light on our path in a dark world, and that it sets forth the way to our eternal well-being.

The first concern of the translators has been the accuracy of the translation and its fidelity to the thought of the biblical writers. They have weighed the significance of the lexical and grammatical details of the Hebrew, Aramaic and Greek texts. At the same time, they have striven for more than a word-for-word translation. Because thought patterns and syntax differ from language to language, faithful communication of the meaning of the writers of the Bible demands frequent modifications in sentence structure and constant regard for the contextual meanings of words.

A sensitive feeling for style does not always accompany scholarship. Accordingly the Committee on Bible Translation submitted the developing version to a number of stylistic consultants. Two of them read every book of both Old and New Testaments twice—once before and once after the last major revision—and made invaluable suggestions. Samples of the translation were tested for clarity and ease of reading by various kinds of people—young and old, highly educated and less well educated, ministers and laymen.

Concern for clear and natural English—that the New International Version should be idiomatic but not idiosyncratic, contemporary but not dated—motivated the translators and consultants. At the same time, they tried to reflect the differing styles of the biblical writers. In view of the international use of English, the translators sought to avoid obvious Americanisms on the one hand and obvious Anglicisms on the other. A British edition reflects the comparatively few differences of significant idiom and of spelling.

As for the traditional pronouns "thou," "thee" and "thine" in reference to the Deity, the translators judged that to use these archaisms (along with the old verb forms such as "doest," "wouldest" and "hadst") would violate accuracy in translation. Neither Hebrew, Aramaic nor Greek uses special pronouns for the persons of the Godhead. A present-day translation is not enhanced by forms that in the time of the King James Version were used in everyday speech, whether referring to God or man.

For the Old Testament the standard Hebrew text, the Masoretic Text as published in the latest editions of *Biblia Hebraica,* was used throughout. The Dead Sea Scrolls contain material bearing on an earlier stage of the Hebrew text. They were consulted, as were the Samaritan Pentateuch and the ancient scribal traditions relating to textual changes. Sometimes a variant Hebrew reading in the margin of the Masoretic Text was followed instead of the text itself. Such instances, being variants within the Masoretic tradition, are not specified by footnotes. In rare cases, words in the consonantal text were divided differently from the way they appear in the Masoretic Text. Footnotes indicate this. The translators also consulted the more important early versions—the Septuagint; Aquila, Symmachus and Theodotion; the Vulgate; the Syriac Peshitta; the Targums; and for the Psalms the *Juxta Hebraica* of Jerome. Readings from these versions were occasionally followed where the Masoretic Text seemed doubtful and where accepted principles of textual criticism showed that one or more of these textual witnesses appeared to provide the correct reading. Such instances are footnoted. Sometimes vowel letters and vowel signs did not, in the judgment of the translators, represent the correct vowels for the original consonantal text. Accordingly some words were read with a different set of vowels. These instances are usually not indicated by footnotes.

The Greek text used in translating the New Testament was an eclectic one. No other piece of ancient literature has such an abundance of manuscript witnesses as does the New Testament. Where existing manuscripts differ, the translators made their choice of readings according to accepted principles of New Testament textual criticism. Footnotes call attention to places where there was uncertainty about what the original text was. The best current printed texts of the Greek New Testament were used.

There is a sense in which the work of translation is never wholly finished. This applies to all great literature and uniquely so to the Bible. In 1973 the New Testament in the New International Version was published. Since then, suggestions for corrections and revisions have been received from various sources. The Committee on Bible Translation carefully considered the suggestions and adopted a number of them. These were incorporated in the first printing of the entire Bible in 1978. Additional revisions were made by the Committee on Bible Translation in 1983 and appear in printings after that date.

As in other ancient documents, the precise meaning of the biblical texts is sometimes uncertain. This is more often the case with the Hebrew and Aramaic texts than with the Greek text. Although archaeological and linguistic discoveries in this century aid in understanding difficult passages, some uncertainties remain. The more significant of these have been called to the reader's attention in the footnotes.

In regard to the divine name *YHWH,* commonly referred to as the *Tetragrammaton,* the translators adopted the device used in most English versions of rendering that name as "LORD" in capital letters to distinguish it from *Adonai,* another Hebrew word rendered "Lord," for which small letters are used. Wherever the two names stand together in the Old Testament as a compound name of God, they are rendered "Sovereign LORD."

Because for most readers today the phrases "the LORD of hosts" and "God of hosts" have little meaning, this version renders them "the LORD Almighty" and "God Almighty." These renderings convey the sense of the Hebrew, namely, "he who is sovereign over all the 'hosts' (powers) in heaven and on earth, especially over the 'hosts' (armies) of Israel." For readers unacquainted with Hebrew this does not make clear the distinction between *Sabaoth* ("hosts" or "Almighty") and *Shaddai* (which can also be translated "Almighty"), but the latter occurs infrequently and is always footnoted. When *Adonai* and *YHWH Sabaoth* occur together, they are rendered "the Lord, the LORD Almighty."

As for other proper nouns, the familiar spellings of the King James Version are generally retained. Names traditionally spelled with "ch," except where it is final, are usually spelled in this translation with "k" or "c," since the biblical languages do not have the sound that "ch" frequently indicates in English—for example, in *chant.* For well-known names such as Zechariah, however, the traditional spelling has been retained. Variation in the spelling of names in the original languages has usually not been indicated. Where a person or place has two or more different names in the Hebrew, Aramaic or Greek texts, the more familiar one has generally been used, with footnotes where needed.

To achieve clarity the translators sometimes supplied words not in the original texts but required by the context. If there was uncertainty about such material, it is enclosed in brackets. Also for the sake of clarity or style, nouns, including some proper nouns, are sometimes substituted for pronouns, and vice versa. And though the Hebrew writers often shifted back and forth between first, second and third personal pronouns without change of antecedent, this translation often makes them uniform, in accordance with English style and without the use of footnotes.

Poetical passages are printed as poetry, that is, with indentation of lines and with separate stanzas. These are generally designed to reflect the structure of Hebrew poetry. This poetry is normally characterized by parallelism in balanced lines. Most of the poetry in the Bible is in the Old Testament, and scholars differ regarding the scansion of Hebrew lines. The translators determined the stanza divisions for the most part by analysis of the subject matter. The stanzas therefore serve as poetic paragraphs.

As an aid to the reader, italicized sectional headings are inserted in most of the books. They are not to be regarded as part of the NIV text, are not for oral reading, and are not intended to dictate the interpretation of the sections they head.

The footnotes in this version are of several kinds, most of which need no explanation. Those giving alternative translations begin with "Or" and generally introduce the alternative with the last word preceding it in the text, except when it is a single-word alternative; in poetry quoted in a footnote a slant mark indicates a line division. Footnotes introduced by "Or" do not have uniform significance. In some cases two possible translations were considered to have about equal validity. In other cases, though the translators were convinced that the translation in the text was correct, they judged that another interpretation was possible and of sufficient importance to be represented in a footnote.

In the New Testament, footnotes that refer to uncertainty regarding the original text are introduced by "Some manuscripts" or similar expressions. In the Old Testament, evidence for the reading chosen is given first and evidence for the alternative is added after a semicolon (for example: Septuagint; Hebrew *father*). In such notes the term "Hebrew" refers to the Masoretic Text.

It should be noted that minerals, flora and fauna, architectural details, articles of clothing and jewelry, musical instruments and other articles cannot always be identified with precision. Also measures of capacity in the biblical period are particularly uncertain (see the table of weights and measures following the text).

Like all translations of the Bible, made as they are by imperfect man, this one undoubtedly falls short of its goals. Yet we are grateful to God for the extent to which he has enabled us to realize these goals and for the strength he has given us and our colleagues to complete our task. We offer this version of the Bible to him in whose name and for whose glory it has been made. We pray that it will lead many into a better understanding of the Holy Scriptures and a fuller knowledge of Jesus Christ the incarnate Word, of whom the Scriptures so faithfully testify.

The Committee on Bible Translation

June 1978
(Revised August 1983)

Names of the translators and editors may be secured
from the International Bible Society,
translation sponsors of the New International Version,
1820 Jet Stream Drive, Colorado Springs, Colorado
80921-3696 U.S.A.

The
Old Testament

The First Book of Moses called

GENESIS

"In the beginning, God . . ." Worship begins with God, not with us. In worship we respond to God, Who has created us and Who seeks to have fellowship with us. The word *genesis* means "beginning." It supplies an apt title for this book, not only because the Bible begins here, but also because the book itself is full of beginnings. God creates the universe, including man and woman. When they rebel against God, the long, sad history of human brokenness begins. Yet the longer, joyous history of God's salvation begins in Genesis as well.

In the first main section (chs. 1—11) we meet the Creator Who evokes our awe by forming the universe out of nothing. God delights in His workmanship, seeing that it is "very good." Human beings, created in the image of God, are central to His good creation. But human disobedience tarnishes His masterpiece. Starting with Adam and Eve, sin spreads like an avalanche, damaging not only humanity but even creation itself. Punishment must come; but as God's judgment upon human sin commences, so does His gracious effort to redeem fallen humanity.

In the second main section of Genesis (chs. 12—50) we encounter God as a covenant-maker who begins, through Abraham and Sarah, to form a great nation. Ultimately, from this holy nation all peoples on earth will be blessed. We know what the first readers of Genesis did not know: that from Israel would come Jesus the Messiah, the Savior of the World.

Worship begins with God, not with us.

God reveals in Genesis that He is not disconnected from His creation. Instead, God interacts with His creatures in ways that reveal His character. The covenant with Abraham, for example, indicates the depth of God's commitment to humanity, a commitment that is ultimately fulfilled on the cross. The covenant also reveals God's desire to be in relationship with us, a special relationship based upon divine initiative and requiring our response of loving obedience.

The concluding narratives of Genesis show how God uses both saints and scoundrels to fulfill His purposes. (And sometimes He uses saints who act like scoundrels!) The sovereign God will not ultimately be frustrated, in spite of our human tendency to seek selfish gain rather than God's glory. God's promises made to Abraham, conferred on us through Jesus Christ, will one day be fulfilled. Meanwhile, like Abraham, we are children of God through faith, who worship God by living obediently, so that His sovereign purposes might be fulfilled in us and through us.

(1:1) You alone exist in the beginning, O God. You alone are the Alpha and Omega, the one "who is, and who was, and who is to come." You alone transcend and embrace even time itself. You alone chose to create all things, to make a world to glorify Yourself and to receive Your love. You alone, in the mystery of Your sovereignty, chose me even before the creation of the world to belong to You as Your special, beloved child. I am amazed, awestruck, humbled, beloved—and I bow before You alone. (Eph 1:4–6; Rev 1:8)

"In the beginning was the Word, and the Word was with God, and the Word was God." (Jn 1:1) God is forever seeking to speak Himself out to His creation . . . He is, by His nature continuously articulate. He fills the world with His speaking voice.

A. W. Tozer (1897-1963)

(1:3) At Your command, O God, light came to be—the visible light that brightens Your creation and the light of truth that illuminates our existence as Your creatures. Your Word is a lamp to our feet and a light to our path. In our struggle to see by Your light, You have come as the Light of the world—Jesus, who turns even the darkness into light for us. O bright and Morning Star, let Your light shine in our hearts to give us the light of the knowledge of the glory of God in the face of Christ! (Ps 18:28; 119:105; Jn 8:12; 2Co 4:6; Rev 22:16)

For the beauty of the earth,
For the glory of the skies,
For the love which from our birth
Over and around us lies,
Lord of all, to Thee we raise
This our hymn of grateful praise.

"For the Beauty of the Earth"
Folliott Sandford Pierpoint (1864)

The Beginning

1 In the beginning God created the heavens and the earth.
2 Now the earth was[a] formless and empty, darkness was over
the surface of the deep, and the Spirit of God was hovering
over the waters.

3 And God said, "Let there be light," and there was light. 4 God
saw that the light was good, and he separated the light from
the darkness. 5 God called the light "day," and the darkness
he called "night." And there was evening, and there was
morning—the first day.
6 And God said, "Let there be an expanse between the waters to
separate water from water." 7 So God made the expanse and
separated the water under the expanse from the water above
it. And it was so. 8 God called the expanse "sky." And there
was evening, and there was morning—the second day.
9 And God said, "Let the water under the sky be gathered to one
place, and let dry ground appear." And it was so. 10 God
called the dry ground "land," and the gathered waters he
called "seas." And God saw that it was good.
11 Then God said, "Let the land produce vegetation: seed-
bearing plants and trees on the land that bear fruit with seed
in it, according to their various kinds." And it was so. 12 The
land produced vegetation: plants bearing seed according to
their kinds and trees bearing fruit with seed in it according
to their kinds. And God saw that it was good. 13 And there
was evening, and there was morning—the third day.
14 And God said, "Let there be lights in the expanse of the sky to
separate the day from the night, and let them serve as signs
to mark seasons and days and years, 15 and let them be lights
in the expanse of the sky to give light on the earth." And it
was so. 16 God made two great lights—the greater light to
govern the day and the lesser light to govern the night. He
also made the stars. 17 God set them in the expanse of the sky
to give light on the earth, 18 to govern the day and the night,
and to separate light from darkness. And God saw that it was
good. 19 And there was evening, and there was morning—
the fourth day.
20 And God said, "Let the water teem with living creatures, and let
birds fly above the earth across the expanse of the sky." 21 So
God created the great creatures of the sea and every living
and moving thing with which the water teems, according to
their kinds, and every winged bird according to its kind. And
God saw that it was good. 22 God blessed them and said, "Be
fruitful and increase in number and fill the water in the seas,
and let the birds increase on the earth." 23 And there was
evening, and there was morning—the fifth day.
24 And God said, "Let the land produce living creatures according
to their kinds: livestock, creatures that move along the
ground, and wild animals, each according to its kind." And
it was so. 25 God made the wild animals according to their
kinds, the livestock according to their kinds, and all the
creatures that move along the ground according to their
kinds. And God saw that it was good.
26 Then God said, "Let us make man in our image, in our

[a] 2 Or possibly *became*

MY BELOVED

Did you know that I created you in My own image? Did you know that I chose you in Christ before the creation of the world to be holy and blameless in My sight? In love I predestined you to be adopted as My child through My Son Jesus, because it pleased Me to do so.

You already know that sin is what separates us from one another. Because of the disobedience of Adam you were made a sinner. But I demonstrated My love for you in this: while you were still a sinner, My Son Jesus died for you. His innocent blood was shed for the forgiveness of your sins—all of your sins. Because of His obedience, you are made righteous. Therefore, we no longer have to be separated from one another.

Anyone who receives Him as Savior and believes on His name is immediately adopted into Our family and becomes My child. It all begins with grace through faith—not with a list of good works or self-help programs. Just believe and receive My Son Jesus Christ, and then follow Him all the days of your life.

Ge 1:27; Jn 1:12; Ro 5:8,12,19; Eph 1:4,5,7; 2:8-9; 1Jn1:12

likeness, and let them rule over the fish of the sea and the
birds of the air, over the livestock, over all the earth,[a] and
over all the creatures that move along the ground."

27 So God created man in his own image,
in the image of God he created him;
male and female he created them.

28 God blessed them and said to them, "Be fruitful and increase in number; fill the earth and subdue it. Rule over the
fish of the sea and the birds of the air and over every living
creature that moves on the ground."
29 Then God said, "I give you every seed-bearing plant on
the face of the whole earth and every tree that has fruit with
seed in it. They will be yours for food. 30 And to all the beasts
of the earth and all the birds of the air and all the creatures
that move on the ground—everything that has the breath of
life in it—I give every green plant for food." And it was so.
31 God saw all that he had made, and it was very good. And
there was evening, and there was morning—the sixth day.

2 Thus the heavens and the earth were completed in all their
vast array.

2 By the seventh day God had finished the work he had been
doing; so on the seventh day he rested[b] from all his work.
3 And God blessed the seventh day and made it holy, because
on it he rested from all the work of creating that he had
done.

Adam and Eve

4 This is the account of the heavens and the earth when they
were created.

When the LORD God made the earth and the heavens— 5 and no
shrub of the field had yet appeared on the earth[c] and no plant of
the field had yet sprung up, for the LORD God had not sent rain on
the earth[c] and there was no man to work the ground, 6 but
streams[d] came up from the earth and watered the whole surface
of the ground— 7 the LORD God formed the man[e] from the dust of
the ground and breathed into his nostrils the breath of life, and
the man became a living being.
8 Now the LORD God had planted a garden in the east, in Eden;
and there he put the man he had formed. 9 And the LORD God made
all kinds of trees grow out of the ground—trees that were pleasing to the eye and good for food. In the middle of the garden were
the tree of life and the tree of the knowledge of good and evil.
10 A river watering the garden flowed from Eden; from there it
was separated into four headwaters. 11 The name of the first is the
Pishon; it winds through the entire land of Havilah, where there is
gold. 12 (The gold of that land is good; aromatic resin[f] and onyx
are also there.) 13 The name of the second river is the Gihon; it
winds through the entire land of Cush.[g] 14 The name of the third
river is the Tigris; it runs along the east side of Asshur. And the
fourth river is the Euphrates.
15 The LORD God took the man and put him in the Garden of

[a] *26* Hebrew; Syriac *all the wild animals* [b] *2* Or *ceased*; also in verse 3 [c] *5* Or *land*; also in verse 6 [d] *6* Or *mist* [e] *7* The Hebrew for *man (adam)* sounds like and may be related to the Hebrew for *ground (adamah)*; it is also the name *Adam* (see Gen. 2:20). [f] *12* Or *good; pearls* [g] *13* Possibly southeast Mesopotamia

If the mind of God as discovered to us in his Word and works is so vast and deep, what must his mind be in all its undisclosed resources in the infinity and eternity of its existence?

John Bate (17th c.)

(1:27) You reveal Yourself to us, God our Creator, as an all-powerful God whose very word calls creation into existence. You are a God of perfection, whose incomprehensible goodness is mirrored in the wonder of Your creation. An even greater wonder is this: We reflect You, having been created in Your image, the very image of God! You have made us a little lower than the heavenly beings. You have crowned us with glory and honor. You have given us authority over Your creation, to fill it and to rule over it for Your purposes. Yet when we allow the magnificence of Your creation to show us just a bit of Your unique majesty, what are we that You are mindful of us? What are we that You should care for us? (Ps 8:1–4)

(2:7) When You formed man in Your image out of the dust of the ground, You were building a temple. And as a creature of dust, I too am a temple. You have placed my name above the door and now You stand at the door and knock, waiting for me to invite You in. Lord of heaven, come and be Lord of this piece of earth. Come and fill this temple with the living breath of Your Holy Spirit. Make it a place of worship. Find Your rest within its walls. Be enthroned on my praises. (Ps 22:3; 132:8,14; 1Co 6:19; Rev 3:20)

Breathe on me, Breath of God,
Fill me with life anew,
That I may love what Thou dost
love,
And do what Thou wouldst do.

"Breathe On Me, Breath of God"
Edwin Hatch (1886)

Eden to work it and take care of it. 16And the LORD God commanded the man, "You are free to eat from any tree in the garden;
17but you must not eat from the tree of the knowledge of good
and evil, for when you eat of it you will surely die."
18The LORD God said, "It is not good for the man to be alone. I
will make a helper suitable for him."
19Now the LORD God had formed out of the ground all the beasts
of the field and all the birds of the air. He brought them to the
man to see what he would name them; and whatever the man
called each living creature, that was its name. 20So the man gave
names to all the livestock, the birds of the air and all the beasts of
the field.
But for Adam[a] no suitable helper was found. 21So the LORD God
caused the man to fall into a deep sleep; and while he was sleeping, he took one of the man's ribs[b] and closed up the place with
flesh. 22Then the LORD God made a woman from the rib[c] he had
taken out of the man, and he brought her to the man.
23The man said,

"This is now bone of my bones
and flesh of my flesh;
she shall be called 'woman,[d]'
for she was taken out of man."

24For this reason a man will leave his father and mother and be
united to his wife, and they will become one flesh.
25The man and his wife were both naked, and they felt no
shame.

The Fall of Man

3 Now the serpent was more crafty than any of the wild animals
the LORD God had made. He said to the woman, "Did God
really say, 'You must not eat from any tree in the garden'?"
2The woman said to the serpent, "We may eat fruit from the
trees in the garden, 3but God did say, 'You must not eat fruit from
the tree that is in the middle of the garden, and you must not touch
it, or you will die.'"
4"You will not surely die," the serpent said to the woman. 5"For
God knows that when you eat of it your eyes will be opened, and
you will be like God, knowing good and evil."
6When the woman saw that the fruit of the tree was good for
food and pleasing to the eye, and also desirable for gaining wisdom, she took some and ate it. She also gave some to her husband, who was with her, and he ate it. 7Then the eyes of both of
them were opened, and they realized they were naked; so they
sewed fig leaves together and made coverings for themselves.
8Then the man and his wife heard the sound of the LORD God as
he was walking in the garden in the cool of the day, and they hid
from the LORD God among the trees of the garden. 9But the LORD
God called to the man, "Where are you?"
10He answered, "I heard you in the garden, and I was afraid because I was naked; so I hid."
11And he said, "Who told you that you were naked? Have you
eaten from the tree that I commanded you not to eat from?"
12The man said, "The woman you put here with me—she gave
me some fruit from the tree, and I ate it."

[a]20 Or *the man* [b]21 Or *took part of the man's side* [c]22 Or *part* [d]23 The Hebrew for *woman* sounds like the Hebrew for *man.*

As in Paradise, God walks in the Holy Scriptures, seeking man.

Saint Ambrose (339-397)

(3:9) You call out to us, "Where are You?" before we ever cry out to You. It is because You initiate relationship that we are able to worship You. You receive our worship because You come looking for us when we hide in our sin. Like a good shepherd, You seek us when we are hopelessly lost. You bring us back when we have strayed. You bind us up when we are injured. You forgive us when we confess our sins against You. Your love never lets us go. You always find us. (Isa 65:1; Eze 34:11–16; Lk 15:4–7; Ro 5:8; 1Jn 1:9)

If God had not called to him, his condition would have been as desperate as that of fallen angels; this lost sheep would have wandered endlessly if the Good Shepherd had not sought after him to bring him back.

Matthew Henry (1662-1714)

The love of God is greater far
Than tongue or pen can ever tell;
It goes beyond the highest star,
And reaches to the lowest hell;
The guilty pair, bowed down with
care,
God gave His Son to win;
His erring child He reconciled,
And pardoned from his sin.

"The Love of God"
F.M. Lehman (1917)

13Then the LORD God said to the woman, "What is this you have
done?"
The woman said, "The serpent deceived me, and I ate."
14So the LORD God said to the serpent, "Because you have done
this,

"Cursed are you above all the livestock
and all the wild animals!
You will crawl on your belly
and you will eat dust
all the days of your life.
15And I will put enmity
between you and the woman,
and between your offspring[a] and hers;
he will crush[b] your head,
and you will strike his heel."

16To the woman he said,

"I will greatly increase your pains in childbearing;
with pain you will give birth to children.
Your desire will be for your husband,
and he will rule over you."

17To Adam he said, "Because you listened to your wife and ate
from the tree about which I commanded you, 'You must not eat
of it,'

"Cursed is the ground because of you;
through painful toil you will eat of it
all the days of your life.
18It will produce thorns and thistles for you,
and you will eat the plants of the field.
19By the sweat of your brow
you will eat your food
until you return to the ground,
since from it you were taken;
for dust you are
and to dust you will return."

20Adam[c] named his wife Eve,[d] because she would become the
mother of all the living.
21The LORD God made garments of skin for Adam and his wife
and clothed them. 22And the LORD God said, "The man has now
become like one of us, knowing good and evil. He must not be allowed to reach out his hand and take also from the tree of life and
eat, and live forever." 23So the LORD God banished him from the
Garden of Eden to work the ground from which he had been
taken. 24After he drove the man out, he placed on the east side[e] of
the Garden of Eden cherubim and a flaming sword flashing back
and forth to guard the way to the tree of life.

Cain and Abel

4 Adam[c] lay with his wife Eve, and she became pregnant and
gave birth to Cain.[f] She said, "With the help of the LORD I have
brought forth[g] a man." 2Later she gave birth to his brother Abel.
Now Abel kept flocks, and Cain worked the soil. 3In the course

[a] 15 Or *seed* [b] 15 Or *strike* [c] 20,1 Or *The man* [d] 20 *Eve* probably means *living.*
[e] 24 Or *placed in front* [f] 1 *Cain* sounds like the Hebrew for *brought forth* or *acquired.*
[g] 1 Or *have acquired*

(3:21) I thank You, O God, that when I stumble and fall, when sin strips me of my innocence, You find me and provide my covering. Adam and Eve clothed themselves with fig leaves. But you made garments of animal skins to cover their nakedness—garments that required the shedding of innocent blood, for "it is the blood that makes atonement for one's life." In the same way, "At just the right time," You shed Your own blood to cover my nakedness with Your righteousness. In spite of my sin, You are my gracious Provider. (Ge 3:7; Lev 17:11; Ro 5:6–8)

You are the garment that covers all nakedness.

Saint Catherine of Siena (1347-1380)

Hide me, Lord, in your holiness,
Every sin I now confess,
Praise to You, forgiving Lord,
Hide me in Your holiness,
Hide me in Your holiness.

"Hide Me In Your Holiness"
Steve Ragsdale (©1986)

of time Cain brought some of the fruits of the soil as an offering to the LORD. 4But Abel brought fat portions from some of
the firstborn of his flock. The LORD looked with favor on Abel
and his offering, 5but on Cain and his offering he did not look
with favor. So Cain was very angry, and his face was downcast.
6Then the LORD said to Cain, "Why are you angry? Why is
your face downcast? 7If you do what is right, will you not be accepted? But if you do not do what is right, sin is crouching at
your door; it desires to have you, but you must master it."
8Now Cain said to his brother Abel, "Let's go out to the
field."[a] And while they were in the field, Cain attacked his
brother Abel and killed him.
9Then the LORD said to Cain, "Where is your brother Abel?"
"I don't know," he replied. "Am I my brother's keeper?"
10The LORD said, "What have you done? Listen! Your brother's blood cries out to me from the ground. 11Now you are
under a curse and driven from the ground, which opened its
mouth to receive your brother's blood from your hand. 12When
you work the ground, it will no longer yield its crops for you.
You will be a restless wanderer on the earth."
13Cain said to the LORD, "My punishment is more than I can
bear. 14Today you are driving me from the land, and I will be
hidden from your presence; I will be a restless wanderer on
the earth, and whoever finds me will kill me."
15But the LORD said to him, "Not so[b]; if anyone kills Cain, he
will suffer vengeance seven times over." Then the LORD put a
mark on Cain so that no one who found him would kill him.
16So Cain went out from the LORD's presence and lived in the
land of Nod,[c] east of Eden.
17Cain lay with his wife, and she became pregnant and gave
birth to Enoch. Cain was then building a city, and he named it
after his son Enoch. 18To Enoch was born Irad, and Irad was
the father of Mehujael, and Mehujael was the father of
Methushael, and Methushael was the father of Lamech.
19Lamech married two women, one named Adah and the
other Zillah. 20Adah gave birth to Jabal; he was the father of
those who live in tents and raise livestock. 21His brother's name
was Jubal; he was the father of all who play the harp and flute.
22Zillah also had a son, Tubal-Cain, who forged all kinds of tools
out of[d] bronze and iron. Tubal-Cain's sister was Naamah.
23Lamech said to his wives,

"Adah and Zillah, listen to me;
wives of Lamech, hear my words.
I have killed[e] a man for wounding me,
a young man for injuring me.
24If Cain is avenged seven times,
then Lamech seventy-seven times."

25Adam lay with his wife again, and she gave birth to a son
and named him Seth,[f] saying, "God has granted me another
child in place of Abel, since Cain killed him." 26Seth also had
a son, and he named him Enosh.
At that time men began to call on[g] the name of the LORD.

[a] 8 Samaritan Pentateuch, Septuagint, Vulgate and Syriac; Masoretic Text does not have *"Let's go out to the field."* [b] 15 Septuagint, Vulgate and Syriac; Hebrew *Very well* [c] 16 *Nod* means *wandering* (see verses 12 and 14). [d] 22 Or *who instructed all who work in* [e] 23 Or *I will kill* [f] 25 *Seth* probably means *granted.* [g] 26 Or *to proclaim*

(4:8) Lord, I cannot escape the fact that one single act of worship produced the first murderer and the first martyr. If my heart is not being transformed by my encounters with You in worship, then it is being hardened. Soften my heart, Lord. Let pure worship flow from the innermost part of my being, from a life that is fully surrendered to You.

For the stroke that came from Cain's hand was not aimed merely at Abel, it was in spirit aimed at God . . . the blood of Abel cried in the ears of the Lord, "O God, the blood shed here was shed for thee. If it were not for love of Thee, this blood had not been shed! If these drops had not been consecrated by devotion, if this blood had not flowed in the veins of man who loved God with all his heart, it had not been poured out upon the ground. O God," cries every drop, "I fell upon the ground for Thee." [And so says the blood of Christ.] "O, God, the Sufferer, Pal in death whose wounds are torn open with the cruel nails, and who's soul is wracked with pain unutterable, dies for Thee. If there had been no God, He need not die. But it is for Thee, for Thee each pang, for Thee each groan, for Thee each drop of blood.

Charles Haddon Spurgeon (1834-1892)

Lord, take my life, and make it
wholly Thine;
Fill my poor heart with Thy great
love divine.
Take all my will, my passion, self and
pride;
I now surrender, Lord
In me abide.

"Cleanse Me"
J. Edwin Orr (1936)

From Adam to Noah

5 This is the written account of Adam's line.
When God created man, he made him in the likeness of God.
2He created them male and female and blessed them. And when
they were created, he called them "man.[a]"
3When Adam had lived 130 years, he had a son in his own likeness, in his own image; and he named him Seth. 4After Seth was
born, Adam lived 800 years and had other sons and daughters.
5Altogether, Adam lived 930 years, and then he died.
6When Seth had lived 105 years, he became the father[b] of
Enosh. 7And after he became the father of Enosh, Seth lived 807
years and had other sons and daughters. 8Altogether, Seth lived
912 years, and then he died.
9When Enosh had lived 90 years, he became the father of
Kenan. 10And after he became the father of Kenan, Enosh lived
815 years and had other sons and daughters. 11Altogether, Enosh
lived 905 years, and then he died.
12When Kenan had lived 70 years, he became the father of Mahalalel. 13And after he became the father of Mahalalel, Kenan lived
840 years and had other sons and daughters. 14Altogether, Kenan
lived 910 years, and then he died.
15When Mahalalel had lived 65 years, he became the father of
Jared. 16And after he became the father of Jared, Mahalalel lived
830 years and had other sons and daughters. 17Altogether, Mahalalel lived 895 years, and then he died.
18When Jared had lived 162 years, he became the father of
Enoch. 19And after he became the father of Enoch, Jared lived 800
years and had other sons and daughters. 20Altogether, Jared lived
962 years, and then he died.
21When Enoch had lived 65 years, he became the father of
Methuselah. 22And after he became the father of Methuselah,
Enoch walked with God 300 years and had other sons and daughters. 23Altogether, Enoch lived 365 years. 24Enoch walked with
God; then he was no more, because God took him away.
25When Methuselah had lived 187 years, he became the father
of Lamech. 26And after he became the father of Lamech, Methuselah lived 782 years and had other sons and daughters. 27Altogeth-
er, Methuselah lived 969 years, and then he died.
28When Lamech had lived 182 years, he had a son. 29He named
him Noah[c] and said, "He will comfort us in the labor and painful
toil of our hands caused by the ground the LORD has cursed."
30After Noah was born, Lamech lived 595 years and had other
sons and daughters. 31Altogether, Lamech lived 777 years, and
then he died.
32After Noah was 500 years old, he became the father of Shem,
Ham and Japheth.

The Flood

6 When men began to increase in number on the earth and
daughters were born to them, 2the sons of God saw that the
daughters of men were beautiful, and they married any of them
they chose. 3Then the LORD said, "My Spirit will not contend with[d]

[a] 2 Hebrew *adam* [b] 6 *Father* may mean *ancestor*; also in verses 7–26.
[c] 29 *Noah* sounds like the Hebrew for *comfort.* [d] 3 Or *My spirit will not remain in*

(5:24) Oh to walk with You each and every day, dear Lord, to walk in the paths of righteousness, to walk by the light of Your Word. Help me to know that even when I walk through the valley of the shadow of death, I need not fear, because You are with me. As I wander through this life, with its trials and temptations, its discouragements and detours, hold me tightly by the hand. Keep me with You, Lord, walking ever by Your side. (Ps 23:4)

O to be like Thee!
O to be like Thee,
Blessed Redeemer,
Pure as Thou art!
Come in Thy sweetness,
Come in Thy fullness;
Stamp Thine own image
Deep on my heart.

"O To Be Like Thee"
Thomas O. Chisholm (1866–1960)

(6:6–7) How tragic, O Lord, that we should cause You grief and fill Your heart with pain! You made us so that we might glorify You and give You delight. But our wickedness is great, polluting even our hidden thoughts. Yet we praise You, O God, that in Your great mercy You have chosen not to wipe us from the face of the earth; rather, You have chosen to wipe away our sins and transgressions. Cleanse us, wash us, free us, so that we might fear You and serve You. May we grieve Your Spirit no longer, but instead bring delight to Your heart. (Ps 51:1,9; 104:31; 147:11; Isa 43:25; Eph 4:30)

There's a wideness in God's mercy
Like the wideness of the sea;
There's a kindness in His justice
Which is more than liberty.
For the love of God is broader
Than the measure of man's mind;
And the heart of the Eternal
Is most wonderfully kind.

"There's a Wideness in God's Mercy"
Frederick W. Faber (1862)

(7:5) How I yearn to be like Noah, who "did all that the LORD commanded him"! What have You asked of me, Master, but to fear You, to walk in all Your ways, to love You, to serve You with all my heart and soul. But how, dear Lord, can I even begin to live so completely for You when I find it so natural to live for myself alone? Only by grace . . . as it transforms me, leading me into those good works for which You have created and redeemed me. Let Your grace take hold of my life, so that I might do all that You have commanded me. (Lev 19:37; Dt 10:12; Eph 2:8–10)

Faith and obedience are bound up in the same bundle. He that obeys God, trusts God; and he that trusts God, obeys God.
Charles Haddon Spurgeon (1834-1892)

man forever, for he is mortal[a]; his days will be a hundred and
twenty years."
[4]The Nephilim were on the earth in those days—and also afterward—when the sons of God went to the daughters of men and
had children by them. They were the heroes of old, men of
renown.
[5]The LORD saw how great man's wickedness on the earth had
become, and that every inclination of the thoughts of his heart was
only evil all the time. [6]The LORD was grieved that he had made man
on the earth, and his heart was filled with pain. [7]So the LORD said,
"I will wipe mankind, whom I have created, from the face of the
earth—men and animals, and creatures that move along the
ground, and birds of the air—for I am grieved that I have made
them." [8]But Noah found favor in the eyes of the LORD.

[9]This is the account of Noah.

Noah was a righteous man, blameless among the people of his
time, and he walked with God. [10]Noah had three sons: Shem, Ham
and Japheth.
[11]Now the earth was corrupt in God's sight and was full of violence. [12]God saw how corrupt the earth had become, for all the
people on earth had corrupted their ways. [13]So God said to Noah,
"I am going to put an end to all people, for the earth is filled with
violence because of them. I am surely going to destroy both them
and the earth. [14]So make yourself an ark of cypress[b] wood; make
rooms in it and coat it with pitch inside and out. [15]This is how you
are to build it: The ark is to be 450 feet long, 75 feet wide and 45
feet high.[c] [16]Make a roof for it and finish[d] the ark to within 18
inches[e] of the top. Put a door in the side of the ark and make
lower, middle and upper decks. [17]I am going to bring floodwaters
on the earth to destroy all life under the heavens, every creature
that has the breath of life in it. Everything on earth will perish.
[18]But I will establish my covenant with you, and you will enter the
ark—you and your sons and your wife and your sons' wives with
you. [19]You are to bring into the ark two of all living creatures,
male and female, to keep them alive with you. [20]Two of every kind
of bird, of every kind of animal and of every kind of creature that
moves along the ground will come to you to be kept alive. [21]You
are to take every kind of food that is to be eaten and store it away
as food for you and for them."
[22]Noah did everything just as God commanded him.
7 The LORD then said to Noah, "Go into the ark, you and your
whole family, because I have found you righteous in this generation. [2]Take with you seven[f] of every kind of clean animal, a
male and its mate, and two of every kind of unclean animal, a male
and its mate, [3]and also seven of every kind of bird, male and female, to keep their various kinds alive throughout the earth.
[4]Seven days from now I will send rain on the earth for forty days
and forty nights, and I will wipe from the face of the earth every
living creature I have made."
[5]And Noah did all that the LORD commanded him.
[6]Noah was six hundred years old when the floodwaters came
on the earth. [7]And Noah and his sons and his wife and his sons'

[a]3 Or *corrupt* [b]14 The meaning of the Hebrew for this word is uncertain.
[c]15 Hebrew *300 cubits long, 50 cubits wide and 30 cubits high* (about 140 meters long, 23 meters wide and 13.5 meters high) [d]16 Or *Make an opening for light by finishing*
[e]16 Hebrew *a cubit* (about 0.5 meter) [f]2 Or *seven pairs*; also in verse 3

wives entered the ark to escape the waters of the flood. 8Pairs of
clean and unclean animals, of birds and of all creatures that move
along the ground, 9male and female, came to Noah and entered
the ark, as God had commanded Noah. 10And after the seven days
the floodwaters came on the earth.
11In the six hundredth year of Noah's life, on the seventeenth
day of the second month—on that day all the springs of the great
deep burst forth, and the floodgates of the heavens were opened.
12And rain fell on the earth forty days and forty nights.
13On that very day Noah and his sons, Shem, Ham and Japheth,
together with his wife and the wives of his three sons, entered the
ark. 14They had with them every wild animal according to its kind,
all livestock according to their kinds, every creature that moves
along the ground according to its kind and every bird according
to its kind, everything with wings. 15Pairs of all creatures that have
the breath of life in them came to Noah and entered the ark. 16The
animals going in were male and female of every living thing, as
God had commanded Noah. Then the LORD shut him in.
17For forty days the flood kept coming on the earth, and as the
waters increased they lifted the ark high above the earth. 18The
waters rose and increased greatly on the earth, and the ark float-
ed on the surface of the water. 19They rose greatly on the earth,
and all the high mountains under the entire heavens were covered. 20The waters rose and covered the mountains to a depth of
more than twenty feet.[a,b] 21Every living thing that moved on the
earth perished—birds, livestock, wild animals, all the creatures
that swarm over the earth, and all mankind. 22Everything on dry
land that had the breath of life in its nostrils died. 23Every living
thing on the face of the earth was wiped out; men and animals and
the creatures that move along the ground and the birds of the air
were wiped from the earth. Only Noah was left, and those with him
in the ark.
24The waters flooded the earth for a hundred and fifty days.

8 But God remembered Noah and all the wild animals and the
livestock that were with him in the ark, and he sent a wind
over the earth, and the waters receded. 2Now the springs of the
deep and the floodgates of the heavens had been closed, and the
rain had stopped falling from the sky. 3The water receded steadily from the earth. At the end of the hundred and fifty days the water
had gone down, 4and on the seventeenth day of the seventh month
the ark came to rest on the mountains of Ararat. 5The waters continued to recede until the tenth month, and on the first day of the
tenth month the tops of the mountains became visible.
6After forty days Noah opened the window he had made in the
ark 7and sent out a raven, and it kept flying back and forth until
the water had dried up from the earth. 8Then he sent out a dove
to see if the water had receded from the surface of the ground.
9But the dove could find no place to set its feet because there was
water over all the surface of the earth; so it returned to Noah in the
ark. He reached out his hand and took the dove and brought it
back to himself in the ark. 10He waited seven more days and again
sent out the dove from the ark. 11When the dove returned to him
in the evening, there in its beak was a freshly plucked olive leaf!
Then Noah knew that the water had receded from the earth. 12He

[a] 20 Hebrew *fifteen cubits* (about 6.9 meters) [b] 20 Or *rose more than twenty feet, and the mountains were covered*

(7:13–16) Lord God, You who are the covenanting One, enclose me in Your grace and carry me over to a safer shore. May I be found secure in Christ, shut in by Your hand, and in Your great love and mercy protected in the cleansing flood. Without sail and without oar, I do not rely on my own craftiness or strength, but I lean wholly on Your hand to pilot me to higher ground.

Jesus, lover of my soul,
Let me to Thy bosom fly,
While the nearer waters roll,
While the tempest still is high:
Hide me, O my Savior, hide,
Till the storm of life is past:
Safe into the haven guide;
O receive my soul at last!

"Jesus, Lover of My Soul"
Charles Wesley (1740)

(8:1) "You, LORD, have never forsaken those who seek you." You did not tell Noah how long he would be in the ark, and You have not told me how long my trial will last either. But I praise You, O God, for Your great faithfulness. You answer me when I am in distress. "Remember your word to your servant, for you have given me hope. My comfort in my suffering is this: Your promise preserves my life." (Ps 9:10; 119:49–50)

He knows when we are spiritually ready to receive the blessing to our profit and His glory. Waiting in the sunshine of His love is what will ripen the soul for His blessing. Waiting under the cloud of trial, that breaks in showers of blessings, is as needful. Be assured that if God waits longer than you could wish, it is only to make the blessing doubly precious. God waited four thousand years, till the fullness of time, ere He sent His Son. Our times are in His hands; He will avenge His elect speedily; He will make haste for our help, and not delay one hour too long.

Andrew Murray (1828-1917)

(8:20–21) As one man's sacrifice was pleasing to You and caused You to show mercy to all mankind, may the aroma of my sacrifice of praise bring You pleasure and turn away Your wrath; and in return may it bring Your favor and mercy to the world around me. "For we are to God the aroma of Christ among those who are being saved and those who are perishing." (2Co 2:15)

Everything I am, everything I have,
Everything I can, I bring to You;
For You alone are worthy,
So I come to give You praise;
And everything I am I bring to You.

"Everything I Am"
Scott Dyer & Joe Horness (©1996)

waited seven more days and sent the dove out again, but this time
it did not return to him.
13By the first day of the first month of Noah's six hundred and
first year, the water had dried up from the earth. Noah then removed the covering from the ark and saw that the surface of the
ground was dry. 14By the twenty-seventh day of the second month
the earth was completely dry.
15Then God said to Noah, 16"Come out of the ark, you and
your wife and your sons and their wives. 17Bring out every kind
of living creature that is with you—the birds, the animals, and
all the creatures that move along the ground—so they can multiply on the earth and be fruitful and increase in number
upon it."
18So Noah came out, together with his sons and his wife and his
sons' wives. 19All the animals and all the creatures that move
along the ground and all the birds—everything that moves on the
earth—came out of the ark, one kind after another.
20Then Noah built an altar to the LORD and, taking some of all
the clean animals and clean birds, he sacrificed burnt offerings on
it. 21The LORD smelled the pleasing aroma and said in his heart:
"Never again will I curse the ground because of man, even
though[a] every inclination of his heart is evil from childhood. And
never again will I destroy all living creatures, as I have done.

22"As long as the earth endures,
seedtime and harvest,
cold and heat,
summer and winter,
day and night
will never cease."

God's Covenant With Noah

9 Then God blessed Noah and his sons, saying to them, "Be
fruitful and increase in number and fill the earth. 2The fear
and dread of you will fall upon all the beasts of the earth and all
the birds of the air, upon every creature that moves along the
ground, and upon all the fish of the sea; they are given into your
hands. 3Everything that lives and moves will be food for you. Just
as I gave you the green plants, I now give you everything.
4"But you must not eat meat that has its lifeblood still in it. 5And
for your lifeblood I will surely demand an accounting. I will demand an accounting from every animal. And from each man, too,
I will demand an accounting for the life of his fellow man.

6"Whoever sheds the blood of man,
by man shall his blood be shed;
for in the image of God
has God made man.

7As for you, be fruitful and increase in number; multiply on the
earth and increase upon it."
8Then God said to Noah and to his sons with him: 9"I now establish my covenant with you and with your descendants after you
10and with every living creature that was with you—the birds, the
livestock and all the wild animals, all those that came out of the
ark with you—every living creature on earth. 11I establish my

[a] 21 Or *man, for*

covenant with you: Never again will all life be cut off by the waters
of a flood; never again will there be a flood to destroy the earth."
12And God said, "This is the sign of the covenant I am making
between me and you and every living creature with you, a covenant
for all generations to come: 13I have set my rainbow in the clouds,
and it will be the sign of the covenant between me and the earth.
14Whenever I bring clouds over the earth and the rainbow appears
in the clouds, 15I will remember my covenant between me and you
and all living creatures of every kind. Never again will the waters
become a flood to destroy all life. 16Whenever the rainbow appears
in the clouds, I will see it and remember the everlasting covenant
between God and all living creatures of every kind on the earth."
17So God said to Noah, "This is the sign of the covenant I have
established between me and all life on the earth."

The Sons of Noah

18The sons of Noah who came out of the ark were Shem, Ham
and Japheth. (Ham was the father of Canaan.) 19These were the
three sons of Noah, and from them came the people who were
scattered over the earth.
20Noah, a man of the soil, proceeded[a] to plant a vineyard.
21When he drank some of its wine, he became drunk and lay uncovered inside his tent. 22Ham, the father of Canaan, saw his father's nakedness and told his two brothers outside. 23But Shem
and Japheth took a garment and laid it across their shoulders;
then they walked in backward and covered their father's nakedness. Their faces were turned the other way so that they would not
see their father's nakedness.
24When Noah awoke from his wine and found out what his
youngest son had done to him, 25he said,

"Cursed be Canaan!
The lowest of slaves
will he be to his brothers."

26He also said,

"Blessed be the LORD, the God of Shem!
May Canaan be the slave of Shem.[b]
27May God extend the territory of Japheth[c];
may Japheth live in the tents of Shem,
and may Canaan be his[d] slave."

28After the flood Noah lived 350 years. 29Altogether, Noah lived
950 years, and then he died.

The Table of Nations

10 This is the account of Shem, Ham and Japheth, Noah's sons,
who themselves had sons after the flood.

The Japhethites

2The sons[e] of Japheth:
Gomer, Magog, Madai, Javan, Tubal, Meshech and Tiras.
3The sons of Gomer:
Ashkenaz, Riphath and Togarmah.
4The sons of Javan:

[a] 20 Or *soil, was the first* [b] 26 Or *be his slave* [c] 27 *Japheth* sounds like the Hebrew for *extend.* [d] 27 Or *their* [e] 2 *Sons* may mean *descendants* or *successors* or *nations*; also in verses 3, 4, 6, 7, 20–23, 29 and 31.

(9:12–16) Having reached the other side of judgment, Noah encountered a glimpse of the glory that surrounds Your throne—the sign of Your covenant. The rainbow of Your grace contains every shade of light to counter every shadow of darkness. It is a constant reminder to us that Your grace is always sufficient and is present in every storm of life. (Eze 1:28)

The thicker the cloud the brighter the bow in the cloud. Thus, as threatening afflictions abound, encouraging consolations much more abound. The rainbow appears when one part of the sky is clear, which intimates mercy remembered in the midst of wrath; and the clouds are hemmed as it were with the rainbow, that they may not overspread the heavens, for the bow is colored rain or the edges of a cloud gilded.
Matthew Henry (1662-1714)

(9:22–27) Save me from the ways of the wicked, from those whose ways are perverse, who leave the straight paths to walk in dark ways. Let me walk in the ways of the upright and keep to the paths of the righteous. Let discretion protect me and understanding guard me. For the upright will live in the land and the blameless will remain in it; but the wicked will be cut off from the land, and the unfaithful will be torn from it. (Pr 2:11–14,20–22)

Elishah, Tarshish, the Kittim and the Rodanim.[a] 5(From
these the maritime peoples spread out into their territories by their clans within their nations, each with its own
language.)

The Hamites

6The sons of Ham:
Cush, Mizraim,[b] Put and Canaan.
7The sons of Cush:
Seba, Havilah, Sabtah, Raamah and Sabteca.
The sons of Raamah:
Sheba and Dedan.

8Cush was the father[c] of Nimrod, who grew to be a mighty warrior on the earth. 9He was a mighty hunter before the LORD; that is
why it is said, "Like Nimrod, a mighty hunter before the LORD."
10The first centers of his kingdom were Babylon, Erech, Akkad
and Calneh, in[d] Shinar.[e] 11From that land he went to Assyria,
where he built Nineveh, Rehoboth Ir,[f] Calah 12and Resen, which is
between Nineveh and Calah; that is the great city.

13Mizraim was the father of
the Ludites, Anamites, Lehabites, Naphtuhites, 14Pathru-
sites, Casluhites (from whom the Philistines came) and
Caphtorites.
15Canaan was the father of
Sidon his firstborn,[g] and of the Hittites, 16Jebusites, Amorites, Girgashites, 17Hivites, Arkites, Sinites, 18Arvadites,
Zemarites and Hamathites.

Later the Canaanite clans scattered 19and the borders of Canaan
reached from Sidon toward Gerar as far as Gaza, and then toward
Sodom, Gomorrah, Admah and Zeboiim, as far as Lasha.
20These are the sons of Ham by their clans and languages, in
their territories and nations.

The Semites

21Sons were also born to Shem, whose older brother was[h] Japheth; Shem was the ancestor of all the sons of Eber.

22The sons of Shem:
Elam, Asshur, Arphaxad, Lud and Aram.
23The sons of Aram:
Uz, Hul, Gether and Meshech.[i]
24Arphaxad was the father of[j] Shelah,
and Shelah the father of Eber.
25Two sons were born to Eber:
One was named Peleg,[k] because in his time the earth was
divided; his brother was named Joktan.
26Joktan was the father of
Almodad, Sheleph, Hazarmaveth, Jerah, 27Hadoram, Uzal,

[a] *4* Some manuscripts of the Masoretic Text and Samaritan Pentateuch (see also Septuagint and 1 Chron. 1:7); most manuscripts of the Masoretic Text *Dodanim* [b] *6* That is, Egypt; also in verse 13 [c] *8* *Father* may mean *ancestor* or *predecessor* or *founder*; also in verses 13, 15, 24 and 26. [d] *10* Or *Erech and Akkad—all of them in* [e] *10* That is, Babylonia [f] *11* Or *Nineveh with its city squares* [g] *15* Or *of the Sidonians, the foremost* [h] *21* Or *Shem, the older brother of* [i] *23* See Septuagint and 1 Chron. 1:17; Hebrew *Mash* [j] *24* Hebrew; Septuagint *father of Cainan, and Cainan was the father of* [k] *25* *Peleg* means *division.*

I have one passion only: It is he! It is he!
Count Nikolaus Ludwig von Zinzendorf (1700–1760)

(10:9) How will I be remembered, Lord, after I have left this earth? What will people say about me? What will be my lasting contribution to the world? Will I be known primarily as a successful entrepreneur, or a faithful disciple? Will I be remembered as a workaholic, or an approved worker for Your kingdom? Will my legacy be a life squandered on trivia, or a life invested in Your mission on earth? Help me to act today so that my life might be remembered as fully and faithfully lived. (2Ti 2:15)

O may all who come behind us find
us faithful;
May the fire of our devotion light
their way.
May the footprints that we leave,
Lead them to believe;
And the lives we live inspire them to
obey.
O may all who come behind us find
us faithful.

"Find Us Faithful"
Jon Mohr (©1987)

Diklah, 28Obal, Abimael, Sheba, 29Ophir, Havilah and
Jobab. All these were sons of Joktan.

30The region where they lived stretched from Mesha toward Sephar, in the eastern hill country.

31These are the sons of Shem by their clans and languages, in their territories and nations.

32These are the clans of Noah's sons, according to their lines of descent, within their nations. From these the nations spread out over the earth after the flood.

The Tower of Babel

11 Now the whole world had one language and a common speech. 2As men moved eastward,[a] they found a plain in Shinar[b] and settled there.

3They said to each other, "Come, let's make bricks and bake them thoroughly." They used brick instead of stone, and tar for
mortar. 4Then they said, "Come, let us build ourselves a city, with a tower that reaches to the heavens, so that we may make a name for ourselves and not be scattered over the face of the whole earth."

5But the LORD came down to see the city and the tower that the
men were building. 6The LORD said, "If as one people speaking the same language they have begun to do this, then nothing they
plan to do will be impossible for them. 7Come, let us go down and
confuse their language so they will not understand each other."

8So the LORD scattered them from there over all the earth, and
they stopped building the city. 9That is why it was called Babel[c]—because there the LORD confused the language of the whole world. From there the LORD scattered them over the face of the whole earth.

From Shem to Abram

10This is the account of Shem.

Two years after the flood, when Shem was 100 years old, he became the father[d] of Arphaxad. 11And after he became the father of Arphaxad, Shem lived 500 years and had other sons and daughters.

12When Arphaxad had lived 35 years, he became the father of
Shelah. 13And after he became the father of Shelah, Arphaxad lived 403 years and had other sons and daughters.[e]

14When Shelah had lived 30 years, he became the father of
Eber. 15And after he became the father of Eber, Shelah lived 403 years and had other sons and daughters.

16When Eber had lived 34 years, he became the father of Peleg.
17And after he became the father of Peleg, Eber lived 430 years and had other sons and daughters.

18When Peleg had lived 30 years, he became the father of Reu.
19And after he became the father of Reu, Peleg lived 209 years and had other sons and daughters.

20When Reu had lived 32 years, he became the father of Serug.

[a] 2 Or *from the east*; or *in the east* [b] 2 That is, Babylonia [c] 9 That is, Babylon; *Babel* sounds like the Hebrew for *confused*. [d] 10 *Father* may mean *ancestor*; also in verses 11–25. [e] 12,13 Hebrew; Septuagint (see also Luke 3:35, 36 and note at Gen. 10:24) *35 years, he became the father of Cainan. 13And after he became the father of Cainan, Arphaxad lived 430 years and had other sons and daughters, and then he died. When Cainan had lived 130 years, he became the father of Shelah. And after he became the father of Shelah, Cainan lived 330 years and had other sons and daughters*

Ancient of Days! Except thou deign
Upon the finished task to smile,
The workman's hand hath toiled in vain,
To hew the rock and rear the pile.
William Cullen Bryant (1794–1878)

(11:4) God, You are the One who searches my heart and examines my mind. You graciously expose my hidden motives, the self-promoting designs I so piously hide from others but cannot keep hidden from You. I confess that, even when I am serving You, Lord, a part of me yearns for human approval, to make a name for myself. "Create in me a pure heart, O God," that I might serve You with genuine humility and full integrity. (Ps 51:10; Jer 17:10; 1Co 4:5)

I want a principle within
Of watchful godly fear,
A sensibility of sin,
A pain to feel it near,
Help me the first approach to feel
Of pride or wrong desire;
To catch the wandering of my will,
And quench the kindling fire.
"I Want a Principle Within"
Charles Wesley (1749)

(12:1) Lord, even as You called Abram to leave his people, so You call us to leave behind our primary loyalties in order to follow You. We respond to this call, sometimes with faith, sometimes with hesitation. It is frightening, Lord, to abandon the semblance of security and "go to the land You will show us." We want to know in advance where the land is and whether we will prosper there. But You simply offer Yourself as one worthy of all trust, and issue the invitation: "Come, follow me." (Mk 1:17)

You know no disturbing voice? God never points out for you a pathway altogether different from the one you had planned? Then, my brother, you are living still in the land of slavery, in the land of darkness.

G. Campbell Morgan (1863–1945)

(12:3) Lord, when You called one particular man and through him chose to bless one particular people, Your vision encompassed all peoples on earth. We marvel at the depth of Your mercy, the breadth of Your grace that brings salvation even to the ends of the earth. May the day come when "all the ends of the earth will remember and turn to [You], and all the families of the nations bow down before [You]." Reveal Your righteousness, O Lord, so that all nations will come and worship You, praising You forever and ever! (Ps 22:27; 45:17; Isa 49:6; Rev 15:4)

21 And after he became the father of Serug, Reu lived 207 years
and had other sons and daughters.
22 When Serug had lived 30 years, he became the father of
Nahor. 23 And after he became the father of Nahor, Serug lived 200
years and had other sons and daughters.
24 When Nahor had lived 29 years, he became the father of
Terah. 25 And after he became the father of Terah, Nahor lived 119
years and had other sons and daughters.
26 After Terah had lived 70 years, he became the father of
Abram, Nahor and Haran.

27 This is the account of Terah.

Terah became the father of Abram, Nahor and Haran. And
Haran became the father of Lot. 28 While his father Terah was still
alive, Haran died in Ur of the Chaldeans, in the land of his birth.
29 Abram and Nahor both married. The name of Abram's wife was
Sarai, and the name of Nahor's wife was Milcah; she was the
daughter of Haran, the father of both Milcah and Iscah. 30 Now
Sarai was barren; she had no children.
31 Terah took his son Abram, his grandson Lot son of Haran,
and his daughter-in-law Sarai, the wife of his son Abram, and together they set out from Ur of the Chaldeans to go to Canaan. But
when they came to Haran, they settled there.
32 Terah lived 205 years, and he died in Haran.

The Call of Abram

12 The LORD had said to Abram, "Leave your country, your people and your father's household and go to the land I will show you.

2 "I will make you into a great nation
and I will bless you;
I will make your name great,
and you will be a blessing.
3 I will bless those who bless you,
and whoever curses you I will curse;
and all peoples on earth
will be blessed through you."

4 So Abram left, as the LORD had told him; and Lot went with
him. Abram was seventy-five years old when he set out from
Haran. 5 He took his wife Sarai, his nephew Lot, all the possessions they had accumulated and the people they had acquired in
Haran, and they set out for the land of Canaan, and they arrived
there.
6 Abram traveled through the land as far as the site of the great
tree of Moreh at Shechem. At that time the Canaanites were in the
land. 7 The LORD appeared to Abram and said, "To your offspring[a]
I will give this land." So he built an altar there to the LORD, who
had appeared to him.
8 From there he went on toward the hills east of Bethel and
pitched his tent, with Bethel on the west and Ai on the east. There
he built an altar to the LORD and called on the name of the LORD.
9 Then Abram set out and continued toward the Negev.

[a] 7 Or *seed*

Abram in Egypt

10Now there was a famine in the land, and Abram went down to
Egypt to live there for a while because the famine was severe. 11As
he was about to enter Egypt, he said to his wife Sarai, "I know
what a beautiful woman you are. 12When the Egyptians see you,
they will say, 'This is his wife.' Then they will kill me but will let
you live. 13Say you are my sister, so that I will be treated well for
your sake and my life will be spared because of you."

14When Abram came to Egypt, the Egyptians saw that she was a
very beautiful woman. 15And when Pharaoh's officials saw her,
they praised her to Pharaoh, and she was taken into his palace.
16He treated Abram well for her sake, and Abram acquired sheep
and cattle, male and female donkeys, menservants and maidservants, and camels.

17But the LORD inflicted serious diseases on Pharaoh and his
household because of Abram's wife Sarai. 18So Pharaoh summoned Abram. "What have you done to me?" he said. "Why didn't
you tell me she was your wife? 19Why did you say, 'She is my sister,' so that I took her to be my wife? Now then, here is your wife.
Take her and go!" 20Then Pharaoh gave orders about Abram to his
men, and they sent him on his way, with his wife and everything he
had.

Abram and Lot Separate

13 So Abram went up from Egypt to the Negev, with his wife
and everything he had, and Lot went with him. 2Abram had
become very wealthy in livestock and in silver and gold.

3From the Negev he went from place to place until he came to
Bethel, to the place between Bethel and Ai where his tent had been
earlier 4and where he had first built an altar. There Abram called
on the name of the LORD.

5Now Lot, who was moving about with Abram, also had flocks
and herds and tents. 6But the land could not support them while
they stayed together, for their possessions were so great that they
were not able to stay together. 7And quarreling arose between
Abram's herdsmen and the herdsmen of Lot. The Canaanites and
Perizzites were also living in the land at that time.

8So Abram said to Lot, "Let's not have any quarreling between
you and me, or between your herdsmen and mine, for we are
brothers. 9Is not the whole land before you? Let's part company. If
you go to the left, I'll go to the right; if you go to the right, I'll go
to the left."

10Lot looked up and saw that the whole plain of the Jordan was
well watered, like the garden of the LORD, like the land of Egypt, toward Zoar. (This was before the LORD destroyed Sodom and Gomorrah.) 11So Lot chose for himself the whole plain of the Jordan
and set out toward the east. The two men parted company:
12Abram lived in the land of Canaan, while Lot lived among the cities of the plain and pitched his tents near Sodom. 13Now the men
of Sodom were wicked and were sinning greatly against the LORD.

14The LORD said to Abram after Lot had parted from him, "Lift
up your eyes from where you are and look north and south, east
and west. 15All the land that you see I will give to you and your offspring[a] forever. 16I will make your offspring like the dust of the
earth, so that if anyone could count the dust, then your offspring

[a] 15 Or *seed*; also in verse 16

(12:11–13) We have just esteemed Abram, the man of faith who left everything familiar because he trusted You, Lord. Now we see the flip side of faith—the struggle, the doubt, the fear. With Your promise of blessing still echoing in his ears, Abram compromised Sarai's wellbeing because he lacked confidence in You. How sad, and how sadly familiar to me. I am like Abram, receiving Your promises in faith one moment, doubting in fear the next. Help me, Lord, to trust You always.

(13:8–16) Thank You, Lord, for Your trustworthiness and justice. When Abram, who had the heart of a true peacemaker, settled a feud by offering Lot any portion of the land he desired, Lot took the most beautiful plain in sight. But You were faithful to Abram and gave him back everything he had lost in his gracious gesture. Teach me to trust You in all things as Abram did, to place relationships above possessions, and to know that all good things come from You. Lord, Your Word confirms that the inheritance you choose for us is better than anything we could gain for ourselves. (Ps 16:1–6; Jas 1:17)

God always gives his very best to those who leave the choice with him.

James Hudson Taylor (1832-1905)

(14:18–20) Our God, You have filled the Old Testament with snapshots that help us to know Jesus, to receive Your gifts of grace, and to worship You in response. Reflected in the mysterious figure of Melchizedek we see Jesus, who is indeed our "Melchizedek," our "King of Righteousness." Even as this priestly king once offered bread and wine to feed hungry bodies, so Jesus offers bread and wine—His broken body and His shed blood—to feed our famished souls. When we meet Jesus, the King of kings and the priest of God Most High, not only are we blessed, but we are also led to bless You for the victory in which we share. Receive our "tenth," O Lord, as a sign that we belong to You completely. We bless You with the offering of our lives! (Ps 110:4; Heb 5:6–10; 6:20; 7:23–27)

could be counted. 17Go, walk through the length and breadth of
the land, for I am giving it to you."
18So Abram moved his tents and went to live near the great
trees of Mamre at Hebron, where he built an altar to the LORD.

Abram Rescues Lot

14 At this time Amraphel king of Shinar,[a] Arioch king of Ellasar, Kedorlaomer king of Elam and Tidal king of Goiim
2went to war against Bera king of Sodom, Birsha king of Gomor-
rah, Shinab king of Admah, Shemeber king of Zeboiim, and the
king of Bela (that is, Zoar). 3All these latter kings joined forces in
the Valley of Siddim (the Salt Sea[b]). 4For twelve years they had
been subject to Kedorlaomer, but in the thirteenth year they rebelled.
5In the fourteenth year, Kedorlaomer and the kings allied with
him went out and defeated the Rephaites in Ashteroth Karnaim,
the Zuzites in Ham, the Emites in Shaveh Kiriathaim 6and the Horites in the hill country of Seir, as far as El Paran near the desert.
7Then they turned back and went to En Mishpat (that is, Kadesh),
and they conquered the whole territory of the Amalekites, as well
as the Amorites who were living in Hazazon Tamar.
8Then the king of Sodom, the king of Gomorrah, the king of
Admah, the king of Zeboiim and the king of Bela (that is, Zoar)
marched out and drew up their battle lines in the Valley of Siddim
9against Kedorlaomer king of Elam, Tidal king of Goiim, Amraphel king of Shinar and Arioch king of Ellasar—four kings against
five. 10Now the Valley of Siddim was full of tar pits, and when the
kings of Sodom and Gomorrah fled, some of the men fell into
them and the rest fled to the hills. 11The four kings seized all the
goods of Sodom and Gomorrah and all their food; then they went
away. 12They also carried off Abram's nephew Lot and his possessions, since he was living in Sodom.
13One who had escaped came and reported this to Abram the
Hebrew. Now Abram was living near the great trees of Mamre the
Amorite, a brother[c] of Eshcol and Aner, all of whom were allied
with Abram. 14When Abram heard that his relative had been taken
captive, he called out the 318 trained men born in his household
and went in pursuit as far as Dan. 15During the night Abram divided his men to attack them and he routed them, pursuing them
as far as Hobah, north of Damascus. 16He recovered all the goods
and brought back his relative Lot and his possessions, together
with the women and the other people.
17After Abram returned from defeating Kedorlaomer and the
kings allied with him, the king of Sodom came out to meet him in
the Valley of Shaveh (that is, the King's Valley).
18Then Melchizedek king of Salem[d] brought out bread and
wine. He was priest of God Most High, 19and he blessed Abram,
saying,

"Blessed be Abram by God Most High,
Creator[e] of heaven and earth.
20And blessed be[f] God Most High,
who delivered your enemies into your hand."

Then Abram gave him a tenth of everything.

[a] *1* That is, Babylonia; also in verse 9 [b] *3* That is, the Dead Sea [c] *13* Or *a relative*; or *an ally* [d] *18* That is, Jerusalem [e] *19* Or *Possessor*; also in verse 22 [f] *20* Or *And praise be to*

21The king of Sodom said to Abram, "Give me the people and
keep the goods for yourself."
22But Abram said to the king of Sodom, "I have raised my hand
to the LORD, God Most High, Creator of heaven and earth, and have
taken an oath 23that I will accept nothing belonging to you, not
even a thread or the thong of a sandal, so that you will never be
able to say, 'I made Abram rich.' 24I will accept nothing but what
my men have eaten and the share that belongs to the men who
went with me—to Aner, Eshcol and Mamre. Let them have their
share."

God's Covenant With Abram

15 After this, the word of the LORD came to Abram in a vision:

"Do not be afraid, Abram.
I am your shield,[a]
your very great reward.[b]"

2But Abram said, "O Sovereign LORD, what can you give me
since I remain childless and the one who will inherit[c] my estate is
Eliezer of Damascus?" 3And Abram said, "You have given me no
children; so a servant in my household will be my heir."
4Then the word of the LORD came to him: "This man will not be
your heir, but a son coming from your own body will be your
heir." 5He took him outside and said, "Look up at the heavens and
count the stars—if indeed you can count them." Then he said to
him, "So shall your offspring be."
6Abram believed the LORD, and he credited it to him as righteousness.
7He also said to him, "I am the LORD, who brought you out of Ur
of the Chaldeans to give you this land to take possession of it."
8But Abram said, "O Sovereign LORD, how can I know that I will
gain possession of it?"
9So the LORD said to him, "Bring me a heifer, a goat and a ram,
each three years old, along with a dove and a young pigeon."
10Abram brought all these to him, cut them in two and
arranged the halves opposite each other; the birds, however, he
did not cut in half. 11Then birds of prey came down on the carcasses, but Abram drove them away.
12As the sun was setting, Abram fell into a deep sleep, and a
thick and dreadful darkness came over him. 13Then the LORD said
to him, "Know for certain that your descendants will be strangers
in a country not their own, and they will be enslaved and mistreated four hundred years. 14But I will punish the nation they
serve as slaves, and afterward they will come out with great possessions. 15You, however, will go to your fathers in peace and be
buried at a good old age. 16In the fourth generation your descendants will come back here, for the sin of the Amorites has not yet
reached its full measure."
17When the sun had set and darkness had fallen, a smoking
firepot with a blazing torch appeared and passed between the
pieces. 18On that day the LORD made a covenant with Abram and
said, "To your descendants I give this land, from the river[d] of
Egypt to the great river, the Euphrates— 19the land of the Kenites,

[a] *1* Or *sovereign* [b] *1* Or *shield; / your reward will be very great* [c] *2* The meaning of the Hebrew for this phrase is uncertain. [d] *18* Or *Wadi*

Why and how is God to be loved? God himself is the reason why; without limit is how.

Saint Bernard of Clairvaux (1090-1153)

(15:1) O God, You are my shield, my helper, my fortress, my deliverer, my strength, my refuge. You are my glorious sword, my eternal protection, my loving God. You are the horn of my salvation, the rock in whom I take refuge, the One who gives glory and lifts my head. My heart trusts in You and leaps for joy! (Ps 3:3; 18:2; 28:7)

The God of Abraham praise,
Who reigns enthroned above;
Ancient of everlasting days,
And God of love.
Jehovah, great I Am,
By earth and heav'n confessed;
I bow and bless the sacred name
Forever blest.

"The God of Abraham Praise"
Thomas Olivers (1770)

(16:13) O God who sees us, nothing in all creation is hidden from Your sight. In Your mercy You look upon those who are like Hagar—the oppressed, the lowly, the alien, the fatherless, the widow. How comforting to remember that Your "seeing" is not just a passing glance or a disinterested observation. It is personal, focused, and continues from the past, through today's sunlight and shadow, and into the future. Your seeing encompasses all the days of our lives, which You have foreseen all along. (Ge 31:42; Ex 3:9; Ps 138:6; 146:9)

No distant Lord have I,
Loving afar to be;
Made flesh for me, he cannot rest
Until he rests in me.
Brother in joy and pain,
Bone of my bone was he,
Now—intimacy closer still,
He dwells himself in me.

Maltbie D. Babcock (1858-1901)

(17:5) To Abram and Sarai You gave new names, Lord. In You they became Abraham and Sarah, names that embodied their new identities. So You continue to do with Your people. Those once called Deserted will be named, "My Delight is In Her," because You delight in Your people. Those once called Desolate will be named "Married," because they will be married to You alone. By Your grace we are also receiving a new name. As children are named for their fathers, so we are being named after You. And so we will be forever, Your people, Your delight, Your beloved. (Isa 62:1–4; Rev 3:12)

Kenizzites, Kadmonites, 20 Hittites, Perizzites, Rephaites, 21 Amorites, Canaanites, Girgashites and Jebusites."

Hagar and Ishmael

16 Now Sarai, Abram's wife, had borne him no children. But
she had an Egyptian maidservant named Hagar; 2 so she said
to Abram, "The LORD has kept me from having children. Go, sleep
with my maidservant; perhaps I can build a family through her."
Abram agreed to what Sarai said. 3 So after Abram had been living in Canaan ten years, Sarai his wife took her Egyptian maidservant Hagar and gave her to her husband to be his wife. 4 He slept
with Hagar, and she conceived.

When she knew she was pregnant, she began to despise her mistress. 5 Then Sarai said to Abram, "You are responsible for the
wrong I am suffering. I put my servant in your arms, and now that
she knows she is pregnant, she despises me. May the LORD judge
between you and me."

6 "Your servant is in your hands," Abram said. "Do with her
whatever you think best." Then Sarai mistreated Hagar; so she fled
from her.

7 The angel of the LORD found Hagar near a spring in the desert;
it was the spring that is beside the road to Shur. 8 And he said,
"Hagar, servant of Sarai, where have you come from, and where
are you going?"

"I'm running away from my mistress Sarai," she answered.

9 Then the angel of the LORD told her, "Go back to your mistress
and submit to her." 10 The angel added, "I will so increase your descendants that they will be too numerous to count."

11 The angel of the LORD also said to her:

"You are now with child
and you will have a son.
You shall name him Ishmael,[a]
for the LORD has heard of your misery.
12 He will be a wild donkey of a man;
his hand will be against everyone
and everyone's hand against him,
and he will live in hostility
toward[b] all his brothers."

13 She gave this name to the LORD who spoke to her: "You are the
God who sees me," for she said, "I have now seen[c] the One who
sees me." 14 That is why the well was called Beer Lahai Roi[d]; it is
still there, between Kadesh and Bered.

15 So Hagar bore Abram a son, and Abram gave the name Ishmael to the son she had borne. 16 Abram was eighty-six years old
when Hagar bore him Ishmael.

The Covenant of Circumcision

17 When Abram was ninety-nine years old, the LORD appeared
to him and said, "I am God Almighty[e]; walk before me and
be blameless. 2 I will confirm my covenant between me and you
and will greatly increase your numbers."

3 Abram fell facedown, and God said to him, 4 "As for me, this is
my covenant with you: You will be the father of many nations. 5 No

[a] *11 Ishmael* means *God hears.* [b] *12* Or *live to the east / of* [c] *13* Or *seen the back of* [d] *14 Beer Lahai Roi* means *well of the Living One who sees me.* [e] *1* Hebrew *El-Shaddai*

longer will you be called Abram[a]; your name will be Abraham,[b] for
I have made you a father of many nations. [6]I will make you very
fruitful; I will make nations of you, and kings will come from you.
[7]I will establish my covenant as an everlasting covenant between
me and you and your descendants after you for the generations to
come, to be your God and the God of your descendants after you.
[8]The whole land of Canaan, where you are now an alien, I will give
as an everlasting possession to you and your descendants after you;
and I will be their God."
[9]Then God said to Abraham, "As for you, you must keep my covenant, you and your descendants after you for the generations to
come. [10]This is my covenant with you and your descendants after
you, the covenant you are to keep: Every male among you shall be
circumcised. [11]You are to undergo circumcision, and it will be the
sign of the covenant between me and you. [12]For the generations to
come every male among you who is eight days old must be circumcised, including those born in your household or bought with
money from a foreigner—those who are not your offspring.
[13]Whether born in your household or bought with your money,
they must be circumcised. My covenant in your flesh is to be an
everlasting covenant. [14]Any uncircumcised male, who has not been
circumcised in the flesh, will be cut off from his people; he has
broken my covenant."
[15]God also said to Abraham, "As for Sarai your wife, you are no
longer to call her Sarai; her name will be Sarah. [16]I will bless her
and will surely give you a son by her. I will bless her so that she will
be the mother of nations; kings of peoples will come from her."
[17]Abraham fell facedown; he laughed and said to himself, "Will
a son be born to a man a hundred years old? Will Sarah bear a
child at the age of ninety?" [18]And Abraham said to God, "If only
Ishmael might live under your blessing!"
[19]Then God said, "Yes, but your wife Sarah will bear you a son,
and you will call him Isaac.[c] I will establish my covenant with him
as an everlasting covenant for his descendants after him. [20]And as
for Ishmael, I have heard you: I will surely bless him; I will make
him fruitful and will greatly increase his numbers. He will be the
father of twelve rulers, and I will make him into a great nation.
[21]But my covenant I will establish with Isaac, whom Sarah will
bear to you by this time next year." [22]When he had finished speaking with Abraham, God went up from him.
[23]On that very day Abraham took his son Ishmael and all those
born in his household or bought with his money, every male in his
household, and circumcised them, as God told him. [24]Abraham
was ninety-nine years old when he was circumcised, [25]and his son
Ishmael was thirteen; [26]Abraham and his son Ishmael were both
circumcised on that same day. [27]And every male in Abraham's
household, including those born in his household or bought from
a foreigner, was circumcised with him.

The Three Visitors

18 The LORD appeared to Abraham near the great trees of
Mamre while he was sitting at the entrance to his tent in
the heat of the day. [2]Abraham looked up and saw three men standing nearby. When he saw them, he hurried from the entrance of
his tent to meet them and bowed low to the ground.

[a] 5 *Abram* means *exalted father.* [b] 5 *Abraham* means *father of many.* [c] 19 *Isaac* means *he laughs.*

(17:7) Sovereign Lord, as it was with Abraham, so it is with us today. You are the God who establishes a covenant with us. We know You, not because of our own efforts but because You have initiated the relationship. Your new covenant depends solely on the blood of Jesus poured out for us on the cross. We cannot earn Your favor or negotiate a deal with You. The terms are still determined by You alone. Praise be to You, Lord, for Your sovereignty and Your grace, by which You have become our God and we have become Your people. (Lk 22:20)

(17:17) In response to Your promise, Mighty God, Abraham did not merely snicker. No, he fell on his face and laughed with fervent unbelief. Once again this man of exceptional faith stumbled, overcome by the ridiculousness of Your grace. I wonder, is Your grace still too generous, too wonderful, too unpredictable? Is my failure to be startled or even to laugh more a sign of my apathy than of my faith? Has Your amazing love become commonplace to me? "Restore to me the joy of your salvation" so that I might be filled with awe and say, "[I] have seen remarkable things today!" (Ps 51:12; Lk 5:26).

God is the great reality. His resources are available and endless. His promises are real and glorious, beyond our wildest dreams.

J. B. Phillips (1906–1982)

(18:14) "Is anything too hard for the LORD?" You once asked this question of Abraham and Sarah as they chuckled in unbelief. And Your Spirit keeps asking me the same, Omnipotent God, when I struggle to trust You. My mind says, "No, of course not. You can do everything." But my hesitant heart often says, "Well, I'm not so sure." Grant to me the faith of Mary, who heard the angel say "Nothing is impossible with God," and responded, "I am the Lord's servant." Give me the confidence of Jeremiah, who prayed, "Ah, Sovereign LORD, . . . nothing is too hard for you!" (Jer 32:17; Lk 1:37–38)

He is able, more than able
To accomplish what concerns me today.
He is able, more than able
To handle anything that comes my way
He is able, more than able
To do much more than I could ever dream.
He is able, more than able
To make me what He wants me to be.

"He is Able"
Rory Noland and
Greg Ferguson (©1989)

3He said, "If I have found favor in your eyes, my lord,[a] do not
pass your servant by. 4Let a little water be brought, and then you
may all wash your feet and rest under this tree. 5Let me get you
something to eat, so you can be refreshed and then go on your
way—now that you have come to your servant."
"Very well," they answered, "do as you say."
6So Abraham hurried into the tent to Sarah. "Quick," he said,
"get three seahs[b] of fine flour and knead it and bake some bread."
7Then he ran to the herd and selected a choice, tender calf and
gave it to a servant, who hurried to prepare it. 8He then brought
some curds and milk and the calf that had been prepared, and set
these before them. While they ate, he stood near them under a tree.
9"Where is your wife Sarah?" they asked him.
"There, in the tent," he said.
10Then the LORD[c] said, "I will surely return to you about this
time next year, and Sarah your wife will have a son."
Now Sarah was listening at the entrance to the tent, which was
behind him. 11Abraham and Sarah were already old and well advanced in years, and Sarah was past the age of childbearing. 12So
Sarah laughed to herself as she thought, "After I am worn out and
my master[d] is old, will I now have this pleasure?"
13Then the LORD said to Abraham, "Why did Sarah laugh and say,
'Will I really have a child, now that I am old?' 14Is anything too
hard for the LORD? I will return to you at the appointed time next
year and Sarah will have a son."
15Sarah was afraid, so she lied and said, "I did not laugh."
But he said, "Yes, you did laugh."

Abraham Pleads for Sodom

16When the men got up to leave, they looked down toward
Sodom, and Abraham walked along with them to see them on their
way. 17Then the LORD said, "Shall I hide from Abraham what I am
about to do? 18Abraham will surely become a great and powerful
nation, and all nations on earth will be blessed through him. 19For
I have chosen him, so that he will direct his children and his
household after him to keep the way of the LORD by doing what is
right and just, so that the LORD will bring about for Abraham what
he has promised him."
20Then the LORD said, "The outcry against Sodom and Gomorrah
is so great and their sin so grievous 21that I will go down and see
if what they have done is as bad as the outcry that has reached me.
If not, I will know."
22The men turned away and went toward Sodom, but Abraham
remained standing before the LORD.[e] 23Then Abraham approached
him and said: "Will you sweep away the righteous with the wicked?
24What if there are fifty righteous people in the city? Will you really
sweep it away and not spare[f] the place for the sake of the fifty righteous people in it? 25Far be it from you to do such a thing—to kill
the righteous with the wicked, treating the righteous and the
wicked alike. Far be it from you! Will not the Judge[g] of all the
earth do right?"
26The LORD said, "If I find fifty righteous people in the city of
Sodom, I will spare the whole place for their sake."

[a] 3 Or *O Lord* [b] 6 That is, probably about 20 quarts (about 22 liters) [c] 10 Hebrew *Then he* [d] 12 Or *husband* [e] 22 Masoretic Text; an ancient Hebrew scribal tradition *but the LORD remained standing before Abraham* [f] 24 Or *forgive*; also in verse 26 [g] 25 Or *Ruler*

27Then Abraham spoke up again: "Now that I have been so bold
as to speak to the Lord, though I am nothing but dust and ashes,
28what if the number of the righteous is five less than fifty? Will you
destroy the whole city because of five people?"

"If I find forty-five there," he said, "I will not destroy it."

29Once again he spoke to him, "What if only forty are found
there?"

He said, "For the sake of forty, I will not do it."

30Then he said, "May the Lord not be angry, but let me speak.
What if only thirty can be found there?"

He answered, "I will not do it if I find thirty there."

31Abraham said, "Now that I have been so bold as to speak to the
Lord, what if only twenty can be found there?"

He said, "For the sake of twenty, I will not destroy it."

32Then he said, "May the Lord not be angry, but let me speak just
once more. What if only ten can be found there?"

He answered, "For the sake of ten, I will not destroy it."

33When the LORD had finished speaking with Abraham, he left,
and Abraham returned home.

Sodom and Gomorrah Destroyed

19 The two angels arrived at Sodom in the evening, and Lot was
sitting in the gateway of the city. When he saw them, he got up
to meet them and bowed down with his face to the ground. 2"My
lords," he said, "please turn aside to your servant's house. You can
wash your feet and spend the night and then go on your way early
in the morning."

"No," they answered, "we will spend the night in the square."

3But he insisted so strongly that they did go with him and entered
his house. He prepared a meal for them, baking bread without yeast,
and they ate. 4Before they had gone to bed, all the men from every
part of the city of Sodom—both young and old—surrounded the
house. 5They called to Lot, "Where are the men who came to you
tonight? Bring them out to us so that we can have sex with them."

6Lot went outside to meet them and shut the door behind him
7and said, "No, my friends. Don't do this wicked thing. 8Look, I
have two daughters who have never slept with a man. Let me bring
them out to you, and you can do what you like with them. But don't
do anything to these men, for they have come under the protection
of my roof."

9"Get out of our way," they replied. And they said, "This fellow
came here as an alien, and now he wants to play the judge! We'll
treat you worse than them." They kept bringing pressure on Lot and
moved forward to break down the door.

10But the men inside reached out and pulled Lot back into the
house and shut the door. 11Then they struck the men who were at
the door of the house, young and old, with blindness so that they
could not find the door.

12The two men said to Lot, "Do you have anyone else here—
sons-in-law, sons or daughters, or anyone else in the city who belongs to you? Get them out of here, 13because we are going to destroy this place. The outcry to the LORD against its people is so great
that he has sent us to destroy it."

14So Lot went out and spoke to his sons-in-law, who were
pledged to marry[a] his daughters. He said, "Hurry and get out of

[a] 14 Or *were married to*

(18:16–33) You alone are God Almighty, incomparable, awesome, Creator of heaven and earth. All Your works are just and true. Yet You confide in those who fear You; and You listen to us! You heed our prayers, our pleadings, our protestations. You hear us even when we question You or argue a case against You. In the mystery of Your will, You teach us to come before You, not only with humility but also with a boldness that is almost brazen. Lord, teach us to pray! (Ps 25:14; Jer 12:1; Hab 1:2–13; Lk 11:1–8; Heb 4:16; Rev 15:3)

More things are wrought by prayer
Than this world dreams of.

Alfred, Lord Tennyson (1809-1892)

this place, because the LORD is about to destroy the city!" But his
sons-in-law thought he was joking.
15With the coming of dawn, the angels urged Lot, saying,
"Hurry! Take your wife and your two daughters who are here, or
you will be swept away when the city is punished."
16When he hesitated, the men grasped his hand and the hands
of his wife and of his two daughters and led them safely out of the
city, for the LORD was merciful to them. 17As soon as they had
brought them out, one of them said, "Flee for your lives! Don't
look back, and don't stop anywhere in the plain! Flee to the mountains or you will be swept away!"
18But Lot said to them, "No, my lords,[a] please! 19Your[b] servant
has found favor in your[b] eyes, and you[b] have shown great kindness to me in sparing my life. But I can't flee to the mountains; this
disaster will overtake me, and I'll die. 20Look, here is a town near
enough to run to, and it is small. Let me flee to it—it is very small,
isn't it? Then my life will be spared."
21He said to him, "Very well, I will grant this request too; I will
not overthrow the town you speak of. 22But flee there quickly, because I cannot do anything until you reach it." (That is why the
town was called Zoar.[c])
23By the time Lot reached Zoar, the sun had risen over the land.
24Then the LORD rained down burning sulfur on Sodom and Gomorrah—from the LORD out of the heavens. 25Thus he overthrew
those cities and the entire plain, including all those living in the
cities—and also the vegetation in the land. 26But Lot's wife looked
back, and she became a pillar of salt.
27Early the next morning Abraham got up and returned to the
place where he had stood before the LORD. 28He looked down toward Sodom and Gomorrah, toward all the land of the plain, and
he saw dense smoke rising from the land, like smoke from a furnace.
29So when God destroyed the cities of the plain, he remembered Abraham, and he brought Lot out of the catastrophe that
overthrew the cities where Lot had lived.

Lot and His Daughters

30Lot and his two daughters left Zoar and settled in the mountains, for he was afraid to stay in Zoar. He and his two daughters
lived in a cave. 31One day the older daughter said to the younger,
"Our father is old, and there is no man around here to lie with us,
as is the custom all over the earth. 32Let's get our father to drink
wine and then lie with him and preserve our family line through
our father."
33That night they got their father to drink wine, and the older
daughter went in and lay with him. He was not aware of it when
she lay down or when she got up.
34The next day the older daughter said to the younger, "Last
night I lay with my father. Let's get him to drink wine again tonight,
and you go in and lie with him so we can preserve our family line
through our father." 35So they got their father to drink wine that
night also, and the younger daughter went and lay with him. Again
he was not aware of it when she lay down or when she got up.
36So both of Lot's daughters became pregnant by their father.
37The older daughter had a son, and she named him Moab[d]; he is

[a] 18 Or *No, Lord*; or *No, my lord* [b] 19 The Hebrew is singular. [c] 22 *Zoar* means *small.* [d] 37 *Moab* sounds like the Hebrew for *from father.*

Fear. His modus operandi is to manipulate you with the mysterious, to taunt you with the unknown. Fear of death, fear of failure, fear of God, fear of tomorrow—his arsenal is vast. His goal? To create cowardly, joyless souls. He doesn't want you to make the journey to the mountain. He figures if he can rattle you enough, you will take your eyes off the peaks and settle for a dull existence in the flatlands.

Max L. Lucado (1955-)

(19:16) How often, Lord, have I heard Your gracious call . . . and hesitated! How often have I begun to act in faith, only to let fear drag me down! But in Your mercy, You reach out to me. You lift me up and lead me in the way of salvation. You are One who says: "I am the LORD, your God, who takes hold of your right hand and says to you, Do not fear; I will help you." Thank You, Lord my God, for showing the wonder of Your great love by saving me with Your strong hand! (Ps 17:7; Isa 41:13)

the father of the Moabites of today. 38The younger daughter also had a son, and she named him Ben-Ammi[a]; he is the father of the Ammonites of today.

Abraham and Abimelech

20 Now Abraham moved on from there into the region of the Negev and lived between Kadesh and Shur. For a while he stayed in Gerar, 2and there Abraham said of his wife Sarah, "She is my sister." Then Abimelech king of Gerar sent for Sarah and took her.

3But God came to Abimelech in a dream one night and said to him, "You are as good as dead because of the woman you have taken; she is a married woman."

4Now Abimelech had not gone near her, so he said, "Lord, will you destroy an innocent nation? 5Did he not say to me, 'She is my sister,' and didn't she also say, 'He is my brother'? I have done this with a clear conscience and clean hands."

6Then God said to him in the dream, "Yes, I know you did this with a clear conscience, and so I have kept you from sinning against me. That is why I did not let you touch her. 7Now return the man's wife, for he is a prophet, and he will pray for you and you will live. But if you do not return her, you may be sure that you and all yours will die."

8Early the next morning Abimelech summoned all his officials, and when he told them all that had happened, they were very much afraid. 9Then Abimelech called Abraham in and said, "What have you done to us? How have I wronged you that you have brought such great guilt upon me and my kingdom? You have done things to me that should not be done." 10And Abimelech asked Abraham, "What was your reason for doing this?"

11Abraham replied, "I said to myself, 'There is surely no fear of God in this place, and they will kill me because of my wife.' 12Besides, she really is my sister, the daughter of my father though not of my mother; and she became my wife. 13And when God had me wander from my father's household, I said to her, 'This is how you can show your love to me: Everywhere we go, say of me, "He is my brother." ' "

14Then Abimelech brought sheep and cattle and male and female slaves and gave them to Abraham, and he returned Sarah his wife to him. 15And Abimelech said, "My land is before you; live wherever you like."

16To Sarah he said, "I am giving your brother a thousand shekels[b] of silver. This is to cover the offense against you before all who are with you; you are completely vindicated."

17Then Abraham prayed to God, and God healed Abimelech, his wife and his slave girls so they could have children again, 18for the LORD had closed up every womb in Abimelech's household because of Abraham's wife Sarah.

The Birth of Isaac

21 Now the LORD was gracious to Sarah as he had said, and the LORD did for Sarah what he had promised. 2Sarah became pregnant and bore a son to Abraham in his old age, at the very time God had promised him. 3Abraham gave the name Isaac[c] to the son Sarah bore him. 4When his son Isaac was eight days old,

[a] *38 Ben-Ammi* means *son of my people.* [b] *16* That is, about 25 pounds (about 11.5 kilograms) [c] *3 Isaac* means *he laughs.*

(20:1–18) We have been here before, haven't we, Lord? Abraham, who once trusted You, now feared for his life. His doubt endangered the safety of his own wife. As You did before in Egypt, once again You not only delivered Abraham and Sarah but also showered blessings upon them. We have been here before, haven't we, Lord . . . in those times when I doubted Your goodness and acted in fear? As You did with Abraham and Sarah, so also You have repeatedly delivered me from my folly and blessed me through Your inexhaustible grace. Thanks be to You, O God, for grace that is greater than all my sin, all my fear, all my foolishness! (Ge 12:11–13)

This is a wise, sane Christian faith: that a man commit himself, his life, and his hopes to God; that God undertakes the special protection of that man; that therefore that man ought not to be afraid of anything.

George MacDonald (1824–1905)

Abraham circumcised him, as God commanded him. 5Abraham was a hundred years old when his son Isaac was born to him.

6Sarah said, "God has brought me laughter, and everyone who hears about this will laugh with me." 7And she added, "Who would have said to Abraham that Sarah would nurse children? Yet I have borne him a son in his old age."

Hagar and Ishmael Sent Away

8The child grew and was weaned, and on the day Isaac was weaned Abraham held a great feast. 9But Sarah saw that the son whom Hagar the Egyptian had borne to Abraham was mocking, 10and she said to Abraham, "Get rid of that slave woman and her son, for that slave woman's son will never share in the inheritance with my son Isaac."

11The matter distressed Abraham greatly because it concerned his son. 12But God said to him, "Do not be so distressed about the boy and your maidservant. Listen to whatever Sarah tells you, because it is through Isaac that your offspring[a] will be reckoned. 13I will make the son of the maidservant into a nation also, because he is your offspring."

14Early the next morning Abraham took some food and a skin of water and gave them to Hagar. He set them on her shoulders and then sent her off with the boy. She went on her way and wandered in the desert of Beersheba.

15When the water in the skin was gone, she put the boy under one of the bushes. 16Then she went off and sat down nearby, about a bowshot away, for she thought, "I cannot watch the boy die." And as she sat there nearby, she[b] began to sob.

17God heard the boy crying, and the angel of God called to Hagar from heaven and said to her, "What is the matter, Hagar? Do not be afraid; God has heard the boy crying as he lies there. 18Lift the boy up and take him by the hand, for I will make him into a great nation."

19Then God opened her eyes and she saw a well of water. So she went and filled the skin with water and gave the boy a drink.

20God was with the boy as he grew up. He lived in the desert and became an archer. 21While he was living in the Desert of Paran, his mother got a wife for him from Egypt.

The Treaty at Beersheba

22At that time Abimelech and Phicol the commander of his forces said to Abraham, "God is with you in everything you do. 23Now swear to me here before God that you will not deal falsely with me or my children or my descendants. Show to me and the country where you are living as an alien the same kindness I have shown to you."

24Abraham said, "I swear it."

25Then Abraham complained to Abimelech about a well of water that Abimelech's servants had seized. 26But Abimelech said, "I don't know who has done this. You did not tell me, and I heard about it only today."

27So Abraham brought sheep and cattle and gave them to Abimelech, and the two men made a treaty. 28Abraham set apart seven ewe lambs from the flock, 29and Abimelech asked Abraham,

[a] 12 Or *seed* [b] 16 Hebrew; Septuagint *the child*

(21:3–7) Oh the tender irony of Your grace, Lord! When Abraham laughed at the absurdity of Your promise, You instructed him to name his son "Isaac," meaning, "he laughs." Though Sarah also snickered in unbelief when hearing that You would give her a son, Your grace was not restrained. She gave birth to Isaac, saying, "God has brought me laughter." O Lord, You turn our sneers into laughter, our doubt into faith. Your goodness, too wonderful to be believed, surprises and delights our hearts. (Ge 17:15–19; 18:12–15)

To believe in God is to know that all the rules will be fair—and that there will be wonderful surprises!

Sister Corita (1918–1986)

(21:17–20) You are the God who gave Ishmael his name, a name that reveals who You are—the "God who hears." Always faithful to Your promises, You heard when Ishmael cried out. Not only did You hear, but You also provided water to quench his thirst. As You were centuries ago, so You are today. Your faithfulness continues still. Your promises endure forever. This very moment You hear the cry of Your people and deliver us from trouble. We praise You, O God who hears us! We praise You for Your faithfulness to all generations! (Ge 16:10–11; Ps 34:17; 145:13)

"What is the meaning of these seven ewe lambs you have set apart
by themselves?"
30He replied, "Accept these seven lambs from my hand as a witness that I dug this well."
31So that place was called Beersheba,[a] because the two men
swore an oath there.
32After the treaty had been made at Beersheba, Abimelech and
Phicol the commander of his forces returned to the land of the
Philistines. 33Abraham planted a tamarisk tree in Beersheba, and
there he called upon the name of the LORD, the Eternal God. 34And
Abraham stayed in the land of the Philistines for a long time.

Abraham Tested

22 Some time later God tested Abraham. He said to him,
"Abraham!"
"Here I am," he replied.
2Then God said, "Take your son, your only son, Isaac, whom
you love, and go to the region of Moriah. Sacrifice him there as a
burnt offering on one of the mountains I will tell you about."
3Early the next morning Abraham got up and saddled his donkey. He took with him two of his servants and his son Isaac. When
he had cut enough wood for the burnt offering, he set out for the
place God had told him about. 4On the third day Abraham looked
up and saw the place in the distance. 5He said to his servants,
"Stay here with the donkey while I and the boy go over there. We
will worship and then we will come back to you."
6Abraham took the wood for the burnt offering and placed it on
his son Isaac, and he himself carried the fire and the knife. As the
two of them went on together, 7Isaac spoke up and said to his father Abraham, "Father?"
"Yes, my son?" Abraham replied.
"The fire and wood are here," Isaac said, "but where is the
lamb for the burnt offering?"
8Abraham answered, "God himself will provide the lamb for the
burnt offering, my son." And the two of them went on together.
9When they reached the place God had told him about, Abraham built an altar there and arranged the wood on it. He bound
his son Isaac and laid him on the altar, on top of the wood. 10Then
he reached out his hand and took the knife to slay his son. 11But
the angel of the LORD called out to him from heaven, "Abraham!
Abraham!"
"Here I am," he replied.
12"Do not lay a hand on the boy," he said. "Do not do anything
to him. Now I know that you fear God, because you have not withheld from me your son, your only son."
13Abraham looked up and there in a thicket he saw a ram[b]
caught by its horns. He went over and took the ram and sacrificed
it as a burnt offering instead of his son. 14So Abraham called that
place The LORD Will Provide. And to this day it is said, "On the
mountain of the LORD it will be provided."
15The angel of the LORD called to Abraham from heaven a second time 16and said, "I swear by myself, declares the LORD, that
because you have done this and have not withheld your son, your
only son, 17I will surely bless you and make your descendants as

[a] 31 *Beersheba* can mean *well of seven* or *well of the oath.* [b] 13 Many manuscripts of the Masoretic Text, Samaritan Pentateuch, Septuagint and Syriac; most manuscripts of the Masoretic Text *a ram behind* ⌞*him*⌟

Your only Son, no sin to hide,
But You have sent Him from Your
side
To walk upon this guilty sod
And to become the Lamb of God.

O Lamb of God, sweet Lamb of God,
I love the holy Lamb of God,
O wash me in His precious blood,
My Jesus Christ, the Lamb of God

"Lamb of God"
Twila Paris (©1985)

(22:8–14) Gracious God, You will provide! When You call me to do that which I cannot begin to accomplish on my own, You will provide. When Your ways confound my understanding, You will provide. When I am weak, hungry and lonely, You will provide. When I realize how lost I am in sin, You will provide. Indeed, You did provide, giving Your one and only Son as a sacrifice so that I might be justified before You and live eternally with You. Loving God, You have always provided, and You will provide again! (Jn 3:16; Ro 3:23–26)

Doth He not know what is best for us, and what conduceth most unto His own glory? So is it to live in the exercise of faith that if God calls us unto any of those things which are peculiarly dreadful unto our natures, He will give us such supplies of spiritual strength and patience as shall enable us to undergo them, if not with ease and joy, yet with peace and quietness beyond our expectation.

John Owen (1616-1683)

numerous as the stars in the sky and as the sand on the seashore.
Your descendants will take possession of the cities of their enemies, 18and through your offspring[a] all nations on earth will be
blessed, because you have obeyed me."
19Then Abraham returned to his servants, and they set off together for Beersheba. And Abraham stayed in Beersheba.

Nahor's Sons

20Some time later Abraham was told, "Milcah is also a mother;
she has borne sons to your brother Nahor: 21Uz the firstborn, Buz
his brother, Kemuel (the father of Aram), 22Kesed, Hazo, Pildash,
Jidlaph and Bethuel." 23Bethuel became the father of Rebekah.
Milcah bore these eight sons to Abraham's brother Nahor. 24His
concubine, whose name was Reumah, also had sons: Tebah,
Gaham, Tahash and Maacah.

The Death of Sarah

23 Sarah lived to be a hundred and twenty-seven years old.
2She died at Kiriath Arba (that is, Hebron) in the land of
Canaan, and Abraham went to mourn for Sarah and to weep over
her.
3Then Abraham rose from beside his dead wife and spoke to
the Hittites.[b] He said, 4"I am an alien and a stranger among you.
Sell me some property for a burial site here so I can bury my
dead."
5The Hittites replied to Abraham, 6"Sir, listen to us. You are a
mighty prince among us. Bury your dead in the choicest of our
tombs. None of us will refuse you his tomb for burying your
dead."
7Then Abraham rose and bowed down before the people of the
land, the Hittites. 8He said to them, "If you are willing to let me
bury my dead, then listen to me and intercede with Ephron son of
Zohar on my behalf 9so he will sell me the cave of Machpelah,
which belongs to him and is at the end of his field. Ask him to sell
it to me for the full price as a burial site among you."
10Ephron the Hittite was sitting among his people and he
replied to Abraham in the hearing of all the Hittites who had come
to the gate of his city. 11"No, my lord," he said. "Listen to me; I
give[c] you the field, and I give[c] you the cave that is in it. I give[c] it to
you in the presence of my people. Bury your dead."
12Again Abraham bowed down before the people of the land
13and he said to Ephron in their hearing, "Listen to me, if you will.
I will pay the price of the field. Accept it from me so I can bury my
dead there."
14Ephron answered Abraham, 15"Listen to me, my lord; the
land is worth four hundred shekels[d] of silver, but what is that between me and you? Bury your dead."
16Abraham agreed to Ephron's terms and weighed out for him
the price he had named in the hearing of the Hittites: four hundred shekels of silver, according to the weight current among the
merchants.
17So Ephron's field in Machpelah near Mamre—both the field
and the cave in it, and all the trees within the borders of the
field—was deeded 18to Abraham as his property in the presence
of all the Hittites who had come to the gate of the city. 19Afterward

[a] 18 Or *seed* [b] 3 Or *the sons of Heth*; also in verses 5, 7, 10, 16, 18 and 20 [c] 11 Or *sell* [d] 15 That is, about 10 pounds (about 4.5 kilograms)

(22:18) Your Word tells us that because of Abraham's faith and obedience You not only blessed him and his family but also blessed all the nations of the earth. It was because of Abraham's faith that You rescued Lot from Sodom. It was because of Abraham's faith that You looked after Isaac and his generations. It is, even today, because of Abraham's faith that we have a relationship with You through Your beloved Son, Who was Abraham's earthly offspring. Give me faith like Abraham's, Lord, and the spirit of obedience that so endeared him to You. Allow my faith to bless others—many others—and to reach beyond myself and my small circle of influence, even into the uttermost parts of the world. (Ge 19:29; 26:4–5; Ro 4; 2Co 10:15; Gal 3:6–9)

Abraham buried his wife Sarah in the cave in the field of Machpelah near Mamre (which is at Hebron) in the land of Canaan.
20So the field and the cave in it were deeded to Abraham by the
Hittites as a burial site.

Isaac and Rebekah

24 Abraham was now old and well advanced in years, and the
LORD had blessed him in every way. 2He said to the chief[a]
servant in his household, the one in charge of all that he had, "Put
your hand under my thigh. 3I want you to swear by the LORD, the
God of heaven and the God of earth, that you will not get a wife for
my son from the daughters of the Canaanites, among whom I am
living, 4but will go to my country and my own relatives and get a
wife for my son Isaac."
5The servant asked him, "What if the woman is unwilling to
come back with me to this land? Shall I then take your son back
to the country you came from?"
6"Make sure that you do not take my son back there," Abraham
said. 7"The LORD, the God of heaven, who brought me out of my father's household and my native land and who spoke to me and
promised me on oath, saying, 'To your offspring[b] I will give this
land'—he will send his angel before you so that you can get a wife
for my son from there. 8If the woman is unwilling to come back
with you, then you will be released from this oath of mine. Only do
not take my son back there." 9So the servant put his hand under
the thigh of his master Abraham and swore an oath to him concerning this matter.
10Then the servant took ten of his master's camels and left, taking with him all kinds of good things from his master. He set out
for Aram Naharaim[c] and made his way to the town of Nahor. 11He
had the camels kneel down near the well outside the town; it was
toward evening, the time the women go out to draw water.
12Then he prayed, "O LORD, God of my master Abraham, give
me success today, and show kindness to my master Abraham.
13See, I am standing beside this spring, and the daughters of the
townspeople are coming out to draw water. 14May it be that when
I say to a girl, 'Please let down your jar that I may have a drink,'
and she says, 'Drink, and I'll water your camels too'—let her be
the one you have chosen for your servant Isaac. By this I will know
that you have shown kindness to my master."
15Before he had finished praying, Rebekah came out with her
jar on her shoulder. She was the daughter of Bethuel son of Milcah, who was the wife of Abraham's brother Nahor. 16The girl was
very beautiful, a virgin; no man had ever lain with her. She went
down to the spring, filled her jar and came up again.
17The servant hurried to meet her and said, "Please give me a
little water from your jar."
18"Drink, my lord," she said, and quickly lowered the jar to
her hands and gave him a drink.
19After she had given him a drink, she said, "I'll draw water for
your camels too, until they have finished drinking." 20So she
quickly emptied her jar into the trough, ran back to the well to
draw more water, and drew enough for all his camels. 21Without
saying a word, the man watched her closely to learn whether or
not the LORD had made his journey successful.

[a] *2* Or *oldest* [b] *7* Or *seed* [c] *10* That is, Northwest Mesopotamia

(24:12–15) Lord, even before Abraham's servant had finished praying You answered his prayer. Sometimes You answer my prayers so quickly that my head spins. I am startled by Your nearness and reminded of Your goodness. Thank You for those astonishing times when Your prompt answers to my prayers bolster my faith and revitalize my efforts to pray.

Between the humble and contrite heart and the majesty of heaven, there are no barriers; the only password is prayer.
Hosea Ballou (1771-1852)

When we are obedient, God guides our steps and our stops.
Corrie ten Boom (1892–1983)

(24:26–27) Thank You for Your faithfulness to faith-filled people. Abraham's servant recognized that his own success was the result of Your faithfulness to Abraham. As with Abraham, may Your favor be so present in my life that it will inspire others to call on Your name. As a result of Your faithfulness to my faith-fullness, may people see Your handiwork and give You praise.

22When the camels had finished drinking, the man took out a
gold nose ring weighing a beka[a] and two gold bracelets weighing
ten shekels.[b] 23Then he asked, "Whose daughter are you? Please
tell me, is there room in your father's house for us to spend the
night?"
24She answered him, "I am the daughter of Bethuel, the son
that Milcah bore to Nahor." 25And she added, "We have plenty of
straw and fodder, as well as room for you to spend the night."
26Then the man bowed down and worshiped the LORD, 27saying,
"Praise be to the LORD, the God of my master Abraham, who has
not abandoned his kindness and faithfulness to my master. As for
me, the LORD has led me on the journey to the house of my master's relatives."
28The girl ran and told her mother's household about these
things. 29Now Rebekah had a brother named Laban, and he hurried out to the man at the spring. 30As soon as he had seen the
nose ring, and the bracelets on his sister's arms, and had heard
Rebekah tell what the man said to her, he went out to the man and
found him standing by the camels near the spring. 31"Come, you
who are blessed by the LORD," he said. "Why are you standing out
here? I have prepared the house and a place for the camels."
32So the man went to the house, and the camels were unloaded.
Straw and fodder were brought for the camels, and water for him
and his men to wash their feet. 33Then food was set before him,
but he said, "I will not eat until I have told you what I have to say."
"Then tell us," ⌞Laban⌟ said.
34So he said, "I am Abraham's servant. 35The LORD has blessed
my master abundantly, and he has become wealthy. He has given
him sheep and cattle, silver and gold, menservants and maidservants, and camels and donkeys. 36My master's wife Sarah has
borne him a son in her[c] old age, and he has given him everything
he owns. 37And my master made me swear an oath, and said, 'You
must not get a wife for my son from the daughters of the Canaanites, in whose land I live, 38but go to my father's family and to my
own clan, and get a wife for my son.'
39"Then I asked my master, 'What if the woman will not come
back with me?'
40"He replied, 'The LORD, before whom I have walked, will send
his angel with you and make your journey a success, so that you
can get a wife for my son from my own clan and from my father's
family. 41Then, when you go to my clan, you will be released from
my oath even if they refuse to give her to you—you will be released from my oath.'
42"When I came to the spring today, I said, 'O LORD, God of my
master Abraham, if you will, please grant success to the journey
on which I have come. 43See, I am standing beside this spring; if
a maiden comes out to draw water and I say to her, "Please let me
drink a little water from your jar," 44and if she says to me, "Drink,
and I'll draw water for your camels too," let her be the one the
LORD has chosen for my master's son.'
45"Before I finished praying in my heart, Rebekah came out,
with her jar on her shoulder. She went down to the spring and
drew water, and I said to her, 'Please give me a drink.'
46"She quickly lowered her jar from her shoulder and said,

[a] 22 That is, about 1/5 ounce (about 5.5 grams) [b] 22 That is, about 4 ounces (about 110 grams) [c] 36 Or *his*

‘Drink, and I’ll water your camels too.’ So I drank, and she watered the camels also.
47 “I asked her, ‘Whose daughter are you?’
“She said, ‘The daughter of Bethuel son of Nahor, whom Milcah
bore to him.’
“Then I put the ring in her nose and the bracelets on her arms,
48 and I bowed down and worshiped the LORD. I praised the LORD,
the God of my master Abraham, who had led me on the right road
to get the granddaughter of my master’s brother for his son.
49 Now if you will show kindness and faithfulness to my master, tell
me; and if not, tell me, so I may know which way to turn.”
50 Laban and Bethuel answered, “This is from the LORD; we can
say nothing to you one way or the other. 51 Here is Rebekah; take
her and go, and let her become the wife of your master’s son, as
the LORD has directed.”
52 When Abraham’s servant heard what they said, he bowed
down to the ground before the LORD. 53 Then the servant brought
out gold and silver jewelry and articles of clothing and gave them
to Rebekah; he also gave costly gifts to her brother and to her
mother. 54 Then he and the men who were with him ate and drank
and spent the night there.
When they got up the next morning, he said, “Send me on my
way to my master.”
55 But her brother and her mother replied, “Let the girl remain
with us ten days or so; then you[a] may go.”
56 But he said to them, “Do not detain me, now that the LORD has
granted success to my journey. Send me on my way so I may go to
my master.”
57 Then they said, “Let’s call the girl and ask her about it.” 58 So
they called Rebekah and asked her, “Will you go with this man?”
“I will go,” she said.
59 So they sent their sister Rebekah on her way, along with her
nurse and Abraham’s servant and his men. 60 And they blessed Rebekah and said to her,

“Our sister, may you increase
to thousands upon thousands;
may your offspring possess
the gates of their enemies.”

61 Then Rebekah and her maids got ready and mounted their
camels and went back with the man. So the servant took Rebekah
and left.
62 Now Isaac had come from Beer Lahai Roi, for he was living in
the Negev. 63 He went out to the field one evening to meditate,[b]
and as he looked up, he saw camels approaching. 64 Rebekah also
looked up and saw Isaac. She got down from her camel 65 and
asked the servant, “Who is that man in the field coming to
meet us?”
“He is my master,” the servant answered. So she took her veil
and covered herself.
66 Then the servant told Isaac all he had done. 67 Isaac brought
her into the tent of his mother Sarah, and he married Rebekah. So
she became his wife, and he loved her; and Isaac was comforted
after his mother’s death.

[a] 55 Or *she* [b] 63 The meaning of the Hebrew for this word is uncertain.

(24:50–51) Thank You, Lord, for those times when You make Your will so clear that I cannot misconstrue it, when all that I can say is, “This is from the LORD.” Yet knowing Your will is one thing; doing it is another. By Your Spirit, help me to do what You command. May my passion be not only to know Your truth but to live it each day. May the prayer of my heart be, “Teach me your way, O LORD, and I will walk in your truth.” (Ps 86:11)

O Will, that willest good alone,
Lead thou the way, thou guidest best;
A silent child, I follow on,
And trusting lean upon thy breast.
And if in gloom I see thee not,
I lean upon thy love unknown;
In me thy blessed will is wrought,
If I will nothing of my own.

Gerhard Tersteegen (1697-1769)

The Death of Abraham

25 Abraham took[a] another wife, whose name was Keturah.
2She bore him Zimran, Jokshan, Medan, Midian, Ishbak
and Shuah. 3Jokshan was the father of Sheba and Dedan; the descendants of Dedan were the Asshurites, the Letushites and the
Leummites. 4The sons of Midian were Ephah, Epher, Hanoch,
Abida and Eldaah. All these were descendants of Keturah.
5Abraham left everything he owned to Isaac. 6But while he was
still living, he gave gifts to the sons of his concubines and sent
them away from his son Isaac to the land of the east.
7Altogether, Abraham lived a hundred and seventy-five years.
8Then Abraham breathed his last and died at a good old age, an
old man and full of years; and he was gathered to his people. 9His
sons Isaac and Ishmael buried him in the cave of Machpelah near
Mamre, in the field of Ephron son of Zohar the Hittite, 10the field
Abraham had bought from the Hittites.[b] There Abraham was
buried with his wife Sarah. 11After Abraham's death, God blessed
his son Isaac, who then lived near Beer Lahai Roi.

Ishmael's Sons

12This is the account of Abraham's son Ishmael, whom Sarah's
maidservant, Hagar the Egyptian, bore to Abraham.
13These are the names of the sons of Ishmael, listed in the
order of their birth: Nebaioth the firstborn of Ishmael, Kedar,
Adbeel, Mibsam, 14Mishma, Dumah, Massa, 15Hadad, Tema,
Jetur, Naphish and Kedemah. 16These were the sons of Ishmael,
and these are the names of the twelve tribal rulers according to
their settlements and camps. 17Altogether, Ishmael lived a hundred and thirty-seven years. He breathed his last and died, and
he was gathered to his people. 18His descendants settled in the
area from Havilah to Shur, near the border of Egypt, as you
go toward Asshur. And they lived in hostility toward[c] all their
brothers.

Jacob and Esau

19This is the account of Abraham's son Isaac.

Abraham became the father of Isaac, 20and Isaac was forty
years old when he married Rebekah daughter of Bethuel the Aramean from Paddan Aram[d] and sister of Laban the Aramean.
21Isaac prayed to the LORD on behalf of his wife, because she
was barren. The LORD answered his prayer, and his wife Rebekah
became pregnant. 22The babies jostled each other within her, and
she said, "Why is this happening to me?" So she went to inquire
of the LORD.
23The LORD said to her,

"Two nations are in your womb,
  and two peoples from within you will be separated;
one people will be stronger than the other,
  and the older will serve the younger."

24When the time came for her to give birth, there were twin
boys in her womb. 25The first to come out was red, and his whole
body was like a hairy garment; so they named him Esau.[e] 26After

(25:22–24) Lord, just as You had specific knowledge about the babies in Rebekah's womb, so Your plans for each of us preceded our birth. You know our appearance and our personalities. You know our future. You know our strengths and weaknesses, and You foresee the relationships we will eventually share. How we thank You for Your ever-present involvement in our lives. We praise You that all our days have been ordained for us by You, "written in Your book before one of them came to be." (Ps 139:16)

[a] *1* Or *had taken* [b] *10* Or *the sons of Heth* [c] *18* Or *lived to the east of* [d] *20* That is, Northwest Mesopotamia [e] *25* *Esau* may mean *hairy*; he was also called Edom, which means *red*.

this, his brother came out, with his hand grasping Esau's heel; so he was named Jacob.[a] Isaac was sixty years old when Rebekah gave birth to them.

27 The boys grew up, and Esau became a skillful hunter, a man of the open country, while Jacob was a quiet man, staying among the tents. 28 Isaac, who had a taste for wild game, loved Esau, but Rebekah loved Jacob.

29 Once when Jacob was cooking some stew, Esau came in from the open country, famished. 30 He said to Jacob, "Quick, let me have some of that red stew! I'm famished!" (That is why he was also called Edom.[b])

31 Jacob replied, "First sell me your birthright."

32 "Look, I am about to die," Esau said. "What good is the birthright to me?"

33 But Jacob said, "Swear to me first." So he swore an oath to him, selling his birthright to Jacob.

34 Then Jacob gave Esau some bread and some lentil stew. He ate and drank, and then got up and left.

So Esau despised his birthright.

Isaac and Abimelech

26 Now there was a famine in the land—besides the earlier famine of Abraham's time—and Isaac went to Abimelech king of the Philistines in Gerar. 2 The LORD appeared to Isaac and said, "Do not go down to Egypt; live in the land where I tell you to live. 3 Stay in this land for a while, and I will be with you and will bless you. For to you and your descendants I will give all these lands and will confirm the oath I swore to your father Abraham. 4 I will make your descendants as numerous as the stars in the sky and will give them all these lands, and through your offspring[c] all nations on earth will be blessed, 5 because Abraham obeyed me and kept my requirements, my commands, my decrees and my laws." 6 So Isaac stayed in Gerar.

7 When the men of that place asked him about his wife, he said, "She is my sister," because he was afraid to say, "She is my wife." He thought, "The men of this place might kill me on account of Rebekah, because she is beautiful."

8 When Isaac had been there a long time, Abimelech king of the Philistines looked down from a window and saw Isaac caressing his wife Rebekah. 9 So Abimelech summoned Isaac and said, "She is really your wife! Why did you say, 'She is my sister'?"

Isaac answered him, "Because I thought I might lose my life on account of her."

10 Then Abimelech said, "What is this you have done to us? One of the men might well have slept with your wife, and you would have brought guilt upon us."

11 So Abimelech gave orders to all the people: "Anyone who molests this man or his wife shall surely be put to death."

12 Isaac planted crops in that land and the same year reaped a hundredfold, because the LORD blessed him. 13 The man became rich, and his wealth continued to grow until he became very wealthy. 14 He had so many flocks and herds and servants that the Philistines envied him. 15 So all the wells that his father's servants had dug in the time of his father Abraham, the Philistines stopped up, filling them with earth.

[a] 26 *Jacob* means *he grasps the heel* (figuratively, *he deceives*). [b] 30 *Edom* means *red.*
[c] 4 Or *seed*

(26:1–11) We have seen this before, Lord. Isaac is his father's boy—like father in faith, like father in fear. Do You ever get tired of us, Lord? Of our redundancy in sinning? Of our tendency to receive Your promises so gladly and then to doubt Your trustworthiness so promptly? Of our penchant for passing on our sins and fears to our children? No, You are a God who does not grow tired or weary, whose unlimited patience endures, whose compassions never fail. Great is Your faithfulness! (Ge 12:10–20; 20:1–17; Isa 40:28; La 3:22–23; 1Ti 1:16)

Our ground of hope is that God does not weary of mankind.

Ralph Washington Sockman (1889-1970)

God incarnate is the end of fear; and the heart that realizes that he is in the midst . . . will be quiet in the midst of alarm.
F. B. Meyer (1847-1929)

(26:24) "Do not be afraid, for I am with you." As You once pledged to Isaac, Lord, so You have always promised to Your people, through Moses to the Israelites, through David to Solomon, through Jesus to the disciples—and to us. What could be better than this? You are always with us, heavenly Father, through Your Son, Immanuel, "God with us," and through Your Spirit, who lives in each of us. Help us to trust Your indwelling presence, so that we might live and serve boldly, without fear. (Dt 31:8; 1Ch 28:20; Mt 1:23; 28:20; Ro 8:9–11)

16 Then Abimelech said to Isaac, "Move away from us; you
have become too powerful for us."
17 So Isaac moved away from there and encamped in the Valley of Gerar and settled there. 18 Isaac reopened the wells that
had been dug in the time of his father Abraham, which the Philistines had stopped up after Abraham died, and he gave them
the same names his father had given them.
19 Isaac's servants dug in the valley and discovered a well of
fresh water there. 20 But the herdsmen of Gerar quarreled with
Isaac's herdsmen and said, "The water is ours!" So he named the
well Esek,[a] because they disputed with him. 21 Then they dug another well, but they quarreled over that one also; so he named it
Sitnah.[b] 22 He moved on from there and dug another well, and
no one quarreled over it. He named it Rehoboth,[c] saying, "Now
the LORD has given us room and we will flourish in the land."
23 From there he went up to Beersheba. 24 That night the LORD
appeared to him and said, "I am the God of your father Abraham. Do not be afraid, for I am with you; I will bless you and will
increase the number of your descendants for the sake of my servant Abraham."
25 Isaac built an altar there and called on the name of the
LORD. There he pitched his tent, and there his servants dug a
well.
26 Meanwhile, Abimelech had come to him from Gerar, with
Ahuzzath his personal adviser and Phicol the commander of his
forces. 27 Isaac asked them, "Why have you come to me, since
you were hostile to me and sent me away?"
28 They answered, "We saw clearly that the LORD was with you;
so we said, 'There ought to be a sworn agreement between us'—
between us and you. Let us make a treaty with you 29 that you will
do us no harm, just as we did not molest you but always treated
you well and sent you away in peace. And now you are blessed by
the LORD."
30 Isaac then made a feast for them, and they ate and drank.
31 Early the next morning the men swore an oath to each other.
Then Isaac sent them on their way, and they left him in peace.
32 That day Isaac's servants came and told him about the well
they had dug. They said, "We've found water!" 33 He called it Shibah,[d] and to this day the name of the town has been Beersheba.[e]
34 When Esau was forty years old, he married Judith daughter
of Beeri the Hittite, and also Basemath daughter of Elon the Hittite. 35 They were a source of grief to Isaac and Rebekah.

Jacob Gets Isaac's Blessing

27 When Isaac was old and his eyes were so weak that he
could no longer see, he called for Esau his older son and
said to him, "My son."
"Here I am," he answered.
2 Isaac said, "I am now an old man and don't know the day of
my death. 3 Now then, get your weapons—your quiver and
bow—and go out to the open country to hunt some wild game
for me. 4 Prepare me the kind of tasty food I like and bring it to
me to eat, so that I may give you my blessing before I die."
5 Now Rebekah was listening as Isaac spoke to his son Esau.

[a] 20 *Esek* means *dispute.* [b] 21 *Sitnah* means *opposition.* [c] 22 *Rehoboth* means *room.* [d] 33 *Shibah* can mean *oath* or *seven.* [e] 33 *Beersheba* can mean *well of the oath* or *well of seven.*

When Esau left for the open country to hunt game and bring it
back, 6Rebekah said to her son Jacob, "Look, I overheard your
father say to your brother Esau, 7'Bring me some game and
prepare me some tasty food to eat, so that I may give you my
blessing in the presence of the LORD before I die.' 8Now, my son,
listen carefully and do what I tell you: 9Go out to the flock and
bring me two choice young goats, so I can prepare some tasty
food for your father, just the way he likes it. 10Then take it to
your father to eat, so that he may give you his blessing before he
dies."

11Jacob said to Rebekah his mother, "But my brother Esau is
a hairy man, and I'm a man with smooth skin. 12What if my father touches me? I would appear to be tricking him and would
bring down a curse on myself rather than a blessing."

13His mother said to him, "My son, let the curse fall on me.
Just do what I say; go and get them for me."

14So he went and got them and brought them to his mother,
and she prepared some tasty food, just the way his father liked it.
15Then Rebekah took the best clothes of Esau her older son,
which she had in the house, and put them on her younger son
Jacob. 16She also covered his hands and the smooth part of his
neck with the goatskins. 17Then she handed to her son Jacob the
tasty food and the bread she had made.

18He went to his father and said, "My father."

"Yes, my son," he answered. "Who is it?"

19Jacob said to his father, "I am Esau your firstborn. I have
done as you told me. Please sit up and eat some of my game so
that you may give me your blessing."

20Isaac asked his son, "How did you find it so quickly, my
son?"

"The LORD your God gave me success," he replied.

21Then Isaac said to Jacob, "Come near so I can touch you,
my son, to know whether you really are my son Esau or not."

22Jacob went close to his father Isaac, who touched him and
said, "The voice is the voice of Jacob, but the hands are the
hands of Esau." 23He did not recognize him, for his hands were
hairy like those of his brother Esau; so he blessed him. 24"Are
you really my son Esau?" he asked.

"I am," he replied.

25Then he said, "My son, bring me some of your game to eat,
so that I may give you my blessing."

Jacob brought it to him and he ate; and he brought some wine
and he drank. 26Then his father Isaac said to him, "Come here,
my son, and kiss me."

27So he went to him and kissed him. When Isaac caught the
smell of his clothes, he blessed him and said,

"Ah, the smell of my son
is like the smell of a field
that the LORD has blessed.
28May God give you of heaven's dew
and of earth's richness—
an abundance of grain and new wine.
29May nations serve you
and peoples bow down to you.
Be lord over your brothers,
and may the sons of your mother bow down to you.

(27:20) Righteous Lord, I see myself in Jacob's deception of his father. How often do I "credit" You with the success of my fleshly endeavors? How often do I invoke Your name over self-centered activities? How often do I attempt to finish in the flesh what You have begun in the Spirit? Father, forgive me. Yet I also see Your amazing sovereignty in Jacob's scheme. These were not perfect people; but they were Your people. In spite of their fallen human nature, You worked through them to advance Your divine purpose of redemption. (Ge 25:23; Gal 3:3)

"O God, stay with me; let no word cross my lips that is not your word, no thoughts enter my mind that are not your thoughts, no deed ever be done or entertained by me that is not your deed. Amen."

Malcolm Muggeridge (1903-1990)

Dear Lord and Father of mankind,
Forgive our foolish ways!
Reclothe us in our rightful mind;
In purer lives Thy service find,
In deeper rev'rence, praise.

"Dear Lord and Father of Mankind"
John G. Whittier (1872)

(27:30–40) I am astounded, Lord, by Your willingness to use our faults, even our sins, in the unfolding of Your sovereign will. Jacob's deceit, Isaac's error, Esau's anger—these You will weave together into the tapestry of salvation. In the mystery of Your providence, what we intend for harm, You intend for good. Even when I falter or fail, Your plans are never in jeopardy. How thankful I am that You are a God who works all things, yes, *all things*, together for good! (Ge 50:20; Ro 8:28)

God is good and God is light,
In this faith I rest secure,
Evil can but serve the right,
Over all shall love endure.
John Greenleaf Whittier (1807-1892)

May those who curse you be cursed
and those who bless you be blessed."

30After Isaac finished blessing him and Jacob had scarcely left
his father's presence, his brother Esau came in from hunting.
31He too prepared some tasty food and brought it to his father.
Then he said to him, "My father, sit up and eat some of my game,
so that you may give me your blessing."
32His father Isaac asked him, "Who are you?"
"I am your son," he answered, "your firstborn, Esau."
33Isaac trembled violently and said, "Who was it, then, that
hunted game and brought it to me? I ate it just before you came
and I blessed him—and indeed he will be blessed!"
34When Esau heard his father's words, he burst out with a loud
and bitter cry and said to his father, "Bless me—me too, my father!"
35But he said, "Your brother came deceitfully and took your
blessing."
36Esau said, "Isn't he rightly named Jacob[a]? He has deceived
me these two times: He took my birthright, and now he's taken my
blessing!" Then he asked, "Haven't you reserved any blessing
for me?"
37Isaac answered Esau, "I have made him lord over you and
have made all his relatives his servants, and I have sustained him
with grain and new wine. So what can I possibly do for you, my
son?"
38Esau said to his father, "Do you have only one blessing, my father? Bless me too, my father!" Then Esau wept aloud.
39His father Isaac answered him,

"Your dwelling will be
away from the earth's richness,
away from the dew of heaven above.
40You will live by the sword
and you will serve your brother.
But when you grow restless,
you will throw his yoke
from off your neck."

Jacob Flees to Laban

41Esau held a grudge against Jacob because of the blessing his
father had given him. He said to himself, "The days of mourning
for my father are near; then I will kill my brother Jacob."
42When Rebekah was told what her older son Esau had said,
she sent for her younger son Jacob and said to him, "Your brother Esau is consoling himself with the thought of killing you. 43Now
then, my son, do what I say: Flee at once to my brother Laban in
Haran. 44Stay with him for a while until your brother's fury subsides. 45When your brother is no longer angry with you and forgets what you did to him, I'll send word for you to come back
from there. Why should I lose both of you in one day?"
46Then Rebekah said to Isaac, "I'm disgusted with living because of these Hittite women. If Jacob takes a wife from among the
women of this land, from Hittite women like these, my life will not
be worth living."

[a] 36 *Jacob* means ***he grasps the heel*** (figuratively, *he deceives*).

28 So Isaac called for Jacob and blessed[a] him and commanded him: "Do not marry a Canaanite woman. 2Go at
once to Paddan Aram,[b] to the house of your mother's father Bethuel. Take a wife for yourself there, from among the daughters of
Laban, your mother's brother. 3May God Almighty[c] bless you and
make you fruitful and increase your numbers until you become a
community of peoples. 4May he give you and your descendants
the blessing given to Abraham, so that you may take possession of
the land where you now live as an alien, the land God gave to
Abraham." 5Then Isaac sent Jacob on his way, and he went to Paddan Aram, to Laban son of Bethuel the Aramean, the brother of
Rebekah, who was the mother of Jacob and Esau.

6Now Esau learned that Isaac had blessed Jacob and had sent
him to Paddan Aram to take a wife from there, and that when he
blessed him he commanded him, "Do not marry a Canaanite
woman," 7and that Jacob had obeyed his father and mother and
had gone to Paddan Aram. 8Esau then realized how displeasing
the Canaanite women were to his father Isaac; 9so he went to Ishmael and married Mahalath, the sister of Nebaioth and daughter
of Ishmael son of Abraham, in addition to the wives he already
had.

Jacob's Dream at Bethel

10Jacob left Beersheba and set out for Haran. 11When he
reached a certain place, he stopped for the night because the sun
had set. Taking one of the stones there, he put it under his head
and lay down to sleep. 12He had a dream in which he saw a stairway[d] resting on the earth, with its top reaching to heaven, and the
angels of God were ascending and descending on it. 13There
above it[e] stood the LORD, and he said: "I am the LORD, the God of
your father Abraham and the God of Isaac. I will give you and your
descendants the land on which you are lying. 14Your descendants
will be like the dust of the earth, and you will spread out to the
west and to the east, to the north and to the south. All peoples on
earth will be blessed through you and your offspring. 15I am with
you and will watch over you wherever you go, and I will bring you
back to this land. I will not leave you until I have done what I have
promised you."

16When Jacob awoke from his sleep, he thought, "Surely the
LORD is in this place, and I was not aware of it." 17He was afraid
and said, "How awesome is this place! This is none other than the
house of God; this is the gate of heaven."

18Early the next morning Jacob took the stone he had placed
under his head and set it up as a pillar and poured oil on top of it.
19He called that place Bethel,[f] though the city used to be called
Luz.

20Then Jacob made a vow, saying, "If God will be with me and
will watch over me on this journey I am taking and will give me
food to eat and clothes to wear 21so that I return safely to my father's house, then the LORD[g] will be my God 22and[h] this stone that
I have set up as a pillar will be God's house, and of all that you give
me I will give you a tenth."

(28:10–17) How often, Lord, have I been wallowing through life, unaware of Your presence, only to exult like Jacob: "Surely the LORD is in this place, and I was not aware of it!" Thank You for not allowing my narrow perception to limit Your work in my life. Thank You for those times when Your gracious activity has exceeded my expectations. Thank You for doing that which I never even thought to ask or imagine. Thank You for the daily surprise of Your compassionate presence. (La 3:22–23; Eph 3:20–21)

[a] *1* Or *greeted* [b] *2* That is, Northwest Mesopotamia; also in verses 5, 6 and 7 [c] *3* Hebrew *El-Shaddai* [d] *12* Or *ladder* [e] *13* Or *There beside him* [f] *19* *Bethel* means *house of God.* [g] *20,21* Or *Since God . . . father's house, the LORD* [h] *21,22* Or *house, and the LORD will be my God, 22then*

Jacob Arrives in Paddan Aram

29 Then Jacob continued on his journey and came to the land
of the eastern peoples. [2]There he saw a well in the field,
with three flocks of sheep lying near it because the flocks were
watered from that well. The stone over the mouth of the well was
large. [3]When all the flocks were gathered there, the shepherds
would roll the stone away from the well's mouth and water the
sheep. Then they would return the stone to its place over the
mouth of the well.

[4]Jacob asked the shepherds, "My brothers, where are you
from?"

"We're from Haran," they replied.

[5]He said to them, "Do you know Laban, Nahor's grandson?"

"Yes, we know him," they answered.

[6]Then Jacob asked them, "Is he well?"

"Yes, he is," they said, "and here comes his daughter Rachel
with the sheep."

[7]"Look," he said, "the sun is still high; it is not time for the
flocks to be gathered. Water the sheep and take them back to pasture."

[8]"We can't," they replied, "until all the flocks are gathered and
the stone has been rolled away from the mouth of the well. Then
we will water the sheep."

[9]While he was still talking with them, Rachel came with her father's sheep, for she was a shepherdess. [10]When Jacob saw Rachel
daughter of Laban, his mother's brother, and Laban's sheep, he
went over and rolled the stone away from the mouth of the well
and watered his uncle's sheep. [11]Then Jacob kissed Rachel and
began to weep aloud. [12]He had told Rachel that he was a relative
of her father and a son of Rebekah. So she ran and told her father.

[13]As soon as Laban heard the news about Jacob, his sister's
son, he hurried to meet him. He embraced him and kissed him
and brought him to his home, and there Jacob told him all these
things. [14]Then Laban said to him, "You are my own flesh and
blood."

Jacob Marries Leah and Rachel

After Jacob had stayed with him for a whole month, [15]Laban
said to him, "Just because you are a relative of mine, should you
work for me for nothing? Tell me what your wages should be."

[16]Now Laban had two daughters; the name of the older was
Leah, and the name of the younger was Rachel. [17]Leah had weak[a]
eyes, but Rachel was lovely in form, and beautiful. [18]Jacob was in
love with Rachel and said, "I'll work for you seven years in return
for your younger daughter Rachel."

[19]Laban said, "It's better that I give her to you than to some
other man. Stay here with me." [20]So Jacob served seven years to
get Rachel, but they seemed like only a few days to him because of
his love for her.

[21]Then Jacob said to Laban, "Give me my wife. My time is completed, and I want to lie with her."

[22]So Laban brought together all the people of the place and
gave a feast. [23]But when evening came, he took his daughter Leah
and gave her to Jacob, and Jacob lay with her. [24]And Laban gave
his servant girl Zilpah to his daughter as her maidservant.

[a] 17 Or *delicate*

(29:20) Creator God, You have created me with the capacity to love deeply. The fervor of true love can even change my perception of time, making years seem like a few days. Oh, that I might love You with such intensity! Ignite my passion for You, so that I might serve You with all of my heart and all of my soul, scarcely noticing how time passes! May I love You with all that I am—heart, soul, mind and strength. (Dt 10:12; Mk 12:30)

Love feels no burden, thinks nothing of trouble, attempts what is above its strength, pleads no excuse of impossibility; for it thinks all things lawful for itself, and all things possible. It is therefore able to undertake all things, and warrants them to take effect, where he who does not love, would faint and lie down.

Thomas à Kempis (c.1380–1471)

MY BELOVED

I am your Father and you are My child. I will never leave you. Never. I will watch over you wherever you go.

I have upheld you since you were conceived, and have carried you since your birth. Even into your old age, when your hair has turned gray and you have grown weak, I will sustain you. I have made you and I will carry you when you cannot go on. Because you love Me, I will rescue you; I will be with you in trouble, I will deliver you and honor you. I will never leave you nor forsake you. So you can say with confidence, "The Lord is my helper; I will not be afraid. What can man do to me?"

Who can separate you from My love? Shall trouble or hardship or persecution or famine or nakedness or danger or sword? No! In all these things you are more than a conqueror through Me because I love you. Nothing in all creation will ever be able to separate you from My love that is in Christ Jesus your Lord.

So be strong and courageous. Do not be afraid, for I am with you. I am your Father and you are My child. I live with you and walk with you. In light of these promises, keep yourself pure from everything that contaminates body and spirit, and walk in holiness out of reverence for Me.

Dt 31:6, 8; Ps 91:14-15; Isa 46:3-4; Ro 8:35, 37-39; 2Co 6:16—7:1; Heb 13:5-6

25When morning came, there was Leah! So Jacob said to Laban,
"What is this you have done to me? I served you for Rachel, didn't
I? Why have you deceived me?"
26Laban replied, "It is not our custom here to give the younger
daughter in marriage before the older one. 27Finish this daughter's bridal week; then we will give you the younger one also, in return for another seven years of work."
28And Jacob did so. He finished the week with Leah, and then
Laban gave him his daughter Rachel to be his wife. 29Laban gave
his servant girl Bilhah to his daughter Rachel as her maidservant.
30Jacob lay with Rachel also, and he loved Rachel more than Leah.
And he worked for Laban another seven years.

Jacob's Children

31When the LORD saw that Leah was not loved, he opened her
womb, but Rachel was barren. 32Leah became pregnant and gave
birth to a son. She named him Reuben,[a] for she said, "It is because the LORD has seen my misery. Surely my husband will love
me now."
33She conceived again, and when she gave birth to a son she
said, "Because the LORD heard that I am not loved, he gave me this
one too." So she named him Simeon.[b]
34Again she conceived, and when she gave birth to a son she
said, "Now at last my husband will become attached to me, because I have borne him three sons." So he was named Levi.[c]
35She conceived again, and when she gave birth to a son she
said, "This time I will praise the LORD." So she named him Judah.[d]
Then she stopped having children.

30 When Rachel saw that she was not bearing Jacob any children, she became jealous of her sister. So she said to
Jacob, "Give me children, or I'll die!"
2Jacob became angry with her and said, "Am I in the place of
God, who has kept you from having children?"
3Then she said, "Here is Bilhah, my maidservant. Sleep with her
so that she can bear children for me and that through her I too
can build a family."
4So she gave him her servant Bilhah as a wife. Jacob slept with
her, 5and she became pregnant and bore him a son. 6Then Rachel
said, "God has vindicated me; he has listened to my plea and given
me a son." Because of this she named him Dan.[e]
7Rachel's servant Bilhah conceived again and bore Jacob a second son. 8Then Rachel said, "I have had a great struggle with my
sister, and I have won." So she named him Naphtali.[f]
9When Leah saw that she had stopped having children, she took
her maidservant Zilpah and gave her to Jacob as a wife. 10Leah's
servant Zilpah bore Jacob a son. 11Then Leah said, "What good
fortune!"[g] So she named him Gad.[h]
12Leah's servant Zilpah bore Jacob a second son. 13Then Leah
said, "How happy I am! The women will call me happy." So she
named him Asher.[i]
14During wheat harvest, Reuben went out into the fields and
found some mandrake plants, which he brought to his mother

[a] 32 *Reuben* sounds like the Hebrew for *he has seen my misery*; the name means *see, a son.* [b] 33 *Simeon* probably means *one who hears.* [c] 34 *Levi* sounds like and may be derived from the Hebrew for *attached.* [d] 35 *Judah* sounds like and may be derived from the Hebrew for *praise.* [e] 6 *Dan* here means *he has vindicated.* [f] 8 *Naphtali* means *my struggle.* [g] 11 Or *"A troop is coming!"* [h] 11 *Gad* can mean *good fortune* or *a troop.* [i] 13 *Asher* means *happy.*

(29:31) O Lord, You keep Your eye upon those who are helpless. You hear the cry of the needy. You lift up those who are bowed down. You "settle the barren woman in her home as a happy mother of children." You are "a father to the fatherless, a defender of widows." There is none like You, Sovereign God, who sits enthroned on high, yet who stoops down to help those who need Your salvation. "Praise be to the LORD, to God our Savior, who daily bears our burdens." (Ps 68:4–10, 19; 69:32–33; 113:5–9; 146:7–10)

Man may dismiss compassion from his heart, but God will never.

William Cowper (1731-1800)

Leah. Rachel said to Leah, "Please give me some of your son's
mandrakes."
15But she said to her, "Wasn't it enough that you took away my
husband? Will you take my son's mandrakes too?"

"Very well," Rachel said, "he can sleep with you tonight in return for your son's mandrakes."
16So when Jacob came in from the fields that evening, Leah
went out to meet him. "You must sleep with me," she said. "I have
hired you with my son's mandrakes." So he slept with her that
night.
17God listened to Leah, and she became pregnant and bore
Jacob a fifth son. 18Then Leah said, "God has rewarded me for
giving my maidservant to my husband." So she named him Issachar.[a]
19Leah conceived again and bore Jacob a sixth son. 20Then
Leah said, "God has presented me with a precious gift. This time
my husband will treat me with honor, because I have borne him
six sons." So she named him Zebulun.[b]
21Some time later she gave birth to a daughter and named her
Dinah.
22Then God remembered Rachel; he listened to her and opened
her womb. 23She became pregnant and gave birth to a son and
said, "God has taken away my disgrace." 24She named him Joseph,[c] and said, "May the LORD add to me another son."

Jacob's Flocks Increase

25After Rachel gave birth to Joseph, Jacob said to Laban, "Send
me on my way so I can go back to my own homeland. 26Give me
my wives and children, for whom I have served you, and I will be
on my way. You know how much work I've done for you."
27But Laban said to him, "If I have found favor in your eyes,
please stay. I have learned by divination that[d] the LORD has blessed
me because of you." 28He added, "Name your wages, and I will
pay them."
29Jacob said to him, "You know how I have worked for you and
how your livestock has fared under my care. 30The little you had
before I came has increased greatly, and the LORD has blessed you
wherever I have been. But now, when may I do something for my
own household?"
31"What shall I give you?" he asked.

"Don't give me anything," Jacob replied. "But if you will do this
one thing for me, I will go on tending your flocks and watching
over them: 32Let me go through all your flocks today and remove
from them every speckled or spotted sheep, every dark-colored
lamb and every spotted or speckled goat. They will be my wages.
33And my honesty will testify for me in the future, whenever you
check on the wages you have paid me. Any goat in my possession
that is not speckled or spotted, or any lamb that is not dark-colored, will be considered stolen."
34"Agreed," said Laban. "Let it be as you have said." 35That
same day he removed all the male goats that were streaked or
spotted, and all the speckled or spotted female goats (all that had
white on them) and all the dark-colored lambs, and he placed
them in the care of his sons. 36Then he put a three-day journey

[a] 18 *Issachar* sounds like the Hebrew for *reward.* [b] 20 *Zebulun* probably means *honor.*
[c] 24 *Joseph* means *may he add.* [d] 27 Or possibly *have become rich and*

(30:15–24) How patient You are with us, Lord. Faithfully, You work Your will through us even as we flounder in pettiness, self-promotion and niggling rivalries. Though Leah and Rachel squabbled in jealous competition, still You listened to Leah; You remembered Rachel. Though their behavior was not worthy of Your patience, nevertheless You graciously worked through them to build Your nation. I too am prone to foolishness and failure. But I praise You and give You thanks that in Your great faithfulness and compassion You respond to my heart cries, remove my disgrace, and work Your good will through my life.

between himself and Jacob, while Jacob continued to tend the rest
of Laban's flocks.
37 Jacob, however, took fresh-cut branches from poplar, almond and plane trees and made white stripes on them by peeling
the bark and exposing the white inner wood of the branches.
38 Then he placed the peeled branches in all the watering troughs,
so that they would be directly in front of the flocks when they came
to drink. When the flocks were in heat and came to drink, 39 they
mated in front of the branches. And they bore young that were
streaked or speckled or spotted. 40 Jacob set apart the young of the
flock by themselves, but made the rest face the streaked and dark-
colored animals that belonged to Laban. Thus he made separate
flocks for himself and did not put them with Laban's animals.
41 Whenever the stronger females were in heat, Jacob would place
the branches in the troughs in front of the animals so they would
mate near the branches, 42 but if the animals were weak, he would
not place them there. So the weak animals went to Laban and the
strong ones to Jacob. 43 In this way the man grew exceedingly
prosperous and came to own large flocks, and maidservants and
menservants, and camels and donkeys.

Jacob Flees From Laban

31 Jacob heard that Laban's sons were saying, "Jacob has
taken everything our father owned and has gained all this
wealth from what belonged to our father." 2 And Jacob noticed that
Laban's attitude toward him was not what it had been.
3 Then the LORD said to Jacob, "Go back to the land of your fathers and to your relatives, and I will be with you."
4 So Jacob sent word to Rachel and Leah to come out to the
fields where his flocks were. 5 He said to them, "I see that your father's attitude toward me is not what it was before, but the God of
my father has been with me. 6 You know that I've worked for your
father with all my strength, 7 yet your father has cheated me by
changing my wages ten times. However, God has not allowed him
to harm me. 8 If he said, 'The speckled ones will be your wages,'
then all the flocks gave birth to speckled young; and if he said,
'The streaked ones will be your wages,' then all the flocks bore
streaked young. 9 So God has taken away your father's livestock
and has given them to me.
10 "In breeding season I once had a dream in which I looked up
and saw that the male goats mating with the flock were streaked,
speckled or spotted. 11 The angel of God said to me in the dream,
'Jacob.' I answered, 'Here I am.' 12 And he said, 'Look up and see
that all the male goats mating with the flock are streaked, speckled or spotted, for I have seen all that Laban has been doing to
you. 13 I am the God of Bethel, where you anointed a pillar and
where you made a vow to me. Now leave this land at once and go
back to your native land.' "
14 Then Rachel and Leah replied, "Do we still have any share in
the inheritance of our father's estate? 15 Does he not regard us as
foreigners? Not only has he sold us, but he has used up what was
paid for us. 16 Surely all the wealth that God took away from our
father belongs to us and our children. So do whatever God has
told you."
17 Then Jacob put his children and his wives on camels, 18 and
he drove all his livestock ahead of him, along with all the goods he

(31:13) You are the God of Bethel, reigning over the angels who serve You. At Bethel You revealed Your heavenly glory to Jacob and renewed the promises You had made to his ancestors. Thank You for those times when Your presence is so palpable that we can only say with Jacob: "Surely the LORD is in this place . . . How awesome is this place!" Thank You for those times when You allow us to see even more of Your glory. Thank You for those times when You reassure us with the promise of life. (Ge 28:10–22; 2Ti 1:1)

had accumulated in Paddan Aram,[a] to go to his father Isaac in the
land of Canaan.
19When Laban had gone to shear his sheep, Rachel stole her
father's household gods. 20Moreover, Jacob deceived Laban the
Aramean by not telling him he was running away. 21So he fled
with all he had, and crossing the River,[b] he headed for the hill
country of Gilead.

Laban Pursues Jacob

22On the third day Laban was told that Jacob had fled. 23Taking
his relatives with him, he pursued Jacob for seven days and caught
up with him in the hill country of Gilead. 24Then God came to
Laban the Aramean in a dream at night and said to him, "Be careful not to say anything to Jacob, either good or bad."
25Jacob had pitched his tent in the hill country of Gilead when
Laban overtook him, and Laban and his relatives camped there
too. 26Then Laban said to Jacob, "What have you done? You've deceived me, and you've carried off my daughters like captives in
war. 27Why did you run off secretly and deceive me? Why didn't
you tell me, so I could send you away with joy and singing to the
music of tambourines and harps? 28You didn't even let me kiss
my grandchildren and my daughters good-by. You have done a
foolish thing. 29I have the power to harm you; but last night the
God of your father said to me, 'Be careful not to say anything to
Jacob, either good or bad.' 30Now you have gone off because you
longed to return to your father's house. But why did you steal my
gods?"
31Jacob answered Laban, "I was afraid, because I thought you
would take your daughters away from me by force. 32But if you
find anyone who has your gods, he shall not live. In the presence
of our relatives, see for yourself whether there is anything of yours
here with me; and if so, take it." Now Jacob did not know that Rachel had stolen the gods.
33So Laban went into Jacob's tent and into Leah's tent and into
the tent of the two maidservants, but he found nothing. After he
came out of Leah's tent, he entered Rachel's tent. 34Now Rachel
had taken the household gods and put them inside her camel's
saddle and was sitting on them. Laban searched through everything in the tent but found nothing.
35Rachel said to her father, "Don't be angry, my lord, that I cannot stand up in your presence; I'm having my period." So he
searched but could not find the household gods.
36Jacob was angry and took Laban to task. "What is my crime?"
he asked Laban. "What sin have I committed that you hunt me
down? 37Now that you have searched through all my goods, what
have you found that belongs to your household? Put it here in front
of your relatives and mine, and let them judge between the two
of us.
38"I have been with you for twenty years now. Your sheep and
goats have not miscarried, nor have I eaten rams from your flocks.
39I did not bring you animals torn by wild beasts; I bore the loss
myself. And you demanded payment from me for whatever was
stolen by day or night. 40This was my situation: The heat consumed me in the daytime and the cold at night, and sleep fled from
my eyes. 41It was like this for the twenty years I was in your house-

[a] *18* That is, Northwest Mesopotamia [b] *21* That is, the Euphrates

When we have nothing left but God, then we become aware that God is enough.
Agnes Maude Royden (1876-1956)

(31:29) O God our Help, You have protected Your people from harm—Jacob from Laban's revenge, the Israelites from Egyptian chariots, the exiles on their way back to Jerusalem. You alone are the Lord, my rock, my fortress and my deliverer. You are my refuge, a strong tower against the enemy. Only in You will my soul find rest, for "the one the LORD loves rests between his shoulders." (Dt 33:12; Jos 24:17; Ezr 8:31; Ps 18:2; 61:3; 62:1–2)

O God, our help in ages past,
Our hope for years to come,
Our shelter from the stormy blast,
And our eternal home!
"O God, Our Help in Ages Past"
Isaac Watts (1719)

hold. I worked for you fourteen years for your two daughters and
six years for your flocks, and you changed my wages ten times.
42If the God of my father, the God of Abraham and the Fear of
Isaac, had not been with me, you would surely have sent me away
empty-handed. But God has seen my hardship and the toil of my
hands, and last night he rebuked you."
43Laban answered Jacob, "The women are my daughters, the
children are my children, and the flocks are my flocks. All you see
is mine. Yet what can I do today about these daughters of mine, or
about the children they have borne? 44Come now, let's make a covenant, you and I, and let it serve as a witness between us."
45So Jacob took a stone and set it up as a pillar. 46He said to his
relatives, "Gather some stones." So they took stones and piled
them in a heap, and they ate there by the heap. 47Laban called it
Jegar Sahadutha,[a] and Jacob called it Galeed.[b]
48Laban said, "This heap is a witness between you and me
today." That is why it was called Galeed. 49It was also called Mizpah,[c] because he said, "May the LORD keep watch between you
and me when we are away from each other. 50If you mistreat my
daughters or if you take any wives besides my daughters, even
though no one is with us, remember that God is a witness between
you and me."
51Laban also said to Jacob, "Here is this heap, and here is this
pillar I have set up between you and me. 52This heap is a witness,
and this pillar is a witness, that I will not go past this heap to your
side to harm you and that you will not go past this heap and pillar
to my side to harm me. 53May the God of Abraham and the God of
Nahor, the God of their father, judge between us."
So Jacob took an oath in the name of the Fear of his father
Isaac. 54He offered a sacrifice there in the hill country and invited
his relatives to a meal. After they had eaten, they spent the night
there.
55Early the next morning Laban kissed his grandchildren and
his daughters and blessed them. Then he left and returned home.

Jacob Prepares to Meet Esau

32 Jacob also went on his way, and the angels of God met him.
2When Jacob saw them, he said, "This is the camp of
God!" So he named that place Mahanaim.[d]
3Jacob sent messengers ahead of him to his brother Esau in the
land of Seir, the country of Edom. 4He instructed them: "This is
what you are to say to my master Esau: 'Your servant Jacob says, I
have been staying with Laban and have remained there till now. 5I
have cattle and donkeys, sheep and goats, menservants and maidservants. Now I am sending this message to my lord, that I may
find favor in your eyes.' "
6When the messengers returned to Jacob, they said, "We went
to your brother Esau, and now he is coming to meet you, and four
hundred men are with him."
7In great fear and distress Jacob divided the people who were
with him into two groups,[e] and the flocks and herds and camels
as well. 8He thought, "If Esau comes and attacks one group,[f] the
group[f] that is left may escape."
9Then Jacob prayed, "O God of my father Abraham, God of my

[a] 47 The Aramaic *Jegar Sahadutha* means *witness heap.* [b] 47 The Hebrew *Galeed* means *witness heap.* [c] 49 *Mizpah* means *watchtower.* [d] 2 *Mahanaim* means *two camps.* [e] 7 Or *camps*; also in verse 10 [f] 8 Or *camp*

(32:1–12) Father God, how like Jacob I am in my fear and faithlessness! You fulfilled Your prophecy to his mother by providing a blessing for his future. You protected him from his conniving father-in-law. You sent angels to encourage him along the way. And yet, as he was about to enter into the fulfillment of Your promised future, he was confronted with his past failures, and fear nearly overwhelmed him. How quickly he—and I—forget Your saving grace and provision. Lord, open my eyes to Your past acts of salvation. Make me aware of Your protective presence today. And give me faith, hope and courage to walk into the future, entrusting all things to Your love and power. (Ge 25:23; 31:42)

He does not need to transplant us into a different field, but right where we are, with just the circumstances that surround us, he makes his sun to shine and his dew to fall upon us, and transforms the very things that were before our greatest hindrances into the chiefest and most blessed means of our growth. No difficulties in your case can baffle him, No dwarfing of your growth in years that are past, no apparent dryness of your inward springs of life, no crookedness or deformity in any of your past development, can in the least mar the perfect work that he will accomplish, if you will only put yourselves absolutely into his hands and let him have his own way with you.

Hannah Whitall Smith (1832-1911)

Open my eyes, that I may see
Glimpses of truth Thou hast for me;
Place in my hands the wonderful key
That shall unclasp and set me free.

Silently now I wait for Thee
Ready, my God, Thy will to see;
Open my eyes, illumine me,
Spirit divine!

"Open My Eyes, That I May See"
Clara H. Scott (1895)

(32:22–32) It is really no contest, Lord, when I struggle with You. There is no doubt about Your superior strength. But, mercifully, You allow me to grapple with You as a child wrestles with a father—to pummel You with my prayers, to disturb You with my doubts, to badger You for yet another blessing. By grace You do bless me through the struggle, sometimes with new humility, sometimes with a new identity, sometimes with new assurance that even as I did not let go of You, so You will never let go of me.

father Isaac, O LORD, who said to me, 'Go back to your country and
your relatives, and I will make you prosper,' [10]I am unworthy of
all the kindness and faithfulness you have shown your servant. I
had only my staff when I crossed this Jordan, but now I have become two groups. [11]Save me, I pray, from the hand of my brother
Esau, for I am afraid he will come and attack me, and also the
mothers with their children. [12]But you have said, 'I will surely
make you prosper and will make your descendants like the sand
of the sea, which cannot be counted.' "

[13]He spent the night there, and from what he had with him he
selected a gift for his brother Esau: [14]two hundred female goats
and twenty male goats, two hundred ewes and twenty rams, [15]thir-
ty female camels with their young, forty cows and ten bulls, and
twenty female donkeys and ten male donkeys. [16]He put them in
the care of his servants, each herd by itself, and said to his servants, "Go ahead of me, and keep some space between the herds."
[17]He instructed the one in the lead: "When my brother Esau
meets you and asks, 'To whom do you belong, and where are you
going, and who owns all these animals in front of you?' [18]then you
are to say, 'They belong to your servant Jacob. They are a gift sent
to my lord Esau, and he is coming behind us.' "

[19]He also instructed the second, the third and all the others
who followed the herds: "You are to say the same thing to Esau
when you meet him. [20]And be sure to say, 'Your servant Jacob is
coming behind us.' " For he thought, "I will pacify him with these
gifts I am sending on ahead; later, when I see him, perhaps he will
receive me." [21]So Jacob's gifts went on ahead of him, but he himself spent the night in the camp.

Jacob Wrestles With God

[22]That night Jacob got up and took his two wives, his two maidservants and his eleven sons and crossed the ford of the Jabbok.
[23]After he had sent them across the stream, he sent over all his
possessions. [24]So Jacob was left alone, and a man wrestled with
him till daybreak. [25]When the man saw that he could not overpower him, he touched the socket of Jacob's hip so that his hip
was wrenched as he wrestled with the man. [26]Then the man said,
"Let me go, for it is daybreak."

But Jacob replied, "I will not let you go unless you bless me."
[27]The man asked him, "What is your name?"

"Jacob," he answered.

[28]Then the man said, "Your name will no longer be Jacob, but
Israel,[a] because you have struggled with God and with men and
have overcome."

[29]Jacob said, "Please tell me your name."

But he replied, "Why do you ask my name?" Then he blessed
him there.

[30]So Jacob called the place Peniel,[b] saying, "It is because I saw
God face to face, and yet my life was spared."

[31]The sun rose above him as he passed Peniel,[c] and he was
limping because of his hip. [32]Therefore to this day the Israelites
do not eat the tendon attached to the socket of the hip, because
the socket of Jacob's hip was touched near the tendon.

[a] *28 Israel* means *he struggles with God.* [b] *30 Peniel* means *face of God.*
[c] *31* Hebrew *Penuel,* a variant of *Peniel*

Jacob Meets Esau

33 Jacob looked up and there was Esau, coming with his four
hundred men; so he divided the children among Leah, Rachel and the two maidservants. 2He put the maidservants and their
children in front, Leah and her children next, and Rachel and Joseph in the rear. 3He himself went on ahead and bowed down to
the ground seven times as he approached his brother.
4But Esau ran to meet Jacob and embraced him; he threw his
arms around his neck and kissed him. And they wept. 5Then Esau
looked up and saw the women and children. "Who are these with
you?" he asked.
Jacob answered, "They are the children God has graciously
given your servant."
6Then the maidservants and their children approached and
bowed down. 7Next, Leah and her children came and bowed
down. Last of all came Joseph and Rachel, and they too bowed
down.
8Esau asked, "What do you mean by all these droves I met?"
"To find favor in your eyes, my lord," he said.
9But Esau said, "I already have plenty, my brother. Keep what
you have for yourself."
10"No, please!" said Jacob. "If I have found favor in your eyes,
accept this gift from me. For to see your face is like seeing the
face of God, now that you have received me favorably. 11Please accept the present that was brought to you, for God has been gracious to me and I have all I need." And because Jacob insisted,
Esau accepted it.
12Then Esau said, "Let us be on our way; I'll accompany you."
13But Jacob said to him, "My lord knows that the children are
tender and that I must care for the ewes and cows that are nursing their young. If they are driven hard just one day, all the animals
will die. 14So let my lord go on ahead of his servant, while I move
along slowly at the pace of the droves before me and that of the
children, until I come to my lord in Seir."
15Esau said, "Then let me leave some of my men with you."
"But why do that?" Jacob asked. "Just let me find favor in the
eyes of my lord."
16So that day Esau started on his way back to Seir. 17Jacob,
however, went to Succoth, where he built a place for himself and
made shelters for his livestock. That is why the place is called Succoth.[a]
18After Jacob came from Paddan Aram,[b] he arrived safely at
the[c] city of Shechem in Canaan and camped within sight of the
city. 19For a hundred pieces of silver,[d] he bought from the sons of
Hamor, the father of Shechem, the plot of ground where he
pitched his tent. 20There he set up an altar and called it El Elohe
Israel.[e]

Dinah and the Shechemites

34 Now Dinah, the daughter Leah had borne to Jacob, went
out to visit the women of the land. 2When Shechem son of
Hamor the Hivite, the ruler of that area, saw her, he took her and
violated her. 3His heart was drawn to Dinah daughter of Jacob,

[a] *17 Succoth* means *shelters.* [b] *18* That is, Northwest Mesopotamia [c] *18* Or *arrived at Shalem, a* [d] *19* Hebrew *hundred kesitahs;* a kesitah was a unit of money of unknown weight and value. [e] *20 El Elohe Israel* can mean *God, the God of Israel* or *mighty is the God of Israel.*

I used to think that God's gifts were on shelves one above the other and that the taller we grew in Christian character the more easily we could reach them. I now find that God's gifts are on shelves one beneath the other and that it is not a question of growing taller but of stooping lower.

F. B. Meyer (1847–1929)

(33:3–4) When Jacob humbled himself before Esau, Esau's heart softened. I thank You, Lord, for Your ability to soften hardened hearts and heal broken relationships when we humble ourselves before others. Lord, in all of my relationships teach me the power of humility. Where I have done wrong to someone else, forgive me, and show me how to make things right. Help me to consider others better than myself, so that You can go before me with grace and peace. (Php 2:3)

Agape love is . . . profound concern for the well-being of another, without any desire to control that other, to be thanked by that other, or to enjoy the process.

Madeleine L'Engle (1918-)

(34:1–31) O Lord, how we have ruined Your good creation. Though You created human love to reflect Your own love, we have perverted Your gift for selfish gain and domination. Though once You created sexual intimacy as a tender expression of devotion, now we use one another, even violating the sanctity of another person's body and destroying a life for a few moments of tawdry pleasure. In seeking our own advantage we deceive and distort the truth. In seeking revenge we injure both the guilty and the innocent. O Lord, forgive us for ruining Your good creation! Come, Lord Jesus, and make all things new! (Rev 21:5)

and he loved the girl and spoke tenderly to her. 4And Shechem
said to his father Hamor, "Get me this girl as my wife."
5When Jacob heard that his daughter Dinah had been defiled,
his sons were in the fields with his livestock; so he kept quiet
about it until they came home.
6Then Shechem's father Hamor went out to talk with Jacob.
7Now Jacob's sons had come in from the fields as soon as they
heard what had happened. They were filled with grief and fury, because Shechem had done a disgraceful thing in[a] Israel by lying
with Jacob's daughter—a thing that should not be done.
8But Hamor said to them, "My son Shechem has his heart set
on your daughter. Please give her to him as his wife. 9Intermarry
with us; give us your daughters and take our daughters for yourselves. 10You can settle among us; the land is open to you. Live in
it, trade[b] in it, and acquire property in it."
11Then Shechem said to Dinah's father and brothers, "Let me
find favor in your eyes, and I will give you whatever you ask.
12Make the price for the bride and the gift I am to bring as great
as you like, and I'll pay whatever you ask me. Only give me the girl
as my wife."
13Because their sister Dinah had been defiled, Jacob's sons
replied deceitfully as they spoke to Shechem and his father Hamor.
14They said to them, "We can't do such a thing; we can't give our
sister to a man who is not circumcised. That would be a disgrace
to us. 15We will give our consent to you on one condition only:
that you become like us by circumcising all your males. 16Then we
will give you our daughters and take your daughters for ourselves.
We'll settle among you and become one people with you. 17But if
you will not agree to be circumcised, we'll take our sister[c]
and go."
18Their proposal seemed good to Hamor and his son Shechem.
19The young man, who was the most honored of all his father's
household, lost no time in doing what they said, because he was
delighted with Jacob's daughter. 20So Hamor and his son Shechem
went to the gate of their city to speak to their fellow townsmen.
21"These men are friendly toward us," they said. "Let them live in
our land and trade in it; the land has plenty of room for them. We
can marry their daughters and they can marry ours. 22But the men
will consent to live with us as one people only on the condition
that our males be circumcised, as they themselves are. 23Won't
their livestock, their property and all their other animals become
ours? So let us give our consent to them, and they will settle
among us."
24All the men who went out of the city gate agreed with Hamor
and his son Shechem, and every male in the city was circumcised.
25Three days later, while all of them were still in pain, two of
Jacob's sons, Simeon and Levi, Dinah's brothers, took their
swords and attacked the unsuspecting city, killing every male.
26They put Hamor and his son Shechem to the sword and took
Dinah from Shechem's house and left. 27The sons of Jacob came
upon the dead bodies and looted the city where[d] their sister had
been defiled. 28They seized their flocks and herds and donkeys
and everything else of theirs in the city and out in the fields.
29They carried off all their wealth and all their women and children, taking as plunder everything in the houses.

[a] 7 Or *against* [b] 10 Or *move about freely*; also in verse 21 [c] 17 Hebrew *daughter*
[d] 27 Or *because*

30 Then Jacob said to Simeon and Levi, "You have brought trouble on me by making me a stench to the Canaanites and Perizzites,
the people living in this land. We are few in number, and if they
join forces against me and attack me, I and my household will be
destroyed."
31 But they replied, "Should he have treated our sister like a
prostitute?"

Jacob Returns to Bethel

35 Then God said to Jacob, "Go up to Bethel and settle there,
and build an altar there to God, who appeared to you when
you were fleeing from your brother Esau."
2 So Jacob said to his household and to all who were with him,
"Get rid of the foreign gods you have with you, and purify yourselves and change your clothes. 3 Then come, let us go up to Bethel, where I will build an altar to God, who answered me in the day
of my distress and who has been with me wherever I have gone."
4 So they gave Jacob all the foreign gods they had and the rings in
their ears, and Jacob buried them under the oak at Shechem.
5 Then they set out, and the terror of God fell upon the towns all
around them so that no one pursued them.
6 Jacob and all the people with him came to Luz (that is, Bethel) in the land of Canaan. 7 There he built an altar, and he called
the place El Bethel,[a] because it was there that God revealed himself to him when he was fleeing from his brother.
8 Now Deborah, Rebekah's nurse, died and was buried under
the oak below Bethel. So it was named Allon Bacuth.[b]
9 After Jacob returned from Paddan Aram,[c] God appeared to
him again and blessed him. 10 God said to him, "Your name is
Jacob,[d] but you will no longer be called Jacob; your name will be
Israel.[e]" So he named him Israel.
11 And God said to him, "I am God Almighty[f]; be fruitful and increase in number. A nation and a community of nations will come
from you, and kings will come from your body. 12 The land I gave
to Abraham and Isaac I also give to you, and I will give this land to
your descendants after you." 13 Then God went up from him at the
place where he had talked with him.
14 Jacob set up a stone pillar at the place where God had talked
with him, and he poured out a drink offering on it; he also poured
oil on it. 15 Jacob called the place where God had talked with him
Bethel.[g]

The Deaths of Rachel and Isaac

16 Then they moved on from Bethel. While they were still some
distance from Ephrath, Rachel began to give birth and had great
difficulty. 17 And as she was having great difficulty in childbirth, the
midwife said to her, "Don't be afraid, for you have another son."
18 As she breathed her last—for she was dying—she named her
son Ben-Oni.[h] But his father named him Benjamin.[i]
19 So Rachel died and was buried on the way to Ephrath (that is,
Bethlehem). 20 Over her tomb Jacob set up a pillar, and to this day
that pillar marks Rachel's tomb.
21 Israel moved on again and pitched his tent beyond Migdal

[a] 7 *El Bethel* means *God of Bethel.* [b] 8 *Allon Bacuth* means *oak of weeping.*
[c] 9 That is, Northwest Mesopotamia; also in verse 26 [d] 10 *Jacob* means *he grasps the heel* (figuratively, *he deceives*). [e] 10 *Israel* means *he struggles with God.*
[f] 11 Hebrew *El-Shaddai* [g] 15 *Bethel* means *house of God.* [h] 18 *Ben-Oni* means *son of my trouble.* [i] 18 *Benjamin* means *son of my right hand.*

*Heavenly Father, from whom all father-
hood in heaven and earth is named, bless,
we beg you, all children, and give to their
parents and to all in whose charge they
may be, your Spirit of wisdom and love; so
that the home in which they grow up may
be to them an image of your kingdom, and
the care of their parents a likeness of your
love; through Jesus Christ our Lord.*

Leslie Hunter (b. 1890)

(35:11–12) God of all generations, as You were known to Abraham and Isaac as El-Shaddai, the Lord Almighty, so You revealed Yourself to Jacob. As You promised to bless Abraham and Isaac, so You promised to bless Jacob. Thank You, Lord, for the blessing of faith passed on from parents to children. And thank You, El-Shaddai, for renewing Your covenant with each generation, for revealing Yourself afresh to those who first learned of You from faithful parents. By Your grace, our faith so carefully passed down is not merely a hand-me-down but something that can be new every morning. (Ge 17:1; 28:3; Dt 4:9; Ps 135:13)

You have been a shelter, Lord,
To every generation,
To every generation.
A sanctuary from the storm,
To every generation,
To every generation, Lord.

You've seen the years pass
In untold numbers,
As in a single night
You've seen the lifetime of man
Fade quickly before the light.

Our years go by before Your eyes;
You know our rebellious ways.
Make us wise to live holy lives
In the balance of our days.

"To Every Generation"
Bill Batstone (©1986)

(36:7) As it was with Abram and Lot years before, so it is with Esau and Jacob. Once again, Lord, You blessed Your chosen ones with riches in abundance. Have You not blessed me even more richly—not with cattle or land, but with life . . . abundant life, eternal life, life with You now and forever, life generously endowed by Your gifts of grace, life in the fellowship of Your family? Thank You, O Living God, for the bountiful blessings of life. (Ge 13:1–9)

For three things I thank God every day of my life: thanks that he has vouchsafed me knowledge of his works; deep thanks that he has set in my darkness the lamp of faith; deep, deepest thanks that I have another life to look forward to—a life joyous with light and flowers and heavenly song.
Helen Adams Keller (1880–1968)

Praise God from whom all blessings flow;
Praise Him, all creatures here below;
Praise Him above, ye heav'nly host;
Praise Father, Son and Holy Ghost.
Doxology
Thomas Ken (1709)

Eder. 22While Israel was living in that region, Reuben went in and
slept with his father's concubine Bilhah, and Israel heard of it.

Jacob had twelve sons:
23The sons of Leah:
Reuben the firstborn of Jacob,
Simeon, Levi, Judah, Issachar and Zebulun.
24The sons of Rachel:
Joseph and Benjamin.
25The sons of Rachel's maidservant Bilhah:
Dan and Naphtali.
26The sons of Leah's maidservant Zilpah:
Gad and Asher.
These were the sons of Jacob, who were born to him in Paddan Aram.

27Jacob came home to his father Isaac in Mamre, near Kiriath
Arba (that is, Hebron), where Abraham and Isaac had stayed.
28Isaac lived a hundred and eighty years. 29Then he breathed his
last and died and was gathered to his people, old and full of years.
And his sons Esau and Jacob buried him.

Esau's Descendants

36 This is the account of Esau (that is, Edom).

2Esau took his wives from the women of Canaan: Adah
daughter of Elon the Hittite, and Oholibamah daughter of
Anah and granddaughter of Zibeon the Hivite— 3also Basemath daughter of Ishmael and sister of Nebaioth.
4Adah bore Eliphaz to Esau, Basemath bore Reuel, 5and
Oholibamah bore Jeush, Jalam and Korah. These were the
sons of Esau, who were born to him in Canaan.
6Esau took his wives and sons and daughters and all the
members of his household, as well as his livestock and all his
other animals and all the goods he had acquired in Canaan,
and moved to a land some distance from his brother Jacob.
7Their possessions were too great for them to remain together; the land where they were staying could not support
them both because of their livestock. 8So Esau (that is,
Edom) settled in the hill country of Seir.

9This is the account of Esau the father of the Edomites in the hill
country of Seir.

10These are the names of Esau's sons:
Eliphaz, the son of Esau's wife Adah, and Reuel, the son of Esau's wife Basemath.
11The sons of Eliphaz:
Teman, Omar, Zepho, Gatam and Kenaz.
12Esau's son Eliphaz also had a concubine named Timna, who bore him Amalek. These were grandsons of Esau's wife Adah.
13The sons of Reuel:
Nahath, Zerah, Shammah and Mizzah. These were grandsons of Esau's wife Basemath.
14The sons of Esau's wife Oholibamah daughter of Anah and granddaughter of Zibeon, whom she bore to Esau:
Jeush, Jalam and Korah.
15These were the chiefs among Esau's descendants:

The sons of Eliphaz the firstborn of Esau:
Chiefs Teman, Omar, Zepho, Kenaz, 16 Korah,[a] Gatam and Amalek. These were the chiefs descended from Eliphaz in Edom; they were grandsons of Adah.
17 The sons of Esau's son Reuel:
Chiefs Nahath, Zerah, Shammah and Mizzah. These were the chiefs descended from Reuel in Edom; they were grandsons of Esau's wife Basemath.
18 The sons of Esau's wife Oholibamah:
Chiefs Jeush, Jalam and Korah. These were the chiefs descended from Esau's wife Oholibamah daughter of Anah.

19 These were the sons of Esau (that is, Edom), and these were their chiefs.

20 These were the sons of Seir the Horite, who were living in the region:
Lotan, Shobal, Zibeon, Anah, 21 Dishon, Ezer and Dishan. These sons of Seir in Edom were Horite chiefs.
22 The sons of Lotan:
Hori and Homam.[b] Timna was Lotan's sister.
23 The sons of Shobal:
Alvan, Manahath, Ebal, Shepho and Onam.
24 The sons of Zibeon:
Aiah and Anah. This is the Anah who discovered the hot springs[c] in the desert while he was grazing the donkeys of his father Zibeon.
25 The children of Anah:
Dishon and Oholibamah daughter of Anah.
26 The sons of Dishon[d]:
Hemdan, Eshban, Ithran and Keran.
27 The sons of Ezer:
Bilhan, Zaavan and Akan.
28 The sons of Dishan:
Uz and Aran.
29 These were the Horite chiefs:
Lotan, Shobal, Zibeon, Anah, 30 Dishon, Ezer and Dishan. These were the Horite chiefs, according to their divisions, in the land of Seir.

The Rulers of Edom

31 These were the kings who reigned in Edom before any Israelite king reigned[e]:
32 Bela son of Beor became king of Edom. His city was named Dinhabah.
33 When Bela died, Jobab son of Zerah from Bozrah succeeded him as king.
34 When Jobab died, Husham from the land of the Temanites succeeded him as king.
35 When Husham died, Hadad son of Bedad, who defeated Midian in the country of Moab, succeeded him as king. His city was named Avith.

[a] *16* Masoretic Text; Samaritan Pentateuch (see also Gen. 36:11 and 1 Chron. 1:36) does not have *Korah.* [b] *22* Hebrew *Hemam,* a variant of *Homam* (see 1 Chron. 1:39)
[c] *24* Vulgate; Syriac *discovered water;* the meaning of the Hebrew for this word is uncertain.
[d] *26* Hebrew *Dishan,* a variant of *Dishon* [e] *31* Or *before an Israelite king reigned over them*

(36:15–35) Once again, Lord, I come upon a list of names: forgotten names, names I can hardly pronounce, names I'd just as soon skip over altogether. But I am reminded today that these names mean something to You. You know each person in this list. You know everything about their lives long since past. They matter to You, even as I matter to You. In a world so large, in a history so long, I often feel tiny, unnoticed, insignificant. But You, O Infinite God, You know my name. You know me. I matter to You. What a wonder!

I have a Maker,
He formed my heart.
Before even time began
My life was in His hand.

He knows my name,
He knows my every thought,
He sees each tear that falls
And hears me when I call.

"He Knows My Name"
Tommy Walker (©1996)

If we need something to buttress us in the inevitable struggles of life, there is nothing that can help us more than the conviction that each one of us is sought by him who made the Pleiades and Orion, that each of us is truly known as no finite men can ever know us, and that, in spite of our feebleness and sin, we can become channels of God's universal love.

D. Elton Trueblood (1900-1994)

(37:5–11) Sovereign Lord, I confess that sometimes my dreams are like those of Joseph: dreams of my own success and glory, dreams of my own power and influence. How easily I can receive Your vision and recast it to my own advantage; and how little do I know what these dreams will cost me! Forgive me for my preoccupation with myself and my own greatness. Give me a humble heart—a heart that bows before You, a heart that seeks Your glory alone. And teach me to leave the fulfillment of my dreams to You.

They that know God will be humble; they that know themselves cannot be proud.
John Flavel (1627-1691)

36 When Hadad died, Samlah from Masrekah succeeded him as king.
37 When Samlah died, Shaul from Rehoboth on the river[a] succeeded him as king.
38 When Shaul died, Baal-Hanan son of Acbor succeeded him as king.
39 When Baal-Hanan son of Acbor died, Hadad[b] succeeded him as king. His city was named Pau, and his wife's name was Mehetabel daughter of Matred, the daughter of Me-Zahab.

40 These were the chiefs descended from Esau, by name, according to their clans and regions:
Timna, Alvah, Jetheth, 41 Oholibamah, Elah, Pinon,
42 Kenaz, Teman, Mibzar, 43 Magdiel and Iram. These were the chiefs of Edom, according to their settlements in the land they occupied.

This was Esau the father of the Edomites.

Joseph's Dreams

37 Jacob lived in the land where his father had stayed, the land of Canaan.

2 This is the account of Jacob.

Joseph, a young man of seventeen, was tending the flocks with his brothers, the sons of Bilhah and the sons of Zilpah, his father's wives, and he brought their father a bad report about them.
3 Now Israel loved Joseph more than any of his other sons, because he had been born to him in his old age; and he made a richly ornamented[c] robe for him. 4 When his brothers saw that their father loved him more than any of them, they hated him and could not speak a kind word to him.
5 Joseph had a dream, and when he told it to his brothers, they hated him all the more. 6 He said to them, "Listen to this dream I had: 7 We were binding sheaves of grain out in the field when suddenly my sheaf rose and stood upright, while your sheaves gathered around mine and bowed down to it."
8 His brothers said to him, "Do you intend to reign over us? Will you actually rule us?" And they hated him all the more because of his dream and what he had said.
9 Then he had another dream, and he told it to his brothers. "Listen," he said, "I had another dream, and this time the sun and moon and eleven stars were bowing down to me."
10 When he told his father as well as his brothers, his father rebuked him and said, "What is this dream you had? Will your mother and I and your brothers actually come and bow down to the ground before you?" 11 His brothers were jealous of him, but his father kept the matter in mind.

Joseph Sold by His Brothers

12 Now his brothers had gone to graze their father's flocks near Shechem, 13 and Israel said to Joseph, "As you know, your broth-

[a] *37* Possibly the Euphrates [b] *39* Many manuscripts of the Masoretic Text, Samaritan Pentateuch and Syriac (see also 1 Chron. 1:50); most manuscripts of the Masoretic Text *Hadar* [c] *3* The meaning of the Hebrew for *richly ornamented* is uncertain; also in verses 23 and 32.

ers are grazing the flocks near Shechem. Come, I am going to
send you to them."
"Very well," he replied.
14So he said to him, "Go and see if all is well with your brothers and with the flocks, and bring word back to me." Then he sent
him off from the Valley of Hebron.
When Joseph arrived at Shechem, 15a man found him wandering around in the fields and asked him, "What are you looking
for?"
16He replied, "I'm looking for my brothers. Can you tell me
where they are grazing their flocks?"
17"They have moved on from here," the man answered. "I
heard them say, 'Let's go to Dothan.' "
So Joseph went after his brothers and found them near Dothan.
18But they saw him in the distance, and before he reached them,
they plotted to kill him.
19"Here comes that dreamer!" they said to each other. 20"Come
now, let's kill him and throw him into one of these cisterns and say
that a ferocious animal devoured him. Then we'll see what comes
of his dreams."
21When Reuben heard this, he tried to rescue him from their
hands. "Let's not take his life," he said. 22"Don't shed any blood.
Throw him into this cistern here in the desert, but don't lay a hand
on him." Reuben said this to rescue him from them and take him
back to his father.
23So when Joseph came to his brothers, they stripped him of
his robe—the richly ornamented robe he was wearing— 24and
they took him and threw him into the cistern. Now the cistern was
empty; there was no water in it.
25As they sat down to eat their meal, they looked up and saw a
caravan of Ishmaelites coming from Gilead. Their camels were
loaded with spices, balm and myrrh, and they were on their way to
take them down to Egypt.
26Judah said to his brothers, "What will we gain if we kill our
brother and cover up his blood? 27Come, let's sell him to the Ishmaelites and not lay our hands on him; after all, he is our brother, our own flesh and blood." His brothers agreed.
28So when the Midianite merchants came by, his brothers
pulled Joseph up out of the cistern and sold him for twenty
shekels[a] of silver to the Ishmaelites, who took him to Egypt.
29When Reuben returned to the cistern and saw that Joseph was
not there, he tore his clothes. 30He went back to his brothers and
said, "The boy isn't there! Where can I turn now?"
31Then they got Joseph's robe, slaughtered a goat and dipped
the robe in the blood. 32They took the ornamented robe back to
their father and said, "We found this. Examine it to see whether it
is your son's robe."
33He recognized it and said, "It is my son's robe! Some ferocious animal has devoured him. Joseph has surely been torn to
pieces."
34Then Jacob tore his clothes, put on sackcloth and mourned
for his son many days. 35All his sons and daughters came to comfort him, but he refused to be comforted. "No," he said, "in
mourning will I go down to the grave[b] to my son." So his father
wept for him.

[a] *28* That is, about 8 ounces (about 0.2 kilogram) [b] *35* Hebrew *Sheol*

(37:17–35) O Lord, this story reeks with the pollution of the human heart: men so filled with hatred that they plot to kill their own flesh and blood; brothers so filled with greed that they sell Joseph into slavery; sons so hardened that they deceive their own father, causing him to grieve inconsolably. Yet You will use these horrors for the salvation of Your chosen ones—including even the very perpetrators. You "have bound all men over to disobedience so that [You] may have mercy on them all. Oh, the depth of the riches of the wisdom and knowledge of God! How unsearchable his judgments, and his paths beyond tracing out!" (Ge 50:20; Ro 11:32–33)

36 Meanwhile, the Midianites[a] sold Joseph in Egypt to Potiphar,
one of Pharaoh's officials, the captain of the guard.

Judah and Tamar

38 At that time, Judah left his brothers and went down to stay
with a man of Adullam named Hirah. 2 There Judah met
the daughter of a Canaanite man named Shua. He married her and
lay with her; 3 she became pregnant and gave birth to a son, who
was named Er. 4 She conceived again and gave birth to a son and
named him Onan. 5 She gave birth to still another son and named
him Shelah. It was at Kezib that she gave birth to him.
6 Judah got a wife for Er, his firstborn, and her name was Tamar.
7 But Er, Judah's firstborn, was wicked in the LORD's sight; so the
LORD put him to death.
8 Then Judah said to Onan, "Lie with your brother's wife and
fulfill your duty to her as a brother-in-law to produce offspring for
your brother." 9 But Onan knew that the offspring would not be
his; so whenever he lay with his brother's wife, he spilled his
semen on the ground to keep from producing offspring for his
brother. 10 What he did was wicked in the LORD's sight; so he put
him to death also.
11 Judah then said to his daughter-in-law Tamar, "Live as a
widow in your father's house until my son Shelah grows up." For
he thought, "He may die too, just like his brothers." So Tamar
went to live in her father's house.
12 After a long time Judah's wife, the daughter of Shua, died.
When Judah had recovered from his grief, he went up to Timnah,
to the men who were shearing his sheep, and his friend Hirah the
Adullamite went with him.
13 When Tamar was told, "Your father-in-law is on his way to
Timnah to shear his sheep," 14 she took off her widow's clothes,
covered herself with a veil to disguise herself, and then sat down
at the entrance to Enaim, which is on the road to Timnah. For she
saw that, though Shelah had now grown up, she had not been
given to him as his wife.
15 When Judah saw her, he thought she was a prostitute, for she
had covered her face. 16 Not realizing that she was his daughter-in-
law, he went over to her by the roadside and said, "Come now, let
me sleep with you."
"And what will you give me to sleep with you?" she asked.
17 "I'll send you a young goat from my flock," he said.
"Will you give me something as a pledge until you send it?" she
asked.
18 He said, "What pledge should I give you?"
"Your seal and its cord, and the staff in your hand," she answered. So he gave them to her and slept with her, and she became pregnant by him. 19 After she left, she took off her veil and
put on her widow's clothes again.
20 Meanwhile Judah sent the young goat by his friend the Adullamite in order to get his pledge back from the woman, but he did
not find her. 21 He asked the men who lived there, "Where is the
shrine prostitute who was beside the road at Enaim?"
"There hasn't been any shrine prostitute here," they said.
22 So he went back to Judah and said, "I didn't find her. Besides,

(37:36) O Lord, when I find myself in desperate straits, be faithful to hear my cry for mercy. "I pray to you, O LORD, in the time of your favor; in your great love, O God, answer me with your sure salvation. Rescue me from the mire, do not let me sink; deliver me from those who hate me, from the deep waters. Do not let the floodwaters engulf me or the depths swallow me up or the pit close its mouth over me. Answer me, O LORD, out of the goodness of your love; in your great mercy turn to me. Do not hide your face from your servant; answer me quickly, for I am in trouble. Come near and rescue me; redeem me because of my foes." (Ps 69:13–18)

[a] *36* Samaritan Pentateuch, Septuagint, Vulgate and Syriac (see also verse 28); Masoretic Text *Medanites*

the men who lived there said, 'There hasn't been any shrine prostitute here.'"

23Then Judah said, "Let her keep what she has, or we will become a laughingstock. After all, I did send her this young goat, but you didn't find her."

24About three months later Judah was told, "Your daughter-in-law Tamar is guilty of prostitution, and as a result she is now pregnant."

Judah said, "Bring her out and have her burned to death!"

25As she was being brought out, she sent a message to her father-in-law. "I am pregnant by the man who owns these," she said. And she added, "See if you recognize whose seal and cord and staff these are."

26Judah recognized them and said, "She is more righteous than I, since I wouldn't give her to my son Shelah." And he did not sleep with her again.

27When the time came for her to give birth, there were twin boys in her womb. 28As she was giving birth, one of them put out his hand; so the midwife took a scarlet thread and tied it on his wrist and said, "This one came out first." 29But when he drew back his hand, his brother came out, and she said, "So this is how you have broken out!" And he was named Perez.[a] 30Then his brother, who had the scarlet thread on his wrist, came out and he was given the name Zerah.[b]

Joseph and Potiphar's Wife

39 Now Joseph had been taken down to Egypt. Potiphar, an Egyptian who was one of Pharaoh's officials, the captain of the guard, bought him from the Ishmaelites who had taken him there.

2The LORD was with Joseph and he prospered, and he lived in the house of his Egyptian master. 3When his master saw that the LORD was with him and that the LORD gave him success in everything he did, 4Joseph found favor in his eyes and became his attendant. Potiphar put him in charge of his household, and he entrusted to his care everything he owned. 5From the time he put him in charge of his household and of all that he owned, the LORD blessed the household of the Egyptian because of Joseph. The blessing of the LORD was on everything Potiphar had, both in the house and in the field. 6So he left in Joseph's care everything he had; with Joseph in charge, he did not concern himself with anything except the food he ate.

Now Joseph was well-built and handsome, 7and after a while his master's wife took notice of Joseph and said, "Come to bed with me!"

8But he refused. "With me in charge," he told her, "my master does not concern himself with anything in the house; everything he owns he has entrusted to my care. 9No one is greater in this house than I am. My master has withheld nothing from me except you, because you are his wife. How then could I do such a wicked thing and sin against God?" 10And though she spoke to Joseph day after day, he refused to go to bed with her or even be with her.

11One day he went into the house to attend to his duties, and none of the household servants was inside. 12She caught him by his cloak and said, "Come to bed with me!" But he left his cloak in her hand and ran out of the house.

[a] 29 *Perez* means *breaking out.* [b] 30 *Zerah* can mean *scarlet* or *brightness.*

(39:12) O Righteous God, in this day when our heroes so readily succumb to the temptations of the flesh, and when these temptations are so often dangled before all of us, help me to be like Joseph. Give me the discernment to know what is right—and what is wrong. Grant me the courage to call sin "sin." Strengthen me to withstand evil. Quicken me to flee from wickedness when it threatens to snare me. Deliver me from the grasp of the evil one. Help me always to turn away from sin and to turn to You, my fortress, my stronghold, my deliverer, my shield. (Ps 18:2; 27:1; Mt 6:13)

The greatest man is he who chooses the right with invincible resolution, who resists the sorest temptations from within and without, who bears the heaviest burdens cheerfully, who is calmest in storms and most fearless under menace and frowns, whose reliance on truth, virtue, on God, is most unfaltering; and is this a greatness which is apt to make a show, or which is most likely to abound in conspicuous station?

William Ellery Channing (1780-1842)

Lord, You are my refuge,
My life is in Your hand.
I know that I can trust You,
And with Your help I'll stand.
I will not be shaken
If Your favor I can see,
I'll stand strong like a mountain
If You just shine Your light on me,
Shine Your light on me.

"I Will Not Be Shaken"
Rick Founds (©1995)

(39:20–23) Even when Joseph was sold into slavery and cast into prison, You were with him, Lord, and You gave him success. Your presence and Your blessings transcend our circumstances. As You were with Abraham, Isaac and Jacob, so You were with Joseph. You have always been with Your people: with Moses, Joshua and the Israelites; with Gideon, Samuel and Your judges and prophets; with David and the kings who sought You; with the disciples of Jesus and Mary His mother. So You will be with us, to bless us, to prosper us, to give us success in whatever we do by Your strength. Thank You, Lord, for the promise that You will be with us always, never failing or forsaking us. (Ge 21:22; 26:2–3; Ex 3:12; Dt 31:6–8; Jos 1:5; Jdg 2:18; 6:12; 2Sa 7:3; 1Ki 11:38; 2Ki 18:5–7; Mt 28:20; Lk 1:28; Jn 14:1–4)

I will be with you,
There's no need to fear.
How can they harm you
When I hold you near?
Your life is in my life
Come peril or sword.
I will be with you,
I will be with you,
For I am the Lord.

"I Will Be With You"
Bill Batstone (©1988)

[13]When she saw that he had left his cloak in her hand and had run out of the house, [14]she called her household servants. "Look," she said to them, "this Hebrew has been brought to us to make sport of us! He came in here to sleep with me, but I screamed. [15]When he heard me scream for help, he left his cloak beside me and ran out of the house."

[16]She kept his cloak beside her until his master came home. [17]Then she told him this story: "That Hebrew slave you brought us came to me to make sport of me. [18]But as soon as I screamed for help, he left his cloak beside me and ran out of the house."

[19]When his master heard the story his wife told him, saying, "This is how your slave treated me," he burned with anger. [20]Joseph's master took him and put him in prison, the place where the king's prisoners were confined.

But while Joseph was there in the prison, [21]the Lord was with him; he showed him kindness and granted him favor in the eyes of the prison warden. [22]So the warden put Joseph in charge of all those held in the prison, and he was made responsible for all that was done there. [23]The warden paid no attention to anything under Joseph's care, because the Lord was with Joseph and gave him success in whatever he did.

The Cupbearer and the Baker

40 Some time later, the cupbearer and the baker of the king of Egypt offended their master, the king of Egypt. [2]Pharaoh was angry with his two officials, the chief cupbearer and the chief baker, [3]and put them in custody in the house of the captain of the guard, in the same prison where Joseph was confined. [4]The captain of the guard assigned them to Joseph, and he attended them.

After they had been in custody for some time, [5]each of the two men—the cupbearer and the baker of the king of Egypt, who were being held in prison—had a dream the same night, and each dream had a meaning of its own.

[6]When Joseph came to them the next morning, he saw that they were dejected. [7]So he asked Pharaoh's officials who were in custody with him in his master's house, "Why are your faces so sad today?"

[8]"We both had dreams," they answered, "but there is no one to interpret them."

Then Joseph said to them, "Do not interpretations belong to God? Tell me your dreams."

[9]So the chief cupbearer told Joseph his dream. He said to him, "In my dream I saw a vine in front of me, [10]and on the vine were three branches. As soon as it budded, it blossomed, and its clusters ripened into grapes. [11]Pharaoh's cup was in my hand, and I took the grapes, squeezed them into Pharaoh's cup and put the cup in his hand."

[12]"This is what it means," Joseph said to him. "The three branches are three days. [13]Within three days Pharaoh will lift up your head and restore you to your position, and you will put Pharaoh's cup in his hand, just as you used to do when you were his cupbearer. [14]But when all goes well with you, remember me and show me kindness; mention me to Pharaoh and get me out of this prison. [15]For I was forcibly carried off from the land of the Hebrews, and even here I have done nothing to deserve being put in a dungeon."

[16]When the chief baker saw that Joseph had given a favorable

interpretation, he said to Joseph, "I too had a dream: On my head
were three baskets of bread.[a] 17In the top basket were all kinds of
baked goods for Pharaoh, but the birds were eating them out of
the basket on my head."
18"This is what it means," Joseph said. "The three baskets are
three days. 19Within three days Pharaoh will lift off your head and
hang you on a tree.[b] And the birds will eat away your flesh."
20Now the third day was Pharaoh's birthday, and he gave a feast
for all his officials. He lifted up the heads of the chief cupbearer
and the chief baker in the presence of his officials: 21He restored
the chief cupbearer to his position, so that he once again put the
cup into Pharaoh's hand, 22but he hanged[c] the chief baker, just as
Joseph had said to them in his interpretation.
23The chief cupbearer, however, did not remember Joseph; he
forgot him.

Pharaoh's Dreams

41 When two full years had passed, Pharaoh had a dream: He
was standing by the Nile, 2when out of the river there came
up seven cows, sleek and fat, and they grazed among the reeds.
3After them, seven other cows, ugly and gaunt, came up out of the
Nile and stood beside those on the riverbank. 4And the cows that
were ugly and gaunt ate up the seven sleek, fat cows. Then Pharaoh woke up.
5He fell asleep again and had a second dream: Seven heads of
grain, healthy and good, were growing on a single stalk. 6After
them, seven other heads of grain sprouted—thin and scorched by
the east wind. 7The thin heads of grain swallowed up the seven
healthy, full heads. Then Pharaoh woke up; it had been a dream.
8In the morning his mind was troubled, so he sent for all the
magicians and wise men of Egypt. Pharaoh told them his dreams,
but no one could interpret them for him.
9Then the chief cupbearer said to Pharaoh, "Today I am reminded of my shortcomings. 10Pharaoh was once angry with his
servants, and he imprisoned me and the chief baker in the house
of the captain of the guard. 11Each of us had a dream the same
night, and each dream had a meaning of its own. 12Now a young
Hebrew was there with us, a servant of the captain of the guard.
We told him our dreams, and he interpreted them for us, giving
each man the interpretation of his dream. 13And things turned out
exactly as he interpreted them to us: I was restored to my position,
and the other man was hanged.[c]"
14So Pharaoh sent for Joseph, and he was quickly brought from
the dungeon. When he had shaved and changed his clothes, he
came before Pharaoh.
15Pharaoh said to Joseph, "I had a dream, and no one can interpret it. But I have heard it said of you that when you hear a
dream you can interpret it."
16"I cannot do it," Joseph replied to Pharaoh, "but God will
give Pharaoh the answer he desires."
17Then Pharaoh said to Joseph, "In my dream I was standing
on the bank of the Nile, 18when out of the river there came up
seven cows, fat and sleek, and they grazed among the reeds.
19After them, seven other cows came up—scrawny and very ugly
and lean. I had never seen such ugly cows in all the land of Egypt.

[a] 16 Or *three wicker baskets* [b] 19 Or *and impale you on a pole* [c] 22,13 Or *impaled*

When a man has no strength, if he leans on God, he becomes powerful.

Dwight Lyman Moody (1837-1899)

(41:16) Joseph could not do it, Lord, but You could. I cannot do that which challenges me now, but You can—through me. Indeed, because You give me strength, I can do everything. So I will boast, not in human wisdom or might, but in You, in the God for whom all things are possible. "I love you, O LORD, my strength." "O my Strength, I sing praise to you; you, O God, are my fortress, my loving God." (Ps 18:1; 59:17; Jer 9:23–24; Mk 10:27; Php 4:13)

I sing th'almighty pow'r of God
That made the mountains rise,
That spread the flowing seas abroad
And built the lofty skies.
I sing the wisdom that ordained
The sun to rule the day;
The moon shines full at His command
And all the stars obey.

"I Sing the Almighty Power of God"
Isaac Watts (1715)

(41:38–40) Holy Spirit, You are God, the third person of the Trinity, worshiped and glorified with the Father and the Son. You were present in the creation, hovering over the waters. You gave wisdom to Joseph, impressing even the godless Pharaoh. You inspired the leaders of Israel, revealing the will of God. You alighted upon Jesus, inaugurating Him for His mission. Now, You have been poured out upon all believers, filling men and women with the very power of God. Holy Spirit, we worship You! Holy Spirit, we offer ourselves to You! Holy Spirit, fill us afresh with Your power. (Ge 1:2; Mk 1:10–11; Ac 2:14–21)

Gracious Spirit, dwell with me:
I myself would gracious be;
And with words that help and heal
Would Thy life in mine reveal;
And with actions bold and meek
Would for Christ my Savior speak.

"Gracious Spirit, Dwell with Me"
Thomas T. Lynch (1855)

20 The lean, ugly cows ate up the seven fat cows that came up first. 21 But even after they ate them, no one could tell that they had done so; they looked just as ugly as before. Then I woke up.

22 "In my dreams I also saw seven heads of grain, full and good, growing on a single stalk. 23 After them, seven other heads sprouted—withered and thin and scorched by the east wind. 24 The thin heads of grain swallowed up the seven good heads. I told this to the magicians, but none could explain it to me."

25 Then Joseph said to Pharaoh, "The dreams of Pharaoh are one and the same. God has revealed to Pharaoh what he is about to do. 26 The seven good cows are seven years, and the seven good heads of grain are seven years; it is one and the same dream. 27 The seven lean, ugly cows that came up afterward are seven years, and so are the seven worthless heads of grain scorched by the east wind: They are seven years of famine.

28 "It is just as I said to Pharaoh: God has shown Pharaoh what he is about to do. 29 Seven years of great abundance are coming throughout the land of Egypt, 30 but seven years of famine will follow them. Then all the abundance in Egypt will be forgotten, and the famine will ravage the land. 31 The abundance in the land will not be remembered, because the famine that follows it will be so severe. 32 The reason the dream was given to Pharaoh in two forms is that the matter has been firmly decided by God, and God will do it soon.

33 "And now let Pharaoh look for a discerning and wise man and put him in charge of the land of Egypt. 34 Let Pharaoh appoint commissioners over the land to take a fifth of the harvest of Egypt during the seven years of abundance. 35 They should collect all the food of these good years that are coming and store up the grain under the authority of Pharaoh, to be kept in the cities for food. 36 This food should be held in reserve for the country, to be used during the seven years of famine that will come upon Egypt, so that the country may not be ruined by the famine."

37 The plan seemed good to Pharaoh and to all his officials. 38 So Pharaoh asked them, "Can we find anyone like this man, one in whom is the spirit of God[a]?"

39 Then Pharaoh said to Joseph, "Since God has made all this known to you, there is no one so discerning and wise as you. 40 You shall be in charge of my palace, and all my people are to submit to your orders. Only with respect to the throne will I be greater than you."

Joseph in Charge of Egypt

41 So Pharaoh said to Joseph, "I hereby put you in charge of the whole land of Egypt." 42 Then Pharaoh took his signet ring from his finger and put it on Joseph's finger. He dressed him in robes of fine linen and put a gold chain around his neck. 43 He had him ride in a chariot as his second-in-command,[b] and men shouted before him, "Make way[c]!" Thus he put him in charge of the whole land of Egypt.

44 Then Pharaoh said to Joseph, "I am Pharaoh, but without your word no one will lift hand or foot in all Egypt." 45 Pharaoh gave Joseph the name Zaphenath-Paneah and gave him Asenath daughter of Potiphera, priest of On,[d] to be his wife. And Joseph went throughout the land of Egypt.

[a] 38 Or *of the gods* [b] 43 Or *in the chariot of his second-in-command*; or *in his second chariot* [c] 43 Or *Bow down* [d] 45 That is, Heliopolis; also in verse 50

46Joseph was thirty years old when he entered the service of
Pharaoh king of Egypt. And Joseph went out from Pharaoh's presence and traveled throughout Egypt. 47During the seven years of
abundance the land produced plentifully. 48Joseph collected all
the food produced in those seven years of abundance in Egypt and
stored it in the cities. In each city he put the food grown in the
fields surrounding it. 49Joseph stored up huge quantities of grain,
like the sand of the sea; it was so much that he stopped keeping
records because it was beyond measure.

50Before the years of famine came, two sons were born to Joseph by Asenath daughter of Potiphera, priest of On. 51Joseph
named his firstborn Manasseh[a] and said, "It is because God has
made me forget all my trouble and all my father's household."
52The second son he named Ephraim[b] and said, "It is because
God has made me fruitful in the land of my suffering."

53The seven years of abundance in Egypt came to an end, 54and
the seven years of famine began, just as Joseph had said. There
was famine in all the other lands, but in the whole land of Egypt
there was food. 55When all Egypt began to feel the famine, the
people cried to Pharaoh for food. Then Pharaoh told all the Egyptians, "Go to Joseph and do what he tells you."

56When the famine had spread over the whole country, Joseph
opened the storehouses and sold grain to the Egyptians, for the
famine was severe throughout Egypt. 57And all the countries came
to Egypt to buy grain from Joseph, because the famine was severe
in all the world.

Joseph's Brothers Go to Egypt

42 When Jacob learned that there was grain in Egypt, he said
to his sons, "Why do you just keep looking at each other?"
2He continued, "I have heard that there is grain in Egypt. Go down
there and buy some for us, so that we may live and not die."

3Then ten of Joseph's brothers went down to buy grain from
Egypt. 4But Jacob did not send Benjamin, Joseph's brother, with
the others, because he was afraid that harm might come to him.
5So Israel's sons were among those who went to buy grain, for the
famine was in the land of Canaan also.

6Now Joseph was the governor of the land, the one who sold
grain to all its people. So when Joseph's brothers arrived, they
bowed down to him with their faces to the ground. 7As soon as Joseph saw his brothers, he recognized them, but he pretended to
be a stranger and spoke harshly to them. "Where do you come
from?" he asked.

"From the land of Canaan," they replied, "to buy food."

8Although Joseph recognized his brothers, they did not recognize him. 9Then he remembered his dreams about them and said
to them, "You are spies! You have come to see where our land is
unprotected."

10"No, my lord," they answered. "Your servants have come to
buy food. 11We are all the sons of one man. Your servants are
honest men, not spies."

12"No!" he said to them. "You have come to see where our land
is unprotected."

13But they replied, "Your servants were twelve brothers, the

[a] 51 *Manasseh* sounds like and may be derived from the Hebrew for *forget.*
[b] 52 *Ephraim* sounds like the Hebrew for *twice fruitful.*

(41:52) Redeemer God, You are indeed the one who makes me fruitful even in the land of suffering. Faithful God, I praise You for never hiding Your face from my suffering but listening to my cry for help. Merciful God, I thank You for the comfort You give in my affliction, for Your promise that preserves my life. Compassionate God, I bless You for pouring out Your love into my heart, so that I might rejoice even in distress. Sovereign God, in the midst of pain and despair, I nevertheless hope in You, confident that through suffering I will be made whole and that I will someday share in Your own resplendent glory. (Ps 22:24; 119:50; Ro 5:3–5; 8:17–18; 2Co 1:5–7; Heb 2:9–10)

It is the fire of suffering which will bring forth the gold of godliness.

Madame Jeanne Marie de La Mothe Guyon (1648–1717)

(42:28) How instinctively we attribute calamities to You, Lord! We name them "acts of God"—hurricanes, tornadoes, floods, earthquakes, catastrophic illnesses. In times of tragic loss, even those who doubt Your existence will cry, "What is this that God has done to us?" Yet how rarely we give You credit for "ordinary entitlements"—waking up each morning, a child's embrace, a radiant sunset. We are so quick to accuse You and so slow to thank You; so quick to shout "unfair" and so slow to share our blessings; so quick to lay blame and so slow to accept responsibility. Forgive us, Lord, when we discredit Your name and ignore Your goodness. Help us to receive each of Your gifts with gratitude and to throw ourselves on Your mercy when troubles come our way.

sons of one man, who lives in the land of Canaan. The youngest is
now with our father, and one is no more."
14Joseph said to them, "It is just as I told you: You are spies!
15And this is how you will be tested: As surely as Pharaoh lives,
you will not leave this place unless your youngest brother comes
here. 16Send one of your number to get your brother; the rest of
you will be kept in prison, so that your words may be tested to see
if you are telling the truth. If you are not, then as surely as Pharaoh lives, you are spies!" 17And he put them all in custody for
three days.
18On the third day, Joseph said to them, "Do this and you will
live, for I fear God: 19If you are honest men, let one of your brothers stay here in prison, while the rest of you go and take grain
back for your starving households. 20But you must bring your
youngest brother to me, so that your words may be verified and
that you may not die." This they proceeded to do.
21They said to one another, "Surely we are being punished because of our brother. We saw how distressed he was when he
pleaded with us for his life, but we would not listen; that's why this
distress has come upon us."
22Reuben replied, "Didn't I tell you not to sin against the boy?
But you wouldn't listen! Now we must give an accounting for his
blood." 23They did not realize that Joseph could understand them,
since he was using an interpreter.
24He turned away from them and began to weep, but then
turned back and spoke to them again. He had Simeon taken from
them and bound before their eyes.
25Joseph gave orders to fill their bags with grain, to put each
man's silver back in his sack, and to give them provisions for their
journey. After this was done for them, 26they loaded their grain on
their donkeys and left.
27At the place where they stopped for the night one of them
opened his sack to get feed for his donkey, and he saw his silver
in the mouth of his sack. 28"My silver has been returned," he said
to his brothers. "Here it is in my sack."

Their hearts sank and they turned to each other trembling and
said, "What is this that God has done to us?"
29When they came to their father Jacob in the land of Canaan,
they told him all that had happened to them. They said, 30"The
man who is lord over the land spoke harshly to us and treated us
as though we were spying on the land. 31But we said to him, 'We
are honest men; we are not spies. 32We were twelve brothers, sons
of one father. One is no more, and the youngest is now with our father in Canaan.'
33"Then the man who is lord over the land said to us, 'This is
how I will know whether you are honest men: Leave one of your
brothers here with me, and take food for your starving households
and go. 34But bring your youngest brother to me so I will know
that you are not spies but honest men. Then I will give your brother back to you, and you can trade[a] in the land.' "
35As they were emptying their sacks, there in each man's sack
was his pouch of silver! When they and their father saw the money
pouches, they were frightened. 36Their father Jacob said to them,
"You have deprived me of my children. Joseph is no more and

[a] 34 Or *move about freely*

Simeon is no more, and now you want to take Benjamin. Everything is against me!"
37 Then Reuben said to his father, "You may put both of my sons
to death if I do not bring him back to you. Entrust him to my care,
and I will bring him back."
38 But Jacob said, "My son will not go down there with you; his
brother is dead and he is the only one left. If harm comes to him
on the journey you are taking, you will bring my gray head down
to the grave[a] in sorrow."

The Second Journey to Egypt

43 Now the famine was still severe in the land. 2 So when they
had eaten all the grain they had brought from Egypt, their
father said to them, "Go back and buy us a little more food."
3 But Judah said to him, "The man warned us solemnly, 'You
will not see my face again unless your brother is with you.' 4 If you
will send our brother along with us, we will go down and buy food
for you. 5 But if you will not send him, we will not go down, because the man said to us, 'You will not see my face again unless
your brother is with you.' "
6 Israel asked, "Why did you bring this trouble on me by telling
the man you had another brother?"
7 They replied, "The man questioned us closely about ourselves
and our family. 'Is your father still living?' he asked us. 'Do you
have another brother?' We simply answered his questions. How
were we to know he would say, 'Bring your brother down here'?"
8 Then Judah said to Israel his father, "Send the boy along with
me and we will go at once, so that we and you and our children
may live and not die. 9 I myself will guarantee his safety; you can
hold me personally responsible for him. If I do not bring him
back to you and set him here before you, I will bear the blame before you all my life. 10 As it is, if we had not delayed, we could have
gone and returned twice."
11 Then their father Israel said to them, "If it must be, then do
this: Put some of the best products of the land in your bags and
take them down to the man as a gift—a little balm and a little
honey, some spices and myrrh, some pistachio nuts and almonds.
12 Take double the amount of silver with you, for you must return
the silver that was put back into the mouths of your sacks. Perhaps
it was a mistake. 13 Take your brother also and go back to the man
at once. 14 And may God Almighty[b] grant you mercy before the
man so that he will let your other brother and Benjamin come
back with you. As for me, if I am bereaved, I am bereaved."
15 So the men took the gifts and double the amount of silver,
and Benjamin also. They hurried down to Egypt and presented
themselves to Joseph. 16 When Joseph saw Benjamin with them, he
said to the steward of his house, "Take these men to my house,
slaughter an animal and prepare dinner; they are to eat with me at
noon."
17 The man did as Joseph told him and took the men to Joseph's
house. 18 Now the men were frightened when they were taken to
his house. They thought, "We were brought here because of the
silver that was put back into our sacks the first time. He wants to
attack us and overpower us and seize us as slaves and take our
donkeys."

[a] 38 Hebrew *Sheol* [b] 14 Hebrew *El-Shaddai*

(43:14) Kyrie eleison! Lord, have mercy! What prayer has resonated more often in the worship of Your people than this one? What prayer could more aptly demonstrate our desperate need of You? What prayer could more simply suggest Your true nature as a merciful God? Indeed, "You are a gracious and merciful God," a God whose mercies are new every morning. In Your "great mercy" You have "given us new birth into a living hope through the resurrection of Jesus Christ from the dead." All praise be to You, God of mercy! (Ps 25:6; Ne 9:31; 1Pe 1:3)

Prostrate before thy throne to lie,
And gaze and gaze on thee!
Frederick William Faber (1814-1863)

(43:28) There was a time, O Lord, when subjects humbled themselves before their human leaders, bowing down in honor. Now, our democratic ideals combined with our leaders' imperfections make such a gesture seem absurd. There was a time, O King, when Your subjects humbled themselves before You, bowing down in body and soul that You might be honored. Now we expect worship to meet our needs, to serve our comfort and convenience. Forgive us for usurping Your place in worship. Restore to us the true essence of worship—the offering of ourselves in humble submission to You, our King of kings and Lord of lords.

19So they went up to Joseph's steward and spoke to him at the
entrance to the house. 20"Please, sir," they said, "we came down
here the first time to buy food. 21But at the place where we
stopped for the night we opened our sacks and each of us found
his silver—the exact weight—in the mouth of his sack. So we
have brought it back with us. 22We have also brought additional
silver with us to buy food. We don't know who put our silver in our
sacks."
23"It's all right," he said. "Don't be afraid. Your God, the God of
your father, has given you treasure in your sacks; I received your
silver." Then he brought Simeon out to them.
24The steward took the men into Joseph's house, gave them
water to wash their feet and provided fodder for their donkeys.
25They prepared their gifts for Joseph's arrival at noon, because
they had heard that they were to eat there.
26When Joseph came home, they presented to him the gifts they
had brought into the house, and they bowed down before him to
the ground. 27He asked them how they were, and then he said,
"How is your aged father you told me about? Is he still living?"
28They replied, "Your servant our father is still alive and well."
And they bowed low to pay him honor.
29As he looked about and saw his brother Benjamin, his own
mother's son, he asked, "Is this your youngest brother, the one
you told me about?" And he said, "God be gracious to you, my
son." 30Deeply moved at the sight of his brother, Joseph hurried
out and looked for a place to weep. He went into his private room
and wept there.
31After he had washed his face, he came out and, controlling
himself, said, "Serve the food."
32They served him by himself, the brothers by themselves, and
the Egyptians who ate with him by themselves, because Egyptians
could not eat with Hebrews, for that is detestable to Egyptians.
33The men had been seated before him in the order of their ages,
from the firstborn to the youngest; and they looked at each other
in astonishment. 34When portions were served to them from Joseph's table, Benjamin's portion was five times as much as anyone
else's. So they feasted and drank freely with him.

A Silver Cup in a Sack

44 Now Joseph gave these instructions to the steward of his
house: "Fill the men's sacks with as much food as they can
carry, and put each man's silver in the mouth of his sack. 2Then
put my cup, the silver one, in the mouth of the youngest one's
sack, along with the silver for his grain." And he did as Joseph
said.
3As morning dawned, the men were sent on their way with their
donkeys. 4They had not gone far from the city when Joseph said to
his steward, "Go after those men at once, and when you catch up
with them, say to them, 'Why have you repaid good with evil? 5Isn't
this the cup my master drinks from and also uses for divination?
This is a wicked thing you have done.' "
6When he caught up with them, he repeated these words to
them. 7But they said to him, "Why does my lord say such things?
Far be it from your servants to do anything like that! 8We even
brought back to you from the land of Canaan the silver we found
inside the mouths of our sacks. So why would we steal silver or
gold from your master's house? 9If any of your servants is found to

have it, he will die; and the rest of us will become my lord's
slaves."
10"Very well, then," he said, "let it be as you say. Whoever is
found to have it will become my slave; the rest of you will be free
from blame."
11Each of them quickly lowered his sack to the ground and
opened it. 12Then the steward proceeded to search, beginning
with the oldest and ending with the youngest. And the cup was
found in Benjamin's sack. 13At this, they tore their clothes. Then
they all loaded their donkeys and returned to the city.
14Joseph was still in the house when Judah and his brothers
came in, and they threw themselves to the ground before him.
15Joseph said to them, "What is this you have done? Don't you
know that a man like me can find things out by divination?"
16"What can we say to my lord?" Judah replied. "What can we
say? How can we prove our innocence? God has uncovered your
servants' guilt. We are now my lord's slaves—we ourselves and
the one who was found to have the cup."
17But Joseph said, "Far be it from me to do such a thing! Only
the man who was found to have the cup will become my slave. The
rest of you, go back to your father in peace."
18Then Judah went up to him and said: "Please, my lord, let
your servant speak a word to my lord. Do not be angry with your
servant, though you are equal to Pharaoh himself. 19My lord
asked his servants, 'Do you have a father or a brother?' 20And we
answered, 'We have an aged father, and there is a young son born
to him in his old age. His brother is dead, and he is the only one
of his mother's sons left, and his father loves him.'
21"Then you said to your servants, 'Bring him down to me so I
can see him for myself.' 22And we said to my lord, 'The boy cannot leave his father; if he leaves him, his father will die.' 23But you
told your servants, 'Unless your youngest brother comes down
with you, you will not see my face again.' 24When we went back to
your servant my father, we told him what my lord had said.
25"Then our father said, 'Go back and buy a little more food.'
26But we said, 'We cannot go down. Only if our youngest brother
is with us will we go. We cannot see the man's face unless our
youngest brother is with us.'
27"Your servant my father said to us, 'You know that my wife
bore me two sons. 28One of them went away from me, and I said,
"He has surely been torn to pieces." And I have not seen him
since. 29If you take this one from me too and harm comes to him,
you will bring my gray head down to the grave[a] in misery.'
30"So now, if the boy is not with us when I go back to your servant my father and if my father, whose life is closely bound up with
the boy's life, 31sees that the boy isn't there, he will die. Your servants will bring the gray head of our father down to the grave in
sorrow. 32Your servant guaranteed the boy's safety to my father. I
said, 'If I do not bring him back to you, I will bear the blame before you, my father, all my life!'
33"Now then, please let your servant remain here as my lord's
slave in place of the boy, and let the boy return with his brothers.
34How can I go back to my father if the boy is not with me? No! Do
not let me see the misery that would come upon my father."

[a] 29 Hebrew *Sheol*; also in verse 31

(44:18–34) O Lord, what a change of heart in Judah! He who once tormented his father with the deception of Joseph's "death" now feels a deep compassion for this same father. What softened his heart, Lord? Time? Suffering? Or the work of Your Spirit in time and through suffering? Indeed, You are the One who removes the heart of stone, replacing it with a heart of flesh. O Lord, take away my selfishness and insensitivity. Father in heaven, make my heart tender, that I might serve others and seek to please You above all else! (Eze 36:24–27)

Give me, O Lord, a steadfast heart,
which no unworthy affection may drag downwards;
Give me an unconquered heart, which no tribulation can wear out;
Give me an upright heart, which no unworthy purpose may tempt aside.
Saint Thomas Aquinas (1225-1274)

Change my heart, oh God,
Make it ever true;
Change my heart, oh God,
May I be like You.

You are the potter,
I am the clay,
Mold me and make me:
This is what I pray.
"Change My Heart, Oh God"
Eddie Espinosa (©1982)

Joseph Makes Himself Known

45 Then Joseph could no longer control himself before all his
attendants, and he cried out, "Have everyone leave my
presence!" So there was no one with Joseph when he made himself known to his brothers. 2And he wept so loudly that the Egyptians heard him, and Pharaoh's household heard about it.
3Joseph said to his brothers, "I am Joseph! Is my father still living?" But his brothers were not able to answer him, because they
were terrified at his presence.
4Then Joseph said to his brothers, "Come close to me." When
they had done so, he said, "I am your brother Joseph, the one you
sold into Egypt! 5And now, do not be distressed and do not be
angry with yourselves for selling me here, because it was to save
lives that God sent me ahead of you. 6For two years now there has
been famine in the land, and for the next five years there will not
be plowing and reaping. 7But God sent me ahead of you to preserve for you a remnant on earth and to save your lives by a great
deliverance.[a]
8"So then, it was not you who sent me here, but God. He made
me father to Pharaoh, lord of his entire household and ruler of all
Egypt. 9Now hurry back to my father and say to him, 'This is what
your son Joseph says: God has made me lord of all Egypt. Come
down to me; don't delay. 10You shall live in the region of Goshen
and be near me—you, your children and grandchildren, your
flocks and herds, and all you have. 11I will provide for you there,
because five years of famine are still to come. Otherwise you and
your household and all who belong to you will become destitute.'
12"You can see for yourselves, and so can my brother Benjamin, that it is really I who am speaking to you. 13Tell my father
about all the honor accorded me in Egypt and about everything
you have seen. And bring my father down here quickly."
14Then he threw his arms around his brother Benjamin and
wept, and Benjamin embraced him, weeping. 15And he kissed all
his brothers and wept over them. Afterward his brothers talked
with him.
16When the news reached Pharaoh's palace that Joseph's
brothers had come, Pharaoh and all his officials were pleased.
17Pharaoh said to Joseph, "Tell your brothers, 'Do this: Load
your animals and return to the land of Canaan, 18and bring your
father and your families back to me. I will give you the best of the
land of Egypt and you can enjoy the fat of the land.'
19"You are also directed to tell them, 'Do this: Take some carts
from Egypt for your children and your wives, and get your father
and come. 20Never mind about your belongings, because the best
of all Egypt will be yours.' "
21So the sons of Israel did this. Joseph gave them carts, as Pharaoh had commanded, and he also gave them provisions for their
journey. 22To each of them he gave new clothing, but to Benjamin
he gave three hundred shekels[b] of silver and five sets of clothes.
23And this is what he sent to his father: ten donkeys loaded with
the best things of Egypt, and ten female donkeys loaded with grain
and bread and other provisions for his journey. 24Then he sent
his brothers away, and as they were leaving he said to them, "Don't
quarrel on the way!"

[a] 7 Or *save you as a great band of survivors* [b] 22 That is, about 7 1/2 pounds (about 3.5 kilograms)

(45:4–7) Is Joseph right, Lord? Did You send him to Egypt? Was it Your will for him to be sold into slavery and cast into prison? Is it not true that You do "not willingly bring affliction or grief to the children of men"? Yet, then again, "Is it not from the mouth of the Most High that both calamities and good things come?" Your ways, Lord, are "too wonderful for me to know." Your providence is perplexing, and profoundly more gracious than anything I can imagine. For, this I confess, that "in all things [You work] for the good of those who love [You]." I adore You, Gracious God, for Your unfathomable goodness. I bow before Your inscrutable sovereignty. (Job 42:3; Ecc 3:11; Isa 40:13–14, 28; La 3:33, 38; Ro 8:28)

Our being is in the hands of omnipotent Goodness, by whom what appears casual to us is directed for ends ultimately kind and merciful; and that nothing can finally hurt him who debars not himself from the divine favour.

Samuel Johnson (1709–1784)

25 So they went up out of Egypt and came to their father Jacob in
the land of Canaan. 26 They told him, "Joseph is still alive! In fact,
he is ruler of all Egypt." Jacob was stunned; he did not believe
them. 27 But when they told him everything Joseph had said to
them, and when he saw the carts Joseph had sent to carry him
back, the spirit of their father Jacob revived. 28 And Israel said,
"I'm convinced! My son Joseph is still alive. I will go and see him
before I die."

Jacob Goes to Egypt

46 So Israel set out with all that was his, and when he
reached Beersheba, he offered sacrifices to the God of his
father Isaac.
2 And God spoke to Israel in a vision at night and said, "Jacob!
Jacob!"
"Here I am," he replied.
3 "I am God, the God of your father," he said. "Do not be afraid
to go down to Egypt, for I will make you into a great nation there.
4 I will go down to Egypt with you, and I will surely bring you back
again. And Joseph's own hand will close your eyes."
5 Then Jacob left Beersheba, and Israel's sons took their father
Jacob and their children and their wives in the carts that Pharaoh
had sent to transport him. 6 They also took with them their livestock and the possessions they had acquired in Canaan, and Jacob
and all his offspring went to Egypt. 7 He took with him to Egypt his
sons and grandsons and his daughters and granddaughters—all
his offspring.

8 These are the names of the sons of Israel (Jacob and his descendants) who went to Egypt:

Reuben the firstborn of Jacob.
9 The sons of Reuben:
Hanoch, Pallu, Hezron and Carmi.
10 The sons of Simeon:
Jemuel, Jamin, Ohad, Jakin, Zohar and Shaul the son of a
Canaanite woman.
11 The sons of Levi:
Gershon, Kohath and Merari.
12 The sons of Judah:
Er, Onan, Shelah, Perez and Zerah (but Er and Onan had
died in the land of Canaan).
The sons of Perez:
Hezron and Hamul.
13 The sons of Issachar:
Tola, Puah,[a] Jashub[b] and Shimron.
14 The sons of Zebulun:
Sered, Elon and Jahleel.
15 These were the sons Leah bore to Jacob in Paddan Aram,[c]
besides his daughter Dinah. These sons and daughters of his were
thirty-three in all.

16 The sons of Gad:
Zephon,[d] Haggi, Shuni, Ezbon, Eri, Arodi and Areli.
17 The sons of Asher:

[a] *13* Samaritan Pentateuch and Syriac (see also 1 Chron. 7:1); Masoretic Text *Puvah*
[b] *13* Samaritan Pentateuch and some Septuagint manuscripts (see also Num. 26:24 and 1 Chron. 7:1); Masoretic Text *Iob* [c] *15* That is, Northwest Mesopotamia
[d] *16* Samaritan Pentateuch and Septuagint (see also Num. 26:15); Masoretic Text *Ziphion*

(46:2–5) You are the God who calls to me and who calls me to do Your will. Your call requires me to say "Here I am, ready to do whatever pleases You." To worship You fully means that I offer not merely the praise of my lips or even the adoration of my heart, but my whole self to You in humble obedience. O Lord, when You call, help me to echo the response of Abraham, Jacob, Moses, Samuel, Isaiah and my Lord Jesus Himself: "Here I am . . . I have come to do your will, O God." Here I am, Sovereign God, here I am for You.
(Ge 22:1; Ex 3:4; 1Sa 3:4; Isa 6:8; Heb 10:7)

There are no disappointments to those whose wills are buried in the will of God.
Frederick William Faber (1814–1863)

Imnah, Ishvah, Ishvi and Beriah.
Their sister was Serah.
The sons of Beriah:
Heber and Malkiel.
18These were the children born to Jacob by Zilpah, whom
Laban had given to his daughter Leah—sixteen in all.

19The sons of Jacob's wife Rachel:
Joseph and Benjamin. 20In Egypt, Manasseh and Ephraim
were born to Joseph by Asenath daughter of Potiphera,
priest of On.[a]
21The sons of Benjamin:
Bela, Beker, Ashbel, Gera, Naaman, Ehi, Rosh, Muppim,
Huppim and Ard.
22These were the sons of Rachel who were born to Jacob—
fourteen in all.

23The son of Dan:
Hushim.
24The sons of Naphtali:
Jahziel, Guni, Jezer and Shillem.
25These were the sons born to Jacob by Bilhah, whom Laban
had given to his daughter Rachel—seven in all.

26All those who went to Egypt with Jacob—those who were his
direct descendants, not counting his sons' wives—numbered
sixty-six persons. 27With the two sons[b] who had been born to Joseph in Egypt, the members of Jacob's family, which went to Egypt,
were seventy[c] in all.

28Now Jacob sent Judah ahead of him to Joseph to get directions to Goshen. When they arrived in the region of Goshen, 29Jo-
seph had his chariot made ready and went to Goshen to meet his
father Israel. As soon as Joseph appeared before him, he threw his
arms around his father[d] and wept for a long time.
30Israel said to Joseph, "Now I am ready to die, since I have
seen for myself that you are still alive."
31Then Joseph said to his brothers and to his father's household, "I will go up and speak to Pharaoh and will say to him, 'My
brothers and my father's household, who were living in the land of
Canaan, have come to me. 32The men are shepherds; they tend
livestock, and they have brought along their flocks and herds and
everything they own.' 33When Pharaoh calls you in and asks,
'What is your occupation?' 34you should answer, 'Your servants
have tended livestock from our boyhood on, just as our fathers
did.' Then you will be allowed to settle in the region of Goshen, for
all shepherds are detestable to the Egyptians."

47 Joseph went and told Pharaoh, "My father and brothers,
with their flocks and herds and everything they own, have
come from the land of Canaan and are now in Goshen." 2He chose
five of his brothers and presented them before Pharaoh.
3Pharaoh asked the brothers, "What is your occupation?"
"Your servants are shepherds," they replied to Pharaoh, "just as
our fathers were." 4They also said to him, "We have come to live
here awhile, because the famine is severe in Canaan and your ser-

[a] 20 That is, Heliopolis [b] 27 Hebrew; Septuagint *the nine children* [c] 27 Hebrew (see also Exodus 1:5 and footnote); Septuagint (see also Acts 7:14) *seventy-five* [d] 29 Hebrew *around him*

(46:29) This poignant reunion between father and son makes me yearn to see You face-to-face, heavenly Father. Before Your singular sovereignty I will someday bow in adoration, only to be ordained to reign with You. As I marvel at Your dazzling glory I will extol You, only to discover that I share even in the glory of Christ. In the presence of Your holiness I will stand amazed, only to realize that I have been made holy and pure by the completed work of Christ in me. Out of love for You I will hope to embrace You, only to find that You have run to me, to enfold me in Your arms and to kiss me as Your own beloved child. (Mt 5:8; Ro 8:17; 1Co 13:12; 1Th 3:13; 2Ti 2:12; Heb 12:14)

Children of the heav'nly Father,
Safely in His bosom gather;
Nestling bird nor star in heaven
Such a refuge e'er was given.

Though He giveth or He taketh,
God His children ne'er forsaketh;
His the loving purpose solely
To preserve them pure and holy.
"Children of the Heavenly Father"
Carolina Sandell Berg (1858)
Trans. Ernest W. Olson (1925)

vants' flocks have no pasture. So now, please let your servants settle in Goshen."
5Pharaoh said to Joseph, "Your father and your brothers have
come to you, 6and the land of Egypt is before you; settle your father and your brothers in the best part of the land. Let them live in
Goshen. And if you know of any among them with special ability,
put them in charge of my own livestock."
7Then Joseph brought his father Jacob in and presented him
before Pharaoh. After Jacob blessed[a] Pharaoh, 8Pharaoh asked
him, "How old are you?"
9And Jacob said to Pharaoh, "The years of my pilgrimage are a
hundred and thirty. My years have been few and difficult, and they
do not equal the years of the pilgrimage of my fathers." 10Then
Jacob blessed[b] Pharaoh and went out from his presence.
11So Joseph settled his father and his brothers in Egypt and
gave them property in the best part of the land, the district of Rameses, as Pharaoh directed. 12Joseph also provided his father and
his brothers and all his father's household with food, according to
the number of their children.

Joseph and the Famine

13There was no food, however, in the whole region because the
famine was severe; both Egypt and Canaan wasted away because of
the famine. 14Joseph collected all the money that was to be found
in Egypt and Canaan in payment for the grain they were buying,
and he brought it to Pharaoh's palace. 15When the money of the
people of Egypt and Canaan was gone, all Egypt came to Joseph
and said, "Give us food. Why should we die before your eyes? Our
money is used up."
16"Then bring your livestock," said Joseph. "I will sell you food
in exchange for your livestock, since your money is gone." 17So
they brought their livestock to Joseph, and he gave them food in
exchange for their horses, their sheep and goats, their cattle and
donkeys. And he brought them through that year with food in exchange for all their livestock.
18When that year was over, they came to him the following year
and said, "We cannot hide from our lord the fact that since our
money is gone and our livestock belongs to you, there is nothing
left for our lord except our bodies and our land. 19Why should we
perish before your eyes—we and our land as well? Buy us and
our land in exchange for food, and we with our land will be in
bondage to Pharaoh. Give us seed so that we may live and not die,
and that the land may not become desolate."
20So Joseph bought all the land in Egypt for Pharaoh. The Egyptians, one and all, sold their fields, because the famine was too severe for them. The land became Pharaoh's, 21and Joseph reduced
the people to servitude,[c] from one end of Egypt to the other.
22However, he did not buy the land of the priests, because they received a regular allotment from Pharaoh and had food enough
from the allotment Pharaoh gave them. That is why they did not
sell their land.
23Joseph said to the people, "Now that I have bought you and
your land today for Pharaoh, here is seed for you so you can plant
the ground. 24But when the crop comes in, give a fifth of it to
Pharaoh. The other four-fifths you may keep as seed for the fields

(47:6–11) Joseph gave the best part of the land to his brothers, who had once thrown him into a cistern. The one who was abandoned blessed those who had once betrayed their own flesh and blood. What a poignant reminder of how You treat us, O gracious Redeemer! We who sent Jesus to the cross by our sin and betrayed the very Son of God—even we have been settled in the "best part" of Your land. You have blessed us in our "Goshen." You have given us the privilege of calling You "*Abba*, Father," the comforting assurance of our salvation in Christ, the empowering presence of Your Spirit, the anticipatory fellowship of Your church, the trustworthy guidance of Your Word, the healing nourishment of Your sacraments. We praise You, O Lord, for the marvelous mystery of Your redemption!

[a] 7 Or *greeted* [b] 10 Or *said farewell to* [c] 21 Samaritan Pentateuch and Septuagint (see also Vulgate); Masoretic Text *and he moved the people into the cities*

and as food for yourselves and your households and your children."
25"You have saved our lives," they said. "May we find favor in
the eyes of our lord; we will be in bondage to Pharaoh."
26So Joseph established it as a law concerning land in Egypt—
still in force today—that a fifth of the produce belongs to Pharaoh. It was only the land of the priests that did not become Pharaoh's.
27Now the Israelites settled in Egypt in the region of Goshen.
They acquired property there and were fruitful and increased
greatly in number.
28Jacob lived in Egypt seventeen years, and the years of his life
were a hundred and forty-seven. 29When the time drew near for
Israel to die, he called for his son Joseph and said to him, "If I
have found favor in your eyes, put your hand under my thigh and
promise that you will show me kindness and faithfulness. Do not
bury me in Egypt, 30but when I rest with my fathers, carry me out
of Egypt and bury me where they are buried."
"I will do as you say," he said.
31"Swear to me," he said. Then Joseph swore to him, and Israel worshiped as he leaned on the top of his staff.[a]

Manasseh and Ephraim

48 Some time later Joseph was told, "Your father is ill." So he
took his two sons Manasseh and Ephraim along with him.
2When Jacob was told, "Your son Joseph has come to you," Israel rallied his strength and sat up on the bed.
3Jacob said to Joseph, "God Almighty[b] appeared to me at Luz in
the land of Canaan, and there he blessed me 4and said to me, 'I
am going to make you fruitful and will increase your numbers. I
will make you a community of peoples, and I will give this land as
an everlasting possession to your descendants after you.'
5"Now then, your two sons born to you in Egypt before I came
to you here will be reckoned as mine; Ephraim and Manasseh
will be mine, just as Reuben and Simeon are mine. 6Any children
born to you after them will be yours; in the territory they inherit
they will be reckoned under the names of their brothers. 7As I
was returning from Paddan,[c] to my sorrow Rachel died in the
land of Canaan while we were still on the way, a little distance
from Ephrath. So I buried her there beside the road to Ephrath"
(that is, Bethlehem).
8When Israel saw the sons of Joseph, he asked, "Who are
these?"
9"They are the sons God has given me here," Joseph said to his
father.
Then Israel said, "Bring them to me so I may bless them."
10Now Israel's eyes were failing because of old age, and he
could hardly see. So Joseph brought his sons close to him, and his
father kissed them and embraced them.
11Israel said to Joseph, "I never expected to see your face
again, and now God has allowed me to see your children too."
12Then Joseph removed them from Israel's knees and bowed
down with his face to the ground. 13And Joseph took both of them,
Ephraim on his right toward Israel's left hand and Manasseh on
his left toward Israel's right hand, and brought them close to him.

[a] *31* Or *Israel bowed down at the head of his bed* [b] *3* Hebrew *El-Shaddai* [c] *7* That is, Northwest Mesopotamia

Faith and sight are set in opposition to each other in Scripture, but not faith and reason . . . True faith is essentially reasonable because it trusts in the character and the promises of God. A believing Christian is one whose mind reflects and rests on these certitudes.

John R. W. Stott (1921-)

(48:3–4) Thank You, Lord, for Your promises! They have sustained me throughout my life as they did for Jacob. They have given me comfort in suffering. Through Your very great and precious promises You have helped me to escape from the corruption of this world in order to participate in Your very nature. You are faithful, O God, to fulfill everything You have promised. All of Your promises are "Yes" in Christ! Hallelujah! (Ps 119:50; 145:13; 2Co 1:20; 2Pe 1:4)

[14]But Israel reached out his right hand and put it on Ephraim's
head, though he was the younger, and crossing his arms, he put
his left hand on Manasseh's head, even though Manasseh was the
firstborn.
[15]Then he blessed Joseph and said,

"May the God before whom my fathers
Abraham and Isaac walked,
the God who has been my shepherd
all my life to this day,
[16]the Angel who has delivered me from all harm
—may he bless these boys.
May they be called by my name
and the names of my fathers Abraham and Isaac,
and may they increase greatly
upon the earth."

[17]When Joseph saw his father placing his right hand on Ephraim's head he was displeased; so he took hold of his father's hand
to move it from Ephraim's head to Manasseh's head. [18]Joseph said
to him, "No, my father, this one is the firstborn; put your right
hand on his head."
[19]But his father refused and said, "I know, my son, I know. He
too will become a people, and he too will become great. Nevertheless, his younger brother will be greater than he, and his descendants will become a group of nations." [20]He blessed them
that day and said,

"In your[a] name will Israel pronounce this blessing:
'May God make you like Ephraim and Manasseh.' "

So he put Ephraim ahead of Manasseh.
[21]Then Israel said to Joseph, "I am about to die, but God will be
with you[b] and take you[b] back to the land of your[b] fathers. [22]And
to you, as one who is over your brothers, I give the ridge of land[c]
I took from the Amorites with my sword and my bow."

Jacob Blesses His Sons

49 Then Jacob called for his sons and said: "Gather around
so I can tell you what will happen to you in days to come.

[2]"Assemble and listen, sons of Jacob;
listen to your father Israel.

[3]"Reuben, you are my firstborn,
my might, the first sign of my strength,
excelling in honor, excelling in power.
[4]Turbulent as the waters, you will no longer excel,
for you went up onto your father's bed,
onto my couch and defiled it.

[5]"Simeon and Levi are brothers—
their swords[d] are weapons of violence.
[6]Let me not enter their council,
let me not join their assembly,
for they have killed men in their anger
and hamstrung oxen as they pleased.

[a] *20* The Hebrew is singular. [b] *21* The Hebrew is plural. [c] *22* Or *And to you I give one portion more than to your brothers—the portion* [d] *5* The meaning of the Hebrew for this word is uncertain.

The Lord my pasture shall prepare,
And feed me with a shepherd's care;
His presence shall my wants supply,
And guard me with a watchful eye.
Joseph Addison (1672-1719)

(48:15–16) Gracious Lord, You are indeed the Shepherd of Your people. Thank You for being my Shepherd, for watching over and protecting me, for providing my sustenance and rest, for guiding me in Your ways and never leaving me. I worship You, Lord Jesus, for being the Good Shepherd. You seek me when I am lost. With You, Good Shepherd, I am found! You have laid down Your life for me, that I might live as one of Your flock. O my Shepherd, I am Yours! "Surely goodness and love will follow me all the days of my life, and I will dwell in the house of the LORD forever." (Ps 23; Lk 15:3–6; Jn 10:11–15)

I look to the Shepherd,
He meets all my needs;
Beside the still waters
He faithfully leads,
Bringing peace to my soul,
As His love makes me whole.

Surely goodness and mercy
Shall follow me, follow me
All the days of my life.
Surely goodness and mercy
Shall follow me
All my life.

"I Look to the Shepherd"
Walt Harrah (©1987)

(49:8–12) I praise you, O God, that this blessing found its fulfillment in our Lord Jesus Christ, who is the Lion of Judah. He has triumphed over sin and death. He holds the scepter of divine power. His kingdom will last forever. All praise be to You, Lion of Judah! You are also the Lamb of God, who takes away the sin of the world. You are the Passover lamb, the perfect sacrifice, without defect or blemish. You are worthy, Lion of Judah, O Lamb of God, "to receive power and wealth and wisdom and strength and honor and glory and praise!" With the hosts of heaven I bow before You in worship. (Lk 1:33; Jn 1:29; 1Co 5:7; 1Pe 1:19; Rev 5:5–13)

Who is He?
Who's the mightiest of all?
Who is He?
Creation trembles at His call.
Who is He?
The lowly sacrifice
Who paid a victim's price;
His name is Jesus.

Jesus, from the Father's own right
hand
Jesus, Son of God and Son of man
Jesus, who died and rose again
Jesus, He's the Lion and the Lamb.

"The Lion and The Lamb"
Anne Barbour and Bill Batstone (©1990)

7 Cursed be their anger, so fierce,
and their fury, so cruel!
I will scatter them in Jacob
and disperse them in Israel.

8 "Judah,[a] your brothers will praise you;
your hand will be on the neck of your enemies;
your father's sons will bow down to you.
9 You are a lion's cub, O Judah;
you return from the prey, my son.
Like a lion he crouches and lies down,
like a lioness—who dares to rouse him?
10 The scepter will not depart from Judah,
nor the ruler's staff from between his feet,
until he comes to whom it belongs[b]
and the obedience of the nations is his.
11 He will tether his donkey to a vine,
his colt to the choicest branch;
he will wash his garments in wine,
his robes in the blood of grapes.
12 His eyes will be darker than wine,
his teeth whiter than milk.[c]
13 "Zebulun will live by the seashore
and become a haven for ships;
his border will extend toward Sidon.

14 "Issachar is a rawboned[d] donkey
lying down between two saddlebags.[e]
15 When he sees how good is his resting place
and how pleasant is his land,
he will bend his shoulder to the burden
and submit to forced labor.
16 "Dan[f] will provide justice for his people
as one of the tribes of Israel.
17 Dan will be a serpent by the roadside,
a viper along the path,
that bites the horse's heels
so that its rider tumbles backward.

18 "I look for your deliverance, O LORD.

19 "Gad[g] will be attacked by a band of raiders,
but he will attack them at their heels.

20 "Asher's food will be rich;
he will provide delicacies fit for a king.

21 "Naphtali is a doe set free
that bears beautiful fawns.[h]

22 "Joseph is a fruitful vine,
a fruitful vine near a spring,
whose branches climb over a wall.[i]
23 With bitterness archers attacked him;

[a] 8 *Judah* sounds like and may be derived from the Hebrew for *praise*. [b] 10 Or *until Shiloh comes*; or *until he comes to whom tribute belongs* [c] 12 Or *will be dull from wine, / his teeth white from milk* [d] 14 Or *strong* [e] 14 Or *campfires* [f] 16 *Dan* here means *he provides justice*. [g] 19 *Gad* can mean *attack* and *band of raiders*. [h] 21 Or *free; / he utters beautiful words* [i] 22 Or *Joseph is a wild colt, / a wild colt near a spring, / a wild donkey on a terraced hill*

they shot at him with hostility.
24 But his bow remained steady,
his strong arms stayed[a] limber,
because of the hand of the Mighty One of Jacob,
because of the Shepherd, the Rock of Israel,
25 because of your father's God, who helps you,
because of the Almighty,[b] who blesses you
with blessings of the heavens above,
blessings of the deep that lies below,
blessings of the breast and womb.
26 Your father's blessings are greater
than the blessings of the ancient mountains,
than[c] the bounty of the age-old hills.
Let all these rest on the head of Joseph,
on the brow of the prince among[d] his brothers.

27 "Benjamin is a ravenous wolf;
in the morning he devours the prey,
in the evening he divides the plunder."

28 All these are the twelve tribes of Israel, and this is what their
father said to them when he blessed them, giving each the blessing appropriate to him.

The Death of Jacob

29 Then he gave them these instructions: "I am about to be gathered to my people. Bury me with my fathers in the cave in the field
of Ephron the Hittite, 30 the cave in the field of Machpelah, near
Mamre in Canaan, which Abraham bought as a burial place from
Ephron the Hittite, along with the field. 31 There Abraham and his
wife Sarah were buried, there Isaac and his wife Rebekah were
buried, and there I buried Leah. 32 The field and the cave in it were
bought from the Hittites.[e]"

33 When Jacob had finished giving instructions to his sons, he
drew his feet up into the bed, breathed his last and was gathered
to his people.

50 Joseph threw himself upon his father and wept over him
and kissed him. 2 Then Joseph directed the physicians
in his service to embalm his father Israel. So the physicians
embalmed him, 3 taking a full forty days, for that was the time
required for embalming. And the Egyptians mourned for him
seventy days.

4 When the days of mourning had passed, Joseph said to Pharaoh's court, "If I have found favor in your eyes, speak to Pharaoh
for me. Tell him, 5 'My father made me swear an oath and said, "I
am about to die; bury me in the tomb I dug for myself in the land
of Canaan." Now let me go up and bury my father; then I will return.' "

6 Pharaoh said, "Go up and bury your father, as he made you
swear to do."

7 So Joseph went up to bury his father. All Pharaoh's officials accompanied him—the dignitaries of his court and all the dignitaries of Egypt— 8 besides all the members of Joseph's household
and his brothers and those belonging to his father's household.
Only their children and their flocks and herds were left in Goshen.

[a] 23,24 Or *archers will attack . . . will shoot . . . will remain . . . will stay* [b] 25 Hebrew *Shaddai* [c] 26 Or *of my progenitors, / as great as* [d] 26 Or *the one separated from* [e] 32 Or *the sons of Heth*

(49:24) "Come, let us sing for joy to the LORD; let us shout aloud to the Rock of our salvation. Let us come before him with thanksgiving and extol him with music and song." O Rock of Refuge, You are my fortress and strong tower. When everything around me feels dangerous and insecure, You are always sure and solid. O Rock eternal, You keep me in perfect peace when I trust in You. O living Stone, though rejected by many and a Stone for their stumbling, You are precious to God. You have finished Your work as the "Rock my Savior." From You I drink the living water of eternal life. "The LORD lives! Praise be to my Rock! Exalted be God, the Rock, my Savior!" (Nu 20:8; 2Sa 22:47; Ps 31:2–3; 89:26; 95:1–2; Isa 26:3–4; 1Co 10:4; 1Pe 2:4)

The true religion is built upon the Rock; the rest are tossed upon the waves of time.

Francis Bacon (1561-1626)

9Chariots and horsemen[a] also went up with him. It was a very
large company.
10When they reached the threshing floor of Atad, near the Jordan, they lamented loudly and bitterly; and there Joseph observed
a seven-day period of mourning for his father. 11When the Canaanites who lived there saw the mourning at the threshing floor of
Atad, they said, "The Egyptians are holding a solemn ceremony of
mourning." That is why that place near the Jordan is called Abel
Mizraim.[b]
12So Jacob's sons did as he had commanded them: 13They carried him to the land of Canaan and buried him in the cave in the
field of Machpelah, near Mamre, which Abraham had bought as a
burial place from Ephron the Hittite, along with the field. 14After
burying his father, Joseph returned to Egypt, together with his
brothers and all the others who had gone with him to bury his
father.

Joseph Reassures His Brothers

15When Joseph's brothers saw that their father was dead, they
said, "What if Joseph holds a grudge against us and pays us back
for all the wrongs we did to him?" 16So they sent word to Joseph,
saying, "Your father left these instructions before he died: 17'This
is what you are to say to Joseph: I ask you to forgive your brothers
the sins and the wrongs they committed in treating you so badly.'
Now please forgive the sins of the servants of the God of your father." When their message came to him, Joseph wept.
18His brothers then came and threw themselves down before
him. "We are your slaves," they said.
19But Joseph said to them, "Don't be afraid. Am I in the place
of God? 20You intended to harm me, but God intended it for good
to accomplish what is now being done, the saving of many lives.
21So then, don't be afraid. I will provide for you and your children." And he reassured them and spoke kindly to them.

The Death of Joseph

22Joseph stayed in Egypt, along with all his father's family. He
lived a hundred and ten years 23and saw the third generation of
Ephraim's children. Also the children of Makir son of Manasseh
were placed at birth on Joseph's knees.[c]
24Then Joseph said to his brothers, "I am about to die. But God
will surely come to your aid and take you up out of this land to the
land he promised on oath to Abraham, Isaac and Jacob." 25And
Joseph made the sons of Israel swear an oath and said, "God will
surely come to your aid, and then you must carry my bones up
from this place."
26So Joseph died at the age of a hundred and ten. And after they
embalmed him, he was placed in a coffin in Egypt.

God is over all things, under all things, outside all, within, but not enclosed, without, but not excluded, above, but not raised up, below, but not depressed, wholly above, presiding, wholly without, embracing, wholly within, filling.

Hildebert of Lavardin (1056-1133)

(50:20) Sovereign Lord, You are holy and wholly other. All Your works are perfect. You do no wrong. Yet in the mystery of Your providence You intend for good that which we intend for evil. You use even our sin against You for the saving of many lives. What a mystery! What a wonder! What a comfort to know that when we fail You are not impeded! According to the mystery of Your will, You will accomplish all that You have purposed. In the day of Christ You will have completed Your good work in us. We will stand before You, blameless, pure and holy. Awesome God, all wise and infinitely good, we bow before You! We worship You! We give You thanks! We praise You for Your glory! (Dt 32:4; Php 1:10; 1Th 3:13)

[a] 9 Or *charioteers* [b] 11 *Abel Mizraim* means *mourning of the Egyptians.* [c] 23 That is, were counted as his

The Second Book of Moses called

EXODUS

The book of Exodus tells the story of the departure of Israel from bondage in Egypt. This "exodus" from slavery is fundamentally the work of Israel's God. In the process of delivering His people He reveals more of His character, thereby clarifying how we are to respond to Him in a life of worship.

God's redemption of the Israelites begins when He hears their cries for deliverance from slavery (ch. 2). God has compassion on His people and remembers His covenant with Abraham. He commences His deliverance by revealing Himself to Moses in the burning bush (ch. 3). He is no mere tribal deity, but a holy God, a God Whose very name, "I AM WHO I AM," exhibits His ultimate sovereignty. Like Moses, in the presence of this God we are awestruck and want to hide our faces. Yet God does not consume us with His fire; rather, He draws us into relationship with Himself and enlists us for His saving purposes.

Through Moses, the Lord saves His people from their bondage in Egypt (chs. 3—14). Along the way God demonstrates His superior power over human tyranny, pagan gods and natural processes. Despite the resistance of Pharaoh, God frees His people. He institutes the celebration of the Passover feast to preserve the lives of Israel's firstborn sons and also to help future generations to remember His gracious deliverance. As Christians, our worship also centers in God's salvation and a meal of remembrance—the salvation through Christ's death which is celebrated in His Supper. Even as the children of Israel rejoiced in song because God had saved them (ch. 15), so we worship with joyful praise because of what God has done for us through Christ.

But God seeks more than the praise of our lips—He expects us to worship Him through our obedience to His commands. After setting His people free, God reaffirms and expands His covenant with them (ch. 19). He reveals the law on Mt. Sinai, a legal code beginning with the Ten Commandments (ch. 20). These are the terms of the covenant.

God seeks more than the praise of our lips—He expects us to worship Him through our obedience to His commands.

God begins His law by claiming His unique right to be worshiped. Other gods and idols are forbidden. God is jealous for worship and shares this honor with no other. When the Israelites worship a golden calf, God's anger burns hot and the people pay a heavy penalty (ch. 32). By this sad tale we are reminded of our own tendency to place other "gods" before the One God Who is worthy of our exclusive worship.

In Exodus we encounter a glorious God. The story ends with the glory of God filling the tabernacle, the center of Israel's worship (ch. 40). God's glory is overwhelming, far beyond our comprehension. Even Moses cannot bear to look upon it (ch. 33). Exodus reminds us that we worship a God Whose glory fills us with awe and Who deserves to have our lives given to Him in reverent, active worship.

God is the God of promise. He keeps his word, even when that seems impossible; even when the circumstances seem to point to the opposite.

Colin Urquhart (1940-)

(1:7) O Lord, You are God! You give life to the dead and call things that are not as though they were. How powerful is Your word of promise. Centuries before, You had promised to make of Abraham and Sarah a great nation. After so long a time, in so unlikely a place, no one would have expected this overwhelming explosion of life! Yet all the while Your powerful promise was unfolding behind the scenes. Teach us Lord, that worship must not depend on our own sense of timing or circumstances, but on Your unwavering word of promise. (Ge 15:5,13–14; Ro 4:17)

What though I wait the live-long
night
And till the dawn appeareth,
My heart still trusteth in God's
might;
It doubteth not nor feareth:
So let the Israelites in heart,
Born of the Spirit, do their part,
And wait till God appeareth.

"Out of the Depths"
Martin Luther (1524)
Trans. Richard Massie (1854)

(2:3) In wisdom Lord, You lead us to the limit of our own resources. Confronted with the onslaught of evil power, we soon come face-to-face with our own weakness and frailty. We do all we can, only to find that our efforts fall short. Lord, how desperate we are for You to act! And so we come to trust, not in ourselves, but in God who raises the dead and delivers from deadly peril. We learn to glory even in our weaknesses, knowing that they will become the showcase for Your saving power. (2Co 1:9–10)

The Israelites Oppressed

These are the names of the sons of Israel who went to Egypt
with Jacob, each with his family: 2Reuben, Simeon, Levi and
Judah; 3Issachar, Zebulun and Benjamin; 4Dan and Naphtali; Gad
and Asher. 5The descendants of Jacob numbered seventy[a] in all;
Joseph was already in Egypt.
6Now Joseph and all his brothers and all that generation died,
7but the Israelites were fruitful and multiplied greatly and became
exceedingly numerous, so that the land was filled with them.
8Then a new king, who did not know about Joseph, came to
power in Egypt. 9"Look," he said to his people, "the Israelites
have become much too numerous for us. 10Come, we must deal
shrewdly with them or they will become even more numerous
and, if war breaks out, will join our enemies, fight against us and
leave the country."
11So they put slave masters over them to oppress them with
forced labor, and they built Pithom and Rameses as store cities
for Pharaoh. 12But the more they were oppressed, the more they
multiplied and spread; so the Egyptians came to dread the Israelites 13and worked them ruthlessly. 14They made their lives bitter
with hard labor in brick and mortar and with all kinds of work in
the fields; in all their hard labor the Egyptians used them ruthlessly.
15The king of Egypt said to the Hebrew midwives, whose names
were Shiphrah and Puah, 16"When you help the Hebrew women in
childbirth and observe them on the delivery stool, if it is a boy, kill
him; but if it is a girl, let her live." 17The midwives, however,
feared God and did not do what the king of Egypt had told them to
do; they let the boys live. 18Then the king of Egypt summoned the
midwives and asked them, "Why have you done this? Why have you
let the boys live?"
19The midwives answered Pharaoh, "Hebrew women are not
like Egyptian women; they are vigorous and give birth before the
midwives arrive."
20So God was kind to the midwives and the people increased
and became even more numerous. 21And because the midwives
feared God, he gave them families of their own.
22Then Pharaoh gave this order to all his people: "Every boy
that is born[b] you must throw into the Nile, but let every girl live."

The Birth of Moses

2 Now a man of the house of Levi married a Levite woman, 2and
she became pregnant and gave birth to a son. When she saw
that he was a fine child, she hid him for three months. 3But when
she could hide him no longer, she got a papyrus basket for him
and coated it with tar and pitch. Then she placed the child in it
and put it among the reeds along the bank of the Nile. 4His sister
stood at a distance to see what would happen to him.
5Then Pharaoh's daughter went down to the Nile to bathe, and
her attendants were walking along the river bank. She saw the basket among the reeds and sent her slave girl to get it. 6She opened
it and saw the baby. He was crying, and she felt sorry for him.
"This is one of the Hebrew babies," she said.

[a] *5* Masoretic Text (see also Gen. 46:27); Dead Sea Scrolls and Septuagint (see also Acts 7:14 and note at Gen. 46:27) *seventy-five* [b] *22* Masoretic Text; Samaritan Pentateuch, Septuagint and Targums *born to the Hebrews*

7 Then his sister asked Pharaoh's daughter, "Shall I go and get
one of the Hebrew women to nurse the baby for you?"
8 "Yes, go," she answered. And the girl went and got the baby's
mother. 9 Pharaoh's daughter said to her, "Take this baby and
nurse him for me, and I will pay you." So the woman took the
baby and nursed him. 10 When the child grew older, she took him
to Pharaoh's daughter and he became her son. She named him
Moses,[a] saying, "I drew him out of the water."

Moses Flees to Midian

11 One day, after Moses had grown up, he went out to where his
own people were and watched them at their hard labor. He saw
an Egyptian beating a Hebrew, one of his own people. 12 Glancing
this way and that and seeing no one, he killed the Egyptian and
hid him in the sand. 13 The next day he went out and saw two Hebrews fighting. He asked the one in the wrong, "Why are you hit-
ting your fellow Hebrew?"
14 The man said, "Who made you ruler and judge over us? Are
you thinking of killing me as you killed the Egyptian?" Then
Moses was afraid and thought, "What I did must have become
known."
15 When Pharaoh heard of this, he tried to kill Moses, but
Moses fled from Pharaoh and went to live in Midian, where he sat
down by a well. 16 Now a priest of Midian had seven daughters,
and they came to draw water and fill the troughs to water their father's flock. 17 Some shepherds came along and drove them away,
but Moses got up and came to their rescue and watered their
flock.
18 When the girls returned to Reuel their father, he asked them,
"Why have you returned so early today?"
19 They answered, "An Egyptian rescued us from the shepherds. He even drew water for us and watered the flock."
20 "And where is he?" he asked his daughters. "Why did you
leave him? Invite him to have something to eat."
21 Moses agreed to stay with the man, who gave his daughter
Zipporah to Moses in marriage. 22 Zipporah gave birth to a son,
and Moses named him Gershom,[b] saying, "I have become an
alien in a foreign land."
23 During that long period, the king of Egypt died. The Israelites groaned in their slavery and cried out, and their cry for help
because of their slavery went up to God. 24 God heard their groaning and he remembered his covenant with Abraham, with Isaac
and with Jacob. 25 So God looked on the Israelites and was concerned about them.

Moses and the Burning Bush

3 Now Moses was tending the flock of Jethro his father-in-law,
the priest of Midian, and he led the flock to the far side of the
desert and came to Horeb, the mountain of God. 2 There the angel
of the LORD appeared to him in flames of fire from within a bush.
Moses saw that though the bush was on fire it did not burn up.
3 So Moses thought, "I will go over and see this strange sight—
why the bush does not burn up."
4 When the LORD saw that he had gone over to look, God called
to him from within the bush, "Moses! Moses!"

[a] 10 *Moses* sounds like the Hebrew for *draw out.* [b] 22 *Gershom* sounds like the Hebrew for *an alien there.*

(2:23) What if my prayer appears unanswered? What if my pain is unrelieved? Shall I place a time limit on You, O God—an expiration date on my prayers? Surely the struggle of Your people can never go unnoticed in heaven. Our prayers rise like incense before Your throne and fill Your senses. You hear! You see! You know! You are ever mindful of Your promise. Here I am before You once again, Lord. I wait in hope. (Rev 5:8–12)

We dare not think that God is absent or daydreaming. The do-nothing God. He's not tucked away in some far corner of the universe, uncaring, unfeeling, unthinking . . . uninvolved. Count on it–God intrudes in glorious and myriad ways.

Joni Eareckson Tada (1949-)

(3:1) Horeb: A desolate, lonely wasteland. But You bless this place with Your presence, Lord, and it becomes the mountain of God. It becomes the place of awesome revelation! Moses: A broken, aimless man. But You bless him with Your presence and he becomes a man of God. He becomes the instrument of Your great work! Here I am, Lord. What can Your presence make of me?

This is holy ground.
We're standing on holy ground.
For the Lord is present,
And where He is, is holy.

These are holy hands.
He's given us holy hands.
He works through these hands
And so these hands are holy.

"Holy Ground"
Christopher Beatty (©1982)

And Moses said, "Here I am."

5 "Do not come any closer," God said. "Take off your sandals, for the place where you are standing is holy ground." 6 Then he said, "I am the God of your father, the God of Abraham, the God of Isaac and the God of Jacob." At this, Moses hid his face, because he was afraid to look at God.

7 The LORD said, "I have indeed seen the misery of my people in Egypt. I have heard them crying out because of their slave drivers, and I am concerned about their suffering. 8 So I have come down to rescue them from the hand of the Egyptians and to bring them up out of that land into a good and spacious land, a land flowing with milk and honey—the home of the Canaanites, Hittites, Amorites, Perizzites, Hivites and Jebusites. 9 And now the cry of the Israelites has reached me, and I have seen the way the Egyptians are oppressing them. 10 So now, go. I am sending you to Pharaoh to bring my people the Israelites out of Egypt."

11 But Moses said to God, "Who am I, that I should go to Pharaoh and bring the Israelites out of Egypt?"

12 And God said, "I will be with you. And this will be the sign to you that it is I who have sent you: When you have brought the people out of Egypt, you[a] will worship God on this mountain."

13 Moses said to God, "Suppose I go to the Israelites and say to them, 'The God of your fathers has sent me to you,' and they ask me, 'What is his name?' Then what shall I tell them?"

14 God said to Moses, "I AM WHO I AM.[b] This is what you are to say to the Israelites: 'I AM has sent me to you.' "

15 God also said to Moses, "Say to the Israelites, 'The LORD,[c] the God of your fathers—the God of Abraham, the God of Isaac and the God of Jacob—has sent me to you.' This is my name forever, the name by which I am to be remembered from generation to generation.

16 "Go, assemble the elders of Israel and say to them, 'The LORD, the God of your fathers—the God of Abraham, Isaac and Jacob—appeared to me and said: I have watched over you and have seen what has been done to you in Egypt. 17 And I have promised to bring you up out of your misery in Egypt into the land of the Canaanites, Hittites, Amorites, Perizzites, Hivites and Jebusites—a land flowing with milk and honey.'

18 "The elders of Israel will listen to you. Then you and the elders are to go to the king of Egypt and say to him, 'The LORD, the God of the Hebrews, has met with us. Let us take a three-day journey into the desert to offer sacrifices to the LORD our God.' 19 But I know that the king of Egypt will not let you go unless a mighty hand compels him. 20 So I will stretch out my hand and strike the Egyptians with all the wonders that I will perform among them. After that, he will let you go.

21 "And I will make the Egyptians favorably disposed toward this people, so that when you leave you will not go empty-handed. 22 Every woman is to ask her neighbor and any woman living in her house for articles of silver and gold and for clothing, which you will put on your sons and daughters. And so you will plunder the Egyptians."

(3:8) What comfort to know that You see, You hear and You know the needs of Your people. But what if seeing and hearing, You did not respond? What if You would not or could not help? But You do help. The firm foundation of our hope and the fiery passion of our worship are caught up in these words: "I have come down." What mystery! What joy! Truly You "stoop down to make me great." Here in the desert You foreshadow the day of ultimate rescue, the day of Christ—God coming down in human form, Immanuel, God with us! (Ps 18:35; Mt 1:23)

(3:15) I tremble before Your presence, Lord. I am both humbled and hopeful at the revelation of Your name and the awesome power of Your being. You are the I AM, the eternal majestic One, Yahweh! But You also name Yourself as the God of committed relationship with imperfect people. You are the God of Abraham, the God of Isaac, and the God of Jacob. This is Your identity forever, my God. I am hopeful in Your love. I will ever honor You for both Your transcendent glory and Your immanent care. Hallowed be Your name.

[a] 12 The Hebrew is plural. [b] 14 Or *I WILL BE WHAT I WILL BE* [c] 15 The Hebrew for *LORD* sounds like and may be derived from the Hebrew for *I AM* in verse 14.

Signs for Moses

4 Moses answered, "What if they do not believe me or listen to
me and say, 'The LORD did not appear to you'?"
2Then the LORD said to him, "What is that in your hand?"
"A staff," he replied.
3The LORD said, "Throw it on the ground."
Moses threw it on the ground and it became a snake, and he
ran from it. 4Then the LORD said to him, "Reach out your hand
and take it by the tail." So Moses reached out and took hold of
the snake and it turned back into a staff in his hand. 5"This," said
the LORD, "is so that they may believe that the LORD, the God of
their fathers—the God of Abraham, the God of Isaac and the God
of Jacob—has appeared to you."
6Then the LORD said, "Put your hand inside your cloak." So
Moses put his hand into his cloak, and when he took it out, it
was leprous,[a] like snow.
7"Now put it back into your cloak," he said. So Moses put his
hand back into his cloak, and when he took it out, it was restored, like the rest of his flesh.
8Then the LORD said, "If they do not believe you or pay attention to the first miraculous sign, they may believe the second.
9But if they do not believe these two signs or listen to you, take
some water from the Nile and pour it on the dry ground. The
water you take from the river will become blood on the ground."
10Moses said to the LORD, "O Lord, I have never been eloquent,
neither in the past nor since you have spoken to your servant. I
am slow of speech and tongue."
11The LORD said to him, "Who gave man his mouth? Who
makes him deaf or mute? Who gives him sight or makes him
blind? Is it not I, the LORD? 12Now go; I will help you speak and
will teach you what to say."
13But Moses said, "O Lord, please send someone else to do it."
14Then the LORD's anger burned against Moses and he said,
"What about your brother, Aaron the Levite? I know he can speak
well. He is already on his way to meet you, and his heart will be
glad when he sees you. 15You shall speak to him and put words
in his mouth; I will help both of you speak and will teach you
what to do. 16He will speak to the people for you, and it will be
as if he were your mouth and as if you were God to him. 17But
take this staff in your hand so you can perform miraculous signs
with it."

Moses Returns to Egypt

18Then Moses went back to Jethro his father-in-law and said to
him, "Let me go back to my own people in Egypt to see if any of
them are still alive."
Jethro said, "Go, and I wish you well."
19Now the LORD had said to Moses in Midian, "Go back to
Egypt, for all the men who wanted to kill you are dead." 20So
Moses took his wife and sons, put them on a donkey and started
back to Egypt. And he took the staff of God in his hand.
21The LORD said to Moses, "When you return to Egypt, see that
you perform before Pharaoh all the wonders I have given you the
power to do. But I will harden his heart so that he will not let the

[a]6 The Hebrew word was used for various diseases affecting the skin—not necessarily leprosy.

(4:12–13) I yield my life to You, Lord. May this be my act of worship. If I encounter You in a powerful way and learn the deep truths of Your nature, yet fail to answer Your call to service, I am no true worshiper. Have I surrendered every part of my life? Every capability of my body? You look not for impressive abilities, but only for a willing heart. You are Master of all creation. You can make much of very little when it is yielded up to Your hand. (Ps 51:17)

If you don't have a willing heart
Ask Him to give you one.
If you can't seem to make a start
Trust in His power.
For the Lord of Love is watching
you;
He sees what you're going through,
And He will make a way
If you want Him to.
Oh, do you want Him to?
Then tell Him so.

"Willing Heart"
Kelly Willard (©1981)

(4:22) Thank You, Lord, for loving me. It is Your love that gives my life its true value. To the Egyptians Israel was nothing more than a vast collection of slaves. But You called Israel Your firstborn son. With that label of love You honored them with immeasurable value. My life may not seem very impressive. But Lord, when I received Christ, You gave me the honor of being called a child of God! Thank You so much, Lord, for this new identity in Christ. (Jn 1:12–13)

In the very beginning, when this great universe lay in the mind of God, like unborn forests in the acorn-cup; long ere the echoes waked the solitudes, before the mountains were brought forth, and long ere the light flashed through the sky, God loved his chosen creatures.

Charles Haddon Spurgeon (1834-1892)

(5:1) So, it is a call to worship that sets the stage for battle! You want my full allegiance, Lord. You will not share Your glory with another. Worship represents conflict of interests, a spiritual battle. What is this struggle going on in my heart? Where is my allegiance? Help me, Lord, to stand firm against those things that have a false claim on my life and my attention. Help me to break free and worship You only, with all my heart, soul and strength.

The dearest idol I have known,
Whate'er that idol be,
Help me to tear it from its throne,
And worship only thee.

William Cowper (1731-1800)

people go. 22Then say to Pharaoh, 'This is what the LORD says: Israel is my firstborn son, 23and I told you, "Let my son go, so he
may worship me." But you refused to let him go; so I will kill your
firstborn son.' "
24At a lodging place on the way, the LORD met ⌞Moses⌟[a] and was
about to kill him. 25But Zipporah took a flint knife, cut off her
son's foreskin and touched ⌞Moses'⌟ feet with it.[b] "Surely you are
a bridegroom of blood to me," she said. 26So the LORD let him
alone. (At that time she said "bridegroom of blood," referring to
circumcision.)
27The LORD said to Aaron, "Go into the desert to meet Moses."
So he met Moses at the mountain of God and kissed him. 28Then
Moses told Aaron everything the LORD had sent him to say, and also
about all the miraculous signs he had commanded him to perform.
29Moses and Aaron brought together all the elders of the Israelites, 30and Aaron told them everything the LORD had said to
Moses. He also performed the signs before the people, 31and they
believed. And when they heard that the LORD was concerned about them and had seen their misery, they bowed down and worshiped.

Bricks Without Straw

5 Afterward Moses and Aaron went to Pharaoh and said, "This is what the LORD, the God of Israel, says: 'Let my people go, so that they may hold a festival to me in the desert.' "
2Pharaoh said, "Who is the LORD, that I should obey him and let Israel go? I do not know the LORD and I will not let Israel go."
3Then they said, "The God of the Hebrews has met with us. Now let us take a three-day journey into the desert to offer sacrifices to the LORD our God, or he may strike us with plagues or with the sword."
4But the king of Egypt said, "Moses and Aaron, why are you tak-
ing the people away from their labor? Get back to your work!"
5Then Pharaoh said, "Look, the people of the land are now numerous, and you are stopping them from working."
6That same day Pharaoh gave this order to the slave drivers and
foremen in charge of the people: 7"You are no longer to supply
the people with straw for making bricks; let them go and gather
their own straw. 8But require them to make the same number of
bricks as before; don't reduce the quota. They are lazy; that is why
they are crying out, 'Let us go and sacrifice to our God.' 9Make the
work harder for the men so that they keep working and pay no attention to lies."
10Then the slave drivers and the foremen went out and said to
the people, "This is what Pharaoh says: 'I will not give you any
more straw. 11Go and get your own straw wherever you can find it,
but your work will not be reduced at all.' " 12So the people scattered all over Egypt to gather stubble to use for straw. 13The slave
drivers kept pressing them, saying, "Complete the work required
of you for each day, just as when you had straw." 14The Israelite
foremen appointed by Pharaoh's slave drivers were beaten and were asked, "Why didn't you meet your quota of bricks yesterday or today, as before?"
15Then the Israelite foremen went and appealed to Pharaoh:
"Why have you treated your servants this way? 16Your servants are

[a] 24 Or ⌞*Moses' son*⌟; Hebrew *him* [b] 25 Or *and drew near* ⌞*Moses'*⌟ *feet*

given no straw, yet we are told, 'Make bricks!' Your servants are being beaten, but the fault is with your own people."

17Pharaoh said, "Lazy, that's what you are—lazy! That is why you keep saying, 'Let us go and sacrifice to the LORD.' 18Now get to work. You will not be given any straw, yet you must produce your full quota of bricks."

19The Israelite foremen realized they were in trouble when they were told, "You are not to reduce the number of bricks required of you for each day." 20When they left Pharaoh, they found Moses and Aaron waiting to meet them, 21and they said, "May the LORD look upon you and judge you! You have made us a stench to Pharaoh and his officials and have put a sword in their hand to kill us."

God Promises Deliverance

22Moses returned to the LORD and said, "O Lord, why have you brought trouble upon this people? Is this why you sent me? 23Ever since I went to Pharaoh to speak in your name, he has brought trouble upon this people, and you have not rescued your people at all."

6 Then the LORD said to Moses, "Now you will see what I will do to Pharaoh: Because of my mighty hand he will let them go; because of my mighty hand he will drive them out of his country."

2God also said to Moses, "I am the LORD. 3I appeared to Abraham, to Isaac and to Jacob as God Almighty,[a] but by my name the LORD[b] I did not make myself known to them.[c] 4I also established my covenant with them to give them the land of Canaan, where they lived as aliens. 5Moreover, I have heard the groaning of the Israelites, whom the Egyptians are enslaving, and I have remembered my covenant.

6"Therefore, say to the Israelites: 'I am the LORD, and I will bring you out from under the yoke of the Egyptians. I will free you from being slaves to them, and I will redeem you with an outstretched arm and with mighty acts of judgment. 7I will take you as my own people, and I will be your God. Then you will know that I am the LORD your God, who brought you out from under the yoke of the Egyptians. 8And I will bring you to the land I swore with uplifted hand to give to Abraham, to Isaac and to Jacob. I will give it to you as a possession. I am the LORD.' "

9Moses reported this to the Israelites, but they did not listen to him because of their discouragement and cruel bondage.

10Then the LORD said to Moses, 11"Go, tell Pharaoh king of Egypt to let the Israelites go out of his country."

12But Moses said to the LORD, "If the Israelites will not listen to me, why would Pharaoh listen to me, since I speak with faltering lips[d]?"

Family Record of Moses and Aaron

13Now the LORD spoke to Moses and Aaron about the Israelites and Pharaoh king of Egypt, and he commanded them to bring the Israelites out of Egypt.

14These were the heads of their families[e]:

[a] 3 Hebrew *El-Shaddai* [b] 3 See note at Exodus 3:15. [c] 3 Or *Almighty, and by my name the LORD did I not let myself be known to them?* [d] 12 Hebrew *I am uncircumcised of lips*; also in verse 30 [e] 14 The Hebrew for *families* here and in verse 25 refers to units larger than clans.

(5:23) Help me, God, when I am confused—when things do not go according to my expectations. My schedule calls for immediate relief from all distress. If You love me and have given Your promise of help, why the delay? Are You playing games with my life? Pain and disappointment cloud my perspective, and I enter this strange place somewhere between trust and accusation. I cry out, "How long, O LORD, will you forget me forever?" Yet still I hope in You, my God. Please be patient with my impatience. (Ps 13:1; Rev 6:10)

Our eternal message of hope is that dawn will come. Our slave foreparents realized this. They were never unmindful of the fact of midnight, for always there was the rawhide whip of the overseer and the auction block where families were torn asunder to remind them of its reality. Faith in the dawn arises from the faith that God is good and just. When one believes this, he knows that the contradictions of life are neither final nor ultimate . . . Even the worst starless midnight may herald the dawn of some great fulfillment.

Martin Luther King, Jr. (1929–1968)

(6:7) The greatest gift You have given is not the gift of freedom, though we long for this precious gift. Nor is it the gift of provision, a blessing undeserved. The greatest gift of all is that You give Yourself to us in loving relationship. What an awesome wonder that You take us to be Your very own! To be "betrothed to the Lord" is the highest honor. To be "the bride of Christ" is the ultimate gift. Your love, O God, makes our freedom complete. (Jer 2:2; Rev 19:7)

(7:1) As I worship, help me to gain Your perspective, Lord. Let me see Your sovereign power. Worldly power intimidates me, even when I know it has no ultimate control. Pharaoh was worshiped as a god by his people, yet he was only a mortal man. But those sent to speak in Your name have all the authority of heaven standing behind them. (Mt 28:18–20)

I walk by faith, each step by faith;
To live by faith, I put my trust in You.
Every step I take is a step of faith;
No weapon formed against me shall prosper.
And every prayer I make is a prayer of faith;
If my God is for me, who can be against me?

"I Walk By Faith"
Chris Falson (©1990)

(7:4) What do You see when You look at Your church, Lord? We seem such a feeble and confused group. Yet You saw Israel, a rag-tag collection of slaves, and You called them "my divisions." You saw in them a great army. What You saw You spoke, and what You spoke they became. What do You see in us, Lord? Do You see us standing as a great army for Christ? "Can these bones live?" Yes! You see in us a great multitude, riding with Jesus on white horses, dressed in fine linen, white and clean. (Eze 37:3,10; Rev 19:14)

The sons of Reuben the firstborn son of Israel were Hanoch and Pallu, Hezron and Carmi. These were the clans of Reuben.
15The sons of Simeon were Jemuel, Jamin, Ohad, Jakin, Zohar and Shaul the son of a Canaanite woman. These were the clans of Simeon.
16These were the names of the sons of Levi according to their records: Gershon, Kohath and Merari. Levi lived 137 years.
17The sons of Gershon, by clans, were Libni and Shimei.
18The sons of Kohath were Amram, Izhar, Hebron and Uzziel. Kohath lived 133 years.
19The sons of Merari were Mahli and Mushi.
These were the clans of Levi according to their records.
20Amram married his father's sister Jochebed, who bore him Aaron and Moses. Amram lived 137 years.
21The sons of Izhar were Korah, Nepheg and Zicri.
22The sons of Uzziel were Mishael, Elzaphan and Sithri.
23Aaron married Elisheba, daughter of Amminadab and sister of Nahshon, and she bore him Nadab and Abihu, Eleazar and Ithamar.
24The sons of Korah were Assir, Elkanah and Abiasaph. These were the Korahite clans.
25Eleazar son of Aaron married one of the daughters of Putiel, and she bore him Phinehas.

These were the heads of the Levite families, clan by clan.
26It was this same Aaron and Moses to whom the LORD said,
"Bring the Israelites out of Egypt by their divisions." 27They were
the ones who spoke to Pharaoh king of Egypt about bringing the Israelites out of Egypt. It was the same Moses and Aaron.

Aaron to Speak for Moses

28Now when the LORD spoke to Moses in Egypt, 29he said to him,
"I am the LORD. Tell Pharaoh king of Egypt everything I tell you."
30But Moses said to the LORD, "Since I speak with faltering lips, why would Pharaoh listen to me?"

7 Then the LORD said to Moses, "See, I have made you like God to Pharaoh, and your brother Aaron will be your prophet.
2You are to say everything I command you, and your brother Aaron is to tell Pharaoh to let the Israelites go out of his country. 3But I
will harden Pharaoh's heart, and though I multiply my miraculous signs and wonders in Egypt, 4he will not listen to you. Then I will lay my hand on Egypt and with mighty acts of judgment I will bring out my divisions, my people the Israelites. 5And the Egyptians will
know that I am the LORD when I stretch out my hand against Egypt and bring the Israelites out of it."
6Moses and Aaron did just as the LORD commanded them.
7Moses was eighty years old and Aaron eighty-three when they spoke to Pharaoh.

Aaron's Staff Becomes a Snake

8The LORD said to Moses and Aaron, 9"When Pharaoh says to you, 'Perform a miracle,' then say to Aaron, 'Take your staff and throw it down before Pharaoh,' and it will become a snake."
10So Moses and Aaron went to Pharaoh and did just as the LORD commanded. Aaron threw his staff down in front of Pharaoh and

his officials, and it became a snake. 11Pharaoh then summoned wise men and sorcerers, and the Egyptian magicians also did the same things by their secret arts: 12Each one threw down his staff and it became a snake. But Aaron's staff swallowed up their staffs. 13Yet Pharaoh's heart became hard and he would not listen to them, just as the LORD had said.

The Plague of Blood

14Then the LORD said to Moses, "Pharaoh's heart is unyielding; he refuses to let the people go. 15Go to Pharaoh in the morning as he goes out to the water. Wait on the bank of the Nile to meet him, and take in your hand the staff that was changed into a snake. 16Then say to him, 'The LORD, the God of the Hebrews, has sent me to say to you: Let my people go, so that they may worship me in the desert. But until now you have not listened. 17This is what the LORD says: By this you will know that I am the LORD: With the staff that is in my hand I will strike the water of the Nile, and it will be changed into blood. 18The fish in the Nile will die, and the river will stink; the Egyptians will not be able to drink its water.' "

19The LORD said to Moses, "Tell Aaron, 'Take your staff and stretch out your hand over the waters of Egypt—over the streams and canals, over the ponds and all the reservoirs'—and they will turn to blood. Blood will be everywhere in Egypt, even in the wooden buckets and stone jars."

20Moses and Aaron did just as the LORD had commanded. He raised his staff in the presence of Pharaoh and his officials and struck the water of the Nile, and all the water was changed into blood. 21The fish in the Nile died, and the river smelled so bad that the Egyptians could not drink its water. Blood was everywhere in Egypt.

22But the Egyptian magicians did the same things by their secret arts, and Pharaoh's heart became hard; he would not listen to Moses and Aaron, just as the LORD had said. 23Instead, he turned and went into his palace, and did not take even this to heart. 24And all the Egyptians dug along the Nile to get drinking water, because they could not drink the water of the river.

The Plague of Frogs

8 25Seven days passed after the LORD struck the Nile. 1Then the LORD said to Moses, "Go to Pharaoh and say to him, 'This is what the LORD says: Let my people go, so that they may worship me. 2If you refuse to let them go, I will plague your whole country with frogs. 3The Nile will teem with frogs. They will come up into your palace and your bedroom and onto your bed, into the houses of your officials and on your people, and into your ovens and kneading troughs. 4The frogs will go up on you and your people and all your officials.' "

5Then the LORD said to Moses, "Tell Aaron, 'Stretch out your hand with your staff over the streams and canals and ponds, and make frogs come up on the land of Egypt.' "

6So Aaron stretched out his hand over the waters of Egypt, and the frogs came up and covered the land. 7But the magicians did the same things by their secret arts; they also made frogs come up on the land of Egypt.

8Pharaoh summoned Moses and Aaron and said, "Pray to the LORD to take the frogs away from me and my people, and I will let your people go to offer sacrifices to the LORD."

(7:11–12) Thank You, Lord, for You have given us all that we need to prevail. We have found that the battle is more involved than we first expected. We have learned that our struggle is not against flesh and blood, but against spiritual forces of evil in heavenly realms. Yet even in this, You have equipped us well for victory. The opposition is fierce and cunning. But we will overcome, because the One who is in us is greater than the one who is in the world! (Eph 6:12; 1Jn 4:4)

God calls us to live a life we cannot live, so that we must depend on him for supernatural ability. We are called to do the impossible, to live beyond our natural ability.

Erwin W. Lutzer (1941-)

(7:15) When Aaron's staff swallowed up all the staffs of the Egyptian sorcerers, it was a decisive moment of victory. That victory foreshadowed each new victory that would follow. You instructed Moses to carry that staff as a symbol of victory into each new conflict. Jesus, Your cross is my ultimate symbol of victory. Through the cross You have crushed the power of evil. Your cross sets the stage for every spiritual victory in my life. Help me, Lord, to hold tight to the cross and to carry it into every spiritual battle I face. (Ex 7:12; 17:9)

(8:22) How grateful we are, Lord, for You have not appointed us to suffer wrath but to receive Your gift of salvation through Jesus Christ! While our lives in this world are not free from difficulties or suffering, we are indeed free from the wrath of Your judgment. We rejoice in being called Your own people, and we delight in the expectation of goodness from Your hand, even in times of great turmoil. (1Th 5:9)

O Jesus Christ, do not delay,
But hasten our salvation;
We often tremble on our way
In fear and tribulation.
Oh hear and grant our fervent plea;
Come, mighty Judge, and set us free
From death and every evil.

"The Day Is Surely Drawing Near"
Bartholomaus Ringwaldt
(c.1532-1600)
Trans. Philip A. Peter (1832-1917)

(8:25) Help us, Lord, to worship without compromise. Partial obedience is only a gesture in the right direction—a tip of the hat to You, while our feet and hands remain in service to our enemy. But You call us to uncompromising worship. We will answer that call on Your terms, Lord, with all that we are and all that we have. So shall we stand as Your servants in true holiness.

To worship is to quicken the conscience by the holiness of God, to feed the mind with the truth of God, to purge the imagination by the beauty of God, to open the heart to the love of God, to devote the will to the purpose of God.

Archbishop William Temple (1881-1944)

9Moses said to Pharaoh, "I leave to you the honor of setting the time for me to pray for you and your officials and your people that you and your houses may be rid of the frogs, except for those that remain in the Nile."

10"Tomorrow," Pharaoh said.

Moses replied, "It will be as you say, so that you may know
there is no one like the LORD our God. 11The frogs will leave you
and your houses, your officials and your people; they will remain only in the Nile."

12After Moses and Aaron left Pharaoh, Moses cried out to the
LORD about the frogs he had brought on Pharaoh. 13And the LORD
did what Moses asked. The frogs died in the houses, in the courtyards and in the fields.
14They were piled into heaps, and the land
reeked of them. 15But when Pharaoh saw that there was relief, he hardened his heart and would not listen to Moses and Aaron, just as the LORD had said.

The Plague of Gnats

16Then the LORD said to Moses, "Tell Aaron, 'Stretch out your staff and strike the dust of the ground,' and throughout the land of
Egypt the dust will become gnats." 17They did this, and when
Aaron stretched out his hand with the staff and struck the dust of the ground, gnats came upon men and animals. All the dust
throughout the land of Egypt became gnats. 18But when the magicians tried to produce gnats by their secret arts, they could not. And the gnats were on men and animals.

19The magicians said to Pharaoh, "This is the finger of God." But Pharaoh's heart was hard and he would not listen, just as the LORD had said.

The Plague of Flies

20Then the LORD said to Moses, "Get up early in the morning and confront Pharaoh as he goes to the water and say to him, 'This is what the LORD says: Let my people go, so that they may worship
me. 21If you do not let my people go, I will send swarms of flies on you and your officials, on your people and into your houses. The houses of the Egyptians will be full of flies, and even the ground where they are.

22" 'But on that day I will deal differently with the land of Goshen, where my people live; no swarms of flies will be there, so
that you will know that I, the LORD, am in this land. 23I will make
a distinction[a] between my people and your people. This miraculous sign will occur tomorrow.' "

24And the LORD did this. Dense swarms of flies poured into Pharaoh's palace and into the houses of his officials, and throughout Egypt the land was ruined by the flies.

25Then Pharaoh summoned Moses and Aaron and said, "Go, sacrifice to your God here in the land."

26But Moses said, "That would not be right. The sacrifices we offer the LORD our God would be detestable to the Egyptians. And if we offer sacrifices that are detestable in their eyes, will they not
stone us? 27We must take a three-day journey into the desert to offer sacrifices to the LORD our God, as he commands us."

28Pharaoh said, "I will let you go to offer sacrifices to the LORD

[a] 23 Septuagint and Vulgate; Hebrew *will put a deliverance*

your God in the desert, but you must not go very far. Now pray
for me."
29 Moses answered, "As soon as I leave you, I will pray to the
LORD, and tomorrow the flies will leave Pharaoh and his officials
and his people. Only be sure that Pharaoh does not act deceitfully again by not letting the people go to offer sacrifices to the LORD."
30 Then Moses left Pharaoh and prayed to the LORD, 31 and the
LORD did what Moses asked: The flies left Pharaoh and his officials
and his people; not a fly remained. 32 But this time also Pharaoh
hardened his heart and would not let the people go.

The Plague on Livestock

9 Then the LORD said to Moses, "Go to Pharaoh and say to him,
'This is what the LORD, the God of the Hebrews, says: "Let my
people go, so that they may worship me." 2 If you refuse to let them
go and continue to hold them back, 3 the hand of the LORD will
bring a terrible plague on your livestock in the field—on your
horses and donkeys and camels and on your cattle and sheep and
goats. 4 But the LORD will make a distinction between the livestock
of Israel and that of Egypt, so that no animal belonging to the Israelites will die.' "
5 The LORD set a time and said, "Tomorrow the LORD will do this
in the land." 6 And the next day the LORD did it: All the livestock of
the Egyptians died, but not one animal belonging to the Israelites
died. 7 Pharaoh sent men to investigate and found that not even
one of the animals of the Israelites had died. Yet his heart was unyielding and he would not let the people go.

The Plague of Boils

8 Then the LORD said to Moses and Aaron, "Take handfuls of soot
from a furnace and have Moses toss it into the air in the presence
of Pharaoh. 9 It will become fine dust over the whole land of Egypt,
and festering boils will break out on men and animals throughout
the land."
10 So they took soot from a furnace and stood before Pharaoh.
Moses tossed it into the air, and festering boils broke out on men
and animals. 11 The magicians could not stand before Moses because of the boils that were on them and on all the Egyptians.
12 But the LORD hardened Pharaoh's heart and he would not listen
to Moses and Aaron, just as the LORD had said to Moses.

The Plague of Hail

13 Then the LORD said to Moses, "Get up early in the morning,
confront Pharaoh and say to him, 'This is what the LORD, the God
of the Hebrews, says: Let my people go, so that they may worship
me, 14 or this time I will send the full force of my plagues against
you and against your officials and your people, so you may know
that there is no one like me in all the earth. 15 For by now I could
have stretched out my hand and struck you and your people with
a plague that would have wiped you off the earth. 16 But I have
raised you up[a] for this very purpose, that I might show you my
power and that my name might be proclaimed in all the earth.
17 You still set yourself against my people and will not let them go.
18 Therefore, at this time tomorrow I will send the worst hailstorm
that has ever fallen on Egypt, from the day it was founded till now.

[a] 16 Or *have spared you*

(9:1) O Lord my God, I count it the highest privilege to be called Your servant. You have waged a war to set me free, and You have prevailed. Now, having been set free, I find my heart captive to Your great goodness and love. Your relentless quest for my liberation has bound me to You in grateful praise and service. And this was Your plan all along. You have set the captives free that they might worship You. Lives given to You in the service of worship are lives that will ever be free!

Worship is not a part of the Christian life; it is the Christian life.

Gerald Vann (1906-1963)

(9:16) How deep is the mystery of Your sovereign will, my God. How unsearchable are Your judgments and Your paths beyond tracing out! Truly You know the hearts and the choices of all of us, even before we are formed. You determine Your plan and bring it to pass in Your time and in Your way. You work even through the rebellious choices of sinful lives, and Your purpose comes to pass. In all of this You remain patient and just. O Lord, we marvel at Your wisdom and Your sovereign power. (Ps 139:4,13–16; Ro 9:17–18; 11:33)

(9:20–30) Grant us hearts of true reverence before You, Lord, for the fear of the Lord is the beginning of wisdom, and the knowledge of the Holy One is understanding. Some come near to the door of wisdom, yet fail to enter in. Others fear the consequences of disobeying Your Word but do not yet have a heart of true reverence for You. Teach us to live in the kind of obedience that flows from genuine reverence, holy Lord. (Pr 9:10)

Of all the ways of awakening inner reverence in man, the best is the contemplation of the works of God. Their transcendent greatness must inspire awe.

Elijah de Vidas (16th c.)

(10:2) The incomparable story of redemption bears repeating. Empower us, Lord, to tell the story often and to tell it well. Through devastating judgments You made a mockery of the pompous splendor of Pharaoh. You set Your people free. It was a story to fill the hearts of generations of Your people. And now an even greater story is ours in Christ. Through the cross You crushed the head of the serpent, making a mockery of the powers of darkness. It is a story that still sets captives free! May we tell it often. May we tell it well. (Col 2:15)

Thanks we give and adoration
For Your Gospel's joyful sound.
May the fruits of Your salvation
In our hearts and lives abound.
Ever faithful, ever faithful
To Your truth may we be found.

"Lord, Dismiss Us with Your Blessing"
John Fawcett (1740–1817)

19 Give an order now to bring your livestock and everything you have
in the field to a place of shelter, because the hail will fall on every
man and animal that has not been brought in and is still out in the
field, and they will die.' "
20 Those officials of Pharaoh who feared the word of the LORD
hurried to bring their slaves and their livestock inside. 21 But those
who ignored the word of the LORD left their slaves and livestock in
the field.
22 Then the LORD said to Moses, "Stretch out your hand toward the
sky so that hail will fall all over Egypt—on men and animals and on
everything growing in the fields of Egypt." 23 When Moses stretched
out his staff toward the sky, the LORD sent thunder and hail, and
lightning flashed down to the ground. So the LORD rained hail on the
land of Egypt; 24 hail fell and lightning flashed back and forth. It was
the worst storm in all the land of Egypt since it had become a nation.
25 Throughout Egypt hail struck everything in the fields—both men
and animals; it beat down everything growing in the fields and
stripped every tree. 26 The only place it did not hail was the land of
Goshen, where the Israelites were.
27 Then Pharaoh summoned Moses and Aaron. "This time I have
sinned," he said to them. "The LORD is in the right, and I and my
people are in the wrong. 28 Pray to the LORD, for we have had enough
thunder and hail. I will let you go; you don't have to stay any longer."
29 Moses replied, "When I have gone out of the city, I will spread
out my hands in prayer to the LORD. The thunder will stop and there
will be no more hail, so you may know that the earth is the LORD's.
30 But I know that you and your officials still do not fear the LORD
God."
31 (The flax and barley were destroyed, since the barley had
headed and the flax was in bloom. 32 The wheat and spelt, however,
were not destroyed, because they ripen later.)
33 Then Moses left Pharaoh and went out of the city. He spread
out his hands toward the LORD; the thunder and hail stopped, and
the rain no longer poured down on the land. 34 When Pharaoh saw
that the rain and hail and thunder had stopped, he sinned again: He
and his officials hardened their hearts. 35 So Pharaoh's heart was
hard and he would not let the Israelites go, just as the LORD had said
through Moses.

The Plague of Locusts

10 Then the LORD said to Moses, "Go to Pharaoh, for I have
hardened his heart and the hearts of his officials so that I
may perform these miraculous signs of mine among them 2 that you
may tell your children and grandchildren how I dealt harshly with
the Egyptians and how I performed my signs among them, and that
you may know that I am the LORD."
3 So Moses and Aaron went to Pharaoh and said to him, "This is
what the LORD, the God of the Hebrews, says: 'How long will you
refuse to humble yourself before me? Let my people go, so that they
may worship me. 4 If you refuse to let them go, I will bring locusts
into your country tomorrow. 5 They will cover the face of the ground
so that it cannot be seen. They will devour what little you have left
after the hail, including every tree that is growing in your fields.
6 They will fill your houses and those of all your officials and all the
Egyptians—something neither your fathers nor your forefathers
have ever seen from the day they settled in this land till now.' " Then
Moses turned and left Pharaoh.

7Pharaoh's officials said to him, "How long will this man be a
snare to us? Let the people go, so that they may worship the LORD
their God. Do you not yet realize that Egypt is ruined?"
8Then Moses and Aaron were brought back to Pharaoh. "Go,
worship the LORD your God," he said. "But just who will be
going?"
9Moses answered, "We will go with our young and old, with
our sons and daughters, and with our flocks and herds, because
we are to celebrate a festival to the LORD."
10Pharaoh said, "The LORD be with you—if I let you go, along
with your women and children! Clearly you are bent on evil.[a]
11No! Have only the men go; and worship the LORD, since that's
what you have been asking for." Then Moses and Aaron were
driven out of Pharaoh's presence.
12And the LORD said to Moses, "Stretch out your hand over
Egypt so that locusts will swarm over the land and devour everything growing in the fields, everything left by the hail."
13So Moses stretched out his staff over Egypt, and the LORD
made an east wind blow across the land all that day and all that
night. By morning the wind had brought the locusts; 14they invaded all Egypt and settled down in every area of the country in
great numbers. Never before had there been such a plague of locusts, nor will there ever be again. 15They covered all the ground
until it was black. They devoured all that was left after the hail—
everything growing in the fields and the fruit on the trees. Nothing green remained on tree or plant in all the land of Egypt.
16Pharaoh quickly summoned Moses and Aaron and said, "I
have sinned against the LORD your God and against you. 17Now
forgive my sin once more and pray to the LORD your God to take
this deadly plague away from me."
18Moses then left Pharaoh and prayed to the LORD. 19And the
LORD changed the wind to a very strong west wind, which caught
up the locusts and carried them into the Red Sea.[b] Not a locust
was left anywhere in Egypt. 20But the LORD hardened Pharaoh's
heart, and he would not let the Israelites go.

The Plague of Darkness

21Then the LORD said to Moses, "Stretch out your hand toward
the sky so that darkness will spread over Egypt—darkness that
can be felt." 22So Moses stretched out his hand toward the sky,
and total darkness covered all Egypt for three days. 23No one
could see anyone else or leave his place for three days. Yet all the
Israelites had light in the places where they lived.
24Then Pharaoh summoned Moses and said, "Go, worship the
LORD. Even your women and children may go with you; only leave
your flocks and herds behind."
25But Moses said, "You must allow us to have sacrifices and
burnt offerings to present to the LORD our God. 26Our livestock
too must go with us; not a hoof is to be left behind. We have to
use some of them in worshiping the LORD our God, and until we
get there we will not know what we are to use to worship the
LORD."
27But the LORD hardened Pharaoh's heart, and he was not willing to let them go. 28Pharaoh said to Moses, "Get out of my sight!

[a] *10* Or *Be careful, trouble is in store for you!* [b] *19* Hebrew *Yam Suph*; that is, Sea of Reeds

(10:21) With You, Lord, is the fountain of life, and in Your light we see light. To turn away from You, Lord, is only darkness—darkness that consumes both heart and mind. How fitting that the last plague before death itself was the plague of darkness. Having refused the clear testimony of Your power and Your will, the Egyptians were thrust into the gloom of night. Lord, even now I am surrounded by the darkness of a world in rebellion against You. How fearful are Your judgments, Lord! How precious is the light You bestow on willing hearts. (Ps 36:9; Jn 8:12; Ro 1:21)

In darkness there is no choice. It is light that enables us to see the differences between things; and it is Christ who gives us light.

Augustus W. Hare (1792-1834)

He comes with rescue speedy
To those who suffer wrong,
To help the poor and needy,
And bid the weak be strong;
To give them songs for sighing,
Their darkness turn to light,
Whose souls, condemned and dying,
Were precious in His sight.

"Hail to the Lord's Anointed"
James Montgomery (1771-1854)

(10:26) Help me to follow the example of Moses: "Not a hoof is to be left behind," he said. In my worship of You, let me freely offer everything I have and am, with nothing held back. As I flee from the slavery of sin, let me not leave anything of myself within its grasp. Free me from any constraints that would hinder my giving to You of my whole self. O Great Redeemer, redeem everything of value in my life so that I may be fully dedicated to the high calling of worship.

"Not a hoof shall remain behind." This is the true attitude of the man of faith. Evil is always suggesting some compromise. To listen to it, is to remain enslaved.

G. Campbell Morgan (1863-1945)

(12:2) I believe that You are the God of new beginnings. I believe that You give the possibility of a new identity, a new life. I believe that You create a strong future that breaks free from bondage to the past. I believe that You bring a decisive moment, a moment orchestrated by Your perfect grace. It is a moment when absolutely everything changes by Your divine, redemptive power. The Passover and the death of the lamb marked the beginning of a new life for Your people. Even so, I thank You for the death and resurrection of Jesus, the Lamb of God, as the beginning of my new life in Christ. For "if anyone is in Christ, he is a new creation; the old has gone, the new has come!" (2Co 5:17).

(12:6) Lord, You have united me with Your people by sacrifice. You have created a new community, a group of people bound together by shared experience. Many things can bind a people together, but there is no other experience in life to match this one! Through the Lamb of God You have created the community of God—a people saved by the blood of the Lamb, each one partaking of that solemn meal. O Lord, unite us in Christ, the Lamb of God. From every nation, tribe and tongue, make us one unique community through the sacrifice of Christ.

Biblically the church is an organism, not an organization—a movement, not a monument. It is not a part of the community; it is a whole new community. It is not an orderly gathering; it is a new order with new values, often in sharp conflict with the values of the surrounding society.

Charles Colson (1931-)

Make sure you do not appear before me again! The day you see my face you will die."

29"Just as you say," Moses replied, "I will never appear before you again."

The Plague on the Firstborn

11 Now the LORD had said to Moses, "I will bring one more plague on Pharaoh and on Egypt. After that, he will let you go from here, and when he does, he will drive you out completely. 2Tell the people that men and women alike are to ask their neighbors for articles of silver and gold." 3(The LORD made the Egyptians favorably disposed toward the people, and Moses himself was highly regarded in Egypt by Pharaoh's officials and by the people.)

4So Moses said, "This is what the LORD says: 'About midnight I will go throughout Egypt. 5Every firstborn son in Egypt will die, from the firstborn son of Pharaoh, who sits on the throne, to the firstborn son of the slave girl, who is at her hand mill, and all the firstborn of the cattle as well. 6There will be loud wailing throughout Egypt—worse than there has ever been or ever will be again. 7But among the Israelites not a dog will bark at any man or animal.' Then you will know that the LORD makes a distinction between Egypt and Israel. 8All these officials of yours will come to me, bowing down before me and saying, 'Go, you and all the people who follow you!' After that I will leave." Then Moses, hot with anger, left Pharaoh.

9The LORD had said to Moses, "Pharaoh will refuse to listen to you—so that my wonders may be multiplied in Egypt." 10Moses and Aaron performed all these wonders before Pharaoh, but the LORD hardened Pharaoh's heart, and he would not let the Israelites go out of his country.

The Passover

12 The LORD said to Moses and Aaron in Egypt, 2"This month is to be for you the first month, the first month of your year. 3Tell the whole community of Israel that on the tenth day of this month each man is to take a lamb[a] for his family, one for each household. 4If any household is too small for a whole lamb, they must share one with their nearest neighbor, having taken into account the number of people there are. You are to determine the amount of lamb needed in accordance with what each person will eat. 5The animals you choose must be year-old males without defect, and you may take them from the sheep or the goats. 6Take care of them until the fourteenth day of the month, when all the people of the community of Israel must slaughter them at twilight. 7Then they are to take some of the blood and put it on the sides and tops of the doorframes of the houses where they eat the lambs. 8That same night they are to eat the meat roasted over the fire, along with bitter herbs, and bread made without yeast. 9Do not eat the meat raw or cooked in water, but roast it over the fire—head, legs and inner parts. 10Do not leave any of it till morning; if some is left till morning, you must burn it. 11This is how you are to eat it: with your cloak tucked into your belt, your sandals on your feet and your staff in your hand. Eat it in haste; it is the LORD's Passover.

[a] 3 The Hebrew word can mean *lamb* or *kid*; also in verse 4.

12"On that same night I will pass through Egypt and strike down every firstborn—both men and animals—and I will bring judgment on all the gods of Egypt. I am the LORD. 13The blood will be a sign for you on the houses where you are; and when I see the blood, I will pass over you. No destructive plague will touch you when I strike Egypt.

14"This is a day you are to commemorate; for the generations to come you shall celebrate it as a festival to the LORD—a lasting ordinance. 15For seven days you are to eat bread made without yeast. On the first day remove the yeast from your houses, for whoever eats anything with yeast in it from the first day through the seventh must be cut off from Israel. 16On the first day hold a sacred assembly, and another one on the seventh day. Do no work at all on these days, except to prepare food for everyone to eat—that is all you may do.

17"Celebrate the Feast of Unleavened Bread, because it was on this very day that I brought your divisions out of Egypt. Celebrate this day as a lasting ordinance for the generations to come. 18In the first month you are to eat bread made without yeast, from the evening of the fourteenth day until the evening of the twenty-first day. 19For seven days no yeast is to be found in your houses. And whoever eats anything with yeast in it must be cut off from the community of Israel, whether he is an alien or native-born. 20Eat nothing made with yeast. Wherever you live, you must eat unleavened bread."

21Then Moses summoned all the elders of Israel and said to them, "Go at once and select the animals for your families and slaughter the Passover lamb. 22Take a bunch of hyssop, dip it into the blood in the basin and put some of the blood on the top and on both sides of the doorframe. Not one of you shall go out the door of his house until morning. 23When the LORD goes through the land to strike down the Egyptians, he will see the blood on the top and sides of the doorframe and will pass over that doorway, and he will not permit the destroyer to enter your houses and strike you down.

24"Obey these instructions as a lasting ordinance for you and your descendants. 25When you enter the land that the LORD will give you as he promised, observe this ceremony. 26And when your children ask you, 'What does this ceremony mean to you?' 27then tell them, 'It is the Passover sacrifice to the LORD, who passed over the houses of the Israelites in Egypt and spared our homes when he struck down the Egyptians.' " Then the people bowed down and worshiped. 28The Israelites did just what the LORD commanded Moses and Aaron.

29At midnight the LORD struck down all the firstborn in Egypt, from the firstborn of Pharaoh, who sat on the throne, to the firstborn of the prisoner, who was in the dungeon, and the firstborn of all the livestock as well. 30Pharaoh and all his officials and all the Egyptians got up during the night, and there was loud wailing in Egypt, for there was not a house without someone dead.

The Exodus

31During the night Pharaoh summoned Moses and Aaron and said, "Up! Leave my people, you and the Israelites! Go, worship the LORD as you have requested. 32Take your flocks and herds, as you have said, and go. And also bless me."

33The Egyptians urged the people to hurry and leave the coun-

(12:13) Merciful God, You give this perfect focal point for assurance. Just outside the door, the terror of Your wrath is unleashed. The feeble walls of a house cannot keep it back. The death decree of Your judgment falls in the street. No wishing or hoping can alter its course. Nevertheless, just outside the door, You turn the terror away. You give the blood of the lamb, which alone stands between destruction and deliverance. Thank You, God, for judgment is surely coming. Yet I am safe because of the blood of Jesus, the Passover Lamb slain for me. (1Co 5:7)

The blood of Christ may seem to be a grim, repulsive subject to those who do not realize its true significance, but to those who have accepted his redemption and have been set free from sin's chains, the blood of Christ is precious.

Billy Graham (1918-)

Where the paschal blood is poured
Death's dread angel sheathes the sword;
Israel's hosts triumphant go
Through the wave that drowns the foe.
Alleluia!

"At the Lamb's High Feast We Sing"
Lutheran Office Hymn (17th c.)
Trans. Robert Campbell (1814-1868)

(12:30) Mighty God, when You struck down the Egyptians' firstborn, pouring out Your wrath on an ungodly people, Your angel of death passed over the houses that were marked with the blood of the Passover lamb. Centuries later, You struck down Your own firstborn Son, our Passover Lamb, pouring out Your wrath on Him instead of us. The firstborn Egyptians were taken in judgment so that Your people could be freed from slavery; Your only Son was given in judgment so that we could be freed from sin and death. Today, in grateful response, I affirm that Jesus Christ is Your one and only Son and that His blood marks the entryway into my heart. I put my full faith in Him as Your chosen means of eternal salvation, and I declare in praise that by His blood I will be spared from the wrath to come. (Jn 3:16)

(12:42) Lord, grant me diligence in remembering! With heart, mind, soul and strength I will cling to the memory of Your redemptive work, Your saving love. Lord Jesus, You kept vigil for me upon the cross and freed me from my guilt and shame. Now, Lord, with broken bread and the cup of communion I will keep vigil to honor the greatness of Your love for me. (Lk 22:19–20)

(13:2) O God, Your mercy is overwhelming. Through sacrifice You have saved us from destruction. How then shall we respond to this awesome gift? We will give our very lives back to You in worship. We offer ourselves to You, Lord, each one a living sacrifice for Your service. Use us, Lord, in any way You will. (Ro 12:1)

Your holy body into death was given,
Life to win for us in heaven.
No greater love than this to You
could bind us;
May this feast of that remind us!
O Lord, have mercy!
Lord, Your kindness so much more
did move You
That Your blood now moves us to
love You.
All our debt You have paid;
Peace with God once more is made.
O Lord, have mercy!

"O Lord, We Praise You"
German Folk Hymn and
Martin Luther (1483–1546)
Trans. The Lutheran Hymnal (©1941)

try. "For otherwise," they said, "we will all die!" 34 So the people
took their dough before the yeast was added, and carried it on
their shoulders in kneading troughs wrapped in clothing. 35 The
Israelites did as Moses instructed and asked the Egyptians for articles of silver and gold and for clothing. 36 The LORD had made the
Egyptians favorably disposed toward the people, and they gave
them what they asked for; so they plundered the Egyptians.

37 The Israelites journeyed from Rameses to Succoth. There
were about six hundred thousand men on foot, besides women
and children. 38 Many other people went up with them, as well as
large droves of livestock, both flocks and herds. 39 With the dough
they had brought from Egypt, they baked cakes of unleavened
bread. The dough was without yeast because they had been driven
out of Egypt and did not have time to prepare food for themselves.

40 Now the length of time the Israelite people lived in Egypt[a] was
430 years. 41 At the end of the 430 years, to the very day, all the
LORD's divisions left Egypt. 42 Because the LORD kept vigil that night
to bring them out of Egypt, on this night all the Israelites are to
keep vigil to honor the LORD for the generations to come.

Passover Restrictions

43 The LORD said to Moses and Aaron, "These are the regulations for the Passover:

"No foreigner is to eat of it. 44 Any slave you have bought may
eat of it after you have circumcised him, 45 but a temporary resident and a hired worker may not eat of it.

46 "It must be eaten inside one house; take none of the meat
outside the house. Do not break any of the bones. 47 The whole
community of Israel must celebrate it.

48 "An alien living among you who wants to celebrate the LORD's
Passover must have all the males in his household circumcised;
then he may take part like one born in the land. No uncircumcised
male may eat of it. 49 The same law applies to the native-born and
to the alien living among you."

50 All the Israelites did just what the LORD had commanded
Moses and Aaron. 51 And on that very day the LORD brought the Israelites out of Egypt by their divisions.

Consecration of the Firstborn

13 The LORD said to Moses, 2 "Consecrate to me every firstborn
male. The first offspring of every womb among the Israelites
belongs to me, whether man or animal."

3 Then Moses said to the people, "Commemorate this day, the
day you came out of Egypt, out of the land of slavery, because the
LORD brought you out of it with a mighty hand. Eat nothing containing yeast. 4 Today, in the month of Abib, you are leaving. 5 When
the LORD brings you into the land of the Canaanites, Hittites, Amorites, Hivites and Jebusites—the land he swore to your forefathers
to give you, a land flowing with milk and honey—you are to observe this ceremony in this month: 6 For seven days eat bread
made without yeast and on the seventh day hold a festival to the
LORD. 7 Eat unleavened bread during those seven days; nothing
with yeast in it is to be seen among you, nor shall any yeast be
seen anywhere within your borders. 8 On that day tell your son, 'I
do this because of what the LORD did for me when I came out of

[a] 40 Masoretic Text; Samaritan Pentateuch and Septuagint *Egypt and Canaan*

Egypt.' 9This observance will be for you like a sign on your hand
and a reminder on your forehead that the law of the LORD is to be
on your lips. For the LORD brought you out of Egypt with his mighty
hand. 10You must keep this ordinance at the appointed time year
after year.

11"After the LORD brings you into the land of the Canaanites and
gives it to you, as he promised on oath to you and your forefathers, 12you are to give over to the LORD the first offspring of every
womb. All the firstborn males of your livestock belong to the LORD.
13Redeem with a lamb every firstborn donkey, but if you do not redeem it, break its neck. Redeem every firstborn among your sons.

14"In days to come, when your son asks you, 'What does this
mean?' say to him, 'With a mighty hand the LORD brought us out of
Egypt, out of the land of slavery. 15When Pharaoh stubbornly refused to let us go, the LORD killed every firstborn in Egypt, both
man and animal. This is why I sacrifice to the LORD the first male
offspring of every womb and redeem each of my firstborn sons.'
16And it will be like a sign on your hand and a symbol on your
forehead that the LORD brought us out of Egypt with his mighty
hand."

Crossing the Sea

17When Pharaoh let the people go, God did not lead them on
the road through the Philistine country, though that was shorter.
For God said, "If they face war, they might change their minds and
return to Egypt." 18So God led the people around by the desert
road toward the Red Sea.[a] The Israelites went up out of Egypt
armed for battle.

19Moses took the bones of Joseph with him because Joseph had
made the sons of Israel swear an oath. He had said, "God will
surely come to your aid, and then you must carry my bones up
with you from this place."[b]

20After leaving Succoth they camped at Etham on the edge of
the desert. 21By day the LORD went ahead of them in a pillar of
cloud to guide them on their way and by night in a pillar of fire to
give them light, so that they could travel by day or night. 22Neither
the pillar of cloud by day nor the pillar of fire by night left its place
in front of the people.

14 Then the LORD said to Moses, 2"Tell the Israelites to turn
back and encamp near Pi Hahiroth, between Migdol and
the sea. They are to encamp by the sea, directly opposite Baal Zephon. 3Pharaoh will think, 'The Israelites are wandering around
the land in confusion, hemmed in by the desert.' 4And I will hard-
en Pharaoh's heart, and he will pursue them. But I will gain glory
for myself through Pharaoh and all his army, and the Egyptians
will know that I am the LORD." So the Israelites did this.

5When the king of Egypt was told that the people had fled, Pharaoh and his officials changed their minds about them and said,
"What have we done? We have let the Israelites go and have lost
their services!" 6So he had his chariot made ready and took his
army with him. 7He took six hundred of the best chariots, along
with all the other chariots of Egypt, with officers over all of them.
8The LORD hardened the heart of Pharaoh king of Egypt, so that he
pursued the Israelites, who were marching out boldly. 9The Egyptians—all Pharaoh's horses and chariots, horsemen[c] and

[a] *18* Hebrew *Yam Suph*; that is, Sea of Reeds [b] *19* See Gen. 50:25. [c] *9* Or *charioteers*; also in verses 17, 18, 23, 26 and 28

(13:18) Your people were armed for battle, but not yet ready for war. You knew it well, Lord, for You know us better than we know ourselves. You see our strengths and our weaknesses, and You give us all that we need for victory. You provide all that we need for life and godliness. You guide us in Your perfect knowledge and wisdom. So lead us, Lord, but not into temptation. Remember our frailty, Lord, and deliver us from evil. (Mt 6:13; 2Pe 1:3)

Faith is not a sense, nor sight, nor reason, but taking God at his Word.

Arthur Benoni Evans (1781–1854)

(13:19) Father, grant me a radical faith: a faith strong enough to hope even beyond the grave. Grant me a faith like that of Joseph, who knew that death itself could not quench Your word of promise, my God. Grant me a faith that looks across the threshold of time and sees the certainty of what You will bring to pass. (Ge 50:25)

Lord, give me faith to live from day to day,
With tranquil heart to do my simple part,
And with my hand in thine just go thy way!
Lord, give me faith to leave it all to thee!
The future is thy gift;
I would not lift
The veil thy love has hung 'twixt it and me.

John Oxenham (1861–1941)

(13:21–22) O God, Your guidance is essential to the pilgrimage of Your people. We would not know where to go, but for the instruction of Your Word. We would not know when to go, but for the wise direction of Your Holy Spirit, prompting us either to sit still or to move forward. We would not know how to go, but for the sense of Your presence, which shines brightest in our darkest hour. Just as the pillar of cloud and fire never left its place in front of Your people, so You have promised never to leave us or forsake us. We praise and thank You for Your everlasting faithfulness.

(14:14) Almighty God, when all hell is breaking loose against me, help me to remember that You are Lord, that You are able, that You are present. Help me to lift my eyes from earthly conflict to see Your heavenly power. Cause me to know the peace that passes understanding, a peace that comes from acknowledging Your lordship in every circumstance of my life. (Php 4:7)

Thou alone art deliverance–absolute safety from every cause and kind of trouble that ever existed, anywhere now exists, or ever can exist in thy universe.

George MacDonald (1824-1905)

(14:27–28) I praise You, saving God, great Deliverer, for that which delivers us also destroys our sworn enemy. Sin, our cruel taskmaster, like Pharaoh, has been buried under the sea of Your mercy. You have provided a way where there was no way, and the terror that once was is no more.

If the Lord had not been on our side,
All our enemies would have
Swallowed us alive.
If the Lord had not been on our side,
All the raging waters,
And the mighty flood,
Would have swept over us.
If the Lord, if the Lord
If the Lord had not been on our side.

Blessed be the Lord,
Blessed be the Lord,
Who has not given us up,
The Lord who is our help,
Maker of heaven and earth.

"If The Lord Had Not Been On Our Side"
Rob Mathes (©1996)

troops—pursued the Israelites and overtook them as they
camped by the sea near Pi Hahiroth, opposite Baal Zephon.
10As Pharaoh approached, the Israelites looked up, and there
were the Egyptians, marching after them. They were terrified and
cried out to the LORD. 11They said to Moses, "Was it because
there were no graves in Egypt that you brought us to the desert
to die? What have you done to us by bringing us out of Egypt?
12Didn't we say to you in Egypt, 'Leave us alone; let us serve the
Egyptians'? It would have been better for us to serve the Egyptians than to die in the desert!"
13Moses answered the people, "Do not be afraid. Stand firm
and you will see the deliverance the LORD will bring you today.
The Egyptians you see today you will never see again. 14The LORD
will fight for you; you need only to be still."
15Then the LORD said to Moses, "Why are you crying out to
me? Tell the Israelites to move on. 16Raise your staff and stretch
out your hand over the sea to divide the water so that the Israelites can go through the sea on dry ground. 17I will harden the
hearts of the Egyptians so that they will go in after them. And I
will gain glory through Pharaoh and all his army, through his
chariots and his horsemen. 18The Egyptians will know that I am
the LORD when I gain glory through Pharaoh, his chariots and
his horsemen."
19Then the angel of God, who had been traveling in front of Israel's army, withdrew and went behind them. The pillar of cloud
also moved from in front and stood behind them, 20coming between the armies of Egypt and Israel. Throughout the night the
cloud brought darkness to the one side and light to the other
side; so neither went near the other all night long.
21Then Moses stretched out his hand over the sea, and all that
night the LORD drove the sea back with a strong east wind and
turned it into dry land. The waters were divided, 22and the Israelites went through the sea on dry ground, with a wall of water
on their right and on their left.
23The Egyptians pursued them, and all Pharaoh's horses and
chariots and horsemen followed them into the sea. 24During the
last watch of the night the LORD looked down from the pillar of
fire and cloud at the Egyptian army and threw it into confusion.
25He made the wheels of their chariots come off[a] so that they
had difficulty driving. And the Egyptians said, "Let's get away
from the Israelites! The LORD is fighting for them against Egypt."
26Then the LORD said to Moses, "Stretch out your hand over
the sea so that the waters may flow back over the Egyptians and
their chariots and horsemen." 27Moses stretched out his hand
over the sea, and at daybreak the sea went back to its place. The
Egyptians were fleeing toward[b] it, and the LORD swept them into
the sea. 28The water flowed back and covered the chariots and
horsemen—the entire army of Pharaoh that had followed the Israelites into the sea. Not one of them survived.
29But the Israelites went through the sea on dry ground, with
a wall of water on their right and on their left. 30That day the
LORD saved Israel from the hands of the Egyptians, and Israel saw
the Egyptians lying dead on the shore. 31And when the Israelites
saw the great power the LORD displayed against the Egyptians, the

[a] 25 Or *He jammed the wheels of their chariots* (see Samaritan Pentateuch, Septuagint and Syriac) [b] 27 Or *from*

people feared the LORD and put their trust in him and in Moses his servant.

The Song of Moses and Miriam

15 Then Moses and the Israelites sang this song to the LORD:

"I will sing to the LORD,
for he is highly exalted.
The horse and its rider
he has hurled into the sea.
2 The LORD is my strength and my song;
he has become my salvation.
He is my God, and I will praise him,
my father's God, and I will exalt him.
3 The LORD is a warrior;
the LORD is his name.
4 Pharaoh's chariots and his army
he has hurled into the sea.
The best of Pharaoh's officers
are drowned in the Red Sea.[a]
5 The deep waters have covered them;
they sank to the depths like a stone.

6 "Your right hand, O LORD,
was majestic in power.
Your right hand, O LORD,
shattered the enemy.
7 In the greatness of your majesty
you threw down those who opposed you.
You unleashed your burning anger;
it consumed them like stubble.
8 By the blast of your nostrils
the waters piled up.
The surging waters stood firm like a wall;
the deep waters congealed in the heart of the sea.

9 "The enemy boasted,
'I will pursue, I will overtake them.
I will divide the spoils;
I will gorge myself on them.
I will draw my sword
and my hand will destroy them.'
10 But you blew with your breath,
and the sea covered them.
They sank like lead
in the mighty waters.

11 "Who among the gods is like you, O LORD?
Who is like you—
majestic in holiness,
awesome in glory,
working wonders?
12 You stretched out your right hand
and the earth swallowed them.

13 "In your unfailing love you will lead
the people you have redeemed.

[a] 4 Hebrew *Yam Suph*; that is, Sea of Reeds; also in verse 22

Make of our hearts a field to raise your praise.

Luci Shaw (1928-)

(15:1–13) Your victorious power brings overwhelming joy; Your strength displayed on behalf of Your people makes us strong in trust and bold in praise. One stroke of Your hand, O God, and everything is changed! The enemy is defeated; the bitterness of slavery is broken; Your people are saved; the hope of new life unfolds. Lord, let me see the greatness of Your victory ever more clearly. You are so faithful to save. Help me to be faithful in praise, always remembering to give You the glory for every victory in my life. Truly You are glorious in holiness, rich in mercy, worthy to be served and worthy to be praised!

(15:13) An unknown world lies before me. You have called me from my old life and brought me into a whole new reality in Christ. I step forward by faith, counting on Your perfect love to guide me. Your steady faithfulness is my constant hope. Having worked in power to redeem my life from death, surely You will strengthen and guide my steps in life. Having begun this good work in my life, surely You will carry it on to completion until the day of Christ Jesus. (Php 1:6)

He leadeth me! O blessed thought!
O words with heav'nly comfort
fraught!
Whate'er I do, where'er I be,
Still 'tis God's hand that leadeth me!

"He Leadeth Me, O Blessed Thought"
Joseph Gilmore (1862)

(15:18) This is my comfort through all the uncertainties of life—that You reign forever, Lord. I cannot say what a day may bring. I only know that You are the Sovereign King of each new day, forever. Kingdoms may rise and fall; the earth itself may crumble, but Your throne stands sure above it all. I bow before Your throne and fix the gaze of my soul on my saving God. "A glorious throne, exalted from the beginning, is the place of our sanctuary." (Jer 17:12)

The kingdom of God does not exist because of your effort or mine. It exists because God reigns. Our part is to enter this kingdom and bring our life under his sovereign will.

T. Z. Koo

(15:26) Lord, You have come that we might have life, and have it to the full. But I have only begun to taste the fullness that You have provided for me. How I long to experience every good thing You have promised for those who love You. Teach me, Lord, to walk in newness of life with You. Free me from the bitterness of unbelief and disobedience. Bring renewal and wholeness to my life, for You are the God who heals. "Heal me, O LORD, and I will be healed; save me and I will be saved, for you are the one I praise." (Jer 17:14; Jn 10:10)

In your strength you will guide them
to your holy dwelling.
14 The nations will hear and tremble;
anguish will grip the people of Philistia.
15 The chiefs of Edom will be terrified,
the leaders of Moab will be seized with trembling,
the people[a] of Canaan will melt away;
16 terror and dread will fall upon them.
By the power of your arm
they will be as still as a stone—
until your people pass by, O LORD,
until the people you bought[b] pass by.
17 You will bring them in and plant them
on the mountain of your inheritance—
the place, O LORD, you made for your dwelling,
the sanctuary, O Lord, your hands established.
18 The LORD will reign
for ever and ever."

19 When Pharaoh's horses, chariots and horsemen[c] went into
the sea, the LORD brought the waters of the sea back over them, but
the Israelites walked through the sea on dry ground. 20 Then Miriam the prophetess, Aaron's sister, took a tambourine in her hand,
and all the women followed her, with tambourines and dancing.
21 Miriam sang to them:

"Sing to the LORD,
for he is highly exalted.
The horse and its rider
he has hurled into the sea."

The Waters of Marah and Elim

22 Then Moses led Israel from the Red Sea and they went into
the Desert of Shur. For three days they traveled in the desert without finding water. 23 When they came to Marah, they could not
drink its water because it was bitter. (That is why the place is
called Marah.[d]) 24 So the people grumbled against Moses, saying,
"What are we to drink?"

25 Then Moses cried out to the LORD, and the LORD showed him
a piece of wood. He threw it into the water, and the water became
sweet.

There the LORD made a decree and a law for them, and there he
tested them. 26 He said, "If you listen carefully to the voice of the
LORD your God and do what is right in his eyes, if you pay attention
to his commands and keep all his decrees, I will not bring on you
any of the diseases I brought on the Egyptians, for I am the LORD,
who heals you."

27 Then they came to Elim, where there were twelve springs and
seventy palm trees, and they camped there near the water.

Manna and Quail

16 The whole Israelite community set out from Elim and came
to the Desert of Sin, which is between Elim and Sinai, on
the fifteenth day of the second month after they had come out of
Egypt. 2 In the desert the whole community grumbled against
Moses and Aaron. 3 The Israelites said to them, "If only we had

[a] *15* Or *rulers* [b] *16* Or *created* [c] *19* Or *charioteers* [d] *23* *Marah* means *bitter.*

died by the LORD's hand in Egypt! There we sat around pots of meat
and ate all the food we wanted, but you have brought us out into
this desert to starve this entire assembly to death."
4Then the LORD said to Moses, "I will rain down bread from
heaven for you. The people are to go out each day and gather
enough for that day. In this way I will test them and see whether
they will follow my instructions. 5On the sixth day they are to prepare what they bring in, and that is to be twice as much as they
gather on the other days."
6So Moses and Aaron said to all the Israelites, "In the evening
you will know that it was the LORD who brought you out of Egypt,
7and in the morning you will see the glory of the LORD, because he
has heard your grumbling against him. Who are we, that you
should grumble against us?" 8Moses also said, "You will know that
it was the LORD when he gives you meat to eat in the evening and
all the bread you want in the morning, because he has heard your
grumbling against him. Who are we? You are not grumbling
against us, but against the LORD."
9Then Moses told Aaron, "Say to the entire Israelite community, 'Come before the LORD, for he has heard your grumbling.' "
10While Aaron was speaking to the whole Israelite community,
they looked toward the desert, and there was the glory of the LORD
appearing in the cloud.
11The LORD said to Moses, 12"I have heard the grumbling of the
Israelites. Tell them, 'At twilight you will eat meat, and in the
morning you will be filled with bread. Then you will know that I
am the LORD your God.' "
13That evening quail came and covered the camp, and in the
morning there was a layer of dew around the camp. 14When the
dew was gone, thin flakes like frost on the ground appeared on
the desert floor. 15When the Israelites saw it, they said to each
other, "What is it?" For they did not know what it was.

Moses said to them, "It is the bread the LORD has given you to
eat. 16This is what the LORD has commanded: 'Each one is to gather as much as he needs. Take an omer[a] for each person you have
in your tent.' "
17The Israelites did as they were told; some gathered much,
some little. 18And when they measured it by the omer, he who
gathered much did not have too much, and he who gathered little
did not have too little. Each one gathered as much as he needed.
19Then Moses said to them, "No one is to keep any of it until
morning."
20However, some of them paid no attention to Moses; they kept
part of it until morning, but it was full of maggots and began to
smell. So Moses was angry with them.
21Each morning everyone gathered as much as he needed, and
when the sun grew hot, it melted away. 22On the sixth day, they
gathered twice as much—two omers[b] for each person—and the
leaders of the community came and reported this to Moses. 23He
said to them, "This is what the LORD commanded: 'Tomorrow is to
be a day of rest, a holy Sabbath to the LORD. So bake what you want
to bake and boil what you want to boil. Save whatever is left and
keep it until morning.' "
24So they saved it until morning, as Moses commanded, and it
did not stink or get maggots in it. 25"Eat it today," Moses said,

[a] *16* That is, probably about 2 quarts (about 2 liters); also in verses 18, 32, 33 and 36
[b] *22* That is, probably about 4 quarts (about 4.5 liters)

(16:4) Heavenly Father, You are perfect in love and perfect in Your provision for Your people. Day by day You give what we need for every dimension of life. We look to You with grateful hearts for our daily bread. Teach us, gracious Lord, to look past the gift to see You, the Giver of all good things. Keep us ever mindful that Your people do not live on bread alone but on every word that comes from your mouth. Guide us by Your Word to Jesus, the true Bread from heaven, the Bread of God that gives life to the world. (Dt 8:3; Mt 6:11; Jn 6:32–35)

Round each habitation hovering,
See the cloud and fire appear
For a glory and a covering,
Showing that the Lord is near!
Thus they march, the pillar leading,
Light by night and shade by day,
Daily on the manna feeding
Which He gives them when they
pray.

"Glorious Things of Thee Are Spoken"
John Newton (1779)

(17:6) Make Your presence ever more real to me! Like the rock and the river that flows from it, let me see Jesus my Savior: Jesus, God in human flesh, smitten with the cross for my sins; Jesus, raised from death to dispense a river of living water, the gift of the Holy Spirit, to all who believe. (Jn 7:38–39)

(17:11) Can it be that my prayer will affect the outcome of the battle? What an awesome privilege; what a heavy responsibility! Will people live or die, evil be contained or spread, Your purpose be advanced or hindered, all because of my prayer? Then I will pray. But send me help, Lord, for my spirit is willing, but my body is weak. I will pray, "Father let Your kingdom come; let Your will be done." Then I will watch to see Your mighty hand prevail! (Mt 6:10; 26:41)

It does not need to be a formal prayer: the most stumbling and broken cry–a sigh, a whisper, anything that tells the heart's loneliness and need and penitence–can find its way to him.

Phillips Brooks (1835-1893)

"because today is a Sabbath to the LORD. You will not find any of it
on the ground today. 26Six days you are to gather it, but on the seventh day, the Sabbath, there will not be any."
27Nevertheless, some of the people went out on the seventh day
to gather it, but they found none. 28Then the LORD said to Moses,
"How long will you[a] refuse to keep my commands and my instructions? 29Bear in mind that the LORD has given you the Sabbath; that is why on the sixth day he gives you bread for two days.
Everyone is to stay where he is on the seventh day; no one is to go
out." 30So the people rested on the seventh day.
31The people of Israel called the bread manna.[b] It was white
like coriander seed and tasted like wafers made with honey.
32Moses said, "This is what the LORD has commanded: 'Take an
omer of manna and keep it for the generations to come, so they
can see the bread I gave you to eat in the desert when I brought
you out of Egypt.'"
33So Moses said to Aaron, "Take a jar and put an omer of
manna in it. Then place it before the LORD to be kept for the generations to come."
34As the LORD commanded Moses, Aaron put the manna in front
of the Testimony, that it might be kept. 35The Israelites ate manna
forty years, until they came to a land that was settled; they ate
manna until they reached the border of Canaan.
36(An omer is one tenth of an ephah.)

Water From the Rock

17 The whole Israelite community set out from the Desert of
Sin, traveling from place to place as the LORD commanded.
They camped at Rephidim, but there was no water for the people
to drink. 2So they quarreled with Moses and said, "Give us water
to drink."
Moses replied, "Why do you quarrel with me? Why do you put
the LORD to the test?"
3But the people were thirsty for water there, and they grumbled
against Moses. They said, "Why did you bring us up out of Egypt to
make us and our children and livestock die of thirst?"
4Then Moses cried out to the LORD, "What am I to do with these
people? They are almost ready to stone me."
5The LORD answered Moses, "Walk on ahead of the people.
Take with you some of the elders of Israel and take in your hand
the staff with which you struck the Nile, and go. 6I will stand there
before you by the rock at Horeb. Strike the rock, and water will
come out of it for the people to drink." So Moses did this in the
sight of the elders of Israel. 7And he called the place Massah[c] and
Meribah[d] because the Israelites quarreled and because they tested the LORD saying, "Is the LORD among us or not?"

The Amalekites Defeated

8The Amalekites came and attacked the Israelites at Rephidim.
9Moses said to Joshua, "Choose some of our men and go out to
fight the Amalekites. Tomorrow I will stand on top of the hill with
the staff of God in my hands."
10So Joshua fought the Amalekites as Moses had ordered, and
Moses, Aaron and Hur went to the top of the hill. 11As long as
Moses held up his hands, the Israelites were winning, but when-

[a] *28* The Hebrew is plural. [b] *31* *Manna* means *What is it?* (see verse 15).
[c] *7* *Massah* means *testing.* [d] *7* *Meribah* means *quarreling.*

ever he lowered his hands, the Amalekites were winning.
12When Moses' hands grew tired, they took a stone and put it
under him and he sat on it. Aaron and Hur held his hands up—
one on one side, one on the other—so that his hands remained
steady till sunset. 13So Joshua overcame the Amalekite army with
the sword.
14Then the LORD said to Moses, "Write this on a scroll as
something to be remembered and make sure that Joshua hears
it, because I will completely blot out the memory of Amalek from
under heaven."
15Moses built an altar and called it The LORD is my Banner.
16He said, "For hands were lifted up to the throne of the LORD.
The[a] LORD will be at war against the Amalekites from generation
to generation."

Jethro Visits Moses

18 Now Jethro, the priest of Midian and father-in-law of Moses,
heard of everything God had done for Moses and for his
people Israel, and how the LORD had brought Israel out of Egypt.
2After Moses had sent away his wife Zipporah, his father-in-law
Jethro received her 3and her two sons. One son was named Gershom,[b] for Moses said, "I have become an alien in a foreign
land"; 4and the other was named Eliezer,[c] for he said, "My father's
God was my helper; he saved me from the sword of Pharaoh."
5Jethro, Moses' father-in-law, together with Moses' sons and
wife, came to him in the desert, where he was camped near the
mountain of God. 6Jethro had sent word to him, "I, your father-in-
law Jethro, am coming to you with your wife and her two sons."
7So Moses went out to meet his father-in-law and bowed down
and kissed him. They greeted each other and then went into the
tent. 8Moses told his father-in-law about everything the LORD had
done to Pharaoh and the Egyptians for Israel's sake and about all
the hardships they had met along the way and how the LORD had
saved them.
9Jethro was delighted to hear about all the good things the LORD
had done for Israel in rescuing them from the hand of the Egyptians. 10He said, "Praise be to the LORD, who rescued you from
the hand of the Egyptians and of Pharaoh, and who rescued the
people from the hand of the Egyptians. 11Now I know that the LORD
is greater than all other gods, for he did this to those who had
treated Israel arrogantly." 12Then Jethro, Moses' father-in-law,
brought a burnt offering and other sacrifices to God, and Aaron
came with all the elders of Israel to eat bread with Moses' father-
in-law in the presence of God.
13The next day Moses took his seat to serve as judge for the
people, and they stood around him from morning till evening.
14When his father-in-law saw all that Moses was doing for the people, he said, "What is this you are doing for the people? Why do
you alone sit as judge, while all these people stand around you
from morning till evening?"
15Moses answered him, "Because the people come to me to
seek God's will. 16Whenever they have a dispute, it is brought to
me, and I decide between the parties and inform them of God's
decrees and laws."
17Moses' father-in-law replied, "What you are doing is not

[a] 16 Or *"Because a hand was against the throne of the LORD, the* [b] 3 *Gershom* sounds like the Hebrew for *an alien there.* [c] 4 *Eliezer* means *my God is helper.*

Today I am one day nearer home than ever before. One day nearer the dawning when the fog will lift, mysteries clear, and all question marks straighten up into exclamation points!

Vance Havner (1901-)

(17:15–16) Lord God, You are the high and holy One, seated upon Your throne. The nations rage; the kings of the earth take their stand against You, against Jesus, Your Anointed One, and against Your church. You will break them to pieces like pottery! Evil cannot prevail against You, O Sovereign King of the universe. In the constant strife of this world, You are my refuge. You are my hope, my victory, my banner. In the conflict of my life, Lord, I will lift my hands to You. (Ps 2:2.9)

Stand up, stand up for Jesus,
As soldiers of the cross,
Lift high His royal banner;
It must not suffer loss.
From vict'ry unto vict'ry
His army He shall lead,
Till ev'ry foe is vanquished
And Christ is Lord indeed.

"Stand Up, Stand Up for Jesus"
George Duffield (1818-1888)

(18:8) Empower me, Father, by Your Holy Spirit, to tell the glorious story of all that You have done through Christ. Grant me boldness to proclaim the wonders of His saving work. Give me words to share the greatness of Your victory and the blessings of Your guidance and care. In every circumstance in which You place me and with each new person You bring my way, empower me by Your Holy Spirit to be Your faithful witness for Christ.

good. 18You and these people who come to you will only wear
yourselves out. The work is too heavy for you; you cannot handle
it alone. 19Listen now to me and I will give you some advice, and
may God be with you. You must be the people's representative before God and bring their disputes to him. 20Teach them the decrees and laws, and show them the way to live and the duties they
are to perform. 21But select capable men from all the people—
men who fear God, trustworthy men who hate dishonest gain—
and appoint them as officials over thousands, hundreds, fifties and
tens. 22Have them serve as judges for the people at all times, but
have them bring every difficult case to you; the simple cases they
can decide themselves. That will make your load lighter, because
they will share it with you. 23If you do this and God so commands,
you will be able to stand the strain, and all these people will go
home satisfied."

24Moses listened to his father-in-law and did everything he said.
25He chose capable men from all Israel and made them leaders of
the people, officials over thousands, hundreds, fifties and tens.
26They served as judges for the people at all times. The difficult
cases they brought to Moses, but the simple ones they decided
themselves.

27Then Moses sent his father-in-law on his way, and Jethro returned to his own country.

At Mount Sinai

19 In the third month after the Israelites left Egypt—on the
very day—they came to the Desert of Sinai. 2After they set
out from Rephidim, they entered the Desert of Sinai, and Israel
camped there in the desert in front of the mountain.

3Then Moses went up to God, and the LORD called to him from
the mountain and said, "This is what you are to say to the house
of Jacob and what you are to tell the people of Israel: 4'You yourselves have seen what I did to Egypt, and how I carried you on eagles' wings and brought you to myself. 5Now if you obey me fully
and keep my covenant, then out of all nations you will be my treasured possession. Although the whole earth is mine, 6you[a] will be
for me a kingdom of priests and a holy nation.' These are the
words you are to speak to the Israelites."

7So Moses went back and summoned the elders of the people
and set before them all the words the LORD had commanded him
to speak. 8The people all responded together, "We will do everything the LORD has said." So Moses brought their answer back to
the LORD.

9The LORD said to Moses, "I am going to come to you in a dense
cloud, so that the people will hear me speaking with you and will
always put their trust in you." Then Moses told the LORD what the
people had said.

10And the LORD said to Moses, "Go to the people and consecrate them today and tomorrow. Have them wash their clothes
11and be ready by the third day, because on that day the LORD will
come down on Mount Sinai in the sight of all the people. 12Put
limits for the people around the mountain and tell them, 'Be careful that you do not go up the mountain or touch the foot of it. Whoever touches the mountain shall surely be put to death. 13He shall
surely be stoned or shot with arrows; not a hand is to be laid on

[a] 5,6 Or *possession, for the whole earth is mine.* 6*You*

(19:5) These people were powerless, captive and unworthy. What, then, did You see that moved Your heart to choose them? And what did You see that moved Your heart to choose me? How awesome! It is Your choice that has given my life its true value, Lord. To belong to You is my highest honor. It is sweeter still to know that I did not choose You but that You chose me. You have appointed me to do good works and to bear fruit that will last and bring You honor. (Jn 15:16; Eph 2:10)

(19:6) You have called us to be "a royal priesthood, a holy nation, a people belonging to God," so that we may declare Your praises. Help me, Lord, to play my part. Help me to live up to this high calling. Teach me to live at the intersection of human need and divine reality. Open my eyes to the hurt of the world and the hope of heaven. Use me, Lord. Make me in daily practice what You have declared me to be by spiritual position—a priest in Your kingdom, set apart to declare Your praise. Touch me that I may touch others. Change me, O God, and help me to change the world in Your name. (1Pe 2:9)

The greatest miracle that God can do today is to take an unholy man out of an unholy world, and make that man holy and put him back into that unholy world and keep him holy in it.

Leonard Ravenhill (1907-1993)

him. Whether man or animal, he shall not be permitted to live.' Only when the ram's horn sounds a long blast may they go up to the mountain."

14After Moses had gone down the mountain to the people, he consecrated them, and they washed their clothes. 15Then he said to the people, "Prepare yourselves for the third day. Abstain from sexual relations."

16On the morning of the third day there was thunder and lightning, with a thick cloud over the mountain, and a very loud trumpet blast. Everyone in the camp trembled. 17Then Moses led the people out of the camp to meet with God, and they stood at the foot of the mountain. 18Mount Sinai was covered with smoke, because the LORD descended on it in fire. The smoke billowed up from it like smoke from a furnace, the whole mountain[a] trembled violently, 19and the sound of the trumpet grew louder and louder. Then Moses spoke and the voice of God answered him.[b]

20The LORD descended to the top of Mount Sinai and called Moses to the top of the mountain. So Moses went up 21and the LORD said to him, "Go down and warn the people so they do not force their way through to see the LORD and many of them perish. 22Even the priests, who approach the LORD, must consecrate themselves, or the LORD will break out against them."

23Moses said to the LORD, "The people cannot come up Mount Sinai, because you yourself warned us, 'Put limits around the mountain and set it apart as holy.' "

24The LORD replied, "Go down and bring Aaron up with you. But the priests and the people must not force their way through to come up to the LORD, or he will break out against them."

25So Moses went down to the people and told them.

The Ten Commandments

20 And God spoke all these words:

2 "I am the LORD your God, who brought you out of Egypt, out of the land of slavery.

3 "You shall have no other gods before[c] me.

4 "You shall not make for yourself an idol in the form of anything in heaven above or on the earth beneath or in the waters below. 5You shall not bow down to them or worship them; for I, the LORD your God, am a jealous God, punishing the children for the sin of the fathers to the third and fourth generation of those who hate me, 6but showing love to a thousand ⌞generations⌟ of those who love me and keep my commandments.

7 "You shall not misuse the name of the LORD your God, for the LORD will not hold anyone guiltless who misuses his name.

8 "Remember the Sabbath day by keeping it holy. 9Six days you shall labor and do all your work, 10but the seventh day is a Sabbath to the LORD your God. On it you shall not do any work, neither you, nor your son or daughter, nor your manservant or maidservant, nor your animals, nor the alien within your gates. 11For in six days the LORD made the heavens and the earth, the sea, and all that is

[a] 18 Most Hebrew manuscripts; a few Hebrew manuscripts and Septuagint *all the people*
[b] 19 Or *and God answered him with thunder* [c] 3 Or *besides*

(20:2) Everything begins with Your awesome work of grace, my God. You have demonstrated Your love through redemption. You have set me free from the slavery of sin. Now it is my turn to respond to Your gracious love. So I will listen for Your Word and walk in obedience to Your will. You alone know what it will take to build this new life. Help me to hear, Lord, to respond, and to continue in this relationship of love that has been founded by Your grace. Lead me in Your way!

As the earth can produce nothing unless it is fertilized by the sun, so we can do nothing without the grace of God.
Saint Jean Baptiste Marie Vianney (1786-1859)

(20:3–8) "Love the Lord your God." Truly the fear of the Lord is the beginning of wisdom, and all who follow Your precepts have good understanding. Sovereign Lord, in light of these first four commandments, teach me first to love You with all of my heart, soul, mind and strength; to fear You; to give You glory; and to worship You. For to do these things, Lord, is to fulfill the eternal gospel. To You belongs eternal praise. (Ps 111:10; Mk 12:30; Rev 14:6–7)

in them, but he rested on the seventh day. Therefore the
LORD blessed the Sabbath day and made it holy.
12 "Honor your father and your mother, so that you may live
long in the land the LORD your God is giving you.
13 "You shall not murder.
14 "You shall not commit adultery.
15 "You shall not steal.
16 "You shall not give false testimony against your neighbor.
17 "You shall not covet your neighbor's house. You shall not
covet your neighbor's wife, or his manservant or maidservant, his ox or donkey, or anything that belongs to
your neighbor."

18 When the people saw the thunder and lightning and heard the
trumpet and saw the mountain in smoke, they trembled with fear.
They stayed at a distance 19 and said to Moses, "Speak to us yourself and we will listen. But do not have God speak to us or we will
die."
20 Moses said to the people, "Do not be afraid. God has come to
test you, so that the fear of God will be with you to keep you from
sinning."
21 The people remained at a distance, while Moses approached
the thick darkness where God was.

Idols and Altars

22 Then the LORD said to Moses, "Tell the Israelites this: 'You
have seen for yourselves that I have spoken to you from heaven:
23 Do not make any gods to be alongside me; do not make for
yourselves gods of silver or gods of gold.
24 " 'Make an altar of earth for me and sacrifice on it your burnt
offerings and fellowship offerings,[a] your sheep and goats and your
cattle. Wherever I cause my name to be honored, I will come to
you and bless you. 25 If you make an altar of stones for me, do not
build it with dressed stones, for you will defile it if you use a tool
on it. 26 And do not go up to my altar on steps, lest your nakedness
be exposed on it.'

21 "These are the laws you are to set before them:

Hebrew Servants

2 "If you buy a Hebrew servant, he is to serve you for six years.
But in the seventh year, he shall go free, without paying anything.
3 If he comes alone, he is to go free alone; but if he has a wife
when he comes, she is to go with him. 4 If his master gives him a
wife and she bears him sons or daughters, the woman and her
children shall belong to her master, and only the man shall go
free.
5 "But if the servant declares, 'I love my master and my wife and
children and do not want to go free,' 6 then his master must take
him before the judges.[b] He shall take him to the door or the doorpost and pierce his ear with an awl. Then he will be his servant for
life.
7 "If a man sells his daughter as a servant, she is not to go free
as menservants do. 8 If she does not please the master who has selected her for himself,[c] he must let her be redeemed. He has no

[a] 24 Traditionally *peace offerings* [b] 6 Or *before God* [c] 8 Or *master so that he does not choose her*

(20:12–17) "Love your neighbor as yourself." These next six commandments teach me to love others. Father, let love for others flow from my love for You. To love You is to yearn to be like You. So I pray that You will give me Your loving heart—Your compassion, Your understanding, Your generosity, so that I will do nothing out of selfishness or vain conceit, but in humility I will consider others better than myself. For only when I have Your love inside me can Your love shine through me, and only then can I fulfill Your law and righteousness. (Mk 12:31; Php 2:3)

Christian love links love of God and love of neighbor in a twofold Great Commandment from which neither element can be dropped, so sin against neighbor through lack of human love is sin against God.
Georgia Harkness (1891-1979)

(20:18–21) O Great Deliverer, as with Your ancient people You have delivered me from the slavery of sin. You have brought me through the sea of fear. You have every right to speak to me as a father to his child—sometimes in sweet words of comfort, sometimes in harsh words of correction, but always from a heart of love. The very fact that You instruct me is proof of Your love for me. Therefore, I will not lose heart when You rebuke me. Though You slay me, still I will hope in You. (Job 13:15; Heb 12:5)

right to sell her to foreigners, because he has broken faith with her. [9]If he selects her for his son, he must grant her the rights of a daughter. [10]If he marries another woman, he must not deprive the first one of her food, clothing and marital rights. [11]If he does not provide her with these three things, she is to go free, without any payment of money.

Personal Injuries

[12]"Anyone who strikes a man and kills him shall surely be put to death. [13]However, if he does not do it intentionally, but God lets it happen, he is to flee to a place I will designate. [14]But if a man schemes and kills another man deliberately, take him away from my altar and put him to death.

[15]"Anyone who attacks[a] his father or his mother must be put to death.

[16]"Anyone who kidnaps another and either sells him or still has him when he is caught must be put to death.

[17]"Anyone who curses his father or mother must be put to death.

[18]"If men quarrel and one hits the other with a stone or with his fist[b] and he does not die but is confined to bed, [19]the one who struck the blow will not be held responsible if the other gets up and walks around outside with his staff; however, he must pay the injured man for the loss of his time and see that he is completely healed.

[20]"If a man beats his male or female slave with a rod and the slave dies as a direct result, he must be punished, [21]but he is not to be punished if the slave gets up after a day or two, since the slave is his property.

[22]"If men who are fighting hit a pregnant woman and she gives birth prematurely[c] but there is no serious injury, the offender must be fined whatever the woman's husband demands and the court allows. [23]But if there is serious injury, you are to take life for life, [24]eye for eye, tooth for tooth, hand for hand, foot for foot, [25]burn for burn, wound for wound, bruise for bruise.

[26]"If a man hits a manservant or maidservant in the eye and destroys it, he must let the servant go free to compensate for the eye. [27]And if he knocks out the tooth of a manservant or maidservant, he must let the servant go free to compensate for the tooth.

[28]"If a bull gores a man or a woman to death, the bull must be stoned to death, and its meat must not be eaten. But the owner of the bull will not be held responsible. [29]If, however, the bull has had the habit of goring and the owner has been warned but has not kept it penned up and it kills a man or woman, the bull must be stoned and the owner also must be put to death. [30]However, if payment is demanded of him, he may redeem his life by paying whatever is demanded. [31]This law also applies if the bull gores a son or daughter. [32]If the bull gores a male or female slave, the owner must pay thirty shekels[d] of silver to the master of the slave, and the bull must be stoned.

[33]"If a man uncovers a pit or digs one and fails to cover it and an ox or a donkey falls into it, [34]the owner of the pit must

[a] 15 Or *kills* [b] 18 Or *with a tool* [c] 22 Or *she has a miscarriage* [d] 32 That is, about 12 ounces (about 0.3 kilogram)

Our sociology reflects our theology.

Rebecca Manley Pippert (1948-)

(21:8–33) Thank You, gracious Lord, for Your care for the innocent victims of poverty, violence, abuse and neglect. You are a help and a defense for those who cannot defend themselves. Give us boldness to rise up on their behalf and bring righteousness and justice into their circumstances.

The greatest thing a man can do for his heavenly Father is to be kind to some of his other children.

Henry Drummond (1851–1897)

(22:1–15) "If . . . if . . . if." You know all that can go wrong in our human relationships, whether deliberate or accidental. You know us better than we know ourselves. You know our propensity for selfishness, our capacity for failure, our vulnerability to loss and mistreatment—and You care. Thank You for instructing us on how to live together. Heavenly Father, help us to live in harmony with one another, to be sympathetic, to love as brothers and sisters, to be compassionate and humble. Help us not to repay evil with evil or insult with insult, but with blessing, because to this You have called us so that we may inherit a blessing. (1Pe 3:8–9)

Beloved, let us love one another,
For love is of God,
And everyone that loveth is born of God,
And knoweth God.
He that loveth not, knoweth not God,
For God is love.
Beloved, let us love one another.

"Beloved (1 John 4:7–8)"
Dennis Ryder (©1974)

pay for the loss; he must pay its owner, and the dead animal will
be his.
35"If a man's bull injures the bull of another and it dies, they
are to sell the live one and divide both the money and the dead
animal equally. 36However, if it was known that the bull had the
habit of goring, yet the owner did not keep it penned up, the
owner must pay, animal for animal, and the dead animal will be
his.

Protection of Property

22 "If a man steals an ox or a sheep and slaughters it or sells
it, he must pay back five head of cattle for the ox and four
sheep for the sheep.
2"If a thief is caught breaking in and is struck so that he dies,
the defender is not guilty of bloodshed; 3but if it happens[a] after
sunrise, he is guilty of bloodshed.
"A thief must certainly make restitution, but if he has nothing,
he must be sold to pay for his theft.
4"If the stolen animal is found alive in his possession—whether
ox or donkey or sheep—he must pay back double.
5"If a man grazes his livestock in a field or vineyard and lets
them stray and they graze in another man's field, he must make
restitution from the best of his own field or vineyard.
6"If a fire breaks out and spreads into thornbushes so that it
burns shocks of grain or standing grain or the whole field, the one
who started the fire must make restitution.
7"If a man gives his neighbor silver or goods for safekeeping
and they are stolen from the neighbor's house, the thief, if he is
caught, must pay back double. 8But if the thief is not found, the
owner of the house must appear before the judges[b] to determine
whether he has laid his hands on the other man's property. 9In all
cases of illegal possession of an ox, a donkey, a sheep, a garment,
or any other lost property about which somebody says, 'This is
mine,' both parties are to bring their cases before the judges. The
one whom the judges declare[c] guilty must pay back double to his
neighbor.
10"If a man gives a donkey, an ox, a sheep or any other animal
to his neighbor for safekeeping and it dies or is injured or is taken
away while no one is looking, 11the issue between them will be
settled by the taking of an oath before the LORD that the neighbor
did not lay hands on the other person's property. The owner is to
accept this, and no restitution is required. 12But if the animal was
stolen from the neighbor, he must make restitution to the owner.
13If it was torn to pieces by a wild animal, he shall bring in the remains as evidence and he will not be required to pay for the torn
animal.
14"If a man borrows an animal from his neighbor and it is injured or dies while the owner is not present, he must make restitution. 15But if the owner is with the animal, the borrower will not
have to pay. If the animal was hired, the money paid for the hire
covers the loss.

Social Responsibility

16"If a man seduces a virgin who is not pledged to be married
and sleeps with her, he must pay the bride-price, and she shall be

[a] 3 Or *if he strikes him* [b] 8 Or *before God*; also in verse 9 [c] 9 Or *whom God declares*

his wife. 17If her father absolutely refuses to give her to him, he must still pay the bride-price for virgins.

18"Do not allow a sorceress to live.

19"Anyone who has sexual relations with an animal must be put to death.

20"Whoever sacrifices to any god other than the LORD must be destroyed.[a]

21"Do not mistreat an alien or oppress him, for you were aliens in Egypt.

22"Do not take advantage of a widow or an orphan. 23If you do and they cry out to me, I will certainly hear their cry. 24My anger will be aroused, and I will kill you with the sword; your wives will become widows and your children fatherless.

25"If you lend money to one of my people among you who is needy, do not be like a moneylender; charge him no interest.[b] 26If you take your neighbor's cloak as a pledge, return it to him by sunset, 27because his cloak is the only covering he has for his body. What else will he sleep in? When he cries out to me, I will hear, for I am compassionate.

28"Do not blaspheme God[c] or curse the ruler of your people.

29"Do not hold back offerings from your granaries or your vats.[d]

"You must give me the firstborn of your sons. 30Do the same with your cattle and your sheep. Let them stay with their mothers for seven days, but give them to me on the eighth day.

31"You are to be my holy people. So do not eat the meat of an animal torn by wild beasts; throw it to the dogs.

Laws of Justice and Mercy

23 "Do not spread false reports. Do not help a wicked man by being a malicious witness.

2"Do not follow the crowd in doing wrong. When you give testimony in a lawsuit, do not pervert justice by siding with the crowd, 3and do not show favoritism to a poor man in his lawsuit.

4"If you come across your enemy's ox or donkey wandering off, be sure to take it back to him. 5If you see the donkey of someone who hates you fallen down under its load, do not leave it there; be sure you help him with it.

6"Do not deny justice to your poor people in their lawsuits. 7Have nothing to do with a false charge and do not put an innocent or honest person to death, for I will not acquit the guilty.

8"Do not accept a bribe, for a bribe blinds those who see and twists the words of the righteous.

9"Do not oppress an alien; you yourselves know how it feels to be aliens, because you were aliens in Egypt.

Sabbath Laws

10"For six years you are to sow your fields and harvest the crops, 11but during the seventh year let the land lie unplowed and unused. Then the poor among your people may get food from it, and the wild animals may eat what they leave. Do the same with your vineyard and your olive grove.

12"Six days do your work, but on the seventh day do not work,

[a] 20 The Hebrew term refers to the irrevocable giving over of things or persons to the LORD, often by totally destroying them. [b] 25 Or *excessive interest* [c] 28 Or *Do not revile the judges* [d] 29 The meaning of the Hebrew for this phrase is uncertain.

(23:2) Stand with me, Jesus, when I turn from the crowd and walk the lonely road. When I break from the group because the group is going in the wrong direction let me know that You are near. The easy way, the wrong way, is often crowded with a loud, enthusiastic throng whose excitement is contagious. Your way is more often traveled alone, or so it seems. But You, Lord, are with me. You will never leave me or forsake me. I am counting on Your presence, Lord, even now.

(23:9) I love Your heart, Lord. Your care extends to every life, in every circumstance. I too was a stranger to Your people and Your promises, without hope and without God in the world. Your heart was inclined toward me and Your eye was upon me even then. Your people embraced me, inviting me into the family of God. Now I rejoice to be a fellow citizen with Your people and a member of Your household. May I now extend a heart of compassion to all those who have yet to come into Your family in Christ. (Eph 2:12,19)

Life is short and we have not too much time for gladdening the hearts of those who are traveling the dark way with us. Oh, be swift to love! Make haste to be kind!

Henri Frédéric Amiel (1821–1881)

All heaven is waiting to help those who will discover the will of God and do it.

J. Robert Ashcroft (1878–1958)

(23:20) I praise You for Your commitment to complete that which You begin. You brought Your people out of slavery, You prepared a place for them, and You provided protection and guidance every step of the way. And You, faithful God, have taken care of everything on my behalf as well. You have set me free. You guide me and protect me. You will see me through to the fulfillment of Your purpose; I need only pay attention and follow. Jesus, Captain of my salvation, my eyes are fixed on You. Lead me, Lord. Your victory ensures my success. Following You I cannot fail. Help me to continue in Your Word; to walk in the obedience that will ever move me forward. (Php 1:6; Heb 12:1–2)

Christ be my leader by night as by day,
Safe through the darkness, for He is the way.
Gladly I follow, my future his care,
Darkness is daylight when Jesus is there.

"Christ Be My Leader"
Timothy Dudley-Smith (©1964)

(23:31) Enlarge my vision, Lord. I am too confined in my perspective. You are God; able to do immeasurably more than all I could ask or even think. What You have in mind is much more glorious than I could ever imagine! Show me the incredible things You have prepared for me—things that no eye has ever seen or mind conceived. Let Your Spirit reveal the true inheritance You have granted me in Christ. Then help me to forget what is behind and press on toward the goal to win the prize for which You have called me heavenward in Christ Jesus! (1Co 2:9–10; Eph 3:20–21; Php 3:13–14)

so that your ox and your donkey may rest and the slave born in
your household, and the alien as well, may be refreshed.
13"Be careful to do everything I have said to you. Do not invoke the names of other gods; do not let them be heard on your
lips.

The Three Annual Festivals

14"Three times a year you are to celebrate a festival to me.
15"Celebrate the Feast of Unleavened Bread; for seven days eat
bread made without yeast, as I commanded you. Do this at the
appointed time in the month of Abib, for in that month you came
out of Egypt.
"No one is to appear before me empty-handed.
16"Celebrate the Feast of Harvest with the firstfruits of the
crops you sow in your field.
"Celebrate the Feast of Ingathering at the end of the year, when
you gather in your crops from the field.
17"Three times a year all the men are to appear before the Sovereign LORD.
18"Do not offer the blood of a sacrifice to me along with anything containing yeast.
"The fat of my festival offerings must not be kept until morning.
19"Bring the best of the firstfruits of your soil to the house of
the LORD your God.
"Do not cook a young goat in its mother's milk.

God's Angel to Prepare the Way

20"See, I am sending an angel ahead of you to guard you along
the way and to bring you to the place I have prepared. 21Pay attention to him and listen to what he says. Do not rebel against
him; he will not forgive your rebellion, since my Name is in him.
22If you listen carefully to what he says and do all that I say, I will
be an enemy to your enemies and will oppose those who oppose
you. 23My angel will go ahead of you and bring you into the land
of the Amorites, Hittites, Perizzites, Canaanites, Hivites and Jebusites, and I will wipe them out. 24Do not bow down before their
gods or worship them or follow their practices. You must demolish them and break their sacred stones to pieces. 25Worship the
LORD your God, and his blessing will be on your food and water.
I will take away sickness from among you, 26and none will miscarry or be barren in your land. I will give you a full life span.
27"I will send my terror ahead of you and throw into confusion
every nation you encounter. I will make all your enemies turn
their backs and run. 28I will send the hornet ahead of you to
drive the Hivites, Canaanites and Hittites out of your way. 29But I
will not drive them out in a single year, because the land would
become desolate and the wild animals too numerous for you.
30Little by little I will drive them out before you, until you have increased enough to take possession of the land.
31"I will establish your borders from the Red Sea[a] to the Sea
of the Philistines,[b] and from the desert to the River.[c] I will hand
over to you the people who live in the land and you will drive
them out before you. 32Do not make a covenant with them or
with their gods. 33Do not let them live in your land, or they will

[a] 31 Hebrew *Yam Suph*; that is, Sea of Reeds [b] 31 That is, the Mediterranean
[c] 31 That is, the Euphrates

cause you to sin against me, because the worship of their gods
will certainly be a snare to you."

The Covenant Confirmed

24 Then he said to Moses, "Come up to the LORD, you and
Aaron, Nadab and Abihu, and seventy of the elders of Israel. You are to worship at a distance, 2but Moses alone is to approach the LORD; the others must not come near. And the people
may not come up with him."
3When Moses went and told the people all the LORD's words and
laws, they responded with one voice, "Everything the LORD has said
we will do." 4Moses then wrote down everything the LORD had
said.
He got up early the next morning and built an altar at the foot
of the mountain and set up twelve stone pillars representing the
twelve tribes of Israel. 5Then he sent young Israelite men, and they
offered burnt offerings and sacrificed young bulls as fellowship
offerings[a] to the LORD. 6Moses took half of the blood and put it in
bowls, and the other half he sprinkled on the altar. 7Then he took
the Book of the Covenant and read it to the people. They responded, "We will do everything the LORD has said; we will obey."
8Moses then took the blood, sprinkled it on the people and
said, "This is the blood of the covenant that the LORD has made
with you in accordance with all these words."
9Moses and Aaron, Nadab and Abihu, and the seventy elders of
Israel went up 10and saw the God of Israel. Under his feet was
something like a pavement made of sapphire,[b] clear as the sky itself. 11But God did not raise his hand against these leaders of the
Israelites; they saw God, and they ate and drank.
12The LORD said to Moses, "Come up to me on the mountain
and stay here, and I will give you the tablets of stone, with the law
and commands I have written for their instruction."
13Then Moses set out with Joshua his aide, and Moses went up
on the mountain of God. 14He said to the elders, "Wait here for us
until we come back to you. Aaron and Hur are with you, and anyone involved in a dispute can go to them."
15When Moses went up on the mountain, the cloud covered it,
16and the glory of the LORD settled on Mount Sinai. For six days the
cloud covered the mountain, and on the seventh day the LORD
called to Moses from within the cloud. 17To the Israelites the glory
of the LORD looked like a consuming fire on top of the mountain.
18Then Moses entered the cloud as he went on up the mountain.
And he stayed on the mountain forty days and forty nights.

Offerings for the Tabernacle

25 The LORD said to Moses, 2"Tell the Israelites to bring me an
offering. You are to receive the offering for me from each
man whose heart prompts him to give. 3These are the offerings
you are to receive from them: gold, silver and bronze; 4blue, purple and scarlet yarn and fine linen; goat hair; 5ram skins dyed red
and hides of sea cows[c]; acacia wood; 6olive oil for the light; spices
for the anointing oil and for the fragrant incense; 7and onyx stones
and other gems to be mounted on the ephod and breastpiece.
8"Then have them make a sanctuary for me, and I will dwell

[a] 5 Traditionally *peace offerings* [b] 10 Or *lapis lazuli* [c] 5 That is, dugongs

(24:2) None of the people dared to step into Your presence, Holy Lord. None of the leaders, except Moses himself, were afforded the honor of approaching You. But now in Christ and through faith in Him I can come before Your presence with freedom and confidence. How I treasure this privilege, granted through faith in Christ alone. It is Your ultimate gift. It is my highest calling. It is amazing grace. Here I am, Lord. I come before You even now with reverence and awe. (Eph 3:12; Heb 12:18–29)

(25:2) When You ask for what I have, surely it is not because of need. All things belong to You, the King of heaven and earth; yet You ask me for an offering all the same. You invite me to participate in the great work that You intend to do. So, here is my best, Lord. Take my heart and my whole life. Take it now. Let this gift be like the perfume that Mary poured on the feet of Christ. Let it bring glory to Your name. Please receive it, Lord, as an offering of worship; please use it, Lord, for the work of the ministry. (Jn 12:3)

You do not have to be rich to be generous. If he has the spirit of true generosity, a pauper can give like a prince.

Corinne U. Wells

among them. 9 Make this tabernacle and all its furnishings exactly
like the pattern I will show you.

The Ark

10 "Have them make a chest of acacia wood—two and a half
cubits long, a cubit and a half wide, and a cubit and a half high.[a]
11 Overlay it with pure gold, both inside and out, and make a gold
molding around it. 12 Cast four gold rings for it and fasten them to
its four feet, with two rings on one side and two rings on the other.
13 Then make poles of acacia wood and overlay them with gold.
14 Insert the poles into the rings on the sides of the chest to carry
it. 15 The poles are to remain in the rings of this ark; they are not
to be removed. 16 Then put in the ark the Testimony, which I will
give you.

17 "Make an atonement cover[b] of pure gold—two and a half
cubits long and a cubit and a half wide.[c] 18 And make two cherubim out of hammered gold at the ends of the cover. 19 Make one
cherub on one end and the second cherub on the other; make the
cherubim of one piece with the cover, at the two ends. 20 The cherubim are to have their wings spread upward, overshadowing the
cover with them. The cherubim are to face each other, looking toward the cover. 21 Place the cover on top of the ark and put in the
ark the Testimony, which I will give you. 22 There, above the cover
between the two cherubim that are over the ark of the Testimony,
I will meet with you and give you all my commands for the Israelites.

The Table

23 "Make a table of acacia wood—two cubits long, a cubit wide
and a cubit and a half high.[d] 24 Overlay it with pure gold and make
a gold molding around it. 25 Also make around it a rim a handbreadth[e] wide and put a gold molding on the rim. 26 Make four
gold rings for the table and fasten them to the four corners, where
the four legs are. 27 The rings are to be close to the rim to hold the
poles used in carrying the table. 28 Make the poles of acacia wood,
overlay them with gold and carry the table with them. 29 And make
its plates and dishes of pure gold, as well as its pitchers and bowls
for the pouring out of offerings. 30 Put the bread of the Presence
on this table to be before me at all times.

The Lampstand

31 "Make a lampstand of pure gold and hammer it out, base and
shaft; its flowerlike cups, buds and blossoms shall be of one piece
with it. 32 Six branches are to extend from the sides of the lampstand—three on one side and three on the other. 33 Three cups
shaped like almond flowers with buds and blossoms are to be on
one branch, three on the next branch, and the same for all six
branches extending from the lampstand. 34 And on the lampstand
there are to be four cups shaped like almond flowers with buds
and blossoms. 35 One bud shall be under the first pair of branches
extending from the lampstand, a second bud under the second
pair, and a third bud under the third pair—six branches in all.

(25:10–16) Hide Your Word in my heart, Lord. As the tablets were stored in the ark, and the ark in the Most Holy Place, so may Your Word be stored in my inmost being so that I might not sin against You. (Ps 119:11)

(25:17–22) This atonement cover, Your "mercy seat," covered the ark, which contained the law. Your mercy is not subjected to the law; rather, the law is covered, indeed subordinated, to Your mercy. And it is at this place, where justice and mercy meet, that You promise to meet with Your people. O merciful God, we praise You that mercy triumphs over judgment. (see NIV footnote on v. 17; Jas 2:13)

Come, ye disconsolate,
Where'er ye languish;
Come to the mercy seat,
Fervently kneel;
Here bring your wounded hearts,
Here tell your anguish;
Earth has no sorrow
That heaven cannot heal.

Come, Ye Disconsolate
Thomas Moore (1824)

[a] *10* That is, about 3 3/4 feet (about 1.1 meters) long and 2 1/4 feet (about 0.7 meter) wide and high [b] *17* Traditionally *a mercy seat* [c] *17* That is, about 3 3/4 feet (about 1.1 meters) long and 2 1/4 feet (about 0.7 meter) wide [d] *23* That is, about 3 feet (about 0.9 meter) long and 1 1/2 feet (about 0.5 meter) wide and 2 1/4 feet (about 0.7 meter) high [e] *25* That is, about 3 inches (about 8 centimeters)

36The buds and branches shall all be of one piece with the lampstand, hammered out of pure gold.
37"Then make its seven lamps and set them up on it so that they
light the space in front of it. 38Its wick trimmers and trays are to
be of pure gold. 39A talent[a] of pure gold is to be used for the
lampstand and all these accessories. 40See that you make them
according to the pattern shown you on the mountain.

The Tabernacle

26 "Make the tabernacle with ten curtains of finely twisted
linen and blue, purple and scarlet yarn, with cherubim
worked into them by a skilled craftsman. 2All the curtains are to
be the same size—twenty-eight cubits long and four cubits wide.[b]
3Join five of the curtains together, and do the same with the other
five. 4Make loops of blue material along the edge of the end curtain in one set, and do the same with the end curtain in the other
set. 5Make fifty loops on one curtain and fifty loops on the end
curtain of the other set, with the loops opposite each other. 6Then
make fifty gold clasps and use them to fasten the curtains together so that the tabernacle is a unit.
7"Make curtains of goat hair for the tent over the tabernacle—
eleven altogether. 8All eleven curtains are to be the same size—
thirty cubits long and four cubits wide.[c] 9Join five of the curtains
together into one set and the other six into another set. Fold the
sixth curtain double at the front of the tent. 10Make fifty loops
along the edge of the end curtain in one set and also along the
edge of the end curtain in the other set. 11Then make fifty bronze
clasps and put them in the loops to fasten the tent together as a
unit. 12As for the additional length of the tent curtains, the half
curtain that is left over is to hang down at the rear of the tabernacle. 13The tent curtains will be a cubit[d] longer on both sides; what
is left will hang over the sides of the tabernacle so as to cover it.
14Make for the tent a covering of ram skins dyed red, and over
that a covering of hides of sea cows.[e]
15"Make upright frames of acacia wood for the tabernacle.
16Each frame is to be ten cubits long and a cubit and a half wide,[f]
17with two projections set parallel to each other. Make all the
frames of the tabernacle in this way. 18Make twenty frames for the
south side of the tabernacle 19and make forty silver bases to go
under them—two bases for each frame, one under each projection. 20For the other side, the north side of the tabernacle, make
twenty frames 21and forty silver bases—two under each frame.
22Make six frames for the far end, that is, the west end of the
tabernacle, 23and make two frames for the corners at the far end.
24At these two corners they must be double from the bottom all
the way to the top, and fitted into a single ring; both shall be like
that. 25So there will be eight frames and sixteen silver bases—two
under each frame.
26"Also make crossbars of acacia wood: five for the frames on
one side of the tabernacle, 27five for those on the other side, and
five for the frames on the west, at the far end of the tabernacle.
28The center crossbar is to extend from end to end at the middle

[a] *39* That is, about 75 pounds (about 34 kilograms) [b] *2* That is, about 42 feet (about 12.5 meters) long and 6 feet (about 1.8 meters) wide [c] *8* That is, about 45 feet (about 13.5 meters) long and 6 feet (about 1.8 meters) wide [d] *13* That is, about 1 1/2 feet (about 0.5 meter) [e] *14* That is, dugongs [f] *16* That is, about 15 feet (about 4.5 meters) long and 2 1/4 feet (about 0.7 meter) wide

Father! Replenish with thy grace this longing heart of mine;
Make it thy quiet dwelling place, thy sacred inmost shrine!

Angelus Silesius (1624–1677)

(26:1–37) Our Merciful God, how graciously You provided for Your people as they followed You through the wilderness. You designed a portable meeting place for a people on a pilgrimage. You gave such intricate detail for the design of this tabernacle, just as You worked in such intimate detail when You formed man from the dust. Today, our bodies are the temple of the Holy Spirit—a transitory meeting place of God with man, veiled in human flesh, yet fully furnished for the service of worship. We praise You, Lord, for this hope we have in Christ Jesus: that once we enter the promised land, there at last will be our permanent meeting place with You. (Ge 2:7; 2Sa 7:5–7; 1Co 6:19)

(26:31–33) This curtain signified the wall of separation between the people and Your holy presence. It was a constant reminder that Your glory, though near, was not to be touched or looked upon. But we praise You, loving God, that the curtain was torn from top to bottom when our Lord was crucified. Now, through the blood of Jesus, we have boldness not just to look in, but to enter into Your holy presence by a new and living way opened for us through the curtain, that is, His flesh. We are no longer kept at a distance; rather, Your love draws us into intimate fellowship with You. (Mt 27:51; Heb 10:19–20)

(27:1) Lord, please sharpen the focus of my eyes of faith. I see in Your Word so many facets of Your glory, so many pictures of Your nature: You are the sacrificial Lamb, the high priest, the curtain of the tabernacle, the Word itself. And here, Lord Jesus Christ, You stand eternally as the true type of the altar of God; for it is the altar that sanctifies the gift, and You are the One who sanctifies me. You are the One who makes me holy. Through You, I present myself daily as a living sacrifice. Only through You is my spiritual act of worship acceptable to the Most High. (Ex 29:37; Lev 20:8; Mt 23:19; Ro 12:1; 1Pe 2:5)

of the frames. 29 Overlay the frames with gold and make gold rings
to hold the crossbars. Also overlay the crossbars with gold.
30 "Set up the tabernacle according to the plan shown you on
the mountain.
31 "Make a curtain of blue, purple and scarlet yarn and finely
twisted linen, with cherubim worked into it by a skilled craftsman.
32 Hang it with gold hooks on four posts of acacia wood overlaid
with gold and standing on four silver bases. 33 Hang the curtain
from the clasps and place the ark of the Testimony behind the curtain. The curtain will separate the Holy Place from the Most Holy
Place. 34 Put the atonement cover on the ark of the Testimony in
the Most Holy Place. 35 Place the table outside the curtain on the
north side of the tabernacle and put the lampstand opposite it on
the south side.
36 "For the entrance to the tent make a curtain of blue, purple
and scarlet yarn and finely twisted linen—the work of an embroiderer. 37 Make gold hooks for this curtain and five posts of acacia
wood overlaid with gold. And cast five bronze bases for them.

The Altar of Burnt Offering

27 "Build an altar of acacia wood, three cubits[a] high; it is to
be square, five cubits long and five cubits wide.[b] 2 Make a
horn at each of the four corners, so that the horns and the altar
are of one piece, and overlay the altar with bronze. 3 Make all its
utensils of bronze—its pots to remove the ashes, and its shovels,
sprinkling bowls, meat forks and firepans. 4 Make a grating for it,
a bronze network, and make a bronze ring at each of the four corners of the network. 5 Put it under the ledge of the altar so that it
is halfway up the altar. 6 Make poles of acacia wood for the altar
and overlay them with bronze. 7 The poles are to be inserted into
the rings so they will be on two sides of the altar when it is carried.
8 Make the altar hollow, out of boards. It is to be made just as you
were shown on the mountain.

The Courtyard

9 "Make a courtyard for the tabernacle. The south side shall be
a hundred cubits[c] long and is to have curtains of finely twisted
linen, 10 with twenty posts and twenty bronze bases and with silver
hooks and bands on the posts. 11 The north side shall also be a
hundred cubits long and is to have curtains, with twenty posts and
twenty bronze bases and with silver hooks and bands on the posts.
12 "The west end of the courtyard shall be fifty cubits[d] wide and
have curtains, with ten posts and ten bases. 13 On the east end, toward the sunrise, the courtyard shall also be fifty cubits wide.
14 Curtains fifteen cubits[e] long are to be on one side of the entrance, with three posts and three bases, 15 and curtains fifteen cubits long are to be on the other side, with three posts and three
bases.
16 "For the entrance to the courtyard, provide a curtain twenty
cubits[f] long, of blue, purple and scarlet yarn and finely twisted
linen—the work of an embroiderer—with four posts and four
bases. 17 All the posts around the courtyard are to have silver
bands and hooks, and bronze bases. 18 The courtyard shall be a

[a] *1* That is, about 4 1/2 feet (about 1.3 meters) [b] *1* That is, about 7 1/2 feet (about 2.3 meters) long and wide [c] *9* That is, about 150 feet (about 46 meters); also in verse 11 [d] *12* That is, about 75 feet (about 23 meters); also in verse 13 [e] *14* That is, about 22 1/2 feet (about 6.9 meters); also in verse 15 [f] *16* That is, about 30 feet (about 9 meters)

hundred cubits long and fifty cubits wide,[a] with curtains of finely
twisted linen five cubits[b] high, and with bronze bases. 19All the
other articles used in the service of the tabernacle, whatever their
function, including all the tent pegs for it and those for the courtyard, are to be of bronze.

Oil for the Lampstand

20"Command the Israelites to bring you clear oil of pressed olives for the light so that the lamps may be kept burning. 21In the
Tent of Meeting, outside the curtain that is in front of the Testimony, Aaron and his sons are to keep the lamps burning before the
LORD from evening till morning. This is to be a lasting ordinance
among the Israelites for the generations to come.

The Priestly Garments

28 "Have Aaron your brother brought to you from among the
Israelites, along with his sons Nadab and Abihu, Eleazar
and Ithamar, so they may serve me as priests. 2Make sacred garments for your brother Aaron, to give him dignity and honor. 3Tell
all the skilled men to whom I have given wisdom in such matters
that they are to make garments for Aaron, for his consecration, so
he may serve me as priest. 4These are the garments they are to
make: a breastpiece, an ephod, a robe, a woven tunic, a turban
and a sash. They are to make these sacred garments for your
brother Aaron and his sons, so they may serve me as priests.
5Have them use gold, and blue, purple and scarlet yarn, and fine
linen.

The Ephod

6"Make the ephod of gold, and of blue, purple and scarlet yarn,
and of finely twisted linen—the work of a skilled craftsman. 7It is
to have two shoulder pieces attached to two of its corners, so it
can be fastened. 8Its skillfully woven waistband is to be like it—
of one piece with the ephod and made with gold, and with blue,
purple and scarlet yarn, and with finely twisted linen.
9"Take two onyx stones and engrave on them the names of the
sons of Israel 10in the order of their birth—six names on one
stone and the remaining six on the other. 11Engrave the names of
the sons of Israel on the two stones the way a gem cutter engraves
a seal. Then mount the stones in gold filigree settings 12and fasten
them on the shoulder pieces of the ephod as memorial stones for
the sons of Israel. Aaron is to bear the names on his shoulders as
a memorial before the LORD. 13Make gold filigree settings 14and
two braided chains of pure gold, like a rope, and attach the chains
to the settings.

The Breastpiece

15"Fashion a breastpiece for making decisions—the work of a
skilled craftsman. Make it like the ephod: of gold, and of blue,
purple and scarlet yarn, and of finely twisted linen. 16It is to be
square—a span[c] long and a span wide—and folded double.
17Then mount four rows of precious stones on it. In the first row
there shall be a ruby, a topaz and a beryl; 18in the second row a
turquoise, a sapphire[d] and an emerald; 19in the third row a ja-

[a] *18* That is, about 150 feet (about 46 meters) long and 75 feet (about 23 meters) wide
[b] *18* That is, about 7 1/2 feet (about 2.3 meters) [c] *16* That is, about 9 inches (about 22 centimeters) [d] *18* Or *lapis lazuli*

(27:21) What good is a lamp if it does not burn? It is like salt with no flavor or a well with no water. Lord, continually fill Your church with the fresh oil of the Holy Spirit. Help us to keep the light of Your life lit brightly at all times for all to see. (Mt 5:13–16)

(28:12) O God, how I need a mediator, someone to arbitrate between You and me, to lay his hand upon us both. Aaron, the high priest, bore the names of the sons of Israel on his shoulders as a memorial. This reminded them of their need for a mediator—someone to intercede for them before You. But it was also a memorial to You, O God, of those whom You called Aaron to serve. By accepting the priest, You accepted the people. And I am now borne on the shoulders of Jesus, my High Priest. Because He is accepted, I am accepted. Thank You, righteous Father, that in Your mercy You have appointed a Mediator for me who pleads with You on my behalf "as a man pleads for his friend." (Job 9:33; 16:19–21)

If I could hear Christ praying for me in the next room, I would not fear a million enemies. Yet distance makes no difference. He is praying for me.

Robert Murray McCheyne (1813–1843)

(28:29) Lord, You call each one of us by name. You know us individually. You are Lord of the universe, yet You are also my God. I belong to You and You are ever mindful of me. I find new strength through this intimate love. In times of trial or discouragement, this is my strength—that You remember me. My name is on Your heart. My life is in Your view.

If I forget,
Yet God remembers! If these hands of mine
Cease from their clinging, yet the hands
divine
Hold me so firmly that I cannot fall;
And if sometimes I am too tired to call
For him to help me, then he reads the
prayer
Unspoken in my heart, and lifts my care.
Robert Browning (1812-1889)

(28:38) O Holy God, please receive my life as a gift, imperfect as it is. I offer it to You in the name of Jesus. Even the best I have to offer is blemished by human failure. For "I find this law at work in me: When I want to do good, evil is right there with me." So I put myself in the hands of Jesus, my perfect heavenly high priest. Receive my life, God, in Jesus' name. May it be cleansed, perfected and made holy by His holy hand. (Ro 7:21)

cinth, an agate and an amethyst; 20 in the fourth row a chrysolite,
an onyx and a jasper.[a] Mount them in gold filigree settings.
21 There are to be twelve stones, one for each of the names of the
sons of Israel, each engraved like a seal with the name of one of
the twelve tribes.
22 "For the breastpiece make braided chains of pure gold, like
a rope. 23 Make two gold rings for it and fasten them to two corners of the breastpiece. 24 Fasten the two gold chains to the rings
at the corners of the breastpiece, 25 and the other ends of the
chains to the two settings, attaching them to the shoulder pieces of
the ephod at the front. 26 Make two gold rings and attach them to
the other two corners of the breastpiece on the inside edge next
to the ephod. 27 Make two more gold rings and attach them to the
bottom of the shoulder pieces on the front of the ephod, close to
the seam just above the waistband of the ephod. 28 The rings of
the breastpiece are to be tied to the rings of the ephod with blue
cord, connecting it to the waistband, so that the breastpiece will
not swing out from the ephod.
29 "Whenever Aaron enters the Holy Place, he will bear the
names of the sons of Israel over his heart on the breastpiece of decision as a continuing memorial before the LORD. 30 Also put the
Urim and the Thummim in the breastpiece, so they may be over
Aaron's heart whenever he enters the presence of the LORD. Thus
Aaron will always bear the means of making decisions for the Israelites over his heart before the LORD.

Other Priestly Garments

31 "Make the robe of the ephod entirely of blue cloth, 32 with an
opening for the head in its center. There shall be a woven edge
like a collar[b] around this opening, so that it will not tear. 33 Make
pomegranates of blue, purple and scarlet yarn around the hem of
the robe, with gold bells between them. 34 The gold bells and the
pomegranates are to alternate around the hem of the robe.
35 Aaron must wear it when he ministers. The sound of the bells
will be heard when he enters the Holy Place before the LORD and
when he comes out, so that he will not die.
36 "Make a plate of pure gold and engrave on it as on a seal:
HOLY TO THE LORD. 37 Fasten a blue cord to it to attach it to the turban; it is to be on the front of the turban. 38 It will be on Aaron's
forehead, and he will bear the guilt involved in the sacred gifts the
Israelites consecrate, whatever their gifts may be. It will be on
Aaron's forehead continually so that they will be acceptable to the
LORD.
39 "Weave the tunic of fine linen and make the turban of fine
linen. The sash is to be the work of an embroiderer. 40 Make tunics, sashes and headbands for Aaron's sons, to give them dignity
and honor. 41 After you put these clothes on your brother Aaron
and his sons, anoint and ordain them. Consecrate them so they
may serve me as priests.
42 "Make linen undergarments as a covering for the body,
reaching from the waist to the thigh. 43 Aaron and his sons must
wear them whenever they enter the Tent of Meeting or approach
the altar to minister in the Holy Place, so that they will not incur
guilt and die.

[a] *20* The precise identification of some of these precious stones is uncertain. [b] *32* The meaning of the Hebrew for this word is uncertain.

"This is to be a lasting ordinance for Aaron and his descendants.

Consecration of the Priests

29 "This is what you are to do to consecrate them, so they
may serve me as priests: Take a young bull and two rams
without defect. 2And from fine wheat flour, without yeast, make
bread, and cakes mixed with oil, and wafers spread with oil. 3Put
them in a basket and present them in it—along with the bull and
the two rams. 4Then bring Aaron and his sons to the entrance to
the Tent of Meeting and wash them with water. 5Take the garments
and dress Aaron with the tunic, the robe of the ephod, the ephod
itself and the breastpiece. Fasten the ephod on him by its skillfully woven waistband. 6Put the turban on his head and attach the sacred diadem to the turban. 7Take the anointing oil and anoint him
by pouring it on his head. 8Bring his sons and dress them in tunics
9and put headbands on them. Then tie sashes on Aaron and his
sons.[a] The priesthood is theirs by a lasting ordinance. In this way
you shall ordain Aaron and his sons.

10"Bring the bull to the front of the Tent of Meeting, and Aaron
and his sons shall lay their hands on its head. 11Slaughter it in the
LORD's presence at the entrance to the Tent of Meeting. 12Take
some of the bull's blood and put it on the horns of the altar with
your finger, and pour out the rest of it at the base of the altar.
13Then take all the fat around the inner parts, the covering of the
liver, and both kidneys with the fat on them, and burn them on the
altar. 14But burn the bull's flesh and its hide and its offal outside
the camp. It is a sin offering.

15"Take one of the rams, and Aaron and his sons shall lay their
hands on its head. 16Slaughter it and take the blood and sprinkle
it against the altar on all sides. 17Cut the ram into pieces and wash
the inner parts and the legs, putting them with the head and the
other pieces. 18Then burn the entire ram on the altar. It is a burnt
offering to the LORD, a pleasing aroma, an offering made to the
LORD by fire.

19"Take the other ram, and Aaron and his sons shall lay their
hands on its head. 20Slaughter it, take some of its blood and put it
on the lobes of the right ears of Aaron and his sons, on the thumbs
of their right hands, and on the big toes of their right feet. Then
sprinkle blood against the altar on all sides. 21And take some of
the blood on the altar and some of the anointing oil and sprinkle
it on Aaron and his garments and on his sons and their garments.
Then he and his sons and their garments will be consecrated.

22"Take from this ram the fat, the fat tail, the fat around the
inner parts, the covering of the liver, both kidneys with the fat on
them, and the right thigh. (This is the ram for the ordination.)
23From the basket of bread made without yeast, which is before
the LORD, take a loaf, and a cake made with oil, and a wafer. 24Put
all these in the hands of Aaron and his sons and wave them before
the LORD as a wave offering. 25Then take them from their hands
and burn them on the altar along with the burnt offering for a
pleasing aroma to the LORD, an offering made to the LORD by fire.
26After you take the breast of the ram for Aaron's ordination, wave
it before the LORD as a wave offering, and it will be your share.

27"Consecrate those parts of the ordination ram that belong to

[a] 9 Hebrew; Septuagint *on them*

(29:10) The priests laid their hands on the head of the sin offering, identifying themselves with the atoning work of the sacrifice, acknowledging that the animal was suffering the punishment they deserved, and giving thanks to You for providing a sacrifice that would make them acceptable in Your sight. Lord, I now come and lay the hands of my faith upon the head of Jesus, the Lamb of God who takes away the sin of the world. Aware of my insufficiency, I lean the full weight of my soul on His all–sufficiency. I confess that I am a sinner in need of a savior. My life is now hidden in His, for I have run to Christ. Through Him alone I find forgiveness of sins. (Jn 1:29; Gal 2:20; Col 3:3)

(29:20) Prepare me for ministry in Your name, O God. Let me serve as one first touched and transformed by Your saving blood. Give me ears to hear with clarity and compassion, for I too am a sinner cleansed by sacrifice. Give me hands to help with gentleness and love—these hands I once used to hurt and hinder, now pardoned by Your grace. Give me feet to walk in all Your ways, feet to follow You. Prepare me now for ministry, Lord. Prepare me head to toe. Let all that I am be an instrument of Your grace.

Teach us, good Lord, to serve thee as thou deservest;
To give and not to count the cost;
To fight and not to heed the wounds;
To toil and not to seek for rest;
To labor and not to ask for any reward,
Save that of knowing that we do thy will.
Amen.

Saint Ignatius of Loyola (1491–1556)

(29:38–39) Our Father in heaven, You ordained daily sacrifices as a constant reminder to us of Your daily mercy. They were offered to You as expressions of worship, love and devotion. Help me every day to come to You with a grateful heart; and help me, through Jesus, to continually offer to You the sacrifice of praise, the fruit of lips that confess His name. (Heb 13:15)

(29:42–43) How great is Your glory, Lord. Your presence transforms a tent into a holy sanctuary. No amount of artistic display can produce the presence of God. But Your living presence makes even a desolate place into the very gate of heaven. When we assemble for worship, we long for Your living presence, Lord. Come with Your divine reality into all our feeble efforts and into our simple earthly meeting places. Fill our churches with Your glory, and fill our hearts as well. May we each become tabernacles of Your living presence by the power of Your Holy Spirit. (Ge 28:17; 1Co 6:19)

If God should give my soul all he ever made or might make, apart from himself, and giving it, he stayed away even by as much as a hairbreadth, my soul would not be satisfied.

Meister Eckhart (c.1260–c.1327)

Aaron and his sons: the breast that was waved and the thigh that
was presented. 28This is always to be the regular share from the
Israelites for Aaron and his sons. It is the contribution the Israelites are to make to the LORD from their fellowship offerings.[a]
29"Aaron's sacred garments will belong to his descendants so
that they can be anointed and ordained in them. 30The son who
succeeds him as priest and comes to the Tent of Meeting to minister in the Holy Place is to wear them seven days.
31"Take the ram for the ordination and cook the meat in a sacred place. 32At the entrance to the Tent of Meeting, Aaron and
his sons are to eat the meat of the ram and the bread that is in
the basket. 33They are to eat these offerings by which atonement
was made for their ordination and consecration. But no one else
may eat them, because they are sacred. 34And if any of the meat
of the ordination ram or any bread is left over till morning, burn
it up. It must not be eaten, because it is sacred.
35"Do for Aaron and his sons everything I have commanded
you, taking seven days to ordain them. 36Sacrifice a bull each
day as a sin offering to make atonement. Purify the altar by making atonement for it, and anoint it to consecrate it. 37For seven
days make atonement for the altar and consecrate it. Then the
altar will be most holy, and whatever touches it will be holy.
38"This is what you are to offer on the altar regularly each
day: two lambs a year old. 39Offer one in the morning and the
other at twilight. 40With the first lamb offer a tenth of an ephah[b]
of fine flour mixed with a quarter of a hin[c] of oil from pressed
olives, and a quarter of a hin of wine as a drink offering. 41Sac-
rifice the other lamb at twilight with the same grain offering and
its drink offering as in the morning—a pleasing aroma, an offering made to the LORD by fire.
42"For the generations to come this burnt offering is to be
made regularly at the entrance to the Tent of Meeting before the
LORD. There I will meet you and speak to you; 43there also I will
meet with the Israelites, and the place will be consecrated by my
glory.
44"So I will consecrate the Tent of Meeting and the altar and
will consecrate Aaron and his sons to serve me as priests.
45Then I will dwell among the Israelites and be their God.
46They will know that I am the LORD their God, who brought
them out of Egypt so that I might dwell among them. I am the
LORD their God.

The Altar of Incense

30 "Make an altar of acacia wood for burning incense. 2It is
to be square, a cubit long and a cubit wide, and two cubits high[d]—its horns of one piece with it. 3Overlay the top and
all the sides and the horns with pure gold, and make a gold
molding around it. 4Make two gold rings for the altar below the
molding—two on opposite sides—to hold the poles used to
carry it. 5Make the poles of acacia wood and overlay them with
gold. 6Put the altar in front of the curtain that is before the ark
of the Testimony—before the atonement cover that is over the
Testimony—where I will meet with you.
7"Aaron must burn fragrant incense on the altar every morn-

[a] *28* Traditionally *peace offerings* [b] *40* That is, probably about 2 quarts (about 2 liters) [c] *40* That is, probably about 1 quart (about 1 liter) [d] *2* That is, about 1 1/2 feet (about 0.5 meter) long and wide and about 3 feet (about 0.9 meter) high

ing when he tends the lamps. 8He must burn incense again when he lights the lamps at twilight so incense will burn regularly before the LORD for the generations to come. 9Do not offer on this altar any other incense or any burnt offering or grain offering, and do not pour a drink offering on it. 10Once a year Aaron shall make atonement on its horns. This annual atonement must be made with the blood of the atoning sin offering for the generations to come. It is most holy to the LORD."

Atonement Money

11Then the LORD said to Moses, 12"When you take a census of the Israelites to count them, each one must pay the LORD a ransom for his life at the time he is counted. Then no plague will come on them when you number them. 13Each one who crosses over to those already counted is to give a half shekel,[a] according to the sanctuary shekel, which weighs twenty gerahs. This half shekel is an offering to the LORD. 14All who cross over, those twenty years old or more, are to give an offering to the LORD. 15The rich are not to give more than a half shekel and the poor are not to give less when you make the offering to the LORD to atone for your lives. 16Receive the atonement money from the Israelites and use it for the service of the Tent of Meeting. It will be a memorial for the Israelites before the LORD, making atonement for your lives."

Basin for Washing

17Then the LORD said to Moses, 18"Make a bronze basin, with its bronze stand, for washing. Place it between the Tent of Meeting and the altar, and put water in it. 19Aaron and his sons are to wash their hands and feet with water from it. 20Whenever they enter the Tent of Meeting, they shall wash with water so that they will not die. Also, when they approach the altar to minister by presenting an offering made to the LORD by fire, 21they shall wash their hands and feet so that they will not die. This is to be a lasting ordinance for Aaron and his descendants for the generations to come."

Anointing Oil

22Then the LORD said to Moses, 23"Take the following fine spices: 500 shekels[b] of liquid myrrh, half as much (that is, 250 shekels) of fragrant cinnamon, 250 shekels of fragrant cane, 24500 shekels of cassia—all according to the sanctuary shekel—and a hin[c] of olive oil. 25Make these into a sacred anointing oil, a fragrant blend, the work of a perfumer. It will be the sacred anointing oil. 26Then use it to anoint the Tent of Meeting, the ark of the Testimony, 27the table and all its articles, the lampstand and its accessories, the altar of incense, 28the altar of burnt offering and all its utensils, and the basin with its stand. 29You shall consecrate them so they will be most holy, and whatever touches them will be holy.

30"Anoint Aaron and his sons and consecrate them so they may serve me as priests. 31Say to the Israelites, 'This is to be my sacred anointing oil for the generations to come. 32Do not pour it on men's bodies and do not make any oil with the same formula. It is sacred, and you are to consider it sacred. 33Whoever

[a] *13* That is, about 1/5 ounce (about 6 grams); also in verse 15 [b] *23* That is, about 12 1/2 pounds (about 6 kilograms) [c] *24* That is, probably about 4 quarts (about 4 liters)

(30:7–10) Let my prayer be set before You like incense, Lord, and may the lifting up of my hands be like the evening sacrifice. For You have called me to prayer—persistent prayer that continues to ask, to seek and to knock at the door of heaven. You have called me to prayer that will acknowledge You day and night. So receive my prayer, Lord. I offer up my requests upon the altar of Christ, within the authority of His shed blood. (Ps 141:2; Mt 7:7)

God bestows many things on us out of his liberality, even without our asking for them. But that he wishes to bestow certain things on us at our asking is for the sake of our good, that we may acquire confidence in having recourse to God, and that we may recognize in him the Author of our goods.

Saint Thomas Aquinas (1225-1274)

Lord, teach us how to pray aright
with reverence and with fear;
Though weak and sinful in your sight,
we may, we must draw near.

We perish if we cease from prayer:
O grant us power to pray;
And when to meet you we prepare,
Lord, meet us by the way.

"Lord, Teach Us How to Pray Aright"
James Montgomery (1823)

(30:21) The impurities of a sinful world have soiled me, Lord: heart, mind, soul and spirit. Wash me, Lord, with the pure water of Your Word. Give me a renewed mind to know Your will. Give me "beautiful feet" to carry the Good News of the gospel. Give me holy hands to lift to You in prayer. How I long to stand before Your presence unashamed; I want to come near in purity. If You do not wash me, then I can have no fellowship with You. So wash me, Lord, that I might draw near every day. (Isa 52:7; Jn 13:8; Ro 12:2; Eph 5:26; 1Ti 2:8)

(31:3) "Not to us, O LORD, not to us but to your name be the glory, because of your love and faithfulness." All that we are and all that we do in Your service comes first from Your hand of grace. We are Your workmanship, created in Christ Jesus to do good works, which You prepared in advance for us to do. This is now our high calling, to be co-workers with You, to accomplish Your divine purpose. Come Holy Spirit! Fill us with skill, ability and knowledge. Empower us, Lord, so that in all things we may show that our work is more than our own; it is the work of Your divine hand in and through us. (Ps 115:1; Eph 2:10)

(31:18) Lord God, I thank You for the certainty of Your covenant with Your people. The Testimony of Your covenant was not just left to the custody of their memory, a memory that fades with time; rather, it was written in stone as a permanent reminder of Your care for them and of their responsibility to You. What an incredible gift! And yet this Testimony of Your covenant, the law written by the finger of God on tablets of stone, would one day be superceded by a new covenant, written by the nail-pierced hands of Christ upon the tablets of our hearts. (Jn 1:17; 2Co 3:3,7–11)

makes perfume like it and whoever puts it on anyone other than
a priest must be cut off from his people.' "

Incense

34 Then the LORD said to Moses, "Take fragrant spices—gum
resin, onycha and galbanum—and pure frankincense, all in
equal amounts, 35 and make a fragrant blend of incense, the
work of a perfumer. It is to be salted and pure and sacred.
36 Grind some of it to powder and place it in front of the Testimony in the Tent of Meeting, where I will meet with you. It shall
be most holy to you. 37 Do not make any incense with this formula for yourselves; consider it holy to the LORD. 38 Whoever
makes any like it to enjoy its fragrance must be cut off from his
people."

Bezalel and Oholiab

31 Then the LORD said to Moses, 2 "See, I have chosen Bezalel son of Uri, the son of Hur, of the tribe of Judah, 3 and
I have filled him with the Spirit of God, with skill, ability and
knowledge in all kinds of crafts— 4 to make artistic designs for
work in gold, silver and bronze, 5 to cut and set stones, to work
in wood, and to engage in all kinds of craftsmanship. 6 Moreover, I have appointed Oholiab son of Ahisamach, of the tribe of
Dan, to help him. Also I have given skill to all the craftsmen to
make everything I have commanded you: 7 the Tent of Meeting,
the ark of the Testimony with the atonement cover on it, and
all the other furnishings of the tent— 8 the table and its articles,
the pure gold lampstand and all its accessories, the altar of incense, 9 the altar of burnt offering and all its utensils, the basin
with its stand— 10 and also the woven garments, both the sacred garments for Aaron the priest and the garments for his
sons when they serve as priests, 11 and the anointing oil and fragrant incense for the Holy Place. They are to make them just as
I commanded you."

The Sabbath

12 Then the LORD said to Moses, 13 "Say to the Israelites, 'You
must observe my Sabbaths. This will be a sign between me and
you for the generations to come, so you may know that I am the
LORD, who makes you holy.[a]
14 " 'Observe the Sabbath, because it is holy to you. Anyone
who desecrates it must be put to death; whoever does any work
on that day must be cut off from his people. 15 For six days,
work is to be done, but the seventh day is a Sabbath of rest, holy
to the LORD. Whoever does any work on the Sabbath day must be
put to death. 16 The Israelites are to observe the Sabbath, celebrating it for the generations to come as a lasting covenant. 17 It
will be a sign between me and the Israelites forever, for in six
days the LORD made the heavens and the earth, and on the seventh day he abstained from work and rested.' "
18 When the LORD finished speaking to Moses on Mount Sinai,
he gave him the two tablets of the Testimony, the tablets of stone
inscribed by the finger of God.

[a] 13 Or *who sanctifies you*; or *who sets you apart as holy*

The Golden Calf

32 When the people saw that Moses was so long in coming
down from the mountain, they gathered around Aaron and
said, "Come, make us gods[a] who will go before us. As for this fellow Moses who brought us up out of Egypt, we don't know what
has happened to him."
2Aaron answered them, "Take off the gold earrings that your
wives, your sons and your daughters are wearing, and bring them
to me." 3So all the people took off their earrings and brought
them to Aaron. 4He took what they handed him and made it into
an idol cast in the shape of a calf, fashioning it with a tool. Then
they said, "These are your gods,[b] O Israel, who brought you up
out of Egypt."
5When Aaron saw this, he built an altar in front of the calf and
announced, "Tomorrow there will be a festival to the LORD." 6So
the next day the people rose early and sacrificed burnt offerings
and presented fellowship offerings.[c] Afterward they sat down to
eat and drink and got up to indulge in revelry.
7Then the LORD said to Moses, "Go down, because your people,
whom you brought up out of Egypt, have become corrupt. 8They
have been quick to turn away from what I commanded them and
have made themselves an idol cast in the shape of a calf. They have
bowed down to it and sacrificed to it and have said, 'These are
your gods, O Israel, who brought you up out of Egypt.'
9"I have seen these people," the LORD said to Moses, "and they
are a stiff-necked people. 10Now leave me alone so that my anger
may burn against them and that I may destroy them. Then I will
make you into a great nation."
11But Moses sought the favor of the LORD his God. "O LORD," he
said, "why should your anger burn against your people, whom you
brought out of Egypt with great power and a mighty hand? 12Why
should the Egyptians say, 'It was with evil intent that he brought
them out, to kill them in the mountains and to wipe them off the
face of the earth'? Turn from your fierce anger; relent and do not
bring disaster on your people. 13Remember your servants Abraham, Isaac and Israel, to whom you swore by your own self: 'I will
make your descendants as numerous as the stars in the sky and I
will give your descendants all this land I promised them, and it
will be their inheritance forever.' " 14Then the LORD relented and
did not bring on his people the disaster he had threatened.
15Moses turned and went down the mountain with the two
tablets of the Testimony in his hands. They were inscribed on both
sides, front and back. 16The tablets were the work of God; the
writing was the writing of God, engraved on the tablets.
17When Joshua heard the noise of the people shouting, he said
to Moses, "There is the sound of war in the camp."
18Moses replied:

"It is not the sound of victory,
it is not the sound of defeat;
it is the sound of singing that I hear."

19When Moses approached the camp and saw the calf and the
dancing, his anger burned and he threw the tablets out of his
hands, breaking them to pieces at the foot of the mountain. 20And

[a] *1* Or *a god*; also in verses 23 and 31 [b] *4* Or *This is your god*; also in verse 8
[c] *6* Traditionally *peace offerings*

(32:1–4) What drives our hearts to forsake You? What do we desire so desperately that we exchange Your truth, O God, for a lie? Turning from You, the fountain of living water, we dig for ourselves broken cisterns that can hold no water. We whitewash walls of doctrine that have no sure foundation. O God of majestic holiness! You are our Maker and our King! But we are looking for a convenient deity, a god that we may control. Rather than serve You as we should, we desire a god to serve us and make no demands. Forgive us, Lord. Come tear these pitiful idols from our wandering hearts. (Jer 2:13; Eze 13:10; Ro 1:25)

(32:32) "Greater love has no one than this, that he lay down his life for his friends." Moses made a stunning offer: his life in exchange for the lives of his people. Did he know the full weight of what he offered? Jesus, You knew the price that You would pay. You knew the terrible weight of judgment that You would endure. Still, You gave up Your life to the cross. What Moses could not do, You have done, my Savior. Your perfect life, in perfect love, given for me. How precious is Your love; how great is Your gift. (Jn 15:13)

(33:5–6) It is time to be honest before You, Lord. I must face the reality of my sin. It is time to confess and change my ways. Look on me, Lord. Tell me what You see. Is there sincerity in my sorrow? Do I have a sense of the pain that I have caused? Do I care? Here I am, Lord, open and exposed before Your gaze. What will You do in the aftermath of my sin? With brokenness of heart I yield to Your correcting love.

In confession . . . we open our lives to the healing, reconciling, restoring, uplifting grace of him who loves us in spite of what we are.

Louis Cassels (1922-1974)

he took the calf they had made and burned it in the fire; then he ground it to powder, scattered it on the water and made the Israelites drink it.

21He said to Aaron, "What did these people do to you, that you led them into such great sin?"

22"Do not be angry, my lord," Aaron answered. "You know how prone these people are to evil. 23They said to me, 'Make us gods who will go before us. As for this fellow Moses who brought us up out of Egypt, we don't know what has happened to him.' 24So I told them, 'Whoever has any gold jewelry, take it off.' Then they gave me the gold, and I threw it into the fire, and out came this calf!"

25Moses saw that the people were running wild and that Aaron had let them get out of control and so become a laughingstock to their enemies. 26So he stood at the entrance to the camp and said, "Whoever is for the LORD, come to me." And all the Levites rallied to him.

27Then he said to them, "This is what the LORD, the God of Israel, says: 'Each man strap a sword to his side. Go back and forth through the camp from one end to the other, each killing his brother and friend and neighbor.' " 28The Levites did as Moses commanded, and that day about three thousand of the people died. 29Then Moses said, "You have been set apart to the LORD today, for you were against your own sons and brothers, and he has blessed you this day."

30The next day Moses said to the people, "You have committed a great sin. But now I will go up to the LORD; perhaps I can make atonement for your sin."

31So Moses went back to the LORD and said, "Oh, what a great sin these people have committed! They have made themselves gods of gold. 32But now, please forgive their sin—but if not, then blot me out of the book you have written."

33The LORD replied to Moses, "Whoever has sinned against me I will blot out of my book. 34Now go, lead the people to the place I spoke of, and my angel will go before you. However, when the time comes for me to punish, I will punish them for their sin."

35And the LORD struck the people with a plague because of what they did with the calf Aaron had made.

33 Then the LORD said to Moses, "Leave this place, you and the people you brought up out of Egypt, and go up to the land I promised on oath to Abraham, Isaac and Jacob, saying, 'I will give it to your descendants.' 2I will send an angel before you and drive out the Canaanites, Amorites, Hittites, Perizzites, Hivites and Jebusites. 3Go up to the land flowing with milk and honey. But I will not go with you, because you are a stiff-necked people and I might destroy you on the way."

4When the people heard these distressing words, they began to mourn and no one put on any ornaments. 5For the LORD had said to Moses, "Tell the Israelites, 'You are a stiff-necked people. If I were to go with you even for a moment, I might destroy you. Now take off your ornaments and I will decide what to do with you.' " 6So the Israelites stripped off their ornaments at Mount Horeb.

The Tent of Meeting

7Now Moses used to take a tent and pitch it outside the camp some distance away, calling it the "tent of meeting." Anyone inquiring of the LORD would go to the tent of meeting outside the

camp. 8And whenever Moses went out to the tent, all the people
rose and stood at the entrances to their tents, watching Moses
until he entered the tent. 9As Moses went into the tent, the pillar of
cloud would come down and stay at the entrance, while the LORD
spoke with Moses. 10Whenever the people saw the pillar of cloud
standing at the entrance to the tent, they all stood and worshiped,
each at the entrance to his tent. 11The LORD would speak to Moses
face to face, as a man speaks with his friend. Then Moses would
return to the camp, but his young aide Joshua son of Nun did not
leave the tent.

Moses and the Glory of the LORD

12Moses said to the LORD, "You have been telling me, 'Lead
these people,' but you have not let me know whom you will send
with me. You have said, 'I know you by name and you have found
favor with me.' 13If you are pleased with me, teach me your ways
so I may know you and continue to find favor with you. Remember that this nation is your people."

14The LORD replied, "My Presence will go with you, and I will
give you rest."

15Then Moses said to him, "If your Presence does not go with
us, do not send us up from here. 16How will anyone know that you
are pleased with me and with your people unless you go with us?
What else will distinguish me and your people from all the other
people on the face of the earth?"

17And the LORD said to Moses, "I will do the very thing you have
asked, because I am pleased with you and I know you by name."

18Then Moses said, "Now show me your glory."

19And the LORD said, "I will cause all my goodness to pass in
front of you, and I will proclaim my name, the LORD, in your presence. I will have mercy on whom I will have mercy, and I will have
compassion on whom I will have compassion. 20But," he said,
"you cannot see my face, for no one may see me and live."

21Then the LORD said, "There is a place near me where you may
stand on a rock. 22When my glory passes by, I will put you in a
cleft in the rock and cover you with my hand until I have passed
by. 23Then I will remove my hand and you will see my back; but
my face must not be seen."

The New Stone Tablets

34 The LORD said to Moses, "Chisel out two stone tablets like
the first ones, and I will write on them the words that were
on the first tablets, which you broke. 2Be ready in the morning,
and then come up on Mount Sinai. Present yourself to me there on
top of the mountain. 3No one is to come with you or be seen anywhere on the mountain; not even the flocks and herds may graze
in front of the mountain."

4So Moses chiseled out two stone tablets like the first ones and
went up Mount Sinai early in the morning, as the LORD had commanded him; and he carried the two stone tablets in his hands.
5Then the LORD came down in the cloud and stood there with him
and proclaimed his name, the LORD. 6And he passed in front of
Moses, proclaiming, "The LORD, the LORD, the compassionate and
gracious God, slow to anger, abounding in love and faithfulness,
7maintaining love to thousands, and forgiving wickedness, rebellion and sin. Yet he does not leave the guilty unpunished; he pun-

(33:11) Bring me close, Lord. Let me see Your face. I have watched others draw close to You in worship and prayer. Let me share that blessing, too. May I draw close like Abraham, Moses and David. May I be like Peter, James and John who stood with Jesus on the mountain and witnessed his glory. Bring me close, Lord. Like Joshua I wait, hoping for a glimpse. The testimony of others is not enough for me. Bring me close, Lord, and let me see Your face. (Mt. 17:1–8)

(34:6) Awesome God, let me see Your glory! Your glory is so much more than raw power or blinding light. When Moses prayed to see the revelation of Your glory, You answered by illuminating the excellencies of Your character, the perfect attributes of Your own nature. Open my eyes to Your glory, Lord! Show me the glory of Your faithfulness and love. With each new day, Lord, show me the glory of Your very nature, revealed in Jesus Christ, the Word made flesh.

Oh God, awesome in power.
Oh God, gentle in love.
Oh God, You are my God,
And I love You.

Oh God, full of compassion.
Oh God, faithful and true.
Oh God, You are my God,
And I love You.

"Awesome In Power"
Rick Founds (©1990)

ishes the children and their children for the sin of the fathers to
the third and fourth generation."
8Moses bowed to the ground at once and worshiped. 9"O Lord,
if I have found favor in your eyes," he said, "then let the Lord go
with us. Although this is a stiff-necked people, forgive our wickedness and our sin, and take us as your inheritance."
10Then the LORD said: "I am making a covenant with you. Before
all your people I will do wonders never before done in any nation
in all the world. The people you live among will see how awesome
is the work that I, the LORD, will do for you. 11Obey what I command you today. I will drive out before you the Amorites, Canaanites, Hittites, Perizzites, Hivites and Jebusites. 12Be careful not to
make a treaty with those who live in the land where you are going,
or they will be a snare among you. 13Break down their altars,
smash their sacred stones and cut down their Asherah poles.[a]
14Do not worship any other god, for the LORD, whose name is Jealous, is a jealous God.
15"Be careful not to make a treaty with those who live in the
land; for when they prostitute themselves to their gods and sacrifice to them, they will invite you and you will eat their sacrifices.
16And when you choose some of their daughters as wives for your
sons and those daughters prostitute themselves to their gods, they
will lead your sons to do the same.
17"Do not make cast idols.
18"Celebrate the Feast of Unleavened Bread. For seven days eat
bread made without yeast, as I commanded you. Do this at the appointed time in the month of Abib, for in that month you came out
of Egypt.
19"The first offspring of every womb belongs to me, including
all the firstborn males of your livestock, whether from herd or
flock. 20Redeem the firstborn donkey with a lamb, but if you do
not redeem it, break its neck. Redeem all your firstborn sons.
"No one is to appear before me empty-handed.
21"Six days you shall labor, but on the seventh day you shall
rest; even during the plowing season and harvest you must rest.
22"Celebrate the Feast of Weeks with the firstfruits of the wheat
harvest, and the Feast of Ingathering at the turn of the year.[b]
23Three times a year all your men are to appear before the Sovereign LORD, the God of Israel. 24I will drive out nations before you
and enlarge your territory, and no one will covet your land when
you go up three times each year to appear before the LORD your
God.
25"Do not offer the blood of a sacrifice to me along with anything containing yeast, and do not let any of the sacrifice from the
Passover Feast remain until morning.
26"Bring the best of the firstfruits of your soil to the house of
the LORD your God.
"Do not cook a young goat in its mother's milk."
27Then the LORD said to Moses, "Write down these words, for in
accordance with these words I have made a covenant with you and
with Israel." 28Moses was there with the LORD forty days and forty
nights without eating bread or drinking water. And he wrote on the
tablets the words of the covenant—the Ten Commandments.

[a] 13 That is, symbols of the goddess Asherah [b] 22 That is, in the fall

(34:14) God of holy love, all Your ways are right. Yours is a heart of perfect passion. You are jealous for this love relationship we share, a love founded in Your goodness and truth. If I worship another I betray our love—I sin against You, against myself, against the truth. To worship another is to break Your heart and to live a lie. Keep watch over this love with perfect care, Lord, and I will devote my heart only to You.

(34:21) Today I cease my frantic striving and endless motion. There is always more to be done, unfinished business that beckons and presses. But today I pause to remember and to worship. "Unless the LORD builds the house, its builders labor in vain." You are God, the creator, sustainer and director of all things. I do not presume to take Your place at the controls! What I do in my own strength amounts to nothing, but under Your benevolent blessing my feeble efforts are strengthened and multiplied. Today I pause to acknowledge You. (Ps 127:1)

The Radiant Face of Moses

29When Moses came down from Mount Sinai with the two
tablets of the Testimony in his hands, he was not aware that his
face was radiant because he had spoken with the LORD. 30When
Aaron and all the Israelites saw Moses, his face was radiant, and
they were afraid to come near him. 31But Moses called to them; so
Aaron and all the leaders of the community came back to him,
and he spoke to them. 32Afterward all the Israelites came near
him, and he gave them all the commands the LORD had given him
on Mount Sinai.

33When Moses finished speaking to them, he put a veil over his
face. 34But whenever he entered the LORD's presence to speak with
him, he removed the veil until he came out. And when he came out
and told the Israelites what he had been commanded, 35they saw
that his face was radiant. Then Moses would put the veil back over
his face until he went in to speak with the LORD.

Sabbath Regulations

35 Moses assembled the whole Israelite community and said
to them, "These are the things the LORD has commanded
you to do: 2For six days, work is to be done, but the seventh day
shall be your holy day, a Sabbath of rest to the LORD. Whoever does
any work on it must be put to death. 3Do not light a fire in any of
your dwellings on the Sabbath day."

Materials for the Tabernacle

4Moses said to the whole Israelite community, "This is what the
LORD has commanded: 5From what you have, take an offering for
the LORD. Everyone who is willing is to bring to the LORD an offering of gold, silver and bronze; 6blue, purple and scarlet yarn and
fine linen; goat hair; 7ram skins dyed red and hides of sea cows[a];
acacia wood; 8olive oil for the light; spices for the anointing oil
and for the fragrant incense; 9and onyx stones and other gems to
be mounted on the ephod and breastpiece.

10"All who are skilled among you are to come and make everything the LORD has commanded: 11the tabernacle with its tent and
its covering, clasps, frames, crossbars, posts and bases; 12the ark
with its poles and the atonement cover and the curtain that shields
it; 13the table with its poles and all its articles and the bread of the
Presence; 14the lampstand that is for light with its accessories,
lamps and oil for the light; 15the altar of incense with its poles, the
anointing oil and the fragrant incense; the curtain for the doorway
at the entrance to the tabernacle; 16the altar of burnt offering with
its bronze grating, its poles and all its utensils; the bronze basin
with its stand; 17the curtains of the courtyard with its posts and
bases, and the curtain for the entrance to the courtyard; 18the tent
pegs for the tabernacle and for the courtyard, and their ropes;
19the woven garments worn for ministering in the sanctuary—
both the sacred garments for Aaron the priest and the garments
for his sons when they serve as priests."

20Then the whole Israelite community withdrew from Moses'
presence, 21and everyone who was willing and whose heart moved
him came and brought an offering to the LORD for the work on the
Tent of Meeting, for all its service, and for the sacred garments.
22All who were willing, men and women alike, came and brought

[a] 7 That is, dugongs; also in verse 23

(34:33–35) Those who look to You, Lord, are radiant. The greatest honor in all of life is to know You: to walk with You and draw near to You in worship. This holy fellowship is uplifting! It enriches my life in every way. It wells up within me and overflows. The radiance that Moses knew was glorious, though veiled and fading. But the radiance of Your Spirit in my heart through Christ is more glorious still. For whenever anyone turns to You, Lord, the veil is taken away. "And we, who with unveiled faces all reflect the Lord's glory, are being transformed into his likeness with ever-increasing glory, which comes from the Lord, who is the Spirit." (Ps 34:5; 2Co 3:10–18)

O Christ, whom now beneath a veil
we see:
May what we thirst for soon our
portion be,
To gaze on Thee unveiled, and see
Thy face,
The vision of Thy glory, and Thy
grace.

"Thee We Adore, O Hidden Savior"
Thomas Aquinas (1227–1274)
Trans. James R. Woodford
(1820–1885)

Spirit-filled souls are ablaze for God. They love with a love that glows. They believe with a faith that kindles. They serve with a devotion that consumes. They hate sin with a fierceness that burns. They rejoice with a joy that radiates. Love is perfected in the fire of God.

Samuel Chadwick (1832–1917)

(35:29) Teach me to "excel in this grace of giving." To give to Your work is to participate in something of infinite value, something that will never fade away. But my eyes are fixed on temporal things. I cling to earthly things as if there were nothing more—no God, no glory, no tomorrow. Touch my heart, Lord. Lift my eyes. Grant me a higher view. Teach me to give, storing up treasure in heaven that will last forever. (2Co 8:7)

I have held many things in my hands, and I have lost them all; but whatever I have placed in God's hands, that I still possess.
Martin Luther (1483-1546)

(36:1–2) When I set out to work in Your name, let it be my best work. Let it be inspired by Your Spirit and pursued with all diligence. Empower me, Lord, to accomplish my God-appointed task. Grace me with special insight and ability. Guide my thoughts and steady my hands. Help me to remember that Your work is the most important work of all.

Every single person has one thing that he can do a little better than most people around him, and he has a sacred obligation to himself to find out what that thing is and to do it. (Most saints, after all, have been men and women, not who soared to heights of achievement, but who sank to depths of service we would not dream of.)
Sydney J. Harris (1917-1986)

gold jewelry of all kinds: brooches, earrings, rings and ornaments. They all presented their gold as a wave offering to the LORD.
23Everyone who had blue, purple or scarlet yarn or fine linen, or goat hair, ram skins dyed red or hides of sea cows brought them.
24Those presenting an offering of silver or bronze brought it as an offering to the LORD, and everyone who had acacia wood for any part of the work brought it. 25Every skilled woman spun with her hands and brought what she had spun—blue, purple or scarlet yarn or fine linen. 26And all the women who were willing and had the skill spun the goat hair. 27The leaders brought onyx stones and other gems to be mounted on the ephod and breastpiece.
28They also brought spices and olive oil for the light and for the anointing oil and for the fragrant incense. 29All the Israelite men and women who were willing brought to the LORD freewill offerings for all the work the LORD through Moses had commanded them to do.

Bezalel and Oholiab

30Then Moses said to the Israelites, "See, the LORD has chosen Bezalel son of Uri, the son of Hur, of the tribe of Judah, 31and he has filled him with the Spirit of God, with skill, ability and knowledge in all kinds of crafts— 32to make artistic designs for work in gold, silver and bronze, 33to cut and set stones, to work in wood and to engage in all kinds of artistic craftsmanship. 34And he has given both him and Oholiab son of Ahisamach, of the tribe of Dan, the ability to teach others. 35He has filled them with skill to do all kinds of work as craftsmen, designers, embroiderers in blue, purple and scarlet yarn and fine linen, and weavers—all of them
36 master craftsmen and designers. 1So Bezalel, Oholiab and every skilled person to whom the LORD has given skill and ability to know how to carry out all the work of constructing the sanctuary are to do the work just as the LORD has commanded."
2Then Moses summoned Bezalel and Oholiab and every skilled person to whom the LORD had given ability and who was willing to come and do the work. 3They received from Moses all the offerings the Israelites had brought to carry out the work of constructing the sanctuary. And the people continued to bring freewill offerings morning after morning. 4So all the skilled craftsmen who were doing all the work on the sanctuary left their work 5and said to Moses, "The people are bringing more than enough for doing the work the LORD commanded to be done."
6Then Moses gave an order and they sent this word throughout the camp: "No man or woman is to make anything else as an offering for the sanctuary." And so the people were restrained from bringing more, 7because what they already had was more than enough to do all the work.

The Tabernacle

8All the skilled men among the workmen made the tabernacle with ten curtains of finely twisted linen and blue, purple and scarlet yarn, with cherubim worked into them by a skilled craftsman.
9All the curtains were the same size—twenty-eight cubits long and four cubits wide.[a] 10They joined five of the curtains together and did the same with the other five. 11Then they made loops of blue material along the edge of the end curtain in one set, and the same

[a] 9 That is, about 42 feet (about 12.5 meters) long and 6 feet (about 1.8 meters) wide

was done with the end curtain in the other set. [12]They also made fifty loops on one curtain and fifty loops on the end curtain of the other set, with the loops opposite each other. [13]Then they made fifty gold clasps and used them to fasten the two sets of curtains together so that the tabernacle was a unit.

[14]They made curtains of goat hair for the tent over the tabernacle—eleven altogether. [15]All eleven curtains were the same size—thirty cubits long and four cubits wide.[a] [16]They joined five of the curtains into one set and the other six into another set. [17]Then they made fifty loops along the edge of the end curtain in one set and also along the edge of the end curtain in the other set. [18]They made fifty bronze clasps to fasten the tent together as a unit. [19]Then they made for the tent a covering of ram skins dyed red, and over that a covering of hides of sea cows.[b]

[20]They made upright frames of acacia wood for the tabernacle. [21]Each frame was ten cubits long and a cubit and a half wide,[c] [22]with two projections set parallel to each other. They made all the frames of the tabernacle in this way. [23]They made twenty frames for the south side of the tabernacle [24]and made forty silver bases to go under them—two bases for each frame, one under each projection. [25]For the other side, the north side of the tabernacle, they made twenty frames [26]and forty silver bases—two under each frame. [27]They made six frames for the far end, that is, the west end of the tabernacle, [28]and two frames were made for the corners of the tabernacle at the far end. [29]At these two corners the frames were double from the bottom all the way to the top and fitted into a single ring; both were made alike. [30]So there were eight frames and sixteen silver bases—two under each frame.

[31]They also made crossbars of acacia wood: five for the frames on one side of the tabernacle, [32]five for those on the other side, and five for the frames on the west, at the far end of the tabernacle. [33]They made the center crossbar so that it extended from end to end at the middle of the frames. [34]They overlaid the frames with gold and made gold rings to hold the crossbars. They also overlaid the crossbars with gold.

[35]They made the curtain of blue, purple and scarlet yarn and finely twisted linen, with cherubim worked into it by a skilled craftsman. [36]They made four posts of acacia wood for it and overlaid them with gold. They made gold hooks for them and cast their four silver bases. [37]For the entrance to the tent they made a curtain of blue, purple and scarlet yarn and finely twisted linen—the work of an embroiderer; [38]and they made five posts with hooks for them. They overlaid the tops of the posts and their bands with gold and made their five bases of bronze.

The Ark

37 Bezalel made the ark of acacia wood—two and a half cubits long, a cubit and a half wide, and a cubit and a half high.[d] [2]He overlaid it with pure gold, both inside and out, and made a gold molding around it. [3]He cast four gold rings for it and fastened them to its four feet, with two rings on one side and two rings on the other. [4]Then he made poles of acacia wood and over-

[a] *15* That is, about 45 feet (about 13.5 meters) long and 6 feet (about 1.8 meters) wide
[b] *19* That is, dugongs [c] *21* That is, about 15 feet (about 4.5 meters) long and 2 1/4 feet (about 0.7 meter) wide [d] *1* That is, about 3 3/4 feet (about 1.1 meters) long and 2 1/4 feet (about 0.7 meter) wide and high

(36:8–38) You, O God, made the world and everything in it. You are the Lord of heaven and earth. You do not live in temples built by hands. We praise You that today Your dwelling place is not made of curtains or even stone, but that we are Your temple, living stones built into a spiritual house on a sure foundation, with Jesus Christ as the chief cornerstone. In him, like the curtains of the tabernacle, we are joined together and rise to become a holy temple in the Lord, a dwelling in which You live by Your Spirit. (Eph 2:19–22; 1 Pe 2:5)

laid them with gold. 5And he inserted the poles into the rings on the sides of the ark to carry it.

6He made the atonement cover of pure gold—two and a half cubits long and a cubit and a half wide.[a] 7Then he made two cherubim out of hammered gold at the ends of the cover. 8He made one cherub on one end and the second cherub on the other; at the two ends he made them of one piece with the cover. 9The cherubim had their wings spread upward, overshadowing the cover with them. The cherubim faced each other, looking toward the cover.

The Table

10They[b] made the table of acacia wood—two cubits long, a cubit wide, and a cubit and a half high.[c] 11Then they overlaid it with pure gold and made a gold molding around it. 12They also made around it a rim a handbreadth[d] wide and put a gold molding on the rim. 13They cast four gold rings for the table and fastened them to the four corners, where the four legs were. 14The rings were put close to the rim to hold the poles used in carrying the table. 15The poles for carrying the table were made of acacia wood and were overlaid with gold. 16And they made from pure gold the articles for the table—its plates and dishes and bowls and its pitchers for the pouring out of drink offerings.

The Lampstand

17They made the lampstand of pure gold and hammered it out, base and shaft; its flowerlike cups, buds and blossoms were of one piece with it. 18Six branches extended from the sides of the lampstand—three on one side and three on the other. 19Three cups shaped like almond flowers with buds and blossoms were on one branch, three on the next branch and the same for all six branches extending from the lampstand. 20And on the lampstand were four cups shaped like almond flowers with buds and blossoms. 21One bud was under the first pair of branches extending from the lampstand, a second bud under the second pair, and a third bud under the third pair—six branches in all. 22The buds and the branches were all of one piece with the lampstand, hammered out of pure gold.

23They made its seven lamps, as well as its wick trimmers and trays, of pure gold. 24They made the lampstand and all its accessories from one talent[e] of pure gold.

The Altar of Incense

25They made the altar of incense out of acacia wood. It was square, a cubit long and a cubit wide, and two cubits high[f]—its horns of one piece with it. 26They overlaid the top and all the sides and the horns with pure gold, and made a gold molding around it. 27They made two gold rings below the molding—two on opposite sides—to hold the poles used to carry it. 28They made the poles of acacia wood and overlaid them with gold.

29They also made the sacred anointing oil and the pure, fragrant incense—the work of a perfumer.

[a] *6* That is, about 3 3/4 feet (about 1.1 meters) long and 2 1/4 feet (about 0.7 meter) wide [b] *10* Or *He*; also in verses 11–29 [c] *10* That is, about 3 feet (about 0.9 meter) long, 1 1/2 feet (about 0.5 meter) wide, and 2 1/4 feet (about 0.7 meter) high [d] *12* That is, about 3 inches (about 8 centimeters) [e] *24* That is, about 75 pounds (about 34 kilograms) [f] *25* That is, about 1 1/2 feet (about 0.5 meter) long and wide, and about 3 feet (about 0.9 meter) high

Christ is the bread for men's souls. In him the church has enough to feed the whole world.

Ian Maclaren (1850-1907)

(37:10) Day by day I need You, Lord. Day by day. As the body hungers for daily bread, so my spirit hungers for Your living presence. You gave Israel this table for the bread of Your presence. You have given me Jesus, the living bread of God, who gives life to the world. Lord, I come to You now. I take You into my heart. Set up Your table deep within and commune with me. (Jn 6:32–35; Rev 3:20).

We taste You, ever Living Bread,
And long to feast upon You still;
We drink of You, the Fountainhead;
Our thirsting souls from You we fill.
"O Jesus, Joy of Loving Hearts"
Bernard of Clairvaux (1091-1153)
Trans. Ray Palmer (1808-1887)

The Altar of Burnt Offering

38 They[a] built the altar of burnt offering of acacia wood,
three cubits[b] high; it was square, five cubits long and five
cubits wide.[c] 2They made a horn at each of the four corners, so
that the horns and the altar were of one piece, and they overlaid
the altar with bronze. 3They made all its utensils of bronze—its
pots, shovels, sprinkling bowls, meat forks and firepans. 4They
made a grating for the altar, a bronze network, to be under its
ledge, halfway up the altar. 5They cast bronze rings to hold the
poles for the four corners of the bronze grating. 6They made the
poles of acacia wood and overlaid them with bronze. 7They inserted the poles into the rings so they would be on the sides of the
altar for carrying it. They made it hollow, out of boards.

Basin for Washing

8They made the bronze basin and its bronze stand from the
mirrors of the women who served at the entrance to the Tent of
Meeting.

The Courtyard

9Next they made the courtyard. The south side was a hundred
cubits[d] long and had curtains of finely twisted linen, 10with twenty posts and twenty bronze bases, and with silver hooks and bands
on the posts. 11The north side was also a hundred cubits long and
had twenty posts and twenty bronze bases, with silver hooks and
bands on the posts.

12The west end was fifty cubits[e] wide and had curtains, with ten
posts and ten bases, with silver hooks and bands on the posts.
13The east end, toward the sunrise, was also fifty cubits wide.
14Curtains fifteen cubits[f] long were on one side of the entrance,
with three posts and three bases, 15and curtains fifteen cubits long
were on the other side of the entrance to the courtyard, with three
posts and three bases. 16All the curtains around the courtyard
were of finely twisted linen. 17The bases for the posts were bronze.
The hooks and bands on the posts were silver, and their tops were
overlaid with silver; so all the posts of the courtyard had silver
bands.

18The curtain for the entrance to the courtyard was of blue,
purple and scarlet yarn and finely twisted linen—the work of an
embroiderer. It was twenty cubits[g] long and, like the curtains of
the courtyard, five cubits[h] high, 19with four posts and four bronze
bases. Their hooks and bands were silver, and their tops were
overlaid with silver. 20All the tent pegs of the tabernacle and of the
surrounding courtyard were bronze.

The Materials Used

21These are the amounts of the materials used for the tabernacle, the tabernacle of the Testimony, which were recorded at
Moses' command by the Levites under the direction of Ithamar
son of Aaron, the priest. 22(Bezalel son of Uri, the son of Hur, of
the tribe of Judah, made everything the LORD commanded Moses;
23with him was Oholiab son of Ahisamach, of the tribe of Dan—

[a] *1* Or *He*; also in verses 2–9 [b] *1* That is, about 4 1/2 feet (about 1.3 meters) [c] *1* That is, about 7 1/2 feet (about 2.3 meters) long and wide [d] *9* That is, about 150 feet (about 46 meters) [e] *12* That is, about 75 feet (about 23 meters) [f] *14* That is, about 22 1/2 feet (about 6.9 meters) [g] *18* That is, about 30 feet (about 9 meters) [h] *18* That is, about 7 1/2 feet (about 2.3 meters)

O my Savior, make me see
How dearly thou hast paid for me.
Richard Crashaw (c.1613-1649)

(38:4) Like the grating of bronze on the altar, so was Your cross, Jesus—a symbol of death as it bore up the sacrifice. On the cross You suffered the death that ought to have been my own; the sacrifice made in my place. It was the gruesome yet saving work of Your mercy. Now, Lord Jesus, Your cross has become a thing of beauty and power to me. "For the message of the cross is foolishness to those who are perishing, but to us who are being saved it is the power of God." (1Co 1:18)

I come to the cross seeking mercy
and grace,
I come to the cross, where You died
in my place.
Out of my weakness and into Your
strength,
Humbly, I come to the cross.

Your arms are open, You call me by
name.
You welcome this child that was
lost.
You paid the price for my guilt and
my shame.
Jesus, I come,
Jesus, I come,
Jesus, I come to the cross.

"I Come To The Cross"
Bob Somma and Bill Batstone (©1996)

(39:6–7) I rejoice in Your attentive love, my Lord. My name is always before You. I am safe, living beneath Your gaze, ever in the view of Your watchful eye. My personal cares are lifted before Your throne, borne up on the shoulders of Jesus. On good days and bad, in every circumstance of life, this will be my confidence, and all my trust will be in You.

Have faith in God when your
  pathway is lonely;
He sees and knows all the way you
  have trod.
Never alone are the least of His
  children;
Have faith in God, have faith in God.

Have faith in God; He's on the
  throne.
Have faith in God; He watches o'er
  His own.
He cannot fail! He must prevail!
Have faith in God, have faith in God.

"Have Faith in God"
B.B. McKinney (©1934, 1962)

a craftsman and designer, and an embroiderer in blue, purple and scarlet yarn and fine linen.) 24 The total amount of the gold from the wave offering used for all the work on the sanctuary was 29 talents and 730 shekels,[a] according to the sanctuary shekel.

25 The silver obtained from those of the community who were counted in the census was 100 talents and 1,775 shekels,[b] according to the sanctuary shekel— 26 one beka per person, that is, half a shekel,[c] according to the sanctuary shekel, from everyone who had crossed over to those counted, twenty years old or more, a total of 603,550 men. 27 The 100 talents[d] of silver were used to cast the bases for the sanctuary and for the curtain—100 bases from the 100 talents, one talent for each base. 28 They used the 1,775 shekels[e] to make the hooks for the posts, to overlay the tops of the posts, and to make their bands.

29 The bronze from the wave offering was 70 talents and 2,400 shekels.[f] 30 They used it to make the bases for the entrance to the Tent of Meeting, the bronze altar with its bronze grating and all its utensils, 31 the bases for the surrounding courtyard and those for its entrance and all the tent pegs for the tabernacle and those for the surrounding courtyard.

The Priestly Garments

39 From the blue, purple and scarlet yarn they made woven garments for ministering in the sanctuary. They also made sacred garments for Aaron, as the LORD commanded Moses.

The Ephod

2 They[g] made the ephod of gold, and of blue, purple and scarlet yarn, and of finely twisted linen. 3 They hammered out thin sheets of gold and cut strands to be worked into the blue, purple and scarlet yarn and fine linen—the work of a skilled craftsman. 4 They made shoulder pieces for the ephod, which were attached to two of its corners, so it could be fastened. 5 Its skillfully woven waistband was like it—of one piece with the ephod and made with gold, and with blue, purple and scarlet yarn, and with finely twisted linen, as the LORD commanded Moses.

6 They mounted the onyx stones in gold filigree settings and engraved them like a seal with the names of the sons of Israel. 7 Then they fastened them on the shoulder pieces of the ephod as memorial stones for the sons of Israel, as the LORD commanded Moses.

The Breastpiece

8 They fashioned the breastpiece—the work of a skilled craftsman. They made it like the ephod: of gold, and of blue, purple and scarlet yarn, and of finely twisted linen. 9 It was square—a span[h] long and a span wide—and folded double. 10 Then they mounted four rows of precious stones on it. In the first row there was a ruby, a topaz and a beryl; 11 in the second row a turquoise, a sapphire[i] and an emerald; 12 in the third row a jacinth, an agate and an amethyst; 13 in the fourth row a chrysolite, an onyx and a

[a] *24* The weight of the gold was a little over one ton (about 1 metric ton). [b] *25* The weight of the silver was a little over 3 3/4 tons (about 3.4 metric tons). [c] *26* That is, about 1/5 ounce (about 5.5 grams) [d] *27* That is, about 3 3/4 tons (about 3.4 metric tons) [e] *28* That is, about 45 pounds (about 20 kilograms) [f] *29* The weight of the bronze was about 2 1/2 tons (about 2.4 metric tons). [g] *2* Or *He*; also in verses 7, 8 and 22 [h] *9* That is, about 9 inches (about 22 centimeters) [i] *11* Or *lapis lazuli*

jasper.[a] They were mounted in gold filigree settings. 14There
were twelve stones, one for each of the names of the sons of Israel, each engraved like a seal with the name of one of the twelve
tribes.
15For the breastpiece they made braided chains of pure gold,
like a rope. 16They made two gold filigree settings and two gold
rings, and fastened the rings to two of the corners of the breastpiece. 17They fastened the two gold chains to the rings at the corners of the breastpiece, 18and the other ends of the chains to the
two settings, attaching them to the shoulder pieces of the ephod
at the front. 19They made two gold rings and attached them to
the other two corners of the breastpiece on the inside edge next
to the ephod. 20Then they made two more gold rings and attached them to the bottom of the shoulder pieces on the front of
the ephod, close to the seam just above the waistband of the
ephod. 21They tied the rings of the breastpiece to the rings of
the ephod with blue cord, connecting it to the waistband so that
the breastpiece would not swing out from the ephod—as the
LORD commanded Moses.

Other Priestly Garments

22They made the robe of the ephod entirely of blue cloth—the
work of a weaver— 23with an opening in the center of the robe
like the opening of a collar,[b] and a band around this opening, so
that it would not tear. 24They made pomegranates of blue, purple
and scarlet yarn and finely twisted linen around the hem of the
robe. 25And they made bells of pure gold and attached them
around the hem between the pomegranates. 26The bells and
pomegranates alternated around the hem of the robe to be worn
for ministering, as the LORD commanded Moses.
27For Aaron and his sons, they made tunics of fine linen—the
work of a weaver— 28and the turban of fine linen, the linen
headbands and the undergarments of finely twisted linen. 29The
sash was of finely twisted linen and blue, purple and scarlet
yarn—the work of an embroiderer—as the LORD commanded
Moses.
30They made the plate, the sacred diadem, out of pure gold
and engraved on it, like an inscription on a seal: HOLY TO THE LORD.
31Then they fastened a blue cord to it to attach it to the turban, as
the LORD commanded Moses.

Moses Inspects the Tabernacle

32So all the work on the tabernacle, the Tent of Meeting, was
completed. The Israelites did everything just as the LORD commanded Moses. 33Then they brought the tabernacle to Moses: the
tent and all its furnishings, its clasps, frames, crossbars, posts
and bases; 34the covering of ram skins dyed red, the covering of
hides of sea cows[c] and the shielding curtain; 35the ark of the Testimony with its poles and the atonement cover; 36the table with all
its articles and the bread of the Presence; 37the pure gold lampstand with its row of lamps and all its accessories, and the oil for
the light; 38the gold altar, the anointing oil, the fragrant incense,
and the curtain for the entrance to the tent; 39the bronze altar
with its bronze grating, its poles and all its utensils; the basin with
its stand; 40the curtains of the courtyard with its posts and bases,

[a] *13* The precise identification of some of these precious stones is uncertain. [b] *23* The meaning of the Hebrew for this word is uncertain. [c] *34* That is, dugongs

(39:32) We praise You, gracious Lord, for Your invitation to Your people to build the Tent of Meeting. You chose to dwell among us: then in a tabernacle made with hands, and now in a temple made without hands. Your people did everything just as You said. By simple obedience to Your instructions, they erected an awesome sanctuary for holy communion with You. What could You do through the members of my church, Lord, if we came each day with hearts of loving obedience to You? Would You build a sanctuary of praise? Would You change the world? Would we find deeper communion with You? Lord, help us to fully obey You so that You can make Your presence known in our lives. (Jn 14:21,23; Ac 17:24)

Gathered here together,
Gathered by Your grace;
Having one desire, to seek Your face.
United in believing
That our faith is true,
Thankful in the knowledge
We belong to You.

We pray, make Your presence
known,
Make Your presence known,
Make Your presence known in our
hearts.

"Make Your Presence Known"
John Barbour (©1993)

(40:13–15) Jesus, Savior, there is no other priest like You. Many were anointed with sacred oil and set apart for God's holy work, but You are above them all, anointed by the Father with the oil of joy! Jesus, Messiah, Anointed One, all my hope rests on You. You are anointed to preach good news to the poor, to bind up the brokenhearted, to proclaim freedom for the captives. Here I am, Lord: poor, brokenhearted, in need of freedom. Save me, Jesus, Anointed Savior, and I shall be saved! (Isa 61:1; Heb 1:9)

(40:20–21) We thank You, Lord, that relationship is at the heart of worship. At the center of the Most Holy Place of worship, the place of Your presence, were the tablets of the Testimony of Your covenant with Your people. There is no true worship, no true communion with You today, that does not have at its core the Testimony of Your new covenant with us—a covenant that You initiated, that You signed with Your own blood, and that You have invited us to enter. So we give You thanks and praise for the blood of the new covenant that makes our worship acceptable to You. (Ex 31:18)

Worship is the highest and noblest act that any person can do. When men worship, God is satisfied! And when you worship, you are fulfilled! Think about this: why did Jesus Christ come? He came to make worshipers out of rebels. We who were once self-centered have to be completely changed so that we can shift our attention outside of ourselves and become able to worship him.

Raymond C. Ortlund (1923-)

and the curtain for the entrance to the courtyard; the ropes and
tent pegs for the courtyard; all the furnishings for the tabernacle,
the Tent of Meeting; 41and the woven garments worn for ministering in the sanctuary, both the sacred garments for Aaron the priest
and the garments for his sons when serving as priests.
42The Israelites had done all the work just as the LORD had
commanded Moses. 43Moses inspected the work and saw that they
had done it just as the LORD had commanded. So Moses blessed
them.

Setting Up the Tabernacle

40 Then the LORD said to Moses: 2"Set up the tabernacle, the
Tent of Meeting, on the first day of the first month. 3Place
the ark of the Testimony in it and shield the ark with the curtain.
4Bring in the table and set out what belongs on it. Then bring in
the lampstand and set up its lamps. 5Place the gold altar of incense in front of the ark of the Testimony and put the curtain at the
entrance to the tabernacle.
6"Place the altar of burnt offering in front of the entrance to
the tabernacle, the Tent of Meeting; 7place the basin between the
Tent of Meeting and the altar and put water in it. 8Set up the courtyard around it and put the curtain at the entrance to the courtyard.
9"Take the anointing oil and anoint the tabernacle and everything in it; consecrate it and all its furnishings, and it will be holy.
10Then anoint the altar of burnt offering and all its utensils; consecrate the altar, and it will be most holy. 11Anoint the basin and
its stand and consecrate them.
12"Bring Aaron and his sons to the entrance to the Tent of Meeting and wash them with water. 13Then dress Aaron in the sacred
garments, anoint him and consecrate him so he may serve me as
priest. 14Bring his sons and dress them in tunics. 15Anoint them
just as you anointed their father, so they may serve me as priests.
Their anointing will be to a priesthood that will continue for all
generations to come." 16Moses did everything just as the LORD
commanded him.
17So the tabernacle was set up on the first day of the first month
in the second year. 18When Moses set up the tabernacle, he put
the bases in place, erected the frames, inserted the crossbars and
set up the posts. 19Then he spread the tent over the tabernacle
and put the covering over the tent, as the LORD commanded him.
20He took the Testimony and placed it in the ark, attached the
poles to the ark and put the atonement cover over it. 21Then he
brought the ark into the tabernacle and hung the shielding curtain
and shielded the ark of the Testimony, as the LORD commanded
him.
22Moses placed the table in the Tent of Meeting on the north
side of the tabernacle outside the curtain 23and set out the bread
on it before the LORD, as the LORD commanded him.
24He placed the lampstand in the Tent of Meeting opposite the
table on the south side of the tabernacle 25and set up the lamps
before the LORD, as the LORD commanded him.
26Moses placed the gold altar in the Tent of Meeting in front of
the curtain 27and burned fragrant incense on it, as the LORD commanded him. 28Then he put up the curtain at the entrance to the
tabernacle.
29He set the altar of burnt offering near the entrance to the

tabernacle, the Tent of Meeting, and offered on it burnt offerings
and grain offerings, as the LORD commanded him.
30He placed the basin between the Tent of Meeting and the altar
and put water in it for washing, 31and Moses and Aaron and his
sons used it to wash their hands and feet. 32They washed whenever they entered the Tent of Meeting or approached the altar, as the
LORD commanded Moses.
33Then Moses set up the courtyard around the tabernacle and
altar and put up the curtain at the entrance to the courtyard. And
so Moses finished the work.

The Glory of the LORD

34Then the cloud covered the Tent of Meeting, and the glory of
the LORD filled the tabernacle. 35Moses could not enter the Tent of
Meeting because the cloud had settled upon it, and the glory of the
LORD filled the tabernacle.
36In all the travels of the Israelites, whenever the cloud lifted
from above the tabernacle, they would set out; 37but if the cloud
did not lift, they did not set out—until the day it lifted. 38So the
cloud of the LORD was over the tabernacle by day, and fire was in
the cloud by night, in the sight of all the house of Israel during all
their travels.

(40:36–38) You have redeemed our lives from slavery, Lord. This is a gift of grace greater than we could have ever imagined. But there is a greater gift of Your grace than this—the gift of Your presence in our hearts. This is the gift that is beyond comprehension, yet we pray to know it, Lord! Please manifest Your presence in our midst today. Lead us step-by-step, day by day, into all that You have for us. Amen.

We will worship and adore You,
We will bow before Your throne,
Let the fruit of our lips be pleasing
to You,
Oh, let Your glory fill this place.

"Let Your Glory Fill This Place"
Denise Graves (©1995)

Leviticus

The Third Book of Moses called

LEVITICUS

In the book of Leviticus we encounter a holy God Who calls us to holiness: "Be holy because I, the LORD your God, am holy" (19:2). To say that God is holy means that He is set apart from everything in creation. God is "wholly other."

The Bible associates God's holiness with His moral perfection. Unlike humanity, God is perfect and is completely without sin. This ethical dimension of His holiness creates a problem for us: How can we, sinners that we are, be holy? How can we have relationship with or worship a holy God when our lips, our actions and our hearts are so profane?

The book of Leviticus reveals the first stage of God's answer to these questions. Because of their sin the Israelites must offer holy sacrifices that signify the gravity of their offense and that symbolize their desire for forgiveness (chs. 1—7). Once each year, a Day of Atonement is set aside for exceptional sacrifices that dramatize Israel's need for "at-one-ment"—reconciliation with God (16:1–34; 23:26–32). The high priest sacrifices a goat as a "sin offering" for Israel. A second goat, a "scapegoat," symbolically carries the sins of the people into the wilderness. During the solemn rituals on the Day of Atonement, the people fast and refrain from work. In this way, "Atonement is to be made once a year for all the sins of the Israelites" (16:34).

Yet Israel's holiness depends not only on sacrifices for sin, but also on living according to God's holy standards. Chapters 17—26 reiterate many of God's commandments for daily life, while adding new ones such as: "Love your neighbor as yourself" (19:18).

The book of Leviticus draws us into a deeper understanding of Christ's sacrifice for us, and therefore into more profound and thankful worship.

Unfortunately, the Israelites could not, nor can we ourselves, live up to God's requirements for holy living. Atoning sacrifices, however powerful they were, could not solve the root problem of human sin. The New Testament book of Hebrews, using the imagery of Leviticus, reveals the next stage of God's solution to this problem. Christ's death on the cross is a "once-for-all" sacrifice that leads to complete atonement with God. Yet Jesus is not only the perfect sacrifice, He is the high priest Who makes a way for us to have intimacy with God. Because Jesus is our high priest, "let us then approach the throne of grace with confidence, so that we may receive mercy and find grace to help us in our time of need" (Heb 4:15–16).

When we have participated through faith in the "once-for-all" sacrifice of Jesus Christ, then we are empowered to live holy lives: "Offer your bodies as living sacrifices, holy and pleasing to God—this is your spiritual act of worship" (Ro 12:1). Even though Christians do not follow the sacrificial laws of Leviticus—believing them to have been fulfilled by Christ—we follow the moral law so that we might offer worship to God in our daily living.

The book of Leviticus draws us into a deeper understanding of Christ's sacrifice for us, and therefore into more profound and thankful worship. This book also charges us to worship God, not merely through song and ceremony but with lives fully devoted to him and offered as holy, living sacrifices.

The Burnt Offering

1 The LORD called to Moses and spoke to him from the Tent of
Meeting. He said, 2"Speak to the Israelites and say to them:
'When any of you brings an offering to the LORD, bring as your offering an animal from either the herd or the flock.
3" 'If the offering is a burnt offering from the herd, he is to offer
a male without defect. He must present it at the entrance to the
Tent of Meeting so that it[a] will be acceptable to the LORD. 4He is to
lay his hand on the head of the burnt offering, and it will be accepted on his behalf to make atonement for him. 5He is to slaughter the young bull before the LORD, and then Aaron's sons the
priests shall bring the blood and sprinkle it against the altar on all
sides at the entrance to the Tent of Meeting. 6He is to skin the
burnt offering and cut it into pieces. 7The sons of Aaron the priest
are to put fire on the altar and arrange wood on the fire. 8Then
Aaron's sons the priests shall arrange the pieces, including the
head and the fat, on the burning wood that is on the altar. 9He is
to wash the inner parts and the legs with water, and the priest is to
burn all of it on the altar. It is a burnt offering, an offering made
by fire, an aroma pleasing to the LORD.
10" 'If the offering is a burnt offering from the flock, from either the sheep or the goats, he is to offer a male without defect.
11He is to slaughter it at the north side of the altar before the LORD,
and Aaron's sons the priests shall sprinkle its blood against the
altar on all sides. 12He is to cut it into pieces, and the priest shall
arrange them, including the head and the fat, on the burning wood
that is on the altar. 13He is to wash the inner parts and the legs
with water, and the priest is to bring all of it and burn it on the
altar. It is a burnt offering, an offering made by fire, an aroma
pleasing to the LORD.
14" 'If the offering to the LORD is a burnt offering of birds, he is
to offer a dove or a young pigeon. 15The priest shall bring it to the
altar, wring off the head and burn it on the altar; its blood shall be
drained out on the side of the altar. 16He is to remove the crop
with its contents[b] and throw it to the east side of the altar, where
the ashes are. 17He shall tear it open by the wings, not severing it
completely, and then the priest shall burn it on the wood that is on
the fire on the altar. It is a burnt offering, an offering made by fire,
an aroma pleasing to the LORD.

The Grain Offering

2 " 'When someone brings a grain offering to the LORD, his offering is to be of fine flour. He is to pour oil on it, put incense
on it 2and take it to Aaron's sons the priests. The priest shall take
a handful of the fine flour and oil, together with all the incense,
and burn this as a memorial portion on the altar, an offering made
by fire, an aroma pleasing to the LORD. 3The rest of the grain offering belongs to Aaron and his sons; it is a most holy part of the
offerings made to the LORD by fire.
4" 'If you bring a grain offering baked in an oven, it is to consist of fine flour: cakes made without yeast and mixed with oil, or[c]
wafers made without yeast and spread with oil. 5If your grain offering is prepared on a griddle, it is to be made of fine flour mixed
with oil, and without yeast. 6Crumble it and pour oil on it; it is a

[a] 3 Or *he* [b] 16 Or *crop and the feathers*; the meaning of the Hebrew for this word is uncertain. [c] 4 Or *and*

(1:4–9) Merciful God, I thank You for providing a way for us to be acceptable before You, "an aroma pleasing to the LORD." For Your people of old, their atonement came through the death of innocent animals. They laid their hands on the animal's head to admit their guilt and identify with its substitutional death. All of this pointed to the one, perfect sacrifice—our Lord Jesus Christ, the spotless Lamb of God Who died so that we might be reconciled to You. O merciful God, today by faith I lay my hand upon the wounded head of Christ, confessing my sins and identifying with His substitutional death for me. Thank You, gracious Father, that I have been crucified with Christ and I now live by faith in Your Son Who loved me and gave Himself for me. Because He is acceptable to You, I am now acceptable to You. (Gal 2:20)

I lay my sins on Jesus,
The spotless Lamb of God;
He bears them all, and frees us
From the accursed load:
I bring my guilt to Jesus,
To wash my crimson stains
White in His blood most precious,
Till not a stain remains.

"I Lay My Sins on Jesus"
Horatius Bonar (1843)

We have not to do with a God who is off there above the sky, who can deal with us only through the violation of physical law. We have instead a God in whom we live and move and are, whose being opens into ours and ours into his, who is the very life of our lives, the matrix of our personality; and there is no separation between us unless we make it ourselves.

Rufus Matthew Jones (1863-1948)

grain offering. 7If your grain offering is cooked in a pan, it is to be
made of fine flour and oil. 8Bring the grain offering made of these
things to the LORD; present it to the priest, who shall take it to the
altar. 9He shall take out the memorial portion from the grain offering and burn it on the altar as an offering made by fire, an aroma
pleasing to the LORD. 10The rest of the grain offering belongs to
Aaron and his sons; it is a most holy part of the offerings made to
the LORD by fire.
11" 'Every grain offering you bring to the LORD must be made
without yeast, for you are not to burn any yeast or honey in an offering made to the LORD by fire. 12You may bring them to the LORD
as an offering of the firstfruits, but they are not to be offered on the
altar as a pleasing aroma. 13Season all your grain offerings with
salt. Do not leave the salt of the covenant of your God out of your
grain offerings; add salt to all your offerings.
14" 'If you bring a grain offering of firstfruits to the LORD, offer
crushed heads of new grain roasted in the fire. 15Put oil and incense on it; it is a grain offering. 16The priest shall burn the memorial portion of the crushed grain and the oil, together with all the
incense, as an offering made to the LORD by fire.

The Fellowship Offering

3 " 'If someone's offering is a fellowship offering,[a] and he offers
an animal from the herd, whether male or female, he is to present before the LORD an animal without defect. 2He is to lay his
hand on the head of his offering and slaughter it at the entrance to
the Tent of Meeting. Then Aaron's sons the priests shall sprinkle the
blood against the altar on all sides. 3From the fellowship offering
he is to bring a sacrifice made to the LORD by fire: all the fat that
covers the inner parts or is connected to them, 4both kidneys with
the fat on them near the loins, and the covering of the liver, which
he will remove with the kidneys. 5Then Aaron's sons are to burn it
on the altar on top of the burnt offering that is on the burning
wood, as an offering made by fire, an aroma pleasing to the LORD.
6" 'If he offers an animal from the flock as a fellowship offering
to the LORD, he is to offer a male or female without defect. 7If he offers a lamb, he is to present it before the LORD. 8He is to lay his
hand on the head of his offering and slaughter it in front of the Tent
of Meeting. Then Aaron's sons shall sprinkle its blood against the
altar on all sides. 9From the fellowship offering he is to bring a
sacrifice made to the LORD by fire: its fat, the entire fat tail cut off
close to the backbone, all the fat that covers the inner parts or is
connected to them, 10both kidneys with the fat on them near the
loins, and the covering of the liver, which he will remove with the
kidneys. 11The priest shall burn them on the altar as food, an offering made to the LORD by fire.
12" 'If his offering is a goat, he is to present it before the LORD.
13He is to lay his hand on its head and slaughter it in front of the
Tent of Meeting. Then Aaron's sons shall sprinkle its blood against
the altar on all sides. 14From what he offers he is to make this offering to the LORD by fire: all the fat that covers the inner parts or is
connected to them, 15both kidneys with the fat on them near the
loins, and the covering of the liver, which he will remove with the
kidneys. 16The priest shall burn them on the altar as food, an offering made by fire, a pleasing aroma. All the fat is the LORD's.

[a] 1 Traditionally *peace offering*; also in verses 3, 6 and 9

(2:13) Yahweh Elohim, Covenanting God, You give life and meaning to common things surrounding us. To Your people of old, salt was not only a preservative, it was a symbol of friendship. You asked that all the grain offerings made to You be seasoned with salt, reminding us that Your covenant is everlasting. So today I present my life as an offering to You. May my speech, the fruit of my life, be full of grace, seasoned with salt, as an acceptable offering of praise to You. (Nu 18:19; Col 4:6; Heb 13:15)

(3:1–16) What can we give You, Lord? You have everything. You created the heavens and the earth. Everything we have comes from your gracious hand. How is it then, that we can bring something that is "pleasing to the LORD?" Our worship of You brings You pleasure. As a father delights in the hugs of his children, so You delight in receiving our offerings of worship. We love You Father and are happy to bring You joy. (1Ch 29:11–14; Ps 8:3–9)

What can I give Him, poor as I am,
Were I a shepherd I'd give Him a lamb,
Were I a king I would do my part,
Since I'm a child, I'll give Him my heart.
Christina Rossetti (1830–1894)

17" 'This is a lasting ordinance for the generations to come,
wherever you live: You must not eat any fat or any blood.' "

The Sin Offering

4 The LORD said to Moses, 2"Say to the Israelites: 'When anyone
sins unintentionally and does what is forbidden in any of the
LORD's commands—

3" 'If the anointed priest sins, bringing guilt on the people, he
must bring to the LORD a young bull without defect as a sin offering for the sin he has committed. 4He is to present the bull at the
entrance to the Tent of Meeting before the LORD. He is to lay his
hand on its head and slaughter it before the LORD. 5Then the
anointed priest shall take some of the bull's blood and carry it into
the Tent of Meeting. 6He is to dip his finger into the blood and
sprinkle some of it seven times before the LORD, in front of the
curtain of the sanctuary. 7The priest shall then put some of the
blood on the horns of the altar of fragrant incense that is before
the LORD in the Tent of Meeting. The rest of the bull's blood he
shall pour out at the base of the altar of burnt offering at the entrance to the Tent of Meeting. 8He shall remove all the fat from the
bull of the sin offering—the fat that covers the inner parts or is
connected to them, 9both kidneys with the fat on them near the
loins, and the covering of the liver, which he will remove with the
kidneys— 10just as the fat is removed from the ox[a] sacrificed as
a fellowship offering.[b] Then the priest shall burn them on the altar
of burnt offering. 11But the hide of the bull and all its flesh, as
well as the head and legs, the inner parts and offal— 12that is, all
the rest of the bull—he must take outside the camp to a place
ceremonially clean, where the ashes are thrown, and burn it in a
wood fire on the ash heap.

13" 'If the whole Israelite community sins unintentionally and
does what is forbidden in any of the LORD's commands, even
though the community is unaware of the matter, they are guilty.
14When they become aware of the sin they committed, the assembly must bring a young bull as a sin offering and present it before
the Tent of Meeting. 15The elders of the community are to lay their
hands on the bull's head before the LORD, and the bull shall be
slaughtered before the LORD. 16Then the anointed priest is to take
some of the bull's blood into the Tent of Meeting. 17He shall dip
his finger into the blood and sprinkle it before the LORD seven
times in front of the curtain. 18He is to put some of the blood on
the horns of the altar that is before the LORD in the Tent of Meeting. The rest of the blood he shall pour out at the base of the altar
of burnt offering at the entrance to the Tent of Meeting. 19He shall
remove all the fat from it and burn it on the altar, 20and do with
this bull just as he did with the bull for the sin offering. In this way
the priest will make atonement for them, and they will be forgiv-
en. 21Then he shall take the bull outside the camp and burn it as
he burned the first bull. This is the sin offering for the community.

22" 'When a leader sins unintentionally and does what is forbidden in any of the commands of the LORD his God, he is guilty.
23When he is made aware of the sin he committed, he must bring
as his offering a male goat without defect. 24He is to lay his hand

[a] *10* The Hebrew word can include both male and female. [b] *10* Traditionally *peace offering*; also in verses 26, 31 and 35

It is not sin as we see it which was laid on Christ, but sin as God sees it; not sin as our conscience feebly reveals it to us, but sin as God beholds it.

Charles Haddon Spurgeon (1834-1892)

(4:2) Lord, there are times when I know the right thing to do and fail to do it. I know I am guilty in those cases. Yet, here I find I am also liable for unintentional sin. Ignorance clearly is no excuse when it comes to holiness. My conscience may be clear, but that does not make me innocent. But I thank You, Father, that in Your mercy, the blood of Jesus Christ purifies me from all sin—deliberate or unintentional; known or unknown; past, present or future. As both my priest and my sacrifice, He ever lives to intercede for me. (1Co 4:4; Heb 7:25; Jas 4:17; 1Jn 1:7)

What can wash away my sin?
Nothing but the blood of Jesus
What can make me whole again?
Nothing but the blood of Jesus

O, precious is the flow
That makes me white as snow
No other fount I know
Nothing but the blood of Jesus

"Nothing But the Blood of Jesus"
Robert Lowry (1876)

(4:6–7, 17–18) Blood was sprinkled on the curtain that led to the Most Holy Place. By this we see that access to Your presence is only through the blood. Blood was smeared on the horns of the altar of incense. Our prayers are as incense to You, and by this we see that they are only effective through the blood. Blood was poured out at the foot of the brazen altar, the place where the offerings were presented. By this we see that there is no fellowship with You except through the blood. Thank You for the blood of Jesus that makes us fully acceptable in Your sight, that empowers our prayers, and that gives us access to Your very presence. (Ps 141:2; Heb 9:12; 10:19–22; Rev 5:8)

on the goat's head and slaughter it at the place where the burnt offering is slaughtered before the LORD. It is a sin offering. 25 Then
the priest shall take some of the blood of the sin offering with his
finger and put it on the horns of the altar of burnt offering and
pour out the rest of the blood at the base of the altar. 26 He shall
burn all the fat on the altar as he burned the fat of the fellowship
offering. In this way the priest will make atonement for the man's
sin, and he will be forgiven.

27 " 'If a member of the community sins unintentionally and
does what is forbidden in any of the LORD's commands, he is guilty.
28 When he is made aware of the sin he committed, he must bring
as his offering for the sin he committed a female goat without defect. 29 He is to lay his hand on the head of the sin offering and
slaughter it at the place of the burnt offering. 30 Then the priest is
to take some of the blood with his finger and put it on the horns
of the altar of burnt offering and pour out the rest of the blood at
the base of the altar. 31 He shall remove all the fat, just as the fat is
removed from the fellowship offering, and the priest shall burn it
on the altar as an aroma pleasing to the LORD. In this way the priest
will make atonement for him, and he will be forgiven.

32 " 'If he brings a lamb as his sin offering, he is to bring a female without defect. 33 He is to lay his hand on its head and
slaughter it for a sin offering at the place where the burnt offering
is slaughtered. 34 Then the priest shall take some of the blood of
the sin offering with his finger and put it on the horns of the altar
of burnt offering and pour out the rest of the blood at the base of
the altar. 35 He shall remove all the fat, just as the fat is removed
from the lamb of the fellowship offering, and the priest shall burn
it on the altar on top of the offerings made to the LORD by fire. In
this way the priest will make atonement for him for the sin he has
committed, and he will be forgiven.

5 " 'If a person sins because he does not speak up when he
hears a public charge to testify regarding something he has
seen or learned about, he will be held responsible.

2 " 'Or if a person touches anything ceremonially unclean—
whether the carcasses of unclean wild animals or of unclean livestock or of unclean creatures that move along the ground—even
though he is unaware of it, he has become unclean and is guilty.

3 " 'Or if he touches human uncleanness—anything that would
make him unclean—even though he is unaware of it, when he
learns of it he will be guilty.

4 " 'Or if a person thoughtlessly takes an oath to do anything,
whether good or evil—in any matter one might carelessly swear
about—even though he is unaware of it, in any case when he
learns of it he will be guilty.

5 " 'When anyone is guilty in any of these ways, he must confess
in what way he has sinned 6 and, as a penalty for the sin he has
committed, he must bring to the LORD a female lamb or goat from
the flock as a sin offering; and the priest shall make atonement for
him for his sin.

7 " 'If he cannot afford a lamb, he is to bring two doves or two
young pigeons to the LORD as a penalty for his sin—one for a sin
offering and the other for a burnt offering. 8 He is to bring them to
the priest, who shall first offer the one for the sin offering. He is
to wring its head from its neck, not severing it completely, 9 and is
to sprinkle some of the blood of the sin offering against the side of

(4:24–35) The life is in the blood; the blood makes atonement for one's sin. When the victim was slain, the blood of the atoning sacrifice was shed, the life was extinguished, and sin was covered. For without the shedding of blood, there is no forgiveness of sin. The cycle went on and on, day after day, year after year, century after century, until Your blood was shed, Lord. As Your flock, we sighed a breath of hope. You, our Lamb of God, provided the perfect, permanent solution to our hopeless situation. (Lev 17:11; Jn 1:29; Heb 10:12–14)

For all the blood of beasts
On ancient altars slain
Could never give the conscience
  peace
Or wash away its stain:

But Christ, the heavenly Lamb,
Takes all our sins away—
A sacrifice of nobler
Name and richer blood than they.

In faith I lay my hand
Upon his head divine
While as a penitent I stand
And there confess my sin.

"What Offering Shall We Give?"
Isaac Watts (1709)

the altar; the rest of the blood must be drained out at the base of
the altar. It is a sin offering. 10The priest shall then offer the
other as a burnt offering in the prescribed way and make atonement for him for the sin he has committed, and he will be forgiven.
11" 'If, however, he cannot afford two doves or two young pigeons, he is to bring as an offering for his sin a tenth of an
ephah[a] of fine flour for a sin offering. He must not put oil or incense on it, because it is a sin offering. 12He is to bring it to the
priest, who shall take a handful of it as a memorial portion and
burn it on the altar on top of the offerings made to the LORD by
fire. It is a sin offering. 13In this way the priest will make atonement for him for any of these sins he has committed, and he will
be forgiven. The rest of the offering will belong to the priest, as
in the case of the grain offering.' "

The Guilt Offering

14The LORD said to Moses: 15"When a person commits a violation and sins unintentionally in regard to any of the LORD's holy
things, he is to bring to the LORD as a penalty a ram from the
flock, one without defect and of the proper value in silver, according to the sanctuary shekel.[b] It is a guilt offering. 16He must
make restitution for what he has failed to do in regard to the
holy things, add a fifth of the value to that and give it all to the
priest, who will make atonement for him with the ram as a guilt
offering, and he will be forgiven.
17"If a person sins and does what is forbidden in any of the
LORD's commands, even though he does not know it, he is guilty
and will be held responsible. 18He is to bring to the priest as a
guilt offering a ram from the flock, one without defect and of the
proper value. In this way the priest will make atonement for him
for the wrong he has committed unintentionally, and he will be
forgiven. 19It is a guilt offering; he has been guilty of[c] wrongdoing against the LORD."

6 The LORD said to Moses: 2"If anyone sins and is unfaithful to
the LORD by deceiving his neighbor about something entrusted to him or left in his care or stolen, or if he cheats him,
3or if he finds lost property and lies about it, or if he swears
falsely, or if he commits any such sin that people may do—
4when he thus sins and becomes guilty, he must return what he
has stolen or taken by extortion, or what was entrusted to him,
or the lost property he found, 5or whatever it was he swore falsely about. He must make restitution in full, add a fifth of the value
to it and give it all to the owner on the day he presents his guilt
offering. 6And as a penalty he must bring to the priest, that is, to
the LORD, his guilt offering, a ram from the flock, one without defect and of the proper value. 7In this way the priest will make
atonement for him before the LORD, and he will be forgiven for
any of these things he did that made him guilty."

The Burnt Offering

8The LORD said to Moses: 9"Give Aaron and his sons this command: 'These are the regulations for the burnt offering: The burnt
offering is to remain on the altar hearth throughout the night, till
morning, and the fire must be kept burning on the altar. 10The

[a] *11* That is, probably about 2 quarts (about 2 liters) [b] *15* That is, about 2/5 ounce (about 11.5 grams) [c] *19* Or *has made full expiation for his*

Anybody who has once been horrified by the dreadfulness of his own sin that nailed Jesus to the cross will no longer be horrified by even the rankest sins of a brother.

Dietrich Bonhoeffer (1906-1945)

(5:11) I praise You, Father, that You provide for all Your children, rich and poor alike. You do not look at the outward appearance, but are instead concerned with the condition of the heart. So You provided an acceptable sacrifice for any who would come to You. All of us are accountable in our relationship to You. Every one of us must acknowledge that we have fallen short of the mark. We praise You again as the God who forgives. Whether we are princes or paupers, pastors or prostitutes, Your grace is sufficient to forgive all of us for all of our sins. (1Sa 16:7; 1Jn 1:8–10)

Marvelous grace of our loving Lord,
Grace that exceeds our sin and our guilt!
Yonder on Calvary's mount outpoured
There where the blood of the Lamb was spilt.

Grace, grace, God's grace,
Grace that will pardon and cleanse within,
Grace, grace, God's grace,
Grace that is greater than all our sin!

"Grace Greater Than Our Sin"
Julia H. Johnston (1849-1919)

(6:9–13) Father, how I need the eternal, purifying fire of Your holiness to consume me as the fire consumed the burnt offering. May all that I am be completely given to You "throughout the night, till morning" and all the days of my life. (Heb 12:29)

(6:16–18) O God, our Provider, You give Your children a share of eternity. In return, we give You our undying thanks. Your priests, the Levites, had no earthly heritage of land in Canaan. Yet You made provision for them to have a share of the offerings made to You. In the same way we, who have all been made priests by our high priest Jesus, have a share in the heritage of heaven. Hallelujah! (Jos 13:14, 33; 18:7; Heb 3:1; 1Pe 2:5)

priest shall then put on his linen clothes, with linen undergarments next to his body, and shall remove the ashes of the burnt
offering that the fire has consumed on the altar and place them
beside the altar. 11Then he is to take off these clothes and put on
others, and carry the ashes outside the camp to a place that is
ceremonially clean. 12The fire on the altar must be kept burning;
it must not go out. Every morning the priest is to add firewood
and arrange the burnt offering on the fire and burn the fat of the
fellowship offerings[a] on it. 13The fire must be kept burning on
the altar continuously; it must not go out.

The Grain Offering

14" 'These are the regulations for the grain offering: Aaron's
sons are to bring it before the LORD, in front of the altar. 15The
priest is to take a handful of fine flour and oil, together with all
the incense on the grain offering, and burn the memorial portion on the altar as an aroma pleasing to the LORD. 16Aaron and
his sons shall eat the rest of it, but it is to be eaten without yeast
in a holy place; they are to eat it in the courtyard of the Tent of
Meeting. 17It must not be baked with yeast; I have given it as
their share of the offerings made to me by fire. Like the sin offering and the guilt offering, it is most holy. 18Any male descendant of Aaron may eat it. It is his regular share of the offerings
made to the LORD by fire for the generations to come. Whatever
touches them will become holy.[b]' "

19The LORD also said to Moses, 20"This is the offering Aaron
and his sons are to bring to the LORD on the day he[c] is anointed: a
tenth of an ephah[d] of fine flour as a regular grain offering, half of
it in the morning and half in the evening. 21Prepare it with oil on
a griddle; bring it well-mixed and present the grain offering broken[e] in pieces as an aroma pleasing to the LORD. 22The son who is
to succeed him as anointed priest shall prepare it. It is the LORD's
regular share and is to be burned completely. 23Every grain offering of a priest shall be burned completely; it must not be eaten."

The Sin Offering

24The LORD said to Moses, 25"Say to Aaron and his sons: 'These
are the regulations for the sin offering: The sin offering is to be
slaughtered before the LORD in the place the burnt offering is
slaughtered; it is most holy. 26The priest who offers it shall eat it;
it is to be eaten in a holy place, in the courtyard of the Tent of
Meeting. 27Whatever touches any of the flesh will become holy,
and if any of the blood is spattered on a garment, you must wash
it in a holy place. 28The clay pot the meat is cooked in must be
broken; but if it is cooked in a bronze pot, the pot is to be scoured
and rinsed with water. 29Any male in a priest's family may eat it; it
is most holy. 30But any sin offering whose blood is brought into
the Tent of Meeting to make atonement in the Holy Place must not
be eaten; it must be burned.

The Guilt Offering

7 " 'These are the regulations for the guilt offering, which is
most holy: 2The guilt offering is to be slaughtered in the place
where the burnt offering is slaughtered, and its blood is to be

[a] 12 Traditionally *peace offerings* [b] 18 Or *Whoever touches them must be holy*; similarly in verse 27 [c] 20 Or *each* [d] 20 That is, probably about 2 quarts (about 2 liters) [e] 21 The meaning of the Hebrew for this word is uncertain.

sprinkled against the altar on all sides. 3All its fat shall be offered: the fat tail and the fat that covers the inner parts, 4both
kidneys with the fat on them near the loins, and the covering
of the liver, which is to be removed with the kidneys. 5The
priest shall burn them on the altar as an offering made to the
LORD by fire. It is a guilt offering. 6Any male in a priest's family may eat it, but it must be eaten in a holy place; it is most
holy.

7" 'The same law applies to both the sin offering and the
guilt offering: They belong to the priest who makes atonement
with them. 8The priest who offers a burnt offering for anyone
may keep its hide for himself. 9Every grain offering baked in
an oven or cooked in a pan or on a griddle belongs to the
priest who offers it, 10and every grain offering, whether mixed
with oil or dry, belongs equally to all the sons of Aaron.

The Fellowship Offering

11" 'These are the regulations for the fellowship offering[a] a
person may present to the LORD:

12" 'If he offers it as an expression of thankfulness, then
along with this thank offering he is to offer cakes of bread made
without yeast and mixed with oil, wafers made without yeast and
spread with oil, and cakes of fine flour well-kneaded and mixed
with oil. 13Along with his fellowship offering of thanksgiving he
is to present an offering with cakes of bread made with yeast.
14He is to bring one of each kind as an offering, a contribution
to the LORD; it belongs to the priest who sprinkles the blood of
the fellowship offerings. 15The meat of his fellowship offering of
thanksgiving must be eaten on the day it is offered; he must
leave none of it till morning.

16" 'If, however, his offering is the result of a vow or is a
freewill offering, the sacrifice shall be eaten on the day he offers
it, but anything left over may be eaten on the next day. 17Any
meat of the sacrifice left over till the third day must be burned
up. 18If any meat of the fellowship offering is eaten on the third
day, it will not be accepted. It will not be credited to the one
who offered it, for it is impure; the person who eats any of it will
be held responsible.

19" 'Meat that touches anything ceremonially unclean must
not be eaten; it must be burned up. As for other meat, anyone
ceremonially clean may eat it. 20But if anyone who is unclean
eats any meat of the fellowship offering belonging to the LORD,
that person must be cut off from his people. 21If anyone touches
something unclean—whether human uncleanness or an unclean animal or any unclean, detestable thing—and then eats
any of the meat of the fellowship offering belonging to the LORD,
that person must be cut off from his people.' "

Eating Fat and Blood Forbidden

22The LORD said to Moses, 23"Say to the Israelites: 'Do not
eat any of the fat of cattle, sheep or goats. 24The fat of an animal found dead or torn by wild animals may be used for any
other purpose, but you must not eat it. 25Anyone who eats the
fat of an animal from which an offering by fire may be[b] made
to the LORD must be cut off from his people. 26And wherever

[a] *11* Traditionally *peace offering*; also in verses 13–37 [b] *25* Or *fire is*

(7:11–12) Thank You, gracious Lord, for giving us the gift of free will. You do not force us to have fellowship with You; rather, You lovingly woo us into relationship. May my worship and praise come from a heart that is filled with thanksgiving to You. I willfully, joyfully, gratefully come to You, not to see what You can do for me, but simply to say thank You, I love You, and to spend time in Your presence.

Christianity isn't only going to church on Sunday. It is living twenty-four hours of every day with Jesus Christ.

Billy Graham (1918-)

you live, you must not eat the blood of any bird or animal. 27If
anyone eats blood, that person must be cut off from his people.' "

The Priests' Share

28The LORD said to Moses, 29"Say to the Israelites: 'Anyone
who brings a fellowship offering to the LORD is to bring part of
it as his sacrifice to the LORD. 30With his own hands he is to
bring the offering made to the LORD by fire; he is to bring the fat,
together with the breast, and wave the breast before the LORD as
a wave offering. 31The priest shall burn the fat on the altar, but
the breast belongs to Aaron and his sons. 32You are to give the
right thigh of your fellowship offerings to the priest as a contribution. 33The son of Aaron who offers the blood and the fat of
the fellowship offering shall have the right thigh as his share.
34From the fellowship offerings of the Israelites, I have taken
the breast that is waved and the thigh that is presented and have
given them to Aaron the priest and his sons as their regular
share from the Israelites.' "

35This is the portion of the offerings made to the LORD by fire
that were allotted to Aaron and his sons on the day they were
presented to serve the LORD as priests. 36On the day they were
anointed, the LORD commanded that the Israelites give this to
them as their regular share for the generations to come.

37These, then, are the regulations for the burnt offering, the
grain offering, the sin offering, the guilt offering, the ordination
offering and the fellowship offering, 38which the LORD gave
Moses on Mount Sinai on the day he commanded the Israelites
to bring their offerings to the LORD, in the Desert of Sinai.

The Ordination of Aaron and His Sons

8 The LORD said to Moses, 2"Bring Aaron and his sons, their
garments, the anointing oil, the bull for the sin offering, the
two rams and the basket containing bread made without yeast,
3and gather the entire assembly at the entrance to the Tent of
Meeting." 4Moses did as the LORD commanded him, and the assembly gathered at the entrance to the Tent of Meeting.

5Moses said to the assembly, "This is what the LORD has commanded to be done." 6Then Moses brought Aaron and his sons
forward and washed them with water. 7He put the tunic on
Aaron, tied the sash around him, clothed him with the robe and
put the ephod on him. He also tied the ephod to him by its skillfully woven waistband; so it was fastened on him. 8He placed
the breastpiece on him and put the Urim and Thummim in the
breastpiece. 9Then he placed the turban on Aaron's head and
set the gold plate, the sacred diadem, on the front of it, as the
LORD commanded Moses.

10Then Moses took the anointing oil and anointed the tabernacle and everything in it, and so consecrated them. 11He
sprinkled some of the oil on the altar seven times, anointing
the altar and all its utensils and the basin with its stand, to consecrate them. 12He poured some of the anointing oil on
Aaron's head and anointed him to consecrate him. 13Then he
brought Aaron's sons forward, put tunics on them, tied sashes
around them and put headbands on them, as the LORD commanded Moses.

(7:37–38) In Your kindness You gave Your people detailed instructions so that their worship would be acceptable to You. Though these sacrifices have been fulfilled in Christ, still it is the attitude of our hearts that matters most to You. "The sacrifices of God are a broken spirit; a broken and contrite heart, O God, you will not despise." What good are the works of our hands or the words of our lips if we do not give You our hearts? For You do not find pleasure in mere ceremony; if our hearts are far from You, then our worship is in vain. May we worship You today with humble hearts and obedient hands so that all we do may be pleasing and acceptable to You. (Ps 51:17; Mt 15:8; Jn 4:23–24; Heb 9:9–10,23–28)

It is possible to be so active in the service of Christ as to forget to love him.

P. T. Forsyth (1848-1921)

14He then presented the bull for the sin offering, and Aaron
and his sons laid their hands on its head. 15Moses slaughtered
the bull and took some of the blood, and with his finger he put it
on all the horns of the altar to purify the altar. He poured out the
rest of the blood at the base of the altar. So he consecrated it to
make atonement for it. 16Moses also took all the fat around the
inner parts, the covering of the liver, and both kidneys and their
fat, and burned it on the altar. 17But the bull with its hide and its
flesh and its offal he burned up outside the camp, as the LORD
commanded Moses.

18He then presented the ram for the burnt offering, and Aaron
and his sons laid their hands on its head. 19Then Moses slaughtered the ram and sprinkled the blood against the altar on all
sides. 20He cut the ram into pieces and burned the head, the
pieces and the fat. 21He washed the inner parts and the legs with
water and burned the whole ram on the altar as a burnt offering,
a pleasing aroma, an offering made to the LORD by fire, as the
LORD commanded Moses.

22He then presented the other ram, the ram for the ordination,
and Aaron and his sons laid their hands on its head. 23Moses
slaughtered the ram and took some of its blood and put it on the
lobe of Aaron's right ear, on the thumb of his right hand and on
the big toe of his right foot. 24Moses also brought Aaron's sons
forward and put some of the blood on the lobes of their right
ears, on the thumbs of their right hands and on the big toes of
their right feet. Then he sprinkled blood against the altar on all
sides. 25He took the fat, the fat tail, all the fat around the inner
parts, the covering of the liver, both kidneys and their fat and the
right thigh. 26Then from the basket of bread made without yeast,
which was before the LORD, he took a cake of bread, and one
made with oil, and a wafer; he put these on the fat portions and
on the right thigh. 27He put all these in the hands of Aaron and
his sons and waved them before the LORD as a wave offering.
28Then Moses took them from their hands and burned them on
the altar on top of the burnt offering as an ordination offering, a
pleasing aroma, an offering made to the LORD by fire. 29He also
took the breast—Moses' share of the ordination ram—and
waved it before the LORD as a wave offering, as the LORD commanded Moses.

30Then Moses took some of the anointing oil and some of the
blood from the altar and sprinkled them on Aaron and his garments and on his sons and their garments. So he consecrated
Aaron and his garments and his sons and their garments.

31Moses then said to Aaron and his sons, "Cook the meat at
the entrance to the Tent of Meeting and eat it there with the
bread from the basket of ordination offerings, as I commanded,
saying,[a] 'Aaron and his sons are to eat it.' 32Then burn up the
rest of the meat and the bread. 33Do not leave the entrance to
the Tent of Meeting for seven days, until the days of your ordination are completed, for your ordination will last seven days.
34What has been done today was commanded by the LORD to
make atonement for you. 35You must stay at the entrance to the
Tent of Meeting day and night for seven days and do what the
LORD requires, so you will not die; for that is what I have been

[a] 31 Or *I was commanded:*

(8:30) Lord, set me apart for Your holy purpose. May I stand before You in the service of worship, clothed with Your garments of salvation and in Your robe of righteousness, clearly marked with the blood of Jesus, and richly anointed with the oil of the Holy Spirit. (1Sa 16:13; Isa 61:10; 1Jn 1:7)

Give of your best to the Master;
Give Him first place in your heart.
Give Him first place in your service;
Consecrate ev'ry part.
Give, and to you will be given;
God his beloved Son gave.
Gratefully seeking to serve Him;
Give Him the best that you have.

"Give of Your Best to the Master"
Howard B. Grose (1851-1939)

commanded." 36So Aaron and his sons did everything the LORD
commanded through Moses.

The Priests Begin Their Ministry

9 On the eighth day Moses summoned Aaron and his sons and
the elders of Israel. 2He said to Aaron, "Take a bull calf for
your sin offering and a ram for your burnt offering, both without
defect, and present them before the LORD. 3Then say to the Israelites: 'Take a male goat for a sin offering, a calf and a lamb—both
a year old and without defect—for a burnt offering, 4and an ox[a]
and a ram for a fellowship offering[b] to sacrifice before the LORD,
together with a grain offering mixed with oil. For today the LORD
will appear to you.' "
5They took the things Moses commanded to the front of the
Tent of Meeting, and the entire assembly came near and stood before the LORD. 6Then Moses said, "This is what the LORD has commanded you to do, so that the glory of the LORD may appear to
you."
7Moses said to Aaron, "Come to the altar and sacrifice your sin
offering and your burnt offering and make atonement for yourself
and the people; sacrifice the offering that is for the people and
make atonement for them, as the LORD has commanded."
8So Aaron came to the altar and slaughtered the calf as a sin offering for himself. 9His sons brought the blood to him, and he
dipped his finger into the blood and put it on the horns of the
altar; the rest of the blood he poured out at the base of the altar.
10On the altar he burned the fat, the kidneys and the covering of
the liver from the sin offering, as the LORD commanded Moses;
11the flesh and the hide he burned up outside the camp.
12Then he slaughtered the burnt offering. His sons handed him
the blood, and he sprinkled it against the altar on all sides. 13They
handed him the burnt offering piece by piece, including the head,
and he burned them on the altar. 14He washed the inner parts and
the legs and burned them on top of the burnt offering on the altar.
15Aaron then brought the offering that was for the people. He
took the goat for the people's sin offering and slaughtered it and
offered it for a sin offering as he did with the first one.
16He brought the burnt offering and offered it in the prescribed
way. 17He also brought the grain offering, took a handful of it and
burned it on the altar in addition to the morning's burnt offering.
18He slaughtered the ox and the ram as the fellowship offering
for the people. His sons handed him the blood, and he sprinkled
it against the altar on all sides. 19But the fat portions of the ox and
the ram—the fat tail, the layer of fat, the kidneys and the covering
of the liver— 20these they laid on the breasts, and then Aaron
burned the fat on the altar. 21Aaron waved the breasts and the
right thigh before the LORD as a wave offering, as Moses commanded.
22Then Aaron lifted his hands toward the people and blessed
them. And having sacrificed the sin offering, the burnt offering and
the fellowship offering, he stepped down.
23Moses and Aaron then went into the Tent of Meeting. When
they came out, they blessed the people; and the glory of the LORD
appeared to all the people. 24Fire came out from the presence of
the LORD and consumed the burnt offering and the fat portions on

[a] 4 The Hebrew word can include both male and female; also in verses 18 and 19.
[b] 4 Traditionally *peace offering*; also in verses 18 and 22

(9:4) Lord of glory, time and again You have chosen to reveal Yourself in unique ways to Your children as they worship You. You are not distant from Your worshipers, but You far surpass anything we can imagine. You are beyond comprehending, but not unknowable. You are everywhere in the universe, yet You desire to be close to us. As we worship through the blood of our perfect Sacrifice, consume us with Your glorious and awesome presence. (Dt 4:7,12; Ps 8:3–4; 139:8–10)

(9:24) So often, God, You were present on this earth in fire, and through it You instilled a godly fear in Your people. You called Moses from the burning bush. You spoke to the Israelites at Mt. Horeb from the fire. You judged Nadab and Abihu with fire from heaven. As Solomon's prayer of dedication ended, fire fell from heaven, consumed the sacrifice, and filled the people with awe. You met Elijah at Mt. Carmel as Your fire consumed the altar. John said believers would be baptized with fire and with the Holy Spirit. Lord, You are described as a consuming fire. We pray that once again the flames of Your holiness would come to our cold hearts and ignite Your holy fire within us. (Ex 3:2; Lev 10:2; Dt 4:12; 1Ki 18:38–39; 2Ch 7:1–3; Mt 3:11; Heb 12:29)

the altar. And when all the people saw it, they shouted for joy and
fell facedown.

The Death of Nadab and Abihu

10 Aaron's sons Nadab and Abihu took their censers, put fire
in them and added incense; and they offered unauthorized
fire before the LORD, contrary to his command. 2So fire came out
from the presence of the LORD and consumed them, and they died
before the LORD. 3Moses then said to Aaron, "This is what the LORD
spoke of when he said:

" 'Among those who approach me
I will show myself holy;
in the sight of all the people
I will be honored.' "

Aaron remained silent.
4Moses summoned Mishael and Elzaphan, sons of Aaron's
uncle Uzziel, and said to them, "Come here; carry your cousins
outside the camp, away from the front of the sanctuary." 5So they
came and carried them, still in their tunics, outside the camp, as
Moses ordered.
6Then Moses said to Aaron and his sons Eleazar and Ithamar,
"Do not let your hair become unkempt,[a] and do not tear your
clothes, or you will die and the LORD will be angry with the whole
community. But your relatives, all the house of Israel, may mourn
for those the LORD has destroyed by fire. 7Do not leave the entrance to the Tent of Meeting or you will die, because the LORD's
anointing oil is on you." So they did as Moses said.
8Then the LORD said to Aaron, 9"You and your sons are not to
drink wine or other fermented drink whenever you go into the
Tent of Meeting, or you will die. This is a lasting ordinance for the
generations to come. 10You must distinguish between the holy and
the common, between the unclean and the clean, 11and you must
teach the Israelites all the decrees the LORD has given them
through Moses."
12Moses said to Aaron and his remaining sons, Eleazar and Ithamar, "Take the grain offering left over from the offerings made to
the LORD by fire and eat it prepared without yeast beside the altar,
for it is most holy. 13Eat it in a holy place, because it is your share
and your sons' share of the offerings made to the LORD by fire; for
so I have been commanded. 14But you and your sons and your
daughters may eat the breast that was waved and the thigh that
was presented. Eat them in a ceremonially clean place; they have
been given to you and your children as your share of the Israelites'
fellowship offerings.[b] 15The thigh that was presented and the
breast that was waved must be brought with the fat portions of the
offerings made by fire, to be waved before the LORD as a wave offering. This will be the regular share for you and your children, as
the LORD has commanded."
16When Moses inquired about the goat of the sin offering and
found that it had been burned up, he was angry with Eleazar and
Ithamar, Aaron's remaining sons, and asked, 17"Why didn't you
eat the sin offering in the sanctuary area? It is most holy; it was
given to you to take away the guilt of the community by making
atonement for them before the LORD. 18Since its blood was not

[a] 6 Or *Do not uncover your heads* [b] 14 Traditionally *peace offerings*

The fear of God is to be united with the love of God; for love without fear makes men remiss, and fear without love makes them servile and desperate.

Johann Gerhard (1582–1637)

(10:1–2) O Holy God, though You are to be loved, You are also to be feared. For "the fear of the LORD is the beginning of wisdom." Help me to never take lightly my privileged position as a priest before You. Help me to never compromise holiness for convenience, or to confuse anointing with talent. Place in me a deep respect for Your holiness. Teach me to worship You acceptably with reverence and awe, for You, my God, are a consuming fire. (Ps 111:10; Mk 7:6; Heb 12:28–29; Rev 1:6)

taken into the Holy Place, you should have eaten the goat in the
sanctuary area, as I commanded."
19 Aaron replied to Moses, "Today they sacrificed their sin offering and their burnt offering before the LORD, but such things as
this have happened to me. Would the LORD have been pleased if I
had eaten the sin offering today?" 20 When Moses heard this, he
was satisfied.

Clean and Unclean Food

11 The LORD said to Moses and Aaron, 2 "Say to the Israelites:
'Of all the animals that live on land, these are the ones you
may eat: 3 You may eat any animal that has a split hoof completely
divided and that chews the cud.
4 " 'There are some that only chew the cud or only have a split
hoof, but you must not eat them. The camel, though it chews the
cud, does not have a split hoof; it is ceremonially unclean for you.
5 The coney,[a] though it chews the cud, does not have a split hoof;
it is unclean for you. 6 The rabbit, though it chews the cud, does
not have a split hoof; it is unclean for you. 7 And the pig, though it
has a split hoof completely divided, does not chew the cud; it is
unclean for you. 8 You must not eat their meat or touch their carcasses; they are unclean for you.
9 " 'Of all the creatures living in the water of the seas and the
streams, you may eat any that have fins and scales. 10 But all creatures in the seas or streams that do not have fins and scales—
whether among all the swarming things or among all the other living creatures in the water—you are to detest. 11 And since you are
to detest them, you must not eat their meat and you must detest
their carcasses. 12 Anything living in the water that does not have
fins and scales is to be detestable to you.
13 " 'These are the birds you are to detest and not eat because
they are detestable: the eagle, the vulture, the black vulture, 14 the
red kite, any kind of black kite, 15 any kind of raven, 16 the horned
owl, the screech owl, the gull, any kind of hawk, 17 the little owl,
the cormorant, the great owl, 18 the white owl, the desert owl, the
osprey, 19 the stork, any kind of heron, the hoopoe and the bat.[b]
20 " 'All flying insects that walk on all fours are to be detestable
to you. 21 There are, however, some winged creatures that walk on
all fours that you may eat: those that have jointed legs for hopping
on the ground. 22 Of these you may eat any kind of locust, katydid,
cricket or grasshopper. 23 But all other winged creatures that have
four legs you are to detest.
24 " 'You will make yourselves unclean by these; whoever
touches their carcasses will be unclean till evening. 25 Whoever
picks up one of their carcasses must wash his clothes, and he will
be unclean till evening.
26 " 'Every animal that has a split hoof not completely divided or
that does not chew the cud is unclean for you; whoever touches
⌞the carcass of⌟ any of them will be unclean. 27 Of all the animals
that walk on all fours, those that walk on their paws are unclean
for you; whoever touches their carcasses will be unclean till
evening. 28 Anyone who picks up their carcasses must wash his
clothes, and he will be unclean till evening. They are unclean for
you.
29 " 'Of the animals that move about on the ground, these are

[a] 5 That is, the hyrax or rock badger [b] 19 The precise identification of some of the birds, insects and animals in this chapter is uncertain.

(11:1–28) Clean and unclean animals, ceremonial law—what was the point, Lord? Was it just to keep Israel distinct and separate? Was the ceremonial law a symbol of something else to come? Even when I do not understand Your ways, help me, Lord, to treat seriously what You consider important. Help me to discern the substance and truth in what You demonstrate. Help me to observe the details of Your call to holy living in Christ. And help me to pay careful attention to the things that matter to You, even when they seem to be harmless to me. Teach me to live by Your standards, and not by the standards of the world. (Isa 55:8–9; 2Co 6:17)

Because our understanding is earth-bound . . . human to the core . . . limited . . . finite . . . we operate in a dimension totally unlike our Lord . . . who knows no such limitations. We see now. He sees forever.

Charles R. Swindoll (1934-)

unclean for you: the weasel, the rat, any kind of great lizard, [30]the
gecko, the monitor lizard, the wall lizard, the skink and the
chameleon. [31]Of all those that move along the ground, these are
unclean for you. Whoever touches them when they are dead will
be unclean till evening. [32]When one of them dies and falls on
something, that article, whatever its use, will be unclean, whether
it is made of wood, cloth, hide or sackcloth. Put it in water; it will
be unclean till evening, and then it will be clean. [33]If one of them
falls into a clay pot, everything in it will be unclean, and you must
break the pot. [34]Any food that could be eaten but has water on it
from such a pot is unclean, and any liquid that could be drunk
from it is unclean. [35]Anything that one of their carcasses falls on
becomes unclean; an oven or cooking pot must be broken up.
They are unclean, and you are to regard them as unclean. [36]A
spring, however, or a cistern for collecting water remains clean,
but anyone who touches one of these carcasses is unclean. [37]If a
carcass falls on any seeds that are to be planted, they remain
clean. [38]But if water has been put on the seed and a carcass falls
on it, it is unclean for you.

[39]" 'If an animal that you are allowed to eat dies, anyone who
touches the carcass will be unclean till evening. [40]Anyone who
eats some of the carcass must wash his clothes, and he will be unclean till evening. Anyone who picks up the carcass must wash his
clothes, and he will be unclean till evening.

[41]" 'Every creature that moves about on the ground is detestable; it is not to be eaten. [42]You are not to eat any creature that
moves about on the ground, whether it moves on its belly or walks
on all fours or on many feet; it is detestable. [43]Do not defile yourselves by any of these creatures. Do not make yourselves unclean
by means of them or be made unclean by them. [44]I am the LORD
your God; consecrate yourselves and be holy, because I am holy.
Do not make yourselves unclean by any creature that moves about
on the ground. [45]I am the LORD who brought you up out of Egypt
to be your God; therefore be holy, because I am holy.

[46]" 'These are the regulations concerning animals, birds, every
living thing that moves in the water and every creature that moves
about on the ground. [47]You must distinguish between the unclean
and the clean, between living creatures that may be eaten and
those that may not be eaten.' "

Purification After Childbirth

12 The LORD said to Moses, [2]"Say to the Israelites: 'A woman
who becomes pregnant and gives birth to a son will be ceremonially unclean for seven days, just as she is unclean during
her monthly period. [3]On the eighth day the boy is to be circumcised. [4]Then the woman must wait thirty-three days to be purified
from her bleeding. She must not touch anything sacred or go to
the sanctuary until the days of her purification are over. [5]If she
gives birth to a daughter, for two weeks the woman will be unclean, as during her period. Then she must wait sixty-six days to
be purified from her bleeding.

[6]" 'When the days of her purification for a son or daughter are
over, she is to bring to the priest at the entrance to the Tent of
Meeting a year-old lamb for a burnt offering and a young pigeon
or a dove for a sin offering. [7]He shall offer them before the LORD
to make atonement for her, and then she will be ceremonially
clean from her flow of blood.

Holiness is inwrought by the Holy Spirit, not because we have suffered, but because we have surrendered.

Richard Shelley Taylor (1912-)

(11:45) We thank You, dear Father, for rescuing us from the dominion of darkness and bringing us into the kingdom of Your Son. Thank You for redemption and forgiveness of sins. Thank You for making us holy, for calling us Your own, and for making Yourself our God. For we did not choose You; You chose us and set us apart for Your purposes. You decreed holiness for us; You are the one who makes us holy. We cannot make ourselves holy; we can only make ourselves unholy. Now, heavenly Father, help us to live a life worthy of You and to please You in every way, to bear fruit in every good work, to grow in our knowledge of You, and to be strengthened with all power according to Your glorious might. (Lev 20:8,26; Jn 15:16; Col 1:10–14)

And You loved me
Before I knew You;
And You knew me for all time.
I've been created
In Your image, Oh Lord,
And You brought me,
And You sought me,
Your blood poured out for me,
A new creation
In Your image, Oh Lord.
You rescued me.

"You Rescued Me"
Geoff Bullock (©1993)

God is a specialist in the sin disease.
Erwin W. Lutzer (1941-)

(13:1–8) Father, why was the victim pronounced "unclean" rather than "unhealthy"? It sounds more like a verdict than a diagnosis, as if the presence of the infection were the evidence of sin. Oh how sin must break Your heart, Father. To see its power not only to isolate us from one another, but from You, and to literally eat us alive. How I thank You, Lord, that now, through the blood of Jesus, You cleanse us not just on the surface, but from the inside out. You cleanse us not just from the symptoms of being unclean, but from the cause. So I present myself to You, my Priest, and pray, "Search me, O God . . . See if there is any offensive way in me." "Cleanse me with hyssop and I will be clean; wash me, and I will be whiter than snow." (Lev 14:1–7; Ps 51:7; 139:23–24; Isa 59:2)

Search me, O God,
And know my heart today;
Try me, O Savior,
Know my thoughts, I pray.
See if there be
Some wicked way in me;
Cleanse me from every sin,
And set me free.

"Cleanse Me"
J. Edwin Orr (1936)

" 'These are the regulations for the woman who gives birth to a boy or a girl. 8If she cannot afford a lamb, she is to bring two doves or two young pigeons, one for a burnt offering and the other for a sin offering. In this way the priest will make atonement for her, and she will be clean.' "

Regulations About Infectious Skin Diseases

13 The LORD said to Moses and Aaron, 2"When anyone has a swelling or a rash or a bright spot on his skin that may become an infectious skin disease,[a] he must be brought to Aaron the priest or to one of his sons[b] who is a priest. 3The priest is to examine the sore on his skin, and if the hair in the sore has turned white and the sore appears to be more than skin deep,[c] it is an infectious skin disease. When the priest examines him, he shall pronounce him ceremonially unclean. 4If the spot on his skin is white but does not appear to be more than skin deep and the hair in it has not turned white, the priest is to put the infected person in isolation for seven days. 5On the seventh day the priest is to examine him, and if he sees that the sore is unchanged and has not spread in the skin, he is to keep him in isolation another seven days. 6On the seventh day the priest is to examine him again, and if the sore has faded and has not spread in the skin, the priest shall pronounce him clean; it is only a rash. The man must wash his clothes, and he will be clean. 7But if the rash does spread in his skin after he has shown himself to the priest to be pronounced clean, he must appear before the priest again. 8The priest is to examine him, and if the rash has spread in the skin, he shall pronounce him unclean; it is an infectious disease.

9"When anyone has an infectious skin disease, he must be brought to the priest. 10The priest is to examine him, and if there is a white swelling in the skin that has turned the hair white and if there is raw flesh in the swelling, 11it is a chronic skin disease and the priest shall pronounce him unclean. He is not to put him in isolation, because he is already unclean.

12"If the disease breaks out all over his skin and, so far as the priest can see, it covers all the skin of the infected person from head to foot, 13the priest is to examine him, and if the disease has covered his whole body, he shall pronounce that person clean. Since it has all turned white, he is clean. 14But whenever raw flesh appears on him, he will be unclean. 15When the priest sees the raw flesh, he shall pronounce him unclean. The raw flesh is unclean; he has an infectious disease. 16Should the raw flesh change and turn white, he must go to the priest. 17The priest is to examine him, and if the sores have turned white, the priest shall pronounce the infected person clean; then he will be clean.

18"When someone has a boil on his skin and it heals, 19and in the place where the boil was, a white swelling or reddish-white spot appears, he must present himself to the priest. 20The priest is to examine it, and if it appears to be more than skin deep and the hair in it has turned white, the priest shall pronounce him unclean. It is an infectious skin disease that has broken out where the boil was. 21But if, when the priest examines it, there is no white hair in it and it is not more than skin deep and has faded, then the priest is to put him in isolation for seven days. 22If it is

[a] 2 Traditionally *leprosy*; the Hebrew word was used for various diseases affecting the skin—not necessarily leprosy; also elsewhere in this chapter. [b] 2 Or *descendants*
[c] 3 Or *be lower than the rest of the skin*; also elsewhere in this chapter

spreading in the skin, the priest shall pronounce him unclean; it
is infectious. 23But if the spot is unchanged and has not spread, it
is only a scar from the boil, and the priest shall pronounce him
clean.
24"When someone has a burn on his skin and a reddish-white
or white spot appears in the raw flesh of the burn, 25the priest is
to examine the spot, and if the hair in it has turned white, and it
appears to be more than skin deep, it is an infectious disease that
has broken out in the burn. The priest shall pronounce him unclean; it is an infectious skin disease. 26But if the priest examines
it and there is no white hair in the spot and if it is not more than
skin deep and has faded, then the priest is to put him in isolation
for seven days. 27On the seventh day the priest is to examine him,
and if it is spreading in the skin, the priest shall pronounce him
unclean; it is an infectious skin disease. 28If, however, the spot is
unchanged and has not spread in the skin but has faded, it is a
swelling from the burn, and the priest shall pronounce him clean;
it is only a scar from the burn.
29"If a man or woman has a sore on the head or on the chin,
30the priest is to examine the sore, and if it appears to be more
than skin deep and the hair in it is yellow and thin, the priest shall
pronounce that person unclean; it is an itch, an infectious disease
of the head or chin. 31But if, when the priest examines this kind of
sore, it does not seem to be more than skin deep and there is no
black hair in it, then the priest is to put the infected person in isolation for seven days. 32On the seventh day the priest is to examine the sore, and if the itch has not spread and there is no yellow
hair in it and it does not appear to be more than skin deep, 33he
must be shaved except for the diseased area, and the priest is to
keep him in isolation another seven days. 34On the seventh day the
priest is to examine the itch, and if it has not spread in the skin
and appears to be no more than skin deep, the priest shall pronounce him clean. He must wash his clothes, and he will be clean.
35But if the itch does spread in the skin after he is pronounced
clean, 36the priest is to examine him, and if the itch has spread in
the skin, the priest does not need to look for yellow hair; the person is unclean. 37If, however, in his judgment it is unchanged and
black hair has grown in it, the itch is healed. He is clean, and the
priest shall pronounce him clean.
38"When a man or woman has white spots on the skin, 39the
priest is to examine them, and if the spots are dull white, it is a
harmless rash that has broken out on the skin; that person is
clean.
40"When a man has lost his hair and is bald, he is clean. 41If
he has lost his hair from the front of his scalp and has a bald
forehead, he is clean. 42But if he has a reddish-white sore on his
bald head or forehead, it is an infectious disease breaking out on
his head or forehead. 43The priest is to examine him, and if the
swollen sore on his head or forehead is reddish-white like an infectious skin disease, 44the man is diseased and is unclean. The
priest shall pronounce him unclean because of the sore on his
head.
45"The person with such an infectious disease must wear torn
clothes, let his hair be unkempt,[a] cover the lower part of his face
and cry out, 'Unclean! Unclean!' 46As long as he has the infection

[a] 45 Or *clothes, uncover his head*

(13:45–46) Father, this seems such cruel treatment for someone in such suffering. Yet we see how important it was for You to protect Your people from the spread of infection. We see the hopelessness of the victim who was cast out of the community. We see the hopelessness of his friends and loved ones who longed to bring him comfort, but could not touch him without also becoming unclean themselves. We see the hopelessness of the priest who could only pronounce the state of health as either clean or unclean, but could not heal the disease itself. Faced with this hopelessness, it is all the more profound when we consider the words and actions of Jesus toward the leper who came to him: Jesus reached out His hand and touched the man. "Be clean," he said. And immediately the man was cured of his leprosy. I praise You, Lord Jesus, for You still touch and cleanse and heal the hopeless. (Mt 8:2–3)

This was all that the law could do, in that it was weak through the flesh; it taught the leper to cry, "Unclean, unclean"; but the gospel has put another cry into the lepers' mouths, "Jesus, Master, have mercy on us." The law only shows us our disease; the gospel shows us our help in Christ.

Matthew Henry (1662-1714)

he remains unclean. He must live alone; he must live outside the
camp.

Regulations About Mildew

47"If any clothing is contaminated with mildew—any woolen
or linen clothing, 48any woven or knitted material of linen or
wool, any leather or anything made of leather— 49and if the contamination in the clothing, or leather, or woven or knitted material, or any leather article, is greenish or reddish, it is a spreading
mildew and must be shown to the priest. 50The priest is to examine the mildew and isolate the affected article for seven days. 51On
the seventh day he is to examine it, and if the mildew has spread
in the clothing, or the woven or knitted material, or the leather,
whatever its use, it is a destructive mildew; the article is unclean.
52He must burn up the clothing, or the woven or knitted material
of wool or linen, or any leather article that has the contamination
in it, because the mildew is destructive; the article must be
burned up.

53"But if, when the priest examines it, the mildew has not
spread in the clothing, or the woven or knitted material, or the
leather article, 54he shall order that the contaminated article be
washed. Then he is to isolate it for another seven days. 55After the
affected article has been washed, the priest is to examine it, and if
the mildew has not changed its appearance, even though it has not
spread, it is unclean. Burn it with fire, whether the mildew has affected one side or the other. 56If, when the priest examines it, the
mildew has faded after the article has been washed, he is to tear
the contaminated part out of the clothing, or the leather, or the
woven or knitted material. 57But if it reappears in the clothing, or
in the woven or knitted material, or in the leather article, it is
spreading, and whatever has the mildew must be burned with fire.
58The clothing, or the woven or knitted material, or any leather
article that has been washed and is rid of the mildew, must be
washed again, and it will be clean."

59These are the regulations concerning contamination by mildew in woolen or linen clothing, woven or knitted material, or any
leather article, for pronouncing them clean or unclean.

Cleansing From Infectious Skin Diseases

14 The LORD said to Moses, 2"These are the regulations for the
diseased person at the time of his ceremonial cleansing,
when he is brought to the priest: 3The priest is to go outside the
camp and examine him. If the person has been healed of his infectious skin disease,[a] 4the priest shall order that two live clean
birds and some cedar wood, scarlet yarn and hyssop be brought
for the one to be cleansed. 5Then the priest shall order that one of
the birds be killed over fresh water in a clay pot. 6He is then to
take the live bird and dip it, together with the cedar wood, the
scarlet yarn and the hyssop, into the blood of the bird that was
killed over the fresh water. 7Seven times he shall sprinkle the one
to be cleansed of the infectious disease and pronounce him clean.
Then he is to release the live bird in the open fields.

8"The person to be cleansed must wash his clothes, shave off all
his hair and bathe with water; then he will be ceremonially clean.
After this he may come into the camp, but he must stay outside his

[a]3 Traditionally *leprosy*; the Hebrew word was used for various diseases affecting the skin—not necessarily leprosy; also elsewhere in this chapter.

Teach me to feel another's woe,
To hide the fault I see;
That mercy I to others show,
That mercy show to me.
Alexander Pope (1688-1744)

(14:3) Father, there are many people in our world today whom we in Your church declare to be "unclean": the street people, the diseased, those who dwell "outside the camp" in the outskirts and back alleys of society, those who bear the physical signs of spiritual failure. Jesus touched "sinners" like these; I confess that I often look the other way, or maybe toss a coin or two in their direction, and then quickly move on so as not to be touched by them. Lord, forgive me, and fill me with the compassion of Jesus to bring healing and restoration and friendship to the hopeless. (Mk 2:15–17; Lk 10:30–37; 2Co 1:3–4)

If I have not charity
If love does not flow from me
I am nothing
Jesus, reduce me to love
"Charity"
Kenn Gulliksen (©1971)

tent for seven days. 9On the seventh day he must shave off all his
hair; he must shave his head, his beard, his eyebrows and the rest
of his hair. He must wash his clothes and bathe himself with water,
and he will be clean.

10"On the eighth day he must bring two male lambs and one
ewe lamb a year old, each without defect, along with three-tenths
of an ephah[a] of fine flour mixed with oil for a grain offering, and
one log[b] of oil. 11The priest who pronounces him clean shall present both the one to be cleansed and his offerings before the LORD
at the entrance to the Tent of Meeting.

12"Then the priest is to take one of the male lambs and offer it
as a guilt offering, along with the log of oil; he shall wave them before the LORD as a wave offering. 13He is to slaughter the lamb in
the holy place where the sin offering and the burnt offering are
slaughtered. Like the sin offering, the guilt offering belongs to the
priest; it is most holy. 14The priest is to take some of the blood of
the guilt offering and put it on the lobe of the right ear of the one
to be cleansed, on the thumb of his right hand and on the big toe
of his right foot. 15The priest shall then take some of the log of oil,
pour it in the palm of his own left hand, 16dip his right forefinger
into the oil in his palm, and with his finger sprinkle some of it before the LORD seven times. 17The priest is to put some of the oil remaining in his palm on the lobe of the right ear of the one to be
cleansed, on the thumb of his right hand and on the big toe of his
right foot, on top of the blood of the guilt offering. 18The rest of
the oil in his palm the priest shall put on the head of the one to be
cleansed and make atonement for him before the LORD.

19"Then the priest is to sacrifice the sin offering and make
atonement for the one to be cleansed from his uncleanness. After
that, the priest shall slaughter the burnt offering 20and offer it on
the altar, together with the grain offering, and make atonement for
him, and he will be clean.

21"If, however, he is poor and cannot afford these, he must take
one male lamb as a guilt offering to be waved to make atonement
for him, together with a tenth of an ephah[c] of fine flour mixed
with oil for a grain offering, a log of oil, 22and two doves or two
young pigeons, which he can afford, one for a sin offering and the
other for a burnt offering.

23"On the eighth day he must bring them for his cleansing to
the priest at the entrance to the Tent of Meeting, before the LORD.
24The priest is to take the lamb for the guilt offering, together with
the log of oil, and wave them before the LORD as a wave offering.
25He shall slaughter the lamb for the guilt offering and take some
of its blood and put it on the lobe of the right ear of the one to be
cleansed, on the thumb of his right hand and on the big toe of his
right foot. 26The priest is to pour some of the oil into the palm of
his own left hand, 27and with his right forefinger sprinkle some of
the oil from his palm seven times before the LORD. 28Some of the
oil in his palm he is to put on the same places he put the blood of
the guilt offering—on the lobe of the right ear of the one to be
cleansed, on the thumb of his right hand and on the big toe of his
right foot. 29The rest of the oil in his palm the priest shall put on
the head of the one to be cleansed, to make atonement for him before the LORD. 30Then he shall sacrifice the doves or the young pi-

[a] *10* That is, probably about 6 quarts (about 6.5 liters) [b] *10* That is, probably about 2/3 pint (about 0.3 liter); also in verses 12, 15, 21 and 24 [c] *21* That is, probably about 2 quarts (about 2 liters)

(14:14) Blood on the right ear, right hand and right foot. Thank You, merciful God, that by this same ceremony both priest and leper were anointed. How we all need to be cleansed in what we hear, what we do, and how we walk. Lord, anoint these areas of my life so that I may be cleansed and forgiven before You. (Lev 8:23–24)

geons, which the person can afford, **31**one[a] as a sin offering and
the other as a burnt offering, together with the grain offering. In
this way the priest will make atonement before the LORD on behalf
of the one to be cleansed."
32These are the regulations for anyone who has an infectious
skin disease and who cannot afford the regular offerings for his
cleansing.

Cleansing From Mildew

33The LORD said to Moses and Aaron, **34**"When you enter the
land of Canaan, which I am giving you as your possession, and I
put a spreading mildew in a house in that land, **35**the owner of
the house must go and tell the priest, 'I have seen something that
looks like mildew in my house.' **36**The priest is to order the
house to be emptied before he goes in to examine the mildew, so
that nothing in the house will be pronounced unclean. After this
the priest is to go in and inspect the house. **37**He is to examine
the mildew on the walls, and if it has greenish or reddish de-
pressions that appear to be deeper than the surface of the wall,
38the priest shall go out the doorway of the house and close it up
for seven days. **39**On the seventh day the priest shall return to inspect the house. If the mildew has spread on the walls, **40**he is to
order that the contaminated stones be torn out and thrown into
an unclean place outside the town. **41**He must have all the inside
walls of the house scraped and the material that is scraped off
dumped into an unclean place outside the town. **42**Then they are
to take other stones to replace these and take new clay and plaster the house.
43"If the mildew reappears in the house after the stones have
been torn out and the house scraped and plastered, **44**the priest
is to go and examine it and, if the mildew has spread in the
house, it is a destructive mildew; the house is unclean. **45**It must
be torn down—its stones, timbers and all the plaster—and taken
out of the town to an unclean place.
46"Anyone who goes into the house while it is closed up will be
unclean till evening. **47**Anyone who sleeps or eats in the house
must wash his clothes.
48"But if the priest comes to examine it and the mildew has not
spread after the house has been plastered, he shall pronounce
the house clean, because the mildew is gone. **49**To purify the
house he is to take two birds and some cedar wood, scarlet yarn
and hyssop. **50**He shall kill one of the birds over fresh water in a
clay pot. **51**Then he is to take the cedar wood, the hyssop, the
scarlet yarn and the live bird, dip them into the blood of the dead
bird and the fresh water, and sprinkle the house seven times.
52He shall purify the house with the bird's blood, the fresh water,
the live bird, the cedar wood, the hyssop and the scarlet yarn.
53Then he is to release the live bird in the open fields outside the
town. In this way he will make atonement for the house, and it
will be clean."
54These are the regulations for any infectious skin disease, for
an itch, **55**for mildew in clothing or in a house, **56**and for a
swelling, a rash or a bright spot, **57**to determine when something
is clean or unclean.

(14:35–47) Father, cleanse my home from the "mildew" of sin. Let righteousness be its foundation; let love be its walls; and let the peace of Christ be its covering. Let all who come here find relief from the destructive influences of the world. Let it be said of my home as it is said of Your church, "THE LORD IS THERE." (Eze 48:35)

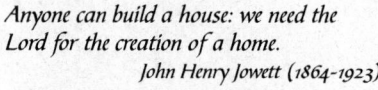

Anyone can build a house: we need the Lord for the creation of a home.
John Henry Jowett (1864-1923)

[a] *31* Septuagint and Syriac; Hebrew *31such as the person can afford, one*

These are the regulations for infectious skin diseases and mildew.

Discharges Causing Uncleanness

15 The LORD said to Moses and Aaron, 2"Speak to the Israelites
and say to them: 'When any man has a bodily discharge, the
discharge is unclean. 3Whether it continues flowing from his body
or is blocked, it will make him unclean. This is how his discharge
will bring about uncleanness:
4" 'Any bed the man with a discharge lies on will be unclean,
and anything he sits on will be unclean. 5Anyone who touches his
bed must wash his clothes and bathe with water, and he will be unclean till evening. 6Whoever sits on anything that the man with a
discharge sat on must wash his clothes and bathe with water, and
he will be unclean till evening.
7" 'Whoever touches the man who has a discharge must wash
his clothes and bathe with water, and he will be unclean till
evening.
8" 'If the man with the discharge spits on someone who is
clean, that person must wash his clothes and bathe with water,
and he will be unclean till evening.
9" 'Everything the man sits on when riding will be unclean,
10and whoever touches any of the things that were under him will
be unclean till evening; whoever picks up those things must wash
his clothes and bathe with water, and he will be unclean till
evening.
11" 'Anyone the man with a discharge touches without rinsing
his hands with water must wash his clothes and bathe with water,
and he will be unclean till evening.
12" 'A clay pot that the man touches must be broken, and any
wooden article is to be rinsed with water.
13" 'When a man is cleansed from his discharge, he is to count
off seven days for his ceremonial cleansing; he must wash his
clothes and bathe himself with fresh water, and he will be clean.
14On the eighth day he must take two doves or two young pigeons
and come before the LORD to the entrance to the Tent of Meeting
and give them to the priest. 15The priest is to sacrifice them, the
one for a sin offering and the other for a burnt offering. In this way
he will make atonement before the LORD for the man because of
his discharge.
16" 'When a man has an emission of semen, he must bathe his
whole body with water, and he will be unclean till evening. 17Any
clothing or leather that has semen on it must be washed with
water, and it will be unclean till evening. 18When a man lies with
a woman and there is an emission of semen, both must bathe
with water, and they will be unclean till evening.
19" 'When a woman has her regular flow of blood, the impurity of her monthly period will last seven days, and anyone who
touches her will be unclean till evening.
20" 'Anything she lies on during her period will be unclean, and
anything she sits on will be unclean. 21Whoever touches her bed
must wash his clothes and bathe with water, and he will be unclean till evening. 22Whoever touches anything she sits on must
wash his clothes and bathe with water, and he will be unclean till
evening. 23Whether it is the bed or anything she was sitting on,
when anyone touches it, he will be unclean till evening.
24" 'If a man lies with her and her monthly flow touches him,

The dying Jesus is the evidence of God's anger toward sin; but the living Jesus is the proof of God's love and forgiveness.

Lorenz Eifert

(15:1–30) O, Lord God, how pure and holy You are. If Your people could be made unclean by physical conditions that were not a matter of conscious choice, how much more heinous must our deliberate sins be to You? Oh how we thank You for our Savior! And how we thank You, Jesus, that we can reach out and touch You, and be cleansed and forgiven. For "if we confess our sins, [you are] faithful and just and will forgive us our sins and purify us from all unrighteousness." (Mk 5:25–34; 1Jn 1:9)

There is a stream that flows from
Calvary,
A crimson tide so deep and wide.
It washes whiter than the purest
snow;
It cleanseth me, I know.

Hallelujah! 'Tis His blood that
cleanseth me;
'Tis His grace that makes me free.
And, my brother, 'tis for thee.
O hallelujah! 'Tis salvation full and
free;
And it cleanseth, yes, it cleanseth
me.

"It Cleanseth Me"
F.L. Snyder (1899)

he will be unclean for seven days; any bed he lies on will be unclean.

25" 'When a woman has a discharge of blood for many days at
a time other than her monthly period or has a discharge that continues beyond her period, she will be unclean as long as she has
the discharge, just as in the days of her period. 26Any bed she lies
on while her discharge continues will be unclean, as is her bed
during her monthly period, and anything she sits on will be unclean, as during her period. 27Whoever touches them will be unclean; he must wash his clothes and bathe with water, and he will
be unclean till evening.

28" 'When she is cleansed from her discharge, she must count
off seven days, and after that she will be ceremonially clean. 29On
the eighth day she must take two doves or two young pigeons and
bring them to the priest at the entrance to the Tent of Meeting.
30The priest is to sacrifice one for a sin offering and the other for
a burnt offering. In this way he will make atonement for her before the LORD for the uncleanness of her discharge.

31" 'You must keep the Israelites separate from things that
make them unclean, so they will not die in their uncleanness for
defiling my dwelling place,[a] which is among them.' "

32These are the regulations for a man with a discharge, for anyone made unclean by an emission of semen, 33for a woman in her
monthly period, for a man or a woman with a discharge, and for
a man who lies with a woman who is ceremonially unclean.

The Day of Atonement

16 The LORD spoke to Moses after the death of the two sons of
Aaron who died when they approached the LORD. 2The LORD
said to Moses: "Tell your brother Aaron not to come whenever he
chooses into the Most Holy Place behind the curtain in front of the
atonement cover on the ark, or else he will die, because I appear
in the cloud over the atonement cover.

3"This is how Aaron is to enter the sanctuary area: with a young
bull for a sin offering and a ram for a burnt offering. 4He is to put
on the sacred linen tunic, with linen undergarments next to his
body; he is to tie the linen sash around him and put on the linen
turban. These are sacred garments; so he must bathe himself with
water before he puts them on. 5From the Israelite community he
is to take two male goats for a sin offering and a ram for a burnt
offering.

6"Aaron is to offer the bull for his own sin offering to make
atonement for himself and his household. 7Then he is to take the
two goats and present them before the LORD at the entrance to the
Tent of Meeting. 8He is to cast lots for the two goats—one lot for
the LORD and the other for the scapegoat.[b] 9Aaron shall bring the
goat whose lot falls to the LORD and sacrifice it for a sin offering.
10But the goat chosen by lot as the scapegoat shall be presented
alive before the LORD to be used for making atonement by sending
it into the desert as a scapegoat.

11"Aaron shall bring the bull for his own sin offering to make
atonement for himself and his household, and he is to slaughter
the bull for his own sin offering. 12He is to take a censer full of
burning coals from the altar before the LORD and two handfuls of
finely ground fragrant incense and take them behind the curtain.

[a] *31* Or *my tabernacle* [b] *8* That is, the goat of removal; Hebrew *azazel*; also in verses 10 and 26

(16:2–3) Most holy God, how I thank You for Your love and mercy. The curtain in the temple separated You from a sinful people. It hid Your presence from the view of the worshipers. Only Aaron could enter the Most Holy Place, and that just one day each year, to behold Your glory. It was truly the most sacred place in all the earth. You warned Aaron not to come at any other time or he would die. But now, through Jesus, You invite me to come at all times so that I might live. And so I come to You, and I praise You for Jesus, my sacrifice and high priest who ushers me straight to Your throne through the torn curtain of His body. (Heb 9:11–14, 24–26; 10:19–22)

Waiting in His holy presence,
Silent now before His throne;
Let us worship Lord Jehovah,
Bringing gifts to Him alone.

We will bow before His majesty,
Loving Him with hearts aflame;
Kings and priests to serve His
righteousness,
We will stand and praise His name.

King and Lord of all creation,
Sov'reign in authority;
We will never cease to praise Him,
Throughout all eternity.

"Let Us Worship Lord Jehovah"
Kirk Dearman (©1987)

13He is to put the incense on the fire before the LORD, and the
smoke of the incense will conceal the atonement cover above
the Testimony, so that he will not die. 14He is to take some of the
bull's blood and with his finger sprinkle it on the front of the
atonement cover; then he shall sprinkle some of it with his finger
seven times before the atonement cover.
15"He shall then slaughter the goat for the sin offering for the
people and take its blood behind the curtain and do with it as he
did with the bull's blood: He shall sprinkle it on the atonement
cover and in front of it. 16In this way he will make atonement for
the Most Holy Place because of the uncleanness and rebellion of
the Israelites, whatever their sins have been. He is to do the same
for the Tent of Meeting, which is among them in the midst of their
uncleanness. 17No one is to be in the Tent of Meeting from the
time Aaron goes in to make atonement in the Most Holy Place
until he comes out, having made atonement for himself, his
household and the whole community of Israel.
18"Then he shall come out to the altar that is before the LORD
and make atonement for it. He shall take some of the bull's blood
and some of the goat's blood and put it on all the horns of the
altar. 19He shall sprinkle some of the blood on it with his finger
seven times to cleanse it and to consecrate it from the uncleanness of the Israelites.
20"When Aaron has finished making atonement for the Most
Holy Place, the Tent of Meeting and the altar, he shall bring forward the live goat. 21He is to lay both hands on the head of the
live goat and confess over it all the wickedness and rebellion of
the Israelites—all their sins—and put them on the goat's head.
He shall send the goat away into the desert in the care of a man
appointed for the task. 22The goat will carry on itself all their sins
to a solitary place; and the man shall release it in the desert.
23"Then Aaron is to go into the Tent of Meeting and take off the
linen garments he put on before he entered the Most Holy Place,
and he is to leave them there. 24He shall bathe himself with water
in a holy place and put on his regular garments. Then he shall
come out and sacrifice the burnt offering for himself and the
burnt offering for the people, to make atonement for himself and
for the people. 25He shall also burn the fat of the sin offering on
the altar.
26"The man who releases the goat as a scapegoat must wash
his clothes and bathe himself with water; afterward he may come
into the camp. 27The bull and the goat for the sin offerings,
whose blood was brought into the Most Holy Place to make
atonement, must be taken outside the camp; their hides, flesh
and offal are to be burned up. 28The man who burns them must
wash his clothes and bathe himself with water; afterward he may
come into the camp.
29"This is to be a lasting ordinance for you: On the tenth day of
the seventh month you must deny yourselves[a] and not do any
work—whether native-born or an alien living among you—
30because on this day atonement will be made for you, to cleanse
you. Then, before the LORD, you will be clean from all your sins.
31It is a sabbath of rest, and you must deny yourselves; it is a lasting ordinance. 32The priest who is anointed and ordained to succeed his father as high priest is to make atonement. He is to put

[a] 29 Or *must fast*; also in verse 31

The Old Testament Hebrew word that we translate "atonement" means literally "to cover up." The animal sacrifices were intended to "cover" a man's sins. In the New Testament, however, the meaning of atoning sacrifice is conveyed by the word expiate, which means "to put away." The blood that Jesus shed in our behalf on the cross at Calvary does not merely cover up our sin, it puts away our sin as though it had never been committed.

Bishop T. W. Wilson (1663-1735)

(16:15–22) Gracious and merciful God, I praise You for atoning for my sins through the blood of Jesus, "the Lamb of God, who takes away the sin of the world!" He paid the price of death for all of my sin—every thought of evil, every look of lust, every act of violence, every word of blasphemy—all sin, the very sin of sinning, was atoned for once and for all by the blood of Jesus. Through Jesus You put to death my sinful nature, and then You erased all record of my sinful past. You laid on Him all of my iniquity, and He removed it as far as the east is from the west. I thank You, Father, that through Jesus, You not only forgave my sins, but You cleansed me from all unrighteousness. (Ps 103:12; Isa 53:6; Jn 1:29; Ro 3:23–25; Gal 5:24; Heb 10:17; 1Jn 1:9)

Thou within the veil hast entered,
Robed in flesh, our great High Priest;
Thou on earth both Priest and
Victim
In the eucharistic feast.

"Alleluia, Sing to Jesus"
William Chatterton Dix (c.1866)

(17:11) Lord, let us never forget that it is the blood of Christ that makes atonement for our lives—it is not His life, or His teaching, or His miracles, or His resurrection, or His second coming—it is His blood, the giving of His life, that brought us forgiveness. Without His death, there is no life. Without the cross, there is no resurrection. Let our worship be, like the worship in heaven, always centered on this fact—the shed blood of Jesus purifies us from all sin. (Rev 5:9–12)

The blood that from the Lord's beloved wounds does flow
Is the most precious dew he will on us bestow.

Angelus Silesius (1624–1677)

(18:3–4) All praise to You, Father, for the new life I have in Christ Jesus. As You brought Your people out of Egypt, so You have brought me out of bondage to sin and death. Through Jesus I have been made holy and have been brought into Your presence. It is because of His sacrifice at Calvary that I am a new creature. I renounce the sins of my past and I plead for Your strength to resist the temptations of the future. Teach me, Father, to walk in the new way of the Spirit—in freedom and obedience. (Ro 5:21; 6:16; 7:6; 8:2; Heb 10:22)

on the sacred linen garments 33and make atonement for the Most
Holy Place, for the Tent of Meeting and the altar, and for the
priests and all the people of the community.
34"This is to be a lasting ordinance for you: Atonement is to be
made once a year for all the sins of the Israelites."
And it was done, as the LORD commanded Moses.

Eating Blood Forbidden

17 The LORD said to Moses, 2"Speak to Aaron and his sons and
to all the Israelites and say to them: 'This is what the LORD
has commanded: 3Any Israelite who sacrifices an ox,[a] a lamb or
a goat in the camp or outside of it 4instead of bringing it to the entrance to the Tent of Meeting to present it as an offering to the
LORD in front of the tabernacle of the LORD—that man shall be
considered guilty of bloodshed; he has shed blood and must be
cut off from his people. 5This is so the Israelites will bring to the
LORD the sacrifices they are now making in the open fields. They
must bring them to the priest, that is, to the LORD, at the entrance
to the Tent of Meeting and sacrifice them as fellowship offerings.[b]
6The priest is to sprinkle the blood against the altar of the LORD at
the entrance to the Tent of Meeting and burn the fat as an aroma
pleasing to the LORD. 7They must no longer offer any of their sacrifices to the goat idols[c] to whom they prostitute themselves. This
is to be a lasting ordinance for them and for the generations to
come.'
8"Say to them: 'Any Israelite or any alien living among them
who offers a burnt offering or sacrifice 9and does not bring it to
the entrance to the Tent of Meeting to sacrifice it to the LORD—that
man must be cut off from his people.
10" 'Any Israelite or any alien living among them who eats any
blood—I will set my face against that person who eats blood and
will cut him off from his people. 11For the life of a creature is in
the blood, and I have given it to you to make atonement for yourselves on the altar; it is the blood that makes atonement for one's
life. 12Therefore I say to the Israelites, "None of you may eat
blood, nor may an alien living among you eat blood."
13" 'Any Israelite or any alien living among you who hunts any
animal or bird that may be eaten must drain out the blood and
cover it with earth, 14because the life of every creature is its blood.
That is why I have said to the Israelites, "You must not eat the
blood of any creature, because the life of every creature is its
blood; anyone who eats it must be cut off."
15" 'Anyone, whether native-born or alien, who eats anything
found dead or torn by wild animals must wash his clothes and
bathe with water, and he will be ceremonially unclean till evening;
then he will be clean. 16But if he does not wash his clothes and
bathe himself, he will be held responsible.' "

Unlawful Sexual Relations

18 The LORD said to Moses, 2"Speak to the Israelites and say to
them: 'I am the LORD your God. 3You must not do as they do
in Egypt, where you used to live, and you must not do as they do
in the land of Canaan, where I am bringing you. Do not follow
their practices. 4You must obey my laws and be careful to follow

[a] 3 The Hebrew word can include both male and female. [b] 5 Traditionally *peace offerings* [c] 7 Or *demons*

my decrees. I am the LORD your God. 5 Keep my decrees and laws,
for the man who obeys them will live by them. I am the LORD.
6 " 'No one is to approach any close relative to have sexual relations. I am the LORD.
7 " 'Do not dishonor your father by having sexual relations with
your mother. She is your mother; do not have relations with her.
8 " 'Do not have sexual relations with your father's wife; that
would dishonor your father.
9 " 'Do not have sexual relations with your sister, either your father's daughter or your mother's daughter, whether she was born
in the same home or elsewhere.
10 " 'Do not have sexual relations with your son's daughter or
your daughter's daughter; that would dishonor you.
11 " 'Do not have sexual relations with the daughter of your father's wife, born to your father; she is your sister.
12 " 'Do not have sexual relations with your father's sister; she is
your father's close relative.
13 " 'Do not have sexual relations with your mother's sister, because she is your mother's close relative.
14 " 'Do not dishonor your father's brother by approaching his
wife to have sexual relations; she is your aunt.
15 " 'Do not have sexual relations with your daughter-in-law. She
is your son's wife; do not have relations with her.
16 " 'Do not have sexual relations with your brother's wife; that
would dishonor your brother.
17 " 'Do not have sexual relations with both a woman and her
daughter. Do not have sexual relations with either her son's
daughter or her daughter's daughter; they are her close relatives.
That is wickedness.
18 " 'Do not take your wife's sister as a rival wife and have sexual relations with her while your wife is living.
19 " 'Do not approach a woman to have sexual relations during
the uncleanness of her monthly period.
20 " 'Do not have sexual relations with your neighbor's wife and
defile yourself with her.
21 " 'Do not give any of your children to be sacrificed[a] to Molech, for you must not profane the name of your God. I am the
LORD.
22 " 'Do not lie with a man as one lies with a woman; that is detestable.
23 " 'Do not have sexual relations with an animal and defile
yourself with it. A woman must not present herself to an animal to
have sexual relations with it; that is a perversion.
24 " 'Do not defile yourselves in any of these ways, because this
is how the nations that I am going to drive out before you became
defiled. 25 Even the land was defiled; so I punished it for its sin,
and the land vomited out its inhabitants. 26 But you must keep my
decrees and my laws. The native-born and the aliens living among
you must not do any of these detestable things, 27 for all these
things were done by the people who lived in the land before you,
and the land became defiled. 28 And if you defile the land, it will
vomit you out as it vomited out the nations that were before you.
29 " 'Everyone who does any of these detestable things—such
persons must be cut off from their people. 30 Keep my requirements and do not follow any of the detestable customs that were

[a] 21 Or *to be passed through ⌊the fire⌋*

(18:5–30) Holy and righteous Father, You made us and You know what is best for us. We are sacred to You. Thank You for not leaving us without instructions. Help us, Father, to keep ourselves undefiled. Give us discernment between what is socially acceptable and what is acceptable to You, and give us strength to live by our convictions. Do what You must to frighten us away from sin, and help us to be as fully committed to You as You are to us. (1Pe 2:9–12)

practiced before you came and do not defile yourselves with them.
I am the LORD your God.' "

Various Laws

19 The LORD said to Moses, 2"Speak to the entire assembly of
Israel and say to them: 'Be holy because I, the LORD your
God, am holy.
3" 'Each of you must respect his mother and father, and you
must observe my Sabbaths. I am the LORD your God.
4" 'Do not turn to idols or make gods of cast metal for yourselves. I am the LORD your God.
5" 'When you sacrifice a fellowship offering[a] to the LORD, sacrifice it in such a way that it will be accepted on your behalf. 6It
shall be eaten on the day you sacrifice it or on the next day; anything left over until the third day must be burned up. 7If any of it
is eaten on the third day, it is impure and will not be accepted.
8Whoever eats it will be held responsible because he has desecrated what is holy to the LORD; that person must be cut off from
his people.
9" 'When you reap the harvest of your land, do not reap to the
very edges of your field or gather the gleanings of your harvest.
10Do not go over your vineyard a second time or pick up the
grapes that have fallen. Leave them for the poor and the alien. I am
the LORD your God.
11" 'Do not steal.
" 'Do not lie.
" 'Do not deceive one another.
12" 'Do not swear falsely by my name and so profane the name
of your God. I am the LORD.
13" 'Do not defraud your neighbor or rob him.
" 'Do not hold back the wages of a hired man overnight.
14" 'Do not curse the deaf or put a stumbling block in front of
the blind, but fear your God. I am the LORD.
15" 'Do not pervert justice; do not show partiality to the poor or
favoritism to the great, but judge your neighbor fairly.
16" 'Do not go about spreading slander among your people.
" 'Do not do anything that endangers your neighbor's life. I am
the LORD.
17" 'Do not hate your brother in your heart. Rebuke your
neighbor frankly so you will not share in his guilt.
18" 'Do not seek revenge or bear a grudge against one of your
people, but love your neighbor as yourself. I am the LORD.
19" 'Keep my decrees.
" 'Do not mate different kinds of animals.
" 'Do not plant your field with two kinds of seed.
" 'Do not wear clothing woven of two kinds of material.
20" 'If a man sleeps with a woman who is a slave girl promised
to another man but who has not been ransomed or given her freedom, there must be due punishment. Yet they are not to be put to
death, because she had not been freed. 21The man, however, must
bring a ram to the entrance to the Tent of Meeting for a guilt offering to the LORD. 22With the ram of the guilt offering the priest is
to make atonement for him before the LORD for the sin he has
committed, and his sin will be forgiven.
23" 'When you enter the land and plant any kind of fruit tree,

[a] 5 Traditionally *peace offering*

The love of our neighbor is the only door out of the dungeon of self.
George MacDonald (1824-1905)

(19:9–18) Thank You, Father, for caring enough about us to tell us how to care for one another. Help us to treasure the gift of people, to treat each other with love and respect, to treat each other the way we want to be treated ourselves. And help us to do it, not just out of a sense of human decency, but out of worship. Help us to love with Your love and in Your way, out of love for You. (Mt 25:31–45; Eph 4:29–32)

MY BELOVED

My entire law is summed up in a single command: "Love your neighbor as yourself." Love does no harm to its neighbor. Therefore love is the fulfillment of the law.

Clothe yourself with compassion, kindness, humility, gentleness and patience. Forgive whatever grievances you may have against anyone. Forgive as I have forgiven you. And over all these virtues put on love, which binds them all together in perfect unity.

Imitate Me as my beloved child, and live a life of love. Endeavor to love others in the way that My Son loved you. If you do this then all people will know that you are His disciple.

Do not repay evil with evil or insult with insult, but with blessing, because this is what I have called you to so that you may inherit My blessing. Do not envy others or keep a record of how they have wronged you. Get rid of all bitterness, rage and anger; for this does not bring about the righteous life that I desire. Do not seek revenge or bear a grudge against your brother. Instead, seek peace and pursue it.

Let the peace of Christ rule in your heart, and let the word of Christ dwell in you richly as you teach and admonish others with all wisdom, and as you sing psalms, hymns and spiritual songs with gratitude in your heart to Me. And whatever you do, whether in word or deed, do it all in the name of the Lord Jesus, giving thanks to Me, your Father, through Him.

Lev 19:18; Jn 13:34-35; Ro 13:10; 1Co 13:4-5; Gal 5:14; Eph 4:31–5:2; Col 3:12-15; Jas 1:20; 1Pe 3:9,11

regard its fruit as forbidden.[a] For three years you are to consider it forbidden[a]; it must not be eaten. 24In the fourth year all its fruit will be holy, an offering of praise to the LORD. 25But in the fifth year you may eat its fruit. In this way your harvest will be increased. I am the LORD your God.

26" 'Do not eat any meat with the blood still in it.

" 'Do not practice divination or sorcery.

27" 'Do not cut the hair at the sides of your head or clip off the edges of your beard.

28" 'Do not cut your bodies for the dead or put tattoo marks on yourselves. I am the LORD.

29" 'Do not degrade your daughter by making her a prostitute, or the land will turn to prostitution and be filled with wickedness.

30" 'Observe my Sabbaths and have reverence for my sanctuary. I am the LORD.

31" 'Do not turn to mediums or seek out spiritists, for you will be defiled by them. I am the LORD your God.

32" 'Rise in the presence of the aged, show respect for the elderly and revere your God. I am the LORD.

33" 'When an alien lives with you in your land, do not mistreat him. 34The alien living with you must be treated as one of your native-born. Love him as yourself, for you were aliens in Egypt. I am the LORD your God.

35" 'Do not use dishonest standards when measuring length, weight or quantity. 36Use honest scales and honest weights, an honest ephah[b] and an honest hin.[c] I am the LORD your God, who brought you out of Egypt.

37" 'Keep all my decrees and all my laws and follow them. I am the LORD.' "

Punishments for Sin

20 The LORD said to Moses, 2"Say to the Israelites: 'Any Israelite or any alien living in Israel who gives[d] any of his children to Molech must be put to death. The people of the community are to stone him. 3I will set my face against that man and I will cut him off from his people; for by giving his children to Molech, he has defiled my sanctuary and profaned my holy name. 4If the people of the community close their eyes when that man gives one of his children to Molech and they fail to put him to death, 5I will set my face against that man and his family and will cut off from their people both him and all who follow him in prostituting themselves to Molech.

6" 'I will set my face against the person who turns to mediums and spiritists to prostitute himself by following them, and I will cut him off from his people.

7" 'Consecrate yourselves and be holy, because I am the LORD your God. 8Keep my decrees and follow them. I am the LORD, who makes you holy.[e]

9" 'If anyone curses his father or mother, he must be put to death. He has cursed his father or his mother, and his blood will be on his own head.

10" 'If a man commits adultery with another man's wife—with the wife of his neighbor—both the adulterer and the adulteress must be put to death.

[a]23 Hebrew *uncircumcised* [b]36 An ephah was a dry measure. [c]36 A hin was a liquid measure. [d]2 Or *sacrifices*; also in verses 3 and 4 [e]8 Or *who sanctifies you*; or *who sets you apart as holy*

(19:33–37) O Lord, how You love righteousness. Fairness and compassion are Your hallmarks. Help us to treat everyone with equal weights of mercy and measurements of forgiveness, equal lengths of patience and quantities of love. Help Your church to welcome every race and social strata with equal acceptance and dignity just as You do. Help us, Lord, to manifest Your character in every relationship. In all our ways, let us bring honor to Your name.

Kindness has converted more sinners than zeal, eloquence, or learning.

Frederick William Faber (1814–1863)

O sweetest Love, Your grace on us
bestow;
Set our hearts with sacred fire
aglow,
That with hearts united we love
each other,
Ev'ry stranger, sister and brother.
Lord, have mercy!

"To God the Holy Spirit Let Us Pray"
Martin Luther (1483–1546)
Trans. Worship Supplement (©1969)

A holy life is not an ascetic, or gloomy, or solitary life, but a life regulated by divine truth and faithful in Christian duty. It is living above the world while we are still in it.

Tryon Edwards (1809-1894)

(20:22–26) As Israel was set apart as a unique and holy nation, so are we, Your church, set apart for Your service. You have set us apart to salt the earth, to bless the nations, to demonstrate righteousness to the world. Oh how we want to please You. Work in our spirits, Lord, so that we will have the strength and wisdom to make Your name great throughout the earth. You have chosen and called us; we are answering. Thank You for making us Your people; now please use us for Jesus' sake. (Mt 5:13; 1Pe 2:9)

Set me apart for yourself,
O Lord,
Deep in my heart, set me apart,
Let me know nothing but more of
You.
Take me Lord, set me apart.
Set me apart from the things that
would hinder me,
Taking attention from You;
I want to serve You with single
devotion,
Wholly committed to You.

"Set Me Apart"
Walt Harrah (©1991)

11“ ‘If a man sleeps with his father's wife, he has dishonored his
father. Both the man and the woman must be put to death; their
blood will be on their own heads.
12“ ‘If a man sleeps with his daughter-in-law, both of them must
be put to death. What they have done is a perversion; their blood
will be on their own heads.
13“ ‘If a man lies with a man as one lies with a woman, both of
them have done what is detestable. They must be put to death; their
blood will be on their own heads.
14“ ‘If a man marries both a woman and her mother, it is
wicked. Both he and they must be burned in the fire, so that no
wickedness will be among you.
15“ ‘If a man has sexual relations with an animal, he must be put
to death, and you must kill the animal.
16“ ‘If a woman approaches an animal to have sexual relations
with it, kill both the woman and the animal. They must be put to
death; their blood will be on their own heads.
17“ ‘If a man marries his sister, the daughter of either his father
or his mother, and they have sexual relations, it is a disgrace. They
must be cut off before the eyes of their people. He has dishonored
his sister and will be held responsible.
18“ ‘If a man lies with a woman during her monthly period and
has sexual relations with her, he has exposed the source of her
flow, and she has also uncovered it. Both of them must be cut off
from their people.
19“ ‘Do not have sexual relations with the sister of either your
mother or your father, for that would dishonor a close relative;
both of you would be held responsible.
20“ ‘If a man sleeps with his aunt, he has dishonored his uncle.
They will be held responsible; they will die childless.
21“ ‘If a man marries his brother's wife, it is an act of impurity;
he has dishonored his brother. They will be childless.
22“ ‘Keep all my decrees and laws and follow them, so that the
land where I am bringing you to live may not vomit you out. 23You
must not live according to the customs of the nations I am going to
drive out before you. Because they did all these things, I abhorred
them. 24But I said to you, "You will possess their land; I will give it
to you as an inheritance, a land flowing with milk and honey." I am
the LORD your God, who has set you apart from the nations.
25“ ‘You must therefore make a distinction between clean and
unclean animals and between unclean and clean birds. Do not defile yourselves by any animal or bird or anything that moves along
the ground—those which I have set apart as unclean for you.
26You are to be holy to me[a] because I, the LORD, am holy, and I
have set you apart from the nations to be my own.
27“ ‘A man or woman who is a medium or spiritist among you
must be put to death. You are to stone them; their blood will be on
their own heads.’ ”

Rules for Priests

21 The LORD said to Moses, "Speak to the priests, the sons of
Aaron, and say to them: 'A priest must not make himself ceremonially unclean for any of his people who die, 2except for a
close relative, such as his mother or father, his son or daughter, his
brother, 3or an unmarried sister who is dependent on him since

[a]26 Or *be my holy ones*

she has no husband—for her he may make himself unclean. 4He
must not make himself unclean for people related to him by marriage,[a] and so defile himself.
5" 'Priests must not shave their heads or shave off the edges of
their beards or cut their bodies. 6They must be holy to their God
and must not profane the name of their God. Because they present
the offerings made to the LORD by fire, the food of their God, they
are to be holy.
7" 'They must not marry women defiled by prostitution or divorced from their husbands, because priests are holy to their God.
8Regard them as holy, because they offer up the food of your God.
Consider them holy, because I the LORD am holy—I who make you
holy.[b]
9" 'If a priest's daughter defiles herself by becoming a prostitute, she disgraces her father; she must be burned in the fire.
10" 'The high priest, the one among his brothers who has had
the anointing oil poured on his head and who has been ordained
to wear the priestly garments, must not let his hair become unkempt[c] or tear his clothes. 11He must not enter a place where
there is a dead body. He must not make himself unclean, even for
his father or mother, 12nor leave the sanctuary of his God or desecrate it, because he has been dedicated by the anointing oil of his
God. I am the LORD.
13" 'The woman he marries must be a virgin. 14He must not
marry a widow, a divorced woman, or a woman defiled by prostitution, but only a virgin from his own people, 15so he will not defile his offspring among his people. I am the LORD, who makes him
holy.[d] ' "
16The LORD said to Moses, 17"Say to Aaron: 'For the generations
to come none of your descendants who has a defect may come
near to offer the food of his God. 18No man who has any defect may
come near: no man who is blind or lame, disfigured or deformed;
19no man with a crippled foot or hand, 20or who is hunchbacked
or dwarfed, or who has any eye defect, or who has festering or running sores or damaged testicles. 21No descendant of Aaron the
priest who has any defect is to come near to present the offerings
made to the LORD by fire. He has a defect; he must not come near
to offer the food of his God. 22He may eat the most holy food of his
God, as well as the holy food; 23yet because of his defect, he must
not go near the curtain or approach the altar, and so desecrate my
sanctuary. I am the LORD, who makes them holy.[e] ' "
24So Moses told this to Aaron and his sons and to all the Israelites.

22 The LORD said to Moses, 2"Tell Aaron and his sons to treat
with respect the sacred offerings the Israelites consecrate to
me, so they will not profane my holy name. I am the LORD.
3"Say to them: 'For the generations to come, if any of your descendants is ceremonially unclean and yet comes near the sacred
offerings that the Israelites consecrate to the LORD, that person
must be cut off from my presence. I am the LORD.
4" 'If a descendant of Aaron has an infectious skin disease[f] or a
bodily discharge, he may not eat the sacred offerings until he is

[a] 4 Or *unclean as a leader among his people* [b] 8 Or *who sanctify you*; or *who set you apart as holy* [c] 10 Or *not uncover his head* [d] 15 Or *who sanctifies him*; or *who sets him apart as holy* [e] 23 Or *who sanctifies them*; or *who sets them apart as holy*
[f] 4 Traditionally *leprosy*; the Hebrew word was used for various diseases affecting the skin—not necessarily leprosy.

(21:1–8) I pray for those whom You have called out from among us to serve as leaders in worship. Help them to conduct their lives in a way that points to Your holiness. May they take leadership in demonstrating a life that is set apart for You.

A person who lives right, and is right, has more power in his silence than another has by words.

Phillips Brooks (1835–1893)

(22:9) You are a God of infinite purity. There is no privilege or level of spiritual achievement that causes You to wink at sin. Help me to be diligent to guard my heart, to put away perversity from my mouth, to keep my eyes looking straight ahead and to take only ways that are firm. Teach me to hate evil and to cling to what is good. Though now I am invited to come to You with confidence, may I never come with presumption or disrespect. Only You are able to keep me from falling and to present me before Your glorious presence without fault and with great joy. And so to You, God my Savior, be glory, majesty, power and authority, through Jesus Christ my Lord, before all ages, now and forevermore! Amen. (Pr 4:23–26; Ecc 5:1; Ro 12:9; Heb 4:16; Jude 1:24–25)

Take time to be holy;
The world rushes on.
Spend much time in secret
With Jesus alone.
By looking to Jesus,
Like Him thou shalt be;
Thy friends in thy conduct
His likeness shall see.

"Take Time to Be Holy"
William D. Longstaff (1882)

cleansed. He will also be unclean if he touches something defiled by
a corpse or by anyone who has an emission of semen, 5or if he
touches any crawling thing that makes him unclean, or any person
who makes him unclean, whatever the uncleanness may be. 6The
one who touches any such thing will be unclean till evening. He
must not eat any of the sacred offerings unless he has bathed himself with water. 7When the sun goes down, he will be clean, and
after that he may eat the sacred offerings, for they are his food. 8He
must not eat anything found dead or torn by wild animals, and so
become unclean through it. I am the LORD.

9" 'The priests are to keep my requirements so that they do not
become guilty and die for treating them with contempt. I am the
LORD, who makes them holy.[a]

10" 'No one outside a priest's family may eat the sacred offering,
nor may the guest of a priest or his hired worker eat it. 11But if a
priest buys a slave with money, or if a slave is born in his household,
that slave may eat his food. 12If a priest's daughter marries anyone
other than a priest, she may not eat any of the sacred contributions.
13But if a priest's daughter becomes a widow or is divorced, yet has
no children, and she returns to live in her father's house as in her
youth, she may eat of her father's food. No unauthorized person,
however, may eat any of it.

14" 'If anyone eats a sacred offering by mistake, he must make
restitution to the priest for the offering and add a fifth of the value
to it. 15The priests must not desecrate the sacred offerings the Israelites present to the LORD 16by allowing them to eat the sacred offerings and so bring upon them guilt requiring payment. I am the
LORD, who makes them holy.' "

Unacceptable Sacrifices

17The LORD said to Moses, 18"Speak to Aaron and his sons and to
all the Israelites and say to them: 'If any of you—either an Israelite
or an alien living in Israel—presents a gift for a burnt offering to the
LORD, either to fulfill a vow or as a freewill offering, 19you must present a male without defect from the cattle, sheep or goats in order
that it may be accepted on your behalf. 20Do not bring anything with
a defect, because it will not be accepted on your behalf. 21When
anyone brings from the herd or flock a fellowship offering[b] to the
LORD to fulfill a special vow or as a freewill offering, it must be without defect or blemish to be acceptable. 22Do not offer to the LORD
the blind, the injured or the maimed, or anything with warts or festering or running sores. Do not place any of these on the altar as an
offering made to the LORD by fire. 23You may, however, present as a
freewill offering an ox[c] or a sheep that is deformed or stunted, but
it will not be accepted in fulfillment of a vow. 24You must not offer
to the LORD an animal whose testicles are bruised, crushed, torn or
cut. You must not do this in your own land, 25and you must not accept such animals from the hand of a foreigner and offer them as
the food of your God. They will not be accepted on your behalf, because they are deformed and have defects.' "

26The LORD said to Moses, 27"When a calf, a lamb or a goat is
born, it is to remain with its mother for seven days. From the eighth
day on, it will be acceptable as an offering made to the LORD by fire.
28Do not slaughter a cow or a sheep and its young on the same day.

[a] *9* Or *who sanctifies them*; or *who sets them apart as holy*; also in verse 16
[b] *21* Traditionally *peace offering* [c] *23* The Hebrew word can include both male and female.

29“When you sacrifice a thank offering to the LORD, sacrifice it
in such a way that it will be accepted on your behalf. 30It must be
eaten that same day; leave none of it till morning. I am the LORD.
31“Keep my commands and follow them. I am the LORD. 32Do
not profane my holy name. I must be acknowledged as holy by the
Israelites. I am the LORD, who makes[a] you holy[b] 33and who
brought you out of Egypt to be your God. I am the LORD.”

23 The LORD said to Moses, 2“Speak to the Israelites and say
to them: ‘These are my appointed feasts, the appointed
feasts of the LORD, which you are to proclaim as sacred assemblies.

The Sabbath

3“ ‘There are six days when you may work, but the seventh day
is a Sabbath of rest, a day of sacred assembly. You are not to do
any work; wherever you live, it is a Sabbath to the LORD.

The Passover and Unleavened Bread

4“ ‘These are the LORD’s appointed feasts, the sacred assemblies
you are to proclaim at their appointed times: 5The LORD’s Passover
begins at twilight on the fourteenth day of the first month. 6On the
fifteenth day of that month the LORD’s Feast of Unleavened Bread
begins; for seven days you must eat bread made without yeast. 7On
the first day hold a sacred assembly and do no regular work. 8For
seven days present an offering made to the LORD by fire. And on the
seventh day hold a sacred assembly and do no regular work.’ ”

Firstfruits

9The LORD said to Moses, 10“Speak to the Israelites and say to
them: ‘When you enter the land I am going to give you and you
reap its harvest, bring to the priest a sheaf of the first grain you
harvest. 11He is to wave the sheaf before the LORD so it will be accepted on your behalf; the priest is to wave it on the day after the
Sabbath. 12On the day you wave the sheaf, you must sacrifice as a
burnt offering to the LORD a lamb a year old without defect, 13to-
gether with its grain offering of two-tenths of an ephah[c] of fine
flour mixed with oil—an offering made to the LORD by fire, a
pleasing aroma—and its drink offering of a quarter of a hin[d] of
wine. 14You must not eat any bread, or roasted or new grain, until
the very day you bring this offering to your God. This is to be a lasting ordinance for the generations to come, wherever you live.

Feast of Weeks

15“ ‘From the day after the Sabbath, the day you brought the
sheaf of the wave offering, count off seven full weeks. 16Count off
fifty days up to the day after the seventh Sabbath, and then present
an offering of new grain to the LORD. 17From wherever you live,
bring two loaves made of two-tenths of an ephah of fine flour,
baked with yeast, as a wave offering of firstfruits to the LORD.
18Present with this bread seven male lambs, each a year old and
without defect, one young bull and two rams. They will be a burnt
offering to the LORD, together with their grain offerings and drink
offerings—an offering made by fire, an aroma pleasing to the

[a] 32 Or *made* [b] 32 Or *who sanctifies you*; or *who sets you apart as holy* [c] 13 That is, probably about 4 quarts (about 4.5 liters); also in verse 17 [d] 13 That is, probably about 1 quart (about 1 liter)

(22:32) Thank You, Father, for the gift of holiness. We are not Yours because we are holy; we are holy because we are Yours. Now help us to live as holy people. Teach us to “purify ourselves from everything that contaminates body and spirit, perfecting holiness out of reverence for God.” And as we grow in Your holiness, righteousness and faith, may we bring glory, honor and praise to Your name. (2Co 7:1; Heb 2:11; 1Pe 1:15–16)

Take time to be holy;
Be calm in thy soul
Each thot and each motive
Beneath His control.
Thus led by His Spirit
To fountains of love,
Thou soon shall be fitted
For service above.

“Take Time to Be Holy”
William D. Longstaff (1882)

Our progress in holiness depends on God and ourselves—on God’s grace and on our will to be holy.

Mother Teresa of Calcutta (1910-1997)

(23:18–40) Thank You, Father, for Your kindness and faithfulness to us. These feasts and assemblies were days of rest—days set apart to gather with the people of faith and to remember Your goodness, to seek Your forgiveness, and to celebrate Your provision year after year. You are an unchanging God, and the memory of past encounters with You builds our faith for future encounters with You. You provided for us, and You will provide again. You forgave us, and You will forgive again. You delivered us, and You will deliver again. Thank You, Father, that we can rest secure in the hope of Your unchanging faithfulness.

LORD. 19Then sacrifice one male goat for a sin offering and two
lambs, each a year old, for a fellowship offering.[a] 20The priest is
to wave the two lambs before the LORD as a wave offering, together with the bread of the firstfruits. They are a sacred offering to
the LORD for the priest. 21On that same day you are to proclaim a
sacred assembly and do no regular work. This is to be a lasting
ordinance for the generations to come, wherever you live.
22" 'When you reap the harvest of your land, do not reap to
the very edges of your field or gather the gleanings of your harvest. Leave them for the poor and the alien. I am the LORD your
God.' "

Feast of Trumpets

23The LORD said to Moses, 24"Say to the Israelites: 'On the first
day of the seventh month you are to have a day of rest, a sacred
assembly commemorated with trumpet blasts. 25Do no regular
work, but present an offering made to the LORD by fire.' "

Day of Atonement

26The LORD said to Moses, 27"The tenth day of this seventh
month is the Day of Atonement. Hold a sacred assembly and
deny yourselves,[b] and present an offering made to the LORD by
fire. 28Do no work on that day, because it is the Day of Atonement, when atonement is made for you before the LORD your
God. 29Anyone who does not deny himself on that day must be
cut off from his people. 30I will destroy from among his people
anyone who does any work on that day. 31You shall do no work
at all. This is to be a lasting ordinance for the generations to
come, wherever you live. 32It is a sabbath of rest for you, and
you must deny yourselves. From the evening of the ninth day of
the month until the following evening you are to observe your
sabbath."

Feast of Tabernacles

33The LORD said to Moses, 34"Say to the Israelites: 'On the fifteenth day of the seventh month the LORD's Feast of Tabernacles
begins, and it lasts for seven days. 35The first day is a sacred assembly; do no regular work. 36For seven days present offerings
made to the LORD by fire, and on the eighth day hold a sacred assembly and present an offering made to the LORD by fire. It is the
closing assembly; do no regular work.
37(" 'These are the LORD's appointed feasts, which you are to
proclaim as sacred assemblies for bringing offerings made to the
LORD by fire—the burnt offerings and grain offerings, sacrifices
and drink offerings required for each day. 38These offerings are
in addition to those for the LORD's Sabbaths and[c] in addition to
your gifts and whatever you have vowed and all the freewill offerings you give to the LORD.)
39" 'So beginning with the fifteenth day of the seventh month,
after you have gathered the crops of the land, celebrate the festival to the LORD for seven days; the first day is a day of rest, and
the eighth day also is a day of rest. 40On the first day you are to
take choice fruit from the trees, and palm fronds, leafy branches
and poplars, and rejoice before the LORD your God for seven
days. 41Celebrate this as a festival to the LORD for seven days each

[a] *19* Traditionally *peace offering* [b] *27* Or *and fast*; also in verses 29 and 32 [c] *38* Or *These feasts are in addition to the LORD's Sabbaths, and these offerings are*

year. This is to be a lasting ordinance for the generations to come;
celebrate it in the seventh month. 42Live in booths for seven days:
All native-born Israelites are to live in booths 43so your descendants will know that I had the Israelites live in booths when I
brought them out of Egypt. I am the LORD your God.' "
44So Moses announced to the Israelites the appointed feasts of
the LORD.

Oil and Bread Set Before the LORD

24 The LORD said to Moses, 2"Command the Israelites to bring
you clear oil of pressed olives for the light so that the
lamps may be kept burning continually. 3Outside the curtain of
the Testimony in the Tent of Meeting, Aaron is to tend the lamps
before the LORD from evening till morning, continually. This is to
be a lasting ordinance for the generations to come. 4The lamps on
the pure gold lampstand before the LORD must be tended continually.
5"Take fine flour and bake twelve loaves of bread, using two-
tenths of an ephah[a] for each loaf. 6Set them in two rows, six in
each row, on the table of pure gold before the LORD. 7Along each
row put some pure incense as a memorial portion to represent the
bread and to be an offering made to the LORD by fire. 8This bread
is to be set out before the LORD regularly, Sabbath after Sabbath, on
behalf of the Israelites, as a lasting covenant. 9It belongs to Aaron
and his sons, who are to eat it in a holy place, because it is a most
holy part of their regular share of the offerings made to the LORD
by fire."

A Blasphemer Stoned

10Now the son of an Israelite mother and an Egyptian father
went out among the Israelites, and a fight broke out in the camp
between him and an Israelite. 11The son of the Israelite woman
blasphemed the Name with a curse; so they brought him to Moses.
(His mother's name was Shelomith, the daughter of Dibri the Danite.) 12They put him in custody until the will of the LORD should be
made clear to them.
13Then the LORD said to Moses: 14"Take the blasphemer outside the camp. All those who heard him are to lay their hands on
his head, and the entire assembly is to stone him. 15Say to the Israelites: 'If anyone curses his God, he will be held responsible;
16anyone who blasphemes the name of the LORD must be put to
death. The entire assembly must stone him. Whether an alien or
native-born, when he blasphemes the Name, he must be put to
death.
17" 'If anyone takes the life of a human being, he must be put to
death. 18Anyone who takes the life of someone's animal must
make restitution—life for life. 19If anyone injures his neighbor,
whatever he has done must be done to him: 20fracture for frac-
ture, eye for eye, tooth for tooth. As he has injured the other, so he
is to be injured. 21Whoever kills an animal must make restitution,
but whoever kills a man must be put to death. 22You are to have
the same law for the alien and the native-born. I am the LORD your
God.' "
23Then Moses spoke to the Israelites, and they took the blas-

[a] 5 That is, probably about 4 quarts (about 4.5 liters)

(24:2) You, Lord, are the light of the world. We are a multitude of little lamps, ignited from Your flame and set on a hill for the world to see. Keep us full of the holy oil of Your Word and Your Spirit. Where our flames have burned low, we rejoice that You will not extinguish us, but will rekindle us and give us hearts ablaze for holiness. We plead for a fresh touch, fresh oil, fresh fire. (Ex 27:21; Isa 42:3; Mt 5:14–16; 12:20)

A holy life will produce the deepest impression. Lighthouses blow no horns; they only shine.

Dwight Lyman Moody (1837–1899)

phemer outside the camp and stoned him. The Israelites did as the
LORD commanded Moses.

The Sabbath Year

25 The LORD said to Moses on Mount Sinai, 2“Speak to the Israelites and say to them: ‘When you enter the land I am
going to give you, the land itself must observe a sabbath to the
LORD. 3For six years sow your fields, and for six years prune your
vineyards and gather their crops. 4But in the seventh year the land
is to have a sabbath of rest, a sabbath to the LORD. Do not sow your
fields or prune your vineyards. 5Do not reap what grows of itself
or harvest the grapes of your untended vines. The land is to have
a year of rest. 6Whatever the land yields during the sabbath year
will be food for you—for yourself, your manservant and maidservant, and the hired worker and temporary resident who live
among you, 7as well as for your livestock and the wild animals in
your land. Whatever the land produces may be eaten.

The Year of Jubilee

8“ ‘Count off seven sabbaths of years—seven times seven
years—so that the seven sabbaths of years amount to a period of
forty-nine years. 9Then have the trumpet sounded everywhere on
the tenth day of the seventh month; on the Day of Atonement
sound the trumpet throughout your land. 10Consecrate the fiftieth
year and proclaim liberty throughout the land to all its inhabitants.
It shall be a jubilee for you; each one of you is to return to his family property and each to his own clan. 11The fiftieth year shall be
a jubilee for you; do not sow and do not reap what grows of itself
or harvest the untended vines. 12For it is a jubilee and is to be
holy for you; eat only what is taken directly from the fields.

13“ ‘In this Year of Jubilee everyone is to return to his own
property.

14“ ‘If you sell land to one of your countrymen or buy any from
him, do not take advantage of each other. 15You are to buy from
your countryman on the basis of the number of years since the Jubilee. And he is to sell to you on the basis of the number of years
left for harvesting crops. 16When the years are many, you are to increase the price, and when the years are few, you are to decrease
the price, because what he is really selling you is the number of
crops. 17Do not take advantage of each other, but fear your God.
I am the LORD your God.

18“ ‘Follow my decrees and be careful to obey my laws, and you
will live safely in the land. 19Then the land will yield its fruit, and
you will eat your fill and live there in safety. 20You may ask, “What
will we eat in the seventh year if we do not plant or harvest our
crops?” 21I will send you such a blessing in the sixth year that the
land will yield enough for three years. 22While you plant during
the eighth year, you will eat from the old crop and will continue to
eat from it until the harvest of the ninth year comes in.

23“ ‘The land must not be sold permanently, because the land is
mine and you are but aliens and my tenants. 24Throughout the
country that you hold as a possession, you must provide for the redemption of the land.

25“ ‘If one of your countrymen becomes poor and sells some of
his property, his nearest relative is to come and redeem what his
countryman has sold. 26If, however, a man has no one to redeem
it for him but he himself prospers and acquires sufficient means

(25:18–23) Everything we have is Yours, O Lord. We are Your tenants, Your servants, the stewards of Your property. You are not a harsh taskmaster. You know our feeble frame, our need for rest, our fear of never having enough, and our propensity to burn ourselves out. We acknowledge gratefully the bounty of Your grace. How marvelous to see that You anticipate our obedience, even rewarding it ahead of time through Your abundant provision! So help us, Lord, to trust You more, to walk in obedience, and to take better care of ourselves and Your world according to Your plan.

We are not our own, anymore than what we possess is our own. We did not make ourselves; we cannot be supreme over ourselves. We cannot be our own masters. We are God's property by creation, by redemption, by regeneration.

Cardinal John Henry Newman (1801–1890)

to redeem it, 27he is to determine the value for the years since he
sold it and refund the balance to the man to whom he sold it; he
can then go back to his own property. 28But if he does not acquire
the means to repay him, what he sold will remain in the possession of the buyer until the Year of Jubilee. It will be returned in the
Jubilee, and he can then go back to his property.
29" 'If a man sells a house in a walled city, he retains the right
of redemption a full year after its sale. During that time he may redeem it. 30If it is not redeemed before a full year has passed, the
house in the walled city shall belong permanently to the buyer and
his descendants. It is not to be returned in the Jubilee. 31But
houses in villages without walls around them are to be considered
as open country. They can be redeemed, and they are to be returned in the Jubilee.
32" 'The Levites always have the right to redeem their houses in
the Levitical towns, which they possess. 33So the property of the
Levites is redeemable—that is, a house sold in any town they
hold—and is to be returned in the Jubilee, because the houses in
the towns of the Levites are their property among the Israelites.
34But the pastureland belonging to their towns must not be sold;
it is their permanent possession.
35" 'If one of your countrymen becomes poor and is unable to
support himself among you, help him as you would an alien or a
temporary resident, so he can continue to live among you. 36Do
not take interest of any kind[a] from him, but fear your God, so that
your countryman may continue to live among you. 37You must not
lend him money at interest or sell him food at a profit. 38I am the
LORD your God, who brought you out of Egypt to give you the land
of Canaan and to be your God.
39" 'If one of your countrymen becomes poor among you and
sells himself to you, do not make him work as a slave. 40He is to
be treated as a hired worker or a temporary resident among you;
he is to work for you until the Year of Jubilee. 41Then he and his
children are to be released, and he will go back to his own clan
and to the property of his forefathers. 42Because the Israelites are
my servants, whom I brought out of Egypt, they must not be sold
as slaves. 43Do not rule over them ruthlessly, but fear your God.
44" 'Your male and female slaves are to come from the nations
around you; from them you may buy slaves. 45You may also buy
some of the temporary residents living among you and members
of their clans born in your country, and they will become your
property. 46You can will them to your children as inherited property and can make them slaves for life, but you must not rule over
your fellow Israelites ruthlessly.
47" 'If an alien or a temporary resident among you becomes
rich and one of your countrymen becomes poor and sells himself
to the alien living among you or to a member of the alien's clan,
48he retains the right of redemption after he has sold himself. One
of his relatives may redeem him: 49An uncle or a cousin or any
blood relative in his clan may redeem him. Or if he prospers, he
may redeem himself. 50He and his buyer are to count the time
from the year he sold himself up to the Year of Jubilee. The price
for his release is to be based on the rate paid to a hired man for
that number of years. 51If many years remain, he must pay for his
redemption a larger share of the price paid for him. 52If only a

[a] *36* Or *take excessive interest*; similarly in verse 37

(25:25–48) O Lord, our Redeemer and the Redeemer of Israel, You provided a way for both property and life to be redeemed in the ancient days of Israel. Those of your children who were in slavery or bondage could be set free by a kinsman-redeemer paying the price of redemption. And that is exactly what You did for us. When we could do nothing, being sold to sin, You stepped in and purchased us with Your own blood, so that You might become our Kinsman-Redeemer. We have forever been set free because of Your sacrificial love. (Ru 4:5–10; Job 19:25; Isa 59:20; Jer 31:11; Ro 3:24–26)

You are worthy to receive all the
honor
You are worthy to receive all the
glory
You are worthy to receive all the
power
You have purchased us
You have purchased us
You have purchased us
With Your blood

"You Have Purchased Us"
Joseph Garlington (©1995)

(26:1–21) Righteous Father, You are fair and just in all Your ways. You reward those who earnestly seek You. With obedience comes abundance of blessing—more than enough to give away. With submission comes safety. With faith comes favor. With worship comes peace and rest. But with disobedience comes discipline. The choice is ours. Thank You, Lord, for the riches of Your kindness, tolerance and patience. (Ro 2:4; Heb 11:6)

Earnestly I seek You
In this weary land,
For Your love is life to me.
In the sanctuary
I will lift my hands
Only to You, my King.
For my soul thirsts for You, oh God,
And my heart yearns for You,
oh God,
My eyes long to see Your face.
For You are holy in power and glory,
In kindness and mercy, oh God.
For You are holy, oh God.

"Earnestly I Seek You"
Beverly Darnall and John Darnall (©1991)

Freedom does not mean I am able to do whatever I want to do. That's the worst kind of bondage. Freedom means I have been set free to become all that God wants me to be, to achieve all that God wants me to achieve, to enjoy all that God wants me to enjoy.

Warren W. Wiersbe (1929-)

few years remain until the Year of Jubilee, he is to compute that
and pay for his redemption accordingly. 53He is to be treated as a
man hired from year to year; you must see to it that his owner
does not rule over him ruthlessly.
54" 'Even if he is not redeemed in any of these ways, he and his
children are to be released in the Year of Jubilee, 55for the Israelites belong to me as servants. They are my servants, whom I
brought out of Egypt. I am the LORD your God.

Reward for Obedience

26 " 'Do not make idols or set up an image or a sacred stone
for yourselves, and do not place a carved stone in your
land to bow down before it. I am the LORD your God.
2" 'Observe my Sabbaths and have reverence for my sanctuary.
I am the LORD.
3" 'If you follow my decrees and are careful to obey my commands, 4I will send you rain in its season, and the ground will
yield its crops and the trees of the field their fruit. 5Your threshing will continue until grape harvest and the grape harvest will
continue until planting, and you will eat all the food you want and
live in safety in your land.
6" 'I will grant peace in the land, and you will lie down and no
one will make you afraid. I will remove savage beasts from the
land, and the sword will not pass through your country. 7You will
pursue your enemies, and they will fall by the sword before you.
8Five of you will chase a hundred, and a hundred of you will chase
ten thousand, and your enemies will fall by the sword before you.
9" 'I will look on you with favor and make you fruitful and increase your numbers, and I will keep my covenant with you. 10You
will still be eating last year's harvest when you will have to move it
out to make room for the new. 11I will put my dwelling place[a]
among you, and I will not abhor you. 12I will walk among you and
be your God, and you will be my people. 13I am the LORD your
God, who brought you out of Egypt so that you would no longer be
slaves to the Egyptians; I broke the bars of your yoke and enabled
you to walk with heads held high.

Punishment for Disobedience

14" 'But if you will not listen to me and carry out all these commands, 15and if you reject my decrees and abhor my laws and fail
to carry out all my commands and so violate my covenant, 16then
I will do this to you: I will bring upon you sudden terror, wasting
diseases and fever that will destroy your sight and drain away your
life. You will plant seed in vain, because your enemies will eat it.
17I will set my face against you so that you will be defeated by your
enemies; those who hate you will rule over you, and you will flee
even when no one is pursuing you.
18" 'If after all this you will not listen to me, I will punish you
for your sins seven times over. 19I will break down your stubborn
pride and make the sky above you like iron and the ground beneath you like bronze. 20Your strength will be spent in vain, because your soil will not yield its crops, nor will the trees of the
land yield their fruit.
21" 'If you remain hostile toward me and refuse to listen to me,
I will multiply your afflictions seven times over, as your sins de-

[a] 11 Or *my tabernacle*

serve. 22I will send wild animals against you, and they will rob you
of your children, destroy your cattle and make you so few in number that your roads will be deserted.
23" 'If in spite of these things you do not accept my correction
but continue to be hostile toward me, 24I myself will be hostile toward you and will afflict you for your sins seven times over. 25And
I will bring the sword upon you to avenge the breaking of the covenant. When you withdraw into your cities, I will send a plague
among you, and you will be given into enemy hands. 26When I cut
off your supply of bread, ten women will be able to bake your
bread in one oven, and they will dole out the bread by weight. You
will eat, but you will not be satisfied.
27" 'If in spite of this you still do not listen to me but continue
to be hostile toward me, 28then in my anger I will be hostile toward you, and I myself will punish you for your sins seven times
over. 29You will eat the flesh of your sons and the flesh of your
daughters. 30I will destroy your high places, cut down your incense altars and pile your dead bodies on the lifeless forms of
your idols, and I will abhor you. 31I will turn your cities into ruins
and lay waste your sanctuaries, and I will take no delight in the
pleasing aroma of your offerings. 32I will lay waste the land, so
that your enemies who live there will be appalled. 33I will scatter
you among the nations and will draw out my sword and pursue
you. Your land will be laid waste, and your cities will lie in ruins.
34Then the land will enjoy its sabbath years all the time that it lies
desolate and you are in the country of your enemies; then the land
will rest and enjoy its sabbaths. 35All the time that it lies desolate,
the land will have the rest it did not have during the sabbaths you
lived in it.
36" 'As for those of you who are left, I will make their hearts so
fearful in the lands of their enemies that the sound of a windblown
leaf will put them to flight. They will run as though fleeing from the
sword, and they will fall, even though no one is pursuing them.
37They will stumble over one another as though fleeing from the
sword, even though no one is pursuing them. So you will not be
able to stand before your enemies. 38You will perish among the
nations; the land of your enemies will devour you. 39Those of you
who are left will waste away in the lands of their enemies because
of their sins; also because of their fathers' sins they will waste
away.
40" 'But if they will confess their sins and the sins of their fathers—their treachery against me and their hostility toward me,
41which made me hostile toward them so that I sent them into the
land of their enemies—then when their uncircumcised hearts are
humbled and they pay for their sin, 42I will remember my covenant with Jacob and my covenant with Isaac and my covenant
with Abraham, and I will remember the land. 43For the land will
be deserted by them and will enjoy its sabbaths while it lies desolate without them. They will pay for their sins because they rejected my laws and abhorred my decrees. 44Yet in spite of this, when
they are in the land of their enemies, I will not reject them or
abhor them so as to destroy them completely, breaking my covenant with them. I am the LORD their God. 45But for their sake I
will remember the covenant with their ancestors whom I brought
out of Egypt in the sight of the nations to be their God. I am the
LORD.' "
46These are the decrees, the laws and the regulations that the

(26:42–46) You, O God, are always faithful. You never leave us hopeless. You know our weaknesses, that we are made of dust, that we are as fickle as we are frail. Even when we rebel against You, You hold out the promise of restoration to us. For You are more willing to show us mercy than we are willing to submit. You are more ready to forgive us than we are ready to repent. You are more eager to restore us than we are eager to return to You. Truly Your grace, O Lord, is far greater than our sin. (Ro 5:20)

Frail children of dust, and feeble as
frail,
In Thee do we trust, nor find Thee
to fail.
Thy mercies how tender, how firm to
the end!
Our Maker, Defender, Redeemer,
and Friend!

"O Worship the King"
Robert Grant (1833)

LORD established on Mount Sinai between himself and the Israelites through Moses.

Redeeming What Is the LORD's

27 The LORD said to Moses, 2"Speak to the Israelites and say
to them: 'If anyone makes a special vow to dedicate persons to the LORD by giving equivalent values, 3set the value of a
male between the ages of twenty and sixty at fifty shekels[a] of silver,
according to the sanctuary shekel[b]; 4and if it is a female, set her
value at thirty shekels.[c] 5If it is a person between the ages of five
and twenty, set the value of a male at twenty shekels[d] and of a female at ten shekels.[e] 6If it is a person between one month and
five years, set the value of a male at five shekels[f] of silver and that
of a female at three shekels[g] of silver. 7If it is a person sixty years
old or more, set the value of a male at fifteen shekels[h] and of a female at ten shekels. 8If anyone making the vow is too poor to pay
the specified amount, he is to present the person to the priest,
who will set the value for him according to what the man making
the vow can afford.

9" 'If what he vowed is an animal that is acceptable as an offering to the LORD, such an animal given to the LORD becomes holy.
10He must not exchange it or substitute a good one for a bad one,
or a bad one for a good one; if he should substitute one animal for
another, both it and the substitute become holy. 11If what he
vowed is a ceremonially unclean animal—one that is not acceptable as an offering to the LORD—the animal must be presented to
the priest, 12who will judge its quality as good or bad. Whatever
value the priest then sets, that is what it will be. 13If the owner
wishes to redeem the animal, he must add a fifth to its value.

14" 'If a man dedicates his house as something holy to the LORD,
the priest will judge its quality as good or bad. Whatever value the
priest then sets, so it will remain. 15If the man who dedicates his
house redeems it, he must add a fifth to its value, and the house
will again become his.

16" 'If a man dedicates to the LORD part of his family land, its
value is to be set according to the amount of seed required for
it—fifty shekels of silver to a homer[i] of barley seed. 17If he dedicates his field during the Year of Jubilee, the value that has been
set remains. 18But if he dedicates his field after the Jubilee, the
priest will determine the value according to the number of years
that remain until the next Year of Jubilee, and its set value will be
reduced. 19If the man who dedicates the field wishes to redeem it,
he must add a fifth to its value, and the field will again become his.
20If, however, he does not redeem the field, or if he has sold it to
someone else, it can never be redeemed. 21When the field is released in the Jubilee, it will become holy, like a field devoted to the
LORD; it will become the property of the priests.[j]

22" 'If a man dedicates to the LORD a field he has bought, which
is not part of his family land, 23the priest will determine its value
up to the Year of Jubilee, and the man must pay its value on that
day as something holy to the LORD. 24In the Year of Jubilee the field
will revert to the person from whom he bought it, the one whose

(27:2–8) Father, please give me a heart that is willing to give to You, not only out of obligation, but out of devotion and gratitude. Help me to give my life to You as freely as You have given Yours to me, not grudgingly but joyfully.

[a] *3* That is, about 1 1/4 pounds (about 0.6 kilogram); also in verse 16 [b] *3* That is, about 2/5 ounce (about 11.5 grams); also in verse 25 [c] *4* That is, about 12 ounces (about 0.3 kilogram) [d] *5* That is, about 8 ounces (about 0.2 kilogram) [e] *5* That is, about 4 ounces (about 110 grams); also in verse 7 [f] *6* That is, about 2 ounces (about 55 grams) [g] *6* That is, about 1 1/4 ounces (about 35 grams) [h] *7* That is, about 6 ounces (about 170 grams) [i] *16* That is, probably about 6 bushels (about 220 liters) [j] *21* Or *priest*

land it was. 25Every value is to be set according to the sanctuary shekel, twenty gerahs to the shekel.

26" 'No one, however, may dedicate the firstborn of an animal, since the firstborn already belongs to the LORD; whether an ox[a] or a sheep, it is the LORD's. 27If it is one of the unclean animals, he may buy it back at its set value, adding a fifth of the value to it. If he does not redeem it, it is to be sold at its set value.

28" 'But nothing that a man owns and devotes[b] to the LORD—whether man or animal or family land—may be sold or redeemed; everything so devoted is most holy to the LORD.

29" 'No person devoted to destruction[c] may be ransomed; he must be put to death.

30" 'A tithe of everything from the land, whether grain from the soil or fruit from the trees, belongs to the LORD; it is holy to the LORD. 31If a man redeems any of his tithe, he must add a fifth of the value to it. 32The entire tithe of the herd and flock—every tenth animal that passes under the shepherd's rod—will be holy to the LORD. 33He must not pick out the good from the bad or make any substitution. If he does make a substitution, both the animal and its substitute become holy and cannot be redeemed.' "

34These are the commands the LORD gave Moses on Mount Sinai for the Israelites.

(27:34) Righteous Judge, I look into the stark light of Your law as one looks into a mirror. And what I see is the absolute impossibility of achieving holiness in my own strength, because of my sinful nature. But I praise You, O God, for "what the law was powerless to do in that it was weakened by the sinful nature," You did by sending Your own Son, Jesus Christ, "in the likeness of sinful man to be a sin offering. And so [you] condemned sin in sinful man, in order that the righteous requirements of the law might be fully met in us, who do not live according to the sinful nature but according to the Spirit." "Therefore, there is now no condemnation for those who are in Christ Jesus, because through Christ Jesus the law of the Spirit of life set me free from the law of sin and death." (Ro 8:1–4; Jas 1:23–24)

[a] *26* The Hebrew word can include both male and female. [b] *28* The Hebrew term refers to the irrevocable giving over of things or persons to the LORD. [c] *29* The Hebrew term refers to the irrevocable giving over of things or persons to the LORD, often by totally destroying them.

The Fourth Book of Moses called

NUMBERS

The name of this book in English comes from the two census countings of the Israelites during their wandering in the desert. However, the Hebrew title, "In the Wilderness," gives a better sense of the whole book. Here we see God's chosen people, recipients of the law, as they advance in fits and starts through the wilderness to inherit the promised land.

In Numbers we encounter the God Who is constantly present with His people, Who guides them and Who provides for their needs. Nothing is too trivial for God's gracious attention.

But the people are not satisfied with God's care. Numbers honestly recounts the Israelites' failure to trust God: They complain and grumble (ch. 11); they doubt God's faithfulness and plot to return to Egypt (ch. 14); they worship Baal (ch. 25); they rebel against God's appointed leaders (ch. 16). Even Moses gets so angry with them that he disobeys God's command (ch. 20).

For their failure to believe God the children of Israel pay a terrible price: They must wander for 40 years in the wilderness, allowing an entire generation to die, rather than entering immediately into the promised land. Nevertheless, "The Lord is slow to anger, abounding in love and forgiving sin and rebellion" (14:18).

> **In Numbers we encounter the God Who is constantly present with His people . . . Nothing is too trivial for God's gracious attention.**

After a long sojourn in the desert, a new generation of God's people is finally ready to enter their land. In spite of their foot-dragging and complaining, God will fulfill His promise by leading the people into "a land flowing with milk and honey" (14:8). Numbers reminds us that God's promises are trustworthy. His providence never fails. His patience prevails.

Numbers challenges our shallow obedience. How often have we experienced seasons "in the wilderness" because our fears have kept us from experiencing God's rich blessings? How often have we grumbled because our circumstances have not matched our narrow expectations? Yet God's patience and provision remain constant for us through Jesus Christ, Who is with us always (Mt 28:20). The book of Numbers encourages us, however, not to presume upon God's mercy but instead to worship God through trusting His Word completely.

God's grace for us is captured wonderfully in the priestly benediction of Numbers 6:24–26: "The Lord bless you and keep you; the Lord make his face shine upon you and be gracious to you; the Lord turn his face toward you and give you peace." In Christ we receive God's bounteous blessings, and we bless Him in return through words of praise and lives of obedience.

The Census

1 The LORD spoke to Moses in the Tent of Meeting in the Desert
of Sinai on the first day of the second month of the second year
after the Israelites came out of Egypt. He said: 2"Take a census of
the whole Israelite community by their clans and families, listing
every man by name, one by one. 3You and Aaron are to number by
their divisions all the men in Israel twenty years old or more who
are able to serve in the army. 4One man from each tribe, each the
head of his family, is to help you. 5These are the names of the men
who are to assist you:

from Reuben, Elizur son of Shedeur;
6from Simeon, Shelumiel son of Zurishaddai;
7from Judah, Nahshon son of Amminadab;
8from Issachar, Nethanel son of Zuar;
9from Zebulun, Eliab son of Helon;
10from the sons of Joseph:
from Ephraim, Elishama son of Ammihud;
from Manasseh, Gamaliel son of Pedahzur;
11from Benjamin, Abidan son of Gideoni;
12from Dan, Ahiezer son of Ammishaddai;
13from Asher, Pagiel son of Ocran;
14from Gad, Eliasaph son of Deuel;
15from Naphtali, Ahira son of Enan."

16These were the men appointed from the community, the leaders of their ancestral tribes. They were the heads of the clans of Israel.
17Moses and Aaron took these men whose names had been
given, 18and they called the whole community together on the first
day of the second month. The people indicated their ancestry by
their clans and families, and the men twenty years old or more
were listed by name, one by one, 19as the LORD commanded
Moses. And so he counted them in the Desert of Sinai:

20From the descendants of Reuben the firstborn son of Israel:
All the men twenty years old or more who were able to
serve in the army were listed by name, one by one, according to the records of their clans and families. 21The
number from the tribe of Reuben was 46,500.

22From the descendants of Simeon:
All the men twenty years old or more who were able to
serve in the army were counted and listed by name, one by
one, according to the records of their clans and families.
23The number from the tribe of Simeon was 59,300.

24From the descendants of Gad:
All the men twenty years old or more who were able to
serve in the army were listed by name, according to the
records of their clans and families. 25The number from
the tribe of Gad was 45,650.

26From the descendants of Judah:
All the men twenty years old or more who were able to
serve in the army were listed by name, according to the
records of their clans and families. 27The number from
the tribe of Judah was 74,600.

28From the descendants of Issachar:

The fellowship of God is delightful beyond all telling. He communes with His redeemed ones in an easy, uninhibited fellowship that is restful and healing to the soul.
A.W. Tozer (1897–1963)

(1:1) "The LORD spoke to Moses in the Tent . . . in the Desert." You graciously provided a place of fellowship in the desert, Father. The tent was Your earthly throne room, the center of Your sovereignty. You spoke with Moses there. I praise You, Lord, that You are not a distant and silent God, but that You are present and intimate. Even now, I invite You to make my body—my "tent"—Your throne room. As I spend time with You in Your Word, I pray that You will speak to me and lead me in my journey of life. I depend on You, Father, to take me by the hand and bring me into the glorious rest of Your kingdom—both here on earth and in heaven. (Ro 12:1; 1Co 6:19–20)

How lovely Your dwelling place,
How precious it is to me,
How my soul is yearning
For the courts of the King.
My heart and my flesh cry out
To dwell in Your house, O Lord;
It is here that my strength is found,
As I'm bowing down to you.

Better is one day in the courts
Of the Living God
Than a thousand years in any other
Time or place.
"How Lovely Your Dwelling Place"
Tommy Walker (©1993)

All the men twenty years old or more who were able to
serve in the army were listed by name, according to the
records of their clans and families. 29The number from
the tribe of Issachar was 54,400.

30From the descendants of Zebulun:
All the men twenty years old or more who were able to
serve in the army were listed by name, according to the
records of their clans and families. 31The number from
the tribe of Zebulun was 57,400.

32From the sons of Joseph:
From the descendants of Ephraim:
All the men twenty years old or more who were able to
serve in the army were listed by name, according to the
records of their clans and families. 33The number from
the tribe of Ephraim was 40,500.

34From the descendants of Manasseh:
All the men twenty years old or more who were able to
serve in the army were listed by name, according to the
records of their clans and families. 35The number from
the tribe of Manasseh was 32,200.

36From the descendants of Benjamin:
All the men twenty years old or more who were able to
serve in the army were listed by name, according to the
records of their clans and families. 37The number from
the tribe of Benjamin was 35,400.

38From the descendants of Dan:
All the men twenty years old or more who were able to
serve in the army were listed by name, according to the
records of their clans and families. 39The number from
the tribe of Dan was 62,700.

40From the descendants of Asher:
All the men twenty years old or more who were able to
serve in the army were listed by name, according to the
records of their clans and families. 41The number from
the tribe of Asher was 41,500.

42From the descendants of Naphtali:
All the men twenty years old or more who were able to
serve in the army were listed by name, according to the
records of their clans and families. 43The number from
the tribe of Naphtali was 53,400.

44These were the men counted by Moses and Aaron and the
twelve leaders of Israel, each one representing his family. 45All the
Israelites twenty years old or more who were able to serve in Israel's army were counted according to their families. 46The total
number was 603,550.

47The families of the tribe of Levi, however, were not counted
along with the others. 48The LORD had said to Moses: 49"You must
not count the tribe of Levi or include them in the census of the
other Israelites. 50Instead, appoint the Levites to be in charge of
the tabernacle of the Testimony—over all its furnishings and
everything belonging to it. They are to carry the tabernacle and all
its furnishings; they are to take care of it and encamp around it.
51Whenever the tabernacle is to move, the Levites are to take it

(1:47–51) Father, You did not allow the families of the tribe of Levi to be counted along with the fighting men. The only blood they were to shed was that of the sacrifice; their warfare was indeed spiritual and not physical. The tabernacle was located at the center of their lives, and as they encamped around it, it was their responsibility to protect it. I thank You for this glorious picture of the responsibility I have in worship. Help me to look after the tabernacle of my heart, to treat it as a treasured possession and to keep my defenses well in place. And as I serve You in worship, Lord, please come and occupy the very center of my life. (2 Cor 10:3-4; Eph 6:12)

down, and whenever the tabernacle is to be set up, the Levites shall do it. Anyone else who goes near it shall be put to death. [52]The Israelites are to set up their tents by divisions, each man in his own camp under his own standard. [53]The Levites, however, are to set up their tents around the tabernacle of the Testimony so that wrath will not fall on the Israelite community. The Levites are to be responsible for the care of the tabernacle of the Testimony."

[54]The Israelites did all this just as the LORD commanded Moses.

The Arrangement of the Tribal Camps

2 The LORD said to Moses and Aaron: [2]"The Israelites are to camp around the Tent of Meeting some distance from it, each man under his standard with the banners of his family."

[3]On the east, toward the sunrise, the divisions of the camp of Judah are to encamp under their standard. The leader of the people of Judah is Nahshon son of Amminadab. [4]His division numbers 74,600.

[5]The tribe of Issachar will camp next to them. The leader of the people of Issachar is Nethanel son of Zuar. [6]His division numbers 54,400.

[7]The tribe of Zebulun will be next. The leader of the people of Zebulun is Eliab son of Helon. [8]His division numbers 57,400.

[9]All the men assigned to the camp of Judah, according to their divisions, number 186,400. They will set out first.

[10]On the south will be the divisions of the camp of Reuben under their standard. The leader of the people of Reuben is Elizur son of Shedeur. [11]His division numbers 46,500.

[12]The tribe of Simeon will camp next to them. The leader of the people of Simeon is Shelumiel son of Zurishaddai. [13]His division numbers 59,300.

[14]The tribe of Gad will be next. The leader of the people of Gad is Eliasaph son of Deuel.[a] [15]His division numbers 45,650.

[16]All the men assigned to the camp of Reuben, according to their divisions, number 151,450. They will set out second.

[17]Then the Tent of Meeting and the camp of the Levites will set out in the middle of the camps. They will set out in the same order as they encamp, each in his own place under his standard.

[18]On the west will be the divisions of the camp of Ephraim under their standard. The leader of the people of Ephraim is Elishama son of Ammihud. [19]His division numbers 40,500.

[20]The tribe of Manasseh will be next to them. The leader of the people of Manasseh is Gamaliel son of Pedahzur. [21]His division numbers 32,200.

[22]The tribe of Benjamin will be next. The leader of the people of Benjamin is Abidan son of Gideoni. [23]His division numbers 35,400.

[24]All the men assigned to the camp of Ephraim, according to their divisions, number 108,100. They will set out third.

[a] *14* Many manuscripts of the Masoretic Text, Samaritan Pentateuch and Vulgate (see also Num. 1:14); most manuscripts of the Masoretic Text *Reuel*

(1:53) I praise You, O God, that Your mercy triumphs over judgment. While You appointed the other tribes to protect Israel from their enemies, You appointed the Levites to protect Israel from Your wrath. At Your command, the worship leaders formed the buffer zone between judgment and mercy, death and life, sin and holiness as they encamped around the tabernacle. Truly, "righteousness and peace kiss[ed] each other" in the encampment of worship. (Ps 85:8–10; Hab 3:2; Jas 2:13)

(2:17) According to Your instructions, O God, the place of worship was at the center of the community and at the center of the journey. Just as Your presence was evident at the heart of the Israelite camp, I pray that it will also be evident at the center of my life.

25 On the north will be the divisions of the camp of Dan,
under their standard. The leader of the people of Dan is
Ahiezer son of Ammishaddai. 26 His division numbers
62,700.
27 The tribe of Asher will camp next to them. The leader
of the people of Asher is Pagiel son of Ocran. 28 His division
numbers 41,500.
29 The tribe of Naphtali will be next. The leader of the
people of Naphtali is Ahira son of Enan. 30 His division
numbers 53,400.
31 All the men assigned to the camp of Dan number
157,600. They will set out last, under their standards.

32 These are the Israelites, counted according to their
families. All those in the camps, by their divisions, number
603,550. 33 The Levites, however, were not counted along
with the other Israelites, as the LORD commanded Moses.

34 So the Israelites did everything the LORD commanded Moses;
that is the way they encamped under their standards, and that is
the way they set out, each with his clan and family.

The Levites

3 This is the account of the family of Aaron and Moses at the
time the LORD talked with Moses on Mount Sinai.
2 The names of the sons of Aaron were Nadab the firstborn and
Abihu, Eleazar and Ithamar. 3 Those were the names of Aaron's
sons, the anointed priests, who were ordained to serve as
priests. 4 Nadab and Abihu, however, fell dead before the LORD
when they made an offering with unauthorized fire before him in
the Desert of Sinai. They had no sons; so only Eleazar and Ithamar served as priests during the lifetime of their father Aaron.
5 The LORD said to Moses, 6 "Bring the tribe of Levi and present
them to Aaron the priest to assist him. 7 They are to perform duties for him and for the whole community at the Tent of Meeting
by doing the work of the tabernacle. 8 They are to take care of all
the furnishings of the Tent of Meeting, fulfilling the obligations of
the Israelites by doing the work of the tabernacle. 9 Give the Levites to Aaron and his sons; they are the Israelites who are to be
given wholly to him.[a] 10 Appoint Aaron and his sons to serve as
priests; anyone else who approaches the sanctuary must be put
to death."
11 The LORD also said to Moses, 12 "I have taken the Levites
from among the Israelites in place of the first male offspring of
every Israelite woman. The Levites are mine, 13 for all the firstborn are mine. When I struck down all the firstborn in Egypt, I
set apart for myself every firstborn in Israel, whether man or animal. They are to be mine. I am the LORD."
14 The LORD said to Moses in the Desert of Sinai, 15 "Count the
Levites by their families and clans. Count every male a month old
or more." 16 So Moses counted them, as he was commanded by
the word of the LORD.
17 These were the names of the sons of Levi:
Gershon, Kohath and Merari.
18 These were the names of the Gershonite clans:
Libni and Shimei.

(3:4) O Most holy God, You did not stand silent as these priests trifled with Your holiness. O Lord who does not change, may I never worship You with a presumptuous spirit. Place within me a deep respect for Your authority. Teach me to worship You acceptably with reverence and awe, for You, my God are a consuming fire. (Heb 12:28–29)

(3:10) Though Israel had a high priest, the people had to keep their distance from Your presence. But now through Christ, our high priest, You invite us to "approach the throne of grace with confidence, so that we may receive mercy and find grace to help us in our time of need." I praise You, Father, that we are no longer kept at a distance, but we are called into closest fellowship with You because we abide in Christ. We no longer live under the threat of death; we now live under the guarantee of life—indeed, life can only be found in Your presence, O God, while death awaits those who keep their distance from You. (Heb 4:14–16)

[a] 9 Most manuscripts of the Masoretic Text; some manuscripts of the Masoretic Text, Samaritan Pentateuch and Septuagint (see also Num. 8:16) *to me*

19 The Kohathite clans:
Amram, Izhar, Hebron and Uzziel.
20 The Merarite clans:
Mahli and Mushi.
These were the Levite clans, according to their families.

21 To Gershon belonged the clans of the Libnites and Shimeites;
these were the Gershonite clans. 22 The number of all the males a
month old or more who were counted was 7,500. 23 The Gershonite clans were to camp on the west, behind the tabernacle.
24 The leader of the families of the Gershonites was Eliasaph son of
Lael. 25 At the Tent of Meeting the Gershonites were responsible
for the care of the tabernacle and tent, its coverings, the curtain at
the entrance to the Tent of Meeting, 26 the curtains of the court-
yard, the curtain at the entrance to the courtyard surrounding the tabernacle and altar, and the ropes—and everything related to their use.

27 To Kohath belonged the clans of the Amramites, Izharites, Hebronites and Uzzielites; these were the Kohathite clans. 28 The
number of all the males a month old or more was 8,600.[a] The Kohathites were responsible for the care of the sanctuary. 29 The Kohathite clans were to camp on the south side of the tabernacle.
30 The leader of the families of the Kohathite clans was Elizaphan
son of Uzziel. 31 They were responsible for the care of the ark, the table, the lampstand, the altars, the articles of the sanctuary used in ministering, the curtain, and everything related to their use.
32 The chief leader of the Levites was Eleazar son of Aaron, the priest. He was appointed over those who were responsible for the care of the sanctuary.

33 To Merari belonged the clans of the Mahlites and the Mu-
shites; these were the Merarite clans. 34 The number of all the
males a month old or more who were counted was 6,200. 35 The
leader of the families of the Merarite clans was Zuriel son of Abihail; they were to camp on the north side of the tabernacle. 36 The
Merarites were appointed to take care of the frames of the tabernacle, its crossbars, posts, bases, all its equipment, and everything
related to their use, 37 as well as the posts of the surrounding courtyard with their bases, tent pegs and ropes.

38 Moses and Aaron and his sons were to camp to the east of the tabernacle, toward the sunrise, in front of the Tent of Meeting. They were responsible for the care of the sanctuary on behalf of the Israelites. Anyone else who approached the sanctuary was to be put to death.

39 The total number of Levites counted at the LORD's command by Moses and Aaron according to their clans, including every male a month old or more, was 22,000.

40 The LORD said to Moses, "Count all the firstborn Israelite
males who are a month old or more and make a list of their
names. 41 Take the Levites for me in place of all the firstborn of the

[a] 28 Hebrew; some Septuagint manuscripts *8,300*

(3:18–35) Almighty God, You communicate Your glory and Your power in so many ways, even in the very names of the leaders of the Levite clans. Many of these names serve as memorials to Your faithfulness and power. "My God has added" (Eliasaph) proclaims that from the fullness of Your grace You add one blessing after another to our lives. "Belonging to God" (Lael) declares the wonderful comfort we have because we are Yours. "My God has protected" (Elizaphan) and "My strength is God" (Uzziel) give us courage in the midst of life's storms. "My Rock is God" (Zuriel) and "my Father is power" (Abihail) prompt us to seek true security in You alone, for You are our Rock and our Redeemer. (Jn 1:16)

(3:39) The total number of Levites counted was 22,000. They were by far the smallest of the tribes. But You took those who seemed to be of least value and gave them the highest honor. Those who were the weakest You held the closest, and surrounded them with the hosts of Your army. Truly, You lifted up the humble and bestowed honor on the least of the brethren. We praise Your wonderful name! (Nu 2:17; 3:11–13)

(3:42–48) The firstborn of Israel were Yours, O God, because the Passover lamb was slain for their sakes in Egypt. They were no longer their own—they were bought at a price. And we are now "the church of the firstborn" because Jesus Christ, our Passover lamb, died for all of us. For we know that "it was not with perishable things such as silver or gold that [we] were redeemed, but with the precious blood of Christ, a lamb without blemish or defect. He was chosen before the creation of the world, but was revealed in these last times for [our] sake." Through Him we belong to You. We are no longer our own—we were bought at a price. (Ex 12:1–13,29; 13:2; 1Co 5:7; 6:19–20; Heb 12:23; 1Pe 1:18–21)

As Christians, therefore, we are not our own, and do not belong to ourselves nor to other people, not even to our own loved ones . . . Our talents are not ours to do with as we please, or as our people please. Our time is not ours to spend as we choose, or as others may wish. All is His. Our spirits are His. Our bodies are His. Our minds, our intelligence, are His. Our talents are His. Our possessions are His. Our children are His. All we are, all we have, all we hold dear, are His and His alone. We are His blood-bought people; the Church of Christ is a blood-bought band.

G. Christian Weiss (1910-)

Son of God, Son of Man,
You became the Spotless Lamb;
Suffering for me,
You showed me mercy,
Now You reign in majesty.

We worship Thee,
O Lamb of God,
The Living Word.
We lift up Your name
And worship Thee.
Ancient of Days,
We give You praise,
O Lamb upon the throne.

"To the Lamb"
Shannon Fogal Wexelberg (©1993)

Israelites, and the livestock of the Levites in place of all the firstborn of the livestock of the Israelites. I am the LORD."
42So Moses counted all the firstborn of the Israelites, as the
LORD commanded him. 43The total number of firstborn males a
month old or more, listed by name, was 22,273.
44The LORD also said to Moses, 45"Take the Levites in place of
all the firstborn of Israel, and the livestock of the Levites in place
of their livestock. The Levites are to be mine. I am the LORD. 46To
redeem the 273 firstborn Israelites who exceed the number of the
Levites, 47collect five shekels[a] for each one, according to the
sanctuary shekel, which weighs twenty gerahs. 48Give the money
for the redemption of the additional Israelites to Aaron and his
sons."
49So Moses collected the redemption money from those who
exceeded the number redeemed by the Levites. 50From the firstborn of the Israelites he collected silver weighing 1,365 shekels,[b]
according to the sanctuary shekel. 51Moses gave the redemption
money to Aaron and his sons, as he was commanded by the word
of the LORD.

The Kohathites

4 The LORD said to Moses and Aaron: 2"Take a census of the Kohathite branch of the Levites by their clans and families.
3Count all the men from thirty to fifty years of age who come to
serve in the work in the Tent of Meeting.
4"This is the work of the Kohathites in the Tent of Meeting: the
care of the most holy things. 5When the camp is to move, Aaron
and his sons are to go in and take down the shielding curtain and
cover the ark of the Testimony with it. 6Then they are to cover this
with hides of sea cows,[c] spread a cloth of solid blue over that and
put the poles in place.
7"Over the table of the Presence they are to spread a blue cloth
and put on it the plates, dishes and bowls, and the jars for drink
offerings; the bread that is continually there is to remain on it.
8Over these they are to spread a scarlet cloth, cover that with
hides of sea cows and put its poles in place.
9"They are to take a blue cloth and cover the lampstand that is
for light, together with its lamps, its wick trimmers and trays, and
all its jars for the oil used to supply it. 10Then they are to wrap it
and all its accessories in a covering of hides of sea cows and put
it on a carrying frame.
11"Over the gold altar they are to spread a blue cloth and cover
that with hides of sea cows and put its poles in place.
12"They are to take all the articles used for ministering in the
sanctuary, wrap them in a blue cloth, cover that with hides of sea
cows and put them on a carrying frame.
13"They are to remove the ashes from the bronze altar and
spread a purple cloth over it. 14Then they are to place on it all the
utensils used for ministering at the altar, including the firepans,
meat forks, shovels and sprinkling bowls. Over it they are to
spread a covering of hides of sea cows and put its poles in place.
15"After Aaron and his sons have finished covering the holy furnishings and all the holy articles, and when the camp is ready to
move, the Kohathites are to come to do the carrying. But they must

[a] 47 That is, about 2 ounces (about 55 grams) [b] 50 That is, about 35 pounds (about 15.5 kilograms) [c] 6 That is, dugongs; also in verses 8, 10, 11, 12, 14 and 25

not touch the holy things or they will die. The Kohathites are to
carry those things that are in the Tent of Meeting.
16"Eleazar son of Aaron, the priest, is to have charge of the oil
for the light, the fragrant incense, the regular grain offering and
the anointing oil. He is to be in charge of the entire tabernacle
and everything in it, including its holy furnishings and articles."
17The LORD said to Moses and Aaron, 18"See that the Kohathite
tribal clans are not cut off from the Levites. 19So that they may live
and not die when they come near the most holy things, do this for
them: Aaron and his sons are to go into the sanctuary and assign
to each man his work and what he is to carry. 20But the Kohathites must not go in to look at the holy things, even for a moment,
or they will die."

The Gershonites

21The LORD said to Moses, 22"Take a census also of the Gershonites by their families and clans. 23Count all the men from thirty to fifty years of age who come to serve in the work at the Tent of
Meeting.
24"This is the service of the Gershonite clans as they work and
carry burdens: 25They are to carry the curtains of the tabernacle,
the Tent of Meeting, its covering and the outer covering of hides of
sea cows, the curtains for the entrance to the Tent of Meeting,
26the curtains of the courtyard surrounding the tabernacle and
altar, the curtain for the entrance, the ropes and all the equipment
used in its service. The Gershonites are to do all that needs to be
done with these things. 27All their service, whether carrying or
doing other work, is to be done under the direction of Aaron and
his sons. You shall assign to them as their responsibility all they
are to carry. 28This is the service of the Gershonite clans at the
Tent of Meeting. Their duties are to be under the direction of Ithamar son of Aaron, the priest.

The Merarites

29"Count the Merarites by their clans and families. 30Count all
the men from thirty to fifty years of age who come to serve in the
work at the Tent of Meeting. 31This is their duty as they perform
service at the Tent of Meeting: to carry the frames of the tabernacle, its crossbars, posts and bases, 32as well as the posts of the
surrounding courtyard with their bases, tent pegs, ropes, all their
equipment and everything related to their use. Assign to each man
the specific things he is to carry. 33This is the service of the Merarite clans as they work at the Tent of Meeting under the direction
of Ithamar son of Aaron, the priest."

The Numbering of the Levite Clans

34Moses, Aaron and the leaders of the community counted the
Kohathites by their clans and families. 35All the men from thirty to
fifty years of age who came to serve in the work in the Tent of
Meeting, 36counted by clans, were 2,750. 37This was the total of
all those in the Kohathite clans who served in the Tent of Meeting.
Moses and Aaron counted them according to the LORD's command
through Moses.
38The Gershonites were counted by their clans and families.
39All the men from thirty to fifty years of age who came to serve in
the work at the Tent of Meeting, 40counted by their clans and families, were 2,630. 41This was the total of those in the Gershonite

(4:15,20) "Blessed are those who have not seen and yet have believed." The Kohathites devoted their lives to carrying that which they could never see with their own eyes or touch with their own hands. But they felt the weight of their burden. They carried a mystery into a mystery, not knowing what they carried, or where they were going, or how long they would travel; and yet they were faithful in their call. Help me, Lord, to "live by faith, not by sight." Even though I cannot see You, I believe in You and I love You. (Jn 20:29; 2Co 5:7; 1Pe 1:8–9)

Though I can't see
Your holy, holy face;
And Your throne in heaven above,
It seems so far away.
Though I can't touch, I can't touch
Your nail-scarred hands,
I have a deep, unspeakable joy
That makes my faith to stand.

Lord, I believe in You,
I'll always believe in You.
Though I can't see
You with my eyes,
Deep in my heart
Your presence I find.
Lord, I believe in You,
And I'll keep my trust in You.
Let the whole world
Say what they may,
No one can take this joy away,
Lord, I believe.

"Lord, I Believe In You"
Tommy Walker (©1996)

(5:3) How can I come before You, pure and holy God? I have so many faults; some painfully visible, others less conspicuous but still condemnable. You have every right, Lord, to send me away, for I am not worthy to stand in Your presence. You cannot tolerate impurity; there can be no uncleanness where You are present. So then wash me, Father, in the precious blood of Your Son Jesus. Because of His redeeming work, I will not receive from You the judgment I deserve. Instead I will experience Your amazing grace, as You declare me pure and holy in Your sight. (Heb 9:12–14; 10:19–22)

I was so lost I should have died,
But You have brought me to Your
side
To be led by Your staff and rod,
And to be called a lamb of God.

O Lamb of God, sweet Lamb of God,
I love the holy Lamb of God,
O wash me in His precious blood,
My Jesus Christ, the Lamb of God.

"Lamb of God"
Twila Paris (©1985)

clans who served at the Tent of Meeting. Moses and Aaron counted them according to the LORD's command.
42 The Merarites were counted by their clans and families. 43 All
the men from thirty to fifty years of age who came to serve in the
work at the Tent of Meeting, 44 counted by their clans, were 3,200.
45 This was the total of those in the Merarite clans. Moses and
Aaron counted them according to the LORD's command through
Moses.
46 So Moses, Aaron and the leaders of Israel counted all the Levites by their clans and families. 47 All the men from thirty to fifty
years of age who came to do the work of serving and carrying the
Tent of Meeting 48 numbered 8,580. 49 At the LORD's command
through Moses, each was assigned his work and told what to
carry.

Thus they were counted, as the LORD commanded Moses.

The Purity of the Camp

5 The LORD said to Moses, 2 "Command the Israelites to send
away from the camp anyone who has an infectious skin disease[a] or a discharge of any kind, or who is ceremonially unclean
because of a dead body. 3 Send away male and female alike; send
them outside the camp so they will not defile their camp, where I
dwell among them." 4 The Israelites did this; they sent them outside the camp. They did just as the LORD had instructed Moses.

Restitution for Wrongs

5 The LORD said to Moses, 6 "Say to the Israelites: 'When a man
or woman wrongs another in any way[b] and so is unfaithful to the
LORD, that person is guilty 7 and must confess the sin he has committed. He must make full restitution for his wrong, add one fifth
to it and give it all to the person he has wronged. 8 But if that person has no close relative to whom restitution can be made for the
wrong, the restitution belongs to the LORD and must be given to the
priest, along with the ram with which atonement is made for him.
9 All the sacred contributions the Israelites bring to a priest will
belong to him. 10 Each man's sacred gifts are his own, but what he
gives to the priest will belong to the priest.' "

The Test for an Unfaithful Wife

11 Then the LORD said to Moses, 12 "Speak to the Israelites and
say to them: 'If a man's wife goes astray and is unfaithful to him
13 by sleeping with another man, and this is hidden from her husband and her impurity is undetected (since there is no witness
against her and she has not been caught in the act), 14 and if feelings of jealousy come over her husband and he suspects his wife
and she is impure—or if he is jealous and suspects her even
though she is not impure— 15 then he is to take his wife to the
priest. He must also take an offering of a tenth of an ephah[c] of
barley flour on her behalf. He must not pour oil on it or put incense on it, because it is a grain offering for jealousy, a reminder
offering to draw attention to guilt.
16 " 'The priest shall bring her and have her stand before the
LORD. 17 Then he shall take some holy water in a clay jar and put
some dust from the tabernacle floor into the water. 18 After the

[a] 2 Traditionally *leprosy*; the Hebrew word was used for various diseases affecting the skin—not necessarily leprosy. [b] 6 Or *woman commits any wrong common to mankind* [c] 15 That is, probably about 2 quarts (about 2 liters)

priest has had the woman stand before the LORD, he shall loosen
her hair and place in her hands the reminder offering, the grain
offering for jealousy, while he himself holds the bitter water that
brings a curse. 19Then the priest shall put the woman under oath
and say to her, "If no other man has slept with you and you have
not gone astray and become impure while married to your husband, may this bitter water that brings a curse not harm you. 20But
if you have gone astray while married to your husband and you
have defiled yourself by sleeping with a man other than your husband"— 21here the priest is to put the woman under this curse of
the oath—"may the LORD cause your people to curse and denounce you when he causes your thigh to waste away and your
abdomen to swell.[a] 22May this water that brings a curse enter
your body so that your abdomen swells and your thigh wastes
away.[b]"

"'Then the woman is to say, "Amen. So be it."

23" 'The priest is to write these curses on a scroll and then
wash them off into the bitter water. 24He shall have the woman
drink the bitter water that brings a curse, and this water will enter
her and cause bitter suffering. 25The priest is to take from her
hands the grain offering for jealousy, wave it before the LORD and
bring it to the altar. 26The priest is then to take a handful of the
grain offering as a memorial offering and burn it on the altar; after
that, he is to have the woman drink the water. 27If she has defiled
herself and been unfaithful to her husband, then when she is made
to drink the water that brings a curse, it will go into her and cause
bitter suffering; her abdomen will swell and her thigh waste away,[c]
and she will become accursed among her people. 28If, however,
the woman has not defiled herself and is free from impurity, she
will be cleared of guilt and will be able to have children.

29" 'This, then, is the law of jealousy when a woman goes astray
and defiles herself while married to her husband, 30or when feelings of jealousy come over a man because he suspects his wife.
The priest is to have her stand before the LORD and is to apply this
entire law to her. 31The husband will be innocent of any wrongdoing, but the woman will bear the consequences of her sin.' "

The Nazirite

6 The LORD said to Moses, 2"Speak to the Israelites and say to
them: 'If a man or woman wants to make a special vow, a
vow of separation to the LORD as a Nazirite, 3he must abstain from
wine and other fermented drink and must not drink vinegar made
from wine or from other fermented drink. He must not drink
grape juice or eat grapes or raisins. 4As long as he is a Nazirite, he
must not eat anything that comes from the grapevine, not even the
seeds or skins.

5" 'During the entire period of his vow of separation no razor
may be used on his head. He must be holy until the period of his
separation to the LORD is over; he must let the hair of his head grow
long. 6Throughout the period of his separation to the LORD he must
not go near a dead body. 7Even if his own father or mother or
brother or sister dies, he must not make himself ceremonially unclean on account of them, because the symbol of his separation to

[a] 21 Or *causes you to have a miscarrying womb and barrenness* [b] 22 Or *body and cause you to be barren and have a miscarrying womb* [c] 27 Or *suffering; she will have barrenness and a miscarrying womb*

(6:1–8) Like the Nazirites of old, I turn my face toward You, Lord, that You may consecrate me to Your service. How I long to be completely devoted to You, not just during a certain season in my life but in every season and in every circumstance. This is my heart's prayer, Father, that I would be set apart as Your humble servant, ready to follow wherever You lead.

Take my life and let it be
Consecrated, Lord, to Thee;
Take my moments and my days
Let them flow in ceaseless praise,
Let them flow in ceaseless praise.

Take my will and make it Thine
It shall be no longer mine;
Take my heart it is Thine own,
It shall be Thy royal throne,
It shall be Thy royal throne.

"Take My Life and Let It Be"
Francis Ridley Havergal (1836–1879)

God is on his head. 8Throughout the period of his separation he is
consecrated to the LORD.
9" 'If someone dies suddenly in his presence, thus defiling the
hair he has dedicated, he must shave his head on the day of his
cleansing—the seventh day. 10Then on the eighth day he must
bring two doves or two young pigeons to the priest at the entrance
to the Tent of Meeting. 11The priest is to offer one as a sin offering and the other as a burnt offering to make atonement for him
because he sinned by being in the presence of the dead body. That
same day he is to consecrate his head. 12He must dedicate himself
to the LORD for the period of his separation and must bring a year-
old male lamb as a guilt offering. The previous days do not count,
because he became defiled during his separation.
13" 'Now this is the law for the Nazirite when the period of his
separation is over. He is to be brought to the entrance to the Tent
of Meeting. 14There he is to present his offerings to the LORD: a
year-old male lamb without defect for a burnt offering, a year-old
ewe lamb without defect for a sin offering, a ram without defect
for a fellowship offering,[a] 15together with their grain offerings and
drink offerings, and a basket of bread made without yeast—cakes
made of fine flour mixed with oil, and wafers spread with oil.
16" 'The priest is to present them before the LORD and make the
sin offering and the burnt offering. 17He is to present the basket of
unleavened bread and is to sacrifice the ram as a fellowship offering to the LORD, together with its grain offering and drink offering.
18" 'Then at the entrance to the Tent of Meeting, the Nazirite
must shave off the hair that he dedicated. He is to take the hair and
put it in the fire that is under the sacrifice of the fellowship offering.
19" 'After the Nazirite has shaved off the hair of his dedication,
the priest is to place in his hands a boiled shoulder of the ram,
and a cake and a wafer from the basket, both made without yeast.
20The priest shall then wave them before the LORD as a wave offering; they are holy and belong to the priest, together with the
breast that was waved and the thigh that was presented. After that,
the Nazirite may drink wine.
21" 'This is the law of the Nazirite who vows his offering to the
LORD in accordance with his separation, in addition to whatever
else he can afford. He must fulfill the vow he has made, according
to the law of the Nazirite.' "

The Priestly Blessing

22The LORD said to Moses, 23"Tell Aaron and his sons, 'This is
how you are to bless the Israelites. Say to them:

24" ' "The LORD bless you
and keep you;
25the LORD make his face shine upon you
and be gracious to you;
26the LORD turn his face toward you
and give you peace." '

27"So they will put my name on the Israelites, and I will bless
them."

[a] *14* Traditionally *peace offering*; also in verses 17 and 18

(6:24–26) This blessing washes over me today like refreshing ocean waves on a scorching summer day. I praise You, my compassionate, merciful God, for granting me Your acceptance and Your favor. I praise You, my strong, tender Father, for giving me Your peace—a peace like no other, a peace that only You can give. I praise You and rest in You today, sweet Lord, as You offer me Your blessing and Your protection. Turn Your face toward me now, I pray, and shine upon me, that I may shine for You.

Do you accept the fact that the Bible's definition of grace–God's unmerited favor shown to people who are totally undeserving of it–applies to you not only in salvation but in your everyday life? The meaning of grace never changes.

Jerry Bridges (1929-)

Offerings at the Dedication of the Tabernacle

7 When Moses finished setting up the tabernacle, he anointed it and consecrated it and all its furnishings. He also anointed and consecrated the altar and all its utensils. 2Then the leaders of Israel, the heads of families who were the tribal leaders in charge of those who were counted, made offerings. 3They brought as their gifts before the LORD six covered carts and twelve oxen—an ox from each leader and a cart from every two. These they presented before the tabernacle.

4The LORD said to Moses, 5"Accept these from them, that they may be used in the work at the Tent of Meeting. Give them to the Levites as each man's work requires."

6So Moses took the carts and oxen and gave them to the Levites. 7He gave two carts and four oxen to the Gershonites, as their work required, 8and he gave four carts and eight oxen to the Merarites, as their work required. They were all under the direction of Ithamar son of Aaron, the priest. 9But Moses did not give any to the Kohathites, because they were to carry on their shoulders the holy things, for which they were responsible.

10When the altar was anointed, the leaders brought their offerings for its dedication and presented them before the altar. 11For the LORD had said to Moses, "Each day one leader is to bring his offering for the dedication of the altar."

12The one who brought his offering on the first day was Nahshon son of Amminadab of the tribe of Judah.

13His offering was one silver plate weighing a hundred and thirty shekels,[a] and one silver sprinkling bowl weighing seventy shekels,[b] both according to the sanctuary shekel, each filled with fine flour mixed with oil as a grain offering; 14one gold dish weighing ten shekels,[c] filled with incense; 15one young bull, one ram and one male lamb a year old, for a burnt offering; 16one male goat for a sin offering; 17and two oxen, five rams, five male goats and five male lambs a year old, to be sacrificed as a fellowship offering.[d] This was the offering of Nahshon son of Amminadab.

18On the second day Nethanel son of Zuar, the leader of Issachar, brought his offering.

19The offering he brought was one silver plate weighing a hundred and thirty shekels, and one silver sprinkling bowl weighing seventy shekels, both according to the sanctuary shekel, each filled with fine flour mixed with oil as a grain offering; 20one gold dish weighing ten shekels, filled with incense; 21one young bull, one ram and one male lamb a year old, for a burnt offering; 22one male goat for a sin offering; 23and two oxen, five rams, five male goats and five male lambs a year old, to be sacrificed as a fellowship offering. This was the offering of Nethanel son of Zuar.

24On the third day, Eliab son of Helon, the leader of the people of Zebulun, brought his offering.

25His offering was one silver plate weighing a hundred and thirty shekels, and one silver sprinkling bowl weighing sev-

[a] 13 That is, about 3 1/4 pounds (about 1.5 kilograms); also elsewhere in this chapter
[b] 13 That is, about 1 3/4 pounds (about 0.8 kilogram); also elsewhere in this chapter
[c] 14 That is, about 4 ounces (about 110 grams); also elsewhere in this chapter
[d] 17 Traditionally *peace offering*; also elsewhere in this chapter

(7:1–5) Gracious Father, we praise You for providing the tabernacle for Your people of old. It was a visible reminder of Your glorious presence among them. It was the place where they presented themselves to You and You presented Yourself to them. You did not dwell in a permanent house—You dwelt among Your people in a tent, just as Your people lived in tents. You condescended to meet with them in their condition; You sympathized with their distresses. Yet You had something even more wonderful in mind. You sent Your precious Son in human flesh, to dwell among us, to meet with us in our condition, to sympathize with our distresses, and to reveal Your glorious presence to us. Through Jesus we present ourselves to You; through Jesus, You present Yourself to us. Sovereign Lord, we bow in humble gratitude this day for Jesus, God incarnate. (Ex 40:34–38; Jn 1:14)

(7:25–53) You met with Your people at Sinai and gave them instructions for holy living. In gratitude and obedience, they brought their offerings for the support of the sanctuary. Even today, each one of Your people has a responsibility, as part of Your community of faith, to contribute to the service of Your church. I want to serve You as an expression of my devotion and love for You. Thank You, Lord God, for the privilege of being Your servant.

Take my silver and my gold
Not a mite would I withhold;
Take my intellect and use
Ev'ry pow'r as Thou shalt choose,
Ev'ry pow'r as Thou shalt choose.

Take my love my Lord, I pour
At Thy feet its treasure store;
Take myself and I will be
Ever, only, all for Thee,
Ever, only, all for Thee.

"Take My Life and Let It Be"
Francis Ridley Havergal (1836-1879)

enty shekels, both according to the sanctuary shekel, each
filled with fine flour mixed with oil as a grain offering; 26one
gold dish weighing ten shekels, filled with incense; 27one
young bull, one ram and one male lamb a year old, for a
burnt offering; 28one male goat for a sin offering; 29and two
oxen, five rams, five male goats and five male lambs a year
old, to be sacrificed as a fellowship offering. This was the offering of Eliab son of Helon.

30On the fourth day Elizur son of Shedeur, the leader of the people of Reuben, brought his offering.

31His offering was one silver plate weighing a hundred and
thirty shekels, and one silver sprinkling bowl weighing seventy shekels, both according to the sanctuary shekel, each
filled with fine flour mixed with oil as a grain offering; 32one
gold dish weighing ten shekels, filled with incense; 33one
young bull, one ram and one male lamb a year old, for a
burnt offering; 34one male goat for a sin offering; 35and two
oxen, five rams, five male goats and five male lambs a year
old, to be sacrificed as a fellowship offering. This was the offering of Elizur son of Shedeur.

36On the fifth day Shelumiel son of Zurishaddai, the leader of the people of Simeon, brought his offering.

37His offering was one silver plate weighing a hundred and
thirty shekels, and one silver sprinkling bowl weighing seventy shekels, both according to the sanctuary shekel, each
filled with fine flour mixed with oil as a grain offering; 38one
gold dish weighing ten shekels, filled with incense; 39one
young bull, one ram and one male lamb a year old, for a
burnt offering; 40one male goat for a sin offering; 41and two
oxen, five rams, five male goats and five male lambs a year
old, to be sacrificed as a fellowship offering. This was the offering of Shelumiel son of Zurishaddai.

42On the sixth day Eliasaph son of Deuel, the leader of the people of Gad, brought his offering.

43His offering was one silver plate weighing a hundred and
thirty shekels, and one silver sprinkling bowl weighing seventy shekels, both according to the sanctuary shekel, each
filled with fine flour mixed with oil as a grain offering; 44one
gold dish weighing ten shekels, filled with incense; 45one
young bull, one ram and one male lamb a year old, for a
burnt offering; 46one male goat for a sin offering; 47and two
oxen, five rams, five male goats and five male lambs a year
old, to be sacrificed as a fellowship offering. This was the offering of Eliasaph son of Deuel.

48On the seventh day Elishama son of Ammihud, the leader of the people of Ephraim, brought his offering.

49His offering was one silver plate weighing a hundred and
thirty shekels, and one silver sprinkling bowl weighing seventy shekels, both according to the sanctuary shekel, each
filled with fine flour mixed with oil as a grain offering; 50one
gold dish weighing ten shekels, filled with incense; 51one
young bull, one ram and one male lamb a year old, for a
burnt offering; 52one male goat for a sin offering; 53and two
oxen, five rams, five male goats and five male lambs a year

old, to be sacrificed as a fellowship offering. This was the offering of Elishama son of Ammihud.

54On the eighth day Gamaliel son of Pedahzur, the leader of the people of Manasseh, brought his offering.

55His offering was one silver plate weighing a hundred and thirty shekels, and one silver sprinkling bowl weighing seventy shekels, both according to the sanctuary shekel, each filled with fine flour mixed with oil as a grain offering; 56one gold dish weighing ten shekels, filled with incense; 57one young bull, one ram and one male lamb a year old, for a burnt offering; 58one male goat for a sin offering; 59and two oxen, five rams, five male goats and five male lambs a year old, to be sacrificed as a fellowship offering. This was the offering of Gamaliel son of Pedahzur.

60On the ninth day Abidan son of Gideoni, the leader of the people of Benjamin, brought his offering.

61His offering was one silver plate weighing a hundred and thirty shekels, and one silver sprinkling bowl weighing seventy shekels, both according to the sanctuary shekel, each filled with fine flour mixed with oil as a grain offering; 62one gold dish weighing ten shekels, filled with incense; 63one young bull, one ram and one male lamb a year old, for a burnt offering; 64one male goat for a sin offering; 65and two oxen, five rams, five male goats and five male lambs a year old, to be sacrificed as a fellowship offering. This was the offering of Abidan son of Gideoni.

66On the tenth day Ahiezer son of Ammishaddai, the leader of the people of Dan, brought his offering.

67His offering was one silver plate weighing a hundred and thirty shekels, and one silver sprinkling bowl weighing seventy shekels, both according to the sanctuary shekel, each filled with fine flour mixed with oil as a grain offering; 68one gold dish weighing ten shekels, filled with incense; 69one young bull, one ram and one male lamb a year old, for a burnt offering; 70one male goat for a sin offering; 71and two oxen, five rams, five male goats and five male lambs a year old, to be sacrificed as a fellowship offering. This was the offering of Ahiezer son of Ammishaddai.

72On the eleventh day Pagiel son of Ocran, the leader of the people of Asher, brought his offering.

73His offering was one silver plate weighing a hundred and thirty shekels, and one silver sprinkling bowl weighing seventy shekels, both according to the sanctuary shekel, each filled with fine flour mixed with oil as a grain offering; 74one gold dish weighing ten shekels, filled with incense; 75one young bull, one ram and one male lamb a year old, for a burnt offering; 76one male goat for a sin offering; 77and two oxen, five rams, five male goats and five male lambs a year old, to be sacrificed as a fellowship offering. This was the offering of Pagiel son of Ocran.

78On the twelfth day Ahira son of Enan, the leader of the people of Naphtali, brought his offering.

79His offering was one silver plate weighing a hundred and thirty shekels, and one silver sprinkling bowl weighing sev-

(7:54–81) What a celebration this must have been, Lord! Every day, for twelve consecutive days, the leader of one of the twelve tribes of Israel brought magnificent offerings and presented them before Your altar. Though each offering was identical, each was received individually by You. Even now You receive our gifts individually, and You take delight in us individually, as a father delights in each of his unique children. May we continue to be faithful to bring our offerings to You and to bring You joy through our thanksgiving and obedience.

In the beginning God established a pattern of sharing for mankind. They were to share with God in bringing him the sacrifice of their first fruits. God's object was not to receive a gift from man, but to receive the giver. God was not to be "paid off," but to receive an acknowledgment of man's love and gratitude.

Giving is the outward expression of love in the heart of every Christian. Our spiritual health depends on that expression of love, or else the love itself will wither and die.

Clarence W. Hatch (1903-1960)

We bring the sacrifice of praise
Into the house of the Lord;
We bring the sacrifice of praise
Into the house of the Lord.
And we offer up to You
The sacrifices of thanksgiving;
And we offer up to You
The sacrifices of joy.

"We Bring The Sacrifice Of Praise"
Kirk Dearman (©1984)

enty shekels, both according to the sanctuary shekel, each
filled with fine flour mixed with oil as a grain offering; 80one
gold dish weighing ten shekels, filled with incense; 81one
young bull, one ram and one male lamb a year old, for a
burnt offering; 82one male goat for a sin offering; 83and two
oxen, five rams, five male goats and five male lambs a year
old, to be sacrificed as a fellowship offering. This was the offering of Ahira son of Enan.

84These were the offerings of the Israelite leaders for the dedication of the altar when it was anointed: twelve silver plates, twelve
silver sprinkling bowls and twelve gold dishes. 85Each silver plate
weighed a hundred and thirty shekels, and each sprinkling bowl
seventy shekels. Altogether, the silver dishes weighed two thousand four hundred shekels,[a] according to the sanctuary shekel.
86The twelve gold dishes filled with incense weighed ten shekels
each, according to the sanctuary shekel. Altogether, the gold
dishes weighed a hundred and twenty shekels.[b] 87The total number of animals for the burnt offering came to twelve young bulls,
twelve rams and twelve male lambs a year old, together with their
grain offering. Twelve male goats were used for the sin offering.
88The total number of animals for the sacrifice of the fellowship
offering came to twenty-four oxen, sixty rams, sixty male goats and
sixty male lambs a year old. These were the offerings for the dedication of the altar after it was anointed.

89When Moses entered the Tent of Meeting to speak with the
LORD, he heard the voice speaking to him from between the two
cherubim above the atonement cover on the ark of the Testimony.
And he spoke with him.

Setting Up the Lamps

8 The LORD said to Moses, 2"Speak to Aaron and say to him,
'When you set up the seven lamps, they are to light the area in
front of the lampstand.' "

3Aaron did so; he set up the lamps so that they faced forward on
the lampstand, just as the LORD commanded Moses. 4This is how
the lampstand was made: It was made of hammered gold—from
its base to its blossoms. The lampstand was made exactly like the
pattern the LORD had shown Moses.

The Setting Apart of the Levites

5The LORD said to Moses: 6"Take the Levites from among the
other Israelites and make them ceremonially clean. 7To purify
them, do this: Sprinkle the water of cleansing on them; then have
them shave their whole bodies and wash their clothes, and so purify themselves. 8Have them take a young bull with its grain offering of fine flour mixed with oil; then you are to take a second
young bull for a sin offering. 9Bring the Levites to the front of the
Tent of Meeting and assemble the whole Israelite community.
10You are to bring the Levites before the LORD, and the Israelites
are to lay their hands on them. 11Aaron is to present the Levites
before the LORD as a wave offering from the Israelites, so that they
may be ready to do the work of the LORD.

12"After the Levites lay their hands on the heads of the bulls, use
the one for a sin offering to the LORD and the other for a burnt of-

[a] *85* That is, about 60 pounds (about 28 kilograms) [b] *86* That is, about 3 pounds (about 1.4 kilograms)

(7:89) How awesome, how incredible to imagine what Moses must have heard in Your presence, O God! In the Tent of Meeting, in the Most Holy Place, from between the wings of the cherubim above the mercy seat, Moses heard Your voice and he spoke with You. Your Old Testament people needed an advocate, someone who could represent them before You. You graciously met that need in the person of Moses. And now, through Jesus our Advocate, I can enter the Most Holy Place. Through Christ's atonement I have received Your mercy. And in Your mercy, You speak to me from Your Word and You listen as I speak to You in prayer. Thank You, Lord, for communing with me. (1Ti 2:5; Heb 10:19–22)

Commune with me,
Commune with me;
Between the wings of the cherubim,
Commune with me.

I worship You,
I worship You;
Between the wings of the cherubim,
I worship You.

"Commune With Me"
Kirk Dearman (©1981)

Children, draw near to your Father and He will embrace you in the arms of love. Come, you poor, stray, wandering sheep, return to your Shepherd! Come, sinners, to your Savior! Come, you who are dull, ignorant and illiterate, and who think yourselves most incapable of prayer. You are most especially adapted for it. Let all without exception come, for Jesus Christ has called all.

Madame Jeanne Marie de la Mothe Guyon (1648–1717)

fering, to make atonement for the Levites. 13Have the Levites stand
in front of Aaron and his sons and then present them as a wave offering to the LORD. 14In this way you are to set the Levites apart from
the other Israelites, and the Levites will be mine.
15"After you have purified the Levites and presented them as a
wave offering, they are to come to do their work at the Tent of Meeting. 16They are the Israelites who are to be given wholly to me. I
have taken them as my own in place of the firstborn, the first male
offspring from every Israelite woman. 17Every firstborn male in Israel, whether man or animal, is mine. When I struck down all the
firstborn in Egypt, I set them apart for myself. 18And I have taken the
Levites in place of all the firstborn sons in Israel. 19Of all the Israelites, I have given the Levites as gifts to Aaron and his sons to do the
work at the Tent of Meeting on behalf of the Israelites and to make
atonement for them so that no plague will strike the Israelites when
they go near the sanctuary."
20Moses, Aaron and the whole Israelite community did with the
Levites just as the LORD commanded Moses. 21The Levites purified
themselves and washed their clothes. Then Aaron presented them as
a wave offering before the LORD and made atonement for them to
purify them. 22After that, the Levites came to do their work at the
Tent of Meeting under the supervision of Aaron and his sons. They
did with the Levites just as the LORD commanded Moses.
23The LORD said to Moses, 24"This applies to the Levites: Men
twenty-five years old or more shall come to take part in the work at
the Tent of Meeting, 25but at the age of fifty, they must retire from
their regular service and work no longer. 26They may assist their
brothers in performing their duties at the Tent of Meeting, but they
themselves must not do the work. This, then, is how you are to assign the responsibilities of the Levites."

The Passover

9 The LORD spoke to Moses in the Desert of Sinai in the first month
of the second year after they came out of Egypt. He said, 2"Have
the Israelites celebrate the Passover at the appointed time. 3Celebrate
it at the appointed time, at twilight on the fourteenth day of this month,
in accordance with all its rules and regulations."
4So Moses told the Israelites to celebrate the Passover, 5and they
did so in the Desert of Sinai at twilight on the fourteenth day of the
first month. The Israelites did everything just as the LORD commanded Moses.
6But some of them could not celebrate the Passover on that day
because they were ceremonially unclean on account of a dead body.
So they came to Moses and Aaron that same day 7and said to Moses,
"We have become unclean because of a dead body, but why should
we be kept from presenting the LORD's offering with the other Israelites at the appointed time?"
8Moses answered them, "Wait until I find out what the LORD commands concerning you."
9Then the LORD said to Moses, 10"Tell the Israelites: 'When any of
you or your descendants are unclean because of a dead body or are
away on a journey, they may still celebrate the LORD's Passover. 11They
are to celebrate it on the fourteenth day of the second month at twilight. They are to eat the lamb, together with unleavened bread and
bitter herbs. 12They must not leave any of it till morning or break any
of its bones. When they celebrate the Passover, they must follow all
the regulations. 13But if a man who is ceremonially clean and not on

(9:1–5) Jesus, You are our Passover Lamb. Your shed blood bought our freedom from slavery to sin and death. You are the blood-stained door between death and life, and Your flesh provides sustenance for our journey. As we feast at Your communion table we remember Your promise: "I tell you the truth, unless you eat the flesh of the Son of Man and drink his blood, you have no life in You. Whoever eats my flesh and drinks my blood has eternal life, and I will raise him up at the last day. For my flesh is real food and my blood is real drink. Whoever eats my flesh and drinks my blood remains in me, and I in him." (Jn 6:53–56)

In the Eucharist, we are reminded of the overarching forgiveness accomplished in Christ's sacrifice that made obsolete the whole Jewish sacrificial system. "For if, when we were God's enemies, we were reconciled to him through the death of his Son, how much more, having been reconciled, shall we be saved through his life!" (Romans 5:10).

Paul Brand (1914-) and Philip Yancey (1949-)

As we drink this cup, we worship
You;
As we eat this bread, we honor You;
And we offer You our lives
As You have offered Yours for us.
We remember all You've done for us;
We remember Your covenant with
us;
We remember and worship You,
O Lord.

"We Remember You"
Kirk Dearman (©1988)

(9:15–23) How we long to be led like the Israelites of old, who set out at Your command and who stopped at Your command. Despite their failures and disobedience during the course of their forty-year journey, Your presence remained with them and Your guidance was unmistakable. Truly Your grace was greater than their sin. Like them, we cannot live without Your presence, faithful God. Be to us the cloud that guides us by day; let the holy fire of Your presence illuminate our spirits at night. Whether we wake or sleep, precious Lord, light up our lives so that we reflect Your glory, so that we point others to You, so that we become the people You want us to be. (Ro 5:20)

Guide me, O Thou great Jehovah,
Pilgrim thro' this barren land.
I am weak, but Thou art mighty;
Hold me with Thy pow'rful hand.
Bread of Heaven, Bread of Heaven,
Feed me till I want no more.
Feed me till I want no more.

Open now the crystal fountain
Whence the healing stream doth
flow.
Let the fire and cloudy pillar
Lead me all my journey thro'.
Strong Deliv'rer, strong Deliv'rer,
Be Thou still my Strength and
Shield.
Be Thou still my Strength and
Shield.

"Guide Me, O Thou Great Jehovah"
William Williams (1745)

a journey fails to celebrate the Passover, that person must be cut off
from his people because he did not present the LORD's offering at the
appointed time. That man will bear the consequences of his sin.
14" 'An alien living among you who wants to celebrate the LORD's
Passover must do so in accordance with its rules and regulations.
You must have the same regulations for the alien and the native-born.' "

The Cloud Above the Tabernacle

15On the day the tabernacle, the Tent of the Testimony, was set up,
the cloud covered it. From evening till morning the cloud above the
tabernacle looked like fire. 16That is how it continued to be; the
cloud covered it, and at night it looked like fire. 17Whenever
the cloud lifted from above the Tent, the Israelites set out; wherever
the cloud settled, the Israelites encamped. 18At the LORD's command the Israelites set out, and at his command they encamped. As
long as the cloud stayed over the tabernacle, they remained in
camp. 19When the cloud remained over the tabernacle a long time,
the Israelites obeyed the LORD's order and did not set out. 20Some-
times the cloud was over the tabernacle only a few days; at the
LORD's command they would encamp, and then at his command they
would set out. 21Sometimes the cloud stayed only from evening till
morning, and when it lifted in the morning, they set out. Whether by
day or by night, whenever the cloud lifted, they set out. 22Whether
the cloud stayed over the tabernacle for two days or a month or a
year, the Israelites would remain in camp and not set out; but when
it lifted, they would set out. 23At the LORD's command they encamped, and at the LORD's command they set out. They obeyed the
LORD's order, in accordance with his command through Moses.

The Silver Trumpets

10 The LORD said to Moses: 2"Make two trumpets of hammered
silver, and use them for calling the community together and
for having the camps set out. 3When both are sounded, the whole
community is to assemble before you at the entrance to the Tent of
Meeting. 4If only one is sounded, the leaders—the heads of the
clans of Israel—are to assemble before you. 5When a trumpet blast
is sounded, the tribes camping on the east are to set out. 6At the
sounding of a second blast, the camps on the south are to set out.
The blast will be the signal for setting out. 7To gather the assembly,
blow the trumpets, but not with the same signal.
8"The sons of Aaron, the priests, are to blow the trumpets. This
is to be a lasting ordinance for you and the generations to come.
9When you go into battle in your own land against an enemy who is
oppressing you, sound a blast on the trumpets. Then you will be remembered by the LORD your God and rescued from your enemies.
10Also at your times of rejoicing—your appointed feasts and New
Moon festivals—you are to sound the trumpets over your burnt offerings and fellowship offerings,[a] and they will be a memorial for
you before your God. I am the LORD your God."

The Israelites Leave Sinai

11On the twentieth day of the second month of the second year, the
cloud lifted from above the tabernacle of the Testimony. 12Then the
Israelites set out from the Desert of Sinai and traveled from place to

[a] 10 Traditionally *peace offerings*

place until the cloud came to rest in the Desert of Paran. 13They set out, this first time, at the LORD's command through Moses.

14The divisions of the camp of Judah went first, under their standard. Nahshon son of Amminadab was in command. 15Nethanel son of Zuar was over the division of the tribe of Issachar, 16and Eliab son of Helon was over the division of the tribe of Zebulun. 17Then the tabernacle was taken down, and the Gershonites and Merarites, who carried it, set out.

18The divisions of the camp of Reuben went next, under their standard. Elizur son of Shedeur was in command. 19Shelumiel son of Zurishaddai was over the division of the tribe of Simeon, 20and Eliasaph son of Deuel was over the division of the tribe of Gad. 21Then the Kohathites set out, carrying the holy things. The tabernacle was to be set up before they arrived.

22The divisions of the camp of Ephraim went next, under their standard. Elishama son of Ammihud was in command. 23Gamaliel son of Pedahzur was over the division of the tribe of Manasseh, 24and Abidan son of Gideoni was over the division of the tribe of Benjamin.

25Finally, as the rear guard for all the units, the divisions of the camp of Dan set out, under their standard. Ahiezer son of Ammishaddai was in command. 26Pagiel son of Ocran was over the division of the tribe of Asher, 27and Ahira son of Enan was over the division of the tribe of Naphtali. 28This was the order of march for the Israelite divisions as they set out.

29Now Moses said to Hobab son of Reuel the Midianite, Moses' father-in-law, "We are setting out for the place about which the LORD said, 'I will give it to you.' Come with us and we will treat you well, for the LORD has promised good things to Israel."

30He answered, "No, I will not go; I am going back to my own land and my own people."

31But Moses said, "Please do not leave us. You know where we should camp in the desert, and you can be our eyes. 32If you come with us, we will share with you whatever good things the LORD gives us."

33So they set out from the mountain of the LORD and traveled for three days. The ark of the covenant of the LORD went before them during those three days to find them a place to rest. 34The cloud of the LORD was over them by day when they set out from the camp.

35Whenever the ark set out, Moses said,

"Rise up, O LORD!
May your enemies be scattered;
may your foes flee before you."

36Whenever it came to rest, he said,

"Return, O LORD,
to the countless thousands of Israel."

Fire From the LORD

11 Now the people complained about their hardships in the hearing of the LORD, and when he heard them his anger was aroused. Then fire from the LORD burned among them and consumed some of the outskirts of the camp. 2When the people cried out to Moses, he prayed to the LORD and the fire died

Wherever we are this moment, chances are as we look about, we can see testimony of God's promise to provide . . . Infinite indeed are His abundant provisions to His people, including the best of all His blessings: His very presence.

Dick Eastman (1944-)
and Jack Hayford (1934-)

(10:29) Lord God, in all the twists and turns of life I am convinced that You are at work for the good of Your people, both corporately and individually. How I long at this very moment to taste and see that You are good. In my life's journey I gratefully look to You for guidance, provision and protection. Feed me today from Your table of plenty; let me drink from Your cup of blessing, and may I eagerly share whatever good things You give to me with those whom I encounter today. (Ps 34:8)

The LORD has promised good to me,
His word my hope secures;
He will my shield and portion be
As long as life endures.

"Amazing Grace"
John Newton (1779)

(11:4–6) Lord, may I never become bored with grace, now that I have been delivered from my slavery to sin. May I never crave the things with which I once tried to satisfy my fleshly appetites. Instead give me a hunger for heavenly food. Jesus, You are the bread of life. Teach me to find in You my daily bread, and to feed upon Your Word. Create in me a heart of submission, a spirit of obedience, an attitude of contentment.

I love Your grace, I love Your mercy.
I love the way You help me when I call.
I love Your truth,
I love the power of Your name.
But You know I love
Your presence most of all.

My soul takes refuge
In the shadow of Your wings.
Close to You is where I want to be.
You are my strength, You are my God,
You are my King.
And all I want is what You want for me.

"I Love Your Grace"
Rick Founds (©1990)

down. 3So that place was called Taberah,[a] because fire from the
LORD had burned among them.

Quail From the LORD

4The rabble with them began to crave other food, and again
the Israelites started wailing and said, "If only we had meat to
eat! 5We remember the fish we ate in Egypt at no cost—also the
cucumbers, melons, leeks, onions and garlic. 6But now we have
lost our appetite; we never see anything but this manna!"
7The manna was like coriander seed and looked like resin.
8The people went around gathering it, and then ground it in a
handmill or crushed it in a mortar. They cooked it in a pot or
made it into cakes. And it tasted like something made with olive
oil. 9When the dew settled on the camp at night, the manna also
came down.
10Moses heard the people of every family wailing, each at the
entrance to his tent. The LORD became exceedingly angry, and
Moses was troubled. 11He asked the LORD, "Why have you
brought this trouble on your servant? What have I done to displease you that you put the burden of all these people on me?
12Did I conceive all these people? Did I give them birth? Why do
you tell me to carry them in my arms, as a nurse carries an infant, to the land you promised on oath to their forefathers?
13Where can I get meat for all these people? They keep wailing
to me, 'Give us meat to eat!' 14I cannot carry all these people by
myself; the burden is too heavy for me. 15If this is how you are
going to treat me, put me to death right now—if I have found
favor in your eyes—and do not let me face my own ruin."
16The LORD said to Moses: "Bring me seventy of Israel's elders
who are known to you as leaders and officials among the people.
Have them come to the Tent of Meeting, that they may stand there
with you. 17I will come down and speak with you there, and I
will take of the Spirit that is on you and put the Spirit on them.
They will help you carry the burden of the people so that you
will not have to carry it alone.
18"Tell the people: 'Consecrate yourselves in preparation for
tomorrow, when you will eat meat. The LORD heard you when you
wailed, "If only we had meat to eat! We were better off in Egypt!"
Now the LORD will give you meat, and you will eat it. 19You will
not eat it for just one day, or two days, or five, ten or twenty days,
20but for a whole month—until it comes out of your nostrils and
you loathe it—because you have rejected the LORD, who is
among you, and have wailed before him, saying, "Why did we
ever leave Egypt?" ' "
21But Moses said, "Here I am among six hundred thousand
men on foot, and you say, 'I will give them meat to eat for a
whole month!' 22Would they have enough if flocks and herds
were slaughtered for them? Would they have enough if all the
fish in the sea were caught for them?"
23The LORD answered Moses, "Is the LORD's arm too short?
You will now see whether or not what I say will come true for
you."
24So Moses went out and told the people what the LORD had
said. He brought together seventy of their elders and had them
stand around the Tent. 25Then the LORD came down in the cloud

[a] 3 *Taberah* means *burning.*

and spoke with him, and he took of the Spirit that was on him and put the Spirit on the seventy elders. When the Spirit rested on them, they prophesied, but they did not do so again.[a]
26However, two men, whose names were Eldad and Medad,
had remained in the camp. They were listed among the elders,
but did not go out to the Tent. Yet the Spirit also rested on them,
and they prophesied in the camp. 27A young man ran and told
Moses, "Eldad and Medad are prophesying in the camp."
28Joshua son of Nun, who had been Moses' aide since youth,
spoke up and said, "Moses, my lord, stop them!"
29But Moses replied, "Are you jealous for my sake? I wish that
all the LORD's people were prophets and that the LORD would put
his Spirit on them!" 30Then Moses and the elders of Israel returned to the camp.
31Now a wind went out from the LORD and drove quail in from
the sea. It brought them[b] down all around the camp to about
three feet[c] above the ground, as far as a day's walk in any direction. 32All that day and night and all the next day the people went
out and gathered quail. No one gathered less than ten homers.[d]
Then they spread them out all around the camp. 33But while the
meat was still between their teeth and before it could be consumed, the anger of the LORD burned against the people, and he
struck them with a severe plague. 34Therefore the place was
named Kibroth Hattaavah,[e] because there they buried the people
who had craved other food.
35From Kibroth Hattaavah the people traveled to Hazeroth and
stayed there.

Miriam and Aaron Oppose Moses

12 Miriam and Aaron began to talk against Moses because of
his Cushite wife, for he had married a Cushite. 2"Has the
LORD spoken only through Moses?" they asked. "Hasn't he also
spoken through us?" And the LORD heard this.
3(Now Moses was a very humble man, more humble than anyone else on the face of the earth.)
4At once the LORD said to Moses, Aaron and Miriam, "Come
out to the Tent of Meeting, all three of you." So the three of them
came out. 5Then the LORD came down in a pillar of cloud; he
stood at the entrance to the Tent and summoned Aaron and Miriam. When both of them stepped forward, 6he said, "Listen to my
words:

"When a prophet of the LORD is among you,
  I reveal myself to him in visions,
  I speak to him in dreams.
7But this is not true of my servant Moses;
  he is faithful in all my house.
8With him I speak face to face,
  clearly and not in riddles;
  he sees the form of the LORD.
Why then were you not afraid
  to speak against my servant Moses?"

9The anger of the LORD burned against them, and he left them.
10When the cloud lifted from above the Tent, there stood Mir-

[a] 25 Or *prophesied and continued to do so* [b] 31 Or *They flew* [c] 31 Hebrew *two cubits* (about 1 meter) [d] 32 That is, probably about 60 bushels (about 2.2 kiloliters)
[e] 34 *Kibroth Hattaavah* means *graves of craving.*

(11:34) I confess, Lord, that I don't always think of my cravings as dangerous. I don't see that my yearnings make me vulnerable to Your judgment. Kibroth Hattaavah reminds me that I need to be careful—satisfying my craving could cost me my soul. My prayer today is that You would not let worldly hungers put a wedge between You and me. Help me to crave eternal fellowship with You more passionately than any temporary pleasure. Let me learn from these people who hungered for "other food," so that I may find contentment in whatever You provide for me on the journey—one day at a time. (Php 4:11–12)

(12:8) Lord, how I long for the day when Moses' experience becomes mine—that day when I will see You face-to-face, and speak with You, and find complete rest in Your glorious presence. As I wait for that day when You welcome me to my eternal home, let me be humble, even as Moses was humble. Let me not seek the praise of others, Lord, but only Your favor. Work in and through me, Your fragile jar of clay, so that Your strength will be made perfect in my weakness. Oh, may Your power rest on me, that I may find joy and purpose in serving You all the days of my life. (2Co 4:7; 12:9)

There is satisfaction in serving the Lord Jesus; sweetness in suffering for His Name; blessing in bearing His reproach; pleasure in becoming a pilgrim; delight in doing His bidding . . . like Moses of old, with lowly heart and veiled face, we shall walk where He leads, shall be thankful for daily manna, shall endure as seeing Him who is invisible, shall believe Him when every other friend fails.

Victor Raymond Edman (1900–1967)

(12:15) You are so gracious, Lord. You were merciful to Miriam, showing her the error of her ways, teaching her a lesson she'd never forget, and yet allowing her to be restored to the community of Your people. And You show mercy to me, too, for I foolishly commit sin after sin, even though I know better. I am so slow to learn, and You would be justified if You were to send me away from Your loving presence permanently. Thank You for displaying Your mercy in my life——a mercy that disciplines me to draw me back to You, so that I can be healed, restored, and made new.

(13:1–2) Just as You invited the Israelites of old to explore the land of promise, so You invite us, precious Lord, to a life of exploration, a life of adventure. You encourage us to discover and unearth the wealth of Your good gifts; to taste and to see that You are good; to experience the richness of salvation that we have in Your Son Jesus; to share with others the wonderful fruit of His righteousness. In this moment of personal worship, Lord, I open myself to You and to the life of exploration You offer. Help me to follow You in the adventure of faith with all the wonder and amazement of a little child. (Lk 18:17)

The time has come to move on? Then break up the camp with a good heart; it is only one more stage on the journey home!

One day we shall break camp for the last time in this world and face the final adventure of death. May we then have so passed the days of our pilgrimage, with the Lord of adventurers by our side, that we may reach, in the end, our eternal home.

W. R. Matthews (1818-1909)

iam—leprous,[a] like snow. Aaron turned toward her and saw
that she had leprosy; 11and he said to Moses, "Please, my lord,
do not hold against us the sin we have so foolishly committed.
12Do not let her be like a stillborn infant coming from its mother's
womb with its flesh half eaten away."

13So Moses cried out to the LORD, "O God, please heal her!"

14The LORD replied to Moses, "If her father had spit in her face,
would she not have been in disgrace for seven days? Confine her
outside the camp for seven days; after that she can be brought
back." 15So Miriam was confined outside the camp for seven days,
and the people did not move on till she was brought back.

16After that, the people left Hazeroth and encamped in the
Desert of Paran.

Exploring Canaan

13 The LORD said to Moses, 2"Send some men to explore the
land of Canaan, which I am giving to the Israelites. From
each ancestral tribe send one of its leaders."

3So at the LORD's command Moses sent them out from the
Desert of Paran. All of them were leaders of the Israelites. 4These
are their names:

from the tribe of Reuben, Shammua son of Zaccur;
5from the tribe of Simeon, Shaphat son of Hori;
6from the tribe of Judah, Caleb son of Jephunneh;
7from the tribe of Issachar, Igal son of Joseph;
8from the tribe of Ephraim, Hoshea son of Nun;
9from the tribe of Benjamin, Palti son of Raphu;
10from the tribe of Zebulun, Gaddiel son of Sodi;
11from the tribe of Manasseh (a tribe of Joseph), Gaddi son of Susi;
12from the tribe of Dan, Ammiel son of Gemalli;
13from the tribe of Asher, Sethur son of Michael;
14from the tribe of Naphtali, Nahbi son of Vophsi;
15from the tribe of Gad, Geuel son of Maki.

16These are the names of the men Moses sent to explore the land.
(Moses gave Hoshea son of Nun the name Joshua.)

17When Moses sent them to explore Canaan, he said, "Go up
through the Negev and on into the hill country. 18See what the land
is like and whether the people who live there are strong or weak,
few or many. 19What kind of land do they live in? Is it good or
bad? What kind of towns do they live in? Are they unwalled or fortified? 20How is the soil? Is it fertile or poor? Are there trees on it
or not? Do your best to bring back some of the fruit of the land."
(It was the season for the first ripe grapes.)

21So they went up and explored the land from the Desert of Zin
as far as Rehob, toward Lebo[b] Hamath. 22They went up through
the Negev and came to Hebron, where Ahiman, Sheshai and Talmai, the descendants of Anak, lived. (Hebron had been built seven
years before Zoan in Egypt.) 23When they reached the Valley of
Eshcol,[c] they cut off a branch bearing a single cluster of grapes.
Two of them carried it on a pole between them, along with some
pomegranates and figs. 24That place was called the Valley of Eshcol because of the cluster of grapes the Israelites cut off there.
25At the end of forty days they returned from exploring the land.

[a] *10* The Hebrew word was used for various diseases affecting the skin—not necessarily leprosy. [b] *21* Or *toward the entrance to* [c] *23* *Eshcol* means *cluster*; also in verse 24.

Report on the Exploration

26They came back to Moses and Aaron and the whole Israelite
community at Kadesh in the Desert of Paran. There they reported
to them and to the whole assembly and showed them the fruit of
the land. 27They gave Moses this account: "We went into the land
to which you sent us, and it does flow with milk and honey! Here
is its fruit. 28But the people who live there are powerful, and the
cities are fortified and very large. We even saw descendants of
Anak there. 29The Amalekites live in the Negev; the Hittites, Jebusites and Amorites live in the hill country; and the Canaanites live
near the sea and along the Jordan."
30Then Caleb silenced the people before Moses and said, "We
should go up and take possession of the land, for we can certainly do it."
31But the men who had gone up with him said, "We can't attack
those people; they are stronger than we are." 32And they spread
among the Israelites a bad report about the land they had explored. They said, "The land we explored devours those living in
it. All the people we saw there are of great size. 33We saw the
Nephilim there (the descendants of Anak come from the Nephilim). We seemed like grasshoppers in our own eyes, and we
looked the same to them."

The People Rebel

14 That night all the people of the community raised their
voices and wept aloud. 2All the Israelites grumbled against
Moses and Aaron, and the whole assembly said to them, "If only
we had died in Egypt! Or in this desert! 3Why is the LORD bringing
us to this land only to let us fall by the sword? Our wives and children will be taken as plunder. Wouldn't it be better for us to go
back to Egypt?" 4And they said to each other, "We should choose
a leader and go back to Egypt."
5Then Moses and Aaron fell facedown in front of the whole Israelite assembly gathered there. 6Joshua son of Nun and Caleb son
of Jephunneh, who were among those who had explored the land,
tore their clothes 7and said to the entire Israelite assembly, "The
land we passed through and explored is exceedingly good. 8If the
LORD is pleased with us, he will lead us into that land, a land flowing with milk and honey, and will give it to us. 9Only do not rebel
against the LORD. And do not be afraid of the people of the land,
because we will swallow them up. Their protection is gone, but the
LORD is with us. Do not be afraid of them."
10But the whole assembly talked about stoning them. Then the
glory of the LORD appeared at the Tent of Meeting to all the Israelites. 11The LORD said to Moses, "How long will these people treat
me with contempt? How long will they refuse to believe in me, in
spite of all the miraculous signs I have performed among them?
12I will strike them down with a plague and destroy them, but I
will make you into a nation greater and stronger than they."
13Moses said to the LORD, "Then the Egyptians will hear about
it! By your power you brought these people up from among them.
14And they will tell the inhabitants of this land about it. They have
already heard that you, O LORD, are with these people and that you,
O LORD, have been seen face to face, that your cloud stays over
them, and that you go before them in a pillar of cloud by day and
a pillar of fire by night. 15If you put these people to death all at
one time, the nations who have heard this report about you will

(13:27–33) I want to be like Caleb, Lord: convinced of Your power; sold on Your goodness; committed to Your service. But all too often I see the obstacles looming out ahead of me. I grow fainthearted and fail to remember that You are walking the path alongside me. Forgive me for not trusting You, for giving in to my fear. Make me like Caleb, Father God. Empower me with Your strength. Convince me of Your faithfulness. Enable me to see You above all else, for with You all things are possible! (Mk 10:27)

God likes His people to believe that there is nothing too hard for Him . . . We are all the time limiting God's power by our own ideas. Let us get our eyes off one another and fix them upon God. There is nothing too hard for Him.

Dwight L. Moody (1837-1899)

When I can't see You, I know You're
here;
When I can't feel You, I will not
fear;
I will trust in You
And I will not be afraid.
And when the battle is close at hand,
I know You're with me to help me
stand;
I will trust in You
And I will not be afraid.
I will not be afraid,
I will not be afraid.
I will trust in You,
I will trust in You.

"I Will Trust in You"
Danny Daniels (©1987)

(14:17–20) Thank You for the powerful gift of prayer. Thank You for hearing us when we call on You. You are so willing to listen, so gracious in Your response, so generous with Your mercy. Moses prayed, "Forgive the sin of these people," to which You replied, "I have forgiven them, as you asked." You displayed Your strength, not in the destruction that You had threatened, but in the forgiveness for which Moses had prayed. Truly, "the prayer of a righteous man is powerful and effective." (Jas 5:16)

Prayer is the noblest exercise of the soul, the most exalted use of our best faculties.
William Law (1686–1761)

say, 16 'The LORD was not able to bring these people into the land he promised them on oath; so he slaughtered them in the desert.'

17 "Now may the Lord's strength be displayed, just as you have declared: 18 'The LORD is slow to anger, abounding in love and forgiving sin and rebellion. Yet he does not leave the guilty unpunished; he punishes the children for the sin of the fathers to the third and fourth generation.' 19 In accordance with your great love, forgive the sin of these people, just as you have pardoned them from the time they left Egypt until now."

20 The LORD replied, "I have forgiven them, as you asked. 21 Nevertheless, as surely as I live and as surely as the glory of the LORD fills the whole earth, 22 not one of the men who saw my glory and the miraculous signs I performed in Egypt and in the desert but who disobeyed me and tested me ten times— 23 not one of them will ever see the land I promised on oath to their forefathers. No one who has treated me with contempt will ever see it. 24 But because my servant Caleb has a different spirit and follows me wholeheartedly, I will bring him into the land he went to, and his descendants will inherit it. 25 Since the Amalekites and Canaanites are living in the valleys, turn back tomorrow and set out toward the desert along the route to the Red Sea.[a]"

26 The LORD said to Moses and Aaron: 27 "How long will this wicked community grumble against me? I have heard the complaints of these grumbling Israelites. 28 So tell them, 'As surely as I live, declares the LORD, I will do to you the very things I heard you say: 29 In this desert your bodies will fall—every one of you twenty years old or more who was counted in the census and who has grumbled against me. 30 Not one of you will enter the land I swore with uplifted hand to make your home, except Caleb son of Jephunneh and Joshua son of Nun. 31 As for your children that you said would be taken as plunder, I will bring them in to enjoy the land you have rejected. 32 But you—your bodies will fall in this desert. 33 Your children will be shepherds here for forty years, suffering for your unfaithfulness, until the last of your bodies lies in the desert. 34 For forty years—one year for each of the forty days you explored the land—you will suffer for your sins and know what it is like to have me against you.' 35 I, the LORD, have spoken, and I will surely do these things to this whole wicked community, which has banded together against me. They will meet their end in this desert; here they will die."

36 So the men Moses had sent to explore the land, who returned and made the whole community grumble against him by spreading a bad report about it— 37 these men responsible for spreading the bad report about the land were struck down and died of a plague before the LORD. 38 Of the men who went to explore the land, only Joshua son of Nun and Caleb son of Jephunneh survived.

39 When Moses reported this to all the Israelites, they mourned bitterly. 40 Early the next morning they went up toward the high hill country. "We have sinned," they said. "We will go up to the place the LORD promised."

41 But Moses said, "Why are you disobeying the LORD's command? This will not succeed! 42 Do not go up, because the LORD is not with you. You will be defeated by your enemies, 43 for the

[a] *25* Hebrew *Yam Suph*; that is, Sea of Reeds

Amalekites and Canaanites will face you there. Because you have
turned away from the LORD, he will not be with you and you will
fall by the sword."
44 Nevertheless, in their presumption they went up toward the
high hill country, though neither Moses nor the ark of the LORD's
covenant moved from the camp. 45 Then the Amalekites and
Canaanites who lived in that hill country came down and attacked them and beat them down all the way to Hormah.

Supplementary Offerings

15 The LORD said to Moses, 2 "Speak to the Israelites and say
to them: 'After you enter the land I am giving you as a
home 3 and you present to the LORD offerings made by fire, from
the herd or the flock, as an aroma pleasing to the LORD—
whether burnt offerings or sacrifices, for special vows or freewill
offerings or festival offerings— 4 then the one who brings his offering shall present to the LORD a grain offering of a tenth of an
ephah[a] of fine flour mixed with a quarter of a hin[b] of oil. 5 With
each lamb for the burnt offering or the sacrifice, prepare a quarter of a hin of wine as a drink offering.
6 " 'With a ram prepare a grain offering of two-tenths of an
ephah[c] of fine flour mixed with a third of a hin[d] of oil, 7 and a
third of a hin of wine as a drink offering. Offer it as an aroma
pleasing to the LORD.
8 " 'When you prepare a young bull as a burnt offering or sacrifice, for a special vow or a fellowship offering[e] to the LORD,
9 bring with the bull a grain offering of three-tenths of an ephah[f]
of fine flour mixed with half a hin[g] of oil. 10 Also bring half a hin
of wine as a drink offering. It will be an offering made by fire, an
aroma pleasing to the LORD. 11 Each bull or ram, each lamb or
young goat, is to be prepared in this manner. 12 Do this for each
one, for as many as you prepare.
13 " 'Everyone who is native-born must do these things in this
way when he brings an offering made by fire as an aroma pleasing to the LORD. 14 For the generations to come, whenever an
alien or anyone else living among you presents an offering made
by fire as an aroma pleasing to the LORD, he must do exactly as
you do. 15 The community is to have the same rules for you and
for the alien living among you; this is a lasting ordinance for the
generations to come. You and the alien shall be the same before
the LORD: 16 The same laws and regulations will apply both to you
and to the alien living among you.' "
17 The LORD said to Moses, 18 "Speak to the Israelites and say to
them: 'When you enter the land to which I am taking you 19 and
you eat the food of the land, present a portion as an offering to
the LORD. 20 Present a cake from the first of your ground meal
and present it as an offering from the threshing floor.
21 Throughout the generations to come you are to give this offering to the LORD from the first of your ground meal.

Offerings for Unintentional Sins

22 " 'Now if you unintentionally fail to keep any of these commands the LORD gave Moses— 23 any of the LORD's commands to

[a] 4 That is, probably about 2 quarts (about 2 liters) [b] 4 That is, probably about 1 quart (about 1 liter); also in verse 5 [c] 6 That is, probably about 4 quarts (about 4.5 liters)
[d] 6 That is, probably about 1 1/4 quarts (about 1.2 liters); also in verse 7
[e] 8 Traditionally *peace offering* [f] 9 That is, probably about 6 quarts (about 6.5 liters)
[g] 9 That is, probably about 2 quarts (about 2 liters); also in verse 10

(15:15) How gracious You are, dear heavenly Father! Just as in ancient times, when You required that aliens be treated the same as Your people, so today You welcome all who respond to Your invitation to come to You in spirit and truth. You are no respecter of persons, Lord. With You, there is neither Jew nor Greek, slave nor free, male nor female, for we are all one in Christ Jesus. He is our peace, who has broken down every barrier, and through Him, we are no longer foreigners and aliens, but fellow citizens with Your people and members of Your household. We worship You, Father, for accepting us into the community of those who are saved through the blood of the Lamb, your precious Son Jesus. (Gal 3:26-28; Eph 2:11-14,19–20)

One by one we're drawn together,
One by one to Jesus' side.
One in Him, we'll live forever,
Strangers He has reconciled.

In His love no walls between us,
In His love a common ground.
Kneeling at the cross of Jesus,
All our pride comes tumbling down.

Let the walls fall down.
Let the walls fall down.
Let the walls fall down.
By His love let the walls fall down.

"Let the Walls Fall Down"
Bill Batstone, Anne Barbour and
John Barbour (©1993)

(15:39) Lord, You know us so well. You know how prone we are to forget—or to deny—things that are important to You. You graciously made provision for Your people to be forgiven for unintentional sins. Now You made a way to help *prevent* unintentional sins. In the days of ancient Israel, these tassels were a visible and tactile reminder to Your people of how they were to live and to whom they belonged. Lord, provide me with a daily reminder—whatever You choose for me—that will help me remember day after day, year after year, to obey all Your commands so that I can bring glory to Your name.

you through him, from the day the LORD gave them and continuing through the generations to come— 24and if this is done unintentionally without the community being aware of it, then the
whole community is to offer a young bull for a burnt offering as
an aroma pleasing to the LORD, along with its prescribed grain
offering and drink offering, and a male goat for a sin offering.
25The priest is to make atonement for the whole Israelite community, and they will be forgiven, for it was not intentional and
they have brought to the LORD for their wrong an offering made
by fire and a sin offering. 26The whole Israelite community and
the aliens living among them will be forgiven, because all the
people were involved in the unintentional wrong.

27" 'But if just one person sins unintentionally, he must bring
a year-old female goat for a sin offering. 28The priest is to make
atonement before the LORD for the one who erred by sinning unintentionally, and when atonement has been made for him, he
will be forgiven. 29One and the same law applies to everyone
who sins unintentionally, whether he is a native-born Israelite or
an alien.

30" 'But anyone who sins defiantly, whether native-born or
alien, blasphemes the LORD, and that person must be cut off from
his people. 31Because he has despised the LORD's word and broken his commands, that person must surely be cut off; his guilt
remains on him.' "

The Sabbath-Breaker Put to Death

32While the Israelites were in the desert, a man was found
gathering wood on the Sabbath day. 33Those who found him
gathering wood brought him to Moses and Aaron and the whole
assembly, 34and they kept him in custody, because it was not
clear what should be done to him. 35Then the LORD said to
Moses, "The man must die. The whole assembly must stone him
outside the camp." 36So the assembly took him outside the camp
and stoned him to death, as the LORD commanded Moses.

Tassels on Garments

37The LORD said to Moses, 38"Speak to the Israelites and say to
them: 'Throughout the generations to come you are to make tassels on the corners of your garments, with a blue cord on each
tassel. 39You will have these tassels to look at and so you will remember all the commands of the LORD, that you may obey them
and not prostitute yourselves by going after the lusts of your own
hearts and eyes. 40Then you will remember to obey all my commands and will be consecrated to your God. 41I am the LORD
your God, who brought you out of Egypt to be your God. I am the
LORD your God.' "

Korah, Dathan and Abiram

16 Korah son of Izhar, the son of Kohath, the son of Levi, and
certain Reubenites—Dathan and Abiram, sons of Eliab,
and On son of Peleth—became insolent[a] 2and rose up against
Moses. With them were 250 Israelite men, well-known community leaders who had been appointed members of the council.
3They came as a group to oppose Moses and Aaron and said to
them, "You have gone too far! The whole community is holy,

[a] 1 Or *Peleth—took* men

every one of them, and the LORD is with them. Why then do you
set yourselves above the LORD's assembly?"
4When Moses heard this, he fell facedown. 5Then he said to
Korah and all his followers: "In the morning the LORD will show
who belongs to him and who is holy, and he will have that person
come near him. The man he chooses he will cause to come near
him. 6You, Korah, and all your followers are to do this: Take
censers 7and tomorrow put fire and incense in them before the
LORD. The man the LORD chooses will be the one who is holy. You
Levites have gone too far!"
8Moses also said to Korah, "Now listen, you Levites! 9Isn't it
enough for you that the God of Israel has separated you from the
rest of the Israelite community and brought you near himself to
do the work at the LORD's tabernacle and to stand before the community and minister to them? 10He has brought you and all your
fellow Levites near himself, but now you are trying to get the
priesthood too. 11It is against the LORD that you and all your followers have banded together. Who is Aaron that you should
grumble against him?"
12Then Moses summoned Dathan and Abiram, the sons of
Eliab. But they said, "We will not come! 13Isn't it enough that you
have brought us up out of a land flowing with milk and honey to
kill us in the desert? And now you also want to lord it over us?
14Moreover, you haven't brought us into a land flowing with milk
and honey or given us an inheritance of fields and vineyards. Will
you gouge out the eyes of[a] these men? No, we will not come!"
15Then Moses became very angry and said to the LORD, "Do
not accept their offering. I have not taken so much as a donkey
from them, nor have I wronged any of them."
16Moses said to Korah, "You and all your followers are to appear before the LORD tomorrow—you and they and Aaron.
17Each man is to take his censer and put incense in it—250
censers in all—and present it before the LORD. You and Aaron
are to present your censers also." 18So each man took his censer,
put fire and incense in it, and stood with Moses and Aaron at the
entrance to the Tent of Meeting. 19When Korah had gathered all
his followers in opposition to them at the entrance to the Tent of
Meeting, the glory of the LORD appeared to the entire assembly.
20The LORD said to Moses and Aaron, 21"Separate yourselves
from this assembly so I can put an end to them at once."
22But Moses and Aaron fell facedown and cried out, "O God,
God of the spirits of all mankind, will you be angry with the entire assembly when only one man sins?"
23Then the LORD said to Moses, 24"Say to the assembly, 'Move
away from the tents of Korah, Dathan and Abiram.' "
25Moses got up and went to Dathan and Abiram, and the elders
of Israel followed him. 26He warned the assembly, "Move back
from the tents of these wicked men! Do not touch anything belonging to them, or you will be swept away because of all their
sins." 27So they moved away from the tents of Korah, Dathan and
Abiram. Dathan and Abiram had come out and were standing
with their wives, children and little ones at the entrances to their
tents.
28Then Moses said, "This is how you will know that the LORD
has sent me to do all these things and that it was not my idea: 29If

[a] 14 Or *you make slaves of;* or *you deceive*

(16:8–11) I ponder the attitudes of Korah, Dathan, Abiram and other leaders of Israel, and I am amazed at their audacity. But it disturbs me even more to see, reflected in their story, my own rebellious spirit. How easy it is, Lord, for me to become self-absorbed, insolent and disrespectful—so centered on myself that I forget Your continuous blessings. I am often dissatisfied with Your guidance and ungrateful for Your generosity. I covet other people's gifts and callings. In this very moment, Lord, I seek Your forgiveness. Purify me with Your holy fire, that I may be cleansed. Do not consume me in Your anger, but preserve me, that I may worship You all the days of my life.

The greatest burden we have to carry in life, the most difficult thing we have to manage, is self. Our own daily round of existence, our bodies and emotions, our private weaknesses and temptations–our inward concerns of every kind: these are the things that worry us more than anything else. These are the cares that most often rob us of our joy.

In laying down your burdens, therefore, the first one you must get rid of is yourself. You must hand over yourself and all your concerns into the care and keeping of your God, and leave them there. He made you; therefore He surely understands you and knows how to manage you, if you will only trust Him to do it.

Catherine Jackson

these men die a natural death and experience only what usually
happens to men, then the LORD has not sent me. 30 But if the LORD
brings about something totally new, and the earth opens its mouth
and swallows them, with everything that belongs to them, and they
go down alive into the grave,[a] then you will know that these men
have treated the LORD with contempt."

31 As soon as he finished saying all this, the ground under them
split apart 32 and the earth opened its mouth and swallowed them,
with their households and all Korah's men and all their possessions. 33 They went down alive into the grave, with everything they
owned; the earth closed over them, and they perished and were
gone from the community. 34 At their cries, all the Israelites
around them fled, shouting, "The earth is going to swallow us
too!"

35 And fire came out from the LORD and consumed the 250 men
who were offering the incense.

36 The LORD said to Moses, 37 "Tell Eleazar son of Aaron, the
priest, to take the censers out of the smoldering remains and scatter the coals some distance away, for the censers are holy— 38 the
censers of the men who sinned at the cost of their lives. Hammer
the censers into sheets to overlay the altar, for they were presented before the LORD and have become holy. Let them be a sign to the
Israelites."

39 So Eleazar the priest collected the bronze censers brought by
those who had been burned up, and he had them hammered out
to overlay the altar, 40 as the LORD directed him through Moses.
This was to remind the Israelites that no one except a descendant
of Aaron should come to burn incense before the LORD, or he
would become like Korah and his followers.

41 The next day the whole Israelite community grumbled against
Moses and Aaron. "You have killed the LORD's people," they said.

42 But when the assembly gathered in opposition to Moses and
Aaron and turned toward the Tent of Meeting, suddenly the cloud
covered it and the glory of the LORD appeared. 43 Then Moses and
Aaron went to the front of the Tent of Meeting, 44 and the LORD said
to Moses, 45 "Get away from this assembly so I can put an end to
them at once." And they fell facedown.

46 Then Moses said to Aaron, "Take your censer and put incense
in it, along with fire from the altar, and hurry to the assembly to
make atonement for them. Wrath has come out from the LORD; the
plague has started." 47 So Aaron did as Moses said, and ran into
the midst of the assembly. The plague had already started among
the people, but Aaron offered the incense and made atonement
for them. 48 He stood between the living and the dead, and the
plague stopped. 49 But 14,700 people died from the plague, in addition to those who had died because of Korah. 50 Then Aaron returned to Moses at the entrance to the Tent of Meeting, for the
plague had stopped.

The Budding of Aaron's Staff

17 The LORD said to Moses, 2 "Speak to the Israelites and get
twelve staffs from them, one from the leader of each of their
ancestral tribes. Write the name of each man on his staff. 3 On the
staff of Levi write Aaron's name, for there must be one staff for the
head of each ancestral tribe. 4 Place them in the Tent of Meeting in

[a] 30 Hebrew *Sheol*; also in verse 33

(16:46–48) Most holy God, Aaron confirmed his calling as the high priest when he stood between the living and the dead and made atonement for the sins of Israel. You, in turn, confirmed his calling by honoring his intercession and stopping Your judgment against the people. While the censers of others brought Your wrath, the censer of Aaron won Your peace. Lord, I pray that I might have a heart like that of Aaron—willing to bless those who persecute me, and to pray for those who mistreat me. (Lev 10:1–3; Lk 6:28)

front of the Testimony, where I meet with you. 5The staff belonging to the man I choose will sprout, and I will rid myself of this
constant grumbling against you by the Israelites."
6So Moses spoke to the Israelites, and their leaders gave him
twelve staffs, one for the leader of each of their ancestral tribes,
and Aaron's staff was among them. 7Moses placed the staffs before
the LORD in the Tent of the Testimony.
8The next day Moses entered the Tent of the Testimony and saw
that Aaron's staff, which represented the house of Levi, had not
only sprouted but had budded, blossomed and produced almonds. 9Then Moses brought out all the staffs from the LORD's
presence to all the Israelites. They looked at them, and each man
took his own staff.
10The LORD said to Moses, "Put back Aaron's staff in front of
the Testimony, to be kept as a sign to the rebellious. This will put
an end to their grumbling against me, so that they will not die."
11Moses did just as the LORD commanded him.
12The Israelites said to Moses, "We will die! We are lost, we are
all lost! 13Anyone who even comes near the tabernacle of the LORD
will die. Are we all going to die?"

Duties of Priests and Levites

18 The LORD said to Aaron, "You, your sons and your father's
family are to bear the responsibility for offenses against the
sanctuary, and you and your sons alone are to bear the responsibility for offenses against the priesthood. 2Bring your fellow Levites from your ancestral tribe to join you and assist you when you
and your sons minister before the Tent of the Testimony. 3They are
to be responsible to you and are to perform all the duties of the
Tent, but they must not go near the furnishings of the sanctuary or
the altar, or both they and you will die. 4They are to join you and
be responsible for the care of the Tent of Meeting—all the work
at the Tent—and no one else may come near where you are.
5"You are to be responsible for the care of the sanctuary and
the altar, so that wrath will not fall on the Israelites again. 6I myself have selected your fellow Levites from among the Israelites as
a gift to you, dedicated to the LORD to do the work at the Tent of
Meeting. 7But only you and your sons may serve as priests in connection with everything at the altar and inside the curtain. I am
giving you the service of the priesthood as a gift. Anyone else who
comes near the sanctuary must be put to death."

Offerings for Priests and Levites

8Then the LORD said to Aaron, "I myself have put you in charge
of the offerings presented to me; all the holy offerings the Israelites give me I give to you and your sons as your portion and regular share. 9You are to have the part of the most holy offerings that
is kept from the fire. From all the gifts they bring me as most holy
offerings, whether grain or sin or guilt offerings, that part belongs
to you and your sons. 10Eat it as something most holy; every male
shall eat it. You must regard it as holy.
11"This also is yours: whatever is set aside from the gifts of all
the wave offerings of the Israelites. I give this to you and your sons
and daughters as your regular share. Everyone in your household
who is ceremonially clean may eat it.
12"I give you all the finest olive oil and all the finest new wine
and grain they give the LORD as the firstfruits of their harvest.

(17:3–10) I praise You, O God, for the significance of Aaron's rod—a sign and symbol of the coming Christ, whose eternal high priesthood was confirmed when You raised Him from the dead. For "Christ has indeed been raised from the dead, the firstfruits of those who have fallen asleep." Like Aaron's rod, the priesthood of the risen Christ bears fruit for today; and its buds and blossoms promise fruitfulness for tomorrow. (1Co 15:20; Heb 2:17; 3:1; 4:14—5:10; 7:1–28)

Jesus lives, and death is now
But my entrance into glory.
Courage then, my soul, for thou
Hast a crown of life before thee;
Thou shalt find thy hopes were just;
Jesus is my hope and trust.

"Jesus Lives and So Shall I"
Christian F. Gellert (1757)
Trans. J.D. Lang (1826)

13All the land's firstfruits that they bring to the LORD will be
yours. Everyone in your household who is ceremonially clean
may eat it.
14"Everything in Israel that is devoted[a] to the LORD is yours.
15The first offspring of every womb, both man and animal, that
is offered to the LORD is yours. But you must redeem every firstborn son and every firstborn male of unclean animals. 16When
they are a month old, you must redeem them at the redemption
price set at five shekels[b] of silver, according to the sanctuary
shekel, which weighs twenty gerahs.
17"But you must not redeem the firstborn of an ox, a sheep or
a goat; they are holy. Sprinkle their blood on the altar and burn
their fat as an offering made by fire, an aroma pleasing to the
LORD. 18Their meat is to be yours, just as the breast of the wave
offering and the right thigh are yours. 19Whatever is set aside
from the holy offerings the Israelites present to the LORD I give to
you and your sons and daughters as your regular share. It is an
everlasting covenant of salt before the LORD for both you and
your offspring."
20The LORD said to Aaron, "You will have no inheritance in
their land, nor will you have any share among them; I am your
share and your inheritance among the Israelites.
21"I give to the Levites all the tithes in Israel as their inheritance in return for the work they do while serving at the Tent of
Meeting. 22From now on the Israelites must not go near the Tent
of Meeting, or they will bear the consequences of their sin and
will die. 23It is the Levites who are to do the work at the Tent of
Meeting and bear the responsibility for offenses against it. This is
a lasting ordinance for the generations to come. They will receive no inheritance among the Israelites. 24Instead, I give to the
Levites as their inheritance the tithes that the Israelites present
as an offering to the LORD. That is why I said concerning them:
'They will have no inheritance among the Israelites.' "
25The LORD said to Moses, 26"Speak to the Levites and say to
them: 'When you receive from the Israelites the tithe I give you
as your inheritance, you must present a tenth of that tithe as the
LORD's offering. 27Your offering will be reckoned to you as grain
from the threshing floor or juice from the winepress. 28In this
way you also will present an offering to the LORD from all the
tithes you receive from the Israelites. From these tithes you must
give the LORD's portion to Aaron the priest. 29You must present
as the LORD's portion the best and holiest part of everything given
to you.'
30"Say to the Levites: 'When you present the best part, it will
be reckoned to you as the product of the threshing floor or the
winepress. 31You and your households may eat the rest of it
anywhere, for it is your wages for your work at the Tent of Meeting. 32By presenting the best part of it you will not be guilty in
this matter; then you will not defile the holy offerings of the Israelites, and you will not die.' "

The Water of Cleansing

19 The LORD said to Moses and Aaron: 2"This is a requirement
of the law that the LORD has commanded: Tell the Israelites
to bring you a red heifer without defect or blemish and that has

[a] *14* The Hebrew term refers to the irrevocable giving over of things or persons to the LORD.
[b] *16* That is, about 2 ounces (about 55 grams)

(18:20) Lord, like Your priests in ancient times, we find our inheritance in You. You provide for us whatever we need, whenever we need it. You have promised to give us the desire of our hearts. And for all eternity, we are joint heirs with Your beloved Son. What greater inheritance could anyone seek than You? Even today, as Your priests, we remember the words of Jesus, "Seek first his kingdom and his righteousness, and all these things will be given to you as well." (Ps 37:4; Mt 6:33; Ro 8:17)

Riches I heed not, nor man's empty
praise,
Thou mine inheritance, now and
always;
Thou and Thou only, first in my
heart,
High King of heaven, my Treasure
Thou art.

"Be Thou My Vision"
Ancient Irish Hymn (8th C.)
Trans. Mary E. Byrne (1880-1931)
Versified by Eleanor H. Hull (1860-1935)

They waste their energies in unrewarding efforts; yet they accomplish nothing, for, setting their affections on created things, they try them all in turn before they dream of trying God from whom all things proceed. Suppose they did get everything they wanted, what would happen then? One treasure after another would fail to satisfy, and then the only object of desire left would be the Cause of all.

Saint Bernard of Clairvaux (1090-1153)

never been under a yoke. 3Give it to Eleazar the priest; it is to be taken outside the camp and slaughtered in his presence. 4Then Eleazar the priest is to take some of its blood on his finger and sprinkle it seven times toward the front of the Tent of Meeting. 5While he watches, the heifer is to be burned—its hide, flesh, blood and offal. 6The priest is to take some cedar wood, hyssop and scarlet wool and throw them onto the burning heifer. 7After that, the priest must wash his clothes and bathe himself with water. He may then come into the camp, but he will be ceremonially unclean till evening. 8The man who burns it must also wash his clothes and bathe with water, and he too will be unclean till evening.

9"A man who is clean shall gather up the ashes of the heifer and put them in a ceremonially clean place outside the camp. They shall be kept by the Israelite community for use in the water of cleansing; it is for purification from sin. 10The man who gathers up the ashes of the heifer must also wash his clothes, and he too will be unclean till evening. This will be a lasting ordinance both for the Israelites and for the aliens living among them.

11"Whoever touches the dead body of anyone will be unclean for seven days. 12He must purify himself with the water on the third day and on the seventh day; then he will be clean. But if he does not purify himself on the third and seventh days, he will not be clean. 13Whoever touches the dead body of anyone and fails to purify himself defiles the LORD's tabernacle. That person must be cut off from Israel. Because the water of cleansing has not been sprinkled on him, he is unclean; his uncleanness remains on him.

14"This is the law that applies when a person dies in a tent: Anyone who enters the tent and anyone who is in it will be unclean for seven days, 15and every open container without a lid fastened on it will be unclean.

16"Anyone out in the open who touches someone who has been killed with a sword or someone who has died a natural death, or anyone who touches a human bone or a grave, will be unclean for seven days.

17"For the unclean person, put some ashes from the burned purification offering into a jar and pour fresh water over them. 18Then a man who is ceremonially clean is to take some hyssop, dip it in the water and sprinkle the tent and all the furnishings and the people who were there. He must also sprinkle anyone who has touched a human bone or a grave or someone who has been killed or someone who has died a natural death. 19The man who is clean is to sprinkle the unclean person on the third and seventh days, and on the seventh day he is to purify him. The person being cleansed must wash his clothes and bathe with water, and that evening he will be clean. 20But if a person who is unclean does not purify himself, he must be cut off from the community, because he has defiled the sanctuary of the LORD. The water of cleansing has not been sprinkled on him, and he is unclean. 21This is a lasting ordinance for them.

"The man who sprinkles the water of cleansing must also wash his clothes, and anyone who touches the water of cleansing will be unclean till evening. 22Anything that an unclean person

(19:9) In Your mercy, Lord, You identified the ashes of a red heifer as the means of cleansing Your Old Testament people. The red heifer was killed before the sin was committed—the payment had already been made and awaited its appropriation. Yet it was only an outward cleansing. The inward cleansing had to wait for the appearance of Your beloved Son Jesus. His blood was shed on the cross before I ever sinned—again, the payment was already made and awaited its appropriation. How can I thank You enough, Father God, for the blood of Jesus that cleanses me inside and out? Jesus died for me before I ever sinned. Now I live with You as though I never sinned. (Heb 9:13–14)

Have you been to Jesus for the
cleansing power?
Are you washed in the blood of the
Lamb?
Are you fully trusting in His grace
this hour?
Are you washed in the blood of the
Lamb?

Lay aside the garments that are
stained with sin,
And be washed in the blood of the
Lamb.
There's a fountain flowing for the
soul unclean,
O be washed in the blood of the
Lamb.

Are you washed in the blood,
In the soul-cleansing blood of the
Lamb?
Are your garments spotless?
Are they white as snow?
Are you washed in the blood of the
Lamb?

"Are You Washed in the Blood?"
Elisha A. Hoffman (1839–1929)

touches becomes unclean, and anyone who touches it becomes
unclean till evening."

Water From the Rock

20 In the first month the whole Israelite community arrived
at the Desert of Zin, and they stayed at Kadesh. There
Miriam died and was buried.
2Now there was no water for the community, and the people
gathered in opposition to Moses and Aaron. 3They quarreled
with Moses and said, "If only we had died when our brothers
fell dead before the LORD! 4Why did you bring the LORD's community into this desert, that we and our livestock should die
here? 5Why did you bring us up out of Egypt to this terrible
place? It has no grain or figs, grapevines or pomegranates. And
there is no water to drink!"
6Moses and Aaron went from the assembly to the entrance to
the Tent of Meeting and fell facedown, and the glory of the LORD
appeared to them. 7The LORD said to Moses, 8"Take the staff, and
you and your brother Aaron gather the assembly together. Speak
to that rock before their eyes and it will pour out its water. You
will bring water out of the rock for the community so they and
their livestock can drink."
9So Moses took the staff from the LORD's presence, just as he
commanded him. 10He and Aaron gathered the assembly together in front of the rock and Moses said to them, "Listen, you
rebels, must we bring you water out of this rock?" 11Then Moses
raised his arm and struck the rock twice with his staff. Water
gushed out, and the community and their livestock drank.
12But the LORD said to Moses and Aaron, "Because you did not
trust in me enough to honor me as holy in the sight of the Israelites, you will not bring this community into the land I give
them."
13These were the waters of Meribah,[a] where the Israelites
quarreled with the LORD and where he showed himself holy
among them.

Edom Denies Israel Passage

14Moses sent messengers from Kadesh to the king of Edom,
saying:

"This is what your brother Israel says: You know about
all the hardships that have come upon us. 15Our forefathers
went down into Egypt, and we lived there many years. The
Egyptians mistreated us and our fathers, 16but when we
cried out to the LORD, he heard our cry and sent an angel
and brought us out of Egypt.
"Now we are here at Kadesh, a town on the edge of your
territory. 17Please let us pass through your country. We will
not go through any field or vineyard, or drink water from
any well. We will travel along the king's highway and not
turn to the right or to the left until we have passed through
your territory."
18But Edom answered:

"You may not pass through here; if you try, we will march
out and attack you with the sword."

[a] 13 *Meribah* means *quarreling*.

Deep humility is a strong bulwark; and as we enter into it, we find safety.
John Woolman (1720–1772)

(20:12) There is no height of spiritual attainment from which I cannot fall, no level of spiritual competency at which I can dictate the means by which You will act. You are always sovereign; I am always subservient. May I never take You for granted or think that I have You all figured out. Keep me attuned to Your voice and help me to be obedient to Your instructions, especially when I think that I know a better way to accomplish Your will. May I never do anything to dishonor You or to jeopardize Your plans for my life.

Teach me Your holy ways, O Lord,
So I can walk in Your truth
Teach me Your holy ways, O Lord,
And make me wholly devoted to
You.

It is the cry of my heart to follow
You
It is the cry of my heart to be close
to You.
It is the cry of my heart to follow,
All of the days of my life.

"Cry of My Heart"
Terry Butler (©1991)

19The Israelites replied:

"We will go along the main road, and if we or our livestock drink any of your water, we will pay for it. We only want to pass through on foot—nothing else."

20Again they answered:

"You may not pass through."

Then Edom came out against them with a large and powerful
army. 21Since Edom refused to let them go through their territory, Israel turned away from them.

The Death of Aaron

22The whole Israelite community set out from Kadesh and
came to Mount Hor. 23At Mount Hor, near the border of Edom,
the LORD said to Moses and Aaron, 24"Aaron will be gathered to
his people. He will not enter the land I give the Israelites, because both of you rebelled against my command at the waters of
Meribah. 25Get Aaron and his son Eleazar and take them up
Mount Hor. 26Remove Aaron's garments and put them on his son
Eleazar, for Aaron will be gathered to his people; he will die
there."

27Moses did as the LORD commanded: They went up Mount
Hor in the sight of the whole community. 28Moses removed
Aaron's garments and put them on his son Eleazar. And Aaron
died there on top of the mountain. Then Moses and Eleazar
came down from the mountain, 29and when the whole community learned that Aaron had died, the entire house of Israel
mourned for him thirty days.

Arad Destroyed

21 When the Canaanite king of Arad, who lived in the Negev,
heard that Israel was coming along the road to Atharim,
he attacked the Israelites and captured some of them. 2Then Israel made this vow to the LORD: "If you will deliver these people
into our hands, we will totally destroy[a] their cities." 3The LORD
listened to Israel's plea and gave the Canaanites over to them.
They completely destroyed them and their towns; so the place
was named Hormah.[b]

The Bronze Snake

4They traveled from Mount Hor along the route to the Red
Sea,[c] to go around Edom. But the people grew impatient on the
way; 5they spoke against God and against Moses, and said, "Why
have you brought us up out of Egypt to die in the desert? There
is no bread! There is no water! And we detest this miserable
food!"

6Then the LORD sent venomous snakes among them; they bit
the people and many Israelites died. 7The people came to Moses
and said, "We sinned when we spoke against the LORD and
against you. Pray that the LORD will take the snakes away from
us." So Moses prayed for the people.

8The LORD said to Moses, "Make a snake and put it up on a
pole; anyone who is bitten can look at it and live." 9So Moses

[a] 2 The Hebrew term refers to the irrevocable giving over of things or persons to the LORD, often by totally destroying them; also in verse 3. [b] 3 *Hormah* means *destruction*.
[c] 4 Hebrew *Yam Suph*; that is, Sea of Reeds

(20:24–26) We thank You, Father, for sovereignly choosing Aaron's successor. You did not leave Your people, even for a moment, without a priest to intercede for them. And we praise You that in the fullness of time You sent Your Son Jesus to be our great high priest. Now there were many priests before, because death prevented them from continuing in office; "but because Jesus lives forever, he has a permanent priesthood." Therefore He is able to save completely those of us who come to You through Him, because He always lives to intercede for us. (Heb 7:23–25)

(21:6–9) "Just as Moses lifted up the snake in the desert, so the Son of Man must be lifted up, that everyone who believes in him may have eternal life." After You said those words, Lord Jesus, You were lifted up high on the cross, and died to remove the curse of sin from all of us. Since then, Your Father has lifted You up to the highest place, far above all rule and authority. And You continue to be lifted high by the preaching of the Word. As we look to You for salvation, we affirm that You were made "in the likeness of sinful man to be a sin offering." Once again, the cure was made in the likeness of the curse. For it is Your Father's will that "everyone who looks to the Son and believes in him shall have eternal life." (Jn 3:14–15; 6:40; Ro 8:3; Eph 1:20–21; Php 2:9)

"Looking" on the Old Testament serpent is identical with "believing" on the New Testament Christ. That is, the looking and believing are the same thing . . . While Israel looked with their external eyes, believing is done with the heart . . . Faith is the gaze of the soul upon a saving God . . . Believing, then, is directing the heart's attention to Jesus. It is lifting the mind to "behold the Lamb of God," and never ceasing that beholding for the rest of our lives.

A. W. Tozer (1897–1963)

Life is offered unto you,
Hallelujah!
Eternal life your soul shall have,
If you'll only look to Him,
Hallelujah!
Look to Jesus, who alone can save.

Look and live, O sinner, live,
Look to Jesus now and live;
'Tis recorded in His word,
Hallelujah!
It is only that You look and live.

"I've a Message From the Lord"
William A. Ogden (1887)

made a bronze snake and put it up on a pole. Then when anyone was bitten by a snake and looked at the bronze snake, he lived.

The Journey to Moab

10The Israelites moved on and camped at Oboth. 11Then they
set out from Oboth and camped in Iye Abarim, in the desert that
faces Moab toward the sunrise. 12From there they moved on and
camped in the Zered Valley. 13They set out from there and
camped alongside the Arnon, which is in the desert extending into Amorite territory. The Arnon is the border of Moab, between
Moab and the Amorites. 14That is why the Book of the Wars of
the LORD says:

"... Waheb in Suphah[a] and the ravines,
the Arnon 15and[b] the slopes of the ravines
that lead to the site of Ar
and lie along the border of Moab."

16From there they continued on to Beer, the well where the LORD said to Moses, "Gather the people together and I will give them water."

17Then Israel sang this song:

"Spring up, O well!
Sing about it,
18about the well that the princes dug,
that the nobles of the people sank—
the nobles with scepters and staffs."

Then they went from the desert to Mattanah, 19from Mattanah to
Nahaliel, from Nahaliel to Bamoth, 20and from Bamoth to the
valley in Moab where the top of Pisgah overlooks the wasteland.

Defeat of Sihon and Og

21Israel sent messengers to say to Sihon king of the Amorites:

22"Let us pass through your country. We will not turn aside into any field or vineyard, or drink water from any well. We will travel along the king's highway until we have passed through your territory."

23But Sihon would not let Israel pass through his territory. He mustered his entire army and marched out into the desert against Israel. When he reached Jahaz, he fought with Israel.
24Israel, however, put him to the sword and took over his land
from the Arnon to the Jabbok, but only as far as the Ammonites,
because their border was fortified. 25Israel captured all the cities of the Amorites and occupied them, including Heshbon and
all its surrounding settlements. 26Heshbon was the city of Sihon
king of the Amorites, who had fought against the former king of Moab and had taken from him all his land as far as the Arnon.

27That is why the poets say:

"Come to Heshbon and let it be rebuilt;
let Sihon's city be restored.

28"Fire went out from Heshbon,
a blaze from the city of Sihon.
It consumed Ar of Moab,

[a] 14 The meaning of the Hebrew for this phrase is uncertain. [b] 14,15 Or *"I have been given from Suphah and the ravines / of the Arnon 15to*

the citizens of Arnon's heights.
29 Woe to you, O Moab!
You are destroyed, O people of Chemosh!
He has given up his sons as fugitives
and his daughters as captives
to Sihon king of the Amorites.

30 "But we have overthrown them;
Heshbon is destroyed all the way to Dibon.
We have demolished them as far as Nophah,
which extends to Medeba."

31 So Israel settled in the land of the Amorites.
32 After Moses had sent spies to Jazer, the Israelites captured
its surrounding settlements and drove out the Amorites who
were there. 33 Then they turned and went up along the road toward Bashan, and Og king of Bashan and his whole army
marched out to meet them in battle at Edrei.
34 The LORD said to Moses, "Do not be afraid of him, for I have
handed him over to you, with his whole army and his land. Do to
him what you did to Sihon king of the Amorites, who reigned in
Heshbon."
35 So they struck him down, together with his sons and his
whole army, leaving them no survivors. And they took possession of his land.

Balak Summons Balaam

22 Then the Israelites traveled to the plains of Moab and
camped along the Jordan across from Jericho.[a]
2 Now Balak son of Zippor saw all that Israel had done to the
Amorites, 3 and Moab was terrified because there were so many
people. Indeed, Moab was filled with dread because of the Israelites.
4 The Moabites said to the elders of Midian, "This horde is going
to lick up everything around us, as an ox licks up the grass of the
field."
So Balak son of Zippor, who was king of Moab at that time,
5 sent messengers to summon Balaam son of Beor, who was at Pethor, near the River,[b] in his native land. Balak said:

"A people has come out of Egypt; they cover the face of the
land and have settled next to me. 6 Now come and put a curse
on these people, because they are too powerful for me. Perhaps then I will be able to defeat them and drive them out of
the country. For I know that those you bless are blessed, and
those you curse are cursed."

7 The elders of Moab and Midian left, taking with them the fee
for divination. When they came to Balaam, they told him what
Balak had said.
8 "Spend the night here," Balaam said to them, "and I will bring
you back the answer the LORD gives me." So the Moabite princes
stayed with him.
9 God came to Balaam and asked, "Who are these men with
you?"
10 Balaam said to God, "Balak son of Zippor, king of Moab,
sent me this message: 11 'A people that has come out of Egypt

[a] 1 Hebrew *Jordan of Jericho*; possibly an ancient name for the Jordan River [b] 5 That is, the Euphrates

(21:34–35) We praise You, Father, for the assurance of Your presence as we move forward in obedience to Your leadership. For Your church corporately and for believers individually, it seems that our spiritual gains are always the result of spiritual conflicts. But we know that when we fight Your battles, we will reap the rewards of Your victories. Lead on, O King eternal! Armed in the power of Your might, Your people are more than conquerors. (Isa 43:11–13; Ro 8:37)

In heavenly armor we'll enter the
land,
The battle belongs to the Lord.
No weapon that's fashioned against
us will stand,
The battle belongs to the Lord.

When your enemy presses in hard,
do not fear,
The battle belongs to the Lord.
Take courage, my friend, your
redemption is near,
The battle belongs to the Lord.

We sing glory, honor,
Power and strength to the Lord.
We sing glory, honor,
Power and strength to the Lord.

"The Battle Belongs to the Lord"
Jamie Owens-Collins (©1984)

(22:10–32) Lord, Your ways are so far above ours. You sent the angel to kill Balaam, then You opened the donkey's mouth to spare Balaam. In reality, Balaam was more stubborn than his donkey. He persisted in his quest for fame and fortune, hoping that somehow You would change Your mind and allow him to curse Israel. But once Balaam started down his stubborn path You would not allow him to change his direction. Instead, You changed his intention. The sword of Your judgment was tempered by mercy. You would have killed him before allowing him to curse Your people. But, far better, You turned what was intended for evil into a blessing for Your people. (Isa 55:8)

I arise today
Through God's strength to pilot me;
God's might to uphold me,
God's wisdom to guide me,
God's eye to look before me,
God' ear to hear me,
God's word to speak for me.
Patrick of Ireland (c.389- c.461)

covers the face of the land. Now come and put a curse on them for me. Perhaps then I will be able to fight them and drive them away.' "

12But God said to Balaam, "Do not go with them. You must not put a curse on those people, because they are blessed."

13The next morning Balaam got up and said to Balak's princes, "Go back to your own country, for the LORD has refused to let me go with you."

14So the Moabite princes returned to Balak and said, "Balaam refused to come with us."

15Then Balak sent other princes, more numerous and more
distinguished than the first. 16They came to Balaam and said:

> "This is what Balak son of Zippor says: Do not let anything keep you from coming to me, 17because I will reward you handsomely and do whatever you say. Come and put a curse on these people for me."

18But Balaam answered them, "Even if Balak gave me his palace filled with silver and gold, I could not do anything great
or small to go beyond the command of the LORD my God. 19Now
stay here tonight as the others did, and I will find out what else the LORD will tell me."

20That night God came to Balaam and said, "Since these men have come to summon you, go with them, but do only what I tell you."

Balaam's Donkey

21Balaam got up in the morning, saddled his donkey and
went with the princes of Moab. 22But God was very angry when
he went, and the angel of the LORD stood in the road to oppose him. Balaam was riding on his donkey, and his two servants
were with him. 23When the donkey saw the angel of the LORD standing in the road with a drawn sword in his hand, she turned off the road into a field. Balaam beat her to get her back on the road.

24Then the angel of the LORD stood in a narrow path between
two vineyards, with walls on both sides. 25When the donkey saw the angel of the LORD, she pressed close to the wall, crushing Balaam's foot against it. So he beat her again.

26Then the angel of the LORD moved on ahead and stood in a narrow place where there was no room to turn, either to the
right or to the left. 27When the donkey saw the angel of the LORD, she lay down under Balaam, and he was angry and beat her with
his staff. 28Then the LORD opened the donkey's mouth, and she said to Balaam, "What have I done to you to make you beat me these three times?"

29Balaam answered the donkey, "You have made a fool of me! If I had a sword in my hand, I would kill you right now."

30The donkey said to Balaam, "Am I not your own donkey, which you have always ridden, to this day? Have I been in the habit of doing this to you?"

"No," he said.

31Then the LORD opened Balaam's eyes, and he saw the angel of the LORD standing in the road with his sword drawn. So he bowed low and fell facedown.

32The angel of the LORD asked him, "Why have you beaten your donkey these three times? I have come here to oppose you

because your path is a reckless one before me.[a] 33The donkey
saw me and turned away from me these three times. If she had
not turned away, I would certainly have killed you by now, but
I would have spared her."
34Balaam said to the angel of the LORD, "I have sinned. I did
not realize you were standing in the road to oppose me. Now if
you are displeased, I will go back."
35The angel of the LORD said to Balaam, "Go with the men, but
speak only what I tell you." So Balaam went with the princes of
Balak.
36When Balak heard that Balaam was coming, he went out to
meet him at the Moabite town on the Arnon border, at the edge
of his territory. 37Balak said to Balaam, "Did I not send you an
urgent summons? Why didn't you come to me? Am I really not
able to reward you?"
38"Well, I have come to you now," Balaam replied. "But can I
say just anything? I must speak only what God puts in my
mouth."
39Then Balaam went with Balak to Kiriath Huzoth. 40Balak sacrificed cattle and sheep, and gave some to Balaam and the princes
who were with him. 41The next morning Balak took Balaam up to
Bamoth Baal, and from there he saw part of the people.

Balaam's First Oracle

23 Balaam said, "Build me seven altars here, and prepare
seven bulls and seven rams for me." 2Balak did as Balaam said, and the two of them offered a bull and a ram on each
altar.
3Then Balaam said to Balak, "Stay here beside your offering
while I go aside. Perhaps the LORD will come to meet with me.
Whatever he reveals to me I will tell you." Then he went off to a
barren height.
4God met with him, and Balaam said, "I have prepared seven
altars, and on each altar I have offered a bull and a ram."
5The LORD put a message in Balaam's mouth and said, "Go
back to Balak and give him this message."
6So he went back to him and found him standing beside his
offering, with all the princes of Moab. 7Then Balaam uttered his
oracle:

"Balak brought me from Aram,
the king of Moab from the eastern mountains.
'Come,' he said, 'curse Jacob for me;
come, denounce Israel.'
8How can I curse
those whom God has not cursed?
How can I denounce
those whom the LORD has not denounced?
9From the rocky peaks I see them,
from the heights I view them.
I see a people who live apart
and do not consider themselves one of the nations.
10Who can count the dust of Jacob
or number the fourth part of Israel?
Let me die the death of the righteous,
and may my end be like theirs!"

[a] 32 The meaning of the Hebrew for this clause is uncertain.

(23:5) Who can oppose You, Almighty God? You do whatever You please. You turned Balak's sorcerer into Your messenger. You chose a Gentile to pronounce blessing on Israel and doom upon his own people. Your choice had nothing to do with his holiness, but it had everything to do with Your sovereignty. If You can speak through a donkey, You can certainly speak through anyone else You choose. But, as Jesus taught us, even if someone prophesies in Your name, that does not necessarily reflect a right relationship with You. (1Sa 19:20–24; Job 23:13; Isa 43:13; Mt 7:21–23)

The believer can each day be pleasing to God only in that which he does through the power of Christ dwelling in him. The daily inflowing of the life-sap of the Holy Spirit is his only power to bring forth fruit. He lives alone in him and is for each moment dependent on him alone . . . Believers, meditate on this until your soul bows to worship.

Andrew Murray (1828-1917)

(23:18–24) These beautiful words pledged hope and destiny for Your people, and affirmed Your great faithfulness. There was no misfortune or misery in sight for Israel; even though they were far from sinless, their sins were covered by the atoning sacrifice. You were jealous for their safety and zealous for their holiness, and You made provision for both. Just as You blessed them with a sure blessing for the future, O bless us today, Lord God. For when You speak Your blessing upon Your people, Your promise cannot be broken.

Pardon for sin,
And a peace that endureth;
Thine own dear presence
To cheer and to guide.
Strength for today,
And bright hope for tomorrow;
Blessings all mine,
With ten thousand beside.

Great is Thy Faithfulness!
Great is Thy Faithfulness!
Morning by morning new mercies I see
All I have needed Thy hand hath provided
Great is Thy Faithfulness
Lord unto me!

"Great Is Thy Faithfulness"
Thomas O. Chisholm (©1923, 1951)

Hope is nothing else than the expectation of the things that faith has believed to be truly promised by God. Thus faith believes God to be truthful: Hope expects that he will show his veracity at the opportune time. Faith believes God to be our Father: Hope expects that he will always act as such toward us.

John Calvin (1509-1564)

11Balak said to Balaam, "What have you done to me? I brought you to curse my enemies, but you have done nothing but bless them!"

12He answered, "Must I not speak what the LORD puts in my mouth?"

Balaam's Second Oracle

13Then Balak said to him, "Come with me to another place where you can see them; you will see only a part but not all of them. And from there, curse them for me." 14So he took him to the field of Zophim on the top of Pisgah, and there he built seven altars and offered a bull and a ram on each altar.

15Balaam said to Balak, "Stay here beside your offering while I meet with him over there."

16The LORD met with Balaam and put a message in his mouth and said, "Go back to Balak and give him this message."

17So he went to him and found him standing beside his offering, with the princes of Moab. Balak asked him, "What did the LORD say?"

18Then he uttered his oracle:

"Arise, Balak, and listen;
hear me, son of Zippor.
19God is not a man, that he should lie,
nor a son of man, that he should change his mind.
Does he speak and then not act?
Does he promise and not fulfill?
20I have received a command to bless;
he has blessed, and I cannot change it.

21"No misfortune is seen in Jacob,
no misery observed in Israel.[a]
The LORD their God is with them;
the shout of the King is among them.
22God brought them out of Egypt;
they have the strength of a wild ox.
23There is no sorcery against Jacob,
no divination against Israel.
It will now be said of Jacob
and of Israel, 'See what God has done!'
24The people rise like a lioness;
they rouse themselves like a lion
that does not rest till he devours his prey
and drinks the blood of his victims."

25Then Balak said to Balaam, "Neither curse them at all nor bless them at all!"

26Balaam answered, "Did I not tell you I must do whatever the LORD says?"

Balaam's Third Oracle

27Then Balak said to Balaam, "Come, let me take you to another place. Perhaps it will please God to let you curse them for me from there." 28And Balak took Balaam to the top of Peor, overlooking the wasteland.

29Balaam said, "Build me seven altars here, and prepare seven

[a] 21 Or *He has not looked on Jacob's offenses / or on the wrongs found in Israel.*

bulls and seven rams for me." 30Balak did as Balaam had said,
and offered a bull and a ram on each altar.

24 Now when Balaam saw that it pleased the LORD to bless Israel, he did not resort to sorcery as at other times, but
turned his face toward the desert. 2When Balaam looked out and
saw Israel encamped tribe by tribe, the Spirit of God came upon
him 3and he uttered his oracle:

"The oracle of Balaam son of Beor,
the oracle of one whose eye sees clearly,
4the oracle of one who hears the words of God,
who sees a vision from the Almighty,[a]
who falls prostrate, and whose eyes are opened:

5"How beautiful are your tents, O Jacob,
your dwelling places, O Israel!

6"Like valleys they spread out,
like gardens beside a river,
like aloes planted by the LORD,
like cedars beside the waters.
7Water will flow from their buckets;
their seed will have abundant water.

"Their king will be greater than Agag;
their kingdom will be exalted.

8"God brought them out of Egypt;
they have the strength of a wild ox.
They devour hostile nations
and break their bones in pieces;
with their arrows they pierce them.
9Like a lion they crouch and lie down,
like a lioness—who dares to rouse them?

"May those who bless you be blessed
and those who curse you be cursed!"

10Then Balak's anger burned against Balaam. He struck his
hands together and said to him, "I summoned you to curse my
enemies, but you have blessed them these three times. 11Now
leave at once and go home! I said I would reward you handsome-
ly, but the LORD has kept you from being rewarded."

12Balaam answered Balak, "Did I not tell the messengers you
sent me, 13'Even if Balak gave me his palace filled with silver and
gold, I could not do anything of my own accord, good or bad, to
go beyond the command of the LORD—and I must say only what
the LORD says'? 14Now I am going back to my people, but come, let
me warn you of what this people will do to your people in days to
come."

Balaam's Fourth Oracle

15Then he uttered his oracle:

"The oracle of Balaam son of Beor,
the oracle of one whose eye sees clearly,
16the oracle of one who hears the words of God,
who has knowledge from the Most High,
who sees a vision from the Almighty,

[a] 4 Hebrew *Shaddai*; also in verse 16

(24:2–9) We praise You, Lord God, for the blessings You have bestowed upon Your people, both then and now. Balaam's oracle was a declaration of Your vision for Israel: beauty, fruitfulness, power and destiny. How we praise You, that we too share these ancient blessings, because they find their ultimate fulfillment in the exalted reign of our King, Jesus Christ. How we thank You for Your great care and provision. You brought us out of spiritual bondage and You will yet bring us into the fullness of spiritual freedom.

I have known what the enjoyments and advantages of this life are, and what the more refined pleasures which learning and intellectual power can bestow; and with all the experience that more than threescore years can give I now, on the eve of my departure, declare to you . . . that health is a great blessing, competence obtained by honourable industry a great blessing, and a great blessing it is to have kind, faithful, and loving friends and relatives; but that the greatest of all blessings, as it is the most ennobling of all privileges, is to be indeed a Christian.

Samuel Taylor Coleridge (1772-1834)

who falls prostrate, and whose eyes are opened:
17 "I see him, but not now;
I behold him, but not near.
A star will come out of Jacob;
a scepter will rise out of Israel.
He will crush the foreheads of Moab,
the skulls[a] of[b] all the sons of Sheth.[c]
18 Edom will be conquered;
Seir, his enemy, will be conquered,
but Israel will grow strong.
19 A ruler will come out of Jacob
and destroy the survivors of the city."

Balaam's Final Oracles

20 Then Balaam saw Amalek and uttered his oracle:

"Amalek was first among the nations,
but he will come to ruin at last."

21 Then he saw the Kenites and uttered his oracle:

"Your dwelling place is secure,
your nest is set in a rock;
22 yet you Kenites will be destroyed
when Asshur takes you captive."

23 Then he uttered his oracle:

"Ah, who can live when God does this?[d]
24 Ships will come from the shores of Kittim;
they will subdue Asshur and Eber,
but they too will come to ruin."

25 Then Balaam got up and returned home and Balak went his own way.

Moab Seduces Israel

25 While Israel was staying in Shittim, the men began to indulge in sexual immorality with Moabite women, 2who invited them to the sacrifices to their gods. The people ate and
bowed down before these gods. 3So Israel joined in worshiping
the Baal of Peor. And the LORD's anger burned against them.
4The LORD said to Moses, "Take all the leaders of these people,
kill them and expose them in broad daylight before the LORD, so
that the LORD's fierce anger may turn away from Israel."
5So Moses said to Israel's judges, "Each of you must put to
death those of your men who have joined in worshiping the Baal
of Peor."
6Then an Israelite man brought to his family a Midianite woman
right before the eyes of Moses and the whole assembly of Israel
while they were weeping at the entrance to the Tent of Meeting.
7When Phinehas son of Eleazar, the son of Aaron, the priest, saw
this, he left the assembly, took a spear in his hand 8and followed
the Israelite into the tent. He drove the spear through both of
them—through the Israelite and into the woman's body. Then the

[a] *17* Samaritan Pentateuch (see also Jer. 48:45); the meaning of the word in the Masoretic Text is uncertain. [b] *17* Or possibly *Moab, / batter* [c] *17* Or *all the noisy boasters*
[d] *23* Masoretic Text; with a different word division of the Hebrew *A people will gather from the north.*

(24:17–19) Father God, we see in this vision the coming of Joshua, who would start the work of conquering the enemy; the coming of David, who would continue the work; and the coming of the Messiah, Jesus, who would perfect the work. This great Messianic promise was not delivered by a Jew to the Jews, but by a Gentile to the Gentiles, so that all of the nations would know that a King is coming at whose feet all of creation will bow and worship. (Php 2:10–11)

At the name of Jesus every knee shall bow,
Every tongue confess Him King of glory now;
'Tis the Father's pleasure we should call Him Lord,
Who from the beginning was the mighty Word.

"At the Name of Jesus"
Caroline Maria Noel (1890)

plague against the Israelites was stopped; [9]but those who died in
the plague numbered 24,000.
[10]The LORD said to Moses, [11]"Phinehas son of Eleazar, the son
of Aaron, the priest, has turned my anger away from the Israelites;
for he was as zealous as I am for my honor among them, so that
in my zeal I did not put an end to them. [12]Therefore tell him I am
making my covenant of peace with him. [13]He and his descendants
will have a covenant of a lasting priesthood, because he was zealous for the honor of his God and made atonement for the Israelites."
[14]The name of the Israelite who was killed with the Midianite
woman was Zimri son of Salu, the leader of a Simeonite family.
[15]And the name of the Midianite woman who was put to death was
Cozbi daughter of Zur, a tribal chief of a Midianite family.
[16]The LORD said to Moses, [17]"Treat the Midianites as enemies
and kill them, [18]because they treated you as enemies when they
deceived you in the affair of Peor and their sister Cozbi, the daughter of a Midianite leader, the woman who was killed when the
plague came as a result of Peor."

The Second Census

26 After the plague the LORD said to Moses and Eleazar son of
Aaron, the priest, [2]"Take a census of the whole Israelite
community by families—all those twenty years old or more who
are able to serve in the army of Israel." [3]So on the plains of Moab
by the Jordan across from Jericho,[a] Moses and Eleazar the priest
spoke with them and said, [4]"Take a census of the men twenty
years old or more, as the LORD commanded Moses."

These were the Israelites who came out of Egypt:

[5]The descendants of Reuben, the firstborn son of Israel, were:
through Hanoch, the Hanochite clan;
through Pallu, the Palluite clan;
[6]through Hezron, the Hezronite clan;
through Carmi, the Carmite clan.
[7]These were the clans of Reuben; those numbered were 43,730.
[8]The son of Pallu was Eliab, [9]and the sons of Eliab were Nemuel, Dathan and Abiram. The same Dathan and Abiram were the
community officials who rebelled against Moses and Aaron and
were among Korah's followers when they rebelled against the
LORD. [10]The earth opened its mouth and swallowed them along
with Korah, whose followers died when the fire devoured the 250
men. And they served as a warning sign. [11]The line of Korah, however, did not die out.

[12]The descendants of Simeon by their clans were:
through Nemuel, the Nemuelite clan;
through Jamin, the Jaminite clan;
through Jakin, the Jakinite clan;
[13]through Zerah, the Zerahite clan;
through Shaul, the Shaulite clan.
[14]These were the clans of Simeon; there were 22,200 men.

[15]The descendants of Gad by their clans were:
through Zephon, the Zephonite clan;
through Haggi, the Haggite clan;

[a] 3 Hebrew *Jordan of Jericho*; possibly an ancient name for the Jordan River; also in verse 63

(25:6–12) "Now these things occurred as examples to keep us from setting our hearts on evil things as they did." Father, let us learn from Phineas' example to be zealous for Your honor. Give us wisdom and courage to "not associate with anyone who calls himself a brother" but who willfully and arrogantly desecrates the sanctity of our fellowship and demonstrates a blatant disregard for holiness. Purify Your church, Lord, so that we may live in Your peace. (1Co 5:11; 10:6–11)

(26:9–11) I am thankful, Lord, for this admonition from Israel's history. It is a warning of Your judgment against rebellion, but it is also a reminder of Your mercy in allowing Korah's lineage to continue. For, long after this episode, David employed the sons of Korah as the doorkeepers of Your house. I do not want to be counted among those who rebel against You and experience Your consuming judgment. Instead, I choose to follow You diligently so that I might receive Your abundant mercy, both in this life and in the life to come. (1Ch 26:19; Ps 84)

(26:20–22) In Your perfect plan, almighty God, You ordained that from the tribe of Judah, from the clan of Perez, through the lineage of David would come the Savior of the world, Your precious Son Jesus. I praise You this day for Your one and only Son, the Word become flesh, Immanuel, God–with–us. I worship You for demonstrating Your love, Your patience, Your grace as You carried out Your plan to bring redemption to fallen humanity, to set us free from the bondage of sin and death. In these moments of personal worship, I rest secure in Your presence, and I submit myself to Your perfect will. (Ge 49:10; Ru 4:18–22; Mt 1:1–6)

O come, O come, Emmanuel,
And ransom captive Israel,
That mourns in lonely exile here,
Until the Son of God appear.

Rejoice! Rejoice! Emmanuel
Shall come to Thee, O Israel!
"O Come, O Come, Emmanuel"
Latin Hymn (12th c.)
Trans. John M. Neale (1818-1866)

through Shuni, the Shunite clan;
16 through Ozni, the Oznite clan;
through Eri, the Erite clan;
17 through Arodi,[a] the Arodite clan;
through Areli, the Arelite clan.
18 These were the clans of Gad; those numbered were 40,500.

19 Er and Onan were sons of Judah, but they died in Canaan.
20 The descendants of Judah by their clans were:
through Shelah, the Shelanite clan;
through Perez, the Perezite clan;
through Zerah, the Zerahite clan.
21 The descendants of Perez were:
through Hezron, the Hezronite clan;
through Hamul, the Hamulite clan.
22 These were the clans of Judah; those numbered were 76,500.

23 The descendants of Issachar by their clans were:
through Tola, the Tolaite clan;
through Puah, the Puite[b] clan;
24 through Jashub, the Jashubite clan;
through Shimron, the Shimronite clan.
25 These were the clans of Issachar; those numbered were 64,300.

26 The descendants of Zebulun by their clans were:
through Sered, the Seredite clan;
through Elon, the Elonite clan;
through Jahleel, the Jahleelite clan.
27 These were the clans of Zebulun; those numbered were 60,500.

28 The descendants of Joseph by their clans through Manasseh and Ephraim were:

29 The descendants of Manasseh:
through Makir, the Makirite clan (Makir was the father of Gilead);
through Gilead, the Gileadite clan.
30 These were the descendants of Gilead:
through Iezer, the Iezerite clan;
through Helek, the Helekite clan;
31 through Asriel, the Asrielite clan;
through Shechem, the Shechemite clan;
32 through Shemida, the Shemidaite clan;
through Hepher, the Hepherite clan.
33 (Zelophehad son of Hepher had no sons; he had only daughters, whose names were Mahlah, Noah, Hoglah, Milcah and Tirzah.)
34 These were the clans of Manasseh; those numbered were 52,700.

35 These were the descendants of Ephraim by their clans:
through Shuthelah, the Shuthelahite clan;
through Beker, the Bekerite clan;
through Tahan, the Tahanite clan.
36 These were the descendants of Shuthelah:
through Eran, the Eranite clan.
37 These were the clans of Ephraim; those numbered were 32,500.

[a] *17* Samaritan Pentateuch and Syriac (see also Gen. 46:16); Masoretic Text *Arod*
[b] *23* Samaritan Pentateuch, Septuagint, Vulgate and Syriac (see also 1 Chron. 7:1); Masoretic Text *through Puvah, the Punite*

These were the descendants of Joseph by their clans.
38 The descendants of Benjamin by their clans were:
through Bela, the Belaite clan;
through Ashbel, the Ashbelite clan;
through Ahiram, the Ahiramite clan;
39 through Shupham,[a] the Shuphamite clan;
through Hupham, the Huphamite clan.
40 The descendants of Bela through Ard and Naaman were:
through Ard,[b] the Ardite clan;
through Naaman, the Naamite clan.
41 These were the clans of Benjamin; those numbered were 45,600.

42 These were the descendants of Dan by their clans:
through Shuham, the Shuhamite clan.
These were the clans of Dan: 43 All of them were Shuhamite clans; and those numbered were 64,400.

44 The descendants of Asher by their clans were:
through Imnah, the Imnite clan;
through Ishvi, the Ishvite clan;
through Beriah, the Beriite clan;
45 and through the descendants of Beriah:
through Heber, the Heberite clan;
through Malkiel, the Malkielite clan.
46 (Asher had a daughter named Serah.)
47 These were the clans of Asher; those numbered were 53,400.

48 The descendants of Naphtali by their clans were:
through Jahzeel, the Jahzeelite clan;
through Guni, the Gunite clan;
49 through Jezer, the Jezerite clan;
through Shillem, the Shillemite clan.
50 These were the clans of Naphtali; those numbered were 45,400.

51 The total number of the men of Israel was 601,730.

52 The LORD said to Moses, 53 "The land is to be allotted to them as an inheritance based on the number of names. 54 To a larger group give a larger inheritance, and to a smaller group a smaller one; each is to receive its inheritance according to the number of those listed. 55 Be sure that the land is distributed by lot. What each group inherits will be according to the names for its ancestral tribe. 56 Each inheritance is to be distributed by lot among the larger and smaller groups."

57 These were the Levites who were counted by their clans:
through Gershon, the Gershonite clan;
through Kohath, the Kohathite clan;
through Merari, the Merarite clan.
58 These also were Levite clans:
the Libnite clan,
the Hebronite clan,
the Mahlite clan,
the Mushite clan,

[a] 39 A few manuscripts of the Masoretic Text, Samaritan Pentateuch, Vulgate and Syriac (see also Septuagint); most manuscripts of the Masoretic Text *Shephupham* [b] 40 Samaritan Pentateuch and Vulgate (see also Septuagint); Masoretic Text does not have *through Ard.*

(26:37–51) Almighty God, we see in this census a picture of both Your patience and Your faithfulness in fulfilling Your promise to Your people. In the midst of the desert's hardships and during times of painful discipline, You did not abandon Your people or forget Your promises to make them a great and fruitful nation. And now, as they stood poised to enter the promised land, they found that their numbers were virtually the same as when they entered the desert 40 years earlier. The old generation had passed away, just as You said they would. A new generation had replaced the old, just as You said they would. And out of 603,550 people, only Joshua and Caleb remained, just as You said they would. In blessing and in judgment, Balaam's words rang true: "God is not a man, that he should lie, nor a son of man, that he should change his mind. Does he speak and then not act? Does he promise and not fulfill?" (Nu 1:46; 14:26–35; 23:19; 26:64–65)

Want of trust is at the root of almost all our sins and all our weaknesses; and how shall we escape it but by looking to Him and observing His faithfulness? . . . How many estimate difficulties in the light of their own resources, and thus attempt little and often fail in the little they attempt! All God's giants have been weak men, who did great things for God because they reckoned on his being with them.

James Hudson Taylor (1832-1905)

the Korahite clan.
(Kohath was the forefather of Amram; 59the name of Amram's wife was Jochebed, a descendant of Levi, who was born to the Levites[a] in Egypt. To Amram she bore Aaron, Moses and their sister Miriam. 60Aaron was the father of Nadab and Abihu, Eleazar and Ithamar. 61But Nadab and Abihu died when they made an offering before the LORD with unauthorized fire.)

62All the male Levites a month old or more numbered 23,000. They were not counted along with the other Israelites because they received no inheritance among them.

63These are the ones counted by Moses and Eleazar the priest when they counted the Israelites on the plains of Moab by the Jordan across from Jericho. 64Not one of them was among those counted by Moses and Aaron the priest when they counted the Israelites in the Desert of Sinai. 65For the LORD had told those Israelites they would surely die in the desert, and not one of them was left except Caleb son of Jephunneh and Joshua son of Nun.

Zelophehad's Daughters

27 The daughters of Zelophehad son of Hepher, the son of Gilead, the son of Makir, the son of Manasseh, belonged to the clans of Manasseh son of Joseph. The names of the daughters were Mahlah, Noah, Hoglah, Milcah and Tirzah. They approached 2the entrance to the Tent of Meeting and stood before Moses, Eleazar the priest, the leaders and the whole assembly, and said, 3"Our father died in the desert. He was not among Korah's followers, who banded together against the LORD, but he died for his own sin and left no sons. 4Why should our father's name disappear from his clan because he had no son? Give us property among our father's relatives."

5So Moses brought their case before the LORD 6and the LORD said to him, 7"What Zelophehad's daughters are saying is right. You must certainly give them property as an inheritance among their father's relatives and turn their father's inheritance over to them.

8"Say to the Israelites, 'If a man dies and leaves no son, turn his inheritance over to his daughter. 9If he has no daughter, give his inheritance to his brothers. 10If he has no brothers, give his inheritance to his father's brothers. 11If his father had no brothers, give his inheritance to the nearest relative in his clan, that he may possess it. This is to be a legal requirement for the Israelites, as the LORD commanded Moses.' "

Joshua to Succeed Moses

12Then the LORD said to Moses, "Go up this mountain in the Abarim range and see the land I have given the Israelites. 13After you have seen it, you too will be gathered to your people, as your brother Aaron was, 14for when the community rebelled at the waters in the Desert of Zin, both of you disobeyed my command to honor me as holy before their eyes." (These were the waters of Meribah Kadesh, in the Desert of Zin.)

15Moses said to the LORD, 16"May the LORD, the God of the spirits of all mankind, appoint a man over this community 17to

(27:1–11) Our God and Father, You see, You hear and You act on behalf of those who turn to You for help. In faith, these women sought an inheritance in the promised land, even though the land was not yet conquered. They knew You as Provider, so they looked to You for provision. They knew You as the Judge, so they looked to You for justice. You were a Father to these who were fatherless; and as they committed their way to You, You made the justice of their cause shine like the noonday sun. (Ps 37:5–6; 68:5)

[a] 59 Or *Jochebed, a daughter of Levi, who was born to Levi*

go out and come in before them, one who will lead them out and
bring them in, so the LORD's people will not be like sheep without a shepherd."
18So the LORD said to Moses, "Take Joshua son of Nun, a man
in whom is the spirit,[a] and lay your hand on him. 19Have him
stand before Eleazar the priest and the entire assembly and
commission him in their presence. 20Give him some of your authority so the whole Israelite community will obey him. 21He is
to stand before Eleazar the priest, who will obtain decisions for
him by inquiring of the Urim before the LORD. At his command he
and the entire community of the Israelites will go out, and at his
command they will come in."
22Moses did as the LORD commanded him. He took Joshua
and had him stand before Eleazar the priest and the whole assembly. 23Then he laid his hands on him and commissioned
him, as the LORD instructed through Moses.

Daily Offerings

28 The LORD said to Moses, 2"Give this command to the Israelites and say to them: 'See that you present to me at
the appointed time the food for my offerings made by fire, as an
aroma pleasing to me.' 3Say to them: 'This is the offering made
by fire that you are to present to the LORD: two lambs a year old
without defect, as a regular burnt offering each day. 4Prepare
one lamb in the morning and the other at twilight, 5together with
a grain offering of a tenth of an ephah[b] of fine flour mixed with
a quarter of a hin[c] of oil from pressed olives. 6This is the regular burnt offering instituted at Mount Sinai as a pleasing aroma,
an offering made to the LORD by fire. 7The accompanying drink
offering is to be a quarter of a hin of fermented drink with each
lamb. Pour out the drink offering to the LORD at the sanctuary.
8Prepare the second lamb at twilight, along with the same kind
of grain offering and drink offering that you prepare in the
morning. This is an offering made by fire, an aroma pleasing to
the LORD.

Sabbath Offerings

9" 'On the Sabbath day, make an offering of two lambs a year
old without defect, together with its drink offering and a grain
offering of two-tenths of an ephah[d] of fine flour mixed with oil.
10This is the burnt offering for every Sabbath, in addition to the
regular burnt offering and its drink offering.

Monthly Offerings

11" 'On the first of every month, present to the LORD a burnt
offering of two young bulls, one ram and seven male lambs a
year old, all without defect. 12With each bull there is to be a
grain offering of three-tenths of an ephah[e] of fine flour mixed
with oil; with the ram, a grain offering of two-tenths of an
ephah of fine flour mixed with oil; 13and with each lamb, a
grain offering of a tenth of an ephah of fine flour mixed with
oil. This is for a burnt offering, a pleasing aroma, an offering
made to the LORD by fire. 14With each bull there is to be a drink

[a] *18* Or *Spirit* [b] *5* That is, probably about 2 quarts (about 2 liters); also in verses 13, 21 and 29 [c] *5* That is, probably about 1 quart (about 1 liter); also in verses 7 and 14
[d] *9* That is, probably about 4 quarts (about 4.5 liters); also in verses 12, 20 and 28
[e] *12* That is, probably about 6 quarts (about 6.5 liters); also in verses 20 and 28

(27:16–20) Moses prayed that You would raise up a leader—one who would intercede for the people and show them the way. It was his prayer that the people would "not be like sheep without a shepherd." You instructed him to "take Joshua . . . commission him . . . and give him some of your authority." Centuries later, Jesus looked upon Israel as "sheep without a shepherd" and prayed that You would raise up workers to show them the way to Your kingdom. Then He commissioned His disciples and gave them some of His authority. Today, Father, we thank You for raising up anointed leaders in our midst who lead under Your authority. Thank You for not allowing us to become like "sheep without a shepherd, harassed and helpless." (Mt 9:36–10:1; 28:18)

There never lived a man who had such a passion for men as Jesus. He lived to win them out of their distressed, sinful, needy lives up to a new level. He died to win them. His last act was dying to win men. His last word was, "Go ye and win men." And His first act when He got back home, all scarred and marred by His contact with earth, was to send down the same Spirit as swayed him those human years to live in us that we might have the same passion for winning men as He.

Dr. Samuel Dickey Gordon (1859-1936)

offering of half a hin[a] of wine; with the ram, a third of a hin[b];
and with each lamb, a quarter of a hin. This is the monthly burnt
offering to be made at each new moon during the year. 15Be-
sides the regular burnt offering with its drink offering, one male
goat is to be presented to the LORD as a sin offering.

The Passover

16“ ‘On the fourteenth day of the first month the LORD’s
Passover is to be held. 17On the fifteenth day of this month there
is to be a festival; for seven days eat bread made without yeast.
18On the first day hold a sacred assembly and do no regular
work. 19Present to the LORD an offering made by fire, a burnt offering of two young bulls, one ram and seven male lambs a year
old, all without defect. 20With each bull prepare a grain offering
of three-tenths of an ephah of fine flour mixed with oil; with the
ram, two-tenths; 21and with each of the seven lambs, one-tenth.
22Include one male goat as a sin offering to make atonement for
you. 23Prepare these in addition to the regular morning burnt
offering. 24In this way prepare the food for the offering made by
fire every day for seven days as an aroma pleasing to the LORD; it
is to be prepared in addition to the regular burnt offering and its
drink offering. 25On the seventh day hold a sacred assembly and
do no regular work.

Feast of Weeks

26“ ‘On the day of firstfruits, when you present to the LORD an
offering of new grain during the Feast of Weeks, hold a sacred
assembly and do no regular work. 27Present a burnt offering of
two young bulls, one ram and seven male lambs a year old as an
aroma pleasing to the LORD. 28With each bull there is to be a
grain offering of three-tenths of an ephah of fine flour mixed
with oil; with the ram, two-tenths; 29and with each of the seven
lambs, one-tenth. 30Include one male goat to make atonement
for you. 31Prepare these together with their drink offerings, in
addition to the regular burnt offering and its grain offering. Be
sure the animals are without defect.

Feast of Trumpets

29 “ ‘On the first day of the seventh month hold a sacred assembly and do no regular work. It is a day for you to
sound the trumpets. 2As an aroma pleasing to the LORD, prepare
a burnt offering of one young bull, one ram and seven male
lambs a year old, all without defect. 3With the bull prepare a
grain offering of three-tenths of an ephah[c] of fine flour mixed
with oil; with the ram, two-tenths[d]; 4and with each of the seven
lambs, one-tenth.[e] 5Include one male goat as a sin offering to
make atonement for you. 6These are in addition to the monthly
and daily burnt offerings with their grain offerings and drink offerings as specified. They are offerings made to the LORD by
fire—a pleasing aroma.

Day of Atonement

7“ ‘On the tenth day of this seventh month hold a sacred as-

(28:16–17) We thank You, Father, for our Lord Jesus Christ, our Passover lamb. His blood has won our freedom. His flesh is our sustenance. As we celebrate His sacrifice for us at the Lord’s table, may we search our hearts for the yeast of sin, and rid ourselves of its influence. May we remember and heed the words of the apostle Paul: “Get rid of the old yeast that you may be a new batch without yeast—as you really are. For Christ, our Passover lamb, has been sacrificed. Therefore let us keep the Festival, not with the old yeast, the yeast of malice and wickedness, but with bread without yeast, the bread of sincerity and truth.” (1Co 5:7–8; 11:27–28)

[a] *14* That is, probably about 2 quarts (about 2 liters) [b] *14* That is, probably about 1 1/4 quarts (about 1.2 liters) [c] *3* That is, probably about 6 quarts (about 6.5 liters); also in verses 9 and 14 [d] *3* That is, probably about 4 quarts (about 4.5 liters); also in verses 9 and 14 [e] *4* That is, probably about 2 quarts (about 2 liters); also in verses 10 and 15

sembly. You must deny yourselves[a] and do no work. 8Present as
an aroma pleasing to the LORD a burnt offering of one young bull,
one ram and seven male lambs a year old, all without defect.
9With the bull prepare a grain offering of three-tenths of an
ephah of fine flour mixed with oil; with the ram, two-tenths;
10and with each of the seven lambs, one-tenth. 11Include one
male goat as a sin offering, in addition to the sin offering for
atonement and the regular burnt offering with its grain offering,
and their drink offerings.

Feast of Tabernacles

12" 'On the fifteenth day of the seventh month, hold a sacred
assembly and do no regular work. Celebrate a festival to the LORD
for seven days. 13Present an offering made by fire as an aroma
pleasing to the LORD, a burnt offering of thirteen young bulls, two
rams and fourteen male lambs a year old, all without defect.
14With each of the thirteen bulls prepare a grain offering of
three-tenths of an ephah of fine flour mixed with oil; with each
of the two rams, two-tenths; 15and with each of the fourteen
lambs, one-tenth. 16Include one male goat as a sin offering, in
addition to the regular burnt offering with its grain offering and
drink offering.
17" 'On the second day prepare twelve young bulls, two rams
and fourteen male lambs a year old, all without defect. 18With
the bulls, rams and lambs, prepare their grain offerings and
drink offerings according to the number specified. 19Include
one male goat as a sin offering, in addition to the regular burnt
offering with its grain offering, and their drink offerings.
20" 'On the third day prepare eleven bulls, two rams and fourteen male lambs a year old, all without defect. 21With the bulls,
rams and lambs, prepare their grain offerings and drink offerings according to the number specified. 22Include one male goat
as a sin offering, in addition to the regular burnt offering with its
grain offering and drink offering.
23" 'On the fourth day prepare ten bulls, two rams and fourteen male lambs a year old, all without defect. 24With the bulls,
rams and lambs, prepare their grain offerings and drink offerings according to the number specified. 25Include one male goat
as a sin offering, in addition to the regular burnt offering with its
grain offering and drink offering.
26" 'On the fifth day prepare nine bulls, two rams and fourteen male lambs a year old, all without defect. 27With the bulls,
rams and lambs, prepare their grain offerings and drink offerings according to the number specified. 28Include one male goat
as a sin offering, in addition to the regular burnt offering with its
grain offering and drink offering.
29" 'On the sixth day prepare eight bulls, two rams and fourteen male lambs a year old, all without defect. 30With the bulls,
rams and lambs, prepare their grain offerings and drink offerings according to the number specified. 31Include one male goat
as a sin offering, in addition to the regular burnt offering with its
grain offering and drink offering.
32" 'On the seventh day prepare seven bulls, two rams and
fourteen male lambs a year old, all without defect. 33With the
bulls, rams and lambs, prepare their grain offerings and drink

[a] 7 Or *must fast*

(29:7–11) We thank You, O God, for the Day of Atonement. These sacrifices were "an annual reminder of sins, because it was impossible for the blood of bulls and goats to take away sins." But we praise You that when Jesus Christ came into the world, He brought true substance to this shadow and became our atoning sacrifice—once and for all—making us holy forever through the sacrifice of His body. Having satisfied Your will, You responded with joy: "'Their sins and lawless acts I will remember no more.' And where these have been forgiven, there is no longer any sacrifice for sin." We praise You, living God, that Your love and mercy endure forever. (Heb 10:1–18)

If he gave Himself to death for our sins, then undoubtedly He is no tyrant or judge which will condemn us for our sins. He is no caster-down of the afflicted, but a raiser-up of those that are fallen, a merciful reliever and comforter of the heavy and the broken-hearted. Else should Paul lie in saying, 'which gave himself for our sins.'

Martin Luther (1483-1546)

The Holy Lamb was stricken,
Abandoned and alone.
He bore the world's affliction,
He bore it as His own.

For me He was forsaken,
For me He died alone.
My sins forever taken
That I might be His own.

"The Holy Heart"
Anne Barbour and Marsha Skidmore
(©1993)

offerings according to the number specified. 34Include one
male goat as a sin offering, in addition to the regular burnt offering with its grain offering and drink offering.
35" 'On the eighth day hold an assembly and do no regular
work. 36Present an offering made by fire as an aroma pleasing to
the LORD, a burnt offering of one bull, one ram and seven male
lambs a year old, all without defect. 37With the bull, the ram and
the lambs, prepare their grain offerings and drink offerings according to the number specified. 38Include one male goat as a
sin offering, in addition to the regular burnt offering with its
grain offering and drink offering.
39" 'In addition to what you vow and your freewill offerings,
prepare these for the LORD at your appointed feasts: your burnt
offerings, grain offerings, drink offerings and fellowship offerings.[a] ' "
40Moses told the Israelites all that the LORD commanded him.

Vows

30 Moses said to the heads of the tribes of Israel: "This is
what the LORD commands: 2When a man makes a vow to
the LORD or takes an oath to obligate himself by a pledge, he
must not break his word but must do everything he said.
3"When a young woman still living in her father's house
makes a vow to the LORD or obligates herself by a pledge 4and
her father hears about her vow or pledge but says nothing to her,
then all her vows and every pledge by which she obligated herself will stand. 5But if her father forbids her when he hears about
it, none of her vows or the pledges by which she obligated herself will stand; the LORD will release her because her father has
forbidden her.
6"If she marries after she makes a vow or after her lips utter
a rash promise by which she obligates herself 7and her husband
hears about it but says nothing to her, then her vows or the
pledges by which she obligated herself will stand. 8But if her
husband forbids her when he hears about it, he nullifies the vow
that obligates her or the rash promise by which she obligates
herself, and the LORD will release her.
9"Any vow or obligation taken by a widow or divorced woman
will be binding on her.
10"If a woman living with her husband makes a vow or obligates herself by a pledge under oath 11and her husband hears
about it but says nothing to her and does not forbid her, then all
her vows or the pledges by which she obligated herself will
stand. 12But if her husband nullifies them when he hears about
them, then none of the vows or pledges that came from her lips
will stand. Her husband has nullified them, and the LORD will release her. 13Her husband may confirm or nullify any vow she
makes or any sworn pledge to deny herself. 14But if her husband
says nothing to her about it from day to day, then he confirms all
her vows or the pledges binding on her. He confirms them by
saying nothing to her when he hears about them. 15If, however,
he nullifies them some time after he hears about them, then he
is responsible for her guilt."
16These are the regulations the LORD gave Moses concerning

[a] 39 Traditionally *peace offerings*

Every business takes inventory. The books are reviewed, the stock examined, and a determination is made of the company's financial condition.

Every believer who is wise in the Kingdom of heaven will cry, "Search me, O God, and know my heart. Try me and know my anxieties" (Psalm 139:23). We frequently need to take a personal inventory to determine if things are right between God and our hearts.

Charles Haddon Spurgeon (1834–1892)

(30:2) Heavenly Father, am I a person of my word? Do I keep my promises to You? Do I do what I say I will do? Your Word forces me to ponder these questions today. I must admit, Lord, that I don't always take seriously Your command to stay true to the words I speak and the promises I make. Help me to be careful in what I say. I want to be known as someone who is reliable, trustworthy, true. You are faithful to me, O Lord. Help me to be faithful to You and to those whom You have placed in my life.

relationships between a man and his wife, and between a father
and his young daughter still living in his house.

Vengeance on the Midianites

31 The LORD said to Moses, 2“Take vengeance on the Midianites for the Israelites. After that, you will be gathered to your
people.”
3So Moses said to the people, “Arm some of your men to go to
war against the Midianites and to carry out the LORD’s vengeance
on them. 4Send into battle a thousand men from each of the tribes
of Israel.” 5So twelve thousand men armed for battle, a thousand
from each tribe, were supplied from the clans of Israel. 6Moses
sent them into battle, a thousand from each tribe, along with Phinehas son of Eleazar, the priest, who took with him articles from the
sanctuary and the trumpets for signaling.
7They fought against Midian, as the LORD commanded Moses,
and killed every man. 8Among their victims were Evi, Rekem, Zur,
Hur and Reba—the five kings of Midian. They also killed Balaam
son of Beor with the sword. 9The Israelites captured the Midianite women and children and took all the Midianite herds, flocks
and goods as plunder. 10They burned all the towns where the Midianites had settled, as well as all their camps. 11They took all the
plunder and spoils, including the people and animals, 12and
brought the captives, spoils and plunder to Moses and Eleazar the
priest and the Israelite assembly at their camp on the plains of
Moab, by the Jordan across from Jericho.[a]
13Moses, Eleazar the priest and all the leaders of the community went to meet them outside the camp. 14Moses was angry with
the officers of the army—the commanders of thousands and commanders of hundreds—who returned from the battle.
15“Have you allowed all the women to live?” he asked them.
16“They were the ones who followed Balaam’s advice and were
the means of turning the Israelites away from the LORD in what
happened at Peor, so that a plague struck the LORD’s people.
17Now kill all the boys. And kill every woman who has slept with
a man, 18but save for yourselves every girl who has never slept
with a man.
19“All of you who have killed anyone or touched anyone who
was killed must stay outside the camp seven days. On the third and
seventh days you must purify yourselves and your captives. 20Pu-
rify every garment as well as everything made of leather, goat hair
or wood.”
21Then Eleazar the priest said to the soldiers who had gone into
battle, “This is the requirement of the law that the LORD gave
Moses: 22Gold, silver, bronze, iron, tin, lead 23and anything else
that can withstand fire must be put through the fire, and then it
will be clean. But it must also be purified with the water of cleansing. And whatever cannot withstand fire must be put through that
water. 24On the seventh day wash your clothes and you will be
clean. Then you may come into the camp.”

Dividing the Spoils

25The LORD said to Moses, 26“You and Eleazar the priest and the
family heads of the community are to count all the people and animals that were captured. 27Divide the spoils between the soldiers

[a] 12 Hebrew *Jordan of Jericho*; possibly an ancient name for the Jordan River

(31:1–18) How difficult it is to reconcile these commands of Yours with Your gracious and forgiving nature—You who are the defender of widows and the Father to the fatherless; You who insisted that Your people treat the aliens among them with respect and dignity. Yet, like a farmer turning over the soil and rooting out every weed—even the seedlings—so You were making preparations for a new planting in the land. And these were a people who had reached the extremes of depravity, in much the same way as Sodom and Gomorrah. Father, if this is the way You chose to deal with wickedness, how shall I then deal with sinful habits, activities, relationships, relics, “harmless” flirtations, or other seeds of sin in my own life? Teach me Lord, from this difficult passage, how to walk in purity before You. (Ex 22:21; Lev 19:33–34; Dt 9:5)

We choose the Fear of the Lord.
We choose the Fear of the Lord,
For the Fear of the Lord
Is to hate all evil.
We choose the Fear of the Lord.
We choose the Fear of the Lord.

He who delights in the Word of the
Lord
Shall be blessed in all of his ways,
For the Friendship of God
Is with those who Fear Him.
So we choose the Fear of the Lord,
We choose the way of the Lord.
We choose the Word of the Lord.

“We Choose The Fear Of The Lord”
Kirk Dearman (©1989)

(31:54) Lord, You have been so gracious to me. What can I give You that would serve as a memorial to Your mercy? My money? My possessions? My family? My talents? My life? It is the desire of my heart to give to You all that I am, all that I have, all that I could ever hope for, so that I may be completely devoted to You. Let me spend my life as a living testimony to Your goodness. May I give as these men gave: freely, joyfully, willingly, and in gratitude for Your great compassion.

What can I give Him, poor as I am?
If I were a shepherd I would bring a
lamb;
If I were a wiseman I would do my
part;
Yet what can I give Him? Give Him
my heart.

"What Can I Give Him?"
Christina Rossetti (1830–1894)

Great works do not always lie in our way, but every moment we may do little ones excellently, that is, with great love. I beg you to remark the saint who gives a cup of water for God's sake to a poor thirsty traveler; he seems to do a small thing; but the intention, the sweetness, the love with which he animates his action, is so excellent that it turns this simple water into the water of life, and of eternal life.

Saint Francis de Sales (1567–1622)

who took part in the battle and the rest of the community. 28From
the soldiers who fought in the battle, set apart as tribute for the
LORD one out of every five hundred, whether persons, cattle, donkeys, sheep or goats. 29Take this tribute from their half share and
give it to Eleazar the priest as the LORD's part. 30From the Israelites' half, select one out of every fifty, whether persons, cattle, donkeys, sheep, goats or other animals. Give them to the Levites, who
are responsible for the care of the LORD's tabernacle." 31So Moses
and Eleazar the priest did as the LORD commanded Moses.

32The plunder remaining from the spoils that the soldiers took
was 675,000 sheep, 3372,000 cattle, 3461,000 donkeys 35and
32,000 women who had never slept with a man.

36The half share of those who fought in the battle was:

337,500 sheep, 37of which the tribute for the LORD was 675;
38 36,000 cattle, of which the tribute for the LORD was 72;
39 30,500 donkeys, of which the tribute for the LORD was 61;
40 16,000 people, of which the tribute for the LORD was 32.

41Moses gave the tribute to Eleazar the priest as the LORD's part,
as the LORD commanded Moses.

42The half belonging to the Israelites, which Moses set apart
from that of the fighting men— 43the community's half—was
337,500 sheep, 4436,000 cattle, 4530,500 donkeys 46and 16,000
people. 47From the Israelites' half, Moses selected one out of
every fifty persons and animals, as the LORD commanded him, and
gave them to the Levites, who were responsible for the care of the
LORD's tabernacle.

48Then the officers who were over the units of the army—the
commanders of thousands and commanders of hundreds—went
to Moses 49and said to him, "Your servants have counted the soldiers under our command, and not one is missing. 50So we have
brought as an offering to the LORD the gold articles each of us acquired—armlets, bracelets, signet rings, earrings and necklaces—to make atonement for ourselves before the LORD."

51Moses and Eleazar the priest accepted from them the gold—
all the crafted articles. 52All the gold from the commanders of
thousands and commanders of hundreds that Moses and Eleazar
presented as a gift to the LORD weighed 16,750 shekels.[a] 53Each
soldier had taken plunder for himself. 54Moses and Eleazar the
priest accepted the gold from the commanders of thousands and
commanders of hundreds and brought it into the Tent of Meeting
as a memorial for the Israelites before the LORD.

The Transjordan Tribes

32 The Reubenites and Gadites, who had very large herds and
flocks, saw that the lands of Jazer and Gilead were suitable
for livestock. 2So they came to Moses and Eleazar the priest and to
the leaders of the community, and said, 3"Ataroth, Dibon, Jazer,
Nimrah, Heshbon, Elealeh, Sebam, Nebo and Beon— 4the land
the LORD subdued before the people of Israel—are suitable for
livestock, and your servants have livestock. 5If we have found favor
in your eyes," they said, "let this land be given to your servants as
our possession. Do not make us cross the Jordan."

6Moses said to the Gadites and Reubenites, "Shall your countrymen go to war while you sit here? 7Why do you discourage the

[a] *52* That is, about 420 pounds (about 190 kilograms)

Israelites from going over into the land the LORD has given them?
8This is what your fathers did when I sent them from Kadesh Barnea to look over the land. 9After they went up to the Valley of
Eshcol and viewed the land, they discouraged the Israelites from
entering the land the LORD had given them. 10The LORD's anger was
aroused that day and he swore this oath: 11'Because they have not
followed me wholeheartedly, not one of the men twenty years old
or more who came up out of Egypt will see the land I promised on
oath to Abraham, Isaac and Jacob— 12not one except Caleb son
of Jephunneh the Kenizzite and Joshua son of Nun, for they followed the LORD wholeheartedly.' 13The LORD's anger burned
against Israel and he made them wander in the desert forty years,
until the whole generation of those who had done evil in his sight
was gone.

14"And here you are, a brood of sinners, standing in the place
of your fathers and making the LORD even more angry with Israel.
15If you turn away from following him, he will again leave all this
people in the desert, and you will be the cause of their destruction."

16Then they came up to him and said, "We would like to build
pens here for our livestock and cities for our women and children. 17But we are ready to arm ourselves and go ahead of the Israelites until we have brought them to their place. Meanwhile our
women and children will live in fortified cities, for protection from
the inhabitants of the land. 18We will not return to our homes until
every Israelite has received his inheritance. 19We will not receive
any inheritance with them on the other side of the Jordan, because
our inheritance has come to us on the east side of the Jordan."

20Then Moses said to them, "If you will do this—if you will arm
yourselves before the LORD for battle, 21and if all of you will go
armed over the Jordan before the LORD until he has driven his enemies out before him— 22then when the land is subdued before
the LORD, you may return and be free from your obligation to the
LORD and to Israel. And this land will be your possession before
the LORD.

23"But if you fail to do this, you will be sinning against the LORD;
and you may be sure that your sin will find you out. 24Build cities
for your women and children, and pens for your flocks, but do
what you have promised."

25The Gadites and Reubenites said to Moses, "We your servants
will do as our lord commands. 26Our children and wives, our
flocks and herds will remain here in the cities of Gilead. 27But
your servants, every man armed for battle, will cross over to fight
before the LORD, just as our lord says."

28Then Moses gave orders about them to Eleazar the priest and
Joshua son of Nun and to the family heads of the Israelite tribes.
29He said to them, "If the Gadites and Reubenites, every man
armed for battle, cross over the Jordan with you before the LORD,
then when the land is subdued before you, give them the land of
Gilead as their possession. 30But if they do not cross over with you
armed, they must accept their possession with you in Canaan."

31The Gadites and Reubenites answered, "Your servants will do
what the LORD has said. 32We will cross over before the LORD into
Canaan armed, but the property we inherit will be on this side of
the Jordan."

33Then Moses gave to the Gadites, the Reubenites and the half-
tribe of Manasseh son of Joseph the kingdom of Sihon king of the

(32:1–33) Lord, what am I holding on to that could be causing me to forfeit something of the fullness of Your grace for me? The Reubenites, the Gadites and the half-tribe of Manasseh settled for something less than Your highest purpose because they saw that the land was suitable to their economy. Their decision cost them dearly in the future, for the first tribes settled were the first tribes displaced by the Assyrians many years later. Show me, Lord, whether I am choosing second best when Your highest plan and purpose is waiting just beyond the next river. As Jesus said, "What good is it for a man to gain the whole world, yet forfeit his soul?" (2Ki 10:32–33; 1Ch 5:26; Mk 8:36)

We judge of things by their present appearance, but the Lord sees them in their consequences; if we could do so likewise, we should be perfectly of His mind; but as we cannot, it is an unspeakable mercy that He will manage for us, whether we are pleased with His management or not; and it is spoken of as one of His heaviest judgments, when He gives any person or people up to the way of their own hearts, and to walk after their own counsels.

John Newton (1725-1807)

My heart, my life, my all I bring
To Christ who loves me so;
He is my Master, Lord and King,
Wherever He leads I'll go.

Wherever He leads I'll go,
Wherever He leads I'll go,
I'll follow my Christ who loves me so,
Wherever He leads I'll go.

"Wherever He Leads I'll Go"
B.B. McKinney (©1936, 1964)

(33:1–33) Each stage of Israel's journey was lit by Your presence in the pillar of fire. You led Your people step-by-step, from place to place, all along the way. You never stopped providing for them. You never stopped defending them. You never left them despite all of the reasons they gave You to do so. I praise You, loving Father, for Your faithfulness and mercy.

O God our Father, history and experience have given us so many evidences of Thy guidance to nations and to individuals that we should not doubt Thy power or Thy willingness to direct us. Give us the faith to believe that when God wants us to do or not to do any particular thing, God finds a way of letting us know it.

May we not make it more difficult for Thee to guide us, but be willing to be led of Thee, that Thy will may be done in us and through us.

Peter Marshall (1902–1949)

Help me then in every tribulation
So to trust Thy promises, O Lord,
That I lose not faith's sweet
consolation
Offered me within Thy holy Word.
Help me, Lord, when toil and trouble
meeting,
E'er to take, as from a father's hand,
One by one, the days, the moments
fleeting,
Till I reach the Promised Land.

"Day By Day"
Carolina Sandell Berg (1865)
Trans. Andrew L. Skoog (1856–1934)

Amorites and the kingdom of Og king of Bashan—the whole land
with its cities and the territory around them.
34 The Gadites built up Dibon, Ataroth, Aroer, 35 Atroth Shophan,
Jazer, Jogbehah, 36 Beth Nimrah and Beth Haran as fortified cities,
and built pens for their flocks. 37 And the Reubenites rebuilt Heshbon, Elealeh and Kiriathaim, 38 as well as Nebo and Baal Meon
(these names were changed) and Sibmah. They gave names to the
cities they rebuilt.
39 The descendants of Makir son of Manasseh went to Gilead,
captured it and drove out the Amorites who were there. 40 So
Moses gave Gilead to the Makirites, the descendants of Manasseh,
and they settled there. 41 Jair, a descendant of Manasseh, captured
their settlements and called them Havvoth Jair.[a] 42 And Nobah captured Kenath and its surrounding settlements and called it Nobah
after himself.

Stages in Israel's Journey

33 Here are the stages in the journey of the Israelites when
they came out of Egypt by divisions under the leadership of
Moses and Aaron. 2 At the LORD's command Moses recorded the
stages in their journey. This is their journey by stages:

3 The Israelites set out from Rameses on the fifteenth day
of the first month, the day after the Passover. They marched
out boldly in full view of all the Egyptians, 4 who were burying all their firstborn, whom the LORD had struck down
among them; for the LORD had brought judgment on their
gods.
5 The Israelites left Rameses and camped at Succoth.
6 They left Succoth and camped at Etham, on the edge of
the desert.
7 They left Etham, turned back to Pi Hahiroth, to the east of
Baal Zephon, and camped near Migdol.
8 They left Pi Hahiroth[b] and passed through the sea into
the desert, and when they had traveled for three days in the
Desert of Etham, they camped at Marah.
9 They left Marah and went to Elim, where there were
twelve springs and seventy palm trees, and they camped
there.
10 They left Elim and camped by the Red Sea.[c]
11 They left the Red Sea and camped in the Desert of Sin.
12 They left the Desert of Sin and camped at Dophkah.
13 They left Dophkah and camped at Alush.
14 They left Alush and camped at Rephidim, where there
was no water for the people to drink.
15 They left Rephidim and camped in the Desert of Sinai.
16 They left the Desert of Sinai and camped at Kibroth Hattaavah.
17 They left Kibroth Hattaavah and camped at Hazeroth.
18 They left Hazeroth and camped at Rithmah.
19 They left Rithmah and camped at Rimmon Perez.
20 They left Rimmon Perez and camped at Libnah.
21 They left Libnah and camped at Rissah.
22 They left Rissah and camped at Kehelathah.

[a] 41 Or *them the settlements of Jair* [b] 8 Many manuscripts of the Masoretic Text, Samaritan Pentateuch and Vulgate; most manuscripts of the Masoretic Text *left from before Hahiroth* [c] 10 Hebrew *Yam Suph*; that is, Sea of Reeds; also in verse 11

[23]They left Kehelathah and camped at Mount Shepher.
[24]They left Mount Shepher and camped at Haradah.
[25]They left Haradah and camped at Makheloth.
[26]They left Makheloth and camped at Tahath.
[27]They left Tahath and camped at Terah.
[28]They left Terah and camped at Mithcah.
[29]They left Mithcah and camped at Hashmonah.
[30]They left Hashmonah and camped at Moseroth.
[31]They left Moseroth and camped at Bene Jaakan.
[32]They left Bene Jaakan and camped at Hor Haggidgad.
[33]They left Hor Haggidgad and camped at Jotbathah.
[34]They left Jotbathah and camped at Abronah.
[35]They left Abronah and camped at Ezion Geber.
[36]They left Ezion Geber and camped at Kadesh, in the Desert of Zin.
[37]They left Kadesh and camped at Mount Hor, on the border of Edom.
[38]At the LORD's command Aaron the priest went
up Mount Hor, where he died on the first day of the fifth
month of the fortieth year after the Israelites came out of
Egypt. [39]Aaron was a hundred and twenty-three years old
when he died on Mount Hor.
[40]The Canaanite king of Arad, who lived in the Negev of Canaan, heard that the Israelites were coming.
[41]They left Mount Hor and camped at Zalmonah.
[42]They left Zalmonah and camped at Punon.
[43]They left Punon and camped at Oboth.
[44]They left Oboth and camped at Iye Abarim, on the border of Moab.
[45]They left Iyim[a] and camped at Dibon Gad.
[46]They left Dibon Gad and camped at Almon Diblathaim.
[47]They left Almon Diblathaim and camped in the mountains of Abarim, near Nebo.
[48]They left the mountains of Abarim and camped on the
plains of Moab by the Jordan across from Jericho.[b] [49]There
on the plains of Moab they camped along the Jordan from
Beth Jeshimoth to Abel Shittim.

[50]On the plains of Moab by the Jordan across from Jericho the
LORD said to Moses, [51]"Speak to the Israelites and say to them:
'When you cross the Jordan into Canaan, [52]drive out all the inhabitants of the land before you. Destroy all their carved images
and their cast idols, and demolish all their high places. [53]Take
possession of the land and settle in it, for I have given you the land
to possess. [54]Distribute the land by lot, according to your clans.
To a larger group give a larger inheritance, and to a smaller group a smaller one. Whatever falls to them by lot will be theirs. Distribute it according to your ancestral tribes.
[55]" 'But if you do not drive out the inhabitants of the land, those
you allow to remain will become barbs in your eyes and thorns in
your sides. They will give you trouble in the land where you will
live. [56]And then I will do to you what I plan to do to them.' "

[a] *45* That is, Iye Abarim [b] *48* Hebrew *Jordan of Jericho*; possibly an ancient name for the Jordan River; also in verse 50

(33:50–56) Almighty God, I pray for Your church throughout the world. As we continue to press on into the fullness of life in Your kingdom, let us give no place to the devil, leave no room for sin, give no thought to temptation, make no compromise with unrighteousness, strike no deal with the world, defend no guilt of our own, retain no memory of wickedness, preserve no relic of idolatry, loosen no standard of morality, and tolerate no alternative to holiness. Help us, rather, to prepare our minds for action; to be self-controlled; to set our hope fully on the grace to be given us when Jesus Christ is revealed. As obedient children, let us not conform to the evil desires we had when we lived in ignorance. But just as You Who called us are holy, so may we be holy in all we do; for it is written: "Be holy, because I am holy." (Lev 19:1; 1Pe 1:13–16)

God doesn't conform to a holy standard; He is the standard. He never does anything wrong. He never errs, He never causes something to happen that isn't right. There are no degrees to his holiness. He is holy, flawless, without error, without sin, fully righteous, utterly, absolutely, infinitely holy.

John MacArthur, Jr. (1939-)

Holy One, Most Holy One,
Your ways are higher than mine.
Holy One, Most Holy One,
May Your ways be mine.

Your ways are higher than the
mountains.
Your love is deeper than the sea.
Your mercy, flowing like a fountain,
Has touched my heart and made me
free.

"Most Holy One"
Kelly Willard and Paul Baloche (©1990)

(34:1–12) As I read of the breadth and width of the land You promised to Your people, I remember that they never took complete possession of it. They settled for less than You were willing to give them. In my own life, Lord, why do I limit Your kindness to me? Why do I fail to take possession of the fullness of life that You intend for me? Are there areas of my life that I assume I will never conquer? Continue to draw me, Lord, into the rich inheritance You have prepared for me. For You have promised, "No eye has seen, no ear has heard, no mind has conceived what God has prepared for those who love him." (1Co 2:9)

Boundaries of Canaan

34 The LORD said to Moses, 2"Command the Israelites and say
to them: 'When you enter Canaan, the land that will be allotted to you as an inheritance will have these boundaries:

3" 'Your southern side will include some of the Desert of Zin
along the border of Edom. On the east, your southern boundary
will start from the end of the Salt Sea,[a] 4cross south of Scorpion[b]
Pass, continue on to Zin and go south of Kadesh Barnea. Then it
will go to Hazar Addar and over to Azmon, 5where it will turn, join
the Wadi of Egypt and end at the Sea.[c]
6" 'Your western boundary will be the coast of the Great Sea.
This will be your boundary on the west.
7" 'For your northern boundary, run a line from the Great Sea
to Mount Hor 8and from Mount Hor to Lebo[d] Hamath. Then the
boundary will go to Zedad, 9continue to Ziphron and end at Hazar
Enan. This will be your boundary on the north.
10" 'For your eastern boundary, run a line from Hazar Enan to
Shepham. 11The boundary will go down from Shepham to Riblah
on the east side of Ain and continue along the slopes east of the
Sea of Kinnereth.[e] 12Then the boundary will go down along the
Jordan and end at the Salt Sea.
" 'This will be your land, with its boundaries on every side.' "
13Moses commanded the Israelites: "Assign this land by lot as
an inheritance. The LORD has ordered that it be given to the nine
and a half tribes, 14because the families of the tribe of Reuben, the
tribe of Gad and the half-tribe of Manasseh have received their inheritance. 15These two and a half tribes have received their inheritance on the east side of the Jordan of Jericho,[f] toward the
sunrise."
16The LORD said to Moses, 17"These are the names of the men
who are to assign the land for you as an inheritance: Eleazar the
priest and Joshua son of Nun. 18And appoint one leader from each
tribe to help assign the land. 19These are their names:

Caleb son of Jephunneh,
  from the tribe of Judah;
20 Shemuel son of Ammihud,
  from the tribe of Simeon;
21 Elidad son of Kislon,
  from the tribe of Benjamin;
22 Bukki son of Jogli,
  the leader from the tribe of Dan;
23 Hanniel son of Ephod,
  the leader from the tribe of Manasseh son of Joseph;
24 Kemuel son of Shiphtan,
  the leader from the tribe of Ephraim son of Joseph;
25 Elizaphan son of Parnach,
  the leader from the tribe of Zebulun;
26 Paltiel son of Azzan,
  the leader from the tribe of Issachar;
27 Ahihud son of Shelomi,
  the leader from the tribe of Asher;
28 Pedahel son of Ammihud,
  the leader from the tribe of Naphtali."

[a] 3 That is, the Dead Sea; also in verse 12 [b] 4 Hebrew *Akrabbim* [c] 5 That is, the Mediterranean; also in verses 6 and 7 [d] 8 Or *to the entrance to* [e] 11 That is, Galilee [f] 15 *Jordan of Jericho* was possibly an ancient name for the Jordan River.

29These are the men the LORD commanded to assign the inheritance to the Israelites in the land of Canaan.

Towns for the Levites

35 On the plains of Moab by the Jordan across from Jericho,[a] the LORD said to Moses, 2"Command the Israelites to give the Levites towns to live in from the inheritance the Israelites will possess. And give them pasturelands around the towns. 3Then they will have towns to live in and pasturelands for their cattle, flocks and all their other livestock.

4"The pasturelands around the towns that you give the Levites will extend out fifteen hundred feet[b] from the town wall. 5Outside the town, measure three thousand feet[c] on the east side, three thousand on the south side, three thousand on the west and three thousand on the north, with the town in the center. They will have this area as pastureland for the towns.

Cities of Refuge

6"Six of the towns you give the Levites will be cities of refuge, to which a person who has killed someone may flee. In addition, give them forty-two other towns. 7In all you must give the Levites forty-eight towns, together with their pasturelands. 8The towns you give the Levites from the land the Israelites possess are to be given in proportion to the inheritance of each tribe: Take many towns from a tribe that has many, but few from one that has few."

9Then the LORD said to Moses: 10"Speak to the Israelites and say to them: 'When you cross the Jordan into Canaan, 11select some towns to be your cities of refuge, to which a person who has killed someone accidentally may flee. 12They will be places of refuge from the avenger, so that a person accused of murder may not die before he stands trial before the assembly. 13These six towns you give will be your cities of refuge. 14Give three on this side of the Jordan and three in Canaan as cities of refuge. 15These six towns will be a place of refuge for Israelites, aliens and any other people living among them, so that anyone who has killed another accidentally can flee there.

16" 'If a man strikes someone with an iron object so that he dies, he is a murderer; the murderer shall be put to death. 17Or if anyone has a stone in his hand that could kill, and he strikes someone so that he dies, he is a murderer; the murderer shall be put to death. 18Or if anyone has a wooden object in his hand that could kill, and he hits someone so that he dies, he is a murderer; the murderer shall be put to death. 19The avenger of blood shall put the murderer to death; when he meets him, he shall put him to death. 20If anyone with malice aforethought shoves another or throws something at him intentionally so that he dies 21or if in hostility he hits him with his fist so that he dies, that person shall be put to death; he is a murderer. The avenger of blood shall put the murderer to death when he meets him.

22" 'But if without hostility someone suddenly shoves another or throws something at him unintentionally 23or, without seeing him, drops a stone on him that could kill him, and he dies, then since he was not his enemy and he did not intend to harm him, 24the assembly must judge between him and the avenger of blood

[a] *1* Hebrew *Jordan of Jericho*; possibly an ancient name for the Jordan River [b] *4* Hebrew *a thousand cubits* (about 450 meters) [c] *5* Hebrew *two thousand cubits* (about 900 meters)

(35:1–4) You are always faithful to Your word, Father. Hundreds of years earlier You foretold through Jacob that the descendents of Levi would be dispersed throughout Israel. What was spoken as a curse by Jacob became a blessing for the entire nation. Here You mandated that the Levites, as Your ministers, should not be relegated to some distant or unique outpost in society, but rather that they should be spread like salt and light throughout the land. And You graciously blessed the Levites in the process. They did not have to "sow or reap or store away in barns" because You, Heavenly Father, fed them from the tithes and offerings of Israel. You turned a curse into a blessing, and gave hope to the hopeless. (Ge 49:7; Mt 6:26; Gal 6:6)

according to these regulations. 25 The assembly must protect the one accused of murder from the avenger of blood and send him back to the city of refuge to which he fled. He must stay there until the death of the high priest, who was anointed with the holy oil.

26 " 'But if the accused ever goes outside the limits of the city of refuge to which he has fled 27 and the avenger of blood finds him outside the city, the avenger of blood may kill the accused without being guilty of murder. 28 The accused must stay in his city of refuge until the death of the high priest; only after the death of the high priest may he return to his own property.

29 " 'These are to be legal requirements for you throughout the generations to come, wherever you live.

30 " 'Anyone who kills a person is to be put to death as a murderer only on the testimony of witnesses. But no one is to be put to death on the testimony of only one witness.

31 " 'Do not accept a ransom for the life of a murderer, who deserves to die. He must surely be put to death.

32 " 'Do not accept a ransom for anyone who has fled to a city of refuge and so allow him to go back and live on his own land before the death of the high priest.

33 " 'Do not pollute the land where you are. Bloodshed pollutes the land, and atonement cannot be made for the land on which blood has been shed, except by the blood of the one who shed it. 34 Do not defile the land where you live and where I dwell, for I, the LORD, dwell among the Israelites.' "

Inheritance of Zelophehad's Daughters

36 The family heads of the clan of Gilead son of Makir, the son of Manasseh, who were from the clans of the descendants of Joseph, came and spoke before Moses and the leaders, the heads of the Israelite families. 2 They said, "When the LORD commanded my lord to give the land as an inheritance to the Israelites by lot, he ordered you to give the inheritance of our brother Zelophehad to his daughters. 3 Now suppose they marry men from other Israelite tribes; then their inheritance will be taken from our ancestral inheritance and added to that of the tribe they marry into. And so part of the inheritance allotted to us will be taken away. 4 When the Year of Jubilee for the Israelites comes, their inheritance will be added to that of the tribe into which they marry, and their property will be taken from the tribal inheritance of our forefathers."

5 Then at the LORD's command Moses gave this order to the Israelites: "What the tribe of the descendants of Joseph is saying is right. 6 This is what the LORD commands for Zelophehad's daughters: They may marry anyone they please as long as they marry within the tribal clan of their father. 7 No inheritance in Israel is to pass from tribe to tribe, for every Israelite shall keep the tribal land inherited from his forefathers. 8 Every daughter who inherits land in any Israelite tribe must marry someone in her father's tribal clan, so that every Israelite will possess the inheritance of his fathers. 9 No inheritance may pass from tribe to tribe, for each Israelite tribe is to keep the land it inherits."

10 So Zelophehad's daughters did as the LORD commanded Moses. 11 Zelophehad's daughters—Mahlah, Tirzah, Hoglah, Milcah and Noah—married their cousins on their father's side. 12 They married within the clans of the descendants of Manasseh

(35:25–27) We praise You, Lord Jesus Christ, for You are our city of refuge. All of us are guilty of manslaughter, for it was our sin that caused Your death. But we hear Your cry to the Father, "Forgive them, for they do not know what they are doing." And we hear Your invitation to us, "Come to me . . . and I will give you rest." Apart from You, we face certain death. So we run to You, Jesus Christ, for refuge. We hide in You, we abide in You, knowing that "there is now no condemnation for those who are in Christ Jesus." (Ps 18:2; 91:2; Pr 18:10; Mt 11:28; Lk 23:34; Ro 8:1)

Other refuge have I none;
Hangs my helpless soul on Thee;
Leave, oh! Leave me not alone,
Still support and comfort me.
All my trust on Thee is stayed,
All my help from Thee I bring;
Cover my defenseless head
With the shadow of Thy wing.

"Jesus, Lover of My Soul"
Charles Wesley (1740)

son of Joseph, and their inheritance remained in their father's clan and tribe.

13These are the commands and regulations the LORD gave through Moses to the Israelites on the plains of Moab by the Jordan across from Jericho.[a]

(36:13) I praise You, Lord, for the lessons in this book. Please open my heart and mind to what You would have me learn from these pages. For I know that "these things occurred as examples to keep us from setting our hearts on evil things as they did;" and that "all Scripture is God-breathed and is useful for teaching, rebuking, correcting and training in righteousness," so that the people of God may be thoroughly equipped for every good work. (1Co 10:6–11; 2Ti 3:16–17)

The God of Abraham, the God of Isaac, the God of Jacob, the God of Christians, is a God of love and consolation, a God who fills the souls and hearts of his own, a God who makes them feel their inward wretchedness and His infinite mercy, who unites Himself to their inmost spirit, filling it with humility and joy, with confidence and love, rendering them incapable of any end other than Himself.

Blaise Pascal (1623-1662)

[a] 13 Hebrew *Jordan of Jericho*; possibly an ancient name for the Jordan River

The Fifth Book of Moses called DEUTERONOMY

Deuteronomy

"Deuteronomy" translates a Greek word meaning "second lawgiving." This title reflects the fact that the book reiterates the law revealed first at Mt. Sinai. But Deuteronomy does not merely repeat what was heard before. Rather, it reconfigures the law in the form of an ancient treaty between an overlord and his subjects. Thus Deuteronomy reminds the Israelites that their special relationship with their Lord demands covenant faithfulness and promises blessings in return. Moses summarizes their obligations by saying, "And now, O Israel, what does the LORD your God ask of you but to fear the LORD your God, to walk in all his ways, to love him, to serve the LORD your God with all your heart and with all your soul, and to observe the LORD's commands and decrees that I am giving you today for your own good?" (10:12–13).

The book consists primarily of three speeches given by Moses shortly before the Israelites begin their conquest of the promised land (1:1—4:40; 4:44—26:19; 29:1—30:20). He reminds the people of how God delivered them from Egypt and revealed the law. He repeats and explains the law, so that the people will be equipped to live in covenant faithfulness after they have taken possession of the land. If they obey God's word, the Israelites will be greatly blessed. But if they disobey, they will suffer horrendous consequences (ch. 28).

As followers of Jesus we ought to worship God with all that we are, and live our lives, not in fear of God's anger, but in response to the love He showed us.

All of this can sound narrowly legalistic when separated from Deuteronomy's emphasis upon love. Because God loved Israel, He delivered His people from Egypt and revealed His law to them (4:37). In response, the people had the high calling and privilege of loving God completely. The core of the law, the essence of covenant faithfulness, is summed up in the "Shema": "Hear [Heb. *shema*], O Israel: The LORD our God, the LORD is one. Love the LORD your God with all your heart and with all your soul and with all your strength" (6:4–5). God's people obeyed the law in response to God's love and as an expression of their love for Him.

So it is for those of us who are God's people through Christ. Jesus Himself quotes the Shema, calling it the greatest commandment (Mt 22:37–38). As followers of Jesus we ought to worship God with all that we are, and live our lives, not in fear of God's anger, but in response to the love He showed us when He "sent his Son as an atoning sacrifice for our sins" (1Jn 4:10). On the cross, Christ "[became] a curse for us," thus saving us, not merely from the curses threatened in Deuteronomy, but also from the curse of death brought on by our sin (Gal 3:13). In this way 'God demonstrates his own love for us . . . While we were still sinners, Christ died for us" (Ro 5:8). Thus we live and worship in response to God's love in Christ by loving God with every part of our being.

The Command to Leave Horeb

1 These are the words Moses spoke to all Israel in the desert
east of the Jordan—that is, in the Arabah—opposite Suph, between Paran and Tophel, Laban, Hazeroth and Dizahab. 2 (It takes
eleven days to go from Horeb to Kadesh Barnea by the Mount Seir
road.)
3 In the fortieth year, on the first day of the eleventh month,
Moses proclaimed to the Israelites all that the LORD had commanded him concerning them. 4 This was after he had defeated
Sihon king of the Amorites, who reigned in Heshbon, and at Edrei
had defeated Og king of Bashan, who reigned in Ashtaroth.
5 East of the Jordan in the territory of Moab, Moses began to expound this law, saying:

6 The LORD our God said to us at Horeb, "You have stayed long
enough at this mountain. 7 Break camp and advance into the hill
country of the Amorites; go to all the neighboring peoples in the
Arabah, in the mountains, in the western foothills, in the Negev
and along the coast, to the land of the Canaanites and to Lebanon,
as far as the great river, the Euphrates. 8 See, I have given you this
land. Go in and take possession of the land that the LORD swore he
would give to your fathers—to Abraham, Isaac and Jacob—and
to their descendants after them."

The Appointment of Leaders

9 At that time I said to you, "You are too heavy a burden for me
to carry alone. 10 The LORD your God has increased your numbers
so that today you are as many as the stars in the sky. 11 May the
LORD, the God of your fathers, increase you a thousand times and
bless you as he has promised! 12 But how can I bear your problems and your burdens and your disputes all by myself? 13 Choose
some wise, understanding and respected men from each of your
tribes, and I will set them over you."
14 You answered me, "What you propose to do is good."
15 So I took the leading men of your tribes, wise and respected
men, and appointed them to have authority over you—as commanders of thousands, of hundreds, of fifties and of tens and as
tribal officials. 16 And I charged your judges at that time: Hear the
disputes between your brothers and judge fairly, whether the case
is between brother Israelites or between one of them and an alien.
17 Do not show partiality in judging; hear both small and great
alike. Do not be afraid of any man, for judgment belongs to God.
Bring me any case too hard for you, and I will hear it. 18 And at
that time I told you everything you were to do.

Spies Sent Out

19 Then, as the LORD our God commanded us, we set out from
Horeb and went toward the hill country of the Amorites through
all that vast and dreadful desert that you have seen, and so we
reached Kadesh Barnea. 20 Then I said to you, "You have reached
the hill country of the Amorites, which the LORD our God is giving
us. 21 See, the LORD your God has given you the land. Go up and
take possession of it as the LORD, the God of your fathers, told you.
Do not be afraid; do not be discouraged."
22 Then all of you came to me and said, "Let us send men ahead
to spy out the land for us and bring back a report about the route
we are to take and the towns we will come to."

(1:8) Gracious Father, as You charged Your people to enter the land You swore to give to their fathers, so You charge me to enter the land of the unsearchable riches of Christ Who came so that I may have life, and have it to the full. Open my eyes that I may fully see the provision of Your promises in Your Word. Strengthen my heart, Lord, to take possession of the unmerited inheritance You have purchased for me through Your Son, Jesus. (Jn 10:10)

We were chaff, now we are wheat;
We were dross, now we are gold;
We were ravens, now we are sheep;
We were thorns, now we are grapes;
We were thistles, now we are lilies;
We were strangers, now we are citizens;
We were harlots, now we are virgins;
Hell was our inheritance, now heaven is
our possession;
We were children of wrath, now we are
sons of mercy;
We were bondslaves to Satan, now we are
heirs of God and co-heirs with Jesus
Christ.

James Bisse

(1:21) Throughout my pilgrimage of faith You speak words of encouragement to me, dear God. My fears and discouragement abate only as I see that it is You who are with me. For if You are with me, who can be against me? My heart grows strong, even in the wilderness and in my weaknesses, as I remember Your promise, "Never will I leave You; never will I forsake You." Indeed, You are my Immanuel. (Ro 8:31; Heb 13:5)

This is a time to remember
The greatness of the Lord;
He has so faithfully led us
As promised in his Word;
He has so bountifully given
His grace like freshening rain;
He has so lovingly pardoned
And made us whole again.

"This Is A Time to Remember"
Bryan Jeffery Leech (©1982)

There is an Arm that never tires,
When human strength gives way.
George Matheson (1842-1906)

(1:30–31) Father, You are forever the Champion of Your people, defending, strengthening and—more often than we know—carrying us in Your everlasting arms. You are mightier than our worst enemies, wiser than our most esteemed sages, and more tenderhearted than any earthly father. How we thank You for being ever-present, for we dare not face the world without You.

Great is the Lord,
And most worthy of praise,
In the city of our God,
The holy place,
The joy of the whole earth.
Great is the Lord
In whom we have the victory,
He aids us against the enemy,
We bow down on our knees.

And Lord, we want to
Lift Your name on high,
And Lord, we want to thank You
For the works You've done in our
lives.
And Lord, we trust in Your unfailing
love,
For You alone are God eternal
Throughout earth and heaven above.
"Great Is The Lord"
Steve McEwan (©1985)

23The idea seemed good to me; so I selected twelve of you, one
man from each tribe. 24They left and went up into the hill country,
and came to the Valley of Eshcol and explored it. 25Taking with
them some of the fruit of the land, they brought it down to us and
reported, "It is a good land that the LORD our God is giving us."

Rebellion Against the LORD

26But you were unwilling to go up; you rebelled against the
command of the LORD your God. 27You grumbled in your tents and
said, "The LORD hates us; so he brought us out of Egypt to deliver
us into the hands of the Amorites to destroy us. 28Where can we
go? Our brothers have made us lose heart. They say, 'The people
are stronger and taller than we are; the cities are large, with walls
up to the sky. We even saw the Anakites there.' "
29Then I said to you, "Do not be terrified; do not be afraid of
them. 30The LORD your God, who is going before you, will fight for
you, as he did for you in Egypt, before your very eyes, 31and in the
desert. There you saw how the LORD your God carried you, as a father carries his son, all the way you went until you reached this
place."
32In spite of this, you did not trust in the LORD your God, 33who
went ahead of you on your journey, in fire by night and in a cloud
by day, to search out places for you to camp and to show you the
way you should go.
34When the LORD heard what you said, he was angry and
solemnly swore: 35"Not a man of this evil generation shall see the
good land I swore to give your forefathers, 36except Caleb son of
Jephunneh. He will see it, and I will give him and his descendants
the land he set his feet on, because he followed the LORD wholeheartedly."
37Because of you the LORD became angry with me also and said,
"You shall not enter it, either. 38But your assistant, Joshua son of
Nun, will enter it. Encourage him, because he will lead Israel to
inherit it. 39And the little ones that you said would be taken captive, your children who do not yet know good from bad—they will
enter the land. I will give it to them and they will take possession
of it. 40But as for you, turn around and set out toward the desert
along the route to the Red Sea.[a]"
41Then you replied, "We have sinned against the LORD. We will
go up and fight, as the LORD our God commanded us." So every
one of you put on his weapons, thinking it easy to go up into the
hill country.
42But the LORD said to me, "Tell them, 'Do not go up and fight,
because I will not be with you. You will be defeated by your enemies.' "
43So I told you, but you would not listen. You rebelled against
the LORD's command and in your arrogance you marched up into
the hill country. 44The Amorites who lived in those hills came out
against you; they chased you like a swarm of bees and beat you
down from Seir all the way to Hormah. 45You came back and wept
before the LORD, but he paid no attention to your weeping and
turned a deaf ear to you. 46And so you stayed in Kadesh many
days—all the time you spent there.

[a] 40 Hebrew *Yam Suph*; that is, Sea of Reeds

Wanderings in the Desert

2 Then we turned back and set out toward the desert along the
route to the Red Sea,[a] as the LORD had directed me. For a long
time we made our way around the hill country of Seir.
2Then the LORD said to me, 3"You have made your way around
this hill country long enough; now turn north. 4Give the people
these orders: 'You are about to pass through the territory of your
brothers the descendants of Esau, who live in Seir. They will be
afraid of you, but be very careful. 5Do not provoke them to war,
for I will not give you any of their land, not even enough to put
your foot on. I have given Esau the hill country of Seir as his own.
6You are to pay them in silver for the food you eat and the water
you drink.'"
7The LORD your God has blessed you in all the work of your
hands. He has watched over your journey through this vast desert.
These forty years the LORD your God has been with you, and you
have not lacked anything.
8So we went on past our brothers the descendants of Esau, who
live in Seir. We turned from the Arabah road, which comes up
from Elath and Ezion Geber, and traveled along the desert road of
Moab.
9Then the LORD said to me, "Do not harass the Moabites or provoke them to war, for I will not give you any part of their land. I
have given Ar to the descendants of Lot as a possession."
10(The Emites used to live there—a people strong and numerous, and as tall as the Anakites. 11Like the Anakites, they too were
considered Rephaites, but the Moabites called them Emites. 12Ho-
rites used to live in Seir, but the descendants of Esau drove them
out. They destroyed the Horites from before them and settled in
their place, just as Israel did in the land the LORD gave them as
their possession.)
13And the LORD said, "Now get up and cross the Zered Valley."
So we crossed the valley.
14Thirty-eight years passed from the time we left Kadesh Barnea
until we crossed the Zered Valley. By then, that entire generation
of fighting men had perished from the camp, as the LORD had
sworn to them. 15The LORD's hand was against them until he had
completely eliminated them from the camp.
16Now when the last of these fighting men among the people
had died, 17the LORD said to me, 18"Today you are to pass by the
region of Moab at Ar. 19When you come to the Ammonites, do not
harass them or provoke them to war, for I will not give you possession of any land belonging to the Ammonites. I have given it as
a possession to the descendants of Lot."
20(That too was considered a land of the Rephaites, who used
to live there; but the Ammonites called them Zamzummites.
21They were a people strong and numerous, and as tall as the Anakites. The LORD destroyed them from before the Ammonites, who
drove them out and settled in their place. 22The LORD had done the
same for the descendants of Esau, who lived in Seir, when he destroyed the Horites from before them. They drove them out and
have lived in their place to this day. 23And as for the Avvites who
lived in villages as far as Gaza, the Caphtorites coming out from
Caphtor[b] destroyed them and settled in their place.)

[a] *1* Hebrew *Yam Suph*; that is, Sea of Reeds [b] *23* That is, Crete

(2:7) By Your divine power You provided for all the needs of Your people. By that same power You have given me everything I need for life and godliness through my knowledge of You. For You have called me by Your own glory and goodness. As Your child I trust Your intimate knowledge of my needs more than I trust my own desires. Keep from me the things I want when they are a cheap and deadly substitute for what I really need. (2Pe 1:3)

You rescued me and picked me up,
A living hope of grace revealed,
A life transformed in righteousness;
Oh Lord, You have rescued me.
Forgiving me, You healed my heart
And set me free from sin and death.
You bought me life,
You've made me whole;
Oh Lord, You have rescued me.
"You Rescued Me"
Geoff Bullock (©1993)

Defeat of Sihon King of Heshbon

24“Set out now and cross the Arnon Gorge. See, I have given into your hand Sihon the Amorite, king of Heshbon, and his country. Begin to take possession of it and engage him in battle. 25This very day I will begin to put the terror and fear of you on all the nations under heaven. They will hear reports of you and will tremble and be in anguish because of you.”

26From the desert of Kedemoth I sent messengers to Sihon king of Heshbon offering peace and saying, 27“Let us pass through your country. We will stay on the main road; we will not turn aside to the right or to the left. 28Sell us food to eat and water to drink for their price in silver. Only let us pass through on foot— 29as the descendants of Esau, who live in Seir, and the Moabites, who live in Ar, did for us—until we cross the Jordan into the land the LORD our God is giving us.” 30But Sihon king of Heshbon refused to let us pass through. For the LORD your God had made his spirit stubborn and his heart obstinate in order to give him into your hands, as he has now done.

31The LORD said to me, “See, I have begun to deliver Sihon and his country over to you. Now begin to conquer and possess his land.”

32When Sihon and all his army came out to meet us in battle at Jahaz, 33the LORD our God delivered him over to us and we struck him down, together with his sons and his whole army. 34At that time we took all his towns and completely destroyed[a] them—men, women and children. We left no survivors. 35But the livestock and the plunder from the towns we had captured we carried off for ourselves. 36From Aroer on the rim of the Arnon Gorge, and from the town in the gorge, even as far as Gilead, not one town was too strong for us. The LORD our God gave us all of them. 37But in accordance with the command of the LORD our God, you did not encroach on any of the land of the Ammonites, neither the land along the course of the Jabbok nor that around the towns in the hills.

Defeat of Og King of Bashan

3 Next we turned and went up along the road toward Bashan, and Og king of Bashan with his whole army marched out to meet us in battle at Edrei. 2The LORD said to me, “Do not be afraid of him, for I have handed him over to you with his whole army and his land. Do to him what you did to Sihon king of the Amorites, who reigned in Heshbon.”

3So the LORD our God also gave into our hands Og king of Bashan and all his army. We struck them down, leaving no survivors. 4At that time we took all his cities. There was not one of the sixty cities that we did not take from them—the whole region of Argob, Og’s kingdom in Bashan. 5All these cities were fortified with high walls and with gates and bars, and there were also a great many unwalled villages. 6We completely destroyed[a] them, as we had done with Sihon king of Heshbon, destroying[a] every city—men, women and children. 7But all the livestock and the plunder from their cities we carried off for ourselves.

8So at that time we took from these two kings of the Amorites the territory east of the Jordan, from the Arnon Gorge as far as

(2:25) O Lord of the nations, You are awesome in all Your ways. None can ultimately thwart Your will—no king, no kingdom. You position Your people in the world with Your Word and Spirit not that we might be great, but that You might be great through us. May humility and expectancy adorn Your people as we follow You into our calling.

(2:30) Almighty God, You are unwilling to settle for anything less than Your perfect will for Your people. You do not compromise. You do not negotiate. Your plans and purposes move forward like a lava flow, and no adversary—not even a king or a pharaoh—can stand in Your way. We praise You for Your irresistible power, Your immeasurable love and Your relentless determination to bless us.

[a] *34,6* The Hebrew term refers to the irrevocable giving over of things or persons to the LORD, often by totally destroying them.

Mount Hermon. 9(Hermon is called Sirion by the Sidonians; the
Amorites call it Senir.) 10We took all the towns on the plateau, and
all Gilead, and all Bashan as far as Salecah and Edrei, towns of
Og's kingdom in Bashan. 11(Only Og king of Bashan was left of the
remnant of the Rephaites. His bed[a] was made of iron and was
more than thirteen feet long and six feet wide.[b] It is still in Rabbah
of the Ammonites.)

Division of the Land

12Of the land that we took over at that time, I gave the Reubenites and the Gadites the territory north of Aroer by the Arnon
Gorge, including half the hill country of Gilead, together with its
towns. 13The rest of Gilead and also all of Bashan, the kingdom of
Og, I gave to the half tribe of Manasseh. (The whole region of
Argob in Bashan used to be known as a land of the Rephaites.
14Jair, a descendant of Manasseh, took the whole region of Argob
as far as the border of the Geshurites and the Maacathites; it was
named after him, so that to this day Bashan is called Havvoth
Jair.[c]) 15And I gave Gilead to Makir. 16But to the Reubenites and
the Gadites I gave the territory extending from Gilead down to the
Arnon Gorge (the middle of the gorge being the border) and out
to the Jabbok River, which is the border of the Ammonites. 17Its
western border was the Jordan in the Arabah, from Kinnereth to
the Sea of the Arabah (the Salt Sea[d]), below the slopes of Pisgah.
18I commanded you at that time: "The LORD your God has given
you this land to take possession of it. But all your able-bodied
men, armed for battle, must cross over ahead of your brother Israelites. 19However, your wives, your children and your livestock
(I know you have much livestock) may stay in the towns I have
given you, 20until the LORD gives rest to your brothers as he has to
you, and they too have taken over the land that the LORD your God
is giving them, across the Jordan. After that, each of you may go
back to the possession I have given you."

Moses Forbidden to Cross the Jordan

21At that time I commanded Joshua: "You have seen with your
own eyes all that the LORD your God has done to these two kings.
The LORD will do the same to all the kingdoms over there where
you are going. 22Do not be afraid of them; the LORD your God himself will fight for you."
23At that time I pleaded with the LORD: 24"O Sovereign LORD,
you have begun to show to your servant your greatness and your
strong hand. For what god is there in heaven or on earth who can
do the deeds and mighty works you do? 25Let me go over and see
the good land beyond the Jordan—that fine hill country and Lebanon."
26But because of you the LORD was angry with me and would not
listen to me. "That is enough," the LORD said. "Do not speak to me
anymore about this matter. 27Go up to the top of Pisgah and look
west and north and south and east. Look at the land with your own
eyes, since you are not going to cross this Jordan. 28But commission Joshua, and encourage and strengthen him, for he will lead
this people across and will cause them to inherit the land that you
will see." 29So we stayed in the valley near Beth Peor.

[a] *11* Or *sarcophagus* [b] *11* Hebrew *nine cubits long and four cubits wide* (about 4 meters long and 1.8 meters wide) [c] *14* Or *called the settlements of Jair* [d] *17* That is, the Dead Sea

(3:18–20) Father in heaven, just as You commanded the Israelites to fight on behalf of their brothers and sisters across the river, so also You call upon us to care for our fellow Christians. Do not allow Your people to be at ease in suburban churches while the grave needs of inner city congregations remain unmet. Do not permit us to become complacent while Your persecuted children around the world struggle against ruthless oppression. Please use us to provide peace and provision for those who need it, Lord, and let us take no rest until Your people everywhere can fully enjoy their promised rest in You.

Do all the good you can,
By all the means you can,
In all the ways you can,
In all the places you can,
At all the times you can,
To all the people you can,
As long as ever you can.

John Wesley (1703-1791)

Rise up, O men of God!
The church for you doth wait,
Her strength unequal to her task,
Rise up, and make her great!

Rise up, the Lord is calling!
Rise up, this is the day;
Rise up, and seize the moment,
Rise up, O men of faith!

"Rise Up, O Men Of God"
William Merrill and
William Walter (c.1911)
New Words by Buddy Owens and
Bill Batstone (©1994)

Obedience Commanded

4 Hear now, O Israel, the decrees and laws I am about to teach
you. Follow them so that you may live and may go in and take
possession of the land that the LORD, the God of your fathers, is giving you. 2Do not add to what I command you and do not subtract
from it, but keep the commands of the LORD your God that I give
you.

3You saw with your own eyes what the LORD did at Baal Peor.
The LORD your God destroyed from among you everyone who followed the Baal of Peor, 4but all of you who held fast to the LORD
your God are still alive today.

5See, I have taught you decrees and laws as the LORD my God
commanded me, so that you may follow them in the land you are
entering to take possession of it. 6Observe them carefully, for this
will show your wisdom and understanding to the nations, who will
hear about all these decrees and say, "Surely this great nation is a
wise and understanding people." 7What other nation is so great as
to have their gods near them the way the LORD our God is near us
whenever we pray to him? 8And what other nation is so great as to
have such righteous decrees and laws as this body of laws I am
setting before you today?

9Only be careful, and watch yourselves closely so that you do
not forget the things your eyes have seen or let them slip from your
heart as long as you live. Teach them to your children and to their
children after them. 10Remember the day you stood before the
LORD your God at Horeb, when he said to me, "Assemble the people before me to hear my words so that they may learn to revere
me as long as they live in the land and may teach them to their
children." 11You came near and stood at the foot of the mountain
while it blazed with fire to the very heavens, with black clouds and
deep darkness. 12Then the LORD spoke to you out of the fire. You
heard the sound of words but saw no form; there was only a voice.
13He declared to you his covenant, the Ten Commandments,
which he commanded you to follow and then wrote them on two
stone tablets. 14And the LORD directed me at that time to teach you
the decrees and laws you are to follow in the land that you are
crossing the Jordan to possess.

Idolatry Forbidden

15You saw no form of any kind the day the LORD spoke to you at
Horeb out of the fire. Therefore watch yourselves very carefully,
16so that you do not become corrupt and make for yourselves an
idol, an image of any shape, whether formed like a man or a
woman, 17or like any animal on earth or any bird that flies in the
air, 18or like any creature that moves along the ground or any fish
in the waters below. 19And when you look up to the sky and see
the sun, the moon and the stars—all the heavenly array—do not
be enticed into bowing down to them and worshiping things the
LORD your God has apportioned to all the nations under heaven.
20But as for you, the LORD took you and brought you out of the
iron-smelting furnace, out of Egypt, to be the people of his inheritance, as you now are.

21The LORD was angry with me because of you, and he solemnly swore that I would not cross the Jordan and enter the good land
the LORD your God is giving you as your inheritance. 22I will die in
this land; I will not cross the Jordan; but you are about to cross
over and take possession of that good land. 23Be careful not to

(4:7) Even as You were near to Your people when Moses led them, we rejoice that You are also in our midst today as we pray to You. In gratitude we lift our hands in Your Presence. We exalt You in songs of praise for Your love and faithfulness.

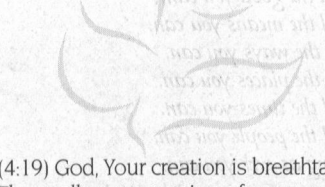

(4:19) God, Your creation is breathtaking. The endless procession of suns, moons and planets proclaims that You are the Master Designer. And all of nature—seas and mountains, fields and forests—attests to Your supreme artistry. But with equal clarity, we also discover Your likeness in what seems at first an unlikely place: in the faces of men, women and children. How incredible that You have made humankind in Your image. How remarkable that to love one another is to worship You.

forget the covenant of the LORD your God that he made with you;
do not make for yourselves an idol in the form of anything the
LORD your God has forbidden. [24]For the LORD your God is a consuming fire, a jealous God.
[25]After you have had children and grandchildren and have lived
in the land a long time—if you then become corrupt and make
any kind of idol, doing evil in the eyes of the LORD your God and
provoking him to anger, [26]I call heaven and earth as witnesses
against you this day that you will quickly perish from the land that
you are crossing the Jordan to possess. You will not live there long
but will certainly be destroyed. [27]The LORD will scatter you among
the peoples, and only a few of you will survive among the nations
to which the LORD will drive you. [28]There you will worship man-
made gods of wood and stone, which cannot see or hear or eat or
smell. [29]But if from there you seek the LORD your God, you will
find him if you look for him with all your heart and with all your
soul. [30]When you are in distress and all these things have happened to you, then in later days you will return to the LORD your
God and obey him. [31]For the LORD your God is a merciful God; he
will not abandon or destroy you or forget the covenant with your
forefathers, which he confirmed to them by oath.

The LORD Is God

[32]Ask now about the former days, long before your time, from
the day God created man on the earth; ask from one end of the
heavens to the other. Has anything so great as this ever happened,
or has anything like it ever been heard of? [33]Has any other people
heard the voice of God[a] speaking out of fire, as you have, and
lived? [34]Has any god ever tried to take for himself one nation out
of another nation, by testings, by miraculous signs and wonders,
by war, by a mighty hand and an outstretched arm, or by great and
awesome deeds, like all the things the LORD your God did for you
in Egypt before your very eyes?
[35]You were shown these things so that you might know that the
LORD is God; besides him there is no other. [36]From heaven he
made you hear his voice to discipline you. On earth he showed
you his great fire, and you heard his words from out of the fire.
[37]Because he loved your forefathers and chose their descendants
after them, he brought you out of Egypt by his Presence and his
great strength, [38]to drive out before you nations greater and
stronger than you and to bring you into their land to give it to you
for your inheritance, as it is today.
[39]Acknowledge and take to heart this day that the LORD is God
in heaven above and on the earth below. There is no other. [40]Keep
his decrees and commands, which I am giving you today, so that it
may go well with you and your children after you and that you may
live long in the land the LORD your God gives you for all time.

Cities of Refuge

[41]Then Moses set aside three cities east of the Jordan, [42]to
which anyone who had killed a person could flee if he had unintentionally killed his neighbor without malice aforethought. He
could flee into one of these cities and save his life. [43]The cities
were these: Bezer in the desert plateau, for the Reubenites; Ra-

[a] 33 Or *of a god*

(4:25–31) O Lord, You are always patient, merciful and forever awaiting our return to You. And once our petty gods have shattered, failing to meet their empty promises, we rush back to You, wholeheartedly seeking reconciliation. Our eyes turn heavenward, and we are stunned at the sight of Your welcoming smile. Your grace and forgiveness reduce us to tears; more than ever we are aware of Your everlasting and unconditional love.

Like the father of the Prodigal Son, God can see repentance coming a great way off and is there to meet it; the repentance is the reconciliation.

Dorothy L. Sayers (1893–1957)

(4:39) Eternal Father, Your love is without measure. Your wisdom extends to the highest heavens, beyond human imagination, and we cannot fathom the depths of Your knowledge. In Your great power and authority You guide the orbits of both galaxies and molecules with but a glance. Yet in Your everlasting love You reach down to guide each of Your children individually, with the gentle touch of a father teaching his beloved babies to walk.

moth in Gilead, for the Gadites; and Golan in Bashan, for the Manassites.

Introduction to the Law

44This is the law Moses set before the Israelites. 45These are the
stipulations, decrees and laws Moses gave them when they came
out of Egypt 46and were in the valley near Beth Peor east of the
Jordan, in the land of Sihon king of the Amorites, who reigned in
Heshbon and was defeated by Moses and the Israelites as they
came out of Egypt. 47They took possession of his land and the land
of Og king of Bashan, the two Amorite kings east of the Jordan.
48This land extended from Aroer on the rim of the Arnon Gorge to
Mount Siyon[a] (that is, Hermon), 49and included all the Arabah
east of the Jordan, as far as the Sea of the Arabah,[b] below the
slopes of Pisgah.

The Ten Commandments

5 Moses summoned all Israel and said:
Hear, O Israel, the decrees and laws I declare in your hearing
today. Learn them and be sure to follow them. 2The LORD our God
made a covenant with us at Horeb. 3It was not with our fathers that
the LORD made this covenant, but with us, with all of us who are
alive here today. 4The LORD spoke to you face to face out of the fire
on the mountain. 5(At that time I stood between the LORD and you
to declare to you the word of the LORD, because you were afraid of
the fire and did not go up the mountain.) And he said:

6"I am the LORD your God, who brought you out of Egypt,
out of the land of slavery.

7"You shall have no other gods before[c] me.

8"You shall not make for yourself an idol in the form of anything in heaven above or on the earth beneath or in the
waters below. 9You shall not bow down to them or worship them; for I, the LORD your God, am a jealous God,
punishing the children for the sin of the fathers to the
third and fourth generation of those who hate me, 10but
showing love to a thousand ⌞generations⌟ of those who
love me and keep my commandments.

11"You shall not misuse the name of the LORD your God, for the
LORD will not hold anyone guiltless who misuses his
name.

12"Observe the Sabbath day by keeping it holy, as the LORD your
God has commanded you. 13Six days you shall labor
and do all your work, 14but the seventh day is a Sabbath
to the LORD your God. On it you shall not do any work,
neither you, nor your son or daughter, nor your
manservant or maidservant, nor your ox, your donkey
or any of your animals, nor the alien within your gates,
so that your manservant and maidservant may rest, as
you do. 15Remember that you were slaves in Egypt and
that the LORD your God brought you out of there with a
mighty hand and an outstretched arm. Therefore the
LORD your God has commanded you to observe the Sabbath day.

16"Honor your father and your mother, as the LORD your God

[a] 48 Hebrew; Syriac (see also Deut. 3:9) *Sirion* [b] 49 That is, the Dead Sea [c] 7 Or *besides*

(5:2–3) Father, how we thank You for the covenant You made with Your people on Mount Horeb, speaking to them through fire and thunder. And we thank You for the covenant You made with us through Jesus. On another mountain called Calvary, in obedience to You, He poured out His priceless blood to seal the New Covenant. We praise You, Father, that we have not just inherited a promise You made to someone else long ago; rather, this New Covenant is a living and active covenant, made with us today through the shed blood of the living Christ.

(5:6–15) God of all ages, You are a Father who cares for His own with tender love, with great wisdom and understanding. You have provided specific laws to guide us, enabling us to live in a loving relationship with You. How well You know that if we do not wholeheartedly love You, neither can we carry on loving relationships with one another. Write Your commandments on the stony tablets of our hearts, lest we forget to love You or one another according to Your perfect will.

In the triangle of love between ourselves, God, and other people, is found the secret of existence, and the best foretaste, I suspect, that we can have on earth of what heaven will probably be like.

Samuel M. Shoemaker (1893–1963)

has commanded you, so that you may live long and that
it may go well with you in the land the LORD your God is
giving you.
17 "You shall not murder.
18 "You shall not commit adultery.
19 "You shall not steal.
20 "You shall not give false testimony against your neighbor.
21 "You shall not covet your neighbor's wife. You shall not set
your desire on your neighbor's house or land, his
manservant or maidservant, his ox or donkey, or anything that belongs to your neighbor."

22These are the commandments the LORD proclaimed in a loud
voice to your whole assembly there on the mountain from out of
the fire, the cloud and the deep darkness; and he added nothing
more. Then he wrote them on two stone tablets and gave them
to me.
23When you heard the voice out of the darkness, while the
mountain was ablaze with fire, all the leading men of your tribes
and your elders came to me.
24And you said, "The LORD our God
has shown us his glory and his majesty, and we have heard his
voice from the fire. Today we have seen that a man can live even if
God speaks with him.
25But now, why should we die? This great
fire will consume us, and we will die if we hear the voice of the
LORD our God any longer.
26For what mortal man has ever heard
the voice of the living God speaking out of fire, as we have, and
survived?
27Go near and listen to all that the LORD our God says.
Then tell us whatever the LORD our God tells you. We will listen and
obey."
28The LORD heard you when you spoke to me and the LORD said
to me, "I have heard what this people said to you. Everything they
said was good.
29Oh, that their hearts would be inclined to fear
me and keep all my commands always, so that it might go well
with them and their children forever!
30"Go, tell them to return to their tents.
31But you stay here
with me so that I may give you all the commands, decrees and
laws you are to teach them to follow in the land I am giving them
to possess."
32So be careful to do what the LORD your God has commanded
you; do not turn aside to the right or to the left.
33Walk in all the
way that the LORD your God has commanded you, so that you may
live and prosper and prolong your days in the land that you will
possess.

Love the LORD Your God

6 These are the commands, decrees and laws the LORD your
God directed me to teach you to observe in the land that you
are crossing the Jordan to possess,
2so that you, your children
and their children after them may fear the LORD your God as long
as you live by keeping all his decrees and commands that I give
you, and so that you may enjoy long life.
3Hear, O Israel, and be
careful to obey so that it may go well with you and that you may increase greatly in a land flowing with milk and honey, just as the
LORD, the God of your fathers, promised you.
4Hear, O Israel: The LORD our God, the LORD is one.[a]
5Love the

[a] 4 Or *The LORD our God is one LORD*; or *The LORD is our God, the LORD is one*; or *The LORD is our God, the LORD alone*

(5:22) Who are we that You should speak to us? That You have chosen to make Your name and will known is overwhelming, Father. Your "loud voice" reveals the passion, love and intensity of Your pursuing heart. How we praise You for Your tenacious involvement in having a people for Yourself and for Your glory. O God, grant us ears to hear You speaking loudly and clearly in Your Word.

If we knew how to listen to God, we should hear him speaking to us, for God does speak. He speaks in his gospel; he speaks also through life—that new gospel to which we ourselves add a page each day.

Michel Quoist (1921-)

We choose the Word of the Lord.
We choose the Word of the Lord,
For the Word of the Lord
Shall endure forever.
We choose the Word of the Lord.
We choose the Word of the Lord.

He who delights in the Word of the
Lord
Shall be blessed in all of his ways,
For the friendship of God
Is with those who fear Him.
So we choose the fear of the Lord,
We choose the way of the Lord.
We choose the Word of the Lord.

"We Choose The Fear Of The Lord"
Kirk Dearman (©1989)

(6:4–9) We praise You, God of our fathers, for ancient words of worship that resound across the centuries and millennia. Along with all who fear You, we reverently add our voices to these timeless words of the *Shema*, joyfully affirming that You are the mighty One. May we never forget, and may our children always remember, that You are the God above all gods, and that You deserve our love above all other loves.

(6:15) Oh, that I would understand how Your jealousy speaks of my worth to You. Who am I and what is my heart that You would be jealous for my affection? Bless You, O Lover of my soul.

LORD your God with all your heart and with all your soul and with
all your strength. 6These commandments that I give you today are
to be upon your hearts. 7Impress them on your children. Talk
about them when you sit at home and when you walk along the
road, when you lie down and when you get up. 8Tie them as symbols on your hands and bind them on your foreheads. 9Write them
on the doorframes of your houses and on your gates.

10When the LORD your God brings you into the land he swore to
your fathers, to Abraham, Isaac and Jacob, to give you—a land
with large, flourishing cities you did not build, 11houses filled with
all kinds of good things you did not provide, wells you did not dig,
and vineyards and olive groves you did not plant—then when you
eat and are satisfied, 12be careful that you do not forget the LORD,
who brought you out of Egypt, out of the land of slavery.

13Fear the LORD your God, serve him only and take your oaths
in his name. 14Do not follow other gods, the gods of the peoples
around you; 15for the LORD your God, who is among you, is a jealous God and his anger will burn against you, and he will destroy
you from the face of the land. 16Do not test the LORD your God as
you did at Massah. 17Be sure to keep the commands of the LORD
your God and the stipulations and decrees he has given you. 18Do
what is right and good in the LORD's sight, so that it may go well
with you and you may go in and take over the good land that the
LORD promised on oath to your forefathers, 19thrusting out all your
enemies before you, as the LORD said.

20In the future, when your son asks you, "What is the meaning
of the stipulations, decrees and laws the LORD our God has commanded you?" 21tell him: "We were slaves of Pharaoh in Egypt,
but the LORD brought us out of Egypt with a mighty hand. 22Before
our eyes the LORD sent miraculous signs and wonders—great and
terrible—upon Egypt and Pharaoh and his whole household.
23But he brought us out from there to bring us in and give us the
land that he promised on oath to our forefathers. 24The LORD commanded us to obey all these decrees and to fear the LORD our God,
so that we might always prosper and be kept alive, as is the case
today. 25And if we are careful to obey all this law before the LORD
our God, as he has commanded us, that will be our righteousness."

Driving Out the Nations

7 When the LORD your God brings you into the land you are entering to possess and drives out before you many nations—
the Hittites, Girgashites, Amorites, Canaanites, Perizzites, Hivites
and Jebusites, seven nations larger and stronger than you— 2and
when the LORD your God has delivered them over to you and you
have defeated them, then you must destroy them totally.[a] Make no
treaty with them, and show them no mercy. 3Do not intermarry
with them. Do not give your daughters to their sons or take their
daughters for your sons, 4for they will turn your sons away from
following me to serve other gods, and the LORD's anger will burn
against you and will quickly destroy you. 5This is what you are to
do to them: Break down their altars, smash their sacred stones,
cut down their Asherah poles[b] and burn their idols in the fire.
6For you are a people holy to the LORD your God. The LORD your

[a] 2 The Hebrew term refers to the irrevocable giving over of things or persons to the LORD, often by totally destroying them; also in verse 26. [b] 5 That is, symbols of the goddess Asherah; here and elsewhere in Deuteronomy

God has chosen you out of all the peoples on the face of the earth to be his people, his treasured possession.

7The LORD did not set his affection on you and choose you because you were more numerous than other peoples, for you were the fewest of all peoples. 8But it was because the LORD loved you and kept the oath he swore to your forefathers that he brought you out with a mighty hand and redeemed you from the land of slavery, from the power of Pharaoh king of Egypt. 9Know therefore that the LORD your God is God; he is the faithful God, keeping his covenant of love to a thousand generations of those who love him and keep his commands. 10But

those who hate him he will repay to their face by
destruction;
he will not be slow to repay to their face those who
hate him.

11Therefore, take care to follow the commands, decrees and laws I give you today.

12If you pay attention to these laws and are careful to follow them, then the LORD your God will keep his covenant of love with you, as he swore to your forefathers. 13He will love you and bless you and increase your numbers. He will bless the fruit of your womb, the crops of your land—your grain, new wine and oil—the calves of your herds and the lambs of your flocks in the land that he swore to your forefathers to give you. 14You will be blessed more than any other people; none of your men or women will be childless, nor any of your livestock without young. 15The LORD will keep you free from every disease. He will not inflict on you the horrible diseases you knew in Egypt, but he will inflict them on all who hate you. 16You must destroy all the peoples the LORD your God gives over to you. Do not look on them with pity and do not serve their gods, for that will be a snare to you.

17You may say to yourselves, "These nations are stronger than we are. How can we drive them out?" 18But do not be afraid of them; remember well what the LORD your God did to Pharaoh and to all Egypt. 19You saw with your own eyes the great trials, the miraculous signs and wonders, the mighty hand and outstretched arm, with which the LORD your God brought you out. The LORD your God will do the same to all the peoples you now fear. 20Moreover, the LORD your God will send the hornet among them until even the survivors who hide from you have perished. 21Do not be terrified by them, for the LORD your God, who is among you, is a great and awesome God. 22The LORD your God will drive out those nations before you, little by little. You will not be allowed to eliminate them all at once, or the wild animals will multiply around you. 23But the LORD your God will deliver them over to you, throwing them into great confusion until they are destroyed. 24He will give their kings into your hand, and you will wipe out their names from under heaven. No one will be able to stand up against you; you will destroy them. 25The images of their gods you are to burn in the fire. Do not covet the silver and gold on them, and do not take it for yourselves, or you will be ensnared by it, for it is detestable to the LORD your God. 26Do not bring a detestable thing into your house or you, like it, will be set apart for destruction. Utterly abhor and detest it, for it is set apart for destruction.

(7:7–8) Father, how we praise You for the revelation of Your sovereign grace! There is nothing in any of Your people that can explain why You have chosen to redeem and love us as You do. You love us simply because You have chosen to love.

(7:17–18) When I am filled with fear concerning the challenges around me and ahead of me, grant that I will be quick to remember Your great deliverances in the past. Blessed Redeemer, You have delivered me from the guilt and consequences of my sin through the death and resurrection of Jesus Christ. You will continue to deliver me until I am safely home in that place that is truly home.

He is able to deliver thee.
He is able to deliver thee.
Tho by sin oppressed,
go to Him for rest.
Our God is able to deliver thee.

"He Is Able To Deliver Thee"
William A. Ogden (1887)

Do Not Forget the LORD

8 Be careful to follow every command I am giving you today, so
that you may live and increase and may enter and possess the
land that the LORD promised on oath to your forefathers. 2Re-
member how the LORD your God led you all the way in the desert
these forty years, to humble you and to test you in order to know
what was in your heart, whether or not you would keep his commands. 3He humbled you, causing you to hunger and then feeding
you with manna, which neither you nor your fathers had known,
to teach you that man does not live on bread alone but on every
word that comes from the mouth of the LORD. 4Your clothes did
not wear out and your feet did not swell during these forty years.
5Know then in your heart that as a man disciplines his son, so the
LORD your God disciplines you.
6Observe the commands of the LORD your God, walking in his
ways and revering him. 7For the LORD your God is bringing you
into a good land—a land with streams and pools of water, with
springs flowing in the valleys and hills; 8a land with wheat and
barley, vines and fig trees, pomegranates, olive oil and honey; 9a
land where bread will not be scarce and you will lack nothing; a
land where the rocks are iron and you can dig copper out of the
hills.
10When you have eaten and are satisfied, praise the LORD your
God for the good land he has given you. 11Be careful that you do
not forget the LORD your God, failing to observe his commands,
his laws and his decrees that I am giving you this day. 12Otherwise,
when you eat and are satisfied, when you build fine houses and
settle down, 13and when your herds and flocks grow large and
your silver and gold increase and all you have is multiplied, 14then
your heart will become proud and you will forget the LORD your
God, who brought you out of Egypt, out of the land of slavery. 15He
led you through the vast and dreadful desert, that thirsty and waterless land, with its venomous snakes and scorpions. He brought
you water out of hard rock. 16He gave you manna to eat in the
desert, something your fathers had never known, to humble and
to test you so that in the end it might go well with you. 17You may
say to yourself, "My power and the strength of my hands have produced this wealth for me." 18But remember the LORD your God,
for it is he who gives you the ability to produce wealth, and so
confirms his covenant, which he swore to your forefathers, as it is
today.
19If you ever forget the LORD your God and follow other gods
and worship and bow down to them, I testify against you today that
you will surely be destroyed. 20Like the nations the LORD destroyed
before you, so you will be destroyed for not obeying the LORD your
God.

Not Because of Israel's Righteousness

9 Hear, O Israel. You are now about to cross the Jordan to go
in and dispossess nations greater and stronger than you, with
large cities that have walls up to the sky. 2The people are strong
and tall—Anakites! You know about them and have heard it said:
"Who can stand up against the Anakites?" 3But be assured today
that the LORD your God is the one who goes across ahead of you
like a devouring fire. He will destroy them; he will subdue them
before you. And you will drive them out and annihilate them
quickly, as the LORD has promised you.

(8:2–5) How wise You are, Father, teaching us not only with words but with unforgettable lessons. How would we understand deep satisfaction if You had not allowed us to hunger? How would we understand faith or hope or patience if You had not required us to wait? Most of all, how would we have recognized You as our Heavenly Father if You had not lovingly carried us in Your arms when we could not walk, and disciplined us as beloved children when we would not obey?

Is He not following thee with daily mercies, moving upon thy soul, providing for thy body, preserving both? Doth He not bear thee continually in the arms of His love, and promise that all things shall work together for thy good, and suit all His dealings to thy greatest advantage, and give His angels charge over thee? And canst thou be taken up with the joys below and forget thy Lord who forgets not thee?

Richard Baxter (1615–1691)

(8:10–20) O God, You did such great things for Your people when You brought them into the land of promise. Then, as now, You provided immense blessings and unimaginable benefits. But now as then, true to human form, our pride overtakes gratitude, arrogance eclipses awe, and we begin to applaud ourselves for having done so well. Forgive our poor memories, heavenly Father. How can we forget that every good and perfect gift comes from Your storehouse? Yet even when we forget You, You are unchanging in Your faithfulness to us. (Jas 1:17)

4After the LORD your God has driven them out before you, do not say to yourself, "The LORD has brought me here to take possession of this land because of my righteousness." No, it is on account of the wickedness of these nations that the LORD is going to drive them out before you. 5It is not because of your righteousness or your integrity that you are going in to take possession of their land; but on account of the wickedness of these nations, the LORD your God will drive them out before you, to accomplish what he swore to your fathers, to Abraham, Isaac and Jacob. 6Understand, then, that it is not because of your righteousness that the LORD your God is giving you this good land to possess, for you are a stiff-necked people.

The Golden Calf

7Remember this and never forget how you provoked the LORD your God to anger in the desert. From the day you left Egypt until you arrived here, you have been rebellious against the LORD. 8At Horeb you aroused the LORD's wrath so that he was angry enough to destroy you. 9When I went up on the mountain to receive the tablets of stone, the tablets of the covenant that the LORD had made with you, I stayed on the mountain forty days and forty nights; I ate no bread and drank no water. 10The LORD gave me two stone tablets inscribed by the finger of God. On them were all the commandments the LORD proclaimed to you on the mountain out of the fire, on the day of the assembly.

11At the end of the forty days and forty nights, the LORD gave me the two stone tablets, the tablets of the covenant. 12Then the LORD told me, "Go down from here at once, because your people whom you brought out of Egypt have become corrupt. They have turned away quickly from what I commanded them and have made a cast idol for themselves."

13And the LORD said to me, "I have seen this people, and they are a stiff-necked people indeed! 14Let me alone, so that I may destroy them and blot out their name from under heaven. And I will make you into a nation stronger and more numerous than they."

15So I turned and went down from the mountain while it was ablaze with fire. And the two tablets of the covenant were in my hands.[a] 16When I looked, I saw that you had sinned against the LORD your God; you had made for yourselves an idol cast in the shape of a calf. You had turned aside quickly from the way that the LORD had commanded you. 17So I took the two tablets and threw them out of my hands, breaking them to pieces before your eyes.

18Then once again I fell prostrate before the LORD for forty days and forty nights; I ate no bread and drank no water, because of all the sin you had committed, doing what was evil in the LORD's sight and so provoking him to anger. 19I feared the anger and wrath of the LORD, for he was angry enough with you to destroy you. But again the LORD listened to me. 20And the LORD was angry enough with Aaron to destroy him, but at that time I prayed for Aaron too. 21Also I took that sinful thing of yours, the calf you had made, and burned it in the fire. Then I crushed it and ground it to powder as fine as dust and threw the dust into a stream that flowed down the mountain.

22You also made the LORD angry at Taberah, at Massah and at Kibroth Hattaavah.

[a] 15 Or *And I had the two tablets of the covenant with me, one in each hand*

(9:6) Since the time of Adam and Eve, You have been generous simply because of the greatness of Your heart. You have been faithful only because You cannot be less than Who You are. You have saved us not because of our goodness, but because of Your grace. In spite of our stubbornness, You have chosen to show us kindness and to lead us to new life. We are Yours, not because we are righteous; we are righteous because we are Yours. (Ro 5:8)

Mine is the sin, but Thine the righteousness;
Mine is the guilt, but Thine the cleansing blood;
Here is my robe, my refuge, and my peace:
Thy blood, Thy righteousness, O Lord, my God.

Here, O My Lord, I See Thee
Horatius Bonar (1808-1889)

Is Christ thy advocate to plead thy cause?
Art thou his client? Such shall never slide.
He never lost his case.

Edward Taylor (c.1645–1729)

(9:22–26) Though You have forgiven me and have chosen not to remember my sin, I still carry in my memory the record of my failures—the things left undone, the steps of faith not taken, the diversions pursued in defiance of Your instruction. I know my transgressions, and my sin is always before me—a constant reminder that my salvation owes itself purely to Your infinite mercy. I thank You that I, like Your people of old, have an Advocate who stands in the way of judgment and pleads the case of the guilty. He is able to save completely because He always lives to make intercession for me. (Heb 7:25)

Does anybody here need Jesus?
Does anybody want the Lord?
Is anybody's heart just breaking?
Jesus feels it. He wants to heal it.
Does anybody want the Lord?

Is your mind filled
With memories that haunt you?
Is the road you're traveling
Coming to an end?
Is there no one left to blame
And your mirror says the same?
Well, just call upon His name,
He will hear you.

"Does Anybody Here Need Jesus?"
Milton Carroll (©1996)

23 And when the LORD sent you out from Kadesh Barnea, he said,
"Go up and take possession of the land I have given you." But you
rebelled against the command of the LORD your God. You did not
trust him or obey him. 24 You have been rebellious against the
LORD ever since I have known you.
25 I lay prostrate before the LORD those forty days and forty
nights because the LORD had said he would destroy you. 26 I prayed
to the LORD and said, "O Sovereign LORD, do not destroy your people, your own inheritance that you redeemed by your great power
and brought out of Egypt with a mighty hand. 27 Remember your
servants Abraham, Isaac and Jacob. Overlook the stubbornness of
this people, their wickedness and their sin. 28 Otherwise, the country from which you brought us will say, 'Because the LORD was not
able to take them into the land he had promised them, and because he hated them, he brought them out to put them to death in
the desert.' 29 But they are your people, your inheritance that you
brought out by your great power and your outstretched arm."

Tablets Like the First Ones

10 At that time the LORD said to me, "Chisel out two stone
tablets like the first ones and come up to me on the mountain. Also make a wooden chest.[a] 2 I will write on the tablets the
words that were on the first tablets, which you broke. Then you
are to put them in the chest."
3 So I made the ark out of acacia wood and chiseled out two
stone tablets like the first ones, and I went up on the mountain
with the two tablets in my hands. 4 The LORD wrote on these tablets
what he had written before, the Ten Commandments he had proclaimed to you on the mountain, out of the fire, on the day of the
assembly. And the LORD gave them to me. 5 Then I came back down
the mountain and put the tablets in the ark I had made, as the
LORD commanded me, and they are there now.
6 (The Israelites traveled from the wells of the Jaakanites to Mo-
serah. There Aaron died and was buried, and Eleazar his son succeeded him as priest. 7 From there they traveled to Gudgodah and
on to Jotbathah, a land with streams of water. 8 At that time the
LORD set apart the tribe of Levi to carry the ark of the covenant of
the LORD, to stand before the LORD to minister and to pronounce
blessings in his name, as they still do today. 9 That is why the Levites have no share or inheritance among their brothers; the LORD
is their inheritance, as the LORD your God told them.)
10 Now I had stayed on the mountain forty days and nights, as I
did the first time, and the LORD listened to me at this time also. It
was not his will to destroy you. 11 "Go," the LORD said to me, "and
lead the people on their way, so that they may enter and possess
the land that I swore to their fathers to give them."

Fear the LORD

12 And now, O Israel, what does the LORD your God ask of you
but to fear the LORD your God, to walk in all his ways, to love him,
to serve the LORD your God with all your heart and with all your
soul, 13 and to observe the LORD's commands and decrees that I am
giving you today for your own good?
14 To the LORD your God belong the heavens, even the highest
heavens, the earth and everything in it. 15 Yet the LORD set his af-

[a] 1 That is, an ark

fection on your forefathers and loved them, and he chose you,
their descendants, above all the nations, as it is today. 16Circum-
cise your hearts, therefore, and do not be stiff-necked any longer.
17For the LORD your God is God of gods and Lord of lords, the
great God, mighty and awesome, who shows no partiality and accepts no bribes. 18He defends the cause of the fatherless and the
widow, and loves the alien, giving him food and clothing. 19And
you are to love those who are aliens, for you yourselves were
aliens in Egypt. 20Fear the LORD your God and serve him. Hold fast
to him and take your oaths in his name. 21He is your praise; he is
your God, who performed for you those great and awesome wonders you saw with your own eyes. 22Your forefathers who went
down into Egypt were seventy in all, and now the LORD your God
has made you as numerous as the stars in the sky.

Love and Obey the LORD

11 Love the LORD your God and keep his requirements, his decrees, his laws and his commands always. 2Remember
today that your children were not the ones who saw and experienced the discipline of the LORD your God: his majesty, his mighty
hand, his outstretched arm; 3the signs he performed and the
things he did in the heart of Egypt, both to Pharaoh king of Egypt
and to his whole country; 4what he did to the Egyptian army, to its
horses and chariots, how he overwhelmed them with the waters of
the Red Sea[a] as they were pursuing you, and how the LORD
brought lasting ruin on them. 5It was not your children who saw
what he did for you in the desert until you arrived at this place,
6and what he did to Dathan and Abiram, sons of Eliab the Reubenite, when the earth opened its mouth right in the middle of all
Israel and swallowed them up with their households, their tents
and every living thing that belonged to them. 7But it was your own
eyes that saw all these great things the LORD has done.

8Observe therefore all the commands I am giving you today, so
that you may have the strength to go in and take over the land that
you are crossing the Jordan to possess, 9and so that you may live
long in the land that the LORD swore to your forefathers to give to
them and their descendants, a land flowing with milk and honey.
10The land you are entering to take over is not like the land of
Egypt, from which you have come, where you planted your seed
and irrigated it by foot as in a vegetable garden. 11But the land you
are crossing the Jordan to take possession of is a land of mountains and valleys that drinks rain from heaven. 12It is a land the
LORD your God cares for; the eyes of the LORD your God are continually on it from the beginning of the year to its end.

13So if you faithfully obey the commands I am giving you
today—to love the LORD your God and to serve him with all your
heart and with all your soul— 14then I will send rain on your land
in its season, both autumn and spring rains, so that you may gather in your grain, new wine and oil. 15I will provide grass in the
fields for your cattle, and you will eat and be satisfied.

16Be careful, or you will be enticed to turn away and worship
other gods and bow down to them. 17Then the LORD's anger will
burn against you, and he will shut the heavens so that it will not
rain and the ground will yield no produce, and you will soon perish from the good land the LORD is giving you. 18Fix these words of

[a] 4 Hebrew *Yam Suph*; that is, Sea of Reeds

(10:14–15) It is astonishing to think that You, the altogether holy and righteous God, the One to whom belongs everything in heaven and earth, would ever set Your affection on a people like us. Father, we praise You for Your great love and unmerited favor.

God excludes none, if they do not exclude themselves.

William Guthrie (1620-1665)

(11:8) This is a paradox Lord, a challenge to the way I generally think about the life of faith and obedience. Usually I pray for You to give me strength to obey. Here You instruct me to obey that I might be strengthened. Your promise to me is powerful. In obeying You I will find all the strength I need to live a life that is pleasing to You.

mine in your hearts and minds; tie them as symbols on your hands
and bind them on your foreheads. 19Teach them to your children,
talking about them when you sit at home and when you walk along
the road, when you lie down and when you get up. 20Write them
on the doorframes of your houses and on your gates, 21so that
your days and the days of your children may be many in the land
that the LORD swore to give your forefathers, as many as the days
that the heavens are above the earth.
22If you carefully observe all these commands I am giving you
to follow—to love the LORD your God, to walk in all his ways and
to hold fast to him— 23then the LORD will drive out all these nations before you, and you will dispossess nations larger and
stronger than you. 24Every place where you set your foot will be
yours: Your territory will extend from the desert to Lebanon, and
from the Euphrates River to the western sea.[a] 25No man will be
able to stand against you. The LORD your God, as he promised you,
will put the terror and fear of you on the whole land, wherever
you go.
26See, I am setting before you today a blessing and a curse—
27the blessing if you obey the commands of the LORD your God that
I am giving you today; 28the curse if you disobey the commands of
the LORD your God and turn from the way that I command you
today by following other gods, which you have not known. 29When
the LORD your God has brought you into the land you are entering
to possess, you are to proclaim on Mount Gerizim the blessings,
and on Mount Ebal the curses. 30As you know, these mountains
are across the Jordan, west of the road,[b] toward the setting sun,
near the great trees of Moreh, in the territory of those Canaanites
living in the Arabah in the vicinity of Gilgal. 31You are about to
cross the Jordan to enter and take possession of the land the LORD
your God is giving you. When you have taken it over and are living
there, 32be sure that you obey all the decrees and laws I am setting before you today.

The One Place of Worship

12 These are the decrees and laws you must be careful to follow in the land that the LORD, the God of your fathers, has
given you to possess—as long as you live in the land. 2Destroy
completely all the places on the high mountains and on the hills
and under every spreading tree where the nations you are dispossessing worship their gods. 3Break down their altars, smash their
sacred stones and burn their Asherah poles in the fire; cut down
the idols of their gods and wipe out their names from those
places.
4You must not worship the LORD your God in their way. 5But you
are to seek the place the LORD your God will choose from among
all your tribes to put his Name there for his dwelling. To that place
you must go; 6there bring your burnt offerings and sacrifices, your
tithes and special gifts, what you have vowed to give and your
freewill offerings, and the firstborn of your herds and flocks.
7There, in the presence of the LORD your God, you and your families shall eat and shall rejoice in everything you have put your
hand to, because the LORD your God has blessed you.
8You are not to do as we do here today, everyone as he sees fit,
9since you have not yet reached the resting place and the inheri-

[a] 24 That is, the Mediterranean [b] 30 Or *Jordan, westward*

(11:18–21) O Holy God, write Your Word on the tablet of my life. May it flood my heart and shine its light of truth into every dark corner of my conscience. May it enlighten my eyes and be the filter through which I see all things. May it fill my mind so that all of my thoughts will be captive to obedience to Christ. May it direct my steps into Your good, pleasing and perfect will. May it guide my hands into the work of the ministry. May it guard the doorway of my life so that all of my comings and goings may pass under the scrutiny of Your divine wisdom. May Your Word, O God, be the constant employer of my spirit, soul and body.

The chief service I owe you, O God, is that every thought and word of mine should speak of you.

Hilary of Poitiers (c.315–368)

(12:2–4) Lord, as You bring me day by day into the fullness of Your resurrection life, I pray that You will destroy every vestige of idolatry—every memory, every vain imagination, every thought and habit that does not please You. Purify my heart and so let my worship be pure and pleasing to You.

tance the LORD your God is giving you. 10But you will cross the
Jordan and settle in the land the LORD your God is giving you as an
inheritance, and he will give you rest from all your enemies
around you so that you will live in safety. 11Then to the place the
LORD your God will choose as a dwelling for his Name—there you
are to bring everything I command you: your burnt offerings and
sacrifices, your tithes and special gifts, and all the choice possessions you have vowed to the LORD. 12And there rejoice before the
LORD your God, you, your sons and daughters, your menservants
and maidservants, and the Levites from your towns, who have no
allotment or inheritance of their own. 13Be careful not to sacrifice
your burnt offerings anywhere you please. 14Offer them only at
the place the LORD will choose in one of your tribes, and there observe everything I command you.

15Nevertheless, you may slaughter your animals in any of your
towns and eat as much of the meat as you want, as if it were
gazelle or deer, according to the blessing the LORD your God gives
you. Both the ceremonially unclean and the clean may eat it.
16But you must not eat the blood; pour it out on the ground like
water. 17You must not eat in your own towns the tithe of your
grain and new wine and oil, or the firstborn of your herds and
flocks, or whatever you have vowed to give, or your freewill offerings or special gifts. 18Instead, you are to eat them in the presence of the LORD your God at the place the LORD your God will
choose—you, your sons and daughters, your menservants and
maidservants, and the Levites from your towns—and you are to
rejoice before the LORD your God in everything you put your hand
to. 19Be careful not to neglect the Levites as long as you live in
your land.

20When the LORD your God has enlarged your territory as he
promised you, and you crave meat and say, "I would like some
meat," then you may eat as much of it as you want. 21If the place
where the LORD your God chooses to put his Name is too far away
from you, you may slaughter animals from the herds and flocks
the LORD has given you, as I have commanded you, and in your
own towns you may eat as much of them as you want. 22Eat them
as you would gazelle or deer. Both the ceremonially unclean and
the clean may eat. 23But be sure you do not eat the blood, because
the blood is the life, and you must not eat the life with the meat.
24You must not eat the blood; pour it out on the ground like water.
25Do not eat it, so that it may go well with you and your children
after you, because you will be doing what is right in the eyes of the
LORD.

26But take your consecrated things and whatever you have
vowed to give, and go to the place the LORD will choose. 27Present
your burnt offerings on the altar of the LORD your God, both the
meat and the blood. The blood of your sacrifices must be poured
beside the altar of the LORD your God, but you may eat the meat.
28Be careful to obey all these regulations I am giving you, so that
it may always go well with you and your children after you, because you will be doing what is good and right in the eyes of the
LORD your God.

29The LORD your God will cut off before you the nations you are
about to invade and dispossess. But when you have driven them
out and settled in their land, 30and after they have been destroyed
before you, be careful not to be ensnared by inquiring about their
gods, saying, "How do these nations serve their gods? We will do

(12:23) Father, since ancient times You have declared that blood represents life. Yet when You sent Your Son to die for us, He instructed us to partake of the bread of His flesh and the cup of His blood in remembrance of His sacrifice. How we thank You for the pulsing, vibrant life You have given us through Him—life that surges into us through faith, revitalizes us through Holy Communion, and empowers us through the great mystery of Christ's indwelling Presence. (Mt 26:26–28)

(12:28) Lord, Your law is perfect, reviving our souls. Your statutes are trustworthy, making even the most simpleminded of us wise. Lord, Your precepts are invariably right, lifting our hearts with joy. Your commands are radiant, flooding our eyes with light. Our fear of You purifies us, both now and forever. In every way, Lord, Your Word is more precious than gold and is sweeter than honey. If we listen it warns us of danger, and when we keep it we are greatly rewarded. (Ps 19:7–11)

God is an omniscient Creator who knows which rules are best for mankind; and these moral laws are a reflection of his nature, imposed on a universe which he created–a universe which functions best when his laws are obeyed.

Erwin W. Lutzer (1941-)

The only sovereign I recognize is he who sets fire to the suns and, with one blow of his hand, can send the worlds rolling in space.

François René (1768-1848)

(13:6–8) Father, although we are fickle and faithless, we long for You to be our first Love. Your great love for us outshines every human love we can ever know. You deserve the best we have to offer, emotionally, physically and intellectually. Help us to remember that no one—father or mother, husband, wife or children, brothers or sisters, or even we ourselves—could ever compete with You and Your sovereignty over our lives. (Lk 14:26–27; Rev 2:4)

Left to ourselves, we surely stray;
Oh, lead us on the narrow way,
With wisest counsel guide us;
And give us steadfastness, that we
May follow You forever free,
No matter who derides us.
Gently heal those hearts now
broken;
Give some token You are near us,
Whom we trust to light and cheer
us.

"O Holy Spirit Enter In"
Michael Schirmer (1606-1673)
Trans. Catherine Winkworth
(1829-1878)

the same." 31You must not worship the LORD your God in their
way, because in worshiping their gods, they do all kinds of detestable things the LORD hates. They even burn their sons and
daughters in the fire as sacrifices to their gods.
32See that you do all I command you; do not add to it or take
away from it.

Worshiping Other Gods

13 If a prophet, or one who foretells by dreams, appears
among you and announces to you a miraculous sign or
wonder, 2and if the sign or wonder of which he has spoken takes
place, and he says, "Let us follow other gods" (gods you have not
known) "and let us worship them," 3you must not listen to the
words of that prophet or dreamer. The LORD your God is testing
you to find out whether you love him with all your heart and with
all your soul. 4It is the LORD your God you must follow, and him
you must revere. Keep his commands and obey him; serve him
and hold fast to him. 5That prophet or dreamer must be put to
death, because he preached rebellion against the LORD your God,
who brought you out of Egypt and redeemed you from the land of
slavery; he has tried to turn you from the way the LORD your God
commanded you to follow. You must purge the evil from among
you.
6If your very own brother, or your son or daughter, or the wife
you love, or your closest friend secretly entices you, saying, "Let us
go and worship other gods" (gods that neither you nor your fathers have known, 7gods of the peoples around you, whether near
or far, from one end of the land to the other), 8do not yield to him
or listen to him. Show him no pity. Do not spare him or shield
him. 9You must certainly put him to death. Your hand must be the
first in putting him to death, and then the hands of all the people.
10Stone him to death, because he tried to turn you away from the
LORD your God, who brought you out of Egypt, out of the land of
slavery. 11Then all Israel will hear and be afraid, and no one
among you will do such an evil thing again.
12If you hear it said about one of the towns the LORD your God
is giving you to live in 13that wicked men have arisen among you
and have led the people of their town astray, saying, "Let us go
and worship other gods" (gods you have not known), 14then you
must inquire, probe and investigate it thoroughly. And if it is true
and it has been proved that this detestable thing has been done
among you, 15you must certainly put to the sword all who live in
that town. Destroy it completely,[a] both its people and its livestock.
16Gather all the plunder of the town into the middle of the public
square and completely burn the town and all its plunder as a
whole burnt offering to the LORD your God. It is to remain a ruin
forever, never to be rebuilt. 17None of those condemned things[a]
shall be found in your hands, so that the LORD will turn from his
fierce anger; he will show you mercy, have compassion on you,
and increase your numbers, as he promised on oath to your forefathers, 18because you obey the LORD your God, keeping all his
commands that I am giving you today and doing what is right in his
eyes.

[a] *15,17* The Hebrew term refers to the irrevocable giving over of things or persons to the LORD, often by totally destroying them.

Clean and Unclean Food

14 You are the children of the LORD your God. Do not cut yourselves or shave the front of your heads for the dead, 2for
you are a people holy to the LORD your God. Out of all the peoples
on the face of the earth, the LORD has chosen you to be his treasured possession.
3Do not eat any detestable thing. 4These are the animals you
may eat: the ox, the sheep, the goat, 5the deer, the gazelle, the roe
deer, the wild goat, the ibex, the antelope and the mountain
sheep.[a] 6You may eat any animal that has a split hoof divided in
two and that chews the cud. 7However, of those that chew the cud
or that have a split hoof completely divided you may not eat the
camel, the rabbit or the coney.[b] Although they chew the cud, they
do not have a split hoof; they are ceremonially unclean for you.
8The pig is also unclean; although it has a split hoof, it does not
chew the cud. You are not to eat their meat or touch their carcasses.
9Of all the creatures living in the water, you may eat any that has
fins and scales. 10But anything that does not have fins and scales
you may not eat; for you it is unclean.
11You may eat any clean bird. 12But these you may not eat: the
eagle, the vulture, the black vulture, 13the red kite, the black kite,
any kind of falcon, 14any kind of raven, 15the horned owl, the
screech owl, the gull, any kind of hawk, 16the little owl, the great
owl, the white owl, 17the desert owl, the osprey, the cormorant,
18the stork, any kind of heron, the hoopoe and the bat.
19All flying insects that swarm are unclean to you; do not eat
them. 20But any winged creature that is clean you may eat.
21Do not eat anything you find already dead. You may give it to
an alien living in any of your towns, and he may eat it, or you may
sell it to a foreigner. But you are a people holy to the LORD your
God.
Do not cook a young goat in its mother's milk.

Tithes

22Be sure to set aside a tenth of all that your fields produce
each year. 23Eat the tithe of your grain, new wine and oil, and the
firstborn of your herds and flocks in the presence of the LORD your
God at the place he will choose as a dwelling for his Name, so that
you may learn to revere the LORD your God always. 24But if that
place is too distant and you have been blessed by the LORD your
God and cannot carry your tithe (because the place where the
LORD will choose to put his Name is so far away), 25then exchange
your tithe for silver, and take the silver with you and go to the
place the LORD your God will choose. 26Use the silver to buy whatever you like: cattle, sheep, wine or other fermented drink, or anything you wish. Then you and your household shall eat there in the
presence of the LORD your God and rejoice. 27And do not neglect
the Levites living in your towns, for they have no allotment or inheritance of their own.
28At the end of every three years, bring all the tithes of that
year's produce and store it in your towns, 29so that the Levites
(who have no allotment or inheritance of their own) and the
aliens, the fatherless and the widows who live in your towns may

[a] 5 The precise identification of some of the birds and animals in this chapter is uncertain.
[b] 7 That is, the hyrax or rock badger

(14:1–2) Gracious Father, You adopted us, not because You needed children but because we were orphans who needed a Father. You made us holy, not because of our own merit but because, like any father, You want Your children to be like You. You chose us, not because we were faithful to You but so that through Your grace we might be so. (Lev 20:7–8; Ro 8:15; Eph 1:4–5)

Father, our God and Father,
You are the Author of Life.
Father, You freely offer
Your healing water of life.
You welcome all the thirsty,
Whose wells have run dry,
To love and tender mercy
Like a river from on high.
Father, the ones who love You
Drink deeply of You,
and never die.

"Father of Life"
Phil Kristianson and Bill Batstone
(©1998)

(15:11) Your eyes, God of all Compassion, are always turned toward the poor, the needy and the broken-hearted. And, recognizing our own poverty of spirit, You have promised that when we meet the needs of others we too will be enriched. How gracious You are to extend Your generosity through our tight-fisted hands. How wise You are to teach us Your ways by allowing us to participate in Your unceasing work of provision. Open our hands as You open our hearts, Lord, and make us like You: cheerful, extravagant givers. (2Co 9:6–15)

The saying is, that he who gives to the poor, lends to the Lord. But it may be said, not improperly, the Lord lends to us to give to the poor.

William Penn (1644-1718)

God's command to love each other
Is required of every man.
Showing mercy to a brother
Mirrors His redemptive plan.
In compassion He has given
Of His love that is divine.
On the cross sins were forgiven;
Joy and peace are fully thine.

"Come, All Christians, Be Committed"
Eva B. Lloyd (©1966)

come and eat and be satisfied, and so that the LORD your God may
bless you in all the work of your hands.

The Year for Canceling Debts

15 At the end of every seven years you must cancel debts. 2This
is how it is to be done: Every creditor shall cancel the loan
he has made to his fellow Israelite. He shall not require payment
from his fellow Israelite or brother, because the LORD's time for
canceling debts has been proclaimed. 3You may require payment
from a foreigner, but you must cancel any debt your brother owes
you. 4However, there should be no poor among you, for in the
land the LORD your God is giving you to possess as your inheritance, he will richly bless you, 5if only you fully obey the LORD your
God and are careful to follow all these commands I am giving you
today. 6For the LORD your God will bless you as he has promised,
and you will lend to many nations but will borrow from none. You
will rule over many nations but none will rule over you.
7If there is a poor man among your brothers in any of the towns
of the land that the LORD your God is giving you, do not be hard-
hearted or tightfisted toward your poor brother. 8Rather be openhanded and freely lend him whatever he needs. 9Be careful not to
harbor this wicked thought: "The seventh year, the year for canceling debts, is near," so that you do not show ill will toward your
needy brother and give him nothing. He may then appeal to the
LORD against you, and you will be found guilty of sin. 10Give generously to him and do so without a grudging heart; then because
of this the LORD your God will bless you in all your work and in
everything you put your hand to. 11There will always be poor people in the land. Therefore I command you to be openhanded toward your brothers and toward the poor and needy in your land.

Freeing Servants

12If a fellow Hebrew, a man or a woman, sells himself to you
and serves you six years, in the seventh year you must let him go
free. 13And when you release him, do not send him away empty-
handed. 14Supply him liberally from your flock, your threshing
floor and your winepress. Give to him as the LORD your God has
blessed you. 15Remember that you were slaves in Egypt and the
LORD your God redeemed you. That is why I give you this command today.
16But if your servant says to you, "I do not want to leave you,"
because he loves you and your family and is well off with you,
17then take an awl and push it through his ear lobe into the door,
and he will become your servant for life. Do the same for your
maidservant.
18Do not consider it a hardship to set your servant free, because his service to you these six years has been worth twice as
much as that of a hired hand. And the LORD your God will bless you
in everything you do.

The Firstborn Animals

19Set apart for the LORD your God every firstborn male of your
herds and flocks. Do not put the firstborn of your oxen to work,
and do not shear the firstborn of your sheep. 20Each year you and
your family are to eat them in the presence of the LORD your God
at the place he will choose. 21If an animal has a defect, is lame or
blind, or has any serious flaw, you must not sacrifice it to the LORD

your God. 22You are to eat it in your own towns. Both the ceremonially unclean and the clean may eat it, as if it were gazelle or
deer. 23But you must not eat the blood; pour it out on the ground
like water.

Passover

16 Observe the month of Abib and celebrate the Passover of
the LORD your God, because in the month of Abib he
brought you out of Egypt by night. 2Sacrifice as the Passover to
the LORD your God an animal from your flock or herd at the place
the LORD will choose as a dwelling for his Name. 3Do not eat it
with bread made with yeast, but for seven days eat unleavened
bread, the bread of affliction, because you left Egypt in haste—so
that all the days of your life you may remember the time of your
departure from Egypt. 4Let no yeast be found in your possession
in all your land for seven days. Do not let any of the meat you sacrifice on the evening of the first day remain until morning.

5You must not sacrifice the Passover in any town the LORD your
God gives you 6except in the place he will choose as a dwelling for
his Name. There you must sacrifice the Passover in the evening,
when the sun goes down, on the anniversary[a] of your departure
from Egypt. 7Roast it and eat it at the place the LORD your God will
choose. Then in the morning return to your tents. 8For six days eat
unleavened bread and on the seventh day hold an assembly to the
LORD your God and do no work.

Feast of Weeks

9Count off seven weeks from the time you begin to put the sickle to the standing grain. 10Then celebrate the Feast of Weeks to the
LORD your God by giving a freewill offering in proportion to the
blessings the LORD your God has given you. 11And rejoice before
the LORD your God at the place he will choose as a dwelling for his
Name—you, your sons and daughters, your menservants and
maidservants, the Levites in your towns, and the aliens, the fatherless and the widows living among you. 12Remember that you were
slaves in Egypt, and follow carefully these decrees.

Feast of Tabernacles

13Celebrate the Feast of Tabernacles for seven days after you
have gathered the produce of your threshing floor and your winepress. 14Be joyful at your Feast—you, your sons and daughters,
your menservants and maidservants, and the Levites, the aliens,
the fatherless and the widows who live in your towns. 15For seven
days celebrate the Feast to the LORD your God at the place the LORD
will choose. For the LORD your God will bless you in all your harvest and in all the work of your hands, and your joy will be complete.

16Three times a year all your men must appear before the LORD
your God at the place he will choose: at the Feast of Unleavened
Bread, the Feast of Weeks and the Feast of Tabernacles. No man
should appear before the LORD empty-handed: 17Each of you must
bring a gift in proportion to the way the LORD your God has blessed
you.

[a]6 Or *down, at the time of day*

(16:1–8) Father, You have established feasts and celebrations to remind us of Your works of power and deliverance. Just as the Passover memorialized Israel's miraculous deliverance from Egypt, we gratefully partake of Holy Communion in remembrance of our deliverance from the consequences of sin. How we thank You for Jesus, our Paschal Lamb, Who died to protect us from death, Who gave His life to provide us with eternal life, once and for all. (1Co 11:23–26)

(17:2–5) Lord, You know us so well. What must You be thinking when we mock ancient idolators, saying, "I would never worship such a thing." Moments later we turn our eyes toward the mirror and begin to serve even less impressive masters: pleasure, pride, prosperity, power. Continue to expose to us the idols we so blatantly worship alongside of You, and sometimes in place of You. Purify our lives so that our worship may be pleasing to You.

Idolatry is not only the adoration of images . . . but also trust in one's own righteousness, works and merits, and putting confidence in riches and power.

Martin Luther (1483-1546)

Judges

18Appoint judges and officials for each of your tribes in every
town the LORD your God is giving you, and they shall judge the people fairly. 19Do not pervert justice or show partiality. Do not accept
a bribe, for a bribe blinds the eyes of the wise and twists the words
of the righteous. 20Follow justice and justice alone, so that you
may live and possess the land the LORD your God is giving you.

Worshiping Other Gods

21Do not set up any wooden Asherah pole[a] beside the altar you
build to the LORD your God, 22and do not erect a sacred stone, for
these the LORD your God hates.

17 Do not sacrifice to the LORD your God an ox or a sheep that
has any defect or flaw in it, for that would be detestable to
him.

2If a man or woman living among you in one of the towns the
LORD gives you is found doing evil in the eyes of the LORD your God
in violation of his covenant, 3and contrary to my command has
worshiped other gods, bowing down to them or to the sun or the
moon or the stars of the sky, 4and this has been brought to your
attention, then you must investigate it thoroughly. If it is true and
it has been proved that this detestable thing has been done in Israel, 5take the man or woman who has done this evil deed to your
city gate and stone that person to death. 6On the testimony of two
or three witnesses a man shall be put to death, but no one shall be
put to death on the testimony of only one witness. 7The hands of
the witnesses must be the first in putting him to death, and then
the hands of all the people. You must purge the evil from among
you.

Law Courts

8If cases come before your courts that are too difficult for you
to judge—whether bloodshed, lawsuits or assaults—take them to
the place the LORD your God will choose. 9Go to the priests, who
are Levites, and to the judge who is in office at that time. Inquire
of them and they will give you the verdict. 10You must act according to the decisions they give you at the place the LORD will choose.
Be careful to do everything they direct you to do. 11Act according
to the law they teach you and the decisions they give you. Do not
turn aside from what they tell you, to the right or to the left. 12The
man who shows contempt for the judge or for the priest who
stands ministering there to the LORD your God must be put to
death. You must purge the evil from Israel. 13All the people will
hear and be afraid, and will not be contemptuous again.

The King

14When you enter the land the LORD your God is giving you and
have taken possession of it and settled in it, and you say, "Let us
set a king over us like all the nations around us," 15be sure to appoint over you the king the LORD your God chooses. He must be
from among your own brothers. Do not place a foreigner over
you, one who is not a brother Israelite. 16The king, moreover,
must not acquire great numbers of horses for himself or make the
people return to Egypt to get more of them, for the LORD has told
you, "You are not to go back that way again." 17He must not take

[a] 21 Or *Do not plant any tree dedicated to Asherah*

many wives, or his heart will be led astray. He must not accumulate large amounts of silver and gold.

18When he takes the throne of his kingdom, he is to write for himself on a scroll a copy of this law, taken from that of the priests, who are Levites. 19It is to be with him, and he is to read it all the days of his life so that he may learn to revere the LORD his God and follow carefully all the words of this law and these decrees 20and not consider himself better than his brothers and turn from the law to the right or to the left. Then he and his descendants will reign a long time over his kingdom in Israel.

Offerings for Priests and Levites

18 The priests, who are Levites—indeed the whole tribe of Levi—are to have no allotment or inheritance with Israel. They shall live on the offerings made to the LORD by fire, for that is their inheritance. 2They shall have no inheritance among their brothers; the LORD is their inheritance, as he promised them.

3This is the share due the priests from the people who sacrifice a bull or a sheep: the shoulder, the jowls and the inner parts. 4You are to give them the firstfruits of your grain, new wine and oil, and the first wool from the shearing of your sheep, 5for the LORD your God has chosen them and their descendants out of all your tribes to stand and minister in the LORD's name always.

6If a Levite moves from one of your towns anywhere in Israel where he is living, and comes in all earnestness to the place the LORD will choose, 7he may minister in the name of the LORD his God like all his fellow Levites who serve there in the presence of the LORD. 8He is to share equally in their benefits, even though he has received money from the sale of family possessions.

Detestable Practices

9When you enter the land the LORD your God is giving you, do not learn to imitate the detestable ways of the nations there. 10Let no one be found among you who sacrifices his son or daughter in[a] the fire, who practices divination or sorcery, interprets omens, engages in witchcraft, 11or casts spells, or who is a medium or spiritist or who consults the dead. 12Anyone who does these things is detestable to the LORD, and because of these detestable practices the LORD your God will drive out those nations before you. 13You must be blameless before the LORD your God.

The Prophet

14The nations you will dispossess listen to those who practice sorcery or divination. But as for you, the LORD your God has not permitted you to do so. 15The LORD your God will raise up for you a prophet like me from among your own brothers. You must listen to him. 16For this is what you asked of the LORD your God at Horeb on the day of the assembly when you said, "Let us not hear the voice of the LORD our God nor see this great fire anymore, or we will die."

17The LORD said to me: "What they say is good. 18I will raise up for them a prophet like you from among their brothers; I will put my words in his mouth, and he will tell them everything I command him. 19If anyone does not listen to my words that the prophet speaks in my name, I myself will call him to account. 20But a

[a] 10 *Or who makes his son or daughter pass through*

(18:2) Lord, Your priests of old did not inherit provision; they inherited the Provider. What greater inheritance could anyone seek than You? With You, there is no shortage. There is no loss. There is no threat of famine or drought. You are, in Yourself, all sufficient. Even today, You provide for us as Your priests whatever we need. And year by year, decade by decade, You give us the desires of our hearts. What more could we ask than to have all things in You? What greater legacy could we pass on to our children than to know You as their Provider?

(18:18) Jesus, You are the promised Prophet, greater even than Moses. Just as Moses was called upon to lead God's people into freedom from slavery and to reveal the Law to them, so also You came into the world to deliver all people from their slavery to sin. You did not come to abolish the Law or the Prophets, but to fulfill them. We praise You for Your finished work of redemption and for Your ongoing ministry as our Prophet, our Priest and our King. (Mt 5:17)

(19:1–3) I praise You, Lord, for Your great mercy. You are a refuge for the oppressed, a stronghold in times of trouble. No one will be condemned who takes refuge in You. So I fix my eyes on You, O Sovereign Lord. "In you, O LORD, I have taken refuge; let me never be put to shame. Rescue me and deliver me in your righteousness; turn your ear to me and save me. Be my rock of refuge, to which I can always go; give the command to save me, for you are my rock and my fortress." (Ps 9:9, 34:22; 71:1–3; 141:8)

What though my joys and comforts die?
The Lord my Savior liveth;
What though the darkness gather round?
Songs in the night he giveth;
No storm can shake my inmost calm,
While to that refuge clinging;
Since Christ is Lord of heaven and earth,
How can I keep from singing?
Robert Lowry (1826-1899)

prophet who presumes to speak in my name anything I have not
commanded him to say, or a prophet who speaks in the name of
other gods, must be put to death."
21You may say to yourselves, "How can we know when a message has not been spoken by the LORD?" 22If what a prophet proclaims in the name of the LORD does not take place or come true,
that is a message the LORD has not spoken. That prophet has spoken presumptuously. Do not be afraid of him.

Cities of Refuge

19 When the LORD your God has destroyed the nations whose
land he is giving you, and when you have driven them out
and settled in their towns and houses, 2then set aside for yourselves three cities centrally located in the land the LORD your God
is giving you to possess. 3Build roads to them and divide into three
parts the land the LORD your God is giving you as an inheritance,
so that anyone who kills a man may flee there.
4This is the rule concerning the man who kills another and
flees there to save his life—one who kills his neighbor unintentionally, without malice aforethought. 5For instance, a man may
go into the forest with his neighbor to cut wood, and as he swings
his ax to fell a tree, the head may fly off and hit his neighbor and
kill him. That man may flee to one of these cities and save his life.
6Otherwise, the avenger of blood might pursue him in a rage,
overtake him if the distance is too great, and kill him even though
he is not deserving of death, since he did it to his neighbor without malice aforethought. 7This is why I command you to set aside
for yourselves three cities.
8If the LORD your God enlarges your territory, as he promised
on oath to your forefathers, and gives you the whole land he
promised them, 9because you carefully follow all these laws I
command you today—to love the LORD your God and to walk always in his ways—then you are to set aside three more cities.
10Do this so that innocent blood will not be shed in your land,
which the LORD your God is giving you as your inheritance, and so
that you will not be guilty of bloodshed.
11But if a man hates his neighbor and lies in wait for him, assaults and kills him, and then flees to one of these cities, 12the elders of his town shall send for him, bring him back from the city,
and hand him over to the avenger of blood to die. 13Show him no
pity. You must purge from Israel the guilt of shedding innocent
blood, so that it may go well with you.
14Do not move your neighbor's boundary stone set up by your
predecessors in the inheritance you receive in the land the LORD
your God is giving you to possess.

Witnesses

15One witness is not enough to convict a man accused of any
crime or offense he may have committed. A matter must be established by the testimony of two or three witnesses.
16If a malicious witness takes the stand to accuse a man of a
crime, 17the two men involved in the dispute must stand in the
presence of the LORD before the priests and the judges who are
in office at the time. 18The judges must make a thorough investigation, and if the witness proves to be a liar, giving false testimony against his brother, 19then do to him as he intended to do
to his brother. You must purge the evil from among you. 20The

rest of the people will hear of this and be afraid, and never again will such an evil thing be done among you. 21 Show no pity: life for life, eye for eye, tooth for tooth, hand for hand, foot for foot.

Going to War

20 When you go to war against your enemies and see horses and chariots and an army greater than yours, do not be afraid of them, because the LORD your God, who brought you up out of Egypt, will be with you. 2 When you are about to go into battle, the priest shall come forward and address the army. 3 He shall say: "Hear, O Israel, today you are going into battle against your enemies. Do not be fainthearted or afraid; do not be terrified or give way to panic before them. 4 For the LORD your God is the one who goes with you to fight for you against your enemies to give you victory."

5 The officers shall say to the army: "Has anyone built a new house and not dedicated it? Let him go home, or he may die in battle and someone else may dedicate it. 6 Has anyone planted a vineyard and not begun to enjoy it? Let him go home, or he may die in battle and someone else enjoy it. 7 Has anyone become pledged to a woman and not married her? Let him go home, or he may die in battle and someone else marry her." 8 Then the officers shall add, "Is any man afraid or fainthearted? Let him go home so that his brothers will not become disheartened too." 9 When the officers have finished speaking to the army, they shall appoint commanders over it.

10 When you march up to attack a city, make its people an offer of peace. 11 If they accept and open their gates, all the people in it shall be subject to forced labor and shall work for you. 12 If they refuse to make peace and they engage you in battle, lay siege to that city. 13 When the LORD your God delivers it into your hand, put to the sword all the men in it. 14 As for the women, the children, the livestock and everything else in the city, you may take these as plunder for yourselves. And you may use the plunder the LORD your God gives you from your enemies. 15 This is how you are to treat all the cities that are at a distance from you and do not belong to the nations nearby.

16 However, in the cities of the nations the LORD your God is giving you as an inheritance, do not leave alive anything that breathes. 17 Completely destroy[a] them—the Hittites, Amorites, Canaanites, Perizzites, Hivites and Jebusites—as the LORD your God has commanded you. 18 Otherwise, they will teach you to follow all the detestable things they do in worshiping their gods, and you will sin against the LORD your God.

19 When you lay siege to a city for a long time, fighting against it to capture it, do not destroy its trees by putting an ax to them, because you can eat their fruit. Do not cut them down. Are the trees of the field people, that you should besiege them?[b] 20 However, you may cut down trees that you know are not fruit trees and use them to build siege works until the city at war with you falls.

[a] *17* The Hebrew term refers to the irrevocable giving over of things or persons to the LORD, often by totally destroying them. [b] *19* Or *down to use in the siege, for the fruit trees are for the benefit of man.*

(20:2–4) Just as Israel faced menacing earthly armies, so we are surrounded by spiritual enemies. In their terrible darkness they sometimes appear to be greater than we are. What courage and hope we find, Lord Jesus, in knowing that You are our victorious High Priest, well-prepared to face the battle with us. Not only are You our Priest, but You are also our warrior King, fearless and invincible, fighting with us and for us. The battle belongs to You, Lord Jesus Christ, and because of You, and the armor of light You provide for us, we are more than conquerors. (Ro 13:12)

When the power of darkness comes
in like a flood;
The battle belongs to the Lord.
He's raised up a standard, the power
of His blood;
The battle belongs to the Lord.
We sing, "Glory, honor, power and
strength to the Lord."
We sing, "Glory, honor, power and
strength to the Lord."

"The Battle Belongs to the Lord"
Jamie Owens-Collins (©1984)

Feed on Christ, and then go and live your life, and it is Christ in you that lives your life, that helps the poor, that tells the truth, that fights the battle, and that wins the crown.

Phillips Brooks (1835-1893)

Atonement for an Unsolved Murder

21 If a man is found slain, lying in a field in the land the LORD
your God is giving you to possess, and it is not known who
killed him, 2your elders and judges shall go out and measure the
distance from the body to the neighboring towns. 3Then the elders
of the town nearest the body shall take a heifer that has never been
worked and has never worn a yoke 4and lead her down to a valley that has not been plowed or planted and where there is a flowing stream. There in the valley they are to break the heifer's neck.
5The priests, the sons of Levi, shall step forward, for the LORD your
God has chosen them to minister and to pronounce blessings in
the name of the LORD and to decide all cases of dispute and assault. 6Then all the elders of the town nearest the body shall wash
their hands over the heifer whose neck was broken in the valley,
7and they shall declare: "Our hands did not shed this blood, nor
did our eyes see it done. 8Accept this atonement for your people
Israel, whom you have redeemed, O LORD, and do not hold your
people guilty of the blood of an innocent man." And the bloodshed
will be atoned for. 9So you will purge from yourselves the guilt of
shedding innocent blood, since you have done what is right in the
eyes of the LORD.

Marrying a Captive Woman

10When you go to war against your enemies and the LORD your
God delivers them into your hands and you take captives, 11if you
notice among the captives a beautiful woman and are attracted to
her, you may take her as your wife. 12Bring her into your home
and have her shave her head, trim her nails 13and put aside the
clothes she was wearing when captured. After she has lived in your
house and mourned her father and mother for a full month, then
you may go to her and be her husband and she shall be your wife.
14If you are not pleased with her, let her go wherever she wishes.
You must not sell her or treat her as a slave, since you have dishonored her.

The Right of the Firstborn

15If a man has two wives, and he loves one but not the other,
and both bear him sons but the firstborn is the son of the wife he
does not love, 16when he wills his property to his sons, he must
not give the rights of the firstborn to the son of the wife he loves in
preference to his actual firstborn, the son of the wife he does not
love. 17He must acknowledge the son of his unloved wife as the
firstborn by giving him a double share of all he has. That son is the
first sign of his father's strength. The right of the firstborn belongs
to him.

A Rebellious Son

18If a man has a stubborn and rebellious son who does not
obey his father and mother and will not listen to them when they
discipline him, 19his father and mother shall take hold of him and
bring him to the elders at the gate of his town. 20They shall say to
the elders, "This son of ours is stubborn and rebellious. He will
not obey us. He is a profligate and a drunkard." 21Then all the
men of his town shall stone him to death. You must purge the evil
from among you. All Israel will hear of it and be afraid.

(21:1–9) For the sin that goes unpunished in our land, Lord, forgive us. You know the guilty party, for nothing is hidden from You. We cannot say the sin is not ours. Even though our consciences may be clear, that does not make us innocent in Your eyes. So we humbly ask You for mercy and forgiveness. (1Co 4:4)

Guilty, vile, and helpless we;
Spotless Lamb of God was He.
Full atonement, can it be?
Hallelujah! What a Savior!

"Hallelujah! What a Savior!"
Phillip P. Bliss (1875)

Various Laws

22If a man guilty of a capital offense is put to death and his body
is hung on a tree, 23you must not leave his body on the tree
overnight. Be sure to bury him that same day, because anyone who
is hung on a tree is under God's curse. You must not desecrate the
land the LORD your God is giving you as an inheritance.

22 If you see your brother's ox or sheep straying, do not ignore it but be sure to take it back to him. 2If the brother
does not live near you or if you do not know who he is, take it
home with you and keep it until he comes looking for it. Then give
it back to him. 3Do the same if you find your brother's donkey or
his cloak or anything he loses. Do not ignore it.

4If you see your brother's donkey or his ox fallen on the road,
do not ignore it. Help him get it to its feet.

5A woman must not wear men's clothing, nor a man wear
women's clothing, for the LORD your God detests anyone who does
this.

6If you come across a bird's nest beside the road, either in a
tree or on the ground, and the mother is sitting on the young or on
the eggs, do not take the mother with the young. 7You may take
the young, but be sure to let the mother go, so that it may go well
with you and you may have a long life.

8When you build a new house, make a parapet around your
roof so that you may not bring the guilt of bloodshed on your
house if someone falls from the roof.

9Do not plant two kinds of seed in your vineyard; if you do, not
only the crops you plant but also the fruit of the vineyard will be
defiled.[a]

10Do not plow with an ox and a donkey yoked together.

11Do not wear clothes of wool and linen woven together.

12Make tassels on the four corners of the cloak you wear.

Marriage Violations

13If a man takes a wife and, after lying with her, dislikes her
14and slanders her and gives her a bad name, saying, "I married
this woman, but when I approached her, I did not find proof of
her virginity," 15then the girl's father and mother shall bring proof
that she was a virgin to the town elders at the gate. 16The girl's father will say to the elders, "I gave my daughter in marriage to this
man, but he dislikes her. 17Now he has slandered her and said, 'I
did not find your daughter to be a virgin.' But here is the proof of
my daughter's virginity." Then her parents shall display the cloth
before the elders of the town, 18and the elders shall take the man
and punish him. 19They shall fine him a hundred shekels of silver[b] and give them to the girl's father, because this man has given
an Israelite virgin a bad name. She shall continue to be his wife; he
must not divorce her as long as he lives.

20If, however, the charge is true and no proof of the girl's virginity can be found, 21she shall be brought to the door of her father's house and there the men of her town shall stone her to
death. She has done a disgraceful thing in Israel by being promiscuous while still in her father's house. You must purge the evil
from among you.

22If a man is found sleeping with another man's wife, both the

[a] *9* Or *be forfeited to the sanctuary* [b] *19* That is, about 2 1/2 pounds (about 1 kilogram)

(21:23) Lord Jesus, how wondrous is Your cross. You, the Prince of Glory, have taken upon Yourself the curse that was ours because of our lawbreaking and unrighteousness. We praise You that, because You were cursed, we will never be cursed for our sin. (Gal 3:13)

We shall never understand anything of our Lord's preaching and ministry unless we continually keep in mind what exactly and exclusively his errand was in this world. Sin was his errand in this world, and it was his only errand. He would never have been in this world, either preaching or doing anything else, but for sin. He could have done everything else for us without coming down into this world at all; everything else but take away our sin.

Alexander Whyte (1836-1921)

I love Thee because
Thou hast first loved me,
And purchased my pardon
On Calvary's tree.
I love Thee for wearing
The thorns on Thy brow.
If ever I loved Thee,
My Jesus, 'tis now.

"My Jesus, I Love Thee"
William R. Featherstone (c.1862)

man who slept with her and the woman must die. You must purge
the evil from Israel.
23If a man happens to meet in a town a virgin pledged to be
married and he sleeps with her, 24you shall take both of them to
the gate of that town and stone them to death—the girl because
she was in a town and did not scream for help, and the man because he violated another man's wife. You must purge the evil
from among you.
25But if out in the country a man happens to meet a girl pledged
to be married and rapes her, only the man who has done this shall
die. 26Do nothing to the girl; she has committed no sin deserving
death. This case is like that of someone who attacks and murders
his neighbor, 27for the man found the girl out in the country, and
though the betrothed girl screamed, there was no one to rescue
her.
28If a man happens to meet a virgin who is not pledged to be
married and rapes her and they are discovered, 29he shall pay the
girl's father fifty shekels of silver.[a] He must marry the girl, for he
has violated her. He can never divorce her as long as he lives.
30A man is not to marry his father's wife; he must not dishonor
his father's bed.

Exclusion From the Assembly

23 No one who has been emasculated by crushing or cutting
may enter the assembly of the LORD.
2No one born of a forbidden marriage[b] nor any of his descendants may enter the assembly of the LORD, even down to the tenth
generation.
3No Ammonite or Moabite or any of his descendants may enter
the assembly of the LORD, even down to the tenth generation. 4For
they did not come to meet you with bread and water on your way
when you came out of Egypt, and they hired Balaam son of Beor
from Pethor in Aram Naharaim[c] to pronounce a curse on you.
5However, the LORD your God would not listen to Balaam but
turned the curse into a blessing for you, because the LORD your
God loves you. 6Do not seek a treaty of friendship with them as
long as you live.
7Do not abhor an Edomite, for he is your brother. Do not abhor
an Egyptian, because you lived as an alien in his country. 8The
third generation of children born to them may enter the assembly
of the LORD.

Uncleanness in the Camp

9When you are encamped against your enemies, keep away
from everything impure. 10If one of your men is unclean because
of a nocturnal emission, he is to go outside the camp and stay
there. 11But as evening approaches he is to wash himself, and at
sunset he may return to the camp.
12Designate a place outside the camp where you can go to relieve yourself. 13As part of your equipment have something to dig
with, and when you relieve yourself, dig a hole and cover up your
excrement. 14For the LORD your God moves about in your camp to
protect you and to deliver your enemies to you. Your camp must
be holy, so that he will not see among you anything indecent and
turn away from you.

[a] 29 That is, about 1 1/4 pounds (about 0.6 kilogram) [b] 2 Or *one of illegitimate birth*
[c] 4 That is, Northwest Mesopotamia

(23:5) God of the Resurrection, You breathe new life into fallen seeds. You exchange beauty for ashes. You reward our long-sown tears with harvests of joy. How often You have reached out to the cursed, the lost, the broken and the outcast and have transformed them into beautiful blessings. You work out all aspects of our lives for good, and You do so simply because You love us. (Ps 126:5; Isa 61:3; Ro 8:28)

Receive every day as a resurrection from death, as a new enjoyment of life . . . let your joyful heart praise and magnify so good and glorious a Creator.

William Law (1686-1761)

Miscellaneous Laws

15 If a slave has taken refuge with you, do not hand him over to
his master. 16 Let him live among you wherever he likes and in
whatever town he chooses. Do not oppress him.

17 No Israelite man or woman is to become a shrine prostitute.
18 You must not bring the earnings of a female prostitute or of a
male prostitute[a] into the house of the LORD your God to pay any
vow, because the LORD your God detests them both.

19 Do not charge your brother interest, whether on money or
food or anything else that may earn interest. 20 You may charge a
foreigner interest, but not a brother Israelite, so that the LORD your
God may bless you in everything you put your hand to in the land
you are entering to possess.

21 If you make a vow to the LORD your God, do not be slow to pay
it, for the LORD your God will certainly demand it of you and you
will be guilty of sin. 22 But if you refrain from making a vow, you
will not be guilty. 23 Whatever your lips utter you must be sure to
do, because you made your vow freely to the LORD your God with
your own mouth.

24 If you enter your neighbor's vineyard, you may eat all the
grapes you want, but do not put any in your basket. 25 If you enter
your neighbor's grainfield, you may pick kernels with your hands,
but you must not put a sickle to his standing grain.

24 If a man marries a woman who becomes displeasing to
him because he finds something indecent about her, and
he writes her a certificate of divorce, gives it to her and sends her
from his house, 2 and if after she leaves his house she becomes the
wife of another man, 3 and her second husband dislikes her and
writes her a certificate of divorce, gives it to her and sends her
from his house, or if he dies, 4 then her first husband, who divorced her, is not allowed to marry her again after she has been
defiled. That would be detestable in the eyes of the LORD. Do not
bring sin upon the land the LORD your God is giving you as an inheritance.

5 If a man has recently married, he must not be sent to war or
have any other duty laid on him. For one year he is to be free to
stay at home and bring happiness to the wife he has married.

6 Do not take a pair of millstones—not even the upper one—as
security for a debt, because that would be taking a man's livelihood as security.

7 If a man is caught kidnapping one of his brother Israelites and
treats him as a slave or sells him, the kidnapper must die. You
must purge the evil from among you.

8 In cases of leprous[b] diseases be very careful to do exactly as
the priests, who are Levites, instruct you. You must follow carefully what I have commanded them. 9 Remember what the LORD your
God did to Miriam along the way after you came out of Egypt.

10 When you make a loan of any kind to your neighbor, do not
go into his house to get what he is offering as a pledge. 11 Stay outside and let the man to whom you are making the loan bring the
pledge out to you. 12 If the man is poor, do not go to sleep with his
pledge in your possession. 13 Return his cloak to him by sunset so
that he may sleep in it. Then he will thank you, and it will be regarded as a righteous act in the sight of the LORD your God.

[a] *18* Hebrew *of a dog* [b] *8* The Hebrew word was used for various diseases affecting the skin—not necessarily leprosy.

(23:19–20) Lord, out of the abundance with which You have so freely blessed me, I will freely bless my brothers and sisters with a generous measure so that nothing will hinder the flow of Your provision in my life. Thank You for Your gracious promise, "Give, and it will be given to you. A good measure, pressed down, shaken together and running over, will be poured into your lap. For with the measure you use, it will be measured to you." (Lk 6:38)

14 Do not take advantage of a hired man who is poor and
needy, whether he is a brother Israelite or an alien living in one
of your towns. 15 Pay him his wages each day before sunset, because he is poor and is counting on it. Otherwise he may cry to
the LORD against you, and you will be guilty of sin.
16 Fathers shall not be put to death for their children, nor children put to death for their fathers; each is to die for his own sin.
17 Do not deprive the alien or the fatherless of justice, or take
the cloak of the widow as a pledge. 18 Remember that you were
slaves in Egypt and the LORD your God redeemed you from there.
That is why I command you to do this.
19 When you are harvesting in your field and you overlook a
sheaf, do not go back to get it. Leave it for the alien, the fatherless and the widow, so that the LORD your God may bless you in
all the work of your hands. 20 When you beat the olives from your
trees, do not go over the branches a second time. Leave what remains for the alien, the fatherless and the widow. 21 When you
harvest the grapes in your vineyard, do not go over the vines
again. Leave what remains for the alien, the fatherless and the
widow. 22 Remember that you were slaves in Egypt. That is why I
command you to do this.

25 When men have a dispute, they are to take it to court and
the judges will decide the case, acquitting the innocent
and condemning the guilty. 2 If the guilty man deserves to be
beaten, the judge shall make him lie down and have him flogged
in his presence with the number of lashes his crime deserves,
3 but he must not give him more than forty lashes. If he is
flogged more than that, your brother will be degraded in your
eyes.
4 Do not muzzle an ox while it is treading out the grain.
5 If brothers are living together and one of them dies without
a son, his widow must not marry outside the family. Her husband's brother shall take her and marry her and fulfill the duty
of a brother-in-law to her. 6 The first son she bears shall carry on
the name of the dead brother so that his name will not be blotted out from Israel.
7 However, if a man does not want to marry his brother's wife,
she shall go to the elders at the town gate and say, "My husband's brother refuses to carry on his brother's name in Israel.
He will not fulfill the duty of a brother-in-law to me." 8 Then the
elders of his town shall summon him and talk to him. If he persists in saying, "I do not want to marry her," 9 his brother's
widow shall go up to him in the presence of the elders, take off
one of his sandals, spit in his face and say, "This is what is done
to the man who will not build up his brother's family line."
10 That man's line shall be known in Israel as The Family of the
Unsandaled.
11 If two men are fighting and the wife of one of them comes
to rescue her husband from his assailant, and she reaches out
and seizes him by his private parts, 12 you shall cut off her hand.
Show her no pity.
13 Do not have two differing weights in your bag—one heavy,
one light. 14 Do not have two differing measures in your
house—one large, one small. 15 You must have accurate and
honest weights and measures, so that you may live long in the
land the LORD your God is giving you. 16 For the LORD your God

(24:19) O Lord our Provider, there is no shortage of Your abundance. You provide so faithfully and generously. All that I have comes from You. Please make me a source of Your provision to others. Help me not to clutch the wealth You bring my way, but to hold it with open hands so that in giving I might receive more, and in receiving I might give again. (1Ch 29:14)

In the just reward of labor,
God's will is done.
In the help we give our neighbor,
God's will is done.
In our worldwide task of caring
For the hungry and despairing,
In the harvests we are sharing,
God's will is done.

"For the Fruit of All Creation"
Fred Pratt Green (©1970)

detests anyone who does these things, anyone who deals dis-
honestly.
17Remember what the Amalekites did to you along the way
when you came out of Egypt. 18When you were weary and worn
out, they met you on your journey and cut off all who were lag-
ging behind; they had no fear of God. 19When the LORD your God
gives you rest from all the enemies around you in the land he is
giving you to possess as an inheritance, you shall blot out the
memory of Amalek from under heaven. Do not forget!

Firstfruits and Tithes

26 When you have entered the land the LORD your God is giving you as an inheritance and have taken possession of it
and settled in it, 2take some of the firstfruits of all that you produce from the soil of the land the LORD your God is giving you and
put them in a basket. Then go to the place the LORD your God will
choose as a dwelling for his Name 3and say to the priest in office
at the time, "I declare today to the LORD your God that I have come
to the land the LORD swore to our forefathers to give us." 4The
priest shall take the basket from your hands and set it down in
front of the altar of the LORD your God. 5Then you shall declare before the LORD your God: "My father was a wandering Aramean, and
he went down into Egypt with a few people and lived there and became a great nation, powerful and numerous. 6But the Egyptians
mistreated us and made us suffer, putting us to hard labor. 7Then
we cried out to the LORD, the God of our fathers, and the LORD
heard our voice and saw our misery, toil and oppression. 8So the
LORD brought us out of Egypt with a mighty hand and an outstretched arm, with great terror and with miraculous signs and
wonders. 9He brought us to this place and gave us this land, a
land flowing with milk and honey; 10and now I bring the firstfruits
of the soil that you, O LORD, have given me." Place the basket before the LORD your God and bow down before him. 11And you and
the Levites and the aliens among you shall rejoice in all the good
things the LORD your God has given to you and your household.
12When you have finished setting aside a tenth of all your produce in the third year, the year of the tithe, you shall give it to the
Levite, the alien, the fatherless and the widow, so that they may eat
in your towns and be satisfied. 13Then say to the LORD your God:
"I have removed from my house the sacred portion and have given
it to the Levite, the alien, the fatherless and the widow, according
to all you commanded. I have not turned aside from your commands nor have I forgotten any of them. 14I have not eaten any of
the sacred portion while I was in mourning, nor have I removed
any of it while I was unclean, nor have I offered any of it to the
dead. I have obeyed the LORD my God; I have done everything you
commanded me. 15Look down from heaven, your holy dwelling
place, and bless your people Israel and the land you have given us
as you promised on oath to our forefathers, a land flowing with
milk and honey."

Follow the LORD's Commands

16The LORD your God commands you this day to follow these
decrees and laws; carefully observe them with all your heart and
with all your soul. 17You have declared this day that the LORD is
your God and that you will walk in his ways, that you will keep his
decrees, commands and laws, and that you will obey him. 18And

(26:9–10) Faithful Provider, accept my offering of firstfruits. There is nothing I have that has not come from You—nothing. You have given me the power to make wealth, to be productive, to be creative, to enjoy rich relationship. Every breath I breathe is a gift from You. May the first thanks I render and the first gift I offer be always unto You. (Dt 8:17–18)

May this life that I live bring You
praise,
Blessing You and Your wonderful
ways,
In the work of my hands, and the
words that I say,
I will worship You, Lord, all my days.

I will sing to Your name when I
wake,
Giving thanks for each breath that I
take,
From the first light I see, to the last
pray'r I pray,
I will worship You, Lord, all my days.

"All My Days"
Bill Batstone and Bob Somma (©1990)

the LORD has declared this day that you are his people, his treasured possession as he promised, and that you are to keep all his
commands. 19 He has declared that he will set you in praise, fame
and honor high above all the nations he has made and that you
will be a people holy to the LORD your God, as he promised.

The Altar on Mount Ebal

27 Moses and the elders of Israel commanded the people:
"Keep all these commands that I give you today. 2 When you
have crossed the Jordan into the land the LORD your God is giving
you, set up some large stones and coat them with plaster. 3 Write
on them all the words of this law when you have crossed over to
enter the land the LORD your God is giving you, a land flowing with
milk and honey, just as the LORD, the God of your fathers, promised you. 4 And when you have crossed the Jordan, set up these
stones on Mount Ebal, as I command you today, and coat them
with plaster. 5 Build there an altar to the LORD your God, an altar of
stones. Do not use any iron tool upon them. 6 Build the altar of the
LORD your God with fieldstones and offer burnt offerings on it to
the LORD your God. 7 Sacrifice fellowship offerings[a] there, eating
them and rejoicing in the presence of the LORD your God. 8 And you
shall write very clearly all the words of this law on these stones you
have set up."

Curses From Mount Ebal

9 Then Moses and the priests, who are Levites, said to all Israel,
"Be silent, O Israel, and listen! You have now become the people
of the LORD your God. 10 Obey the LORD your God and follow his
commands and decrees that I give you today."
11 On the same day Moses commanded the people:
12 When you have crossed the Jordan, these tribes shall stand on
Mount Gerizim to bless the people: Simeon, Levi, Judah, Issachar,
Joseph and Benjamin. 13 And these tribes shall stand on Mount
Ebal to pronounce curses: Reuben, Gad, Asher, Zebulun, Dan and
Naphtali.
14 The Levites shall recite to all the people of Israel in a loud voice:

15 "Cursed is the man who carves an image or casts an
idol—a thing detestable to the LORD, the work of the craftsman's hands—and sets it up in secret."

Then all the people shall say, "Amen!"

16 "Cursed is the man who dishonors his father or his
mother."

Then all the people shall say, "Amen!"

17 "Cursed is the man who moves his neighbor's boundary
stone."

Then all the people shall say, "Amen!"

18 "Cursed is the man who leads the blind astray on the
road."

Then all the people shall say, "Amen!"

19 "Cursed is the man who withholds justice from the
alien, the fatherless or the widow."

Then all the people shall say, "Amen!"

20 "Cursed is the man who sleeps with his father's wife, for
he dishonors his father's bed."

Then all the people shall say, "Amen!"

[a] 7 Traditionally *peace offerings*

(26:18) Of all the things You have made, Father, and from among all the people who have ever lived You call us Your treasured possession. We were bought at a price. We are not our own. What privilege, what honor, what attainment, real or imagined, can possibly compare with being Your treasure? Help us always to bring You joy. (1Co 6:19–20)

May this life that I live make You glad,
Help me praise You with all that I have.
May the thoughts of my heart bring a smile to Your face,
I will worship You, Lord, all my days.

Ev'ry day is a gift from Your hand,
You're the Author of all that I am.
Let my story be told in this heart-spoken phrase:
I will worship You, Lord, all my days.

"All My Days"
Bill Batstone and Bob Somma (©1990)

21"Cursed is the man who has sexual relations with any animal."

Then all the people shall say, "Amen!"

22"Cursed is the man who sleeps with his sister, the daughter of his father or the daughter of his mother."

Then all the people shall say, "Amen!"

23"Cursed is the man who sleeps with his mother-in-law."

Then all the people shall say, "Amen!"

24"Cursed is the man who kills his neighbor secretly."

Then all the people shall say, "Amen!"

25"Cursed is the man who accepts a bribe to kill an innocent person."

Then all the people shall say, "Amen!"

26"Cursed is the man who does not uphold the words of this law by carrying them out."

Then all the people shall say, "Amen!"

Blessings for Obedience

28 If you fully obey the LORD your God and carefully follow all his commands I give you today, the LORD your God will set you high above all the nations on earth.
2All these blessings will come upon you and accompany you if you obey the LORD your God:

3You will be blessed in the city and blessed in the country.

4The fruit of your womb will be blessed, and the crops of your land and the young of your livestock—the calves of your herds and the lambs of your flocks.

5Your basket and your kneading trough will be blessed.

6You will be blessed when you come in and blessed when you go out.

7The LORD will grant that the enemies who rise up against you will be defeated before you. They will come at you from one direction but flee from you in seven.

8The LORD will send a blessing on your barns and on everything you put your hand to. The LORD your God will bless you in the land he is giving you.

9The LORD will establish you as his holy people, as he promised you on oath, if you keep the commands of the LORD your God and walk in his ways.
10Then all the peoples on earth will see that you are called by the name of the LORD, and they will fear you.
11The LORD will grant you abundant prosperity—in the fruit of your womb, the young of your livestock and the crops of your ground—in the land he swore to your forefathers to give you.

12The LORD will open the heavens, the storehouse of his bounty, to send rain on your land in season and to bless all the work of your hands. You will lend to many nations but will borrow from none.
13The LORD will make you the head, not the tail. If you pay attention to the commands of the LORD your God that I give you this day and carefully follow them, you will always be at the top, never at the bottom.
14Do not turn aside from any of the commands I give you today, to the right or to the left, following other gods and serving them.

(28:1–13) Dear heavenly Father, how You yearn to bless Your people. You pour Your grace upon us when we humble ourselves before You; grace upon grace to meet our every need: victory, destiny, dignity, sanity, prosperity and spiritual vitality. In response to Your loving-kindness, we gratefully offer You our loving obedience.

There shall be showers of blessing:
This is the promise of love.
There shall be seasons refreshing,
Sent from the Savior above.

"There Shall Be Showers of Blessing"
Daniel W. Whittle (1840-1901)

Curses for Disobedience

15However, if you do not obey the LORD your God and do not carefully follow all his commands and decrees I am giving you today, all these curses will come upon you and overtake you:

16You will be cured in the city and cursed in the country.
17Your basket and your kneading trough will be cursed.
18The fruit of your womb will be cursed, and the crops of your land, and the calves of your herds and the lambs of your flocks.
19You will be cursed when you come in and cursed when you go out.

20The LORD will send on you curses, confusion and rebuke in everything you put your hand to, until you are destroyed and come to sudden ruin because of the evil you have done in forsaking
him.[a] 21The LORD will plague you with diseases until he has de-
stroyed you from the land you are entering to possess. 22The LORD
will strike you with wasting disease, with fever and inflammation, with scorching heat and drought, with blight and mildew, which
will plague you until you perish. 23The sky over your head will be
bronze, the ground beneath you iron. 24The LORD will turn the rain of your country into dust and powder; it will come down from the skies until you are destroyed.
25The LORD will cause you to be defeated before your enemies. You will come at them from one direction but flee from them in seven, and you will become a thing of horror to all the kingdoms
on earth. 26Your carcasses will be food for all the birds of the air and the beasts of the earth, and there will be no one to frighten
them away. 27The LORD will afflict you with the boils of Egypt and with tumors, festering sores and the itch, from which you cannot
be cured. 28The LORD will afflict you with madness, blindness and
confusion of mind. 29At midday you will grope about like a blind man in the dark. You will be unsuccessful in everything you do; day after day you will be oppressed and robbed, with no one to rescue you.
30You will be pledged to be married to a woman, but another will take her and ravish her. You will build a house, but you will not live in it. You will plant a vineyard, but you will not even begin
to enjoy its fruit. 31Your ox will be slaughtered before your eyes, but you will eat none of it. Your donkey will be forcibly taken from you and will not be returned. Your sheep will be given to your enemies, and no one will rescue them. 32Your sons and daughters will be given to another nation, and you will wear out your eyes
watching for them day after day, powerless to lift a hand. 33A peo-
ple that you do not know will eat what your land and labor produce, and you will have nothing but cruel oppression all your
days. 34The sights you see will drive you mad. 35The LORD will af-
flict your knees and legs with painful boils that cannot be cured, spreading from the soles of your feet to the top of your head.
36The LORD will drive you and the king you set over you to a nation unknown to you or your fathers. There you will worship other
gods, gods of wood and stone. 37You will become a thing of hor-
ror and an object of scorn and ridicule to all the nations where the LORD will drive you.
38You will sow much seed in the field but you will harvest little,

[a] 20 Hebrew *me*

(28:15) Father, Your gifts to us are as numerous and varied as the stars You have hung in the sky. And one of them is the gift of warning. We thank You for Your clear warnings to us. If You never spoke to us about the tragic consequences of disobedience, we would surely drift into the misery of rebellion more often than we do. We are indebted to You for Your faithful advice and admonition.

The voice of God is a friendly voice. No one need fear to listen to it unless he has already made up his mind to resist it.

A.W. Tozer (1897–1963)

I want a godly fear,
A quick discerning eye
That looks to Thee when sin is near
And sees the tempter fly;
A spirit still prepared
And armed with jealous care,
Forever standing on its guard
And watching unto prayer.

"Jesus, My Strength, My Hope"
Charles Wesley (1742)

because locusts will devour it. 39You will plant vineyards and cultivate them but you will not drink the wine or gather the grapes, because worms will eat them. 40You will have olive trees throughout your country but you will not use the oil, because the olives will drop off. 41You will have sons and daughters but you will not keep them, because they will go into captivity. 42Swarms of locusts will take over all your trees and the crops of your land.

43The alien who lives among you will rise above you higher and higher, but you will sink lower and lower. 44He will lend to you, but you will not lend to him. He will be the head, but you will be the tail.

45All these curses will come upon you. They will pursue you and overtake you until you are destroyed, because you did not obey the LORD your God and observe the commands and decrees he gave you. 46They will be a sign and a wonder to you and your descendants forever. 47Because you did not serve the LORD your God joyfully and gladly in the time of prosperity, 48therefore in hunger and thirst, in nakedness and dire poverty, you will serve the enemies the LORD sends against you. He will put an iron yoke on your neck until he has destroyed you.

49The LORD will bring a nation against you from far away, from the ends of the earth, like an eagle swooping down, a nation whose language you will not understand, 50a fierce-looking nation without respect for the old or pity for the young. 51They will devour the young of your livestock and the crops of your land until you are destroyed. They will leave you no grain, new wine or oil, nor any calves of your herds or lambs of your flocks until you are ruined. 52They will lay siege to all the cities throughout your land until the high fortified walls in which you trust fall down. They will besiege all the cities throughout the land the LORD your God is giving you.

53Because of the suffering that your enemy will inflict on you during the siege, you will eat the fruit of the womb, the flesh of the sons and daughters the LORD your God has given you. 54Even the most gentle and sensitive man among you will have no compassion on his own brother or the wife he loves or his surviving children, 55and he will not give to one of them any of the flesh of his children that he is eating. It will be all he has left because of the suffering your enemy will inflict on you during the siege of all your cities. 56The most gentle and sensitive woman among you—so sensitive and gentle that she would not venture to touch the ground with the sole of her foot—will begrudge the husband she loves and her own son or daughter 57the afterbirth from her womb and the children she bears. For she intends to eat them secretly during the siege and in the distress that your enemy will inflict on you in your cities.

58If you do not carefully follow all the words of this law, which are written in this book, and do not revere this glorious and awesome name—the LORD your God— 59the LORD will send fearful plagues on you and your descendants, harsh and prolonged disasters, and severe and lingering illnesses. 60He will bring upon you all the diseases of Egypt that you dreaded, and they will cling to you. 61The LORD will also bring on you every kind of sickness and disaster not recorded in this Book of the Law, until you are destroyed. 62You who were as numerous as the stars in the sky will be left but few in number, because you did not obey the LORD your God. 63Just as it pleased the LORD to make you prosper and

We all sin by needlessly disobeying the apostolic injunction to rejoice as much as by anything else.

C.S. Lewis (1898-1963)

(28:47–48) Gracious Father, You have given to us joyfully, so we will serve You with joy. We return to You not only the gifts that You have placed in our hands, but also the love that You have placed in our hearts. We give thanks to You for our prosperity; and we give to You from our prosperity with thanksgiving. Help us always to be thankful and so worship You acceptably with reverence and awe. (Heb 12:28)

increase in number, so it will please him to ruin and destroy you.
You will be uprooted from the land you are entering to possess.
64Then the LORD will scatter you among all nations, from one
end of the earth to the other. There you will worship other gods—
gods of wood and stone, which neither you nor your fathers have
known. 65Among those nations you will find no repose, no resting
place for the sole of your foot. There the LORD will give you an anxious mind, eyes weary with longing, and a despairing heart. 66You
will live in constant suspense, filled with dread both night and day,
never sure of your life. 67In the morning you will say, "If only it
were evening!" and in the evening, "If only it were morning!"—
because of the terror that will fill your hearts and the sights that
your eyes will see. 68The LORD will send you back in ships to Egypt
on a journey I said you should never make again. There you will
offer yourselves for sale to your enemies as male and female
slaves, but no one will buy you.

Renewal of the Covenant

29 These are the terms of the covenant the LORD commanded
Moses to make with the Israelites in Moab, in addition to
the covenant he had made with them at Horeb.
2Moses summoned all the Israelites and said to them:

Your eyes have seen all that the LORD did in Egypt to Pharaoh, to
all his officials and to all his land. 3With your own eyes you saw
those great trials, those miraculous signs and great wonders. 4But
to this day the LORD has not given you a mind that understands or
eyes that see or ears that hear. 5During the forty years that I led
you through the desert, your clothes did not wear out, nor did the
sandals on your feet. 6You ate no bread and drank no wine or
other fermented drink. I did this so that you might know that I am
the LORD your God.
7When you reached this place, Sihon king of Heshbon and Og
king of Bashan came out to fight against us, but we defeated them.
8We took their land and gave it as an inheritance to the Reubenites, the Gadites and the half-tribe of Manasseh.
9Carefully follow the terms of this covenant, so that you may
prosper in everything you do. 10All of you are standing today in the
presence of the LORD your God—your leaders and chief men, your
elders and officials, and all the other men of Israel, 11together
with your children and your wives, and the aliens living in your
camps who chop your wood and carry your water. 12You are
standing here in order to enter into a covenant with the LORD your
God, a covenant the LORD is making with you this day and sealing
with an oath, 13to confirm you this day as his people, that he may
be your God as he promised you and as he swore to your fathers,
Abraham, Isaac and Jacob. 14I am making this covenant, with its
oath, not only with you 15who are standing here with us today in
the presence of the LORD our God but also with those who are not
here today.
16You yourselves know how we lived in Egypt and how we
passed through the countries on the way here. 17You saw among
them their detestable images and idols of wood and stone, of silver and gold. 18Make sure there is no man or woman, clan or
tribe among you today whose heart turns away from the LORD our
God to go and worship the gods of those nations; make sure there
is no root among you that produces such bitter poison.
19When such a person hears the words of this oath, he invokes

(29:3–6) Sovereign Lord, through blessing or discipline You alone are the One true living and loving God. You whisper in my pain and shout in my success, "I am the Lord; there is no other!"

Divine love can admit no rival.
Johann Tauler (c.1300-1361)

(29:12–13) All of Your covenants are covenants of grace. If it were not for Your grace, we would never have a covenant with You. All would be lost if it were not for Your great love and compassion. Again and again, You reach beyond human frailty and extend Your hand of mercy. God of peace, Lord of love, why do You love us so much?

a blessing on himself and therefore thinks, "I will be safe, even
though I persist in going my own way." This will bring disaster on
the watered land as well as the dry.[a] 20The LORD will never be willing to forgive him; his wrath and zeal will burn against that man.
All the curses written in this book will fall upon him, and the LORD
will blot out his name from under heaven. 21The LORD will single
him out from all the tribes of Israel for disaster, according to all
the curses of the covenant written in this Book of the Law.

22Your children who follow you in later generations and foreigners who come from distant lands will see the calamities that
have fallen on the land and the diseases with which the LORD has
afflicted it. 23The whole land will be a burning waste of salt and
sulfur—nothing planted, nothing sprouting, no vegetation growing on it. It will be like the destruction of Sodom and Gomorrah,
Admah and Zeboiim, which the LORD overthrew in fierce anger.
24All the nations will ask: "Why has the LORD done this to this land?
Why this fierce, burning anger?"

25And the answer will be: "It is because this people abandoned
the covenant of the LORD, the God of their fathers, the covenant he
made with them when he brought them out of Egypt. 26They went
off and worshiped other gods and bowed down to them, gods they
did not know, gods he had not given them. 27Therefore the LORD's
anger burned against this land, so that he brought on it all the
curses written in this book. 28In furious anger and in great wrath
the LORD uprooted them from their land and thrust them into another land, as it is now."

29The secret things belong to the LORD our God, but the things
revealed belong to us and to our children forever, that we may follow all the words of this law.

Prosperity After Turning to the LORD

30 When all these blessings and curses I have set before you
come upon you and you take them to heart wherever the
LORD your God disperses you among the nations, 2and when you
and your children return to the LORD your God and obey him with
all your heart and with all your soul according to everything I
command you today, 3then the LORD your God will restore your
fortunes[b] and have compassion on you and gather you again from
all the nations where he scattered you. 4Even if you have been
banished to the most distant land under the heavens, from there
the LORD your God will gather you and bring you back. 5He will
bring you to the land that belonged to your fathers, and you will
take possession of it. He will make you more prosperous and numerous than your fathers. 6The LORD your God will circumcise
your hearts and the hearts of your descendants, so that you may
love him with all your heart and with all your soul, and live. 7The
LORD your God will put all these curses on your enemies who hate
and persecute you. 8You will again obey the LORD and follow all his
commands I am giving you today. 9Then the LORD your God will
make you most prosperous in all the work of your hands and in
the fruit of your womb, the young of your livestock and the crops
of your land. The LORD will again delight in you and make you
prosperous, just as he delighted in your fathers, 10if you obey the
LORD your God and keep his commands and decrees that are writ-

[a] *19* Or *way, in order to add drunkenness to thirst."* [b] *3* Or *will bring you back from captivity*

(29:29) Eternally wise and loving Father, I am grateful for the things that You have chosen to make plain to Your children in Your Word. May these revelations of grace and truth be sufficient for now as I anticipate the Day when I will know fully even as I am fully known. The secret things are Yours; the revealed things, mine. I will rest content. (Ps 25:14; 1Co 13:12)

(30:5–9) You have loved us with an everlasting love, heavenly Father, just as You have loved Your people in every generation. Why have You delighted Yourself in us and committed Yourself to our blessing? Certainly not because of our good behavior! No, Your kindness and love have providentially appeared in our lives, and You have saved us, not because of righteous things we have done, but because of Your mercy. (Tit 3:5)

ten in this Book of the Law and turn to the LORD your God with all your heart and with all your soul.

The Offer of Life or Death

11 Now what I am commanding you today is not too difficult for you or beyond your reach. 12 It is not up in heaven, so that you have to ask, "Who will ascend into heaven to get it and proclaim it to us so we may obey it?" 13 Nor is it beyond the sea, so that you have to ask, "Who will cross the sea to get it and proclaim it to us so we may obey it?" 14 No, the word is very near you; it is in your mouth and in your heart so you may obey it.

15 See, I set before you today life and prosperity, death and destruction. 16 For I command you today to love the LORD your God, to walk in his ways, and to keep his commands, decrees and laws; then you will live and increase, and the LORD your God will bless you in the land you are entering to possess.

17 But if your heart turns away and you are not obedient, and if you are drawn away to bow down to other gods and worship them, 18 I declare to you this day that you will certainly be destroyed. You will not live long in the land you are crossing the Jordan to enter and possess.

19 This day I call heaven and earth as witnesses against you that I have set before you life and death, blessings and curses. Now choose life, so that you and your children may live 20 and that you may love the LORD your God, listen to his voice, and hold fast to him. For the LORD is your life, and he will give you many years in the land he swore to give to your fathers, Abraham, Isaac and Jacob.

Joshua to Succeed Moses

31 Then Moses went out and spoke these words to all Israel: 2 "I am now a hundred and twenty years old and I am no longer able to lead you. The LORD has said to me, 'You shall not cross the Jordan.' 3 The LORD your God himself will cross over ahead of you. He will destroy these nations before you, and you will take possession of their land. Joshua also will cross over ahead of you, as the LORD said. 4 And the LORD will do to them what he did to Sihon and Og, the kings of the Amorites, whom he destroyed along with their land. 5 The LORD will deliver them to you, and you must do to them all that I have commanded you. 6 Be strong and courageous. Do not be afraid or terrified because of them, for the LORD your God goes with you; he will never leave you nor forsake you."

7 Then Moses summoned Joshua and said to him in the presence of all Israel, "Be strong and courageous, for you must go with this people into the land that the LORD swore to their forefathers to give them, and you must divide it among them as their inheritance. 8 The LORD himself goes before you and will be with you; he will never leave you nor forsake you. Do not be afraid; do not be discouraged."

The Reading of the Law

9 So Moses wrote down this law and gave it to the priests, the sons of Levi, who carried the ark of the covenant of the LORD, and to all the elders of Israel. 10 Then Moses commanded them: "At the end of every seven years, in the year for canceling debts, during the Feast of Tabernacles, 11 when all Israel comes to appear before

The Bible holds up before us ideals that are within sight of the weakest and the lowliest, and yet so high that the best and the noblest are kept with their faces turned ever upward.

William Jennings Bryan (1860–1925)

(30:11–14) Thank You, Father, for making Your commandments clear and accessible to me. Thank You for inspiring writers to record them for me to read, and for engraving them upon my soul so that I can remember them. "May the words of my mouth and the meditation of my heart be pleasing in Your sight, O LORD, my Rock and my Redeemer." (Ps 19:14)

(31:3) As You promised Your people of old, so You promise me today, "Never will I leave You, never will I forsake You." Lord, I want to be where You are. Go before me to prepare the way. Stay with me to direct my every step. Surround me with Your presence so that I may say with confidence, "The Lord is my helper; I will not be afraid. What can man do to me?" (Heb 13:5–6)

Abide with me!
Fast falls the eventide;
The darkness deepens:
Lord, with me abide!
When other helpers fail,
And comforts flee,
Help of the helpless
Oh, abide with me!

"Abide With Me"
Henry F. Lyte (1793-1847)

the LORD your God at the place he will choose, you shall read this
law before them in their hearing. 12Assemble the people—men,
women and children, and the aliens living in your towns—so they
can listen and learn to fear the LORD your God and follow carefully all the words of this law. 13Their children, who do not know this
law, must hear it and learn to fear the LORD your God as long as
you live in the land you are crossing the Jordan to possess."

Israel's Rebellion Predicted

14The LORD said to Moses, "Now the day of your death is near.
Call Joshua and present yourselves at the Tent of Meeting, where I
will commission him." So Moses and Joshua came and presented
themselves at the Tent of Meeting.

15Then the LORD appeared at the Tent in a pillar of cloud, and
the cloud stood over the entrance to the Tent. 16And the LORD said
to Moses: "You are going to rest with your fathers, and these people will soon prostitute themselves to the foreign gods of the land
they are entering. They will forsake me and break the covenant I
made with them. 17On that day I will become angry with them and
forsake them; I will hide my face from them, and they will be destroyed. Many disasters and difficulties will come upon them, and
on that day they will ask, 'Have not these disasters come upon us
because our God is not with us?' 18And I will certainly hide my
face on that day because of all their wickedness in turning to other
gods.

19"Now write down for yourselves this song and teach it to the
Israelites and have them sing it, so that it may be a witness for me
against them. 20When I have brought them into the land flowing
with milk and honey, the land I promised on oath to their forefathers, and when they eat their fill and thrive, they will turn to other
gods and worship them, rejecting me and breaking my covenant.
21And when many disasters and difficulties come upon them, this
song will testify against them, because it will not be forgotten by
their descendants. I know what they are disposed to do, even before I bring them into the land I promised them on oath." 22So
Moses wrote down this song that day and taught it to the Israelites.

23The LORD gave this command to Joshua son of Nun: "Be
strong and courageous, for you will bring the Israelites into the
land I promised them on oath, and I myself will be with you."

24After Moses finished writing in a book the words of this law
from beginning to end, 25he gave this command to the Levites who
carried the ark of the covenant of the LORD: 26"Take this Book of
the Law and place it beside the ark of the covenant of the LORD
your God. There it will remain as a witness against you. 27For I
know how rebellious and stiff-necked you are. If you have been
rebellious against the LORD while I am still alive and with you, how
much more will you rebel after I die! 28Assemble before me all the
elders of your tribes and all your officials, so that I can speak
these words in their hearing and call heaven and earth to testify
against them. 29For I know that after my death you are sure to become utterly corrupt and to turn from the way I have commanded
you. In days to come, disaster will fall upon you because you will
do evil in the sight of the LORD and provoke him to anger by what
your hands have made."

(31:20–21) Merciful God, how well You know the human heart—our propensities and fickleness. And yet, in Your love, You always protect, trust, hope and persevere. Even Your most severe acts of discipline are motivated by Your kindness, in the hope that we will come to repentance. (Ro 2:4; 1Co 13:6)

Our Father knows our weaknesses even better than we do, and he does not expect us to become saints overnight. But he does demand that we keep moving in that direction, or as the good old Methodist phrase puts it, that we continue "groaning toward perfection." At each step of the journey, the question that really matters is not whether we are a little farther along than some of our friends and neighbors, but how far we have progressed since yesterday.

Louis Cassels (1922-1974)

All the way my Savior leads me;
Cheers each winding path I tread,
Gives me grace for every trial,
Feeds me with the living bread;
Though my weary steps may falter,
And my soul a-thirst may be,
Gushing from the rock before me,
Lo! A spring of joy I see.

"All the Way My Savior Leads Me"
Fanny J. Crosby (1875)

The Song of Moses

30 And Moses recited the words of this song from beginning to end in the hearing of the whole assembly of Israel:

32 Listen, O heavens, and I will speak;
hear, O earth, the words of my mouth.
2 Let my teaching fall like rain
and my words descend like dew,
like showers on new grass,
like abundant rain on tender plants.

3 I will proclaim the name of the LORD.
Oh, praise the greatness of our God!
4 He is the Rock, his works are perfect,
and all his ways are just.
A faithful God who does no wrong,
upright and just is he.

5 They have acted corruptly toward him;
to their shame they are no longer his children,
but a warped and crooked generation.[a]
6 Is this the way you repay the LORD,
O foolish and unwise people?
Is he not your Father, your Creator,[b]
who made you and formed you?

7 Remember the days of old;
consider the generations long past.
Ask your father and he will tell you,
your elders, and they will explain to you.
8 When the Most High gave the nations their inheritance,
when he divided all mankind,
he set up boundaries for the peoples
according to the number of the sons of Israel.[c]
9 For the LORD's portion is his people,
Jacob his allotted inheritance.

10 In a desert land he found him,
in a barren and howling waste.
He shielded him and cared for him;
he guarded him as the apple of his eye,
11 like an eagle that stirs up its nest
and hovers over its young,
that spreads its wings to catch them
and carries them on its pinions.
12 The LORD alone led him;
no foreign god was with him.

13 He made him ride on the heights of the land
and fed him with the fruit of the fields.
He nourished him with honey from the rock,
and with oil from the flinty crag,
14 with curds and milk from herd and flock
and with fattened lambs and goats,
with choice rams of Bashan
and the finest kernels of wheat.
You drank the foaming blood of the grape.

[a] 5 Or *Corrupt are they and not his children, / a generation warped and twisted to their shame* [b] 6 Or *Father, who bought you* [c] 8 Masoretic Text; Dead Sea Scrolls (see also Septuagint) *sons of God*

(32:1–14) Lord God, we praise You for Your faithfulness to those whom You have chosen to be Your inheritance. Just as You brought ancient Israel through a dangerous wasteland, so You have also rescued us. You have brooded over us, nudged us along, and finally taught us to fly on the wings of the Spirit. Your nurturing care and gracious provision have strengthened and satisfied us. You alone are our God and Father. Apart from You, there is no savior.

Out of my shameful failure and loss,
Jesus, I come, Jesus, I come;
Into the glorious gain of Thy cross,
Jesus, I come to Thee.
Out of earth's sorrows into Thy balm,
Out of life's storms and into Thy calm,
Out of distress to jubilant psalm,
Jesus, I come to Thee.

"Jesus, I Come"
William T. Sleeper (1887)

15 Jeshurun[a] grew fat and kicked;
filled with food, he became heavy and sleek.
He abandoned the God who made him
and rejected the Rock his Savior.
16 They made him jealous with their foreign gods
and angered him with their detestable idols.
17 They sacrificed to demons, which are not God—
gods they had not known,
gods that recently appeared,
gods your fathers did not fear.
18 You deserted the Rock, who fathered you;
you forgot the God who gave you birth.

19 The LORD saw this and rejected them
because he was angered by his sons and daughters.
20 "I will hide my face from them," he said,
"and see what their end will be;
for they are a perverse generation,
children who are unfaithful.
21 They made me jealous by what is no god
and angered me with their worthless idols.
I will make them envious by those who are not a people;
I will make them angry by a nation that has no understanding.
22 For a fire has been kindled by my wrath,
one that burns to the realm of death[b] below.
It will devour the earth and its harvests
and set afire the foundations of the mountains.

23 "I will heap calamities upon them
and spend my arrows against them.
24 I will send wasting famine against them,
consuming pestilence and deadly plague;
I will send against them the fangs of wild beasts,
the venom of vipers that glide in the dust.
25 In the street the sword will make them childless;
in their homes terror will reign.
Young men and young women will perish,
infants and gray-haired men.
26 I said I would scatter them
and blot out their memory from mankind,
27 but I dreaded the taunt of the enemy,
lest the adversary misunderstand
and say, 'Our hand has triumphed;
the LORD has not done all this.'"

28 They are a nation without sense,
there is no discernment in them.
29 If only they were wise and would understand this
and discern what their end will be!
30 How could one man chase a thousand,
or two put ten thousand to flight,
unless their Rock had sold them,
unless the LORD had given them up?
31 For their rock is not like our Rock,
as even our enemies concede.

[a] *15 Jeshurun* means *the upright one*, that is, Israel. [b] *22* Hebrew *to Sheol*

Our salvation, thank God, depends much more on his love of us than on our love of him.

Father Andrew (1869-1946)

(32:15–30) God of our fathers, as we read about the unfaithfulness of Your people of old, we stand condemned along with them. In our prosperity, we too have turned our eyes away from You. Like them, we have allowed worthless idols and diabolical powers to deceive us. We have surely angered You with our spiritual promiscuity. But though we deserve Your wrath, Lord, we have received Your mercy. Jesus died in our place. We are unspeakably grateful, for You have laid upon Him the iniquity of us all. (Isa 53:6; Jnh 2:8)

O how the world to evil allures me!
O how my heart is tempted to sin!
I must tell Jesus, and He will help me
Over the world the vict'ry to win!

"I Must Tell Jesus"
Elisha A. Hoffman (1894)

It is but right that our hearts should be on God, when the heart of God is so much on us.

Richard Baxter (1615-1691)

(32:31–47) O Lord, Your love for Your people is stronger than death. Your jealousy is more determined than the grave. Your love burns like a mighty flame: the greatest oceans cannot quench it; all the rivers in the world cannot wash it away. In fierce love and severe mercy, You have allowed us to be wounded, only to raise us up, restore us to new life, and destroy our enemy in the process. How can we even begin to respond to Your everlasting love but through awe, humility and obedience? (SS 8:6–7)

Out of my bondage, sorrow and
night,
Jesus, I come, Jesus, I come;
Into Thy freedom, gladness and light,
Jesus, I come to Thee.
Out of my sickness into Thy health,
Out of my want and into Thy
wealth,
Out of my sin and into Thyself,
Jesus, I come to Thee.

"Jesus, I Come"
William T. Sleeper (1887)

32 Their vine comes from the vine of Sodom
and from the fields of Gomorrah.
Their grapes are filled with poison,
and their clusters with bitterness.
33 Their wine is the venom of serpents,
the deadly poison of cobras.

34 "Have I not kept this in reserve
and sealed it in my vaults?
35 It is mine to avenge; I will repay.
In due time their foot will slip;
their day of disaster is near
and their doom rushes upon them."

36 The LORD will judge his people
and have compassion on his servants
when he sees their strength is gone
and no one is left, slave or free.
37 He will say: "Now where are their gods,
the rock they took refuge in,
38 the gods who ate the fat of their sacrifices
and drank the wine of their drink offerings?
Let them rise up to help you!
Let them give you shelter!

39 "See now that I myself am He!
There is no god besides me.
I put to death and I bring to life,
I have wounded and I will heal,
and no one can deliver out of my hand.
40 I lift my hand to heaven and declare:
As surely as I live forever,
41 when I sharpen my flashing sword
and my hand grasps it in judgment,
I will take vengeance on my adversaries
and repay those who hate me.
42 I will make my arrows drunk with blood,
while my sword devours flesh:
the blood of the slain and the captives,
the heads of the enemy leaders."

43 Rejoice, O nations, with his people,[a,b]
for he will avenge the blood of his servants;
he will take vengeance on his enemies
and make atonement for his land and people.

44 Moses came with Joshua[c] son of Nun and spoke all the words
of this song in the hearing of the people. 45 When Moses finished
reciting all these words to all Israel, 46 he said to them, "Take to
heart all the words I have solemnly declared to you this day, so
that you may command your children to obey carefully all the
words of this law. 47 They are not just idle words for you—they are
your life. By them you will live long in the land you are crossing
the Jordan to possess."

[a] 43 Or *Make his people rejoice, O nations* [b] 43 Masoretic Text; Dead Sea Scrolls (see also Septuagint) *people, / and let all the angels worship him /* [c] 44 Hebrew *Hoshea*, a variant of *Joshua*

Moses to Die on Mount Nebo

48On that same day the LORD told Moses, 49"Go up into the Abarim Range to Mount Nebo in Moab, across from Jericho, and
view Canaan, the land I am giving the Israelites as their own possession. 50There on the mountain that you have climbed you will
die and be gathered to your people, just as your brother Aaron
died on Mount Hor and was gathered to his people. 51This is because both of you broke faith with me in the presence of the Israelites at the waters of Meribah Kadesh in the Desert of Zin and
because you did not uphold my holiness among the Israelites.
52Therefore, you will see the land only from a distance; you will
not enter the land I am giving to the people of Israel."

Moses Blesses the Tribes

33 This is the blessing that Moses the man of God pronounced on the Israelites before his death. 2He said:

"The LORD came from Sinai
and dawned over them from Seir;
he shone forth from Mount Paran.
He came with[a] myriads of holy ones
from the south, from his mountain slopes.[b]
3Surely it is you who love the people;
all the holy ones are in your hand.
At your feet they all bow down,
and from you receive instruction,
4the law that Moses gave us,
the possession of the assembly of Jacob.
5He was king over Jeshurun[c]
when the leaders of the people assembled,
along with the tribes of Israel.

6"Let Reuben live and not die,
nor[d] his men be few."

7And this he said about Judah:

"Hear, O LORD, the cry of Judah;
bring him to his people.
With his own hands he defends his cause.
Oh, be his help against his foes!"

8About Levi he said:

"Your Thummim and Urim belong
to the man you favored.
You tested him at Massah;
you contended with him at the waters of Meribah.
9He said of his father and mother,
'I have no regard for them.'
He did not recognize his brothers
or acknowledge his own children,
but he watched over your word
and guarded your covenant.
10He teaches your precepts to Jacob
and your law to Israel.
He offers incense before you

[a]2 Or *from* [b]2 The meaning of the Hebrew for this phrase is uncertain.
[c]5 *Jeshurun* means *the upright one,* that is, Israel; also in verse 26. [d]6 Or *but let*

(32:48–52) Lord God, You and Your will are unfathomable. You have mercy on whom You have mercy, and You have compassion on whom You have compassion. Your dealings with Your servant Moses are mysterious, but in Your holiness You can do nothing but what is right and just. As the Psalmist has written: "One thing God has spoken, two things have I heard: that you, O God, are strong, and that you , O Lord, are loving. Surely You will reward each person according to what he has done." (Ps 62:11–12; Ro 9:15)

Self-will should be so completely poured out of the vessel of the soul into the ocean of the will of God, that whatever God may will, that at once the soul should will; and that whatever God may allow, that the soul should at once willingly embrace, whether it may be in itself sweet or bitter.

Louis de Blois (1506-1566)

(33:1–29) Father in heaven, just as Moses bestowed on each of Israel's tribes a specific blessing based on their particular characteristics, so You bless every one of us individually, honoring our unique personalities. Thank You for encouraging us in our areas of frailty, empowering us in our areas of strength, and enriching our talents and capabilities with Your supernatural power. You have made each of us a one-of-a-kind work of art, created in Christ Jesus to do good works, which You have prepared in advance for us to do. (Eph 2:10)

God gives to every man the virtue, temper, understanding, taste that lifts him into life and lets him fall just in the niche he was ordained to fall.
William Cowper (1731-1800)

and whole burnt offerings on your altar.
11 Bless all his skills, O LORD,
and be pleased with the work of his hands.
Smite the loins of those who rise up against him;
strike his foes till they rise no more."

12 About Benjamin he said:

"Let the beloved of the LORD rest secure in him,
for he shields him all day long,
and the one the LORD loves rests between his shoulders."

13 About Joseph he said:

"May the LORD bless his land
with the precious dew from heaven above
and with the deep waters that lie below;
14 with the best the sun brings forth
and the finest the moon can yield;
15 with the choicest gifts of the ancient mountains
and the fruitfulness of the everlasting hills;
16 with the best gifts of the earth and its fullness
and the favor of him who dwelt in the burning bush.
Let all these rest on the head of Joseph,
on the brow of the prince among[a] his brothers.
17 In majesty he is like a firstborn bull;
his horns are the horns of a wild ox.
With them he will gore the nations,
even those at the ends of the earth.
Such are the ten thousands of Ephraim;
such are the thousands of Manasseh."

18 About Zebulun he said:

"Rejoice, Zebulun, in your going out,
and you, Issachar, in your tents.
19 They will summon peoples to the mountain
and there offer sacrifices of righteousness;
they will feast on the abundance of the seas,
on the treasures hidden in the sand."

20 About Gad he said:

"Blessed is he who enlarges Gad's domain!
Gad lives there like a lion,
tearing at arm or head.
21 He chose the best land for himself;
the leader's portion was kept for him.
When the heads of the people assembled,
he carried out the LORD's righteous will,
and his judgments concerning Israel."

22 About Dan he said:

"Dan is a lion's cub,
springing out of Bashan."

23 About Naphtali he said:

"Naphtali is abounding with the favor of the LORD

[a] 16 Or *of the one separated from*

MY BELOVED

I am the eternal God, your Refuge. And underneath you are My everlasting arms.

My grace is sufficient for you, for My power is made perfect in weakness.

So do not be anxious about anything, but in everything, by prayer and petition, with thanksgiving, present your requests to Me. And My peace, which transcends understanding, will stand guard over your heart and your mind.

When you were in great need I saved you. Be at rest once more, My child, for I have been good to you. I have delivered your soul from death, your eyes from tears, your feet from stumbling so that you may walk before Me in the land of the living.

When the cords of death entangle you, when the anguish of the grave comes upon you, when you are overcome with trouble and sorrow, call upon My name.

I will reach down from on high and take hold of you; I will draw you out of the deep waters. I will rescue you from your powerful enemy, from your foes who are too strong for you. Though they confront you in the day of your disaster, I will be your support. I will bring you into a spacious place; I will rescue you because I delight in you. I will quiet you with My love; I will rejoice over you with singing.

So, My loved one, rest secure in Me, for I will shield you all day long. You are the one I love; come rest between My shoulders.

Dt 33:12,27; Ps 18:16-19; 116:3-5,6-9; Zep 3:17; 2Co 12:9; Php 4:6-7

and is full of his blessing;
he will inherit southward to the lake."

24 About Asher he said:

"Most blessed of sons is Asher;
let him be favored by his brothers,
and let him bathe his feet in oil.
25 The bolts of your gates will be iron and bronze,
and your strength will equal your days.

26 "There is no one like the God of Jeshurun,
who rides on the heavens to help you
and on the clouds in his majesty.
27 The eternal God is your refuge,
and underneath are the everlasting arms.
He will drive out your enemy before you,
saying, 'Destroy him!'
28 So Israel will live in safety alone;
Jacob's spring is secure
in a land of grain and new wine,
where the heavens drop dew.
29 Blessed are you, O Israel!
Who is like you,
a people saved by the LORD?
He is your shield and helper
and your glorious sword.
Your enemies will cower before you,
and you will trample down their high places.[a]"

The Death of Moses

34 Then Moses climbed Mount Nebo from the plains of Moab
to the top of Pisgah, across from Jericho. There the LORD
showed him the whole land—from Gilead to Dan, 2 all of Naphtali,
the territory of Ephraim and Manasseh, all the land of Judah as far
as the western sea,[b] 3 the Negev and the whole region from the Valley of Jericho, the City of Palms, as far as Zoar. 4 Then the LORD said
to him, "This is the land I promised on oath to Abraham, Isaac and
Jacob when I said, 'I will give it to your descendants.' I have let you
see it with your eyes, but you will not cross over into it."
5 And Moses the servant of the LORD died there in Moab, as the
LORD had said. 6 He buried him[c] in Moab, in the valley opposite
Beth Peor, but to this day no one knows where his grave is. 7 Moses
was a hundred and twenty years old when he died, yet his eyes were
not weak nor his strength gone. 8 The Israelites grieved for Moses
in the plains of Moab thirty days, until the time of weeping and
mourning was over.
9 Now Joshua son of Nun was filled with the spirit[d] of wisdom because Moses had laid his hands on him. So the Israelites listened to
him and did what the LORD had commanded Moses.
10 Since then, no prophet has risen in Israel like Moses, whom
the LORD knew face to face, 11 who did all those miraculous signs
and wonders the LORD sent him to do in Egypt—to Pharaoh and to
all his officials and to his whole land. 12 For no one has ever shown
the mighty power or performed the awesome deeds that Moses
did in the sight of all Israel.

[a] 29 Or *will tread upon their bodies* [b] 2 That is, the Mediterranean [c] 6 Or *He was buried* [d] 9 Or *Spirit*

(34:1–12) God, You stand forever with Your arms outstretched between heaven and earth, meting out eternal justice with one hand, extending tender mercies with the other. Before Moses closed his eyes in death, You showed him the land of promise, a land he would never enter because of his disobedience. Then You gently buried him Yourself, in a secret place known only to You—a sacred interment befitting one who had known You face to face. How You loved him, in spite of his failings! And how You love each of us, sparing us our own well-deserved death sentence; having buried and raised to eternal life Your only begotten Son.

Our faults are like a grain of sand beside the great mountain of the mercies of God.
Saint Jean Baptiste Marie Vianney (1786–1859)

Eternal life, raise me from death;
Eternal brightness, help me see;
Eternal Spirit, give me breath;
Eternal Savior, come to me.

Until by Your most costly grace,
Invited by Your holy Word,
At last I come before Your face
To know You, my eternal God.
"Eternal Light, Shine in My Heart"
Christopher Idle (©1982)

Joshua

The Book of JOSHUA

God is the original promise maker and promise keeper. That which He had promised to Abraham, and then to Moses, begins to be fulfilled in the book of Joshua. In this book we encounter God as the faithful Lord Who keeps all of His promises (23:10).

This book focuses on the conquest (1:1—12:24) and division (13:1—19:51) of Canaan. For the Israelites, this land is more than real estate. It is a gift from God, the inheritance that God had promised in His foundational covenant with Abraham: "On that day the LORD made a covenant with Abram and said, 'To your descendants I give this land' " (Ge 15:18). In the land God's people can worship Him as a "kingdom of priests and a holy nation" (Ex 19:6). From this land God will ultimately bless all the nations of the earth (Ge 12:3).

This ultimate blessing seems far away from the immediate story of Joshua, however, where God commands Israel to destroy the Canaanites completely (e.g., 10:40). We wonder: How can God have willed such destruction? Knowing the abominations of the Canaanites and their cancerous Baal worship helps us answer this question. But we must also remember just how much God seeks worship that is guided by His word alone and not tainted by the idolatries of any culture. In fact, our struggle to understand God's actions in Joshua protects us from our own cultural idol—a cuddly lap dog "god" who happily permits us to have many other divine pets. The God of Joshua is a warrior, a judge and a jealous God who will never share His people or their worship with other "gods."

Our commitment to God is not some relic from the past worthy of our reminiscence, but a living relationship that deserves regular renewal.

The story of Joshua ends with his farewell address, in which he reminds the people of how God has kept all of His promises (ch. 23). Joshua calls the Israelites to do everything written in the law as their loving response. Gathering all the tribes together at Shechem (ch 24), he challenges them to choose whom they will serve, either the true God or the pagan gods. Having been warned by Joshua of the penalties for breaking the covenant, the Israelites reaffirm their commitment to serve God alone. In their act of covenant renewal we are reminded that our commitment to God is not some relic from the past worthy of our reminiscence, but a living relationship that deserves regular renewal.

Through faith in Christ we share in the promises of God once made to Israel (Eph 3:6). Moreover, through Christ we experience God's ultimate promise keeping: "For no matter how many promises God has made, they are 'Yes' in Christ" (2Co 1:20). Though we live in this world as aliens, we are citizens of heaven who will one day be fully transformed into heavenly glory (Php 3:20–21). Thus we worship God in gratitude for His grace poured out in Christ, and in hope of a glorious future in His promised land.

The LORD Commands Joshua

1 After the death of Moses the servant of the LORD, the LORD said to Joshua son of Nun, Moses' aide: 2"Moses my servant is dead. Now then, you and all these people, get ready to cross the Jordan River into the land I am about to give to them—to the Israelites. 3I will give you every place where you set your foot, as I promised Moses. 4Your territory will extend from the desert to Lebanon, and from the great river, the Euphrates—all the Hittite country—to the Great Sea[a] on the west. 5No one will be able to stand up against you all the days of your life. As I was with Moses, so I will be with you; I will never leave you nor forsake you.

6"Be strong and courageous, because you will lead these people to inherit the land I swore to their forefathers to give them. 7Be strong and very courageous. Be careful to obey all the law my servant Moses gave you; do not turn from it to the right or to the left, that you may be successful wherever you go. 8Do not let this Book of the Law depart from your mouth; meditate on it day and night, so that you may be careful to do everything written in it. Then you will be prosperous and successful. 9Have I not commanded you? Be strong and courageous. Do not be terrified; do not be discouraged, for the LORD your God will be with you wherever you go."

10So Joshua ordered the officers of the people: 11"Go through the camp and tell the people, 'Get your supplies ready. Three days from now you will cross the Jordan here to go in and take possession of the land the LORD your God is giving you for your own.' "

12But to the Reubenites, the Gadites and the half-tribe of Manasseh, Joshua said, 13"Remember the command that Moses the servant of the LORD gave you: 'The LORD your God is giving you rest and has granted you this land.' 14Your wives, your children and your livestock may stay in the land that Moses gave you east of the Jordan, but all your fighting men, fully armed, must cross over ahead of your brothers. You are to help your brothers 15until the LORD gives them rest, as he has done for you, and until they too have taken possession of the land that the LORD your God is giving them. After that, you may go back and occupy your own land, which Moses the servant of the LORD gave you east of the Jordan toward the sunrise."

16Then they answered Joshua, "Whatever you have commanded us we will do, and wherever you send us we will go. 17Just as we fully obeyed Moses, so we will obey you. Only may the LORD your God be with you as he was with Moses. 18Whoever rebels against your word and does not obey your words, whatever you may command them, will be put to death. Only be strong and courageous!"

Rahab and the Spies

2 Then Joshua son of Nun secretly sent two spies from Shittim. "Go, look over the land," he said, "especially Jericho." So they went and entered the house of a prostitute[b] named Rahab and stayed there.

2The king of Jericho was told, "Look! Some of the Israelites have come here tonight to spy out the land." 3So the king of Jericho sent this message to Rahab: "Bring out the men who came to

[a] 4 That is, the Mediterranean [b] 1 Or possibly *an innkeeper*

(1:1–5) Thank You, Lord, that You are always moving forward—never static, always dynamic. You are the constant One. Your servants come and go, but You are always with us. I praise You that even for me today Your awesome promise holds true: "As I was with Moses, so I will be with you; I will never leave you nor forsake you."

(1:6–9) Almighty God, again and again You have said, "Be strong and courageous." You have reminded me that fear of anything or anyone but You is unfit for me. You and You alone are to be feared, and Your Word is the compass that will guide me into the way of life. How I thank You for the courage I draw from Your mighty presence and for the wisdom and direction Your Word provides. Apart from You I can do nothing; but I can do everything through Christ who gives me strength. (Jn 15:5; Php 4:13)

Therefore with mind entire, faith firm, courage undaunted, love thorough, let us be ready for whatever God wills; faithfully keeping His commandment, having innocence in simplicity, peaceableness in love, modesty in lowliness, diligence in ministering, mercifulness in helping the poor, firmness in standing for truth, and sternness in keeping of discipline.

Bede the Venerable (673-735)

Be bold, be strong
For the Lord thy God is with thee
Do not be afraid
Do not be dismayed
Walk in faith and victory
For the Lord thy God is with thee
Run through the camp
Tell everybody, "Get ready! Get ready!"
Are you ready to take the land?
Are you ready to take a stand?
Are you ready to take this land for the Lord?
I'm bold, I'm strong
For the Lord my God is with me
I am not afraid
I am not dismayed
I'm walking in faith and victory
For the Lord my God is with me.

"Be Bold, Be Strong"
Morris Chapman (©1984)

(2:4–14) How marvelous, my God, that in Your plans You make space and place for people like Rahab, the one-time harlot. Surely, then, there is place for me with all my sins and shortcomings. Take me, make me, use even me in the fulfillment of Your mysterious plans and purposes.

We're not to spend our days in watching our own vices, in gazing at our own sins, in stirring and raking up all the mud of our past lives; but to lift our thoughts from our own corrupt nature to Him who put on that nature in order to deliver it from corruption, and to fix our contemplations and our affections on Him who came to clothe us in His perfect righteousness, and through whom and in whom, if we are united to Him by a living faith, we too become righteous.

Augustus Hare (1792-1834)
and Julius Charles Hare (1795-1855)

(2:21) Lord, we praise You for remembering us, for rescuing us, for redeeming us. For every generation You have been a saving God. In spite of our sin, You have looked for the scarlet cord, the crimson mark of the Passover lamb, the covering of Jesus' blood. And when You see evidence of our faith, Your grace and mercy save us. Father, we praise you today for your surprising and awesome salvation.

you and entered your house, because they have come to spy out
the whole land."
4But the woman had taken the two men and hidden them. She
said, "Yes, the men came to me, but I did not know where they
had come from. 5At dusk, when it was time to close the city gate,
the men left. I don't know which way they went. Go after them
quickly. You may catch up with them." 6(But she had taken them
up to the roof and hidden them under the stalks of flax she had
laid out on the roof.) 7So the men set out in pursuit of the spies
on the road that leads to the fords of the Jordan, and as soon as
the pursuers had gone out, the gate was shut.
8Before the spies lay down for the night, she went up on the
roof 9and said to them, "I know that the LORD has given this land
to you and that a great fear of you has fallen on us, so that all who
live in this country are melting in fear because of you. 10We have
heard how the LORD dried up the water of the Red Sea[a] for you
when you came out of Egypt, and what you did to Sihon and Og,
the two kings of the Amorites east of the Jordan, whom you completely destroyed.[b] 11When we heard of it, our hearts melted and
everyone's courage failed because of you, for the LORD your God is
God in heaven above and on the earth below. 12Now then, please
swear to me by the LORD that you will show kindness to my family,
because I have shown kindness to you. Give me a sure sign 13that
you will spare the lives of my father and mother, my brothers and
sisters, and all who belong to them, and that you will save us from
death."
14"Our lives for your lives!" the men assured her. "If you don't
tell what we are doing, we will treat you kindly and faithfully when
the LORD gives us the land."
15So she let them down by a rope through the window, for the
house she lived in was part of the city wall. 16Now she had said to
them, "Go to the hills so the pursuers will not find you. Hide yourselves there three days until they return, and then go on your way."
17The men said to her, "This oath you made us swear will not
be binding on us 18unless, when we enter the land, you have tied
this scarlet cord in the window through which you let us down,
and unless you have brought your father and mother, your brothers and all your family into your house. 19If anyone goes outside
your house into the street, his blood will be on his own head; we
will not be responsible. As for anyone who is in the house with
you, his blood will be on our head if a hand is laid on him. 20But
if you tell what we are doing, we will be released from the oath you
made us swear."
21"Agreed," she replied. "Let it be as you say." So she sent them
away and they departed. And she tied the scarlet cord in the window.
22When they left, they went into the hills and stayed there three
days, until the pursuers had searched all along the road and returned without finding them. 23Then the two men started back.
They went down out of the hills, forded the river and came to Joshua son of Nun and told him everything that had happened to them.
24They said to Joshua, "The LORD has surely given the whole land
into our hands; all the people are melting in fear because of us."

[a] 10 Hebrew *Yam Suph*; that is, Sea of Reeds [b] 10 The Hebrew term refers to the irrevocable giving over of things or persons to the LORD, often by totally destroying them.

Crossing the Jordan

3 Early in the morning Joshua and all the Israelites set out from Shittim and went to the Jordan, where they camped before crossing over. 2After three days the officers went throughout the camp, 3giving orders to the people: "When you see the ark of the covenant of the LORD your God, and the priests, who are Levites, carrying it, you are to move out from your positions and follow it. 4Then you will know which way to go, since you have never been this way before. But keep a distance of about a thousand yards[a] between you and the ark; do not go near it."

5Joshua told the people, "Consecrate yourselves, for tomorrow the LORD will do amazing things among you."

6Joshua said to the priests, "Take up the ark of the covenant and pass on ahead of the people." So they took it up and went ahead of them.

7And the LORD said to Joshua, "Today I will begin to exalt you in the eyes of all Israel, so they may know that I am with you as I was with Moses. 8Tell the priests who carry the ark of the covenant: 'When you reach the edge of the Jordan's waters, go and stand in the river.' "

9Joshua said to the Israelites, "Come here and listen to the words of the LORD your God. 10This is how you will know that the living God is among you and that he will certainly drive out before you the Canaanites, Hittites, Hivites, Perizzites, Girgashites, Amorites and Jebusites. 11See, the ark of the covenant of the Lord of all the earth will go into the Jordan ahead of you. 12Now then, choose twelve men from the tribes of Israel, one from each tribe. 13And as soon as the priests who carry the ark of the LORD—the Lord of all the earth—set foot in the Jordan, its waters flowing downstream will be cut off and stand up in a heap."

14So when the people broke camp to cross the Jordan, the priests carrying the ark of the covenant went ahead of them. 15Now the Jordan is at flood stage all during harvest. Yet as soon as the priests who carried the ark reached the Jordan and their feet touched the water's edge, 16the water from upstream stopped flowing. It piled up in a heap a great distance away, at a town called Adam in the vicinity of Zarethan, while the water flowing down to the Sea of the Arabah (the Salt Sea[b]) was completely cut off. So the people crossed over opposite Jericho. 17The priests who carried the ark of the covenant of the LORD stood firm on dry ground in the middle of the Jordan, while all Israel passed by until the whole nation had completed the crossing on dry ground.

4 When the whole nation had finished crossing the Jordan, the LORD said to Joshua, 2"Choose twelve men from among the people, one from each tribe, 3and tell them to take up twelve stones from the middle of the Jordan from right where the priests stood and to carry them over with you and put them down at the place where you stay tonight."

4So Joshua called together the twelve men he had appointed from the Israelites, one from each tribe, 5and said to them, "Go over before the ark of the LORD your God into the middle of the Jordan. Each of you is to take up a stone on his shoulder, according to the number of the tribes of the Israelites, 6to serve as a sign among you. In the future, when your children ask you,

[a] *4* Hebrew *about two thousand cubits* (about 900 meters) [b] *16* That is, the Dead Sea

(3:17) Father, I have my own Jordans to cross—formidable obstacles and challenges to face. I know You have good plans for me, but You will not take me further than I am willing to go. Help me to be strong and courageous, Father. I want to move forward, to plant my feet in the unpredictable waters, to step into the future You have planned for me. May Your presence go before me, move within me and press in behind me, until I take that first terrifying step of faith and I am on my way. Without You I can do nothing.

If God wants you to do something, he'll make it possible for you to do it, but the grace he provides comes only with the task and cannot be stockpiled beforehand. We are dependent on him from hour to hour, and the greater our awareness of this fact, the less likely we are to faint or fail in a crisis.

Louis Cassels (1922–1974)

When I tread the verge of Jordan,
Bid my anxious fears subside;
Death of death and hell's
destruction,
Land me safe on Canaan's side.
Songs and praises, songs and praises,
I will raise forevermore,
I will raise forevermore.

"Guide Me, O Thou Great Jehovah"
William Williams (1717–1791)

'What do these stones mean?' 7tell them that the flow of the Jordan was cut off before the ark of the covenant of the LORD. When
it crossed the Jordan, the waters of the Jordan were cut off.
These stones are to be a memorial to the people of Israel
forever."

8So the Israelites did as Joshua commanded them. They took
twelve stones from the middle of the Jordan, according to the
number of the tribes of the Israelites, as the LORD had told Joshua; and they carried them over with them to their camp, where
they put them down. 9Joshua set up the twelve stones that had
been[a] in the middle of the Jordan at the spot where the priests
who carried the ark of the covenant had stood. And they are there
to this day.

10Now the priests who carried the ark remained standing in
the middle of the Jordan until everything the LORD had commanded Joshua was done by the people, just as Moses had directed Joshua. The people hurried over, 11and as soon as all of
them had crossed, the ark of the LORD and the priests came to the
other side while the people watched. 12The men of Reuben, Gad
and the half-tribe of Manasseh crossed over, armed, in front of
the Israelites, as Moses had directed them. 13About forty thousand armed for battle crossed over before the LORD to the plains
of Jericho for war.

14That day the LORD exalted Joshua in the sight of all Israel;
and they revered him all the days of his life, just as they had revered Moses.

15Then the LORD said to Joshua, 16"Command the priests carrying the ark of the Testimony to come up out of the Jordan."

17So Joshua commanded the priests, "Come up out of the Jordan."

18And the priests came up out of the river carrying the ark of
the covenant of the LORD. No sooner had they set their feet on the
dry ground than the waters of the Jordan returned to their place
and ran at flood stage as before.

19On the tenth day of the first month the people went up from
the Jordan and camped at Gilgal on the eastern border of Jericho.
20And Joshua set up at Gilgal the twelve stones they had taken out
of the Jordan. 21He said to the Israelites, "In the future when your
descendants ask their fathers, 'What do these stones mean?' 22tell
them, 'Israel crossed the Jordan on dry ground.' 23For the LORD
your God dried up the Jordan before you until you had crossed
over. The LORD your God did to the Jordan just what he had done
to the Red Sea[b] when he dried it up before us until we had
crossed over. 24He did this so that all the peoples of the earth
might know that the hand of the LORD is powerful and so that you
might always fear the LORD your God."

Circumcision at Gilgal

5 Now when all the Amorite kings west of the Jordan and all the
Canaanite kings along the coast heard how the LORD had
dried up the Jordan before the Israelites until we had crossed
over, their hearts melted and they no longer had the courage to
face the Israelites.

2At that time the LORD said to Joshua, "Make flint knives and

(4:7–9) Lord, help us to remember the mighty things You have done for us. Sometimes, like the Israelites, we are blind to Your great favors; we fail to remember your works in our lives. At other times we are so overwhelmed by Your works that we assume we will always remember and that we need no memorial. In either case, we eventually forget. Teach us, therefore, to put in place some tokens of remembrance, recalling all You have done for us: in words, or art, or song, or even sculpted stone. May we never forget Your mighty deeds of love and grace.

If we keep silent
The rocks will cry out,
Blessed be the King.
And if we don't praise Him
The earth will shout:
Blessed be the King.

Sing hallelujah, sing hallelujah,
Let all the world
Sing praises to the King.

"Let All the World Sing Praises"
Chris Falson (©1996)

[a] 9 Or *Joshua also set up twelve stones* [b] 23 Hebrew *Yam Suph*; that is, Sea of Reeds

circumcise the Israelites again." 3So Joshua made flint knives and circumcised the Israelites at Gibeath Haaraloth.[a]

4Now this is why he did so: All those who came out of Egypt—all the men of military age—died in the desert on the way after leaving Egypt. 5All the people that came out had been circumcised, but all the people born in the desert during the journey from Egypt had not. 6The Israelites had moved about in the desert forty years until all the men who were of military age when they left Egypt had died, since they had not obeyed the LORD. For the LORD had sworn to them that they would not see the land that he had solemnly promised their fathers to give us, a land flowing with milk and honey. 7So he raised up their sons in their place, and these were the ones Joshua circumcised. They were still uncircumcised because they had not been circumcised on the way. 8And after the whole nation had been circumcised, they remained where they were in camp until they were healed.

9Then the LORD said to Joshua, "Today I have rolled away the reproach of Egypt from you." So the place has been called Gilgal[b] to this day.

10On the evening of the fourteenth day of the month, while camped at Gilgal on the plains of Jericho, the Israelites celebrated the Passover. 11The day after the Passover, that very day, they ate some of the produce of the land: unleavened bread and roasted grain. 12The manna stopped the day after[c] they ate this food from the land; there was no longer any manna for the Israelites, but that year they ate of the produce of Canaan.

The Fall of Jericho

13Now when Joshua was near Jericho, he looked up and saw a man standing in front of him with a drawn sword in his hand. Joshua went up to him and asked, "Are you for us or for our enemies?"

14"Neither," he replied, "but as commander of the army of the LORD I have now come." Then Joshua fell facedown to the ground in reverence, and asked him, "What message does my Lord[d] have for his servant?"

15The commander of the LORD's army replied, "Take off your sandals, for the place where you are standing is holy." And Joshua did so.

6 Now Jericho was tightly shut up because of the Israelites. No one went out and no one came in.

2Then the LORD said to Joshua, "See, I have delivered Jericho into your hands, along with its king and its fighting men. 3March around the city once with all the armed men. Do this for six days. 4Have seven priests carry trumpets of rams' horns in front of the ark. On the seventh day, march around the city seven times, with the priests blowing the trumpets. 5When you hear them sound a long blast on the trumpets, have all the people give a loud shout; then the wall of the city will collapse and the people will go up, every man straight in."

6So Joshua son of Nun called the priests and said to them, "Take up the ark of the covenant of the LORD and have seven priests carry trumpets in front of it." 7And he ordered the people, "Advance! March around the city, with the armed guard going ahead of the ark of the LORD."

[a] 3 *Gibeath Haaraloth* means *hill of foreskins.* [b] 9 *Gilgal* sounds like the Hebrew for *roll.* [c] 12 Or *the day* [d] 14 Or *lord*

What we need in religion is not new light, but new sight; not new paths, but new strength to walk in the old ones; not new duties, but new strength from on high to fulfill those that are plain to us.

Tryon Edwards (1809-1894)

(5:4–9) Lord, I am overwhelmed when I consider how negligent I can be in my wilderness times. Yet Your grace is always abundant. Thank You, heavenly Father, that You are the God of the second chance. Circumcise my heart, Lord. Roll away the reproach of my slavery to sin so that I may love You with all my heart and soul. (Dt 30:6)

(5:14—6:2) O Commander of the hosts of heaven, O Lord, mighty in battle, You do not come to take sides—You come to take over! Only You are holy, and You only fight for holy causes—Your causes. You do not align Yourself with our purposes; rather, we must align ourselves with Yours and cooperate with You in what You are doing on the earth. The coming battle at Jericho was not Joshua's battle—it was Yours. You planned the strategy, You chose the timing, You gave the orders and You brought the ultimate victory. Today, in the struggles we face as Your church and as Your children, help us to follow Your command. Come and take over. Induct us into Your army and use us as weapons in Your spiritual battle.

Those know best how to command that know how to obey.

Matthew Henry (1662-1714)

To accept the will of God never leads to the miserable feeling that it is useless to strive anymore. God does not ask for the dull, weak, sleepy acquiescence of indolence. He asks for something vivid and strong. He asks us to cooperate with him, actively willing what he wills, our only aim his glory.

Amy Carmichael (1867-1951)

(6:1–21) Lord, Your power is amazing—it takes my breath away. You can do anything You want, through whomever You wish to use. It is astonishing to think that the huge walls of a fortified city could crumble while Your people simply marched around it, blew on trumpets and shouted. In simple human terms, Your instructions seem absurd. Yet You accomplished Your purposes through the simple obedience of Your people. Teach me today to listen to Your instructions and to obey, no matter how little I understand. And I will praise You as I stand and see Your will accomplished through my life. Now to You who are able to do immeasurably more than all I ask or imagine, according to Your power that is at work within me, to You be glory in the church and in Christ Jesus throughout all generations, for ever and ever. Amen. (Eph 3:20–21)

8When Joshua had spoken to the people, the seven priests carrying the seven trumpets before the LORD went forward, blowing their trumpets, and the ark of the LORD's covenant followed them. 9The armed guard marched ahead of the priests who blew the trumpets, and the rear guard followed the ark. All this time the trumpets were sounding. 10But Joshua had commanded the people, "Do not give a war cry, do not raise your voices, do not say a word until the day I tell you to shout. Then shout!" 11So he had the ark of the LORD carried around the city, circling it once. Then the people returned to camp and spent the night there.

12Joshua got up early the next morning and the priests took up the ark of the LORD. 13The seven priests carrying the seven trumpets went forward, marching before the ark of the LORD and blowing the trumpets. The armed men went ahead of them and the rear guard followed the ark of the LORD, while the trumpets kept sounding. 14So on the second day they marched around the city once and returned to the camp. They did this for six days.

15On the seventh day, they got up at daybreak and marched around the city seven times in the same manner, except that on that day they circled the city seven times. 16The seventh time around, when the priests sounded the trumpet blast, Joshua commanded the people, "Shout! For the LORD has given you the city! 17The city and all that is in it are to be devoted[a] to the LORD. Only Rahab the prostitute[b] and all who are with her in her house shall be spared, because she hid the spies we sent. 18But keep away from the devoted things, so that you will not bring about your own destruction by taking any of them. Otherwise you will make the camp of Israel liable to destruction and bring trouble on it. 19All the silver and gold and the articles of bronze and iron are sacred to the LORD and must go into his treasury."

20When the trumpets sounded, the people shouted, and at the sound of the trumpet, when the people gave a loud shout, the wall collapsed; so every man charged straight in, and they took the city. 21They devoted the city to the LORD and destroyed with the sword every living thing in it—men and women, young and old, cattle, sheep and donkeys.

22Joshua said to the two men who had spied out the land, "Go into the prostitute's house and bring her out and all who belong to her, in accordance with your oath to her." 23So the young men who had done the spying went in and brought out Rahab, her father and mother and brothers and all who belonged to her. They brought out her entire family and put them in a place outside the camp of Israel.

24Then they burned the whole city and everything in it, but they put the silver and gold and the articles of bronze and iron into the treasury of the LORD's house. 25But Joshua spared Rahab the prostitute, with her family and all who belonged to her, because she hid the men Joshua had sent as spies to Jericho—and she lives among the Israelites to this day.

26At that time Joshua pronounced this solemn oath: "Cursed before the LORD is the man who undertakes to rebuild this city, Jericho:

"At the cost of his firstborn son

[a] *17* The Hebrew term refers to the irrevocable giving over of things or persons to the LORD, often by totally destroying them; also in verses 18 and 21. [b] *17* Or possibly *innkeeper*; also in verses 22 and 25

will he lay its foundations;
at the cost of his youngest
will he set up its gates."

27 So the LORD was with Joshua, and his fame spread throughout the land.

Achan's Sin

7 But the Israelites acted unfaithfully in regard to the devoted things[a]; Achan son of Carmi, the son of Zimri,[b] the son of Zerah, of the tribe of Judah, took some of them. So the LORD's anger burned against Israel.

2 Now Joshua sent men from Jericho to Ai, which is near Beth Aven to the east of Bethel, and told them, "Go up and spy out the region." So the men went up and spied out Ai.

3 When they returned to Joshua, they said, "Not all the people will have to go up against Ai. Send two or three thousand men to take it and do not weary all the people, for only a few men are there." 4 So about three thousand men went up; but they were routed by the men of Ai, 5 who killed about thirty-six of them. They chased the Israelites from the city gate as far as the stone quarries[c] and struck them down on the slopes. At this the hearts of the people melted and became like water.

6 Then Joshua tore his clothes and fell facedown to the ground before the ark of the LORD, remaining there till evening. The elders of Israel did the same, and sprinkled dust on their heads. 7 And Joshua said, "Ah, Sovereign LORD, why did you ever bring this people across the Jordan to deliver us into the hands of the Amorites to destroy us? If only we had been content to stay on the other side of the Jordan! 8 O Lord, what can I say, now that Israel has been routed by its enemies? 9 The Canaanites and the other people of the country will hear about this and they will surround us and wipe out our name from the earth. What then will you do for your own great name?"

10 The LORD said to Joshua, "Stand up! What are you doing down on your face? 11 Israel has sinned; they have violated my covenant, which I commanded them to keep. They have taken some of the devoted things; they have stolen, they have lied, they have put them with their own possessions. 12 That is why the Israelites cannot stand against their enemies; they turn their backs and run because they have been made liable to destruction. I will not be with you anymore unless you destroy whatever among you is devoted to destruction.

13 "Go, consecrate the people. Tell them, 'Consecrate yourselves in preparation for tomorrow; for this is what the LORD, the God of Israel, says: That which is devoted is among you, O Israel. You cannot stand against your enemies until you remove it.

14 " 'In the morning, present yourselves tribe by tribe. The tribe that the LORD takes shall come forward clan by clan; the clan that the LORD takes shall come forward family by family; and the family that the LORD takes shall come forward man by man. 15 He who is caught with the devoted things shall be destroyed by fire, along with all that belongs to him. He has violated the covenant of the LORD and has done a disgraceful thing in Israel!' "

[a] *1* The Hebrew term refers to the irrevocable giving over of things or persons to the LORD, often by totally destroying them; also in verses 11, 12, 13 and 15. [b] *1* See Septuagint and 1 Chron. 2:6; Hebrew *Zabdi*; also in verses 17 and 18. [c] *5* Or *as far as Shebarim*

(7:1–21) You brought to light what was hidden in darkness and exposed the motives of Achan's heart. Sin had entered the camp through one man, and death through sin, in that many died through Achan's disobedience. If it were not for Your great mercy and the gift of Your grace through Jesus Christ, we too would be consumed by Your anger. For You have set our iniquities before You, our secret sins in the light of Your presence. Lord, spare me from the sin of Achan. May I never take for myself what is rightfully Yours. May I never be deceived by wealth or serve the god of materialism. Help me to walk in obedience to You so that nothing in my life will hinder the flow of blessing to those around me. (Ps 90:7–8; Ro 5:12–15; 1Co 4:5)

Dark is the stain that we cannot hide
What can avail to wash it away?
Look! There is flowing a crimson tide;
Whiter than snow you may be today.

Grace, grace, God's grace,
Grace that will pardon and cleanse within!
Grace, grace, God's grace,
Grace that is greater than all our sin!

"Grace Greater Than Our Sin"
Julia H. Johnston (1849–1919)

16Early the next morning Joshua had Israel come forward by tribes, and Judah was taken. 17The clans of Judah came forward, and he took the Zerahites. He had the clan of the Zerahites come forward by families, and Zimri was taken. 18Joshua had his family come forward man by man, and Achan son of Carmi, the son of Zimri, the son of Zerah, of the tribe of Judah, was taken.

19Then Joshua said to Achan, "My son, give glory to the LORD,[a] the God of Israel, and give him the praise.[b] Tell me what you have done; do not hide it from me."

20Achan replied, "It is true! I have sinned against the LORD, the God of Israel. This is what I have done: 21When I saw in the plunder a beautiful robe from Babylonia,[c] two hundred shekels[d] of silver and a wedge of gold weighing fifty shekels,[e] I coveted them and took them. They are hidden in the ground inside my tent, with the silver underneath."

22So Joshua sent messengers, and they ran to the tent, and there it was, hidden in his tent, with the silver underneath. 23They took the things from the tent, brought them to Joshua and all the Israelites and spread them out before the LORD.

24Then Joshua, together with all Israel, took Achan son of Zerah, the silver, the robe, the gold wedge, his sons and daughters, his cattle, donkeys and sheep, his tent and all that he had, to the Valley of Achor. 25Joshua said, "Why have you brought this trouble on us? The LORD will bring trouble on you today."

Then all Israel stoned him, and after they had stoned the rest, they burned them. 26Over Achan they heaped up a large pile of rocks, which remains to this day. Then the LORD turned from his fierce anger. Therefore that place has been called the Valley of Achor[f] ever since.

Ai Destroyed

8 Then the LORD said to Joshua, "Do not be afraid; do not be discouraged. Take the whole army with you, and go up and attack Ai. For I have delivered into your hands the king of Ai, his people, his city and his land. 2You shall do to Ai and its king as you did to Jericho and its king, except that you may carry off their plunder and livestock for yourselves. Set an ambush behind the city."

3So Joshua and the whole army moved out to attack Ai. He chose thirty thousand of his best fighting men and sent them out at night 4with these orders: "Listen carefully. You are to set an ambush behind the city. Don't go very far from it. All of you be on the alert. 5I and all those with me will advance on the city, and when the men come out against us, as they did before, we will flee from them. 6They will pursue us until we have lured them away from the city, for they will say, 'They are running away from us as they did before.' So when we flee from them, 7you are to rise up from ambush and take the city. The LORD your God will give it into your hand. 8When you have taken the city, set it on fire. Do what the LORD has commanded. See to it; you have my orders."

9Then Joshua sent them off, and they went to the place of ambush and lay in wait between Bethel and Ai, to the west of Ai—but Joshua spent that night with the people.

10Early the next morning Joshua mustered his men, and he and

[a] *19* A solemn charge to tell the truth [b] *19* Or *and confess to him* [c] *21* Hebrew *Shinar* [d] *21* That is, about 5 pounds (about 2.3 kilograms) [e] *21* That is, about 1 1/4 pounds (about 0.6 kilogram) [f] *26* *Achor* means *trouble.*

(8:1–2) Lord, sometimes we can accomplish Your tasks by ourselves. Sometimes Your work requires a few more individuals. But at other times we must "take the whole army" and move together with all Your people. I praise You for the church, the earthly body of Christ, and for its power and effectiveness when all members move together to accomplish Your work. As long as I live, Lord, keep me with Your people and make our hands strong to accomplish the things You call us to do together.

(8:9) God, You are the master strategist. In one battle You supernaturally brought down city walls with a trumpet blast and a shout. In another You defeated an enemy through ordinary military operations. By whatever means You choose to employ, Your triumph requires but one human contribution: our humble obedience.

the leaders of Israel marched before them to Ai. 11The entire force that was with him marched up and approached the city and arrived in front of it. They set up camp north of Ai, with the valley between them and the city. 12Joshua had taken about five thousand men and set them in ambush between Bethel and Ai, to the west of the city. 13They had the soldiers take up their positions—all those in the camp to the north of the city and the ambush to the west of it. That night Joshua went into the valley.

14When the king of Ai saw this, he and all the men of the city hurried out early in the morning to meet Israel in battle at a certain place overlooking the Arabah. But he did not know that an ambush had been set against him behind the city. 15Joshua and all Israel let themselves be driven back before them, and they fled toward the desert. 16All the men of Ai were called to pursue them, and they pursued Joshua and were lured away from the city. 17Not a man remained in Ai or Bethel who did not go after Israel. They left the city open and went in pursuit of Israel.

18Then the LORD said to Joshua, "Hold out toward Ai the javelin that is in your hand, for into your hand I will deliver the city." So Joshua held out his javelin toward Ai. 19As soon as he did this, the men in the ambush rose quickly from their position and rushed forward. They entered the city and captured it and quickly set it on fire.

20The men of Ai looked back and saw the smoke of the city rising against the sky, but they had no chance to escape in any direction, for the Israelites who had been fleeing toward the desert had turned back against their pursuers. 21For when Joshua and all Israel saw that the ambush had taken the city and that smoke was going up from the city, they turned around and attacked the men of Ai. 22The men of the ambush also came out of the city against them, so that they were caught in the middle, with Israelites on both sides. Israel cut them down, leaving them neither survivors nor fugitives. 23But they took the king of Ai alive and brought him to Joshua.

24When Israel had finished killing all the men of Ai in the fields and in the desert where they had chased them, and when every one of them had been put to the sword, all the Israelites returned to Ai and killed those who were in it. 25Twelve thousand men and women fell that day—all the people of Ai. 26For Joshua did not draw back the hand that held out his javelin until he had destroyed[a] all who lived in Ai. 27But Israel did carry off for themselves the livestock and plunder of this city, as the LORD had instructed Joshua.

28So Joshua burned Ai and made it a permanent heap of ruins, a desolate place to this day. 29He hung the king of Ai on a tree and left him there until evening. At sunset, Joshua ordered them to take his body from the tree and throw it down at the entrance of the city gate. And they raised a large pile of rocks over it, which remains to this day.

The Covenant Renewed at Mount Ebal

30Then Joshua built on Mount Ebal an altar to the LORD, the God of Israel, 31as Moses the servant of the LORD had commanded the Israelites. He built it according to what is written in the Book of the Law of Moses—an altar of uncut stones, on which no iron tool

I used to ask God to help me. Then I asked if I might help him. I ended up by asking him to do his work through me.
James Hudson Taylor (1832-1905)

(8:14–19) O holy God, when the Israelites first attacked Ai they failed to seek Your counsel or Your cleansing. Instead, they devised their own plan and harbored secret sin in their midst. If they had only asked You first, You might have exposed their hidden sin and spared them their disaster. For when they humbly sought Your face and rid themselves of the sin in their camp, You led them to victory. O Lord, cleanse Your church today from secret sins. Bring to light what is hidden in darkness and expose the motives of our hearts. Purify us so that we can move forward in Your righteousness from victory to victory. (Jos 7:1–5; 1Co 4:5)

Lead on, O King Eternal,
The day of march has come;
Henceforth in fields of conquest
Thy tents shall be our home.
Thro' days of preparation
Thy grace has made us strong;
And now, O King Eternal,
We lift our battle song.
"Lead On, O King Eternal"
Ernest W. Shurtleff (1862-1917)

[a] 26 The Hebrew term refers to the irrevocable giving over of things or persons to the LORD, often by totally destroying them.

had been used. On it they offered to the LORD burnt offerings and
sacrificed fellowship offerings.[a] **32**There, in the presence of the
Israelites, Joshua copied on stones the law of Moses, which he
had written. **33**All Israel, aliens and citizens alike, with their elders, officials and judges, were standing on both sides of the ark
of the covenant of the LORD, facing those who carried it—the
priests, who were Levites. Half of the people stood in front of
Mount Gerizim and half of them in front of Mount Ebal, as Moses
the servant of the LORD had formerly commanded when he gave instructions to bless the people of Israel.

34Afterward, Joshua read all the words of the law—the blessings and the curses—just as it is written in the Book of the Law.
35There was not a word of all that Moses had commanded that
Joshua did not read to the whole assembly of Israel, including the
women and children, and the aliens who lived among them.

The Gibeonite Deception

9 Now when all the kings west of the Jordan heard about these
things—those in the hill country, in the western foothills, and
along the entire coast of the Great Sea[b] as far as Lebanon (the
kings of the Hittites, Amorites, Canaanites, Perizzites, Hivites and
Jebusites)— **2**they came together to make war against Joshua and
Israel.

3However, when the people of Gibeon heard what Joshua had
done to Jericho and Ai, **4**they resorted to a ruse: They went as a
delegation whose donkeys were loaded[c] with worn-out sacks and
old wineskins, cracked and mended. **5**The men put worn and
patched sandals on their feet and wore old clothes. All the bread
of their food supply was dry and moldy. **6**Then they went to Joshua in the camp at Gilgal and said to him and the men of Israel,
"We have come from a distant country; make a treaty with us."

7The men of Israel said to the Hivites, "But perhaps you live
near us. How then can we make a treaty with you?"

8"We are your servants," they said to Joshua.

But Joshua asked, "Who are you and where do you come
from?"

9They answered: "Your servants have come from a very distant
country because of the fame of the LORD your God. For we have
heard reports of him: all that he did in Egypt, **10**and all that he did
to the two kings of the Amorites east of the Jordan—Sihon king of
Heshbon, and Og king of Bashan, who reigned in Ashtaroth. **11**And
our elders and all those living in our country said to us, 'Take provisions for your journey; go and meet them and say to them, "We
are your servants; make a treaty with us." ' **12**This bread of ours
was warm when we packed it at home on the day we left to come
to you. But now see how dry and moldy it is. **13**And these wineskins that we filled were new, but see how cracked they are. And
our clothes and sandals are worn out by the very long journey."

14The men of Israel sampled their provisions but did not inquire of the LORD. **15**Then Joshua made a treaty of peace with them
to let them live, and the leaders of the assembly ratified it by oath.

16Three days after they made the treaty with the Gibeonites, the
Israelites heard that they were neighbors, living near them. **17**So
the Israelites set out and on the third day came to their cities: Gib-

[a] *31* Traditionally *peace offerings* [b] *1* That is, the Mediterranean [c] *4* Most Hebrew manuscripts; some Hebrew manuscripts, Vulgate and Syriac (see also Septuagint) *They prepared provisions and loaded their donkeys*

(8:34–35) Joshua remembered Your instruction, Lord: "Be careful to obey all the law . . . not turn from it to the right or to the left." And once he had come to a respite from the battle, he faithfully read Your word to Your people. As You did with Joshua, place in me a reverence for Your Word and for Your ways. Teach me to hear You clearly and to obey You completely. (Jos 1:7)

(9:3–4) Lord, when Your people are deceived the consequences are far-reaching and destructive. This is sobering, because we know all too well how clever our enemy is and how susceptible we are to his ploys. Please, Lord, give us discernment, that we might recognize the deceptions that would lead us astray or deter us from walking in the center Your will.

(9:14) O God, You are the source of wisdom and understanding. I need Your guidance so desperately. All I have to do is ask, and You will give it generously. Help me not to rely on my own insights. Hear me, Lord, and answer me, as I seek Your will and direction in every situation of my life. (Jas 1:5)

eon, Kephirah, Beeroth and Kiriath Jearim. 18 But the Israelites did
not attack them, because the leaders of the assembly had sworn an
oath to them by the LORD, the God of Israel.

The whole assembly grumbled against the leaders, 19 but all the
leaders answered, "We have given them our oath by the LORD, the
God of Israel, and we cannot touch them now. 20 This is what we
will do to them: We will let them live, so that wrath will not fall on
us for breaking the oath we swore to them." 21 They continued,
"Let them live, but let them be woodcutters and water carriers for
the entire community." So the leaders' promise to them was kept.

22 Then Joshua summoned the Gibeonites and said, "Why did
you deceive us by saying, 'We live a long way from you,' while actually you live near us? 23 You are now under a curse: You will
never cease to serve as woodcutters and water carriers for the
house of my God."

24 They answered Joshua, "Your servants were clearly told how
the LORD your God had commanded his servant Moses to give you
the whole land and to wipe out all its inhabitants from before you.
So we feared for our lives because of you, and that is why we did
this. 25 We are now in your hands. Do to us whatever seems good
and right to you."

26 So Joshua saved them from the Israelites, and they did not
kill them. 27 That day he made the Gibeonites woodcutters and
water carriers for the community and for the altar of the LORD at
the place the LORD would choose. And that is what they are to this
day.

The Sun Stands Still

10 Now Adoni-Zedek king of Jerusalem heard that Joshua had
taken Ai and totally destroyed[a] it, doing to Ai and its king as
he had done to Jericho and its king, and that the people of Gibeon had made a treaty of peace with Israel and were living near
them. 2 He and his people were very much alarmed at this, because Gibeon was an important city, like one of the royal cities; it
was larger than Ai, and all its men were good fighters. 3 So Adoni-
Zedek king of Jerusalem appealed to Hoham king of Hebron,
Piram king of Jarmuth, Japhia king of Lachish and Debir king of
Eglon. 4 "Come up and help me attack Gibeon," he said, "because
it has made peace with Joshua and the Israelites."

5 Then the five kings of the Amorites—the kings of Jerusalem,
Hebron, Jarmuth, Lachish and Eglon—joined forces. They moved
up with all their troops and took up positions against Gibeon and
attacked it.

6 The Gibeonites then sent word to Joshua in the camp at Gilgal:
"Do not abandon your servants. Come up to us quickly and save
us! Help us, because all the Amorite kings from the hill country
have joined forces against us."

7 So Joshua marched up from Gilgal with his entire army, including all the best fighting men. 8 The LORD said to Joshua, "Do
not be afraid of them; I have given them into your hand. Not one
of them will be able to withstand you."

9 After an all-night march from Gilgal, Joshua took them by surprise. 10 The LORD threw them into confusion before Israel, who
defeated them in a great victory at Gibeon. Israel pursued them
along the road going up to Beth Horon and cut them down all the

[a] 1 The Hebrew term refers to the irrevocable giving over of things or persons to the LORD, often by totally destroying them; also in verses 28, 35, 37, 39 and 40.

(10:8) Lord God, just as Israel failed to inquire of You about the Gibeonites, so I have not always pleased You or submitted to Your authority. Father, You and I both know that the consequences of my sins have been costly. But even as I have sought to remain faithful to my unwise commitments, You have stood alongside me, strengthening my hand, protecting my interests and even working out all my foolishness for the best because of Your love and mercy. Thank You, heavenly Father, for being greater than my greatest mistakes. (Ro 8:28)

Ever and everywhere a mighty battle is raging around us, a battle in which we are all volunteers, aye, and enrolled soldiers on either side the great silent internal battle, of lust against purity, of truth against falsehood, of right against wrong. It needs no splendid occasion, no stately amphitheater, no pomp and prodigality of outward circumstances: for its seat is in the human heart. But its effects and issues are in the world.

Frederick William Faber (1814–1863)

Nature is but a name for an effect whose cause is God.

William Cowper (1731-1800)

(10:12–13) Almighty God, when You fight for Your people all of the forces of the universe are at Your command. You can choose to arrest a heavenly body as readily as You can halt an earthly one. I marvel and worship that here You heard the voice of a man who dared to ask the impossible. He asked boldly and You acted powerfully. You did not let the sun go down on Your wrath, and You left no foothold for the enemies of Your people. Israel brought this fight upon themselves because they did not seek Your guidance in their relationship with the Gibeonites, yet You were faithful to fight for them and secure their peace. (Eph 4:26–27)

Holy, holy, holy
Is our Lord God Almighty
He alone is worthy,
Awesome Lord, Mighty King.

He reigns through all the universe,
His glory covers all the earth.
His pow'r displayed in mighty works,
And we proclaim Him as our Lord
and King.

"He Reigns"
Janet Grossman (©1988)

way to Azekah and Makkedah. 11As they fled before Israel on the
road down from Beth Horon to Azekah, the LORD hurled large hailstones down on them from the sky, and more of them died from
the hailstones than were killed by the swords of the Israelites.
12On the day the LORD gave the Amorites over to Israel, Joshua
said to the LORD in the presence of Israel:

"O sun, stand still over Gibeon,
O moon, over the Valley of Aijalon."
13So the sun stood still,
and the moon stopped,
till the nation avenged itself on[a] its enemies,

as it is written in the Book of Jashar.

The sun stopped in the middle of the sky and delayed going
down about a full day. 14There has never been a day like it before
or since, a day when the LORD listened to a man. Surely the LORD
was fighting for Israel!
15Then Joshua returned with all Israel to the camp at Gilgal.

Five Amorite Kings Killed

16Now the five kings had fled and hidden in the cave at Makkedah. 17When Joshua was told that the five kings had been found
hiding in the cave at Makkedah, 18he said, "Roll large rocks up to
the mouth of the cave, and post some men there to guard it. 19But
don't stop! Pursue your enemies, attack them from the rear and
don't let them reach their cities, for the LORD your God has given
them into your hand."

20So Joshua and the Israelites destroyed them completely—almost to a man—but the few who were left reached their fortified
cities. 21The whole army then returned safely to Joshua in the
camp at Makkedah, and no one uttered a word against the Israelites.
22Joshua said, "Open the mouth of the cave and bring those five
kings out to me." 23So they brought the five kings out of the
cave—the kings of Jerusalem, Hebron, Jarmuth, Lachish and
Eglon. 24When they had brought these kings to Joshua, he summoned all the men of Israel and said to the army commanders
who had come with him, "Come here and put your feet on the
necks of these kings." So they came forward and placed their feet
on their necks.
25Joshua said to them, "Do not be afraid; do not be discouraged. Be strong and courageous. This is what the LORD will do to
all the enemies you are going to fight." 26Then Joshua struck and
killed the kings and hung them on five trees, and they were left
hanging on the trees until evening.
27At sunset Joshua gave the order and they took them down
from the trees and threw them into the cave where they had been
hiding. At the mouth of the cave they placed large rocks, which are
there to this day.
28That day Joshua took Makkedah. He put the city and its king
to the sword and totally destroyed everyone in it. He left no survivors. And he did to the king of Makkedah as he had done to the
king of Jericho.

[a] 13 Or *nation triumphed over*

Southern Cities Conquered

29Then Joshua and all Israel with him moved on from Makkedah to Libnah and attacked it. 30The LORD also gave that city and
its king into Israel's hand. The city and everyone in it Joshua put
to the sword. He left no survivors there. And he did to its king as
he had done to the king of Jericho.

31Then Joshua and all Israel with him moved on from Libnah to
Lachish; he took up positions against it and attacked it. 32The LORD
handed Lachish over to Israel, and Joshua took it on the second
day. The city and everyone in it he put to the sword, just as he had
done to Libnah. 33Meanwhile, Horam king of Gezer had come up
to help Lachish, but Joshua defeated him and his army—until no
survivors were left.

34Then Joshua and all Israel with him moved on from Lachish
to Eglon; they took up positions against it and attacked it. 35They
captured it that same day and put it to the sword and totally destroyed everyone in it, just as they had done to Lachish.

36Then Joshua and all Israel with him went up from Eglon to
Hebron and attacked it. 37They took the city and put it to the
sword, together with its king, its villages and everyone in it. They
left no survivors. Just as at Eglon, they totally destroyed it and
everyone in it.

38Then Joshua and all Israel with him turned around and attacked Debir. 39They took the city, its king and its villages, and put
them to the sword. Everyone in it they totally destroyed. They left
no survivors. They did to Debir and its king as they had done to
Libnah and its king and to Hebron.

40So Joshua subdued the whole region, including the hill country, the Negev, the western foothills and the mountain slopes, together with all their kings. He left no survivors. He totally destroyed all who breathed, just as the LORD, the God of Israel, had
commanded. 41Joshua subdued them from Kadesh Barnea to Gaza
and from the whole region of Goshen to Gibeon. 42All these kings
and their lands Joshua conquered in one campaign, because the
LORD, the God of Israel, fought for Israel.

43Then Joshua returned with all Israel to the camp at Gilgal.

Northern Kings Defeated

11 When Jabin king of Hazor heard of this, he sent word to
Jobab king of Madon, to the kings of Shimron and Acshaph,
2and to the northern kings who were in the mountains, in the Arabah south of Kinnereth, in the western foothills and in Naphoth
Dor[a] on the west; 3to the Canaanites in the east and west; to the
Amorites, Hittites, Perizzites and Jebusites in the hill country; and
to the Hivites below Hermon in the region of Mizpah. 4They came
out with all their troops and a large number of horses and chariots—a huge army, as numerous as the sand on the seashore. 5All
these kings joined forces and made camp together at the Waters of
Merom, to fight against Israel.

6The LORD said to Joshua, "Do not be afraid of them, because by
this time tomorrow I will hand all of them over to Israel, slain. You
are to hamstring their horses and burn their chariots."

7So Joshua and his whole army came against them suddenly at
the Waters of Merom and attacked them, 8and the LORD gave them
into the hand of Israel. They defeated them and pursued them all

[a]2 Or *in the heights of Dor*

(10:30–43) After Your people's failure to consult with You about the Gibeonites, they seemed all the more committed to Your will. And as they carefully submitted to You, You fought for them and gave them glorious success. Teach me, Lord, to learn from my failures. If You have stood beside me in spite of my disobedience, how much more will You help me when I obey?

(11:1–6) Lord, You are mighty in battle, and the battle is Yours, not mine. No foe can stand against You. So help me not to be afraid or discouraged in the face of adversity. Strengthen me as I take up my position, and grant me faith and courage as I stand firm and watch Your deliverance. Help me to fight the good fight of the faith and to do all that You direct me to do. (1Ti 6:12)

The Bible nowhere indicates that God withdraws us from the troubles of life. In fact, we become more involved in life's troubles when we come to Christ. But he gives us power to go on with the battle.

Billy Graham (1918-)

(11:20) O Lord, at times I wonder why You allow so many obstacles to stand in my way. I would gladly ignore them, negotiate with them or take a different course, but You require that I confront them anyway. Then, after the conflict is over, I see that You have raised those obstacles up in order to destroy them, once and for all, so that my future peace will not be threatened. How I thank You for Your foresight, Your wisdom, and Your determination to complete the good work that You have begun in my life. (Php 1:6)

God knows, not I, the reason why
His winds of storm drive through my door;
I am content to live or die
Just knowing this, nor knowing more.
My Father's hand appointing me
My days and ways, so I am free.

Margaret Sangster (1838–1912)

the way to Greater Sidon, to Misrephoth Maim, and to the Valley of
Mizpah on the east, until no survivors were left. [9]Joshua did to
them as the LORD had directed: He hamstrung their horses and
burned their chariots.

[10]At that time Joshua turned back and captured Hazor and put
its king to the sword. (Hazor had been the head of all these kingdoms.) [11]Everyone in it they put to the sword. They totally destroyed[a] them, not sparing anything that breathed, and he burned
up Hazor itself.

[12]Joshua took all these royal cities and their kings and put them
to the sword. He totally destroyed them, as Moses the servant of the
LORD had commanded. [13]Yet Israel did not burn any of the cities
built on their mounds—except Hazor, which Joshua burned. [14]The
Israelites carried off for themselves all the plunder and livestock of
these cities, but all the people they put to the sword until they completely destroyed them, not sparing anyone that breathed. [15]As the
LORD commanded his servant Moses, so Moses commanded Joshua, and Joshua did it; he left nothing undone of all that the LORD
commanded Moses.

[16]So Joshua took this entire land: the hill country, all the Negev,
the whole region of Goshen, the western foothills, the Arabah and
the mountains of Israel with their foothills, [17]from Mount Halak,
which rises toward Seir, to Baal Gad in the Valley of Lebanon below
Mount Hermon. He captured all their kings and struck them down,
putting them to death. [18]Joshua waged war against all these kings
for a long time. [19]Except for the Hivites living in Gibeon, not one city
made a treaty of peace with the Israelites, who took them all in battle. [20]For it was the LORD himself who hardened their hearts to wage
war against Israel, so that he might destroy them totally, extermi-
nating them without mercy, as the LORD had commanded Moses.

[21]At that time Joshua went and destroyed the Anakites from the
hill country: from Hebron, Debir and Anab, from all the hill country of Judah, and from all the hill country of Israel. Joshua totally
destroyed them and their towns. [22]No Anakites were left in Israelite territory; only in Gaza, Gath and Ashdod did any survive. [23]So
Joshua took the entire land, just as the LORD had directed Moses,
and he gave it as an inheritance to Israel according to their tribal
divisions.

Then the land had rest from war.

List of Defeated Kings

12 These are the kings of the land whom the Israelites had defeated and whose territory they took over east of the Jordan,
from the Arnon Gorge to Mount Hermon, including all the eastern
side of the Arabah:

[2]Sihon king of the Amorites,
who reigned in Heshbon. He ruled from Aroer on the rim of
the Arnon Gorge—from the middle of the gorge—to the Jabbok River, which is the border of the Ammonites. This included half of Gilead. [3]He also ruled over the eastern Arabah
from the Sea of Kinnereth[b] to the Sea of the Arabah (the Salt
Sea[c]), to Beth Jeshimoth, and then southward below the
slopes of Pisgah.

[a] *11* The Hebrew term refers to the irrevocable giving over of things or persons to the LORD, often by totally destroying them; also in verses 12, 20 and 21. [b] *3* That is, Galilee
[c] *3* That is, the Dead Sea

4 And the territory of Og king of Bashan,
one of the last of the Rephaites, who reigned in Ashtaroth
and Edrei. 5 He ruled over Mount Hermon, Salecah, all of Bashan to the border of the people of Geshur and Maacah, and
half of Gilead to the border of Sihon king of Heshbon.

6 Moses, the servant of the LORD, and the Israelites conquered
them. And Moses the servant of the LORD gave their land to the
Reubenites, the Gadites and the half-tribe of Manasseh to be their
possession.

7 These are the kings of the land that Joshua and the Israelites
conquered on the west side of the Jordan, from Baal Gad in the
Valley of Lebanon to Mount Halak, which rises toward Seir (their
lands Joshua gave as an inheritance to the tribes of Israel according to their tribal divisions— 8 the hill country, the western
foothills, the Arabah, the mountain slopes, the desert and the
Negev—the lands of the Hittites, Amorites, Canaanites, Perizzites,
Hivites and Jebusites):

9 the king of Jericho	one
the king of Ai (near Bethel)	one
10 the king of Jerusalem	one
the king of Hebron	one
11 the king of Jarmuth	one
the king of Lachish	one
12 the king of Eglon	one
the king of Gezer	one
13 the king of Debir	one
the king of Geder	one
14 the king of Hormah	one
the king of Arad	one
15 the king of Libnah	one
the king of Adullam	one
16 the king of Makkedah	one
the king of Bethel	one
17 the king of Tappuah	one
the king of Hepher	one
18 the king of Aphek	one
the king of Lasharon	one
19 the king of Madon	one
the king of Hazor	one
20 the king of Shimron Meron	one
the king of Acshaph	one
21 the king of Taanach	one
the king of Megiddo	one
22 the king of Kedesh	one
the king of Jokneam in Carmel	one
23 the king of Dor (in Naphoth Dor[a])	one
the king of Goyim in Gilgal	one
24 the king of Tirzah	one

thirty-one kings in all.

Land Still to Be Taken

13 When Joshua was old and well advanced in years, the LORD said to him, "You are very old, and there are still very large areas of land to be taken over.

[a] 23 Or *in the heights of Dor*

God's actual divine essence and his will, administration and works—are absolutely beyond all human thought, human understanding or wisdom; in short, that they are and ever will be incomprehensible, inscrutable, and altogether hidden to human reason.

Martin Luther (1483-1546)

(12:7–24) These 31 kings represent 31 peoples who were utterly destroyed. Lord, the violent death of so many is difficult to understand, even though Your Word says that their sin required it. But You did not give the land to Your people because of their righteousness. Rather, You used Your people as an instrument to punish the Canaanites for their wickedness. Hundreds of years earlier You foretold the destruction of the Canaanites. But in Your compassion You were slow to bring judgment. Indeed, You take no pleasure in the death of the wicked. Now, after more than 600 years, the time had come. How awesome it is to know You as a God of mercy; but how terrible when Your ways are endlessly violated and when Your mercy goes unheeded. (Ge 15:16; Dt 9:4; Eze 33:11)

Lord, when I endeavour any great matter, help me to remember that it is not the beginning but the continuing of the same until it has been thoroughly finished which yieldeth the true glory, through Jesus Christ our Lord.

Sir Francis Drake (1540-1596)

Our commitment to Christ, however genuine and whole-hearted it may be today, must be renewed tomorrow . . . and the day after that . . . and the day after that . . . until the path comes at last to the river.
Louis Cassels (1922–1974)

(13:13) The Israelites did not finish what they had started. They compromised and had to live with the consequences of their disobedience. Lord, help me to be faithful to Your instructions and to leave no place for compromise with evil. Give me the courage to demolish every pretense that sets itself up against You. Give me the discipline to take captive every thought to make it obedient to Christ. (2Co 10:5–6)

So send I you–by grace made strong
to triumph
O'er hosts of hell, o'er darkness,
death and sin,
My name to bear and in that name
to conquer
So send I you, My victory to win.
"So Send I You–by Grace Made Strong"
Margaret Clarkson (©1964)

2"This is the land that remains: all the regions of the Philistines and Geshurites: 3from the Shihor River on the east of
Egypt to the territory of Ekron on the north, all of it counted
as Canaanite (the territory of the five Philistine rulers in
Gaza, Ashdod, Ashkelon, Gath and Ekron—that of the Avvites); 4from the south, all the land of the Canaanites, from
Arah of the Sidonians as far as Aphek, the region of the Amorites, 5the area of the Gebalites[a]; and all Lebanon to the
east, from Baal Gad below Mount Hermon to Lebo[b] Hamath.

6"As for all the inhabitants of the mountain regions from Lebanon to Misrephoth Maim, that is, all the Sidonians, I myself will
drive them out before the Israelites. Be sure to allocate this land
to Israel for an inheritance, as I have instructed you, 7and divide
it as an inheritance among the nine tribes and half of the tribe of
Manasseh."

Division of the Land East of the Jordan

8The other half of Manasseh,[c] the Reubenites and the Gadites had
received the inheritance that Moses had given them east of the Jordan, as he, the servant of the LORD, had assigned it to them.

9It extended from Aroer on the rim of the Arnon Gorge, and
from the town in the middle of the gorge, and included the
whole plateau of Medeba as far as Dibon, 10and all the towns
of Sihon king of the Amorites, who ruled in Heshbon, out to
the border of the Ammonites. 11It also included Gilead, the
territory of the people of Geshur and Maacah, all of Mount
Hermon and all Bashan as far as Salecah— 12that is, the
whole kingdom of Og in Bashan, who had reigned in Ashtaroth and Edrei and had survived as one of the last of the
Rephaites. Moses had defeated them and taken over their
land. 13But the Israelites did not drive out the people of Geshur and Maacah, so they continue to live among the Israelites to this day.

14But to the tribe of Levi he gave no inheritance, since the offerings made by fire to the LORD, the God of Israel, are their inheritance, as he promised them.

15This is what Moses had given to the tribe of Reuben, clan by
clan:

16The territory from Aroer on the rim of the Arnon Gorge,
and from the town in the middle of the gorge, and the whole
plateau past Medeba 17to Heshbon and all its towns on the
plateau, including Dibon, Bamoth Baal, Beth Baal Meon,
18Jahaz, Kedemoth, Mephaath, 19Kiriathaim, Sibmah, Zereth
Shahar on the hill in the valley, 20Beth Peor, the slopes of Pisgah, and Beth Jeshimoth 21—all the towns on the plateau
and the entire realm of Sihon king of the Amorites, who
ruled at Heshbon. Moses had defeated him and the Midianite chiefs, Evi, Rekem, Zur, Hur and Reba—princes allied
with Sihon—who lived in that country. 22In addition to those
slain in battle, the Israelites had put to the sword Balaam son
of Beor, who practiced divination. 23The boundary of the
Reubenites was the bank of the Jordan. These towns and

[a]5 That is, the area of Byblos [b]5 Or *to the entrance to* [c]8 Hebrew *With it* (that is, with the other half of Manasseh)

their villages were the inheritance of the Reubenites, clan by
clan.
24 This is what Moses had given to the tribe of Gad, clan by clan:

25 The territory of Jazer, all the towns of Gilead and half the
Ammonite country as far as Aroer, near Rabbah; 26 and from
Heshbon to Ramath Mizpah and Betonim, and from Mahanaim to the territory of Debir; 27 and in the valley, Beth
Haram, Beth Nimrah, Succoth and Zaphon with the rest of
the realm of Sihon king of Heshbon (the east side of the Jordan, the territory up to the end of the Sea of Kinnereth[a]).
28 These towns and their villages were the inheritance of the
Gadites, clan by clan.

29 This is what Moses had given to the half-tribe of Manasseh, that
is, to half the family of the descendants of Manasseh, clan by clan:

30 The territory extending from Mahanaim and including all
of Bashan, the entire realm of Og king of Bashan—all the
settlements of Jair in Bashan, sixty towns, 31 half of Gilead,
and Ashtaroth and Edrei (the royal cities of Og in Bashan).
This was for the descendants of Makir son of Manasseh—for
half of the sons of Makir, clan by clan.

32 This is the inheritance Moses had given when he was in the
plains of Moab across the Jordan east of Jericho. 33 But to the tribe
of Levi, Moses had given no inheritance; the LORD, the God of Israel, is their inheritance, as he promised them.

Division of the Land West of the Jordan

14 Now these are the areas the Israelites received as an inheritance in the land of Canaan, which Eleazar the priest, Joshua son of Nun and the heads of the tribal clans of Israel allotted to
them. 2 Their inheritances were assigned by lot to the nine-and-a-
half tribes, as the LORD had commanded through Moses. 3 Moses
had granted the two-and-a-half tribes their inheritance east of the
Jordan but had not granted the Levites an inheritance among the
rest, 4 for the sons of Joseph had become two tribes—Manasseh
and Ephraim. The Levites received no share of the land but only
towns to live in, with pasturelands for their flocks and herds. 5 So
the Israelites divided the land, just as the LORD had commanded
Moses.

Hebron Given to Caleb

6 Now the men of Judah approached Joshua at Gilgal, and Caleb
son of Jephunneh the Kenizzite said to him, "You know what the
LORD said to Moses the man of God at Kadesh Barnea about you
and me. 7 I was forty years old when Moses the servant of the LORD
sent me from Kadesh Barnea to explore the land. And I brought
him back a report according to my convictions, 8 but my brothers
who went up with me made the hearts of the people melt with fear.
I, however, followed the LORD my God wholeheartedly. 9 So on that
day Moses swore to me, 'The land on which your feet have walked
will be your inheritance and that of your children forever, because
you have followed the LORD my God wholeheartedly.'[b]
10 "Now then, just as the LORD promised, he has kept me alive
for forty-five years since the time he said this to Moses, while Is-

[a] 27 That is, Galilee [b] 9 Deut. 1:36

(13:33) Lord God, as a priest in Your kingdom, I thank You that You are my final inheritance and my portion. Not land, or a position, or worldly wealth, but You—the Provider, the Creator, the Redeemer—You are my portion. (1Pe 2:9)

God is so good that he only awaits our desire to overwhelm us with the gift of himself.

François Fénelon (1651-1715)

rael moved about in the desert. So here I am today, eighty-five
years old! 11I am still as strong today as the day Moses sent me
out; I'm just as vigorous to go out to battle now as I was then.
12Now give me this hill country that the LORD promised me that
day. You yourself heard then that the Anakites were there and their
cities were large and fortified, but, the LORD helping me, I will
drive them out just as he said."

13Then Joshua blessed Caleb son of Jephunneh and gave him
Hebron as his inheritance. 14So Hebron has belonged to Caleb
son of Jephunneh the Kenizzite ever since, because he followed
the LORD, the God of Israel, wholeheartedly. 15(Hebron used to be
called Kiriath Arba after Arba, who was the greatest man among
the Anakites.)

Then the land had rest from war.

Allotment for Judah

15 The allotment for the tribe of Judah, clan by clan, extended
down to the territory of Edom, to the Desert of Zin in the extreme south.

2Their southern boundary started from the bay at the
southern end of the Salt Sea,[a] 3crossed south of Scorpion[b]
Pass, continued on to Zin and went over to the south of Kadesh Barnea. Then it ran past Hezron up to Addar and
curved around to Karka. 4It then passed along to Azmon and
joined the Wadi of Egypt, ending at the sea. This is their[c]
southern boundary.

5The eastern boundary is the Salt Sea as far as the mouth
of the Jordan.

The northern boundary started from the bay of the sea at
the mouth of the Jordan, 6went up to Beth Hoglah and continued north of Beth Arabah to the Stone of Bohan son of
Reuben. 7The boundary then went up to Debir from the Valley of Achor and turned north to Gilgal, which faces the Pass
of Adummim south of the gorge. It continued along to the
waters of En Shemesh and came out at En Rogel. 8Then it
ran up the Valley of Ben Hinnom along the southern slope of
the Jebusite city (that is, Jerusalem). From there it climbed
to the top of the hill west of the Hinnom Valley at the northern end of the Valley of Rephaim. 9From the hilltop the
boundary headed toward the spring of the waters of Nephtoah, came out at the towns of Mount Ephron and went down
toward Baalah (that is, Kiriath Jearim). 10Then it curved
westward from Baalah to Mount Seir, ran along the northern
slope of Mount Jearim (that is, Kesalon), continued down to
Beth Shemesh and crossed to Timnah. 11It went to the northern slope of Ekron, turned toward Shikkeron, passed along
to Mount Baalah and reached Jabneel. The boundary ended
at the sea.

12The western boundary is the coastline of the Great Sea.[d]
These are the boundaries around the people of Judah by their
clans.

13In accordance with the LORD's command to him, Joshua gave
to Caleb son of Jephunneh a portion in Judah—Kiriath Arba, that
is, Hebron. (Arba was the forefather of Anak.) 14From Hebron

[a] 2 That is, the Dead Sea; also in verse 5 [b] 3 Hebrew *Akrabbim* [c] 4 Hebrew *your*
[d] 12 That is, the Mediterranean; also in verse 47

In essence, there is only one thing God asks of us—that we be . . . people for whom God is everything and for whom God is enough.
Brennan Manning (1934-)

(14:6–15) Give me the spirit of Caleb, Lord God, who was wholehearted, enthusiastic and courageous. Caleb's towering faith in You reduced danger down to its proper size; like David, he knew that no giant could stand against Almighty God. Even in old age Caleb was fearless and utterly reliant upon You to finish the work You had begun so many years before. Like him, teach me to trust You completely and to boldly step into the future with hope, joy and an assurance of peace.

Caleb drove out the three Anakites—Sheshai, Ahiman and Talmai—descendants of Anak. 15From there he marched against the
people living in Debir (formerly called Kiriath Sepher). 16And
Caleb said, "I will give my daughter Acsah in marriage to the man
who attacks and captures Kiriath Sepher." 17Othniel son of Kenaz,
Caleb's brother, took it; so Caleb gave his daughter Acsah to him
in marriage.

18One day when she came to Othniel, she urged him[a] to ask her
father for a field. When she got off her donkey, Caleb asked her,
"What can I do for you?"

19She replied, "Do me a special favor. Since you have given me
land in the Negev, give me also springs of water." So Caleb gave
her the upper and lower springs.

20This is the inheritance of the tribe of Judah, clan by clan:

21The southernmost towns of the tribe of Judah in the Negev toward the boundary of Edom were:

Kabzeel, Eder, Jagur, 22Kinah, Dimonah, Adadah, 23Ke-
desh, Hazor, Ithnan, 24Ziph, Telem, Bealoth, 25Hazor Ha-
dattah, Kerioth Hezron (that is, Hazor), 26Amam, Shema,
Moladah, 27Hazar Gaddah, Heshmon, Beth Pelet, 28Hazar
Shual, Beersheba, Biziothiah, 29Baalah, Iim, Ezem, 30Elto-
lad, Kesil, Hormah, 31Ziklag, Madmannah, Sansannah, 32Le-
baoth, Shilhim, Ain and Rimmon—a total of twenty-nine
towns and their villages.

33In the western foothills:

Eshtaol, Zorah, Ashnah, 34Zanoah, En Gannim, Tappuah,
Enam, 35Jarmuth, Adullam, Socoh, Azekah, 36Shaaraim, Ad-
ithaim and Gederah (or Gederothaim)[b]—fourteen towns
and their villages.

37Zenan, Hadashah, Migdal Gad, 38Dilean, Mizpah, Joktheel, 39Lachish, Bozkath, Eglon, 40Cabbon, Lahmas, Kitlish,
41Gederoth, Beth Dagon, Naamah and Makkedah—sixteen
towns and their villages.

42Libnah, Ether, Ashan, 43Iphtah, Ashnah, Nezib, 44Keilah,
Aczib and Mareshah—nine towns and their villages.

45Ekron, with its surrounding settlements and villages;
46west of Ekron, all that were in the vicinity of Ashdod, together with their villages; 47Ashdod, its surrounding settlements and villages; and Gaza, its settlements and villages, as
far as the Wadi of Egypt and the coastline of the Great Sea.

48In the hill country:

Shamir, Jattir, Socoh, 49Dannah, Kiriath Sannah (that is,
Debir), 50Anab, Eshtemoh, Anim, 51Goshen, Holon and
Giloh—eleven towns and their villages.

52Arab, Dumah, Eshan, 53Janim, Beth Tappuah, Aphekah,
54Humtah, Kiriath Arba (that is, Hebron) and Zior—nine
towns and their villages.

55Maon, Carmel, Ziph, Juttah, 56Jezreel, Jokdeam, Zanoah, 57Kain, Gibeah and Timnah—ten towns and their villages.

58Halhul, Beth Zur, Gedor, 59Maarath, Beth Anoth and El-
tekon—six towns and their villages.

[a] *18* Hebrew and some Septuagint manuscripts; other Septuagint manuscripts (see also note at Judges 1:14) *Othniel, he urged her* [b] *36* Or *Gederah and Gederothaim*

(15:14) My Lord, Father and Friend: You know the power of the enemy's forces—different kinds of "sons of Anak" who can and do come against me. You know "the rulers, the authorities, the powers of this dark world and the spiritual forces of evil in the heavenly realms" that are arrayed against me. Help me to put on the whole armor of God and to be strong in You and in the strength of Your might, so that I may drive out such forces and make them release any hold upon my life. Grant me victory over them, so that I may enter into my inheritance in You. (Eph 6:12–13)

The weapons of our warfare
Are not made with human hands;
And the enemy we face
Is not the flesh and blood of man;
But we serve a mighty captain
With a wondrous battle plan;
He's already won the victory;
Yet He calls us now to stand.
Hear the battle cry,
Put your armor on,
We must occupy the land
Until the kingdom comes.

"Hear The Battle Cry"
Jamie Owens-Collins (©1991)

60 Kiriath Baal (that is, Kiriath Jearim) and Rabbah—two
towns and their villages.
61 In the desert:
Beth Arabah, Middin, Secacah, 62 Nibshan, the City of Salt
and En Gedi—six towns and their villages.
63 Judah could not dislodge the Jebusites, who were living in Jerusalem; to this day the Jebusites live there with the people of
Judah.

Allotment for Ephraim and Manasseh

16 The allotment for Joseph began at the Jordan of Jericho,[a] east of the waters of Jericho, and went up from
there through the desert into the hill country of Bethel. 2 It
went on from Bethel (that is, Luz),[b] crossed over to the territory of the Arkites in Ataroth, 3 descended westward to the
territory of the Japhletites as far as the region of Lower Beth
Horon and on to Gezer, ending at the sea.
4 So Manasseh and Ephraim, the descendants of Joseph, received
their inheritance.

5 This was the territory of Ephraim, clan by clan:
The boundary of their inheritance went from Ataroth
Addar in the east to Upper Beth Horon 6 and continued to the
sea. From Micmethath on the north it curved eastward to Ta-
anath Shiloh, passing by it to Janoah on the east. 7 Then it
went down from Janoah to Ataroth and Naarah, touched Jericho and came out at the Jordan. 8 From Tappuah the border
went west to the Kanah Ravine and ended at the sea. This was
the inheritance of the tribe of the Ephraimites, clan by clan.
9 It also included all the towns and their villages that were set
aside for the Ephraimites within the inheritance of the Manassites.
10 They did not dislodge the Canaanites living in Gezer; to this day
the Canaanites live among the people of Ephraim but are required
to do forced labor.

17 This was the allotment for the tribe of Manasseh as Joseph's
firstborn, that is, for Makir, Manasseh's firstborn. Makir
was the ancestor of the Gileadites, who had received Gilead and
Bashan because the Makirites were great soldiers. 2 So this allotment was for the rest of the people of Manasseh—the clans of
Abiezer, Helek, Asriel, Shechem, Hepher and Shemida. These are
the other male descendants of Manasseh son of Joseph by their
clans.
3 Now Zelophehad son of Hepher, the son of Gilead, the son of
Makir, the son of Manasseh, had no sons but only daughters,
whose names were Mahlah, Noah, Hoglah, Milcah and Tirzah.
4 They went to Eleazar the priest, Joshua son of Nun, and the leaders and said, "The LORD commanded Moses to give us an inheritance among our brothers." So Joshua gave them an inheritance
along with the brothers of their father, according to the LORD's
command. 5 Manasseh's share consisted of ten tracts of land besides Gilead and Bashan east of the Jordan, 6 because the daughters of the tribe of Manasseh received an inheritance among the
sons. The land of Gilead belonged to the rest of the descendants of
Manasseh.

[a] 1 *Jordan of Jericho* was possibly an ancient name for the Jordan River. [b] 2 Septuagint; Hebrew *Bethel to Luz*

(15:63;16:10) Lord God, You faithfully fulfill Your covenant promises to us, but we do not always fulfill ours to You. Please forgive us when we don't drive out sin's occupying forces from our hearts. When we allow them to remain there, eventually they wreak havoc. Save us, Lord, from our unfaithfulness and its consequences.

As long as we be meddling with any part of sin, we shall never see clearly the blissful countenance of our Lord.

Julian of Norwich (c.1342-1423)

7The territory of Manasseh extended from Asher to
Micmethath east of Shechem. The boundary ran southward
from there to include the people living at En Tappuah. 8(Manasseh had the land of Tappuah, but Tappuah itself, on the
boundary of Manasseh, belonged to the Ephraimites.) 9Then
the boundary continued south to the Kanah Ravine. There
were towns belonging to Ephraim lying among the towns of
Manasseh, but the boundary of Manasseh was the northern
side of the ravine and ended at the sea. 10On the south the
land belonged to Ephraim, on the north to Manasseh. The
territory of Manasseh reached the sea and bordered Asher
on the north and Issachar on the east.

11Within Issachar and Asher, Manasseh also had Beth
Shan, Ibleam and the people of Dor, Endor, Taanach and Megiddo, together with their surrounding settlements (the third
in the list is Naphoth[a]).
12Yet the Manassites were not able to occupy these towns, for the
Canaanites were determined to live in that region. 13However,
when the Israelites grew stronger, they subjected the Canaanites to
forced labor but did not drive them out completely.
14The people of Joseph said to Joshua, "Why have you given us
only one allotment and one portion for an inheritance? We are a
numerous people and the LORD has blessed us abundantly."
15"If you are so numerous," Joshua answered, "and if the hill
country of Ephraim is too small for you, go up into the forest and
clear land for yourselves there in the land of the Perizzites and
Rephaites."
16The people of Joseph replied, "The hill country is not enough
for us, and all the Canaanites who live in the plain have iron chariots, both those in Beth Shan and its settlements and those in the
Valley of Jezreel."
17But Joshua said to the house of Joseph—to Ephraim and
Manasseh—"You are numerous and very powerful. You will have
not only one allotment 18but the forested hill country as well.
Clear it, and its farthest limits will be yours; though the Canaanites have iron chariots and though they are strong, you can drive
them out."

Division of the Rest of the Land

18 The whole assembly of the Israelites gathered at Shiloh and
set up the Tent of Meeting there. The country was brought
under their control, 2but there were still seven Israelite tribes who
had not yet received their inheritance.
3So Joshua said to the Israelites: "How long will you wait before
you begin to take possession of the land that the LORD, the God of
your fathers, has given you? 4Appoint three men from each tribe.
I will send them out to make a survey of the land and to write a description of it, according to the inheritance of each. Then they will
return to me. 5You are to divide the land into seven parts. Judah
is to remain in its territory on the south and the house of Joseph
in its territory on the north. 6After you have written descriptions of
the seven parts of the land, bring them here to me and I will cast
lots for you in the presence of the LORD our God. 7The Levites,
however, do not get a portion among you, because the priestly service of the LORD is their inheritance. And Gad, Reuben and the

[a] 11 That is, Naphoth Dor

(17:12–18) Almighty God, give Your church boldness to stand against the powers of the world. Give us tenacity to resist compromise with the ways of the ungodly. Help us to move out in faith and obedience to Your leading, in spite of the obstacles the world places before us. We declare in faith that You, the One who lives within us, are far greater than he that is in the world. (1Jn 4:4)

Faith is a strong power, mastering any difficulty in the strength of the Lord who made heaven and earth.

Corrie ten Boom (1892–1983)

(18:3) Like Your people of old, I too struggle with weakness of will. Keep me from becoming complacent in my spiritual growth. Deliver me, O Lord, from stubbornness and disobedience. Free me from laziness and procrastination. Forgive me for putting off until tomorrow the full measure of obedience You require of me from day to day. Please give me singleness of heart and action so that through my complete obedience I might worship You in spirit and truth. (Jer 32:39)

(18:8–10) Shiloh was the name of the place where You met with Your people. Shiloh was also a name by which the people referred to their Messiah. How appropriate that their offerings of worship and Your allotment of their inheritance should both take place at Shiloh. It is the same in Your church today, O God. Our offerings of worship are presented to You through our Messiah; and Your gifts of grace are presented to us through our Messiah. Our Messiah, our Shiloh, our meeting place with You, is Jesus Christ, God in the flesh. (See NIV footnote at Ge 49:10; Heb 13:15–21)

half-tribe of Manasseh have already received their inheritance on
the east side of the Jordan. Moses the servant of the LORD gave it to
them."
8As the men started on their way to map out the land, Joshua instructed them, "Go and make a survey of the land and write a description of it. Then return to me, and I will cast lots for you here
at Shiloh in the presence of the LORD." 9So the men left and went
through the land. They wrote its description on a scroll, town by
town, in seven parts, and returned to Joshua in the camp at Shiloh.
10Joshua then cast lots for them in Shiloh in the presence of the
LORD, and there he distributed the land to the Israelites according
to their tribal divisions.

Allotment for Benjamin

11The lot came up for the tribe of Benjamin, clan by clan. Their allotted territory lay between the tribes of Judah and Joseph:
12On the north side their boundary began at the Jordan,
passed the northern slope of Jericho and headed west into
the hill country, coming out at the desert of Beth Aven.
13From there it crossed to the south slope of Luz (that is,
Bethel) and went down to Ataroth Addar on the hill south of
Lower Beth Horon.
14From the hill facing Beth Horon on the south the boundary turned south along the western side and came out at Kiriath Baal (that is, Kiriath Jearim), a town of the people of
Judah. This was the western side.
15The southern side began at the outskirts of Kiriath Jearim on the west, and the boundary came out at the spring of
the waters of Nephtoah. 16The boundary went down to the
foot of the hill facing the Valley of Ben Hinnom, north of the
Valley of Rephaim. It continued down the Hinnom Valley
along the southern slope of the Jebusite city and so to En
Rogel. 17It then curved north, went to En Shemesh, continued to Geliloth, which faces the Pass of Adummim, and ran
down to the Stone of Bohan son of Reuben. 18It continued to
the northern slope of Beth Arabah[a] and on down into the Arabah. 19It then went to the northern slope of Beth Hoglah
and came out at the northern bay of the Salt Sea,[b] at the
mouth of the Jordan in the south. This was the southern
boundary.
20The Jordan formed the boundary on the eastern side.
These were the boundaries that marked out the inheritance of the
clans of Benjamin on all sides.

21The tribe of Benjamin, clan by clan, had the following cities:
Jericho, Beth Hoglah, Emek Keziz, 22Beth Arabah, Zemaraim, Bethel, 23Avvim, Parah, Ophrah, 24Kephar Ammoni,
Ophni and Geba—twelve towns and their villages.
25Gibeon, Ramah, Beeroth, 26Mizpah, Kephirah, Mozah,
27Rekem, Irpeel, Taralah, 28Zelah, Haeleph, the Jebusite city
(that is, Jerusalem), Gibeah and Kiriath—fourteen towns
and their villages.
This was the inheritance of Benjamin for its clans.

[a] *18* Septuagint; Hebrew *slope facing the Arabah* [b] *19* That is, the Dead Sea

Allotment for Simeon

19 The second lot came out for the tribe of Simeon, clan by clan. Their inheritance lay within the territory of Judah. 2It included:

Beersheba (or Sheba),[a] Moladah, 3Hazar Shual, Balah, Ezem, 4Eltolad, Bethul, Hormah, 5Ziklag, Beth Marcaboth, Hazar Susah, 6Beth Lebaoth and Sharuhen—thirteen towns and their villages;

7Ain, Rimmon, Ether and Ashan—four towns and their villages— 8and all the villages around these towns as far as Baalath Beer (Ramah in the Negev).

This was the inheritance of the tribe of the Simeonites, clan by clan. 9The inheritance of the Simeonites was taken from the share of Judah, because Judah's portion was more than they needed. So the Simeonites received their inheritance within the territory of Judah.

Allotment for Zebulun

10The third lot came up for Zebulun, clan by clan:

The boundary of their inheritance went as far as Sarid. 11Going west it ran to Maralah, touched Dabbesheth, and extended to the ravine near Jokneam. 12It turned east from Sarid toward the sunrise to the territory of Kisloth Tabor and went on to Daberath and up to Japhia. 13Then it continued eastward to Gath Hepher and Eth Kazin; it came out at Rimmon and turned toward Neah. 14There the boundary went around on the north to Hannathon and ended at the Valley of Iphtah El. 15Included were Kattath, Nahalal, Shimron, Idalah and Bethlehem. There were twelve towns and their villages.

16These towns and their villages were the inheritance of Zebulun, clan by clan.

Allotment for Issachar

17The fourth lot came out for Issachar, clan by clan. 18Their territory included:

Jezreel, Kesulloth, Shunem, 19Hapharaim, Shion, Anaharath, 20Rabbith, Kishion, Ebez, 21Remeth, En Gannim, En Haddah and Beth Pazzez. 22The boundary touched Tabor, Shahazumah and Beth Shemesh, and ended at the Jordan. There were sixteen towns and their villages.

23These towns and their villages were the inheritance of the tribe of Issachar, clan by clan.

Allotment for Asher

24The fifth lot came out for the tribe of Asher, clan by clan. 25Their territory included:

Helkath, Hali, Beten, Acshaph, 26Allammelech, Amad and Mishal. On the west the boundary touched Carmel and Shihor Libnath. 27It then turned east toward Beth Dagon, touched Zebulun and the Valley of Iphtah El, and went north to Beth Emek and Neiel, passing Cabul on the left. 28It went to Abdon,[b] Rehob, Hammon and Kanah, as far as Greater Sidon. 29The boundary then turned back toward Ramah and went to the fortified city of Tyre, turned toward Hosah and

[a] *2* Or *Beersheba, Sheba*; 1 Chron. 4:28 does not have *Sheba*. [b] *28* Some Hebrew manuscripts (see also Joshua 21:30); most Hebrew manuscripts *Ebron*

(19:1–29) Thank You for Your faithfulness to people of these ancient tribes: to communities, leaders, families and individuals. They were established in a new home that held great significance as the end result of your ancient promises. How they must have rejoiced and worshiped You for fulfilling Your promises in such a remarkable way!

(20:1–6) Merciful God, we thank You for the cities of refuge that provided safe haven for those who sinned unintentionally. For though in their minds they were innocent, their hands were nonetheless guilty. And You have provided for us an even greater refuge, a place more sure and lasting. Christ is our refuge, and there is no condemnation for those who are in Him. By faith we come to Him for mercy and forgiveness. By grace we will abide in Him forever. (Ro 8:1)

O Lord, turn not away thy face
From him that lies prostrate,
Lamenting sore his sinful life,
Before thy mercy gate;
Mercy, good Lord, mercy I ask,
This is the total sum;
For mercy, Lord, is all my suit:
Lord, let thy mercy come.

John Marckant

Lord, You are my refuge,
You are my hiding place.
O Lord, You are my refuge
And I will rest in Your saving grace.
You're the Rock of my salvation,
You're the One who calms the
storm;
Lord, You set my feet on higher
ground.
I will worship and adore You,
I will lift my voice on high,
For only in Your presence will I find:
Lord, You are my refuge,
You are my hiding place.
O Lord, You are my refuge
And I will rest in Your saving grace.

"You Are My Refuge"
Lenny LeBlanc and Greg Gulley (©1990)

came out at the sea in the region of Aczib, [30]Ummah, Aphek
and Rehob. There were twenty-two towns and their villages.
[31]These towns and their villages were the inheritance of the tribe
of Asher, clan by clan.

Allotment for Naphtali

[32]The sixth lot came out for Naphtali, clan by clan:
[33]Their boundary went from Heleph and the large tree in
Zaanannim, passing Adami Nekeb and Jabneel to Lakkum
and ending at the Jordan. [34]The boundary ran west through
Aznoth Tabor and came out at Hukkok. It touched Zebulun
on the south, Asher on the west and the Jordan[a] on the east.
[35]The fortified cities were Ziddim, Zer, Hammath, Rakkath,
Kinnereth, [36]Adamah, Ramah, Hazor, [37]Kedesh, Edrei, En
Hazor, [38]Iron, Migdal El, Horem, Beth Anath and Beth Shemesh.
There were nineteen towns and their villages.
[39]These towns and their villages were the inheritance of the tribe
of Naphtali, clan by clan.

Allotment for Dan

[40]The seventh lot came out for the tribe of Dan, clan by clan.
[41]The territory of their inheritance included:
Zorah, Eshtaol, Ir Shemesh, [42]Shaalabbin, Aijalon, Ithlah,
[43]Elon, Timnah, Ekron, [44]Eltekeh, Gibbethon, Baalath, [45]Jehud,
Bene Berak, Gath Rimmon, [46]Me Jarkon and Rakkon,
with the area facing Joppa.
[47](But the Danites had difficulty taking possession of their territory,
so they went up and attacked Leshem, took it, put it to the
sword and occupied it. They settled in Leshem and named it Dan
after their forefather.)
[48]These towns and their villages were the inheritance of the tribe
of Dan, clan by clan.

Allotment for Joshua

[49]When they had finished dividing the land into its allotted portions,
the Israelites gave Joshua son of Nun an inheritance among
them, [50]as the LORD had commanded. They gave him the town he
asked for—Timnath Serah[b] in the hill country of Ephraim. And he
built up the town and settled there.
[51]These are the territories that Eleazar the priest, Joshua son of
Nun and the heads of the tribal clans of Israel assigned by lot at
Shiloh in the presence of the LORD at the entrance to the Tent of
Meeting. And so they finished dividing the land.

Cities of Refuge

20 Then the LORD said to Joshua: [2]"Tell the Israelites to designate
the cities of refuge, as I instructed you through
Moses, [3]so that anyone who kills a person accidentally and unintentionally
may flee there and find protection from the avenger of
blood.
[4]"When he flees to one of these cities, he is to stand in the entrance
of the city gate and state his case before the elders of that
city. Then they are to admit him into their city and give him a place
to live with them. [5]If the avenger of blood pursues him, they must
not surrender the one accused, because he killed his neighbor

[a] 34 Septuagint; Hebrew *west, and Judah, the Jordan,* [b] 50 Also known as *Timnath Heres* (see Judges 2:9)

unintentionally and without malice aforethought. 6He is to stay in
that city until he has stood trial before the assembly and until the
death of the high priest who is serving at that time. Then he may
go back to his own home in the town from which he fled."

7So they set apart Kedesh in Galilee in the hill country of Naphtali, Shechem in the hill country of Ephraim, and Kiriath Arba (that
is, Hebron) in the hill country of Judah. 8On the east side of the
Jordan of Jericho[a] they designated Bezer in the desert on the plateau in the tribe of Reuben, Ramoth in Gilead in the tribe of Gad,
and Golan in Bashan in the tribe of Manasseh. 9Any of the Israelites or any alien living among them who killed someone accidentally could flee to these designated cities and not be killed by the
avenger of blood prior to standing trial before the assembly.

Towns for the Levites

21 Now the family heads of the Levites approached Eleazar the
priest, Joshua son of Nun, and the heads of the other tribal
families of Israel 2at Shiloh in Canaan and said to them, "The LORD
commanded through Moses that you give us towns to live in, with
pasturelands for our livestock." 3So, as the LORD had commanded,
the Israelites gave the Levites the following towns and pasturelands
out of their own inheritance:

4The first lot came out for the Kohathites, clan by clan. The Levites who were descendants of Aaron the priest were allotted thirteen towns from the tribes of Judah, Simeon and Benjamin. 5The
rest of Kohath's descendants were allotted ten towns from the
clans of the tribes of Ephraim, Dan and half of Manasseh.

6The descendants of Gershon were allotted thirteen towns from
the clans of the tribes of Issachar, Asher, Naphtali and the half-
tribe of Manasseh in Bashan.

7The descendants of Merari, clan by clan, received twelve towns
from the tribes of Reuben, Gad and Zebulun.

8So the Israelites allotted to the Levites these towns and their
pasturelands, as the LORD had commanded through Moses.

9From the tribes of Judah and Simeon they allotted the following
towns by name 10(these towns were assigned to the descendants
of Aaron who were from the Kohathite clans of the Levites, because the first lot fell to them):

11They gave them Kiriath Arba (that is, Hebron), with its
surrounding pastureland, in the hill country of Judah. (Arba
was the forefather of Anak.) 12But the fields and villages
around the city they had given to Caleb son of Jephunneh as
his possession.

13So to the descendants of Aaron the priest they gave Hebron (a city of refuge for one accused of murder), Libnah,
14Jattir, Eshtemoa, 15Holon, Debir, 16Ain, Juttah and Beth
Shemesh, together with their pasturelands—nine towns
from these two tribes.

17And from the tribe of Benjamin they gave them Gibeon,
Geba, 18Anathoth and Almon, together with their pasturelands—four towns.

19All the towns for the priests, the descendants of Aaron, were
thirteen, together with their pasturelands.

[a] 8 *Jordan of Jericho* was possibly an ancient name for the Jordan River.

(21:1–8) Lord God, just as You called the Levites to be priests, so You have also called us to be priests among the people who surround us. We are not intended to be an elite caste with our own spiritual secrets. Instead we are to be lights for the darkness, salt for the earth. You have not called us to abandon our earthly communities but to serve You in their midst. Teach us to wholeheartedly reflect You in the world, while striving to remain untarnished by it. (Jn 17:15–18; 1Pe 2:9)

They serve God well, who serve his creatures.

Caroline Sheridan Norton (1808-1877)

Priests of the world, Christ sends us
forth
This world of time to consecrate,
This world of sin by grace to heal,
Christ's world in Christ to recreate.

"Forth in the Peace of Christ We Go"
James Quinn SJ (©1969)

True have his promises been; not one has failed. I want none beside him. In life he is my life, and in death he shall be the death of death; in poverty, Christ is my riches; in sickness, he makes my bed; in darkness, he is my star, and in brightness, he is my sun; he is the manna of the camp in the wilderness, and he shall be the new corn of the host when they come to Canaan. Jesus is to me all grace and no wrath, all truth and no falsehood; and of truth and grace he is full, infinitely full.

Charles Haddon Spurgeon (1834–1892)

(21:45) God, You are so faithful! Your promises never fail; Your words never return to You without accomplishing their purpose. Help me to believe and to trust You beyond any shadow of a doubt. For surely, if You can fulfill Your promises to an entire nation, You can fulfill Your promises to me. (Isa 55:11; Php 1:6)

Like the sun that rises every day,
You are so faithful,
Lord, You are faithful.
Like the rain that You send
And every breath that I breathe,
You are so faithful, Lord.

Like a rose that comes alive every spring,
You are so faithful,
Lord, You are faithful.
Like the life that You give
To every beat of my heart,
You are so faithful, Lord.

"You Are So Faithful"
Lenny LeBlanc and Greg Gulley (©1989)

20The rest of the Kohathite clans of the Levites were allotted towns
from the tribe of Ephraim:
21In the hill country of Ephraim they were given Shechem
(a city of refuge for one accused of murder) and Gezer,
22Kibzaim and Beth Horon, together with their pasturelands—four towns.
23Also from the tribe of Dan they received Eltekeh, Gibbethon, 24Aijalon and Gath Rimmon, together with their pasturelands—four towns.
25From half the tribe of Manasseh they received Taanach
and Gath Rimmon, together with their pasturelands—two
towns.
26All these ten towns and their pasturelands were given to the rest
of the Kohathite clans.

27The Levite clans of the Gershonites were given:
from the half-tribe of Manasseh,
Golan in Bashan (a city of refuge for one accused of murder)
and Be Eshtarah, together with their pasturelands—two
towns;
28from the tribe of Issachar,
Kishion, Daberath, 29Jarmuth and En Gannim, together with
their pasturelands—four towns;
30from the tribe of Asher,
Mishal, Abdon, 31Helkath and Rehob, together with their
pasturelands—four towns;
32from the tribe of Naphtali,
Kedesh in Galilee (a city of refuge for one accused of murder), Hammoth Dor and Kartan, together with their pasturelands—three towns.
33All the towns of the Gershonite clans were thirteen, together
with their pasturelands.

34The Merarite clans (the rest of the Levites) were given:
from the tribe of Zebulun,
Jokneam, Kartah, 35Dimnah and Nahalal, together with their
pasturelands—four towns;
36from the tribe of Reuben,
Bezer, Jahaz, 37Kedemoth and Mephaath, together with their
pasturelands—four towns;
38from the tribe of Gad,
Ramoth in Gilead (a city of refuge for one accused of murder), Mahanaim, 39Heshbon and Jazer, together with their
pasturelands—four towns in all.
40All the towns allotted to the Merarite clans, who were the rest of
the Levites, were twelve.
41The towns of the Levites in the territory held by the Israelites
were forty-eight in all, together with their pasturelands. 42Each of
these towns had pasturelands surrounding it; this was true for all
these towns.

43So the LORD gave Israel all the land he had sworn to give their
forefathers, and they took possession of it and settled there. 44The
LORD gave them rest on every side, just as he had sworn to their
forefathers. Not one of their enemies withstood them; the LORD
handed all their enemies over to them. 45Not one of all the LORD's
good promises to the house of Israel failed; every one was fulfilled.

Eastern Tribes Return Home

22 Then Joshua summoned the Reubenites, the Gadites and
the half-tribe of Manasseh 2and said to them, "You have
done all that Moses the servant of the LORD commanded, and you
have obeyed me in everything I commanded. 3For a long time
now—to this very day—you have not deserted your brothers but
have carried out the mission the LORD your God gave you. 4Now
that the LORD your God has given your brothers rest as he promised, return to your homes in the land that Moses the servant of
the LORD gave you on the other side of the Jordan. 5But be very
careful to keep the commandment and the law that Moses the servant of the LORD gave you: to love the LORD your God, to walk in all
his ways, to obey his commands, to hold fast to him and to serve
him with all your heart and all your soul."

6Then Joshua blessed them and sent them away, and they went
to their homes. 7(To the half-tribe of Manasseh Moses had given
land in Bashan, and to the other half of the tribe Joshua gave land
on the west side of the Jordan with their brothers.) When Joshua
sent them home, he blessed them, 8saying, "Return to your homes
with your great wealth—with large herds of livestock, with silver,
gold, bronze and iron, and a great quantity of clothing—and divide with your brothers the plunder from your enemies."

9So the Reubenites, the Gadites and the half-tribe of Manasseh
left the Israelites at Shiloh in Canaan to return to Gilead, their own
land, which they had acquired in accordance with the command
of the LORD through Moses.

10When they came to Geliloth near the Jordan in the land of Canaan, the Reubenites, the Gadites and the half-tribe of Manasseh
built an imposing altar there by the Jordan. 11And when the Israelites heard that they had built the altar on the border of Canaan
at Geliloth near the Jordan on the Israelite side, 12the whole assembly of Israel gathered at Shiloh to go to war against them.

13So the Israelites sent Phinehas son of Eleazar, the priest, to
the land of Gilead—to Reuben, Gad and the half-tribe of Manasseh. 14With him they sent ten of the chief men, one for each of the
tribes of Israel, each the head of a family division among the Israelite clans.

15When they went to Gilead—to Reuben, Gad and the half-tribe
of Manasseh—they said to them: 16"The whole assembly of the
LORD says: 'How could you break faith with the God of Israel like
this? How could you turn away from the LORD and build yourselves
an altar in rebellion against him now? 17Was not the sin of Peor
enough for us? Up to this very day we have not cleansed ourselves
from that sin, even though a plague fell on the community of the
LORD! 18And are you now turning away from the LORD?

" 'If you rebel against the LORD today, tomorrow he will be angry
with the whole community of Israel. 19If the land you possess is
defiled, come over to the LORD's land, where the LORD's tabernacle
stands, and share the land with us. But do not rebel against the
LORD or against us by building an altar for yourselves, other than
the altar of the LORD our God. 20When Achan son of Zerah acted
unfaithfully regarding the devoted things,[a] did not wrath come
upon the whole community of Israel? He was not the only one who
died for his sin.' "

(22:3) Lord, give me grace, understanding and loyalty to stand by my family, my friends and all my Christian brothers and sisters. Let me not forsake or desert those who need me. I know that the greatest thing I could ever do is to carry out the loving and caring tasks You have given me both in serving You and in serving others. Grant me discernment as to what those tasks entail, diligence in doing them and perseverance to complete them according to Your will.

Make a rule and pray to God to help you to keep it, never, if possible, to lie down at night without being able to say: "I have made one human being at least a little wiser, or a little happier, or at least a little better this day."

Charles Kingsley (1819-1875)

[a] 20 The Hebrew term refers to the irrevocable giving over of things or persons to the LORD, often by totally destroying them.

21 Then Reuben, Gad and the half-tribe of Manasseh replied to
the heads of the clans of Israel: 22 "The Mighty One, God, the LORD!
The Mighty One, God, the LORD! He knows! And let Israel know! If
this has been in rebellion or disobedience to the LORD, do not
spare us this day. 23 If we have built our own altar to turn away
from the LORD and to offer burnt offerings and grain offerings, or
to sacrifice fellowship offerings[a] on it, may the LORD himself call
us to account.

24 "No! We did it for fear that some day your descendants might
say to ours, 'What do you have to do with the LORD, the God of Israel? 25 The LORD has made the Jordan a boundary between us and
you—you Reubenites and Gadites! You have no share in the LORD.'
So your descendants might cause ours to stop fearing the LORD.

26 "That is why we said, 'Let us get ready and build an altar—
but not for burnt offerings or sacrifices.' 27 On the contrary, it is to
be a witness between us and you and the generations that follow,
that we will worship the LORD at his sanctuary with our burnt offerings, sacrifices and fellowship offerings. Then in the future your
descendants will not be able to say to ours, 'You have no share in
the LORD.'

28 "And we said, 'If they ever say this to us, or to our descendants, we will answer: Look at the replica of the LORD's altar, which
our fathers built, not for burnt offerings and sacrifices, but as a
witness between us and you.'

29 "Far be it from us to rebel against the LORD and turn away
from him today by building an altar for burnt offerings, grain offerings and sacrifices, other than the altar of the LORD our God that
stands before his tabernacle."

30 When Phinehas the priest and the leaders of the community—the heads of the clans of the Israelites—heard what Reuben,
Gad and Manasseh had to say, they were pleased. 31 And Phinehas
son of Eleazar, the priest, said to Reuben, Gad and Manasseh,
"Today we know that the LORD is with us, because you have not
acted unfaithfully toward the LORD in this matter. Now you have
rescued the Israelites from the LORD's hand."

32 Then Phinehas son of Eleazar, the priest, and the leaders returned to Canaan from their meeting with the Reubenites and Gadites in Gilead and reported to the Israelites. 33 They were glad to
hear the report and praised God. And they talked no more about
going to war against them to devastate the country where the Reubenites and the Gadites lived.

34 And the Reubenites and the Gadites gave the altar this name:
A Witness Between Us that the LORD is God.

Joshua's Farewell to the Leaders

23 After a long time had passed and the LORD had given Israel rest from all their enemies around them, Joshua, by then
old and well advanced in years, 2 summoned all Israel—their elders, leaders, judges and officials—and said to them: "I am old
and well advanced in years. 3 You yourselves have seen everything
the LORD your God has done to all these nations for your sake; it
was the LORD your God who fought for you. 4 Remember how I
have allotted as an inheritance for your tribes all the land of the
nations that remain—the nations I conquered—between the Jordan and the Great Sea[b] in the west. 5 The LORD your God himself

[a] 23 Traditionally *peace offerings*; also in verse 27 [b] 4 That is, the Mediterranean

(22:21–34) How quickly we judge the motives of others, and how easily we criticize their manner of worship. Forgive us, Lord! Rather than believing the best of our brothers and sisters in Christ, we rush to find fault with them while fervently defending our own traditions. O God, please pardon our arrogance, teach us to suppress our spiritual pride, and help us to gracefully seek common ground with those who know and love Your only Son.

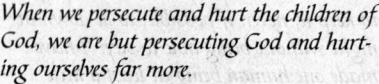

When we persecute and hurt the children of God, we are but persecuting God and hurting ourselves far more.

Albert Benjamin Simpson (1843-1919)

will drive them out of your way. He will push them out before you,
and you will take possession of their land, as the LORD your God
promised you.
6"Be very strong; be careful to obey all that is written in the
Book of the Law of Moses, without turning aside to the right or to
the left. 7Do not associate with these nations that remain among
you; do not invoke the names of their gods or swear by them. You
must not serve them or bow down to them. 8But you are to hold
fast to the LORD your God, as you have until now.
9"The LORD has driven out before you great and powerful nations; to this day no one has been able to withstand you. 10One of
you routs a thousand, because the LORD your God fights for you,
just as he promised. 11So be very careful to love the LORD your
God.
12"But if you turn away and ally yourselves with the survivors
of these nations that remain among you and if you intermarry
with them and associate with them, 13then you may be sure that
the LORD your God will no longer drive out these nations before
you. Instead, they will become snares and traps for you, whips on
your backs and thorns in your eyes, until you perish from this
good land, which the LORD your God has given you.
14"Now I am about to go the way of all the earth. You know
with all your heart and soul that not one of all the good promises
the LORD your God gave you has failed. Every promise has been
fulfilled; not one has failed. 15But just as every good promise of
the LORD your God has come true, so the LORD will bring on you
all the evil he has threatened, until he has destroyed you from
this good land he has given you. 16If you violate the covenant of
the LORD your God, which he commanded you, and go and serve
other gods and bow down to them, the LORD's anger will burn
against you, and you will quickly perish from the good land he
has given you."

The Covenant Renewed at Shechem

24 Then Joshua assembled all the tribes of Israel at Shechem. He summoned the elders, leaders, judges and officials of Israel, and they presented themselves before God.
2Joshua said to all the people, "This is what the LORD, the God
of Israel, says: 'Long ago your forefathers, including Terah the father of Abraham and Nahor, lived beyond the River[a] and worshiped other gods. 3But I took your father Abraham from the land
beyond the River and led him throughout Canaan and gave him
many descendants. I gave him Isaac, 4and to Isaac I gave Jacob
and Esau. I assigned the hill country of Seir to Esau, but Jacob
and his sons went down to Egypt.
5" 'Then I sent Moses and Aaron, and I afflicted the Egyptians
by what I did there, and I brought you out. 6When I brought your
fathers out of Egypt, you came to the sea, and the Egyptians pursued them with chariots and horsemen[b] as far as the Red Sea.[c]
7But they cried to the LORD for help, and he put darkness between
you and the Egyptians; he brought the sea over them and covered
them. You saw with your own eyes what I did to the Egyptians.
Then you lived in the desert for a long time.
8" 'I brought you to the land of the Amorites who lived east of
the Jordan. They fought against you, but I gave them into your

[a] 2 That is, the Euphrates; also in verses 3, 14 and 15 [b] 6 Or *charioteers* [c] 6 Hebrew *Yam Suph*; that is, Sea of Reeds

(23:10–11) My Lord, I do love You for so many reasons, one of which is for Your extraordinary and supernatural equation: In the power of Your Spirit, I as one individual believer can put to flight enormous powers of evil darkness. I praise You too that Your people, as we see in the early church, can succeed against enormous opposition despite being in the minority. Grant that in these days too Your church may still prevail over the great odds against us. I pray it in the Name that is above every Name, the Name of Jesus Christ, our Conquering Lord and King. Amen.

Believing God's promises the Christian is taken through difficulties of every shape and size–and arrives safely.

Richard C. Halverson (1916-)

(24:2–8) How wonderful, O God of Moses and Joshua, that You still lead us today. You are the God of history; and now and forever You have good plans for Your people. Teach us to fear You, to serve You, to follow You in faithfulness, God of our Fathers, wherever You lead. Guide us into the promised land You have chosen for us.

God has no need of marionettes. He pays men the compliment of allowing them to live without him if they choose. But if they live without him in this life, they must also live without him in the next.

Leon Morris (1914-)

(24:15) Lord God, I have seen the idols that surround me—idols of wealth, power, fear and desire. But You, O Lord, have all good things in Your hand, and You have promised to provide all that I need. What could I desire more than You? Who else should I turn to? Where else would I go? I will serve You, Lord, because I love You and I fear You. I acknowledge You as the God above all gods. You alone deserve my worship, my devotion, my praise.

Come and fill our homes
With Your presence;
You alone are worthy
Of our reverence.
As for me and my house,
We will serve the Lord.

Lord, we vow to live holy,
Bowing our knees to You only.
As for me and my house,
We will serve the Lord.

Staying together, praying together,
Any storm we can weather,
Trusting in God's Word.
We need each other,
Fathers and mothers,
Sisters and brothers
In harmony and love.

"The Family Prayer Song"
Morris Chapman (©1994)

hands. I destroyed them from before you, and you took possession of their land. 9When Balak son of Zippor, the king of Moab,
prepared to fight against Israel, he sent for Balaam son of Beor to
put a curse on you. 10But I would not listen to Balaam, so he
blessed you again and again, and I delivered you out of his hand.
11" 'Then you crossed the Jordan and came to Jericho. The citizens of Jericho fought against you, as did also the Amorites, Perizzites, Canaanites, Hittites, Girgashites, Hivites and Jebusites, but
I gave them into your hands. 12I sent the hornet ahead of you,
which drove them out before you—also the two Amorite kings.
You did not do it with your own sword and bow. 13So I gave you
a land on which you did not toil and cities you did not build; and
you live in them and eat from vineyards and olive groves that you
did not plant.'
14"Now fear the LORD and serve him with all faithfulness.
Throw away the gods your forefathers worshiped beyond the
River and in Egypt, and serve the LORD. 15But if serving the LORD
seems undesirable to you, then choose for yourselves this day
whom you will serve, whether the gods your forefathers served
beyond the River, or the gods of the Amorites, in whose land you
are living. But as for me and my household, we will serve the
LORD."
16Then the people answered, "Far be it from us to forsake the
LORD to serve other gods! 17It was the LORD our God himself who
brought us and our fathers up out of Egypt, from that land of slavery, and performed those great signs before our eyes. He protected us on our entire journey and among all the nations
through which we traveled. 18And the LORD drove out before us
all the nations, including the Amorites, who lived in the land. We
too will serve the LORD, because he is our God."
19Joshua said to the people, "You are not able to serve the
LORD. He is a holy God; he is a jealous God. He will not forgive
your rebellion and your sins. 20If you forsake the LORD and serve
foreign gods, he will turn and bring disaster on you and make an
end of you, after he has been good to you."
21But the people said to Joshua, "No! We will serve the LORD."
22Then Joshua said, "You are witnesses against yourselves that
you have chosen to serve the LORD."
"Yes, we are witnesses," they replied.
23"Now then," said Joshua, "throw away the foreign gods that
are among you and yield your hearts to the LORD, the God of Israel."
24And the people said to Joshua, "We will serve the LORD our
God and obey him."
25On that day Joshua made a covenant for the people, and
there at Shechem he drew up for them decrees and laws. 26And
Joshua recorded these things in the Book of the Law of God. Then
he took a large stone and set it up there under the oak near the
holy place of the LORD.
27"See!" he said to all the people. "This stone will be a witness
against us. It has heard all the words the LORD has said to us. It
will be a witness against you if you are untrue to your God."

Buried in the Promised Land

28Then Joshua sent the people away, each to his own inheritance.
29After these things, Joshua son of Nun, the servant of the LORD,

died at the age of a hundred and ten. 30 And they buried him in the land of his inheritance, at Timnath Serah[a] in the hill country of Ephraim, north of Mount Gaash.

31 Israel served the LORD throughout the lifetime of Joshua and of the elders who outlived him and who had experienced everything the LORD had done for Israel.

32 And Joseph's bones, which the Israelites had brought up from Egypt, were buried at Shechem in the tract of land that Jacob bought for a hundred pieces of silver[b] from the sons of Hamor, the father of Shechem. This became the inheritance of Joseph's descendants.

33 And Eleazar son of Aaron died and was buried at Gibeah, which had been allotted to his son Phinehas in the hill country of Ephraim.

(24:31) Eternal God, may I leave a legacy of godliness that will inspire those around me and those who follow after I am gone to serve You with greater heart and deeper zeal. Amen.

God the Father, name we treasure,
Each new generation draws
From the past that You have given
For the future that is Yours:
May these children, in Your
keeping,
Love Your ways, obey Your laws.

"God the Father, Name We Treasure"
Rev. Basil E. Bridge (©1975)

[a] *30* Also known as *Timnath Heres* (see Judges 2:9) [b] *32* Hebrew ***hundred kesitahs***; a kesitah was a unit of money of unknown weight and value.

The Book of JUDGES

The book of Judges begins to tell the story of God's relationship with Israel following the conquest of Canaan. The chosen people now live in the promised land, although their compromises with its pagan inhabitants lead to a lifestyle far inferior to what God had intended. Even though they dwell in their divine inheritance, the Israelites repeatedly fall into sin and need God's deliverance.

Unlike other nations, Israel has no human king during the era of the judges. The government is truly theocratic—with the Lord as King. Though this sounds like an ideal arrangement, the reality is far from ideal. Time and again the people forget their divine King and choose rather to serve the gods of their pagan neighbors. As a result God lifts His protection from the people and they fall under the oppressive hand of Gentile kings.

As the Israelites groan in agony, they cry out to God Who hears their prayers. In compassion the Lord raises up "judges" to save the people from their oppressors. Though traditionally translated as "judge," the Hebrew term *shophet* actually means "leader." Through His leaders God delivers Israel from foreign domination and guides His people into a period of stability and blessing. But, sadly and predictably, once a judge dies the Israelites return to their spiritually adulterous and disastrous ways. Then, after additional years of suffering, God once again raises up another judge to save His people. But this salvation lasts only as long as the judge remains alive.

Jesus Christ has fulfilled the role of the final Judge. When we who know Christ fall back into sin, we do not need a new savior, but rather a new experience of the salvation we already have in Christ.

Many of us can relate to the sorry but merciful cycle of Israel's sin and God's deliverance. Even those of us who have been saved through Jesus Christ can wander away from God. We are tempted to worship other "gods" such as success, materialism, physical attractiveness, sexual immorality or moral relativism. Yet when we chase after our sinful idols, like the Israelites we reap the fruit of sin and groan in our suffering. And, as He did repeatedly so long ago, God shows compassion to us and delivers us from our bondage.

But, though God can use human agents to assist in our deliverance, He does not need to send new "judges." Jesus Christ has fulfilled the role of the final Judge (Ac 10:42–43), pronouncing upon us the sentence of "guilty," and then taking that sentence upon Himself. Thus He has set us free once and for all from sin and its sorry effects. When we who know Christ fall back into sin, we do not need a new savior, but rather a new experience of the salvation we already have in Christ.

Our worship regularly reflects the saving work of Jesus Christ. We continually thank Him for His gracious redemption. For though we still sin, "If we confess our sins, he is faithful and just and will forgive us our sins and purify us from all unrighteousness" (1Jn 1:9). In the Lord's Supper we remember the supreme act by which our Judge has delivered us. In every aspect of worship we exalt Jesus Christ, our ultimate Judge, Leader and Savior.

Israel Fights the Remaining Canaanites

1 After the death of Joshua, the Israelites asked the LORD, "Who
will be the first to go up and fight for us against the Canaanites?"
2The LORD answered, "Judah is to go; I have given the land into
their hands."
3Then the men of Judah said to the Simeonites their brothers,
"Come up with us into the territory allotted to us, to fight against
the Canaanites. We in turn will go with you into yours." So the Simeonites went with them.
4When Judah attacked, the LORD gave the Canaanites and Perizzites into their hands and they struck down ten thousand men at
Bezek. 5It was there that they found Adoni-Bezek and fought
against him, putting to rout the Canaanites and Perizzites. 6Adoni-
Bezek fled, but they chased him and caught him, and cut off his
thumbs and big toes.
7Then Adoni-Bezek said, "Seventy kings with their thumbs and
big toes cut off have picked up scraps under my table. Now God
has paid me back for what I did to them." They brought him to Jerusalem, and he died there.
8The men of Judah attacked Jerusalem also and took it. They
put the city to the sword and set it on fire.
9After that, the men of Judah went down to fight against the
Canaanites living in the hill country, the Negev and the western
foothills. 10They advanced against the Canaanites living in Hebron
(formerly called Kiriath Arba) and defeated Sheshai, Ahiman and
Talmai.
11From there they advanced against the people living in Debir
(formerly called Kiriath Sepher). 12And Caleb said, "I will give my
daughter Acsah in marriage to the man who attacks and captures
Kiriath Sepher." 13Othniel son of Kenaz, Caleb's younger brother,
took it; so Caleb gave his daughter Acsah to him in marriage.
14One day when she came to Othniel, she urged him[a] to ask her
father for a field. When she got off her donkey, Caleb asked her,
"What can I do for you?"
15She replied, "Do me a special favor. Since you have given me
land in the Negev, give me also springs of water." Then Caleb gave
her the upper and lower springs.
16The descendants of Moses' father-in-law, the Kenite, went up
from the City of Palms[b] with the men of Judah to live among the
people of the Desert of Judah in the Negev near Arad.
17Then the men of Judah went with the Simeonites their brothers and attacked the Canaanites living in Zephath, and they totally
destroyed[c] the city. Therefore it was called Hormah.[d] 18The men
of Judah also took[e] Gaza, Ashkelon and Ekron—each city with its
territory.
19The LORD was with the men of Judah. They took possession of
the hill country, but they were unable to drive the people from the
plains, because they had iron chariots. 20As Moses had promised,
Hebron was given to Caleb, who drove from it the three sons of
Anak. 21The Benjamites, however, failed to dislodge the Jebusites,
who were living in Jerusalem; to this day the Jebusites live there
with the Benjamites.

[a] *14* Hebrew; Septuagint and Vulgate *Othniel, he urged her* [b] *16* That is, Jericho
[c] *17* The Hebrew term refers to the irrevocable giving over of things or persons to the LORD, often by totally destroying them. [d] *17 Hormah* means *destruction.* [e] *18* Hebrew; Septuagint *Judah did not take*

(1:1–21) After the death of Joshua, Your people asked You for a leader. And as You had foretold in Jacob's blessing many centuries before, the tribe of Judah would rise to prominence and lead the people into victory. But even under the direction of Your appointed leaders, Your people would falter in their quest for victory because of their lack of obedience to You. O Lord, in our day—indeed, in my day—may I be faithful to Your covenant and see the enemy's influence vanquished from every area of my life. (Ge 49:8–10)

Christ engaged the powers of darkness first, and foiled them, which animates us for our conflicts; and it is in him that we are more than conquerors.

Matthew Henry (1662-1714)

22Now the house of Joseph attacked Bethel, and the LORD was
with them. 23When they sent men to spy out Bethel (formerly
called Luz), 24the spies saw a man coming out of the city and they
said to him, "Show us how to get into the city and we will see that
you are treated well." 25So he showed them, and they put the city
to the sword but spared the man and his whole family. 26He then
went to the land of the Hittites, where he built a city and called it
Luz, which is its name to this day.
27But Manasseh did not drive out the people of Beth Shan or
Taanach or Dor or Ibleam or Megiddo and their surrounding settlements, for the Canaanites were determined to live in that land.
28When Israel became strong, they pressed the Canaanites into
forced labor but never drove them out completely. 29Nor did
Ephraim drive out the Canaanites living in Gezer, but the Canaanites continued to live there among them. 30Neither did Zebulun
drive out the Canaanites living in Kitron or Nahalol, who remained
among them; but they did subject them to forced labor. 31Nor did
Asher drive out those living in Acco or Sidon or Ahlab or Aczib or
Helbah or Aphek or Rehob, 32and because of this the people of
Asher lived among the Canaanite inhabitants of the land. 33Neither
did Naphtali drive out those living in Beth Shemesh or Beth Anath;
but the Naphtalites too lived among the Canaanite inhabitants of
the land, and those living in Beth Shemesh and Beth Anath became
forced laborers for them. 34The Amorites confined the Danites to
the hill country, not allowing them to come down into the plain.
35And the Amorites were determined also to hold out in Mount
Heres, Aijalon and Shaalbim, but when the power of the house of
Joseph increased, they too were pressed into forced labor. 36The
boundary of the Amorites was from Scorpion[a] Pass to Sela and
beyond.

The Angel of the LORD at Bokim

2 The angel of the LORD went up from Gilgal to Bokim and said,
"I brought you up out of Egypt and led you into the land that
I swore to give to your forefathers. I said, 'I will never break my
covenant with you, 2and you shall not make a covenant with the
people of this land, but you shall break down their altars.' Yet you
have disobeyed me. Why have you done this? 3Now therefore I tell
you that I will not drive them out before you; they will be ⌞thorns⌟
in your sides and their gods will be a snare to you."
4When the angel of the LORD had spoken these things to all the
Israelites, the people wept aloud, 5and they called that place
Bokim.[b] There they offered sacrifices to the LORD.

Disobedience and Defeat

6After Joshua had dismissed the Israelites, they went to take
possession of the land, each to his own inheritance. 7The people
served the LORD throughout the lifetime of Joshua and of the elders
who outlived him and who had seen all the great things the LORD
had done for Israel.
8Joshua son of Nun, the servant of the LORD, died at the age of a
hundred and ten. 9And they buried him in the land of his inheritance, at Timnath Heres[c] in the hill country of Ephraim, north of
Mount Gaash.
10After that whole generation had been gathered to their fa-

(1:27—2:3) O God, I confess that in my own strength and self-confidence I allow certain sins to linger uncontested in my life. I presume that I have them under control; that I am the master and not the slave. Yet the things I tolerate are the very things that become thorns in my side. Convinced that I can stand, how soon I fall! Forgive me Lord, and empower me with holy tenacity to drive out completely those things that hold me back from being all You have created me to be. (Jn 8:34)

[a] 36 Hebrew *Akrabbim* [b] 5 *Bokim* means *weepers.* [c] 9 Also known as *Timnath Serah* (see Joshua 19:50 and 24:30)

thers, another generation grew up, who knew neither the LORD nor
what he had done for Israel. 11Then the Israelites did evil in the
eyes of the LORD and served the Baals. 12They forsook the LORD,
the God of their fathers, who had brought them out of Egypt. They
followed and worshiped various gods of the peoples around them.
They provoked the LORD to anger 13because they forsook him and
served Baal and the Ashtoreths. 14In his anger against Israel the
LORD handed them over to raiders who plundered them. He sold
them to their enemies all around, whom they were no longer able
to resist. 15Whenever Israel went out to fight, the hand of the LORD
was against them to defeat them, just as he had sworn to them.
They were in great distress.

16Then the LORD raised up judges,[a] who saved them out of the
hands of these raiders. 17Yet they would not listen to their judges
but prostituted themselves to other gods and worshiped them. Unlike their fathers, they quickly turned from the way in which their
fathers had walked, the way of obedience to the LORD's commands.
18Whenever the LORD raised up a judge for them, he was with the
judge and saved them out of the hands of their enemies as long as
the judge lived; for the LORD had compassion on them as they
groaned under those who oppressed and afflicted them. 19But
when the judge died, the people returned to ways even more corrupt than those of their fathers, following other gods and serving
and worshiping them. They refused to give up their evil practices
and stubborn ways.

20Therefore the LORD was very angry with Israel and said, "Because this nation has violated the covenant that I laid down for
their forefathers and has not listened to me, 21I will no longer
drive out before them any of the nations Joshua left when he died.
22I will use them to test Israel and see whether they will keep the
way of the LORD and walk in it as their forefathers did." 23The LORD
had allowed those nations to remain; he did not drive them out at
once by giving them into the hands of Joshua.

3 These are the nations the LORD left to test all those Israelites
who had not experienced any of the wars in Canaan 2(he did
this only to teach warfare to the descendants of the Israelites who
had not had previous battle experience): 3the five rulers of the
Philistines, all the Canaanites, the Sidonians, and the Hivites living
in the Lebanon mountains from Mount Baal Hermon to Lebo[b] Hamath. 4They were left to test the Israelites to see whether they
would obey the LORD's commands, which he had given their forefathers through Moses.

5The Israelites lived among the Canaanites, Hittites, Amorites,
Perizzites, Hivites and Jebusites. 6They took their daughters in
marriage and gave their own daughters to their sons, and served
their gods.

Othniel

7The Israelites did evil in the eyes of the LORD; they forgot the
LORD their God and served the Baals and the Asherahs. 8The anger
of the LORD burned against Israel so that he sold them into the
hands of Cushan-Rishathaim king of Aram Naharaim,[c] to whom
the Israelites were subject for eight years. 9But when they cried
out to the LORD, he raised up for them a deliverer, Othniel son of
Kenaz, Caleb's younger brother, who saved them. 10The Spirit of

[a] 16 Or *leaders*; similarly in verses 17–19 [b] 3 Or *to the entrance to* [c] 8 That is, Northwest Mesopotamia

(2:22—3:2) O Lord, when I encounter adversity or resistance in my spiritual growth, help me to look beyond the immediate test to see the outcome You desire. Help me to look to You in faith even as You look to me for faithfulness. May I be found faithful in the midst of the trial, and may I be proven worthy of the calling I have received. (Hab 2:4; Eph 4:1)

The Christian who through identification with Christ in death and resurrection enters into the Promised Land of a life of fullness and of victory finds himself up against the forces of Hell pitted against Christ and His Church . . . He comes to realize as never before that here in this world, whose head is the Prince of Darkness, he is living in enemy territory and that he is going to be made to feel it . . .

He must now fashion a strategy of a very different order. Carnal weapons are now of no value. They must be weapons mighty through God to the pulling down of strongholds (2 Cor 10:4).

Frederick Julius Huegel (1889–1971)

(3:12–15) Father, I praise You for Your great faithfulness to Your people. Again and again they sinned against You. Again and again You disciplined them. Again and again they cried out to You in repentance. And again and again You sent a deliverer to save them from their torment. So the pattern continued: disobedience, discipline, distress, deliverance. And so it continues even among Your people today. How quickly we turn from Your way. Yet how faithfully You lead us—and sometimes drive us—back to the fold. Thank You, Father, for Your mercy and for Your kindness that leads us to repentance. (Jdg 2:11–19; Ro 2:4)

We have to learn that we are dependent upon the enabling power of the Holy Spirit to attain any degree of holiness. Then, as we look to Him, we will see Him working in us–revealing our sin, creating a desire for holiness, and giving us the strength to respond to Him in obedience.

Jerry Bridges (1929-)

the LORD came upon him, so that he became Israel's judge[a] and
went to war. The LORD gave Cushan-Rishathaim king of Aram into
the hands of Othniel, who overpowered him. 11So the land had
peace for forty years, until Othniel son of Kenaz died.

Ehud

12Once again the Israelites did evil in the eyes of the LORD, and
because they did this evil the LORD gave Eglon king of Moab power
over Israel. 13Getting the Ammonites and Amalekites to join him,
Eglon came and attacked Israel, and they took possession of the
City of Palms.[b] 14The Israelites were subject to Eglon king of
Moab for eighteen years.

15Again the Israelites cried out to the LORD, and he gave them a
deliverer—Ehud, a left-handed man, the son of Gera the Benjamite. The Israelites sent him with tribute to Eglon king of Moab.
16Now Ehud had made a double-edged sword about a foot and a
half[c] long, which he strapped to his right thigh under his clothing.
17He presented the tribute to Eglon king of Moab, who was a very
fat man. 18After Ehud had presented the tribute, he sent on their
way the men who had carried it. 19At the idols[d] near Gilgal he
himself turned back and said, "I have a secret message for you,
O king."

The king said, "Quiet!" And all his attendants left him.

20Ehud then approached him while he was sitting alone in the
upper room of his summer palace[e] and said, "I have a message
from God for you." As the king rose from his seat, 21Ehud reached
with his left hand, drew the sword from his right thigh and
plunged it into the king's belly. 22Even the handle sank in after the
blade, which came out his back. Ehud did not pull the sword out,
and the fat closed in over it. 23Then Ehud went out to the porch[f];
he shut the doors of the upper room behind him and locked them.

24After he had gone, the servants came and found the doors of
the upper room locked. They said, "He must be relieving himself
in the inner room of the house." 25They waited to the point of em-
barrassment, but when he did not open the doors of the room,
they took a key and unlocked them. There they saw their lord fall-
en to the floor, dead.

26While they waited, Ehud got away. He passed by the idols and
escaped to Seirah. 27When he arrived there, he blew a trumpet in
the hill country of Ephraim, and the Israelites went down with him
from the hills, with him leading them.

28"Follow me," he ordered, "for the LORD has given Moab, your
enemy, into your hands." So they followed him down and, taking
possession of the fords of the Jordan that led to Moab, they allowed no one to cross over. 29At that time they struck down about
ten thousand Moabites, all vigorous and strong; not a man escaped. 30That day Moab was made subject to Israel, and the land
had peace for eighty years.

Shamgar

31After Ehud came Shamgar son of Anath, who struck down six
hundred Philistines with an oxgoad. He too saved Israel.

[a] *10* Or *leader* [b] *13* That is, Jericho [c] *16* Hebrew *a cubit* (about 0.5 meter)
[d] *19* Or *the stone quarries*; also in verse 26 [e] *20* The meaning of the Hebrew for this phrase is uncertain. [f] *23* The meaning of the Hebrew for this word is uncertain.

Deborah

4 After Ehud died, the Israelites once again did evil in the eyes
of the LORD. 2So the LORD sold them into the hands of Jabin, a
king of Canaan, who reigned in Hazor. The commander of his
army was Sisera, who lived in Harosheth Haggoyim. 3Because he
had nine hundred iron chariots and had cruelly oppressed the Israelites for twenty years, they cried to the LORD for help.
4Deborah, a prophetess, the wife of Lappidoth, was leading[a] Israel at that time. 5She held court under the Palm of Deborah between Ramah and Bethel in the hill country of Ephraim, and the
Israelites came to her to have their disputes decided. 6She sent for
Barak son of Abinoam from Kedesh in Naphtali and said to him,
"The LORD, the God of Israel, commands you: 'Go, take with you
ten thousand men of Naphtali and Zebulun and lead the way to
Mount Tabor. 7I will lure Sisera, the commander of Jabin's army,
with his chariots and his troops to the Kishon River and give him
into your hands.' "
8Barak said to her, "If you go with me, I will go; but if you don't
go with me, I won't go."
9"Very well," Deborah said, "I will go with you. But because of
the way you are going about this,[b] the honor will not be yours, for
the LORD will hand Sisera over to a woman." So Deborah went with
Barak to Kedesh, 10where he summoned Zebulun and Naphtali.
Ten thousand men followed him, and Deborah also went with him.
11Now Heber the Kenite had left the other Kenites, the descendants of Hobab, Moses' brother-in-law,[c] and pitched his tent by
the great tree in Zaanannim near Kedesh.
12When they told Sisera that Barak son of Abinoam had gone up
to Mount Tabor, 13Sisera gathered together his nine hundred iron
chariots and all the men with him, from Harosheth Haggoyim to
the Kishon River.
14Then Deborah said to Barak, "Go! This is the day the LORD has
given Sisera into your hands. Has not the LORD gone ahead of you?"
So Barak went down Mount Tabor, followed by ten thousand men.
15At Barak's advance, the LORD routed Sisera and all his chariots
and army by the sword, and Sisera abandoned his chariot and fled
on foot. 16But Barak pursued the chariots and army as far as
Harosheth Haggoyim. All the troops of Sisera fell by the sword;
not a man was left.
17Sisera, however, fled on foot to the tent of Jael, the wife of
Heber the Kenite, because there were friendly relations between
Jabin king of Hazor and the clan of Heber the Kenite.
18Jael went out to meet Sisera and said to him, "Come, my lord,
come right in. Don't be afraid." So he entered her tent, and she
put a covering over him.
19"I'm thirsty," he said. "Please give me some water." She
opened a skin of milk, gave him a drink, and covered him up.
20"Stand in the doorway of the tent," he told her. "If someone
comes by and asks you, 'Is anyone here?' say 'No.' "
21But Jael, Heber's wife, picked up a tent peg and a hammer
and went quietly to him while he lay fast asleep, exhausted. She
drove the peg through his temple into the ground, and he died.
22Barak came by in pursuit of Sisera, and Jael went out to meet
him. "Come," she said, "I will show you the man you're looking

[a] 4 Traditionally *judging* [b] 9 Or *But on the expedition you are undertaking* [c] 11 Or *father-in-law*

Ever and anon in the long history of God's patient dealing with men, we find him raising up some woman to lead, to guide, to inspire; and always there is this same element of enthusiasm and force. The one great message of the story seems to be that it warns us to take heed that we do not imagine ourselves to be wiser than God. When he calls and equips a woman to high service, let us beware lest we dishonor him by refusing to recognize her, or cooperate with her.

G. Campbell Morgan (1863-1945)

(4:4—5:31) Lord, I thank You for raising up Deborah, and for the crucial role she played in preserving and protecting Your covenant people. As a prophetess she knew Your voice; as a leader she knew Your way. Lord, raise up Deborahs in our day—godly women who are strong, wise, courageous, filled with faith, and diligent in their service to You and Your people.

for." So he went in with her, and there lay Sisera with the tent peg through his temple—dead.

23 On that day God subdued Jabin, the Canaanite king, before the Israelites. 24 And the hand of the Israelites grew stronger and stronger against Jabin, the Canaanite king, until they destroyed him.

The Song of Deborah

5 On that day Deborah and Barak son of Abinoam sang this song:

2 "When the princes in Israel take the lead,
when the people willingly offer themselves—
praise the LORD!

3 "Hear this, you kings! Listen, you rulers!
I will sing to[a] the LORD, I will sing;
I will make music to[b] the LORD, the God of Israel.

4 "O LORD, when you went out from Seir,
when you marched from the land of Edom,
the earth shook, the heavens poured,
the clouds poured down water.
5 The mountains quaked before the LORD, the One of Sinai,
before the LORD, the God of Israel.

6 "In the days of Shamgar son of Anath,
in the days of Jael, the roads were abandoned;
travelers took to winding paths.
7 Village life[c] in Israel ceased,
ceased until I,[d] Deborah, arose,
arose a mother in Israel.
8 When they chose new gods,
war came to the city gates,
and not a shield or spear was seen
among forty thousand in Israel.
9 My heart is with Israel's princes,
with the willing volunteers among the people.
Praise the LORD!

10 "You who ride on white donkeys,
sitting on your saddle blankets,
and you who walk along the road,
consider 11 the voice of the singers[e] at the watering places.
They recite the righteous acts of the LORD,
the righteous acts of his warriors[f] in Israel.

"Then the people of the LORD
went down to the city gates.
12 'Wake up, wake up, Deborah!
Wake up, wake up, break out in song!
Arise, O Barak!
Take captive your captives, O son of Abinoam.'
13 "Then the men who were left
came down to the nobles;

[a] *3* Or *of* [b] *3* Or */ with song I will praise* [c] *7* Or *Warriors* [d] *7* Or *you* [e] *11* Or *archers*; the meaning of the Hebrew for this word is uncertain. [f] *11* Or *villagers*

(5:2) Lord, I see the beauty and simplicity of Your plan. The princes take the lead, the people willingly offer themselves, and You are greatly praised! Restore Your church so that we will function according to Your design rather than our own. O God, raise up leaders in our day—men and women of humility, faith, courage and influence—so that Your people will be faithful in service and Your name will be honored not only among us, but because of us, throughout this world.

There is a Lord to this harvest. There is a great Commander-in-chief to this campaign. He has the whole campaign for a world carefully planned out. And each man's part in it is planned too. He knows best what needs to be done. He sees keenly the strategic points, and the emergencies. If only He could but depend on our ears being trained to know His voice, and our wills trained to simple, full obedience, how much difference it would make to Him.

Dr. Samuel Dickey Gordon (1859–1936)

the people of the LORD
came to me with the mighty.
14 Some came from Ephraim, whose roots were in
Amalek;
Benjamin was with the people who followed you.
From Makir captains came down,
from Zebulun those who bear a commander's staff.
15 The princes of Issachar were with Deborah;
yes, Issachar was with Barak,
rushing after him into the valley.
In the districts of Reuben
there was much searching of heart.
16 Why did you stay among the campfires[a]
to hear the whistling for the flocks?
In the districts of Reuben
there was much searching of heart.
17 Gilead stayed beyond the Jordan.
And Dan, why did he linger by the ships?
Asher remained on the coast
and stayed in his coves.
18 The people of Zebulun risked their very lives;
so did Naphtali on the heights of the field.

19 "Kings came, they fought;
the kings of Canaan fought
at Taanach by the waters of Megiddo,
but they carried off no silver, no plunder.
20 From the heavens the stars fought,
from their courses they fought against Sisera.
21 The river Kishon swept them away,
the age-old river, the river Kishon.
March on, my soul; be strong!
22 Then thundered the horses' hoofs—
galloping, galloping go his mighty steeds.
23 'Curse Meroz,' said the angel of the LORD.
'Curse its people bitterly,
because they did not come to help the LORD,
to help the LORD against the mighty.'

24 "Most blessed of women be Jael,
the wife of Heber the Kenite,
most blessed of tent-dwelling women.
25 He asked for water, and she gave him milk;
in a bowl fit for nobles she brought him curdled
milk.
26 Her hand reached for the tent peg,
her right hand for the workman's hammer.
She struck Sisera, she crushed his head,
she shattered and pierced his temple.
27 At her feet he sank,
he fell; there he lay.
At her feet he sank, he fell;
where he sank, there he fell—dead.

28 "Through the window peered Sisera's mother;
behind the lattice she cried out,

[a] 16 Or *saddlebags*

(5:16–18) O God, forbid that I should "stay among the campfires" while others are risking their very lives in sacrificial service to Your name. Forbid that I should "linger by the ships" when others fearlessly race inland with the claims of Your sovereign grace and saving power. Grant me faith to hear Your Word and courage to do Your will when decisive obedience is required. Call me out from my place of comfort and security; let me join those who dare to do Your will—even in the face of strong opposition.

Am I a soldier of the cross,
A follower of the Lamb,
And shall I fear to own his cause,
Or blush to speak his name?

Must I be carried to the skies
On flowery beds of ease,
While others fought to win the
prize,
And sailed through bloody seas?

"Am I a Soldier of the Cross"
Isaac Watts (c.1724)

(6:2–12) Lord, stir Your people to arise from their hiding places and come into the light! Do not let human oppression or the satanic schemes of darkness cause us to cower in fear and unbelief. Speak, Lord, to those whom You see as mighty warriors! Speak as You spoke to Gideon. Call us to trust in You, and anoint us with a fearless faith that destroys idols, rallies warriors and vanquishes Your enemies. O God, turn cowards into conquerors for the sake of Your kingdom. Amen.

Encamped along the hills of light,
Ye Christian soldiers, rise
And press the battle ere the night
Shall veil the glowing skies.
Against the foe in vales below
Let all our strength be hurled;
Faith is the victory, we know,
That overcomes the world.

Faith is the victory!
Faith is the victory!
O glorious victory
That overcomes the world!

"Faith Is the Victory"
John H. Yates (1837-1900)

(6:14) I praise You, Father, that You use us in spite of our failures, our fears, our sins and our weaknesses. You use imperfect people to accomplish Your perfect will. We go in faith, "in the strength [we] have," and You are with us. I thank You for not looking for people who have it all together. Instead, You use people who are willing to say yes, to take the risk and follow Your direction. As it was with Gideon, so it is with us today: You use us in spite of ourselves, so that all of the glory goes to You. Praise Your holy name. (2Co 12:9; Heb 11:32–34)

It is not my ability, but my response to God's ability, that counts.
Corrie ten Boom (1892-1983)

'Why is his chariot so long in coming?
Why is the clatter of his chariots delayed?'
29 The wisest of her ladies answer her;
indeed, she keeps saying to herself,
30 'Are they not finding and dividing the spoils:
a girl or two for each man,
colorful garments as plunder for Sisera,
colorful garments embroidered,
highly embroidered garments for my neck—
all this as plunder?'

31 "So may all your enemies perish, O LORD!
But may they who love you be like the sun
when it rises in its strength."

Then the land had peace forty years.

Gideon

6 Again the Israelites did evil in the eyes of the LORD, and for seven years he gave them into the hands of the Midianites. 2Because the power of Midian was so oppressive, the Israelites prepared shelters for themselves in mountain clefts, caves and strongholds. 3Whenever the Israelites planted their crops, the Midianites, Amalekites and other eastern peoples invaded the country. 4They camped on the land and ruined the crops all the way to Gaza and did not spare a living thing for Israel, neither sheep nor cattle nor donkeys. 5They came up with their livestock and their tents like swarms of locusts. It was impossible to count the men and their camels; they invaded the land to ravage it. 6Midian so impoverished the Israelites that they cried out to the LORD for help.

7When the Israelites cried to the LORD because of Midian, 8he sent them a prophet, who said, "This is what the LORD, the God of Israel, says: I brought you up out of Egypt, out of the land of slavery. 9I snatched you from the power of Egypt and from the hand of all your oppressors. I drove them from before you and gave you their land. 10I said to you, 'I am the LORD your God; do not worship the gods of the Amorites, in whose land you live.' But you have not listened to me."

11The angel of the LORD came and sat down under the oak in Ophrah that belonged to Joash the Abiezrite, where his son Gideon was threshing wheat in a winepress to keep it from the Midianites. 12When the angel of the LORD appeared to Gideon, he said, "The LORD is with you, mighty warrior."

13"But sir," Gideon replied, "if the LORD is with us, why has all this happened to us? Where are all his wonders that our fathers told us about when they said, 'Did not the LORD bring us up out of Egypt?' But now the LORD has abandoned us and put us into the hand of Midian."

14The LORD turned to him and said, "Go in the strength you have and save Israel out of Midian's hand. Am I not sending you?"

15"But Lord,[a]" Gideon asked, "how can I save Israel? My clan is the weakest in Manasseh, and I am the least in my family."

16The LORD answered, "I will be with you, and you will strike down all the Midianites together."

17Gideon replied, "If now I have found favor in your eyes, give

[a] 15 Or *sir*

me a sign that it is really you talking to me. 18Please do not go
away until I come back and bring my offering and set it before
you."

And the LORD said, "I will wait until you return."

19Gideon went in, prepared a young goat, and from an ephah[a]
of flour he made bread without yeast. Putting the meat in a basket and its broth in a pot, he brought them out and offered them
to him under the oak.

20The angel of God said to him, "Take the meat and the unleavened bread, place them on this rock, and pour out the
broth." And Gideon did so. 21With the tip of the staff that was in
his hand, the angel of the LORD touched the meat and the unleavened bread. Fire flared from the rock, consuming the meat
and the bread. And the angel of the LORD disappeared. 22When
Gideon realized that it was the angel of the LORD, he exclaimed,
"Ah, Sovereign LORD! I have seen the angel of the LORD face to
face!"

23But the LORD said to him, "Peace! Do not be afraid. You are
not going to die."

24So Gideon built an altar to the LORD there and called it The
LORD is Peace. To this day it stands in Ophrah of the Abiezrites.

25That same night the LORD said to him, "Take the second bull
from your father's herd, the one seven years old.[b] Tear down
your father's altar to Baal and cut down the Asherah pole[c] beside
it. 26Then build a proper kind of[d] altar to the LORD your God on
the top of this height. Using the wood of the Asherah pole that
you cut down, offer the second[e] bull as a burnt offering."

27So Gideon took ten of his servants and did as the LORD told
him. But because he was afraid of his family and the men of the
town, he did it at night rather than in the daytime.

28In the morning when the men of the town got up, there was
Baal's altar, demolished, with the Asherah pole beside it cut
down and the second bull sacrificed on the newly built altar!

29They asked each other, "Who did this?"

When they carefully investigated, they were told, "Gideon son
of Joash did it."

30The men of the town demanded of Joash, "Bring out your
son. He must die, because he has broken down Baal's altar and
cut down the Asherah pole beside it."

31But Joash replied to the hostile crowd around him, "Are you
going to plead Baal's cause? Are you trying to save him? Whoever fights for him shall be put to death by morning! If Baal really
is a god, he can defend himself when someone breaks down his
altar." 32So that day they called Gideon "Jerub-Baal,[f]" saying,
"Let Baal contend with him," because he broke down Baal's
altar.

33Now all the Midianites, Amalekites and other eastern peoples joined forces and crossed over the Jordan and camped in
the Valley of Jezreel. 34Then the Spirit of the LORD came upon
Gideon, and he blew a trumpet, summoning the Abiezrites to follow him. 35He sent messengers throughout Manasseh, calling
them to arms, and also into Asher, Zebulun and Naphtali, so that
they too went up to meet them.

[a] *19* That is, probably about 3/5 bushel (about 22 liters) [b] *25* Or *Take a full-grown, mature bull from your father's herd* [c] *25* That is, a symbol of the goddess Asherah; here and elsewhere in Judges [d] *26* Or *build with layers of stone an* [e] *26* Or *full-grown*; also in verse 28 [f] *32* *Jerub-Baal* means *let Baal contend.*

(6:16) "I will be with You." The promise of Your presence gives us comfort and courage for the task ahead. With these words You commissioned Moses, Joshua and Gideon. With these same words Jesus commissioned us. Thank You, Lord, that when You call us into Your service You do not leave us on our own. Though at times You hide Yourself in the shadows, we can trust in Your promise that You will always be with us. (Ex 3:12, Jos 1:5,9; Mt 28:20)

I will be with you, I'll be on your side.
Your prayer for deliverance will not
be denied.
I'll fight the battle that evil might
wage.
And I will be with you, I will be with
you
'Til the end of the age.

"I Will Be With You"
Bill Batstone (©1988)

(6:25–35) Before Gideon could vanquish the enemies from his homeland, he had to vanquish the idols from his household. Lord, please purify me from anything that might cause me to forfeit Your anointing in my life. Open my eyes to see the false gods that I have brought into my household, and give me courage to take whatever steps are necessary to follow You in complete obedience.

I had been used to hearing Christians talk about consecration to the will of God as being such a high religious attainment that only a few extra devout souls could hope to reach it. But with my discovery of the infinite unselfishness of God, I came to realize that consecration to Him was not an attainment but a priceless privilege; and I cannot but feel sure that if people only knew the loveliness of His will, not a devout few only, but every soul in the universe would rush eagerly to choose it for every moment of their lives.

Hannah Whitall Smith (1832-1911)

36Gideon said to God, "If you will save Israel by my hand as
you have promised— 37look, I will place a wool fleece on the
threshing floor. If there is dew only on the fleece and all the
ground is dry, then I will know that you will save Israel by my
hand, as you said." 38And that is what happened. Gideon rose
early the next day; he squeezed the fleece and wrung out the
dew—a bowlful of water.
39Then Gideon said to God, "Do not be angry with me. Let me
make just one more request. Allow me one more test with the
fleece. This time make the fleece dry and the ground covered with
dew." 40That night God did so. Only the fleece was dry; all the
ground was covered with dew.

Gideon Defeats the Midianites

7 Early in the morning, Jerub-Baal (that is, Gideon) and all his
men camped at the spring of Harod. The camp of Midian was
north of them in the valley near the hill of Moreh. 2The LORD said
to Gideon, "You have too many men for me to deliver Midian into
their hands. In order that Israel may not boast against me that her
own strength has saved her, 3announce now to the people, 'Anyone who trembles with fear may turn back and leave Mount
Gilead.' " So twenty-two thousand men left, while ten thousand
remained.
4But the LORD said to Gideon, "There are still too many men.
Take them down to the water, and I will sift them for you there. If
I say, 'This one shall go with you,' he shall go; but if I say, 'This
one shall not go with you,' he shall not go."
5So Gideon took the men down to the water. There the LORD
told him, "Separate those who lap the water with their tongues
like a dog from those who kneel down to drink." 6Three hundred men lapped with their hands to their mouths. All the rest got
down on their knees to drink.
7The LORD said to Gideon, "With the three hundred men that
lapped I will save you and give the Midianites into your hands. Let
all the other men go, each to his own place." 8So Gideon sent the
rest of the Israelites to their tents but kept the three hundred,
who took over the provisions and trumpets of the others.
Now the camp of Midian lay below him in the valley. 9During
that night the LORD said to Gideon, "Get up, go down against the
camp, because I am going to give it into your hands. 10If you are
afraid to attack, go down to the camp with your servant Purah
11and listen to what they are saying. Afterward, you will be encouraged to attack the camp." So he and Purah his servant went
down to the outposts of the camp. 12The Midianites, the Amalekites and all the other eastern peoples had settled in the valley,
thick as locusts. Their camels could no more be counted than
the sand on the seashore.
13Gideon arrived just as a man was telling a friend his dream.
"I had a dream," he was saying. "A round loaf of barley bread
came tumbling into the Midianite camp. It struck the tent with
such force that the tent overturned and collapsed."
14His friend responded, "This can be nothing other than the
sword of Gideon son of Joash, the Israelite. God has given the
Midianites and the whole camp into his hands."
15When Gideon heard the dream and its interpretation, he
worshiped God. He returned to the camp of Israel and called out,
"Get up! The LORD has given the Midianite camp into your hands."

(6:36–40) Lord, like Gideon, I need Your constant reassurance. Please forgive the weakness of my faith. It's not that I doubt You or Your faithfulness or power. Rather, I doubt myself. I often think I know what You want me to do. But then I have second thoughts—am I making things up in my own imagination? Is that really You, Lord? My heart is deceitful and desperately wicked, but I want so much to know Your will. Lord, I believe. Help my unbelief! And please be patient with me in the process.

(7:2–8) Thank You, God, that You do not allow me to become deceived by my resources. Whether great or small, whether weak or strong, I will always need You. I cannot help but think how astounded Gideon must have been at the thought of going into battle with only 300 men. And how awestruck and overjoyed he must have been at the sight of Your amazing deliverance. Lord, do in me anything You need to do so that You can do through me everything You want to do.

16Dividing the three hundred men into three companies, he placed trumpets and empty jars in the hands of all of them, with torches inside.
17"Watch me," he told them. "Follow my lead. When I get to the edge of the camp, do exactly as I do. 18When I and all who are with me blow our trumpets, then from all around the camp blow yours and shout, 'For the LORD and for Gideon.' "
19Gideon and the hundred men with him reached the edge of the camp at the beginning of the middle watch, just after they had changed the guard. They blew their trumpets and broke the jars that were in their hands. 20The three companies blew the trumpets and smashed the jars. Grasping the torches in their left hands and holding in their right hands the trumpets they were to blow, they shouted, "A sword for the LORD and for Gideon!" 21While each man held his position around the camp, all the Midianites ran, crying out as they fled.
22When the three hundred trumpets sounded, the LORD caused the men throughout the camp to turn on each other with their swords. The army fled to Beth Shittah toward Zererah as far as the border of Abel Meholah near Tabbath. 23Israelites from Naphtali, Asher and all Manasseh were called out, and they pursued the Midianites. 24Gideon sent messengers throughout the hill country of Ephraim, saying, "Come down against the Midianites and seize the waters of the Jordan ahead of them as far as Beth Barah."

So all the men of Ephraim were called out and they took the waters of the Jordan as far as Beth Barah. 25They also captured two of the Midianite leaders, Oreb and Zeeb. They killed Oreb at the rock of Oreb, and Zeeb at the winepress of Zeeb. They pursued the Midianites and brought the heads of Oreb and Zeeb to Gideon, who was by the Jordan.

Zebah and Zalmunna

8 Now the Ephraimites asked Gideon, "Why have you treated us like this? Why didn't you call us when you went to fight Midian?" And they criticized him sharply.
2But he answered them, "What have I accomplished compared to you? Aren't the gleanings of Ephraim's grapes better than the full grape harvest of Abiezer? 3God gave Oreb and Zeeb, the Midianite leaders, into your hands. What was I able to do compared to you?" At this, their resentment against him subsided.
4Gideon and his three hundred men, exhausted yet keeping up the pursuit, came to the Jordan and crossed it. 5He said to the men of Succoth, "Give my troops some bread; they are worn out, and I am still pursuing Zebah and Zalmunna, the kings of Midian."
6But the officials of Succoth said, "Do you already have the hands of Zebah and Zalmunna in your possession? Why should we give bread to your troops?"
7Then Gideon replied, "Just for that, when the LORD has given Zebah and Zalmunna into my hand, I will tear your flesh with desert thorns and briers."
8From there he went up to Peniel[a] and made the same request of them, but they answered as the men of Succoth had. 9So he said to the men of Peniel, "When I return in triumph, I will tear down this tower."
10Now Zebah and Zalmunna were in Karkor with a force of

[a] 8 Hebrew *Penuel,* a variant of *Peniel*; also in verses 9 and 17

(7:17) O Lord, our need for godly leaders is great! Give us men and women who exemplify in their character and conduct the qualities that command respect, allegiance and unswerving courage. Let those now step forward who can say, "Watch me. Follow my lead. Do exactly as I do." And, Lord, if it is not presumptuous of me to ask, let me be such a leader in this day. (1Co 4:16; Heb 13:7)

God has never had on his side a majority of men and women. He does not need a majority to work wonders in history, but he does need a minority fully committed to him and his purpose.

Ernest Fremont Tittle (1885-1949)

(8:4) Lord, may it be said of me as it was said of Gideon that I kept up the pursuit even though I was exhausted. Give me fortitude, patience and joy so that my life will be pleasing to You and inspiring to those with whom I have influence. Forbid that I should serve You in any half-hearted way. Do not allow me to settle for one victory when You would give me one hundred! Give me no rest if I give rest to the enemies of my soul! Lead on, Lord, and make me a pursuer of Your perfect will. (Heb 6:9–12)

(8:23–27) O Lord, a little fox can spoil the vine. A little folly can shame a reputation. And a little treasure can become a snare to even the greatest of leaders. And if a man like Gideon should fall, what chance then do I have in the face of such subtle temptations? O Lord, set a guard upon my heart. Let me not wander from the truth of Your Lordship, nor permit my thoughts to become enticed with taking just a little glory for myself. Let me learn from Gideon's fall, so that I may in this day stand tall.

Let us remember that God looks in our actions only for the motive. The world judges us by appearance; God counts for nothing what is most dazzling to men. What He desires is a pure intention, true docility, and a sincere self-renunciation. All this is exercised more frequently, and in a way that tries us more severely on common than on great occasions . . . We are more easily led away by little things, because we believe them more innocent and imagine that we are less attracted to them; nevertheless, when God deprives us of them, we soon discover, from the pain of deprivation, how excessive and inexcusable was our attachment to them.

François Fénelon (1651–1715)

about fifteen thousand men, all that were left of the armies of the
eastern peoples; a hundred and twenty thousand swordsmen had
fallen. 11Gideon went up by the route of the nomads east of Nobah
and Jogbehah and fell upon the unsuspecting army. 12Zebah and
Zalmunna, the two kings of Midian, fled, but he pursued them and
captured them, routing their entire army.
13Gideon son of Joash then returned from the battle by the Pass
of Heres. 14He caught a young man of Succoth and questioned
him, and the young man wrote down for him the names of the seventy-seven officials of Succoth, the elders of the town. 15Then Gideon came and said to the men of Succoth, "Here are Zebah and
Zalmunna, about whom you taunted me by saying, 'Do you already
have the hands of Zebah and Zalmunna in your possession? Why
should we give bread to your exhausted men?' " 16He took the el-
ders of the town and taught the men of Succoth a lesson by punishing them with desert thorns and briers. 17He also pulled down
the tower of Peniel and killed the men of the town.
18Then he asked Zebah and Zalmunna, "What kind of men did
you kill at Tabor?"

"Men like you," they answered, "each one with the bearing of a prince."

19Gideon replied, "Those were my brothers, the sons of my
own mother. As surely as the LORD lives, if you had spared their
lives, I would not kill you." 20Turning to Jether, his oldest son, he
said, "Kill them!" But Jether did not draw his sword, because he
was only a boy and was afraid.
21Zebah and Zalmunna said, "Come, do it yourself. 'As is the
man, so is his strength.' " So Gideon stepped forward and killed
them, and took the ornaments off their camels' necks.

Gideon's Ephod

22The Israelites said to Gideon, "Rule over us—you, your son
and your grandson—because you have saved us out of the hand of
Midian."
23But Gideon told them, "I will not rule over you, nor will my
son rule over you. The LORD will rule over you." 24And he said, "I
do have one request, that each of you give me an earring from
your share of the plunder." (It was the custom of the Ishmaelites
to wear gold earrings.)
25They answered, "We'll be glad to give them." So they spread
out a garment, and each man threw a ring from his plunder onto
it. 26The weight of the gold rings he asked for came to seventeen
hundred shekels,[a] not counting the ornaments, the pendants and
the purple garments worn by the kings of Midian or the chains
that were on their camels' necks. 27Gideon made the gold into an
ephod, which he placed in Ophrah, his town. All Israel prostituted themselves by worshiping it there, and it became a snare to
Gideon and his family.

Gideon's Death

28Thus Midian was subdued before the Israelites and did not
raise its head again. During Gideon's lifetime, the land enjoyed
peace forty years.
29Jerub-Baal son of Joash went back home to live. 30He had
seventy sons of his own, for he had many wives. 31His concubine,

[a] *26* That is, about 43 pounds (about 19.5 kilograms)

who lived in Shechem, also bore him a son, whom he named Abimelech. 32Gideon son of Joash died at a good old age and was buried in the tomb of his father Joash in Ophrah of the Abiezrites.

33No sooner had Gideon died than the Israelites again prostituted themselves to the Baals. They set up Baal-Berith as their god and 34did not remember the LORD their God, who had rescued them from the hands of all their enemies on every side. 35They also failed to show kindness to the family of Jerub-Baal (that is, Gideon) for all the good things he had done for them.

Abimelech

9 Abimelech son of Jerub-Baal went to his mother's brothers in Shechem and said to them and to all his mother's clan, 2"Ask all the citizens of Shechem, 'Which is better for you: to have all seventy of Jerub-Baal's sons rule over you, or just one man?' Remember, I am your flesh and blood."

3When the brothers repeated all this to the citizens of Shechem, they were inclined to follow Abimelech, for they said, "He is our brother." 4They gave him seventy shekels[a] of silver from the temple of Baal-Berith, and Abimelech used it to hire reckless adventurers, who became his followers. 5He went to his father's home in Ophrah and on one stone murdered his seventy brothers, the sons of Jerub-Baal. But Jotham, the youngest son of Jerub-Baal, escaped by hiding. 6Then all the citizens of Shechem and Beth Millo gathered beside the great tree at the pillar in Shechem to crown Abimelech king.

7When Jotham was told about this, he climbed up on the top of Mount Gerizim and shouted to them, "Listen to me, citizens of Shechem, so that God may listen to you. 8One day the trees went out to anoint a king for themselves. They said to the olive tree, 'Be our king.'

9"But the olive tree answered, 'Should I give up my oil, by which both gods and men are honored, to hold sway over the trees?'

10"Next, the trees said to the fig tree, 'Come and be our king.'

11"But the fig tree replied, 'Should I give up my fruit, so good and sweet, to hold sway over the trees?'

12"Then the trees said to the vine, 'Come and be our king.'

13"But the vine answered, 'Should I give up my wine, which cheers both gods and men, to hold sway over the trees?'

14"Finally all the trees said to the thornbush, 'Come and be our king.'

15"The thornbush said to the trees, 'If you really want to anoint me king over you, come and take refuge in my shade; but if not, then let fire come out of the thornbush and consume the cedars of Lebanon!'

16"Now if you have acted honorably and in good faith when you made Abimelech king, and if you have been fair to Jerub-Baal and his family, and if you have treated him as he deserves— 17and to think that my father fought for you, risked his life to rescue you from the hand of Midian 18(but today you have revolted against my father's family, murdered his seventy sons on a single stone, and made Abimelech, the son of his slave girl, king over the citizens of Shechem because he is your brother)— 19if then you have acted honorably and in good faith toward Jerub-Baal and his family

[a] 4 That is, about 1 3/4 pounds (about 0.8 kilogram)

(8:33—9:6) Father, Your people were hostile toward You in their worship, so they became hostile in their relationships. They turned away from the God of peace and embraced a violent leader. And in so doing they became living examples of Biblical truth: "The mind of sinful man is death, but the mind controlled by the Spirit is life and peace; the sinful mind is hostile to God. It does not submit to God's law, nor can it do so. Those controlled by the sinful nature cannot please God." (Ro 8:6–8)

Who has a right to go into God's presence? Who has a right to draw near? Those who seek Him with clean hands and a pure heart; that is, those who worship God acceptably. Those who receive righteousness from God, or those who are redeemed. The two characteristics are inseparable. One does not become a true worshiper apart from redemption, and one who is genuinely redeemed becomes a true worshiper. He is done with superficial religion and false gods and adores the living and true God.

John MacArthur, Jr. (1939-)

today, may Abimelech be your joy, and may you be his, too! 20But
if you have not, let fire come out from Abimelech and consume
you, citizens of Shechem and Beth Millo, and let fire come out
from you, citizens of Shechem and Beth Millo, and consume
Abimelech!"
21Then Jotham fled, escaping to Beer, and he lived there because he was afraid of his brother Abimelech.
22After Abimelech had governed Israel three years, 23God sent
an evil spirit between Abimelech and the citizens of Shechem, who
acted treacherously against Abimelech. 24God did this in order
that the crime against Jerub-Baal's seventy sons, the shedding of
their blood, might be avenged on their brother Abimelech and on
the citizens of Shechem, who had helped him murder his brothers. 25In opposition to him these citizens of Shechem set men on
the hilltops to ambush and rob everyone who passed by, and this
was reported to Abimelech.
26Now Gaal son of Ebed moved with his brothers into Shechem,
and its citizens put their confidence in him. 27After they had gone
out into the fields and gathered the grapes and trodden them, they
held a festival in the temple of their god. While they were eating
and drinking, they cursed Abimelech. 28Then Gaal son of Ebed
said, "Who is Abimelech, and who is Shechem, that we should be
subject to him? Isn't he Jerub-Baal's son, and isn't Zebul his
deputy? Serve the men of Hamor, Shechem's father! Why should we
serve Abimelech? 29If only this people were under my command!
Then I would get rid of him. I would say to Abimelech, 'Call out
your whole army!' "[a]
30When Zebul the governor of the city heard what Gaal son of
Ebed said, he was very angry. 31Under cover he sent messengers
to Abimelech, saying, "Gaal son of Ebed and his brothers have
come to Shechem and are stirring up the city against you. 32Now
then, during the night you and your men should come and lie in
wait in the fields. 33In the morning at sunrise, advance against the
city. When Gaal and his men come out against you, do whatever
your hand finds to do."
34So Abimelech and all his troops set out by night and took up
concealed positions near Shechem in four companies. 35Now Gaal
son of Ebed had gone out and was standing at the entrance to the
city gate just as Abimelech and his soldiers came out from their
hiding place.
36When Gaal saw them, he said to Zebul, "Look, people are
coming down from the tops of the mountains!"

Zebul replied, "You mistake the shadows of the mountains for
men."
37But Gaal spoke up again: "Look, people are coming down
from the center of the land, and a company is coming from the direction of the soothsayers' tree."
38Then Zebul said to him, "Where is your big talk now, you who
said, 'Who is Abimelech that we should be subject to him?' Aren't
these the men you ridiculed? Go out and fight them!"
39So Gaal led out[b] the citizens of Shechem and fought Abimelech. 40Abimelech chased him, and many fell wounded in the
flight—all the way to the entrance to the gate. 41Abimelech stayed
in Arumah, and Zebul drove Gaal and his brothers out of Shechem.

[a] 29 Septuagint; Hebrew *him." Then he said to Abimelech, "Call out your whole army!"*
[b] 39 Or *Gaal went out in the sight of*

(9:23–25) O God, in Your great wisdom You can use the fickle loyalties of wicked people to cause them to devour one another. Truly, vengeance belongs to You, Lord. You avenged the shedding of innocent blood, and You did not allow the guilty to go unpunished. Thank You, Father, for Your righteous judgments. (Dt 32:43)

Lord, I feel so helpless in dealing with what I am up against. I have made the mistake of focusing exclusively on my vulnerability, rather than also trusting you with final outcomes. I am strengthened today in knowing anew you have the last word because you have the greater power.

George O. Wood (1941-)

42The next day the people of Shechem went out to the fields, and this was reported to Abimelech. 43So he took his men, divided them into three companies and set an ambush in the fields. When he saw the people coming out of the city, he rose to attack them. 44Abimelech and the companies with him rushed forward to a position at the entrance to the city gate. Then two companies rushed upon those in the fields and struck them down. 45All that day Abimelech pressed his attack against the city until he had captured it and killed its people. Then he destroyed the city and scattered salt over it.

46On hearing this, the citizens in the tower of Shechem went into the stronghold of the temple of El-Berith. 47When Abimelech heard that they had assembled there, 48he and all his men went up Mount Zalmon. He took an ax and cut off some branches, which he lifted to his shoulders. He ordered the men with him, "Quick! Do what you have seen me do!" 49So all the men cut branches and followed Abimelech. They piled them against the stronghold and set it on fire over the people inside. So all the people in the tower of Shechem, about a thousand men and women, also died.

50Next Abimelech went to Thebez and besieged it and captured it. 51Inside the city, however, was a strong tower, to which all the men and women—all the people of the city—fled. They locked themselves in and climbed up on the tower roof. 52Abimelech went to the tower and stormed it. But as he approached the entrance to the tower to set it on fire, 53a woman dropped an upper millstone on his head and cracked his skull.

54Hurriedly he called to his armor-bearer, "Draw your sword and kill me, so that they can't say, 'A woman killed him.' " So his servant ran him through, and he died. 55When the Israelites saw that Abimelech was dead, they went home.

56Thus God repaid the wickedness that Abimelech had done to his father by murdering his seventy brothers. 57God also made the men of Shechem pay for all their wickedness. The curse of Jotham son of Jerub-Baal came on them.

Tola

10 After the time of Abimelech a man of Issachar, Tola son of Puah, the son of Dodo, rose to save Israel. He lived in Shamir, in the hill country of Ephraim. 2He led[a] Israel twenty-three years; then he died, and was buried in Shamir.

Jair

3He was followed by Jair of Gilead, who led Israel twenty-two years. 4He had thirty sons, who rode thirty donkeys. They controlled thirty towns in Gilead, which to this day are called Havvoth Jair.[b] 5When Jair died, he was buried in Kamon.

Jephthah

6Again the Israelites did evil in the eyes of the LORD. They served the Baals and the Ashtoreths, and the gods of Aram, the gods of Sidon, the gods of Moab, the gods of the Ammonites and the gods of the Philistines. And because the Israelites forsook the LORD and no longer served him, 7he became angry with them. He sold them into the hands of the Philistines and the Ammonites,

[a] 2 Traditionally *judged*; also in verse 3 [b] 4 Or *called the settlements of Jair*

(9:56) How I thank You, God, for the witness of Your Word—for the record it bears to Your faithfulness in performing what You promise. Indeed, You are not a God who can be mocked. You reward every person according to his or her deeds. Though some may go unchastised for a season, nevertheless You answer their unrepentant ways with justice. And I praise You, O God, that You show favor and lovingkindness to those who trust in You. (Gal 6:10)

8who that year shattered and crushed them. For eighteen years they oppressed all the Israelites on the east side of the Jordan in Gilead, the land of the Amorites. 9The Ammonites also crossed the Jordan to fight against Judah, Benjamin and the house of Ephraim; and Israel was in great distress. 10Then the Israelites cried out to the LORD, "We have sinned against you, forsaking our God and serving the Baals."

11The LORD replied, "When the Egyptians, the Amorites, the Ammonites, the Philistines, 12the Sidonians, the Amalekites and the Maonites[a] oppressed you and you cried to me for help, did I not save you from their hands? 13But you have forsaken me and served other gods, so I will no longer save you. 14Go and cry out to the gods you have chosen. Let them save you when you are in trouble!"

15But the Israelites said to the LORD, "We have sinned. Do with us whatever you think best, but please rescue us now." 16Then they got rid of the foreign gods among them and served the LORD. And he could bear Israel's misery no longer.

17When the Ammonites were called to arms and camped in Gilead, the Israelites assembled and camped at Mizpah. 18The leaders of the people of Gilead said to each other, "Whoever will launch the attack against the Ammonites will be the head of all those living in Gilead."

11 Jephthah the Gileadite was a mighty warrior. His father was Gilead; his mother was a prostitute. 2Gilead's wife also bore him sons, and when they were grown up, they drove Jephthah away. "You are not going to get any inheritance in our family," they said, "because you are the son of another woman." 3So Jephthah fled from his brothers and settled in the land of Tob, where a group of adventurers gathered around him and followed him.

4Some time later, when the Ammonites made war on Israel, 5the elders of Gilead went to get Jephthah from the land of Tob. 6"Come," they said, "be our commander, so we can fight the Ammonites."

7Jephthah said to them, "Didn't you hate me and drive me from my father's house? Why do you come to me now, when you're in trouble?"

8The elders of Gilead said to him, "Nevertheless, we are turning to you now; come with us to fight the Ammonites, and you will be our head over all who live in Gilead."

9Jephthah answered, "Suppose you take me back to fight the Ammonites and the LORD gives them to me—will I really be your head?"

10The elders of Gilead replied, "The LORD is our witness; we will certainly do as you say." 11So Jephthah went with the elders of Gilead, and the people made him head and commander over them. And he repeated all his words before the LORD in Mizpah.

12Then Jephthah sent messengers to the Ammonite king with the question: "What do you have against us that you have attacked our country?"

13The king of the Ammonites answered Jephthah's messengers, "When Israel came up out of Egypt, they took away my land from the Arnon to the Jabbok, all the way to the Jordan. Now give it back peaceably."

[a] *12* Hebrew; some Septuagint manuscripts *Midianites*

Events and circumstances awaken our religion, as though there were no need to pray to God except in illness and sorrow. As soon as affairs take a turn for the better and the danger is past, our devotion vanishes; the most we think of doing is to thank God for the successful end of our troubles; after a short act of gratitude we forget him and think of nothing but our pleasures.

Jean Nicolas Grou (1731–1803)

(10:11–16) Lord, what is Your love that You overlook the shallow and superficial confessions of a people who turn to You only because they are in trouble, and who will surely turn from You after You have delivered them? What strength is in Your heart to continually show Yourself faithful, even when You are dealt with so faithlessly? O what a great and awesome God You are! I praise You for Your perfect love that "always protects, always trusts, always hopes, always perseveres," and that never fails. (1Co 13:7–8)

He is the hope of the captive's heart,
He is the power that sets them free,
It's in His life that we receive
The wonder of His love.

And His love endures forever,
Unchanging always true.
And His love endures forever,
Forever, for all time.
Yes, His love endures forever,
Love divine.

"His Love Endures Forever"
Bob Wilson (©1995)

[14]Jephthah sent back messengers to the Ammonite king, [15]saying:

"This is what Jephthah says: Israel did not take the land of Moab or the land of the Ammonites. [16]But when they came up out of Egypt, Israel went through the desert to the Red Sea[a] and on to Kadesh. [17]Then Israel sent messengers to the king of Edom, saying, 'Give us permission to go through your country,' but the king of Edom would not listen. They sent also to the king of Moab, and he refused. So Israel stayed at Kadesh.

[18]"Next they traveled through the desert, skirted the lands of Edom and Moab, passed along the eastern side of the country of Moab, and camped on the other side of the Arnon. They did not enter the territory of Moab, for the Arnon was its border.

[19]"Then Israel sent messengers to Sihon king of the Amorites, who ruled in Heshbon, and said to him, 'Let us pass through your country to our own place.' [20]Sihon, however, did not trust Israel[b] to pass through his territory. He mustered all his men and encamped at Jahaz and fought with Israel.

[21]"Then the LORD, the God of Israel, gave Sihon and all his men into Israel's hands, and they defeated them. Israel took over all the land of the Amorites who lived in that country, [22]capturing all of it from the Arnon to the Jabbok and from the desert to the Jordan.

[23]"Now since the LORD, the God of Israel, has driven the Amorites out before his people Israel, what right have you to take it over? [24]Will you not take what your god Chemosh gives you? Likewise, whatever the LORD our God has given us, we will possess. [25]Are you better than Balak son of Zippor, king of Moab? Did he ever quarrel with Israel or fight with them? [26]For three hundred years Israel occupied Heshbon, Aroer, the surrounding settlements and all the towns along the Arnon. Why didn't you retake them during that time? [27]I have not wronged you, but you are doing me wrong by waging war against me. Let the LORD, the Judge,[c] decide the dispute this day between the Israelites and the Ammonites."

[28]The king of Ammon, however, paid no attention to the message Jephthah sent him.

[29]Then the Spirit of the LORD came upon Jephthah. He crossed Gilead and Manasseh, passed through Mizpah of Gilead, and from there he advanced against the Ammonites. [30]And Jephthah made a vow to the LORD: "If you give the Ammonites into my hands, [31]whatever comes out of the door of my house to meet me when I return in triumph from the Ammonites will be the LORD's, and I will sacrifice it as a burnt offering."

[32]Then Jephthah went over to fight the Ammonites, and the LORD gave them into his hands. [33]He devastated twenty towns from Aroer to the vicinity of Minnith, as far as Abel Keramim. Thus Israel subdued Ammon.

[34]When Jephthah returned to his home in Mizpah, who should come out to meet him but his daughter, dancing to the sound of tambourines! She was an only child. Except for her he had neither

[a] *16* Hebrew *Yam Suph*; that is, Sea of Reeds [b] *20* Or *however, would not make an agreement for Israel* [c] *27* Or *Ruler*

(11:30–31) Lord, keep me from making foolish vows. And forgive me for being so presumptuous in thinking that I could bargain for Your blessings or impress You with promises of what I will do for you, in return for what I hope You will do for me. And Lord, spare those around me from the consequence of my undisciplined imagination and reckless tongue. Let me be one who is content simply to trust You without trying to impress You.

The lips are the double gates that open to let forth words, and the prayer is that God would set at that gateway a guard and sentinel (Psalms 141:3) . . . Our tongues hang loosely and swing easily without our knowing it. We are betrayed into hasty and wicked words; hence the need of a divine sentinel to keep watch. This doorkeeper demands the countersign of each word that would go forth—the countersign of its right to leave us, the proof that it is not an enemy to betray, but a servant of God and man, to fulfill some holy mission. It is also to be remembered that while warriors and others who go out from a gate may return through the same gate, no words ever go back into the city of Mansoul. When once they leave those gates, it is forever, whether to execute some good work, or to wander hither and thither as messengers of evil.

Arthur T. Pierson (1837-1911)

(12:1–3) The Ephraimites were not willing to fight for their country; neither were they content to live in peace with their countrymen. When they were called, they did not answer; when they were not called, they were offended. They were slow to make war against their enemies, but they were quick to make war against their brothers. And because they were not content to live in peace, they would die by the sword—all for the sake of pride, all under the influence of jealousy. O God, deliver us from the power of pride. Teach us to rejoice in the victories of our brothers and sisters in Christ, and to serve one another in love. Give us wisdom to heed Your warning: "If you keep on biting and devouring each other, watch out or you will be destroyed by each other." (Gal 5:13–15)

Jealousy is an insidious attitude that creeps into our hearts when we take our eyes off God and put them onto others. We can be jealous of each other's gifts or position in a church or group, or of the high profile another's ministry has compared to ours. The Bible says that measuring ourselves against each other is not wise (2 Cor. 10:12).

Floyd McClung, Jr. (1945-)

son nor daughter. [35]When he saw her, he tore his clothes and cried, "Oh! My daughter! You have made me miserable and wretched, because I have made a vow to the LORD that I cannot break."

[36]"My father," she replied, "you have given your word to the LORD. Do to me just as you promised, now that the LORD has avenged you of your enemies, the Ammonites. [37]But grant me this one request," she said. "Give me two months to roam the hills and weep with my friends, because I will never marry."

[38]"You may go," he said. And he let her go for two months. She and the girls went into the hills and wept because she would never marry. [39]After the two months, she returned to her father and he did to her as he had vowed. And she was a virgin.

From this comes the Israelite custom [40]that each year the young women of Israel go out for four days to commemorate the daughter of Jephthah the Gileadite.

Jephthah and Ephraim

12 The men of Ephraim called out their forces, crossed over to Zaphon and said to Jephthah, "Why did you go to fight the Ammonites without calling us to go with you? We're going to burn down your house over your head."

[2]Jephthah answered, "I and my people were engaged in a great struggle with the Ammonites, and although I called, you didn't save me out of their hands. [3]When I saw that you wouldn't help, I took my life in my hands and crossed over to fight the Ammonites, and the LORD gave me the victory over them. Now why have you come up today to fight me?"

[4]Jephthah then called together the men of Gilead and fought against Ephraim. The Gileadites struck them down because the Ephraimites had said, "You Gileadites are renegades from Ephraim and Manasseh." [5]The Gileadites captured the fords of the Jordan leading to Ephraim, and whenever a survivor of Ephraim said, "Let me cross over," the men of Gilead asked him, "Are you an Ephraimite?" If he replied, "No," [6]they said, "All right, say 'Shibboleth.' " If he said, "Sibboleth," because he could not pronounce the word correctly, they seized him and killed him at the fords of the Jordan. Forty-two thousand Ephraimites were killed at that time.

[7]Jephthah led[a] Israel six years. Then Jephthah the Gileadite died, and was buried in a town in Gilead.

Ibzan, Elon and Abdon

[8]After him, Ibzan of Bethlehem led Israel. [9]He had thirty sons and thirty daughters. He gave his daughters away in marriage to those outside his clan, and for his sons he brought in thirty young women as wives from outside his clan. Ibzan led Israel seven years. [10]Then Ibzan died, and was buried in Bethlehem.

[11]After him, Elon the Zebulunite led Israel ten years. [12]Then Elon died, and was buried in Aijalon in the land of Zebulun.

[13]After him, Abdon son of Hillel, from Pirathon, led Israel. [14]He had forty sons and thirty grandsons, who rode on seventy donkeys. He led Israel eight years. [15]Then Abdon son of Hillel died, and was buried at Pirathon in Ephraim, in the hill country of the Amalekites.

[a] 7 Traditionally *judged*; also in verses 8–14

The Birth of Samson

13 Again the Israelites did evil in the eyes of the LORD, so the LORD delivered them into the hands of the Philistines for forty years.

2 A certain man of Zorah, named Manoah, from the clan of the Danites, had a wife who was sterile and remained childless. 3 The angel of the LORD appeared to her and said, "You are sterile and childless, but you are going to conceive and have a son. 4 Now see to it that you drink no wine or other fermented drink and that you do not eat anything unclean, 5 because you will conceive and give birth to a son. No razor may be used on his head, because the boy is to be a Nazirite, set apart to God from birth, and he will begin the deliverance of Israel from the hands of the Philistines."

6 Then the woman went to her husband and told him, "A man of God came to me. He looked like an angel of God, very awesome. I didn't ask him where he came from, and he didn't tell me his name. 7 But he said to me, 'You will conceive and give birth to a son. Now then, drink no wine or other fermented drink and do not eat anything unclean, because the boy will be a Nazirite of God from birth until the day of his death.' "

8 Then Manoah prayed to the LORD: "O Lord, I beg you, let the man of God you sent to us come again to teach us how to bring up the boy who is to be born."

9 God heard Manoah, and the angel of God came again to the woman while she was out in the field; but her husband Manoah was not with her. 10 The woman hurried to tell her husband, "He's here! The man who appeared to me the other day!"

11 Manoah got up and followed his wife. When he came to the man, he said, "Are you the one who talked to my wife?"

"I am," he said.

12 So Manoah asked him, "When your words are fulfilled, what is to be the rule for the boy's life and work?"

13 The angel of the LORD answered, "Your wife must do all that I have told her. 14 She must not eat anything that comes from the grapevine, nor drink any wine or other fermented drink nor eat anything unclean. She must do everything I have commanded her."

15 Manoah said to the angel of the LORD, "We would like you to stay until we prepare a young goat for you."

16 The angel of the LORD replied, "Even though you detain me, I will not eat any of your food. But if you prepare a burnt offering, offer it to the LORD." (Manoah did not realize that it was the angel of the LORD.)

17 Then Manoah inquired of the angel of the LORD, "What is your name, so that we may honor you when your word comes true?"

18 He replied, "Why do you ask my name? It is beyond understanding.[a]" 19 Then Manoah took a young goat, together with the grain offering, and sacrificed it on a rock to the LORD. And the LORD did an amazing thing while Manoah and his wife watched: 20 As the flame blazed up from the altar toward heaven, the angel of the LORD ascended in the flame. Seeing this, Manoah and his wife fell with their faces to the ground. 21 When the angel of the LORD did not show himself again to Manoah and his wife, Manoah realized that it was the angel of the LORD.

[a] 18 Or *is wonderful*

(13:1–5) I praise You, Lord, for Your favor toward Samson's mother. You stepped into her hopeless situation and miraculously gave her a son. But as is so often the case, with Your favor comes a test. Your promise tested her faith; Your instructions tested her faithfulness. Lord, help me to pass the tests of faith and faithfulness that so often accompany Your favor in my life. And may I dedicate the fruit of Your favor to Your sovereign use. As for Your people, they brought their distress upon themselves. But in Your great mercy, after the appointed time, You miraculously raised up a deliverer to free them from their oppressors. Thank You, dear Father, that even when we abandon You, You do not abandon us.

"Count your many blessings," says the old hymn, "and it will surprise you what the Lord hath done." This prayer should end in glad and solemn resolve: "Lord, seal this gratitude upon my face, my words, my generous concern for my neighbors, my every outward thought and act."

George A. Buttrick (1892-1980)

The steadfast love of the Lord
Never ceases;
His mercies never come to an end.
They are new ev'ry morning,
New ev'ry morning;
Great is Thy faithfulness, O Lord.
Great is Thy faithfulness.

"The Steadfast Love Of The Lord"
Edith McNeill (©1974)

22“We are doomed to die!” he said to his wife. “We have seen
God!”
23But his wife answered, “If the LORD had meant to kill us, he
would not have accepted a burnt offering and grain offering from
our hands, nor shown us all these things or now told us this.”
24The woman gave birth to a boy and named him Samson. He
grew and the LORD blessed him, 25and the Spirit of the LORD began
to stir him while he was in Mahaneh Dan, between Zorah and Eshtaol.

Samson's Marriage

14 Samson went down to Timnah and saw there a young Philistine woman. 2When he returned, he said to his father and
mother, “I have seen a Philistine woman in Timnah; now get her for
me as my wife.”
3His father and mother replied, “Isn't there an acceptable
woman among your relatives or among all our people? Must you go
to the uncircumcised Philistines to get a wife?”
But Samson said to his father, “Get her for me. She's the right
one for me.” 4(His parents did not know that this was from the
LORD, who was seeking an occasion to confront the Philistines; for
at that time they were ruling over Israel.) 5Samson went down to
Timnah together with his father and mother. As they approached
the vineyards of Timnah, suddenly a young lion came roaring toward him. 6The Spirit of the LORD came upon him in power so that
he tore the lion apart with his bare hands as he might have torn a
young goat. But he told neither his father nor his mother what he
had done. 7Then he went down and talked with the woman, and he
liked her.
8Some time later, when he went back to marry her, he turned
aside to look at the lion's carcass. In it was a swarm of bees and
some honey, 9which he scooped out with his hands and ate as he
went along. When he rejoined his parents, he gave them some, and
they too ate it. But he did not tell them that he had taken the honey
from the lion's carcass.
10Now his father went down to see the woman. And Samson
made a feast there, as was customary for bridegrooms. 11When he
appeared, he was given thirty companions.
12“Let me tell you a riddle,” Samson said to them. “If you can
give me the answer within the seven days of the feast, I will give you
thirty linen garments and thirty sets of clothes. 13If you can't tell me
the answer, you must give me thirty linen garments and thirty sets
of clothes.”
“Tell us your riddle,” they said. “Let's hear it.”
14He replied,

> “Out of the eater, something to eat;
> out of the strong, something sweet.”

For three days they could not give the answer.
15On the fourth[a] day, they said to Samson's wife, “Coax your
husband into explaining the riddle for us, or we will burn you and
your father's household to death. Did you invite us here to rob us?”
16Then Samson's wife threw herself on him, sobbing, “You hate
me! You don't really love me. You've given my people a riddle, but
you haven't told me the answer.”

[a] 15 Some Septuagint manuscripts and Syriac; Hebrew *seventh*

In the lion of trial we find the honey of communion.
Charles Haddon Spurgeon (1834–1892)

(14:6–9) Father God, how I long for Your Holy Spirit to move upon me with power, as You moved upon Samson, Gideon and Othniel. For I am Your workmanship, created in Christ Jesus to do good works, which You prepared in advance for me to do. Please give me courage not to shrink back even in the face of overwhelming odds. You look for those through whom You can do the impossible. Don't ever let me settle for only those things I can do myself. (Jdg 3:10; 6:34; 14:6; Eph 2:10; Heb 10:35–39)

How my heart wonders
At the vastness of Your call,
When all that I have
In my hand seems so small,
I have known Your power
In my life,
The mighty hand that created all.
So won't You hear my prayer
And strengthen my hands?

Strengthen my hands,
Place in my heart
The wisdom to see
And to do my part.
Give me the grace
To accomplish the task;
See that I'm ready,

And I'm willing, Lord,
Strengthen my hands.
"Strengthen My Hands"
Paddy Graves and Denise Graves (©1996)

"I haven't even explained it to my father or mother," he replied,
"so why should I explain it to you?" 17She cried the whole seven
days of the feast. So on the seventh day he finally told her, because
she continued to press him. She in turn explained the riddle to her
people.
18Before sunset on the seventh day the men of the town said to
him,

"What is sweeter than honey?
What is stronger than a lion?"

Samson said to them,

"If you had not plowed with my heifer,
you would not have solved my riddle."

19Then the Spirit of the LORD came upon him in power. He went
down to Ashkelon, struck down thirty of their men, stripped them
of their belongings and gave their clothes to those who had explained the riddle. Burning with anger, he went up to his father's
house. 20And Samson's wife was given to the friend who had attended him at his wedding.

Samson's Vengeance on the Philistines

15 Later on, at the time of wheat harvest, Samson took a young
goat and went to visit his wife. He said, "I'm going to my
wife's room." But her father would not let him go in.
2"I was so sure you thoroughly hated her," he said, "that I gave
her to your friend. Isn't her younger sister more attractive? Take
her instead."
3Samson said to them, "This time I have a right to get even with
the Philistines; I will really harm them." 4So he went out and
caught three hundred foxes and tied them tail to tail in pairs. He
then fastened a torch to every pair of tails, 5lit the torches and let
the foxes loose in the standing grain of the Philistines. He burned
up the shocks and standing grain, together with the vineyards and
olive groves.
6When the Philistines asked, "Who did this?" they were told,
"Samson, the Timnite's son-in-law, because his wife was given to
his friend."
So the Philistines went up and burned her and her father to
death. 7Samson said to them, "Since you've acted like this, I won't
stop until I get my revenge on you." 8He attacked them viciously
and slaughtered many of them. Then he went down and stayed in a
cave in the rock of Etam.
9The Philistines went up and camped in Judah, spreading out
near Lehi. 10The men of Judah asked, "Why have you come to
fight us?"
"We have come to take Samson prisoner," they answered, "to do
to him as he did to us."
11Then three thousand men from Judah went down to the cave
in the rock of Etam and said to Samson, "Don't you realize that the
Philistines are rulers over us? What have you done to us?"
He answered, "I merely did to them what they did to me."
12They said to him, "We've come to tie you up and hand you
over to the Philistines."
Samson said, "Swear to me that you won't kill me yourselves."
13"Agreed," they answered. "We will only tie you up and hand
you over to them. We will not kill you." So they bound him with two

(14:16–19) In spite of Samson's foolishness and selfishness, You anointed him to bring vengeance against Your enemies. Though his methods seem barbaric and difficult to understand, still it was Your Spirit upon him that enabled him to accomplish these amazing feats. I praise You, Lord, that in Your sovereignty You choose and use whomever You wish to fulfill Your divine purposes.

Blessed be the glory of the Lord for his Godhead, his mysteriousness, his sovereignty, his almightiness, his eternity, and his providence.

Lancelot Andrews (1555–1626)

Spirit of the Lord, come upon me in power.
Spirit of the Lord, descend on me.
In your strength, I am strong;
Live and move in me my whole life long.

"Spirit of the Lord"
Walt Harrah (©1998)

new ropes and led him up from the rock. 14As he approached Lehi, the Philistines came toward him shouting. The Spirit of the LORD came upon him in power. The ropes on his arms became like charred flax, and the bindings dropped from his hands. 15Finding a fresh jawbone of a donkey, he grabbed it and struck down a thousand men.

16Then Samson said,

"With a donkey's jawbone
I have made donkeys of them.[a]
With a donkey's jawbone
I have killed a thousand men."

17When he finished speaking, he threw away the jawbone; and the place was called Ramath Lehi.[b]

18Because he was very thirsty, he cried out to the LORD, "You have given your servant this great victory. Must I now die of thirst and fall into the hands of the uncircumcised?" 19Then God opened up the hollow place in Lehi, and water came out of it. When Samson drank, his strength returned and he revived. So the spring was called En Hakkore,[c] and it is still there in Lehi.

20Samson led[d] Israel for twenty years in the days of the Philistines.

Samson and Delilah

16 One day Samson went to Gaza, where he saw a prostitute. He went in to spend the night with her. 2The people of Gaza were told, "Samson is here!" So they surrounded the place and lay in wait for him all night at the city gate. They made no move during the night, saying, "At dawn we'll kill him."

3But Samson lay there only until the middle of the night. Then he got up and took hold of the doors of the city gate, together with the two posts, and tore them loose, bar and all. He lifted them to his shoulders and carried them to the top of the hill that faces Hebron.

4Some time later, he fell in love with a woman in the Valley of Sorek whose name was Delilah. 5The rulers of the Philistines went to her and said, "See if you can lure him into showing you the secret of his great strength and how we can overpower him so we may tie him up and subdue him. Each one of us will give you eleven hundred shekels[e] of silver."

6So Delilah said to Samson, "Tell me the secret of your great strength and how you can be tied up and subdued."

7Samson answered her, "If anyone ties me with seven fresh thongs[f] that have not been dried, I'll become as weak as any other man."

8Then the rulers of the Philistines brought her seven fresh thongs that had not been dried, and she tied him with them. 9With men hidden in the room, she called to him, "Samson, the Philistines are upon you!" But he snapped the thongs as easily as a piece of string snaps when it comes close to a flame. So the secret of his strength was not discovered.

10Then Delilah said to Samson, "You have made a fool of me; you lied to me. Come now, tell me how you can be tied."

[a] *16* Or *made a heap or two*; the Hebrew for *donkey* sounds like the Hebrew for *heap.*
[b] *17* *Ramath Lehi* means *jawbone hill.* [c] *19* *En Hakkore* means *caller's spring.*
[d] *20* Traditionally *judged* [e] *5* That is, about 28 pounds (about 13 kilograms) [f] *7* Or *bowstrings*; also in verses 8 and 9

(16:4–6) Lord, protect me from the seductive lure of the world. Alert me to the flattery and deception that seeks only my ruin. Forbid me to linger long in the embrace of treachery. You have blessed me with gifts and abilities that are wonderful. You have placed Your hand upon me and given me measures of success. But what good are these things if I do not have strength of character? Now I pray You will keep my soul from presumptuous sin and subtle pride. Teach me to guard my heart, for it is the wellspring of life. (Pr 4:23)

O to grace how great a debtor
Daily I'm constrained to be!
Let Thy goodness, like a fetter,
Bind my wand'ring heart to Thee:
Prone to wander, Lord, I feel it,
Prone to leave the God I love;
Here's my heart, O take and seal it;
Seal it for Thy courts above.

"Come, Thou Fount of Every Blessing"
Robert Robinson (1735-1790)

The rule that governs my life is this: Anything that dims my vision of Christ, or takes away my taste for Bible study, or cramps my prayer life, or makes Christian work difficult, is wrong for me, and I must, as a Christian, turn away from it.

J. Wilbur Chapman (1859-1918)

11 He said, "If anyone ties me securely with new ropes that have
never been used, I'll become as weak as any other man."
12 So Delilah took new ropes and tied him with them. Then, with
men hidden in the room, she called to him, "Samson, the Philistines are upon you!" But he snapped the ropes off his arms as if
they were threads.
13 Delilah then said to Samson, "Until now, you have been making a fool of me and lying to me. Tell me how you can be tied."
He replied, "If you weave the seven braids of my head into the
fabric ⌊on the loom⌋ and tighten it with the pin, I'll become as
weak as any other man." So while he was sleeping, Delilah took
the seven braids of his head, wove them into the fabric 14 and[a]
tightened it with the pin.
Again she called to him, "Samson, the Philistines are upon
you!" He awoke from his sleep and pulled up the pin and the
loom, with the fabric.
15 Then she said to him, "How can you say, 'I love you,' when
you won't confide in me? This is the third time you have made a
fool of me and haven't told me the secret of your great strength."
16 With such nagging she prodded him day after day until he was
tired to death.
17 So he told her everything. "No razor has ever been used on
my head," he said, "because I have been a Nazirite set apart to
God since birth. If my head were shaved, my strength would leave
me, and I would become as weak as any other man."
18 When Delilah saw that he had told her everything, she sent
word to the rulers of the Philistines, "Come back once more; he
has told me everything." So the rulers of the Philistines returned
with the silver in their hands. 19 Having put him to sleep on her
lap, she called a man to shave off the seven braids of his hair, and
so began to subdue him.[b] And his strength left him.
20 Then she called, "Samson, the Philistines are upon you!"
He awoke from his sleep and thought, "I'll go out as before and
shake myself free." But he did not know that the LORD had left him.
21 Then the Philistines seized him, gouged out his eyes and took
him down to Gaza. Binding him with bronze shackles, they set him
to grinding in the prison. 22 But the hair on his head began to grow
again after it had been shaved.

The Death of Samson

23 Now the rulers of the Philistines assembled to offer a great
sacrifice to Dagon their god and to celebrate, saying, "Our god
has delivered Samson, our enemy, into our hands."
24 When the people saw him, they praised their god, saying,

"Our god has delivered our enemy
  into our hands,
the one who laid waste our land
  and multiplied our slain."

25 While they were in high spirits, they shouted, "Bring out Samson to entertain us." So they called Samson out of the prison, and
he performed for them.
When they stood him among the pillars, 26 Samson said to the
servant who held his hand, "Put me where I can feel the pillars

[a] *13,14* Some Septuagint manuscripts; Hebrew "⌊*I can*⌋ *if you weave the seven braids of my head into the fabric* ⌊*on the loom*⌋." [14]*So she* [b] *19* Hebrew; some Septuagint manuscripts *and he began to weaken*

(16:20–21) Father, as I look at the record of Samson's life, I ask You to take inventory of my own. What is the condition of my heart? Do I think I can flirt with temptation without falling? Do I think I can play with fire without getting burned? Is it possible that You could leave me and I would not even know it? Do I rely on my own strength—the strength You have given to me—to the point that I no longer rely on You? Have I been weakened by disobedience and blinded by sin? O God, deliver me from the self-deception of pride.

I call to You from out of the deep,
O Lord, most high,
Aware of my sin and the distance I
  keep
From the light, O Lord;
But there is forgiveness with Thee
And in wonder I fall on my knees.

My soul waits for the Lord
In the hope of His promise,
In the hope of His promise
Deliverance will come
My soul waits for the Lord
Through the night 'til the morning
Like a night watchman waiting
For the coming of the dawn.

"My Soul Waits"
Bill Batstone (©1986)

(17:6) Jesus, You are Lord. You alone can govern my soul and keep me from doing those things that may seem right to me but only end in death. Be exalted in my life and reign over my thoughts, my dreams, my hopes and my decisions. Let Your Word be established as the standard for my faith and conduct, and let Your Spirit lead me into doing only those things that please You and bring life to others. (Pr 14:12)

Lord, I lift my heart in full
surrender.
All that I hold dear I give to You.
Purify my heart and make me holy,
So I might walk the way
That's pleasing You.

"To Be Pleasing You"
Teresa Muller (©1984)

that support the temple, so that I may lean against them." 27 Now
the temple was crowded with men and women; all the rulers of the
Philistines were there, and on the roof were about three thousand
men and women watching Samson perform. 28 Then Samson
prayed to the LORD, "O Sovereign LORD, remember me. O God,
please strengthen me just once more, and let me with one blow
get revenge on the Philistines for my two eyes." 29 Then Samson
reached toward the two central pillars on which the temple stood.
Bracing himself against them, his right hand on the one and his
left hand on the other, 30 Samson said, "Let me die with the Philistines!" Then he pushed with all his might, and down came the
temple on the rulers and all the people in it. Thus he killed many
more when he died than while he lived.

31 Then his brothers and his father's whole family went down to
get him. They brought him back and buried him between Zorah
and Eshtaol in the tomb of Manoah his father. He had led[a] Israel
twenty years.

Micah's Idols

17 Now a man named Micah from the hill country of Ephraim
2 said to his mother, "The eleven hundred shekels[b] of silver
that were taken from you and about which I heard you utter a
curse—I have that silver with me; I took it."

Then his mother said, "The LORD bless you, my son!"

3 When he returned the eleven hundred shekels of silver to his
mother, she said, "I solemnly consecrate my silver to the LORD for
my son to make a carved image and a cast idol. I will give it back
to you."

4 So he returned the silver to his mother, and she took two hundred shekels[c] of silver and gave them to a silversmith, who made
them into the image and the idol. And they were put in Micah's
house.

5 Now this man Micah had a shrine, and he made an ephod and
some idols and installed one of his sons as his priest. 6 In those
days Israel had no king; everyone did as he saw fit.

7 A young Levite from Bethlehem in Judah, who had been living
within the clan of Judah, 8 left that town in search of some other
place to stay. On his way[d] he came to Micah's house in the hill
country of Ephraim.

9 Micah asked him, "Where are you from?"

"I'm a Levite from Bethlehem in Judah," he said, "and I'm looking for a place to stay."

10 Then Micah said to him, "Live with me and be my father and
priest, and I'll give you ten shekels[e] of silver a year, your clothes
and your food." 11 So the Levite agreed to live with him, and the
young man was to him like one of his sons. 12 Then Micah installed
the Levite, and the young man became his priest and lived in his
house. 13 And Micah said, "Now I know that the LORD will be good
to me, since this Levite has become my priest."

Danites Settle in Laish

18 In those days Israel had no king.
And in those days the tribe of the Danites was seeking a
place of their own where they might settle, because they had not

[a] *31* Traditionally *judged* [b] *2* That is, about 28 pounds (about 13 kilograms) [c] *4* That is, about 5 pounds (about 2.3 kilograms) [d] *8* Or *To carry on his profession* [e] *10* That is, about 4 ounces (about 110 grams)

yet come into an inheritance among the tribes of Israel. 2So the
Danites sent five warriors from Zorah and Eshtaol to spy out the
land and explore it. These men represented all their clans. They
told them, "Go, explore the land."
The men entered the hill country of Ephraim and came to the
house of Micah, where they spent the night. 3When they were near
Micah's house, they recognized the voice of the young Levite; so
they turned in there and asked him, "Who brought you here? What
are you doing in this place? Why are you here?"
4He told them what Micah had done for him, and said, "He has
hired me and I am his priest."
5Then they said to him, "Please inquire of God to learn whether
our journey will be successful."
6The priest answered them, "Go in peace. Your journey has the
LORD's approval."
7So the five men left and came to Laish, where they saw that the
people were living in safety, like the Sidonians, unsuspecting and
secure. And since their land lacked nothing, they were prosperous.[a] Also, they lived a long way from the Sidonians and had no
relationship with anyone else.[b]
8When they returned to Zorah and Eshtaol, their brothers asked
them, "How did you find things?"
9They answered, "Come on, let's attack them! We have seen that
the land is very good. Aren't you going to do something? Don't hesitate to go there and take it over. 10When you get there, you will
find an unsuspecting people and a spacious land that God has put
into your hands, a land that lacks nothing whatever."
11Then six hundred men from the clan of the Danites, armed
for battle, set out from Zorah and Eshtaol. 12On their way they set
up camp near Kiriath Jearim in Judah. This is why the place west
of Kiriath Jearim is called Mahaneh Dan[c] to this day. 13From there
they went on to the hill country of Ephraim and came to Micah's
house.
14Then the five men who had spied out the land of Laish said to
their brothers, "Do you know that one of these houses has an
ephod, other household gods, a carved image and a cast idol? Now
you know what to do." 15So they turned in there and went to the
house of the young Levite at Micah's place and greeted him. 16The
six hundred Danites, armed for battle, stood at the entrance to the
gate. 17The five men who had spied out the land went inside and
took the carved image, the ephod, the other household gods and
the cast idol while the priest and the six hundred armed men
stood at the entrance to the gate.
18When these men went into Micah's house and took the carved
image, the ephod, the other household gods and the cast idol, the
priest said to them, "What are you doing?"
19They answered him, "Be quiet! Don't say a word. Come with
us, and be our father and priest. Isn't it better that you serve a
tribe and clan in Israel as priest rather than just one man's household?" 20Then the priest was glad. He took the ephod, the other
household gods and the carved image and went along with the
people. 21Putting their little children, their livestock and their possessions in front of them, they turned away and left.
22When they had gone some distance from Micah's house, the
men who lived near Micah were called together and overtook the

[a] 7 The meaning of the Hebrew for this clause is uncertain. [b] 7 Hebrew; some Septuagint manuscripts *with the Arameans* [c] 12 *Mahaneh Dan* means *Dan's camp.*

It does not take keen insight to see that most people are working to gather the treasures of earth, without much concern for the treasures of heaven. Yes, if Jesus had said, "Seek ye first the things of the earth, and the kingdom of heaven shall be given to you," many people could not follow that rule more assiduously than they are doing it now.

But isn't it strange? Almost all people know that moth and rust will destroy their earthly treasures and that sooner or later these will be taken from them. And they know that only the heavenly and eternal things remain forever theirs. Still people continue tirelessly to seek earthly treasures, and do not move a finger to get heavenly riches. How can we explain such foolishness?

J. N. Kildahl (1857-1920)

(18:18–20) O Lord, I pray for those who are in ministry today. May they resist all temptation to dilute true worship or to compromise with the ways of the world. Please grant them the integrity never to sell out to materialism or give in to the pressures of prestige and vanity. Help them to guide us into pure expressions of worship and service for Your sake.

With my whole heart
I have sought You Lord.
With my whole heart
I have sought You Lord.
Turn my heart toward Your
commandments,
Away from selfish gain.
Turn my eyes from all that's
worthless
Revive me in Your way
Here today.

"With My Whole Heart"
Scott V. Smith (©1996)

(18:29–31) Though You had allowed them this victory, the Danites continued in their idolatry. They confused their prosperity with Your pleasure. O Lord, keep our hearts pure before You. For "what good is it for a man to gain the whole world, yet forfeit his soul?" (Mk 8:36)

When we see the reality of our sin, when we come face to face with it and look into the raging fire of hell itself, and when we then repent and believe and are delivered from that plight, our entire being is filled with unspeakable gratitude to the God Who sent His Son to that cross for us.

We must express that gratitude. But how? Simply stated: by living the way He commands. By obedience. That is what the Scripture means by holiness or sanctification–believers are set apart for holy living. Therefore, holiness is the only possible response to God's grace. Holy living is loving God.

Charles Colson (1931-)

Danites. 23 As they shouted after them, the Danites turned and said to Micah, "What's the matter with you that you called out your men to fight?"

24 He replied, "You took the gods I made, and my priest, and went away. What else do I have? How can you ask, 'What's the matter with you?' "

25 The Danites answered, "Don't argue with us, or some hot-tempered men will attack you, and you and your family will lose your lives." 26 So the Danites went their way, and Micah, seeing that they were too strong for him, turned around and went back home.

27 Then they took what Micah had made, and his priest, and went on to Laish, against a peaceful and unsuspecting people. They attacked them with the sword and burned down their city. 28 There was no one to rescue them because they lived a long way from Sidon and had no relationship with anyone else. The city was in a valley near Beth Rehob.

The Danites rebuilt the city and settled there. 29 They named it Dan after their forefather Dan, who was born to Israel—though the city used to be called Laish. 30 There the Danites set up for themselves the idols, and Jonathan son of Gershom, the son of Moses,[a] and his sons were priests for the tribe of Dan until the time of the captivity of the land. 31 They continued to use the idols Micah had made, all the time the house of God was in Shiloh.

A Levite and His Concubine

19 In those days Israel had no king.

Now a Levite who lived in a remote area in the hill country of Ephraim took a concubine from Bethlehem in Judah. 2 But she was unfaithful to him. She left him and went back to her father's house in Bethlehem, Judah. After she had been there four months, 3 her husband went to her to persuade her to return. He had with him his servant and two donkeys. She took him into her father's house, and when her father saw him, he gladly welcomed him. 4 His father-in-law, the girl's father, prevailed upon him to stay; so he remained with him three days, eating and drinking, and sleeping there.

5 On the fourth day they got up early and he prepared to leave, but the girl's father said to his son-in-law, "Refresh yourself with something to eat; then you can go." 6 So the two of them sat down to eat and drink together. Afterward the girl's father said, "Please stay tonight and enjoy yourself." 7 And when the man got up to go, his father-in-law persuaded him, so he stayed there that night. 8 On the morning of the fifth day, when he rose to go, the girl's father said, "Refresh yourself. Wait till afternoon!" So the two of them ate together.

9 Then when the man, with his concubine and his servant, got up to leave, his father-in-law, the girl's father, said, "Now look, it's almost evening. Spend the night here; the day is nearly over. Stay and enjoy yourself. Early tomorrow morning you can get up and be on your way home." 10 But, unwilling to stay another night, the man left and went toward Jebus (that is, Jerusalem), with his two saddled donkeys and his concubine.

11 When they were near Jebus and the day was almost gone, the

[a] *30* An ancient Hebrew scribal tradition, some Septuagint manuscripts and Vulgate; Masoretic Text *Manasseh*

servant said to his master, "Come, let's stop at this city of the Jebusites and spend the night."
12His master replied, "No. We won't go into an alien city, whose
people are not Israelites. We will go on to Gibeah." 13He added,
"Come, let's try to reach Gibeah or Ramah and spend the night in
one of those places." 14So they went on, and the sun set as they
neared Gibeah in Benjamin. 15There they stopped to spend the
night. They went and sat in the city square, but no one took them
into his home for the night.
16That evening an old man from the hill country of Ephraim,
who was living in Gibeah (the men of the place were Benjamites),
came in from his work in the fields. 17When he looked and saw
the traveler in the city square, the old man asked, "Where are you
going? Where did you come from?"
18He answered, "We are on our way from Bethlehem in Judah
to a remote area in the hill country of Ephraim where I live. I have
been to Bethlehem in Judah and now I am going to the house of
the LORD. No one has taken me into his house. 19We have both
straw and fodder for our donkeys and bread and wine for ourselves your servants—me, your maidservant, and the young man
with us. We don't need anything."
20"You are welcome at my house," the old man said. "Let me
supply whatever you need. Only don't spend the night in the
square." 21So he took him into his house and fed his donkeys.
After they had washed their feet, they had something to eat and
drink.
22While they were enjoying themselves, some of the wicked
men of the city surrounded the house. Pounding on the door, they
shouted to the old man who owned the house, "Bring out the man
who came to your house so we can have sex with him."
23The owner of the house went outside and said to them, "No,
my friends, don't be so vile. Since this man is my guest, don't do
this disgraceful thing. 24Look, here is my virgin daughter, and his
concubine. I will bring them out to you now, and you can use them
and do to them whatever you wish. But to this man, don't do such
a disgraceful thing."
25But the men would not listen to him. So the man took his
concubine and sent her outside to them, and they raped her and
abused her throughout the night, and at dawn they let her go.
26At daybreak the woman went back to the house where her
master was staying, fell down at the door and lay there until daylight.
27When her master got up in the morning and opened the door
of the house and stepped out to continue on his way, there lay his
concubine, fallen in the doorway of the house, with her hands on
the threshold. 28He said to her, "Get up; let's go." But there was no
answer. Then the man put her on his donkey and set out for home.
29When he reached home, he took a knife and cut up his concubine, limb by limb, into twelve parts and sent them into all the
areas of Israel. 30Everyone who saw it said, "Such a thing has
never been seen or done, not since the day the Israelites came up
out of Egypt. Think about it! Consider it! Tell us what to do!"

Israelites Fight the Benjamites

20 Then all the Israelites from Dan to Beersheba and from the
land of Gilead came out as one man and assembled before
the LORD in Mizpah. 2The leaders of all the people of the tribes of

(19:12–15) O God, how often have I turned a cold shoulder to the needs of a brother or sister—or to You—when I have ignored the needs of a stranger? What protection has not been afforded because of my indifference? What warmth has not been shared because of my coldness? What kindness has not been shown because of my selfishness? What love has been driven off by my fear? Lord, forgive me. Help me to live according to Your words of truth: "Whatever you did for one of the least of these brothers of mine, you did for me." (Mt 25:35–45; 1Jn 4:18)

It is Christ who pines when the poor are hungry; it is Christ who is repulsed when strangers are not welcome; it is Christ who suffers when rags fail to keep out the cold; it is Christ who is in anguish in the long-drawn illness; it is Christ who waits behind the prison doors. You come upon one of those who have been broken by the tempests of life, and if you look with eyes of Christian faith and love, he will lift a brow "luminous and imperial from the rags," and you will know that you are standing before the King of kings, Lord of lords.

Archbishop William Temple (1628-1699)

Brother, let me be your servant,
Let me be as Christ to you.
Pray that I might have the grace
To let you be my servant too.

We are pilgrims on a journey,
We are brothers on the road;
We are here to help each other
Walk the mile and bear the load.

"The Servant Song"
Richard Gillard (©1977)

Israel took their places in the assembly of the people of God, four
hundred thousand soldiers armed with swords. 3 (The Benjamites
heard that the Israelites had gone up to Mizpah.) Then the Israelites said, "Tell us how this awful thing happened."
4So the Levite, the husband of the murdered woman, said, "I
and my concubine came to Gibeah in Benjamin to spend the night.
5During the night the men of Gibeah came after me and surrounded the house, intending to kill me. They raped my concubine, and she died. 6I took my concubine, cut her into pieces and
sent one piece to each region of Israel's inheritance, because they
committed this lewd and disgraceful act in Israel. 7Now, all you Israelites, speak up and give your verdict."
8All the people rose as one man, saying, "None of us will go
home. No, not one of us will return to his house. 9But now this is
what we'll do to Gibeah: We'll go up against it as the lot directs.
10We'll take ten men out of every hundred from all the tribes of Israel, and a hundred from a thousand, and a thousand from ten
thousand, to get provisions for the army. Then, when the army arrives at Gibeah[a] in Benjamin, it can give them what they deserve
for all this vileness done in Israel." 11So all the men of Israel got
together and united as one man against the city.
12The tribes of Israel sent men throughout the tribe of Benjamin, saying, "What about this awful crime that was committed
among you? 13Now surrender those wicked men of Gibeah so that
we may put them to death and purge the evil from Israel."
But the Benjamites would not listen to their fellow Israelites.
14From their towns they came together at Gibeah to fight against
the Israelites. 15At once the Benjamites mobilized twenty-six thousand swordsmen from their towns, in addition to seven hundred
chosen men from those living in Gibeah. 16Among all these soldiers there were seven hundred chosen men who were left-handed, each of whom could sling a stone at a hair and not miss.
17Israel, apart from Benjamin, mustered four hundred thousand swordsmen, all of them fighting men.
18The Israelites went up to Bethel[b] and inquired of God. They
said, "Who of us shall go first to fight against the Benjamites?"
The LORD replied, "Judah shall go first."
19The next morning the Israelites got up and pitched camp near
Gibeah. 20The men of Israel went out to fight the Benjamites and
took up battle positions against them at Gibeah. 21The Benjamites
came out of Gibeah and cut down twenty-two thousand Israelites
on the battlefield that day. 22But the men of Israel encouraged one
another and again took up their positions where they had stationed themselves the first day. 23The Israelites went up and wept
before the LORD until evening, and they inquired of the LORD. They
said, "Shall we go up again to battle against the Benjamites, our
brothers?"
The LORD answered, "Go up against them."
24Then the Israelites drew near to Benjamin the second day.
25This time, when the Benjamites came out from Gibeah to oppose them, they cut down another eighteen thousand Israelites,
all of them armed with swords.
26Then the Israelites, all the people, went up to Bethel, and
there they sat weeping before the LORD. They fasted that day until
evening and presented burnt offerings and fellowship offerings[c] to

(20:3–26) O Father, I know that You never intended for people to live this way. Your intention was for sinlessness, holiness, pure and undefiled fellowship from person to person, and between You and us. But when worship is defiled, morality collapses and relationships are destroyed. Sin spreads like cancer. There is no way out but through Your divine, gracious intervention. O God, I pray for Your church today: Purify us and deliver us from evil.

[a] *10* One Hebrew manuscript; most Hebrew manuscripts *Geba,* a variant of *Gibeah*
[b] *18* Or *to the house of God*; also in verse 26 [c] *26* Traditionally *peace offerings*

the LORD. [27]And the Israelites inquired of the LORD. (In those days the ark of the covenant of God was there, [28]with Phinehas son of Eleazar, the son of Aaron, ministering before it.) They asked, "Shall we go up again to battle with Benjamin our brother, or not?"

The LORD responded, "Go, for tomorrow I will give them into your hands."

[29]Then Israel set an ambush around Gibeah. [30]They went up against the Benjamites on the third day and took up positions against Gibeah as they had done before. [31]The Benjamites came out to meet them and were drawn away from the city. They began to inflict casualties on the Israelites as before, so that about thirty men fell in the open field and on the roads—the one leading to Bethel and the other to Gibeah.

[32]While the Benjamites were saying, "We are defeating them as before," the Israelites were saying, "Let's retreat and draw them away from the city to the roads."

[33]All the men of Israel moved from their places and took up positions at Baal Tamar, and the Israelite ambush charged out of its place on the west[a] of Gibeah.[b] [34]Then ten thousand of Israel's finest men made a frontal attack on Gibeah. The fighting was so heavy that the Benjamites did not realize how near disaster was. [35]The LORD defeated Benjamin before Israel, and on that day the Israelites struck down 25,100 Benjamites, all armed with swords. [36]Then the Benjamites saw that they were beaten.

Now the men of Israel had given way before Benjamin, because they relied on the ambush they had set near Gibeah. [37]The men who had been in ambush made a sudden dash into Gibeah, spread out and put the whole city to the sword. [38]The men of Israel had arranged with the ambush that they should send up a great cloud of smoke from the city, [39]and then the men of Israel would turn in the battle.

The Benjamites had begun to inflict casualties on the men of Israel (about thirty), and they said, "We are defeating them as in the first battle." [40]But when the column of smoke began to rise from the city, the Benjamites turned and saw the smoke of the whole city going up into the sky. [41]Then the men of Israel turned on them, and the men of Benjamin were terrified, because they realized that disaster had come upon them. [42]So they fled before the Israelites in the direction of the desert, but they could not escape the battle. And the men of Israel who came out of the towns cut them down there. [43]They surrounded the Benjamites, chased them and easily[c] overran them in the vicinity of Gibeah on the east. [44]Eighteen thousand Benjamites fell, all of them valiant fighters. [45]As they turned and fled toward the desert to the rock of Rimmon, the Israelites cut down five thousand men along the roads. They kept pressing after the Benjamites as far as Gidom and struck down two thousand more.

[46]On that day twenty-five thousand Benjamite swordsmen fell, all of them valiant fighters. [47]But six hundred men turned and fled into the desert to the rock of Rimmon, where they stayed four months. [48]The men of Israel went back to Benjamin and put all the towns to the sword, including the animals and everything else they found. All the towns they came across they set on fire.

(20:27–48) O God, how we need Your mercy. The atrocities recorded on these pages did not take place in some pagan land; this was among Your people. Benjamin, the "son of my right hand," was not willing to cut out the infection of sin, so the entire hand was severed. It breaks my heart, and I know it breaks Yours, to consider how far and how quickly we can fall into sin. O how we need a Savior to save us from our sins, to save us from our stubbornness, to save us from ourselves (see footnote Ge 35:18).

If we will ask, He'll show us mercy.
If we bow down and humbly pray,
Joining our hands,
Turning our hearts to Him,
He will hear us once again.

For this one reason,
For this one cause,
We stand together
In the calling of our God:
To lift our voices,
To lift our hands,
And pray to heaven
For a healing in this land.

"For This One Reason"
John Barbour and Marsha Skidmore
(©1996)

[a]33 Some Septuagint manuscripts and Vulgate; the meaning of the Hebrew for this word is uncertain. [b]33 Hebrew *Geba,* a variant of *Gibeah* [c]43 The meaning of the Hebrew for this word is uncertain.

Even necessary justice is to be done with compassion. God does not punish with delight, nor should men.

Matthew Henry (1662-1714)

(21:2–3) Lord, let me never rejoice in the demise of a brother. May I remember Paul's admonition to restore the one who has been disciplined by You: "The punishment inflicted on him by the majority is sufficient for him. Now instead, you ought to forgive and comfort him, so that he will not be overwhelmed by excessive sorrow. I urge you, therefore, to reaffirm your love for him. The reason I wrote you was to see if you would stand the test and be obedient in everything. If you forgive anyone, I also forgive him. And what I have forgiven—if there was anything to forgive—I have forgiven in the sight of Christ for your sake, in order that Satan might not outwit us." (2Co 2:6–11)

Wives for the Benjamites

21 The men of Israel had taken an oath at Mizpah: "Not one of
us will give his daughter in marriage to a Benjamite."
2 The people went to Bethel,[a] where they sat before God until
evening, raising their voices and weeping bitterly. 3 "O LORD, the
God of Israel," they cried, "why has this happened to Israel? Why
should one tribe be missing from Israel today?"
4 Early the next day the people built an altar and presented
burnt offerings and fellowship offerings.[b]
5 Then the Israelites asked, "Who from all the tribes of Israel
has failed to assemble before the LORD?" For they had taken a
solemn oath that anyone who failed to assemble before the LORD at
Mizpah should certainly be put to death.
6 Now the Israelites grieved for their brothers, the Benjamites.
"Today one tribe is cut off from Israel," they said. 7 "How can we
provide wives for those who are left, since we have taken an oath
by the LORD not to give them any of our daughters in marriage?"
8 Then they asked, "Which one of the tribes of Israel failed to assemble before the LORD at Mizpah?" They discovered that no one
from Jabesh Gilead had come to the camp for the assembly. 9 For
when they counted the people, they found that none of the people
of Jabesh Gilead were there.
10 So the assembly sent twelve thousand fighting men with instructions to go to Jabesh Gilead and put to the sword those living
there, including the women and children. 11 "This is what you are
to do," they said. "Kill every male and every woman who is not a
virgin." 12 They found among the people living in Jabesh Gilead
four hundred young women who had never slept with a man, and
they took them to the camp at Shiloh in Canaan.
13 Then the whole assembly sent an offer of peace to the Benjamites at the rock of Rimmon. 14 So the Benjamites returned at
that time and were given the women of Jabesh Gilead who had
been spared. But there were not enough for all of them.
15 The people grieved for Benjamin, because the LORD had made
a gap in the tribes of Israel. 16 And the elders of the assembly said,
"With the women of Benjamin destroyed, how shall we provide
wives for the men who are left? 17 The Benjamite survivors must
have heirs," they said, "so that a tribe of Israel will not be wiped
out. 18 We can't give them our daughters as wives, since we Israelites have taken this oath: 'Cursed be anyone who gives a wife to a
Benjamite.' 19 But look, there is the annual festival of the LORD in
Shiloh, to the north of Bethel, and east of the road that goes from
Bethel to Shechem, and to the south of Lebonah."
20 So they instructed the Benjamites, saying, "Go and hide in the
vineyards 21 and watch. When the girls of Shiloh come out to join
in the dancing, then rush from the vineyards and each of you seize
a wife from the girls of Shiloh and go to the land of Benjamin.
22 When their fathers or brothers complain to us, we will say to
them, 'Do us a kindness by helping them, because we did not get
wives for them during the war, and you are innocent, since you did
not give your daughters to them.' "
23 So that is what the Benjamites did. While the girls were dancing, each man caught one and carried her off to be his wife. Then
they returned to their inheritance and rebuilt the towns and settled
in them.

[a] 2 Or *to the house of God* [b] 4 Traditionally *peace offerings*

24At that time the Israelites left that place and went home to their tribes and clans, each to his own inheritance.
25In those days Israel had no king; everyone did as he saw fit.

(21:24–25) Heavenly Father, I read in these final, sobering words Your own editorial comment upon the true condition of a nation and the cause for the many inexplicable and outrageous things they did in Your name. I shudder to think that I myself could live in such a way as to merit the same epitaph for my own life! O Lord, You are my King. Reign over me so that I may live only and always as You see fit. Amen.

You have a duel citizenry. You live both in time and eternity. Your highest loyalty is to God, and not to the mores or folkways, the state or the nation, or any man-made institutions. If any earthly institution or custom conflicts with God's will, it is your Christian duty to oppose it. You must never allow the transitory, evanescent demands of man-made institutions to take precedence over the eternal demands of the Almighty God. In a time when men are surrendering the high values of the faith you must cling to them, and despite the pressure of an alien generation preserve them for children yet unborn. You must be willing to challenge unjust mores, to champion unpopular causes, and to buck the status quo. You are called to be the salt of the earth. You are to be the light of the world. You are to be that vitally active leaven in the lump of the nation.

Martin Luther King, Jr. (1929-1968)

The Book of RUTH

The story of Ruth takes place during the time of the judges. She is memorable not only because her tale is emotionally and morally satisfying, but also because she is a Gentile who chooses to be devoted to the God of Israel. Recently widowed, Ruth the Moabitess remains with her Hebrew mother-in-law Naomi rather than living with her native people: "Your people will be my people and your God my God" (1:16). This act of faithfulness to Naomi and to the Lord leads to a providential meeting with a distant relative of Ruth's deceased husband, a righteous man named Boaz. After showing kindness to Ruth, Boaz ultimately redeems her husband's property and marries her. God richly rewards Ruth's faithfulness.

The account of Ruth may seem at first glance to be nothing more than a moralizing tale of how "good things happen to good people." But the real story of Ruth concerns God's amazing grace in the lives of ordinary people going through difficult times. First, we encounter the grace of God that extends to someone who is not a member of the chosen people. Although she is a Moabitess, Ruth shares in God's promises. By her example we are reminded to thank God that His love includes us regardless of our race.

In Ruth we see that there are no "mere coincidences" in the lives of God's people; His fingerprints can be found on even the most seemingly trivial events.

Second, the book of Ruth provides us with several models of faithfulness. In this story, loyalty is sacrificial and commitment is costly. Ruth, Naomi and Boaz demonstrate the kind of covenant faithfulness—to people and to the Lord—that leads to the full inheritance of God's blessings.

Third, we see in Boaz a "type" of Christ—one whose activity foreshadows that of our Lord. In faithfulness to the Mosaic Law (Lev 25:25; Dt 25:5–10), Boaz redeems Ruth's helpless estate and brings this Gentile woman into the household of God. By taking her to be his bride, he also makes her a co-heir of his own estate. Similarly, Jesus Christ, our "Kinsman-Redeemer," has paid the price to redeem us from sin and death. He has brought us into the family of God and has made us His Bride so that we can share in His inheritance (Ro 8:16–17; Rev 21:2,9).

Finally, in Ruth we see that there are no "mere coincidences" in the lives of God's people; His fingerprints can be found on even the most seemingly trivial events. Certainly God acts to bless Ruth, but the extent of His blessing reaches far beyond her "happily ever after" life with Boaz. Matthew's Gospel reminds us that Ruth is the great-grandmother of David, the great king of Israel. Therefore, Jesus, the Son of David, is a descendant of Ruth, a Gentile (Mt 1:5–6).

Even though Ruth was not born among the chosen people, she nevertheless took refuge under God's wings (2:12). Here she found protection, nourishment and blessing. Through Jesus Christ, those of us who, like Ruth, have also been born as Gentiles, take refuge in the Lord (Ps 91:3–4). In our worship we luxuriate in God's faithfulness to us while offering thanks for His gracious protection.

Naomi and Ruth

1 In the days when the judges ruled,[a] there was a famine in the
land, and a man from Bethlehem in Judah, together with his
wife and two sons, went to live for a while in the country of
Moab. 2The man's name was Elimelech, his wife's name Naomi,
and the names of his two sons were Mahlon and Kilion. They
were Ephrathites from Bethlehem, Judah. And they went to Moab
and lived there.
3Now Elimelech, Naomi's husband, died, and she was left with
her two sons. 4They married Moabite women, one named Orpah
and the other Ruth. After they had lived there about ten years,
5both Mahlon and Kilion also died, and Naomi was left without
her two sons and her husband.
6When she heard in Moab that the LORD had come to the aid
of his people by providing food for them, Naomi and her daughters-in-law prepared to return home from there. 7With her two
daughters-in-law she left the place where she had been living
and set out on the road that would take them back to the land of
Judah.
8Then Naomi said to her two daughters-in-law, "Go back,
each of you, to your mother's home. May the LORD show kindness to you, as you have shown to your dead and to me. 9May the
LORD grant that each of you will find rest in the home of another
husband."
Then she kissed them and they wept aloud 10and said to her,
"We will go back with you to your people."
11But Naomi said, "Return home, my daughters. Why would
you come with me? Am I going to have any more sons, who could
become your husbands? 12Return home, my daughters; I am too
old to have another husband. Even if I thought there was still
hope for me—even if I had a husband tonight and then gave
birth to sons— 13would you wait until they grew up? Would you
remain unmarried for them? No, my daughters. It is more bitter
for me than for you, because the LORD's hand has gone out
against me!"
14At this they wept again. Then Orpah kissed her mother-in-
law good-by, but Ruth clung to her.
15"Look," said Naomi, "your sister-in-law is going back to her
people and her gods. Go back with her."
16But Ruth replied, "Don't urge me to leave you or to turn
back from you. Where you go I will go, and where you stay I will
stay. Your people will be my people and your God my God.
17Where you die I will die, and there I will be buried. May the
LORD deal with me, be it ever so severely, if anything but death
separates you and me." 18When Naomi realized that Ruth was
determined to go with her, she stopped urging her.
19So the two women went on until they came to Bethlehem.
When they arrived in Bethlehem, the whole town was stirred because of them, and the women exclaimed, "Can this be Naomi?"
20"Don't call me Naomi,[b]" she told them. "Call me Mara,[c] because the Almighty[d] has made my life very bitter. 21I went away
full, but the LORD has brought me back empty. Why call me
Naomi? The LORD has afflicted[e] me; the Almighty has brought
misfortune upon me."

[a] 1 Traditionally *judged* [b] 20 *Naomi* means *pleasant*; also in verse 21. [c] 20 *Mara* means *bitter.* [d] 20 Hebrew *Shaddai*; also in verse 21 [e] 21 Or *has testified against*

(1:13,20–22) Your wisdom, O Lord, extends far beyond my understanding. If I could see what You see and know what You know, I would realize that even affliction and misfortune can be blessings, and that Your hand is always a hand of compassion and mercy for those who love You. Help me to see beyond pain, heartache and loss to the future You are preparing for me. Help me to believe that in due time, as you led Naomi, so You will lead me from the place of barrenness to fruitfulness. (Ps 138:8)

O Love that will not let me go,
I rest my weary soul in Thee.
I give Thee back the life I owe,
That in Thine ocean depths its flow
May richer, fuller be.

O Joy that seekest me thro' pain,
I cannot close my heart to Thee.
I trace the rainbow thro' the rain,
And feel the promise is not vain
That morn shall tearless be.

"O Love That Will Not Let Me Go"
George Matheson (1842-1906)

Receive every inward and outward trouble, every disappointment, pain, uneasiness, temptation, darkness, and desolation, with both thy hands, as a true opportunity and blessed occasion of dying to self, and entering into a fuller fellowship with thy self-denying, suffering Savior. Look at no inward or outward trouble in any other view; reject every other thought about it, and then every kind of trial and distress will become the blessed day of thy prosperity. That state is best, which exerciseth the highest faith in and fullest resignation to God.

William Law (1686-1761)

22 So Naomi returned from Moab accompanied by Ruth the
Moabitess, her daughter-in-law, arriving in Bethlehem as the barley harvest was beginning.

Ruth Meets Boaz

2 Now Naomi had a relative on her husband's side, from the
clan of Elimelech, a man of standing, whose name was Boaz.
2 And Ruth the Moabitess said to Naomi, "Let me go to the
fields and pick up the leftover grain behind anyone in whose
eyes I find favor."

Naomi said to her, "Go ahead, my daughter." 3 So she went out
and began to glean in the fields behind the harvesters. As it
turned out, she found herself working in a field belonging to
Boaz, who was from the clan of Elimelech.

4 Just then Boaz arrived from Bethlehem and greeted the harvesters, "The LORD be with you!"

"The LORD bless you!" they called back.

5 Boaz asked the foreman of his harvesters, "Whose young
woman is that?"

6 The foreman replied, "She is the Moabitess who came back
from Moab with Naomi. 7 She said, 'Please let me glean and gather among the sheaves behind the harvesters.' She went into the
field and has worked steadily from morning till now, except for
a short rest in the shelter."

8 So Boaz said to Ruth, "My daughter, listen to me. Don't go
and glean in another field and don't go away from here. Stay
here with my servant girls. 9 Watch the field where the men are
harvesting, and follow along after the girls. I have told the men
not to touch you. And whenever you are thirsty, go and get a
drink from the water jars the men have filled."

10 At this, she bowed down with her face to the ground. She
exclaimed, "Why have I found such favor in your eyes that you
notice me—a foreigner?"

11 Boaz replied, "I've been told all about what you have done
for your mother-in-law since the death of your husband—how
you left your father and mother and your homeland and came to
live with a people you did not know before. 12 May the LORD
repay you for what you have done. May you be richly rewarded
by the LORD, the God of Israel, under whose wings you have come
to take refuge."

13 "May I continue to find favor in your eyes, my lord," she
said. "You have given me comfort and have spoken kindly to
your servant—though I do not have the standing of one of your
servant girls."

14 At mealtime Boaz said to her, "Come over here. Have some
bread and dip it in the wine vinegar."

When she sat down with the harvesters, he offered her some
roasted grain. She ate all she wanted and had some left over.
15 As she got up to glean, Boaz gave orders to his men, "Even if
she gathers among the sheaves, don't embarrass her. 16 Rather,
pull out some stalks for her from the bundles and leave them
for her to pick up, and don't rebuke her."

17 So Ruth gleaned in the field until evening. Then she
threshed the barley she had gathered, and it amounted to about
an ephah.[a] 18 She carried it back to town, and her mother-in-law

[a] 17 That is, probably about 3/5 bushel (about 22 liters)

(2:3–5) Great and marvelous Lord, I praise You for the way You orchestrate the "circumstances" of our lives. Ruth "found herself" in Boaz's field, and "just then Boaz arrived . . ." You knew that from this meeting of a Jewish man and a Gentile woman there would in time come the Messiah Who would reconcile both the Jews and the Gentiles to You and to one another. Truly, in all things You work for the good of those who love You, who have been called according to Your purpose. (Ru 4:21–22; Mt 1:1–16; Ro 8:28; Eph 2:11–18)

(2:12) My Father, Your wings are a place of safety, of refreshment, of stillness in the storm. You provide help, joy and hope in the midst of the most fearful circumstances. You are my shelter, my hiding place; in You I am safe, regardless of what happens around me. In You, O Lord, do I put my trust. I truly have found refuge under the shadow of Your wings. (Ps 17:8–9; 36:7–8; 57:1; 63:7; 91:4)

Under His wings I am safely abiding.
Tho' the night deepens and tempests are wild,
Still I can trust Him; I know He will keep me.
He has redeemed me, and I am His child.

Under His wings, under His wings,
Who from His love can sever?
Under His wings my soul shall abide,
Safely abide forever.

"Under His Wings"
William O. Cushing (1823-1902)

saw how much she had gathered. Ruth also brought out and gave her what she had left over after she had eaten enough.

19 Her mother-in-law asked her, "Where did you glean today? Where did you work? Blessed be the man who took notice of you!"

Then Ruth told her mother-in-law about the one at whose place she had been working. "The name of the man I worked with today is Boaz," she said.

20 "The LORD bless him!" Naomi said to her daughter-in-law. "He has not stopped showing his kindness to the living and the dead." She added, "That man is our close relative; he is one of our kinsman-redeemers."

21 Then Ruth the Moabitess said, "He even said to me, 'Stay with my workers until they finish harvesting all my grain.' "

22 Naomi said to Ruth her daughter-in-law, "It will be good for you, my daughter, to go with his girls, because in someone else's field you might be harmed."

23 So Ruth stayed close to the servant girls of Boaz to glean until the barley and wheat harvests were finished. And she lived with her mother-in-law.

Ruth and Boaz at the Threshing Floor

3 One day Naomi her mother-in-law said to her, "My daughter, should I not try to find a home[a] for you, where you will be well provided for? 2 Is not Boaz, with whose servant girls you have been, a kinsman of ours? Tonight he will be winnowing barley on the threshing floor. 3 Wash and perfume yourself, and put on your best clothes. Then go down to the threshing floor, but don't let him know you are there until he has finished eating and drinking. 4 When he lies down, note the place where he is lying. Then go and uncover his feet and lie down. He will tell you what to do."

5 "I will do whatever you say," Ruth answered. 6 So she went down to the threshing floor and did everything her mother-in-law told her to do.

7 When Boaz had finished eating and drinking and was in good spirits, he went over to lie down at the far end of the grain pile. Ruth approached quietly, uncovered his feet and lay down. 8 In the middle of the night something startled the man, and he turned and discovered a woman lying at his feet.

9 "Who are you?" he asked.

"I am your servant Ruth," she said. "Spread the corner of your garment over me, since you are a kinsman-redeemer."

10 "The LORD bless you, my daughter," he replied. "This kindness is greater than that which you showed earlier: You have not run after the younger men, whether rich or poor. 11 And now, my daughter, don't be afraid. I will do for you all you ask. All my fellow townsmen know that you are a woman of noble character. 12 Although it is true that I am near of kin, there is a kinsman-redeemer nearer than I. 13 Stay here for the night, and in the morning if he wants to redeem, good; let him redeem. But if he is not willing, as surely as the LORD lives I will do it. Lie here until morning."

14 So she lay at his feet until morning, but got up before any-

[a] 1 Hebrew *find rest* (see Ruth 1:9)

(3:9) Lord Jesus, You are my Kinsman-Redeemer, the true substance of this shadow. You took me as Your own and covered me with Your righteousness. You brought me into Your covenant, into Your care, and into the fellowship of saints. I had nothing to offer You except my spiritual poverty; but You clothed me with the riches of Your grace. Afresh this day, I lay myself at Your feet and pray, "Cover me; spread Your garment over me, for You are my nearest Kinsman." I surrender myself to You, acknowledge my need for You, and receive Your covering, Your protection and Your gracious provision. (Isa 54:5; 61:10)

How blessed would it be, if, in wandering in the field of meditation tonight, our [happenstance] should be to "light" on the place where our next Kinsman will reveal himself to us! O Spirit of God, guide us to him. We would sooner glean in his field than bear away the whole harvest from any other.

Charles Haddon Spurgeon (1834-1892)

I love the Lord,
For He heard my voice;
He heard my cry for mercy.
I love the Lord
Because He turned His ear to me.
I will call on Him as long as I live.

The Lord is gracious and righteous.
Our God is full of compassion.
The Lord protects the simple-
hearted.
He has become my salvation.

"I Love The Lord"
Kelly Willard and Jeff Jansen (©1998)

(4:6–10) How I bless You, Lord Jesus, that when You came to redeem us You took no thought for Your own estate. Though You were rich, for our sake You became poor, so that through Your poverty we might become rich. You were willing to give up everything to make us Your own and to restore our lost inheritance. You purchased us, not to make us slaves but to make us Your bride. And now, Lord, as Your bride, may we bear much fruit for Your glory. (Isa 61:10; Ro 7:4; 2Co 8:9; Rev 21:10)

Lord in Your faithfulness
You have pursued me.
Gently and tenderly,
Lord, you have wooed me.
Who could imagine I would find
All of the riches that are mine.

So great a salvation,
So costly a gift,
So great a redemption
So the dying might live.
So great a salvation,
So high the price,
So kind a Redeemer,
Supreme sacrifice.
Great is your love!
Great is your love!
Great is your love!

"So Great A Salvation"
David Durham and Becky Durham
(©1998)

one could be recognized; and he said, "Don't let it be known that a woman came to the threshing floor."

15He also said, "Bring me the shawl you are wearing and hold it out." When she did so, he poured into it six measures of barley and put it on her. Then he[a] went back to town.

16When Ruth came to her mother-in-law, Naomi asked, "How did it go, my daughter?"

Then she told her everything Boaz had done for her 17and added, "He gave me these six measures of barley, saying, 'Don't go back to your mother-in-law empty-handed.' "

18Then Naomi said, "Wait, my daughter, until you find out what happens. For the man will not rest until the matter is settled today."

Boaz Marries Ruth

4 Meanwhile Boaz went up to the town gate and sat there. When the kinsman-redeemer he had mentioned came along, Boaz said, "Come over here, my friend, and sit down." So he went over and sat down.

2Boaz took ten of the elders of the town and said, "Sit here," and they did so. 3Then he said to the kinsman-redeemer, "Naomi, who has come back from Moab, is selling the piece of land that belonged to our brother Elimelech. 4I thought I should bring the matter to your attention and suggest that you buy it in the presence of these seated here and in the presence of the elders of my people. If you will redeem it, do so. But if you[b] will not, tell me, so I will know. For no one has the right to do it except you, and I am next in line."

"I will redeem it," he said.

5Then Boaz said, "On the day you buy the land from Naomi and from Ruth the Moabitess, you acquire[c] the dead man's widow, in order to maintain the name of the dead with his property."

6At this, the kinsman-redeemer said, "Then I cannot redeem it because I might endanger my own estate. You redeem it yourself. I cannot do it."

7(Now in earlier times in Israel, for the redemption and transfer of property to become final, one party took off his sandal and gave it to the other. This was the method of legalizing transactions in Israel.)

8So the kinsman-redeemer said to Boaz, "Buy it yourself." And he removed his sandal.

9Then Boaz announced to the elders and all the people, "Today you are witnesses that I have bought from Naomi all the property of Elimelech, Kilion and Mahlon. 10I have also acquired Ruth the Moabitess, Mahlon's widow, as my wife, in order to maintain the name of the dead with his property, so that his name will not disappear from among his family or from the town records. Today you are witnesses!"

11Then the elders and all those at the gate said, "We are witnesses. May the LORD make the woman who is coming into your home like Rachel and Leah, who together built up the house of Israel. May you have standing in Ephrathah and be famous in Bethlehem. 12Through the offspring the LORD gives you by this young

[a] 15 Most Hebrew manuscripts; many Hebrew manuscripts, Vulgate and Syriac *she*
[b] 4 Many Hebrew manuscripts, Septuagint, Vulgate and Syriac; most Hebrew manuscripts *he*
[c] 5 Hebrew; Vulgate and Syriac *Naomi, you acquire Ruth the Moabitess,*

woman, may your family be like that of Perez, whom Tamar bore
to Judah."

The Genealogy of David

13So Boaz took Ruth and she became his wife. Then he went to
her, and the LORD enabled her to conceive, and she gave birth to a
son. 14The women said to Naomi: "Praise be to the LORD, who this
day has not left you without a kinsman-redeemer. May he become
famous throughout Israel! 15He will renew your life and sustain
you in your old age. For your daughter-in-law, who loves you and
who is better to you than seven sons, has given him birth."
16Then Naomi took the child, laid him in her lap and cared for
him. 17The women living there said, "Naomi has a son." And they
named him Obed. He was the father of Jesse, the father of David.
18This, then, is the family line of Perez:

Perez was the father of Hezron,
19 Hezron the father of Ram,
Ram the father of Amminadab,
20 Amminadab the father of Nahshon,
Nahshon the father of Salmon,[a]
21 Salmon the father of Boaz,
Boaz the father of Obed,
22 Obed the father of Jesse,
and Jesse the father of David.

[a] 20 A few Hebrew manuscripts, some Septuagint manuscripts and Vulgate (see also verse 21 and Septuagint of 1 Chron. 2:11); most Hebrew manuscripts *Salma*

More are the tender thoughts, the inspired potential actions, in God, than the stars in the heavens. Innumerable are the sweet influences that he sends down from his realm above. More and purer are his blessings than the drops of dew that night shakes down on the flowers and grass.

He penetrates and pervades the world with more saving mercies than does the sun with particles of light and heat. He declares that his nature in himself is boundless—that his heart of mercy is inexhaustible—that his work of comfort is endless.

Henry Ward Beecher (1813–1887)

(4:12–22) Thank You, Father, for this great lesson of hope—hope for a redeemer, hope for a future, hope for a fruitful destiny. What a wonder it is that You would choose a poor, Gentile widow—an alien to your covenant—to be a part of the family line of our Savior. And what a wonder it is that You would choose me to be a part of the continuing lineage of the Lord Jesus Christ, my kinsman-redeemer. Truly You raise up the poor to seat them with princes; indeed, You have raised me up to be seated with Christ, the Prince of Peace. (Ps 113:7–8; Eph 2:6–10)

Under His wings O what precious
enjoyment!
There will I hide till life's trials are
o'er;
Sheltered, protected, no evil can
harm me.
Resting in Jesus, I'm safe evermore.

"Under His Wings"
William O. Cushing (1823–1902)

1 & 2 Samuel

The First & Second Books of
SAMUEL

The books of 1 and 2 Samuel recount Israel's transformation from a theocracy (ruled by God through judges) to a monarchy (ruled by a king). First Samuel begins with the career of Samuel, the last of the judges. With God's consent, Samuel anoints Saul as Israel's first king. But Saul's rule is tarnished by his failure to obey God and by his selfish conflict with David. Second Samuel begins with the death of Saul and David's succession to the throne. The book narrates David's kingly rule, failures and all. At the end of 2 Samuel David and his family are securely enthroned in Israel.

When the aged Samuel steps down as judge, the Israelites clamor for a king so that they can be just like the other nations (1Sa 8). Samuel does not welcome the transition from theocratic to monarchic rule; he foresees the oppressive possibilities in human tyranny. God helps Samuel to see that the people are not rejecting Samuel so much as they are rejecting God as their King. Nevertheless, God instructs Samuel to give them the king they desire.

Among the three main characters of 1 and 2 Samuel—Samuel, Saul and David—David plays the starring role. He is introduced as a man after God's own heart (1Sa 13:14). As a boy, David demonstrates extraordinary trust in God when confronting Goliath (1Sa 17). As a man, David acknowledges God as the source of his strength and protection: "The Lord is my rock, my fortress and my deliverer; my God is my rock, in whom I take refuge, my shield and the horn of my salvation" (2Sa 22:2–3).

Authentic worship includes not only joyful praise, but also the explicit acknowledgment of our sin.

But this great man of God is also a vile sinner. King David not only commits adultery with another man's wife but also makes sure that this man, one of David's "mighty men" (2Sa 23:8, 39) and an officer in David's army, is killed in battle (2Sa 11). Yet even though enmeshed in sin, David is praiseworthy still for his genuine repentance. When confronted with his transgressions, he confesses and turns to God with his whole heart. David's excellence lies not in moral perfection but in his ultimate commitment to seek the Lord.

As a king, David becomes a "type" of Jesus, a picture that foreshadows the true Son of David, the One Who comes as Messiah to reign over Israel—and all the earth. We worship King Jesus in humble submission, just as one would bow before a human sovereign. As a forgiven sinner, David reminds us of the necessity of confession and true repentance. Authentic worship includes not only joyful praise, but also the explicit acknowledgment of our sin. As a composer of praise, David helps us to lose ourselves in the overpowering majesty of God: "The Lord lives! Praise be to my Rock! Exalted be God, the Rock, my Savior!" (2Sa 22:47).

The Birth of Samuel

1 There was a certain man from Ramathaim, a Zuphite[a] from
the hill country of Ephraim, whose name was Elkanah son of
Jeroham, the son of Elihu, the son of Tohu, the son of Zuph, an
Ephraimite. 2He had two wives; one was called Hannah and the
other Peninnah. Peninnah had children, but Hannah had none.
3Year after year this man went up from his town to worship and
sacrifice to the LORD Almighty at Shiloh, where Hophni and Phinehas, the two sons of Eli, were priests of the LORD. 4Whenever the
day came for Elkanah to sacrifice, he would give portions of the
meat to his wife Peninnah and to all her sons and daughters. 5But
to Hannah he gave a double portion because he loved her, and the
LORD had closed her womb. 6And because the LORD had closed her
womb, her rival kept provoking her in order to irritate her. 7This
went on year after year. Whenever Hannah went up to the house of
the LORD, her rival provoked her till she wept and would not eat.
8Elkanah her husband would say to her, "Hannah, why are you
weeping? Why don't you eat? Why are you downhearted? Don't I
mean more to you than ten sons?"
9Once when they had finished eating and drinking in Shiloh,
Hannah stood up. Now Eli the priest was sitting on a chair by the
doorpost of the LORD's temple.[b] 10In bitterness of soul Hannah
wept much and prayed to the LORD. 11And she made a vow, saying,
"O LORD Almighty, if you will only look upon your servant's misery
and remember me, and not forget your servant but give her a son,
then I will give him to the LORD for all the days of his life, and no
razor will ever be used on his head."
12As she kept on praying to the LORD, Eli observed her mouth.
13Hannah was praying in her heart, and her lips were moving but
her voice was not heard. Eli thought she was drunk 14and said to
her, "How long will you keep on getting drunk? Get rid of your
wine."
15"Not so, my lord," Hannah replied, "I am a woman who is
deeply troubled. I have not been drinking wine or beer; I was
pouring out my soul to the LORD. 16Do not take your servant for a
wicked woman; I have been praying here out of my great anguish
and grief."
17Eli answered, "Go in peace, and may the God of Israel grant
you what you have asked of him."
18She said, "May your servant find favor in your eyes." Then
she went her way and ate something, and her face was no longer
downcast.
19Early the next morning they arose and worshiped before the
LORD and then went back to their home at Ramah. Elkanah lay with
Hannah his wife, and the LORD remembered her. 20So in the
course of time Hannah conceived and gave birth to a son. She
named him Samuel,[c] saying, "Because I asked the LORD for him."

Hannah Dedicates Samuel

21When the man Elkanah went up with all his family to offer the
annual sacrifice to the LORD and to fulfill his vow, 22Hannah did
not go. She said to her husband, "After the boy is weaned, I will
take him and present him before the LORD, and he will live there
always."

[a] 1 Or *from Ramathaim Zuphim* [b] 9 That is, tabernacle [c] 20 *Samuel* sounds like the Hebrew for *heard of God.*

One need not cry out very loudly; He is nearer to us than we think.

Brother Lawrence of the Resurrection (c.1605-1691)

(1:6–17) Lord, sometimes life seems unfair. Bad things can happen to good people while good things happen to bad people. It can be so hard to believe that You are in control, or even that You care. Yet You are always there. You are always at work. In Your time You will turn my disappointments into joys, my failures into successes. Help me to trust You, even though Your deliverance has not yet come and seems so far away. Gracious God, surprise me once again with another breathtaking demonstration of Your goodness and faithfulness.

In His time, in His time.
He makes all things beautiful
In His time.
Lord, please show me ev'ry day
As You're teaching me Your way,
That You do just what You say
In Your time.

"In His Time"
Diane Ball (©1978)

(2:4–8) O Holy God, I join Hannah in praising You for Your power to alter the condition of Your creation. You weaken the strong and strengthen the weak. The full become hungry and the hungry You fill with food. You raise the poor from the dust and seat them with princes. Indeed, You hold power over life and death. I praise You for being a God of redemption, re-creation, and renewal. As Your glory is revealed, "every valley shall be raised up, every mountain and hill made low." May Your kingdom come, Sovereign Lord! May Your will be done! (Isa 40:4–5; Mt 6:10)

He upholds the whole creation, founded the earth, and still sustains it by the word of his power. What cannot he do in the affairs of families and kingdoms, far beyond our conception and expectation, who hangs the earth upon nothing?

Matthew Henry (1662-1714)

23 "Do what seems best to you," Elkanah her husband told her.
"Stay here until you have weaned him; only may the LORD make
good his[a] word." So the woman stayed at home and nursed her
son until she had weaned him.
24 After he was weaned, she took the boy with her, young as he
was, along with a three-year-old bull,[b] an ephah[c] of flour and a
skin of wine, and brought him to the house of the LORD at Shiloh.
25 When they had slaughtered the bull, they brought the boy to Eli,
26 and she said to him, "As surely as you live, my lord, I am the
woman who stood here beside you praying to the LORD. 27 I prayed
for this child, and the LORD has granted me what I asked of him.
28 So now I give him to the LORD. For his whole life he will be given
over to the LORD." And he worshiped the LORD there.

Hannah's Prayer

2 Then Hannah prayed and said:

"My heart rejoices in the LORD;
in the LORD my horn[d] is lifted high.
My mouth boasts over my enemies,
for I delight in your deliverance.

2 "There is no one holy[e] like the LORD;
there is no one besides you;
there is no Rock like our God.

3 "Do not keep talking so proudly
or let your mouth speak such arrogance,
for the LORD is a God who knows,
and by him deeds are weighed.

4 "The bows of the warriors are broken,
but those who stumbled are armed with strength.
5 Those who were full hire themselves out for food,
but those who were hungry hunger no more.
She who was barren has borne seven children,
but she who has had many sons pines away.

6 "The LORD brings death and makes alive;
he brings down to the grave[f] and raises up.
7 The LORD sends poverty and wealth;
he humbles and he exalts.
8 He raises the poor from the dust
and lifts the needy from the ash heap;
he seats them with princes
and has them inherit a throne of honor.

"For the foundations of the earth are the LORD's;
upon them he has set the world.
9 He will guard the feet of his saints,
but the wicked will be silenced in darkness.

"It is not by strength that one prevails;
10 those who oppose the LORD will be shattered.
He will thunder against them from heaven;
the LORD will judge the ends of the earth.

[a] 23 Masoretic Text; Dead Sea Scrolls, Septuagint and Syriac *your* [b] 24 Dead Sea Scrolls, Septuagint and Syriac; Masoretic Text *with three bulls* [c] 24 That is, probably about 3/5 bushel (about 22 liters) [d] *1 Horn* here symbolizes strength; also in verse 10. [e] 2 Or *no Holy One* [f] 6 Hebrew *Sheol*

"He will give strength to his king
and exalt the horn of his anointed."

11Then Elkanah went home to Ramah, but the boy ministered
before the LORD under Eli the priest.

Eli's Wicked Sons

12Eli's sons were wicked men; they had no regard for the LORD.
13Now it was the practice of the priests with the people that whenever anyone offered a sacrifice and while the meat was being
boiled, the servant of the priest would come with a three-pronged
fork in his hand. 14He would plunge it into the pan or kettle or
caldron or pot, and the priest would take for himself whatever the
fork brought up. This is how they treated all the Israelites who
came to Shiloh. 15But even before the fat was burned, the servant
of the priest would come and say to the man who was sacrificing,
"Give the priest some meat to roast; he won't accept boiled meat
from you, but only raw."

16If the man said to him, "Let the fat be burned up first, and
then take whatever you want," the servant would then answer, "No,
hand it over now; if you don't, I'll take it by force."

17This sin of the young men was very great in the LORD's sight,
for they[a] were treating the LORD's offering with contempt.
18But Samuel was ministering before the LORD—a boy wearing
a linen ephod. 19Each year his mother made him a little robe and
took it to him when she went up with her husband to offer the annual sacrifice. 20Eli would bless Elkanah and his wife, saying,
"May the LORD give you children by this woman to take the place
of the one she prayed for and gave to the LORD." Then they would
go home. 21And the LORD was gracious to Hannah; she conceived
and gave birth to three sons and two daughters. Meanwhile, the
boy Samuel grew up in the presence of the LORD.

22Now Eli, who was very old, heard about everything his sons
were doing to all Israel and how they slept with the women who
served at the entrance to the Tent of Meeting. 23So he said to them,
"Why do you do such things? I hear from all the people about
these wicked deeds of yours. 24No, my sons; it is not a good report
that I hear spreading among the LORD's people. 25If a man sins
against another man, God[b] may mediate for him; but if a man sins
against the LORD, who will intercede for him?" His sons, however,
did not listen to their father's rebuke, for it was the LORD's will to
put them to death.

26And the boy Samuel continued to grow in stature and in favor
with the LORD and with men.

Prophecy Against the House of Eli

27Now a man of God came to Eli and said to him, "This is what
the LORD says: 'Did I not clearly reveal myself to your father's
house when they were in Egypt under Pharaoh? 28I chose your father out of all the tribes of Israel to be my priest, to go up to my
altar, to burn incense, and to wear an ephod in my presence. I
also gave your father's house all the offerings made with fire by the
Israelites. 29Why do you[c] scorn my sacrifice and offering that I
prescribed for my dwelling? Why do you honor your sons more
than me by fattening yourselves on the choice parts of every offering made by my people Israel?'

[a] 17 Or *men* [b] 25 Or *the judges* [c] 29 The Hebrew is plural.

(2:18–21) O Giving God, how Hannah's heart must have ached as she brought a little robe to her beloved son in their yearly visit. Yet she was faithful to her vow, and thereby she blessed the entire nation. Help me to be so faithful! Teach me to trust You with my greatest treasures. Help me to give all that I am to You without holding back, so that others may be blessed through my obedience. Loving God, I trust in Your faithfulness. For even as You blessed Hannah with five more children, so You promise to bless me with abundant, eternal life as I surrender my life to You. Help me to be willing to give up my rights so that I can freely receive Your blessings. (Mt 16:25; Lk 9:23–25; Ro 12:1–2)

If we are not our own, but the Lord's, it is clear to what purpose all our deeds must be directed. We are not our own, therefore neither our reason nor our will should guide us in our thoughts and actions. We are not our own, therefore we should not seek what is only expedient to the flesh. We are not our own, therefore let us forget ourselves and our own interests as far as possible.

We are God's own; to him, therefore, let us live and die. We are God's own; therefore let his wisdom and will dominate all our actions. We are God's own; therefore let every part of our existence be directed towards him as our only legitimate goal.

John Calvin (1509–1564)

All to Thee is yielded,
I am not my own;
Blissful, glad surrender,
I am Thine alone.

Fill me with the knowledge
Of Thy glorious will;
All Thine own good pleasure
In my life fulfill.

"Speak, Lord in the Stillness"
May E. Grimes (1920)

30"Therefore the LORD, the God of Israel, declares: 'I promised
that your house and your father's house would minister before me
forever.' But now the LORD declares: 'Far be it from me! Those who
honor me I will honor, but those who despise me will be disdained.
31The time is coming when I will cut short your strength and the
strength of your father's house, so that there will not be an old man
in your family line 32and you will see distress in my dwelling. Although good will be done to Israel, in your family line there will
never be an old man. 33Every one of you that I do not cut off from
my altar will be spared only to blind your eyes with tears and to
grieve your heart, and all your descendants will die in the prime of
life.

34" 'And what happens to your two sons, Hophni and Phinehas,
will be a sign to you—they will both die on the same day. 35I will
raise up for myself a faithful priest, who will do according to what
is in my heart and mind. I will firmly establish his house, and he
will minister before my anointed one always. 36Then everyone left
in your family line will come and bow down before him for a piece
of silver and a crust of bread and plead, "Appoint me to some
priestly office so I can have food to eat." ' "

The LORD Calls Samuel

3 The boy Samuel ministered before the LORD under Eli. In those
days the word of the LORD was rare; there were not many visions.

2One night Eli, whose eyes were becoming so weak that he could
barely see, was lying down in his usual place. 3The lamp of God
had not yet gone out, and Samuel was lying down in the temple[a] of
the LORD, where the ark of God was. 4Then the LORD called Samuel.

Samuel answered, "Here I am." 5And he ran to Eli and said,
"Here I am; you called me."

But Eli said, "I did not call; go back and lie down." So he went
and lay down.

6Again the LORD called, "Samuel!" And Samuel got up and went
to Eli and said, "Here I am; you called me."

"My son," Eli said, "I did not call; go back and lie down."

7Now Samuel did not yet know the LORD: The word of the LORD
had not yet been revealed to him.

8The LORD called Samuel a third time, and Samuel got up and
went to Eli and said, "Here I am; you called me."

Then Eli realized that the LORD was calling the boy. 9So Eli told
Samuel, "Go and lie down, and if he calls you, say, 'Speak, LORD, for
your servant is listening.' " So Samuel went and lay down in his
place.

10The LORD came and stood there, calling as at the other times,
"Samuel! Samuel!"

Then Samuel said, "Speak, for your servant is listening."

11And the LORD said to Samuel: "See, I am about to do something
in Israel that will make the ears of everyone who hears of it tingle.
12At that time I will carry out against Eli everything I spoke against
his family—from beginning to end. 13For I told him that I would
judge his family forever because of the sin he knew about; his sons
made themselves contemptible,[b] and he failed to restrain them.
14Therefore, I swore to the house of Eli, 'The guilt of Eli's house
will never be atoned for by sacrifice or offering.' "

[a] *3* That is, tabernacle [b] *13* Masoretic Text; an ancient Hebrew scribal tradition and Septuagint *sons blasphemed God*

(3:8–9) When You speak to me, Lord, I often fail to hear. And when I hear, I often fail to understand. And when I understand, I often fail to obey. The clamorous world around me obscures Your voice. Yet even in silence, my noisy soul can drown out the gentle whisper of Your Spirit. Give me, I pray, the wisdom of Eli, who knew when Your voice was calling. And then give me the obedient heart of Samuel, that I might say to You: "Speak, for Your servant is listening!" (1Ki 19:12–13)

Speak, Lord, in the stillness
While I wait on Thee;
Hushed my heart to listen
In expectancy.

Speak, O blessed Master,
In this quiet hour;
Let me see Thy face, Lord,
Feel Thy touch of power.

"Speak, Lord in the Stillness"
May E. Grimes (1920)

15 Samuel lay down until morning and then opened the doors of
the house of the LORD. He was afraid to tell Eli the vision, 16 but Eli
called him and said, "Samuel, my son."
Samuel answered, "Here I am."
17 "What was it he said to you?" Eli asked. "Do not hide it from
me. May God deal with you, be it ever so severely, if you hide from
me anything he told you." 18 So Samuel told him everything, hiding
nothing from him. Then Eli said, "He is the LORD; let him do what
is good in his eyes."
19 The LORD was with Samuel as he grew up, and he let none of
his words fall to the ground. 20 And all Israel from Dan to Beersheba recognized that Samuel was attested as a prophet of the
LORD. 21 The LORD continued to appear at Shiloh, and there he revealed himself to Samuel through his word.
4 And Samuel's word came to all Israel.

The Philistines Capture the Ark

Now the Israelites went out to fight against the Philistines. The
Israelites camped at Ebenezer, and the Philistines at Aphek. 2 The
Philistines deployed their forces to meet Israel, and as the battle
spread, Israel was defeated by the Philistines, who killed about
four thousand of them on the battlefield. 3 When the soldiers returned to camp, the elders of Israel asked, "Why did the LORD
bring defeat upon us today before the Philistines? Let us bring the
ark of the LORD's covenant from Shiloh, so that it[a] may go with us
and save us from the hand of our enemies."
4 So the people sent men to Shiloh, and they brought back the
ark of the covenant of the LORD Almighty, who is enthroned between the cherubim. And Eli's two sons, Hophni and Phinehas,
were there with the ark of the covenant of God.
5 When the ark of the LORD's covenant came into the camp, all
Israel raised such a great shout that the ground shook. 6 Hearing
the uproar, the Philistines asked, "What's all this shouting in the
Hebrew camp?"
When they learned that the ark of the LORD had come into the
camp, 7 the Philistines were afraid. "A god has come into the
camp," they said. "We're in trouble! Nothing like this has happened before. 8 Woe to us! Who will deliver us from the hand of
these mighty gods? They are the gods who struck the Egyptians
with all kinds of plagues in the desert. 9 Be strong, Philistines! Be
men, or you will be subject to the Hebrews, as they have been to
you. Be men, and fight!"
10 So the Philistines fought, and the Israelites were defeated and
every man fled to his tent. The slaughter was very great; Israel lost
thirty thousand foot soldiers. 11 The ark of God was captured, and
Eli's two sons, Hophni and Phinehas, died.

Death of Eli

12 That same day a Benjamite ran from the battle line and went
to Shiloh, his clothes torn and dust on his head. 13 When he arrived, there was Eli sitting on his chair by the side of the road,
watching, because his heart feared for the ark of God. When the
man entered the town and told what had happened, the whole
town sent up a cry.

[a] 3 Or *he*

(3:17–18) Your Word, Almighty God, does not always comfort. At times it cuts deeply, dividing soul and spirit, joints and marrow. It judges the thoughts of my heart, and I am found guilty. At other times Your Word promises a season of discipline under Your parental hand. When Your Word is hard to hear, give me the submissive spirit of Eli, who received Your bad news by acknowledging Your sovereignty and goodness. Help me to listen to the harsh words of Your judgment, so that I might receive with joy Your gracious words of correction. Help me to submit to Your discipline, so that I might share in your holiness. (Heb 4:12–13; 12:10)

His usual agent of correction is his living Word . . . The Scriptures encourage and guide us, but they frequently do so by pointing out our misconceptions, blunders, and deficiencies.

Our response should be one of immense thanksgiving that through the ministry of his Word God is able to correct our erroneous course. Rather than becoming discouraged, hurt, or combative when God examines us, we should be quick to examine ourselves, repent, and allow the Holy Spirit to direct our steps in his straight path.

Charles Stanley (1932-)

14 Eli heard the outcry and asked, "What is the meaning of this
uproar?"
The man hurried over to Eli, 15 who was ninety-eight years old
and whose eyes were set so that he could not see. 16 He told Eli, "I
have just come from the battle line; I fled from it this very day."
Eli asked, "What happened, my son?"
17 The man who brought the news replied, "Israel fled before
the Philistines, and the army has suffered heavy losses. Also your
two sons, Hophni and Phinehas, are dead, and the ark of God has
been captured."
18 When he mentioned the ark of God, Eli fell backward off his
chair by the side of the gate. His neck was broken and he died, for
he was an old man and heavy. He had led[a] Israel forty years.
19 His daughter-in-law, the wife of Phinehas, was pregnant and
near the time of delivery. When she heard the news that the ark of
God had been captured and that her father-in-law and her husband were dead, she went into labor and gave birth, but was
overcome by her labor pains. 20 As she was dying, the women attending her said, "Don't despair; you have given birth to a son."
But she did not respond or pay any attention.
21 She named the boy Ichabod,[b] saying, "The glory has departed from Israel"—because of the capture of the ark of God and the
deaths of her father-in-law and her husband. 22 She said, "The
glory has departed from Israel, for the ark of God has been captured."

The Ark in Ashdod and Ekron

5 After the Philistines had captured the ark of God, they took it
from Ebenezer to Ashdod. 2 Then they carried the ark into
Dagon's temple and set it beside Dagon. 3 When the people of Ashdod rose early the next day, there was Dagon, fallen on his face on
the ground before the ark of the LORD! They took Dagon and put
him back in his place. 4 But the following morning when they rose,
there was Dagon, fallen on his face on the ground before the ark
of the LORD! His head and hands had been broken off and were
lying on the threshold; only his body remained. 5 That is why to
this day neither the priests of Dagon nor any others who enter
Dagon's temple at Ashdod step on the threshold.
6 The LORD's hand was heavy upon the people of Ashdod and its
vicinity; he brought devastation upon them and afflicted them with
tumors.[c] 7 When the men of Ashdod saw what was happening, they
said, "The ark of the god of Israel must not stay here with us, because his hand is heavy upon us and upon Dagon our god." 8 So
they called together all the rulers of the Philistines and asked
them, "What shall we do with the ark of the god of Israel?"
They answered, "Have the ark of the god of Israel moved to
Gath." So they moved the ark of the God of Israel.
9 But after they had moved it, the LORD's hand was against that
city, throwing it into a great panic. He afflicted the people of the
city, both young and old, with an outbreak of tumors.[d] 10 So they
sent the ark of God to Ekron.
As the ark of God was entering Ekron, the people of Ekron
cried out, "They have brought the ark of the god of Israel around
to us to kill us and our people." 11 So they called together all the

[a] 18 Traditionally *judged* [b] 21 *Ichabod* means *no glory.* [c] 6 Hebrew; Septuagint and Vulgate *tumors. And rats appeared in their land, and death and destruction were throughout the city* [d] 9 Or *with tumors in the groin* (see Septuagint)

(4:17–18) Heavenly Father, how tragic was Eli's death! A man who served Your people for 40 years died with ghastly news ringing in his ears: His sons had been killed and the ark of God captured. We all hope to die in peace, with the strands of our lives neatly tied together. We dream of leaving behind a worthy legacy, including healthy, God-fearing children. But we cannot choose the occasion of our death. Nor can we force our children to live holy lives. What can we do as we consider the hour of our death? We can live each moment seeking always to do Your will: to act justly, to love mercy, and to walk humbly with You, O God. (Mic 6:8)

(4:21–22) I praise You, O God, that Your glory is no longer contained in an ark made with human hands. Your glory has been revealed in the person of Jesus Christ and has been given to all who believe through the Spirit of Christ dwelling in our hearts. Christ in me is my hope of glory, and no enemy can ever take that away. (Col 1:27)

rulers of the Philistines and said, "Send the ark of the god of Israel away; let it go back to its own place, or it[a] will kill us and our people." For death had filled the city with panic; God's hand was very heavy upon it. 12Those who did not die were afflicted with tumors, and the outcry of the city went up to heaven.

The Ark Returned to Israel

6 When the ark of the LORD had been in Philistine territory seven months, 2the Philistines called for the priests and the diviners and said, "What shall we do with the ark of the LORD? Tell us how we should send it back to its place."

3They answered, "If you return the ark of the god of Israel, do not send it away empty, but by all means send a guilt offering to him. Then you will be healed, and you will know why his hand has not been lifted from you."

4The Philistines asked, "What guilt offering should we send to him?"

They replied, "Five gold tumors and five gold rats, according to the number of the Philistine rulers, because the same plague has struck both you and your rulers. 5Make models of the tumors and of the rats that are destroying the country, and pay honor to Israel's god. Perhaps he will lift his hand from you and your gods and your land. 6Why do you harden your hearts as the Egyptians and Pharaoh did? When he[b] treated them harshly, did they not send the Israelites out so they could go on their way?

7"Now then, get a new cart ready, with two cows that have calved and have never been yoked. Hitch the cows to the cart, but take their calves away and pen them up. 8Take the ark of the LORD and put it on the cart, and in a chest beside it put the gold objects you are sending back to him as a guilt offering. Send it on its way, 9but keep watching it. If it goes up to its own territory, toward Beth Shemesh, then the LORD has brought this great disaster on us. But if it does not, then we will know that it was not his hand that struck us and that it happened to us by chance."

10So they did this. They took two such cows and hitched them to the cart and penned up their calves. 11They placed the ark of the LORD on the cart and along with it the chest containing the gold rats and the models of the tumors. 12Then the cows went straight up toward Beth Shemesh, keeping on the road and lowing all the way; they did not turn to the right or to the left. The rulers of the Philistines followed them as far as the border of Beth Shemesh.

13Now the people of Beth Shemesh were harvesting their wheat in the valley, and when they looked up and saw the ark, they rejoiced at the sight. 14The cart came to the field of Joshua of Beth Shemesh, and there it stopped beside a large rock. The people chopped up the wood of the cart and sacrificed the cows as a burnt offering to the LORD. 15The Levites took down the ark of the LORD, together with the chest containing the gold objects, and placed them on the large rock. On that day the people of Beth Shemesh offered burnt offerings and made sacrifices to the LORD. 16The five rulers of the Philistines saw all this and then returned that same day to Ekron.

17These are the gold tumors the Philistines sent as a guilt offering to the LORD—one each for Ashdod, Gaza, Ashkelon, Gath and

[a] *11* Or *he* [b] *6* That is, God

(5:11—6:17) Your ark, O God, brought judgment to the lost and convinced them of their guilt. But it brought joy to Israel. Today, it is the same way for the glory of the Gospel, the aroma of Christ in us: It is the smell of death to those who are perishing, the fragrance of life to those who are being saved. (2Co 2:15–16)

Ekron. 18And the number of the gold rats was according to the number of Philistine towns belonging to the five rulers—the fortified towns with their country villages. The large rock, on which[a] they set the ark of the LORD, is a witness to this day in the field of Joshua of Beth Shemesh.

19But God struck down some of the men of Beth Shemesh, putting seventy[b] of them to death because they had looked into the ark of the LORD. The people mourned because of the heavy blow the LORD had dealt them, 20and the men of Beth Shemesh asked, "Who can stand in the presence of the LORD, this holy God? To whom will the ark go up from here?"

21Then they sent messengers to the people of Kiriath Jearim, saying, "The Philistines have returned the ark of the LORD. Come

7 down and take it up to your place." 1So the men of Kiriath Jearim came and took up the ark of the LORD. They took it to Abinadab's house on the hill and consecrated Eleazar his son to guard the ark of the LORD.

Samuel Subdues the Philistines at Mizpah

2It was a long time, twenty years in all, that the ark remained at Kiriath Jearim, and all the people of Israel mourned and sought after the LORD. 3And Samuel said to the whole house of Israel, "If you are returning to the LORD with all your hearts, then rid yourselves of the foreign gods and the Ashtoreths and commit yourselves to the LORD and serve him only, and he will deliver you out of the hand of the Philistines." 4So the Israelites put away their Baals and Ashtoreths, and served the LORD only.

5Then Samuel said, "Assemble all Israel at Mizpah and I will intercede with the LORD for you." 6When they had assembled at Mizpah, they drew water and poured it out before the LORD. On that day they fasted and there they confessed, "We have sinned against the LORD." And Samuel was leader[c] of Israel at Mizpah.

7When the Philistines heard that Israel had assembled at Mizpah, the rulers of the Philistines came up to attack them. And when the Israelites heard of it, they were afraid because of the Philistines. 8They said to Samuel, "Do not stop crying out to the LORD our God for us, that he may rescue us from the hand of the Philistines." 9Then Samuel took a suckling lamb and offered it up as a whole burnt offering to the LORD. He cried out to the LORD on Israel's behalf, and the LORD answered him.

10While Samuel was sacrificing the burnt offering, the Philistines drew near to engage Israel in battle. But that day the LORD thundered with loud thunder against the Philistines and threw them into such a panic that they were routed before the Israelites. 11The men of Israel rushed out of Mizpah and pursued the Philistines, slaughtering them along the way to a point below Beth Car.

12Then Samuel took a stone and set it up between Mizpah and Shen. He named it Ebenezer,[d] saying, "Thus far has the LORD helped us." 13So the Philistines were subdued and did not invade Israelite territory again.

Throughout Samuel's lifetime, the hand of the LORD was against the Philistines. 14The towns from Ekron to Gath that the Philis-

[a] 18 A few Hebrew manuscripts (see also Septuagint); most Hebrew manuscripts *villages as far as Greater Abel, where* [b] 19 A few Hebrew manuscripts; most Hebrew manuscripts and Septuagint *50,070* [c] 6 Traditionally *judge* [d] 12 *Ebenezer* means *stone of help.*

(7:2–4) Exalted God, I too need to hear Samuel's pointed exhortation: If you are returning to the Lord with all your heart, then get rid of other gods and commit yourself only to the Lord. Like Your people so long ago, I confess that my loyalties are divided. I want You, Lord, and financial security. I want You, Lord, and the freedom to run my own life. I want You, Lord, but with my personal priorities intact. But I know now that to be completely free I must be completely Yours. So please forgive me, gracious God, for compromising my commitment to You. Deliver me from my infidelity and give me an undivided heart. (Ps 86:11)

If I'm to live in truth and love
To glorify Your name;
If for a living sacrifice to be;
To share the joy, the grace and peace
Your Spirit does impart;
Lord, I need an undivided heart.
That I might know You,
That I might serve You,
That I might worship You as King,
To see the Morning Star,
To know how great You are,
Lord, I need an undivided heart.

"Undivided Heart"
Dan Marks (©1996)

tines had captured from Israel were restored to her, and Israel
delivered the neighboring territory from the power of the Philistines. And there was peace between Israel and the Amorites.
15Samuel continued as judge over Israel all the days of his life.
16From year to year he went on a circuit from Bethel to Gilgal to
Mizpah, judging Israel in all those places. 17But he always went
back to Ramah, where his home was, and there he also judged Israel. And he built an altar there to the LORD.

Israel Asks for a King

8 When Samuel grew old, he appointed his sons as judges for
Israel. 2The name of his firstborn was Joel and the name of
his second was Abijah, and they served at Beersheba. 3But his
sons did not walk in his ways. They turned aside after dishonest
gain and accepted bribes and perverted justice.
4So all the elders of Israel gathered together and came to Samuel at Ramah. 5They said to him, "You are old, and your sons do
not walk in your ways; now appoint a king to lead[a] us, such as all
the other nations have."
6But when they said, "Give us a king to lead us," this displeased Samuel; so he prayed to the LORD. 7And the LORD told
him: "Listen to all that the people are saying to you; it is not you
they have rejected, but they have rejected me as their king. 8As
they have done from the day I brought them up out of Egypt until
this day, forsaking me and serving other gods, so they are doing
to you. 9Now listen to them; but warn them solemnly and let them
know what the king who will reign over them will do."
10Samuel told all the words of the LORD to the people who were
asking him for a king. 11He said, "This is what the king who will
reign over you will do: He will take your sons and make them
serve with his chariots and horses, and they will run in front of
his chariots. 12Some he will assign to be commanders of thousands and commanders of fifties, and others to plow his ground
and reap his harvest, and still others to make weapons of war and
equipment for his chariots. 13He will take your daughters to be
perfumers and cooks and bakers. 14He will take the best of your
fields and vineyards and olive groves and give them to his attendants. 15He will take a tenth of your grain and of your vintage and
give it to his officials and attendants. 16Your menservants and
maidservants and the best of your cattle[b] and donkeys he will
take for his own use. 17He will take a tenth of your flocks, and
you yourselves will become his slaves. 18When that day comes,
you will cry out for relief from the king you have chosen, and the
LORD will not answer you in that day."
19But the people refused to listen to Samuel. "No!" they said.
"We want a king over us. 20Then we will be like all the other nations, with a king to lead us and to go out before us and fight our
battles."
21When Samuel heard all that the people said, he repeated it
before the LORD. 22The LORD answered, "Listen to them and give
them a king."
Then Samuel said to the men of Israel, "Everyone go back to
his town."

[a] 5 Traditionally *judge*; also in verses 6 and 20 [b] 16 Septuagint; Hebrew *young men*

(8:4–22) All-powerful, all-knowing God, it grieves me to see the Creator rejected by His creation, the Lover of our souls spurned by His beloved. But this was no surprise to You. You had even warned Moses hundreds of years earlier that this was coming. You know our sinful desire to imitate the world, our stubborn pride that makes us think we know better than You. But You are not limited by worldly systems; You can rule through priests or kings. It was for the people's sake and not Your own that You warned them against a monarchy. Yet even in their rebellion You were laying the foundation for our high priest, the King of kings, Jesus Christ, who would one day come and bring harmony between the throne and the temple. (Dt 17:14–20; Zec 6:13)

O Lord, come quickly and reign on thy throne, for now often something rises up within me, and tries to take possession of thy throne; pride, covetousness, uncleanness, and sloth want to be my kings; and then evil-speaking, anger, hatred, and the whole train of vices join with me in warring against myself, and try to reign over me. I resist them, and say, "I have no other king than Christ." O King of Peace, come and reign in me, for I will have no king but thee! Amen.

Saint Bernard of Clairvaux (1090–1153)

(9:1–17) Lord, how often Your great and surprising work in us starts with small beginnings. Saul never would have guessed that a search for donkeys would lead to a monarchy. Yet even as he scoured the countryside, You were executing Your grand plans for Saul. O God, when I resent the humble tasks of my life, remind me of Saul and the donkeys. Teach me to be faithful in small things, so that You might entrust me with more of Your kingdom work. (Ps 115:13; Lk 19:12–26)

Samuel Anoints Saul

9 There was a Benjamite, a man of standing, whose name was Kish son of Abiel, the son of Zeror, the son of Becorath, the son of Aphiah of Benjamin. 2He had a son named Saul, an impressive young man without equal among the Israelites—a head taller than any of the others.

3Now the donkeys belonging to Saul's father Kish were lost, and Kish said to his son Saul, "Take one of the servants with you and go and look for the donkeys." 4So he passed through the hill country of Ephraim and through the area around Shalisha, but they did not find them. They went on into the district of Shaalim, but the donkeys were not there. Then he passed through the territory of Benjamin, but they did not find them.

5When they reached the district of Zuph, Saul said to the servant who was with him, "Come, let's go back, or my father will stop thinking about the donkeys and start worrying about us."

6But the servant replied, "Look, in this town there is a man of God; he is highly respected, and everything he says comes true. Let's go there now. Perhaps he will tell us what way to take."

7Saul said to his servant, "If we go, what can we give the man? The food in our sacks is gone. We have no gift to take to the man of God. What do we have?"

8The servant answered him again. "Look," he said, "I have a quarter of a shekel[a] of silver. I will give it to the man of God so that he will tell us what way to take." 9(Formerly in Israel, if a man went to inquire of God, he would say, "Come, let us go to the seer," because the prophet of today used to be called a seer.)

10"Good," Saul said to his servant. "Come, let's go." So they set out for the town where the man of God was.

11As they were going up the hill to the town, they met some girls coming out to draw water, and they asked them, "Is the seer here?"

12"He is," they answered. "He's ahead of you. Hurry now; he has just come to our town today, for the people have a sacrifice at the high place. 13As soon as you enter the town, you will find him before he goes up to the high place to eat. The people will not begin eating until he comes, because he must bless the sacrifice; afterward, those who are invited will eat. Go up now; you should find him about this time."

14They went up to the town, and as they were entering it, there was Samuel, coming toward them on his way up to the high place.

15Now the day before Saul came, the LORD had revealed this to Samuel: 16"About this time tomorrow I will send you a man from the land of Benjamin. Anoint him leader over my people Israel; he will deliver my people from the hand of the Philistines. I have looked upon my people, for their cry has reached me."

17When Samuel caught sight of Saul, the LORD said to him, "This is the man I spoke to you about; he will govern my people."

18Saul approached Samuel in the gateway and asked, "Would you please tell me where the seer's house is?"

19"I am the seer," Samuel replied. "Go up ahead of me to the high place, for today you are to eat with me, and in the morning I will let you go and will tell you all that is in your heart. 20As for the donkeys you lost three days ago, do not worry about them; they

[a] *8* That is, about 1/10 ounce (about 3 grams)

have been found. And to whom is all the desire of Israel turned, if
not to you and all your father's family?"
21Saul answered, "But am I not a Benjamite, from the smallest
tribe of Israel, and is not my clan the least of all the clans of the
tribe of Benjamin? Why do you say such a thing to me?"
22Then Samuel brought Saul and his servant into the hall and
seated them at the head of those who were invited—about thirty
in number. 23Samuel said to the cook, "Bring the piece of meat I
gave you, the one I told you to lay aside."
24So the cook took up the leg with what was on it and set it in
front of Saul. Samuel said, "Here is what has been kept for you.
Eat, because it was set aside for you for this occasion, from the
time I said, 'I have invited guests.' " And Saul dined with Samuel
that day.
25After they came down from the high place to the town, Samuel talked with Saul on the roof of his house. 26They rose about
daybreak and Samuel called to Saul on the roof, "Get ready, and I
will send you on your way." When Saul got ready, he and Samuel
went outside together. 27As they were going down to the edge of
the town, Samuel said to Saul, "Tell the servant to go on ahead of
us"—and the servant did so—"but you stay here awhile, so that I
may give you a message from God."

10 Then Samuel took a flask of oil and poured it on Saul's
head and kissed him, saying, "Has not the LORD anointed
you leader over his inheritance?[a] 2When you leave me today, you
will meet two men near Rachel's tomb, at Zelzah on the border of
Benjamin. They will say to you, 'The donkeys you set out to look
for have been found. And now your father has stopped thinking
about them and is worried about you. He is asking, "What shall I
do about my son?" '
3"Then you will go on from there until you reach the great tree
of Tabor. Three men going up to God at Bethel will meet you there.
One will be carrying three young goats, another three loaves of
bread, and another a skin of wine. 4They will greet you and offer
you two loaves of bread, which you will accept from them.
5"After that you will go to Gibeah of God, where there is a
Philistine outpost. As you approach the town, you will meet a procession of prophets coming down from the high place with lyres,
tambourines, flutes and harps being played before them, and they
will be prophesying. 6The Spirit of the LORD will come upon you in
power, and you will prophesy with them; and you will be changed
into a different person. 7Once these signs are fulfilled, do whatever your hand finds to do, for God is with you.
8"Go down ahead of me to Gilgal. I will surely come down to
you to sacrifice burnt offerings and fellowship offerings,[b] but you
must wait seven days until I come to you and tell you what you are
to do."

Saul Made King

9As Saul turned to leave Samuel, God changed Saul's heart, and
all these signs were fulfilled that day. 10When they arrived at Gibeah, a procession of prophets met him; the Spirit of God came
upon him in power, and he joined in their prophesying. 11When

[a] 1 Hebrew; Septuagint and Vulgate *over his people Israel? You will reign over the LORD's people and save them from the power of their enemies round about. And this will be a sign to you that the LORD has anointed you leader over his inheritance:*
[b] 8 Traditionally *peace offerings*

(10:1–10) When Your Spirit comes upon us, Lord, we are changed. As You once did for Your servant Saul, so I pray You will do for me today. May Your Holy Spirit come upon me in power so that I may boldly proclaim Your Word and declare Your glory. Remove my heart of stone and give me a heart of flesh and a new spirit. I praise You for being a God who makes all things new—even me! (Eze 36:26–27; Ac 1:8; 2Co 5:17; Rev 21:5)

Holy Spirit,
Send Your anointing,
Stir the gift You've placed inside.
From this hour
Release Your power;
Through my life be glorified.

Breath of heaven,
Breath of heaven,
Breathe on me.

"Breath Of Heaven"
Buddy Owens and Morris Chapman
(©1999)

(10:11–27) When Saul was selected as king, some people were puzzled, some were impressed, some were offended, but all of them were wrong. The choice of Saul was Your choice, not theirs. For You reached Your sovereign hand even into their decline into the ways of the world, and You directed the course of the nation. I praise You, Almighty God, that Your acts of grace are not dependent on our faithfulness but are solely the result of Yours.

all those who had formerly known him saw him prophesying with the prophets, they asked each other, "What is this that has happened to the son of Kish? Is Saul also among the prophets?"
12 A man who lived there answered, "And who is their father?" So
it became a saying: "Is Saul also among the prophets?" 13 After Saul
stopped prophesying, he went to the high place.
14 Now Saul's uncle asked him and his servant, "Where have you been?"

"Looking for the donkeys," he said. "But when we saw they were not to be found, we went to Samuel."
15 Saul's uncle said, "Tell me what Samuel said to you."
16 Saul replied, "He assured us that the donkeys had been found." But he did not tell his uncle what Samuel had said about the kingship.
17 Samuel summoned the people of Israel to the LORD at Mizpah
18 and said to them, "This is what the LORD, the God of Israel, says:
'I brought Israel up out of Egypt, and I delivered you from the power
of Egypt and all the kingdoms that oppressed you.' 19 But you have
now rejected your God, who saves you out of all your calamities and distresses. And you have said, 'No, set a king over us.' So now present yourselves before the LORD by your tribes and clans."
20 When Samuel brought all the tribes of Israel near, the tribe of
Benjamin was chosen. 21 Then he brought forward the tribe of Ben-
jamin, clan by clan, and Matri's clan was chosen. Finally Saul son of Kish was chosen. But when they looked for him, he was not to be
found. 22 So they inquired further of the LORD, "Has the man come here yet?"

And the LORD said, "Yes, he has hidden himself among the baggage."
23 They ran and brought him out, and as he stood among the
people he was a head taller than any of the others. 24 Samuel said
to all the people, "Do you see the man the LORD has chosen? There is no one like him among all the people."

Then the people shouted, "Long live the king!"
25 Samuel explained to the people the regulations of the kingship. He wrote them down on a scroll and deposited it before the LORD. Then Samuel dismissed the people, each to his own home.
26 Saul also went to his home in Gibeah, accompanied by valiant
men whose hearts God had touched. 27 But some troublemakers
said, "How can this fellow save us?" They despised him and brought him no gifts. But Saul kept silent.

Saul Rescues the City of Jabesh

11 Nahash the Ammonite went up and besieged Jabesh Gilead. And all the men of Jabesh said to him, "Make a treaty with us, and we will be subject to you."
2 But Nahash the Ammonite replied, "I will make a treaty with you only on the condition that I gouge out the right eye of every one of you and so bring disgrace on all Israel."
3 The elders of Jabesh said to him, "Give us seven days so we can send messengers throughout Israel; if no one comes to rescue us, we will surrender to you."
4 When the messengers came to Gibeah of Saul and reported
these terms to the people, they all wept aloud. 5 Just then Saul was
returning from the fields, behind his oxen, and he asked, "What is wrong with the people? Why are they weeping?" Then they repeated to him what the men of Jabesh had said.

6 When Saul heard their words, the Spirit of God came upon him
in power, and he burned with anger. 7 He took a pair of oxen, cut
them into pieces, and sent the pieces by messengers throughout
Israel, proclaiming, "This is what will be done to the oxen of anyone who does not follow Saul and Samuel." Then the terror of the
LORD fell on the people, and they turned out as one man. 8 When
Saul mustered them at Bezek, the men of Israel numbered three
hundred thousand and the men of Judah thirty thousand.

9 They told the messengers who had come, "Say to the men of Jabesh Gilead, 'By the time the sun is hot tomorrow, you will be delivered.'" When the messengers went and reported this to the men
of Jabesh, they were elated. 10 They said to the Ammonites, "Tomorrow we will surrender to you, and you can do to us whatever
seems good to you."

11 The next day Saul separated his men into three divisions; during the last watch of the night they broke into the camp of the Ammonites and slaughtered them until the heat of the day. Those who
survived were scattered, so that no two of them were left together.

Saul Confirmed as King

12 The people then said to Samuel, "Who was it that asked, 'Shall
Saul reign over us?' Bring these men to us and we will put them to
death."

13 But Saul said, "No one shall be put to death today, for this day
the LORD has rescued Israel."

14 Then Samuel said to the people, "Come, let us go to Gilgal and
there reaffirm the kingship." 15 So all the people went to Gilgal and
confirmed Saul as king in the presence of the LORD. There they sacrificed fellowship offerings[a] before the LORD, and Saul and all the
Israelites held a great celebration.

Samuel's Farewell Speech

12 Samuel said to all Israel, "I have listened to everything you
said to me and have set a king over you. 2 Now you have a
king as your leader. As for me, I am old and gray, and my sons are
here with you. I have been your leader from my youth until this
day. 3 Here I stand. Testify against me in the presence of the LORD
and his anointed. Whose ox have I taken? Whose donkey have I
taken? Whom have I cheated? Whom have I oppressed? From
whose hand have I accepted a bribe to make me shut my eyes? If I
have done any of these, I will make it right."

4 "You have not cheated or oppressed us," they replied. "You
have not taken anything from anyone's hand."

5 Samuel said to them, "The LORD is witness against you, and also
his anointed is witness this day, that you have not found anything in
my hand."

"He is witness," they said.

6 Then Samuel said to the people, "It is the LORD who appointed
Moses and Aaron and brought your forefathers up out of Egypt.
7 Now then, stand here, because I am going to confront you with evidence before the LORD as to all the righteous acts performed by the
LORD for you and your fathers.

8 "After Jacob entered Egypt, they cried to the LORD for help, and
the LORD sent Moses and Aaron, who brought your forefathers out
of Egypt and settled them in this place.

[a] 15 Traditionally *peace offerings*

(12:1–5) Dear Lord, in our time, as in the days of Samuel, it would be so easy to testify against those in authority over us. Our attention quickly focuses on the obvious and numerous failings of our leaders. Yet, we confess that too often we have forgotten to take notice of those who lead with integrity. Even in this day we are blessed with leaders who serve faithfully according to Your standards. Thank You, Lord, for pastors and elders, mayors and principals, bosses and business owners who walk in Your ways. Thank You for leaders who, like Samuel, have served us—and, indeed, who have served You—not for selfish gain, but for the common good and for Your glory.

(12:19–25) Sovereign Lord, as You once chose the children of Israel to be Your people, so You have also chosen us through Jesus Christ. You have made us Your own possession, not because of any superlative worth we possess but because it gives You pleasure. And You will never reject us, not only because You love us but also because our very existence as a people glorifies Your great name. Indeed, may Your name be exalted through us, not only in principle but also in fact. May we serve You faithfully with all of our hearts, living each moment for the praise of Your glory. (Dt 7:6–10; Eph 1:3–9; 1Pe 2:9)

Come, let us worship and bow down,
Let us kneel before the Lord, our
God, our Maker.
Come, let us worship and bow down,
Let us kneel before the Lord, our
God, our Maker.
For He is our God,
And we are the people of His
pasture,
And the sheep of His hand,
Just the sheep of His hand.
"Come, Let Us Worship And Bow Down"
Dave Doherty (©1980)

9"But they forgot the LORD their God; so he sold them into the
hand of Sisera, the commander of the army of Hazor, and into the
hands of the Philistines and the king of Moab, who fought against
them. 10They cried out to the LORD and said, 'We have sinned; we
have forsaken the LORD and served the Baals and the Ashtoreths.
But now deliver us from the hands of our enemies, and we will
serve you.' 11Then the LORD sent Jerub-Baal,[a] Barak,[b] Jephthah
and Samuel,[c] and he delivered you from the hands of your enemies on every side, so that you lived securely.
12"But when you saw that Nahash king of the Ammonites was
moving against you, you said to me, 'No, we want a king to rule
over us'—even though the LORD your God was your king. 13Now
here is the king you have chosen, the one you asked for; see, the
LORD has set a king over you. 14If you fear the LORD and serve and
obey him and do not rebel against his commands, and if both you
and the king who reigns over you follow the LORD your God—
good! 15But if you do not obey the LORD, and if you rebel against
his commands, his hand will be against you, as it was against your
fathers.
16"Now then, stand still and see this great thing the LORD is
about to do before your eyes! 17Is it not wheat harvest now? I will
call upon the LORD to send thunder and rain. And you will realize
what an evil thing you did in the eyes of the LORD when you asked
for a king."
18Then Samuel called upon the LORD, and that same day the
LORD sent thunder and rain. So all the people stood in awe of the
LORD and of Samuel.
19The people all said to Samuel, "Pray to the LORD your God for
your servants so that we will not die, for we have added to all our
other sins the evil of asking for a king."
20"Do not be afraid," Samuel replied. "You have done all this
evil; yet do not turn away from the LORD, but serve the LORD with all
your heart. 21Do not turn away after useless idols. They can do
you no good, nor can they rescue you, because they are useless.
22For the sake of his great name the LORD will not reject his people, because the LORD was pleased to make you his own. 23As for
me, far be it from me that I should sin against the LORD by failing
to pray for you. And I will teach you the way that is good and right.
24But be sure to fear the LORD and serve him faithfully with all your
heart; consider what great things he has done for you. 25Yet if you
persist in doing evil, both you and your king will be swept away."

Samuel Rebukes Saul

13 Saul was ⌞thirty⌟[d] years old when he became king, and he
reigned over Israel ⌞forty-⌟[e] two years.
2Saul[f] chose three thousand men from Israel; two thousand
were with him at Micmash and in the hill country of Bethel, and a
thousand were with Jonathan at Gibeah in Benjamin. The rest of
the men he sent back to their homes.
3Jonathan attacked the Philistine outpost at Geba, and the Philistines heard about it. Then Saul had the trumpet blown throughout the land and said, "Let the Hebrews hear!" 4So all Israel heard
the news: "Saul has attacked the Philistine outpost, and now Isra-

[a] 11 Also called *Gideon* [b] 11 Some Septuagint manuscripts and Syriac; Hebrew *Bedan* [c] 11 Hebrew; some Septuagint manuscripts and Syriac *Samson* [d] 1 A few late manuscripts of the Septuagint; Hebrew does not have *thirty.* [e] 1 See the round number in Acts 13:21; Hebrew does not have *forty-.* [f] 1,2 Or *and when he had reigned over Israel two years, 2he*

el has become a stench to the Philistines." And the people were
summoned to join Saul at Gilgal.
5The Philistines assembled to fight Israel, with three thousand[a]
chariots, six thousand charioteers, and soldiers as numerous as
the sand on the seashore. They went up and camped at Micmash,
east of Beth Aven. 6When the men of Israel saw that their situation
was critical and that their army was hard pressed, they hid in
caves and thickets, among the rocks, and in pits and cisterns.
7Some Hebrews even crossed the Jordan to the land of Gad and
Gilead.

Saul remained at Gilgal, and all the troops with him were quaking with fear. 8He waited seven days, the time set by Samuel; but
Samuel did not come to Gilgal, and Saul's men began to scatter.
9So he said, "Bring me the burnt offering and the fellowship offerings.[b]" And Saul offered up the burnt offering. 10Just as he finished making the offering, Samuel arrived, and Saul went out to
greet him.
11"What have you done?" asked Samuel.

Saul replied, "When I saw that the men were scattering, and
that you did not come at the set time, and that the Philistines were
assembling at Micmash, 12I thought, 'Now the Philistines will
come down against me at Gilgal, and I have not sought the LORD's
favor.' So I felt compelled to offer the burnt offering."
13"You acted foolishly," Samuel said. "You have not kept the
command the LORD your God gave you; if you had, he would have
established your kingdom over Israel for all time. 14But now your
kingdom will not endure; the LORD has sought out a man after his
own heart and appointed him leader of his people, because you
have not kept the LORD's command."
15Then Samuel left Gilgal[c] and went up to Gibeah in Benjamin,
and Saul counted the men who were with him. They numbered
about six hundred.

Israel Without Weapons

16Saul and his son Jonathan and the men with them were staying in Gibeah[d] in Benjamin, while the Philistines camped at Micmash. 17Raiding parties went out from the Philistine camp in three
detachments. One turned toward Ophrah in the vicinity of Shual,
18another toward Beth Horon, and the third toward the border-
land overlooking the Valley of Zeboim facing the desert.
19Not a blacksmith could be found in the whole land of Israel,
because the Philistines had said, "Otherwise the Hebrews will
make swords or spears!" 20So all Israel went down to the Philistines to have their plowshares, mattocks, axes and sickles[e] sharpened. 21The price was two thirds of a shekel[f] for sharpening
plowshares and mattocks, and a third of a shekel[g] for sharpening
forks and axes and for repointing goads.
22So on the day of the battle not a soldier with Saul and Jonathan had a sword or spear in his hand; only Saul and his son Jonathan had them.

[a] 5 Some Septuagint manuscripts and Syriac; Hebrew *thirty thousand* [b] 9 Traditionally *peace offerings* [c] 15 Hebrew; Septuagint *Gilgal and went his way; the rest of the people went after Saul to meet the army, and they went out of Gilgal* [d] 16 Two Hebrew manuscripts; most Hebrew manuscripts *Geba,* a variant of *Gibeah* [e] 20 Septuagint; Hebrew *plowshares* [f] 21 Hebrew *pim;* that is, about 1/4 ounce (about 8 grams) [g] 21 That is, about 1/8 ounce (about 4 grams)

(13:13–14) Holy God, when Saul disobeyed Your command You sought out a man after Your own heart to lead Your people. A man after Your own heart! How I long to be such a person, someone whose inner being reflects Your own nature. By Your Spirit, transform my stubborn, hardened heart. Teach me to think Your thoughts after You. Move me to feel with Your holy passion. Help me to choose each day to live as a new person, newly created in Christ to be like You, in true righteousness and holiness. (Eze 36:26; Eph 4:24)

As for me, I will behold Thy face
In righteousness,
I will be satisfied when I awake
With Thy likeness.
I want to be just like You, Lord,
So as for me, I will behold Thy face.

"As For Me"
Dan Marks (©1982)

This year I have started out trying to live all my waking moments in conscious listening to the inner voice, asking without ceasing, "What, Father, do you desire said? What, Father, do you desire done this minute?" . . . I seem to have to make sure of only one thing now, and every other thing "takes care of itself," or I prefer to say what is more true, God takes care of all the rest. My part is to live in this hour in continuous inner conversation with God and in perfect responsiveness to his will. To make this hour gloriously rich. This seems to be all I need to think about.

Frank Laubach (1884-1970)

(14:6) Sovereign Lord, You are "mighty to save." No power in heaven or on earth can stop You from saving us when You choose to do so. Your salvation comes from Your very nature as a God who is jealous for His people. You are our shield and defender—"the LORD mighty in battle." With the multitudes of heaven we shout: "Hallelujah! Salvation and glory and power belong to our God!" (Ps 24:8; Zep 3:17; Rev 19:1)

Lead on, O King Eternal,
We follow, not with fears;
For gladness breaks like morning
Where'er Your face appears;
Your cross is lifted o'er us;
We journey in its light;
The crown awaits the conquest;
Lead on, O God of might.

Lead On, O King Eternal
Ernest W. Shurtleff (1887)

Jonathan Attacks the Philistines

23Now a detachment of Philistines had gone out to the pass at
14 Micmash. 1One day Jonathan son of Saul said to the young
man bearing his armor, "Come, let's go over to the Philistine outpost on the other side." But he did not tell his father.
2Saul was staying on the outskirts of Gibeah under a pomegranate tree in Migron. With him were about six hundred men,
3among whom was Ahijah, who was wearing an ephod. He was a
son of Ichabod's brother Ahitub son of Phinehas, the son of Eli,
the LORD's priest in Shiloh. No one was aware that Jonathan had
left.
4On each side of the pass that Jonathan intended to cross to
reach the Philistine outpost was a cliff; one was called Bozez, and
the other Seneh. 5One cliff stood to the north toward Micmash, the
other to the south toward Geba.
6Jonathan said to his young armor-bearer, "Come, let's go over
to the outpost of those uncircumcised fellows. Perhaps the LORD
will act in our behalf. Nothing can hinder the LORD from saving,
whether by many or by few."
7"Do all that you have in mind," his armor-bearer said. "Go
ahead; I am with you heart and soul."
8Jonathan said, "Come, then; we will cross over toward the men
and let them see us. 9If they say to us, 'Wait there until we come
to you,' we will stay where we are and not go up to them. 10But if
they say, 'Come up to us,' we will climb up, because that will be
our sign that the LORD has given them into our hands."
11So both of them showed themselves to the Philistine outpost.
"Look!" said the Philistines. "The Hebrews are crawling out of the
holes they were hiding in." 12The men of the outpost shouted to
Jonathan and his armor-bearer, "Come up to us and we'll teach
you a lesson."
So Jonathan said to his armor-bearer, "Climb up after me; the
LORD has given them into the hand of Israel."
13Jonathan climbed up, using his hands and feet, with his
armor-bearer right behind him. The Philistines fell before Jonathan, and his armor-bearer followed and killed behind him. 14In
that first attack Jonathan and his armor-bearer killed some twenty men in an area of about half an acre.[a]

Israel Routs the Philistines

15Then panic struck the whole army—those in the camp and
field, and those in the outposts and raiding parties—and the
ground shook. It was a panic sent by God.[b]
16Saul's lookouts at Gibeah in Benjamin saw the army melting
away in all directions. 17Then Saul said to the men who were with
him, "Muster the forces and see who has left us." When they did,
it was Jonathan and his armor-bearer who were not there.
18Saul said to Ahijah, "Bring the ark of God." (At that time it
was with the Israelites.)[c] 19While Saul was talking to the priest,
the tumult in the Philistine camp increased more and more. So
Saul said to the priest, "Withdraw your hand."
20Then Saul and all his men assembled and went to the battle.
They found the Philistines in total confusion, striking each other
with their swords. 21Those Hebrews who had previously been with

[a] *14* Hebrew *half a yoke*; a "yoke" was the land plowed by a yoke of oxen in one day.
[b] *15* Or *a terrible panic* [c] *18* Hebrew; Septuagint *"Bring the ephod." (At that time he wore the ephod before the Israelites.)*

the Philistines and had gone up with them to their camp went over
to the Israelites who were with Saul and Jonathan. 22When all the
Israelites who had hidden in the hill country of Ephraim heard
that the Philistines were on the run, they joined the battle in hot
pursuit. 23So the LORD rescued Israel that day, and the battle
moved on beyond Beth Aven.

Jonathan Eats Honey

24Now the men of Israel were in distress that day, because Saul
had bound the people under an oath, saying, "Cursed be any man
who eats food before evening comes, before I have avenged myself
on my enemies!" So none of the troops tasted food.
25The entire army[a] entered the woods, and there was honey on
the ground. 26When they went into the woods, they saw the honey
oozing out, yet no one put his hand to his mouth, because they
feared the oath. 27But Jonathan had not heard that his father had
bound the people with the oath, so he reached out the end of the
staff that was in his hand and dipped it into the honeycomb. He
raised his hand to his mouth, and his eyes brightened.[b] 28Then
one of the soldiers told him, "Your father bound the army under
a strict oath, saying, 'Cursed be any man who eats food today!'
That is why the men are faint."
29Jonathan said, "My father has made trouble for the country.
See how my eyes brightened[c] when I tasted a little of this honey.
30How much better it would have been if the men had eaten today
some of the plunder they took from their enemies. Would not the
slaughter of the Philistines have been even greater?"
31That day, after the Israelites had struck down the Philistines
from Micmash to Aijalon, they were exhausted. 32They pounced
on the plunder and, taking sheep, cattle and calves, they
butchered them on the ground and ate them, together with the
blood. 33Then someone said to Saul, "Look, the men are sinning
against the LORD by eating meat that has blood in it."
"You have broken faith," he said. "Roll a large stone over here
at once." 34Then he said, "Go out among the men and tell them,
'Each of you bring me your cattle and sheep, and slaughter them
here and eat them. Do not sin against the LORD by eating meat with
blood still in it.' "
So everyone brought his ox that night and slaughtered it there.
35Then Saul built an altar to the LORD; it was the first time he had
done this.
36Saul said, "Let us go down after the Philistines by night and
plunder them till dawn, and let us not leave one of them alive."
"Do whatever seems best to you," they replied.
But the priest said, "Let us inquire of God here."
37So Saul asked God, "Shall I go down after the Philistines? Will
you give them into Israel's hand?" But God did not answer him
that day.
38Saul therefore said, "Come here, all you who are leaders of
the army, and let us find out what sin has been committed today.
39As surely as the LORD who rescues Israel lives, even if it lies with
my son Jonathan, he must die." But not one of the men said a
word.
40Saul then said to all the Israelites, "You stand over there; I
and Jonathan my son will stand over here."

[a] 25 Or *Now all the people of the land* [b] 27 Or *his strength was renewed* [c] 29 Or *my strength was renewed*

(14:24–35) Saul was careless with his words, careless with his people, and careless with his God. His foolish vows and foolish threats forced his men to obey their leader; but in their weakness they sinned against You. They followed Saul's unreasonable command but compromised Your holy command; they feared Saul more than they feared You. Lord, give us wisdom to guard our tongues and to not place unreasonable demands on ourselves or on those who are under our authority. Help us to add to our faith goodness; "and to goodness, knowledge; and to knowledge, self-control; and to self-control, perseverance; and to perseverance, godliness; and to godliness, brotherly kindness; and to brotherly kindness, love." Guide us in Your ways, O Lord, and keep us from presumptuous sin. (2Pe 1:5–8)

Beloved, let us mark it well. Let us not miss the warning. Let us remember forever that no man can rule others until he himself is absolutely led of God, that no man can conquer foes till he first is conquered, that no man can lead in triumph . . . until he himself is led in triumph the willing captive of the Saviour's love and the Master's will.

Albert Benjamin Simpson (1843-1919)

"Do what seems best to you," the men replied.
41Then Saul prayed to the LORD, the God of Israel, "Give me the
right answer."[a] And Jonathan and Saul were taken by lot, and the
men were cleared. 42Saul said, "Cast the lot between me and Jonathan my son." And Jonathan was taken.
43Then Saul said to Jonathan, "Tell me what you have done."
So Jonathan told him, "I merely tasted a little honey with the
end of my staff. And now must I die?"
44Saul said, "May God deal with me, be it ever so severely, if you
do not die, Jonathan."
45But the men said to Saul, "Should Jonathan die—he who has
brought about this great deliverance in Israel? Never! As surely as
the LORD lives, not a hair of his head will fall to the ground, for he
did this today with God's help." So the men rescued Jonathan, and
he was not put to death.
46Then Saul stopped pursuing the Philistines, and they withdrew to their own land.
47After Saul had assumed rule over Israel, he fought against
their enemies on every side: Moab, the Ammonites, Edom, the
kings[b] of Zobah, and the Philistines. Wherever he turned, he inflicted punishment on them.[c] 48He fought valiantly and defeated
the Amalekites, delivering Israel from the hands of those who had
plundered them.

Saul's Family

49Saul's sons were Jonathan, Ishvi and Malki-Shua. The name of
his older daughter was Merab, and that of the younger was Michal.
50His wife's name was Ahinoam daughter of Ahimaaz. The name of
the commander of Saul's army was Abner son of Ner, and Ner was
Saul's uncle. 51Saul's father Kish and Abner's father Ner were sons
of Abiel.
52All the days of Saul there was bitter war with the Philistines,
and whenever Saul saw a mighty or brave man, he took him into
his service.

The LORD Rejects Saul as King

15 Samuel said to Saul, "I am the one the LORD sent to anoint
you king over his people Israel; so listen now to the message from the LORD. 2This is what the LORD Almighty says: 'I will
punish the Amalekites for what they did to Israel when they way-
laid them as they came up from Egypt. 3Now go, attack the Amalekites and totally destroy[d] everything that belongs to them. Do not
spare them; put to death men and women, children and infants,
cattle and sheep, camels and donkeys.' "
4So Saul summoned the men and mustered them at Telaim—
two hundred thousand foot soldiers and ten thousand men from
Judah. 5Saul went to the city of Amalek and set an ambush in the
ravine. 6Then he said to the Kenites, "Go away, leave the Amalekites so that I do not destroy you along with them; for you showed
kindness to all the Israelites when they came up out of Egypt." So
the Kenites moved away from the Amalekites.
7Then Saul attacked the Amalekites all the way from Havilah to

[a] *41* Hebrew; Septuagint *"Why have you not answered your servant today? If the fault is in me or my son Jonathan, respond with Urim, but if the men of Israel are at fault, respond with Thummim."* [b] *47* Masoretic Text; Dead Sea Scrolls and Septuagint *king*
[c] *47* Hebrew; Septuagint *he was victorious* [d] *3* The Hebrew term refers to the irrevocable giving over of things or persons to the LORD, often by totally destroying them; also in verses 8, 9, 15, 18, 20 and 21.

(15:2–3) Your will, O God, continues from generation to generation. When Your people first entered the wilderness after leaving Egypt, the Amalekites attacked them from behind and abused the stragglers—those who were slow or lame or sick or with little children. And You responded by saying that You would "completely blot out the memory of Amalek from under heaven." You are a God of justice, a God who does not forget the sins committed against You or the crimes committed against Your people. Vengeance is Yours; You will repay. Before Your judgment all people are humbled. But You, Almighty God, are exalted in Your justice. We bow before You, O awesome Judge! We lift up Your holy name before all people! (Ex 17:8–16; Dt 25:17–19; 32:41; Isa 5:16)

The thunders of His hand
Keep the wide world in awe;
His wrath and justice stand
To guard His holy law.
And where His love resolves to bless,
His truth confirms and seals the
grace.

Thro' all His mighty works
Amazing wisdom shines
Subdues the pow'rs of hell,
Confounds their dark designs.
Strong is His arm, and shall fulfill
His great decrees and sov'reign will.

"The Lord Jehovah Reigns"
Isaac Watts (1709)

Shur, to the east of Egypt. 8He took Agag king of the Amalekites
alive, and all his people he totally destroyed with the sword. 9But
Saul and the army spared Agag and the best of the sheep and cattle, the fat calves[a] and lambs—everything that was good. These
they were unwilling to destroy completely, but everything that was
despised and weak they totally destroyed.
10Then the word of the LORD came to Samuel: 11"I am grieved
that I have made Saul king, because he has turned away from me
and has not carried out my instructions." Samuel was troubled,
and he cried out to the LORD all that night.
12Early in the morning Samuel got up and went to meet Saul,
but he was told, "Saul has gone to Carmel. There he has set up a
monument in his own honor and has turned and gone on down to
Gilgal."
13When Samuel reached him, Saul said, "The LORD bless you! I
have carried out the LORD's instructions."
14But Samuel said, "What then is this bleating of sheep in my
ears? What is this lowing of cattle that I hear?"
15Saul answered, "The soldiers brought them from the Amalekites; they spared the best of the sheep and cattle to sacrifice to the
LORD your God, but we totally destroyed the rest."
16"Stop!" Samuel said to Saul. "Let me tell you what the LORD
said to me last night."
"Tell me," Saul replied.
17Samuel said, "Although you were once small in your own
eyes, did you not become the head of the tribes of Israel? The LORD
anointed you king over Israel. 18And he sent you on a mission,
saying, 'Go and completely destroy those wicked people, the Amalekites; make war on them until you have wiped them out.' 19Why
did you not obey the LORD? Why did you pounce on the plunder
and do evil in the eyes of the LORD?"
20"But I did obey the LORD," Saul said. "I went on the mission
the LORD assigned me. I completely destroyed the Amalekites and
brought back Agag their king. 21The soldiers took sheep and cattle from the plunder, the best of what was devoted to God, in order
to sacrifice them to the LORD your God at Gilgal."
22But Samuel replied:

"Does the LORD delight in burnt offerings and sacrifices
as much as in obeying the voice of the LORD?
To obey is better than sacrifice,
and to heed is better than the fat of rams.
23For rebellion is like the sin of divination,
and arrogance like the evil of idolatry.
Because you have rejected the word of the LORD,
he has rejected you as king."

24Then Saul said to Samuel, "I have sinned. I violated the LORD's
command and your instructions. I was afraid of the people and so
I gave in to them. 25Now I beg you, forgive my sin and come back
with me, so that I may worship the LORD."
26But Samuel said to him, "I will not go back with you. You
have rejected the word of the LORD, and the LORD has rejected you
as king over Israel!"
27As Samuel turned to leave, Saul caught hold of the hem of his
robe, and it tore. 28Samuel said to him, "The LORD has torn the

[a] 9 Or *the grown bulls*; the meaning of the Hebrew for this phrase is uncertain.

(15:22) O God, how much easier it is for me to worship with religious acts than with a life of obedience! Though You delight in my songs and hymns and spiritual songs, how much more are You honored by the music of my submission to Your will. Help me to worship You with all that I am and with all the instruments at my disposal. May You be praised by the harmony between my words of worship and my deeds of obedience! (Ps 51:16–17)

Sacrifice is but a feeble attempt to take that away which obedience would have prevented.

Matthew Henry (1662–1714)

kingdom of Israel from you today and has given it to one of your
neighbors—to one better than you. 29He who is the Glory of Israel does not lie or change his mind; for he is not a man, that he
should change his mind."
30Saul replied, "I have sinned. But please honor me before the
elders of my people and before Israel; come back with me, so that
I may worship the LORD your God." 31So Samuel went back with
Saul, and Saul worshiped the LORD.
32Then Samuel said, "Bring me Agag king of the Amalekites."
Agag came to him confidently,[a] thinking, "Surely the bitterness
of death is past."
33But Samuel said,

"As your sword has made women childless,
so will your mother be childless among women."

And Samuel put Agag to death before the LORD at Gilgal.
34Then Samuel left for Ramah, but Saul went up to his home in
Gibeah of Saul. 35Until the day Samuel died, he did not go to see
Saul again, though Samuel mourned for him. And the LORD was
grieved that he had made Saul king over Israel.

Samuel Anoints David

16 The LORD said to Samuel, "How long will you mourn for
Saul, since I have rejected him as king over Israel? Fill your
horn with oil and be on your way; I am sending you to Jesse of
Bethlehem. I have chosen one of his sons to be king."
2But Samuel said, "How can I go? Saul will hear about it and
kill me."
The LORD said, "Take a heifer with you and say, 'I have come to
sacrifice to the LORD.' 3Invite Jesse to the sacrifice, and I will show
you what to do. You are to anoint for me the one I indicate."
4Samuel did what the LORD said. When he arrived at Bethlehem,
the elders of the town trembled when they met him. They asked,
"Do you come in peace?"
5Samuel replied, "Yes, in peace; I have come to sacrifice to the
LORD. Consecrate yourselves and come to the sacrifice with me."
Then he consecrated Jesse and his sons and invited them to the
sacrifice.
6When they arrived, Samuel saw Eliab and thought, "Surely the
LORD's anointed stands here before the LORD."
7But the LORD said to Samuel, "Do not consider his appearance
or his height, for I have rejected him. The LORD does not look at
the things man looks at. Man looks at the outward appearance,
but the LORD looks at the heart."
8Then Jesse called Abinadab and had him pass in front of Samuel. But Samuel said, "The LORD has not chosen this one either."
9Jesse then had Shammah pass by, but Samuel said, "Nor has the
LORD chosen this one." 10Jesse had seven of his sons pass before
Samuel, but Samuel said to him, "The LORD has not chosen these."
11So he asked Jesse, "Are these all the sons you have?"
"There is still the youngest," Jesse answered, "but he is tending
the sheep."
Samuel said, "Send for him; we will not sit down[b] until he arrives."

[a] 32 Or *him trembling, yet* [b] 11 Some Septuagint manuscripts; Hebrew *not gather around*

The world judges us by appearance; God counts for nothing what is most dazzling to men. What he desires is a pure intention, true docility, and a sincere self-renunciation.

Francois Fénelon (1651–1715)

(16:7) When You look at my heart, O Lord, what do You see? Do You see a heart eager for You or one satisfied with earthly delights? Do You see a heart grieved by sin or one hardened by habitual disobedience? Do You see a heart open to transformation or one defended against Your healing intervention? "O Lord, you have searched me and you know me." Nothing about me is hidden from You. So, gracious Lord, where You see darkness in me, shine Your light. Where You see sin, please forgive. Where dross remains, purge it away. Where You see an old heart of stone, give me a new heart of flesh. (Ps 139:1; Eze 36:26)

12So he sent and had him brought in. He was ruddy, with a fine
appearance and handsome features.
Then the LORD said, "Rise and anoint him; he is the one."
13So Samuel took the horn of oil and anointed him in the presence of his brothers, and from that day on the Spirit of the LORD
came upon David in power. Samuel then went to Ramah.

David in Saul's Service

14Now the Spirit of the LORD had departed from Saul, and an
evil[a] spirit from the LORD tormented him.
15Saul's attendants said to him, "See, an evil spirit from God is
tormenting you. 16Let our lord command his servants here to
search for someone who can play the harp. He will play when the
evil spirit from God comes upon you, and you will feel better."
17So Saul said to his attendants, "Find someone who plays well
and bring him to me."
18One of the servants answered, "I have seen a son of Jesse of
Bethlehem who knows how to play the harp. He is a brave man
and a warrior. He speaks well and is a fine-looking man. And the
LORD is with him."
19Then Saul sent messengers to Jesse and said, "Send me your
son David, who is with the sheep." 20So Jesse took a donkey
loaded with bread, a skin of wine and a young goat and sent them
with his son David to Saul.
21David came to Saul and entered his service. Saul liked him
very much, and David became one of his armor-bearers. 22Then
Saul sent word to Jesse, saying, "Allow David to remain in my service, for I am pleased with him."
23Whenever the spirit from God came upon Saul, David would
take his harp and play. Then relief would come to Saul; he would
feel better, and the evil spirit would leave him.

David and Goliath

17 Now the Philistines gathered their forces for war and assembled at Socoh in Judah. They pitched camp at Ephes
Dammim, between Socoh and Azekah. 2Saul and the Israelites assembled and camped in the Valley of Elah and drew up their battle line to meet the Philistines. 3The Philistines occupied one hill
and the Israelites another, with the valley between them.
4A champion named Goliath, who was from Gath, came out of the
Philistine camp. He was over nine feet[b] tall. 5He had a bronze helmet on his head and wore a coat of scale armor of bronze weighing
five thousand shekels[c]; 6on his legs he wore bronze greaves, and a
bronze javelin was slung on his back. 7His spear shaft was like a
weaver's rod, and its iron point weighed six hundred shekels.[d] His
shield bearer went ahead of him.
8Goliath stood and shouted to the ranks of Israel, "Why do you
come out and line up for battle? Am I not a Philistine, and are you
not the servants of Saul? Choose a man and have him come down
to me. 9If he is able to fight and kill me, we will become your subjects; but if I overcome him and kill him, you will become our
subjects and serve us." 10Then the Philistine said, "This day I defy
the ranks of Israel! Give me a man and let us fight each other."

[a] *14* Or *injurious*; also in verses 15, 16 and 23 [b] *4* Hebrew *was six cubits and a span* (about 3 meters) [c] *5* That is, about 125 pounds (about 57 kilograms) [d] *7* That is, about 15 pounds (about 7 kilograms)

(17:8–11) How easily we become "dismayed and terrified" in the face of danger, dear Lord. How quickly we forget Your promise to care for us. Like the Israelites, our first response to the "Goliaths" in our life is fear. Forgive us, patient God, when we forget Your faithfulness. Pardon us when we cower before "giants" that shrink in comparison to Your exalted majesty. Cleanse us from fear, that we might trust in You with all of our hearts, no matter what threatens us. Help us to sing with the Psalmist: "In God, whose word I praise, in God I trust; I will not be afraid." (Ps 56:4; Pr 3:5)

It is possible for you and for me to live in this world as sure that the Lord is with us as we can be sure of anything—
to have no fear at all
to be able to anticipate tomorrow with a thrill of delight
to have no fear of anything—neither of sickness
nor unemployment
nor loneliness
nor death
nor anything at all.

Peter Marshall (1902-1949)

(17:23–26) O Lord, when the soldiers saw a giant, David saw a mere mortal who stood outside of Your covenant promises. When the Israelites trembled because a giant defied Israel, David was incensed that he defied the armies of the living God. David experienced the world, not as mere human activity, but as a stage for Your divine drama. His world was shaped, not by powerful people with loud voices, but by Your presence and promises. Help me, Lord, to see the world as You see it, to hear with Your ears and to feel with Your heart. May I live each day in the reality of relationship with You, O Living God!

Learn your lessons well in the schoolroom of obscurity. God is preparing you as his chosen arrow. As yet your shaft is hidden in his quiver, in the shadows . . . but at the precise moment at which it will tell with the greatest effect, he will reach for you and launch you to that place of his appointment.

Charles R. Swindoll (1934-)

11On hearing the Philistine's words, Saul and all the Israelites were dismayed and terrified.

12Now David was the son of an Ephrathite named Jesse, who was from Bethlehem in Judah. Jesse had eight sons, and in Saul's time he was old and well advanced in years. **13**Jesse's three oldest sons had followed Saul to the war: The firstborn was Eliab; the second, Abinadab; and the third, Shammah. **14**David was the youngest. The three oldest followed Saul, **15**but David went back and forth from Saul to tend his father's sheep at Bethlehem.

16For forty days the Philistine came forward every morning and evening and took his stand.

17Now Jesse said to his son David, "Take this ephah[a] of roasted grain and these ten loaves of bread for your brothers and hurry to their camp. **18**Take along these ten cheeses to the commander of their unit.[b] See how your brothers are and bring back some assurance[c] from them. **19**They are with Saul and all the men of Israel in the Valley of Elah, fighting against the Philistines."

20Early in the morning David left the flock with a shepherd, loaded up and set out, as Jesse had directed. He reached the camp as the army was going out to its battle positions, shouting the war cry. **21**Israel and the Philistines were drawing up their lines facing each other. **22**David left his things with the keeper of supplies, ran to the battle lines and greeted his brothers. **23**As he was talking with them, Goliath, the Philistine champion from Gath, stepped out from his lines and shouted his usual defiance, and David heard it. **24**When the Israelites saw the man, they all ran from him in great fear.

25Now the Israelites had been saying, "Do you see how this man keeps coming out? He comes out to defy Israel. The king will give great wealth to the man who kills him. He will also give him his daughter in marriage and will exempt his father's family from taxes in Israel."

26David asked the men standing near him, "What will be done for the man who kills this Philistine and removes this disgrace from Israel? Who is this uncircumcised Philistine that he should defy the armies of the living God?"

27They repeated to him what they had been saying and told him, "This is what will be done for the man who kills him."

28When Eliab, David's oldest brother, heard him speaking with the men, he burned with anger at him and asked, "Why have you come down here? And with whom did you leave those few sheep in the desert? I know how conceited you are and how wicked your heart is; you came down only to watch the battle."

29"Now what have I done?" said David. "Can't I even speak?" **30**He then turned away to someone else and brought up the same matter, and the men answered him as before. **31**What David said was overheard and reported to Saul, and Saul sent for him.

32David said to Saul, "Let no one lose heart on account of this Philistine; your servant will go and fight him."

33Saul replied, "You are not able to go out against this Philistine and fight him; you are only a boy, and he has been a fighting man from his youth."

34But David said to Saul, "Your servant has been keeping his father's sheep. When a lion or a bear came and carried off a sheep from the flock, **35**I went after it, struck it and rescued the sheep

[a] *17* That is, probably about 3/5 bushel (about 22 liters) [b] *18* Hebrew *thousand*
[c] *18* Or *some token*; or *some pledge of spoils*

from its mouth. When it turned on me, I seized it by its hair, struck
it and killed it. 36 Your servant has killed both the lion and the
bear; this uncircumcised Philistine will be like one of them, because he has defied the armies of the living God. 37 The LORD who
delivered me from the paw of the lion and the paw of the bear will
deliver me from the hand of this Philistine."

Saul said to David, "Go, and the LORD be with you."

38 Then Saul dressed David in his own tunic. He put a coat of
armor on him and a bronze helmet on his head. 39 David fastened
on his sword over the tunic and tried walking around, because he
was not used to them.

"I cannot go in these," he said to Saul, "because I am not used
to them." So he took them off. 40 Then he took his staff in his hand,
chose five smooth stones from the stream, put them in the pouch
of his shepherd's bag and, with his sling in his hand, approached
the Philistine.

41 Meanwhile, the Philistine, with his shield bearer in front of
him, kept coming closer to David. 42 He looked David over and
saw that he was only a boy, ruddy and handsome, and he despised
him. 43 He said to David, "Am I a dog, that you come at me with
sticks?" And the Philistine cursed David by his gods. 44 "Come
here," he said, "and I'll give your flesh to the birds of the air and
the beasts of the field!"

45 David said to the Philistine, "You come against me with sword
and spear and javelin, but I come against you in the name of the
LORD Almighty, the God of the armies of Israel, whom you have defied. 46 This day the LORD will hand you over to me, and I'll strike
you down and cut off your head. Today I will give the carcasses of
the Philistine army to the birds of the air and the beasts of the
earth, and the whole world will know that there is a God in Israel.
47 All those gathered here will know that it is not by sword or spear
that the LORD saves; for the battle is the LORD's, and he will give all
of you into our hands."

48 As the Philistine moved closer to attack him, David ran quickly toward the battle line to meet him. 49 Reaching into his bag and
taking out a stone, he slung it and struck the Philistine on the forehead. The stone sank into his forehead, and he fell facedown on
the ground.

50 So David triumphed over the Philistine with a sling and a
stone; without a sword in his hand he struck down the Philistine
and killed him.

51 David ran and stood over him. He took hold of the Philistine's
sword and drew it from the scabbard. After he killed him, he cut
off his head with the sword.

When the Philistines saw that their hero was dead, they turned
and ran. 52 Then the men of Israel and Judah surged forward with
a shout and pursued the Philistines to the entrance of Gath[a] and
to the gates of Ekron. Their dead were strewn along the Shaaraim
road to Gath and Ekron. 53 When the Israelites returned from
chasing the Philistines, they plundered their camp. 54 David took
the Philistine's head and brought it to Jerusalem, and he put the
Philistine's weapons in his own tent.

55 As Saul watched David going out to meet the Philistine, he
said to Abner, commander of the army, "Abner, whose son is that
young man?"

[a] 52 Some Septuagint manuscripts; Hebrew *a valley*

(17:47) In every challenge of life, O Lord, the battle is Yours. Whether we face disease or depression, injustice or unbelief, heresy or hatred, the battle is still Yours. You are a mighty warrior who fights on our side. And when we enter the battle as Your soldiers, we fight by Your power. No matter how desperate our situation may appear, no matter how large the "giants" that confront us, in the end You will be victorious, and we will share in Your victory. Even now we celebrate Your ultimate victory through Jesus Christ. With the host of heaven we shout: "Hallelujah! For our Lord God Almighty reigns. Let us rejoice and be glad and give him glory!" (Ps 24:8; Isa 42:13; Jer 20:11; Rev 19:6–7)

I am only one, but I am one.
I can't do everything, but
I can do something.
And what I can do, I ought to do.
And what I ought to do, by the
Grace of God, I shall do.

Edward Everett Hale (1822–1909)

Stand and see what the Lord will do.
In the struggle you face He will fight
for you.
By the power of His arm He will
bring you through.
Stand and see what the Lord will do.

"Stand and See"
Bill Batstone and Phil Kristianson
(©1994)

Abner replied, "As surely as you live, O king, I don't know."
56The king said, "Find out whose son this young man is."
57As soon as David returned from killing the Philistine, Abner
took him and brought him before Saul, with David still holding
the Philistine's head.
58"Whose son are you, young man?" Saul asked him.
David said, "I am the son of your servant Jesse of Bethlehem."

Saul's Jealousy of David

18 After David had finished talking with Saul, Jonathan became
one in spirit with David, and he loved him as himself.
2From that day Saul kept David with him and did not let him return to his father's house. 3And Jonathan made a covenant with
David because he loved him as himself. 4Jonathan took off the
robe he was wearing and gave it to David, along with his tunic, and
even his sword, his bow and his belt.
5Whatever Saul sent him to do, David did it so successfully[a] that
Saul gave him a high rank in the army. This pleased all the people,
and Saul's officers as well.
6When the men were returning home after David had killed the
Philistine, the women came out from all the towns of Israel to
meet King Saul with singing and dancing, with joyful songs and
with tambourines and lutes. 7As they danced, they sang:

"Saul has slain his thousands,
and David his tens of thousands."

8Saul was very angry; this refrain galled him. "They have credited David with tens of thousands," he thought, "but me with only
thousands. What more can he get but the kingdom?" 9And from
that time on Saul kept a jealous eye on David.
10The next day an evil[b] spirit from God came forcefully upon
Saul. He was prophesying in his house, while David was playing
the harp, as he usually did. Saul had a spear in his hand 11and he
hurled it, saying to himself, "I'll pin David to the wall." But David
eluded him twice.
12Saul was afraid of David, because the LORD was with David
but had left Saul. 13So he sent David away from him and gave him
command over a thousand men, and David led the troops in their
campaigns. 14In everything he did he had great success,[c] because
the LORD was with him. 15When Saul saw how successful[d] he was,
he was afraid of him. 16But all Israel and Judah loved David, because he led them in their campaigns.
17Saul said to David, "Here is my older daughter Merab. I will
give her to you in marriage; only serve me bravely and fight the
battles of the LORD." For Saul said to himself, "I will not raise a
hand against him. Let the Philistines do that!"
18But David said to Saul, "Who am I, and what is my family or
my father's clan in Israel, that I should become the king's son-in-
law?" 19So[e] when the time came for Merab, Saul's daughter, to be
given to David, she was given in marriage to Adriel of Meholah.
20Now Saul's daughter Michal was in love with David, and when
they told Saul about it, he was pleased. 21"I will give her to him,"
he thought, "so that she may be a snare to him and so that the
hand of the Philistines may be against him." So Saul said to David,
"Now you have a second opportunity to become my son-in-law."

[a] 5 Or *wisely* [b] 10 Or *injurious* [c] 14 Or *he was very wise* [d] 15 Or *wise*
[e] 19 Or *However,*

(18:12–14) David succeeded in all he did because You were with him, dear Lord. But no matter how glorious his accomplishments, nothing could be better than the mere fact of Your presence. Simply to have You with me, Heavenly Father, is glory enough! With You I find unfailing love. With You I find unsurpassed rest and peace. With You my life has eternal meaning, whether this world considers me a great success or a dismal failure. How I thank You for being with me always, my God, Immanuel! (Ex 33:14; Ps 130:7; Mt 1:23; 28:20)

When we are faithful in keeping ourselves in his holy presence, keeping him always before us, this not only prevents our offending him or doing something displeasing in his sight (at least willfully), but it also brings to us a holy freedom, and if I may say so, a familiarity with God wherein we may ask and receive the graces we are so desperately in need of.

Brother Lawrence of the Resurrection (1611-1691)

22Then Saul ordered his attendants: "Speak to David privately and say, 'Look, the king is pleased with you, and his attendants all like you; now become his son-in-law.'"
23They repeated these words to David. But David said, "Do you think it is a small matter to become the king's son-in-law? I'm only a poor man and little known."
24When Saul's servants told him what David had said, 25Saul
replied, "Say to David, 'The king wants no other price for the bride than a hundred Philistine foreskins, to take revenge on his enemies.'" Saul's plan was to have David fall by the hands of the Philistines.
26When the attendants told David these things, he was pleased to become the king's son-in-law. So before the allotted time elapsed,
27David and his men went out and killed two hundred Philistines. He brought their foreskins and presented the full number to the king so that he might become the king's son-in-law. Then Saul gave him his daughter Michal in marriage.
28When Saul realized that the LORD was with David and that his daughter Michal loved David, 29Saul became still more afraid of him, and he remained his enemy the rest of his days.
30The Philistine commanders continued to go out to battle, and as often as they did, David met with more success[a] than the rest of Saul's officers, and his name became well known.

Saul Tries to Kill David

19 Saul told his son Jonathan and all the attendants to kill David. But Jonathan was very fond of David 2and warned him, "My
father Saul is looking for a chance to kill you. Be on your guard tomorrow morning; go into hiding and stay there. 3I will go out and
stand with my father in the field where you are. I'll speak to him about you and will tell you what I find out."
4Jonathan spoke well of David to Saul his father and said to him, "Let not the king do wrong to his servant David; he has not wronged you, and what he has done has benefited you greatly. 5He took his
life in his hands when he killed the Philistine. The LORD won a great victory for all Israel, and you saw it and were glad. Why then would you do wrong to an innocent man like David by killing him for no reason?"
6Saul listened to Jonathan and took this oath: "As surely as the LORD lives, David will not be put to death."
7So Jonathan called David and told him the whole conversation. He brought him to Saul, and David was with Saul as before.
8Once more war broke out, and David went out and fought the Philistines. He struck them with such force that they fled before him.
9But an evil[b] spirit from the LORD came upon Saul as he was sitting in his house with his spear in his hand. While David was playing the harp, 10Saul tried to pin him to the wall with his spear, but
David eluded him as Saul drove the spear into the wall. That night David made good his escape.
11Saul sent men to David's house to watch it and to kill him in the morning. But Michal, David's wife, warned him, "If you don't run for your life tonight, tomorrow you'll be killed." 12So Michal let
David down through a window, and he fled and escaped. 13Then
Michal took an idol[c] and laid it on the bed, covering it with a garment and putting some goats' hair at the head.

[a] 30 Or *David acted more wisely* [b] 9 Or *injurious* [c] 13 Hebrew *teraphim*; also in verse 16

(19:11–12) O God, when I am pursued by my enemies, please give me a heart like David's to pursue You with prayer and worship. And may David's psalm be the song in my heart: "Deliver me from my enemies, O God; protect me from those who rise up against me. Deliver me from evildoers and save me from bloodthirsty men. See how they lie in wait for me! Fierce men conspire against me for no offense or sin of mine, O Lord . . . Arise to help me; look on my plight! . . . O my Strength, I watch for you; you, O God, are my fortress . . . I will sing of your strength, in the morning I will sing of your love; for you are my fortress, my refuge in times of trouble. O my Strength, I sing praise to you; you, O God, are my fortress, my loving God." (Ps 59:1–4,9,16–17)

Hear my prayer, O Lord,
From the ends of the earth I cry.
Your peace will lead me to the Rock
That is higher than I.

For You have been my strength
In times of trouble,
A tower above my enemies.
And Lord, I will abide with You
Forever
In the shelter of Your wings.

"Hear My Prayer"
Debbie Owens (©1993)

14 When Saul sent the men to capture David, Michal said, "He is
ill."
15 Then Saul sent the men back to see David and told them,
"Bring him up to me in his bed so that I may kill him." 16 But when
the men entered, there was the idol in the bed, and at the head
was some goats' hair.
17 Saul said to Michal, "Why did you deceive me like this and
send my enemy away so that he escaped?"
Michal told him, "He said to me, 'Let me get away. Why should
I kill you?' "
18 When David had fled and made his escape, he went to Samuel at Ramah and told him all that Saul had done to him. Then he
and Samuel went to Naioth and stayed there. 19 Word came to Saul:
"David is in Naioth at Ramah"; 20 so he sent men to capture him.
But when they saw a group of prophets prophesying, with Samuel
standing there as their leader, the Spirit of God came upon Saul's
men and they also prophesied. 21 Saul was told about it, and he
sent more men, and they prophesied too. Saul sent men a third
time, and they also prophesied. 22 Finally, he himself left for
Ramah and went to the great cistern at Secu. And he asked,
"Where are Samuel and David?"
"Over in Naioth at Ramah," they said.
23 So Saul went to Naioth at Ramah. But the Spirit of God came
even upon him, and he walked along prophesying until he came to
Naioth. 24 He stripped off his robes and also prophesied in Samuel's presence. He lay that way all that day and night. This is why
people say, "Is Saul also among the prophets?"

David and Jonathan

20 Then David fled from Naioth at Ramah and went to Jonathan and asked, "What have I done? What is my crime?
How have I wronged your father, that he is trying to take my life?"
2 "Never!" Jonathan replied. "You are not going to die! Look,
my father doesn't do anything, great or small, without confiding in
me. Why would he hide this from me? It's not so!"
3 But David took an oath and said, "Your father knows very well
that I have found favor in your eyes, and he has said to himself,
'Jonathan must not know this or he will be grieved.' Yet as surely
as the LORD lives and as you live, there is only a step between me
and death."
4 Jonathan said to David, "Whatever you want me to do, I'll do
for you."
5 So David said, "Look, tomorrow is the New Moon festival, and
I am supposed to dine with the king; but let me go and hide in the
field until the evening of the day after tomorrow. 6 If your father
misses me at all, tell him, 'David earnestly asked my permission to
hurry to Bethlehem, his hometown, because an annual sacrifice is
being made there for his whole clan.' 7 If he says, 'Very well,' then
your servant is safe. But if he loses his temper, you can be sure
that he is determined to harm me. 8 As for you, show kindness to
your servant, for you have brought him into a covenant with you
before the LORD. If I am guilty, then kill me yourself! Why hand me
over to your father?"
9 "Never!" Jonathan said. "If I had the least inkling that my father was determined to harm you, wouldn't I tell you?"
10 David asked, "Who will tell me if your father answers you
harshly?"

(19:18–24) Almighty God, Your ways are wise and mysterious. Who can withstand Your power? Saul and his men prophesied, but it had nothing to do with their holiness—it had everything to do with Your sovereign choice to overpower them at the moment. As Jesus taught us, not everyone who prophesies will enter the kingdom of heaven, but only those who do Your will. Good works and religious activities are never a substitute for a holy heart. Holy God, overwhelm my evil intentions with Your Spirit; have Your way in my soul, and bend my selfish will to Your sovereign will. (Mt 7:21–23)

The holiness of God is an exceedingly high standard, a perfect standard. But it is nevertheless one that He holds us to. He cannot do less. While it is true that He accepts us solely through the merit of Christ, God's standard for our character, our attitudes, affections, and actions is, "Be holy, because I am holy."

Jerry Bridges (1929-)

11“Come,” Jonathan said, “let’s go out into the field.” So they
went there together.
12Then Jonathan said to David: “By the LORD, the God of Israel, I will surely sound out my father by this time the day after tomorrow! If he is favorably disposed toward you, will I not send
you word and let you know? 13But if my father is inclined to harm
you, may the LORD deal with me, be it ever so severely, if I do not
let you know and send you away safely. May the LORD be with you
as he has been with my father. 14But show me unfailing kindness
like that of the LORD as long as I live, so that I may not be killed,
15and do not ever cut off your kindness from my family—not
even when the LORD has cut off every one of David’s enemies from
the face of the earth.”
16So Jonathan made a covenant with the house of David, saying,
“May the LORD call David’s enemies to account.” 17And Jonathan
had David reaffirm his oath out of love for him, because he loved
him as he loved himself.
18Then Jonathan said to David: “Tomorrow is the New Moon
festival. You will be missed, because your seat will be empty. 19The
day after tomorrow, toward evening, go to the place where you hid
when this trouble began, and wait by the stone Ezel. 20I will shoot
three arrows to the side of it, as though I were shooting at a target. 21Then I will send a boy and say, ‘Go, find the arrows.’ If I say
to him, ‘Look, the arrows are on this side of you; bring them here,’
then come, because, as surely as the LORD lives, you are safe; there
is no danger. 22But if I say to the boy, ‘Look, the arrows are beyond you,’ then you must go, because the LORD has sent you away.
23And about the matter you and I discussed—remember, the LORD
is witness between you and me forever.”
24So David hid in the field, and when the New Moon festival
came, the king sat down to eat. 25He sat in his customary place by
the wall, opposite Jonathan,[a] and Abner sat next to Saul, but
David’s place was empty. 26Saul said nothing that day, for he
thought, “Something must have happened to David to make him
ceremonially unclean—surely he is unclean.” 27But the next day,
the second day of the month, David’s place was empty again. Then
Saul said to his son Jonathan, “Why hasn’t the son of Jesse come
to the meal, either yesterday or today?”
28Jonathan answered, “David earnestly asked me for permission to go to Bethlehem. 29He said, ‘Let me go, because our family is observing a sacrifice in the town and my brother has ordered
me to be there. If I have found favor in your eyes, let me get away
to see my brothers.’ That is why he has not come to the king’s
table.”
30Saul’s anger flared up at Jonathan and he said to him, “You
son of a perverse and rebellious woman! Don’t I know that you
have sided with the son of Jesse to your own shame and to the
shame of the mother who bore you? 31As long as the son of Jesse
lives on this earth, neither you nor your kingdom will be established. Now send and bring him to me, for he must die!”
32“Why should he be put to death? What has he done?” Jonathan asked his father. 33But Saul hurled his spear at him to kill
him. Then Jonathan knew that his father intended to kill David.
34Jonathan got up from the table in fierce anger; on that second

[a] 25 Septuagint; Hebrew *wall. Jonathan arose*

God-ordained friendships are sharp tools for producing Christlikeness in our lives. You cannot think of David apart from Jonathan; Elisha without Elijah; or Paul without Timothy, Barnabas, or Silas.

Charles Stanley (1932-)

(20:12–17) Thank You, gracious Father, for the gift of loyal friendships. David was vulnerable—Jonathan could have betrayed him and given up David’s hiding place. Jonathan was vulnerable—he risked his own life for the safety of his friend. Lord, help me to be a loyal friend, even at the risk of personal loss. May I always be a friend who can be trusted. (Jn 15:13)

(21:1–6) Holy God, You established the sacrificial system so that You might be worshiped in righteousness. Yet You called Your people to worship You, not merely in outward observance, but from the heart. Even Your own sacrificial precepts matter less to You than the merciful heart of the one who sacrifices: "I desire mercy, not sacrifice, and acknowledgment of God rather than burnt offerings." Help us, O God, never to let our styles and structures of worship, however inspired they may be, limit our freedom to be merciful. May our priorities for worship always mirror Your own! (Hos 6:6; Mt 12:3–8)

day of the month he did not eat, because he was grieved at his father's shameful treatment of David.
35In the morning Jonathan went out to the field for his meeting
with David. He had a small boy with him, 36and he said to the boy,
"Run and find the arrows I shoot." As the boy ran, he shot an
arrow beyond him. 37When the boy came to the place where Jonathan's arrow had fallen, Jonathan called out after him, "Isn't the
arrow beyond you?" 38Then he shouted, "Hurry! Go quickly! Don't
stop!" The boy picked up the arrow and returned to his master.
39(The boy knew nothing of all this; only Jonathan and David
knew.) 40Then Jonathan gave his weapons to the boy and said,
"Go, carry them back to town."
41After the boy had gone, David got up from the south side ⌞of
the stone⌟ and bowed down before Jonathan three times, with his
face to the ground. Then they kissed each other and wept together—but David wept the most.
42Jonathan said to David, "Go in peace, for we have sworn
friendship with each other in the name of the LORD, saying, 'The
LORD is witness between you and me, and between your descendants and my descendants forever.' " Then David left, and Jonathan went back to the town.

David at Nob

21 David went to Nob, to Ahimelech the priest. Ahimelech
trembled when he met him, and asked, "Why are you alone?
Why is no one with you?"
2David answered Ahimelech the priest, "The king charged me
with a certain matter and said to me, 'No one is to know anything
about your mission and your instructions.' As for my men, I have
told them to meet me at a certain place. 3Now then, what do you
have on hand? Give me five loaves of bread, or whatever you can
find."
4But the priest answered David, "I don't have any ordinary
bread on hand; however, there is some consecrated bread here—
provided the men have kept themselves from women."
5David replied, "Indeed women have been kept from us, as usual
whenever[a] I set out. The men's things[b] are holy even on missions
that are not holy. How much more so today!" 6So the priest gave
him the consecrated bread, since there was no bread there except
the bread of the Presence that had been removed from before the
LORD and replaced by hot bread on the day it was taken away.
7Now one of Saul's servants was there that day, detained before
the LORD; he was Doeg the Edomite, Saul's head shepherd.
8David asked Ahimelech, "Don't you have a spear or a sword
here? I haven't brought my sword or any other weapon, because
the king's business was urgent."
9The priest replied, "The sword of Goliath the Philistine, whom
you killed in the Valley of Elah, is here; it is wrapped in a cloth behind the ephod. If you want it, take it; there is no sword here but
that one."
David said, "There is none like it; give it to me."

David at Gath

10That day David fled from Saul and went to Achish king of
Gath. 11But the servants of Achish said to him, "Isn't this David,

[a] 5 Or *from us in the past few days since* [b] 5 Or *bodies*

the king of the land? Isn't he the one they sing about in their
dances:

" 'Saul has slain his thousands,
and David his tens of thousands'?"

12David took these words to heart and was very much afraid
of Achish king of Gath. 13So he pretended to be insane in their
presence; and while he was in their hands he acted like a madman, making marks on the doors of the gate and letting saliva
run down his beard.
14Achish said to his servants, "Look at the man! He is insane!
Why bring him to me? 15Am I so short of madmen that you have
to bring this fellow here to carry on like this in front of me? Must
this man come into my house?"

David at Adullam and Mizpah

22 David left Gath and escaped to the cave of Adullam. When
his brothers and his father's household heard about it,
they went down to him there. 2All those who were in distress or
in debt or discontented gathered around him, and he became
their leader. About four hundred men were with him.
3From there David went to Mizpah in Moab and said to the
king of Moab, "Would you let my father and mother come and
stay with you until I learn what God will do for me?" 4So he left
them with the king of Moab, and they stayed with him as long as
David was in the stronghold.
5But the prophet Gad said to David, "Do not stay in the stronghold. Go into the land of Judah." So David left and went to the
forest of Hereth.

Saul Kills the Priests of Nob

6Now Saul heard that David and his men had been discovered.
And Saul, spear in hand, was seated under the tamarisk tree on
the hill at Gibeah, with all his officials standing around him.
7Saul said to them, "Listen, men of Benjamin! Will the son of
Jesse give all of you fields and vineyards? Will he make all of you
commanders of thousands and commanders of hundreds? 8Is
that why you have all conspired against me? No one tells me
when my son makes a covenant with the son of Jesse. None of
you is concerned about me or tells me that my son has incited
my servant to lie in wait for me, as he does today."
9But Doeg the Edomite, who was standing with Saul's officials,
said, "I saw the son of Jesse come to Ahimelech son of Ahitub at
Nob. 10Ahimelech inquired of the LORD for him; he also gave him
provisions and the sword of Goliath the Philistine."
11Then the king sent for the priest Ahimelech son of Ahitub
and his father's whole family, who were the priests at Nob, and
they all came to the king. 12Saul said, "Listen now, son of Ahitub."
"Yes, my lord," he answered.
13Saul said to him, "Why have you conspired against me, you
and the son of Jesse, giving him bread and a sword and inquiring of God for him, so that he has rebelled against me and lies in
wait for me, as he does today?"
14Ahimelech answered the king, "Who of all your servants is
as loyal as David, the king's son-in-law, captain of your bodyguard and highly respected in your household? 15Was that day

(22:1–5) O Lord, when I am in distress, please turn my heart to worship and hear my prayer for mercy as You surely heard David's psalm from the cave: "I cry aloud to the LORD; I lift up my voice to the LORD for mercy. I pour out my complaint before him; before him I tell my trouble. When my spirit grows faint within me, it is you who know my way . . . I cry to you, O Lord; I say, 'You are my refuge, my portion in the land of the living.' Listen to my cry, for I am in desperate need; rescue me from those who pursue me, for they are too strong for me. Set me free from my prison, that I may praise your name." (Ps 142:1–3,5–7)

O merciful God, be unto me a strong tower of defense; give me grace to await your leisure and patiently to bear what you are doing to me; nothing doubting or mistrusting your goodness towards me, for you know what is good for me better than I do. Therefore do with me in all things what you will; only arm me, I beseech you, with your armor, that I may stand fast; above all things, taking to me the shield of faith; praying always that I may refer myself wholly to your will, abiding your pleasure and comforting myself in these troubles which it shall please you to send me, seeing such troubles are profitable for me; and I am assuredly persuaded that all you do cannot but be well; and unto you be all honor and glory. Amen.

Lady Jane Grey (1537-1554)

I have been driven many times to my knees by the overwhelming conviction that I had nowhere else to go. My own wisdom, and that of all about me, seemed insufficient for the day.

Abraham Lincoln (1809-1865)

(23:1–5) Sovereign Lord, David and his soldiers had good reason to be afraid to attack the Philistines at Keilah. Vulnerable against the superior power of Saul, now they would arouse the anger of the Philistines as well. But Your command was clear: "Go!" So David and his men went to Keilah, yielding not to reasonable fears and trusting not in human wisdom, but putting their faith in Your Word alone. May I be a person of such faith! When I am afraid, especially when I have every reason to fear, help me to hold on to Your Word and follow You obediently.

Anywhere with Jesus I can safely go,
Anywhere He leads me in this world below.
Anywhere without Him dearest joys would fade.
Anywhere with Jesus I am not afraid.

Anywhere! Anywhere!
Fear I cannot know.
Anywhere with Jesus
I can safely go.

"Anywhere with Jesus"
Jessie B. Pounds (1887)

the first time I inquired of God for him? Of course not! Let not the king accuse your servant or any of his father's family, for your servant knows nothing at all about this whole affair."

16But the king said, "You will surely die, Ahimelech, you and your father's whole family."

17Then the king ordered the guards at his side: "Turn and kill the priests of the LORD, because they too have sided with David. They knew he was fleeing, yet they did not tell me."

But the king's officials were not willing to raise a hand to strike the priests of the LORD.

18The king then ordered Doeg, "You turn and strike down the priests." So Doeg the Edomite turned and struck them down. That
day he killed eighty-five men who wore the linen ephod. 19He
also put to the sword Nob, the town of the priests, with its men and women, its children and infants, and its cattle, donkeys and sheep.

20But Abiathar, a son of Ahimelech son of Ahitub, escaped and
fled to join David. 21He told David that Saul had killed the priests
of the LORD. 22Then David said to Abiathar: "That day, when Doeg the Edomite was there, I knew he would be sure to tell Saul. I am
responsible for the death of your father's whole family. 23Stay with
me; don't be afraid; the man who is seeking your life is seeking mine also. You will be safe with me."

David Saves Keilah

23 When David was told, "Look, the Philistines are fighting
against Keilah and are looting the threshing floors," 2he
inquired of the LORD, saying, "Shall I go and attack these Philistines?"

The LORD answered him, "Go, attack the Philistines and save Keilah."

3But David's men said to him, "Here in Judah we are afraid. How much more, then, if we go to Keilah against the Philistine forces!"

4Once again David inquired of the LORD, and the LORD answered
him, "Go down to Keilah, for I am going to give the Philistines into
your hand." 5So David and his men went to Keilah, fought the Philistines and carried off their livestock. He inflicted heavy losses on
the Philistines and saved the people of Keilah. 6(Now Abiathar son
of Ahimelech had brought the ephod down with him when he fled to David at Keilah.)

Saul Pursues David

7Saul was told that David had gone to Keilah, and he said, "God has handed him over to me, for David has imprisoned himself by
entering a town with gates and bars." 8And Saul called up all his
forces for battle, to go down to Keilah to besiege David and his men.

9When David learned that Saul was plotting against him, he said
to Abiathar the priest, "Bring the ephod." 10David said, "O LORD,
God of Israel, your servant has heard definitely that Saul plans to
come to Keilah and destroy the town on account of me. 11Will the
citizens of Keilah surrender me to him? Will Saul come down, as your servant has heard? O LORD, God of Israel, tell your servant."

And the LORD said, "He will."

12Again David asked, "Will the citizens of Keilah surrender me
and my men to Saul?"

And the LORD said, "They will."
13So David and his men, about six hundred in number, left
Keilah and kept moving from place to place. When Saul was told
that David had escaped from Keilah, he did not go there.
14David stayed in the desert strongholds and in the hills of the
Desert of Ziph. Day after day Saul searched for him, but God did
not give David into his hands.
15While David was at Horesh in the Desert of Ziph, he learned
that Saul had come out to take his life. 16And Saul's son Jonathan
went to David at Horesh and helped him find strength in God.
17"Don't be afraid," he said. "My father Saul will not lay a hand
on you. You will be king over Israel, and I will be second to you.
Even my father Saul knows this." 18The two of them made a covenant before the LORD. Then Jonathan went home, but David remained at Horesh.
19The Ziphites went up to Saul at Gibeah and said, "Is not
David hiding among us in the strongholds at Horesh, on the hill
of Hakilah, south of Jeshimon? 20Now, O king, come down whenever it pleases you to do so, and we will be responsible for handing him over to the king."
21Saul replied, "The LORD bless you for your concern for me.
22Go and make further preparation. Find out where David usually goes and who has seen him there. They tell me he is very
crafty. 23Find out about all the hiding places he uses and come
back to me with definite information.[a] Then I will go with you; if
he is in the area, I will track him down among all the clans of
Judah."
24So they set out and went to Ziph ahead of Saul. Now David
and his men were in the Desert of Maon, in the Arabah south of
Jeshimon. 25Saul and his men began the search, and when David
was told about it, he went down to the rock and stayed in the
Desert of Maon. When Saul heard this, he went into the Desert of
Maon in pursuit of David.
26Saul was going along one side of the mountain, and David
and his men were on the other side, hurrying to get away from
Saul. As Saul and his forces were closing in on David and his
men to capture them, 27a messenger came to Saul, saying,
"Come quickly! The Philistines are raiding the land." 28Then
Saul broke off his pursuit of David and went to meet the Philis-
tines. That is why they call this place Sela Hammahlekoth.[b]
29And David went up from there and lived in the strongholds of
En Gedi.

David Spares Saul's Life

24 After Saul returned from pursuing the Philistines, he was
told, "David is in the Desert of En Gedi." 2So Saul took
three thousand chosen men from all Israel and set out to look
for David and his men near the Crags of the Wild Goats.
3He came to the sheep pens along the way; a cave was there,
and Saul went in to relieve himself. David and his men were far
back in the cave. 4The men said, "This is the day the LORD spoke
of when he said[c] to you, 'I will give your enemy into your hands
for you to deal with as you wish.' " Then David crept up unnoticed and cut off a corner of Saul's robe.
5Afterward, David was conscience-stricken for having cut off

[a] 23 Or *me at Nacon* [b] 28 *Sela Hammahlekoth* means *rock of parting.* [c] 4 Or *"Today the LORD is saying*

(23:12–14) You are so dependable, Lord. Whenever David sought Your guidance, even in small things, You instructed him. And because he trusted in You he was delivered again and again from his enemies. As You were with David, so You are with us—the same yesterday, today and forever. Though we may not hear Your voice as clearly as David did, You faithfully guide us if we seek You. And though we may not face a human opponent, You protect us from the supernatural enemy who seeks to devour us. Thank You for being such a trustworthy God, One who delivers us from the evil one. (Mt 6:13; Heb 13; 1Pe 5:8)

Victories for God's people come in all shapes and sizes. Sometimes it even seems that God sets up certain situations to show His sovereignty. From His vantage point the view is always victory.

Dick Eastman (1944-) and
Jack Hayford (1934-)

a corner of his robe. [6]He said to his men, "The LORD forbid that I
should do such a thing to my master, the LORD's anointed, or lift
my hand against him; for he is the anointed of the LORD." [7]With
these words David rebuked his men and did not allow them to attack Saul. And Saul left the cave and went his way.
[8]Then David went out of the cave and called out to Saul, "My
lord the king!" When Saul looked behind him, David bowed down
and prostrated himself with his face to the ground. [9]He said to
Saul, "Why do you listen when men say, 'David is bent on harming
you'? [10]This day you have seen with your own eyes how the LORD
delivered you into my hands in the cave. Some urged me to kill
you, but I spared you; I said, 'I will not lift my hand against my
master, because he is the LORD's anointed.' [11]See, my father, look
at this piece of your robe in my hand! I cut off the corner of your
robe but did not kill you. Now understand and recognize that I am
not guilty of wrongdoing or rebellion. I have not wronged you, but
you are hunting me down to take my life. [12]May the LORD judge between you and me. And may the LORD avenge the wrongs you have
done to me, but my hand will not touch you. [13]As the old saying
goes, 'From evildoers come evil deeds,' so my hand will not touch
you.
[14]"Against whom has the king of Israel come out? Whom are
you pursuing? A dead dog? A flea? [15]May the LORD be our judge
and decide between us. May he consider my cause and uphold it;
may he vindicate me by delivering me from your hand."
[16]When David finished saying this, Saul asked, "Is that your
voice, David my son?" And he wept aloud. [17]"You are more righteous than I," he said. "You have treated me well, but I have treated you badly. [18]You have just now told me of the good you did to
me; the LORD delivered me into your hands, but you did not kill
me. [19]When a man finds his enemy, does he let him get away unharmed? May the LORD reward you well for the way you treated me
today. [20]I know that you will surely be king and that the kingdom
of Israel will be established in your hands. [21]Now swear to me by
the LORD that you will not cut off my descendants or wipe out my
name from my father's family."
[22]So David gave his oath to Saul. Then Saul returned home, but
David and his men went up to the stronghold.

David, Nabal and Abigail

25 Now Samuel died, and all Israel assembled and mourned
for him; and they buried him at his home in Ramah.
Then David moved down into the Desert of Maon.[a] [2]A certain
man in Maon, who had property there at Carmel, was very wealthy.
He had a thousand goats and three thousand sheep, which he was
shearing in Carmel. [3]His name was Nabal and his wife's name was
Abigail. She was an intelligent and beautiful woman, but her husband, a Calebite, was surly and mean in his dealings.
[4]While David was in the desert, he heard that Nabal was shearing sheep. [5]So he sent ten young men and said to them, "Go up to
Nabal at Carmel and greet him in my name. [6]Say to him: 'Long life
to you! Good health to you and your household! And good health
to all that is yours!
[7]" 'Now I hear that it is sheep-shearing time. When your shepherds were with us, we did not mistreat them, and the whole time

[a] 1 Some Septuagint manuscripts; Hebrew *Paran*

The true meaning of love dawns on us when we find ourselves required to love someone who has hurt us or mistreated us. Perhaps one of our greatest needs is the motivation to love such people . . . .

The Scriptures teach that we cannot live the Christian life with integrity unless we love people when they are impossible to get along with.

The challenge is to love and keep on loving, even when it is hard.

Floyd McClung, Jr. (1945-)

(24:8–21) What a stirring display of mercy, Lord! Though Saul badly mistreated David and sought his life, when David had the opportunity to kill Saul he did not do so. We see once again how David's heart had been shaped by Your own: He blessed the one who persecuted him. He did not repay evil with evil but did all he could to live at peace with his enemy. He overcame evil with good. He did not take revenge but left room for You to avenge his cause. O God of grace and mercy, help me to learn from David's example of godly character. (Ac 13:22; Ro 12:14–21)

they were at Carmel nothing of theirs was missing. 8Ask your own
servants and they will tell you. Therefore be favorable toward my
young men, since we come at a festive time. Please give your servants and your son David whatever you can find for them.' "
9When David's men arrived, they gave Nabal this message in
David's name. Then they waited.
10Nabal answered David's servants, "Who is this David? Who is
this son of Jesse? Many servants are breaking away from their masters these days. 11Why should I take my bread and water, and the
meat I have slaughtered for my shearers, and give it to men coming from who knows where?"
12David's men turned around and went back. When they arrived, they reported every word. 13David said to his men, "Put on
your swords!" So they put on their swords, and David put on his.
About four hundred men went up with David, while two hundred
stayed with the supplies.
14One of the servants told Nabal's wife Abigail: "David sent messengers from the desert to give our master his greetings, but he
hurled insults at them. 15Yet these men were very good to us. They
did not mistreat us, and the whole time we were out in the fields
near them nothing was missing. 16Night and day they were a wall
around us all the time we were herding our sheep near them.
17Now think it over and see what you can do, because disaster is
hanging over our master and his whole household. He is such a
wicked man that no one can talk to him."
18Abigail lost no time. She took two hundred loaves of bread,
two skins of wine, five dressed sheep, five seahs[a] of roasted grain,
a hundred cakes of raisins and two hundred cakes of pressed figs,
and loaded them on donkeys. 19Then she told her servants, "Go
on ahead; I'll follow you." But she did not tell her husband Nabal.
20As she came riding her donkey into a mountain ravine, there
were David and his men descending toward her, and she met
them. 21David had just said, "It's been useless—all my watching
over this fellow's property in the desert so that nothing of his was
missing. He has paid me back evil for good. 22May God deal with
David,[b] be it ever so severely, if by morning I leave alive one male
of all who belong to him!"
23When Abigail saw David, she quickly got off her donkey and
bowed down before David with her face to the ground. 24She fell
at his feet and said: "My lord, let the blame be on me alone. Please
let your servant speak to you; hear what your servant has to say.
25May my lord pay no attention to that wicked man Nabal. He is
just like his name—his name is Fool, and folly goes with him. But
as for me, your servant, I did not see the men my master sent.
26"Now since the LORD has kept you, my master, from bloodshed and from avenging yourself with your own hands, as surely as
the LORD lives and as you live, may your enemies and all who intend to harm my master be like Nabal. 27And let this gift, which
your servant has brought to my master, be given to the men who
follow you. 28Please forgive your servant's offense, for the LORD
will certainly make a lasting dynasty for my master, because he
fights the LORD's battles. Let no wrongdoing be found in you as
long as you live. 29Even though someone is pursuing you to take
your life, the life of my master will be bound securely in the bundle of the living by the LORD your God. But the lives of your ene-

[a] *18* That is, probably about a bushel (about 37 liters) [b] *22* Some Septuagint manuscripts; Hebrew *with David's enemies*

(25:21–28) How quickly and rashly David spoke in his anger toward Nabal! I am reminded, Lord, of times when I too have spoken hastily. Even though I have not promised to kill innocent people, I have used words to hurt. I have entertained thoughts of vengeance. I have spoken from an insulted pride rather than a trusting heart. Forgive me, Lord, for being so quick to utter hurtful and vain words. Teach me to fight only Your battles and to let You fight mine. (1Sa 25:36–39; Mt 5:22; Jas 3:8–11)

We must meet our hurts, our disappointments, our frustrations, the malice of our enemies, the provoking habits of our friends–our trials and temptations of every sort–with an attitude of active and practical surrender and trust. Only then will we be able to spread our wings and fly above them all to the "heavenly places in Christ." From that vantage point we will be able to see our problems through the eyes of Jesus, and they will lose their power to harm or distress us.

Catherine Jackson

mies he will hurl away as from the pocket of a sling. 30When the
LORD has done for my master every good thing he promised concerning him and has appointed him leader over Israel, 31my
master will not have on his conscience the staggering burden of
needless bloodshed or of having avenged himself. And when the
LORD has brought my master success, remember your servant."
32David said to Abigail, "Praise be to the LORD, the God of Israel, who has sent you today to meet me. 33May you be blessed for
your good judgment and for keeping me from bloodshed this day
and from avenging myself with my own hands. 34Otherwise, as
surely as the LORD, the God of Israel, lives, who has kept me from
harming you, if you had not come quickly to meet me, not one
male belonging to Nabal would have been left alive by daybreak."
35Then David accepted from her hand what she had brought
him and said, "Go home in peace. I have heard your words and
granted your request."
36When Abigail went to Nabal, he was in the house holding a
banquet like that of a king. He was in high spirits and very drunk.
So she told him nothing until daybreak. 37Then in the morning,
when Nabal was sober, his wife told him all these things, and his
heart failed him and he became like a stone. 38About ten days
later, the LORD struck Nabal and he died.
39When David heard that Nabal was dead, he said, "Praise be to
the LORD, who has upheld my cause against Nabal for treating me
with contempt. He has kept his servant from doing wrong and has
brought Nabal's wrongdoing down on his own head."
Then David sent word to Abigail, asking her to become his wife.
40His servants went to Carmel and said to Abigail, "David has sent
us to you to take you to become his wife."
41She bowed down with her face to the ground and said, "Here
is your maidservant, ready to serve you and wash the feet of my
master's servants." 42Abigail quickly got on a donkey and, attended by her five maids, went with David's messengers and became
his wife. 43David had also married Ahinoam of Jezreel, and they
both were his wives. 44But Saul had given his daughter Michal,
David's wife, to Paltiel[a] son of Laish, who was from Gallim.

David Again Spares Saul's Life

26 The Ziphites went to Saul at Gibeah and said, "Is not David
hiding on the hill of Hakilah, which faces Jeshimon?"
2So Saul went down to the Desert of Ziph, with his three thousand chosen men of Israel, to search there for David. 3Saul made
his camp beside the road on the hill of Hakilah facing Jeshimon,
but David stayed in the desert. When he saw that Saul had followed
him there, 4he sent out scouts and learned that Saul had definitely arrived.[b]
5Then David set out and went to the place where Saul had
camped. He saw where Saul and Abner son of Ner, the commander of the army, had lain down. Saul was lying inside the camp, with
the army encamped around him.
6David then asked Ahimelech the Hittite and Abishai son of Zeruiah, Joab's brother, "Who will go down into the camp with me to
Saul?"
"I'll go with you," said Abishai.
7So David and Abishai went to the army by night, and there was

[a] 44 Hebrew *Palti*, a variant of *Paltiel* [b] 4 Or *had come to Nacon*

(25:32–39) How gracious You are, Lord, to keep us from fulfilling our foolish vows and following our self-destructive instincts! In his anger David pledged to spill innocent blood. But through the intercession of Abigail You delivered him from his sinful folly. I wonder how often You have kept me from evil—often without my awareness of Your merciful intervention. Thank You, dear Lord, for protecting me from myself. Thank You for working behind the scenes of my life so that I might walk faithfully along Your paths. (Ps 19:13)

Godly self-mastery of the passions not only represents the highest beauty and conquest, but the truest preparation for service. It means Godlikeness of character, for God Himself is "slow to anger." These words express, very feebly, the fact that He is unchanging in moral character, subject to no impulsive and sudden outbreaks of passion–eternally calm, while yet eternally angry with sin.

Arthur T. Pierson (1837-1911)

Saul, lying asleep inside the camp with his spear stuck in the ground near his head. Abner and the soldiers were lying around him.

8Abishai said to David, "Today God has delivered your enemy into your hands. Now let me pin him to the ground with one thrust of my spear; I won't strike him twice."

9But David said to Abishai, "Don't destroy him! Who can lay a
hand on the LORD's anointed and be guiltless? 10As surely as the
LORD lives," he said, "the LORD himself will strike him; either his time will come and he will die, or he will go into battle and perish. 11But the LORD forbid that I should lay a hand on the LORD's
anointed. Now get the spear and water jug that are near his head, and let's go."

12So David took the spear and water jug near Saul's head, and they left. No one saw or knew about it, nor did anyone wake up. They were all sleeping, because the LORD had put them into a deep sleep.

13Then David crossed over to the other side and stood on top of the hill some distance away; there was a wide space between
them. 14He called out to the army and to Abner son of Ner, "Aren't
you going to answer me, Abner?"

Abner replied, "Who are you who calls to the king?"

15David said, "You're a man, aren't you? And who is like you in Israel? Why didn't you guard your lord the king? Someone came to
destroy your lord the king. 16What you have done is not good. As
surely as the LORD lives, you and your men deserve to die, because you did not guard your master, the LORD's anointed. Look around you. Where are the king's spear and water jug that were near his head?"

17Saul recognized David's voice and said, "Is that your voice, David my son?"

David replied, "Yes it is, my lord the king." 18And he added,
"Why is my lord pursuing his servant? What have I done, and what
wrong am I guilty of? 19Now let my lord the king listen to his ser-
vant's words. If the LORD has incited you against me, then may he accept an offering. If, however, men have done it, may they be cursed before the LORD! They have now driven me from my share in the LORD's inheritance and have said, 'Go, serve other gods.'
20Now do not let my blood fall to the ground far from the pres-
ence of the LORD. The king of Israel has come out to look for a flea—as one hunts a partridge in the mountains."

21Then Saul said, "I have sinned. Come back, David my son.
Because you considered my life precious today, I will not try to harm you again. Surely I have acted like a fool and have erred greatly."

22"Here is the king's spear," David answered. "Let one of your
young men come over and get it. 23The LORD rewards every man
for his righteousness and faithfulness. The LORD delivered you into my hands today, but I would not lay a hand on the LORD's anointed. 24As surely as I valued your life today, so may the LORD value
my life and deliver me from all trouble."

25Then Saul said to David, "May you be blessed, my son David;
you will do great things and surely triumph."

So David went on his way, and Saul returned home.

O Lord, you have called us to overcome evil with good and to pray for our enemies. I ask, Lord, that you have pity on my enemies, just as you have pity on me. Lead them, together with me, into your heavenly kingdom.

Lancelot Andrews (1555-1626)

(26:8–24) Thank You, Father, for David's example of righteousness and faithfulness. You delivered David's enemy into his hands; David returned him unharmed into Yours. O God of mercy, O God of justice, help me to walk in Your ways as David did. Help me to show mercy so that I may receive mercy. Help me to forgive so that I may be forgiven. Help me to release my enemies into Your hands so that my hands might be free to serve You. (Jer 11:20; Mt 5:7; 6:14; Jas 2:13)

David Among the Philistines

27 But David thought to himself, "One of these days I will be
destroyed by the hand of Saul. The best thing I can do is
to escape to the land of the Philistines. Then Saul will give up
searching for me anywhere in Israel, and I will slip out of his
hand."
2So David and the six hundred men with him left and went over
to Achish son of Maoch king of Gath. 3David and his men settled
in Gath with Achish. Each man had his family with him, and David
had his two wives: Ahinoam of Jezreel and Abigail of Carmel, the
widow of Nabal. 4When Saul was told that David had fled to Gath,
he no longer searched for him.
5Then David said to Achish, "If I have found favor in your eyes,
let a place be assigned to me in one of the country towns, that I
may live there. Why should your servant live in the royal city with
you?"
6So on that day Achish gave him Ziklag, and it has belonged to
the kings of Judah ever since. 7David lived in Philistine territory
a year and four months.
8Now David and his men went up and raided the Geshurites,
the Girzites and the Amalekites. (From ancient times these peoples had lived in the land extending to Shur and Egypt.) 9When-
ever David attacked an area, he did not leave a man or woman
alive, but took sheep and cattle, donkeys and camels, and
clothes. Then he returned to Achish.
10When Achish asked, "Where did you go raiding today?"
David would say, "Against the Negev of Judah" or "Against the
Negev of Jerahmeel" or "Against the Negev of the Kenites." 11He
did not leave a man or woman alive to be brought to Gath, for he
thought, "They might inform on us and say, 'This is what David
did.' " And such was his practice as long as he lived in Philistine
territory. 12Achish trusted David and said to himself, "He has become so odious to his people, the Israelites, that he will be my
servant forever."

Saul and the Witch of Endor

28 In those days the Philistines gathered their forces to fight
against Israel. Achish said to David, "You must understand that you and your men will accompany me in the army."
2David said, "Then you will see for yourself what your servant
can do."
Achish replied, "Very well, I will make you my bodyguard for
life."
3Now Samuel was dead, and all Israel had mourned for him
and buried him in his own town of Ramah. Saul had expelled the
mediums and spiritists from the land.
4The Philistines assembled and came and set up camp at Shunem, while Saul gathered all the Israelites and set up camp at Gilboa. 5When Saul saw the Philistine army, he was afraid; terror
filled his heart. 6He inquired of the LORD, but the LORD did not answer him by dreams or Urim or prophets. 7Saul then said to his
attendants, "Find me a woman who is a medium, so I may go and
inquire of her."
"There is one in Endor," they said.
8So Saul disguised himself, putting on other clothes, and at
night he and two men went to the woman. "Consult a spirit for
me," he said, "and bring up for me the one I name."

(28:5–8) Gracious God, I find it so easy to look down upon Saul—until I realize how much I am like him at times. How often have I come to You for guidance, only to be distressed when You expect me to wait? How often have I found other ways to fabricate Your direction? Forgive me, Sovereign Lord, for my rationalizations, my quick solutions, my tendency to rush ahead of Your Spirit. Forgive me for failing to wait quietly upon You in silence and for filling Your silence with my own empty words.

Do not run impetuously before the Lord; learn to wait His time; the minute-hand as well as the hour-hand must point the exact moment for action.

Lettie B. Cowman (1870–1960)

Have Faith in God when your pray'rs
are unanswered;
Your earnest plea He will never
forget.
Wait on the Lord; trust His Word
and be patient.
Have Faith in God; He'll answer yet.

"Have Faith in God"
B.B. McKinney (©1934, 1962)

9 But the woman said to him, "Surely you know what Saul has
done. He has cut off the mediums and spiritists from the land.
Why have you set a trap for my life to bring about my death?"
10 Saul swore to her by the LORD, "As surely as the LORD lives,
you will not be punished for this."
11 Then the woman asked, "Whom shall I bring up for you?"
"Bring up Samuel," he said.
12 When the woman saw Samuel, she cried out at the top of her
voice and said to Saul, "Why have you deceived me? You are
Saul!"
13 The king said to her, "Don't be afraid. What do you see?"
The woman said, "I see a spirit[a] coming up out of the ground."
14 "What does he look like?" he asked.
"An old man wearing a robe is coming up," she said.
Then Saul knew it was Samuel, and he bowed down and prostrated himself with his face to the ground.
15 Samuel said to Saul, "Why have you disturbed me by bringing me up?"
"I am in great distress," Saul said. "The Philistines are fighting
against me, and God has turned away from me. He no longer answers me, either by prophets or by dreams. So I have called on
you to tell me what to do."
16 Samuel said, "Why do you consult me, now that the LORD has
turned away from you and become your enemy? 17 The LORD has
done what he predicted through me. The LORD has torn the kingdom out of your hands and given it to one of your neighbors—to
David. 18 Because you did not obey the LORD or carry out his
fierce wrath against the Amalekites, the LORD has done this to you
today. 19 The LORD will hand over both Israel and you to the Philistines, and tomorrow you and your sons will be with me. The
LORD will also hand over the army of Israel to the Philistines."
20 Immediately Saul fell full length on the ground, filled with
fear because of Samuel's words. His strength was gone, for he
had eaten nothing all that day and night.
21 When the woman came to Saul and saw that he was greatly
shaken, she said, "Look, your maidservant has obeyed you. I took
my life in my hands and did what you told me to do. 22 Now please
listen to your servant and let me give you some food so you may
eat and have the strength to go on your way."
23 He refused and said, "I will not eat."
But his men joined the woman in urging him, and he listened
to them. He got up from the ground and sat on the couch.
24 The woman had a fattened calf at the house, which she
butchered at once. She took some flour, kneaded it and baked
bread without yeast. 25 Then she set it before Saul and his men,
and they ate. That same night they got up and left.

Achish Sends David Back to Ziklag

29 The Philistines gathered all their forces at Aphek, and Israel camped by the spring in Jezreel. 2 As the Philistine
rulers marched with their units of hundreds and thousands,
David and his men were marching at the rear with Achish. 3 The
commanders of the Philistines asked, "What about these Hebrews?"
Achish replied, "Is this not David, who was an officer of Saul

[a] 13 Or *see spirits*; or *see gods*

What are we without God? What are we without the constant influence of the Spirit who makes us fruitful? Oh believer, learn to reject pride. In you there is no room for it. Whoever you are, whatever you have accomplished, you have nothing to make you proud. The more you have the more you are in debt to God, and there is no reason to be proud that you are in debt.

Charles Haddon Spurgeon (1834–1892)

(28:15–20) O Father, help me to learn from Saul's life. His pride and impatience were his downfall. Saul would not listen to You in his prosperity; now he lamented Your silence in his adversity. Once he was Your anointed one; now he was Your enemy. O God, hear my prayer. Please, give me a heart to listen and obey. Help me to be a faithful servant and an obedient child. "Search me, O God, and know my heart; test me and know my anxious thoughts. See if there is any offensive way in me, and lead me in the way everlasting." (Ps 139:23–24)

king of Israel? He has already been with me for over a year, and
from the day he left Saul until now, I have found no fault in him."
4But the Philistine commanders were angry with him and said,
"Send the man back, that he may return to the place you assigned
him. He must not go with us into battle, or he will turn against us
during the fighting. How better could he regain his master's favor
than by taking the heads of our own men? 5Isn't this the David
they sang about in their dances:

" 'Saul has slain his thousands,
and David his tens of thousands'?"

6So Achish called David and said to him, "As surely as the LORD
lives, you have been reliable, and I would be pleased to have you
serve with me in the army. From the day you came to me until now,
I have found no fault in you, but the rulers don't approve of you.
7Turn back and go in peace; do nothing to displease the Philistine
rulers."
8"But what have I done?" asked David. "What have you found
against your servant from the day I came to you until now? Why
can't I go and fight against the enemies of my lord the king?"
9Achish answered, "I know that you have been as pleasing in
my eyes as an angel of God; nevertheless, the Philistine commanders have said, 'He must not go up with us into battle.' 10Now get up
early, along with your master's servants who have come with you,
and leave in the morning as soon as it is light."
11So David and his men got up early in the morning to go back
to the land of the Philistines, and the Philistines went up to Jezreel.

David Destroys the Amalekites

30 David and his men reached Ziklag on the third day. Now
the Amalekites had raided the Negev and Ziklag. They had
attacked Ziklag and burned it, 2and had taken captive the women
and all who were in it, both young and old. They killed none of
them, but carried them off as they went on their way.
3When David and his men came to Ziklag, they found it destroyed by fire and their wives and sons and daughters taken captive. 4So David and his men wept aloud until they had no strength
left to weep. 5David's two wives had been captured—Ahinoam of
Jezreel and Abigail, the widow of Nabal of Carmel. 6David was
greatly distressed because the men were talking of stoning him;
each one was bitter in spirit because of his sons and daughters.
But David found strength in the LORD his God.
7Then David said to Abiathar the priest, the son of Ahimelech,
"Bring me the ephod." Abiathar brought it to him, 8and David inquired of the LORD, "Shall I pursue this raiding party? Will I overtake them?"
"Pursue them," he answered. "You will certainly overtake them
and succeed in the rescue."
9David and the six hundred men with him came to the Besor
Ravine, where some stayed behind, 10for two hundred men were
too exhausted to cross the ravine. But David and four hundred
men continued the pursuit.
11They found an Egyptian in a field and brought him to David.
They gave him water to drink and food to eat— 12part of a cake
of pressed figs and two cakes of raisins. He ate and was revived,

When life caves in, you do not need reasons—you need comfort. You do not need some answers—you need someone. And Jesus does not come to us with an explanation—He comes to us with His presence.

Bob Benson (1930-1986)

(30:1–6) In the time of intense mourning David found strength in You. When his life was threatened by his friends, he turned to You for sustenance. O God, there is no other way to cope with the pains and crises of this life. When the doctor says "malignancy," I find strength in You alone. When the casket is lowered into the ground, I turn to You for solace. When my family is shattered, when my career plans are dashed, when violence rips our society apart, when injustice prevails, when all hope seems lost, only in You do I find the power to go on. You alone are my rock, my fortress, my deliverer. You are my shield, the horn of my salvation, my stronghold. In You alone do I trust, for Your compassions never fail! (Ps 18:2; La 3:22)

His strength is perfect when our
strength is gone;
He'll carry us when we can't carry
on.
Raised in His power, the weak
become strong;
His strength is perfect, His
strength is perfect.

"His Strength is Perfect"
Steven Curtis Chapman and Jerry Salley
(©1988)

for he had not eaten any food or drunk any water for three days
and three nights.
13David asked him, "To whom do you belong, and where do you
come from?"
He said, "I am an Egyptian, the slave of an Amalekite. My master
abandoned me when I became ill three days ago. 14We raided the
Negev of the Kerethites and the territory belonging to Judah and
the Negev of Caleb. And we burned Ziklag."
15David asked him, "Can you lead me down to this raiding
party?"
He answered, "Swear to me before God that you will not kill me
or hand me over to my master, and I will take you down to them."
16He led David down, and there they were, scattered over the
countryside, eating, drinking and reveling because of the great
amount of plunder they had taken from the land of the Philistines
and from Judah. 17David fought them from dusk until the evening
of the next day, and none of them got away, except four hundred
young men who rode off on camels and fled. 18David recovered
everything the Amalekites had taken, including his two wives.
19Nothing was missing: young or old, boy or girl, plunder or anything else they had taken. David brought everything back. 20He
took all the flocks and herds, and his men drove them ahead of the
other livestock, saying, "This is David's plunder."
21Then David came to the two hundred men who had been too
exhausted to follow him and who were left behind at the Besor
Ravine. They came out to meet David and the people with him. As
David and his men approached, he greeted them. 22But all the evil
men and troublemakers among David's followers said, "Because
they did not go out with us, we will not share with them the plunder we recovered. However, each man may take his wife and children and go."
23David replied, "No, my brothers, you must not do that with
what the LORD has given us. He has protected us and handed over
to us the forces that came against us. 24Who will listen to what you
say? The share of the man who stayed with the supplies is to be the
same as that of him who went down to the battle. All will share
alike." 25David made this a statute and ordinance for Israel from
that day to this.
26When David arrived in Ziklag, he sent some of the plunder to
the elders of Judah, who were his friends, saying, "Here is a present for you from the plunder of the LORD's enemies."
27He sent it to those who were in Bethel, Ramoth Negev and Jattir; 28to those in Aroer, Siphmoth, Eshtemoa 29and Racal; to those
in the towns of the Jerahmeelites and the Kenites; 30to those in
Hormah, Bor Ashan, Athach 31and Hebron; and to those in all the
other places where David and his men had roamed.

Saul Takes His Life

31 Now the Philistines fought against Israel; the Israelites fled
before them, and many fell slain on Mount Gilboa. 2The Philistines pressed hard after Saul and his sons, and they killed his
sons Jonathan, Abinadab and Malki-Shua. 3The fighting grew fierce
around Saul, and when the archers overtook him, they wounded
him critically.
4Saul said to his armor-bearer, "Draw your sword and run me
through, or these uncircumcised fellows will come and run me
through and abuse me."

(30:21–25) Gracious God, "every good and perfect gift is from above." Even that which appears to result from human effort is, indeed, a gift from Your hand. In David's response to Your bounty we see how Your grace transforms us. When we experience life's benefits as Your good gifts, we are set free to share them with others—even those who, by selfish human standards, do not deserve them. Thank You, dear Lord, for Your endless generosity. May Your grace so transform us that we give away freely that which we have received from You. (Mt 10:8; Jas 1:17)

Since devotion consists in a certain degree of eminent charity, it not only makes us prompt, active, and faithful in observance of God's commands, but in addition it arouses us to do quickly and lovingly as many good works as possible, both those commanded and those merely counseled or inspired.

Saint Francis de Sales (1567-1622)

But his armor-bearer was terrified and would not do it; so Saul
took his own sword and fell on it. 5When the armor-bearer saw
that Saul was dead, he too fell on his sword and died with him. 6So
Saul and his three sons and his armor-bearer and all his men died
together that same day.
7When the Israelites along the valley and those across the Jordan saw that the Israelite army had fled and that Saul and his sons
had died, they abandoned their towns and fled. And the Philistines
came and occupied them.
8The next day, when the Philistines came to strip the dead, they
found Saul and his three sons fallen on Mount Gilboa. 9They cut
off his head and stripped off his armor, and they sent messengers
throughout the land of the Philistines to proclaim the news in the
temple of their idols and among their people. 10They put his
armor in the temple of the Ashtoreths and fastened his body to the
wall of Beth Shan.
11When the people of Jabesh Gilead heard of what the Philistines had done to Saul, 12all their valiant men journeyed through
the night to Beth Shan. They took down the bodies of Saul and his
sons from the wall of Beth Shan and went to Jabesh, where they
burned them. 13Then they took their bones and buried them
under a tamarisk tree at Jabesh, and they fasted seven days.

(31:4–13) So what will be the final measure of my life, O God? When the fire of Your judgment tests the quality of my life, what will remain after the dross is consumed? Will I have lived for Your glory, storing up treasures in heaven? Or will I escape from the flames of judgment with nothing left but my life spared by Your grace? I do not want to finish my days like Saul: dishonored, detached from You—a colossal disappointment. Draw me to Yourself so that I might press on with singular focus toward the goal of knowing and serving Christ. In the day of Your judgment may I be found worthy to receive the prize of Your pleasure in my life. Even now, "take my life and let it be consecrated, Lord, to Thee"—and Thee alone! Amen. (Ps 39:4; Mt 6:20; 1Co 3:12–15; Php 3:8–14)

We never reach a place in the Christian life where it is no longer necessary to watch and pray lest we fall into temptation. A constant coming back in spirit to our Center which is Christ the Lord, is our only safeguard.

Frederick Julius Huegel (1889–1971)

Consecrate me now to Thy service,
Lord, by the power of grace divine.
Let my soul look up with a steadfast
hope,
And my will be lost in Thine.

"I Am Thine, O Lord"
Fanny J. Crosby (1875)

David Hears of Saul's Death

1 After the death of Saul, David returned from defeating the Amalekites and stayed in Ziklag two days. 2On the third day a man
arrived from Saul's camp, with his clothes torn and with dust on
his head. When he came to David, he fell to the ground to pay him
honor.

3"Where have you come from?" David asked him.

He answered, "I have escaped from the Israelite camp."

4"What happened?" David asked. "Tell me."

He said, "The men fled from the battle. Many of them fell and died. And Saul and his son Jonathan are dead."

5Then David said to the young man who brought him the report, "How do you know that Saul and his son Jonathan are
dead?"

6"I happened to be on Mount Gilboa," the young man said,
"and there was Saul, leaning on his spear, with the chariots and
riders almost upon him. 7When he turned around and saw me, he
called out to me, and I said, 'What can I do?'

8"He asked me, 'Who are you?'

" 'An Amalekite,' I answered.

9"Then he said to me, 'Stand over me and kill me! I am in the throes of death, but I'm still alive.'

10"So I stood over him and killed him, because I knew that after he had fallen he could not survive. And I took the crown that was on his head and the band on his arm and have brought them here to my lord."

11Then David and all the men with him took hold of their
clothes and tore them. 12They mourned and wept and fasted till
evening for Saul and his son Jonathan, and for the army of the
LORD and the house of Israel, because they had fallen by the sword.

13David said to the young man who brought him the report, "Where are you from?"

"I am the son of an alien, an Amalekite," he answered.

14David asked him, "Why were you not afraid to lift your hand to destroy the LORD's anointed?"

15Then David called one of his men and said, "Go, strike him
down!" So he struck him down, and he died. 16For David had said
to him, "Your blood be on your own head. Your own mouth testified against you when you said, 'I killed the LORD's anointed.' "

David's Lament for Saul and Jonathan

17David took up this lament concerning Saul and his son Jonathan, 18and ordered that the men of Judah be taught this lament of
the bow (it is written in the Book of Jashar):

19"Your glory, O Israel, lies slain on your heights.
How the mighty have fallen!

20"Tell it not in Gath,
proclaim it not in the streets of Ashkelon,
lest the daughters of the Philistines be glad,
lest the daughters of the uncircumcised rejoice.

21"O mountains of Gilboa,
may you have neither dew nor rain,
nor fields that yield offerings ⌊of grain⌋.
For there the shield of the mighty was defiled,
the shield of Saul—no longer rubbed with oil.

(1:17–21) O God, our hearts break with Yours when one of Your anointed goes down in ruin. We lift up a prayer for Your appointed leaders right now: May they follow the path of righteousness. Protect them from foolish pride. Dress them in Your full armor, so that when the day of evil comes they may be able to stand their ground—for Your glory, Holy One of Israel. (Eph 6:13)

Every full-time Christian worker needs a prayer team standing with him, strengthening him, and covering him with intercession . . . Blessed is that person or ministry that has not only enlisted the aid of prayer helpers, but has intercessor-watchmen who carry a continual burden for the ministry . . . When God entrusts you with a special prayer burden, accept it with joy and be faithful to it. It is a special commission from the Lord.

Wesley L. Duewel (1916-)

Friends, our life is love and peace and tenderness. We are called to bear one another's burdens, forgive one another, and never judge or accuse one another. Instead, we must pray for one another, helping one another up with a tender hand if there has been any slip or fall.

Isaac Penington (1617–1680)

(1:22–24) Even in Saul's death, David was kind to him and treated him with great honor. David grieved the loss of the Lord's anointed even though Saul had tried repeatedly to kill him. In this he demonstrated something of Your heart, O God, for You "take no pleasure in the death of anyone," but "rather that they turn from their ways and live." Help me to learn from David's example to love my enemies and to bless, rather than curse, those who persecute me. (Eze 18:32; 33:11; Mt 5:44; Ro 12:14)

22 From the blood of the slain,
from the flesh of the mighty,
the bow of Jonathan did not turn back,
the sword of Saul did not return unsatisfied.

23 "Saul and Jonathan—
in life they were loved and gracious,
and in death they were not parted.
They were swifter than eagles,
they were stronger than lions.

24 "O daughters of Israel,
weep for Saul,
who clothed you in scarlet and finery,
who adorned your garments with ornaments of gold.

25 "How the mighty have fallen in battle!
Jonathan lies slain on your heights.
26 I grieve for you, Jonathan my brother;
you were very dear to me.
Your love for me was wonderful,
more wonderful than that of women.

27 "How the mighty have fallen!
The weapons of war have perished!"

David Anointed King Over Judah

2 In the course of time, David inquired of the LORD. "Shall I go
up to one of the towns of Judah?" he asked.
The LORD said, "Go up."
David asked, "Where shall I go?"
"To Hebron," the LORD answered.
2 So David went up there with his two wives, Ahinoam of Jezreel and Abigail, the widow of Nabal of Carmel. 3 David also took the
men who were with him, each with his family, and they settled in
Hebron and its towns. 4 Then the men of Judah came to Hebron
and there they anointed David king over the house of Judah.
When David was told that it was the men of Jabesh Gilead who
had buried Saul, 5 he sent messengers to the men of Jabesh Gilead
to say to them, "The LORD bless you for showing this kindness to
Saul your master by burying him. 6 May the LORD now show you
kindness and faithfulness, and I too will show you the same favor
because you have done this. 7 Now then, be strong and brave, for
Saul your master is dead, and the house of Judah has anointed me
king over them."

War Between the Houses of David and Saul

8 Meanwhile, Abner son of Ner, the commander of Saul's army,
had taken Ish-Bosheth son of Saul and brought him over to Mahanaim. 9 He made him king over Gilead, Ashuri[a] and Jezreel, and
also over Ephraim, Benjamin and all Israel.
10 Ish-Bosheth son of Saul was forty years old when he became
king over Israel, and he reigned two years. The house of Judah,
however, followed David. 11 The length of time David was king in
Hebron over the house of Judah was seven years and six months.
12 Abner son of Ner, together with the men of Ish-Bosheth son of
Saul, left Mahanaim and went to Gibeon. 13 Joab son of Zeruiah

[a] 9 Or *Asher*

and David's men went out and met them at the pool of Gibeon.
One group sat down on one side of the pool and one group on
the other side.
14Then Abner said to Joab, "Let's have some of the young men
get up and fight hand to hand in front of us."
"All right, let them do it," Joab said.
15So they stood up and were counted off—twelve men for
Benjamin and Ish-Bosheth son of Saul, and twelve for David.
16Then each man grabbed his opponent by the head and thrust
his dagger into his opponent's side, and they fell down together.
So that place in Gibeon was called Helkath Hazzurim.[a]
17The battle that day was very fierce, and Abner and the men of
Israel were defeated by David's men.
18The three sons of Zeruiah were there: Joab, Abishai and Asahel. Now Asahel was as fleet-footed as a wild gazelle. 19He
chased Abner, turning neither to the right nor to the left as he
pursued him. 20Abner looked behind him and asked, "Is that
you, Asahel?"
"It is," he answered.
21Then Abner said to him, "Turn aside to the right or to the
left; take on one of the young men and strip him of his weapons."
But Asahel would not stop chasing him.
22Again Abner warned Asahel, "Stop chasing me! Why should I
strike you down? How could I look your brother Joab in the
face?"
23But Asahel refused to give up the pursuit; so Abner thrust the
butt of his spear into Asahel's stomach, and the spear came out
through his back. He fell there and died on the spot. And every
man stopped when he came to the place where Asahel had fallen
and died.
24But Joab and Abishai pursued Abner, and as the sun was setting, they came to the hill of Ammah, near Giah on the way to the
wasteland of Gibeon. 25Then the men of Benjamin rallied behind
Abner. They formed themselves into a group and took their stand
on top of a hill.
26Abner called out to Joab, "Must the sword devour forever?
Don't you realize that this will end in bitterness? How long before
you order your men to stop pursuing their brothers?"
27Joab answered, "As surely as God lives, if you had not spoken, the men would have continued the pursuit of their brothers
until morning.[b]"
28So Joab blew the trumpet, and all the men came to a halt;
they no longer pursued Israel, nor did they fight anymore.
29All that night Abner and his men marched through the Arabah. They crossed the Jordan, continued through the whole Bith-
ron[c] and came to Mahanaim.
30Then Joab returned from pursuing Abner and assembled all
his men. Besides Asahel, nineteen of David's men were found
missing. 31But David's men had killed three hundred and sixty
Benjamites who were with Abner. 32They took Asahel and buried
him in his father's tomb at Bethlehem. Then Joab and his men
marched all night and arrived at Hebron by daybreak.

[a] *16 Helkath Hazzurim* means *field of daggers* or *field of hostilities.* [b] *27* Or *spoken this morning, the men would not have taken up the pursuit of their brothers*; or *spoken, the men would have given up the pursuit of their brothers by morning* [c] *29* Or *morning*; or *ravine*; the meaning of the Hebrew for this word is uncertain.

Of every idle word that we speak we must give account in the day of judgment. Fearful thought! What but the most callous heart can forget that . . . what sort of a memorial are you and I preparing against that day. Think how much we say—how little to any good purpose. How many words are spoken vainly, foolishly, wickedly—in pride, in envy, in malice, in anger, in hatred!

Arthur T. Pierson (1837-1911)

(2:26) Must the sword of division devour Your people forever, O God? Must we always destroy each other with ill-spoken words of accusation or criticism? When will we realize that if we keep on biting and devouring each other we will be destroyed by each other? Make me an instrument of Your peace, Lord of love, rather than a sower of discord. "How good and pleasant it is when brothers live together in unity!" (Ps 133:1; Gal 5:15)

Oh, let us be the generation
Of reconciliation and peace,
And let us build on one foundation
'Til He comes
And the wars of men shall cease.
Let us share the love of Jesus
Without hypocrisy,
Let mercy and forgiveness
Begin with you and me.
Let us be the generation
Of reconciliation and peace.

"The Reconciliation Song"
Morris Chapman, Buddy Owens and Claire Cloninger (©1995)

The Lord is my strength, my strong rock,
my defense, my deliverer, the horn of my
salvation, and my refuge. Amen.
Lancelot Andrews (1555-1626)

(3:17–18) Just as David was raised up to rescue Your people from all their enemies, so I praise You, Jesus Christ, Son of David, for being my Deliverer, the One who rescues me from sin, Satan and death. I proclaim this day that You are King of my life; and in my heart I set You apart as Lord. (Heb 2:14–15; 1Pe 3:15)

3 The war between the house of Saul and the house of David
lasted a long time. David grew stronger and stronger, while
the house of Saul grew weaker and weaker.
2 Sons were born to David in Hebron:

His firstborn was Amnon the son of Ahinoam of Jezreel;
3 his second, Kileab the son of Abigail the widow of Nabal of Carmel;
the third, Absalom the son of Maacah daughter of Talmai king of Geshur;
4 the fourth, Adonijah the son of Haggith;
the fifth, Shephatiah the son of Abital;
5 and the sixth, Ithream the son of David's wife Eglah.
These were born to David in Hebron.

Abner Goes Over to David

6 During the war between the house of Saul and the house of
David, Abner had been strengthening his own position in the
house of Saul. 7 Now Saul had had a concubine named Rizpah
daughter of Aiah. And Ish-Bosheth said to Abner, "Why did you
sleep with my father's concubine?"
8 Abner was very angry because of what Ish-Bosheth said and he
answered, "Am I a dog's head—on Judah's side? This very day I
am loyal to the house of your father Saul and to his family and
friends. I haven't handed you over to David. Yet now you accuse
me of an offense involving this woman! 9 May God deal with Abner,
be it ever so severely, if I do not do for David what the LORD promised him on oath 10 and transfer the kingdom from the house of
Saul and establish David's throne over Israel and Judah from Dan
to Beersheba." 11 Ish-Bosheth did not dare to say another word to
Abner, because he was afraid of him.
12 Then Abner sent messengers on his behalf to say to David,
"Whose land is it? Make an agreement with me, and I will help you
bring all Israel over to you."
13 "Good," said David. "I will make an agreement with you. But
I demand one thing of you: Do not come into my presence unless
you bring Michal daughter of Saul when you come to see me."
14 Then David sent messengers to Ish-Bosheth son of Saul, demanding, "Give me my wife Michal, whom I betrothed to myself
for the price of a hundred Philistine foreskins."
15 So Ish-Bosheth gave orders and had her taken away from her
husband Paltiel son of Laish. 16 Her husband, however, went with
her, weeping behind her all the way to Bahurim. Then Abner said
to him, "Go back home!" So he went back.
17 Abner conferred with the elders of Israel and said, "For some
time you have wanted to make David your king. 18 Now do it! For
the LORD promised David, 'By my servant David I will rescue my
people Israel from the hand of the Philistines and from the hand
of all their enemies.' "
19 Abner also spoke to the Benjamites in person. Then he went
to Hebron to tell David everything that Israel and the whole house
of Benjamin wanted to do. 20 When Abner, who had twenty men
with him, came to David at Hebron, David prepared a feast for
him and his men. 21 Then Abner said to David, "Let me go at once
and assemble all Israel for my lord the king, so that they may
make a compact with you, and that you may rule over all that your
heart desires." So David sent Abner away, and he went in peace.

Joab Murders Abner

22Just then David's men and Joab returned from a raid and
brought with them a great deal of plunder. But Abner was no
longer with David in Hebron, because David had sent him away,
and he had gone in peace. 23When Joab and all the soldiers with
him arrived, he was told that Abner son of Ner had come to the
king and that the king had sent him away and that he had gone in
peace.

24So Joab went to the king and said, "What have you done?
Look, Abner came to you. Why did you let him go? Now he is gone!
25You know Abner son of Ner; he came to deceive you and observe your movements and find out everything you are doing."

26Joab then left David and sent messengers after Abner, and
they brought him back from the well of Sirah. But David did not
know it. 27Now when Abner returned to Hebron, Joab took him
aside into the gateway, as though to speak with him privately. And
there, to avenge the blood of his brother Asahel, Joab stabbed him
in the stomach, and he died.

28Later, when David heard about this, he said, "I and my kingdom are forever innocent before the LORD concerning the blood of
Abner son of Ner. 29May his blood fall upon the head of Joab and
upon all his father's house! May Joab's house never be without
someone who has a running sore or leprosy[a] or who leans on a
crutch or who falls by the sword or who lacks food."

30(Joab and his brother Abishai murdered Abner because he
had killed their brother Asahel in the battle at Gibeon.)

31Then David said to Joab and all the people with him, "Tear
your clothes and put on sackcloth and walk in mourning in front
of Abner." King David himself walked behind the bier. 32They
buried Abner in Hebron, and the king wept aloud at Abner's tomb.
All the people wept also.

33The king sang this lament for Abner:

"Should Abner have died as the lawless die?
34 Your hands were not bound,
your feet were not fettered.
You fell as one falls before wicked men."

And all the people wept over him again.

35Then they all came and urged David to eat something while it
was still day; but David took an oath, saying, "May God deal with
me, be it ever so severely, if I taste bread or anything else before
the sun sets!"

36All the people took note and were pleased; indeed, everything
the king did pleased them. 37So on that day all the people and all
Israel knew that the king had no part in the murder of Abner son
of Ner.

38Then the king said to his men, "Do you not realize that a
prince and a great man has fallen in Israel this day? 39And today,
though I am the anointed king, I am weak, and these sons of Zeruiah are too strong for me. May the LORD repay the evildoer according to his evil deeds!"

[a] 29 The Hebrew word was used for various diseases affecting the skin—not necessarily leprosy.

(3:22–27) Abner killed Joab's brother in self defense during a civil war. Therefore, Joab's act of killing Abner was not justified. Father God, protect me from self-deceit. Keep me from rationalizing my own selfish desires based on my perception of the greater sins or faults of others. Prevent me from having a spirit of revenge, and help me to leave the matter of judgment in Your hands alone. In fact, may I even desire to "feed my enemy"—thereby overcoming evil with good rather than being overcome by evil. (2Sa 2:17–28; Ro 12:17–21; 1Pe 3:8–12)

Ish-Bosheth Murdered

4 When Ish-Bosheth son of Saul heard that Abner had died
in Hebron, he lost courage, and all Israel became
alarmed. 2Now Saul's son had two men who were leaders of
raiding bands. One was named Baanah and the other Recab;
they were sons of Rimmon the Beerothite from the tribe of
Benjamin—Beeroth is considered part of Benjamin, 3because
the people of Beeroth fled to Gittaim and have lived there as
aliens to this day.

4(Jonathan son of Saul had a son who was lame in both feet.
He was five years old when the news about Saul and Jonathan
came from Jezreel. His nurse picked him up and fled, but as
she hurried to leave, he fell and became crippled. His name
was Mephibosheth.)

5Now Recab and Baanah, the sons of Rimmon the Beerothite, set out for the house of Ish-Bosheth, and they arrived there
in the heat of the day while he was taking his noonday rest.
6They went into the inner part of the house as if to get some
wheat, and they stabbed him in the stomach. Then Recab and
his brother Baanah slipped away.

7They had gone into the house while he was lying on the
bed in his bedroom. After they stabbed and killed him, they
cut off his head. Taking it with them, they traveled all night by
way of the Arabah. 8They brought the head of Ish-Bosheth to
David at Hebron and said to the king, "Here is the head of Ish-
Bosheth son of Saul, your enemy, who tried to take your life.
This day the LORD has avenged my lord the king against Saul
and his offspring."

9David answered Recab and his brother Baanah, the sons of
Rimmon the Beerothite, "As surely as the LORD lives, who has
delivered me out of all trouble, 10when a man told me, 'Saul is
dead,' and thought he was bringing good news, I seized him
and put him to death in Ziklag. That was the reward I gave him
for his news! 11How much more—when wicked men have
killed an innocent man in his own house and on his own
bed—should I not now demand his blood from your hand and
rid the earth of you!"

12So David gave an order to his men, and they killed them.
They cut off their hands and feet and hung the bodies by the
pool in Hebron. But they took the head of Ish-Bosheth and
buried it in Abner's tomb at Hebron.

David Becomes King Over Israel

5 All the tribes of Israel came to David at Hebron and said,
"We are your own flesh and blood. 2In the past, while Saul
was king over us, you were the one who led Israel on their military campaigns. And the LORD said to you, 'You will shepherd
my people Israel, and you will become their ruler.' "

3When all the elders of Israel had come to King David at Hebron, the king made a compact with them at Hebron before the
LORD, and they anointed David king over Israel.

4David was thirty years old when he became king, and he
reigned forty years. 5In Hebron he reigned over Judah seven
years and six months, and in Jerusalem he reigned over all Israel and Judah thirty-three years.

(5:1–3) We honor You, King Jesus—Who as to Your human nature are the Son of David, and Who through the Spirit of holiness and by Your resurrection from the dead were declared with power to be the Son of God. Thank You for taking on our own flesh and blood—for becoming one of us—so that You can be our merciful and faithful high priest as well as our victorious King. Thank You for being the Good Shepherd Who so freely and wondrously laid down Your life for Your sheep. (Jn 10:11; Ro 1:3–4; Heb 2:14–18)

All divine names and titles are applied to Him. He is called God, the mighty God, the great God, God over all; Jehovah; Lord; the Lord of lords and King of kings. All divine attributes are ascribed to Him. He is declared to be omnipresent, omniscient, almighty, and immutable, the same yesterday, today, and forever. He is set forth as the creator and upholder and ruler of the universe. All things were created by Him and for Him; and by Him all things consist. He is the object of worship to all intelligent creatures, even the highest; all the angels (i.e., all creatures between man and God) are commanded to prostrate themselves before Him.

Charles Hodge (1823–1886)

The King of love my Shepherd is,
Whose goodness faileth never;
I nothing lack if I am His
And He is mine forever.

And so thro' all the length of days
Thy goodness faileth never:
Good Shepherd, may I sing Thy
praise
Within Thy house forever.

"The King of Love My Shepherd Is"
Henry W. Baker (1821–1877)

David Conquers Jerusalem

6The king and his men marched to Jerusalem to attack the Jebusites, who lived there. The Jebusites said to David, "You will
not get in here; even the blind and the lame can ward you off."
They thought, "David cannot get in here." 7Nevertheless, David
captured the fortress of Zion, the City of David.
8On that day, David said, "Anyone who conquers the Jebusites will have to use the water shaft[a] to reach those 'lame and
blind' who are David's enemies.[b]" That is why they say, "The
'blind and lame' will not enter the palace."
9David then took up residence in the fortress and called it
the City of David. He built up the area around it, from the supporting terraces[c] inward. 10And he became more and more
powerful, because the LORD God Almighty was with him.
11Now Hiram king of Tyre sent messengers to David, along
with cedar logs and carpenters and stonemasons, and they
built a palace for David. 12And David knew that the LORD had
established him as king over Israel and had exalted his kingdom for the sake of his people Israel.
13After he left Hebron, David took more concubines and
wives in Jerusalem, and more sons and daughters were born to
him. 14These are the names of the children born to him there:
Shammua, Shobab, Nathan, Solomon, 15Ibhar, Elishua, Nepheg, Japhia, 16Elishama, Eliada and Eliphelet.

David Defeats the Philistines

17When the Philistines heard that David had been anointed
king over Israel, they went up in full force to search for him, but
David heard about it and went down to the stronghold. 18Now
the Philistines had come and spread out in the Valley of Rephaim; 19so David inquired of the LORD, "Shall I go and attack the
Philistines? Will you hand them over to me?"
The LORD answered him, "Go, for I will surely hand the Philistines over to you."
20So David went to Baal Perazim, and there he defeated them.
He said, "As waters break out, the LORD has broken out against
my enemies before me." So that place was called Baal Perazim.[d] 21The Philistines abandoned their idols there, and David
and his men carried them off.
22Once more the Philistines came up and spread out in the
Valley of Rephaim; 23so David inquired of the LORD, and he answered, "Do not go straight up, but circle around behind them
and attack them in front of the balsam trees. 24As soon as you
hear the sound of marching in the tops of the balsam trees,
move quickly, because that will mean the LORD has gone out in
front of you to strike the Philistine army." 25So David did as the
LORD commanded him, and he struck down the Philistines all
the way from Gibeon[e] to Gezer.

The Ark Brought to Jerusalem

6 David again brought together out of Israel chosen men,
thirty thousand in all. 2He and all his men set out from Baalah of Judah[f] to bring up from there the ark of God, which is

[a] 8 Or *use scaling books* [b] 8 Or *are hated by David* [c] 9 Or *the Millo* [d] 20 *Baal Perazim* means *the lord who breaks out.* [e] 25 Septuagint (see also 1 Chron. 14:16); Hebrew *Geba* [f] 2 That is, Kiriath Jearim; Hebrew *Baale Judah*, a variant of *Baalah of Judah*

(5:6–9) "Extol the LORD, O Jerusalem; praise your God, O Zion, for he strengthens the bars of your gates and blesses your people within you." The Holy City of Your presence is the fortress of my life. I will remain in that fortress until the time You have appointed for my residence in the new Jerusalem— where there will be no more death or mourning or crying or pain. Your works are glorious, and in Your presence there is joy forever! (Ps 147:12–13; Rev 21:2–4)

Since every Christian is a steward, everyone should better understand stewardship and its implications. For the majority of people, all areas of life except the financial are left untouched by its principles. Yet it is in the stewardship of the whole of life that abundant living comes–that life for which the heart hungers and which it does not know how to find. Christ came to bring us that richer, fuller life. His plan and purpose for us will be accomplished only when he can work through every department of our lives. Do we know how to develop and make available to Christ our abilities so that he may direct and use them for the good of all mankind?

Clarence W. Hatch

(5:10–12) Whatever power, position, prestige or possessions I have, I acknowledge that they are gifts from You. I offer these temporal things back to You for the sake of Your kingdom and Your people.

called by the Name,[a] the name of the LORD Almighty, who is
enthroned between the cherubim that are on the ark. 3They
set the ark of God on a new cart and brought it from the
house of Abinadab, which was on the hill. Uzzah and Ahio,
sons of Abinadab, were guiding the new cart 4with the ark of
God on it,[b] and Ahio was walking in front of it. 5David and the
whole house of Israel were celebrating with all their might
before the LORD, with songs[c] and with harps, lyres, tambourines, sistrums and cymbals.

6When they came to the threshing floor of Nacon, Uzzah
reached out and took hold of the ark of God, because the oxen
stumbled. 7The LORD's anger burned against Uzzah because of
his irreverent act; therefore God struck him down and he died
there beside the ark of God.

8Then David was angry because the LORD's wrath had broken
out against Uzzah, and to this day that place is called Perez
Uzzah.[d]

9David was afraid of the LORD that day and said, "How can
the ark of the LORD ever come to me?" 10He was not willing to
take the ark of the LORD to be with him in the City of David. Instead, he took it aside to the house of Obed-Edom the Gittite.
11The ark of the LORD remained in the house of Obed-Edom the
Gittite for three months, and the LORD blessed him and his entire household.

12Now King David was told, "The LORD has blessed the
household of Obed-Edom and everything he has, because of the
ark of God." So David went down and brought up the ark of God
from the house of Obed-Edom to the City of David with rejoicing. 13When those who were carrying the ark of the LORD had
taken six steps, he sacrificed a bull and a fattened calf. 14David,
wearing a linen ephod, danced before the LORD with all his
might, 15while he and the entire house of Israel brought up the
ark of the LORD with shouts and the sound of trumpets.

16As the ark of the LORD was entering the City of David, Michal daughter of Saul watched from a window. And when she
saw King David leaping and dancing before the LORD, she despised him in her heart.

17They brought the ark of the LORD and set it in its place inside the tent that David had pitched for it, and David sacrificed
burnt offerings and fellowship offerings[e] before the LORD.
18After he had finished sacrificing the burnt offerings and fellowship offerings, he blessed the people in the name of the
LORD Almighty. 19Then he gave a loaf of bread, a cake of dates
and a cake of raisins to each person in the whole crowd of Israelites, both men and women. And all the people went to their
homes.

20When David returned home to bless his household, Michal
daughter of Saul came out to meet him and said, "How the king
of Israel has distinguished himself today, disrobing in the sight
of the slave girls of his servants as any vulgar fellow would!"

21David said to Michal, "It was before the LORD, who chose
me rather than your father or anyone from his house when he

[a] 2 Hebrew; Septuagint and Vulgate do not have *the Name.* [b] 3,4 Dead Sea Scrolls and some Septuagint manuscripts; Masoretic Text *cart* [4]*and they brought it with the ark of God from the house of Abinadab, which was on the hill* [c] 5 See Dead Sea Scrolls, Septuagint and 1 Chronicles 13:8; Masoretic Text *celebrating before the LORD with all kinds of instruments made of pine.* [d] 8 *Perez Uzzah* means *outbreak against Uzzah.*
[e] 17 Traditionally *peace offerings*; also in verse 18

(6:1–8) David and Uzzah should have known better. They should have known that they were not transporting the ark of the Lord according to Your instructions. I should know better too. I should know better than to treat You casually. I should know better than to presume upon Your grace. Please teach me to worship You in both the fear of the Lord and in the joy of my salvation.

Lord, I am grateful for who you are and what you have done for me. I need your wisdom every day. Bring together the pieces of my life with a new appreciation for your Word and a fresh commitment to obedience. I know that fearing you does not mean I am afraid of you but that I respect and revere your majestic name. You have promised that you will give me the discernment and insight I need as I grow in my reverence for you. I am excited about building my life on the wisdom of your Word.
Charles Stanley (1932-)

(6:9–11) O Lord, take up residence in my house. As the ark contained the tablets of the law, so let my home be a place of the Word. May my family experience Your blessing as Your presence dwells among us. (Ps 119:11)

appointed me ruler over the LORD's people Israel—I will celebrate before the LORD. 22I will become even more undignified
than this, and I will be humiliated in my own eyes. But by these
slave girls you spoke of, I will be held in honor."
23And Michal daughter of Saul had no children to the day of
her death.

God's Promise to David

7 After the king was settled in his palace and the LORD had given
him rest from all his enemies around him, 2he said to Nathan
the prophet, "Here I am, living in a palace of cedar, while the ark
of God remains in a tent."
3Nathan replied to the king, "Whatever you have in mind, go
ahead and do it, for the LORD is with you."
4That night the word of the LORD came to Nathan, saying:

5"Go and tell my servant David, 'This is what the LORD says:
Are you the one to build me a house to dwell in? 6I have not
dwelt in a house from the day I brought the Israelites up out
of Egypt to this day. I have been moving from place to place
with a tent as my dwelling. 7Wherever I have moved with all
the Israelites, did I ever say to any of their rulers whom I
commanded to shepherd my people Israel, "Why have you
not built me a house of cedar?"'
8"Now then, tell my servant David, 'This is what the LORD
Almighty says: I took you from the pasture and from following the flock to be ruler over my people Israel. 9I have been
with you wherever you have gone, and I have cut off all your
enemies from before you. Now I will make your name great,
like the names of the greatest men of the earth. 10And I will
provide a place for my people Israel and will plant them so
that they can have a home of their own and no longer be disturbed. Wicked people will not oppress them anymore, as
they did at the beginning 11and have done ever since the time
I appointed leaders[a] over my people Israel. I will also give
you rest from all your enemies.
" 'The LORD declares to you that the LORD himself will establish a house for you: 12When your days are over and you
rest with your fathers, I will raise up your offspring to succeed
you, who will come from your own body, and I will establish
his kingdom. 13He is the one who will build a house for my
Name, and I will establish the throne of his kingdom forever.
14I will be his father, and he will be my son. When he does
wrong, I will punish him with the rod of men, with floggings
inflicted by men. 15But my love will never be taken away from
him, as I took it away from Saul, whom I removed from before you. 16Your house and your kingdom will endure forever before me[b]; your throne will be established forever.' "

17Nathan reported to David all the words of this entire revelation.

David's Prayer

18Then King David went in and sat before the LORD, and he said:

"Who am I, O Sovereign LORD, and what is my family, that

[a] *11* Traditionally *judges* [b] *16* Some Hebrew manuscripts and Septuagint; most Hebrew manuscripts *you*

(7:11–16) O the glory of Your covenant with David! O the glory of the kingdom You planned through David's wonderful Son Jesus, our Messiah. For it is He who fulfills completely Your promises made to David. For You have given Him "the throne of his father David, and he will reign over the house of Jacob forever; his kingdom will never end." He is indeed the Messiah, the Son of the Most High, Who fulfills the hope of David; and He is building the spiritual house of the Lord. (Isa 9:6–7; Lk 1:32–33; Ro 1:3–4; 1Pe 2:5)

Hail to the Lord's anointed,
Great David's greater Son!
Hail, in the time appointed,
His reign on earth begun!
He comes to break oppression,
To set the captive free,
To take away transgression
And rule in equity.

Kings shall fall down before Him,
And gold and incense bring;
All nations shall adore Him,
His praise all people sing.
To Him shall prayer unceasing
And daily vows ascend;
His kingdom still increasing,
A kingdom without end.

"Hail to the Lord's Anointed"
James Montgomery (1771-1854)

(7:18–22) Who am I, O Sovereign Lord, that You have brought me this far? You know me completely, just like You knew David. "You have searched me and you know me. You know when I sit and when I rise . . . You are familiar with all my ways." Yet for the sake of Your Word and because of Your enduring love You have blessed me with every spiritual blessing in Christ. You have lavished upon me the riches of Your grace. How great You are, O Sovereign Lord! There is none like You. (Ps 139:1–3; Eph 1:3,7–8)

You are deserving
Of all the praises, Lord.
And I am yearning
To be in Your presence once more.
Deep inside my heart is burning.
I want to give You more;
For You're the only one that I adore.

How great You are.
How great You are.
You are the mighty King
And You've come to reign in me.
How great You are.
How great You are.
I give You all the praises of my
heart.

"How Great You Are"
Shannon Wexelberg (©1993)

you have brought me this far? [19]And as if this were not
enough in your sight, O Sovereign LORD, you have also spoken about the future of the house of your servant. Is this
your usual way of dealing with man, O Sovereign LORD?
[20]"What more can David say to you? For you know your
servant, O Sovereign LORD. [21]For the sake of your word and
according to your will, you have done this great thing and
made it known to your servant.
[22]"How great you are, O Sovereign LORD! There is no one
like you, and there is no God but you, as we have heard with
our own ears. [23]And who is like your people Israel—the
one nation on earth that God went out to redeem as a people for himself, and to make a name for himself, and to perform great and awesome wonders by driving out nations and
their gods from before your people, whom you redeemed
from Egypt?[a] [24]You have established your people Israel as
your very own forever, and you, O LORD, have become their
God.
[25]"And now, LORD God, keep forever the promise you
have made concerning your servant and his house. Do as
you promised, [26]so that your name will be great forever.
Then men will say, 'The LORD Almighty is God over Israel!'
And the house of your servant David will be established before you.
[27]"O LORD Almighty, God of Israel, you have revealed this
to your servant, saying, 'I will build a house for you.' So your
servant has found courage to offer you this prayer. [28]O Sovereign LORD, you are God! Your words are trustworthy, and
you have promised these good things to your servant. [29]Now
be pleased to bless the house of your servant, that it may
continue forever in your sight; for you, O Sovereign LORD,
have spoken, and with your blessing the house of your servant will be blessed forever."

David's Victories

8 In the course of time, David defeated the Philistines and
subdued them, and he took Metheg Ammah from the control of the Philistines.
[2]David also defeated the Moabites. He made them lie down
on the ground and measured them off with a length of cord.
Every two lengths of them were put to death, and the third length
was allowed to live. So the Moabites became subject to David
and brought tribute.
[3]Moreover, David fought Hadadezer son of Rehob, king of
Zobah, when he went to restore his control along the Euphrates
River. [4]David captured a thousand of his chariots, seven thousand charioteers[b] and twenty thousand foot soldiers. He hamstrung all but a hundred of the chariot horses.
[5]When the Arameans of Damascus came to help Hadadezer
king of Zobah, David struck down twenty-two thousand of them.
[6]He put garrisons in the Aramean kingdom of Damascus, and

[a] 23 See Septuagint and 1 Chron. 17:21; Hebrew *wonders for your land and before your people, whom you redeemed from Egypt, from the nations and their gods.*
[b] 4 Septuagint (see also Dead Sea Scrolls and 1 Chron. 18:4); Masoretic Text *captured seventeen hundred of his charioteers*

the Arameans became subject to him and brought tribute. The
LORD gave David victory wherever he went.
7David took the gold shields that belonged to the officers of
Hadadezer and brought them to Jerusalem. 8From Tebah[a] and Be-
rothai, towns that belonged to Hadadezer, King David took a great
quantity of bronze.
9When Tou[b] king of Hamath heard that David had defeated the
entire army of Hadadezer, 10he sent his son Joram[c] to King David
to greet him and congratulate him on his victory in battle over
Hadadezer, who had been at war with Tou. Joram brought with
him articles of silver and gold and bronze.
11King David dedicated these articles to the LORD, as he had
done with the silver and gold from all the nations he had subdued:
12Edom[d] and Moab, the Ammonites and the Philistines, and Amalek. He also dedicated the plunder taken from Hadadezer son of
Rehob, king of Zobah.
13And David became famous after he returned from striking
down eighteen thousand Edomites[e] in the Valley of Salt.
14He put garrisons throughout Edom, and all the Edomites became subject to David. The LORD gave David victory wherever he
went.

David's Officials

15David reigned over all Israel, doing what was just and right
for all his people. 16Joab son of Zeruiah was over the army; Jehoshaphat son of Ahilud was recorder; 17Zadok son of Ahitub and
Ahimelech son of Abiathar were priests; Seraiah was secretary;
18Benaiah son of Jehoiada was over the Kerethites and Pelethites;
and David's sons were royal advisers.[f]

David and Mephibosheth

9 David asked, "Is there anyone still left of the house of Saul to
whom I can show kindness for Jonathan's sake?"
2Now there was a servant of Saul's household named Ziba. They
called him to appear before David, and the king said to him, "Are
you Ziba?"
"Your servant," he replied.
3The king asked, "Is there no one still left of the house of Saul
to whom I can show God's kindness?"
Ziba answered the king, "There is still a son of Jonathan; he is
crippled in both feet."
4"Where is he?" the king asked.
Ziba answered, "He is at the house of Makir son of Ammiel in
Lo Debar."
5So King David had him brought from Lo Debar, from the house
of Makir son of Ammiel.
6When Mephibosheth son of Jonathan, the son of Saul, came to
David, he bowed down to pay him honor.
David said, "Mephibosheth!"
"Your servant," he replied.
7"Don't be afraid," David said to him, "for I will surely show
you kindness for the sake of your father Jonathan. I will restore to

[a] 8 See some Septuagint manuscripts (see also 1 Chron. 18:8); Hebrew *Betah.*
[b] 9 Hebrew *Toi,* a variant of *Tou;* also in verse 10 [c] 10 A variant of *Hadoram*
[d] 12 Some Hebrew manuscripts, Septuagint and Syriac (see also 1 Chron. 18:11); most Hebrew manuscripts *Aram* [e] 13 A few Hebrew manuscripts, Septuagint and Syriac (see also 1 Chron. 18:12); most Hebrew manuscripts *Aram* (that is, Arameans) [f] 18 Or *were priests*

If I were to ask, "Where did you fall in love with Him?," without exception every child of God would say, "I fell in love with the Lord Jesus at the place called Calvary where He met my foe, faced my battles, and won my victory."

Harold Wildish

(8:6,14) "The LORD gave David victory wherever he went." Today we continue to rely on You to fight our battles. We look forward to that final conflict, when Jesus Christ hands over the kingdom to You after He has destroyed all dominion, authority and power—the last enemy to be destroyed being death. "Some trust in chariots and some in horses, but we trust in the name of the LORD our God." (Ps 20:7; 1Co 15:24–26)

you all the land that belonged to your grandfather Saul, and you
will always eat at my table."
8Mephibosheth bowed down and said, "What is your servant,
that you should notice a dead dog like me?"
9Then the king summoned Ziba, Saul's servant, and said to him,
"I have given your master's grandson everything that belonged to
Saul and his family. 10You and your sons and your servants are to
farm the land for him and bring in the crops, so that your master's
grandson may be provided for. And Mephibosheth, grandson of
your master, will always eat at my table." (Now Ziba had fifteen
sons and twenty servants.)
11Then Ziba said to the king, "Your servant will do whatever my
lord the king commands his servant to do." So Mephibosheth ate
at David's[a] table like one of the king's sons.
12Mephibosheth had a young son named Mica, and all the
members of Ziba's household were servants of Mephibosheth.
13And Mephibosheth lived in Jerusalem, because he always ate at
the king's table, and he was crippled in both feet.

David Defeats the Ammonites

10 In the course of time, the king of the Ammonites died, and
his son Hanun succeeded him as king. 2David thought, "I
will show kindness to Hanun son of Nahash, just as his father
showed kindness to me." So David sent a delegation to express his
sympathy to Hanun concerning his father.
When David's men came to the land of the Ammonites, 3the Ammonite nobles said to Hanun their lord, "Do you think David is
honoring your father by sending men to you to express sympathy?
Hasn't David sent them to you to explore the city and spy it out and
overthrow it?" 4So Hanun seized David's men, shaved off half of
each man's beard, cut off their garments in the middle at the buttocks, and sent them away.
5When David was told about this, he sent messengers to meet
the men, for they were greatly humiliated. The king said, "Stay at
Jericho till your beards have grown, and then come back."
6When the Ammonites realized that they had become a stench
in David's nostrils, they hired twenty thousand Aramean foot soldiers from Beth Rehob and Zobah, as well as the king of Maacah
with a thousand men, and also twelve thousand men from Tob.
7On hearing this, David sent Joab out with the entire army of
fighting men. 8The Ammonites came out and drew up in battle formation at the entrance to their city gate, while the Arameans of
Zobah and Rehob and the men of Tob and Maacah were by themselves in the open country.
9Joab saw that there were battle lines in front of him and behind him; so he selected some of the best troops in Israel and deployed them against the Arameans. 10He put the rest of the men
under the command of Abishai his brother and deployed them
against the Ammonites. 11Joab said, "If the Arameans are too
strong for me, then you are to come to my rescue; but if the Ammonites are too strong for you, then I will come to rescue you.
12Be strong and let us fight bravely for our people and the cities
of our God. The LORD will do what is good in his sight."
13Then Joab and the troops with him advanced to fight the Arameans, and they fled before him. 14When the Ammonites saw that

[a] 11 Septuagint; Hebrew *my*

He was desirous to show kindness to the house of Saul, not only because he trusted in God and feared not what they could do unto him, but because he was of a charitable disposition, and forgave what they had done to him. We must not be backward to do any office of love and goodwill to those that have done us many an injury. This is the way to overcome evil, and to find mercy for ourselves and ours, when we or they need it.

Matthew Henry (1662-1714)

(9:7–11) Lord, I see in David's kindness a picture of Your kindness to me. For I, like Mephibosheth, was broken by a fall, living in fear and shame. But You sought me out, not for judgment but for blessing; and You brought me into communion with You at Your own table, "like one of the kings sons." You restored my heavenly inheritance and gave me dignity and joy. In gratitude, and by Your grace, I will seek to show this same kind of love and forgiveness to my enemies and to repay evil with blessing. (Mt 5:44; Jn 1:12; 1Pe 3:9)

You're all that I ever wanted,
You're all that I ever need;
And though I wasn't looking
You were after me.
For Your love for me is eternal,
And this I know is true,
I could never repay the debt
Of love I owe to You.

For who is like the Lord, my God?
Compassionate and full of mercy.
Who compares to Your great love?
There's none in all the earth.
I will sing of Your love and grace
That covers all my guilt and shame.
In all the earth
Who is like the Lord?

"Who Is Like the Lord?"
Holland Davis (©1998)

the Arameans were fleeing, they fled before Abishai and went inside the city. So Joab returned from fighting the Ammonites and
came to Jerusalem.
15After the Arameans saw that they had been routed by Israel,
they regrouped. 16Hadadezer had Arameans brought from beyond the River[a]; they went to Helam, with Shobach the commander of Hadadezer's army leading them.
17When David was told of this, he gathered all Israel, crossed
the Jordan and went to Helam. The Arameans formed their battle lines to meet David and fought against him. 18But they fled
before Israel, and David killed seven hundred of their charioteers and forty thousand of their foot soldiers.[b] He also struck
down Shobach the commander of their army, and he died there.
19When all the kings who were vassals of Hadadezer saw that
they had been defeated by Israel, they made peace with the Israelites and became subject to them.
So the Arameans were afraid to help the Ammonites anymore.

David and Bathsheba

11 In the spring, at the time when kings go off to war, David
sent Joab out with the king's men and the whole Israelite
army. They destroyed the Ammonites and besieged Rabbah. But
David remained in Jerusalem.
2One evening David got up from his bed and walked around
on the roof of the palace. From the roof he saw a woman
bathing. The woman was very beautiful, 3and David sent someone to find out about her. The man said, "Isn't this Bathsheba,
the daughter of Eliam and the wife of Uriah the Hittite?" 4Then
David sent messengers to get her. She came to him, and he slept
with her. (She had purified herself from her uncleanness.)
Then[c] she went back home. 5The woman conceived and sent
word to David, saying, "I am pregnant."
6So David sent this word to Joab: "Send me Uriah the Hittite."
And Joab sent him to David. 7When Uriah came to him, David
asked him how Joab was, how the soldiers were and how the
war was going. 8Then David said to Uriah, "Go down to your
house and wash your feet." So Uriah left the palace, and a gift
from the king was sent after him. 9But Uriah slept at the entrance
to the palace with all his master's servants and did not go down
to his house.
10When David was told, "Uriah did not go home," he asked
him, "Haven't you just come from a distance? Why didn't you go
home?"
11Uriah said to David, "The ark and Israel and Judah are staying in tents, and my master Joab and my lord's men are camped
in the open fields. How could I go to my house to eat and drink
and lie with my wife? As surely as you live, I will not do such a
thing!"
12Then David said to him, "Stay here one more day, and tomorrow I will send you back." So Uriah remained in Jerusalem
that day and the next. 13At David's invitation, he ate and drank
with him, and David made him drunk. But in the evening Uriah
went out to sleep on his mat among his master's servants; he did
not go home.
14In the morning David wrote a letter to Joab and sent it with

[a] *16* That is, the Euphrates [b] *18* Some Septuagint manuscripts (see also 1 Chron. 19:18); Hebrew *horsemen* [c] *4* Or *with her. When she purified herself from her uncleanness,*

Remember, no one is so holy that he or she does not have to deal with temptations.

We will do better in dealing with temptations if we keep an eye on them in the very beginning. Temptations are more easily overcome if they are never allowed to enter our minds. Meet them at the door as soon as they knock, and do not let them in.

Thomas à Kempis (c.1380-1471)

(11:1–5) O God, I so desperately need Your help to resist sexual temptation. Opportunities for voyeurism abound everywhere: on television, at the newsstand, on the Internet. Living in this "adulterous and sinful generation," may I never assume I am immune from the temptation of an illicit affair. I choose today to flee from sexual immorality and to honor You with my body. Please keep me from deliberate or naïve behavior that might cause someone else to stumble. Lead me not into temptation, Lord, but deliver me from the evil one. (Mt 6:13; 1Co 6:18–20)

Pure and holy I would be,
Worthy of Your love for me.
Teach me while Your light is clear;
Change me while my heart is near.

Holy, holy, holy Lord.

"Pure and Holy"
Mike Hudson and Bob Farnsworth
(©1985)

Uriah. 15In it he wrote, "Put Uriah in the front line where the
fighting is fiercest. Then withdraw from him so he will be struck
down and die."

16So while Joab had the city under siege, he put Uriah at a
place where he knew the strongest defenders were. 17When the
men of the city came out and fought against Joab, some of the
men in David's army fell; moreover, Uriah the Hittite died.

18Joab sent David a full account of the battle. 19He instructed the messenger: "When you have finished giving the king this
account of the battle, 20the king's anger may flare up, and he
may ask you, 'Why did you get so close to the city to fight?
Didn't you know they would shoot arrows from the wall? 21Who
killed Abimelech son of Jerub-Besheth[a]? Didn't a woman throw
an upper millstone on him from the wall, so that he died in
Thebez? Why did you get so close to the wall?' If he asks you
this, then say to him, 'Also, your servant Uriah the Hittite is
dead.'"

22The messenger set out, and when he arrived he told David
everything Joab had sent him to say. 23The messenger said to
David, "The men overpowered us and came out against us in the
open, but we drove them back to the entrance to the city gate.
24Then the archers shot arrows at your servants from the wall,
and some of the king's men died. Moreover, your servant Uriah
the Hittite is dead."

25David told the messenger, "Say this to Joab: 'Don't let this
upset you; the sword devours one as well as another. Press the
attack against the city and destroy it.' Say this to encourage
Joab."

26When Uriah's wife heard that her husband was dead, she
mourned for him. 27After the time of mourning was over, David
had her brought to his house, and she became his wife and
bore him a son. But the thing David had done displeased the
LORD.

Nathan Rebukes David

12 The LORD sent Nathan to David. When he came to him, he
said, "There were two men in a certain town, one rich and
the other poor. 2The rich man had a very large number of sheep
and cattle, 3but the poor man had nothing except one little ewe
lamb he had bought. He raised it, and it grew up with him and
his children. It shared his food, drank from his cup and even
slept in his arms. It was like a daughter to him.

4"Now a traveler came to the rich man, but the rich man refrained from taking one of his own sheep or cattle to prepare a
meal for the traveler who had come to him. Instead, he took the
ewe lamb that belonged to the poor man and prepared it for the
one who had come to him."

5David burned with anger against the man and said to Nathan,
"As surely as the LORD lives, the man who did this deserves to
die! 6He must pay for that lamb four times over, because he did
such a thing and had no pity."

7Then Nathan said to David, "You are the man! This is what
the LORD, the God of Israel, says: 'I anointed you king over Israel, and I delivered you from the hand of Saul. 8I gave your master's house to you, and your master's wives into your arms. I gave

[a] *21* Also known as *Jerub-Baal* (that is, Gideon)

(11:26–27) "But the thing David had done displeased the Lord." It is the desire of my heart, Heavenly Father, not to displease You. And yet I so easily get entangled in the web of sin. I know all too well what Paul meant when he wrote: "I do not understand what I do. For what I want to do I do not do, but what I hate I do." I cry out to You for mercy and strength. Please "forgive my hidden faults. Keep Your servant also from willful sins; may they not rule over me." (Ps 19:12–13; Ro 7:15; Heb 12:1)

We must correct and chasten one another when it is needed. We must not let our love for brothers or sisters cool when they sin; but neither must we speak as though all is well when it is not. True love shows itself not only by smiling at one another and speaking pleasantly. Real love desires the eternal welfare of our brothers, and it may become necessary at times to speak stern, unpleasant truths. I am not grateful to the brother who would see me go astray without trying to rescue me. "Brethren, if any of you do err from the truth, and one convert him; let him know, that he which converteth the sinner from the error of his way shall save a soul from death, and shall hide a multitude of sins" (James 5:19-20).

J. N. Kildahl (1857-1920)

(12:1–7) "You are the man!" How those words must have pierced David's soul! Your Word is sharper than any double-edged sword, judging the thoughts and attitudes of the heart. In what way do I need my soul pierced? I invite Your Word, Your Spirit, Your human messengers, to search me and confront me. And I pray with David: "Search me, O God, and know my heart; test me and know my anxious thoughts. See if there is any offensive way in me, and lead me in the way everlasting." (Ps 139:23–24; Heb 4:12)

you the house of Israel and Judah. And if all this had been too little, I would have given you even more. **9**Why did you despise the
word of the LORD by doing what is evil in his eyes? You struck
down Uriah the Hittite with the sword and took his wife to be your
own. You killed him with the sword of the Ammonites. **10**Now,
therefore, the sword will never depart from your house, because
you despised me and took the wife of Uriah the Hittite to be your
own.'

11"This is what the LORD says: 'Out of your own household I am
going to bring calamity upon you. Before your very eyes I will take
your wives and give them to one who is close to you, and he will
lie with your wives in broad daylight. **12**You did it in secret, but I
will do this thing in broad daylight before all Israel.' "

13Then David said to Nathan, "I have sinned against the LORD."

Nathan replied, "The LORD has taken away your sin. You are not
going to die. **14**But because by doing this you have made the enemies of the LORD show utter contempt,[a] the son born to you will
die."

15After Nathan had gone home, the LORD struck the child that
Uriah's wife had borne to David, and he became ill. **16**David pleaded with God for the child. He fasted and went into his house and
spent the nights lying on the ground. **17**The elders of his household stood beside him to get him up from the ground, but he refused, and he would not eat any food with them.

18On the seventh day the child died. David's servants were
afraid to tell him that the child was dead, for they thought, "While
the child was still living, we spoke to David but he would not listen to us. How can we tell him the child is dead? He may do something desperate."

19David noticed that his servants were whispering among themselves and he realized the child was dead. "Is the child dead?" he
asked.

"Yes," they replied, "he is dead."

20Then David got up from the ground. After he had washed, put
on lotions and changed his clothes, he went into the house of the
LORD and worshiped. Then he went to his own house, and at his
request they served him food, and he ate.

21His servants asked him, "Why are you acting this way? While
the child was alive, you fasted and wept, but now that the child is
dead, you get up and eat!"

22He answered, "While the child was still alive, I fasted and
wept. I thought, 'Who knows? The LORD may be gracious to me
and let the child live.' **23**But now that he is dead, why should I fast?
Can I bring him back again? I will go to him, but he will not return
to me."

24Then David comforted his wife Bathsheba, and he went to her
and lay with her. She gave birth to a son, and they named him Solomon. The LORD loved him; **25**and because the LORD loved him, he
sent word through Nathan the prophet to name him Jedidiah.[b]

26Meanwhile Joab fought against Rabbah of the Ammonites and
captured the royal citadel. **27**Joab then sent messengers to David,
saying, "I have fought against Rabbah and taken its water supply.
28Now muster the rest of the troops and besiege the city and capture it. Otherwise I will take the city, and it will be named
after me."

[a] *14* Masoretic Text; an ancient Hebrew scribal tradition *this you have shown utter contempt for the LORD* [b] *25 Jedidiah* means *loved by the LORD.*

(12:13a) "I have sinned against the Lord." Like David, I accept responsibility for my sin. Rather than a worldly sorrow that laments getting caught, may I have a godly sorrow that brings repentance. Please hear my prayer, O God; and when You hear, forgive: "Against you, you only, have I sinned and done what is evil in your sight, so that you are proved right when you speak and justified when you judge. Create in me a pure heart, O God, and renew a steadfast spirit within me. Do not cast me from your presence or take your Holy Spirit from me. Restore to me the joy of your salvation and grant me a willing spirit, to sustain me." (1Ki8:30; Ps 51:4,10–12; 2Co 7:10)

(12:13b) "The LORD has taken away your sin. You are not going to die." Though David's acts of adultery and murder deserved the death penalty, in Your mercy You forgave him, Lord. David himself would testify, "Blessed is he whose transgressions are forgiven, whose sins are covered." I too give You thanks today for Your blessed promise that, if we confess our sins, You are "faithful and just and will forgive us our sins and purify us from all unrighteousness." (Ps 32:1; 1Jn 1:9)

(12:14–20) I do not always understand Your judgments, God. Why did this baby have to die? Was it a necessary message to "the enemies of the Lord"? I acknowledge that Your ways are higher than my ways and Your thoughts than my thoughts. Help me to have a heart like David—to trust You and to worship You even in the midst of grief. (Isa 55:9; Gal 6:7; Heb 12:5–7)

[29]So David mustered the entire army and went to Rabbah, and attacked and captured it. [30]He took the crown from the head of their king[a]—its weight was a talent[b] of gold, and it was set with precious stones—and it was placed on David's head. He took a great quantity of plunder from the city [31]and brought out the people who were there, consigning them to labor with saws and with iron picks and axes, and he made them work at brickmaking.[c] He did this to all the Ammonite towns. Then David and his entire army returned to Jerusalem.

Amnon and Tamar

13 In the course of time, Amnon son of David fell in love with Tamar, the beautiful sister of Absalom son of David.

[2]Amnon became frustrated to the point of illness on account of his sister Tamar, for she was a virgin, and it seemed impossible for him to do anything to her.

[3]Now Amnon had a friend named Jonadab son of Shimeah, David's brother. Jonadab was a very shrewd man. [4]He asked Amnon, "Why do you, the king's son, look so haggard morning after morning? Won't you tell me?"

Amnon said to him, "I'm in love with Tamar, my brother Absalom's sister."

[5]"Go to bed and pretend to be ill," Jonadab said. "When your father comes to see you, say to him, 'I would like my sister Tamar to come and give me something to eat. Let her prepare the food in my sight so I may watch her and then eat it from her hand.' "

[6]So Amnon lay down and pretended to be ill. When the king came to see him, Amnon said to him, "I would like my sister Tamar to come and make some special bread in my sight, so I may eat from her hand."

[7]David sent word to Tamar at the palace: "Go to the house of your brother Amnon and prepare some food for him." [8]So Tamar went to the house of her brother Amnon, who was lying down. She took some dough, kneaded it, made the bread in his sight and baked it. [9]Then she took the pan and served him the bread, but he refused to eat.

"Send everyone out of here," Amnon said. So everyone left him. [10]Then Amnon said to Tamar, "Bring the food here into my bedroom so I may eat from your hand." And Tamar took the bread she had prepared and brought it to her brother Amnon in his bedroom. [11]But when she took it to him to eat, he grabbed her and said, "Come to bed with me, my sister."

[12]"Don't, my brother!" she said to him. "Don't force me. Such a thing should not be done in Israel! Don't do this wicked thing. [13]What about me? Where could I get rid of my disgrace? And what about you? You would be like one of the wicked fools in Israel. Please speak to the king; he will not keep me from being married to you." [14]But he refused to listen to her, and since he was stronger than she, he raped her.

[15]Then Amnon hated her with intense hatred. In fact, he hated her more than he had loved her. Amnon said to her, "Get up and get out!"

[16]"No!" she said to him. "Sending me away would be a greater wrong than what you have already done to me."

But he refused to listen to her. [17]He called his personal servant

[a] *30* Or *of Milcom* (that is, Molech) [b] *30* That is, about 75 pounds (about 34 kilograms)
[c] *31* The meaning of the Hebrew for this clause is uncertain.

(13:1–15) Lord, You warned David through Nathan that trouble would come upon him from within his own house. And here was the beginning of David's trouble. Sexual immorality, violence and murder had been David's sins; now those sins took root in his children as Amnon raped Tamar and Absalom later murdered Amnon in revenge. O God, deliver us from the curse of sin. Don't let our children follow the pathway of our mistakes. In Your mercy, and through the blood of Christ, break the yoke of bondage before the yoke entraps our children. (2Sa 12:10–11; 13:23–29; La 1:14; Gal 5:1)

and said, "Get this woman out of here and bolt the door after her."
18So his servant put her out and bolted the door after her. She was
wearing a richly ornamented[a] robe, for this was the kind of garment the virgin daughters of the king wore. 19Tamar put ashes on
her head and tore the ornamented[b] robe she was wearing. She
put her hand on her head and went away, weeping aloud as she
went.
20Her brother Absalom said to her, "Has that Amnon, your
brother, been with you? Be quiet now, my sister; he is your brother. Don't take this thing to heart." And Tamar lived in her brother
Absalom's house, a desolate woman.
21When King David heard all this, he was furious. 22Absalom
never said a word to Amnon, either good or bad; he hated Amnon
because he had disgraced his sister Tamar.

Absalom Kills Amnon

23Two years later, when Absalom's sheepshearers were at Baal
Hazor near the border of Ephraim, he invited all the king's sons to
come there. 24Absalom went to the king and said, "Your servant
has had shearers come. Will the king and his officials please
join me?"
25"No, my son," the king replied. "All of us should not go; we
would only be a burden to you." Although Absalom urged him, he
still refused to go, but gave him his blessing.
26Then Absalom said, "If not, please let my brother Amnon
come with us."
The king asked him, "Why should he go with you?" 27But Absalom urged him, so he sent with him Amnon and the rest of the
king's sons.
28Absalom ordered his men, "Listen! When Amnon is in high
spirits from drinking wine and I say to you, 'Strike Amnon down,'
then kill him. Don't be afraid. Have not I given you this order? Be
strong and brave." 29So Absalom's men did to Amnon what Absalom had ordered. Then all the king's sons got up, mounted their
mules and fled.
30While they were on their way, the report came to David: "Absalom has struck down all the king's sons; not one of them is left."
31The king stood up, tore his clothes and lay down on the ground;
and all his servants stood by with their clothes torn.
32But Jonadab son of Shimeah, David's brother, said, "My lord
should not think that they killed all the princes; only Amnon is
dead. This has been Absalom's expressed intention ever since the
day Amnon raped his sister Tamar. 33My lord the king should not
be concerned about the report that all the king's sons are dead.
Only Amnon is dead."
34Meanwhile, Absalom had fled.
Now the man standing watch looked up and saw many people
on the road west of him, coming down the side of the hill. The
watchman went and told the king, "I see men in the direction of
Horonaim, on the side of the hill."[c]
35Jonadab said to the king, "See, the king's sons are here; it
has happened just as your servant said."
36As he finished speaking, the king's sons came in, wailing
loudly. The king, too, and all his servants wept very bitterly.

[a] *18* The meaning of the Hebrew for this phrase is uncertain. [b] *19* The meaning of the Hebrew for this word is uncertain. [c] *34* Septuagint; Hebrew does not have this sentence.

(13:20) My heart aches, as I know Yours does, Father, for those who have been sexually abused. I pray that those who have been violated will not feel like "spoiled goods," desolate for the rest of their lives. And do not let those of us in the Christian community give victims of sexual abuse the kind of message Absalom spoke: "Be quiet now . . . Don't take this thing to heart." Rather, let us help them express their pain. Make us conduits of Your healing instead of perpetuators of their shame.

There is a place of quiet rest,
Near to the heart of God.
A place where sin cannot molest,
Near to the heart of God.

O Jesus, blest Redeemer,
Sent from the heart of God,
Hold us, who wait before Thee,
Near to the heart of God.

"Near to the Heart of God"
Cleland Boyd McAfee (1901)

As the Lord's followers, we're to assemble together, encourage others toward good works, rejoice and weep as a family, and bear one another's burdens. In effect, we are to be God's messengers to one another, depositing His hope and truth into hearts.

Judith Couchman (1953-)

(13:37–14:14) Lord, the love You give parents for their children is a wondrous thing. How much greater is Your marvelous love for us! As shown to us in Jesus' parable of the lost son, You long for each of us as David longed for his wayward son. Thank You for devising "ways so that a banished person may not remain estranged" from You. Thank You for always seeking after us, even when we are not seeking after You. Thank You, heavenly Father, for Your love that will never let us go. (Lk 15:20; Jn 10:27–29)

Softly and tenderly, Jesus is calling,
Calling for you and for me;
See, on the portals,
He's waiting and watching,
Watching for you and for me.

Come home, come home,
You who are weary come home;
Earnestly, tenderly, Jesus is calling,
Calling, "O sinner, come home!"

O for the wonderful love He has
promised,
Promised for you and for me!
Though we have sinned,
He has mercy and pardon,
Pardon for you and for me.

"Softly and Tenderly"
Will L. Thompson (1847-1909)

Let us, then, as we have such examples before us, be of good cheer and keep from despair. For God is not so well pleased with being our Master as he is with being our Father; he is not so pleased with our being his slaves as he is with our being his children. This is what God truly wants. This is why he did all that he has done, not sparing his only begotten Son, that we, as adopted sons and daughters, might love him as a Father.

Saint John Chrysostom (345-407)

37 Absalom fled and went to Talmai son of Ammihud, the king of
Geshur. But King David mourned for his son every day.
38 After Absalom fled and went to Geshur, he stayed there three
years. 39 And the spirit of the king[a] longed to go to Absalom, for he
was consoled concerning Amnon's death.

Absalom Returns to Jerusalem

14 Joab son of Zeruiah knew that the king's heart longed for
Absalom. 2 So Joab sent someone to Tekoa and had a wise
woman brought from there. He said to her, "Pretend you are in
mourning. Dress in mourning clothes, and don't use any cosmet-
ic lotions. Act like a woman who has spent many days grieving for
the dead. 3 Then go to the king and speak these words to him."
And Joab put the words in her mouth.
4 When the woman from Tekoa went[b] to the king, she fell with
her face to the ground to pay him honor, and she said, "Help me,
O king!"
5 The king asked her, "What is troubling you?"
She said, "I am indeed a widow; my husband is dead. 6 I your
servant had two sons. They got into a fight with each other in the
field, and no one was there to separate them. One struck the other
and killed him. 7 Now the whole clan has risen up against your
servant; they say, 'Hand over the one who struck his brother down,
so that we may put him to death for the life of his brother whom
he killed; then we will get rid of the heir as well.' They would put
out the only burning coal I have left, leaving my husband neither
name nor descendant on the face of the earth."
8 The king said to the woman, "Go home, and I will issue an
order in your behalf."
9 But the woman from Tekoa said to him, "My lord the king, let
the blame rest on me and on my father's family, and let the king
and his throne be without guilt."
10 The king replied, "If anyone says anything to you, bring him
to me, and he will not bother you again."
11 She said, "Then let the king invoke the LORD his God to prevent the avenger of blood from adding to the destruction, so that
my son will not be destroyed."
"As surely as the LORD lives," he said, "not one hair of your
son's head will fall to the ground."
12 Then the woman said, "Let your servant speak a word to my
lord the king."
"Speak," he replied.
13 The woman said, "Why then have you devised a thing like this
against the people of God? When the king says this, does he not
convict himself, for the king has not brought back his banished
son? 14 Like water spilled on the ground, which cannot be recovered, so we must die. But God does not take away life; instead, he
devises ways so that a banished person may not remain estranged
from him.
15 "And now I have come to say this to my lord the king because
the people have made me afraid. Your servant thought, 'I will
speak to the king; perhaps he will do what his servant asks. 16 Perhaps the king will agree to deliver his servant from the hand of the

[a] 39 Dead Sea Scrolls and some Septuagint manuscripts; Masoretic Text *But ⌊the spirit of⌋ David the king* [b] 4 Many Hebrew manuscripts, Septuagint, Vulgate and Syriac; most Hebrew manuscripts *spoke*

man who is trying to cut off both me and my son from the inheritance God gave us.'
17 "And now your servant says, 'May the word of my lord the
king bring me rest, for my lord the king is like an angel of God
in discerning good and evil. May the LORD your God be with
you.' "
18 Then the king said to the woman, "Do not keep from me
the answer to what I am going to ask you."
"Let my lord the king speak," the woman said.
19 The king asked, "Isn't the hand of Joab with you in all
this?"
The woman answered, "As surely as you live, my lord the
king, no one can turn to the right or to the left from anything my
lord the king says. Yes, it was your servant Joab who instructed
me to do this and who put all these words into the mouth of
your servant. 20 Your servant Joab did this to change the present
situation. My lord has wisdom like that of an angel of God—he
knows everything that happens in the land."
21 The king said to Joab, "Very well, I will do it. Go, bring
back the young man Absalom."
22 Joab fell with his face to the ground to pay him honor, and
he blessed the king. Joab said, "Today your servant knows that
he has found favor in your eyes, my lord the king, because the
king has granted his servant's request."
23 Then Joab went to Geshur and brought Absalom back to Jerusalem. 24 But the king said, "He must go to his own house; he
must not see my face." So Absalom went to his own house and
did not see the face of the king.
25 In all Israel there was not a man so highly praised for his
handsome appearance as Absalom. From the top of his head to
the sole of his foot there was no blemish in him. 26 Whenever he
cut the hair of his head—he used to cut his hair from time to
time when it became too heavy for him—he would weigh it, and
its weight was two hundred shekels[a] by the royal standard.
27 Three sons and a daughter were born to Absalom. The
daughter's name was Tamar, and she became a beautiful
woman.
28 Absalom lived two years in Jerusalem without seeing the
king's face. 29 Then Absalom sent for Joab in order to send him
to the king, but Joab refused to come to him. So he sent a second time, but he refused to come. 30 Then he said to his servants, "Look, Joab's field is next to mine, and he has barley
there. Go and set it on fire." So Absalom's servants set the field
on fire.
31 Then Joab did go to Absalom's house and he said to him,
"Why have your servants set my field on fire?"
32 Absalom said to Joab, "Look, I sent word to you and said,
'Come here so I can send you to the king to ask, "Why have I
come from Geshur? It would be better for me if I were still
there!" ' Now then, I want to see the king's face, and if I am
guilty of anything, let him put me to death."
33 So Joab went to the king and told him this. Then the king
summoned Absalom, and he came in and bowed down with his
face to the ground before the king. And the king kissed Absalom.

[a] *26* That is, about 5 pounds (about 2.3 kilograms)

(14:23–33) Though David was a man after Your own heart, he was a failure as a father. A father disciplines the child he loves. But David's lack of fatherly discipline and sovereign justice only allowed his sons to continue in their destructive ways. Therefore, they had no fear of God or of justice, nor did they show their father any respect. Amnon, Absalom and Adonijah were all destroyed because of their rebellious, undisciplined hearts. Please help me, Father, to learn from David's mistakes as well as from his successes. Show me how to raise up children who will fear You and love You and serve You all their lives. (1Ki 1:6; Pr 3:12; Ac 13:22; Heb 12:7–9)

O give us homes built firm upon the
Savior,
Where Christ is Head and
Counselor and Guide;
Where every child is taught His love
and favor
And gives his heart to Christ, the
Crucified:
How sweet to know that, tho' his
footsteps waver,
His faithful Lord is walking by his
side!

"A Christian Home"
Barbara B. Hart (©1965)

Absalom's Conspiracy

15 In the course of time, Absalom provided himself with a chariot and horses and with fifty men to run ahead of him. **2**He would get up early and stand by the side of the road leading to the city gate. Whenever anyone came with a complaint to be placed before the king for a decision, Absalom would call out to him, "What town are you from?" He would answer, "Your servant is from one of the tribes of Israel." **3**Then Absalom would say to him, "Look, your claims are valid and proper, but there is no representative of the king to hear you." **4**And Absalom would add, "If only I were appointed judge in the land! Then everyone who has a complaint or case could come to me and I would see that he gets justice."

5Also, whenever anyone approached him to bow down before him, Absalom would reach out his hand, take hold of him and kiss him. **6**Absalom behaved in this way toward all the Israelites who came to the king asking for justice, and so he stole the hearts of the men of Israel.

7At the end of four[a] years, Absalom said to the king, "Let me go to Hebron and fulfill a vow I made to the LORD. **8**While your servant was living at Geshur in Aram, I made this vow: 'If the LORD takes me back to Jerusalem, I will worship the LORD in Hebron.[b]' "

9The king said to him, "Go in peace." So he went to Hebron.

10Then Absalom sent secret messengers throughout the tribes of Israel to say, "As soon as you hear the sound of the trumpets, then say, 'Absalom is king in Hebron.' " **11**Two hundred men from Jerusalem had accompanied Absalom. They had been invited as guests and went quite innocently, knowing nothing about the matter. **12**While Absalom was offering sacrifices, he also sent for Ahithophel the Gilonite, David's counselor, to come from Giloh, his hometown. And so the conspiracy gained strength, and Absalom's following kept on increasing.

David Flees

13A messenger came and told David, "The hearts of the men of Israel are with Absalom."

14Then David said to all his officials who were with him in Jerusalem, "Come! We must flee, or none of us will escape from Absalom. We must leave immediately, or he will move quickly to overtake us and bring ruin upon us and put the city to the sword."

15The king's officials answered him, "Your servants are ready to do whatever our lord the king chooses."

16The king set out, with his entire household following him; but he left ten concubines to take care of the palace. **17**So the king set out, with all the people following him, and they halted at a place some distance away. **18**All his men marched past him, along with all the Kerethites and Pelethites; and all the six hundred Gittites who had accompanied him from Gath marched before the king.

19The king said to Ittai the Gittite, "Why should you come along with us? Go back and stay with King Absalom. You are a foreigner, an exile from your homeland. **20**You came only yester-

[a] *7* Some Septuagint manuscripts, Syriac and Josephus; Hebrew *forty* [b] *8* Some Septuagint manuscripts; Hebrew does not have *in Hebron.*

(15:1–6) Protect me from deceitfully stealing the hearts of people like Absalom did: producing pompous outward impressions, making groundless promises, denigrating those who are in authority, or ingratiating myself with others through flattery and feigned affection. I realize that I cannot be both a people-pleaser and a servant of Christ. I refuse to resort to the ways of the world; I will follow Your pure and unpretentious ways, O Lord. (Gal 1:10; Jas 3:16)

day. And today shall I make you wander about with us, when I do
not know where I am going? Go back, and take your countrymen.
May kindness and faithfulness be with you."
21 But Ittai replied to the king, "As surely as the LORD lives, and
as my lord the king lives, wherever my lord the king may be,
whether it means life or death, there will your servant be."
22 David said to Ittai, "Go ahead, march on." So Ittai the Gittite
marched on with all his men and the families that were with him.
23 The whole countryside wept aloud as all the people passed
by. The king also crossed the Kidron Valley, and all the people
moved on toward the desert.
24 Zadok was there, too, and all the Levites who were with him
were carrying the ark of the covenant of God. They set down the
ark of God, and Abiathar offered sacrifices[a] until all the people
had finished leaving the city.
25 Then the king said to Zadok, "Take the ark of God back into
the city. If I find favor in the LORD's eyes, he will bring me back and
let me see it and his dwelling place again. 26 But if he says, 'I am
not pleased with you,' then I am ready; let him do to me whatever
seems good to him."
27 The king also said to Zadok the priest, "Aren't you a seer? Go
back to the city in peace, with your son Ahimaaz and Jonathan son
of Abiathar. You and Abiathar take your two sons with you. 28 I will
wait at the fords in the desert until word comes from you to inform
me." 29 So Zadok and Abiathar took the ark of God back to Jerusalem and stayed there.
30 But David continued up the Mount of Olives, weeping as he
went; his head was covered and he was barefoot. All the people
with him covered their heads too and were weeping as they went
up. 31 Now David had been told, "Ahithophel is among the con-
spirators with Absalom." So David prayed, "O LORD, turn Ahithophel's counsel into foolishness."
32 When David arrived at the summit, where people used to
worship God, Hushai the Arkite was there to meet him, his robe
torn and dust on his head. 33 David said to him, "If you go with me,
you will be a burden to me. 34 But if you return to the city and say
to Absalom, 'I will be your servant, O king; I was your father's servant in the past, but now I will be your servant,' then you can help
me by frustrating Ahithophel's advice. 35 Won't the priests Zadok
and Abiathar be there with you? Tell them anything you hear in the
king's palace. 36 Their two sons, Ahimaaz son of Zadok and Jonathan son of Abiathar, are there with them. Send them to me with
anything you hear."
37 So David's friend Hushai arrived at Jerusalem as Absalom was
entering the city.

David and Ziba

16 When David had gone a short distance beyond the summit,
there was Ziba, the steward of Mephibosheth, waiting to
meet him. He had a string of donkeys saddled and loaded with
two hundred loaves of bread, a hundred cakes of raisins, a hundred cakes of figs and a skin of wine.
2 The king asked Ziba, "Why have you brought these?"
Ziba answered, "The donkeys are for the king's household to

[a] 24 Or *Abiathar went up*

That we may not complain of what is, let us see God's hand in all events; and, that we may not be afraid of what shall be, let us see all events in God's hand.

Matthew Henry (1662-1714)

(15:25–26) "Let him do to me whatever seems good to him." O to have a heart like David's. He trusted completely in Your wisdom and Your justice. He submitted his will to Yours and placed himself in Your hands. "Blessed is the man who makes the LORD his trust." (Ps 40:4)

And when in the valley of deepest
despair,
I look to the Shepherd,
His presence is there
Bringing peace to my soul,
As His love makes me whole.

Surely goodness and mercy shall
follow me,
Follow me all the days of my life.
Surely goodness and mercy shall
follow me,
All my life.

"I Look to the Shepherd"
Walt Harrah (©1987)

ride on, the bread and fruit are for the men to eat, and the wine is
to refresh those who become exhausted in the desert."
3The king then asked, "Where is your master's grandson?"
Ziba said to him, "He is staying in Jerusalem, because he thinks,
'Today the house of Israel will give me back my grandfather's kingdom.' "
4Then the king said to Ziba, "All that belonged to Mephibosheth
is now yours."
"I humbly bow," Ziba said. "May I find favor in your eyes, my
lord the king."

Shimei Curses David

5As King David approached Bahurim, a man from the same
clan as Saul's family came out from there. His name was Shimei
son of Gera, and he cursed as he came out. 6He pelted David and
all the king's officials with stones, though all the troops and the
special guard were on David's right and left. 7As he cursed,
Shimei said, "Get out, get out, you man of blood, you scoundrel!
8The LORD has repaid you for all the blood you shed in the
household of Saul, in whose place you have reigned. The LORD
has handed the kingdom over to your son Absalom. You have
come to ruin because you are a man of blood!"
9Then Abishai son of Zeruiah said to the king, "Why should
this dead dog curse my lord the king? Let me go over and cut off
his head."
10But the king said, "What do you and I have in common, you
sons of Zeruiah? If he is cursing because the LORD said to him,
'Curse David,' who can ask, 'Why do you do this?' "
11David then said to Abishai and all his officials, "My son, who
is of my own flesh, is trying to take my life. How much more,
then, this Benjamite! Leave him alone; let him curse, for the LORD
has told him to. 12It may be that the LORD will see my distress and
repay me with good for the cursing I am receiving today."
13So David and his men continued along the road while Shimei was going along the hillside opposite him, cursing as he went
and throwing stones at him and showering him with dirt. 14The
king and all the people with him arrived at their destination exhausted. And there he refreshed himself.

(16:5–13) Lord Jesus, grant me self-control when I am insulted or ridiculed. Help me to follow Your example: When You were insulted, You did not retaliate; when You suffered, You made no threats. Give me the kind of attitude David had: the recognition that I am not necessarily innocent. If I suffer, may it be because of the name of Christ rather than because of my own sins. May I commit myself to You, my faithful Creator, and continue to do good. (1Pe 2:23; 4:14–19)

The Advice of Hushai and Ahithophel

15Meanwhile, Absalom and all the men of Israel came to Jerusalem, and Ahithophel was with him. 16Then Hushai the Arkite,
David's friend, went to Absalom and said to him, "Long live the
king! Long live the king!"
17Absalom asked Hushai, "Is this the love you show your
friend? Why didn't you go with your friend?"
18Hushai said to Absalom, "No, the one chosen by the LORD, by
these people, and by all the men of Israel—his I will be, and I will
remain with him. 19Furthermore, whom should I serve? Should I
not serve the son? Just as I served your father, so I will serve you."
20Absalom said to Ahithophel, "Give us your advice. What
should we do?"
21Ahithophel answered, "Lie with your father's concubines
whom he left to take care of the palace. Then all Israel will hear
that you have made yourself a stench in your father's nostrils, and
the hands of everyone with you will be strengthened." 22So they

pitched a tent for Absalom on the roof, and he lay with his father's
concubines in the sight of all Israel.
23 Now in those days the advice Ahithophel gave was like that of
one who inquires of God. That was how both David and Absalom
regarded all of Ahithophel's advice.
17 Ahithophel said to Absalom, "I would[a] choose twelve thousand men and set out tonight in pursuit of David. 2 I would[b]
attack him while he is weary and weak. I would[b] strike him with
terror, and then all the people with him will flee. I would[b] strike
down only the king 3 and bring all the people back to you. The
death of the man you seek will mean the return of all; all the people will be unharmed." 4 This plan seemed good to Absalom and to
all the elders of Israel.
5 But Absalom said, "Summon also Hushai the Arkite, so we can
hear what he has to say." 6 When Hushai came to him, Absalom
said, "Ahithophel has given this advice. Should we do what he
says? If not, give us your opinion."
7 Hushai replied to Absalom, "The advice Ahithophel has given
is not good this time. 8 You know your father and his men; they are
fighters, and as fierce as a wild bear robbed of her cubs. Besides,
your father is an experienced fighter; he will not spend the night
with the troops. 9 Even now, he is hidden in a cave or some other
place. If he should attack your troops first,[c] whoever hears about
it will say, 'There has been a slaughter among the troops who follow Absalom.' 10 Then even the bravest soldier, whose heart is like
the heart of a lion, will melt with fear, for all Israel knows that
your father is a fighter and that those with him are brave.
11 "So I advise you: Let all Israel, from Dan to Beersheba—as
numerous as the sand on the seashore—be gathered to you, with
you yourself leading them into battle. 12 Then we will attack him
wherever he may be found, and we will fall on him as dew settles
on the ground. Neither he nor any of his men will be left alive. 13 If
he withdraws into a city, then all Israel will bring ropes to that city,
and we will drag it down to the valley until not even a piece of it
can be found."
14 Absalom and all the men of Israel said, "The advice of Hushai
the Arkite is better than that of Ahithophel." For the LORD had determined to frustrate the good advice of Ahithophel in order to
bring disaster on Absalom.
15 Hushai told Zadok and Abiathar, the priests, "Ahithophel has
advised Absalom and the elders of Israel to do such and such, but
I have advised them to do so and so. 16 Now send a message immediately and tell David, 'Do not spend the night at the fords in the
desert; cross over without fail, or the king and all the people with
him will be swallowed up.' "
17 Jonathan and Ahimaaz were staying at En Rogel. A servant girl
was to go and inform them, and they were to go and tell King
David, for they could not risk being seen entering the city. 18 But a
young man saw them and told Absalom. So the two of them left
quickly and went to the house of a man in Bahurim. He had a well
in his courtyard, and they climbed down into it. 19 His wife took a
covering and spread it out over the opening of the well and scattered grain over it. No one knew anything about it.
20 When Absalom's men came to the woman at the house, they
asked, "Where are Ahimaaz and Jonathan?"

[a] 1 Or *Let me* [b] 2 Or *will* [c] 9 Or *When some of the men fall at the first attack*

(17:14) You, Lord, determine the course of history. You do as You please with the peoples of the earth and their rulers. There is no advice, no plan, that can succeed against You. As I think about global events today, as well as the events of my own daily routine, I rest in Your sovereignty. I trust You, King of kings, in the affairs of international significance. I trust You, heavenly Father, in the affairs of my personal life. Big or small, I cast all my concerns and anxieties on You. (Da 4:35; Pr 21:30; Mt 10:29–31; 1Pe 5:7)

Any voice we recognize as God's in the field of life must be the same voice we hear in the Bible. If we haven't cultivated our familiarity with God's powerfully comforting voice behind closed doors, we are in danger of mistaking many field voices as God's. Much of what we hear, even in our Christian circles, sounds good, but it does not come from God. Or, even though it reflects God's truth, it may not be God's timely instruction for us. We can tie ourselves in knots when, because we do not hear God, we try to follow all the right-sounding voices, all the ones that claim God's direction.

Our ability to hear God's voice is a gift from Him that must be cultivated in private with a focus on God in His Word, and practiced everywhere.

Martha Thatcher (1950–)

The woman answered them, "They crossed over the brook."[a] The men searched but found no one, so they returned to Jerusalem.

21 After the men had gone, the two climbed out of the well and went to inform King David. They said to him, "Set out and cross the river at once; Ahithophel has advised such and such against you." 22 So David and all the people with him set out and crossed the Jordan. By daybreak, no one was left who had not crossed the Jordan.

23 When Ahithophel saw that his advice had not been followed, he saddled his donkey and set out for his house in his hometown. He put his house in order and then hanged himself. So he died and was buried in his father's tomb.

24 David went to Mahanaim, and Absalom crossed the Jordan with all the men of Israel. 25 Absalom had appointed Amasa over the army in place of Joab. Amasa was the son of a man named Jether,[b] an Israelite[c] who had married Abigail,[d] the daughter of Nahash and sister of Zeruiah the mother of Joab. 26 The Israelites and Absalom camped in the land of Gilead.

27 When David came to Mahanaim, Shobi son of Nahash from Rabbah of the Ammonites, and Makir son of Ammiel from Lo Debar, and Barzillai the Gileadite from Rogelim 28 brought bedding and bowls and articles of pottery. They also brought wheat and barley, flour and roasted grain, beans and lentils,[e] 29 honey and curds, sheep, and cheese from cows' milk for David and his people to eat. For they said, "The people have become hungry and tired and thirsty in the desert."

Absalom's Death

18 David mustered the men who were with him and appointed over them commanders of thousands and commanders of hundreds. 2 David sent the troops out—a third under the command of Joab, a third under Joab's brother Abishai son of Zeruiah, and a third under Ittai the Gittite. The king told the troops, "I myself will surely march out with you."

3 But the men said, "You must not go out; if we are forced to flee, they won't care about us. Even if half of us die, they won't care; but you are worth ten thousand of us.[f] It would be better now for you to give us support from the city."

4 The king answered, "I will do whatever seems best to you."

So the king stood beside the gate while all the men marched out in units of hundreds and of thousands. 5 The king commanded Joab, Abishai and Ittai, "Be gentle with the young man Absalom for my sake." And all the troops heard the king giving orders concerning Absalom to each of the commanders.

6 The army marched into the field to fight Israel, and the battle took place in the forest of Ephraim. 7 There the army of Israel was defeated by David's men, and the casualties that day were great—twenty thousand men. 8 The battle spread out over the whole countryside, and the forest claimed more lives that day than the sword.

9 Now Absalom happened to meet David's men. He was riding his mule, and as the mule went under the thick branches of a large

(18:5) How should David have felt about his rebellious son? How do You feel, God, about what people today call "tough love"? Under what circumstances is it right or wrong to be gentle? Give me wisdom, like You gave the apostle Paul, so that I can be gentle when I need to be and "tough" when I need to be. (1Co 4:21; 2Co 13:10)

[a] 20 Or *"They passed by the sheep pen toward the water."* [b] 25 Hebrew *Ithra,* a variant of *Jether* [c] 25 Hebrew and some Septuagint manuscripts; other Septuagint manuscripts (see also 1 Chron. 2:17) *Ishmaelite* or *Jezreelite* [d] 25 Hebrew *Abigal,* a variant of *Abigail* [e] 28 Most Septuagint manuscripts and Syriac; Hebrew *lentils, and roasted grain* [f] 3 Two Hebrew manuscripts, some Septuagint manuscripts and Vulgate; most Hebrew manuscripts *care; for now there are ten thousand like us*

oak, Absalom's head got caught in the tree. He was left hanging in midair, while the mule he was riding kept on going.

10When one of the men saw this, he told Joab, "I just saw Absalom hanging in an oak tree."

11Joab said to the man who had told him this, "What! You saw him? Why didn't you strike him to the ground right there? Then I would have had to give you ten shekels[a] of silver and a warrior's belt."

12But the man replied, "Even if a thousand shekels[b] were weighed out into my hands, I would not lift my hand against the king's son. In our hearing the king commanded you and Abishai and Ittai, 'Protect the young man Absalom for my sake.[c]' 13And if
I had put my life in jeopardy[d]—and nothing is hidden from the king—you would have kept your distance from me."

14Joab said, "I'm not going to wait like this for you." So he took three javelins in his hand and plunged them into Absalom's heart while Absalom was still alive in the oak tree. 15And ten of
Joab's armor-bearers surrounded Absalom, struck him and killed him.

16Then Joab sounded the trumpet, and the troops stopped pursuing Israel, for Joab halted them. 17They took Absalom, threw
him into a big pit in the forest and piled up a large heap of rocks over him. Meanwhile, all the Israelites fled to their homes.

18During his lifetime Absalom had taken a pillar and erected it in the King's Valley as a monument to himself, for he thought, "I have no son to carry on the memory of my name." He named the pillar after himself, and it is called Absalom's Monument to this day.

David Mourns

19Now Ahimaaz son of Zadok said, "Let me run and take the news to the king that the LORD has delivered him from the hand of his enemies."

20"You are not the one to take the news today," Joab told him. "You may take the news another time, but you must not do so today, because the king's son is dead."

21Then Joab said to a Cushite, "Go, tell the king what you have seen." The Cushite bowed down before Joab and ran off.

22Ahimaaz son of Zadok again said to Joab, "Come what may, please let me run behind the Cushite."

But Joab replied, "My son, why do you want to go? You don't have any news that will bring you a reward."

23He said, "Come what may, I want to run."

So Joab said, "Run!" Then Ahimaaz ran by way of the plain[e] and outran the Cushite.

24While David was sitting between the inner and outer gates, the watchman went up to the roof of the gateway by the wall. As he looked out, he saw a man running alone. 25The watchman
called out to the king and reported it.

The king said, "If he is alone, he must have good news." And the man came closer and closer.

26Then the watchman saw another man running, and he called down to the gatekeeper, "Look, another man running alone!"

[a] *11* That is, about 4 ounces (about 115 grams) [b] *12* That is, about 25 pounds (about 11 kilograms) [c] *12* A few Hebrew manuscripts, Septuagint, Vulgate and Syriac; most Hebrew manuscripts may be translated *Absalom, whoever you may be.* [d] *13* Or *Otherwise, if I had acted treacherously toward him* [e] *23* That is, the plain of the Jordan

(18:9–18) You have declared, Lord, that at times You punish people as their deeds deserve. The end of Absalom's life reveals Your ironic justice. His handsome head was his downfall. And the pillar that Absalom erected as a monument to himself stood in sharp contrast to the heap of rocks that was piled over his dead body. Father, protect me from vanity and pride. Don't let my ego be my undoing. Don't let me erect any "monuments" to myself. I choose instead to humble myself before You, Lord, and to let You lift me up. (2Sa 14:25–26; Jer 21:14; Jas 4:10)

(18:33) Despite all the evil that Absalom had planned against his father, David's heart was broken over the death of Absalom. How much greater is Your love for us, Father? We have rebelled against You. We have rejected Your love and attempted to place ourselves on Your rightful throne in our lives. Yet in spite of our sin—in fact, because of our sin—You sent Jesus to die for us so that we would not have to be separated from You. For this, I am forever grateful. (Jn 3:16; Ro 5:8)

Christ died in my place. I was indeed a dead man but for Christ. He died my death. "Who his own self bore our sins in his own body on the tree, that we, being dead to sins, should live unto righteousness" (1 Pe 2:24).

L. E. Maxwell (1895-1984)

The king said, "He must be bringing good news, too."
27The watchman said, "It seems to me that the first one runs
like Ahimaaz son of Zadok."
"He's a good man," the king said. "He comes with good news."
28Then Ahimaaz called out to the king, "All is well!" He bowed
down before the king with his face to the ground and said,
"Praise be to the LORD your God! He has delivered up the men
who lifted their hands against my lord the king."
29The king asked, "Is the young man Absalom safe?"
Ahimaaz answered, "I saw great confusion just as Joab was
about to send the king's servant and me, your servant, but I don't
know what it was."
30The king said, "Stand aside and wait here." So he stepped
aside and stood there.
31Then the Cushite arrived and said, "My lord the king, hear
the good news! The LORD has delivered you today from all who
rose up against you."
32The king asked the Cushite, "Is the young man Absalom
safe?"
The Cushite replied, "May the enemies of my lord the king and
all who rise up to harm you be like that young man."
33The king was shaken. He went up to the room over the gateway and wept. As he went, he said: "O my son Absalom! My son,
my son Absalom! If only I had died instead of you—O Absalom,
my son, my son!"
19 Joab was told, "The king is weeping and mourning for Absalom." 2And for the whole army the victory that day was
turned into mourning, because on that day the troops heard it
said, "The king is grieving for his son." 3The men stole into the
city that day as men steal in who are ashamed when they flee from
battle. 4The king covered his face and cried aloud, "O my son
Absalom! O Absalom, my son, my son!"
5Then Joab went into the house to the king and said, "Today
you have humiliated all your men, who have just saved your life
and the lives of your sons and daughters and the lives of your
wives and concubines. 6You love those who hate you and hate
those who love you. You have made it clear today that the commanders and their men mean nothing to you. I see that you would
be pleased if Absalom were alive today and all of us were dead.
7Now go out and encourage your men. I swear by the LORD that if
you don't go out, not a man will be left with you by nightfall. This
will be worse for you than all the calamities that have come upon
you from your youth till now."
8So the king got up and took his seat in the gateway. When the
men were told, "The king is sitting in the gateway," they all came
before him.

David Returns to Jerusalem

Meanwhile, the Israelites had fled to their homes. 9Throughout
the tribes of Israel, the people were all arguing with each other,
saying, "The king delivered us from the hand of our enemies; he
is the one who rescued us from the hand of the Philistines. But
now he has fled the country because of Absalom; 10and Absalom,
whom we anointed to rule over us, has died in battle. So why do
you say nothing about bringing the king back?"
11King David sent this message to Zadok and Abiathar, the
priests: "Ask the elders of Judah, 'Why should you be the last to

bring the king back to his palace, since what is being said throughout Israel has reached the king at his quarters? 12You are my brothers, my own flesh and blood. So why should you be the last to bring back the king?' 13And say to Amasa, 'Are you not my own flesh and blood? May God deal with me, be it ever so severely, if from now on you are not the commander of my army in place of Joab.' "

14He won over the hearts of all the men of Judah as though they were one man. They sent word to the king, "Return, you and all your men." 15Then the king returned and went as far as the Jordan.

Now the men of Judah had come to Gilgal to go out and meet the king and bring him across the Jordan. 16Shimei son of Gera, the Benjamite from Bahurim, hurried down with the men of Judah to meet King David. 17With him were a thousand Benjamites, along with Ziba, the steward of Saul's household, and his fifteen sons and twenty servants. They rushed to the Jordan, where the king was. 18They crossed at the ford to take the king's household over and to do whatever he wished.

When Shimei son of Gera crossed the Jordan, he fell prostrate before the king 19and said to him, "May my lord not hold me guilty. Do not remember how your servant did wrong on the day my lord the king left Jerusalem. May the king put it out of his mind. 20For I your servant know that I have sinned, but today I have come here as the first of the whole house of Joseph to come down and meet my lord the king."

21Then Abishai son of Zeruiah said, "Shouldn't Shimei be put to death for this? He cursed the LORD's anointed."

22David replied, "What do you and I have in common, you sons of Zeruiah? This day you have become my adversaries! Should anyone be put to death in Israel today? Do I not know that today I am king over Israel?" 23So the king said to Shimei, "You shall not die." And the king promised him on oath.

24Mephibosheth, Saul's grandson, also went down to meet the king. He had not taken care of his feet or trimmed his mustache or washed his clothes from the day the king left until the day he returned safely. 25When he came from Jerusalem to meet the king, the king asked him, "Why didn't you go with me, Mephibosheth?"

26He said, "My lord the king, since I your servant am lame, I said, 'I will have my donkey saddled and will ride on it, so I can go with the king.' But Ziba my servant betrayed me. 27And he has slandered your servant to my lord the king. My lord the king is like an angel of God; so do whatever pleases you. 28All my grandfather's descendants deserved nothing but death from my lord the king, but you gave your servant a place among those who eat at your table. So what right do I have to make any more appeals to the king?"

29The king said to him, "Why say more? I order you and Ziba to divide the fields."

30Mephibosheth said to the king, "Let him take everything, now that my lord the king has arrived home safely."

31Barzillai the Gileadite also came down from Rogelim to cross the Jordan with the king and to send him on his way from there.
32Now Barzillai was a very old man, eighty years of age. He had provided for the king during his stay in Mahanaim, for he was a

(19:11–30) When David fled from Absalom, he cried out to You to defend and deliver him: "Arise, O Lord! Deliver me, O my God! Strike all my enemies on the jaw; break the teeth of the wicked." But when You delivered David and he had the chance to strike out in revenge, he chose instead to show mercy and called for a day of amnesty. You "lifted up" David's head; therefore, he spared the heads of his enemies, Amasa and Shimei, and showed kindness to those who had treated him with treachery. O Lord, help me to forgive as I have been forgiven. Teach me to show mercy as I have received mercy. (Ps 3:7–8; Mt 18:32–33; Jas 2:13)

We become like those with whom we associate. A man's ideals mold him. Living with Jesus makes us look like Himself . . . "We all with open face reflecting as in a mirror the glory of the Lord are changed" (2 Co 3:18). We stand between Him and those who don't know Him. We are the mirror catching the rays of his face and sending them down to those around. And not only do those around see the light–his light–in us, but we are being changed all the while. For others' sake as well as our own, the mirror should be kept clean and well polished so the reflection will be distinct and true.

Dr. Samuel Dickey Gordon (1859-1936)

(19:40—20:1) Protect Your church today, Lord, from division and strife. Keep us from bristling with wounded pride. Keep our spiritual leaders united in You, and keep the people from turning against them or pitting one leader against another. Guard us from following voices of contention. (Jn 17:20–21)

Oh, let us be the generation
Of reconciliation and peace,
And let us pray for restoration
And seek the Lord
Together on our knees.
Let us keep our hearts from evil
And cling to what is good.
Let us honor one another
And love the brotherhood.
Let us be the generation
Of reconciliation and peace.

The Reconciliation Song
Morris Chapman, Buddy Owens and
Claire Cloninger (©1995)

Jesus had one objective in life. He wanted to glorify the Father. His attention was on the Father. He came to do the Father's will. Think of how far we have drifted from Jesus' objective.

Ron Auch (1951-)

very wealthy man. 33The king said to Barzillai, "Cross over with
me and stay with me in Jerusalem, and I will provide for you."
34But Barzillai answered the king, "How many more years will
I live, that I should go up to Jerusalem with the king? 35I am now
eighty years old. Can I tell the difference between what is good
and what is not? Can your servant taste what he eats and drinks?
Can I still hear the voices of men and women singers? Why should
your servant be an added burden to my lord the king? 36Your servant will cross over the Jordan with the king for a short distance,
but why should the king reward me in this way? 37Let your servant
return, that I may die in my own town near the tomb of my father
and mother. But here is your servant Kimham. Let him cross over
with my lord the king. Do for him whatever pleases you."
38The king said, "Kimham shall cross over with me, and I will
do for him whatever pleases you. And anything you desire from me
I will do for you."
39So all the people crossed the Jordan, and then the king
crossed over. The king kissed Barzillai and gave him his blessing,
and Barzillai returned to his home.
40When the king crossed over to Gilgal, Kimham crossed with
him. All the troops of Judah and half the troops of Israel had taken
the king over.
41Soon all the men of Israel were coming to the king and saying to him, "Why did our brothers, the men of Judah, steal the
king away and bring him and his household across the Jordan, together with all his men?"
42All the men of Judah answered the men of Israel, "We did this
because the king is closely related to us. Why are you angry about
it? Have we eaten any of the king's provisions? Have we taken anything for ourselves?"
43Then the men of Israel answered the men of Judah, "We have
ten shares in the king; and besides, we have a greater claim on
David than you have. So why do you treat us with contempt? Were
we not the first to speak of bringing back our king?"
But the men of Judah responded even more harshly than the
men of Israel.

Sheba Rebels Against David

20 Now a troublemaker named Sheba son of Bicri, a Benjamite, happened to be there. He sounded the trumpet and
shouted,

"We have no share in David,
no part in Jesse's son!
Every man to his tent, O Israel!"

2So all the men of Israel deserted David to follow Sheba son of
Bicri. But the men of Judah stayed by their king all the way from
the Jordan to Jerusalem.
3When David returned to his palace in Jerusalem, he took the
ten concubines he had left to take care of the palace and put them
in a house under guard. He provided for them, but did not lie with
them. They were kept in confinement till the day of their death, living as widows.
4Then the king said to Amasa, "Summon the men of Judah to
come to me within three days, and be here yourself." 5But when
Amasa went to summon Judah, he took longer than the time the
king had set for him.

6David said to Abishai, "Now Sheba son of Bicri will do us more
harm than Absalom did. Take your master's men and pursue him,
or he will find fortified cities and escape from us." 7So Joab's men
and the Kerethites and Pelethites and all the mighty warriors went
out under the command of Abishai. They marched out from Jerusalem to pursue Sheba son of Bicri.

8While they were at the great rock in Gibeon, Amasa came to meet them. Joab was wearing his military tunic, and strapped over it at his waist was a belt with a dagger in its sheath. As he stepped forward, it dropped out of its sheath.

9Joab said to Amasa, "How are you, my brother?" Then Joab
took Amasa by the beard with his right hand to kiss him. 10Amasa
was not on his guard against the dagger in Joab's hand, and Joab plunged it into his belly, and his intestines spilled out on the ground. Without being stabbed again, Amasa died. Then Joab and his brother Abishai pursued Sheba son of Bicri.

11One of Joab's men stood beside Amasa and said, "Whoever
favors Joab, and whoever is for David, let him follow Joab!"
12Amasa lay wallowing in his blood in the middle of the road, and the man saw that all the troops came to a halt there. When he realized that everyone who came up to Amasa stopped, he dragged
him from the road into a field and threw a garment over him.
13After Amasa had been removed from the road, all the men went on with Joab to pursue Sheba son of Bicri.

14Sheba passed through all the tribes of Israel to Abel Beth Maacah[a] and through the entire region of the Berites, who gathered
together and followed him. 15All the troops with Joab came and besieged Sheba in Abel Beth Maacah. They built a siege ramp up to the city, and it stood against the outer fortifications. While they
were battering the wall to bring it down, 16a wise woman called
from the city, "Listen! Listen! Tell Joab to come here so I can speak
to him." 17He went toward her, and she asked, "Are you Joab?"

"I am," he answered.

She said, "Listen to what your servant has to say."

"I'm listening," he said.

18She continued, "Long ago they used to say, 'Get your answer
at Abel,' and that settled it. 19We are the peaceful and faithful in Israel. You are trying to destroy a city that is a mother in Israel. Why do you want to swallow up the LORD's inheritance?"

20"Far be it from me!" Joab replied, "Far be it from me to swal-
low up or destroy! 21That is not the case. A man named Sheba son of Bicri, from the hill country of Ephraim, has lifted up his hand against the king, against David. Hand over this one man, and I'll withdraw from the city."

The woman said to Joab, "His head will be thrown to you from the wall."

22Then the woman went to all the people with her wise advice, and they cut off the head of Sheba son of Bicri and threw it to Joab. So he sounded the trumpet, and his men dispersed from the city, each returning to his home. And Joab went back to the king in Jerusalem.

23Joab was over Israel's entire army; Benaiah son of Jehoiada
was over the Kerethites and Pelethites; 24Adoniram[b] was in charge
of forced labor; Jehoshaphat son of Ahilud was recorder; 25Sheva

[a] 14 Or *Abel, even Beth Maacah*; also in verse 15 [b] 24 Some Septuagint manuscripts (see also 1 Kings 4:6 and 5:14); Hebrew *Adoram*

(20:14–22) Lord, how often have I harbored an enemy of the King by giving place to sin in my life? Help me, like the people of Abel, to recognize the danger I am in and to renounce all allegiances that are offensive to You. Bring Your forces to bear against me until I willingly give up my sinful ways and make peace with You.

Our Father, we are beginning to understand at last that the things that are wrong with our world are the sum total of all the things that are wrong with us as individuals. Thou hast made us after Thine image, and our hearts can find no rest until they rest in Thee.

We are too Christian really to enjoy sinning and too fond of sinning really to enjoy Christianity. Most of us know perfectly well what we ought to do; our trouble is that we do not want to do it. Thy help is our only hope. Make us want to do what is right, and give us the ability to do it.

In the name of Christ our Lord. Amen.

Peter Marshall (1902–1949)

was secretary; Zadok and Abiathar were priests; 26and Ira the Jairite was David's priest.

The Gibeonites Avenged

21 During the reign of David, there was a famine for three successive years; so David sought the face of the LORD. The LORD said, "It is on account of Saul and his blood-stained house; it is because he put the Gibeonites to death."

2The king summoned the Gibeonites and spoke to them. (Now the Gibeonites were not a part of Israel but were survivors of the Amorites; the Israelites had sworn to ⌞spare⌟ them, but Saul in his zeal for Israel and Judah had tried to annihilate them.) 3David asked the Gibeonites, "What shall I do for you? How shall I make amends so that you will bless the LORD's inheritance?"

4The Gibeonites answered him, "We have no right to demand silver or gold from Saul or his family, nor do we have the right to put anyone in Israel to death."

"What do you want me to do for you?" David asked.

5They answered the king, "As for the man who destroyed us and plotted against us so that we have been decimated and have no place anywhere in Israel, 6let seven of his male descendants be given to us to be killed and exposed before the LORD at Gibeah of Saul—the LORD's chosen one."

So the king said, "I will give them to you."

7The king spared Mephibosheth son of Jonathan, the son of Saul, because of the oath before the LORD between David and Jonathan son of Saul. 8But the king took Armoni and Mephibosheth, the two sons of Aiah's daughter Rizpah, whom she had borne to Saul, together with the five sons of Saul's daughter Merab,[a] whom she had borne to Adriel son of Barzillai the Meholathite. 9He handed them over to the Gibeonites, who killed and exposed them on a hill before the LORD. All seven of them fell together; they were put to death during the first days of the harvest, just as the barley harvest was beginning.

10Rizpah daughter of Aiah took sackcloth and spread it out for herself on a rock. From the beginning of the harvest till the rain poured down from the heavens on the bodies, she did not let the birds of the air touch them by day or the wild animals by night. 11When David was told what Aiah's daughter Rizpah, Saul's concubine, had done, 12he went and took the bones of Saul and his son Jonathan from the citizens of Jabesh Gilead. (They had taken them secretly from the public square at Beth Shan, where the Philistines had hung them after they struck Saul down on Gilboa.) 13David brought the bones of Saul and his son Jonathan from there, and the bones of those who had been killed and exposed were gathered up.

14They buried the bones of Saul and his son Jonathan in the tomb of Saul's father Kish, at Zela in Benjamin, and did everything the king commanded. After that, God answered prayer in behalf of the land.

Wars Against the Philistines

15Once again there was a battle between the Philistines and Israel. David went down with his men to fight against the Philistines, and he became exhausted. 16And Ishbi-Benob, one of the descen-

(21:1) Saul violated a covenant and shed innocent blood. But time does not erode the guilt of sin. There is no statute of limitations on Your justice, O God. Sin must be dealt with through confession and repentance. The timing and the severity of the penalty are Yours to decide. Truly You defend the innocent and uphold the justice of their cause. (Jos 9:15–20)

[a] 8 Two Hebrew manuscripts, some Septuagint manuscripts and Syriac (see also 1 Samuel 18:19); most Hebrew and Septuagint manuscripts *Michal*

dants of Rapha, whose bronze spearhead weighed three hundred shekels[a] and who was armed with a new ⌞sword⌟, said he would kill David. 17But Abishai son of Zeruiah came to David's rescue; he struck the Philistine down and killed him. Then David's men swore to him, saying, "Never again will you go out with us to battle, so that the lamp of Israel will not be extinguished."

18In the course of time, there was another battle with the Philistines, at Gob. At that time Sibbecai the Hushathite killed Saph, one of the descendants of Rapha.

19In another battle with the Philistines at Gob, Elhanan son of Jaare-Oregim[b] the Bethlehemite killed Goliath[c] the Gittite, who had a spear with a shaft like a weaver's rod.

20In still another battle, which took place at Gath, there was a huge man with six fingers on each hand and six toes on each foot—twenty-four in all. He also was descended from Rapha.
21When he taunted Israel, Jonathan son of Shimeah, David's brother, killed him.

22These four were descendants of Rapha in Gath, and they fell at the hands of David and his men.

David's Song of Praise

22 David sang to the LORD the words of this song when the LORD delivered him from the hand of all his enemies and from the hand of Saul. 2He said:

"The LORD is my rock, my fortress and my
  deliverer;
3 my God is my rock, in whom I take refuge,
  my shield and the horn[d] of my salvation.
He is my stronghold, my refuge and my savior—
  from violent men you save me.
4I call to the LORD, who is worthy of praise,
  and I am saved from my enemies.

5"The waves of death swirled about me;
  the torrents of destruction overwhelmed me.
6The cords of the grave[e] coiled around me;
  the snares of death confronted me.
7In my distress I called to the LORD;
  I called out to my God.
From his temple he heard my voice;
  my cry came to his ears.

8"The earth trembled and quaked,
  the foundations of the heavens[f] shook;
  they trembled because he was angry.
9Smoke rose from his nostrils;
  consuming fire came from his mouth,
  burning coals blazed out of it.
10He parted the heavens and came down;
  dark clouds were under his feet.
11He mounted the cherubim and flew;
  he soared[g] on the wings of the wind.
12He made darkness his canopy around him—

[a] *16* That is, about 7 1/2 pounds (about 3.5 kilograms) [b] *19* Or *son of Jair the weaver* [c] *19* Hebrew and Septuagint; 1 Chron. 20:5 *son of Jair killed Lahmi the brother of Goliath* [d] *3 Horn* here symbolizes strength. [e] *6* Hebrew *Sheol* [f] *8* Hebrew; Vulgate and Syriac (see also Psalm 18:7) *mountains* [g] *11* Many Hebrew manuscripts (see also Psalm 18:10); most Hebrew manuscripts *appeared*

(21:17) Lord, just as David needed the help of his friend to save him from his enemy, so I need my friends to fight for me in prayer when I face an adversary who is too strong for me. At those times, I pray, raise up brothers and sisters in Christ who will join in the spiritual fray and fight for me in prayer.

When we hold up the life of another before God, when we expose it to God's love, when we pray for its release from drowsiness, for the quickening of its inner health, for the power to throw off a destructive habit, for the restoration of its free and vital relationship with its fellows, for its strength to resist temptation, for its courage to continue against sharp opposition—only then do we sense what it means to share in God's work, in his concern.

Douglas V. Steere (1901-)

(22:1–7) Like David, I sing a song of praise to You, Lord. You are indeed my strength and my salvation. When the hordes of sin and despair try to destroy me, I call to You and You save me from these enemies. My hope comes from You, O God. You are my fortress, and I will not be shaken. My salvation and honor depend on You, for You are my rock, my refuge. (Ps 62:5–7; 118:14)

There is no Rock,
There is no God like our God.
No other name
Worthy of all our praise.
The Rock of Salvation
That cannot be moved,
He's proven Himself
To be faithful and true.
There is no Rock,
There is no God like ours.

"Rock of Ages"
Rita Baloche (©1997)

(22:26) Thank You, Lord, for giving us Your Spirit to enable us to walk in Your ways. "To the faithful you show yourself faithful." And even if I am faithless, You remain faithful because You never change. You are the same yesterday and today and forever. (2Ti 2:13; Heb 13:8)

(22:29) King David was referred to as "the lamp of Israel." But he knew that You were his lamp, O Lord. You are light, and in You there is no darkness at all. Your Word is a lamp to our feet and a light for our path. Your Son, Jesus Christ, is the light of the world, and whoever follows Him will have the light of life. Thank You, Father, for rescuing me from the dominion of darkness and bringing me into the kingdom of light—the kingdom of Your Son! (2Sa 21:17; Ps 119:105; Jn 8:12; Col 1:12–13; 1Jn 1:5)

Through the tender mercy of our God, the dayspring from on high has visited us. Glory be to Thee, O Lord; glory to you, Creator of the light, Enlightener of the world. God is the Lord who has shown us the light.

Glory be to you for the visible light: the sun's radiance, the flame of fire; day and night, evening and morning. For the light invisible and intellectual: that which may be known of God, that which is written in the law, oracles of prophets, melody of psalms, instruction of proverbs, experience of histories–a light which never sets.

Lancelot Andrews (1555–1626)

the dark[a] rain clouds of the sky.
13 Out of the brightness of his presence
bolts of lightning blazed forth.
14 The LORD thundered from heaven;
the voice of the Most High resounded.
15 He shot arrows and scattered ⌞the enemies⌟,
bolts of lightning and routed them.
16 The valleys of the sea were exposed
and the foundations of the earth laid bare
at the rebuke of the LORD,
at the blast of breath from his nostrils.

17 "He reached down from on high and took hold of me;
he drew me out of deep waters.
18 He rescued me from my powerful enemy,
from my foes, who were too strong for me.
19 They confronted me in the day of my disaster,
but the LORD was my support.
20 He brought me out into a spacious place;
he rescued me because he delighted in me.

21 "The LORD has dealt with me according to my righteousness;
according to the cleanness of my hands he has rewarded me.
22 For I have kept the ways of the LORD;
I have not done evil by turning from my God.
23 All his laws are before me;
I have not turned away from his decrees.
24 I have been blameless before him
and have kept myself from sin.
25 The LORD has rewarded me according to my righteousness,
according to my cleanness[b] in his sight.

26 "To the faithful you show yourself faithful,
to the blameless you show yourself blameless,
27 to the pure you show yourself pure,
but to the crooked you show yourself shrewd.
28 You save the humble,
but your eyes are on the haughty to bring them low.
29 You are my lamp, O LORD;
the LORD turns my darkness into light.
30 With your help I can advance against a troop[c];
with my God I can scale a wall.

31 "As for God, his way is perfect;
the word of the LORD is flawless.
He is a shield
for all who take refuge in him.
32 For who is God besides the LORD?
And who is the Rock except our God?
33 It is God who arms me with strength[d]
and makes my way perfect.
34 He makes my feet like the feet of a deer;

[a] *12* Septuagint and Vulgate (see also Psalm 18:11); Hebrew *massed* [b] *25* Hebrew; Septuagint and Vulgate (see also Psalm 18:24) *to the cleanness of my hands* [c] *30* Or *can run through a barricade* [d] *33* Dead Sea Scrolls, some Septuagint manuscripts, Vulgate and Syriac (see also Psalm 18:32); Masoretic Text *who is my strong refuge*

he enables me to stand on the heights.
35 He trains my hands for battle;
my arms can bend a bow of bronze.
36 You give me your shield of victory;
you stoop down to make me great.
37 You broaden the path beneath me,
so that my ankles do not turn.

38 "I pursued my enemies and crushed them;
I did not turn back till they were destroyed.
39 I crushed them completely, and they could not rise;
they fell beneath my feet.
40 You armed me with strength for battle;
you made my adversaries bow at my feet.
41 You made my enemies turn their backs in flight,
and I destroyed my foes.
42 They cried for help, but there was no one to save them—
to the LORD, but he did not answer.
43 I beat them as fine as the dust of the earth;
I pounded and trampled them like mud in the streets.

44 "You have delivered me from the attacks of my people;
you have preserved me as the head of nations.
People I did not know are subject to me,
45 and foreigners come cringing to me;
as soon as they hear me, they obey me.
46 They all lose heart;
they come trembling[a] from their strongholds.

47 "The LORD lives! Praise be to my Rock!
Exalted be God, the Rock, my Savior!
48 He is the God who avenges me,
who puts the nations under me,
49 who sets me free from my enemies.
You exalted me above my foes;
from violent men you rescued me.
50 Therefore I will praise you, O LORD, among the nations;
I will sing praises to your name.
51 He gives his king great victories;
he shows unfailing kindness to his anointed,
to David and his descendants forever."

The Last Words of David

23 These are the last words of David:

"The oracle of David son of Jesse,
the oracle of the man exalted by the Most High,
the man anointed by the God of Jacob,
Israel's singer of songs[b]:

2 "The Spirit of the LORD spoke through me;
his word was on my tongue.
3 The God of Israel spoke,
the Rock of Israel said to me:
'When one rules over men in righteousness,

[a] 46 Some Septuagint manuscripts and Vulgate (see also Psalm 18:45); Masoretic Text *they arm themselves.* [b] 1 Or *Israel's beloved singer*

(22:35–41) You have armed me with strength for spiritual battle. I know that my real struggle is not against flesh and blood, but against the spiritual forces of evil in the heavenly realms. I accept and put on the full armor of God so that I can take my stand against the devil's schemes. I will stand firm, wearing the belt of truth, the breastplate of righteousness, the shield of faith, the helmet of salvation and the sword of the Spirit, which is the Word of God. (Eph 6:10–17)

(22:47–50) "The Lord lives!" Your deliverance in David's life, as well as my own, demonstrates beyond doubt that You are the living God! Therefore I will praise You among the nations. I anticipate the day when a great multitude from every nation, tribe, people and language will stand before Your throne and cry out: "Salvation belongs to our God, who sits on the throne, and to the Lamb." (Rev 7:9–10)

(22:51) Praise be to Your name, Lord, for the great victories You gave to David. They were a foreshadowing of the greater victories You have given Jesus Christ, the Son of David! In Your great power You have given Him victory over all powers and authorities. He has won the war against sin and temptation, Satan and his demons, and hell and death. I will sing praises to Your name. (Col 2:15)

(23:2–4) With these words of David, I give You praise, Holy Spirit of God; I give You praise, our Father, the God of Israel; I give You praise, Lord Jesus Christ, the Rock of Israel—blessed Trinity. Though David spoke of his own reign, he also spoke prophetically of the sovereignty of a coming King—Jesus, the King of kings, the Son of the Most High. He is both the Son and Lord of David, both the Root and the fruit of Jesse. He is the Fear of Isaac, the Lord Our Righteousness, the righteous Branch of David. He is the bright Morning Star and the Light of the world. Come, Lord Jesus, and rule over all the earth! (Ge 31:53; Isa 11:1–10; Jer 23:5–6; Mt 21:9; 22:42–46; Lk 1:32–33; Jn 8:12; Ro 15:12; 1Co 10:4; Rev 22:16)

All hail, King Jesus,
All hail, Emmanuel;
King of kings, Lord of lords,
Bright Morning Star.
And throughout eternity I'll sing His praises,
And I'll reign with Him throughout eternity.

"All Hail King Jesus"
Dave Moody (©1981)

when he rules in the fear of God,
4 he is like the light of morning at sunrise
on a cloudless morning,
like the brightness after rain
that brings the grass from the earth.'

5 "Is not my house right with God?
Has he not made with me an everlasting covenant,
arranged and secured in every part?
Will he not bring to fruition my salvation
and grant me my every desire?
6 But evil men are all to be cast aside like thorns,
which are not gathered with the hand.
7 Whoever touches thorns
uses a tool of iron or the shaft of a spear;
they are burned up where they lie."

David's Mighty Men

8 These are the names of David's mighty men:
Josheb-Basshebeth,[a] a Tahkemonite,[b] was chief of the Three; he raised his spear against eight hundred men, whom he killed[c] in one encounter.
9 Next to him was Eleazar son of Dodai the Ahohite. As one of
the three mighty men, he was with David when they taunted the
Philistines gathered ⌞at Pas Dammim⌟[d] for battle. Then the men
of Israel retreated, 10 but he stood his ground and struck down
the Philistines till his hand grew tired and froze to the sword. The LORD brought about a great victory that day. The troops returned to Eleazar, but only to strip the dead.
11 Next to him was Shammah son of Agee the Hararite. When
the Philistines banded together at a place where there was a field
full of lentils, Israel's troops fled from them. 12 But Shammah
took his stand in the middle of the field. He defended it and struck the Philistines down, and the LORD brought about a great victory.
13 During harvest time, three of the thirty chief men came down to David at the cave of Adullam, while a band of Philistines
was encamped in the Valley of Rephaim. 14 At that time David was
in the stronghold, and the Philistine garrison was at Bethlehem.
15 David longed for water and said, "Oh, that someone would get me a drink of water from the well near the gate of Bethlehem!"
16 So the three mighty men broke through the Philistine lines, drew water from the well near the gate of Bethlehem and carried it back to David. But he refused to drink it; instead, he poured it
out before the LORD. 17 "Far be it from me, O LORD, to do this!" he said. "Is it not the blood of men who went at the risk of their lives?" And David would not drink it.
Such were the exploits of the three mighty men.
18 Abishai the brother of Joab son of Zeruiah was chief of the Three.[e] He raised his spear against three hundred men, whom

[a] 8 Hebrew; some Septuagint manuscripts suggest *Ish-Bosheth,* that is, *Esh-Baal* (see also 1 Chron. 11:11 *Jashobeam*). [b] 8 Probably a variant of *Hacmonite* (see 1 Chron. 11:11) [c] 8 Some Septuagint manuscripts (see also 1 Chron. 11:11); Hebrew and other Septuagint manuscripts *Three; it was Adino the Eznite who killed eight hundred men* [d] 9 See 1 Chron. 11:13; Hebrew *gathered there.* [e] 18 Most Hebrew manuscripts (see also 1 Chron. 11:20); two Hebrew manuscripts and Syriac *Thirty*

MY BELOVED

Do not make light of My discipline, and do not lose heart when I rebuke you, because I discipline those I love. No discipline seems pleasant at the time, but painful. Later on, however, it produces a harvest of righteousness and peace for those who have been trained by it.

I am the God of peace. Through the blood of My eternal covenant, I will equip you with everything good for doing My will, and I will work in you what is pleasing to Me, through My Son, Jesus.

You have been reconciled to Me without blemish; you are free from accusation. But you must continue in your faith, established and firm, not moved from the hope you hold onto in the gospel. So throw off everything that hinders you and the sin that so easily entangles, and run with perseverance the race marked out for you. Run in such a way as to get the prize. Forgetting what is behind and straining toward what is ahead, press on toward the goal to win the prize for which I have called you heavenward in Christ Jesus.

As you follow My ways, I will sanctify you through and through. Your whole spirit, soul and body will be kept blameless at the coming of My Son, Jesus Christ. I have begun this good work in you and I will complete it. I am the One who calls you; I am faithful and I will do it.

2Sa 23:5; 1Co 9:24; Php 1:6; 3:13-14; Col 1:22-23; 1Th 5:23-24; Heb 12:5,11; 13:20-21

he killed, and so he became as famous as the Three. 19Was he
not held in greater honor than the Three? He became their commander, even though he was not included among them.

20Benaiah son of Jehoiada was a valiant fighter from Kabzeel,
who performed great exploits. He struck down two of Moab's
best men. He also went down into a pit on a snowy day and killed
a lion. 21And he struck down a huge Egyptian. Although the Egyptian had a spear in his hand, Benaiah went against him with a
club. He snatched the spear from the Egyptian's hand and killed
him with his own spear. 22Such were the exploits of Benaiah son
of Jehoiada; he too was as famous as the three mighty men. 23He
was held in greater honor than any of the Thirty, but he was not
included among the Three. And David put him in charge of his
bodyguard.

24Among the Thirty were:
Asahel the brother of Joab,
Elhanan son of Dodo from Bethlehem,
25Shammah the Harodite,
Elika the Harodite,
26Helez the Paltite,
Ira son of Ikkesh from Tekoa,
27Abiezer from Anathoth,
Mebunnai[a] the Hushathite,
28Zalmon the Ahohite,
Maharai the Netophathite,
29Heled[b] son of Baanah the Netophathite,
Ithai son of Ribai from Gibeah in Benjamin,
30Benaiah the Pirathonite,
Hiddai[c] from the ravines of Gaash,
31Abi-Albon the Arbathite,
Azmaveth the Barhumite,
32Eliahba the Shaalbonite,
the sons of Jashen,
Jonathan 33son of[d] Shammah the Hararite,
Ahiam son of Sharar[e] the Hararite,
34Eliphelet son of Ahasbai the Maacathite,
Eliam son of Ahithophel the Gilonite,
35Hezro the Carmelite,
Paarai the Arbite,
36Igal son of Nathan from Zobah,
the son of Hagri,[f]
37Zelek the Ammonite,
Naharai the Beerothite, the armor-bearer of Joab son of Zeruiah,
38Ira the Ithrite,
Gareb the Ithrite
39and Uriah the Hittite.
There were thirty-seven in all.

[a] 27 Hebrew; some Septuagint manuscripts (see also 1 Chron. 11:29) *Sibbecai*
[b] 29 Some Hebrew manuscripts and Vulgate (see also 1 Chron. 11:30); most Hebrew manuscripts *Heleb* [c] 30 Hebrew; some Septuagint manuscripts (see also 1 Chron. 11:32) *Hurai* [d] 33 Some Septuagint manuscripts (see also 1 Chron. 11:34); Hebrew does not have *son of.* [e] 33 Hebrew; some Septuagint manuscripts (see also 1 Chron. 11:35) *Sacar*
[f] 36 Some Septuagint manuscripts (see also 1 Chron. 11:38); Hebrew *Haggadi*

(23:24–39) Almighty One, may I be included in Your listing of "Who's Who" in spiritual might! I ask this not for worldly accolades or for the sake of my ego, but for Your glory and the sake of Your kingdom. In humility I acknowledge the source of my strength: " 'Not by might nor by power, but by my Spirit,' says the LORD Almighty." (Zec 4:6)

Christ, the Son of David, has his worthies too, who, like David's, are influenced by his example, fight his battles against the spiritual enemies of his kingdom, and in his strength are more than conquerors . . . all the good soldiers of Jesus Christ have their names better preserved than even these worthies have; for they are written in heaven.

Matthew Henry (1662-1714)

David Counts the Fighting Men

24 Again the anger of the LORD burned against Israel, and he
incited David against them, saying, "Go and take a census
of Israel and Judah."
2So the king said to Joab and the army commanders[a] with him,
"Go throughout the tribes of Israel from Dan to Beersheba and enroll the fighting men, so that I may know how many there are."
3But Joab replied to the king, "May the LORD your God multiply
the troops a hundred times over, and may the eyes of my lord the
king see it. But why does my lord the king want to do such a
thing?"
4The king's word, however, overruled Joab and the army commanders; so they left the presence of the king to enroll the fighting men of Israel.
5After crossing the Jordan, they camped near Aroer, south of
the town in the gorge, and then went through Gad and on to Jazer.
6They went to Gilead and the region of Tahtim Hodshi, and on to
Dan Jaan and around toward Sidon. 7Then they went toward the
fortress of Tyre and all the towns of the Hivites and Canaanites. Finally, they went on to Beersheba in the Negev of Judah.
8After they had gone through the entire land, they came back to
Jerusalem at the end of nine months and twenty days.
9Joab reported the number of the fighting men to the king: In
Israel there were eight hundred thousand able-bodied men who
could handle a sword, and in Judah five hundred thousand.
10David was conscience-stricken after he had counted the fighting men, and he said to the LORD, "I have sinned greatly in what I
have done. Now, O LORD, I beg you, take away the guilt of your servant. I have done a very foolish thing."
11Before David got up the next morning, the word of the LORD
had come to Gad the prophet, David's seer: 12"Go and tell David,
'This is what the LORD says: I am giving you three options. Choose
one of them for me to carry out against you.' "
13So Gad went to David and said to him, "Shall there come
upon you three[b] years of famine in your land? Or three months of
fleeing from your enemies while they pursue you? Or three days of
plague in your land? Now then, think it over and decide how I
should answer the one who sent me."
14David said to Gad, "I am in deep distress. Let us fall into the
hands of the LORD, for his mercy is great; but do not let me fall into
the hands of men."
15So the LORD sent a plague on Israel from that morning until
the end of the time designated, and seventy thousand of the people from Dan to Beersheba died. 16When the angel stretched out
his hand to destroy Jerusalem, the LORD was grieved because of the
calamity and said to the angel who was afflicting the people,
"Enough! Withdraw your hand." The angel of the LORD was then at
the threshing floor of Araunah the Jebusite.
17When David saw the angel who was striking down the people,
he said to the LORD, "I am the one who has sinned and done
wrong. These are but sheep. What have they done? Let your hand
fall upon me and my family."

[a] 2 Septuagint (see also verse 4 and 1 Chron. 21:2); Hebrew *Joab the army commander*
[b] 13 Septuagint (see also 1 Chron. 21:12); Hebrew *seven*

(24:14–17) Even before David cried out, "Let your hand fall upon me and my family," You had already told the angel of judgment: "Enough! Withdraw your hand." Thank You, Lord, that even before we cry out to You, Your mercy is already at work. "While we were still sinners, Christ died for us." (Isa 65:1; Ro 5:8)

Because of what Jesus has done–His dying, His substitutionary sufferings, His vicarious obedience–the Lord our God accepts us. What preciousness there is in Him to make up for our lack of preciousness. What a sweet aroma to put away our bitterness. What a cleansing in His blood to take away sin like ours. What a glory in His righteousness to make such unacceptable creatures accepted in the Beloved! . . . Jehovah's gracious eye never looks on you in anger when he looks at you through Christ, for then He sees no sin. Though you still struggle with sin, you are always accepted in Christ, always blessed, and always dear to the Father's heart.

Charles Haddon Spurgeon (1834-1892)

David Builds an Altar

18On that day Gad went to David and said to him, "Go up and
build an altar to the LORD on the threshing floor of Araunah the
Jebusite." 19So David went up, as the LORD had commanded
through Gad. 20When Araunah looked and saw the king and his
men coming toward him, he went out and bowed down before the
king with his face to the ground.
21Araunah said, "Why has my lord the king come to his servant?"

"To buy your threshing floor," David answered, "so I can build an altar to the LORD, that the plague on the people may be stopped."

22Araunah said to David, "Let my lord the king take whatever
pleases him and offer it up. Here are oxen for the burnt offering,
and here are threshing sledges and ox yokes for the wood. 23O
king, Araunah gives all this to the king." Araunah also said to him,
"May the LORD your God accept you."
24But the king replied to Araunah, "No, I insist on paying you
for it. I will not sacrifice to the LORD my God burnt offerings that
cost me nothing."

So David bought the threshing floor and the oxen and paid fifty
shekels[a] of silver for them. 25David built an altar to the LORD there
and sacrificed burnt offerings and fellowship offerings.[b] Then the
LORD answered prayer in behalf of the land, and the plague on Israel was stopped.

(24:18–25) In Your sovereignty, Lord, You instructed David to build an altar at the very place that would later become the site of the temple. I rejoice that true repentance results in pure worship. I thank You that this book does not end with judgment and destruction but with deliverance and blessing. The name of the Lord be praised! (2Ch 3:1)

Throughout the Scriptures we find confirmation of this basic truth that God's primary activity has always been the seeking of true worshipers. From God's Word we see that all of history consummates in heaven, where the whole of that eternal domain of the redeemed resounds with worship. The sole purpose of our being in heaven is that we might worship God rightly and forever. We, along with the redeemed of all ages, are saved to that glorious and unending end.

John MacArthur, Jr. (1939-)

[a] *24* That is, about 1 1/4 pounds (about 0.6 kilogram) [b] *25* Traditionally *peace offerings*

1 & 2 Kings

The First & Second Books of the KINGS

First and Second Kings tell what happened to God's people from the pinnacle of Israel's power under Solomon to the conquest of Judah by Babylon four centuries later. These two books, originally written as a single document, explain why God's chosen people lost their sovereignty, their land and their temple.

As 1 Kings begins, David's rule passes to his son Solomon, under whose reign the nation thrives (1Ki 1–4; 9:15–28). King Solomon completes the sacred task of building a temple for God, a place that represents God's presence with His people (1Ki 5–10). The establishment of the temple in Jerusalem completes Israel's settlement of the promised land.

But God's presence does not guarantee His unqualified blessing. If Solomon and his sons continue to serve God faithfully, He will bless them. But if they turn to other gods, Israel will be cut off from the promised land (1Ki 9:1–9). Sadly, this warning fails to keep Solomon from ignoring the Lord and worshiping foreign gods (1Ki 11).

After Solomon's death the northern tribes secede from the rule of David's line in Judah. The northern kingdom, often called Israel, establishes its own kingship—with dire consequences. To a man, the northern kings "[do] evil in the eyes of the LORD" (e.g., 1Ki 15:26). Because they chase after foreign gods, the kings bring God's promised discipline upon Israel, ultimately in the form of the Assyrian conquest in 722 B.C.

First and Second Kings reveal God's gracious attempts to woo His rebellious people back into intimate relationship with Himself.

The southern kingdom of Judah fares better than the northern kingdom, in part because several of Judah's kings faithfully serve the Lord (e.g., Hezekiah [2Ki 18—20] and Josiah [2Ki 22:1—23:30]). But the covenant loyalty of a few godly kings cannot make up for the disloyalty of the majority. Though Judah outlasts Israel, God eventually delivers Judah over to Babylon in 586 B.C. With this final blow to God's people, the books of 1 and 2 Kings come to a dreary end.

These books warn us about the dreadful consequences of spiritual adultery. Though our "baals" are not the same as those of ancient paganism, we can easily be tempted to chase after the "gods" of our culture. Yet as King Josiah honored God by following "the Book of the Law" (2Ki 22—23), so we can glorify Him by making Scripture the unique authority for our faith and worship.

First and Second Kings reveal God's gracious attempts to woo His rebellious people back into intimate relationship with Himself. Though these books focus on the kings, they also show the prophets calling the Israelites back to God. Even when we wander away from the Lord, His goodness reaches out to draw us home. In Jesus Christ God has reached all the way to the cross, causing Him to become sin for us so that we might become God's own righteousness (2Co 5:21). In gratitude, awe and obedience, we worship a God whose love will never let us go!

Adonijah Sets Himself Up as King

1 When King David was old and well advanced in years, he
could not keep warm even when they put covers over him.
2So his servants said to him, "Let us look for a young virgin to attend the king and take care of him. She can lie beside him so that
our lord the king may keep warm."
3Then they searched throughout Israel for a beautiful girl and
found Abishag, a Shunammite, and brought her to the king. 4The
girl was very beautiful; she took care of the king and waited on
him, but the king had no intimate relations with her.
5Now Adonijah, whose mother was Haggith, put himself forward and said, "I will be king." So he got chariots and horses[a]
ready, with fifty men to run ahead of him. 6(His father had never
interfered with him by asking, "Why do you behave as you do?"
He was also very handsome and was born next after Absalom.)
7Adonijah conferred with Joab son of Zeruiah and with Abiathar the priest, and they gave him their support. 8But Zadok the
priest, Benaiah son of Jehoiada, Nathan the prophet, Shimei and
Rei[b] and David's special guard did not join Adonijah.
9Adonijah then sacrificed sheep, cattle and fattened calves at
the Stone of Zoheleth near En Rogel. He invited all his brothers,
the king's sons, and all the men of Judah who were royal officials,
10but he did not invite Nathan the prophet or Benaiah or the special guard or his brother Solomon.
11Then Nathan asked Bathsheba, Solomon's mother, "Have you
not heard that Adonijah, the son of Haggith, has become king
without our lord David's knowing it? 12Now then, let me advise
you how you can save your own life and the life of your son Solomon. 13Go in to King David and say to him, 'My lord the king, did
you not swear to me your servant: "Surely Solomon your son shall
be king after me, and he will sit on my throne"? Why then has Adonijah become king?' 14While you are still there talking to the
king, I will come in and confirm what you have said."
15So Bathsheba went to see the aged king in his room, where
Abishag the Shunammite was attending him. 16Bathsheba bowed
low and knelt before the king.
"What is it you want?" the king asked.
17She said to him, "My lord, you yourself swore to me your
servant by the LORD your God: 'Solomon your son shall be king
after me, and he will sit on my throne.' 18But now Adonijah has
become king, and you, my lord the king, do not know about it.
19He has sacrificed great numbers of cattle, fattened calves, and
sheep, and has invited all the king's sons, Abiathar the priest and
Joab the commander of the army, but he has not invited Solomon
your servant. 20My lord the king, the eyes of all Israel are on you,
to learn from you who will sit on the throne of my lord the king
after him. 21Otherwise, as soon as my lord the king is laid to rest
with his fathers, I and my son Solomon will be treated as criminals."
22While she was still speaking with the king, Nathan the prophet arrived. 23And they told the king, "Nathan the prophet is here."
So he went before the king and bowed with his face to the ground.
24Nathan said, "Have you, my lord the king, declared that Adonijah shall be king after you, and that he will sit on your throne?
25Today he has gone down and sacrificed great numbers of cat-

[a] 5 Or *charioteers* [b] 8 Or *and his friends*

(1:5–6) Father, we know that You humble the proud but give grace to the humble. Because David failed to teach his son humility, he would now reap the harvest of his son's pride. Make us wise, Lord, not only as parents who must dispense discipline, but also as Your children, who must receive it. Teach us to submit to You, Heavenly Father, for if You love us, You will surely chasten us, humble us and bring us under Your authority. (Pr 3:12; Jas 4:6)

Like a concerned parent, God corrects his children who are on a wayward path: "The Lord disciplines those he loves, and he punishes everyone he accepts as a son" (Heb 12:6).

Does that change your view of admonition? Do you see that God's sometimes painful dealings with you are but an extension of his fatherhood? Do you understand that his rebuke only affirms your glorious position as a child of God, who loves you enough to place his disciplining hand on your life?

Charles Stanley (1832-)

Who is the man to whom
The Lord will have regard?
He who is broken
And has a humble heart.
God is not impressed
With the loftiness of man,
For everything was made for Him,
And comes from His own hand.

Humble yourself before your Lord
and King,
Give Him your heart, offer your
everything.
There's no limit on the love He has
for you,
So humble yourself and see what
God will do.

"Humble Yourself"
Kelly Willard (©1985)

tle, fattened calves, and sheep. He has invited all the king's sons,
the commanders of the army and Abiathar the priest. Right now
they are eating and drinking with him and saying, 'Long live King
Adonijah!' 26But me your servant, and Zadok the priest, and Benaiah son of Jehoiada, and your servant Solomon he did not invite. 27Is this something my lord the king has done without letting
his servants know who should sit on the throne of my lord the
king after him?"

David Makes Solomon King

28Then King David said, "Call in Bathsheba." So she came into
the king's presence and stood before him.

29The king then took an oath: "As surely as the LORD lives, who
has delivered me out of every trouble, 30I will surely carry out
today what I swore to you by the LORD, the God of Israel: Solomon
your son shall be king after me, and he will sit on my throne in
my place."

31Then Bathsheba bowed low with her face to the ground and,
kneeling before the king, said, "May my lord King David live forever!"

32King David said, "Call in Zadok the priest, Nathan the prophet and Benaiah son of Jehoiada." When they came before the
king, 33he said to them: "Take your lord's servants with you and
set Solomon my son on my own mule and take him down to
Gihon. 34There have Zadok the priest and Nathan the prophet
anoint him king over Israel. Blow the trumpet and shout, 'Long
live King Solomon!' 35Then you are to go up with him, and he is
to come and sit on my throne and reign in my place. I have appointed him ruler over Israel and Judah."

36Benaiah son of Jehoiada answered the king, "Amen! May the
LORD, the God of my lord the king, so declare it. 37As the LORD was
with my lord the king, so may he be with Solomon to make his
throne even greater than the throne of my lord King David!"

38So Zadok the priest, Nathan the prophet, Benaiah son of Jehoiada, the Kerethites and the Pelethites went down and put Solomon on King David's mule and escorted him to Gihon. 39Zadok
the priest took the horn of oil from the sacred tent and anointed
Solomon. Then they sounded the trumpet and all the people
shouted, "Long live King Solomon!" 40And all the people went up
after him, playing flutes and rejoicing greatly, so that the ground
shook with the sound.

41Adonijah and all the guests who were with him heard it as
they were finishing their feast. On hearing the sound of the trumpet, Joab asked, "What's the meaning of all the noise in the city?"

42Even as he was speaking, Jonathan son of Abiathar the priest
arrived. Adonijah said, "Come in. A worthy man like you must be
bringing good news."

43"Not at all!" Jonathan answered. "Our lord King David has
made Solomon king. 44The king has sent with him Zadok the
priest, Nathan the prophet, Benaiah son of Jehoiada, the Kerethites and the Pelethites, and they have put him on the king's mule,
45and Zadok the priest and Nathan the prophet have anointed
him king at Gihon. From there they have gone up cheering, and
the city resounds with it. That's the noise you hear. 46Moreover,
Solomon has taken his seat on the royal throne. 47Also, the royal
officials have come to congratulate our lord King David, saying,
'May your God make Solomon's name more famous than yours

(1:29–30) O God, our great Redeemer, You are faithful to those who love You. You assured David many years earlier that he would have a son named Solomon and that You would establish Solomon's throne forever. Now as David looked to the future of the kingdom, he remembered Your faithfulness in the past, and he himself was faithful to act according to Your desire. O Lord, as I face decisions that will impact the future, help me to remember Your faithfulness, to seek Your will and to be faithful to act according to Your desire. (1Ch 22:9–10)

God has been and continues to be faithful to his creation . . . Jesus' unfailing faithfulness is expressed in a most profound way by the Cross, in his willingness to take our deaths and our sins upon himself and to die for us. The Cross shows us that Jesus is faithful to us even when we deny him, forsake him, betray him, and even put him to death. Jesus' death on a cross is the supreme expression of God's faithfulness to you and me . . . God is trustworthy.

Jeffrey T. Wild

and his throne greater than yours!' And the king bowed in worship on his bed 48 and said, 'Praise be to the LORD, the God of Israel, who has allowed my eyes to see a successor on my throne
today.'"
49 At this, all Adonijah's guests rose in alarm and dispersed.
50 But Adonijah, in fear of Solomon, went and took hold of the
horns of the altar. 51 Then Solomon was told, "Adonijah is afraid
of King Solomon and is clinging to the horns of the altar. He says,
'Let King Solomon swear to me today that he will not put his servant to death with the sword.'"
52 Solomon replied, "If he shows himself to be a worthy man,
not a hair of his head will fall to the ground; but if evil is found in
him, he will die." 53 Then King Solomon sent men, and they
brought him down from the altar. And Adonijah came and bowed
down to King Solomon, and Solomon said, "Go to your home."

David's Charge to Solomon

2 When the time drew near for David to die, he gave a charge
to Solomon his son.
2 "I am about to go the way of all the earth," he said. "So be
strong, show yourself a man, 3 and observe what the LORD your
God requires: Walk in his ways, and keep his decrees and commands, his laws and requirements, as written in the Law of
Moses, so that you may prosper in all you do and wherever you
go, 4 and that the LORD may keep his promise to me: 'If your descendants watch how they live, and if they walk faithfully before
me with all their heart and soul, you will never fail to have a man
on the throne of Israel.'
5 "Now you yourself know what Joab son of Zeruiah did to
me—what he did to the two commanders of Israel's armies,
Abner son of Ner and Amasa son of Jether. He killed them, shedding their blood in peacetime as if in battle, and with that blood
stained the belt around his waist and the sandals on his feet.
6 Deal with him according to your wisdom, but do not let his gray
head go down to the grave[a] in peace.
7 "But show kindness to the sons of Barzillai of Gilead and let
them be among those who eat at your table. They stood by me
when I fled from your brother Absalom.
8 "And remember, you have with you Shimei son of Gera, the
Benjamite from Bahurim, who called down bitter curses on me
the day I went to Mahanaim. When he came down to meet me at
the Jordan, I swore to him by the LORD: 'I will not put you to death
by the sword.' 9 But now, do not consider him innocent. You are
a man of wisdom; you will know what to do to him. Bring his gray
head down to the grave in blood."
10 Then David rested with his fathers and was buried in the City
of David. 11 He had reigned forty years over Israel—seven years
in Hebron and thirty-three in Jerusalem. 12 So Solomon sat on the
throne of his father David, and his rule was firmly established.

Solomon's Throne Established

13 Now Adonijah, the son of Haggith, went to Bathsheba, Solomon's mother. Bathsheba asked him, "Do you come peacefully?"
He answered, "Yes, peacefully." 14 Then he added, "I have
something to say to you."

[a] 6 Hebrew *Sheol*; also in verse 9

Let each, in his own age, successively, keep God's charge, and then God will be sure to continue his word. We never let fall the promise till we let fall the precept. God had promised David that the Messiah should come from his loins, and that promise was absolute: but the promise that there should not fail him a man on the throne of Israel was conditional—if his seed behave themselves, as they should. If Solomon, in his day, fulfill the condition, he does his part towards the perpetuating of the promise. The condition is that he walk before God in all his institutions, in sincerity, with zeal and resolution.

Matthew Henry (1662-1714)

(2:1–4) O God, help me to pass on to my children a godly heritage. May they learn to fear You as their all-powerful God, and to love You as their all-merciful Father. May they walk in Your ways so that they might live in Your blessing; and may none of them ever fail to be found seated with Christ and reigning with him. (Ps 78:4–7; Eph 1:20; 2:6; 2Ti 2:12)

"You may say it," she replied.
15"As you know," he said, "the kingdom was mine. All Israel
looked to me as their king. But things changed, and the kingdom
has gone to my brother; for it has come to him from the LORD.
16Now I have one request to make of you. Do not refuse me."
"You may make it," she said.
17So he continued, "Please ask King Solomon—he will not
refuse you—to give me Abishag the Shunammite as my wife."
18"Very well," Bathsheba replied, "I will speak to the king for
you."
19When Bathsheba went to King Solomon to speak to him for
Adonijah, the king stood up to meet her, bowed down to her and
sat down on his throne. He had a throne brought for the king's
mother, and she sat down at his right hand.
20"I have one small request to make of you," she said. "Do not
refuse me."
The king replied, "Make it, my mother; I will not refuse you."
21So she said, "Let Abishag the Shunammite be given in marriage to your brother Adonijah."
22King Solomon answered his mother, "Why do you request
Abishag the Shunammite for Adonijah? You might as well request
the kingdom for him—after all, he is my older brother—yes, for
him and for Abiathar the priest and Joab son of Zeruiah!"
23Then King Solomon swore by the LORD: "May God deal with
me, be it ever so severely, if Adonijah does not pay with his life for
this request! 24And now, as surely as the LORD lives—he who has
established me securely on the throne of my father David and has
founded a dynasty for me as he promised—Adonijah shall be put
to death today!" 25So King Solomon gave orders to Benaiah son of
Jehoiada, and he struck down Adonijah and he died.
26To Abiathar the priest the king said, "Go back to your fields
in Anathoth. You deserve to die, but I will not put you to death
now, because you carried the ark of the Sovereign LORD before my
father David and shared all my father's hardships." 27So Solomon
removed Abiathar from the priesthood of the LORD, fulfilling the
word the LORD had spoken at Shiloh about the house of Eli.
28When the news reached Joab, who had conspired with Adonijah though not with Absalom, he fled to the tent of the LORD and
took hold of the horns of the altar. 29King Solomon was told that
Joab had fled to the tent of the LORD and was beside the altar.
Then Solomon ordered Benaiah son of Jehoiada, "Go, strike him
down!"
30So Benaiah entered the tent of the LORD and said to Joab,
"The king says, 'Come out!' "
But he answered, "No, I will die here."
Benaiah reported to the king, "This is how Joab answered me."
31Then the king commanded Benaiah, "Do as he says. Strike
him down and bury him, and so clear me and my father's house
of the guilt of the innocent blood that Joab shed. 32The LORD will
repay him for the blood he shed, because without the knowledge
of my father David he attacked two men and killed them with the
sword. Both of them—Abner son of Ner, commander of Israel's
army, and Amasa son of Jether, commander of Judah's army—
were better men and more upright than he. 33May the guilt of
their blood rest on the head of Joab and his descendants forever.
But on David and his descendants, his house and his throne, may
there be the LORD's peace forever."

(2:13–33) "The acts of the sinful nature are obvious . . . hatred, discord, jealousy, fits of rage, selfish ambition, dissentions, factions and envy . . . Those who live like this will not inherit the kingdom of God." Blind ambition was Adonijah's downfall. Not only did it cost him his own life, but it unleashed a fury of violence that removed all other potential rivals from Solomon's court. Teach us, Lord, to entrust the future to You and to allow You to lift us up or humble us according to Your plans and purposes. Your Word makes the alternative all too clear—"pride goes before destruction, a haughty spirit before a fall." (Pr 16:18; Gal 5:19–21)

Out of unrest and arrogant pride,
Jesus, I come; Jesus, I come.
Into Thy blessed will to abide,
Jesus, I come to Thee.
Out of myself to dwell in Thy love,
Out of despair into raptures above,
Upward for aye on wings like a dove,
Jesus, I come to Thee.

Jesus, I Come
William T. Sleeper (1887)

34So Benaiah son of Jehoiada went up and struck down Joab
and killed him, and he was buried on his own land[a] in the desert.
35The king put Benaiah son of Jehoiada over the army in Joab's
position and replaced Abiathar with Zadok the priest.

36Then the king sent for Shimei and said to him, "Build yourself a house in Jerusalem and live there, but do not go anywhere
else. 37The day you leave and cross the Kidron Valley, you can be
sure you will die; your blood will be on your own head."

38Shimei answered the king, "What you say is good. Your servant will do as my lord the king has said." And Shimei stayed in Jerusalem for a long time.

39But three years later, two of Shimei's slaves ran off to Achish son of Maacah, king of Gath, and Shimei was told, "Your slaves
are in Gath." 40At this, he saddled his donkey and went to Achish at Gath in search of his slaves. So Shimei went away and brought the slaves back from Gath.

41When Solomon was told that Shimei had gone from Jerusalem to Gath and had returned,
42the king summoned Shimei and said to him, "Did I not make you swear by the LORD and warn you, 'On the day you leave to go anywhere else, you can be sure you will die'? At that time you said to me, 'What you say is good. I will obey.'
43Why then did you not keep your oath to the LORD and obey the command I gave you?"

44The king also said to Shimei, "You know in your heart all the wrong you did to my father David. Now the LORD will repay you for your wrongdoing.
45But King Solomon will be blessed, and David's throne will remain secure before the LORD forever."

46Then the king gave the order to Benaiah son of Jehoiada, and he went out and struck Shimei down and killed him.

The kingdom was now firmly established in Solomon's hands.

Solomon Asks for Wisdom

3 Solomon made an alliance with Pharaoh king of Egypt and married his daughter. He brought her to the City of David until he finished building his palace and the temple of the LORD, and the wall around Jerusalem.
2The people, however, were still sacrificing at the high places, because a temple had not yet been built for the Name of the LORD.
3Solomon showed his love for the LORD by walking according to the statutes of his father David, except that he offered sacrifices and burned incense on the high places.

4The king went to Gibeon to offer sacrifices, for that was the most important high place, and Solomon offered a thousand burnt offerings on that altar.
5At Gibeon the LORD appeared to Solomon during the night in a dream, and God said, "Ask for whatever you want me to give you."

6Solomon answered, "You have shown great kindness to your servant, my father David, because he was faithful to you and righteous and upright in heart. You have continued this great kindness to him and have given him a son to sit on his throne this very day.

7"Now, O LORD my God, you have made your servant king in place of my father David. But I am only a little child and do not know how to carry out my duties.
8Your servant is here among the people you have chosen, a great people, too numerous to

[a]34 Or *buried in his tomb*

(3:3) Solomon loved You. He showed that he loved You not just "with words or tongue but with actions and in truth." He loved You in such a way that everyone else knew it. Lord, would anyone who watched my life be surprised to learn that I love You? Do my actions speak louder than my words? Am I an embarrassed Christian? Are You an embarrassed God? (1Jn 3:18)

God is entitled to our love. Why? Because he gave himself for us despite the fact that we are so undeserving. What better could he have given? If we ask why God is entitled to our love, we should answer, "Because he first loved us." God is clearly deserving of our love, especially if we consider who he is that loves us, who we are that he loves, and how much he loves us.

And who is God? Is he not the one to whom every spirit bears witness: "Thou art my God"? God has no need of our worldly possessions. True love is precisely this: that it does not seek its own interests. And how much does he love us? He so loved the world that he gave his only Son; he laid down his life for us.

Bernard of Clairvaux (1090-1153)

(3:9–15) All wisdom comes from You, Father. Solomon's request for Your wisdom revealed the longing in his heart to serve You and to please You. He did not seek wealth or power or love, but he simply asked for Your gift of wisdom, knowing that all else would follow. In much the same way, You have said that it is wise for us to seek Your kingdom and righteousness first. You have promised that when we do so, everything else we need will be given to us as well. (Mt 6:33)

The greatest demonstration of God's Father heart is revealed in His attention to the details of our lives. He longs to surprise us with the "extras," those little pleasures and treasures that only a father would know we desire. God is not stingy, possessive, or materialistic. We often use people as things; He uses things to bless people. And He manifests His generosity through more important gifts than just material goods. He freely gives us the priceless intangibles of forgiveness, mercy, and love.

Floyd McClung, Jr. (1945-)

Seek ye first the kingdom of God
And His righteousness;
And all these things shall
Be added unto you,
Allelu, Alleluia.

"Seek Ye First"
Karen Lafferty (©1972)

count or number. 9So give your servant a discerning heart to govern your people and to distinguish between right and wrong. For
who is able to govern this great people of yours?"
10The Lord was pleased that Solomon had asked for this. 11So
God said to him, "Since you have asked for this and not for long
life or wealth for yourself, nor have asked for the death of your
enemies but for discernment in administering justice, 12I will do
what you have asked. I will give you a wise and discerning heart,
so that there will never have been anyone like you, nor will there
ever be. 13Moreover, I will give you what you have not asked
for—both riches and honor—so that in your lifetime you will
have no equal among kings. 14And if you walk in my ways and
obey my statutes and commands as David your father did, I will
give you a long life." 15Then Solomon awoke—and he realized it
had been a dream.

He returned to Jerusalem, stood before the ark of the Lord's covenant and sacrificed burnt offerings and fellowship offerings.[a] Then he gave a feast for all his court.

A Wise Ruling

16Now two prostitutes came to the king and stood before him.
17One of them said, "My lord, this woman and I live in the same
house. I had a baby while she was there with me. 18The third day
after my child was born, this woman also had a baby. We were
alone; there was no one in the house but the two of us.
19"During the night this woman's son died because she lay on
him. 20So she got up in the middle of the night and took my son
from my side while I your servant was asleep. She put him by her
breast and put her dead son by my breast. 21The next morning, I
got up to nurse my son—and he was dead! But when I looked at
him closely in the morning light, I saw that it wasn't the son I had
borne."
22The other woman said, "No! The living one is my son; the
dead one is yours."

But the first one insisted, "No! The dead one is yours; the living one is mine." And so they argued before the king.

23The king said, "This one says, 'My son is alive and your son
is dead,' while that one says, 'No! Your son is dead and mine is
alive.' "
24Then the king said, "Bring me a sword." So they brought a
sword for the king. 25He then gave an order: "Cut the living child
in two and give half to one and half to the other."
26The woman whose son was alive was filled with compassion
for her son and said to the king, "Please, my lord, give her the living baby! Don't kill him!"

But the other said, "Neither I nor you shall have him. Cut him in two!"

27Then the king gave his ruling: "Give the living baby to the
first woman. Do not kill him; she is his mother."
28When all Israel heard the verdict the king had given, they
held the king in awe, because they saw that he had wisdom from
God to administer justice.

[a] 15 Traditionally *peace offerings*

Solomon's Officials and Governors

4 So King Solomon ruled over all Israel. 2And these were his chief officials:

Azariah son of Zadok—the priest;
3Elihoreph and Ahijah, sons of Shisha—secretaries;
Jehoshaphat son of Ahilud—recorder;
4Benaiah son of Jehoiada—commander in chief;
Zadok and Abiathar—priests;
5Azariah son of Nathan—in charge of the district officers;
Zabud son of Nathan—a priest and personal adviser to the king;
6Ahishar—in charge of the palace;
Adoniram son of Abda—in charge of forced labor.

7Solomon also had twelve district governors over all Israel, who supplied provisions for the king and the royal household. Each one had to provide supplies for one month in the year.
8These are their names:

Ben-Hur—in the hill country of Ephraim;
9Ben-Deker—in Makaz, Shaalbim, Beth Shemesh and Elon Bethhanan;
10Ben-Hesed—in Arubboth (Socoh and all the land of Hepher were his);
11Ben-Abinadab—in Naphoth Dor[a] (he was married to Taphath daughter of Solomon);
12Baana son of Ahilud—in Taanach and Megiddo, and in all of Beth Shan next to Zarethan below Jezreel, from Beth Shan to Abel Meholah across to Jokmeam;
13Ben-Geber—in Ramoth Gilead (the settlements of Jair son of Manasseh in Gilead were his, as well as the district of Argob in Bashan and its sixty large walled cities with bronze gate bars);
14Ahinadab son of Iddo—in Mahanaim;
15Ahimaaz—in Naphtali (he had married Basemath daughter of Solomon);
16Baana son of Hushai—in Asher and in Aloth;
17Jehoshaphat son of Paruah—in Issachar;
18Shimei son of Ela—in Benjamin;
19Geber son of Uri—in Gilead (the country of Sihon king of the Amorites and the country of Og king of Bashan). He was the only governor over the district.

Solomon's Daily Provisions

20The people of Judah and Israel were as numerous as the
sand on the seashore; they ate, they drank and they were happy.
21And Solomon ruled over all the kingdoms from the River[b] to
the land of the Philistines, as far as the border of Egypt. These
countries brought tribute and were Solomon's subjects all his life.
22Solomon's daily provisions were thirty cors[c] of fine flour and
sixty cors[d] of meal, 23ten head of stall-fed cattle, twenty of pas-
ture-fed cattle and a hundred sheep and goats, as well as deer, gazelles, roebucks and choice fowl. 24For he ruled over all the
kingdoms west of the River, from Tiphsah to Gaza, and had peace

[a] *11* Or *in the heights of Dor* [b] *21* That is, the Euphrates; also in verse 24 [c] *22* That is, probably about 185 bushels (about 6.6 kiloliters) [d] *22* That is, probably about 375 bushels (about 13.2 kiloliters)

(4:20–25) Father, I praise You for always keeping Your promises. As You promised Abraham, the people of Judah and Israel were "as numerous as the sand of the seashore," and they had "[taken] possession of the cities of their enemies." As You promised David, You granted Israel peace and quiet during Solomon's reign. And as You promised Solomon, You gave him a wise and discerning heart and great riches and honor so that he had no equal among kings. Truly, "the LORD bestows favor and honor; no good thing does he withhold from those whose walk is blameless." (Ge 22:17; 1Ki 3:13; 1Ch 22:9; Ps 84:11)

No one yet has ever set out to test God's promises fairly, thoroughly, and humbly, and had to report that God's promises don't work.

On the contrary, given a fair opportunity, God always surprises and overwhelms those who truly seek, with His bounty and His power.

Peter Marshall (1902-1949)

You underscored in Your Word how appropriate it was that Solomon, having the choice of asking anything he wished, asked for wisdom rather than riches.

Now, as I come before You today, Lord, I feel very unlike Solomon. I am too inclined to seek a shortcut to solutions. I am too quick to suppose easy answers are forthcoming. But I'm here to make the one request You've taught me for such situations: "Ask in faith (for wisdom), nothing doubting." And I'm encouraged to believe—in fact, Father, I do—I do believe You are ready this moment to give me wisdom for today, wisdom for its decisions, wisdom for my conversations, and wisdom for touching others with Your love. And the reason I do believe is not only because You have said You will give freely to those who ask, but because You have made Jesus to become wisdom for me and unto me. And it is in His name I pray. Amen.

Dick Eastman (1944-) and Jack Hayford (1934-)

(4:29–34) Father, I marvel at the wisdom You gave to Solomon—wisdom as measureless "as the sand on the seashore" to lead a people who were "as numerous as the sand on the seashore." You fully equipped him for the task that You assigned him. But as powerful and as wise as Solomon was, there would one day be another king, a descendant of Solomon's line, the Lord Jesus Christ, the "one greater than Solomon" who would himself be "the power of God and the wisdom of God." Lord Jesus, I worship You as the King of kings. (1Ki 4:20; Mt 12:42; 1Co 1:24; Heb 13:21)

on all sides. 25During Solomon's lifetime Judah and Israel, from
Dan to Beersheba, lived in safety, each man under his own vine
and fig tree.
26Solomon had four[a] thousand stalls for chariot horses, and
twelve thousand horses.[b]
27The district officers, each in his month, supplied provisions
for King Solomon and all who came to the king's table. They saw
to it that nothing was lacking. 28They also brought to the proper
place their quotas of barley and straw for the chariot horses and
the other horses.

Solomon's Wisdom

29God gave Solomon wisdom and very great insight, and a
breadth of understanding as measureless as the sand on the
seashore. 30Solomon's wisdom was greater than the wisdom of all
the men of the East, and greater than all the wisdom of Egypt.
31He was wiser than any other man, including Ethan the Ezrahite—wiser than Heman, Calcol and Darda, the sons of Mahol.
And his fame spread to all the surrounding nations. 32He spoke
three thousand proverbs and his songs numbered a thousand and
five. 33He described plant life, from the cedar of Lebanon to the
hyssop that grows out of walls. He also taught about animals and
birds, reptiles and fish. 34Men of all nations came to listen to Solomon's wisdom, sent by all the kings of the world, who had heard
of his wisdom.

Preparations for Building the Temple

5 When Hiram king of Tyre heard that Solomon had been
anointed king to succeed his father David, he sent his envoys
to Solomon, because he had always been on friendly terms with
David. 2Solomon sent back this message to Hiram:

3"You know that because of the wars waged against my father David from all sides, he could not build a temple for the
Name of the LORD his God until the LORD put his enemies
under his feet. 4But now the LORD my God has given me rest
on every side, and there is no adversary or disaster. 5I intend, therefore, to build a temple for the Name of the LORD
my God, as the LORD told my father David, when he said,
'Your son whom I will put on the throne in your place will
build the temple for my Name.'
6"So give orders that cedars of Lebanon be cut for me. My
men will work with yours, and I will pay you for your men
whatever wages you set. You know that we have no one so
skilled in felling timber as the Sidonians."

7When Hiram heard Solomon's message, he was greatly
pleased and said, "Praise be to the LORD today, for he has given
David a wise son to rule over this great nation."
8So Hiram sent word to Solomon:

"I have received the message you sent me and will do all
you want in providing the cedar and pine logs. 9My men will
haul them down from Lebanon to the sea, and I will float
them in rafts by sea to the place you specify. There I will sep-

[a] *26* Some Septuagint manuscripts (see also 2 Chron. 9:25); Hebrew *forty* [b] *26* Or *charioteers*

arate them and you can take them away. And you are to grant
my wish by providing food for my royal household."
10 In this way Hiram kept Solomon supplied with all the cedar
and pine logs he wanted, 11 and Solomon gave Hiram twenty thousand cors[a] of wheat as food for his household, in addition to twenty thousand baths[b,c] of pressed olive oil. Solomon continued to
do this for Hiram year after year. 12 The LORD gave Solomon wisdom, just as he had promised him. There were peaceful relations
between Hiram and Solomon, and the two of them made a treaty.
13 King Solomon conscripted laborers from all Israel—thirty
thousand men. 14 He sent them off to Lebanon in shifts of ten thousand a month, so that they spent one month in Lebanon and two
months at home. Adoniram was in charge of the forced labor.
15 Solomon had seventy thousand carriers and eighty thousand
stonecutters in the hills, 16 as well as thirty-three hundred[d] foremen who supervised the project and directed the workmen. 17 At
the king's command they removed from the quarry large blocks of
quality stone to provide a foundation of dressed stone for the temple. 18 The craftsmen of Solomon and Hiram and the men of
Gebal[e] cut and prepared the timber and stone for the building of
the temple.

Solomon Builds the Temple

6 In the four hundred and eightieth[f] year after the Israelites
had come out of Egypt, in the fourth year of Solomon's reign
over Israel, in the month of Ziv, the second month, he began to
build the temple of the LORD.
2 The temple that King Solomon built for the LORD was sixty cubits long, twenty wide and thirty high.[g] 3 The portico at the front of
the main hall of the temple extended the width of the temple, that
is twenty cubits,[h] and projected ten cubits[i] from the front of the
temple. 4 He made narrow clerestory windows in the temple.
5 Against the walls of the main hall and inner sanctuary he built a
structure around the building, in which there were side rooms.
6 The lowest floor was five cubits[j] wide, the middle floor six cubits[k] and the third floor seven.[l] He made offset ledges around the
outside of the temple so that nothing would be inserted into the
temple walls.
7 In building the temple, only blocks dressed at the quarry were
used, and no hammer, chisel or any other iron tool was heard at
the temple site while it was being built.
8 The entrance to the lowest[m] floor was on the south side of the
temple; a stairway led up to the middle level and from there to the
third. 9 So he built the temple and completed it, roofing it with
beams and cedar planks. 10 And he built the side rooms all along
the temple. The height of each was five cubits, and they were attached to the temple by beams of cedar.
11 The word of the LORD came to Solomon: 12 "As for this temple
you are building, if you follow my decrees, carry out my regula-

[a] *11* That is, probably about 125,000 bushels (about 4,400 kiloliters) [b] *11* Septuagint (see also 2 Chron. 2:10); Hebrew *twenty cors* [c] *11* That is, about 115,000 gallons (about 440 kiloliters) [d] *16* Hebrew; some Septuagint manuscripts (see also 2 Chron. 2:2, 18) *thirty-six hundred* [e] *18* That is, Byblos [f] *1* Hebrew; Septuagint *four hundred and fortieth* [g] *2* That is, about 90 feet (about 27 meters) long and 30 feet (about 9 meters) wide and 45 feet (about 13.5 meters) high [h] *3* That is, about 30 feet (about 9 meters) [i] *3* That is, about 15 feet (about 4.5 meters) [j] *6* That is, about 7 1/2 feet (about 2.3 meters); also in verses 10 and 24 [k] *6* That is, about 9 feet (about 2.7 meters) [l] *6* That is, about 10 1/2 feet (about 3.1 meters) [m] *8* Septuagint; Hebrew *middle*

(6:1–13) It was Solomon's dream to build a temple for You, Lord, and he set out to do so on a grand scale. He spared no expense, overlooked no detail, and brought into service every person he could find to complete the task. Today, in another time and place, You have promised to make Your temple in our hearts. Should we be less enthusiastic, less committed as we prepare our hearts to worship You in spirit and in truth? (Jn 4:24)

We dedicate this temple,
O Father, unto Thee
The God of ancient ages
And ages yet to be:
That here our hearts may worship
And here our songs ascend
In loving adoration
And praise that knows no end.

"We Dedicate This Temple"
Ernest K. Emurian (©1952)

All genuine worship is . . . heartfelt response to the truth of God and His Word. Truth is the objective factor in worship, and spirit is the subjective. Both must come together . . . The nature of worship, then, is to offer God worship from the depths of our inner beings in praise, prayer, song, giving, and living, always based upon His revealed truth. The person who would worship God must therefore have a faithful commitment to the Word of God. Worship does not happen by a zap out of heaven that makes us fall down. It is the overflow of our understanding of God as He has revealed Himself in the Scriptures. That is worshiping in spirit and in truth.

John MacArthur, Jr. (1939-)

(6:14–38) The glory of Your presence was reflected in Solomon's temple. It bore witness to the awe and reverence Your people felt for You. The most exquisite gold, wood and stone were used to make Your house a masterpiece of fine art. Gifted artisans and craftsmen presented their skills to You as offerings of praise. Even today, as we dedicate our efforts to Your service, may we generously bring our best gifts, for all things belong to You, and You have called us to invest our talents wisely in Your worship. (Mt 25:14–30)

There are many who profess to love God and his cause but are not dedicated to it. They go to church regularly. They read their Bibles. They pray that the work of the Lord will be carried to all corners of the earth. They give tithes and offerings on occasion. They participate in the church services and call themselves Christian, but are they actually willing to share, to give their best for Christ's cause? On every hand there is need for an understanding of the importance of all-out consecration of the faculties God has given us. Without this consecration, God cannot work in us and through us to accomplish his purpose in our lives or in the world.

Clarence W. Hatch

Of your time and talents give ye
They are gifts from God above
To be used by Christians freely
To proclaim His wondrous love.
Come again to serve the Savior;
Tithes and off'rings with you bring.
In your work, with Him find favor,
And with joy His praises sing.

"Come, All Christians Be Committed"
Eva B. Lloyd (©1966)

tions and keep all my commands and obey them, I will fulfill
through you the promise I gave to David your father. 13And I will
live among the Israelites and will not abandon my people Israel."
14So Solomon built the temple and completed it. 15He lined its
interior walls with cedar boards, paneling them from the floor of
the temple to the ceiling, and covered the floor of the temple with
planks of pine. 16He partitioned off twenty cubits[a] at the rear of
the temple with cedar boards from floor to ceiling to form within the temple an inner sanctuary, the Most Holy Place. 17The main
hall in front of this room was forty cubits[b] long. 18The inside of
the temple was cedar, carved with gourds and open flowers.
Everything was cedar; no stone was to be seen.
19He prepared the inner sanctuary within the temple to set the
ark of the covenant of the LORD there. 20The inner sanctuary was
twenty cubits long, twenty wide and twenty high.[c] He overlaid the
inside with pure gold, and he also overlaid the altar of cedar.
21Solomon covered the inside of the temple with pure gold, and
he extended gold chains across the front of the inner sanctuary,
which was overlaid with gold. 22So he overlaid the whole interior with gold. He also overlaid with gold the altar that belonged to
the inner sanctuary.
23In the inner sanctuary he made a pair of cherubim of olive
wood, each ten cubits[d] high. 24One wing of the first cherub was
five cubits long, and the other wing five cubits—ten cubits from
wing tip to wing tip. 25The second cherub also measured ten cubits, for the two cherubim were identical in size and shape. 26The
height of each cherub was ten cubits. 27He placed the cherubim
inside the innermost room of the temple, with their wings spread
out. The wing of one cherub touched one wall, while the wing of
the other touched the other wall, and their wings touched each
other in the middle of the room. 28He overlaid the cherubim with
gold.
29On the walls all around the temple, in both the inner and
outer rooms, he carved cherubim, palm trees and open flowers.
30He also covered the floors of both the inner and outer rooms of
the temple with gold.
31For the entrance of the inner sanctuary he made doors of
olive wood with five-sided jambs. 32And on the two olive wood
doors he carved cherubim, palm trees and open flowers, and
overlaid the cherubim and palm trees with beaten gold. 33In the
same way he made four-sided jambs of olive wood for the entrance to the main hall. 34He also made two pine doors, each having two leaves that turned in sockets. 35He carved cherubim,
palm trees and open flowers on them and overlaid them with gold
hammered evenly over the carvings.
36And he built the inner courtyard of three courses of dressed
stone and one course of trimmed cedar beams.
37The foundation of the temple of the LORD was laid in the
fourth year, in the month of Ziv. 38In the eleventh year in the
month of Bul, the eighth month, the temple was finished in all its
details according to its specifications. He had spent seven years
building it.

[a] *16* That is, about 30 feet (about 9 meters) [b] *17* That is, about 60 feet (about 18 meters) [c] *20* That is, about 30 feet (about 9 meters) long, wide and high [d] *23* That is, about 15 feet (about 4.5 meters)

Solomon Builds His Palace

7 It took Solomon thirteen years, however, to complete the
construction of his palace. [2]He built the Palace of the Forest
of Lebanon a hundred cubits long, fifty wide and thirty high,[a] with
four rows of cedar columns supporting trimmed cedar beams.
[3]It was roofed with cedar above the beams that rested on the
columns—forty-five beams, fifteen to a row. [4]Its windows were
placed high in sets of three, facing each other. [5]All the doorways
had rectangular frames; they were in the front part in sets of
three, facing each other.[b]

[6]He made a colonnade fifty cubits long and thirty wide.[c] In
front of it was a portico, and in front of that were pillars and an
overhanging roof.

[7]He built the throne hall, the Hall of Justice, where he was to
judge, and he covered it with cedar from floor to ceiling.[d] [8]And
the palace in which he was to live, set farther back, was similar in
design. Solomon also made a palace like this hall for Pharaoh's
daughter, whom he had married.

[9]All these structures, from the outside to the great courtyard
and from foundation to eaves, were made of blocks of high-grade
stone cut to size and trimmed with a saw on their inner and outer
faces. [10]The foundations were laid with large stones of good quality, some measuring ten cubits[e] and some eight.[f] [11]Above were
high-grade stones, cut to size, and cedar beams. [12]The great
courtyard was surrounded by a wall of three courses of dressed
stone and one course of trimmed cedar beams, as was the inner
courtyard of the temple of the LORD with its portico.

The Temple's Furnishings

[13]King Solomon sent to Tyre and brought Huram,[g] [14]whose
mother was a widow from the tribe of Naphtali and whose father
was a man of Tyre and a craftsman in bronze. Huram was highly
skilled and experienced in all kinds of bronze work. He came to
King Solomon and did all the work assigned to him.

[15]He cast two bronze pillars, each eighteen cubits high and
twelve cubits around,[h] by line. [16]He also made two capitals of
cast bronze to set on the tops of the pillars; each capital was five
cubits[i] high. [17]A network of interwoven chains festooned the capitals on top of the pillars, seven for each capital. [18]He made
pomegranates in two rows[j] encircling each network to decorate
the capitals on top of the pillars.[k] He did the same for each capital. [19]The capitals on top of the pillars in the portico were in the
shape of lilies, four cubits[l] high. [20]On the capitals of both pillars,
above the bowl-shaped part next to the network, were the two
hundred pomegranates in rows all around. [21]He erected the pillars at the portico of the temple. The pillar to the south he named
Jakin[m] and the one to the north Boaz.[n] [22]The capitals on top

[a] *2* That is, about 150 feet (about 46 meters) long, 75 feet (about 23 meters) wide and 45 feet (about 13.5 meters) high [b] *5* The meaning of the Hebrew for this verse is uncertain. [c] *6* That is, about 75 feet (about 23 meters) long and 45 feet (about 13.5 meters) wide [d] *7* Vulgate and Syriac; Hebrew *floor* [e] *10* That is, about 15 feet (about 4.5 meters) [f] *10* That is, about 12 feet (about 3.6 meters) [g] *13* Hebrew *Hiram*, a variant of *Huram*; also in verses 40 and 45 [h] *15* That is, about 27 feet (about 8.1 meters) high and 18 feet (about 5.4 meters) around [i] *16* That is, about 7 1/2 feet (about 2.3 meters); also in verse 23 [j] *18* Two Hebrew manuscripts and Septuagint; most Hebrew manuscripts *made the pillars, and there were two rows* [k] *18* Many Hebrew manuscripts and Syriac; most Hebrew manuscripts *pomegranates* [l] *19* That is, about 6 feet (about 1.8 meters); also in verse 38 [m] *21* *Jakin* probably means *he establishes.* [n] *21* *Boaz* probably means *in him is strength.*

He is the living God, that clothes the earth with grass and herbs, causes the trees to grow and bring forth food for you, and makes the fishes of the sea to breathe and live. He makes the fowls of the air to breed and causes the buck and the doe, the creatures, and all the beasts to bring forth whereby they may be food for you. He is the living God, that causes the sun to give warmth to you, to nourish you when you are cold. He is the living God, that causes the snow and frost to melt and causes the rain to water the plants. He is the living God, that made heaven and earth, the clouds, causes the springs to break out of the rocks, and divided the great sea from the earth. He divides the light from the darkness, by which it is called day and the darkness night . . . He is to be worshiped that does this. He is the living God that gives you breath, life, and strength and gives you beasts and cattle whereby you may be fed and clothed. He is the living God, and he is to be worshiped.

This is the King of Kings and Lord of Lords, in whose hand is the breath of all mankind.

George Fox (1624–1691)

(7:13–21) Lord God, we long to worship You with excellence. Huram was an engraver and a craftsman—one of the great artists of the ancient world. He generously poured his immense talent into the furnishing of Your house. Nothing was too good for You during that time of history—but it is not always so today. Lord, restore our sense of reverence. Teach us to offer our very best to You in the service of worship.

We dedicate this temple,
This labor of our hands,
To Father, Son, and Spirit,
Whose temple ever stands
In hearts that learn to love Thee
And minds that comprehend,
In wills empow'red to witness
Thy kingdom without end!

"We Dedicate This Temple"
Ernest K. Emurian (©1952)

were in the shape of lilies. And so the work on the pillars was
completed.
23He made the Sea of cast metal, circular in shape, measuring
ten cubits[a] from rim to rim and five cubits high. It took a line of
thirty cubits[b] to measure around it. 24Below the rim, gourds encircled it—ten to a cubit. The gourds were cast in two rows in
one piece with the Sea.
25The Sea stood on twelve bulls, three facing north, three facing west, three facing south and three facing east. The Sea rested
on top of them, and their hindquarters were toward the center.
26It was a handbreadth[c] in thickness, and its rim was like the rim
of a cup, like a lily blossom. It held two thousand baths.[d]
27He also made ten movable stands of bronze; each was four
cubits long, four wide and three high.[e] 28This is how the stands
were made: They had side panels attached to uprights. 29On the
panels between the uprights were lions, bulls and cherubim—
and on the uprights as well. Above and below the lions and bulls
were wreaths of hammered work. 30Each stand had four bronze
wheels with bronze axles, and each had a basin resting on four
supports, cast with wreaths on each side. 31On the inside of the
stand there was an opening that had a circular frame one cubit[f]
deep. This opening was round, and with its basework it measured
a cubit and a half.[g] Around its opening there was engraving. The
panels of the stands were square, not round. 32The four wheels
were under the panels, and the axles of the wheels were attached
to the stand. The diameter of each wheel was a cubit and a half.
33The wheels were made like chariot wheels; the axles, rims,
spokes and hubs were all of cast metal.
34Each stand had four handles, one on each corner, projecting
from the stand. 35At the top of the stand there was a circular band
half a cubit[h] deep. The supports and panels were attached to the
top of the stand. 36He engraved cherubim, lions and palm trees
on the surfaces of the supports and on the panels, in every available space, with wreaths all around. 37This is the way he made
the ten stands. They were all cast in the same molds and were
identical in size and shape.
38He then made ten bronze basins, each holding forty baths[i]
and measuring four cubits across, one basin to go on each of the
ten stands. 39He placed five of the stands on the south side of the
temple and five on the north. He placed the Sea on the south side,
at the southeast corner of the temple. 40He also made the basins
and shovels and sprinkling bowls.
So Huram finished all the work he had undertaken for King
Solomon in the temple of the LORD:

41the two pillars;
the two bowl-shaped capitals on top of the pillars;
the two sets of network decorating the two bowl-shaped capitals on top of the pillars;
42the four hundred pomegranates for the two sets of network (two rows of pomegranates for each network, decorating the bowl-shaped capitals on top of the pillars);

(7:23–26) Holy and righteous God, the great Sea that Solomon designed for Your temple speaks of our enormous need for cleansing. All the water in the world could not wash away our sinful nature. But by Your grace, the blood of Your Lamb has cleansed us from all unrighteousness. How we thank You that one day we will stand in His presence beside a great heavenly sea, saying, "Worthy is the Lamb, who was slain, to receive power and wealth and wisdom and strength and honor and glory and praise!" (Rev 4:6; 5:12)

[a] *23* That is, about 15 feet (about 4.5 meters) [b] *23* That is, about 45 feet (about 13.5 meters) [c] *26* That is, about 3 inches (about 8 centimeters) [d] *26* That is, probably about 11,500 gallons (about 44 kiloliters); the Septuagint does not have this sentence. [e] *27* That is, about 6 feet (about 1.8 meters) long and wide and about 4 1/2 feet (about 1.3 meters) high [f] *31* That is, about 1 1/2 feet (about 0.5 meter) [g] *31* That is, about 2 1/4 feet (about 0.7 meter); also in verse 32 [h] *35* That is, about 3/4 foot (about 0.2 meter) [i] *38* That is, about 230 gallons (about 880 liters)

43 the ten stands with their ten basins;
44 the Sea and the twelve bulls under it;
45 the pots, shovels and sprinkling bowls.

All these objects that Huram made for King Solomon for the
temple of the LORD were of burnished bronze. 46 The king had
them cast in clay molds in the plain of the Jordan between Succoth and Zarethan. 47 Solomon left all these things unweighed,
because there were so many; the weight of the bronze was not
determined.

48 Solomon also made all the furnishings that were in the LORD's
temple:

the golden altar;
the golden table on which was the bread of the Presence;
49 the lampstands of pure gold (five on the right and five on the
left, in front of the inner sanctuary);
the gold floral work and lamps and tongs;
50 the pure gold basins, wick trimmers, sprinkling bowls,
dishes and censers;
and the gold sockets for the doors of the innermost room,
the Most Holy Place, and also for the doors of the main
hall of the temple.

51 When all the work King Solomon had done for the temple of
the LORD was finished, he brought in the things his father David
had dedicated—the silver and gold and the furnishings—and he
placed them in the treasuries of the LORD's temple.

The Ark Brought to the Temple

8 Then King Solomon summoned into his presence at Jerusalem the elders of Israel, all the heads of the tribes and the
chiefs of the Israelite families, to bring up the ark of the LORD's
covenant from Zion, the City of David. 2 All the men of Israel came
together to King Solomon at the time of the festival in the month
of Ethanim, the seventh month.

3 When all the elders of Israel had arrived, the priests took up
the ark, 4 and they brought up the ark of the LORD and the Tent of
Meeting and all the sacred furnishings in it. The priests and Levites carried them up, 5 and King Solomon and the entire assembly of Israel that had gathered about him were before the ark,
sacrificing so many sheep and cattle that they could not be
recorded or counted.

6 The priests then brought the ark of the LORD's covenant to its
place in the inner sanctuary of the temple, the Most Holy Place,
and put it beneath the wings of the cherubim. 7 The cherubim
spread their wings over the place of the ark and overshadowed
the ark and its carrying poles. 8 These poles were so long that
their ends could be seen from the Holy Place in front of the inner
sanctuary, but not from outside the Holy Place; and they are still
there today. 9 There was nothing in the ark except the two stone
tablets that Moses had placed in it at Horeb, where the LORD made
a covenant with the Israelites after they came out of Egypt.

10 When the priests withdrew from the Holy Place, the cloud
filled the temple of the LORD. 11 And the priests could not perform
their service because of the cloud, for the glory of the LORD filled
his temple.

12 Then Solomon said, "The LORD has said that he would dwell

God of wonder, God of splendor,
God of all the earth adored.
God of light and my salvation,
Holy are You, Lord.

God of glory, God of mercy,
God, Emmanuel proclaimed
Shining light to ev'ry nation,
Holy is Your name.

You alone are worthy,
You alone are worthy,
You alone are worthy of our praise.

"God of Wonder"
Steve McEwan (©1996)

(8:1–11) Lord, just as Your visible presence descended on the tabernacle in the wilderness, so You came to dwell in Solomon's temple. Your cloud once again provided clear evidence of Your willingness to dwell in the midst of Your people. As I prepare the temple of my heart for You, I offer You my best gifts and my finest possessions. I invite You to come and dwell in me, and I pray that Your glory may be clearly evident in my life, for all the world to see. (Ex 40:34–35; 2Co 3:18; Col 1:27)

Open your soul and entertain the glory of God and after a while that glory will be reflected in the world about you and in the very clouds above your head.

Frank Laubach (1884–1970)

(8:27–30) You are too great, Sovereign Lord, to dwell in a house made with human hands. You are too vast for us to comprehend. Yet because of Your immeasurable love You condescend to dwell in our hearts. You hear our prayers; You forgive our sins. We are now the temples of the Holy Spirit, and because of Your presence in our lives we now bear the name and the likeness of Christ. Praise Your holy name. (Isa 66:1–2; 1Co 6:19–20; 2Co 3:18)

The Temple of Solomon was absolutely surrendered to God when it was dedicated to Him. And every one of us is a temple of God, in which God will dwell and work mightily on one condition–absolute surrender to Him. God claims it, God is worthy of it, and without it God cannot work His blessed work in us.

God not only claims it, but God will work it Himself . . . If there is anything holding you back, or any sacrifice you are afraid of making, come to God now, and prove how gracious your God is, and be not afraid that He will command from you what He will not bestow.

Andrew Murray (1828-1917)

in a dark cloud; 13I have indeed built a magnificent temple for
you, a place for you to dwell forever."
14While the whole assembly of Israel was standing there, the
king turned around and blessed them. 15Then he said:

"Praise be to the LORD, the God of Israel, who with his
own hand has fulfilled what he promised with his own
mouth to my father David. For he said, 16'Since the day I
brought my people Israel out of Egypt, I have not chosen a
city in any tribe of Israel to have a temple built for my Name
to be there, but I have chosen David to rule my people Israel.'

17"My father David had it in his heart to build a temple for
the Name of the LORD, the God of Israel. 18But the LORD said
to my father David, 'Because it was in your heart to build a
temple for my Name, you did well to have this in your heart.
19Nevertheless, you are not the one to build the temple, but
your son, who is your own flesh and blood—he is the one
who will build the temple for my Name.'

20"The LORD has kept the promise he made: I have succeeded David my father and now I sit on the throne of Israel, just as the LORD promised, and I have built the temple for
the Name of the LORD, the God of Israel. 21I have provided a
place there for the ark, in which is the covenant of the LORD
that he made with our fathers when he brought them out of
Egypt."

Solomon's Prayer of Dedication

22Then Solomon stood before the altar of the LORD in front of
the whole assembly of Israel, spread out his hands toward heaven 23and said:

"O LORD, God of Israel, there is no God like you in heaven above or on earth below—you who keep your covenant
of love with your servants who continue wholeheartedly in
your way. 24You have kept your promise to your servant
David my father; with your mouth you have promised and
with your hand you have fulfilled it—as it is today.
25"Now LORD, God of Israel, keep for your servant David
my father the promises you made to him when you said,
'You shall never fail to have a man to sit before me on the
throne of Israel, if only your sons are careful in all they do
to walk before me as you have done.' 26And now, O God of
Israel, let your word that you promised your servant David
my father come true.
27"But will God really dwell on earth? The heavens, even
the highest heaven, cannot contain you. How much less this
temple I have built! 28Yet give attention to your servant's
prayer and his plea for mercy, O LORD my God. Hear the cry
and the prayer that your servant is praying in your presence
this day. 29May your eyes be open toward this temple night
and day, this place of which you said, 'My Name shall be
there,' so that you will hear the prayer your servant prays toward this place. 30Hear the supplication of your servant and
of your people Israel when they pray toward this place. Hear
from heaven, your dwelling place, and when you hear, forgive.
31"When a man wrongs his neighbor and is required to

take an oath and he comes and swears the oath before your
altar in this temple, 32then hear from heaven and act. Judge
between your servants, condemning the guilty and bringing
down on his own head what he has done. Declare the innocent not guilty, and so establish his innocence.
33"When your people Israel have been defeated by an
enemy because they have sinned against you, and when they
turn back to you and confess your name, praying and making supplication to you in this temple, 34then hear from
heaven and forgive the sin of your people Israel and bring
them back to the land you gave to their fathers.
35"When the heavens are shut up and there is no rain because your people have sinned against you, and when they
pray toward this place and confess your name and turn from
their sin because you have afflicted them, 36then hear from
heaven and forgive the sin of your servants, your people Israel. Teach them the right way to live, and send rain on the
land you gave your people for an inheritance.
37"When famine or plague comes to the land, or blight or
mildew, locusts or grasshoppers, or when an enemy be-
sieges them in any of their cities, whatever disaster or disease may come, 38and when a prayer or plea is made by any
of your people Israel—each one aware of the afflictions of
his own heart, and spreading out his hands toward this temple— 39then hear from heaven, your dwelling place. Forgive and act; deal with each man according to all he does,
since you know his heart (for you alone know the hearts of
all men), 40so that they will fear you all the time they live in
the land you gave our fathers.
41"As for the foreigner who does not belong to your people Israel but has come from a distant land because of your
name— 42for men will hear of your great name and your
mighty hand and your outstretched arm—when he comes
and prays toward this temple, 43then hear from heaven, your
dwelling place, and do whatever the foreigner asks of you,
so that all the peoples of the earth may know your name and
fear you, as do your own people Israel, and may know that
this house I have built bears your Name.
44"When your people go to war against their enemies,
wherever you send them, and when they pray to the LORD toward the city you have chosen and the temple I have built for
your Name, 45then hear from heaven their prayer and their
plea, and uphold their cause.
46"When they sin against you—for there is no one who
does not sin—and you become angry with them and give
them over to the enemy, who takes them captive to his own
land, far away or near; 47and if they have a change of heart
in the land where they are held captive, and repent and
plead with you in the land of their conquerors and say, 'We
have sinned, we have done wrong, we have acted wickedly';
48and if they turn back to you with all their heart and soul in
the land of their enemies who took them captive, and pray to
you toward the land you gave their fathers, toward the city
you have chosen and the temple I have built for your Name;
49then from heaven, your dwelling place, hear their prayer
and their plea, and uphold their cause. 50And forgive your
people, who have sinned against you; forgive all the offenses

If my people's hearts are humbled,
If they pray and seek my face,
If they turn away from evil,
I will not withhold my grace.
I will hear their prayers from heaven;
I will pardon every sin.
If my people's hearts are humbled,
I will surely heal their land.

"If My People's Hearts Are Humbled"
Claire Cloninger (©1986)

(8:33–50) Lord God, if You do not forgive us for our many sins, we will be unable to survive in this world or face You in the world to come. If You do not hear us when we pray, we will be helpless. Our lives are fully dependent upon You for both provision and protection. Solomon's prayer is wise and perceptive. Because of our human nature, we often sin against You. How grateful we are for Your promise that, "if we confess our sins, [You are] faithful and just and will forgive us our sins and purify us from all unrighteousness." (1Jn 1:9)

Merciful and pitiful Lord, long-suffering and full of compassion: I have sinned, Lord, I have sinned against Thee. O wretched man that I am, I have sinned, Lord, against you grievously, as I have participated in false vanities.

I conceal nothing from you, Lord. I make no excuses. I denounce against myself my sins. Indeed, I have sinned against the Lord . . . and call to mind those particular sins I wish to confess.

Lancelot Andrews (1555-1626)

they have committed against you, and cause their conquerors to show them mercy; 51for they are your people and
your inheritance, whom you brought out of Egypt, out of that
iron-smelting furnace.
52"May your eyes be open to your servant's plea and to
the plea of your people Israel, and may you listen to them
whenever they cry out to you. 53For you singled them out
from all the nations of the world to be your own inheritance,
just as you declared through your servant Moses when you,
O Sovereign LORD, brought our fathers out of Egypt."

54When Solomon had finished all these prayers and supplications
to the LORD, he rose from before the altar of the LORD, where he had
been kneeling with his hands spread out toward heaven. 55He stood
and blessed the whole assembly of Israel in a loud voice, saying:
56"Praise be to the LORD, who has given rest to his people Israel just as he promised. Not one word has failed of all the
good promises he gave through his servant Moses. 57May the
LORD our God be with us as he was with our fathers; may he
never leave us nor forsake us. 58May he turn our hearts to
him, to walk in all his ways and to keep the commands, decrees and regulations he gave our fathers. 59And may these
words of mine, which I have prayed before the LORD, be near
to the LORD our God day and night, that he may uphold the
cause of his servant and the cause of his people Israel according to each day's need, 60so that all the peoples of the earth
may know that the LORD is God and that there is no other. 61But
your hearts must be fully committed to the LORD our God, to
live by his decrees and obey his commands, as at this time."

The Dedication of the Temple

62Then the king and all Israel with him offered sacrifices before the LORD. 63Solomon offered a sacrifice of fellowship offerings[a] to the LORD: twenty-two thousand cattle and a hundred and
twenty thousand sheep and goats. So the king and all the Israelites dedicated the temple of the LORD.
64On that same day the king consecrated the middle part of the
courtyard in front of the temple of the LORD, and there he offered
burnt offerings, grain offerings and the fat of the fellowship offerings, because the bronze altar before the LORD was too small to
hold the burnt offerings, the grain offerings and the fat of the fellowship offerings.
65So Solomon observed the festival at that time, and all Israel
with him—a vast assembly, people from Lebo[b] Hamath to the
Wadi of Egypt. They celebrated it before the LORD our God for
seven days and seven days more, fourteen days in all. 66On the
following day he sent the people away. They blessed the king and
then went home, joyful and glad in heart for all the good things
the LORD had done for his servant David and his people Israel.

The LORD Appears to Solomon

9 When Solomon had finished building the temple of the LORD
and the royal palace, and had achieved all he had desired to
do, 2the LORD appeared to him a second time, as he had appeared
to him at Gibeon. 3The LORD said to him:

[a] 63 Traditionally *peace offerings*; also in verse 64 [b] 65 Or *from the entrance to*

(8:65–66) We have much to celebrate, Lord, when we remember the astonishing provisions You have made for us, the indescribable blessings You have poured out on us, the unexplainable interventions You have made for us. Teach us to rejoice, Lord—to get up off our knees, wipe away our tears and lift our hands in praise and thanksgiving before You. It is good for us to be reminded, "The joy of the LORD is [our] strength." (Ne 8:10)

Joyful, joyful, we adore Thee,
God of glory, Lord of love;
Hearts unfold like flowers before
Thee,
Opening to the sun above.
Melt the clouds of sin and sadness;
Drive the dark of doubt away.
Giver of immortal gladness,
Fill us with the light of day!

"Joyful, Joyful We Adore Thee"
Henry Van Dyke (1907)

A lecturer to a group of businessmen displayed a sheet of white paper on which was one blot. He asked what they saw. All answered, "A blot." The test was unfair: it invited the wrong answer. Nevertheless, there is an ingratitude in human nature by which we notice the black disfigurement and forget the widespread mercy.

We need deliberately to call to mind the joys of our journey. Perhaps we should try to write down the blessings of one day. We might begin; we could never end; there are not pens or paper enough in all the world.

George A. Buttrick (1892-1980)

"I have heard the prayer and plea you have made before
me; I have consecrated this temple, which you have built,
by putting my Name there forever. My eyes and my heart will
always be there.
4"As for you, if you walk before me in integrity of heart
and uprightness, as David your father did, and do all I command and observe my decrees and laws, 5I will establish
your royal throne over Israel forever, as I promised David
your father when I said, 'You shall never fail to have a man
on the throne of Israel.'
6"But if you[a] or your sons turn away from me and do
not observe the commands and decrees I have given you[a]
and go off to serve other gods and worship them, 7then I
will cut off Israel from the land I have given them and will
reject this temple I have consecrated for my Name. Israel
will then become a byword and an object of ridicule
among all peoples. 8And though this temple is now imposing, all who pass by will be appalled and will scoff and say,
'Why has the LORD done such a thing to this land and to
this temple?' 9People will answer, 'Because they have forsaken the LORD their God, who brought their fathers out of
Egypt, and have embraced other gods, worshiping and
serving them—that is why the LORD brought all this disaster on them.' "

Solomon's Other Activities

10At the end of twenty years, during which Solomon built these
two buildings—the temple of the LORD and the royal palace—
11King Solomon gave twenty towns in Galilee to Hiram king of
Tyre, because Hiram had supplied him with all the cedar and
pine and gold he wanted. 12But when Hiram went from Tyre to
see the towns that Solomon had given him, he was not pleased
with them. 13"What kind of towns are these you have given me,
my brother?" he asked. And he called them the Land of Cabul,[b]
a name they have to this day. 14Now Hiram had sent to the king
120 talents[c] of gold.
15Here is the account of the forced labor King Solomon conscripted to build the LORD's temple, his own palace, the supporting terraces,[d] the wall of Jerusalem, and Hazor, Megiddo and
Gezer. 16(Pharaoh king of Egypt had attacked and captured
Gezer. He had set it on fire. He killed its Canaanite inhabitants
and then gave it as a wedding gift to his daughter, Solomon's
wife. 17And Solomon rebuilt Gezer.) He built up Lower Beth
Horon, 18Baalath, and Tadmor[e] in the desert, within his land,
19as well as all his store cities and the towns for his chariots and
for his horses[f]—whatever he desired to build in Jerusalem, in
Lebanon and throughout all the territory he ruled.
20All the people left from the Amorites, Hittites, Perizzites,
Hivites and Jebusites (these peoples were not Israelites), 21that
is, their descendants remaining in the land, whom the Israelites
could not exterminate[g]—these Solomon conscripted for his
slave labor force, as it is to this day. 22But Solomon did not
make slaves of any of the Israelites; they were his fighting men,

[a] *6* The Hebrew is plural. [b] *13* *Cabul* sounds like the Hebrew for *good-for-nothing.*
[c] *14* That is, about 4 1/2 tons (about 4 metric tons) [d] *15* Or *the Millo*; also in verse 24
[e] *18* The Hebrew may also be read *Tamar.* [f] *19* Or *charioteers* [g] *21* The Hebrew term refers to the irrevocable giving over of things or persons to the LORD, often by totally destroying them.

(9:1–9) You appeared to Solomon because he had invited You to be at the heart of his kingdom. And You promised to stay in the midst of Your people as long as You were welcome there. As for us, You have promised never to leave us or forsake us; yet how often do we forsake You? You know all too well that at times we walk away from You, refusing to heed Your instructions or honor Your name. God, help us to remain faithful to You, as You are faithful to us. Please make Your home with us all the days of our lives. (Heb 13:5)

Father in Heaven! What are we without You! What is all that we know, vast accumulation though it be, but a chipped fragment if we do not know You! What is all our striving, could it ever encompass a world, but a half-finished work if we do not know You: You, the One, who is one thing and who is all!

Søren Kierkegaard (1813-1855)

his government officials, his officers, his captains, and the commanders of his chariots and charioteers. 23They were also the
chief officials in charge of Solomon's projects—550 officials
supervising the men who did the work.
24After Pharaoh's daughter had come up from the City of David
to the palace Solomon had built for her, he constructed the supporting terraces.
25Three times a year Solomon sacrificed burnt offerings and
fellowship offerings[a] on the altar he had built for the LORD, burning incense before the LORD along with them, and so fulfilled the
temple obligations.
26King Solomon also built ships at Ezion Geber, which is near
Elath in Edom, on the shore of the Red Sea.[b] 27And Hiram sent
his men—sailors who knew the sea—to serve in the fleet with
Solomon's men. 28They sailed to Ophir and brought back 420 talents[c] of gold, which they delivered to King Solomon.

The Queen of Sheba Visits Solomon

10 When the queen of Sheba heard about the fame of Solomon and his relation to the name of the LORD, she came to
test him with hard questions. 2Arriving at Jerusalem with a very
great caravan—with camels carrying spices, large quantities of
gold, and precious stones—she came to Solomon and talked
with him about all that she had on her mind. 3Solomon answered
all her questions; nothing was too hard for the king to explain to
her. 4When the queen of Sheba saw all the wisdom of Solomon
and the palace he had built, 5the food on his table, the seating of
his officials, the attending servants in their robes, his cupbearers,
and the burnt offerings he made at[d] the temple of the LORD, she
was overwhelmed.
6She said to the king, "The report I heard in my own country
about your achievements and your wisdom is true. 7But I did not
believe these things until I came and saw with my own eyes. Indeed, not even half was told me; in wisdom and wealth you have
far exceeded the report I heard. 8How happy your men must be!
How happy your officials, who continually stand before you and
hear your wisdom! 9Praise be to the LORD your God, who has delighted in you and placed you on the throne of Israel. Because of
the LORD's eternal love for Israel, he has made you king, to maintain justice and righteousness."
10And she gave the king 120 talents[e] of gold, large quantities of
spices, and precious stones. Never again were so many spices
brought in as those the queen of Sheba gave to King Solomon.
11(Hiram's ships brought gold from Ophir; and from there they
brought great cargoes of almugwood[f] and precious stones. 12The
king used the almugwood to make supports for the temple of
the LORD and for the royal palace, and to make harps and lyres for
the musicians. So much almugwood has never been imported or
seen since that day.)
13King Solomon gave the queen of Sheba all she desired and
asked for, besides what he had given her out of his royal bounty.
Then she left and returned with her retinue to her own country.

[a] *25* Traditionally *peace offerings* [b] *26* Hebrew *Yam Suph*; that is, Sea of Reeds
[c] *28* That is, about 16 tons (about 14.5 metric tons) [d] *5* Or *the ascent by which he went up to* [e] *10* That is, about 4 1/2 tons (about 4 metric tons) [f] *11* Probably a variant of *algumwood*; also in verse 12

(10:1–9) When You prosper Your people, Lord, You are glorified in their abundance. When You provide wisdom, Your name is lifted up through Your people's words and actions. When You place men and women in roles of power and influence, Your authority radiates through them. Make us worthy of Your favor, Lord, that we might be living illustrations of Your grace and mercy to a watching world.

Your kingdom come
Around and through and in me,
Your power and glory,
Let them shine through me;
Your hallowed name,
O, may I bear with honor,
And may Your living
Kingdom come in me.
The Bread of Life,
O may I share with honor,
And may You feed
A hungry world through me.

"I Then Shall Live"
Gloria Gaither (©1981)

Solomon's Splendor

14 The weight of the gold that Solomon received yearly was 666 talents,[a] 15 not including the revenues from merchants and traders and from all the Arabian kings and the governors of the land.

16 King Solomon made two hundred large shields of hammered gold; six hundred bekas[b] of gold went into each shield. 17 He also made three hundred small shields of hammered gold, with three minas[c] of gold in each shield. The king put them in the Palace of the Forest of Lebanon.

18 Then the king made a great throne inlaid with ivory and overlaid with fine gold. 19 The throne had six steps, and its back had a rounded top. On both sides of the seat were armrests, with a lion standing beside each of them. 20 Twelve lions stood on the six steps, one at either end of each step. Nothing like it had ever been made for any other kingdom. 21 All King Solomon's goblets were gold, and all the household articles in the Palace of the Forest of Lebanon were pure gold. Nothing was made of silver, because silver was considered of little value in Solomon's days. 22 The king had a fleet of trading ships[d] at sea along with the ships of Hiram. Once every three years it returned, carrying gold, silver and ivory, and apes and baboons.

23 King Solomon was greater in riches and wisdom than all the other kings of the earth. 24 The whole world sought audience with Solomon to hear the wisdom God had put in his heart. 25 Year after year, everyone who came brought a gift—articles of silver and gold, robes, weapons and spices, and horses and mules.

26 Solomon accumulated chariots and horses; he had fourteen hundred chariots and twelve thousand horses,[e] which he kept in the chariot cities and also with him in Jerusalem. 27 The king made silver as common in Jerusalem as stones, and cedar as plentiful as sycamore-fig trees in the foothills. 28 Solomon's horses were imported from Egypt[f] and from Kue[g]—the royal merchants purchased them from Kue. 29 They imported a chariot from Egypt for six hundred shekels[h] of silver, and a horse for a hundred and fifty.[i] They also exported them to all the kings of the Hittites and of the Arameans.

Solomon's Wives

11 King Solomon, however, loved many foreign women besides Pharaoh's daughter—Moabites, Ammonites, Edomites, Sidonians and Hittites. 2 They were from nations about which the LORD had told the Israelites, "You must not intermarry with them, because they will surely turn your hearts after their gods." Nevertheless, Solomon held fast to them in love. 3 He had seven hundred wives of royal birth and three hundred concubines, and his wives led him astray. 4 As Solomon grew old, his wives turned his heart after other gods, and his heart was not fully devoted to the LORD his God, as the heart of David his father had been. 5 He followed Ashtoreth the goddess of the Sidonians, and Molech[j] the detestable god of the Ammonites. 6 So Solomon did evil in the eyes of the LORD; he did not follow the LORD completely, as David his father had done.

7 On a hill east of Jerusalem, Solomon built a high place for Che-

[a] *14* That is, about 25 tons (about 23 metric tons) [b] *16* That is, about 7 1/2 pounds (about 3.5 kilograms) [c] *17* That is, about 3 3/4 pounds (about 1.7 kilograms)
[d] *22* Hebrew *of ships of Tarshish* [e] *26* Or *charioteers* [f] *28* Or possibly *Muzur*, a region in Cilicia; also in verse 29 [g] *28* Probably *Cilicia* [h] *29* That is, about 15 pounds (about 7 kilograms) [i] *29* That is, about 3 3/4 pounds (about 1.7 kilograms)
[j] *5* Hebrew *Milcom*; also in verse 33

(11:1–6) O Lord, You demand our single-minded devotion. No matter how carefully we try to obey Your instructions, if our hearts are not completely Yours we will surely lose our way. We may be faithful in every other aspect of life, but if, like Solomon, we do not allow our appetites and emotions to be ruled by Your Spirit, we are in grave danger. Teach us to guard our hearts, Sovereign Lord, for You have taught us that the heart is the wellspring of life. (Pr 4:23)

What folly to fear to be too entirely God's! It is to fear to be too happy. It is to fear to love God's will in all things. It is to fear to have too much courage in the crosses which are inevitable, too much comfort in God's love, and too much detachment from the passions which make us miserable . . . woe unto those weak and timid souls who are divided between God and their world!

François Fénelon (1651-1715)

(11:7–11) You call me to measure myself by Your Word, Lord God, in order to stay in close communion with You. Solomon knew all the answers. He could advise others. He could discern between truth and falsehood. But Solomon was blind to his own folly, and as a result his relationship with You was broken. Lord, do not allow me to be like him—like one who looks at his face in a mirror and then goes away and immediately forgets what he looks like. Instead, teach me to look intently into Your Word—the perfect law that gives freedom—and to continue to do this, not forgetting what I have heard, but doing it. (Jas 1:23–25)

The heart is also deceitful. It excuses, rationalizes, and justifies our actions. It blinds us to entire areas of sin in our lives. It causes us to deal with sin using only halfway measures, or to think that mental assent to the Word of God is the same as obedience (James 1:22).

Jerry Bridges (1929-)

Take time to be holy,
Speak oft with Thy Lord;
Abide in Him always,
And feed on His Word.
Make friends of God's children;
Help those who are weak,
Forgetting in nothing
His blessing to seek.

"Take Time to Be Holy"
William D. Longstaff (1882)

mosh the detestable god of Moab, and for Molech the detestable god of the Ammonites. 8He did the same for all his foreign wives, who burned incense and offered sacrifices to their gods.

9The LORD became angry with Solomon because his heart had turned away from the LORD, the God of Israel, who had appeared to him twice. 10Although he had forbidden Solomon to follow other gods, Solomon did not keep the LORD's command. 11So the LORD said to Solomon, "Since this is your attitude and you have not kept my covenant and my decrees, which I commanded you, I will most certainly tear the kingdom away from you and give it to one of your subordinates. 12Nevertheless, for the sake of David your father, I will not do it during your lifetime. I will tear it out of the hand of your son. 13Yet I will not tear the whole kingdom from him, but will give him one tribe for the sake of David my servant and for the sake of Jerusalem, which I have chosen."

Solomon's Adversaries

14Then the LORD raised up against Solomon an adversary, Hadad the Edomite, from the royal line of Edom. 15Earlier when David was fighting with Edom, Joab the commander of the army, who had gone up to bury the dead, had struck down all the men in Edom. 16Joab and all the Israelites stayed there for six months, until they had destroyed all the men in Edom. 17But Hadad, still only a boy, fled to Egypt with some Edomite officials who had served his father. 18They set out from Midian and went to Paran. Then taking men from Paran with them, they went to Egypt, to Pharaoh king of Egypt, who gave Hadad a house and land and provided him with food.

19Pharaoh was so pleased with Hadad that he gave him a sister of his own wife, Queen Tahpenes, in marriage. 20The sister of Tahpenes bore him a son named Genubath, whom Tahpenes brought up in the royal palace. There Genubath lived with Pharaoh's own children.

21While he was in Egypt, Hadad heard that David rested with his fathers and that Joab the commander of the army was also dead. Then Hadad said to Pharaoh, "Let me go, that I may return to my own country."

22"What have you lacked here that you want to go back to your own country?" Pharaoh asked.

"Nothing," Hadad replied, "but do let me go!"

23And God raised up against Solomon another adversary, Rezon son of Eliada, who had fled from his master, Hadadezer king of Zobah. 24He gathered men around him and became the leader of a band of rebels when David destroyed the forces[a] ⌊of Zobah⌋; the rebels went to Damascus, where they settled and took control. 25Rezon was Israel's adversary as long as Solomon lived, adding to the trouble caused by Hadad. So Rezon ruled in Aram and was hostile toward Israel.

Jeroboam Rebels Against Solomon

26Also, Jeroboam son of Nebat rebelled against the king. He was one of Solomon's officials, an Ephraimite from Zeredah, and his mother was a widow named Zeruah.

27Here is the account of how he rebelled against the king: Solomon had built the supporting terraces[b] and had filled in the gap

[a] 24 Hebrew *destroyed them* [b] 27 Or *the Millo*

in the wall of the city of David his father. 28Now Jeroboam was a man of standing, and when Solomon saw how well the young man did his work, he put him in charge of the whole labor force of the house of Joseph.

29About that time Jeroboam was going out of Jerusalem, and Ahijah the prophet of Shiloh met him on the way, wearing a new cloak. The two of them were alone out in the country, 30and Ahijah took hold of the new cloak he was wearing and tore it into twelve pieces. 31Then he said to Jeroboam, "Take ten pieces for yourself, for this is what the LORD, the God of Israel, says: 'See, I am going to tear the kingdom out of Solomon's hand and give you ten tribes. 32But for the sake of my servant David and the city of Jerusalem, which I have chosen out of all the tribes of Israel, he will have one tribe. 33I will do this because they have[a] forsaken me and worshiped Ashtoreth the goddess of the Sidonians, Chemosh the god of the Moabites, and Molech the god of the Ammonites, and have not walked in my ways, nor done what is right in my eyes, nor kept my statutes and laws as David, Solomon's father, did.

34" 'But I will not take the whole kingdom out of Solomon's hand; I have made him ruler all the days of his life for the sake of David my servant, whom I chose and who observed my commands and statutes. 35I will take the kingdom from his son's hands and give you ten tribes. 36I will give one tribe to his son so that David my servant may always have a lamp before me in Jerusalem, the city where I chose to put my Name. 37However, as for you, I will take you, and you will rule over all that your heart desires; you will be king over Israel. 38If you do whatever I command you and walk in my ways and do what is right in my eyes by keeping my statutes and commands, as David my servant did, I will be with you. I will build you a dynasty as enduring as the one I built for David and will give Israel to you. 39I will humble David's descendants because of this, but not forever.' "

40Solomon tried to kill Jeroboam, but Jeroboam fled to Egypt, to Shishak the king, and stayed there until Solomon's death.

Solomon's Death

41As for the other events of Solomon's reign—all he did and the wisdom he displayed—are they not written in the book of the annals of Solomon? 42Solomon reigned in Jerusalem over all Israel forty years. 43Then he rested with his fathers and was buried in the city of David his father. And Rehoboam his son succeeded him as king.

Israel Rebels Against Rehoboam

12 Rehoboam went to Shechem, for all the Israelites had gone there to make him king. 2When Jeroboam son of Nebat heard this (he was still in Egypt, where he had fled from King Solomon), he returned from[b] Egypt. 3So they sent for Jeroboam, and he and the whole assembly of Israel went to Rehoboam and said to him: 4"Your father put a heavy yoke on us, but now lighten the harsh labor and the heavy yoke he put on us, and we will serve you."

5Rehoboam answered, "Go away for three days and then come back to me." So the people went away.

(11:28–40) Your continuing loyalty to David bears witness to the integrity of Your Word. Although You had actually appeared to Solomon on two occasions, he refused to heed Your warnings and obey You. Even then, You preserved a portion of his kingdom because of Your love for his father, David. I praise You because You are so faithful, Lord, always longing to bless, always desiring reconciliation and restored relationship with Your people.

[a] 33 Hebrew; Septuagint, Vulgate and Syriac *because he has* [b] 2 Or *he remained in*

(12:6–16) Lord, You despise pride and arrogance, and so should we, for they are so often the precursors of cruelty and abuse. You have warned us to humble ourselves so that You can lift us up and honor us. And yet, throughout the centuries, there have been those who have sought to glorify themselves, and in doing so have sorely mistreated those around them. Teach us humility, Lord, as an expression of obedience to You, for only where there is humility can there be peace. (1Co 13:4; Jas 4:10)

The way to rule is to serve, to do good, and stoop to do it, to become all things to all men and so win their hearts.

Matthew Henry (1662-1714)

6Then King Rehoboam consulted the elders who had served his father Solomon during his lifetime. "How would you advise me to answer these people?" he asked.

7They replied, "If today you will be a servant to these people and serve them and give them a favorable answer, they will always be your servants."

8But Rehoboam rejected the advice the elders gave him and consulted the young men who had grown up with him and were
serving him. 9He asked them, "What is your advice? How should we answer these people who say to me, 'Lighten the yoke your father put on us'?"

10The young men who had grown up with him replied, "Tell these people who have said to you, 'Your father put a heavy yoke on us, but make our yoke lighter'—tell them, 'My little finger is
thicker than my father's waist. 11My father laid on you a heavy yoke; I will make it even heavier. My father scourged you with whips; I will scourge you with scorpions.' "

12Three days later Jeroboam and all the people returned to Rehoboam, as the king had said, "Come back to me in three days."
13The king answered the people harshly. Rejecting the advice
given him by the elders, 14he followed the advice of the young men and said, "My father made your yoke heavy; I will make it even heavier. My father scourged you with whips; I will scourge
you with scorpions." 15So the king did not listen to the people, for this turn of events was from the LORD, to fulfill the word the LORD had spoken to Jeroboam son of Nebat through Ahijah the Shilonite.

16When all Israel saw that the king refused to listen to them, they answered the king:

"What share do we have in David,
what part in Jesse's son?
To your tents, O Israel!
Look after your own house, O David!"

So the Israelites went home. 17But as for the Israelites who were living in the towns of Judah, Rehoboam still ruled over them.

18King Rehoboam sent out Adoniram,[a] who was in charge of forced labor, but all Israel stoned him to death. King Rehoboam, however, managed to get into his chariot and escape to Jerusalem. 19So Israel has been in rebellion against the house of David to this day.

20When all the Israelites heard that Jeroboam had returned, they sent and called him to the assembly and made him king over all Israel. Only the tribe of Judah remained loyal to the house of David.

21When Rehoboam arrived in Jerusalem, he mustered the whole house of Judah and the tribe of Benjamin—a hundred and eighty thousand fighting men—to make war against the house of Israel and to regain the kingdom for Rehoboam son of Solomon.

22But this word of God came to Shemaiah the man of God:
23"Say to Rehoboam son of Solomon king of Judah, to the whole
house of Judah and Benjamin, and to the rest of the people,
24'This is what the LORD says: Do not go up to fight against your brothers, the Israelites. Go home, every one of you, for this is my

[a] *18* Some Septuagint manuscripts and Syriac (see also 1 Kings 4:6 and 5:14); Hebrew *Adoram*

doing.' " So they obeyed the word of the LORD and went home again, as the LORD had ordered.

Golden Calves at Bethel and Dan

25Then Jeroboam fortified Shechem in the hill country of
Ephraim and lived there. From there he went out and built up Peniel.[a]
26Jeroboam thought to himself, "The kingdom will now likely
revert to the house of David. 27If these people go up to offer sacrifices at the temple of the LORD in Jerusalem, they will again give
their allegiance to their lord, Rehoboam king of Judah. They will
kill me and return to King Rehoboam."
28After seeking advice, the king made two golden calves. He
said to the people, "It is too much for you to go up to Jerusalem.
Here are your gods, O Israel, who brought you up out of Egypt."
29One he set up in Bethel, and the other in Dan. 30And this thing
became a sin; the people went even as far as Dan to worship the
one there.
31Jeroboam built shrines on high places and appointed priests
from all sorts of people, even though they were not Levites. 32He
instituted a festival on the fifteenth day of the eighth month, like
the festival held in Judah, and offered sacrifices on the altar. This
he did in Bethel, sacrificing to the calves he had made. And at
Bethel he also installed priests at the high places he had made.
33On the fifteenth day of the eighth month, a month of his own
choosing, he offered sacrifices on the altar he had built at Bethel. So he instituted the festival for the Israelites and went up to the altar to make offerings.

The Man of God From Judah

13 By the word of the LORD a man of God came from Judah to
Bethel, as Jeroboam was standing by the altar to make an
offering. 2He cried out against the altar by the word of the LORD:
"O altar, altar! This is what the LORD says: 'A son named Josiah will
be born to the house of David. On you he will sacrifice the priests
of the high places who now make offerings here, and human
bones will be burned on you.' " 3That same day the man of God
gave a sign: "This is the sign the LORD has declared: The altar will
be split apart and the ashes on it will be poured out."
4When King Jeroboam heard what the man of God cried out
against the altar at Bethel, he stretched out his hand from the
altar and said, "Seize him!" But the hand he stretched out toward
the man shriveled up, so that he could not pull it back. 5Also, the
altar was split apart and its ashes poured out according to the
sign given by the man of God by the word of the LORD.
6Then the king said to the man of God, "Intercede with the
LORD your God and pray for me that my hand may be restored."
So the man of God interceded with the LORD, and the king's hand
was restored and became as it was before.
7The king said to the man of God, "Come home with me and
have something to eat, and I will give you a gift."
8But the man of God answered the king, "Even if you were to
give me half your possessions, I would not go with you, nor would
I eat bread or drink water here. 9For I was commanded by the
word of the LORD: 'You must not eat bread or drink water or re-

[a] 25 Hebrew *Penuel,* a variant of *Peniel*

The empire of Caesar is gone; the legions of Rome are smouldering in the dust; the avalanches that Napoleon hurled upon Europe have melted away; the prince of the Pharaohs is fallen; the pyramids they raised to be their tombs are sinking every day in the desert sands; Tyre is a rock for bleaching fisherman's nets; Sidon has scarcely left a wreck behind; but the Word of God still survives. All things that threatened to extinguish it have only aided it; and it proves every day how transient is the noblest monument that men can build, how enduring is the least word that God has spoken.

Albert Baird Cummins (1850-1926)

(13:1–3) So often, Lord, You speak Your Word through anonymous people, ordinary folks who have no credentials except that You have chosen them to carry Your message. This prophet wasn't perfect in Your eyes—his name isn't even mentioned—yet through him came a stunning prophecy about the future King Josiah that was precisely fulfilled some 300 years later. This prophet died in disgrace, yet Your glorious Word came through him and continued long after him. And, as always, You kept Your word. (2Ki 23:15–16)

God has spoken by His prophets,
Spoken His unchanging Word,
Each from age to age proclaiming
God, the One, the righteous Lord.
In the world's despair and turmoil
One firm anchor holds us fast:
God is King, His throne eternal,
God the first, and God the last.

"God Has Spoken by His Prophets"
George W. Briggs (©1953)

When we are willing to do His will it is not difficult to find out His will, but if willfully we make our plans and ask Him to sanction them, we can so easily move off the highway into the byways.
Harold Wildish

(13:11–32) Sovereign Lord, You demand obedience from Your children. No matter how hungry this prophet may have been, and no matter how cleverly he was deceived, he simply did not submit to Your authority, and it cost him his life. Teach me to listen, to hear and to obey You, Father, for I am often hungry for things I should not have, and I am often deceived by words I should not believe. Lord, have mercy on me.

turn by the way you came.' " 10So he took another road and did
not return by the way he had come to Bethel.
11Now there was a certain old prophet living in Bethel, whose
sons came and told him all that the man of God had done there
that day. They also told their father what he had said to the king.
12Their father asked them, "Which way did he go?" And his sons
showed him which road the man of God from Judah had taken.
13So he said to his sons, "Saddle the donkey for me." And when
they had saddled the donkey for him, he mounted it 14and rode
after the man of God. He found him sitting under an oak tree and
asked, "Are you the man of God who came from Judah?"
"I am," he replied.
15So the prophet said to him, "Come home with me and eat."
16The man of God said, "I cannot turn back and go with you,
nor can I eat bread or drink water with you in this place. 17I have
been told by the word of the LORD: 'You must not eat bread or
drink water there or return by the way you came.' "
18The old prophet answered, "I too am a prophet, as you are.
And an angel said to me by the word of the LORD: 'Bring him back
with you to your house so that he may eat bread and drink
water.' " (But he was lying to him.) 19So the man of God returned
with him and ate and drank in his house.
20While they were sitting at the table, the word of the LORD
came to the old prophet who had brought him back. 21He cried
out to the man of God who had come from Judah, "This is what
the LORD says: 'You have defied the word of the LORD and have not
kept the command the LORD your God gave you. 22You came back
and ate bread and drank water in the place where he told you not
to eat or drink. Therefore your body will not be buried in the
tomb of your fathers.' "
23When the man of God had finished eating and drinking, the
prophet who had brought him back saddled his donkey for him.
24As he went on his way, a lion met him on the road and killed
him, and his body was thrown down on the road, with both the
donkey and the lion standing beside it. 25Some people who
passed by saw the body thrown down there, with the lion standing beside the body, and they went and reported it in the city
where the old prophet lived.
26When the prophet who had brought him back from his journey heard of it, he said, "It is the man of God who defied the word
of the LORD. The LORD has given him over to the lion, which has
mauled him and killed him, as the word of the LORD had warned
him."
27The prophet said to his sons, "Saddle the donkey for me,"
and they did so. 28Then he went out and found the body thrown
down on the road, with the donkey and the lion standing beside
it. The lion had neither eaten the body nor mauled the donkey.
29So the prophet picked up the body of the man of God, laid it on
the donkey, and brought it back to his own city to mourn for him
and bury him. 30Then he laid the body in his own tomb, and they
mourned over him and said, "Oh, my brother!"
31After burying him, he said to his sons, "When I die, bury me
in the grave where the man of God is buried; lay my bones beside
his bones. 32For the message he declared by the word of the LORD
against the altar in Bethel and against all the shrines on the high
places in the towns of Samaria will certainly come true."
33Even after this, Jeroboam did not change his evil ways, but

once more appointed priests for the high places from all sorts of
people. Anyone who wanted to become a priest he consecrated
for the high places. 34This was the sin of the house of Jeroboam
that led to its downfall and to its destruction from the face of the
earth.

Ahijah's Prophecy Against Jeroboam

14 At that time Abijah son of Jeroboam became ill, 2and Jeroboam said to his wife, "Go, disguise yourself, so you won't
be recognized as the wife of Jeroboam. Then go to Shiloh. Ahijah
the prophet is there—the one who told me I would be king over
this people. 3Take ten loaves of bread with you, some cakes and
a jar of honey, and go to him. He will tell you what will happen to
the boy." 4So Jeroboam's wife did what he said and went to Ahijah's house in Shiloh.
Now Ahijah could not see; his sight was gone because of his
age. 5But the LORD had told Ahijah, "Jeroboam's wife is coming to
ask you about her son, for he is ill, and you are to give her such
and such an answer. When she arrives, she will pretend to be
someone else."
6So when Ahijah heard the sound of her footsteps at the door,
he said, "Come in, wife of Jeroboam. Why this pretense? I have
been sent to you with bad news. 7Go, tell Jeroboam that this is
what the LORD, the God of Israel, says: 'I raised you up from
among the people and made you a leader over my people Israel.
8I tore the kingdom away from the house of David and gave it to
you, but you have not been like my servant David, who kept my
commands and followed me with all his heart, doing only what
was right in my eyes. 9You have done more evil than all who lived
before you. You have made for yourself other gods, idols made of
metal; you have provoked me to anger and thrust me behind your
back.
10" 'Because of this, I am going to bring disaster on the house
of Jeroboam. I will cut off from Jeroboam every last male in Israel—slave or free. I will burn up the house of Jeroboam as one
burns dung, until it is all gone. 11Dogs will eat those belonging to
Jeroboam who die in the city, and the birds of the air will feed on
those who die in the country. The LORD has spoken!'
12"As for you, go back home. When you set foot in your city,
the boy will die. 13All Israel will mourn for him and bury him. He
is the only one belonging to Jeroboam who will be buried, because he is the only one in the house of Jeroboam in whom the
LORD, the God of Israel, has found anything good.
14"The LORD will raise up for himself a king over Israel who
will cut off the family of Jeroboam. This is the day! What? Yes,
even now.[a] 15And the LORD will strike Israel, so that it will be like
a reed swaying in the water. He will uproot Israel from this good
land that he gave to their forefathers and scatter them beyond the
River,[b] because they provoked the LORD to anger by making Asherah poles.[c] 16And he will give Israel up because of the sins Jeroboam has committed and has caused Israel to commit."
17Then Jeroboam's wife got up and left and went to Tirzah. As
soon as she stepped over the threshold of the house, the boy died.
18They buried him, and all Israel mourned for him, as the LORD
had said through his servant the prophet Ahijah.

[a] *14* The meaning of the Hebrew for this sentence is uncertain. [b] *15* That is, the Euphrates [c] *15* That is, symbols of the goddess Asherah; here and elsewhere in 1 Kings

(14:7–9) Though Your people had neglected You, You would not neglect them, for You still called Yourself "the Lord, the God of Israel." But in Your jealousy You punished the one who had led Your people in their adulterous ways. Truly, "if anyone causes one of these little ones who believe in me to sin, it would be better for him to have a large millstone hung around his neck and to be drowned in the depths of the sea." Thank You, Lord, for Your jealous love for us. Thank You for not turning Your back on us when we are unfaithful to You. Let us never take Your grace for granted or forget the kindness You have shown us. (Mt 18:6)

(15:3–5) O God, may I have a heart for You like David had. In spite of his sins and failures You continued to honor him from generation to generation. His life was the benchmark of godly living. Teach me to study the lives of faithful men and women in whom You have been well pleased. Help me to "consider the outcome of their way of life and imitate their faith" so that I might please You in all that I do. (Heb 13:7)

What He is today we shall find Him tomorrow and the next day and the next year. He is quick to overlook imperfections when he knows we meant to do His will. He loves us for ourselves and values our love more than galaxies of new created worlds.

. . . He remembers our frame and knows that we are dust. He may sometimes chasten us, it is true, but even this He does with a smile, the proud, tender smile of a Father Who is bursting with pleasure over an imperfect but promising son who is coming every day to look more and more like the One Whose child he is.

A.W. Tozer (1897-1963)

Lord, I want to live my life to please
 You,
I bring my heart before You to
 remold;
Make of me a vessel fit for honor
That I might shine for You as
 sparkling gold.

To be pleasing You, pleasing You;
This is all I really want to do.
To be pleasing You, pleasing You;
This is all I really want to do.

"To Be Pleasing You"
Teresa Muller (©1984)

19 The other events of Jeroboam's reign, his wars and how he
ruled, are written in the book of the annals of the kings of Israel.
20 He reigned for twenty-two years and then rested with his fathers. And Nadab his son succeeded him as king.

Rehoboam King of Judah

21 Rehoboam son of Solomon was king in Judah. He was forty-
one years old when he became king, and he reigned seventeen
years in Jerusalem, the city the LORD had chosen out of all the
tribes of Israel in which to put his Name. His mother's name was
Naamah; she was an Ammonite.

22 Judah did evil in the eyes of the LORD. By the sins they committed they stirred up his jealous anger more than their fathers
had done. 23 They also set up for themselves high places, sacred
stones and Asherah poles on every high hill and under every
spreading tree. 24 There were even male shrine prostitutes in the
land; the people engaged in all the detestable practices of the nations the LORD had driven out before the Israelites.

25 In the fifth year of King Rehoboam, Shishak king of Egypt attacked Jerusalem. 26 He carried off the treasures of the temple of
the LORD and the treasures of the royal palace. He took everything,
including all the gold shields Solomon had made. 27 So King Rehoboam made bronze shields to replace them and assigned these
to the commanders of the guard on duty at the entrance to the
royal palace. 28 Whenever the king went to the LORD's temple, the
guards bore the shields, and afterward they returned them to
the guardroom.

29 As for the other events of Rehoboam's reign, and all he did,
are they not written in the book of the annals of the kings of
Judah? 30 There was continual warfare between Rehoboam and
Jeroboam. 31 And Rehoboam rested with his fathers and was
buried with them in the City of David. His mother's name was Naamah; she was an Ammonite. And Abijah[a] his son succeeded him
as king.

Abijah King of Judah

15 In the eighteenth year of the reign of Jeroboam son of
Nebat, Abijah[b] became king of Judah, 2 and he reigned in
Jerusalem three years. His mother's name was Maacah daughter
of Abishalom.[c]

3 He committed all the sins his father had done before him; his
heart was not fully devoted to the LORD his God, as the heart of
David his forefather had been. 4 Nevertheless, for David's sake the
LORD his God gave him a lamp in Jerusalem by raising up a son to
succeed him and by making Jerusalem strong. 5 For David had
done what was right in the eyes of the LORD and had not failed to
keep any of the LORD's commands all the days of his life—except
in the case of Uriah the Hittite.

6 There was war between Rehoboam[d] and Jeroboam throughout ⌊Abijah's⌋ lifetime. 7 As for the other events of Abijah's reign,
and all he did, are they not written in the book of the annals of the
kings of Judah? There was war between Abijah and Jeroboam.

[a] *31* Some Hebrew manuscripts and Septuagint (see also 2 Chron. 12:16); most Hebrew manuscripts *Abijam* [b] *1* Some Hebrew manuscripts and Septuagint (see also 2 Chron. 12:16); most Hebrew manuscripts *Abijam*; also in verses 7 and 8 [c] *2* A variant of *Absalom*; also in verse 10 [d] *6* Most Hebrew manuscripts; some Hebrew manuscripts and Syriac *Abijam* (that is, Abijah)

8And Abijah rested with his fathers and was buried in the City of
David. And Asa his son succeeded him as king.

Asa King of Judah

9In the twentieth year of Jeroboam king of Israel, Asa became
king of Judah, 10and he reigned in Jerusalem forty-one years. His
grandmother's name was Maacah daughter of Abishalom.
11Asa did what was right in the eyes of the LORD, as his father
David had done. 12He expelled the male shrine prostitutes from
the land and got rid of all the idols his fathers had made. 13He
even deposed his grandmother Maacah from her position as
queen mother, because she had made a repulsive Asherah pole.
Asa cut the pole down and burned it in the Kidron Valley. 14Al-
though he did not remove the high places, Asa's heart was fully
committed to the LORD all his life. 15He brought into the temple of
the LORD the silver and gold and the articles that he and his father
had dedicated.
16There was war between Asa and Baasha king of Israel
throughout their reigns. 17Baasha king of Israel went up against
Judah and fortified Ramah to prevent anyone from leaving or entering the territory of Asa king of Judah.
18Asa then took all the silver and gold that was left in the treasuries of the LORD's temple and of his own palace. He entrusted it
to his officials and sent them to Ben-Hadad son of Tabrimmon,
the son of Hezion, the king of Aram, who was ruling in Damascus.
19"Let there be a treaty between me and you," he said, "as there
was between my father and your father. See, I am sending you a
gift of silver and gold. Now break your treaty with Baasha king of
Israel so he will withdraw from me."
20Ben-Hadad agreed with King Asa and sent the commanders
of his forces against the towns of Israel. He conquered Ijon, Dan,
Abel Beth Maacah and all Kinnereth in addition to Naphtali.
21When Baasha heard this, he stopped building Ramah and withdrew to Tirzah. 22Then King Asa issued an order to all Judah—no
one was exempt—and they carried away from Ramah the stones
and timber Baasha had been using there. With them King Asa built
up Geba in Benjamin, and also Mizpah.
23As for all the other events of Asa's reign, all his achievements,
all he did and the cities he built, are they not written in the book
of the annals of the kings of Judah? In his old age, however, his
feet became diseased. 24Then Asa rested with his fathers and was
buried with them in the city of his father David. And Jehoshaphat
his son succeeded him as king.

Nadab King of Israel

25Nadab son of Jeroboam became king of Israel in the second
year of Asa king of Judah, and he reigned over Israel two years.
26He did evil in the eyes of the LORD, walking in the ways of his father and in his sin, which he had caused Israel to commit.
27Baasha son of Ahijah of the house of Issachar plotted against
him, and he struck him down at Gibbethon, a Philistine town,
while Nadab and all Israel were besieging it. 28Baasha killed
Nadab in the third year of Asa king of Judah and succeeded him
as king.
29As soon as he began to reign, he killed Jeroboam's whole
family. He did not leave Jeroboam anyone that breathed, but destroyed them all, according to the word of the LORD given through

(15:11–14) Lord God, how I long to be remembered by You as a person who did what was right in Your eyes. You long for me to please You, but I cannot do so unless You change me from within. Remove from my life everything that offends You, and strengthen me to do Your will. Transform me, Lord, by the renewing of my mind, and may my heart be fully committed to You all the days of my life. (Ro 12:2)

I delight to do Thy will, O God;
Thy law is within my heart.
Many are the wonders Thou hast done,
There is none to compare with Thee.
Fill my heart with Thy loving kindness,
Breathe on me breath of the Living God.
How I love to sing Thy praises,
How I love to bless Thy holy name!
How I love to sing Thy praises,
How I love to bless Thy holy name!

"I Delight To Do Thy Will"
John Sellers (©1989)

When God created man, to find his blessedness in entire dependence upon Him, and in receiving all life and goodness each moment from Him, humility was the one condition of his continuing in that blessed state. When man disobeyed and fell it was self-exaltation that drew him from God and became the ruling power of his life and the cause of all sin and wretchedness.
Andrew Murray (1828-1917)

(16:1–4) O God, keep me from the stubborn pride of Baasha. You warned him of his coming destruction, yet he did not repent. In spite of the great things You had done for him, he neglected to serve You. Instead, he deliberately walked in Jeroboam's sins; therefore, he suffered Jeroboam's fate. Lord, You warn us so that You will not have to destroy us, for You do not delight in the death of sinners. Help me to heed Your warnings when You speak to me. Help me to walk faithfully in Your ways and to worship You with a humble heart. (1Ki 14:10–11)

his servant Ahijah the Shilonite— [30]because of the sins Jeroboam had committed and had caused Israel to commit, and because he provoked the LORD, the God of Israel, to anger.

[31]As for the other events of Nadab's reign, and all he did, are they not written in the book of the annals of the kings of Israel? [32]There was war between Asa and Baasha king of Israel throughout their reigns.

Baasha King of Israel

[33]In the third year of Asa king of Judah, Baasha son of Ahijah became king of all Israel in Tirzah, and he reigned twenty-four years. [34]He did evil in the eyes of the LORD, walking in the ways of Jeroboam and in his sin, which he had caused Israel to commit.

16 Then the word of the LORD came to Jehu son of Hanani against Baasha: [2]"I lifted you up from the dust and made you leader of my people Israel, but you walked in the ways of Jeroboam and caused my people Israel to sin and to provoke me to anger by their sins. [3]So I am about to consume Baasha and his house, and I will make your house like that of Jeroboam son of Nebat. [4]Dogs will eat those belonging to Baasha who die in the city, and the birds of the air will feed on those who die in the country."

[5]As for the other events of Baasha's reign, what he did and his achievements, are they not written in the book of the annals of the kings of Israel? [6]Baasha rested with his fathers and was buried in Tirzah. And Elah his son succeeded him as king.

[7]Moreover, the word of the LORD came through the prophet Jehu son of Hanani to Baasha and his house, because of all the evil he had done in the eyes of the LORD, provoking him to anger by the things he did, and becoming like the house of Jeroboam—and also because he destroyed it.

Elah King of Israel

[8]In the twenty-sixth year of Asa king of Judah, Elah son of Baasha became king of Israel, and he reigned in Tirzah two years.

[9]Zimri, one of his officials, who had command of half his chariots, plotted against him. Elah was in Tirzah at the time, getting drunk in the home of Arza, the man in charge of the palace at Tirzah. [10]Zimri came in, struck him down and killed him in the twenty-seventh year of Asa king of Judah. Then he succeeded him as king.

[11]As soon as he began to reign and was seated on the throne, he killed off Baasha's whole family. He did not spare a single male, whether relative or friend. [12]So Zimri destroyed the whole family of Baasha, in accordance with the word of the LORD spoken against Baasha through the prophet Jehu— [13]because of all the sins Baasha and his son Elah had committed and had caused Israel to commit, so that they provoked the LORD, the God of Israel, to anger by their worthless idols.

[14]As for the other events of Elah's reign, and all he did, are they not written in the book of the annals of the kings of Israel?

Zimri King of Israel

[15]In the twenty-seventh year of Asa king of Judah, Zimri reigned in Tirzah seven days. The army was encamped near Gibbethon, a Philistine town. [16]When the Israelites in the camp heard that Zimri had plotted against the king and murdered him,

they proclaimed Omri, the commander of the army, king over
Israel that very day there in the camp. 17 Then Omri and all the
Israelites with him withdrew from Gibbethon and laid siege to Tirzah. 18 When Zimri saw that the city was taken, he went into the
citadel of the royal palace and set the palace on fire around him.
So he died, 19 because of the sins he had committed, doing evil in
the eyes of the LORD and walking in the ways of Jeroboam and in
the sin he had committed and had caused Israel to commit.
20 As for the other events of Zimri's reign, and the rebellion he
carried out, are they not written in the book of the annals of the
kings of Israel?

Omri King of Israel

21 Then the people of Israel were split into two factions; half
supported Tibni son of Ginath for king, and the other half supported Omri. 22 But Omri's followers proved stronger than those
of Tibni son of Ginath. So Tibni died and Omri became king.
23 In the thirty-first year of Asa king of Judah, Omri became
king of Israel, and he reigned twelve years, six of them in Tirzah.
24 He bought the hill of Samaria from Shemer for two talents[a] of
silver and built a city on the hill, calling it Samaria, after Shemer,
the name of the former owner of the hill.
25 But Omri did evil in the eyes of the LORD and sinned more
than all those before him. 26 He walked in all the ways of Jeroboam son of Nebat and in his sin, which he had caused Israel to
commit, so that they provoked the LORD, the God of Israel, to
anger by their worthless idols.
27 As for the other events of Omri's reign, what he did and the
things he achieved, are they not written in the book of the annals
of the kings of Israel? 28 Omri rested with his fathers and was
buried in Samaria. And Ahab his son succeeded him as king.

Ahab Becomes King of Israel

29 In the thirty-eighth year of Asa king of Judah, Ahab son of
Omri became king of Israel, and he reigned in Samaria over Israel twenty-two years. 30 Ahab son of Omri did more evil in the
eyes of the LORD than any of those before him. 31 He not only considered it trivial to commit the sins of Jeroboam son of Nebat, but
he also married Jezebel daughter of Ethbaal king of the Sidonians, and began to serve Baal and worship him. 32 He set up an
altar for Baal in the temple of Baal that he built in Samaria.
33 Ahab also made an Asherah pole and did more to provoke the
LORD, the God of Israel, to anger than did all the kings of Israel
before him.
34 In Ahab's time, Hiel of Bethel rebuilt Jericho. He laid its
foundations at the cost of his firstborn son Abiram, and he set up
its gates at the cost of his youngest son Segub, in accordance with
the word of the LORD spoken by Joshua son of Nun.

Elijah Fed by Ravens

17 Now Elijah the Tishbite, from Tishbe[b] in Gilead, said to
Ahab, "As the LORD, the God of Israel, lives, whom I serve,
there will be neither dew nor rain in the next few years except at
my word."
2 Then the word of the LORD came to Elijah: 3 "Leave here, turn

[a] 24 That is, about 150 pounds (about 70 kilograms) [b] 1 Or *Tishbite, of the settlers*

Some value the opinion of others; they court applause—ambitious to be thought patterns of honest, virtuous demeanor and dignified deportment. Others crave an approving verdict from history, caring less what is said of them now by contemporaries than for immortal honors after they die.

The Word of God, however, teaches us to emphasize character far more than reputation, and to "exercise ourselves to have always a conscience void of offence toward God and toward men" (Acts 24:16).

Arthur T. Pierson (1837–1911)

(16:34) Joshua's words may have been long forgotten by Ahab's rebellious subjects, but not by You, Lord God. "Cursed before the LORD is the man who undertakes to rebuild this city, Jericho," Joshua said after his resounding victory. "At the cost of his firstborn son will he lay its foundations; at the cost of his youngest will he set up its gates." Lord, teach us to remember Your prophetic words to Your people, so that we might not offend You in what we do—or in what we leave undone. (Jos 6:26)

(17:7–15) O Lord, You have chosen "the foolish things of the world to shame the wise," and "the weak things of the world to shame the strong." To fully trust You often requires us to set aside our "common" sense and to choose instead uncommon obedience. The widow's simple faith in the words of Your prophet caused her to "foolishly" give up the last of her food. In doing so, she saved her own life and the life of her son. O Lord, give me this kind of "foolish" faith, the kind of faith that says, "Here, take everything," so that I may see the wonders of Your power. (1Co 1:27)

Your Father holds the purse strings. What we lose for His sake He can repay a thousand times. If you obey His will, rest assured that He will provide.

Charles Haddon Spurgeon (1834–1892)

Lord of past ages, Lord of this
morning,
Lord of the future, help us we pray:
Teach us to trust You, love and obey
You,
Crown You each moment Lord of
today.

"God of the Ages"
Margaret Clarkson (©1982)

eastward and hide in the Kerith Ravine, east of the Jordan. 4You
will drink from the brook, and I have ordered the ravens to feed
you there."
5So he did what the LORD had told him. He went to the Kerith
Ravine, east of the Jordan, and stayed there. 6The ravens brought
him bread and meat in the morning and bread and meat in the
evening, and he drank from the brook.

The Widow at Zarephath

7Some time later the brook dried up because there had been
no rain in the land. 8Then the word of the LORD came to him:
9"Go at once to Zarephath of Sidon and stay there. I have commanded a widow in that place to supply you with food." 10So he
went to Zarephath. When he came to the town gate, a widow was
there gathering sticks. He called to her and asked, "Would you
bring me a little water in a jar so I may have a drink?" 11As she
was going to get it, he called, "And bring me, please, a piece of
bread."
12"As surely as the LORD your God lives," she replied, "I don't
have any bread—only a handful of flour in a jar and a little oil in
a jug. I am gathering a few sticks to take home and make a meal
for myself and my son, that we may eat it—and die."
13Elijah said to her, "Don't be afraid. Go home and do as you
have said. But first make a small cake of bread for me from what
you have and bring it to me, and then make something for yourself and your son. 14For this is what the LORD, the God of Israel,
says: 'The jar of flour will not be used up and the jug of oil will
not run dry until the day the LORD gives rain on the land.' "
15She went away and did as Elijah had told her. So there was
food every day for Elijah and for the woman and her family. 16For
the jar of flour was not used up and the jug of oil did not run dry,
in keeping with the word of the LORD spoken by Elijah.
17Some time later the son of the woman who owned the house
became ill. He grew worse and worse, and finally stopped breathing. 18She said to Elijah, "What do you have against me, man of
God? Did you come to remind me of my sin and kill my son?"
19"Give me your son," Elijah replied. He took him from her
arms, carried him to the upper room where he was staying, and
laid him on his bed. 20Then he cried out to the LORD, "O LORD my
God, have you brought tragedy also upon this widow I am staying
with, by causing her son to die?" 21Then he stretched himself out
on the boy three times and cried to the LORD, "O LORD my God, let
this boy's life return to him!"
22The LORD heard Elijah's cry, and the boy's life returned to
him, and he lived. 23Elijah picked up the child and carried him
down from the room into the house. He gave him to his mother
and said, "Look, your son is alive!"
24Then the woman said to Elijah, "Now I know that you are a
man of God and that the word of the LORD from your mouth is the
truth."

Elijah and Obadiah

18 After a long time, in the third year, the word of the LORD
came to Elijah: "Go and present yourself to Ahab, and I
will send rain on the land." 2So Elijah went to present himself to
Ahab.
Now the famine was severe in Samaria, 3and Ahab had sum-

moned Obadiah, who was in charge of his palace. (Obadiah was
a devout believer in the LORD. 4While Jezebel was killing off the
LORD's prophets, Obadiah had taken a hundred prophets and hidden them in two caves, fifty in each, and had supplied them with
food and water.) 5Ahab had said to Obadiah, "Go through the
land to all the springs and valleys. Maybe we can find some grass
to keep the horses and mules alive so we will not have to kill any
of our animals." 6So they divided the land they were to cover,
Ahab going in one direction and Obadiah in another.

7As Obadiah was walking along, Elijah met him. Obadiah recognized him, bowed down to the ground, and said, "Is it really
you, my lord Elijah?"

8"Yes," he replied. "Go tell your master, 'Elijah is here.' "

9"What have I done wrong," asked Obadiah, "that you are
handing your servant over to Ahab to be put to death? 10As surely as the LORD your God lives, there is not a nation or kingdom
where my master has not sent someone to look for you. And
whenever a nation or kingdom claimed you were not there, he
made them swear they could not find you. 11But now you tell me
to go to my master and say, 'Elijah is here.' 12I don't know where
the Spirit of the LORD may carry you when I leave you. If I go and
tell Ahab and he doesn't find you, he will kill me. Yet I your servant have worshiped the LORD since my youth. 13Haven't you
heard, my lord, what I did while Jezebel was killing the prophets
of the LORD? I hid a hundred of the LORD's prophets in two caves,
fifty in each, and supplied them with food and water. 14And now
you tell me to go to my master and say, 'Elijah is here.' He will
kill me!"

15Elijah said, "As the LORD Almighty lives, whom I serve, I will
surely present myself to Ahab today."

Elijah on Mount Carmel

16So Obadiah went to meet Ahab and told him, and Ahab went
to meet Elijah. 17When he saw Elijah, he said to him, "Is that you,
you troubler of Israel?"

18"I have not made trouble for Israel," Elijah replied. "But you
and your father's family have. You have abandoned the LORD's
commands and have followed the Baals. 19Now summon the people from all over Israel to meet me on Mount Carmel. And bring
the four hundred and fifty prophets of Baal and the four hundred
prophets of Asherah, who eat at Jezebel's table."

20So Ahab sent word throughout all Israel and assembled the
prophets on Mount Carmel. 21Elijah went before the people and
said, "How long will you waver between two opinions? If the LORD
is God, follow him; but if Baal is God, follow him."

But the people said nothing.

22Then Elijah said to them, "I am the only one of the LORD's
prophets left, but Baal has four hundred and fifty prophets. 23Get
two bulls for us. Let them choose one for themselves, and let
them cut it into pieces and put it on the wood but not set fire to
it. I will prepare the other bull and put it on the wood but not set
fire to it. 24Then you call on the name of your god, and I will call
on the name of the LORD. The god who answers by fire—he is
God."

Then all the people said, "What you say is good."

25Elijah said to the prophets of Baal, "Choose one of the bulls
and prepare it first, since there are so many of you. Call on the

Once to every man and nation
Comes the moment to decide,
In the strife of truth with falsehood,
For the good or evil side;
Some great cause, some great
  decision,
Off'ring each the bloom or blight,
And the choice goes by forever
'Twixt that darkness and that light.

Though the cause of evil prosper,
Yet the truth alone is strong;
Though her portion be the scaffold,
And upon the throne be wrong,
Yet that scaffold sways the future,
And, behind the dim unknown,
Standeth God within the shadow,
Keeping watch above His own.

"Once to Every Man and Nation"
James Russell Lowell (1819-1891)

(18:1–15) Lord, You have good plans for us, but we must learn to listen and to trust Your intentions. Sometimes You want to use us anonymously; sometimes You expose us for all the world to see. Obadiah did well to hide Your prophets from the evil hand of Jezebel, but You had other plans for Elijah. It was Your will to place him at center stage, in full view of everyone, and to work Your wonders through him. Teach us to obey You, Lord, whether You wish us to be seen or unseen, known or unknown, for both our glory and our protection lie in our submission to Your perfect will.

It may seem a very terrible thing for the soul to yield itself wholly and unreservedly to the will of Christ. "What is going to happen? What about tomorrow? Will He not put a very heavy burden upon me if I yield, if I take the yoke?" Ah, you have not known my Master; you have not looked into His face; you have not realized His infinite love for you. Why, God's will for you means your fullest happiness!

Lettie B. Cowman (1870-1960)

(18:26–40) O God, as Elijah prepared the sacrifice and cried out to You in prayer, so I offer You my heart this day. Let Your fire fall on me until I am fully consumed. I abhor every false way and renounce everything that is not of You. Put to death every sin that lingers in my life and every ungodly influence that seeks to raise itself above Your name. Let none of it remain—no unholy compromises, no "managed" sins, no hedged bets. And after You have sent the fire, then send the rain of Your spirit to quench the parched ground in my soul.

Jesus, my strength, my hope,
On Thee I cast my care,
With humble confidence look up,
And know Thou hear'st my prayer.
Give me on Thee to wait
Till I can all things do;
On Thee, almighty to create,
Almighty to renew.

I want a true regard,
A single steady aim,
Unmoved by threat'ning or reward,
To Thee and Thy great name;
A jealous, just concern
For Thine immortal praise;
A pure desire that all may learn
And glorify Thy grace.

"Jesus, My Strength, My Hope"
Charles Wesley (1742)

name of your god, but do not light the fire." 26 So they took the
bull given them and prepared it.
Then they called on the name of Baal from morning till noon.
"O Baal, answer us!" they shouted. But there was no response; no
one answered. And they danced around the altar they had made.
27 At noon Elijah began to taunt them. "Shout louder!" he said.
"Surely he is a god! Perhaps he is deep in thought, or busy, or
traveling. Maybe he is sleeping and must be awakened." 28 So they
shouted louder and slashed themselves with swords and spears,
as was their custom, until their blood flowed. 29 Midday passed,
and they continued their frantic prophesying until the time for the
evening sacrifice. But there was no response, no one answered,
no one paid attention.
30 Then Elijah said to all the people, "Come here to me." They
came to him, and he repaired the altar of the LORD, which was in
ruins. 31 Elijah took twelve stones, one for each of the tribes descended from Jacob, to whom the word of the LORD had come,
saying, "Your name shall be Israel." 32 With the stones he built an
altar in the name of the LORD, and he dug a trench around it large
enough to hold two seahs[a] of seed. 33 He arranged the wood, cut
the bull into pieces and laid it on the wood. Then he said to them,
"Fill four large jars with water and pour it on the offering and on
the wood."
34 "Do it again," he said, and they did it again.
"Do it a third time," he ordered, and they did it the third time.
35 The water ran down around the altar and even filled the trench.
36 At the time of sacrifice, the prophet Elijah stepped forward
and prayed: "O LORD, God of Abraham, Isaac and Israel, let it be
known today that you are God in Israel and that I am your servant
and have done all these things at your command. 37 Answer me,
O LORD, answer me, so these people will know that you, O LORD,
are God, and that you are turning their hearts back again."
38 Then the fire of the LORD fell and burned up the sacrifice, the
wood, the stones and the soil, and also licked up the water in the
trench.
39 When all the people saw this, they fell prostrate and cried,
"The LORD—he is God! The LORD—he is God!"
40 Then Elijah commanded them, "Seize the prophets of Baal.
Don't let anyone get away!" They seized them, and Elijah had
them brought down to the Kishon Valley and slaughtered there.
41 And Elijah said to Ahab, "Go, eat and drink, for there is the
sound of a heavy rain." 42 So Ahab went off to eat and drink, but
Elijah climbed to the top of Carmel, bent down to the ground and
put his face between his knees.
43 "Go and look toward the sea," he told his servant. And he
went up and looked.
"There is nothing there," he said.
Seven times Elijah said, "Go back."
44 The seventh time the servant reported, "A cloud as small as
a man's hand is rising from the sea."
So Elijah said, "Go and tell Ahab, 'Hitch up your chariot and go
down before the rain stops you.'"
45 Meanwhile, the sky grew black with clouds, the wind rose, a
heavy rain came on and Ahab rode off to Jezreel. 46 The power of

[a] 32 That is, probably about 13 quarts (about 15 liters)

the LORD came upon Elijah and, tucking his cloak into his belt, he
ran ahead of Ahab all the way to Jezreel.

Elijah Flees to Horeb

19 Now Ahab told Jezebel everything Elijah had done and how
he had killed all the prophets with the sword. 2 So Jezebel
sent a messenger to Elijah to say, "May the gods deal with me, be
it ever so severely, if by this time tomorrow I do not make your
life like that of one of them."
3 Elijah was afraid[a] and ran for his life. When he came to Beersheba in Judah, he left his servant there, 4 while he himself went
a day's journey into the desert. He came to a broom tree, sat
down under it and prayed that he might die. "I have had enough,
LORD," he said. "Take my life; I am no better than my ancestors."
5 Then he lay down under the tree and fell asleep.
All at once an angel touched him and said, "Get up and eat."
6 He looked around, and there by his head was a cake of bread
baked over hot coals, and a jar of water. He ate and drank and
then lay down again.
7 The angel of the LORD came back a second time and touched
him and said, "Get up and eat, for the journey is too much for
you." 8 So he got up and ate and drank. Strengthened by that food,
he traveled forty days and forty nights until he reached Horeb, the
mountain of God. 9 There he went into a cave and spent the night.

The LORD Appears to Elijah

And the word of the LORD came to him: "What are you doing
here, Elijah?"
10 He replied, "I have been very zealous for the LORD God
Almighty. The Israelites have rejected your covenant, broken
down your altars, and put your prophets to death with the sword.
I am the only one left, and now they are trying to kill me too."
11 The LORD said, "Go out and stand on the mountain in the
presence of the LORD, for the LORD is about to pass by."
Then a great and powerful wind tore the mountains apart and
shattered the rocks before the LORD, but the LORD was not in the
wind. After the wind there was an earthquake, but the LORD was
not in the earthquake. 12 After the earthquake came a fire, but the
LORD was not in the fire. And after the fire came a gentle whisper.
13 When Elijah heard it, he pulled his cloak over his face and went
out and stood at the mouth of the cave.
Then a voice said to him, "What are you doing here, Elijah?"
14 He replied, "I have been very zealous for the LORD God
Almighty. The Israelites have rejected your covenant, broken
down your altars, and put your prophets to death with the sword.
I am the only one left, and now they are trying to kill me too."
15 The LORD said to him, "Go back the way you came, and go to
the Desert of Damascus. When you get there, anoint Hazael king
over Aram. 16 Also, anoint Jehu son of Nimshi king over Israel,
and anoint Elisha son of Shaphat from Abel Meholah to succeed
you as prophet. 17 Jehu will put to death any who escape the
sword of Hazael, and Elisha will put to death any who escape the
sword of Jehu. 18 Yet I reserve seven thousand in Israel—all
whose knees have not bowed down to Baal and all whose mouths
have not kissed him."

[a] 3 Or *Elijah saw*

(19:3–18) You know me so well, Lord. You know my fears and my limitations. And, like Elijah, sometimes the journey is just too much for me. Lord, when I am afraid and ready to quit, let me feast on the bread of Your Word and the water of Your Spirit. Visit me with Your manifest presence and speak to me with Your still small voice. Renew my vision and send me on in this great adventure of faith. (Isa 50:4–5; Mt 4:4; Jn 7:38–39)

O let me hear Thee speaking
In accents clear and still,
Above the storms of passion,
The murmurs of self-will.
O speak to reassure me,
To hasten or control;
O speak, and make me listen,
Thou Guardian of my soul.

"O Jesus, I Have Promised"
John E. Bode (1866)

We read in the Word, "He loved us and gave Himself for us." It was not what we were worth in ourselves, but what we were worth to His own fathomless love, that led Him to shed His blood for our redemption.

But the fact remains, He bought us and we belong to Him. Dare we withhold ourselves from the One who bought us and Whose we actually are?

George Christian Weiss (1910-)

(19:19–21) When You call us into Your service, Lord, it is an event worth celebrating. Elisha burned the plow and gave everything away for the sake of a heavenly treasure. Indeed, "no one who has left home or wife or brothers or parents or children for the sake of the kingdom of God will fail to receive many times as much in this age and, in the age to come, eternal life." Thank You for the great privilege of serving Your Kingdom, for You are a just and holy King, and there is no greater honor than to do Your bidding and carry Your message to the world. (Lk 18:29–30)

Skills and time are ours for pressing
T'ward the goals of Christ, Thy Son:
Men at peace in health and
Freedom,
Races joined, the Church made one.
Now direct our daily labor,
Lest we strive for self alone;
Born with talents, make us servants
Fit to answer at Thy throne.

"God, Whose Giving Knows No Ending"
Robert Lansing Edwards (©1961)

The Call of Elisha

19So Elijah went from there and found Elisha son of Shaphat.
He was plowing with twelve yoke of oxen, and he himself was
driving the twelfth pair. Elijah went up to him and threw his cloak
around him. 20Elisha then left his oxen and ran after Elijah. "Let
me kiss my father and mother good-by," he said, "and then I will
come with you."
"Go back," Elijah replied. "What have I done to you?"
21So Elisha left him and went back. He took his yoke of oxen
and slaughtered them. He burned the plowing equipment to cook
the meat and gave it to the people, and they ate. Then he set out
to follow Elijah and became his attendant.

Ben-Hadad Attacks Samaria

20 Now Ben-Hadad king of Aram mustered his entire army.
Accompanied by thirty-two kings with their horses and
chariots, he went up and besieged Samaria and attacked it. 2He
sent messengers into the city to Ahab king of Israel, saying, "This
is what Ben-Hadad says: 3'Your silver and gold are mine, and the
best of your wives and children are mine.' "
4The king of Israel answered, "Just as you say, my lord the
king. I and all I have are yours."
5The messengers came again and said, "This is what Ben-
Hadad says: 'I sent to demand your silver and gold, your wives
and your children. 6But about this time tomorrow I am going to
send my officials to search your palace and the houses of your officials. They will seize everything you value and carry it away.' "
7The king of Israel summoned all the elders of the land and
said to them, "See how this man is looking for trouble! When he
sent for my wives and my children, my silver and my gold, I did
not refuse him."
8The elders and the people all answered, "Don't listen to him
or agree to his demands."
9So he replied to Ben-Hadad's messengers, "Tell my lord the
king, 'Your servant will do all you demanded the first time, but
this demand I cannot meet.' " They left and took the answer back
to Ben-Hadad.
10Then Ben-Hadad sent another message to Ahab: "May the
gods deal with me, be it ever so severely, if enough dust remains
in Samaria to give each of my men a handful."
11The king of Israel answered, "Tell him: 'One who puts on his
armor should not boast like one who takes it off.' "
12Ben-Hadad heard this message while he and the kings were
drinking in their tents,[a] and he ordered his men: "Prepare to attack." So they prepared to attack the city.

Ahab Defeats Ben-Hadad

13Meanwhile a prophet came to Ahab king of Israel and announced, "This is what the LORD says: 'Do you see this vast army?
I will give it into your hand today, and then you will know that I
am the LORD.' "
14"But who will do this?" asked Ahab.
The prophet replied, "This is what the LORD says: 'The young
officers of the provincial commanders will do it.' "
"And who will start the battle?" he asked.

[a] *12* Or *in Succoth*; also in verse 16

The prophet answered, "You will."
15So Ahab summoned the young officers of the provincial commanders, 232 men. Then he assembled the rest of the Israelites, 7,000 in all. 16They set out at noon while Ben-Hadad and
the 32 kings allied with him were in their tents getting drunk.
17The young officers of the provincial commanders went out first.
Now Ben-Hadad had dispatched scouts, who reported, "Men
are advancing from Samaria."
18He said, "If they have come out for peace, take them alive; if
they have come out for war, take them alive."
19The young officers of the provincial commanders marched
out of the city with the army behind them 20and each one struck
down his opponent. At that, the Arameans fled, with the Israelites
in pursuit. But Ben-Hadad king of Aram escaped on horseback
with some of his horsemen. 21The king of Israel advanced and
overpowered the horses and chariots and inflicted heavy losses
on the Arameans.
22Afterward, the prophet came to the king of Israel and said,
"Strengthen your position and see what must be done, because
next spring the king of Aram will attack you again."
23Meanwhile, the officials of the king of Aram advised him,
"Their gods are gods of the hills. That is why they were too strong
for us. But if we fight them on the plains, surely we will be
stronger than they. 24Do this: Remove all the kings from their
commands and replace them with other officers. 25You must also
raise an army like the one you lost—horse for horse and chariot
for chariot—so we can fight Israel on the plains. Then surely we
will be stronger than they." He agreed with them and acted accordingly.
26The next spring Ben-Hadad mustered the Arameans and
went up to Aphek to fight against Israel. 27When the Israelites
were also mustered and given provisions, they marched out to
meet them. The Israelites camped opposite them like two small
flocks of goats, while the Arameans covered the countryside.
28The man of God came up and told the king of Israel, "This is
what the LORD says: 'Because the Arameans think the LORD is a
god of the hills and not a god of the valleys, I will deliver this vast
army into your hands, and you will know that I am the LORD.' "
29For seven days they camped opposite each other, and on the
seventh day the battle was joined. The Israelites inflicted a hundred thousand casualties on the Aramean foot soldiers in one day.
30The rest of them escaped to the city of Aphek, where the wall
collapsed on twenty-seven thousand of them. And Ben-Hadad fled
to the city and hid in an inner room.
31His officials said to him, "Look, we have heard that the kings
of the house of Israel are merciful. Let us go to the king of Israel
with sackcloth around our waists and ropes around our heads.
Perhaps he will spare your life."
32Wearing sackcloth around their waists and ropes around
their heads, they went to the king of Israel and said, "Your servant
Ben-Hadad says: 'Please let me live.' "
The king answered, "Is he still alive? He is my brother."
33The men took this as a good sign and were quick to pick up
his word. "Yes, your brother Ben-Hadad!" they said.
"Go and get him," the king said. When Ben-Hadad came out,
Ahab had him come up into his chariot.
34"I will return the cities my father took from your father,"

(20:27–30) Almighty God, I give You praise. Your ways are far beyond human reason: You enable the weak to confound the strong; You enable one to put a thousand to flight and two to vanquish ten thousand. Truly, You are our shield and our defender. You give us the victory for the sake of Your great name. (Dt 32:30)

God . . . is not in the business of helping the humanly strong become stronger; rather he takes the weak and makes them strong in himself.

Erwin W. Lutzer (1941-)

God's commandments are uncompromising, inexorable, unqualified, and our obedience must be inflexible, absolute and complete. The faintest reservation is really the very soul of disobedience.

Albert Benjamin Simpson (1843-1919)

(20:32–43) Ahab did not consult You, his covenant God, before he covenanted with his enemy. O God, keep me from such foolish presumption. Let there be no unholy alliances in my life. May I always seek Your will in every relationship, be it personal or professional, and may I never compromise what is right for what is convenient.

Ben-Hadad offered. "You may set up your own market areas in Damascus, as my father did in Samaria."

⌊Ahab said,⌋ "On the basis of a treaty I will set you free." So he made a treaty with him, and let him go.

A Prophet Condemns Ahab

35By the word of the LORD one of the sons of the prophets said to his companion, "Strike me with your weapon," but the man refused.

36So the prophet said, "Because you have not obeyed the LORD, as soon as you leave me a lion will kill you." And after the man went away, a lion found him and killed him.

37The prophet found another man and said, "Strike me, please." So the man struck him and wounded him.
38Then the prophet went and stood by the road waiting for the king. He disguised himself with his headband down over his eyes.
39As the king passed by, the prophet called out to him, "Your servant went into the thick of the battle, and someone came to me with a captive and said, 'Guard this man. If he is missing, it will be your life for his life, or you must pay a talent[a] of silver.'
40While your servant was busy here and there, the man disappeared."

"That is your sentence," the king of Israel said. "You have pronounced it yourself."

41Then the prophet quickly removed the headband from his eyes, and the king of Israel recognized him as one of the prophets.
42He said to the king, "This is what the LORD says: 'You have set free a man I had determined should die.[b] Therefore it is your life for his life, your people for his people.' "
43Sullen and angry, the king of Israel went to his palace in Samaria.

Naboth's Vineyard

21 Some time later there was an incident involving a vineyard belonging to Naboth the Jezreelite. The vineyard was in Jezreel, close to the palace of Ahab king of Samaria.
2Ahab said to Naboth, "Let me have your vineyard to use for a vegetable garden, since it is close to my palace. In exchange I will give you a better vineyard or, if you prefer, I will pay you whatever it is worth."

3But Naboth replied, "The LORD forbid that I should give you the inheritance of my fathers."

4So Ahab went home, sullen and angry because Naboth the Jezreelite had said, "I will not give you the inheritance of my fathers." He lay on his bed sulking and refused to eat.

5His wife Jezebel came in and asked him, "Why are you so sullen? Why won't you eat?"

6He answered her, "Because I said to Naboth the Jezreelite, 'Sell me your vineyard; or if you prefer, I will give you another vineyard in its place.' But he said, 'I will not give you my vineyard.' "

7Jezebel his wife said, "Is this how you act as king over Israel? Get up and eat! Cheer up. I'll get you the vineyard of Naboth the Jezreelite."

8So she wrote letters in Ahab's name, placed his seal on them, and sent them to the elders and nobles who lived in Naboth's city with him.
9In those letters she wrote:

[a] 39 That is, about 75 pounds (about 34 kilograms) [b] 42 The Hebrew term refers to the irrevocable giving over of things or persons to the LORD, often by totally destroying them.

"Proclaim a day of fasting and seat Naboth in a prominent place among the people. 10But seat two scoundrels opposite him and have them testify that he has cursed both God and the king. Then take him out and stone him to death."

11So the elders and nobles who lived in Naboth's city did as Jezebel directed in the letters she had written to them. 12They proclaimed a fast and seated Naboth in a prominent place among the people. 13Then two scoundrels came and sat opposite him and brought charges against Naboth before the people, saying, "Naboth has cursed both God and the king." So they took him outside the city and stoned him to death. 14Then they sent word to Jezebel: "Naboth has been stoned and is dead."

15As soon as Jezebel heard that Naboth had been stoned to death, she said to Ahab, "Get up and take possession of the vineyard of Naboth the Jezreelite that he refused to sell you. He is no longer alive, but dead." 16When Ahab heard that Naboth was dead, he got up and went down to take possession of Naboth's vineyard.

17Then the word of the LORD came to Elijah the Tishbite: 18"Go down to meet Ahab king of Israel, who rules in Samaria. He is now in Naboth's vineyard, where he has gone to take possession of it. 19Say to him, 'This is what the LORD says: Have you not murdered a man and seized his property?' Then say to him, 'This is what the LORD says: In the place where dogs licked up Naboth's blood, dogs will lick up your blood—yes, yours!' "

20Ahab said to Elijah, "So you have found me, my enemy!"

"I have found you," he answered, "because you have sold yourself to do evil in the eyes of the LORD. 21'I am going to bring disaster on you. I will consume your descendants and cut off from Ahab every last male in Israel—slave or free. 22I will make your house like that of Jeroboam son of Nebat and that of Baasha son of Ahijah, because you have provoked me to anger and have caused Israel to sin.'

23"And also concerning Jezebel the LORD says: 'Dogs will devour Jezebel by the wall of[a] Jezreel.'

24"Dogs will eat those belonging to Ahab who die in the city, and the birds of the air will feed on those who die in the country."

25(There was never a man like Ahab, who sold himself to do evil in the eyes of the LORD, urged on by Jezebel his wife. 26He behaved in the vilest manner by going after idols, like the Amorites the LORD drove out before Israel.)

27When Ahab heard these words, he tore his clothes, put on sackcloth and fasted. He lay in sackcloth and went around meekly.

28Then the word of the LORD came to Elijah the Tishbite: 29"Have you noticed how Ahab has humbled himself before me? Because he has humbled himself, I will not bring this disaster in his day, but I will bring it on his house in the days of his son."

Micaiah Prophesies Against Ahab

22 For three years there was no war between Aram and Israel. 2But in the third year Jehoshaphat king of Judah went down to see the king of Israel. 3The king of Israel had said to his

[a] *23* Most Hebrew manuscripts; a few Hebrew manuscripts, Vulgate and Syriac (see also 2 Kings 9:26) *the plot of ground at*

(21:9–16) Lord, I confess that I sometimes do not understand You. When I see the fate of Naboth, I have to ask, as the prophet Habakkuk once asked, "Why then do you tolerate the treacherous? Why are you silent while the wicked swallow up those more righteous than themselves?" Why didn't You prevent this? O God, when life seems unfair, when power is on the side of the oppressors, when the righteous get what the wicked deserve and the wicked get what the righteous deserve, help me to trust in Your sovereignty. (Ecc 4:1; 8:14; Hab 1:13)

Forgive us, Lord, that as we grow to maturity, our faith is blighted with doubts, withered with worry, tainted with sophistication. We pray that thou wilt make us like children again in faith—not childish, but childlike in the simplicity of a faith that is willing to trust thee even though we cannot see what tomorrow will bring.

We ask thee to give to each of us that childlike faith, that simplicity of mind which is willing to lay aside all egotism and conceit, which recognizes vanity for what it is—an empty show, which knows that we are incapable of thinking the thoughts of God, which is willing to be humble again.

Peter Marshall (1902–1949)

officials, "Don't you know that Ramoth Gilead belongs to us and
yet we are doing nothing to retake it from the king of Aram?"
4So he asked Jehoshaphat, "Will you go with me to fight against
Ramoth Gilead?"
Jehoshaphat replied to the king of Israel, "I am as you are, my
people as your people, my horses as your horses." 5But Jehoshaphat also said to the king of Israel, "First seek the counsel of the
LORD."
6So the king of Israel brought together the prophets—about
four hundred men—and asked them, "Shall I go to war against
Ramoth Gilead, or shall I refrain?"
"Go," they answered, "for the Lord will give it into the king's
hand."
7But Jehoshaphat asked, "Is there not a prophet of the LORD
here whom we can inquire of?"
8The king of Israel answered Jehoshaphat, "There is still one
man through whom we can inquire of the LORD, but I hate him because he never prophesies anything good about me, but always
bad. He is Micaiah son of Imlah."
"The king should not say that," Jehoshaphat replied.
9So the king of Israel called one of his officials and said, "Bring
Micaiah son of Imlah at once."
10Dressed in their royal robes, the king of Israel and Jehoshaphat king of Judah were sitting on their thrones at the threshing
floor by the entrance of the gate of Samaria, with all the prophets
prophesying before them. 11Now Zedekiah son of Kenaanah had
made iron horns and he declared, "This is what the LORD says:
'With these you will gore the Arameans until they are destroyed.' "
12All the other prophets were prophesying the same thing. "Attack Ramoth Gilead and be victorious," they said, "for the LORD
will give it into the king's hand."
13The messenger who had gone to summon Micaiah said to
him, "Look, as one man the other prophets are predicting success
for the king. Let your word agree with theirs, and speak favorably."
14But Micaiah said, "As surely as the LORD lives, I can tell him
only what the LORD tells me."
15When he arrived, the king asked him, "Micaiah, shall we go
to war against Ramoth Gilead, or shall I refrain?"
"Attack and be victorious," he answered, "for the LORD will give
it into the king's hand."
16The king said to him, "How many times must I make you
swear to tell me nothing but the truth in the name of the LORD?"
17Then Micaiah answered, "I saw all Israel scattered on the
hills like sheep without a shepherd, and the LORD said, 'These people have no master. Let each one go home in peace.' "
18The king of Israel said to Jehoshaphat, "Didn't I tell you that
he never prophesies anything good about me, but only bad?"
19Micaiah continued, "Therefore hear the word of the LORD: I
saw the LORD sitting on his throne with all the host of heaven standing around him on his right and on his left. 20And the LORD said,
'Who will entice Ahab into attacking Ramoth Gilead and going to
his death there?'
"One suggested this, and another that. 21Finally, a spirit came
forward, stood before the LORD and said, 'I will entice him.'
22" 'By what means?' the LORD asked.
" 'I will go out and be a lying spirit in the mouths of all his
prophets,' he said.

(22:14) Father, I long to have integrity and courage like Micaiah. Whether I am called upon to speak to a neighbor, a boss, or a king, help me to remember that I serve a greater king, the King of kings, who is dressed in whiter robes and is seated upon a more glorious throne than any earthly power. Let me never be afraid or ashamed to speak the truth in the name of the Lord.

(22:17) In Ahab's previous battle with the Arameans, the sheep put the wolves to flight. This time around, the sheep were scattered on the hills. O God, victory is Yours to give to the humble and Yours to withhold from the proud.

" 'You will succeed in enticing him,' said the LORD. 'Go and
do it.'
23"So now the LORD has put a lying spirit in the mouths of all
these prophets of yours. The LORD has decreed disaster for you."
24Then Zedekiah son of Kenaanah went up and slapped Micaiah in the face. "Which way did the spirit from[a] the LORD go when
he went from me to speak to you?" he asked.
25Micaiah replied, "You will find out on the day you go to hide
in an inner room."
26The king of Israel then ordered, "Take Micaiah and send him
back to Amon the ruler of the city and to Joash the king's son
27and say, 'This is what the king says: Put this fellow in prison
and give him nothing but bread and water until I return safely.' "
28Micaiah declared, "If you ever return safely, the LORD has not
spoken through me." Then he added, "Mark my words, all you
people!"

Ahab Killed at Ramoth Gilead

29So the king of Israel and Jehoshaphat king of Judah went up
to Ramoth Gilead. 30The king of Israel said to Jehoshaphat, "I
will enter the battle in disguise, but you wear your royal robes."
So the king of Israel disguised himself and went into battle.
31Now the king of Aram had ordered his thirty-two chariot
commanders, "Do not fight with anyone, small or great, except
the king of Israel." 32When the chariot commanders saw Jehoshaphat, they thought, "Surely this is the king of Israel." So they
turned to attack him, but when Jehoshaphat cried out, 33the chariot commanders saw that he was not the king of Israel and
stopped pursuing him.
34But someone drew his bow at random and hit the king of Israel between the sections of his armor. The king told his chariot
driver, "Wheel around and get me out of the fighting. I've been
wounded." 35All day long the battle raged, and the king was
propped up in his chariot facing the Arameans. The blood from
his wound ran onto the floor of the chariot, and that evening he
died. 36As the sun was setting, a cry spread through the army:
"Every man to his town; everyone to his land!"
37So the king died and was brought to Samaria, and they
buried him there. 38They washed the chariot at a pool in Samaria
(where the prostitutes bathed),[b] and the dogs licked up his
blood, as the word of the LORD had declared.
39As for the other events of Ahab's reign, including all he did,
the palace he built and inlaid with ivory, and the cities he fortified,
are they not written in the book of the annals of the kings of Israel? 40Ahab rested with his fathers. And Ahaziah his son succeeded him as king.

Jehoshaphat King of Judah

41Jehoshaphat son of Asa became king of Judah in the fourth
year of Ahab king of Israel. 42Jehoshaphat was thirty-five years
old when he became king, and he reigned in Jerusalem twenty-
five years. His mother's name was Azubah daughter of Shilhi. 43In
everything he walked in the ways of his father Asa and did not
stray from them; he did what was right in the eyes of the LORD. The
high places, however, were not removed, and the people contin-

[a] 24 Or *Spirit of* [b] 38 Or *Samaria and cleaned the weapons*

God is a great king above all kings, and has a throne above all the thrones of earthly princes. The rise and fall of princes, the issues of war, and all the great affairs of state, which are the subject of the consultations of wise and great men, are no more above God's direction than the meanest concerns of the poorest cottages are below his notice. It is not without the divine permission that the devil deceives men, and even thereby God serves his purposes.

Matthew Henry (1662-1714)

(22:20–23) Ahab was enticed because he "refused to love the truth and so be saved." For this reason You sent him a powerful delusion so that he would believe the lie; for indeed "all will be condemned who have not believed the truth but have delighted in wickedness." "To God belong wisdom and power; counsel and understanding are his. What he tears down cannot be rebuilt; the man he imprisons cannot be released . . . To him belong strength and victory; both deceived and deceiver are his." (Job 12:13–16; 2Th 2:9–12)

ued to offer sacrifices and burn incense there. 44 Jehoshaphat was
also at peace with the king of Israel.
45 As for the other events of Jehoshaphat's reign, the things he
achieved and his military exploits, are they not written in the
book of the annals of the kings of Judah? 46 He rid the land of the
rest of the male shrine prostitutes who remained there even after
the reign of his father Asa. 47 There was then no king in Edom; a
deputy ruled.
48 Now Jehoshaphat built a fleet of trading ships[a] to go to Ophir
for gold, but they never set sail—they were wrecked at Ezion
Geber. 49 At that time Ahaziah son of Ahab said to Jehoshaphat,
"Let my men sail with your men," but Jehoshaphat refused.
50 Then Jehoshaphat rested with his fathers and was buried
with them in the city of David his father. And Jehoram his son succeeded him.

Ahaziah King of Israel

51 Ahaziah son of Ahab became king of Israel in Samaria in the
seventeenth year of Jehoshaphat king of Judah, and he reigned
over Israel two years. 52 He did evil in the eyes of the LORD, because he walked in the ways of his father and mother and in the
ways of Jeroboam son of Nebat, who caused Israel to sin. 53 He
served and worshiped Baal and provoked the LORD, the God of Israel, to anger, just as his father had done.

Most of us read the Bible the way a mouse tries to remove the cheese from the trap without getting caught. Some of us have mastered that. We have read the story as though it were about someone else a long time ago; that way we don't get caught.
Søren Kierkegaard (1813-1855)

(22:45–53) I thank You, Father, for the written record of the lives of those who have gone before us. By them You teach us the lessons of faith and godliness; and by them You warn us of the consequences of sin. "For everything that was written in the past was written to teach us, so that through endurance and the encouragement of the Scriptures we might have hope." (Ro 15:4; 1Co 10:6,11)

[a] 48 Hebrew *of ships of Tarshish*

The LORD's Judgment on Ahaziah

1 After Ahab's death, Moab rebelled against Israel. 2Now Ahaziah had fallen through the lattice of his upper room in Samaria
and injured himself. So he sent messengers, saying to them, "Go
and consult Baal-Zebub, the god of Ekron, to see if I will recover
from this injury."
3But the angel of the LORD said to Elijah the Tishbite, "Go up
and meet the messengers of the king of Samaria and ask them, 'Is
it because there is no God in Israel that you are going off to consult Baal-Zebub, the god of Ekron?' 4Therefore this is what the
LORD says: 'You will not leave the bed you are lying on. You will
certainly die!' " So Elijah went.
5When the messengers returned to the king, he asked them,
"Why have you come back?"
6"A man came to meet us," they replied. "And he said to us,
'Go back to the king who sent you and tell him, "This is what the
LORD says: Is it because there is no God in Israel that you are
sending men to consult Baal-Zebub, the god of Ekron? Therefore
you will not leave the bed you are lying on. You will certainly
die!" ' "
7The king asked them, "What kind of man was it who came to
meet you and told you this?"
8They replied, "He was a man with a garment of hair and with
a leather belt around his waist."
The king said, "That was Elijah the Tishbite."
9Then he sent to Elijah a captain with his company of fifty men.
The captain went up to Elijah, who was sitting on the top of a hill,
and said to him, "Man of God, the king says, 'Come down!' "
10Elijah answered the captain, "If I am a man of God, may fire
come down from heaven and consume you and your fifty men!"
Then fire fell from heaven and consumed the captain and his
men.
11At this the king sent to Elijah another captain with his fifty
men. The captain said to him, "Man of God, this is what the king
says, 'Come down at once!' "
12"If I am a man of God," Elijah replied, "may fire come down
from heaven and consume you and your fifty men!" Then the fire
of God fell from heaven and consumed him and his fifty men.
13So the king sent a third captain with his fifty men. This third
captain went up and fell on his knees before Elijah. "Man of
God," he begged, "please have respect for my life and the lives of
these fifty men, your servants! 14See, fire has fallen from heaven
and consumed the first two captains and all their men. But now
have respect for my life!"
15The angel of the LORD said to Elijah, "Go down with him; do
not be afraid of him." So Elijah got up and went down with him
to the king.
16He told the king, "This is what the LORD says: Is it because
there is no God in Israel for you to consult that you have sent
messengers to consult Baal-Zebub, the god of Ekron? Because
you have done this, you will never leave the bed you are lying on.
You will certainly die!" 17So he died, according to the word of the
LORD that Elijah had spoken.
Because Ahaziah had no son, Joram[a] succeeded him as king in
the second year of Jehoram son of Jehoshaphat king of Judah.

[a] *17* Hebrew *Jehoram,* a variant of *Joram*

Lord Jehovah reigns in majesty,
We will bow before His throne;
We will worship Him in
righteousness,
We will worship Him alone.

"We Will Glorify"
Twila Paris (©1982)

(1:1–3,16–17) Lord, I declare that You are the one and only true God over Israel, over the church, over the nations. You are my Creator and Redeemer, and You are the only God of whom I will inquire. I come with humility and amazement at Your availability, to seek Your face and give You worship, and to listen for Your voice.

18As for all the other events of Ahaziah's reign, and what he did,
are they not written in the book of the annals of the kings of
Israel?

Elijah Taken Up to Heaven

2 When the LORD was about to take Elijah up to heaven in a
whirlwind, Elijah and Elisha were on their way from Gilgal.
2Elijah said to Elisha, "Stay here; the LORD has sent me to Bethel."
But Elisha said, "As surely as the LORD lives and as you live, I
will not leave you." So they went down to Bethel.
3The company of the prophets at Bethel came out to Elisha and
asked, "Do you know that the LORD is going to take your master
from you today?"
"Yes, I know," Elisha replied, "but do not speak of it."
4Then Elijah said to him, "Stay here, Elisha; the LORD has sent
me to Jericho."
And he replied, "As surely as the LORD lives and as you live, I
will not leave you." So they went to Jericho.
5The company of the prophets at Jericho went up to Elisha and
asked him, "Do you know that the LORD is going to take your master from you today?"
"Yes, I know," he replied, "but do not speak of it."
6Then Elijah said to him, "Stay here; the LORD has sent me to
the Jordan."
And he replied, "As surely as the LORD lives and as you live, I
will not leave you." So the two of them walked on.
7Fifty men of the company of the prophets went and stood at a
distance, facing the place where Elijah and Elisha had stopped at
the Jordan. 8Elijah took his cloak, rolled it up and struck the
water with it. The water divided to the right and to the left, and the
two of them crossed over on dry ground.
9When they had crossed, Elijah said to Elisha, "Tell me, what
can I do for you before I am taken from you?"
"Let me inherit a double portion of your spirit," Elisha replied.
10"You have asked a difficult thing," Elijah said, "yet if you see
me when I am taken from you, it will be yours—otherwise not."
11As they were walking along and talking together, suddenly a
chariot of fire and horses of fire appeared and separated the two
of them, and Elijah went up to heaven in a whirlwind. 12Elisha
saw this and cried out, "My father! My father! The chariots and
horsemen of Israel!" And Elisha saw him no more. Then he took
hold of his own clothes and tore them apart.
13He picked up the cloak that had fallen from Elijah and went
back and stood on the bank of the Jordan. 14Then he took the
cloak that had fallen from him and struck the water with it.
"Where now is the LORD, the God of Elijah?" he asked. When he
struck the water, it divided to the right and to the left, and he
crossed over.
15The company of the prophets from Jericho, who were watching, said, "The spirit of Elijah is resting on Elisha." And they went
to meet him and bowed to the ground before him. 16"Look," they
said, "we your servants have fifty able men. Let them go and look
for your master. Perhaps the Spirit of the LORD has picked him up
and set him down on some mountain or in some valley."
"No," Elisha replied, "do not send them."
17But they persisted until he was too ashamed to refuse. So he
said, "Send them." And they sent fifty men, who searched for

(2:1–15) O Lord, You are the same yesterday, today and forever. Your miraculous power has never dissipated. Just as Elisha followed Elijah, teach me to follow You, so that I might become a recipient of Your anointing. You are the true fountain of grace, redemption and power. Shape me, even today, into Your image, that I may be able to do Your works and glorify Your name. (Jn 14:12; Heb 13:8)

O to be like Thee! Blessed Redeemer,
This is my constant longing and prayer.
Gladly I'll forfeit all of earth's treasures,
Jesus, Thy perfect likeness to wear.

O to be like Thee!
O to be like Thee,
Blessed Redeemer,
Pure as Thou art!
Come in Thy sweetness,
Come in Thy fullness;
Stamp Thine own image
Deep on my heart.

"O To Be Like Thee"
Thomas O. Chisholm (1866-1960)

three days but did not find him. 18When they returned to Elisha,
who was staying in Jericho, he said to them, "Didn't I tell you not
to go?"

Healing of the Water

19The men of the city said to Elisha, "Look, our lord, this town
is well situated, as you can see, but the water is bad and the land
is unproductive."
20"Bring me a new bowl," he said, "and put salt in it." So they
brought it to him.
21Then he went out to the spring and threw the salt into it, saying, "This is what the LORD says: 'I have healed this water. Never
again will it cause death or make the land unproductive.' " 22And
the water has remained wholesome to this day, according to the
word Elisha had spoken.

Elisha Is Jeered

23From there Elisha went up to Bethel. As he was walking
along the road, some youths came out of the town and jeered at
him. "Go on up, you baldhead!" they said. "Go on up, you baldhead!" 24He turned around, looked at them and called down a
curse on them in the name of the LORD. Then two bears came out
of the woods and mauled forty-two of the youths. 25And he went
on to Mount Carmel and from there returned to Samaria.

Moab Revolts

3 Joram[a] son of Ahab became king of Israel in Samaria in the
eighteenth year of Jehoshaphat king of Judah, and he reigned
twelve years. 2He did evil in the eyes of the LORD, but not as his father and mother had done. He got rid of the sacred stone of Baal
that his father had made. 3Nevertheless he clung to the sins of
Jeroboam son of Nebat, which he had caused Israel to commit; he
did not turn away from them.
4Now Mesha king of Moab raised sheep, and he had to supply
the king of Israel with a hundred thousand lambs and with the
wool of a hundred thousand rams. 5But after Ahab died, the king
of Moab rebelled against the king of Israel. 6So at that time King
Joram set out from Samaria and mobilized all Israel. 7He also
sent this message to Jehoshaphat king of Judah: "The king of
Moab has rebelled against me. Will you go with me to fight against
Moab?"
"I will go with you," he replied. "I am as you are, my people as
your people, my horses as your horses."
8"By what route shall we attack?" he asked.
"Through the Desert of Edom," he answered.
9So the king of Israel set out with the king of Judah and the
king of Edom. After a roundabout march of seven days, the army
had no more water for themselves or for the animals with them.
10"What!" exclaimed the king of Israel. "Has the LORD called us
three kings together only to hand us over to Moab?"
11But Jehoshaphat asked, "Is there no prophet of the LORD
here, that we may inquire of the LORD through him?"
An officer of the king of Israel answered, "Elisha son of Shaphat is here. He used to pour water on the hands of Elijah.[b]"
12Jehoshaphat said, "The word of the LORD is with him." So the

[a] *1* Hebrew *Jehoram*, a variant of *Joram*; also in verse 6 [b] *11* That is, he was Elijah's personal servant.

(2:19–22) Father, just as You miraculously purified the waters of Jericho, so I pray that You will purify the outflow of my life. Fill my speech with Your Word and season it with the salt of grace, so that it may bring life and fruitfulness to the world around me. (Col 4:6)

May the mind of Christ my Savior
Live in me from day to day,
By His love and power controlling
All I do and say.

May the Word of God dwell richly
In my heart from hour to hour,
So that all may see I triumph
Only through His power.

"May the Mind of Christ My Savior"
Kate B. Wilkinson (1925)

king of Israel and Jehoshaphat and the king of Edom went down
to him.
13Elisha said to the king of Israel, "What do we have to do
with each other? Go to the prophets of your father and the
prophets of your mother."
"No," the king of Israel answered, "because it was the LORD
who called us three kings together to hand us over to Moab."
14Elisha said, "As surely as the LORD Almighty lives, whom I
serve, if I did not have respect for the presence of Jehoshaphat
king of Judah, I would not look at you or even notice you. 15But
now bring me a harpist."
While the harpist was playing, the hand of the LORD came upon
Elisha 16and he said, "This is what the LORD says: Make this valley full of ditches. 17For this is what the LORD says: You will see
neither wind nor rain, yet this valley will be filled with water, and
you, your cattle and your other animals will drink. 18This is an
easy thing in the eyes of the LORD; he will also hand Moab over to
you. 19You will overthrow every fortified city and every major
town. You will cut down every good tree, stop up all the springs,
and ruin every good field with stones."
20The next morning, about the time for offering the sacrifice,
there it was—water flowing from the direction of Edom! And the
land was filled with water.
21Now all the Moabites had heard that the kings had come to
fight against them; so every man, young and old, who could bear
arms was called up and stationed on the border. 22When they
got up early in the morning, the sun was shining on the water. To
the Moabites across the way, the water looked red—like blood.
23"That's blood!" they said. "Those kings must have fought and
slaughtered each other. Now to the plunder, Moab!"
24But when the Moabites came to the camp of Israel, the Israelites rose up and fought them until they fled. And the Israelites invaded the land and slaughtered the Moabites. 25They destroyed the towns, and each man threw a stone on every good
field until it was covered. They stopped up all the springs and cut
down every good tree. Only Kir Hareseth was left with its stones
in place, but men armed with slings surrounded it and attacked
it as well.
26When the king of Moab saw that the battle had gone against
him, he took with him seven hundred swordsmen to break
through to the king of Edom, but they failed. 27Then he took his
firstborn son, who was to succeed him as king, and offered him
as a sacrifice on the city wall. The fury against Israel was great;
they withdrew and returned to their own land.

The Widow's Oil

4 The wife of a man from the company of the prophets cried
out to Elisha, "Your servant my husband is dead, and you
know that he revered the LORD. But now his creditor is coming to
take my two boys as his slaves."
2Elisha replied to her, "How can I help you? Tell me, what do
you have in your house?"
"Your servant has nothing there at all," she said, "except a little oil."
3Elisha said, "Go around and ask all your neighbors for empty
jars. Don't ask for just a few. 4Then go inside and shut the door

(3:18–24) Father, we rejoice that the divine provisions, the unexpected strategies, the interventions of heaven that seem almost impossible to believe are but "an easy thing in the eyes of the Lord." O God, pour the faith of Elisha upon Your church. Help us to reach boldly for miracles that will confuse and confound the enemy and deliver our generation from bondage and unbelief.

Faith in God is like believing a man can walk over Niagara Falls on a tightrope while pushing a wheelbarrow. Trust in God is like getting into the wheelbarrow! To believe God can do something miraculous is one thing; to risk his willingness to do it in your life is another.

James C. Dobson (1936-)

The view is clear from where I stand,
I can see the imprint of God's hand.
From who I was to who I'll be,
His love and grace have delivered me.
Guiding me, guarding me,
Leading me, loving me.

Isn't He good? Isn't He good?
Hasn't He done all He said He would?
All that we have, all that we are,
Comes from above.
Isn't He good? Isn't He good?
He met the need like only He could.
Faithful and true to me and you,
Isn't He good?

"Isn't He Good"
Beverly Darnall (©1992)

behind you and your sons. Pour oil into all the jars, and as each
is filled, put it to one side."
5She left him and afterward shut the door behind her and her
sons. They brought the jars to her and she kept pouring. 6When
all the jars were full, she said to her son, "Bring me another
one."
But he replied, "There is not a jar left." Then the oil stopped
flowing.
7She went and told the man of God, and he said, "Go, sell the
oil and pay your debts. You and your sons can live on what is
left."

The Shunammite's Son Restored to Life

8One day Elisha went to Shunem. And a well-to-do woman was
there, who urged him to stay for a meal. So whenever he came
by, he stopped there to eat. 9She said to her husband, "I know
that this man who often comes our way is a holy man of God.
10Let's make a small room on the roof and put in it a bed and a
table, a chair and a lamp for him. Then he can stay there whenever he comes to us."
11One day when Elisha came, he went up to his room and lay
down there. 12He said to his servant Gehazi, "Call the Shunammite." So he called her, and she stood before him. 13Elisha said
to him, "Tell her, 'You have gone to all this trouble for us. Now
what can be done for you? Can we speak on your behalf to the
king or the commander of the army?' "
She replied, "I have a home among my own people."
14"What can be done for her?" Elisha asked.
Gehazi said, "Well, she has no son and her husband is old."
15Then Elisha said, "Call her." So he called her, and she stood
in the doorway. 16"About this time next year," Elisha said, "you
will hold a son in your arms."
"No, my lord," she objected. "Don't mislead your servant, O
man of God!"
17But the woman became pregnant, and the next year about
that same time she gave birth to a son, just as Elisha had told her.
18The child grew, and one day he went out to his father, who
was with the reapers. 19"My head! My head!" he said to his father.
His father told a servant, "Carry him to his mother." 20After
the servant had lifted him up and carried him to his mother, the
boy sat on her lap until noon, and then he died. 21She went up
and laid him on the bed of the man of God, then shut the door
and went out.
22She called her husband and said, "Please send me one of
the servants and a donkey so I can go to the man of God quickly
and return."
23"Why go to him today?" he asked. "It's not the New Moon or
the Sabbath."
"It's all right," she said.
24She saddled the donkey and said to her servant, "Lead on;
don't slow down for me unless I tell you." 25So she set out and
came to the man of God at Mount Carmel.
When he saw her in the distance, the man of God said to his
servant Gehazi, "Look! There's the Shunammite! 26Run to meet
her and ask her, 'Are you all right? Is your husband all right? Is
your child all right?' "

"I believe in God the Father Almighty, Maker of heaven and earth." What does this mean? I believe that God has made me and all creatures; that he has given and still preserves to me my body and soul, eyes, ears, and all my members, my reason and all my senses; also clothing and shoes, meat and drink, house and home, wife and child, land, cattle and all my goods; that he richly and daily provides me with all that I need for this body and life, protects me against all danger and guards and keeps me from all evil; and all this purely out of fatherly, divine goodness and mercy, without merit or worthiness in me; for all of which I am in duty bound to thank and praise, to serve and obey him.

Martin Luther (1483-1546)

(4:5–7) Yahweh Jireh, I acknowledge that You are indeed God Who Provides. Your provision is limited only by my ability to receive. If I provided more vessels, would You not continue to pour out more oil? Help me to keep knocking, asking and receiving so that my soul and body may be filled with the bounty of Your Spirit, and that my heart and mouth may be filled with thanksgiving. (Mt 7:7–8)

It is ours to offer what we can, God's to supply what we cannot.

Saint Jerome (c.374–c.420)

(4:42–44) Lord, I praise You for Your mercy and power. There is no shortage of Your abundance. In every need, You have always been and always will be my Provider and Protector. If I am faithful in my offerings to You, then You will multiply what little I have to meet the needs of many others. Teach me to trust You more, Lord. Let me be a source of blessing to those in need around me. (Mk 6:37–44)

You are my God,
I am Your servant.
You are my King,
My Lord and Savior.
You are my friend,
My joy and comfort.
You are my Lord,
You are my God.

Hear, hear the angels sing,
All creation brings You the glory.
And I will lift my heart in faith,
Lift my eyes to see You
In holiness, in righteousness,
In majesty; You are my God.

"You Are My God"
Geoff Bullock and Gail Dunshea (©1992)

"Everything is all right," she said.
27When she reached the man of God at the mountain, she took
hold of his feet. Gehazi came over to push her away, but the man
of God said, "Leave her alone! She is in bitter distress, but the
LORD has hidden it from me and has not told me why."
28"Did I ask you for a son, my lord?" she said. "Didn't I tell
you, 'Don't raise my hopes'?"
29Elisha said to Gehazi, "Tuck your cloak into your belt, take
my staff in your hand and run. If you meet anyone, do not greet
him, and if anyone greets you, do not answer. Lay my staff on the
boy's face."
30But the child's mother said, "As surely as the LORD lives and
as you live, I will not leave you." So he got up and followed her.
31Gehazi went on ahead and laid the staff on the boy's face, but
there was no sound or response. So Gehazi went back to meet Elisha and told him, "The boy has not awakened."
32When Elisha reached the house, there was the boy lying dead
on his couch. 33He went in, shut the door on the two of them and
prayed to the LORD. 34Then he got on the bed and lay upon the
boy, mouth to mouth, eyes to eyes, hands to hands. As he
stretched himself out upon him, the boy's body grew warm. 35Eli-
sha turned away and walked back and forth in the room and then
got on the bed and stretched out upon him once more. The boy
sneezed seven times and opened his eyes.
36Elisha summoned Gehazi and said, "Call the Shunammite."
And he did. When she came, he said, "Take your son." 37She
came in, fell at his feet and bowed to the ground. Then she took
her son and went out.

Death in the Pot

38Elisha returned to Gilgal and there was a famine in that region. While the company of the prophets was meeting with him,
he said to his servant, "Put on the large pot and cook some stew
for these men."
39One of them went out into the fields to gather herbs and
found a wild vine. He gathered some of its gourds and filled the
fold of his cloak. When he returned, he cut them up into the pot
of stew, though no one knew what they were. 40The stew was
poured out for the men, but as they began to eat it, they cried out,
"O man of God, there is death in the pot!" And they could not
eat it.
41Elisha said, "Get some flour." He put it into the pot and said,
"Serve it to the people to eat." And there was nothing harmful in
the pot.

Feeding of a Hundred

42A man came from Baal Shalishah, bringing the man of God
twenty loaves of barley bread baked from the first ripe grain,
along with some heads of new grain. "Give it to the people to eat,"
Elisha said.
43"How can I set this before a hundred men?" his servant
asked.
But Elisha answered, "Give it to the people to eat. For this is
what the LORD says: 'They will eat and have some left over.' "
44Then he set it before them, and they ate and had some left over,
according to the word of the LORD.

Naaman Healed of Leprosy

5 Now Naaman was commander of the army of the king of
Aram. He was a great man in the sight of his master and highly regarded, because through him the LORD had given victory to
Aram. He was a valiant soldier, but he had leprosy.[a]
2Now bands from Aram had gone out and had taken captive a
young girl from Israel, and she served Naaman's wife. 3She said
to her mistress, "If only my master would see the prophet who is
in Samaria! He would cure him of his leprosy."
4Naaman went to his master and told him what the girl from Israel had said. 5"By all means, go," the king of Aram replied. "I
will send a letter to the king of Israel." So Naaman left, taking
with him ten talents[b] of silver, six thousand shekels[c] of gold and
ten sets of clothing. 6The letter that he took to the king of Israel
read: "With this letter I am sending my servant Naaman to you so
that you may cure him of his leprosy."
7As soon as the king of Israel read the letter, he tore his robes
and said, "Am I God? Can I kill and bring back to life? Why does
this fellow send someone to me to be cured of his leprosy? See
how he is trying to pick a quarrel with me!"
8When Elisha the man of God heard that the king of Israel had
torn his robes, he sent him this message: "Why have you torn
your robes? Have the man come to me and he will know that there
is a prophet in Israel." 9So Naaman went with his horses and
chariots and stopped at the door of Elisha's house. 10Elisha sent
a messenger to say to him, "Go, wash yourself seven times in the
Jordan, and your flesh will be restored and you will be cleansed."
11But Naaman went away angry and said, "I thought that he
would surely come out to me and stand and call on the name of
the LORD his God, wave his hand over the spot and cure me of my
leprosy. 12Are not Abana and Pharpar, the rivers of Damascus,
better than any of the waters of Israel? Couldn't I wash in them
and be cleansed?" So he turned and went off in a rage.
13Naaman's servants went to him and said, "My father, if the
prophet had told you to do some great thing, would you not have
done it? How much more, then, when he tells you, 'Wash and be
cleansed'!" 14So he went down and dipped himself in the Jordan
seven times, as the man of God had told him, and his flesh was restored and became clean like that of a young boy.
15Then Naaman and all his attendants went back to the man of
God. He stood before him and said, "Now I know that there is no
God in all the world except in Israel. Please accept now a gift
from your servant."
16The prophet answered, "As surely as the LORD lives, whom I
serve, I will not accept a thing." And even though Naaman urged
him, he refused.
17"If you will not," said Naaman, "please let me, your servant,
be given as much earth as a pair of mules can carry, for your servant will never again make burnt offerings and sacrifices to any
other god but the LORD. 18But may the LORD forgive your servant
for this one thing: When my master enters the temple of Rimmon
to bow down and he is leaning on my arm and I bow there also—
when I bow down in the temple of Rimmon, may the LORD forgive
your servant for this."

[a] *1* The Hebrew word was used for various diseases affecting the skin—not necessarily leprosy; also in verses 3, 6, 7, 11 and 27. [b] *5* That is, about 750 pounds (about 340 kilograms) [c] *5* That is, about 150 pounds (about 70 kilograms)

(5:8–14) I worship You, my Healer and Deliverer. I know Your heart's desire is to cleanse and deliver the whole world. Yet so often we struggle to find our own remedies, like a patient trying to prescribe his treatment to the doctor. Our pride keeps us from Your provision. Surely, we think, the message of the gospel is too simple—washing in the blood of Christ is too easy to affect transformation. And yet it does. It has made me whole. Bless the name of the Savior forever!

All we want in Christ, we shall find in Christ. If we want little, we shall find little. If we want much, we shall find much; but if, in utter helplessness, we cast our all on Christ, he will be to us the whole treasury of God.

Henry Benjamin Whipple (1822-1901)

19“Go in peace,” Elisha said.
After Naaman had traveled some distance, 20Gehazi, the servant of Elisha the man of God, said to himself, “My master was too
easy on Naaman, this Aramean, by not accepting from him what
he brought. As surely as the LORD lives, I will run after him and get
something from him.”
21So Gehazi hurried after Naaman. When Naaman saw him
running toward him, he got down from the chariot to meet him.
“Is everything all right?” he asked.
22“Everything is all right,” Gehazi answered. “My master sent
me to say, ‘Two young men from the company of the prophets
have just come to me from the hill country of Ephraim. Please
give them a talent[a] of silver and two sets of clothing.’ ”
23“By all means, take two talents,” said Naaman. He urged Gehazi to accept them, and then tied up the two talents of silver in
two bags, with two sets of clothing. He gave them to two of his servants, and they carried them ahead of Gehazi. 24When Gehazi
came to the hill, he took the things from the servants and put
them away in the house. He sent the men away and they left.
25Then he went in and stood before his master Elisha.
“Where have you been, Gehazi?” Elisha asked.
“Your servant didn’t go anywhere,” Gehazi answered.
26But Elisha said to him, “Was not my spirit with you when the
man got down from his chariot to meet you? Is this the time to
take money, or to accept clothes, olive groves, vineyards, flocks,
herds, or menservants and maidservants? 27Naaman’s leprosy will
cling to you and to your descendants forever.” Then Gehazi went
from Elisha’s presence and he was leprous, as white as snow.

An Axhead Floats

6 The company of the prophets said to Elisha, “Look, the
place where we meet with you is too small for us. 2Let us go
to the Jordan, where each of us can get a pole; and let us build
a place there for us to live.”
And he said, “Go.”
3Then one of them said, “Won’t you please come with your
servants?”
“I will,” Elisha replied. 4And he went with them.
They went to the Jordan and began to cut down trees. 5As one
of them was cutting down a tree, the iron axhead fell into the
water. “Oh, my lord,” he cried out, “it was borrowed!”
6The man of God asked, “Where did it fall?” When he showed
him the place, Elisha cut a stick and threw it there, and made the
iron float. 7“Lift it out,” he said. Then the man reached out his
hand and took it.

Elisha Traps Blinded Arameans

8Now the king of Aram was at war with Israel. After conferring
with his officers, he said, “I will set up my camp in such and
such a place.”
9The man of God sent word to the king of Israel: “Beware of
passing that place, because the Arameans are going down there.”
10So the king of Israel checked on the place indicated by the
man of God. Time and again Elisha warned the king, so that he
was on his guard in such places.

[a] 22 That is, about 75 pounds (about 34 kilograms)

Ahab sold himself for a vineyard; Judas, a bag of silver; Achan, a wedge and a garment; Gehazi, silver and raiment. Are you for sale?

Orin Philip Gifford (b. 1847)

(5:20–27) Greed, deception and lies—a trilogy that inevitably brings judgment and destruction. Deliver me, O God, from these sins of Gehazi, Judas and Ananias, and instead give me a heart whose treasure lies in heaven. You are my treasure, O Lord, magnificent with splendor, everlasting and eternal. (Mt 26:14; 27:3–5; Ac 5:1–5)

11This enraged the king of Aram. He summoned his officers
and demanded of them, "Will you not tell me which of us is on
the side of the king of Israel?"

12"None of us, my lord the king," said one of his officers, "but
Elisha, the prophet who is in Israel, tells the king of Israel the
very words you speak in your bedroom."

13"Go, find out where he is," the king ordered, "so I can send
men and capture him." The report came back: "He is in Dothan." 14Then he sent horses and chariots and a strong force
there. They went by night and surrounded the city.

15When the servant of the man of God got up and went out
early the next morning, an army with horses and chariots had
surrounded the city. "Oh, my lord, what shall we do?" the servant
asked.

16"Don't be afraid," the prophet answered. "Those who are
with us are more than those who are with them."

17And Elisha prayed, "O LORD, open his eyes so he may see."
Then the LORD opened the servant's eyes, and he looked and saw
the hills full of horses and chariots of fire all around Elisha.

18As the enemy came down toward him, Elisha prayed to the
LORD, "Strike these people with blindness." So he struck them
with blindness, as Elisha had asked.

19Elisha told them, "This is not the road and this is not the
city. Follow me, and I will lead you to the man you are looking
for." And he led them to Samaria.

20After they entered the city, Elisha said, "LORD, open the eyes
of these men so they can see." Then the LORD opened their eyes
and they looked, and there they were, inside Samaria.

21When the king of Israel saw them, he asked Elisha, "Shall I
kill them, my father? Shall I kill them?"

22"Do not kill them," he answered. "Would you kill men you
have captured with your own sword or bow? Set food and water
before them so that they may eat and drink and then go back to
their master." 23So he prepared a great feast for them, and after
they had finished eating and drinking, he sent them away, and
they returned to their master. So the bands from Aram stopped
raiding Israel's territory.

Famine in Besieged Samaria

24Some time later, Ben-Hadad king of Aram mobilized his entire army and marched up and laid siege to Samaria. 25There
was a great famine in the city; the siege lasted so long that a donkey's head sold for eighty shekels[a] of silver, and a quarter of a
cab[b] of seed pods[c] for five shekels.[d]

26As the king of Israel was passing by on the wall, a woman
cried to him, "Help me, my lord the king!"

27The king replied, "If the LORD does not help you, where can
I get help for you? From the threshing floor? From the winepress?" 28Then he asked her, "What's the matter?"

She answered, "This woman said to me, 'Give up your son so
we may eat him today, and tomorrow we'll eat my son.' 29So we
cooked my son and ate him. The next day I said to her, 'Give up
your son so we may eat him,' but she had hidden him."

30When the king heard the woman's words, he tore his robes.

[a]25 That is, about 2 pounds (about 1 kilogram) [b]25 That is, probably about 1/2 pint (about 0.3 liter) [c]25 Or *of dove's dung* [d]25 That is, about 2 ounces (about 55 grams)

O Lord God, in whom we live and move and have our being, open our eyes that we may behold your fatherly presence ever about us. Teach us to be anxious for nothing, and when we have done what you have given us to do, help us, O God our Savior, to leave the issue to your wisdom, knowing that all things are possible to us through your Son our Savior, Jesus Christ.

Richard Meux Benson (1824-1915)

(6:11–17) In our spiritual warfare, Lord, give us hearing ears that alert us to the enemy's plans and show us how to thwart them. Give us eyes of faith that perceive the heavenly chariots of fire around us. Put the strength of Your joy in our hearts. Place the sword of Your Word in our hands. Fill our mouths with songs of praise. And above all, Lord, teach us to pray. Then we will triumph gloriously in the power of Your name! (Ps 149:5–9; Eph 6:12–18)

As he went along the wall, the people looked, and there, underneath, he had sackcloth on his body. 31He said, "May God deal with me, be it ever so severely, if the head of Elisha son of Shaphat remains on his shoulders today!"

32Now Elisha was sitting in his house, and the elders were sitting with him. The king sent a messenger ahead, but before he arrived, Elisha said to the elders, "Don't you see how this murderer is sending someone to cut off my head? Look, when the messenger comes, shut the door and hold it shut against him. Is not the sound of his master's footsteps behind him?"

33While he was still talking to them, the messenger came down to him. And ⌞the king⌟ said, "This disaster is from the LORD. Why should I wait for the LORD any longer?"

7 Elisha said, "Hear the word of the LORD. This is what the LORD says: About this time tomorrow, a seah[a] of flour will sell for a shekel[b] and two seahs[c] of barley for a shekel at the gate of Samaria."

2The officer on whose arm the king was leaning said to the man of God, "Look, even if the LORD should open the floodgates of the heavens, could this happen?"

"You will see it with your own eyes," answered Elisha, "but you will not eat any of it!"

The Siege Lifted

3Now there were four men with leprosy[d] at the entrance of the city gate. They said to each other, "Why stay here until we die? 4If we say, 'We'll go into the city'—the famine is there, and we will die. And if we stay here, we will die. So let's go over to the camp of the Arameans and surrender. If they spare us, we live; if they kill us, then we die."

5At dusk they got up and went to the camp of the Arameans. When they reached the edge of the camp, not a man was there, 6for the Lord had caused the Arameans to hear the sound of chariots and horses and a great army, so that they said to one another, "Look, the king of Israel has hired the Hittite and Egyptian kings to attack us!" 7So they got up and fled in the dusk and abandoned their tents and their horses and donkeys. They left the camp as it was and ran for their lives.

8The men who had leprosy reached the edge of the camp and entered one of the tents. They ate and drank, and carried away silver, gold and clothes, and went off and hid them. They returned and entered another tent and took some things from it and hid them also.

9Then they said to each other, "We're not doing right. This is a day of good news and we are keeping it to ourselves. If we wait until daylight, punishment will overtake us. Let's go at once and report this to the royal palace."

10So they went and called out to the city gatekeepers and told them, "We went into the Aramean camp and not a man was there—not a sound of anyone—only tethered horses and donkeys, and the tents left just as they were." 11The gatekeepers shouted the news, and it was reported within the palace.

12The king got up in the night and said to his officers, "I will

[a] *1* That is, probably about 7 quarts (about 7.3 liters); also in verses 16 and 18 [b] *1* That is, about 2/5 ounce (about 11 grams); also in verses 16 and 18 [c] *1* That is, probably about 13 quarts (about 15 liters); also in verses 16 and 18 [d] *3* The Hebrew word is used for various diseases affecting the skin—not necessarily leprosy; also in verse 8.

(7:1–10) Teach me, Lord, to wait in faith. Help me never to doubt Your Word, no matter how appalling my circumstances may seem, or how impossible my chances of deliverance. Your plans for my rescue are immeasurably greater than all I could ask or imagine. God of mercy and miracles, by Your wisdom, by Your own methods, You make my enemies flee when none pursues them, and I am saved. Nothing, nothing is too hard for You. (Jer 32:17; Eph 3:20)

Praise, my soul, the King of heaven;
To His feet your tribute bring.
Ransomed, healed, restored, forgiven,
Evermore His praises sing.
Alleluia! Alleluia!
Praise the everlasting King!

Praise Him for His grace and favor
To our fathers in distress;
Praise Him, still the same as ever,
Slow to chide and swift to bless.
Alleluia! Alleluia!
Glorious in His faithfulness!

Praise, My Soul, The King Of Heaven
Henry F. Lyte (1834)

tell you what the Arameans have done to us. They know we are
starving; so they have left the camp to hide in the countryside,
thinking, 'They will surely come out, and then we will take them
alive and get into the city.' "
13One of his officers answered, "Have some men take five of
the horses that are left in the city. Their plight will be like that of
all the Israelites left here—yes, they will only be like all these Israelites who are doomed. So let us send them to find out what
happened."
14So they selected two chariots with their horses, and the king
sent them after the Aramean army. He commanded the drivers,
"Go and find out what has happened." 15They followed them as
far as the Jordan, and they found the whole road strewn with the
clothing and equipment the Arameans had thrown away in their
headlong flight. So the messengers returned and reported to the
king. 16Then the people went out and plundered the camp of the
Arameans. So a seah of flour sold for a shekel, and two seahs of
barley sold for a shekel, as the LORD had said.
17Now the king had put the officer on whose arm he leaned in
charge of the gate, and the people trampled him in the gateway,
and he died, just as the man of God had foretold when the king
came down to his house. 18It happened as the man of God had
said to the king: "About this time tomorrow, a seah of flour will
sell for a shekel and two seahs of barley for a shekel at the gate
of Samaria."
19The officer had said to the man of God, "Look, even if the
LORD should open the floodgates of the heavens, could this happen?" The man of God had replied, "You will see it with your own
eyes, but you will not eat any of it!" 20And that is exactly what
happened to him, for the people trampled him in the gateway,
and he died.

The Shunammite's Land Restored

8 Now Elisha had said to the woman whose son he had restored to life, "Go away with your family and stay for a while
wherever you can, because the LORD has decreed a famine in the
land that will last seven years." 2The woman proceeded to do as
the man of God said. She and her family went away and stayed in
the land of the Philistines seven years.
3At the end of the seven years she came back from the land of
the Philistines and went to the king to beg for her house and land.
4The king was talking to Gehazi, the servant of the man of God,
and had said, "Tell me about all the great things Elisha has done."
5Just as Gehazi was telling the king how Elisha had restored the
dead to life, the woman whose son Elisha had brought back to life
came to beg the king for her house and land.
Gehazi said, "This is the woman, my lord the king, and this is
her son whom Elisha restored to life." 6The king asked the
woman about it, and she told him.
Then he assigned an official to her case and said to him, "Give
back everything that belonged to her, including all the income
from her land from the day she left the country until now."

Hazael Murders Ben-Hadad

7Elisha went to Damascus, and Ben-Hadad king of Aram was
ill. When the king was told, "The man of God has come all the way
up here," 8he said to Hazael, "Take a gift with you and go to meet

Holy, holy, holy
Is the Lord Almighty;
Glory and honor and power
Belong unto our God.

Holy and righteous and true,
We give our praises to You;
Merciful heavenly Father,
There is no other like You.

"Our God"
Harlan Rogers (©1992)

(8:1–6) Famine. Barrenness. Fruitlessness. Just as with Israel, so today our disobedience can make our world a place of both physical and spiritual famine, barren and wasted. Although Your judgments are certain and severe, yet in Your wrath You remember mercy toward those who love You. For those who seek Your face and heed Your instructions, there is divine protection and provision and, always, restoration. Thank You, Father. You are mercy itself. And You are too wonderful for words. (Hab 3:2)

O heavenly Father, your hand replenishes all living creatures with blessing and gives meat to the hungry in due season; we acknowledge our meat and drink to be your gifts, prepared by your fatherly providence to be received by us for the comfort of our bodies with thanksgiving: We most humbly beg you to bless us and our food and to give us grace so to use these your benefits that we may be thankful to you and liberal to our poor neighbors, through Jesus Christ our Lord. Amen.

Thomas Becon (c.1511–1567)

Of all commentaries on the Scriptures, good examples are the best.

John Donne (1572–1631)

(8:16–18) O God, give us wisdom to walk only in the ways of the righteous. Break every ungodly bond that ties us to wicked forebears. By virtue of our new birth, You are our Father and our model. Teach us to walk in Your ways. By Your Spirit's power, work Your virtue in us and through us. May we leave a heritage of godliness and blessing throughout the earth. May we bring glory and honor and praise to Your name forever. And may we leave a well-worn path to Your throne for the generations that follow us. (Eph 5:1; Heb 13:7)

the man of God. Consult the LORD through him; ask him, 'Will I recover from this illness?' "
9Hazael went to meet Elisha, taking with him as a gift forty camel-loads of all the finest wares of Damascus. He went in and stood before him, and said, "Your son Ben-Hadad king of Aram has sent me to ask, 'Will I recover from this illness?' "
10Elisha answered, "Go and say to him, 'You will certainly recover'; but[a] the LORD has revealed to me that he will in fact die."
11He stared at him with a fixed gaze until Hazael felt ashamed. Then the man of God began to weep.
12"Why is my lord weeping?" asked Hazael.
"Because I know the harm you will do to the Israelites," he answered. "You will set fire to their fortified places, kill their young men with the sword, dash their little children to the ground, and rip open their pregnant women."
13Hazael said, "How could your servant, a mere dog, accomplish such a feat?"
"The LORD has shown me that you will become king of Aram," answered Elisha.
14Then Hazael left Elisha and returned to his master. When Ben-Hadad asked, "What did Elisha say to you?" Hazael replied, "He told me that you would certainly recover." 15But the next day
he took a thick cloth, soaked it in water and spread it over the king's face, so that he died. Then Hazael succeeded him as king.

Jehoram King of Judah

16In the fifth year of Joram son of Ahab king of Israel, when Jehoshaphat was king of Judah, Jehoram son of Jehoshaphat began his reign as king of Judah. 17He was thirty-two years old when he
became king, and he reigned in Jerusalem eight years. 18He
walked in the ways of the kings of Israel, as the house of Ahab had done, for he married a daughter of Ahab. He did evil in the eyes of the LORD. 19Nevertheless, for the sake of his servant David, the LORD was not willing to destroy Judah. He had promised to maintain a lamp for David and his descendants forever.
20In the time of Jehoram, Edom rebelled against Judah and set
up its own king. 21So Jehoram[b] went to Zair with all his chariots. The Edomites surrounded him and his chariot commanders, but he rose up and broke through by night; his army, however, fled back home. 22To this day Edom has been in rebellion against Judah. Libnah revolted at the same time.
23As for the other events of Jehoram's reign, and all he did, are they not written in the book of the annals of the kings of Judah?
24Jehoram rested with his fathers and was buried with them in the City of David. And Ahaziah his son succeeded him as king.

Ahaziah King of Judah

25In the twelfth year of Joram son of Ahab king of Israel, Ahaziah son of Jehoram king of Judah began to reign. 26Ahaziah was
twenty-two years old when he became king, and he reigned in Jerusalem one year. His mother's name was Athaliah, a granddaughter of Omri king of Israel. 27He walked in the ways of the
house of Ahab and did evil in the eyes of the LORD, as the house of Ahab had done, for he was related by marriage to Ahab's family.
28Ahaziah went with Joram son of Ahab to war against Hazael

[a] 10 The Hebrew may also be read *Go and say, 'You will certainly not recover,' for.*
[b] 21 Hebrew *Joram,* a variant of *Jehoram;* also in verses 23 and 24

king of Aram at Ramoth Gilead. The Arameans wounded Joram;
29so King Joram returned to Jezreel to recover from the wounds
the Arameans had inflicted on him at Ramoth[a] in his battle with
Hazael king of Aram.

Then Ahaziah son of Jehoram king of Judah went down to Jezreel to see Joram son of Ahab, because he had been wounded.

Jehu Anointed King of Israel

9 The prophet Elisha summoned a man from the company of
the prophets and said to him, "Tuck your cloak into your
belt, take this flask of oil with you and go to Ramoth Gilead.
2When you get there, look for Jehu son of Jehoshaphat, the son of
Nimshi. Go to him, get him away from his companions and take
him into an inner room. 3Then take the flask and pour the oil on
his head and declare, 'This is what the LORD says: I anoint you
king over Israel.' Then open the door and run; don't delay!"
4So the young man, the prophet, went to Ramoth Gilead.
5When he arrived, he found the army officers sitting together. "I
have a message for you, commander," he said.

"For which of us?" asked Jehu.

"For you, commander," he replied.

6Jehu got up and went into the house. Then the prophet
poured the oil on Jehu's head and declared, "This is what the
LORD, the God of Israel, says: 'I anoint you king over the LORD's
people Israel. 7You are to destroy the house of Ahab your master,
and I will avenge the blood of my servants the prophets and the
blood of all the LORD's servants shed by Jezebel. 8The whole house
of Ahab will perish. I will cut off from Ahab every last male in Israel—slave or free. 9I will make the house of Ahab like the house
of Jeroboam son of Nebat and like the house of Baasha son of
Ahijah. 10As for Jezebel, dogs will devour her on the plot of
ground at Jezreel, and no one will bury her.' " Then he opened
the door and ran.

11When Jehu went out to his fellow officers, one of them asked
him, "Is everything all right? Why did this madman come to you?"

"You know the man and the sort of things he says," Jehu
replied.

12"That's not true!" they said. "Tell us."

Jehu said, "Here is what he told me: 'This is what the LORD says:
I anoint you king over Israel.' "

13They hurried and took their cloaks and spread them under
him on the bare steps. Then they blew the trumpet and shouted,
"Jehu is king!"

Jehu Kills Joram and Ahaziah

14So Jehu son of Jehoshaphat, the son of Nimshi, conspired
against Joram. (Now Joram and all Israel had been defending Ramoth Gilead against Hazael king of Aram, 15but King Joram[b] had
returned to Jezreel to recover from the wounds the Arameans had
inflicted on him in the battle with Hazael king of Aram.) Jehu
said, "If this is the way you feel, don't let anyone slip out of the
city to go and tell the news in Jezreel." 16Then he got into his
chariot and rode to Jezreel, because Joram was resting there and
Ahaziah king of Judah had gone down to see him.

[a] 29 Hebrew *Ramah,* a variant of *Ramoth* [b] 15 Hebrew *Jehoram,* a variant of *Joram;* also in verses 17 and 21–24

(9:7–10) When I see Your outraged judgment uprooting and destroying those who have flagrantly sinned against You, I can only cry out my fervent thanks for the Redeemer. Your Son has atoned for my many transgressions with His own blood; He has purchased my peace with You. By sacrificing Himself He has saved me from Your wrath. How I praise You for Your love and mercy. How I thank You that I am Yours forever.

17 When the lookout standing on the tower in Jezreel saw Jehu's troops approaching, he called out, "I see some troops coming."

"Get a horseman," Joram ordered. "Send him to meet them and ask, 'Do you come in peace?' "

18 The horseman rode off to meet Jehu and said, "This is what the king says: 'Do you come in peace?' "

"What do you have to do with peace?" Jehu replied. "Fall in behind me."

The lookout reported, "The messenger has reached them, but he isn't coming back."

19 So the king sent out a second horseman. When he came to them he said, "This is what the king says: 'Do you come in peace?' "

Jehu replied, "What do you have to do with peace? Fall in behind me."

20 The lookout reported, "He has reached them, but he isn't coming back either. The driving is like that of Jehu son of Nimshi—he drives like a madman."

21 "Hitch up my chariot," Joram ordered. And when it was hitched up, Joram king of Israel and Ahaziah king of Judah rode out, each in his own chariot, to meet Jehu. They met him at the plot of ground that had belonged to Naboth the Jezreelite. 22 When Joram saw Jehu he asked, "Have you come in peace, Jehu?"

"How can there be peace," Jehu replied, "as long as all the idolatry and witchcraft of your mother Jezebel abound?"

23 Joram turned about and fled, calling out to Ahaziah, "Treachery, Ahaziah!"

24 Then Jehu drew his bow and shot Joram between the shoulders. The arrow pierced his heart and he slumped down in his chariot. 25 Jehu said to Bidkar, his chariot officer, "Pick him up and throw him on the field that belonged to Naboth the Jezreelite. Remember how you and I were riding together in chariots behind Ahab his father when the LORD made this prophecy about him: 26 'Yesterday I saw the blood of Naboth and the blood of his sons, declares the LORD, and I will surely make you pay for it on this plot of ground, declares the LORD.'[a] Now then, pick him up and throw him on that plot, in accordance with the word of the LORD."

27 When Ahaziah king of Judah saw what had happened, he fled up the road to Beth Haggan.[b] Jehu chased him, shouting, "Kill him too!" They wounded him in his chariot on the way up to Gur near Ibleam, but he escaped to Megiddo and died there. 28 His servants took him by chariot to Jerusalem and buried him with his fathers in his tomb in the City of David. 29 (In the eleventh year of Joram son of Ahab, Ahaziah had become king of Judah.)

Jezebel Killed

30 Then Jehu went to Jezreel. When Jezebel heard about it, she painted her eyes, arranged her hair and looked out of a window. 31 As Jehu entered the gate, she asked, "Have you come in peace, Zimri, you murderer of your master?"[c]

32 He looked up at the window and called out, "Who is on my side? Who?" Two or three eunuchs looked down at him. 33 "Throw her down!" Jehu said. So they threw her down, and some of her

(9:24–33) When You choose to move in judgment, Father God, there are no walls high enough, no caves deep enough, no eons long enough to hide us—monarchs and commoners alike—from Your all-seeing eyes. Each of us could count on detection and consequent justice, but for Your own merciful intervention. Only in Your grace lies our hope, our shelter, our salvation.

[a] *26* See 1 Kings 21:19. [b] *27* Or *fled by way of the garden house* [c] *31* Or *"Did Zimri have peace, who murdered his master?"*

blood spattered the wall and the horses as they trampled her underfoot.

34Jehu went in and ate and drank. "Take care of that cursed woman," he said, "and bury her, for she was a king's daughter." 35But when they went out to bury her, they found nothing except her skull, her feet and her hands. 36They went back and told Jehu, who said, "This is the word of the LORD that he spoke through his servant Elijah the Tishbite: On the plot of ground at Jezreel dogs will devour Jezebel's flesh.[a] 37Jezebel's body will be like refuse on the ground in the plot at Jezreel, so that no one will be able to say, 'This is Jezebel.' "

Ahab's Family Killed

10 Now there were in Samaria seventy sons of the house of Ahab. So Jehu wrote letters and sent them to Samaria: to the officials of Jezreel,[b] to the elders and to the guardians of Ahab's children. He said, 2"As soon as this letter reaches you, since your master's sons are with you and you have chariots and horses, a fortified city and weapons, 3choose the best and most worthy of your master's sons and set him on his father's throne. Then fight for your master's house."

4But they were terrified and said, "If two kings could not resist him, how can we?"

5So the palace administrator, the city governor, the elders and the guardians sent this message to Jehu: "We are your servants and we will do anything you say. We will not appoint anyone as king; you do whatever you think best."

6Then Jehu wrote them a second letter, saying, "If you are on my side and will obey me, take the heads of your master's sons and come to me in Jezreel by this time tomorrow."

Now the royal princes, seventy of them, were with the leading men of the city, who were rearing them. 7When the letter arrived, these men took the princes and slaughtered all seventy of them. They put their heads in baskets and sent them to Jehu in Jezreel. 8When the messenger arrived, he told Jehu, "They have brought the heads of the princes."

Then Jehu ordered, "Put them in two piles at the entrance of the city gate until morning."

9The next morning Jehu went out. He stood before all the people and said, "You are innocent. It was I who conspired against my master and killed him, but who killed all these? 10Know then, that not a word the LORD has spoken against the house of Ahab will fail. The LORD has done what he promised through his servant Elijah." 11So Jehu killed everyone in Jezreel who remained of the house of Ahab, as well as all his chief men, his close friends and his priests, leaving him no survivor.

12Jehu then set out and went toward Samaria. At Beth Eked of the Shepherds, 13he met some relatives of Ahaziah king of Judah and asked, "Who are you?"

They said, "We are relatives of Ahaziah, and we have come down to greet the families of the king and of the queen mother."

14"Take them alive!" he ordered. So they took them alive and slaughtered them by the well of Beth Eked—forty-two men. He left no survivor.

15After he left there, he came upon Jehonadab son of Recab,

[a] *36* See 1 Kings 21:23. [b] *1* Hebrew; some Septuagint manuscripts and Vulgate *of the city*

(9:34—10:17) Lord, I see the fulfillment of the prophetic word You spoke to Elijah concerning Ahab and Jezebel, and I shake my head in wonder. I am appalled when I think of the depths of wickedness to which we can fall, a wickedness so deep that it would cause You to destroy an entire family and all its descendants. But You are sovereign, Lord, and You are holy. All of Your judgments are righteous. (1Ki 21:17–26; 2Ki 9:7–10)

who was on his way to meet him. Jehu greeted him and said, "Are
you in accord with me, as I am with you?"
"I am," Jehonadab answered.
"If so," said Jehu, "give me your hand." So he did, and Jehu
helped him up into the chariot. 16 Jehu said, "Come with me and
see my zeal for the LORD." Then he had him ride along in his
chariot.
17 When Jehu came to Samaria, he killed all who were left there
of Ahab's family; he destroyed them, according to the word of the
LORD spoken to Elijah.

Ministers of Baal Killed

18 Then Jehu brought all the people together and said to them,
"Ahab served Baal a little; Jehu will serve him much. 19 Now summon all the prophets of Baal, all his ministers and all his priests.
See that no one is missing, because I am going to hold a great
sacrifice for Baal. Anyone who fails to come will no longer live."
But Jehu was acting deceptively in order to destroy the ministers
of Baal.
20 Jehu said, "Call an assembly in honor of Baal." So they proclaimed it. 21 Then he sent word throughout Israel, and all the
ministers of Baal came; not one stayed away. They crowded into
the temple of Baal until it was full from one end to the other.
22 And Jehu said to the keeper of the wardrobe, "Bring robes for
all the ministers of Baal." So he brought out robes for them.
23 Then Jehu and Jehonadab son of Recab went into the temple
of Baal. Jehu said to the ministers of Baal, "Look around and see
that no servants of the LORD are here with you—only ministers of
Baal." 24 So they went in to make sacrifices and burnt offerings.
Now Jehu had posted eighty men outside with this warning: "If
one of you lets any of the men I am placing in your hands escape,
it will be your life for his life."
25 As soon as Jehu had finished making the burnt offering, he
ordered the guards and officers: "Go in and kill them; let no one
escape." So they cut them down with the sword. The guards and
officers threw the bodies out and then entered the inner shrine of
the temple of Baal. 26 They brought the sacred stone out of the
temple of Baal and burned it. 27 They demolished the sacred stone
of Baal and tore down the temple of Baal, and people have used
it for a latrine to this day.
28 So Jehu destroyed Baal worship in Israel. 29 However, he did
not turn away from the sins of Jeroboam son of Nebat, which he
had caused Israel to commit—the worship of the golden calves at
Bethel and Dan.
30 The LORD said to Jehu, "Because you have done well in accomplishing what is right in my eyes and have done to the house
of Ahab all I had in mind to do, your descendants will sit on the
throne of Israel to the fourth generation." 31 Yet Jehu was not
careful to keep the law of the LORD, the God of Israel, with all his
heart. He did not turn away from the sins of Jeroboam, which he
had caused Israel to commit.
32 In those days the LORD began to reduce the size of Israel.
Hazael overpowered the Israelites throughout their territory
33 east of the Jordan in all the land of Gilead (the region of Gad,
Reuben and Manasseh), from Aroer by the Arnon Gorge through
Gilead to Bashan.
34 As for the other events of Jehu's reign, all he did, and all his

Repentance means the opportunity of a new start, the chance to correct what man had left crooked, to fill that which is wanting in one's life.

Abba Hillel Silver (1893-1963)

(10:28–32) Search my soul, O Lord. Cleanse me from the hypocrisy of condemning other people's sins and idolatries while failing to fully keep my own heart pure. Release my hands from the worthless idols that cause me to forfeit the fullness of Your grace. I offer You every thought, every ambition, every lust, every self-indulgence that conflicts with Your holiness in my life. I bow down gladly in Your awesome presence and invite You alone to fill every chamber of my being. (Jnh 2:8, 2Co 10:5)

Purify my heart,
Touch me with Your cleansing fire.
Take me to the cross,
Your holiness is my desire.

Breathe Your life in me,
Kindle a love that
Flows from Your throne.
Oh, purify my heart,
Purify my heart.

"Purify My Heart"
Jeff Nelson (©1992)

achievements, are they not written in the book of the annals of the kings of Israel?
35Jehu rested with his fathers and was buried in Samaria. And
Jehoahaz his son succeeded him as king. 36The time that Jehu
reigned over Israel in Samaria was twenty-eight years.

Athaliah and Joash

11 When Athaliah the mother of Ahaziah saw that her son was
dead, she proceeded to destroy the whole royal family. 2But
Jehosheba, the daughter of King Jehoram[a] and sister of Ahaziah, took Joash son of Ahaziah and stole him away from among the royal princes, who were about to be murdered. She put him and his nurse in a bedroom to hide him from Athaliah; so he was not
killed. 3He remained hidden with his nurse at the temple of the
LORD for six years while Athaliah ruled the land.
4In the seventh year Jehoiada sent for the commanders of units of a hundred, the Carites and the guards and had them brought to him at the temple of the LORD. He made a covenant with them and put them under oath at the temple of the LORD. Then he showed
them the king's son. 5He commanded them, saying, "This is what
you are to do: You who are in the three companies that are going on duty on the Sabbath—a third of you guarding the royal palace,
6a third at the Sur Gate, and a third at the gate behind the guard,
who take turns guarding the temple— 7and you who are in the
other two companies that normally go off Sabbath duty are all to
guard the temple for the king. 8Station yourselves around the king,
each man with his weapon in his hand. Anyone who approaches your ranks[b] must be put to death. Stay close to the king wherever he goes."
9The commanders of units of a hundred did just as Jehoiada the priest ordered. Each one took his men—those who were going on duty on the Sabbath and those who were going off duty—and came
to Jehoiada the priest. 10Then he gave the commanders the spears
and shields that had belonged to King David and that were in the
temple of the LORD. 11The guards, each with his weapon in his
hand, stationed themselves around the king—near the altar and the temple, from the south side to the north side of the temple.
12Jehoiada brought out the king's son and put the crown on him; he presented him with a copy of the covenant and proclaimed him king. They anointed him, and the people clapped their hands and shouted, "Long live the king!"
13When Athaliah heard the noise made by the guards and the
people, she went to the people at the temple of the LORD. 14She
looked and there was the king, standing by the pillar, as the custom was. The officers and the trumpeters were beside the king, and all the people of the land were rejoicing and blowing trumpets. Then Athaliah tore her robes and called out, "Treason! Treason!"
15Jehoiada the priest ordered the commanders of units of a hundred, who were in charge of the troops: "Bring her out between the ranks[c] and put to the sword anyone who follows her." For the priest had said, "She must not be put to death in the temple of
the LORD." 16So they seized her as she reached the place where the
horses enter the palace grounds, and there she was put to death.
17Jehoiada then made a covenant between the LORD and the king and people that they would be the LORD's people. He also

[a] 2 Hebrew *Joram,* a variant of *Jehoram* [b] 8 Or *approaches the precincts* [c] 15 Or *out from the precincts*

God's promises are like the stars; the darker the night the brighter they shine.
David Nicholas (c.1978)

(11:1–16) We praise You, our covenanting God, for Your great faithfulness to keep Your promise to David that he would never fail to have a son on the throne of Israel. Athalia, the daughter of Jezebel, in her own wicked ambition had all but destroyed David's line. But in Your wisdom and sovereignty You preserved one child and kept him hidden in the safety of Your own house. And the words of praise from David's heart again rang true for the life of this son of David: "In the day of trouble he will keep me safe in his dwelling; he will hide me in the shelter of his tabernacle." (1Ki 2:4; Ps 27:5)

The Lord is my light and my
salvation,
The Lord is the strength of my life.
The Lord is my light and my
salvation,
The Lord is the strength of my life.
So I will not be afraid,
No, I will not be afraid;
Because the Lord is my light,
The Lord is my light,
The Lord is my light.

In the day of trouble
He will hide me;
He will keep me safe,
He will guide me through.

In the darkest hour
He will keep me;
Evil has no power when
He shelters me.

"The Lord is My Light"
Walt Harrah (©1987)

There are three kinds of giving: grudge giving, duty giving, and thanksgiving. Grudge giving says, "I hate to," duty giving says, "I ought to," thanksgiving says, "I want to." The first comes from constraint, the second from a sense of obligation, the third from a full heart. Nothing much is conveyed in grudge giving since "the gift without the giver is bare." Something more happens in duty giving, but there is no song in it. Thanksgiving is an open gate into the love of God.

Robert N. Rodenmayer (1909–1979)

(12:1–14) Lord, teach us to faithfully bring our tithes and offerings to be used for the continual building of Your kingdom. And help us to be good stewards of the resources of the church. May we never squander them or use them foolishly. Just as our praise is the sacrifice of our lips, so may our money be the sacrifice of our labor, offered to You in devoted worship. As we give freely, generously and joyfully we pray that You will use our gifts to build up the church and win the lost. (2 Co 9:6–7; Heb 13:15)

Savior, Thy dying love Thou gavest
me,
Nor should I aught withhold,
Dear Lord, from Thee;
In love my soul would bow,
My heart fulfill its vow,
Some off'ring bring Thee now,
Something for Thee.

"Something for Thee"
Sylvanus D. Phelps (1816–1895)

made a covenant between the king and the people. 18All the people of the land went to the temple of Baal and tore it down. They
smashed the altars and idols to pieces and killed Mattan the
priest of Baal in front of the altars.
Then Jehoiada the priest posted guards at the temple of the
LORD. 19He took with him the commanders of hundreds, the Carites, the guards and all the people of the land, and together they
brought the king down from the temple of the LORD and went into
the palace, entering by way of the gate of the guards. The king
then took his place on the royal throne, 20and all the people of
the land rejoiced. And the city was quiet, because Athaliah had
been slain with the sword at the palace.
21Joash[a] was seven years old when he began to reign.

Joash Repairs the Temple

12 In the seventh year of Jehu, Joash[b] became king, and he
reigned in Jerusalem forty years. His mother's name was
Zibiah; she was from Beersheba. 2Joash did what was right in the
eyes of the LORD all the years Jehoiada the priest instructed him.
3The high places, however, were not removed; the people continued to offer sacrifices and burn incense there.
4Joash said to the priests, "Collect all the money that is brought
as sacred offerings to the temple of the LORD—the money collected in the census, the money received from personal vows and
the money brought voluntarily to the temple. 5Let every priest receive the money from one of the treasurers, and let it be used to
repair whatever damage is found in the temple."
6But by the twenty-third year of King Joash the priests still had
not repaired the temple. 7Therefore King Joash summoned Jehoiada the priest and the other priests and asked them, "Why
aren't you repairing the damage done to the temple? Take no
more money from your treasurers, but hand it over for repairing
the temple." 8The priests agreed that they would not collect any
more money from the people and that they would not repair the
temple themselves.
9Jehoiada the priest took a chest and bored a hole in its lid. He
placed it beside the altar, on the right side as one enters the temple of the LORD. The priests who guarded the entrance put into the
chest all the money that was brought to the temple of the LORD.
10Whenever they saw that there was a large amount of money in
the chest, the royal secretary and the high priest came, counted
the money that had been brought into the temple of the LORD and
put it into bags. 11When the amount had been determined, they
gave the money to the men appointed to supervise the work on
the temple. With it they paid those who worked on the temple of
the LORD—the carpenters and builders, 12the masons and stonecutters. They purchased timber and dressed stone for the repair
of the temple of the LORD, and met all the other expenses of
restoring the temple.
13The money brought into the temple was not spent for making
silver basins, wick trimmers, sprinkling bowls, trumpets or any
other articles of gold or silver for the temple of the LORD; 14it was
paid to the workmen, who used it to repair the temple. 15They did
not require an accounting from those to whom they gave the
money to pay the workers, because they acted with complete hon-

[a] 21 Hebrew *Jehoash,* a variant of *Joash*   [b] 1 Hebrew *Jehoash,* a variant of *Joash*; also in verses 2, 4, 6, 7 and 18

esty. 16The money from the guilt offerings and sin offerings was
not brought into the temple of the LORD; it belonged to the priests.
17About this time Hazael king of Aram went up and attacked
Gath and captured it. Then he turned to attack Jerusalem. 18But
Joash king of Judah took all the sacred objects dedicated by his
fathers—Jehoshaphat, Jehoram and Ahaziah, the kings of
Judah—and the gifts he himself had dedicated and all the gold
found in the treasuries of the temple of the LORD and of the royal
palace, and he sent them to Hazael king of Aram, who then withdrew from Jerusalem.
19As for the other events of the reign of Joash, and all he did,
are they not written in the book of the annals of the kings of
Judah? 20His officials conspired against him and assassinated him
at Beth Millo, on the road down to Silla. 21The officials who murdered him were Jozabad son of Shimeath and Jehozabad son of
Shomer. He died and was buried with his fathers in the City of
David. And Amaziah his son succeeded him as king.

Jehoahaz King of Israel

13 In the twenty-third year of Joash son of Ahaziah king of
Judah, Jehoahaz son of Jehu became king of Israel in
Samaria, and he reigned seventeen years. 2He did evil in the eyes
of the LORD by following the sins of Jeroboam son of Nebat, which
he had caused Israel to commit, and he did not turn away from
them. 3So the LORD's anger burned against Israel, and for a long
time he kept them under the power of Hazael king of Aram and
Ben-Hadad his son.
4Then Jehoahaz sought the LORD's favor, and the LORD listened
to him, for he saw how severely the king of Aram was oppressing
Israel. 5The LORD provided a deliverer for Israel, and they escaped from the power of Aram. So the Israelites lived in their own
homes as they had before. 6But they did not turn away from the
sins of the house of Jeroboam, which he had caused Israel to
commit; they continued in them. Also, the Asherah pole[a] remained standing in Samaria.
7Nothing had been left of the army of Jehoahaz except fifty
horsemen, ten chariots and ten thousand foot soldiers, for the
king of Aram had destroyed the rest and made them like the dust
at threshing time.
8As for the other events of the reign of Jehoahaz, all he did and
his achievements, are they not written in the book of the annals of
the kings of Israel? 9Jehoahaz rested with his fathers and was
buried in Samaria. And Jehoash[b] his son succeeded him as king.

Jehoash King of Israel

10In the thirty-seventh year of Joash king of Judah, Jehoash son
of Jehoahaz became king of Israel in Samaria, and he reigned sixteen years. 11He did evil in the eyes of the LORD and did not turn
away from any of the sins of Jeroboam son of Nebat, which he
had caused Israel to commit; he continued in them.
12As for the other events of the reign of Jehoash, all he did and
his achievements, including his war against Amaziah king of
Judah, are they not written in the book of the annals of the kings
of Israel? 13Jehoash rested with his fathers, and Jeroboam suc-

[a] *6* That is, a symbol of the goddess Asherah; here and elsewhere in 2 Kings [b] *9* Hebrew *Joash,* a variant of *Jehoash;* also in verses 12–14 and 25

(13:1–5) Even in the midst of Your wrath and discipline, You listen for our cry. Your heart is hopeful and tender. Your longsuffering is vast and Your mercy truly endures forever. When we, like Jehoahaz, were unable to save ourselves, we earnestly sought Your help. In Your grace You listened, provided a Savior and delivered us from the power of the enemy. Teach us to abandon all other gods and give You our allegiance all the days of our lives.

Like a dove when hunted, frightened,
As a wounded fawn was I;
Broken hearted, yet He healed me.
He will heed the sinner's cry.

"He the Pearly Gates Will Open"
Frederick A. Blom (c.1917)
Trans. Nathaniel Carlson (c.1935)

ceeded him on the throne. Jehoash was buried in Samaria with
the kings of Israel.
14Now Elisha was suffering from the illness from which he
died. Jehoash king of Israel went down to see him and wept over
him. "My father! My father!" he cried. "The chariots and horsemen of Israel!"
15Elisha said, "Get a bow and some arrows," and he did so.
16"Take the bow in your hands," he said to the king of Israel.
When he had taken it, Elisha put his hands on the king's hands.
17"Open the east window," he said, and he opened it. "Shoot!"
Elisha said, and he shot. "The LORD's arrow of victory, the arrow
of victory over Aram!" Elisha declared. "You will completely destroy the Arameans at Aphek."
18Then he said, "Take the arrows," and the king took them.
Elisha told him, "Strike the ground." He struck it three times and
stopped. 19The man of God was angry with him and said, "You
should have struck the ground five or six times; then you would
have defeated Aram and completely destroyed it. But now you will
defeat it only three times."
20Elisha died and was buried.
Now Moabite raiders used to enter the country every spring.
21Once while some Israelites were burying a man, suddenly they
saw a band of raiders; so they threw the man's body into Elisha's
tomb. When the body touched Elisha's bones, the man came to
life and stood up on his feet.
22Hazael king of Aram oppressed Israel throughout the reign
of Jehoahaz. 23But the LORD was gracious to them and had compassion and showed concern for them because of his covenant
with Abraham, Isaac and Jacob. To this day he has been unwilling
to destroy them or banish them from his presence.
24Hazael king of Aram died, and Ben-Hadad his son succeeded him as king. 25Then Jehoash son of Jehoahaz recaptured from
Ben-Hadad son of Hazael the towns he had taken in battle from
his father Jehoahaz. Three times Jehoash defeated him, and so he
recovered the Israelite towns.

Amaziah King of Judah

14 In the second year of Jehoash[a] son of Jehoahaz king of Israel, Amaziah son of Joash king of Judah began to reign.
2He was twenty-five years old when he became king, and he
reigned in Jerusalem twenty-nine years. His mother's name was
Jehoaddin; she was from Jerusalem. 3He did what was right in
the eyes of the LORD, but not as his father David had done. In
everything he followed the example of his father Joash. 4The high
places, however, were not removed; the people continued to offer
sacrifices and burn incense there.
5After the kingdom was firmly in his grasp, he executed the officials who had murdered his father the king. 6Yet he did not put
the sons of the assassins to death, in accordance with what is
written in the Book of the Law of Moses where the LORD commanded: "Fathers shall not be put to death for their children, nor
children put to death for their fathers; each is to die for his own
sins."[b]
7He was the one who defeated ten thousand Edomites in the

[a] 1 Hebrew *Joash*, a variant of *Jehoash*; also in verses 13, 23 and 27 [b] 6 Deut. 24:16

Let us work as if success depended upon ourselves alone; but with heartfelt conviction that we are doing nothing and God everything.

Saint Ignatius of Loyola (1491–1556)

(13:15–19) "Praise be to the LORD my Rock, who trains my hands for war, my fingers for battle." In the spiritual struggles we face, Lord God, You are our leader, full of wisdom and power. You have given us weapons and authority, now give us the skill and courage to use them. Anoint us with the Holy Spirit, that we may be strong in the Lord and in his mighty power. Teach us to pray and keep on praying, to resist and keep on resisting, to praise and keep on praising until the power of the evil one is completely destroyed. (Ps 144:1; Eph 6:10–18; Jas 4:7; 1Pe 5:8–9)

Be strong in the Lord,
And be of good courage;
Your mighty Commander
Will vanquish the foe.
Fear not the battle
For the victory is always His;
He will protect you
Wherever you go.

"Be Strong in the Lord"
Linda Lee Johnson (©1979)

Valley of Salt and captured Sela in battle, calling it Joktheel, the name it has to this day.
8Then Amaziah sent messengers to Jehoash son of Jehoahaz, the son of Jehu, king of Israel, with the challenge: "Come, meet me face to face."
9But Jehoash king of Israel replied to Amaziah king of Judah: "A thistle in Lebanon sent a message to a cedar in Lebanon, 'Give your daughter to my son in marriage.' Then a wild beast in Lebanon came along and trampled the thistle underfoot.
10You have indeed defeated Edom and now you are arrogant. Glory in your victory, but stay at home! Why ask for trouble and cause your own downfall and that of Judah also?"
11Amaziah, however, would not listen, so Jehoash king of Israel attacked. He and Amaziah king of Judah faced each other at Beth Shemesh in Judah.
12Judah was routed by Israel, and every man fled to his home.
13Jehoash king of Israel captured Amaziah king of Judah, the son of Joash, the son of Ahaziah, at Beth Shemesh. Then Jehoash went to Jerusalem and broke down the wall of Jerusalem from the Ephraim Gate to the Corner Gate—a section about six hundred feet long.[a]
14He took all the gold and silver and all the articles found in the temple of the LORD and in the treasuries of the royal palace. He also took hostages and returned to Samaria.
15As for the other events of the reign of Jehoash, what he did and his achievements, including his war against Amaziah king of Judah, are they not written in the book of the annals of the kings of Israel?
16Jehoash rested with his fathers and was buried in Samaria with the kings of Israel. And Jeroboam his son succeeded him as king.
17Amaziah son of Joash king of Judah lived for fifteen years after the death of Jehoash son of Jehoahaz king of Israel.
18As for the other events of Amaziah's reign, are they not written in the book of the annals of the kings of Judah?
19They conspired against him in Jerusalem, and he fled to Lachish, but they sent men after him to Lachish and killed him there.
20He was brought back by horse and was buried in Jerusalem with his fathers, in the City of David.
21Then all the people of Judah took Azariah,[b] who was sixteen years old, and made him king in place of his father Amaziah.
22He was the one who rebuilt Elath and restored it to Judah after Amaziah rested with his fathers.

Jeroboam II King of Israel

23In the fifteenth year of Amaziah son of Joash king of Judah, Jeroboam son of Jehoash king of Israel became king in Samaria, and he reigned forty-one years.
24He did evil in the eyes of the LORD and did not turn away from any of the sins of Jeroboam son of Nebat, which he had caused Israel to commit.
25He was the one who restored the boundaries of Israel from Lebo[c] Hamath to the Sea of the Arabah,[d] in accordance with the word of the LORD, the God of Israel, spoken through his servant Jonah son of Amittai, the prophet from Gath Hepher.
26The LORD had seen how bitterly everyone in Israel, whether slave or free, was suffering; there was no one to help them.
27And since the LORD had not said he would blot out the name of Israel

(14:8–14) Father, deliver me from arrogance and presumption that can lead me into conflicts I would do better to avoid. Help me to stay attuned to Your voice and humble in my spirit. Keep my heart faithful to You in worship. Like Jesus, I want to do only those things I see You doing. Then I can be sure of my ground and confident of victory. (2Ch 25:14–27; Pr 18:6; Jn 5:19)

[a] *13* Hebrew *four hundred cubits* (about 180 meters) [b] *21* Also called *Uzziah*
[c] *25* Or *from the entrance to* [d] *25* That is, the Dead Sea

from under heaven, he saved them by the hand of Jeroboam son
of Jehoash.
28As for the other events of Jeroboam's reign, all he did, and
his military achievements, including how he recovered for Israel
both Damascus and Hamath, which had belonged to Yaudi,[a] are
they not written in the book of the annals of the kings of Israel?
29Jeroboam rested with his fathers, the kings of Israel. And
Zechariah his son succeeded him as king.

Azariah King of Judah

15 In the twenty-seventh year of Jeroboam king of Israel, Azariah
son of Amaziah king of Judah began to reign. **2**He was sixteen
years old when he became king, and he reigned in Jerusalem fifty-
two years. His mother's name was Jecoliah; she was from Jerusalem.
3He did what was right in the eyes of the LORD, just as his father Amaziah had done. **4**The high places, however, were not removed; the
people continued to offer sacrifices and burn incense there.
5The LORD afflicted the king with leprosy[b] until the day he died,
and he lived in a separate house.[c] Jotham the king's son had
charge of the palace and governed the people of the land.
6As for the other events of Azariah's reign, and all he did, are
they not written in the book of the annals of the kings of Judah?
7Azariah rested with his fathers and was buried near them in the
City of David. And Jotham his son succeeded him as king.

Zechariah King of Israel

8In the thirty-eighth year of Azariah king of Judah, Zechariah
son of Jeroboam became king of Israel in Samaria, and he
reigned six months. **9**He did evil in the eyes of the LORD, as his fathers had done. He did not turn away from the sins of Jeroboam
son of Nebat, which he had caused Israel to commit.
10Shallum son of Jabesh conspired against Zechariah. He attacked him in front of the people,[d] assassinated him and succeeded him as king. **11**The other events of Zechariah's reign are
written in the book of the annals of the kings of Israel. **12**So the
word of the LORD spoken to Jehu was fulfilled: "Your descendants
will sit on the throne of Israel to the fourth generation."[e]

Shallum King of Israel

13Shallum son of Jabesh became king in the thirty-ninth year of
Uzziah king of Judah, and he reigned in Samaria one month.
14Then Menahem son of Gadi went from Tirzah up to Samaria. He
attacked Shallum son of Jabesh in Samaria, assassinated him and
succeeded him as king.
15The other events of Shallum's reign, and the conspiracy he
led, are written in the book of the annals of the kings of Israel.
16At that time Menahem, starting out from Tirzah, attacked
Tiphsah and everyone in the city and its vicinity, because they refused to open their gates. He sacked Tiphsah and ripped open all
the pregnant women.

Menahem King of Israel

17In the thirty-ninth year of Azariah king of Judah, Menahem
son of Gadi became king of Israel, and he reigned in Samaria ten

[a] 28 Or *Judah* [b] 5 The Hebrew word was used for various diseases affecting the skin—not necessarily leprosy. [c] 5 Or *in a house where he was relieved of responsibility* [d] 10 Hebrew; some Septuagint manuscripts *in Ibleam* [e] 12 2 Kings 10:30

(15:1–5) How many of us began our spiritual lives by carefully doing what was right in Your eyes, Lord? And how many of us have failed to obey fully and have experienced the strong discipline of Your tough love? I worshipfully submit to that discipline, Lord, knowing that Your correction ultimately strengthens my soul. Lord, cleanse me from all unrighteousness and make me a fully devoted follower of Yours, so that my last days may be stronger, holier and more full of glory than my first days. (2Ch 26; Heb 12:11)

Holy Spirit, Pow'r divine,
Cleanse this guilty heart of mine.
Long hath sin without control
Held dominion o'er my soul.

Holy Spirit, all divine,
Dwell within this heart of mine.
Cast down every idol throne;
Reign supreme, and reign alone.

"Holy Spirit, Light Divine"
Andrew Reed (1787-1862)

years. 18He did evil in the eyes of the LORD. During his entire reign
he did not turn away from the sins of Jeroboam son of Nebat,
which he had caused Israel to commit.
19Then Pul[a] king of Assyria invaded the land, and Menahem
gave him a thousand talents[b] of silver to gain his support and
strengthen his own hold on the kingdom. 20Menahem exacted
this money from Israel. Every wealthy man had to contribute fifty
shekels[c] of silver to be given to the king of Assyria. So the king of
Assyria withdrew and stayed in the land no longer.
21As for the other events of Menahem's reign, and all he did,
are they not written in the book of the annals of the kings of Israel? 22Menahem rested with his fathers. And Pekahiah his son
succeeded him as king.

Pekahiah King of Israel

23In the fiftieth year of Azariah king of Judah, Pekahiah son of
Menahem became king of Israel in Samaria, and he reigned two
years. 24Pekahiah did evil in the eyes of the LORD. He did not turn
away from the sins of Jeroboam son of Nebat, which he had
caused Israel to commit. 25One of his chief officers, Pekah son of
Remaliah, conspired against him. Taking fifty men of Gilead with
him, he assassinated Pekahiah, along with Argob and Arieh, in
the citadel of the royal palace at Samaria. So Pekah killed Pekahiah and succeeded him as king.
26The other events of Pekahiah's reign, and all he did, are written in the book of the annals of the kings of Israel.

Pekah King of Israel

27In the fifty-second year of Azariah king of Judah, Pekah son
of Remaliah became king of Israel in Samaria, and he reigned
twenty years. 28He did evil in the eyes of the LORD. He did not turn
away from the sins of Jeroboam son of Nebat, which he had
caused Israel to commit.
29In the time of Pekah king of Israel, Tiglath-Pileser king of
Assyria came and took Ijon, Abel Beth Maacah, Janoah, Kedesh
and Hazor. He took Gilead and Galilee, including all the land of
Naphtali, and deported the people to Assyria. 30Then Hoshea son
of Elah conspired against Pekah son of Remaliah. He attacked
and assassinated him, and then succeeded him as king in the
twentieth year of Jotham son of Uzziah.
31As for the other events of Pekah's reign, and all he did,
are they not written in the book of the annals of the kings of Israel?

Jotham King of Judah

32In the second year of Pekah son of Remaliah king of Israel,
Jotham son of Uzziah king of Judah began to reign. 33He was
twenty-five years old when he became king, and he reigned in Jerusalem sixteen years. His mother's name was Jerusha daughter
of Zadok. 34He did what was right in the eyes of the LORD, just as
his father Uzziah had done. 35The high places, however, were not
removed; the people continued to offer sacrifices and burn incense there. Jotham rebuilt the Upper Gate of the temple of the
LORD.
36As for the other events of Jotham's reign, and what he did,

If evil is not something directly willed by God and not something wholly outside of his control, but something in his good world which he has temporarily permitted to exist while he calls for volunteers to oppose and correct it, then the task of overcoming evil is never a hopeless one.

Walter Marshall Horton (1895-1966)

(15:17–31) Your Word is so plain, Your warnings, by both judgments and mercies, are so clear. Yet today as yesterday world leaders make the fatal choices that lead to bloodshed, chaos and despair. You have called Your people to pray for those who rule over us, and so we ask You to give us leaders with hearts that are inclined to godliness. Open their eyes to Your ways and their ears to Your voice. Surround them with godly counsel. And through the darkness, let an obedient church light the world with the love and blessing of God.

We open our hearts
And our lives to You, Oh God.
Create within us a servant heart
So that we can show Your love.
Where all hope has been lost
Let Your Spirit bring new life.
To those in need, bring prosperity;
Where there's darkness, shine Your light.

We pray for this city we live in.
We pray that our sins be forgiven.
Do Your will right here as in heaven;
Father, we call on Your name.

We pray for our children.
We pray for our leaders.
We pray for our families.
Oh, bless us, Lord, we pray.

"Prayer For The City"
Tore Aas and Scott V. Smith (©1995)

a 19 Also called *Tiglath-Pileser* b 19 That is, about 37 tons (about 34 metric tons)
c 20 That is, about 1 1/4 pounds (about 0.6 kilogram)

Those will soon come to make nothing of God that will not be content to make him their all.

Matthew Henry (1662–1714)

(16:10–15) It is not enough for worship to be right in our own eyes—it must be right in Your eyes, or it cannot be right at all. God forbid that I, Your temple, should allow any altar in my heart but the altar that is Christ; for the altar sanctifies the gift, and only through Christ is my worship sanctified. God forbid that we, Your church, should ever replace the plain and simple truth of Christ with an elaborate substitute, or exchange the truth of the gospel for popular theories or humanistic doctrines. Give us boldness to resist the temptation to imitate the ways of the world, no matter how beautiful or well-intentioned they seem. You have called us to be lights to the world. But if the light within us is darkness, how great is that darkness! O Lord, have mercy on us. (Mt 5:14; 6:23; 23:19; 2Co 6:16)

are they not written in the book of the annals of the kings of
Judah? 37 (In those days the LORD began to send Rezin king of
Aram and Pekah son of Remaliah against Judah.) 38 Jotham rested with his fathers and was buried with them in the City of David,
the city of his father. And Ahaz his son succeeded him as king.

Ahaz King of Judah

16 In the seventeenth year of Pekah son of Remaliah, Ahaz
son of Jotham king of Judah began to reign. 2 Ahaz was
twenty years old when he became king, and he reigned in Jerusalem sixteen years. Unlike David his father, he did not do what was
right in the eyes of the LORD his God. 3 He walked in the ways of
the kings of Israel and even sacrificed his son in[a] the fire, following the detestable ways of the nations the LORD had driven out
before the Israelites. 4 He offered sacrifices and burned incense at
the high places, on the hilltops and under every spreading tree.
5 Then Rezin king of Aram and Pekah son of Remaliah king of
Israel marched up to fight against Jerusalem and besieged Ahaz,
but they could not overpower him. 6 At that time, Rezin king of
Aram recovered Elath for Aram by driving out the men of Judah.
Edomites then moved into Elath and have lived there to this day.
7 Ahaz sent messengers to say to Tiglath-Pileser king of Assyria,
"I am your servant and vassal. Come up and save me out of the
hand of the king of Aram and of the king of Israel, who are attacking me." 8 And Ahaz took the silver and gold found in the temple of the LORD and in the treasuries of the royal palace and sent
it as a gift to the king of Assyria. 9 The king of Assyria complied by
attacking Damascus and capturing it. He deported its inhabitants
to Kir and put Rezin to death.
10 Then King Ahaz went to Damascus to meet Tiglath-Pileser
king of Assyria. He saw an altar in Damascus and sent to Uriah the
priest a sketch of the altar, with detailed plans for its construction. 11 So Uriah the priest built an altar in accordance with all the
plans that King Ahaz had sent from Damascus and finished it
before King Ahaz returned. 12 When the king came back from Damascus and saw the altar, he approached it and presented offerings[b] on it. 13 He offered up his burnt offering and grain offering,
poured out his drink offering, and sprinkled the blood of his fellowship offerings[c] on the altar. 14 The bronze altar that stood
before the LORD he brought from the front of the temple—from
between the new altar and the temple of the LORD—and put it on
the north side of the new altar.
15 King Ahaz then gave these orders to Uriah the priest: "On the
large new altar, offer the morning burnt offering and the evening
grain offering, the king's burnt offering and his grain offering,
and the burnt offering of all the people of the land, and their
grain offering and their drink offering. Sprinkle on the altar all
the blood of the burnt offerings and sacrifices. But I will use the
bronze altar for seeking guidance." 16 And Uriah the priest did
just as King Ahaz had ordered.
17 King Ahaz took away the side panels and removed the basins
from the movable stands. He removed the Sea from the bronze
bulls that supported it and set it on a stone base. 18 He took away
the Sabbath canopy[d] that had been built at the temple and re-

[a] 3 Or *even made his son pass through* [b] 12 Or *and went up* [c] 13 Traditionally *peace offerings* [d] 18 Or *the dais of his throne* (see Septuagint)

moved the royal entryway outside the temple of the LORD, in def-
erence to the king of Assyria.
19As for the other events of the reign of Ahaz, and what he did,
are they not written in the book of the annals of the kings of
Judah? 20Ahaz rested with his fathers and was buried with them
in the City of David. And Hezekiah his son succeeded him as
king.

Hoshea Last King of Israel

17 In the twelfth year of Ahaz king of Judah, Hoshea son of
Elah became king of Israel in Samaria, and he reigned
nine years. 2He did evil in the eyes of the LORD, but not like the
kings of Israel who preceded him.
3Shalmaneser king of Assyria came up to attack Hoshea, who
had been Shalmaneser's vassal and had paid him tribute. 4But
the king of Assyria discovered that Hoshea was a traitor, for he
had sent envoys to So[a] king of Egypt, and he no longer paid tribute to the king of Assyria, as he had done year by year. Therefore
Shalmaneser seized him and put him in prison. 5The king of Assyria invaded the entire land, marched against Samaria and laid
siege to it for three years. 6In the ninth year of Hoshea, the king
of Assyria captured Samaria and deported the Israelites to Assyria. He settled them in Halah, in Gozan on the Habor River and
in the towns of the Medes.

Israel Exiled Because of Sin

7All this took place because the Israelites had sinned against
the LORD their God, who had brought them up out of Egypt from
under the power of Pharaoh king of Egypt. They worshiped other
gods 8and followed the practices of the nations the LORD had
driven out before them, as well as the practices that the kings of
Israel had introduced. 9The Israelites secretly did things against
the LORD their God that were not right. From watchtower to fortified city they built themselves high places in all their towns.
10They set up sacred stones and Asherah poles on every high hill
and under every spreading tree. 11At every high place they
burned incense, as the nations whom the LORD had driven out
before them had done. They did wicked things that provoked the
LORD to anger. 12They worshiped idols, though the LORD had said,
"You shall not do this."[b] 13The LORD warned Israel and Judah
through all his prophets and seers: "Turn from your evil ways.
Observe my commands and decrees, in accordance with the entire Law that I commanded your fathers to obey and that I delivered to you through my servants the prophets."
14But they would not listen and were as stiff-necked as their
fathers, who did not trust in the LORD their God. 15They rejected
his decrees and the covenant he had made with their fathers and
the warnings he had given them. They followed worthless idols
and themselves became worthless. They imitated the nations
around them although the LORD had ordered them, "Do not do as
they do," and they did the things the LORD had forbidden them
to do.
16They forsook all the commands of the LORD their God and
made for themselves two idols cast in the shape of calves, and an
Asherah pole. They bowed down to all the starry hosts, and they

[a] 4 Or *to Sais, to the*; *So* is possibly an abbreviation for *Osorkon*. [b] 12 Exodus 20:4, 5

We never do anything so secretly but that it is in the presence of two witnesses: God and our own conscience.

Benjamin Whichcote (1609–1683)

(17:9–15) "'Can anyone hide in secret places so that I cannot see him?' declares the LORD. 'Do not I fill heaven and earth?' declares the LORD." We think our sins are hidden; we are careful to keep them in the secret recesses of our hearts. But our souls are as glass to You, O Lord; You see everything. "You have set our iniquities before you, our secret sins in the light of your presence." We have no one to blame when Your discipline comes, as it surely does. We cannot say, "We didn't know! No one told us!" Your prophets and pastors have faithfully warned and pled from street corner and pulpit. And they have shown the way of cleansing and forgiveness. Open the ears and hearts of our nation. Awaken us again and bring us safely to the cross. (Dt 27:15; Ps 90:8; Jer 23:24; Eze 8:12)

Sinning is nothing but turning from God one's face
And having turned it thus, turning it toward death.

Angelus Silesius (1624–1677)

(17:22–23) What could be more devastating, more barren and hopeless than to be removed from Your presence by our disobedience? Our lives would be without light, without joy, without growth or fruitfulness. We would be like exiles in a dry and desolate land of the spirit. God, we recognize Your sovereignty, Your uncompromising holiness, authority and power. We run into Your presence as obedient sons and daughters who worship You with love and awe. And we thank You for the wonder of Your great mercy, for when we repent You forgive and restore.

If we will call, the Lord will answer.
He will forgive and draw us near.
And when we bow in repentance,
He will lift us up again.

For this one reason,
For this one cause,
We stand together
In the calling of our God:
To lift our voices,
To lift our hands,
And pray to heaven
For a healing in this land.

"For This One Reason"
John Barbour and Marsha Skidmore
(©1996)

worshiped Baal. 17They sacrificed their sons and daughters in[a]
the fire. They practiced divination and sorcery and sold themselves to do evil in the eyes of the LORD, provoking him to anger.
18So the LORD was very angry with Israel and removed them
from his presence. Only the tribe of Judah was left, 19and even
Judah did not keep the commands of the LORD their God. They
followed the practices Israel had introduced. 20Therefore the
LORD rejected all the people of Israel; he afflicted them and gave
them into the hands of plunderers, until he thrust them from
his presence.
21When he tore Israel away from the house of David, they
made Jeroboam son of Nebat their king. Jeroboam enticed Israel away from following the LORD and caused them to commit
a great sin. 22The Israelites persisted in all the sins of Jeroboam
and did not turn away from them 23until the LORD removed them
from his presence, as he had warned through all his servants
the prophets. So the people of Israel were taken from their
homeland into exile in Assyria, and they are still there.

Samaria Resettled

24The king of Assyria brought people from Babylon, Cuthah,
Avva, Hamath and Sepharvaim and settled them in the towns of
Samaria to replace the Israelites. They took over Samaria and
lived in its towns. 25When they first lived there, they did not
worship the LORD; so he sent lions among them and they killed
some of the people. 26It was reported to the king of Assyria:
"The people you deported and resettled in the towns of Samaria
do not know what the god of that country requires. He has sent
lions among them, which are killing them off, because the people do not know what he requires."
27Then the king of Assyria gave this order: "Have one of the
priests you took captive from Samaria go back to live there and
teach the people what the god of the land requires." 28So one of
the priests who had been exiled from Samaria came to live in
Bethel and taught them how to worship the LORD.
29Nevertheless, each national group made its own gods in the
several towns where they settled, and set them up in the shrines
the people of Samaria had made at the high places. 30The men
from Babylon made Succoth Benoth, the men from Cuthah
made Nergal, and the men from Hamath made Ashima; 31the Avvites made Nibhaz and Tartak, and the Sepharvites burned their
children in the fire as sacrifices to Adrammelech and Anam-
melech, the gods of Sepharvaim. 32They worshiped the LORD,
but they also appointed all sorts of their own people to officiate
for them as priests in the shrines at the high places. 33They worshiped the LORD, but they also served their own gods in accordance with the customs of the nations from which they had been
brought.
34To this day they persist in their former practices. They
neither worship the LORD nor adhere to the decrees and ordinances, the laws and commands that the LORD gave the descendants of Jacob, whom he named Israel. 35When the LORD made
a covenant with the Israelites, he commanded them: "Do not
worship any other gods or bow down to them, serve them or
sacrifice to them. 36But the LORD, who brought you up out of

[a] 17 Or *They made their sons and daughters pass through*

MY BELOVED

Do not let your communication with Me be limited to a cry for help. I also want to hear from you when you aren't in trouble.

During your good days, come before Me singing songs of joy and thanksgiving. Remember that it is I Who delivered you from trouble. It is I Who defended you from the attack of others.

Your salvation comes from Me. When you cry out for help, I hear your cry and comfort you. When you come to Me in need of protection, I hide you in the shelter of My presence. I cover you with My love.

At the dawn of creation, I formed the heavens with all their galaxies. I made the land and seas, and I alone gave life to everything. But though the multitudes of heaven worship Me, still I long for your worship.

As your Creator, I have chosen you to be My own. You are My treasured possession. I surround you with favor as with a shield. So praise My name, My beloved. Praise Me, for I am good. When you sing praises to My name, I am pleased. So sing a joyful song . . . even now!

2Ki 17:39; Ne 9:6; Ps 5:12; 27:5; 31:20; 100:2-3; 107:22; 135:1-4; Jn 4:23

Egypt with mighty power and outstretched arm, is the one you
must worship. To him you shall bow down and to him offer sacrifices. 37You must always be careful to keep the decrees and
ordinances, the laws and commands he wrote for you. Do not
worship other gods. 38Do not forget the covenant I have made
with you, and do not worship other gods. 39Rather, worship the
LORD your God; it is he who will deliver you from the hand of all
your enemies."
40They would not listen, however, but persisted in their former
practices. 41Even while these people were worshiping the LORD,
they were serving their idols. To this day their children and
grandchildren continue to do as their fathers did.

Hezekiah King of Judah

18 In the third year of Hoshea son of Elah king of Israel, Hezekiah son of Ahaz king of Judah began to reign. 2He was
twenty-five years old when he became king, and he reigned in Jerusalem twenty-nine years. His mother's name was Abijah[a]
daughter of Zechariah. 3He did what was right in the eyes of the
LORD, just as his father David had done. 4He removed the high
places, smashed the sacred stones and cut down the Asherah
poles. He broke into pieces the bronze snake Moses had made,
for up to that time the Israelites had been burning incense to it.
(It was called[b] Nehushtan.[c])
5Hezekiah trusted in the LORD, the God of Israel. There was no
one like him among all the kings of Judah, either before him or
after him. 6He held fast to the LORD and did not cease to follow
him; he kept the commands the LORD had given Moses. 7And the
LORD was with him; he was successful in whatever he undertook.
He rebelled against the king of Assyria and did not serve him.
8From watchtower to fortified city, he defeated the Philistines, as
far as Gaza and its territory.
9In King Hezekiah's fourth year, which was the seventh year of
Hoshea son of Elah king of Israel, Shalmaneser king of Assyria
marched against Samaria and laid siege to it. 10At the end of three
years the Assyrians took it. So Samaria was captured in Hezekiah's sixth year, which was the ninth year of Hoshea king of Israel.
11The king of Assyria deported Israel to Assyria and settled them
in Halah, in Gozan on the Habor River and in towns of the Medes.
12This happened because they had not obeyed the LORD their God,
but had violated his covenant—all that Moses the servant of the
LORD commanded. They neither listened to the commands nor
carried them out.
13In the fourteenth year of King Hezekiah's reign, Sennacherib
king of Assyria attacked all the fortified cities of Judah and captured them. 14So Hezekiah king of Judah sent this message to the
king of Assyria at Lachish: "I have done wrong. Withdraw from
me, and I will pay whatever you demand of me." The king of Assyria exacted from Hezekiah king of Judah three hundred talents[d]
of silver and thirty talents[e] of gold. 15So Hezekiah gave him all the
silver that was found in the temple of the LORD and in the treasuries of the royal palace.
16At this time Hezekiah king of Judah stripped off the gold with

[a] 2 Hebrew *Abi*, a variant of *Abijah* [b] 4 Or *He called it* [c] 4 *Nehushtan* sounds like the Hebrew for *bronze* and *snake* and *unclean thing*. [d] 14 That is, about 11 tons (about 10 metric tons) [e] 14 That is, about 1 ton (about 1 metric ton)

(18:4) Even good and holy things can become objects of idolatry when they become the focus of our adoration. Even ministers and ministries can consume our attention, our devotion and our love. O Lord, keep my worship focused on You. Let me never confuse symbols with reality or the work with its Initiator. You alone are my Lord, my love, and my purpose for being.

which he had covered the doors and doorposts of the temple of
the LORD, and gave it to the king of Assyria.

Sennacherib Threatens Jerusalem

17The king of Assyria sent his supreme commander, his chief
officer and his field commander with a large army, from Lachish
to King Hezekiah at Jerusalem. They came up to Jerusalem and
stopped at the aqueduct of the Upper Pool, on the road to the
Washerman's Field. 18They called for the king; and Eliakim son of
Hilkiah the palace administrator, Shebna the secretary, and Joah
son of Asaph the recorder went out to them.
19The field commander said to them, "Tell Hezekiah:

" 'This is what the great king, the king of Assyria, says: On
what are you basing this confidence of yours? 20You say you
have strategy and military strength—but you speak only
empty words. On whom are you depending, that you rebel
against me? 21Look now, you are depending on Egypt, that
splintered reed of a staff, which pierces a man's hand and
wounds him if he leans on it! Such is Pharaoh king of Egypt
to all who depend on him. 22And if you say to me, "We are
depending on the LORD our God"—isn't he the one whose
high places and altars Hezekiah removed, saying to Judah
and Jerusalem, "You must worship before this altar in Jerusalem"?

23" 'Come now, make a bargain with my master, the king
of Assyria: I will give you two thousand horses—if you can
put riders on them! 24How can you repulse one officer of
the least of my master's officials, even though you are depending on Egypt for chariots and horsemen[a]? 25Further-
more, have I come to attack and destroy this place without
word from the LORD? The LORD himself told me to march
against this country and destroy it.' "

26Then Eliakim son of Hilkiah, and Shebna and Joah said to
the field commander, "Please speak to your servants in Aramaic,
since we understand it. Don't speak to us in Hebrew in the hearing of the people on the wall."
27But the commander replied, "Was it only to your master and
you that my master sent me to say these things, and not to the
men sitting on the wall—who, like you, will have to eat their own
filth and drink their own urine?"
28Then the commander stood and called out in Hebrew: "Hear
the word of the great king, the king of Assyria! 29This is what the
king says: Do not let Hezekiah deceive you. He cannot deliver you
from my hand. 30Do not let Hezekiah persuade you to trust in the
LORD when he says, 'The LORD will surely deliver us; this city will
not be given into the hand of the king of Assyria.'
31"Do not listen to Hezekiah. This is what the king of Assyria
says: Make peace with me and come out to me. Then every one of
you will eat from his own vine and fig tree and drink water from
his own cistern, 32until I come and take you to a land like your
own, a land of grain and new wine, a land of bread and vineyards,
a land of olive trees and honey. Choose life and not death!
"Do not listen to Hezekiah, for he is misleading you when he
says, 'The LORD will deliver us.' 33Has the god of any nation ever

[a] 24 Or *charioteers*

Temptation is the devil looking through the keyhole; yielding is opening the door and inviting him in.

Billy Sunday (1862-1935)

(18:16–33) O Lord, My Deliverer, help me to resist the temptation to give up, pay off or sell out to the enemy. When I surrender holy things to him, it is an open door for terror. Only You can offer me true blessing and protection—all other promises of pleasure are counterfeits, "a land like your own." When the enemy seems too strong for me, help me to hold fast to Your truth and to my faith.

You are my hiding place.
You always fill my heart
With songs of deliverance.
Whenever I am afraid
I will trust in You.

I will trust in You.
Let the weak say
I am strong in the
Strength of the Lord.
I will trust in You.

"You Are My Hiding Place"
Michael Ledner (©1981)

delivered his land from the hand of the king of Assyria? 34Where
are the gods of Hamath and Arpad? Where are the gods of Sepharvaim, Hena and Ivvah? Have they rescued Samaria from my hand?
35Who of all the gods of these countries has been able to save his
land from me? How then can the LORD deliver Jerusalem from my
hand?"

36But the people remained silent and said nothing in reply, because the king had commanded, "Do not answer him."

37Then Eliakim son of Hilkiah the palace administrator,
Shebna the secretary and Joah son of Asaph the recorder went
to Hezekiah, with their clothes torn, and told him what the field
commander had said.

Jerusalem's Deliverance Foretold

19 When King Hezekiah heard this, he tore his clothes and put
on sackcloth and went into the temple of the LORD. 2He
sent Eliakim the palace administrator, Shebna the secretary and
the leading priests, all wearing sackcloth, to the prophet Isaiah
son of Amoz. 3They told him, "This is what Hezekiah says: This
day is a day of distress and rebuke and disgrace, as when children come to the point of birth and there is no strength to deliver them. 4It may be that the LORD your God will hear all the words
of the field commander, whom his master, the king of Assyria, has
sent to ridicule the living God, and that he will rebuke him for the
words the LORD your God has heard. Therefore pray for the remnant that still survives."

5When King Hezekiah's officials came to Isaiah, 6Isaiah said to
them, "Tell your master, 'This is what the LORD says: Do not be
afraid of what you have heard—those words with which the un-
derlings of the king of Assyria have blasphemed me. 7Listen! I am
going to put such a spirit in him that when he hears a certain report, he will return to his own country, and there I will have him
cut down with the sword.' "

8When the field commander heard that the king of Assyria
had left Lachish, he withdrew and found the king fighting
against Libnah.

9Now Sennacherib received a report that Tirhakah, the Cushite[a] king ⌞of Egypt⌟, was marching out to fight against him. So he
again sent messengers to Hezekiah with this word: 10"Say to Hezekiah king of Judah: Do not let the god you depend on deceive
you when he says, 'Jerusalem will not be handed over to the king
of Assyria.' 11Surely you have heard what the kings of Assyria have
done to all the countries, destroying them completely. And will
you be delivered? 12Did the gods of the nations that were destroyed by my forefathers deliver them: the gods of Gozan, Haran,
Rezeph and the people of Eden who were in Tel Assar? 13Where
is the king of Hamath, the king of Arpad, the king of the city of
Sepharvaim, or of Hena or Ivvah?"

Hezekiah's Prayer

14Hezekiah received the letter from the messengers and read
it. Then he went up to the temple of the LORD and spread it out before the LORD. 15And Hezekiah prayed to the LORD: "O LORD, God
of Israel, enthroned between the cherubim, you alone are God
over all the kingdoms of the earth. You have made heaven and

[a] 9 That is, from the upper Nile region

Lo, the great King of kings,
With healing in His wings,
To every captive soul
A full deliv'rance brings;
And thro' the vacant cells
The song of triumph rings:
The Comforter has come!

"The Comforter Has Come"
Frank Bottome (1823–1894)

(19:5–15) I praise You, Father, for Your jealous love for us. You take personally the threats our enemy throws at us, and You come to our rescue when we humbly cry out to You for help. No other god can, or will, call forth the reserves of heaven for the deliverance of his people. You are the one, the only, the mighty and glorious Savior. (Ps 86:7–10; 135:15–18)

God has set a Savior against sin, a heaven against a hell, light against darkness, good against evil, and the breadth and length and depth and height of grace that is in himself for my good, against all the power and strength and subtlety of every enemy.

John Bunyan (1628–1688)

(19:21) After all their unfaithfulness, worshiping foreign gods and chasing after unholy alliances, You still spoke of Your wayward people as the "Virgin Daughter of Zion." Lord, Your love is certainly not blind, yet You continually look at Your people through eyes of hope, seeing all that You created us to be. I pledge myself to You alone, Father. Purify me, shape me, fill me. Complete the work You have begun that I might truly fulfill the dreams You have for me. (1Co 13:4–7; Php 1:6)

I belong to You, my Lord and King,
And I know that Your desire is for
me.
And Your love falls like sweet
refreshing rain,
Gently flowing down again so free.
Lead me to the place
Where I can hear Your words of
healing;
Where the fragrance of Your love
consumes my soul.
Where my heart is overwhelmed
With the mercy that You've given;
Where I hear Your gentle voice call
to me,
You are my beloved.
And many waters cannot quench the
burning flame;
Rivers cannot wash away Your love.
And I know that in You I am safe;
You call me by my name,
Your beloved one.

"My Beloved"
Holland Davis (©1996)

earth. 16Give ear, O LORD, and hear; open your eyes, O LORD, and
see; listen to the words Sennacherib has sent to insult the living
God.
17"It is true, O LORD, that the Assyrian kings have laid waste
these nations and their lands. 18They have thrown their gods into
the fire and destroyed them, for they were not gods but only wood
and stone, fashioned by men's hands. 19Now, O LORD our God,
deliver us from his hand, so that all kingdoms on earth may know
that you alone, O LORD, are God."

Isaiah Prophesies Sennacherib's Fall

20Then Isaiah son of Amoz sent a message to Hezekiah: "This
is what the LORD, the God of Israel, says: I have heard your prayer
concerning Sennacherib king of Assyria. 21This is the word that
the LORD has spoken against him:

" 'The Virgin Daughter of Zion
despises you and mocks you.
The Daughter of Jerusalem
tosses her head as you flee.
22Who is it you have insulted and blasphemed?
Against whom have you raised your voice
and lifted your eyes in pride?
Against the Holy One of Israel!
23By your messengers
you have heaped insults on the Lord.
And you have said,
"With my many chariots
I have ascended the heights of the mountains,
the utmost heights of Lebanon.
I have cut down its tallest cedars,
the choicest of its pines.
I have reached its remotest parts,
the finest of its forests.
24I have dug wells in foreign lands
and drunk the water there.
With the soles of my feet
I have dried up all the streams of Egypt."

25" 'Have you not heard?
Long ago I ordained it.
In days of old I planned it;
now I have brought it to pass,
that you have turned fortified cities
into piles of stone.
26Their people, drained of power,
are dismayed and put to shame.
They are like plants in the field,
like tender green shoots,
like grass sprouting on the roof,
scorched before it grows up.

27" 'But I know where you stay
and when you come and go
and how you rage against me.
28Because you rage against me
and your insolence has reached my ears,
I will put my hook in your nose
and my bit in your mouth,

and I will make you return
by the way you came.'

29"This will be the sign for you, O Hezekiah:

"This year you will eat what grows by itself,
and the second year what springs from that.
But in the third year sow and reap,
plant vineyards and eat their fruit.
30 Once more a remnant of the house of Judah
will take root below and bear fruit above.
31 For out of Jerusalem will come a remnant,
and out of Mount Zion a band of survivors.
The zeal of the LORD Almighty will accomplish this.

32"Therefore this is what the LORD says concerning the king of
Assyria:

"He will not enter this city
or shoot an arrow here.
He will not come before it with shield
or build a siege ramp against it.
33 By the way that he came he will return;
he will not enter this city,
declares the LORD.
34 I will defend this city and save it,
for my sake and for the sake of David my servant."

35That night the angel of the LORD went out and put to death a
hundred and eighty-five thousand men in the Assyrian camp.
When the people got up the next morning—there were all the
dead bodies! 36So Sennacherib king of Assyria broke camp and
withdrew. He returned to Nineveh and stayed there.
37One day, while he was worshiping in the temple of his god
Nisroch, his sons Adrammelech and Sharezer cut him down with
the sword, and they escaped to the land of Ararat. And Esarhaddon his son succeeded him as king.

Hezekiah's Illness

20 In those days Hezekiah became ill and was at the point of
death. The prophet Isaiah son of Amoz went to him and
said, "This is what the LORD says: Put your house in order, because you are going to die; you will not recover."
2Hezekiah turned his face to the wall and prayed to the LORD,
3"Remember, O LORD, how I have walked before you faithfully and
with wholehearted devotion and have done what is good in your
eyes." And Hezekiah wept bitterly.
4Before Isaiah had left the middle court, the word of the LORD
came to him: 5"Go back and tell Hezekiah, the leader of my people, 'This is what the LORD, the God of your father David, says: I
have heard your prayer and seen your tears; I will heal you. On
the third day from now you will go up to the temple of the LORD.
6I will add fifteen years to your life. And I will deliver you and this
city from the hand of the king of Assyria. I will defend this city for
my sake and for the sake of my servant David.' "
7Then Isaiah said, "Prepare a poultice of figs." They did so and
applied it to the boil, and he recovered.
8Hezekiah had asked Isaiah, "What will be the sign that the

(20:1–6) Lord, it seems as though You sometimes make a pronouncement just to provoke prayer. In spite of Your words through Isaiah, You answered the cries of Hezekiah. In Your great mercy You did for him what You might not have done had he not asked. How often do I give in to the seemingly inevitable when You are just waiting to step in on my behalf if I will only ask? Thank You for really listening to my prayers and for allowing Your heart to be moved by them. (Jas 4:2; 5:16)

Prayer is not overcoming God's reluctance; it is laying hold of his highest willingness.
Archbishop Richard Chenevix Trench (1807–1886)

LORD will heal me and that I will go up to the temple of the LORD
on the third day from now?"
9Isaiah answered, "This is the LORD's sign to you that the LORD
will do what he has promised: Shall the shadow go forward ten
steps, or shall it go back ten steps?"
10"It is a simple matter for the shadow to go forward ten
steps," said Hezekiah. "Rather, have it go back ten steps."
11Then the prophet Isaiah called upon the LORD, and the LORD
made the shadow go back the ten steps it had gone down on the
stairway of Ahaz.

Envoys From Babylon

12At that time Merodach-Baladan son of Baladan king of Babylon sent Hezekiah letters and a gift, because he had heard of
Hezekiah's illness. 13Hezekiah received the messengers and
showed them all that was in his storehouses—the silver, the gold,
the spices and the fine oil—his armory and everything found
among his treasures. There was nothing in his palace or in all his
kingdom that Hezekiah did not show them.
14Then Isaiah the prophet went to King Hezekiah and asked,
"What did those men say, and where did they come from?"
"From a distant land," Hezekiah replied. "They came from
Babylon."
15The prophet asked, "What did they see in your palace?"
"They saw everything in my palace," Hezekiah said. "There is
nothing among my treasures that I did not show them."
16Then Isaiah said to Hezekiah, "Hear the word of the LORD:
17The time will surely come when everything in your palace, and
all that your fathers have stored up until this day, will be carried
off to Babylon. Nothing will be left, says the LORD. 18And some of
your descendants, your own flesh and blood, that will be born to
you, will be taken away, and they will become eunuchs in the
palace of the king of Babylon."
19"The word of the LORD you have spoken is good," Hezekiah
replied. For he thought, "Will there not be peace and security in
my lifetime?"
20As for the other events of Hezekiah's reign, all his achievements and how he made the pool and the tunnel by which he
brought water into the city, are they not written in the book of the
annals of the kings of Judah? 21Hezekiah rested with his fathers.
And Manasseh his son succeeded him as king.

Manasseh King of Judah

21 Manasseh was twelve years old when he became king, and
he reigned in Jerusalem fifty-five years. His mother's name
was Hephzibah. 2He did evil in the eyes of the LORD, following the
detestable practices of the nations the LORD had driven out before
the Israelites. 3He rebuilt the high places his father Hezekiah had
destroyed; he also erected altars to Baal and made an Asherah
pole, as Ahab king of Israel had done. He bowed down to all the
starry hosts and worshiped them. 4He built altars in the temple of
the LORD, of which the LORD had said, "In Jerusalem I will put my
Name." 5In both courts of the temple of the LORD, he built altars
to all the starry hosts. 6He sacrificed his own son in[a] the fire,
practiced sorcery and divination, and consulted mediums and

Prayer is weakness leaning on omnipotence.

W. S. Bowden

(20:9–11) Hezekiah, Gideon and Elijah all put You to the test, making their requests as difficult as they thought possible so that no one could doubt it was You who answered them. Yet even these were "simple matters" to You. I praise You, gracious Lord, that the more difficult my circumstances become, the more Your glory is evident as You do what no one else can do; and I can say what Jesus said: "With man this is impossible, but with God all things are possible." (Jdg 6:36–40; 1Ki 18:32–38; Mt 19:26)

[a] 6 Or *He made his own son pass through*

spiritists. He did much evil in the eyes of the LORD, provoking him to anger.

7He took the carved Asherah pole he had made and put it in the temple, of which the LORD had said to David and to his son Solomon, "In this temple and in Jerusalem, which I have chosen out of all the tribes of Israel, I will put my Name forever. 8I will not again make the feet of the Israelites wander from the land I gave their forefathers, if only they will be careful to do everything I commanded them and will keep the whole Law that my servant Moses gave them." 9But the people did not listen. Manasseh led them astray, so that they did more evil than the nations the LORD had destroyed before the Israelites.

10The LORD said through his servants the prophets: 11"Manasseh king of Judah has committed these detestable sins. He has done more evil than the Amorites who preceded him and has led Judah into sin with his idols. 12Therefore this is what the LORD, the God of Israel, says: I am going to bring such disaster on Jerusalem and Judah that the ears of everyone who hears of it will tingle. 13I will stretch out over Jerusalem the measuring line used against Samaria and the plumb line used against the house of Ahab. I will wipe out Jerusalem as one wipes a dish, wiping it and turning it upside down. 14I will forsake the remnant of my inheritance and hand them over to their enemies. They will be looted and plundered by all their foes, 15because they have done evil in my eyes and have provoked me to anger from the day their forefathers came out of Egypt until this day."

16Moreover, Manasseh also shed so much innocent blood that he filled Jerusalem from end to end—besides the sin that he had caused Judah to commit, so that they did evil in the eyes of the LORD.

17As for the other events of Manasseh's reign, and all he did, including the sin he committed, are they not written in the book of the annals of the kings of Judah? 18Manasseh rested with his fathers and was buried in his palace garden, the garden of Uzza. And Amon his son succeeded him as king.

Amon King of Judah

19Amon was twenty-two years old when he became king, and he reigned in Jerusalem two years. His mother's name was Meshullemeth daughter of Haruz; she was from Jotbah. 20He did evil in the eyes of the LORD, as his father Manasseh had done. 21He walked in all the ways of his father; he worshiped the idols his father had worshiped, and bowed down to them. 22He forsook the LORD, the God of his fathers, and did not walk in the way of the LORD.

23Amon's officials conspired against him and assassinated the king in his palace. 24Then the people of the land killed all who had plotted against King Amon, and they made Josiah his son king in his place.

25As for the other events of Amon's reign, and what he did, are they not written in the book of the annals of the kings of Judah? 26He was buried in his grave in the garden of Uzza. And Josiah his son succeeded him as king.

The Book of the Law Found

22 Josiah was eight years old when he became king, and he reigned in Jerusalem thirty-one years. His mother's name was Jedidah daughter of Adaiah; she was from Bozkath. 2He

(21:7–22) Regardless of our upbringing, You give each of us the opportunity to choose the path we will follow—the path of life unto life, or of death unto death. And You hold us accountable for our decisions. For those who live according to Your ways, You promise blessing and fulfillment. In Your promises, Lord, we see the desires of Your heart toward Your people. You long to give us a place, a home, security in relationship with You. You, the Creator of the universe, desire to identify us with Your name as a father gives his name to his children. Help us to walk obediently and humbly before You as loving children who make their Father happy and proud. (Eze 18:1–20; Jn 14:23; Ac 3:19; Ro 2:6)

did what was right in the eyes of the LORD and walked in all the
ways of his father David, not turning aside to the right or to the
left.
3In the eighteenth year of his reign, King Josiah sent the secretary, Shaphan son of Azaliah, the son of Meshullam, to the
temple of the LORD. He said: 4"Go up to Hilkiah the high priest
and have him get ready the money that has been brought into
the temple of the LORD, which the doorkeepers have collected
from the people. 5Have them entrust it to the men appointed to
supervise the work on the temple. And have these men pay the
workers who repair the temple of the LORD— 6the carpenters,
the builders and the masons. Also have them purchase timber
and dressed stone to repair the temple. 7But they need not account for the money entrusted to them, because they are acting
faithfully."
8Hilkiah the high priest said to Shaphan the secretary, "I
have found the Book of the Law in the temple of the LORD." He
gave it to Shaphan, who read it. 9Then Shaphan the secretary
went to the king and reported to him: "Your officials have paid
out the money that was in the temple of the LORD and have entrusted it to the workers and supervisors at the temple."
10Then Shaphan the secretary informed the king, "Hilkiah the
priest has given me a book." And Shaphan read from it in the
presence of the king.
11When the king heard the words of the Book of the Law, he
tore his robes. 12He gave these orders to Hilkiah the priest,
Ahikam son of Shaphan, Acbor son of Micaiah, Shaphan the
secretary and Asaiah the king's attendant: 13"Go and inquire of
the LORD for me and for the people and for all Judah about what
is written in this book that has been found. Great is the LORD's
anger that burns against us because our fathers have not
obeyed the words of this book; they have not acted in accordance with all that is written there concerning us."
14Hilkiah the priest, Ahikam, Acbor, Shaphan and Asaiah
went to speak to the prophetess Huldah, who was the wife of
Shallum son of Tikvah, the son of Harhas, keeper of the
wardrobe. She lived in Jerusalem, in the Second District.
15She said to them, "This is what the LORD, the God of Israel, says: Tell the man who sent you to me, 16'This is what the
LORD says: I am going to bring disaster on this place and its
people, according to everything written in the book the king of
Judah has read. 17Because they have forsaken me and burned
incense to other gods and provoked me to anger by all the
idols their hands have made,[a] my anger will burn against this
place and will not be quenched.' 18Tell the king of Judah, who
sent you to inquire of the LORD, 'This is what the LORD, the God
of Israel, says concerning the words you heard: 19Because your
heart was responsive and you humbled yourself before the LORD
when you heard what I have spoken against this place and its
people, that they would become accursed and laid waste, and
because you tore your robes and wept in my presence, I have
heard you, declares the LORD. 20Therefore I will gather you to
your fathers, and you will be buried in peace. Your eyes will
not see all the disaster I am going to bring on this place.' "
So they took her answer back to the king.

[a] 17 Or *by everything they have done*

(22:8) Like a defiant flower breaking its way through a crack in the concrete, so Your Word can break through the rubble of dead religion and the ruin of abandoned faith. As I give Your Word its proper place in my life, restore and renew this temple that Your glory might be displayed in all its color and beauty. (1Co 3:16)

Enlighten us, O God, by your Spirit, in the understanding of your Word, and grant us the grace to receive it in true fear and humility, that we may learn to put our trust in you, to fear and honor you, by glorifying your Holy Name in all our life, and to yield you the love and obedience which faithful servants owe to their master and children to their fathers, seeing it has led you to call us to the number of your servants and children.

John Calvin (1509–1564)

(22:11,18–19) Your Word shines a holy light on our lives, revealing behaviors and loyalties that are displeasing to You and destructive to us. You are searching for a heart that is responsive and humble, that You might pour out Your grace, not Your judgment. Thank You for the merciful gift of Your Word, Lord, that opens our eyes to the truth and leads us to life-giving repentance. (Ps 119:11,105; Jas 1:22–25)

Josiah Renews the Covenant

23 Then the king called together all the elders of Judah and
Jerusalem. 2He went up to the temple of the LORD with
the men of Judah, the people of Jerusalem, the priests and the
prophets—all the people from the least to the greatest. He
read in their hearing all the words of the Book of the Covenant,
which had been found in the temple of the LORD. 3The king
stood by the pillar and renewed the covenant in the presence of
the LORD—to follow the LORD and keep his commands, regulations and decrees with all his heart and all his soul, thus con-
firming the words of the covenant written in this book. Then all
the people pledged themselves to the covenant.
4The king ordered Hilkiah the high priest, the priests next in
rank and the doorkeepers to remove from the temple of the
LORD all the articles made for Baal and Asherah and all the starry hosts. He burned them outside Jerusalem in the fields of the
Kidron Valley and took the ashes to Bethel. 5He did away with
the pagan priests appointed by the kings of Judah to burn incense on the high places of the towns of Judah and on those
around Jerusalem—those who burned incense to Baal, to the
sun and moon, to the constellations and to all the starry hosts.
6He took the Asherah pole from the temple of the LORD to the
Kidron Valley outside Jerusalem and burned it there. He
ground it to powder and scattered the dust over the graves of
the common people. 7He also tore down the quarters of the
male shrine prostitutes, which were in the temple of the LORD
and where women did weaving for Asherah.
8Josiah brought all the priests from the towns of Judah and
desecrated the high places, from Geba to Beersheba, where the
priests had burned incense. He broke down the shrines[a] at the
gates—at the entrance to the Gate of Joshua, the city governor,
which is on the left of the city gate. 9Although the priests of the
high places did not serve at the altar of the LORD in Jerusalem,
they ate unleavened bread with their fellow priests.
10He desecrated Topheth, which was in the Valley of Ben
Hinnom, so no one could use it to sacrifice his son or daughter in[b] the fire to Molech. 11He removed from the entrance to
the temple of the LORD the horses that the kings of Judah had
dedicated to the sun. They were in the court near the room of
an official named Nathan-Melech. Josiah then burned the chariots dedicated to the sun.
12He pulled down the altars the kings of Judah had erected
on the roof near the upper room of Ahaz, and the altars Manasseh had built in the two courts of the temple of the LORD. He
removed them from there, smashed them to pieces and threw
the rubble into the Kidron Valley. 13The king also desecrated
the high places that were east of Jerusalem on the south of the
Hill of Corruption—the ones Solomon king of Israel had built
for Ashtoreth the vile goddess of the Sidonians, for Chemosh
the vile god of Moab, and for Molech[c] the detestable god of the
people of Ammon. 14Josiah smashed the sacred stones and cut
down the Asherah poles and covered the sites with human
bones.

[a] 8 Or *high places* [b] 10 Or *to make his son or daughter pass through* [c] 13 Hebrew *Milcom*

(23:4–14) Just as Josiah destroyed all vestiges of idolatry from the temple, so You desire a complete abandonment of the dark deeds of my past. Even their residue so easily becomes a stumbling block for me. Father, I turn whole-heartedly from those things that displease and dishonor You, so that no trappings of sin would remain to remind either of us of my past. (Eph 4:22–24)

I will never be the same again,
I can never return, I've closed the
door.
I will walk the path, I'll run the race,
And I will never be the same again.

Fall like fire, soak like rain;
Flow like mighty waters again and
again.
Sweep away the darkness,
Burn away the chaff,
And let a flame burn to glorify Your
Name.

"I Will Never Be (The Same Again)"
Geoff Bullock (©1995)

(23:15–18) I worship You, Father, for Your faithfulness to keep Your word. You had spoken of this destruction some 350 years earlier, in specific detail; and in Your perfect time, and by Your prescribed methods, You brought this to pass. If You are this faithful to fulfill Your warnings of judgment against those who reject You, how much more faithful are You to fulfill Your promises to those who love You? I praise You, Lord, with the words of the Psalmist: "Your promises have been thoroughly tested, and Your servant loves them." (Jos 21:45; 1Ki 13:1–5; Ps 119:140; 2Co 7:1; 2Pe 1:4)

Faith, mighty faith, the promise sees,
And looks to that alone;
Laughs at impossibilities,
And cries it shall be done.
Charles Wesley (1707–1788)

15 Even the altar at Bethel, the high place made by Jeroboam
son of Nebat, who had caused Israel to sin—even that altar and
high place he demolished. He burned the high place and ground
it to powder, and burned the Asherah pole also. 16 Then Josiah
looked around, and when he saw the tombs that were there on
the hillside, he had the bones removed from them and burned on
the altar to defile it, in accordance with the word of the LORD proclaimed by the man of God who foretold these things.
17 The king asked, "What is that tombstone I see?"
The men of the city said, "It marks the tomb of the man of God
who came from Judah and pronounced against the altar of Bethel the very things you have done to it."
18 "Leave it alone," he said. "Don't let anyone disturb his
bones." So they spared his bones and those of the prophet who
had come from Samaria.
19 Just as he had done at Bethel, Josiah removed and defiled all
the shrines at the high places that the kings of Israel had built in
the towns of Samaria that had provoked the LORD to anger. 20 Josiah slaughtered all the priests of those high places on the altars
and burned human bones on them. Then he went back to Jerusalem.
21 The king gave this order to all the people: "Celebrate the
Passover to the LORD your God, as it is written in this Book of the
Covenant." 22 Not since the days of the judges who led Israel, nor
throughout the days of the kings of Israel and the kings of Judah,
had any such Passover been observed. 23 But in the eighteenth
year of King Josiah, this Passover was celebrated to the LORD in Jerusalem.
24 Furthermore, Josiah got rid of the mediums and spiritists,
the household gods, the idols and all the other detestable things
seen in Judah and Jerusalem. This he did to fulfill the requirements of the law written in the book that Hilkiah the priest had
discovered in the temple of the LORD. 25 Neither before nor after
Josiah was there a king like him who turned to the LORD as he
did—with all his heart and with all his soul and with all his
strength, in accordance with all the Law of Moses.
26 Nevertheless, the LORD did not turn away from the heat of his
fierce anger, which burned against Judah because of all that Manasseh had done to provoke him to anger. 27 So the LORD said, "I
will remove Judah also from my presence as I removed Israel,
and I will reject Jerusalem, the city I chose, and this temple,
about which I said, 'There shall my Name be.'[a]"
28 As for the other events of Josiah's reign, and all he did, are
they not written in the book of the annals of the kings of Judah?
29 While Josiah was king, Pharaoh Neco king of Egypt went up
to the Euphrates River to help the king of Assyria. King Josiah
marched out to meet him in battle, but Neco faced him and killed
him at Megiddo. 30 Josiah's servants brought his body in a chariot from Megiddo to Jerusalem and buried him in his own tomb.
And the people of the land took Jehoahaz son of Josiah and
anointed him and made him king in place of his father.

Jehoahaz King of Judah

31 Jehoahaz was twenty-three years old when he became king,
and he reigned in Jerusalem three months. His mother's name

[a] 27 1 Kings 8:29

was Hamutal daughter of Jeremiah; she was from Libnah. [32]He did evil in the eyes of the LORD, just as his fathers had done. [33]Pharaoh Neco put him in chains at Riblah in the land of Hamath[a] so that he might not reign in Jerusalem, and he imposed on Judah a levy of a hundred talents[b] of silver and a talent[c] of gold. [34]Pharaoh Neco made Eliakim son of Josiah king in place of his father Josiah and changed Eliakim's name to Jehoiakim. But he took Jehoahaz and carried him off to Egypt, and there he died. [35]Jehoiakim paid Pharaoh Neco the silver and gold he demanded. In order to do so, he taxed the land and exacted the silver and gold from the people of the land according to their assessments.

Jehoiakim King of Judah

[36]Jehoiakim was twenty-five years old when he became king, and he reigned in Jerusalem eleven years. His mother's name was Zebidah daughter of Pedaiah; she was from Rumah. [37]And he did evil in the eyes of the LORD, just as his fathers had done.

24 During Jehoiakim's reign, Nebuchadnezzar king of Babylon invaded the land, and Jehoiakim became his vassal for three years. But then he changed his mind and rebelled against Nebuchadnezzar. [2]The LORD sent Babylonian,[d] Aramean, Moabite and Ammonite raiders against him. He sent them to destroy Judah, in accordance with the word of the LORD proclaimed by his servants the prophets. [3]Surely these things happened to Judah according to the LORD's command, in order to remove them from his presence because of the sins of Manasseh and all he had done, [4]including the shedding of innocent blood. For he had filled Jerusalem with innocent blood, and the LORD was not willing to forgive.

[5]As for the other events of Jehoiakim's reign, and all he did, are they not written in the book of the annals of the kings of Judah? [6]Jehoiakim rested with his fathers. And Jehoiachin his son succeeded him as king.

[7]The king of Egypt did not march out from his own country again, because the king of Babylon had taken all his territory, from the Wadi of Egypt to the Euphrates River.

Jehoiachin King of Judah

[8]Jehoiachin was eighteen years old when he became king, and he reigned in Jerusalem three months. His mother's name was Nehushta daughter of Elnathan; she was from Jerusalem. [9]He did evil in the eyes of the LORD, just as his father had done.

[10]At that time the officers of Nebuchadnezzar king of Babylon advanced on Jerusalem and laid siege to it, [11]and Nebuchadnezzar himself came up to the city while his officers were besieging it. [12]Jehoiachin king of Judah, his mother, his attendants, his nobles and his officials all surrendered to him.

In the eighth year of the reign of the king of Babylon, he took Jehoiachin prisoner. [13]As the LORD had declared, Nebuchadnezzar removed all the treasures from the temple of the LORD and from the royal palace, and took away all the gold articles that Solomon king of Israel had made for the temple of the LORD. [14]He carried into exile all Jerusalem: all the officers and fighting men,

[a] *33* Hebrew; Septuagint (see also 2 Chron. 36:3) *Neco at Riblah in Hamath removed him* [b] *33* That is, about 3 3/4 tons (about 3.4 metric tons) [c] *33* That is, about 75 pounds (about 34 kilograms) [d] *2* Or *Chaldean*

(24:1–4) Lord, how often do we leave ourselves vulnerable to the attacks of the enemy because of our disobedience and stubbornness? How often do we show contempt for the riches of Your kindness, tolerance and patience, not realizing that Your kindness leads us toward repentance? May it never be necessary, as it once was in the Corinthian church, for anyone of us to be handed "over to Satan, so that the sinful nature may be destroyed and his spirit saved on the day of the Lord." Lord, spare us from the destructive power of sin. Stir up within us the desire for holiness. (2Ki 21:1–9; Ro 2:4; 1Co 5:1–5)

Yield not to temptation,
For yielding is sin.
Each vict'ry will help you
Some other to win.
Fight manfully onward;
Dark passions subdue.
Look ever to Jesus;
He'll carry you thro'.

Ask the Savior to help you,
Comfort, strengthen, and keep you.
He is willing to aid you;
He will carry you through.

"Yield Not to Temptation"
Horatio R. Palmer (1868)

and all the craftsmen and artisans—a total of ten thousand. Only
the poorest people of the land were left.
15 Nebuchadnezzar took Jehoiachin captive to Babylon. He also
took from Jerusalem to Babylon the king's mother, his wives, his
officials and the leading men of the land. 16 The king of Babylon
also deported to Babylon the entire force of seven thousand fighting men, strong and fit for war, and a thousand craftsmen and artisans. 17 He made Mattaniah, Jehoiachin's uncle, king in his place
and changed his name to Zedekiah.

Zedekiah King of Judah

18 Zedekiah was twenty-one years old when he became king,
and he reigned in Jerusalem eleven years. His mother's name was
Hamutal daughter of Jeremiah; she was from Libnah. 19 He did
evil in the eyes of the LORD, just as Jehoiakim had done. 20 It was
because of the LORD's anger that all this happened to Jerusalem
and Judah, and in the end he thrust them from his presence.

The Fall of Jerusalem

Now Zedekiah rebelled against the king of Babylon.
25 So in the ninth year of Zedekiah's reign, on the tenth day
of the tenth month, Nebuchadnezzar king of Babylon
marched against Jerusalem with his whole army. He encamped
outside the city and built siege works all around it. 2 The city was
kept under siege until the eleventh year of King Zedekiah. 3 By the
ninth day of the ⌊fourth⌋[a] month the famine in the city had become so severe that there was no food for the people to eat.
4 Then the city wall was broken through, and the whole army fled
at night through the gate between the two walls near the king's
garden, though the Babylonians[b] were surrounding the city. They
fled toward the Arabah,[c] 5 but the Babylonian[d] army pursued the
king and overtook him in the plains of Jericho. All his soldiers
were separated from him and scattered, 6 and he was captured.
He was taken to the king of Babylon at Riblah, where sentence
was pronounced on him. 7 They killed the sons of Zedekiah before his eyes. Then they put out his eyes, bound him with bronze
shackles and took him to Babylon.
8 On the seventh day of the fifth month, in the nineteenth year of
Nebuchadnezzar king of Babylon, Nebuzaradan commander of
the imperial guard, an official of the king of Babylon, came to Jerusalem. 9 He set fire to the temple of the LORD, the royal palace
and all the houses of Jerusalem. Every important building he
burned down. 10 The whole Babylonian army, under the commander of the imperial guard, broke down the walls around Jerusalem. 11 Nebuzaradan the commander of the guard carried
into exile the people who remained in the city, along with the rest
of the populace and those who had gone over to the king of Babylon. 12 But the commander left behind some of the poorest people of the land to work the vineyards and fields.
13 The Babylonians broke up the bronze pillars, the movable
stands and the bronze Sea that were at the temple of the LORD and
they carried the bronze to Babylon. 14 They also took away the
pots, shovels, wick trimmers, dishes and all the bronze articles
used in the temple service. 15 The commander of the imperial

[a] 3 See Jer. 52:6. [b] 4 Or *Chaldeans*; also in verses 13, 25 and 26 [c] 4 Or *the Jordan Valley* [d] 5 Or *Chaldean*; also in verses 10 and 24

(24:12–20) Lord, You are righteous and just in all Your ways. Your people robbed You of their loyalty; You denied them their wealth, their protection, their freedom and their identity. Ultimately, Father, You denied them Your presence. How it must have broken Your heart to see them impoverished by sin. But even when they were without Your presence, they were not without Your promise. For You promised through the prophet Ezekiel that You would bring Your people back from their captivity and restore their relationship with You. I praise You, Lord, that Your faithful covenant love endures forever and that You will not abandon the work of Your hands. (Ps 138:8; Eze 36:17–38)

guard took away the censers and sprinkling bowls—all that were made of pure gold or silver.

16The bronze from the two pillars, the Sea and the movable stands, which Solomon had made for the temple of the LORD, was more than could be weighed. 17Each pillar was twenty-seven feet[a] high. The bronze capital on top of one pillar was four and a half feet[b] high and was decorated with a network and pomegranates of bronze all around. The other pillar, with its network, was similar.

18The commander of the guard took as prisoners Seraiah the chief priest, Zephaniah the priest next in rank and the three doorkeepers. 19Of those still in the city, he took the officer in charge of the fighting men and five royal advisers. He also took the secretary who was chief officer in charge of conscripting the people of the land and sixty of his men who were found in the city. 20Nebuzaradan the commander took them all and brought them to the king of Babylon at Riblah. 21There at Riblah, in the land of Hamath, the king had them executed.

So Judah went into captivity, away from her land.

22Nebuchadnezzar king of Babylon appointed Gedaliah son of Ahikam, the son of Shaphan, to be over the people he had left behind in Judah. 23When all the army officers and their men heard that the king of Babylon had appointed Gedaliah as governor, they came to Gedaliah at Mizpah—Ishmael son of Nethaniah, Johanan son of Kareah, Seraiah son of Tanhumeth the Netophathite, Jaazaniah the son of the Maacathite, and their men. 24Gedaliah took an oath to reassure them and their men. "Do not be afraid of the Babylonian officials," he said. "Settle down in the land and serve the king of Babylon, and it will go well with you."

25In the seventh month, however, Ishmael son of Nethaniah, the son of Elishama, who was of royal blood, came with ten men and assassinated Gedaliah and also the men of Judah and the Babylonians who were with him at Mizpah. 26At this, all the people from the least to the greatest, together with the army officers, fled to Egypt for fear of the Babylonians.

Jehoiachin Released

27In the thirty-seventh year of the exile of Jehoiachin king of Judah, in the year Evil-Merodach[c] became king of Babylon, he released Jehoiachin from prison on the twenty-seventh day of the twelfth month. 28He spoke kindly to him and gave him a seat of honor higher than those of the other kings who were with him in Babylon. 29So Jehoiachin put aside his prison clothes and for the rest of his life ate regularly at the king's table. 30Day by day the king gave Jehoiachin a regular allowance as long as he lived.

[a] 17 Hebrew *eighteen cubits* (about 8.1 meters) [b] 17 Hebrew *three cubits* (about 1.3 meters) [c] 27 Also called *Amel-Marduk*

(25:27–29) Although Your judgment was fiercely enacted against those who disobeyed You, the king of Judah was spared, and Your promise to David was kept. Even exile could not destroy Your people, the line of David, and the promise of a Messiah who would save the world from sin. You are faithful, Lord, both in great things and in small, accomplishing Your will in a sinful world, bringing forth Your plan of redemption, and in wrath, remembering mercy. (Hab 3:2)

God's investment in us is so great he could not possibly abandon us.

Erwin W. Lutzer (1941-)

1 & 2 Chronicles

The First & Second Books of the

CHRONICLES

First and Second Chronicles recast the history of Israel from a unique perspective. Using Biblical books (including Samuel and Kings) and other ancient sources, the "Chronicler" writes to encourage the Jews who have returned from exile in Babylon. He recounts sacred history to explain why they have become a subject people and how they can live righteously in hope of full restoration in the future.

After a lengthy genealogical presentation (1Ch 1—9) Chronicles depicts the royal activities of David and Solomon. Showing only modest interest in military accomplishments, Chronicles focuses on the centralization and organization of temple worship in Jerusalem (1Ch 13—29; 2Ch 3—7). These efforts culminate in the dedication of the temple, which is filled twice with God's glory (2Ch 5:13–14; 7:1–3). In his dedication prayer Solomon acknowledges that no earthly structure can ever contain God (2Ch 6:18). Nevertheless, the temple is God's house. It serves as a tangible reminder of God's presence in Judah and as a place where people can seek right relationship with God through sacrifices.

The centrality of the temple in Chronicles foreshadows the centrality of Jesus Christ. As the temple embodied God's presence in Israel, so Jesus is the incarnation of the Word of God. As the glory of God filled Solomon's temple, so Jesus uniquely reveals the glory of the Lord (Jn 1:14). As the priests entered the temple on behalf of the people, so Jesus is our great high priest who has entered into the very presence of God for our sake (Heb 4:14; 9:24–25). As temple sacrifices symbolized reconciliation between God and Israel, the once-for-all sacrifice of Jesus fully reconciles us to God (Heb 9:26). In the days of Solomon's temple, the worship of God's people centered in that building. In the days of Jesus Christ—in which we live today—the worship of God's people finds its true center in Christ alone.

The Lord is forever at work, guiding His chosen people to worship Him—whether in the Jerusalem temple, or in the "temple" of Christian community, or in the "temples" of our own lives.

From the high point of the temple dedication, Chronicles follows the downward spiral of Israel, though focusing almost exclusively upon the southern kingdom of Judah. Several righteous Judean kings feature prominently in the story, but no human or divine effort can stop the people's downfall. As Chronicles summarizes: "The LORD . . . sent word to them through his messengers again and again, because he had pity on his people and on his dwelling place. But they mocked God's messengers, despised his words and scoffed at his prophets until the wrath of the LORD was aroused against his people and there was no remedy" (2Ch 36:15–16).

But Chronicles concludes with a distinct note of hope. By the command of Cyrus, king of Persia, the Israelites are free to return from Babylon and to rebuild the temple in Jerusalem (2Ch 36:22–23). Beyond God's just punishment of His rebellious children stands His restoring mercy. The Lord is forever at work, guiding His chosen people to worship Him—whether in the Jerusalem temple, or in the "temple" of Christian community (1Co 3:16–17), or in the "temples" of our own lives (1Co 6:19–20).

Historical Records From Adam to Abraham

To Noah's Sons

1 Adam, Seth, Enosh, 2Kenan, Mahalalel, Jared, 3Enoch,
Methuselah, Lamech, Noah.

4The sons of Noah:[a]
Shem, Ham and Japheth.

The Japhethites

5The sons[b] of Japheth:
Gomer, Magog, Madai, Javan, Tubal, Meshech and Tiras.
6The sons of Gomer:
Ashkenaz, Riphath[c] and Togarmah.
7The sons of Javan:
Elishah, Tarshish, the Kittim and the Rodanim.

The Hamites

8The sons of Ham:
Cush, Mizraim,[d] Put and Canaan.
9The sons of Cush:
Seba, Havilah, Sabta, Raamah and Sabteca.
The sons of Raamah:
Sheba and Dedan.
10Cush was the father[e] of
Nimrod, who grew to be a mighty warrior on earth.
11Mizraim was the father of
the Ludites, Anamites, Lehabites, Naphtuhites, 12Pathru-
sites, Casluhites (from whom the Philistines came) and Caphtorites.
13Canaan was the father of
Sidon his firstborn,[f] and of the Hittites, 14Jebusites, Amorites, Girgashites, 15Hivites, Arkites, Sinites, 16Arvadites,
Zemarites and Hamathites.

The Semites

17The sons of Shem:
Elam, Asshur, Arphaxad, Lud and Aram.
The sons of Aram[g]:
Uz, Hul, Gether and Meshech.
18Arphaxad was the father of Shelah,
and Shelah the father of Eber.
19Two sons were born to Eber:
One was named Peleg,[h] because in his time the earth was divided; his brother was named Joktan.
20Joktan was the father of
Almodad, Sheleph, Hazarmaveth, Jerah, 21Hadoram, Uzal,
Diklah, 22Obal,[i] Abimael, Sheba, 23Ophir, Havilah and
Jobab. All these were sons of Joktan.

[a] *4* Septuagint; Hebrew does not have *The sons of Noah:* [b] *5 Sons* may mean *descendants* or *successors* or *nations*; also in verses 6–10, 17 and 20. [c] *6* Many Hebrew manuscripts and Vulgate (see also Septuagint and Gen. 10:3); most Hebrew manuscripts *Diphath* [d] *8* That is, Egypt; also in verse 11 [e] *10 Father* may mean *ancestor* or *predecessor* or *founder*; also in verses 11, 13, 18 and 20. [f] *13* Or *of the Sidonians, the foremost* [g] *17* One Hebrew manuscript and some Septuagint manuscripts (see also Gen. 10:23); most Hebrew manuscripts do not have this line. [h] *19 Peleg* means *division.* [i] *22* Some Hebrew manuscripts and Syriac (see also Gen. 10:28); most Hebrew manuscripts *Ebal*

(1:1) God of our fathers, You said, "Let us make man in our image." You made us that we might reflect Your glory. You know us all, even our most remote ancestors. You remember their names, a thousand generations past. And You know every one of us by name, even in this generation. "For a thousand years in Your sight are like a day that has just gone by, or like a watch in the night." In all the night watches, remember me, O Lord. (Ge 1:26; Ps 90:4)

O God, our help in ages past,
Our hope for years to come,
Our shelter from the stormy blast,
And our eternal home!

"O God, Our Help in Ages Past"
Isaac Watts (1719)

(1:8) Lord God, our Creator, we marvel at the variety of peoples whom You have created to worship You. We look forward to the day when we will all worship You with one voice. From the rising to the setting of the sun, in every place incense and pure offerings will be brought to Your name, because Your name will be great among the nations. (Mal 1:11)

We are all by nature the seed of Adam. Let us see to it that by faith, we become the seed of Abraham.

Matthew Henry (1662-1714)

(1:34) Father, we thank You that we are all children of Abraham, Isaac and Israel. Through Christ we have been grafted into this sacred family tree. Through Abraham, we are children of faith. Through Isaac, we are children of promise. Through Israel, we are children of destiny. (Ro 4:11–12; 11:17–18; Gal 4:21–31)

24 Shem, Arphaxad,[a] Shelah,
25 Eber, Peleg, Reu,
26 Serug, Nahor, Terah
27 and Abram (that is, Abraham).

The Family of Abraham

28 The sons of Abraham:
Isaac and Ishmael.

Descendants of Hagar

29 These were their descendants:
Nebaioth the firstborn of Ishmael, Kedar, Adbeel, Mibsam,
30 Mishma, Dumah, Massa, Hadad, Tema, 31 Jetur, Naphish and Kedemah. These were the sons of Ishmael.

Descendants of Keturah

32 The sons born to Keturah, Abraham's concubine:
Zimran, Jokshan, Medan, Midian, Ishbak and Shuah.
The sons of Jokshan:
Sheba and Dedan.
33 The sons of Midian:
Ephah, Epher, Hanoch, Abida and Eldaah.
All these were descendants of Keturah.

Descendants of Sarah

34 Abraham was the father of Isaac.
The sons of Isaac:
Esau and Israel.

Esau's Sons

35 The sons of Esau:
Eliphaz, Reuel, Jeush, Jalam and Korah.
36 The sons of Eliphaz:
Teman, Omar, Zepho,[b] Gatam and Kenaz;
by Timna: Amalek.[c]
37 The sons of Reuel:
Nahath, Zerah, Shammah and Mizzah.

The People of Seir in Edom

38 The sons of Seir:
Lotan, Shobal, Zibeon, Anah, Dishon, Ezer and Dishan.
39 The sons of Lotan:
Hori and Homam. Timna was Lotan's sister.
40 The sons of Shobal:
Alvan,[d] Manahath, Ebal, Shepho and Onam.
The sons of Zibeon:
Aiah and Anah.
41 The son of Anah:
Dishon.
The sons of Dishon:
Hemdan,[e] Eshban, Ithran and Keran.

[a] *24* Hebrew; some Septuagint manuscripts *Arphaxad, Cainan* (see also note at Gen. 11:10) [b] *36* Many Hebrew manuscripts, some Septuagint manuscripts and Syriac (see also Gen. 36:11); most Hebrew manuscripts *Zephi* [c] *36* Some Septuagint manuscripts (see also Gen. 36:12); Hebrew *Gatam, Kenaz, Timna and Amalek* [d] *40* Many Hebrew manuscripts and some Septuagint manuscripts (see also Gen. 36:23); most Hebrew manuscripts *Alian* [e] *41* Many Hebrew manuscripts and some Septuagint manuscripts (see also Gen. 36:26); most Hebrew manuscripts *Hamran*

42 The sons of Ezer:
Bilhan, Zaavan and Akan.[a]
The sons of Dishan[b]:
Uz and Aran.

The Rulers of Edom

43 These were the kings who reigned in Edom before any Israelite king reigned[c]:
Bela son of Beor, whose city was named Dinhabah.
44 When Bela died, Jobab son of Zerah from Bozrah succeeded him as king.
45 When Jobab died, Husham from the land of the Temanites succeeded him as king.
46 When Husham died, Hadad son of Bedad, who defeated Midian in the country of Moab, succeeded him as king. His city was named Avith.
47 When Hadad died, Samlah from Masrekah succeeded him as king.
48 When Samlah died, Shaul from Rehoboth on the river[d] succeeded him as king.
49 When Shaul died, Baal-Hanan son of Acbor succeeded him as king.
50 When Baal-Hanan died, Hadad succeeded him as king. His city was named Pau,[e] and his wife's name was Mehetabel daughter of Matred, the daughter of Me-Zahab. 51 Hadad also died.

The chiefs of Edom were:
Timna, Alvah, Jetheth, 52 Oholibamah, Elah, Pinon, 53 Kenaz, Teman, Mibzar, 54 Magdiel and Iram. These were the chiefs of Edom.

Israel's Sons

2 These were the sons of Israel:
Reuben, Simeon, Levi, Judah, Issachar, Zebulun, 2 Dan, Joseph, Benjamin, Naphtali, Gad and Asher.

Judah

To Hezron's Sons

3 The sons of Judah:
Er, Onan and Shelah. These three were born to him by a Canaanite woman, the daughter of Shua. Er, Judah's firstborn, was wicked in the LORD's sight; so the LORD put him to death. 4 Tamar, Judah's daughter-in-law, bore him Perez and Zerah. Judah had five sons in all.

5 The sons of Perez:
Hezron and Hamul.
6 The sons of Zerah:
Zimri, Ethan, Heman, Calcol and Darda[f]—five in all.
7 The son of Carmi:

(2:1–2) From everlasting to everlasting Your love, O Lord, is with those who fear You, and Your righteousness with their children's children—with those who keep Your covenant and remember to obey Your precepts. (Ps 103:17–18)

God, our help and constant refuge,
Ever present in our need!
Though the earth be ever changing,
Though it fall into the sea,
Rock secure, ever sure
Through all tumult You endure.
"God, Our Help and Constant Refuge"
Fred R. Anderson (©1986)

[a] *42* Many Hebrew and Septuagint manuscripts (see also Gen. 36:27); most Hebrew manuscripts *Zaavan, Jaakan* [b] *42* Hebrew *Dishon,* a variant of *Dishan* [c] *43* Or *before an Israelite king reigned over them* [d] *48* Possibly the Euphrates [e] *50* Many Hebrew manuscripts, some Septuagint manuscripts, Vulgate and Syriac (see also Gen. 36:39); most Hebrew manuscripts *Pai* [f] *6* Many Hebrew manuscripts, some Septuagint manuscripts and Syriac (see also 1 Kings 4:31); most Hebrew manuscripts *Dara*

(2:10–17) These are Your roots, O Son of David, our Lord Jesus Christ. You are the grand offspring of Judah, the shoot that has come up from the stump of Jesse, the righteous Branch that has sprouted from David's line. You have branched out from this place and built the spiritual temple of the Lord. You are clothed with majesty, and You will sit and rule forever as a priest on Your throne, with the glory and power of a king and with the tenderness and compassion of a priest. (1Ch 2:3; Isa 11:1; Jer 33:15; Zec 6:12–13; Mt 1:3)

Lo, how a rose e'er blooming
From tender stem hath sprung.
Of Jesse's lineage coming,
By faithful prophets sung.
It came a floweret bright,
Amid the cold of winter,
When half-spent was the night.

This Flower, whose fragrance tender
With sweetness fills the air,
Dispels with glorious splendor
The darkness everywhere.
True man, yet very God,
From sin and death He saves us
And lightens every load.

"Lo, How a Rose E'er Blooming"
German Carol (16th c.)
Trans. Theodore Baker (1851-1934),
stanza 1 and
Harriet Krauth Spaeth (1845-1925),
stanza 3

Alexander, Caesar, Charlemagne, and myself founded empires; but upon what did we rest the creations of our genius? Upon force. Jesus Christ alone founded his empire upon love, and at this hour millions of men would die for him.

Napoleon Bonaparte (1769-1821)

Achar,[a] who brought trouble on Israel by violating the
ban on taking devoted things.[b]
8 The son of Ethan:
Azariah.
9 The sons born to Hezron were:
Jerahmeel, Ram and Caleb.[c]

From Ram Son of Hezron

10 Ram was the father of
Amminadab, and Amminadab the father of Nahshon, the
leader of the people of Judah. 11 Nahshon was the father
of Salmon,[d] Salmon the father of Boaz, 12 Boaz the father
of Obed and Obed the father of Jesse.
13 Jesse was the father of
Eliab his firstborn; the second son was Abinadab, the
third Shimea, 14 the fourth Nethanel, the fifth Raddai,
15 the sixth Ozem and the seventh David. 16 Their sisters
were Zeruiah and Abigail. Zeruiah's three sons were
Abishai, Joab and Asahel. 17 Abigail was the mother of
Amasa, whose father was Jether the Ishmaelite.

Caleb Son of Hezron

18 Caleb son of Hezron had children by his wife Azubah (and
by Jerioth). These were her sons: Jesher, Shobab and
Ardon. 19 When Azubah died, Caleb married Ephrath, who
bore him Hur. 20 Hur was the father of Uri, and Uri the father of Bezalel.
21 Later, Hezron lay with the daughter of Makir the father of
Gilead (he had married her when he was sixty years old),
and she bore him Segub. 22 Segub was the father of Jair,
who controlled twenty-three towns in Gilead. 23 (But Geshur and Aram captured Havvoth Jair,[e] as well as Kenath
with its surrounding settlements—sixty towns.) All these
were descendants of Makir the father of Gilead.
24 After Hezron died in Caleb Ephrathah, Abijah the wife of
Hezron bore him Ashhur the father[f] of Tekoa.

Jerahmeel Son of Hezron

25 The sons of Jerahmeel the firstborn of Hezron:
Ram his firstborn, Bunah, Oren, Ozem and[g] Ahijah. 26 Jerahmeel had another wife, whose name was Atarah; she
was the mother of Onam.
27 The sons of Ram the firstborn of Jerahmeel:
Maaz, Jamin and Eker.
28 The sons of Onam:
Shammai and Jada.
The sons of Shammai:
Nadab and Abishur.
29 Abishur's wife was named Abihail, who bore him Ahban and
Molid.
30 The sons of Nadab:

[a] 7 *Achar* means *trouble*; *Achar* is called *Achan* in Joshua. [b] 7 The Hebrew term refers to the irrevocable giving over of things or persons to the LORD, often by totally destroying them. [c] 9 Hebrew *Kelubai,* a variant of *Caleb* [d] 11 Septuagint (see also Ruth 4:21); Hebrew *Salma* [e] 23 Or *captured the settlements of Jair* [f] 24 *Father* may mean *civic leader* or *military leader*; also in verses 42, 45, 49–52 and possibly elsewhere. [g] 25 Or *Oren and Ozem, by*

Seled and Appaim. Seled died without children.
31 The son of Appaim:
Ishi, who was the father of Sheshan.
Sheshan was the father of Ahlai.
32 The sons of Jada, Shammai's brother:
Jether and Jonathan. Jether died without children.
33 The sons of Jonathan:
Peleth and Zaza.
These were the descendants of Jerahmeel.
34 Sheshan had no sons—only daughters.
He had an Egyptian servant named Jarha. 35 Sheshan gave
his daughter in marriage to his servant Jarha, and she
bore him Attai.
36 Attai was the father of Nathan,
Nathan the father of Zabad,
37 Zabad the father of Ephlal,
Ephlal the father of Obed,
38 Obed the father of Jehu,
Jehu the father of Azariah,
39 Azariah the father of Helez,
Helez the father of Eleasah,
40 Eleasah the father of Sismai,
Sismai the father of Shallum,
41 Shallum the father of Jekamiah,
and Jekamiah the father of Elishama.

The Clans of Caleb

42 The sons of Caleb the brother of Jerahmeel:
Mesha his firstborn, who was the father of Ziph, and his
son Mareshah,[a] who was the father of Hebron.
43 The sons of Hebron:
Korah, Tappuah, Rekem and Shema. 44 Shema was the father of Raham, and Raham the father of Jorkeam. Rekem
was the father of Shammai. 45 The son of Shammai was
Maon, and Maon was the father of Beth Zur.
46 Caleb's concubine Ephah was the mother of Haran, Moza
and Gazez. Haran was the father of Gazez.
47 The sons of Jahdai:
Regem, Jotham, Geshan, Pelet, Ephah and Shaaph.
48 Caleb's concubine Maacah was the mother of Sheber and
Tirhanah. 49 She also gave birth to Shaaph the father of
Madmannah and to Sheva the father of Macbenah and
Gibea. Caleb's daughter was Acsah. 50 These were the descendants of Caleb.

The sons of Hur the firstborn of Ephrathah:
Shobal the father of Kiriath Jearim, 51 Salma the father of
Bethlehem, and Hareph the father of Beth Gader.
52 The descendants of Shobal the father of Kiriath Jearim
were:
Haroeh, half the Manahathites, 53 and the clans of Kiriath
Jearim: the Ithrites, Puthites, Shumathites and Mishra-
ites. From these descended the Zorathites and Eshtao-
lites.
54 The descendants of Salma:
Bethlehem, the Netophathites, Atroth Beth Joab, half the

[a] 42 The meaning of the Hebrew for this phrase is uncertain.

If gratitude is due from children to their earthly parent, how much more is the gratitude of the great family of men due to our Father in heaven.

Hosea Ballou (1771-1852)

(2:42) Eternal God and Father, "One generation will commend your works to another; they will tell of your mighty acts. Your kingdom is an everlasting kingdom, and your dominion endures through all generations." (Ps 145:4,13)

You have been a shelter, Lord,
To ev'ry generation,
To ev'ry generation.
A sanctuary from the storm,
To ev'ry generation,
To ev'ry generation, Lord.

You've seen the years pass in untold
numbers,
As in a single night
You've seen the lifetime of man
Fade quickly before the light.

Our years go by before Your eyes;
You know our rebellious ways.
Make us wise to live holy lives
In the balance of our days.

"To Every Generation"
Bill Batstone (©1986)

Manahathites, the Zorites, 55and the clans of scribes[a]
who lived at Jabez: the Tirathites, Shimeathites and Su-
cathites. These are the Kenites who came from Hammath,
the father of the house of Recab.[b]

The Sons of David

3 These were the sons of David born to him in Hebron:
The firstborn was Amnon the son of Ahinoam of Jezreel;
the second, Daniel the son of Abigail of Carmel;
2 the third, Absalom the son of Maacah daughter of Talmai
king of Geshur;
the fourth, Adonijah the son of Haggith;
3 the fifth, Shephatiah the son of Abital;
and the sixth, Ithream, by his wife Eglah.
4 These six were born to David in Hebron, where he
reigned seven years and six months.
David reigned in Jerusalem thirty-three years, 5and these were
the children born to him there:
Shammua,[c] Shobab, Nathan and Solomon. These four
were by Bathsheba[d] daughter of Ammiel. 6There were
also Ibhar, Elishua,[e] Eliphelet, 7Nogah, Nepheg, Japhia,
8Elishama, Eliada and Eliphelet—nine in all. 9All these
were the sons of David, besides his sons by his concubines. And Tamar was their sister.

(3:10–16) Righteous Judge, of these kings who followed after Solomon, only eight did what was right in Your eyes. What good is an inheritance without godly character? Indeed, "what good is it for a man to gain the whole world, yet forfeit his soul?" "Search me O God, and know my heart; test me and know my anxious thoughts. See if there is any offensive way in me, and lead me in the way everlasting (Ps 139:23–24; Mk 8:36)

The Kings of Judah

10 Solomon's son was Rehoboam,
Abijah his son,
Asa his son,
Jehoshaphat his son,
11 Jehoram[f] his son,
Ahaziah his son,
Joash his son,
12 Amaziah his son,
Azariah his son,
Jotham his son,
13 Ahaz his son,
Hezekiah his son,
Manasseh his son,
14 Amon his son,
Josiah his son.
15 The sons of Josiah:
Johanan the firstborn,
Jehoiakim the second son,
Zedekiah the third,
Shallum the fourth.
16 The successors of Jehoiakim:
Jehoiachin[g] his son,
and Zedekiah.

[a] *55* Or *of the Sopherites* [b] *55* Or *father of Beth Recab* [c] *5* Hebrew *Shimea,* a variant of *Shammua* [d] *5* One Hebrew manuscript and Vulgate (see also Septuagint and 2 Samuel 11:3); most Hebrew manuscripts *Bathshua* [e] *6* Two Hebrew manuscripts (see also 2 Samuel 5:15 and 1 Chron. 14:5); most Hebrew manuscripts *Elishama*
[f] *11* Hebrew *Joram,* a variant of *Jehoram* [g] *16* Hebrew *Jeconiah,* a variant of *Jehoiachin*; also in verse 17

The Royal Line After the Exile

17 The descendants of Jehoiachin the captive:
Shealtiel his son, 18 Malkiram, Pedaiah, Shenazzar, Jekamiah, Hoshama and Nedabiah.
19 The sons of Pedaiah:
Zerubbabel and Shimei.
The sons of Zerubbabel:
Meshullam and Hananiah.
Shelomith was their sister.
20 There were also five others:
Hashubah, Ohel, Berekiah, Hasadiah and Jushab-Hesed.
21 The descendants of Hananiah:
Pelatiah and Jeshaiah, and the sons of Rephaiah, of Arnan, of Obadiah and of Shecaniah.
22 The descendants of Shecaniah:
Shemaiah and his sons:
Hattush, Igal, Bariah, Neariah and Shaphat—six in all.
23 The sons of Neariah:
Elioenai, Hizkiah and Azrikam—three in all.
24 The sons of Elioenai:
Hodaviah, Eliashib, Pelaiah, Akkub, Johanan, Delaiah and Anani—seven in all.

Other Clans of Judah

4 The descendants of Judah:
Perez, Hezron, Carmi, Hur and Shobal.
2 Reaiah son of Shobal was the father of Jahath, and Jahath the father of Ahumai and Lahad. These were the clans of the Zorathites.
3 These were the sons[a] of Etam:
Jezreel, Ishma and Idbash. Their sister was named Hazzelelponi.
4 Penuel was the father of Gedor, and Ezer the father of Hushah.
These were the descendants of Hur, the firstborn of Ephrathah and father[b] of Bethlehem.
5 Ashhur the father of Tekoa had two wives, Helah and Naarah.
6 Naarah bore him Ahuzzam, Hepher, Temeni and Haahashtari. These were the descendants of Naarah.
7 The sons of Helah:
Zereth, Zohar, Ethnan, 8 and Koz, who was the father of Anub and Hazzobebah and of the clans of Aharhel son of Harum.

9 Jabez was more honorable than his brothers. His mother had named him Jabez,[c] saying, "I gave birth to him in pain."
10 Jabez cried out to the God of Israel, "Oh, that you would bless me and enlarge my territory! Let your hand be with me, and keep me from harm so that I will be free from pain." And God granted his request.

11 Kelub, Shuhah's brother, was the father of Mehir, who was the father of Eshton.
12 Eshton was the father of Beth Rapha, Paseah and Tehinnah the father of Ir Nahash.[d] These were the men of Recah.

13 The sons of Kenaz:

[a] 3 Some Septuagint manuscripts (see also Vulgate); Hebrew *father* [b] 4 *Father* may mean *civic leader* or *military leader*; also in verses 12, 14, 17, 18 and possibly elsewhere. [c] 9 *Jabez* sounds like the Hebrew for *pain*. [d] 12 Or *of the city of Nahash*

(4:9–10) Whether I was born in praise, as Judah, or born in pain, as Jabez, may I be found honorable before You. You Who save, save me. You Who bless, bless me. Enlarge my heart, and so enlarge my portion in You. Let Your hand be with me to guide, protect, comfort and correct. I pray for my brothers and sisters who are suffering: As You remembered Abraham and so brought Lot out of his catastrophe, even so remember Your favor toward me and save my loved ones from pain. (Ge 19:29)

I know not by what methods rare,
But this I know: God answers prayer.
I know not if the blessing sought
Will come in just the guise I thought.
I leave my prayer to him alone
Whose will is wiser than my own.

Eliza M. Hickok

(4:22) O Ancient of Days, these records from antiquity remind us of a timeless truth: "Lord, you have been our dwelling place throughout all generations. Before the mountains were born or you brought forth the earth and the world, from everlasting to everlasting you are God. You turn men back to dust, saying, 'Return to dust, O sons of men.' For a thousand years in your sight are like a day that has just gone by, or like a watch in the night. You sweep men away in the sleep of death; they are like the new grass of the morning—though in the morning it springs up new, by evening it is dry and withered . . . Teach us to number our days aright, that we may gain a heart of wisdom." (Ps 90:1–6,12)

Othniel and Seraiah.
The sons of Othniel:
Hathath and Meonothai.[a] 14Meonothai was the father of Ophrah.
Seraiah was the father of Joab,
the father of Ge Harashim.[b] It was called this because its people were craftsmen.
15The sons of Caleb son of Jephunneh:
Iru, Elah and Naam.
The son of Elah:
Kenaz.
16The sons of Jehallelel:
Ziph, Ziphah, Tiria and Asarel.
17The sons of Ezrah:
Jether, Mered, Epher and Jalon. One of Mered's wives gave birth to Miriam, Shammai and Ishbah the father of Eshtemoa. 18(His Judean wife gave birth to Jered the father of Gedor, Heber the father of Soco, and Jekuthiel the father of Zanoah.) These were the children of Pharaoh's daughter Bithiah, whom Mered had married.
19The sons of Hodiah's wife, the sister of Naham:
the father of Keilah the Garmite, and Eshtemoa the Maacathite.
20The sons of Shimon:
Amnon, Rinnah, Ben-Hanan and Tilon.
The descendants of Ishi:
Zoheth and Ben-Zoheth.
21The sons of Shelah son of Judah:
Er the father of Lecah, Laadah the father of Mareshah and the clans of the linen workers at Beth Ashbea, 22Jokim, the men of Cozeba, and Joash and Saraph, who ruled in Moab and Jashubi Lehem. (These records are from ancient times.) 23They were the potters who lived at Netaim and Gederah; they stayed there and worked for the king.

Simeon

24The descendants of Simeon:
Nemuel, Jamin, Jarib, Zerah and Shaul;
25Shallum was Shaul's son, Mibsam his son and Mishma his son.
26The descendants of Mishma:
Hammuel his son, Zaccur his son and Shimei his son.
27Shimei had sixteen sons and six daughters, but his brothers
did not have many children; so their entire clan did not become
as numerous as the people of Judah. 28They lived in Beersheba,
Moladah, Hazar Shual, 29Bilhah, Ezem, Tolad, 30Bethuel, Hormah, Ziklag, 31Beth Marcaboth, Hazar Susim, Beth Biri and Shaaraim. These were their towns until the reign of David. 32Their
surrounding villages were Etam, Ain, Rimmon, Token and
Ashan—five towns— 33and all the villages around these towns as
far as Baalath.[c] These were their settlements. And they kept a genealogical record.

34Meshobab, Jamlech, Joshah son of Amaziah, 35Joel, Jehu

[a] 13 Some Septuagint manuscripts and Vulgate; Hebrew does not have *and Meonothai.*
[b] 14 *Ge Harashim* means *valley of craftsmen.* [c] 33 Some Septuagint manuscripts (see also Joshua 19:8); Hebrew *Baal*

son of Joshibiah, the son of Seraiah, the son of Asiel, 36 also
Elioenai, Jaakobah, Jeshohaiah, Asaiah, Adiel, Jesimiel, Be-
naiah, 37 and Ziza son of Shiphi, the son of Allon, the son of
Jedaiah, the son of Shimri, the son of Shemaiah.

38 The men listed above by name were leaders of their clans.
Their families increased greatly, 39 and they went to the outskirts
of Gedor to the east of the valley in search of pasture for their
flocks. 40 They found rich, good pasture, and the land was spacious, peaceful and quiet. Some Hamites had lived there formerly.

41 The men whose names were listed came in the days of Hezekiah king of Judah. They attacked the Hamites in their dwellings
and also the Meunites who were there and completely destroyed[a]
them, as is evident to this day. Then they settled in their place, because there was pasture for their flocks. 42 And five hundred of
these Simeonites, led by Pelatiah, Neariah, Rephaiah and Uzziel,
the sons of Ishi, invaded the hill country of Seir. 43 They killed the
remaining Amalekites who had escaped, and they have lived there
to this day.

My soul is like a mirror in which the glory of God is reflected, but sin, however insignificant, covers the mirror with smoke.

Saint Teresa of Avila (1515-1582)

Reuben

5 The sons of Reuben the firstborn of Israel (he was the firstborn, but when he defiled his father's marriage bed, his
rights as firstborn were given to the sons of Joseph son of Israel;
so he could not be listed in the genealogical record in accordance with his birthright, 2 and though Judah was the strongest of
his brothers and a ruler came from him, the rights of the firstborn belonged to Joseph)— 3 the sons of Reuben the firstborn of
Israel:

Hanoch, Pallu, Hezron and Carmi.

4 The descendants of Joel:

Shemaiah his son, Gog his son,
Shimei his son, 5 Micah his son,
Reaiah his son, Baal his son,
6 and Beerah his son, whom Tiglath-Pileser[b] king of Assyria took into exile. Beerah was a leader of the Reubenites.

7 Their relatives by clans, listed according to their genealogical records:

Jeiel the chief, Zechariah, 8 and Bela son of Azaz, the son
of Shema, the son of Joel. They settled in the area from
Aroer to Nebo and Baal Meon. 9 To the east they occupied
the land up to the edge of the desert that extends to the
Euphrates River, because their livestock had increased in
Gilead.

10 During Saul's reign they waged war against the Hagrites,
who were defeated at their hands; they occupied the
dwellings of the Hagrites throughout the entire region east
of Gilead.

(5:1–3) Gracious Father, grant that Your glory will not be obscured in this world by the sins of Your people. Purify us that our service may be pure and that in truth we may serve Your glory. Grant that the disorder of our houses will not hide the beauty of Your holy house. Grant that we will reflect Your glory in the peace and justice of the household of faith.

Gad

11 The Gadites lived next to them in Bashan, as far as Salecah:
12 Joel was the chief, Shapham the second, then Janai and
Shaphat, in Bashan.

[a] *41* The Hebrew term refers to the irrevocable giving over of things or persons to the LORD, often by totally destroying them. [b] *6* Hebrew *Tilgath-Pilneser,* a variant of *Tiglath-Pileser;* also in verse 26

13 Their relatives, by families, were:
Michael, Meshullam, Sheba, Jorai, Jacan, Zia and Eber—seven in all.
14 These were the sons of Abihail son of Huri, the son of Jaroah, the son of Gilead, the son of Michael, the son of Jeshishai, the son of Jahdo, the son of Buz.
15 Ahi son of Abdiel, the son of Guni, was head of their family.
16 The Gadites lived in Gilead, in Bashan and its outlying villages, and on all the pasturelands of Sharon as far as they extended.
17 All these were entered in the genealogical records during the reigns of Jotham king of Judah and Jeroboam king of Israel.
18 The Reubenites, the Gadites and the half-tribe of Manasseh
had 44,760 men ready for military service—able-bodied men
who could handle shield and sword, who could use a bow, and
who were trained for battle. 19 They waged war against the Hagrites, Jetur, Naphish and Nodab. 20 They were helped in fighting
them, and God handed the Hagrites and all their allies over to
them, because they cried out to him during the battle. He answered their prayers, because they trusted in him. 21 They seized
the livestock of the Hagrites—fifty thousand camels, two hundred
fifty thousand sheep and two thousand donkeys. They also took
one hundred thousand people captive, 22 and many others fell
slain, because the battle was God's. And they occupied the land
until the exile.

The Half-Tribe of Manasseh

23 The people of the half-tribe of Manasseh were numerous; they settled in the land from Bashan to Baal Hermon, that is, to Senir (Mount Hermon).
24 These were the heads of their families: Epher, Ishi, Eliel, Az-
riel, Jeremiah, Hodaviah and Jahdiel. They were brave warriors,
famous men, and heads of their families. 25 But they were unfaithful to the God of their fathers and prostituted themselves to
the gods of the peoples of the land, whom God had destroyed before them. 26 So the God of Israel stirred up the spirit of Pul king
of Assyria (that is, Tiglath-Pileser king of Assyria), who took the
Reubenites, the Gadites and the half-tribe of Manasseh into exile.
He took them to Halah, Habor, Hara and the river of Gozan,
where they are to this day.

Levi

6 The sons of Levi:
Gershon, Kohath and Merari.
2 The sons of Kohath:
Amram, Izhar, Hebron and Uzziel.
3 The children of Amram:
Aaron, Moses and Miriam.
The sons of Aaron:
Nadab, Abihu, Eleazar and Ithamar.
4 Eleazar was the father of Phinehas,
Phinehas the father of Abishua,
5 Abishua the father of Bukki,
Bukki the father of Uzzi,
6 Uzzi the father of Zerahiah,
Zerahiah the father of Meraioth,

(5:18–26) "Blessed is the man who makes the LORD his trust, who does not look to the proud, to those who turn aside to false gods."

O Lord, as we read of the faith and the unfaithfulness of Your people, we are reminded of these judgments of David. When we call to You in distress, You answer our prayers because we trust in You. You give us aid against the enemy, for the help of humans is worthless. When our battles are Your battles, then Your victories are our victories. How much of our undoing is the result of our unfaithfulness! How quick we are to forget the God Who saves us. You give grace when we are humble, yet You resist us when we are proud. And so we humbly pray, O Lord, save us. O Lord, forgive us. O Lord, restore us. (Ps 40:4; 60:11; Pr 3:34; Jas 4:6)

Do not trust in your own knowledge, nor in the cleverness of any man living, but rather in the grace of God, who aids the humble, and humbles the proud.

Thomas à Kempis (c.1380-1471)

7 Meraioth the father of Amariah,
Amariah the father of Ahitub,
8 Ahitub the father of Zadok,
Zadok the father of Ahimaaz,
9 Ahimaaz the father of Azariah,
Azariah the father of Johanan,
10 Johanan the father of Azariah (it was he who served as
priest in the temple Solomon built in Jerusalem),
11 Azariah the father of Amariah,
Amariah the father of Ahitub,
12 Ahitub the father of Zadok,
Zadok the father of Shallum,
13 Shallum the father of Hilkiah,
Hilkiah the father of Azariah,
14 Azariah the father of Seraiah,
and Seraiah the father of Jehozadak.
15 Jehozadak was deported when the LORD sent Judah and Jerusalem into exile by the hand of Nebuchadnezzar.

16 The sons of Levi:
Gershon,[a] Kohath and Merari.
17 These are the names of the sons of Gershon:
Libni and Shimei.
18 The sons of Kohath:
Amram, Izhar, Hebron and Uzziel.
19 The sons of Merari:
Mahli and Mushi.
These are the clans of the Levites listed according to their fa-
thers:
20 Of Gershon:
Libni his son, Jehath his son,
Zimmah his son, 21 Joah his son,
Iddo his son, Zerah his son
and Jeatherai his son.
22 The descendants of Kohath:
Amminadab his son, Korah his son,
Assir his son, 23 Elkanah his son,
Ebiasaph his son, Assir his son,
24 Tahath his son, Uriel his son,
Uzziah his son and Shaul his son.
25 The descendants of Elkanah:
Amasai, Ahimoth,
26 Elkanah his son,[b] Zophai his son,
Nahath his son, 27 Eliab his son,
Jeroham his son, Elkanah his son
and Samuel his son.[c]
28 The sons of Samuel:
Joel[d] the firstborn
and Abijah the second son.
29 The descendants of Merari:
Mahli, Libni his son,
Shimei his son, Uzzah his son,

[a] *16* Hebrew *Gershom,* a variant of *Gershon*; also in verses 17, 20, 43, 62 and 71
[b] *26* Some Hebrew manuscripts, Septuagint and Syriac; most Hebrew manuscripts *Ahimoth* *26and Elkanah. The sons of Elkanah:*
[c] *27* Some Septuagint manuscripts (see also 1 Samuel 1:19,20 and 1 Chron. 6:33,34); Hebrew does not have *and Samuel his son.*
[d] *28* Some Septuagint manuscripts and Syriac (see also 1 Samuel 8:2 and 1 Chron. 6:33); Hebrew does not have *Joel.*

(6:16) What is the meaning of all this genealogy? Why should I read through this list of long-gone people, families, clans and tribes? These are the generations of those whom You entrusted with Your sacred service. These are the people whom You called to meet with You in Your tabernacle, Your tent of meeting. These are the generations of those who sought the face of God. These are the living stones of the priesthood, joined together by the mortar of the covenant.

Each of the redeemed shall forever know and praise some one aspect of the divine beauty better than any other creature can. Why else were individuals created, but that God, loving all infinitely, should love each differently? . . . If all experience God in the same way and returned him an identical worship, the song of the church triumphant would have no symphony, it would be like an orchestra in which all the instruments played the same note.

C.S. Lewis (1898-1963)

I will give my love to You,
The One who first loved me.
Through ev'ry moment of my life,
With ev'ry breath I breathe.

I will sing my song to You,
You're the reason for each rhyme.
Your Spirit's captured all of me:
Strength and soul and mind.

With all of my heart,
With all of my heart,
I will praise You, Lord,
With all of my heart.

"With All Of My Heart"
Bill Batstone and Morris Chapman
(©1990)

(6:31–32) "Blessed are those who dwell in Your house; they are ever praising You." Surely when I worship You my praise is joined to that of the cherubim and seraphim, angels and archangels, and all the company of heavenly hosts singing, "Holy, Holy, Holy." My worship is also joined to that of all the tribes and families of Israel arranged in order about the tabernacle, so long ago. You are surrounded by the song of angel choirs and the myriad saints who have gone before me, yet You delight in the sound of my voice. (Ps 84:4; Isa 6:3)

The Lord is in His holy temple.
And we are in His presence now!
The ones who've gone
Before have gathered;
As one before the Lord we bow:

Singing alleluia, alleluia, alleluia,
Singing alleluia, alleluia, alleluia.
We Sing Alleluia"
Walt Harrah (©1988)

(6:49) O God of our fathers, help us to leave a legacy of worship. May we pass on to our children the secret of setting the fire of devotion to their spiritual gifts and lifting up the incense of prayer. (Ps 71:17–18; Isa 38:19)

The best way for a child to learn to fear God is to know a real Christian. The best way for a child to learn to pray is to live with a father and mother who know a life of friendship with God and who truly pray.
Johann Heinrich Pestalozzi (1746-1827)

30 Shimea his son, Haggiah his son
and Asaiah his son.

The Temple Musicians

31 These are the men David put in charge of the music in the
house of the LORD after the ark came to rest there. 32 They ministered with music before the tabernacle, the Tent of Meeting, until
Solomon built the temple of the LORD in Jerusalem. They performed their duties according to the regulations laid down for
them.
33 Here are the men who served, together with their sons:
From the Kohathites:
Heman, the musician,
the son of Joel, the son of Samuel,
34 the son of Elkanah, the son of Jeroham,
the son of Eliel, the son of Toah,
35 the son of Zuph, the son of Elkanah,
the son of Mahath, the son of Amasai,
36 the son of Elkanah, the son of Joel,
the son of Azariah, the son of Zephaniah,
37 the son of Tahath, the son of Assir,
the son of Ebiasaph, the son of Korah,
38 the son of Izhar, the son of Kohath,
the son of Levi, the son of Israel;
39 and Heman's associate Asaph, who served at his right hand:
Asaph son of Berekiah, the son of Shimea,
40 the son of Michael, the son of Baaseiah,[a]
the son of Malkijah, 41 the son of Ethni,
the son of Zerah, the son of Adaiah,
42 the son of Ethan, the son of Zimmah,
the son of Shimei, 43 the son of Jahath,
the son of Gershon, the son of Levi;
44 and from their associates, the Merarites, at his left hand:
Ethan son of Kishi, the son of Abdi,
the son of Malluch, 45 the son of Hashabiah,
the son of Amaziah, the son of Hilkiah,
46 the son of Amzi, the son of Bani,
the son of Shemer, 47 the son of Mahli,
the son of Mushi, the son of Merari,
the son of Levi.

48 Their fellow Levites were assigned to all the other duties of
the tabernacle, the house of God. 49 But Aaron and his descendants were the ones who presented offerings on the altar of burnt
offering and on the altar of incense in connection with all that
was done in the Most Holy Place, making atonement for Israel, in
accordance with all that Moses the servant of God had commanded.

50 These were the descendants of Aaron:
Eleazar his son, Phinehas his son,
Abishua his son, 51 Bukki his son,
Uzzi his son, Zerahiah his son,
52 Meraioth his son, Amariah his son,
Ahitub his son, 53 Zadok his son
and Ahimaaz his son.

[a] 40 Most Hebrew manuscripts; some Hebrew manuscripts, one Septuagint manuscript and Syriac *Maaseiah*

[54]These were the locations of their settlements allotted as their
territory (they were assigned to the descendants of Aaron who
were from the Kohathite clan, because the first lot was for them):
[55]They were given Hebron in Judah with its surrounding
pasturelands. [56]But the fields and villages around the city
were given to Caleb son of Jephunneh.
[57]So the descendants of Aaron were given Hebron (a city
of refuge), and Libnah,[a] Jattir, Eshtemoa, [58]Hilen, Debir,
[59]Ashan, Juttah[b] and Beth Shemesh, together with their pasturelands. [60]And from the tribe of Benjamin they were given
Gibeon,[c] Geba, Alemeth and Anathoth, together with their
pasturelands.

These towns, which were distributed among the Kohathite clans, were thirteen in all.

[61]The rest of Kohath's descendants were allotted ten towns from the clans of half the tribe of Manasseh.

[62]The descendants of Gershon, clan by clan, were allotted thirteen towns from the tribes of Issachar, Asher and Naphtali, and from the part of the tribe of Manasseh that is in Bashan.

[63]The descendants of Merari, clan by clan, were allotted twelve towns from the tribes of Reuben, Gad and Zebulun.

[64]So the Israelites gave the Levites these towns and their pasturelands. [65]From the tribes of Judah, Simeon and Benjamin they
allotted the previously named towns.

[66]Some of the Kohathite clans were given as their territory towns from the tribe of Ephraim.

[67]In the hill country of Ephraim they were given Shechem
(a city of refuge), and Gezer,[d] [68]Jokmeam, Beth Horon,
[69]Aijalon and Gath Rimmon, together with their pasturelands.

[70]And from half the tribe of Manasseh the Israelites gave Aner and Bileam, together with their pasturelands, to the rest of the Kohathite clans.

[71]The Gershonites received the following:
From the clan of the half-tribe of Manasseh
they received Golan in Bashan and also Ashtaroth, together with their pasturelands;
[72]from the tribe of Issachar
they received Kedesh, Daberath, [73]Ramoth and Anem, together with their pasturelands;
[74]from the tribe of Asher
they received Mashal, Abdon, [75]Hukok and Rehob, together with their pasturelands;
[76]and from the tribe of Naphtali
they received Kedesh in Galilee, Hammon and Kiriathaim, together with their pasturelands.

[77]The Merarites (the rest of the Levites) received the following:
From the tribe of Zebulun
they received Jokneam, Kartah,[e] Rimmono and Tabor, together with their pasturelands;

[a] 57 See Joshua 21:13; Hebrew *given the cities of refuge: Hebron, Libnah.* [b] 59 Syriac (see also Septuagint and Joshua 21:16); Hebrew does not have *Juttah.* [c] 60 See Joshua 21:17; Hebrew does not have *Gibeon.* [d] 67 See Joshua 21:21; Hebrew *given the cities of refuge: Shechem, Gezer.* [e] 77 See Septuagint and Joshua 21:34; Hebrew does not have *Jokneam, Kartah.*

Ministry is a communal and mutual experience. Somehow we have come to believe that good leadership requires a safe distance from those we are called to lead. Christian leaders are called to live the Incarnation, that is, to live in the body, not only in their own bodies but also in the corporate body of the community, and to discover there the presence of the Holy Spirit.

Henri Nouwen (1932–1996)

(6:54–81) In every corner of our world and in every area of our lives, may we attend to Your service, Lord. May we never be elitist or remote from the concerns of life. For it is here, amid the daily struggle, that we are to live out the life of Christ. May it truly be evident that the kingdom of God is within us and among us. (Lk 17:21)

78 from the tribe of Reuben across the Jordan east of Jericho
they received Bezer in the desert, Jahzah, 79 Kedemoth
and Mephaath, together with their pasturelands;
80 and from the tribe of Gad
they received Ramoth in Gilead, Mahanaim, 81 Heshbon
and Jazer, together with their pasturelands.

Issachar

7 The sons of Issachar:
Tola, Puah, Jashub and Shimron—four in all.
2 The sons of Tola:
Uzzi, Rephaiah, Jeriel, Jahmai, Ibsam and Samuel—
heads of their families. During the reign of David, the descendants of Tola listed as fighting men in their genealogy numbered 22,600.
3 The son of Uzzi:
Izrahiah.
The sons of Izrahiah:
Michael, Obadiah, Joel and Isshiah. All five of them were
chiefs. 4 According to their family genealogy, they had
36,000 men ready for battle, for they had many wives and children.
5 The relatives who were fighting men belonging to all the clans of Issachar, as listed in their genealogy, were 87,000 in all.

Benjamin

6 Three sons of Benjamin:
Bela, Beker and Jediael.
7 The sons of Bela:
Ezbon, Uzzi, Uzziel, Jerimoth and Iri, heads of families—five in all. Their genealogical record listed 22,034 fighting men.
8 The sons of Beker:
Zemirah, Joash, Eliezer, Elioenai, Omri, Jeremoth, Abijah,
Anathoth and Alemeth. All these were the sons of Beker.
9 Their genealogical record listed the heads of families and 20,200 fighting men.
10 The son of Jediael:
Bilhan.
The sons of Bilhan:
Jeush, Benjamin, Ehud, Kenaanah, Zethan, Tarshish and
Ahishahar. 11 All these sons of Jediael were heads of families.
There were 17,200 fighting men ready to go out to war.
12 The Shuppites and Huppites were the descendants of Ir, and the Hushites the descendants of Aher.

Naphtali

13 The sons of Naphtali:
Jahziel, Guni, Jezer and Shillem[a]—the descendants of Bilhah.

Manasseh

14 The descendants of Manasseh:
Asriel was his descendant through his Aramean concu-

[a] *13* Some Hebrew and Septuagint manuscripts (see also Gen. 46:24 and Num. 26:49); most Hebrew manuscripts *Shallum*

(7:1–13) I will tell the next generation Your praiseworthy deeds, O LORD, Your power, and the wonders You have done. I will teach my children Your Word, so the next generation will know it, even the children yet to be born, and they in turn will tell their children. Then they will put their trust in You, O God, and will not forget Your deeds but will keep Your commands. (Ps 78:4–7)

Give the Bible to the people, unadulterated, pure, unaltered, unexplained, uncheapened, and then see it work through the whole nature. It is very difficult indeed for a man or for a boy who knows the Scriptures ever to get away from it. It follows him like the memory of his mother. It haunts him like an old song. It reminds him like the word of an old and revered teacher. It forms a part of the warp and woof of his life.
Woodrow Wilson (1856-1924)

O teach me, Lord, that I may teach
The precious things Thou dost
impart;
And wing my words that they may
reach
The hidden depths of many a heart.
"Lord, Speak to Me"
Frances Ridley Havergal (1872)

bine. She gave birth to Makir the father of Gilead. 15 Makir
took a wife from among the Huppites and Shuppites. His sister's name was Maacah.

Another descendant was named Zelophehad, who had
only daughters.

16 Makir's wife Maacah gave birth to a son and named him
Peresh. His brother was named Sheresh, and his sons were
Ulam and Rakem.

17 The son of Ulam:
Bedan.

These were the sons of Gilead son of Makir, the son of Manasseh. 18 His sister Hammoleketh gave birth to Ishhod,
Abiezer and Mahlah.

19 The sons of Shemida were:
Ahian, Shechem, Likhi and Aniam.

Ephraim

20 The descendants of Ephraim:
Shuthelah, Bered his son,
Tahath his son, Eleadah his son,
Tahath his son, 21 Zabad his son
and Shuthelah his son.

Ezer and Elead were killed by the native-born men of
Gath, when they went down to seize their livestock. 22 Their
father Ephraim mourned for them many days, and his relatives came to comfort him. 23 Then he lay with his wife again,
and she became pregnant and gave birth to a son. He named
him Beriah,[a] because there had been misfortune in his family. 24 His daughter was Sheerah, who built Lower and Upper
Beth Horon as well as Uzzen Sheerah.

25 Rephah was his son, Resheph his son,[b]
Telah his son, Tahan his son,
26 Ladan his son, Ammihud his son,
Elishama his son, 27 Nun his son
and Joshua his son.

28 Their lands and settlements included Bethel and its surrounding villages, Naaran to the east, Gezer and its villages to the
west, and Shechem and its villages all the way to Ayyah and its villages. 29 Along the borders of Manasseh were Beth Shan, Taanach,
Megiddo and Dor, together with their villages. The descendants of
Joseph son of Israel lived in these towns.

Asher

30 The sons of Asher:
Imnah, Ishvah, Ishvi and Beriah. Their sister was Serah.

31 The sons of Beriah:
Heber and Malkiel, who was the father of Birzaith.

32 Heber was the father of Japhlet, Shomer and Hotham and of
their sister Shua.

33 The sons of Japhlet:
Pasach, Bimhal and Ashvath.
These were Japhlet's sons.

34 The sons of Shomer:
Ahi, Rohgah,[c] Hubbah and Aram.

[a] *23 Beriah* sounds like the Hebrew for *misfortune.* [b] *25* Some Septuagint manuscripts; Hebrew does not have *his son.* [c] *34* Or *of his brother Shomer: Rohgah*

(7:21) Lord, You told Your people to possess the land of the Philistines and to drive out their enemies. But some were faithless, and their obedience was incomplete. They settled for something less. You have told me to possess that which You have given me and to resist the enemy of my soul. But I have turned back from the task. Instead, like Ezer and Elead, I have behaved like a horse thief. You want me to go boldly into my destiny and to take hold of Your promises to me. I am content just to nit-pick—to manage sin and steal its fruit, rather than drive it out of my life. I confess to You that at times I behave as one who has no fear of God before his eyes. For in my own eyes I flatter myself too much to detect or hate my sin. Lord, have mercy on me, a sinner. Forgive me for being faithless. Cleanse me from my stubbornness and rebellion. Give me boldness to obey You completely. (Ex 23:31; Ps 36:1–2)

35 The sons of his brother Helem:
Zophah, Imna, Shelesh and Amal.
36 The sons of Zophah:
Suah, Harnepher, Shual, Beri, Imrah, 37 Bezer, Hod,
Shamma, Shilshah, Ithran[a] and Beera.
38 The sons of Jether:
Jephunneh, Pispah and Ara.
39 The sons of Ulla:
Arah, Hanniel and Rizia.
40 All these were descendants of Asher—heads of families,
choice men, brave warriors and outstanding leaders. The number
of men ready for battle, as listed in their genealogy, was 26,000.

The Genealogy of Saul the Benjamite

8 Benjamin was the father of Bela his firstborn,
Ashbel the second son, Aharah the third,
2 Nohah the fourth and Rapha the fifth.
3 The sons of Bela were:
Addar, Gera, Abihud,[b] 4 Abishua, Naaman, Ahoah, 5 Gera,
Shephuphan and Huram.
6 These were the descendants of Ehud, who were heads of
families of those living in Geba and were deported to
Manahath:
7 Naaman, Ahijah, and Gera, who deported them and who
was the father of Uzza and Ahihud.
8 Sons were born to Shaharaim in Moab after he had divorced
his wives Hushim and Baara. 9 By his wife Hodesh he had
Jobab, Zibia, Mesha, Malcam, 10 Jeuz, Sakia and Mirmah.
These were his sons, heads of families. 11 By Hushim he
had Abitub and Elpaal.
12 The sons of Elpaal:
Eber, Misham, Shemed (who built Ono and Lod with its
surrounding villages), 13 and Beriah and Shema, who
were heads of families of those living in Aijalon and who
drove out the inhabitants of Gath.
14 Ahio, Shashak, Jeremoth, 15 Zebadiah, Arad, Eder, 16 Michael, Ishpah and Joha were the sons of Beriah.
17 Zebadiah, Meshullam, Hizki, Heber, 18 Ishmerai, Izliah and
Jobab were the sons of Elpaal.
19 Jakim, Zicri, Zabdi, 20 Elienai, Zillethai, Eliel, 21 Adaiah, Ber-
aiah and Shimrath were the sons of Shimei.
22 Ishpan, Eber, Eliel, 23 Abdon, Zicri, Hanan, 24 Hananiah,
Elam, Anthothijah, 25 Iphdeiah and Penuel were the sons
of Shashak.
26 Shamsherai, Shehariah, Athaliah, 27 Jaareshiah, Elijah and
Zicri were the sons of Jeroham.
28 All these were heads of families, chiefs as listed in their genealogy, and they lived in Jerusalem.
29 Jeiel[c] the father[d] of Gibeon lived in Gibeon.
His wife's name was Maacah, 30 and his firstborn son was
Abdon, followed by Zur, Kish, Baal, Ner,[e] Nadab, 31 Gedor,
Ahio, Zeker 32 and Mikloth, who was the father of Shimeah. They too lived near their relatives in Jerusalem.

[a] *37* Possibly a variant of *Jether* [b] *3* Or *Gera the father of Ehud* [c] *29* Some Septuagint manuscripts (see also 1 Chron. 9:35); Hebrew does not have *Jeiel.*
[d] *29* *Father* may mean *civic leader* or *military leader.* [e] *30* Some Septuagint manuscripts (see also 1 Chron. 9:36); Hebrew does not have *Ner.*

(8:1) When we survey these genealogies, O Faithful Father, we see Your hand protecting Your children through the ages. We see Your loving remembrance of their names. We behold Your continuing purpose in their families. And we catch a glimpse of something more. These old lists remind us of our transcendent family of which You are the heavenly Father. These names written here with such care remind us that our names are written down with even greater care in the Lamb's book of life. Each of us, from generation to generation, carries forward the faith of the living Christ—each of us with a destiny to fulfill, each of us with a legacy to leave behind. (Rev 21:27)

(8:29–39) Father, I am caught with sadness as I peruse the names of the Benjaminites who are of the family of Saul. I weep with David at the memory of the anointed of Yahweh who died in ignominy rather than in glory. I reflect on the sadness of the life of Jonathan, one son on whom the sins of the father truly did rest. I grieve for what might have been. And I pray, loving Father, that such a story would not be written of my own life. By Your grace, hold me in Your loyal love. And by Your grace, help me to remain loyal to You. (Ex 20:5–6; 2Sa 1:17–27)

33 Ner was the father of Kish, Kish the father of Saul, and Saul the father of Jonathan, Malki-Shua, Abinadab and Esh-Baal.[a]
34 The son of Jonathan:
Merib-Baal,[b] who was the father of Micah.
35 The sons of Micah:
Pithon, Melech, Tarea and Ahaz.
36 Ahaz was the father of Jehoaddah, Jehoaddah was the father of Alemeth, Azmaveth and Zimri, and Zimri was the father of Moza. 37 Moza was the father of Binea; Raphah was his son, Eleasah his son and Azel his son.
38 Azel had six sons, and these were their names:
Azrikam, Bokeru, Ishmael, Sheariah, Obadiah and Hanan. All these were the sons of Azel.
39 The sons of his brother Eshek:
Ulam his firstborn, Jeush the second son and Eliphelet the third. 40 The sons of Ulam were brave warriors who could handle the bow. They had many sons and grandsons—150 in all.
All these were the descendants of Benjamin.

9 All Israel was listed in the genealogies recorded in the book of the kings of Israel.

The People in Jerusalem

The people of Judah were taken captive to Babylon because of their unfaithfulness. 2 Now the first to resettle on their own property in their own towns were some Israelites, priests, Levites and temple servants.

3 Those from Judah, from Benjamin, and from Ephraim and Manasseh who lived in Jerusalem were:
4 Uthai son of Ammihud, the son of Omri, the son of Imri, the son of Bani, a descendant of Perez son of Judah.
5 Of the Shilonites:
Asaiah the firstborn and his sons.
6 Of the Zerahites:
Jeuel.
The people from Judah numbered 690.
7 Of the Benjamites:
Sallu son of Meshullam, the son of Hodaviah, the son of Hassenuah;
8 Ibneiah son of Jeroham; Elah son of Uzzi, the son of Micri; and Meshullam son of Shephatiah, the son of Reuel, the son of Ibnijah.
9 The people from Benjamin, as listed in their genealogy, numbered 956. All these men were heads of their families.
10 Of the priests:
Jedaiah; Jehoiarib; Jakin;
11 Azariah son of Hilkiah, the son of Meshullam, the son of Zadok, the son of Meraioth, the son of Ahitub, the official in charge of the house of God;
12 Adaiah son of Jeroham, the son of Pashhur, the son of Malkijah; and Maasai son of Adiel, the son of Jahzerah, the son of Meshullam, the son of Meshillemith, the son of Immer.

[a] 33 Also known as *Ish-Bosheth* [b] 34 Also known as *Mephibosheth*

(9:1) The most solemn contrasts in Your Word concern the righteous and the wicked. On the one hand I affirm the hope that Your righteous ones will live by their faith. But with sadness I also affirm the worst. For Your wrath has been revealed from heaven against all ungodliness and wickedness of unfaithful men who suppressed the truth by their wickedness. Although they knew You, they neither glorified You nor gave thanks to You. Their thinking became futile. Their foolish hearts were darkened. Thinking they were wise, they became fools, and exchanged the truth of God for a lie. They worshiped and served created things rather than You, the Creator. Because of this, You gave them over to their captors. Therefore, I have no excuse when I pass judgment on others, if I practice the same sins for which I so eagerly judge them—greed, depravity, envy, murder, strife, deceit, malice, gossip, slander, arrogance. How can I escape Your judgment if I show contempt for You? In Your kindness, Lord, lead me to repentance. (Hab 2:4; Ro 1:18—2:4)

O Lord, forgive me for what I have been, sanctify what I am, and order what I shall be.

Frederick MacNutt (1873-1949)

(9:17–19) God and Father of our Lord Jesus Christ, let me be "a doorkeeper in the house of my God." In the service of Christ make me a steward of all that is sacred. In the spiritual temple of my heart, the temple made without hands, teach me to guard with care the holy things You have hidden there. And may the psalm of the sons of Korah become the prayer of my heart as well: "How lovely is Your dwelling place, O LORD Almighty! My soul yearns, even faints for the courts of the LORD; my heart and my flesh cry out for the living God. Blessed are those who dwell in your house; they are ever praising you. Better is one day in your courts than a thousand elsewhere; I would rather be a doorkeeper in the house of my God than dwell in the tents of the wicked." (Ps 84)

Who may ascend
To the hill of the Lord?
And who may stand
In His holy place?
He who has clean hands
And a pure heart
May ascend to the hill,
May ascend to the hill,
May ascend to the hill of the Lord.

Cleanse my hands
And my heart, oh Lord,
Come and purify me
In Your love
Fill my life
With Your righteousness
So that I may ascend to Your hill.

"Who May Ascend to the Hill of the Lord"
Kirk Dearman (©1989)

The highest service may be prepared for and done in the humblest surroundings. In silence, in waiting, in obscure, unnoticed offices, in years of uneventful, unrecorded duties, the Son of God grew and waxed strong.

Inscription in the Stanford University Chapel

13 The priests, who were heads of families, numbered
1,760. They were able men, responsible for ministering
in the house of God.
14 Of the Levites:
Shemaiah son of Hasshub, the son of Azrikam, the son of
Hashabiah, a Merarite; 15 Bakbakkar, Heresh, Galal and
Mattaniah son of Mica, the son of Zicri, the son of Asaph;
16 Obadiah son of Shemaiah, the son of Galal, the son of
Jeduthun; and Berekiah son of Asa, the son of Elkanah,
who lived in the villages of the Netophathites.
17 The gatekeepers:
Shallum, Akkub, Talmon, Ahiman and their brothers, Shallum their chief 18 being stationed at the King's Gate on the
east, up to the present time. These were the gatekeepers
belonging to the camp of the Levites. 19 Shallum son of
Kore, the son of Ebiasaph, the son of Korah, and his fellow
gatekeepers from his family (the Korahites) were responsible for guarding the thresholds of the Tent[a] just as their
fathers had been responsible for guarding the entrance to
the dwelling of the LORD. 20 In earlier times Phinehas son of
Eleazar was in charge of the gatekeepers, and the LORD was
with him. 21 Zechariah son of Meshelemiah was the gatekeeper at the entrance to the Tent of Meeting.
22 Altogether, those chosen to be gatekeepers at the thresholds
numbered 212. They were registered by genealogy in their villages. The gatekeepers had been assigned to their positions of
trust by David and Samuel the seer. 23 They and their descendants
were in charge of guarding the gates of the house of the LORD—
the house called the Tent. 24 The gatekeepers were on the four
sides: east, west, north and south. 25 Their brothers in their villages had to come from time to time and share their duties for
seven-day periods. 26 But the four principal gatekeepers, who
were Levites, were entrusted with the responsibility for the rooms
and treasuries in the house of God. 27 They would spend the night
stationed around the house of God, because they had to guard it;
and they had charge of the key for opening it each morning.
28 Some of them were in charge of the articles used in the temple service; they counted them when they were brought in and
when they were taken out. 29 Others were assigned to take care of
the furnishings and all the other articles of the sanctuary, as well
as the flour and wine, and the oil, incense and spices. 30 But some
of the priests took care of mixing the spices. 31 A Levite named
Mattithiah, the firstborn son of Shallum the Korahite, was entrusted with the responsibility for baking the offering bread.
32 Some of their Kohathite brothers were in charge of preparing
for every Sabbath the bread set out on the table.
33 Those who were musicians, heads of Levite families, stayed
in the rooms of the temple and were exempt from other duties
because they were responsible for the work day and night.
34 All these were heads of Levite families, chiefs as listed in
their genealogy, and they lived in Jerusalem.

The Genealogy of Saul

35 Jeiel the father[b] of Gibeon lived in Gibeon.
His wife's name was Maacah, 36 and his firstborn son was

[a] 19 That is, the temple; also in verses 21 and 23 [b] 35 *Father* may mean *civic leader* or *military leader.*

Abdon, followed by Zur, Kish, Baal, Ner, Nadab, 37 Gedor, Ahio, Zechariah and Mikloth. 38 Mikloth was the father of Shimeam. They too lived near their relatives in Jerusalem.

39 Ner was the father of Kish, Kish the father of Saul, and Saul the father of Jonathan, Malki-Shua, Abinadab and Esh-Baal.[a]

40 The son of Jonathan:

Merib-Baal,[b] who was the father of Micah.

41 The sons of Micah:

Pithon, Melech, Tahrea and Ahaz.[c]

42 Ahaz was the father of Jadah, Jadah[d] was the father of Alemeth, Azmaveth and Zimri, and Zimri was the father of Moza. 43 Moza was the father of Binea; Rephaiah was his son, Eleasah his son and Azel his son.

44 Azel had six sons, and these were their names:

Azrikam, Bokeru, Ishmael, Sheariah, Obadiah and Hanan. These were the sons of Azel.

Saul Takes His Life

10 Now the Philistines fought against Israel; the Israelites fled before them, and many fell slain on Mount Gilboa. 2 The Philistines pressed hard after Saul and his sons, and they killed his sons Jonathan, Abinadab and Malki-Shua. 3 The fighting grew fierce around Saul, and when the archers overtook him, they wounded him.

4 Saul said to his armor-bearer, "Draw your sword and run me through, or these uncircumcised fellows will come and abuse me."

But his armor-bearer was terrified and would not do it; so Saul took his own sword and fell on it. 5 When the armor-bearer saw that Saul was dead, he too fell on his sword and died. 6 So Saul and his three sons died, and all his house died together.

7 When all the Israelites in the valley saw that the army had fled and that Saul and his sons had died, they abandoned their towns and fled. And the Philistines came and occupied them.

8 The next day, when the Philistines came to strip the dead, they found Saul and his sons fallen on Mount Gilboa. 9 They stripped him and took his head and his armor, and sent messengers throughout the land of the Philistines to proclaim the news among their idols and their people. 10 They put his armor in the temple of their gods and hung up his head in the temple of Dagon.

11 When all the inhabitants of Jabesh Gilead heard of everything the Philistines had done to Saul, 12 all their valiant men went and took the bodies of Saul and his sons and brought them to Jabesh. Then they buried their bones under the great tree in Jabesh, and they fasted seven days.

13 Saul died because he was unfaithful to the LORD; he did not keep the word of the LORD and even consulted a medium for guidance, 14 and did not inquire of the LORD. So the LORD put him to death and turned the kingdom over to David son of Jesse.

[a] *39* Also known as *Ish-Bosheth* [b] *40* Also known as *Mephibosheth* [c] *41* Vulgate and Syriac (see also Septuagint and 1 Chron. 8:35); Hebrew does not have *and Ahaz.*
[d] *42* Some Hebrew manuscripts and Septuagint (see also 1 Chron. 8:36); most Hebrew manuscripts *Jarah, Jarah*

(10:8–10) Lord, how the wicked rage when I am unfaithful to You. How they love to see You disgraced! Keep me humble and obedient to You so that I never give Your enemies opportunity to mock You.

(10:13–14) Holy God, I repent of all that disqualifies me from sacred service to Your kingdom. Help me to keep Your Word. Put to death all that is unfaithful in me. Strengthen faith within me that my service to You may be pure. And may the kingdom of my world become the kingdom of my Lord and of His Christ—Jesus, the son of David. (Rev 11:15)

(11:1–3) Jesus, son of David, You are the Lord's Anointed, the Messiah. We are now Your people, and You are not ashamed to call us Your brothers and sisters. We pledge our loyalty to You. We lift You up as our King. Be our Shepherd. Be our Ruler. Be our Savior. Be our Lord. (Heb 2:11)

His name is Wonderful, His name is
Wonderful,
His name is Wonderful, Jesus, my
Lord,
He is the mighty King, Master of
everything,
His name is Wonderful, Jesus, my
Lord.
He's the great Shepherd, the Rock
of all ages,
Almighty God is He;
Bow down before Him, love and
adore Him;
His name is Wonderful, Jesus, my
Lord.

"His Name Is Wonderful"
Audrey Mieir (©1959, 1987)

(11:7) King Jesus, come take up residence in this once hostile fortress of my heart.

God has two dwellings: one in heaven, and the other in a meek and thankful heart.
Izaak Walton (1593-1683)

David Becomes King Over Israel

11 All Israel came together to David at Hebron and said, "We
are your own flesh and blood. 2In the past, even while Saul
was king, you were the one who led Israel on their military campaigns. And the LORD your God said to you, 'You will shepherd my
people Israel, and you will become their ruler.' "
3When all the elders of Israel had come to King David at Hebron, he made a compact with them at Hebron before the LORD,
and they anointed David king over Israel, as the LORD had promised through Samuel.

David Conquers Jerusalem

4David and all the Israelites marched to Jerusalem (that is,
Jebus). The Jebusites who lived there 5said to David, "You will
not get in here." Nevertheless, David captured the fortress of
Zion, the City of David.
6David had said, "Whoever leads the attack on the Jebusites
will become commander-in-chief." Joab son of Zeruiah went up
first, and so he received the command.
7David then took up residence in the fortress, and so it was
called the City of David. 8He built up the city around it, from the
supporting terraces[a] to the surrounding wall, while Joab restored
the rest of the city. 9And David became more and more powerful,
because the LORD Almighty was with him.

David's Mighty Men

10These were the chiefs of David's mighty men—they, together
with all Israel, gave his kingship strong support to extend it over
the whole land, as the LORD had promised— 11this is the list of
David's mighty men:
Jashobeam,[b] a Hacmonite, was chief of the officers[c]; he raised
his spear against three hundred men, whom he killed in one encounter.
12Next to him was Eleazar son of Dodai the Ahohite, one of the
three mighty men. 13He was with David at Pas Dammim when the
Philistines gathered there for battle. At a place where there was a
field full of barley, the troops fled from the Philistines. 14But they
took their stand in the middle of the field. They defended it and
struck the Philistines down, and the LORD brought about a great
victory.
15Three of the thirty chiefs came down to David to the rock at
the cave of Adullam, while a band of Philistines was encamped in
the Valley of Rephaim. 16At that time David was in the stronghold,
and the Philistine garrison was at Bethlehem. 17David longed for
water and said, "Oh, that someone would get me a drink of water
from the well near the gate of Bethlehem!" 18So the Three broke
through the Philistine lines, drew water from the well near the
gate of Bethlehem and carried it back to David. But he refused to
drink it; instead, he poured it out before the LORD. 19"God forbid
that I should do this!" he said. "Should I drink the blood of these
men who went at the risk of their lives?" Because they risked their
lives to bring it back, David would not drink it.
Such were the exploits of the three mighty men.
20Abishai the brother of Joab was chief of the Three. He raised

[a] 8 Or *the Millo* [b] 11 Possibly a variant of *Jashob-Baal* [c] 11 Or *Thirty*; some Septuagint manuscripts *Three* (see also 2 Samuel 23:8)

his spear against three hundred men, whom he killed, and so he
became as famous as the Three. 21He was doubly honored above
the Three and became their commander, even though he was not
included among them.

22Benaiah son of Jehoiada was a valiant fighter from Kabzeel,
who performed great exploits. He struck down two of Moab's best
men. He also went down into a pit on a snowy day and killed a
lion. 23And he struck down an Egyptian who was seven and a half
feet[a] tall. Although the Egyptian had a spear like a weaver's rod in
his hand, Benaiah went against him with a club. He snatched the
spear from the Egyptian's hand and killed him with his own spear.
24Such were the exploits of Benaiah son of Jehoiada; he too was
as famous as the three mighty men. 25He was held in greater
honor than any of the Thirty, but he was not included among the
Three. And David put him in charge of his bodyguard.

26The mighty men were:
Asahel the brother of Joab,
Elhanan son of Dodo from Bethlehem,
27Shammoth the Harorite,
Helez the Pelonite,
28Ira son of Ikkesh from Tekoa,
Abiezer from Anathoth,
29Sibbecai the Hushathite,
Ilai the Ahohite,
30Maharai the Netophathite,
Heled son of Baanah the Netophathite,
31Ithai son of Ribai from Gibeah in Benjamin,
Benaiah the Pirathonite,
32Hurai from the ravines of Gaash,
Abiel the Arbathite,
33Azmaveth the Baharumite,
Eliahba the Shaalbonite,
34the sons of Hashem the Gizonite,
Jonathan son of Shagee the Hararite,
35Ahiam son of Sacar the Hararite,
Eliphal son of Ur,
36Hepher the Mekerathite,
Ahijah the Pelonite,
37Hezro the Carmelite,
Naarai son of Ezbai,
38Joel the brother of Nathan,
Mibhar son of Hagri,
39Zelek the Ammonite,
Naharai the Berothite, the armor-bearer of Joab son of Zeruiah,
40Ira the Ithrite,
Gareb the Ithrite,
41Uriah the Hittite,
Zabad son of Ahlai,
42Adina son of Shiza the Reubenite, who was chief of the Reubenites, and the thirty with him,
43Hanan son of Maacah,
Joshaphat the Mithnite,
44Uzzia the Ashterathite,
Shama and Jeiel the sons of Hotham the Aroerite,

[a] 23 Hebrew *five cubits* (about 2.3 meters)

(11:26) Ascended One, we thank You that in times past You raised up mighty men and women in the midst of Your people for the service of righteousness. And we thank You for the mighty men and women You have given to Your church today: the apostles, prophets, evangelists, pastors and teachers—and others who are strong in the spiritual battles of our times. Because of their ministry we who were once Your enemies are now Your loyal servants. Bless them as they expand Your kingdom territory and prepare Your people for works of service. (Eph 4:10–13)

45Jediael son of Shimri,
his brother Joha the Tizite,
46Eliel the Mahavite,
Jeribai and Joshaviah the sons of Elnaam,
Ithmah the Moabite,
47Eliel, Obed and Jaasiel the Mezobaite.

Warriors Join David

12 These were the men who came to David at Ziklag, while he
was banished from the presence of Saul son of Kish (they
were among the warriors who helped him in battle; 2they were
armed with bows and were able to shoot arrows or to sling stones
right-handed or left-handed; they were kinsmen of Saul from the
tribe of Benjamin):

3Ahiezer their chief and Joash the sons of Shemaah the
Gibeathite; Jeziel and Pelet the sons of Azmaveth; Beracah,
Jehu the Anathothite, 4and Ishmaiah the Gibeonite, a mighty
man among the Thirty, who was a leader of the Thirty; Jeremiah, Jahaziel, Johanan, Jozabad the Gederathite, 5Eluzai,
Jerimoth, Bealiah, Shemariah and Shephatiah the Haruphite;
6Elkanah, Isshiah, Azarel, Joezer and Jashobeam the Korahites; 7and Joelah and Zebadiah the sons of Jeroham from
Gedor.

8Some Gadites defected to David at his stronghold in the
desert. They were brave warriors, ready for battle and able to
handle the shield and spear. Their faces were the faces of lions,
and they were as swift as gazelles in the mountains.

9Ezer was the chief,
Obadiah the second in command, Eliab the third,
10Mishmannah the fourth, Jeremiah the fifth,
11Attai the sixth, Eliel the seventh,
12Johanan the eighth, Elzabad the ninth,
13Jeremiah the tenth and Macbannai the eleventh.

14These Gadites were army commanders; the least was a match
for a hundred, and the greatest for a thousand. 15It was they who
crossed the Jordan in the first month when it was overflowing all
its banks, and they put to flight everyone living in the valleys, to
the east and to the west.

16Other Benjamites and some men from Judah also came to
David in his stronghold. 17David went out to meet them and said
to them, "If you have come to me in peace, to help me, I am ready
to have you unite with me. But if you have come to betray me to
my enemies when my hands are free from violence, may the God
of our fathers see it and judge you."

18Then the Spirit came upon Amasai, chief of the Thirty, and he
said:

"We are yours, O David!
We are with you, O son of Jesse!
Success, success to you,
and success to those who help you,
for your God will help you."

So David received them and made them leaders of his raiding
bands.

19Some of the men of Manasseh defected to David when he
went with the Philistines to fight against Saul. (He and his men did

(12:18) These men joined David because they knew he was the Lord's anointed. And so I join myself to You, Lord Christ, the Anointed One, the true Messiah. Among people of this world, You are not yet recognized as the great King; their allegiance is to another prince. But I come to You in peace, O Prince of Peace. I join You in the fellowship of Your suffering, knowing that if I endure, I will also reign with You in Your kingdom. (Php 3:10–11; 2Ti 2:12)

Blessed master, we are at peace with Thee so completely as to be at one with Thee. What Thou sayest we believe; what Thou doest we admire, what Thou commandest we obey; what Thou claimest we resign; what Thou forbiddest we forego. We yield ourselves up to Thee wholly, and are at perfect peace with Thee in all Thy purposes, and designs and acts. Peace, peace to Thee.

Charles Haddon Spurgeon (1834–1892)

I am resolved to follow the Savior,
Faithful and true each day.
Heed what He sayeth, do what He
willeth;
He is the Living Way.

"I Am Resolved"
Palmer Hartsough (1844–1932)

not help the Philistines because, after consultation, their rulers
sent him away. They said, "It will cost us our heads if he deserts
to his master Saul.") 20When David went to Ziklag, these were
the men of Manasseh who defected to him: Adnah, Jozabad, Jediael, Michael, Jozabad, Elihu and Zillethai, leaders of units of a
thousand in Manasseh. 21They helped David against raiding
bands, for all of them were brave warriors, and they were commanders in his army. 22Day after day men came to help David,
until he had a great army, like the army of God.[a]

Others Join David at Hebron

23These are the numbers of the men armed for battle who
came to David at Hebron to turn Saul's kingdom over to him, as
the LORD had said:

24men of Judah, carrying shield and spear—6,800 armed for battle;

25men of Simeon, warriors ready for battle—7,100;

26men of Levi—4,600, 27including Jehoiada, leader of the
family of Aaron, with 3,700 men, 28and Zadok, a brave
young warrior, with 22 officers from his family;

29men of Benjamin, Saul's kinsmen—3,000, most of whom had remained loyal to Saul's house until then;

30men of Ephraim, brave warriors, famous in their own clans—20,800;

31men of half the tribe of Manasseh, designated by name to come and make David king—18,000;

32men of Issachar, who understood the times and knew what Israel should do—200 chiefs, with all their relatives under their command;

33men of Zebulun, experienced soldiers prepared for battle with every type of weapon, to help David with undivided loyalty—50,000;

34men of Naphtali—1,000 officers, together with 37,000 men carrying shields and spears;

35men of Dan, ready for battle—28,600;

36men of Asher, experienced soldiers prepared for battle—40,000;

37and from east of the Jordan, men of Reuben, Gad and the half-tribe of Manasseh, armed with every type of weapon—120,000.

38All these were fighting men who volunteered to serve in the
ranks. They came to Hebron fully determined to make David king
over all Israel. All the rest of the Israelites were also of one mind
to make David king. 39The men spent three days there with David,
eating and drinking, for their families had supplied provisions for
them. 40Also, their neighbors from as far away as Issachar, Zebulun and Naphtali came bringing food on donkeys, camels, mules
and oxen. There were plentiful supplies of flour, fig cakes, raisin
cakes, wine, oil, cattle and sheep, for there was joy in Israel.

Bringing Back the Ark

13 David conferred with each of his officers, the commanders
of thousands and commanders of hundreds. 2He then said
to the whole assembly of Israel, "If it seems good to you and if it
is the will of the LORD our God, let us send word far and wide to

[a] 22 Or *a great and mighty army*

(12:22) As we go forward, followers of a greater King even than David of old, championing the cause of Christ, we thank You, Lord, for adding to our number daily those who are being saved. (Ac 2:47)

Fierce may be the conflict,
Strong may be the foe,
But the King's own army
None can overthrow.
Round His standard ranging;
Vict'ry is secure;
For His truth unchanging
Makes the triumph sure.
Joyfully enlisting
By Thy grace divine,
We are on the Lord's side,
Savior, we are Thine.

"Who Is On the Lord's Side?"
Frances Ridley Havergal (1836–1879)

(12:38–40) Just as Your people gathered together to celebrate the rule of King David, we Your people today, who are scattered throughout the earth, look forward to the day when we will feast together in the joy of Your table and celebrate our covenant with You. There we will proclaim Christ as King of kings and Lord of lords of the earth. In the meantime, I celebrate my relationship with You and invite You to take Your rightful place on the throne of my heart.

Wherever God rules over the human heart as King, there is the kingdom of God established.

Paul W. Harrison (1883-)

the rest of our brothers throughout the territories of Israel, and
also to the priests and Levites who are with them in their towns
and pasturelands, to come and join us. 3Let us bring the ark of our
God back to us, for we did not inquire of[a] it[b] during the reign of
Saul." 4The whole assembly agreed to do this, because it seemed
right to all the people.
5So David assembled all the Israelites, from the Shihor River in
Egypt to Lebo[c] Hamath, to bring the ark of God from Kiriath Jearim. 6David and all the Israelites with him went to Baalah of Judah
(Kiriath Jearim) to bring up from there the ark of God the LORD,
who is enthroned between the cherubim—the ark that is called by
the Name.
7They moved the ark of God from Abinadab's house on a new
cart, with Uzzah and Ahio guiding it. 8David and all the Israelites
were celebrating with all their might before God, with songs and
with harps, lyres, tambourines, cymbals and trumpets.
9When they came to the threshing floor of Kidon, Uzzah reached
out his hand to steady the ark, because the oxen stumbled. 10The
LORD's anger burned against Uzzah, and he struck him down because he had put his hand on the ark. So he died there before God.
11Then David was angry because the LORD's wrath had broken
out against Uzzah, and to this day that place is called Perez Uzzah.[d]
12David was afraid of God that day and asked, "How can I ever
bring the ark of God to me?" 13He did not take the ark to be with
him in the City of David. Instead, he took it aside to the house of
Obed-Edom the Gittite. 14The ark of God remained with the family of Obed-Edom in his house for three months, and the LORD
blessed his household and everything he had.

David's House and Family

14 Now Hiram king of Tyre sent messengers to David, along
with cedar logs, stonemasons and carpenters to build a
palace for him. 2And David knew that the LORD had established
him as king over Israel and that his kingdom had been highly exalted for the sake of his people Israel.
3In Jerusalem David took more wives and became the father of
more sons and daughters. 4These are the names of the children
born to him there: Shammua, Shobab, Nathan, Solomon, 5Ibhar,
Elishua, Elpelet, 6Nogah, Nepheg, Japhia, 7Elishama, Beeliada[e]
and Eliphelet.

David Defeats the Philistines

8When the Philistines heard that David had been anointed king
over all Israel, they went up in full force to search for him, but
David heard about it and went out to meet them. 9Now the Philistines had come and raided the Valley of Rephaim; 10so David inquired of God: "Shall I go and attack the Philistines? Will you hand
them over to me?"
The LORD answered him, "Go, I will hand them over to you."
11So David and his men went up to Baal Perazim, and there he
defeated them. He said, "As waters break out, God has broken out
against my enemies by my hand." So that place was called Baal Perazim.[f] 12The Philistines had abandoned their gods there, and David
gave orders to burn them in the fire.

[a] 3 Or *we neglected* [b] 3 Or *him* [c] 5 Or *to the entrance to* [d] 11 *Perez Uzzah* means *outbreak against Uzzah.* [e] 7 A variant of *Eliada* [f] 11 *Baal Perazim* means *the lord who breaks out.*

(13:3) Father in heaven, we have sought Your King, that Your kingdom may come. Now we seek Your wisdom, that Your will may be done.

(13:10) I confess to You, O Lord, that at times I have been careless as I have handled sacred things. Yet, in Your mercy, You have not broken out upon me as You did upon Uzzah when he grabbed the ark with his hand. Help me to be more careful as I handle sacred things, particularly as I minister Your Word among Your people in Your house. Help me to balance the joy of the Lord with the fear of the Lord. Purify me so that I might serve You in worship that is in spirit and in truth. (Ps 2:11)

(14:12) All that the world relies on will be abandoned in the fray. All idols will become fuel for the fire of Your judgment. King Jesus, lead the way in the battle against my enemies: sin, despair, self-reliance, doubt. Take all of the idols that I have relied on and throw them into the fire. There is no God but the one true God—the God and Father of our Lord Jesus Christ.

13Once more the Philistines raided the valley; 14so David inquired of God again, and God answered him, "Do not go straight up, but circle around them and attack them in front of the balsam trees. 15As soon as you hear the sound of marching in the tops of the balsam trees, move out to battle, because that will mean God has gone out in front of you to strike the Philistine army." 16So David did as God commanded him, and they struck down the Philistine army, all the way from Gibeon to Gezer.

17So David's fame spread throughout every land, and the LORD made all the nations fear him.

The Ark Brought to Jerusalem

15 After David had constructed buildings for himself in the City of David, he prepared a place for the ark of God and pitched a tent for it. 2Then David said, "No one but the Levites may carry the ark of God, because the LORD chose them to carry the ark of the LORD and to minister before him forever."

3David assembled all Israel in Jerusalem to bring up the ark of the LORD to the place he had prepared for it. 4He called together the descendants of Aaron and the Levites:

5From the descendants of Kohath,
Uriel the leader and 120 relatives;
6from the descendants of Merari,
Asaiah the leader and 220 relatives;
7from the descendants of Gershon,[a]
Joel the leader and 130 relatives;
8from the descendants of Elizaphan,
Shemaiah the leader and 200 relatives;
9from the descendants of Hebron,
Eliel the leader and 80 relatives;
10from the descendants of Uzziel,
Amminadab the leader and 112 relatives.

11Then David summoned Zadok and Abiathar the priests, and Uriel, Asaiah, Joel, Shemaiah, Eliel and Amminadab the Levites. 12He said to them, "You are the heads of the Levitical families; you and your fellow Levites are to consecrate yourselves and bring up the ark of the LORD, the God of Israel, to the place I have prepared for it. 13It was because you, the Levites, did not bring it up the first time that the LORD our God broke out in anger against us. We did not inquire of him about how to do it in the prescribed way." 14So the priests and Levites consecrated themselves in order to bring up the ark of the LORD, the God of Israel. 15And the Levites carried the ark of God with the poles on their shoulders, as Moses had commanded in accordance with the word of the LORD.

16David told the leaders of the Levites to appoint their brothers as singers to sing joyful songs, accompanied by musical instruments: lyres, harps and cymbals.

17So the Levites appointed Heman son of Joel; from his brothers, Asaph son of Berekiah; and from their brothers the Merarites, Ethan son of Kushaiah; 18and with them their brothers next in rank: Zechariah,[b] Jaaziel, Shemiramoth, Jehiel, Unni, Eliab, Benaiah, Maaseiah, Mattithiah, Eliphelehu, Mikneiah, Obed-Edom and Jeiel,[c] the gatekeepers.

[a] 7 Hebrew *Gershom,* a variant of *Gershon* [b] 18 Three Hebrew manuscripts and most Septuagint manuscripts (see also verse 20 and 1 Chron. 16:5); most Hebrew manuscripts *Zechariah son and* or *Zechariah, Ben and* [c] 18 Hebrew; Septuagint (see also verse 21) *Jeiel and Azaziah*

(14:13–16) Again and again I encounter the same enemies. But I will not lean on my own understanding, nor will I presume upon my past experiences of Your grace. I will humble myself and seek Your saving hand once again. As You are the storehouse of my daily bread, so You will be the strategist of my daily battles. In all my ways I will acknowledge You, and I will marvel as You direct my paths. (Pr 3:5–6)

(15:3) The ark of the covenant was a solemn, wondrous symbol of Your presence in Israel. It contained the tablets of Your gracious Law. With joyful celebration, David transported the ark to Jerusalem that Your Word and Your presence might rest at the center of Your people. And so today, we declare with Your servant David that we have hidden Your Word in our hearts, that it may be at the center of our community with one another, at the center of our commerce with the world, and at the center of our covenant with You.

19 The musicians Heman, Asaph and Ethan were to sound the
bronze cymbals; 20 Zechariah, Aziel, Shemiramoth, Jehiel, Unni,
Eliab, Maaseiah and Benaiah were to play the lyres according to
alamoth,[a] 21 and Mattithiah, Eliphelehu, Mikneiah, Obed-Edom,
Jeiel and Azaziah were to play the harps, directing according to
sheminith.[a] 22 Kenaniah the head Levite was in charge of the
singing; that was his responsibility because he was skillful at it.
23 Berekiah and Elkanah were to be doorkeepers for the ark.
24 Shebaniah, Joshaphat, Nethanel, Amasai, Zechariah, Benaiah
and Eliezer the priests were to blow trumpets before the ark of
God. Obed-Edom and Jehiah were also to be doorkeepers for the
ark.

25 So David and the elders of Israel and the commanders of
units of a thousand went to bring up the ark of the covenant of the
LORD from the house of Obed-Edom, with rejoicing. 26 Because
God had helped the Levites who were carrying the ark of the covenant of the LORD, seven bulls and seven rams were sacrificed.
27 Now David was clothed in a robe of fine linen, as were all the
Levites who were carrying the ark, and as were the singers, and
Kenaniah, who was in charge of the singing of the choirs. David
also wore a linen ephod. 28 So all Israel brought up the ark of the
covenant of the LORD with shouts, with the sounding of rams'
horns and trumpets, and of cymbals, and the playing of lyres and
harps.

29 As the ark of the covenant of the LORD was entering the City
of David, Michal daughter of Saul watched from a window. And
when she saw King David dancing and celebrating, she despised
him in her heart.

16 They brought the ark of God and set it inside the tent that
David had pitched for it, and they presented burnt offerings and fellowship offerings[b] before God. 2 After David had finished sacrificing the burnt offerings and fellowship offerings, he
blessed the people in the name of the LORD. 3 Then he gave a loaf
of bread, a cake of dates and a cake of raisins to each Israelite
man and woman.

4 He appointed some of the Levites to minister before the ark of
the LORD, to make petition, to give thanks, and to praise the LORD,
the God of Israel: 5 Asaph was the chief, Zechariah second, then
Jeiel, Shemiramoth, Jehiel, Mattithiah, Eliab, Benaiah, Obed-
Edom and Jeiel. They were to play the lyres and harps, Asaph was
to sound the cymbals, 6 and Benaiah and Jahaziel the priests were
to blow the trumpets regularly before the ark of the covenant of
God.

David's Psalm of Thanks

7 That day David first committed to Asaph and his associates
this psalm of thanks to the LORD:

8 Give thanks to the LORD, call on his name;
make known among the nations what he has done.
9 Sing to him, sing praise to him;
tell of all his wonderful acts.
10 Glory in his holy name;
let the hearts of those who seek the LORD rejoice.
11 Look to the LORD and his strength;
seek his face always.

[a] *20,21* Probably a musical term [b] *1* Traditionally *peace offerings*; also in verse 2

(15:29) I wonder why Michal despised her husband, David, when he danced before the ark of the covenant with such abandon? Was it because she recognized that he had a spiritual anointing that her father, Saul, once had enjoyed, but then had lost? Was it because she recognized that David had an all-absorbing devotion to You, his Lord, which offended her? I wonder why it is that the worldly-wise find the godly so unbearable. O Lord, may my personal sense of appropriate worship never impose itself on the joy of others.

(16:1–3) When You are present, Lord, in the midst of Your people, what can we do but bring sacrifices of praise to You and pledge ourselves to Your service? Take me, O God. I offer my body, my mind and my soul as a living sacrifice. (Ro 12:1)

(16:7–36) With Your ancient people Israel, we who know You implore You to make Your name known among the nations. Will You be pleased to use us in this task? We magnify Your name, O Yahweh. We praise Your name, O living Jesus.

MY BELOVED

I know that you have grown weary. Look to Me for strength and seek My face always. Trust in Me and do not be afraid.

Lift your eyes and look to the heavens: Who created all this? I bring out the starry host one by one and call them each by name. Because of My great power and mighty strength, not one of them is missing. So why do you say, "God doesn't see me; He has disregarded my cause"?

Don't you know? Haven't you heard? I am the everlasting God, the Creator of the ends of the earth. I will not grow tired or weary, and My understanding no one can fathom. I give strength to the weary and increase the power of the weak. So I will strengthen you and help you. With My right hand I will hold you up. When you run you will not stumble or fall. In fact, you will feel like an eagle soaring above the world and all its problems.

So sing of My love and strength in the morning and of My faithfulness at night. For I am your Fortress; I am your Refuge in times of trouble. I am your God, and I love you.

I am your Strength. I am your Song. I am your Salvation. Trust in Me and do not be afraid. When your soul is weary with sorrow, I will strengthen you according to My Word.

Ps 59:16-17; 92:2; 118:14; 119:28; Isa 12:2; 40:26-31; 41:10

12 Remember the wonders he has done,
his miracles, and the judgments he pronounced,
13 O descendants of Israel his servant,
O sons of Jacob, his chosen ones.

14 He is the LORD our God;
his judgments are in all the earth.
15 He remembers[a] his covenant forever,
the word he commanded, for a thousand generations,
16 the covenant he made with Abraham,
the oath he swore to Isaac.
17 He confirmed it to Jacob as a decree,
to Israel as an everlasting covenant:
18 "To you I will give the land of Canaan
as the portion you will inherit."

19 When they were but few in number,
few indeed, and strangers in it,
20 they[b] wandered from nation to nation,
from one kingdom to another.
21 He allowed no man to oppress them;
for their sake he rebuked kings:
22 "Do not touch my anointed ones;
do my prophets no harm."

23 Sing to the LORD, all the earth;
proclaim his salvation day after day.
24 Declare his glory among the nations,
his marvelous deeds among all peoples.
25 For great is the LORD and most worthy of praise;
he is to be feared above all gods.
26 For all the gods of the nations are idols,
but the LORD made the heavens.
27 Splendor and majesty are before him;
strength and joy in his dwelling place.
28 Ascribe to the LORD, O families of nations,
ascribe to the LORD glory and strength,
29 ascribe to the LORD the glory due his name.
Bring an offering and come before him;
worship the LORD in the splendor of his[c] holiness.
30 Tremble before him, all the earth!
The world is firmly established; it cannot be moved.
31 Let the heavens rejoice, let the earth be glad;
let them say among the nations, "The LORD reigns!"
32 Let the sea resound, and all that is in it;
let the fields be jubilant, and everything in them!
33 Then the trees of the forest will sing,
they will sing for joy before the LORD,
for he comes to judge the earth.

34 Give thanks to the LORD, for he is good;
his love endures forever.
35 Cry out, "Save us, O God our Savior;

[a] *15* Some Septuagint manuscripts (see also Psalm 105:8); Hebrew *Remember*
[b] *18–20* One Hebrew manuscript, Septuagint and Vulgate (see also Psalm 105:12); most Hebrew manuscripts *inherit, / 19though you are but few in number, / few indeed, and strangers in it." / 20They*
[c] *29* Or *LORD with the splendor of*

(16:15–25) Blessed are You, O God and Father of my Lord Jesus Christ. You have made me Yours and joined me to Yourself in the covenant You made with Abraham, Isaac and Jacob, together with Your people for a thousand generations. It is my covenant responsibility to remember Your mighty acts of redemption and Your judgments, and to recount the story of Your wonderful works. It is my covenant responsibility to worship You by remembering Your promises and rejoicing in their fulfillment. It is my covenant responsibility to declare Your glory among the nations, Your marvelous deeds among all peoples. For You are great and most worthy of praise.

We declare Your majesty,
We proclaim that Your name is exalted!
For You reign magnificently,
Rule victoriously
And Your power is shown
Throughout the earth.

And we exclaim:
"Our God is mighty!"
Lift up Your name,
For You are holy!
Sing it again,
All honor and glory!
In adoration we bow
Before Your throne!

"We Declare Your Majesty"
Malcolm duPlessis (©1985)

gather us and deliver us from the nations,
that we may give thanks to your holy name,
that we may glory in your praise."
36 Praise be to the LORD, the God of Israel,
from everlasting to everlasting.

Then all the people said "Amen" and "Praise the LORD."

37 David left Asaph and his associates before the ark of the covenant of the LORD to minister there regularly, according to each day's requirements.
38 He also left Obed-Edom and his sixty-eight associates to minister with them. Obed-Edom son of Jeduthun, and also Hosah, were gatekeepers.

39 David left Zadok the priest and his fellow priests before the tabernacle of the LORD at the high place in Gibeon
40 to present burnt offerings to the LORD on the altar of burnt offering regularly, morning and evening, in accordance with everything written in the Law of the LORD, which he had given Israel.
41 With them were Heman and Jeduthun and the rest of those chosen and designated by name to give thanks to the LORD, "for his love endures forever."
42 Heman and Jeduthun were responsible for the sounding of the trumpets and cymbals and for the playing of the other instruments for sacred song. The sons of Jeduthun were stationed at the gate.

43 Then all the people left, each for his own home, and David returned home to bless his family.

(17:4–10) You raised up David, the shepherd king, and gave him a name that was great among the nations. Now You have raised up Jesus, the Son of David, as our Shepherd King. You have exalted Him to the highest place and have given Him the name that is above every name. You will subdue His enemies and make them a footstool for His feet. You will build a house for Him, and Your people will live in peace. Glory to God in the highest! (Ps 110:1; Eze 40—48; Zep 3:14–20; Php 2:9–11)

God's Promise to David

17 After David was settled in his palace, he said to Nathan the prophet, "Here I am, living in a palace of cedar, while the ark of the covenant of the LORD is under a tent."

2 Nathan replied to David, "Whatever you have in mind, do it, for God is with you."

3 That night the word of God came to Nathan, saying:

4 "Go and tell my servant David, 'This is what the LORD says: You are not the one to build me a house to dwell in.
5 I have not dwelt in a house from the day I brought Israel up out of Egypt to this day. I have moved from one tent site to another, from one dwelling place to another.
6 Wherever I have moved with all the Israelites, did I ever say to any of their leaders[a] whom I commanded to shepherd my people, "Why have you not built me a house of cedar?" '

7 "Now then, tell my servant David, 'This is what the LORD Almighty says: I took you from the pasture and from following the flock, to be ruler over my people Israel.
8 I have been with you wherever you have gone, and I have cut off all your enemies from before you. Now I will make your name like the names of the greatest men of the earth.
9 And I will provide a place for my people Israel and will plant them so that they can have a home of their own and no longer be disturbed. Wicked people will not oppress them anymore, as they did at the beginning
10 and have done ever since the time I appointed leaders over my people Israel. I will also subdue all your enemies.

" 'I declare to you that the LORD will build a house for you:
11 When your days are over and you go to be with your

[a] 6 Traditionally *judges*; also in verse 10

fathers, I will raise up your offspring to succeed you, one
of your own sons, and I will establish his kingdom. 12He is
the one who will build a house for me, and I will establish
his throne forever. 13I will be his father, and he will be my
son. I will never take my love away from him, as I took it
away from your predecessor. 14I will set him over my
house and my kingdom forever; his throne will be established forever.' "
15Nathan reported to David all the words of this entire revelation.

David's Prayer

16Then King David went in and sat before the LORD, and he
said:

"Who am I, O LORD God, and what is my family, that you
have brought me this far? 17And as if this were not enough in
your sight, O God, you have spoken about the future of the
house of your servant. You have looked on me as though I
were the most exalted of men, O LORD God.
18"What more can David say to you for honoring your
servant? For you know your servant, 19O LORD. For the sake
of your servant and according to your will, you have done
this great thing and made known all these great promises.
20"There is no one like you, O LORD, and there is no God
but you, as we have heard with our own ears. 21And who is
like your people Israel—the one nation on earth whose God
went out to redeem a people for himself, and to make a
name for yourself, and to perform great and awesome wonders by driving out nations from before your people, whom
you redeemed from Egypt? 22You made your people Israel
your very own forever, and you, O LORD, have become their
God.
23"And now, LORD, let the promise you have made concerning your servant and his house be established forever.
Do as you promised, 24so that it will be established and that
your name will be great forever. Then men will say, 'The
LORD Almighty, the God over Israel, is Israel's God!' And the
house of your servant David will be established before you.
25"You, my God, have revealed to your servant that you
will build a house for him. So your servant has found
courage to pray to you. 26O LORD, you are God! You have
promised these good things to your servant. 27Now you have
been pleased to bless the house of your servant, that it may
continue forever in your sight; for you, O LORD, have blessed
it, and it will be blessed forever."

David's Victories

18 In the course of time, David defeated the Philistines and
subdued them, and he took Gath and its surrounding villages from the control of the Philistines.
2David also defeated the Moabites, and they became subject to
him and brought tribute.
3Moreover, David fought Hadadezer king of Zobah, as far as
Hamath, when he went to establish his control along the Euphrates River. 4David captured a thousand of his chariots, seven thou-

(17:11–14) Oh the depth of the love You had for David. Oh the heights to which You esteemed him. And what deeper love and greater esteem You have for the Son of David! For it is He who fulfills completely all the promises You made to David. His name is Jesus, and He is truly the Son of the Most High. For You have given Him "the throne of his father David, and he will reign over the house of Jacob forever; his kingdom will never end." He is indeed the Messiah who fulfills the hope of David; and He will build the house of the Lord. (Lk 1:32–33)

(17:16) O God, I confess with David that I am unworthy of any of Your mercies. Yet You have called me to come and join myself to Christ, the long-promised Son of David, the Prince of the house of Israel. Why have You chosen my family and me? That You should call me is a wondrous mystery. All I can do in return is to acknowledge Your wonder and live in joyful response to Your grace.

(18:9–11) Lord God, You prospered the work of David's hand, and David dedicated his prosperity to the work of Your service. In all the victories of my life, I dedicate to You the riches and the honor, for though they are in part the rewards of the sweat of my brow, they are ultimately and truly the gift of Your hand.

Savior, Thy dying love Thou gavest
me,
Nor should I aught withhold,
Dear Lord, from Thee;
In love my soul would bow,
My heart fulfill its vow,
Some off'ring bring Thee now,
Something for Thee.

"Something for Thee"
Sylvanus D. Phelps (1816-1895)

(18:14–17) Lord God, You are most righteous in all Your judgments. You called David to administer justice and equity to all his people. Now we Your people find justice and equity in Jesus Christ, the Son of David. In Him is the perfect rule of life. We take Jesus Christ as our Captain of Salvation and Prince of Peace. May He lead us to victory in our life and peace in the world to come.

sand charioteers and twenty thousand foot soldiers. He hamstrung all but a hundred of the chariot horses.

5 When the Arameans of Damascus came to help Hadadezer king of Zobah, David struck down twenty-two thousand of them. 6 He put garrisons in the Aramean kingdom of Damascus, and the Arameans became subject to him and brought tribute. The LORD gave David victory everywhere he went.

7 David took the gold shields carried by the officers of Hadadezer and brought them to Jerusalem. 8 From Tebah[a] and Cun, towns that belonged to Hadadezer, David took a great quantity of bronze, which Solomon used to make the bronze Sea, the pillars and various bronze articles.

9 When Tou king of Hamath heard that David had defeated the entire army of Hadadezer king of Zobah, 10 he sent his son Hadoram to King David to greet him and congratulate him on his victory in battle over Hadadezer, who had been at war with Tou. Hadoram brought all kinds of articles of gold and silver and bronze.

11 King David dedicated these articles to the LORD, as he had done with the silver and gold he had taken from all these nations: Edom and Moab, the Ammonites and the Philistines, and Amalek.

12 Abishai son of Zeruiah struck down eighteen thousand Edomites in the Valley of Salt. 13 He put garrisons in Edom, and all the Edomites became subject to David. The LORD gave David victory everywhere he went.

David's Officials

14 David reigned over all Israel, doing what was just and right for all his people. 15 Joab son of Zeruiah was over the army; Jehoshaphat son of Ahilud was recorder; 16 Zadok son of Ahitub and Ahimelech[b] son of Abiathar were priests; Shavsha was secretary; 17 Benaiah son of Jehoiada was over the Kerethites and Pelethites; and David's sons were chief officials at the king's side.

The Battle Against the Ammonites

19 In the course of time, Nahash king of the Ammonites died, and his son succeeded him as king. 2 David thought, "I will show kindness to Hanun son of Nahash, because his father showed kindness to me." So David sent a delegation to express his sympathy to Hanun concerning his father.

When David's men came to Hanun in the land of the Ammonites to express sympathy to him, 3 the Ammonite nobles said to Hanun, "Do you think David is honoring your father by sending men to you to express sympathy? Haven't his men come to you to explore and spy out the country and overthrow it?" 4 So Hanun seized David's men, shaved them, cut off their garments in the middle at the buttocks, and sent them away.

5 When someone came and told David about the men, he sent messengers to meet them, for they were greatly humiliated. The king said, "Stay at Jericho till your beards have grown, and then come back."

6 When the Ammonites realized that they had become a stench in David's nostrils, Hanun and the Ammonites sent a thousand talents[c] of silver to hire chariots and charioteers from Aram Naharaim,[d] Aram Maacah and Zobah. 7 They hired thirty-two thou-

[a] 8 Hebrew *Tibhath,* a variant of *Tebah* [b] 16 Some Hebrew manuscripts, Vulgate and Syriac (see also 2 Samuel 8:17); most Hebrew manuscripts *Abimelech* [c] 6 That is, about 37 tons (about 34 metric tons) [d] 6 That is, Northwest Mesopotamia

sand chariots and charioteers, as well as the king of Maacah with his troops, who came and camped near Medeba, while the Ammonites were mustered from their towns and moved out for battle.

8On hearing this, David sent Joab out with the entire army of fighting men. 9The Ammonites came out and drew up in battle formation at the entrance to their city, while the kings who had come were by themselves in the open country.

10Joab saw that there were battle lines in front of him and behind him; so he selected some of the best troops in Israel and deployed them against the Arameans. 11He put the rest of the men under the command of Abishai his brother, and they were deployed against the Ammonites. 12Joab said, "If the Arameans are too strong for me, then you are to rescue me; but if the Ammonites are too strong for you, then I will rescue you. 13Be strong and let us fight bravely for our people and the cities of our God. The LORD will do what is good in his sight."

14Then Joab and the troops with him advanced to fight the Arameans, and they fled before him. 15When the Ammonites saw that the Arameans were fleeing, they too fled before his brother Abishai and went inside the city. So Joab went back to Jerusalem.

16After the Arameans saw that they had been routed by Israel, they sent messengers and had Arameans brought from beyond the River,[a] with Shophach the commander of Hadadezer's army leading them.

17When David was told of this, he gathered all Israel and crossed the Jordan; he advanced against them and formed his battle lines opposite them. David formed his lines to meet the Arameans in battle, and they fought against him. 18But they fled before Israel, and David killed seven thousand of their charioteers and forty thousand of their foot soldiers. He also killed Shophach the commander of their army.

19When the vassals of Hadadezer saw that they had been defeated by Israel, they made peace with David and became subject to him.

So the Arameans were not willing to help the Ammonites anymore.

The Capture of Rabbah

20 In the spring, at the time when kings go off to war, Joab led out the armed forces. He laid waste the land of the Ammonites and went to Rabbah and besieged it, but David remained in Jerusalem. Joab attacked Rabbah and left it in ruins.
2David took the crown from the head of their king[b]—its weight was found to be a talent[c] of gold, and it was set with precious stones—and it was placed on David's head. He took a great quantity of plunder from the city 3and brought out the people who were there, consigning them to labor with saws and with iron picks and axes. David did this to all the Ammonite towns. Then David and his entire army returned to Jerusalem.

War With the Philistines

4In the course of time, war broke out with the Philistines, at Gezer. At that time Sibbecai the Hushathite killed Sippai, one of

[a] *16* That is, the Euphrates [b] *2* Or *of Milcom,* that is, Molech [c] *2* That is, about 75 pounds (about 34 kilograms)

(19:12–13) As with Joab, so may the commitment of my heart be to stand firm in faith and courage, to be strong and to do everything in love. May I fight bravely for Your people on the battlefield of the spirit, waging a war of passionate prayer for Your kingdom. Lord, hear my prayers of intercession and do what is good in Your sight. (1Co 16:13–14)

(20:1) "But David remained in Jerusalem." At times, O Lord, our sins are so well known that it is not necessary to speak of them in detail; a brief phrase may be a shadow that covers the horror. Yet, in Your mercy, such sins may be forgiven and lost forever in the sea of Your forgetfulness. (2Sa 11)

It is not only temptation that tries the generous Christian, but at times sin also; he may have a heavy fall, one that he had thought impossible, so deep and strong had seemed his love for the Lord. And having fallen, he is likely to become discouraged. Never before has he understood to such an extent the ugliness of sin—because he has now a greater understanding of the love of God.

All is grace. This fall will make him realize that he cannot rely on himself at all. It will put him in his place—at the bottom. But with this mistrust of himself must go a greater confidence in God, the Father.

Michel Quoist (1921-)

There's a wideness in God's mercy
Like the wideness of the sea;
There's a kindness in His justice
Which is more than liberty.

There is welcome for the sinner
And more graces for the good;
There is mercy with the Savior;
There is healing in His blood.

For the love of God is broader
Than the measure of man's mind;
And the heart of the Eternal
Is most wonderfully kind.

"There's a Wideness in God's Mercy"
Frederick W. Faber (1862)

(21:1) "Our Father in heaven . . . lead us not into temptation" In my service to You, do not let Satan stand up against me and incite me to do evil. Even Your most devout followers can be deceived by the enemy of our souls. Let me never be so proud as to think that I am out of the reach of temptation. Lord, have mercy. (Mt 6:9,13)

(21:7) O Lord, from whom all true power and might come, I confess that I spend too much time counting my troops, assessing my abilities, reckoning how much strength I have in my own hands. I confess that too often I count on my power rather than on Your power. Cleanse me from pride. Deliver me from self-reliance. Forgive me for even imagining that my victories are the reward of my own righteousness. To You belong all might and power. Yours is the victory.

(21:13–15) "Enough! Withdraw your hand." When we put ourselves in Your hands, O Lord, even in Your wrath You show us mercy. For judgment is ever Your "strange work." You will not always accuse, neither will You harbor Your anger forever. In this sacred place, the threshing floor of Araunah, on Mt. Moriah, the place of Your covenant with Abraham, You stayed the sword of punishment and extended Your hand of grace. (Ge 22; Ps 103:9; Isa 28:21; Hab 3:2)

the descendants of the Rephaites, and the Philistines were subjugated.
5In another battle with the Philistines, Elhanan son of Jair
killed Lahmi the brother of Goliath the Gittite, who had a spear
with a shaft like a weaver's rod.
6In still another battle, which took place at Gath, there was a
huge man with six fingers on each hand and six toes on each
foot—twenty-four in all. He also was descended from Rapha.
7When he taunted Israel, Jonathan son of Shimea, David's brother, killed him.
8These were descendants of Rapha in Gath, and they fell at the
hands of David and his men.

David Numbers the Fighting Men

21 Satan rose up against Israel and incited David to take a
census of Israel. 2So David said to Joab and the commanders of the troops, "Go and count the Israelites from Beersheba to
Dan. Then report back to me so that I may know how many there
are."
3But Joab replied, "May the LORD multiply his troops a hundred times over. My lord the king, are they not all my lord's subjects? Why does my lord want to do this? Why should he bring
guilt on Israel?"
4The king's word, however, overruled Joab; so Joab left and
went throughout Israel and then came back to Jerusalem. 5Joab
reported the number of the fighting men to David: In all Israel
there were one million one hundred thousand men who could
handle a sword, including four hundred and seventy thousand in
Judah.
6But Joab did not include Levi and Benjamin in the numbering,
because the king's command was repulsive to him. 7This command was also evil in the sight of God; so he punished Israel.
8Then David said to God, "I have sinned greatly by doing this.
Now, I beg you, take away the guilt of your servant. I have done a
very foolish thing."
9The LORD said to Gad, David's seer, 10"Go and tell David, 'This
is what the LORD says: I am giving you three options. Choose one
of them for me to carry out against you.' "
11So Gad went to David and said to him, "This is what the LORD
says: 'Take your choice: 12three years of famine, three months of
being swept away[a] before your enemies, with their swords overtaking you, or three days of the sword of the LORD—days of
plague in the land, with the angel of the LORD ravaging every part
of Israel.' Now then, decide how I should answer the one who
sent me."
13David said to Gad, "I am in deep distress. Let me fall into the
hands of the LORD, for his mercy is very great; but do not let me
fall into the hands of men."
14So the LORD sent a plague on Israel, and seventy thousand
men of Israel fell dead. 15And God sent an angel to destroy Jerusalem. But as the angel was doing so, the LORD saw it and was
grieved because of the calamity and said to the angel who was destroying the people, "Enough! Withdraw your hand." The angel of
the LORD was then standing at the threshing floor of Araunah[b] the
Jebusite.

[a] *12* Hebrew; Septuagint and Vulgate (see also 2 Samuel 24:13) *of fleeing* [b] *15* Hebrew *Ornan,* a variant of *Araunah*; also in verses 18–28

16David looked up and saw the angel of the LORD standing between heaven and earth, with a drawn sword in his hand extended over Jerusalem. Then David and the elders, clothed in
sackcloth, fell facedown.
17David said to God, "Was it not I who ordered the fighting
men to be counted? I am the one who has sinned and done
wrong. These are but sheep. What have they done? O LORD my
God, let your hand fall upon me and my family, but do not let this
plague remain on your people."
18Then the angel of the LORD ordered Gad to tell David to go up
and build an altar to the LORD on the threshing floor of Araunah
the Jebusite. 19So David went up in obedience to the word that
Gad had spoken in the name of the LORD.
20While Araunah was threshing wheat, he turned and saw the
angel; his four sons who were with him hid themselves. 21Then
David approached, and when Araunah looked and saw him, he
left the threshing floor and bowed down before David with his
face to the ground.
22David said to him, "Let me have the site of your threshing
floor so I can build an altar to the LORD, that the plague on the
people may be stopped. Sell it to me at the full price."
23Araunah said to David, "Take it! Let my lord the king do
whatever pleases him. Look, I will give the oxen for the burnt offerings, the threshing sledges for the wood, and the wheat for the
grain offering. I will give all this."
24But King David replied to Araunah, "No, I insist on paying the
full price. I will not take for the LORD what is yours, or sacrifice a
burnt offering that costs me nothing."
25So David paid Araunah six hundred shekels[a] of gold for the
site. 26David built an altar to the LORD there and sacrificed burnt
offerings and fellowship offerings.[b] He called on the LORD, and
the LORD answered him with fire from heaven on the altar of burnt
offering.
27Then the LORD spoke to the angel, and he put his sword back
into its sheath. 28At that time, when David saw that the LORD had
answered him on the threshing floor of Araunah the Jebusite, he
offered sacrifices there. 29The tabernacle of the LORD, which
Moses had made in the desert, and the altar of burnt offering
were at that time on the high place at Gibeon. 30But David could
not go before it to inquire of God, because he was afraid of the
sword of the angel of the LORD.

22 Then David said, "The house of the LORD God is to be here,
and also the altar of burnt offering for Israel."

Preparations for the Temple

2So David gave orders to assemble the aliens living in Israel,
and from among them he appointed stonecutters to prepare
dressed stone for building the house of God. 3He provided a large
amount of iron to make nails for the doors of the gateways and
for the fittings, and more bronze than could be weighed. 4He also
provided more cedar logs than could be counted, for the Sidonians and Tyrians had brought large numbers of them to David.
5David said, "My son Solomon is young and inexperienced,
and the house to be built for the LORD should be of great magnificence and fame and splendor in the sight of all the nations.

[a]25 That is, about 15 pounds (about 7 kilograms) [b]26 Traditionally *peace offerings*

(21:15—22:1) What was it about this place that You would choose it for Your temple? Help me to see with eyes of faith: This place was where the wheat was separated from the chaff. It was a place with a history, for on this same hill Abraham bound up Isaac in the act of sacrifice to You. It was a place that would have a glorious future as Mt. Zion, the mountain of the Lord. It was a place where judgment met mercy. It was a place of humble confession and repentance. It was here that David took full responsibility for his actions and pleaded for those who suffered because of his sin. It was here that peace was made with You through the offering of acceptable sacrifices. This was a fearful place. It was Your chosen place. It became a holy place. This place was bought at a price. But still, Lord, why this place?

And why me, Lord? Why would You choose to build Your temple in me? For my body is now the temple of the Holy Spirit. I am no longer my own; I was bought at a price. Instead of judgment, I found Your mercy. In humility, I confessed my sin and repented before You. I accepted full responsibility for my actions and I pleaded for Your mercy on those who suffered because of my sin. Through the sacrifice of Christ, the ultimate offering, I made my peace with You. Now this fearful place—Your chosen place—has become a holy place. I dedicate the altar of my heart for the worship of my God, and offer You the sacrifice of praise as an act of faith. (Ge 22:1–14; 1Co 6:19–20; Heb 13:15)

The temple of glory is built on the threshing-floor of affliction.

Charles Haddon Spurgeon (1834-1892)

(22:17–19) God of our Fathers, grant that my children might serve You better than I. Give them discretion and understanding that they might live by Your Word. Grant that I may pass on to them the heritage of spiritual treasures with which You have blessed me. May they use these treasures wisely for the work of the ministry. May they set their minds and hearts to seek the Lord their God. For it is from You, O God, that all wisdom and prosperity come.

O give us homes where Christ is
Lord and Master,
The Bible read, the precious hymns
still sung;
Where pray'r comes first in peace or
in disaster,
And praise is natural speech to every
tongue;
Where mountains move before a
faith that's vaster,
And Christ sufficient is for old and
young.

"A Christian Home"
Barbara B. Hart (©1965)

I believe I should have been swept by the flood of French infidelity, if it had not been for one thing, the remembrance of the time when my mother used to make me kneel by her side, and taking my little hand in hers, taught me to repeat the Lord's Prayer.

John Randolph (1773–1833)

Therefore I will make preparations for it." So David made extensive preparations before his death.
6Then he called for his son Solomon and charged him to build
a house for the LORD, the God of Israel. 7David said to Solomon:
"My son, I had it in my heart to build a house for the Name of the
LORD my God. 8But this word of the LORD came to me: 'You have
shed much blood and have fought many wars. You are not to
build a house for my Name, because you have shed much blood
on the earth in my sight. 9But you will have a son who will be a
man of peace and rest, and I will give him rest from all his enemies on every side. His name will be Solomon,[a] and I will grant
Israel peace and quiet during his reign. 10He is the one who will
build a house for my Name. He will be my son, and I will be his
father. And I will establish the throne of his kingdom over Israel
forever.'
11"Now, my son, the LORD be with you, and may you have success and build the house of the LORD your God, as he said you
would. 12May the LORD give you discretion and understanding
when he puts you in command over Israel, so that you may keep
the law of the LORD your God. 13Then you will have success if you
are careful to observe the decrees and laws that the LORD gave
Moses for Israel. Be strong and courageous. Do not be afraid or
discouraged.
14"I have taken great pains to provide for the temple of the
LORD a hundred thousand talents[b] of gold, a million talents[c] of silver, quantities of bronze and iron too great to be weighed, and
wood and stone. And you may add to them. 15You have many
workmen: stonecutters, masons and carpenters, as well as men
skilled in every kind of work 16in gold and silver, bronze and
iron—craftsmen beyond number. Now begin the work, and the
LORD be with you."
17Then David ordered all the leaders of Israel to help his son
Solomon. 18He said to them, "Is not the LORD your God with you?
And has he not granted you rest on every side? For he has handed the inhabitants of the land over to me, and the land is subject
to the LORD and to his people. 19Now devote your heart and soul
to seeking the LORD your God. Begin to build the sanctuary of the
LORD God, so that you may bring the ark of the covenant of the
LORD and the sacred articles belonging to God into the temple that
will be built for the Name of the LORD."

The Levites

23 When David was old and full of years, he made his son
Solomon king over Israel.
2He also gathered together all the leaders of Israel, as well as
the priests and Levites. 3The Levites thirty years old or more were
counted, and the total number of men was thirty-eight thousand.
4David said, "Of these, twenty-four thousand are to supervise the
work of the temple of the LORD and six thousand are to be officials
and judges. 5Four thousand are to be gatekeepers and four thousand are to praise the LORD with the musical instruments I have
provided for that purpose."
6David divided the Levites into groups corresponding to the
sons of Levi: Gershon, Kohath and Merari.

[a] 9 *Solomon* sounds like and may be derived from the Hebrew for *peace*. [b] 14 That is, about 3,750 tons (about 3,450 metric tons) [c] 14 That is, about 37,500 tons (about 34,500 metric tons)

Gershonites

7Belonging to the Gershonites:
Ladan and Shimei.
8The sons of Ladan:
Jehiel the first, Zetham and Joel—three in all.
9The sons of Shimei:
Shelomoth, Haziel and Haran—three in all.
These were the heads of the families of Ladan.
10And the sons of Shimei:
Jahath, Ziza,[a] Jeush and Beriah.
These were the sons of Shimei—four in all.
11Jahath was the first and Ziza the second, but Jeush and Beriah did not have many sons; so they were counted as one family with one assignment.

Kohathites

12The sons of Kohath:
Amram, Izhar, Hebron and Uzziel—four in all.
13The sons of Amram:
Aaron and Moses.
Aaron was set apart, he and his descendants forever, to consecrate the most holy things, to offer sacrifices before the LORD, to minister before him and to pronounce bless-
ings in his name forever. 14The sons of Moses the man of
God were counted as part of the tribe of Levi.
15The sons of Moses:
Gershom and Eliezer.
16The descendants of Gershom:
Shubael was the first.
17The descendants of Eliezer:
Rehabiah was the first.
Eliezer had no other sons, but the sons of Rehabiah were very numerous.
18The sons of Izhar:
Shelomith was the first.
19The sons of Hebron:
Jeriah the first, Amariah the second, Jahaziel the third and Jekameam the fourth.
20The sons of Uzziel:
Micah the first and Isshiah the second.

Merarites

21The sons of Merari:
Mahli and Mushi.
The sons of Mahli:
Eleazar and Kish.
22Eleazar died without having sons: he had only daughters. Their cousins, the sons of Kish, married them.
23The sons of Mushi:
Mahli, Eder and Jerimoth—three in all.

24These were the descendants of Levi by their families—the heads of families as they were registered under their names and counted individually, that is, the workers twenty years old or
more who served in the temple of the LORD. 25For David had said,

[a] *10* One Hebrew manuscript, Septuagint and Vulgate (see also verse 11); most Hebrew manuscripts *Zina*

(23:12–13) Thank You, Father God, for Your gift of spiritual leaders to every generation of Your people. From Aaron the high priest You provided a fruitful line of priests to serve You and to minister to Your people Israel. And now, Lord Jesus, You are our great high priest. You sacrificed for our sins once for all when You offered Yourself on the altar of the cross. Because You live forever, You have a permanent priesthood. You are able to save completely those who come to God through You, because You always live to intercede for us. The blood of Your sacrifice speaks far more eloquently than any of Aaron's sacrifices. It is through You, dear Jesus, that we are accepted and draw near to God with confidence. Through You, we offer our prayers to God. And through You, God offers His blessings to us. (Heb 4:14–16; 7:22–25; 12:24)

"Since the LORD, the God of Israel, has granted rest to his people
and has come to dwell in Jerusalem forever, 26the Levites no
longer need to carry the tabernacle or any of the articles used in
its service." 27According to the last instructions of David, the Levites were counted from those twenty years old or more.

28The duty of the Levites was to help Aaron's descendants in
the service of the temple of the LORD: to be in charge of the courtyards, the side rooms, the purification of all sacred things and
the performance of other duties at the house of God. 29They
were in charge of the bread set out on the table, the flour for the
grain offerings, the unleavened wafers, the baking and the mixing, and all measurements of quantity and size. 30They were also
to stand every morning to thank and praise the LORD. They were
to do the same in the evening 31and whenever burnt offerings
were presented to the LORD on Sabbaths and at New Moon festivals and at appointed feasts. They were to serve before the LORD
regularly in the proper number and in the way prescribed for
them.

32And so the Levites carried out their responsibilities for the
Tent of Meeting, for the Holy Place and, under their brothers the
descendants of Aaron, for the service of the temple of the LORD.

The Divisions of Priests

24 These were the divisions of the sons of Aaron:
The sons of Aaron were Nadab, Abihu, Eleazar and Ithamar. 2But Nadab and Abihu died before their father did, and they
had no sons; so Eleazar and Ithamar served as the priests. 3With
the help of Zadok a descendant of Eleazar and Ahimelech a descendant of Ithamar, David separated them into divisions for their
appointed order of ministering. 4A larger number of leaders were
found among Eleazar's descendants than among Ithamar's, and
they were divided accordingly: sixteen heads of families from Eleazar's descendants and eight heads of families from Ithamar's
descendants. 5They divided them impartially by drawing lots, for
there were officials of the sanctuary and officials of God among
the descendants of both Eleazar and Ithamar.

6The scribe Shemaiah son of Nethanel, a Levite, recorded
their names in the presence of the king and of the officials:
Zadok the priest, Ahimelech son of Abiathar and the heads of
families of the priests and of the Levites—one family being taken
from Eleazar and then one from Ithamar.

7The first lot fell to Jehoiarib,
the second to Jedaiah,
8the third to Harim,
the fourth to Seorim,
9the fifth to Malkijah,
the sixth to Mijamin,
10the seventh to Hakkoz,
the eighth to Abijah,
11the ninth to Jeshua,
the tenth to Shecaniah,
12the eleventh to Eliashib,
the twelfth to Jakim,
13the thirteenth to Huppah,
the fourteenth to Jeshebeab,
14the fifteenth to Bilgah,
the sixteenth to Immer,

(24:1) It is Yours to choose whom You will have serve You. We may wonder why You selected the priesthood by genealogy, but we acknowledge Your wisdom. We might like to choose by popularity, by merit, or at random, yet You reserve the right to call those whom You have chosen. In that splendid mystery of Your sovereignty, we find ourselves the most blessed of all. We are priests because of rebirth, not because of our own righteousness. As You did with the Levites, so You have done with us. We, Your children, have all become Your royal priesthood. (1Pe 2:9)

God did not choose us because we were worthy, but by choosing us he makes us worthy.

Thomas Watson (c.1557-1592)

Stand up and bless the Lord,
Ye people of His choice;
Stand up and bless the Lord your
God
With heart and soul and voice.

Stand up and bless the Lord;
The Lord your God adore.
Stand up and bless His glorious name
Henceforth forevermore.

"Stand Up and Bless the Lord"
James Montgomery (1824)

15 the seventeenth to Hezir,
the eighteenth to Happizzez,
16 the nineteenth to Pethahiah,
the twentieth to Jehezkel,
17 the twenty-first to Jakin,
the twenty-second to Gamul,
18 the twenty-third to Delaiah
and the twenty-fourth to Maaziah.

19 This was their appointed order of ministering when they entered the temple of the LORD, according to the regulations prescribed for them by their forefather Aaron, as the LORD, the God of Israel, had commanded him.

The Rest of the Levites

20 As for the rest of the descendants of Levi:
from the sons of Amram: Shubael;
from the sons of Shubael: Jehdeiah.
21 As for Rehabiah, from his sons:
Isshiah was the first.
22 From the Izharites: Shelomoth;
from the sons of Shelomoth: Jahath.
23 The sons of Hebron: Jeriah the first,[a] Amariah the second,
Jahaziel the third and Jekameam the fourth.
24 The son of Uzziel: Micah;
from the sons of Micah: Shamir.
25 The brother of Micah: Isshiah;
from the sons of Isshiah: Zechariah.
26 The sons of Merari: Mahli and Mushi.
The son of Jaaziah: Beno.
27 The sons of Merari:
from Jaaziah: Beno, Shoham, Zaccur and Ibri.
28 From Mahli: Eleazar, who had no sons.
29 From Kish: the son of Kish:
Jerahmeel.
30 And the sons of Mushi: Mahli, Eder and Jerimoth.

These were the Levites, according to their families. 31 They also cast lots, just as their brothers the descendants of Aaron did, in the presence of King David and of Zadok, Ahimelech, and the heads of families of the priests and of the Levites. The families of the oldest brother were treated the same as those of the youngest.

The Singers

25 David, together with the commanders of the army, set apart some of the sons of Asaph, Heman and Jeduthun for the ministry of prophesying, accompanied by harps, lyres and cymbals. Here is the list of the men who performed this service:

2 From the sons of Asaph:
Zaccur, Joseph, Nethaniah and Asarelah. The sons of Asaph were under the supervision of Asaph, who prophesied under the king's supervision.
3 As for Jeduthun, from his sons:
Gedaliah, Zeri, Jeshaiah, Shimei,[b] Hashabiah and Mattithiah,

[a] 23 Two Hebrew manuscripts and some Septuagint manuscripts (see also 1 Chron. 23:19); most Hebrew manuscripts *The sons of Jeriah:* [b] 3 One Hebrew manuscript and some Septuagint manuscripts (see also verse 17); most Hebrew manuscripts do not have *Shimei.*

In worship we meet the power of God and stand in its strengthening.
Nels F. S. Ferré (1769–1821)

(25:1) David was committed to worship as a matter of national security. Almighty God, in our preparation for the warfare of the Spirit, let us not neglect the prophetic ministry of the song of worship as a strategic, spiritual weapon. Help us to give ourselves to it as diligently and skillfully as to every other aspect of prayer. "For though we live in the world, we do not wage war as the world does. The weapons we fight with are not the weapons of the world. On the contrary, they have divine power to demolish strongholds." (Ps 144:1; 149:6; 2Co 10:3–4)

Lifting high the royal banners,
We proclaim His kingdom reign;
We will crown Him king forever,
We exalt His glorious name.

King and Lord of all creation,
Sovereign in authority;
We will never cease to praise Him,
Throughout all eternity.

"Let Us Worship Lord Jehovah"
Kirk Dearman (©1987)

six in all, under the supervision of their father Jeduthun, who prophesied, using the harp in thanking and praising the LORD.

4 As for Heman, from his sons:
Bukkiah, Mattaniah, Uzziel, Shubael and Jerimoth; Hananiah, Hanani, Eliathah, Giddalti and Romamti-Ezer; Joshbekashah, Mallothi, Hothir and Mahazioth. 5 All these were sons
of Heman the king's seer. They were given him through the
promises of God to exalt him.[a] God gave Heman fourteen
sons and three daughters.

6 All these men were under the supervision of their fathers for
the music of the temple of the LORD, with cymbals, lyres and
harps, for the ministry at the house of God. Asaph, Jeduthun and
Heman were under the supervision of the king. 7 Along with their
relatives—all of them trained and skilled in music for the LORD—
they numbered 288. 8 Young and old alike, teacher as well as student, cast lots for their duties.

9 The first lot, which was for Asaph, fell to Joseph,
his sons and relatives,[b] 12[c]
the second to Gedaliah,
he and his relatives and sons, 12
10 the third to Zaccur,
his sons and relatives, 12
11 the fourth to Izri,[d]
his sons and relatives, 12
12 the fifth to Nethaniah,
his sons and relatives, 12
13 the sixth to Bukkiah,
his sons and relatives, 12
14 the seventh to Jesarelah,[e]
his sons and relatives, 12
15 the eighth to Jeshaiah,
his sons and relatives, 12
16 the ninth to Mattaniah,
his sons and relatives, 12
17 the tenth to Shimei,
his sons and relatives, 12
18 the eleventh to Azarel,[f]
his sons and relatives, 12
19 the twelfth to Hashabiah,
his sons and relatives, 12
20 the thirteenth to Shubael,
his sons and relatives, 12
21 the fourteenth to Mattithiah,
his sons and relatives, 12
22 the fifteenth to Jerimoth,
his sons and relatives, 12
23 the sixteenth to Hananiah,
his sons and relatives, 12
24 the seventeenth to Joshbekashah,
his sons and relatives, 12
25 the eighteenth to Hanani,
his sons and relatives, 12

(25:9–31) When the lot falls on me to sing the praises of Your name, I want it to be a spiritual act of worship according to Your Word. I will sing and make music in my heart to You, O Lord, for I have been called out to serve Your glory. My chief end is to glorify You and in doing that I will enjoy You forever. (Ro 12:1; Eph 5:19)

I will bless Thee as long as I live,
I will sing praises to Thy name!
And my mouth speaks Your praises
With joyful lips
In the shadow of Your wings
I sing for joy!
"I Will Bless Thee As Long As I Live"
John Sellers (©1989)

[a] 5 Hebrew *exalt the horn* [b] 9 See Septuagint; Hebrew does not have *his sons and relatives.* [c] 9 See the total in verse 7; Hebrew does not have *twelve.* [d] 11 A variant of *Zeri* [e] 14 A variant of *Asarelah* [f] 18 A variant of *Uzziel*

26 the nineteenth to Mallothi,
his sons and relatives, 12
27 the twentieth to Eliathah,
his sons and relatives, 12
28 the twenty-first to Hothir,
his sons and relatives, 12
29 the twenty-second to Giddalti,
his sons and relatives, 12
30 the twenty-third to Mahazioth,
his sons and relatives, 12
31 the twenty-fourth to Romamti-Ezer,
his sons and relatives, 12

The Gatekeepers

26 The divisions of the gatekeepers:

From the Korahites: Meshelemiah son of Kore, one of the sons of Asaph.
2 Meshelemiah had sons:
Zechariah the firstborn,
Jediael the second,
Zebadiah the third,
Jathniel the fourth,
3 Elam the fifth,
Jehohanan the sixth
and Eliehoenai the seventh.
4 Obed-Edom also had sons:
Shemaiah the firstborn,
Jehozabad the second,
Joah the third,
Sacar the fourth,
Nethanel the fifth,
5 Ammiel the sixth,
Issachar the seventh
and Peullethai the eighth.
(For God had blessed Obed-Edom.)
6 His son Shemaiah also had sons, who were leaders in their father's family because they were very capable men.
7 The sons of Shemaiah: Othni, Rephael, Obed and Elzabad; his relatives Elihu and Semakiah were also able men.
8 All these were descendants of Obed-Edom; they and their sons and their relatives were capable men with the strength to do the work—descendants of Obed-Edom, 62 in all.
9 Meshelemiah had sons and relatives, who were able men—18 in all.
10 Hosah the Merarite had sons: Shimri the first (although he was not the firstborn, his father had appointed him the first),
11 Hilkiah the second, Tabaliah the third and Zechariah the fourth. The sons and relatives of Hosah were 13 in all.
12 These divisions of the gatekeepers, through their chief men, had duties for ministering in the temple of the LORD, just as their relatives had.
13 Lots were cast for each gate, according to their families, young and old alike.

(26:1) Holy God, help me to serve well as a gatekeeper in the temple of my heart, to allow in only that which is pleasing to You. Help me to be alert as I stand watch at the gate of my eyes, the gate of my ears, the gate of my hands, the gate of my feet and the gate of my mind. Help me to not be slack in my duty to guard the treasures You have stored inside.

[14]The lot for the East Gate fell to Shelemiah.[a] Then lots were cast for his son Zechariah, a wise counselor, and the lot for the North Gate fell to him. [15]The lot for the South Gate fell to Obed-Edom, and the lot for the storehouse fell to his sons. [16]The lots for the West Gate and the Shalleketh Gate on the upper road fell to Shuppim and Hosah.

Guard was alongside of guard: [17]There were six Levites a day on the east, four a day on the north, four a day on the south and two at a time at the storehouse. [18]As for the court to the west, there were four at the road and two at the court itself.

[19]These were the divisions of the gatekeepers who were descendants of Korah and Merari.

The Treasurers and Other Officials

[20]Their fellow Levites were[b] in charge of the treasuries of the house of God and the treasuries for the dedicated things.

[21]The descendants of Ladan, who were Gershonites through Ladan and who were heads of families belonging to Ladan the Gershonite, were Jehieli, [22]the sons of Jehieli, Zetham and his brother Joel. They were in charge of the treasuries of the temple of the LORD.

[23]From the Amramites, the Izharites, the Hebronites and the Uzzielites:

24 Shubael, a descendant of Gershom son of Moses, was the officer in charge of the treasuries. [25]His relatives through Eliezer: Rehabiah his son, Jeshaiah his son, Joram his son, Zicri his son and Shelomith his son. [26]Shelomith and his relatives were in charge of all the treasuries for the things dedicated by King David, by the heads of families who were the commanders of thousands and commanders of hundreds, and by the other army commanders. [27]Some of the plunder taken in battle they dedicated for the repair of the temple of the LORD. [28]And everything dedicated by Samuel the seer and by Saul son of Kish, Abner son of Ner and Joab son of Zeruiah, and all the other dedicated things were in the care of Shelomith and his relatives.

29 From the Izharites: Kenaniah and his sons were assigned duties away from the temple, as officials and judges over Israel.

30 From the Hebronites: Hashabiah and his relatives—seventeen hundred able men—were responsible in Israel west of the Jordan for all the work of the LORD and for the king's service. [31]As for the Hebronites, Jeriah was their chief according to the genealogical records of their families. In the fortieth year of David's reign a search was made in the records, and capable men among the Hebronites were found at Jazer in Gilead. [32]Jeriah had twenty-seven hundred relatives, who were able men and heads of families, and King David put them in charge of the Reubenites, the Gadites and the half-tribe of Manasseh for every matter pertaining to God and for the affairs of the king.

[a] 14 A variant of *Meshelemiah* [b] 20 Septuagint; Hebrew *As for the Levites, Ahijah was*

(26:20) Holy God, You have put me in charge of the temple of the Holy Spirit, for indeed my body is Your temple. And You have filled this temple with talents and treasures. Help me to be a wise steward of my body, my time and my talents. I offer myself to You as a living sacrifice, holy and pleasing to You, for this is the spiritual worship You have asked of me. (Ro 12:1; 1Co 6:19)

We give thee but thine own,
Whate'er the gift may be;
All that we have is thine alone,
A trust, O Lord, from thee.
William Walsham How (1823–1897)

(26:27) Mighty God, when you led your people into battle You not only brought them victory, but at times You also gave them the wealth of the wicked. When Israel was thinking rightly, they took no pride in their own strength, nor did they take credit for their success. Instead, in joy they would bring a portion of the plunder back to You as a gift of worship. O Lord, may I live my life in this way, acknowledging that any victories I win are won by You. Out of the abundance with which You bless my life, help me to be faithful in dedicating a portion of my wealth to the service of Your house.

Army Divisions

27 This is the list of the Israelites—heads of families, commanders of thousands and commanders of hundreds, and their officers, who served the king in all that concerned the army divisions that were on duty month by month throughout the year. Each division consisted of 24,000 men.

2 In charge of the first division, for the first month, was Jashobeam son of Zabdiel. There were 24,000 men in his division. 3 He was a descendant of Perez and chief of all the army officers for the first month.
4 In charge of the division for the second month was Dodai the Ahohite; Mikloth was the leader of his division. There were 24,000 men in his division.
5 The third army commander, for the third month, was Benaiah son of Jehoiada the priest. He was chief and there were 24,000 men in his division. 6 This was the Benaiah who was a mighty man among the Thirty and was over the Thirty. His son Ammizabad was in charge of his division.
7 The fourth, for the fourth month, was Asahel the brother of Joab; his son Zebadiah was his successor. There were 24,000 men in his division.
8 The fifth, for the fifth month, was the commander Shamhuth the Izrahite. There were 24,000 men in his division.
9 The sixth, for the sixth month, was Ira the son of Ikkesh the Tekoite. There were 24,000 men in his division.
10 The seventh, for the seventh month, was Helez the Pelonite, an Ephraimite. There were 24,000 men in his division.
11 The eighth, for the eighth month, was Sibbecai the Hushathite, a Zerahite. There were 24,000 men in his division.
12 The ninth, for the ninth month, was Abiezer the Anathothite, a Benjamite. There were 24,000 men in his division.
13 The tenth, for the tenth month, was Maharai the Netophathite, a Zerahite. There were 24,000 men in his division.
14 The eleventh, for the eleventh month, was Benaiah the Pirathonite, an Ephraimite. There were 24,000 men in his division.
15 The twelfth, for the twelfth month, was Heldai the Netophathite, from the family of Othniel. There were 24,000 men in his division.

Officers of the Tribes

16 The officers over the tribes of Israel:

over the Reubenites: Eliezer son of Zicri;
over the Simeonites: Shephatiah son of Maacah;
17 over Levi: Hashabiah son of Kemuel;
over Aaron: Zadok;
18 over Judah: Elihu, a brother of David;
over Issachar: Omri son of Michael;
19 over Zebulun: Ishmaiah son of Obadiah;
over Naphtali: Jerimoth son of Azriel;
20 over the Ephraimites: Hoshea son of Azaziah;
over half the tribe of Manasseh: Joel son of Pedaiah;
21 over the half-tribe of Manasseh in Gilead: Iddo son of Zechariah;
over Benjamin: Jaasiel son of Abner;

(27:1) Almighty God, You commanded the armies of Israel through David, Your servant. Now You lead Your people through Christ our Lord, the Son of David, who is seated at Your right hand. You have promised that Your troops will be willing on Your day of battle. Pour out Your Spirit on us today that we would willingly enlist in the great army of witnesses professing our faith in Your saving power. Pour out upon Your kingdom today leaders from every land and every tribe for every season and every time, that Your Kingdom may prosper to Your eternal glory. (Ps 110:1–3)

(27:33) Among those who served David was one known as a "friend of the King." King Jesus, Son of David, Friend of sinners, may You know me among Your servants as one who is Your friend.

You cannot say that you are friendless when Christ has said, "Henceforth I call you not servants . . . but I have called you friends" (Jn 15:15).

Billy Graham (1918-)

Lord You are amazing,
Clothed in majesty;
All of heaven and earth
Declare Your glory.
Lord, I want to know You
Much better than I do,
Draw me into the secret place
With You.

For the more I know You
The more I love You, Lord.
The more I know You
The more I hunger for Your Word.
And as You lead me day by day,
I pray my heart will never stray.
For the more I know You
The more I love You Lord,
I love You Lord.

"The More I Know You"
Pamela Fadness and Greg Fadness (©1999)

22 over Dan: Azarel son of Jeroham.
These were the officers over the tribes of Israel.

23 David did not take the number of the men twenty years old or
less, because the LORD had promised to make Israel as numerous
as the stars in the sky. 24 Joab son of Zeruiah began to count the
men but did not finish. Wrath came on Israel on account of this
numbering, and the number was not entered in the book[a] of the
annals of King David.

The King's Overseers

25 Azmaveth son of Adiel was in charge of the royal storehouses.
Jonathan son of Uzziah was in charge of the storehouses in the
outlying districts, in the towns, the villages and the watchtowers.
26 Ezri son of Kelub was in charge of the field workers who
farmed the land.
27 Shimei the Ramathite was in charge of the vineyards.
Zabdi the Shiphmite was in charge of the produce of the vineyards for the wine vats.
28 Baal-Hanan the Gederite was in charge of the olive and sycamore-fig trees in the western foothills.
Joash was in charge of the supplies of olive oil.
29 Shitrai the Sharonite was in charge of the herds grazing in
Sharon.
Shaphat son of Adlai was in charge of the herds in the valleys.
30 Obil the Ishmaelite was in charge of the camels.
Jehdeiah the Meronothite was in charge of the donkeys.
31 Jaziz the Hagrite was in charge of the flocks.
All these were the officials in charge of King David's property.
32 Jonathan, David's uncle, was a counselor, a man of insight
and a scribe. Jehiel son of Hacmoni took care of the king's sons.
33 Ahithophel was the king's counselor.
Hushai the Arkite was the king's friend. 34 Ahithophel was succeeded by Jehoiada son of Benaiah and by Abiathar.
Joab was the commander of the royal army.

David's Plans for the Temple

28 David summoned all the officials of Israel to assemble at
Jerusalem: the officers over the tribes, the commanders of
the divisions in the service of the king, the commanders of thousands and commanders of hundreds, and the officials in charge
of all the property and livestock belonging to the king and his
sons, together with the palace officials, the mighty men and all the
brave warriors.

2 King David rose to his feet and said: "Listen to me, my brothers and my people. I had it in my heart to build a house as a place
of rest for the ark of the covenant of the LORD, for the footstool of
our God, and I made plans to build it. 3 But God said to me, 'You
are not to build a house for my Name, because you are a warrior
and have shed blood.'

4 "Yet the LORD, the God of Israel, chose me from my whole
family to be king over Israel forever. He chose Judah as leader,
and from the house of Judah he chose my family, and from my father's sons he was pleased to make me king over all Israel. 5 Of all
my sons—and the LORD has given me many—he has chosen my

[a] 24 Septuagint; Hebrew *number*

son Solomon to sit on the throne of the kingdom of the LORD over
Israel. 6He said to me: 'Solomon your son is the one who will
build my house and my courts, for I have chosen him to be my
son, and I will be his father. 7I will establish his kingdom forever
if he is unswerving in carrying out my commands and laws, as is
being done at this time.'
8"So now I charge you in the sight of all Israel and of the assembly of the LORD, and in the hearing of our God: Be careful to
follow all the commands of the LORD your God, that you may possess this good land and pass it on as an inheritance to your descendants forever.
9"And you, my son Solomon, acknowledge the God of your father, and serve him with wholehearted devotion and with a willing mind, for the LORD searches every heart and understands
every motive behind the thoughts. If you seek him, he will be
found by you; but if you forsake him, he will reject you forever.
10Consider now, for the LORD has chosen you to build a temple as
a sanctuary. Be strong and do the work."
11Then David gave his son Solomon the plans for the portico of
the temple, its buildings, its storerooms, its upper parts, its inner
rooms and the place of atonement. 12He gave him the plans of all
that the Spirit had put in his mind for the courts of the temple of
the LORD and all the surrounding rooms, for the treasuries of the
temple of God and for the treasuries for the dedicated things.
13He gave him instructions for the divisions of the priests and Levites, and for all the work of serving in the temple of the LORD, as
well as for all the articles to be used in its service. 14He designated the weight of gold for all the gold articles to be used in various
kinds of service, and the weight of silver for all the silver articles
to be used in various kinds of service: 15the weight of gold for the
gold lampstands and their lamps, with the weight for each lampstand and its lamps; and the weight of silver for each silver lampstand and its lamps, according to the use of each lampstand;
16the weight of gold for each table for consecrated bread; the
weight of silver for the silver tables; 17the weight of pure gold for
the forks, sprinkling bowls and pitchers; the weight of gold for
each gold dish; the weight of silver for each silver dish; 18and the
weight of the refined gold for the altar of incense. He also gave
him the plan for the chariot, that is, the cherubim of gold that
spread their wings and shelter the ark of the covenant of the LORD.
19"All this," David said, "I have in writing from the hand of the
LORD upon me, and he gave me understanding in all the details of
the plan."
20David also said to Solomon his son, "Be strong and courageous, and do the work. Do not be afraid or discouraged, for the
LORD God, my God, is with you. He will not fail you or forsake you
until all the work for the service of the temple of the LORD is finished. 21The divisions of the priests and Levites are ready for all
the work on the temple of God, and every willing man skilled in
any craft will help you in all the work. The officials and all the
people will obey your every command."

Gifts for Building the Temple

29 Then King David said to the whole assembly: "My son Solomon, the one whom God has chosen, is young and inexperienced. The task is great, because this palatial structure is not
for man but for the LORD God. 2With all my resources I have pro-

(28:9–10) Gracious Father, You have given me a trust, just as David made with his son Solomon. I want to be found faithful to that trust. I want to live a life that is worthy of the calling I have received from You. I want to serve You out of a pure heart and a clean conscience. Yet, even if my conscience were clean, that would not mean that I am innocent. And as Job once declared, "though I were innocent . . . I could only plead with my Judge for mercy." You know me much better than I know myself. So I will seek You, Lord, that You might bring to light what is hidden in darkness and expose the motives of my heart. Oh how I want to be clean before You, without fear and with nothing to hide. (1Co 4:2–5)

(29:3) From whom You've given much, You require much. And I, like David, want to give You more than just the requirements. What I have set aside for the building of my personal kingdom, I now give to You for the building of Yours. I willingly, joyfully, sacrificially dedicate myself to You as an act of worship.

All I once held dear, built my life
  upon,
All this world reveres and wars to
  own.
All I once thought gain
I have counted loss,
Spent and worthless now
Compared to this.

Knowing You, Jesus, knowing You,
There is no greater thing.
You're my all, You're the best,
You're my joy, my righteousness,
And I love You, Lord.

"Knowing You (All I Once Held Dear)"
Graham Kendrick (©1993)

There is no portion of our time that is our time, and the rest God's; there is no portion of money that is our money, and the rest God's money. It is all his; he made it all, gives it all, and he has simply trusted it to us for his service. A servant has two purses, the master's and his own, but we have only one.

Adolphe Monod (1800–1856)

(29:16–17) O Yahweh Yireh ("Jehovah Jireh"), we praise You for meeting the needs of Your ancient people Israel as they sought to worship You in their holy Temple. And You are still "Yahweh-Who-Provides," seeing to the needs of Your church by blessing Your people today. We are the storehouses of Your provision. Through the sacrifice of our time, talents and wealth we gladly give back to You what is rightfully Yours. Please receive our worship. (Ge 22:14)

vided for the temple of my God—gold for the gold work, silver
for the silver, bronze for the bronze, iron for the iron and wood
for the wood, as well as onyx for the settings, turquoise,[a] stones
of various colors, and all kinds of fine stone and marble—all of
these in large quantities. 3Besides, in my devotion to the temple
of my God I now give my personal treasures of gold and silver for
the temple of my God, over and above everything I have provided
for this holy temple: 4three thousand talents[b] of gold (gold of
Ophir) and seven thousand talents[c] of refined silver, for the over-
laying of the walls of the buildings, 5for the gold work and the silver work, and for all the work to be done by the craftsmen. Now,
who is willing to consecrate himself today to the LORD?"
6Then the leaders of families, the officers of the tribes of Israel, the commanders of thousands and commanders of hundreds,
and the officials in charge of the king's work gave willingly. 7They
gave toward the work on the temple of God five thousand talents[d]
and ten thousand darics[e] of gold, ten thousand talents[f] of silver,
eighteen thousand talents[g] of bronze and a hundred thousand talents[h] of iron. 8Any who had precious stones gave them to the
treasury of the temple of the LORD in the custody of Jehiel the Gershonite. 9The people rejoiced at the willing response of their
leaders, for they had given freely and wholeheartedly to the LORD.
David the king also rejoiced greatly.

David's Prayer

10David praised the LORD in the presence of the whole assembly, saying,

"Praise be to you, O LORD,
  God of our father Israel,
  from everlasting to everlasting.
11Yours, O LORD, is the greatness and the power
  and the glory and the majesty and the splendor,
  for everything in heaven and earth is yours.
Yours, O LORD, is the kingdom;
  you are exalted as head over all.
12Wealth and honor come from you;
  you are the ruler of all things.
In your hands are strength and power
  to exalt and give strength to all.
13Now, our God, we give you thanks,
  and praise your glorious name.

14"But who am I, and who are my people, that we should be
able to give as generously as this? Everything comes from you,
and we have given you only what comes from your hand. 15We
are aliens and strangers in your sight, as were all our forefathers.
Our days on earth are like a shadow, without hope. 16O LORD our
God, as for all this abundance that we have provided for building
you a temple for your Holy Name, it comes from your hand, and
all of it belongs to you. 17I know, my God, that you test the heart
and are pleased with integrity. All these things have I given willingly and with honest intent. And now I have seen with joy how

[a] 2 The meaning of the Hebrew for this word is uncertain. [b] 4 That is, about 110 tons (about 100 metric tons) [c] 4 That is, about 260 tons (about 240 metric tons) [d] 7 That is, about 190 tons (about 170 metric tons) [e] 7 That is, about 185 pounds (about 84 kilograms) [f] 7 That is, about 375 tons (about 345 metric tons) [g] 7 That is, about 675 tons (about 610 metric tons) [h] 7 That is, about 3,750 tons (about 3,450 metric tons)

willingly your people who are here have given to you. 18O LORD,
God of our fathers Abraham, Isaac and Israel, keep this desire in
the hearts of your people forever, and keep their hearts loyal to
you. 19And give my son Solomon the wholehearted devotion to
keep your commands, requirements and decrees and to do everything to build the palatial structure for which I have provided."
20Then David said to the whole assembly, "Praise the LORD your
God." So they all praised the LORD, the God of their fathers; they
bowed low and fell prostrate before the LORD and the king.

Solomon Acknowledged as King

21The next day they made sacrifices to the LORD and presented
burnt offerings to him: a thousand bulls, a thousand rams and a
thousand male lambs, together with their drink offerings, and
other sacrifices in abundance for all Israel. 22They ate and drank
with great joy in the presence of the LORD that day.
Then they acknowledged Solomon son of David as king a second time, anointing him before the LORD to be ruler and Zadok to
be priest. 23So Solomon sat on the throne of the LORD as king in
place of his father David. He prospered and all Israel obeyed him.
24All the officers and mighty men, as well as all of King David's
sons, pledged their submission to King Solomon.
25The LORD highly exalted Solomon in the sight of all Israel and
bestowed on him royal splendor such as no king over Israel ever
had before.

The Death of David

26David son of Jesse was king over all Israel. 27He ruled over
Israel forty years—seven in Hebron and thirty-three in Jerusalem. 28He died at a good old age, having enjoyed long life, wealth
and honor. His son Solomon succeeded him as king.
29As for the events of King David's reign, from beginning to
end, they are written in the records of Samuel the seer, the
records of Nathan the prophet and the records of Gad the seer,
30together with the details of his reign and power, and the circumstances that surrounded him and Israel and the kingdoms of
all the other lands.

(29:18) Most gracious God and Father, as it was with Your people of old, so my desire to serve You sacrificially is precious to You. Indeed, my desire itself is a gift from Your hand. Store this desire in the treasury of my heart; hold it there for safekeeping. And then guard my heart with the gift of loyalty.

Grace binds you with far stronger cords than the cords of duty or obligation can bind you. Grace is free, but when once you take it, you are bound forever to the Giver and bound to catch the spirit of the Giver. Like produces like. Grace makes you gracious, the Giver makes you give.

E. Stanley Jones (1884–1973)

(29:21–22) Praise be to You, O Lord. To You Whom Solomon worshiped in great joy and devotion; to You Whom Jesus has taught us to call, "Our Father in heaven," we bring our praise. What else can we do but be thankful? What else can we give but thanksgiving? "Everything comes from you, and we have given you only what comes from your hand." And who am I, O Lord, and what are we as a people, except by Your grace poured out to us through Jesus Christ? We are nothing in ourselves. We are nothing except by His victory over death and His gift of new and eternal life. And so to You we offer ourselves freely. Yours is the kingdom and the power and the glory. Yours is the greatness and the victory and the majesty. To You alone we give our praise. Amen! (1Ch 29:14; Mt 6:9)

Solomon Asks for Wisdom

1 Solomon son of David established himself firmly over his
kingdom, for the LORD his God was with him and made him
exceedingly great.
2Then Solomon spoke to all Israel—to the commanders of
thousands and commanders of hundreds, to the judges and to
all the leaders in Israel, the heads of families— 3and Solomon
and the whole assembly went to the high place at Gibeon, for
God's Tent of Meeting was there, which Moses the LORD's servant had made in the desert. 4Now David had brought up the
ark of God from Kiriath Jearim to the place he had prepared
for it, because he had pitched a tent for it in Jerusalem. 5But
the bronze altar that Bezalel son of Uri, the son of Hur, had
made was in Gibeon in front of the tabernacle of the LORD; so
Solomon and the assembly inquired of him there. 6Solomon
went up to the bronze altar before the LORD in the Tent of Meeting and offered a thousand burnt offerings on it.
7That night God appeared to Solomon and said to him, "Ask
for whatever you want me to give you."
8Solomon answered God, "You have shown great kindness to
David my father and have made me king in his place. 9Now,
LORD God, let your promise to my father David be confirmed,
for you have made me king over a people who are as numerous
as the dust of the earth. 10Give me wisdom and knowledge, that
I may lead this people, for who is able to govern this great people of yours?"
11God said to Solomon, "Since this is your heart's desire and
you have not asked for wealth, riches or honor, nor for the
death of your enemies, and since you have not asked for a long
life but for wisdom and knowledge to govern my people over
whom I have made you king, 12therefore wisdom and knowledge will be given you. And I will also give you wealth, riches
and honor, such as no king who was before you ever had and
none after you will have."
13Then Solomon went to Jerusalem from the high place at
Gibeon, from before the Tent of Meeting. And he reigned over
Israel.
14Solomon accumulated chariots and horses; he had fourteen hundred chariots and twelve thousand horses,[a] which he
kept in the chariot cities and also with him in Jerusalem. 15The
king made silver and gold as common in Jerusalem as stones,
and cedar as plentiful as sycamore-fig trees in the foothills.
16Solomon's horses were imported from Egypt[b] and from
Kue[c]—the royal merchants purchased them from Kue. 17They
imported a chariot from Egypt for six hundred shekels[d] of silver, and a horse for a hundred and fifty.[e] They also exported
them to all the kings of the Hittites and of the Arameans.

Preparations for Building the Temple

2 Solomon gave orders to build a temple for the Name of the
LORD and a royal palace for himself. 2He conscripted seventy thousand men as carriers and eighty thousand as stonecutters in the hills and thirty-six hundred as foremen over
them.

[a] 14 Or *charioteers* [b] 16 Or possibly *Muzur,* a region in Cilicia; also in verse 17 [c] 16 Probably Cilicia [d] 17 That is, about 15 pounds (about 7 kilograms) [e] 17 That is, about 3 3/4 pounds (about 1.7 kilograms)

(1:7–13) You, O Lord, are the only wise God. You are the source of all wisdom and understanding. Thank You for Solomon's living example of Your gracious invitation to us: "If any of you lacks wisdom, he should ask God, who gives generously to all without finding fault, and it will be given to him." To You, O God, be all blessing and glory! Amen. (Pr 2:6; Ro 16:27; Jas 1:5)

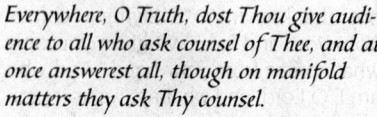

Everywhere, O Truth, dost Thou give audience to all who ask counsel of Thee, and at once answerest all, though on manifold matters they ask Thy counsel.

Saint Augustine of Hippo (354-430)

3 Solomon sent this message to Hiram[a] king of Tyre:
"Send me cedar logs as you did for my father David when
you sent him cedar to build a palace to live in. 4 Now I am
about to build a temple for the Name of the LORD my God
and to dedicate it to him for burning fragrant incense before him, for setting out the consecrated bread regularly,
and for making burnt offerings every morning and evening
and on Sabbaths and New Moons and at the appointed
feasts of the LORD our God. This is a lasting ordinance for
Israel.
5 "The temple I am going to build will be great, because
our God is greater than all other gods. 6 But who is able to
build a temple for him, since the heavens, even the highest
heavens, cannot contain him? Who then am I to build a temple for him, except as a place to burn sacrifices before him?
7 "Send me, therefore, a man skilled to work in gold and
silver, bronze and iron, and in purple, crimson and blue
yarn, and experienced in the art of engraving, to work in
Judah and Jerusalem with my skilled craftsmen, whom my
father David provided.
8 "Send me also cedar, pine and algum[b] logs from Lebanon, for I know that your men are skilled in cutting timber
there. My men will work with yours 9 to provide me with
plenty of lumber, because the temple I build must be large
and magnificent. 10 I will give your servants, the woodsmen
who cut the timber, twenty thousand cors[c] of ground wheat,
twenty thousand cors of barley, twenty thousand baths[d] of
wine and twenty thousand baths of olive oil."

11 Hiram king of Tyre replied by letter to Solomon:
"Because the LORD loves his people, he has made you
their king."

12 And Hiram added:
"Praise be to the LORD, the God of Israel, who made heav-
en and earth! He has given King David a wise son, endowed
with intelligence and discernment, who will build a temple
for the LORD and a palace for himself.
13 "I am sending you Huram-Abi, a man of great skill,
14 whose mother was from Dan and whose father was from
Tyre. He is trained to work in gold and silver, bronze and
iron, stone and wood, and with purple and blue and crimson yarn and fine linen. He is experienced in all kinds of
engraving and can execute any design given to him. He will
work with your craftsmen and with those of my lord, David
your father.
15 "Now let my lord send his servants the wheat and barley and the olive oil and wine he promised, 16 and we will
cut all the logs from Lebanon that you need and will float
them in rafts by sea down to Joppa. You can then take them
up to Jerusalem."

17 Solomon took a census of all the aliens who were in Israel,
after the census his father David had taken; and they were found

[a] *3* Hebrew *Huram*, a variant of *Hiram*; also in verses 11 and 12 [b] *8* Probably a variant of *algum*; possibly juniper [c] *10* That is, probably about 125,000 bushels (about 4,400 kiloliters) [d] *10* That is, probably about 115,000 gallons (about 440 kiloliters)

(2:1–6) You called Solomon to build a house for You. He was wise enough to understand that no building could contain You, for You do not dwell in a house made with human hands. But I praise You, O God, that now because of Jesus Christ my body is a temple of Your Holy Spirit. The highest heaven cannot contain You, yet You dwell within me and establish Your rule in my heart. (2Ch 6:18; Isa 66:1–2; Ac 17:24–25; 1Co 6:19–20)

(2:13) Creator God, I see Your workmanship everywhere. You created humanity in Your image; and in our artistry and craftsmanship we reflect Your infinite creativity. Give me wisdom to use my skills to Your glory, my King.

to be 153,600. [18]He assigned 70,000 of them to be carriers and
80,000 to be stonecutters in the hills, with 3,600 foremen over
them to keep the people working.

Solomon Builds the Temple

3 Then Solomon began to build the temple of the LORD in Jerusalem on Mount Moriah, where the LORD had appeared to
his father David. It was on the threshing floor of Araunah[a] the
Jebusite, the place provided by David. [2]He began building on
the second day of the second month in the fourth year of his
reign.

[3]The foundation Solomon laid for building the temple of God
was sixty cubits long and twenty cubits wide[b] (using the cubit of
the old standard). [4]The portico at the front of the temple was
twenty cubits[c] long across the width of the building and twenty
cubits[d] high.

He overlaid the inside with pure gold. [5]He paneled the main
hall with pine and covered it with fine gold and decorated it with
palm tree and chain designs. [6]He adorned the temple with precious stones. And the gold he used was gold of Parvaim. [7]He
overlaid the ceiling beams, doorframes, walls and doors of the
temple with gold, and he carved cherubim on the walls.

[8]He built the Most Holy Place, its length corresponding to the
width of the temple—twenty cubits long and twenty cubits wide.
He overlaid the inside with six hundred talents[e] of fine gold.
[9]The gold nails weighed fifty shekels.[f] He also overlaid the
upper parts with gold.

[10]In the Most Holy Place he made a pair of sculptured cherubim and overlaid them with gold. [11]The total wingspan of the
cherubim was twenty cubits. One wing of the first cherub was
five cubits[g] long and touched the temple wall, while its other
wing, also five cubits long, touched the wing of the other cherub. [12]Similarly one wing of the second cherub was five cubits
long and touched the other temple wall, and its other wing, also
five cubits long, touched the wing of the first cherub. [13]The
wings of these cherubim extended twenty cubits. They stood on
their feet, facing the main hall.[h]

[14]He made the curtain of blue, purple and crimson yarn and
fine linen, with cherubim worked into it.

[15]In the front of the temple he made two pillars, which ⌊to-
gether⌋ were thirty-five cubits[i] long, each with a capital on top
measuring five cubits. [16]He made interwoven chains[j] and put
them on top of the pillars. He also made a hundred pomegranates and attached them to the chains. [17]He erected the pillars in
the front of the temple, one to the south and one to the north.
The one to the south he named Jakin[k] and the one to the north
Boaz.[l]

Let your thoughts be psalms, your prayers incense, and your breath praise.
Charles Haddon Spurgeon (1834-1892)

(3:1–2) I praise You, O God, that Your temple was built at the place where judgment met mercy, where sacrifice met restoration, where confession met forgiveness. The house of worship was built on a foundation of atonement. And so it is today. We, Your church, the "house" of worship, are built on the atoning sacrifice of Jesus Christ, the Lamb of God. "In him the whole building is joined together and rises to become a holy temple" in which You live by Your Spirit. (Eph 2:21–22)

The Church's one foundation
Is Jesus Christ her Lord;
She is His new creation
By water and the Word:
From heaven He came and sought her
To be His holy bride;
With His own blood He bought her,
And for her life He died.
"The Church's One Foundation"
Samuel T. Stone (1868)

[a] *1* Hebrew *Ornan,* a variant of *Araunah* [b] *3* That is, about 90 feet (about 27 meters) long and 30 feet (about 9 meters) wide [c] *4* That is, about 30 feet (about 9 meters); also in verses 8, 11 and 13 [d] *4* Some Septuagint and Syriac manuscripts; Hebrew *and a hundred and twenty* [e] *8* That is, about 23 tons (about 21 metric tons) [f] *9* That is, about 1 1/4 pounds (about 0.6 kilogram) [g] *11* That is, about 7 1/2 feet (about 2.3 meters); also in verse 15 [h] *13* Or *facing inward* [i] *15* That is, about 52 feet (about 16 meters) [j] *16* Or possibly *made chains in the inner sanctuary*; the meaning of the Hebrew for this phrase is uncertain. [k] *17* *Jakin* probably means *he establishes.* [l] *17* *Boaz* probably means *in him is strength.*

The Temple's Furnishings

4 He made a bronze altar twenty cubits long, twenty cubits
wide and ten cubits high.[a] 2He made the Sea of cast metal,
circular in shape, measuring ten cubits from rim to rim and five
cubits[b] high. It took a line of thirty cubits[c] to measure around it.
3Below the rim, figures of bulls encircled it—ten to a cubit.[d] The
bulls were cast in two rows in one piece with the Sea.

4The Sea stood on twelve bulls, three facing north, three facing
west, three facing south and three facing east. The Sea rested on
top of them, and their hindquarters were toward the center. 5It
was a handbreadth[e] in thickness, and its rim was like the rim of
a cup, like a lily blossom. It held three thousand baths.[f]

6He then made ten basins for washing and placed five on the
south side and five on the north. In them the things to be used for
the burnt offerings were rinsed, but the Sea was to be used by the
priests for washing.

7He made ten gold lampstands according to the specifications
for them and placed them in the temple, five on the south side
and five on the north.

8He made ten tables and placed them in the temple, five on the
south side and five on the north. He also made a hundred gold
sprinkling bowls.

9He made the courtyard of the priests, and the large court and
the doors for the court, and overlaid the doors with bronze. 10He
placed the Sea on the south side, at the southeast corner.

11He also made the pots and shovels and sprinkling bowls.
So Huram finished the work he had undertaken for King Solomon in the temple of God:

12the two pillars;
the two bowl-shaped capitals on top of the pillars;
the two sets of network decorating the two bowl-shaped capitals on top of the pillars;
13the four hundred pomegranates for the two sets of network
(two rows of pomegranates for each network, decorating
the bowl-shaped capitals on top of the pillars);
14the stands with their basins;
15the Sea and the twelve bulls under it;
16the pots, shovels, meat forks and all related articles.

All the objects that Huram-Abi made for King Solomon for the
temple of the LORD were of polished bronze. 17The king had them
cast in clay molds in the plain of the Jordan between Succoth and
Zarethan.[g] 18All these things that Solomon made amounted to so
much that the weight of the bronze was not determined.

19Solomon also made all the furnishings that were in God's
temple:

the golden altar;
the tables on which was the bread of the Presence;
20the lampstands of pure gold with their lamps, to burn in
front of the inner sanctuary as prescribed;
21the gold floral work and lamps and tongs (they were solid
gold);

[a] *1* That is, about 30 feet (about 9 meters) long and wide, and about 15 feet (about 4.5 meters) high [b] *2* That is, about 7 1/2 feet (about 2.3 meters) [c] *2* That is, about 45 feet (about 13.5 meters) [d] *3* That is, about 1 1/2 feet (about 0.5 meter) [e] *5* That is, about 3 inches (about 8 centimeters) [f] *5* That is, about 17,500 gallons (about 66 kiloliters) [g] *17* Hebrew *Zeredatha,* a variant of *Zarethan*

(4:1–22) What a wonderful sight Your temple must have been, O Lord. Every item was filled with meaning and pointed the worshipers' attention to You. Yet these things and this place were only hints of Your heavenly dwelling place. If this was glorious, then what is coming is far more glorious. If this was but an artist's rendering, how much more beautiful must Your heavenly temple be? You are indeed an awesome God.

Blessed are they who shall at length behold what as yet mortal eye hath not seen and faith only enjoys! Those wonderful things of the new world are even now as they shall be then. They are immortal and eternal; and the souls who shall then be made conscious of them will see them in their calmness and their majesty where they have ever been. But who can express the surprise and rapture which will come upon those who then at last apprehend them for the first time, and to whose perceptions they are new!

Cardinal John Henry Newman (1801-1890)

(5:11–14) The completion of the temple was cause for celebration. What an amazing spectacle it must have been when Your presence filled the place! The cloud of Your glory surely made it more splendid than did all the gold and precious stones. How we long for a similar experience of Your presence in worship. Lord, come into our midst as we gather in Your name. Unite us "as with one voice, to give praise and thanks" to You. Indeed You are good, O Lord, and Your love endures forever!

We will worship and adore You,
We will bow before Your throne,
Let the fruit of our lips be pleasing
to You,
Oh, let Your glory fill this place.

"Let Your Glory Fill This Place"
Denise Graves (©1995)

22the pure gold wick trimmers, sprinkling bowls, dishes and
censers; and the gold doors of the temple: the inner
doors to the Most Holy Place and the doors of the main
hall.

5 When all the work Solomon had done for the temple of the
LORD was finished, he brought in the things his father David
had dedicated—the silver and gold and all the furnishings—and
he placed them in the treasuries of God's temple.

The Ark Brought to the Temple

2Then Solomon summoned to Jerusalem the elders of Israel,
all the heads of the tribes and the chiefs of the Israelite families,
to bring up the ark of the LORD's covenant from Zion, the City of
David. 3And all the men of Israel came together to the king at the
time of the festival in the seventh month.

4When all the elders of Israel had arrived, the Levites took up
the ark, 5and they brought up the ark and the Tent of Meeting
and all the sacred furnishings in it. The priests, who were Levites,
carried them up; 6and King Solomon and the entire assembly of
Israel that had gathered about him were before the ark, sacrificing so many sheep and cattle that they could not be recorded or
counted.

7The priests then brought the ark of the LORD's covenant to its
place in the inner sanctuary of the temple, the Most Holy Place,
and put it beneath the wings of the cherubim. 8The cherubim
spread their wings over the place of the ark and covered the ark
and its carrying poles. 9These poles were so long that their ends,
extending from the ark, could be seen from in front of the inner
sanctuary, but not from outside the Holy Place; and they are still
there today. 10There was nothing in the ark except the two tablets
that Moses had placed in it at Horeb, where the LORD made a covenant with the Israelites after they came out of Egypt.

11The priests then withdrew from the Holy Place. All the priests
who were there had consecrated themselves, regardless of their
divisions. 12All the Levites who were musicians—Asaph, Heman,
Jeduthun and their sons and relatives—stood on the east side of
the altar, dressed in fine linen and playing cymbals, harps and
lyres. They were accompanied by 120 priests sounding trumpets.
13The trumpeters and singers joined in unison, as with one voice,
to give praise and thanks to the LORD. Accompanied by trumpets,
cymbals and other instruments, they raised their voices in praise
to the LORD and sang:

"He is good;
his love endures forever."

Then the temple of the LORD was filled with a cloud, 14and the
priests could not perform their service because of the cloud, for
the glory of the LORD filled the temple of God.

6 Then Solomon said, "The LORD has said that he would dwell
in a dark cloud; 2I have built a magnificent temple for you,
a place for you to dwell forever."

3While the whole assembly of Israel was standing there, the
king turned around and blessed them. 4Then he said:

"Praise be to the LORD, the God of Israel, who with his
hands has fulfilled what he promised with his mouth to my
father David. For he said, 5'Since the day I brought my peo-

ple out of Egypt, I have not chosen a city in any tribe of Israel to have a temple built for my Name to be there, nor have I
chosen anyone to be the leader over my people Israel. 6But
now I have chosen Jerusalem for my Name to be there, and I
have chosen David to rule my people Israel.'

7"My father David had it in his heart to build a temple for
the Name of the LORD, the God of Israel. 8But the LORD said to
my father David, 'Because it was in your heart to build a temple for my Name, you did well to have this in your heart. 9Nev-
ertheless, you are not the one to build the temple, but your
son, who is your own flesh and blood—he is the one who will
build the temple for my Name.'

10"The LORD has kept the promise he made. I have succeeded David my father and now I sit on the throne of Israel,
just as the LORD promised, and I have built the temple for the
Name of the LORD, the God of Israel. 11There I have placed
the ark, in which is the covenant of the LORD that he made
with the people of Israel."

Solomon's Prayer of Dedication

12Then Solomon stood before the altar of the LORD in front of the
whole assembly of Israel and spread out his hands. 13Now he had
made a bronze platform, five cubits[a] long, five cubits wide and
three cubits[b] high, and had placed it in the center of the outer
court. He stood on the platform and then knelt down before the
whole assembly of Israel and spread out his hands toward heaven.
14He said:

"O LORD, God of Israel, there is no God like you in heaven
or on earth—you who keep your covenant of love with your
servants who continue wholeheartedly in your way. 15You
have kept your promise to your servant David my father; with
your mouth you have promised and with your hand you have
fulfilled it—as it is today.

16"Now LORD, God of Israel, keep for your servant David
my father the promises you made to him when you said, 'You
shall never fail to have a man to sit before me on the throne
of Israel, if only your sons are careful in all they do to walk
before me according to my law, as you have done.' 17And
now, O LORD, God of Israel, let your word that you promised
your servant David come true.

18"But will God really dwell on earth with men? The heavens, even the highest heavens, cannot contain you. How much
less this temple I have built! 19Yet give attention to your servant's prayer and his plea for mercy, O LORD my God. Hear the
cry and the prayer that your servant is praying in your presence. 20May your eyes be open toward this temple day and
night, this place of which you said you would put your Name
there. May you hear the prayer your servant prays toward this
place. 21Hear the supplications of your servant and of your
people Israel when they pray toward this place. Hear from
heaven, your dwelling place; and when you hear, forgive.

22"When a man wrongs his neighbor and is required to
take an oath and he comes and swears the oath before your
altar in this temple, 23then hear from heaven and act. Judge

[a] 13 That is, about 7 1/2 feet (about 2.3 meters) [b] 13 That is, about 4 1/2 feet (about 1.3 meters)

(6:1–11) Blessed are You, Lord God of Israel. For You have kept Your covenant that You made with David long ago. Today Jesus Christ, the Son of David, reigns over Your people. He serves You as our High Priest, bringing our prayers to Your heavenly altar. So we bring our praise and prayer to You in His name. (Heb 4:14)

Those that set God always before them and walk before him with all their hearts, shall find him as good as his word and better; he will both keep covenant with them and show mercy to them.

Matthew Henry (1662-1714)

(6:14–21) O Lord, there is no god like You. Your presence filled Solomon's temple. You have dwelt in our midst in Jesus Christ, and now You dwell in my heart through Your Holy Spirit. You watch me from heaven and know my innermost thoughts and fears; You hear my cries and answer my prayers with Your mercy. I will follow You all the days of my life.

between your servants, repaying the guilty by bringing down
on his own head what he has done. Declare the innocent not
guilty and so establish his innocence.
24“When your people Israel have been defeated by an
enemy because they have sinned against you and when they
turn back and confess your name, praying and making supplication before you in this temple, 25then hear from heav-
en and forgive the sin of your people Israel and bring them
back to the land you gave to them and their fathers.
26“When the heavens are shut up and there is no rain because your people have sinned against you, and when they
pray toward this place and confess your name and turn from
their sin because you have afflicted them, 27then hear from
heaven and forgive the sin of your servants, your people Israel. Teach them the right way to live, and send rain on the
land you gave your people for an inheritance.
28“When famine or plague comes to the land, or blight or
mildew, locusts or grasshoppers, or when enemies besiege
them in any of their cities, whatever disaster or disease may
come, 29and when a prayer or plea is made by any of your
people Israel—each one aware of his afflictions and pains,
and spreading out his hands toward this temple— 30then
hear from heaven, your dwelling place. Forgive, and deal
with each man according to all he does, since you know his
heart (for you alone know the hearts of men), 31so that they
will fear you and walk in your ways all the time they live in
the land you gave our fathers.
32“As for the foreigner who does not belong to your people Israel but has come from a distant land because of your
great name and your mighty hand and your outstretched
arm—when he comes and prays toward this temple, 33then
hear from heaven, your dwelling place, and do whatever the
foreigner asks of you, so that all the peoples of the earth may
know your name and fear you, as do your own people Israel, and may know that this house I have built bears your
Name.
34“When your people go to war against their enemies,
wherever you send them, and when they pray to you toward
this city you have chosen and the temple I have built for your
Name, 35then hear from heaven their prayer and their plea,
and uphold their cause.
36“When they sin against you—for there is no one who
does not sin—and you become angry with them and give
them over to the enemy, who takes them captive to a land far
away or near; 37and if they have a change of heart in the
land where they are held captive, and repent and plead with
you in the land of their captivity and say, ‘We have sinned, we
have done wrong and acted wickedly’; 38and if they turn
back to you with all their heart and soul in the land of their
captivity where they were taken, and pray toward the land
you gave their fathers, toward the city you have chosen and
toward the temple I have built for your Name; 39then from
heaven, your dwelling place, hear their prayer and their
pleas, and uphold their cause. And forgive your people, who
have sinned against you.
40“Now, my God, may your eyes be open and your ears attentive to the prayers offered in this place.

Listen! You who think yourselves to be so dull and fit for nothing! By prayer you may live on God Himself with less difficulty or interruption than you live in the vital air. Wouldn't it seem, then, to be highly sinful to neglect prayer?

Madame Jeanne Marie de la Mothe Guyon
(1648-1717)

(6:24–31) Father, thank You that I can call upon You when I am defeated and discouraged. Thank You for Your promise to hear my prayers of earnest repentance and confession. My hope comes from knowing that You will deal with me graciously and mercifully. You know all about me, Father, and I will give You the praise and honor You deserve.

Lord, look upon my need.
I need You, I need You.
Lord, have mercy now on me.
Forgive me, O Lord, forgive me,
And I will be clean.
O Lord, You are familiar with my ways;
There is nothing hid from You.
O Lord, You know the number of my days.
I want to live my life for You.

"I Need You"
Rick Founds (©1989)

MY BELOVED

Celebrate My abundant goodness! Joyfully sing of My righteousness! I have saved you! So rejoice in My salvation. When you call on Me I will be with you. From My own hand I will satisfy your heart's desire when you reverently fear Me.

Every good and perfect gift comes from Me. For I am gracious and compassionate, slow to anger and rich in love. I am good to you and have compassion on you. I uphold you when you fall and lift you up when you are under a great load.

I am the Lord, Who remains faithful forever. I uphold the cause of the oppressed and give food to the hungry. I set prisoners free. I give sight to the blind and lift up those who are bowed down. I love the righteous. I watch over the homeless and sustain the fatherless and the widow.

I will watch over you because you love Me. I will deal well with you for the sake of My name. Because I love you, I will deliver you! In your time of distress, I will hear your cry and save you. This is a promise to you.

So be confident of this, My beloved: You will see and experience My goodness while you live. For I am faithful to My promises, and My love abounds toward you. I love you.

Ps 27:13; 109:21; 145:7-9,13-14,16,18-20; 146:6-9; Jas 1:17

41 "Now arise, O LORD God, and come to your resting place,
you and the ark of your might.
May your priests, O LORD God, be clothed with salvation,
may your saints rejoice in your goodness.
42 O LORD God, do not reject your anointed one.
Remember the great love promised to David your servant."

The Dedication of the Temple

7 When Solomon finished praying, fire came down from heav-
en and consumed the burnt offering and the sacrifices, and
the glory of the LORD filled the temple. 2The priests could not
enter the temple of the LORD because the glory of the LORD filled
it. 3When all the Israelites saw the fire coming down and the glory
of the LORD above the temple, they knelt on the pavement with
their faces to the ground, and they worshiped and gave thanks to
the LORD, saying,

"He is good;
his love endures forever."

4Then the king and all the people offered sacrifices before the
LORD. 5And King Solomon offered a sacrifice of twenty-two thousand head of cattle and a hundred and twenty thousand sheep
and goats. So the king and all the people dedicated the temple of
God. 6The priests took their positions, as did the Levites with the
LORD's musical instruments, which King David had made for
praising the LORD and which were used when he gave thanks, saying, "His love endures forever." Opposite the Levites, the priests
blew their trumpets, and all the Israelites were standing.
7Solomon consecrated the middle part of the courtyard in
front of the temple of the LORD, and there he offered burnt offerings and the fat of the fellowship offerings,[a] because the bronze
altar he had made could not hold the burnt offerings, the grain
offerings and the fat portions.
8So Solomon observed the festival at that time for seven days,
and all Israel with him—a vast assembly, people from Lebo[b] Hamath to the Wadi of Egypt. 9On the eighth day they held an assembly, for they had celebrated the dedication of the altar for
seven days and the festival for seven days more. 10On the twenty-
third day of the seventh month he sent the people to their homes,
joyful and glad in heart for the good things the LORD had done for
David and Solomon and for his people Israel.

The LORD Appears to Solomon

11When Solomon had finished the temple of the LORD and the
royal palace, and had succeeded in carrying out all he had in
mind to do in the temple of the LORD and in his own palace, 12the
LORD appeared to him at night and said:

"I have heard your prayer and have chosen this place for
myself as a temple for sacrifices.
13"When I shut up the heavens so that there is no rain, or
command locusts to devour the land or send a plague
among my people, 14if my people, who are called by my

[a] 7 Traditionally *peace offerings* [b] 8 Or *from the entrance to*

(7:1–10) Lord, the extravagant and heartfelt celebration that Solomon led must have pleased You. We regret how often we just go through the motions of worship to get it over with. Please restore to your church the joy of salvation. Rekindle our passion for You so that our worship will be pleasing in Your sight.

(7:14) Thank You, Father, for these wonderful words of assurance. Thank You for the privilege You give to us by allowing us to seek You, and by honoring the sincere prayers of Your people. Thank You for Your promise to hear us. Thank You for Your promise to forgive us. Thank You for Your promise to heal us. You are truly "the compassionate and gracious God, slow to anger, abounding in love and faithfulness, maintaining love to thousands, and forgiving wickedness, rebellion and sin." (Ex 34:6–7)

Stretch out Your hand
And heal this nation,
Stretch out Your hand
And bring restoration.
Let Your mercy overflow us
Like a never failing stream,
By the blood of Jesus, cleanse us,
Oh Lord, it's You we seek.
Cause Your face to shine
Upon us again.

"Stretch Out Your Hand"
Scott V. Smith and Malcolm duPlessis
(©1995)

When the Church spends much time praying, it begins to see what God does and does not approve of, and through that people are led to repentance . . . But that's still just the beginning. It's the repentance of the Church as a whole that leads to revival. As the revival sweeps the land, even non-Christians begin to repent. Soon you have a mighty move of God in the country. It all starts with prayer, and it all continues in prayer.

Ron Auch (1951-)

name, will humble themselves and pray and seek my face and turn from their wicked ways, then will I hear from heaven and will forgive their sin and will heal their land. 15Now my eyes will be open and my ears attentive to the prayers offered in this place. 16I have chosen and consecrated this temple so that my Name may be there forever. My eyes and my heart will always be there.

17"As for you, if you walk before me as David your father did, and do all I command, and observe my decrees and laws, 18I will establish your royal throne, as I covenanted with David your father when I said, 'You shall never fail to have a man to rule over Israel.'

19"But if you[a] turn away and forsake the decrees and commands I have given you[a] and go off to serve other gods and worship them, 20then I will uproot Israel from my land, which I have given them, and will reject this temple I have consecrated for my Name. I will make it a byword and an object of ridicule among all peoples. 21And though this temple is now so imposing, all who pass by will be appalled and say, 'Why has the LORD done such a thing to this land and to this temple?' 22People will answer, 'Because they have forsaken the LORD, the God of their fathers, who brought them out of Egypt, and have embraced other gods, worshiping and serving them—that is why he brought all this disaster on them.' "

Solomon's Other Activities

8 At the end of twenty years, during which Solomon built the temple of the LORD and his own palace, 2Solomon rebuilt the villages that Hiram[b] had given him, and settled Israelites in them. 3Solomon then went to Hamath Zobah and captured it. 4He also built up Tadmor in the desert and all the store cities he had built in Hamath. 5He rebuilt Upper Beth Horon and Lower Beth Horon as fortified cities, with walls and with gates and bars, 6as well as Baalath and all his store cities, and all the cities for his chariots and for his horses[c]—whatever he desired to build in Jerusalem, in Lebanon and throughout all the territory he ruled.

7All the people left from the Hittites, Amorites, Perizzites, Hivites and Jebusites (these peoples were not Israelites), 8that is, their descendants remaining in the land, whom the Israelites had not destroyed—these Solomon conscripted for his slave labor force, as it is to this day. 9But Solomon did not make slaves of the Israelites for his work; they were his fighting men, commanders of his captains, and commanders of his chariots and charioteers. 10They were also King Solomon's chief officials—two hundred and fifty officials supervising the men.

11Solomon brought Pharaoh's daughter up from the City of David to the palace he had built for her, for he said, "My wife must not live in the palace of David king of Israel, because the places the ark of the LORD has entered are holy."

12On the altar of the LORD that he had built in front of the portico, Solomon sacrificed burnt offerings to the LORD, 13according to the daily requirement for offerings commanded by Moses for Sabbaths, New Moons and the three annual feasts—the Feast of Unleavened Bread, the Feast of Weeks and the Feast of Tabernacles. 14In keeping with the ordinance of his father David, he ap-

[a] *19* The Hebrew is plural. [b] *2* Hebrew *Huram,* a variant of *Hiram*; also in verse 18
[c] *6* Or *charioteers*

(8:2–10) I praise You, Father, for blessing Solomon with unprecedented success. He was a great ruler as well as a great worship leader. His glorious kingdom foreshadowed an even greater Kingdom that is made up of all the tribes of the earth, which Your own Son rules with perfect peace and justice. I thank You for bringing me into the eternal kingdom of the Lord Jesus Christ. (Col 1:13–14; Heb 1:8)

All hail to the King!
In splendor enthroned;
Glad praises we bring,
Thy wonders make known.
Returning victorious,
Great conqueror of sin,
King Jesus, all glorious,
Our vict'ry will win.

"O Worship the King"
David Guthrie (©1997)

pointed the divisions of the priests for their duties, and the Levites to lead the praise and to assist the priests according to each day's requirement. He also appointed the gatekeepers by divisions for the various gates, because this was what David the man of God had ordered. 15They did not deviate from the king's commands to the priests or to the Levites in any matter, including that of the treasuries.

16All Solomon's work was carried out, from the day the foundation of the temple of the LORD was laid until its completion. So the temple of the LORD was finished.

17Then Solomon went to Ezion Geber and Elath on the coast of Edom. 18And Hiram sent him ships commanded by his own officers, men who knew the sea. These, with Solomon's men, sailed to Ophir and brought back four hundred and fifty talents[a] of gold, which they delivered to King Solomon.

The Queen of Sheba Visits Solomon

9 When the queen of Sheba heard of Solomon's fame, she came to Jerusalem to test him with hard questions. Arriving with a very great caravan—with camels carrying spices, large quantities of gold, and precious stones—she came to Solomon and talked with him about all she had on her mind. 2Solomon answered all her questions; nothing was too hard for him to explain to her. 3When the queen of Sheba saw the wisdom of Solomon, as well as the palace he had built, 4the food on his table, the seating of his officials, the attending servants in their robes, the cupbearers in their robes and the burnt offerings he made at[b] the temple of the LORD, she was overwhelmed.

5She said to the king, "The report I heard in my own country about your achievements and your wisdom is true. 6But I did not believe what they said until I came and saw with my own eyes. Indeed, not even half the greatness of your wisdom was told me; you have far exceeded the report I heard. 7How happy your men must be! How happy your officials, who continually stand before you and hear your wisdom! 8Praise be to the LORD your God, who has delighted in you and placed you on his throne as king to rule for the LORD your God. Because of the love of your God for Israel and his desire to uphold them forever, he has made you king over them, to maintain justice and righteousness."

9Then she gave the king 120 talents[c] of gold, large quantities of spices, and precious stones. There had never been such spices as those the queen of Sheba gave to King Solomon.

10(The men of Hiram and the men of Solomon brought gold from Ophir; they also brought algumwood[d] and precious stones. 11The king used the algumwood to make steps for the temple of the LORD and for the royal palace, and to make harps and lyres for the musicians. Nothing like them had ever been seen in Judah.)

12King Solomon gave the queen of Sheba all she desired and asked for; he gave her more than she had brought to him. Then she left and returned with her retinue to her own country.

[a] *18* That is, about 17 tons (about 16 metric tons) [b] *4* Or *the ascent by which he went up to* [c] *9* That is, about 4 1/2 tons (about 4 metric tons) [d] *10* Probably a variant of *almugwood*

(9:8) Jesus Christ, Son of David, You are enthroned as the eternal King! As You said Yourself, if the queen of Sheba was impressed by the wisdom of Solomon, how much more should people respond to You who are so much greater than Solomon! You reign on David's throne and over his kingdom, establishing and upholding it with justice and righteousness forever. (Isa 9:7; Mt 12:42)

Solomon's Splendor

13The weight of the gold that Solomon received yearly was 666 talents,[a] 14not including the revenues brought in by merchants and traders. Also all the kings of Arabia and the governors of the land brought gold and silver to Solomon.

15King Solomon made two hundred large shields of hammered gold; six hundred bekas[b] of hammered gold went into each shield. 16He also made three hundred small shields of hammered gold, with three hundred bekas[c] of gold in each shield. The king put them in the Palace of the Forest of Lebanon.

17Then the king made a great throne inlaid with ivory and overlaid with pure gold. 18The throne had six steps, and a footstool of gold was attached to it. On both sides of the seat were armrests, with a lion standing beside each of them. 19Twelve lions stood on the six steps, one at either end of each step. Nothing like it had ever been made for any other kingdom. 20All King Solomon's goblets were gold, and all the household articles in the Palace of the Forest of Lebanon were pure gold. Nothing was made of silver, because silver was considered of little value in Solomon's day. 21The king had a fleet of trading ships[d] manned by Hiram's[e] men. Once every three years it returned, carrying gold, silver and ivory, and apes and baboons.

22King Solomon was greater in riches and wisdom than all the other kings of the earth. 23All the kings of the earth sought audience with Solomon to hear the wisdom God had put in his heart. 24Year after year, everyone who came brought a gift—articles of silver and gold, and robes, weapons and spices, and horses and mules.

25Solomon had four thousand stalls for horses and chariots, and twelve thousand horses,[f] which he kept in the chariot cities and also with him in Jerusalem. 26He ruled over all the kings from the River[g] to the land of the Philistines, as far as the border of Egypt. 27The king made silver as common in Jerusalem as stones, and cedar as plentiful as sycamore-fig trees in the foothills. 28Solomon's horses were imported from Egypt[h] and from all other countries.

Solomon's Death

29As for the other events of Solomon's reign, from beginning to end, are they not written in the records of Nathan the prophet, in the prophecy of Ahijah the Shilonite and in the visions of Iddo the seer concerning Jeroboam son of Nebat? 30Solomon reigned in Jerusalem over all Israel forty years. 31Then he rested with his fathers and was buried in the city of David his father. And Rehoboam his son succeeded him as king.

Israel Rebels Against Rehoboam

10 Rehoboam went to Shechem, for all the Israelites had gone there to make him king. 2When Jeroboam son of Nebat heard this (he was in Egypt, where he had fled from King Solomon), he returned from Egypt. 3So they sent for Jeroboam, and he and all Israel went to Rehoboam and said to him: 4"Your fa-

[a] 13 That is, about 25 tons (about 23 metric tons) [b] 15 That is, about 7 1/2 pounds (about 3.5 kilograms) [c] 16 That is, about 3 3/4 pounds (about 1.7 kilograms) [d] 21 Hebrew *of ships that could go to Tarshish* [e] 21 Hebrew *Huram,* a variant of *Hiram* [f] 25 Or *charioteers* [g] 26 That is, the Euphrates [h] 28 Or possibly *Muzur,* a region in Cilicia

(9:13–28) Father, as I read of Solomon's wealth and grandeur, his opulence and extravagance, I remember the words of Jesus: "And why do you worry about clothes? See how the lilies of the field grow. They do not labor or spin. Yet I tell you that not even Solomon in all his splendor was dressed like one of these. If that is how God clothes the grass of the field, which is here today and tomorrow is thrown into the fire, will he not much more clothe you, O you of little faith?" I praise You, O Lord, for the unsurpassed beauty of Your creation. And I thank You for Your faithfulness to provide everything I need. (Mt 6:28–30)

Worldly cares are not a part of our discipleship, but distinct and subordinate concerns. Before we start taking thought for our life, our food and clothing, our work and families, we must seek the righteousness of Christ . . . If we follow Jesus and look only to his righteousness, we are in his hands and under the protection of him and his Father.

Dietrich Bonhoeffer (1906-1945)

Praise to the Lord, who o'er all
Things so wondrously reigneth,
Shelters thee under His wings,
Yea, so gently sustaineth!
Hast thou not seen
How thy desires e'er have been
Granted in what He ordaineth?

"Praise to the Lord, the Almighty"
Joachim Neander (1680)
Trans. Catherine Winkworth (1827-1878)

ther put a heavy yoke on us, but now lighten the harsh labor and
the heavy yoke he put on us, and we will serve you."
5Rehoboam answered, "Come back to me in three days." So
the people went away.
6Then King Rehoboam consulted the elders who had served
his father Solomon during his lifetime. "How would you advise
me to answer these people?" he asked.
7They replied, "If you will be kind to these people and please
them and give them a favorable answer, they will always be your
servants."
8But Rehoboam rejected the advice the elders gave him and
consulted the young men who had grown up with him and were
serving him. 9He asked them, "What is your advice? How should
we answer these people who say to me, 'Lighten the yoke your father put on us'?"
10The young men who had grown up with him replied, "Tell
the people who have said to you, 'Your father put a heavy yoke on
us, but make our yoke lighter'—tell them, 'My little finger is
thicker than my father's waist. 11My father laid on you a heavy
yoke; I will make it even heavier. My father scourged you with
whips; I will scourge you with scorpions.' "
12Three days later Jeroboam and all the people returned to Rehoboam, as the king had said, "Come back to me in three days."
13The king answered them harshly. Rejecting the advice of the elders, 14he followed the advice of the young men and said, "My father made your yoke heavy; I will make it even heavier. My father
scourged you with whips; I will scourge you with scorpions."
15So the king did not listen to the people, for this turn of events
was from God, to fulfill the word the LORD had spoken to Jeroboam son of Nebat through Ahijah the Shilonite.
16When all Israel saw that the king refused to listen to them,
they answered the king:

"What share do we have in David,
what part in Jesse's son?
To your tents, O Israel!
Look after your own house, O David!"

So all the Israelites went home. 17But as for the Israelites who
were living in the towns of Judah, Rehoboam still ruled over
them.
18King Rehoboam sent out Adoniram,[a] who was in charge of
forced labor, but the Israelites stoned him to death. King Rehoboam, however, managed to get into his chariot and escape to Jerusalem. 19So Israel has been in rebellion against the house of
David to this day.

11 When Rehoboam arrived in Jerusalem, he mustered the
house of Judah and Benjamin—a hundred and eighty thousand fighting men—to make war against Israel and to regain the
kingdom for Rehoboam.
2But this word of the LORD came to Shemaiah the man of God:
3"Say to Rehoboam son of Solomon king of Judah and to all the
Israelites in Judah and Benjamin, 4'This is what the LORD says: Do
not go up to fight against your brothers. Go home, every one of
you, for this is my doing.' " So they obeyed the words of the LORD
and turned back from marching against Jeroboam.

[a] *18* Hebrew *Hadoram,* a variant of *Adoniram*

(10:15) The division of the kingdom was Your doing, Lord. It was the fulfillment of Your word to Solomon when he turned away from You. You determine the course of nations, O God, for all authority is in Your hand. "Wealth and honor come from you; you are the ruler of all things. In your hands are strength and power to exalt and give strength to all." (1Ki 11:9–11,29–37; 1Ch 29:12)

(11:13–17) O Lord, I pray that I would be like these faithful priests and Levites from the northern kingdom of Israel who refused to compromise or give in to false worship. Even if it means abandoning my home and property, I want to be steadfast for You. No matter what those around me are doing or what my culture accepts, I will set my heart on seeking You. (1Ki 12:26–30)

When Jesus has become great and precious and indispensable to the heart, one no longer counts it a great sacrifice to give up everything else for the privilege of following Him.

J. N. Kildahl (1857-1920)

Who is on the Lord's side?
Who will serve the King?
Who will be His helpers,
Other lives to bring?
Who will leave the world's side?
Who will face the foe?
Who is on the Lord's side?
Who for Him will go?
By Thy call of mercy,
By Thy grace divine,
We are on the Lord's side,
Savior, we are Thine.

"Who Is on the Lord's Side?"
Frances Ridley Havergal (1836-1879)

Rehoboam Fortifies Judah

[5]Rehoboam lived in Jerusalem and built up towns for defense in Judah: [6]Bethlehem, Etam, Tekoa, [7]Beth Zur, Soco, Adullam, [8]Gath, Mareshah, Ziph, [9]Adoraim, Lachish, Azekah, [10]Zorah, Aijalon and Hebron. These were fortified cities in Judah and Benjamin. [11]He strengthened their defenses and put commanders in them, with supplies of food, olive oil and wine. [12]He put shields and spears in all the cities, and made them very strong. So Judah and Benjamin were his.

[13]The priests and Levites from all their districts throughout Israel sided with him. [14]The Levites even abandoned their pasturelands and property, and came to Judah and Jerusalem because Jeroboam and his sons had rejected them as priests of the LORD. [15]And he appointed his own priests for the high places and for the goat and calf idols he had made. [16]Those from every tribe of Israel who set their hearts on seeking the LORD, the God of Israel, followed the Levites to Jerusalem to offer sacrifices to the LORD, the God of their fathers. [17]They strengthened the kingdom of Judah and supported Rehoboam son of Solomon three years, walking in the ways of David and Solomon during this time.

Rehoboam's Family

[18]Rehoboam married Mahalath, who was the daughter of David's son Jerimoth and of Abihail, the daughter of Jesse's son Eliab. [19]She bore him sons: Jeush, Shemariah and Zaham. [20]Then he married Maacah daughter of Absalom, who bore him Abijah, Attai, Ziza and Shelomith. [21]Rehoboam loved Maacah daughter of Absalom more than any of his other wives and concubines. In all, he had eighteen wives and sixty concubines, twenty-eight sons and sixty daughters.

[22]Rehoboam appointed Abijah son of Maacah to be the chief prince among his brothers, in order to make him king. [23]He acted wisely, dispersing some of his sons throughout the districts of Judah and Benjamin, and to all the fortified cities. He gave them abundant provisions and took many wives for them.

Shishak Attacks Jerusalem

12 After Rehoboam's position as king was established and he had become strong, he and all Israel[a] with him abandoned the law of the LORD. [2]Because they had been unfaithful to the LORD, Shishak king of Egypt attacked Jerusalem in the fifth year of King Rehoboam. [3]With twelve hundred chariots and sixty thousand horsemen and the innumerable troops of Libyans, Sukkites and Cushites[b] that came with him from Egypt, [4]he captured the fortified cities of Judah and came as far as Jerusalem.

[5]Then the prophet Shemaiah came to Rehoboam and to the leaders of Judah who had assembled in Jerusalem for fear of Shishak, and he said to them, "This is what the LORD says, 'You have abandoned me; therefore, I now abandon you to Shishak.' "

[6]The leaders of Israel and the king humbled themselves and said, "The LORD is just."

[7]When the LORD saw that they humbled themselves, this word of the LORD came to Shemaiah: "Since they have humbled themselves, I will not destroy them but will soon give them deliver-

[a] *1* That is, Judah, as frequently in 2 Chronicles [b] *3* That is, people from the upper Nile region

ance. My wrath will not be poured out on Jerusalem through Shishak. 8They will, however, become subject to him, so that they
may learn the difference between serving me and serving the
kings of other lands."
9When Shishak king of Egypt attacked Jerusalem, he carried
off the treasures of the temple of the LORD and the treasures of the
royal palace. He took everything, including the gold shields Solomon had made. 10So King Rehoboam made bronze shields to replace them and assigned these to the commanders of the guard
on duty at the entrance to the royal palace. 11Whenever the king
went to the LORD's temple, the guards went with him, bearing the
shields, and afterward they returned them to the guardroom.
12Because Rehoboam humbled himself, the LORD's anger
turned from him, and he was not totally destroyed. Indeed, there
was some good in Judah.
13King Rehoboam established himself firmly in Jerusalem and
continued as king. He was forty-one years old when he became
king, and he reigned seventeen years in Jerusalem, the city the
LORD had chosen out of all the tribes of Israel in which to put his
Name. His mother's name was Naamah; she was an Ammonite.
14He did evil because he had not set his heart on seeking the
LORD.
15As for the events of Rehoboam's reign, from beginning to
end, are they not written in the records of Shemaiah the prophet
and of Iddo the seer that deal with genealogies? There was continual warfare between Rehoboam and Jeroboam. 16Rehoboam
rested with his fathers and was buried in the City of David. And
Abijah his son succeeded him as king.

Abijah King of Judah

13 In the eighteenth year of the reign of Jeroboam, Abijah became king of Judah, 2and he reigned in Jerusalem three
years. His mother's name was Maacah,[a] a daughter[b] of Uriel of
Gibeah.
There was war between Abijah and Jeroboam. 3Abijah went
into battle with a force of four hundred thousand able fighting
men, and Jeroboam drew up a battle line against him with eight
hundred thousand able troops.
4Abijah stood on Mount Zemaraim, in the hill country of
Ephraim, and said, "Jeroboam and all Israel, listen to me! 5Don't
you know that the LORD, the God of Israel, has given the kingship
of Israel to David and his descendants forever by a covenant of
salt? 6Yet Jeroboam son of Nebat, an official of Solomon son of
David, rebelled against his master. 7Some worthless scoundrels
gathered around him and opposed Rehoboam son of Solomon
when he was young and indecisive and not strong enough to resist them.
8"And now you plan to resist the kingdom of the LORD, which
is in the hands of David's descendants. You are indeed a vast army
and have with you the golden calves that Jeroboam made to be
your gods. 9But didn't you drive out the priests of the LORD, the
sons of Aaron, and the Levites, and make priests of your own as
the peoples of other lands do? Whoever comes to consecrate himself with a young bull and seven rams may become a priest of
what are not gods.

[a] 2 Most Septuagint manuscripts and Syriac (see also 2 Chron. 11:20 and 1 Kings 15:2); Hebrew *Micaiah* [b] 2 Or *granddaughter*

(12:1–12) Holy God, You are just and compassionate. Though Judah turned its back on You, You did not stop calling out to Your people, warning them of the consequences of their sins. They repented and You protected them from total destruction. They lost their glory, but You saved their lives. Lord, do not let me be slow to repent and return to You. Do not let my pride or my shame keep me from setting my heart on seeking You.

If my people's hearts are humbled,
If they pray and seek My face,
If they turn away from evil,
I will not withhold my grace.
I will hear their prayers from heaven;
I will pardon every sin.
If my people's hearts are humbled,
I will surely heal their land.

Then my eyes will see their sorrow,
Then my ears will hear their plea;
If my people's hearts are humbled
I will set their nation free.
If my people's hearts are humbled,
If they pray and seek my face;
If they turn away from evil,
I will not withhold my grace.

"If My People's Hearts Are Humbled"
Claire Cloninger (©1986)

Break off every known sin, come out boldly from the world; cry mightily to God in prayer; cast yourself wholly and unreservedly on the Lord Jesus for time and eternity; lay aside every weight. Cling to nothing, however dear, which interferes with our soul's salvation; give up everything, however precious, which comes between you and heaven. This old shipwrecked world is fast sinking beneath your feet: the one thing needful is to have a place in the lifeboat and get safe to shore.

J. C. Ryle (1816-1900)

10"As for us, the LORD is our God, and we have not forsaken
him. The priests who serve the LORD are sons of Aaron, and the Levites assist them. 11Every morning and evening they present burnt
offerings and fragrant incense to the LORD. They set out the bread
on the ceremonially clean table and light the lamps on the gold
lampstand every evening. We are observing the requirements of
the LORD our God. But you have forsaken him. 12God is with us; he
is our leader. His priests with their trumpets will sound the battle
cry against you. Men of Israel, do not fight against the LORD, the
God of your fathers, for you will not succeed."
13Now Jeroboam had sent troops around to the rear, so that
while he was in front of Judah the ambush was behind them.
14Judah turned and saw that they were being attacked at both front
and rear. Then they cried out to the LORD. The priests blew their
trumpets 15and the men of Judah raised the battle cry. At the
sound of their battle cry, God routed Jeroboam and all Israel before Abijah and Judah. 16The Israelites fled before Judah, and God
delivered them into their hands. 17Abijah and his men inflicted
heavy losses on them, so that there were five hundred thousand
casualties among Israel's able men. 18The men of Israel were subdued on that occasion, and the men of Judah were victorious because they relied on the LORD, the God of their fathers.
19Abijah pursued Jeroboam and took from him the towns of
Bethel, Jeshanah and Ephron, with their surrounding villages.
20Jeroboam did not regain power during the time of Abijah. And
the LORD struck him down and he died.
21But Abijah grew in strength. He married fourteen wives and
had twenty-two sons and sixteen daughters.
22The other events of Abijah's reign, what he did and what he
said, are written in the annotations of the prophet Iddo.

14 And Abijah rested with his fathers and was buried in the
City of David. Asa his son succeeded him as king, and in his
days the country was at peace for ten years.

Asa King of Judah

2Asa did what was good and right in the eyes of the LORD his
God. 3He removed the foreign altars and the high places, smashed
the sacred stones and cut down the Asherah poles.[a] 4He commanded Judah to seek the LORD, the God of their fathers, and to
obey his laws and commands. 5He removed the high places and
incense altars in every town in Judah, and the kingdom was at
peace under him. 6He built up the fortified cities of Judah, since
the land was at peace. No one was at war with him during those
years, for the LORD gave him rest.
7"Let us build up these towns," he said to Judah, "and put walls
around them, with towers, gates and bars. The land is still ours,
because we have sought the LORD our God; we sought him and he
has given us rest on every side." So they built and prospered.
8Asa had an army of three hundred thousand men from Judah,
equipped with large shields and with spears, and two hundred and
eighty thousand from Benjamin, armed with small shields and with
bows. All these were brave fighting men.
9Zerah the Cushite marched out against them with a vast army[b]
and three hundred chariots, and came as far as Mareshah. 10Asa

[a] 3 That is, symbols of the goddess Asherah; here and elsewhere in 2 Chronicles
[b] 9 Hebrew *with an army of a thousand thousands* or *with an army of thousands upon thousands*

(14:1–8) God of our fathers, Abijah desired to leave a legacy of faithfulness to You. You blessed Your people by giving them Asa as heir to his throne. May I invest myself in Your purposes, O Lord, that those who come after me might enjoy the benefits of Your blessing.

Believe it, Christians, for a certain truth that, when you come to die, your thoughts will not be: What a figure have I made in the world; how pleasantly have I passed my days; what pleasures have I enjoyed; and what wealth do I leave behind me? No, no. But . . . How have I spent my life; how have I employed my time; how have I improved the talents with which God entrusted me; what good have I done in the world; have I brought up my children in the fear of God; have I been kind and helpful to poor and needy people; have I lived in the fear of God and worshipped Him both in public and in private, according to my ability?

Bishop Thomas Wilson (1663-1735)

went out to meet him, and they took up battle positions in the
Valley of Zephathah near Mareshah.
11Then Asa called to the LORD his God and said, "LORD, there
is no one like you to help the powerless against the mighty. Help
us, O LORD our God, for we rely on you, and in your name we
have come against this vast army. O LORD, you are our God; do
not let man prevail against you."
12The LORD struck down the Cushites before Asa and Judah.
The Cushites fled, 13and Asa and his army pursued them as far
as Gerar. Such a great number of Cushites fell that they could
not recover; they were crushed before the LORD and his forces.
The men of Judah carried off a large amount of plunder. 14They
destroyed all the villages around Gerar, for the terror of the
LORD had fallen upon them. They plundered all these villages,
since there was much booty there. 15They also attacked the
camps of the herdsmen and carried off droves of sheep and
goats and camels. Then they returned to Jerusalem.

Asa's Reform

15 The Spirit of God came upon Azariah son of Oded. 2He
went out to meet Asa and said to him, "Listen to me, Asa
and all Judah and Benjamin. The LORD is with you when you are
with him. If you seek him, he will be found by you, but if you
forsake him, he will forsake you. 3For a long time Israel was
without the true God, without a priest to teach and without the
law. 4But in their distress they turned to the LORD, the God of Israel, and sought him, and he was found by them. 5In those days
it was not safe to travel about, for all the inhabitants of the lands
were in great turmoil. 6One nation was being crushed by another and one city by another, because God was troubling them
with every kind of distress. 7But as for you, be strong and do not
give up, for your work will be rewarded."
8When Asa heard these words and the prophecy of Azariah
son of[a] Oded the prophet, he took courage. He removed the detestable idols from the whole land of Judah and Benjamin and
from the towns he had captured in the hills of Ephraim. He repaired the altar of the LORD that was in front of the portico of the
LORD's temple.
9Then he assembled all Judah and Benjamin and the people
from Ephraim, Manasseh and Simeon who had settled among
them, for large numbers had come over to him from Israel
when they saw that the LORD his God was with him.
10They assembled at Jerusalem in the third month of the fifteenth year of Asa's reign. 11At that time they sacrificed to the
LORD seven hundred head of cattle and seven thousand sheep
and goats from the plunder they had brought back. 12They entered into a covenant to seek the LORD, the God of their fathers,
with all their heart and soul. 13All who would not seek the LORD,
the God of Israel, were to be put to death, whether small or
great, man or woman. 14They took an oath to the LORD with loud
acclamation, with shouting and with trumpets and horns. 15All
Judah rejoiced about the oath because they had sworn it wholeheartedly. They sought God eagerly, and he was found by them.
So the LORD gave them rest on every side.

[a] 8 Vulgate and Syriac (see also Septuagint and verse 1); Hebrew does not have *Azariah son of.*

Thank you, Father, that you still speak to me today through your Word, my circumstances, and other people. I need to hear your voice. Teach me to be quiet and alert. I will wait on you and follow your counsel.

Charles Stanley (1932-)

(15:1–19) Glorious God, what a wonder Your Word is. You gave courage to King Asa through Your prophet Azariah, and he led the people in spiritual renewal. Let Your Word resound in Your church today, Lord, so that many will take courage to seek You and to commit themselves to You.

God's Word is our great heritage
And shall be ours forevermore;
To spread its light from age to age
Shall be our chief endeavor.
Through life it guides our way;
In death it is our stay.
Lord, grant while time shall last
Your Church may hold it fast
Throughout all generations.

"God's Word Is Our Great Heritage"
Nikolai F.S. Grundtvig (1783-1872)
Trans. Ole G. Belsheim (1861-1925)

16King Asa also deposed his grandmother Maacah from her
position as queen mother, because she had made a repulsive
Asherah pole. Asa cut the pole down, broke it up and burned it
in the Kidron Valley. 17Although he did not remove the high
places from Israel, Asa's heart was fully committed ⌊to the
LORD⌋ all his life. 18He brought into the temple of God the silver and gold and the articles that he and his father had dedicated.
19There was no more war until the thirty-fifth year of Asa's
reign.

Asa's Last Years

16 In the thirty-sixth year of Asa's reign Baasha king of Israel went up against Judah and fortified Ramah to prevent
anyone from leaving or entering the territory of Asa king of
Judah.
2Asa then took the silver and gold out of the treasuries of the
LORD's temple and of his own palace and sent it to Ben-Hadad
king of Aram, who was ruling in Damascus. 3"Let there be a
treaty between me and you," he said, "as there was between my
father and your father. See, I am sending you silver and gold.
Now break your treaty with Baasha king of Israel so he will withdraw from me."
4Ben-Hadad agreed with King Asa and sent the commanders
of his forces against the towns of Israel. They conquered Ijon,
Dan, Abel Maim[a] and all the store cities of Naphtali. 5When Baasha heard this, he stopped building Ramah and abandoned his
work. 6Then King Asa brought all the men of Judah, and they
carried away from Ramah the stones and timber Baasha had
been using. With them he built up Geba and Mizpah.
7At that time Hanani the seer came to Asa king of Judah and
said to him: "Because you relied on the king of Aram and not on
the LORD your God, the army of the king of Aram has escaped
from your hand. 8Were not the Cushites[b] and Libyans a mighty
army with great numbers of chariots and horsemen[c]? Yet when
you relied on the LORD, he delivered them into your hand. 9For
the eyes of the LORD range throughout the earth to strengthen
those whose hearts are fully committed to him. You have done
a foolish thing, and from now on you will be at war."
10Asa was angry with the seer because of this; he was so enraged that he put him in prison. At the same time Asa brutally
oppressed some of the people.
11The events of Asa's reign, from beginning to end, are written in the book of the kings of Judah and Israel. 12In the thirty-
ninth year of his reign Asa was afflicted with a disease in his
feet. Though his disease was severe, even in his illness he did
not seek help from the LORD, but only from the physicians.
13Then in the forty-first year of his reign Asa died and rested
with his fathers. 14They buried him in the tomb that he had cut
out for himself in the City of David. They laid him on a bier covered with spices and various blended perfumes, and they made
a huge fire in his honor.

(16:1–10) "LORD, there is no one like you to help the powerless against the mighty. Help us, O LORD our God, for we rely on you, and in your name we have come against this vast army." How easily Asa forgot his own prayer. How quickly he forgot the lessons of past victories. And how often, like Asa, do I forget Your faithfulness when I face adversity. Lord, deliver me from the temptation to take matters into my own hands, to solve perplexing problems in my life without Your divine guidance. Give me humility to hear and to follow clear words of warning from Your servants, for You give grace to the humble, but You resist those who resist You. (2Ch 14:11; Pr 3:34)

Quite possibly you are standing at a fork in life's pathway and do not know whether you should turn to the right or to the left? Perhaps the decision that must be made today, or tomorrow at the latest, seems somewhat trivial; nevertheless, you sense intuitively that great issues are involved. You may never come again to this same parting of the ways, and life will be different in the tomorrows because of the decision of today . . . You will find that to ask wisdom of the Highest, to wait for His indication of the way, and to obey Him without hesitation is to be led in the right way, at His time, and for His glory.

Victor Raymond Edman (1900–1967)

[a] 4 Also known as *Abel Beth Maacah* [b] 8 That is, people from the upper Nile region
[c] 8 Or *charioteers*

Jehoshaphat King of Judah

17 Jehoshaphat his son succeeded him as king and strengthened himself against Israel. 2He stationed troops in all the
fortified cities of Judah and put garrisons in Judah and in the
towns of Ephraim that his father Asa had captured.
3The LORD was with Jehoshaphat because in his early years
he walked in the ways his father David had followed. He did not
consult the Baals 4but sought the God of his father and followed
his commands rather than the practices of Israel. 5The LORD established the kingdom under his control; and all Judah brought
gifts to Jehoshaphat, so that he had great wealth and honor. 6His
heart was devoted to the ways of the LORD; furthermore, he removed the high places and the Asherah poles from Judah.
7In the third year of his reign he sent his officials Ben-Hail,
Obadiah, Zechariah, Nethanel and Micaiah to teach in the
towns of Judah. 8With them were certain Levites—Shemaiah,
Nethaniah, Zebadiah, Asahel, Shemiramoth, Jehonathan, Adonijah, Tobijah and Tob-Adonijah—and the priests Elishama
and Jehoram. 9They taught throughout Judah, taking with them
the Book of the Law of the LORD; they went around to all the
towns of Judah and taught the people.
10The fear of the LORD fell on all the kingdoms of the lands
surrounding Judah, so that they did not make war with Jehoshaphat. 11Some Philistines brought Jehoshaphat gifts and silver
as tribute, and the Arabs brought him flocks: seven thousand
seven hundred rams and seven thousand seven hundred goats.
12Jehoshaphat became more and more powerful; he built
forts and store cities in Judah 13and had large supplies in the
towns of Judah. He also kept experienced fighting men in Jerusalem. 14Their enrollment by families was as follows:

From Judah, commanders of units of 1,000:
  Adnah the commander, with 300,000 fighting men;
15next, Jehohanan the commander, with 280,000;
16next, Amasiah son of Zicri, who volunteered himself for
  the service of the LORD, with 200,000.
17From Benjamin:
  Eliada, a valiant soldier, with 200,000 men armed with
  bows and shields;
18next, Jehozabad, with 180,000 men armed for battle.

19These were the men who served the king, besides those he
stationed in the fortified cities throughout Judah.

Micaiah Prophesies Against Ahab

18 Now Jehoshaphat had great wealth and honor, and he allied himself with Ahab by marriage. 2Some years later he
went down to visit Ahab in Samaria. Ahab slaughtered many sheep
and cattle for him and the people with him and urged him to attack Ramoth Gilead. 3Ahab king of Israel asked Jehoshaphat king
of Judah, "Will you go with me against Ramoth Gilead?"
Jehoshaphat replied, "I am as you are, and my people as your
people; we will join you in the war." 4But Jehoshaphat also said
to the king of Israel, "First seek the counsel of the LORD."
5So the king of Israel brought together the prophets—four
hundred men—and asked them, "Shall we go to war against
Ramoth Gilead, or shall I refrain?"
"Go," they answered, "for God will give it into the king's hand."

(17:3–9) God of Israel, You are the God of Your people in every age. You blessed Jehoshaphat because he walked in the ways of his ancestor, King David. We pray that You will give us leaders who will lead us in peaceful and godly ways. May they have courage to follow You and trust in Your Word. (1Ti 2:1–2)

(18:4–17) Father, though I may not be a prophet like Micaiah, You still require integrity from me when I am pressured to conform to the ways of the world. O Lord, give me strength and courage to speak the truth at all times, rather than caving in to my desire to say what people want to hear. I also pray for the leaders of Your church today: May they resist the temptation to compromise truth in order to gain approval or avoid conflict.

I am resolved to enter the Kingdom,
Leaving the paths of sin.
Friends may oppose me,
Foes may beset me;
Still will I enter in.

I am resolved, and who will go with me?
Come, friends without delay;
Taught by the Bible, led by the Spirit,
We'll walk the heav'nly way.

"I Am Resolved"
Palmer Hartsough (1844–1932)

6 But Jehoshaphat asked, "Is there not a prophet of the LORD
here whom we can inquire of?"
7 The king of Israel answered Jehoshaphat, "There is still one
man through whom we can inquire of the LORD, but I hate him because he never prophesies anything good about me, but always
bad. He is Micaiah son of Imlah."
"The king should not say that," Jehoshaphat replied.
8 So the king of Israel called one of his officials and said,
"Bring Micaiah son of Imlah at once."
9 Dressed in their royal robes, the king of Israel and Jehoshaphat king of Judah were sitting on their thrones at the threshing
floor by the entrance to the gate of Samaria, with all the prophets
prophesying before them. 10 Now Zedekiah son of Kenaanah had
made iron horns, and he declared, "This is what the LORD says:
'With these you will gore the Arameans until they are destroyed.' "
11 All the other prophets were prophesying the same thing. "Attack Ramoth Gilead and be victorious," they said, "for the LORD
will give it into the king's hand."
12 The messenger who had gone to summon Micaiah said to
him, "Look, as one man the other prophets are predicting success for the king. Let your word agree with theirs, and speak favorably."
13 But Micaiah said, "As surely as the LORD lives, I can tell him
only what my God says."
14 When he arrived, the king asked him, "Micaiah, shall we go
to war against Ramoth Gilead, or shall I refrain?"
"Attack and be victorious," he answered, "for they will be given
into your hand."
15 The king said to him, "How many times must I make you
swear to tell me nothing but the truth in the name of the LORD?"
16 Then Micaiah answered, "I saw all Israel scattered on the
hills like sheep without a shepherd, and the LORD said, 'These
people have no master. Let each one go home in peace.' "
17 The king of Israel said to Jehoshaphat, "Didn't I tell you that
he never prophesies anything good about me, but only bad?"
18 Micaiah continued, "Therefore hear the word of the LORD: I
saw the LORD sitting on his throne with all the host of heaven
standing on his right and on his left. 19 And the LORD said, 'Who
will entice Ahab king of Israel into attacking Ramoth Gilead and
going to his death there?'
"One suggested this, and another that. 20 Finally, a spirit came
forward, stood before the LORD and said, 'I will entice him.'
" 'By what means?' the LORD asked.
21 " 'I will go and be a lying spirit in the mouths of all his
prophets,' he said.
" 'You will succeed in enticing him,' said the LORD. 'Go and
do it.'
22 "So now the LORD has put a lying spirit in the mouths of these
prophets of yours. The LORD has decreed disaster for you."
23 Then Zedekiah son of Kenaanah went up and slapped Micaiah in the face. "Which way did the spirit from[a] the LORD go when
he went from me to speak to you?" he asked.
24 Micaiah replied, "You will find out on the day you go to hide
in an inner room."
25 The king of Israel then ordered, "Take Micaiah and send him

[a] 23 Or *Spirit of*

back to Amon the ruler of the city and to Joash the king's son,
[26]and say, 'This is what the king says: Put this fellow in prison
and give him nothing but bread and water until I return safely.' "

[27]Micaiah declared, "If you ever return safely, the LORD has not
spoken through me." Then he added, "Mark my words, all you
people!"

Ahab Killed at Ramoth Gilead

[28]So the king of Israel and Jehoshaphat king of Judah went up
to Ramoth Gilead. [29]The king of Israel said to Jehoshaphat, "I
will enter the battle in disguise, but you wear your royal robes."
So the king of Israel disguised himself and went into battle.

[30]Now the king of Aram had ordered his chariot commanders,
"Do not fight with anyone, small or great, except the king of Israel." [31]When the chariot commanders saw Jehoshaphat, they
thought, "This is the king of Israel." So they turned to attack him,
but Jehoshaphat cried out, and the LORD helped him. God drew
them away from him, [32]for when the chariot commanders saw
that he was not the king of Israel, they stopped pursuing him.

[33]But someone drew his bow at random and hit the king of Israel between the sections of his armor. The king told the chariot
driver, "Wheel around and get me out of the fighting. I've been
wounded." [34]All day long the battle raged, and the king of Israel
propped himself up in his chariot facing the Arameans until
evening. Then at sunset he died.

19 When Jehoshaphat king of Judah returned safely to his
palace in Jerusalem, [2]Jehu the seer, the son of Hanani,
went out to meet him and said to the king, "Should you help the
wicked and love[a] those who hate the LORD? Because of this, the
wrath of the LORD is upon you. [3]There is, however, some good in
you, for you have rid the land of the Asherah poles and have set
your heart on seeking God."

Jehoshaphat Appoints Judges

[4]Jehoshaphat lived in Jerusalem, and he went out again among
the people from Beersheba to the hill country of Ephraim and
turned them back to the LORD, the God of their fathers. [5]He appointed judges in the land, in each of the fortified cities of Judah.
[6]He told them, "Consider carefully what you do, because you are
not judging for man but for the LORD, who is with you whenever
you give a verdict. [7]Now let the fear of the LORD be upon you.
Judge carefully, for with the LORD our God there is no injustice or
partiality or bribery."

[8]In Jerusalem also, Jehoshaphat appointed some of the Levites,
priests and heads of Israelite families to administer the law of the
LORD and to settle disputes. And they lived in Jerusalem. [9]He gave
them these orders: "You must serve faithfully and wholeheartedly
in the fear of the LORD. [10]In every case that comes before you
from your fellow countrymen who live in the cities—whether
bloodshed or other concerns of the law, commands, decrees or
ordinances—you are to warn them not to sin against the LORD;
otherwise his wrath will come on you and your brothers. Do this,
and you will not sin.

[11]"Amariah the chief priest will be over you in any matter concerning the LORD, and Zebadiah son of Ishmael, the leader of the

[a]2 Or *and make alliances with*

(19:4-7) You are righteous and just in all Your ways, heavenly Judge. Your law is perfect. You bless those who uphold justice and mercy. May we be counted among those who have concern for the oppressed. Teach us to "follow justice and justice alone" so that we may live and possess the land that You have given us. We look forward to that great day when Your justice will "roll on like a river," and "righteousness like a never-failing stream." (Dt 16:20; Am 5:24)

tribe of Judah, will be over you in any matter concerning the king, and the Levites will serve as officials before you. Act with courage, and may the LORD be with those who do well."

Jehoshaphat Defeats Moab and Ammon

20 After this, the Moabites and Ammonites with some of the
Meunites[a] came to make war on Jehoshaphat.
2Some men came and told Jehoshaphat, "A vast army is coming against you from Edom,[b] from the other side of the Sea.[c] It is
already in Hazazon Tamar" (that is, En Gedi). 3Alarmed, Jehoshaphat resolved to inquire of the LORD, and he proclaimed a fast
for all Judah. 4The people of Judah came together to seek help
from the LORD; indeed, they came from every town in Judah to
seek him.
5Then Jehoshaphat stood up in the assembly of Judah and Jerusalem at the temple of the LORD in the front of the new courtyard 6and said:
"O LORD, God of our fathers, are you not the God who is
in heaven? You rule over all the kingdoms of the nations.
Power and might are in your hand, and no one can withstand you. 7O our God, did you not drive out the inhabitants
of this land before your people Israel and give it forever to
the descendants of Abraham your friend? 8They have lived in
it and have built in it a sanctuary for your Name, saying, 9'If
calamity comes upon us, whether the sword of judgment, or
plague or famine, we will stand in your presence before this
temple that bears your Name and will cry out to you in our
distress, and you will hear us and save us.'
10"But now here are men from Ammon, Moab and Mount
Seir, whose territory you would not allow Israel to invade
when they came from Egypt; so they turned away from them
and did not destroy them. 11See how they are repaying us by
coming to drive us out of the possession you gave us as an
inheritance. 12O our God, will you not judge them? For we
have no power to face this vast army that is attacking us. We
do not know what to do, but our eyes are upon you."
13All the men of Judah, with their wives and children and little
ones, stood there before the LORD.
14Then the Spirit of the LORD came upon Jahaziel son of
Zechariah, the son of Benaiah, the son of Jeiel, the son of Mattaniah, a Levite and descendant of Asaph, as he stood in the assembly.
15He said: "Listen, King Jehoshaphat and all who live in Judah
and Jerusalem! This is what the LORD says to you: 'Do not be afraid
or discouraged because of this vast army. For the battle is not
yours, but God's. 16Tomorrow march down against them. They
will be climbing up by the Pass of Ziz, and you will find them at
the end of the gorge in the Desert of Jeruel. 17You will not have
to fight this battle. Take up your positions; stand firm and see the
deliverance the LORD will give you, O Judah and Jerusalem. Do
not be afraid; do not be discouraged. Go out to face them tomorrow, and the LORD will be with you.'"
18Jehoshaphat bowed with his face to the ground, and all the
people of Judah and Jerusalem fell down in worship before the

[a] *1* Some Septuagint manuscripts; Hebrew *Ammonites* [b] *2* One Hebrew manuscript; most Hebrew manuscripts, Septuagint and Vulgate *Aram* [c] *2* That is, the Dead Sea

(20:5–13) O God, You are my security in times of tribulation. You are my defender when I am afraid. Through trials and uncertainties, You are an ever-present help. You are not waiting for me on the other side of trouble; You are right here, in the middle of it all, guiding my steps, lighting the way, savoring each moment as though it were Your only chance to display Your greatness. I praise You, Almighty God, my Rock, my Fortress and my Redeemer. I know that You hear my cry and that You will answer my prayer for deliverance. (Ps 43:1–5; 116:1–9)

Our loving Lord is not just present, but nearer than thought can imagine—so near that a whisper can reach Him . . . our Very Present Help will not disappoint us. For Thou, Lord, hast never failed them that seek Thee.

Amy Carmichael (1867-1951)

When the power of darkness comes
in like a flood.
The battle belongs to the Lord.
He's raised up a standard, the power
of His blood,
The battle belongs to the Lord.

We sing glory, honor,
Power and strength to the Lord.
We sing glory, honor,
Power and strength to the Lord.

"The Battle Belongs to the Lord"
Jamie Owens-Collins (©1984)

LORD. 19Then some Levites from the Kohathites and Korahites stood
up and praised the LORD, the God of Israel, with very loud voice.
20Early in the morning they left for the Desert of Tekoa. As they
set out, Jehoshaphat stood and said, "Listen to me, Judah and people of Jerusalem! Have faith in the LORD your God and you will be
upheld; have faith in his prophets and you will be successful."
21After consulting the people, Jehoshaphat appointed men to sing
to the LORD and to praise him for the splendor of his[a] holiness as
they went out at the head of the army, saying:

"Give thanks to the LORD,
for his love endures forever."

22As they began to sing and praise, the LORD set ambushes
against the men of Ammon and Moab and Mount Seir who were invading Judah, and they were defeated. 23The men of Ammon and
Moab rose up against the men from Mount Seir to destroy and annihilate them. After they finished slaughtering the men from Seir,
they helped to destroy one another.
24When the men of Judah came to the place that overlooks the
desert and looked toward the vast army, they saw only dead bodies
lying on the ground; no one had escaped. 25So Jehoshaphat and his
men went to carry off their plunder, and they found among them a
great amount of equipment and clothing[b] and also articles of
value—more than they could take away. There was so much plunder that it took three days to collect it. 26On the fourth day they assembled in the Valley of Beracah, where they praised the LORD. This
is why it is called the Valley of Beracah[c] to this day.
27Then, led by Jehoshaphat, all the men of Judah and Jerusalem
returned joyfully to Jerusalem, for the LORD had given them cause
to rejoice over their enemies. 28They entered Jerusalem and went
to the temple of the LORD with harps and lutes and trumpets.
29The fear of God came upon all the kingdoms of the countries
when they heard how the LORD had fought against the enemies of Israel. 30And the kingdom of Jehoshaphat was at peace, for his God
had given him rest on every side.

The End of Jehoshaphat's Reign

31So Jehoshaphat reigned over Judah. He was thirty-five years
old when he became king of Judah, and he reigned in Jerusalem
twenty-five years. His mother's name was Azubah daughter of Shilhi. 32He walked in the ways of his father Asa and did not stray from
them; he did what was right in the eyes of the LORD. 33The high
places, however, were not removed, and the people still had not set
their hearts on the God of their fathers.
34The other events of Jehoshaphat's reign, from beginning to
end, are written in the annals of Jehu son of Hanani, which are
recorded in the book of the kings of Israel.
35Later, Jehoshaphat king of Judah made an alliance with Ahaziah king of Israel, who was guilty of wickedness. 36He agreed with
him to construct a fleet of trading ships.[d] After these were built at
Ezion Geber, 37Eliezer son of Dodavahu of Mareshah prophesied
against Jehoshaphat, saying, "Because you have made an alliance
with Ahaziah, the LORD will destroy what you have made." The ships
were wrecked and were not able to set sail to trade.[e]

(20:20–23) Troubles come and go, but Your love endures forever. Nations rise and fall, but Your love endures forever. Enemies rage, the wicked threaten and boast, but Your love endures forever. Lord, in my darkest hour, help me to remember this lesson. In every spiritual battle (and every battle is spiritual), I will sing praise to Your name and give You thanks, for Your love endures forever. (1Jn 5:4)

For God has won the victory
And set His people free,
His Word has slain the enemy.
The earth shall stand and see that:

Through our God, we shall do
valiantly,
It is He who will tread down our
enemies,
We'll sing and shout His victory,
Christ is King!

"Victory Song"
Dale Garratt (©1979)

[a] 21 Or *him with the splendor of* [b] 25 Some Hebrew manuscripts and Vulgate; most Hebrew manuscripts *corpses* [c] 26 *Beracah* means *praise.* [d] 36 Hebrew *of ships that could go to Tarshish* [e] 37 Hebrew *sail for Tarshish*

21 Then Jehoshaphat rested with his fathers and was buried
with them in the City of David. And Jehoram his son succeeded him as king. 2Jehoram's brothers, the sons of Jehoshaphat, were Azariah, Jehiel, Zechariah, Azariahu, Michael and
Shephatiah. All these were sons of Jehoshaphat king of Israel.[a]
3Their father had given them many gifts of silver and gold and
articles of value, as well as fortified cities in Judah, but he had
given the kingdom to Jehoram because he was his firstborn
son.

Jehoram King of Judah

4When Jehoram established himself firmly over his father's
kingdom, he put all his brothers to the sword along with some of
the princes of Israel. 5Jehoram was thirty-two years old when he
became king, and he reigned in Jerusalem eight years. 6He
walked in the ways of the kings of Israel, as the house of Ahab had
done, for he married a daughter of Ahab. He did evil in the eyes
of the LORD. 7Nevertheless, because of the covenant the LORD had
made with David, the LORD was not willing to destroy the house of
David. He had promised to maintain a lamp for him and his descendants forever.
8In the time of Jehoram, Edom rebelled against Judah and set
up its own king. 9So Jehoram went there with his officers and all
his chariots. The Edomites surrounded him and his chariot commanders, but he rose up and broke through by night. 10To this
day Edom has been in rebellion against Judah.
Libnah revolted at the same time, because Jehoram had forsaken the LORD, the God of his fathers. 11He had also built high
places on the hills of Judah and had caused the people of Jerusalem to prostitute themselves and had led Judah astray.
12Jehoram received a letter from Elijah the prophet, which
said:

"This is what the LORD, the God of your father David, says:
'You have not walked in the ways of your father Jehoshaphat
or of Asa king of Judah. 13But you have walked in the ways
of the kings of Israel, and you have led Judah and the people of Jerusalem to prostitute themselves, just as the house
of Ahab did. You have also murdered your own brothers,
members of your father's house, men who were better than
you. 14So now the LORD is about to strike your people, your
sons, your wives and everything that is yours, with a heavy
blow. 15You yourself will be very ill with a lingering disease
of the bowels, until the disease causes your bowels to come
out.' "

16The LORD aroused against Jehoram the hostility of the Philistines and of the Arabs who lived near the Cushites. 17They attacked Judah, invaded it and carried off all the goods found in the
king's palace, together with his sons and wives. Not a son was left
to him except Ahaziah,[b] the youngest.
18After all this, the LORD afflicted Jehoram with an incurable
disease of the bowels. 19In the course of time, at the end of the
second year, his bowels came out because of the disease, and he
died in great pain. His people made no fire in his honor, as they
had for his fathers.

(21:4–11) O God, how could Jehoram, the son of a good king like Jehoshaphat, turn out so bad? How could he murder his own brothers? How could he forsake the way of his father and lead Your people into idolatry? How is it that godly parents can have ungodly children? Please help us to instill the fear of the Lord into our children's hearts. Help us to do all that we can to "bring them up in the training and instruction of the Lord," and then entrust them into Your hands as their loving heavenly Father. (Pr 22:6; Eph 6:4)

God, give us Christian homes!
Homes where the Bible is loved and
taught,
Homes where the Master's will is
sought,
Homes crowned with beauty
Your love has wrought;
God, give us Christian homes;
God, give us Christian homes!

God, give us Christian homes!
Homes where the children are led to
know
Christ in His beauty who loves them
so,
Homes where the altar fires burn
and glow;
God, give us Christian homes;
God, give us Christian homes!

"God, Give Us Christian Homes"
B.B. McKinney (1886-1952)

[a]2 That is, Judah, as frequently in 2 Chronicles [b]17 Hebrew *Jehoahaz,* a variant of *Ahaziah*

20Jehoram was thirty-two years old when he became king, and
he reigned in Jerusalem eight years. He passed away, to no one's
regret, and was buried in the City of David, but not in the tombs
of the kings.

Ahaziah King of Judah

22 The people of Jerusalem made Ahaziah, Jehoram's
youngest son, king in his place, since the raiders, who
came with the Arabs into the camp, had killed all the older sons.
So Ahaziah son of Jehoram king of Judah began to reign.
2Ahaziah was twenty-two[a] years old when he became king, and
he reigned in Jerusalem one year. His mother's name was Athaliah, a granddaughter of Omri.
3He too walked in the ways of the house of Ahab, for his mother encouraged him in doing wrong. 4He did evil in the eyes of the
LORD, as the house of Ahab had done, for after his father's death
they became his advisers, to his undoing. 5He also followed their
counsel when he went with Joram[b] son of Ahab king of Israel to
war against Hazael king of Aram at Ramoth Gilead. The Arameans
wounded Joram; 6so he returned to Jezreel to recover from the
wounds they had inflicted on him at Ramoth[c] in his battle with
Hazael king of Aram.
Then Ahaziah[d] son of Jehoram king of Judah went down to Jezreel to see Joram son of Ahab because he had been wounded.
7Through Ahaziah's visit to Joram, God brought about Ahaziah's downfall. When Ahaziah arrived, he went out with Joram to
meet Jehu son of Nimshi, whom the LORD had anointed to destroy
the house of Ahab. 8While Jehu was executing judgment on the
house of Ahab, he found the princes of Judah and the sons of Ahaziah's relatives, who had been attending Ahaziah, and he killed
them. 9He then went in search of Ahaziah, and his men captured
him while he was hiding in Samaria. He was brought to Jehu and
put to death. They buried him, for they said, "He was a son of Jehoshaphat, who sought the LORD with all his heart." So there was
no one in the house of Ahaziah powerful enough to retain the
kingdom.

Athaliah and Joash

10When Athaliah the mother of Ahaziah saw that her son was
dead, she proceeded to destroy the whole royal family of the
house of Judah. 11But Jehosheba,[e] the daughter of King Jehoram,
took Joash son of Ahaziah and stole him away from among the
royal princes who were about to be murdered and put him and
his nurse in a bedroom. Because Jehosheba,[e] the daughter of
King Jehoram and wife of the priest Jehoiada, was Ahaziah's sister, she hid the child from Athaliah so she could not kill him.
12He remained hidden with them at the temple of God for six
years while Athaliah ruled the land.

23 In the seventh year Jehoiada showed his strength. He
made a covenant with the commanders of units of a hundred: Azariah son of Jeroham, Ishmael son of Jehohanan, Azariah son of Obed, Maaseiah son of Adaiah, and Elishaphat son of
Zicri. 2They went throughout Judah and gathered the Levites and

[a] 2 Some Septuagint manuscripts and Syriac (see also 2 Kings 8:26); Hebrew *forty-two*
[b] 5 Hebrew *Jehoram,* a variant of *Joram;* also in verses 6 and 7 [c] 6 Hebrew *Ramah,* a variant of *Ramoth* [d] 6 Some Hebrew manuscripts, Septuagint, Vulgate and Syriac (see also 2 Kings 8:29); most Hebrew manuscripts *Azariah* [e] 11 Hebrew *Jehoshabeath,* a variant of *Jehosheba*

(22:1–12) These were dark times for Your people, Lord. The leaders of Judah and Israel did not seek Your ways, and they were both slain in judgment on the same day. Ahaziah's wicked mother then tried to murder all the rightful heirs to David's throne. Yet Your covenant with David was protected; You wouldn't allow his house to be destroyed. Thank You, Lord, that You are at work even in the darkest times, and that no promise of Yours will ever fail. (2Ki 11:1–16; 2Chr 21:7; Ps 32:7)

Praise the Lord! For He is glorious;
Never shall His promise fail.
God hath made His saints victorious;
Sin and death shall not prevail.
Praise the God of our salvation!
Hosts on high, His pow'r proclaim.
Heav'n and earth, and all creation,
Laud and magnify His name.

"Praise the Lord! Ye Heaven's Adore Him"
Foundling Hospital Collection (1796)

Oh! What need there is that up out of this darkness and trouble and sadness, out of these calamities, there should be exalted, somewhere, an image that writes upon itself, "I am the God of comfort." That brings God right home to man's need. The world would die if it had no hope of finding such a God.

Henry Ward Beecher (1813-1887)

(23:16–17) Holy Lord, I thank You for Your jealous love. There can be no other gods before You. You will not tolerate divided loyalties among Your people. Refocus my commitment to You, and help me to eliminate anything from my life that compromises my worship. May I continually acknowledge and honor my covenant with You, just as You continually acknowledge and honor Your covenant with me. (Ex 20:3)

the heads of Israelite families from all the towns. When they
came to Jerusalem, 3the whole assembly made a covenant with
the king at the temple of God.
Jehoiada said to them, "The king's son shall reign, as the
LORD promised concerning the descendants of David. 4Now this
is what you are to do: A third of you priests and Levites who are
going on duty on the Sabbath are to keep watch at the doors, 5a
third of you at the royal palace and a third at the Foundation
Gate, and all the other men are to be in the courtyards of the
temple of the LORD. 6No one is to enter the temple of the LORD
except the priests and Levites on duty; they may enter because
they are consecrated, but all the other men are to guard what
the LORD has assigned to them.[a] 7The Levites are to station
themselves around the king, each man with his weapons in his
hand. Anyone who enters the temple must be put to death. Stay
close to the king wherever he goes."
8The Levites and all the men of Judah did just as Jehoiada the
priest ordered. Each one took his men—those who were going
on duty on the Sabbath and those who were going off duty—for
Jehoiada the priest had not released any of the divisions. 9Then
he gave the commanders of units of a hundred the spears and
the large and small shields that had belonged to King David and
that were in the temple of God. 10He stationed all the men, each
with his weapon in his hand, around the king—near the altar
and the temple, from the south side to the north side of the temple.
11Jehoiada and his sons brought out the king's son and put
the crown on him; they presented him with a copy of the covenant and proclaimed him king. They anointed him and shouted, "Long live the king!"
12When Athaliah heard the noise of the people running and
cheering the king, she went to them at the temple of the LORD.
13She looked, and there was the king, standing by his pillar at
the entrance. The officers and the trumpeters were beside the
king, and all the people of the land were rejoicing and blowing
trumpets, and singers with musical instruments were leading
the praises. Then Athaliah tore her robes and shouted, "Treason! Treason!"
14Jehoiada the priest sent out the commanders of units of a
hundred, who were in charge of the troops, and said to them:
"Bring her out between the ranks[b] and put to the sword anyone
who follows her." For the priest had said, "Do not put her to
death at the temple of the LORD." 15So they seized her as she
reached the entrance of the Horse Gate on the palace grounds,
and there they put her to death.
16Jehoiada then made a covenant that he and the people and
the king[c] would be the LORD's people. 17All the people went to
the temple of Baal and tore it down. They smashed the altars
and idols and killed Mattan the priest of Baal in front of the altars.
18Then Jehoiada placed the oversight of the temple of the
LORD in the hands of the priests, who were Levites, to whom
David had made assignments in the temple, to present the burnt
offerings of the LORD as written in the Law of Moses, with re-

[a] 6 Or *to observe the LORD's command ⌞not to enter⌟* [b] 14 Or *out from the precincts*
[c] 16 Or *covenant between ⌞the LORD⌟ and the people and the king that they* (see 2 Kings 11:17)

joicing and singing, as David had ordered. 19He also stationed doorkeepers at the gates of the LORD's temple so that no one who was in any way unclean might enter.

20He took with him the commanders of hundreds, the nobles, the rulers of the people and all the people of the land and brought the king down from the temple of the LORD. They went into the palace through the Upper Gate and seated the king on the royal throne, 21and all the people of the land rejoiced. And the city was quiet, because Athaliah had been slain with the sword.

Joash Repairs the Temple

24 Joash was seven years old when he became king, and he reigned in Jerusalem forty years. His mother's name was Zibiah; she was from Beersheba. 2Joash did what was right in the eyes of the LORD all the years of Jehoiada the priest. 3Jehoiada chose two wives for him, and he had sons and daughters.

4Some time later Joash decided to restore the temple of the LORD. 5He called together the priests and Levites and said to them, "Go to the towns of Judah and collect the money due annually from all Israel, to repair the temple of your God. Do it now." But the Levites did not act at once.

6Therefore the king summoned Jehoiada the chief priest and said to him, "Why haven't you required the Levites to bring in from Judah and Jerusalem the tax imposed by Moses the servant of the LORD and by the assembly of Israel for the Tent of the Testimony?"

7Now the sons of that wicked woman Athaliah had broken into the temple of God and had used even its sacred objects for the Baals.

8At the king's command, a chest was made and placed outside, at the gate of the temple of the LORD. 9A proclamation was then issued in Judah and Jerusalem that they should bring to the LORD the tax that Moses the servant of God had required of Israel in the desert. 10All the officials and all the people brought their contributions gladly, dropping them into the chest until it was full. 11Whenever the chest was brought in by the Levites to the king's officials and they saw that there was a large amount of money, the royal secretary and the officer of the chief priest would come and empty the chest and carry it back to its place. They did this regularly and collected a great amount of money. 12The king and Jehoiada gave it to the men who carried out the work required for the temple of the LORD. They hired masons and carpenters to restore the LORD's temple, and also workers in iron and bronze to repair the temple.

13The men in charge of the work were diligent, and the repairs progressed under them. They rebuilt the temple of God according to its original design and reinforced it. 14When they had finished, they brought the rest of the money to the king and Jehoiada, and with it were made articles for the LORD's temple: articles for the service and for the burnt offerings, and also dishes and other objects of gold and silver. As long as Jehoiada lived, burnt offerings were presented continually in the temple of the LORD.

15Now Jehoiada was old and full of years, and he died at the age of a hundred and thirty. 16He was buried with the kings in the City of David, because of the good he had done in Israel for God and his temple.

(23:19) To honor Your holiness, Jehoiada stationed doorkeepers to prevent those who were ceremonially unclean from entering Your temple. Thank You, righteous Father, that the death of Your Son Jesus has made it possible for all to enter Your holy presence—both literally and symbolically. For at the moment of His death, the curtain of the temple before the Most Holy Place was torn in two. Since doorkeepers are no longer needed to keep people out of Your presence, make me a doorkeeper to help people enter into Your presence. (Mt 27:51; Heb 4:16; 10:19–22)

I will enter His gates
With thanksgiving in my heart,
I will enter His courts with praise.
I will say, "This is the day
That the Lord has made!"
I will rejoice for He has made me glad.

He has made me glad,
He has made me glad,
I will rejoice for He has made me glad.
He has made me glad,
He has made me glad,
I will rejoice for He has made me glad.

"He Has Made Me Glad"
Leona Von Brethorst (©1976)

(24:17–21) Lord, we praise You for Your prophets of old who served You faithfully and courageously. Strengthen us in our day to proclaim the truth with boldness, and help us not to lose heart when others resist Your Word. And should we suffer for our faith, then let us not be ashamed but commit ourselves to You and continue to do good, knowing that if we die with You, we will also live with You, and if we endure with You, we will also reign with You. (2Ti 2:11–12; 1Pe 4:15–19)

Let the world despise and leave me,
They have left my Savior too;
Human hearts and looks deceive me;
Thou art not, like man, untrue;
And, while Thou shalt smile upon me,
God of wisdom, love, and might,
Foes may hate and friends may shun me;
Show Thy face, and all is bright.

"Jesus, I My Cross Have Taken"
Henry F. Lyte (1824)

The Wickedness of Joash

17 After the death of Jehoiada, the officials of Judah came and paid homage to the king, and he listened to them. 18 They abandoned the temple of the LORD, the God of their fathers, and worshiped Asherah poles and idols. Because of their guilt, God's anger came upon Judah and Jerusalem. 19 Although the LORD sent prophets to the people to bring them back to him, and though they testified against them, they would not listen.

20 Then the Spirit of God came upon Zechariah son of Jehoiada the priest. He stood before the people and said, "This is what God says: 'Why do you disobey the LORD's commands? You will not prosper. Because you have forsaken the LORD, he has forsaken you.'"

21 But they plotted against him, and by order of the king they stoned him to death in the courtyard of the LORD's temple. 22 King Joash did not remember the kindness Zechariah's father Jehoiada had shown him but killed his son, who said as he lay dying, "May the LORD see this and call you to account."

23 At the turn of the year,[a] the army of Aram marched against Joash; it invaded Judah and Jerusalem and killed all the leaders of the people. They sent all the plunder to their king in Damascus. 24 Although the Aramean army had come with only a few men, the LORD delivered into their hands a much larger army. Because Judah had forsaken the LORD, the God of their fathers, judgment was executed on Joash. 25 When the Arameans withdrew, they left Joash severely wounded. His officials conspired against him for murdering the son of Jehoiada the priest, and they killed him in his bed. So he died and was buried in the City of David, but not in the tombs of the kings.

26 Those who conspired against him were Zabad,[b] son of Shimeath an Ammonite woman, and Jehozabad, son of Shimrith[c] a Moabite woman. 27 The account of his sons, the many prophecies about him, and the record of the restoration of the temple of God are written in the annotations on the book of the kings. And Amaziah his son succeeded him as king.

Amaziah King of Judah

25 Amaziah was twenty-five years old when he became king, and he reigned in Jerusalem twenty-nine years. His mother's name was Jehoaddin[d]; she was from Jerusalem. 2 He did what was right in the eyes of the LORD, but not wholeheartedly. 3 After the kingdom was firmly in his control, he executed the officials who had murdered his father the king. 4 Yet he did not put their sons to death, but acted in accordance with what is written in the Law, in the Book of Moses, where the LORD commanded: "Fathers shall not be put to death for their children, nor children put to death for their fathers; each is to die for his own sins."[e]

5 Amaziah called the people of Judah together and assigned them according to their families to commanders of thousands and commanders of hundreds for all Judah and Benjamin. He then mustered those twenty years old or more and found that there were three hundred thousand men ready for military service, able to handle the spear and shield. 6 He also hired a hun-

[a] 23 Probably in the spring [b] 26 A variant of *Jozabad* [c] 26 A variant of *Shomer*
[d] 1 Hebrew *Jehoaddan,* a variant of *Jehoaddin* [e] 4 Deut. 24:16

dred thousand fighting men from Israel for a hundred talents[a] of silver.
7But a man of God came to him and said, "O king, these troops from Israel must not march with you, for the LORD is not with Israel—not with any of the people of Ephraim.
8Even if you go and fight courageously in battle, God will overthrow you before the enemy, for God has the power to help or to overthrow."
9Amaziah asked the man of God, "But what about the hundred talents I paid for these Israelite troops?"

The man of God replied, "The LORD can give you much more than that."
10So Amaziah dismissed the troops who had come to him from Ephraim and sent them home. They were furious with Judah and left for home in a great rage.
11Amaziah then marshaled his strength and led his army to the Valley of Salt, where he killed ten thousand men of Seir.
12The army of Judah also captured ten thousand men alive, took them to the top of a cliff and threw them down so that all were dashed to pieces.
13Meanwhile the troops that Amaziah had sent back and had not allowed to take part in the war raided Judean towns from Samaria to Beth Horon. They killed three thousand people and carried off great quantities of plunder.
14When Amaziah returned from slaughtering the Edomites, he brought back the gods of the people of Seir. He set them up as his own gods, bowed down to them and burned sacrifices to them.
15The anger of the LORD burned against Amaziah, and he sent a prophet to him, who said, "Why do you consult this people's gods, which could not save their own people from your hand?"
16While he was still speaking, the king said to him, "Have we appointed you an adviser to the king? Stop! Why be struck down?"

So the prophet stopped but said, "I know that God has determined to destroy you, because you have done this and have not listened to my counsel."
17After Amaziah king of Judah consulted his advisers, he sent this challenge to Jehoash[b] son of Jehoahaz, the son of Jehu, king of Israel: "Come, meet me face to face."
18But Jehoash king of Israel replied to Amaziah king of Judah: "A thistle in Lebanon sent a message to a cedar in Lebanon, 'Give your daughter to my son in marriage.' Then a wild beast in Lebanon came along and trampled the thistle underfoot.
19You say to yourself that you have defeated Edom, and now you are arrogant and proud. But stay at home! Why ask for trouble and cause your own downfall and that of Judah also?"
20Amaziah, however, would not listen, for God so worked that he might hand them over to ⌊Jehoash⌋, because they sought the gods of Edom.
21So Jehoash king of Israel attacked. He and Amaziah king of Judah faced each other at Beth Shemesh in Judah.
22Judah was routed by Israel, and every man fled to his home.
23Jehoash king of Israel captured Amaziah king of Judah, the son of Joash, the son of Ahaziah,[c] at Beth Shemesh. Then Jehoash brought him to Jerusalem and broke down the wall of Jerusalem from the Ephraim Gate to the Corner Gate—a section about six hundred feet[d] long.
24He took all the gold and silver and all the

[a] *6* That is, about 3 3/4 tons (about 3.4 metric tons); also in verse 9 [b] *17* Hebrew *Joash,* a variant of *Jehoash*; also in verses 18, 21, 23 and 25 [c] *23* Hebrew *Jehoahaz,* a variant of *Ahaziah* [d] *23* Hebrew *four hundred cubits* (about 180 meters)

(25:6–16) Father, we thank You for the warnings You give to us in Your Word. They are lessons of both grace and judgment. In the day of adversity, Amaziah listened to Your prophet. He validated his loyalty to You and ended his unholy alliance. But in the day of victory, Amaziah rejected Your prophet. He violated his loyalty to You and ended his holy alliance. O God, help me to remain always faithful to You, just as You are always faithful to me.

God is still sifting men for service. He will use gladly every man who is willing to be used. When a man stands the first test well, there comes a second. That, stood well, means others. These are our promotion tests. He lets those who stand all testings into the thickest of the fight and up to the highest heights of victory. Master, help us to endure every test as seeing Him who is invisible.

Dr. Samuel Dickey Gordon (1859-1936)

Unshakable, immovable,
Faithful and true;
Full of wisdom, strength and beauty:
These things are true of You.
Fearless, courageous,
Righteousness shines
Through in all You do;
Yet You're so humble,
You laid down Your life:
These things are true of You.

And as I turn my face to You,
Oh Lord, I ask and pray,
By the power of Your love and grace,
Make these things true of me, too.
Make these things true of me, too.

"These Things are True of You"
Tommy Walker (©1996)

articles found in the temple of God that had been in the care of
Obed-Edom, together with the palace treasures and the hostages,
and returned to Samaria.
[25]Amaziah son of Joash king of Judah lived for fifteen years
after the death of Jehoash son of Jehoahaz king of Israel. [26]As for
the other events of Amaziah's reign, from beginning to end, are
they not written in the book of the kings of Judah and Israel?
[27]From the time that Amaziah turned away from following the
LORD, they conspired against him in Jerusalem and he fled to Lachish, but they sent men after him to Lachish and killed him
there. [28]He was brought back by horse and was buried with his
fathers in the City of Judah.

Uzziah King of Judah

26 Then all the people of Judah took Uzziah,[a] who was sixteen years old, and made him king in place of his father
Amaziah. [2]He was the one who rebuilt Elath and restored it to
Judah after Amaziah rested with his fathers.
[3]Uzziah was sixteen years old when he became king, and he
reigned in Jerusalem fifty-two years. His mother's name was Jecoliah; she was from Jerusalem. [4]He did what was right in the
eyes of the LORD, just as his father Amaziah had done. [5]He sought
God during the days of Zechariah, who instructed him in the
fear[b] of God. As long as he sought the LORD, God gave him success.
[6]He went to war against the Philistines and broke down the
walls of Gath, Jabneh and Ashdod. He then rebuilt towns near
Ashdod and elsewhere among the Philistines. [7]God helped him
against the Philistines and against the Arabs who lived in Gur
Baal and against the Meunites. [8]The Ammonites brought tribute
to Uzziah, and his fame spread as far as the border of Egypt, because he had become very powerful.
[9]Uzziah built towers in Jerusalem at the Corner Gate, at the
Valley Gate and at the angle of the wall, and he fortified them.
[10]He also built towers in the desert and dug many cisterns, because he had much livestock in the foothills and in the plain. He
had people working his fields and vineyards in the hills and in
the fertile lands, for he loved the soil.
[11]Uzziah had a well-trained army, ready to go out by divisions
according to their numbers as mustered by Jeiel the secretary
and Maaseiah the officer under the direction of Hananiah, one of
the royal officials. [12]The total number of family leaders over the
fighting men was 2,600. [13]Under their command was an army of
307,500 men trained for war, a powerful force to support the
king against his enemies. [14]Uzziah provided shields, spears, helmets, coats of armor, bows and slingstones for the entire army.
[15]In Jerusalem he made machines designed by skillful men for
use on the towers and on the corner defenses to shoot arrows
and hurl large stones. His fame spread far and wide, for he was
greatly helped until he became powerful.
[16]But after Uzziah became powerful, his pride led to his
downfall. He was unfaithful to the LORD his God, and entered the
temple of the LORD to burn incense on the altar of incense. [17]Az-
ariah the priest with eighty other courageous priests of the LORD
followed him in. [18]They confronted him and said, "It is not right

(26:3–5) "Seek the LORD while he may be found; call on him while he is near." May I, like Uzziah, seek You, O Lord. May I have a teachable spirit so that godly people like Zechariah can instruct me in "the fear of God." I resolve to seek Your kingdom and Your righteousness, confident that whatever measure of success You want me to have will be given to me as well. (Isa 55:6; Mt 6:33)

[a] *1* Also called *Azariah* [b] *5* Many Hebrew manuscripts, Septuagint and Syriac; other Hebrew manuscripts *vision*

MY BELOVED

If you accept My words and treasure My commands, if you turn your full attention to the pursuit of wisdom and apply your heart and mind to understanding, and if you call out to Me for insight and look for it as for silver and search for it as for hidden treasure, then you will understand the reverence and worshipful fear of the Lord and find the knowledge of God. For I am the source of wisdom; true knowledge and understanding come from Me.

You will understand what is right and just and fair—every good path. For wisdom will enter your heart, and knowledge will be pleasant to your soul. Discretion will protect you, and understanding will guard you. My wisdom will save you from the ways of the world.

For I look down from heaven to see if there are any who understand, any who seek Me, and to strengthen those whose hearts are fully committed to Me. So let your heart rejoice as you seek Me. Look to Me and My strength. Seek My face always.

Do not forget My teaching, but keep My commands in your heart, for they will prolong your life many years and bring you prosperity. Let love and faithfulness never leave you; bind them around your neck; write them on the tablet of your heart. Then you will win favor and a good name in My sight and in the sight of others.

2Ch 16:9; Ps 53:2; 105:3-4; Pr 2:1-6,9-12; 3:1-4

for you, Uzziah, to burn incense to the LORD. That is for the
priests, the descendants of Aaron, who have been consecrated to
burn incense. Leave the sanctuary, for you have been unfaithful;
and you will not be honored by the LORD God."
19Uzziah, who had a censer in his hand ready to burn incense,
became angry. While he was raging at the priests in their presence
before the incense altar in the LORD's temple, leprosy[a] broke out
on his forehead. 20When Azariah the chief priest and all the other
priests looked at him, they saw that he had leprosy on his forehead, so they hurried him out. Indeed, he himself was eager to
leave, because the LORD had afflicted him.
21King Uzziah had leprosy until the day he died. He lived in a
separate house[b]—leprous, and excluded from the temple of the
LORD. Jotham his son had charge of the palace and governed the
people of the land.
22The other events of Uzziah's reign, from beginning to end,
are recorded by the prophet Isaiah son of Amoz. 23Uzziah rested
with his fathers and was buried near them in a field for burial
that belonged to the kings, for people said, "He had leprosy." And
Jotham his son succeeded him as king.

Jotham King of Judah

27 Jotham was twenty-five years old when he became king,
and he reigned in Jerusalem sixteen years. His mother's
name was Jerusha daughter of Zadok. 2He did what was right in
the eyes of the LORD, just as his father Uzziah had done, but unlike
him he did not enter the temple of the LORD. The people, however, continued their corrupt practices. 3Jotham rebuilt the Upper
Gate of the temple of the LORD and did extensive work on the wall
at the hill of Ophel. 4He built towns in the Judean hills and forts
and towers in the wooded areas.
5Jotham made war on the king of the Ammonites and conquered them. That year the Ammonites paid him a hundred talents[c] of silver, ten thousand cors[d] of wheat and ten thousand cors
of barley. The Ammonites brought him the same amount also in
the second and third years.
6Jotham grew powerful because he walked steadfastly before
the LORD his God.
7The other events in Jotham's reign, including all his wars and
the other things he did, are written in the book of the kings of Israel and Judah. 8He was twenty-five years old when he became
king, and he reigned in Jerusalem sixteen years. 9Jotham rested
with his fathers and was buried in the City of David. And Ahaz his
son succeeded him as king.

Ahaz King of Judah

28 Ahaz was twenty years old when he became king, and he
reigned in Jerusalem sixteen years. Unlike David his father, he did not do what was right in the eyes of the LORD. 2He
walked in the ways of the kings of Israel and also made cast idols
for worshiping the Baals. 3He burned sacrifices in the Valley of
Ben Hinnom and sacrificed his sons in the fire, following the detestable ways of the nations the LORD had driven out before the Is-

[a] *19* The Hebrew word was used for various diseases affecting the skin—not necessarily leprosy; also in verses 20, 21 and 23. [b] *21* Or *in a house where he was relieved of responsibilities* [c] *5* That is, about 3 3/4 tons (about 3.4 metric tons) [d] *5* That is, probably about 62,000 bushels (about 2,200 kiloliters)

(26:16–21) Gracious Lord, prosperity and success are Yours to give. You helped Uzziah greatly when he invaded foreign lands. But when he invaded Your temple You punished him for his impudence. He did not come in humility and the fear of the Lord, but rather in pride and disrespect for Your sovereignty. His pride cost him the fellowship of his God and his people. Truly, "pride goes before destruction, a haughty spirit before a fall." (Pr 16:18)

Know of a truth that if thine own honour is of more importance to thee and dearer than that of another man, thou doest wrongfully . . . It is God's nature to give; and He lives and moves that He may give unto us when we are humble.

Johann Tauler (1300-1361)

raelites. 4He offered sacrifices and burned incense at the high
places, on the hilltops and under every spreading tree.
5Therefore the LORD his God handed him over to the king of
Aram. The Arameans defeated him and took many of his people
as prisoners and brought them to Damascus.
He was also given into the hands of the king of Israel, who inflicted heavy casualties on him. 6In one day Pekah son of Remaliah killed a hundred and twenty thousand soldiers in Judah—
because Judah had forsaken the LORD, the God of their fathers.
7Zicri, an Ephraimite warrior, killed Maaseiah the king's son,
Azrikam the officer in charge of the palace, and Elkanah, second to the king. 8The Israelites took captive from their kinsmen
two hundred thousand wives, sons and daughters. They also
took a great deal of plunder, which they carried back to
Samaria.
9But a prophet of the LORD named Oded was there, and he
went out to meet the army when it returned to Samaria. He said
to them, "Because the LORD, the God of your fathers, was angry
with Judah, he gave them into your hand. But you have slaughtered them in a rage that reaches to heaven. 10And now you intend to make the men and women of Judah and Jerusalem your
slaves. But aren't you also guilty of sins against the LORD your
God? 11Now listen to me! Send back your fellow countrymen you
have taken as prisoners, for the LORD's fierce anger rests on
you."
12Then some of the leaders in Ephraim—Azariah son of Jehohanan, Berekiah son of Meshillemoth, Jehizkiah son of Shallum,
and Amasa son of Hadlai—confronted those who were arriving
from the war. 13"You must not bring those prisoners here," they
said, "or we will be guilty before the LORD. Do you intend to add
to our sin and guilt? For our guilt is already great, and his fierce
anger rests on Israel."
14So the soldiers gave up the prisoners and plunder in the
presence of the officials and all the assembly. 15The men designated by name took the prisoners, and from the plunder they
clothed all who were naked. They provided them with clothes
and sandals, food and drink, and healing balm. All those who
were weak they put on donkeys. So they took them back to their
fellow countrymen at Jericho, the City of Palms, and returned to
Samaria.
16At that time King Ahaz sent to the king[a] of Assyria for help.
17The Edomites had again come and attacked Judah and carried
away prisoners, 18while the Philistines had raided towns in the
foothills and in the Negev of Judah. They captured and occupied
Beth Shemesh, Aijalon and Gederoth, as well as Soco, Timnah
and Gimzo, with their surrounding villages. 19The LORD had
humbled Judah because of Ahaz king of Israel,[b] for he had promoted wickedness in Judah and had been most unfaithful to the
LORD. 20Tiglath-Pileser[c] king of Assyria came to him, but he gave
him trouble instead of help. 21Ahaz took some of the things
from the temple of the LORD and from the royal palace and from
the princes and presented them to the king of Assyria, but that
did not help him.
22In his time of trouble King Ahaz became even more un-

(28:1–8) Ahaz worshiped the gods of the Gentiles, so You "handed him over" to a Gentile king. He walked in the ways of the wicked kings of Israel, so "he was also given into the hands of the king of Israel." When we reject You as our God, we also reject You as our Protector. "Those who cling to worthless idols forfeit the grace that could be theirs. But I, with a song of thanksgiving, will sacrifice to you. What I have vowed I will make good. Salvation comes from the LORD." (Jnh 2:8–9; Ro 1:18–32)

Let us therefore desire nothing else, wish for nothing else, and let nothing please and delight us except our Creator and Redeemer, and Savior, the only true God, who is full of good, all good, entire good, the true and supreme good, who alone is good, merciful and kind, gentle and sweet, who alone is holy, just, true, and upright, who alone is benign, pure, and clean, grace, all glory of all penitents and of the just, and of all the blessed rejoicing in heaven. Let nothing therefore hinder us, let nothing separate us, let nothing come between us.

Francis of Assisi (1181-1226)

[a] *16* One Hebrew manuscript, Septuagint and Vulgate (see also 2 Kings 16:7); most Hebrew manuscripts *kings* [b] *19* That is, Judah, as frequently in 2 Chronicles [c] *20* Hebrew *Tilgath-Pilneser,* a variant of *Tiglath-Pileser*

faithful to the LORD. 23 He offered sacrifices to the gods of Damascus, who had defeated him; for he thought, "Since the gods of the
kings of Aram have helped them, I will sacrifice to them so they will
help me." But they were his downfall and the downfall of all Israel.
24 Ahaz gathered together the furnishings from the temple of God
and took them away.[a] He shut the doors of the LORD's temple and
set up altars at every street corner in Jerusalem. 25 In every town in
Judah he built high places to burn sacrifices to other gods and provoked the LORD, the God of his fathers, to anger.
26 The other events of his reign and all his ways, from beginning
to end, are written in the book of the kings of Judah and Israel.
27 Ahaz rested with his fathers and was buried in the city of Jerusalem, but he was not placed in the tombs of the kings of Israel. And
Hezekiah his son succeeded him as king.

Hezekiah Purifies the Temple

29 Hezekiah was twenty-five years old when he became king,
and he reigned in Jerusalem twenty-nine years. His mother's name was Abijah daughter of Zechariah. 2 He did what was
right in the eyes of the LORD, just as his father David had done.
3 In the first month of the first year of his reign, he opened the
doors of the temple of the LORD and repaired them. 4 He brought in
the priests and the Levites, assembled them in the square on the
east side 5 and said: "Listen to me, Levites! Consecrate yourselves
now and consecrate the temple of the LORD, the God of your fathers.
Remove all defilement from the sanctuary. 6 Our fathers were unfaithful; they did evil in the eyes of the LORD our God and forsook
him. They turned their faces away from the LORD's dwelling place
and turned their backs on him. 7 They also shut the doors of the
portico and put out the lamps. They did not burn incense or present any burnt offerings at the sanctuary to the God of Israel.
8 Therefore, the anger of the LORD has fallen on Judah and Jerusalem; he has made them an object of dread and horror and scorn,
as you can see with your own eyes. 9 This is why our fathers have
fallen by the sword and why our sons and daughters and our wives
are in captivity. 10 Now I intend to make a covenant with the LORD,
the God of Israel, so that his fierce anger will turn away from us.
11 My sons, do not be negligent now, for the LORD has chosen you to
stand before him and serve him, to minister before him and to
burn incense."
12 Then these Levites set to work:
from the Kohathites,
Mahath son of Amasai and Joel son of Azariah;
from the Merarites,
Kish son of Abdi and Azariah son of Jehallelel;
from the Gershonites,
Joah son of Zimmah and Eden son of Joah;
13 from the descendants of Elizaphan,
Shimri and Jeiel;
from the descendants of Asaph,
Zechariah and Mattaniah;
14 from the descendants of Heman,
Jehiel and Shimei;
from the descendants of Jeduthun,
Shemaiah and Uzziel.

[a] 24 Or *and cut them up*

(28:22–25) Dear Lord, protect me from continually going the wrong direction like Ahaz did in his blind stubbornness. In times of trouble, I want to turn toward You rather than away from You. Even if I become discouraged or disillusioned, I want to keep my hope in You, Lord, "for with the LORD is unfailing love and with him is full redemption." (Ps 130:7)

(29:15–19) Now, O Lord, is the time for the cleansing of Your house. Wash away the sin that so easily entangles us. Purify our lives and help us to live each day as the temple of Your Holy Spirit. We choose to be holy, as You are holy. (Lev 19:2; Mt 5:48; Heb 12:1)

Oh Lord, we come before You now,
We're asking You
To show us who You are.
And let us leave all the things
That keep us from You
Outside this place today.
Oh Lord, we come to worship You.
"We Come to Worship You"
Tim Taber and Robert Stafford (©1997)

(29:25–30) Thank You, majestic Lord, for the wonderful gift of music: for instruments to play and voices to raise in praise and adoration to You. As we visualize the children of Israel worshiping You through song, how much more should we—who have been made holy through the once-for-all sacrifice of Jesus Christ—worship You with songs of gladness and gratitude! (Ps 5:11; Isa 35:10; Col 3:16; Heb 10:10)

15When they had assembled their brothers and consecrated
themselves, they went in to purify the temple of the LORD, as the
king had ordered, following the word of the LORD. 16The priests
went into the sanctuary of the LORD to purify it. They brought out
to the courtyard of the LORD's temple everything unclean that they
found in the temple of the LORD. The Levites took it and carried it
out to the Kidron Valley. 17They began the consecration on the
first day of the first month, and by the eighth day of the month
they reached the portico of the LORD. For eight more days they
consecrated the temple of the LORD itself, finishing on the sixteenth day of the first month.

18Then they went in to King Hezekiah and reported: "We have
purified the entire temple of the LORD, the altar of burnt offering
with all its utensils, and the table for setting out the consecrated
bread, with all its articles. 19We have prepared and consecrated
all the articles that King Ahaz removed in his unfaithfulness while
he was king. They are now in front of the LORD's altar."

20Early the next morning King Hezekiah gathered the city officials together and went up to the temple of the LORD. 21They
brought seven bulls, seven rams, seven male lambs and seven
male goats as a sin offering for the kingdom, for the sanctuary
and for Judah. The king commanded the priests, the descendants
of Aaron, to offer these on the altar of the LORD. 22So they slaughtered the bulls, and the priests took the blood and sprinkled it on
the altar; next they slaughtered the rams and sprinkled their
blood on the altar; then they slaughtered the lambs and sprinkled
their blood on the altar. 23The goats for the sin offering were
brought before the king and the assembly, and they laid their
hands on them. 24The priests then slaughtered the goats and presented their blood on the altar for a sin offering to atone for all Israel, because the king had ordered the burnt offering and the sin
offering for all Israel.

25He stationed the Levites in the temple of the LORD with cymbals, harps and lyres in the way prescribed by David and Gad the
king's seer and Nathan the prophet; this was commanded by the
LORD through his prophets. 26So the Levites stood ready with
David's instruments, and the priests with their trumpets.

27Hezekiah gave the order to sacrifice the burnt offering on
the altar. As the offering began, singing to the LORD began also, accompanied by trumpets and the instruments of David king of Israel. 28The whole assembly bowed in worship, while the singers
sang and the trumpeters played. All this continued until the sacrifice of the burnt offering was completed.

29When the offerings were finished, the king and everyone
present with him knelt down and worshiped. 30King Hezekiah
and his officials ordered the Levites to praise the LORD with the
words of David and of Asaph the seer. So they sang praises with
gladness and bowed their heads and worshiped.

31Then Hezekiah said, "You have now dedicated yourselves to
the LORD. Come and bring sacrifices and thank offerings to the
temple of the LORD." So the assembly brought sacrifices and thank
offerings, and all whose hearts were willing brought burnt offerings.

32The number of burnt offerings the assembly brought was
seventy bulls, a hundred rams and two hundred male lambs—all
of them for burnt offerings to the LORD. 33The animals consecrated as sacrifices amounted to six hundred bulls and three

thousand sheep and goats. 34The priests, however, were too few to skin all the burnt offerings; so their kinsmen the Levites helped them until the task was finished and until other priests had been consecrated, for the Levites had been more conscientious in consecrating themselves than the priests had been. 35There were burnt offerings in abundance, together with the fat of the fellowship offerings[a] and the drink offerings that accompanied the burnt offerings.

So the service of the temple of the LORD was reestablished. 36Hezekiah and all the people rejoiced at what God had brought about for his people, because it was done so quickly.

Hezekiah Celebrates the Passover

30 Hezekiah sent word to all Israel and Judah and also wrote letters to Ephraim and Manasseh, inviting them to come to the temple of the LORD in Jerusalem and celebrate the Passover to the LORD, the God of Israel. 2The king and his officials and the whole assembly in Jerusalem decided to celebrate the Passover in the second month. 3They had not been able to celebrate it at the regular time because not enough priests had consecrated themselves and the people had not assembled in Jerusalem. 4The plan seemed right both to the king and to the whole assembly. 5They decided to send a proclamation throughout Israel, from Beersheba to Dan, calling the people to come to Jerusalem and celebrate the Passover to the LORD, the God of Israel. It had not been celebrated in large numbers according to what was written.

6At the king's command, couriers went throughout Israel and Judah with letters from the king and from his officials, which read:

"People of Israel, return to the LORD, the God of Abraham, Isaac and Israel, that he may return to you who are left, who have escaped from the hand of the kings of Assyria. 7Do not be like your fathers and brothers, who were unfaithful to the LORD, the God of their fathers, so that he made them an object of horror, as you see. 8Do not be stiff-necked, as your fathers were; submit to the LORD. Come to the sanctuary, which he has consecrated forever. Serve the LORD your God, so that his fierce anger will turn away from you. 9If you return to the LORD, then your brothers and your children will be shown compassion by their captors and will come back to this land, for the LORD your God is gracious and compassionate. He will not turn his face from you if you return to him."

10The couriers went from town to town in Ephraim and Manasseh, as far as Zebulun, but the people scorned and ridiculed them. 11Nevertheless, some men of Asher, Manasseh and Zebulun humbled themselves and went to Jerusalem. 12Also in Judah the hand of God was on the people to give them unity of mind to carry out what the king and his officials had ordered, following the word of the LORD.

13A very large crowd of people assembled in Jerusalem to celebrate the Feast of Unleavened Bread in the second month. 14They removed the altars in Jerusalem and cleared away the incense altars and threw them into the Kidron Valley.

[a] 35 Traditionally *peace offerings*

(30:1–5) It is sad, Lord, that Your people had failed to celebrate Passover as a nation for over two hundred years, "since the days of Solomon." Show Your people today how to honor You in the celebrations and traditions that have been handed down to us. In our zeal to be relevant and contemporary, prevent us from neglecting or violating those things You desire to transfer throughout the generations. (2Chr 30:26)

The Lord accepts our obedience in attending to the rituals of worship He has ordained . . . But we must avoid becoming mechanical or rote in our relationship to Him. What good is our attendance at church, faithfulness in spiritual disciplines, regular Bible reading and prayer—if we don't trust Him?

George O. Wood (1941-)

15They slaughtered the Passover lamb on the fourteenth day of
the second month. The priests and the Levites were ashamed and
consecrated themselves and brought burnt offerings to the temple
of the LORD. 16Then they took up their regular positions as prescribed in the Law of Moses the man of God. The priests sprinkled the blood handed to them by the Levites. 17Since many in the
crowd had not consecrated themselves, the Levites had to kill the
Passover lambs for all those who were not ceremonially clean
and could not consecrate ⌞their lambs⌟ to the LORD. 18Although
most of the many people who came from Ephraim, Manasseh, Issachar and Zebulun had not purified themselves, yet they ate the
Passover, contrary to what was written. But Hezekiah prayed for
them, saying, "May the LORD, who is good, pardon everyone
19who sets his heart on seeking God—the LORD, the God of his fathers—even if he is not clean according to the rules of the sanctuary." 20And the LORD heard Hezekiah and healed the people.
21The Israelites who were present in Jerusalem celebrated the
Feast of Unleavened Bread for seven days with great rejoicing,
while the Levites and priests sang to the LORD every day, accompanied by the LORD's instruments of praise.[a]
22Hezekiah spoke encouragingly to all the Levites, who showed
good understanding of the service of the LORD. For the seven days
they ate their assigned portion and offered fellowship offerings[b]
and praised the LORD, the God of their fathers.
23The whole assembly then agreed to celebrate the festival
seven more days; so for another seven days they celebrated joyfully. 24Hezekiah king of Judah provided a thousand bulls and seven
thousand sheep and goats for the assembly, and the officials provided them with a thousand bulls and ten thousand sheep and
goats. A great number of priests consecrated themselves. 25The
entire assembly of Judah rejoiced, along with the priests and Levites and all who had assembled from Israel, including the aliens
who had come from Israel and those who lived in Judah. 26There
was great joy in Jerusalem, for since the days of Solomon son of
David king of Israel there had been nothing like this in Jerusalem.
27The priests and the Levites stood to bless the people, and God
heard them, for their prayer reached heaven, his holy dwelling
place.

31 When all this had ended, the Israelites who were there went
out to the towns of Judah, smashed the sacred stones and
cut down the Asherah poles. They destroyed the high places and
the altars throughout Judah and Benjamin and in Ephraim
and Manasseh. After they had destroyed all of them, the Israelites
returned to their own towns and to their own property.

Contributions for Worship

2Hezekiah assigned the priests and Levites to divisions—each
of them according to their duties as priests or Levites—to offer
burnt offerings and fellowship offerings,[b] to minister, to give
thanks and to sing praises at the gates of the LORD's dwelling. 3The
king contributed from his own possessions for the morning and
evening burnt offerings and for the burnt offerings on the Sabbaths, New Moons and appointed feasts as written in the Law of
the LORD. 4He ordered the people living in Jerusalem to give the
portion due the priests and Levites so they could devote them-

[a] 21 Or *priests praised the LORD every day with resounding instruments belonging to the LORD* [b] 22,2 Traditionally *peace offerings*

(31:1) Lord, as Your people experienced Your transforming power in worship, they were filled with zeal for You. Today, as we encounter You in spirit and in truth, stir us to do any necessary housecleaning—by destroying the things in our lives that displease You. Deepen our devotion to You, and make us passionate for Your holiness.

When a person sincerely spends time in God's presence, he can't help but begin to clean house. He starts to see things from God's perspective, not just from man's. The more time he spends in His presence, the more he begins to think like God. He deals with more and more issues in his life that require repentance. Without consistency in prayer, there are some issues we will never deal with.

Ron Auch (1951-)

Oh, holy Fire,
Love's purest light,
Burn all desires
Till You are my one delight.
My love for You will never die,
Jesus, You are my life.

I come to You,
I run to You,
There's no greater joy
Than knowing You.

Oh, conquering King
Conquer my heart,
And make of me
A pleasing gift to God.
My love for You will never die,
Jesus, You are my life.

"Jesus, You Are My Life"
Steve Fry (©1996)

selves to the Law of the LORD. 5 As soon as the order went out, the
Israelites generously gave the firstfruits of their grain, new wine,
oil and honey and all that the fields produced. They brought a
great amount, a tithe of everything. 6 The men of Israel and Judah
who lived in the towns of Judah also brought a tithe of their herds
and flocks and a tithe of the holy things dedicated to the LORD
their God, and they piled them in heaps. 7 They began doing this
in the third month and finished in the seventh month. 8 When Hezekiah and his officials came and saw the heaps, they praised the
LORD and blessed his people Israel.

9 Hezekiah asked the priests and Levites about the heaps; 10 and
Azariah the chief priest, from the family of Zadok, answered,
"Since the people began to bring their contributions to the temple of the LORD, we have had enough to eat and plenty to spare,
because the LORD has blessed his people, and this great amount is
left over."

11 Hezekiah gave orders to prepare storerooms in the temple of
the LORD, and this was done. 12 Then they faithfully brought in the
contributions, tithes and dedicated gifts. Conaniah, a Levite, was
in charge of these things, and his brother Shimei was next in
rank. 13 Jehiel, Azaziah, Nahath, Asahel, Jerimoth, Jozabad, Eliel,
Ismakiah, Mahath and Benaiah were supervisors under Conaniah
and Shimei his brother, by appointment of King Hezekiah and Azariah the official in charge of the temple of God.

14 Kore son of Imnah the Levite, keeper of the East Gate, was in
charge of the freewill offerings given to God, distributing the contributions made to the LORD and also the consecrated gifts.
15 Eden, Miniamin, Jeshua, Shemaiah, Amariah and Shecaniah assisted him faithfully in the towns of the priests, distributing to
their fellow priests according to their divisions, old and young
alike.

16 In addition, they distributed to the males three years old or
more whose names were in the genealogical records—all who
would enter the temple of the LORD to perform the daily duties of
their various tasks, according to their responsibilities and their
divisions. 17 And they distributed to the priests enrolled by their
families in the genealogical records and likewise to the Levites
twenty years old or more, according to their responsibilities and
their divisions. 18 They included all the little ones, the wives, and
the sons and daughters of the whole community listed in these genealogical records. For they were faithful in consecrating themselves.

19 As for the priests, the descendants of Aaron, who lived on
the farm lands around their towns or in any other towns, men
were designated by name to distribute portions to every male
among them and to all who were recorded in the genealogies of
the Levites.

20 This is what Hezekiah did throughout Judah, doing what was
good and right and faithful before the LORD his God. 21 In everything that he undertook in the service of God's temple and in obedience to the law and the commands, he sought his God and
worked wholeheartedly. And so he prospered.

Sennacherib Threatens Jerusalem

32 After all that Hezekiah had so faithfully done, Sennacherib
king of Assyria came and invaded Judah. He laid siege to
the fortified cities, thinking to conquer them for himself. 2 When

(31:9–11) Father, may Your people today be generous so that the needs of Your servants in ministry will be met, with plenty to spare. Everything comes from You, and we can give You only what comes from Your hand. So teach us to give joyfully, willingly and sacrificially. (1Ch 29:14–16)

As saints of old their first fruits
brought,
Of orchard, flock, and field,
To God the Giver of all good,
The Source of bounteous yield,
So we today first fruits would bring;
The wealth of this good land,
Of farm and market, shop and home,
Of mind, and heart, and hand.

In gratitude and humble trust,
We bring our best today,
To serve your cause and share
Your love with all along life's way.
O God, who gave yourself to us,
In Jesus Christ, your Son,
Teach us to give ourselves each day
Until life's work is done.

"As Saints of Old"
Frank von Christierson (©1961)

(32:1–8) "After all that Hezekiah had so faithfully done," he still suffered trials and hardships. I thank You, Father, for my trials of faith because they are opportunities for You to display Your great power. You will never abandon me as long as I look to You for help. "Though an army besiege me, my heart will not fear; though war break out against me, even then will I be confident," for the One Who is in me is greater than the one who is in the world. (Jos 1:9; Ps 27:1–3; Jas 1:2–4; 1Jn 4:4)

Stand up, stand up for Jesus;
Stand in His strength alone.
The arm of flesh will fail you
Ye dare not trust your own.
Put on the gospel armor
And, watching unto prayer,
Where duty calls or danger,
Be never wanting there.

Stand up, stand up for Jesus.
The strife will not be long;
This day the noise of battle,
The next, the victor's song.
To him who overcometh
A crown of life shall be;
He with the King of Glory
Shall reign eternally.

"Stand Up, Stand Up for Jesus"
George Duffield (1818-1888)

Paths chosen for us by God all lead onward and upward, even when they seem to us to turn about in inextricable confusion, and to move downward to the valleys of humiliation and suffering. He is the All-Wise, and to him, wisdom is the way by which Love gains his victory.

G. Campbell Morgan (1863-1945)

Hezekiah saw that Sennacherib had come and that he intended to
make war on Jerusalem, 3he consulted with his officials and military staff about blocking off the water from the springs outside
the city, and they helped him. 4A large force of men assembled,
and they blocked all the springs and the stream that flowed
through the land. "Why should the kings[a] of Assyria come and
find plenty of water?" they said. 5Then he worked hard repairing
all the broken sections of the wall and building towers on it. He
built another wall outside that one and reinforced the supporting
terraces[b] of the City of David. He also made large numbers of
weapons and shields.
6He appointed military officers over the people and assembled
them before him in the square at the city gate and encouraged
them with these words: 7"Be strong and courageous. Do not be
afraid or discouraged because of the king of Assyria and the vast
army with him, for there is a greater power with us than with him.
8With him is only the arm of flesh, but with us is the LORD our God
to help us and to fight our battles." And the people gained confidence from what Hezekiah the king of Judah said.
9Later, when Sennacherib king of Assyria and all his forces
were laying siege to Lachish, he sent his officers to Jerusalem with
this message for Hezekiah king of Judah and for all the people of
Judah who were there:

10"This is what Sennacherib king of Assyria says: On what
are you basing your confidence, that you remain in Jerusalem under siege? 11When Hezekiah says, 'The LORD our God
will save us from the hand of the king of Assyria,' he is misleading you, to let you die of hunger and thirst. 12Did not
Hezekiah himself remove this god's high places and altars,
saying to Judah and Jerusalem, 'You must worship before
one altar and burn sacrifices on it'?
13"Do you not know what I and my fathers have done to
all the peoples of the other lands? Were the gods of those nations ever able to deliver their land from my hand? 14Who of
all the gods of these nations that my fathers destroyed has
been able to save his people from me? How then can your
god deliver you from my hand? 15Now do not let Hezekiah
deceive you and mislead you like this. Do not believe him,
for no god of any nation or kingdom has been able to deliver his people from my hand or the hand of my fathers. How
much less will your god deliver you from my hand!"

16Sennacherib's officers spoke further against the LORD God
and against his servant Hezekiah. 17The king also wrote letters insulting the LORD, the God of Israel, and saying this against him:
"Just as the gods of the peoples of the other lands did not rescue
their people from my hand, so the god of Hezekiah will not rescue his people from my hand." 18Then they called out in Hebrew
to the people of Jerusalem who were on the wall, to terrify them
and make them afraid in order to capture the city. 19They spoke
about the God of Jerusalem as they did about the gods of the other
peoples of the world—the work of men's hands.
20King Hezekiah and the prophet Isaiah son of Amoz cried out
in prayer to heaven about this. 21And the LORD sent an angel, who
annihilated all the fighting men and the leaders and officers in

[a] 4 Hebrew; Septuagint and Syriac *king* [b] 5 Or *the Millo*

the camp of the Assyrian king. So he withdrew to his own land in disgrace. And when he went into the temple of his god, some of his sons cut him down with the sword.

22So the LORD saved Hezekiah and the people of Jerusalem from the hand of Sennacherib king of Assyria and from the hand of all others. He took care of them[a] on every side. 23Many brought offerings to Jerusalem for the LORD and valuable gifts for Hezekiah king of Judah. From then on he was highly regarded by all the nations.

Hezekiah's Pride, Success and Death

24In those days Hezekiah became ill and was at the point of death. He prayed to the LORD, who answered him and gave him a miraculous sign. 25But Hezekiah's heart was proud and he did not respond to the kindness shown him; therefore the LORD's wrath was on him and on Judah and Jerusalem. 26Then Hezekiah repented of the pride of his heart, as did the people of Jerusalem; therefore the LORD's wrath did not come upon them during the days of Hezekiah.

27Hezekiah had very great riches and honor, and he made treasuries for his silver and gold and for his precious stones, spices, shields and all kinds of valuables. 28He also made buildings to store the harvest of grain, new wine and oil; and he made stalls for various kinds of cattle, and pens for the flocks. 29He built villages and acquired great numbers of flocks and herds, for God had given him very great riches.

30It was Hezekiah who blocked the upper outlet of the Gihon spring and channeled the water down to the west side of the City of David. He succeeded in everything he undertook. 31But when envoys were sent by the rulers of Babylon to ask him about the miraculous sign that had occurred in the land, God left him to test him and to know everything that was in his heart.

32The other events of Hezekiah's reign and his acts of devotion are written in the vision of the prophet Isaiah son of Amoz in the book of the kings of Judah and Israel. 33Hezekiah rested with his fathers and was buried on the hill where the tombs of David's descendants are. All Judah and the people of Jerusalem honored him when he died. And Manasseh his son succeeded him as king.

Manasseh King of Judah

33 Manasseh was twelve years old when he became king, and he reigned in Jerusalem fifty-five years. 2He did evil in the eyes of the LORD, following the detestable practices of the nations the LORD had driven out before the Israelites. 3He rebuilt the high places his father Hezekiah had demolished; he also erected altars to the Baals and made Asherah poles. He bowed down to all the starry hosts and worshiped them. 4He built altars in the temple of the LORD, of which the LORD had said, "My Name will remain in Jerusalem forever." 5In both courts of the temple of the LORD, he built altars to all the starry hosts. 6He sacrificed his sons in[b] the fire in the Valley of Ben Hinnom, practiced sorcery, divination and witchcraft, and consulted mediums and spiritists. He did much evil in the eyes of the LORD, provoking him to anger.

7He took the carved image he had made and put it in God's temple, of which God had said to David and to his son Solomon,

[a] 22 Hebrew; Septuagint and Vulgate *He gave them rest* [b] 6 Or *He made his sons pass through*

(32:24–26) Father, You are merciful and patient with Your people. Even when we are overcome by pride, You are faithful to us. Keep us humble, Lord. Please help us not to think more highly of ourselves than we should or to flatter ourselves so much that we cannot detect or hate our sin. And may we never show contempt for the riches of Your kindness, tolerance and patience, for it is Your kindness that leads us toward repentance. (Ps 36:2; Ro 2:4; 12:3)

As Jesus Christ does not only teach humility, but also bestows it, let us begin by asking Him to give us a love for that virtue . . . No prayer could be more pleasing to Jesus Christ; we can feel sure of that; He will infallibly grant our request if we sincerely wish it to be granted.

Jean Nicolas Grou (1731-1803)

"In this temple and in Jerusalem, which I have chosen out of all the tribes of Israel, I will put my Name forever. **8**I will not again make the feet of the Israelites leave the land I assigned to your forefathers, if only they will be careful to do everything I commanded them concerning all the laws, decrees and ordinances given through Moses." **9**But Manasseh led Judah and the people of Jerusalem astray, so that they did more evil than the nations the LORD had destroyed before the Israelites.

10The LORD spoke to Manasseh and his people, but they paid no attention. **11**So the LORD brought against them the army commanders of the king of Assyria, who took Manasseh prisoner, put a hook in his nose, bound him with bronze shackles and took him to Babylon. **12**In his distress he sought the favor of the LORD his God and humbled himself greatly before the God of his fathers. **13**And when he prayed to him, the LORD was moved by his entreaty and listened to his plea; so he brought him back to Jerusalem and to his kingdom. Then Manasseh knew that the LORD is God.

14Afterward he rebuilt the outer wall of the City of David, west of the Gihon spring in the valley, as far as the entrance of the Fish Gate and encircling the hill of Ophel; he also made it much higher. He stationed military commanders in all the fortified cities in Judah.

15He got rid of the foreign gods and removed the image from the temple of the LORD, as well as all the altars he had built on the temple hill and in Jerusalem; and he threw them out of the city. **16**Then he restored the altar of the LORD and sacrificed fellowship offerings[a] and thank offerings on it, and told Judah to serve the LORD, the God of Israel. **17**The people, however, continued to sacrifice at the high places, but only to the LORD their God.

18The other events of Manasseh's reign, including his prayer to his God and the words the seers spoke to him in the name of the LORD, the God of Israel, are written in the annals of the kings of Israel.[b] **19**His prayer and how God was moved by his entreaty, as well as all his sins and unfaithfulness, and the sites where he built high places and set up Asherah poles and idols before he humbled himself—all are written in the records of the seers.[c] **20**Manasseh rested with his fathers and was buried in his palace. And Amon his son succeeded him as king.

Amon King of Judah

21Amon was twenty-two years old when he became king, and he reigned in Jerusalem two years. **22**He did evil in the eyes of the LORD, as his father Manasseh had done. Amon worshiped and offered sacrifices to all the idols Manasseh had made. **23**But unlike his father Manasseh, he did not humble himself before the LORD; Amon increased his guilt.

24Amon's officials conspired against him and assassinated him in his palace. **25**Then the people of the land killed all who had plotted against King Amon, and they made Josiah his son king in his place.

(33:9–17) You are a God of mercy. Even though Manasseh led Your people into idolatry, You were "moved by his entreaty and listened to his plea;" and so You restored him to his throne. Thank You for loving us enough to humble us. And thank You for blessing us with Your grace when we are humble.

If only we knew how much we need God's grace, we would never lose touch with him. Believe me. Make a commitment never to deliberately stray from him, to live the rest of your life in his holy presence. Don't do this in expectation of receiving heavenly comforts; simply do it out of love for him.

Brother Lawrence of the Resurrection (1611-1691)

[a] *16* Traditionally *peace offerings* [b] *18* That is, Judah, as frequently in 2 Chronicles
[c] *19* One Hebrew manuscript and Septuagint; most Hebrew manuscripts *of Hozai*

Josiah's Reforms

34 Josiah was eight years old when he became king, and he reigned in Jerusalem thirty-one years. 2He did what was right in the eyes of the LORD and walked in the ways of his father David, not turning aside to the right or to the left.

3In the eighth year of his reign, while he was still young, he began to seek the God of his father David. In his twelfth year he began to purge Judah and Jerusalem of high places, Asherah poles, carved idols and cast images. 4Under his direction the altars of the Baals were torn down; he cut to pieces the incense altars that were above them, and smashed the Asherah poles, the idols and the images. These he broke to pieces and scattered over the graves of those who had sacrificed to them. 5He burned the bones of the priests on their altars, and so he purged Judah and Jerusalem. 6In the towns of Manasseh, Ephraim and Simeon, as far as Naphtali, and in the ruins around them, 7he tore down the altars and the Asherah poles and crushed the idols to powder and cut to pieces all the incense altars throughout Israel. Then he went back to Jerusalem.

8In the eighteenth year of Josiah's reign, to purify the land and the temple, he sent Shaphan son of Azaliah and Maaseiah the ruler of the city, with Joah son of Joahaz, the recorder, to repair the temple of the LORD his God.

9They went to Hilkiah the high priest and gave him the money that had been brought into the temple of God, which the Levites who were the doorkeepers had collected from the people of Manasseh, Ephraim and the entire remnant of Israel and from all the people of Judah and Benjamin and the inhabitants of Jerusalem. 10Then they entrusted it to the men appointed to supervise the work on the LORD's temple. These men paid the workers who repaired and restored the temple. 11They also gave money to the carpenters and builders to purchase dressed stone, and timber for joists and beams for the buildings that the kings of Judah had allowed to fall into ruin.

12The men did the work faithfully. Over them to direct them were Jahath and Obadiah, Levites descended from Merari, and Zechariah and Meshullam, descended from Kohath. The Levites—all who were skilled in playing musical instruments—13had charge of the laborers and supervised all the workers from job to job. Some of the Levites were secretaries, scribes and doorkeepers.

The Book of the Law Found

14While they were bringing out the money that had been taken into the temple of the LORD, Hilkiah the priest found the Book of the Law of the LORD that had been given through Moses. 15Hilkiah said to Shaphan the secretary, "I have found the Book of the Law in the temple of the LORD." He gave it to Shaphan.

16Then Shaphan took the book to the king and reported to him: "Your officials are doing everything that has been committed to them. 17They have paid out the money that was in the temple of the LORD and have entrusted it to the supervisors and workers." 18Then Shaphan the secretary informed the king, "Hilkiah the priest has given me a book." And Shaphan read from it in the presence of the king.

19When the king heard the words of the Law, he tore his robes. 20He gave these orders to Hilkiah, Ahikam son of Shaphan,

(34:1–7) Our Father, may young people today follow the example of Josiah. May they seek You and not turn aside to the right or to the left. May they devote themselves fully to You and courageously resist the idols of our culture. Bring revival to Your church through our young people. (1Ti 4:12)

Abdon son of Micah,[a] Shaphan the secretary and Asaiah the
king's attendant: 21“Go and inquire of the LORD for me and for the
remnant in Israel and Judah about what is written in this book
that has been found. Great is the LORD's anger that is poured out
on us because our fathers have not kept the word of the LORD;
they have not acted in accordance with all that is written in this
book.”
22Hilkiah and those the king had sent with him[b] went to speak
to the prophetess Huldah, who was the wife of Shallum son of
Tokhath,[c] the son of Hasrah,[d] keeper of the wardrobe. She lived
in Jerusalem, in the Second District.
23She said to them, “This is what the LORD, the God of Israel,
says: Tell the man who sent you to me, 24‘This is what the LORD
says: I am going to bring disaster on this place and its people—
all the curses written in the book that has been read in the presence of the king of Judah. 25Because they have forsaken me and
burned incense to other gods and provoked me to anger by all
that their hands have made,[e] my anger will be poured out on this
place and will not be quenched.’ 26Tell the king of Judah, who
sent you to inquire of the LORD, ‘This is what the LORD, the God of
Israel, says concerning the words you heard: 27Because your
heart was responsive and you humbled yourself before God when
you heard what he spoke against this place and its people, and
because you humbled yourself before me and tore your robes
and wept in my presence, I have heard you, declares the LORD.
28Now I will gather you to your fathers, and you will be buried in
peace. Your eyes will not see all the disaster I am going to bring
on this place and on those who live here.’ ”
So they took her answer back to the king.
29Then the king called together all the elders of Judah and Jerusalem. 30He went up to the temple of the LORD with the men of
Judah, the people of Jerusalem, the priests and the Levites—all
the people from the least to the greatest. He read in their hearing
all the words of the Book of the Covenant, which had been found
in the temple of the LORD. 31The king stood by his pillar and renewed the covenant in the presence of the LORD—to follow the
LORD and keep his commands, regulations and decrees with all
his heart and all his soul, and to obey the words of the covenant
written in this book.
32Then he had everyone in Jerusalem and Benjamin pledge
themselves to it; the people of Jerusalem did this in accordance
with the covenant of God, the God of their fathers.
33Josiah removed all the detestable idols from all the territory
belonging to the Israelites, and he had all who were present in Israel serve the LORD their God. As long as he lived, they did not fail
to follow the LORD, the God of their fathers.

Josiah Celebrates the Passover

35 Josiah celebrated the Passover to the LORD in Jerusalem,
and the Passover lamb was slaughtered on the fourteenth
day of the first month. 2He appointed the priests to their duties
and encouraged them in the service of the LORD's temple. 3He said
to the Levites, who instructed all Israel and who had been consecrated to the LORD: “Put the sacred ark in the temple that Solo-

[a] 20 Also called *Acbor son of Micaiah* [b] 22 One Hebrew manuscript, Vulgate and Syriac; most Hebrew manuscripts do not have *had sent with him.* [c] 22 Also called *Tikvah* [d] 22 Also called *Harhas* [e] 25 Or *by everything they have done*

Revelation is the first step to holiness, and consecration is the second. A day comes in our lives, as definite as the day of our conversion, when we give up all right to ourselves and submit to the absolute Lordship of Jesus Christ.

Watchman Nee (1903-1972)

(34:29–33) “Come, let us return to the LORD.” May all Your people today—“from the least to the greatest”—respond to Your covenant of love and faithfulness. May we with one voice pledge to follow You and obey Your words. O that we would love You, dear God, with all our heart and with all our soul and with all our mind and with all our strength. (Ex 24:3,7; Hos 6:1; Mk 12:30)

Jesus call us from the worship
Of the vain world's golden store,
From each idol that would keep us,
Saying, “Christian, love Me more.”

Jesus calls us: by Thy mercies,
Savior, may we hear Thy call,
Give our hearts to Thine obedience,
Serve and love Thee best of all.

“Jesus Calls Us O'er the Tumult”
Cecil F. Alexander (1852)

mon son of David king of Israel built. It is not to be carried about
on your shoulders. Now serve the LORD your God and his people
Israel. 4Prepare yourselves by families in your divisions, according to the directions written by David king of Israel and by his
son Solomon.
5"Stand in the holy place with a group of Levites for each sub-
division of the families of your fellow countrymen, the lay people.
6Slaughter the Passover lambs, consecrate yourselves and prepare ⌊the lambs⌋ for your fellow countrymen, doing what the LORD
commanded through Moses."
7Josiah provided for all the lay people who were there a total
of thirty thousand sheep and goats for the Passover offerings, and
also three thousand cattle—all from the king's own possessions.
8His officials also contributed voluntarily to the people and the
priests and Levites. Hilkiah, Zechariah and Jehiel, the administrators of God's temple, gave the priests twenty-six hundred
Passover offerings and three hundred cattle. 9Also Conaniah
along with Shemaiah and Nethanel, his brothers, and Hashabiah,
Jeiel and Jozabad, the leaders of the Levites, provided five thousand Passover offerings and five hundred head of cattle for the Levites.
10The service was arranged and the priests stood in their
places with the Levites in their divisions as the king had ordered.
11The Passover lambs were slaughtered, and the priests sprinkled the blood handed to them, while the Levites skinned the animals. 12They set aside the burnt offerings to give them to the
subdivisions of the families of the people to offer to the LORD, as
is written in the Book of Moses. They did the same with the cattle. 13They roasted the Passover animals over the fire as prescribed, and boiled the holy offerings in pots, caldrons and pans
and served them quickly to all the people. 14After this, they made
preparations for themselves and for the priests, because the
priests, the descendants of Aaron, were sacrificing the burnt offerings and the fat portions until nightfall. So the Levites made
preparations for themselves and for the Aaronic priests.
15The musicians, the descendants of Asaph, were in the places
prescribed by David, Asaph, Heman and Jeduthun the king's seer.
The gatekeepers at each gate did not need to leave their posts, because their fellow Levites made the preparations for them.
16So at that time the entire service of the LORD was carried out
for the celebration of the Passover and the offering of burnt offerings on the altar of the LORD, as King Josiah had ordered. 17The
Israelites who were present celebrated the Passover at that time
and observed the Feast of Unleavened Bread for seven days. 18The
Passover had not been observed like this in Israel since the days
of the prophet Samuel; and none of the kings of Israel had ever
celebrated such a Passover as did Josiah, with the priests, the Levites and all Judah and Israel who were there with the people of
Jerusalem. 19This Passover was celebrated in the eighteenth year
of Josiah's reign.

The Death of Josiah

20After all this, when Josiah had set the temple in order, Neco
king of Egypt went up to fight at Carchemish on the Euphrates,
and Josiah marched out to meet him in battle. 21But Neco sent
messengers to him, saying, "What quarrel is there between you
and me, O king of Judah? It is not you I am attacking at this time,

(35:7–19) O Lord, what an awesome event this Passover must have been! Yet there was to be an even more glorious Passover—in which only one lamb, rather than thousands, would be slain! Lord Jesus, at that Passover You offered Yourself as our Passover lamb. So we keep the feast of Your table in celebration of Your redeeming love. We anxiously anticipate the day when we will share fellowship with You in the coming wedding supper of the Lamb. Hallelujah! All glory and honor and praise be to You! (Mk 14:12–25; 1Co 5:7; Rev 19:6–9)

but the house with which I am at war. God has told me to hurry;
so stop opposing God, who is with me, or he will destroy you."
22 Josiah, however, would not turn away from him, but disguised himself to engage him in battle. He would not listen to
what Neco had said at God's command but went to fight him on
the plain of Megiddo.
23 Archers shot King Josiah, and he told his officers, "Take me
away; I am badly wounded." 24 So they took him out of his chariot, put him in the other chariot he had and brought him to Jerusalem, where he died. He was buried in the tombs of his fathers,
and all Judah and Jerusalem mourned for him.
25 Jeremiah composed laments for Josiah, and to this day all
the men and women singers commemorate Josiah in the laments.
These became a tradition in Israel and are written in the Laments.
26 The other events of Josiah's reign and his acts of devotion,
according to what is written in the Law of the LORD— 27 all the
events, from beginning to end, are written in the book of the
36 kings of Israel and Judah. 1 And the people of the land
took Jehoahaz son of Josiah and made him king in Jerusalem in place of his father.

Jehoahaz King of Judah

2 Jehoahaz[a] was twenty-three years old when he became king,
and he reigned in Jerusalem three months. 3 The king of Egypt de-
throned him in Jerusalem and imposed on Judah a levy of a hundred talents[b] of silver and a talent[c] of gold. 4 The king of Egypt
made Eliakim, a brother of Jehoahaz, king over Judah and Jerusalem and changed Eliakim's name to Jehoiakim. But Neco took
Eliakim's brother Jehoahaz and carried him off to Egypt.

Jehoiakim King of Judah

5 Jehoiakim was twenty-five years old when he became king,
and he reigned in Jerusalem eleven years. He did evil in the eyes
of the LORD his God. 6 Nebuchadnezzar king of Babylon attacked
him and bound him with bronze shackles to take him to Babylon.
7 Nebuchadnezzar also took to Babylon articles from the temple of
the LORD and put them in his temple[d] there.
8 The other events of Jehoiakim's reign, the detestable things
he did and all that was found against him, are written in the book
of the kings of Israel and Judah. And Jehoiachin his son succeeded him as king.

Jehoiachin King of Judah

9 Jehoiachin was eighteen[e] years old when he became king,
and he reigned in Jerusalem three months and ten days. He did
evil in the eyes of the LORD. 10 In the spring, King Nebuchadnezzar
sent for him and brought him to Babylon, together with articles of
value from the temple of the LORD, and he made Jehoiachin's
uncle,[f] Zedekiah, king over Judah and Jerusalem.

Zedekiah King of Judah

11 Zedekiah was twenty-one years old when he became king,
and he reigned in Jerusalem eleven years. 12 He did evil in the

[a] 2 Hebrew *Joahaz,* a variant of *Jehoahaz*; also in verse 4 [b] 3 That is, about 3 3/4 tons (about 3.4 metric tons) [c] 3 That is, about 75 pounds (about 34 kilograms) [d] 7 Or *palace* [e] 9 One Hebrew manuscript, some Septuagint manuscripts and Syriac (see also 2 Kings 24:8); most Hebrew manuscripts *eight* [f] 10 Hebrew *brother,* that is, relative (see 2 Kings 24:17)

(35:22–24) Lord, it is sad to see the demise of good people. Josiah "walked in the ways of his father David, not turning aside to the right or to the left." "Neither before nor after Josiah was there a king like him who turned to the LORD as he did—with all his heart and with all his soul and with all his strength." Yet even Josiah had his weaknesses; his poor judgment was his downfall. He rushed into harm's way unnecessarily. Lord, spare me from poor judgment, for I know that sometimes I can be my own worst enemy. Please teach me to seek You before I enter any conflict or confrontation. (2Ki 23:25; 2Ch 34:2)

Father, I don't often look before I leap. My landings are not pretty. Help me to take the time to look things over thoroughly when making important decisions. Let me know what you want, and I will trust you for the outcome.

Charles Stanley (1932-)

eyes of the LORD his God and did not humble himself before Jeremiah the prophet, who spoke the word of the LORD. 13He also rebelled against King Nebuchadnezzar, who had made him take an
oath in God's name. He became stiff-necked and hardened his
heart and would not turn to the LORD, the God of Israel. 14Fur-
thermore, all the leaders of the priests and the people became
more and more unfaithful, following all the detestable practices
of the nations and defiling the temple of the LORD, which he had
consecrated in Jerusalem.

The Fall of Jerusalem

15The LORD, the God of their fathers, sent word to them through
his messengers again and again, because he had pity on his people and on his dwelling place. 16But they mocked God's messengers, despised his words and scoffed at his prophets until the
wrath of the LORD was aroused against his people and there was
no remedy. 17He brought up against them the king of the Babylonians,[a] who killed their young men with the sword in the sanctuary, and spared neither young man nor young woman, old man or
aged. God handed all of them over to Nebuchadnezzar. 18He carried to Babylon all the articles from the temple of God, both large
and small, and the treasures of the LORD's temple and the treasures of the king and his officials. 19They set fire to God's temple
and broke down the wall of Jerusalem; they burned all the palaces and destroyed everything of value there.
20He carried into exile to Babylon the remnant, who escaped
from the sword, and they became servants to him and his sons
until the kingdom of Persia came to power. 21The land enjoyed its
sabbath rests; all the time of its desolation it rested, until the seventy years were completed in fulfillment of the word of the LORD
spoken by Jeremiah.
22In the first year of Cyrus king of Persia, in order to fulfill the
word of the LORD spoken by Jeremiah, the LORD moved the heart
of Cyrus king of Persia to make a proclamation throughout his
realm and to put it in writing:
23"This is what Cyrus king of Persia says:

" 'The LORD, the God of heaven, has given me all the kingdoms of the earth and he has appointed me to build a temple for him at Jerusalem in Judah. Anyone of his people among you—may the LORD his God be with him, and let him go up.' "

[a] 17 Or *Chaldeans*

(36:11–19) Father God, it is frightening to read how Your people so abused Your mercy. Because of Your pity You sent Your prophets to them again and again. But Your people not only ignored Your messengers, they also persecuted them. Finally there remained "no remedy" except destruction and exile. May Your people today learn the lessons of this tragic story. May we give heed to the warnings in Your Word and may our hearts be humble toward You.

(36:20–23) Thank You, Lord, that even in these darkest of times You had a plan—a plan of hope and restoration. Thank You for always preserving a remnant. Thank You for preserving the promised land for seventy years, reserving it for Your people's return. Thank You that in our darkest times, You are with us. We rejoice that absolutely nothing can separate us from Your love! (Ro 8:35–39)

The source of our security lies in what we trust. When you place your security in other persons or things, your source of security is temporary at best. Jesus triumphed by trusting the Father with His life. Even His detractors at the cross admitted, "He trusts in God" (Matthew 27:43). Can the same thing be said about us, even in our own darkest hour?

George O. Wood (1941-)

Ezra–Nehemiah

The Books of EZRA & NEHEMIAH

The books of Ezra and Nehemiah, originally a single work, narrate the restoration of Israel following the Babylonian exile. Shortly after Persia has overthrown Babylon, the Persian king Cyrus decrees that the Jews can return to Jerusalem to rebuild the temple (Ezr 1:1–4). In spite of opposition from Judah's neighbors, the restoration project is ultimately successful (Ezr 3–6). For the first time in decades, sacrifices are offered to God in His "house."

The fact that God begins His restoration of Israel with the temple underscores the priority of worship. Worship must never be an afterthought, or simply a "warm-up" for the "real meat" of preaching. The core of our faithful response to God is the offering of worship.

The next sections of Ezra–Nehemiah focus on a period of time over 50 years after the completion of the temple. Now the leadership of Ezra (Ezr 7—10; Ne 8—10) and Nehemiah (Ne 1—7; 11—13) figures prominently in the ongoing restoration of the covenant people. Ezra, a priest and "teacher" of the law, facilitates the spiritual restoration of Judah through applying and teaching God's commands. Nehemiah, a Hebrew member of the Persian royal court, oversees the physical and political restoration of Judah by motivating the people to rebuild the wall of Jerusalem and by serving as governor. Like Ezra, Nehemiah is a man of prayer with a passionate heart for God (Ne 1).

Worship must never be an afterthought, or simply a "warm-up" for the "real meat" of preaching. The core of our faithful response to God is the offering of worship.

The pinnacle of restoration in Ezra–Nehemiah comes after the temple and wall have been rebuilt. Ezra and Nehemiah then join forces to lead the whole nation in covenant renewal. The revival begins as Ezra reads God's law to the people. Their first response is to weep, probably with tears of grief over their sin. But, though repentance and grief are certainly appropriate at times (Ezr 10:1; Ne 1:4), Ezra and Nehemiah call the people first to rejoice because "the joy of the LORD is your strength" (Ne 8:10). After a joyful celebration, which includes the Feast of Booths, the children of Israel gather once again, this time to confess their corporate sins to God (Ne 9:1–38). After confession they renew their covenant with God by making specific commitments to keep the law, especially as it pertains to temple worship (Ne 10:1-39).

In Ezra–Nehemiah God is revealed as the unique, glorious, holy Lord Who calls together His chosen people and faithfully blesses them (Ne 9). The perpetual unfaithfulness of the people ultimately brings God's judgment as He "hand[s] them over to the neighboring peoples" (Ne 9:30). But even then, "in [His] great mercy [He] did not put an end to them or abandon them, for [He is] a gracious and merciful God" (Ne 9:31). Our gracious God is a restoring God, One Who gives new life to spiritual dry bones. Like the Israelites, we will be renewed as we listen to God's Word, celebrate His saving works, confess our sins and commit ourselves to live and to worship each day in the new covenant of Christ.

Cyrus Helps the Exiles to Return

1 In the first year of Cyrus king of Persia, in order to fulfill the word of the LORD spoken by Jeremiah, the LORD moved the heart of Cyrus king of Persia to make a proclamation throughout his realm and to put it in writing:

2“This is what Cyrus king of Persia says:

“ ‘The LORD, the God of heaven, has given me all the kingdoms of the earth and he has appointed me to build a temple for him at Jerusalem in Judah. 3Anyone of his people among you—may his God be with him, and let him go up to Jerusalem in Judah and build the temple of the LORD, the God of Israel, the God who is in Jerusalem. 4And the people of any place where survivors may now be living are to provide him with silver and gold, with goods and livestock, and with freewill offerings for the temple of God in Jerusalem.’ ”

5Then the family heads of Judah and Benjamin, and the priests and Levites—everyone whose heart God had moved—prepared to go up and build the house of the LORD in Jerusalem. 6All their neighbors assisted them with articles of silver and gold, with goods and livestock, and with valuable gifts, in addition to all the freewill offerings. 7Moreover, King Cyrus brought out the articles belonging to the temple of the LORD, which Nebuchadnezzar had carried away from Jerusalem and had placed in the temple of his god.[a] 8Cyrus king of Persia had them brought by Mithredath the treasurer, who counted them out to Sheshbazzar the prince of Judah.

9This was the inventory:

gold dishes	30
silver dishes	1,000
silver pans[b]	29
10gold bowls	30
matching silver bowls	410
other articles	1,000

11In all, there were 5,400 articles of gold and of silver. Sheshbazzar brought all these along when the exiles came up from Babylon to Jerusalem.

The List of the Exiles Who Returned

2 Now these are the people of the province who came up from the captivity of the exiles, whom Nebuchadnezzar king of Babylon had taken captive to Babylon (they returned to Jerusalem and Judah, each to his own town, 2in company with Zerubbabel, Jeshua, Nehemiah, Seraiah, Reelaiah, Mordecai, Bilshan, Mispar, Bigvai, Rehum and Baanah):

The list of the men of the people of Israel:

3the descendants of Parosh	2,172
4of Shephatiah	372
5of Arah	775
6of Pahath-Moab (through the line of Jeshua and Joab)	2,812
7of Elam	1,254
8of Zattu	945

[a] 7 Or *gods* [b] 9 The meaning of the Hebrew for this word is uncertain.

The promises of Scriptures are not mere pious hopes or sanctified guesses. They are more than sentimental words to be printed on decorated cards for Sunday School children.

They are eternal verities.
They are true.
There is no perhaps about them.

Peter Marshall (1902-1949)

(1:1–5) I worship You, Almighty God. You are the King of kings. You rule over all the nations of the earth. You have the power to move the hearts of kings and commoners, captors and captives. The prophet Isaiah foretold nearly 150 years earlier that a ruler named Cyrus would one day allow Your captive people to return to Jerusalem and rebuild the city and Your temple. The prophet Jeremiah also foretold the return of the remnant of Israel after 70 years of captivity. Now, Your Word came to pass, just as the prophets said it would. Truly, You are the God who "carries out the words of his servants and fulfills the predictions of his messengers." (Isa 44:26–28; Jer 29:10)

The work is Yours and not our own;
Oh, come, and make Your presence known;
Our prayers accept, our off'rings bless,
Our labors crown with due success.

We are the people of Your choice,
And while we in this grace rejoice,
Our prayer is this, our constant care,
That others too our bliss may share.

"Great God, a Blessing From Your Throne"
Conrad H.L. Schuette (1843-1926)

(2:9–48) This long list of names reminds us of another list of names, written in the Lamb's book of life. In that book is the permanent record of those of us who have been released from captivity to sin and death by our Lord Jesus Christ. To us You have made an even greater promise of a more glorious temple, a temple made without hands, that is built out of living stones upon the foundation of Jesus Christ. We, Your people, are the temple of the Lord, more glorious than any building made with human hands. We have been fashioned by Your own hands, purchased with Your own blood, and set apart to be Your residence on the earth. Bless us and guide us, Lord, as we set ourselves to the task of preparing our hearts to be places of worship. (Ac 7:48; 17:24; 1Co 6:19–20; 1Pe 2:5; Rev 21:27)

The church is not a building made with stone. It is a building made with living flesh. We believers are living stones in God's temple, and when we come together we constitute a place of worship where God manifests Himself in ways that He cannot manifest Himself when we are alone. Believers become the living temple of God, offering to Him spiritual sacrifices not possible anywhere other than in the assembly of the redeemed church.

John MacArthur, Jr. (1939-)

9 of Zaccai	760
10 of Bani	642
11 of Bebai	623
12 of Azgad	1,222
13 of Adonikam	666
14 of Bigvai	2,056
15 of Adin	454
16 of Ater (through Hezekiah)	98
17 of Bezai	323
18 of Jorah	112
19 of Hashum	223
20 of Gibbar	95
21 the men of Bethlehem	123
22 of Netophah	56
23 of Anathoth	128
24 of Azmaveth	42
25 of Kiriath Jearim,[a] Kephirah and Beeroth	743
26 of Ramah and Geba	621
27 of Micmash	122
28 of Bethel and Ai	223
29 of Nebo	52
30 of Magbish	156
31 of the other Elam	1,254
32 of Harim	320
33 of Lod, Hadid and Ono	725
34 of Jericho	345
35 of Senaah	3,630

36 The priests:

the descendants of Jedaiah (through the family of Jeshua)	973
37 of Immer	1,052
38 of Pashhur	1,247
39 of Harim	1,017

40 The Levites:

the descendants of Jeshua and Kadmiel (through the line of Hodaviah)	74

41 The singers:

the descendants of Asaph	128

42 The gatekeepers of the temple:

the descendants of Shallum, Ater, Talmon, Akkub, Hatita and Shobai	139

43 The temple servants:

the descendants of
Ziha, Hasupha, Tabbaoth,
44 Keros, Siaha, Padon,
45 Lebanah, Hagabah, Akkub,
46 Hagab, Shalmai, Hanan,
47 Giddel, Gahar, Reaiah,
48 Rezin, Nekoda, Gazzam,

[a] 25 See Septuagint (see also Neh. 7:29); Hebrew *Kiriath Arim.*

[49]Uzza, Paseah, Besai,
[50]Asnah, Meunim, Nephussim,
[51]Bakbuk, Hakupha, Harhur,
[52]Bazluth, Mehida, Harsha,
[53]Barkos, Sisera, Temah,
[54]Neziah and Hatipha

[55]The descendants of the servants of Solomon:

the descendants of
Sotai, Hassophereth, Peruda,
[56]Jaala, Darkon, Giddel,
[57]Shephatiah, Hattil,
Pokereth-Hazzebaim and Ami

[58]The temple servants and the descendants of the servants of Solomon 392

[59]The following came up from the towns of Tel Melah, Tel Harsha, Kerub, Addon and Immer, but they could not show that their families were descended from Israel:

[60]The descendants of
Delaiah, Tobiah and Nekoda 652

[61]And from among the priests:

The descendants of
Hobaiah, Hakkoz and Barzillai (a man who had married a daughter of Barzillai the Gileadite and was called by that name).

[62]These searched for their family records, but they could not find them and so were excluded from the priesthood as unclean. [63]The governor ordered them not to eat any of the most sacred food until there was a priest ministering with the Urim and Thummim.

[64]The whole company numbered 42,360, [65]besides their 7,337 menservants and maidservants; and they also had 200 men and women singers. [66]They had 736 horses, 245 mules, [67]435 camels and 6,720 donkeys.

[68]When they arrived at the house of the LORD in Jerusalem, some of the heads of the families gave freewill offerings toward the rebuilding of the house of God on its site. [69]According to their ability they gave to the treasury for this work 61,000 drachmas[a] of gold, 5,000 minas[b] of silver and 100 priestly garments.

[70]The priests, the Levites, the singers, the gatekeepers and the temple servants settled in their own towns, along with some of the other people, and the rest of the Israelites settled in their towns.

Rebuilding the Altar

3 When the seventh month came and the Israelites had settled
in their towns, the people assembled as one man in Jerusalem. [2]Then Jeshua son of Jozadak and his fellow priests and Zerubbabel son of Shealtiel and his associates began to build the
altar of the God of Israel to sacrifice burnt offerings on it, in accordance with what is written in the Law of Moses the man of God.
[3]Despite their fear of the peoples around them, they built the altar

[a] 69 That is, about 1,100 pounds (about 500 kilograms) [b] 69 That is, about 3 tons (about 2.9 metric tons)

Christ is made the sure foundation,
Christ the head and cornerstone,
Chosen of the Lord and precious,
Binding all the Church in one,
Holy Zion's help forever,
And her confidence alone.

"Christ Is Made the Sure Foundation"
Latin Hymn (7th c.)
Trans. John M. Neale (1818–1866)

(3:1–3) Your people built the altar on its original foundation. Lord, let the worship in Your church today be built on a sure foundation, the original foundation of Christ as revealed in Your holy Scriptures. Despite our fear of the people around us, let us be committed to worship in spirit and truth, without compromise and without shame. For "this is what the Sovereign LORD says: 'See, I lay a stone in Zion, a tested stone, a precious cornerstone for a sure foundation; the one who trusts will never be dismayed.' " (Isa 28:16; 1Pe 2:6)

This day with this prayer I ask that this name dominate all that concerns me: Jesus—the Cornerstone. I want to build upon You, knowing that Your surprises are better than my carefully laid plans.

Dick Eastman (1944-) and
Jack Hayford (1934-)

(4:1–4) O God, as I build my new life in Christ, help me to be careful with the alliances I make. Protect me from false allies who claim to help me—from "friends" who claim to know the way, yet who are not guided by Your Holy Spirit. And I pray for Your church, Lord, that You will protect us from "false apostles, deceitful workmen, masquerading as apostles of Christ . . . for Satan himself masquerades as an angel of light. It is not surprising, then, if his servants masquerade as servants of righteousness." O God, give us wisdom and discernment as we build our churches. (2Co 11:13–15)

We must remember that we deal with a crafty enemy. If we were suddenly aware of a serpent nestling in our bed, we would go to great lengths to kill it. But when the devil nestles in our souls, we tell ourselves we are in no danger, and thus we lie at ease. Why? Because we do not see him and his intent with our mortal eyes . . . Fighting an enemy we can see makes it easy to be on guard, but one that cannot be seen we will not easily escape. Also, know that the devil has no desire for open combat (for he would surely be defeated), but rather, under the appearance of friendship, intends to insinuate the venom of his malice.

Saint John Chrysostom (345-407)

on its foundation and sacrificed burnt offerings on it to the LORD,
both the morning and evening sacrifices. 4Then in accordance
with what is written, they celebrated the Feast of Tabernacles with
the required number of burnt offerings prescribed for each day.
5After that, they presented the regular burnt offerings, the New
Moon sacrifices and the sacrifices for all the appointed sacred
feasts of the LORD, as well as those brought as freewill offerings to
the LORD. 6On the first day of the seventh month they began to offer
burnt offerings to the LORD, though the foundation of the LORD's
temple had not yet been laid.

Rebuilding the Temple

7Then they gave money to the masons and carpenters, and gave
food and drink and oil to the people of Sidon and Tyre, so that they
would bring cedar logs by sea from Lebanon to Joppa, as authorized by Cyrus king of Persia.

8In the second month of the second year after their arrival at
the house of God in Jerusalem, Zerubbabel son of Shealtiel, Jeshua son of Jozadak and the rest of their brothers (the priests and
the Levites and all who had returned from the captivity to Jerusalem) began the work, appointing Levites twenty years of age and
older to supervise the building of the house of the LORD. 9Jeshua
and his sons and brothers and Kadmiel and his sons (descendants
of Hodaviah[a]) and the sons of Henadad and their sons and brothers—all Levites—joined together in supervising those working on
the house of God.

10When the builders laid the foundation of the temple of the
LORD, the priests in their vestments and with trumpets, and the Levites (the sons of Asaph) with cymbals, took their places to praise
the LORD, as prescribed by David king of Israel. 11With praise and
thanksgiving they sang to the LORD:

"He is good;
his love to Israel endures forever."

And all the people gave a great shout of praise to the LORD, because the foundation of the house of the LORD was laid. 12But many
of the older priests and Levites and family heads, who had seen the
former temple, wept aloud when they saw the foundation of this
temple being laid, while many others shouted for joy. 13No one
could distinguish the sound of the shouts of joy from the sound of
weeping, because the people made so much noise. And the sound
was heard far away.

Opposition to the Rebuilding

4 When the enemies of Judah and Benjamin heard that the exiles were building a temple for the LORD, the God of Israel,
2they came to Zerubbabel and to the heads of the families and
said, "Let us help you build because, like you, we seek your God
and have been sacrificing to him since the time of Esarhaddon
king of Assyria, who brought us here."

3But Zerubbabel, Jeshua and the rest of the heads of the families of Israel answered, "You have no part with us in building a
temple to our God. We alone will build it for the LORD, the God of
Israel, as King Cyrus, the king of Persia, commanded us."

4Then the peoples around them set out to discourage the peo-

[a] 9 Hebrew *Yehudah,* probably a variant of *Hodaviah*

ple of Judah and make them afraid to go on building.[a] 5They hired counselors to work against them and frustrate their plans during the entire reign of Cyrus king of Persia and down to the reign of Darius king of Persia.

Later Opposition Under Xerxes and Artaxerxes

6At the beginning of the reign of Xerxes,[b] they lodged an accusation against the people of Judah and Jerusalem.

7And in the days of Artaxerxes king of Persia, Bishlam, Mithredath, Tabeel and the rest of his associates wrote a letter to Artaxerxes. The letter was written in Aramaic script and in the Aramaic language.[c,d]

8Rehum the commanding officer and Shimshai the secretary wrote a letter against Jerusalem to Artaxerxes the king as follows:

9Rehum the commanding officer and Shimshai the secretary, together with the rest of their associates—the judges and officials over the men from Tripolis, Persia,[e] Erech and Babylon, the Elamites of Susa, 10and the other people whom the great and honorable Ashurbanipal[f] deported and settled in the city of Samaria and elsewhere in Trans-Euphrates.

11(This is a copy of the letter they sent him.)

To King Artaxerxes,

From your servants, the men of Trans-Euphrates:

12The king should know that the Jews who came up to us from you have gone to Jerusalem and are rebuilding that rebellious and wicked city. They are restoring the walls and repairing the foundations.

13Furthermore, the king should know that if this city is built and its walls are restored, no more taxes, tribute or duty will be paid, and the royal revenues will suffer. 14Now since we are under obligation to the palace and it is not proper for us to see the king dishonored, we are sending this message to inform the king, 15so that a search may be made in the archives of your predecessors. In these records you will find that this city is a rebellious city, troublesome to kings and provinces, a place of rebellion from ancient times. That is why this city was destroyed. 16We inform the king that if this city is built and its walls are restored, you will be left with nothing in Trans-Euphrates.

17The king sent this reply:

To Rehum the commanding officer, Shimshai the secretary and the rest of their associates living in Samaria and elsewhere in Trans-Euphrates:

Greetings.

18The letter you sent us has been read and translated in my presence. 19I issued an order and a search was made, and it was found that this city has a long history of revolt against kings and has been a place of rebellion and sedition.

[a] 4 Or *and troubled them as they built* [b] 6 Hebrew *Ahasuerus,* a variant of Xerxes' Persian name [c] 7 Or *written in Aramaic and translated* [d] 7 The text of Ezra 4:8—6:18 is in Aramaic. [e] 9 Or *officials, magistrates and governors over the men from* [f] 10 Aramaic *Osnappar,* a variant of *Ashurbanipal*

(4:4–16) Lord, when my faith is challenged, when I face discouragement and opposition on every side, help me to remember Your words from Hebrews: "Remember those earlier days after you had received the light, when you stood your ground in a great contest in the face of suffering. Sometimes you were publicly exposed to insult and persecution; at other times you stood side by side with those who were so treated . . . So do not throw away your confidence; it will be richly rewarded. You need to persevere so that when you have done the will of God, you will receive what he has promised." (Heb 10:32–36)

Did we in our own strength confide,
Our striving would be losing,
Were not the right man on our side,
The man of God's own choosing.
Dost ask who that may be?
Christ Jesus, it is He.
Lord Sabaoth His name,
From age to age the same,
And He must win the battle.

"A Mighty Fortress Is Our God"
Martin Luther (1483-1546)
Trans. Frederick Henry Hedge (1805-1890)

Our all-knowing, all-wise God is also our all-seeing God. His presence permeates all we do. We live and move and have our being in him. We walk before him each day, our hearts opened before him. He sees our pain, our discouragement, our confusion, our heartache, our struggles. And in the seeing, he comes to our rescue with amazing grace.

Understanding that every detail of our lives is laid bare before our heavenly Father and that we are in his all-sufficient care should move us to profound awe and adoration.

Charles Stanley (1932-)

(5:5) O God, help me to ignore the voice of the accuser, the one who would dash my hopes or challenge the validity of the work You are doing in my life. Make me strong in the new life You have given me, so that I will not fear the taunts or threats, but remain faithful and diligent to the task at hand. And as I fix my gaze upon You, may I find that Your gaze is fixed on me. Just knowing that You are watching gives me comfort and courage to carry on. (Ps 33:18)

And though this world with devils
filled
Should threaten to undo us.
We will not fear, for God hath
willed
His truth to triumph through us.
The prince of darkness grim,
We tremble not for him
His rage we can endure,
For lo, his doom is sure:
One little word shall fell him.

"A Mighty Fortress Is Our God"
Martin Luther (1483-1546)
Trans. Frederick Henry Hedge (1805-1890)

20Jerusalem has had powerful kings ruling over the whole of
Trans-Euphrates, and taxes, tribute and duty were paid to
them. 21Now issue an order to these men to stop work, so
that this city will not be rebuilt until I so order. 22Be careful
not to neglect this matter. Why let this threat grow, to the
detriment of the royal interests?

23As soon as the copy of the letter of King Artaxerxes was read
to Rehum and Shimshai the secretary and their associates, they
went immediately to the Jews in Jerusalem and compelled them
by force to stop.

24Thus the work on the house of God in Jerusalem came to a
standstill until the second year of the reign of Darius king of
Persia.

Tattenai's Letter to Darius

5 Now Haggai the prophet and Zechariah the prophet, a descendant of Iddo, prophesied to the Jews in Judah and Jerusalem in the name of the God of Israel, who was over them. 2Then
Zerubbabel son of Shealtiel and Jeshua son of Jozadak set to work
to rebuild the house of God in Jerusalem. And the prophets of
God were with them, helping them.
3At that time Tattenai, governor of Trans-Euphrates, and Shethar-Bozenai and their associates went to them and asked, "Who
authorized you to rebuild this temple and restore this structure?"
4They also asked, "What are the names of the men constructing
this building?"[a] 5But the eye of their God was watching over the
elders of the Jews, and they were not stopped until a report could
go to Darius and his written reply be received.
6This is a copy of the letter that Tattenai, governor of Trans-Euphrates, and Shethar-Bozenai and their associates, the officials of
Trans-Euphrates, sent to King Darius. 7The report they sent him
read as follows:

To King Darius:

Cordial greetings.

8The king should know that we went to the district of
Judah, to the temple of the great God. The people are building it with large stones and placing the timbers in the walls.
The work is being carried on with diligence and is making
rapid progress under their direction.
9We questioned the elders and asked them, "Who authorized you to rebuild this temple and restore this structure?"
10We also asked them their names, so that we could write
down the names of their leaders for your information.
11This is the answer they gave us:

"We are the servants of the God of heaven and earth, and
we are rebuilding the temple that was built many years ago,
one that a great king of Israel built and finished. 12But because our fathers angered the God of heaven, he handed
them over to Nebuchadnezzar the Chaldean, king of Babylon, who destroyed this temple and deported the people to
Babylon.

[a] 4 See Septuagint; Aramaic [4]*We told them the names of the men constructing this building.*

[13]"However, in the first year of Cyrus king of Babylon, King Cyrus issued a decree to rebuild this house of God. [14]He even removed from the temple[a] of Babylon the gold and silver articles of the house of God, which Nebuchadnezzar had taken from the temple in Jerusalem and brought to the temple[a] in Babylon.

"Then King Cyrus gave them to a man named Sheshbazzar, whom he had appointed governor, [15]and he told him, 'Take these articles and go and deposit them in the temple in Jerusalem. And rebuild the house of God on its site.' [16]So this Sheshbazzar came and laid the foundations of the house of God in Jerusalem. From that day to the present it has been under construction but is not yet finished."

[17]Now if it pleases the king, let a search be made in the royal archives of Babylon to see if King Cyrus did in fact issue a decree to rebuild this house of God in Jerusalem. Then let the king send us his decision in this matter.

The Decree of Darius

6 King Darius then issued an order, and they searched in the archives stored in the treasury at Babylon. [2]A scroll was found in the citadel of Ecbatana in the province of Media, and this was written on it:

Memorandum:

[3]In the first year of King Cyrus, the king issued a decree concerning the temple of God in Jerusalem:

Let the temple be rebuilt as a place to present sacrifices, and let its foundations be laid. It is to be ninety feet[b] high and ninety feet wide, [4]with three courses of large stones and one of timbers. The costs are to be paid by the royal treasury. [5]Also, the gold and silver articles of the house of God, which Nebuchadnezzar took from the temple in Jerusalem and brought to Babylon, are to be returned to their places in the temple in Jerusalem; they are to be deposited in the house of God.

[6]Now then, Tattenai, governor of Trans-Euphrates, and Shethar-Bozenai and you, their fellow officials of that province, stay away from there. [7]Do not interfere with the work on this temple of God. Let the governor of the Jews and the Jewish elders rebuild this house of God on its site.

[8]Moreover, I hereby decree what you are to do for these elders of the Jews in the construction of this house of God:

The expenses of these men are to be fully paid out of the royal treasury, from the revenues of Trans-Euphrates, so that the work will not stop. [9]Whatever is needed—young bulls, rams, male lambs for burnt offerings to the God of heaven, and wheat, salt, wine and oil, as requested by the priests in Jerusalem—must be given them daily without fail, [10]so that they may offer sacrifices pleasing to the God of heaven and pray for the well-being of the king and his sons.

[11]Furthermore, I decree that if anyone changes this edict, a beam is to be pulled from his house and he is to be lifted

[a]*14* Or *palace* [b]*3* Aramaic *sixty cubits* (about 27 meters)

(6:6–12) "A sinner's wealth is stored up for the righteous." O God, You are our faithful Provider. I praise You for Your wonderful ways. Not only were Your people allowed to continue the work, but their oppressors had to pay for it! What a wonderful example of Your divine irony and Your divine provision for the needs of Your people as they labored to do Your will. May it be the same with us who diligently labor in this modern day, for You are an unchanging God. Praise be to You! (Pr 13:22)

All God's gifts are prepared in advance and reserved for wants foreseen. He knows our future needs, and out of the fullness of Christ Jesus He provides from His goodness. You may therefore trust Him for all your future needs. He has infallible foreknowledge about every one of them. He can say to you in any condition, "I knew that you would need this."

Charles Haddon Spurgeon (1834–1892)

In the season of our plenty,
In the season of our need;
We will find His grace sufficient,
We will find His love complete.

Safe within His hands that guide us,
Hidden in His healing wings;
Day by day His love provides us
Ev'ry good and perfect thing.

In thanksgiving, let us praise Him;
In thanksgiving, let us sing
Songs of praise and adoration
To our gracious Lord and King.

"In Thanksgiving Let Us Praise Him"
Claire Cloninger (©1986)

(6:19–22) You, O God, are the fountain from which all of our joy flows. Today, I celebrate my Passover Lamb as Your people celebrated so long ago. I sing to You the words of the prophet Isaiah: "The ransomed of the LORD will return. They will enter Zion with singing; everlasting joy will crown their heads. Gladness and joy will overtake them, and sorrow and sighing will flee away." (Isa 35:10; 1Co 5:7)

(7:6–10) Heavenly Father, may I, like Ezra, see the evidence of Your gracious hand on my life as I devote myself to study, to do and to teach Your Word. (Ps 1:1–3)

Study, while demanding, is never grievous. The outcome of learning the Bible is a love for its content and a respect for its relevancy. The Word which comes to dwell in our lives is itself the parent of joy. Remember the great first Psalm? It blessed the man whose delight was in the Law of the Lord, especially if the man meditated upon the Word of the Lord.

Calvin Miller (1936-)

I will delight in the law of the Lord,
I will meditate day and night.
Then, like a tree firmly planted,
I'll be grounded in Your Word.

Blessed is the one
Who follows the way of the Lord;
Blessed is the one.

"I Will Delight"
Walt Harrah and John A. Schreiner (©1991)

up and impaled on it. And for this crime his house is to be
made a pile of rubble. 12May God, who has caused his Name
to dwell there, overthrow any king or people who lifts a hand
to change this decree or to destroy this temple in Jerusalem.

I Darius have decreed it. Let it be carried out with diligence.

Completion and Dedication of the Temple

13Then, because of the decree King Darius had sent, Tattenai,
governor of Trans-Euphrates, and Shethar-Bozenai and their associates carried it out with diligence. 14So the elders of the Jews continued to build and prosper under the preaching of Haggai the
prophet and Zechariah, a descendant of Iddo. They finished building the temple according to the command of the God of Israel and
the decrees of Cyrus, Darius and Artaxerxes, kings of Persia. 15The
temple was completed on the third day of the month Adar, in the
sixth year of the reign of King Darius.

16Then the people of Israel—the priests, the Levites and the
rest of the exiles—celebrated the dedication of the house of God
with joy. 17For the dedication of this house of God they offered a
hundred bulls, two hundred rams, four hundred male lambs and,
as a sin offering for all Israel, twelve male goats, one for each of
the tribes of Israel. 18And they installed the priests in their divi-
sions and the Levites in their groups for the service of God at Jerusalem, according to what is written in the Book of Moses.

The Passover

19On the fourteenth day of the first month, the exiles celebrated the Passover. 20The priests and Levites had purified themselves
and were all ceremonially clean. The Levites slaughtered the
Passover lamb for all the exiles, for their brothers the priests and
for themselves. 21So the Israelites who had returned from the exile
ate it, together with all who had separated themselves from the unclean practices of their Gentile neighbors in order to seek the
LORD, the God of Israel. 22For seven days they celebrated with joy
the Feast of Unleavened Bread, because the LORD had filled them
with joy by changing the attitude of the king of Assyria, so that he
assisted them in the work on the house of God, the God of Israel.

Ezra Comes to Jerusalem

7 After these things, during the reign of Artaxerxes king of Persia, Ezra son of Seraiah, the son of Azariah, the son of Hilkiah, 2the son of Shallum, the son of Zadok, the son of Ahitub, 3the
son of Amariah, the son of Azariah, the son of Meraioth, 4the son
of Zerahiah, the son of Uzzi, the son of Bukki, 5the son of Abishua, the son of Phinehas, the son of Eleazar, the son of Aaron the
chief priest— 6this Ezra came up from Babylon. He was a teacher
well versed in the Law of Moses, which the LORD, the God of Israel, had given. The king had granted him everything he asked, for
the hand of the LORD his God was on him. 7Some of the Israelites,
including priests, Levites, singers, gatekeepers and temple servants, also came up to Jerusalem in the seventh year of King Artaxerxes.

8Ezra arrived in Jerusalem in the fifth month of the seventh year
of the king. 9He had begun his journey from Babylon on the first
day of the first month, and he arrived in Jerusalem on the first day
of the fifth month, for the gracious hand of his God was on him.

10For Ezra had devoted himself to the study and observance of the
Law of the LORD, and to teaching its decrees and laws in Israel.

King Artaxerxes' Letter to Ezra

11This is a copy of the letter King Artaxerxes had given to Ezra
the priest and teacher, a man learned in matters concerning the
commands and decrees of the LORD for Israel:

12[a] Artaxerxes, king of kings,

To Ezra the priest, a teacher of the Law of the God of heav-
en:

Greetings.

13Now I decree that any of the Israelites in my kingdom,
including priests and Levites, who wish to go to Jerusalem
with you, may go. 14You are sent by the king and his seven
advisers to inquire about Judah and Jerusalem with regard
to the Law of your God, which is in your hand. 15Moreover,
you are to take with you the silver and gold that the king and
his advisers have freely given to the God of Israel, whose
dwelling is in Jerusalem, 16together with all the silver and
gold you may obtain from the province of Babylon, as well as
the freewill offerings of the people and priests for the temple of their God in Jerusalem. 17With this money be sure to
buy bulls, rams and male lambs, together with their grain offerings and drink offerings, and sacrifice them on the altar
of the temple of your God in Jerusalem.
18You and your brother Jews may then do whatever seems
best with the rest of the silver and gold, in accordance with
the will of your God. 19Deliver to the God of Jerusalem all
the articles entrusted to you for worship in the temple of
your God. 20And anything else needed for the temple of your
God that you may have occasion to supply, you may provide
from the royal treasury.
21Now I, King Artaxerxes, order all the treasurers of
Trans-Euphrates to provide with diligence whatever Ezra the
priest, a teacher of the Law of the God of heaven, may ask of
you— 22up to a hundred talents[b] of silver, a hundred cors[c]
of wheat, a hundred baths[d] of wine, a hundred baths[d] of
olive oil, and salt without limit. 23Whatever the God of heav-
en has prescribed, let it be done with diligence for the temple of the God of heaven. Why should there be wrath against
the realm of the king and of his sons? 24You are also to
know that you have no authority to impose taxes, tribute or
duty on any of the priests, Levites, singers, gatekeepers, temple servants or other workers at this house of God.
25And you, Ezra, in accordance with the wisdom of your
God, which you possess, appoint magistrates and judges to
administer justice to all the people of Trans-Euphrates—all
who know the laws of your God. And you are to teach any
who do not know them. 26Whoever does not obey the law of
your God and the law of the king must surely be punished by
death, banishment, confiscation of property, or imprisonment.

Commonly there are three stages in work for God: Impossible, Difficult, Done!
James Hudson Taylor (1832–1905)

(7:11–28) I praise You, Lord, for the favor that was given to Ezra by this pagan king. And I pray, according to Your Word, "for kings and all those in authority" in all the nations of the world, that You would incline their hearts favorably toward Your ministers of the gospel. Open doors that no mortal can open; make a way where there is no way, so that Your church may be established and Your Word may be proclaimed with freedom and boldness in the uttermost parts of the earth. (1Ti 2:1–4)

[a] *12* The text of Ezra 7:12–26 is in Aramaic. [b] *22* That is, about 3 3/4 tons (about 3.4 metric tons) [c] *22* That is, probably about 600 bushels (about 22 kiloliters) [d] *22* That is, probably about 600 gallons (about 2.2 kiloliters)

[27]Praise be to the LORD, the God of our fathers, who has put it
into the king's heart to bring honor to the house of the LORD in
Jerusalem in this way [28]and who has extended his good favor to
me before the king and his advisers and all the king's powerful
officials. Because the hand of the LORD my God was on me, I took
courage and gathered leading men from Israel to go up with me.

List of the Family Heads Returning With Ezra

8 These are the family heads and those registered with them who came up with me from Babylon during the reign of King Artaxerxes:

[2]of the descendants of Phinehas, Gershom;
of the descendants of Ithamar, Daniel;
of the descendants of David, Hattush [3]of the descendants of Shecaniah;
of the descendants of Parosh, Zechariah, and with him were registered 150 men;
[4]of the descendants of Pahath-Moab, Eliehoenai son of Zerahiah, and with him 200 men;
[5]of the descendants of Zattu,[a] Shecaniah son of Jahaziel, and with him 300 men;
[6]of the descendants of Adin, Ebed son of Jonathan, and with him 50 men;
[7]of the descendants of Elam, Jeshaiah son of Athaliah, and with him 70 men;
[8]of the descendants of Shephatiah, Zebadiah son of Michael, and with him 80 men;
[9]of the descendants of Joab, Obadiah son of Jehiel, and with him 218 men;
[10]of the descendants of Bani,[b] Shelomith son of Josiphiah, and with him 160 men;
[11]of the descendants of Bebai, Zechariah son of Bebai, and with him 28 men;
[12]of the descendants of Azgad, Johanan son of Hakkatan, and with him 110 men;
[13]of the descendants of Adonikam, the last ones, whose names were Eliphelet, Jeuel and Shemaiah, and with them 60 men;
[14]of the descendants of Bigvai, Uthai and Zaccur, and with them 70 men.

The Return to Jerusalem

[15]I assembled them at the canal that flows toward Ahava, and
we camped there three days. When I checked among the people
and the priests, I found no Levites there. [16]So I summoned Eliezer, Ariel, Shemaiah, Elnathan, Jarib, Elnathan, Nathan, Zechariah and Meshullam, who were leaders, and Joiarib and Elnathan,
who were men of learning, [17]and I sent them to Iddo, the leader
in Casiphia. I told them what to say to Iddo and his kinsmen, the
temple servants in Casiphia, so that they might bring attendants to
us for the house of our God. [18]Because the gracious hand of our
God was on us, they brought us Sherebiah, a capable man, from
the descendants of Mahli son of Levi, the son of Israel, and Sherebiah's sons and brothers, 18 men; [19]and Hashabiah, together

[a] *5* Some Septuagint manuscripts (also 1 Esdras 8:32); Hebrew does not have *Zattu.*
[b] *10* Some Septuagint manuscripts (also 1 Esdras 8:36); Hebrew does not have *Bani.*

(7:27—8:18) O God, raise up leaders like Ezra in our day, who can inspire our hearts to follow them in Your ways. And give us eyes to recognize Your hand in the lives of godly leaders, so that in following them we will see that we are following You.

Every man is a centre of perpetual radiation like a luminous body; he is, as it were, a beacon which entices a ship upon the rocks if it does not guide it into port. Every man is a priest, even involuntarily; his conduct is an unspoken sermon, which is forever preaching to others–but there are priests of Baal, of Moloch, and of all the false gods. Such is the high importance of example. Thence comes the terrible responsibility which weighs upon us all.

Henri-Frederic Amiel (1821-1881)

with Jeshaiah from the descendants of Merari, and his brothers
and nephews, 20 men. 20They also brought 220 of the temple servants—a body that David and the officials had established to assist the Levites. All were registered by name.
21There, by the Ahava Canal, I proclaimed a fast, so that we
might humble ourselves before our God and ask him for a safe
journey for us and our children, with all our possessions. 22I was
ashamed to ask the king for soldiers and horsemen to protect us
from enemies on the road, because we had told the king, "The
gracious hand of our God is on everyone who looks to him, but
his great anger is against all who forsake him." 23So we fasted
and petitioned our God about this, and he answered our prayer.
24Then I set apart twelve of the leading priests, together with
Sherebiah, Hashabiah and ten of their brothers, 25and I weighed
out to them the offering of silver and gold and the articles that the
king, his advisers, his officials and all Israel present there had
donated for the house of our God. 26I weighed out to them 650
talents[a] of silver, silver articles weighing 100 talents,[b] 100 talents[b] of gold, 2720 bowls of gold valued at 1,000 darics,[c] and
two fine articles of polished bronze, as precious as gold.
28I said to them, "You as well as these articles are consecrated to the LORD. The silver and gold are a freewill offering to the
LORD, the God of your fathers. 29Guard them carefully until you
weigh them out in the chambers of the house of the LORD in Jerusalem before the leading priests and the Levites and the family
heads of Israel." 30Then the priests and Levites received the silver and gold and sacred articles that had been weighed out to be
taken to the house of our God in Jerusalem.
31On the twelfth day of the first month we set out from the
Ahava Canal to go to Jerusalem. The hand of our God was on us,
and he protected us from enemies and bandits along the way.
32So we arrived in Jerusalem, where we rested three days.
33On the fourth day, in the house of our God, we weighed out
the silver and gold and the sacred articles into the hands of Meremoth son of Uriah, the priest. Eleazar son of Phinehas was with
him, and so were the Levites Jozabad son of Jeshua and Noadiah
son of Binnui. 34Everything was accounted for by number and
weight, and the entire weight was recorded at that time.
35Then the exiles who had returned from captivity sacrificed
burnt offerings to the God of Israel: twelve bulls for all Israel,
ninety-six rams, seventy-seven male lambs and, as a sin offering,
twelve male goats. All this was a burnt offering to the LORD. 36They
also delivered the king's orders to the royal satraps and to the
governors of Trans-Euphrates, who then gave assistance to the
people and to the house of God.

Ezra's Prayer About Intermarriage

9 After these things had been done, the leaders came to me
and said, "The people of Israel, including the priests and the
Levites, have not kept themselves separate from the neighboring
peoples with their detestable practices, like those of the Canaanites, Hittites, Perizzites, Jebusites, Ammonites, Moabites, Egyptians and Amorites. 2They have taken some of their daughters as
wives for themselves and their sons, and have mingled the holy

[a]26 That is, about 25 tons (about 22 metric tons) [b]26 That is, about 3 3/4 tons (about 3.4 metric tons) [c]27 That is, about 19 pounds (about 8.5 kilograms)

(8:21–23) Lord, let us learn from Ezra's example that before we set out on any major undertaking, we first need to submit ourselves to You in humility and seek Your gracious hand of blessing. We praise You and thank You for the great privilege we have in fasting and prayer. May we never take it for granted or neglect our responsibility to fast and pray.

Those who seek God are safe under the shadow of his wings, even in their greatest dangers, but those who forsake him are continually exposed, even when they are most secure.

Matthew Henry (1662–1714)

Oh, Protector of my soul,
You will stand against the foe;
In the dark You'll be a light for me.
Oh, Protector of my soul.

"Protector Of My Soul"
Anne Barbour (©1990)

(9:5–15) Protect us, O God, from any compromise with the idolatry so common to our culture. Keep us pure in our devotion to You and prevent the enticement of sin from entering our homes and families. Make us a holy people, O Lord, in all that we are and all that we do. Let us live for the sake of Your glory alone.

If I'm to be whom You desire,
All throughout my life,
A vessel unto honor, Lord, to Thee;
And before Your throne
To hear You say
That I have done my part,
Lord, I need an undivided heart.

That I might know You,
That I might serve You,
That I might worship You as King,
To see the Morning Star,
To know how great You are,
Lord, I need an undivided heart.

"Undivided Heart"
Dan Marks (©1996)

The well-defined spiritual life is not only the highest life, but it is also the most easily lived. The whole cross is more easily carried than the half. It is the man who tries to make the best of both worlds who makes nothing of either. And he who seeks to serve two masters misses the benediction of both. But he who has taken his stand, who has drawn a boundary-line sharp and deep about his religious life, who has marked off all beyond as forever forbidden ground to him, finds the yoke easy and the burden light.

Henry Drummond (1851–1897)

race with the peoples around them. And the leaders and officials
have led the way in this unfaithfulness."
3When I heard this, I tore my tunic and cloak, pulled hair from
my head and beard and sat down appalled. 4Then everyone who
trembled at the words of the God of Israel gathered around me
because of this unfaithfulness of the exiles. And I sat there appalled until the evening sacrifice.
5Then, at the evening sacrifice, I rose from my self-abasement,
with my tunic and cloak torn, and fell on my knees with my hands
spread out to the LORD my God 6and prayed:

"O my God, I am too ashamed and disgraced to lift up my
face to you, my God, because our sins are higher than our
heads and our guilt has reached to the heavens. 7From the
days of our forefathers until now, our guilt has been great.
Because of our sins, we and our kings and our priests have
been subjected to the sword and captivity, to pillage and humiliation at the hand of foreign kings, as it is today.
8"But now, for a brief moment, the LORD our God has
been gracious in leaving us a remnant and giving us a firm
place in his sanctuary, and so our God gives light to our eyes
and a little relief in our bondage. 9Though we are slaves,
our God has not deserted us in our bondage. He has shown
us kindness in the sight of the kings of Persia: He has granted us new life to rebuild the house of our God and repair its
ruins, and he has given us a wall of protection in Judah and
Jerusalem.
10"But now, O our God, what can we say after this? For we
have disregarded the commands 11you gave through your
servants the prophets when you said: 'The land you are entering to possess is a land polluted by the corruption of its
peoples. By their detestable practices they have filled it with
their impurity from one end to the other. 12Therefore, do
not give your daughters in marriage to their sons or take
their daughters for your sons. Do not seek a treaty of friendship with them at any time, that you may be strong and eat
the good things of the land and leave it to your children as
an everlasting inheritance.'
13"What has happened to us is a result of our evil deeds
and our great guilt, and yet, our God, you have punished us
less than our sins have deserved and have given us a remnant like this. 14Shall we again break your commands and
intermarry with the peoples who commit such detestable
practices? Would you not be angry enough with us to destroy
us, leaving us no remnant or survivor? 15O LORD, God of Israel, you are righteous! We are left this day as a remnant.
Here we are before you in our guilt, though because of it
not one of us can stand in your presence."

The People's Confession of Sin

10 While Ezra was praying and confessing, weeping and
throwing himself down before the house of God, a large
crowd of Israelites—men, women and children—gathered
around him. They too wept bitterly. 2Then Shecaniah son of Jehiel, one of the descendants of Elam, said to Ezra, "We have been
unfaithful to our God by marrying foreign women from the peoples around us. But in spite of this, there is still hope for Israel.
3Now let us make a covenant before our God to send away all

these women and their children, in accordance with the counsel of my lord and of those who fear the commands of our God. Let it be done according to the Law. 4Rise up; this matter is in your hands. We will support you, so take courage and do it."

5So Ezra rose up and put the leading priests and Levites and all Israel under oath to do what had been suggested. And they took the oath. 6Then Ezra withdrew from before the house of God and went to the room of Jehohanan son of Eliashib. While he was there, he ate no food and drank no water, because he continued to mourn over the unfaithfulness of the exiles.

7A proclamation was then issued throughout Judah and Jerusalem for all the exiles to assemble in Jerusalem. 8Anyone who failed to appear within three days would forfeit all his property, in accordance with the decision of the officials and elders, and would himself be expelled from the assembly of the exiles.

9Within the three days, all the men of Judah and Benjamin had gathered in Jerusalem. And on the twentieth day of the ninth month, all the people were sitting in the square before the house of God, greatly distressed by the occasion and because of the rain. 10Then Ezra the priest stood up and said to them, "You have been unfaithful; you have married foreign women, adding to Israel's guilt. 11Now make confession to the LORD, the God of your fathers, and do his will. Separate yourselves from the peoples around you and from your foreign wives."

12The whole assembly responded with a loud voice: "You are right! We must do as you say. 13But there are many people here and it is the rainy season; so we cannot stand outside. Besides, this matter cannot be taken care of in a day or two, because we have sinned greatly in this thing. 14Let our officials act for the whole assembly. Then let everyone in our towns who has married a foreign woman come at a set time, along with the elders and judges of each town, until the fierce anger of our God in this matter is turned away from us." 15Only Jonathan son of Asahel and Jahzeiah son of Tikvah, supported by Meshullam and Shabbethai the Levite, opposed this.

16So the exiles did as was proposed. Ezra the priest selected men who were family heads, one from each family division, and all of them designated by name. On the first day of the tenth month they sat down to investigate the cases, 17and by the first day of the first month they finished dealing with all the men who had married foreign women.

Those Guilty of Intermarriage

18Among the descendants of the priests, the following had married foreign women:

From the descendants of Jeshua son of Jozadak, and his brothers: Maaseiah, Eliezer, Jarib and Gedaliah. 19(They all gave their hands in pledge to put away their wives, and for their guilt they each presented a ram from the flock as a guilt offering.)

20From the descendants of Immer:
Hanani and Zebadiah.

21From the descendants of Harim:
Maaseiah, Elijah, Shemaiah, Jehiel and Uzziah.

22From the descendants of Pashhur:

(10:3–17) I look at this situation and I grieve for the people of Israel. Father, I confess that I do not always understand the ways of Your people of old. It often seems that our attempts to remedy the results of our sinful choices only serve to worsen the results of those choices. I pray for those in Your church today who are married to unbelievers. I pray that You will use their living witness to lead their spouses to Christ. And I thank You for Your words of instruction from the apostle Paul in his first letter to the Corinthians when he addressed this very issue. O Lord, give us wisdom in our time of need. (1Co 7:12–17)

(10:23–44) Father, after all You have done for us to save us and restore us to fellowship with You, please help us to "make every effort to be found spotless, blameless and at peace" with You. Teach us to be on our guard so that we may not be carried away by the error of lawless men and fall from our secure position. May we grow in the grace and knowledge of our Lord and Savior Jesus Christ. To Him be glory both now and forever! Amen. (2Pe 3:14,17–18)

Most great and mighty God, you are the sovereign Lord of heaven and earth, the Creator, the Preserver and Governor of all things. You dwell in that light which no mortal eye can approach, and yet you do not disdain to behold our darkened souls. Look down, we beg you, on us your unworthy creatures. We humbly thank you for your daily care of us. We beg your pardon for whatsoever you have seen amiss in us this day, in our thoughts, words, or actions. Strengthen us in every good purpose and resolution. Reform whatsoever you see amiss in the temper and disposition of our minds or in any of the habits of our lives; that we may love you more and serve you better, and do your will with greater care and diligence than we have yet done. In the name of Jesus Christ our only Lord and Savior.

Warren Hastings (1732-1818)

Elioenai, Maaseiah, Ishmael, Nethanel, Jozabad and Elasah.

23 Among the Levites:

Jozabad, Shimei, Kelaiah (that is, Kelita), Pethahiah, Judah and Eliezer.

24 From the singers:

Eliashib.

From the gatekeepers:

Shallum, Telem and Uri.

25 And among the other Israelites:

From the descendants of Parosh:

Ramiah, Izziah, Malkijah, Mijamin, Eleazar, Malkijah and Benaiah.

26 From the descendants of Elam:

Mattaniah, Zechariah, Jehiel, Abdi, Jeremoth and Elijah.

27 From the descendants of Zattu:

Elioenai, Eliashib, Mattaniah, Jeremoth, Zabad and Aziza.

28 From the descendants of Bebai:

Jehohanan, Hananiah, Zabbai and Athlai.

29 From the descendants of Bani:

Meshullam, Malluch, Adaiah, Jashub, Sheal and Jeremoth.

30 From the descendants of Pahath-Moab:

Adna, Kelal, Benaiah, Maaseiah, Mattaniah, Bezalel, Binnui and Manasseh.

31 From the descendants of Harim:

Eliezer, Ishijah, Malkijah, Shemaiah, Shimeon,
32 Benjamin, Malluch and Shemariah.

33 From the descendants of Hashum:

Mattenai, Mattattah, Zabad, Eliphelet, Jeremai, Manasseh and Shimei.

34 From the descendants of Bani:

Maadai, Amram, Uel,
35 Benaiah, Bedeiah, Keluhi,
36 Vaniah, Meremoth, Eliashib,
37 Mattaniah, Mattenai and Jaasu.

38 From the descendants of Binnui:[a]

Shimei,
39 Shelemiah, Nathan, Adaiah,
40 Macnadebai, Shashai, Sharai,
41 Azarel, Shelemiah, Shemariah,
42 Shallum, Amariah and Joseph.

43 From the descendants of Nebo:

Jeiel, Mattithiah, Zabad, Zebina, Jaddai, Joel and Benaiah.

44 All these had married foreign women, and some of them had children by these wives.[b]

[a] 37,38 See Septuagint (also 1 Esdras 9:34); Hebrew *Jaasu* [38] *and Bani and Binnui,*
[b] 44 Or *and they sent them away with their children*

Nehemiah's Prayer

1 The words of Nehemiah son of Hacaliah:

In the month of Kislev in the twentieth year, while I was in the citadel of Susa, [2]Hanani, one of my brothers, came from Judah with some other men, and I questioned them about the Jewish remnant that survived the exile, and also about Jerusalem.

[3]They said to me, "Those who survived the exile and are back in the province are in great trouble and disgrace. The wall of Jerusalem is broken down, and its gates have been burned with fire."

[4]When I heard these things, I sat down and wept. For some days I mourned and fasted and prayed before the God of heaven. [5]Then I said:

"O LORD, God of heaven, the great and awesome God, who keeps his covenant of love with those who love him and obey his commands, [6]let your ear be attentive and your eyes open to hear the prayer your servant is praying before you day and night for your servants, the people of Israel. I confess the sins we Israelites, including myself and my father's house, have committed against you. [7]We have acted very wickedly toward you. We have not obeyed the commands, decrees and laws you gave your servant Moses.

[8]"Remember the instruction you gave your servant Moses, saying, 'If you are unfaithful, I will scatter you among the nations, [9]but if you return to me and obey my commands, then even if your exiled people are at the farthest horizon, I will gather them from there and bring them to the place I have chosen as a dwelling for my Name.'

[10]"They are your servants and your people, whom you redeemed by your great strength and your mighty hand. [11]O Lord, let your ear be attentive to the prayer of this your servant and to the prayer of your servants who delight in revering your name. Give your servant success today by granting him favor in the presence of this man."

I was cupbearer to the king.

Artaxerxes Sends Nehemiah to Jerusalem

2 In the month of Nisan in the twentieth year of King Artaxerxes, when wine was brought for him, I took the wine and gave it to the king. I had not been sad in his presence before; [2]so the king asked me, "Why does your face look so sad when you are not ill? This can be nothing but sadness of heart."

I was very much afraid, [3]but I said to the king, "May the king live forever! Why should my face not look sad when the city where my fathers are buried lies in ruins, and its gates have been destroyed by fire?"

[4]The king said to me, "What is it you want?"

Then I prayed to the God of heaven, [5]and I answered the king, "If it pleases the king and if your servant has found favor in his sight, let him send me to the city in Judah where my fathers are buried so that I can rebuild it."

[6]Then the king, with the queen sitting beside him, asked me, "How long will your journey take, and when will you get back?" It pleased the king to send me; so I set a time.

[7]I also said to him, "If it pleases the king, may I have letters to

(1:1–11) "By the rivers of Babylon we sat and wept when we remembered Zion." Out of their disgrace and oppression your people cried out to You, and You listened. I thank you, Father, that because of Your covenant love we can pray to You in spite of our failures. Though we turn our backs on You, You will never abandon us or fail to be our God. Have mercy upon us, O Lord, when we fail to live as Your people. (Dt 4:31; Ps 137:1)

(2:1–7) You are the great and awesome God; You keep Your covenant with those who love You and keep Your commandments. Your patience with Your people is marvelous. You graciously support us when we serve You. You hear us when we bring our needs before You. Your providence is wonderful. You move the hearts of rulers and give Your people favor in their sight. (Ezr 1:1–3; Pr 21:1)

(2:11–18) You stirred Nehemiah's heart to rebuild the broken-down walls of the city. Stir my heart as well. Give me a passion for building Your kingdom, Lord. Point out where You want me to work and what You want me to do. Give me confidence that Your hand is with me, and may my efforts bring You honor and glory.

Difficulty is the very atmosphere of miracle–it is miracle in its first stage. If it is to be a great miracle, the condition is not difficulty but impossibility.

Lettie B. Cowman (1870-1960)

(2:19–20) God of heaven and earth, You are truly great and awesome! You promise ultimate success to those who serve You. Keep us from us being discouraged by those who oppose us. Let us build on the true foundation of Your prophets and apostles, with Christ Jesus himself as the chief Cornerstone. (Eph 2:20)

the governors of Trans-Euphrates, so that they will provide me
safe-conduct until I arrive in Judah? 8And may I have a letter to
Asaph, keeper of the king's forest, so he will give me timber to
make beams for the gates of the citadel by the temple and for the
city wall and for the residence I will occupy?" And because the
gracious hand of my God was upon me, the king granted my requests. 9So I went to the governors of Trans-Euphrates and gave
them the king's letters. The king had also sent army officers and
cavalry with me.

10When Sanballat the Horonite and Tobiah the Ammonite official heard about this, they were very much disturbed that someone had come to promote the welfare of the Israelites.

Nehemiah Inspects Jerusalem's Walls

11I went to Jerusalem, and after staying there three days 12I set
out during the night with a few men. I had not told anyone what
my God had put in my heart to do for Jerusalem. There were no
mounts with me except the one I was riding on.

13By night I went out through the Valley Gate toward the Jackal[a] Well and the Dung Gate, examining the walls of Jerusalem,
which had been broken down, and its gates, which had been destroyed by fire. 14Then I moved on toward the Fountain Gate and
the King's Pool, but there was not enough room for my mount to
get through; 15so I went up the valley by night, examining the
wall. Finally, I turned back and reentered through the Valley Gate.
16The officials did not know where I had gone or what I was
doing, because as yet I had said nothing to the Jews or the priests
or nobles or officials or any others who would be doing the work.

17Then I said to them, "You see the trouble we are in: Jerusalem lies in ruins, and its gates have been burned with fire. Come,
let us rebuild the wall of Jerusalem, and we will no longer be in
disgrace." 18I also told them about the gracious hand of my God
upon me and what the king had said to me.

They replied, "Let us start rebuilding." So they began this good
work.

19But when Sanballat the Horonite, Tobiah the Ammonite official and Geshem the Arab heard about it, they mocked and
ridiculed us. "What is this you are doing?" they asked. "Are you
rebelling against the king?"

20I answered them by saying, "The God of heaven will give us
success. We his servants will start rebuilding, but as for you, you
have no share in Jerusalem or any claim or historic right to it."

Builders of the Wall

3 Eliashib the high priest and his fellow priests went to work
and rebuilt the Sheep Gate. They dedicated it and set its
doors in place, building as far as the Tower of the Hundred,
which they dedicated, and as far as the Tower of Hananel. 2The
men of Jericho built the adjoining section, and Zaccur son of Imri
built next to them.

3The Fish Gate was rebuilt by the sons of Hassenaah. They laid
its beams and put its doors and bolts and bars in place. 4Mere-
moth son of Uriah, the son of Hakkoz, repaired the next section.
Next to him Meshullam son of Berekiah, the son of Meshezabel,
made repairs, and next to him Zadok son of Baana also made re-

[a] *13* Or *Serpent* or *Fig*

pairs. 5The next section was repaired by the men of Tekoa, but
their nobles would not put their shoulders to the work under
their supervisors.[a]

6The Jeshanah[b] Gate was repaired by Joiada son of Paseah and
Meshullam son of Besodeiah. They laid its beams and put its
doors and bolts and bars in place. 7Next to them, repairs were
made by men from Gibeon and Mizpah—Melatiah of Gibeon and
Jadon of Meronoth—places under the authority of the governor
of Trans-Euphrates. 8Uzziel son of Harhaiah, one of the goldsmiths, repaired the next section; and Hananiah, one of the
perfume-makers, made repairs next to that. They restored[c] Jerusalem as far as the Broad Wall. 9Rephaiah son of Hur, ruler of a
half-district of Jerusalem, repaired the next section. 10Adjoining
this, Jedaiah son of Harumaph made repairs opposite his house,
and Hattush son of Hashabneiah made repairs next to him.
11Malkijah son of Harim and Hasshub son of Pahath-Moab repaired another section and the Tower of the Ovens. 12Shallum
son of Hallohesh, ruler of a half-district of Jerusalem, repaired
the next section with the help of his daughters.

13The Valley Gate was repaired by Hanun and the residents of
Zanoah. They rebuilt it and put its doors and bolts and bars in
place. They also repaired five hundred yards[d] of the wall as far as
the Dung Gate.

14The Dung Gate was repaired by Malkijah son of Recab, ruler
of the district of Beth Hakkerem. He rebuilt it and put its doors
and bolts and bars in place.

15The Fountain Gate was repaired by Shallun son of Col-Hozeh,
ruler of the district of Mizpah. He rebuilt it, roofing it over and
putting its doors and bolts and bars in place. He also repaired the
wall of the Pool of Siloam,[e] by the King's Garden, as far as the
steps going down from the City of David. 16Beyond him, Nehemiah son of Azbuk, ruler of a half-district of Beth Zur, made repairs
up to a point opposite the tombs[f] of David, as far as the artificial
pool and the House of the Heroes.

17Next to him, the repairs were made by the Levites under
Rehum son of Bani. Beside him, Hashabiah, ruler of half the district of Keilah, carried out repairs for his district. 18Next to him,
the repairs were made by their countrymen under Binnui[g] son of
Henadad, ruler of the other half-district of Keilah. 19Next to him,
Ezer son of Jeshua, ruler of Mizpah, repaired another section,
from a point facing the ascent to the armory as far as the angle.
20Next to him, Baruch son of Zabbai zealously repaired another
section, from the angle to the entrance of the house of Eliashib
the high priest. 21Next to him, Meremoth son of Uriah, the son of
Hakkoz, repaired another section, from the entrance of Eliashib's
house to the end of it.

22The repairs next to him were made by the priests from the
surrounding region. 23Beyond them, Benjamin and Hasshub
made repairs in front of their house; and next to them, Azariah
son of Maaseiah, the son of Ananiah, made repairs beside his

The work of God happens when the people of God labor.

Mark Roberts (1957-)

(3:5–23) Sovereign Lord, we praise You for the dignity You give to each of us by assigning us our roles and our places in building up Your kingdom. You know our names and You know our work. Please give all of Your people in the community of faith a sense of united purpose and destiny. Help us to "stand firm in one spirit, contending as one man for the faith of the gospel without being frightened in any way" by those who oppose us. (Php 1:27–28)

[a] *5* Or *their Lord* or *the governor* [b] *6* Or *Old* [c] *8* Or *They left out part of*
[d] *13* Hebrew *a thousand cubits* (about 450 meters) [e] *15* Hebrew *Shelah,* a variant of *Shiloah,* that is, Siloam [f] *16* Hebrew; Septuagint, some Vulgate manuscripts and Syriac *tomb* [g] *18* Two Hebrew manuscripts and Syriac (see also Septuagint and verse 24); most Hebrew manuscripts *Bavvai*

(4:6–12) "The people worked with all their heart," yet they worried about the risks and became discouraged at the size of their task. Father, You know how often I am tempted to give in to my fears and frustrations, and to give up on Your work. As I pursue Your will for my life, O Lord, please increase my confidence in Your protection and Your promise of success.

God gives us the grace to accomplish what He calls us to do. His commands are also His promise of victory.

Sometimes you might feel that it is impossible to endure to the end. That may be right! But when we come to the end of what is possible for us, then we can see God do the impossible. Faith has not begun until we believe God for the impossible. We don't need faith to do what is possible. So if you are facing impossible situations in your life, praise God, for now you can begin to exercise your faith.

Floyd McClung, Jr. (1945-)

He is able, more than able
To accomplish what concerns me
today.
He is able, more than able
To handle anything that comes my
way.
He is able, more than able
To do much more than I could ever
dream.
He is able, more than able
To make me what He wants me to
be.

"He is Able"
Rory Noland and Greg Ferguson (©1989)

house. 24Next to him, Binnui son of Henadad repaired another section, from Azariah's house to the angle and the corner, 25and Palal son of Uzai worked opposite the angle and the tower projecting from the upper palace near the court of the guard. Next to him, Pedaiah son of Parosh 26and the temple servants living on the hill of Ophel made repairs up to a point opposite the Water Gate toward the east and the projecting tower. 27Next to them, the men of Tekoa repaired another section, from the great projecting tower to the wall of Ophel.

28Above the Horse Gate, the priests made repairs, each in front of his own house. 29Next to them, Zadok son of Immer made repairs opposite his house. Next to him, Shemaiah son of Shecaniah, the guard at the East Gate, made repairs. 30Next to him, Hananiah son of Shelemiah, and Hanun, the sixth son of Zalaph, repaired another section. Next to them, Meshullam son of Berekiah made repairs opposite his living quarters. 31Next to him, Malkijah, one of the goldsmiths, made repairs as far as the house of the temple servants and the merchants, opposite the Inspection Gate, and as far as the room above the corner; 32and between the room above the corner and the Sheep Gate the goldsmiths and merchants made repairs.

Opposition to the Rebuilding

4 When Sanballat heard that we were rebuilding the wall, he became angry and was greatly incensed. He ridiculed the Jews, 2and in the presence of his associates and the army of Samaria, he said, "What are those feeble Jews doing? Will they restore their wall? Will they offer sacrifices? Will they finish in a day? Can they bring the stones back to life from those heaps of rubble—burned as they are?"

3Tobiah the Ammonite, who was at his side, said, "What they are building—if even a fox climbed up on it, he would break down their wall of stones!"

4Hear us, O our God, for we are despised. Turn their insults back on their own heads. Give them over as plunder in a land of captivity. 5Do not cover up their guilt or blot out their sins from your sight, for they have thrown insults in the face of[a] the builders.

6So we rebuilt the wall till all of it reached half its height, for the people worked with all their heart.

7But when Sanballat, Tobiah, the Arabs, the Ammonites and the men of Ashdod heard that the repairs to Jerusalem's walls had gone ahead and that the gaps were being closed, they were very angry. 8They all plotted together to come and fight against Jerusalem and stir up trouble against it. 9But we prayed to our God and posted a guard day and night to meet this threat.

10Meanwhile, the people in Judah said, "The strength of the laborers is giving out, and there is so much rubble that we cannot rebuild the wall."

11Also our enemies said, "Before they know it or see us, we will be right there among them and will kill them and put an end to the work."

12Then the Jews who lived near them came and told us ten times over, "Wherever you turn, they will attack us."

[a] 5 Or *have provoked you to anger before*

13 Therefore I stationed some of the people behind the lowest
points of the wall at the exposed places, posting them by families,
with their swords, spears and bows. 14 After I looked things over,
I stood up and said to the nobles, the officials and the rest of the
people, "Don't be afraid of them. Remember the Lord, who is
great and awesome, and fight for your brothers, your sons and
your daughters, your wives and your homes."
15 When our enemies heard that we were aware of their plot
and that God had frustrated it, we all returned to the wall, each to
his own work.
16 From that day on, half of my men did the work, while the
other half were equipped with spears, shields, bows and armor.
The officers posted themselves behind all the people of Judah
17 who were building the wall. Those who carried materials did
their work with one hand and held a weapon in the other, 18 and
each of the builders wore his sword at his side as he worked. But
the man who sounded the trumpet stayed with me.
19 Then I said to the nobles, the officials and the rest of the people, "The work is extensive and spread out, and we are widely
separated from each other along the wall. 20 Wherever you hear
the sound of the trumpet, join us there. Our God will fight for us!"
21 So we continued the work with half the men holding spears,
from the first light of dawn till the stars came out. 22 At that time I
also said to the people, "Have every man and his helper stay inside Jerusalem at night, so they can serve us as guards by night
and workmen by day." 23 Neither I nor my brothers nor my men
nor the guards with me took off our clothes; each had his
weapon, even when he went for water.[a]

Nehemiah Helps the Poor

5 Now the men and their wives raised a great outcry against
their Jewish brothers. 2 Some were saying, "We and our sons
and daughters are numerous; in order for us to eat and stay alive,
we must get grain."
3 Others were saying, "We are mortgaging our fields, our vineyards and our homes to get grain during the famine."
4 Still others were saying, "We have had to borrow money to
pay the king's tax on our fields and vineyards. 5 Although we are
of the same flesh and blood as our countrymen and though our
sons are as good as theirs, yet we have to subject our sons and
daughters to slavery. Some of our daughters have already been
enslaved, but we are powerless, because our fields and our vineyards belong to others."
6 When I heard their outcry and these charges, I was very angry.
7 I pondered them in my mind and then accused the nobles and
officials. I told them, "You are exacting usury from your own
countrymen!" So I called together a large meeting to deal with
them 8 and said: "As far as possible, we have bought back our
Jewish brothers who were sold to the Gentiles. Now you are selling your brothers, only for them to be sold back to us!" They kept
quiet, because they could find nothing to say.
9 So I continued, "What you are doing is not right. Shouldn't
you walk in the fear of our God to avoid the reproach of our Gentile enemies? 10 I and my brothers and my men are also lending
the people money and grain. But let the exacting of usury stop!

[a] 23 The meaning of the Hebrew for this clause is uncertain.

Spiritual strength and courage are very necessary for our spiritual warfare. We have no sufficient strength of our own. All our sufficiency is of God. In his strength we must go forth and go on. We must fetch in grace and help from heaven to enable us to do that which of ourselves we cannot do in our Christian work and warfare.

Matthew Henry (1662-1714)

(4:16–18) As long as we are engaged in spiritual work, we will also be engaged in spiritual warfare. We praise You, our God and Father, that You equip us with spiritual gifts for our work and with spiritual weapons for our warfare. Now please teach us to work diligently, to pray fervently, and to serve faithfully in the power of Your Spirit (2Co 10:3–4; Eph 6:10–18)

Face to face, brother to brother,
Face to face, one friend to another.
Growing together
We're building the kingdom of God.

Man to man, shoulder to shoulder,
Man to man, serving each other.
Working together
We're building the kingdom of God

Brother to brother, we'll strengthen
each other,
And stand for the truth side by side
Brother to brother, we'll honor each
other
As men of the kingdom on high.

Back to back, warrior to warrior,
Back to back, defending each other.
Standing together
We're building the kingdom of God.

"Face To Face"
Buddy Owens and Bill Batstone (©1993)

11 Give back to them immediately their fields, vineyards, olive groves and houses, and also the usury you are charging them—the hundredth part of the money, grain, new wine and oil."

12 "We will give it back," they said. "And we will not demand anything more from them. We will do as you say."

Then I summoned the priests and made the nobles and officials take an oath to do what they had promised. 13 I also shook out the folds of my robe and said, "In this way may God shake out of his house and possessions every man who does not keep this promise. So may such a man be shaken out and emptied!"

At this the whole assembly said, "Amen," and praised the LORD. And the people did as they had promised.

14 Moreover, from the twentieth year of King Artaxerxes, when I was appointed to be their governor in the land of Judah, until his thirty-second year—twelve years—neither I nor my brothers ate the food allotted to the governor. 15 But the earlier governors—those preceding me—placed a heavy burden on the people and took forty shekels[a] of silver from them in addition to food and wine. Their assistants also lorded it over the people. But out of reverence for God I did not act like that. 16 Instead, I devoted myself to the work on this wall. All my men were assembled there for the work; we[b] did not acquire any land.

17 Furthermore, a hundred and fifty Jews and officials ate at my table, as well as those who came to us from the surrounding nations. 18 Each day one ox, six choice sheep and some poultry were prepared for me, and every ten days an abundant supply of wine of all kinds. In spite of all this, I never demanded the food allotted to the governor, because the demands were heavy on these people.

19 Remember me with favor, O my God, for all I have done for these people.

Further Opposition to the Rebuilding

6 When word came to Sanballat, Tobiah, Geshem the Arab and the rest of our enemies that I had rebuilt the wall and not a gap was left in it—though up to that time I had not set the doors in the gates— 2 Sanballat and Geshem sent me this message: "Come, let us meet together in one of the villages[c] on the plain of Ono."

But they were scheming to harm me; 3 so I sent messengers to them with this reply: "I am carrying on a great project and cannot go down. Why should the work stop while I leave it and go down to you?" 4 Four times they sent me the same message, and each time I gave them the same answer.

5 Then, the fifth time, Sanballat sent his aide to me with the same message, and in his hand was an unsealed letter 6 in which was written:

> "It is reported among the nations—and Geshem[d] says it is true—that you and the Jews are plotting to revolt, and therefore you are building the wall. Moreover, according to these reports you are about to become their king 7 and have even appointed prophets to make this proclamation about

(5:14–19) We pray for our leaders, O Lord, that You would protect them from greed. Give us leaders who are honest and dedicated to the work to which You have called them. We need men and women who will not use their power for personal gain, but who are committed to the welfare of the people they serve.

Lord Jesus, think on me,
And purge away my sin;
From earthborn passions set me free
And make me pure within.

Lord Jesus, think on me,
With care and woe oppressed;
Let me Thy loving servant be
And gain Thy promised rest.

"Lord Jesus, Think on Me"
Synesius of Cyrene (c.410)
Trans. Allen W. Chatfield (1876)

[a] 15 That is, about 1 pound (about 0.5 kilogram) [b] 16 Most Hebrew manuscripts; some Hebrew manuscripts, Septuagint, Vulgate and Syriac *I* [c] 2 Or *in Kephirim* [d] 6 Hebrew *Gashmu*, a variant of *Geshem*

you in Jerusalem: 'There is a king in Judah!' Now this report
will get back to the king; so come, let us confer together."
8 I sent him this reply: "Nothing like what you are saying is happening; you are just making it up out of your head."
9 They were all trying to frighten us, thinking, "Their hands will
get too weak for the work, and it will not be completed."
⌞But I prayed,⌟ "Now strengthen my hands."
10 One day I went to the house of Shemaiah son of Delaiah, the
son of Mehetabel, who was shut in at his home. He said, "Let us
meet in the house of God, inside the temple, and let us close the
temple doors, because men are coming to kill you—by night they
are coming to kill you."
11 But I said, "Should a man like me run away? Or should one
like me go into the temple to save his life? I will not go!" 12 I realized that God had not sent him, but that he had prophesied
against me because Tobiah and Sanballat had hired him. 13 He
had been hired to intimidate me so that I would commit a sin by
doing this, and then they would give me a bad name to
discredit me.

14 Remember Tobiah and Sanballat, O my God, because of what
they have done; remember also the prophetess Noadiah and the
rest of the prophets who have been trying to intimidate me.

The Completion of the Wall

15 So the wall was completed on the twenty-fifth of Elul, in fifty-
two days. 16 When all our enemies heard about this, all the
surrounding nations were afraid and lost their self-confidence,
because they realized that this work had been done with the help
of our God.
17 Also, in those days the nobles of Judah were sending many
letters to Tobiah, and replies from Tobiah kept coming to them.
18 For many in Judah were under oath to him, since he was son-
in-law to Shecaniah son of Arah, and his son Jehohanan had married the daughter of Meshullam son of Berekiah. 19 Moreover,
they kept reporting to me his good deeds and then telling him
what I said. And Tobiah sent letters to intimidate me.
7 After the wall had been rebuilt and I had set the doors in
place, the gatekeepers and the singers and the Levites were
appointed. 2 I put in charge of Jerusalem my brother Hanani,
along with[a] Hananiah the commander of the citadel, because he
was a man of integrity and feared God more than most men do. 3 I
said to them, "The gates of Jerusalem are not to be opened until
the sun is hot. While the gatekeepers are still on duty, have them
shut the doors and bar them. Also appoint residents of Jerusalem
as guards, some at their posts and some near their own houses."

The List of the Exiles Who Returned

4 Now the city was large and spacious, but there were few people in it, and the houses had not yet been rebuilt. 5 So my God put
it into my heart to assemble the nobles, the officials and the common people for registration by families. I found the genealogical
record of those who had been the first to return. This is what I
found written there:

6 These are the people of the province who came up from

[a]2 Or *Hanani, that is,*

(6:15–16) Lord, as Your people continued to work in spite of opposition, so may we in Your church continue faithfully in the work You have given to us. Help us to work with focus and determination, to "be strong in the Lord and in his mighty power." In everything we do, may we set "an example by doing what is good" through our "integrity, seriousness and soundness of speech that cannot be condemned, so that those who oppose [us] may be ashamed." (Eph 6:10; Tit 2:7–8)

He giveth more grace
When the burdens grow greater;
He sendeth more strength
When the labors increase.
To added affliction
He addeth His mercy;
To multiplied trials,
His multiplied peace.

His love has no limit;
His grace has no measure;
His power has no boundary
Known unto men.
For out of His infinite riches in Jesus,
He giveth, and giveth, and giveth
again!

"He Giveth More Grace"
Annie Johnson Flint (©1941, 1969)

the captivity of the exiles whom Nebuchadnezzar king of Babylon had taken captive (they returned to Jerusalem and Judah, each to his own town, 7in company with Zerubbabel, Jeshua, Nehemiah, Azariah, Raamiah, Nahamani, Mordecai, Bilshan, Mispereth, Bigvai, Nehum and Baanah):

The list of the men of Israel:

8the descendants of Parosh	2,172
9of Shephatiah	372
10of Arah	652
11of Pahath-Moab (through the line of Jeshua and Joab)	2,818
12of Elam	1,254
13of Zattu	845
14of Zaccai	760
15of Binnui	648
16of Bebai	628
17of Azgad	2,322
18of Adonikam	667
19of Bigvai	2,067
20of Adin	655
21of Ater (through Hezekiah)	98
22of Hashum	328
23of Bezai	324
24of Hariph	112
25of Gibeon	95
26the men of Bethlehem and Netophah	188
27of Anathoth	128
28of Beth Azmaveth	42
29of Kiriath Jearim, Kephirah and Beeroth	743
30of Ramah and Geba	621
31of Micmash	122
32of Bethel and Ai	123
33of the other Nebo	52
34of the other Elam	1,254
35of Harim	320
36of Jericho	345
37of Lod, Hadid and Ono	721
38of Senaah	3,930

39The priests:

the descendants of Jedaiah (through the family of Jeshua)	973
40of Immer	1,052
41of Pashhur	1,247
42of Harim	1,017

43The Levites:

the descendants of Jeshua (through Kadmiel through the line of Hodaviah)	74

44The singers:

the descendants of Asaph	148

45The gatekeepers:

the descendants of

(7:6–45) Saving God, each of these names, recorded so carefully, reminds us that You know the names of every one of us whom You have freed from the captivity of sin. We give You thanks, Father, for You have "qualified [us] to share in the inheritance of the saints in the kingdom of light." You have "rescued us from the dominion of darkness and brought us into the kingdom of the Son [You love], in whom we have redemption, the forgiveness of sins." (Col 1:12–14)

There is rich blessing and encouragement for us in our salvation, but it is all for God's glory and for the pleasure of His Son, Jesus Christ. Since in Christ we are more than conquerors (Ro 8:37), we can receive the promise that Christ Himself has given: "To him who overcomes, I will give the right to sit with me on my throne, just as I overcame and sat down with my Father on his throne" (Rev 3:21). Then the blessings of the covenant that God makes with all His sons will be fulfilled: "He who overcomes will inherit all this, and I will be his God and he will be my son" (Rev 21:7).

Sinclair B. Ferguson (1948-)

Shallum, Ater, Talmon, Akkub, Hatita and Shobai 138

46 The temple servants:

the descendants of
Ziha, Hasupha, Tabbaoth,
47 Keros, Sia, Padon,
48 Lebana, Hagaba, Shalmai,
49 Hanan, Giddel, Gahar,
50 Reaiah, Rezin, Nekoda,
51 Gazzam, Uzza, Paseah,
52 Besai, Meunim, Nephussim,
53 Bakbuk, Hakupha, Harhur,
54 Bazluth, Mehida, Harsha,
55 Barkos, Sisera, Temah,
56 Neziah and Hatipha

57 The descendants of the servants of Solomon:

the descendants of
Sotai, Sophereth, Perida,
58 Jaala, Darkon, Giddel,
59 Shephatiah, Hattil,
Pokereth-Hazzebaim and Amon

60 The temple servants and the descendants of the
servants of Solomon 392

61 The following came up from the towns of Tel Melah, Tel
Harsha, Kerub, Addon and Immer, but they could not show
that their families were descended from Israel:

62 the descendants of
Delaiah, Tobiah and Nekoda 642

63 And from among the priests:

the descendants of
Hobaiah, Hakkoz and Barzillai (a man who had
married a daughter of Barzillai the Gileadite and
was called by that name).

64 These searched for their family records, but they could
not find them and so were excluded from the priesthood as
unclean. 65 The governor, therefore, ordered them not to eat
any of the most sacred food until there should be a priest
ministering with the Urim and Thummim.

66 The whole company numbered 42,360, 67 besides their
7,337 menservants and maidservants; and they also had 245
men and women singers. 68 There were 736 horses, 245
mules,[a] 69 435 camels and 6,720 donkeys.

70 Some of the heads of the families contributed to the
work. The governor gave to the treasury 1,000 drachmas[b] of
gold, 50 bowls and 530 garments for priests. 71 Some of the
heads of the families gave to the treasury for the work
20,000 drachmas[c] of gold and 2,200 minas[d] of silver. 72 The
total given by the rest of the people was 20,000 drachmas of
gold, 2,000 minas[e] of silver and 67 garments for priests.

[a] *68* Some Hebrew manuscripts (see also Ezra 2:66); most Hebrew manuscripts do not have this verse. [b] *70* That is, about 19 pounds (about 8.5 kilograms) [c] *71* That is, about 375 pounds (about 170 kilograms); also in verse 72 [d] *71* That is, about 1 1/3 tons (about 1.2 metric tons) [e] *72* That is, about 1 1/4 tons (about 1.1 metric tons)

(7:46–60) Heavenly Father, when you call all your people home, what a glorious company will be gathered into Your city, the heavenly Jerusalem. That number will be far greater than those who came to the restored city long ago. We long for the day when we will gather from every nation and every race to behold Your glory and majesty. On that great day, every tongue will confess that Jesus Christ is Lord. (Php 2:10–11; Rev 5:9–10)

Christ has prayed that we may share in His glory! Not only so, but the ultimate reason for our salvation and spiritual transformation further guarantees that we will successfully pass through the dangers and trials of the Christian life. For God's purpose is that Christ should be the first-born in an innummerable company of brothers!

Sinclair B. Ferguson (1948-)

73The priests, the Levites, the gatekeepers, the singers
and the temple servants, along with certain of the people
and the rest of the Israelites, settled in their own towns.

Ezra Reads the Law

When the seventh month came and the Israelites had settled in
8 their towns, 1all the people assembled as one man in the
square before the Water Gate. They told Ezra the scribe to
bring out the Book of the Law of Moses, which the LORD had
commanded for Israel.
2So on the first day of the seventh month Ezra the priest
brought the Law before the assembly, which was made up of men
and women and all who were able to understand. 3He read it
aloud from daybreak till noon as he faced the square before the
Water Gate in the presence of the men, women and others who
could understand. And all the people listened attentively to the
Book of the Law.
4Ezra the scribe stood on a high wooden platform built for the
occasion. Beside him on his right stood Mattithiah, Shema, Anaiah, Uriah, Hilkiah and Maaseiah; and on his left were Pedaiah,
Mishael, Malkijah, Hashum, Hashbaddanah, Zechariah and Meshullam.
5Ezra opened the book. All the people could see him because
he was standing above them; and as he opened it, the people all
stood up. 6Ezra praised the LORD, the great God; and all the people lifted their hands and responded, "Amen! Amen!" Then they
bowed down and worshiped the LORD with their faces to the
ground.
7The Levites—Jeshua, Bani, Sherebiah, Jamin, Akkub, Shabbethai, Hodiah, Maaseiah, Kelita, Azariah, Jozabad, Hanan and
Pelaiah—instructed the people in the Law while the people were
standing there. 8They read from the Book of the Law of God,
making it clear[a] and giving the meaning so that the people could
understand what was being read.
9Then Nehemiah the governor, Ezra the priest and scribe, and
the Levites who were instructing the people said to them all, "This
day is sacred to the LORD your God. Do not mourn or weep." For
all the people had been weeping as they listened to the words of
the Law.
10Nehemiah said, "Go and enjoy choice food and sweet drinks,
and send some to those who have nothing prepared. This day is
sacred to our Lord. Do not grieve, for the joy of the LORD is your
strength."
11The Levites calmed all the people, saying, "Be still, for this is
a sacred day. Do not grieve."
12Then all the people went away to eat and drink, to send portions of food and to celebrate with great joy, because they now
understood the words that had been made known to them.
13On the second day of the month, the heads of all the families,
along with the priests and the Levites, gathered around Ezra the
scribe to give attention to the words of the Law. 14They found
written in the Law, which the LORD had commanded through
Moses, that the Israelites were to live in booths during the feast of
the seventh month 15and that they should proclaim this word and
spread it throughout their towns and in Jerusalem: "Go out into

[a] 8 Or *God, translating it*

Lord Jesus, in the events of this day may I find myself in the path of the blessed. Keep my heart from evil—from walking, standing, or sitting in the places of the heart and mind where I ought not to be. May I delight in you and your Word, and may my inner thoughts be open to and upon you moment by moment.

George O. Wood (1941-)

(8:1–12) "The precepts of the LORD are right, giving joy to the heart." We thank You, Father, for the gift of Your written Word to us. It informs our minds and transforms our hearts. It judges our thoughts and attitudes. Your Word brings order and direction to our lives, and through it You teach us how to live in our newfound freedom. Father, may we be people who not only listen to Your Word, but who also joyfully do what it says. (Ps 19:7–11; Heb 4:12)

I will celebrate,
Sing unto the Lord,
Sing to the Lord a new song.
I will celebrate,
Sing unto the Lord,
Sing to the Lord a new song.

With my heart rejoicing within,
With my mind focused on Him.
With my hands raised to the
heavens,
All I am, worshiping Him.

"I Will Celebrate"
Rita Baloche (©1990)

the hill country and bring back branches from olive and wild
olive trees, and from myrtles, palms and shade trees, to make
booths"—as it is written.[a]
16So the people went out and brought back branches and built
themselves booths on their own roofs, in their courtyards, in the
courts of the house of God and in the square by the Water Gate
and the one by the Gate of Ephraim. 17The whole company that
had returned from exile built booths and lived in them. From the
days of Joshua son of Nun until that day, the Israelites had not
celebrated it like this. And their joy was very great.
18Day after day, from the first day to the last, Ezra read from
the Book of the Law of God. They celebrated the feast for seven
days, and on the eighth day, in accordance with the regulation,
there was an assembly.

The Israelites Confess Their Sins

9 On the twenty-fourth day of the same month, the Israelites
gathered together, fasting and wearing sackcloth and having
dust on their heads. 2Those of Israelite descent had separated
themselves from all foreigners. They stood in their places and
confessed their sins and the wickedness of their fathers. 3They
stood where they were and read from the Book of the Law of the
LORD their God for a quarter of the day, and spent another quarter in confession and in worshiping the LORD their God. 4Standing
on the stairs were the Levites—Jeshua, Bani, Kadmiel, Shebaniah,
Bunni, Sherebiah, Bani and Kenani—who called with loud voices
to the LORD their God. 5And the Levites—Jeshua, Kadmiel, Bani,
Hashabneiah, Sherebiah, Hodiah, Shebaniah and Pethahiah—
said: "Stand up and praise the LORD your God, who is from everlasting to everlasting.[b]"

"Blessed be your glorious name, and may it be exalted
above all blessing and praise. 6You alone are the LORD. You
made the heavens, even the highest heavens, and all their
starry host, the earth and all that is on it, the seas and all that
is in them. You give life to everything, and the multitudes of
heaven worship you.
7"You are the LORD God, who chose Abram and brought
him out of Ur of the Chaldeans and named him Abraham.
8You found his heart faithful to you, and you made a covenant with him to give to his descendants the land of the
Canaanites, Hittites, Amorites, Perizzites, Jebusites and Girgashites. You have kept your promise because you are righteous.
9"You saw the suffering of our forefathers in Egypt; you
heard their cry at the Red Sea.[c] 10You sent miraculous signs
and wonders against Pharaoh, against all his officials and all
the people of his land, for you knew how arrogantly the
Egyptians treated them. You made a name for yourself,
which remains to this day. 11You divided the sea before
them, so that they passed through it on dry ground, but you
hurled their pursuers into the depths, like a stone into
mighty waters. 12By day you led them with a pillar of cloud,
and by night with a pillar of fire to give them light on the
way they were to take.

[a] 15 See Lev. 23:37–40. [b] 5 Or *God for ever and ever* [c] 9 Hebrew *Yam Suph*; that is, Sea of Reeds

(9:5–12) O Lord my God, I join my voice with Your people of old and praise You for Your mighty acts. Your covenant love is indeed an active love. And You are not just a God who did great things for them; You are the God who does great things for us. Blessed be Your glorious name!

Stand up and bless the Lord,
You people of his choice,
Stand up and bless the Lord your God
With heart and soul and voice.

Stand up and bless the Lord,
The Lord your God adore;
Stand up and bless his glorious name,
Both now and evermore.

"Stand Up and Bless the Lord"
James Montgomery (1824)

Grant almighty God, that as you have, in various ways, testified and daily also prove how dear and precious to you is humanity as we enjoy daily so many and so remarkable proofs of your goodness and favor—O grant that we learn to rely wholly on your goodness, so many examples of which you set before us, and which you would have us continually to experience, that we may not only pass through our earthly course, but also confidently aspire to the hope of that blessed and celestial life which is laid up for us in heaven, through Christ alone our Lord. Amen.

John Calvin (1509–1564)

(9:13–28) Gracious and forgiving God, You are always faithful, in spite of my failures. Though my sins seem endless, Your grace is boundless. You are indeed a great and merciful God, abounding in compassion and love for me. You are always ready to forgive, always eager to restore, always willing to give me another chance and to set me on the path of righteousness. I confess my sinfulness; I acknowledge Your faithfulness; I humbly offer my thanks to You, O merciful, loving Father. (1Jn 1:9)

Merciful Lord, it does not surprise me that you forget completely the sins of those who repent. I am not surprised that you remain faithful to those who hate and revile you. The mercy which pours forth from you fills the whole world . . . It was by your mercy that we were created, and by your mercy that you redeemed us by sending your Son. Your mercy is the light in which sinners find you and good people come back to you...Your justice is constantly tempered with mercy, so you refuse to punish us as we deserve.

Saint Catherine of Siena (1347-1380)

All the way my Savior leads me.
What have I to ask beside?
Can I doubt His tender mercy
Who thro' life has been my Guide?
Heav'nly peace, divinest comfort,
Here by faith in Him to dwell!
For I know, whate'er befall me,
Jesus doeth all things well.

All the way my Savior leads me,
Cheers each winding path I tread,
Gives me grace for ev'ry trial,
Feeds me with the living bread.
Tho' my weary steps may falter,
And my soul athirst may be,
Gushing from the Rock before me,
Lo! a spring of joy I see.

"All the Way My Savior Leads Me"
Fanny J. Crosby (1875)

13"You came down on Mount Sinai; you spoke to them
from heaven. You gave them regulations and laws that are
just and right, and decrees and commands that are good.
14You made known to them your holy Sabbath and gave
them commands, decrees and laws through your servant
Moses. 15In their hunger you gave them bread from heaven
and in their thirst you brought them water from the rock;
you told them to go in and take possession of the land you
had sworn with uplifted hand to give them.
16"But they, our forefathers, became arrogant and stiff-
necked, and did not obey your commands. 17They refused
to listen and failed to remember the miracles you performed
among them. They became stiff-necked and in their rebellion appointed a leader in order to return to their slavery.
But you are a forgiving God, gracious and compassionate,
slow to anger and abounding in love. Therefore you did not
desert them, 18even when they cast for themselves an image
of a calf and said, 'This is your god, who brought you up out
of Egypt,' or when they committed awful blasphemies.
19"Because of your great compassion you did not abandon them in the desert. By day the pillar of cloud did not
cease to guide them on their path, nor the pillar of fire by
night to shine on the way they were to take. 20You gave your
good Spirit to instruct them. You did not withhold your
manna from their mouths, and you gave them water for their
thirst. 21For forty years you sustained them in the desert;
they lacked nothing, their clothes did not wear out nor did
their feet become swollen.
22"You gave them kingdoms and nations, allotting to them
even the remotest frontiers. They took over the country of
Sihon[a] king of Heshbon and the country of Og king of Bashan. 23You made their sons as numerous as the stars in the
sky, and you brought them into the land that you told their
fathers to enter and possess. 24Their sons went in and took
possession of the land. You subdued before them the
Canaanites, who lived in the land; you handed the Canaanites
over to them, along with their kings and the peoples of the
land, to deal with them as they pleased. 25They captured fortified cities and fertile land; they took possession of houses
filled with all kinds of good things, wells already dug, vineyards, olive groves and fruit trees in abundance. They ate to
the full and were well-nourished; they reveled in your great
goodness.
26"But they were disobedient and rebelled against you;
they put your law behind their backs. They killed your
prophets, who had admonished them in order to turn them
back to you; they committed awful blasphemies. 27So you
handed them over to their enemies, who oppressed them.
But when they were oppressed they cried out to you. From
heaven you heard them, and in your great compassion you
gave them deliverers, who rescued them from the hand of
their enemies.
28"But as soon as they were at rest, they again did what
was evil in your sight. Then you abandoned them to the hand
of their enemies so that they ruled over them. And when they

[a] 22 One Hebrew manuscript and Septuagint; most Hebrew manuscripts *Sihon, that is, the country of the*

cried out to you again, you heard from heaven, and in your
compassion you delivered them time after time.
29 "You warned them to return to your law, but they became arrogant and disobeyed your commands. They sinned
against your ordinances, by which a man will live if he obeys
them. Stubbornly they turned their backs on you, became
stiff-necked and refused to listen. 30 For many years you
were patient with them. By your Spirit you admonished them
through your prophets. Yet they paid no attention, so you
handed them over to the neighboring peoples. 31 But in your
great mercy you did not put an end to them or abandon
them, for you are a gracious and merciful God.
32 "Now therefore, O our God, the great, mighty and awesome God, who keeps his covenant of love, do not let all this
hardship seem trifling in your eyes—the hardship that has
come upon us, upon our kings and leaders, upon our
priests and prophets, upon our fathers and all your people,
from the days of the kings of Assyria until today. 33 In all that
has happened to us, you have been just; you have acted faithfully, while we did wrong. 34 Our kings, our leaders, our
priests and our fathers did not follow your law; they did not
pay attention to your commands or the warnings you gave
them. 35 Even while they were in their kingdom, enjoying
your great goodness to them in the spacious and fertile land
you gave them, they did not serve you or turn from their evil
ways.
36 "But see, we are slaves today, slaves in the land you
gave our forefathers so they could eat its fruit and the other
good things it produces. 37 Because of our sins, its abundant
harvest goes to the kings you have placed over us. They rule
over our bodies and our cattle as they please. We are in
great distress.

The Agreement of the People

38 "In view of all this, we are making a binding agreement,
putting it in writing, and our leaders, our Levites and our priests
are affixing their seals to it."

10 Those who sealed it were:

Nehemiah the governor, the son of Hacaliah.

Zedekiah, 2 Seraiah, Azariah, Jeremiah,
3 Pashhur, Amariah, Malkijah,
4 Hattush, Shebaniah, Malluch,
5 Harim, Meremoth, Obadiah,
6 Daniel, Ginnethon, Baruch,
7 Meshullam, Abijah, Mijamin,
8 Maaziah, Bilgai and Shemaiah.
These were the priests.

9 The Levites:
Jeshua son of Azaniah, Binnui of the sons of Henadad, Kadmiel,
10 and their associates: Shebaniah,
Hodiah, Kelita, Pelaiah, Hanan,
11 Mica, Rehob, Hashabiah,
12 Zaccur, Sherebiah, Shebaniah,

It is amazing that a poor human creature is able to speak with God's high Majesty in heaven and not be afraid. When we pray, the heart and the conscience must not pull away from God because of our sins and our unworthiness, or stand in doubt, or be scared away. When we pray we must hold fast and believe that God has heard our prayer. It was for this reason that the ancients defined prayer as an Ascensus mentis ad Deum, "a climbing up of the heart unto God."

Martin Luther (1483-1546)

(9:33) You are faithful and true, Lord. You are the same in every age. Unfortunately, we are also the same in every age: rebellious, sinful, stubborn, ungrateful and proud. But in Your kindness, You lead us to repentance. And so I repent. "Have mercy on me, O God, according to your unfailing love; according to your great compassion blot out my transgressions. Wash away all my iniquity and cleanse me from my sin. For I know my transgressions, and my sin is always before me. Against you, you only, have I sinned and done what is evil in your sight, so that you are proved right when you speak and justified when you judge." (Ps 51:1–4)

O Lord, hear,
O Lord, forgive us.
We have lost the awe of You.
Have mercy, have mercy.
O Lord, cleanse
Our hearts which are divided.
Stir the faith that we once knew.
We're thirsty, we're thirsty.

O Lord, restore
The church that bears Your name.
O Spirit, send
A revival to this nation.
Breathe on us again,
Breathe on us again.

"Breathe On Us Again"
Steve Fry (©1997)

(10:29–37) In light of the great things You have done for us and the immeasurable mercies and protections You have poured over us, it is only right that we commit ourselves to follow Your ways and live according to Your Word. Lord, we promise this day to keep ourselves free from unholy alliances; to carefully guard our hearts against the tactics of the enemy; to conduct our lives in a way that is pleasing to You; to faithfully fulfill our responsibilities in worship through giving tithes and offerings for the ongoing work of the ministry. Lord, please bless the work of our hands as we devote the fruit of our labors to Your purposes.

If you have ever loved a person enough to find joy in making sacrifices for that person—then I beg you to give Jesus this kind of love. He Himself is longing for you to do so. He loves you with more than the love of friendship. He loves you the way a bridegroom loves his bride, and nothing but total surrender will satisfy Him. He has given you all of Himself, and He asks for all of you in return. For you to hold back anything will grieve Him to the heart. For your sake He poured out all He had, and for His sake you must do the same. Be generous in your surrender! Meet His measureless devotion for you with a measureless devotion to Him.

Catherine Jackson

13 Hodiah, Bani and Beninu.

14 The leaders of the people:

Parosh, Pahath-Moab, Elam, Zattu, Bani,
15 Bunni, Azgad, Bebai,
16 Adonijah, Bigvai, Adin,
17 Ater, Hezekiah, Azzur,
18 Hodiah, Hashum, Bezai,
19 Hariph, Anathoth, Nebai,
20 Magpiash, Meshullam, Hezir,
21 Meshezabel, Zadok, Jaddua,
22 Pelatiah, Hanan, Anaiah,
23 Hoshea, Hananiah, Hasshub,
24 Hallohesh, Pilha, Shobek,
25 Rehum, Hashabnah, Maaseiah,
26 Ahiah, Hanan, Anan,
27 Malluch, Harim and Baanah.

28 "The rest of the people—priests, Levites, gatekeepers,
singers, temple servants and all who separated themselves
from the neighboring peoples for the sake of the Law of God,
together with their wives and all their sons and daughters
who are able to understand— 29 all these now join their
brothers the nobles, and bind themselves with a curse and an
oath to follow the Law of God given through Moses the servant of God and to obey carefully all the commands, regulations and decrees of the LORD our Lord.

30 "We promise not to give our daughters in marriage to
the peoples around us or take their daughters for our sons.

31 "When the neighboring peoples bring merchandise or
grain to sell on the Sabbath, we will not buy from them on the Sabbath or on any holy day. Every seventh year we will forgo working the land and will cancel all debts.

32 "We assume the responsibility for carrying out the commands to give a third of a shekel[a] each year for the service of
the house of our God: 33 for the bread set out on the table; for
the regular grain offerings and burnt offerings; for the offerings on the Sabbaths, New Moon festivals and appointed feasts; for the holy offerings; for sin offerings to make atonement for Israel; and for all the duties of the house of our God.

34 "We—the priests, the Levites and the people—have cast lots to determine when each of our families is to bring to the house of our God at set times each year a contribution of wood to burn on the altar of the LORD our God, as it is written in the Law.

35 "We also assume responsibility for bringing to the house of the LORD each year the firstfruits of our crops and of every fruit tree.

36 "As it is also written in the Law, we will bring the firstborn of our sons and of our cattle, of our herds and of our flocks to the house of our God, to the priests ministering there.

37 "Moreover, we will bring to the storerooms of the house of our God, to the priests, the first of our ground meal, of our

[a] *32* That is, about 1/8 ounce (about 4 grams)

⌞grain⌟ offerings, of the fruit of all our trees and of our new wine and oil. And we will bring a tithe of our crops to the Levites, for it is the Levites who collect the tithes in all the towns
where we work. 38A priest descended from Aaron is to accompany the Levites when they receive the tithes, and the Levites are to bring a tenth of the tithes up to the house of our
God, to the storerooms of the treasury. 39The people of Israel, including the Levites, are to bring their contributions of grain, new wine and oil to the storerooms where the articles for the sanctuary are kept and where the ministering priests, the gatekeepers and the singers stay.

"We will not neglect the house of our God."

The New Residents of Jerusalem

11 Now the leaders of the people settled in Jerusalem, and the rest of the people cast lots to bring one out of every ten to live in Jerusalem, the holy city, while the remaining nine were to
stay in their own towns. 2The people commended all the men who volunteered to live in Jerusalem.

3These are the provincial leaders who settled in Jerusalem (now some Israelites, priests, Levites, temple servants and descendants of Solomon's servants lived in the towns of Judah, each
on his own property in the various towns, 4while other people from both Judah and Benjamin lived in Jerusalem):

From the descendants of Judah:

Athaiah son of Uzziah, the son of Zechariah, the son of Amariah, the son of Shephatiah, the son of Mahalalel, a descendant of Perez; 5and Maaseiah son of Baruch, the son of Col-Hozeh, the son of Hazaiah, the son of Adaiah, the son of
Joiarib, the son of Zechariah, a descendant of Shelah. 6The descendants of Perez who lived in Jerusalem totaled 468 able men.

7From the descendants of Benjamin:

Sallu son of Meshullam, the son of Joed, the son of Pedaiah, the son of Kolaiah, the son of Maaseiah, the son of Ithiel, the
son of Jeshaiah, 8and his followers, Gabbai and Sallai—928
men. 9Joel son of Zicri was their chief officer, and Judah son of Hassenuah was over the Second District of the city.

10From the priests:

Jedaiah; the son of Joiarib; Jakin; 11Seraiah son of Hilkiah, the son of Meshullam, the son of Zadok, the son of Meraioth, the
son of Ahitub, supervisor in the house of God, 12and their associates, who carried on work for the temple—822 men; Adaiah son of Jeroham, the son of Pelaliah, the son of Amzi, the son of Zechariah, the son of Pashhur, the son of Malkijah,
13and his associates, who were heads of families—242 men; Amashsai son of Azarel, the son of Ahzai, the son of Meshillemoth, the son of Immer,
14and his[a] associates, who were able men—128. Their chief officer was Zabdiel son of Haggedolim.

15From the Levites:

Shemaiah son of Hasshub, the son of Azrikam, the son of

[a] 14 Most Septuagint manuscripts; Hebrew *their*

(10:37—11:4) Father, some of Your people left the comfort of their rural surroundings to move their families to Jerusalem in order that Your city might be populated. While many were chosen for this task, others went voluntarily. The sacrifice of these families exceeded the sacrifice of normal tithes—they packed up everything and moved into an area fraught with uncertainty. In view of Your faithfulness and in gratitude for Your mercy, I covenant with You, my God, to joyfully do my part in giving to Your church for the work of the ministry. Father, give me their courage and dedication that I and my family might follow wherever you lead.

We can adopt a lifestyle of giving because God has first given to us. His divine resources are available to us through our relationship with Christ and the presence of the Holy Spirit. Our first step toward becoming generous people is giving to God. It is our means of acknowledging his lordship and demonstrating our dependence on him. A good beginning is to give a tithe, a tenth of what we earn. This becomes easier when we understand that everything rightfully belongs to God. Returning a fraction of his liberality should delight us. We are to give gleefully, gratefully, humbly.

Charles Stanley (1932-)

We give Thee but Thine own,
What e'er the gift may be.
All that we have is Thine alone
A trust, O Lord, from Thee.

May we Thy bounties thus
As stewards true receive,
And gladly as Thou blessest us,
To Thee our first fruits give.

"We Give Thee But Thine Own"
William W. How (1823-1897)

(12:1–9) God of our fathers, in every generation You have faithfully raised up individuals to serve You by leading others in worship. We thank You for those whom You have called in our day to lead us in our corporate expressions of praise and thanksgiving. We pray that You will bless them for their dedicated service to Your church.

O Lord, be my God, and let there be no other before you. Grant me to worship you and serve you according to your commandments: with truth in my spirit, with reverence in my body, with the blessing upon my lips–both in private and in public. Help me to show honor and submission to those who have been put over me. Help me to show affection for and care for those who have been put in my charge.

Lancelot Andrews (1555-1626)

Hashabiah, the son of Bunni; 16 Shabbethai and Jozabad, two
of the heads of the Levites, who had charge of the outside
work of the house of God; 17 Mattaniah son of Mica, the son of
Zabdi, the son of Asaph, the director who led in thanksgiving
and prayer; Bakbukiah, second among his associates; and
Abda son of Shammua, the son of Galal, the son of Jeduthun.
18 The Levites in the holy city totaled 284.

19 The gatekeepers:

Akkub, Talmon and their associates, who kept watch at the
gates—172 men.

20 The rest of the Israelites, with the priests and Levites, were in
all the towns of Judah, each on his ancestral property.
21 The temple servants lived on the hill of Ophel, and Ziha and
Gishpa were in charge of them.
22 The chief officer of the Levites in Jerusalem was Uzzi son of
Bani, the son of Hashabiah, the son of Mattaniah, the son of Mica.
Uzzi was one of Asaph's descendants, who were the singers responsible for the service of the house of God. 23 The singers were
under the king's orders, which regulated their daily activity.
24 Pethahiah son of Meshezabel, one of the descendants of Zerah
son of Judah, was the king's agent in all affairs relating to the people.
25 As for the villages with their fields, some of the people of Judah
lived in Kiriath Arba and its surrounding settlements, in Dibon and
its settlements, in Jekabzeel and its villages, 26 in Jeshua, in Moladah,
in Beth Pelet, 27 in Hazar Shual, in Beersheba and its settlements,
28 in Ziklag, in Meconah and its settlements, 29 in En Rimmon, in
Zorah, in Jarmuth, 30 Zanoah, Adullam and their villages, in Lachish
and its fields, and in Azekah and its settlements. So they were living
all the way from Beersheba to the Valley of Hinnom.
31 The descendants of the Benjamites from Geba lived in Micmash, Aija, Bethel and its settlements, 32 in Anathoth, Nob and Ananiah, 33 in Hazor, Ramah and Gittaim, 34 in Hadid, Zeboim and
Neballat, 35 in Lod and Ono, and in the Valley of the Craftsmen.
36 Some of the divisions of the Levites of Judah settled in Benjamin.

Priests and Levites

12 These were the priests and Levites who returned with Zerubbabel son of Shealtiel and with Jeshua:

Seraiah, Jeremiah, Ezra,
2 Amariah, Malluch, Hattush,
3 Shecaniah, Rehum, Meremoth,
4 Iddo, Ginnethon,[a] Abijah,
5 Mijamin,[b] Moadiah, Bilgah,
6 Shemaiah, Joiarib, Jedaiah,
7 Sallu, Amok, Hilkiah and Jedaiah.

These were the leaders of the priests and their associates in the
days of Jeshua.
8 The Levites were Jeshua, Binnui, Kadmiel, Sherebiah, Judah,
and also Mattaniah, who, together with his associates, was in
charge of the songs of thanksgiving. 9 Bakbukiah and Unni, their
associates, stood opposite them in the services.

[a] 4 Many Hebrew manuscripts and Vulgate (see also Neh. 12:16); most Hebrew manuscripts *Ginnethoi* [b] 5 A variant of *Miniamin*

[10]Jeshua was the father of Joiakim, Joiakim the father of Eliashib, Eliashib the father of Joiada, [11]Joiada the father of Jonathan, and Jonathan the father of Jaddua.

[12]In the days of Joiakim, these were the heads of the priestly families:

of Seraiah's family, Meraiah;
of Jeremiah's, Hananiah;
13 of Ezra's, Meshullam;
of Amariah's, Jehohanan;
14 of Malluch's, Jonathan;
of Shecaniah's,[a] Joseph;
15 of Harim's, Adna;
of Meremoth's,[b] Helkai;
16 of Iddo's, Zechariah;
of Ginnethon's, Meshullam;
17 of Abijah's, Zicri;
of Miniamin's and of Moadiah's, Piltai;
18 of Bilgah's, Shammua;
of Shemaiah's, Jehonathan;
19 of Joiarib's, Mattenai;
of Jedaiah's, Uzzi;
20 of Sallu's, Kallai;
of Amok's, Eber;
21 of Hilkiah's, Hashabiah;
of Jedaiah's, Nethanel.

[22]The family heads of the Levites in the days of Eliashib, Joiada, Johanan and Jaddua, as well as those of the priests, were recorded in the reign of Darius the Persian. [23]The family heads among the descendants of Levi up to the time of Johanan son of Eliashib were recorded in the book of the annals. [24]And the leaders of the Levites were Hashabiah, Sherebiah, Jeshua son of Kadmiel, and their associates, who stood opposite them to give praise and thanksgiving, one section responding to the other, as prescribed by David the man of God.

[25]Mattaniah, Bakbukiah, Obadiah, Meshullam, Talmon and Akkub were gatekeepers who guarded the storerooms at the gates. [26]They served in the days of Joiakim son of Jeshua, the son of Jozadak, and in the days of Nehemiah the governor and of Ezra the priest and scribe.

Dedication of the Wall of Jerusalem

[27]At the dedication of the wall of Jerusalem, the Levites were sought out from where they lived and were brought to Jerusalem to celebrate joyfully the dedication with songs of thanksgiving and with the music of cymbals, harps and lyres. [28]The singers also were brought together from the region around Jerusalem—from the villages of the Netophathites, [29]from Beth Gilgal, and from the area of Geba and Azmaveth, for the singers had built villages for themselves around Jerusalem. [30]When the priests and Levites had purified themselves ceremonially, they purified the people, the gates and the wall.

[31]I had the leaders of Judah go up on top[c] of the wall. I also assigned two large choirs to give thanks. One was to proceed on top[d]

[a] *14* Very many Hebrew manuscripts, some Septuagint manuscripts and Syriac (see also Neh. 12:3); most Hebrew manuscripts *Shebaniah's* [b] *15* Some Septuagint manuscripts (see also Neh. 12:3); Hebrew *Meraioth's* [c] *31* Or *go alongside* [d] *31* Or *proceed alongside*

(12:30) I thank You, Father, that true holiness pertains not just to my "religious life" but to every aspect of life—every relationship, every transaction, every point of contact with the world. Help me to purify the gates of my eyes and my ears and my mouth against the ungodly influences of the culture around me. Strengthen me against the onslaught of temptation. May all of my relationships be conducted with purity and holiness, with order and self-control. I want to be like a "city on a hill"; a city whose walls and gates have been purified; a city that contains the temple of the Lord. (Mt 5:14)

This is true perfection: not to avoid a wicked life because like slaves we servilely fear punishment, nor to do good because we hope for rewards, as if cashing in on the virtuous life by some business-like arrangement. On the contrary, disregarding all those things for which we hope and which have been reserved by promise, we regard falling from God's friendship as the only thing dreadful and we consider becoming God's friend the only thing worthy of honor and desire.

Gregory of Nyssa (331-396)

(12:32–43) What a great day it was when the people of Jerusalem dedicated their rebuilt wall! This wall was evidence to all the surrounding nations that You were at work in the lives of Your people. Their enemies were struck with fear at the presence of the wall, and probably shuddered to hear the sounds of the celebration. But this celebration was only a glimpse of the celebration to come within the magnificent walls of Your new Jerusalem. On that day fear and trembling will cease, and the gates on all sides will receive Your joyous and thankful people from every nation. We will enter with songs of praise and thanksgiving. We will give thanks to You, O Lord, for Your steadfast love endures forever. (Ps 118:1; Rev 21:10–21)

O God, our Heavenly Father, we thank thee for this golden privilege to worship thee, the only true God of the universe. We come to thee today, grateful that thou hast kept us through the long night of the past and ushered us into the challenge of the present and the bright hope of the future. We are mindful, O God, that man cannot save himself, for man is not the measure of things and humanity is not God. Bound by our chains of sins and finiteness, we know we need a Savior . . . Keep us, we pray, in perfect peace, help us to walk together, pray together, sing together, and live together until that day when all God's children, Black, White, Red, and Yellow, will rejoice in one common band of humanity in the kingdom of our Lord and of our God, we pray. Amen.

Martin Luther King, Jr. (1929-1968)

Break into songs of joy
In the honor of the Lord on high.
With praises, lift your voice,
Let ev'ry instrument and all creation
Now rejoice, rejoice!

"Break Into Songs of Joy"
Bill Batstone (©1986)

of the wall to the right, toward the Dung Gate. 32Hoshaiah and
half the leaders of Judah followed them, 33along with Azariah,
Ezra, Meshullam, 34Judah, Benjamin, Shemaiah, Jeremiah, 35as
well as some priests with trumpets, and also Zechariah son of
Jonathan, the son of Shemaiah, the son of Mattaniah, the son of
Micaiah, the son of Zaccur, the son of Asaph, 36and his associates—Shemaiah, Azarel, Milalai, Gilalai, Maai, Nethanel, Judah
and Hanani—with musical instruments ⌊prescribed by⌋ David the
man of God. Ezra the scribe led the procession. 37At the Fountain
Gate they continued directly up the steps of the City of David on
the ascent to the wall and passed above the house of David to the
Water Gate on the east.

38The second choir proceeded in the opposite direction. I followed them on top[a] of the wall, together with half the people—
past the Tower of the Ovens to the Broad Wall, 39over the Gate of
Ephraim, the Jeshanah[b] Gate, the Fish Gate, the Tower of Hananel
and the Tower of the Hundred, as far as the Sheep Gate. At the
Gate of the Guard they stopped.

40The two choirs that gave thanks then took their places in the
house of God; so did I, together with half the officials, 41as well
as the priests—Eliakim, Maaseiah, Miniamin, Micaiah, Elioenai,
Zechariah and Hananiah with their trumpets— 42and also Maaseiah, Shemaiah, Eleazar, Uzzi, Jehohanan, Malkijah, Elam and
Ezer. The choirs sang under the direction of Jezrahiah. 43And on
that day they offered great sacrifices, rejoicing because God had
given them great joy. The women and children also rejoiced. The
sound of rejoicing in Jerusalem could be heard far away.

44At that time men were appointed to be in charge of the storerooms for the contributions, firstfruits and tithes. From the fields
around the towns they were to bring into the storerooms the portions required by the Law for the priests and the Levites, for Judah
was pleased with the ministering priests and Levites. 45They performed the service of their God and the service of purification, as
did also the singers and gatekeepers, according to the commands
of David and his son Solomon. 46For long ago, in the days of
David and Asaph, there had been directors for the singers and for
the songs of praise and thanksgiving to God. 47So in the days of
Zerubbabel and of Nehemiah, all Israel contributed the daily portions for the singers and gatekeepers. They also set aside the portion for the other Levites, and the Levites set aside the portion for
the descendants of Aaron.

Nehemiah's Final Reforms

13 On that day the Book of Moses was read aloud in the hearing of the people and there it was found written that no
Ammonite or Moabite should ever be admitted into the assembly
of God, 2because they had not met the Israelites with food and
water but had hired Balaam to call a curse down on them. (Our
God, however, turned the curse into a blessing.) 3When the people heard this law, they excluded from Israel all who were of foreign descent.

4Before this, Eliashib the priest had been put in charge of the
storerooms of the house of our God. He was closely associated
with Tobiah, 5and he had provided him with a large room formerly used to store the grain offerings and incense and temple ar-

[a] 38 Or *them alongside* [b] 39 Or *Old*

ticles, and also the tithes of grain, new wine and oil prescribed
for the Levites, singers and gatekeepers, as well as the contributions for the priests.
6But while all this was going on, I was not in Jerusalem, for in
the thirty-second year of Artaxerxes king of Babylon I had returned to the king. Some time later I asked his permission 7and
came back to Jerusalem. Here I learned about the evil thing Eliashib had done in providing Tobiah a room in the courts of the
house of God. 8I was greatly displeased and threw all Tobiah's
household goods out of the room. 9I gave orders to purify the
rooms, and then I put back into them the equipment of the house
of God, with the grain offerings and the incense.
10I also learned that the portions assigned to the Levites had
not been given to them, and that all the Levites and singers responsible for the service had gone back to their own fields. 11So
I rebuked the officials and asked them, "Why is the house of God
neglected?" Then I called them together and stationed them at
their posts.
12All Judah brought the tithes of grain, new wine and oil into
the storerooms. 13I put Shelemiah the priest, Zadok the scribe,
and a Levite named Pedaiah in charge of the storerooms and
made Hanan son of Zaccur, the son of Mattaniah, their assistant,
because these men were considered trustworthy. They were made
responsible for distributing the supplies to their brothers.

14Remember me for this, O my God, and do not blot out what
I have so faithfully done for the house of my God and its services.

15In those days I saw men in Judah treading winepresses on
the Sabbath and bringing in grain and loading it on donkeys, together with wine, grapes, figs and all other kinds of loads. And
they were bringing all this into Jerusalem on the Sabbath. Therefore I warned them against selling food on that day. 16Men from
Tyre who lived in Jerusalem were bringing in fish and all kinds of
merchandise and selling them in Jerusalem on the Sabbath to the
people of Judah. 17I rebuked the nobles of Judah and said to
them, "What is this wicked thing you are doing—desecrating the
Sabbath day? 18Didn't your forefathers do the same things, so that
our God brought all this calamity upon us and upon this city? Now
you are stirring up more wrath against Israel by desecrating the
Sabbath."
19When evening shadows fell on the gates of Jerusalem before
the Sabbath, I ordered the doors to be shut and not opened until
the Sabbath was over. I stationed some of my own men at the
gates so that no load could be brought in on the Sabbath day.
20Once or twice the merchants and sellers of all kinds of goods
spent the night outside Jerusalem. 21But I warned them and said,
"Why do you spend the night by the wall? If you do this again, I
will lay hands on you." From that time on they no longer came on
the Sabbath. 22Then I commanded the Levites to purify themselves and go and guard the gates in order to keep the Sabbath
day holy.

Remember me for this also, O my God, and show mercy to me
according to your great love.

23Moreover, in those days I saw men of Judah who had married women from Ashdod, Ammon and Moab. 24Half of their children spoke the language of Ashdod or the language of one of the

(13:4–9) Search me, O God. What am I storing in the temple of my heart? Is it filled with the fruit of Your Spirit's work in my life, or am I making room for the adversary by setting aside little hiding places to harbor secret sins? Help me to feel the grief of Your Spirit and to respond quickly and decisively with confession and repentance whenever You point out areas of compromise. Purify my heart, Lord, and fill it with Your Spirit. Sanctify it and make it holy.

Search me, O God, and know my
heart today;
Try me, O Savior, know my
thoughts, I pray.
See if there be some wicked way in
me;
Cleanse me from ev'ry sin, and set
me free.

"Cleanse Me"
J. Edwin Orr (1936)

other peoples, and did not know how to speak the language of
Judah. 25I rebuked them and called curses down on them. I beat
some of the men and pulled out their hair. I made them take an
oath in God's name and said: "You are not to give your daughters
in marriage to their sons, nor are you to take their daughters in
marriage for your sons or for yourselves. 26Was it not because of
marriages like these that Solomon king of Israel sinned? Among
the many nations there was no king like him. He was loved by his
God, and God made him king over all Israel, but even he was led
into sin by foreign women. 27Must we hear now that you too are
doing all this terrible wickedness and are being unfaithful to our
God by marrying foreign women?"

28One of the sons of Joiada son of Eliashib the high priest was
son-in-law to Sanballat the Horonite. And I drove him away
from me.

29Remember them, O my God, because they defiled the priestly office and the covenant of the priesthood and of the Levites.

30So I purified the priests and the Levites of everything foreign,
and assigned them duties, each to his own task. 31I also made
provision for contributions of wood at designated times, and for
the firstfruits.

Remember me with favor, O my God.

When we see God as holy, our instant and only reaction is to see ourselves as unholy. Between God's holiness and man's unholiness is a gulf. And until a man understands the holiness of God he can never know the depth of his own sin . . . Without such a vision of God's holiness, true worship is not possible. Worship is not giddy. It does not rush into God's presence unprepared and insensitive to His majesty. It is not shallow, superficial, or flippant. Worship is life lived in the presence of an infinitely righteous and omnipresent God by one utterly aware of His holiness and consequently overwhelmed with his own unholiness.

John MacArthur, Jr. (1939-)

(13:30) O holy God, make me a pure vessel for Your service. Whether You call me to preach before thousands, or simply to bring a word of comfort to a hurting soul, may I do so from a position of personal holiness. May I never come casually or presumptuously into Your presence. Rather remind me of Paul's exhortation to "purify [myself] from everything that contaminates body and spirit, perfecting holiness out of reverence for God." (2Co 7:1; Heb 9:14)

The Book of ESTHER

An old Scottish saying goes, "A coincidence is a minor miracle in which God chooses to remain anonymous." The book of Esther reminds us that, although we may not always see it, God is at work in the lives of His people. God can use seemingly ordinary events to accomplish extraordinary things.

Esther

The book of Esther is an engaging story with fascinating characters and a suspenseful plot. There are four main sections. The first section (chs. 1—2) introduces a young Jewish woman, Esther, who is cared for by her cousin Mordecai and who becomes a wife of Xerxes, king of Persia. The following section (chs. 3—4) focuses on the opportunistic and anti-Jewish Haman, who threatens the Jews and endangers their royal protection. When Haman sees Mordecai failing to honor him as a royal nobleman, he contrives to have Mordecai exposed as a traitor and all Jews in the Persian empire killed. In the next section (chs. 5—8), Esther cleverly intercedes for her people by getting the king in a mood to hear her case favorably. Meanwhile, Haman prepares for Mordecai's execution. The story climaxes in the final section (chapters 9—10), when Esther exposes Haman's plot to her husband, King Xerxes. Haman, not Mordecai, turns out to be the real traitor, for the Jews are loyal to the king. Ironically, Haman is hanged on the very gallows he has built for Mordecai, while the Jews enjoy a new season of royal favor. They respond by the institution of a new feast, Purim, which commemorates Jewish deliverance at the hands of Esther and Mordecai.

For Christian (and many Jewish) readers, Esther presents the puzzle of God's invisibility. The book never mentions God directly. Even the celebration of Purim, as described in chapter 9, does not explicitly credit the Lord for Jewish deliverance. Of course we can easily see God's hidden hand behind the "coincidences" of Esther. When Mordecai asks Esther, "And who knows but that you have come to royal position for such a time as this?" (4:14), we understand that God has been directing the affairs, not only of Esther, but of the Persian empire as well.

The book of Esther reminds us that, although we may not always see it, God is at work in the lives of His people. God can use seemingly ordinary events to accomplish extraordinary things.

Yet the inclusion of Esther in the canon of Scripture challenges us to worship a God Whose presence is not always evident. At times we see God's hand plainly and hear His voice clearly. At times we do not. Nevertheless, God continues to be at work whether or not we sense His activity. We worship God, not simply when we experience Him immediately, but because of Who He is and of what He has done in history as well as in our lives. Even when we are not feeling God's presence, we worship Him because He deserves it. As His creatures, we are most fully alive when we serve our main task in life, which is to "glorify God and enjoy him forever."*

* Westminster Shorter Catechism, Question and Answer 1

(1:1) In every place, in every age, You have been present, Lord. Whether we have seen You, whether we have acknowledged You, You have been there. You have cut a path through our circumstances and left Your fingerprints on our lives. O Father, open our eyes and hearts to Your presence that we may see You and hear You and know You as our God today.

God is in all things and in every place. There is not a place in the world in which he is not most truly present. Just as birds, wherever they fly, always meet with the air, so we, wherever we go, or wherever we are, always find God present.
Saint Francis of Sales (1567-1622)

God ruleth on high, almighty to save.
And still He is nigh; His presence we have.
The great congregation His triumph shall sing,
Ascribing salvation to Jesus our King.
Ye Servants of God
Charles Wesley (1744)

(1:4–8) O Lord, when I see the vanity with which the world displays its riches, draw my eyes upward to gaze on Your beauty. When the world spreads its banquet table before me, teach me to hunger for the food of Your truth, and to thirst for the wine of Your presence.

Queen Vashti Deposed

1 This is what happened during the time of Xerxes,[a] the Xerxes
who ruled over 127 provinces stretching from India to Cush[b]:
2At that time King Xerxes reigned from his royal throne in the
citadel of Susa, 3and in the third year of his reign he gave a banquet
for all his nobles and officials. The military leaders of Persia and
Media, the princes, and the nobles of the provinces were present.
4For a full 180 days he displayed the vast wealth of his kingdom
and the splendor and glory of his majesty. 5When these days were
over, the king gave a banquet, lasting seven days, in the enclosed
garden of the king's palace, for all the people from the least to the
greatest, who were in the citadel of Susa. 6The garden had hangings
of white and blue linen, fastened with cords of white linen and purple material to silver rings on marble pillars. There were couches
of gold and silver on a mosaic pavement of porphyry, marble,
mother-of-pearl and other costly stones. 7Wine was served in goblets of gold, each one different from the other, and the royal wine
was abundant, in keeping with the king's liberality. 8By the king's
command each guest was allowed to drink in his own way, for the
king instructed all the wine stewards to serve each man what he
wished.
9Queen Vashti also gave a banquet for the women in the royal
palace of King Xerxes.
10On the seventh day, when King Xerxes was in high spirits from
wine, he commanded the seven eunuchs who served him—Mehuman, Biztha, Harbona, Bigtha, Abagtha, Zethar and Carcas— 11to
bring before him Queen Vashti, wearing her royal crown, in order
to display her beauty to the people and nobles, for she was lovely
to look at. 12But when the attendants delivered the king's com-
mand, Queen Vashti refused to come. Then the king became furious and burned with anger.
13Since it was customary for the king to consult experts in
matters of law and justice, he spoke with the wise men who understood the times 14and were closest to the king—Carshena, Shethar, Admatha, Tarshish, Meres, Marsena and Memucan, the seven
nobles of Persia and Media who had special access to the king and
were highest in the kingdom.
15"According to law, what must be done to Queen Vashti?" he
asked. "She has not obeyed the command of King Xerxes that the
eunuchs have taken to her."
16Then Memucan replied in the presence of the king and the
nobles, "Queen Vashti has done wrong, not only against the king
but also against all the nobles and the peoples of all the provinces
of King Xerxes. 17For the queen's conduct will become known to all
the women, and so they will despise their husbands and say, 'King
Xerxes commanded Queen Vashti to be brought before him, but
she would not come.' 18This very day the Persian and Median
women of the nobility who have heard about the queen's conduct
will respond to all the king's nobles in the same way. There will be
no end of disrespect and discord.
19"Therefore, if it pleases the king, let him issue a royal decree
and let it be written in the laws of Persia and Media, which cannot
be repealed, that Vashti is never again to enter the presence of King
Xerxes. Also let the king give her royal position to someone else

[a] 1 Hebrew *Ahasuerus,* a variant of Xerxes' Persian name; here and throughout Esther
[b] 1 That is, the upper Nile region

who is better than she. 20Then when the king's edict is proclaimed throughout all his vast realm, all the women will respect their husbands, from the least to the greatest."

21The king and his nobles were pleased with this advice, so the king did as Memucan proposed. 22He sent dispatches to all parts of the kingdom, to each province in its own script and to each people in its own language, proclaiming in each people's tongue that every man should be ruler over his own household.

Esther Made Queen

2 Later when the anger of King Xerxes had subsided, he remembered Vashti and what she had done and what he had decreed about her. 2Then the king's personal attendants proposed, "Let a search be made for beautiful young virgins for the king. 3Let the king appoint commissioners in every province of his realm to bring all these beautiful girls into the harem at the citadel of Susa. Let them be placed under the care of Hegai, the king's eunuch, who is in charge of the women; and let beauty treatments be given to them. 4Then let the girl who pleases the king be queen instead of Vashti." This advice appealed to the king, and he followed it.

5Now there was in the citadel of Susa a Jew of the tribe of Benjamin, named Mordecai son of Jair, the son of Shimei, the son of Kish, 6who had been carried into exile from Jerusalem by Nebuchadnezzar king of Babylon, among those taken captive with Jehoiachin[a] king of Judah. 7Mordecai had a cousin named Hadassah, whom he had brought up because she had neither father nor mother. This girl, who was also known as Esther, was lovely in form and features, and Mordecai had taken her as his own daughter when her father and mother died.

8When the king's order and edict had been proclaimed, many girls were brought to the citadel of Susa and put under the care of Hegai. Esther also was taken to the king's palace and entrusted to Hegai, who had charge of the harem. 9The girl pleased him and won his favor. Immediately he provided her with her beauty treatments and special food. He assigned to her seven maids selected from the king's palace and moved her and her maids into the best place in the harem.

10Esther had not revealed her nationality and family background, because Mordecai had forbidden her to do so. 11Every day he walked back and forth near the courtyard of the harem to find out how Esther was and what was happening to her.

12Before a girl's turn came to go in to King Xerxes, she had to complete twelve months of beauty treatments prescribed for the women, six months with oil of myrrh and six with perfumes and cosmetics. 13And this is how she would go to the king: Anything she wanted was given her to take with her from the harem to the king's palace. 14In the evening she would go there and in the morning return to another part of the harem to the care of Shaashgaz, the king's eunuch who was in charge of the concubines. She would not return to the king unless he was pleased with her and summoned her by name.

15When the turn came for Esther (the girl Mordecai had adopted, the daughter of his uncle Abihail) to go to the king, she asked for nothing other than what Hegai, the king's eunuch who was in charge of the harem, suggested. And Esther won the favor of

[a] 6 Hebrew *Jeconiah,* a variant of *Jehoiachin*

(2:2–4,15) O Lord, I see how sovereignly You set the stage for Your will to be done. You humble the proud and exalt the humble. You open doors and call us to walk through them into the center of Your plans for us. Then You give us free will to follow You or to turn away. Today, I choose to embrace Your will for me, to walk through the doors You open, and to cooperate with the plans You have laid, plans to prosper and not to harm me, plans to give me a future and a hope. My life is in Your hands. (Jer 29:11)

Oh what it is to know
You are with me,
Oh what it is to know
You are there,
You are forever goodness and mercy,
Beside me where e'er I go,
And how wonderful it is to know.

I call upon You,
Gracious Redeemer,
My Lord, You hear.
I call upon You,
Gracious Redeemer,
I know You're near.

"Oh What It Is To Know"
Rob Mathes (©1996)

(2:10) Speak clearly to me, Lord. Reveal to me those times when You would have me speak out about my faith and those times when You would have me remain quiet. Then give me the courage to obey You. Let discretion be my protection and understanding be my guard. (Pr 2:11)

If Jesus Christ is God and died for me, then no sacrifice can be too great for me to make for him.

Charles Thomas Studd (1862–1931)

(3:2) When people all around me are bowing down to worship the world, give me the courage to stand up for You. Though choosing You may enrage those who are in authority, keep me steadfast. So engulf me in Your love, O Lord, that my heart would break before it would dishonor You.

I would be true,
For there are those who trust me.
I would be pure,
For there are those who care.
I would be strong,
For there is much to suffer.
I would be brave,
For there is much to dare.
I would be brave,
For there is much to dare.

I would be prayerful
Thro' each busy moment.
I would be constantly
In touch with God.
I would be tuned to
Hear His slightest whisper.
I would have faith
To keep the path Christ trod.
I would have faith
To keep the path Christ trod.

"I Would Be True"
Howard A. Walter (1907)

everyone who saw her. 16She was taken to King Xerxes in the royal residence in the tenth month, the month of Tebeth, in the seventh year of his reign.

17Now the king was attracted to Esther more than to any of the other women, and she won his favor and approval more than any of the other virgins. So he set a royal crown on her head and made her queen instead of Vashti. 18And the king gave a great banquet, Esther's banquet, for all his nobles and officials. He proclaimed a holiday throughout the provinces and distributed gifts with royal liberality.

Mordecai Uncovers a Conspiracy

19When the virgins were assembled a second time, Mordecai was sitting at the king's gate. 20But Esther had kept secret her family background and nationality just as Mordecai had told her to do, for she continued to follow Mordecai's instructions as she had done when he was bringing her up.

21During the time Mordecai was sitting at the king's gate, Bigthana[a] and Teresh, two of the king's officers who guarded the doorway, became angry and conspired to assassinate King Xerxes. 22But Mordecai found out about the plot and told Queen Esther, who in turn reported it to the king, giving credit to Mordecai. 23And when the report was investigated and found to be true, the two officials were hanged on a gallows.[b] All this was recorded in the book of the annals in the presence of the king.

Haman's Plot to Destroy the Jews

3 After these events, King Xerxes honored Haman son of Hammedatha, the Agagite, elevating him and giving him a seat of honor higher than that of all the other nobles. 2All the royal officials at the king's gate knelt down and paid honor to Haman, for the king had commanded this concerning him. But Mordecai would not kneel down or pay him honor.

3Then the royal officials at the king's gate asked Mordecai, "Why do you disobey the king's command?" 4Day after day they spoke to him but he refused to comply. Therefore they told Haman about it to see whether Mordecai's behavior would be tolerated, for he had told them he was a Jew.

5When Haman saw that Mordecai would not kneel down or pay him honor, he was enraged. 6Yet having learned who Mordecai's people were, he scorned the idea of killing only Mordecai. Instead Haman looked for a way to destroy all Mordecai's people, the Jews, throughout the whole kingdom of Xerxes.

7In the twelfth year of King Xerxes, in the first month, the month of Nisan, they cast the *pur* (that is, the lot) in the presence of Haman to select a day and month. And the lot fell on[c] the twelfth month, the month of Adar.

8Then Haman said to King Xerxes, "There is a certain people dispersed and scattered among the peoples in all the provinces of your kingdom whose customs are different from those of all other people and who do not obey the king's laws; it is not in the king's best interest to tolerate them. 9If it pleases the king, let a decree be issued to destroy them, and I will put ten thousand talents[d] of silver into the royal treasury for the men who carry out this business."

[a] 21 Hebrew *Bigthan,* a variant of *Bigthana* [b] 23 Or *were hung* (or *impaled*) *on poles*; similarly elsewhere in Esther [c] 7 Septuagint; Hebrew does not have *And the lot fell on.* [d] 9 That is, about 375 tons (about 345 metric tons)

10So the king took his signet ring from his finger and gave it to
Haman son of Hammedatha, the Agagite, the enemy of the Jews.
11"Keep the money," the king said to Haman, "and do with the people as you please."
12Then on the thirteenth day of the first month the royal secretaries were summoned. They wrote out in the script of each province and in the language of each people all Haman's orders to the
king's satraps, the governors of the various provinces and the nobles of the various peoples. These were written in the name of King
Xerxes himself and sealed with his own ring. 13Dispatches were
sent by couriers to all the king's provinces with the order to destroy, kill and annihilate all the Jews—young and old, women and
little children—on a single day, the thirteenth day of the twelfth
month, the month of Adar, and to plunder their goods. 14A copy of
the text of the edict was to be issued as law in every province and
made known to the people of every nationality so they would be
ready for that day.
15Spurred on by the king's command, the couriers went out, and
the edict was issued in the citadel of Susa. The king and Haman sat
down to drink, but the city of Susa was bewildered.

Mordecai Persuades Esther to Help

4 When Mordecai learned of all that had been done, he tore his
clothes, put on sackcloth and ashes, and went out into the city,
wailing loudly and bitterly. 2But he went only as far as the king's
gate, because no one clothed in sackcloth was allowed to enter it.
3In every province to which the edict and order of the king came,
there was great mourning among the Jews, with fasting, weeping
and wailing. Many lay in sackcloth and ashes.
4When Esther's maids and eunuchs came and told her about
Mordecai, she was in great distress. She sent clothes for him to put
on instead of his sackcloth, but he would not accept them. 5Then
Esther summoned Hathach, one of the king's eunuchs assigned to
attend her, and ordered him to find out what was troubling Mordecai and why.
6So Hathach went out to Mordecai in the open square of the city
in front of the king's gate. 7Mordecai told him everything that had
happened to him, including the exact amount of money Haman had
promised to pay into the royal treasury for the destruction of the
Jews. 8He also gave him a copy of the text of the edict for their annihilation, which had been published in Susa, to show to Esther
and explain it to her, and he told him to urge her to go into the
king's presence to beg for mercy and plead with him for her people.
9Hathach went back and reported to Esther what Mordecai had
said. 10Then she instructed him to say to Mordecai, 11"All the
king's officials and the people of the royal provinces know that for
any man or woman who approaches the king in the inner court
without being summoned the king has but one law: that he be put
to death. The only exception to this is for the king to extend the
gold scepter to him and spare his life. But thirty days have passed
since I was called to go to the king."
12When Esther's words were reported to Mordecai, 13he sent
back this answer: "Do not think that because you are in the king's
house you alone of all the Jews will escape. 14For if you remain
silent at this time, relief and deliverance for the Jews will arise from
another place, but you and your father's family will perish. And

(4:1) Lord, if my faithfulness to You puts others at risk, I pray You will have mercy. I will lift my voice to You and cry out for help. I will clothe my soul in sackcloth and my heart in ashes. You alone are my hope when all seems hopeless. You alone are my help in the day of trouble. Apart from You I know I cannot face what I must face. But with You, my Lord and my God, all things are possible. (Ps 27:5; Mt 19:26)

(4:14) Lord God, You brought Esther to a place where she could be Your means for the deliverance of her nation. And You still bring people into times and places for Your own specific purposes. I do not want to miss those purposes in my own life, Lord. I am Your workmanship, created in Christ Jesus to do good works, which You prepared in advance for me to do. I want to be the instrument of Your Holy Spirit as He works in and through me, bringing Your plans to completion on the earth. Give me the courage and vision I will need to be Your person at this time and in this place, knowing that You have called me, You are faithful and You will do it. (Eph 2:10; 1Th 5:24)

Give us ears to hear that still, small
voice;
And give us lips forever willing to
rejoice.
And may our eyes be lit with wisdom,
May we know the path that's true;
And we'll march with hearts
Courageous after You.

We're marching on with hearts
courageous;
We'll follow anywhere You want us
to.
And should You lead us where the
battle rages,
Let us march with hearts
courageous after You.

"Hearts Courageous"
Jamie Owens-Collins (©1984)

Not only for every idle word must man give an account, but for every idle silence.
Saint Ambrose (339-397)

(4:15–17) Father, as I consider Esther's courage in the face of death, I must stop and examine my own character. What would I do? Would I be faithful? Would I rely on the power of prayer and fasting? I remember the words and experiences of the apostle Paul: "We were under great pressure, far beyond our ability to endure, so that we despaired even of life. Indeed, in our hearts we felt the sentence of death. But this happened that we might not rely on ourselves but on God, who raises the dead. He has delivered us from such a deadly peril, and he will deliver us. On him we have set our hope that he will continue to deliver us, as you help us by your prayers. Then many will give thanks on our behalf for the gracious favor granted us in answer to the prayers of many." Lord, should I ever be in such circumstances, may I, with such boldness, dare to do what is right in Your eyes. (2Co 1:8–11)

(5:14) When I see the world erect its gallows and they cast their shadow on my soul, come, O light of Christ, and dispel those shadows. For Your love that is in me is greater than the hate that is in the world, and Your power to deliver is greater than the world's power to destroy.

who knows but that you have come to royal position for such a time as this?"

15Then Esther sent this reply to Mordecai: 16"Go, gather together all the Jews who are in Susa, and fast for me. Do not eat or drink for three days, night or day. I and my maids will fast as you do. When this is done, I will go to the king, even though it is against the law. And if I perish, I perish."

17So Mordecai went away and carried out all of Esther's instructions.

Esther's Request to the King

5 On the third day Esther put on her royal robes and stood in the inner court of the palace, in front of the king's hall. The king was sitting on his royal throne in the hall, facing the entrance. 2When he saw Queen Esther standing in the court, he was pleased with her and held out to her the gold scepter that was in his hand. So Esther approached and touched the tip of the scepter.

3Then the king asked, "What is it, Queen Esther? What is your request? Even up to half the kingdom, it will be given you."

4"If it pleases the king," replied Esther, "let the king, together with Haman, come today to a banquet I have prepared for him."

5"Bring Haman at once," the king said, "so that we may do what Esther asks."

So the king and Haman went to the banquet Esther had prepared. 6As they were drinking wine, the king again asked Esther, "Now what is your petition? It will be given you. And what is your request? Even up to half the kingdom, it will be granted."

7Esther replied, "My petition and my request is this: 8If the king regards me with favor and if it pleases the king to grant my petition and fulfill my request, let the king and Haman come tomorrow to the banquet I will prepare for them. Then I will answer the king's question."

Haman's Rage Against Mordecai

9Haman went out that day happy and in high spirits. But when he saw Mordecai at the king's gate and observed that he neither rose nor showed fear in his presence, he was filled with rage against Mordecai. 10Nevertheless, Haman restrained himself and went home.

Calling together his friends and Zeresh, his wife, 11Haman boasted to them about his vast wealth, his many sons, and all the ways the king had honored him and how he had elevated him above the other nobles and officials. 12"And that's not all," Haman added. "I'm the only person Queen Esther invited to accompany the king to the banquet she gave. And she has invited me along with the king tomorrow. 13But all this gives me no satisfaction as long as I see that Jew Mordecai sitting at the king's gate."

14His wife Zeresh and all his friends said to him, "Have a gallows built, seventy-five feet[a] high, and ask the king in the morning to have Mordecai hanged on it. Then go with the king to the dinner and be happy." This suggestion delighted Haman, and he had the gallows built.

[a] *14* Hebrew *fifty cubits* (about 23 meters)

Mordecai Honored

6 That night the king could not sleep; so he ordered the
book of the chronicles, the record of his reign, to be
brought in and read to him. 2It was found recorded there that
Mordecai had exposed Bigthana and Teresh, two of the king's
officers who guarded the doorway, who had conspired to assassinate King Xerxes.
3"What honor and recognition has Mordecai received for
this?" the king asked.
"Nothing has been done for him," his attendants answered.
4The king said, "Who is in the court?" Now Haman had just
entered the outer court of the palace to speak to the king about
hanging Mordecai on the gallows he had erected for him.
5His attendants answered, "Haman is standing in the court."
"Bring him in," the king ordered.
6When Haman entered, the king asked him, "What should
be done for the man the king delights to honor?"
Now Haman thought to himself, "Who is there that the king
would rather honor than me?" 7So he answered the king, "For
the man the king delights to honor, 8have them bring a royal
robe the king has worn and a horse the king has ridden, one
with a royal crest placed on its head. 9Then let the robe and
horse be entrusted to one of the king's most noble princes. Let
them robe the man the king delights to honor, and lead him on
the horse through the city streets, proclaiming before him,
'This is what is done for the man the king delights to honor!' "
10"Go at once," the king commanded Haman. "Get the robe
and the horse and do just as you have suggested for Mordecai
the Jew, who sits at the king's gate. Do not neglect anything you
have recommended."
11So Haman got the robe and the horse. He robed Mordecai,
and led him on horseback through the city streets, proclaiming
before him, "This is what is done for the man the king delights
to honor!"
12Afterward Mordecai returned to the king's gate. But
Haman rushed home, with his head covered in grief, 13and told
Zeresh his wife and all his friends everything that had happened to him.
His advisers and his wife Zeresh said to him, "Since Mordecai, before whom your downfall has started, is of Jewish origin,
you cannot stand against him—you will surely come to ruin!"
14While they were still talking with him, the king's eunuchs arrived and hurried Haman away to the banquet Esther had prepared.

Haman Hanged

7 So the king and Haman went to dine with Queen Esther,
2and as they were drinking wine on that second day, the
king again asked, "Queen Esther, what is your petition? It will be
given you. What is your request? Even up to half the kingdom, it
will be granted."
3Then Queen Esther answered, "If I have found favor with
you, O king, and if it pleases your majesty, grant me my life—
this is my petition. And spare my people—this is my request.
4For I and my people have been sold for destruction and
slaughter and annihilation. If we had merely been sold as male

(6:1–11) Lord, I praise You that at times Your divine justice is truly comic! And You are always just. At times You hoist the wicked with their own hooks. At other times I begin to wonder whether the wicked will ever be punished. Yet, as with Mordecai, Your justice will ultimately prevail. I can be sure that You are at work in the lives of those who love You, bringing right from wrong and working all things, even evil things, together for good. (Ro 8:28)

(7:3) As Esther was willing to lay down her life for her people, so You ask me to be willing to lay down my life for my brothers and sisters. But apart from You and the indwelling power of Your Spirit, I am not capable of anything nearly so good or noble. Therefore fill me, Lord, with all that You are—all the courage, all the power, all the faith and hope and love that I will need to live sacrificially. Teach me to intercede for my brothers and sisters, to plead for them, to put my life at risk for them if it is ever called for. And teach me to trust You to operate in and through me to do every good work. (Php 2:13)

Father, I abandon myself into Your hands; do with me what You will. Whatever You may do, I thank you: I am ready for all, I accept all. Let only Your will be done in me and in all Your creatures–I wish no more than this, Lord.

Venerable Charles de Foucauld (1858-1916)

and female slaves, I would have kept quiet, because no such distress would justify disturbing the king.[a]"
5King Xerxes asked Queen Esther, "Who is he? Where is the
man who has dared to do such a thing?"
6Esther said, "The adversary and enemy is this vile Haman."
Then Haman was terrified before the king and queen. 7The
king got up in a rage, left his wine and went out into the palace
garden. But Haman, realizing that the king had already decided
his fate, stayed behind to beg Queen Esther for his life.
8Just as the king returned from the palace garden to the banquet hall, Haman was falling on the couch where Esther was reclining.
The king exclaimed, "Will he even molest the queen while she
is with me in the house?"
As soon as the word left the king's mouth, they covered
Haman's face. 9Then Harbona, one of the eunuchs attending the
king, said, "A gallows seventy-five feet[b] high stands by Haman's
house. He had it made for Mordecai, who spoke up to help the
king."
The king said, "Hang him on it!" 10So they hanged Haman on
the gallows he had prepared for Mordecai. Then the king's fury
subsided.

The King's Edict in Behalf of the Jews

8 That same day King Xerxes gave Queen Esther the estate of
Haman, the enemy of the Jews. And Mordecai came into the
presence of the king, for Esther had told how he was related to
her. 2The king took off his signet ring, which he had reclaimed
from Haman, and presented it to Mordecai. And Esther appointed him over Haman's estate.
3Esther again pleaded with the king, falling at his feet and
weeping. She begged him to put an end to the evil plan of Haman
the Agagite, which he had devised against the Jews. 4Then the
king extended the gold scepter to Esther and she arose and stood
before him.
5"If it pleases the king," she said, "and if he regards me with
favor and thinks it the right thing to do, and if he is pleased with
me, let an order be written overruling the dispatches that Haman
son of Hammedatha, the Agagite, devised and wrote to destroy the
Jews in all the king's provinces. 6For how can I bear to see disaster fall on my people? How can I bear to see the destruction of
my family?"
7King Xerxes replied to Queen Esther and to Mordecai the Jew,
"Because Haman attacked the Jews, I have given his estate to Esther, and they have hanged him on the gallows. 8Now write another decree in the king's name in behalf of the Jews as seems
best to you, and seal it with the king's signet ring—for no document written in the king's name and sealed with his ring can be
revoked."
9At once the royal secretaries were summoned—on the twenty-third day of the third month, the month of Sivan. They wrote
out all Mordecai's orders to the Jews, and to the satraps, governors and nobles of the 127 provinces stretching from India to
Cush.[c] These orders were written in the script of each province

[a] 4 Or *quiet, but the compensation our adversary offers cannot be compared with the loss the king would suffer* [b] 9 Hebrew *fifty cubits* (about 23 meters) [c] 9 That is, the upper Nile region

(7:9–10) Holy God, Your saving work is amazing. I will trust only in You. When the wicked plot against me and carry out their schemes, I will be still and wait patiently for You, for You are powerful against the forces of wickedness. You laugh at the wicked, for You know their day is coming. They draw the sword and bend the bow to bring down the poor and needy, to slay those whose ways are upright. But their swords will pierce their own hearts, and their bows will be broken. You are indeed the Redeemer of Your people. (Ps 37:5–15)

Faith in time of adversity makes the serpent swallow itself!

Norman Grubb (1895–1995)

(8:5–6) O Lord, you are the Savior of Your people, yesterday, today and forever. When we consider our own deliverance, how can we help but praise You? Once there was a death sentence on our family, the human family, because every one of us had sinned and fallen far short of Your glory. But because You loved us, You were not content to lose us. And so You sent Your own Son to plead our case. He was born as a baby, lived innocently among us, was wrongly accused, beaten and bruised and brutalized, and finally crucified on the hard wood of a cross so that our death sentence could be rescinded. His blood pleads for us, and by His blood we find favor in Your sight. All honor and glory and praise be to You, O God, our Redeemer.

and the language of each people and also to the Jews in their own script and language. 10Mordecai wrote in the name of King Xerxes, sealed the dispatches with the king's signet ring, and sent them by mounted couriers, who rode fast horses especially bred for the king.

11The king's edict granted the Jews in every city the right to assemble and protect themselves; to destroy, kill and annihilate any armed force of any nationality or province that might attack them and their women and children; and to plunder the property of their enemies. 12The day appointed for the Jews to do this in all the provinces of King Xerxes was the thirteenth day of the twelfth month, the month of Adar. 13A copy of the text of the edict was to be issued as law in every province and made known to the people of every nationality so that the Jews would be ready on that day to avenge themselves on their enemies.

14The couriers, riding the royal horses, raced out, spurred on by the king's command. And the edict was also issued in the citadel of Susa.

15Mordecai left the king's presence wearing royal garments of blue and white, a large crown of gold and a purple robe of fine linen. And the city of Susa held a joyous celebration. 16For the Jews it was a time of happiness and joy, gladness and honor. 17In every province and in every city, wherever the edict of the king went, there was joy and gladness among the Jews, with feasting and celebrating. And many people of other nationalities became Jews because fear of the Jews had seized them.

Triumph of the Jews

9 On the thirteenth day of the twelfth month, the month of Adar, the edict commanded by the king was to be carried out. On this day the enemies of the Jews had hoped to overpower them, but now the tables were turned and the Jews got the upper hand over those who hated them. 2The Jews assembled in their cities in all the provinces of King Xerxes to attack those seeking their destruction. No one could stand against them, because the people of all the other nationalities were afraid of them. 3And all the nobles of the provinces, the satraps, the governors and the king's administrators helped the Jews, because fear of Mordecai had seized them. 4Mordecai was prominent in the palace; his reputation spread throughout the provinces, and he became more and more powerful.

5The Jews struck down all their enemies with the sword, killing and destroying them, and they did what they pleased to those who hated them. 6In the citadel of Susa, the Jews killed and destroyed five hundred men. 7They also killed Parshandatha, Dalphon, Aspatha, 8Poratha, Adalia, Aridatha, 9Parmashta, Arisai, Aridai and Vaizatha, 10the ten sons of Haman son of Hammedatha, the enemy of the Jews. But they did not lay their hands on the plunder.

11The number of those slain in the citadel of Susa was reported to the king that same day. 12The king said to Queen Esther, "The Jews have killed and destroyed five hundred men and the ten sons of Haman in the citadel of Susa. What have they done in the rest of the king's provinces? Now what is your petition? It will be given you. What is your request? It will also be granted."

13"If it pleases the king," Esther answered, "give the Jews in Susa permission to carry out this day's edict tomorrow also, and let Haman's ten sons be hanged on gallows."

(8:9–14) Sovereign Lord, we praise You for Your royal edicts, Your written promises sealed by the Holy Spirit, that grant us the right and the power to defend ourselves against the enemy. In ancient times, O Lord, You gave Your people victory with the hard implements of sword, bow and spear. And in our day You have not left us defenseless. You have equipped us for battle with spiritual armor: the helmet of salvation, the breastplate of righteousness, the belt of truth, the shoes of Good News, the shield of faith and the sword of the Spirit, which is the Word of God. You have put in our hearts the power of prayer, and You have covered us with the shed blood of the Lamb. You have caused the light of Your love to shine within us and through us—the light against which no darkness can ultimately prevail. We praise You, our Captain and our King. (Eph 6:10–18)

(8:15–17) How like You, O Lord, to turn mourning into dancing, fear into wondrous joy. In Your mercy, Lord, You also lift me. You hear the cry of my heart. You heal my deepest wounds. You clothe me in garments of righteousness, praise and salvation. In grace You set a place for me at Your table and welcome me. You teach me Your song of praise and You call me Your child. I will praise You forever and ever. Amen! (Ps 132:9; Isa 61:3,10)

Thou hast given so much to me
Give one thing more–a grateful heart;
Not thankful when it pleaseth me,
As if thy blessings had spare days,
But such a heart whose pulse may be
Thy praise.

George Herbert (1593-1633)

14So the king commanded that this be done. An edict was issued in Susa, and they hanged the ten sons of Haman. 15The Jews
in Susa came together on the fourteenth day of the month of Adar,
and they put to death in Susa three hundred men, but they did not
lay their hands on the plunder.

16Meanwhile, the remainder of the Jews who were in the king's
provinces also assembled to protect themselves and get relief
from their enemies. They killed seventy-five thousand of them but
did not lay their hands on the plunder. 17This happened on the
thirteenth day of the month of Adar, and on the fourteenth they
rested and made it a day of feasting and joy.

Purim Celebrated

18The Jews in Susa, however, had assembled on the thirteenth
and fourteenth, and then on the fifteenth they rested and made it
a day of feasting and joy.

19That is why rural Jews—those living in villages—observe the
fourteenth of the month of Adar as a day of joy and feasting, a day
for giving presents to each other.

20Mordecai recorded these events, and he sent letters to all the
Jews throughout the provinces of King Xerxes, near and far, 21to
have them celebrate annually the fourteenth and fifteenth days of
the month of Adar 22as the time when the Jews got relief from
their enemies, and as the month when their sorrow was turned
into joy and their mourning into a day of celebration. He wrote
them to observe the days as days of feasting and joy and giving
presents of food to one another and gifts to the poor.

23So the Jews agreed to continue the celebration they had
begun, doing what Mordecai had written to them. 24For Haman
son of Hammedatha, the Agagite, the enemy of all the Jews, had
plotted against the Jews to destroy them and had cast the *pur*
(that is, the lot) for their ruin and destruction. 25But when the
plot came to the king's attention,[a] he issued written orders that
the evil scheme Haman had devised against the Jews should come
back onto his own head, and that he and his sons should be
hanged on the gallows. 26(Therefore these days were called
Purim, from the word *pur*.) Because of everything written in this
letter and because of what they had seen and what had happened
to them, 27the Jews took it upon themselves to establish the custom that they and their descendants and all who join them should
without fail observe these two days every year, in the way prescribed and at the time appointed. 28These days should be remembered and observed in every generation by every family, and
in every province and in every city. And these days of Purim
should never cease to be celebrated by the Jews, nor should the
memory of them die out among their descendants.

29So Queen Esther, daughter of Abihail, along with Mordecai
the Jew, wrote with full authority to confirm this second letter
concerning Purim. 30And Mordecai sent letters to all the Jews in
the 127 provinces of the kingdom of Xerxes—words of goodwill
and assurance— 31to establish these days of Purim at their designated times, as Mordecai the Jew and Queen Esther had decreed for them, and as they had established for themselves and
their descendants in regard to their times of fasting and lamenta-

[a] 25 Or *when Esther came before the king*

Gratitude is born in hearts that take time to count up past mercies.

Charles Edward Jefferson (1860–1937)

(9:27–32) Lord, I never want to forget Your goodness to me. I want to write it indelibly on my heart, sing it in songs and relive it in my memories. I want to talk about it to my family when we are seated at the table, when we are walking together and when we have guests in our home. I want Your goodness, Your deliverance, Your faithfulness to me and my family to be spoken of and celebrated throughout all of our years together, so that our children's children and their children for generations to come will know and love and honor You as their God. (Dt 6:4–9)

I will celebrate,
Sing unto the Lord,
Sing to the Lord a new song.
With my heart rejoicing within,
With my mind focused on Him.
With my hands raised to the
heavens,
All I am, worshiping Him.

"I Will Celebrate"
Rita Baloche (©1990)

tion. 32Esther's decree confirmed these regulations about Purim, and it was written down in the records.

The Greatness of Mordecai

10 King Xerxes imposed tribute throughout the empire, to its
distant shores. 2And all his acts of power and might, to-
gether with a full account of the greatness of Mordecai to which the king had raised him, are they not written in the book of the annals of the kings of Media and Persia? 3Mordecai the Jew was
second in rank to King Xerxes, preeminent among the Jews, and held in high esteem by his many fellow Jews, because he worked for the good of his people and spoke up for the welfare of all the Jews.

Consecration is handing God a blank sheet to fill in with your name signed at the bottom.

M. H. Miller (1904-)

(10:1–3) Thank You, Lord, for the history handed down to us that tells of Your working in the hearts and lives of men and women through the ages. Thank You that Your love is still at work, that Your Spirit is still active wherever hearts are open to You. Lord, I open my heart today. I invite You to move into the center of my life and write a new chapter in me. I want to walk in the great adventure of Your will. By the power of Your Holy Spirit, have Your way in my life. Amen.

What a glorious wonder my Lord is.
What a glorious wonder my Lord is.
My light and salvation,
My strength and shield.
What a glorious wonder my Lord is.

"Glorious Wonder"
Rob Mathes (©1996)

The Book of JOB

Why does God allow good people to suffer? Questions like this often ring in our ears—and in our hearts. For centuries God's people have turned to the book of Job for answers to this question and for encouragement during seasons of personal suffering.

There are six main parts in the book of Job. Part one (chs. 1—2) introduces Job as a righteous, God-fearing man. When Satan insists that Job's faith is simply a response to his blessed life, God allows Satan to bring suffering upon Job. And suffer Job does, with unspeakably heart-wrenching losses. In part two (chs. 3—27) three of Job's friends attempt to "help" him by making him see that his own sin has caused his suffering. But Job rejects their counsel, defending his integrity before God. In part three (chs. 28—31) Job maintains his defense, while meditating upon God's wisdom and calling out for divine help. In the fourth part (chs. 32—37) a new speaker offers more advice to Job, but without resolving his dilemma. Then God speaks to Job out of the whirlwind, challenging his meager wisdom. In this fifth part (chs. 38—41) the Lord overwhelms Job with His majesty and mystery. In the sixth part (ch. 42) Job admits that he has spoken of "things I did not understand, things too wonderful for me" (42:3). He repents of his arrogance and is exonerated and restored by God, Who accuses Job's friends of speaking theological falsehoods. But when Job intercedes with his friends, God deals graciously with them even as He blesses Job magnificently (42:7–10).

We worship a God Who does not answer all of our questions, but Who meets our deepest needs by offering Himself, His love and His salvation.

In Job we are confronted by the inscrutability of suffering. Simplistic solutions melt in the heat of human pain and then evaporate in the presence of Almighty God. This book obliterates the deep-seated prejudice that regards all suffering as evidence of individual sin and divine displeasure. Though human sinfulness in general is the root of all suffering, that does not imply that each person who suffers receives precisely what his or her actions deserve. Sometimes the righteous suffer; sometimes God appears to "smile on the schemes of the wicked" (10:3).

The example of Job encourages us to be authentic in our communication with God. Sometimes we can act as though God just is not big enough to handle our anger or disappointment with Him. But Job teaches us that God welcomes complete honesty with Him. Like Jesus on the cross, there may be times when we ought to pray: "My God, my God, why have you forsaken me?" (Mk 15:34).

The cross of Christ also presents God's final solution to the problem of suffering. God takes our suffering upon Himself in Jesus; the Righteous One bears what He does not deserve so that we who are unrighteous might receive the fullness of grace. We worship a God Who does not answer all of our questions, but Who meets our deepest needs by offering Himself, His love and His salvation.

Prologue

1 In the land of Uz there lived a man whose name was Job. This
man was blameless and upright; he feared God and shunned
evil. 2He had seven sons and three daughters, 3and he owned
seven thousand sheep, three thousand camels, five hundred yoke
of oxen and five hundred donkeys, and had a large number of servants. He was the greatest man among all the people of the East.
4His sons used to take turns holding feasts in their homes, and
they would invite their three sisters to eat and drink with them.
5When a period of feasting had run its course, Job would send and
have them purified. Early in the morning he would sacrifice a
burnt offering for each of them, thinking, "Perhaps my children
have sinned and cursed God in their hearts." This was Job's regular custom.

Job's First Test

6One day the angels[a] came to present themselves before the
LORD, and Satan[b] also came with them. 7The LORD said to Satan,
"Where have you come from?"
Satan answered the LORD, "From roaming through the earth and
going back and forth in it."
8Then the LORD said to Satan, "Have you considered my servant
Job? There is no one on earth like him; he is blameless and upright, a man who fears God and shuns evil."
9"Does Job fear God for nothing?" Satan replied. 10"Have you
not put a hedge around him and his household and everything he
has? You have blessed the work of his hands, so that his flocks and
herds are spread throughout the land. 11But stretch out your hand
and strike everything he has, and he will surely curse you to your
face."
12The LORD said to Satan, "Very well, then, everything he has is
in your hands, but on the man himself do not lay a finger."
Then Satan went out from the presence of the LORD.
13One day when Job's sons and daughters were feasting and
drinking wine at the oldest brother's house, 14a messenger came
to Job and said, "The oxen were plowing and the donkeys were
grazing nearby, 15and the Sabeans attacked and carried them off.
They put the servants to the sword, and I am the only one who has
escaped to tell you!"
16While he was still speaking, another messenger came and
said, "The fire of God fell from the sky and burned up the sheep
and the servants, and I am the only one who has escaped to tell
you!"
17While he was still speaking, another messenger came and
said, "The Chaldeans formed three raiding parties and swept down
on your camels and carried them off. They put the servants to the
sword, and I am the only one who has escaped to tell you!"
18While he was still speaking, yet another messenger came and
said, "Your sons and daughters were feasting and drinking wine at
the oldest brother's house, 19when suddenly a mighty wind swept
in from the desert and struck the four corners of the house. It collapsed on them and they are dead, and I am the only one who has
escaped to tell you!"
20At this, Job got up and tore his robe and shaved his head.
Then he fell to the ground in worship 21and said:

[a] 6 Hebrew *the sons of God* [b] 6 *Satan* means *accuser.*

If thankfulness arises through prosperity, well and good. But what are you going to do when the prosperity fails? If thankfulness springs up through health, well and good. But what will you do when disease makes you bedridden? Must you then become glum or bitter? But now, supposing it is through our dear Lord Christ that you cultivate the fine art of thanksgiving, then what? Then money in the bank, however useful, does not have me at its mercy: if I lose it, I can still offer thanks.

Paul Stromberg Rees (1900–)

(1:9) Holy and loving God, I am a part of a world and a culture that feeds and fuels this very lie of Satan. Why do I love You? Why do I have an affectionate reverence for You? Is it only because of the good things that You do for me, the blessings that You have brought into my life? Oh, may it be that I love You simply because You alone are worthy of my affection, my attention, my allegiance, my all.

Does Jesus care when I've said
goodbye
To the dearest on earth to me,
And my sad heart aches till it nearly
breaks.
Is it aught to Him? Does He see?

O yes, He cares; I know He cares,
His heart is touched with my grief;
When the days are weary,
The long nights dreary,
I know my Savior cares.

"Does Jesus Care?"
Frank E. Graeff (1901)

(1:20–21) Father, my Provider, all things come from You. Family, health, protection, wealth—all the joyful treasures I hold so dear are Yours, loaned to me but for a season. They are Yours to give and Yours to take away. Though some might curse You for their losses, I choose, like Job, to praise Your name and worship You for Your sovereignty. You are God; I am human. The rules are set. In the give and take of life, may I never doubt Your love, and may I never lose the gift of faith.

(2:6) Sovereign Lord, Your confidence in Job is a mystery. Do You have the same confidence in me? I must confess that I really do not want to know the answer to that question. I want to be found faithful, but I do not want to be *proven* faithful. Forgive me for my fear—for doubting that Your grace is sufficient to meet every challenge. Forgive me for not living in complete surrender to Your will. Lord, I do believe that You want only the best for my life. Please help me in my unbelief.

(2:10) Lord, I relinquish to You all right to define "good" and "trouble." I have walked with You long enough to know that many things I call "trouble" turn out for my good, and many things I have perceived as "good" have proven to be otherwise. Who am I to say anything but "thank You" for what comes to me from Your hand? For I know that in all things You work for the good of those who love You. I want to be more willing to accept from You whatever will bring glory to Yourself and Christ-likeness in my soul. (La 3:38; Ro 8:28)

When peace, like a river
Attendeth my way,
When sorrows like sea billows roll;
Whatever my lot,
Thou hast taught me to say,
"It is well, it is well with my soul."

"It Is Well With My Soul"
Horatio G. Spafford (1873)

"Naked I came from my mother's womb,
and naked I will depart.[a]
The LORD gave and the LORD has taken away;
may the name of the LORD be praised."

22In all this, Job did not sin by charging God with wrongdoing.

Job's Second Test

2 On another day the angels[b] came to present themselves before the LORD, and Satan also came with them to present himself before him. 2And the LORD said to Satan, "Where have you
come from?"

Satan answered the LORD, "From roaming through the earth
and going back and forth in it."

3Then the LORD said to Satan, "Have you considered my servant
Job? There is no one on earth like him; he is blameless and upright, a man who fears God and shuns evil. And he still maintains
his integrity, though you incited me against him to ruin him without any reason."

4"Skin for skin!" Satan replied. "A man will give all he has for
his own life. 5But stretch out your hand and strike his flesh and
bones, and he will surely curse you to your face."

6The LORD said to Satan, "Very well, then, he is in your hands;
but you must spare his life."

7So Satan went out from the presence of the LORD and afflicted
Job with painful sores from the soles of his feet to the top of his
head. 8Then Job took a piece of broken pottery and scraped himself with it as he sat among the ashes.

9His wife said to him, "Are you still holding on to your integrity? Curse God and die!"

10He replied, "You are talking like a foolish[c] woman. Shall we
accept good from God, and not trouble?"

In all this, Job did not sin in what he said.

Job's Three Friends

11When Job's three friends, Eliphaz the Temanite, Bildad the
Shuhite and Zophar the Naamathite, heard about all the troubles
that had come upon him, they set out from their homes and met
together by agreement to go and sympathize with him and comfort him. 12When they saw him from a distance, they could hardly recognize him; they began to weep aloud, and they tore their
robes and sprinkled dust on their heads. 13Then they sat on the
ground with him for seven days and seven nights. No one said a
word to him, because they saw how great his suffering was.

Job Speaks

3 After this, Job opened his mouth and cursed the day of his
birth. 2He said:

3"May the day of my birth perish,
and the night it was said, 'A boy is born!'
4That day—may it turn to darkness;
may God above not care about it;
may no light shine upon it.
5May darkness and deep shadow[d] claim it once more;
may a cloud settle over it;

[a] 21 Or *will return there* [b] 1 Hebrew *the sons of God* [c] 10 The Hebrew word rendered *foolish* denotes moral deficiency. [d] 5 Or *and the shadow of death*

may blackness overwhelm its light.
6 That night—may thick darkness seize it;
may it not be included among the days of the year
nor be entered in any of the months.
7 May that night be barren;
may no shout of joy be heard in it.
8 May those who curse days[a] curse that day,
those who are ready to rouse Leviathan.
9 May its morning stars become dark;
may it wait for daylight in vain
and not see the first rays of dawn,
10 for it did not shut the doors of the womb on me
to hide trouble from my eyes.

11 "Why did I not perish at birth,
and die as I came from the womb?
12 Why were there knees to receive me
and breasts that I might be nursed?
13 For now I would be lying down in peace;
I would be asleep and at rest
14 with kings and counselors of the earth,
who built for themselves places now lying in ruins,
15 with rulers who had gold,
who filled their houses with silver.
16 Or why was I not hidden in the ground like a stillborn child,
like an infant who never saw the light of day?
17 There the wicked cease from turmoil,
and there the weary are at rest.
18 Captives also enjoy their ease;
they no longer hear the slave driver's shout.
19 The small and the great are there,
and the slave is freed from his master.

20 "Why is light given to those in misery,
and life to the bitter of soul,
21 to those who long for death that does not come,
who search for it more than for hidden treasure,
22 who are filled with gladness
and rejoice when they reach the grave?
23 Why is life given to a man
whose way is hidden,
whom God has hedged in?
24 For sighing comes to me instead of food;
my groans pour out like water.
25 What I feared has come upon me;
what I dreaded has happened to me.
26 I have no peace, no quietness;
I have no rest, but only turmoil."

Eliphaz

4 Then Eliphaz the Temanite replied:

2 "If someone ventures a word with you, will you be impatient?
But who can keep from speaking?

[a] 8 Or *the sea*

(3:20–26) Patient and forbearing Father, I praise You for not judging me quickly, even when I question Your ways. In my suffering I may come to You with words that I later regret. But You understand that my pain and confusion prompt these words. You have called me to worship You in spirit and truth; You have required of me authenticity, so I have spoken from the depths of my heart. Thank You for listening to my greatest hurts. Thank You for Your loving arms, which are always open. (Jn 4:24)

I lay my "whys"
before your cross
in worship kneeling,
my mind too numb
for thought,
my heart beyond
all feeling:
And worshiping,
realize that I
in knowing you
don't need a "why."

Ruth Bell Graham (1920-)

I've tasted all the things
That come against you, my child;
They fell to the ground beneath
Golgotha's tree.
My name is Faithful,
And oh, the love that I have for you,
My child.

Can you hear me?
Will you answer?
Can you hear me?
Will you follow, follow Me?

"Message From A King"
Harlan Rogers (©1986)

We habitually stand in our now and look back by faith to see the past filled with God. We look forward and see Him inhabiting our future; but our now is uninhabited except for ourselves. Thus we are guilty of a kind of pro tem atheism which leaves us alone in the universe while, for the time, God is not. We talk of Him much and loudly, but we secretly think of Him as being absent, and we think of ourselves as inhabiting a parenthetic interval between the God who was and the God who will be.

A.W. Tozer (1897-1963)

(5:1) Lord, sometimes I wonder where You are. I cry out to You and I wait but find only silence. I pray, but I hear no answer. Are You listening, Lord? Some say You are not there; Your Word calls such people fools. But who could feel more foolish than I when You seem to ignore my pleading? God in heaven, take pity on me! You are my only hope. Without You I have no place to turn. So I will cling to You and will not let You go. My only comfort in my suffering is this: Your promise preserves my life. (Ps 119:50)

While life's dark maze I tread,
And griefs around me spread,
Be Thou my guide;
Bid darkness turn to day,
Wipe sorrow's tears away,
Nor let me ever stray
From Thee aside.

"My Faith Looks Up To Thee"
Ray Palmer (1830)

3 Think how you have instructed many,
how you have strengthened feeble hands.
4 Your words have supported those who stumbled;
you have strengthened faltering knees.
5 But now trouble comes to you, and you are discouraged;
it strikes you, and you are dismayed.
6 Should not your piety be your confidence
and your blameless ways your hope?

7 "Consider now: Who, being innocent, has ever perished?
Where were the upright ever destroyed?
8 As I have observed, those who plow evil
and those who sow trouble reap it.
9 At the breath of God they are destroyed;
at the blast of his anger they perish.
10 The lions may roar and growl,
yet the teeth of the great lions are broken.
11 The lion perishes for lack of prey,
and the cubs of the lioness are scattered.

12 "A word was secretly brought to me,
my ears caught a whisper of it.
13 Amid disquieting dreams in the night,
when deep sleep falls on men,
14 fear and trembling seized me
and made all my bones shake.
15 A spirit glided past my face,
and the hair on my body stood on end.
16 It stopped,
but I could not tell what it was.
A form stood before my eyes,
and I heard a hushed voice:
17 'Can a mortal be more righteous than God?
Can a man be more pure than his Maker?
18 If God places no trust in his servants,
if he charges his angels with error,
19 how much more those who live in houses of clay,
whose foundations are in the dust,
who are crushed more readily than a moth!
20 Between dawn and dusk they are broken to pieces;
unnoticed, they perish forever.
21 Are not the cords of their tent pulled up,
so that they die without wisdom?'[a]

5 "Call if you will, but who will answer you?
To which of the holy ones will you turn?
2 Resentment kills a fool,
and envy slays the simple.
3 I myself have seen a fool taking root,
but suddenly his house was cursed.
4 His children are far from safety,
crushed in court without a defender.
5 The hungry consume his harvest,
taking it even from among thorns,

[a] 21 Some interpreters end the quotation after verse 17.

and the thirsty pant after his wealth.
6 For hardship does not spring from the soil,
nor does trouble sprout from the ground.
7 Yet man is born to trouble
as surely as sparks fly upward.

8 "But if it were I, I would appeal to God;
I would lay my cause before him.
9 He performs wonders that cannot be fathomed,
miracles that cannot be counted.
10 He bestows rain on the earth;
he sends water upon the countryside.
11 The lowly he sets on high,
and those who mourn are lifted to safety.
12 He thwarts the plans of the crafty,
so that their hands achieve no success.
13 He catches the wise in their craftiness,
and the schemes of the wily are swept away.
14 Darkness comes upon them in the daytime;
at noon they grope as in the night.
15 He saves the needy from the sword in their mouth;
he saves them from the clutches of the powerful.
16 So the poor have hope,
and injustice shuts its mouth.

17 "Blessed is the man whom God corrects;
so do not despise the discipline of the Almighty.[a]
18 For he wounds, but he also binds up;
he injures, but his hands also heal.
19 From six calamities he will rescue you;
in seven no harm will befall you.
20 In famine he will ransom you from death,
and in battle from the stroke of the sword.
21 You will be protected from the lash of the tongue,
and need not fear when destruction comes.
22 You will laugh at destruction and famine,
and need not fear the beasts of the earth.
23 For you will have a covenant with the stones of the field,
and the wild animals will be at peace with you.
24 You will know that your tent is secure;
you will take stock of your property and find nothing missing.
25 You will know that your children will be many,
and your descendants like the grass of the earth.
26 You will come to the grave in full vigor,
like sheaves gathered in season.

27 "We have examined this, and it is true.
So hear it and apply it to yourself."

Job 6

Then Job replied:

2 "If only my anguish could be weighed
and all my misery be placed on the scales!
3 It would surely outweigh the sand of the seas—

[a] 17 Hebrew *Shaddai*; here and throughout Job

(5:17–18) God, You are Sovereign. You can do with me what You will; I am Yours. I will not make light of Your discipline or lose heart when You rebuke me, because You discipline those You love. If my suffering is a trial by Your design, then let my faith be proven genuine and result in Your praise. If I receive a wound from Your hand, then bind it up, Father. Heal me, and help me to learn my lesson well, as a cherished child who is taught by a gracious Parent. (Heb 12:5–6; 1Pe 1:6–7)

Lord, I'm in Your hands,
Lord, I'm in Your heart,
In Your thoughts, in Your plans,
Never on my own.
Lord, I'm in Your hands,
Lord, I'm in Your heart,
In Your thoughts, in Your plans,
Never left alone.

And when the darkness closes in
And fear begins to rise,
Help me to remember
You're always by my side.

"Lord, I'm in Your Hands"
Tim Weeks (©1994)

Give no place to despondency. God's designs regarding you, and his methods of bringing about these designs, are infinitely wise.

Madame Jeanne Marie de La Mothe Guyon (1648–1717)

no wonder my words have been impetuous.
4 The arrows of the Almighty are in me,
my spirit drinks in their poison;
God's terrors are marshaled against me.
5 Does a wild donkey bray when it has grass,
or an ox bellow when it has fodder?
6 Is tasteless food eaten without salt,
or is there flavor in the white of an egg[a]?
7 I refuse to touch it;
such food makes me ill.

8 "Oh, that I might have my request,
that God would grant what I hope for,
9 that God would be willing to crush me,
to let loose his hand and cut me off!
10 Then I would still have this consolation—
my joy in unrelenting pain—
that I had not denied the words of the Holy One.

(6:8–10) Father, I am humbled by Job's loyalty to You, that he would rather face death than deny Your Word. When my turn comes to face hardship, help me to be true to You and to hold on to Your Word. Though I may not understand your actions in my life, help me not to let go of my faith in your love for me.

11 "What strength do I have, that I should still hope?
What prospects, that I should be patient?
12 Do I have the strength of stone?
Is my flesh bronze?
13 Do I have any power to help myself,
now that success has been driven from me?

14 "A despairing man should have the devotion of his friends,
even though he forsakes the fear of the Almighty.
15 But my brothers are as undependable as intermittent streams,
as the streams that overflow
16 when darkened by thawing ice
and swollen with melting snow,
17 but that cease to flow in the dry season,
and in the heat vanish from their channels.
18 Caravans turn aside from their routes;
they go up into the wasteland and perish.
19 The caravans of Tema look for water,
the traveling merchants of Sheba look in hope.
20 They are distressed, because they had been confident;
they arrive there, only to be disappointed.
21 Now you too have proved to be of no help;
you see something dreadful and are afraid.
22 Have I ever said, 'Give something on my behalf,
pay a ransom for me from your wealth,
23 deliver me from the hand of the enemy,
ransom me from the clutches of the ruthless'?

(6:14–15) Lord, when I lose hope and am tempted to forsake You, You will not forsake me. Thank You, Jesus, that You are the Friend who sticks closer than a brother. You are the Friend born for adversity. Though all others may depart in my seasons of unbelief and dark struggle, You will never leave me nor forsake me. Jesus, what a Friend for sinners—Jesus, lover of my soul! (Pr 18:24; Heb 13:5)

24 "Teach me, and I will be quiet;
show me where I have been wrong.
25 How painful are honest words!
But what do your arguments prove?
26 Do you mean to correct what I say,
and treat the words of a despairing man as wind?
27 You would even cast lots for the fatherless
and barter away your friend.

(6:25–26) Compassionate Lord, teach me to listen not just to the words of those who are hurting in my world but also to their hearts. How often I rush to judgment, hearing only what is said and not what is meant. Help me to be quick to listen and slow to speak, so that when I do speak I will bring words of life and healing. (Jas 1:19)

[a] 6 The meaning of the Hebrew for this phrase is uncertain.

28 "But now be so kind as to look at me.
Would I lie to your face?
29 Relent, do not be unjust;
reconsider, for my integrity is at stake.[a]
30 Is there any wickedness on my lips?
Can my mouth not discern malice?

7 "Does not man have hard service on earth?
Are not his days like those of a hired man?
2 Like a slave longing for the evening shadows,
or a hired man waiting eagerly for his wages,
3 so I have been allotted months of futility,
and nights of misery have been assigned to me.
4 When I lie down I think, 'How long before I get up?'
The night drags on, and I toss till dawn.
5 My body is clothed with worms and scabs,
my skin is broken and festering.

6 "My days are swifter than a weaver's shuttle,
and they come to an end without hope.
7 Remember, O God, that my life is but a breath;
my eyes will never see happiness again.
8 The eye that now sees me will see me no longer;
you will look for me, but I will be no more.
9 As a cloud vanishes and is gone,
so he who goes down to the grave[b] does not return.
10 He will never come to his house again;
his place will know him no more.

11 "Therefore I will not keep silent;
I will speak out in the anguish of my spirit,
I will complain in the bitterness of my soul.
12 Am I the sea, or the monster of the deep,
that you put me under guard?
13 When I think my bed will comfort me
and my couch will ease my complaint,
14 even then you frighten me with dreams
and terrify me with visions,
15 so that I prefer strangling and death,
rather than this body of mine.
16 I despise my life; I would not live forever.
Let me alone; my days have no meaning.

17 "What is man that you make so much of him,
that you give him so much attention,
18 that you examine him every morning
and test him every moment?
19 Will you never look away from me,
or let me alone even for an instant?
20 If I have sinned, what have I done to you,
O watcher of men?
Why have you made me your target?
Have I become a burden to you?[c]
21 Why do you not pardon my offenses
and forgive my sins?

[a] 29 Or *my righteousness still stands* [b] 9 Hebrew *Sheol* [c] 20 A few manuscripts of the Masoretic Text, an ancient Hebrew scribal tradition and Septuagint; most manuscripts of the Masoretic Text *I have become a burden to myself.*

(7:5) Merciful Father, I confess that in the presence of physical suffering of this nature I tend to become the priest or the Levite who walks by on the other side of the street. It is far easier for me to pray and offer a Scripture than to roll up my sleeves and touch the seething wound. Have mercy on a small-hearted person like me. Free me to love sacrificially, as Jesus loves me. (Lk 10:30–37)

I expect to pass through life but once. If therefore, there be any kindness that I can show, or any good thing I can do to any fellow being, let me do it now, and not defer or neglect it, as I shall not pass this way again.

Stephen Grellet (1773-1855)

(7:21) Dear God, at those times when I am most tempted to believe the accusations of the enemy, to hear and receive his condemnation, bring the cross of Jesus before the eyes of my heart. You have pardoned my offenses. You have forgiven all of my sins. Jesus has paid the full price of my redemption.

(8:1–6) These graceless words must grieve You, Lord. To imply that Job's sufferings were the result of his unrighteousness was like rubbing salt in his wounds. Job was blameless and upright in Your eyes, but still he suffered. What could anyone ever do to earn Your favor or force Your hand? Nothing. But what love, what compassion, what incredible grace that You would rouse Yourself on our behalf, not because of our purity or uprightness, but in spite of our impurity and unrighteousness. For You demonstrated Your own love for us in this: While we were still sinners, Christ died for us to restore us to a right relationship with You. (Job 2:3; Ro 5:8)

Never a trial that He is not there,
Never a burden that He doth not
bear,
Never a sorrow that He doth not
share;
Moment by moment I'm under His
care.

"Moment by Moment"
Daniel W. Whittle (1893)

For I will soon lie down in the dust;
you will search for me, but I will be no more."

Bildad

8 Then Bildad the Shuhite replied:

2 "How long will you say such things?
Your words are a blustering wind.
3 Does God pervert justice?
Does the Almighty pervert what is right?
4 When your children sinned against him,
he gave them over to the penalty of their sin.
5 But if you will look to God
and plead with the Almighty,
6 if you are pure and upright,
even now he will rouse himself on your behalf
and restore you to your rightful place.
7 Your beginnings will seem humble,
so prosperous will your future be.

8 "Ask the former generations
and find out what their fathers learned,
9 for we were born only yesterday and know
nothing,
and our days on earth are but a shadow.
10 Will they not instruct you and tell you?
Will they not bring forth words from their
understanding?
11 Can papyrus grow tall where there is no marsh?
Can reeds thrive without water?
12 While still growing and uncut,
they wither more quickly than grass.
13 Such is the destiny of all who forget God;
so perishes the hope of the godless.
14 What he trusts in is fragile[a];
what he relies on is a spider's web.
15 He leans on his web, but it gives way;
he clings to it, but it does not hold.
16 He is like a well-watered plant in the sunshine,
spreading its shoots over the garden;
17 it entwines its roots around a pile of rocks
and looks for a place among the stones.
18 But when it is torn from its spot,
that place disowns it and says, 'I never saw you.'
19 Surely its life withers away,
and[b] from the soil other plants grow.

20 "Surely God does not reject a blameless man
or strengthen the hands of evildoers.
21 He will yet fill your mouth with laughter
and your lips with shouts of joy.
22 Your enemies will be clothed in shame,
and the tents of the wicked will be no more."

[a] 14 The meaning of the Hebrew for this word is uncertain. [b] 19 Or *Surely all the joy it has / is that*

Job

9

Then Job replied:

2"Indeed, I know that this is true.
But how can a mortal be righteous before God?
3Though one wished to dispute with him,
he could not answer him one time out of a thousand.
4His wisdom is profound, his power is vast.
Who has resisted him and come out unscathed?
5He moves mountains without their knowing it
and overturns them in his anger.
6He shakes the earth from its place
and makes its pillars tremble.
7He speaks to the sun and it does not shine;
he seals off the light of the stars.
8He alone stretches out the heavens
and treads on the waves of the sea.
9He is the Maker of the Bear and Orion,
the Pleiades and the constellations of the south.
10He performs wonders that cannot be fathomed,
miracles that cannot be counted.
11When he passes me, I cannot see him;
when he goes by, I cannot perceive him.
12If he snatches away, who can stop him?
Who can say to him, 'What are you doing?'
13God does not restrain his anger;
even the cohorts of Rahab cowered at his feet.

14"How then can I dispute with him?
How can I find words to argue with him?
15Though I were innocent, I could not answer him;
I could only plead with my Judge for mercy.
16Even if I summoned him and he responded,
I do not believe he would give me a hearing.
17He would crush me with a storm
and multiply my wounds for no reason.
18He would not let me regain my breath
but would overwhelm me with misery.
19If it is a matter of strength, he is mighty!
And if it is a matter of justice, who will summon him[a]?
20Even if I were innocent, my mouth would condemn me;
if I were blameless, it would pronounce me guilty.

21"Although I am blameless,
I have no concern for myself;
I despise my own life.
22It is all the same; that is why I say,
'He destroys both the blameless and the wicked.'
23When a scourge brings sudden death,
he mocks the despair of the innocent.
24When a land falls into the hands of the wicked,
he blindfolds its judges.
If it is not he, then who is it?

[a] 19 See Septuagint; Hebrew *me*.

(9:2) Holy God, all of us have sinned and fallen short of Your glory. But I praise You that in Your grace a righteousness has been revealed from heaven, which is by faith, from first to last. Abraham's faith was his righteousness. Job's faith was his righteousness. By your grace and by faith You clothe sinful mortals like me in the perfect righteousness of the Lord Jesus. (Ro 3:10–26; 4:3)

(9:15) Job knew that in the light of Your holiness his innocence could not be defended. His righteousness was like filthy rags. And so is mine. Righteous Judge, even Your harshest judgment is merciful, for You could cast me into uttermost darkness without a word of explanation. I do not claim innocence, for among all generations only Your Son is innocent. I can only plead for mercy. I call on the name of Jesus; I claim the innocence He bestows upon me. I trust in Christ alone for hope, for help and for healing. (Isa 64:6)

(9:32–35) Jesus, You are the answer to Job's longing. And You are the answer to mine. You are God in the flesh. You became human like me. You became my Arbitrator. You became my Peacemaker. I worship You for being the one true Mediator between God and humanity, the Reconciler, the Advocate I need before the Father. Through Your death upon the cross You have taken the rod of God's judgment for me and for all who trust in You. Hallelujah, what a Savior! (Job 16:19; 19:25; 1Ti 2:5)

He wrestled with justice, that thou mightest have rest; he wept and mourned, that thou mightest laugh and rejoice; he was betrayed, that thou mightest go free; was apprehended, that thou mightest escape; he was condemned, that thou mightest be justified, and was killed, that thou mightest live; he wore a crown of thorns, that thou mightest wear a crown of glory; and was nailed to the cross with his arms wide open, to show with what freeness all his merits shall be bestowed on the coming soul, and how heartily he will receive it into his bosom.

John Bunyan (1628-1688)

(10:2) Gracious Father, if not for my Savior I might speak just as Job. But through faith in Christ, today and forever, I receive Your glorious declaration, "Therefore, there is now no condemnation for those who are in Christ Jesus." Because of Jesus You will never condemn me for my sins. It will not happen. It cannot happen. I am acquitted of all charges. Because of Jesus I am free. (Ro 8:1)

25 "My days are swifter than a runner;
they fly away without a glimpse of joy.
26 They skim past like boats of papyrus,
like eagles swooping down on their prey.
27 If I say, 'I will forget my complaint,
I will change my expression, and smile,'
28 I still dread all my sufferings,
for I know you will not hold me innocent.
29 Since I am already found guilty,
why should I struggle in vain?
30 Even if I washed myself with soap[a]
and my hands with washing soda,
31 you would plunge me into a slime pit
so that even my clothes would detest me.

32 "He is not a man like me that I might answer him,
that we might confront each other in court.
33 If only there were someone to arbitrate between us,
to lay his hand upon us both,
34 someone to remove God's rod from me,
so that his terror would frighten me no more.
35 Then I would speak up without fear of him,
but as it now stands with me, I cannot.

10 "I loathe my very life;
therefore I will give free rein to my complaint
and speak out in the bitterness of my soul.
2 I will say to God: Do not condemn me,
but tell me what charges you have against me.
3 Does it please you to oppress me,
to spurn the work of your hands,
while you smile on the schemes of the wicked?
4 Do you have eyes of flesh?
Do you see as a mortal sees?
5 Are your days like those of a mortal
or your years like those of a man,
6 that you must search out my faults
and probe after my sin—
7 though you know that I am not guilty
and that no one can rescue me from your hand?

8 "Your hands shaped me and made me.
Will you now turn and destroy me?
9 Remember that you molded me like clay.
Will you now turn me to dust again?
10 Did you not pour me out like milk
and curdle me like cheese,
11 clothe me with skin and flesh
and knit me together with bones and sinews?
12 You gave me life and showed me kindness,
and in your providence watched over my spirit.

13 "But this is what you concealed in your heart,
and I know that this was in your mind:
14 If I sinned, you would be watching me
and would not let my offense go unpunished.
15 If I am guilty—woe to me!

[a] 30 Or *snow*

Even if I am innocent, I cannot lift my head,
for I am full of shame
and drowned in[a] my affliction.
16 If I hold my head high, you stalk me like a lion
and again display your awesome power against me.
17 You bring new witnesses against me
and increase your anger toward me;
your forces come against me wave upon wave.

18 "Why then did you bring me out of the womb?
I wish I had died before any eye saw me.
19 If only I had never come into being,
or had been carried straight from the womb to the grave!
20 Are not my few days almost over?
Turn away from me so I can have a moment's joy
21 before I go to the place of no return,
to the land of gloom and deep shadow,[b]
22 to the land of deepest night,
of deep shadow and disorder,
where even the light is like darkness."

Zophar

11 Then Zophar the Naamathite replied:

2 "Are all these words to go unanswered?
Is this talker to be vindicated?
3 Will your idle talk reduce men to silence?
Will no one rebuke you when you mock?
4 You say to God, 'My beliefs are flawless
and I am pure in your sight.'
5 Oh, how I wish that God would speak,
that he would open his lips against you
6 and disclose to you the secrets of wisdom,
for true wisdom has two sides.
Know this: God has even forgotten some of your sin.

7 "Can you fathom the mysteries of God?
Can you probe the limits of the Almighty?
8 They are higher than the heavens—what can you do?
They are deeper than the depths of the grave[c]—
what can you know?
9 Their measure is longer than the earth
and wider than the sea.

10 "If he comes along and confines you in prison
and convenes a court, who can oppose him?
11 Surely he recognizes deceitful men;
and when he sees evil, does he not take note?
12 But a witless man can no more become wise
than a wild donkey's colt can be born a man.[d]

13 "Yet if you devote your heart to him
and stretch out your hands to him,
14 if you put away the sin that is in your hand
and allow no evil to dwell in your tent,
15 then you will lift up your face without shame;

[a] 15 Or *and aware of* [b] 21 Or *and the shadow of death*; also in verse 22
[c] 8 Hebrew *than Sheol* [d] 12 Or *wild donkey can be born tame*

(11:6) Out of the depths I cry to You: O Lord, hear my voice. Let Your ears be attentive to my cry for mercy. If You, O Lord, kept a record of sins, who could stand? But with You there is forgiveness; therefore You are feared. I wait for You, Lord; my soul waits, and in Your word I put my hope. (Ps 130:1–5)

No one understands like Jesus;
He's a Friend beyond compare.
Meet Him at the throne of mercy;
He is waiting for you there.

No one understands like Jesus
When you falter on the way.
Tho' you fail Him, sadly fail Him,
He will pardon you today.

"No One Understands Like Jesus"
John W. Peterson (©1952)

(12:4–5) I love You, Lord, because You hear my voice; You hear my cry for mercy. Because You turn Your ear to me, I will call on You as long as I live. For You are gracious and righteous and full of compassion. I will be at rest because You are good to me. For You do not have contempt for my suffering; rather, it is in my suffering that I know Your closest fellowship. (Ps 116:1–7; Php 3:10)

God puts his ear so closely down to your lips that he can hear your faintest whisper. It is not God away off up yonder; it is God away down here, close up—so close up that when you pray to him, it is more a kiss than a whisper.

Thomas De Witt Talmage (1832-1902)

(12:7–9) God of Creation, all Your works speak of Your glory and wisdom, of Your eternal power and divine nature. You have carefully and intricately designed every creature, human or animal, great or small, with Your skillful hands. How fearfully and wonderfully you have made us! Lord, when we look upon Your creation and fail to see Your fingerprint revealed in it, we have no excuse. (Ps 139:13–16; Ro 1:20)

you will stand firm and without fear.
16 You will surely forget your trouble,
recalling it only as waters gone by.
17 Life will be brighter than noonday,
and darkness will become like morning.
18 You will be secure, because there is hope;
you will look about you and take your rest in safety.
19 You will lie down, with no one to make you afraid,
and many will court your favor.
20 But the eyes of the wicked will fail,
and escape will elude them;
their hope will become a dying gasp."

Job 12

Then Job replied:

2 "Doubtless you are the people,
and wisdom will die with you!
3 But I have a mind as well as you;
I am not inferior to you.
Who does not know all these things?

4 "I have become a laughingstock to my friends,
though I called upon God and he answered—
a mere laughingstock, though righteous and blameless!
5 Men at ease have contempt for misfortune
as the fate of those whose feet are slipping.
6 The tents of marauders are undisturbed,
and those who provoke God are secure—
those who carry their god in their hands.[a]

7 "But ask the animals, and they will teach you,
or the birds of the air, and they will tell you;
8 or speak to the earth, and it will teach you,
or let the fish of the sea inform you.
9 Which of all these does not know
that the hand of the LORD has done this?
10 In his hand is the life of every creature
and the breath of all mankind.
11 Does not the ear test words
as the tongue tastes food?
12 Is not wisdom found among the aged?
Does not long life bring understanding?

13 "To God belong wisdom and power;
counsel and understanding are his.
14 What he tears down cannot be rebuilt;
the man he imprisons cannot be released.
15 If he holds back the waters, there is drought;
if he lets them loose, they devastate the land.
16 To him belong strength and victory;
both deceived and deceiver are his.
17 He leads counselors away stripped
and makes fools of judges.
18 He takes off the shackles put on by kings

[a] 6 Or *secure / in what God's hand brings them*

and ties a loincloth[a] around their waist.
19 He leads priests away stripped
and overthrows men long established.
20 He silences the lips of trusted advisers
and takes away the discernment of elders.
21 He pours contempt on nobles
and disarms the mighty.
22 He reveals the deep things of darkness
and brings deep shadows into the light.
23 He makes nations great, and destroys them;
he enlarges nations, and disperses them.
24 He deprives the leaders of the earth of their reason;
he sends them wandering through a trackless waste.
25 They grope in darkness with no light;
he makes them stagger like drunkards.

13 "My eyes have seen all this,
my ears have heard and understood it.
2 What you know, I also know;
I am not inferior to you.
3 But I desire to speak to the Almighty
and to argue my case with God.
4 You, however, smear me with lies;
you are worthless physicians, all of you!
5 If only you would be altogether silent!
For you, that would be wisdom.
6 Hear now my argument;
listen to the plea of my lips.
7 Will you speak wickedly on God's behalf?
Will you speak deceitfully for him?
8 Will you show him partiality?
Will you argue the case for God?
9 Would it turn out well if he examined you?
Could you deceive him as you might deceive men?
10 He would surely rebuke you
if you secretly showed partiality.
11 Would not his splendor terrify you?
Would not the dread of him fall on you?
12 Your maxims are proverbs of ashes;
your defenses are defenses of clay.

13 "Keep silent and let me speak;
then let come to me what may.
14 Why do I put myself in jeopardy
and take my life in my hands?
15 Though he slay me, yet will I hope in him;
I will surely[b] defend my ways to his face.
16 Indeed, this will turn out for my deliverance,
for no godless man would dare come before him!
17 Listen carefully to my words;
let your ears take in what I say.
18 Now that I have prepared my case,
I know I will be vindicated.
19 Can anyone bring charges against me?
If so, I will be silent and die.

[a] 18 Or *shackles of kings / and ties a belt* [b] 15 Or *He will surely slay me; I have no hope — / yet I will*

(12:23) How tragic it is, Father, when we, Your people, live in fear of world powers and rulers who do not acknowledge You. What are they but mere mortals? You have taught us not to fear those who can only kill the body. Eternity is in Your hands. The boundaries of the nations have been set. We bow in awe before You. (Mt 10:28)

(13:15–19) Help me to trust You as Job trusted You in the face of adversity. Give me strength to cling to Your promise that the one You love will rest between Your shoulders. Help me to live a life of integrity and obedience so that I may come before You with a clean conscience. Righteous and merciful God, I look to You alone for deliverance, vindication and peace. (Dt 33:12)

My way is very simple. My soul lives on God, by a glance of love between him and myself. By this glance God gives himself to me, and I give myself to him. This is my habitual state, that in which God has placed me. I neither can nor should turn myself from it on account of suffering. This I accept as inseparable from love here below. Love suffers as the voice sings.

Lucie Christine (1858-1916)

(14:5) Sovereign Lord, You hold my times and my seasons in Your mighty hands. No amount of worrying can add a single hour to my life. So I will not fret about tomorrow, but I will seek You and Your righteousness, releasing the outcome of my life's pilgrimage to You. Thank You for being a wise and trustworthy Steward of my days and a sovereign Protector of my appointed years. (Ecc 3:1–8; Mt 6:27,33–34)

Have Faith in God.
Let your hope rest on the Faith
He has placed in your heart.
Never give up,
Never let go of the Faith
He has placed in your heart.

"Have Faith in God"
Geoff Bullock (©1993)

(14:14) Heavenly Father, because You have raised Jesus from the dead, we who die in Him will be raised to a new life with You. You have taken the sting from death, and You have turned death's defeat into victory. Thank You for the power of Christ's resurrection, and for making it available to us. (1 Co 15:54)

20 "Only grant me these two things, O God,
and then I will not hide from you:
21 Withdraw your hand far from me,
and stop frightening me with your terrors.
22 Then summon me and I will answer,
or let me speak, and you reply.
23 How many wrongs and sins have I committed?
Show me my offense and my sin.
24 Why do you hide your face
and consider me your enemy?
25 Will you torment a windblown leaf?
Will you chase after dry chaff?
26 For you write down bitter things against me
and make me inherit the sins of my youth.
27 You fasten my feet in shackles;
you keep close watch on all my paths
by putting marks on the soles of my feet.

28 "So man wastes away like something rotten,
like a garment eaten by moths.

14 "Man born of woman
is of few days and full of trouble.
2 He springs up like a flower and withers away;
like a fleeting shadow, he does not endure.
3 Do you fix your eye on such a one?
Will you bring him[a] before you for judgment?
4 Who can bring what is pure from the impure?
No one!
5 Man's days are determined;
you have decreed the number of his months
and have set limits he cannot exceed.
6 So look away from him and let him alone,
till he has put in his time like a hired man.
7 "At least there is hope for a tree:
If it is cut down, it will sprout again,
and its new shoots will not fail.
8 Its roots may grow old in the ground
and its stump die in the soil,
9 yet at the scent of water it will bud
and put forth shoots like a plant.
10 But man dies and is laid low;
he breathes his last and is no more.
11 As water disappears from the sea
or a riverbed becomes parched and dry,
12 so man lies down and does not rise;
till the heavens are no more, men will not
awake
or be roused from their sleep.

13 "If only you would hide me in the grave[b]
and conceal me till your anger has passed!
If only you would set me a time
and then remember me!
14 If a man dies, will he live again?
All the days of my hard service

[a] *3* Septuagint, Vulgate and Syriac; Hebrew *me* [b] *13* Hebrew *Sheol*

I will wait for my renewal[a] to come.
15 You will call and I will answer you;
you will long for the creature your hands have made.
16 Surely then you will count my steps
but not keep track of my sin.
17 My offenses will be sealed up in a bag;
you will cover over my sin.

18 "But as a mountain erodes and crumbles
and as a rock is moved from its place,
19 as water wears away stones
and torrents wash away the soil,
so you destroy man's hope.
20 You overpower him once for all, and he is gone;
you change his countenance and send him away.
21 If his sons are honored, he does not know it;
if they are brought low, he does not see it.
22 He feels but the pain of his own body
and mourns only for himself."

Eliphaz

15 Then Eliphaz the Temanite replied:

2 "Would a wise man answer with empty notions
or fill his belly with the hot east wind?
3 Would he argue with useless words,
with speeches that have no value?
4 But you even undermine piety
and hinder devotion to God.
5 Your sin prompts your mouth;
you adopt the tongue of the crafty.
6 Your own mouth condemns you, not mine;
your own lips testify against you.

7 "Are you the first man ever born?
Were you brought forth before the hills?
8 Do you listen in on God's council?
Do you limit wisdom to yourself?
9 What do you know that we do not know?
What insights do you have that we do not have?
10 The gray-haired and the aged are on our side,
men even older than your father.
11 Are God's consolations not enough for you,
words spoken gently to you?
12 Why has your heart carried you away,
and why do your eyes flash,
13 so that you vent your rage against God
and pour out such words from your mouth?

14 "What is man, that he could be pure,
or one born of woman, that he could be righteous?
15 If God places no trust in his holy ones,
if even the heavens are not pure in his eyes,
16 how much less man, who is vile and corrupt,
who drinks up evil like water!

[a] 14 Or *release*

(14:17) Lord Jesus, Lamb of God, You have once and for all covered my sins by the blood that You shed on the cross. Because of what You have done for me God will never treat me as my sins deserve or repay me according to my iniquity. How can I ever praise You enough? (Ps 103:10; Mic 7:18–20)

(15:2–6) Father, You have not spoken kindly to those, like Job's friends, who trust in their own righteousness. You have firmly warned me to remove the plank from my own eye before I concern myself with another's vision. Thank You for Your refusal to tolerate human pride and for sending Your Spirit to detect it in my heart. Cleanse me from self-righteousness. Make me humble, so that You can be fully glorified, and, as I learn humility, lift me up in due season according to Your purposes—not according to mine. (Lk 6:41–42)

He whose garments are the whitest will best perceive the spots upon them. He whose crown shines the brightest will know when he has lost a jewel. He who gives the most light to the world will always be able to discover his own darkness.

Charles Haddon Spurgeon (1834-1892)

17 "Listen to me and I will explain to you;
let me tell you what I have seen,
18 what wise men have declared,
hiding nothing received from their fathers
19 (to whom alone the land was given
when no alien passed among them):
20 All his days the wicked man suffers torment,
the ruthless through all the years stored up for him.
21 Terrifying sounds fill his ears;
when all seems well, marauders attack him.
22 He despairs of escaping the darkness;
he is marked for the sword.
23 He wanders about—food for vultures[a];
he knows the day of darkness is at hand.
24 Distress and anguish fill him with terror;
they overwhelm him, like a king poised to attack,
25 because he shakes his fist at God
and vaunts himself against the Almighty,
26 defiantly charging against him
with a thick, strong shield.

27 "Though his face is covered with fat
and his waist bulges with flesh,
28 he will inhabit ruined towns
and houses where no one lives,
houses crumbling to rubble.
29 He will no longer be rich and his wealth will not endure,
nor will his possessions spread over the land.
30 He will not escape the darkness;
a flame will wither his shoots,
and the breath of God's mouth will carry him away.
31 Let him not deceive himself by trusting what is worthless,
for he will get nothing in return.
32 Before his time he will be paid in full,
and his branches will not flourish.
33 He will be like a vine stripped of its unripe grapes,
like an olive tree shedding its blossoms.
34 For the company of the godless will be barren,
and fire will consume the tents of those who love bribes.
35 They conceive trouble and give birth to evil;
their womb fashions deceit."

Job
16

Then Job replied:

2 "I have heard many things like these;
miserable comforters are you all!
3 Will your long-winded speeches never end?
What ails you that you keep on arguing?
4 I also could speak like you,
if you were in my place;

(16:2–3) God of all comfort, give me well-spoken words of grace and truth for those whom You place under my care. How well I know that the tongue has the power of life and the power of death. I want to be a means of mercy, not a means of misery, to the broken. As You fill my heart with Your glory, so also fill my mouth with Your wisdom. (Pr 18:21; 2Co 1:3–4; Jas 3:1–12)

[a] 23 Or *about, looking for food*

I could make fine speeches against you
and shake my head at you.
5 But my mouth would encourage you;
comfort from my lips would bring you relief.

6 "Yet if I speak, my pain is not relieved;
and if I refrain, it does not go away.
7 Surely, O God, you have worn me out;
you have devastated my entire household.
8 You have bound me—and it has become a witness;
my gauntness rises up and testifies against me.
9 God assails me and tears me in his anger
and gnashes his teeth at me;
my opponent fastens on me his piercing eyes.
10 Men open their mouths to jeer at me;
they strike my cheek in scorn
and unite together against me.
11 God has turned me over to evil men
and thrown me into the clutches of the wicked.
12 All was well with me, but he shattered me;
he seized me by the neck and crushed me.
He has made me his target;
13 his archers surround me.
Without pity, he pierces my kidneys
and spills my gall on the ground.
14 Again and again he bursts upon me;
he rushes at me like a warrior.

15 "I have sewed sackcloth over my skin
and buried my brow in the dust.
16 My face is red with weeping,
deep shadows ring my eyes;
17 yet my hands have been free of violence
and my prayer is pure.

18 "O earth, do not cover my blood;
may my cry never be laid to rest!
19 Even now my witness is in heaven;
my advocate is on high.
20 My intercessor is my friend[a]
as my eyes pour out tears to God;
21 on behalf of a man he pleads with God
as a man pleads for his friend.

22 "Only a few years will pass
before I go on the journey of no return.

17 1 My spirit is broken,
my days are cut short,
the grave awaits me.
2 Surely mockers surround me;
my eyes must dwell on their hostility.

3 "Give me, O God, the pledge you demand.
Who else will put up security for me?
4 You have closed their minds to understanding;
therefore you will not let them triumph.
5 If a man denounces his friends for reward,

[a] 20 Or *My friends treat me with scorn*

Usually prayer is a question of groaning rather than speaking, tears rather than words. For He sets our tears in His sight, and our groaning is not hidden from Him who made all things by His Word and does not ask for words of man.

Saint Augustine of Hippo (354–430)

(16:20–21) Job's cry for an advocate in suffering is a cry that has echoed throughout all of human history. And it is a cry that has echoed throughout my history as well. Jesus, my Friend, You are my Advocate. You intercede for me day and night, pleading with the Father on my behalf. In doing so You are able to save me completely. How I thank You for Your eternal friendship and for taking up my case and presenting it to God. (Lam 3:58; Heb 7:24–26)

Alleluia! Bread of angels,
Thou on earth our food, our stay!
Alleluia! Here the sinful
Flee to Thee from day to day.
Intercessor, Friend of sinners,
Earth's Redeemer, plead for me,
Where the songs of all the sinless
Sweep across the crystal sea.

"Alleluia! Sing to Jesus!"
William Chatterton Dix (1866)

(17:13–15) I have great hope in Your saving power, O God. For You are present with me in the depths of despair. If I spread out my bed in darkness, "even the darkness will not be dark to you; the night will shine like the day, for darkness is as light to you." So even in death there is hope: hope for peace with You; hope in seeing Your face; hope in hearing Your voice; hope for the resurrection; hope in Your promise that You will one day wipe every tear from my eyes. (Ps 139:12; Rev 21:4)

Death is not the end; it is only a new beginning. Death is not the master of the house; he is only the porter at the King's lodge, appointed to open the gate and let the King's guests into the realm of eternal day.

John Henry Jowett (1864-1923)

Like a child in the womb,
Like the Son of God concealed
within the tomb,
Light will come once again.
The dark is just the middle, not the
end.

"Seasons of the Soul"
Jamie Owens-Collins (©1996)

the eyes of his children will fail.

6 "God has made me a byword to everyone,
a man in whose face people spit.
7 My eyes have grown dim with grief;
my whole frame is but a shadow.
8 Upright men are appalled at this;
the innocent are aroused against the ungodly.
9 Nevertheless, the righteous will hold to their ways,
and those with clean hands will grow stronger.

10 "But come on, all of you, try again!
I will not find a wise man among you.
11 My days have passed, my plans are shattered,
and so are the desires of my heart.
12 These men turn night into day;
in the face of darkness they say, 'Light is near.'
13 If the only home I hope for is the grave,[a]
if I spread out my bed in darkness,
14 if I say to corruption, 'You are my father,'
and to the worm, 'My mother' or 'My sister,'
15 where then is my hope?
Who can see any hope for me?
16 Will it go down to the gates of death[a]?
Will we descend together into the dust?"

Bildad

18 Then Bildad the Shuhite replied:

2 "When will you end these speeches?
Be sensible, and then we can talk.
3 Why are we regarded as cattle
and considered stupid in your sight?
4 You who tear yourself to pieces in your anger,
is the earth to be abandoned for your sake?
Or must the rocks be moved from their place?

5 "The lamp of the wicked is snuffed out;
the flame of his fire stops burning.
6 The light in his tent becomes dark;
the lamp beside him goes out.
7 The vigor of his step is weakened;
his own schemes throw him down.
8 His feet thrust him into a net
and he wanders into its mesh.
9 A trap seizes him by the heel;
a snare holds him fast.
10 A noose is hidden for him on the ground;
a trap lies in his path.
11 Terrors startle him on every side
and dog his every step.
12 Calamity is hungry for him;
disaster is ready for him when he falls.
13 It eats away parts of his skin;
death's firstborn devours his limbs.
14 He is torn from the security of his tent
and marched off to the king of terrors.

[a] *13,16* Hebrew *Sheol*

15 Fire resides[a] in his tent;
burning sulfur is scattered over his dwelling.
16 His roots dry up below
and his branches wither above.
17 The memory of him perishes from the earth;
he has no name in the land.
18 He is driven from light into darkness
and is banished from the world.
19 He has no offspring or descendants among his people,
no survivor where once he lived.
20 Men of the west are appalled at his fate;
men of the east are seized with horror.
21 Surely such is the dwelling of an evil man;
such is the place of one who knows not God."

Job

19 Then Job replied:

2 "How long will you torment me
and crush me with words?
3 Ten times now you have reproached me;
shamelessly you attack me.
4 If it is true that I have gone astray,
my error remains my concern alone.
5 If indeed you would exalt yourselves above me
and use my humiliation against me,
6 then know that God has wronged me
and drawn his net around me.

7 "Though I cry, 'I've been wronged!' I get no response;
though I call for help, there is no justice.
8 He has blocked my way so I cannot pass;
he has shrouded my paths in darkness.
9 He has stripped me of my honor
and removed the crown from my head.
10 He tears me down on every side till I am gone;
he uproots my hope like a tree.
11 His anger burns against me;
he counts me among his enemies.
12 His troops advance in force;
they build a siege ramp against me
and encamp around my tent.

13 "He has alienated my brothers from me;
my acquaintances are completely estranged from me.
14 My kinsmen have gone away;
my friends have forgotten me.
15 My guests and my maidservants count me a stranger;
they look upon me as an alien.
16 I summon my servant, but he does not answer,
though I beg him with my own mouth.
17 My breath is offensive to my wife;
I am loathsome to my own brothers.
18 Even the little boys scorn me;
when I appear, they ridicule me.

[a] 15 Or *Nothing he had remains*

I wonder many times that ever a child of God should have a sad heart, considering what the Lord is preparing for him.
Samuel Rutherford (1600-1661)

(19:7–12) How often have I blamed You for my hardships? If in my frustration and pain I have lashed out at You and accused You of wrong, please forgive me, Father. Help me to trust You. Give me faith to see, as the apostle Paul saw, that "our present sufferings are not worth comparing with the glory that will be revealed in us." While I wait for deliverance, send Your Holy Spirit to help me in my weakness. When I do not know how to pray and my words have given way to groanings, may Your Spirit intercede for me in accordance with Your will. Give me strength to cling to Your promise that in all things You work for the good of those who love You, conforming us into the likeness of Your Son. (Ro 8:18–29)

(19:25–27) Lord, I have this same confidence: "I know that my Redeemer lives." His name is Jesus, and He is alive forevermore. No matter what else I am in doubt about, no matter what mysteries remain unsolved, no matter what I know only in part or see from afar, this I know in full today: Lord Jesus, You have redeemed me from sin and death and You are alive! And one day, I will see You in all of Your glory.

I know that my Redeemer lives:
What joy this blest assurance gives!
He lives, He lives, who once was
dead;
He lives, my everlasting Head!

He lives, to bless me with His love;
He lives to plead for me above;
He lives, my hungry soul to feed;
He lives, to help in time of need.

He lives, and grants me daily breath;
He lives, and I shall conquer death;
He lives, my future to prepare;
He lives, to bring me safely there.

"I Know That My Redeemer Lives"
Samuel Medley (1738-1799)

19 All my intimate friends detest me;
those I love have turned against me.
20 I am nothing but skin and bones;
I have escaped with only the skin of my teeth.[a]

21 "Have pity on me, my friends, have pity,
for the hand of God has struck me.
22 Why do you pursue me as God does?
Will you never get enough of my flesh?

23 "Oh, that my words were recorded,
that they were written on a scroll,
24 that they were inscribed with an iron tool on[b] lead,
or engraved in rock forever!
25 I know that my Redeemer[c] lives,
and that in the end he will stand upon the earth.[d]
26 And after my skin has been destroyed,
yet[e] in[f] my flesh I will see God;
27 I myself will see him
with my own eyes—I, and not another.
How my heart yearns within me!

28 "If you say, 'How we will hound him,
since the root of the trouble lies in him,[g]'
29 you should fear the sword yourselves;
for wrath will bring punishment by the sword,
and then you will know that there is judgment.[h]"

Zophar

20

Then Zophar the Naamathite replied:

2 "My troubled thoughts prompt me to answer
because I am greatly disturbed.
3 I hear a rebuke that dishonors me,
and my understanding inspires me to reply.

4 "Surely you know how it has been from of old,
ever since man[i] was placed on the earth,
5 that the mirth of the wicked is brief,
the joy of the godless lasts but a moment.
6 Though his pride reaches to the heavens
and his head touches the clouds,
7 he will perish forever, like his own dung;
those who have seen him will say, 'Where is he?'
8 Like a dream he flies away, no more to be found,
banished like a vision of the night.
9 The eye that saw him will not see him again;
his place will look on him no more.
10 His children must make amends to the poor;
his own hands must give back his wealth.
11 The youthful vigor that fills his bones
will lie with him in the dust.

12 "Though evil is sweet in his mouth
and he hides it under his tongue,
13 though he cannot bear to let it go

[a] 20 Or *only my gums* [b] 24 Or *and* [c] 25 Or *defender* [d] 25 Or *upon my grave* [e] 26 Or *And after I awake, / though this ⌊body⌋ has been destroyed, / then* [f] 26 Or / *apart from* [g] 28 Many Hebrew manuscripts, Septuagint and Vulgate; most Hebrew manuscripts *me* [h] 29 Or / *that you may come to know the Almighty* [i] 4 Or *Adam*

and keeps it in his mouth,
14 yet his food will turn sour in his stomach;
it will become the venom of serpents within him.
15 He will spit out the riches he swallowed;
God will make his stomach vomit them up.
16 He will suck the poison of serpents;
the fangs of an adder will kill him.
17 He will not enjoy the streams,
the rivers flowing with honey and cream.
18 What he toiled for he must give back uneaten;
he will not enjoy the profit from his trading.
19 For he has oppressed the poor and left them
destitute;
he has seized houses he did not build.

20 "Surely he will have no respite from his craving;
he cannot save himself by his treasure.
21 Nothing is left for him to devour;
his prosperity will not endure.
22 In the midst of his plenty, distress will overtake him;
the full force of misery will come upon him.
23 When he has filled his belly,
God will vent his burning anger against him
and rain down his blows upon him.
24 Though he flees from an iron weapon,
a bronze-tipped arrow pierces him.
25 He pulls it out of his back,
the gleaming point out of his liver.
Terrors will come over him;
26 total darkness lies in wait for his treasures.
A fire unfanned will consume him
and devour what is left in his tent.
27 The heavens will expose his guilt;
the earth will rise up against him.
28 A flood will carry off his house,
rushing waters[a] on the day of God's wrath.
29 Such is the fate God allots the wicked,
the heritage appointed for them by God."

Job 21

Then Job replied:

2 "Listen carefully to my words;
let this be the consolation you give me.
3 Bear with me while I speak,
and after I have spoken, mock on.

4 "Is my complaint directed to man?
Why should I not be impatient?
5 Look at me and be astonished;
clap your hand over your mouth.
6 When I think about this, I am terrified;
trembling seizes my body.
7 Why do the wicked live on,
growing old and increasing in power?
8 They see their children established around them,

[a] 28 Or *The possessions in his house will be carried off, / washed away*

(20:29) Holy and righteous God, like all humans I am tainted with evil. My spirit is warped by sin, and my character is twisted by selfishness. Have mercy on me, Lord God, for the sake of Your Son Jesus. He paid the price for my unworthy nature. He redeemed me from Your judgment; he rescued me from my appropriate fate. Hear Him as He pleads for me, Father. Forgive my unrighteousness as You look upon His perfect sacrifice. (Heb 7:25)

Christ's death on the cross included a sacrifice for all our sins, past, present, and future. Every sin that you will ever commit has already been paid for. All of our sins were future when Christ died two thousand years ago. There is no sin that you will ever commit that has not already been included in Christ's death.

Erwin W. Lutzer (1941-)

(21:5) Until I am willing to acknowledge the depth of the misery of the broken, I am in no position to counsel them, Father. Forgive me when I would attempt to heal painful wounds in a light and superficial way. Free me to weep with those who weep and to comfort those who mourn.

(21:7–15) "Better a poor man whose walk is blameless than a rich man whose ways are perverse." Father, why do the wicked prosper? Those who care the least about Your ways seem to enjoy the most prosperity. Those who worry the least about pleasing You seem to have the fewest anxieties. Those who refuse to share their wealth seem to have the most luxuries to flaunt. Remember me, Father, and keep me from discouragement. You are a righteous Judge, O God, and Your eyes look from eternity to this present world. Deliver me from shortsightedness, teach me to pray for the everlasting souls of my enemies, and reassure me of Your favor. (Pr 28:6)

(21:27) It has often been said that we, Your people, are the only army that shoots its own wounded. How sad, how tragic indeed. What must the watching world think of us as they see the graceless ways in which we bite and devour one another? And worse, what do they think of You in light of our unloving ways? Father, forgive us. Father, forgive me.

Mercy imitates God and disappoints Satan.

Saint John Chrysostom (c.347-407)

their offspring before their eyes.
9 Their homes are safe and free from fear;
the rod of God is not upon them.
10 Their bulls never fail to breed;
their cows calve and do not miscarry.
11 They send forth their children as a flock;
their little ones dance about.
12 They sing to the music of tambourine and harp;
they make merry to the sound of the flute.
13 They spend their years in prosperity
and go down to the grave[a] in peace.[b]
14 Yet they say to God, 'Leave us alone!
We have no desire to know your ways.
15 Who is the Almighty, that we should serve him?
What would we gain by praying to him?'
16 But their prosperity is not in their own hands,
so I stand aloof from the counsel of the wicked.

17 "Yet how often is the lamp of the wicked snuffed out?
How often does calamity come upon them,
the fate God allots in his anger?
18 How often are they like straw before the wind,
like chaff swept away by a gale?
19 ⌊It is said,⌋ 'God stores up a man's punishment for his sons.'
Let him repay the man himself, so that he will know it!
20 Let his own eyes see his destruction;
let him drink of the wrath of the Almighty.[c]
21 For what does he care about the family he leaves behind
when his allotted months come to an end?

22 "Can anyone teach knowledge to God,
since he judges even the highest?
23 One man dies in full vigor,
completely secure and at ease,
24 his body[d] well nourished,
his bones rich with marrow.
25 Another man dies in bitterness of soul,
never having enjoyed anything good.
26 Side by side they lie in the dust,
and worms cover them both.

27 "I know full well what you are thinking,
the schemes by which you would wrong me.
28 You say, 'Where now is the great man's house,
the tents where wicked men lived?'
29 Have you never questioned those who travel?
Have you paid no regard to their accounts—
30 that the evil man is spared from the day of calamity,
that he is delivered from[e] the day of wrath?
31 Who denounces his conduct to his face?

[a] *13* Hebrew *Sheol* [b] *13* Or *in an instant* [c] *17–20* Verses 17 and 18 may be taken as exclamations and 19 and 20 as declarations. [d] *24* The meaning of the Hebrew for this word is uncertain. [e] *30* Or *man is reserved for the day of calamity, / that he is brought forth to*

Who repays him for what he has done?
32 He is carried to the grave,
and watch is kept over his tomb.
33 The soil in the valley is sweet to him;
all men follow after him,
and a countless throng goes[a] before him.

34 "So how can you console me with your nonsense?
Nothing is left of your answers but falsehood!"

Eliphaz

22 Then Eliphaz the Temanite replied:

2 "Can a man be of benefit to God?
Can even a wise man benefit him?
3 What pleasure would it give the Almighty if you were righteous?
What would he gain if your ways were blameless?

4 "Is it for your piety that he rebukes you
and brings charges against you?
5 Is not your wickedness great?
Are not your sins endless?
6 You demanded security from your brothers for no reason;
you stripped men of their clothing, leaving them naked.
7 You gave no water to the weary
and you withheld food from the hungry,
8 though you were a powerful man, owning land—
an honored man, living on it.
9 And you sent widows away empty-handed
and broke the strength of the fatherless.
10 That is why snares are all around you,
why sudden peril terrifies you,
11 why it is so dark you cannot see,
and why a flood of water covers you.

12 "Is not God in the heights of heaven?
And see how lofty are the highest stars!
13 Yet you say, 'What does God know?
Does he judge through such darkness?
14 Thick clouds veil him, so he does not see us
as he goes about in the vaulted heavens.'
15 Will you keep to the old path
that evil men have trod?
16 They were carried off before their time,
their foundations washed away by a flood.
17 They said to God, 'Leave us alone!
What can the Almighty do to us?'
18 Yet it was he who filled their houses with good things,
so I stand aloof from the counsel of the wicked.

19 "The righteous see their ruin and rejoice;
the innocent mock them, saying,
20 'Surely our foes are destroyed,
and fire devours their wealth.'

[a] 33 Or / *as a countless throng went*

The closer one is to God, the more one feels a sinner.

Louis Evely (1910-)

(22:5) Merciful God, I know that my sins are endless. If You were to number my sins I would be overwhelmed. If You were to show me the fullness of my wickedness I would be undone. But You are compassionate and gracious, slow to anger, abounding in love. You do not treat me as my sins deserve or repay me according to my iniquities. As far as the east is from the west, so far have You removed my transgressions from me. How can I ever praise You enough? (Ps 103:8–14)

All my life was full of sin when Jesus found me,
All my heart was full of misery and woe;
Jesus placed His strong and loving arms around me,
And He led me in the way I ought to go.

"No One Ever Cared for Me Like Jesus"
Charles F. Weigle (©1932)

(22:21) Gracious Father, there is no peace except that which comes through the work of Your Son upon the cross. There is no peace in my law keeping. There is no peace in my tearful penance. There is no peace in my vain promises of moral reform. There is no peace in my striving to merit Your forgiveness and acceptance. Jesus has done for me what I could never have done for myself. He has saved me! He is my peace, Father. I rest my weary and sinful soul fully upon Him.

(23:3) At times I feel as if You are absent, Father. Scripture tells me that You have gone nowhere, for You have promised never to leave me or forsake me, and You cannot lie. Yet at times I cannot seem to find You. My mind swirls with words of truth, but my heart feels so empty and cold. Be gracious unto me then, Lord, when my heart tells me one thing while my mind affirms another. This is my comfort—that Your grasp of me is far greater and stronger than my grasp of You. So I will rest even in my restlessness.

(23:10) Eternal God, Your crucible purifies me; Your flame blazes bright and hot. In Your wisdom You burn away old ways of thinking, past habits and worthless idols. In Your jealousy You incinerate those things that tarnish Your reflection on my heart. I thank You for Your severe mercy, Lord of heaven. You would not do this if I had no value to You. Cleanse my heart, and let what remains in me be a treasure worthy of Your household.

21 "Submit to God and be at peace with him;
in this way prosperity will come to you.
22 Accept instruction from his mouth
and lay up his words in your heart.
23 If you return to the Almighty, you will be restored:
If you remove wickedness far from your tent
24 and assign your nuggets to the dust,
your gold of Ophir to the rocks in the ravines,
25 then the Almighty will be your gold,
the choicest silver for you.
26 Surely then you will find delight in the Almighty
and will lift up your face to God.
27 You will pray to him, and he will hear you,
and you will fulfill your vows.
28 What you decide on will be done,
and light will shine on your ways.
29 When men are brought low and you say, 'Lift them up!'
then he will save the downcast.
30 He will deliver even one who is not innocent,
who will be delivered through the cleanness of your hands."

Job

23

Then Job replied:

2 "Even today my complaint is bitter;
his hand[a] is heavy in spite of[b] my groaning.
3 If only I knew where to find him;
if only I could go to his dwelling!
4 I would state my case before him
and fill my mouth with arguments.
5 I would find out what he would answer me,
and consider what he would say.
6 Would he oppose me with great power?
No, he would not press charges against me.
7 There an upright man could present his case before him,
and I would be delivered forever from my judge.

8 "But if I go to the east, he is not there;
if I go to the west, I do not find him.
9 When he is at work in the north, I do not see him;
when he turns to the south, I catch no glimpse of him.
10 But he knows the way that I take;
when he has tested me, I will come forth as gold.
11 My feet have closely followed his steps;
I have kept to his way without turning aside.
12 I have not departed from the commands of his lips;
I have treasured the words of his mouth more than my daily bread.

13 "But he stands alone, and who can oppose him?
He does whatever he pleases.

[a] 2 Septuagint and Syriac; Hebrew / *the hand on me* [b] 2 Or *heavy on me in*

14 He carries out his decree against me,
and many such plans he still has in store.
15 That is why I am terrified before him;
when I think of all this, I fear him.
16 God has made my heart faint;
the Almighty has terrified me.
17 Yet I am not silenced by the darkness,
by the thick darkness that covers my face.

24 "Why does the Almighty not set times for judgment?
Why must those who know him look in vain for such days?
2 Men move boundary stones;
they pasture flocks they have stolen.
3 They drive away the orphan's donkey
and take the widow's ox in pledge.
4 They thrust the needy from the path
and force all the poor of the land into hiding.
5 Like wild donkeys in the desert,
the poor go about their labor of foraging food;
the wasteland provides food for their children.
6 They gather fodder in the fields
and glean in the vineyards of the wicked.
7 Lacking clothes, they spend the night naked;
they have nothing to cover themselves in the cold.
8 They are drenched by mountain rains
and hug the rocks for lack of shelter.
9 The fatherless child is snatched from the breast;
the infant of the poor is seized for a debt.
10 Lacking clothes, they go about naked;
they carry the sheaves, but still go hungry.
11 They crush olives among the terraces[a];
they tread the winepresses, yet suffer thirst.
12 The groans of the dying rise from the city,
and the souls of the wounded cry out for help.
But God charges no one with wrongdoing.

13 "There are those who rebel against the light,
who do not know its ways
or stay in its paths.
14 When daylight is gone, the murderer rises up
and kills the poor and needy;
in the night he steals forth like a thief.
15 The eye of the adulterer watches for dusk;
he thinks, 'No eye will see me,'
and he keeps his face concealed.
16 In the dark, men break into houses,
but by day they shut themselves in;
they want nothing to do with the light.
17 For all of them, deep darkness is their morning[b];
they make friends with the terrors of darkness.[c]

18 "Yet they are foam on the surface of the water;
their portion of the land is cursed,

[a] *11* Or *olives between the millstones*; the meaning of the Hebrew for this word is uncertain. [b] *17* Or *them, their morning is like the shadow of death* [c] *17* Or *of the shadow of death*

Why stand we here trembling around calling on God for help, and not ourselves, in whom God dwells, stretching a hand to save the falling man?
William Blake (1757-1827)

(24:5–9) Loving Lord, my heart does not feel the plight of the poor and the defenseless the way Yours does. I hear You say, "The poor you will always have with you," and I become calloused and indifferent. I judge them. I ignore them. Forgive me, Lord; free this selfish heart of mine to give as freely as I have received. (Mt 26:11)

Soften my heart, Lord,
Soften my heart,
From all indifference set me apart,
To feel Your compassion,
To weep with Your tears,
Come soften my heart, oh Lord,
Soften my heart.

"Soften My Heart"
Graham Kendrick (©1987)

(25:3–6) Almighty God, Your forces are numberless, yet You choose to make peace with us. You have the right and the power to destroy us, but it is Your pleasure to show mercy. We are sustained by Your grace alone. The light of our righteousness is not even a flickering candle in the blazing sun of Your glory. Therefore, we have no reason to be proud before You, but we have every reason to be humble.

(26:4) Gracious Lord, help me to be quick to listen and slow to speak. Give me an instructed tongue and a sensitive heart to know the word that sustains the weary. Open my ears to listen to those who mourn, to those who are in distress, to those who need hope. O God, help me to listen like one being taught. Gentle Savior, may the Comforter in me bring comfort to the brokenhearted. (Isa 50:4; Jas 1:19)

One reason we can hardly bear to remain silent is that it makes us feel so helpless. We are so accustomed to relying upon words to manage and control others. If we are silent, who will take control? God will take control; but we will never let him take control until we trust him. Silence is intimately related to trust.

Richard J. Foster (1942-)

so that no one goes to the vineyards.
19 As heat and drought snatch away the melted snow,
so the grave[a] snatches away those who have sinned.
20 The womb forgets them,
the worm feasts on them;
evil men are no longer remembered
but are broken like a tree.
21 They prey on the barren and childless woman,
and to the widow show no kindness.
22 But God drags away the mighty by his power;
though they become established, they have no assurance of life.
23 He may let them rest in a feeling of security,
but his eyes are on their ways.
24 For a little while they are exalted, and then they are gone;
they are brought low and gathered up like all others;
they are cut off like heads of grain.
25 "If this is not so, who can prove me false
and reduce my words to nothing?"

Bildad

25 Then Bildad the Shuhite replied:

2 "Dominion and awe belong to God;
he establishes order in the heights of heaven.
3 Can his forces be numbered?
Upon whom does his light not rise?
4 How then can a man be righteous before God?
How can one born of woman be pure?
5 If even the moon is not bright
and the stars are not pure in his eyes,
6 how much less man, who is but a maggot—
a son of man, who is only a worm!"

Job

26 Then Job replied:

2 "How you have helped the powerless!
How you have saved the arm that is feeble!
3 What advice you have offered to one without wisdom!
And what great insight you have displayed!
4 Who has helped you utter these words?
And whose spirit spoke from your mouth?
5 "The dead are in deep anguish,
those beneath the waters and all that live in them.
6 Death[a] is naked before God;
Destruction[b] lies uncovered.
7 He spreads out the northern ⌞skies⌟ over empty space;
he suspends the earth over nothing.
8 He wraps up the waters in his clouds,
yet the clouds do not burst under their weight.
9 He covers the face of the full moon,

[a] *19,6* Hebrew *Sheol* [b] *6* Hebrew *Abaddon*

spreading his clouds over it.
10 He marks out the horizon on the face of the waters
for a boundary between light and darkness.
11 The pillars of the heavens quake,
aghast at his rebuke.
12 By his power he churned up the sea;
by his wisdom he cut Rahab to pieces.
13 By his breath the skies became fair;
his hand pierced the gliding serpent.
14 And these are but the outer fringe of his works;
how faint the whisper we hear of him!
Who then can understand the thunder of his
power?"

27

And Job continued his discourse:

2 "As surely as God lives, who has denied me justice,
the Almighty, who has made me taste bitterness of
soul,
3 as long as I have life within me,
the breath of God in my nostrils,
4 my lips will not speak wickedness,
and my tongue will utter no deceit.
5 I will never admit you are in the right;
till I die, I will not deny my integrity.
6 I will maintain my righteousness and never let go of it;
my conscience will not reproach me as long as I live.

7 "May my enemies be like the wicked,
my adversaries like the unjust!
8 For what hope has the godless when he is cut off,
when God takes away his life?
9 Does God listen to his cry
when distress comes upon him?
10 Will he find delight in the Almighty?
Will he call upon God at all times?

11 "I will teach you about the power of God;
the ways of the Almighty I will not conceal.
12 You have all seen this yourselves.
Why then this meaningless talk?

13 "Here is the fate God allots to the wicked,
the heritage a ruthless man receives from the
Almighty:
14 However many his children, their fate is the sword;
his offspring will never have enough to eat.
15 The plague will bury those who survive him,
and their widows will not weep for them.
16 Though he heaps up silver like dust
and clothes like piles of clay,
17 what he lays up the righteous will wear,
and the innocent will divide his silver.
18 The house he builds is like a moth's cocoon,
like a hut made by a watchman.
19 He lies down wealthy, but will do so no more;
when he opens his eyes, all is gone.
20 Terrors overtake him like a flood;

God, having made man to look upward, has therefore garnished the heavens, to invite him to look upward, that, by pleasing his eye with the dazzling light of the sun and the sparkling light of the stars, their number, order, and various magnitudes, which, as so many golden studs, beautify the canopy drawn over our heads, he may be led to admire the great Creator, the Father and fountain of lights, and to say, "If the pavement be so richly inlaid, what must the palace be!"

Matthew Henry (1662-1714)

(27:5–6) I pray for those who suffer on Your behalf, O Lord. I plead for those in prisons, in labor camps, in brutal circumstances all around the world, those who refuse to deny Your name, those who are captives of conscience. And God, as I pray for them, I pray for myself. Grant me the courage to die for You, and grant me the integrity to live for You, knowing that if I am faithful, even to the point of death, You will give me the crown of life. (Rev 2:10)

(28:12) Lord, You have charged me in all of my seeking to seek wisdom and understanding, to value them above gold and silver. You have given me an inexhaustible supply of riches in Your written Word and in the living Word, the Lord Jesus. I choose to live not as a fool but as Your child; help me as I seek that which You call lasting treasure. (Pr 3:13–14)

(28:20–23) Father, there is such a vast difference between Your wisdom and the wisdom of the world. There is no comparison, only contrast. And You have made it clear that the way to true wisdom, lasting wisdom, essential wisdom is found only in the cross of Your Son, Jesus. By the cross You have made foolish all of the so-called wisdom of this age. I will boast only in the cross and in its wisdom. (1Co 2:1–5)

a tempest snatches him away in the night.
21 The east wind carries him off, and he is gone;
it sweeps him out of his place.
22 It hurls itself against him without mercy
as he flees headlong from its power.
23 It claps its hands in derision
and hisses him out of his place.

28 "There is a mine for silver
and a place where gold is refined.
2 Iron is taken from the earth,
and copper is smelted from ore.
3 Man puts an end to the darkness;
he searches the farthest recesses
for ore in the blackest darkness.
4 Far from where people dwell he cuts a shaft,
in places forgotten by the foot of man;
far from men he dangles and sways.
5 The earth, from which food comes,
is transformed below as by fire;
6 sapphires[a] come from its rocks,
and its dust contains nuggets of gold.
7 No bird of prey knows that hidden path,
no falcon's eye has seen it.
8 Proud beasts do not set foot on it,
and no lion prowls there.
9 Man's hand assaults the flinty rock
and lays bare the roots of the mountains.
10 He tunnels through the rock;
his eyes see all its treasures.
11 He searches[b] the sources of the rivers
and brings hidden things to light.

12 "But where can wisdom be found?
Where does understanding dwell?
13 Man does not comprehend its worth;
it cannot be found in the land of the living.
14 The deep says, 'It is not in me';
the sea says, 'It is not with me.'
15 It cannot be bought with the finest gold,
nor can its price be weighed in silver.
16 It cannot be bought with the gold of Ophir,
with precious onyx or sapphires.
17 Neither gold nor crystal can compare with it,
nor can it be had for jewels of gold.
18 Coral and jasper are not worthy of mention;
the price of wisdom is beyond rubies.
19 The topaz of Cush cannot compare with it;
it cannot be bought with pure gold.

20 "Where then does wisdom come from?
Where does understanding dwell?
21 It is hidden from the eyes of every living thing,
concealed even from the birds of the air.
22 Destruction[c] and Death say,
'Only a rumor of it has reached our ears.'

[a] 6 Or *lapis lazuli*; also in verse 16 [b] 11 Septuagint, Aquila and Vulgate; Hebrew *He dams up* [c] 22 Hebrew *Abaddon*

23 God understands the way to it
and he alone knows where it dwells,
24 for he views the ends of the earth
and sees everything under the heavens.
25 When he established the force of the wind
and measured out the waters,
26 when he made a decree for the rain
and a path for the thunderstorm,
27 then he looked at wisdom and appraised it;
he confirmed it and tested it.
28 And he said to man,
'The fear of the Lord—that is wisdom,
and to shun evil is understanding.' "

29 Job continued his discourse:

2 "How I long for the months gone by,
for the days when God watched over me,
3 when his lamp shone upon my head
and by his light I walked through darkness!
4 Oh, for the days when I was in my prime,
when God's intimate friendship blessed my house,
5 when the Almighty was still with me
and my children were around me,
6 when my path was drenched with cream
and the rock poured out for me streams of olive oil.

7 "When I went to the gate of the city
and took my seat in the public square,
8 the young men saw me and stepped aside
and the old men rose to their feet;
9 the chief men refrained from speaking
and covered their mouths with their hands;
10 the voices of the nobles were hushed,
and their tongues stuck to the roof of their mouths.
11 Whoever heard me spoke well of me,
and those who saw me commended me,
12 because I rescued the poor who cried for help,
and the fatherless who had none to assist him.
13 The man who was dying blessed me;
I made the widow's heart sing.
14 I put on righteousness as my clothing;
justice was my robe and my turban.
15 I was eyes to the blind
and feet to the lame.
16 I was a father to the needy;
I took up the case of the stranger.
17 I broke the fangs of the wicked
and snatched the victims from their teeth.

18 "I thought, 'I will die in my own house,
my days as numerous as the grains of sand.
19 My roots will reach to the water,
and the dew will lie all night on my branches.
20 My glory will remain fresh in me,
the bow ever new in my hand.'

21 "Men listened to me expectantly,

(28:28) The truth You revealed to Job is still truth today—the fear of the Lord is wisdom. Lord, I long to live before You every day with affectionate reverence, with the awe and respect of which You are so worthy. Through the perfect love of Jesus, You have freed me from the fear of being rejected by You. Because I am now free from sin, I want to flee from sin. Keep my heart humble even as You have made my heart glad. This is wisdom indeed.

(29:2–5) Lord, You have always been there to lead me—a light shining in the darkness, a Friend who sticks closer than a brother. But in the seasons of my life, at times the skies have seemed to be made of steel and Your voice has been only a distant memory. Father, give me greater compassion for those who, like Job, are called to just such a place in their journey. Out of the comfort You have given me, help me to comfort Your children. As You lead them through the dark night of the soul, help them to remember that joy will come in the morning. Help them to endure so that the trial of their faith may result in praise; and as You strengthen their faith, so deepen Your friendship with them. (Ps 30:5; Pr 18:24; 2Co 1:3–4)

Those who can sit in silence with their fellowman, not knowing what to say but knowing that they should be there, can bring new life in a dying heart. Those who are not afraid to hold a hand in gratitude, to shed tears in grief and to let a sigh of distress arise straight from the heart can break through paralyzing boundaries and witness the birth of a new fellowship, the fellowship of the broken.

Henri J. M. Nouwen (1932-1996)

(29:23—30:23) Perhaps the most grievous aspect to our suffering is that it makes us contemptible to the ungodly. But I thank You, Lord, that You sympathize with our suffering, for You Yourself have suffered immeasurably more than Job or any other human. You endured the affliction of men. You endured the affliction of the cross. You endured the affliction of God Himself. For though Your suffering was at the hands of men, it was in the plan of God. I praise You, Lord Jesus, that in your great love for me and for Your Father you willingly endured unimaginable agony to save my soul from the agony of hell.

Suffering love, the cross, stands at the heart of the church.

T.Z. Koo

Upon the cross of Jesus
Mine eyes at times can see
The very dying form of One
Who suffered there for me.
And from my smitten heart, with
tears,
These wonders I confess:
The wonder of His glorious love,
And my unworthiness.

"Beneath the Cross of Jesus"
Elizabeth C. Clephane (1872)

waiting in silence for my counsel.
22 After I had spoken, they spoke no more;
my words fell gently on their ears.
23 They waited for me as for showers
and drank in my words as the spring rain.
24 When I smiled at them, they scarcely believed it;
the light of my face was precious to them.[a]
25 I chose the way for them and sat as their chief;
I dwelt as a king among his troops;
I was like one who comforts mourners.

30 "But now they mock me,
men younger than I,
whose fathers I would have disdained
to put with my sheep dogs.
2 Of what use was the strength of their hands to me,
since their vigor had gone from them?
3 Haggard from want and hunger,
they roamed[b] the parched land
in desolate wastelands at night.
4 In the brush they gathered salt herbs,
and their food[c] was the root of the broom tree.
5 They were banished from their fellow men,
shouted at as if they were thieves.
6 They were forced to live in the dry stream beds,
among the rocks and in holes in the ground.
7 They brayed among the bushes
and huddled in the undergrowth.
8 A base and nameless brood,
they were driven out of the land.

9 "And now their sons mock me in song;
I have become a byword among them.
10 They detest me and keep their distance;
they do not hesitate to spit in my face.
11 Now that God has unstrung my bow and afflicted me,
they throw off restraint in my presence.
12 On my right the tribe[d] attacks;
they lay snares for my feet,
they build their siege ramps against me.
13 They break up my road;
they succeed in destroying me—
without anyone's helping them.[e]
14 They advance as through a gaping breach;
amid the ruins they come rolling in.
15 Terrors overwhelm me;
my dignity is driven away as by the wind,
my safety vanishes like a cloud.

16 "And now my life ebbs away;
days of suffering grip me.
17 Night pierces my bones;
my gnawing pains never rest.
18 In his great power ⌞God⌟ becomes like clothing to me[f];
he binds me like the neck of my garment.

[a] *24* The meaning of the Hebrew for this clause is uncertain. [b] *3* Or *gnawed* [c] *4* Or *fuel* [d] *12* The meaning of the Hebrew for this word is uncertain. [e] *13* Or *me. / 'No one can help him,' ⌞they say⌟.* [f] *18* Hebrew; Septuagint *⌞God⌟ grasps my clothing*

19 He throws me into the mud,
and I am reduced to dust and ashes.

20 "I cry out to you, O God, but you do not answer;
I stand up, but you merely look at me.
21 You turn on me ruthlessly;
with the might of your hand you attack me.
22 You snatch me up and drive me before the wind;
you toss me about in the storm.
23 I know you will bring me down to death,
to the place appointed for all the living.

24 "Surely no one lays a hand on a broken man
when he cries for help in his distress.
25 Have I not wept for those in trouble?
Has not my soul grieved for the poor?
26 Yet when I hoped for good, evil came;
when I looked for light, then came darkness.
27 The churning inside me never stops;
days of suffering confront me.
28 I go about blackened, but not by the sun;
I stand up in the assembly and cry for help.
29 I have become a brother of jackals,
a companion of owls.
30 My skin grows black and peels;
my body burns with fever.
31 My harp is tuned to mourning,
and my flute to the sound of wailing.

31 "I made a covenant with my eyes
not to look lustfully at a girl.
2 For what is man's lot from God above,
his heritage from the Almighty on high?
3 Is it not ruin for the wicked,
disaster for those who do wrong?
4 Does he not see my ways
and count my every step?

5 "If I have walked in falsehood
or my foot has hurried after deceit—
6 let God weigh me in honest scales
and he will know that I am blameless—
7 if my steps have turned from the path,
if my heart has been led by my eyes,
or if my hands have been defiled,
8 then may others eat what I have sown,
and may my crops be uprooted.

9 "If my heart has been enticed by a woman,
or if I have lurked at my neighbor's door,
10 then may my wife grind another man's grain,
and may other men sleep with her.
11 For that would have been shameful,
a sin to be judged.
12 It is a fire that burns to Destruction[a];
it would have uprooted my harvest.

[a] 12 Hebrew *Abaddon*

(31:4) Sovereign Lord, even if I were innocent I could only ask You for mercy. You see my ways and count my every step. You know where You are taking me, and You know what I must go through to get there. Let each trial of my faith bring forth praise, glory and honor to You. If I survive, may it be in Your strength. If I fall, may it be into Your grace. Have mercy on me, Lord, and in Your mercy have Your way with me. (Job 9:15; 1Co 4:4; 1Pe 1:6–7)

Have Thine own way, Lord!
Have Thine own way!
Search me and try me,
Master, today.
Whiter than snow, Lord,
Wash me just now,
As in Thy presence
Humbly I bow.

"Have Thine Own Way, Lord!"
Adelaide A. Pollard (1902)

(31:24–28) Father, help me not to look for security in wealth. I do not want to be like the rich fool who built bigger barns for himself. Rather, I want to be rich toward You. True wealth does not consist of an abundance of possessions. True wealth consists in the knowledge of You. (Lk 12:18–20)

(31:29–30) Job knew that sinning against others is sinning against You. So out of his desire to live rightly before You, he lived rightly before others. Help me, Lord, to live this way before You. Forgive me for the times that I have sinned against my enemies. Though I knew You would show mercy, I have secretly longed for revenge, wishing upon them the suffering that I experienced. What is worse? To openly curse another or to secretly hope, even pray, for my enemies' destruction? God have mercy on me. Forgive me, for I have sinned against You. Possess my heart and fill it with the Holy Spirit so that words of love will flow from me.

13 "If I have denied justice to my menservants and maidservants
when they had a grievance against me,
14 what will I do when God confronts me?
What will I answer when called to account?
15 Did not he who made me in the womb make them?
Did not the same one form us both within our mothers?

16 "If I have denied the desires of the poor
or let the eyes of the widow grow weary,
17 if I have kept my bread to myself,
not sharing it with the fatherless—
18 but from my youth I reared him as would a father,
and from my birth I guided the widow—
19 if I have seen anyone perishing for lack of clothing,
or a needy man without a garment,
20 and his heart did not bless me
for warming him with the fleece from my sheep,
21 if I have raised my hand against the fatherless,
knowing that I had influence in court,
22 then let my arm fall from the shoulder,
let it be broken off at the joint.
23 For I dreaded destruction from God,
and for fear of his splendor I could not do such things.

24 "If I have put my trust in gold
or said to pure gold, 'You are my security,'
25 if I have rejoiced over my great wealth,
the fortune my hands had gained,
26 if I have regarded the sun in its radiance
or the moon moving in splendor,
27 so that my heart was secretly enticed
and my hand offered them a kiss of homage,
28 then these also would be sins to be judged,
for I would have been unfaithful to God on high.

29 "If I have rejoiced at my enemy's misfortune
or gloated over the trouble that came to him—
30 I have not allowed my mouth to sin
by invoking a curse against his life—
31 if the men of my household have never said,
'Who has not had his fill of Job's meat?'—
32 but no stranger had to spend the night in the street,
for my door was always open to the traveler—
33 if I have concealed my sin as men do,[a]
by hiding my guilt in my heart
34 because I so feared the crowd
and so dreaded the contempt of the clans
that I kept silent and would not go outside

35 ("Oh, that I had someone to hear me!
I sign now my defense—let the Almighty answer me;
let my accuser put his indictment in writing.
36 Surely I would wear it on my shoulder,
I would put it on like a crown.

[a] 33 Or *as Adam did*

37 I would give him an account of my every step;
like a prince I would approach him.)—
38 "if my land cries out against me
and all its furrows are wet with tears,
39 if I have devoured its yield without payment
or broken the spirit of its tenants,
40 then let briers come up instead of wheat
and weeds instead of barley."

The words of Job are ended.

Elihu

32 So these three men stopped answering Job, because he
was righteous in his own eyes. 2 But Elihu son of Barakel
the Buzite, of the family of Ram, became very angry with Job for
justifying himself rather than God. 3 He was also angry with the
three friends, because they had found no way to refute Job, and
yet had condemned him.[a] 4 Now Elihu had waited before speaking to Job because they were older than he. 5 But when he saw that
the three men had nothing more to say, his anger was aroused.
6 So Elihu son of Barakel the Buzite said:

"I am young in years,
and you are old;
that is why I was fearful,
not daring to tell you what I know.
7 I thought, 'Age should speak;
advanced years should teach wisdom.'
8 But it is the spirit[b] in a man,
the breath of the Almighty, that gives him
understanding.
9 It is not only the old[c] who are wise,
not only the aged who understand what is right.

10 "Therefore I say: Listen to me;
I too will tell you what I know.
11 I waited while you spoke,
I listened to your reasoning;
while you were searching for words,
12 I gave you my full attention.
But not one of you has proved Job wrong;
none of you has answered his arguments.
13 Do not say, 'We have found wisdom;
let God refute him, not man.'
14 But Job has not marshaled his words against me,
and I will not answer him with your arguments.

15 "They are dismayed and have no more to say;
words have failed them.
16 Must I wait, now that they are silent,
now that they stand there with no reply?
17 I too will have my say;
I too will tell what I know.
18 For I am full of words,
and the spirit within me compels me;
19 inside I am like bottled-up wine,

(32:8) Omniscient God, source of wisdom, breathe on me. Fill me with Your Spirit and so fill me with understanding. Renew my mind with the mind of Christ. As You lead me through the lessons of life, let me come through them with a deeper understanding of Your ways and a deeper respect for the suffering of others.

[a] *3* Masoretic Text; an ancient Hebrew scribal tradition *Job, and so had condemned God*
[b] *8* Or *Spirit*; also in verse 18 [c] *9* Or *many*; or *great*

like new wineskins ready to burst.
20 I must speak and find relief;
I must open my lips and reply.
21 I will show partiality to no one,
nor will I flatter any man;
22 for if I were skilled in flattery,
my Maker would soon take me away.

33 "But now, Job, listen to my words;
pay attention to everything I say.
2 I am about to open my mouth;
my words are on the tip of my tongue.
3 My words come from an upright heart;
my lips sincerely speak what I know.
4 The Spirit of God has made me;
the breath of the Almighty gives me life.
5 Answer me then, if you can;
prepare yourself and confront me.
6 I am just like you before God;
I too have been taken from clay.
7 No fear of me should alarm you,
nor should my hand be heavy upon you.

8 "But you have said in my hearing—
I heard the very words—
9 'I am pure and without sin;
I am clean and free from guilt.
10 Yet God has found fault with me;
he considers me his enemy.
11 He fastens my feet in shackles;
he keeps close watch on all my paths.'

12 "But I tell you, in this you are not right,
for God is greater than man.
13 Why do you complain to him
that he answers none of man's words[a]?
14 For God does speak—now one way, now another—
though man may not perceive it.
15 In a dream, in a vision of the night,
when deep sleep falls on men
as they slumber in their beds,
16 he may speak in their ears
and terrify them with warnings,
17 to turn man from wrongdoing
and keep him from pride,
18 to preserve his soul from the pit,[b]
his life from perishing by the sword.[c]
19 Or a man may be chastened on a bed of pain
with constant distress in his bones,
20 so that his very being finds food repulsive
and his soul loathes the choicest meal.
21 His flesh wastes away to nothing,
and his bones, once hidden, now stick out.
22 His soul draws near to the pit,[d]
and his life to the messengers of death.[e]

[a] 13 Or *that he does not answer for any of his actions* [b] 18 Or *preserve him from the grave* [c] 18 Or *from crossing the River* [d] 22 Or *He draws near to the grave* [e] 22 Or *to the dead*

(33:14) When You speak I do not always listen. Lord, give me ears to hear, a heart to receive and a mind to understand Your words of truth. Awaken my spirit to be attentive, receptive and submissive to everything You say.

We need not, when a-bed, lie awake to talk with God. He can visit us while we sleep, and cause us then to hear His voice. Our heart oft times wakes when we sleep, and God can speak to that, either by words, by proverbs, by signs and similitudes, as well as if one was awake.

John Bunyan (1628-1688)

23 "Yet if there is an angel on his side
as a mediator, one out of a thousand,
to tell a man what is right for him,
24 to be gracious to him and say,
'Spare him from going down to the pit[a];
I have found a ransom for him'—
25 then his flesh is renewed like a child's;
it is restored as in the days of his youth.
26 He prays to God and finds favor with him,
he sees God's face and shouts for joy;
he is restored by God to his righteous state.
27 Then he comes to men and says,
'I sinned, and perverted what was right,
but I did not get what I deserved.
28 He redeemed my soul from going down to the pit,[b]
and I will live to enjoy the light.'

29 "God does all these things to a man—
twice, even three times—
30 to turn back his soul from the pit,[c]
that the light of life may shine on him.

31 "Pay attention, Job, and listen to me;
be silent, and I will speak.
32 If you have anything to say, answer me;
speak up, for I want you to be cleared.
33 But if not, then listen to me;
be silent, and I will teach you wisdom."

34 Then Elihu said:

2 "Hear my words, you wise men;
listen to me, you men of learning.
3 For the ear tests words
as the tongue tastes food.
4 Let us discern for ourselves what is right;
let us learn together what is good.

5 "Job says, 'I am innocent,
but God denies me justice.
6 Although I am right,
I am considered a liar;
although I am guiltless,
his arrow inflicts an incurable wound.'
7 What man is like Job,
who drinks scorn like water?
8 He keeps company with evildoers;
he associates with wicked men.
9 For he says, 'It profits a man nothing
when he tries to please God.'

10 "So listen to me, you men of understanding.
Far be it from God to do evil,
from the Almighty to do wrong.
11 He repays a man for what he has done;
he brings upon him what his conduct deserves.
12 It is unthinkable that God would do wrong,

[a] 24 Or *grave* [b] 28 Or *redeemed me from going down to the grave* [c] 30 Or *turn him back from the grave*

(33:23–24) What Elihu could only long for has now become a reality. Lord Jesus Christ—Mediator, Messenger of God, the Word made flesh—no words can ever express Your worth. Lord Jesus Christ—commissioned by the Father, trusted by God Himself to accomplish the task of redemption, and trusted by people to perfect that which You have begun—You hear our cries for mercy, You sympathize with our weaknesses, and You plead our case before the Righteous Judge. What greater advocate could there be than the One who is Himself sent by God to be the ransom for us? (1Ti 2:5–6; Heb 7:25)

Oh, blessed Interpreter! Mighty with God, so that the heart of God is affected with the woes and griefs of men; mighty with men so that the great love of God, which is an ocean without a bottom or shore, is made intelligible to us!

Charles Haddon Spurgeon (1834–1892)

(33:27–28) O wonderful, merciful Savior, I thank You for not giving me what my sins have deserved. Instead of condemnation I have received pardon. Instead of banishment I have been adopted. I am in awe of the promise that Your mercies will never come to an end! I will declare the hope of Your saving grace to the world.

It is impossible for that man to despair who remembers that his Helper is omnipotent.

Jeremy Taylor (1613-1667)

(34:14–15) Almighty God, You uphold all things by Your power. The breath of life is still Yours to give. It is by Your will and grace that things continue as they do. The orbit of the planets, the gravity of the earth and the beating of every heart depend on You. There is nothing over which You are not Lord; there is nothing about which You cannot say, "Mine"! And in Your absolute reign You show absolute love. What a wonder!

that the Almighty would pervert justice.
13 Who appointed him over the earth?
Who put him in charge of the whole world?
14 If it were his intention
and he withdrew his spirit[a] and breath,
15 all mankind would perish together
and man would return to the dust.

16 "If you have understanding, hear this;
listen to what I say.
17 Can he who hates justice govern?
Will you condemn the just and mighty One?
18 Is he not the One who says to kings, 'You are worthless,'
and to nobles, 'You are wicked,'
19 who shows no partiality to princes
and does not favor the rich over the poor,
for they are all the work of his hands?
20 They die in an instant, in the middle of the night;
the people are shaken and they pass away;
the mighty are removed without human hand.

21 "His eyes are on the ways of men;
he sees their every step.
22 There is no dark place, no deep shadow,
where evildoers can hide.
23 God has no need to examine men further,
that they should come before him for judgment.
24 Without inquiry he shatters the mighty
and sets up others in their place.
25 Because he takes note of their deeds,
he overthrows them in the night and they are crushed.
26 He punishes them for their wickedness
where everyone can see them,
27 because they turned from following him
and had no regard for any of his ways.
28 They caused the cry of the poor to come before him,
so that he heard the cry of the needy.
29 But if he remains silent, who can condemn him?
If he hides his face, who can see him?
Yet he is over man and nation alike,
30 to keep a godless man from ruling,
from laying snares for the people.

31 "Suppose a man says to God,
'I am guilty but will offend no more.
32 Teach me what I cannot see;
if I have done wrong, I will not do so again.'
33 Should God then reward you on your terms,
when you refuse to repent?
You must decide, not I;
so tell me what you know.

34 "Men of understanding declare,
wise men who hear me say to me,
35 'Job speaks without knowledge;

[a] 14 Or *Spirit*

his words lack insight.'
36 Oh, that Job might be tested to the utmost
for answering like a wicked man!
37 To his sin he adds rebellion;
scornfully he claps his hands among us
and multiplies his words against God."

35 Then Elihu said:

2 "Do you think this is just?
You say, 'I will be cleared by God.[a]'
3 Yet you ask him, 'What profit is it to me,[b]
and what do I gain by not sinning?'

4 "I would like to reply to you
and to your friends with you.
5 Look up at the heavens and see;
gaze at the clouds so high above you.
6 If you sin, how does that affect him?
If your sins are many, what does that do to him?
7 If you are righteous, what do you give to him,
or what does he receive from your hand?
8 Your wickedness affects only a man like yourself,
and your righteousness only the sons of men.

9 "Men cry out under a load of oppression;
they plead for relief from the arm of the powerful.
10 But no one says, 'Where is God my Maker,
who gives songs in the night,
11 who teaches more to us than to[c] the beasts of the earth
and makes us wiser than[d] the birds of the air?'
12 He does not answer when men cry out
because of the arrogance of the wicked.
13 Indeed, God does not listen to their empty plea;
the Almighty pays no attention to it.
14 How much less, then, will he listen
when you say that you do not see him,
that your case is before him
and you must wait for him,
15 and further, that his anger never punishes
and he does not take the least notice of wickedness.[e]
16 So Job opens his mouth with empty talk;
without knowledge he multiplies words."

36 Elihu continued:

2 "Bear with me a little longer and I will show you
that there is more to be said in God's behalf.
3 I get my knowledge from afar;
I will ascribe justice to my Maker.
4 Be assured that my words are not false;
one perfect in knowledge is with you.

5 "God is mighty, but does not despise men;
he is mighty, and firm in his purpose.

[a] 2 Or *My righteousness is more than God's* [b] 3 Or *you* [c] 11 Or *teaches us by* [d] 11 Or *us wise by* [e] 15 Symmachus, Theodotion and Vulgate; the meaning of the Hebrew for this word is uncertain.

(35:2–3) Lord, what shall we do about our sinful habits? Shall we go ahead and sin because we are not under law but under grace? Shall we continue to be slaves to sin, obeying it on demand? No, Lord, You have delivered us from our slavery to sin, and You will continue to deliver us. (Ro 6:15–18)

(36:4) Father, forgive me for the times when I present myself in this way to my friends, as the all-knowing one. What insufferable arrogance! It is the fool who is wise in his own eyes. There is only One Who is perfect in knowledge, and that is You. What I know You have taught me, Father; and what I know I only know in part.

The first test of a truly great man is his humility. I do not mean by humility, doubt of his own power. But really great men have a curious feeling that the greatness is not in them, but through them. And they see something divine in every other man and are endlessly, foolishly, incredibly merciful.

John Ruskin (1819-1900)

6 He does not keep the wicked alive
but gives the afflicted their rights.
7 He does not take his eyes off the righteous;
he enthrones them with kings
and exalts them forever.
8 But if men are bound in chains,
held fast by cords of affliction,
9 he tells them what they have done—
that they have sinned arrogantly.
10 He makes them listen to correction
and commands them to repent of their evil.
11 If they obey and serve him,
they will spend the rest of their days in prosperity
and their years in contentment.
12 But if they do not listen,
they will perish by the sword[a]
and die without knowledge.

13 "The godless in heart harbor resentment;
even when he fetters them, they do not cry for help.
14 They die in their youth,
among male prostitutes of the shrines.
15 But those who suffer he delivers in their suffering;
he speaks to them in their affliction.

16 "He is wooing you from the jaws of distress
to a spacious place free from restriction,
to the comfort of your table laden with choice food.
17 But now you are laden with the judgment due the
wicked;
judgment and justice have taken hold of you.
18 Be careful that no one entices you by riches;
do not let a large bribe turn you aside.
19 Would your wealth
or even all your mighty efforts
sustain you so you would not be in distress?
20 Do not long for the night,
to drag people away from their homes.[b]
21 Beware of turning to evil,
which you seem to prefer to affliction.

22 "God is exalted in his power.
Who is a teacher like him?
23 Who has prescribed his ways for him,
or said to him, 'You have done wrong'?
24 Remember to extol his work,
which men have praised in song.
25 All mankind has seen it;
men gaze on it from afar.
26 How great is God—beyond our understanding!
The number of his years is past finding out.

27 "He draws up the drops of water,
which distill as rain to the streams[c];
28 the clouds pour down their moisture
and abundant showers fall on mankind.
29 Who can understand how he spreads out the clouds,

(36:15–16) Sometimes You deliver us *out* of our suffering; sometimes You deliver us *in* our suffering. But You are always faithful to deliver. While You may not remove the thorn in my flesh, You will always supply sufficient grace for me to deal with it. I praise You that Your power is made perfect in my weakness, and I praise You for Your wisdom and fatherly care. (2Co 12:7–9)

(36:22–26) O Great Creator, You existed before time began. Before You scattered galaxies across the heavens, before You synchronized the planets, before You formed humans in Your image—You were God of all. Your love, power and wisdom already extended beyond infinity. Today, Your creation as we know it is complete, and You govern millions of unknown worlds with the touch of Your hand. How is it that a God so vast, so unfathomable, so timeless, would seek to live in my heart?

I have a Maker,
He formed my heart.
Before even time began
My life was in His hand.

He knows my name,
He knows my every thought,
He sees each tear that falls
And hears me when I call.

"He Knows My Name"
Tommy Walker (©1996)

[a] 12 Or *will cross the River* [b] 20 The meaning of the Hebrew for verses 18–20 is uncertain. [c] 27 Or *distill from the mist as rain*

how he thunders from his pavilion?
30 See how he scatters his lightning about him,
bathing the depths of the sea.
31 This is the way he governs[a] the nations
and provides food in abundance.
32 He fills his hands with lightning
and commands it to strike its mark.
33 His thunder announces the coming storm;
even the cattle make known its approach.[b]

37 "At this my heart pounds
and leaps from its place.
2 Listen! Listen to the roar of his voice,
to the rumbling that comes from his mouth.
3 He unleashes his lightning beneath the whole heaven
and sends it to the ends of the earth.
4 After that comes the sound of his roar;
he thunders with his majestic voice.
When his voice resounds,
he holds nothing back.
5 God's voice thunders in marvelous ways;
he does great things beyond our understanding.
6 He says to the snow, 'Fall on the earth,'
and to the rain shower, 'Be a mighty downpour.'
7 So that all men he has made may know his work,
he stops every man from his labor.[c]
8 The animals take cover;
they remain in their dens.
9 The tempest comes out from its chamber,
the cold from the driving winds.
10 The breath of God produces ice,
and the broad waters become frozen.
11 He loads the clouds with moisture;
he scatters his lightning through them.
12 At his direction they swirl around
over the face of the whole earth
to do whatever he commands them.
13 He brings the clouds to punish men,
or to water his earth[d] and show his love.

14 "Listen to this, Job;
stop and consider God's wonders.
15 Do you know how God controls the clouds
and makes his lightning flash?
16 Do you know how the clouds hang poised,
those wonders of him who is perfect in knowledge?
17 You who swelter in your clothes
when the land lies hushed under the south wind,
18 can you join him in spreading out the skies,
hard as a mirror of cast bronze?

19 "Tell us what we should say to him;
we cannot draw up our case because of our
darkness.
20 Should he be told that I want to speak?
Would any man ask to be swallowed up?

[a] 31 Or *nourishes* [b] 33 Or *announces his coming— / the One zealous against evil*
[c] 7 Or / *he fills all men with fear by his power* [d] 13 Or *to favor them*

(37:13) Oh the wisdom and power of Your ways! Sovereign God, with the same cloudburst You bring judgment on some men and great blessing on others. You cause the rain to fall on the just and the unjust at the same time with different purposes and ends. Great and marvelous are Your ways!

21 Now no one can look at the sun,
bright as it is in the skies
after the wind has swept them clean.
22 Out of the north he comes in golden splendor;
God comes in awesome majesty.
23 The Almighty is beyond our reach and exalted in power;
in his justice and great righteousness, he does not oppress.
24 Therefore, men revere him,
for does he not have regard for all the wise in heart?[a]"

God doesn't reveal his grand design. He reveals himself.

Frederick Buechner (1926-)

The LORD Speaks

38 Then the LORD answered Job out of the storm. He said:

2 "Who is this that darkens my counsel
with words without knowledge?
3 Brace yourself like a man;
I will question you,
and you shall answer me.

4 "Where were you when I laid the earth's foundation?
Tell me, if you understand.
5 Who marked off its dimensions? Surely you know!
Who stretched a measuring line across it?
6 On what were its footings set,
or who laid its cornerstone—
7 while the morning stars sang together
and all the angels[b] shouted for joy?

8 "Who shut up the sea behind doors
when it burst forth from the womb,
9 when I made the clouds its garment
and wrapped it in thick darkness,
10 when I fixed limits for it
and set its doors and bars in place,
11 when I said, 'This far you may come and no farther;
here is where your proud waves halt'?

12 "Have you ever given orders to the morning,
or shown the dawn its place,
13 that it might take the earth by the edges
and shake the wicked out of it?
14 The earth takes shape like clay under a seal;
its features stand out like those of a garment.
15 The wicked are denied their light,
and their upraised arm is broken.

16 "Have you journeyed to the springs of the sea
or walked in the recesses of the deep?
17 Have the gates of death been shown to you?
Have you seen the gates of the shadow of death[c]?
18 Have you comprehended the vast expanses of the earth?
Tell me, if you know all this.

(38:1–3) It is amazing that You should answer anyone, gracious Father! Yet You stooped to speak to Job in a remarkable demonstration of Your enduring love. And I am filled with wonder when I think that You welcome me into Your presence, that You are always pursuing me, that You dialogue with me, asking searching questions not to humiliate me but to humble me, not to shame me but to silence my presumptuous heart! What a profound comfort to know that You would stoop so low as to make Yourself known to me.

(38:4) Lord, when You laid the foundation of the earth I was in Your mind as one small thought, one flickering idea, one story yet to be told. And while I took form in my mother's womb, even then You knew my future; You had already read the diary of my decades yet to come. "How precious to me are your thoughts, O God! How vast is the sum of them!" (Ps 139:15–17)

[a] 24 Or *for he does not have regard for any who think they are wise.* [b] 7 Hebrew *the sons of God* [c] 17 Or *gates of deep shadows*

19 "What is the way to the abode of light?
And where does darkness reside?
20 Can you take them to their places?
Do you know the paths to their dwellings?
21 Surely you know, for you were already born!
You have lived so many years!

22 "Have you entered the storehouses of the snow
or seen the storehouses of the hail,
23 which I reserve for times of trouble,
for days of war and battle?
24 What is the way to the place where the lightning is dispersed,
or the place where the east winds are scattered over the earth?
25 Who cuts a channel for the torrents of rain,
and a path for the thunderstorm,
26 to water a land where no man lives,
a desert with no one in it,
27 to satisfy a desolate wasteland
and make it sprout with grass?
28 Does the rain have a father?
Who fathers the drops of dew?
29 From whose womb comes the ice?
Who gives birth to the frost from the heavens
30 when the waters become hard as stone,
when the surface of the deep is frozen?

31 "Can you bind the beautiful[a] Pleiades?
Can you loose the cords of Orion?
32 Can you bring forth the constellations in their seasons[b]
or lead out the Bear[c] with its cubs?
33 Do you know the laws of the heavens?
Can you set up ⌊God's[d]⌋ dominion over the earth?

34 "Can you raise your voice to the clouds
and cover yourself with a flood of water?
35 Do you send the lightning bolts on their way?
Do they report to you, 'Here we are'?
36 Who endowed the heart[e] with wisdom
or gave understanding to the mind[e]?
37 Who has the wisdom to count the clouds?
Who can tip over the water jars of the heavens
38 when the dust becomes hard
and the clods of earth stick together?

39 "Do you hunt the prey for the lioness
and satisfy the hunger of the lions
40 when they crouch in their dens
or lie in wait in a thicket?
41 Who provides food for the raven
when its young cry out to God
and wander about for lack of food?

39 "Do you know when the mountain goats give birth?
Do you watch when the doe bears her fawn?
2 Do you count the months till they bear?

[a] 31 Or *the twinkling*; or *the chains of the* [b] 32 Or *the morning star in its season* [c] 32 Or *out Leo* [d] 33 Or *his*; or *their* [e] 36 The meaning of the Hebrew for this word is uncertain.

(38:31–32) Lord, at the dawn of creation You spoke the stars into being. They sang as You made the world; and to this day You call them all by name. Dazzling and glorious as the stars may be, somehow I find myself closer yet to Your heart. For You have promised never to leave me or forsake me, and You have engraved my name on the palms of Your hands. (Dt 31:6; Job 38:7; Ps 147:4; Isa 49:14–16)

(38:36) O great Provider, You who filled the endless heavens with stars; You who filled the thunderous clouds with rain; You who filled the earth and seas with life—You stopped, and You stooped, to fill the lowly human heart with wisdom. Indeed, the whole earth is filled with Your glory.

Ye storms howl out his greatness; let your thunders roll like drums in the march of God's armies! Let your lightning write his name in fire on the midnight darkness; let the illimitable void of space become one mouth for song; and let the unnavigated ether, through its shoreless depths, bear through the infinite remote the name of him whose goodness endureth forever!

Charles Haddon Spurgeon (1834–1892)

(39:4) Heavenly Father, great Creator, Your eyes are upon Your creatures as they are born, as they mate, as they give birth, as they die. You notice the unique characteristics of all species; You recognize each habit; You understand every behavior. You watch the solitary hawk as it soars heavenward, and You know when every sparrow falls to the earth. How much more, Father, do You love and care for us, Your people? You have numbered the hairs of our heads; You have met our needs before we have asked; and above all else You have given Your Son's life as a ransom for ours. (Mt 10:29–31)

Do you know the time they give birth?
3 They crouch down and bring forth their young;
their labor pains are ended.
4 Their young thrive and grow strong in the wilds;
they leave and do not return.

5 "Who let the wild donkey go free?
Who untied his ropes?
6 I gave him the wasteland as his home,
the salt flats as his habitat.
7 He laughs at the commotion in the town;
he does not hear a driver's shout.
8 He ranges the hills for his pasture
and searches for any green thing.

9 "Will the wild ox consent to serve you?
Will he stay by your manger at night?
10 Can you hold him to the furrow with a harness?
Will he till the valleys behind you?
11 Will you rely on him for his great strength?
Will you leave your heavy work to him?
12 Can you trust him to bring in your grain
and gather it to your threshing floor?

13 "The wings of the ostrich flap joyfully,
but they cannot compare with the pinions and feathers of the stork.
14 She lays her eggs on the ground
and lets them warm in the sand,
15 unmindful that a foot may crush them,
that some wild animal may trample them.
16 She treats her young harshly, as if they were not hers;
she cares not that her labor was in vain,
17 for God did not endow her with wisdom
or give her a share of good sense.
18 Yet when she spreads her feathers to run,
she laughs at horse and rider.

19 "Do you give the horse his strength
or clothe his neck with a flowing mane?
20 Do you make him leap like a locust,
striking terror with his proud snorting?
21 He paws fiercely, rejoicing in his strength,
and charges into the fray.
22 He laughs at fear, afraid of nothing;
he does not shy away from the sword.
23 The quiver rattles against his side,
along with the flashing spear and lance.
24 In frenzied excitement he eats up the ground;
he cannot stand still when the trumpet sounds.
25 At the blast of the trumpet he snorts, 'Aha!'
He catches the scent of battle from afar,
the shout of commanders and the battle cry.

26 "Does the hawk take flight by your wisdom
and spread his wings toward the south?
27 Does the eagle soar at your command
and build his nest on high?

28 He dwells on a cliff and stays there at night;
a rocky crag is his stronghold.
29 From there he seeks out his food;
his eyes detect it from afar.
30 His young ones feast on blood,
and where the slain are, there is he."

40 The LORD said to Job:

2 "Will the one who contends with the Almighty correct him?
Let him who accuses God answer him!"

3 Then Job answered the LORD:

4 "I am unworthy—how can I reply to you?
I put my hand over my mouth.
5 I spoke once, but I have no answer—
twice, but I will say no more."

6 Then the LORD spoke to Job out of the storm:

7 "Brace yourself like a man;
I will question you,
and you shall answer me.

8 "Would you discredit my justice?
Would you condemn me to justify yourself?
9 Do you have an arm like God's,
and can your voice thunder like his?
10 Then adorn yourself with glory and splendor,
and clothe yourself in honor and majesty.
11 Unleash the fury of your wrath,
look at every proud man and bring him low,
12 look at every proud man and humble him,
crush the wicked where they stand.
13 Bury them all in the dust together;
shroud their faces in the grave.
14 Then I myself will admit to you
that your own right hand can save you.

15 "Look at the behemoth,[a]
which I made along with you
and which feeds on grass like an ox.
16 What strength he has in his loins,
what power in the muscles of his belly!
17 His tail[b] sways like a cedar;
the sinews of his thighs are close-knit.
18 His bones are tubes of bronze,
his limbs like rods of iron.
19 He ranks first among the works of God,
yet his Maker can approach him with his sword.
20 The hills bring him their produce,
and all the wild animals play nearby.
21 Under the lotus plants he lies,
hidden among the reeds in the marsh.
22 The lotuses conceal him in their shadow;
the poplars by the stream surround him.

[a] 15 Possibly the hippopotamus or the elephant [b] 17 Possibly trunk

(40:4) God of heaven, how unworthy I am to stand before You. In the privacy of my room I spew out my complaints. I arrogantly speak my mind to You as if I were Your equal, arguing and fretting and defending myself, exhorting You to speak, demanding that You act on my behalf. But one glimpse of Your glory, one hint of Your power and I, like Job, am rendered speechless. You are holy; I am sinful. You are all-wise; I am foolish. You are all-powerful; I am weak and helpless. Forgive my presumption, merciful Lord, and teach me the discipline of silent adoration and worshipful listening.

Be still and know
That He is God.
Be still and know
That He is God.
There is no other,
There is no other.

Rest quietly, oh my soul,
Be still and listen
For the comfort of His voice.
Be confident the Lord
Is on your side.
Your salvation's drawing nigh.

"Be Still And Know"
Shannon Wexelberg (©1998)

Is God all-wise? Then the darkest providences have meaning. We will set ourselves as God's interpreters, and because we cannot make straight lines out of our crooked lot, we think that God has turned our life into inextricable confusion. The darkest hours in our life have some intent, and it is really not needful that we should know all at once what that intent is. Let us keep within our own little sphere, and live a day at a time, and breathe a breath at a time, and be content with one pulsation at a time, and interpretation will come when God pleases, and as he pleases.

Joseph Parker (1830-1902)

23 When the river rages, he is not alarmed;
he is secure, though the Jordan should surge
against his mouth.
24 Can anyone capture him by the eyes,[a]
or trap him and pierce his nose?

41

"Can you pull in the leviathan[b] with a fishhook
or tie down his tongue with a rope?
2 Can you put a cord through his nose
or pierce his jaw with a hook?
3 Will he keep begging you for mercy?
Will he speak to you with gentle words?
4 Will he make an agreement with you
for you to take him as your slave for life?
5 Can you make a pet of him like a bird
or put him on a leash for your girls?
6 Will traders barter for him?
Will they divide him up among the merchants?
7 Can you fill his hide with harpoons
or his head with fishing spears?
8 If you lay a hand on him,
you will remember the struggle and never do it
again!
9 Any hope of subduing him is false;
the mere sight of him is overpowering.
10 No one is fierce enough to rouse him.
Who then is able to stand against me?
11 Who has a claim against me that I must pay?
Everything under heaven belongs to me.

12 "I will not fail to speak of his limbs,
his strength and his graceful form.
13 Who can strip off his outer coat?
Who would approach him with a bridle?
14 Who dares open the doors of his mouth,
ringed about with his fearsome teeth?
15 His back has[c] rows of shields
tightly sealed together;
16 each is so close to the next
that no air can pass between.
17 They are joined fast to one another;
they cling together and cannot be parted.
18 His snorting throws out flashes of light;
his eyes are like the rays of dawn.
19 Firebrands stream from his mouth;
sparks of fire shoot out.
20 Smoke pours from his nostrils
as from a boiling pot over a fire of reeds.
21 His breath sets coals ablaze,
and flames dart from his mouth.
22 Strength resides in his neck;
dismay goes before him.
23 The folds of his flesh are tightly joined;
they are firm and immovable.
24 His chest is hard as rock,
hard as a lower millstone.

[a] 24 Or *by a water hole* [b] 1 Possibly the crocodile [c] 15 Or *His pride is his*

(41:11) "Praise be to you, O Lord, God of our fathers, from everlasting to everlasting. Yours, O Lord, is the greatness and the power and the glory and the majesty and the splendor, for everything in heaven and earth is yours. Yours, O Lord, is the kingdom; you are exalted as head over all. Wealth and honor come from you; you are the ruler of all things. In your hands are strength and power to exalt and give strength to all." Now, my God, I give You thanks and praise Your glorious name. (1Ch 29:10–13)

In vain our haughty reason swells,
For nothing's found in thee
But boundless inconceivables
And vast eternity.

Isaac Watts (1674–1748)

25 When he rises up, the mighty are terrified;
they retreat before his thrashing.
26 The sword that reaches him has no effect,
nor does the spear or the dart or the
javelin.
27 Iron he treats like straw
and bronze like rotten wood.
28 Arrows do not make him flee;
slingstones are like chaff to him.
29 A club seems to him but a piece of straw;
he laughs at the rattling of the lance.
30 His undersides are jagged potsherds,
leaving a trail in the mud like a threshing
sledge.
31 He makes the depths churn like a boiling caldron
and stirs up the sea like a pot of ointment.
32 Behind him he leaves a glistening wake;
one would think the deep had white hair.
33 Nothing on earth is his equal—
a creature without fear.
34 He looks down on all that are haughty;
he is king over all that are proud."

Job

42 Then Job replied to the LORD:

2 "I know that you can do all things;
no plan of yours can be thwarted.
3 ⌊You asked,⌋ 'Who is this that obscures my counsel
without knowledge?'
Surely I spoke of things I did not
understand,
things too wonderful for me to know.

4 ⌊"You said,⌋ 'Listen now, and I will speak;
I will question you,
and you shall answer me.'
5 My ears had heard of you
but now my eyes have seen you.
6 Therefore I despise myself
and repent in dust and ashes."

Epilogue

7 After the LORD had said these things to Job, he said to Eliphaz
the Temanite, "I am angry with you and your two friends, because
you have not spoken of me what is right, as my servant Job has.
8 So now take seven bulls and seven rams and go to my servant
Job and sacrifice a burnt offering for yourselves. My servant
Job will pray for you, and I will accept his prayer and not deal
with you according to your folly. You have not spoken of me what
is right, as my servant Job has." 9 So Eliphaz the Temanite, Bildad
the Shuhite and Zophar the Naamathite did what the LORD told
them; and the LORD accepted Job's prayer.
10 After Job had prayed for his friends, the LORD made him
prosperous again and gave him twice as much as he had before.
11 All his brothers and sisters and everyone who had known him
before came and ate with him in his house. They comforted and

(42:5–6) Job longed to see You. He thought he would be vindicated. But when he finally did see You he could no longer defend himself. Where he had once despised his condition and mourned in dust and ashes, now he despised himself and repented in dust and ashes. Truly he was a man who feared You more than he loved himself. Father, help me to imitate his devotion to You as long as I live, no matter what happens. Give me the same kind of unshakable faith in Your unshakable love for me. (Job 2:10; 19:27)

(42:7–10) As I read of Job, I look to You, Lord. This man who was so greatly mistreated by his friends became the merciful priest who interceded on their behalf. Shall I do less? You have led me through heartache and loss; hear me now as I plead for those who robbed me. You have walked with me through the valley of the shadow of death; listen now, as I plead for others who abandoned me there. You have led me with Your nail-scarred hand; stoop now, and extend that hand to those who have not yet reached for You. Lord Jesus, You have instructed me to pray for my enemies, just as You prayed for Yours, and I have obeyed. So now will You, who live to intercede for Your people, please pray for me? (Lk 6:27–28)

There is nothing that makes us love a man so much as praying for him; and when you can once do this sincerely for any man, you have fitted your soul for the performance of everything that is kind and civil towards him . . . By considering yourself as an advocate with God for your neighbours or acquaintance you would never find it hard to be at peace with them yourself. It would be easy to you to bear with and forgive those for whom you particularly implored the divine mercy and forgiveness.

William Law (1686-1761)

(42:11) O Lord, Job's graciousness astounds me. That he would be so kind and forgiving to those who had abandoned him is truly a reflection of a man who is "blameless and upright, a man who fears God and shuns evil." But You are far greater than Job, and You suffered far more deeply. O Holy One, Lord Jesus, at the hand of God You were made perfect through Your suffering. You were despised and rejected by us, and yet You welcome us to feast with You. You have made us holy; You are not ashamed to call us Your family. What pure, forgiving love You have for us. (Job 1:8; Heb 2:10–11)

God is a master Artist. And there are aspects of your life and character–good, quality things–he wants others to notice. So without using blatant tricks or obvious gimmicks, God brings the cool, dark contrast of suffering into your life. That contrast, laid up against the golden character of Christ within you, will draw attention . . . to him. Light against darkness. Beauty against affliction. Joy against sorrow. A sweet, patient spirit against pain and disappointment–major contrasts that have a way of attracting notice. You are the canvas on which he paints glorious truths, sharing beauty, and inspiring others. So that people might see him.

Joni Eareckson Tada (1949-)

Help me then in every tribulation
So to trust Thy promises, O Lord,
That I lose not faith's sweet
consolation
Offered me within Thy holy Word.
Help me, Lord, when toil and trouble
meeting,
E'er to take, as from a father's hand,
One by one, the days, the moments
fleeting,
Till I reach the promised land.

"Day By Day and With Each Passing Moment"
Carolina Sandell Berg (1865)
Trans. Andrew L. Skoog (1856-1934)

(42:16–17) May the rest of my years, whether many or few, be full of Your love, compassion, wisdom and freedom. Amen.

consoled him over all the trouble the LORD had brought upon
him, and each one gave him a piece of silver[a] and a gold ring.
12The LORD blessed the latter part of Job's life more than the
first. He had fourteen thousand sheep, six thousand camels, a
thousand yoke of oxen and a thousand donkeys. 13And he also
had seven sons and three daughters. 14The first daughter he
named Jemimah, the second Keziah and the third Keren-Hap-
puch. 15Nowhere in all the land were there found women as
beautiful as Job's daughters, and their father granted them an inheritance along with their brothers.
16After this, Job lived a hundred and forty years; he saw his
children and their children to the fourth generation. 17And so he
died, old and full of years.

[a] *11* Hebrew *him a kesitah*; a kesitah was a unit of money of unknown weight and value.

The
PSALMS

The book of Psalms is a book of worship. Each psalm captures the writer's response to God from a variety of perspectives. The composers, including David, Asaph and others, are not limited to a narrow range of worship expressions. Among their compositions we find exuberant praise and overflowing gratitude. God is adored, exalted and glorified. But the psalmists also pour out their laments to God—their fears, heartaches and disappointments. In desperation, they call out for God's help even as they confess the certainty of His salvation.

For good reason, the book of Psalms has been called "the church's first hymnal." We find excerpts of this book throughout the New Testament, from the anguished cry of Jesus on the cross (Mk 15:34, par. Ps 22:1) to the joyful praise of Revelation (Rev 15:4, par. Ps 86:9). Today, many of our greatest hymns and worship songs find their inspiration in the these Biblical treasures.

More than any other single book, Biblical or otherwise, the book of Psalms teaches us how to worship. Each psalm expresses, not merely the heart of the composer, but also the heart of the Holy Spirit Who inspired the composition. The more we read, study, meditate upon, sing and pray the psalms, the more we will worship with authenticity and ardor. The psalms invite us to go deeper with the Lord than we have gone before—and they expand the horizons of our heart for God as well.

Each psalm expresses, not merely the heart of the composer, but also the heart of the Holy Spirit Who inspired the composition.

Because the psalms are God's masterpieces of worship, the editors of *The NIV Worship Bible* faced a unique challenge. To write prayers based on the psalms is surely a worthy exercise. But to print those prayers alongside the originals seemed inappropriate. Instead, we decided to reserve the column for a better purpose. Rather than filling the page with our prayers, we encourage you to fill it with yours—in a sense, to make the Book of Psalms your own personal psalter. As you write your prayers, may we suggest that you date them. By doing so, you will be creating memorials to remind you of your past encounters with God in the Scriptures.

As you pray through the psalms, pay attention to the notes under the chapter headings that tell us who the original authors were and under what circumstances the psalms were composed (e.g. Ps 3, 18, 34, 51, etc.). When read in their historic context, the psalms reveal a deeper level of meaning and emotion. Though we do not know the circumstances under which all of the psalms were composed, there are enough clues scattered throughout the psalms to give us a picture of how Biblical worshipers have responded to God in the midst of both trials and victories.

Above all, the psalms teach us that worship is for God. Though we are blessed as we worship, the goal of worship is not our gain, but God's glory. In the timeless words of Psalm 108:3-5: "I will praise you, O Lord, among the nations; I will sing of you among the peoples. For great is your love, higher than the heavens; your faithfulness reaches to the skies. Be exalted, O God, above the heavens, and let your glory be over all the earth."

Psalms

Hear My Prayer

BOOK I

Psalms 1–41

Psalm 1

1 Blessed is the man
who does not walk in the counsel of the wicked
or stand in the way of sinners
or sit in the seat of mockers.
2 But his delight is in the law of the LORD,
and on his law he meditates day and night.
3 He is like a tree planted by streams of water,
which yields its fruit in season
and whose leaf does not wither.
Whatever he does prospers.

4 Not so the wicked!
They are like chaff
that the wind blows away.
5 Therefore the wicked will not stand in the judgment,
nor sinners in the assembly of the righteous.

6 For the LORD watches over the way of the righteous,
but the way of the wicked will perish.

Psalm 2

1 Why do the nations conspire[a]
and the peoples plot in vain?
2 The kings of the earth take their stand
and the rulers gather together
against the LORD
and against his Anointed One.[b]
3 "Let us break their chains," they say,
"and throw off their fetters."

4 The One enthroned in heaven laughs;
the Lord scoffs at them.
5 Then he rebukes them in his anger
and terrifies them in his wrath, saying,
6 "I have installed my King[c]
on Zion, my holy hill."

7 I will proclaim the decree of the LORD:

He said to me, "You are my Son[d];
today I have become your Father.[e]
8 Ask of me,
and I will make the nations your inheritance,
the ends of the earth your possession.
9 You will rule them with an iron scepter[f];
you will dash them to pieces like pottery."

10 Therefore, you kings, be wise;
be warned, you rulers of the earth.
11 Serve the LORD with fear
and rejoice with trembling.
12 Kiss the Son, lest he be angry

[a] *1* Hebrew; Septuagint *rage* [b] *2* Or *anointed one* [c] *6* Or *king* [d] *7* Or *son*; also in verse 12 [e] *7* Or *have begotten you* [f] *9* Or *will break them with a rod of iron*

and you be destroyed in your way,
for his wrath can flare up in a moment.
Blessed are all who take refuge in him.

Psalm 3

A psalm of David. When he fled from his son Absalom.

1 O LORD, how many are my foes!
How many rise up against me!
2 Many are saying of me,
"God will not deliver him." *Selah*[a]

3 But you are a shield around me, O LORD;
you bestow glory on me and lift[b] up my head.
4 To the LORD I cry aloud,
and he answers me from his holy hill. *Selah*

5 I lie down and sleep;
I wake again, because the LORD sustains me.
6 I will not fear the tens of thousands
drawn up against me on every side.

7 Arise, O LORD!
Deliver me, O my God!
Strike all my enemies on the jaw;
break the teeth of the wicked.

8 From the LORD comes deliverance.
May your blessing be on your people. *Selah*

Psalm 4

For the director of music. With stringed instruments.
A psalm of David.

1 Answer me when I call to you,
O my righteous God.
Give me relief from my distress;
be merciful to me and hear my prayer.

2 How long, O men, will you turn my glory into
shame[c]?
How long will you love delusions and seek false
gods[d]? *Selah*
3 Know that the LORD has set apart the godly for
himself;
the LORD will hear when I call to him.

4 In your anger do not sin;
when you are on your beds,
search your hearts and be silent. *Selah*
5 Offer right sacrifices
and trust in the LORD.

6 Many are asking, "Who can show us any good?"
Let the light of your face shine upon us, O LORD.
7 You have filled my heart with greater joy
than when their grain and new wine abound.

[a] 2 A word of uncertain meaning, occurring frequently in the Psalms; possibly a musical term [b] 3 Or *LORD, / my Glorious One, who lifts* [c] 2 Or *you dishonor my Glorious One* [d] 2 Or *seek lies*

Hear My Prayer

Hear My Prayer

8 I will lie down and sleep in peace,
for you alone, O LORD,
make me dwell in safety.

Psalm 5

For the director of music. For flutes. A psalm of David.

1 Give ear to my words, O LORD,
consider my sighing.
2 Listen to my cry for help,
my King and my God,
for to you I pray.
3 In the morning, O LORD, you hear my voice;
in the morning I lay my requests before you
and wait in expectation.
4 You are not a God who takes pleasure in evil;
with you the wicked cannot dwell.
5 The arrogant cannot stand in your presence;
you hate all who do wrong.
6 You destroy those who tell lies;
bloodthirsty and deceitful men
the LORD abhors.
7 But I, by your great mercy,
will come into your house;
in reverence will I bow down
toward your holy temple.
8 Lead me, O LORD, in your righteousness
because of my enemies—
make straight your way before me.
9 Not a word from their mouth can be trusted;
their heart is filled with destruction.
Their throat is an open grave;
with their tongue they speak deceit.
10 Declare them guilty, O God!
Let their intrigues be their downfall.
Banish them for their many sins,
for they have rebelled against you.
11 But let all who take refuge in you be glad;
let them ever sing for joy.
Spread your protection over them,
that those who love your name may rejoice in you.
12 For surely, O LORD, you bless the righteous;
you surround them with your favor as with a
shield.

Psalm 6

For the director of music. With stringed instruments.
According to *sheminith.*[a] A psalm of David.

1 O LORD, do not rebuke me in your anger
or discipline me in your wrath.
2 Be merciful to me, LORD, for I am faint;
O LORD, heal me, for my bones are in agony.

[a] Title: Probably a musical term

3 My soul is in anguish.
How long, O LORD, how long?

4 Turn, O LORD, and deliver me;
save me because of your unfailing love.
5 No one remembers you when he is dead.
Who praises you from the grave[a]?

6 I am worn out from groaning;
all night long I flood my bed with weeping
and drench my couch with tears.
7 My eyes grow weak with sorrow;
they fail because of all my foes.

8 Away from me, all you who do evil,
for the LORD has heard my weeping.
9 The LORD has heard my cry for mercy;
the LORD accepts my prayer.
10 All my enemies will be ashamed and dismayed;
they will turn back in sudden disgrace.

Psalm 7

A *shiggaion*[b] of David, which he sang to the LORD concerning Cush, a Benjamite.

1 O LORD my God, I take refuge in you;
save and deliver me from all who pursue me,
2 or they will tear me like a lion
and rip me to pieces with no one to rescue me.

3 O LORD my God, if I have done this
and there is guilt on my hands—
4 if I have done evil to him who is at peace with me
or without cause have robbed my foe—
5 then let my enemy pursue and overtake me;
let him trample my life to the ground
and make me sleep in the dust. *Selah*

6 Arise, O LORD, in your anger;
rise up against the rage of my enemies.
Awake, my God; decree justice.
7 Let the assembled peoples gather around you.
Rule over them from on high;
8 let the LORD judge the peoples.
Judge me, O LORD, according to my righteousness,
according to my integrity, O Most High.
9 O righteous God,
who searches minds and hearts,
bring to an end the violence of the wicked
and make the righteous secure.

10 My shield[c] is God Most High,
who saves the upright in heart.
11 God is a righteous judge,
a God who expresses his wrath every day.
12 If he does not relent,
he[d] will sharpen his sword;

Hear My Prayer

[a] 5 Hebrew *Sheol* [b] Title: Probably a literary or musical term [c] 10 Or *sovereign*
[d] 12 Or *If a man does not repent, / God*

Hear My Prayer

he will bend and string his bow.
13 He has prepared his deadly weapons;
he makes ready his flaming arrows.

14 He who is pregnant with evil
and conceives trouble gives birth to disillusionment.
15 He who digs a hole and scoops it out
falls into the pit he has made.
16 The trouble he causes recoils on himself;
his violence comes down on his own head.

17 I will give thanks to the LORD because of his righteousness
and will sing praise to the name of the LORD Most High.

Psalm 8

For the director of music. According to *gittith.*[a] A psalm of David.

1 O LORD, our Lord,
how majestic is your name in all the earth!

You have set your glory
above the heavens.
2 From the lips of children and infants
you have ordained praise[b]
because of your enemies,
to silence the foe and the avenger.

3 When I consider your heavens,
the work of your fingers,
the moon and the stars,
which you have set in place,
4 what is man that you are mindful of him,
the son of man that you care for him?
5 You made him a little lower than the heavenly beings[c]
and crowned him with glory and honor.

6 You made him ruler over the works of your hands;
you put everything under his feet:
7 all flocks and herds,
and the beasts of the field,
8 the birds of the air,
and the fish of the sea,
all that swim the paths of the seas.

9 O LORD, our Lord,
how majestic is your name in all the earth!

Psalm 9[d]

For the director of music. To ⌞the tune of⌟ "The Death of the Son." A psalm of David.

1 I will praise you, O LORD, with all my heart;
I will tell of all your wonders.

[a] Title: Probably a musical term [b] 2 Or *strength* [c] 5 Or *than God* [d] Psalms 9 and 10 may have been originally a single acrostic poem, the stanzas of which begin with the successive letters of the Hebrew alphabet. In the Septuagint they constitute one psalm.

2 I will be glad and rejoice in you;
I will sing praise to your name, O Most High.

3 My enemies turn back;
they stumble and perish before you.
4 For you have upheld my right and my cause;
you have sat on your throne, judging righteously.
5 You have rebuked the nations and destroyed the wicked;
you have blotted out their name for ever and ever.
6 Endless ruin has overtaken the enemy,
you have uprooted their cities;
even the memory of them has perished.

7 The LORD reigns forever;
he has established his throne for judgment.
8 He will judge the world in righteousness;
he will govern the peoples with justice.
9 The LORD is a refuge for the oppressed,
a stronghold in times of trouble.
10 Those who know your name will trust in you,
for you, LORD, have never forsaken those who seek you.

11 Sing praises to the LORD, enthroned in Zion;
proclaim among the nations what he has done.
12 For he who avenges blood remembers;
he does not ignore the cry of the afflicted.

13 O LORD, see how my enemies persecute me!
Have mercy and lift me up from the gates of death,
14 that I may declare your praises
in the gates of the Daughter of Zion
and there rejoice in your salvation.
15 The nations have fallen into the pit they have dug;
their feet are caught in the net they have hidden.
16 The LORD is known by his justice;
the wicked are ensnared by the work of their hands. *Higgaion.*[a] *Selah*
17 The wicked return to the grave,[b]
all the nations that forget God.
18 But the needy will not always be forgotten,
nor the hope of the afflicted ever perish.

19 Arise, O LORD, let not man triumph;
let the nations be judged in your presence.
20 Strike them with terror, O LORD;
let the nations know they are but men. *Selah*

Psalm 10[c]

1 Why, O LORD, do you stand far off?
Why do you hide yourself in times of trouble?

2 In his arrogance the wicked man hunts down the weak,

[a] *16* Or *Meditation*; possibly a musical notation [b] *17* Hebrew *Sheol* [c] Psalms 9 and 10 may have been originally a single acrostic poem, the stanzas of which begin with the successive letters of the Hebrew alphabet. In the Septuagint they constitute one psalm.

Hear My Prayer

Hear My Prayer

who are caught in the schemes he devises.
3 He boasts of the cravings of his heart;
he blesses the greedy and reviles the LORD.
4 In his pride the wicked does not seek him;
in all his thoughts there is no room for God.
5 His ways are always prosperous;
he is haughty and your laws are far from him;
he sneers at all his enemies.
6 He says to himself, "Nothing will shake me;
I'll always be happy and never have trouble."
7 His mouth is full of curses and lies and threats;
trouble and evil are under his tongue.
8 He lies in wait near the villages;
from ambush he murders the innocent,
watching in secret for his victims.
9 He lies in wait like a lion in cover;
he lies in wait to catch the helpless;
he catches the helpless and drags them off in his net.
10 His victims are crushed, they collapse;
they fall under his strength.
11 He says to himself, "God has forgotten;
he covers his face and never sees."

12 Arise, LORD! Lift up your hand, O God.
Do not forget the helpless.
13 Why does the wicked man revile God?
Why does he say to himself,
"He won't call me to account"?
14 But you, O God, do see trouble and grief;
you consider it to take it in hand.
The victim commits himself to you;
you are the helper of the fatherless.
15 Break the arm of the wicked and evil man;
call him to account for his wickedness
that would not be found out.

16 The LORD is King for ever and ever;
the nations will perish from his land.
17 You hear, O LORD, the desire of the afflicted;
you encourage them, and you listen to their cry,
18 defending the fatherless and the oppressed,
in order that man, who is of the earth, may terrify no more.

Psalm 11

For the director of music. Of David.

1 In the LORD I take refuge.
How then can you say to me:
"Flee like a bird to your mountain.
2 For look, the wicked bend their bows;
they set their arrows against the strings
to shoot from the shadows
at the upright in heart.

3 When the foundations are being destroyed,
what can the righteous do[a]?"
4 The LORD is in his holy temple;
the LORD is on his heavenly throne.
He observes the sons of men;
his eyes examine them.
5 The LORD examines the righteous,
but the wicked[b] and those who love violence
his soul hates.
6 On the wicked he will rain
fiery coals and burning sulfur;
a scorching wind will be their lot.

7 For the LORD is righteous,
he loves justice;
upright men will see his face.

Psalm 12

For the director of music. According to *sheminith.*[c]
A psalm of David.

1 Help, LORD, for the godly are no more;
the faithful have vanished from among men.
2 Everyone lies to his neighbor;
their flattering lips speak with deception.

3 May the LORD cut off all flattering lips
and every boastful tongue
4 that says, "We will triumph with our tongues;
we own our lips[d]—who is our master?"

5 "Because of the oppression of the weak
and the groaning of the needy,
I will now arise," says the LORD.
"I will protect them from those who malign
them."
6 And the words of the LORD are flawless,
like silver refined in a furnace of clay,
purified seven times.

7 O LORD, you will keep us safe
and protect us from such people forever.
8 The wicked freely strut about
when what is vile is honored among men.

Psalm 13

For the director of music. A psalm of David.

1 How long, O LORD? Will you forget me forever?
How long will you hide your face from me?
2 How long must I wrestle with my thoughts
and every day have sorrow in my heart?
How long will my enemy triumph over me?

3 Look on me and answer, O LORD my God.

[a] 3 Or *what is the Righteous One doing* [b] 5 Or *The LORD, the Righteous One, examines the wicked, /* [c] Title: Probably a musical term [d] 4 Or */ our lips are our plowshares*

Hear My Prayer

Hear My Prayer

Give light to my eyes, or I will sleep in death;
4 my enemy will say, "I have overcome him,"
and my foes will rejoice when I fall.

5 But I trust in your unfailing love;
my heart rejoices in your salvation.
6 I will sing to the LORD,
for he has been good to me.

Psalm 14

For the director of music. Of David.

1 The fool[a] says in his heart,
"There is no God."
They are corrupt, their deeds are vile;
there is no one who does good.

2 The LORD looks down from heaven
on the sons of men
to see if there are any who understand,
any who seek God.
3 All have turned aside,
they have together become corrupt;
there is no one who does good,
not even one.

4 Will evildoers never learn—
those who devour my people as men eat bread
and who do not call on the LORD?
5 There they are, overwhelmed with dread,
for God is present in the company of the
righteous.
6 You evildoers frustrate the plans of the poor,
but the LORD is their refuge.

7 Oh, that salvation for Israel would come out of
Zion!
When the LORD restores the fortunes of his
people,
let Jacob rejoice and Israel be glad!

Psalm 15

A psalm of David.

1 LORD, who may dwell in your sanctuary?
Who may live on your holy hill?

2 He whose walk is blameless
and who does what is righteous,
who speaks the truth from his heart
3 and has no slander on his tongue,
who does his neighbor no wrong
and casts no slur on his fellowman,
4 who despises a vile man
but honors those who fear the LORD,
who keeps his oath
even when it hurts,

[a] *1* The Hebrew words rendered *fool* in Psalms denote one who is morally deficient.

5 who lends his money without usury
and does not accept a bribe against the
innocent.

He who does these things
will never be shaken.

Psalm 16

A *miktam*[a] of David.

1 Keep me safe, O God,
for in you I take refuge.

2 I said to the LORD, "You are my Lord;
apart from you I have no good thing."
3 As for the saints who are in the land,
they are the glorious ones in whom is all my
delight.[b]
4 The sorrows of those will increase
who run after other gods.
I will not pour out their libations of blood
or take up their names on my lips.

5 LORD, you have assigned me my portion and my
cup;
you have made my lot secure.
6 The boundary lines have fallen for me in pleasant
places;
surely I have a delightful inheritance.

7 I will praise the LORD, who counsels me;
even at night my heart instructs me.
8 I have set the LORD always before me.
Because he is at my right hand,
I will not be shaken.

9 Therefore my heart is glad and my tongue rejoices;
my body also will rest secure,
10 because you will not abandon me to the grave,[c]
nor will you let your Holy One[d] see decay.
11 You have made[e] known to me the path of life;
you will fill me with joy in your presence,
with eternal pleasures at your right hand.

Psalm 17

A prayer of David.

1 Hear, O LORD, my righteous plea;
listen to my cry.
Give ear to my prayer—
it does not rise from deceitful lips.
2 May my vindication come from you;
may your eyes see what is right.

3 Though you probe my heart and examine me
at night,

Hear My Prayer

[a] Title: Probably a literary or musical term [b] 3 Or *As for the pagan priests who are in the land / and the nobles in whom all delight, I said:* [c] 10 Hebrew *Sheol* [d] 10 Or *your faithful one* [e] 11 Or *You will make*

Hear My Prayer

though you test me, you will find nothing;
I have resolved that my mouth will not sin.
4 As for the deeds of men—
by the word of your lips
I have kept myself
from the ways of the violent.
5 My steps have held to your paths;
my feet have not slipped.

6 I call on you, O God, for you will answer me;
give ear to me and hear my prayer.
7 Show the wonder of your great love,
you who save by your right hand
those who take refuge in you from their foes.
8 Keep me as the apple of your eye;
hide me in the shadow of your wings
9 from the wicked who assail me,
from my mortal enemies who surround me.

10 They close up their callous hearts,
and their mouths speak with arrogance.
11 They have tracked me down, they now surround me,
with eyes alert, to throw me to the ground.
12 They are like a lion hungry for prey,
like a great lion crouching in cover.

13 Rise up, O LORD, confront them, bring them down;
rescue me from the wicked by your sword.
14 O LORD, by your hand save me from such men,
from men of this world whose reward is in this life.

You still the hunger of those you cherish;
their sons have plenty,
and they store up wealth for their children.
15 And I—in righteousness I will see your face;
when I awake, I will be satisfied with seeing your likeness.

Psalm 18

For the director of music. Of David the servant of the LORD. He sang to the LORD the words of this song when the LORD delivered him from the hand of all his enemies and from the hand of Saul. He said:

1 I love you, O LORD, my strength.

2 The LORD is my rock, my fortress and my deliverer;
my God is my rock, in whom I take refuge.
He is my shield and the horn[a] of my salvation, my stronghold.
3 I call to the LORD, who is worthy of praise,
and I am saved from my enemies.

4 The cords of death entangled me;
the torrents of destruction overwhelmed me.
5 The cords of the grave[b] coiled around me;
the snares of death confronted me.

[a] *2 Horn* here symbolizes strength. [b] *5* Hebrew *Sheol*

6 In my distress I called to the LORD;
I cried to my God for help.
From his temple he heard my voice;
my cry came before him, into his ears.
7 The earth trembled and quaked,
and the foundations of the mountains shook;
they trembled because he was angry.
8 Smoke rose from his nostrils;
consuming fire came from his mouth,
burning coals blazed out of it.
9 He parted the heavens and came down;
dark clouds were under his feet.
10 He mounted the cherubim and flew;
he soared on the wings of the wind.
11 He made darkness his covering, his canopy around him—
the dark rain clouds of the sky.
12 Out of the brightness of his presence clouds advanced,
with hailstones and bolts of lightning.
13 The LORD thundered from heaven;
the voice of the Most High resounded.[a]
14 He shot his arrows and scattered ⌊the enemies⌋,
great bolts of lightning and routed them.
15 The valleys of the sea were exposed
and the foundations of the earth laid bare
at your rebuke, O LORD,
at the blast of breath from your nostrils.

16 He reached down from on high and took hold of me;
he drew me out of deep waters.
17 He rescued me from my powerful enemy,
from my foes, who were too strong for me.
18 They confronted me in the day of my disaster,
but the LORD was my support.
19 He brought me out into a spacious place;
he rescued me because he delighted in me.

20 The LORD has dealt with me according to my righteousness;
according to the cleanness of my hands he has rewarded me.
21 For I have kept the ways of the LORD;
I have not done evil by turning from my God.
22 All his laws are before me;
I have not turned away from his decrees.
23 I have been blameless before him
and have kept myself from sin.
24 The LORD has rewarded me according to my righteousness,
according to the cleanness of my hands in his sight.

25 To the faithful you show yourself faithful,
to the blameless you show yourself blameless,

[a] *13* Some Hebrew manuscripts and Septuagint (see also 2 Samuel 22:14); most Hebrew manuscripts *resounded, / amid hailstones and bolts of lightning*

Hear My Prayer

Hear My Prayer

26 to the pure you show yourself pure,
but to the crooked you show yourself shrewd.
27 You save the humble
but bring low those whose eyes are haughty.
28 You, O LORD, keep my lamp burning;
my God turns my darkness into light.
29 With your help I can advance against a troop[a];
with my God I can scale a wall.

30 As for God, his way is perfect;
the word of the LORD is flawless.
He is a shield
for all who take refuge in him.
31 For who is God besides the LORD?
And who is the Rock except our God?
32 It is God who arms me with strength
and makes my way perfect.
33 He makes my feet like the feet of a deer;
he enables me to stand on the heights.
34 He trains my hands for battle;
my arms can bend a bow of bronze.
35 You give me your shield of victory,
and your right hand sustains me;
you stoop down to make me great.
36 You broaden the path beneath me,
so that my ankles do not turn.

37 I pursued my enemies and overtook them;
I did not turn back till they were destroyed.
38 I crushed them so that they could not rise;
they fell beneath my feet.
39 You armed me with strength for battle;
you made my adversaries bow at my feet.
40 You made my enemies turn their backs in flight,
and I destroyed my foes.
41 They cried for help, but there was no one to save
them—
to the LORD, but he did not answer.
42 I beat them as fine as dust borne on the wind;
I poured them out like mud in the streets.

43 You have delivered me from the attacks of the
people;
you have made me the head of nations;
people I did not know are subject to me.
44 As soon as they hear me, they obey me;
foreigners cringe before me.
45 They all lose heart;
they come trembling from their strongholds.

46 The LORD lives! Praise be to my Rock!
Exalted be God my Savior!
47 He is the God who avenges me,
who subdues nations under me,
48 who saves me from my enemies.
You exalted me above my foes;
from violent men you rescued me.

[a] 29 Or *can run through a barricade*

49 Therefore I will praise you among the nations, O LORD;
I will sing praises to your name.
50 He gives his king great victories;
he shows unfailing kindness to his anointed,
to David and his descendants forever.

Psalm 19

For the director of music. A psalm of David.

1 The heavens declare the glory of God;
the skies proclaim the work of his hands.
2 Day after day they pour forth speech;
night after night they display knowledge.
3 There is no speech or language
where their voice is not heard.[a]
4 Their voice[b] goes out into all the earth,
their words to the ends of the world.

In the heavens he has pitched a tent for the sun,
5 which is like a bridegroom coming forth from his pavilion,
like a champion rejoicing to run his course.
6 It rises at one end of the heavens
and makes its circuit to the other;
nothing is hidden from its heat.

7 The law of the LORD is perfect,
reviving the soul.
The statutes of the LORD are trustworthy,
making wise the simple.
8 The precepts of the LORD are right,
giving joy to the heart.
The commands of the LORD are radiant,
giving light to the eyes.
9 The fear of the LORD is pure,
enduring forever.
The ordinances of the LORD are sure
and altogether righteous.
10 They are more precious than gold,
than much pure gold;
they are sweeter than honey,
than honey from the comb.
11 By them is your servant warned;
in keeping them there is great reward.

12 Who can discern his errors?
Forgive my hidden faults.
13 Keep your servant also from willful sins;
may they not rule over me.
Then will I be blameless,
innocent of great transgression.

14 May the words of my mouth and the meditation of my heart
be pleasing in your sight,
O LORD, my Rock and my Redeemer.

[a] 3 Or *They have no speech, there are no words; / no sound is heard from them*
[b] 4 Septuagint, Jerome and Syriac; Hebrew *line*

Hear My Prayer

Hear My Prayer

Psalm 20

For the director of music. A psalm of David.

1 May the LORD answer you when you are in
distress;
may the name of the God of Jacob protect you.
2 May he send you help from the sanctuary
and grant you support from Zion.
3 May he remember all your sacrifices
and accept your burnt offerings. *Selah*
4 May he give you the desire of your heart
and make all your plans succeed.
5 We will shout for joy when you are victorious
and will lift up our banners in the name of
our God.
May the LORD grant all your requests.

6 Now I know that the LORD saves his anointed;
he answers him from his holy heaven
with the saving power of his right hand.
7 Some trust in chariots and some in horses,
but we trust in the name of the LORD our God.
8 They are brought to their knees and fall,
but we rise up and stand firm.

9 O LORD, save the king!
Answer[a] us when we call!

Psalm 21

For the director of music. A psalm of David.

1 O LORD, the king rejoices in your strength.
How great is his joy in the victories you give!
2 You have granted him the desire of his heart
and have not withheld the request of his
lips. *Selah*
3 You welcomed him with rich blessings
and placed a crown of pure gold on his head.
4 He asked you for life, and you gave it to him—
length of days, for ever and ever.
5 Through the victories you gave, his glory is great;
you have bestowed on him splendor and
majesty.
6 Surely you have granted him eternal blessings
and made him glad with the joy of your
presence.
7 For the king trusts in the LORD;
through the unfailing love of the Most High
he will not be shaken.

8 Your hand will lay hold on all your enemies;
your right hand will seize your foes.
9 At the time of your appearing
you will make them like a fiery furnace.
In his wrath the LORD will swallow them up,
and his fire will consume them.

[a] *9* Or *save! / O King, answer*

10 You will destroy their descendants from the
earth,
their posterity from mankind.
11 Though they plot evil against you
and devise wicked schemes, they cannot succeed;
12 for you will make them turn their backs
when you aim at them with drawn bow.

13 Be exalted, O LORD, in your strength;
we will sing and praise your might.

Psalm 22

For the director of music. To ⌞the tune of⌟ "The Doe of the Morning." A psalm of David.

1 My God, my God, why have you forsaken me?
Why are you so far from saving me,
so far from the words of my groaning?
2 O my God, I cry out by day, but you do not answer,
by night, and am not silent.

3 Yet you are enthroned as the Holy One;
you are the praise of Israel.[a]
4 In you our fathers put their trust;
they trusted and you delivered them.
5 They cried to you and were saved;
in you they trusted and were not disappointed.

6 But I am a worm and not a man,
scorned by men and despised by the people.
7 All who see me mock me;
they hurl insults, shaking their heads:
8 "He trusts in the LORD;
let the LORD rescue him.
Let him deliver him,
since he delights in him."

9 Yet you brought me out of the womb;
you made me trust in you
even at my mother's breast.
10 From birth I was cast upon you;
from my mother's womb you have been my God.
11 Do not be far from me,
for trouble is near
and there is no one to help.

12 Many bulls surround me;
strong bulls of Bashan encircle me.
13 Roaring lions tearing their prey
open their mouths wide against me.
14 I am poured out like water,
and all my bones are out of joint.
My heart has turned to wax;
it has melted away within me.
15 My strength is dried up like a potsherd,
and my tongue sticks to the roof of my mouth;
you lay me[b] in the dust of death.

[a] 3 Or *Yet you are holy, / enthroned on the praises of Israel* [b] 15 Or */ I am laid*

Hear My Prayer

Hear My Prayer

16 Dogs have surrounded me;
a band of evil men has encircled me,
they have pierced[a] my hands and my feet.
17 I can count all my bones;
people stare and gloat over me.
18 They divide my garments among them
and cast lots for my clothing.

19 But you, O LORD, be not far off;
O my Strength, come quickly to help me.
20 Deliver my life from the sword,
my precious life from the power of the dogs.
21 Rescue me from the mouth of the lions;
save[b] me from the horns of the wild oxen.

22 I will declare your name to my brothers;
in the congregation I will praise you.
23 You who fear the LORD, praise him!
All you descendants of Jacob, honor him!
Revere him, all you descendants of Israel!
24 For he has not despised or disdained
the suffering of the afflicted one;
he has not hidden his face from him
but has listened to his cry for help.

25 From you comes the theme of my praise in the great assembly;
before those who fear you[c] will I fulfill my vows.
26 The poor will eat and be satisfied;
they who seek the LORD will praise him—
may your hearts live forever!
27 All the ends of the earth
will remember and turn to the LORD,
and all the families of the nations
will bow down before him,
28 for dominion belongs to the LORD
and he rules over the nations.

29 All the rich of the earth will feast and worship;
all who go down to the dust will kneel before him—
those who cannot keep themselves alive.
30 Posterity will serve him;
future generations will be told about the Lord.
31 They will proclaim his righteousness
to a people yet unborn—
for he has done it.

Psalm 23

A psalm of David.

1 The LORD is my shepherd, I shall not be in want.
2 He makes me lie down in green pastures,
he leads me beside quiet waters,
3 he restores my soul.

[a] *16* Some Hebrew manuscripts, Septuagint and Syriac; most Hebrew manuscripts */ like the lion,* [b] *21* Or */ you have heard* [c] *25* Hebrew *him*

He guides me in paths of righteousness
for his name's sake.
4 Even though I walk
through the valley of the shadow of death,[a]
I will fear no evil,
for you are with me;
your rod and your staff,
they comfort me.

5 You prepare a table before me
in the presence of my enemies.
You anoint my head with oil;
my cup overflows.
6 Surely goodness and love will follow me
all the days of my life,
and I will dwell in the house of the LORD
forever.

Psalm 24

Of David. A psalm.

1 The earth is the LORD's, and everything in it,
the world, and all who live in it;
2 for he founded it upon the seas
and established it upon the waters.

3 Who may ascend the hill of the LORD?
Who may stand in his holy place?
4 He who has clean hands and a pure heart,
who does not lift up his soul to an idol
or swear by what is false.[b]
5 He will receive blessing from the LORD
and vindication from God his Savior.
6 Such is the generation of those who seek him,
who seek your face, O God of Jacob.[c] *Selah*

7 Lift up your heads, O you gates;
be lifted up, you ancient doors,
that the King of glory may come in.
8 Who is this King of glory?
The LORD strong and mighty,
the LORD mighty in battle.
9 Lift up your heads, O you gates;
lift them up, you ancient doors,
that the King of glory may come in.
10 Who is he, this King of glory?
The LORD Almighty—
he is the King of glory. *Selah*

Psalm 25[d]

Of David.

1 To you, O LORD, I lift up my soul;
2 in you I trust, O my God.

[a] 4 Or *through the darkest valley* [b] 4 Or *swear falsely* [c] 6 Two Hebrew manuscripts and Syriac (see also Septuagint); most Hebrew manuscripts *face, Jacob* [d] This psalm is an acrostic poem, the verses of which begin with the successive letters of the Hebrew alphabet.

Hear My Prayer

Hear My Prayer

Do not let me be put to shame,
 nor let my enemies triumph over me.
3 No one whose hope is in you
 will ever be put to shame,
but they will be put to shame
 who are treacherous without excuse.

4 Show me your ways, O LORD,
 teach me your paths;
5 guide me in your truth and teach me,
 for you are God my Savior,
 and my hope is in you all day long.
6 Remember, O LORD, your great mercy and love,
 for they are from of old.
7 Remember not the sins of my youth
 and my rebellious ways;
according to your love remember me,
 for you are good, O LORD.

8 Good and upright is the LORD;
 therefore he instructs sinners in his ways.
9 He guides the humble in what is right
 and teaches them his way.
10 All the ways of the LORD are loving and faithful
 for those who keep the demands of his covenant.
11 For the sake of your name, O LORD,
 forgive my iniquity, though it is great.
12 Who, then, is the man that fears the LORD?
 He will instruct him in the way chosen for him.
13 He will spend his days in prosperity,
 and his descendants will inherit the land.
14 The LORD confides in those who fear him;
 he makes his covenant known to them.
15 My eyes are ever on the LORD,
 for only he will release my feet from the snare.

16 Turn to me and be gracious to me,
 for I am lonely and afflicted.
17 The troubles of my heart have multiplied;
 free me from my anguish.
18 Look upon my affliction and my distress
 and take away all my sins.
19 See how my enemies have increased
 and how fiercely they hate me!
20 Guard my life and rescue me;
 let me not be put to shame,
 for I take refuge in you.
21 May integrity and uprightness protect me,
 because my hope is in you.

22 Redeem Israel, O God,
 from all their troubles!

Psalm 26

Of David.

1 Vindicate me, O LORD,
 for I have led a blameless life;
I have trusted in the LORD

without wavering.
2 Test me, O LORD, and try me,
examine my heart and my mind;
3 for your love is ever before me,
and I walk continually in your truth.
4 I do not sit with deceitful men,
nor do I consort with hypocrites;
5 I abhor the assembly of evildoers
and refuse to sit with the wicked.
6 I wash my hands in innocence,
and go about your altar, O LORD,
7 proclaiming aloud your praise
and telling of all your wonderful deeds.
8 I love the house where you live, O LORD,
the place where your glory dwells.

9 Do not take away my soul along with sinners,
my life with bloodthirsty men,
10 in whose hands are wicked schemes,
whose right hands are full of bribes.
11 But I lead a blameless life;
redeem me and be merciful to me.

12 My feet stand on level ground;
in the great assembly I will praise the LORD.

Psalm 27

Of David.

1 The LORD is my light and my salvation—
whom shall I fear?
The LORD is the stronghold of my life—
of whom shall I be afraid?
2 When evil men advance against me
to devour my flesh,[a]
when my enemies and my foes attack me,
they will stumble and fall.
3 Though an army besiege me,
my heart will not fear;
though war break out against me,
even then will I be confident.

4 One thing I ask of the LORD,
this is what I seek:
that I may dwell in the house of the LORD
all the days of my life,
to gaze upon the beauty of the LORD
and to seek him in his temple.
5 For in the day of trouble
he will keep me safe in his dwelling;
he will hide me in the shelter of his tabernacle
and set me high upon a rock.
6 Then my head will be exalted
above the enemies who surround me;
at his tabernacle will I sacrifice with shouts of joy;
I will sing and make music to the LORD.

[a] 2 Or *to slander me*

Hear My Prayer

Hear My Prayer

7 Hear my voice when I call, O LORD;
be merciful to me and answer me.
8 My heart says of you, "Seek his[a] face!"
Your face, LORD, I will seek.
9 Do not hide your face from me,
do not turn your servant away in anger;
you have been my helper.
Do not reject me or forsake me,
O God my Savior.
10 Though my father and mother forsake me,
the LORD will receive me.
11 Teach me your way, O LORD;
lead me in a straight path
because of my oppressors.
12 Do not turn me over to the desire of my foes,
for false witnesses rise up against me,
breathing out violence.

13 I am still confident of this:
I will see the goodness of the LORD
in the land of the living.
14 Wait for the LORD;
be strong and take heart
and wait for the LORD.

Psalm 28

Of David.

1 To you I call, O LORD my Rock;
do not turn a deaf ear to me.
For if you remain silent,
I will be like those who have gone down to the pit.
2 Hear my cry for mercy
as I call to you for help,
as I lift up my hands
toward your Most Holy Place.
3 Do not drag me away with the wicked,
with those who do evil,
who speak cordially with their neighbors
but harbor malice in their hearts.
4 Repay them for their deeds
and for their evil work;
repay them for what their hands have done
and bring back upon them what they deserve.
5 Since they show no regard for the works of the LORD
and what his hands have done,
he will tear them down
and never build them up again.

6 Praise be to the LORD,
for he has heard my cry for mercy.
7 The LORD is my strength and my shield;
my heart trusts in him, and I am helped.
My heart leaps for joy
and I will give thanks to him in song.

[a] 8 Or *To you, O my heart, he has said, "Seek my*

8 The LORD is the strength of his people,
a fortress of salvation for his anointed one.
9 Save your people and bless your inheritance;
be their shepherd and carry them forever.

Psalm 29

A psalm of David.

1 Ascribe to the LORD, O mighty ones,
ascribe to the LORD glory and strength.
2 Ascribe to the LORD the glory due his name;
worship the LORD in the splendor of his[a]
holiness.

3 The voice of the LORD is over the waters;
the God of glory thunders,
the LORD thunders over the mighty waters.
4 The voice of the LORD is powerful;
the voice of the LORD is majestic.
5 The voice of the LORD breaks the cedars;
the LORD breaks in pieces the cedars of
Lebanon.
6 He makes Lebanon skip like a calf,
Sirion[b] like a young wild ox.
7 The voice of the LORD strikes
with flashes of lightning.
8 The voice of the LORD shakes the desert;
the LORD shakes the Desert of Kadesh.
9 The voice of the LORD twists the oaks[c]
and strips the forests bare.
And in his temple all cry, "Glory!"

10 The LORD sits[d] enthroned over the flood;
the LORD is enthroned as King forever.
11 The LORD gives strength to his people;
the LORD blesses his people with peace.

Psalm 30

A psalm. A song. For the dedication of the temple.[e]
Of David.

1 I will exalt you, O LORD,
for you lifted me out of the depths
and did not let my enemies gloat over me.
2 O LORD my God, I called to you for help
and you healed me.
3 O LORD, you brought me up from the grave[f];
you spared me from going down into the pit.

4 Sing to the LORD, you saints of his;
praise his holy name.
5 For his anger lasts only a moment,
but his favor lasts a lifetime;
weeping may remain for a night,
but rejoicing comes in the morning.

[a] 2 Or *LORD with the splendor of* [b] 6 That is, Mount Hermon [c] 9 Or *LORD makes the deer give birth* [d] 10 Or *sat* [e] Title: Or *palace* [f] 3 Hebrew *Sheol*

Hear My Prayer

Hear My Prayer

6 When I felt secure, I said,
"I will never be shaken."
7 O LORD, when you favored me,
you made my mountain[a] stand firm;
but when you hid your face,
I was dismayed.

8 To you, O LORD, I called;
to the Lord I cried for mercy:
9 "What gain is there in my destruction,[b]
in my going down into the pit?
Will the dust praise you?
Will it proclaim your faithfulness?
10 Hear, O LORD, and be merciful to me;
O LORD, be my help."
11 You turned my wailing into dancing;
you removed my sackcloth and clothed me with joy,
12 that my heart may sing to you and not be silent.
O LORD my God, I will give you thanks forever.

Psalm 31

For the director of music. A psalm of David.

1 In you, O LORD, I have taken refuge;
let me never be put to shame;
deliver me in your righteousness.
2 Turn your ear to me,
come quickly to my rescue;
be my rock of refuge,
a strong fortress to save me.
3 Since you are my rock and my fortress,
for the sake of your name lead and guide me.
4 Free me from the trap that is set for me,
for you are my refuge.
5 Into your hands I commit my spirit;
redeem me, O LORD, the God of truth.

6 I hate those who cling to worthless idols;
I trust in the LORD.
7 I will be glad and rejoice in your love,
for you saw my affliction
and knew the anguish of my soul.
8 You have not handed me over to the enemy
but have set my feet in a spacious place.

9 Be merciful to me, O LORD, for I am in distress;
my eyes grow weak with sorrow,
my soul and my body with grief.
10 My life is consumed by anguish
and my years by groaning;
my strength fails because of my affliction,[c]
and my bones grow weak.
11 Because of all my enemies,
I am the utter contempt of my neighbors;
I am a dread to my friends—

[a] 7 Or *hill country* [b] 9 Or *there if I am silenced* [c] 10 Or *guilt*

those who see me on the street flee from me.
12 I am forgotten by them as though I were dead;
I have become like broken pottery.
13 For I hear the slander of many;
there is terror on every side;
they conspire against me
and plot to take my life.

14 But I trust in you, O LORD;
I say, "You are my God."
15 My times are in your hands;
deliver me from my enemies
and from those who pursue me.
16 Let your face shine on your servant;
save me in your unfailing love.
17 Let me not be put to shame, O LORD,
for I have cried out to you;
but let the wicked be put to shame
and lie silent in the grave.[a]
18 Let their lying lips be silenced,
for with pride and contempt
they speak arrogantly against the righteous.

19 How great is your goodness,
which you have stored up for those who fear you,
which you bestow in the sight of men
on those who take refuge in you.
20 In the shelter of your presence you hide them
from the intrigues of men;
in your dwelling you keep them safe
from accusing tongues.

21 Praise be to the LORD,
for he showed his wonderful love to me
when I was in a besieged city.
22 In my alarm I said,
"I am cut off from your sight!"
Yet you heard my cry for mercy
when I called to you for help.

23 Love the LORD, all his saints!
The LORD preserves the faithful,
but the proud he pays back in full.
24 Be strong and take heart,
all you who hope in the LORD.

Psalm 32

Of David. A *maskil.*[b]

1 Blessed is he
whose transgressions are forgiven,
whose sins are covered.
2 Blessed is the man
whose sin the LORD does not count against him
and in whose spirit is no deceit.

3 When I kept silent,
my bones wasted away

[a] *17* Hebrew *Sheol* [b] Title: Probably a literary or musical term

Hear My Prayer

Hear My Prayer

through my groaning all day long.
4 For day and night
your hand was heavy upon me;
my strength was sapped
as in the heat of summer. *Selah*
5 Then I acknowledged my sin to you
and did not cover up my iniquity.
I said, "I will confess
my transgressions to the LORD"—
and you forgave
the guilt of my sin. *Selah*

6 Therefore let everyone who is godly pray to you
while you may be found;
surely when the mighty waters rise,
they will not reach him.
7 You are my hiding place;
you will protect me from trouble
and surround me with songs of deliverance. *Selah*

8 I will instruct you and teach you in the way you should go;
I will counsel you and watch over you.
9 Do not be like the horse or the mule,
which have no understanding
but must be controlled by bit and bridle
or they will not come to you.
10 Many are the woes of the wicked,
but the LORD's unfailing love
surrounds the man who trusts in him.

11 Rejoice in the LORD and be glad, you righteous;
sing, all you who are upright in heart!

Psalm 33

1 Sing joyfully to the LORD, you righteous;
it is fitting for the upright to praise him.
2 Praise the LORD with the harp;
make music to him on the ten-stringed lyre.
3 Sing to him a new song;
play skillfully, and shout for joy.

4 For the word of the LORD is right and true;
he is faithful in all he does.
5 The LORD loves righteousness and justice;
the earth is full of his unfailing love.

6 By the word of the LORD were the heavens made,
their starry host by the breath of his mouth.
7 He gathers the waters of the sea into jars[a];
he puts the deep into storehouses.
8 Let all the earth fear the LORD;
let all the people of the world revere him.
9 For he spoke, and it came to be;
he commanded, and it stood firm.
10 The LORD foils the plans of the nations;
he thwarts the purposes of the peoples.

[a] 7 Or *sea as into a heap*

11 But the plans of the LORD stand firm forever,
the purposes of his heart through all generations.

12 Blessed is the nation whose God is the LORD,
the people he chose for his inheritance.
13 From heaven the LORD looks down
and sees all mankind;
14 from his dwelling place he watches
all who live on earth—
15 he who forms the hearts of all,
who considers everything they do.
16 No king is saved by the size of his army;
no warrior escapes by his great strength.
17 A horse is a vain hope for deliverance;
despite all its great strength it cannot save.
18 But the eyes of the LORD are on those who fear him,
on those whose hope is in his unfailing love,
19 to deliver them from death
and keep them alive in famine.

20 We wait in hope for the LORD;
he is our help and our shield.
21 In him our hearts rejoice,
for we trust in his holy name.
22 May your unfailing love rest upon us, O LORD,
even as we put our hope in you.

Psalm 34[a]

Of David. When he pretended to be insane before Abimelech, who drove him away, and he left.

1 I will extol the LORD at all times;
his praise will always be on my lips.
2 My soul will boast in the LORD;
let the afflicted hear and rejoice.
3 Glorify the LORD with me;
let us exalt his name together.

4 I sought the LORD, and he answered me;
he delivered me from all my fears.
5 Those who look to him are radiant;
their faces are never covered with shame.
6 This poor man called, and the LORD heard him;
he saved him out of all his troubles.
7 The angel of the LORD encamps around those who fear him,
and he delivers them.

8 Taste and see that the LORD is good;
blessed is the man who takes refuge in him.
9 Fear the LORD, you his saints,
for those who fear him lack nothing.
10 The lions may grow weak and hungry,
but those who seek the LORD lack no good thing.

11 Come, my children, listen to me;
I will teach you the fear of the LORD.

[a] This psalm is an acrostic poem, the verses of which begin with the successive letters of the Hebrew alphabet.

Hear My Prayer

Hear My Prayer

12 Whoever of you loves life
and desires to see many good days,
13 keep your tongue from evil
and your lips from speaking lies.
14 Turn from evil and do good;
seek peace and pursue it.

15 The eyes of the LORD are on the righteous
and his ears are attentive to their cry;
16 the face of the LORD is against those who do evil,
to cut off the memory of them from the earth.

17 The righteous cry out, and the LORD hears them;
he delivers them from all their troubles.
18 The LORD is close to the brokenhearted
and saves those who are crushed in spirit.

19 A righteous man may have many troubles,
but the LORD delivers him from them all;
20 he protects all his bones,
not one of them will be broken.

21 Evil will slay the wicked;
the foes of the righteous will be condemned.
22 The LORD redeems his servants;
no one will be condemned who takes refuge in him.

Psalm 35

Of David.

1 Contend, O LORD, with those who contend with me;
fight against those who fight against me.
2 Take up shield and buckler;
arise and come to my aid.
3 Brandish spear and javelin[a]
against those who pursue me.
Say to my soul,
"I am your salvation."

4 May those who seek my life
be disgraced and put to shame;
may those who plot my ruin
be turned back in dismay.
5 May they be like chaff before the wind,
with the angel of the LORD driving them away;
6 may their path be dark and slippery,
with the angel of the LORD pursuing them.
7 Since they hid their net for me without cause
and without cause dug a pit for me,
8 may ruin overtake them by surprise—
may the net they hid entangle them,
may they fall into the pit, to their ruin.
9 Then my soul will rejoice in the LORD
and delight in his salvation.
10 My whole being will exclaim,
"Who is like you, O LORD?

[a] 3 Or *and block the way*

You rescue the poor from those too strong for them,
the poor and needy from those who rob them."
11 Ruthless witnesses come forward;
they question me on things I know nothing about.
12 They repay me evil for good
and leave my soul forlorn.
13 Yet when they were ill, I put on sackcloth
and humbled myself with fasting.
When my prayers returned to me unanswered,
14 I went about mourning
as though for my friend or brother.
I bowed my head in grief
as though weeping for my mother.
15 But when I stumbled, they gathered in glee;
attackers gathered against me when I was
unaware.
They slandered me without ceasing.
16 Like the ungodly they maliciously mocked[a];
they gnashed their teeth at me.
17 O Lord, how long will you look on?
Rescue my life from their ravages,
my precious life from these lions.
18 I will give you thanks in the great assembly;
among throngs of people I will praise you.

19 Let not those gloat over me
who are my enemies without cause;
let not those who hate me without reason
maliciously wink the eye.
20 They do not speak peaceably,
but devise false accusations
against those who live quietly in the land.
21 They gape at me and say, "Aha! Aha!
With our own eyes we have seen it."

22 O LORD, you have seen this; be not silent.
Do not be far from me, O Lord.
23 Awake, and rise to my defense!
Contend for me, my God and Lord.
24 Vindicate me in your righteousness, O LORD
my God;
do not let them gloat over me.
25 Do not let them think, "Aha, just what we
wanted!"
or say, "We have swallowed him up."

26 May all who gloat over my distress
be put to shame and confusion;
may all who exalt themselves over me
be clothed with shame and disgrace.
27 May those who delight in my vindication
shout for joy and gladness;
may they always say, "The LORD be exalted,
who delights in the well-being of his servant."
28 My tongue will speak of your righteousness
and of your praises all day long.

[a] *16* Septuagint; Hebrew may mean *ungodly circle of mockers.*

Hear My Prayer

Hear My Prayer

Psalm 36

For the director of music. Of David the servant of the LORD.

1 An oracle is within my heart
concerning the sinfulness of the wicked:[a]
There is no fear of God
before his eyes.
2 For in his own eyes he flatters himself
too much to detect or hate his sin.
3 The words of his mouth are wicked and deceitful;
he has ceased to be wise and to do good.
4 Even on his bed he plots evil;
he commits himself to a sinful course
and does not reject what is wrong.

5 Your love, O LORD, reaches to the heavens,
your faithfulness to the skies.
6 Your righteousness is like the mighty mountains,
your justice like the great deep.
O LORD, you preserve both man and beast.
7 How priceless is your unfailing love!
Both high and low among men
find[b] refuge in the shadow of your wings.
8 They feast on the abundance of your house;
you give them drink from your river of delights.
9 For with you is the fountain of life;
in your light we see light.

10 Continue your love to those who know you,
your righteousness to the upright in heart.
11 May the foot of the proud not come against me,
nor the hand of the wicked drive me away.
12 See how the evildoers lie fallen—
thrown down, not able to rise!

Psalm 37[c]

Of David.

1 Do not fret because of evil men
or be envious of those who do wrong;
2 for like the grass they will soon wither,
like green plants they will soon die away.

3 Trust in the LORD and do good;
dwell in the land and enjoy safe pasture.
4 Delight yourself in the LORD
and he will give you the desires of your heart.

5 Commit your way to the LORD;
trust in him and he will do this:
6 He will make your righteousness shine like the dawn,
the justice of your cause like the noonday sun.

7 Be still before the LORD and wait patiently for him;
do not fret when men succeed in their ways,
when they carry out their wicked schemes.

[a] *1* Or *heart: / Sin proceeds from the wicked.* [b] *7* Or *love, O God! / Men find*; or *love! / Both heavenly beings and men / find* [c] This psalm is an acrostic poem, the stanzas of which begin with the successive letters of the Hebrew alphabet.

8 Refrain from anger and turn from wrath;
do not fret—it leads only to evil.
9 For evil men will be cut off,
but those who hope in the LORD will inherit the land.

10 A little while, and the wicked will be no more;
though you look for them, they will not be found.
11 But the meek will inherit the land
and enjoy great peace.

12 The wicked plot against the righteous
and gnash their teeth at them;
13 but the Lord laughs at the wicked,
for he knows their day is coming.

14 The wicked draw the sword
and bend the bow
to bring down the poor and needy,
to slay those whose ways are upright.
15 But their swords will pierce their own hearts,
and their bows will be broken.

16 Better the little that the righteous have
than the wealth of many wicked;
17 for the power of the wicked will be broken,
but the LORD upholds the righteous.

18 The days of the blameless are known to the LORD,
and their inheritance will endure forever.
19 In times of disaster they will not wither;
in days of famine they will enjoy plenty.

20 But the wicked will perish:
The LORD's enemies will be like the beauty of the fields,
they will vanish—vanish like smoke.

21 The wicked borrow and do not repay,
but the righteous give generously;
22 those the LORD blesses will inherit the land,
but those he curses will be cut off.

23 If the LORD delights in a man's way,
he makes his steps firm;
24 though he stumble, he will not fall,
for the LORD upholds him with his hand.

25 I was young and now I am old,
yet I have never seen the righteous forsaken
or their children begging bread.
26 They are always generous and lend freely;
their children will be blessed.

27 Turn from evil and do good;
then you will dwell in the land forever.
28 For the LORD loves the just
and will not forsake his faithful ones.
They will be protected forever,
but the offspring of the wicked will be cut off;
29 the righteous will inherit the land
and dwell in it forever.

Hear My Prayer

Hear My Prayer

30 The mouth of the righteous man utters wisdom,
and his tongue speaks what is just.
31 The law of his God is in his heart;
his feet do not slip.

32 The wicked lie in wait for the righteous,
seeking their very lives;
33 but the LORD will not leave them in their power
or let them be condemned when brought to trial.

34 Wait for the LORD
and keep his way.
He will exalt you to inherit the land;
when the wicked are cut off, you will see it.

35 I have seen a wicked and ruthless man
flourishing like a green tree in its native soil,
36 but he soon passed away and was no more;
though I looked for him, he could not be found.

37 Consider the blameless, observe the upright;
there is a future[a] for the man of peace.
38 But all sinners will be destroyed;
the future[b] of the wicked will be cut off.

39 The salvation of the righteous comes from the LORD;
he is their stronghold in time of trouble.
40 The LORD helps them and delivers them;
he delivers them from the wicked and saves them,
because they take refuge in him.

Psalm 38

A psalm of David. A petition.

1 O LORD, do not rebuke me in your anger
or discipline me in your wrath.
2 For your arrows have pierced me,
and your hand has come down upon me.
3 Because of your wrath there is no health in my body;
my bones have no soundness because of my sin.
4 My guilt has overwhelmed me
like a burden too heavy to bear.

5 My wounds fester and are loathsome
because of my sinful folly.
6 I am bowed down and brought very low;
all day long I go about mourning.
7 My back is filled with searing pain;
there is no health in my body.
8 I am feeble and utterly crushed;
I groan in anguish of heart.

9 All my longings lie open before you, O Lord;
my sighing is not hidden from you.
10 My heart pounds, my strength fails me;
even the light has gone from my eyes.
11 My friends and companions avoid me because of my
wounds;

[a] 37 Or *there will be posterity* [b] 38 Or *posterity*

my neighbors stay far away.
12 Those who seek my life set their traps,
those who would harm me talk of my ruin;
all day long they plot deception.

13 I am like a deaf man, who cannot hear,
like a mute, who cannot open his mouth;
14 I have become like a man who does not hear,
whose mouth can offer no reply.
15 I wait for you, O LORD;
you will answer, O Lord my God.
16 For I said, "Do not let them gloat
or exalt themselves over me when my foot slips."

17 For I am about to fall,
and my pain is ever with me.
18 I confess my iniquity;
I am troubled by my sin.
19 Many are those who are my vigorous enemies;
those who hate me without reason are numerous.
20 Those who repay my good with evil
slander me when I pursue what is good.

21 O LORD, do not forsake me;
be not far from me, O my God.
22 Come quickly to help me,
O Lord my Savior.

Psalm 39

For the director of music. For Jeduthun. A psalm of David.

1 I said, "I will watch my ways
and keep my tongue from sin;
I will put a muzzle on my mouth
as long as the wicked are in my presence."
2 But when I was silent and still,
not even saying anything good,
my anguish increased.
3 My heart grew hot within me,
and as I meditated, the fire burned;
then I spoke with my tongue:

4 "Show me, O LORD, my life's end
and the number of my days;
let me know how fleeting is my life.
5 You have made my days a mere handbreadth;
the span of my years is as nothing before you.
Each man's life is but a breath. *Selah*
6 Man is a mere phantom as he goes to and fro:
He bustles about, but only in vain;
he heaps up wealth, not knowing who will get it.

7 "But now, Lord, what do I look for?
My hope is in you.
8 Save me from all my transgressions;
do not make me the scorn of fools.
9 I was silent; I would not open my mouth,
for you are the one who has done this.
10 Remove your scourge from me;

Hear My Prayer

Hear My Prayer

I am overcome by the blow of your hand.
11 You rebuke and discipline men for their sin;
you consume their wealth like a moth—
each man is but a breath. *Selah*

12 "Hear my prayer, O LORD,
listen to my cry for help;
be not deaf to my weeping.
For I dwell with you as an alien,
a stranger, as all my fathers were.
13 Look away from me, that I may rejoice again
before I depart and am no more."

Psalm 40

For the director of music. Of David. A psalm.

1 I waited patiently for the LORD;
he turned to me and heard my cry.
2 He lifted me out of the slimy pit,
out of the mud and mire;
he set my feet on a rock
and gave me a firm place to stand.
3 He put a new song in my mouth,
a hymn of praise to our God.
Many will see and fear
and put their trust in the LORD.

4 Blessed is the man
who makes the LORD his trust,
who does not look to the proud,
to those who turn aside to false gods.[a]
5 Many, O LORD my God,
are the wonders you have done.
The things you planned for us
no one can recount to you;
were I to speak and tell of them,
they would be too many to declare.

6 Sacrifice and offering you did not desire,
but my ears you have pierced[b,c];
burnt offerings and sin offerings
you did not require.
7 Then I said, "Here I am, I have come—
it is written about me in the scroll.[d]
8 I desire to do your will, O my God;
your law is within my heart."

9 I proclaim righteousness in the great
assembly;
I do not seal my lips,
as you know, O LORD.
10 I do not hide your righteousness in my heart;
I speak of your faithfulness and salvation.
I do not conceal your love and your truth
from the great assembly.

[a] 4 Or *to falsehood* [b] 6 Hebrew; Septuagint *but a body you have prepared for me* (see also Symmachus and Theodotion) [c] 6 Or *opened* [d] 7 Or *come / with the scroll written for me*

11 Do not withhold your mercy from me, O LORD;
may your love and your truth always protect me.
12 For troubles without number surround me;
my sins have overtaken me, and I cannot see.
They are more than the hairs of my head,
and my heart fails within me.

13 Be pleased, O LORD, to save me;
O LORD, come quickly to help me.
14 May all who seek to take my life
be put to shame and confusion;
may all who desire my ruin
be turned back in disgrace.
15 May those who say to me, "Aha! Aha!"
be appalled at their own shame.
16 But may all who seek you
rejoice and be glad in you;
may those who love your salvation always say,
"The LORD be exalted!"

17 Yet I am poor and needy;
may the Lord think of me.
You are my help and my deliverer;
O my God, do not delay.

Psalm 41

For the director of music. A psalm of David.

1 Blessed is he who has regard for the weak;
the LORD delivers him in times of trouble.
2 The LORD will protect him and preserve his life;
he will bless him in the land
and not surrender him to the desire of his foes.
3 The LORD will sustain him on his sickbed
and restore him from his bed of illness.

4 I said, "O LORD, have mercy on me;
heal me, for I have sinned against you."
5 My enemies say of me in malice,
"When will he die and his name perish?"
6 Whenever one comes to see me,
he speaks falsely, while his heart gathers slander;
then he goes out and spreads it abroad.

7 All my enemies whisper together against me;
they imagine the worst for me, saying,
8 "A vile disease has beset him;
he will never get up from the place where he
lies."
9 Even my close friend, whom I trusted,
he who shared my bread,
has lifted up his heel against me.

10 But you, O LORD, have mercy on me;
raise me up, that I may repay them.
11 I know that you are pleased with me,
for my enemy does not triumph over me.
12 In my integrity you uphold me
and set me in your presence forever.

Hear My Prayer

Hear My Prayer

13 Praise be to the LORD, the God of Israel,
from everlasting to everlasting.
Amen and Amen.

BOOK II

Psalms 42–72

Psalm 42[a]

For the director of music. A *maskil*[b] of the Sons of Korah.

1 As the deer pants for streams of water,
so my soul pants for you, O God.
2 My soul thirsts for God, for the living God.
When can I go and meet with God?
3 My tears have been my food
day and night,
while men say to me all day long,
"Where is your God?"
4 These things I remember
as I pour out my soul:
how I used to go with the multitude,
leading the procession to the house of God,
with shouts of joy and thanksgiving
among the festive throng.

5 Why are you downcast, O my soul?
Why so disturbed within me?
Put your hope in God,
for I will yet praise him,
my Savior and 6 my God.

My[c] soul is downcast within me;
therefore I will remember you
from the land of the Jordan,
the heights of Hermon—from Mount Mizar.
7 Deep calls to deep
in the roar of your waterfalls;
all your waves and breakers
have swept over me.

8 By day the LORD directs his love,
at night his song is with me—
a prayer to the God of my life.

9 I say to God my Rock,
"Why have you forgotten me?
Why must I go about mourning,
oppressed by the enemy?"
10 My bones suffer mortal agony
as my foes taunt me,
saying to me all day long,
"Where is your God?"

11 Why are you downcast, O my soul?
Why so disturbed within me?

[a] In many Hebrew manuscripts Psalms 42 and 43 constitute one psalm. [b] Title: Probably a literary or musical term [c] *5,6* A few Hebrew manuscripts, Septuagint and Syriac; most Hebrew manuscripts *praise him for his saving help. / 6O my God, my*

Put your hope in God,
for I will yet praise him,
my Savior and my God.

Psalm 43[a]

1 Vindicate me, O God,
and plead my cause against an ungodly nation;
rescue me from deceitful and wicked men.
2 You are God my stronghold.
Why have you rejected me?
Why must I go about mourning,
oppressed by the enemy?
3 Send forth your light and your truth,
let them guide me;
let them bring me to your holy mountain,
to the place where you dwell.
4 Then will I go to the altar of God,
to God, my joy and my delight.
I will praise you with the harp,
O God, my God.

5 Why are you downcast, O my soul?
Why so disturbed within me?
Put your hope in God,
for I will yet praise him,
my Savior and my God.

Psalm 44

For the director of music. Of the Sons of Korah.
A *maskil.*[b]

1 We have heard with our ears, O God;
our fathers have told us
what you did in their days,
in days long ago.
2 With your hand you drove out the nations
and planted our fathers;
you crushed the peoples
and made our fathers flourish.
3 It was not by their sword that they won the land,
nor did their arm bring them victory;
it was your right hand, your arm,
and the light of your face, for you loved them.

4 You are my King and my God,
who decrees[c] victories for Jacob.
5 Through you we push back our enemies;
through your name we trample our foes.
6 I do not trust in my bow,
my sword does not bring me victory;
7 but you give us victory over our enemies,
you put our adversaries to shame.
8 In God we make our boast all day long,
and we will praise your name forever. *Selah*

[a] In many Hebrew manuscripts Psalms 42 and 43 constitute one psalm. [b] Title: Probably a literary or musical term [c] 4 Septuagint, Aquila and Syriac; Hebrew *King, O God; / command*

Hear My Prayer

Hear My Prayer

9 But now you have rejected and humbled us;
you no longer go out with our armies.
10 You made us retreat before the enemy,
and our adversaries have plundered us.
11 You gave us up to be devoured like sheep
and have scattered us among the nations.
12 You sold your people for a pittance,
gaining nothing from their sale.

13 You have made us a reproach to our neighbors,
the scorn and derision of those around us.
14 You have made us a byword among the nations;
the peoples shake their heads at us.
15 My disgrace is before me all day long,
and my face is covered with shame
16 at the taunts of those who reproach and revile me,
because of the enemy, who is bent on revenge.

17 All this happened to us,
though we had not forgotten you
or been false to your covenant.
18 Our hearts had not turned back;
our feet had not strayed from your path.
19 But you crushed us and made us a haunt for jackals
and covered us over with deep darkness.

20 If we had forgotten the name of our God
or spread out our hands to a foreign god,
21 would not God have discovered it,
since he knows the secrets of the heart?
22 Yet for your sake we face death all day long;
we are considered as sheep to be slaughtered.

23 Awake, O Lord! Why do you sleep?
Rouse yourself! Do not reject us forever.
24 Why do you hide your face
and forget our misery and oppression?

25 We are brought down to the dust;
our bodies cling to the ground.
26 Rise up and help us;
redeem us because of your unfailing love.

Psalm 45

For the director of music. To ⌞the tune of⌟ "Lilies." Of the Sons of Korah. A *maskil.* [a] A wedding song.

1 My heart is stirred by a noble theme
as I recite my verses for the king;
my tongue is the pen of a skillful writer.

2 You are the most excellent of men
and your lips have been anointed with grace,
since God has blessed you forever.
3 Gird your sword upon your side, O mighty one;
clothe yourself with splendor and majesty.
4 In your majesty ride forth victoriously
in behalf of truth, humility and righteousness;

[a] Title: Probably a literary or musical term

let your right hand display awesome deeds.
5 Let your sharp arrows pierce the hearts of the king's enemies;
let the nations fall beneath your feet.
6 Your throne, O God, will last for ever and ever;
a scepter of justice will be the scepter of your kingdom.
7 You love righteousness and hate wickedness;
therefore God, your God, has set you above your companions
by anointing you with the oil of joy.
8 All your robes are fragrant with myrrh and aloes and cassia;
from palaces adorned with ivory
the music of the strings makes you glad.
9 Daughters of kings are among your honored women;
at your right hand is the royal bride in gold of Ophir.

10 Listen, O daughter, consider and give ear:
Forget your people and your father's house.
11 The king is enthralled by your beauty;
honor him, for he is your lord.
12 The Daughter of Tyre will come with a gift,[a]
men of wealth will seek your favor.

13 All glorious is the princess within ⌞her chamber⌟;
her gown is interwoven with gold.
14 In embroidered garments she is led to the king;
her virgin companions follow her
and are brought to you.
15 They are led in with joy and gladness;
they enter the palace of the king.

16 Your sons will take the place of your fathers;
you will make them princes throughout the land.
17 I will perpetuate your memory through all generations;
therefore the nations will praise you for ever and ever.

Psalm 46

For the director of music. Of the Sons of Korah. According to *alamoth*.[b] A song.

1 God is our refuge and strength,
an ever-present help in trouble.
2 Therefore we will not fear, though the earth give way
and the mountains fall into the heart of the sea,
3 though its waters roar and foam
and the mountains quake with their surging. *Selah*

4 There is a river whose streams make glad the city of God,
the holy place where the Most High dwells.
5 God is within her, she will not fall;
God will help her at break of day.

[a] 12 Or *A Tyrian robe is among the gifts* [b] Title: Probably a musical term

Hear My Prayer

Hear My Prayer

6 Nations are in uproar, kingdoms fall;
he lifts his voice, the earth melts.

7 The LORD Almighty is with us;
the God of Jacob is our fortress. *Selah*

8 Come and see the works of the LORD,
the desolations he has brought on the earth.
9 He makes wars cease to the ends of the earth;
he breaks the bow and shatters the spear,
he burns the shields[a] with fire.
10 "Be still, and know that I am God;
I will be exalted among the nations,
I will be exalted in the earth."

11 The LORD Almighty is with us;
the God of Jacob is our fortress. *Selah*

Psalm 47

For the director of music. Of the Sons of Korah. A psalm.

1 Clap your hands, all you nations;
shout to God with cries of joy.
2 How awesome is the LORD Most High,
the great King over all the earth!
3 He subdued nations under us,
peoples under our feet.
4 He chose our inheritance for us,
the pride of Jacob, whom he loved. *Selah*

5 God has ascended amid shouts of joy,
the LORD amid the sounding of trumpets.
6 Sing praises to God, sing praises;
sing praises to our King, sing praises.

7 For God is the King of all the earth;
sing to him a psalm[b] of praise.
8 God reigns over the nations;
God is seated on his holy throne.
9 The nobles of the nations assemble
as the people of the God of Abraham,
for the kings[c] of the earth belong to God;
he is greatly exalted.

Psalm 48

A song. A psalm of the Sons of Korah.

1 Great is the LORD, and most worthy of praise,
in the city of our God, his holy mountain.
2 It is beautiful in its loftiness,
the joy of the whole earth.
Like the utmost heights of Zaphon[d] is Mount Zion,
the[e] city of the Great King.
3 God is in her citadels;
he has shown himself to be her fortress.

[a] 9 Or *chariots* [b] 7 Or *a maskil* (probably a literary or musical term) [c] 9 Or *shields* [d] 2 *Zaphon* can refer to a sacred mountain or the direction north. [e] 2 Or *earth, / Mount Zion, on the northern side / of the*

4 When the kings joined forces,
when they advanced together,
5 they saw ⌞her⌟ and were astounded;
they fled in terror.
6 Trembling seized them there,
pain like that of a woman in labor.
7 You destroyed them like ships of Tarshish
shattered by an east wind.

8 As we have heard,
so have we seen
in the city of the LORD Almighty,
in the city of our God:
God makes her secure forever. *Selah*

9 Within your temple, O God,
we meditate on your unfailing love.
10 Like your name, O God,
your praise reaches to the ends of the earth;
your right hand is filled with righteousness.
11 Mount Zion rejoices,
the villages of Judah are glad
because of your judgments.

12 Walk about Zion, go around her,
count her towers,
13 consider well her ramparts,
view her citadels,
that you may tell of them to the next generation.
14 For this God is our God for ever and ever;
he will be our guide even to the end.

Psalm 49

For the director of music. Of the Sons of Korah. A psalm.

1 Hear this, all you peoples;
listen, all who live in this world,
2 both low and high,
rich and poor alike:
3 My mouth will speak words of wisdom;
the utterance from my heart will give
understanding.
4 I will turn my ear to a proverb;
with the harp I will expound my riddle:

5 Why should I fear when evil days come,
when wicked deceivers surround me—
6 those who trust in their wealth
and boast of their great riches?
7 No man can redeem the life of another
or give to God a ransom for him—
8 the ransom for a life is costly,
no payment is ever enough—
9 that he should live on forever
and not see decay.

10 For all can see that wise men die;
the foolish and the senseless alike perish
and leave their wealth to others.

Hear My Prayer

Hear My Prayer

11 Their tombs will remain their houses[a] forever,
their dwellings for endless generations,
though they had[b] named lands after themselves.

12 But man, despite his riches, does not endure;
he is[c] like the beasts that perish.

13 This is the fate of those who trust in themselves,
and of their followers, who approve their
sayings. *Selah*

14 Like sheep they are destined for the grave,[d]
and death will feed on them.
The upright will rule over them in the morning;
their forms will decay in the grave,[d]
far from their princely mansions.

15 But God will redeem my life[e] from the grave;
he will surely take me to himself. *Selah*

16 Do not be overawed when a man grows rich,
when the splendor of his house increases;
17 for he will take nothing with him when he dies,
his splendor will not descend with him.
18 Though while he lived he counted himself blessed—
and men praise you when you prosper—
19 he will join the generation of his fathers,
who will never see the light ⌞of life⌟.

20 A man who has riches without understanding
is like the beasts that perish.

Psalm 50

A psalm of Asaph.

1 The Mighty One, God, the LORD,
speaks and summons the earth
from the rising of the sun to the place where it
sets.
2 From Zion, perfect in beauty,
God shines forth.
3 Our God comes and will not be silent;
a fire devours before him,
and around him a tempest rages.
4 He summons the heavens above,
and the earth, that he may judge his people:
5 "Gather to me my consecrated ones,
who made a covenant with me by sacrifice."
6 And the heavens proclaim his righteousness,
for God himself is judge. *Selah*

7 "Hear, O my people, and I will speak,
O Israel, and I will testify against you:
I am God, your God.
8 I do not rebuke you for your sacrifices
or your burnt offerings, which are ever before me.
9 I have no need of a bull from your stall
or of goats from your pens,

[a] *11* Septuagint and Syriac; Hebrew *In their thoughts their houses will remain* [b] *11* Or */ for they have* [c] *12* Hebrew; Septuagint and Syriac read verse 12 the same as verse 20. [d] *14* Hebrew *Sheol*; also in verse 15 [e] *15* Or *soul*

MY BELOVED

Do not be fooled by the evil one. He will try to convince you that you have wandered too far from Me and that you cannot come back. That is never true. I am compassionate and gracious, slow to anger, and abounding in love. If you confess your sins, I am faithful and just and will forgive your sins and purify you from all unrighteousness.

Have you ever wondered how high the heavens reach? My love for you is higher than that. And how far do you think the east is from the west? That is how far I have removed your sins from you. They are gone. So do not go looking for them; do not even try to remember them, because I do not.

Be glad when you come before Me. I love to hear you sing joyful songs of praise. Just think of all the benefits you enjoy as My child. And as you rejoice and give thanks to Me even in difficult times, I will fill you with a peace that you cannot explain.

So do not listen any more to the evil one. He only wants to rob you of your joy . . . joy you will find in My presence. Come into My presence. Approach My throne of grace with confidence, and you will receive mercy and find grace to help you in your time of need. Come even now . . . I am waiting for you.

Ps 16:11; 98:1-4; 100:2; 103:2,5,8,11,12; Php 4:4-7; Heb 10:17; 1Jn 1:9

10 for every animal of the forest is mine,
and the cattle on a thousand hills.
11 I know every bird in the mountains,
and the creatures of the field are mine.
12 If I were hungry I would not tell you,
for the world is mine, and all that is in it.
13 Do I eat the flesh of bulls
or drink the blood of goats?
14 Sacrifice thank offerings to God,
fulfill your vows to the Most High,
15 and call upon me in the day of trouble;
I will deliver you, and you will honor me."

16 But to the wicked, God says:

"What right have you to recite my laws
or take my covenant on your lips?
17 You hate my instruction
and cast my words behind you.
18 When you see a thief, you join with him;
you throw in your lot with adulterers.
19 You use your mouth for evil
and harness your tongue to deceit.
20 You speak continually against your brother
and slander your own mother's son.
21 These things you have done and I kept silent;
you thought I was altogether[a] like you.
But I will rebuke you
and accuse you to your face.

22 "Consider this, you who forget God,
or I will tear you to pieces, with none to rescue:
23 He who sacrifices thank offerings honors me,
and he prepares the way
so that I may show him[b] the salvation of God."

Psalm 51

For the director of music. A psalm of David. When the prophet Nathan came to him after David had committed adultery with Bathsheba.

1 Have mercy on me, O God,
according to your unfailing love;
according to your great compassion
blot out my transgressions.
2 Wash away all my iniquity
and cleanse me from my sin.

3 For I know my transgressions,
and my sin is always before me.
4 Against you, you only, have I sinned
and done what is evil in your sight,
so that you are proved right when you speak
and justified when you judge.
5 Surely I was sinful at birth,
sinful from the time my mother conceived me.

[a] 21 Or *thought the 'I AM' was*

[b] 23 Or *and to him who considers his way / I will show*

Hear My Prayer

Hear My Prayer

6 Surely you desire truth in the inner parts[a];
you teach[b] me wisdom in the inmost place.

7 Cleanse me with hyssop, and I will be clean;
wash me, and I will be whiter than snow.
8 Let me hear joy and gladness;
let the bones you have crushed rejoice.
9 Hide your face from my sins
and blot out all my iniquity.

10 Create in me a pure heart, O God,
and renew a steadfast spirit within me.
11 Do not cast me from your presence
or take your Holy Spirit from me.
12 Restore to me the joy of your salvation
and grant me a willing spirit, to sustain me.

13 Then I will teach transgressors your ways,
and sinners will turn back to you.
14 Save me from bloodguilt, O God,
the God who saves me,
and my tongue will sing of your righteousness.
15 O Lord, open my lips,
and my mouth will declare your praise.
16 You do not delight in sacrifice, or I would bring it;
you do not take pleasure in burnt offerings.
17 The sacrifices of God are[c] a broken spirit;
a broken and contrite heart,
O God, you will not despise.

18 In your good pleasure make Zion prosper;
build up the walls of Jerusalem.
19 Then there will be righteous sacrifices,
whole burnt offerings to delight you;
then bulls will be offered on your altar.

Psalm 52

For the director of music. A *maskil*[d] of David. When Doeg the Edomite had gone to Saul and told him: "David has gone to the house of Ahimelech."

1 Why do you boast of evil, you mighty man?
Why do you boast all day long,
you who are a disgrace in the eyes of God?
2 Your tongue plots destruction;
it is like a sharpened razor,
you who practice deceit.
3 You love evil rather than good,
falsehood rather than speaking the truth. *Selah*
4 You love every harmful word,
O you deceitful tongue!

5 Surely God will bring you down to everlasting ruin:
He will snatch you up and tear you from your tent;
he will uproot you from the land of the living.
Selah

[a] *6* The meaning of the Hebrew for this phrase is uncertain. [b] *6* Or *you desired . . .; / you taught* [c] *17* Or *My sacrifice, O God, is* [d] Title: Probably a literary or musical term

6 The righteous will see and fear;
they will laugh at him, saying,
7 "Here now is the man
who did not make God his stronghold
but trusted in his great wealth
and grew strong by destroying others!"
8 But I am like an olive tree
flourishing in the house of God;
I trust in God's unfailing love
for ever and ever.
9 I will praise you forever for what you have done;
in your name I will hope, for your name is good.
I will praise you in the presence of your saints.

Psalm 53

For the director of music. According to *mahalath.*[a]
A *maskil*[b] of David.

1 The fool says in his heart,
"There is no God."
They are corrupt, and their ways are vile;
there is no one who does good.
2 God looks down from heaven
on the sons of men
to see if there are any who understand,
any who seek God.
3 Everyone has turned away,
they have together become corrupt;
there is no one who does good,
not even one.
4 Will the evildoers never learn—
those who devour my people as men eat bread
and who do not call on God?
5 There they were, overwhelmed with dread,
where there was nothing to dread.
God scattered the bones of those who attacked you;
you put them to shame, for God despised them.
6 Oh, that salvation for Israel would come out of Zion!
When God restores the fortunes of his people,
let Jacob rejoice and Israel be glad!

Psalm 54

For the director of music. With stringed instruments. A *maskil*[b]
of David. When the Ziphites had gone to Saul and said, "Is not
David hiding among us?"

1 Save me, O God, by your name;
vindicate me by your might.
2 Hear my prayer, O God;
listen to the words of my mouth.
3 Strangers are attacking me;
ruthless men seek my life—
men without regard for God. *Selah*

[a] Title: Probably a musical term [b] Title: Probably a literary or musical term

Hear My Prayer

Hear My Prayer

4 Surely God is my help;
the Lord is the one who sustains me.

5 Let evil recoil on those who slander me;
in your faithfulness destroy them.

6 I will sacrifice a freewill offering to you;
I will praise your name, O LORD,
for it is good.
7 For he has delivered me from all my troubles,
and my eyes have looked in triumph on my foes.

Psalm 55

For the director of music. With stringed instruments.
A *maskil*[a] of David.

1 Listen to my prayer, O God,
do not ignore my plea;
2 hear me and answer me.
My thoughts trouble me and I am distraught
3 at the voice of the enemy,
at the stares of the wicked;
for they bring down suffering upon me
and revile me in their anger.

4 My heart is in anguish within me;
the terrors of death assail me.
5 Fear and trembling have beset me;
horror has overwhelmed me.
6 I said, "Oh, that I had the wings of a dove!
I would fly away and be at rest—
7 I would flee far away
and stay in the desert; *Selah*
8 I would hurry to my place of shelter,
far from the tempest and storm."

9 Confuse the wicked, O Lord, confound their speech,
for I see violence and strife in the city.
10 Day and night they prowl about on its walls;
malice and abuse are within it.
11 Destructive forces are at work in the city;
threats and lies never leave its streets.

12 If an enemy were insulting me,
I could endure it;
if a foe were raising himself against me,
I could hide from him.
13 But it is you, a man like myself,
my companion, my close friend,
14 with whom I once enjoyed sweet fellowship
as we walked with the throng at the house of God.

15 Let death take my enemies by surprise;
let them go down alive to the grave,[b]
for evil finds lodging among them.

16 But I call to God,
and the LORD saves me.

[a] Title: Probably a literary or musical term [b] 15 Hebrew *Sheol*

17 Evening, morning and noon
I cry out in distress,
and he hears my voice.
18 He ransoms me unharmed
from the battle waged against me,
even though many oppose me.
19 God, who is enthroned forever,
will hear them and afflict them— *Selah*
men who never change their ways
and have no fear of God.

20 My companion attacks his friends;
he violates his covenant.
21 His speech is smooth as butter,
yet war is in his heart;
his words are more soothing than oil,
yet they are drawn swords.

22 Cast your cares on the LORD
and he will sustain you;
he will never let the righteous fall.
23 But you, O God, will bring down the wicked
into the pit of corruption;
bloodthirsty and deceitful men
will not live out half their days.

But as for me, I trust in you.

Psalm 56

For the director of music. To ⌊the tune of⌋ "A Dove on Distant Oaks." Of David. A *miktam*.[a] When the Philistines had seized him in Gath.

1 Be merciful to me, O God, for men hotly pursue me;
all day long they press their attack.
2 My slanderers pursue me all day long;
many are attacking me in their pride.

3 When I am afraid,
I will trust in you.
4 In God, whose word I praise,
in God I trust; I will not be afraid.
What can mortal man do to me?

5 All day long they twist my words;
they are always plotting to harm me.
6 They conspire, they lurk,
they watch my steps,
eager to take my life.

7 On no account let them escape;
in your anger, O God, bring down the nations.
8 Record my lament;
list my tears on your scroll[b]—
are they not in your record?

9 Then my enemies will turn back
when I call for help.
By this I will know that God is for me.

[a] Title: Probably a literary or musical term [b] 8 Or / *put my tears in your wineskin*

Hear My Prayer

Hear My Prayer

10 In God, whose word I praise,
in the LORD, whose word I praise—
11 in God I trust; I will not be afraid.
What can man do to me?

12 I am under vows to you, O God;
I will present my thank offerings to you.
13 For you have delivered me[a] from death
and my feet from stumbling,
that I may walk before God
in the light of life.[b]

Psalm 57

For the director of music. ⌊To the tune of⌋ "Do Not Destroy." Of David. A *miktam.*[c] When he had fled from Saul into the cave.

1 Have mercy on me, O God, have mercy on me,
for in you my soul takes refuge.
I will take refuge in the shadow of your wings
until the disaster has passed.

2 I cry out to God Most High,
to God, who fulfills ⌊his purpose⌋ for me.
3 He sends from heaven and saves me,
rebuking those who hotly pursue me; *Selah*
God sends his love and his faithfulness.

4 I am in the midst of lions;
I lie among ravenous beasts—
men whose teeth are spears and arrows,
whose tongues are sharp swords.

5 Be exalted, O God, above the heavens;
let your glory be over all the earth.

6 They spread a net for my feet—
I was bowed down in distress.
They dug a pit in my path—
but they have fallen into it themselves. *Selah*

7 My heart is steadfast, O God,
my heart is steadfast;
I will sing and make music.
8 Awake, my soul!
Awake, harp and lyre!
I will awaken the dawn.

9 I will praise you, O Lord, among the nations;
I will sing of you among the peoples.
10 For great is your love, reaching to the heavens;
your faithfulness reaches to the skies.

11 Be exalted, O God, above the heavens;
let your glory be over all the earth.

[a] *13* Or *my soul* [b] *13* Or *the land of the living* [c] Title: Probably a literary or musical term

Psalm 58

For the director of music. ⌊To the tune of⌋ "Do Not Destroy." Of David. A *miktam*. [a]

1 Do you rulers indeed speak justly?
Do you judge uprightly among men?
2 No, in your heart you devise injustice,
and your hands mete out violence on the earth.
3 Even from birth the wicked go astray;
from the womb they are wayward and speak lies.
4 Their venom is like the venom of a snake,
like that of a cobra that has stopped its ears,
5 that will not heed the tune of the charmer,
however skillful the enchanter may be.

6 Break the teeth in their mouths, O God;
tear out, O LORD, the fangs of the lions!
7 Let them vanish like water that flows away;
when they draw the bow, let their arrows be
blunted.
8 Like a slug melting away as it moves along,
like a stillborn child, may they not see the sun.

9 Before your pots can feel ⌊the heat of⌋ the thorns—
whether they be green or dry—the wicked will be
swept away. [b]
10 The righteous will be glad when they are avenged,
when they bathe their feet in the blood of the
wicked.
11 Then men will say,
"Surely the righteous still are rewarded;
surely there is a God who judges the earth."

Psalm 59

For the director of music. ⌊To the tune of⌋ "Do Not Destroy." Of David. A *miktam*. [a] When Saul had sent men to watch David's house in order to kill him.

1 Deliver me from my enemies, O God;
protect me from those who rise up against me.
2 Deliver me from evildoers
and save me from bloodthirsty men.

3 See how they lie in wait for me!
Fierce men conspire against me
for no offense or sin of mine, O LORD.
4 I have done no wrong, yet they are ready to attack
me.
Arise to help me; look on my plight!
5 O LORD God Almighty, the God of Israel,
rouse yourself to punish all the nations;
show no mercy to wicked traitors. *Selah*

6 They return at evening,
snarling like dogs,
and prowl about the city.

[a] Title: Probably a literary or musical term [b] 9 The meaning of the Hebrew for this verse is uncertain.

Hear My Prayer

Hear My Prayer

7 See what they spew from their mouths—
they spew out swords from their lips,
and they say, "Who can hear us?"
8 But you, O LORD, laugh at them;
you scoff at all those nations.

9 O my Strength, I watch for you;
you, O God, are my fortress, 10 my loving God.

God will go before me
and will let me gloat over those who slander me.
11 But do not kill them, O Lord our shield,[a]
or my people will forget.
In your might make them wander about,
and bring them down.
12 For the sins of their mouths,
for the words of their lips,
let them be caught in their pride.
For the curses and lies they utter,
13 consume them in wrath,
consume them till they are no more.
Then it will be known to the ends of the earth
that God rules over Jacob. *Selah*

14 They return at evening,
snarling like dogs,
and prowl about the city.
15 They wander about for food
and howl if not satisfied.
16 But I will sing of your strength,
in the morning I will sing of your love;
for you are my fortress,
my refuge in times of trouble.

17 O my Strength, I sing praise to you;
you, O God, are my fortress, my loving God.

Psalm 60

For the director of music. To ⌞the tune of⌟ "The Lily of the Covenant." A *miktam*[b] of David. For teaching. When he fought Aram Naharaim[c] and Aram Zobah,[d] and when Joab returned and struck down twelve thousand Edomites in the Valley of Salt.

1 You have rejected us, O God, and burst forth upon us;
you have been angry—now restore us!
2 You have shaken the land and torn it open;
mend its fractures, for it is quaking.
3 You have shown your people desperate times;
you have given us wine that makes us stagger.
4 But for those who fear you, you have raised a banner
to be unfurled against the bow. *Selah*
5 Save us and help us with your right hand,
that those you love may be delivered.

[a] *11* Or *sovereign* [b] Title: Probably a literary or musical term [c] Title: That is, Arameans of Northwest Mesopotamia [d] Title: That is, Arameans of central Syria

6 God has spoken from his sanctuary:
"In triumph I will parcel out Shechem
and measure off the Valley of Succoth.
7 Gilead is mine, and Manasseh is mine;
Ephraim is my helmet,
Judah my scepter.
8 Moab is my washbasin,
upon Edom I toss my sandal;
over Philistia I shout in triumph."

9 Who will bring me to the fortified city?
Who will lead me to Edom?
10 Is it not you, O God, you who have rejected us
and no longer go out with our armies?
11 Give us aid against the enemy,
for the help of man is worthless.
12 With God we will gain the victory,
and he will trample down our enemies.

Psalm 61

For the director of music. With stringed instruments. Of David.

1 Hear my cry, O God;
listen to my prayer.

2 From the ends of the earth I call to you,
I call as my heart grows faint;
lead me to the rock that is higher than I.
3 For you have been my refuge,
a strong tower against the foe.

4 I long to dwell in your tent forever
and take refuge in the shelter of your wings. *Selah*
5 For you have heard my vows, O God;
you have given me the heritage of those who fear your name.

6 Increase the days of the king's life,
his years for many generations.
7 May he be enthroned in God's presence forever;
appoint your love and faithfulness to protect him.

8 Then will I ever sing praise to your name
and fulfill my vows day after day.

Psalm 62

For the director of music. For Jeduthun. A psalm of David.

1 My soul finds rest in God alone;
my salvation comes from him.
2 He alone is my rock and my salvation;
he is my fortress, I will never be shaken.

3 How long will you assault a man?
Would all of you throw him down—
this leaning wall, this tottering fence?
4 They fully intend to topple him
from his lofty place;

Hear My Prayer

Hear My Prayer

they take delight in lies.
With their mouths they bless,
but in their hearts they curse. *Selah*

5 Find rest, O my soul, in God alone;
my hope comes from him.
6 He alone is my rock and my salvation;
he is my fortress, I will not be shaken.
7 My salvation and my honor depend on God[a];
he is my mighty rock, my refuge.
8 Trust in him at all times, O people;
pour out your hearts to him,
for God is our refuge. *Selah*

9 Lowborn men are but a breath,
the highborn are but a lie;
if weighed on a balance, they are nothing;
together they are only a breath.
10 Do not trust in extortion
or take pride in stolen goods;
though your riches increase,
do not set your heart on them.
11 One thing God has spoken,
two things have I heard:
that you, O God, are strong,
12 and that you, O Lord, are loving.
Surely you will reward each person
according to what he has done.

Psalm 63

A psalm of David. When he was in the Desert of Judah.

1 O God, you are my God,
earnestly I seek you;
my soul thirsts for you,
my body longs for you,
in a dry and weary land
where there is no water.

2 I have seen you in the sanctuary
and beheld your power and your glory.
3 Because your love is better than life,
my lips will glorify you.
4 I will praise you as long as I live,
and in your name I will lift up my hands.
5 My soul will be satisfied as with the richest of foods;
with singing lips my mouth will praise you.
6 On my bed I remember you;
I think of you through the watches of the night.
7 Because you are my help,
I sing in the shadow of your wings.
8 My soul clings to you;
your right hand upholds me.
9 They who seek my life will be destroyed;
they will go down to the depths of the earth.

[a] 7 Or / *God Most High is my salvation and my honor*

10 They will be given over to the sword
and become food for jackals.

11 But the king will rejoice in God;
all who swear by God's name will praise him,
while the mouths of liars will be silenced.

Psalm 64

For the director of music. A psalm of David.

1 Hear me, O God, as I voice my complaint;
protect my life from the threat of the enemy.
2 Hide me from the conspiracy of the wicked,
from that noisy crowd of evildoers.

3 They sharpen their tongues like swords
and aim their words like deadly arrows.
4 They shoot from ambush at the innocent man;
they shoot at him suddenly, without fear.

5 They encourage each other in evil plans,
they talk about hiding their snares;
they say, "Who will see them[a]?"
6 They plot injustice and say,
"We have devised a perfect plan!"
Surely the mind and heart of man are cunning.

7 But God will shoot them with arrows;
suddenly they will be struck down.
8 He will turn their own tongues against them
and bring them to ruin;
all who see them will shake their heads in scorn.

9 All mankind will fear;
they will proclaim the works of God
and ponder what he has done.
10 Let the righteous rejoice in the LORD
and take refuge in him;
let all the upright in heart praise him!

Psalm 65

For the director of music. A psalm of David. A song.

1 Praise awaits[b] you, O God, in Zion;
to you our vows will be fulfilled.
2 O you who hear prayer,
to you all men will come.
3 When we were overwhelmed by sins,
you forgave[c] our transgressions.
4 Blessed are those you choose
and bring near to live in your courts!
We are filled with the good things of your house,
of your holy temple.

5 You answer us with awesome deeds of righteousness,
O God our Savior,
the hope of all the ends of the earth

[a] 5 Or *us* [b] 1 Or *befits*; the meaning of the Hebrew for this word is uncertain. [c] 3 Or *made atonement for*

Hear My Prayer

Hear My Prayer

and of the farthest seas,
6 who formed the mountains by your power,
having armed yourself with strength,
7 who stilled the roaring of the seas,
the roaring of their waves,
and the turmoil of the nations.
8 Those living far away fear your wonders;
where morning dawns and evening fades
you call forth songs of joy.

9 You care for the land and water it;
you enrich it abundantly.
The streams of God are filled with water
to provide the people with grain,
for so you have ordained it.[a]
10 You drench its furrows
and level its ridges;
you soften it with showers
and bless its crops.
11 You crown the year with your bounty,
and your carts overflow with abundance.
12 The grasslands of the desert overflow;
the hills are clothed with gladness.
13 The meadows are covered with flocks
and the valleys are mantled with grain;
they shout for joy and sing.

Psalm 66

For the director of music. A song. A psalm.

1 Shout with joy to God, all the earth!
2 Sing the glory of his name;
make his praise glorious!
3 Say to God, "How awesome are your deeds!
So great is your power
that your enemies cringe before you.
4 All the earth bows down to you;
they sing praise to you,
they sing praise to your name." *Selah*

5 Come and see what God has done,
how awesome his works in man's behalf!
6 He turned the sea into dry land,
they passed through the waters on foot—
come, let us rejoice in him.
7 He rules forever by his power,
his eyes watch the nations—
let not the rebellious rise up against him. *Selah*

8 Praise our God, O peoples,
let the sound of his praise be heard;
9 he has preserved our lives
and kept our feet from slipping.
10 For you, O God, tested us;
you refined us like silver.
11 You brought us into prison
and laid burdens on our backs.

[a] 9 Or *for that is how you prepare the land*

12 You let men ride over our heads;
we went through fire and water,
but you brought us to a place of abundance.

13 I will come to your temple with burnt offerings
and fulfill my vows to you—
14 vows my lips promised and my mouth spoke
when I was in trouble.
15 I will sacrifice fat animals to you
and an offering of rams;
I will offer bulls and goats. *Selah*
16 Come and listen, all you who fear God;
let me tell you what he has done for me.
17 I cried out to him with my mouth;
his praise was on my tongue.
18 If I had cherished sin in my heart,
the Lord would not have listened;
19 but God has surely listened
and heard my voice in prayer.
20 Praise be to God,
who has not rejected my prayer
or withheld his love from me!

Psalm 67

For the director of music. With stringed instruments. A psalm. A song.

1 May God be gracious to us and bless us
and make his face shine upon us, *Selah*
2 that your ways may be known on earth,
your salvation among all nations.

3 May the peoples praise you, O God;
may all the peoples praise you.
4 May the nations be glad and sing for joy,
for you rule the peoples justly
and guide the nations of the earth. *Selah*
5 May the peoples praise you, O God;
may all the peoples praise you.

6 Then the land will yield its harvest,
and God, our God, will bless us.
7 God will bless us,
and all the ends of the earth will fear him.

Psalm 68

For the director of music. Of David. A psalm. A song.

1 May God arise, may his enemies be scattered;
may his foes flee before him.
2 As smoke is blown away by the wind,
may you blow them away;
as wax melts before the fire,
may the wicked perish before God.
3 But may the righteous be glad
and rejoice before God;
may they be happy and joyful.

Hear My Prayer

Hear My Prayer

4 Sing to God, sing praise to his name,
extol him who rides on the clouds[a]—
his name is the LORD—
and rejoice before him.
5 A father to the fatherless, a defender of widows,
is God in his holy dwelling.
6 God sets the lonely in families,[b]
he leads forth the prisoners with singing;
but the rebellious live in a sun-scorched land.

7 When you went out before your people, O God,
when you marched through the wasteland, *Selah*
8 the earth shook,
the heavens poured down rain,
before God, the One of Sinai,
before God, the God of Israel.
9 You gave abundant showers, O God;
you refreshed your weary inheritance.
10 Your people settled in it,
and from your bounty, O God, you provided for the poor.

11 The Lord announced the word,
and great was the company of those who proclaimed it:
12 "Kings and armies flee in haste;
in the camps men divide the plunder.
13 Even while you sleep among the campfires,[c]
the wings of ⌊my⌋ dove are sheathed with silver,
its feathers with shining gold."
14 When the Almighty[d] scattered the kings in the land,
it was like snow fallen on Zalmon.

15 The mountains of Bashan are majestic mountains;
rugged are the mountains of Bashan.
16 Why gaze in envy, O rugged mountains,
at the mountain where God chooses to reign,
where the LORD himself will dwell forever?
17 The chariots of God are tens of thousands
and thousands of thousands;
the Lord ⌊has come⌋ from Sinai into his sanctuary.
18 When you ascended on high,
you led captives in your train;
you received gifts from men,
even from[e] the rebellious—
that you,[f] O LORD God, might dwell there.

19 Praise be to the Lord, to God our Savior,
who daily bears our burdens. *Selah*
20 Our God is a God who saves;
from the Sovereign LORD comes escape from death.

21 Surely God will crush the heads of his enemies,
the hairy crowns of those who go on in their sins.
22 The Lord says, "I will bring them from Bashan;
I will bring them from the depths of the sea,

[a] 4 Or */ prepare the way for him who rides through the deserts* [b] 6 Or *the desolate in a homeland* [c] 13 Or *saddlebags* [d] 14 Hebrew *Shaddai* [e] 18 Or *gifts for men, / even* [f] 18 Or *they*

23 that you may plunge your feet in the blood of your
 foes,
 while the tongues of your dogs have their share."

24 Your procession has come into view, O God,
 the procession of my God and King into the
 sanctuary.
25 In front are the singers, after them the musicians;
 with them are the maidens playing tambourines.
26 Praise God in the great congregation;
 praise the LORD in the assembly of Israel.
27 There is the little tribe of Benjamin, leading them,
 there the great throng of Judah's princes,
 and there the princes of Zebulun and of Naphtali.

28 Summon your power, O God[a];
 show us your strength, O God, as you have done
 before.
29 Because of your temple at Jerusalem
 kings will bring you gifts.
30 Rebuke the beast among the reeds,
 the herd of bulls among the calves of the nations.
Humbled, may it bring bars of silver.
 Scatter the nations who delight in war.
31 Envoys will come from Egypt;
 Cush[b] will submit herself to God.

32 Sing to God, O kingdoms of the earth,
 sing praise to the Lord, *Selah*
33 to him who rides the ancient skies above,
 who thunders with mighty voice.
34 Proclaim the power of God,
 whose majesty is over Israel,
 whose power is in the skies.
35 You are awesome, O God, in your sanctuary;
 the God of Israel gives power and strength to his
 people.

Praise be to God!

Psalm 69

For the director of music. To ⌞the tune of⌟ "Lilies."
Of David.

1 Save me, O God,
 for the waters have come up to my neck.
2 I sink in the miry depths,
 where there is no foothold.
I have come into the deep waters;
 the floods engulf me.
3 I am worn out calling for help;
 my throat is parched.
My eyes fail,
 looking for my God.
4 Those who hate me without reason
 outnumber the hairs of my head;

[a] 28 Many Hebrew manuscripts, Septuagint and Syriac; most Hebrew manuscripts *Your God has summoned power for you* [b] 31 That is, the upper Nile region

Hear My Prayer

Hear My Prayer

many are my enemies without cause,
those who seek to destroy me.
I am forced to restore
what I did not steal.

5 You know my folly, O God;
my guilt is not hidden from you.

6 May those who hope in you
not be disgraced because of me,
O Lord, the LORD Almighty;
may those who seek you
not be put to shame because of me,
O God of Israel.
7 For I endure scorn for your sake,
and shame covers my face.
8 I am a stranger to my brothers,
an alien to my own mother's sons;
9 for zeal for your house consumes me,
and the insults of those who insult you fall on me.
10 When I weep and fast,
I must endure scorn;
11 when I put on sackcloth,
people make sport of me.
12 Those who sit at the gate mock me,
and I am the song of the drunkards.

13 But I pray to you, O LORD,
in the time of your favor;
in your great love, O God,
answer me with your sure salvation.
14 Rescue me from the mire,
do not let me sink;
deliver me from those who hate me,
from the deep waters.
15 Do not let the floodwaters engulf me
or the depths swallow me up
or the pit close its mouth over me.
16 Answer me, O LORD, out of the goodness of your love;
in your great mercy turn to me.
17 Do not hide your face from your servant;
answer me quickly, for I am in trouble.
18 Come near and rescue me;
redeem me because of my foes.

19 You know how I am scorned, disgraced and shamed;
all my enemies are before you.
20 Scorn has broken my heart
and has left me helpless;
I looked for sympathy, but there was none,
for comforters, but I found none.
21 They put gall in my food
and gave me vinegar for my thirst.

22 May the table set before them become a snare;
may it become retribution and[a] a trap.
23 May their eyes be darkened so they cannot see,
and their backs be bent forever.

[a] 22 Or *snare / and their fellowship become*

24 Pour out your wrath on them;
let your fierce anger overtake them.
25 May their place be deserted;
let there be no one to dwell in their tents.
26 For they persecute those you wound
and talk about the pain of those you hurt.
27 Charge them with crime upon crime;
do not let them share in your salvation.
28 May they be blotted out of the book of life
and not be listed with the righteous.

29 I am in pain and distress;
may your salvation, O God, protect me.

30 I will praise God's name in song
and glorify him with thanksgiving.
31 This will please the LORD more than an ox,
more than a bull with its horns and hoofs.
32 The poor will see and be glad—
you who seek God, may your hearts live!
33 The LORD hears the needy
and does not despise his captive people.

34 Let heaven and earth praise him,
the seas and all that move in them,
35 for God will save Zion
and rebuild the cities of Judah.
Then people will settle there and possess it;
36 the children of his servants will inherit it,
and those who love his name will dwell there.

Psalm 70

For the director of music. Of David. A petition.

1 Hasten, O God, to save me;
O LORD, come quickly to help me.
2 May those who seek my life
be put to shame and confusion;
may all who desire my ruin
be turned back in disgrace.
3 May those who say to me, "Aha! Aha!"
turn back because of their shame.
4 But may all who seek you
rejoice and be glad in you;
may those who love your salvation always say,
"Let God be exalted!"

5 Yet I am poor and needy;
come quickly to me, O God.
You are my help and my deliverer;
O LORD, do not delay.

Psalm 71

1 In you, O LORD, I have taken refuge;
let me never be put to shame.
2 Rescue me and deliver me in your righteousness;
turn your ear to me and save me.
3 Be my rock of refuge,

Hear My Prayer

Hear My Prayer

to which I can always go;
give the command to save me,
for you are my rock and my fortress.
4 Deliver me, O my God, from the hand of the wicked,
from the grasp of evil and cruel men.

5 For you have been my hope, O Sovereign LORD,
my confidence since my youth.
6 From birth I have relied on you;
you brought me forth from my mother's womb.
I will ever praise you.
7 I have become like a portent to many,
but you are my strong refuge.
8 My mouth is filled with your praise,
declaring your splendor all day long.

9 Do not cast me away when I am old;
do not forsake me when my strength is gone.
10 For my enemies speak against me;
those who wait to kill me conspire together.
11 They say, "God has forsaken him;
pursue him and seize him,
for no one will rescue him."
12 Be not far from me, O God;
come quickly, O my God, to help me.
13 May my accusers perish in shame;
may those who want to harm me
be covered with scorn and disgrace.

14 But as for me, I will always have hope;
I will praise you more and more.
15 My mouth will tell of your righteousness,
of your salvation all day long,
though I know not its measure.
16 I will come and proclaim your mighty acts,
O Sovereign LORD;
I will proclaim your righteousness, yours alone.
17 Since my youth, O God, you have taught me,
and to this day I declare your marvelous deeds.
18 Even when I am old and gray,
do not forsake me, O God,
till I declare your power to the next generation,
your might to all who are to come.

19 Your righteousness reaches to the skies, O God,
you who have done great things.
Who, O God, is like you?
20 Though you have made me see troubles, many and
bitter,
you will restore my life again;
from the depths of the earth
you will again bring me up.
21 You will increase my honor
and comfort me once again.

22 I will praise you with the harp
for your faithfulness, O my God;
I will sing praise to you with the lyre,
O Holy One of Israel.

23 My lips will shout for joy
when I sing praise to you—
I, whom you have redeemed.
24 My tongue will tell of your righteous acts
all day long,
for those who wanted to harm me
have been put to shame and confusion.

Psalm 72

Of Solomon.

1 Endow the king with your justice, O God,
the royal son with your righteousness.
2 He will[a] judge your people in righteousness,
your afflicted ones with justice.
3 The mountains will bring prosperity to the people,
the hills the fruit of righteousness.
4 He will defend the afflicted among the people
and save the children of the needy;
he will crush the oppressor.

5 He will endure[b] as long as the sun,
as long as the moon, through all generations.
6 He will be like rain falling on a mown field,
like showers watering the earth.
7 In his days the righteous will flourish;
prosperity will abound till the moon is no more.

8 He will rule from sea to sea
and from the River[c] to the ends of the earth.[d]
9 The desert tribes will bow before him
and his enemies will lick the dust.
10 The kings of Tarshish and of distant shores
will bring tribute to him;
the kings of Sheba and Seba
will present him gifts.
11 All kings will bow down to him
and all nations will serve him.

12 For he will deliver the needy who cry out,
the afflicted who have no one to help.
13 He will take pity on the weak and the needy
and save the needy from death.
14 He will rescue them from oppression and violence,
for precious is their blood in his sight.

15 Long may he live!
May gold from Sheba be given him.
May people ever pray for him
and bless him all day long.
16 Let grain abound throughout the land;
on the tops of the hills may it sway.
Let its fruit flourish like Lebanon;
let it thrive like the grass of the field.
17 May his name endure forever;
may it continue as long as the sun.

[a] 2 Or *May be*; similarly in verses 3–11 and 17 [b] 5 Septuagint; Hebrew *You will be feared* [c] 8 That is, the Euphrates [d] 8 Or *the end of the land*

Hear My Prayer

Hear My Prayer

All nations will be blessed through him,
and they will call him blessed.

18 Praise be to the LORD God, the God of Israel,
who alone does marvelous deeds.
19 Praise be to his glorious name forever;
may the whole earth be filled with his glory.
Amen and Amen.

20 This conclues the prayers of David son of Jesse.

BOOK III
Psalms 73–89

Psalm 73

A psalm of Asaph.

1 Surely God is good to Israel,
to those who are pure in heart.

2 But as for me, my feet had almost slipped;
I had nearly lost my foothold.
3 For I envied the arrogant
when I saw the prosperity of the wicked.

4 They have no struggles;
their bodies are healthy and strong.[a]
5 They are free from the burdens common to man;
they are not plagued by human ills.
6 Therefore pride is their necklace;
they clothe themselves with violence.
7 From their callous hearts comes iniquity[b];
the evil conceits of their minds know no limits.
8 They scoff, and speak with malice;
in their arrogance they threaten oppression.
9 Their mouths lay claim to heaven,
and their tongues take possession of the earth.
10 Therefore their people turn to them
and drink up waters in abundance.[c]
11 They say, "How can God know?
Does the Most High have knowledge?"

12 This is what the wicked are like—
always carefree, they increase in wealth.

13 Surely in vain have I kept my heart pure;
in vain have I washed my hands in innocence.
14 All day long I have been plagued;
I have been punished every morning.

15 If I had said, "I will speak thus,"
I would have betrayed your children.
16 When I tried to understand all this,
it was oppressive to me
17 till I entered the sanctuary of God;
then I understood their final destiny.

[a] *4* With a different word division of the Hebrew; Masoretic Text *struggles at their death; / their bodies are healthy* [b] *7* Syriac (see also Septuagint); Hebrew *Their eyes bulge with fat* [c] *10* The meaning of the Hebrew for this verse is uncertain.

18 Surely you place them on slippery ground;
you cast them down to ruin.
19 How suddenly are they destroyed,
completely swept away by terrors!
20 As a dream when one awakes,
so when you arise, O Lord,
you will despise them as fantasies.

21 When my heart was grieved
and my spirit embittered,
22 I was senseless and ignorant;
I was a brute beast before you.
23 Yet I am always with you;
you hold me by my right hand.
24 You guide me with your counsel,
and afterward you will take me into glory.
25 Whom have I in heaven but you?
And earth has nothing I desire besides you.
26 My flesh and my heart may fail,
but God is the strength of my heart
and my portion forever.

27 Those who are far from you will perish;
you destroy all who are unfaithful to you.
28 But as for me, it is good to be near God.
I have made the Sovereign LORD my refuge;
I will tell of all your deeds.

Psalm 74

A *maskil*[a] of Asaph.

1 Why have you rejected us forever, O God?
Why does your anger smolder against the sheep of
your pasture?
2 Remember the people you purchased of old,
the tribe of your inheritance, whom you
redeemed—
Mount Zion, where you dwelt.
3 Turn your steps toward these everlasting ruins,
all this destruction the enemy has brought on the
sanctuary.

4 Your foes roared in the place where you met
with us;
they set up their standards as signs.
5 They behaved like men wielding axes
to cut through a thicket of trees.
6 They smashed all the carved paneling
with their axes and hatchets.
7 They burned your sanctuary to the ground;
they defiled the dwelling place of your Name.
8 They said in their hearts, "We will crush them
completely!"
They burned every place where God was worshiped
in the land.
9 We are given no miraculous signs;

[a] Title: Probably a literary or musical term

Hear My Prayer

Hear My Prayer

no prophets are left,
and none of us knows how long this will be.

10 How long will the enemy mock you, O God?
Will the foe revile your name forever?
11 Why do you hold back your hand, your right hand?
Take it from the folds of your garment and destroy them!

12 But you, O God, are my king from of old;
you bring salvation upon the earth.
13 It was you who split open the sea by your power;
you broke the heads of the monster in the waters.
14 It was you who crushed the heads of Leviathan
and gave him as food to the creatures of the desert.
15 It was you who opened up springs and streams;
you dried up the ever flowing rivers.
16 The day is yours, and yours also the night;
you established the sun and moon.
17 It was you who set all the boundaries of the earth;
you made both summer and winter.

18 Remember how the enemy has mocked you, O LORD,
how foolish people have reviled your name.
19 Do not hand over the life of your dove to wild beasts;
do not forget the lives of your afflicted people forever.
20 Have regard for your covenant,
because haunts of violence fill the dark places of the land.
21 Do not let the oppressed retreat in disgrace;
may the poor and needy praise your name.
22 Rise up, O God, and defend your cause;
remember how fools mock you all day long.
23 Do not ignore the clamor of your adversaries,
the uproar of your enemies, which rises continually.

Psalm 75

For the director of music. ⌊To the tune of⌋ "Do Not Destroy."
A psalm of Asaph. A song.

1 We give thanks to you, O God,
we give thanks, for your Name is near;
men tell of your wonderful deeds.

2 You say, "I choose the appointed time;
it is I who judge uprightly.
3 When the earth and all its people quake,
it is I who hold its pillars firm. *Selah*
4 To the arrogant I say, 'Boast no more,'
and to the wicked, 'Do not lift up your horns.
5 Do not lift your horns against heaven;
do not speak with outstretched neck.' "

6 No one from the east or the west
or from the desert can exalt a man.

7 But it is God who judges:
He brings one down, he exalts another.
8 In the hand of the LORD is a cup
full of foaming wine mixed with spices;
he pours it out, and all the wicked of the earth
drink it down to its very dregs.

9 As for me, I will declare this forever;
I will sing praise to the God of Jacob.
10 I will cut off the horns of all the wicked,
but the horns of the righteous will be lifted up.

Psalm 76

For the director of music. With stringed instruments. A psalm of Asaph. A song.

1 In Judah God is known;
his name is great in Israel.
2 His tent is in Salem,
his dwelling place in Zion.
3 There he broke the flashing arrows,
the shields and the swords, the weapons of war. *Selah*

4 You are resplendent with light,
more majestic than mountains rich with game.
5 Valiant men lie plundered,
they sleep their last sleep;
not one of the warriors
can lift his hands.
6 At your rebuke, O God of Jacob,
both horse and chariot lie still.
7 You alone are to be feared.
Who can stand before you when you are angry?
8 From heaven you pronounced judgment,
and the land feared and was quiet—
9 when you, O God, rose up to judge,
to save all the afflicted of the land. *Selah*
10 Surely your wrath against men brings you praise,
and the survivors of your wrath are restrained.[a]

11 Make vows to the LORD your God and fulfill them;
let all the neighboring lands
bring gifts to the One to be feared.
12 He breaks the spirit of rulers;
he is feared by the kings of the earth.

Psalm 77

For the director of music. For Jeduthun. Of Asaph. A psalm.

1 I cried out to God for help;
I cried out to God to hear me.
2 When I was in distress, I sought the Lord;
at night I stretched out untiring hands
and my soul refused to be comforted.

[a] 10 Or *Surely the wrath of men brings you praise, / and with the remainder of wrath you arm yourself*

Hear My Prayer

Hear My Prayer

3 I remembered you, O God, and I groaned;
I mused, and my spirit grew faint. *Selah*
4 You kept my eyes from closing;
I was too troubled to speak.
5 I thought about the former days,
the years of long ago;
6 I remembered my songs in the night.
My heart mused and my spirit inquired:

7 "Will the Lord reject forever?
Will he never show his favor again?
8 Has his unfailing love vanished forever?
Has his promise failed for all time?
9 Has God forgotten to be merciful?
Has he in anger withheld his compassion?" *Selah*

10 Then I thought, "To this I will appeal:
the years of the right hand of the Most High."
11 I will remember the deeds of the LORD;
yes, I will remember your miracles of long ago.
12 I will meditate on all your works
and consider all your mighty deeds.

13 Your ways, O God, are holy.
What god is so great as our God?
14 You are the God who performs miracles;
you display your power among the peoples.
15 With your mighty arm you redeemed your people,
the descendants of Jacob and Joseph. *Selah*

16 The waters saw you, O God,
the waters saw you and writhed;
the very depths were convulsed.
17 The clouds poured down water,
the skies resounded with thunder;
your arrows flashed back and forth.
18 Your thunder was heard in the whirlwind,
your lightning lit up the world;
the earth trembled and quaked.
19 Your path led through the sea,
your way through the mighty waters,
though your footprints were not seen.

20 You led your people like a flock
by the hand of Moses and Aaron.

Psalm 78

A *maskil*[a] of Asaph.

1 O my people, hear my teaching;
listen to the words of my mouth.
2 I will open my mouth in parables,
I will utter hidden things, things from of old—
3 what we have heard and known,
what our fathers have told us.
4 We will not hide them from their children;
we will tell the next generation
the praiseworthy deeds of the LORD,

[a] Title: Probably a literary or musical term

his power, and the wonders he has done.
5 He decreed statutes for Jacob
and established the law in Israel,
which he commanded our forefathers
to teach their children,
6 so the next generation would know them,
even the children yet to be born,
and they in turn would tell their children.
7 Then they would put their trust in God
and would not forget his deeds
but would keep his commands.
8 They would not be like their forefathers—
a stubborn and rebellious generation,
whose hearts were not loyal to God,
whose spirits were not faithful to him.

9 The men of Ephraim, though armed with bows,
turned back on the day of battle;
10 they did not keep God's covenant
and refused to live by his law.
11 They forgot what he had done,
the wonders he had shown them.
12 He did miracles in the sight of their fathers
in the land of Egypt, in the region of Zoan.
13 He divided the sea and led them through;
he made the water stand firm like a wall.
14 He guided them with the cloud by day
and with light from the fire all night.
15 He split the rocks in the desert
and gave them water as abundant as the seas;
16 he brought streams out of a rocky crag
and made water flow down like rivers.

17 But they continued to sin against him,
rebelling in the desert against the Most High.
18 They willfully put God to the test
by demanding the food they craved.
19 They spoke against God, saying,
"Can God spread a table in the desert?
20 When he struck the rock, water gushed out,
and streams flowed abundantly.
But can he also give us food?
Can he supply meat for his people?"
21 When the LORD heard them, he was very angry;
his fire broke out against Jacob,
and his wrath rose against Israel,
22 for they did not believe in God
or trust in his deliverance.
23 Yet he gave a command to the skies above
and opened the doors of the heavens;
24 he rained down manna for the people to eat,
he gave them the grain of heaven.
25 Men ate the bread of angels;
he sent them all the food they could eat.
26 He let loose the east wind from the heavens
and led forth the south wind by his power.
27 He rained meat down on them like dust,
flying birds like sand on the seashore.

Hear My Prayer

Hear My Prayer

28 He made them come down inside their camp,
all around their tents.
29 They ate till they had more than enough,
for he had given them what they craved.
30 But before they turned from the food they craved,
even while it was still in their mouths,
31 God's anger rose against them;
he put to death the sturdiest among them,
cutting down the young men of Israel.

32 In spite of all this, they kept on sinning;
in spite of his wonders, they did not believe.
33 So he ended their days in futility
and their years in terror.
34 Whenever God slew them, they would seek him;
they eagerly turned to him again.
35 They remembered that God was their Rock,
that God Most High was their Redeemer.
36 But then they would flatter him with their mouths,
lying to him with their tongues;
37 their hearts were not loyal to him,
they were not faithful to his covenant.
38 Yet he was merciful;
he forgave their iniquities
and did not destroy them.
Time after time he restrained his anger
and did not stir up his full wrath.
39 He remembered that they were but flesh,
a passing breeze that does not return.

40 How often they rebelled against him in the desert
and grieved him in the wasteland!
41 Again and again they put God to the test;
they vexed the Holy One of Israel.
42 They did not remember his power—
the day he redeemed them from the oppressor,
43 the day he displayed his miraculous signs in Egypt,
his wonders in the region of Zoan.
44 He turned their rivers to blood;
they could not drink from their streams.
45 He sent swarms of flies that devoured them,
and frogs that devastated them.
46 He gave their crops to the grasshopper,
their produce to the locust.
47 He destroyed their vines with hail
and their sycamore-figs with sleet.
48 He gave over their cattle to the hail,
their livestock to bolts of lightning.
49 He unleashed against them his hot anger,
his wrath, indignation and hostility—
a band of destroying angels.
50 He prepared a path for his anger;
he did not spare them from death
but gave them over to the plague.
51 He struck down all the firstborn of Egypt,
the firstfruits of manhood in the tents of Ham.
52 But he brought his people out like a flock;
he led them like sheep through the desert.

53 He guided them safely, so they were unafraid;
but the sea engulfed their enemies.
54 Thus he brought them to the border of his holy land,
to the hill country his right hand had taken.
55 He drove out nations before them
and allotted their lands to them as an inheritance;
he settled the tribes of Israel in their homes.

56 But they put God to the test
and rebelled against the Most High;
they did not keep his statutes.
57 Like their fathers they were disloyal and faithless,
as unreliable as a faulty bow.
58 They angered him with their high places;
they aroused his jealousy with their idols.
59 When God heard them, he was very angry;
he rejected Israel completely.
60 He abandoned the tabernacle of Shiloh,
the tent he had set up among men.
61 He sent ⌊the ark of⌋ his might into captivity,
his splendor into the hands of the enemy.
62 He gave his people over to the sword;
he was very angry with his inheritance.
63 Fire consumed their young men,
and their maidens had no wedding songs;
64 their priests were put to the sword,
and their widows could not weep.

65 Then the Lord awoke as from sleep,
as a man wakes from the stupor of wine.
66 He beat back his enemies;
he put them to everlasting shame.
67 Then he rejected the tents of Joseph,
he did not choose the tribe of Ephraim;
68 but he chose the tribe of Judah,
Mount Zion, which he loved.
69 He built his sanctuary like the heights,
like the earth that he established forever.
70 He chose David his servant
and took him from the sheep pens;
71 from tending the sheep he brought him
to be the shepherd of his people Jacob,
of Israel his inheritance.
72 And David shepherded them with integrity of heart;
with skillful hands he led them.

Psalm 79

A psalm of Asaph.

1 O God, the nations have invaded your inheritance;
they have defiled your holy temple,
they have reduced Jerusalem to rubble.
2 They have given the dead bodies of your servants
as food to the birds of the air,
the flesh of your saints to the beasts of the earth.
3 They have poured out blood like water
all around Jerusalem,
and there is no one to bury the dead.

Hear My Prayer

Hear My Prayer

4 We are objects of reproach to our neighbors,
of scorn and derision to those around us.

5 How long, O LORD? Will you be angry forever?
How long will your jealousy burn like fire?
6 Pour out your wrath on the nations
that do not acknowledge you,
on the kingdoms
that do not call on your name;
7 for they have devoured Jacob
and destroyed his homeland.
8 Do not hold against us the sins of the fathers;
may your mercy come quickly to meet us,
for we are in desperate need.

9 Help us, O God our Savior,
for the glory of your name;
deliver us and forgive our sins
for your name's sake.
10 Why should the nations say,
"Where is their God?"
Before our eyes, make known among the nations
that you avenge the outpoured blood of your servants.
11 May the groans of the prisoners come before you;
by the strength of your arm
preserve those condemned to die.

12 Pay back into the laps of our neighbors seven times
the reproach they have hurled at you, O Lord.
13 Then we your people, the sheep of your pasture,
will praise you forever;
from generation to generation
we will recount your praise.

Psalm 80

For the director of music. To ⌞the tune of⌟ "The Lilies of the Covenant." Of Asaph. A psalm.

1 Hear us, O Shepherd of Israel,
you who lead Joseph like a flock;
you who sit enthroned between the cherubim, shine forth
2 before Ephraim, Benjamin and Manasseh.
Awaken your might;
come and save us.

3 Restore us, O God;
make your face shine upon us,
that we may be saved.

4 O LORD God Almighty,
how long will your anger smolder
against the prayers of your people?
5 You have fed them with the bread of tears;
you have made them drink tears by the bowlful.
6 You have made us a source of contention to our neighbors,
and our enemies mock us.

7 Restore us, O God Almighty;
make your face shine upon us,
that we may be saved.

8 You brought a vine out of Egypt;
you drove out the nations and planted it.
9 You cleared the ground for it,
and it took root and filled the land.
10 The mountains were covered with its shade,
the mighty cedars with its branches.
11 It sent out its boughs to the Sea,[a]
its shoots as far as the River.[b]

12 Why have you broken down its walls
so that all who pass by pick its grapes?
13 Boars from the forest ravage it
and the creatures of the field feed on it.
14 Return to us, O God Almighty!
Look down from heaven and see!
Watch over this vine,
15 the root your right hand has planted,
the son[c] you have raised up for yourself.

16 Your vine is cut down, it is burned with fire;
at your rebuke your people perish.
17 Let your hand rest on the man at your right hand,
the son of man you have raised up for yourself.
18 Then we will not turn away from you;
revive us, and we will call on your name.

19 Restore us, O LORD God Almighty;
make your face shine upon us,
that we may be saved.

Psalm 81

For the director of music. According to *gittith*.[d]
Of Asaph.

1 Sing for joy to God our strength;
shout aloud to the God of Jacob!
2 Begin the music, strike the tambourine,
play the melodious harp and lyre.

3 Sound the ram's horn at the New Moon,
and when the moon is full, on the day of our
Feast;
4 this is a decree for Israel,
an ordinance of the God of Jacob.
5 He established it as a statute for Joseph
when he went out against Egypt,
where we heard a language we did not
understand.[e]

6 He says, "I removed the burden from their
shoulders;
their hands were set free from the basket.
7 In your distress you called and I rescued you,

[a] *11* Probably the Mediterranean [b] *11* That is, the Euphrates [c] *15* Or *branch*
[d] Title: Probably a musical term [e] *5* Or / *and we heard a voice we had not known*

Hear My Prayer

Hear My Prayer

I answered you out of a thundercloud;
I tested you at the waters of Meribah. *Selah*

8 "Hear, O my people, and I will warn you—
if you would but listen to me, O Israel!
9 You shall have no foreign god among you;
you shall not bow down to an alien god.
10 I am the LORD your God,
who brought you up out of Egypt.
Open wide your mouth and I will fill it.

11 "But my people would not listen to me;
Israel would not submit to me.
12 So I gave them over to their stubborn hearts
to follow their own devices.

13 "If my people would but listen to me,
if Israel would follow my ways,
14 how quickly would I subdue their enemies
and turn my hand against their foes!
15 Those who hate the LORD would cringe before him,
and their punishment would last forever.
16 But you would be fed with the finest of wheat;
with honey from the rock I would satisfy you."

Psalm 82

A psalm of Asaph.

1 God presides in the great assembly;
he gives judgment among the "gods":

2 "How long will you[a] defend the unjust
and show partiality to the wicked? *Selah*
3 Defend the cause of the weak and fatherless;
maintain the rights of the poor and oppressed.
4 Rescue the weak and needy;
deliver them from the hand of the wicked.

5 "They know nothing, they understand nothing.
They walk about in darkness;
all the foundations of the earth are shaken.

6 "I said, 'You are "gods";
you are all sons of the Most High.'
7 But you will die like mere men;
you will fall like every other ruler."

8 Rise up, O God, judge the earth,
for all the nations are your inheritance.

Psalm 83

A song. A psalm of Asaph.

1 O God, do not keep silent;
be not quiet, O God, be not still.
2 See how your enemies are astir,
how your foes rear their heads.
3 With cunning they conspire against your people;

[a] *2* The Hebrew is plural.

they plot against those you cherish.
4 "Come," they say, "let us destroy them as a nation,
that the name of Israel be remembered no more."

5 With one mind they plot together;
they form an alliance against you—
6 the tents of Edom and the Ishmaelites,
of Moab and the Hagrites,
7 Gebal,[a] Ammon and Amalek,
Philistia, with the people of Tyre.
8 Even Assyria has joined them
to lend strength to the descendants of Lot. *Selah*

9 Do to them as you did to Midian,
as you did to Sisera and Jabin at the river Kishon,
10 who perished at Endor
and became like refuse on the ground.
11 Make their nobles like Oreb and Zeeb,
all their princes like Zebah and Zalmunna,
12 who said, "Let us take possession
of the pasturelands of God."

13 Make them like tumbleweed, O my God,
like chaff before the wind.
14 As fire consumes the forest
or a flame sets the mountains ablaze,
15 so pursue them with your tempest
and terrify them with your storm.
16 Cover their faces with shame
so that men will seek your name, O LORD.

17 May they ever be ashamed and dismayed;
may they perish in disgrace.
18 Let them know that you, whose name is the LORD—
that you alone are the Most High over all the
earth.

Psalm 84

For the director of music. According to *gittith*.[b] Of the Sons of Korah. A psalm.

1 How lovely is your dwelling place,
O LORD Almighty!
2 My soul yearns, even faints,
for the courts of the LORD;
my heart and my flesh cry out
for the living God.

3 Even the sparrow has found a home,
and the swallow a nest for herself,
where she may have her young—
a place near your altar,
O LORD Almighty, my King and my God.
4 Blessed are those who dwell in your house;
they are ever praising you. *Selah*

5 Blessed are those whose strength is in you,
who have set their hearts on pilgrimage.

[a] 7 That is, Byblos [b] Title: Probably a musical term

Hear My Prayer

Hear My Prayer

6 As they pass through the Valley of Baca,
they make it a place of springs;
the autumn rains also cover it with pools.[a]
7 They go from strength to strength,
till each appears before God in Zion.

8 Hear my prayer, O LORD God Almighty;
listen to me, O God of Jacob. *Selah*
9 Look upon our shield,[b] O God;
look with favor on your anointed one.

10 Better is one day in your courts
than a thousand elsewhere;
I would rather be a doorkeeper in the house of
my God
than dwell in the tents of the wicked.
11 For the LORD God is a sun and shield;
the LORD bestows favor and honor;
no good thing does he withhold
from those whose walk is blameless.

12 O LORD Almighty,
blessed is the man who trusts in you.

Psalm 85

For the director of music. Of the Sons of Korah.
A psalm.

1 You showed favor to your land, O LORD;
you restored the fortunes of Jacob.
2 You forgave the iniquity of your people
and covered all their sins. *Selah*
3 You set aside all your wrath
and turned from your fierce anger.

4 Restore us again, O God our Savior,
and put away your displeasure toward us.
5 Will you be angry with us forever?
Will you prolong your anger through all
generations?
6 Will you not revive us again,
that your people may rejoice in you?
7 Show us your unfailing love, O LORD,
and grant us your salvation.

8 I will listen to what God the LORD will say;
he promises peace to his people, his
saints—
but let them not return to folly.
9 Surely his salvation is near those who fear him,
that his glory may dwell in our land.

10 Love and faithfulness meet together;
righteousness and peace kiss each other.
11 Faithfulness springs forth from the earth,
and righteousness looks down from heaven.
12 The LORD will indeed give what is good,
and our land will yield its harvest.

[a] 6 Or *blessings* [b] 9 Or *sovereign*

13 Righteousness goes before him
and prepares the way for his steps.

Psalm 86

A prayer of David.

1 Hear, O LORD, and answer me,
for I am poor and needy.
2 Guard my life, for I am devoted to you.
You are my God; save your servant
who trusts in you.
3 Have mercy on me, O Lord,
for I call to you all day long.
4 Bring joy to your servant,
for to you, O Lord,
I lift up my soul.

5 You are forgiving and good, O Lord,
abounding in love to all who call to you.
6 Hear my prayer, O LORD;
listen to my cry for mercy.
7 In the day of my trouble I will call to you,
for you will answer me.

8 Among the gods there is none like you, O Lord;
no deeds can compare with yours.
9 All the nations you have made
will come and worship before you, O Lord;
they will bring glory to your name.
10 For you are great and do marvelous deeds;
you alone are God.

11 Teach me your way, O LORD,
and I will walk in your truth;
give me an undivided heart,
that I may fear your name.
12 I will praise you, O Lord my God, with all my
heart;
I will glorify your name forever.
13 For great is your love toward me;
you have delivered me from the depths of the
grave.[a]

14 The arrogant are attacking me, O God;
a band of ruthless men seeks my life—
men without regard for you.
15 But you, O Lord, are a compassionate and gracious
God,
slow to anger, abounding in love and
faithfulness.
16 Turn to me and have mercy on me;
grant your strength to your servant
and save the son of your maidservant.[b]
17 Give me a sign of your goodness,
that my enemies may see it and be put to shame,
for you, O LORD, have helped me and comforted
me.

[a] 13 Hebrew *Sheol* [b] 16 Or *save your faithful son*

Hear My Prayer

Hear My Prayer

Psalm 87

Of the Sons of Korah. A psalm. A song.

1 He has set his foundation on the holy mountain;
2 the LORD loves the gates of Zion
more than all the dwellings of Jacob.
3 Glorious things are said of you,
O city of God: *Selah*
4 "I will record Rahab[a] and Babylon
among those who acknowledge me—
Philistia too, and Tyre, along with Cush[b]—
and will say, 'This[c] one was born in Zion.' "

5 Indeed, of Zion it will be said,
"This one and that one were born in her,
and the Most High himself will establish her."
6 The LORD will write in the register of the peoples:
"This one was born in Zion." *Selah*
7 As they make music they will sing,
"All my fountains are in you."

Psalm 88

A song. A psalm of the Sons of Korah. For the director of music. According to *mahalath leannoth.*[d] A *maskil*[e] of Heman the Ezrahite.

1 O LORD, the God who saves me,
day and night I cry out before you.
2 May my prayer come before you;
turn your ear to my cry.

3 For my soul is full of trouble
and my life draws near the grave.[f]
4 I am counted among those who go down to the pit;
I am like a man without strength.
5 I am set apart with the dead,
like the slain who lie in the grave,
whom you remember no more,
who are cut off from your care.

6 You have put me in the lowest pit,
in the darkest depths.
7 Your wrath lies heavily upon me;
you have overwhelmed me with all your waves.
Selah
8 You have taken from me my closest friends
and have made me repulsive to them.
I am confined and cannot escape;
9 my eyes are dim with grief.

I call to you, O LORD, every day;
I spread out my hands to you.
10 Do you show your wonders to the dead?
Do those who are dead rise up and praise you?
Selah

[a] *4* A poetic name for Egypt [b] *4* That is, the upper Nile region [c] *4* Or *"O Rahab and Babylon, / Philistia, Tyre and Cush, / I will record concerning those who acknowledge me: / 'This* [d] Title: Possibly a tune, "The Suffering of Affliction" [e] Title: Probably a literary or musical term [f] *3* Hebrew *Sheol*

11 Is your love declared in the grave,
your faithfulness in Destruction[a]?
12 Are your wonders known in the place of darkness,
or your righteous deeds in the land of oblivion?

13 But I cry to you for help, O LORD;
in the morning my prayer comes before you.
14 Why, O LORD, do you reject me
and hide your face from me?

15 From my youth I have been afflicted and close to death;
I have suffered your terrors and am in despair.
16 Your wrath has swept over me;
your terrors have destroyed me.
17 All day long they surround me like a flood;
they have completely engulfed me.
18 You have taken my companions and loved ones from me;
the darkness is my closest friend.

Psalm 89

A *maskil*[b] of Ethan the Ezrahite.

1 I will sing of the LORD's great love forever;
with my mouth I will make your faithfulness known through all generations.
2 I will declare that your love stands firm forever,
that you established your faithfulness in heaven itself.

3 You said, "I have made a covenant with my chosen one,
I have sworn to David my servant,
4 'I will establish your line forever
and make your throne firm through all generations.' " *Selah*

5 The heavens praise your wonders, O LORD,
your faithfulness too, in the assembly of the holy ones.
6 For who in the skies above can compare with the LORD?
Who is like the LORD among the heavenly beings?
7 In the council of the holy ones God is greatly feared;
he is more awesome than all who surround him.
8 O LORD God Almighty, who is like you?
You are mighty, O LORD, and your faithfulness surrounds you.

9 You rule over the surging sea;
when its waves mount up, you still them.
10 You crushed Rahab like one of the slain;
with your strong arm you scattered your enemies.
11 The heavens are yours, and yours also the earth;
you founded the world and all that is in it.
12 You created the north and the south;
Tabor and Hermon sing for joy at your name.

[a] *11* Hebrew *Abaddon* [b] Title: Probably a literary or musical term

Hear My Prayer

Hear My Prayer

13 Your arm is endued with power;
your hand is strong, your right hand exalted.

14 Righteousness and justice are the foundation of your throne;
love and faithfulness go before you.
15 Blessed are those who have learned to acclaim you,
who walk in the light of your presence, O LORD.
16 They rejoice in your name all day long;
they exult in your righteousness.
17 For you are their glory and strength,
and by your favor you exalt our horn.[a]
18 Indeed, our shield[b] belongs to the LORD,
our king to the Holy One of Israel.

19 Once you spoke in a vision,
to your faithful people you said:
"I have bestowed strength on a warrior;
I have exalted a young man from among the people.
20 I have found David my servant;
with my sacred oil I have anointed him.
21 My hand will sustain him;
surely my arm will strengthen him.
22 No enemy will subject him to tribute;
no wicked man will oppress him.
23 I will crush his foes before him
and strike down his adversaries.
24 My faithful love will be with him,
and through my name his horn[c] will be exalted.
25 I will set his hand over the sea,
his right hand over the rivers.
26 He will call out to me, 'You are my Father,
my God, the Rock my Savior.'
27 I will also appoint him my firstborn,
the most exalted of the kings of the earth.
28 I will maintain my love to him forever,
and my covenant with him will never fail.
29 I will establish his line forever,
his throne as long as the heavens endure.

30 "If his sons forsake my law
and do not follow my statutes,
31 if they violate my decrees
and fail to keep my commands,
32 I will punish their sin with the rod,
their iniquity with flogging;
33 but I will not take my love from him,
nor will I ever betray my faithfulness.
34 I will not violate my covenant
or alter what my lips have uttered.
35 Once for all, I have sworn by my holiness—
and I will not lie to David—
36 that his line will continue forever
and his throne endure before me like the sun;
37 it will be established forever like the moon,
the faithful witness in the sky." *Selah*

[a] *17 Horn* here symbolizes strong one. [b] *18* Or *sovereign* [c] *24 Horn* here symbolizes strength.

38 But you have rejected, you have spurned,
you have been very angry with your anointed one.
39 You have renounced the covenant with your servant
and have defiled his crown in the dust.
40 You have broken through all his walls
and reduced his strongholds to ruins.
41 All who pass by have plundered him;
he has become the scorn of his neighbors.
42 You have exalted the right hand of his foes;
you have made all his enemies rejoice.
43 You have turned back the edge of his sword
and have not supported him in battle.
44 You have put an end to his splendor
and cast his throne to the ground.
45 You have cut short the days of his youth;
you have covered him with a mantle of shame.
Selah

46 How long, O LORD? Will you hide yourself forever?
How long will your wrath burn like fire?
47 Remember how fleeting is my life.
For what futility you have created all men!
48 What man can live and not see death,
or save himself from the power of the grave[a]?
Selah
49 O Lord, where is your former great love,
which in your faithfulness you swore to David?
50 Remember, Lord, how your servant has[b] been
mocked,
how I bear in my heart the taunts of all the
nations,
51 the taunts with which your enemies have mocked,
O LORD,
with which they have mocked every step of your
anointed one.

52 Praise be to the LORD forever!
Amen and Amen.

BOOK IV

Psalms 90–106

Psalm 90

A prayer of Moses the man of God.

1 Lord, you have been our dwelling place
throughout all generations.
2 Before the mountains were born
or you brought forth the earth and the world,
from everlasting to everlasting you are God.

3 You turn men back to dust,
saying, "Return to dust, O sons of men."
4 For a thousand years in your sight
are like a day that has just gone by,
or like a watch in the night.

Hear My Prayer

[a] 48 Hebrew *Sheol* [b] 50 Or *your servants have*

Hear My Prayer

5 You sweep men away in the sleep of death;
they are like the new grass of the morning—
6 though in the morning it springs up new,
by evening it is dry and withered.

7 We are consumed by your anger
and terrified by your indignation.
8 You have set our iniquities before you,
our secret sins in the light of your presence.
9 All our days pass away under your wrath;
we finish our years with a moan.
10 The length of our days is seventy years—
or eighty, if we have the strength;
yet their span[a] is but trouble and sorrow,
for they quickly pass, and we fly away.
11 Who knows the power of your anger?
For your wrath is as great as the fear that is due
you.
12 Teach us to number our days aright,
that we may gain a heart of wisdom.

13 Relent, O LORD! How long will it be?
Have compassion on your servants.
14 Satisfy us in the morning with your unfailing love,
that we may sing for joy and be glad all our days.
15 Make us glad for as many days as you have afflicted
us,
for as many years as we have seen trouble.
16 May your deeds be shown to your servants,
your splendor to their children.

17 May the favor[b] of the Lord our God rest upon us;
establish the work of our hands for us—
yes, establish the work of our hands.

Psalm 91

1 He who dwells in the shelter of the Most High
will rest in the shadow of the Almighty.[c]
2 I will say[d] of the LORD, "He is my refuge and my
fortress,
my God, in whom I trust."

3 Surely he will save you from the fowler's snare
and from the deadly pestilence.
4 He will cover you with his feathers,
and under his wings you will find refuge;
his faithfulness will be your shield and rampart.
5 You will not fear the terror of night,
nor the arrow that flies by day,
6 nor the pestilence that stalks in the darkness,
nor the plague that destroys at midday.
7 A thousand may fall at your side,
ten thousand at your right hand,
but it will not come near you.
8 You will only observe with your eyes
and see the punishment of the wicked.

[a] *10* Or *yet the best of them* [b] *17* Or *beauty* [c] *1* Hebrew *Shaddai* [d] *2* Or *He says*

MY BELOVED

Have no fear of sudden disaster. When it comes, proclaim that I am your Refuge and your Fortress, your God, in Whom you place your trust. Then I will save you from the impossible places . . . places where death is waiting to take you. I will cover you with My feathers, and under My wings you will find refuge. I will protect you from trouble and surround you with songs of deliverance.

I will demonstrate My faithfulness to you and to those around you. The knowledge of My love for you will protect you physically and emotionally. And when you have discovered this shelter . . . stay there. You will always be safe if you do what is righteous and speak the truth from your heart.

You will no longer fear the terror that night brings, nor the violence that walks the streets, nor the evil that stalks in darkness, nor even an untimely death.

I will command My angels to guard you in all your ways. Then you will go on your way in safety, and your foot will not stumble; when you lie down, you will not be afraid; when you lie down, your sleep will be sweet. I alone will cause you to dwell in safety. For I am your God.

Ps 4:8; 15:2; 32:7; 91:1-6,11; Pr 3:23-26

9 If you make the Most High your dwelling—
even the LORD, who is my refuge—
10 then no harm will befall you,
no disaster will come near your tent.
11 For he will command his angels concerning you
to guard you in all your ways;
12 they will lift you up in their hands,
so that you will not strike your foot against a
stone.
13 You will tread upon the lion and the cobra;
you will trample the great lion and the serpent.

14 "Because he loves me," says the LORD, "I will rescue
him;
I will protect him, for he acknowledges my name.
15 He will call upon me, and I will answer him;
I will be with him in trouble,
I will deliver him and honor him.
16 With long life will I satisfy him
and show him my salvation."

Psalm 92

A psalm. A song. For the Sabbath day.

1 It is good to praise the LORD
and make music to your name, O Most High,
2 to proclaim your love in the morning
and your faithfulness at night,
3 to the music of the ten-stringed lyre
and the melody of the harp.

4 For you make me glad by your deeds, O LORD;
I sing for joy at the works of your hands.
5 How great are your works, O LORD,
how profound your thoughts!
6 The senseless man does not know,
fools do not understand,
7 that though the wicked spring up like grass
and all evildoers flourish,
they will be forever destroyed.

8 But you, O LORD, are exalted forever.

9 For surely your enemies, O LORD,
surely your enemies will perish;
all evildoers will be scattered.
10 You have exalted my horn[a] like that of a wild ox;
fine oils have been poured upon me.
11 My eyes have seen the defeat of my adversaries;
my ears have heard the rout of my wicked foes.

12 The righteous will flourish like a palm tree,
they will grow like a cedar of Lebanon;
13 planted in the house of the LORD,
they will flourish in the courts of our God.
14 They will still bear fruit in old age,
they will stay fresh and green,

[a] 10 *Horn* here symbolizes strength.

Hear My Prayer

Hear My Prayer

15 proclaiming, "The LORD is upright;
he is my Rock, and there is no wickedness in him."

Psalm 93

1 The LORD reigns, he is robed in majesty;
the LORD is robed in majesty
and is armed with strength.
The world is firmly established;
it cannot be moved.
2 Your throne was established long ago;
you are from all eternity.

3 The seas have lifted up, O LORD,
the seas have lifted up their voice;
the seas have lifted up their pounding waves.
4 Mightier than the thunder of the great waters,
mightier than the breakers of the sea—
the LORD on high is mighty.

5 Your statutes stand firm;
holiness adorns your house
for endless days, O LORD.

Psalm 94

1 O LORD, the God who avenges,
O God who avenges, shine forth.
2 Rise up, O Judge of the earth;
pay back to the proud what they deserve.
3 How long will the wicked, O LORD,
how long will the wicked be jubilant?

4 They pour out arrogant words;
all the evildoers are full of boasting.
5 They crush your people, O LORD;
they oppress your inheritance.
6 They slay the widow and the alien;
they murder the fatherless.
7 They say, "The LORD does not see;
the God of Jacob pays no heed."

8 Take heed, you senseless ones among the people;
you fools, when will you become wise?
9 Does he who implanted the ear not hear?
Does he who formed the eye not see?
10 Does he who disciplines nations not punish?
Does he who teaches man lack knowledge?
11 The LORD knows the thoughts of man;
he knows that they are futile.

12 Blessed is the man you discipline, O LORD,
the man you teach from your law;
13 you grant him relief from days of trouble,
till a pit is dug for the wicked.
14 For the LORD will not reject his people;
he will never forsake his inheritance.
15 Judgment will again be founded on righteousness,
and all the upright in heart will follow it.

16 Who will rise up for me against the wicked?

Who will take a stand for me against evildoers?
17 Unless the LORD had given me help,
I would soon have dwelt in the silence of death.
18 When I said, "My foot is slipping,"
your love, O LORD, supported me.
19 When anxiety was great within me,
your consolation brought joy to my soul.

20 Can a corrupt throne be allied with you—
one that brings on misery by its decrees?
21 They band together against the righteous
and condemn the innocent to death.
22 But the LORD has become my fortress,
and my God the rock in whom I take refuge.
23 He will repay them for their sins
and destroy them for their wickedness;
the LORD our God will destroy them.

Psalm 95

1 Come, let us sing for joy to the LORD;
let us shout aloud to the Rock of our salvation.
2 Let us come before him with thanksgiving
and extol him with music and song.

3 For the LORD is the great God,
the great King above all gods.
4 In his hand are the depths of the earth,
and the mountain peaks belong to him.
5 The sea is his, for he made it,
and his hands formed the dry land.

6 Come, let us bow down in worship,
let us kneel before the LORD our Maker;
7 for he is our God
and we are the people of his pasture,
the flock under his care.

Today, if you hear his voice,
8 do not harden your hearts as you did at Meribah,[a]
as you did that day at Massah[b] in the desert,
9 where your fathers tested and tried me,
though they had seen what I did.
10 For forty years I was angry with that generation;
I said, "They are a people whose hearts go astray,
and they have not known my ways."
11 So I declared on oath in my anger,
"They shall never enter my rest."

Psalm 96

1 Sing to the LORD a new song;
sing to the LORD, all the earth.
2 Sing to the LORD, praise his name;
proclaim his salvation day after day.
3 Declare his glory among the nations,
his marvelous deeds among all peoples.

[a] 8 *Meribah* means *quarreling.* [b] 8 *Massah* means *testing.*

Hear My Prayer

Hear My Prayer

4 For great is the LORD and most worthy of praise;
he is to be feared above all gods.
5 For all the gods of the nations are idols,
but the LORD made the heavens.
6 Splendor and majesty are before him;
strength and glory are in his sanctuary.

7 Ascribe to the LORD, O families of nations,
ascribe to the LORD glory and strength.
8 Ascribe to the LORD the glory due his name;
bring an offering and come into his courts.
9 Worship the LORD in the splendor of his[a] holiness;
tremble before him, all the earth.

10 Say among the nations, "The LORD reigns."
The world is firmly established, it cannot be moved;
he will judge the peoples with equity.
11 Let the heavens rejoice, let the earth be glad;
let the sea resound, and all that is in it;
12 let the fields be jubilant, and everything in them.
Then all the trees of the forest will sing for joy;
13 they will sing before the LORD, for he comes,
he comes to judge the earth.
He will judge the world in righteousness
and the peoples in his truth.

Psalm 97

1 The LORD reigns, let the earth be glad;
let the distant shores rejoice.

2 Clouds and thick darkness surround him;
righteousness and justice are the foundation of his throne.
3 Fire goes before him
and consumes his foes on every side.
4 His lightning lights up the world;
the earth sees and trembles.
5 The mountains melt like wax before the LORD,
before the Lord of all the earth.
6 The heavens proclaim his righteousness,
and all the peoples see his glory.

7 All who worship images are put to shame,
those who boast in idols—
worship him, all you gods!

8 Zion hears and rejoices
and the villages of Judah are glad
because of your judgments, O LORD.
9 For you, O LORD, are the Most High over all the earth;
you are exalted far above all gods.

10 Let those who love the LORD hate evil,
for he guards the lives of his faithful ones
and delivers them from the hand of the wicked.
11 Light is shed upon the righteous

[a] 9 Or *LORD with the splendor of*

and joy on the upright in heart.
12 Rejoice in the LORD, you who are righteous,
and praise his holy name.

Psalm 98

A psalm.

1 Sing to the LORD a new song,
for he has done marvelous things;
his right hand and his holy arm
have worked salvation for him.
2 The LORD has made his salvation known
and revealed his righteousness to the nations.
3 He has remembered his love
and his faithfulness to the house of Israel;
all the ends of the earth have seen
the salvation of our God.

4 Shout for joy to the LORD, all the earth,
burst into jubilant song with music;
5 make music to the LORD with the harp,
with the harp and the sound of singing,
6 with trumpets and the blast of the ram's horn—
shout for joy before the LORD, the King.

7 Let the sea resound, and everything in it,
the world, and all who live in it.
8 Let the rivers clap their hands,
let the mountains sing together for joy;
9 let them sing before the LORD,
for he comes to judge the earth.
He will judge the world in righteousness
and the peoples with equity.

Psalm 99

1 The LORD reigns,
let the nations tremble;
he sits enthroned between the cherubim,
let the earth shake.
2 Great is the LORD in Zion;
he is exalted over all the nations.
3 Let them praise your great and awesome name—
he is holy.

4 The King is mighty, he loves justice—
you have established equity;
in Jacob you have done
what is just and right.
5 Exalt the LORD our God
and worship at his footstool;
he is holy.

6 Moses and Aaron were among his priests,
Samuel was among those who called on his
name;
they called on the LORD
and he answered them.
7 He spoke to them from the pillar of cloud;

Hear My Prayer

Hear My Prayer

they kept his statutes and the decrees he gave
them.

8 O LORD our God,
you answered them;
you were to Israel[a] a forgiving God,
though you punished their misdeeds.[b]
9 Exalt the LORD our God
and worship at his holy mountain,
for the LORD our God is holy.

Psalm 100

A psalm. For giving thanks.

1 Shout for joy to the LORD, all the earth.
2 Worship the LORD with gladness;
come before him with joyful songs.
3 Know that the LORD is God.
It is he who made us, and we are his[c];
we are his people, the sheep of his pasture.

4 Enter his gates with thanksgiving
and his courts with praise;
give thanks to him and praise his name.
5 For the LORD is good and his love endures forever;
his faithfulness continues through all generations.

Psalm 101

Of David. A psalm.

1 I will sing of your love and justice;
to you, O LORD, I will sing praise.
2 I will be careful to lead a blameless life—
when will you come to me?

I will walk in my house
with blameless heart.
3 I will set before my eyes
no vile thing.

The deeds of faithless men I hate;
they will not cling to me.
4 Men of perverse heart shall be far from me;
I will have nothing to do with evil.

5 Whoever slanders his neighbor in secret,
him will I put to silence;
whoever has haughty eyes and a proud heart,
him will I not endure.

6 My eyes will be on the faithful in the land,
that they may dwell with me;
he whose walk is blameless
will minister to me.

7 No one who practices deceit
will dwell in my house;

[a] 8 Hebrew *them* [b] 8 Or / *an avenger of the wrongs done to them* [c] 3 Or *and not we ourselves*

no one who speaks falsely
will stand in my presence.

8 Every morning I will put to silence
all the wicked in the land;
I will cut off every evildoer
from the city of the LORD.

Psalm 102

A prayer of an afflicted man. When he is faint and pours out his lament before the LORD.

1 Hear my prayer, O LORD;
let my cry for help come to you.
2 Do not hide your face from me
when I am in distress.
Turn your ear to me;
when I call, answer me quickly.

3 For my days vanish like smoke;
my bones burn like glowing embers.
4 My heart is blighted and withered like grass;
I forget to eat my food.
5 Because of my loud groaning
I am reduced to skin and bones.
6 I am like a desert owl,
like an owl among the ruins.
7 I lie awake; I have become
like a bird alone on a roof.
8 All day long my enemies taunt me;
those who rail against me use my name as a curse.
9 For I eat ashes as my food
and mingle my drink with tears
10 because of your great wrath,
for you have taken me up and thrown me aside.
11 My days are like the evening shadow;
I wither away like grass.

12 But you, O LORD, sit enthroned forever;
your renown endures through all generations.
13 You will arise and have compassion on Zion,
for it is time to show favor to her;
the appointed time has come.
14 For her stones are dear to your servants;
her very dust moves them to pity.
15 The nations will fear the name of the LORD,
all the kings of the earth will revere your glory.
16 For the LORD will rebuild Zion
and appear in his glory.
17 He will respond to the prayer of the destitute;
he will not despise their plea.
18 Let this be written for a future generation,
that a people not yet created may praise the LORD:
19 "The LORD looked down from his sanctuary on high,
from heaven he viewed the earth,
20 to hear the groans of the prisoners
and release those condemned to death."

Hear My Prayer

Hear My Prayer

21 So the name of the LORD will be declared in Zion
and his praise in Jerusalem
22 when the peoples and the kingdoms
assemble to worship the LORD.

23 In the course of my life[a] he broke my strength;
he cut short my days.
24 So I said:
"Do not take me away, O my God, in the midst of
my days;
your years go on through all generations.
25 In the beginning you laid the foundations of the
earth,
and the heavens are the work of your hands.
26 They will perish, but you remain;
they will all wear out like a garment.
Like clothing you will change them
and they will be discarded.
27 But you remain the same,
and your years will never end.
28 The children of your servants will live in your
presence;
their descendants will be established before you."

Psalm 103

Of David.

1 Praise the LORD, O my soul;
all my inmost being, praise his holy name.
2 Praise the LORD, O my soul,
and forget not all his benefits—
3 who forgives all your sins
and heals all your diseases,
4 who redeems your life from the pit
and crowns you with love and compassion,
5 who satisfies your desires with good things
so that your youth is renewed like the eagle's.

6 The LORD works righteousness
and justice for all the oppressed.

7 He made known his ways to Moses,
his deeds to the people of Israel:
8 The LORD is compassionate and gracious,
slow to anger, abounding in love.
9 He will not always accuse,
nor will he harbor his anger forever;
10 he does not treat us as our sins deserve
or repay us according to our iniquities.
11 For as high as the heavens are above the earth,
so great is his love for those who fear him;
12 as far as the east is from the west,
so far has he removed our transgressions from us.
13 As a father has compassion on his children,
so the LORD has compassion on those who fear him;
14 for he knows how we are formed,

[a] 23 Or *By his power*

he remembers that we are dust.
15 As for man, his days are like grass,
he flourishes like a flower of the field;
16 the wind blows over it and it is gone,
and its place remembers it no more.
17 But from everlasting to everlasting
the LORD's love is with those who fear him,
and his righteousness with their children's
children—
18 with those who keep his covenant
and remember to obey his precepts.

19 The LORD has established his throne in heaven,
and his kingdom rules over all.

20 Praise the LORD, you his angels,
you mighty ones who do his bidding,
who obey his word.
21 Praise the LORD, all his heavenly hosts,
you his servants who do his will.
22 Praise the LORD, all his works
everywhere in his dominion.

Praise the LORD, O my soul.

Psalm 104

1 Praise the LORD, O my soul.

O LORD my God, you are very great;
you are clothed with splendor and majesty.
2 He wraps himself in light as with a garment;
he stretches out the heavens like a tent
3 and lays the beams of his upper chambers on their
waters.
He makes the clouds his chariot
and rides on the wings of the wind.
4 He makes winds his messengers,[a]
flames of fire his servants.

5 He set the earth on its foundations;
it can never be moved.
6 You covered it with the deep as with a garment;
the waters stood above the mountains.
7 But at your rebuke the waters fled,
at the sound of your thunder they took to flight;
8 they flowed over the mountains,
they went down into the valleys,
to the place you assigned for them.
9 You set a boundary they cannot cross;
never again will they cover the earth.

10 He makes springs pour water into the ravines;
it flows between the mountains.
11 They give water to all the beasts of the field;
the wild donkeys quench their thirst.
12 The birds of the air nest by the waters;
they sing among the branches.
13 He waters the mountains from his upper chambers;

Hear My Prayer

[a] 4 Or *angels*

Hear My Prayer

the earth is satisfied by the fruit of his work.
14 He makes grass grow for the cattle,
and plants for man to cultivate—
bringing forth food from the earth:
15 wine that gladdens the heart of man,
oil to make his face shine,
and bread that sustains his heart.
16 The trees of the LORD are well watered,
the cedars of Lebanon that he planted.
17 There the birds make their nests;
the stork has its home in the pine trees.
18 The high mountains belong to the wild goats;
the crags are a refuge for the coneys.[a]

19 The moon marks off the seasons,
and the sun knows when to go down.
20 You bring darkness, it becomes night,
and all the beasts of the forest prowl.
21 The lions roar for their prey
and seek their food from God.
22 The sun rises, and they steal away;
they return and lie down in their dens.
23 Then man goes out to his work,
to his labor until evening.

24 How many are your works, O LORD!
In wisdom you made them all;
the earth is full of your creatures.
25 There is the sea, vast and spacious,
teeming with creatures beyond number—
living things both large and small.
26 There the ships go to and fro,
and the leviathan, which you formed to frolic there.

27 These all look to you
to give them their food at the proper time.
28 When you give it to them,
they gather it up;
when you open your hand,
they are satisfied with good things.
29 When you hide your face,
they are terrified;
when you take away their breath,
they die and return to the dust.
30 When you send your Spirit,
they are created,
and you renew the face of the earth.

31 May the glory of the LORD endure forever;
may the LORD rejoice in his works—
32 he who looks at the earth, and it trembles,
who touches the mountains, and they smoke.

33 I will sing to the LORD all my life;
I will sing praise to my God as long as I live.
34 May my meditation be pleasing to him,
as I rejoice in the LORD.

[a] *18* That is, the hyrax or rock badger

35 But may sinners vanish from the earth
and the wicked be no more.

Praise the LORD, O my soul.

Praise the LORD.[a]

Psalm 105

1 Give thanks to the LORD, call on his name;
make known among the nations what he has done.
2 Sing to him, sing praise to him;
tell of all his wonderful acts.
3 Glory in his holy name;
let the hearts of those who seek the LORD rejoice.
4 Look to the LORD and his strength;
seek his face always.

5 Remember the wonders he has done,
his miracles, and the judgments he pronounced,
6 O descendants of Abraham his servant,
O sons of Jacob, his chosen ones.
7 He is the LORD our God;
his judgments are in all the earth.

8 He remembers his covenant forever,
the word he commanded, for a thousand generations,
9 the covenant he made with Abraham,
the oath he swore to Isaac.
10 He confirmed it to Jacob as a decree,
to Israel as an everlasting covenant:
11 "To you I will give the land of Canaan
as the portion you will inherit."

12 When they were but few in number,
few indeed, and strangers in it,
13 they wandered from nation to nation,
from one kingdom to another.
14 He allowed no one to oppress them;
for their sake he rebuked kings:
15 "Do not touch my anointed ones;
do my prophets no harm."

16 He called down famine on the land
and destroyed all their supplies of food;
17 and he sent a man before them—
Joseph, sold as a slave.
18 They bruised his feet with shackles,
his neck was put in irons,
19 till what he foretold came to pass,
till the word of the LORD proved him true.
20 The king sent and released him,
the ruler of peoples set him free.
21 He made him master of his household,
ruler over all he possessed,
22 to instruct his princes as he pleased
and teach his elders wisdom.

[a] 35 Hebrew *Hallelu Yah*; in the Septuagint this line stands at the beginning of Psalm 105.

Hear My Prayer

Hear My Prayer

23 Then Israel entered Egypt;
Jacob lived as an alien in the land of Ham.
24 The Lord made his people very fruitful;
he made them too numerous for their foes,
25 whose hearts he turned to hate his people,
to conspire against his servants.
26 He sent Moses his servant,
and Aaron, whom he had chosen.
27 They performed his miraculous signs among them,
his wonders in the land of Ham.
28 He sent darkness and made the land dark—
for had they not rebelled against his words?
29 He turned their waters into blood,
causing their fish to die.
30 Their land teemed with frogs,
which went up into the bedrooms of their rulers.
31 He spoke, and there came swarms of flies,
and gnats throughout their country.
32 He turned their rain into hail,
with lightning throughout their land;
33 he struck down their vines and fig trees
and shattered the trees of their country.
34 He spoke, and the locusts came,
grasshoppers without number;
35 they ate up every green thing in their land,
ate up the produce of their soil.
36 Then he struck down all the firstborn in their land,
the firstfruits of all their manhood.

37 He brought out Israel, laden with silver and gold,
and from among their tribes no one faltered.
38 Egypt was glad when they left,
because dread of Israel had fallen on them.
39 He spread out a cloud as a covering,
and a fire to give light at night.
40 They asked, and he brought them quail
and satisfied them with the bread of heaven.
41 He opened the rock, and water gushed out;
like a river it flowed in the desert.

42 For he remembered his holy promise
given to his servant Abraham.
43 He brought out his people with rejoicing,
his chosen ones with shouts of joy;
44 he gave them the lands of the nations,
and they fell heir to what others had toiled for—
45 that they might keep his precepts
and observe his laws.

Praise the Lord.[a]

Psalm 106

1 Praise the Lord.[b]

Give thanks to the Lord, for he is good;
his love endures forever.
2 Who can proclaim the mighty acts of the Lord

[a] *45* Hebrew *Hallelu Yah*   [b] *1* Hebrew *Hallelu Yah*; also in verse 48

or fully declare his praise?
3 Blessed are they who maintain justice,
who constantly do what is right.
4 Remember me, O LORD, when you show favor to your people,
come to my aid when you save them,
5 that I may enjoy the prosperity of your chosen ones,
that I may share in the joy of your nation
and join your inheritance in giving praise.

6 We have sinned, even as our fathers did;
we have done wrong and acted wickedly.
7 When our fathers were in Egypt,
they gave no thought to your miracles;
they did not remember your many kindnesses,
and they rebelled by the sea, the Red Sea.[a]
8 Yet he saved them for his name's sake,
to make his mighty power known.
9 He rebuked the Red Sea, and it dried up;
he led them through the depths as through a desert.
10 He saved them from the hand of the foe;
from the hand of the enemy he redeemed them.
11 The waters covered their adversaries;
not one of them survived.
12 Then they believed his promises
and sang his praise.

13 But they soon forgot what he had done
and did not wait for his counsel.
14 In the desert they gave in to their craving;
in the wasteland they put God to the test.
15 So he gave them what they asked for,
but sent a wasting disease upon them.

16 In the camp they grew envious of Moses
and of Aaron, who was consecrated to the LORD.
17 The earth opened up and swallowed Dathan;
it buried the company of Abiram.
18 Fire blazed among their followers;
a flame consumed the wicked.

19 At Horeb they made a calf
and worshiped an idol cast from metal.
20 They exchanged their Glory
for an image of a bull, which eats grass.
21 They forgot the God who saved them,
who had done great things in Egypt,
22 miracles in the land of Ham
and awesome deeds by the Red Sea.
23 So he said he would destroy them—
had not Moses, his chosen one,
stood in the breach before him
to keep his wrath from destroying them.

24 Then they despised the pleasant land;
they did not believe his promise.

[a] 7 Hebrew *Yam Suph*; that is, Sea of Reeds; also in verses 9 and 22

Hear My Prayer

Hear My Prayer

25 They grumbled in their tents
and did not obey the LORD.
26 So he swore to them with uplifted hand
that he would make them fall in the desert,
27 make their descendants fall among the nations
and scatter them throughout the lands.

28 They yoked themselves to the Baal of Peor
and ate sacrifices offered to lifeless gods;
29 they provoked the LORD to anger by their wicked deeds,
and a plague broke out among them.
30 But Phinehas stood up and intervened,
and the plague was checked.
31 This was credited to him as righteousness
for endless generations to come.

32 By the waters of Meribah they angered the LORD,
and trouble came to Moses because of them;
33 for they rebelled against the Spirit of God,
and rash words came from Moses' lips.[a]

34 They did not destroy the peoples
as the LORD had commanded them,
35 but they mingled with the nations
and adopted their customs.
36 They worshiped their idols,
which became a snare to them.
37 They sacrificed their sons
and their daughters to demons.
38 They shed innocent blood,
the blood of their sons and daughters,
whom they sacrificed to the idols of Canaan,
and the land was desecrated by their blood.
39 They defiled themselves by what they did;
by their deeds they prostituted themselves.

40 Therefore the LORD was angry with his people
and abhorred his inheritance.
41 He handed them over to the nations,
and their foes ruled over them.
42 Their enemies oppressed them
and subjected them to their power.
43 Many times he delivered them,
but they were bent on rebellion
and they wasted away in their sin.

44 But he took note of their distress
when he heard their cry;
45 for their sake he remembered his covenant
and out of his great love he relented.
46 He caused them to be pitied
by all who held them captive.

47 Save us, O LORD our God,
and gather us from the nations,
that we may give thanks to your holy name
and glory in your praise.

[a] *33* Or *against his spirit, / and rash words came from his lips*

48 Praise be to the LORD, the God of Israel,
from everlasting to everlasting.
Let all the people say, "Amen!"

Praise the LORD.

BOOK V
Psalms 107–150

Psalm 107

1 Give thanks to the LORD, for he is good;
his love endures forever.
2 Let the redeemed of the LORD say this—
those he redeemed from the hand of the foe,
3 those he gathered from the lands,
from east and west, from north and south.[a]

4 Some wandered in desert wastelands,
finding no way to a city where they could settle.
5 They were hungry and thirsty,
and their lives ebbed away.
6 Then they cried out to the LORD in their trouble,
and he delivered them from their distress.
7 He led them by a straight way
to a city where they could settle.
8 Let them give thanks to the LORD for his unfailing
love
and his wonderful deeds for men,
9 for he satisfies the thirsty
and fills the hungry with good things.

10 Some sat in darkness and the deepest gloom,
prisoners suffering in iron chains,
11 for they had rebelled against the words of God
and despised the counsel of the Most High.
12 So he subjected them to bitter labor;
they stumbled, and there was no one to help.
13 Then they cried to the LORD in their trouble,
and he saved them from their distress.
14 He brought them out of darkness and the deepest
gloom
and broke away their chains.
15 Let them give thanks to the LORD for his unfailing
love
and his wonderful deeds for men,
16 for he breaks down gates of bronze
and cuts through bars of iron.

17 Some became fools through their rebellious ways
and suffered affliction because of their iniquities.
18 They loathed all food
and drew near the gates of death.
19 Then they cried to the LORD in their trouble,
and he saved them from their distress.
20 He sent forth his word and healed them;
he rescued them from the grave.

[a] 3 Hebrew *north and the sea*

Hear My Prayer

Hear My Prayer

21 Let them give thanks to the LORD for his unfailing
love
and his wonderful deeds for men.
22 Let them sacrifice thank offerings
and tell of his works with songs of joy.

23 Others went out on the sea in ships;
they were merchants on the mighty waters.
24 They saw the works of the LORD,
his wonderful deeds in the deep.
25 For he spoke and stirred up a tempest
that lifted high the waves.
26 They mounted up to the heavens and went down to
the depths;
in their peril their courage melted away.
27 They reeled and staggered like drunken men;
they were at their wits' end.
28 Then they cried out to the LORD in their trouble,
and he brought them out of their distress.
29 He stilled the storm to a whisper;
the waves of the sea were hushed.
30 They were glad when it grew calm,
and he guided them to their desired haven.
31 Let them give thanks to the LORD for his unfailing
love
and his wonderful deeds for men.
32 Let them exalt him in the assembly of the people
and praise him in the council of the elders.

33 He turned rivers into a desert,
flowing springs into thirsty ground,
34 and fruitful land into a salt waste,
because of the wickedness of those who lived
there.
35 He turned the desert into pools of water
and the parched ground into flowing springs;
36 there he brought the hungry to live,
and they founded a city where they could
settle.
37 They sowed fields and planted vineyards
that yielded a fruitful harvest;
38 he blessed them, and their numbers greatly
increased,
and he did not let their herds diminish.

39 Then their numbers decreased, and they were
humbled
by oppression, calamity and sorrow;
40 he who pours contempt on nobles
made them wander in a trackless waste.
41 But he lifted the needy out of their affliction
and increased their families like flocks.
42 The upright see and rejoice,
but all the wicked shut their mouths.

43 Whoever is wise, let him heed these things
and consider the great love of the LORD.

Psalm 108

A song. A psalm of David.

1 My heart is steadfast, O God;
I will sing and make music with all my soul.
2 Awake, harp and lyre!
I will awaken the dawn.
3 I will praise you, O LORD, among the nations;
I will sing of you among the peoples.
4 For great is your love, higher than the heavens;
your faithfulness reaches to the skies.
5 Be exalted, O God, above the heavens,
and let your glory be over all the earth.

6 Save us and help us with your right hand,
that those you love may be delivered.
7 God has spoken from his sanctuary:
"In triumph I will parcel out Shechem
and measure off the Valley of Succoth.
8 Gilead is mine, Manasseh is mine;
Ephraim is my helmet,
Judah my scepter.
9 Moab is my washbasin,
upon Edom I toss my sandal;
over Philistia I shout in triumph."

10 Who will bring me to the fortified city?
Who will lead me to Edom?
11 Is it not you, O God, you who have rejected us
and no longer go out with our armies?
12 Give us aid against the enemy,
for the help of man is worthless.
13 With God we will gain the victory,
and he will trample down our enemies.

Psalm 109

For the director of music. Of David. A psalm.

1 O God, whom I praise,
do not remain silent,
2 for wicked and deceitful men
have opened their mouths against me;
they have spoken against me with lying tongues.
3 With words of hatred they surround me;
they attack me without cause.
4 In return for my friendship they accuse me,
but I am a man of prayer.
5 They repay me evil for good,
and hatred for my friendship.

6 Appoint[a] an evil man[b] to oppose him;
let an accuser[c] stand at his right hand.
7 When he is tried, let him be found guilty,
and may his prayers condemn him.
8 May his days be few;

[a] 6 Or ⌊*They say:*⌋ "*Appoint* (with quotation marks at the end of verse 19) [b] 6 Or *the Evil One* [c] 6 Or *let Satan*

Hear My Prayer

Hear My Prayer

may another take his place of leadership.
9 May his children be fatherless
and his wife a widow.
10 May his children be wandering beggars;
may they be driven[a] from their ruined homes.
11 May a creditor seize all he has;
may strangers plunder the fruits of his labor.
12 May no one extend kindness to him
or take pity on his fatherless children.
13 May his descendants be cut off,
their names blotted out from the next generation.
14 May the iniquity of his fathers be remembered before
the LORD;
may the sin of his mother never be blotted out.
15 May their sins always remain before the LORD,
that he may cut off the memory of them from the
earth.

16 For he never thought of doing a kindness,
but hounded to death the poor
and the needy and the brokenhearted.
17 He loved to pronounce a curse—
may it[b] come on him;
he found no pleasure in blessing—
may it be[c] far from him.
18 He wore cursing as his garment;
it entered into his body like water,
into his bones like oil.
19 May it be like a cloak wrapped about him,
like a belt tied forever around him.
20 May this be the LORD's payment to my accusers,
to those who speak evil of me.

21 But you, O Sovereign LORD,
deal well with me for your name's sake;
out of the goodness of your love, deliver me.
22 For I am poor and needy,
and my heart is wounded within me.
23 I fade away like an evening shadow;
I am shaken off like a locust.
24 My knees give way from fasting;
my body is thin and gaunt.
25 I am an object of scorn to my accusers;
when they see me, they shake their heads.

26 Help me, O LORD my God;
save me in accordance with your love.
27 Let them know that it is your hand,
that you, O LORD, have done it.
28 They may curse, but you will bless;
when they attack they will be put to shame,
but your servant will rejoice.
29 My accusers will be clothed with disgrace
and wrapped in shame as in a cloak.
30 With my mouth I will greatly extol the LORD;
in the great throng I will praise him.

[a] *10* Septuagint; Hebrew *sought* [b] *17* Or *curse, / and it has* [c] *17* Or *blessing, / and it is*

31 For he stands at the right hand of the needy one,
to save his life from those who condemn him.

Psalm 110

Of David. A psalm.

1 The LORD says to my Lord:
"Sit at my right hand
until I make your enemies
a footstool for your feet."

2 The LORD will extend your mighty scepter from Zion;
you will rule in the midst of your enemies.
3 Your troops will be willing
on your day of battle.
Arrayed in holy majesty,
from the womb of the dawn
you will receive the dew of your youth.[a]

4 The LORD has sworn
and will not change his mind:
"You are a priest forever,
in the order of Melchizedek."

5 The Lord is at your right hand;
he will crush kings on the day of his wrath.
6 He will judge the nations, heaping up the dead
and crushing the rulers of the whole earth.
7 He will drink from a brook beside the way[b];
therefore he will lift up his head.

Psalm 111[c]

1 Praise the LORD.[d]

I will extol the LORD with all my heart
in the council of the upright and in the assembly.

2 Great are the works of the LORD;
they are pondered by all who delight in them.
3 Glorious and majestic are his deeds,
and his righteousness endures forever.
4 He has caused his wonders to be remembered;
the LORD is gracious and compassionate.
5 He provides food for those who fear him;
he remembers his covenant forever.
6 He has shown his people the power of his works,
giving them the lands of other nations.
7 The works of his hands are faithful and just;
all his precepts are trustworthy.
8 They are steadfast for ever and ever,
done in faithfulness and uprightness.
9 He provided redemption for his people;
he ordained his covenant forever—
holy and awesome is his name.

10 The fear of the LORD is the beginning of wisdom;

[a] *3* Or / *your young men will come to you like the dew* [b] *7* Or / *The One who grants succession will set him in authority* [c] This psalm is an acrostic poem, the lines of which begin with the successive letters of the Hebrew alphabet. [d] *1* Hebrew *Hallelu Yah*

Hear My Prayer

Hear My Prayer

all who follow his precepts have good
understanding.
To him belongs eternal praise.

Psalm 112[a]

1 Praise the LORD.[b]

Blessed is the man who fears the LORD,
who finds great delight in his commands.

2 His children will be mighty in the land;
the generation of the upright will be blessed.
3 Wealth and riches are in his house,
and his righteousness endures forever.
4 Even in darkness light dawns for the upright,
for the gracious and compassionate and righteous
man.[c]
5 Good will come to him who is generous and lends
freely,
who conducts his affairs with justice.
6 Surely he will never be shaken;
a righteous man will be remembered forever.
7 He will have no fear of bad news;
his heart is steadfast, trusting in the LORD.
8 His heart is secure, he will have no fear;
in the end he will look in triumph on his foes.
9 He has scattered abroad his gifts to the poor,
his righteousness endures forever;
his horn[d] will be lifted high in honor.

10 The wicked man will see and be vexed,
he will gnash his teeth and waste away;
the longings of the wicked will come to nothing.

Psalm 113

1 Praise the LORD.[e]

Praise, O servants of the LORD,
praise the name of the LORD.
2 Let the name of the LORD be praised,
both now and forevermore.
3 From the rising of the sun to the place where it sets,
the name of the LORD is to be praised.

4 The LORD is exalted over all the nations,
his glory above the heavens.
5 Who is like the LORD our God,
the One who sits enthroned on high,
6 who stoops down to look
on the heavens and the earth?

7 He raises the poor from the dust
and lifts the needy from the ash heap;
8 he seats them with princes,
with the princes of their people.

[a] This psalm is an acrostic poem, the lines of which begin with the successive letters of the Hebrew alphabet. [b] *1* Hebrew *Hallelu Yah* [c] *4* Or / *for* ⌞*the* LORD⌟ *is gracious and compassionate and righteous* [d] *9* *Horn* here symbolizes dignity. [e] *1* Hebrew *Hallelu Yah*; also in verse 9

9 He settles the barren woman in her home
as a happy mother of children.

Praise the LORD.

Psalm 114

1 When Israel came out of Egypt,
the house of Jacob from a people of foreign tongue,
2 Judah became God's sanctuary,
Israel his dominion.

3 The sea looked and fled,
the Jordan turned back;
4 the mountains skipped like rams,
the hills like lambs.

5 Why was it, O sea, that you fled,
O Jordan, that you turned back,
6 you mountains, that you skipped like rams,
you hills, like lambs?

7 Tremble, O earth, at the presence of the Lord,
at the presence of the God of Jacob,
8 who turned the rock into a pool,
the hard rock into springs of water.

Psalm 115

1 Not to us, O LORD, not to us
but to your name be the glory,
because of your love and faithfulness.

2 Why do the nations say,
"Where is their God?"
3 Our God is in heaven;
he does whatever pleases him.
4 But their idols are silver and gold,
made by the hands of men.
5 They have mouths, but cannot speak,
eyes, but they cannot see;
6 they have ears, but cannot hear,
noses, but they cannot smell;
7 they have hands, but cannot feel,
feet, but they cannot walk;
nor can they utter a sound with their throats.
8 Those who make them will be like them,
and so will all who trust in them.

9 O house of Israel, trust in the LORD—
he is their help and shield.
10 O house of Aaron, trust in the LORD—
he is their help and shield.
11 You who fear him, trust in the LORD—
he is their help and shield.

12 The LORD remembers us and will bless us:
He will bless the house of Israel,
he will bless the house of Aaron,
13 he will bless those who fear the LORD—
small and great alike.

Hear My Prayer

Hear My Prayer

14 May the LORD make you increase,
both you and your children.
15 May you be blessed by the LORD,
the Maker of heaven and earth.

16 The highest heavens belong to the LORD,
but the earth he has given to man.
17 It is not the dead who praise the LORD,
those who go down to silence;
18 it is we who extol the LORD,
both now and forevermore.

Praise the LORD.[a]

Psalm 116

1 I love the LORD, for he heard my voice;
he heard my cry for mercy.
2 Because he turned his ear to me,
I will call on him as long as I live.

3 The cords of death entangled me,
the anguish of the grave[b] came upon me;
I was overcome by trouble and sorrow.
4 Then I called on the name of the LORD:
"O LORD, save me!"

5 The LORD is gracious and righteous;
our God is full of compassion.
6 The LORD protects the simplehearted;
when I was in great need, he saved me.

7 Be at rest once more, O my soul,
for the LORD has been good to you.

8 For you, O LORD, have delivered my soul from death,
my eyes from tears,
my feet from stumbling,
9 that I may walk before the LORD
in the land of the living.
10 I believed; therefore[c] I said,
"I am greatly afflicted."
11 And in my dismay I said,
"All men are liars."

12 How can I repay the LORD
for all his goodness to me?
13 I will lift up the cup of salvation
and call on the name of the LORD.
14 I will fulfill my vows to the LORD
in the presence of all his people.

15 Precious in the sight of the LORD
is the death of his saints.
16 O LORD, truly I am your servant;
I am your servant, the son of your maidservant[d];
you have freed me from my chains.

17 I will sacrifice a thank offering to you

[a] 18 Hebrew *Hallelu Yah* [b] 3 Hebrew *Sheol* [c] 10 Or *believed even when* [d] 16 Or *servant, your faithful son*

and call on the name of the LORD.
18 I will fulfill my vows to the LORD
in the presence of all his people,
19 in the courts of the house of the LORD—
in your midst, O Jerusalem.

Praise the LORD.[a]

Psalm 117

1 Praise the LORD, all you nations;
extol him, all you peoples.
2 For great is his love toward us,
and the faithfulness of the LORD endures forever.

Praise the LORD.[a]

Psalm 118

1 Give thanks to the LORD, for he is good;
his love endures forever.

2 Let Israel say:
"His love endures forever."
3 Let the house of Aaron say:
"His love endures forever."
4 Let those who fear the LORD say:
"His love endures forever."

5 In my anguish I cried to the LORD,
and he answered by setting me free.
6 The LORD is with me; I will not be afraid.
What can man do to me?
7 The LORD is with me; he is my helper.
I will look in triumph on my enemies.

8 It is better to take refuge in the LORD
than to trust in man.
9 It is better to take refuge in the LORD
than to trust in princes.

10 All the nations surrounded me,
but in the name of the LORD I cut them off.
11 They surrounded me on every side,
but in the name of the LORD I cut them off.
12 They swarmed around me like bees,
but they died out as quickly as burning thorns;
in the name of the LORD I cut them off.

13 I was pushed back and about to fall,
but the LORD helped me.
14 The LORD is my strength and my song;
he has become my salvation.

15 Shouts of joy and victory
resound in the tents of the righteous:
"The LORD's right hand has done mighty things!
16 The LORD's right hand is lifted high;
the LORD's right hand has done mighty things!"

[a] *19,2* Hebrew *Hallelu Yah*

Hear My Prayer

Hear My Prayer

17 I will not die but live,
and will proclaim what the LORD has done.
18 The LORD has chastened me severely,
but he has not given me over to death.

19 Open for me the gates of righteousness;
I will enter and give thanks to the LORD.
20 This is the gate of the LORD
through which the righteous may enter.
21 I will give you thanks, for you answered me;
you have become my salvation.

22 The stone the builders rejected
has become the capstone;
23 the LORD has done this,
and it is marvelous in our eyes.
24 This is the day the LORD has made;
let us rejoice and be glad in it.

25 O LORD, save us;
O LORD, grant us success.
26 Blessed is he who comes in the name of the LORD.
From the house of the LORD we bless you.[a]
27 The LORD is God,
and he has made his light shine upon us.
With boughs in hand, join in the festal procession
up[b] to the horns of the altar.

28 You are my God, and I will give you thanks;
you are my God, and I will exalt you.

29 Give thanks to the LORD, for he is good;
his love endures forever.

Psalm 119[c]

א Aleph

1 Blessed are they whose ways are blameless,
who walk according to the law of the LORD.
2 Blessed are they who keep his statutes
and seek him with all their heart.
3 They do nothing wrong;
they walk in his ways.
4 You have laid down precepts
that are to be fully obeyed.
5 Oh, that my ways were steadfast
in obeying your decrees!
6 Then I would not be put to shame
when I consider all your commands.
7 I will praise you with an upright heart
as I learn your righteous laws.
8 I will obey your decrees;
do not utterly forsake me.

ב Beth

9 How can a young man keep his way pure?
By living according to your word.

[a] *26* The Hebrew is plural. [b] *27* Or *Bind the festal sacrifice with ropes / and take it*
[c] This psalm is an acrostic poem; the verses of each stanza begin with the same letter of the Hebrew alphabet.

10 I seek you with all my heart;
do not let me stray from your commands.
11 I have hidden your word in my heart
that I might not sin against you.
12 Praise be to you, O LORD;
teach me your decrees.
13 With my lips I recount
all the laws that come from your mouth.
14 I rejoice in following your statutes
as one rejoices in great riches.
15 I meditate on your precepts
and consider your ways.
16 I delight in your decrees;
I will not neglect your word.

ג Gimel

17 Do good to your servant, and I will live;
I will obey your word.
18 Open my eyes that I may see
wonderful things in your law.
19 I am a stranger on earth;
do not hide your commands from me.
20 My soul is consumed with longing
for your laws at all times.
21 You rebuke the arrogant, who are cursed
and who stray from your commands.
22 Remove from me scorn and contempt,
for I keep your statutes.
23 Though rulers sit together and slander me,
your servant will meditate on your decrees.
24 Your statutes are my delight;
they are my counselors.

ד Daleth

25 I am laid low in the dust;
preserve my life according to your word.
26 I recounted my ways and you answered me;
teach me your decrees.
27 Let me understand the teaching of your precepts;
then I will meditate on your wonders.
28 My soul is weary with sorrow;
strengthen me according to your word.
29 Keep me from deceitful ways;
be gracious to me through your law.
30 I have chosen the way of truth;
I have set my heart on your laws.
31 I hold fast to your statutes, O LORD;
do not let me be put to shame.
32 I run in the path of your commands,
for you have set my heart free.

ה He

33 Teach me, O LORD, to follow your decrees;
then I will keep them to the end.
34 Give me understanding, and I will keep your law
and obey it with all my heart.
35 Direct me in the path of your commands,

Hear My Prayer

Hear My Prayer

for there I find delight.
36 Turn my heart toward your statutes
and not toward selfish gain.
37 Turn my eyes away from worthless things;
preserve my life according to your word.[a]
38 Fulfill your promise to your servant,
so that you may be feared.
39 Take away the disgrace I dread,
for your laws are good.
40 How I long for your precepts!
Preserve my life in your righteousness.

ו Waw

41 May your unfailing love come to me, O LORD,
your salvation according to your promise;
42 then I will answer the one who taunts me,
for I trust in your word.
43 Do not snatch the word of truth from my mouth,
for I have put my hope in your laws.
44 I will always obey your law,
for ever and ever.
45 I will walk about in freedom,
for I have sought out your precepts.
46 I will speak of your statutes before kings
and will not be put to shame,
47 for I delight in your commands
because I love them.
48 I lift up my hands to[b] your commands, which I love,
and I meditate on your decrees.

ז Zayin

49 Remember your word to your servant,
for you have given me hope.
50 My comfort in my suffering is this:
Your promise preserves my life.
51 The arrogant mock me without restraint,
but I do not turn from your law.
52 I remember your ancient laws, O LORD,
and I find comfort in them.
53 Indignation grips me because of the wicked,
who have forsaken your law.
54 Your decrees are the theme of my song
wherever I lodge.
55 In the night I remember your name, O LORD,
and I will keep your law.
56 This has been my practice:
I obey your precepts.

ח Heth

57 You are my portion, O LORD;
I have promised to obey your words.
58 I have sought your face with all my heart;
be gracious to me according to your promise.
59 I have considered my ways
and have turned my steps to your statutes.

[a] *37* Two manuscripts of the Masoretic Text and Dead Sea Scrolls; most manuscripts of the Masoretic Text *life in your way* [b] *48* Or *for*

60 I will hasten and not delay
to obey your commands.
61 Though the wicked bind me with ropes,
I will not forget your law.
62 At midnight I rise to give you thanks
for your righteous laws.
63 I am a friend to all who fear you,
to all who follow your precepts.
64 The earth is filled with your love, O LORD;
teach me your decrees.

ט Teth

65 Do good to your servant
according to your word, O LORD.
66 Teach me knowledge and good judgment,
for I believe in your commands.
67 Before I was afflicted I went astray,
but now I obey your word.
68 You are good, and what you do is good;
teach me your decrees.
69 Though the arrogant have smeared me with lies,
I keep your precepts with all my heart.
70 Their hearts are callous and unfeeling,
but I delight in your law.
71 It was good for me to be afflicted
so that I might learn your decrees.
72 The law from your mouth is more precious to me
than thousands of pieces of silver and gold.

י Yodh

73 Your hands made me and formed me;
give me understanding to learn your commands.
74 May those who fear you rejoice when they see me,
for I have put my hope in your word.
75 I know, O LORD, that your laws are righteous,
and in faithfulness you have afflicted me.
76 May your unfailing love be my comfort,
according to your promise to your servant.
77 Let your compassion come to me that I may live,
for your law is my delight.
78 May the arrogant be put to shame for wronging me
without cause;
but I will meditate on your precepts.
79 May those who fear you turn to me,
those who understand your statutes.
80 May my heart be blameless toward your decrees,
that I may not be put to shame.

כ Kaph

81 My soul faints with longing for your salvation,
but I have put my hope in your word.
82 My eyes fail, looking for your promise;
I say, "When will you comfort me?"
83 Though I am like a wineskin in the smoke,
I do not forget your decrees.
84 How long must your servant wait?
When will you punish my persecutors?

Hear My Prayer

Hear My Prayer

85 The arrogant dig pitfalls for me,
contrary to your law.
86 All your commands are trustworthy;
help me, for men persecute me without cause.
87 They almost wiped me from the earth,
but I have not forsaken your precepts.
88 Preserve my life according to your love,
and I will obey the statutes of your mouth.

ל Lamedh

89 Your word, O LORD, is eternal;
it stands firm in the heavens.
90 Your faithfulness continues through all generations;
you established the earth, and it endures.
91 Your laws endure to this day,
for all things serve you.
92 If your law had not been my delight,
I would have perished in my affliction.
93 I will never forget your precepts,
for by them you have preserved my life.
94 Save me, for I am yours;
I have sought out your precepts.
95 The wicked are waiting to destroy me,
but I will ponder your statutes.
96 To all perfection I see a limit;
but your commands are boundless.

מ Mem

97 Oh, how I love your law!
I meditate on it all day long.
98 Your commands make me wiser than my enemies,
for they are ever with me.
99 I have more insight than all my teachers,
for I meditate on your statutes.
100 I have more understanding than the elders,
for I obey your precepts.
101 I have kept my feet from every evil path
so that I might obey your word.
102 I have not departed from your laws,
for you yourself have taught me.
103 How sweet are your words to my taste,
sweeter than honey to my mouth!
104 I gain understanding from your precepts;
therefore I hate every wrong path.

נ Nun

105 Your word is a lamp to my feet
and a light for my path.
106 I have taken an oath and confirmed it,
that I will follow your righteous laws.
107 I have suffered much;
preserve my life, O LORD, according to your word.
108 Accept, O LORD, the willing praise of my mouth,
and teach me your laws.
109 Though I constantly take my life in my hands,
I will not forget your law.
110 The wicked have set a snare for me,

but I have not strayed from your precepts.
111 Your statutes are my heritage forever;
they are the joy of my heart.
112 My heart is set on keeping your decrees
to the very end.

ס Samekh

113 I hate double-minded men,
but I love your law.
114 You are my refuge and my shield;
I have put my hope in your word.
115 Away from me, you evildoers,
that I may keep the commands of my God!
116 Sustain me according to your promise, and I will live;
do not let my hopes be dashed.
117 Uphold me, and I will be delivered;
I will always have regard for your decrees.
118 You reject all who stray from your decrees,
for their deceitfulness is in vain.
119 All the wicked of the earth you discard like dross;
therefore I love your statutes.
120 My flesh trembles in fear of you;
I stand in awe of your laws.

ע Ayin

121 I have done what is righteous and just;
do not leave me to my oppressors.
122 Ensure your servant's well-being;
let not the arrogant oppress me.
123 My eyes fail, looking for your salvation,
looking for your righteous promise.
124 Deal with your servant according to your love
and teach me your decrees.
125 I am your servant; give me discernment
that I may understand your statutes.
126 It is time for you to act, O LORD;
your law is being broken.
127 Because I love your commands
more than gold, more than pure gold,
128 and because I consider all your precepts right,
I hate every wrong path.

פ Pe

129 Your statutes are wonderful;
therefore I obey them.
130 The unfolding of your words gives light;
it gives understanding to the simple.
131 I open my mouth and pant,
longing for your commands.
132 Turn to me and have mercy on me,
as you always do to those who love your name.
133 Direct my footsteps according to your word;
let no sin rule over me.
134 Redeem me from the oppression of men,
that I may obey your precepts.
135 Make your face shine upon your servant
and teach me your decrees.

Hear My Prayer

Hear My Prayer

136 Streams of tears flow from my eyes,
for your law is not obeyed.

צ Tsadhe

137 Righteous are you, O LORD,
and your laws are right.
138 The statutes you have laid down are righteous;
they are fully trustworthy.
139 My zeal wears me out,
for my enemies ignore your words.
140 Your promises have been thoroughly tested,
and your servant loves them.
141 Though I am lowly and despised,
I do not forget your precepts.
142 Your righteousness is everlasting
and your law is true.
143 Trouble and distress have come upon me,
but your commands are my delight.
144 Your statutes are forever right;
give me understanding that I may live.

ק Qoph

145 I call with all my heart; answer me, O LORD,
and I will obey your decrees.
146 I call out to you; save me
and I will keep your statutes.
147 I rise before dawn and cry for help;
I have put my hope in your word.
148 My eyes stay open through the watches of the night,
that I may meditate on your promises.
149 Hear my voice in accordance with your love;
preserve my life, O LORD, according to your laws.
150 Those who devise wicked schemes are near,
but they are far from your law.
151 Yet you are near, O LORD,
and all your commands are true.
152 Long ago I learned from your statutes
that you established them to last forever.

ר Resh

153 Look upon my suffering and deliver me,
for I have not forgotten your law.
154 Defend my cause and redeem me;
preserve my life according to your promise.
155 Salvation is far from the wicked,
for they do not seek out your decrees.
156 Your compassion is great, O LORD;
preserve my life according to your laws.
157 Many are the foes who persecute me,
but I have not turned from your statutes.
158 I look on the faithless with loathing,
for they do not obey your word.
159 See how I love your precepts;
preserve my life, O LORD, according to your
love.
160 All your words are true;
all your righteous laws are eternal.

ש Sin and Shin

161 Rulers persecute me without cause,
but my heart trembles at your word.
162 I rejoice in your promise
like one who finds great spoil.
163 I hate and abhor falsehood
but I love your law.
164 Seven times a day I praise you
for your righteous laws.
165 Great peace have they who love your law,
and nothing can make them stumble.
166 I wait for your salvation, O LORD,
and I follow your commands.
167 I obey your statutes,
for I love them greatly.
168 I obey your precepts and your statutes,
for all my ways are known to you.

ת Taw

169 May my cry come before you, O LORD;
give me understanding according to your word.
170 May my supplication come before you;
deliver me according to your promise.
171 May my lips overflow with praise,
for you teach me your decrees.
172 May my tongue sing of your word,
for all your commands are righteous.
173 May your hand be ready to help me,
for I have chosen your precepts.
174 I long for your salvation, O LORD,
and your law is my delight.
175 Let me live that I may praise you,
and may your laws sustain me.
176 I have strayed like a lost sheep.
Seek your servant,
for I have not forgotten your commands.

Psalm 120

A song of ascents.

1 I call on the LORD in my distress,
and he answers me.
2 Save me, O LORD, from lying lips
and from deceitful tongues.

3 What will he do to you,
and what more besides, O deceitful tongue?
4 He will punish you with a warrior's sharp
arrows,
with burning coals of the broom tree.

5 Woe to me that I dwell in Meshech,
that I live among the tents of Kedar!
6 Too long have I lived
among those who hate peace.
7 I am a man of peace;
but when I speak, they are for war.

Hear My Prayer

Hear My Prayer

Psalm 121

A song of ascents.

1 I lift up my eyes to the hills—
where does my help come from?
2 My help comes from the LORD,
the Maker of heaven and earth.

3 He will not let your foot slip—
he who watches over you will not slumber;
4 indeed, he who watches over Israel
will neither slumber nor sleep.

5 The LORD watches over you—
the LORD is your shade at your right hand;
6 the sun will not harm you by day,
nor the moon by night.

7 The LORD will keep you from all harm—
he will watch over your life;
8 the LORD will watch over your coming and going
both now and forevermore.

Psalm 122

A song of ascents. Of David.

1 I rejoiced with those who said to me,
"Let us go to the house of the LORD."
2 Our feet are standing
in your gates, O Jerusalem.

3 Jerusalem is built like a city
that is closely compacted together.
4 That is where the tribes go up,
the tribes of the LORD,
to praise the name of the LORD
according to the statute given to Israel.
5 There the thrones for judgment stand,
the thrones of the house of David.

6 Pray for the peace of Jerusalem:
"May those who love you be secure.
7 May there be peace within your walls
and security within your citadels."
8 For the sake of my brothers and friends,
I will say, "Peace be within you."
9 For the sake of the house of the LORD our God,
I will seek your prosperity.

Psalm 123

A song of ascents.

1 I lift up my eyes to you,
to you whose throne is in heaven.
2 As the eyes of slaves look to the hand of their
master,
as the eyes of a maid look to the hand of her
mistress,

so our eyes look to the LORD our God,
till he shows us his mercy.

3 Have mercy on us, O LORD, have mercy on us,
for we have endured much contempt.
4 We have endured much ridicule from the proud,
much contempt from the arrogant.

Psalm 124

A song of ascents. Of David.

1 If the LORD had not been on our side—
let Israel say—
2 if the LORD had not been on our side
when men attacked us,
3 when their anger flared against us,
they would have swallowed us alive;
4 the flood would have engulfed us,
the torrent would have swept over us,
5 the raging waters
would have swept us away.

6 Praise be to the LORD,
who has not let us be torn by their teeth.
7 We have escaped like a bird
out of the fowler's snare;
the snare has been broken,
and we have escaped.
8 Our help is in the name of the LORD,
the Maker of heaven and earth.

Psalm 125

A song of ascents.

1 Those who trust in the LORD are like Mount Zion,
which cannot be shaken but endures forever.
2 As the mountains surround Jerusalem,
so the LORD surrounds his people
both now and forevermore.

3 The scepter of the wicked will not remain
over the land allotted to the righteous,
for then the righteous might use
their hands to do evil.

4 Do good, O LORD, to those who are good,
to those who are upright in heart.
5 But those who turn to crooked ways
the LORD will banish with the evildoers.

Peace be upon Israel.

Psalm 126

A song of ascents.

1 When the LORD brought back the captives to[a] Zion,
we were like men who dreamed.[b]

[a] *1* Or *LORD restored the fortunes of*   [b] *1* Or *men restored to health*

Hear My Prayer

Hear My Prayer

2 Our mouths were filled with laughter,
our tongues with songs of joy.
Then it was said among the nations,
"The LORD has done great things for them."
3 The LORD has done great things for us,
and we are filled with joy.

4 Restore our fortunes,[a] O LORD,
like streams in the Negev.
5 Those who sow in tears
will reap with songs of joy.
6 He who goes out weeping,
carrying seed to sow,
will return with songs of joy,
carrying sheaves with him.

Psalm 127

A song of ascents. Of Solomon.

1 Unless the LORD builds the house,
its builders labor in vain.
Unless the LORD watches over the city,
the watchmen stand guard in vain.
2 In vain you rise early
and stay up late,
toiling for food to eat—
for he grants sleep to[b] those he loves.

3 Sons are a heritage from the LORD,
children a reward from him.
4 Like arrows in the hands of a warrior
are sons born in one's youth.
5 Blessed is the man
whose quiver is full of them.
They will not be put to shame
when they contend with their enemies in the gate.

Psalm 128

A song of ascents.

1 Blessed are all who fear the LORD,
who walk in his ways.
2 You will eat the fruit of your labor;
blessings and prosperity will be yours.
3 Your wife will be like a fruitful vine
within your house;
your sons will be like olive shoots
around your table.
4 Thus is the man blessed
who fears the LORD.

5 May the LORD bless you from Zion
all the days of your life;
may you see the prosperity of Jerusalem,
6 and may you live to see your children's children.
Peace be upon Israel.

[a] 4 Or *Bring back our captives* [b] 2 Or *eat— / for while they sleep he provides for*

Psalm 129

A song of ascents.

1 They have greatly oppressed me from my
youth—
let Israel say—
2 they have greatly oppressed me from my
youth,
but they have not gained the victory over me.
3 Plowmen have plowed my back
and made their furrows long.
4 But the LORD is righteous;
he has cut me free from the cords of the
wicked.

5 May all who hate Zion
be turned back in shame.
6 May they be like grass on the roof,
which withers before it can grow;
7 with it the reaper cannot fill his hands,
nor the one who gathers fill his arms.
8 May those who pass by not say,
"The blessing of the LORD be upon you;
we bless you in the name of the LORD."

Psalm 130

A song of ascents.

1 Out of the depths I cry to you, O LORD;
2 O Lord, hear my voice.
Let your ears be attentive
to my cry for mercy.

3 If you, O LORD, kept a record of sins,
O Lord, who could stand?
4 But with you there is forgiveness;
therefore you are feared.

5 I wait for the LORD, my soul waits,
and in his word I put my hope.
6 My soul waits for the Lord
more than watchmen wait for the morning,
more than watchmen wait for the morning.

7 O Israel, put your hope in the LORD,
for with the LORD is unfailing love
and with him is full redemption.
8 He himself will redeem Israel
from all their sins.

Psalm 131

A song of ascents. Of David.

1 My heart is not proud, O LORD,
my eyes are not haughty;
I do not concern myself with great matters
or things too wonderful for me.
2 But I have stilled and quieted my soul;

Hear My Prayer

Hear My Prayer

like a weaned child with its mother,
like a weaned child is my soul within me.

3 O Israel, put your hope in the LORD
both now and forevermore.

Psalm 132

A song of ascents.

1 O LORD, remember David
and all the hardships he endured.

2 He swore an oath to the LORD
and made a vow to the Mighty One of Jacob:
3 "I will not enter my house
or go to my bed—
4 I will allow no sleep to my eyes,
no slumber to my eyelids,
5 till I find a place for the LORD,
a dwelling for the Mighty One of Jacob."

6 We heard it in Ephrathah,
we came upon it in the fields of Jaar:[a, b]
7 "Let us go to his dwelling place;
let us worship at his footstool—
8 arise, O LORD, and come to your resting place,
you and the ark of your might.
9 May your priests be clothed with righteousness;
may your saints sing for joy."

10 For the sake of David your servant,
do not reject your anointed one.

11 The LORD swore an oath to David,
a sure oath that he will not revoke:
"One of your own descendants
I will place on your throne—
12 if your sons keep my covenant
and the statutes I teach them,
then their sons will sit
on your throne for ever and ever."

13 For the LORD has chosen Zion,
he has desired it for his dwelling:
14 "This is my resting place for ever and ever;
here I will sit enthroned, for I have
desired it—
15 I will bless her with abundant provisions;
her poor will I satisfy with food.
16 I will clothe her priests with salvation,
and her saints will ever sing for joy.

17 "Here I will make a horn[c] grow for David
and set up a lamp for my anointed one.
18 I will clothe his enemies with shame,
but the crown on his head will be
resplendent."

[a] 6 That is, Kiriath Jearim [b] 6 Or *heard of it in Ephrathah, / we found it in the fields of Jaar.* (And no quotes around verses 7–9) [c] 17 *Horn* here symbolizes strong one, that is, king.

MY BELOVED

As a father has compassion on his children, even so do I have compassion on those who fear Me. I do not treat you as your sins deserve or repay you according to your iniquities. Instead, I have swept away your offenses like a cloud, your sins like the morning mist.

So stop dwelling in the past. You spend too much time reviewing your sins of days gone by. I keep no record of such matters. If I did, you truly would not be able to stand. But I have forgiven you of your sins. All of them!

Or do you think that I may have missed something? Don't do this to yourself. You need to know, once and for all, that the blood of Jesus has paid the price for your sins. Confess your sins to Me, rather than rehearsing them to yourself over and over again. Acknowledge your sin to Me and do not cover up your iniquity. Confess your transgressions to Me and I will forgive the guilt of your sin. And I mean all sin.

Do not trivialize the death and sacrifice of My Son with self-condemnation. Instead, trust in Jesus and receive forgiveness of your sins through His name.

If my Son sets you free, you are free indeed. So forget the former things. Do not dwell on your past failings. If I do not remember your sin anymore, then why should you?

Ps 32:5; 103:10,13; 130:3-4; Isa 43:18,25; 44:22; Jn 8:36; Ac 10:43; 1Jn 1:7

Psalm 133

A song of ascents. Of David.

1 How good and pleasant it is
when brothers live together in unity!
2 It is like precious oil poured on the head,
running down on the beard,
running down on Aaron's beard,
down upon the collar of his robes.
3 It is as if the dew of Hermon
were falling on Mount Zion.
For there the LORD bestows his blessing,
even life forevermore.

Psalm 134

A song of ascents.

1 Praise the LORD, all you servants of the LORD
who minister by night in the house of the LORD.
2 Lift up your hands in the sanctuary
and praise the LORD.

3 May the LORD, the Maker of heaven and earth,
bless you from Zion.

Psalm 135

1 Praise the LORD.[a]

Praise the name of the LORD;
praise him, you servants of the LORD,
2 you who minister in the house of the LORD,
in the courts of the house of our God.

3 Praise the LORD, for the LORD is good;
sing praise to his name, for that is pleasant.
4 For the LORD has chosen Jacob to be his own,
Israel to be his treasured possession.

5 I know that the LORD is great,
that our Lord is greater than all gods.
6 The LORD does whatever pleases him,
in the heavens and on the earth,
in the seas and all their depths.
7 He makes clouds rise from the ends of the earth;
he sends lightning with the rain
and brings out the wind from his storehouses.

8 He struck down the firstborn of Egypt,
the firstborn of men and animals.
9 He sent his signs and wonders into your midst,
O Egypt,
against Pharaoh and all his servants.
10 He struck down many nations
and killed mighty kings—
11 Sihon king of the Amorites,
Og king of Bashan
and all the kings of Canaan—

[a] *1* Hebrew *Hallelu Yah*; also in verses 3 and 21

Hear My Prayer

Hear My Prayer

12 and he gave their land as an inheritance,
an inheritance to his people Israel.

13 Your name, O LORD, endures forever,
your renown, O LORD, through all generations.
14 For the LORD will vindicate his people
and have compassion on his servants.

15 The idols of the nations are silver and gold,
made by the hands of men.
16 They have mouths, but cannot speak,
eyes, but they cannot see;
17 they have ears, but cannot hear,
nor is there breath in their mouths.
18 Those who make them will be like them,
and so will all who trust in them.

19 O house of Israel, praise the LORD;
O house of Aaron, praise the LORD;
20 O house of Levi, praise the LORD;
you who fear him, praise the LORD.
21 Praise be to the LORD from Zion,
to him who dwells in Jerusalem.

Praise the LORD.

Psalm 136

1 Give thanks to the LORD, for he is good.
His love endures forever.
2 Give thanks to the God of gods.
His love endures forever.
3 Give thanks to the Lord of lords:
His love endures forever.

4 to him who alone does great wonders,
His love endures forever.
5 who by his understanding made the heavens,
His love endures forever.
6 who spread out the earth upon the waters,
His love endures forever.
7 who made the great lights—
His love endures forever.
8 the sun to govern the day,
His love endures forever.
9 the moon and stars to govern the night;
His love endures forever.

10 to him who struck down the firstborn of Egypt
His love endures forever.
11 and brought Israel out from among them
His love endures forever.
12 with a mighty hand and outstretched arm;
His love endures forever.

13 to him who divided the Red Sea[a] asunder
His love endures forever.
14 and brought Israel through the midst of it,
His love endures forever.

[a] *13* Hebrew *Yam Suph*; that is, Sea of Reeds; also in verse 15

15 but swept Pharaoh and his army into the
Red Sea;
His love endures forever.
16 to him who led his people through the desert,
His love endures forever.
17 who struck down great kings,
His love endures forever.
18 and killed mighty kings—
His love endures forever.
19 Sihon king of the Amorites
His love endures forever.
20 and Og king of Bashan—
His love endures forever.
21 and gave their land as an inheritance,
His love endures forever.
22 an inheritance to his servant Israel;
His love endures forever.
23 to the One who remembered us in our low
estate
His love endures forever.
24 and freed us from our enemies,
His love endures forever.
25 and who gives food to every creature.
His love endures forever.

26 Give thanks to the God of heaven.
His love endures forever.

Psalm 137

1 By the rivers of Babylon we sat and wept
when we remembered Zion.
2 There on the poplars
we hung our harps,
3 for there our captors asked us for songs,
our tormentors demanded songs of joy;
they said, "Sing us one of the songs of Zion!"

4 How can we sing the songs of the LORD
while in a foreign land?
5 If I forget you, O Jerusalem,
may my right hand forget ⌊its skill⌋.
6 May my tongue cling to the roof of my mouth
if I do not remember you,
if I do not consider Jerusalem
my highest joy.

7 Remember, O LORD, what the Edomites did
on the day Jerusalem fell.
"Tear it down," they cried,
"tear it down to its foundations!"

8 O Daughter of Babylon, doomed to destruction,
happy is he who repays you
for what you have done to us—
9 he who seizes your infants
and dashes them against the rocks.

Hear My Prayer

Hear My Prayer

Psalm 138

Of David.

1 I will praise you, O LORD, with all my heart;
before the "gods" I will sing your praise.
2 I will bow down toward your holy temple
and will praise your name
for your love and your faithfulness,
for you have exalted above all things
your name and your word.
3 When I called, you answered me;
you made me bold and stouthearted.

4 May all the kings of the earth praise you, O LORD,
when they hear the words of your mouth.
5 May they sing of the ways of the LORD,
for the glory of the LORD is great.

6 Though the LORD is on high, he looks upon the
lowly,
but the proud he knows from afar.
7 Though I walk in the midst of trouble,
you preserve my life;
you stretch out your hand against the anger of my
foes,
with your right hand you save me.
8 The LORD will fulfill ⌊his purpose⌋ for me;
your love, O LORD, endures forever—
do not abandon the works of your hands.

Psalm 139

For the director of music. Of David. A psalm.

1 O LORD, you have searched me
and you know me.
2 You know when I sit and when I rise;
you perceive my thoughts from afar.
3 You discern my going out and my lying down;
you are familiar with all my ways.
4 Before a word is on my tongue
you know it completely, O LORD.

5 You hem me in—behind and before;
you have laid your hand upon me.
6 Such knowledge is too wonderful for me,
too lofty for me to attain.

7 Where can I go from your Spirit?
Where can I flee from your presence?
8 If I go up to the heavens, you are there;
if I make my bed in the depths,[a] you are there.
9 If I rise on the wings of the dawn,
if I settle on the far side of the sea,
10 even there your hand will guide me,
your right hand will hold me fast.

11 If I say, "Surely the darkness will hide me

[a] 8 Hebrew *Sheol*

and the light become night around me,"
12 even the darkness will not be dark to you;
the night will shine like the day,
for darkness is as light to you.

13 For you created my inmost being;
you knit me together in my mother's womb.
14 I praise you because I am fearfully and wonderfully made;
your works are wonderful,
I know that full well.
15 My frame was not hidden from you
when I was made in the secret place.
When I was woven together in the depths of the earth,
16 your eyes saw my unformed body.
All the days ordained for me
were written in your book
before one of them came to be.

17 How precious to[a] me are your thoughts, O God!
How vast is the sum of them!
18 Were I to count them,
they would outnumber the grains of sand.
When I awake,
I am still with you.

19 If only you would slay the wicked, O God!
Away from me, you bloodthirsty men!
20 They speak of you with evil intent;
your adversaries misuse your name.
21 Do I not hate those who hate you, O LORD,
and abhor those who rise up against you?
22 I have nothing but hatred for them;
I count them my enemies.

23 Search me, O God, and know my heart;
test me and know my anxious thoughts.
24 See if there is any offensive way in me,
and lead me in the way everlasting.

Psalm 140

For the director of music. A psalm of David.

1 Rescue me, O LORD, from evil men;
protect me from men of violence,
2 who devise evil plans in their hearts
and stir up war every day.
3 They make their tongues as sharp as a serpent's;
the poison of vipers is on their lips. *Selah*

4 Keep me, O LORD, from the hands of the wicked;
protect me from men of violence
who plan to trip my feet.
5 Proud men have hidden a snare for me;
they have spread out the cords of their net
and have set traps for me along my path. *Selah*

[a] 17 Or *concerning*

Hear My Prayer

Hear My Prayer

6 O LORD, I say to you, "You are my God."
Hear, O LORD, my cry for mercy.
7 O Sovereign LORD, my strong deliverer,
who shields my head in the day of battle—
8 do not grant the wicked their desires, O LORD;
do not let their plans succeed,
or they will become proud. *Selah*
9 Let the heads of those who surround me
be covered with the trouble their lips have
caused.
10 Let burning coals fall upon them;
may they be thrown into the fire,
into miry pits, never to rise.
11 Let slanderers not be established in the land;
may disaster hunt down men of violence.

12 I know that the LORD secures justice for the poor
and upholds the cause of the needy.
13 Surely the righteous will praise your name
and the upright will live before you.

Psalm 141

A psalm of David.

1 O LORD, I call to you; come quickly to me.
Hear my voice when I call to you.
2 May my prayer be set before you like incense;
may the lifting up of my hands be like the evening
sacrifice.

3 Set a guard over my mouth, O LORD;
keep watch over the door of my lips.
4 Let not my heart be drawn to what is evil,
to take part in wicked deeds
with men who are evildoers;
let me not eat of their delicacies.

5 Let a righteous man[a] strike me—it is a kindness;
let him rebuke me—it is oil on my head.
My head will not refuse it.

Yet my prayer is ever against the deeds of evildoers;
6 their rulers will be thrown down from the cliffs,
and the wicked will learn that my words were well
spoken.
7 ⌊They will say,⌋ "As one plows and breaks up the
earth,
so our bones have been scattered at the mouth of
the grave.[b]"
8 But my eyes are fixed on you, O Sovereign LORD;
in you I take refuge—do not give me over to
death.
9 Keep me from the snares they have laid for me,
from the traps set by evildoers.
10 Let the wicked fall into their own nets,
while I pass by in safety.

[a] 5 Or *Let the Righteous One* [b] 7 Hebrew *Sheol*

Psalm 142

A *maskil*[a] of David. When he was in the cave. A prayer.

1 I cry aloud to the LORD;
I lift up my voice to the LORD for mercy.
2 I pour out my complaint before him;
before him I tell my trouble.

3 When my spirit grows faint within me,
it is you who know my way.
In the path where I walk
men have hidden a snare for me.
4 Look to my right and see;
no one is concerned for me.
I have no refuge;
no one cares for my life.

5 I cry to you, O LORD;
I say, "You are my refuge,
my portion in the land of the living."
6 Listen to my cry,
for I am in desperate need;
rescue me from those who pursue me,
for they are too strong for me.
7 Set me free from my prison,
that I may praise your name.

Then the righteous will gather about me
because of your goodness to me.

Psalm 143

A psalm of David.

1 O LORD, hear my prayer,
listen to my cry for mercy;
in your faithfulness and righteousness
come to my relief.
2 Do not bring your servant into judgment,
for no one living is righteous before you.

3 The enemy pursues me,
he crushes me to the ground;
he makes me dwell in darkness
like those long dead.
4 So my spirit grows faint within me;
my heart within me is dismayed.

5 I remember the days of long ago;
I meditate on all your works
and consider what your hands have done.
6 I spread out my hands to you;
my soul thirsts for you like a parched land. *Selah*

7 Answer me quickly, O LORD;
my spirit fails.
Do not hide your face from me
or I will be like those who go down to the pit.

[a] Title: Probably a literary or musical term

Hear My Prayer

Hear My Prayer

8 Let the morning bring me word of your unfailing love,
for I have put my trust in you.
Show me the way I should go,
for to you I lift up my soul.
9 Rescue me from my enemies, O LORD,
for I hide myself in you.
10 Teach me to do your will,
for you are my God;
may your good Spirit
lead me on level ground.

11 For your name's sake, O LORD, preserve my life;
in your righteousness, bring me out of trouble.
12 In your unfailing love, silence my enemies;
destroy all my foes,
for I am your servant.

Psalm 144

Of David.

1 Praise be to the LORD my Rock,
who trains my hands for war,
my fingers for battle.
2 He is my loving God and my fortress,
my stronghold and my deliverer,
my shield, in whom I take refuge,
who subdues peoples[a] under me.

3 O LORD, what is man that you care for him,
the son of man that you think of him?
4 Man is like a breath;
his days are like a fleeting shadow.

5 Part your heavens, O LORD, and come down;
touch the mountains, so that they smoke.
6 Send forth lightning and scatter ⌊the enemies⌋;
shoot your arrows and rout them.
7 Reach down your hand from on high;
deliver me and rescue me
from the mighty waters,
from the hands of foreigners
8 whose mouths are full of lies,
whose right hands are deceitful.

9 I will sing a new song to you, O God;
on the ten-stringed lyre I will make music to you,
10 to the One who gives victory to kings,
who delivers his servant David from the deadly
sword.

11 Deliver me and rescue me
from the hands of foreigners
whose mouths are full of lies,
whose right hands are deceitful.

12 Then our sons in their youth
will be like well-nurtured plants,

[a] 2 Many manuscripts of the Masoretic Text, Dead Sea Scrolls, Aquila, Jerome and Syriac; most manuscripts of the Masoretic Text *subdues my people*

and our daughters will be like pillars
carved to adorn a palace.
13 Our barns will be filled
with every kind of provision.
Our sheep will increase by thousands,
by tens of thousands in our fields;
14 our oxen will draw heavy loads.[a]
There will be no breaching of walls,
no going into captivity,
no cry of distress in our streets.

15 Blessed are the people of whom this is true;
blessed are the people whose God is the LORD.

Psalm 145[b]

A psalm of praise. Of David.

1 I will exalt you, my God the King;
I will praise your name for ever and ever.
2 Every day I will praise you
and extol your name for ever and ever.

3 Great is the LORD and most worthy of praise;
his greatness no one can fathom.
4 One generation will commend your works to
another;
they will tell of your mighty acts.
5 They will speak of the glorious splendor of your
majesty,
and I will meditate on your wonderful works.[c]
6 They will tell of the power of your awesome works,
and I will proclaim your great deeds.
7 They will celebrate your abundant goodness
and joyfully sing of your righteousness.

8 The LORD is gracious and compassionate,
slow to anger and rich in love.
9 The LORD is good to all;
he has compassion on all he has made.
10 All you have made will praise you, O LORD;
your saints will extol you.
11 They will tell of the glory of your kingdom
and speak of your might,
12 so that all men may know of your mighty acts
and the glorious splendor of your kingdom.
13 Your kingdom is an everlasting kingdom,
and your dominion endures through all
generations.

The LORD is faithful to all his promises
and loving toward all he has made.[d]
14 The LORD upholds all those who fall
and lifts up all who are bowed down.

[a] *14* Or *our chieftains will be firmly established* [b] This psalm is an acrostic poem, the verses of which (including verse 13b) begin with the successive letters of the Hebrew alphabet. [c] *5* Dead Sea Scrolls and Syriac (see also Septuagint); Masoretic Text *On the glorious splendor of your majesty / and on your wonderful works I will meditate* [d] *13* One manuscript of the Masoretic Text, Dead Sea Scrolls and Syriac (see also Septuagint); most manuscripts of the Masoretic Text do not have the last two lines of verse 13.

Hear My Prayer

Hear My Prayer

15 The eyes of all look to you,
and you give them their food at the proper time.
16 You open your hand
and satisfy the desires of every living thing.

17 The LORD is righteous in all his ways
and loving toward all he has made.
18 The LORD is near to all who call on him,
to all who call on him in truth.
19 He fulfills the desires of those who fear him;
he hears their cry and saves them.
20 The LORD watches over all who love him,
but all the wicked he will destroy.

21 My mouth will speak in praise of the LORD.
Let every creature praise his holy name
for ever and ever.

Psalm 146

1 Praise the LORD.[a]

Praise the LORD, O my soul.
2 I will praise the LORD all my life;
I will sing praise to my God as long as I live.

3 Do not put your trust in princes,
in mortal men, who cannot save.
4 When their spirit departs, they return to the ground;
on that very day their plans come to nothing.

5 Blessed is he whose help is the God of Jacob,
whose hope is in the LORD his God,
6 the Maker of heaven and earth,
the sea, and everything in them—
the LORD, who remains faithful forever.
7 He upholds the cause of the oppressed
and gives food to the hungry.
The LORD sets prisoners free,
8 the LORD gives sight to the blind,
the LORD lifts up those who are bowed down,
the LORD loves the righteous.
9 The LORD watches over the alien
and sustains the fatherless and the widow,
but he frustrates the ways of the wicked.

10 The LORD reigns forever,
your God, O Zion, for all generations.

Praise the LORD.

Psalm 147

1 Praise the LORD.[b]

How good it is to sing praises to our God,
how pleasant and fitting to praise him!

2 The LORD builds up Jerusalem;
he gathers the exiles of Israel.

[a] *1* Hebrew *Hallelu Yah*; also in verse 10 [b] *1* Hebrew *Hallelu Yah*; also in verse 20

3 He heals the brokenhearted
and binds up their wounds.

4 He determines the number of the stars
and calls them each by name.
5 Great is our Lord and mighty in power;
his understanding has no limit.
6 The LORD sustains the humble
but casts the wicked to the ground.

7 Sing to the LORD with thanksgiving;
make music to our God on the harp.
8 He covers the sky with clouds;
he supplies the earth with rain
and makes grass grow on the hills.
9 He provides food for the cattle
and for the young ravens when they call.

10 His pleasure is not in the strength of the horse,
nor his delight in the legs of a man;
11 the LORD delights in those who fear him,
who put their hope in his unfailing love.

12 Extol the LORD, O Jerusalem;
praise your God, O Zion,
13 for he strengthens the bars of your gates
and blesses your people within you.
14 He grants peace to your borders
and satisfies you with the finest of wheat.

15 He sends his command to the earth;
his word runs swiftly.
16 He spreads the snow like wool
and scatters the frost like ashes.
17 He hurls down his hail like pebbles.
Who can withstand his icy blast?
18 He sends his word and melts them;
he stirs up his breezes, and the waters flow.

19 He has revealed his word to Jacob,
his laws and decrees to Israel.
20 He has done this for no other nation;
they do not know his laws.

Praise the LORD.

Psalm 148

1 Praise the LORD.[a]

Praise the LORD from the heavens,
praise him in the heights above.
2 Praise him, all his angels,
praise him, all his heavenly hosts.
3 Praise him, sun and moon,
praise him, all you shining stars.
4 Praise him, you highest heavens
and you waters above the skies.
5 Let them praise the name of the LORD,
for he commanded and they were created.

a 1 Hebrew *Hallelu Yah*; also in verse 14

Hear My Prayer

Hear My Prayer

6 He set them in place for ever and ever;
he gave a decree that will never pass away.

7 Praise the LORD from the earth,
you great sea creatures and all ocean depths,
8 lightning and hail, snow and clouds,
stormy winds that do his bidding,
9 you mountains and all hills,
fruit trees and all cedars,
10 wild animals and all cattle,
small creatures and flying birds,
11 kings of the earth and all nations,
you princes and all rulers on earth,
12 young men and maidens,
old men and children.

13 Let them praise the name of the LORD,
for his name alone is exalted;
his splendor is above the earth and the heavens.
14 He has raised up for his people a horn,[a]
the praise of all his saints,
of Israel, the people close to his heart.

Praise the LORD.

Psalm 149

1 Praise the LORD.[b]

Sing to the LORD a new song,
his praise in the assembly of the saints.

2 Let Israel rejoice in their Maker;
let the people of Zion be glad in their King.
3 Let them praise his name with dancing
and make music to him with tambourine and harp.
4 For the LORD takes delight in his people;
he crowns the humble with salvation.
5 Let the saints rejoice in this honor
and sing for joy on their beds.

6 May the praise of God be in their mouths
and a double-edged sword in their hands,
7 to inflict vengeance on the nations
and punishment on the peoples,
8 to bind their kings with fetters,
their nobles with shackles of iron,
9 to carry out the sentence written against them.
This is the glory of all his saints.

Praise the LORD.

Psalm 150

1 Praise the LORD.[c]

Praise God in his sanctuary;
praise him in his mighty heavens.

[a] 14 *Horn* here symbolizes strong one, that is, king. [b] 1 Hebrew *Hallelu Yah*; also in verse 9 [c] 1 Hebrew *Hallelu Yah*; also in verse 6

2 Praise him for his acts of power;
praise him for his surpassing greatness.
3 Praise him with the sounding of the trumpet,
praise him with the harp and lyre,
4 praise him with tambourine and dancing,
praise him with the strings and flute,
5 praise him with the clash of cymbals,
praise him with resounding cymbals.

6 Let everything that has breath praise the LORD.

Praise the LORD.

Hear My Prayer

Proverbs

The PROVERBS

"The fear of the LORD is the beginning of wisdom, and knowledge of the Holy One is understanding" (9:10). If we want to be wise, we should seek God. If we want to grow in discernment, we should set our hearts to revere God. As we do, we will receive both practical direction and an exalted vision of God's eternal wisdom.

The book of Proverbs contains the sayings of King Solomon and others who were well known for their wisdom. There are three main sections. The first part (chaps. 1—9) is an extended meditation on the virtues of wisdom, here personified as a teacher who seeks students who will learn from her. The second part (10:1—22:16) includes the proverbs of Solomon. The final part (22:17—31:31) consists of more sayings by several different sages.

A proverb is a brief statement of a moral truth. The purpose of Proverbs is not simply to give advice, although many proverbs are very practical in their application. The deeper intention of the book is to shape godly character with divine wisdom. Behind Proverbs is the only wise God, the source of all true wisdom. The wise person worships God, praising Him for His wisdom and thanking Him for the guidance of His commandments for daily life. The fool, by contrast, ignores the teaching of wisdom and fails to worship God.

The book of Proverbs stresses worship in action. We worship God by seeking His wisdom and living according to His Word. "The LORD detests the sacrifice of the wicked, but the prayer of the upright pleases him" (15:8); "To do what is right and just is more acceptable to the LORD than sacrifice" (21:3).

Behind Proverbs is the only wise God, the source of all true wisdom. The wise person worships God, praising Him for His wisdom and thanking Him for the guidance of His commandments for daily life.

Though Christians can certainly profit from the practical wisdom of Proverbs, we also see in God's wisdom a type of Christ. As Wisdom called people to her for instruction, so Jesus echoes: "Come to me, all you who are weary and burdened, and I will give you rest. Take my yoke upon you and learn from me, for I am gentle and humble in heart, and you will find rest for your souls. For my yoke is easy and my burden is light" (Mt 11:28–30). Jesus is the Word and Wisdom of God made flesh. When we praise God for wisdom, we praise Him for Jesus Christ. When we seek more of divine wisdom, we seek more of Christ.

Prologue: Purpose and Theme

1 The proverbs of Solomon son of David, king of Israel:

2 for attaining wisdom and discipline;
for understanding words of insight;
3 for acquiring a disciplined and prudent life,
doing what is right and just and fair;
4 for giving prudence to the simple,
knowledge and discretion to the young—
5 let the wise listen and add to their learning,
and let the discerning get guidance—
6 for understanding proverbs and parables,
the sayings and riddles of the wise.

7 The fear of the LORD is the beginning of
knowledge,
but fools[a] despise wisdom and discipline.

Exhortations to Embrace Wisdom

Warning Against Enticement

8 Listen, my son, to your father's instruction
and do not forsake your mother's teaching.
9 They will be a garland to grace your head
and a chain to adorn your neck.

10 My son, if sinners entice you,
do not give in to them.
11 If they say, "Come along with us;
let's lie in wait for someone's blood,
let's waylay some harmless soul;
12 let's swallow them alive, like the grave,[b]
and whole, like those who go down to the pit;
13 we will get all sorts of valuable things
and fill our houses with plunder;
14 throw in your lot with us,
and we will share a common purse"—
15 my son, do not go along with them,
do not set foot on their paths;
16 for their feet rush into sin,
they are swift to shed blood.
17 How useless to spread a net
in full view of all the birds!
18 These men lie in wait for their own blood;
they waylay only themselves!
19 Such is the end of all who go after ill-gotten gain;
it takes away the lives of those who get it.

Warning Against Rejecting Wisdom

20 Wisdom calls aloud in the street,
she raises her voice in the public squares;
21 at the head of the noisy streets[c] she cries out,
in the gateways of the city she makes her speech:

[a] 7 The Hebrew words rendered *fool* in Proverbs, and often elsewhere in the Old Testament, denote one who is morally deficient. [b] *12* Hebrew *Sheol* [c] *21* Hebrew; Septuagint / *on the tops of the walls*

(1:1–7) Wonderful Counselor, You have provided simple guidelines for every dimension of our lives—principles that bring peace, justice and good sense to everything we do. Thank You for being aware of the ordinary aspects of our earthly existence—the buying and selling, the winning and losing, the joys and sorrows. You are a Father Who advises His children carefully and kindly. Help us always to put You first and to seek Your will instead of our own.

O Word of God incarnate
O Wisdom from on high,
O Truth unchanged, unchanging,
O Light of our dark sky;
We praise You for the radiance
That from the hallowed page,
A lantern to our footsteps,
Shines on from age to age.
"O Word of God Incarnate"
William H. How (1823-1897)

(2:1–8) Sovereign Lord, You are the Almighty Creator, the Holy and Righteous One. You are the Eternal Father, the infinite Source of all life. In Your Presence are truth and wisdom. Righteousness and justice surround Your throne. I worship You, my God and Father, with reverence and awe. Please keep me close to Your side so that I may hear Your voice, learn Your ways and live a life that is pleasing to You.

It seems to me that true fidelity consists in obeying God in all things, and in following the light which points out our duty, and the grace which guides us; taking as our rule of life the intention to please God in all things, and to do always not only what is acceptable to Him, but, if possible, what is most acceptable.

Francois Fenelon (1651–1715)

22 "How long will you simple ones[a] love your simple
ways?
How long will mockers delight in mockery
and fools hate knowledge?
23 If you had responded to my rebuke,
I would have poured out my heart to you
and made my thoughts known to you.
24 But since you rejected me when I called
and no one gave heed when I stretched out my
hand,
25 since you ignored all my advice
and would not accept my rebuke,
26 I in turn will laugh at your disaster;
I will mock when calamity overtakes you—
27 when calamity overtakes you like a storm,
when disaster sweeps over you like a whirlwind,
when distress and trouble overwhelm you.

28 "Then they will call to me but I will not answer;
they will look for me but will not find me.
29 Since they hated knowledge
and did not choose to fear the LORD,
30 since they would not accept my advice
and spurned my rebuke,
31 they will eat the fruit of their ways
and be filled with the fruit of their schemes.
32 For the waywardness of the simple will kill them,
and the complacency of fools will destroy them;
33 but whoever listens to me will live in safety
and be at ease, without fear of harm."

Moral Benefits of Wisdom

2 My son, if you accept my words
and store up my commands within you,
2 turning your ear to wisdom
and applying your heart to understanding,
3 and if you call out for insight
and cry aloud for understanding,
4 and if you look for it as for silver
and search for it as for hidden treasure,
5 then you will understand the fear of the LORD
and find the knowledge of God.
6 For the LORD gives wisdom,
and from his mouth come knowledge and
understanding.
7 He holds victory in store for the upright,
he is a shield to those whose walk is blameless,
8 for he guards the course of the just
and protects the way of his faithful ones.

9 Then you will understand what is right and just
and fair—every good path.
10 For wisdom will enter your heart,
and knowledge will be pleasant to your soul.
11 Discretion will protect you,
and understanding will guard you.

[a] 22 The Hebrew word rendered *simple* in Proverbs generally denotes one without moral direction and inclined to evil.

12 Wisdom will save you from the ways of wicked men,
from men whose words are perverse,
13 who leave the straight paths
to walk in dark ways,
14 who delight in doing wrong
and rejoice in the perverseness of evil,
15 whose paths are crooked
and who are devious in their ways.

16 It will save you also from the adulteress,
from the wayward wife with her seductive words,
17 who has left the partner of her youth
and ignored the covenant she made before God.[a]
18 For her house leads down to death
and her paths to the spirits of the dead.
19 None who go to her return
or attain the paths of life.

20 Thus you will walk in the ways of good men
and keep to the paths of the righteous.
21 For the upright will live in the land,
and the blameless will remain in it;
22 but the wicked will be cut off from the land,
and the unfaithful will be torn from it.

Further Benefits of Wisdom

3 My son, do not forget my teaching,
but keep my commands in your heart,
2 for they will prolong your life many years
and bring you prosperity.

3 Let love and faithfulness never leave you;
bind them around your neck,
write them on the tablet of your heart.
4 Then you will win favor and a good name
in the sight of God and man.

5 Trust in the LORD with all your heart
and lean not on your own understanding;
6 in all your ways acknowledge him,
and he will make your paths straight.[b]

7 Do not be wise in your own eyes;
fear the LORD and shun evil.
8 This will bring health to your body
and nourishment to your bones.

9 Honor the LORD with your wealth,
with the firstfruits of all your crops;
10 then your barns will be filled to overflowing,
and your vats will brim over with new wine.

11 My son, do not despise the LORD's discipline
and do not resent his rebuke,
12 because the LORD disciplines those he loves,
as a father[c] the son he delights in.

13 Blessed is the man who finds wisdom,
the man who gains understanding,

[a] 17 Or *covenant of her God* [b] 6 Or *will direct your paths* [c] 12 Hebrew; Septuagint */ and he punishes*

Lord, there is no refuge from You. You will always find me no matter how far I may seek to get from You. I cannot outrun Your presence or Your judgment. I am grateful, however, that if there is not refuge from You, there is refuge in You. May I be among those who submit to your authority (Ps 2:11-12) rather than those who rebel against you (Ps 2:1-3).

George O. Wood (1941-)

(3:11–12) Father, how You cherish Your children! Your love for us is relentless and undeserved. Even Your discipline is motivated by compassion. Teach me to accept Your correction with humble gratitude. I do not ask You to withhold Your discipline; I only ask that You grant me the wisdom and humility to learn the lessons quickly.

Trust in the Lord with all your
heart,
This is God's gracious command;
In all your ways acknowledge Him,
So shall you dwell in the land.

Trust in the Lord, O troubled soul,
Rest in the arms of His care;
Whatever your lot, it mattereth
not,
For nothing can trouble you there;
Trust in the Lord, O troubled soul,
Nothing can trouble you there.

Trust in the Lord—His eye will guide
All thro your pathway ahead,
He hath redeemed and He will keep,
Trust Him and be not afraid.

"Trust in the Lord with All Your Heart"
Thomas O. Chisholm
(©1937, 1965)

(3:19–20) Father God, we are in awe of Your creation. You found great pleasure in designing this beautiful and complex world for us to inhabit. You suspended it like a jewel in the vastness of the heavens. Our universe teems with countless galaxies. The planets move in procession through space in perfect harmony, displaying Your matchless wisdom. With equal skill, You have ordered our lives, working all things together for good in accordance with Your will. How great is Your mind! How vast is Your understanding! We worship You in wonder, in delight and in gratitude that You love us and provide good plans for us, both now and forever. (Jer 29:11; Ro 8:28)

God must not be confined to one particular section of time nor must we imagine Him as the local god of this planet or even only of the Universe that astronomical survey has so far discovered. It is not, of course, physical size that we are trying to establish in our minds . . . It is rather to see the immensely broad sweep of the Creator's activity, the astonishing complexity of His mental processes which science laboriously uncovers.

J. B. Phillips (1906–1982)

Great is the Lord God, and most worthy,
All of His greatness no one can fathom;
All generations will tell of His wonders,
They will declare His mighty acts.

The Lord is gracious, full of compassion,
Slow to anger, rich in mercy,
So now we join with all of creation
And proclaim His wondrous praise.

How glorious the splendor
Of all Your majesty, O God!
All of Your works shall praise Thee,
All of Your saints now sing.

"How Glorious the Splendor"
Tommy Walker (©1996)

14 for she is more profitable than silver
and yields better returns than gold.
15 She is more precious than rubies;
nothing you desire can compare with her.
16 Long life is in her right hand;
in her left hand are riches and honor.
17 Her ways are pleasant ways,
and all her paths are peace.
18 She is a tree of life to those who embrace her;
those who lay hold of her will be blessed.

19 By wisdom the LORD laid the earth's foundations,
by understanding he set the heavens in place;
20 by his knowledge the deeps were divided,
and the clouds let drop the dew.

21 My son, preserve sound judgment and discernment,
do not let them out of your sight;
22 they will be life for you,
an ornament to grace your neck.
23 Then you will go on your way in safety,
and your foot will not stumble;
24 when you lie down, you will not be afraid;
when you lie down, your sleep will be sweet.
25 Have no fear of sudden disaster
or of the ruin that overtakes the wicked,
26 for the LORD will be your confidence
and will keep your foot from being snared.

27 Do not withhold good from those who deserve it,
when it is in your power to act.
28 Do not say to your neighbor,
"Come back later; I'll give it tomorrow"—
when you now have it with you.
29 Do not plot harm against your neighbor,
who lives trustfully near you.
30 Do not accuse a man for no reason—
when he has done you no harm.

31 Do not envy a violent man
or choose any of his ways,
32 for the LORD detests a perverse man
but takes the upright into his confidence.
33 The LORD's curse is on the house of the wicked,
but he blesses the home of the righteous.
34 He mocks proud mockers
but gives grace to the humble.
35 The wise inherit honor,
but fools he holds up to shame.

Wisdom Is Supreme

4 Listen, my sons, to a father's instruction;
pay attention and gain understanding.
2 I give you sound learning,
so do not forsake my teaching.
3 When I was a boy in my father's house,
still tender, and an only child of my mother,
4 he taught me and said,

MY BELOVED

Do not be wise in your own eyes; but reverently fear Me and flee from evil. This will bring you a much healthier life.

I am the only living God. All of the world's wisdom is foolishness to Me, but even my foolishness is wiser than the world's best wisdom. So listen carefully to My words. Pay close attention to My instructions. Focus on them and treasure them in your heart.

If you will delight in My Word and meditate on it day and night, then you will be like a tree planted by streams of water, which yields its fruit in season and whose leaf does not wither. And whatever you do will prosper.

My Word will bring you life and will help you in your time of need. It is powerful, more powerful than the hopelessness that may invade your soul. So turn to it now. Never forget that I only desire good for you!

I know at times you will face terrible crises, but I also know that My heart for you is to have you discover hope in the midst of your crisis. So turn to Me. And as you reach out to Me, you will discover My love for you. I will restore to you a joy greater than you could imagine. I want your life to be full, for you are Mine.

Ex 15:26; Ps 1:2-3; 103:5; 107:9,20; Pr 3:7-8; 4:20-22; Lk 11:13; 1Co 3:19; 3Jn 2

"Lay hold of my words with all your heart;
keep my commands and you will live.
5 Get wisdom, get understanding;
do not forget my words or swerve from them.
6 Do not forsake wisdom, and she will protect you;
love her, and she will watch over you.
7 Wisdom is supreme; therefore get wisdom.
Though it cost all you have,[a] get understanding.
8 Esteem her, and she will exalt you;
embrace her, and she will honor you.
9 She will set a garland of grace on your head
and present you with a crown of splendor."

10 Listen, my son, accept what I say,
and the years of your life will be many.
11 I guide you in the way of wisdom
and lead you along straight paths.
12 When you walk, your steps will not be hampered;
when you run, you will not stumble.
13 Hold on to instruction, do not let it go;
guard it well, for it is your life.
14 Do not set foot on the path of the wicked
or walk in the way of evil men.
15 Avoid it, do not travel on it;
turn from it and go on your way.
16 For they cannot sleep till they do evil;
they are robbed of slumber till they make someone fall.
17 They eat the bread of wickedness
and drink the wine of violence.

18 The path of the righteous is like the first gleam of dawn,
shining ever brighter till the full light of day.
19 But the way of the wicked is like deep darkness;
they do not know what makes them stumble.

20 My son, pay attention to what I say;
listen closely to my words.
21 Do not let them out of your sight,
keep them within your heart;
22 for they are life to those who find them
and health to a man's whole body.
23 Above all else, guard your heart,
for it is the wellspring of life.
24 Put away perversity from your mouth;
keep corrupt talk far from your lips.
25 Let your eyes look straight ahead,
fix your gaze directly before you.
26 Make level[b] paths for your feet
and take only ways that are firm.
27 Do not swerve to the right or the left;
keep your foot from evil.

Warning Against Adultery

5 My son, pay attention to my wisdom,
listen well to my words of insight,
2 that you may maintain discretion

[a] 7 Or *Whatever else you get* [b] 26 Or *Consider the*

(4:18) Thank You, Lord, for Your light of truth that makes my way both safe and pleasant. With the light of Your presence You warm my heart. With the light of Your wisdom You enlighten my mind. With the light of Your Word You illuminate my path. How I long for the full light of that great and glorious Day when we, Your people, will reach our destination around Your throne. There we will not need the light of a lamp or the light of the sun, for You, O Lord, will give us light. And we will reign with You forever and ever. (Ps 43:3; 89:15; Rev 22:5)

Christ, whose glory fills the skies,
Christ, the true, the only light,
Sun of righteousness, arise,
Triumph over shades of night:
Dayspring from on high, be near,
Daystar, in my heart appear!

Visit then this soul of mine,
Pierce the gloom of sin and grief;
Fill me, radiancy divine,
Scatter all my unbelief:
More and more yourself display,
Shining to the perfect day!

"Christ, Whose Glory Fills the Skies"
Charles Wesley (1740)

God intends the Christian life to be a life of joy—not drudgery. The idea that holiness is associated with a dour disposition is a caricature of the worst sort. In fact, just the opposite is true. Only those who walk in holiness experience true joy.

Jerry Bridges (1929-)

(5:15–21) Thank You, Father, for the joy of marriage and the wonder of love and faithfulness. May these words of counsel ring true in Your church today—Father, please protect the sanctity of marriage. May the joy You have intended for marriage never be compromised by unfaithfulness, whether in thought or deed. For if we cannot be true to those whom we have seen, how can we be true to You Whom we have not seen? (1Co 6:18–20)

and your lips may preserve knowledge.
3 For the lips of an adulteress drip honey,
and her speech is smoother than oil;
4 but in the end she is bitter as gall,
sharp as a double-edged sword.
5 Her feet go down to death;
her steps lead straight to the grave.[a]
6 She gives no thought to the way of life;
her paths are crooked, but she knows it not.

7 Now then, my sons, listen to me;
do not turn aside from what I say.
8 Keep to a path far from her,
do not go near the door of her house,
9 lest you give your best strength to others
and your years to one who is cruel,
10 lest strangers feast on your wealth
and your toil enrich another man's house.
11 At the end of your life you will groan,
when your flesh and body are spent.
12 You will say, "How I hated discipline!
How my heart spurned correction!
13 I would not obey my teachers
or listen to my instructors.
14 I have come to the brink of utter ruin
in the midst of the whole assembly."

15 Drink water from your own cistern,
running water from your own well.
16 Should your springs overflow in the streets,
your streams of water in the public squares?
17 Let them be yours alone,
never to be shared with strangers.
18 May your fountain be blessed,
and may you rejoice in the wife of your youth.
19 A loving doe, a graceful deer—
may her breasts satisfy you always,
may you ever be captivated by her love.
20 Why be captivated, my son, by an adulteress?
Why embrace the bosom of another man's wife?

21 For a man's ways are in full view of the LORD,
and he examines all his paths.
22 The evil deeds of a wicked man ensnare him;
the cords of his sin hold him fast.
23 He will die for lack of discipline,
led astray by his own great folly.

Warnings Against Folly

6 My son, if you have put up security for your neighbor,
if you have struck hands in pledge for another,
2 if you have been trapped by what you said,
ensnared by the words of your mouth,
3 then do this, my son, to free yourself,
since you have fallen into your neighbor's hands:
Go and humble yourself;
press your plea with your neighbor!

[a] 5 Hebrew *Sheol*

4 Allow no sleep to your eyes,
no slumber to your eyelids.
5 Free yourself, like a gazelle from the hand of the hunter,
like a bird from the snare of the fowler.

6 Go to the ant, you sluggard;
consider its ways and be wise!
7 It has no commander,
no overseer or ruler,
8 yet it stores its provisions in summer
and gathers its food at harvest.

9 How long will you lie there, you sluggard?
When will you get up from your sleep?
10 A little sleep, a little slumber,
a little folding of the hands to rest—
11 and poverty will come on you like a bandit
and scarcity like an armed man.[a]

12 A scoundrel and villain,
who goes about with a corrupt mouth,
13 who winks with his eye,
signals with his feet
and motions with his fingers,
14 who plots evil with deceit in his heart—
he always stirs up dissension.
15 Therefore disaster will overtake him in an instant;
he will suddenly be destroyed—without remedy.

16 There are six things the LORD hates,
seven that are detestable to him:
17 haughty eyes,
a lying tongue,
hands that shed innocent blood,
18 a heart that devises wicked schemes,
feet that are quick to rush into evil,
19 a false witness who pours out lies
and a man who stirs up dissension among brothers.

Warning Against Adultery

20 My son, keep your father's commands
and do not forsake your mother's teaching.
21 Bind them upon your heart forever;
fasten them around your neck.
22 When you walk, they will guide you;
when you sleep, they will watch over you;
when you awake, they will speak to you.
23 For these commands are a lamp,
this teaching is a light,
and the corrections of discipline
are the way to life,
24 keeping you from the immoral woman,
from the smooth tongue of the wayward wife.
25 Do not lust in your heart after her beauty
or let her captivate you with her eyes,

[a] 11 Or *like a vagrant / and scarcity like a beggar*

(6:6–11) Thank You, Father, for the gift of work. It is truly a blessing from You. May I glorify You through the work of my hands and give You thanks for the fruit of my labor. And in whatever You give me to do, may I always work at it with all my heart, remembering that it is You Whom I am serving. (Pr 10:4; 14:23; Col 3:17, 23–24)

May this life that I live bring You praise,
Blessing You and Your wonderful ways,
In the work of my hands, and the words that I say,
I will worship You, Lord, all my days.

I will sing to Your name when I wake,
Giving thanks for each breath that I take,
From the first light I see, to the last pray'r I pray,
I will worship You, Lord, all my days.

"All My Days"

Bill Batstone and Bob Somma (©1990)

At an early age He was about His Father's business (Lk 2:49) . . . Can we not follow His footsteps, filled with His Spirit, to finish the task appointed, with heart aglow and hurrying feet, with strong hands and steady mind, with shield of faith and sword of the Spirit, with patience to run the race that is set before us? Can we not trust Him for grace that is sufficient, for strength that is perfected in weakness, for help that is sure, and for faithfulness that will not fail, in order that we may know the discipline of doing our duty?

Victor Raymond Edman (1900-1967)

The Bible is one of God's greatest love gifts to you. It is the world's greatest literary treasure. It is the foundation of the church and your faith. But there is always the danger that you may forget how personally God wants to give it specifically to you. He desires you to use it daily as your spiritual food, your personal prayer resource, and your weapon for spiritual conquest.

Wesley L. Duewel (1916-)

(7:1–3) My Father, You have said "store up my commands within you." So I will feast daily on Your Word and hide it in my heart. Then in the day of trouble, when I am weak and tempted, I will recall Your instructions. They will be to me as spiritual food to nourish my soul and give me strength for the battle. (Ps 119:11–16)

I will delight in the law of the Lord,
I will meditate day and night.
Then, like a tree firmly planted
I'll be grounded in Your Word.

Blessed is the one
Who follows the way of the Lord;
Blessed is the one.

"I Will Delight"
Walt Harrah and
John A. Schreiner (©1991)

26 for the prostitute reduces you to a loaf of bread,
and the adulteress preys upon your very life.
27 Can a man scoop fire into his lap
without his clothes being burned?
28 Can a man walk on hot coals
without his feet being scorched?
29 So is he who sleeps with another man's wife;
no one who touches her will go unpunished.

30 Men do not despise a thief if he steals
to satisfy his hunger when he is starving.
31 Yet if he is caught, he must pay sevenfold,
though it costs him all the wealth of his house.
32 But a man who commits adultery lacks judgment;
whoever does so destroys himself.
33 Blows and disgrace are his lot,
and his shame will never be wiped away;
34 for jealousy arouses a husband's fury,
and he will show no mercy when he takes revenge.
35 He will not accept any compensation;
he will refuse the bribe, however great it is.

Warning Against the Adulteress

7 My son, keep my words
and store up my commands within you.
2 Keep my commands and you will live;
guard my teachings as the apple of your eye.
3 Bind them on your fingers;
write them on the tablet of your heart.
4 Say to wisdom, "You are my sister,"
and call understanding your kinsman;
5 they will keep you from the adulteress,
from the wayward wife with her seductive words.

6 At the window of my house
I looked out through the lattice.
7 I saw among the simple,
I noticed among the young men,
a youth who lacked judgment.
8 He was going down the street near her corner,
walking along in the direction of her house
9 at twilight, as the day was fading,
as the dark of night set in.

10 Then out came a woman to meet him,
dressed like a prostitute and with crafty intent.
11 (She is loud and defiant,
her feet never stay at home;
12 now in the street, now in the squares,
at every corner she lurks.)
13 She took hold of him and kissed him
and with a brazen face she said:

14 "I have fellowship offerings[a] at home;
today I fulfilled my vows.
15 So I came out to meet you;
I looked for you and have found you!

[a] 14 Traditionally *peace offerings*

16 I have covered my bed
with colored linens from Egypt.
17 I have perfumed my bed
with myrrh, aloes and cinnamon.
18 Come, let's drink deep of love till morning;
let's enjoy ourselves with love!
19 My husband is not at home;
he has gone on a long journey.
20 He took his purse filled with money
and will not be home till full moon."

21 With persuasive words she led him astray;
she seduced him with her smooth talk.
22 All at once he followed her
like an ox going to the slaughter,
like a deer[a] stepping into a noose[b]
23 till an arrow pierces his liver,
like a bird darting into a snare,
little knowing it will cost him his life.

24 Now then, my sons, listen to me;
pay attention to what I say.
25 Do not let your heart turn to her ways
or stray into her paths.
26 Many are the victims she has brought down;
her slain are a mighty throng.
27 Her house is a highway to the grave,[c]
leading down to the chambers of death.

Wisdom's Call

8 Does not wisdom call out?
Does not understanding raise her voice?
2 On the heights along the way,
where the paths meet, she takes her stand;
3 beside the gates leading into the city,
at the entrances, she cries aloud:
4 "To you, O men, I call out;
I raise my voice to all mankind.
5 You who are simple, gain prudence;
you who are foolish, gain understanding.
6 Listen, for I have worthy things to say;
I open my lips to speak what is right.
7 My mouth speaks what is true,
for my lips detest wickedness.
8 All the words of my mouth are just;
none of them is crooked or perverse.
9 To the discerning all of them are right;
they are faultless to those who have knowledge.
10 Choose my instruction instead of silver,
knowledge rather than choice gold,
11 for wisdom is more precious than rubies,
and nothing you desire can compare with her.

12 "I, wisdom, dwell together with prudence;
I possess knowledge and discretion.
13 To fear the LORD is to hate evil;

[a] 22 Syriac (see also Septuagint); Hebrew *fool* [b] 22 The meaning of the Hebrew for this line is uncertain. [c] 27 Hebrew *Sheol*

(8:1–11) I thank You, Father, for the voice of wisdom. It calls to us, it seeks us out and does not remain hidden. Its voice can be heard by anyone who will listen. Please give me ears to hear and a heart to understand, so that I may live by Your truth, walk in Your light, and grow in Your grace and knowledge. (Isa 6:10; 2Pe 3:18)

You are the living Truth;
All wisdom dwells in You,
The source of ev'ry skill,
The One Eternal true!
O great I AM, in You we rest,
Sure answer to our ev'ry quest.

You only are true Life;
To know You is to live
The more abundant life
That earth can never give.
O risen Lord, we live in You;
In us each day Your life renew!

"We Come, O Christ, to You"
Margaret Clarkson (©1957, 1985)

(8:22–31) I add my voice to wisdom's great hymn, and I praise You, O Lord. I extol Your wonders. Your glory explodes across the expanse of the sky. Your peace settles into the tranquility of the valleys. Your power gently stirs the wind in the trees. Your image is recorded upon the face of children, women and men. You are the Creator of all, the Giver of life, the Wonderful Counselor, the Mighty God, the Everlasting Father, the Prince of Peace. The voice of wisdom teaches me to worship You, Lord, and I do so, with all my heart. (Isa 9:6)

Now, I pray our Lord to grant that by the blessed Spirit we may always be sensitive of the presence of God wherever we are. His are the beauties of nature, His the sunshine which is bringing on the harvest, His the perfume which loads the air from multitudes of flowers, His the insects which glitter around us like living gems, and yet the Creator and Sustainer of all these is far too little perceived.
Charles Haddon Spurgeon (1834-1892)

All creatures of our God and King,
Lift up your voice and with us sing
Alleluia! Alleluia!
Thou burning sun with golden beam,
Thou silver moon with softer gleam,
Alleluia! Alleluia!
Alleluia! Alleluia! Alleluia!

Thou rushing wind that art so
strong,
Ye clouds that sail in heaven along,
O sing ye! Alleluia!
Thou rising morn in praise rejoice,
Ye lights of evening, find a voice,
Alleluia! Alleluia!
Alleluia! Alleluia! Alleluia!
"All Creatures of Our God and King"
Francis of Assisi (1225)
Trans. William H. Draper (1855-1933)

I hate pride and arrogance,
evil behavior and perverse speech.
14 Counsel and sound judgment are mine;
I have understanding and power.
15 By me kings reign
and rulers make laws that are just;
16 by me princes govern,
and all nobles who rule on earth.[a]
17 I love those who love me,
and those who seek me find me.
18 With me are riches and honor,
enduring wealth and prosperity.
19 My fruit is better than fine gold;
what I yield surpasses choice silver.
20 I walk in the way of righteousness,
along the paths of justice,
21 bestowing wealth on those who love me
and making their treasuries full.

22 "The LORD brought me forth as the first of his works,[b,c]
before his deeds of old;
23 I was appointed[d] from eternity,
from the beginning, before the world began.
24 When there were no oceans, I was given birth,
when there were no springs abounding with water;
25 before the mountains were settled in place,
before the hills, I was given birth,
26 before he made the earth or its fields
or any of the dust of the world.
27 I was there when he set the heavens in place,
when he marked out the horizon on the face of the deep,
28 when he established the clouds above
and fixed securely the fountains of the deep,
29 when he gave the sea its boundary
so the waters would not overstep his command,
and when he marked out the foundations of the earth.
30 Then I was the craftsman at his side.
I was filled with delight day after day,
rejoicing always in his presence,
31 rejoicing in his whole world
and delighting in mankind.

32 "Now then, my sons, listen to me;
blessed are those who keep my ways.
33 Listen to my instruction and be wise;
do not ignore it.
34 Blessed is the man who listens to me,
watching daily at my doors,
waiting at my doorway.
35 For whoever finds me finds life
and receives favor from the LORD.

[a] *16* Many Hebrew manuscripts and Septuagint; most Hebrew manuscripts *and nobles—all righteous rulers* [b] *22* Or *way*; or *dominion* [c] *22* Or *The LORD possessed me at the beginning of his work*; or *The LORD brought me forth at the beginning of his work* [d] *23* Or *fashioned*

36 But whoever fails to find me harms himself;
all who hate me love death."

Invitations of Wisdom and of Folly

9 Wisdom has built her house;
she has hewn out its seven pillars.
2 She has prepared her meat and mixed her wine;
she has also set her table.
3 She has sent out her maids, and she calls
from the highest point of the city.
4 "Let all who are simple come in here!"
she says to those who lack judgment.
5 "Come, eat my food
and drink the wine I have mixed.
6 Leave your simple ways and you will live;
walk in the way of understanding.

7 "Whoever corrects a mocker invites insult;
whoever rebukes a wicked man incurs abuse.
8 Do not rebuke a mocker or he will hate you;
rebuke a wise man and he will love you.
9 Instruct a wise man and he will be wiser still;
teach a righteous man and he will add to his
learning.

10 "The fear of the LORD is the beginning of wisdom,
and knowledge of the Holy One is understanding.
11 For through me your days will be many,
and years will be added to your life.
12 If you are wise, your wisdom will reward you;
if you are a mocker, you alone will suffer."

13 The woman Folly is loud;
she is undisciplined and without knowledge.
14 She sits at the door of her house,
on a seat at the highest point of the city,
15 calling out to those who pass by,
who go straight on their way.
16 "Let all who are simple come in here!"
she says to those who lack judgment.
17 "Stolen water is sweet;
food eaten in secret is delicious!"
18 But little do they know that the dead are there,
that her guests are in the depths of the grave.[a]

Proverbs of Solomon

10 The proverbs of Solomon:

A wise son brings joy to his father,
but a foolish son grief to his mother.

2 Ill-gotten treasures are of no value,
but righteousness delivers from death.

3 The LORD does not let the righteous go hungry
but he thwarts the craving of the wicked.

4 Lazy hands make a man poor,
but diligent hands bring wealth.

[a] 18 Hebrew *Sheol*

(9:1–18) Wisdom calls out: "Let all who are simple come in here!" Folly calls out with the same invitation. One path leads to life, the other to death. O Father, let me not be deceived by the voice of folly. Lead me in the path of righteousness and truth—the path that leads to life.

What a loving, faithful Father,
Mighty God who knows each need.
All His paths are truth and kindness
When we daily let Him lead.
Father God, I stand before You
Pardoned, cleansed, and reconciled.
Help me live as in Your presence:
Caring Father, trusting child.

"Raised From Death to Love and Living"
Ken Bible (©1984)

The decision behind every decision must always be: "Jesus is Lord! I will try to be faithful to Him as Lord in this set of circumstances." When we have difficult decisions to make and are not sure what is right, we start by consciously deciding again that we belong to Him and are called to be responsible to Him . . . Jesus is the norm by which everyone and everything in life is measured.

William P. Barker (1927-)

(10:22–25) You alone are the source of all true goodness, Father. The real blessings in life come from You. You reward me according to my faith, not according to my fears. You fulfill my heart's desires in Your perfect timing. Both the righteous and the wicked experience hardships; but I stand confident in You, Father, grateful for the shelter You provide during turbulent times, and for the blessings You so generously pour out to me. (Ecc 3:11; Ro 1:17; Jas 1:17)

What comes from the love of God has the grace of God as its companion.
Matthew Henry (1662-1714)

Come, Thou Fount of every blessing,
Tune my heart to sing Thy grace;
Streams of mercy, never ceasing,
Call for songs of loudest praise.
Teach me some melodious sonnet,
Sung by flaming tongues above;
Praise His name—I'm fixed upon it
Name of God's redeeming love.
"Come Thou Fount of Every Blessing"
Robert Robinson (1735-1790)

5 He who gathers crops in summer is a wise son,
but he who sleeps during harvest is a disgraceful son.

6 Blessings crown the head of the righteous,
but violence overwhelms the mouth of the wicked.[a]

7 The memory of the righteous will be a blessing,
but the name of the wicked will rot.

8 The wise in heart accept commands,
but a chattering fool comes to ruin.

9 The man of integrity walks securely,
but he who takes crooked paths will be found out.

10 He who winks maliciously causes grief,
and a chattering fool comes to ruin.

11 The mouth of the righteous is a fountain of life,
but violence overwhelms the mouth of the wicked.

12 Hatred stirs up dissension,
but love covers over all wrongs.

13 Wisdom is found on the lips of the discerning,
but a rod is for the back of him who lacks judgment.

14 Wise men store up knowledge,
but the mouth of a fool invites ruin.

15 The wealth of the rich is their fortified city,
but poverty is the ruin of the poor.

16 The wages of the righteous bring them life,
but the income of the wicked brings them punishment.

17 He who heeds discipline shows the way to life,
but whoever ignores correction leads others astray.

18 He who conceals his hatred has lying lips,
and whoever spreads slander is a fool.

19 When words are many, sin is not absent,
but he who holds his tongue is wise.

20 The tongue of the righteous is choice silver,
but the heart of the wicked is of little value.

21 The lips of the righteous nourish many,
but fools die for lack of judgment.

22 The blessing of the LORD brings wealth,
and he adds no trouble to it.

23 A fool finds pleasure in evil conduct,
but a man of understanding delights in wisdom.

24 What the wicked dreads will overtake him;
what the righteous desire will be granted.

25 When the storm has swept by, the wicked are gone,
but the righteous stand firm forever.

[a] 6 Or *but the mouth of the wicked conceals violence*; also in verse 11

26 As vinegar to the teeth and smoke to the eyes,
so is a sluggard to those who send him.

27 The fear of the LORD adds length to life,
but the years of the wicked are cut short.

28 The prospect of the righteous is joy,
but the hopes of the wicked come to nothing.

29 The way of the LORD is a refuge for the righteous,
but it is the ruin of those who do evil.

30 The righteous will never be uprooted,
but the wicked will not remain in the land.

31 The mouth of the righteous brings forth wisdom,
but a perverse tongue will be cut out.

32 The lips of the righteous know what is fitting,
but the mouth of the wicked only what is perverse.

11 The LORD abhors dishonest scales,
but accurate weights are his delight.

2 When pride comes, then comes disgrace,
but with humility comes wisdom.

3 The integrity of the upright guides them,
but the unfaithful are destroyed by their duplicity.

4 Wealth is worthless in the day of wrath,
but righteousness delivers from death.

5 The righteousness of the blameless makes a straight
way for them,
but the wicked are brought down by their own
wickedness.

6 The righteousness of the upright delivers them,
but the unfaithful are trapped by evil desires.

7 When a wicked man dies, his hope perishes;
all he expected from his power comes to nothing.

8 The righteous man is rescued from trouble,
and it comes on the wicked instead.

9 With his mouth the godless destroys his neighbor,
but through knowledge the righteous escape.

10 When the righteous prosper, the city rejoices;
when the wicked perish, there are shouts of joy.

11 Through the blessing of the upright a city is exalted,
but by the mouth of the wicked it is destroyed.

12 A man who lacks judgment derides his neighbor,
but a man of understanding holds his tongue.

13 A gossip betrays a confidence,
but a trustworthy man keeps a secret.

14 For lack of guidance a nation falls,
but many advisers make victory sure.

15 He who puts up security for another will surely suffer,

(11:2) Wisdom is a gift of Your grace, and Your grace is given only to the humble. Pride repels Your grace; but humility protects us from temptation, preserves our peace and prepares us for Your blessing. Thank You, Father, for telling us how to live in the way that pleases You. (Jas 4:6)

Wisdom cannot be reduced to a formula. It is a right relationship with Christ that provides a biblical context so that we can make wise decisions for every phase of living. However, there is a sacred principle that constitutes an eternal equation for receiving and applying God's wisdom: The degree of wisdom we possess from God is directly proportional to our spirit of humility.

A wise person is not a proud one. Pride and vanity are like poison to the spirit of wisdom. Whoever thinks he is wise is disqualified from God's classroom, where wisdom is given to the contrite of spirit and humble of heart.

Charles Stanley (1932-)

(11:24–28) You, O God, are the great Provider, and we are the storehouses of Your provision. You faithfully provide for us so that You may graciously provide through us. Nothing is ever lost when it is given in Your name, Lord. You multiply our offerings and feed not only others but us as well. Open my grip on what little I have so that I might receive from Your boundless wealth. Let me be Your hand of blessing to a needy world. May compassion and generosity accompany my confession of the gospel of Christ, and result in thanksgiving to You.

O to be like Thee! Full of
compassion,
Loving, forgiving, tender and kind;
Helping the helpless, cheering the
fainting,
Seeking the wand'ring sinner to find.

O to be like Thee!
O to be like Thee,
Blessed Redeemer,
Pure as Thou art!
Come in Thy sweetness,
Come in Thy fullness;
Stamp Thine own image
Deep on my heart.

"O to Be Like Thee"
Thomas O. Chisholm (1866-1960)

We can study and discuss what Jesus came to do for mankind. We can learn all the prophecies about Jesus and give our assent to them. They can even become our creeds and beliefs. But it is when we realize that He knows we do not have any bread, and that He is starting it down the table to us, that we suddenly know Who He is. He has been with us in our journey. He has been there all the time.

Bob Benson (1930-1986)

but whoever refuses to strike hands in pledge is safe.

16 A kindhearted woman gains respect,
but ruthless men gain only wealth.

17 A kind man benefits himself,
but a cruel man brings trouble on himself.

18 The wicked man earns deceptive wages,
but he who sows righteousness reaps a sure reward.

19 The truly righteous man attains life,
but he who pursues evil goes to his death.

20 The LORD detests men of perverse heart
but he delights in those whose ways are blameless.

21 Be sure of this: The wicked will not go unpunished,
but those who are righteous will go free.

22 Like a gold ring in a pig's snout
is a beautiful woman who shows no discretion.

23 The desire of the righteous ends only in good,
but the hope of the wicked only in wrath.

24 One man gives freely, yet gains even more;
another withholds unduly, but comes to poverty.

25 A generous man will prosper;
he who refreshes others will himself be refreshed.

26 People curse the man who hoards grain,
but blessing crowns him who is willing to sell.

27 He who seeks good finds goodwill,
but evil comes to him who searches for it.

28 Whoever trusts in his riches will fall,
but the righteous will thrive like a green leaf.

29 He who brings trouble on his family will inherit only wind,
and the fool will be servant to the wise.

30 The fruit of the righteous is a tree of life,
and he who wins souls is wise.

31 If the righteous receive their due on earth,
how much more the ungodly and the sinner!

12 Whoever loves discipline loves knowledge,
but he who hates correction is stupid.

2 A good man obtains favor from the LORD,
but the LORD condemns a crafty man.

3 A man cannot be established through wickedness,
but the righteous cannot be uprooted.

4 A wife of noble character is her husband's crown,
but a disgraceful wife is like decay in his bones.

5 The plans of the righteous are just,
but the advice of the wicked is deceitful.

6 The words of the wicked lie in wait for blood,

but the speech of the upright rescues them.

7 Wicked men are overthrown and are no more,
but the house of the righteous stands firm.

8 A man is praised according to his wisdom,
but men with warped minds are despised.

9 Better to be a nobody and yet have a servant
than pretend to be somebody and have no food.

10 A righteous man cares for the needs of his animal,
but the kindest acts of the wicked are cruel.

11 He who works his land will have abundant food,
but he who chases fantasies lacks judgment.

12 The wicked desire the plunder of evil men,
but the root of the righteous flourishes.

13 An evil man is trapped by his sinful talk,
but a righteous man escapes trouble.

14 From the fruit of his lips a man is filled with good things
as surely as the work of his hands rewards him.

15 The way of a fool seems right to him,
but a wise man listens to advice.

16 A fool shows his annoyance at once,
but a prudent man overlooks an insult.

17 A truthful witness gives honest testimony,
but a false witness tells lies.

18 Reckless words pierce like a sword,
but the tongue of the wise brings healing.

19 Truthful lips endure forever,
but a lying tongue lasts only a moment.

20 There is deceit in the hearts of those who plot evil,
but joy for those who promote peace.

21 No harm befalls the righteous,
but the wicked have their fill of trouble.

22 The LORD detests lying lips,
but he delights in men who are truthful.

23 A prudent man keeps his knowledge to himself,
but the heart of fools blurts out folly.

24 Diligent hands will rule,
but laziness ends in slave labor.

25 An anxious heart weighs a man down,
but a kind word cheers him up.

26 A righteous man is cautious in friendship,[a]
but the way of the wicked leads them astray.

27 The lazy man does not roast[b] his game,
but the diligent man prizes his possessions.

[a] 26 Or *man is a guide to his neighbor* [b] 27 The meaning of the Hebrew for this word is uncertain.

One good deed is worth more than a thousand brilliant theories. Don't wait for greater opportunities or for a different kind of work. Just do the things you find to do day by day . . .

Do it promptly. Do not waste your life thinking about what you intend to do tomorrow. No one ever served God by doing things tomorrow. If we honor Christ and are blessed, it is with the things we do today.

Charles Haddon Spurgeon (1834-1892)

(12:11) All good things come from You, dear Father. Yet You have made it clear that I am not to sit idly and wait for Your blessings to find their way to my front door. Help me to be prudent and productive with the time You have given me. Teach me to "work the land" You have given to me—to make the most of what I have, rather than daydream about what I do not have. Teach me to build my plans on Your foundations—not on foolish infatuations, or on speculations that will never materialize. Please keep me in touch with reality and bring me into alignment with Your wisdom. (Pr 6:9–11; 12:24; Jas 1:17)

God does not show us the whole way but only the next step. His promise is, "I will counsel you with my eye upon you" (Ps 32:8 RSV).

Ingrid Trobisch (1926-)

(13:18–20) Thank You, Lord, for Your constant correction, and for keeping me on the right path. Please give me the discernment to recognize the gentle touch of Your guiding hand, and the humility to follow wherever You lead me. You have graciously provided me with wise counsel—please give me ears to recognize Your voice among all the others, and to walk the path You have chosen for me. (Isa 30:18–21)

28 In the way of righteousness there is life;
along that path is immortality.

13 A wise son heeds his father's instruction,
but a mocker does not listen to rebuke.

2 From the fruit of his lips a man enjoys good things,
but the unfaithful have a craving for violence.

3 He who guards his lips guards his life,
but he who speaks rashly will come to ruin.

4 The sluggard craves and gets nothing,
but the desires of the diligent are fully satisfied.

5 The righteous hate what is false,
but the wicked bring shame and disgrace.

6 Righteousness guards the man of integrity,
but wickedness overthrows the sinner.

7 One man pretends to be rich, yet has nothing;
another pretends to be poor, yet has great wealth.

8 A man's riches may ransom his life,
but a poor man hears no threat.

9 The light of the righteous shines brightly,
but the lamp of the wicked is snuffed out.

10 Pride only breeds quarrels,
but wisdom is found in those who take advice.

11 Dishonest money dwindles away,
but he who gathers money little by little makes it grow.

12 Hope deferred makes the heart sick,
but a longing fulfilled is a tree of life.

13 He who scorns instruction will pay for it,
but he who respects a command is rewarded.

14 The teaching of the wise is a fountain of life,
turning a man from the snares of death.

15 Good understanding wins favor,
but the way of the unfaithful is hard.[a]

16 Every prudent man acts out of knowledge,
but a fool exposes his folly.

17 A wicked messenger falls into trouble,
but a trustworthy envoy brings healing.

18 He who ignores discipline comes to poverty and shame,
but whoever heeds correction is honored.

19 A longing fulfilled is sweet to the soul,
but fools detest turning from evil.

20 He who walks with the wise grows wise,
but a companion of fools suffers harm.

21 Misfortune pursues the sinner,

[a] 15 Or *unfaithful does not endure*

but prosperity is the reward of the righteous.

22 A good man leaves an inheritance for his children's
children,
but a sinner's wealth is stored up for the
righteous.

23 A poor man's field may produce abundant food,
but injustice sweeps it away.

24 He who spares the rod hates his son,
but he who loves him is careful to discipline
him.

25 The righteous eat to their hearts' content,
but the stomach of the wicked goes hungry.

14 The wise woman builds her house,
but with her own hands the foolish one tears hers
down.

2 He whose walk is upright fears the LORD,
but he whose ways are devious despises him.

3 A fool's talk brings a rod to his back,
but the lips of the wise protect them.

4 Where there are no oxen, the manger is empty,
but from the strength of an ox comes an abundant
harvest.

5 A truthful witness does not deceive,
but a false witness pours out lies.

6 The mocker seeks wisdom and finds none,
but knowledge comes easily to the discerning.

7 Stay away from a foolish man,
for you will not find knowledge on his lips.

8 The wisdom of the prudent is to give thought to their
ways,
but the folly of fools is deception.

9 Fools mock at making amends for sin,
but goodwill is found among the upright.

10 Each heart knows its own bitterness,
and no one else can share its joy.

11 The house of the wicked will be destroyed,
but the tent of the upright will flourish.

12 There is a way that seems right to a man,
but in the end it leads to death.

13 Even in laughter the heart may ache,
and joy may end in grief.

14 The faithless will be fully repaid for their ways,
and the good man rewarded for his.

15 A simple man believes anything,
but a prudent man gives thought to his steps.

16 A wise man fears the LORD and shuns evil,
but a fool is hotheaded and reckless.

(13:21) Father God, You faithfully reward those who serve You with integrity. Even if righteousness costs me my life, I know that You will reward me with abundant eternal life. May I always seek to do what is right, not because I am chasing after prosperity, but out of love and gratitude to You. "For the LORD God is a sun and shield; the LORD bestows favor and honor; no good thing does he withhold from those whose walk is blameless. O LORD Almighty, blessed is the man who trusts in you." (Ps 84:11–12)

(14:21,31) I praise You, Father, for Your great compassion. You care for us when we are poor and outcast, needy and neglected. You know our weary state, and You send forth Your blessing to us through Your people. I take comfort in the words of Your Son, Jesus: "'For I was hungry and you gave me something to eat, I was thirsty and you gave me something to drink, I was a stranger and you invited me in, I needed clothes and you clothed me, I was sick and you looked after me, I was in prison and you came to visit me.'" When did we do these things for You, Lord? "'I tell you the truth, whatever you did for one of the least of these brothers of mine, you did for me.'" (Mt 25:35–40)

17 A quick-tempered man does foolish things,
and a crafty man is hated.

18 The simple inherit folly,
but the prudent are crowned with knowledge.

19 Evil men will bow down in the presence of the good,
and the wicked at the gates of the righteous.

20 The poor are shunned even by their neighbors,
but the rich have many friends.

21 He who despises his neighbor sins,
but blessed is he who is kind to the needy.

22 Do not those who plot evil go astray?
But those who plan what is good find[a] love and faithfulness.

23 All hard work brings a profit,
but mere talk leads only to poverty.

24 The wealth of the wise is their crown,
but the folly of fools yields folly.

25 A truthful witness saves lives,
but a false witness is deceitful.

26 He who fears the LORD has a secure fortress,
and for his children it will be a refuge.

27 The fear of the LORD is a fountain of life,
turning a man from the snares of death.

28 A large population is a king's glory,
but without subjects a prince is ruined.

29 A patient man has great understanding,
but a quick-tempered man displays folly.

30 A heart at peace gives life to the body,
but envy rots the bones.

31 He who oppresses the poor shows contempt for their Maker,
but whoever is kind to the needy honors God.

32 When calamity comes, the wicked are brought down,
but even in death the righteous have a refuge.

33 Wisdom reposes in the heart of the discerning
and even among fools she lets herself be known.[b]

34 Righteousness exalts a nation,
but sin is a disgrace to any people.

35 A king delights in a wise servant,
but a shameful servant incurs his wrath.

15 A gentle answer turns away wrath,
but a harsh word stirs up anger.

2 The tongue of the wise commends knowledge,
but the mouth of the fool gushes folly.

[a] 22 Or *show* [b] 33 Hebrew; Septuagint and Syriac / *but in the heart of fools she is not known*

3 The eyes of the LORD are everywhere,
keeping watch on the wicked and the good.

4 The tongue that brings healing is a tree of life,
but a deceitful tongue crushes the spirit.

5 A fool spurns his father's discipline,
but whoever heeds correction shows prudence.

6 The house of the righteous contains great treasure,
but the income of the wicked brings them trouble.

7 The lips of the wise spread knowledge;
not so the hearts of fools.

8 The LORD detests the sacrifice of the wicked,
but the prayer of the upright pleases him.

9 The LORD detests the way of the wicked
but he loves those who pursue righteousness.

10 Stern discipline awaits him who leaves the path;
he who hates correction will die.

11 Death and Destruction[a] lie open before the LORD—
how much more the hearts of men!

12 A mocker resents correction;
he will not consult the wise.

13 A happy heart makes the face cheerful,
but heartache crushes the spirit.

14 The discerning heart seeks knowledge,
but the mouth of a fool feeds on folly.

15 All the days of the oppressed are wretched,
but the cheerful heart has a continual feast.

16 Better a little with the fear of the LORD
than great wealth with turmoil.

17 Better a meal of vegetables where there is love
than a fattened calf with hatred.

18 A hot-tempered man stirs up dissension,
but a patient man calms a quarrel.

19 The way of the sluggard is blocked with thorns,
but the path of the upright is a highway.

20 A wise son brings joy to his father,
but a foolish man despises his mother.

21 Folly delights a man who lacks judgment,
but a man of understanding keeps a straight course.

22 Plans fail for lack of counsel,
but with many advisers they succeed.

23 A man finds joy in giving an apt reply—
and how good is a timely word!

24 The path of life leads upward for the wise
to keep him from going down to the grave.[b]

[a] 11 Hebrew *Sheol and Abaddon* [b] 24 Hebrew *Sheol*

(15:4) Gracious Lord, make me Your messenger of hope and healing. Fill my mouth with words of life. Give me "an instructed tongue, to know the word that sustains the weary." Open my ears to listen to those who mourn, to those who are in distress, to those who need hope. Gentle Savior, may the Comforter bring comfort through me to the brokenhearted. (Isa 50:4)

Take my voice and let me sing
Always, only, for my King;
Take my lips and let them be
Filled with messages from Thee,
Filled with messages from Thee.

"Take My Life and Let It Be"
Francis Ridley Havergal (1836–1879)

In God's plan there are no accidental meetings. In each encounter God has a purpose for both the needy person and you. You may be the one who can really help and counsel the person.

Determine to be an encouragement to everyone whom God brings across your path. It costs little to say a kind word and to communicate a sense of support . . .

We never know where a kindness will lead, because only God can see the potential of the man or woman in our presence.

Jerry White (1937-)

(15:28) Lord, help me to guard my tongue. Teach me the weight of words. More than that, teach me to guard my heart. For "the good man brings good things out of the good stored up in his heart, and the evil man brings evil things out of the evil stored up in his heart. For out of the overflow of his heart his mouth speaks." (Pr 4:23; Lk 6:45; Jas 1:26; 3:5–9)

More like You,
Jesus, more like You,
Fill my heart with Your desire
To make me more like You.
More like You,
Jesus, more like You,
Touch my lips with holy fire,
And make me more like You.

"More Like You"
Scott Wesley Brown (©1997)

The tongue will not be likely to heap up malice, work mischief, and bring us and others to misery, if our hearts be full of kindly affections and right dispositions. Neither will our utterance be apt to lack wisdom or grace if we be truly lovers of truth and God. Let us, then, resort to David's prayer: "Set a watch, O Lord, before my mouth; keep the door of my lips" (Ps 141:3).

Arthur T. Pierson (1837-1911)

25 The LORD tears down the proud man's house
but he keeps the widow's boundaries intact.

26 The LORD detests the thoughts of the wicked,
but those of the pure are pleasing to him.

27 A greedy man brings trouble to his family,
but he who hates bribes will live.

28 The heart of the righteous weighs its answers,
but the mouth of the wicked gushes evil.

29 The LORD is far from the wicked
but he hears the prayer of the righteous.

30 A cheerful look brings joy to the heart,
and good news gives health to the bones.

31 He who listens to a life-giving rebuke
will be at home among the wise.

32 He who ignores discipline despises himself,
but whoever heeds correction gains
understanding.

33 The fear of the LORD teaches a man wisdom,[a]
and humility comes before honor.

16 To man belong the plans of the heart,
but from the LORD comes the reply of the tongue.

2 All a man's ways seem innocent to him,
but motives are weighed by the LORD.

3 Commit to the LORD whatever you do,
and your plans will succeed.

4 The LORD works out everything for his own ends—
even the wicked for a day of disaster.

5 The LORD detests all the proud of heart.
Be sure of this: They will not go unpunished.

6 Through love and faithfulness sin is atoned for;
through the fear of the LORD a man avoids evil.

7 When a man's ways are pleasing to the LORD,
he makes even his enemies live at peace with
him.

8 Better a little with righteousness
than much gain with injustice.

9 In his heart a man plans his course,
but the LORD determines his steps.

10 The lips of a king speak as an oracle,
and his mouth should not betray justice.

11 Honest scales and balances are from the LORD;
all the weights in the bag are of his making.

12 Kings detest wrongdoing,
for a throne is established through
righteousness.

[a] 33 Or *Wisdom teaches the fear of the LORD*

13 Kings take pleasure in honest lips;
they value a man who speaks the truth.

14 A king's wrath is a messenger of death,
but a wise man will appease it.

15 When a king's face brightens, it means life;
his favor is like a rain cloud in spring.

16 How much better to get wisdom than gold,
to choose understanding rather than silver!

17 The highway of the upright avoids evil;
he who guards his way guards his life.

18 Pride goes before destruction,
a haughty spirit before a fall.

19 Better to be lowly in spirit and among the oppressed
than to share plunder with the proud.

20 Whoever gives heed to instruction prospers,
and blessed is he who trusts in the LORD.

21 The wise in heart are called discerning,
and pleasant words promote instruction.[a]

22 Understanding is a fountain of life to those who have it,
but folly brings punishment to fools.

23 A wise man's heart guides his mouth,
and his lips promote instruction.[b]

24 Pleasant words are a honeycomb,
sweet to the soul and healing to the bones.

25 There is a way that seems right to a man,
but in the end it leads to death.

26 The laborer's appetite works for him;
his hunger drives him on.

27 A scoundrel plots evil,
and his speech is like a scorching fire.

28 A perverse man stirs up dissension,
and a gossip separates close friends.

29 A violent man entices his neighbor
and leads him down a path that is not good.

30 He who winks with his eye is plotting perversity;
he who purses his lips is bent on evil.

31 Gray hair is a crown of splendor;
it is attained by a righteous life.

32 Better a patient man than a warrior,
a man who controls his temper than one who takes a city.

33 The lot is cast into the lap,
but its every decision is from the LORD.

[a] 21 Or *words make a man persuasive* [b] 23 Or *mouth / and makes his lips persuasive*

(16:16) Wealth can be lost or stolen. But wisdom, once gained, can never be lost or taken away. Wealth when given away is depleted by the giving. But wisdom when given away becomes even more our possession. Wealth is fleeting and evasive—who is ever satisfied with enough of it? But wisdom flows freely from You to those who ask You for it, and there is always more than enough. (Jas 1:5)

It is comforting, Father, so inspiring to my faith to read Your Word, which says, "If any of you lacks wisdom, let him ask of God, who gives to all liberally and without reproach, and it will be given to him" (Jas 1:5). You knew it all along, of course, that more than anything, other than forgiveness, we needed wisdom.

Dick Eastman (1944-) and Jack Hayford (1934-)

(17:3) Our hearts are more valuable to You than silver and gold are to us. You test them and purify them and improve their worth through the trials of our faith. So I thank You, Father, for the hard times, because I know they will only serve to make me more like Christ.

Lord Jesus, we come to Thee now as little children. Dress us again in clean pinafores; make us tidy once more with the tidiness of true remorse and confession. Oh, wash our hearts, that they may be clean again. Make us to know the strengthening joys of the Spirit, and the newness of life which only Thou can give. Amen.

Peter Marshall (1902-1949)

17 Better a dry crust with peace and quiet
than a house full of feasting,[a] with strife.

2 A wise servant will rule over a disgraceful son,
and will share the inheritance as one of the brothers.

3 The crucible for silver and the furnace for gold,
but the LORD tests the heart.

4 A wicked man listens to evil lips;
a liar pays attention to a malicious tongue.

5 He who mocks the poor shows contempt for their Maker;
whoever gloats over disaster will not go unpunished.

6 Children's children are a crown to the aged,
and parents are the pride of their children.

7 Arrogant[b] lips are unsuited to a fool—
how much worse lying lips to a ruler!

8 A bribe is a charm to the one who gives it;
wherever he turns, he succeeds.

9 He who covers over an offense promotes love,
but whoever repeats the matter separates close friends.

10 A rebuke impresses a man of discernment
more than a hundred lashes a fool.

11 An evil man is bent only on rebellion;
a merciless official will be sent against him.

12 Better to meet a bear robbed of her cubs
than a fool in his folly.

13 If a man pays back evil for good,
evil will never leave his house.

14 Starting a quarrel is like breaching a dam;
so drop the matter before a dispute breaks out.

15 Acquitting the guilty and condemning the innocent—
the LORD detests them both.

16 Of what use is money in the hand of a fool,
since he has no desire to get wisdom?

17 A friend loves at all times,
and a brother is born for adversity.

18 A man lacking in judgment strikes hands in pledge
and puts up security for his neighbor.

19 He who loves a quarrel loves sin;
he who builds a high gate invites destruction.

20 A man of perverse heart does not prosper;
he whose tongue is deceitful falls into trouble.

[a] *1* Hebrew *sacrifices* [b] *7* Or *Eloquent*

21 To have a fool for a son brings grief;
there is no joy for the father of a fool.

22 A cheerful heart is good medicine,
but a crushed spirit dries up the bones.

23 A wicked man accepts a bribe in secret
to pervert the course of justice.

24 A discerning man keeps wisdom in view,
but a fool's eyes wander to the ends of the earth.

25 A foolish son brings grief to his father
and bitterness to the one who bore him.

26 It is not good to punish an innocent man,
or to flog officials for their integrity.

27 A man of knowledge uses words with restraint,
and a man of understanding is even-tempered.

28 Even a fool is thought wise if he keeps silent,
and discerning if he holds his tongue.

18 An unfriendly man pursues selfish ends;
he defies all sound judgment.

2 A fool finds no pleasure in understanding
but delights in airing his own opinions.

3 When wickedness comes, so does contempt,
and with shame comes disgrace.

4 The words of a man's mouth are deep waters,
but the fountain of wisdom is a bubbling brook.

5 It is not good to be partial to the wicked
or to deprive the innocent of justice.

6 A fool's lips bring him strife,
and his mouth invites a beating.

7 A fool's mouth is his undoing,
and his lips are a snare to his soul.

8 The words of a gossip are like choice morsels;
they go down to a man's inmost parts.

9 One who is slack in his work
is brother to one who destroys.

10 The name of the LORD is a strong tower;
the righteous run to it and are safe.

11 The wealth of the rich is their fortified city;
they imagine it an unscalable wall.

12 Before his downfall a man's heart is proud,
but humility comes before honor.

13 He who answers before listening—
that is his folly and his shame.

14 A man's spirit sustains him in sickness,
but a crushed spirit who can bear?

15 The heart of the discerning acquires knowledge;
the ears of the wise seek it out.

(18:10) Your name contains the fullness of everything I need. Your name is Creator, Provider, Savior, Healer, Father, Sustainer, Deliverer, Redeemer, Friend. In Your name I find rest when I am weary, strength when I am weak, safety when I am pursued, hope when I am discouraged, and joy when I am sorrowful. "I will praise you as long as I live, and in your name I will lift up my hands." (Ps 63:4)

Jesus, Your name is power,
Jesus, Your name is might.
Jesus, Your name will break every
stronghold;
Jesus, Your name is life.

Jesus, Your name is healing,
Jesus, Your name gives sight.
Jesus, Your name will free every
captive;
Jesus, Your name is life.

Jesus, Your name is holy,
Jesus, Your name brings light.
Jesus, Your name above every other,
Jesus, Your name is life.

"Jesus, Your Name"
Morris Chapman and
Claire Cloninger (©1990)

(19:8) Lord, teach me to fear You so that I may begin to gain true wisdom. For You, O God, are "a rich store of salvation and wisdom and knowledge; the fear of the LORD is the key to this treasure." And in Christ "are hidden all the treasures of wisdom and knowledge." O God, may I remain hidden in Christ so that I might explore the bountiful riches of this storehouse. (Job 12:13; Isa 33:6; Col 2:2–3)

Be Thou my wisdom,
And Thou my true Word;
I ever with Thee
And Thou with me, Lord;
Thou my great Father,
I Thy true son,
Thou in me dwelling,
And I with Thee one.

"Be Thou My Vision"
Ancient Irish Poem (8th c.)
Trans. Mary E. Byrne (1880-1931)
Versified by Eleanor H. Hull (1860-1935)

16 A gift opens the way for the giver
and ushers him into the presence of the great.

17 The first to present his case seems right,
till another comes forward and questions him.

18 Casting the lot settles disputes
and keeps strong opponents apart.

19 An offended brother is more unyielding than a fortified city,
and disputes are like the barred gates of a citadel.

20 From the fruit of his mouth a man's stomach is filled;
with the harvest from his lips he is satisfied.

21 The tongue has the power of life and death,
and those who love it will eat its fruit.

22 He who finds a wife finds what is good
and receives favor from the LORD.

23 A poor man pleads for mercy,
but a rich man answers harshly.

24 A man of many companions may come to ruin,
but there is a friend who sticks closer than a brother.

19 Better a poor man whose walk is blameless
than a fool whose lips are perverse.

2 It is not good to have zeal without knowledge,
nor to be hasty and miss the way.

3 A man's own folly ruins his life,
yet his heart rages against the LORD.

4 Wealth brings many friends,
but a poor man's friend deserts him.

5 A false witness will not go unpunished,
and he who pours out lies will not go free.

6 Many curry favor with a ruler,
and everyone is the friend of a man who gives gifts.

7 A poor man is shunned by all his relatives—
how much more do his friends avoid him!
Though he pursues them with pleading,
they are nowhere to be found.[a]

8 He who gets wisdom loves his own soul;
he who cherishes understanding prospers.

9 A false witness will not go unpunished,
and he who pours out lies will perish.

10 It is not fitting for a fool to live in luxury—
how much worse for a slave to rule over princes!

11 A man's wisdom gives him patience;
it is to his glory to overlook an offense.

[a] 7 The meaning of the Hebrew for this sentence is uncertain.

12 A king's rage is like the roar of a lion,
but his favor is like dew on the grass.

13 A foolish son is his father's ruin,
and a quarrelsome wife is like a constant dripping.

14 Houses and wealth are inherited from parents,
but a prudent wife is from the LORD.

15 Laziness brings on deep sleep,
and the shiftless man goes hungry.

16 He who obeys instructions guards his life,
but he who is contemptuous of his ways will die.

17 He who is kind to the poor lends to the LORD,
and he will reward him for what he has done.

18 Discipline your son, for in that there is hope;
do not be a willing party to his death.

19 A hot-tempered man must pay the penalty;
if you rescue him, you will have to do it again.

20 Listen to advice and accept instruction,
and in the end you will be wise.

21 Many are the plans in a man's heart,
but it is the LORD's purpose that prevails.

22 What a man desires is unfailing love[a];
better to be poor than a liar.

23 The fear of the LORD leads to life:
Then one rests content, untouched by trouble.

24 The sluggard buries his hand in the dish;
he will not even bring it back to his mouth!

25 Flog a mocker, and the simple will learn prudence;
rebuke a discerning man, and he will gain
knowledge.

26 He who robs his father and drives out his mother
is a son who brings shame and disgrace.

27 Stop listening to instruction, my son,
and you will stray from the words of knowledge.

28 A corrupt witness mocks at justice,
and the mouth of the wicked gulps down evil.

29 Penalties are prepared for mockers,
and beatings for the backs of fools.

20

Wine is a mocker and beer a brawler;
whoever is led astray by them is not wise.

2 A king's wrath is like the roar of a lion;
he who angers him forfeits his life.

3 It is to a man's honor to avoid strife,
but every fool is quick to quarrel.

4 A sluggard does not plow in season;
so at harvest time he looks but finds nothing.

[a] 22 Or *A man's greed is his shame*

What the world needs is more believers who want to do God's will as much as unbelievers want to do their own will . . . It is wonderful to see what miracles God can work in wills that are completely surrendered to Him. He makes hard things easy and bitter things sweet. It isn't that He puts an easy thing in the place of the hard one; He actually changes the hard thing into an easy one.

Catherine Jackson

(19:21) Sovereign Lord, as the heavens are higher than the earth, so are Your ways higher than our ways and Your thoughts than our thoughts. So I surrender my will to Your will and I pray that only Your purposes will be accomplished in my life. "Not my will, but yours be done." (Lk 22:42)

(20:22) "I waited patiently for the LORD; he turned to me and heard my cry." O Lord, vengeance is Yours, and so is mercy. How many times could You could have said to me, "I'll pay you back for this wrong!" Instead You showed me forgiveness. So who am I to demand revenge or vindication? O Lord, when I am mistreated please give me patience to wait for You—not for vengeance, but for deliverance. And I pray that You will give me the grace to forgive my enemies just as You forgave me when I was Your enemy. (Ps 40:1; Ro 5:8)

Once we understand the depth of our sin and the distance it put between us and God and once we get a glimpse of the sacrifice God made to restore fellowship with us, we should not hesitate to get involved in the process of forgiveness. To understand what God did for us and then to refuse to forgive those who have wronged us is to be like the wicked, ungrateful slave Jesus described in Matthew 18:23-34.

Charles Stanley (1932-)

5 The purposes of a man's heart are deep waters,
but a man of understanding draws them out.

6 Many a man claims to have unfailing love,
but a faithful man who can find?

7 The righteous man leads a blameless life;
blessed are his children after him.

8 When a king sits on his throne to judge,
he winnows out all evil with his eyes.

9 Who can say, "I have kept my heart pure;
I am clean and without sin"?

10 Differing weights and differing measures—
the LORD detests them both.

11 Even a child is known by his actions,
by whether his conduct is pure and right.

12 Ears that hear and eyes that see—
the LORD has made them both.

13 Do not love sleep or you will grow poor;
stay awake and you will have food to spare.

14 "It's no good, it's no good!" says the buyer;
then off he goes and boasts about his purchase.

15 Gold there is, and rubies in abundance,
but lips that speak knowledge are a rare jewel.

16 Take the garment of one who puts up security for a stranger;
hold it in pledge if he does it for a wayward woman.

17 Food gained by fraud tastes sweet to a man,
but he ends up with a mouth full of gravel.

18 Make plans by seeking advice;
if you wage war, obtain guidance.

19 A gossip betrays a confidence;
so avoid a man who talks too much.

20 If a man curses his father or mother,
his lamp will be snuffed out in pitch darkness.

21 An inheritance quickly gained at the beginning
will not be blessed at the end.

22 Do not say, "I'll pay you back for this wrong!"
Wait for the LORD, and he will deliver you.

23 The LORD detests differing weights,
and dishonest scales do not please him.

24 A man's steps are directed by the LORD.
How then can anyone understand his own way?

25 It is a trap for a man to dedicate something rashly
and only later to consider his vows.

26 A wise king winnows out the wicked;
he drives the threshing wheel over them.

27 The lamp of the LORD searches the spirit of a man[a];
it searches out his inmost being.

28 Love and faithfulness keep a king safe;
through love his throne is made secure.

29 The glory of young men is their strength,
gray hair the splendor of the old.

30 Blows and wounds cleanse away evil,
and beatings purge the inmost being.

21 The king's heart is in the hand of the LORD;
he directs it like a watercourse wherever he pleases.

2 All a man's ways seem right to him,
but the LORD weighs the heart.

3 To do what is right and just
is more acceptable to the LORD than sacrifice.

4 Haughty eyes and a proud heart,
the lamp of the wicked, are sin!

5 The plans of the diligent lead to profit
as surely as haste leads to poverty.

6 A fortune made by a lying tongue
is a fleeting vapor and a deadly snare.[b]

7 The violence of the wicked will drag them away,
for they refuse to do what is right.

8 The way of the guilty is devious,
but the conduct of the innocent is upright.

9 Better to live on a corner of the roof
than share a house with a quarrelsome wife.

10 The wicked man craves evil;
his neighbor gets no mercy from him.

11 When a mocker is punished, the simple gain wisdom;
when a wise man is instructed, he gets knowledge.

12 The Righteous One[c] takes note of the house of the wicked
and brings the wicked to ruin.

13 If a man shuts his ears to the cry of the poor,
he too will cry out and not be answered.

14 A gift given in secret soothes anger,
and a bribe concealed in the cloak pacifies great wrath.

15 When justice is done, it brings joy to the righteous
but terror to evildoers.

16 A man who strays from the path of understanding
comes to rest in the company of the dead.

17 He who loves pleasure will become poor;
whoever loves wine and oil will never be rich.

[a] 27 Or *The spirit of man is the LORD's lamp* [b] 6 Some Hebrew manuscripts, Septuagint and Vulgate; most Hebrew manuscripts *vapor for those who seek death* [c] 12 Or *The righteous man*

(21:2–3) Father, You know my heart better than I do. Nothing is hidden from You. For You search every heart and understand every motive behind our thoughts. You have shown us what You require of us—that we act justly and love mercy and walk humbly with You. So I pray, "Search me, O God, and know my heart; test me and know my anxious thoughts. See if there is any offensive way in me, and lead me in the way everlasting." (1Ch 28:9; Ps 139:23–24; Jer 17:10; Mic 6:8; Mk 12:33)

I praise Thee, Lord,
For cleansing me from sin.
Fulfill Thy Word,
And make me pure within.
Fill me with fire,
Where once I burned with shame.
Grant my desire
To magnify Thy name.

"Cleanse Me"
J. Edwin Orr (1936)

O God, I want an inner being with "no part dark," no part unredeemed. My heart tingles at the thought that I can have an inner life which will be wholly full of light. I take it. Amen.

E. Stanley Jones (1884–1973)

(21:30–31) Almighty, sovereign Lord, no plan can succeed against You and no plan can succeed without You. Please give me the meekness to surrender to You without a fight, the faith to trust in You without a doubt, and the sense to commit everything to You without exception. Indeed, "many are the plans in a man's heart, but it is the LORD's purpose that prevails." (Pr 16:3–4; 19:21; 1Co 3:19–20)

Jesus says, "Yoke up with Me. Let's pull together, you and I." And if we will pull steadily along, content to be by His side, and to be hearing His quiet voice, and always to keep His pace, step by step with Him, without regard to seeing results, all will be well, and by and by the best results and the largest will be found to have come.

Samuel Dickey Gordon (1859–1936)

18 The wicked become a ransom for the righteous,
and the unfaithful for the upright.

19 Better to live in a desert
than with a quarrelsome and ill-tempered wife.

20 In the house of the wise are stores of choice food and oil,
but a foolish man devours all he has.

21 He who pursues righteousness and love
finds life, prosperity[a] and honor.

22 A wise man attacks the city of the mighty
and pulls down the stronghold in which they trust.

23 He who guards his mouth and his tongue
keeps himself from calamity.

24 The proud and arrogant man—"Mocker" is his name;
he behaves with overweening pride.

25 The sluggard's craving will be the death of him,
because his hands refuse to work.
26 All day long he craves for more,
but the righteous give without sparing.

27 The sacrifice of the wicked is detestable—
how much more so when brought with evil intent!

28 A false witness will perish,
and whoever listens to him will be destroyed forever.[b]

29 A wicked man puts up a bold front,
but an upright man gives thought to his ways.

30 There is no wisdom, no insight, no plan
that can succeed against the LORD.

31 The horse is made ready for the day of battle,
but victory rests with the LORD.

22 A good name is more desirable than great riches;
to be esteemed is better than silver or gold.

2 Rich and poor have this in common:
The LORD is the Maker of them all.

3 A prudent man sees danger and takes refuge,
but the simple keep going and suffer for it.

4 Humility and the fear of the LORD
bring wealth and honor and life.

5 In the paths of the wicked lie thorns and snares,
but he who guards his soul stays far from them.

6 Train[c] a child in the way he should go,
and when he is old he will not turn from it.

7 The rich rule over the poor,
and the borrower is servant to the lender.

[a] 21 Or *righteousness* [b] 28 Or */ but the words of an obedient man will live on*
[c] 6 Or *Start*

8 He who sows wickedness reaps trouble,
and the rod of his fury will be destroyed.

9 A generous man will himself be blessed,
for he shares his food with the poor.

10 Drive out the mocker, and out goes strife;
quarrels and insults are ended.

11 He who loves a pure heart and whose speech is
gracious
will have the king for his friend.

12 The eyes of the LORD keep watch over knowledge,
but he frustrates the words of the unfaithful.

13 The sluggard says, "There is a lion outside!"
or, "I will be murdered in the streets!"

14 The mouth of an adulteress is a deep pit;
he who is under the LORD's wrath will fall into it.

15 Folly is bound up in the heart of a child,
but the rod of discipline will drive it far from him.

16 He who oppresses the poor to increase his wealth
and he who gives gifts to the rich—both come to
poverty.

Sayings of the Wise

17 Pay attention and listen to the sayings of the wise;
apply your heart to what I teach,
18 for it is pleasing when you keep them in your heart
and have all of them ready on your lips.
19 So that your trust may be in the LORD,
I teach you today, even you.
20 Have I not written thirty[a] sayings for you,
sayings of counsel and knowledge,
21 teaching you true and reliable words,
so that you can give sound answers
to him who sent you?

22 Do not exploit the poor because they are poor
and do not crush the needy in court,
23 for the LORD will take up their case
and will plunder those who plunder them.

24 Do not make friends with a hot-tempered man,
do not associate with one easily angered,
25 or you may learn his ways
and get yourself ensnared.

26 Do not be a man who strikes hands in pledge
or puts up security for debts;
27 if you lack the means to pay,
your very bed will be snatched from under you.

28 Do not move an ancient boundary stone
set up by your forefathers.

29 Do you see a man skilled in his work?

[a] 20 Or *not formerly written*; or *not written excellent*

(22:17–21) I thank You, O God, that Your instructions are not like those of a master to a slave; rather, they are like those of a teacher to a student. They are as much for our benefit as they are for Your pleasure, and when we live by them we satisfy both our needs and Your desires. Only as we "pay attention" and apply our hearts to Your Word can we walk in wisdom, and only then will our conversation be "full of grace, seasoned with salt," so that we may know how to answer everyone. (Col 4:5–6)

He will serve before kings;
he will not serve before obscure men.

23 When you sit to dine with a ruler,
note well what[a] is before you,
2 and put a knife to your throat
if you are given to gluttony.
3 Do not crave his delicacies,
for that food is deceptive.

4 Do not wear yourself out to get rich;
have the wisdom to show restraint.
5 Cast but a glance at riches, and they are gone,
for they will surely sprout wings
and fly off to the sky like an eagle.

6 Do not eat the food of a stingy man,
do not crave his delicacies;
7 for he is the kind of man
who is always thinking about the cost.[b]
"Eat and drink," he says to you,
but his heart is not with you.
8 You will vomit up the little you have eaten
and will have wasted your compliments.

9 Do not speak to a fool,
for he will scorn the wisdom of your words.

10 Do not move an ancient boundary stone
or encroach on the fields of the fatherless,
11 for their Defender is strong;
he will take up their case against you.

12 Apply your heart to instruction
and your ears to words of knowledge.

13 Do not withhold discipline from a child;
if you punish him with the rod, he will not die.
14 Punish him with the rod
and save his soul from death.[c]

15 My son, if your heart is wise,
then my heart will be glad;
16 my inmost being will rejoice
when your lips speak what is right.

17 Do not let your heart envy sinners,
but always be zealous for the fear of the LORD.
18 There is surely a future hope for you,
and your hope will not be cut off.

19 Listen, my son, and be wise,
and keep your heart on the right path.
20 Do not join those who drink too much wine
or gorge themselves on meat,
21 for drunkards and gluttons become poor,
and drowsiness clothes them in rags.

22 Listen to your father, who gave you life,
and do not despise your mother when she is old.

[a] *1* Or *who* [b] *7* Or *for as he thinks within himself, / so he is*; or *for as he puts on a feast, / so he is* [c] *14* Hebrew *Sheol*

(23:17–18) True happiness, Lord, is found in belonging to You, not in acquiring possessions or in fulfilling goals or in achieving fame or fortune. In Your awesome love, You have secured my future. In Your Word, I find real hope. Better is one day in Your courts than a thousand elsewhere; I would rather be a doorkeeper in Your house than dwell luxuriously with the wicked. (Ps 84:10)

23 Buy the truth and do not sell it;
get wisdom, discipline and understanding.
24 The father of a righteous man has great joy;
he who has a wise son delights in him.
25 May your father and mother be glad;
may she who gave you birth rejoice!

26 My son, give me your heart
and let your eyes keep to my ways,
27 for a prostitute is a deep pit
and a wayward wife is a narrow well.
28 Like a bandit she lies in wait,
and multiplies the unfaithful among men.

29 Who has woe? Who has sorrow?
Who has strife? Who has complaints?
Who has needless bruises? Who has bloodshot eyes?
30 Those who linger over wine,
who go to sample bowls of mixed wine.
31 Do not gaze at wine when it is red,
when it sparkles in the cup,
when it goes down smoothly!
32 In the end it bites like a snake
and poisons like a viper.
33 Your eyes will see strange sights
and your mind imagine confusing things.
34 You will be like one sleeping on the high seas,
lying on top of the rigging.
35 "They hit me," you will say, "but I'm not hurt!
They beat me, but I don't feel it!
When will I wake up
so I can find another drink?"

24 Do not envy wicked men,
do not desire their company;
2 for their hearts plot violence,
and their lips talk about making trouble.

3 By wisdom a house is built,
and through understanding it is established;
4 through knowledge its rooms are filled
with rare and beautiful treasures.

5 A wise man has great power,
and a man of knowledge increases strength;
6 for waging war you need guidance,
and for victory many advisers.

7 Wisdom is too high for a fool;
in the assembly at the gate he has nothing to say.

8 He who plots evil
will be known as a schemer.
9 The schemes of folly are sin,
and men detest a mocker.

10 If you falter in times of trouble,
how small is your strength!

11 Rescue those being led away to death;
hold back those staggering toward slaughter.

(24:3–4) Father God, help us build our houses upon the firm foundation of Your Word. And provide us with the understanding and love we need to live at peace in our homes. The rich blessings Your wisdom provides are more precious than fine furnishings, more delightful than the best food and wine. Your treasures are rare and remarkable, and they become ours when we humble ourselves and receive what You have chosen for us.

(24:17–18) You are a God of great compassion and mercy. You love us with a love that is not rude, not self-seeking, not easily angered—a love that keeps no record of wrongs. This is the love of Christ. And it is to this kind of love that You call us, because it is with this kind of love that You love us. Lord, help me to love others the way You love me. (Ps 35:12–14; Mt 5:44–48; Lk 6:27–28; Jn 13:34; 1Co 13:5)

When you realize that God has taken you from the gutter, so to speak, and made you a son in His own house—you, a miraculously pardoned offender, guilty, ungrateful, defiant, perverse as you were—your sense of God's 'love beyond degree' is more than words can express.

J. I. Packer (1926-)

Your love compels me, Lord,
To give as You would give,
To speak as You would speak,
To live as You would live.
Your love compels me, Lord,
To see as You would see,
To serve as You would serve,
To be what You would be.

"Your Love Compels Me"
Doug Holck (©1982)

12 If you say, "But we knew nothing about this,"
does not he who weighs the heart perceive it?
Does not he who guards your life know it?
Will he not repay each person according to what he has done?

13 Eat honey, my son, for it is good;
honey from the comb is sweet to your taste.
14 Know also that wisdom is sweet to your soul;
if you find it, there is a future hope for you,
and your hope will not be cut off.

15 Do not lie in wait like an outlaw against a righteous man's house,
do not raid his dwelling place;
16 for though a righteous man falls seven times, he rises again,
but the wicked are brought down by calamity.

17 Do not gloat when your enemy falls;
when he stumbles, do not let your heart rejoice,
18 or the LORD will see and disapprove
and turn his wrath away from him.

19 Do not fret because of evil men
or be envious of the wicked,
20 for the evil man has no future hope,
and the lamp of the wicked will be snuffed out.

21 Fear the LORD and the king, my son,
and do not join with the rebellious,
22 for those two will send sudden destruction upon them,
and who knows what calamities they can bring?

Further Sayings of the Wise

23 These also are sayings of the wise:

To show partiality in judging is not good:
24 Whoever says to the guilty, "You are innocent"—
peoples will curse him and nations denounce him.
25 But it will go well with those who convict the guilty,
and rich blessing will come upon them.

26 An honest answer
is like a kiss on the lips.

27 Finish your outdoor work
and get your fields ready;
after that, build your house.

28 Do not testify against your neighbor without cause,
or use your lips to deceive.
29 Do not say, "I'll do to him as he has done to me;
I'll pay that man back for what he did."

30 I went past the field of the sluggard,
past the vineyard of the man who lacks judgment;
31 thorns had come up everywhere,
the ground was covered with weeds,
and the stone wall was in ruins.
32 I applied my heart to what I observed
and learned a lesson from what I saw:

33 A little sleep, a little slumber,
a little folding of the hands to rest—
34 and poverty will come on you like a bandit
and scarcity like an armed man.[a]

More Proverbs of Solomon

25 These are more proverbs of Solomon, copied by the men of Hezekiah king of Judah:

2 It is the glory of God to conceal a matter;
to search out a matter is the glory of kings.

3 As the heavens are high and the earth is deep,
so the hearts of kings are unsearchable.

4 Remove the dross from the silver,
and out comes material for[b] the silversmith;
5 remove the wicked from the king's presence,
and his throne will be established through
righteousness.

6 Do not exalt yourself in the king's presence,
and do not claim a place among great men;
7 it is better for him to say to you, "Come up here,"
than for him to humiliate you before a nobleman.

What you have seen with your eyes
8 do not bring[c] hastily to court,
for what will you do in the end
if your neighbor puts you to shame?

9 If you argue your case with a neighbor,
do not betray another man's confidence,
10 or he who hears it may shame you
and you will never lose your bad reputation.

11 A word aptly spoken
is like apples of gold in settings of silver.

12 Like an earring of gold or an ornament of fine gold
is a wise man's rebuke to a listening ear.

13 Like the coolness of snow at harvest time
is a trustworthy messenger to those who send him;
he refreshes the spirit of his masters.

14 Like clouds and wind without rain
is a man who boasts of gifts he does not give.

15 Through patience a ruler can be persuaded,
and a gentle tongue can break a bone.

16 If you find honey, eat just enough—
too much of it, and you will vomit.
17 Seldom set foot in your neighbor's house—
too much of you, and he will hate you.

18 Like a club or a sword or a sharp arrow
is the man who gives false testimony against his
neighbor.

[a] 34 Or *like a vagrant / and scarcity like a beggar* [b] 4 Or *comes a vessel from* [c] 7,8 Or *nobleman / on whom you had set your eyes. / [8]Do not go*

(25:2) The heavens declare Your glory, O God; the skies proclaim the work of Your hands. Day after day they pour forth speech; night after night they display knowledge. There is no speech or language where their voice is not heard. Their voice goes out into all the earth, their words to the ends of the world. Since the creation of the world Your invisible qualities—Your eternal power and divine nature—have been made clear and intelligible through the things that You have made. And these are but the outer fringe of Your works; how faint the whisper we hear of You! Who then can understand the thunder of Your power? Oh, the depth of the riches of Your wisdom and knowledge! How unsearchable Your judgments, and Your paths beyond tracing out! (Job 26:14; Ps 19:1–4; Ro 1:19–20; 11:33)

You are beautiful beyond
description,
Too marvelous for words.
Too wonderful for comprehension,
Like nothing ever seen or heard.
Who can grasp Your infinite
wisdom?
Who can fathom the depth of Your
love?
You are beautiful beyond
description,
Majesty enthroned above.
And I stand, I stand in awe of You,
I stand, I stand in awe of You,
Holy God to whom all praise is due,
I stand in awe of You.

"I Stand in Awe"
Mark Altrogge (©1988)

In the silence of the sky and the depths of the sea, in the solitude of the forest and in the peace of home—everywhere—is felt the marvelous movement of his all-controlling and ever-living personality . . . In the silent hours of the night we stand and gaze at the moon, the stars, and the aurora borealis; we feel the rhythmic swing of things in the conflicts and achievements of man; and deep down in our souls we know that Jesus was right, and that God is not far away.

Calvin Weiss Laufer (1874–1938)

Broken by all the times I've failed,
And the days I've hung my head in shame.
Time and again I'm driven to my knees,
And I find Your great compassion there for me.

I'm amazed at all You've done for me;
Who am I, that You'd bless me so.
I stand in awe of all Your wondrous deeds;
You've dealt with me so graciously.

I'm Amazed
Rory Noland (©1991)

(25:21–22) Lord, You fed and clothed me even though I was Your enemy. You met my needs even though I did not say thank You. You spoke words of love to me even though I cursed You. And You died for me even though I sinned against You. These are the things You did for me. Now please fill me with Your love for my enemies. Help me to see them through Your eyes and to treat them with Your mercy and kindness, so that they might also come to know Your love for them in Christ Jesus. (2Ki 6:22–23; Mt 6:14–15; Ro 12:20–21)

To reconcile himself to us, and us to himself, and Jews, Gentiles and other hostile groups to each other, cost him nothing less than the painful shame of the cross. We have no right to expect, therefore, that we shall be able to engage in conciliation work at no cost to ourselves, whether our involvement in the dispute is as the offending or offended party, or as a third party anxious to help enemies to become friends again.

John R. W. Stott (1921-)

19 Like a bad tooth or a lame foot
is reliance on the unfaithful in times of trouble.

20 Like one who takes away a garment on a cold day,
or like vinegar poured on soda,
is one who sings songs to a heavy heart.

21 If your enemy is hungry, give him food to eat;
if he is thirsty, give him water to drink.
22 In doing this, you will heap burning coals on his head,
and the LORD will reward you.

23 As a north wind brings rain,
so a sly tongue brings angry looks.

24 Better to live on a corner of the roof
than share a house with a quarrelsome wife.

25 Like cold water to a weary soul
is good news from a distant land.

26 Like a muddied spring or a polluted well
is a righteous man who gives way to the wicked.

27 It is not good to eat too much honey,
nor is it honorable to seek one's own honor.

28 Like a city whose walls are broken down
is a man who lacks self-control.

26 Like snow in summer or rain in harvest,
honor is not fitting for a fool.

2 Like a fluttering sparrow or a darting swallow,
an undeserved curse does not come to rest.

3 A whip for the horse, a halter for the donkey,
and a rod for the backs of fools!

4 Do not answer a fool according to his folly,
or you will be like him yourself.

5 Answer a fool according to his folly,
or he will be wise in his own eyes.

6 Like cutting off one's feet or drinking violence
is the sending of a message by the hand of a fool.

7 Like a lame man's legs that hang limp
is a proverb in the mouth of a fool.

8 Like tying a stone in a sling
is the giving of honor to a fool.

9 Like a thornbush in a drunkard's hand
is a proverb in the mouth of a fool.

10 Like an archer who wounds at random
is he who hires a fool or any passer-by.

11 As a dog returns to its vomit,
so a fool repeats his folly.

12 Do you see a man wise in his own eyes?
There is more hope for a fool than for him.

13 The sluggard says, "There is a lion in the road,

a fierce lion roaming the streets!"

14 As a door turns on its hinges,
so a sluggard turns on his bed.

15 The sluggard buries his hand in the dish;
he is too lazy to bring it back to his mouth.

16 The sluggard is wiser in his own eyes
than seven men who answer discreetly.

17 Like one who seizes a dog by the ears
is a passer-by who meddles in a quarrel not his own.

18 Like a madman shooting
firebrands or deadly arrows
19 is a man who deceives his neighbor
and says, "I was only joking!"

20 Without wood a fire goes out;
without gossip a quarrel dies down.

21 As charcoal to embers and as wood to fire,
so is a quarrelsome man for kindling strife.

22 The words of a gossip are like choice morsels;
they go down to a man's inmost parts.

23 Like a coating of glaze[a] over earthenware
are fervent lips with an evil heart.

24 A malicious man disguises himself with his lips,
but in his heart he harbors deceit.
25 Though his speech is charming, do not believe him,
for seven abominations fill his heart.
26 His malice may be concealed by deception,
but his wickedness will be exposed in the assembly.

27 If a man digs a pit, he will fall into it;
if a man rolls a stone, it will roll back on him.

28 A lying tongue hates those it hurts,
and a flattering mouth works ruin.

27 Do not boast about tomorrow,
for you do not know what a day may bring forth.

2 Let another praise you, and not your own mouth;
someone else, and not your own lips.

3 Stone is heavy and sand a burden,
but provocation by a fool is heavier than both.

4 Anger is cruel and fury overwhelming,
but who can stand before jealousy?

5 Better is open rebuke
than hidden love.

6 Wounds from a friend can be trusted,
but an enemy multiplies kisses.

7 He who is full loathes honey,
but to the hungry even what is bitter tastes sweet.

[a] 23 With a different word division of the Hebrew; Masoretic Text *of silver dross*

(27:1) "My frame was not hidden from you when I was made in the secret place. When I was woven together in the depths of the earth, your eyes saw my unformed body. All the days ordained for me were written in your book before one of them came to be." I do not know the path of the wind, or how the spirit enters the body when it is formed in a mother's womb, so I surely cannot understand the work of God, the Maker of all things. I do not even know what the next moment will bring. The future is in Your hands, Lord. So let me make the most of every day You give to me, and let me live my life to bring You pleasure. (Ps 139:15–16; Ecc 11:5)

May this life that I live make You glad,
Help me praise You with all that I have.
May the thoughts of my heart
Bring a smile to Your face,
I will worship You, Lord, all my days.

Ev'ry day is a gift from Your hand,
You're the Author of all that I am.
Let my story be told
In this heart-spoken phrase:
I will worship You, Lord, all my days.

"All My Days"
Bill Batstone and Bob Somma (©1990)

We know not what event may be in the teeming womb of time; it is a secret till it is born . . . God has wisely kept us in the dark concerning future events and reserved for himself the knowledge of them, that he may train us up in a dependence upon himself and a continued readiness for every event.

Matthew Henry (1662-1714)

When we take God's Word seriously, our hands hover over our Bibles in anticipation . . . God's Word comes to nourish and refresh, to make fruitful and effective. The Bible is not ineffectual; we can expect something to happen when we receive God's message to us (Isa 55:10-11).
Jean Fleming (1941-)

(27:19) O Lord, You do not look at our outward appearance—You look at our hearts. So how can I see the condition of my heart? By looking into the mirror of Your Word. Your Word reveals to me my own thoughts, motives and values. It exposes the contents of my heart and shows me the kind of person I truly am. But Lord, it is my deepest desire that my heart reflect the heart of Christ so that those who see me will catch a glimpse of His reflection. (2Co 3:18; Heb 4:12–13; Jas 1:23–24)

Christ in us be glorified,
Christ in us be lifted high,
Let His love be shown
And His praises be known,
Let Christ be glorified.
Let Christ be glorified.

In every song we sing,
In the praises that we bring,
Let Christ be glorified.
In the service that we give,
And the lives that we live,
Let Christ be glorified.
"Christ In Us Be Glorified"
Morris Chapman (©1995)

8 Like a bird that strays from its nest
is a man who strays from his home.

9 Perfume and incense bring joy to the heart,
and the pleasantness of one's friend springs from his earnest counsel.

10 Do not forsake your friend and the friend of your father,
and do not go to your brother's house when disaster strikes you—
better a neighbor nearby than a brother far away.

11 Be wise, my son, and bring joy to my heart;
then I can answer anyone who treats me with contempt.

12 The prudent see danger and take refuge,
but the simple keep going and suffer for it.

13 Take the garment of one who puts up security for a stranger;
hold it in pledge if he does it for a wayward woman.

14 If a man loudly blesses his neighbor early in the morning,
it will be taken as a curse.

15 A quarrelsome wife is like
a constant dripping on a rainy day;
16 restraining her is like restraining the wind
or grasping oil with the hand.

17 As iron sharpens iron,
so one man sharpens another.

18 He who tends a fig tree will eat its fruit,
and he who looks after his master will be honored.

19 As water reflects a face,
so a man's heart reflects the man.

20 Death and Destruction[a] are never satisfied,
and neither are the eyes of man.

21 The crucible for silver and the furnace for gold,
but man is tested by the praise he receives.

22 Though you grind a fool in a mortar,
grinding him like grain with a pestle,
you will not remove his folly from him.

23 Be sure you know the condition of your flocks,
give careful attention to your herds;
24 for riches do not endure forever,
and a crown is not secure for all generations.
25 When the hay is removed and new growth appears
and the grass from the hills is gathered in,
26 the lambs will provide you with clothing,
and the goats with the price of a field.

[a] 20 Hebrew *Sheol and Abaddon*

27 You will have plenty of goats' milk
to feed you and your family
and to nourish your servant girls.

28 The wicked man flees though no one pursues,
but the righteous are as bold as a lion.

2 When a country is rebellious, it has many rulers,
but a man of understanding and knowledge
maintains order.

3 A ruler[a] who oppresses the poor
is like a driving rain that leaves no crops.

4 Those who forsake the law praise the wicked,
but those who keep the law resist them.

5 Evil men do not understand justice,
but those who seek the LORD understand it fully.

6 Better a poor man whose walk is blameless
than a rich man whose ways are perverse.

7 He who keeps the law is a discerning son,
but a companion of gluttons disgraces his father.

8 He who increases his wealth by exorbitant interest
amasses it for another, who will be kind to the poor.

9 If anyone turns a deaf ear to the law,
even his prayers are detestable.

10 He who leads the upright along an evil path
will fall into his own trap,
but the blameless will receive a good inheritance.

11 A rich man may be wise in his own eyes,
but a poor man who has discernment sees through
him.

12 When the righteous triumph, there is great elation;
but when the wicked rise to power, men go into
hiding.

13 He who conceals his sins does not prosper,
but whoever confesses and renounces them finds
mercy.

14 Blessed is the man who always fears the LORD,
but he who hardens his heart falls into trouble.

15 Like a roaring lion or a charging bear
is a wicked man ruling over a helpless people.

16 A tyrannical ruler lacks judgment,
but he who hates ill-gotten gain will enjoy a long
life.

17 A man tormented by the guilt of murder
will be a fugitive till death;
let no one support him.

18 He whose walk is blameless is kept safe,
but he whose ways are perverse will suddenly fall.

[a] 3 Or *A poor man*

"I have trusted in Thy mercy [leaned on Thy mercy]" which has loved us with an everlasting love, which pardons and cleanses and will never tire of us. "He that trusteth in the LORD [leaneth on the LORD], mercy shall compass him about" (Ps 32:10 KJV). Is it not like Him to let us know that He wants us to lean, not only on His mercy, but on His very Self?

Amy Carmichael (1867–1951)

(28:13–14) "Blessed is he whose transgressions are forgiven, whose sins are covered. Blessed is the man whose sin the LORD does not count against him and in whose spirit is no deceit. When I kept silent, my bones wasted away through my groaning all day long. For day and night your hand was heavy upon me; my strength was sapped as in the heat of summer. Then I acknowledged my sin to you and did not cover up my iniquity. I said, 'I will confess my transgressions to the LORD'—and you forgave the guilt of my sin." How I thank You, Father, that when we confess our sins You are faithful and just to forgive us our sins and to purify us from all unrighteousness. (Ps 32:1–5; 1Jn 1:9)

If we confess our sins, He is faithful;
If we confess our sins, He is just.
If we confess our sins, He is faithful;
He is faithful, He is faithful to
Forgive.

"He Is Faithful"
Walt Harrah (©1987)

(28:26) Lord God, in a society that reveres self-made men and women, that applauds self-fulfillment and encourages self-aggrandizement, now and then we find ourselves feeling weak and foolish for our reliance upon You. Some people say that our faith in You is a "crutch," but Your Word tells us that we are fools if we trust in ourselves. And we have learned both from Your Son and from hard experience that apart from You we can do nothing. So teach us Your ways, Lord, for in You the weak are strong, and with You all things are possible. (Mt 17:20; 19:26; Jn 5:19; 15:5; 2Co 12:9)

Frail children of dust, and feeble as
 frail,
In Thee do we trust, nor find Thee
 to fail;
Thy mercies how tender, how firm to
 the end,
Our Maker, Defender, Redeemer
 and Friend.

"O Worship the King"
Robert Grant (1833)

When we trust ourselves we are doing the wrong thing. We can fall into the error of spiritual pride on the one hand or discouragement on the other. We are really strong when we are weak; weak when we are strong. So following in the footsteps of Jesus, taking the steps—yes, and the jumps into the unknown—we can become paratroopers. We can storm the enemy's territory and win souls for Jesus.

Corrie ten Boom (1892–1983)

19 He who works his land will have abundant food,
but the one who chases fantasies will have his fill of poverty.

20 A faithful man will be richly blessed,
but one eager to get rich will not go unpunished.

21 To show partiality is not good—
yet a man will do wrong for a piece of bread.

22 A stingy man is eager to get rich
and is unaware that poverty awaits him.

23 He who rebukes a man will in the end gain more favor
than he who has a flattering tongue.

24 He who robs his father or mother
and says, "It's not wrong"—
he is partner to him who destroys.

25 A greedy man stirs up dissension,
but he who trusts in the LORD will prosper.

26 He who trusts in himself is a fool,
but he who walks in wisdom is kept safe.

27 He who gives to the poor will lack nothing,
but he who closes his eyes to them receives many curses.

28 When the wicked rise to power, people go into hiding;
but when the wicked perish, the righteous thrive.

29 A man who remains stiff-necked after many rebukes
will suddenly be destroyed—without remedy.

2 When the righteous thrive, the people rejoice;
when the wicked rule, the people groan.

3 A man who loves wisdom brings joy to his father,
but a companion of prostitutes squanders his wealth.

4 By justice a king gives a country stability,
but one who is greedy for bribes tears it down.

5 Whoever flatters his neighbor
is spreading a net for his feet.

6 An evil man is snared by his own sin,
but a righteous one can sing and be glad.

7 The righteous care about justice for the poor,
but the wicked have no such concern.

8 Mockers stir up a city,
but wise men turn away anger.

9 If a wise man goes to court with a fool,
the fool rages and scoffs, and there is no peace.

10 Bloodthirsty men hate a man of integrity
and seek to kill the upright.

11 A fool gives full vent to his anger,
but a wise man keeps himself under control.

12 If a ruler listens to lies,
all his officials become wicked.

13 The poor man and the oppressor have this in common:
The LORD gives sight to the eyes of both.

14 If a king judges the poor with fairness,
his throne will always be secure.

15 The rod of correction imparts wisdom,
but a child left to himself disgraces his mother.

16 When the wicked thrive, so does sin,
but the righteous will see their downfall.

17 Discipline your son, and he will give you peace;
he will bring delight to your soul.

18 Where there is no revelation, the people cast off restraint;
but blessed is he who keeps the law.

19 A servant cannot be corrected by mere words;
though he understands, he will not respond.

20 Do you see a man who speaks in haste?
There is more hope for a fool than for him.

21 If a man pampers his servant from youth,
he will bring grief[a] in the end.

22 An angry man stirs up dissension,
and a hot-tempered one commits many sins.

23 A man's pride brings him low,
but a man of lowly spirit gains honor.

24 The accomplice of a thief is his own enemy;
he is put under oath and dare not testify.

25 Fear of man will prove to be a snare,
but whoever trusts in the LORD is kept safe.

26 Many seek an audience with a ruler,
but it is from the LORD that man gets justice.

27 The righteous detest the dishonest;
the wicked detest the upright.

Sayings of Agur

30 The sayings of Agur son of Jakeh—an oracle[b]:

This man declared to Ithiel,
to Ithiel and to Ucal:[c]

2 "I am the most ignorant of men;
I do not have a man's understanding.
3 I have not learned wisdom,
nor have I knowledge of the Holy One.
4 Who has gone up to heaven and come down?

[a] *21* The meaning of the Hebrew for this word is uncertain. [b] *1* Or *Jakeh of Massa*
[c] *1* Masoretic Text; with a different word division of the Hebrew *declared, "I am weary, O God; / I am weary, O God, and faint.*

(29:25) You, O Lord, are my salvation. Why should I fear those who can only kill the body and after that can do no more? For fear of man, Abraham denied his wife, Saul forfeited his kingdom, and Peter betrayed his Savior. All of these were foolish deeds, provoked by misplaced fear. But to fear You, my Lord, is the beginning of wisdom. So I will put my trust in You, and I will not be afraid of what anyone else can do to me. (Ge 20:1–11; 1Sa 15:23–24; Ps 111:10; Lk 12:4–7; 22:54–62)

When we were children, the monsters of the dark seemed real and fanged, lurking in the hallway just outside our door. We heard the thunderous footfalls in the gloom. But they turned out to be only our father who heard us crying and came to comfort us. We never saw him in the darkness. But we felt his touch and knew he was there. The universe is vast and sometimes dark, but we are not alone.

Calvin Miller (1936-)

(30:4) We praise Your glorious name: Yahweh, "I AM WHO I AM." It is the name that we adore, though we do not understand it; the name that we cherish, though we cannot measure its value; the name that we fear, though we have seen only a trace of its power. And we exalt the name of Your glorious Son, Jesus, *Yashua*, "Yahweh saves." He has reconciled heaven and earth. "Salvation is found in no one else, for there is no other name under heaven given to men by which we must be saved." You have exalted Him to the highest place and have given Him "the name that is above every name, that at the name of Jesus every knee should bow, in heaven and on earth and under the earth, and every tongue confess that Jesus Christ is Lord, to the glory of God the Father." (Ac 4:12; Php 2:9–11)

O For a thousand tongues to sing
My great Redeemer's praise;
The glories of my God and King,
The triumphs of His grace.

Jesus, the name that charms our fears,
That bids our sorrow cease;
'Tis music in the sinner's ears,
'Tis life and health and peace.

My gracious Master and my God,
Assist me to proclaim,
To spread through all the earth abroad
The honors of Thy name.

"O For A Thousand Tongues To Sing"
Charles Wesley (1739)

When Moses talked with God and asked His name, God replied, "I AM." "I am all that you will need as the occasion arises," He promised Moses. He is all that is needed as our occasions arise as well!

. . . God wants us to know Him. His name assures us that He made us capable of knowing enough to experience His salvation.

Jill Briscoe (1935-)

Who has gathered up the wind in the hollow of his hands?
Who has wrapped up the waters in his cloak?
Who has established all the ends of the earth?
What is his name, and the name of his son?
Tell me if you know!

5 "Every word of God is flawless;
he is a shield to those who take refuge in him.
6 Do not add to his words,
or he will rebuke you and prove you a liar.

7 "Two things I ask of you, O LORD;
do not refuse me before I die:
8 Keep falsehood and lies far from me;
give me neither poverty nor riches,
but give me only my daily bread.
9 Otherwise, I may have too much and disown you
and say, 'Who is the LORD?'
Or I may become poor and steal,
and so dishonor the name of my God.

10 "Do not slander a servant to his master,
or he will curse you, and you will pay for it.

11 "There are those who curse their fathers
and do not bless their mothers;
12 those who are pure in their own eyes
and yet are not cleansed of their filth;
13 those whose eyes are ever so haughty,
whose glances are so disdainful;
14 those whose teeth are swords
and whose jaws are set with knives
to devour the poor from the earth,
the needy from among mankind.

15 "The leech has two daughters.
'Give! Give!' they cry.

"There are three things that are never satisfied,
four that never say, 'Enough!':
16 the grave,[a] the barren womb,
land, which is never satisfied with water,
and fire, which never says, 'Enough!'

17 "The eye that mocks a father,
that scorns obedience to a mother,
will be pecked out by the ravens of the valley,
will be eaten by the vultures.

18 "There are three things that are too amazing for me,
four that I do not understand:
19 the way of an eagle in the sky,
the way of a snake on a rock,
the way of a ship on the high seas,
and the way of a man with a maiden.

20 "This is the way of an adulteress:

[a] *16* Hebrew *Sheol*

She eats and wipes her mouth
and says, 'I've done nothing wrong.'

21 "Under three things the earth trembles,
under four it cannot bear up:
22 a servant who becomes king,
a fool who is full of food,
23 an unloved woman who is married,
and a maidservant who displaces her mistress.

24 "Four things on earth are small,
yet they are extremely wise:
25 Ants are creatures of little strength,
yet they store up their food in the summer;
26 coneys[a] are creatures of little power,
yet they make their home in the crags;
27 locusts have no king,
yet they advance together in ranks;
28 a lizard can be caught with the hand,
yet it is found in kings' palaces.

29 "There are three things that are stately in their stride,
four that move with stately bearing:
30 a lion, mighty among beasts,
who retreats before nothing;
31 a strutting rooster, a he-goat,
and a king with his army around him.[b]

32 "If you have played the fool and exalted yourself,
or if you have planned evil,
clap your hand over your mouth!
33 For as churning the milk produces butter,
and as twisting the nose produces blood,
so stirring up anger produces strife."

Sayings of King Lemuel

31 The sayings of King Lemuel—an oracle[c] his mother taught
him:

2 "O my son, O son of my womb,
O son of my vows,[d]
3 do not spend your strength on women,
your vigor on those who ruin kings.

4 "It is not for kings, O Lemuel—
not for kings to drink wine,
not for rulers to crave beer,
5 lest they drink and forget what the law decrees,
and deprive all the oppressed of their rights.
6 Give beer to those who are perishing,
wine to those who are in anguish;
7 let them drink and forget their poverty
and remember their misery no more.

8 "Speak up for those who cannot speak for themselves,
for the rights of all who are destitute.
9 Speak up and judge fairly;
defend the rights of the poor and needy."

[a] *26* That is, the hyrax or rock badger [b] *31* Or *king secure against revolt* [c] *1* Or *of Lemuel king of Massa, which* [d] *2* Or */ the answer to my prayers*

(31:8) Lord, I am so grateful that You love us, regardless of our appearance, our wealth, our social or political status. We cannot impress You, nor do we need to. You have chosen those who are poor in the eyes of the world to be rich in faith and to inherit the kingdom. In light of this, Father God, give me a compassionate heart. Help me to be as impartial in my love of others as You have been in loving me. (Jas 2:1–5)

It can be so easy at times to say we love people, and be completely honest and sincere in our expression. But so often we don't see the lonely person in the crowd, or the sick or destitute man or woman whose only hope of escape may be the love we can give through Christ. The love God would have us show reaches down to each person.

Billy Graham (1918-)

Epilogue: The Wife of Noble Character

10[a] A wife of noble character who can find?
She is worth far more than rubies.
11 Her husband has full confidence in her
and lacks nothing of value.
12 She brings him good, not harm,
all the days of her life.
13 She selects wool and flax
and works with eager hands.
14 She is like the merchant ships,
bringing her food from afar.
15 She gets up while it is still dark;
she provides food for her family
and portions for her servant girls.
16 She considers a field and buys it;
out of her earnings she plants a vineyard.
17 She sets about her work vigorously;
her arms are strong for her tasks.
18 She sees that her trading is profitable,
and her lamp does not go out at night.
19 In her hand she holds the distaff
and grasps the spindle with her fingers.
20 She opens her arms to the poor
and extends her hands to the needy.
21 When it snows, she has no fear for her household;
for all of them are clothed in scarlet.
22 She makes coverings for her bed;
she is clothed in fine linen and purple.
23 Her husband is respected at the city gate,
where he takes his seat among the elders of the land.
24 She makes linen garments and sells them,
and supplies the merchants with sashes.
25 She is clothed with strength and dignity;
she can laugh at the days to come.
26 She speaks with wisdom,
and faithful instruction is on her tongue.
27 She watches over the affairs of her household
and does not eat the bread of idleness.
28 Her children arise and call her blessed;
her husband also, and he praises her:
29 "Many women do noble things,
but you surpass them all."
30 Charm is deceptive, and beauty is fleeting;
but a woman who fears the LORD is to be praised.
31 Give her the reward she has earned,
and let her works bring her praise at the city gate.

(31:30) Free me, Lord, from the world's distorted standards. I am too easily enchanted by a charming smile, attracted to fashionable clothing and seduced by beautiful faces. You never intended that I see the world—or myself—through the eyes of the flesh, but I do it anyway. Give me Your eyes, Your wisdom and Your insight. Your Word has taught me that You do not look at the outward appearance; rather, You look at the heart. Please, make my heart right before You, Lord, so that You will be pleased with what You see. (1Sa 16:7)

John defines the believer's victory over the world as "our faith." In a general sense, our faith includes the whole body of revealed truth which has come to us by the revelation of God. Our faith overcomes the world in this sense by the inner assimilation of God's revealed Word. [As the believer becomes grounded in the faith through his understanding of God's Word, all worldly values are measured and overcome by the truth of the Word.]

Mark I. Bubeck (1928-)

[a] *10* Verses 10–31 are an acrostic, each verse beginning with a successive letter of the Hebrew alphabet.

ECCLESIATES

or, The Teacher

Ecclesiastes

"'Meaningless! Meaningless!' says the Teacher. 'Utterly meaningless! Everything is meaningless'" (1:1). How can such cynical expressions belong to the Bible? Scripture acknowledges the authentic disillusionment that many feel after searching fruitlessly for personal fulfillment. "Yet when I surveyed all that my hands had done and what I had toiled to achieve, everything was meaningless, a chasing after the wind; nothing was gained under the sun" (2:11).

The author of Ecclesiastes is known only as "the Teacher" (Heb. *Qoheleth*), although tradition and textual cues connect him with King Solomon. The book contains a lengthy speech (1:12—12:8), preceded by a brief introduction (1:1–11) and followed by an epilogue (12:8–14).

The Teacher's message is a bracing confession of his struggle to find meaning in life. His view of the world is often cynical and jaded. His gut-wrenching honesty enlightens our own struggle for a purposeful life. It also models for us how to be honest with God about our own doubts. The Teacher's message may seem shocking to us, but it doesn't offend God. God is more interested in the things on our hearts, however rough, than He is in the polished words we use to impress Him. For all of his cynicism, the Teacher does not question his relationship to God or deny God's goodness.

God is more interested in the things on our hearts, however rough, than He is in the polished words we use to impress Him.

Ecclesiastes also reminds us to cultivate humility before God. We who know God through Jesus Christ and through the Bible must not forget how much bigger God is than our pint-sized conceptions of Him. We must guard against undue self-confidence when we worship a God Who is free and sovereign. His ways are mysterious. Ecclesiastes is an antidote to the venom of glib platitudes and repetitious chatter in worship. As the Teacher says: "Guard your steps when you go to the house of God. Go near to listen rather than to offer the sacrifice of fools, who do not know that they do wrong. Do not be quick with your mouth, do not be hasty in your heart to utter anything before God. God is in heaven and you are on earth, so let your words be few" (5:1–2).

The Preacher's message prepares us for the coming of Christ, the only source of true, lasting meaning. Dillard and Longman observe, "As we turn to the New Testament, we see that Jesus Christ is the one who redeems us from the vanity, the meaninglessness under which Qoheleth suffered. Jesus is the Son of God, but nonetheless He experienced the vanity of the world so that He could free us from it." How thankful we are that God has come in Christ to show us what life is all about and to deliver us from the quicksand of meaninglessness.

*Dillard, Raymond and Longman, Tremper. *An Introduction to the Old Testament.* © 1994, Zondervan Publishing House; p. 255.

(1:1–18) "Forget the former things; do not dwell on the past. See, I am doing a new thing! Now it springs up; do you not perceive it? I am making a way in the desert and streams in the wasteland." Almighty God, apart from You there is nothing new. There is no refreshment. All things are meaningless. We are discontented with what we have and dissatisfied with what we get. We confess our appetites and our emptiness, our frailty and our futility, our faithlessness and our failures. But Your compassions never fail. They are new every morning. Open our eyes to see the new things You are doing today. Help us to forget the former things and press on toward the goal so that we may live a new life and serve in the new way of the Spirit. (Isa 43:18–19; La 3:22–23; Ro 6:4; 7:6; Php 3:13–14)

You are the living Truth;
All wisdom dwells in You,
The source of ev'ry skill,
The One Eternal true!
O great I AM, in You we rest,
Sure answer to our ev'ry quest.

"We Come, O Christ, to You"
Margaret Clarkson (©1957, 1985)

Everything Is Meaningless

1 The words of the Teacher,[a] son of David, king in Jerusalem:

2 "Meaningless! Meaningless!"
says the Teacher.
"Utterly meaningless!
Everything is meaningless."
3 What does man gain from all his labor
at which he toils under the sun?
4 Generations come and generations go,
but the earth remains forever.
5 The sun rises and the sun sets,
and hurries back to where it rises.
6 The wind blows to the south
and turns to the north;
round and round it goes,
ever returning on its course.
7 All streams flow into the sea,
yet the sea is never full.
To the place the streams come from,
there they return again.
8 All things are wearisome,
more than one can say.
The eye never has enough of seeing,
nor the ear its fill of hearing.
9 What has been will be again,
what has been done will be done again;
there is nothing new under the sun.
10 Is there anything of which one can say,
"Look! This is something new"?
It was here already, long ago;
it was here before our time.
11 There is no remembrance of men of old,
and even those who are yet to come
will not be remembered
by those who follow.

Wisdom Is Meaningless

12 I, the Teacher, was king over Israel in Jerusalem. 13 I devoted myself to study and to explore by wisdom all that is done under
heaven. What a heavy burden God has laid on men! 14 I have seen
all the things that are done under the sun; all of them are meaningless, a chasing after the wind.

15 What is twisted cannot be straightened;
what is lacking cannot be counted.

16 I thought to myself, "Look, I have grown and increased in
wisdom more than anyone who has ruled over Jerusalem before
me; I have experienced much of wisdom and knowledge." 17 Then
I applied myself to the understanding of wisdom, and also of
madness and folly, but I learned that this, too, is a chasing after
the wind.

18 For with much wisdom comes much sorrow;
the more knowledge, the more grief.

[a] 1 Or *leader of the assembly*; also in verses 2 and 12

Pleasures Are Meaningless

2 I thought in my heart, "Come now, I will test you with pleasure to find out what is good." But that also proved to be
meaningless. 2"Laughter," I said, "is foolish. And what does pleasure accomplish?" 3I tried cheering myself with wine, and embracing folly—my mind still guiding me with wisdom. I wanted to
see what was worthwhile for men to do under heaven during the
few days of their lives.

4I undertook great projects: I built houses for myself and
planted vineyards. 5I made gardens and parks and planted all
kinds of fruit trees in them. 6I made reservoirs to water groves of
flourishing trees. 7I bought male and female slaves and had other
slaves who were born in my house. I also owned more herds and
flocks than anyone in Jerusalem before me. 8I amassed silver and
gold for myself, and the treasure of kings and provinces. I acquired men and women singers, and a harem[a] as well—the delights of the heart of man. 9I became greater by far than anyone
in Jerusalem before me. In all this my wisdom stayed with me.

10I denied myself nothing my eyes desired;
   I refused my heart no pleasure.
My heart took delight in all my work,
   and this was the reward for all my labor.
11Yet when I surveyed all that my hands had done
   and what I had toiled to achieve,
everything was meaningless, a chasing after the wind;
   nothing was gained under the sun.

Wisdom and Folly Are Meaningless

12Then I turned my thoughts to consider wisdom,
   and also madness and folly.
What more can the king's successor do
   than what has already been done?
13I saw that wisdom is better than folly,
   just as light is better than darkness.
14The wise man has eyes in his head,
   while the fool walks in the darkness;
but I came to realize
   that the same fate overtakes them both.

15Then I thought in my heart,

"The fate of the fool will overtake me also.
   What then do I gain by being wise?"
I said in my heart,
   "This too is meaningless."
16For the wise man, like the fool, will not be long
      remembered;
   in days to come both will be forgotten.
Like the fool, the wise man too must die!

Toil Is Meaningless

17So I hated life, because the work that is done under the sun
was grievous to me. All of it is meaningless, a chasing after the
wind. 18I hated all the things I had toiled for under the sun, because I must leave them to the one who comes after me. 19And
who knows whether he will be a wise man or a fool? Yet he will

[a] 8 The meaning of the Hebrew for this phrase is uncertain.

(2:10–11) How often I delight in what I have done: my achievements, my victories, my possessions, my family . . . my, my, my. But what is it all worth apart from You, Holy God? "Unless the Lord builds the house, its builders labor in vain." Unless You work through me, my labors will be empty. Unless I abide in You, I can do nothing that matters. Unless I do Your bidding, my life will never bear fruit that will last. But when I live by Your grace and for Your glory, then my toil will not be in vain. Help me, Lord, to devote my life to doing Your will, for then I will have treasures in heaven, treasures that will last for eternity. (Ps 127:1; Isa 65:19–23; Mt 6:19–21; Jn 15:5)

Not as I will, but as thou wilt. To be able to say these words and truly mean them is the highest point we can ever hope to attain. Then, indeed, we have broken out of time's hard shell to breathe, not its stale air, but the fresh, exhilarating atmosphere of eternity.

Malcolm Muggeridge (1903-1990)

God and man exist for each other and neither is satisfied without the other.

A.W. Tozer (1897-1963)

In His time, in His time.
He makes all things beautiful
In His time.
Lord, please show me every day
As You're teaching me Your way,
That You do just what You say
In Your time.

"In His Time"
Diane Ball (©1978)

(3:10–14) You have set eternity in my heart, O God. Even as I drink deeply from the cup of human happiness poured for me from Your hand, I yearn with a more profound thirst. Your good gifts—of food and drink, of work and rest—provide temporary delight. Yet they also give me a longing for that which will never pass away. Through the joys of my life I hunger for an even greater joy: to revere You all of my days and to dwell in Your house forever. Nothing compares to You, everlasting Lord. Nothing satisfies as You alone can satisfy. (Ps 84:4,10)

You have eternal life
Implanted in the soul;
Your love shall be our strength and stay,
While ages roll.
We praise You, living God!
We praise Your holy name;
The first, the last, beyond all thought,
And still the same!

"The God of Abraham Praise"
Daniel ben Judah (1404)
Trans. Max Landsberg and Newton Mann (1855)

have control over all the work into which I have poured my effort
and skill under the sun. This too is meaningless. 20So my heart
began to despair over all my toilsome labor under the sun. 21For
a man may do his work with wisdom, knowledge and skill, and
then he must leave all he owns to someone who has not worked
for it. This too is meaningless and a great misfortune. 22What
does a man get for all the toil and anxious striving with which he
labors under the sun? 23All his days his work is pain and grief;
even at night his mind does not rest. This too is meaningless.
24A man can do nothing better than to eat and drink and find
satisfaction in his work. This too, I see, is from the hand of God,
25for without him, who can eat or find enjoyment? 26To the man
who pleases him, God gives wisdom, knowledge and happiness,
but to the sinner he gives the task of gathering and storing up
wealth to hand it over to the one who pleases God. This too is
meaningless, a chasing after the wind.

A Time for Everything

3 There is a time for everything,
and a season for every activity under heaven:

2 a time to be born and a time to die,
a time to plant and a time to uproot,
3 a time to kill and a time to heal,
a time to tear down and a time to build,
4 a time to weep and a time to laugh,
a time to mourn and a time to dance,
5 a time to scatter stones and a time to gather them,
a time to embrace and a time to refrain,
6 a time to search and a time to give up,
a time to keep and a time to throw away,
7 a time to tear and a time to mend,
a time to be silent and a time to speak,
8 a time to love and a time to hate,
a time for war and a time for peace.

9What does the worker gain from his toil? 10I have seen the
burden God has laid on men. 11He has made everything beautiful
in its time. He has also set eternity in the hearts of men; yet they
cannot fathom what God has done from beginning to end. 12I
know that there is nothing better for men than to be happy and do
good while they live. 13That everyone may eat and drink, and find
satisfaction in all his toil—this is the gift of God. 14I know that
everything God does will endure forever; nothing can be added to
it and nothing taken from it. God does it so that men will revere
him.

15Whatever is has already been,
and what will be has been before;
and God will call the past to account.[a]

16And I saw something else under the sun:

In the place of judgment—wickedness was there,
in the place of justice—wickedness was there.

17I thought in my heart,
"God will bring to judgment

[a] 15 Or *God calls back the past*

both the righteous and the wicked,
for there will be a time for every activity,
a time for every deed."

18 I also thought, "As for men, God tests them so that they may
see that they are like the animals. 19 Man's fate is like that of the
animals; the same fate awaits them both: As one dies, so dies the
other. All have the same breath[a]; man has no advantage over the
animal. Everything is meaningless. 20 All go to the same place; all
come from dust, and to dust all return. 21 Who knows if the spirit of man rises upward and if the spirit of the animal[b] goes down
into the earth?"

22 So I saw that there is nothing better for a man than to enjoy
his work, because that is his lot. For who can bring him to see
what will happen after him?

Oppression, Toil, Friendlessness

4 Again I looked and saw all the oppression that was taking place under the sun:

I saw the tears of the oppressed—
and they have no comforter;
power was on the side of their oppressors—
and they have no comforter.
2 And I declared that the dead,
who had already died,
are happier than the living,
who are still alive.
3 But better than both
is he who has not yet been,
who has not seen the evil
that is done under the sun.

4 And I saw that all labor and all achievement spring from
man's envy of his neighbor. This too is meaningless, a chasing
after the wind.

5 The fool folds his hands
and ruins himself.
6 Better one handful with tranquillity
than two handfuls with toil
and chasing after the wind.

7 Again I saw something meaningless under the sun:
8 There was a man all alone;
he had neither son nor brother.
There was no end to his toil,
yet his eyes were not content with his wealth.
"For whom am I toiling," he asked,
"and why am I depriving myself of enjoyment?"
This too is meaningless—
a miserable business!

9 Two are better than one,
because they have a good return for their work:
10 If one falls down,
his friend can help him up.

[a] 19 Or *spirit* [b] 21 Or *Who knows the spirit of man, which rises upward, or the spirit of the animal, which*

Surely God would not have created such a being as man . . . to exist only for a day! No, no, man was made for immortality.
Abraham Lincoln (1809-1865)

(3:18–21) God of the first creation, You formed us from the dust and breathed into us the breath of life. You made us to live forever in perfect fellowship with You. But we turned our backs on You and on Your design for us. Our dusty nature became dirty as we wallowed in sin. Rather than enjoying eternal life, we became mired in the quicksand of death. So, as we have come from dust, to dust we shall return. But, by Your grace, physical death is not the end. Indeed, at the last trumpet we shall be changed. Through Christ our perishable bodies will be clothed with the imperishable, our mortal flesh with immortality. Thanks be to You, God of the new creation! You give us the victory through our Lord Jesus Christ. (1Co 15:51–57).

Finish, then, Thy new creation;
Pure and spotless let us be;
Let us see Thy great salvation
Perfectly restored in Thee;
Changed from glory into glory,
Till in heaven we take our place,
Till we cast our crowns before Thee,
Lost in wonder, love, and praise.
"Love Divine, All Loves Excelling"
Charles Wesley (1747)

There is hardly ever a complete silence in our soul. God is whispering to us well-nigh incessantly. Whenever the sounds of the world die out in the soul, or sink low, then we hear these whisperings of God. He is always whispering to us, only we do not always hear because of the noise, hurry, and the distraction that life causes as it rushes on.

Frederick William Faber (1814-1863)

(5:1–7) Awesome God, I confess my inclination to rush into Your presence overflowing with many words. My private devotions are filled with my agendas for You. My public worship can be so flooded with noise that You would not be able to get a word in edgewise. I confess my failure to listen for Your voice. Too seldom do I wait in silence before You as a servant waits before a king. Help me, O Word of God, to learn to listen to You. Teach me to still my soul as a child with its mother. Give me a renewed vision of Your holiness, so that when I speak to You it might be with reverence and respect. (Ps 131:2; Hab 2:20)

Let all mortal flesh keep silence,
And with fear and trembling stand;
Ponder nothing worldly minded,
For with blessing in His hand
Christ our God to earth descendeth,
Our full homage to demand.

"Let All Mortal Flesh Keep Silence"
Liturgy of St. James (4th c.)
Trans. Gerard Moultrie (1829-1885)

But pity the man who falls
and has no one to help him up!
11 Also, if two lie down together, they will keep warm.
But how can one keep warm alone?
12 Though one may be overpowered,
two can defend themselves.
A cord of three strands is not quickly broken.

Advancement Is Meaningless

13 Better a poor but wise youth than an old but foolish king who
no longer knows how to take warning. 14 The youth may have
come from prison to the kingship, or he may have been born in
poverty within his kingdom. 15 I saw that all who lived and walked
under the sun followed the youth, the king's successor. 16 There
was no end to all the people who were before them. But those
who came later were not pleased with the successor. This too is
meaningless, a chasing after the wind.

Stand in Awe of God

5 Guard your steps when you go to the house of God. Go near
to listen rather than to offer the sacrifice of fools, who do not
know that they do wrong.

2 Do not be quick with your mouth,
do not be hasty in your heart
to utter anything before God.
God is in heaven
and you are on earth,
so let your words be few.
3 As a dream comes when there are many cares,
so the speech of a fool when there are many
words.

4 When you make a vow to God, do not delay in fulfilling it. He
has no pleasure in fools; fulfill your vow. 5 It is better not to vow
than to make a vow and not fulfill it. 6 Do not let your mouth lead
you into sin. And do not protest to the ⌊temple⌋ messenger, "My
vow was a mistake." Why should God be angry at what you say
and destroy the work of your hands? 7 Much dreaming and many
words are meaningless. Therefore stand in awe of God.

Riches Are Meaningless

8 If you see the poor oppressed in a district, and justice and
rights denied, do not be surprised at such things; for one official
is eyed by a higher one, and over them both are others higher
still. 9 The increase from the land is taken by all; the king himself
profits from the fields.

10 Whoever loves money never has money enough;
whoever loves wealth is never satisfied with his
income.
This too is meaningless.

11 As goods increase,
so do those who consume them.
And what benefit are they to the owner
except to feast his eyes on them?

12 The sleep of a laborer is sweet,
whether he eats little or much,

but the abundance of a rich man
permits him no sleep.

13 I have seen a grievous evil under the sun:

wealth hoarded to the harm of its owner,
14 or wealth lost through some misfortune,
so that when he has a son
there is nothing left for him.
15 Naked a man comes from his mother's womb,
and as he comes, so he departs.
He takes nothing from his labor
that he can carry in his hand.

16 This too is a grievous evil:

As a man comes, so he departs,
and what does he gain,
since he toils for the wind?
17 All his days he eats in darkness,
with great frustration, affliction and anger.

18 Then I realized that it is good and proper for a man to eat
and drink, and to find satisfaction in his toilsome labor under the
sun during the few days of life God has given him—for this is his
lot. 19 Moreover, when God gives any man wealth and possessions,
and enables him to enjoy them, to accept his lot and be happy in
his work—this is a gift of God. 20 He seldom reflects on the days
of his life, because God keeps him occupied with gladness of
heart.

6 I have seen another evil under the sun, and it weighs heavily on men:
2 God gives a man wealth, possessions and honor,
so that he lacks nothing his heart desires, but God does not enable him to enjoy them, and a stranger enjoys them instead. This
is meaningless, a grievous evil.
3 A man may have a hundred children and live many years; yet
no matter how long he lives, if he cannot enjoy his prosperity and
does not receive proper burial, I say that a stillborn child is better off than he.
4 It comes without meaning, it departs in darkness, and in darkness its name is shrouded.
5 Though it never saw
the sun or knew anything, it has more rest than does that man—
6 even if he lives a thousand years twice over but fails to enjoy his
prosperity. Do not all go to the same place?

7 All man's efforts are for his mouth,
yet his appetite is never satisfied.
8 What advantage has a wise man
over a fool?
What does a poor man gain
by knowing how to conduct himself before others?
9 Better what the eye sees
than the roving of the appetite.
This too is meaningless,
a chasing after the wind.
10 Whatever exists has already been named,
and what man is has been known;
no man can contend
with one who is stronger than he.
11 The more the words,

God's gifts put man's best dreams to shame.

Elizabeth Barrett Browning (1806-1861)

(5:18–19) Gracious God, thank You for the gift of perspective that these verses bring. Thank You for the gift of life, for the joys of each new day. Thank You for simple gifts of food to eat and water to drink. Thank You for work to do, even when that work is hard or monotonous. Thank You for the grace to be content in all circumstances, both in times of plenty and in times of need. And when You give extra blessings, whether they be material or spiritual, thank You for the ability to enjoy them. Indeed, all good gifts, including the gift of satisfaction, come from You. Thank You, Heavenly Father, for Your boundless generosity! (Php 4:11–12; 1Ti 6:6–10; Jas 1:17)

Now thank we all our God
With heart and hands and voices,
Who wondrous things hath done,
In whom His world rejoices;
Who, from our mother's arms,
Hath blessed us on our way
With countless gifts of love,
And still is ours today.

O may this bounteous God
Through all our life be near us,
With ever joyful hearts
And blessed peace to cheer us;
And keep us in His grace
And guide us when perplexed,
And free us from all ills
In this world and the next

"Now Thank We All Our God"
Martin Rinkart (1636)
Trans. Catherine Winkworth (1829-1878)

the less the meaning,
and how does that profit anyone?

12 For who knows what is good for a man in life, during the few and meaningless days he passes through like a shadow? Who can tell him what will happen under the sun after he is gone?

Wisdom

7 A good name is better than fine perfume,
and the day of death better than the day of birth.
2 It is better to go to a house of mourning
than to go to a house of feasting,
for death is the destiny of every man;
the living should take this to heart.
3 Sorrow is better than laughter,
because a sad face is good for the heart.
4 The heart of the wise is in the house of mourning,
but the heart of fools is in the house of pleasure.
5 It is better to heed a wise man's rebuke
than to listen to the song of fools.
6 Like the crackling of thorns under the pot,
so is the laughter of fools.
This too is meaningless.
7 Extortion turns a wise man into a fool,
and a bribe corrupts the heart.
8 The end of a matter is better than its beginning,
and patience is better than pride.
9 Do not be quickly provoked in your spirit,
for anger resides in the lap of fools.
10 Do not say, "Why were the old days better than these?"
For it is not wise to ask such questions.
11 Wisdom, like an inheritance, is a good thing
and benefits those who see the sun.
12 Wisdom is a shelter
as money is a shelter,
but the advantage of knowledge is this:
that wisdom preserves the life of its possessor.
13 Consider what God has done:

Who can straighten
what he has made crooked?
14 When times are good, be happy;
but when times are bad, consider:
God has made the one
as well as the other.
Therefore, a man cannot discover
anything about his future.

15 In this meaningless life of mine I have seen both of these:

a righteous man perishing in his righteousness,
and a wicked man living long in his wickedness.
16 Do not be overrighteous,
neither be overwise—
why destroy yourself?
17 Do not be overwicked,
and do not be a fool—

If God does not know what is best for us, who would?
Erwin W. Lutzer (1941-)

(6:12) Who knows what is good for me in this life, O Lord? Surely not I. For how often have my best laid plans brought me to despair? Surely this world does not know what is good for me. The promised freedom of its moral relativism has led me into bondage. The clever philosophies and self-realizing therapies of my culture have failed to satisfy. So, who knows what is good for me? Surely You do, all-knowing God. Even before the foundation of the world You had my ultimate purpose in mind. When You saved me by grace, You created me anew for good works that are to be my way of life. (Eph 2:8–10)

why die before your time?
18 It is good to grasp the one
and not let go of the other.
The man who fears God will avoid all ⌊extremes⌋.[a]

19 Wisdom makes one wise man more powerful
than ten rulers in a city.

20 There is not a righteous man on earth
who does what is right and never sins.

21 Do not pay attention to every word people say,
or you may hear your servant cursing you—
22 for you know in your heart
that many times you yourself have cursed others.

23 All this I tested by wisdom and I said,
"I am determined to be wise"—
but this was beyond me.
24 Whatever wisdom may be,
it is far off and most profound—
who can discover it?
25 So I turned my mind to understand,
to investigate and to search out wisdom and the scheme of things
and to understand the stupidity of wickedness
and the madness of folly.

26 I find more bitter than death
the woman who is a snare,
whose heart is a trap
and whose hands are chains.
The man who pleases God will escape her,
but the sinner she will ensnare.

27 "Look," says the Teacher,[b] "this is what I have discovered:

"Adding one thing to another to discover the scheme of things—
28 while I was still searching
but not finding—
I found one ⌊upright⌋ man among a thousand,
but not one ⌊upright⌋ woman among them all.
29 This only have I found:
God made mankind upright,
but men have gone in search of many schemes."

8 Who is like the wise man?
Who knows the explanation of things?
Wisdom brightens a man's face
and changes its hard appearance.

Obey the King

2 Obey the king's command, I say, because you took an oath before God. 3 Do not be in a hurry to leave the king's presence. Do not stand up for a bad cause, for he will do whatever he pleases. 4 Since a king's word is supreme, who can say to him, "What are you doing?"

[a] 18 Or *will follow them both* [b] 27 Or *leader of the assembly*

The simple shepherds heard the voice of an angel and found their Lamb; the wise men saw the light of a star and found their Wisdom.

Archbishop Fulton J. Sheen (1895-1979)

(7:23–24) Your wisdom, O God, is higher than I can reach and deeper than I can fathom. How then can I hope to comprehend it? How can I become wise if Your wisdom is so far away? Praise be to You, Gracious God, for Christ Jesus is Your gift of wisdom to us. Your Word became flesh in Jesus and lived among us. In the incarnation You bridged the chasm of our ignorance. Help me to know Christ, so that in Him I might receive and walk in Your otherwise incomprehensible wisdom. (Jn 1:14; 1Cor 1:20–30; Jas 1:5)

Be Thou my Wisdom and Thou my true Word;
I ever with Thee and Thou with me, Lord;
Thou my great Father, I thy true son;
Thou in me dwelling and I with Thee one.

"Be Thou My Vision"
Ancient Irish Hymn (8th c.)
Trans. Mary E. Byrne (1880-1931)
Versified by Eleanor H. Hull (1860-1935)

5 Whoever obeys his command will come to no harm,
and the wise heart will know the proper time and procedure.
6 For there is a proper time and procedure for every matter,
though a man's misery weighs heavily upon him.

7 Since no man knows the future,
who can tell him what is to come?
8 No man has power over the wind to contain it[a];
so no one has power over the day of his death.
As no one is discharged in time of war,
so wickedness will not release those who practice it.

9 All this I saw, as I applied my mind to everything done under
the sun. There is a time when a man lords it over others to his
own[b] hurt. 10 Then too, I saw the wicked buried—those who
used to come and go from the holy place and receive praise[c] in
the city where they did this. This too is meaningless.
11 When the sentence for a crime is not quickly carried out, the
hearts of the people are filled with schemes to do wrong. 12 Although a wicked man commits a hundred crimes and still lives a
long time, I know that it will go better with God-fearing men, who
are reverent before God. 13 Yet because the wicked do not fear
God, it will not go well with them, and their days will not length-
en like a shadow.
14 There is something else meaningless that occurs on earth:
righteous men who get what the wicked deserve, and wicked men
who get what the righteous deserve. This too, I say, is meaningless. 15 So I commend the enjoyment of life, because nothing is
better for a man under the sun than to eat and drink and be glad.
Then joy will accompany him in his work all the days of the life
God has given him under the sun.
16 When I applied my mind to know wisdom and to observe
man's labor on earth—his eyes not seeing sleep day or night—
17 then I saw all that God has done. No one can comprehend what
goes on under the sun. Despite all his efforts to search it out, man
cannot discover its meaning. Even if a wise man claims he knows,
he cannot really comprehend it.

(8:15) Thank You, blessed and blessing God, for all the joys of human life—for the playful repast of a summer picnic, for the fragrant bounty of a holiday dinner around the family table, for the joyful feasting of a wedding reception. In these simple, human delights we sample a foretaste of heaven, when we will sit at Your table in glory. O Jesus, who once enriched a wedding feast with a gift of fine wine, I thirst for the new wine of Your kingdom. I long to dine with You at the heavenly feast that will never come to an end! (Lk 14:15; Jn 2:1–11)

A Common Destiny for All

9 So I reflected on all this and concluded that the righteous
and the wise and what they do are in God's hands, but no
man knows whether love or hate awaits him. 2 All share a common destiny—the righteous and the wicked, the good and the
bad,[d] the clean and the unclean, those who offer sacrifices and
those who do not.

As it is with the good man,
so with the sinner;
as it is with those who take oaths,
so with those who are afraid to take them.

3 This is the evil in everything that happens under the sun: The
same destiny overtakes all. The hearts of men, moreover, are full

[a] 8 Or *over his spirit to retain it* [b] 9 Or *to their* [c] 10 Some Hebrew manuscripts and Septuagint (Aquila); most Hebrew manuscripts *and are forgotten* [d] 2 Septuagint (Aquila), Vulgate and Syriac; Hebrew does not have *and the bad.*

of evil and there is madness in their hearts while they live, and
afterward they join the dead. [4]Anyone who is among the living
has hope[a]—even a live dog is better off than a dead lion!

[5]For the living know that they will die,
but the dead know nothing;
they have no further reward,
and even the memory of them is
forgotten.
[6]Their love, their hate
and their jealousy have long since vanished;
never again will they have a part
in anything that happens under the sun.

[7]Go, eat your food with gladness, and drink your wine with a
joyful heart, for it is now that God favors what you do. [8]Always
be clothed in white, and always anoint your head with oil.
[9]Enjoy life with your wife, whom you love, all the days of this
meaningless life that God has given you under the sun— all
your meaningless days. For this is your lot in life and in your
toilsome labor under the sun. [10]Whatever your hand finds to
do, do it with all your might, for in the grave,[b] where you are
going, there is neither working nor planning nor knowledge nor
wisdom.

[11]I have seen something else under the sun:

The race is not to the swift
or the battle to the strong,
nor does food come to the wise
or wealth to the brilliant
or favor to the learned;
but time and chance happen to them all.

[12]Moreover, no man knows when his hour will come:

As fish are caught in a cruel net,
or birds are taken in a snare,
so men are trapped by evil times
that fall unexpectedly upon them.

Wisdom Better Than Folly

[13]I also saw under the sun this example of wisdom that greatly impressed me: [14]There was once a small city with only a few
people in it. And a powerful king came against it, surrounded it
and built huge siegeworks against it. [15]Now there lived in that
city a man poor but wise, and he saved the city by his wisdom.
But nobody remembered that poor man. [16]So I said, "Wisdom
is better than strength." But the poor man's wisdom is despised,
and his words are no longer heeded.

[17]The quiet words of the wise are more to be heeded
than the shouts of a ruler of fools.
[18]Wisdom is better than weapons of war,
but one sinner destroys much good.

10 As dead flies give perfume a bad smell,
so a little folly outweighs wisdom and honor.
[2]The heart of the wise inclines to the right,

[a] 4 Or *What then is to be chosen? With all who live, there is hope* [b] 10 Hebrew *Sheol*

(9:14–16) Though we are called to serve our loved ones, our neighbors, and our country, let us not live for the fleeting accolades or fickle memory of humanity; rather, let us live for the pleasure of the One who never forgets. Let us find our fulfillment in the assurance that it is You we are serving, and that You know our every thought and deed, our every intention and motive. You are a just God; You will not forget our work and the love we have shown You as we have helped others. Surely You will reward each person according to what he has done. (Ps 62:12; Jer 17:10; Mt 6:1; 16:27; Col 3:23–24; Heb 6:10; Rev 22:12)

O perfect life of Christ, my Lord!
I want to be like Jesus.
My recompense and my reward
That I may be like Jesus.
His Spirit fill my hung'ring soul,
His power all my life control.
My deepest prayer, my highest goal
That I may be like Jesus.

"I Want to Be Like Jesus"
Thomas O. Chisholm (©1945, 1973)

Nothing that is God's is obtainable by money.

Tertullian (c.160–after 220)

(10:19) Almighty God, money can make such a difference. It buys food and clothing, enrichment and entertainment. It pays for medical care and Christian ministry. It feeds the poor and shelters the homeless. Yet for all of its benefits, money is absolutely worthless when compared to You. For "what good is it for a man to gain the whole world, yet forfeit his soul? Or what can a man give in exchange for his soul?" When we struggle in poverty, You offer the free gift of grace, saying: "Come, all you who are thirsty, come to the waters; and you who have no money, come, buy and eat! Come, buy wine and milk without money and without cost." For the benefits of money we give You thanks, O Lord. For Your all-surpassing value we lift up our praise. For the free gift of Your grace we offer ourselves in return, as a precious sacrifice to You. (Ps 19:9–10; Pr 8:10–11; Isa 55:1–2; Mk 8:34–37; Ro 12:–2)

O the unsearchable riches of Christ!
Wealth that can never be told!
Riches exhaustless of mercy and
grace,
Precious, more precious than gold!

"Unsearchable Riches"
Fanny J. Crosby (1820-1915)

but the heart of the fool to the left.
3 Even as he walks along the road,
the fool lacks sense
and shows everyone how stupid he is.
4 If a ruler's anger rises against you,
do not leave your post;
calmness can lay great errors to rest.

5 There is an evil I have seen under the sun,
the sort of error that arises from a ruler:
6 Fools are put in many high positions,
while the rich occupy the low ones.
7 I have seen slaves on horseback,
while princes go on foot like slaves.

8 Whoever digs a pit may fall into it;
whoever breaks through a wall may be bitten by a snake.
9 Whoever quarries stones may be injured by them;
whoever splits logs may be endangered by them.
10 If the ax is dull
and its edge unsharpened,
more strength is needed
but skill will bring success.

11 If a snake bites before it is charmed,
there is no profit for the charmer.

12 Words from a wise man's mouth are gracious,
but a fool is consumed by his own lips.
13 At the beginning his words are folly;
at the end they are wicked madness—
14 and the fool multiplies words.

No one knows what is coming—
who can tell him what will happen after him?

15 A fool's work wearies him;
he does not know the way to town.

16 Woe to you, O land whose king was a servant[a]
and whose princes feast in the morning.
17 Blessed are you, O land whose king is of noble birth
and whose princes eat at a proper time—
for strength and not for drunkenness.

18 If a man is lazy, the rafters sag;
if his hands are idle, the house leaks.

19 A feast is made for laughter,
and wine makes life merry,
but money is the answer for everything.

20 Do not revile the king even in your thoughts,
or curse the rich in your bedroom,
because a bird of the air may carry your words,
and a bird on the wing may report what you say.

[a] 16 Or *king is a child*

Bread Upon the Waters

11 Cast your bread upon the waters,
for after many days you will find it again.
2 Give portions to seven, yes to eight,
for you do not know what disaster may come upon the land.
3 If clouds are full of water,
they pour rain upon the earth.
Whether a tree falls to the south or to the north,
in the place where it falls, there will it lie.
4 Whoever watches the wind will not plant;
whoever looks at the clouds will not reap.
5 As you do not know the path of the wind,
or how the body is formed[a] in a mother's womb,
so you cannot understand the work of God,
the Maker of all things.
6 Sow your seed in the morning,
and at evening let not your hands be idle,
for you do not know which will succeed,
whether this or that,
or whether both will do equally well.

Remember Your Creator While Young

7 Light is sweet,
and it pleases the eyes to see the sun.
8 However many years a man may live,
let him enjoy them all.
But let him remember the days of darkness,
for they will be many.
Everything to come is meaningless.
9 Be happy, young man, while you are young,
and let your heart give you joy in the days of your youth.
Follow the ways of your heart
and whatever your eyes see,
but know that for all these things
God will bring you to judgment.
10 So then, banish anxiety from your heart
and cast off the troubles of your body,
for youth and vigor are meaningless.

12 Remember your Creator
in the days of your youth,
before the days of trouble come
and the years approach when you will say,
"I find no pleasure in them"—
2 before the sun and the light
and the moon and the stars grow dark,
and the clouds return after the rain;
3 when the keepers of the house tremble,
and the strong men stoop,
when the grinders cease because they are few,
and those looking through the windows grow dim;
4 when the doors to the street are closed

[a]5 Or *know how life* (or *the spirit*) */ enters the body being formed*

(11:5) How and when does the soul enter the body? Where does the wind begin? Eternal God and Creator, if we cannot fully explain those things that can be seen or felt or heard, how can we hope to explain You, the Source and Sustainer of all creation? You are beyond explanation or understanding. You are bigger than our complex theories and theologies—bigger than any box we try to fit You in. While we look to Your Word and wait on Your Spirit to guide us in Your truth, let us be content with Your "unknowableness." Let us take comfort in knowing that our God, Who is bigger than life, is also closer than life. If we sought to love and trust You even half as much as we try to explain You, I am certain we would all be much wiser in the end. (Job 36:26; Isa 40:12–31; Jn 16:13; Ro 11:33)

Only to our intellect is God incomprehensible, not to our love.

The Cloud of Unknowing (1370)

Though I can't see
Your holy, holy face
And Your throne in heaven above,
It seems so far away.
Though I can't touch, I can't touch
Your nail-scarred hands,
I have a deep, unspeakable joy
That makes my faith to stand.

Lord, I believe in You,
I'll always believe in You.
Though I can't see
You with my eyes,
Deep in my heart
Your presence I find.
Lord, I believe in You,
And I'll keep my trust in You.
Let the whole world
Say what they may,
No one can take this joy away,
Lord, I believe.

"Lord, I Believe In You"
Tommy Walker (©1996)

God is more real to me than any thought or thing or person. I feel him in the sunshine or rain; and all mingled with a delicious restfulness most nearly describes my feelings. I talk to him as to a companion in prayer and praise, and our communion is delightful. He answers me again and again, often in words so clearly spoken that it seems my outer ear must have carried the tone, but generally in strong mental impressions. Usually a text of Scripture, unfolding some new view of him and his love for me, and care for my safety . . . That he is mine and I am his never leaves me; it is an abiding joy. Without it life would be a blank, a desert, a shoreless, trackless waste.

William James (1842-1910)

(12:8) "Meaningless! Meaningless! Everything is meaningless!" O Divine Word, apart from You life has no meaning. Please help me to think Your thoughts, so that I might understand the meaning You have given to my life. As You honor me with Your love, give my life divine value. Show me why You have created me, so that I might live for the praise of Your glory. O God "who fills everything in every way," our hearts are empty until You dwell within us. Please fill me with Your Spirit, that my cup might overflow with You all the days of my life. Give substance to my life on this earth, and by Your grace in Christ, receive me into eternal life with You. Amen. (Eph 1:22–23)

and the sound of grinding fades;
when men rise up at the sound of birds,
but all their songs grow faint;
5 when men are afraid of heights
and of dangers in the streets;
when the almond tree blossoms
and the grasshopper drags himself along
and desire no longer is stirred.
Then man goes to his eternal home
and mourners go about the streets.

6 Remember him—before the silver cord is severed,
or the golden bowl is broken;
before the pitcher is shattered at the spring,
or the wheel broken at the well,
7 and the dust returns to the ground it came from,
and the spirit returns to God who gave it.

8 "Meaningless! Meaningless!" says the Teacher.[a]
"Everything is meaningless!"

The Conclusion of the Matter

9 Not only was the Teacher wise, but also he imparted knowledge to the people. He pondered and searched out and set in
order many proverbs. 10 The Teacher searched to find just the
right words, and what he wrote was upright and true.
11 The words of the wise are like goads, their collected sayings
like firmly embedded nails—given by one Shepherd. 12 Be
warned, my son, of anything in addition to them.

Of making many books there is no end, and much study wearies the body.

13 Now all has been heard;
here is the conclusion of the matter:
Fear God and keep his commandments,
for this is the whole ⌞duty⌟ of man.
14 For God will bring every deed into judgment,
including every hidden thing,
whether it is good or evil.

[a] 8 Or *the leader of the assembly*; also in verses 9 and 10

The SONG *of* SONGS

The Song of Songs celebrates the passions of romantic love between a man and a woman. With rich imagery and unabashed sensuality, the lovers praise each other's physical attractiveness and share their yearnings for physical intimacy: "Let him kiss me with the kisses of his mouth—for your love is more delightful than wine" (1:2). Though not a formal drama, Song of Songs is structured with dramatic tension as the lovers move toward the culmination of their desire.

Readers have wondered for centuries what to do with this collection of love poems. Some in Jewish and Christian history who felt uncomfortable with public discussion of human sexuality stumbled over the Song's exuberant and sometimes graphic language. They avoided its scandal by seeing it only as an allegory of the love of God for His people or the love of Christ for His church. And, indeed, there are other Scripture passages that support this kind of interpretation. (Eze 16; 23; Hos 2). Other scholars, however, reject the allegorical interpretation out of hand and take the Song only at its face value.

So how are we to understand this unique Biblical book? How might it inspire our worship? On the one hand we ought to take the Song at face value, as a collection of poems that applaud romantic love. The love between man and woman, completed through sexual intimacy within marriage, is one of God's good gifts, and for this gift He deserves our gratitude.

> **Without minimizing the original sense of the Song, we can allow it to draw us to the intimate love of God for us.**

But we can also allow the imagery of the Song to lead us into deeper intimacy with God. Whether or not the original writer had this in mind as a primary purpose, nevertheless human love provides a fitting analogy for the divine-human relationship. After all, we are the bride of Christ, and Christ's love for the church is like that of a husband for his wife (Eph 5:25–32). So the passionate love in Song of Songs shows us something of how zealously Christ loves His own bride, the church. When the man in the Song calls, " 'Arise, my darling, my beautiful one, and come with me' " (2:10), we hear not only the invitation of a lover but also the beckoning love of Jesus, Who says to us: "Come to me" (Mt 11:28). So, without minimizing the original sense of the Song, we can allow it to draw us to the intimate love of God for us. Our worship, like that of the beloved, returns love for love, as we adore God with all our being.

Song of Songs

(1:2–4) O Lord, in this magnificent song of covenant love in marriage, we also hear the music of Your covenant love for Your people, Your church, the Bride of Christ. And I thank You that You have written me into Your love story. You have called me out of my dead-end dreams and into Your adventure of faith. You have reached out Your hand to me and have brought me into the shared joy of an overcoming life. The sound of Your name sings in my spirit, and the presence of Your love quenches the deepest thirsting of my soul. (1Jn 5:4)

Accustom yourself to the wonderful thought that God loves you with a tenderness, a generosity, and an intimacy which surpasses all your dreams. Give yourself up with joy to a loving confidence in God and have courage to believe firmly that God's action towards you is a masterpiece of partiality and love. Rest tranquilly in this abiding conviction.

Abbe Henri de Tourville (1842-1903)

(1:7) Lord Jesus, You are my Shepherd, leading my heart into safe, green fields and beside quiet pools. I choose to follow You out of the chaos of the world's noisy traffic. I choose to listen to Your strong, calm voice rather than to the voices of the world that stir up anxiety and fear within me. I choose to take my place with Your family and seek pasture with Your flock now and forever. (Ps 23; Jn 10:11)

Fairest Lord Jesus,
Ruler of all nature,
O Thou of God and man the Son:
Thee will I cherish,
Thee will I honor,
Thou my soul's glory, joy, and crown.

Fair are the meadows,
Fairer still the woodlands,
Robed in the blooming garb of spring:
Jesus is fairer,
Jesus is purer,
Who makes the woeful heart to sing.

"Fairest Lord Jesus"
Anonymous German Hymn (1677)
Trans. Anonymous (1850)

1 Solomon's Song of Songs.

Beloved[a]

2 Let him kiss me with the kisses of his mouth—
for your love is more delightful than wine.
3 Pleasing is the fragrance of your perfumes;
your name is like perfume poured out.
No wonder the maidens love you!
4 Take me away with you—let us hurry!
Let the king bring me into his chambers.

Friends

We rejoice and delight in you[b];
we will praise your love more than wine.

Beloved

How right they are to adore you!

5 Dark am I, yet lovely,
O daughters of Jerusalem,
dark like the tents of Kedar,
like the tent curtains of Solomon.[c]
6 Do not stare at me because I am dark,
because I am darkened by the sun.
My mother's sons were angry with me
and made me take care of the vineyards;
my own vineyard I have neglected.
7 Tell me, you whom I love, where you graze your flock
and where you rest your sheep at midday.
Why should I be like a veiled woman
beside the flocks of your friends?

Friends

8 If you do not know, most beautiful of women,
follow the tracks of the sheep
and graze your young goats
by the tents of the shepherds.

Lover

9 I liken you, my darling, to a mare
harnessed to one of the chariots of Pharaoh.
10 Your cheeks are beautiful with earrings,
your neck with strings of jewels.
11 We will make you earrings of gold,
studded with silver.

Beloved

12 While the king was at his table,
my perfume spread its fragrance.
13 My lover is to me a sachet of myrrh
resting between my breasts.
14 My lover is to me a cluster of henna blossoms
from the vineyards of En Gedi.

[a] Primarily on the basis of the gender of the Hebrew pronouns used, male and female speakers are indicated in the margins by the captions *Lover* and *Beloved* respectively. The words of others are marked *Friends*. In some instances the divisions and their captions are debatable. [b] 4 The Hebrew is masculine singular. [c] 5 Or *Salma*

Lover

15 How beautiful you are, my darling!
Oh, how beautiful!
Your eyes are doves.

Beloved

16 How handsome you are, my lover!
Oh, how charming!
And our bed is verdant.

Lover

17 The beams of our house are cedars;
our rafters are firs.

Beloved[a]

2 I am a rose[b] of Sharon,
a lily of the valleys.

Lover

2 Like a lily among thorns
is my darling among the maidens.

Beloved

3 Like an apple tree among the trees of the forest
is my lover among the young men.
I delight to sit in his shade,
and his fruit is sweet to my taste.
4 He has taken me to the banquet hall,
and his banner over me is love.
5 Strengthen me with raisins,
refresh me with apples,
for I am faint with love.
6 His left arm is under my head,
and his right arm embraces me.
7 Daughters of Jerusalem, I charge you
by the gazelles and by the does of the field:
Do not arouse or awaken love
until it so desires.
8 Listen! My lover!
Look! Here he comes,
leaping across the mountains,
bounding over the hills.
9 My lover is like a gazelle or a young stag.
Look! There he stands behind our wall,
gazing through the windows,
peering through the lattice.
10 My lover spoke and said to me,
"Arise, my darling,
my beautiful one, and come with me.
11 See! The winter is past;
the rains are over and gone.
12 Flowers appear on the earth;
the season of singing has come,
the cooing of doves
is heard in our land.

[a] *1* Or *Lover* [b] *1* Possibly a member of the crocus family

(2:1–2) O Lord, my strength amounts to nothing. I am like a tiny flower planted on the side of a mountain, facing into treacherous winds. But Your love fills me with the power to live as You did: to bloom like a rose among the thorns of human callousness, to shed petals of compassion though they may be crushed beneath the sole of human betrayal. Your love draws my roots down deep into the soil of Who You are so that I can blossom with new life that is not my own, but Yours. (2Co 12:9–10)

There's a place at Your table for me
There's a grace that is able to set
my soul free
By the wine and the bread, I am
healed and I'm fed
There's a place at Your table for me.

There's a place at Your table for me
Where the hand of Your mercy
meets all of my needs
Where Your banner of love flies
forever above
There's a place at Your table for me.

"There's a Place at Your Table for Me"
Claire Cloninger (©1998)

(2:10–13) O Lord, Yours is the voice of new beginnings that calls me out of the chaos of the tomb of hopelessness. Yours is the hand that sweeps away the dead leaves of winter and brings forth the majesty of spring. Yours is the call to leave my disappointments in the past and follow You into the promise of tomorrow. Yours are the plans to prosper me and not to harm me, to give me hope and a future. Father God, today I choose to step through the door of hope and into the future with You. (Jer 29:11)

(3:1–4) Lord, sometimes I cry out for You and cannot hear Your answer. Sometimes I look for You and cannot find You there. Yet I know You have not moved. So in the dry seasons of my soul I will ask and keep on asking, seek and keep on seeking, knock and keep on knocking. And when I find Your love that's been waiting all the while, I will hold You as my heart's most precious treasure. I will welcome You into every secret chamber of my being. For You are my Lord and my friend. (Lk 11:9–10)

There is no need to plead that the love of God shall fill our heart as though he were unwilling to fill us. He is willing as light is willing to flood a room that is opened to its brightness; willing as water is willing to flow into an emptied channel. Love is pressing round us on all sides like air. Cease to resist, and instantly love takes possession.

Amy Carmichael (1867-1951)

Loved with everlasting love,
Led by grace that love to know;
Gracious Spirit from above,
Thou has taught me it is so!
O this full and perfect peace!
O this transport all divine!
In a love which cannot cease,
I am His, and He is mine.

Things that once were wild alarms
Cannot now disturb my rest,
Closed in everlasting arms,
Pillowed on the loving breast.
O to lie forever here,
Doubt and care and self resign,
While He whispers in my ear,
I am His, and He is mine.

"I Am His, and He Is Mine"
George W. Robinson (1890)

13 The fig tree forms its early fruit;
the blossoming vines spread their fragrance.
Arise, come, my darling;
my beautiful one, come with me."

Lover

14 My dove in the clefts of the rock,
in the hiding places on the mountainside,
show me your face,
let me hear your voice;
for your voice is sweet,
and your face is lovely.
15 Catch for us the foxes,
the little foxes
that ruin the vineyards,
our vineyards that are in bloom.

Beloved

16 My lover is mine and I am his;
he browses among the lilies.
17 Until the day breaks
and the shadows flee,
turn, my lover,
and be like a gazelle
or like a young stag
on the rugged hills.[a]

3

All night long on my bed
I looked for the one my heart loves;
I looked for him but did not find him.
2 I will get up now and go about the city,
through its streets and squares;
I will search for the one my heart loves.
So I looked for him but did not find him.
3 The watchmen found me
as they made their rounds in the city.
"Have you seen the one my heart loves?"
4 Scarcely had I passed them
when I found the one my heart loves.
I held him and would not let him go
till I had brought him to my mother's house,
to the room of the one who conceived me.
5 Daughters of Jerusalem, I charge you
by the gazelles and by the does of the field:
Do not arouse or awaken love
until it so desires.

6 Who is this coming up from the desert
like a column of smoke,
perfumed with myrrh and incense
made from all the spices of the merchant?
7 Look! It is Solomon's carriage,
escorted by sixty warriors,
the noblest of Israel,
8 all of them wearing the sword,
all experienced in battle,

[a] 17 Or *the hills of Bether*

each with his sword at his side,
prepared for the terrors of the night.
9 King Solomon made for himself the carriage;
he made it of wood from Lebanon.
10 Its posts he made of silver,
its base of gold.
Its seat was upholstered with purple,
its interior lovingly inlaid
by[a] the daughters of Jerusalem.
11 Come out, you daughters of Zion,
and look at King Solomon wearing the crown,
the crown with which his mother crowned him
on the day of his wedding,
the day his heart rejoiced.

Lover

4 How beautiful you are, my darling!
Oh, how beautiful!
Your eyes behind your veil are doves.
Your hair is like a flock of goats
descending from Mount Gilead.
2 Your teeth are like a flock of sheep just shorn,
coming up from the washing.
Each has its twin;
not one of them is alone.
3 Your lips are like a scarlet ribbon;
your mouth is lovely.
Your temples behind your veil
are like the halves of a pomegranate.
4 Your neck is like the tower of David,
built with elegance[b];
on it hang a thousand shields,
all of them shields of warriors.
5 Your two breasts are like two fawns,
like twin fawns of a gazelle
that browse among the lilies.
6 Until the day breaks
and the shadows flee,
I will go to the mountain of myrrh
and to the hill of incense.
7 All beautiful you are, my darling;
there is no flaw in you.

8 Come with me from Lebanon, my bride,
come with me from Lebanon.
Descend from the crest of Amana,
from the top of Senir, the summit of Hermon,
from the lions' dens
and the mountain haunts of the leopards.
9 You have stolen my heart, my sister, my bride;
you have stolen my heart
with one glance of your eyes,
with one jewel of your necklace.
10 How delightful is your love, my sister, my bride!
How much more pleasing is your love than wine,

[a] *10* Or *its inlaid interior a gift of love / from* [b] *4* The meaning of the Hebrew for this word is uncertain.

(4:9–10) Lord, we are Your bride, Your church, Your own. If only we could see ourselves as You do, we would never know another moment of defeat. For You look on us with delight. You have betrothed Yourself to us with everlasting love, and in the end You will return to take us with You. Forgive us when we fail to grasp our destiny. Touch our eyes so we can see what joy awaits us, for we want to be prepared for Your return. (Jer 31:3; Rev 19:7)

and the fragrance of your perfume than any spice!
11 Your lips drop sweetness as the honeycomb, my bride;
milk and honey are under your tongue.
The fragrance of your garments is like that of Lebanon.
12 You are a garden locked up, my sister, my bride;
you are a spring enclosed, a sealed fountain.
13 Your plants are an orchard of pomegranates
with choice fruits,
with henna and nard,
14 nard and saffron,
calamus and cinnamon,
with every kind of incense tree,
with myrrh and aloes
and all the finest spices.
15 You are[a] a garden fountain,
a well of flowing water
streaming down from Lebanon.

Beloved

16 Awake, north wind,
and come, south wind!
Blow on my garden,
that its fragrance may spread abroad.
Let my lover come into his garden
and taste its choice fruits.

Lover

5 I have come into my garden, my sister, my bride;
I have gathered my myrrh with my spice.
I have eaten my honeycomb and my honey;
I have drunk my wine and my milk.

Friends

Eat, O friends, and drink;
drink your fill, O lovers.

Beloved

2 I slept but my heart was awake.
Listen! My lover is knocking:
"Open to me, my sister, my darling,
my dove, my flawless one.
My head is drenched with dew,
my hair with the dampness of the night."
3 I have taken off my robe—
must I put it on again?
I have washed my feet—
must I soil them again?
4 My lover thrust his hand through the latch-opening;
my heart began to pound for him.
5 I arose to open for my lover,
and my hands dripped with myrrh,
my fingers with flowing myrrh,
on the handles of the lock.
6 I opened for my lover,
but my lover had left; he was gone.

(4:12–16) My garden is locked. My heart is hard and barren. Come, hand of God, unlock the gate. Break up the stony ground. Come, grace of God, plant the seeds of the Spirit deep within me so that my life may yield a harvest of peace and joy. Come, love of God, bring forth in me springs of living water that will never fail. Come, breath of God, blow on my life so the fragrance of Jesus may touch all who are near. Come, Son of God, meet me each day in the garden of my heart where I may share my life with You forever. (Mk 4:4–8; Jn 4:5–15; Gal 5:22)

(5:2–6) O Lord, You are always knocking on my heart's door—always waiting so patiently, so lovingly, for me to let You in. Forgive me for making You wait. Forgive me for putting off any precious chance to share my life with You. Don't let me miss another moment. I give You the keys to my heart, Lord. Come and make it Your dwelling place. (Rev 3:20)

[a] *15* Or *I am* (spoken by the *Beloved*)

MY BELOVED

Oh, how beautiful you are to Me! I love you as a husband loves his bride. In My eyes, there is no flaw in you. You are without stain or wrinkle or any other blemish. You are holy and blameless in My sight. You have stolen My heart as a bride steals her husband's heart.

I am the One Who gave you life and made you grow like a plant of the field. You grew up and developed and became the most beautiful of jewels. I spread the corner of My garment over you and covered you. I gave you My solemn oath and entered into a covenant with you, and you became Mine. I saved you and called you to a holy life—not because of anything you have done but because of My own purpose and grace.

I have committed Myself to you forever, in righteousness and justice, in love and compassion. I have raised My banner of love over you. I take great delight in you; I quiet you with My love and rejoice over you with singing.

I have prepared a special place for you in My house. It is far greater than anything you could imagine. And that is where we will live, together, forever and ever. I love you.

Ps 23:6; SS 4:1,7,9; Eze 16:6-8; Hos 2:19; Zep 3:17; Jn 14:2-3; Eph 5:25-27; 2Ti 1:9

My heart sank at his departure.[a]
I looked for him but did not find him.
I called him but he did not answer.
7 The watchmen found me
as they made their rounds in the city.
They beat me, they bruised me;
they took away my cloak,
those watchmen of the walls!
8 O daughters of Jerusalem, I charge you—
if you find my lover,
what will you tell him?
Tell him I am faint with love.

Friends

9 How is your beloved better than others,
most beautiful of women?
How is your beloved better than others,
that you charge us so?

Beloved

10 My lover is radiant and ruddy,
outstanding among ten thousand.
11 His head is purest gold;
his hair is wavy
and black as a raven.
12 His eyes are like doves
by the water streams,
washed in milk,
mounted like jewels.
13 His cheeks are like beds of spice
yielding perfume.
His lips are like lilies
dripping with myrrh.
14 His arms are rods of gold
set with chrysolite.
His body is like polished ivory
decorated with sapphires.[b]
15 His legs are pillars of marble
set on bases of pure gold.
His appearance is like Lebanon,
choice as its cedars.
16 His mouth is sweetness itself;
he is altogether lovely.
This is my lover, this my friend,
O daughters of Jerusalem.

Friends

6 Where has your lover gone,
most beautiful of women?
Which way did your lover turn,
that we may look for him with you?

Beloved

2 My lover has gone down to his garden,
to the beds of spices,

[a] 6 Or *heart had gone out to him when he spoke* [b] 14 Or *lapis lazuli*

(5:10–16) O my Savior, my Lord, the lover of my life and the shepherd of my soul, I am awed by the reality of Who You are. In all the heights of heaven, there is none like You. In all the expanse of earth, there is none like You. You are seated on the throne of life at the center of God's city where angels and mortals continually praise You. And yet You desire to spend Your time with me. O my Savior and my Friend, You're the fairest of ten thousand to my soul. (Rev 7:9–15)

His name has been to me as a civet-box, yea, sweeter than all perfumes. His Voice to me has been most sweet, and his Countenance I have desired more than they that have most desired the light of the sun. His Word I did use to gather for my food, and for antidotes against my faintings. He has held me, and I have kept me from mine iniquities. Yea, my steps hath he strengthened in the way.

John Bunyan (1628–1688)

Precious Lord, all I want is You;
No one else fills my heart
Like You do.
My hands I will raise;
My voice sings Your praise.
All I want, precious Lord,
Is You.

"Precious Lord"
Jean Munsey (©1996)

(6:3) Jesus, all my life I have yearned to know that I belong. I have hungered for the affirmation that I am cherished, cared for, totally loved. Now I have no doubt. I am Yours and You are mine. There is no compromise in this fact, for You love me with an all-consuming and a jealous love. I surrender to Your love, O Lord. I choose to walk in this relationship, to belong totally to You, to be possessed by the power and the passion of Your covenant love for me. (Dt 4:24)

Earnestly I seek You
In this weary land,
For Your love is life to me.
In the sanctuary
I will lift my hands
Only to You, my King.
For my soul thirsts for You, oh God,
And my heart yearns for You, oh God,
My eyes long to see Your face.
For You are holy in power and glory,
In kindness and mercy, oh God.
For You are holy, oh God.

"Earnestly I Seek You"
Beverly Darnall and John Darnall (©1991)

(6:8–9) You know every person on this planet, yet You recognize the singular rhythm of my heart. Above the symphony of Your whole creation—the roar of the thunder, the crashing of the waves, the song of the wind—You hear my small voice call to You, and You answer. You put me together in my mother's womb, and You were pleased with Your work. I do not have to compete for Your love or Your attention. I am unique in Your sight, and You love me for myself, just as I am. (Ps 139)

to browse in the gardens
and to gather lilies.
3 I am my lover's and my lover is mine;
he browses among the lilies.

Lover

4 You are beautiful, my darling, as Tirzah,
lovely as Jerusalem,
majestic as troops with banners.
5 Turn your eyes from me;
they overwhelm me.
Your hair is like a flock of goats
descending from Gilead.
6 Your teeth are like a flock of sheep
coming up from the washing.
Each has its twin,
not one of them is alone.
7 Your temples behind your veil
are like the halves of a pomegranate.
8 Sixty queens there may be,
and eighty concubines,
and virgins beyond number;
9 but my dove, my perfect one, is unique,
the only daughter of her mother,
the favorite of the one who bore her.
The maidens saw her and called her blessed;
the queens and concubines praised her.

Friends

10 Who is this that appears like the dawn,
fair as the moon, bright as the sun,
majestic as the stars in procession?

Lover

11 I went down to the grove of nut trees
to look at the new growth in the valley,
to see if the vines had budded
or the pomegranates were in bloom.
12 Before I realized it,
my desire set me among the royal chariots of my people.[a]

Friends

13 Come back, come back, O Shulammite;
come back, come back, that we may gaze on you!

Lover

Why would you gaze on the Shulammite
as on the dance of Mahanaim?

7 How beautiful your sandaled feet,
O prince's daughter!
Your graceful legs are like jewels,
the work of a craftsman's hands.
2 Your navel is a rounded goblet

[a] 12 Or *among the chariots of Amminadab*; or *among the chariots of the people of the prince*

that never lacks blended wine.
Your waist is a mound of wheat
encircled by lilies.
3 Your breasts are like two fawns,
twins of a gazelle.
4 Your neck is like an ivory tower.
Your eyes are the pools of Heshbon
by the gate of Bath Rabbim.
Your nose is like the tower of Lebanon
looking toward Damascus.
5 Your head crowns you like Mount Carmel.
Your hair is like royal tapestry;
the king is held captive by its tresses.
6 How beautiful you are and how pleasing,
O love, with your delights!
7 Your stature is like that of the palm,
and your breasts like clusters of fruit.
8 I said, "I will climb the palm tree;
I will take hold of its fruit."
May your breasts be like the clusters of the vine,
the fragrance of your breath like apples,
9 and your mouth like the best wine.

Beloved

May the wine go straight to my lover,
flowing gently over lips and teeth.[a]
10 I belong to my lover,
and his desire is for me.
11 Come, my lover, let us go to the countryside,
let us spend the night in the villages.[b]
12 Let us go early to the vineyards
to see if the vines have budded,
if their blossoms have opened,
and if the pomegranates are in bloom—
there I will give you my love.
13 The mandrakes send out their fragrance,
and at our door is every delicacy,
both new and old,
that I have stored up for you, my lover.

8 If only you were to me like a brother,
who was nursed at my mother's breasts!
Then, if I found you outside,
I would kiss you,
and no one would despise me.
2 I would lead you
and bring you to my mother's house—
she who has taught me.
I would give you spiced wine to drink,
the nectar of my pomegranates.
3 His left arm is under my head
and his right arm embraces me.
4 Daughters of Jerusalem, I charge you:
Do not arouse or awaken love
until it so desires.

[a] *9* Septuagint, Aquila, Vulgate and Syriac; Hebrew *lips of sleepers* [b] *11* Or *henna bushes*

You're calling me to a deeper place,
You're calling me to come away.
This is the day that You have made
To walk in Your love and Your
grace.
And I will sing
To You, my King, forever and ever.
I will rise up
And worship Your holiness.
I will sing a song of
Your faithfulness.
On the mountains,
And through the valleys,
Your love will be my peace,
And I will sing of Your love for me.

"I Will Rise Up"
Mike Ash (©1997)

(7:12) I will rise early to meet You, Lord. I will spend time alone with You, whispering the secrets of my heart. I will wait for Your assurance and celebrate Your presence. In the vineyard of Your love I will be satisfied. For You are the Vine and I am the branch. Abiding in You, I receive all that I require to live as Your child in this world—all the peace, the power, the grace, the hope, the mercy, the love. So I will rush to Your vineyard in the early hours, where I know I will find You waiting. (Jn 15:4–7)

In the quiet of the morning,
I will worship Your name.
I will lift my voice with singing
To praise You again.
For it fills my heart with gladness
That remains through the day.
In the quiet of the morning,
I will worship Your name.

"In The Quiet of the Morning"
Wes Tuttle (©1988)

(8:6–7) Thank You, Lord, for the joy of intimacy between a man and a woman in the covenant of marriage. It is a gift that we treasure. And we know, Lord, that this is but a shadow of the love that You have for Your bride, Your church. How we thank You for Your covenant love for us—a love that is indeed stronger than death and more determined than the grave. For death has lost its sting, and the grave will one day lose its hold, but Your love will never let us go. (Isa 26:19; 1Co 15:55; 1Th 4:16)

Set me as a seal upon Your heart,
Lord
Make my life a love song that You
sing
Set my soul on fire with Your
compassion
Make my praise a pleasing offering.

For Your love is stronger than my
dying
And Your grace runs deeper than
my sin
Many floods could never quench its
mercy
Or the holy flame that burns within.

You have laid Your life down as a
ransom
Purchasing my pardon with Your
blood
Pouring out Your joy in place of
ashes
Lifting me forever in Your love.

And I will praise You, and I will
worship You
And I will soar upon Your love like
eagle's wings
And I will praise You, and I will
worship You
For You are Lord of lords and King
of kings.

"A Seal Upon Your Heart"
Claire Cloninger (©1998)

Friends

5 Who is this coming up from the desert
leaning on her lover?

Beloved

Under the apple tree I roused you;
there your mother conceived you,
there she who was in labor gave you birth.
6 Place me like a seal over your heart,
like a seal on your arm;
for love is as strong as death,
its jealousy[a] unyielding as the grave.[b]
It burns like blazing fire,
like a mighty flame.[c]
7 Many waters cannot quench love;
rivers cannot wash it away.
If one were to give
all the wealth of his house for love,
it[d] would be utterly scorned.

Friends

8 We have a young sister,
and her breasts are not yet grown.
What shall we do for our sister
for the day she is spoken for?
9 If she is a wall,
we will build towers of silver on her.
If she is a door,
we will enclose her with panels of cedar.

Beloved

10 I am a wall,
and my breasts are like towers.
Thus I have become in his eyes
like one bringing contentment.
11 Solomon had a vineyard in Baal Hamon;
he let out his vineyard to tenants.
Each was to bring for its fruit
a thousand shekels[e] of silver.
12 But my own vineyard is mine to give;
the thousand shekels are for you, O Solomon,
and two hundred[f] are for those who tend its fruit.

Lover

13 You who dwell in the gardens
with friends in attendance,
let me hear your voice!

Beloved

14 Come away, my lover,
and be like a gazelle
or like a young stag
on the spice-laden mountains.

[a] 6 Or *ardor* [b] 6 Hebrew *Sheol* [c] 6 Or */ like the very flame of the* LORD [d] 7 Or *he* [e] 11 That is, about 25 pounds (about 11.5 kilograms); also in verse 12 [f] 12 That is, about 5 pounds (about 2.3 kilograms)

The Book of the Prophet

ISAIAH

Isaiah

More than any other book of the Bible, Isaiah reveals God to be the "Holy One of Israel," before whom we confess our sin, bow in humble submission, and offer our lives in obedient service. In Isaiah we worship on our knees (45:23).

The holy God is the Savior of Israel (43:3). His people respond to His salvation with faith and joy: " 'Surely God is my salvation; I will trust and not be afraid . . . ' With joy you will draw water from the wells of salvation" (12:2–3). But the experience of God's saving grace and the joy this experience evokes are not limited to Israel. Isaiah prophecies that, at the end of time, all nations will be drawn to worship God: "Listen! Your watchmen lift up their voices; together they shout for joy. When the LORD returns to Zion, they will see it with their own eyes. Burst into songs of joy together, you ruins of Jerusalem, for the LORD has comforted his people, he has redeemed Jerusalem. The LORD will lay bare his holy arm in the sight of all the nations, and all the ends of the earth will see the salvation of our God" (52:8–10). God's glory cannot be contained within one nation, and neither can the joyful worship His glory elicits (6:3; 42:8–10).

According to Isaiah, even Gentiles will find their burnt offerings and sacrifices accepted by God (56:6–7). But this book continually asserts that mere religious observance is worthless apart from a life of obedience (1:1–17). Moreover, songs and prayers to God mean nothing if they do not flow from the heart (29:13). We will worship the God of Isaiah only when we offer everything on the altar: our confessions, our praise, our hearts, our lives.

More than any other book of the Bible, Isaiah reveals God to be the "Holy One of Israel," before whom we confess our sin, bow in humble submission, and offer our lives in obedient service. In Isaiah we worship on our knees.

Isaiah prepares us to worship God through His Servant, our Savior, Jesus Christ. Chapters 40—53 introduce this Servant, God's chosen One who brings justice to nations. Though the Servant is intimately connected to the nation of Israel, His saving work will impact all nations (49:6). The Servant's inclusiveness increases in chapters 52—53, where He accomplishes salvation by suffering for the sins of many. The Holy One of Israel will judge all peoples, but He will also provide a means by which we can experience everlasting peace and healing (53:5).

Isaiah calls us to sing joyfully as we celebrate God's redeeming work through Jesus, His Servant. "Shout for joy, O heavens; rejoice, O earth; burst into song, O mountains! For the LORD comforts his people and will have compassion on his afflicted ones" (49:13).

1 The vision concerning Judah and Jerusalem that Isaiah son of Amoz saw during the reigns of Uzziah, Jotham, Ahaz and Hezekiah, kings of Judah.

A Rebellious Nation

2 Hear, O heavens! Listen, O earth!
For the LORD has spoken:
"I reared children and brought them up,
but they have rebelled against me.
3 The ox knows his master,
the donkey his owner's manger,
but Israel does not know,
my people do not understand."

4 Ah, sinful nation,
a people loaded with guilt,
a brood of evildoers,
children given to corruption!
They have forsaken the LORD;
they have spurned the Holy One of Israel
and turned their backs on him.

5 Why should you be beaten anymore?
Why do you persist in rebellion?
Your whole head is injured,
your whole heart afflicted.
6 From the sole of your foot to the top of your head
there is no soundness—
only wounds and welts
and open sores,
not cleansed or bandaged
or soothed with oil.
7 Your country is desolate,
your cities burned with fire;
your fields are being stripped by foreigners
right before you,
laid waste as when overthrown by strangers.
8 The Daughter of Zion is left
like a shelter in a vineyard,
like a hut in a field of melons,
like a city under siege.
9 Unless the LORD Almighty
had left us some survivors,
we would have become like Sodom,
we would have been like Gomorrah.

10 Hear the word of the LORD,
you rulers of Sodom;
listen to the law of our God,
you people of Gomorrah!
11 "The multitude of your sacrifices—
what are they to me?" says the LORD.
"I have more than enough of burnt offerings,
of rams and the fat of fattened animals;
I have no pleasure
in the blood of bulls and lambs and goats.
12 When you come to appear before me,
who has asked this of you,

(1:4) As it was with Israel of old, so it is with us: Our sin and corruption have not gone unnoticed; Your sentence already is spoken. But Your restoring grace is still available to a repentant people who call on You. So I pray, forgive us; spare us, O marvelous and powerful God, in Your mercy. Fill our hearts again with worship and the testimony of Your salvation. Let that testimony begin today, with me. (2Ch 7:14)

(1:11–16) Create in me a clean heart, O God, and renew a right spirit within me so that my worship will be without hypocrisy. I want to honor You with a pure heart and a righteous life. Help me, Lord. You are my strength and my perfecter. You are the source of my joy and the reason for my worship. (Ps 51:10)

this trampling of my courts?
13 Stop bringing meaningless offerings!
Your incense is detestable to me.
New Moons, Sabbaths and convocations—
I cannot bear your evil assemblies.
14 Your New Moon festivals and your appointed feasts
my soul hates.
They have become a burden to me;
I am weary of bearing them.
15 When you spread out your hands in prayer,
I will hide my eyes from you;
even if you offer many prayers,
I will not listen.
Your hands are full of blood;
16 wash and make yourselves clean.
Take your evil deeds
out of my sight!
Stop doing wrong,
17 learn to do right!
Seek justice,
encourage the oppressed.[a]
Defend the cause of the fatherless,
plead the case of the widow.

18 "Come now, let us reason together,"
says the LORD.
"Though your sins are like scarlet,
they shall be as white as snow;
though they are red as crimson,
they shall be like wool.
19 If you are willing and obedient,
you will eat the best from the land;
20 but if you resist and rebel,
you will be devoured by the sword."
For the mouth of the LORD has spoken.

21 See how the faithful city
has become a harlot!
She once was full of justice;
righteousness used to dwell in her—
but now murderers!
22 Your silver has become dross,
your choice wine is diluted with water.
23 Your rulers are rebels,
companions of thieves;
they all love bribes
and chase after gifts.
They do not defend the cause of the fatherless;
the widow's case does not come before them.
24 Therefore the Lord, the LORD Almighty,
the Mighty One of Israel, declares:
"Ah, I will get relief from my foes
and avenge myself on my enemies.
25 I will turn my hand against you;
I will thoroughly purge away your dross
and remove all your impurities.

[a] 17 Or / *rebuke the oppressor*

(1:16–17) Powerful and merciful God, my Restorer and Redeemer, who else can purge me of sin and uncleanness? You save the weak and helpless ones who cry out to You. You confound the unrepentant, the self-righteous and the self-reliant. Deliver me from the hypocrisy of empty words and empty ritual. Help me to worship You honestly, with pure lips, a compassionate heart and hands full of the works of mercy.

(1:18) God of our salvation, You call us to reason with You. But is it reasonable that my sins, blatant as neon in the night, should be washed white as snow in the blood of God Himself? Is it reasonable that one who lives in constant rebellion would be saved by the very One against Whom he or she has rebelled? No, loving God, it is not reasonable, but it is absolutely true. There, on the altar of a cross, hung a willing Lamb with thorns upon His brow: my redeeming sacrifice. How I praise You for the wonder of this sacrificial act, for it is the world's only hope of eternal life. (1Jn 1:7)

White as snow,
White as snow,
Though my sins were as scarlet,
Lord, I know,
Lord, I know
That I'm clean and forgiven.

Through the power of Your blood,
Through the wonder of Your love,
Through faith in You
I know that I can be
White as snow.

"White As Snow"
Leon Olguin (©1990)

(2:4–5) I believe the words of this anointed prophet, and I rejoice in the vision of Your coming kingdom—a world without war, filled with a people who walk in the light of their Lord. Darkness, hatred and pain will be forgotten. Desperation and loss will be forever wiped away in the joy and comfort of Your presence. O God, I thank You, bless You and praise You for Your sure promise, and I look forward with longing toward its glorious fulfillment.

O God of every nation,
Of every race and land,
Redeem the whole creation
With Your almighty hand;
Where hate and fear divide us
And bitter threats are hurled,
In love and mercy guide us,
And heal our strife-torn world.
"O God of Every Nation"
William W. Reid, Jr. (©1958, 1986)

(2:6–8) Is this not like my nation, Lord? We have silver and gold, securities and possessions, fearsome military capability, and incredible technological skills. But these God-given blessings have taken our eyes off of You, our eternal Provider. These things have become our security, our gods. How quickly we are willing to trade national righteousness for national prosperity. Lord, open our eyes. Show us the pit that yawns before us. I plead for Your revelation, mercy and cleansing in our nation. Nothing is too hard for You, so I worship You and call upon Your omnipotence on behalf of my needy country.

26 I will restore your judges as in days of old,
your counselors as at the beginning.
Afterward you will be called
the City of Righteousness,
the Faithful City."

27 Zion will be redeemed with justice,
her penitent ones with righteousness.
28 But rebels and sinners will both be broken,
and those who forsake the LORD will perish.

29 "You will be ashamed because of the sacred oaks
in which you have delighted;
you will be disgraced because of the gardens
that you have chosen.
30 You will be like an oak with fading leaves,
like a garden without water.
31 The mighty man will become tinder
and his work a spark;
both will burn together,
with no one to quench the fire."

The Mountain of the LORD

2 This is what Isaiah son of Amoz saw concerning Judah and Jerusalem:

2 In the last days

the mountain of the LORD's temple will be established
as chief among the mountains;
it will be raised above the hills,
and all nations will stream to it.

3 Many peoples will come and say,

"Come, let us go up to the mountain of the LORD,
to the house of the God of Jacob.
He will teach us his ways,
so that we may walk in his paths."
The law will go out from Zion,
the word of the LORD from Jerusalem.
4 He will judge between the nations
and will settle disputes for many peoples.
They will beat their swords into plowshares
and their spears into pruning hooks.
Nation will not take up sword against nation,
nor will they train for war anymore.

5 Come, O house of Jacob,
let us walk in the light of the LORD.

The Day of the LORD

6 You have abandoned your people,
the house of Jacob.
They are full of superstitions from the East;
they practice divination like the Philistines
and clasp hands with pagans.
7 Their land is full of silver and gold;
there is no end to their treasures.
Their land is full of horses;
there is no end to their chariots.

8 Their land is full of idols;
they bow down to the work of their hands,
to what their fingers have made.
9 So man will be brought low
and mankind humbled—
do not forgive them.[a]

10 Go into the rocks,
hide in the ground
from dread of the LORD
and the splendor of his majesty!
11 The eyes of the arrogant man will be humbled
and the pride of men brought low;
the LORD alone will be exalted in that day.

12 The LORD Almighty has a day in store
for all the proud and lofty,
for all that is exalted
(and they will be humbled),
13 for all the cedars of Lebanon, tall and lofty,
and all the oaks of Bashan,
14 for all the towering mountains
and all the high hills,
15 for every lofty tower
and every fortified wall,
16 for every trading ship[b]
and every stately vessel.
17 The arrogance of man will be brought low
and the pride of men humbled;
the LORD alone will be exalted in that day,
18 and the idols will totally disappear.

19 Men will flee to caves in the rocks
and to holes in the ground
from dread of the LORD
and the splendor of his majesty,
when he rises to shake the earth.
20 In that day men will throw away
to the rodents and bats
their idols of silver and idols of gold,
which they made to worship.
21 They will flee to caverns in the rocks
and to the overhanging crags
from dread of the LORD
and the splendor of his majesty,
when he rises to shake the earth.

22 Stop trusting in man,
who has but a breath in his nostrils.
Of what account is he?

Judgment on Jerusalem and Judah

3 See now, the Lord,
the LORD Almighty,
is about to take from Jerusalem and Judah
both supply and support:
all supplies of food and all supplies of water,

[a] 9 Or *not raise them up* [b] 16 Hebrew *every ship of Tarshish*

(2:17–21) Shall we praise You only when You comfort and satisfy us? Forbid it, Lord. No, we will praise You for Your judgments, too; they are true and righteous altogether. There is no injustice in You. Again and again You have reached out in compassion across time and space and offered redemption and restoration to a rebellious and willful world. We acknowledge and praise You for Your longsuffering mercy and perfect justice. (Job 2:10; Isa 5:16)

If his justice were such as could be adjudged just by human reckoning, it clearly would not be divine; it would in no way differ from human justice. But inasmuch as he is the one true God, wholly incomprehensible and inaccessible to man's understanding, it is reasonable, indeed inevitable, that his justice also should be incomprehensible.

Martin Luther (1483-1546)

He is exalted,
The King is exalted on high,
I will praise Him.
He is exalted, forever exalted
And I will praise His name.

He is the Lord,
Forever His truth shall reign.
Heaven and earth
Rejoice in His holy name.
He is exalted,
The King is exalted on high.

"He Is Exalted"
Twila Paris (©1985)

(3:13–15) Lord, I now intercede on behalf of our spiritual and governmental leaders. How the devil seeks to deceive them and pervert their best intentions! Come, all-powerful, all-wise, all-seeing God and defend them from the evil one. Give them strength and wisdom to deny their own ambitions and the cravings of the flesh. Even today, begin a work of revelation and restoration in the men and women whom You have placed in positions of authority. We need a miracle, Lord. Only You can do it.

To You, eternal Three in One;
Our songs shall rise in unison;
Those whom You ransom and
restore
Preserve and govern evermore.

"The Royal Banners Forward Go"
Venantius Honorius Fortunatus (530–609)
Trans. John M. Neale (1818–1866)

2 the hero and warrior,
the judge and prophet,
the soothsayer and elder,
3 the captain of fifty and man of rank,
the counselor, skilled craftsman and clever enchanter.

4 I will make boys their officials;
mere children will govern them.
5 People will oppress each other—
man against man, neighbor against neighbor.
The young will rise up against the old,
the base against the honorable.

6 A man will seize one of his brothers
at his father's home, and say,
"You have a cloak, you be our leader;
take charge of this heap of ruins!"
7 But in that day he will cry out,
"I have no remedy.
I have no food or clothing in my house;
do not make me the leader of the people."

8 Jerusalem staggers,
Judah is falling;
their words and deeds are against the LORD,
defying his glorious presence.
9 The look on their faces testifies against them;
they parade their sin like Sodom;
they do not hide it.
Woe to them!
They have brought disaster upon themselves.

10 Tell the righteous it will be well with them,
for they will enjoy the fruit of their deeds.
11 Woe to the wicked! Disaster is upon them!
They will be paid back for what their hands have done.

12 Youths oppress my people,
women rule over them.
O my people, your guides lead you astray;
they turn you from the path.

13 The LORD takes his place in court;
he rises to judge the people.
14 The LORD enters into judgment
against the elders and leaders of his people:
"It is you who have ruined my vineyard;
the plunder from the poor is in your houses.
15 What do you mean by crushing my people
and grinding the faces of the poor?"
declares the Lord, the LORD Almighty.

16 The LORD says,
"The women of Zion are haughty,
walking along with outstretched necks,
flirting with their eyes,
tripping along with mincing steps,
with ornaments jingling on their ankles.
17 Therefore the Lord will bring sores on the heads of the
women of Zion;
the LORD will make their scalps bald."

18In that day the Lord will snatch away their finery: the bangles and headbands and crescent necklaces, 19the earrings and bracelets and veils, 20the headdresses and ankle chains and sashes, the perfume bottles and charms, 21the signet rings and nose rings, 22the fine robes and the capes and cloaks, the purses 23and mirrors, and the linen garments and tiaras and shawls.

24Instead of fragrance there will be a stench;
instead of a sash, a rope;
instead of well-dressed hair, baldness;
instead of fine clothing, sackcloth;
instead of beauty, branding.
25Your men will fall by the sword,
your warriors in battle.
26The gates of Zion will lament and mourn;
destitute, she will sit on the ground.

4 In that day seven women
will take hold of one man
and say, "We will eat our own food
and provide our own clothes;
only let us be called by your name.
Take away our disgrace!"

The Branch of the LORD

2In that day the Branch of the LORD will be beautiful and glorious, and the fruit of the land will be the pride and glory of the
survivors in Israel. 3Those who are left in Zion, who remain in Jerusalem, will be called holy, all who are recorded among the living in Jerusalem. 4The Lord will wash away the filth of the women
of Zion; he will cleanse the bloodstains from Jerusalem by a spirit[a] of judgment and a spirit[a] of fire. 5Then the LORD will create
over all of Mount Zion and over those who assemble there a
cloud of smoke by day and a glow of flaming fire by night; over all
the glory will be a canopy. 6It will be a shelter and shade from the
heat of the day, and a refuge and hiding place from the storm and
rain.

The Song of the Vineyard

5 I will sing for the one I love
a song about his vineyard:
My loved one had a vineyard
on a fertile hillside.
2He dug it up and cleared it of stones
and planted it with the choicest vines.
He built a watchtower in it
and cut out a winepress as well.
Then he looked for a crop of good grapes,
but it yielded only bad fruit.

3"Now you dwellers in Jerusalem and men of Judah,
judge between me and my vineyard.
4What more could have been done for my vineyard
than I have done for it?
When I looked for good grapes,
why did it yield only bad?
5Now I will tell you

[a] 4 Or *the Spirit*

(4:2) I long for the day when the beautiful and glorious Branch of the Lord, The Lord Our Righteousness, will rule and do wisely and execute judgment in the land. On that day, O God, Your people will dwell in safety and worship You together. While I wait for that great Day, I invite You to come this day and receive my thanksgiving and worship. Come, Lord Jesus. Amen. (Jer 23:5–6; Rev 22:20)

(4:5–6) Thank You, Lord, for Your protective covering. Thank You for Your abiding spirit, a sheltering cloud in the heat of the day and a beacon of fire in the darkness. Help me to walk close to You, continually under Your living canopy. You alone are my Guide, my Help, my Strength, my Provider and my Deliverer. Please receive my thanks and love.

(5:1–5) Lord, I pray that I may never hear these words from you. Even though I resist, plow up the hard places in my heart. Dig out the stones of bitterness and burn off the prickly entanglements of sin. Today, this very hour, I yield this piece of earth that is my flesh. Tend it, work it, break it down so that it may flourish with the good fruit of Your Spirit.

Theirs is an endless road, a hopeless maze, who seek for goods before they seek for God.

Bernard of Clairvaux (1090–1153)

(5:8–10) Righteous Lord, true blessing and success come from You. Great gain without obedience to You, the Giver of Life, is destined to become desolate and futile. Deliver me, Lord, from materialism and greed, from always wanting more, bigger, better. The temptation is so subtle; how quickly I become accustomed to comfort and arrogantly expect it as my due. Keep me from pride that turns Your face away from me. I ask You for a humble heart, because it is the gateway to grace. Help me to walk in obedience to Your Word so that I might enjoy the fruitfulness of Your ways.

Humble thyself in the sight of the
Lord,
Humble thyself in the sight of the
Lord.
And He shall lift you up
Higher and higher,
And He shall lift you up.
"Humble Thyself in the Sight of the Lord"
Bob Hudson (©1978)

what I am going to do to my vineyard:
I will take away its hedge,
and it will be destroyed;
I will break down its wall,
and it will be trampled.
6 I will make it a wasteland,
neither pruned nor cultivated,
and briers and thorns will grow there.
I will command the clouds
not to rain on it."

7 The vineyard of the LORD Almighty
is the house of Israel,
and the men of Judah
are the garden of his delight.
And he looked for justice, but saw bloodshed;
for righteousness, but heard cries of distress.

Woes and Judgments

8 Woe to you who add house to house
and join field to field
till no space is left
and you live alone in the land.

9 The LORD Almighty has declared in my hearing:
"Surely the great houses will become desolate,
the fine mansions left without occupants.
10 A ten-acre[a] vineyard will produce only a bath[b] of wine,
a homer[c] of seed only an ephah[d] of grain."
11 Woe to those who rise early in the morning
to run after their drinks,
who stay up late at night
till they are inflamed with wine.
12 They have harps and lyres at their banquets,
tambourines and flutes and wine,
but they have no regard for the deeds of the LORD,
no respect for the work of his hands.
13 Therefore my people will go into exile
for lack of understanding;
their men of rank will die of hunger
and their masses will be parched with thirst.
14 Therefore the grave[e] enlarges its appetite
and opens its mouth without limit;
into it will descend their nobles and masses
with all their brawlers and revelers.
15 So man will be brought low
and mankind humbled,
the eyes of the arrogant humbled.
16 But the LORD Almighty will be exalted by his justice,
and the holy God will show himself holy by his
righteousness.
17 Then sheep will graze as in their own pasture;
lambs will feed[f] among the ruins of the rich.

[a] *10* Hebrew *ten-yoke,* that is, the land plowed by 10 yoke of oxen in one day [b] *10* That is, probably about 6 gallons (about 22 liters) [c] *10* That is, probably about 6 bushels (about 220 liters) [d] *10* That is, probably about 3/5 bushel (about 22 liters) [e] *14* Hebrew *Sheol* [f] *17* Septuagint; Hebrew / *strangers will eat*

18 Woe to those who draw sin along with cords of
deceit,
and wickedness as with cart ropes,
19 to those who say, "Let God hurry,
let him hasten his work
so we may see it.
Let it approach,
let the plan of the Holy One of Israel come,
so we may know it."

20 Woe to those who call evil good
and good evil,
who put darkness for light
and light for darkness,
who put bitter for sweet
and sweet for bitter.
21 Woe to those who are wise in their own eyes
and clever in their own sight.

22 Woe to those who are heroes at drinking wine
and champions at mixing drinks,
23 who acquit the guilty for a bribe,
but deny justice to the innocent.
24 Therefore, as tongues of fire lick up straw
and as dry grass sinks down in the flames,
so their roots will decay
and their flowers blow away like dust;
for they have rejected the law of the LORD Almighty
and spurned the word of the Holy One of Israel.
25 Therefore the LORD's anger burns against his people;
his hand is raised and he strikes them down.
The mountains shake,
and the dead bodies are like refuse in the streets.

Yet for all this, his anger is not turned away,
his hand is still upraised.

26 He lifts up a banner for the distant nations,
he whistles for those at the ends of the earth.
Here they come,
swiftly and speedily!
27 Not one of them grows tired or stumbles,
not one slumbers or sleeps;
not a belt is loosened at the waist,
not a sandal thong is broken.
28 Their arrows are sharp,
all their bows are strung;
their horses' hoofs seem like flint,
their chariot wheels like a whirlwind.
29 Their roar is like that of the lion,
they roar like young lions;
they growl as they seize their prey
and carry it off with no one to rescue.
30 In that day they will roar over it
like the roaring of the sea.
And if one looks at the land,
he will see darkness and distress;
even the light will be darkened by the clouds.

(5:20) Your Word shows plainly what is good and what is evil. What is truth today will be truth forever. Give me courage to speak the truth and live it. Let me not be moved by the so-called wisdom of the world or the deceitfulness of any human philosophy. Guard my heart and mind, Holy Spirit. May I never pervert the ways of God.

It is contrary to reason for a thirsty person to turn from a pure, sparkling mountain stream to quench his thirst at a stale, putrid cistern—yet that is what the human race does when it rejects God's truth and standards in favor of the devil's impure philosophies.

Billy Graham (1918-)

(5:24) Your Word brings health and hope and life. Rejecting Your Word brings destruction and rottenness to the very roots of the soul. But Lord, we are not among those who scorn Your divine, amazing gift. To think that You Who have created the cosmos have bothered to communicate Your Word to us is beyond all understanding. Help us to feast on it with praise, that it may nourish our souls and give us strength to obey with joy. Even though our days are fleeting, Lord, Your Word gives us hope for eternal life. Use us, we pray, to attract others to Your life-giving Word.

I see the Lord
Seated on the throne, exalted,
And the train of His robe
Fills the temple with glory;
And the whole earth is filled,
And the whole earth is filled,
And the whole earth is filled
With His glory.
Holy, holy, holy, holy
Holy is the Lord.

"I See the Lord"
Chris Falson (©1993)

It is not the constant thought of their sins, but the vision of the holiness of God that makes the saints aware of their own sinfulness.

Archbishop Anthony Bloom (1914-)

(6:1–8) O God, give us a new manifestation of Your white-hot holiness—one that will bring us face-to-the floor in repentance, so that You may cleanse us and call us. Give us a vision of Your will, and the courage to be the kind of worshipers You are looking for—those who worship from the heart; those who live sacrificially; those who will win the world; those who will lay their lives down and say, "Here am I, Lord. Send me!" (Jn 4:23–24; Ro 12:1)

Here am I, send me.
Here am I, send me,
Until every nation knows
The power of Your love.
Give me a hunger to know
Where it is You want me to go.
Father, I'm saying
Here am I, send me.

I will go where there's a need.
I will go, Lord, send me.
I will go where You lead,
Even to the ends of the earth.

"Send Me"
Denise Graves (©1995)

Isaiah's Commission

6 In the year that King Uzziah died, I saw the Lord seated on a
throne, high and exalted, and the train of his robe filled the
temple. 2Above him were seraphs, each with six wings: With two
wings they covered their faces, with two they covered their feet,
and with two they were flying. 3And they were calling to one another:

"Holy, holy, holy is the LORD Almighty;
the whole earth is full of his glory."

4At the sound of their voices the doorposts and thresholds shook
and the temple was filled with smoke.
5"Woe to me!" I cried. "I am ruined! For I am a man of unclean lips, and I live among a people of unclean lips, and my eyes
have seen the King, the LORD Almighty."
6Then one of the seraphs flew to me with a live coal in his
hand, which he had taken with tongs from the altar. 7With it he
touched my mouth and said, "See, this has touched your lips;
your guilt is taken away and your sin atoned for."
8Then I heard the voice of the Lord saying, "Whom shall I
send? And who will go for us?"
And I said, "Here am I. Send me!"
9He said, "Go and tell this people:

" 'Be ever hearing, but never understanding;
be ever seeing, but never perceiving.'
10 Make the heart of this people calloused;
make their ears dull
and close their eyes.[a]
Otherwise they might see with their eyes,
hear with their ears,
understand with their hearts,
and turn and be healed."

11Then I said, "For how long, O Lord?"
And he answered:

"Until the cities lie ruined
and without inhabitant,
until the houses are left deserted
and the fields ruined and ravaged,
12 until the LORD has sent everyone far away
and the land is utterly forsaken.
13 And though a tenth remains in the land,
it will again be laid waste.
But as the terebinth and oak
leave stumps when they are cut down,
so the holy seed will be the stump in the land."

The Sign of Immanuel

7 When Ahaz son of Jotham, the son of Uzziah, was king of
Judah, King Rezin of Aram and Pekah son of Remaliah king
of Israel marched up to fight against Jerusalem, but they could
not overpower it.
2Now the house of David was told, "Aram has allied itself

[a] 9,10 Hebrew; Septuagint *'You will be ever hearing, but never understanding; / you will be ever seeing, but never perceiving.' / 10This people's heart has become calloused; / they hardly hear with their ears, / and they have closed their eyes*

with[a] Ephraim"; so the hearts of Ahaz and his people were shak-
en, as the trees of the forest are shaken by the wind.
3Then the LORD said to Isaiah, "Go out, you and your son Shear-
Jashub,[b] to meet Ahaz at the end of the aqueduct of the Upper
Pool, on the road to the Washerman's Field. 4Say to him, 'Be
careful, keep calm and don't be afraid. Do not lose heart because
of these two smoldering stubs of firewood—because of the fierce
anger of Rezin and Aram and of the son of Remaliah. 5Aram,
Ephraim and Remaliah's son have plotted your ruin, saying, 6"Let
us invade Judah; let us tear it apart and divide it among ourselves,
and make the son of Tabeel king over it." 7Yet this is what the
Sovereign LORD says:

" 'It will not take place,
it will not happen,
8for the head of Aram is Damascus,
and the head of Damascus is only Rezin.
Within sixty-five years
Ephraim will be too shattered to be a people.
9The head of Ephraim is Samaria,
and the head of Samaria is only Remaliah's son.
If you do not stand firm in your faith,
you will not stand at all.' "

10Again the LORD spoke to Ahaz, 11"Ask the LORD your God for
a sign, whether in the deepest depths or in the highest heights."
12But Ahaz said, "I will not ask; I will not put the LORD to the
test."
13Then Isaiah said, "Hear now, you house of David! Is it not
enough to try the patience of men? Will you try the patience of my
God also? 14Therefore the Lord himself will give you[c] a sign: The
virgin will be with child and will give birth to a son, and[d] will call
him Immanuel.[e] 15He will eat curds and honey when he knows
enough to reject the wrong and choose the right. 16But before
the boy knows enough to reject the wrong and choose the right,
the land of the two kings you dread will be laid waste. 17The LORD
will bring on you and on your people and on the house of your father a time unlike any since Ephraim broke away from Judah—
he will bring the king of Assyria."
18In that day the LORD will whistle for flies from the distant
streams of Egypt and for bees from the land of Assyria. 19They
will all come and settle in the steep ravines and in the crevices in
the rocks, on all the thornbushes and at all the water holes. 20In
that day the Lord will use a razor hired from beyond the River[f]—
the king of Assyria—to shave your head and the hair of your legs,
and to take off your beards also. 21In that day, a man will keep
alive a young cow and two goats. 22And because of the abundance
of the milk they give, he will have curds to eat. All who remain in
the land will eat curds and honey. 23In that day, in every place
where there were a thousand vines worth a thousand silver
shekels,[g] there will be only briers and thorns. 24Men will go there
with bow and arrow, for the land will be covered with briers and
thorns. 25As for all the hills once cultivated by the hoe, you will

[a] 2 Or *has set up camp in* [b] 3 *Shear-Jashub* means *a remnant will return.*
[c] 14 The Hebrew is plural. [d] 14 Masoretic Text; Dead Sea Scrolls *and he* or *and they*
[e] 14 *Immanuel* means *God with us.* [f] 20 That is, the Euphrates [g] 23 That is, about
25 pounds (about 11.5 kilograms)

One of the ways that our faith expresses itself is by our ability to be still, to be present, and not to panic or lose perspective. God still does his best work in the most difficult of circumstances.

Tim Hansel (1941-)

(7:3–9) Lord, how different my earthly challenges and spiritual battles look from Your perspective! Why should I fear anyone who comes against Your plans for me? I look to You, the initiator and finisher of my faith, for I know that "if I do not stand firm in my faith, I will not stand at all." Here is my heart, Lord; I go to Your Word and come into Your presence to be filled again with the faith that conquers everything.

Be calm my soul, faint not with care
Though burdens deep our hearts
would tear;
He is the Lord, all He commands,
He holdeth me safe in His hands.

"Be Calm My Soul"
Gloria Roe (©1960)

(7:14) A sign! A sign! Immanuel, here predicted, has come to earth, ascended to heaven and will come again. Yet through His Spirit He is continually here: God with us. I honor You, Lord God, because Your words are always true and Your promises are sure, though they may be a long time in coming. "For the revelation awaits an appointed time; it speaks of the end and will not prove false. Though it linger, wait for it; it will certainly come and will not delay." (Hab 2:2–3)

(8:11–14) Even in the midst of national catastrophe, You, Lord, speak peace to those who love You. We need not fear what the ungodly fear or live in terror of our enemies. You alone are the One to fear; You alone are the One to dread. Let only Your enemies be afraid. Why should we fear? To us You are a sanctuary. (Ps 91:7–8; 1Pe 3:13)

My peace I give unto you.
It's a peace that the world
Cannot give.
It's a peace that the world
Cannot understand.
Peace to know, peace to live.
My peace I give unto You.

"My Peace"
Keith Routledge (©1975)

no longer go there for fear of the briers and thorns; they will become places where cattle are turned loose and where sheep run.

Assyria, the LORD's Instrument

8 The LORD said to me, "Take a large scroll and write on it with an ordinary pen: Maher-Shalal-Hash-Baz.[a] 2And I will call in Uriah the priest and Zechariah son of Jeberekiah as reliable witnesses for me."

3Then I went to the prophetess, and she conceived and gave birth to a son. And the LORD said to me, "Name him Maher-Shalal-Hash-Baz. 4Before the boy knows how to say 'My father' or 'My mother,' the wealth of Damascus and the plunder of Samaria will be carried off by the king of Assyria."

5The LORD spoke to me again:

6"Because this people has rejected
the gently flowing waters of Shiloah
and rejoices over Rezin
and the son of Remaliah,
7therefore the Lord is about to bring against them
the mighty floodwaters of the River[b]—
the king of Assyria with all his pomp.
It will overflow all its channels,
run over all its banks
8and sweep on into Judah, swirling over it,
passing through it and reaching up to the neck.
Its outspread wings will cover the breadth of your land,
O Immanuel[c]!"
9Raise the war cry,[d] you nations, and be shattered!
Listen, all you distant lands.
Prepare for battle, and be shattered!
Prepare for battle, and be shattered!
10Devise your strategy, but it will be thwarted;
propose your plan, but it will not stand,
for God is with us.[e]

Fear God

11The LORD spoke to me with his strong hand upon me, warning me not to follow the way of this people. He said:

12"Do not call conspiracy
everything that these people call conspiracy[f];
do not fear what they fear,
and do not dread it.
13The LORD Almighty is the one you are to regard as holy,
he is the one you are to fear,
he is the one you are to dread,
14and he will be a sanctuary;
but for both houses of Israel he will be
a stone that causes men to stumble
and a rock that makes them fall.
And for the people of Jerusalem he will be
a trap and a snare.

[a] *1 Maher-Shalal-Hash-Baz* means *quick to the plunder, swift to the spoil*; also in verse 3. [b] *7* That is, the Euphrates [c] *8 Immanuel* means *God with us.* [d] *9* Or *Do your worst* [e] *10* Hebrew *Immanuel* [f] *12* Or *Do not call for a treaty / every time these people call for a treaty*

15 Many of them will stumble;
they will fall and be broken,
they will be snared and captured."

16 Bind up the testimony
and seal up the law among my disciples.
17 I will wait for the LORD,
who is hiding his face from the house of Jacob.
I will put my trust in him.

18 Here am I, and the children the LORD has given me. We are
signs and symbols in Israel from the LORD Almighty, who dwells
on Mount Zion.
19 When men tell you to consult mediums and spiritists, who
whisper and mutter, should not a people inquire of their God?
Why consult the dead on behalf of the living? 20 To the law and to
the testimony! If they do not speak according to this word, they
have no light of dawn. 21 Distressed and hungry, they will roam
through the land; when they are famished, they will become enraged and, looking upward, will curse their king and their God.
22 Then they will look toward the earth and see only distress and
darkness and fearful gloom, and they will be thrust into utter
darkness.

To Us a Child Is Born

9 Nevertheless, there will be no more gloom for those who were in distress. In the past he humbled the land of Zebulun and the land of Naphtali, but in the future he will honor Galilee of the Gentiles, by the way of the sea, along the Jordan—

2 The people walking in darkness
have seen a great light;
on those living in the land of the shadow of death[a]
a light has dawned.
3 You have enlarged the nation
and increased their joy;
they rejoice before you
as people rejoice at the harvest,
as men rejoice
when dividing the plunder.
4 For as in the day of Midian's defeat,
you have shattered
the yoke that burdens them,
the bar across their shoulders,
the rod of their oppressor.
5 Every warrior's boot used in battle
and every garment rolled in blood
will be destined for burning,
will be fuel for the fire.
6 For to us a child is born,
to us a son is given,
and the government will be on his shoulders.
And he will be called
Wonderful Counselor,[b] Mighty God,
Everlasting Father, Prince of Peace.
7 Of the increase of his government and peace
there will be no end.

[a] 2 Or *land of darkness* [b] 6 Or *Wonderful, Counselor*

(9:2–6) Who is this child? Who is this Wonderful Counselor? He is a son of man Who has walked in our shoes, felt our pains and struggled with our temptations. Moreover, He walks with us now, every step of the way. How could we not love Him? O Light of the World, prophesied deliverer of Israel, You have truly come. You are my deliverer and the light of my world as well. With joy I acknowledge Your right to every righteous and holy title and to every place of authority. Come, Lord Jesus, Messiah, and rule over us with justice and peace. Do it even now in me. I welcome You gratefully to the throne of my life. (Isa 30:21; Jn 1:4–9; 8:12; Heb 4:15)

Born Thy people to deliver,
Born a child and yet a King,
Born to reign in us forever,
Now Thy gracious kingdom bring.
By Thine own eternal Spirit
Rule in all our hearts alone;
By Thine all sufficient merit
Raise us to Thy glorious throne.
"Come, Thou Long Expected Jesus"
Charles Wesley (1744)

(9:7) Our world cries out for justice. We hunger and thirst for truth and integrity. We wait with eager hearts for Your coming, O Prince of Peace. As we wait, let us shine with the light of righteousness and encroach on the rule of darkness. We pray that You will live in us, and be righteous in us. Yours is the light that will cause even the blind to see and glorify God. (Mt.5:14; 28:18–20)

He will reign on David's throne
and over his kingdom,
establishing and upholding it
with justice and righteousness
from that time on and forever.
The zeal of the LORD Almighty
will accomplish this.

The LORD's Anger Against Israel

8 The Lord has sent a message against Jacob;
it will fall on Israel.
9 All the people will know it—
Ephraim and the inhabitants of Samaria—
who say with pride
and arrogance of heart,
10 "The bricks have fallen down,
but we will rebuild with dressed stone;
the fig trees have been felled,
but we will replace them with cedars."
11 But the LORD has strengthened Rezin's foes against them
and has spurred their enemies on.
12 Arameans from the east and Philistines from the west
have devoured Israel with open mouth.

Yet for all this, his anger is not turned away,
his hand is still upraised.

13 But the people have not returned to him who struck them,
nor have they sought the LORD Almighty.
14 So the LORD will cut off from Israel both head and tail,
both palm branch and reed in a single day;
15 the elders and prominent men are the head,
the prophets who teach lies are the tail.
16 Those who guide this people mislead them,
and those who are guided are led astray.
17 Therefore the Lord will take no pleasure in the young men,
nor will he pity the fatherless and widows,
for everyone is ungodly and wicked,
every mouth speaks vileness.

Yet for all this, his anger is not turned away,
his hand is still upraised.

18 Surely wickedness burns like a fire;
it consumes briers and thorns,
it sets the forest thickets ablaze,
so that it rolls upward in a column of smoke.
19 By the wrath of the LORD Almighty
the land will be scorched
and the people will be fuel for the fire;
no one will spare his brother.
20 On the right they will devour,
but still be hungry;
on the left they will eat,
but not be satisfied.

Each will feed on the flesh of his own offspring[a]:
21 Manasseh will feed on Ephraim, and Ephraim on Manasseh;
together they will turn against Judah.

Yet for all this, his anger is not turned away,
his hand is still upraised.

10 Woe to those who make unjust laws,
to those who issue oppressive decrees,
2 to deprive the poor of their rights
and withhold justice from the oppressed of my people,
making widows their prey
and robbing the fatherless.
3 What will you do on the day of reckoning,
when disaster comes from afar?
To whom will you run for help?
Where will you leave your riches?
4 Nothing will remain but to cringe among the captives
or fall among the slain.

Yet for all this, his anger is not turned away,
his hand is still upraised.

God's Judgment on Assyria

5 "Woe to the Assyrian, the rod of my anger,
in whose hand is the club of my wrath!
6 I send him against a godless nation,
I dispatch him against a people who anger me,
to seize loot and snatch plunder,
and to trample them down like mud in the streets.
7 But this is not what he intends,
this is not what he has in mind;
his purpose is to destroy,
to put an end to many nations.
8 'Are not my commanders all kings?' he says.
9 'Has not Calno fared like Carchemish?
Is not Hamath like Arpad,
and Samaria like Damascus?
10 As my hand seized the kingdoms of the idols,
kingdoms whose images excelled those of Jerusalem and Samaria—
11 shall I not deal with Jerusalem and her images
as I dealt with Samaria and her idols?' "

12 When the Lord has finished all his work against Mount Zion and Jerusalem, he will say, "I will punish the king of Assyria for the willful pride of his heart and the haughty look in his eyes.
13 For he says:

" 'By the strength of my hand I have done this,
and by my wisdom, because I have understanding.
I removed the boundaries of nations,
I plundered their treasures;
like a mighty one I subdued[b] their kings.
14 As one reaches into a nest,
so my hand reached for the wealth of the nations;

The love of worldly possessions is a sort of birdline, which entangles the soul and prevents it flying to God.
Saint Augustine of Hippo (354-430)

(10:3) "Where will you leave your riches?" You ask this question of us, too. This is the choice: Gain the world now and lose our souls and, in the eternal process, lose everything, or lay up our treasures in heaven and gain our souls and all else beside. Where our treasure is, there will our hearts be also. I choose to put my worldly goods at Your disposal as a continual act of worship. Let me be Your hand of blessing to a lost and desperate world. All I ask is that many will receive Your mercy through me and give You thanks. (Mk 8:36, Lk 12:34; 2Co 9:9–11)

[a] 20 Or *arm* [b] 13 Or / *I subdued the mighty,*

(10:20–21) This is how You are, Lord—always watching for the prodigals to return. How many times You could have disowned me when I walked away in foolishness or rebellion. Instead, when I came home shamefaced, You forgave, disciplined and restored me like a faithful parent. I praise and honor You for Your gracious provision for me, Your wayward child. May I never forget the hopelessness of wandering from You. And may I never take for granted the joy of being in Your presence. (Lk 15:22–24)

Again and again the towers of the Father's house light up as we tread the dust of the far country.

Helmut Thielicke (1908-1986)

as men gather abandoned eggs,
so I gathered all the countries;
not one flapped a wing,
or opened its mouth to chirp.' "

15 Does the ax raise itself above him who swings it,
or the saw boast against him who uses it?
As if a rod were to wield him who lifts it up,
or a club brandish him who is not wood!
16 Therefore, the Lord, the LORD Almighty,
will send a wasting disease upon his sturdy warriors;
under his pomp a fire will be kindled
like a blazing flame.
17 The Light of Israel will become a fire,
their Holy One a flame;
in a single day it will burn and consume
his thorns and his briers.
18 The splendor of his forests and fertile fields
it will completely destroy,
as when a sick man wastes away.
19 And the remaining trees of his forests will be so few
that a child could write them down.

The Remnant of Israel

20 In that day the remnant of Israel,
the survivors of the house of Jacob,
will no longer rely on him
who struck them down
but will truly rely on the LORD,
the Holy One of Israel.
21 A remnant will return,[a] a remnant of Jacob
will return to the Mighty God.
22 Though your people, O Israel, be like the sand by the sea,
only a remnant will return.
Destruction has been decreed,
overwhelming and righteous.
23 The Lord, the LORD Almighty, will carry out
the destruction decreed upon the whole land.
24 Therefore, this is what the Lord, the LORD Almighty, says:

"O my people who live in Zion,
do not be afraid of the Assyrians,
who beat you with a rod
and lift up a club against you, as Egypt did.
25 Very soon my anger against you will end
and my wrath will be directed to their destruction."

26 The LORD Almighty will lash them with a whip,
as when he struck down Midian at the rock of Oreb;
and he will raise his staff over the waters,
as he did in Egypt.
27 In that day their burden will be lifted from your shoulders,
their yoke from your neck;

[a] 21 Hebrew *shear-jashub*; also in verse 22

the yoke will be broken
because you have grown so fat.[a]

28 They enter Aiath;
they pass through Migron;
they store supplies at Micmash.
29 They go over the pass, and say,
"We will camp overnight at Geba."
Ramah trembles;
Gibeah of Saul flees.
30 Cry out, O Daughter of Gallim!
Listen, O Laishah!
Poor Anathoth!
31 Madmenah is in flight;
the people of Gebim take cover.
32 This day they will halt at Nob;
they will shake their fist
at the mount of the Daughter of Zion,
at the hill of Jerusalem.

33 See, the Lord, the LORD Almighty,
will lop off the boughs with great power.
The lofty trees will be felled,
the tall ones will be brought low.
34 He will cut down the forest thickets with an ax;
Lebanon will fall before the Mighty One.

The Branch From Jesse

11 A shoot will come up from the stump of Jesse;
from his roots a Branch will bear fruit.
2 The Spirit of the LORD will rest on him—
the Spirit of wisdom and of understanding,
the Spirit of counsel and of power,
the Spirit of knowledge and of the fear of the
LORD—
3 and he will delight in the fear of the LORD.

He will not judge by what he sees with his eyes,
or decide by what he hears with his ears;
4 but with righteousness he will judge the needy,
with justice he will give decisions for the poor of the
earth.
He will strike the earth with the rod of his mouth;
with the breath of his lips he will slay the
wicked.
5 Righteousness will be his belt
and faithfulness the sash around his waist.

6 The wolf will live with the lamb,
the leopard will lie down with the goat,
the calf and the lion and the yearling[b] together;
and a little child will lead them.
7 The cow will feed with the bear,
their young will lie down together,
and the lion will eat straw like the ox.
8 The infant will play near the hole of the cobra,

[a] 27 Hebrew; Septuagint *broken / from your shoulders* [b] 6 Hebrew; Septuagint *lion will feed*

(11:1–9) The Righteous One has come and will come again. The Spirit of the Lord will rest on Him; every decision He makes will be godly, every judgment just. This is the One Who comes with the Spirit of wisdom, knowledge, power, understanding, counsel and the fear of the Lord—and the heritage of peace. This is my Lord Jesus. (Jn 8:28)

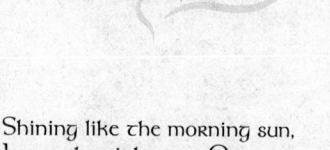

Shining like the morning sun,
Jesus, the righteous One.
Clothed in majesty, splendor, and glory,
Jesus, the righteous One.

Righteous One, Holy Son,
Flow through this vessel of mine.

"Righteous One"
Bruce Muller and Teresa Muller (©1991)

and the young child put his hand into the viper's
nest.
9 They will neither harm nor destroy
on all my holy mountain,
for the earth will be full of the knowledge of
the LORD
as the waters cover the sea.

10 In that day the Root of Jesse will stand as a banner for the
peoples; the nations will rally to him, and his place of rest will
be glorious. 11 In that day the Lord will reach out his hand a second time to reclaim the remnant that is left of his people from
Assyria, from Lower Egypt, from Upper Egypt,[a] from Cush,[b]
from Elam, from Babylonia,[c] from Hamath and from the islands
of the sea.

(11:10–12) I worship You, Root of Jesse, Messiah, Lord. I praise You for giving Your prophet this vision that gave hope to Your people Israel and that gives hope to the nations today. For You will one day be lifted up as a banner over all nations; the wounded and the exiled will rally to Your ensign; the weary and battle-scarred will enter into Your rest. Lord Jesus Christ, this is the certain hope, the heavenly vision, that carries me through the mundane and the discouraging.

12 He will raise a banner for the nations
and gather the exiles of Israel;
he will assemble the scattered people of Judah
from the four quarters of the earth.
13 Ephraim's jealousy will vanish,
and Judah's enemies[d] will be cut off;
Ephraim will not be jealous of Judah,
nor Judah hostile toward Ephraim.
14 They will swoop down on the slopes of Philistia to the
west;
together they will plunder the people to the east.
They will lay hands on Edom and Moab,
and the Ammonites will be subject to them.
15 The LORD will dry up
the gulf of the Egyptian sea;
with a scorching wind he will sweep his hand
over the Euphrates River.[e]
He will break it up into seven streams
so that men can cross over in sandals.
16 There will be a highway for the remnant of his
people
that is left from Assyria,
as there was for Israel
when they came up from Egypt.

Songs of Praise

12 In that day you will say:

"I will praise you, O LORD.
Although you were angry with me,
your anger has turned away
and you have comforted me.
2 Surely God is my salvation;
I will trust and not be afraid.
The LORD, the LORD, is my strength and my song;
he has become my salvation."
3 With joy you will draw water
from the wells of salvation.

(12:3) I am so often—too often—dry, Lord. Oh, refresh me today. Restore to me the joy of my salvation, and renew a right spirit within me. Overfill Your well of living water inside of me and let it overflow to a thirsty world. I have nothing, Lord, except what You give me. I come to You in all humility to receive living water again by faith. (Ps 51:10–12; Jn 4:13–14)

4 In that day you will say:

[a] *11* Hebrew *from Pathros* [b] *11* That is, the upper Nile region [c] *11* Hebrew *Shinar*
[d] *13* Or *hostility* [e] *15* Hebrew *the River*

"Give thanks to the LORD, call on his name;
make known among the nations what he has done,
and proclaim that his name is exalted.
5 Sing to the LORD, for he has done glorious things;
let this be known to all the world.
6 Shout aloud and sing for joy, people of Zion,
for great is the Holy One of Israel among you."

A Prophecy Against Babylon

13 An oracle concerning Babylon that Isaiah son of Amoz saw:

2 Raise a banner on a bare hilltop,
shout to them;
beckon to them
to enter the gates of the nobles.
3 I have commanded my holy ones;
I have summoned my warriors to carry out my wrath—
those who rejoice in my triumph.

4 Listen, a noise on the mountains,
like that of a great multitude!
Listen, an uproar among the kingdoms,
like nations massing together!
The LORD Almighty is mustering
an army for war.
5 They come from faraway lands,
from the ends of the heavens—
the LORD and the weapons of his wrath—
to destroy the whole country.

6 Wail, for the day of the LORD is near;
it will come like destruction from the Almighty.[a]
7 Because of this, all hands will go limp,
every man's heart will melt.
8 Terror will seize them,
pain and anguish will grip them;
they will writhe like a woman in labor.
They will look aghast at each other,
their faces aflame.

9 See, the day of the LORD is coming
—a cruel day, with wrath and fierce anger—
to make the land desolate
and destroy the sinners within it.
10 The stars of heaven and their constellations
will not show their light.
The rising sun will be darkened
and the moon will not give its light.
11 I will punish the world for its evil,
the wicked for their sins.
I will put an end to the arrogance of the haughty
and will humble the pride of the ruthless.
12 I will make man scarcer than pure gold,
more rare than the gold of Ophir.
13 Therefore I will make the heavens tremble;
and the earth will shake from its place

[a] 6 Hebrew *Shaddai*

(12:4–6) My glorious God and King! Today I will lay down my pride and inhibitions. I will shout aloud and sing for joy. My prayer closet will become a noisy, holy place of rejoicing. Never mind what the neighbors think; I will let the nations hear what great things You have done.

I love thee so, I know not how
My transport to control;
Thy love is like a burning fire
Within my very soul.
Frederick William Faber (1814-1863)

(14:1–7) You are the great, compassionate, faithful God. Your promises of forgiveness and restoration are our hope and our consolation. Your promises of peace give us joy in the tumult. You give us courage for our struggle with darkness, and authority to triumph over every spiritual enemy. We praise You and thank You, God of peace, for You will soon crush Satan under our feet. (Ro 16:20)

at the wrath of the LORD Almighty,
in the day of his burning anger.

14 Like a hunted gazelle,
like sheep without a shepherd,
each will return to his own people,
each will flee to his native land.
15 Whoever is captured will be thrust through;
all who are caught will fall by the sword.
16 Their infants will be dashed to pieces before their eyes;
their houses will be looted and their wives ravished.
17 See, I will stir up against them the Medes,
who do not care for silver
and have no delight in gold.
18 Their bows will strike down the young men;
they will have no mercy on infants
nor will they look with compassion on children.
19 Babylon, the jewel of kingdoms,
the glory of the Babylonians'[a] pride,
will be overthrown by God
like Sodom and Gomorrah.
20 She will never be inhabited
or lived in through all generations;
no Arab will pitch his tent there,
no shepherd will rest his flocks there.
21 But desert creatures will lie there,
jackals will fill her houses;
there the owls will dwell,
and there the wild goats will leap about.
22 Hyenas will howl in her strongholds,
jackals in her luxurious palaces.
Her time is at hand,
and her days will not be prolonged.

14 The LORD will have compassion on Jacob;
once again he will choose Israel
and will settle them in their own land.
Aliens will join them
and unite with the house of Jacob.
2 Nations will take them
and bring them to their own place.
And the house of Israel will possess the nations
as menservants and maidservants in the LORD's land.
They will make captives of their captors
and rule over their oppressors.

3 On the day the LORD gives you relief from suffering and turmoil and cruel bondage, 4 you will take up this taunt against the king of Babylon:

How the oppressor has come to an end!
How his fury[b] has ended!
5 The LORD has broken the rod of the wicked,

[a] 19 Or *Chaldeans'* [b] 4 Dead Sea Scrolls, Septuagint and Syriac; the meaning of the word in the Masoretic Text is uncertain.

the scepter of the rulers,
6 which in anger struck down peoples
with unceasing blows,
and in fury subdued nations
with relentless aggression.
7 All the lands are at rest and at peace;
they break into singing.
8 Even the pine trees and the cedars of Lebanon
exult over you and say,
"Now that you have been laid low,
no woodsman comes to cut us down."

9 The grave[a] below is all astir
to meet you at your coming;
it rouses the spirits of the departed to greet you—
all those who were leaders in the world;
it makes them rise from their thrones—
all those who were kings over the nations.
10 They will all respond,
they will say to you,
"You also have become weak, as we are;
you have become like us."
11 All your pomp has been brought down to the grave,
along with the noise of your harps;
maggots are spread out beneath you
and worms cover you.

12 How you have fallen from heaven,
O morning star, son of the dawn!
You have been cast down to the earth,
you who once laid low the nations!
13 You said in your heart,
"I will ascend to heaven;
I will raise my throne
above the stars of God;
I will sit enthroned on the mount of assembly,
on the utmost heights of the sacred mountain.[b]
14 I will ascend above the tops of the clouds;
I will make myself like the Most High."
15 But you are brought down to the grave,
to the depths of the pit.

16 Those who see you stare at you,
they ponder your fate:
"Is this the man who shook the earth
and made kingdoms tremble,
17 the man who made the world a desert,
who overthrew its cities
and would not let his captives go home?"

18 All the kings of the nations lie in state,
each in his own tomb.
19 But you are cast out of your tomb
like a rejected branch;
you are covered with the slain,
with those pierced by the sword,
those who descend to the stones of the pit.

[a] 9 Hebrew *Sheol*; also in verses 11 and 15 [b] 13 Or *the north*; Hebrew *Zaphon*

(14:9–20) All praise to You, O God! Our enemy, Your enemy, is laid low. Though he struggles against his destiny, his judgment is sealed. Though he still rages, his time is short; his doom is sure. And the day is just over the horizon when the pain and suffering of Your people will be relieved, and ultimate justice will rise like the dawn over the earth. Because of Your grace, O God, even now our hearts begin the celebration.

Envious of us Christians, [demons] meddle with all things in their desire to frustrate our journey into heaven so that we might not ascend to the place from which they fell.

Anthony of Egypt (c.251-356)

God is so powerful that he can direct any evil to a good end.
Saint Thomas Aquinas (1225-1274)

(14:24–27) Who can thwart You, God, or turn back the hand that You have stretched out against Your enemies, against those who would oppress Your people? Who can change the judgment You have determined? No one. But in the very midst of Your judgment on the wicked, You bring deliverance, restoration and blessing to Your people. You are truly a faithful and awesome God. (Ps 91:7–8)

God is working His purpose out,
As year succeeds to year:
God is working His purpose out,
And the time is drawing near:
Nearer and nearer draws the time,
The time that shall surely be,
When the earth shall be filled
With the glory of God
As the waters cover the sea.
"God Is Working His Purpose Out"
Arthur C. Ainger (1894)

Like a corpse trampled underfoot,
20 you will not join them in burial,
for you have destroyed your land
and killed your people.

The offspring of the wicked
will never be mentioned again.
21 Prepare a place to slaughter his sons
for the sins of their forefathers;
they are not to rise to inherit the land
and cover the earth with their cities.

22 "I will rise up against them,"
declares the LORD Almighty.
"I will cut off from Babylon her name and survivors,
her offspring and descendants,"
declares the LORD.
23 "I will turn her into a place for owls
and into swampland;
I will sweep her with the broom of destruction,"
declares the LORD Almighty.

A Prophecy Against Assyria

24 The LORD Almighty has sworn,

"Surely, as I have planned, so it will be,
and as I have purposed, so it will stand.
25 I will crush the Assyrian in my land;
on my mountains I will trample him down.
His yoke will be taken from my people,
and his burden removed from their shoulders."
26 This is the plan determined for the whole world;
this is the hand stretched out over all nations.
27 For the LORD Almighty has purposed, and who can thwart him?
His hand is stretched out, and who can turn it back?

A Prophecy Against the Philistines

28 This oracle came in the year King Ahaz died:

29 Do not rejoice, all you Philistines,
that the rod that struck you is broken;
from the root of that snake will spring up a viper,
its fruit will be a darting, venomous serpent.
30 The poorest of the poor will find pasture,
and the needy will lie down in safety.
But your root I will destroy by famine;
it will slay your survivors.

31 Wail, O gate! Howl, O city!
Melt away, all you Philistines!
A cloud of smoke comes from the north,
and there is not a straggler in its ranks.
32 What answer shall be given
to the envoys of that nation?
"The LORD has established Zion,
and in her his afflicted people will find refuge."

A Prophecy Against Moab

15 An oracle concerning Moab:

Ar in Moab is ruined,
destroyed in a night!
Kir in Moab is ruined,
destroyed in a night!
2 Dibon goes up to its temple,
to its high places to weep;
Moab wails over Nebo and Medeba.
Every head is shaved
and every beard cut off.
3 In the streets they wear sackcloth;
on the roofs and in the public squares
they all wail,
prostrate with weeping.
4 Heshbon and Elealeh cry out,
their voices are heard all the way to Jahaz.
Therefore the armed men of Moab cry out,
and their hearts are faint.

5 My heart cries out over Moab;
her fugitives flee as far as Zoar,
as far as Eglath Shelishiyah.
They go up the way to Luhith,
weeping as they go;
on the road to Horonaim
they lament their destruction.
6 The waters of Nimrim are dried up
and the grass is withered;
the vegetation is gone
and nothing green is left.
7 So the wealth they have acquired and stored up
they carry away over the Ravine of the Poplars.
8 Their outcry echoes along the border of Moab;
their wailing reaches as far as Eglaim,
their lamentation as far as Beer Elim.
9 Dimon's[a] waters are full of blood,
but I will bring still more upon Dimon[a]—
a lion upon the fugitives of Moab
and upon those who remain in the land.

16 Send lambs as tribute
to the ruler of the land,
from Sela, across the desert,
to the mount of the Daughter of Zion.
2 Like fluttering birds
pushed from the nest,
so are the women of Moab
at the fords of the Arnon.

3 "Give us counsel,
render a decision.
Make your shadow like night—
at high noon.
Hide the fugitives,

[a] 9 Masoretic Text; Dead Sea Scrolls, some Septuagint manuscripts and Vulgate *Dibon*

Prayer moves the arm which moves the world,
And brings salvation down.
James Montgomery (1771-1854)

(15:5) Lord, help me to cry over needy nations as Your prophet cried over Moab. So many are lost and destined for judgment. Pour out revelation so they may believe and be saved. You are the ultimate authority over all nations, so to You I plead for pity and intervention on their behalf. Not so they may continue safely in their sin, but to buy time for the lost before You bring down the final curtain. For You, Lord, "take no pleasure in the death of the wicked, but rather that they turn from their ways and live." (Eze 33:11)

We are not a post-war generation, but a pre-peace generation. Jesus is coming.
Corrie ten Boom (1892–1983)

(16:5) Imagine One Who rules in mercy and lovingkindness, a judge Who seeks justice and speeds the cause of righteousness, a deliverer Who will banish the oppressor and aggressor from the land forever. O God, I rejoice to know that such a King is coming. Even so, come quickly, Lord Jesus.

(16:9) Forgive me, Lord, for my lack of tears for the nations. Knowing Your power to intervene in their troubles and turmoil, knowing that You wait only for the prayers of Your intercessors to move in mercy, I confess I have been unfaithful to what I know to be my duty. My heart is hard. Holy Spirit of God, put Your compassion in me. Fill my eyes with Your tears. Fill my heart with Your pain for the lost.

do not betray the refugees.
4 Let the Moabite fugitives stay with you;
be their shelter from the destroyer."

The oppressor will come to an end,
and destruction will cease;
the aggressor will vanish from the land.
5 In love a throne will be established;
in faithfulness a man will sit on it—
one from the house[a] of David—
one who in judging seeks justice
and speeds the cause of righteousness.

6 We have heard of Moab's pride—
her overweening pride and conceit,
her pride and her insolence—
but her boasts are empty.
7 Therefore the Moabites wail,
they wail together for Moab.
Lament and grieve
for the men[b] of Kir Hareseth.
8 The fields of Heshbon wither,
the vines of Sibmah also.
The rulers of the nations
have trampled down the choicest vines,
which once reached Jazer
and spread toward the desert.
Their shoots spread out
and went as far as the sea.
9 So I weep, as Jazer weeps,
for the vines of Sibmah.
O Heshbon, O Elealeh,
I drench you with tears!
The shouts of joy over your ripened fruit
and over your harvests have been stilled.
10 Joy and gladness are taken away from the orchards;
no one sings or shouts in the vineyards;
no one treads out wine at the presses,
for I have put an end to the shouting.
11 My heart laments for Moab like a harp,
my inmost being for Kir Hareseth.
12 When Moab appears at her high place,
she only wears herself out;
when she goes to her shrine to pray,
it is to no avail.

13 This is the word the LORD has already spoken concerning
Moab. 14 But now the LORD says: "Within three years, as a servant
bound by contract would count them, Moab's splendor and all
her many people will be despised, and her survivors will be very
few and feeble."

An Oracle Against Damascus

17 An oracle concerning Damascus:

"See, Damascus will no longer be a city
but will become a heap of ruins.

[a] 5 Hebrew *tent* [b] 7 Or "*raisin cakes*," a wordplay

2The cities of Aroer will be deserted
and left to flocks, which will lie down,
with no one to make them afraid.
3The fortified city will disappear from Ephraim,
and royal power from Damascus;
the remnant of Aram will be
like the glory of the Israelites,"
declares the LORD Almighty.

4"In that day the glory of Jacob will fade;
the fat of his body will waste away.
5It will be as when a reaper gathers the standing grain
and harvests the grain with his arm—
as when a man gleans heads of grain
in the Valley of Rephaim.
6Yet some gleanings will remain,
as when an olive tree is beaten,
leaving two or three olives on the topmost
branches,
four or five on the fruitful boughs,"
declares the LORD, the God of Israel.

7In that day men will look to their Maker
and turn their eyes to the Holy One of Israel.
8They will not look to the altars,
the work of their hands,
and they will have no regard for the Asherah poles[a]
and the incense altars their fingers have made.

9In that day their strong cities, which they left because of the
Israelites, will be like places abandoned to thickets and undergrowth. And all will be desolation.

10You have forgotten God your Savior;
you have not remembered the Rock, your
fortress.
Therefore, though you set out the finest plants
and plant imported vines,
11though on the day you set them out, you make them
grow,
and on the morning when you plant them, you bring
them to bud,
yet the harvest will be as nothing
in the day of disease and incurable pain.

12Oh, the raging of many nations—
they rage like the raging sea!
Oh, the uproar of the peoples—
they roar like the roaring of great waters!
13Although the peoples roar like the roar of surging
waters,
when he rebukes them they flee far away,
driven before the wind like chaff on the hills,
like tumbleweed before a gale.
14In the evening, sudden terror!
Before the morning, they are gone!
This is the portion of those who loot us,
the lot of those who plunder us.

[a] 8 That is, symbols of the goddess Asherah

(17:7–8) Father, so often I fool myself into thinking that I can create my own security. The lack of adversity in my life gives me the sense that I have everything under control. Lord, I pray that You will show me the path to absolute dependence on You. If I have committed the error of creating idols in my heart, forgive me. Help me to see that no other gods, no works of my own hands, nothing I have stored up against calamity can rescue or bless me. You alone are God, Deliverer, Lord, Redeemer. I put my trust in You.

(17:10–13) Do we never learn? You are our one sure Rock, our one place of safety. Yet we foolishly choose to walk in independence. Then when things go wrong, as they always do, we roar and rage at You. Let it be far from me, Lord. You are my everlasting Helper, my one sure Hope, my Provider. Without You I am a lost cause. You alone are always faithful, always willing to pardon, always ready to restore, always there.

(19:1) When You rise up, O God, everything else falls down. Idols melt and idolaters flee in the face of Your awesome presence. Blessed are You, Lord God, in Your terrifying majesty! I confess that I am completely unable to stand before You in my own strength. You are too holy, too pure, too amazing; against Your light the darkness in my soul is laid bare. But through Your infinite grace and mercy, You have chosen to redeem me. Although I cannot stand before You, You lift me up through the blood of Your Son. Hallelujah!

A Prophecy Against Cush

18 Woe to the land of whirring wings[a]
along the rivers of Cush,[b]
2 which sends envoys by sea
in papyrus boats over the water.

Go, swift messengers,
to a people tall and smooth-skinned,
to a people feared far and wide,
an aggressive nation of strange speech,
whose land is divided by rivers.

3 All you people of the world,
you who live on the earth,
when a banner is raised on the mountains,
you will see it,
and when a trumpet sounds,
you will hear it.
4 This is what the LORD says to me:
"I will remain quiet and will look on from my dwelling place,
like shimmering heat in the sunshine,
like a cloud of dew in the heat of harvest."
5 For, before the harvest, when the blossom is gone
and the flower becomes a ripening grape,
he will cut off the shoots with pruning knives,
and cut down and take away the spreading branches.
6 They will all be left to the mountain birds of prey
and to the wild animals;
the birds will feed on them all summer,
the wild animals all winter.

7 At that time gifts will be brought to the LORD Almighty

from a people tall and smooth-skinned,
from a people feared far and wide,
an aggressive nation of strange speech,
whose land is divided by rivers—

the gifts will be brought to Mount Zion, the place of the Name of the LORD Almighty.

A Prophecy About Egypt

19 An oracle concerning Egypt:

See, the LORD rides on a swift cloud
and is coming to Egypt.
The idols of Egypt tremble before him,
and the hearts of the Egyptians melt within them.

2 "I will stir up Egyptian against Egyptian—
brother will fight against brother,
neighbor against neighbor,
city against city,
kingdom against kingdom.
3 The Egyptians will lose heart,
and I will bring their plans to nothing;

[a] *1* Or *of locusts* [b] *1* That is, the upper Nile region

they will consult the idols and the spirits of the
dead,
the mediums and the spiritists.
4 I will hand the Egyptians over
to the power of a cruel master,
and a fierce king will rule over them,"
declares the Lord, the LORD Almighty.
5 The waters of the river will dry up,
and the riverbed will be parched and dry.
6 The canals will stink;
the streams of Egypt will dwindle and dry up.
The reeds and rushes will wither,
7 also the plants along the Nile,
at the mouth of the river.
Every sown field along the Nile
will become parched, will blow away and be no
more.
8 The fishermen will groan and lament,
all who cast hooks into the Nile;
those who throw nets on the water
will pine away.
9 Those who work with combed flax will despair,
the weavers of fine linen will lose hope.
10 The workers in cloth will be dejected,
and all the wage earners will be sick at heart.

11 The officials of Zoan are nothing but fools;
the wise counselors of Pharaoh give senseless
advice.
How can you say to Pharaoh,
"I am one of the wise men,
a disciple of the ancient kings"?
12 Where are your wise men now?
Let them show you and make known
what the LORD Almighty
has planned against Egypt.
13 The officials of Zoan have become fools,
the leaders of Memphis[a] are deceived;
the cornerstones of her peoples
have led Egypt astray.
14 The LORD has poured into them
a spirit of dizziness;
they make Egypt stagger in all that she does,
as a drunkard staggers around in his vomit.
15 There is nothing Egypt can do—
head or tail, palm branch or reed.

16 In that day the Egyptians will be like women. They will
shudder with fear at the uplifted hand that the LORD Almighty
raises against them. 17 And the land of Judah will bring terror to
the Egyptians; everyone to whom Judah is mentioned will be terrified, because of what the LORD Almighty is planning against
them.
18 In that day five cities in Egypt will speak the language of

[a] 13 Hebrew *Noph*

(19:3) Lord, I too live in the midst of a culture dedicated to idols. Search my heart and remove my love for every idolatrous thing: money, power and status symbols that make me feel important but create an obstruction in our communication. You are my God; I will come to You alone for security and wisdom. Every spirit that is not Yours, I forswear. Every advisor that is not in tune with Your Word and filled with Your Spirit, I reject. Give me only wisdom from above. (Col 3:5; Jas.1:5)

Farewell, vain world;
My soul bids you adieu;
My savior taught me
To abandon you.
Your charms may gratify
A sensual mind,
But cannot please
A soul for God designed.

David Brainerd (1718-1747)

(19:19–24) I give You praise, O God, for You truly love all the nations. Though You bruise them to bring them to repentance, You restore them abundantly when they give You allegiance. Though You strike, You will heal. For You do not willingly bring affliction and grief to the children of men, nor do You delight in the death of anyone. Thank You, Lord, for Your unfailing mercy. (La 3:33; Eze 18:23,32)

(20:3–6) Lord, I trust only in You! Every other tower will crumble, every other ally will fail, every other spiritual power will fall. I see what happens to those who rely on other helpers, who trust in human wisdom and strength. Sooner or later they will be stripped of everything and their idolatry will be exposed. But You are a sure refuge. Lord, I trust only in You!

When you have no helpers, see all your helpers in God. When you have many helpers, see God in all your helpers. When you have nothing but God, see all in God. When you have everything, see God in everything. Under all conditions, stay thy heart only on the Lord.

Charles Haddon Spurgeon (1834–1892)

Canaan and swear allegiance to the LORD Almighty. One of them
will be called the City of Destruction.[a]
19 In that day there will be an altar to the LORD in the heart of
Egypt, and a monument to the LORD at its border. 20 It will be a
sign and witness to the LORD Almighty in the land of Egypt. When
they cry out to the LORD because of their oppressors, he will send
them a savior and defender, and he will rescue them. 21 So the
LORD will make himself known to the Egyptians, and in that day
they will acknowledge the LORD. They will worship with sacrifices
and grain offerings; they will make vows to the LORD and keep
them. 22 The LORD will strike Egypt with a plague; he will strike
them and heal them. They will turn to the LORD, and he will respond to their pleas and heal them.
23 In that day there will be a highway from Egypt to Assyria. The
Assyrians will go to Egypt and the Egyptians to Assyria. The Egyptians and Assyrians will worship together. 24 In that day Israel will
be the third, along with Egypt and Assyria, a blessing on the earth.
25 The LORD Almighty will bless them, saying, "Blessed be Egypt
my people, Assyria my handiwork, and Israel my inheritance."

A Prophecy Against Egypt and Cush

20 In the year that the supreme commander, sent by Sargon
king of Assyria, came to Ashdod and attacked and captured it— 2 at that time the LORD spoke through Isaiah son of
Amoz. He said to him, "Take off the sackcloth from your body
and the sandals from your feet." And he did so, going around
stripped and barefoot.
3 Then the LORD said, "Just as my servant Isaiah has gone
stripped and barefoot for three years, as a sign and portent
against Egypt and Cush,[b] 4 so the king of Assyria will lead away
stripped and barefoot the Egyptian captives and Cushite exiles,
young and old, with buttocks bared—to Egypt's shame. 5 Those
who trusted in Cush and boasted in Egypt will be afraid and put to
shame. 6 In that day the people who live on this coast will say, 'See
what has happened to those we relied on, those we fled to for
help and deliverance from the king of Assyria! How then can we
escape?' "

A Prophecy Against Babylon

21 An oracle concerning the Desert by the Sea:

Like whirlwinds sweeping through the southland,
  an invader comes from the desert,
  from a land of terror.
2 A dire vision has been shown to me:
  The traitor betrays, the looter takes loot.
Elam, attack! Media, lay siege!
  I will bring to an end all the groaning she caused.
3 At this my body is racked with pain,
  pangs seize me, like those of a woman in labor;
I am staggered by what I hear,
  I am bewildered by what I see.
4 My heart falters,

[a] *18* Most manuscripts of the Masoretic Text; some manuscripts of the Masoretic Text, Dead Sea Scrolls and Vulgate *City of the Sun* (that is, Heliopolis) [b] *3* That is, the upper Nile region; also in verse 5

fear makes me tremble;
the twilight I longed for
has become a horror to me.
5 They set the tables,
they spread the rugs,
they eat, they drink!
Get up, you officers,
oil the shields!

6 This is what the Lord says to me:

"Go, post a lookout
and have him report what he sees.
7 When he sees chariots
with teams of horses,
riders on donkeys
or riders on camels,
let him be alert,
fully alert."

8 And the lookout[a] shouted,

"Day after day, my lord, I stand on the watchtower;
every night I stay at my post.
9 Look, here comes a man in a chariot
with a team of horses.
And he gives back the answer:
'Babylon has fallen, has fallen!
All the images of its gods
lie shattered on the ground!' "

10 O my people, crushed on the threshing floor,
I tell you what I have heard
from the LORD Almighty,
from the God of Israel.

A Prophecy Against Edom

11 An oracle concerning Dumah[b]:

Someone calls to me from Seir,
"Watchman, what is left of the night?
Watchman, what is left of the night?"
12 The watchman replies,
"Morning is coming, but also the night.
If you would ask, then ask;
and come back yet again."

A Prophecy Against Arabia

13 An oracle concerning Arabia:

You caravans of Dedanites,
who camp in the thickets of Arabia,
14 bring water for the thirsty;
you who live in Tema,
bring food for the fugitives.
15 They flee from the sword,
from the drawn sword,

[a] 8 Dead Sea Scrolls and Syriac; Masoretic Text *A lion* [b] 11 *Dumah* means *silence* or *stillness,* a wordplay on *Edom.*

As it is the business of tailors to make clothes and of cobblers to mend shoes, so it is the business of Christians to pray.
Martin Luther (1483-1546)

(21:6–8) In my spirit, I will post myself on the watchtower of prayer and listen for Your signals. I want to be alert to Your Word and Your actions. Speak to me and give me clear direction, I pray. I want to stay when You stay, move when You move and never, never fall asleep at my post. (Hab 2:1)

Wake, awake, for night is flying,
The watchmen on the heights are crying;
Awake, Jerusalem, at last.
Midnight hears the welcome voices,
And at the thrilling cry rejoices:
"Come forth, you maidens! Night is past.
The bridegroom comes!
Awake; your lamps with gladness take!"
Alleluia!
Prepare yourselves to meet the Lord,
Whose light has stirred the waiting guard.
"Wake, Awake, for Night Is Flying"
Philipp Nicolai (1599)
Trans. Catherine Winkworth (1858)

(22:3) Lord, prepare me to stand my ground in the spiritual war that rages in the world around me. Give me courage and faith, Lord, to stand and fight the enemy with Your Word and with worship. I will speak the high praises of God, declaring Your majesty and authority over every spiritual power. Thus, I will see the enemy defeated and my warfare triumphant. (Ps 149:6,8–9)

(22:8–13) Father, You are the only sure defense in time of trouble. Time and again we look to our own strategies and resources for help; and time and again we fail. You are poised to send the resources of heaven to our aid; You wait only for us to come to You with repentance and petition. You wait for our serious intercession—our tears and fasting and prayer. Help us to humble ourselves and put sackcloth on our souls. (Jas 4:2)

from the bent bow
and from the heat of battle.

16 This is what the Lord says to me: "Within one year, as a servant bound by contract would count it, all the pomp of Kedar will come to an end.
17 The survivors of the bowmen, the warriors of Kedar, will be few." The LORD, the God of Israel, has spoken.

A Prophecy About Jerusalem

22 An oracle concerning the Valley of Vision:

What troubles you now,
that you have all gone up on the roofs,
2 O town full of commotion,
O city of tumult and revelry?
Your slain were not killed by the sword,
nor did they die in battle.
3 All your leaders have fled together;
they have been captured without using the bow.
All you who were caught were taken prisoner together,
having fled while the enemy was still far away.
4 Therefore I said, "Turn away from me;
let me weep bitterly.
Do not try to console me
over the destruction of my people."

5 The Lord, the LORD Almighty, has a day
of tumult and trampling and terror
in the Valley of Vision,
a day of battering down walls
and of crying out to the mountains.
6 Elam takes up the quiver,
with her charioteers and horses;
Kir uncovers the shield.
7 Your choicest valleys are full of chariots,
and horsemen are posted at the city gates;
8 the defenses of Judah are stripped away.

And you looked in that day
to the weapons in the Palace of the Forest;
9 you saw that the City of David
had many breaches in its defenses;
you stored up water
in the Lower Pool.
10 You counted the buildings in Jerusalem
and tore down houses to strengthen the wall.
11 You built a reservoir between the two walls
for the water of the Old Pool,
but you did not look to the One who made it,
or have regard for the One who planned it long ago.

12 The Lord, the LORD Almighty,
called you on that day
to weep and to wail,
to tear out your hair and put on sackcloth.
13 But see, there is joy and revelry,

slaughtering of cattle and killing of sheep,
eating of meat and drinking of wine!
"Let us eat and drink," you say,
"for tomorrow we die!"

14The LORD Almighty has revealed this in my hearing: "Till your dying day this sin will not be atoned for," says the Lord, the LORD Almighty.

15This is what the Lord, the LORD Almighty, says:

"Go, say to this steward,
to Shebna, who is in charge of the palace:
16What are you doing here and who gave you permission
to cut out a grave for yourself here,
hewing your grave on the height
and chiseling your resting place in the rock?
17"Beware, the LORD is about to take firm hold of you
and hurl you away, O you mighty man.
18He will roll you up tightly like a ball
and throw you into a large country.
There you will die
and there your splendid chariots will remain—
you disgrace to your master's house!
19I will depose you from your office,
and you will be ousted from your position.

20"In that day I will summon my servant, Eliakim son of Hilkiah. 21I will clothe him with your robe and fasten your sash
around him and hand your authority over to him. He will be a father to those who live in Jerusalem and to the house of Judah. 22I
will place on his shoulder the key to the house of David; what he
opens no one can shut, and what he shuts no one can open. 23I
will drive him like a peg into a firm place; he will be a seat[a] of
honor for the house of his father. 24All the glory of his family will
hang on him: its offspring and offshoots—all its lesser vessels,
from the bowls to all the jars.

25"In that day," declares the LORD Almighty, "the peg driven
into the firm place will give way; it will be sheared off and will
fall, and the load hanging on it will be cut down." The LORD has
spoken.

A Prophecy About Tyre

23 An oracle concerning Tyre:

Wail, O ships of Tarshish!
For Tyre is destroyed
and left without house or harbor.
From the land of Cyprus[b]
word has come to them.

2Be silent, you people of the island
and you merchants of Sidon,
whom the seafarers have enriched.
3On the great waters
came the grain of the Shihor;

[a] 23 Or *throne* [b] 1 Hebrew *Kittim*

(22:17–22) You determine the fate of the nations. You raise up leaders and pull them down according to their acceptance or rejection of Your rule. The nations are at the disposal of Your wisdom and will. Their fate is in Your hands alone. No power on earth but prayer can change their destiny. (Dt 28:47–48; Jnh 3:7–10)

Before Jehovah's awesome throne,
Ye nations, bow with sacred joy;
Know that the Lord is God alone,
He can create, and He destroy.
"Before Jehovah's Awesome Throne"
Isaac Watts (1674–1748)

the harvest of the Nile[a] was the revenue of Tyre,
and she became the marketplace of the nations.

4 Be ashamed, O Sidon, and you, O fortress of the sea,
for the sea has spoken:
"I have neither been in labor nor given birth;
I have neither reared sons nor brought up
daughters."
5 When word comes to Egypt,
they will be in anguish at the report from Tyre.

6 Cross over to Tarshish;
wail, you people of the island.
7 Is this your city of revelry,
the old, old city,
whose feet have taken her
to settle in far-off lands?
8 Who planned this against Tyre,
the bestower of crowns,
whose merchants are princes,
whose traders are renowned in the earth?
9 The LORD Almighty planned it,
to bring low the pride of all glory
and to humble all who are renowned on the earth.

10 Till[b] your land as along the Nile,
O Daughter of Tarshish,
for you no longer have a harbor.
11 The LORD has stretched out his hand over the sea
and made its kingdoms tremble.
He has given an order concerning Phoenicia[c]
that her fortresses be destroyed.
12 He said, "No more of your reveling,
O Virgin Daughter of Sidon, now crushed!
"Up, cross over to Cyprus[d];
even there you will find no rest."
13 Look at the land of the Babylonians,[e]
this people that is now of no account!
The Assyrians have made it
a place for desert creatures;
they raised up their siege towers,
they stripped its fortresses bare
and turned it into a ruin.

14 Wail, you ships of Tarshish;
your fortress is destroyed!

15 At that time Tyre will be forgotten for seventy years, the span
of a king's life. But at the end of these seventy years, it will happen to Tyre as in the song of the prostitute:

16 "Take up a harp, walk through the city,
O prostitute forgotten;
play the harp well, sing many a song,
so that you will be remembered."

[a] *2,3* Masoretic Text; one Dead Sea Scroll *Sidon, / who cross over the sea; / your envoys* *3are on the great waters. / The grain of the Shihor, / the harvest of the Nile,*
[b] *10* Dead Sea Scrolls and some Septuagint manuscripts; Masoretic Text *Go through*
[c] *11* Hebrew *Canaan* [d] *12* Hebrew *Kittim* [e] *13* Or *Chaldeans*

God permits the wicked, but not forever.
Sir Thomas Fuller (1608–1661)

(23:8–9) No people on earth are too rich or powerful to try Your patience forever and remain unscathed. You will humble the proud; Your judgments will fall, and they are just. Your wrath, O God, is revealed from heaven against the godlessness and wickedness of men. For since the creation, Your eternal power and divine nature have been clearly seen, being understood from what has been made, so that men are without excuse. I pray that my nation will abandon pride and run to You for mercy. (Ro 1:18–21)

O God of earth and altar,
Bow down and hear our cry;
Our earthly rulers falter,
Our people drift and die;
The walls of gold entomb us;
The swords of scorn divide.
Take not thy thunder from us,
But take away our pride.
"O God of Earth and Altar"
Gilbert K. Chesterson (1874–1936)

17 At the end of seventy years, the LORD will deal with Tyre. She will return to her hire as a prostitute and will ply her trade with all the kingdoms on the face of the earth. 18 Yet her profit and her earnings will be set apart for the LORD; they will not be stored up or hoarded. Her profits will go to those who live before the LORD, for abundant food and fine clothes.

The LORD's Devastation of the Earth

24 See, the LORD is going to lay waste the earth
and devastate it;
he will ruin its face
and scatter its inhabitants—
2 it will be the same
for priest as for people,
for master as for servant,
for mistress as for maid,
for seller as for buyer,
for borrower as for lender,
for debtor as for creditor.
3 The earth will be completely laid waste
and totally plundered.
The LORD has spoken this word.

4 The earth dries up and withers,
the world languishes and withers,
the exalted of the earth languish.
5 The earth is defiled by its people;
they have disobeyed the laws,
violated the statutes
and broken the everlasting covenant.
6 Therefore a curse consumes the earth;
its people must bear their guilt.
Therefore earth's inhabitants are burned up,
and very few are left.
7 The new wine dries up and the vine withers;
all the merrymakers groan.
8 The gaiety of the tambourines is stilled,
the noise of the revelers has stopped,
the joyful harp is silent.
9 No longer do they drink wine with a song;
the beer is bitter to its drinkers.
10 The ruined city lies desolate;
the entrance to every house is barred.
11 In the streets they cry out for wine;
all joy turns to gloom,
all gaiety is banished from the earth.
12 The city is left in ruins,
its gate is battered to pieces.
13 So will it be on the earth
and among the nations,
as when an olive tree is beaten,
or as when gleanings are left after the grape harvest.

14 They raise their voices, they shout for joy;
from the west they acclaim the LORD's majesty.
15 Therefore in the east give glory to the LORD;
exalt the name of the LORD, the God of Israel,
in the islands of the sea.

(24:1–6) Even the earth suffers from the curse of our sins. We who were created to bless and tend her have defiled her instead. Give Your people holy hearts that will delight You and bring blessing to our world in our time. (Ro 8:19–21)

(24:14–16) After Your judgments there is always a godly remnant who still shout for joy, who give worship and praise for Your justice and mercy and glory. You have declared that there is coming a final, climactic day when Your majesty will be praised in a holy uproar that will thunder and echo and resound through the universe. And today my own soul cries out, "Glory, glory to the Lord!" (Rev 19:1–8)

(24:21–22) Wonderful God, Your presence is everywhere, permeating the heavens and the earth. Neither the kings of earth nor the powers in heaven can find a hiding place in the day of Your wrath. Your omnipresence is a terror for Your enemies—but a blessing for Your people. For me, Your inescapable presence is my lifeline. There is no depth so dark, no place so hidden, no trial so interminable, that You are not there with me always. (Mt 28:20)

God is an infinite circle whose center is everywhere and whose circumference is nowhere.

Saint Augustine of Hippo (354-430)

(25:4–5) If not for Your power and mercy, all the world would fall prey to the wicked and ruthless. But You are the shelter and refuge of all who turn to You. You promise to give relief to those who suffer the storms of injustice and feel the heat of oppression. You pledge that You will silence the voices of the ruthless. Because of Your faithfulness, we can wait out the storms with the certain hope of our release and restoration. We bless Your name.

16 From the ends of the earth we hear singing:
"Glory to the Righteous One."

But I said, "I waste away, I waste away!
Woe to me!
The treacherous betray!
With treachery the treacherous betray!"
17 Terror and pit and snare await you,
O people of the earth.
18 Whoever flees at the sound of terror
will fall into a pit;
whoever climbs out of the pit
will be caught in a snare.

The floodgates of the heavens are opened,
the foundations of the earth shake.
19 The earth is broken up,
the earth is split asunder,
the earth is thoroughly shaken.
20 The earth reels like a drunkard,
it sways like a hut in the wind;
so heavy upon it is the guilt of its rebellion
that it falls—never to rise again.

21 In that day the LORD will punish
the powers in the heavens above
and the kings on the earth below.
22 They will be herded together
like prisoners bound in a dungeon;
they will be shut up in prison
and be punished[a] after many days.
23 The moon will be abashed, the sun
ashamed;
for the LORD Almighty will reign
on Mount Zion and in Jerusalem,
and before its elders, gloriously.

Praise to the LORD

25 O LORD, you are my God;
I will exalt you and praise your name,
for in perfect faithfulness
you have done marvelous things,
things planned long ago.
2 You have made the city a heap of rubble,
the fortified town a ruin,
the foreigners' stronghold a city no more;
it will never be rebuilt.
3 Therefore strong peoples will honor you;
cities of ruthless nations will revere you.
4 You have been a refuge for the poor,
a refuge for the needy in his distress,
a shelter from the storm
and a shade from the heat.
For the breath of the ruthless
is like a storm driving against a wall
5 and like the heat of the desert.
You silence the uproar of foreigners;

[a] 22 Or *released*

as heat is reduced by the shadow of a cloud,
so the song of the ruthless is stilled.

6 On this mountain the LORD Almighty will prepare
a feast of rich food for all peoples,
a banquet of aged wine—
the best of meats and the finest of wines.
7 On this mountain he will destroy
the shroud that enfolds all peoples,
the sheet that covers all nations;
8 he will swallow up death forever.
The Sovereign LORD will wipe away the tears
from all faces;
he will remove the disgrace of his people
from all the earth.
The LORD has spoken.

9 In that day they will say,

"Surely this is our God;
we trusted in him, and he saved us.
This is the LORD, we trusted in him;
let us rejoice and be glad in his salvation."

10 The hand of the LORD will rest on this mountain;
but Moab will be trampled under him
as straw is trampled down in the manure.
11 They will spread out their hands in it,
as a swimmer spreads out his hands to swim.
God will bring down their pride
despite the cleverness[a] of their hands.
12 He will bring down your high fortified walls
and lay them low;
he will bring them down to the ground,
to the very dust.

A Song of Praise

26 In that day this song will be sung in the land of Judah:

We have a strong city;
God makes salvation
its walls and ramparts.
2 Open the gates
that the righteous nation may enter,
the nation that keeps faith.
3 You will keep in perfect peace
him whose mind is steadfast,
because he trusts in you.
4 Trust in the LORD forever,
for the LORD, the LORD, is the Rock eternal.
5 He humbles those who dwell on high,
he lays the lofty city low;
he levels it to the ground
and casts it down to the dust.
6 Feet trample it down—
the feet of the oppressed,
the footsteps of the poor.

[a] 11 The meaning of the Hebrew for this word is uncertain.

Jesus was a walking invitation to a Great Banquet. Just accept the invitation. "Moses is going. David is going. Queen Esther is going. Jeremiah is going. The whole gang's going to be there. Why not me?"

Laurie Beth Jones (1933-)

(25:6–8) I, too, am going to a great banquet prepared by the Lord for all peoples who belong to Him. It will be a celebration—a wedding feast like none ever seen or imagined. There the shroud of mourning will be lifted off the earth, death destroyed, tears gone forever; for You, O Lord, have spoken, and it shall be done! (Mt 8:11; Lk 13:29; Rev 19:9; 21:4)

(26:3) You are the God who sustains me. You carry me and rescue me, and I rest between Your shoulders. Though the mountains be shaken and the hills be removed, yet Your unfailing love for me will not be shaken nor will Your covenant of peace be removed, for You have compassion on me. So I will fix the gaze of my soul on You, O God, for You are my help and salvation. I will not be anxious about anything, but in everything, by prayer and petition, with thanksgiving, I will present my requests to You. And Your peace, O God, which transcends all understanding, will stand guard over my heart and mind in Christ Jesus. (Dt 33:12; Isa 46:4; 54:10; Php 4:6–7)

(26:7–9) Direct me, Lord, to Your level, smooth paths of righteousness. Let me escape the rough road of sin. You are the only Way, the only true and safe Path. You are my righteousness; bring me closer and closer to You. The desire of my heart is that my life will bring glory and esteem to Your name. Hold on tight to me, Lord, so You will never have cause to be ashamed of me. (Jn 14:6)

(26:19) The wicked die, never to know Your eternal life. Only those whom You have redeemed and made righteous through the Son will rise from their graves, singing. What a morning! Resurrection and life; shouts of praise; pure joy unleashed into the universe. Death is a womb from which the Lifegiver will once again raise His own from the dust and restore them into His image. Thanks be to God forever. (Isa 26;13–14; Jn 6:40; 10:28; 17:3)

7 The path of the righteous is level;
O upright One, you make the way of the righteous smooth.
8 Yes, LORD, walking in the way of your laws,[a]
we wait for you;
your name and renown
are the desire of our hearts.
9 My soul yearns for you in the night;
in the morning my spirit longs for you.
When your judgments come upon the earth,
the people of the world learn righteousness.
10 Though grace is shown to the wicked,
they do not learn righteousness;
even in a land of uprightness they go on doing evil
and regard not the majesty of the LORD.
11 O LORD, your hand is lifted high,
but they do not see it.
Let them see your zeal for your people and be put to shame;
let the fire reserved for your enemies consume them.

12 LORD, you establish peace for us;
all that we have accomplished you have done for us.
13 O LORD, our God, other lords besides you have ruled over us,
but your name alone do we honor.
14 They are now dead, they live no more;
those departed spirits do not rise.
You punished them and brought them to ruin;
you wiped out all memory of them.
15 You have enlarged the nation, O LORD;
you have enlarged the nation.
You have gained glory for yourself;
you have extended all the borders of the land.

16 LORD, they came to you in their distress;
when you disciplined them,
they could barely whisper a prayer.[b]
17 As a woman with child and about to give birth
writhes and cries out in her pain,
so were we in your presence, O LORD.
18 We were with child, we writhed in pain,
but we gave birth to wind.
We have not brought salvation to the earth;
we have not given birth to people of the world.

19 But your dead will live;
their bodies will rise.
You who dwell in the dust,
wake up and shout for joy.
Your dew is like the dew of the morning;
the earth will give birth to her dead.

20 Go, my people, enter your rooms
and shut the doors behind you;
hide yourselves for a little while
until his wrath has passed by.

[a] 8 Or *judgments* [b] 16 The meaning of the Hebrew for this clause is uncertain.

MY BELOVED

I know that you have become weary and feel the weight of the world on your shoulders. Come to Me and I will give you rest. Bring all your anxiety and fear to Me and leave them with Me. I will keep you in perfect peace when you keep your mind on Me and trust Me. I care about you.

Know that I have given you My peace. I do not give to you as the world gives . . . and then takes away. So do not let your heart be troubled and do not be afraid. I will fill you with joy and peace if you will trust in Me.

Instead of dwelling on confusion and anxiety, present your concerns to Me in prayer. And be thankful. Then let your mind dwell on things that are true and noble, things that are right and pure, things that are lovely and admirable—all that is excellent and praiseworthy. And the peace you will have—My peace—you will not be able to explain to others. No one can understand it, but you can have it.

Live your life according to My instructions, and I will be with you; because I am the God of peace, My peace will stand guard over your heart and mind in Christ Jesus.

Isa 26:3; Mt 11:28; Jn 14:27; Ro 15:13; Php 4:6-9; 1Pe 5:7

21 See, the LORD is coming out of his dwelling
to punish the people of the earth for their sins.
The earth will disclose the blood shed upon her;
she will conceal her slain no longer.

Deliverance of Israel

27 In that day,

the LORD will punish with his sword,
his fierce, great and powerful sword,
Leviathan the gliding serpent,
Leviathan the coiling serpent;
he will slay the monster of the sea.

2 In that day—

"Sing about a fruitful vineyard:
3 I, the LORD, watch over it;
I water it continually.
I guard it day and night
so that no one may harm it.
4 I am not angry.
If only there were briers and thorns confronting me!
I would march against them in battle;
I would set them all on fire.
5 Or else let them come to me for refuge;
let them make peace with me,
yes, let them make peace with me."

6 In days to come Jacob will take root,
Israel will bud and blossom
and fill all the world with fruit.

7 Has ⌊the LORD⌋ struck her
as he struck down those who struck her?
Has she been killed
as those were killed who killed her?
8 By warfare[a] and exile you contend with her—
with his fierce blast he drives her out,
as on a day the east wind blows.
9 By this, then, will Jacob's guilt be atoned for,
and this will be the full fruitage of the removal of his sin:
When he makes all the altar stones
to be like chalk stones crushed to pieces,
no Asherah poles[b] or incense altars
will be left standing.
10 The fortified city stands desolate,
an abandoned settlement, forsaken like the desert;
there the calves graze,
there they lie down;
they strip its branches bare.
11 When its twigs are dry, they are broken off
and women come and make fires with them.
For this is a people without understanding;
so their Maker has no compassion on them,
and their Creator shows them no favor.

[a] 8 See Septuagint; the meaning of the Hebrew for this word is uncertain. [b] 9 That is, symbols of the goddess Asherah

The devil cannot lord it over those who are servants of God with their whole heart and who place their hope in him. The devil can wrestle with but not overcome them.

Shepherd of Hermas (c.155)

(27:1–3,6) Lord, your servant spoke this word against the evil nations of his day, but we are plagued with another serpent: the father of Leviathan, the force behind all of this world's evil. The day is coming not only for Israel, but for all Your people, Lord, when this hideous serpent will be slain at last. From the time of Eden, he has watched and waited in fear for the fulfillment of Your curse. But no hole in hell will be deep enough to hide him when You speak that final word. When You set the world free from him at last, our lives will become like a fertile, fruitful vineyard, tended and protected by Your own hand. (Ge 3:15)

(27:9) Deliver me and cleanse me, Lord God. Even though I profess my love for You, My heart is wayward. Day after day I find idols left inside that turn my eyes toward the paths of death. O Deliverer, by Your grace, I will tear them down and abandon them all. Let no altars to other gods be left standing in my soul. No other gods before You: this will be the full fruit of my redemption.

12 In that day the LORD will thresh from the flowing Euphrates[a]
to the Wadi of Egypt, and you, O Israelites, will be gathered up
one by one. 13 And in that day a great trumpet will sound. Those
who were perishing in Assyria and those who were exiled in Egypt
will come and worship the LORD on the holy mountain in Jerusalem.

Woe to Ephraim

28 Woe to that wreath, the pride of Ephraim's drunkards,
to the fading flower, his glorious beauty,
set on the head of a fertile valley—
to that city, the pride of those laid low by wine!
2 See, the Lord has one who is powerful and strong.
Like a hailstorm and a destructive wind,
like a driving rain and a flooding downpour,
he will throw it forcefully to the ground.
3 That wreath, the pride of Ephraim's drunkards,
will be trampled underfoot.
4 That fading flower, his glorious beauty,
set on the head of a fertile valley,
will be like a fig ripe before harvest—
as soon as someone sees it and takes it in his hand,
he swallows it.

5 In that day the LORD Almighty
will be a glorious crown,
a beautiful wreath
for the remnant of his people.
6 He will be a spirit of justice
to him who sits in judgment,
a source of strength
to those who turn back the battle at the gate.

7 And these also stagger from wine
and reel from beer:
Priests and prophets stagger from beer
and are befuddled with wine;
they reel from beer,
they stagger when seeing visions,
they stumble when rendering decisions.
8 All the tables are covered with vomit
and there is not a spot without filth.

9 "Who is it he is trying to teach?
To whom is he explaining his message?
To children weaned from their milk,
to those just taken from the breast?
10 For it is:
Do and do, do and do,
rule on rule, rule on rule[b];
a little here, a little there."
11 Very well then, with foreign lips and strange tongues
God will speak to this people,
12 to whom he said,
"This is the resting place, let the weary rest";

(28:9–13) Lord, how You long to lead me into a place of spiritual rest and victory. Rest and power to overcome lie in my relationship with You. But sometimes I ignore Your words to me as if they were incoherent babble; I pride myself in my knowledge and find security in the way I live my life, thinking I know what it takes to live righteously. Expose my hypocrisy, Lord. Show me that I need to measure myself against Your standards, not those of my peers, my pastor, or of my own conscience. Make known to me the reality of my spiritual poverty, so that I may become more fully reliant on Your grace and mercy. (See NIV footnote on v. 10; Isa 29:13–14)

Lord Jesus, think on me,
By anxious thoughts oppressed;
Let me Your loving servant be
And taste Your promised rest.

"Lord Jesus, Think on Me"
Synesius of Cyrene (c.375–430)
Trans. Allen W. Chatfield (1876)

[a] 12 Hebrew *River* [b] 10 Hebrew / *sav lasav sav lasav / kav lakav kav lakav* (possibly meaningless sounds; perhaps a mimicking of the prophet's words); also in verse 13

and, "This is the place of repose"—
but they would not listen.
13 So then, the word of the LORD to them will become:
Do and do, do and do,
rule on rule, rule on rule;
a little here, a little there—
so that they will go and fall backward,
be injured and snared and captured.

14 Therefore hear the word of the LORD, you scoffers
who rule this people in Jerusalem.
15 You boast, "We have entered into a covenant with death,
with the grave[a] we have made an agreement.
When an overwhelming scourge sweeps by,
it cannot touch us,
for we have made a lie our refuge
and falsehood[b] our hiding place."

16 So this is what the Sovereign LORD says:

"See, I lay a stone in Zion,
a tested stone,
a precious cornerstone for a sure foundation;
the one who trusts will never be dismayed.
17 I will make justice the measuring line
and righteousness the plumb line;
hail will sweep away your refuge, the lie,
and water will overflow your hiding place.
18 Your covenant with death will be annulled;
your agreement with the grave will not stand.
When the overwhelming scourge sweeps by,
you will be beaten down by it.
19 As often as it comes it will carry you away;
morning after morning, by day and by night,
it will sweep through."

The understanding of this message
will bring sheer terror.
20 The bed is too short to stretch out on,
the blanket too narrow to wrap around you.
21 The LORD will rise up as he did at Mount Perazim,
he will rouse himself as in the Valley of Gibeon—
to do his work, his strange work,
and perform his task, his alien task.
22 Now stop your mocking,
or your chains will become heavier;
the Lord, the LORD Almighty, has told me
of the destruction decreed against the whole land.

23 Listen and hear my voice;
pay attention and hear what I say.
24 When a farmer plows for planting, does he plow continually?
Does he keep on breaking up and harrowing the soil?
25 When he has leveled the surface,
does he not sow caraway and scatter cummin?

[a] 15 Hebrew *Sheol*; also in verse 18 [b] 15 Or *false gods*

Nothing before, nothing behind;
The steps of faith
Fall on the seeming void, and find
The rock beneath.

John Greenleaf Whittier (1807-1892)

(28:16) Praise to You, our God and Father, for the sure foundation You have laid for Your church. The cornerstone of hope for Your people of old was the covenant You made with Abraham, that You would be their God and that they would be Your people. Our cornerstone of hope today is the covenant of salvation through Jesus Christ. To all who receive Him, to all who believe in His name, He gives the right to become the children of God. He is our foundation; upon this rock You are building Your church. Those of us who trust in Him will never be dismayed. (John 1:12; 1Pe 2:6–8)

How firm a foundation,
Ye saints of the Lord,
Is laid for your faith
In God's excellent Word!
What more can be said
Than to you God hath said,
To you who for refuge
To Jesus have fled?

"How Firm a Foundation"
Rippon's Selection of Hymns (1787)

(28:24–29) You do the plowing, Lord. You do it thoroughly and You know when to stop. You know what kind of soil we are made of and what seed will grow best in our lives. And when the harvest is ready to be put to good use, You thresh out that which is of eternal value from that which will burn up in Your fire of testing. Your discipline is never more than is necessary for our own good; it is never out of unkindness, but always for the purpose of fruitfulness and ministry. You indeed are "wonderful in counsel and magnificent in wisdom."

Let us never forget that the Husbandman is never so near the land as when He is plowing it, the very time when we are tempted to think He hath forsaken us. His plowing is a proof that He thinks you of value, and worth chastening: for He does not waste His plowing on the barren sand. He will not plow continually, but only for a time, and for a definite purpose . . . Soon, aye soon, we shall, through these painful processes and by His gentle showers of grace, become His fruitful land.
Lettie B. Cowman (1870–1960)

Does he not plant wheat in its place,[a]
barley in its plot,[a]
and spelt in its field?
26 His God instructs him
and teaches him the right way.

27 Caraway is not threshed with a sledge,
nor is a cartwheel rolled over cummin;
caraway is beaten out with a rod,
and cummin with a stick.
28 Grain must be ground to make bread;
so one does not go on threshing it forever.
Though he drives the wheels of his threshing cart
over it,
his horses do not grind it.
29 All this also comes from the LORD Almighty,
wonderful in counsel and magnificent in wisdom.

Woe to David's City

29 Woe to you, Ariel, Ariel,
the city where David settled!
Add year to year
and let your cycle of festivals go on.
2 Yet I will besiege Ariel;
she will mourn and lament,
she will be to me like an altar hearth.[b]
3 I will encamp against you all around;
I will encircle you with towers
and set up my siege works against you.
4 Brought low, you will speak from the ground;
your speech will mumble out of the dust.
Your voice will come ghostlike from the earth;
out of the dust your speech will whisper.

5 But your many enemies will become like fine dust,
the ruthless hordes like blown chaff.
Suddenly, in an instant,
6 the LORD Almighty will come
with thunder and earthquake and great noise,
with windstorm and tempest and flames of a
devouring fire.
7 Then the hordes of all the nations that fight against
Ariel,
that attack her and her fortress and besiege her,
will be as it is with a dream,
with a vision in the night—
8 as when a hungry man dreams that he is eating,
but he awakens, and his hunger remains;
as when a thirsty man dreams that he is drinking,
but he awakens faint, with his thirst unquenched.
So will it be with the hordes of all the nations
that fight against Mount Zion.

9 Be stunned and amazed,
blind yourselves and be sightless;
be drunk, but not from wine,

[a] *25* The meaning of the Hebrew for this word is uncertain. [b] *2* The Hebrew for *altar hearth* sounds like the Hebrew for *Ariel.*

stagger, but not from beer.
10 The LORD has brought over you a deep sleep:
He has sealed your eyes (the prophets);
he has covered your heads (the seers).

11 For you this whole vision is nothing but words sealed in a scroll. And if you give the scroll to someone who can read, and say to him, "Read this, please," he will answer, "I can't; it is sealed." 12 Or if you give the scroll to someone who cannot read, and say, "Read this, please," he will answer, "I don't know how to read."

13 The Lord says:

"These people come near to me with their mouth
and honor me with their lips,
but their hearts are far from me.
Their worship of me
is made up only of rules taught by men.[a]
14 Therefore once more I will astound these people
with wonder upon wonder;
the wisdom of the wise will perish,
the intelligence of the intelligent will vanish."
15 Woe to those who go to great depths
to hide their plans from the LORD,
who do their work in darkness and think,
"Who sees us? Who will know?"
16 You turn things upside down,
as if the potter were thought to be like the clay!
Shall what is formed say to him who formed it,
"He did not make me"?
Can the pot say of the potter,
"He knows nothing"?

17 In a very short time, will not Lebanon be turned into a fertile field
and the fertile field seem like a forest?
18 In that day the deaf will hear the words of the scroll,
and out of gloom and darkness
the eyes of the blind will see.
19 Once more the humble will rejoice in the LORD;
the needy will rejoice in the Holy One of Israel.
20 The ruthless will vanish,
the mockers will disappear,
and all who have an eye for evil will be cut down—
21 those who with a word make a man out to be guilty,
who ensnare the defender in court
and with false testimony deprive the innocent of justice.

22 Therefore this is what the LORD, who redeemed Abraham, says to the house of Jacob:

"No longer will Jacob be ashamed;
no longer will their faces grow pale.
23 When they see among them their children,
the work of my hands,
they will keep my name holy;

[a] *13* Hebrew; Septuagint *They worship me in vain; / their teachings are but rules taught by men*

In prayer it is better to have a heart without words, than words without a heart.

John Bunyan (1628-1688)

(29:13) Father, forgive me when I speak words of worship with my mouth, but keep my heart at a distance from Your holy presence. Forgive me when I act out the proper church roles—speaking pious words, shedding superficial tears—but I do not submit my will to You or subject my thoughts and actions to Your scrutiny. Forgive me, Father, when my religion is a display and my spiritual condition is a disgrace. May my words of worship flow from a heart that is hungry for You, connected with You, and overflowing with You.

Worship isn't listening to a sermon, appreciating the harmony of the choir, and joining in singing hymns! It isn't even prayer, for prayer can be the selfish expression of an unbroken spirit. Worship goes deeper. Since God is spirit, we fellowship with him with our spirit; that is, the immortal and invisible part of us meets with God, who is immortal and invisible.

Erwin W. Lutzer (1941-)

Lord, I lay my heart before Your throne;
Lord, I bow my knee to You alone.
And though I know I'm guilty,
You forgive my sin;
Cleanse me with Your blood,
So I may enter in.
In Your presence,
That's where I want to be;
In Your presence for all eternity.
And though I know I'm guilty,
You forgive my sin;
Cleanse me with Your blood,
So I may enter in
To Your presence.

"In Your Presence"
Debbie Cissna (©1998)

(30:1) "Woe to the obstinate children," You said. Whether You deal with individuals or with nations, Your principles do not change: only obedience to You brings us into blessing. You have The Plan. You have The Strategy—for my little life, for Your church, and for all of creation. Almighty God, by Your help and grace I will not yoke myself unequally with unbelieving people; I will consult You alone for wisdom; I will show my love for You by obeying Your commands with joy. (Jn 14:21; 2Co 6:14; Jas 1:5)

Success is neither fame, wealth, nor power; rather it is seeking, knowing, loving, and obeying God. If you seek, you will know; if you know, you will love; if you love, you will obey.

Charles Habib Malik (1906-)

Jesus calls us! In Your mercy,
Savior, make us hear Your call,
Give our hearts to Your obedience,
Serve and love You best of all.

Jesus Calls Us O'er the Tumult
Cecil F. Alexander (1852)

they will acknowledge the holiness of the Holy One
of Jacob,
and will stand in awe of the God of Israel.
24 Those who are wayward in spirit will gain
understanding;
those who complain will accept instruction."

Woe to the Obstinate Nation

30 "Woe to the obstinate children,"
declares the LORD,
"to those who carry out plans that are not mine,
forming an alliance, but not by my Spirit,
heaping sin upon sin;
2 who go down to Egypt
without consulting me;
who look for help to Pharaoh's protection,
to Egypt's shade for refuge.
3 But Pharaoh's protection will be to your shame,
Egypt's shade will bring you disgrace.
4 Though they have officials in Zoan
and their envoys have arrived in Hanes,
5 everyone will be put to shame
because of a people useless to them,
who bring neither help nor advantage,
but only shame and disgrace."

6 An oracle concerning the animals of the Negev:

Through a land of hardship and distress,
of lions and lionesses,
of adders and darting snakes,
the envoys carry their riches on donkeys' backs,
their treasures on the humps of camels,
to that unprofitable nation,
7 to Egypt, whose help is utterly useless.
Therefore I call her
Rahab the Do-Nothing.

8 Go now, write it on a tablet for them,
inscribe it on a scroll,
that for the days to come
it may be an everlasting witness.
9 These are rebellious people, deceitful children,
children unwilling to listen to the LORD's instruction.
10 They say to the seers,
"See no more visions!"
and to the prophets,
"Give us no more visions of what is right!
Tell us pleasant things,
prophesy illusions.
11 Leave this way,
get off this path,
and stop confronting us
with the Holy One of Israel!"

12 Therefore, this is what the Holy One of Israel says:

"Because you have rejected this message,
relied on oppression
and depended on deceit,

13 this sin will become for you
like a high wall, cracked and bulging,
that collapses suddenly, in an instant.
14 It will break in pieces like pottery,
shattered so mercilessly
that among its pieces not a fragment will be found
for taking coals from a hearth
or scooping water out of a cistern."

15 This is what the Sovereign LORD, the Holy One of Israel, says:

"In repentance and rest is your salvation,
in quietness and trust is your strength,
but you would have none of it.
16 You said, 'No, we will flee on horses.'
Therefore you will flee!
You said, 'We will ride off on swift horses.'
Therefore your pursuers will be swift!
17 A thousand will flee
at the threat of one;
at the threat of five
you will all flee away,
till you are left
like a flagstaff on a mountaintop,
like a banner on a hill."

18 Yet the LORD longs to be gracious to you;
he rises to show you compassion.
For the LORD is a God of justice.
Blessed are all who wait for him!

19 O people of Zion, who live in Jerusalem, you will weep no
more. How gracious he will be when you cry for help! As soon as
he hears, he will answer you. 20 Although the Lord gives you the
bread of adversity and the water of affliction, your teachers will
be hidden no more; with your own eyes you will see them.
21 Whether you turn to the right or to the left, your ears will hear
a voice behind you, saying, "This is the way; walk in it." 22 Then
you will defile your idols overlaid with silver and your images
covered with gold; you will throw them away like a menstrual
cloth and say to them, "Away with you!"

23 He will also send you rain for the seed you sow in the
ground, and the food that comes from the land will be rich and
plentiful. In that day your cattle will graze in broad meadows.
24 The oxen and donkeys that work the soil will eat fodder and
mash, spread out with fork and shovel. 25 In the day of great
slaughter, when the towers fall, streams of water will flow on
every high mountain and every lofty hill. 26 The moon will shine
like the sun, and the sunlight will be seven times brighter, like
the light of seven full days, when the LORD binds up the bruises of
his people and heals the wounds he inflicted.

27 See, the Name of the LORD comes from afar,
with burning anger and dense clouds of smoke;
his lips are full of wrath,
and his tongue is a consuming fire.
28 His breath is like a rushing torrent,
rising up to the neck.
He shakes the nations in the sieve of destruction;

(30:15–21) Not through hard work and strife; not through self-inflicted punishments; not through great acts of valor; rather, the way of salvation is through repentance and rest. When we confess our sins, You are faithful and just to forgive our sins and to cleanse us from all unrighteousness. And when we are confronted with Your fatherly discipline, our strength will be found in quietly trusting You. Though we are fed the bread of adversity, we know that it comes from Your gracious hand; though we strain to see any vision of hope, we know we will soon hear Your words of assurance. O compassionate heavenly Father, help us to be ready for the blessing that comes from patiently, faithfully submitting ourselves to You. (1Jn 1:9)

If you make a compromise with surrender, you can remain interested in the abundant life, all the riches of freedom, love, and peace, but it is the same as looking at a display in a shop window. You look through the window but do not go in and buy. You will not pay the price–surrender.

E. Stanley Jones (1884-1973)

(31:4–5) Just as You have promised to defend Jerusalem in times of trouble, so we look to You to be our defender today, O God. Be to us as a great lion or a powerful bird of prey, guarding Your people, warding off the enemy and bringing him down to defeat. We need Your shield over us every day, every moment. With worship, we come for Your covering.

When the work presses, and the battle thickens, and the day seems long in coming, it is good for the heart to remember that the present conflict is with defeated foes, and that there is no room for question as to the final issue, for the Man of Nazareth is not only seated in the place of authority, he carries forward the work of active administration.

G. Campbell Morgan (1863-1945)

he places in the jaws of the peoples
a bit that leads them astray.
29 And you will sing
as on the night you celebrate a holy festival;
your hearts will rejoice
as when people go up with flutes
to the mountain of the LORD,
to the Rock of Israel.
30 The LORD will cause men to hear his majestic voice
and will make them see his arm coming down
with raging anger and consuming fire,
with cloudburst, thunderstorm and hail.
31 The voice of the LORD will shatter Assyria;
with his scepter he will strike them down.
32 Every stroke the LORD lays on them
with his punishing rod
will be to the music of tambourines and harps,
as he fights them in battle with the blows of his arm.
33 Topheth has long been prepared;
it has been made ready for the king.
Its fire pit has been made deep and wide,
with an abundance of fire and wood;
the breath of the LORD,
like a stream of burning sulfur,
sets it ablaze.

Woe to Those Who Rely on Egypt

31 Woe to those who go down to Egypt for help,
who rely on horses,
who trust in the multitude of their chariots
and in the great strength of their horsemen,
but do not look to the Holy One of Israel,
or seek help from the LORD.
2 Yet he too is wise and can bring disaster;
he does not take back his words.
He will rise up against the house of the wicked,
against those who help evildoers.
3 But the Egyptians are men and not God;
their horses are flesh and not spirit.
When the LORD stretches out his hand,
he who helps will stumble,
he who is helped will fall;
both will perish together.
4 This is what the LORD says to me:

"As a lion growls,
a great lion over his prey—
and though a whole band of shepherds
is called together against him,
he is not frightened by their shouts
or disturbed by their clamor—
so the LORD Almighty will come down
to do battle on Mount Zion and on its heights.
5 Like birds hovering overhead,
the LORD Almighty will shield Jerusalem;
he will shield it and deliver it,
he will 'pass over' it and will rescue it."

6Return to him you have so greatly revolted against, O Israelites. 7For in that day every one of you will reject the idols of silver and gold your sinful hands have made.

8"Assyria will fall by a sword that is not of man;
a sword, not of mortals, will devour them.
They will flee before the sword
and their young men will be put to forced labor.
9Their stronghold will fall because of terror;
at sight of the battle standard their commanders will panic,"
declares the LORD,
whose fire is in Zion,
whose furnace is in Jerusalem.

The Kingdom of Righteousness

32 See, a king will reign in righteousness
and rulers will rule with justice.
2Each man will be like a shelter from the wind
and a refuge from the storm,
like streams of water in the desert
and the shadow of a great rock in a thirsty land.

3Then the eyes of those who see will no longer be closed,
and the ears of those who hear will listen.
4The mind of the rash will know and understand,
and the stammering tongue will be fluent and clear.
5No longer will the fool be called noble
nor the scoundrel be highly respected.
6For the fool speaks folly,
his mind is busy with evil:
He practices ungodliness
and spreads error concerning the LORD;
the hungry he leaves empty
and from the thirsty he withholds water.
7The scoundrel's methods are wicked,
he makes up evil schemes
to destroy the poor with lies,
even when the plea of the needy is just.
8But the noble man makes noble plans,
and by noble deeds he stands.

The Women of Jerusalem

9You women who are so complacent,
rise up and listen to me;
you daughters who feel secure,
hear what I have to say!
10In little more than a year
you who feel secure will tremble;
the grape harvest will fail,
and the harvest of fruit will not come.
11Tremble, you complacent women;
shudder, you daughters who feel secure!
Strip off your clothes,
put sackcloth around your waists.
12Beat your breasts for the pleasant fields,
for the fruitful vines

(32:1–5) I long for the day when You will reign in righteousness and all whom You appoint to leadership will rule justly. Instead of being bruised by tyranny, the people will be blessed and sheltered by their leaders. You, O God, will turn everything right-side up. No longer will fools be called noble; no longer will evil be called good. You will give clear vision and revelation to the world. I give You praise even now, Lord God, for I know that great day is coming. (Isa 5:20)

This was the strength of the first Christians, that they lived not in one world only, but in two, and found in consequence not tension alone, but power, the vision of a world unshaken and unshakable.

Harry Emerson Fosdick (1878-1969)

(32:15–18) Father in heaven, pour out Your Spirit! Until He comes, our lives are a wilderness and a wasteland. All our works produce briars and thorns. Pour out Your Spirit! Only then will our fields become fertile, our lives bear fruit and our homes become peaceful. Pour out Your Spirit! We wait on You for a fresh outpouring, a new touch. We long for the "quietness and confidence" that You offer in the midst of our ever-changing world.

13 and for the land of my people,
a land overgrown with thorns and briers—
yes, mourn for all houses of merriment
and for this city of revelry.
14 The fortress will be abandoned,
the noisy city deserted;
citadel and watchtower will become a wasteland forever,
the delight of donkeys, a pasture for flocks,
15 till the Spirit is poured upon us from on high,
and the desert becomes a fertile field,
and the fertile field seems like a forest.
16 Justice will dwell in the desert
and righteousness live in the fertile field.
17 The fruit of righteousness will be peace;
the effect of righteousness will be quietness and confidence forever.
18 My people will live in peaceful dwelling places,
in secure homes,
in undisturbed places of rest.
19 Though hail flattens the forest
and the city is leveled completely,
20 how blessed you will be,
sowing your seed by every stream,
and letting your cattle and donkeys range free.

Distress and Help

33 Woe to you, O destroyer,
you who have not been destroyed!
Woe to you, O traitor,
you who have not been betrayed!
When you stop destroying,
you will be destroyed;
when you stop betraying,
you will be betrayed.

2 O LORD, be gracious to us;
we long for you.
Be our strength every morning,
our salvation in time of distress.
3 At the thunder of your voice, the peoples flee;
when you rise up, the nations scatter.
4 Your plunder, O nations, is harvested as by young locusts;
like a swarm of locusts men pounce on it.

5 The LORD is exalted, for he dwells on high;
he will fill Zion with justice and righteousness.
6 He will be the sure foundation for your times,
a rich store of salvation and wisdom and knowledge;
the fear of the LORD is the key to this treasure.[a]

7 Look, their brave men cry aloud in the streets;
the envoys of peace weep bitterly.
8 The highways are deserted,
no travelers are on the roads.

[a] 6 Or *is a treasure from him*

The treaty is broken,
its witnesses[a] are despised,
no one is respected.
9 The land mourns[b] and wastes away,
Lebanon is ashamed and withers;
Sharon is like the Arabah,
and Bashan and Carmel drop their leaves.

10 "Now will I arise," says the LORD.
"Now will I be exalted;
now will I be lifted up.
11 You conceive chaff,
you give birth to straw;
your breath is a fire that consumes you.
12 The peoples will be burned as if to lime;
like cut thornbushes they will be set ablaze."

13 You who are far away, hear what I have done;
you who are near, acknowledge my power!
14 The sinners in Zion are terrified;
trembling grips the godless:
"Who of us can dwell with the consuming fire?
Who of us can dwell with everlasting burning?"
15 He who walks righteously
and speaks what is right,
who rejects gain from extortion
and keeps his hand from accepting bribes,
who stops his ears against plots of murder
and shuts his eyes against contemplating evil—
16 this is the man who will dwell on the heights,
whose refuge will be the mountain fortress.
His bread will be supplied,
and water will not fail him.

17 Your eyes will see the king in his beauty
and view a land that stretches afar.
18 In your thoughts you will ponder the former terror:
"Where is that chief officer?
Where is the one who took the revenue?
Where is the officer in charge of the towers?"
19 You will see those arrogant people no more,
those people of an obscure speech,
with their strange, incomprehensible tongue.

20 Look upon Zion, the city of our festivals;
your eyes will see Jerusalem,
a peaceful abode, a tent that will not be moved;
its stakes will never be pulled up,
nor any of its ropes broken.
21 There the LORD will be our Mighty One.
It will be like a place of broad rivers and streams.
No galley with oars will ride them,
no mighty ship will sail them.
22 For the LORD is our judge,
the LORD is our lawgiver,
the LORD is our king;
it is he who will save us.

[a] 8 Dead Sea Scrolls; Masoretic Text / *the cities* [b] 9 Or *dries up*

(33:18–19) Surely the time is coming when terror will be only a memory, a history long past. As I hear about current world events, I think of this promise often and long for the day when You will cry, "Enough!" and depose all brutes and tyrants, small and great. Perhaps sooner than we know, they will be wiped away and their arrogance forgotten. I know Your timetable is right, so I can wait with a heart full of hopeful certainty for Your ultimate, eternal justice.

God will have the last word, and it will be good.

Robert Harold Schuller (1926-)

Keep bright in us the vision
Of days when war shall cease,
When hatred and division
Give way to love and peace,
Till dawns the morning glorious
When truth and justice reign,
And Christ shall rule victorious
O'er all the world's domain.

"O God of Every Nation"
William W. Reid, Jr. (©1958, 1986)

(34:1–11) Righteous Judge, You have given the world fair warning about judgment. You have written it down; You have sent out Your prophets; You have called us to repentance; You have offered us mercy. Some have scoffed, mistaking Your longsuffering for a false alarm. But You are not slow in keeping Your promise. You are patient, not wanting any to perish, but all to come to repentance. Since everything will be destroyed, what kind of people ought we to be? Holy and godly, looking forward to a new heaven and a new earth. Merciful God, I repent and worship You in the shelter of the cross. (2Pe 3:9–13)

The day is surely drawing near
When Jesus, God's anointed,
In all His power shall appear
As Judge whom God appointed.
Then fright shall banish idle mirth,
And hungry flames shall ravage
earth,
As Scripture long has warned us.

O Jesus Christ, do not delay,
But hasten our salvation;
We often tremble on our way
In fear and tribulation.
Oh hear and grant our fervent plea;
Come, mighty Judge, and set us free
From death and every evil.

"The Day Is Surely Drawing Near"
Bartholomaus Ringwaldt (c.1532-1600)
Trans. Philip A. Peter (1832-1917)

23 Your rigging hangs loose:
The mast is not held secure,
the sail is not spread.
Then an abundance of spoils will be divided
and even the lame will carry off plunder.
24 No one living in Zion will say, "I am ill";
and the sins of those who dwell there will be
forgiven.

Judgment Against the Nations

34 Come near, you nations, and listen;
pay attention, you peoples!
Let the earth hear, and all that is in it,
the world, and all that comes out of it!
2 The LORD is angry with all nations;
his wrath is upon all their armies.
He will totally destroy[a] them,
he will give them over to slaughter.
3 Their slain will be thrown out,
their dead bodies will send up a stench;
the mountains will be soaked with their blood.
4 All the stars of the heavens will be dissolved
and the sky rolled up like a scroll;
all the starry host will fall
like withered leaves from the vine,
like shriveled figs from the fig tree.

5 My sword has drunk its fill in the heavens;
see, it descends in judgment on Edom,
the people I have totally destroyed.
6 The sword of the LORD is bathed in blood,
it is covered with fat—
the blood of lambs and goats,
fat from the kidneys of rams.
For the LORD has a sacrifice in Bozrah
and a great slaughter in Edom.
7 And the wild oxen will fall with them,
the bull calves and the great bulls.
Their land will be drenched with blood,
and the dust will be soaked with fat.

8 For the LORD has a day of vengeance,
a year of retribution, to uphold Zion's cause.
9 Edom's streams will be turned into pitch,
her dust into burning sulfur;
her land will become blazing pitch!
10 It will not be quenched night and day;
its smoke will rise forever.
From generation to generation it will lie desolate;
no one will ever pass through it again.
11 The desert owl[b] and screech owl[b] will possess it;
the great owl[b] and the raven will nest there.
God will stretch out over Edom
the measuring line of chaos
and the plumb line of desolation.

[a] *2* The Hebrew term refers to the irrevocable giving over of things or persons to the LORD, often by totally destroying them; also in verse 5. [b] *11* The precise identification of these birds is uncertain.

12 Her nobles will have nothing there to be called a
kingdom,
all her princes will vanish away.
13 Thorns will overrun her citadels,
nettles and brambles her strongholds.
She will become a haunt for jackals,
a home for owls.
14 Desert creatures will meet with hyenas,
and wild goats will bleat to each other;
there the night creatures will also repose
and find for themselves places of rest.
15 The owl will nest there and lay eggs,
she will hatch them, and care for her young under
the shadow of her wings;
there also the falcons will gather,
each with its mate.

16 Look in the scroll of the LORD and read:
None of these will be missing,
not one will lack her mate.
For it is his mouth that has given the order,
and his Spirit will gather them together.
17 He allots their portions;
his hand distributes them by measure.
They will possess it forever
and dwell there from generation to generation.

Joy of the Redeemed

35 The desert and the parched land will be glad;
the wilderness will rejoice and blossom.
Like the crocus, 2 it will burst into bloom;
it will rejoice greatly and shout for joy.
The glory of Lebanon will be given to it,
the splendor of Carmel and Sharon;
they will see the glory of the LORD,
the splendor of our God.

3 Strengthen the feeble hands,
steady the knees that give way;
4 say to those with fearful hearts,
"Be strong, do not fear;
your God will come,
he will come with vengeance;
with divine retribution
he will come to save you."
5 Then will the eyes of the blind be opened
and the ears of the deaf unstopped.
6 Then will the lame leap like a deer,
and the mute tongue shout for joy.
Water will gush forth in the wilderness
and streams in the desert.
7 The burning sand will become a pool,
the thirsty ground bubbling springs.
In the haunts where jackals once lay,
grass and reeds and papyrus will grow.
8 And a highway will be there;
it will be called the Way of Holiness.

(35:3–4) Thank You, Lord, for the hope of freedom. I will lift up my feeble hands to You in praise and bow my trembling knees in worship. Strengthen my faint heart as I wait for You to come and save me. Then I will see with my own eyes the deliverance and glory of the Lord.

Strengthen feeble hands and knees,
Fainting hearts, be cheerful!
God who comes for such as these
Seeks and saves the fearful;
Deaf ears, hear the silent tongues
Sing away their weeping;
Blind eyes, see the lifeless ones
Walking, running, leaping!

"When the King Shall Come Again"
Christopher Idle (©1982)

(35:5–7) The Day of the Lord will be a wild, hilarious day of seeing and hearing, of leaping and dancing and shouting and singing. No staid, inhibited praises there. The earth, too, will open its mouth with joy and drink and become a garden like the first morning of earth. Come quickly, Lord Jesus!

What a day for this poor old sin-ruined, storm-torn, heartbroken, groping-in-the-blind world, when He shall take His rightful throne and reign in all hearts and over all lives for ever and ever!

Elmer Ellsworth Helms (b. 1863)

If you wish to be disappointed, look to others. If you wish to be downhearted, look to yourself. If you wish to be encouraged . . . look upon Jesus Christ.

Erich Sauer

(36:4) Some trust in themselves, some trust in the strength of others, but I place my trust solely in You, Lord Jesus Christ. In You is all the fullness of the Godhead, and in You I am complete. I look to You for salvation—salvation from sin and death, and salvation from the judgment to come. I place all of my hope and trust in Your name, Jesus, "for there is no other name under heaven given to men by which we must be saved." (Ac 4:12; Col 2:9–10)

The unclean will not journey on it;
it will be for those who walk in that Way;
wicked fools will not go about on it.[a]
9 No lion will be there,
nor will any ferocious beast get up on it;
they will not be found there.
But only the redeemed will walk there,
10 and the ransomed of the LORD will return.
They will enter Zion with singing;
everlasting joy will crown their heads.
Gladness and joy will overtake them,
and sorrow and sighing will flee away.

Sennacherib Threatens Jerusalem

36 In the fourteenth year of King Hezekiah's reign, Sennacherib king of Assyria attacked all the fortified cities of
Judah and captured them. 2 Then the king of Assyria sent his field
commander with a large army from Lachish to King Hezekiah at
Jerusalem. When the commander stopped at the aqueduct of the
Upper Pool, on the road to the Washerman's Field, 3 Eliakim son
of Hilkiah the palace administrator, Shebna the secretary, and
Joah son of Asaph the recorder went out to him.
4 The field commander said to them, "Tell Hezekiah,

" 'This is what the great king, the king of Assyria, says: On
what are you basing this confidence of yours? 5 You say you
have strategy and military strength—but you speak only
empty words. On whom are you depending, that you rebel
against me? 6 Look now, you are depending on Egypt, that
splintered reed of a staff, which pierces a man's hand and
wounds him if he leans on it! Such is Pharaoh king of Egypt
to all who depend on him. 7 And if you say to me, "We are
depending on the LORD our God"—isn't he the one whose
high places and altars Hezekiah removed, saying to Judah
and Jerusalem, "You must worship before this altar"?
8 " 'Come now, make a bargain with my master, the king of
Assyria: I will give you two thousand horses—if you can put
riders on them! 9 How then can you repulse one officer of
the least of my master's officials, even though you are depending on Egypt for chariots and horsemen? 10 Furthermore, have I come to attack and destroy this land without
the LORD? The LORD himself told me to march against this
country and destroy it.' "

11 Then Eliakim, Shebna and Joah said to the field commander,
"Please speak to your servants in Aramaic, since we understand
it. Don't speak to us in Hebrew in the hearing of the people on the
wall."
12 But the commander replied, "Was it only to your master and
you that my master sent me to say these things, and not to the
men sitting on the wall—who, like you, will have to eat their own
filth and drink their own urine?"
13 Then the commander stood and called out in Hebrew, "Hear
the words of the great king, the king of Assyria! 14 This is what the
king says: Do not let Hezekiah deceive you. He cannot deliver you!
15 Do not let Hezekiah persuade you to trust in the LORD when he

[a] 8 Or / *the simple will not stray from it*

says, 'The LORD will surely deliver us; this city will not be given
into the hand of the king of Assyria.'
16"Do not listen to Hezekiah. This is what the king of Assyria
says: Make peace with me and come out to me. Then every one of
you will eat from his own vine and fig tree and drink water from
his own cistern, 17until I come and take you to a land like your
own—a land of grain and new wine, a land of bread and vineyards.
18"Do not let Hezekiah mislead you when he says, 'The LORD
will deliver us.' Has the god of any nation ever delivered his land
from the hand of the king of Assyria? 19Where are the gods of Hamath and Arpad? Where are the gods of Sepharvaim? Have they
rescued Samaria from my hand? 20Who of all the gods of these
countries has been able to save his land from me? How then can
the LORD deliver Jerusalem from my hand?"
21But the people remained silent and said nothing in reply, because the king had commanded, "Do not answer him."
22Then Eliakim son of Hilkiah the palace administrator, Shebna the secretary, and Joah son of Asaph the recorder went to
Hezekiah, with their clothes torn, and told him what the field
commander had said.

Jerusalem's Deliverance Foretold

37 When King Hezekiah heard this, he tore his clothes and
put on sackcloth and went into the temple of the LORD.
2He sent Eliakim the palace administrator, Shebna the secretary,
and the leading priests, all wearing sackcloth, to the prophet Isaiah son of Amoz. 3They told him, "This is what Hezekiah says:
This day is a day of distress and rebuke and disgrace, as when
children come to the point of birth and there is no strength to deliver them. 4It may be that the LORD your God will hear the words
of the field commander, whom his master, the king of Assyria, has
sent to ridicule the living God, and that he will rebuke him for the
words the LORD your God has heard. Therefore pray for the remnant that still survives."
5When King Hezekiah's officials came to Isaiah, 6Isaiah said to
them, "Tell your master, 'This is what the LORD says: Do not be
afraid of what you have heard—those words with which the un-
derlings of the king of Assyria have blasphemed me. 7Listen! I am
going to put a spirit in him so that when he hears a certain report,
he will return to his own country, and there I will have him cut
down with the sword.' "
8When the field commander heard that the king of Assyria had
left Lachish, he withdrew and found the king fighting against Libnah.
9Now Sennacherib received a report that Tirhakah, the Cushite[a] king ⌞of Egypt⌟, was marching out to fight against him. When
he heard it, he sent messengers to Hezekiah with this word:
10"Say to Hezekiah king of Judah: Do not let the god you depend
on deceive you when he says, 'Jerusalem will not be handed over
to the king of Assyria.' 11Surely you have heard what the kings of
Assyria have done to all the countries, destroying them completely. And will you be delivered? 12Did the gods of the nations that
were destroyed by my forefathers deliver them—the gods of
Gozan, Haran, Rezeph and the people of Eden who were in Tel

[a] 9 That is, from the upper Nile region

(36:16–21) I praise You, O God, for You are the one and only true God, and Your way is the only way to real freedom and fruitfulness. All other gods and worldly ways are counterfeits, and their promises of peace and fulfillment are counterfeits too. Lord, give Your people discernment to know the difference between Your voice and the voice of the enemy. Give us courage to never compromise what we know to be true for that which is convenient, even when the truth leads us into harm's way.

There is no detour to holiness. Jesus came to the resurrection through the cross, not around it.

Leighton Ford (1931–)

Assar? 13Where is the king of Hamath, the king of Arpad, the king
of the city of Sepharvaim, or of Hena or Ivvah?"

Hezekiah's Prayer

14Hezekiah received the letter from the messengers and read
it. Then he went up to the temple of the LORD and spread it out before the LORD. 15And Hezekiah prayed to the LORD: 16"O LORD
Almighty, God of Israel, enthroned between the cherubim, you
alone are God over all the kingdoms of the earth. You have made
heaven and earth. 17Give ear, O LORD, and hear; open your eyes,
O LORD, and see; listen to all the words Sennacherib has sent to
insult the living God.

18"It is true, O LORD, that the Assyrian kings have laid waste all
these peoples and their lands. 19They have thrown their gods into
the fire and destroyed them, for they were not gods but only wood
and stone, fashioned by human hands. 20Now, O LORD our God,
deliver us from his hand, so that all kingdoms on earth may know
that you alone, O LORD, are God.[a]"

Sennacherib's Fall

21Then Isaiah son of Amoz sent a message to Hezekiah: "This
is what the LORD, the God of Israel, says: Because you have prayed
to me concerning Sennacherib king of Assyria, 22this is the word
the LORD has spoken against him:

"The Virgin Daughter of Zion
despises and mocks you.
The Daughter of Jerusalem
tosses her head as you flee.
23Who is it you have insulted and blasphemed?
Against whom have you raised your voice
and lifted your eyes in pride?
Against the Holy One of Israel!
24By your messengers
you have heaped insults on the Lord.
And you have said,
'With my many chariots
I have ascended the heights of the mountains,
the utmost heights of Lebanon.
I have cut down its tallest cedars,
the choicest of its pines.
I have reached its remotest heights,
the finest of its forests.
25I have dug wells in foreign lands[b]
and drunk the water there.
With the soles of my feet
I have dried up all the streams of Egypt.'

26"Have you not heard?
Long ago I ordained it.
In days of old I planned it;
now I have brought it to pass,
that you have turned fortified cities
into piles of stone.
27Their people, drained of power,

[a] *20* Dead Sea Scrolls (see also 2 Kings 19:19); Masoretic Text *alone are the LORD*
[b] *25* Dead Sea Scrolls (see also 2 Kings 19:24); Masoretic Text does not have *in foreign lands.*

(37:14–23) I praise You, my God, that the enemy's attacks against us are attacks against You. You are always near, always watching, always listening and attentive to our prayers. You see the work of our adversary. You hear his threats against us. You know his power and You know our weakness. But You are a jealous God; and in Your jealousy You will avenge us. So we call on You to save and defend us. May the world see Your salvation and know that You are jealous for Your people.

You are the Rock of my salvation,
You are the strength of my life.
You are my hope and my inspiration,
Lord, unto You will I cry.

I believe in You, believe in You,
For Your faithful love to me.
You have been my help in time of
need;
Lord, unto You will I cleave.

"Rock of My Salvation"
Teresa Muller (©1982)

O Lord God, Thou art our refuge and our hope; on Thee alone we rest, for we find all to be weak and insufficient but Thee. Many friends cannot profit, nor strong helpers assist, nor prudent counselors advise, nor the books of the learned afford comfort, nor any precious substance deliver, nor any place give shelter, unless Thou Thyself dost assist, strengthen, console, instruct, and guard us.

James Martineau (1805-1900)

are dismayed and put to shame.
They are like plants in the field,
like tender green shoots,
like grass sprouting on the roof,
scorched[a] before it grows up.

28 "But I know where you stay
and when you come and go
and how you rage against me.
29 Because you rage against me
and because your insolence has reached my ears,
I will put my hook in your nose
and my bit in your mouth,
and I will make you return
by the way you came.

30 "This will be the sign for you, O Hezekiah:

"This year you will eat what grows by itself,
and the second year what springs from that.
But in the third year sow and reap,
plant vineyards and eat their fruit.
31 Once more a remnant of the house of Judah
will take root below and bear fruit above.
32 For out of Jerusalem will come a remnant,
and out of Mount Zion a band of survivors.
The zeal of the LORD Almighty
will accomplish this.

33 "Therefore this is what the LORD says concerning the king of Assyria:

"He will not enter this city
or shoot an arrow here.
He will not come before it with shield
or build a siege ramp against it.
34 By the way that he came he will return;
he will not enter this city,"
declares the LORD.
35 "I will defend this city and save it,
for my sake and for the sake of David my servant!"

36 Then the angel of the LORD went out and put to death a hundred and eighty-five thousand men in the Assyrian camp. When the people got up the next morning—there were all the dead
bodies! 37 So Sennacherib king of Assyria broke camp and withdrew. He returned to Nineveh and stayed there.
38 One day, while he was worshiping in the temple of his god Nisroch, his sons Adrammelech and Sharezer cut him down with the sword, and they escaped to the land of Ararat. And Esarhaddon his son succeeded him as king.

Hezekiah's Illness

38 In those days Hezekiah became ill and was at the point of death. The prophet Isaiah son of Amoz went to him and said, "This is what the LORD says: Put your house in order, because you are going to die; you will not recover."

[a] 27 Some manuscripts of the Masoretic Text, Dead Sea Scrolls and some Septuagint manuscripts (see also 2 Kings 19:26); most manuscripts of the Masoretic Text *roof / and terraced fields*

(37:28–29) Nothing is hidden from You, Lord. You know the ways of all humanity. You know where we live, where we go, what we do. You hear us when we bless and when we rage—against You and one another. You know all the fleshly struggles of saints and sinners alike. O great Redeemer, in Your mercy redeem both the oppressed and the oppressors. Forgive us for our pride and insolence. Deliver us from the "hooks and bits" of Your discipline. Save us, Lord, from our own sins, and from the sinfulness of others.

[2]Hezekiah turned his face to the wall and prayed to the LORD,
[3]"Remember, O LORD, how I have walked before you faithfully and
with wholehearted devotion and have done what is good in your
eyes." And Hezekiah wept bitterly.

[4]Then the word of the LORD came to Isaiah: [5]"Go and tell Hezekiah, 'This is what the LORD, the God of your father David, says:
I have heard your prayer and seen your tears; I will add fifteen
years to your life. [6]And I will deliver you and this city from the
hand of the king of Assyria. I will defend this city.

[7]" 'This is the LORD's sign to you that the LORD will do what he
has promised: [8]I will make the shadow cast by the sun go back
the ten steps it has gone down on the stairway of Ahaz.' " So the
sunlight went back the ten steps it had gone down.

[9]A writing of Hezekiah king of Judah after his illness and recovery:

[10]I said, "In the prime of my life
must I go through the gates of death[a]
and be robbed of the rest of my years?"
[11]I said, "I will not again see the LORD,
the LORD, in the land of the living;
no longer will I look on mankind,
or be with those who now dwell in this world.[b]
[12]Like a shepherd's tent my house
has been pulled down and taken from me.
Like a weaver I have rolled up my life,
and he has cut me off from the loom;
day and night you made an end of me.
[13]I waited patiently till dawn,
but like a lion he broke all my bones;
day and night you made an end of me.
[14]I cried like a swift or thrush,
I moaned like a mourning dove.
My eyes grew weak as I looked to the heavens.
I am troubled; O Lord, come to my aid!"

[15]But what can I say?
He has spoken to me, and he himself has done this.
I will walk humbly all my years
because of this anguish of my soul.
[16]Lord, by such things men live;
and my spirit finds life in them too.
You restored me to health
and let me live.
[17]Surely it was for my benefit
that I suffered such anguish.
In your love you kept me
from the pit of destruction;
you have put all my sins
behind your back.
[18]For the grave[a] cannot praise you,
death cannot sing your praise;
those who go down to the pit
cannot hope for your faithfulness.
[19]The living, the living—they praise you,

[a] *10,18* Hebrew *Sheol* [b] *11* A few Hebrew manuscripts; most Hebrew manuscripts *in the place of cessation*

As a physician, I have seen men, after all other therapy had failed, lifted out of disease and melancholy by the serene effort of prayer.

Alexis Carrel (1873-1944)

(38:15–20) Thank You, gracious Father, for the victories that arise from the valley of anguish. Teach me to give thanks in the dark places and in the light. Teach me to give thanks for the simple things: bed and board, health and love; to give thanks for the cosmic things: the incredible heavens, the nurturing earth; and to give thanks for the miraculous things: the incarnation, the blood of the Lamb, and sins forgiven. Grant me the faith to be joyful always, to pray continually and to give thanks in all circumstances. (1Th 5:16–18)

as I am doing today;
fathers tell their children
about your faithfulness.

20 The LORD will save me,
and we will sing with stringed instruments
all the days of our lives
in the temple of the LORD.

21 Isaiah had said, "Prepare a poultice of figs and apply it to the boil, and he will recover."

22 Hezekiah had asked, "What will be the sign that I will go up to the temple of the LORD?"

Envoys From Babylon

39 At that time Merodach-Baladan son of Baladan king of
Babylon sent Hezekiah letters and a gift, because he had
heard of his illness and recovery. 2 Hezekiah received the envoys
gladly and showed them what was in his storehouses—the silver,
the gold, the spices, the fine oil, his entire armory and everything
found among his treasures. There was nothing in his palace or in
all his kingdom that Hezekiah did not show them.

3 Then Isaiah the prophet went to King Hezekiah and asked,
"What did those men say, and where did they come from?"

"From a distant land," Hezekiah replied. "They came to me
from Babylon."

4 The prophet asked, "What did they see in your palace?"

"They saw everything in my palace," Hezekiah said. "There is
nothing among my treasures that I did not show them."

5 Then Isaiah said to Hezekiah, "Hear the word of the LORD
Almighty: 6 The time will surely come when everything in your
palace, and all that your fathers have stored up until this day, will
be carried off to Babylon. Nothing will be left, says the LORD. 7 And
some of your descendants, your own flesh and blood who will be
born to you, will be taken away, and they will become eunuchs in
the palace of the king of Babylon."

8 "The word of the LORD you have spoken is good," Hezekiah
replied. For he thought, "There will be peace and security in my
lifetime."

Comfort for God's People

40 Comfort, comfort my people,
says your God.
2 Speak tenderly to Jerusalem,
and proclaim to her
that her hard service has been completed,
that her sin has been paid for,
that she has received from the LORD's hand
double for all her sins.

3 A voice of one calling:
"In the desert prepare
the way for the LORD[a];
make straight in the wilderness
a highway for our God.[b]
4 Every valley shall be raised up,

[a] 3 Or *A voice of one calling in the desert: / "Prepare the way for the LORD*
[b] 3 Hebrew; Septuagint *make straight the paths of our God*

(40:3–5) This voice finally came, crying in the wilderness, dressed in camel hair and eating locusts. The theologians were too learned and the rich people too grand to receive such a messenger. But He came for the poor and humble, for those with ears to hear, for those repentant for sin, for those who hungered for truth however it was packaged. Help me, Lord, to keep my spirit alert and my eyes open so I will never miss Your voice or fail to recognize Your messengers. (Mt 3:1–4; 11:7–12; Lk 7:24–30)

Make you straight what long was
crooked,
Make the rougher places plain;
Let your hearts be true and humble,
As befits God's holy reign.
For the glory of the Lord
Now o'er earth is shed abroad;
And all flesh shall see the token
That God's word is never broken.

"Comfort, Comfort You My People"
Johannes Olearius (1671)
Trans. Catherine Winkworth (1827-1878)

Our good Shepherd is impartial in His care for all His sheep, and the weakest lamb is as dear to Him as the most advanced of the flock. Lambs are wont to lag behind, prone to wander, and apt to grow weary, but from all the danger of these infirmities the Shepherd protects them with His own arm of power. He finds new-born souls, like young lambs, ready to perish—He nourishes them till life becomes vigorous; He finds weak minds ready to faint and die—He consoles them and renews their strength. All the little ones He gathers, for it is not the will of our heavenly Father that one of them should perish.

Charles Haddon Spurgeon (1834-1892)

(40:10–12) The hand that measured out the seas and marked off the heavens is the hand that holds me close to the heart of God. The hand that laid the earth's foundation and directed the stars to their places is the hand that directs me to mine. The hand that shaped the mountains and leveled the plains is the hand that defends me. The hand that was nailed to the cross is the hand that wipes away my tears. The hand that holds all things together is the hand that will never let me go.

Lord, I'm in Your hands
Lord, I'm in Your heart
In Your thoughts, in Your plans
Never left alone.

And when the darkness closes in
And fear begins to rise
Help me to remember
You're always by my side.

"Lord, I'm in Your Hands"
Tim Weeks (©1994)

every mountain and hill made low;
the rough ground shall become level,
the rugged places a plain.
5 And the glory of the LORD will be revealed,
and all mankind together will see it.
For the mouth of the LORD has spoken."

6 A voice says, "Cry out."
And I said, "What shall I cry?"
"All men are like grass,
and all their glory is like the flowers of the field.
7 The grass withers and the flowers fall,
because the breath of the LORD blows on them.
Surely the people are grass.
8 The grass withers and the flowers fall,
but the word of our God stands forever."

9 You who bring good tidings to Zion,
go up on a high mountain.
You who bring good tidings to Jerusalem,[a]
lift up your voice with a shout,
lift it up, do not be afraid;
say to the towns of Judah,
"Here is your God!"
10 See, the Sovereign LORD comes with power,
and his arm rules for him.
See, his reward is with him,
and his recompense accompanies him.
11 He tends his flock like a shepherd:
He gathers the lambs in his arms
and carries them close to his heart;
he gently leads those that have young.

12 Who has measured the waters in the hollow of his hand,
or with the breadth of his hand marked off the heavens?
Who has held the dust of the earth in a basket,
or weighed the mountains on the scales
and the hills in a balance?
13 Who has understood the mind[b] of the LORD,
or instructed him as his counselor?
14 Whom did the LORD consult to enlighten him,
and who taught him the right way?
Who was it that taught him knowledge
or showed him the path of understanding?

15 Surely the nations are like a drop in a bucket;
they are regarded as dust on the scales;
he weighs the islands as though they were fine dust.
16 Lebanon is not sufficient for altar fires,
nor its animals enough for burnt offerings.
17 Before him all the nations are as nothing;
they are regarded by him as worthless
and less than nothing.

18 To whom, then, will you compare God?
What image will you compare him to?

[a] 9 Or *O Zion, bringer of good tidings, / go up on a high mountain. / O Jerusalem, bringer of good tidings* [b] 13 Or *Spirit*; or *spirit*

19 As for an idol, a craftsman casts it,
and a goldsmith overlays it with gold
and fashions silver chains for it.
20 A man too poor to present such an offering
selects wood that will not rot.
He looks for a skilled craftsman
to set up an idol that will not topple.
21 Do you not know?
Have you not heard?
Has it not been told you from the beginning?
Have you not understood since the earth was
founded?
22 He sits enthroned above the circle of the earth,
and its people are like grasshoppers.
He stretches out the heavens like a canopy,
and spreads them out like a tent to live in.
23 He brings princes to naught
and reduces the rulers of this world to nothing.
24 No sooner are they planted,
no sooner are they sown,
no sooner do they take root in the ground,
than he blows on them and they wither,
and a whirlwind sweeps them away like chaff.

25 "To whom will you compare me?
Or who is my equal?" says the Holy One.
26 Lift your eyes and look to the heavens:
Who created all these?
He who brings out the starry host one by one,
and calls them each by name.
Because of his great power and mighty strength,
not one of them is missing.

27 Why do you say, O Jacob,
and complain, O Israel,
"My way is hidden from the LORD;
my cause is disregarded by my God"?
28 Do you not know?
Have you not heard?
The LORD is the everlasting God,
the Creator of the ends of the earth.
He will not grow tired or weary,
and his understanding no one can fathom.
29 He gives strength to the weary
and increases the power of the weak.
30 Even youths grow tired and weary,
and young men stumble and fall;
31 but those who hope in the LORD
will renew their strength.
They will soar on wings like eagles;
they will run and not grow weary,
they will walk and not be faint.

The Helper of Israel

41 "Be silent before me, you islands!
Let the nations renew their strength!
Let them come forward and speak;
let us meet together at the place of judgment.

(40:25–31) How wonderful it is to know that the God Who calls each of the stars by name knows each of us by name. The God Who brings order to creation brings order to our lives. The God Who designed the planets and keeps them on their paths has designed a destiny for us and keeps us on our path. Lord, when I am too burdened to soar, too weary to run, too faint to stand, I look to You to carry me from strength to strength, from faith to faith, from glory to glory. (Ps 84:5–7)

Hold me close,
Let Your love surround me;
Bring me near,
Draw me to Your side.
And as I wait,
I'll rise up like the eagle,
And I will soar with You,
Your Spirit leads me on
In the power of Your love.

The Power Of Your Love
Geoff Bullock (©1992)

Jesus never sends a man ahead alone. He blazes a clear way through every thicket and woods, and then softly calls, "Follow me. Let's go on together, you and I." He has been everywhere that we are called to go. His feet have trodden down smooth a path through every experience that comes to us. He knows each road, and knows it well: the valley road of disappointment with its dark shadows; the steep path of temptation down through the rocky ravines and slippery gullies; the narrow path of pain, with the brambly thorn bushes so close on each side, with their slash and sting; the dizzy road along the heights of victory; the old beaten road of common-place daily routine. Everyday paths he has trodden and glorified, and will walk anew with each of us. The only safe way to travel is with Him alongside and in control.

Dr. Samuel Dickey Gordon (1859-1936)

(41:8–10) By faith I too am a descendant of Abraham, a part of Your spiritual Israel. Would I be presumptuous to claim Your loving promises, given here to Israel, as my own? You are my God, too. So calm the fears of this servant and worshiper, and infuse me with strength. Help and uphold me. Please, condescend to be with me; more than anything, I need Your divine friendship. (Gal 3:7,29)

"I myself will help you," declares the Lord. O my soul, is not this enough? Dost thou need more strength than the omnipotence of the United Trinity? Dost thou want more wisdom than exists in the Father, more love than displays itself in the Son, or more power than is manifest in the influences of the Spirit? Bring hither thine empty pitcher! Surely this well will fill it. Haste, gather up thy wants, and bring them here–thine emptiness, thy woes, thy needs. Behold, this river of God is full for thy supply; what canst thou desire beside? Go forth, my soul, in this thy might. The Eternal God is thine helper!

Charles Haddon Spurgeon (1834-1892)

(41:11–14) Our enemies are not flesh and blood, but they are real. Come and fight through us, Lord. Then when the enemy comes in like a flood, we will obey Your call to battle. We will stand in Your strength, invoke Your presence and declare Your authority. Help us not to fear the day of adversity, but to walk in faith and in the power of Your name. (Eph 6:12–18)

Well You know I'm not a fighter,
  Lord
And the hosts of hell are strong.
So fill me with Your Spirit,
Help me put my armor on.
And when I face the enemy
All that he will see
Is me standing there in You
And You standing there in me.

"The Warrior"
Jimmy Owens and Carol Owens (©1984)

2 "Who has stirred up one from the east,
  calling him in righteousness to his service[a]?
He hands nations over to him
  and subdues kings before him.
He turns them to dust with his sword,
  to windblown chaff with his bow.
3 He pursues them and moves on unscathed,
  by a path his feet have not traveled before.
4 Who has done this and carried it through,
  calling forth the generations from the beginning?
I, the LORD—with the first of them
  and with the last—I am he."

5 The islands have seen it and fear;
  the ends of the earth tremble.
They approach and come forward;
6   each helps the other
  and says to his brother, "Be strong!"
7 The craftsman encourages the goldsmith,
  and he who smooths with the hammer
  spurs on him who strikes the anvil.
He says of the welding, "It is good."
  He nails down the idol so it will not topple.

8 "But you, O Israel, my servant,
  Jacob, whom I have chosen,
  you descendants of Abraham my friend,
9 I took you from the ends of the earth,
  from its farthest corners I called you.
I said, 'You are my servant';
  I have chosen you and have not rejected you.
10 So do not fear, for I am with you;
  do not be dismayed, for I am your God.
I will strengthen you and help you;
  I will uphold you with my righteous right hand.

11 "All who rage against you
  will surely be ashamed and disgraced;
those who oppose you
  will be as nothing and perish.
12 Though you search for your enemies,
  you will not find them.
Those who wage war against you
  will be as nothing at all.
13 For I am the LORD, your God,
  who takes hold of your right hand
and says to you, Do not fear;
  I will help you.
14 Do not be afraid, O worm Jacob,
  O little Israel,
for I myself will help you," declares the LORD,
  your Redeemer, the Holy One of Israel.
15 "See, I will make you into a threshing sledge,
  new and sharp, with many teeth.
You will thresh the mountains and crush them,
  and reduce the hills to chaff.

[a] 2 Or / *whom victory meets at every step*

16 You will winnow them, the wind will pick them up,
and a gale will blow them away.
But you will rejoice in the LORD
and glory in the Holy One of Israel.

17 "The poor and needy search for water,
but there is none;
their tongues are parched with thirst.
But I the LORD will answer them;
I, the God of Israel, will not forsake them.
18 I will make rivers flow on barren heights,
and springs within the valleys.
I will turn the desert into pools of water,
and the parched ground into springs.
19 I will put in the desert
the cedar and the acacia, the myrtle and the olive.
I will set pines in the wasteland,
the fir and the cypress together,
20 so that people may see and know,
may consider and understand,
that the hand of the LORD has done this,
that the Holy One of Israel has created it.

21 "Present your case," says the LORD.
"Set forth your arguments," says Jacob's King.
22 "Bring in ⌞your idols⌟ to tell us
what is going to happen.
Tell us what the former things were,
so that we may consider them
and know their final outcome.
Or declare to us the things to come,
23 tell us what the future holds,
so we may know that you are gods.
Do something, whether good or bad,
so that we will be dismayed and filled with fear.
24 But you are less than nothing
and your works are utterly worthless;
he who chooses you is detestable.

25 "I have stirred up one from the north, and he
comes—
one from the rising sun who calls on my name.
He treads on rulers as if they were mortar,
as if he were a potter treading the clay.
26 Who told of this from the beginning, so we could
know,
or beforehand, so we could say, 'He was right'?
No one told of this,
no one foretold it,
no one heard any words from you.
27 I was the first to tell Zion, 'Look, here they are!'
I gave to Jerusalem a messenger of good tidings.
28 I look but there is no one—
no one among them to give counsel,
no one to give answer when I ask them.
29 See, they are all false!
Their deeds amount to nothing;
their images are but wind and confusion.

(41:18–20) O God, "my soul thirsts for you, my body longs for you, in a dry and weary land where there is no water." You listen to the poor and needy, You see the plight of the downcast and humble. You bring us water where we least expect it—in the desolate places. You bring not just a drop of water, not just a single drink, but a river to which we can return over and over again, a source that not only quenches our thirst, but that makes everything around us fruitful and beautiful. O Lord, I thank You that when I am poor in spirit, when I reach the desolate places of the journey, You meet me there with the living water of Your Spirit. (Ps 63:1)

See the streams of living waters,
Springing from eternal love,
Well supply Thy sons and daughters,
And all fear of want remove:
Who can faint, while such a river
Ever flows their thirst to assuage?
Grace which, like the Lord, the
Giver,
Never fails from age to age.

"Glories of Your Name Are Spoken"
John Newton (1779)

We are profoundly impressed with the unlimited resources of the God of the Bible. He never does anything small. When He makes an ocean He makes it so deep that no man can fathom it. When He makes a mountain he makes it so large that no one can measure or weigh it. When He makes flowers, He scatters multiplied millions of them where there is no one to admire them but Himself. When He makes grace, He makes it without sides or bottom and leaves the top off. Instead of giving salvation with a medicine dropper, he pours it forth like a river.

When God sets out to do a thing for us, He does it with a prodigality of love-prompted abundance that fairly staggers one who reckons things by the coldly calculating standards of earth.

Lettie B. Cowman (1870-1960)

(42:3) Thank You, Lord, that when I am bowed with failure or depression, when I am bruised and embittered by disappointments or betrayal, You do not despise or discard me. You bind up my wounds and heal me. When I am fighting doubt and my flame has grown weak, You do not snuff me out. You patiently fan the fire to life again. I love You, Lord.

Christ is building His kingdom with earth's broken things. Men want only the strong, the successful, the victorious, the unbroken, in building their kingdoms; but God is the God of the unsuccessful, of those who have failed. Heaven is filling with earth's broken lives, and there is no bruised reed that Christ cannot take and restore to glorious blessedness and beauty. He can take the life crushed by pain or sorrow and make it into a harp whose music shall be all praise. He can lift earth's saddest failure up to heaven's glory.

James Russell Miller (1840–1912)

(42:6–7) You declared a new thing and I rejoice for it. If not for Your new covenant, how many would have died in the darkness? Thank You for bringing Your light to all people. Because of Your grace, I too can sing the new song and proclaim Your praise from the ends of the earth.

The Servant of the LORD

42 "Here is my servant, whom I uphold,
my chosen one in whom I delight;
I will put my Spirit on him
and he will bring justice to the nations.
2 He will not shout or cry out,
or raise his voice in the streets.
3 A bruised reed he will not break,
and a smoldering wick he will not snuff out.
In faithfulness he will bring forth justice;
4 he will not falter or be discouraged
till he establishes justice on earth.
In his law the islands will put their hope."

5 This is what God the LORD says—
he who created the heavens and stretched them out,
who spread out the earth and all that comes out of it,
who gives breath to its people,
and life to those who walk on it:
6 "I, the LORD, have called you in righteousness;
I will take hold of your hand.
I will keep you and will make you
to be a covenant for the people
and a light for the Gentiles,
7 to open eyes that are blind,
to free captives from prison
and to release from the dungeon those who sit in darkness.

8 "I am the LORD; that is my name!
I will not give my glory to another
or my praise to idols.
9 See, the former things have taken place,
and new things I declare;
before they spring into being
I announce them to you."

Song of Praise to the LORD

10 Sing to the LORD a new song,
his praise from the ends of the earth,
you who go down to the sea, and all that is in it,
you islands, and all who live in them.
11 Let the desert and its towns raise their voices;
let the settlements where Kedar lives rejoice.
Let the people of Sela sing for joy;
let them shout from the mountaintops.
12 Let them give glory to the LORD
and proclaim his praise in the islands.
13 The LORD will march out like a mighty man,
like a warrior he will stir up his zeal;
with a shout he will raise the battle cry
and will triumph over his enemies.

14 "For a long time I have kept silent,
I have been quiet and held myself back.
But now, like a woman in childbirth,
I cry out, I gasp and pant.

15 I will lay waste the mountains and hills
and dry up all their vegetation;
I will turn rivers into islands
and dry up the pools.
16 I will lead the blind by ways they have not known,
along unfamiliar paths I will guide them;
I will turn the darkness into light before them
and make the rough places smooth.
These are the things I will do;
I will not forsake them.
17 But those who trust in idols,
who say to images, 'You are our gods,'
will be turned back in utter shame.

Israel Blind and Deaf

18 "Hear, you deaf;
look, you blind, and see!
19 Who is blind but my servant,
and deaf like the messenger I send?
Who is blind like the one committed to me,
blind like the servant of the LORD?
20 You have seen many things, but have paid no attention;
your ears are open, but you hear nothing."
21 It pleased the LORD
for the sake of his righteousness
to make his law great and glorious.
22 But this is a people plundered and looted,
all of them trapped in pits
or hidden away in prisons.
They have become plunder,
with no one to rescue them;
they have been made loot,
with no one to say, "Send them back."

23 Which of you will listen to this
or pay close attention in time to come?
24 Who handed Jacob over to become loot,
and Israel to the plunderers?
Was it not the LORD,
against whom we have sinned?
For they would not follow his ways;
they did not obey his law.
25 So he poured out on them his burning anger,
the violence of war.
It enveloped them in flames, yet they did not
understand;
it consumed them, but they did not take it to heart.

Israel's Only Savior

43 But now, this is what the LORD says—
he who created you, O Jacob,
he who formed you, O Israel:
"Fear not, for I have redeemed you;
I have summoned you by name; you are mine.
2 When you pass through the waters,
I will be with you;
and when you pass through the rivers,
they will not sweep over you.

(42:16) In the midst of judgment on the ungodly, You are still a shepherd to Your people. You never forsake us. You lead us by ways we never knew existed, away from the destruction and chaos, around the rocks and pitfalls. You direct us as we walk on darkened pathways. Your Word becomes our light. We do not need to see the way; we only need listening ears. (Ps 23:1–4)

Faith is blind—except upward. It is blind to impossibilities and deaf to doubt. It listens only to God.
Dr. Samuel Dickey Gordon (1859-1936)

Well spoke that soldier, who asked what he would do if he became too weak to cling to Christ, answered, "Then I will pray him to cling to me."

Christina Georgina Rossetti (1830-1894)

(43:1–12) O Lord, my Creator, my Redeemer, my Comforter and Friend, You do love me. You called me by name and saved me. To think that my name is in Your mind and on Your lips—it is mercy too deep to fathom. You have proclaimed from the heavens that I am Yours, and that You are not ashamed to be mine. You are my Rock, the anchor of my life. You never, ever, abandon me. I will cling to You when the floods rise and the fires rage. I will proclaim to the whole world that You are the only, the everlasting, the irresistible God Who has redeemed me with Your own life. (Heb 11:16)

"When through deep waters I call
thee to go,
The rivers of sorrow shall not
overflow;
For I will be near thee, thy troubles
to bless,
And sanctify to thee thy deepest
distress.

"When through fiery trials, thy
pathway shall lie,
My grace, all sufficient, shall be thy
supply;
The flame shall not hurt thee, I only
design
Thy dross to consume, and thy gold
to refine.

"The soul that on Jesus hath leaned
for repose,
I will not, I will not desert to its
foes;
That soul, though all hell should
endeavor to shake,
I'll never, no never, no, never forsake!"

"How Firm a Foundation"
Rippon's Selection of Hymns (1787)

When you walk through the fire,
you will not be burned;
the flames will not set you ablaze.
3 For I am the LORD, your God,
the Holy One of Israel, your Savior;
I give Egypt for your ransom,
Cush[a] and Seba in your stead.
4 Since you are precious and honored in my sight,
and because I love you,
I will give men in exchange for you,
and people in exchange for your life.
5 Do not be afraid, for I am with you;
I will bring your children from the east
and gather you from the west.
6 I will say to the north, 'Give them up!'
and to the south, 'Do not hold them back.'
Bring my sons from afar
and my daughters from the ends of the earth—
7 everyone who is called by my name,
whom I created for my glory,
whom I formed and made."
8 Lead out those who have eyes but are blind,
who have ears but are deaf.
9 All the nations gather together
and the peoples assemble.
Which of them foretold this
and proclaimed to us the former things?
Let them bring in their witnesses to prove they were
right,
so that others may hear and say, "It is true."
10 "You are my witnesses," declares the LORD,
"and my servant whom I have chosen,
so that you may know and believe me
and understand that I am he.
Before me no god was formed,
nor will there be one after me.
11 I, even I, am the LORD,
and apart from me there is no savior.
12 I have revealed and saved and proclaimed—
I, and not some foreign god among you.
You are my witnesses," declares the LORD, "that I
am God.
13 Yes, and from ancient days I am he.
No one can deliver out of my hand.
When I act, who can reverse it?"

God's Mercy and Israel's Unfaithfulness

14 This is what the LORD says—
your Redeemer, the Holy One of Israel:
"For your sake I will send to Babylon
and bring down as fugitives all the Babylonians,[b]
in the ships in which they took pride.
15 I am the LORD, your Holy One,
Israel's Creator, your King."

[a] 3 That is, the upper Nile region [b] 14 Or *Chaldeans*

16 This is what the LORD says—
he who made a way through the sea,
a path through the mighty waters,
17 who drew out the chariots and horses,
the army and reinforcements together,
and they lay there, never to rise again,
extinguished, snuffed out like a wick:
18 "Forget the former things;
do not dwell on the past.
19 See, I am doing a new thing!
Now it springs up; do you not perceive it?
I am making a way in the desert
and streams in the wasteland.
20 The wild animals honor me,
the jackals and the owls,
because I provide water in the desert
and streams in the wasteland,
to give drink to my people, my chosen,
21 the people I formed for myself
that they may proclaim my praise.

22 "Yet you have not called upon me, O Jacob,
you have not wearied yourselves for me, O Israel.
23 You have not brought me sheep for burnt offerings,
nor honored me with your sacrifices.
I have not burdened you with grain offerings
nor wearied you with demands for incense.
24 You have not bought any fragrant calamus for me,
or lavished on me the fat of your sacrifices.
But you have burdened me with your sins
and wearied me with your offenses.

25 "I, even I, am he who blots out
your transgressions, for my own sake,
and remembers your sins no more.
26 Review the past for me,
let us argue the matter together;
state the case for your innocence.
27 Your first father sinned;
your spokesmen rebelled against me.
28 So I will disgrace the dignitaries of your temple,
and I will consign Jacob to destruction[a]
and Israel to scorn.

Israel the Chosen

44 "But now listen, O Jacob, my servant,
Israel, whom I have chosen.
2 This is what the LORD says—
he who made you, who formed you in the womb,
and who will help you:
Do not be afraid, O Jacob, my servant,
Jeshurun, whom I have chosen.
3 For I will pour water on the thirsty land,
and streams on the dry ground;
I will pour out my Spirit on your offspring,
and my blessing on your descendants.

[a] 28 The Hebrew term refers to the irrevocable giving over of things or persons to the LORD, often by totally destroying them.

(43:16–21) Lord, please open my eyes of faith. Help me to see the new things You are doing. Help me to let go of my past successes as well as my failures. Please do not allow me to lean on my own strength, or to use my weakness as an excuse; but help me to be fully dependent on You for this day, this hour, this moment. You can make a way through the overwhelming floods, and You can make a way through the desolate places as well. So I come to You today, Father, and I ask You to quench the thirst in my soul. Give me a drink from the spring of living water, and fill my heart with praise. (Php 3:13–14)

Lord, I hear of show'rs of blessing
Thou art scatt'ring full and free;
Show'rs the thirsty land refreshing;
Let some drops now fall on me;
Even me, even me,
Let some drops now fall on me

"Lord, I Hear of Showers of Blessing"
Elizabeth Codner (1860)

A person may go to heaven without health, without riches, without honors, without learning, without friends, but he can never go there without Christ.

John Dyer (1699–1757)

(44:8–16) O Lord God, there are many ways that lead to hell, but only one way that leads to heaven. All other paths are dead ends; all other gods are worthless idols. Those who follow them profess life, but they do not possess life. Let us be Your witnesses to the nations that there is no other God but You, and there is no other name under heaven by which we must be saved but the great and exalted name of Jesus Christ. Jesus is the way; Jesus is the truth; Jesus is the life. No one can come to You, Father, unless they come through Jesus. (Pr 14:12; Jnh 2:8; Jn 14:6; Ac 4:12)

Son of God, eternal Savior,
Source of life and truth and grace,
Word made flesh, whose birth among us
Hallows all our human race,
You our head, who, enthroned in glory,
For Your own will ever plead:
Fill us with Your love and pity,
Heal our wrongs, and help our need.

"Son of God, Eternal Savior"
Somerset C. Lowry (1855–1932)

4 They will spring up like grass in a meadow,
like poplar trees by flowing streams.
5 One will say, 'I belong to the LORD';
another will call himself by the name of Jacob;
still another will write on his hand, 'The LORD's,'
and will take the name Israel.

The LORD, Not Idols

6 "This is what the LORD says—
Israel's King and Redeemer, the LORD Almighty:
I am the first and I am the last;
apart from me there is no God.
7 Who then is like me? Let him proclaim it.
Let him declare and lay out before me
what has happened since I established my ancient people,
and what is yet to come—
yes, let him foretell what will come.
8 Do not tremble, do not be afraid.
Did I not proclaim this and foretell it long ago?
You are my witnesses. Is there any God besides me?
No, there is no other Rock; I know not one."
9 All who make idols are nothing,
and the things they treasure are worthless.
Those who would speak up for them are blind;
they are ignorant, to their own shame.
10 Who shapes a god and casts an idol,
which can profit him nothing?
11 He and his kind will be put to shame;
craftsmen are nothing but men.
Let them all come together and take their stand;
they will be brought down to terror and infamy.

12 The blacksmith takes a tool
and works with it in the coals;
he shapes an idol with hammers,
he forges it with the might of his arm.
He gets hungry and loses his strength;
he drinks no water and grows faint.
13 The carpenter measures with a line
and makes an outline with a marker;
he roughs it out with chisels
and marks it with compasses.
He shapes it in the form of man,
of man in all his glory,
that it may dwell in a shrine.
14 He cut down cedars,
or perhaps took a cypress or oak.
He let it grow among the trees of the forest,
or planted a pine, and the rain made it grow.
15 It is man's fuel for burning;
some of it he takes and warms himself,
he kindles a fire and bakes bread.
But he also fashions a god and worships it;
he makes an idol and bows down to it.
16 Half of the wood he burns in the fire;
over it he prepares his meal,

he roasts his meat and eats his fill.
He also warms himself and says,
"Ah! I am warm; I see the fire."
17 From the rest he makes a god, his idol;
he bows down to it and worships.
He prays to it and says,
"Save me; you are my god."
18 They know nothing, they understand nothing;
their eyes are plastered over so they cannot see,
and their minds closed so they cannot understand.
19 No one stops to think,
no one has the knowledge or understanding to say,
"Half of it I used for fuel;
I even baked bread over its coals,
I roasted meat and I ate.
Shall I make a detestable thing from what is left?
Shall I bow down to a block of wood?"
20 He feeds on ashes, a deluded heart misleads him;
he cannot save himself, or say,
"Is not this thing in my right hand a lie?"

21 "Remember these things, O Jacob,
for you are my servant, O Israel.
I have made you, you are my servant;
O Israel, I will not forget you.
22 I have swept away your offenses like a cloud,
your sins like the morning mist.
Return to me,
for I have redeemed you."

23 Sing for joy, O heavens, for the LORD has done this;
shout aloud, O earth beneath.
Burst into song, you mountains,
you forests and all your trees,
for the LORD has redeemed Jacob,
he displays his glory in Israel.

Jerusalem to Be Inhabited

24 "This is what the LORD says—
your Redeemer, who formed you in the womb:

I am the LORD,
who has made all things,
who alone stretched out the heavens,
who spread out the earth by myself,

25 who foils the signs of false prophets
and makes fools of diviners,
who overthrows the learning of the wise
and turns it into nonsense,
26 who carries out the words of his servants
and fulfills the predictions of his messengers,

who says of Jerusalem, 'It shall be inhabited,'
of the towns of Judah, 'They shall be built,'
and of their ruins, 'I will restore them,'
27 who says to the watery deep, 'Be dry,
and I will dry up your streams,'
28 who says of Cyrus, 'He is my shepherd
and will accomplish all that I please;

(44:22) Compassionate, merciful God, we are so grateful for these words of hope and comfort. These were not words of reassurance to those who were safely in the fold. They were words of grace to those who had sinned against You. But, Hallelujah! They had sinned against a forgiving God. And still today, You offer forgiveness before we repent; You look for us before we look for You. For "while we were still sinners, Christ died for us." We return to You because You redeemed us. We love You because You first loved us. Thank You for the priceless gift of Your amazing grace. (Ro 5:8; 1Jn 4:19)

(44:28—45:7) Dominion belongs to You, Lord, and You rule over the nations. You can harden the heart of a leader, as You did with Pharaoh, or You can soften the heart of leader, as You did with Cyrus, in order to bless Your people. Time and again, You raised leaders over Your people to discipline them when they sinned and to deliver them when they repented. We know that You are sovereign over the kingdoms of earth and that You give them to whomever You wish. You depose one leader and appoint another to accomplish Your purposes. O Lord, we pray that You will give us leaders who will call us to repentance, leaders who will raise the standard of righteousness over our land, so "that we may live peaceful and quiet lives in all godliness and holiness." (2Ch 7:14–22; Ps 22:28; Isa 22:17–21; Da 4:32; Ro 13:1–5; 1Ti 2:1–2)

(45:9) You, Lord, are the master Artisan of my soul. You undertake the job of reshaping me, which sometimes requires that You break me first. But Father, I bow and submit to You. Please make me into a vessel of beauty to carry the water of life.

he will say of Jerusalem, "Let it be rebuilt,"
and of the temple, "Let its foundations be laid." '

45 "This is what the LORD says to his anointed,
to Cyrus, whose right hand I take hold of
to subdue nations before him
and to strip kings of their armor,
to open doors before him
so that gates will not be shut:
2 I will go before you
and will level the mountains[a];
I will break down gates of bronze
and cut through bars of iron.
3 I will give you the treasures of darkness,
riches stored in secret places,
so that you may know that I am the LORD,
the God of Israel, who summons you by name.
4 For the sake of Jacob my servant,
of Israel my chosen,
I summon you by name
and bestow on you a title of honor,
though you do not acknowledge me.
5 I am the LORD, and there is no other;
apart from me there is no God.
I will strengthen you,
though you have not acknowledged me,
6 so that from the rising of the sun
to the place of its setting
men may know there is none besides me.
I am the LORD, and there is no other.
7 I form the light and create darkness,
I bring prosperity and create disaster;
I, the LORD, do all these things.

8 "You heavens above, rain down righteousness;
let the clouds shower it down.
Let the earth open wide,
let salvation spring up,
let righteousness grow with it;
I, the LORD, have created it.

9 "Woe to him who quarrels with his Maker,
to him who is but a potsherd among the potsherds
on the ground.
Does the clay say to the potter,
'What are you making?'
Does your work say,
'He has no hands'?
10 Woe to him who says to his father,
'What have you begotten?'
or to his mother,
'What have you brought to birth?'

11 "This is what the LORD says—
the Holy One of Israel, and its Maker:
Concerning things to come,

[a] 2 Dead Sea Scrolls and Septuagint; the meaning of the word in the Masoretic Text is uncertain.

do you question me about my children,
or give me orders about the work of my hands?
12 It is I who made the earth
and created mankind upon it.
My own hands stretched out the heavens;
I marshaled their starry hosts.
13 I will raise up Cyrus[a] in my righteousness:
I will make all his ways straight.
He will rebuild my city
and set my exiles free,
but not for a price or reward,
says the LORD Almighty."

14 This is what the LORD says:

"The products of Egypt and the merchandise of Cush,[b]
and those tall Sabeans—
they will come over to you
and will be yours;
they will trudge behind you,
coming over to you in chains.
They will bow down before you
and plead with you, saying,
'Surely God is with you, and there is no other;
there is no other god.'"

15 Truly you are a God who hides himself,
O God and Savior of Israel.
16 All the makers of idols will be put to shame and disgraced;
they will go off into disgrace together.
17 But Israel will be saved by the LORD
with an everlasting salvation;
you will never be put to shame or disgraced,
to ages everlasting.

18 For this is what the LORD says—
he who created the heavens,
he is God;
he who fashioned and made the earth,
he founded it;
he did not create it to be empty,
but formed it to be inhabited—
he says:
"I am the LORD,
and there is no other.
19 I have not spoken in secret,
from somewhere in a land of darkness;
I have not said to Jacob's descendants,
'Seek me in vain.'
I, the LORD, speak the truth;
I declare what is right.

20 "Gather together and come;
assemble, you fugitives from the nations.
Ignorant are those who carry about idols of wood,
who pray to gods that cannot save.
21 Declare what is to be, present it—

(45:18–19) How amazing it is to know that You, the transcendent God, the all-knowing, all-powerful, all sufficient Creator of the universe, are my intimate friend. You are bigger than life, and You are closer than life. You gave the sun its light and the earth its flight, and yet You know when a single sparrow falls to the ground. You have the power to create and the means to sustain Your creation. You invite us, even me, into relationship with You. You ask us to seek You, not in vain, but in great hope. For You have promised that when we seek You, we will find You; when we knock, You will open Your door; when we ask, You will answer. And You will meet all our needs according to Your glorious riches in Christ Jesus. (Mt 10:29; Lk 11:9; Php 4:19)

In the Lord, the Lord alone
Are righteousness and strength:
The height and breadth and length
Of love is found in Him.
In the Lord, the Lord alone
Are righteousness and strength;
In the Lord, in the Lord alone.

In the Lord, the Lord alone
Are life and health and peace:
His mercies and His loving kindness
Never cease.
In the Lord, the Lord alone
Are life and health and peace;
In the Lord, in the Lord alone.

"In the Lord Alone"
Walt Harrah (©1989)

[a] 13 Hebrew *him* [b] 14 That is, the upper Nile region

(46:3–4) You are astounding, O Lord: God of the cosmos and God of the tiniest details. We are humbled to know that nothing about Your children is hidden from You or goes without Your care. Before our birth, You know us all and call us by name. In the impetuousness and inexperience of our youth, You forgive our blunders, redirect our steps and empower us by Your spirit. In our old age You renew us and give us wings to fly. And then You give us eternity. We look to You, Lord, for salvation. All our hope is in You. (Isa 40:28–31)

let them take counsel together.
Who foretold this long ago,
who declared it from the distant past?
Was it not I, the LORD?
And there is no God apart from me,
a righteous God and a Savior;
there is none but me.

22 "Turn to me and be saved,
all you ends of the earth;
for I am God, and there is no other.
23 By myself I have sworn,
my mouth has uttered in all integrity
a word that will not be revoked:
Before me every knee will bow;
by me every tongue will swear.
24 They will say of me, 'In the LORD alone
are righteousness and strength.' "
All who have raged against him
will come to him and be put to shame.
25 But in the LORD all the descendants of Israel
will be found righteous and will exult.

Gods of Babylon

46 Bel bows down, Nebo stoops low;
their idols are borne by beasts of burden.[a]
The images that are carried about are burdensome,
a burden for the weary.
2 They stoop and bow down together;
unable to rescue the burden,
they themselves go off into captivity.

3 "Listen to me, O house of Jacob,
all you who remain of the house of Israel,
you whom I have upheld since you were conceived,
and have carried since your birth.
4 Even to your old age and gray hairs
I am he, I am he who will sustain you.
I have made you and I will carry you;
I will sustain you and I will rescue you.

5 "To whom will you compare me or count me equal?
To whom will you liken me that we may be compared?
6 Some pour out gold from their bags
and weigh out silver on the scales;
they hire a goldsmith to make it into a god,
and they bow down and worship it.
7 They lift it to their shoulders and carry it;
they set it up in its place, and there it stands.
From that spot it cannot move.
Though one cries out to it, it does not answer;
it cannot save him from his troubles.

8 "Remember this, fix it in mind,
take it to heart, you rebels.
9 Remember the former things, those of long ago;
I am God, and there is no other;

[a] 1 Or *are but beasts and cattle*

I am God, and there is none like me.
10 I make known the end from the beginning,
from ancient times, what is still to come.
I say: My purpose will stand,
and I will do all that I please.
11 From the east I summon a bird of prey;
from a far-off land, a man to fulfill my purpose.
What I have said, that will I bring about;
what I have planned, that will I do.
12 Listen to me, you stubborn-hearted,
you who are far from righteousness.
13 I am bringing my righteousness near,
it is not far away;
and my salvation will not be delayed.
I will grant salvation to Zion,
my splendor to Israel.

The Fall of Babylon

47 "Go down, sit in the dust,
Virgin Daughter of Babylon;
sit on the ground without a throne,
Daughter of the Babylonians.[a]
No more will you be called
tender or delicate.
2 Take millstones and grind flour;
take off your veil.
Lift up your skirts, bare your legs,
and wade through the streams.
3 Your nakedness will be exposed
and your shame uncovered.
I will take vengeance;
I will spare no one."

4 Our Redeemer—the LORD Almighty is his name—
is the Holy One of Israel.

5 "Sit in silence, go into darkness,
Daughter of the Babylonians;
no more will you be called
queen of kingdoms.
6 I was angry with my people
and desecrated my inheritance;
I gave them into your hand,
and you showed them no mercy.
Even on the aged
you laid a very heavy yoke.
7 You said, 'I will continue forever—
the eternal queen!'
But you did not consider these things
or reflect on what might happen.

8 "Now then, listen, you wanton creature,
lounging in your security
and saying to yourself,
'I am, and there is none besides me.
I will never be a widow
or suffer the loss of children.'

[a] *1* Or *Chaldeans*; also in verse 5

Surrender your will to God. He will never take advantage of you.
Evan Henry Hopkins (1837-1918)

(46:9–10) When I remember Your faithfulness through the ages and through the pages of this book, when I consider Your countless acts of kindness to Your people and to me, I can truly say that there is none like You. You save us. You protect us. You provide for us. These are the things You are pleased to do; and You always do exactly as You please. So, Lord, I surrender myself to the sovereignty of Your will, so that I might live in the pleasure of Your will. (Ps 135:6; Mt 6:10; Php 2:13)

There is none like You, O God;
Your glory fills the heavens.
There is none like You, O God;
Your love enfolds, Your virtue flows,
All that I need is in Your hands.
There is none like You.
"None Like You, O God"
Debbie Cissna (©1998)

9 Both of these will overtake you
in a moment, on a single day:
loss of children and widowhood.
They will come upon you in full measure,
in spite of your many sorceries
and all your potent spells.
10 You have trusted in your wickedness
and have said, 'No one sees me.'
Your wisdom and knowledge mislead you
when you say to yourself,
'I am, and there is none besides me.'
11 Disaster will come upon you,
and you will not know how to conjure it away.
A calamity will fall upon you
that you cannot ward off with a ransom;
a catastrophe you cannot foresee
will suddenly come upon you.

12 "Keep on, then, with your magic spells
and with your many sorceries,
which you have labored at since childhood.
Perhaps you will succeed,
perhaps you will cause terror.
13 All the counsel you have received has only worn you out!
Let your astrologers come forward,
those stargazers who make predictions month by month,
let them save you from what is coming upon you.
14 Surely they are like stubble;
the fire will burn them up.
They cannot even save themselves
from the power of the flame.
Here are no coals to warm anyone;
here is no fire to sit by.
15 That is all they can do for you—
these you have labored with
and trafficked with since childhood.
Each of them goes on in his error;
there is not one that can save you.

Stubborn Israel

48 "Listen to this, O house of Jacob,
you who are called by the name of Israel
and come from the line of Judah,
you who take oaths in the name of the LORD
and invoke the God of Israel—
but not in truth or righteousness—
2 you who call yourselves citizens of the holy city
and rely on the God of Israel—
the LORD Almighty is his name:
3 I foretold the former things long ago,
my mouth announced them and I made them known;
then suddenly I acted, and they came to pass.
4 For I knew how stubborn you were;
the sinews of your neck were iron,
your forehead was bronze.

(47:10) Righteous Judge, the wicked trust in wickedness and say, "No one sees me." What a dire and eternal mistake. Your omnipresence is a sure snare for the wicked. There is simply no place to hide from You. "You have set our iniquities before you, our secret sins in the light of your presence," and You "will bring every deed into judgment, including every hidden thing, whether it is good or evil." Nothing in all creation is hidden from Your sight. "Everything is uncovered and laid bare before the eyes of him to whom we must give account." Indeed, our sins cannot hide us from You, O God, but they might just hide You from us. (Ps 90:8; Ecc 12:14; Jer 23:24; Heb 4:13)

5 Therefore I told you these things long ago;
before they happened I announced them to you
so that you could not say,
'My idols did them;
my wooden image and metal god ordained them.'
6 You have heard these things; look at them all.
Will you not admit them?

"From now on I will tell you of new things,
of hidden things unknown to you.
7 They are created now, and not long ago;
you have not heard of them before today.
So you cannot say,
'Yes, I knew of them.'
8 You have neither heard nor understood;
from of old your ear has not been open.
Well do I know how treacherous you are;
you were called a rebel from birth.
9 For my own name's sake I delay my wrath;
for the sake of my praise I hold it back from you,
so as not to cut you off.
10 See, I have refined you, though not as silver;
I have tested you in the furnace of affliction.
11 For my own sake, for my own sake, I do this.
How can I let myself be defamed?
I will not yield my glory to another.

Israel Freed

12 "Listen to me, O Jacob,
Israel, whom I have called:
I am he;
I am the first and I am the last.
13 My own hand laid the foundations of the earth,
and my right hand spread out the heavens;
when I summon them,
they all stand up together.

14 "Come together, all of you, and listen:
Which of ⌊the idols⌋ has foretold these things?
The LORD's chosen ally
will carry out his purpose against Babylon;
his arm will be against the Babylonians.[a]
15 I, even I, have spoken;
yes, I have called him.
I will bring him,
and he will succeed in his mission.

16 "Come near me and listen to this:

"From the first announcement I have not spoken in secret;
at the time it happens, I am there."

And now the Sovereign LORD has sent me,
with his Spirit.

17 This is what the LORD says—
your Redeemer, the Holy One of Israel:

[a] 14 Or *Chaldeans*; also in verse 20

(48:10) Even Your refining fire is merciful, O God. You could justly destroy us in our sins and be done with it. But, if we surrender to Your fire, You bring us to repentance and to a new plateau of spiritual maturity. Thank You, Father, for the adversity that tests and refines our character. But thank You most of all, Father, for walking with us through the fire.

As sure as ever God puts his children in the furnace, he will be in the furnace with them.

Charles Haddon Spurgeon (1834-1892)

(49:6) Father, how inexpressibly grateful I am that You extended salvation not just to Your beloved Israel, but to all people. O Jesus, Light of the world, when You came, You came to us all. Your brightness flared into the darkness and continues to enlighten and to bless everyone who will run to its shining. Whoever follows You has the light of life. Jesus, Light of the World, ignite my candle from Your flame. (Lk 1:78–79; Jn 8:12; 12:46)

"I am the LORD your God,
who teaches you what is best for you,
who directs you in the way you should go.
18 If only you had paid attention to my commands,
your peace would have been like a river,
your righteousness like the waves of the sea.
19 Your descendants would have been like the sand,
your children like its numberless grains;
their name would never be cut off
nor destroyed from before me."

20 Leave Babylon,
flee from the Babylonians!
Announce this with shouts of joy
and proclaim it.
Send it out to the ends of the earth;
say, "The LORD has redeemed his servant Jacob."
21 They did not thirst when he led them through the deserts;
he made water flow for them from the rock;
he split the rock
and water gushed out.

22 "There is no peace," says the LORD, "for the wicked."

The Servant of the LORD

49 Listen to me, you islands;
hear this, you distant nations:
Before I was born the LORD called me;
from my birth he has made mention of my name.
2 He made my mouth like a sharpened sword,
in the shadow of his hand he hid me;
he made me into a polished arrow
and concealed me in his quiver.
3 He said to me, "You are my servant,
Israel, in whom I will display my splendor."
4 But I said, "I have labored to no purpose;
I have spent my strength in vain and for nothing.
Yet what is due me is in the LORD's hand,
and my reward is with my God."

5 And now the LORD says—
he who formed me in the womb to be his servant
to bring Jacob back to him
and gather Israel to himself,
for I am honored in the eyes of the LORD
and my God has been my strength—
6 he says:
"It is too small a thing for you to be my servant
to restore the tribes of Jacob
and bring back those of Israel I have kept.
I will also make you a light for the Gentiles,
that you may bring my salvation to the ends of the earth."

7 This is what the LORD says—
the Redeemer and Holy One of Israel—
to him who was despised and abhorred by the nation,
to the servant of rulers:

MY BELOVED

If you live according to My Word, then I will guide you always. I will satisfy all your needs and will make you strong. You will be like a well-watered garden, like a spring whose waters never fail. So trust Me with all your heart and lean not on your own understanding. Acknowledge Me in everything you do, and I will make your journey easier.

I will guide you in the way of wisdom and lead you along straight paths. When you walk, your steps will not be hampered; when you run, you will not stumble.

I am your Rock and your Fortress; because I am your God, I will lead and guide you. If you will listen, I will instruct you and teach you the way you should go; I will counsel you and watch over you. I am your God forever and ever, and I promise I will be your guide—even to the end of time.

When you cannot see the way, I will lead you through unfamiliar territory; I will turn the darkness into light before you and make the rough places smooth. These things I will do. I will not forsake you. Once again, I am the Lord your God, Who teaches you what is best for you, Who directs you in the way you should go. You are not alone.

Ps 31:3; 32:8; 48:14; Pr 3:5-6; 4:11-12; Isa 42:16; 48:17; 58:11

"Kings will see you and rise up,
princes will see and bow down,
because of the LORD, who is faithful,
the Holy One of Israel, who has chosen you."

Restoration of Israel

8 This is what the LORD says:

"In the time of my favor I will answer you,
and in the day of salvation I will help you;
I will keep you and will make you
to be a covenant for the people,
to restore the land
and to reassign its desolate inheritances,
9 to say to the captives, 'Come out,'
and to those in darkness, 'Be free!'

"They will feed beside the roads
and find pasture on every barren hill.
10 They will neither hunger nor thirst,
nor will the desert heat or the sun beat upon them.
He who has compassion on them will guide them
and lead them beside springs of water.
11 I will turn all my mountains into roads,
and my highways will be raised up.
12 See, they will come from afar—
some from the north, some from the west,
some from the region of Aswan.[a]"

13 Shout for joy, O heavens;
rejoice, O earth;
burst into song, O mountains!
For the LORD comforts his people
and will have compassion on his afflicted ones.

14 But Zion said, "The LORD has forsaken me,
the Lord has forgotten me."

15 "Can a mother forget the baby at her breast
and have no compassion on the child she has borne?
Though she may forget,
I will not forget you!
16 See, I have engraved you on the palms of my hands;
your walls are ever before me.
17 Your sons hasten back,
and those who laid you waste depart from you.
18 Lift up your eyes and look around;
all your sons gather and come to you.
As surely as I live," declares the LORD,
"you will wear them all as ornaments;
you will put them on, like a bride.

19 "Though you were ruined and made desolate
and your land laid waste,
now you will be too small for your people,
and those who devoured you will be far away.

[a] 12 Dead Sea Scrolls; Masoretic Text *Sinim*

(49:16) What an incredibly powerful image for Your people of all times and places! O Jesus, my Savior and my God, I am humbled to know that my name is engraved on the hands that were nailed to the cross. You bear on Your hands the memory of the price You paid, and the memory of the reward You won. It is comforting to know that I am never farther from You than Your own hands. I am never beyond Your reach or out of Your sight. What greater hope can there be than this? The hands that create, the hands that heal, the hands that provide and defend and comfort and correct—the very hands of God—have my name written on them.

Arise, my soul, arise!
Shake off your guilty fears;
The bleeding Sacrifice
In my behalf appears.
Before the throne my Surety stands;
My name is written on His hands,
My name is written on His hands.

"Arise, My Soul, Arise"
Charles Wesley (1742)

(49:24–25) It seems so daunting sometimes to try to encroach on enemy territory, to take back spiritual captives and plunder the enemy camp. But we look beyond the power of the devil and the limitations of our humanity and gaze with wonder and adoration upon You. You, O God, will fight for us and through us. You will give us the victory through our Lord Jesus Christ. (1Co 15:57)

(50:2) You have long arms, God. They reach all the way from heaven into my world. You have the strength to overwhelm all my foes and the wisdom to solve my problems. Thank You for the priceless gift of prayer that makes all of heaven's resources available on my behalf.

The ability of God is beyond our prayers, beyond our largest prayers! I have been thinking of some of the petitions that have entered into my supplication innumerable times. What have I asked for? I have asked for a cupful, and the ocean remains! I have asked for a sunbeam, and the sun abides! My best asking falls immeasurably short of my Father's giving: it is beyond that we can ask.

John Henry Jowett (1864–1923)

20 The children born during your bereavement
will yet say in your hearing,
'This place is too small for us;
give us more space to live in.'
21 Then you will say in your heart,
'Who bore me these?
I was bereaved and barren;
I was exiled and rejected.
Who brought these up?
I was left all alone,
but these—where have they come from?' "

22 This is what the Sovereign LORD says:

"See, I will beckon to the Gentiles,
I will lift up my banner to the peoples;
they will bring your sons in their arms
and carry your daughters on their shoulders.
23 Kings will be your foster fathers,
and their queens your nursing mothers.
They will bow down before you with their faces to the ground;
they will lick the dust at your feet.
Then you will know that I am the LORD;
those who hope in me will not be disappointed."

24 Can plunder be taken from warriors,
or captives rescued from the fierce[a]?

25 But this is what the LORD says:

"Yes, captives will be taken from warriors,
and plunder retrieved from the fierce;
I will contend with those who contend with you,
and your children I will save.
26 I will make your oppressors eat their own flesh;
they will be drunk on their own blood, as with wine.
Then all mankind will know
that I, the LORD, am your Savior,
your Redeemer, the Mighty One of Jacob."

Israel's Sin and the Servant's Obedience

50 This is what the LORD says:

"Where is your mother's certificate of divorce
with which I sent her away?
Or to which of my creditors
did I sell you?
Because of your sins you were sold;
because of your transgressions your mother was sent away.
2 When I came, why was there no one?
When I called, why was there no one to answer?
Was my arm too short to ransom you?
Do I lack the strength to rescue you?
By a mere rebuke I dry up the sea,
I turn rivers into a desert;

[a] 24 Dead Sea Scrolls, Vulgate and Syriac (see also Septuagint and verse 25); Masoretic Text *righteous*

their fish rot for lack of water
and die of thirst.
3 I clothe the sky with darkness
and make sackcloth its covering."
4 The Sovereign LORD has given me an instructed tongue,
to know the word that sustains the weary.
He wakens me morning by morning,
wakens my ear to listen like one being taught.
5 The Sovereign LORD has opened my ears,
and I have not been rebellious;
I have not drawn back.
6 I offered my back to those who beat me,
my cheeks to those who pulled out my beard;
I did not hide my face
from mocking and spitting.
7 Because the Sovereign LORD helps me,
I will not be disgraced.
Therefore have I set my face like flint,
and I know I will not be put to shame.
8 He who vindicates me is near.
Who then will bring charges against me?
Let us face each other!
Who is my accuser?
Let him confront me!
9 It is the Sovereign LORD who helps me.
Who is he that will condemn me?
They will all wear out like a garment;
the moths will eat them up.

10 Who among you fears the LORD
and obeys the word of his servant?
Let him who walks in the dark,
who has no light,
trust in the name of the LORD
and rely on his God.
11 But now, all you who light fires
and provide yourselves with flaming torches,
go, walk in the light of your fires
and of the torches you have set ablaze.
This is what you shall receive from my hand:
You will lie down in torment.

Everlasting Salvation for Zion

51 "Listen to me, you who pursue righteousness
and who seek the LORD:
Look to the rock from which you were cut
and to the quarry from which you were hewn;
2 look to Abraham, your father,
and to Sarah, who gave you birth.
When I called him he was but one,
and I blessed him and made him many.
3 The LORD will surely comfort Zion
and will look with compassion on all her ruins;
he will make her deserts like Eden,
her wastelands like the garden of the LORD.
Joy and gladness will be found in her,
thanksgiving and the sound of singing.

(51:1–2) Thank You, Lord, for the men and women who have blazed a trail of faith for us to follow. They give us courage. They show us the results of a living faith. They reveal to us the power of the merciful God who gives imperfect people, just like us, the grace and strength to make it through the wilderness and into the promised land. Help us to remember our leaders and to imitate their faith. (Heb 13:7)

I pray to God this day to make me an extraordinary Christian.

George Whitefield (1714–1770)

4 "Listen to me, my people;
hear me, my nation:
The law will go out from me;
my justice will become a light to the nations.
5 My righteousness draws near speedily,
my salvation is on the way,
and my arm will bring justice to the nations.
The islands will look to me
and wait in hope for my arm.
6 Lift up your eyes to the heavens,
look at the earth beneath;
the heavens will vanish like smoke,
the earth will wear out like a garment
and its inhabitants die like flies.
But my salvation will last forever,
my righteousness will never fail.
7 "Hear me, you who know what is right,
you people who have my law in your hearts:
Do not fear the reproach of men
or be terrified by their insults.
8 For the moth will eat them up like a garment;
the worm will devour them like wool.
But my righteousness will last forever,
my salvation through all generations."

9 Awake, awake! Clothe yourself with strength,
O arm of the LORD;
awake, as in days gone by,
as in generations of old.
Was it not you who cut Rahab to pieces,
who pierced that monster through?
10 Was it not you who dried up the sea,
the waters of the great deep,
who made a road in the depths of the sea
so that the redeemed might cross over?
11 The ransomed of the LORD will return.
They will enter Zion with singing;
everlasting joy will crown their heads.
Gladness and joy will overtake them,
and sorrow and sighing will flee away.

12 "I, even I, am he who comforts you.
Who are you that you fear mortal men,
the sons of men, who are but grass,
13 that you forget the LORD your Maker,
who stretched out the heavens
and laid the foundations of the earth,
that you live in constant terror every day
because of the wrath of the oppressor,
who is bent on destruction?
For where is the wrath of the oppressor?
14 The cowering prisoners will soon be set free;
they will not die in their dungeon,
nor will they lack bread.
15 For I am the LORD your God,
who churns up the sea so that its waves roar—
the LORD Almighty is his name.

Fear of God can deliver us from the fear of man.

John Witherspoon (1723-1794)

(51:12–13) You are the one I fear, Lord; I am in awe of Your divinity. Help me to remember You when I am intimidated by other people. The comparison doesn't bear thinking about. You are sublimely marvelous . . . and very, very frightening in Your power. But You love me. You are my comforter and protector. Why should I fear any other?

16 I have put my words in your mouth
and covered you with the shadow of my hand—
I who set the heavens in place,
who laid the foundations of the earth,
and who say to Zion, 'You are my people.' "

The Cup of the LORD's Wrath

17 Awake, awake!
Rise up, O Jerusalem,
you who have drunk from the hand of the LORD
the cup of his wrath,
you who have drained to its dregs
the goblet that makes men stagger.
18 Of all the sons she bore
there was none to guide her;
of all the sons she reared
there was none to take her by the hand.
19 These double calamities have come upon you—
who can comfort you?—
ruin and destruction, famine and sword—
who can[a] console you?
20 Your sons have fainted;
they lie at the head of every street,
like antelope caught in a net.
They are filled with the wrath of the LORD
and the rebuke of your God.

21 Therefore hear this, you afflicted one,
made drunk, but not with wine.
22 This is what your Sovereign LORD says,
your God, who defends his people:
"See, I have taken out of your hand
the cup that made you stagger;
from that cup, the goblet of my wrath,
you will never drink again.
23 I will put it into the hands of your tormentors,
who said to you,
'Fall prostrate that we may walk over you.'
And you made your back like the ground,
like a street to be walked over."

52 Awake, awake, O Zion,
clothe yourself with strength.
Put on your garments of splendor,
O Jerusalem, the holy city.
The uncircumcised and defiled
will not enter you again.
2 Shake off your dust;
rise up, sit enthroned, O Jerusalem.
Free yourself from the chains on your neck,
O captive Daughter of Zion.

3 For this is what the LORD says:
"You were sold for nothing,
and without money you will be redeemed."

4 For this is what the Sovereign LORD says:

(52:3) Once I was a slave to sin. I sold myself out for nothing, but all the money in the world could not buy my freedom. So You bought me back with Your own life and set me free. Sin made me worthless, but to You I am priceless. I praise You, my Redeemer.

a 19 Dead Sea Scrolls, Septuagint, Vulgate and Syriac; Masoretic Text / *how can I*

(52:7–8) Lord, give me feet that run swiftly and steadily with the Good News of the Gospel. May Your message of salvation be the central focus of my life. May its peace and goodness accompany me as naturally as my soul accompanies my body. Father, I want to be a courier of Your grace, a fountain of Your salvation.

If we want to have these beautiful feet, we must have the tidings ready which they are to bear.

Frances Ridley Havergal (1836-1879)

(52:11) Our world is so polluted; how can we be pure? Lord, help us. You have set us free from sin; now teach us to flee from sin. You have made us holy; now teach us to walk in holiness. Go before us and show us the way—"lead us not into temptation." Follow after us and protect us from the sins of the past—"deliver us from evil." Help us to worship You with clean hands and pure hearts as we set our sights on Your kingdom.

"At first my people went down to Egypt to live;
lately, Assyria has oppressed them.

5 "And now what do I have here?" declares the LORD.

"For my people have been taken away for nothing,
and those who rule them mock,[a]"
declares the LORD.

"And all day long
my name is constantly blasphemed.
6 Therefore my people will know my name;
therefore in that day they will know
that it is I who foretold it.
Yes, it is I."

7 How beautiful on the mountains
are the feet of those who bring good news,
who proclaim peace,
who bring good tidings,
who proclaim salvation,
who say to Zion,
"Your God reigns!"
8 Listen! Your watchmen lift up their voices;
together they shout for joy.
When the LORD returns to Zion,
they will see it with their own eyes.
9 Burst into songs of joy together,
you ruins of Jerusalem,
for the LORD has comforted his people,
he has redeemed Jerusalem.
10 The LORD will lay bare his holy arm
in the sight of all the nations,
and all the ends of the earth will see
the salvation of our God.

11 Depart, depart, go out from there!
Touch no unclean thing!
Come out from it and be pure,
you who carry the vessels of the LORD.
12 But you will not leave in haste
or go in flight;
for the LORD will go before you,
the God of Israel will be your rear guard.

The Suffering and Glory of the Servant

13 See, my servant will act wisely[b];
he will be raised and lifted up and highly exalted.
14 Just as there were many who were appalled at him[c]—
his appearance was so disfigured beyond that of any man
and his form marred beyond human likeness—
15 so will he sprinkle many nations,[d]
and kings will shut their mouths because of him.
For what they were not told, they will see,
and what they have not heard, they will understand.

[a] 5 Dead Sea Scrolls and Vulgate; Masoretic Text *wail* [b] 13 Or *will prosper*
[c] 14 Hebrew *you* [d] 15 Hebrew; Septuagint *so will many nations marvel at him*

53 Who has believed our message
and to whom has the arm of the LORD been revealed?
2 He grew up before him like a tender shoot,
and like a root out of dry ground.
He had no beauty or majesty to attract us to him,
nothing in his appearance that we should desire him.
3 He was despised and rejected by men,
a man of sorrows, and familiar with suffering.
Like one from whom men hide their faces
he was despised, and we esteemed him not.

4 Surely he took up our infirmities
and carried our sorrows,
yet we considered him stricken by God,
smitten by him, and afflicted.
5 But he was pierced for our transgressions,
he was crushed for our iniquities;
the punishment that brought us peace was upon him,
and by his wounds we are healed.
6 We all, like sheep, have gone astray,
each of us has turned to his own way;
and the LORD has laid on him
the iniquity of us all.

7 He was oppressed and afflicted,
yet he did not open his mouth;
he was led like a lamb to the slaughter,
and as a sheep before her shearers is silent,
so he did not open his mouth.
8 By oppression[a] and judgment he was taken away.
And who can speak of his descendants?
For he was cut off from the land of the living;
for the transgression of my people he was stricken.[b]
9 He was assigned a grave with the wicked,
and with the rich in his death,
though he had done no violence,
nor was any deceit in his mouth.

10 Yet it was the LORD's will to crush him and cause him to suffer,
and though the LORD makes[c] his life a guilt offering,
he will see his offspring and prolong his days,
and the will of the LORD will prosper in his hand.
11 After the suffering of his soul,
he will see the light ⌞of life⌟[d] and be satisfied[e];
by his knowledge[f] my righteous servant will justify many,
and he will bear their iniquities.
12 Therefore I will give him a portion among the great,[g]
and he will divide the spoils with the strong,[h]

[a] 8 Or *From arrest* [b] 8 Or *away. / Yet who of his generation considered / that he was cut off from the land of the living / for the transgression of my people, / to whom the blow was due?* [c] 10 Hebrew *though you make* [d] 11 Dead Sea Scrolls (see also Septuagint); Masoretic Text does not have *the light ⌞of life⌟.* [e] 11 Or (with Masoretic Text) *11He will see the result of the suffering of his soul / and be satisfied* [f] 11 Or *by knowledge of him* [g] 12 Or *many* [h] 12 Or *numerous*

(53:1–12) Not a quick, antiseptic death by lethal injection; rather, endless hours of torture, filth, blood and searing pain. No placard bearers begging for repeal of the death penalty; rather, shouts and jeers and spittle. No clear, smooth martyr's face; rather, a marred and grotesque visage that caused sensitive women to hide their faces and coarse men to mock Your humiliation. Of course, not one of them had any idea how You would look three days later.

The head that once was crowned with thorns is crowned with glory now.
Thomas Kelley (1769-1855)

"Man of Sorrows," what a name
For the Son of God, Who came
Ruined sinners to reclaim!
Hallelujah! What a Savior!

Bearing shame and scoffing rude,
In my place condemned He stood;
Sealed my pardon with His blood:
Hallelujah! What a Savior!

"Hallelujah! What a Savior!"
Phillip P. Bliss (1875)

(54:6–8) When our sins hide Your face from us, all hope and light and joy is gone. How, Lord, can we live without Your manifest presence? When You abandon us to our own ways, waiting for our repentance, may we remember Your mercy and rush to You with open confession and real contrition. There, if our hearts are true, we will receive unfailing compassion, grace and restoration.

My heart needs Thee, O Lord, my heart needs Thee! No part of my being needs Thee like my heart. All else within me can be filled by Thy gifts. My hunger can be satisfied by daily bread. My thirst can be allayed by earthly waters. My cold can be removed by household fires. My weariness can be relieved by outward rest. But no outward thing can make my heart pure.

George Matheson (1842–1906)

because he poured out his life unto death,
and was numbered with the transgressors.
For he bore the sin of many,
and made intercession for the transgressors.

The Future Glory of Zion

54 "Sing, O barren woman,
you who never bore a child;
burst into song, shout for joy,
you who were never in labor;
because more are the children of the desolate woman
than of her who has a husband,"
says the LORD.

2 "Enlarge the place of your tent,
stretch your tent curtains wide,
do not hold back;
lengthen your cords,
strengthen your stakes.
3 For you will spread out to the right and to the left;
your descendants will dispossess nations
and settle in their desolate cities.

4 "Do not be afraid; you will not suffer shame.
Do not fear disgrace; you will not be humiliated.
You will forget the shame of your youth
and remember no more the reproach of your widowhood.
5 For your Maker is your husband—
the LORD Almighty is his name—
the Holy One of Israel is your Redeemer;
he is called the God of all the earth.
6 The LORD will call you back
as if you were a wife deserted and distressed in spirit—
a wife who married young,
only to be rejected," says your God.
7 "For a brief moment I abandoned you,
but with deep compassion I will bring you back.
8 In a surge of anger
I hid my face from you for a moment,
but with everlasting kindness
I will have compassion on you,"
says the LORD your Redeemer.

9 "To me this is like the days of Noah,
when I swore that the waters of Noah would never again cover the earth.
So now I have sworn not to be angry with you,
never to rebuke you again.
10 Though the mountains be shaken
and the hills be removed,
yet my unfailing love for you will not be shaken
nor my covenant of peace be removed,"
says the LORD, who has compassion on you.

11 "O afflicted city, lashed by storms and not
comforted,
I will build you with stones of turquoise,[a]
your foundations with sapphires.[b]
12 I will make your battlements of rubies,
your gates of sparkling jewels,
and all your walls of precious stones.
13 All your sons will be taught by the LORD,
and great will be your children's peace.
14 In righteousness you will be established:
Tyranny will be far from you;
you will have nothing to fear.
Terror will be far removed;
it will not come near you.
15 If anyone does attack you, it will not be my doing;
whoever attacks you will surrender to you.

16 "See, it is I who created the blacksmith
who fans the coals into flame
and forges a weapon fit for its work.
And it is I who have created the destroyer to work
havoc;
17 no weapon forged against you will prevail,
and you will refute every tongue that accuses you.
This is the heritage of the servants of the LORD,
and this is their vindication from me,"
declares the LORD.

Invitation to the Thirsty

55 "Come, all you who are thirsty,
come to the waters;
and you who have no money,
come, buy and eat!
Come, buy wine and milk
without money and without cost.
2 Why spend money on what is not bread,
and your labor on what does not satisfy?
Listen, listen to me, and eat what is good,
and your soul will delight in the richest of fare.
3 Give ear and come to me;
hear me, that your soul may live.
I will make an everlasting covenant with you,
my faithful love promised to David.
4 See, I have made him a witness to the peoples,
a leader and commander of the peoples.
5 Surely you will summon nations you know not,
and nations that do not know you will hasten to
you,
because of the LORD your God,
the Holy One of Israel,
for he has endowed you with splendor."

6 Seek the LORD while he may be found;
call on him while he is near.
7 Let the wicked forsake his way
and the evil man his thoughts.

[a] 11 The meaning of the Hebrew for this word is uncertain. [b] 11 Or *lapis lazuli*

(55:1–3) I hear You, Lord, crying, "Come, listen, buy and eat." You have everything my soul needs: living water for my thirst, the bread of life for my hunger, refreshment for my fainting spirit. So I come to You, Lord, without money or virtue of my own, to seek Your face and sit with You at Your banqueting table.

Lord, look upon my need.
I need You, I need You.
Lord, have mercy now on me.
Forgive me, O Lord, forgive me
And I will be clean.

O Lord, You are familiar with my
ways;
There is nothing hid from You.
O Lord, You know the number of
my days.
I want to live my life for You.

"I Need You"
Rick Founds (©1989)

(55:6–7) Do You hear me calling, Lord? I'm calling upon You in obedience to Your invitation. I lay at the cross every known wicked way and every evil thought and forsake them all, so that I may worship today in Your manifest presence.

(55:9–13) Your Word is alive and creative. Like rain and snow, it goes forth from You in productive power, fulfills its destiny and returns to You again overflowing with its harvest: the high praises of Your people whom You save, deliver and bless. Drench us, Father, in your Word. Nurture us in its instruction and power so that we can discern Your will for our lives. (Heb 4:12)

God did not write a book and send it by messenger to be read at a distance by unaided minds. He spoke a book and lives in his spoken words, constantly speaking his words and causing the power of them to persist across the years.

A.W. Tozer (1897-1963)

Let him turn to the LORD, and he will have mercy on him,
and to our God, for he will freely pardon.

8 "For my thoughts are not your thoughts,
neither are your ways my ways,"
declares the LORD.

9 "As the heavens are higher than the earth,
so are my ways higher than your ways
and my thoughts than your thoughts.

10 As the rain and the snow
come down from heaven,
and do not return to it
without watering the earth
and making it bud and flourish,
so that it yields seed for the sower and bread for the eater,

11 so is my word that goes out from my mouth:
It will not return to me empty,
but will accomplish what I desire
and achieve the purpose for which I sent it.

12 You will go out in joy
and be led forth in peace;
the mountains and hills
will burst into song before you,
and all the trees of the field
will clap their hands.

13 Instead of the thornbush will grow the pine tree,
and instead of briers the myrtle will grow.
This will be for the LORD's renown,
for an everlasting sign,
which will not be destroyed."

Salvation for Others

56 This is what the LORD says:

"Maintain justice
and do what is right,
for my salvation is close at hand
and my righteousness will soon be revealed.

2 Blessed is the man who does this,
the man who holds it fast,
who keeps the Sabbath without desecrating it,
and keeps his hand from doing any evil."

3 Let no foreigner who has bound himself to the LORD say,
"The LORD will surely exclude me from his people."
And let not any eunuch complain,
"I am only a dry tree."

4 For this is what the LORD says:

"To the eunuchs who keep my Sabbaths,
who choose what pleases me
and hold fast to my covenant—

5 to them I will give within my temple and its walls
a memorial and a name
better than sons and daughters;

I will give them an everlasting name
that will not be cut off.
6 And foreigners who bind themselves to the LORD
to serve him,
to love the name of the LORD,
and to worship him,
all who keep the Sabbath without desecrating it
and who hold fast to my covenant—
7 these I will bring to my holy mountain
and give them joy in my house of prayer.
Their burnt offerings and sacrifices
will be accepted on my altar;
for my house will be called
a house of prayer for all nations."
8 The Sovereign LORD declares—
he who gathers the exiles of Israel:
"I will gather still others to them
besides those already gathered."

God's Accusation Against the Wicked

9 Come, all you beasts of the field,
come and devour, all you beasts of the forest!
10 Israel's watchmen are blind,
they all lack knowledge;
they are all mute dogs,
they cannot bark;
they lie around and dream,
they love to sleep.
11 They are dogs with mighty appetites;
they never have enough.
They are shepherds who lack understanding;
they all turn to their own way,
each seeks his own gain.
12 "Come," each one cries, "let me get wine!
Let us drink our fill of beer!
And tomorrow will be like today,
or even far better."

57 The righteous perish,
and no one ponders it in his heart;
devout men are taken away,
and no one understands
that the righteous are taken away
to be spared from evil.
2 Those who walk uprightly
enter into peace;
they find rest as they lie in death.

3 "But you—come here, you sons of a sorceress,
you offspring of adulterers and prostitutes!
4 Whom are you mocking?
At whom do you sneer
and stick out your tongue?
Are you not a brood of rebels,
the offspring of liars?
5 You burn with lust among the oaks
and under every spreading tree;
you sacrifice your children in the ravines

(56:6–8) How just and fair You are, Lord. No one ever needs to be excluded from Your love and blessing. There are no requirements of race, beauty, intellect or achievement. Whoever loves You, whoever loves Your Word, whoever seeks Your face, whoever calls on Your name, will be a recipient of Your grace. Thank You, Lord, for the hope we have in Your saving love.

My hope is built on nothing less
Than Jesus' blood and righteousness;
No merit of my own I claim,
But wholly lean on Jesus' name.

"The Solid Rock"
Edward Mote (1834)

and under the overhanging crags.
6 ⌊The idols⌋ among the smooth stones of the ravines are
your portion;
they, they are your lot.
Yes, to them you have poured out drink offerings
and offered grain offerings.
In the light of these things, should I relent?
7 You have made your bed on a high and lofty hill;
there you went up to offer your sacrifices.
8 Behind your doors and your doorposts
you have put your pagan symbols.
Forsaking me, you uncovered your bed,
you climbed into it and opened it wide;
you made a pact with those whose beds you love,
and you looked on their nakedness.
9 You went to Molech[a] with olive oil
and increased your perfumes.
You sent your ambassadors[b] far away;
you descended to the grave[c] itself!
10 You were wearied by all your ways,
but you would not say, 'It is hopeless.'
You found renewal of your strength,
and so you did not faint.

11 "Whom have you so dreaded and feared
that you have been false to me,
and have neither remembered me
nor pondered this in your hearts?
Is it not because I have long been silent
that you do not fear me?
12 I will expose your righteousness and your works,
and they will not benefit you.
13 When you cry out for help,
let your collection ⌊of idols⌋ save you!
The wind will carry all of them off,
a mere breath will blow them away.
But the man who makes me his refuge
will inherit the land
and possess my holy mountain."

Comfort for the Contrite

14 And it will be said:

"Build up, build up, prepare the road!
Remove the obstacles out of the way of my
people."
15 For this is what the high and lofty One says—
he who lives forever, whose name is holy:
"I live in a high and holy place,
but also with him who is contrite and lowly in spirit,
to revive the spirit of the lowly
and to revive the heart of the contrite.
16 I will not accuse forever,
nor will I always be angry,
for then the spirit of man would grow faint
before me—

[a]9 Or *to the king* [b]9 Or *idols* [c]9 Hebrew *Sheol*

(57:15) God, high and holy, You came to us in humility and servanthood. You bound Yourself to the confines of a human body to experience all that we experience, to teach us, to wash our feet and forgive our sins. You will make us like Yourself if only we are not too self-loving to ask. You look for the lowly, teachable spirit on whom You can shower Your grace. I pray that You will find what You are looking for in me.

O for a heart to praise my God,
A heart from sin set free,
A heart that always feels Thy blood
So freely shed for me!

A humble, lowly, contrite heart,
Believing, true and clean,
Which neither life nor death can
part
From Him that dwells within.

A heart in every thought renewed,
And full of love divine;
Perfect and right and pure and good,
A copy, Lord, of Thine!

"O for a Heart to Praise My God"
Charles Wesley (1742)

Humility, that is lowliness or self-abasement, is an inward bowing down or prostrating of the heart and of the conscience before God's transcendent worth. Righteousness demands and orders this, and through charity a loving heart cannot leave it undone.

John of Ruysbroeck (1293-1381)

the breath of man that I have created.
17 I was enraged by his sinful greed;
I punished him, and hid my face in anger,
yet he kept on in his willful ways.
18 I have seen his ways, but I will heal him;
I will guide him and restore comfort to him,
19 creating praise on the lips of the mourners in Israel.
Peace, peace, to those far and near,"
says the LORD. "And I will heal them."
20 But the wicked are like the tossing sea,
which cannot rest,
whose waves cast up mire and mud.
21 "There is no peace," says my God, "for the wicked."

True Fasting

58 "Shout it aloud, do not hold back.
Raise your voice like a trumpet.
Declare to my people their rebellion
and to the house of Jacob their sins.
2 For day after day they seek me out;
they seem eager to know my ways,
as if they were a nation that does what is right
and has not forsaken the commands of its God.
They ask me for just decisions
and seem eager for God to come near them.
3 'Why have we fasted,' they say,
'and you have not seen it?
Why have we humbled ourselves,
and you have not noticed?'

"Yet on the day of your fasting, you do as you please
and exploit all your workers.
4 Your fasting ends in quarreling and strife,
and in striking each other with wicked fists.
You cannot fast as you do today
and expect your voice to be heard on high.
5 Is this the kind of fast I have chosen,
only a day for a man to humble himself?
Is it only for bowing one's head like a reed
and for lying on sackcloth and ashes?
Is that what you call a fast,
a day acceptable to the LORD?

6 "Is not this the kind of fasting I have chosen:
to loose the chains of injustice
and untie the cords of the yoke,
to set the oppressed free
and break every yoke?
7 Is it not to share your food with the hungry
and to provide the poor wanderer with shelter—
when you see the naked, to clothe him,
and not to turn away from your own flesh and blood?
8 Then your light will break forth like the dawn,
and your healing will quickly appear;
then your righteousness[a] will go before you,

[a] 8 Or *your righteous One*

(57:19) Merciful, loving God, You have forgiven our sins and healed our souls. You have disciplined us and then comforted and restored us. You have created praise in our hearts and on our lips. We offer that as a sacrifice to You. But more than lip service, we offer You our obedience as the demonstration of worship given by our hearts. (Ro 12:1; Heb 13:15)

(58:9–12) God of mercy, lover of justice, fountain of plenty, please make me like You. In obedience, as an act of worship, I renounce injustice, exploitation and prejudice, not only because they are wrong, but to meet fully Your requirements for answered prayer. May I be a flowing fountain of praise and petition, and may my intercession for my lost and sinful nation be acceptable to You. In obedience, as an act of worship, I offer my hands to You. May they be hands of blessing to a lost and desperate world. I want to be a generous agent of bread for the body, and a clear and bountiful supply of the Bread of Life. May I be a rebuilder of the broken walls of my society, in the name of the Lord. (Mt 25:35–45)

and the glory of the LORD will be your rear guard.
9 Then you will call, and the LORD will answer;
you will cry for help, and he will say: Here am I.

"If you do away with the yoke of oppression,
with the pointing finger and malicious talk,
10 and if you spend yourselves in behalf of the hungry
and satisfy the needs of the oppressed,
then your light will rise in the darkness,
and your night will become like the noonday.
11 The LORD will guide you always;
he will satisfy your needs in a sun-scorched land
and will strengthen your frame.
You will be like a well-watered garden,
like a spring whose waters never fail.
12 Your people will rebuild the ancient ruins
and will raise up the age-old foundations;
you will be called Repairer of Broken Walls,
Restorer of Streets with Dwellings.

13 "If you keep your feet from breaking the Sabbath
and from doing as you please on my holy day,
if you call the Sabbath a delight
and the LORD's holy day honorable,
and if you honor it by not going your own way
and not doing as you please or speaking idle words,
14 then you will find your joy in the LORD,
and I will cause you to ride on the heights of the land
and to feast on the inheritance of your father Jacob."
The mouth of the LORD has spoken.

Sin, Confession and Redemption

59 Surely the arm of the LORD is not too short to save,
nor his ear too dull to hear.
2 But your iniquities have separated
you from your God;
your sins have hidden his face from you,
so that he will not hear.
3 For your hands are stained with blood,
your fingers with guilt.
Your lips have spoken lies,
and your tongue mutters wicked things.
4 No one calls for justice;
no one pleads his case with integrity.
They rely on empty arguments and speak lies;
they conceive trouble and give birth to evil.
5 They hatch the eggs of vipers
and spin a spider's web.
Whoever eats their eggs will die,
and when one is broken, an adder is hatched.
6 Their cobwebs are useless for clothing;
they cannot cover themselves with what they make.
Their deeds are evil deeds,
and acts of violence are in their hands.
7 Their feet rush into sin;
they are swift to shed innocent blood.

Their thoughts are evil thoughts;
ruin and destruction mark their ways.
8 The way of peace they do not know;
there is no justice in their paths.
They have turned them into crooked roads;
no one who walks in them will know peace.
9 So justice is far from us,
and righteousness does not reach us.
We look for light, but all is darkness;
for brightness, but we walk in deep shadows.
10 Like the blind we grope along the wall,
feeling our way like men without eyes.
At midday we stumble as if it were twilight;
among the strong, we are like the dead.
11 We all growl like bears;
we moan mournfully like doves.
We look for justice, but find none;
for deliverance, but it is far away.

12 For our offenses are many in your sight,
and our sins testify against us.
Our offenses are ever with us,
and we acknowledge our iniquities:
13 rebellion and treachery against the LORD,
turning our backs on our God,
fomenting oppression and revolt,
uttering lies our hearts have conceived.
14 So justice is driven back,
and righteousness stands at a distance;
truth has stumbled in the streets,
honesty cannot enter.
15 Truth is nowhere to be found,
and whoever shuns evil becomes a prey.

The LORD looked and was displeased
that there was no justice.
16 He saw that there was no one,
he was appalled that there was no one to
intervene;
so his own arm worked salvation for him,
and his own righteousness sustained him.
17 He put on righteousness as his breastplate,
and the helmet of salvation on his head;
he put on the garments of vengeance
and wrapped himself in zeal as in a cloak.
18 According to what they have done,
so will he repay
wrath to his enemies
and retribution to his foes;
he will repay the islands their due.
19 From the west, men will fear the name of the LORD,
and from the rising of the sun, they will revere his
glory.
For he will come like a pent-up flood
that the breath of the LORD drives along.[a]

[a] 19 Or *When the enemy comes in like a flood, / the Spirit of the LORD will put him to flight*

Seek the truth
Listen to the truth
Teach the truth
Love the truth
Abide by the truth
And defend the truth
Unto the death.

John Huss (c.1370–1415)

(59:15–16) O Jesus our Savior, teach us to be like You. Give us courage to speak up and step out on behalf of justice. Help us to speak the truth in love; to right wrongs, heal wounds, and champion the cause of the dispossessed. May we stand in Your righteousness to intervene and intercede for our own stumbling nation and a world in turmoil. (Eze 22:29–30)

Arise, shine, for your light has come.
Arise, shine, for your light has come.

Nations will come and kings will bow
As the glory of God shines on you.
Lift up your hearts, lift up your voice.
See the King of kings, the Lord of lords,
See the Prince of Peace shine on you.

Arise, shine, for your light has come.
Arise, shine, for your light has come.

"Arise, Shine"
Chris O'Brien and
Margaret Davis (©1996)

(60:1–3) O Lord, I find great hope in these words to Israel, these words to Your church, these words to all who believe. For we have received "the light of the knowledge of the glory of God in the face of Christ." O Lord, You have given us the light of Your presence, Your very own glory, to shine on us, in us, through us, and around us. And now in these days when darkness covers the earth, You call us to action—to shine before all humanity, that they may see our good deeds and give praise to You, Father. While we await the ultimate consummation of this promise in the coming of our Messiah, help us to do all we can to dispel the darkness from the world around us. (Mt 5:14–16; 2Co 4:6)

There is simply no room for passivity in the Christian faith. Life in Christ is one long string of action verbs: grow . . . praise . . . love . . . learn . . . stretch . . . reach . . . put on . . . put off . . . press on . . . follow . . . hold . . . cleave . . . run . . . weep . . . produce . . . stand . . . fight.

Joni Eareckson Tada (1949-)

20 "The Redeemer will come to Zion,
to those in Jacob who repent of their sins,"
declares the LORD.

21 "As for me, this is my covenant with them," says the LORD.
"My Spirit, who is on you, and my words that I have put in your
mouth will not depart from your mouth, or from the mouths of
your children, or from the mouths of their descendants from this
time on and forever," says the LORD.

The Glory of Zion

60 "Arise, shine, for your light has come,
and the glory of the LORD rises upon you.
2 See, darkness covers the earth
and thick darkness is over the peoples,
but the LORD rises upon you
and his glory appears over you.
3 Nations will come to your light,
and kings to the brightness of your dawn.

4 "Lift up your eyes and look about you:
All assemble and come to you;
your sons come from afar,
and your daughters are carried on the arm.
5 Then you will look and be radiant,
your heart will throb and swell with joy;
the wealth on the seas will be brought to you,
to you the riches of the nations will come.
6 Herds of camels will cover your land,
young camels of Midian and Ephah.
And all from Sheba will come,
bearing gold and incense
and proclaiming the praise of the LORD.
7 All Kedar's flocks will be gathered to you,
the rams of Nebaioth will serve you;
they will be accepted as offerings on my altar,
and I will adorn my glorious temple.

8 "Who are these that fly along like clouds,
like doves to their nests?
9 Surely the islands look to me;
in the lead are the ships of Tarshish,[a]
bringing your sons from afar,
with their silver and gold,
to the honor of the LORD your God,
the Holy One of Israel,
for he has endowed you with splendor.

10 "Foreigners will rebuild your walls,
and their kings will serve you.
Though in anger I struck you,
in favor I will show you compassion.
11 Your gates will always stand open,
they will never be shut, day or night,
so that men may bring you the wealth of the nations—
their kings led in triumphal procession.

[a] 9 Or *the trading ships*

12 For the nation or kingdom that will not serve you will
perish;
it will be utterly ruined.
13 "The glory of Lebanon will come to you,
the pine, the fir and the cypress together,
to adorn the place of my sanctuary;
and I will glorify the place of my feet.
14 The sons of your oppressors will come bowing before
you;
all who despise you will bow down at your feet
and will call you the City of the LORD,
Zion of the Holy One of Israel.
15 "Although you have been forsaken and hated,
with no one traveling through,
I will make you the everlasting pride
and the joy of all generations.
16 You will drink the milk of nations
and be nursed at royal breasts.
Then you will know that I, the LORD, am your Savior,
your Redeemer, the Mighty One of Jacob.
17 Instead of bronze I will bring you gold,
and silver in place of iron.
Instead of wood I will bring you bronze,
and iron in place of stones.
I will make peace your governor
and righteousness your ruler.
18 No longer will violence be heard in your land,
nor ruin or destruction within your borders,
but you will call your walls Salvation
and your gates Praise.
19 The sun will no more be your light by day,
nor will the brightness of the moon shine on you,
for the LORD will be your everlasting light,
and your God will be your glory.
20 Your sun will never set again,
and your moon will wane no more;
the LORD will be your everlasting light,
and your days of sorrow will end.
21 Then will all your people be righteous
and they will possess the land forever.
They are the shoot I have planted,
the work of my hands,
for the display of my splendor.
22 The least of you will become a thousand,
the smallest a mighty nation.
I am the LORD;
in its time I will do this swiftly."

The Year of the LORD's Favor

61 The Spirit of the Sovereign LORD is on me,
because the LORD has anointed me
to preach good news to the poor.
He has sent me to bind up the brokenhearted,
to proclaim freedom for the captives
and release from darkness for the prisoners,[a]

[a] 1 Hebrew; Septuagint *the blind*

(60:12–22) When we grow weary, Lord, bring to our remembrance the New Jerusalem. Give us a vision of the righteousness, the peace and justice, the beauty and plenty that are to come. Lift up our eyes and our hearts. Refresh our spirits with the sure expectancy of the glorious reality that is on the way.

Life is the preparation, the training ground, the place where God begins his work of making us into what he wants us to be. But it is not our home.

J.B. Phillips (1906–1982)

Every year, I might almost say every day, that I live, I seem to see more clearly how all the rest and gladness and power of our Christian life hinges on one thing; and that is, taking God at His word, believing that He really means exactly what He says, and accepting the very words in which He reveals His goodness and grace, without substituting others or altering the precise modes and tenses which He has seen fit to use.

Frances Ridley Havergal (1836–1879)

(61:1–11) What a long time Your people waited for Your deliverance. But Your Word is true and at last You came, Lord Jesus Christ, with an anointing of truth and power that has lasted to this day. Still You bind up our broken hearts and deliver us from our sinful bondage. You comfort us and fill us with joy. You restore our losses and give us new purpose and hope. Now we worship and wait once more with faith for You to come again in power and glory. (Lk 4:18–21)

He gave me beauty for ashes,
The oil of joy for mourning,
The garment of praise
For the spirit of heaviness,
That we might be trees of
righteousness,
The planting of the Lord,
That He might be glorified.

"Beauty for Ashes"
Robert Manzano (©1979)

2 to proclaim the year of the LORD's favor
and the day of vengeance of our God,
to comfort all who mourn,
3 and provide for those who grieve in Zion—
to bestow on them a crown of beauty
instead of ashes,
the oil of gladness
instead of mourning,
and a garment of praise
instead of a spirit of despair.
They will be called oaks of righteousness,
a planting of the LORD
for the display of his splendor.

4 They will rebuild the ancient ruins
and restore the places long devastated;
they will renew the ruined cities
that have been devastated for generations.
5 Aliens will shepherd your flocks;
foreigners will work your fields and vineyards.
6 And you will be called priests of the LORD,
you will be named ministers of our God.
You will feed on the wealth of nations,
and in their riches you will boast.

7 Instead of their shame
my people will receive a double portion,
and instead of disgrace
they will rejoice in their inheritance;
and so they will inherit a double portion in their land,
and everlasting joy will be theirs.

8 "For I, the LORD, love justice;
I hate robbery and iniquity.
In my faithfulness I will reward them
and make an everlasting covenant with them.
9 Their descendants will be known among the nations
and their offspring among the peoples.
All who see them will acknowledge
that they are a people the LORD has blessed."

10 I delight greatly in the LORD;
my soul rejoices in my God.
For he has clothed me with garments of salvation
and arrayed me in a robe of righteousness,
as a bridegroom adorns his head like a priest,
and as a bride adorns herself with her jewels.
11 For as the soil makes the sprout come up
and a garden causes seeds to grow,
so the Sovereign LORD will make righteousness and praise
spring up before all nations.

Zion's New Name

62 For Zion's sake I will not keep silent,
for Jerusalem's sake I will not remain quiet,
till her righteousness shines out like the dawn,
her salvation like a blazing torch.
2 The nations will see your righteousness,

and all kings your glory;
you will be called by a new name
that the mouth of the LORD will bestow.
3 You will be a crown of splendor in the LORD's hand,
a royal diadem in the hand of your God.
4 No longer will they call you Deserted,
or name your land Desolate.
But you will be called Hephzibah,[a]
and your land Beulah[b];
for the LORD will take delight in you,
and your land will be married.
5 As a young man marries a maiden,
so will your sons[c] marry you;
as a bridegroom rejoices over his bride,
so will your God rejoice over you.

6 I have posted watchmen on your walls, O Jerusalem;
they will never be silent day or night.
You who call on the LORD,
give yourselves no rest,
7 and give him no rest till he establishes Jerusalem
and makes her the praise of the earth.

8 The LORD has sworn by his right hand
and by his mighty arm:
"Never again will I give your grain
as food for your enemies,
and never again will foreigners drink the new wine
for which you have toiled;
9 but those who harvest it will eat it
and praise the LORD,
and those who gather the grapes will drink it
in the courts of my sanctuary."

10 Pass through, pass through the gates!
Prepare the way for the people.
Build up, build up the highway!
Remove the stones.
Raise a banner for the nations.

11 The LORD has made proclamation
to the ends of the earth:
"Say to the Daughter of Zion,
'See, your Savior comes!
See, his reward is with him,
and his recompense accompanies him.'"
12 They will be called the Holy People,
the Redeemed of the LORD;
and you will be called Sought After,
the City No Longer Deserted.

God's Day of Vengeance and Redemption

63 Who is this coming from Edom,
from Bozrah, with his garments stained crimson?
Who is this, robed in splendor,
striding forward in the greatness of his strength?

(62:6) Lord, just as You posted spiritual watchmen for Jerusalem, let us be watchmen for our needy nation. Give us eyes to seek Your face, and ears to hear Your voice. Give us boldness to declare the Word of the Lord; and hear us as we humble ourselves and cry out to You for mercy. You are omniscient and sovereign over all circumstances, and so we pray, "Let Your will be done in our land even as it is in heaven." We will wait on You, Lord, and pursue You with our intercession; we will pray without ceasing and listen for Your instruction. Tell us how to pray the prayers that are on Your heart, the prayers You long to answer. (Eze 33:2–7)

[a] 4 *Hephzibah* means *my delight is in her.* [b] 4 *Beulah* means *married.* [c] 5 Or *Builder*

"It is I, speaking in righteousness,
mighty to save."

2 Why are your garments red,
like those of one treading the winepress?

3 "I have trodden the winepress alone;
from the nations no one was with me.
I trampled them in my anger
and trod them down in my wrath;
their blood spattered my garments,
and I stained all my clothing.
4 For the day of vengeance was in my heart,
and the year of my redemption has come.
5 I looked, but there was no one to help,
I was appalled that no one gave support;
so my own arm worked salvation for me,
and my own wrath sustained me.
6 I trampled the nations in my anger;
in my wrath I made them drunk
and poured their blood on the ground."

Praise and Prayer

7 I will tell of the kindnesses of the LORD,
the deeds for which he is to be praised,
according to all the LORD has done for us—
yes, the many good things he has done
for the house of Israel,
according to his compassion and many kindnesses.
8 He said, "Surely they are my people,
sons who will not be false to me";
and so he became their Savior.
9 In all their distress he too was distressed,
and the angel of his presence saved them.
In his love and mercy he redeemed them;
he lifted them up and carried them
all the days of old.
10 Yet they rebelled
and grieved his Holy Spirit.
So he turned and became their enemy
and he himself fought against them.

11 Then his people recalled[a] the days of old,
the days of Moses and his people—
where is he who brought them through the sea,
with the shepherd of his flock?
Where is he who set
his Holy Spirit among them,
12 who sent his glorious arm of power
to be at Moses' right hand,
who divided the waters before them,
to gain for himself everlasting renown,
13 who led them through the depths?
Like a horse in open country,
they did not stumble;
14 like cattle that go down to the plain,
they were given rest by the Spirit of the LORD.

[a] 11 Or *But may he recall*

(63:1–6) King of kings, Lord of lords, Righteous Judge, Faithful and True, You are mighty and fearsome in Your wrath. The Day is coming when we will see You robed in garments of vengeance, garments stained in blood—not Your own this time, but the blood of Your enemies. You will come to put an end to sin and oppression, and to restore the rule of God over all the earth. While we wait for that great Day, give us boldness to proclaim Your coming judgment, and compassion to call the lost to Your fountain of grace while there is still time. (Isa 55:6–7; 59:17–18; Heb 3:13; 4:7; Rev 19:11–16)

(63:8–13) Thank You Lord for Your compassionate care. How we need Your Spirit to deliver us in our distresses. We need You to carry us where the road is too rocky or the path too faint for us to follow. Lord, we cry to You for Your manifest presence. Help us to keep the highway clear between our hearts and Yours.

This is how you guided your people
to make for yourself a glorious name.

15 Look down from heaven and see
from your lofty throne, holy and glorious.
Where are your zeal and your might?
Your tenderness and compassion are withheld from us.
16 But you are our Father,
though Abraham does not know us
or Israel acknowledge us;
you, O LORD, are our Father,
our Redeemer from of old is your name.
17 Why, O LORD, do you make us wander from your ways
and harden our hearts so we do not revere you?
Return for the sake of your servants,
the tribes that are your inheritance.
18 For a little while your people possessed your holy place,
but now our enemies have trampled down your sanctuary.
19 We are yours from of old;
but you have not ruled over them,
they have not been called by your name.[a]

64

1 Oh, that you would rend the heavens and come down,
that the mountains would tremble before you!
2 As when fire sets twigs ablaze
and causes water to boil,
come down to make your name known to your enemies
and cause the nations to quake before you!
3 For when you did awesome things that we did not expect,
you came down, and the mountains trembled before you.
4 Since ancient times no one has heard,
no ear has perceived,
no eye has seen any God besides you,
who acts on behalf of those who wait for him.
5 You come to the help of those who gladly do right,
who remember your ways.
But when we continued to sin against them,
you were angry.
How then can we be saved?
6 All of us have become like one who is unclean,
and all our righteous acts are like filthy rags;
we all shrivel up like a leaf,
and like the wind our sins sweep us away.
7 No one calls on your name
or strives to lay hold of you;
for you have hidden your face from us
and made us waste away because of our sins.
8 Yet, O LORD, you are our Father.
We are the clay, you are the potter;

[a] 19 Or *We are like those you have never ruled, / like those never called by your name*

(64:4–9) I worship You, Father, for Your great love and compassion, Your tender mercy, Your patience and kindness, Your restoration and forgiveness. You know our weaknesses and our propensity for sin. You see our helplessness, and You act on our behalf. As a father has compassion on his children, so You, our Father, have compassion on us. Your mercies never fail; Your love endures forever; You will never forsake us. You will always be true to Your name: Everlasting Father, Savior, Provider, Healer, Counselor, Prince of Peace, Mighty God, Friend. (Ps 103:13–17, La 3:22)

God is not affected by our mutability; our changes do not alter him. When we are restless, he remains serene and calm; when we are low, selfish, mean, or dispirited, he is still the unalterable I Am. The same yesterday, today, and forever, in whom is no variableness, neither shadow of turning. What God is in himself, not what we may chance to feel him in this or that moment to be, that is our hope.

Frederick William Robertson (1816-1853)

(65:8) O Lord, I thank You that You see green life flowing deep within the parched brown stems of our vineyards. You observe the remnant of sweetness and nourishment somewhere inside the neglected, shriveled fruit of our lives. You patiently prune us and prop us up. You faithfully feed us and nurture us, determined that the good seed You planted will bear fruit that will reach its full potential in glory. How we thank You, Father, for Your infinite patience with us.

Have Thine own way, Lord!
Have Thine own way!
Hold o'er my being
Absolute sway!
Fill with Thy Spirit
Till all shall see
Christ only, always,
Living in me!

"Have Thine Own Way, Lord!"
Adelaide A. Pollard (1902)

we are all the work of your hand.
9 Do not be angry beyond measure, O LORD;
do not remember our sins forever.
Oh, look upon us, we pray,
for we are all your people.
10 Your sacred cities have become a desert;
even Zion is a desert, Jerusalem a desolation.
11 Our holy and glorious temple, where our fathers praised you,
has been burned with fire,
and all that we treasured lies in ruins.
12 After all this, O LORD, will you hold yourself back?
Will you keep silent and punish us beyond measure?

Judgment and Salvation

65 "I revealed myself to those who did not ask for me;
I was found by those who did not seek me.
To a nation that did not call on my name,
I said, 'Here am I, here am I.'
2 All day long I have held out my hands
to an obstinate people,
who walk in ways not good,
pursuing their own imaginations—
3 a people who continually provoke me
to my very face,
offering sacrifices in gardens
and burning incense on altars of brick;
4 who sit among the graves
and spend their nights keeping secret vigil;
who eat the flesh of pigs,
and whose pots hold broth of unclean meat;
5 who say, 'Keep away; don't come near me,
for I am too sacred for you!'
Such people are smoke in my nostrils,
a fire that keeps burning all day.

6 "See, it stands written before me:
I will not keep silent but will pay back in full;
I will pay it back into their laps—
7 both your sins and the sins of your fathers,"
says the LORD.
"Because they burned sacrifices on the mountains
and defied me on the hills,
I will measure into their laps
the full payment for their former deeds."

8 This is what the LORD says:

"As when juice is still found in a cluster of grapes
and men say, 'Don't destroy it,
there is yet some good in it,'
so will I do in behalf of my servants;
I will not destroy them all.
9 I will bring forth descendants from Jacob,
and from Judah those who will possess my mountains;
my chosen people will inherit them,
and there will my servants live.

10 Sharon will become a pasture for flocks,
and the Valley of Achor a resting place for herds,
for my people who seek me.
11 "But as for you who forsake the LORD
and forget my holy mountain,
who spread a table for Fortune
and fill bowls of mixed wine for Destiny,
12 I will destine you for the sword,
and you will all bend down for the slaughter;
for I called but you did not answer,
I spoke but you did not listen.
You did evil in my sight
and chose what displeases me."

13 Therefore this is what the Sovereign LORD says:

"My servants will eat,
but you will go hungry;
my servants will drink,
but you will go thirsty;
my servants will rejoice,
but you will be put to shame.
14 My servants will sing
out of the joy of their hearts,
but you will cry out
from anguish of heart
and wail in brokenness of spirit.
15 You will leave your name
to my chosen ones as a curse;
the Sovereign LORD will put you to death,
but to his servants he will give another name.
16 Whoever invokes a blessing in the land
will do so by the God of truth;
he who takes an oath in the land
will swear by the God of truth.
For the past troubles will be forgotten
and hidden from my eyes.

New Heavens and a New Earth

17 "Behold, I will create
new heavens and a new earth.
The former things will not be remembered,
nor will they come to mind.
18 But be glad and rejoice forever
in what I will create,
for I will create Jerusalem to be a delight
and its people a joy.
19 I will rejoice over Jerusalem
and take delight in my people;
the sound of weeping and of crying
will be heard in it no more.

20 "Never again will there be in it
an infant who lives but a few days,
or an old man who does not live out his
years;
he who dies at a hundred
will be thought a mere youth;

(65:10) Lord, thank You for Your promise that if we seek You in the Valley of Achor—the place of trouble—You will make it a resting place and a door of hope. There we will find pastures of peace, strength and joy in Your presence. We will find first love renewed, joyful, exciting and fresh. We only have to come and worship. (Jos 7:24–26; Hos 2:15)

(65:17–19) Lord, I actually dream of this. Sometimes it brings me to tears with homesickness. This is my golden goal. This is the vision that keeps me going in the desert: to forget the former things—the pain, the tears—and to rejoice forever and ever in the new world You will create. By Your grace, this is my destiny. (Rev 21:1–5)

Thou art making ready for me. This is too good for truth, yet also too good not to be all truth. Thou hast promised, and Thou keepest faith with the puniest of Thy children; wherefore I take great, sure encouragement. Heaven is my home. I am tried betimes and almost spent with the stress of battle and of climbing the rugged way; but thou dost promise a rest for the people of God, among whom I humbly hope God may have counted me. The soul's everlasting rest! How high the word and topless! I shall meet Thee in the morning, and my dear ones, "Loved long since and lost awhile."

How sweet the meeting! I shall be faint with the long march, and with blood spilt in the long war; but one look on Thee (for we shall see Him as He is) will refresh me more than a plunge in the fountain of life.

Bishop Quayle (1860-1925)

(66:1–2) Almighty, holy God, Creator of heaven and earth, life is in Your breath, time is in Your hands, creation is at the tip of Your tongue. Where, indeed, will we build Your home? In heaven? Heaven is Your chair. On the earth? Earth is Your footrest. And if we could build Your temple, what would we make it with? Wood that burns? Stone that crumbles? Gold that melts? Gold is but the asphalt of heaven. Indeed, how could we contain the uncontainable? How could we give You anything of value? You do not dwell in structures that are built by our hands. Rather, You dwell in people who are broken by Your grace; people whose hearts are mangers, not mansions; people who have no worthiness or righteousness of their own; people who fear You as their God and love You as their Father. O Lord, give me a heart that looks like home to You. Make me a temple for Your Holy Spirit. (Isa 57:15; Ac 7:48; 1Co 6:19–20; Rev 21:21)

And what kind of habitation pleases God? What must our natures be like before he can feel at home within us? He asks nothing but a pure heart and a single mind. He asks no rich paneling, no rugs from the Orient, no art treasures from afar. He desires but sincerity, transparency, humility, and love. He will see to the rest.

A.W. Tozer (1897-1963)

he who fails to reach[a] a hundred
will be considered accursed.
21 They will build houses and dwell in them;
they will plant vineyards and eat their fruit.
22 No longer will they build houses and others live in them,
or plant and others eat.
For as the days of a tree,
so will be the days of my people;
my chosen ones will long enjoy
the works of their hands.
23 They will not toil in vain
or bear children doomed to misfortune;
for they will be a people blessed by the LORD,
they and their descendants with them.
24 Before they call I will answer;
while they are still speaking I will hear.
25 The wolf and the lamb will feed together,
and the lion will eat straw like the ox,
but dust will be the serpent's food.
They will neither harm nor destroy
on all my holy mountain,"
says the LORD.

Judgment and Hope

66 This is what the LORD says:

"Heaven is my throne,
and the earth is my footstool.
Where is the house you will build for me?
Where will my resting place be?
2 Has not my hand made all these things,
and so they came into being?"
declares the LORD.

"This is the one I esteem:
he who is humble and contrite in spirit,
and trembles at my word.
3 But whoever sacrifices a bull
is like one who kills a man,
and whoever offers a lamb,
like one who breaks a dog's neck;
whoever makes a grain offering
is like one who presents pig's blood,
and whoever burns memorial incense,
like one who worships an idol.
They have chosen their own ways,
and their souls delight in their abominations;
4 so I also will choose harsh treatment for them
and will bring upon them what they dread.
For when I called, no one answered,
when I spoke, no one listened.
They did evil in my sight
and chose what displeases me."

5 Hear the word of the LORD,
you who tremble at his word:

[a] 20 Or / *the sinner who reaches*

"Your brothers who hate you,
and exclude you because of my name, have said,
'Let the LORD be glorified,
that we may see your joy!'
Yet they will be put to shame.
6 Hear that uproar from the city,
hear that noise from the temple!
It is the sound of the LORD
repaying his enemies all they deserve.
7 "Before she goes into labor,
she gives birth;
before the pains come upon her,
she delivers a son.
8 Who has ever heard of such a thing?
Who has ever seen such things?
Can a country be born in a day
or a nation be brought forth in a moment?
Yet no sooner is Zion in labor
than she gives birth to her children.
9 Do I bring to the moment of birth
and not give delivery?" says the LORD.
"Do I close up the womb
when I bring to delivery?" says your God.
10 "Rejoice with Jerusalem and be glad for her,
all you who love her;
rejoice greatly with her,
all you who mourn over her.
11 For you will nurse and be satisfied
at her comforting breasts;
you will drink deeply
and delight in her overflowing abundance."

12 For this is what the LORD says:

"I will extend peace to her like a river,
and the wealth of nations like a flooding stream;
you will nurse and be carried on her arm
and dandled on her knees.
13 As a mother comforts her child,
so will I comfort you;
and you will be comforted over Jerusalem."

14 When you see this, your heart will rejoice
and you will flourish like grass;
the hand of the LORD will be made known to his servants,
but his fury will be shown to his foes.
15 See, the LORD is coming with fire,
and his chariots are like a whirlwind;
he will bring down his anger with fury,
and his rebuke with flames of fire.
16 For with fire and with his sword
the LORD will execute judgment upon all men,
and many will be those slain by the LORD.

17 "Those who consecrate and purify themselves to go into the
gardens, following the one in the midst of[a] those who eat the flesh

[a] 17 Or *gardens behind one of your temples, and*

(66:7–9) Your Word, O God, always achieves the purpose for which You send it. You always bring to birth what You have conceived—no stillborn purposes, no aborted plans. Whether it is the birth of the Messiah, the birth of Your church, the birth of a nation, or something You are birthing in me, I believe and declare in faith that all You have designed will be accomplished, and all You begin will be perfectly completed. In its time, You will do it swiftly. (Isa 55:11; 60:22; Php 1:6)

(66:22–23) What You have already fashioned, though fallen and marred, is so marvelous that it is hard to imagine anything more beautiful than the heavens and earth as they now exist. But You will create it. It is already formed in Your mind and in Your heart: a stunning, exquisite work worthy of the magnificence of Your Son. And it is ours, too—all of us who belong to You. O God, we lift up worship and thanksgiving to You now, and with saints and angels ascribe endless glory and honor to Your name. Amen.

Who has not marked even here the glory of God as seen in the great sunset. Rivers of glory wind through meadows of gold. Lakes of glory lie embedded in the evening sky. Seas of glory lap eternal shores with their shimmering waves. Mountains of glory rear themselves to the heavens with cloud-capped summits tipped with the splendor of the dying day. Earth too is flooded with the glory. It falls in the dim aisles of great forests and illumines them with its splendor. It dances among the wind-tossed leaves. It splotches the trunks of giant trees. It bathes in light the upturned faces of those who watch and worship as the climaxing splendor of earth, sea, and sky turns the heart to God our Father who is Himself the glory of all creation and who deigns to give us, in the lavish, golden glory of the sunset the faint forth-shadowing of the glory of the Father's House.

But if the earthly glory is such, what must be the glory of the heavenly city?

James McConkey (1853-1937)

of pigs and rats and other abominable things—they will meet
their end together," declares the LORD.
18"And I, because of their actions and their imaginations, am
about to come[a] and gather all nations and tongues, and they will
come and see my glory.
19"I will set a sign among them, and I will send some of those
who survive to the nations—to Tarshish, to the Libyans[b] and Lydians (famous as archers), to Tubal and Greece, and to the distant
islands that have not heard of my fame or seen my glory. They will
proclaim my glory among the nations. **20**And they will bring all
your brothers, from all the nations, to my holy mountain in Jerusalem as an offering to the LORD—on horses, in chariots and wagons, and on mules and camels," says the LORD. "They will bring
them, as the Israelites bring their grain offerings, to the temple of
the LORD in ceremonially clean vessels. **21**And I will select some of
them also to be priests and Levites," says the LORD.

22"As the new heavens and the new earth that I make will endure before me," declares the LORD, "so will your name and descendants endure. **23**From one New Moon to another and from
one Sabbath to another, all mankind will come and bow down
before me," says the LORD. **24**"And they will go out and look upon
the dead bodies of those who rebelled against me; their worm
will not die, nor will their fire be quenched, and they will be
loathsome to all mankind."

[a] *18* The meaning of the Hebrew for this clause is uncertain. [b] *19* Some Septuagint manuscripts *Put* (Libyans); Hebrew *Pul*

The Book of the Prophet

JEREMIAH

"How can we sing the songs of the LORD while in a foreign land?" (Ps 137:4). So cries an unknown psalmist during Judah's sixth-century exile in Babylon. Though our context differs, we can feel the passion and perplexity of this question. How can we sing praise to God at times when God seems distant? How can we "hope in God" when hope has disappeared from our hearts?

God sends the prophet Jeremiah to help His people make sense of their conquest by Babylon in 586 B.C. and their exile around this time. Though at first Jeremiah calls the people to repentance with the promise of God's blessing (7:5–7), increasingly the prophet reveals that nothing can save Judah from the Babylonian invasion. The people's sins are too profound, their "wound is incurable" (30:12). God will use His "servant," King Nebuchadnezzar, to punish the people for their unfaithfulness (25:9). The Lord is no mere national deity, but the King of the nations under Whom all peoples are humbled. Unlike pagan idols, the Lord is the true God; He is the living God, the eternal King. When He is angry, the earth trembles. When we read Jeremiah we face the mighty, awesome, incomparably holy God (10:10). We reject our tendency to trivialize God. We join the nations in humble, trembling submission before our King.

Jeremiah reminds us that sometimes God's apparent absence from our lives is a result of our own sin. He encourages us to worship God by passionate obedience to God's will. When our hearts are too heavy to exult with praise, we can still worship God by doing His will.

When our hearts are too heavy to exult with praise, we can still worship God by doing His will.

Yet Jeremiah reveals our own inability to know God by human efforts. God alone can give us a heart to know Him (24:7). God alone can heal our incurable wound (30:12–17). When we realize how desperately we need God's mercy, we turn to Him for deliverance. And He promises to restore us: "'You will seek me and find me when you seek me with all your heart. I will be found by you' declares the LORD, 'and will bring you back'" (29:13–14). Though we are not political captives, we seek God for salvation from the captivity of sin and death.

Through Jeremiah God promises to make a new covenant with His people by which He will write His law upon human hearts so that we might know Him (31:31–34). As Christians we experience the fulfillment of this promise. Through Jesus Christ and His death we have been drawn into a new covenant with God, a covenant of grace and forgiveness. We have been redeemed—not from Babylon, but from the bondage to sin. When we worship God through Jesus Christ we realize the fulfillment of the promise once given to the Judean exiles. Even in hard times we can still sing songs of praise to God because of what He has done through Jesus Christ. As new covenant people, we "shout for joy on the heights of Zion" and "rejoice in the bounty of the LORD," for God has turned our "mourning into gladness" (31:12–13).

(1:5) Creator God, I am humbled and amazed that You would take Your eternal purposes and wrap them up in people. Just as You had a unique plan for Jeremiah, so I believe You have imprinted my life with the design of destiny. You have woven significance into the very fabric of who I am. "I praise You because I am fearfully and wonderfully made. When I was woven together in the depths of the earth, Your eyes saw my unformed body. All the days ordained for me were written in Your book before one of them came to be." (Ps 139:13–16)

It does not matter where he places me or how. That is rather for him to consider than for me. For the easiest positions he must give grace; and in the most difficult his grace is sufficient. So, if God places me in great perplexity, must he not give me much guidance? In positions of great difficulty, much grace? In circumstances of great pressure and trial, much strength? As to work, mine was never so plentiful, so responsible, or so difficult; but the weight and strain are all gone. His resources are mine, for he is mine.

James Hudson Taylor (1832-1905)

(1:7–8) Thank You, gracious Father, for raising up men and women in every generation to boldly carry Your Word to Your people. How I long for You to use me in my generation. Sovereign Lord, send forth Your Word in my flesh. Because You are Immanuel, God with us, God with me, I will be Your servant for whatever purpose You design. (Mt 1:23)

So send I you to hearts made hard
by hatred,
To eyes made blind because they will
not see,
To spend, tho' it be blood, to spend
and spare not;
So send I you to taste of Calvary.
"So Send I You–by Grace Made Strong"
Margaret Clarkson (©1964)

1 The words of Jeremiah son of Hilkiah, one of the priests at Anathoth in the territory of Benjamin.
2The word of the LORD came to him in the thirteenth year of the reign of Josiah son of Amon king of Judah,
3and through the reign of Jehoiakim son of Josiah king of Judah, down to the fifth month of the eleventh year of Zedekiah son of Josiah king of Judah, when the people of Jerusalem went into exile.

The Call of Jeremiah

4The word of the LORD came to me, saying,

5"Before I formed you in the womb I knew[a] you,
before you were born I set you apart;
I appointed you as a prophet to the nations."

6"Ah, Sovereign LORD," I said, "I do not know how to speak; I am only a child."
7But the LORD said to me, "Do not say, 'I am only a child.' You must go to everyone I send you to and say whatever I command you.
8Do not be afraid of them, for I am with you and will rescue you," declares the LORD.
9Then the LORD reached out his hand and touched my mouth and said to me, "Now, I have put my words in your mouth.
10See, today I appoint you over nations and kingdoms to uproot and tear down, to destroy and overthrow, to build and to plant."
11The word of the LORD came to me: "What do you see, Jeremiah?"
"I see the branch of an almond tree," I replied.
12The LORD said to me, "You have seen correctly, for I am watching[b] to see that my word is fulfilled."
13The word of the LORD came to me again: "What do you see?"
"I see a boiling pot, tilting away from the north," I answered.
14The LORD said to me, "From the north disaster will be poured out on all who live in the land.
15I am about to summon all the peoples of the northern kingdoms," declares the LORD.

"Their kings will come and set up their thrones
in the entrance of the gates of Jerusalem;
they will come against all her surrounding walls
and against all the towns of Judah.
16I will pronounce my judgments on my people
because of their wickedness in forsaking me,
in burning incense to other gods
and in worshiping what their hands have made.

17"Get yourself ready! Stand up and say to them whatever I command you. Do not be terrified by them, or I will terrify you before them.
18Today I have made you a fortified city, an iron pillar and a bronze wall to stand against the whole land—against the kings of Judah, its officials, its priests and the people of the land.
19They will fight against you but will not overcome you, for I am with you and will rescue you," declares the LORD.

Israel Forsakes God

2 The word of the LORD came to me:
2"Go and proclaim in the hearing of Jerusalem:

[a] 5 Or *chose* [b] *12* The Hebrew for *watching* sounds like the Hebrew for *almond tree.*

MY BELOVED

Before you were born, you were special to Me. I knew you before you were conceived in your mother's womb. With My own hands I fearfully and wonderfully created every detail that makes you unique. I knit together your body, soul and spirit.

I saw you long before you ever existed. I watched every day of your life. So I know you. I know where you have been, where you are, and where you are going.

If only you knew the thoughts I have toward you. Did you know My thoughts for you outnumber the grains of sand on all the beaches of the world? You are the apple of My eye. When trouble approaches, I hide you in the shadow of My wings. I have even engraved you on the palms of My hands.

It is My love for you that makes you precious and honored in My sight. I created you for My glory, and I will never abandon what I have formed and made. My goodness and love will follow you every day of your life. So do not fret; I will fulfill My purpose for your life. And always remember . . . My love endures forever and ever!

Ps 17:8; 23:6; 100:5; 138:8; 139:13-18; Isa 43:4,7; 49:16; Jer 1:5

" 'I remember the devotion of your youth,
how as a bride you loved me
and followed me through the desert,
through a land not sown.
3 Israel was holy to the LORD,
the firstfruits of his harvest;
all who devoured her were held guilty,
and disaster overtook them,' "
declares the LORD.

4 Hear the word of the LORD, O house of Jacob,
all you clans of the house of Israel.

5 This is what the LORD says:

"What fault did your fathers find in me,
that they strayed so far from me?
They followed worthless idols
and became worthless themselves.
6 They did not ask, 'Where is the LORD,
who brought us up out of Egypt
and led us through the barren wilderness,
through a land of deserts and rifts,
a land of drought and darkness,[a]
a land where no one travels and no one
lives?'
7 I brought you into a fertile land
to eat its fruit and rich produce.
But you came and defiled my land
and made my inheritance detestable.
8 The priests did not ask,
'Where is the LORD?'
Those who deal with the law did not know me;
the leaders rebelled against me.
The prophets prophesied by Baal,
following worthless idols.
9 "Therefore I bring charges against you again,"
declares the LORD.
"And I will bring charges against your children's
children.
10 Cross over to the coasts of Kittim[b] and look,
send to Kedar[c] and observe closely;
see if there has ever been anything like this:
11 Has a nation ever changed its gods?
(Yet they are not gods at all.)
But my people have exchanged their[d] Glory
for worthless idols.
12 Be appalled at this, O heavens,
and shudder with great horror,"
declares the LORD.
13 "My people have committed two sins:
They have forsaken me,
the spring of living water,
and have dug their own cisterns,
broken cisterns that cannot hold water.

[a] 6 Or *and the shadow of death* [b] 10 That is, Cyprus and western coastlands [c] 10 The home of Bedouin tribes in the Syro-Arabian desert [d] 11 Masoretic Text; an ancient Hebrew scribal tradition *my*

(2:2) Restore me, O God, to my first love. As a young bride faithfully follows her beloved, so in faith I will follow You. In times of disaster I will not wither; in days of famine I will enjoy plenty. For You will lead me through the desert into a fertile land where I will eat its fruit and rich produce. (Ps 37:19; Jer 2:7; 1Co 13:7; Heb 11:1)

(2:5) Father, as Your people of old, I have become hardened to Your goodness. I have taken Your mercy for granted. I have strayed from You like a prodigal son into a distant country. I have squandered all that You have given to me in the pursuit of worthless idols. I have sinned against heaven and against You, and I am no longer worthy to be called Your child. Loving father, please restore me, as Your child. Please restore me as Your servant. As You have suffered disgrace for my sin, may I be counted worthy of suffering disgrace for Your Name. Help me to live a life worthy of Your calling, pleasing to You in every way. (Lk 15:13,21; Ac 5:41; Eph 4:1)

Penitence does not grow by our looking gloomily on our own badness, but by looking up to God's loveliness, God's love for us.

William Congreve (1670–1729)

(2:13) Springs or cisterns? The flowing life of Your abundance, or my own stagnant, leaky attempts to make life work? That is the choice, and only I can make it. Forgive me, Giver of Life, for pursuing my own plans and solutions that leave me thirsty and unsatisfied. You are the Spring—refreshing, renewing and replenishing. Fill me with Your Spirit. Replace my stagnant waters of rebellion with the deep springs of Your living water. (Jn 4:13–14)

(2:19) O holy God, let me never lose the sense of awe that accompanies Your righteousness, Your wrath and Your mercy; the awe I feel in Your presence as I worship You. Restore to me the wonder, the wide-eyed amazement at Who You are. Such awe will draw me back to You and away from sin.

(2:22) O God, we are an unclean people, soiled and stained with sin. We have tried and failed to cleanse ourselves. Forgive our foolishness in dealing with guilt and shame on our terms, not Yours. Forgive our rationalizations and excuses, which lead us into greater sin and leave us more unclean than ever. You and You alone can purify us, God. Cleanse us with hyssop and we will be clean. Wash us, and we will be whiter than snow. (Ps 51:7)

14 Is Israel a servant, a slave by birth?
    Why then has he become plunder?
15 Lions have roared;
    they have growled at him.
They have laid waste his land;
    his towns are burned and deserted.
16 Also, the men of Memphis[a] and Tahpanhes
    have shaved the crown of your head.[b]
17 Have you not brought this on yourselves
    by forsaking the LORD your God
    when he led you in the way?
18 Now why go to Egypt
    to drink water from the Shihor[c]?
And why go to Assyria
    to drink water from the River[d]?
19 Your wickedness will punish you;
    your backsliding will rebuke you.
Consider then and realize
    how evil and bitter it is for you
when you forsake the LORD your God
    and have no awe of me,"
        declares the Lord, the LORD Almighty.

20 "Long ago you broke off your yoke
    and tore off your bonds;
    you said, 'I will not serve you!'
Indeed, on every high hill
    and under every spreading tree
    you lay down as a prostitute.
21 I had planted you like a choice vine
    of sound and reliable stock.
How then did you turn against me
    into a corrupt, wild vine?
22 Although you wash yourself with soda
    and use an abundance of soap,
    the stain of your guilt is still before me,"
        declares the Sovereign LORD.
23 "How can you say, 'I am not defiled;
    I have not run after the Baals'?
See how you behaved in the valley;
    consider what you have done.
You are a swift she-camel
    running here and there,
24 a wild donkey accustomed to the desert,
    sniffing the wind in her craving—
    in her heat who can restrain her?
Any males that pursue her need not tire
        themselves;
    at mating time they will find her.
25 Do not run until your feet are bare
    and your throat is dry.
But you said, 'It's no use!
    I love foreign gods,
    and I must go after them.'

26 "As a thief is disgraced when he is caught,

[a] 16 Hebrew *Noph* [b] 16 Or *have cracked your skull* [c] 18 That is, a branch of the Nile [d] 18 That is, the Euphrates

so the house of Israel is disgraced—
they, their kings and their officials,
their priests and their prophets.
27 They say to wood, 'You are my father,'
and to stone, 'You gave me birth.'
They have turned their backs to me
and not their faces;
yet when they are in trouble, they say,
'Come and save us!'
28 Where then are the gods you made for yourselves?
Let them come if they can save you
when you are in trouble!
For you have as many gods
as you have towns, O Judah.

29 "Why do you bring charges against me?
You have all rebelled against me,"
declares the LORD.
30 "In vain I punished your people;
they did not respond to correction.
Your sword has devoured your prophets
like a ravening lion.

31 "You of this generation, consider the word of the LORD:

"Have I been a desert to Israel
or a land of great darkness?
Why do my people say, 'We are free to roam;
we will come to you no more'?
32 Does a maiden forget her jewelry,
a bride her wedding ornaments?
Yet my people have forgotten me,
days without number.
33 How skilled you are at pursuing love!
Even the worst of women can learn from your ways.
34 On your clothes men find
the lifeblood of the innocent poor,
though you did not catch them breaking in.
Yet in spite of all this
35 you say, 'I am innocent;
he is not angry with me.'
But I will pass judgment on you
because you say, 'I have not sinned.'
36 Why do you go about so much,
changing your ways?
You will be disappointed by Egypt
as you were by Assyria.
37 You will also leave that place
with your hands on your head,
for the LORD has rejected those you trust;
you will not be helped by them.

3 "If a man divorces his wife
and she leaves him and marries another man,
should he return to her again?
Would not the land be completely defiled?

(2:35) Your people claimed innocence even as they flung their rebellion in Your face. Protect me, my God, from the insidious deception of self-righteousness. Lord, even if I were innocent, I would plead for Your mercy. How much more, in all my sin and guilt, do I need Your grace? I have sinned! Do not allow me to posture as an innocent victim. Help me to humble myself, to be contrite and to tremble at Your word. (Job 9:15; Isa 66:2b).

When the mask of self-righteousness has been torn from us and we stand stripped of all our accustomed defenses, we are candidates for God's generous grace.
Erwin W. Lutzer (1941-)

But you have lived as a prostitute with many
lovers—
would you now return to me?"
declares the LORD.
2"Look up to the barren heights and see.
Is there any place where you have not been
ravished?
By the roadside you sat waiting for lovers,
sat like a nomad[a] in the desert.
You have defiled the land
with your prostitution and wickedness.
3Therefore the showers have been withheld,
and no spring rains have fallen.
Yet you have the brazen look of a prostitute;
you refuse to blush with shame.
4Have you not just called to me:
'My Father, my friend from my youth,
5will you always be angry?
Will your wrath continue forever?'
This is how you talk,
but you do all the evil you can."

Lord, revive the church—beginning with me.
Samuel M. Shoemaker (1893-1963)

Unfaithful Israel

6During the reign of King Josiah, the LORD said to me, "Have
you seen what faithless Israel has done? She has gone up on every
high hill and under every spreading tree and has committed adultery there. 7I thought that after she had done all this she would
return to me but she did not, and her unfaithful sister Judah saw
it. 8I gave faithless Israel her certificate of divorce and sent her
away because of all her adulteries. Yet I saw that her unfaithful
sister Judah had no fear; she also went out and committed adultery. 9Because Israel's immorality mattered so little to her, she
defiled the land and committed adultery with stone and wood.
10In spite of all this, her unfaithful sister Judah did not return to
me with all her heart, but only in pretense," declares the LORD.
11The LORD said to me, "Faithless Israel is more righteous than
unfaithful Judah. 12Go, proclaim this message toward the north:

(3:6–13) Lord, spare me from pretense in my worship. When I come before You, help me to come in humility, in confession and in repentance. Teach me to despise my sins, to fully submit to Your ways, and to receive from You Your incomparable gift of mercy.

" 'Return, faithless Israel,' declares the LORD,
'I will frown on you no longer,
for I am merciful,' declares the LORD,
'I will not be angry forever.
13Only acknowledge your guilt—
you have rebelled against the LORD your God,
you have scattered your favors to foreign gods
under every spreading tree,
and have not obeyed me,' "
declares the LORD.

Give deep humility;
The sense of godly sorrow give;
A strong desire, with confidence,
To hear Your voice and live.
"Lord, Teach Us How to Pray Aright"
James Montgomery (1823)

14"Return, faithless people," declares the LORD, "for I am your
husband. I will choose you—one from a town and two from a
clan—and bring you to Zion. 15Then I will give you shepherds
after my own heart, who will lead you with knowledge and understanding. 16In those days, when your numbers have increased
greatly in the land," declares the LORD, "men will no longer say,
'The ark of the covenant of the LORD.' It will never enter their

[a]2 Or *an Arab*

minds or be remembered; it will not be missed, nor will another
one be made. 17At that time they will call Jerusalem The Throne
of the LORD, and all nations will gather in Jerusalem to honor the
name of the LORD. No longer will they follow the stubbornness of
their evil hearts. 18In those days the house of Judah will join the
house of Israel, and together they will come from a northern land
to the land I gave your forefathers as an inheritance.

19"I myself said,

" 'How gladly would I treat you like sons
and give you a desirable land,
the most beautiful inheritance of any nation.'
I thought you would call me 'Father'
and not turn away from following me.
20But like a woman unfaithful to her husband,
so you have been unfaithful to me, O house of Israel,"
declares the LORD.

21A cry is heard on the barren heights,
the weeping and pleading of the people of Israel,
because they have perverted their ways
and have forgotten the LORD their God.

22"Return, faithless people;
I will cure you of backsliding."

"Yes, we will come to you,
for you are the LORD our God.
23Surely the ⌊idolatrous⌋ commotion on the hills
and mountains is a deception;
surely in the LORD our God
is the salvation of Israel.
24From our youth shameful gods have consumed
the fruits of our fathers' labor—
their flocks and herds,
their sons and daughters.
25Let us lie down in our shame,
and let our disgrace cover us.
We have sinned against the LORD our God,
both we and our fathers;
from our youth till this day
we have not obeyed the LORD our God."

4 "If you will return, O Israel,
return to me,"
declares the LORD.
"If you put your detestable idols out of my sight
and no longer go astray,
2and if in a truthful, just and righteous way
you swear, 'As surely as the LORD lives,'
then the nations will be blessed by him
and in him they will glory."

3This is what the LORD says to the men of Judah and to Jerusalem:

"Break up your unplowed ground
and do not sow among thorns.
4Circumcise yourselves to the LORD,

(3:17) O Great God, I praise You that You will have the last word in our world. I thank You that Jerusalem, the place of past disobedience, will someday be called The Throne of the LORD, and that the kingdoms of this world will become Your kingdom. King of kings, extend Your reign right here today over my stubborn heart. Take authority over my will. Rule my wayward spirit forever and ever. (Rev. 11:15)

(3:19–22) God, we are so unfaithful! We call You "Father" when we want only what You can give. But once we set our eyes on earthly desires and ungodly destinations, we forget You. Yet even when our faithless folly seems to have burned every bridge back to You, Lord, there You still are, arms outstretched, with love in Your eyes and that simple invitation on Your lips: "Return." Thank You for Your healing promise, "I will cure you of backsliding." Cure us, O Father. Make a way back to You as You hear our answer, "Yes, we will come to you, for you are the LORD our God."

(4:3) Oh, Jesus, soften the soil of my heart. Remove the rocks, uproot the weeds and prepare this piece of earth for the seed of Your Word. Plant it deep in me, and let it take root in my soul. Make me fruitful, Lord. Find good soil, good crops and a good return for Your labor. (Mt 13:1–9)

God soon turns from his wrath, but he never turns from his love.
Charles Haddon Spurgeon (1834-1892)

(4:8) Holy God, I thank You for Your wrath, the severe side of Your mercy, that pursues me until my heart turns in repentance and I stand face-to-face with You—terrified by Your holiness, appalled by my sin, amazed by Your grace, captured at last by Your love at the foot of the cross.

Alas! and did my Savior bleed,
And did my sovereign die?
Would He devote that sacred Head
For such a worm as I?

Thus might I hide my blushing face
While His dear cross appears,
Dissolve my heart in thankfulness,
And melt mine eyes to tears.

But drops of grief can ne'er repay
The debt of love I owe:
Here, Lord, I give myself away
'Tis all that I can do!
"Alas! and Did My Savior Bleed"
Isaac Watts (1707)

circumcise your hearts,
you men of Judah and people of Jerusalem,
or my wrath will break out and burn like fire
because of the evil you have done—
burn with no one to quench it.

Disaster From the North

5 "Announce in Judah and proclaim in Jerusalem and say:
'Sound the trumpet throughout the land!'
Cry aloud and say:
'Gather together!
Let us flee to the fortified cities!'
6 Raise the signal to go to Zion!
Flee for safety without delay!
For I am bringing disaster from the north,
even terrible destruction."

7 A lion has come out of his lair;
a destroyer of nations has set out.
He has left his place
to lay waste your land.
Your towns will lie in ruins
without inhabitant.
8 So put on sackcloth,
lament and wail,
for the fierce anger of the LORD
has not turned away from us.

9 "In that day," declares the LORD,
"the king and the officials will lose heart,
the priests will be horrified,
and the prophets will be appalled."

10 Then I said, "Ah, Sovereign LORD, how completely you have deceived this people and Jerusalem by saying, 'You will have peace,' when the sword is at our throats."

11 At that time this people and Jerusalem will be told, "A scorching wind from the barren heights in the desert blows toward my people, but not to winnow or cleanse; 12 a wind too strong for that comes from me.[a] Now I pronounce my judgments against them."

13 Look! He advances like the clouds,
his chariots come like a whirlwind,
his horses are swifter than eagles.
Woe to us! We are ruined!
14 O Jerusalem, wash the evil from your heart and be saved.
How long will you harbor wicked thoughts?
15 A voice is announcing from Dan,
proclaiming disaster from the hills of Ephraim.
16 "Tell this to the nations,
proclaim it to Jerusalem:
'A besieging army is coming from a distant land,
raising a war cry against the cities of Judah.
17 They surround her like men guarding a field,

[a] 12 Or *comes at my command*

because she has rebelled against me,' "
declares the LORD.
18 "Your own conduct and actions
have brought this upon you.
This is your punishment.
How bitter it is!
How it pierces to the heart!"
19 Oh, my anguish, my anguish!
I writhe in pain.
Oh, the agony of my heart!
My heart pounds within me,
I cannot keep silent.
For I have heard the sound of the trumpet;
I have heard the battle cry.
20 Disaster follows disaster;
the whole land lies in ruins.
In an instant my tents are destroyed,
my shelter in a moment.
21 How long must I see the battle standard
and hear the sound of the trumpet?

22 "My people are fools;
they do not know me.
They are senseless children;
they have no understanding.
They are skilled in doing evil;
they know not how to do good."

23 I looked at the earth,
and it was formless and empty;
and at the heavens,
and their light was gone.
24 I looked at the mountains,
and they were quaking;
all the hills were swaying.
25 I looked, and there were no people;
every bird in the sky had flown away.
26 I looked, and the fruitful land was a desert;
all its towns lay in ruins
before the LORD, before his fierce anger.

27 This is what the LORD says:

"The whole land will be ruined,
though I will not destroy it completely.
28 Therefore the earth will mourn
and the heavens above grow dark,
because I have spoken and will not relent,
I have decided and will not turn back."

29 At the sound of horsemen and archers
every town takes to flight.
Some go into the thickets;
some climb up among the rocks.
All the towns are deserted;
no one lives in them.

30 What are you doing, O devastated one?
Why dress yourself in scarlet
and put on jewels of gold?

(4:22) How Your heart must grieve, loving and faithful Father. We are Your own, and yet we are so insensitive in knowing You and so skillful in hurting You. If You did not love us, You would not care. But the immensity of Your love only fuels the fire of Your wrath. Purify us, Lord, with holy fire!

(4:27) Thank You, Lord, for the thread of mercy that You weave through even Your harshest acts of discipline. You did not cast Your people off forever; though You brought grief to discipline them, You showed compassion out of Your great, unfailing love. "For [You do not] willingly bring affliction or grief to the children of men." And thank You for not giving up on me, Lord. You see beyond my failures and prepare me for my future "No discipline seems pleasant at the time, but painful. Later on, however, it produces a harvest of righteousness and peace for those who have been trained by it." (La 3:31–33; Heb 12:11)

(5:7) Indeed, Lord, why should You forgive anyone? Not one of us deserves Your forgiveness. But we praise You, Lord, that You do not treat us as our sins deserve, or repay us according to our iniquities. If You did, not one of us would survive. You are patient with us, understanding and forgiving in the face of our shameless disobedience. In Your perfect justice You are extravagantly merciful. (Ps 103:10)

For as high as the heavens are above
the earth,
So great is His mercy to me;
And as far as the east is from the
west,
So far are my sins from me!

Great is the Lord,
His mercy endures forever, forever.
Great is the Lord,
His mercy endures forever, forever.

Great is the Lord
Rita Baloche (©1989)

Why shade your eyes with paint?
You adorn yourself in vain.
Your lovers despise you;
they seek your life.

31 I hear a cry as of a woman in labor,
a groan as of one bearing her first child—
the cry of the Daughter of Zion gasping for breath,
stretching out her hands and saying,
"Alas! I am fainting;
my life is given over to murderers."

Not One Is Upright

5 "Go up and down the streets of Jerusalem,
look around and consider,
search through her squares.
If you can find but one person
who deals honestly and seeks the truth,
I will forgive this city.
2 Although they say, 'As surely as the LORD lives,'
still they are swearing falsely."

3 O LORD, do not your eyes look for truth?
You struck them, but they felt no pain;
you crushed them, but they refused correction.
They made their faces harder than stone
and refused to repent.
4 I thought, "These are only the poor;
they are foolish,
for they do not know the way of the LORD,
the requirements of their God.
5 So I will go to the leaders
and speak to them;
surely they know the way of the LORD,
the requirements of their God."
But with one accord they too had broken off the yoke
and torn off the bonds.
6 Therefore a lion from the forest will attack them,
a wolf from the desert will ravage them,
a leopard will lie in wait near their towns
to tear to pieces any who venture out,
for their rebellion is great
and their backslidings many.

7 "Why should I forgive you?
Your children have forsaken me
and sworn by gods that are not gods.
I supplied all their needs,
yet they committed adultery
and thronged to the houses of prostitutes.
8 They are well-fed, lusty stallions,
each neighing for another man's wife.
9 Should I not punish them for this?"
declares the LORD.
"Should I not avenge myself
on such a nation as this?

10 "Go through her vineyards and ravage them,
but do not destroy them completely.

Strip off her branches,
for these people do not belong to the LORD.
11 The house of Israel and the house of Judah
have been utterly unfaithful to me,"
declares the LORD.

12 They have lied about the LORD;
they said, "He will do nothing!
No harm will come to us;
we will never see sword or famine.
13 The prophets are but wind
and the word is not in them;
so let what they say be done to them."

14 Therefore this is what the LORD God Almighty says:

"Because the people have spoken these words,
I will make my words in your mouth a fire
and these people the wood it consumes.
15 O house of Israel," declares the LORD,
"I am bringing a distant nation against you—
an ancient and enduring nation,
a people whose language you do not know,
whose speech you do not understand.
16 Their quivers are like an open grave;
all of them are mighty warriors.
17 They will devour your harvests and food,
devour your sons and daughters;
they will devour your flocks and herds,
devour your vines and fig trees.
With the sword they will destroy
the fortified cities in which you trust.

18 "Yet even in those days," declares the LORD, "I will not destroy you completely.
19 And when the people ask, 'Why has the
LORD our God done all this to us?' you will tell them, 'As you have
forsaken me and served foreign gods in your own land, so now
you will serve foreigners in a land not your own.'

20 "Announce this to the house of Jacob
and proclaim it in Judah:
21 Hear this, you foolish and senseless people,
who have eyes but do not see,
who have ears but do not hear:
22 Should you not fear me?" declares the LORD.
"Should you not tremble in my presence?
I made the sand a boundary for the sea,
an everlasting barrier it cannot cross.
The waves may roll, but they cannot prevail;
they may roar, but they cannot cross it.
23 But these people have stubborn and rebellious hearts;
they have turned aside and gone away.
24 They do not say to themselves,
'Let us fear the LORD our God,
who gives autumn and spring rains in season,
who assures us of the regular weeks of harvest.'
25 Your wrongdoings have kept these away;
your sins have deprived you of good.

26 "Among my people are wicked men

(5:23–25) Forgive us, Lord, for blaming You for disasters that come our way when our sin has deprived us of good. You are faithful—all good things come from Your hand. You do not withhold good from those whose walk is blameless. Forgive us, cleanse us, and restore us to the fountain of Your faithfulness. (Ps 84:11)

(5:28–29) Thank You, God of all power, that You would concern Yourself with the case of the fatherless and the rights of the poor. Your power never corrupts Your compassion. When You see trouble and grief, O God, You take it in hand. And just as we look to You for our defense, may You also be able to look to us to defend those who cannot defend themselves. (Ps 10:14)

(6:8) Lord, the very fact that You warn us of impending judgment speaks of Your mercy, of Your patience, of Your longing to see true change in our hearts. You do not want anyone to perish, Father, but for everyone to come to repentance. (2Pe 3:9)

who lie in wait like men who snare birds
and like those who set traps to catch men.
27 Like cages full of birds,
their houses are full of deceit;
they have become rich and powerful
28 and have grown fat and sleek.
Their evil deeds have no limit;
they do not plead the case of the fatherless to win it,
they do not defend the rights of the poor.
29 Should I not punish them for this?"
declares the LORD.
"Should I not avenge myself
on such a nation as this?

30 "A horrible and shocking thing
has happened in the land:
31 The prophets prophesy lies,
the priests rule by their own authority,
and my people love it this way.
But what will you do in the end?

Jerusalem Under Siege

6 "Flee for safety, people of Benjamin!
Flee from Jerusalem!
Sound the trumpet in Tekoa!
Raise the signal over Beth Hakkerem!
For disaster looms out of the north,
even terrible destruction.
2 I will destroy the Daughter of Zion,
so beautiful and delicate.
3 Shepherds with their flocks will come against her;
they will pitch their tents around her,
each tending his own portion."
4 "Prepare for battle against her!
Arise, let us attack at noon!
But, alas, the daylight is fading,
and the shadows of evening grow long.
5 So arise, let us attack at night
and destroy her fortresses!"

6 This is what the LORD Almighty says:

"Cut down the trees
and build siege ramps against Jerusalem.
This city must be punished;
it is filled with oppression.
7 As a well pours out its water,
so she pours out her wickedness.
Violence and destruction resound in her;
her sickness and wounds are ever before me.
8 Take warning, O Jerusalem,
or I will turn away from you
and make your land desolate
so no one can live in it."

9 This is what the LORD Almighty says:

"Let them glean the remnant of Israel
as thoroughly as a vine;

pass your hand over the branches again,
like one gathering grapes."

10 To whom can I speak and give warning?
Who will listen to me?
Their ears are closed[a]
so they cannot hear.
The word of the LORD is offensive to them;
they find no pleasure in it.
11 But I am full of the wrath of the LORD,
and I cannot hold it in.

"Pour it out on the children in the street
and on the young men gathered together;
both husband and wife will be caught in it,
and the old, those weighed down with years.
12 Their houses will be turned over to others,
together with their fields and their wives,
when I stretch out my hand
against those who live in the land,"
declares the LORD.
13 "From the least to the greatest,
all are greedy for gain;
prophets and priests alike,
all practice deceit.
14 They dress the wound of my people
as though it were not serious.
'Peace, peace,' they say,
when there is no peace.
15 Are they ashamed of their loathsome conduct?
No, they have no shame at all;
they do not even know how to blush.
So they will fall among the fallen;
they will be brought down when I punish them,"
says the LORD.

16 This is what the LORD says:

"Stand at the crossroads and look;
ask for the ancient paths,
ask where the good way is, and walk in it,
and you will find rest for your souls.
But you said, 'We will not walk in it.'
17 I appointed watchmen over you and said,
'Listen to the sound of the trumpet!'
But you said, 'We will not listen.'
18 Therefore hear, O nations;
observe, O witnesses,
what will happen to them.
19 Hear, O earth:
I am bringing disaster on this people,
the fruit of their schemes,
because they have not listened to my words
and have rejected my law.
20 What do I care about incense from Sheba
or sweet calamus from a distant land?
Your burnt offerings are not acceptable;
your sacrifices do not please me."

[a] 10 Hebrew *uncircumcised*

(6:16–20) How can I expect You to receive my worship if I will not receive Your instruction? Father, forgive me! When I abandon the safe paths that keep me within Your will; when I close my ears to Your clear, penetrating words of guidance; when I raise my hands without bowing my heart—forgive my hypocrisy Lord, and teach me to worship You in spirit and in truth.

We choose the fear of the Lord.
We choose the fear of the Lord,
For the fear of the Lord
Is to hate all evil.
We choose the fear of the Lord.
We choose the fear of the Lord.

We choose the way of the Lord.
We choose the way of the Lord,
For the way of the Lord
Is the way of wisdom.
We choose the way of the Lord.
We choose the way of the Lord.

We choose the Word of the Lord.
We choose the Word of the Lord,
For the Word of the Lord
Shall endure forever.
We choose the Word of the Lord.
We choose the Word of the Lord.

"We Choose The Fear Of The Lord"
Kirk Dearman (©1989)

(7:2–4) Your people never dreamed that You would destroy the temple that bore the honor of Your own name. But You would, and You did. You had no use for the house if You could not have their hearts. It wasn't enough for them just to say religious words; You required that they live holy lives. Lord, You are the God of truth, and You require truth in my inner parts and integrity in my words and ways. So keep me from praise without purity, sacrifice without sincerity, religion without relationship, liturgy without love, and worship without wonder. First claim my heart as Yours, Father; then teach me the meaning of true worship.

Holy Spirit of God, who prefers before all temples the upright heart and pure, instruct us in all truth; what is dark, illumine; what is low, raise and support; what is shallow, deepen; that every chapter in our lives may witness to your power and justify the ways of God to men. In the name of Jesus, giver of all grace. Amen.

John Milton (1608-1674)

21 Therefore this is what the LORD says:

"I will put obstacles before this people.
Fathers and sons alike will stumble over them;
neighbors and friends will perish."

22 This is what the LORD says:

"Look, an army is coming
from the land of the north;
a great nation is being stirred up
from the ends of the earth.
23 They are armed with bow and spear;
they are cruel and show no mercy.
They sound like the roaring sea
as they ride on their horses;
they come like men in battle formation
to attack you, O Daughter of Zion."

24 We have heard reports about them,
and our hands hang limp.
Anguish has gripped us,
pain like that of a woman in labor.
25 Do not go out to the fields
or walk on the roads,
for the enemy has a sword,
and there is terror on every side.
26 O my people, put on sackcloth
and roll in ashes;
mourn with bitter wailing
as for an only son,
for suddenly the destroyer
will come upon us.

27 "I have made you a tester of metals
and my people the ore,
that you may observe
and test their ways.
28 They are all hardened rebels,
going about to slander.
They are bronze and iron;
they all act corruptly.
29 The bellows blow fiercely
to burn away the lead with fire,
but the refining goes on in vain;
the wicked are not purged out.
30 They are called rejected silver,
because the LORD has rejected them."

False Religion Worthless

7 This is the word that came to Jeremiah from the LORD:
2 "Stand at the gate of the LORD's house and there proclaim
this message:

" 'Hear the word of the LORD, all you people of Judah who
come through these gates to worship the LORD. 3 This is what the
LORD Almighty, the God of Israel, says: Reform your ways and your
actions, and I will let you live in this place. 4 Do not trust in deceptive words and say, "This is the temple of the LORD, the temple
of the LORD, the temple of the LORD!" 5 If you really change your

ways and your actions and deal with each other justly, 6if you do
not oppress the alien, the fatherless or the widow and do not shed
innocent blood in this place, and if you do not follow other gods
to your own harm, 7then I will let you live in this place, in the
land I gave your forefathers for ever and ever. 8But look, you are
trusting in deceptive words that are worthless.

9" 'Will you steal and murder, commit adultery and perjury,[a]
burn incense to Baal and follow other gods you have not known,
10and then come and stand before me in this house, which bears
my Name, and say, "We are safe"—safe to do all these detestable
things? 11Has this house, which bears my Name, become a den of
robbers to you? But I have been watching! declares the LORD.

12" 'Go now to the place in Shiloh where I first made a
dwelling for my Name, and see what I did to it because of the
wickedness of my people Israel. 13While you were doing all these
things, declares the LORD, I spoke to you again and again, but you
did not listen; I called you, but you did not answer. 14Therefore,
what I did to Shiloh I will now do to the house that bears my
Name, the temple you trust in, the place I gave to you and your fathers. 15I will thrust you from my presence, just as I did all your
brothers, the people of Ephraim.'

16"So do not pray for this people nor offer any plea or petition
for them; do not plead with me, for I will not listen to you. 17Do
you not see what they are doing in the towns of Judah and in the
streets of Jerusalem? 18The children gather wood, the fathers
light the fire, and the women knead the dough and make cakes of
bread for the Queen of Heaven. They pour out drink offerings to
other gods to provoke me to anger. 19But am I the one they are
provoking? declares the LORD. Are they not rather harming themselves, to their own shame?

20" 'Therefore this is what the Sovereign LORD says: My anger
and my wrath will be poured out on this place, on man and beast,
on the trees of the field and on the fruit of the ground, and it will
burn and not be quenched.

21" 'This is what the LORD Almighty, the God of Israel, says: Go
ahead, add your burnt offerings to your other sacrifices and eat
the meat yourselves! 22For when I brought your forefathers out of
Egypt and spoke to them, I did not just give them commands
about burnt offerings and sacrifices, 23but I gave them this command: Obey me, and I will be your God and you will be my people. Walk in all the ways I command you, that it may go well with
you. 24But they did not listen or pay attention; instead, they followed the stubborn inclinations of their evil hearts. They went
backward and not forward. 25From the time your forefathers left
Egypt until now, day after day, again and again I sent you my
servants the prophets. 26But they did not listen to me or pay attention. They were stiff-necked and did more evil than their forefathers.'

27"When you tell them all this, they will not listen to you; when
you call to them, they will not answer. 28Therefore say to them,
'This is the nation that has not obeyed the LORD its God or responded to correction. Truth has perished; it has vanished from
their lips. 29Cut off your hair and throw it away; take up a lament
on the barren heights, for the LORD has rejected and abandoned
this generation that is under his wrath.

[a] 9 Or *and swear by false gods*

(7:23–24) Gracious Father, You give us commands because You love us. When we turn from Your commands, we turn from Your love. Forgive us, Father, for our stubborn refusal to follow You. Reveal to us again Your Son Jesus. He did what we have never been able to do—He obeyed You fully. So clothe us in Christ's righteousness and empower us through His resurrection, O God. Apart from Him, we can do nothing. (Jn 15:5)

To be like Christ. That is our goal, plain and simple. It sounds like a peaceful, relaxing, easy objective. But stop and think. He learned obedience by the things he suffered. So must we. It is neither easy nor quick nor natural. It is impossible in the flesh, slow in coming, and supernatural in scope. Only Christ can accomplish it within us.

Charles R. Swindoll (1934-)

(8:1–2) Almighty God, how great and holy You are. How foolishly Your people turned their eyes from You to lesser objects of worship. They exchanged Your truth for a lie and worshiped created things rather than You, the Creator. Lord, keep us from false gods. Help us to let go of the worthless idols that cause us to forfeit the fullness of Your grace. (Jnh 2:8; Ro 1:25)

You alone are worthy of glory.
Creation hails you, omnipotent
King.
You alone deserve our allegiance,
Before your presence
And standing as servants we sing.
For you are King of kings,
Making our praise Your throne;
Into Your courts with joy we
approach
And humbly exalt you alone.

"You Alone"
Mark Roberts (©2000)

The Valley of Slaughter

30" 'The people of Judah have done evil in my eyes, declares
the LORD. They have set up their detestable idols in the house that
bears my Name and have defiled it. 31They have built the high
places of Topheth in the Valley of Ben Hinnom to burn their sons
and daughters in the fire—something I did not command, nor
did it enter my mind. 32So beware, the days are coming, declares
the LORD, when people will no longer call it Topheth or the Valley
of Ben Hinnom, but the Valley of Slaughter, for they will bury the
dead in Topheth until there is no more room. 33Then the carcasses of this people will become food for the birds of the air and
the beasts of the earth, and there will be no one to frighten them
away. 34I will bring an end to the sounds of joy and gladness and
to the voices of bride and bridegroom in the towns of Judah and
the streets of Jerusalem, for the land will become desolate.

8 " 'At that time, declares the LORD, the bones of the kings and
officials of Judah, the bones of the priests and prophets, and
the bones of the people of Jerusalem will be removed from their
graves. 2They will be exposed to the sun and the moon and all the
stars of the heavens, which they have loved and served and which
they have followed and consulted and worshiped. They will not be
gathered up or buried, but will be like refuse lying on the ground.
3Wherever I banish them, all the survivors of this evil nation will
prefer death to life, declares the LORD Almighty.'

Sin and Punishment

4"Say to them, 'This is what the LORD says:

" 'When men fall down, do they not get up?
When a man turns away, does he not return?
5 Why then have these people turned away?
Why does Jerusalem always turn away?
They cling to deceit;
they refuse to return.
6 I have listened attentively,
but they do not say what is right.
No one repents of his wickedness,
saying, "What have I done?"
Each pursues his own course
like a horse charging into battle.
7 Even the stork in the sky
knows her appointed seasons,
and the dove, the swift and the thrush
observe the time of their migration.
But my people do not know
the requirements of the LORD.

8" 'How can you say, "We are wise,
for we have the law of the LORD,"
when actually the lying pen of the scribes
has handled it falsely?
9 The wise will be put to shame;
they will be dismayed and trapped.
Since they have rejected the word of the LORD,
what kind of wisdom do they have?
10 Therefore I will give their wives to other men
and their fields to new owners.
From the least to the greatest,

all are greedy for gain;
prophets and priests alike,
all practice deceit.
11 They dress the wound of my people
as though it were not serious.
"Peace, peace," they say,
when there is no peace.
12 Are they ashamed of their loathsome conduct?
No, they have no shame at all;
they do not even know how to blush.
So they will fall among the fallen;
they will be brought down when they are
punished,
says the LORD.

13 " 'I will take away their harvest,
declares the LORD.
There will be no grapes on the vine.
There will be no figs on the tree,
and their leaves will wither.
What I have given them
will be taken from them.[a]' "

14 "Why are we sitting here?
Gather together!
Let us flee to the fortified cities
and perish there!
For the LORD our God has doomed us to perish
and given us poisoned water to drink,
because we have sinned against him.
15 We hoped for peace
but no good has come,
for a time of healing
but there was only terror.
16 The snorting of the enemy's horses
is heard from Dan;
at the neighing of their stallions
the whole land trembles.
They have come to devour
the land and everything in it,
the city and all who live there."

17 "See, I will send venomous snakes among you,
vipers that cannot be charmed,
and they will bite you,"
declares the LORD.

18 O my Comforter[b] in sorrow,
my heart is faint within me.
19 Listen to the cry of my people
from a land far away:
"Is the LORD not in Zion?
Is her King no longer there?"

"Why have they provoked me to anger with their
images,
with their worthless foreign idols?"

[a] *13* The meaning of the Hebrew for this sentence is uncertain. [b] *18* The meaning of the Hebrew for this word is uncertain.

(8:12) How often Your people have been gravely wounded because they have denied their sin. Lord, teach me the value of shame—not the shallow humiliation that accompanies human disapproval, but Your priceless gift of true shame, which so often precedes repentance. I pray that You will use godly shame to reveal my sin and confront my pride. Lord, open my eyes and heal my heart.

To You, omniscient Lord of all,
With grief and shame I humbly call;
I see my sins against You, Lord,
The sins of thought, of deed, and
word.
They press me sore; to You I flee:
O God, be merciful to me!

My Lord and God, to You I pray,
Oh, cast me not in wrath away;
Let Your good Spirit ne'er depart,
But let Him draw to You my heart
That truly penitent I be:
O God, be merciful to me!

"To You, Omniscient Lord of All"
Magnus B. Landstad (1802–1880)
Trans. Carl Doving (1867–1937)

(8:19) Your people rejected Your presence. Then they lamented Your absence. Lord, help me to seek You while You may be found and to call on You while You are near. Help me to forsake all wickedness and turn to You. Have mercy on me and pardon my sins. Draw me close to Your heart and keep me there, Father. May I never give You cause to withdraw Your hand from me. (Isa 55:6–7)

(8:21–22) With Jeremiah, Your servant, I lament for those who have rebelled against You. Their lives are shattered: they are broken, devastated and in great pain. You, Who were bruised for their iniquity, hold them in Your nail-scarred hands. You have allowed them to be torn to pieces; now please heal them. You have not prevented their injury; now, Great Physician, bind up their wounds. (Hos 6:1)

Let us not underestimate how hard it is to be compassionate. Compassion is hard because it requires the inner disposition to go with others to the place where they are weak, vulnerable, lonely, and broken. But this is not our spontaneous response to suffering. What we desire most is to do away with suffering by fleeing from it or finding a quick cure for it.

Henri Nouwen (1932-1996)

20 "The harvest is past,
the summer has ended,
and we are not saved."

21 Since my people are crushed, I am crushed;
I mourn, and horror grips me.
22 Is there no balm in Gilead?
Is there no physician there?
Why then is there no healing
for the wound of my people?

9

1 Oh, that my head were a spring of water
and my eyes a fountain of tears!
I would weep day and night
for the slain of my people.
2 Oh, that I had in the desert
a lodging place for travelers,
so that I might leave my people
and go away from them;
for they are all adulterers,
a crowd of unfaithful people.

3 "They make ready their tongue
like a bow, to shoot lies;
it is not by truth
that they triumph[a] in the land.
They go from one sin to another;
they do not acknowledge me,"
declares the LORD.
4 "Beware of your friends;
do not trust your brothers.
For every brother is a deceiver,[b]
and every friend a slanderer.
5 Friend deceives friend,
and no one speaks the truth.
They have taught their tongues to lie;
they weary themselves with sinning.
6 You[c] live in the midst of deception;
in their deceit they refuse to acknowledge me,"
declares the LORD.

7 Therefore this is what the LORD Almighty says:

"See, I will refine and test them,
for what else can I do
because of the sin of my people?
8 Their tongue is a deadly arrow;
it speaks with deceit.
With his mouth each speaks cordially to his neighbor,
but in his heart he sets a trap for him.
9 Should I not punish them for this?"
declares the LORD.
"Should I not avenge myself
on such a nation as this?"

10 I will weep and wail for the mountains
and take up a lament concerning the desert
pastures.

[a] 3 Or *lies; / they are not valiant for truth* [b] 4 Or *a deceiving Jacob* [c] 6 That is, Jeremiah (the Hebrew is singular)

They are desolate and untraveled,
 and the lowing of cattle is not heard.
The birds of the air have fled
 and the animals are gone.

11 "I will make Jerusalem a heap of ruins,
 a haunt of jackals;
and I will lay waste the towns of Judah
 so no one can live there."

12 What man is wise enough to understand this? Who has been
instructed by the LORD and can explain it? Why has the land been
ruined and laid waste like a desert that no one can cross?
13 The LORD said, "It is because they have forsaken my law,
which I set before them; they have not obeyed me or followed my
law. 14 Instead, they have followed the stubbornness of their
hearts; they have followed the Baals, as their fathers taught them."
15 Therefore, this is what the LORD Almighty, the God of Israel,
says: "See, I will make this people eat bitter food and drink poisoned water. 16 I will scatter them among nations that neither they
nor their fathers have known, and I will pursue them with the
sword until I have destroyed them."

17 This is what the LORD Almighty says:

"Consider now! Call for the wailing women to come;
 send for the most skillful of them.
18 Let them come quickly
 and wail over us
till our eyes overflow with tears
 and water streams from our eyelids.
19 The sound of wailing is heard from Zion:
 'How ruined we are!
 How great is our shame!
We must leave our land
 because our houses are in ruins.' "

20 Now, O women, hear the word of the LORD;
 open your ears to the words of his mouth.
Teach your daughters how to wail;
 teach one another a lament.
21 Death has climbed in through our windows
 and has entered our fortresses;
it has cut off the children from the streets
 and the young men from the public squares.

22 Say, "This is what the LORD declares:

" 'The dead bodies of men will lie
 like refuse on the open field,
like cut grain behind the reaper,
 with no one to gather them.' "

23 This is what the LORD says:

"Let not the wise man boast of his wisdom
 or the strong man boast of his strength
 or the rich man boast of his riches,
24 but let him who boasts boast about this:
 that he understands and knows me,
that I am the LORD, who exercises kindness,

(9:23–24) Father, I praise You for the ways in which You make Yourself known. I will not boast in my wisdom, because You have chosen the foolish things of the world to shame the wise. I will not boast in strength, because You have chosen the weak things of the world to shame the strong. You have chosen lowly women, men of ill repute, powerless people from nowhere, ordinary folks without human credentials, anonymous people—people like me—to show the world that You are indeed a kind, just and righteous God.

Transfixed with thanks, folded in love, I cannot adore enough.
Myrna Reid Grant (1934-)

(10:6) Because no one is like You, O Lord, I worship You and make You my refuge. Your power overcomes my problems. The authority of Your name overrules all that would defeat me. I praise You that You have no competitor or peer. "Who among the gods is like you, O LORD? Who is like you—majestic in holiness, awesome in glory, working wonders?" (Ex 15:11)

These foolish earthly pow'rs
Parading their might,
Can't match the majesty
Of one starry night.
You gave the word,
And the universe was made.
You'll give the word when it's
through.
There is nobody else, Oh Lord,
Nobody like You.

"Nobody Like You"
Bill Batstone (©1988)

(10:10) In a world that markets innumerable false gods, I acknowledge You, O Lord, as the only true God. In a world that lives as though You were dead, I choose to walk in Christ's resurrection life, for You are the living King. In a world bound by time and quickly passing away, I embrace Your gift of everlasting life. Sovereign Lord, I gratefully worship You in the beauty of all that You are—true, living and eternal.

justice and righteousness on earth,
for in these I delight,"
declares the LORD.

25 "The days are coming," declares the LORD, "when I will punish all who are circumcised only in the flesh— 26 Egypt, Judah,
Edom, Ammon, Moab and all who live in the desert in distant
places.[a] For all these nations are really uncircumcised, and even
the whole house of Israel is uncircumcised in heart."

God and Idols

10 Hear what the LORD says to you, O house of Israel. 2 This is
what the LORD says:

"Do not learn the ways of the nations
or be terrified by signs in the sky,
though the nations are terrified by them.
3 For the customs of the peoples are worthless;
they cut a tree out of the forest,
and a craftsman shapes it with his chisel.
4 They adorn it with silver and gold;
they fasten it with hammer and nails
so it will not totter.
5 Like a scarecrow in a melon patch,
their idols cannot speak;
they must be carried
because they cannot walk.
Do not fear them;
they can do no harm
nor can they do any good."

6 No one is like you, O LORD;
you are great,
and your name is mighty in power.
7 Who should not revere you,
O King of the nations?
This is your due.
Among all the wise men of the nations
and in all their kingdoms,
there is no one like you.
8 They are all senseless and foolish;
they are taught by worthless wooden idols.
9 Hammered silver is brought from Tarshish
and gold from Uphaz.
What the craftsman and goldsmith have made
is then dressed in blue and purple—
all made by skilled workers.
10 But the LORD is the true God;
he is the living God, the eternal King.
When he is angry, the earth trembles;
the nations cannot endure his wrath.

11 "Tell them this: 'These gods, who did not make the heavens
and the earth, will perish from the earth and from under the
heavens.' "[b]

12 But God made the earth by his power;

[a] 26 Or *desert and who clip the hair by their foreheads* [b] 11 The text of this verse is in Aramaic.

he founded the world by his wisdom
and stretched out the heavens by his
understanding.
13 When he thunders, the waters in the heavens roar;
he makes clouds rise from the ends of the earth.
He sends lightning with the rain
and brings out the wind from his storehouses.
14 Everyone is senseless and without knowledge;
every goldsmith is shamed by his idols.
His images are a fraud;
they have no breath in them.
15 They are worthless, the objects of mockery;
when their judgment comes, they will perish.
16 He who is the Portion of Jacob is not like these,
for he is the Maker of all things,
including Israel, the tribe of his inheritance—
the LORD Almighty is his name.

Coming Destruction

17 Gather up your belongings to leave the land,
you who live under siege.
18 For this is what the LORD says:
"At this time I will hurl out
those who live in this land;
I will bring distress on them
so that they may be captured."
19 Woe to me because of my injury!
My wound is incurable!
Yet I said to myself,
"This is my sickness, and I must endure it."
20 My tent is destroyed;
all its ropes are snapped.
My sons are gone from me and are no more;
no one is left now to pitch my tent
or to set up my shelter.
21 The shepherds are senseless
and do not inquire of the LORD;
so they do not prosper
and all their flock is scattered.
22 Listen! The report is coming—
a great commotion from the land of the north!
It will make the towns of Judah desolate,
a haunt of jackals.

Jeremiah's Prayer

23 I know, O LORD, that a man's life is not his own;
it is not for man to direct his steps.
24 Correct me, LORD, but only with justice—
not in your anger,
lest you reduce me to nothing.
25 Pour out your wrath on the nations
that do not acknowledge you,
on the peoples who do not call on your name.
For they have devoured Jacob;
they have devoured him completely
and destroyed his homeland.

(10:16) My Maker and my Portion, I honor You. As my Maker, You are my source; as my Portion, You are my sufficiency. As my Maker, You have fashioned me; as my Portion, You will fill me. I rest in You, I worship You, and I draw life from You. You alone merit the name, "The LORD Almighty."

We pay God honor and reverence, not for his sake (because he is of himself full of glory to which no creature can add anything), but for our own sake.

Saint Thomas Aquinas (1225-1274)

(10:24) Thank You, Lord, for the riches of Your mercy. Thank You for Your patience with my weaknesses. Thank You for choosing to use justice rather than anger to correct me. Thank You for choosing to build me up through Your discipline rather than crush me in Your rage. Thank You for Your love and kindness that leads me to repentance. (Ro 2:4)

(11:3–8) Lord, You know the human heart. We are all inclined to disobedience. Your people violated Your covenant and brought on themselves the judgment that You had foretold. My heart is also inclined to disobedience, and I also deserve Your judgment. I have all too often violated Your good will toward me. But I thank You, merciful God, for the new covenant in the blood of Jesus. By it You pardon me, protect me, provide for me, and prize me as Your own.

Come to Calvary's holy mountain,
Sinners, ruined by the Fall;
Here a pure and healing fountain
Flows to you, to me, to all,
In a full perpetual tide,
Opened when our Savior died.

Those who drink shall live forever;
'Tis a soul renewing flood.
God is faithful; God will never
Break His covenant of blood,
Signed when our Redeemer died,
Sealed when He was glorified.

"Come to Calvary's Holy Mountain"
James Montgomery (1771–1854)

The Covenant Is Broken

11 This is the word that came to Jeremiah from the LORD:
2"Listen to the terms of this covenant and tell them to the
people of Judah and to those who live in Jerusalem. 3Tell them
that this is what the LORD, the God of Israel, says: 'Cursed is the
man who does not obey the terms of this covenant— 4the terms
I commanded your forefathers when I brought them out of Egypt,
out of the iron-smelting furnace.' I said, 'Obey me and do everything I command you, and you will be my people, and I will be
your God. 5Then I will fulfill the oath I swore to your forefathers,
to give them a land flowing with milk and honey'—the land you possess today."

I answered, "Amen, LORD."

6The LORD said to me, "Proclaim all these words in the towns
of Judah and in the streets of Jerusalem: 'Listen to the terms of
this covenant and follow them. 7From the time I brought your forefathers up from Egypt until today, I warned them again and
again, saying, "Obey me." 8But they did not listen or pay attention; instead, they followed the stubbornness of their evil hearts. So I brought on them all the curses of the covenant I had commanded them to follow but that they did not keep.' "

9Then the LORD said to me, "There is a conspiracy among the
people of Judah and those who live in Jerusalem. 10They have returned to the sins of their forefathers, who refused to listen to my words. They have followed other gods to serve them. Both the house of Israel and the house of Judah have broken the covenant
I made with their forefathers. 11Therefore this is what the LORD says: 'I will bring on them a disaster they cannot escape. Although
they cry out to me, I will not listen to them. 12The towns of Judah
and the people of Jerusalem will go and cry out to the gods to whom they burn incense, but they will not help them at all when
disaster strikes. 13You have as many gods as you have towns, O Judah; and the altars you have set up to burn incense to that shameful god Baal are as many as the streets of Jerusalem.'

14"Do not pray for this people nor offer any plea or petition for them, because I will not listen when they call to me in the time of their distress.

15"What is my beloved doing in my temple
as she works out her evil schemes with many?
Can consecrated meat avert ⌞your punishment⌟?
When you engage in your wickedness,
then you rejoice.[a]"

16The LORD called you a thriving olive tree
with fruit beautiful in form.
But with the roar of a mighty storm
he will set it on fire,
and its branches will be broken.

17The LORD Almighty, who planted you, has decreed disaster for you, because the house of Israel and the house of Judah have done evil and provoked me to anger by burning incense to Baal.

Plot Against Jeremiah

18Because the LORD revealed their plot to me, I knew it, for at
that time he showed me what they were doing. 19I had been like

[a] 15 Or *Could consecrated meat avert your punishment? / Then you would rejoice*

a gentle lamb led to the slaughter; I did not realize that they had plotted against me, saying,

"Let us destroy the tree and its fruit;
  let us cut him off from the land of the living,
  that his name be remembered no more."
20 But, O LORD Almighty, you who judge righteously
  and test the heart and mind,
let me see your vengeance upon them,
  for to you I have committed my cause.

21 "Therefore this is what the LORD says about the men of Anathoth who are seeking your life and saying, 'Do not prophesy in the name of the LORD or you will die by our hands'— 22 therefore this is what the LORD Almighty says: 'I will punish them. Their young men will die by the sword, their sons and daughters by famine. 23 Not even a remnant will be left to them, because I will bring disaster on the men of Anathoth in the year of their punishment.' "

Jeremiah's Complaint

12 You are always righteous, O LORD,
  when I bring a case before you.
Yet I would speak with you about your justice:
  Why does the way of the wicked prosper?
  Why do all the faithless live at ease?
2 You have planted them, and they have taken root;
  they grow and bear fruit.
You are always on their lips
  but far from their hearts.
3 Yet you know me, O LORD;
  you see me and test my thoughts about you.
Drag them off like sheep to be butchered!
  Set them apart for the day of slaughter!
4 How long will the land lie parched[a]
  and the grass in every field be withered?
Because those who live in it are wicked,
  the animals and birds have perished.
Moreover, the people are saying,
  "He will not see what happens to us."

God's Answer

5 "If you have raced with men on foot
  and they have worn you out,
  how can you compete with horses?
If you stumble in safe country,[b]
  how will you manage in the thickets by[c] the Jordan?
6 Your brothers, your own family—
  even they have betrayed you;
  they have raised a loud cry against you.
Do not trust them,
  though they speak well of you.

7 "I will forsake my house,
  abandon my inheritance;
I will give the one I love

[a] 4 Or *land mourn* [b] 5 Or *If you put your trust in a land of safety* [c] 5 Or *the flooding of*

(11:20) Thank You, Almighty God, for Your saving acts of grace. You revealed the plot of the wicked to Jeremiah, and he committed his case into Your hand. They tried to silence Jeremiah, and in so doing, to silence the voice of God. But Your Word would stand and Your enemies would fall. You are the righteous Judge Who pleads the cause of the innocent. Your justice is a terror to the ungodly but a comfort to those who trust in You.

(12:1) You are always righteous, O Lord. Even when I do not understand Your ways or decisions, You are right. Your wisdom is far above mine. Your ideas of prosperity and value are beyond my limited comprehension; You are not dependent on my counsel. Though clouds and thick darkness may surround You, Your throne sits on a foundation of righteousness and justice that cannot be shaken. You are holy and wise. I put my trust in You. (Ps 97:2)

(12:15–17) Lord, Your mercy is amazing. You are the God of second chances. Not only did You promise to bless Your own people, but You also promised to redeem their enemies if they would learn Your ways from Your people. Jesus demonstrated this marvelous principle when He prayed not only for His followers, but also for those who would believe in Him through their message. You did not set Your people apart to isolate them from the world; You set them apart to evangelize the world. You did not send Your Son into the world to condemn the world. You sent Him so that the world, through Him, might be saved. O Lord, send Your Son into my world through me today. Set me apart as an instrument of salvation. (Jn 3:17; 17:17–21)

(13:1–10) Grace is the reward of humility. Pride makes us useless to You; therefore, pride is useless to us. Thank You, Lord, for humbling us just so You can pour Your grace out to us. Thank You, Lord, for loving us enough to ruin our pride. (Jas 4:6)

Let me give you the history of pride in three small chapters. The beginning of pride was in heaven. The continuance of pride is on earth. The end of pride is in hell. This history shows how unprofitable it is.

Richard Newton (1813-1887)

into the hands of her enemies.
8 My inheritance has become to me
like a lion in the forest.
She roars at me;
therefore I hate her.
9 Has not my inheritance become to me
like a speckled bird of prey
that other birds of prey surround and attack?
Go and gather all the wild beasts;
bring them to devour.
10 Many shepherds will ruin my vineyard
and trample down my field;
they will turn my pleasant field
into a desolate wasteland.
11 It will be made a wasteland,
parched and desolate before me;
the whole land will be laid waste
because there is no one who cares.
12 Over all the barren heights in the desert
destroyers will swarm,
for the sword of the LORD will devour
from one end of the land to the other;
no one will be safe.
13 They will sow wheat but reap thorns;
they will wear themselves out but gain nothing.
So bear the shame of your harvest
because of the LORD's fierce anger."

14 This is what the LORD says: "As for all my wicked neighbors
who seize the inheritance I gave my people Israel, I will uproot
them from their lands and I will uproot the house of Judah from
among them. 15 But after I uproot them, I will again have compassion and will bring each of them back to his own inheritance
and his own country. 16 And if they learn well the ways of my people and swear by my name, saying, 'As surely as the LORD lives'—
even as they once taught my people to swear by Baal—then they
will be established among my people. 17 But if any nation does
not listen, I will completely uproot and destroy it," declares the
LORD.

A Linen Belt

13 This is what the LORD said to me: "Go and buy a linen belt
and put it around your waist, but do not let it touch water."
2 So I bought a belt, as the LORD directed, and put it around my
waist.

3 Then the word of the LORD came to me a second time: 4 "Take
the belt you bought and are wearing around your waist, and go
now to Perath[a] and hide it there in a crevice in the rocks." 5 So I
went and hid it at Perath, as the LORD told me.

6 Many days later the LORD said to me, "Go now to Perath and
get the belt I told you to hide there." 7 So I went to Perath and dug
up the belt and took it from the place where I had hidden it, but
now it was ruined and completely useless.

8 Then the word of the LORD came to me: 9 "This is what the
LORD says: 'In the same way I will ruin the pride of Judah and the
great pride of Jerusalem. 10 These wicked people, who refuse to

[a] 4 Or possibly *the Euphrates*; also in verses 5–7

listen to my words, who follow the stubbornness of their hearts
and go after other gods to serve and worship them, will be like
this belt—completely useless! 11For as a belt is bound around a
man's waist, so I bound the whole house of Israel and the whole
house of Judah to me,' declares the LORD, 'to be my people for my
renown and praise and honor. But they have not listened.'

Wineskins

12"Say to them: 'This is what the LORD, the God of Israel, says:
Every wineskin should be filled with wine.' And if they say to you,
'Don't we know that every wineskin should be filled with wine?'
13then tell them, 'This is what the LORD says: I am going to fill
with drunkenness all who live in this land, including the kings
who sit on David's throne, the priests, the prophets and all those
living in Jerusalem. 14I will smash them one against the other, fathers and sons alike, declares the LORD. I will allow no pity or
mercy or compassion to keep me from destroying them.' "

Threat of Captivity

15 Hear and pay attention,
do not be arrogant,
for the LORD has spoken.
16 Give glory to the LORD your God
before he brings the darkness,
before your feet stumble
on the darkening hills.
You hope for light,
but he will turn it to thick darkness
and change it to deep gloom.
17 But if you do not listen,
I will weep in secret
because of your pride;
my eyes will weep bitterly,
overflowing with tears,
because the LORD's flock will be taken captive.

18 Say to the king and to the queen mother,
"Come down from your thrones,
for your glorious crowns
will fall from your heads."
19 The cities in the Negev will be shut up,
and there will be no one to open them.
All Judah will be carried into exile,
carried completely away.

20 Lift up your eyes and see
those who are coming from the north.
Where is the flock that was entrusted to you,
the sheep of which you boasted?
21 What will you say when ⌊the LORD⌋ sets over you
those you cultivated as your special allies?
Will not pain grip you
like that of a woman in labor?
22 And if you ask yourself,
"Why has this happened to me?"—
it is because of your many sins
that your skirts have been torn off
and your body mistreated.

(13:11) Your people rebelled against You, so You removed them like a garment. Bind me to Yourself, O Lord, and let my life be lived only for Your praise. Hold me to Yourself and let me hear the whispers of Your heart. Surround me with the glory of Your grace and let me radiate the light of Your life. Make Your faithfulness my fortress, and Your transforming power my story. I am Yours, and I worship You for all that You are to me.

Direct, control, suggest, this day,
All I design, or do, or say,
That all my powers with all their might,
In thy sole glory may unite.

Bishop Thomas Ken (1637-1711)

(14:3) The sins of Your people had caused You to withhold the rain. They had cut themselves off from the Source of all blessing, and now they were paying the price. How many times have I cut myself off from You, only to find my soul parched and unfulfilled? Forgive me, Lord. Upon the dry ground of my spiritual barrenness, pour out Your waters of life. Let me drink again from the wells of Your strength. Fill me up, and fulfill in me the promise of Christ: "If anyone is thirsty, let him come to me and drink. Whoever believes in me, as the Scripture has said, streams of living water will flow from within him." (Jn 7:37b–38)

Draw me to the well to drink,
For I know in me dwells
No good thing.
Draw me to the well to drink,
For it is in You I find my strength.

Wash away all earthly ties,
Any love I've held as mine;
Bind me to Your heart alone,
Where streams of love are flowing
From Your throne.

Waters deep and endless,
Always for the asking;
Rivers pure and living,
Flowing there for me.

"Draw Me to the Well"
Kelly Willard (©1999)

23 Can the Ethiopian[a] change his skin
or the leopard its spots?
Neither can you do good
who are accustomed to doing evil.

24 "I will scatter you like chaff
driven by the desert wind.
25 This is your lot,
the portion I have decreed for you,"
declares the LORD,
"because you have forgotten me
and trusted in false gods.
26 I will pull up your skirts over your face
that your shame may be seen—
27 your adulteries and lustful neighings,
your shameless prostitution!
I have seen your detestable acts
on the hills and in the fields.
Woe to you, O Jerusalem!
How long will you be unclean?"

Drought, Famine, Sword

14 This is the word of the LORD to Jeremiah concerning the drought:

2 "Judah mourns,
her cities languish;
they wail for the land,
and a cry goes up from Jerusalem.
3 The nobles send their servants for water;
they go to the cisterns
but find no water.
They return with their jars unfilled;
dismayed and despairing,
they cover their heads.
4 The ground is cracked
because there is no rain in the land;
the farmers are dismayed
and cover their heads.
5 Even the doe in the field
deserts her newborn fawn
because there is no grass.
6 Wild donkeys stand on the barren heights
and pant like jackals;
their eyesight fails
for lack of pasture."

7 Although our sins testify against us,
O LORD, do something for the sake of your name.
For our backsliding is great;
we have sinned against you.
8 O Hope of Israel,
its Savior in times of distress,
why are you like a stranger in the land,
like a traveler who stays only a night?
9 Why are you like a man taken by surprise,
like a warrior powerless to save?

[a] 23 Hebrew *Cushite* (probably a person from the upper Nile region)

You are among us, O LORD,
and we bear your name;
do not forsake us!

10 This is what the LORD says about this people:

"They greatly love to wander;
they do not restrain their feet.
So the LORD does not accept them;
he will now remember their wickedness
and punish them for their sins."

11 Then the LORD said to me, "Do not pray for the well-being of
this people. 12 Although they fast, I will not listen to their cry;
though they offer burnt offerings and grain offerings, I will not accept them. Instead, I will destroy them with the sword, famine
and plague."
13 But I said, "Ah, Sovereign LORD, the prophets keep telling
them, 'You will not see the sword or suffer famine. Indeed, I will
give you lasting peace in this place.' "
14 Then the LORD said to me, "The prophets are prophesying lies
in my name. I have not sent them or appointed them or spoken to
them. They are prophesying to you false visions, divinations, idolatries[a] and the delusions of their own minds. 15 Therefore, this is
what the LORD says about the prophets who are prophesying in my
name: I did not send them, yet they are saying, 'No sword or
famine will touch this land.' Those same prophets will perish by
sword and famine. 16 And the people they are prophesying to will
be thrown out into the streets of Jerusalem because of the famine
and sword. There will be no one to bury them or their wives, their
sons or their daughters. I will pour out on them the calamity they
deserve.

17 "Speak this word to them:

" 'Let my eyes overflow with tears
night and day without ceasing;
for my virgin daughter—my people—
has suffered a grievous wound,
a crushing blow.
18 If I go into the country,
I see those slain by the sword;
if I go into the city,
I see the ravages of famine.
Both prophet and priest
have gone to a land they know not.' "

19 Have you rejected Judah completely?
Do you despise Zion?
Why have you afflicted us
so that we cannot be healed?
We hoped for peace
but no good has come,
for a time of healing
but there is only terror.
20 O LORD, we acknowledge our wickedness
and the guilt of our fathers;
we have indeed sinned against you.

[a] 14 Or *visions, worthless divinations*

(14:14) A time had come when Your people would not put up with sound doctrine. Instead, to suit their own desires, they gathered around them a great number of teachers to say what their itching ears wanted to hear. But who am I to point a finger of judgment? I know that, if left to my own designs, I will hear only what I want to hear. Help me to recognize Your voice, O Lord. Give me discernment to distinguish between the counsel that comes from Your heart and the agendas that spring from my heart. Help me to sort through the many voices that cry for my attention. Speak Your Word to me—not just what I want to hear, but what You want to say. (2Ti 4:3)

(14:17) Gracious Lord, loving Father, You are full of compassion and mercy. Your heart toward Your people is truly a wonder. Despite their unfaithfulness, despite their spiritual adultery, despite their flaunting of their sin before Your eyes, in Your heart of hearts You still saw them as Your virgin daughter. What forgiveness. What love. What vision. O my great, unchanging God, despite my weakness and failure and rebellion, how do You see me? Redeem me, Lord, and transform me into what You envision me to be.

(15:1–6) Sovereign Lord, Your mind was made up. Your patience had reached its unexplored end. No mediator could stay Your judgment. Under Manasseh, Your people had sinned against You by shedding innocent blood. And so, like Cain, they would be driven from Your presence. But though they were out of Your presence, they were not beyond Your sight. You would restore them at the proper time. You are righteous in all Your ways, O God. (Ge 4:10–14; 2Ki 24:3–4; Jer 16:14–15)

Miserable is the case of those who have sinned so long against God's mercy that at length sinned it away.

Matthew Henry (1662-1714)

The clouds of judgment gather;
The time is growing late;
Be sober and be watchful;
Our Judge is at the gate:
The Judge who comes in mercy,
The Judge who comes in might
To put an end to evil
And diadem the right.

"The Clouds of Judgment Gather"
Bernard of Cluny (12th c.)
Trans. Hymnal Version (©1978)

21 For the sake of your name do not despise us;
do not dishonor your glorious throne.
Remember your covenant with us
and do not break it.
22 Do any of the worthless idols of the nations bring rain?
Do the skies themselves send down showers?
No, it is you, O LORD our God.
Therefore our hope is in you,
for you are the one who does all this.

15 Then the LORD said to me: "Even if Moses and Samuel were
to stand before me, my heart would not go out to this people. Send them away from my presence! Let them go!
2 And if they ask you, 'Where shall we go?' tell them, 'This is what the LORD says:

"'Those destined for death, to death;
those for the sword, to the sword;
those for starvation, to starvation;
those for captivity, to captivity.'

3 "I will send four kinds of destroyers against them," declares
the LORD, "the sword to kill and the dogs to drag away and the
birds of the air and the beasts of the earth to devour and destroy.
4 I will make them abhorrent to all the kingdoms of the earth because of what Manasseh son of Hezekiah king of Judah did in Jerusalem.

5 "Who will have pity on you, O Jerusalem?
Who will mourn for you?
Who will stop to ask how you are?
6 You have rejected me," declares the LORD.
"You keep on backsliding.
So I will lay hands on you and destroy you;
I can no longer show compassion.
7 I will winnow them with a winnowing fork
at the city gates of the land.
I will bring bereavement and destruction on my
people,
for they have not changed their ways.
8 I will make their widows more numerous
than the sand of the sea.
At midday I will bring a destroyer
against the mothers of their young men;
suddenly I will bring down on them
anguish and terror.
9 The mother of seven will grow faint
and breathe her last.
Her sun will set while it is still day;
she will be disgraced and humiliated.
I will put the survivors to the sword
before their enemies,"
declares the LORD.

10 Alas, my mother, that you gave me birth,
a man with whom the whole land strives and
contends!
I have neither lent nor borrowed,
yet everyone curses me.

11 The LORD said,

"Surely I will deliver you for a good purpose;
surely I will make your enemies plead with you
in times of disaster and times of distress.

12 "Can a man break iron—
iron from the north—or bronze?
13 Your wealth and your treasures
I will give as plunder, without charge,
because of all your sins
throughout your country.
14 I will enslave you to your enemies
in[a] a land you do not know,
for my anger will kindle a fire
that will burn against you."

15 You understand, O LORD;
remember me and care for me.
Avenge me on my persecutors.
You are long-suffering—do not take me away;
think of how I suffer reproach for your sake.
16 When your words came, I ate them;
they were my joy and my heart's delight,
for I bear your name,
O LORD God Almighty.
17 I never sat in the company of revelers,
never made merry with them;
I sat alone because your hand was on me
and you had filled me with indignation.
18 Why is my pain unending
and my wound grievous and incurable?
Will you be to me like a deceptive brook,
like a spring that fails?

19 Therefore this is what the LORD says:

"If you repent, I will restore you
that you may serve me;
if you utter worthy, not worthless, words,
you will be my spokesman.
Let this people turn to you,
but you must not turn to them.
20 I will make you a wall to this people,
a fortified wall of bronze;
they will fight against you
but will not overcome you,
for I am with you
to rescue and save you,"
declares the LORD.

21 "I will save you from the hands of the wicked
and redeem you from the grasp of the cruel."

Day of Disaster

16 Then the word of the LORD came to me: 2 "You must not
marry and have sons or daughters in this place." 3 For this
is what the LORD says about the sons and daughters born in this
land and about the women who are their mothers and the men
who are their fathers: 4 "They will die of deadly diseases. They will

[a] 14 Some Hebrew manuscripts, Septuagint and Syriac (see also Jer. 17:4); most Hebrew manuscripts *I will cause your enemies to bring you / into*

(15:16–17) Lord, I praise You for setting me apart as Your own. You have called me by Your name. You have chosen me to represent You and Your kingdom in the world. You have placed Your Word and Your purposes in my otherwise empty heart, filling it with meaning and delight. Thank You for who I am in You, and for Who You are in me.

(15:19) I come to You, my God, in humble repentance. Forgive me for every degree to which my interests have outweighed Your interests. Wash the self-pity out of my heart and the complaining out of my mouth. Give me a will that is bent to You and not enslaved to the approval of others. Put something of worth on my lips to speak for You. Restore me, I pray. I will serve You, for I am Your servant.

Murmur at nothing: if our ills are irreparable, it is ungrateful; if remediless, it is in vain. A Christian builds his fortitude on a better foundation than stoicism; he is pleased with everything that happens because he knows it could not happen unless it had first pleased God, and that which pleases him must be the best.

Charles Caleb Colton (1780-1832)

(16:14–15) Father in heaven, thank You for keeping Your hand of protection, provision and discipline upon Your people, year after year, generation after generation. Thank You for the power You have demonstrated in the lives of our forefathers, and for Your faithfulness to our parents. But thank You most of all for Your relentless grace and mercy to us, and for Your unfailing help in our time of need—yesterday, today and tomorrow. (Heb 4:16)

(16:19) Thank You, Lord, that one day all the nations will yield to Your dominion. Thank You that everything false and worthless will be exposed for what it is. Thank You that a day will come when the worship of ourselves and our idols will cease, and that You alone will be worshiped as our Fortress and Refuge. Receive my praise, O King, and come to reign in me today.

not be mourned or buried but will be like refuse lying on the
ground. They will perish by sword and famine, and their dead
bodies will become food for the birds of the air and the beasts of
the earth."

5 For this is what the LORD says: "Do not enter a house where
there is a funeral meal; do not go to mourn or show sympathy, because I have withdrawn my blessing, my love and my pity from
this people," declares the LORD. 6 "Both high and low will die in
this land. They will not be buried or mourned, and no one will cut
himself or shave his head for them. 7 No one will offer food to
comfort those who mourn for the dead—not even for a father or
a mother—nor will anyone give them a drink to console them.

8 "And do not enter a house where there is feasting and sit
down to eat and drink. 9 For this is what the LORD Almighty, the
God of Israel, says: Before your eyes and in your days I will bring
an end to the sounds of joy and gladness and to the voices of
bride and bridegroom in this place.

10 "When you tell these people all this and they ask you, 'Why
has the LORD decreed such a great disaster against us? What
wrong have we done? What sin have we committed against the
LORD our God?' 11 then say to them, 'It is because your fathers forsook me,' declares the LORD, 'and followed other gods and served
and worshiped them. They forsook me and did not keep my law.
12 But you have behaved more wickedly than your fathers. See
how each of you is following the stubbornness of his evil heart instead of obeying me. 13 So I will throw you out of this land into a
land neither you nor your fathers have known, and there you will
serve other gods day and night, for I will show you no favor.'

14 "However, the days are coming," declares the LORD, "when
men will no longer say, 'As surely as the LORD lives, who brought
the Israelites up out of Egypt,' 15 but they will say, 'As surely as the
LORD lives, who brought the Israelites up out of the land of the
north and out of all the countries where he had banished them.'
For I will restore them to the land I gave their forefathers.

16 "But now I will send for many fishermen," declares the LORD,
"and they will catch them. After that I will send for many hunters,
and they will hunt them down on every mountain and hill and
from the crevices of the rocks. 17 My eyes are on all their ways;
they are not hidden from me, nor is their sin concealed from my
eyes. 18 I will repay them double for their wickedness and their
sin, because they have defiled my land with the lifeless forms of
their vile images and have filled my inheritance with their detestable idols."

19 O LORD, my strength and my fortress,
  my refuge in time of distress,
to you the nations will come
  from the ends of the earth and say,
"Our fathers possessed nothing but false gods,
  worthless idols that did them no good.
20 Do men make their own gods?
  Yes, but they are not gods!"

21 "Therefore I will teach them—
  this time I will teach them
  my power and might.
Then they will know
  that my name is the LORD.

17 "Judah's sin is engraved with an iron tool,
inscribed with a flint point,
on the tablets of their hearts
and on the horns of their altars.
2 Even their children remember
their altars and Asherah poles[a]
beside the spreading trees
and on the high hills.
3 My mountain in the land
and your[b] wealth and all your treasures
I will give away as plunder,
together with your high places,
because of sin throughout your country.
4 Through your own fault you will lose
the inheritance I gave you.
I will enslave you to your enemies
in a land you do not know,
for you have kindled my anger,
and it will burn forever."

5 This is what the LORD says:

"Cursed is the one who trusts in man,
who depends on flesh for his strength
and whose heart turns away from the LORD.
6 He will be like a bush in the wastelands;
he will not see prosperity when it comes.
He will dwell in the parched places of the desert,
in a salt land where no one lives.
7 "But blessed is the man who trusts in the LORD,
whose confidence is in him.
8 He will be like a tree planted by the water
that sends out its roots by the stream.
It does not fear when heat comes;
its leaves are always green.
It has no worries in a year of drought
and never fails to bear fruit."
9 The heart is deceitful above all things
and beyond cure.
Who can understand it?

10 "I the LORD search the heart
and examine the mind,
to reward a man according to his conduct,
according to what his deeds deserve."
11 Like a partridge that hatches eggs it did not lay
is the man who gains riches by unjust means.
When his life is half gone, they will desert him,
and in the end he will prove to be a fool.

12 A glorious throne, exalted from the beginning,
is the place of our sanctuary.
13 O LORD, the hope of Israel,
all who forsake you will be put to shame.

[a] 2 That is, symbols of the goddess Asherah [b] 2,3 Or *hills* / [3] *and the mountains of the land. / Your*

(17:5–9) Caring and righteous Father, You know our ways and You understand our hearts far better than we do. You see our stubbornness. You know that the inclination of our hearts is to do evil. Yet You counsel us on what is right, and graciously warn us of the consequences of going our own way. In Your great mercy, You offer blessing in the face of cursing. We choose this day to trust in You, not in ourselves or any other person. There is no blessing except in You, and that blessing is so undeserved, so unearned; it is simply the result of trust. And with Your blessing comes life, strength, fruitfulness, protection and assurance. (Ge 8:21; 2Ti 1:12–14)

Those who turn away from you will be written in the dust
because they have forsaken the LORD,
the spring of living water.

14 Heal me, O LORD, and I will be healed;
save me and I will be saved,
for you are the one I praise.
15 They keep saying to me,
"Where is the word of the LORD?
Let it now be fulfilled!"
16 I have not run away from being your shepherd;
you know I have not desired the day of despair.
What passes my lips is open before you.
17 Do not be a terror to me;
you are my refuge in the day of disaster.
18 Let my persecutors be put to shame,
but keep me from shame;
let them be terrified,
but keep me from terror.
Bring on them the day of disaster;
destroy them with double destruction.

(17:14) Lord, You are more than my Maker. You are also my Healer and my Savior. My life is secure from both the powers of darkness and the judgment of Your hand. You are, indeed, everything to me: health and salvation, hope and sustenance, wholeness and strength. I lift grateful praise to You from a heart of growing faith.

Keeping the Sabbath Holy

19 This is what the LORD said to me: "Go and stand at the gate of
the people, through which the kings of Judah go in and out; stand
also at all the other gates of Jerusalem. 20 Say to them, 'Hear the
word of the LORD, O kings of Judah and all people of Judah and
everyone living in Jerusalem who come through these gates.
21 This is what the LORD says: Be careful not to carry a load on the
Sabbath day or bring it through the gates of Jerusalem. 22 Do not
bring a load out of your houses or do any work on the Sabbath,
but keep the Sabbath day holy, as I commanded your forefathers.
23 Yet they did not listen or pay attention; they were stiff-necked
and would not listen or respond to discipline. 24 But if you are
careful to obey me, declares the LORD, and bring no load through
the gates of this city on the Sabbath, but keep the Sabbath day
holy by not doing any work on it, 25 then kings who sit on David's
throne will come through the gates of this city with their officials.
They and their officials will come riding in chariots and on
horses, accompanied by the men of Judah and those living in Jerusalem, and this city will be inhabited forever. 26 People will
come from the towns of Judah and the villages around Jerusalem,
from the territory of Benjamin and the western foothills, from the
hill country and the Negev, bringing burnt offerings and sacrifices, grain offerings, incense and thank offerings to the house of
the LORD. 27 But if you do not obey me to keep the Sabbath day
holy by not carrying any load as you come through the gates of Jerusalem on the Sabbath day, then I will kindle an unquenchable
fire in the gates of Jerusalem that will consume her fortresses.' "

(18:1–6) Take my life into Your hands, O Lord. I am the clay, rich with possibilities by Your grace, but marred beyond usefulness by my own failures. So break me down and apply to my heart the water of Your Spirit. Knead the resistance out of me and make me pliable again. With Your skillful hands reshape me to Your liking, just as the potter would reform the clay into an object of beauty and usefulness. Master Potter, You are the God of second chances. Do not give up on me, but make me a vessel fit for Your honor. (2Ti 2:20–21).

At the Potter's House

18 This is the word that came to Jeremiah from the LORD:
2 "Go down to the potter's house, and there I will give you
my message." 3 So I went down to the potter's house, and I saw
him working at the wheel. 4 But the pot he was shaping from the
clay was marred in his hands; so the potter formed it into another pot, shaping it as seemed best to him.

Have Thine own way, Lord!
Have Thine own way!
Thou art the potter,
I am the clay!
Mold me and make me
After Thy will,
While I am waiting,
Yielded and still.

"Have Thine Own Way, Lord!"
Adelaide A. Pollard (1902)

5Then the word of the LORD came to me: 6"O house of Israel,
can I not do with you as this potter does?" declares the LORD.
"Like clay in the hand of the potter, so are you in my hand, O
house of Israel. 7If at any time I announce that a nation or kingdom is to be uprooted, torn down and destroyed, 8and if that nation I warned repents of its evil, then I will relent and not inflict
on it the disaster I had planned. 9And if at another time I announce that a nation or kingdom is to be built up and planted,
10and if it does evil in my sight and does not obey me, then I will
reconsider the good I had intended to do for it.

11"Now therefore say to the people of Judah and those living in
Jerusalem, 'This is what the LORD says: Look! I am preparing a disaster for you and devising a plan against you. So turn from your
evil ways, each one of you, and reform your ways and your actions.'
12But they will reply, 'It's no use. We will continue with our own
plans; each of us will follow the stubbornness of his evil heart.' "

13Therefore this is what the LORD says:

"Inquire among the nations:
Who has ever heard anything like this?
A most horrible thing has been done
by Virgin Israel.
14Does the snow of Lebanon
ever vanish from its rocky slopes?
Do its cool waters from distant sources
ever cease to flow?[a]
15Yet my people have forgotten me;
they burn incense to worthless idols,
which made them stumble in their ways
and in the ancient paths.
They made them walk in bypaths
and on roads not built up.
16Their land will be laid waste,
an object of lasting scorn;
all who pass by will be appalled
and will shake their heads.
17Like a wind from the east,
I will scatter them before their enemies;
I will show them my back and not my face
in the day of their disaster."

18They said, "Come, let's make plans against Jeremiah; for the
teaching of the law by the priest will not be lost, nor will counsel
from the wise, nor the word from the prophets. So come, let's attack him with our tongues and pay no attention to anything he
says."

19Listen to me, O LORD;
hear what my accusers are saying!
20Should good be repaid with evil?
Yet they have dug a pit for me.
Remember that I stood before you
and spoke in their behalf
to turn your wrath away from them.
21So give their children over to famine;
hand them over to the power of the sword.

[a] 14 The meaning of the Hebrew for this sentence is uncertain.

(18:7–12) We thank You, Lord, that judgment is always a strange and alien task for You. You do not wish for harm to come to us. You warn us again and again, "Look! I am preparing a disaster . . . So turn." In Your patience, You give us chance after chance. In Your kindness You lead us to repentance—You call to us and woo us to righteousness. We also thank You, O Lord, that when we show contempt for Your kindness, tolerance and patience, Your punishment is just and effective. We can never say we were not warned. Help us, Lord, to recognize the time of Your mercy and turn from our evil ways. May we repent and turn to You, so that our sins may be wiped out, and that times of refreshing may come to us from Your hand. (Isa 28:21; Ac 3:19; Ro 2:4)

Thou hast promised to receive us,
Poor and sinful though we be;
Thou hast mercy to relieve us,
Grace to cleanse, and pow'r to free:
Blessed Jesus, blessed Jesus,
Early let us turn to Thee;
Blessed Jesus, blessed Jesus,
Early let us turn to Thee.

"Savior, Like a Shepherd Lead Us"
Dorothy A. Thrupp (1836)

Let their wives be made childless and widows;
  let their men be put to death,
  their young men slain by the sword in battle.
22 Let a cry be heard from their houses
  when you suddenly bring invaders against them,
for they have dug a pit to capture me
  and have hidden snares for my feet.
23 But you know, O LORD,
  all their plots to kill me.
Do not forgive their crimes
  or blot out their sins from your sight.
Let them be overthrown before you;
  deal with them in the time of your anger.

19 This is what the LORD says: "Go and buy a clay jar from a
potter. Take along some of the elders of the people and of
the priests 2and go out to the Valley of Ben Hinnom, near the entrance of the Potsherd Gate. There proclaim the words I tell you,
3and say, 'Hear the word of the LORD, O kings of Judah and people of Jerusalem. This is what the LORD Almighty, the God of Israel, says: Listen! I am going to bring a disaster on this place that
will make the ears of everyone who hears of it tingle. 4For they
have forsaken me and made this a place of foreign gods; they
have burned sacrifices in it to gods that neither they nor their fathers nor the kings of Judah ever knew, and they have filled this
place with the blood of the innocent. 5They have built the high
places of Baal to burn their sons in the fire as offerings to Baal—
something I did not command or mention, nor did it enter my
mind. 6So beware, the days are coming, declares the LORD, when
people will no longer call this place Topheth or the Valley of Ben
Hinnom, but the Valley of Slaughter.

7" 'In this place I will ruin[a] the plans of Judah and Jerusalem.
I will make them fall by the sword before their enemies, at the
hands of those who seek their lives, and I will give their carcasses
as food to the birds of the air and the beasts of the earth. 8I will
devastate this city and make it an object of scorn; all who pass by
will be appalled and will scoff because of all its wounds. 9I will
make them eat the flesh of their sons and daughters, and they will
eat one another's flesh during the stress of the siege imposed on
them by the enemies who seek their lives.'

10"Then break the jar while those who go with you are watching, 11and say to them, 'This is what the LORD Almighty says: I will
smash this nation and this city just as this potter's jar is smashed
and cannot be repaired. They will bury the dead in Topheth until
there is no more room. 12This is what I will do to this place and
to those who live here, declares the LORD. I will make this city like
Topheth. 13The houses in Jerusalem and those of the kings of
Judah will be defiled like this place, Topheth—all the houses
where they burned incense on the roofs to all the starry hosts and
poured out drink offerings to other gods.' "

14Jeremiah then returned from Topheth, where the LORD had
sent him to prophesy, and stood in the court of the LORD's temple
and said to all the people, 15"This is what the LORD Almighty, the
God of Israel, says: 'Listen! I am going to bring on this city and the
villages around it every disaster I pronounced against them, because they were stiff-necked and would not listen to my words.' "

[a] 7 The Hebrew for *ruin* sounds like the Hebrew for *jar* (see verses 1 and 10).

(19:5) O God, some of the sins of Your people were so appalling that, because of Your holiness, they were virtually inconceivable to You. What evil the human mind is capable of imagining! Purify us, O Lord. Have mercy on us. Renew our minds with the mind of Christ. Transform us, O God, through the work of Your Holy Spirit, into His image and likeness, and remove from us the unthinkable, the unconscionable, the unspeakable thoughts and ways that so gravely distance us from You. (1Co 2:9–16)

O God! O God! That it were possible
To undo things done; to call back yesterday!
That Time could turn up his swift sandy glass,
To untell the days, and to redeem these hours.

Thomas Heywood (c.1574–1641)

Jesus calls us from the worship
Of the vain world's golden store,
From each idol that would keep us,
Saying, "Christian, love Me more."

"Jesus Calls Us O'er the Tumult"
Cecil F. Alexander (1852)

Jeremiah and Pashhur

20 When the priest Pashhur son of Immer, the chief officer in
the temple of the LORD, heard Jeremiah prophesying these
things, 2he had Jeremiah the prophet beaten and put in the stocks
at the Upper Gate of Benjamin at the LORD's temple. 3The next day,
when Pashhur released him from the stocks, Jeremiah said to
him, "The LORD's name for you is not Pashhur, but Magor-Missabib.[a] 4For this is what the LORD says: 'I will make you a terror to
yourself and to all your friends; with your own eyes you will see
them fall by the sword of their enemies. I will hand all Judah over
to the king of Babylon, who will carry them away to Babylon or
put them to the sword. 5I will hand over to their enemies all the
wealth of this city—all its products, all its valuables and all the
treasures of the kings of Judah. They will take it away as plunder
and carry it off to Babylon. 6And you, Pashhur, and all who live in
your house will go into exile to Babylon. There you will die and
be buried, you and all your friends to whom you have prophesied
lies.' "

Jeremiah's Complaint

7 O LORD, you deceived[b] me, and I was deceived[b];
you overpowered me and prevailed.
I am ridiculed all day long;
everyone mocks me.
8 Whenever I speak, I cry out
proclaiming violence and destruction.
So the word of the LORD has brought me
insult and reproach all day long.
9 But if I say, "I will not mention him
or speak any more in his name,"
his word is in my heart like a fire,
a fire shut up in my bones.
I am weary of holding it in;
indeed, I cannot.
10 I hear many whispering,
"Terror on every side!
Report him! Let's report him!"
All my friends
are waiting for me to slip, saying,
"Perhaps he will be deceived;
then we will prevail over him
and take our revenge on him."
11 But the LORD is with me like a mighty warrior;
so my persecutors will stumble and not prevail.
They will fail and be thoroughly disgraced;
their dishonor will never be forgotten.
12 O LORD Almighty, you who examine the righteous
and probe the heart and mind,
let me see your vengeance upon them,
for to you I have committed my cause.
13 Sing to the LORD!
Give praise to the LORD!
He rescues the life of the needy
from the hands of the wicked.

[a] 3 *Magor-Missabib* means *terror on every side.* [b] 7 Or *persuaded*

(20:9) When I am tempted to quit, give me a heart like Jeremiah's. Let me find Your grace sufficient to overcome every obstacle. Ignite my otherwise fearful and faithless bones with Your unquenchable flame. Burn away self-interest and leave me with no choice but to speak about what I have seen and heard of You. Let me burn with the fire of Your Spirit. (Ac 4:18–20)

I will never be the same again,
I can never return, I've closed the
door.
I will walk the path, I'll run the race,
And I will never be the same again.

Fall like fire, soak like rain;
Flow like mighty waters again and
again.
Sweep away the darkness,
Burn away the chaff,
And let a flame burn to glorify Your
Name.

"I Will Never Be (The Same Again)"
Geoff Bullock (©1995)

(20:11–13) Great Warrior, Prince of Peace, I exalt You and surrender to Your strength. Lord, You are the help and hope of my life. In Your presence I sing to You songs of faith and delight, because Your power is perfected at every point of my weakness. (2 Co 12:9)

(20:14–18) Sovereign God, in the darkest hour You are there. All of life's purpose and value is wrapped up in Who You are, not in the ebb and flow of my emotions. You have called me and redeemed me. I acclaim You as the Guide and Guardian of my days. All things, good and bad, are given meaning, worth and purpose by the loving touch of Your hand.

(21:8–10) Loving Father, You have set before us life and death. By submitting to Your discipline, we choose life, that we and our children may live forever in Your presence. We love You as our God. We listen to Your voice. We hold fast to You, even in times of chastisement; for through Your hand of discipline You affirm Your love and commitment to us. (Dt 30:19–20; Heb 12:5–11)

14 Cursed be the day I was born!
May the day my mother bore me not be blessed!
15 Cursed be the man who brought my father the news,
who made him very glad, saying,
"A child is born to you—a son!"
16 May that man be like the towns
the LORD overthrew without pity.
May he hear wailing in the morning,
a battle cry at noon.
17 For he did not kill me in the womb,
with my mother as my grave,
her womb enlarged forever.
18 Why did I ever come out of the womb
to see trouble and sorrow
and to end my days in shame?

God Rejects Zedekiah's Request

21 The word came to Jeremiah from the LORD when King Zedekiah sent to him Pashhur son of Malkijah and the priest Zephaniah son of Maaseiah. They said:
2 "Inquire now of the LORD for us because Nebuchadnezzar[a] king of Babylon is attacking us. Perhaps the LORD will perform wonders for us as in times past so that he will withdraw from us."

3 But Jeremiah answered them, "Tell Zedekiah,
4 'This is what the LORD, the God of Israel, says: I am about to turn against you the weapons of war that are in your hands, which you are using to fight the king of Babylon and the Babylonians[b] who are outside the wall besieging you. And I will gather them inside this city.
5 I myself will fight against you with an outstretched hand and a mighty arm in anger and fury and great wrath.
6 I will strike down those who live in this city—both men and animals—and they will die of a terrible plague.
7 After that, declares the LORD, I will hand over Zedekiah king of Judah, his officials and the people in this city who survive the plague, sword and famine, to Nebuchadnezzar king of Babylon and to their enemies who seek their lives. He will put them to the sword; he will show them no mercy or pity or compassion.'

8 "Furthermore, tell the people, 'This is what the LORD says: See, I am setting before you the way of life and the way of death.
9 Whoever stays in this city will die by the sword, famine or plague. But whoever goes out and surrenders to the Babylonians who are besieging you will live; he will escape with his life.
10 I have determined to do this city harm and not good, declares the LORD. It will be given into the hands of the king of Babylon, and he will destroy it with fire.'

11 "Moreover, say to the royal house of Judah, 'Hear the word of the LORD;
12 O house of David, this is what the LORD says:

" 'Administer justice every morning;
rescue from the hand of his oppressor
the one who has been robbed,
or my wrath will break out and burn like fire
because of the evil you have done—
burn with no one to quench it.
13 I am against you, ⌞Jerusalem,⌟

[a] 2 Hebrew *Nebuchadrezzar,* of which *Nebuchadnezzar* is a variant; here and often in Jeremiah and Ezekiel [b] 4 Or *Chaldeans*; also in verse 9

you who live above this valley
on the rocky plateau,
declares the LORD—
you who say, "Who can come against us?
Who can enter our refuge?"
14 I will punish you as your deeds deserve,
declares the LORD.
I will kindle a fire in your forests
that will consume everything around you.' "

Judgment Against Evil Kings

22 This is what the LORD says: "Go down to the palace of the
king of Judah and proclaim this message there: 2 'Hear the
word of the LORD, O king of Judah, you who sit on David's
throne—you, your officials and your people who come through
these gates. 3 This is what the LORD says: Do what is just and right.
Rescue from the hand of his oppressor the one who has been
robbed. Do no wrong or violence to the alien, the fatherless or
the widow, and do not shed innocent blood in this place. 4 For if
you are careful to carry out these commands, then kings who sit
on David's throne will come through the gates of this palace, riding in chariots and on horses, accompanied by their officials and
their people. 5 But if you do not obey these commands, declares
the LORD, I swear by myself that this palace will become a ruin.' "
6 For this is what the LORD says about the palace of the king of
Judah:

"Though you are like Gilead to me,
like the summit of Lebanon,
I will surely make you like a desert,
like towns not inhabited.
7 I will send destroyers against you,
each man with his weapons,
and they will cut up your fine cedar beams
and throw them into the fire.

8 "People from many nations will pass by this city and will ask
one another, 'Why has the LORD done such a thing to this great
city?' 9 And the answer will be: 'Because they have forsaken the
covenant of the LORD their God and have worshiped and served
other gods.' "

10 Do not weep for the dead ⌞king⌟ or mourn his loss;
rather, weep bitterly for him who is exiled,
because he will never return
nor see his native land again.

11 For this is what the LORD says about Shallum[a] son of Josiah,
who succeeded his father as king of Judah but has gone from this
place: "He will never return. 12 He will die in the place where they
have led him captive; he will not see this land again."

13 "Woe to him who builds his palace by
unrighteousness,
his upper rooms by injustice,
making his countrymen work for nothing,
not paying them for their labor.
14 He says, 'I will build myself a great palace

[a] 11 Also called *Jehoahaz*

(22:3) Thank You, Lord, for that which You champion—justice, righteousness, compassion, care for the vulnerable and the victim. Here I find Your heart. You came to serve the least important of us, even though You are the greatest of all. I honor You, servant King; Your kingdom turns my worldly ideas upside down, making those who seem to be the most insignificant people on earth the greatest in Your eyes. (Mt 20:26–28)

with spacious upper rooms.'
So he makes large windows in it,
panels it with cedar
and decorates it in red.

15 "Does it make you a king
to have more and more cedar?
Did not your father have food and drink?
He did what was right and just,
so all went well with him.
16 He defended the cause of the poor and needy,
and so all went well.
Is that not what it means to know me?"
declares the LORD.
17 "But your eyes and your heart
are set only on dishonest gain,
on shedding innocent blood
and on oppression and extortion."
18 Therefore this is what the LORD says about Jehoiakim son of Josiah king of Judah:

"They will not mourn for him:
'Alas, my brother! Alas, my sister!'
They will not mourn for him:
'Alas, my master! Alas, his splendor!'
19 He will have the burial of a donkey—
dragged away and thrown
outside the gates of Jerusalem."

20 "Go up to Lebanon and cry out,
let your voice be heard in Bashan,
cry out from Abarim,
for all your allies are crushed.
21 I warned you when you felt secure,
but you said, 'I will not listen!'
This has been your way from your youth;
you have not obeyed me.
22 The wind will drive all your shepherds away,
and your allies will go into exile.
Then you will be ashamed and disgraced
because of all your wickedness.
23 You who live in 'Lebanon,[a]'
who are nestled in cedar buildings,
how you will groan when pangs come upon you,
pain like that of a woman in labor!

24 "As surely as I live," declares the LORD, "even if you, Jehoiachin[b] son of Jehoiakim king of Judah, were a signet ring on
my right hand, I would still pull you off. 25 I will hand you over to
those who seek your life, those you fear—to Nebuchadnezzar
king of Babylon and to the Babylonians.[c] 26 I will hurl you and the
mother who gave you birth into another country, where neither of
you was born, and there you both will die. 27 You will never come
back to the land you long to return to."

28 Is this man Jehoiachin a despised, broken pot,
an object no one wants?

(22:16) Show me, O Lord, what it means to know Your heart. That is my highest aim and my greatest good. Give me Your compassion for the lowliest and neediest among us. Let the neglected be welcome in the circle of my concern. If they are close to Your heart, then let them be close to mine as well. In loving them, let me discover what it means to truly love You.

[a] *23* That is, the palace in Jerusalem (see 1 Kings 7:2) [b] *24* Hebrew *Coniah,* a variant of *Jehoiachin*; also in verse 28 [c] *25* Or *Chaldeans*

Why will he and his children be hurled out,
cast into a land they do not know?
29 O land, land, land,
hear the word of the LORD!
30 This is what the LORD says:
"Record this man as if childless,
a man who will not prosper in his lifetime,
for none of his offspring will prosper,
none will sit on the throne of David
or rule anymore in Judah."

The Righteous Branch

23 "Woe to the shepherds who are destroying and scattering
the sheep of my pasture!" declares the LORD. 2Therefore
this is what the LORD, the God of Israel, says to the shepherds who
tend my people: "Because you have scattered my flock and driven
them away and have not bestowed care on them, I will bestow
punishment on you for the evil you have done," declares the LORD.
3"I myself will gather the remnant of my flock out of all the countries where I have driven them and will bring them back to their
pasture, where they will be fruitful and increase in number. 4I
will place shepherds over them who will tend them, and they will
no longer be afraid or terrified, nor will any be missing," declares the LORD.

5 "The days are coming," declares the LORD,
"when I will raise up to David[a] a righteous
Branch,
a King who will reign wisely
and do what is just and right in the land.
6 In his days Judah will be saved
and Israel will live in safety.
This is the name by which he will be called:
The LORD Our Righteousness.

7"So then, the days are coming," declares the LORD, "when people will no longer say, 'As surely as the LORD lives, who brought
the Israelites up out of Egypt,' 8but they will say, 'As surely as the
LORD lives, who brought the descendants of Israel up out of the
land of the north and out of all the countries where he had banished them.' Then they will live in their own land."

Lying Prophets

9Concerning the prophets:

My heart is broken within me;
all my bones tremble.
I am like a drunken man,
like a man overcome by wine,
because of the LORD
and his holy words.
10 The land is full of adulterers;
because of the curse[b] the land lies parched[c]
and the pastures in the desert are withered.
The ⌊prophets⌋ follow an evil course
and use their power unjustly.

[a] 5 Or *up from David's line* [b] 10 Or *because of these things* [c] 10 Or *land mourns*

I have a great need for Christ; I have a great Christ for my need.
Charles Haddon Spurgeon (1834–1892)

(23:5–6) God, we thank You for Jesus, Your promised "righteous Branch." During His time on earth, Your Spirit was upon Him, the Spirit of wisdom and understanding, the Spirit of counsel and power, the Spirit of knowledge and of the fear of the Lord. Your Son looked beyond the superficial and judged the deep needs of His people. Thank You that He continues, even now, to make right decisions on behalf of the poor in Spirit. Thank You that He will come again to reign in righteousness over all the earth. Maranatha! Come, Lord Jesus. (Isa 11:1–5)

Brothers, this Lord Jesus shall
return again,
With His Father's glory o'er the
earth to reign;
For all wreaths of empire meet upon
His brow,
And our hearts confess Him King of
Glory now.

"At the Name of Jesus"
Caroline Maria Noel (1890)

(23:18) Lord God, let me stand in the counsel of Your Word. Help me to see and hear what You are saying because Your Word accomplishes the purposes of Your heart. Speak to me, Lord, and enable me to hear You distinctly and directly, that I might know what You would have me do.

Speak, Lord, in the stillness
While I wait on Thee;
Hushed my heart to listen
In expectancy.

For the words You give me,
They are life indeed;
Living Bread from heaven,
Now my spirit feed.

Fill me with the knowledge
Of Your glorious will;
All Your own good pleasure
In my life fulfill.

"Speak, Lord in the Stillness"
May E. Grimes (1920)

11 "Both prophet and priest are godless;
even in my temple I find their wickedness,"
declares the LORD.
12 "Therefore their path will become slippery;
they will be banished to darkness
and there they will fall.
I will bring disaster on them
in the year they are punished,"
declares the LORD.

13 "Among the prophets of Samaria
I saw this repulsive thing:
They prophesied by Baal
and led my people Israel astray.
14 And among the prophets of Jerusalem
I have seen something horrible:
They commit adultery and live a lie.
They strengthen the hands of evildoers,
so that no one turns from his wickedness.
They are all like Sodom to me;
the people of Jerusalem are like Gomorrah."

15 Therefore, this is what the LORD Almighty says concerning the prophets:

"I will make them eat bitter food
and drink poisoned water,
because from the prophets of Jerusalem
ungodliness has spread throughout the land."

16 This is what the LORD Almighty says:

"Do not listen to what the prophets are prophesying
to you;
they fill you with false hopes.
They speak visions from their own minds,
not from the mouth of the LORD.
17 They keep saying to those who despise me,
'The LORD says: You will have peace.'
And to all who follow the stubbornness of their
hearts
they say, 'No harm will come to you.'
18 But which of them has stood in the council of
the LORD
to see or to hear his word?
Who has listened and heard his word?
19 See, the storm of the LORD
will burst out in wrath,
a whirlwind swirling down
on the heads of the wicked.
20 The anger of the LORD will not turn back
until he fully accomplishes
the purposes of his heart.
In days to come
you will understand it clearly.
21 I did not send these prophets,
yet they have run with their message;
I did not speak to them,
yet they have prophesied.

22 But if they had stood in my council,
they would have proclaimed my words to my people
and would have turned them from their evil ways
and from their evil deeds.

23 "Am I only a God nearby,"
declares the LORD,
"and not a God far away?
24 Can anyone hide in secret places
so that I cannot see him?"
declares the LORD.
"Do not I fill heaven and earth?"
declares the LORD.

25 "I have heard what the prophets say who prophesy lies in my
name. They say, 'I had a dream! I had a dream!' 26 How long will
this continue in the hearts of these lying prophets, who prophesy
the delusions of their own minds? 27 They think the dreams they
tell one another will make my people forget my name, just as
their fathers forgot my name through Baal worship. 28 Let the
prophet who has a dream tell his dream, but let the one who has
my word speak it faithfully. For what has straw to do with grain?"
declares the LORD. 29 "Is not my word like fire," declares the LORD,
"and like a hammer that breaks a rock in pieces?
30 "Therefore," declares the LORD, "I am against the prophets
who steal from one another words supposedly from me. 31 Yes,"
declares the LORD, "I am against the prophets who wag their own
tongues and yet declare, 'The LORD declares.' 32 Indeed, I am
against those who prophesy false dreams," declares the LORD.
"They tell them and lead my people astray with their reckless lies,
yet I did not send or appoint them. They do not benefit these people in the least," declares the LORD.

False Oracles and False Prophets

33 "When these people, or a prophet or a priest, ask you, 'What
is the oracle[a] of the LORD?' say to them, 'What oracle?[b] I will forsake you, declares the LORD.' 34 If a prophet or a priest or anyone
else claims, 'This is the oracle of the LORD,' I will punish that man
and his household. 35 This is what each of you keeps on saying to
his friend or relative: 'What is the LORD's answer?' or 'What has
the LORD spoken?' 36 But you must not mention 'the oracle of the
LORD' again, because every man's own word becomes his oracle
and so you distort the words of the living God, the LORD Almighty,
our God. 37 This is what you keep saying to a prophet: 'What is the
LORD's answer to you?' or 'What has the LORD spoken?' 38 Although
you claim, 'This is the oracle of the LORD,' this is what the LORD
says: You used the words, 'This is the oracle of the LORD,' even
though I told you that you must not claim, 'This is the oracle of
the LORD.' 39 Therefore, I will surely forget you and cast you out of
my presence along with the city I gave to you and your fathers. 40 I
will bring upon you everlasting disgrace—everlasting shame that
will not be forgotten."

[a] *33* Or *burden* (see Septuagint and Vulgate) [b] *33* Hebrew; Septuagint and Vulgate *'You are the burden.* (The Hebrew for *oracle* and *burden* is the same.)

(23:23–24) Almighty God, You fill heaven and earth with Your presence. You rule heaven and earth with Your power. You sustain heaven and earth with Your providence. I praise You, Lord, that though You are the God most high, You are also the God most nigh.

(23:29) Your Word is like fire, O Lord. Take my doubts and delusions, and make them like straw that is consumed in the flame of Your truth. Where my heart is hard, make Your Word a hammer to shatter my self-will and resistance. Lord, soften my heart and purify me. (Jer 5:14)

God does not discipline us to subdue us, but to condition us for a life of usefulness and blessedness.

Billy Graham (1918-)

(24:6–7) Father, You have promised that if I will submit to Your discipline, then Your eyes will follow me; they will watch over me to protect from me harm and lead me to goodness. Whatever I have forfeited through foolish failure, You can restore. Your vision is to build me up, not tear me down; to plant me deeply in Your love, not uproot me and toss me away. Even the desire to know You comes as a gift from Your hand. With all of my heart I thank You for loving me enough to discipline me as Your child. (Heb 12:5–7)

I bind unto myself today
The pow'r of God to hold and lead,
His eye to watch, His might to stay,
His ear to hearken to my need,
The wisdom of my God to teach,
His hand to guide, His shield to
ward,
The Word of God to give me speech,
His heav'nly host to be my guard.

"I Bind Unto Myself Today"
St. Patrick (c.372-466)
Para. Cecil Frances Alexander (1889)

Two Baskets of Figs

24 After Jehoiachin[a] son of Jehoiakim king of Judah and the officials, the craftsmen and the artisans of Judah were carried into exile from Jerusalem to Babylon by Nebuchadnezzar king of Babylon, the LORD showed me two baskets of figs placed in front of the temple of the LORD. 2One basket had very good figs, like those that ripen early; the other basket had very poor figs, so bad they could not be eaten.

3Then the LORD asked me, "What do you see, Jeremiah?"

"Figs," I answered. "The good ones are very good, but the poor ones are so bad they cannot be eaten."

4Then the word of the LORD came to me: 5"This is what the LORD, the God of Israel, says: 'Like these good figs, I regard as good the exiles from Judah, whom I sent away from this place to the land of the Babylonians.[b] 6My eyes will watch over them for their good, and I will bring them back to this land. I will build them up and not tear them down; I will plant them and not uproot them. 7I will give them a heart to know me, that I am the LORD. They will be my people, and I will be their God, for they will return to me with all their heart.

8" 'But like the poor figs, which are so bad they cannot be eaten,' says the LORD, 'so will I deal with Zedekiah king of Judah, his officials and the survivors from Jerusalem, whether they remain in this land or live in Egypt. 9I will make them abhorrent and an offense to all the kingdoms of the earth, a reproach and a byword, an object of ridicule and cursing, wherever I banish them. 10I will send the sword, famine and plague against them until they are destroyed from the land I gave to them and their fathers.' "

Seventy Years of Captivity

25 The word came to Jeremiah concerning all the people of Judah in the fourth year of Jehoiakim son of Josiah king of Judah, which was the first year of Nebuchadnezzar king of Babylon. 2So Jeremiah the prophet said to all the people of Judah and to all those living in Jerusalem: 3For twenty-three years—from the thirteenth year of Josiah son of Amon king of Judah until this very day—the word of the LORD has come to me and I have spoken to you again and again, but you have not listened.

4And though the LORD has sent all his servants the prophets to you again and again, you have not listened or paid any attention. 5They said, "Turn now, each of you, from your evil ways and your evil practices, and you can stay in the land the LORD gave to you and your fathers for ever and ever. 6Do not follow other gods to serve and worship them; do not provoke me to anger with what your hands have made. Then I will not harm you."

7"But you did not listen to me," declares the LORD, "and you have provoked me with what your hands have made, and you have brought harm to yourselves."

8Therefore the LORD Almighty says this: "Because you have not listened to my words, 9I will summon all the peoples of the north and my servant Nebuchadnezzar king of Babylon," declares the LORD, "and I will bring them against this land and its inhabitants and against all the surrounding nations. I will completely

[a] *1* Hebrew *Jeconiah,* a variant of *Jehoiachin* [b] *5* Or *Chaldeans*

destroy[a] them and make them an object of horror and scorn,
and an everlasting ruin. 10 I will banish from them the sounds of
joy and gladness, the voices of bride and bridegroom, the sound
of millstones and the light of the lamp. 11 This whole country will
become a desolate wasteland, and these nations will serve the
king of Babylon seventy years.
12 "But when the seventy years are fulfilled, I will punish the
king of Babylon and his nation, the land of the Babylonians,[b] for
their guilt," declares the LORD, "and will make it desolate forever.
13 I will bring upon that land all the things I have spoken against
it, all that are written in this book and prophesied by Jeremiah
against all the nations. 14 They themselves will be enslaved by
many nations and great kings; I will repay them according to their
deeds and the work of their hands."

The Cup of God's Wrath

15 This is what the LORD, the God of Israel, said to me: "Take
from my hand this cup filled with the wine of my wrath and make
all the nations to whom I send you drink it. 16 When they drink it,
they will stagger and go mad because of the sword I will send
among them."
17 So I took the cup from the LORD's hand and made all the nations to whom he sent me drink it: 18 Jerusalem and the towns of
Judah, its kings and officials, to make them a ruin and an object
of horror and scorn and cursing, as they are today; 19 Pharaoh
king of Egypt, his attendants, his officials and all his people,
20 and all the foreign people there; all the kings of Uz; all the kings
of the Philistines (those of Ashkelon, Gaza, Ekron, and the people
left at Ashdod); 21 Edom, Moab and Ammon; 22 all the kings of
Tyre and Sidon; the kings of the coastlands across the sea;
23 Dedan, Tema, Buz and all who are in distant places[c]; 24 all the
kings of Arabia and all the kings of the foreign people who live in
the desert; 25 all the kings of Zimri, Elam and Media; 26 and all the
kings of the north, near and far, one after the other—all the kingdoms on the face of the earth. And after all of them, the king of
Sheshach[d] will drink it too.
27 "Then tell them, 'This is what the LORD Almighty, the God of
Israel, says: Drink, get drunk and vomit, and fall to rise no more
because of the sword I will send among you.' 28 But if they refuse
to take the cup from your hand and drink, tell them, 'This is what
the LORD Almighty says: You must drink it! 29 See, I am beginning
to bring disaster on the city that bears my Name, and will you indeed go unpunished? You will not go unpunished, for I am calling down a sword upon all who live on the earth, declares the
LORD Almighty.'
30 "Now prophesy all these words against them and say to them:

"'The LORD will roar from on high;
he will thunder from his holy dwelling
and roar mightily against his land.
He will shout like those who tread the grapes,
shout against all who live on the earth.
31 The tumult will resound to the ends of the earth,
for the LORD will bring charges against the nations;

[a] 9 The Hebrew term refers to the irrevocable giving over of things or persons to the LORD, often by totally destroying them. [b] 12 Or *Chaldeans* [c] 23 Or *who clip the hair by their foreheads* [d] 26 *Sheshach* is a cryptogram for Babylon.

(25:15–29) God of Israel, You held in Your hand a cup filled with the wine of Your wrath, a cup prepared for every idolater and lawless one to drink. And drink it they did, reeling under the judgment they deserved. But there came a day when You passed that cup of wrath on to Your own Son, undeserving as He was of it. Although He prayed, "Take this cup from me," He also said, "Yet not what I will, but what you will." And so He faced death. Thank You, Lord, for allowing Your Son to endure the cross and to drink Your cup of wrath, to the last dregs, for me. (Mk 14:36)

O God, Father in heaven,
Have mercy upon us.
Your heart, O God, is grieved,
We know, by ev'ry evil, ev'ry woe;
Upon Your cross forsaken Son
Our death is laid,
And peace is won.

"Your Heart, O God, Is Grieved"
Jiri Tranovsky (1591-1637)
Trans. Jaroslav J. Vajda (©1970)

(26:3) Sovereign Lord, my salvation lies in repentance and rest: repentance from my sins, and rest within Your everlasting arms. My strength is in quietness and confidence. Yet so often I have rejected Your ways, and in my impatience I have devised my own solutions. Forgive my presumption, Lord, and allow me to return to You. For You long to be gracious to me. Your heart's desire is to show me Your compassion. (Isa 30:15–18)

No man is ever more than four steps from God: conviction, repentance, consecration, and faith.

Roy Lemon Smith (1887–1963)

he will bring judgment on all mankind
and put the wicked to the sword,' "
declares the LORD.

32 This is what the LORD Almighty says:
"Look! Disaster is spreading
from nation to nation;
a mighty storm is rising
from the ends of the earth."

33 At that time those slain by the LORD will be everywhere—from
one end of the earth to the other. They will not be mourned or
gathered up or buried, but will be like refuse lying on the ground.

34 Weep and wail, you shepherds;
roll in the dust, you leaders of the flock.
For your time to be slaughtered has come;
you will fall and be shattered like fine pottery.
35 The shepherds will have nowhere to flee,
the leaders of the flock no place to escape.
36 Hear the cry of the shepherds,
the wailing of the leaders of the flock,
for the LORD is destroying their pasture.
37 The peaceful meadows will be laid waste
because of the fierce anger of the LORD.
38 Like a lion he will leave his lair,
and their land will become desolate
because of the sword[a] of the oppressor
and because of the LORD's fierce anger.

Jeremiah Threatened With Death

26 Early in the reign of Jehoiakim son of Josiah king of
Judah, this word came from the LORD: 2 "This is what the
LORD says: Stand in the courtyard of the LORD's house and speak to
all the people of the towns of Judah who come to worship in the
house of the LORD. Tell them everything I command you; do not
omit a word. 3 Perhaps they will listen and each will turn from his
evil way. Then I will relent and not bring on them the disaster I
was planning because of the evil they have done. 4 Say to them,
'This is what the LORD says: If you do not listen to me and follow
my law, which I have set before you, 5 and if you do not listen to
the words of my servants the prophets, whom I have sent to you
again and again (though you have not listened), 6 then I will make
this house like Shiloh and this city an object of cursing among all
the nations of the earth.' "

7 The priests, the prophets and all the people heard Jeremiah
speak these words in the house of the LORD. 8 But as soon as Jeremiah finished telling all the people everything the LORD had commanded him to say, the priests, the prophets and all the people
seized him and said, "You must die! 9 Why do you prophesy in the
LORD's name that this house will be like Shiloh and this city will be
desolate and deserted?" And all the people crowded around Jeremiah in the house of the LORD.

10 When the officials of Judah heard about these things, they
went up from the royal palace to the house of the LORD and took
their places at the entrance of the New Gate of the LORD's house.

[a] 38 Some Hebrew manuscripts and Septuagint (see also Jer. 46:16 and 50:16); most Hebrew manuscripts *anger*

11 Then the priests and the prophets said to the officials and all
the people, "This man should be sentenced to death because he
has prophesied against this city. You have heard it with your own
ears!"
12 Then Jeremiah said to all the officials and all the people:
"The LORD sent me to prophesy against this house and this city all
the things you have heard. 13 Now reform your ways and your actions and obey the LORD your God. Then the LORD will relent and
not bring the disaster he has pronounced against you. 14 As for
me, I am in your hands; do with me whatever you think is good
and right. 15 Be assured, however, that if you put me to death, you
will bring the guilt of innocent blood on yourselves and on this
city and on those who live in it, for in truth the LORD has sent me
to you to speak all these words in your hearing."
16 Then the officials and all the people said to the priests and
the prophets, "This man should not be sentenced to death! He
has spoken to us in the name of the LORD our God."
17 Some of the elders of the land stepped forward and said to
the entire assembly of people, 18 "Micah of Moresheth prophesied in the days of Hezekiah king of Judah. He told all the people
of Judah, 'This is what the LORD Almighty says:

" 'Zion will be plowed like a field,
Jerusalem will become a heap of rubble,
the temple hill a mound overgrown with thickets.'[a]

19 "Did Hezekiah king of Judah or anyone else in Judah put him to
death? Did not Hezekiah fear the LORD and seek his favor? And
did not the LORD relent, so that he did not bring the disaster he
pronounced against them? We are about to bring a terrible disaster on ourselves!"
20 (Now Uriah son of Shemaiah from Kiriath Jearim was another man who prophesied in the name of the LORD; he prophesied
the same things against this city and this land as Jeremiah did.
21 When King Jehoiakim and all his officers and officials heard his
words, the king sought to put him to death. But Uriah heard of it
and fled in fear to Egypt. 22 King Jehoiakim, however, sent Elnathan son of Acbor to Egypt, along with some other men. 23 They
brought Uriah out of Egypt and took him to King Jehoiakim, who
had him struck down with a sword and his body thrown into the
burial place of the common people.)
24 Furthermore, Ahikam son of Shaphan supported Jeremiah,
and so he was not handed over to the people to be put to death.

Judah to Serve Nebuchadnezzar

27 Early in the reign of Zedekiah[b] son of Josiah king of
Judah, this word came to Jeremiah from the LORD: 2 This is
what the LORD said to me: "Make a yoke out of straps and crossbars and put it on your neck. 3 Then send word to the kings of
Edom, Moab, Ammon, Tyre and Sidon through the envoys who
have come to Jerusalem to Zedekiah king of Judah. 4 Give them a
message for their masters and say, 'This is what the LORD Almighty,
the God of Israel, says: "Tell this to your masters: 5 With my great
power and outstretched arm I made the earth and its people and
the animals that are on it, and I give it to anyone I please. 6 Now I

[a] *18* Micah 3:12 [b] *1* A few Hebrew manuscripts and Syriac (see also Jer. 27:3, 12 and 28:1); most Hebrew manuscripts *Jehoiakim* (Most Septuagint manuscripts do not have this verse.)

(27:5) You, Eternal One, are the magnificent Creator, Maker of the universe and the first cause of all that is. The invisible qualities of Your eternal power and divine nature are clearly seen and understood from what You have made. There is no more convincing witness of Your sovereignty. Creation exists for Your glory and testifies of Your freedom to do whatever You want, even in me. I glorify You and give You praise. (Ro 1:20)

A thousand worlds which roll around us
brightly,
Thee in their orbits bless;
Ten thousand suns which shine above us
nightly,
Proclaim thy righteousness.
Thou didst create the world—'twas the
proud mandate
That woke it unto day;
And the same power that measured,
weighed, and spanned it,
Shall bid that world decay.

Sir John Bowring (1792-1872)

(27:15–17) Your words of truth, O Lord, even when painful or frightening to hear, are filled with the promise of life. The prophets told the king only what he wanted to hear. The king believed only what he wanted to believe. But You were promising a way, not out of the turmoil, but through the turmoil. Help me, Lord, to have ears to hear the truth, and the humility of spirit to submit to Your plans, even when they seem to be for my harm. When the only way *out* is *through*, help me to follow You. For only in Your truth will I find real freedom. (Jn 8:32)

I looked up to the heavens once more, and the quietness of the stars seemed to reproach me. "We are safe up here," they seemed to say. "We shine, fearless and confident, for the God who gave the primrose its rough leaves to hide it from the blast of uneven spring, hangs us in the awful hollows of space. We cannot fall out of his safety. Lift up your eyes on high, and behold!"

George MacDonald (1824-1905)

I've had many tears and sorrows,
I've had questions for tomorrow,
There've been times I didn't know
Right from wrong.
But in ev'ry situation,
God gave blessed consolation
That my trials come to only make
me strong.

Through it all,
Through it all,
Oh, I've learned to trust in Jesus,
I've learned to trust in God.
Through it all,
Through it all,
I've learned to depend upon His
Word.

"Through It All"
Andraé Crouch (©1971)

will hand all your countries over to my servant Nebuchadnezzar
king of Babylon; I will make even the wild animals subject to him.
7All nations will serve him and his son and his grandson until the
time for his land comes; then many nations and great kings will
subjugate him.
8" ' "If, however, any nation or kingdom will not serve Nebuchadnezzar king of Babylon or bow its neck under his yoke, I will
punish that nation with the sword, famine and plague, declares
the LORD, until I destroy it by his hand. 9So do not listen to your
prophets, your diviners, your interpreters of dreams, your mediums or your sorcerers who tell you, 'You will not serve the king
of Babylon.' 10They prophesy lies to you that will only serve to remove you far from your lands; I will banish you and you will perish. 11But if any nation will bow its neck under the yoke of the
king of Babylon and serve him, I will let that nation remain in its
own land to till it and to live there, declares the LORD." ' "
12I gave the same message to Zedekiah king of Judah. I said,
"Bow your neck under the yoke of the king of Babylon; serve him
and his people, and you will live. 13Why will you and your people
die by the sword, famine and plague with which the LORD has
threatened any nation that will not serve the king of Babylon? 14Do
not listen to the words of the prophets who say to you, 'You will
not serve the king of Babylon,' for they are prophesying lies to you.
15'I have not sent them,' declares the LORD. 'They are prophesying
lies in my name. Therefore, I will banish you and you will perish,
both you and the prophets who prophesy to you.' "
16Then I said to the priests and all these people, "This is what
the LORD says: Do not listen to the prophets who say, 'Very soon
now the articles from the LORD's house will be brought back from
Babylon.' They are prophesying lies to you. 17Do not listen to
them. Serve the king of Babylon, and you will live. Why should
this city become a ruin? 18If they are prophets and have the word
of the LORD, let them plead with the LORD Almighty that the furnishings remaining in the house of the LORD and in the palace of
the king of Judah and in Jerusalem not be taken to Babylon. 19For
this is what the LORD Almighty says about the pillars, the Sea, the
movable stands and the other furnishings that are left in this city,
20which Nebuchadnezzar king of Babylon did not take away when
he carried Jehoiachin[a] son of Jehoiakim king of Judah into exile
from Jerusalem to Babylon, along with all the nobles of Judah and
Jerusalem— 21yes, this is what the LORD Almighty, the God of Israel, says about the things that are left in the house of the LORD
and in the palace of the king of Judah and in Jerusalem: 22'They
will be taken to Babylon and there they will remain until the day
I come for them,' declares the LORD. 'Then I will bring them back
and restore them to this place.' "

The False Prophet Hananiah

28 In the fifth month of that same year, the fourth year, early
in the reign of Zedekiah king of Judah, the prophet Hananiah son of Azzur, who was from Gibeon, said to me in the house
of the LORD in the presence of the priests and all the people:
2"This is what the LORD Almighty, the God of Israel, says: 'I will
break the yoke of the king of Babylon. 3Within two years I will
bring back to this place all the articles of the LORD's house that

[a] 20 Hebrew *Jeconiah,* a variant of *Jehoiachin*

Nebuchadnezzar king of Babylon removed from here and took to
Babylon. 4I will also bring back to this place Jehoiachin[a] son of
Jehoiakim king of Judah and all the other exiles from Judah who
went to Babylon,' declares the LORD, 'for I will break the yoke of
the king of Babylon.' "

5Then the prophet Jeremiah replied to the prophet Hananiah
before the priests and all the people who were standing in the
house of the LORD. 6He said, "Amen! May the LORD do so! May the
LORD fulfill the words you have prophesied by bringing the articles
of the LORD's house and all the exiles back to this place from Babylon. 7Nevertheless, listen to what I have to say in your hearing
and in the hearing of all the people: 8From early times the prophets who preceded you and me have prophesied war, disaster and
plague against many countries and great kingdoms. 9But the
prophet who prophesies peace will be recognized as one truly
sent by the LORD only if his prediction comes true."

10Then the prophet Hananiah took the yoke off the neck of the
prophet Jeremiah and broke it, 11and he said before all the people, "This is what the LORD says: 'In the same way will I break the
yoke of Nebuchadnezzar king of Babylon off the neck of all the
nations within two years.' " At this, the prophet Jeremiah went on
his way.

12Shortly after the prophet Hananiah had broken the yoke off
the neck of the prophet Jeremiah, the word of the LORD came to
Jeremiah: 13"Go and tell Hananiah, 'This is what the LORD says:
You have broken a wooden yoke, but in its place you will get a
yoke of iron. 14This is what the LORD Almighty, the God of Israel,
says: I will put an iron yoke on the necks of all these nations to
make them serve Nebuchadnezzar king of Babylon, and they will
serve him. I will even give him control over the wild animals.' "

15Then the prophet Jeremiah said to Hananiah the prophet,
"Listen, Hananiah! The LORD has not sent you, yet you have per-
suaded this nation to trust in lies. 16Therefore, this is what the
LORD says: 'I am about to remove you from the face of the earth.
This very year you are going to die, because you have preached
rebellion against the LORD.' "

17In the seventh month of that same year, Hananiah the prophet died.

A Letter to the Exiles

29 This is the text of the letter that the prophet Jeremiah sent
from Jerusalem to the surviving elders among the exiles
and to the priests, the prophets and all the other people Nebuchadnezzar had carried into exile from Jerusalem to Babylon.
2(This was after King Jehoiachin[a] and the queen mother, the
court officials and the leaders of Judah and Jerusalem, the craftsmen and the artisans had gone into exile from Jerusalem.) 3He
entrusted the letter to Elasah son of Shaphan and to Gemariah
son of Hilkiah, whom Zedekiah king of Judah sent to King Nebuchadnezzar in Babylon. It said:

4This is what the LORD Almighty, the God of Israel, says to
all those I carried into exile from Jerusalem to Babylon:
5"Build houses and settle down; plant gardens and eat what
they produce. 6Marry and have sons and daughters; find
wives for your sons and give your daughters in marriage, so

[a] 4,2 Hebrew *Jeconiah,* a variant of *Jehoiachin*

(28:15–17) Hananiah tried to minimize the severity of the sins of Your people by minimizing the severity of the punishment. Instead, You minimized the influence of this false prophet by minimizing his life. Thank You, Lord of the last word, that You are sovereign in Your ways, serious about Your purposes, and certain in Your determination that those purposes will prevail. Teach us to honor Your truth, and to never put our trust in lies.

Man cannot cover what God would reveal.
Thomas Campbell (1733-1795)

(29:11–14) Thank You, Lord, for the magnificent plans and promises You have in store for those who trust in You, for those who do not resist Your discipline but fully submit to Your sovereignty. O Lord, when Your hand seems heavy against us, in Your time, in Your way, restore our visions and renew our dreams. Fill our hearts with laughter and our mouths with songs of joy. Let even those who watch us from a distance say, "It is obvious that their God is blessing them." We have spent so much time in tears, in grief and in desperation. Breathe new life into our hopes, God of the resurrection. Fill our arms with the priceless treasures we thought we had lost forever. (Ps 126)

I love the Lord,
For He heard my voice;
He heard my cry for mercy.
I love the Lord
Because He turned His ear to me.
I will call on Him as long as I live.

The Lord is gracious and righteous.
Our God is full of compassion.
The Lord protects the simple-
hearted.
He has become my salvation.

"I Love The Lord"
Kelly Willard and Jeff Jansen (©1998)

that they too may have sons and daughters. Increase in number there; do not decrease. 7Also, seek the peace and prosperity of the city to which I have carried you into exile. Pray to the LORD for it, because if it prospers, you too will prosper." 8Yes, this is what the LORD Almighty, the God of Israel, says: "Do not let the prophets and diviners among you deceive you. Do not listen to the dreams you encourage them to have. 9They are prophesying lies to you in my name. I have not sent them," declares the LORD.

10This is what the LORD says: "When seventy years are completed for Babylon, I will come to you and fulfill my gracious promise to bring you back to this place. 11For I know the plans I have for you," declares the LORD, "plans to prosper you and not to harm you, plans to give you hope and a future. 12Then you will call upon me and come and pray to me, and I will listen to you. 13You will seek me and find me when you seek me with all your heart. 14I will be found by you," declares the LORD, "and will bring you back from captivity.[a] I will gather you from all the nations and places where I have banished you," declares the LORD, "and will bring you back to the place from which I carried you into exile."

15You may say, "The LORD has raised up prophets for us in Babylon," 16but this is what the LORD says about the king who sits on David's throne and all the people who remain in this city, your countrymen who did not go with you into exile— 17yes, this is what the LORD Almighty says: "I will send the sword, famine and plague against them and I will make them like poor figs that are so bad they cannot be eaten. 18I will pursue them with the sword, famine and plague and will make them abhorrent to all the kingdoms of the earth and an object of cursing and horror, of scorn and reproach, among all the nations where I drive them. 19For they have not listened to my words," declares the LORD, "words that I sent to them again and again by my servants the prophets. And you exiles have not listened either," declares the LORD.

20Therefore, hear the word of the LORD, all you exiles whom I have sent away from Jerusalem to Babylon. 21This is what the LORD Almighty, the God of Israel, says about Ahab son of Kolaiah and Zedekiah son of Maaseiah, who are prophesying lies to you in my name: "I will hand them over to Nebuchadnezzar king of Babylon, and he will put them to death before your very eyes. 22Because of them, all the exiles from Judah who are in Babylon will use this curse: 'The LORD treat you like Zedekiah and Ahab, whom the king of Babylon burned in the fire.' 23For they have done outrageous things in Israel; they have committed adultery with their neighbors' wives and in my name have spoken lies, which I did not tell them to do. I know it and am a witness to it," declares the LORD.

Message to Shemaiah

24Tell Shemaiah the Nehelamite, 25"This is what the LORD Almighty, the God of Israel, says: You sent letters in your own name to all the people in Jerusalem, to Zephaniah son of Maase-

[a] 14 Or *will restore your fortunes*

iah the priest, and to all the other priests. You said to Zephaniah,
26 'The LORD has appointed you priest in place of Jehoiada to be in
charge of the house of the LORD; you should put any madman who
acts like a prophet into the stocks and neck-irons. 27 So why have
you not reprimanded Jeremiah from Anathoth, who poses as a
prophet among you? 28 He has sent this message to us in Babylon:
It will be a long time. Therefore build houses and settle down;
plant gardens and eat what they produce.' "

29 Zephaniah the priest, however, read the letter to Jeremiah
the prophet. 30 Then the word of the LORD came to Jeremiah:
31 "Send this message to all the exiles: 'This is what the LORD says
about Shemaiah the Nehelamite: Because Shemaiah has prophesied to you, even though I did not send him, and has led you to
believe a lie, 32 this is what the LORD says: I will surely punish Shemaiah the Nehelamite and his descendants. He will have no one
left among this people, nor will he see the good things I will do
for my people, declares the LORD, because he has preached rebellion against me.' "

Restoration of Israel

30 This is the word that came to Jeremiah from the LORD:
2 "This is what the LORD, the God of Israel, says: 'Write in
a book all the words I have spoken to you. 3 The days are coming,'
declares the LORD, 'when I will bring my people Israel and Judah
back from captivity[a] and restore them to the land I gave their
forefathers to possess,' says the LORD."

4 These are the words the LORD spoke concerning Israel and
Judah: 5 "This is what the LORD says:

" 'Cries of fear are heard—
terror, not peace.
6 Ask and see:
Can a man bear children?
Then why do I see every strong man
with his hands on his stomach like a woman in labor,
every face turned deathly pale?
7 How awful that day will be!
None will be like it.
It will be a time of trouble for Jacob,
but he will be saved out of it.

8 " 'In that day,' declares the LORD Almighty,
'I will break the yoke off their necks
and will tear off their bonds;
no longer will foreigners enslave them.
9 Instead, they will serve the LORD their God
and David their king,
whom I will raise up for them.

10 " 'So do not fear, O Jacob my servant;
do not be dismayed, O Israel,'
declares the LORD.
'I will surely save you out of a distant place,
your descendants from the land of their exile.
Jacob will again have peace and security,
and no one will make him afraid.

[a] 3 Or *will restore the fortunes of my people Israel and Judah*

(30:1–11) O God, Your love for us requires that You discipline us. And yet You always restrain the full force of Your hand, waiting, listening for a hint of remorse, for a whisper of repentance. In Your righteousness, You cannot overlook our wrongdoing, yet You never punish us as our sins deserve, knowing that we would be utterly destroyed. Thank You that Your compassions never fail; that they are new every morning. Great is Your faithfulness. (La 3:22–23)

God giveth his wrath by weight, but his mercy without measure.
Sir Thomas Fuller (1608-1661)

He offers all His treasure
Of justice, truth, and righteousness,
His love beyond our measure,
His yearning pity o'er distress;
Nor treats us as we merit,
But sets His anger by.
The poor and contrite spirit
Finds His compassion nigh;
And high as heav'n above us,
As break from close of day,
So far, since He has loved us,
He puts our sins away.
"My Soul, Now Praise Your Maker!"
Johann Gramman (1487-1541)
Trans. Catherine Winkworth (1829-1878)

(30:19) Songs of thanksgiving and sounds of rejoicing: these are what please and fill Your heart, O Lord. We were created to worship You. Our hearts were made to sing. You called for all that have breath to praise You, the Giver of breath itself. When decrease and shame should have marked our lives, You instead brought increase and honor. In so doing You prepared for Yourself a people of praise. So hear the melodies of our hearts and the praises of our lips. These are our songs of gratefulness and sounds of rejoicing. (Ps 150:6)

(30:21–22) Lord Jesus, our Leader, You are one of us. You came in the flesh, lived in the flesh, suffered and died in the flesh, and after Your resurrection You ascended to heaven in Your glorified flesh where You prepare a place for us. You sympathize with our weaknesses, for You have been tempted in every way just as we are. Yet You triumphed over sin and death and are now seated at the right hand of the Father. You devoted Yourself fully to reconciling all flesh to God so that we may come close to Him in confidence. Through You, we are His. Through You, He is ours. (Jn 14:2–3; Ro 5:10–11; Heb 4:15–16)

11 I am with you and will save you,'
declares the LORD.
'Though I completely destroy all the nations
among which I scatter you,
I will not completely destroy you.
I will discipline you but only with justice;
I will not let you go entirely unpunished.'

12 "This is what the LORD says:

" 'Your wound is incurable,
your injury beyond healing.
13 There is no one to plead your cause,
no remedy for your sore,
no healing for you.
14 All your allies have forgotten you;
they care nothing for you.
I have struck you as an enemy would
and punished you as would the cruel,
because your guilt is so great
and your sins so many.
15 Why do you cry out over your wound,
your pain that has no cure?
Because of your great guilt and many sins
I have done these things to you.
16 " 'But all who devour you will be devoured;
all your enemies will go into exile.
Those who plunder you will be plundered;
all who make spoil of you I will despoil.
17 But I will restore you to health
and heal your wounds,'
declares the LORD,
'because you are called an outcast,
Zion for whom no one cares.'

18 "This is what the LORD says:

" 'I will restore the fortunes of Jacob's tents
and have compassion on his dwellings;
the city will be rebuilt on her ruins,
and the palace will stand in its proper place.
19 From them will come songs of thanksgiving
and the sound of rejoicing.
I will add to their numbers,
and they will not be decreased;
I will bring them honor,
and they will not be disdained.
20 Their children will be as in days of old,
and their community will be established before me;
I will punish all who oppress them.
21 Their leader will be one of their own;
their ruler will arise from among them.
I will bring him near and he will come close to me,
for who is he who will devote himself
to be close to me?'
declares the LORD.
22 " 'So you will be my people,
and I will be your God.' "

23 See, the storm of the LORD
will burst out in wrath,
a driving wind swirling down
on the heads of the wicked.
24 The fierce anger of the LORD will not turn back
until he fully accomplishes
the purposes of his heart.
In days to come
you will understand this.

31 "At that time," declares the LORD, "I will be the God of all the clans of Israel, and they will be my people."
2 This is what the LORD says:

"The people who survive the sword
will find favor in the desert;
I will come to give rest to Israel."

3 The LORD appeared to us in the past,[a] saying:

"I have loved you with an everlasting love;
I have drawn you with loving-kindness.
4 I will build you up again
and you will be rebuilt, O Virgin Israel.
Again you will take up your tambourines
and go out to dance with the joyful.
5 Again you will plant vineyards
on the hills of Samaria;
the farmers will plant them
and enjoy their fruit.
6 There will be a day when watchmen cry out
on the hills of Ephraim,
'Come, let us go up to Zion,
to the LORD our God.' "

7 This is what the LORD says:

"Sing with joy for Jacob;
shout for the foremost of the nations.
Make your praises heard, and say,
'O LORD, save your people,
the remnant of Israel.'
8 See, I will bring them from the land of the north
and gather them from the ends of the earth.
Among them will be the blind and the lame,
expectant mothers and women in labor;
a great throng will return.
9 They will come with weeping;
they will pray as I bring them back.
I will lead them beside streams of water
on a level path where they will not stumble,
because I am Israel's father,
and Ephraim is my firstborn son.

10 "Hear the word of the LORD, O nations;
proclaim it in distant coastlands:
'He who scattered Israel will gather them
and will watch over his flock like a shepherd.'
11 For the LORD will ransom Jacob

[a] 3 Or *LORD has appeared to us from afar*

(31:3) I worship You, God of grace. Your everlasting love and Your divine kindness intertwine to form a cord of "loving-kindness," drawing me ever closer to You. To You Who remembered me in my low estate, Who freed me from my enemies, Who provides for my every need—to You, God of heaven, Whose love endures forever, I give thanks. (Ps 136:23–25)

Loved with everlasting love,
Led by grace that love to know;
Gracious Spirit from above,
Thou has taught me it is so!
O, this full and perfect peace!
O, this transport all divine!
In a love which cannot cease,
I am His, and He is mine.

His forever, only His;
Who the Lord and me shall part?
Ah, with what a rest of bliss
Christ can fill the loving heart!
Heav'n and earth may fade and flee,
First born light in gloom decline;
But while God and I shall be,
I am His, and He is mine.

"I Am His, and He Is Mine"
George W. Robinson (1890)

If He could grow weary of me, He would have been tired of me long before now. If He had not loved me with a love as deep as hell, and as strong as death, He would have turned from me long ago. Oh, joy above all joys, to know that I am His everlasting and inalienable inheritance, given to Him by His Father e'er the earth was! Everlasting love shall be the pillow for my head this night.

Charles Haddon Spurgeon (1834–1892)

(31:18–19) Lord, hear my prayer as You heard the prayer of Your people long ago: "Restore me, and I will return." I praise You, loving Father, that You initiate restoration. I do not have to try to prove my worth to You to begin the process of restoration. Instead, I come to You because You have already offered restoration to me; for while I was still a sinner, Christ died for me. Please receive my repentance as my act of worship—my grateful response to a forgiving God. (Ro 5:8)

Grant, almighty God, that, since the dullness and harshness of our flesh is so great that it is needful for us in various ways to be afflicted, we may patiently bear your chastisement, and under a deep feeling of sorrow flee to your mercy displayed to us in Christ; and that, not depending upon the earthly blessings of this perishable life, but relying only upon your Word, we may go forward in the course of our calling; until at length we are gathered to that blessed rest which is laid up for us in heaven; through Jesus Christ our Lord.

John Calvin (1509-1564)

My soul He doth restore again;
And me to walk doth make
Within the paths of righteousness,
E'en for His own name's sake.
"The Lord's My Shepherd, I'll Not Want"
Scottish Psalter (1650)

and redeem them from the hand of those stronger than they.
12 They will come and shout for joy on the heights of Zion;
they will rejoice in the bounty of the LORD—
the grain, the new wine and the oil,
the young of the flocks and herds.
They will be like a well-watered garden,
and they will sorrow no more.
13 Then maidens will dance and be glad,
young men and old as well.
I will turn their mourning into gladness;
I will give them comfort and joy instead of sorrow.
14 I will satisfy the priests with abundance,
and my people will be filled with my bounty,"
declares the LORD.

15 This is what the LORD says:

"A voice is heard in Ramah,
mourning and great weeping,
Rachel weeping for her children
and refusing to be comforted,
because her children are no more."

16 This is what the LORD says:

"Restrain your voice from weeping
and your eyes from tears,
for your work will be rewarded,"
declares the LORD.
"They will return from the land of the enemy.
17 So there is hope for your future,"
declares the LORD.
"Your children will return to their own land.

18 "I have surely heard Ephraim's moaning:
'You disciplined me like an unruly calf,
and I have been disciplined.
Restore me, and I will return,
because you are the LORD my God.
19 After I strayed,
I repented;
after I came to understand,
I beat my breast.
I was ashamed and humiliated
because I bore the disgrace of my youth.'
20 Is not Ephraim my dear son,
the child in whom I delight?
Though I often speak against him,
I still remember him.
Therefore my heart yearns for him;
I have great compassion for him,"
declares the LORD.

21 "Set up road signs;
put up guideposts.
Take note of the highway,
the road that you take.
Return, O Virgin Israel,

return to your towns.
22 How long will you wander,
O unfaithful daughter?
The LORD will create a new thing on earth—
a woman will surround[a] a man."

23 This is what the LORD Almighty, the God of Israel, says: "When
I bring them back from captivity,[b] the people in the land of Judah
and in its towns will once again use these words: 'The LORD bless
you, O righteous dwelling, O sacred mountain.' 24 People will live
together in Judah and all its towns—farmers and those who move
about with their flocks. 25 I will refresh the weary and satisfy the
faint."
26 At this I awoke and looked around. My sleep had been pleasant to me.
27 "The days are coming," declares the LORD, "when I will plant
the house of Israel and the house of Judah with the offspring of
men and of animals. 28 Just as I watched over them to uproot and
tear down, and to overthrow, destroy and bring disaster, so I will
watch over them to build and to plant," declares the LORD. 29 "In
those days people will no longer say,

'The fathers have eaten sour grapes,
and the children's teeth are set on edge.'

30 Instead, everyone will die for his own sin; whoever eats sour
grapes—his own teeth will be set on edge.

31 "The time is coming," declares the LORD,
"when I will make a new covenant
with the house of Israel
and with the house of Judah.
32 It will not be like the covenant
I made with their forefathers
when I took them by the hand
to lead them out of Egypt,
because they broke my covenant,
though I was a husband to[c] them,[d]"
declares the LORD.
33 "This is the covenant I will make with the house of
Israel
after that time," declares the LORD.
"I will put my law in their minds
and write it on their hearts.
I will be their God,
and they will be my people.
34 No longer will a man teach his neighbor,
or a man his brother, saying, 'Know the LORD,'
because they will all know me,
from the least of them to the greatest,"
declares the LORD.
"For I will forgive their wickedness
and will remember their sins no more."

35 This is what the LORD says,

he who appoints the sun

[a] 22 Or *will go about* ⌞*seeking*⌟; or *will protect* [b] 23 Or *I restore their fortunes* [c] 32 Hebrew; Septuagint and Syriac / *and I turned away from* [d] 32 Or *was their master*

(31:23–28) Thank You, Father, that You do not leave Your people without hope. When You discipline us, You do not abandon us. You watch over us through the hard times, rooting up and tearing down our sinfulness, making room for fruitfulness and restoration. Refresh us in our weariness, O Lord, and strengthen us when we are weak.

(31:33–34) Lord Jesus Christ, You are the fulfillment of this new covenant. We worship You for what You have made possible through Your broken body and Your shed blood. By the life-changing power of Your death and resurrection, we are covered with Your righteousness and forgiven of our sins. You have changed us on the inside, enabling us to love what You love and hate what You hate. Instead of hearing about You from a distance, we can now know You personally and intimately. The New Covenant is Your triumph alone, Lord Jesus. We are Yours only because of what You have done.

O the deep, deep, love of Jesus,
Vast, unmeasured, boundless, free!
Rolling as a mighty ocean
In its fullness over me,
Underneath me, all around me,
Is the current of Thy love;
Leading onward, leading homeward
To Thy glorious rest above.

"O The Deep, Deep Love Of Jesus"
Samuel T. Francis (1890)

(31:37) Your love is so faithful, Lord of Life, that the immeasurable would have to be measured and the unsearchable found for that love ever to fail. And amazingly, at the heart of Your unfailing love, I find a place for me. In spite of all that I have done to offend You, You have called me to Yourself. Because Your love is unconditional, there is nothing I could do to make You love me more or to make You love me less. You are the God of perfect love.

I love You, Lord, and I lift my voice
To worship You, O my soul rejoice.
Take joy, my King, in what You hear,
May it be a sweet, sweet sound
In Your ear.

"I Love You, Lord"
Laurie Klein (©1978, 1980)

to shine by day,
who decrees the moon and stars
to shine by night,
who stirs up the sea
so that its waves roar—
the LORD Almighty is his name:
36 "Only if these decrees vanish from my sight,"
declares the LORD,
"will the descendants of Israel ever cease
to be a nation before me."

37 This is what the LORD says:

"Only if the heavens above can be measured
and the foundations of the earth below be searched out
will I reject all the descendants of Israel
because of all they have done,"
declares the LORD.

38 "The days are coming," declares the LORD, "when this city
will be rebuilt for me from the Tower of Hananel to the Corner
Gate. 39 The measuring line will stretch from there straight to the
hill of Gareb and then turn to Goah. 40 The whole valley where
dead bodies and ashes are thrown, and all the terraces out to the
Kidron Valley on the east as far as the corner of the Horse Gate,
will be holy to the LORD. The city will never again be uprooted or
demolished."

Jeremiah Buys a Field

32 This is the word that came to Jeremiah from the LORD in
the tenth year of Zedekiah king of Judah, which was the
eighteenth year of Nebuchadnezzar. 2 The army of the king of Babylon was then besieging Jerusalem, and Jeremiah the prophet was
confined in the courtyard of the guard in the royal palace of
Judah.

3 Now Zedekiah king of Judah had imprisoned him there, saying, "Why do you prophesy as you do? You say, 'This is what the
LORD says: I am about to hand this city over to the king of Babylon,
and he will capture it. 4 Zedekiah king of Judah will not escape
out of the hands of the Babylonians[a] but will certainly be handed
over to the king of Babylon, and will speak with him face to face
and see him with his own eyes. 5 He will take Zedekiah to Babylon, where he will remain until I deal with him, declares the
LORD. If you fight against the Babylonians, you will not succeed.' "

6 Jeremiah said, "The word of the LORD came to me: 7 Hanamel
son of Shallum your uncle is going to come to you and say, 'Buy
my field at Anathoth, because as nearest relative it is your right
and duty to buy it.'

8 "Then, just as the LORD had said, my cousin Hanamel came to
me in the courtyard of the guard and said, 'Buy my field at Anathoth in the territory of Benjamin. Since it is your right to redeem
it and possess it, buy it for yourself.'

"I knew that this was the word of the LORD; 9 so I bought the
field at Anathoth from my cousin Hanamel and weighed out for
him seventeen shekels[b] of silver. 10 I signed and sealed the deed,

[a] 4 Or *Chaldeans*; also in verses 5, 24, 25, 28, 29 and 43 [b] 9 That is, about 7 ounces (about 200 grams)

had it witnessed, and weighed out the silver on the scales. 11I
took the deed of purchase—the sealed copy containing the terms
and conditions, as well as the unsealed copy— 12and I gave this
deed to Baruch son of Neriah, the son of Mahseiah, in the presence of my cousin Hanamel and of the witnesses who had signed
the deed and of all the Jews sitting in the courtyard of the guard.
13"In their presence I gave Baruch these instructions: 14'This
is what the LORD Almighty, the God of Israel, says: Take these documents, both the sealed and unsealed copies of the deed of purchase, and put them in a clay jar so they will last a long time.
15For this is what the LORD Almighty, the God of Israel, says:
Houses, fields and vineyards will again be bought in this land.'
16"After I had given the deed of purchase to Baruch son of Neriah, I prayed to the LORD:

17"Ah, Sovereign LORD, you have made the heavens and the
earth by your great power and outstretched arm. Nothing is
too hard for you. 18You show love to thousands but bring
the punishment for the fathers' sins into the laps of their
children after them. O great and powerful God, whose name
is the LORD Almighty, 19great are your purposes and mighty
are your deeds. Your eyes are open to all the ways of men;
you reward everyone according to his conduct and as his
deeds deserve. 20You performed miraculous signs and wonders in Egypt and have continued them to this day, both in
Israel and among all mankind, and have gained the renown
that is still yours. 21You brought your people Israel out of
Egypt with signs and wonders, by a mighty hand and an outstretched arm and with great terror. 22You gave them this
land you had sworn to give their forefathers, a land flowing
with milk and honey. 23They came in and took possession of
it, but they did not obey you or follow your law; they did not
do what you commanded them to do. So you brought all this
disaster upon them.

24"See how the siege ramps are built up to take the city.
Because of the sword, famine and plague, the city will be
handed over to the Babylonians who are attacking it. What
you said has happened, as you now see. 25And though the
city will be handed over to the Babylonians, you, O Sovereign LORD, say to me, 'Buy the field with silver and have the
transaction witnessed.' "

26Then the word of the LORD came to Jeremiah: 27"I am the
LORD, the God of all mankind. Is anything too hard for me?
28Therefore, this is what the LORD says: I am about to hand this
city over to the Babylonians and to Nebuchadnezzar king of Babylon, who will capture it. 29The Babylonians who are attacking
this city will come in and set it on fire; they will burn it down,
along with the houses where the people provoked me to anger by
burning incense on the roofs to Baal and by pouring out drink offerings to other gods.
30"The people of Israel and Judah have done nothing but evil in
my sight from their youth; indeed, the people of Israel have done
nothing but provoke me with what their hands have made, declares the LORD. 31From the day it was built until now, this city has
so aroused my anger and wrath that I must remove it from my
sight. 32The people of Israel and Judah have provoked me by all
the evil they have done—they, their kings and officials, their

(32:17) Almighty God, when my world falls apart, when my most precious dreams have died, when I cannot see beyond my trouble, how beautiful is the sound of the prophet's words: "Nothing is too hard for you." You are able to do immeasurably more than I could ask or imagine. I give You praise, O God, for with You all things are possible. (Mt 19:26; Eph 3:20)

If all things are possible with God, then all things are possible to him who believes in him.

Corrie ten Boom (1892-1983)

He is able, more than able,
To accomplish what concerns me today.
He is able, more than able,
To handle anything that comes my way.
He is able, more than able,
To do much more than I could ever dream.
He is able, more than able,
To make me what He wants me to be.

"He is Able"
Rory Noland and Greg Ferguson (©1989)

(32:39–41) Faithful, loving God, You are fully devoted to Your people. Please give me a heart that is fully devoted to You, and the integrity to live according to my convictions.

(33:1–11) God, Your Word is living and active. It will not return to You empty; it will accomplish what You desire; it will achieve the purpose for which You sent it. In Your great and unsearchable mind, You have foreseen our restoration—health and healing, peace and security, freedom and renewal, cleansing and forgiveness—and You have spoken it into existence. You have done so not only for our sakes, but also for Your own renown, for an everlasting sign of Your incomprehensible wisdom. (Isa 55:10–13; Heb 4:12)

priests and prophets, the men of Judah and the people of Jerusalem. 33They turned their backs to me and not their faces; though
I taught them again and again, they would not listen or respond to
discipline. 34They set up their abominable idols in the house that
bears my Name and defiled it. 35They built high places for Baal in
the Valley of Ben Hinnom to sacrifice their sons and daughters[a] to
Molech, though I never commanded, nor did it enter my mind,
that they should do such a detestable thing and so make Judah sin.
36"You are saying about this city, 'By the sword, famine and
plague it will be handed over to the king of Babylon'; but this is
what the LORD, the God of Israel, says: 37I will surely gather them
from all the lands where I banish them in my furious anger and
great wrath; I will bring them back to this place and let them live
in safety. 38They will be my people, and I will be their God. 39I
will give them singleness of heart and action, so that they will always fear me for their own good and the good of their children
after them. 40I will make an everlasting covenant with them: I will
never stop doing good to them, and I will inspire them to fear
me, so that they will never turn away from me. 41I will rejoice in
doing them good and will assuredly plant them in this land with
all my heart and soul.
42"This is what the LORD says: As I have brought all this great
calamity on this people, so I will give them all the prosperity I
have promised them. 43Once more fields will be bought in this
land of which you say, 'It is a desolate waste, without men or animals, for it has been handed over to the Babylonians.' 44Fields
will be bought for silver, and deeds will be signed, sealed and witnessed in the territory of Benjamin, in the villages around Jerusalem, in the towns of Judah and in the towns of the hill country, of
the western foothills and of the Negev, because I will restore their
fortunes,[b] declares the LORD."

Promise of Restoration

33 While Jeremiah was still confined in the courtyard of the
guard, the word of the LORD came to him a second time:
2"This is what the LORD says, he who made the earth, the LORD
who formed it and established it—the LORD is his name: 3'Call to
me and I will answer you and tell you great and unsearchable
things you do not know.' 4For this is what the LORD, the God of Israel, says about the houses in this city and the royal palaces of
Judah that have been torn down to be used against the siege
ramps and the sword 5in the fight with the Babylonians[c]: 'They
will be filled with the dead bodies of the men I will slay in my
anger and wrath. I will hide my face from this city because of all
its wickedness.
6" 'Nevertheless, I will bring health and healing to it; I will heal
my people and will let them enjoy abundant peace and security. 7I
will bring Judah and Israel back from captivity[d] and will rebuild
them as they were before. 8I will cleanse them from all the sin
they have committed against me and will forgive all their sins of
rebellion against me. 9Then this city will bring me renown, joy,
praise and honor before all nations on earth that hear of all the
good things I do for it; and they will be in awe and will tremble at
the abundant prosperity and peace I provide for it.'

[a] 35 Or *to make their sons and daughters pass through ⌞the fire⌟* [b] 44 Or *will bring them back from captivity* [c] 5 Or *Chaldeans* [d] 7 Or *will restore the fortunes of Judah and Israel*

10 "This is what the LORD says: 'You say about this place, "It is a
desolate waste, without men or animals." Yet in the towns of
Judah and the streets of Jerusalem that are deserted, inhabited by
neither men nor animals, there will be heard once more 11 the
sounds of joy and gladness, the voices of bride and bridegroom,
and the voices of those who bring thank offerings to the house of
the LORD, saying,

"Give thanks to the LORD Almighty,
for the LORD is good;
his love endures forever."

For I will restore the fortunes of the land as they were before,'
says the LORD.
12 "This is what the LORD Almighty says: 'In this place, desolate
and without men or animals—in all its towns there will again be
pastures for shepherds to rest their flocks. 13 In the towns of the
hill country, of the western foothills and of the Negev, in the territory of Benjamin, in the villages around Jerusalem and in the
towns of Judah, flocks will again pass under the hand of the one
who counts them,' says the LORD.
14 " 'The days are coming,' declares the LORD, 'when I will fulfill the gracious promise I made to the house of Israel and to the
house of Judah.

15 " 'In those days and at that time
I will make a righteous Branch sprout from David's line;
he will do what is just and right in the land.
16 In those days Judah will be saved
and Jerusalem will live in safety.
This is the name by which it[a] will be called:
The LORD Our Righteousness.'

17 For this is what the LORD says: 'David will never fail to have a
man to sit on the throne of the house of Israel, 18 nor will the
priests, who are Levites, ever fail to have a man to stand before
me continually to offer burnt offerings, to burn grain offerings
and to present sacrifices.' "
19 The word of the LORD came to Jeremiah: 20 "This is what the
LORD says: 'If you can break my covenant with the day and my covenant with the night, so that day and night no longer come at their
appointed time, 21 then my covenant with David my servant—and
my covenant with the Levites who are priests ministering before
me—can be broken and David will no longer have a descendant
to reign on his throne. 22 I will make the descendants of David my
servant and the Levites who minister before me as countless as the
stars of the sky and as measureless as the sand on the seashore.' "
23 The word of the LORD came to Jeremiah: 24 "Have you not noticed that these people are saying, 'The LORD has rejected the two
kingdoms[b] he chose'? So they despise my people and no longer
regard them as a nation. 25 This is what the LORD says: 'If I have
not established my covenant with day and night and the fixed laws
of heaven and earth, 26 then I will reject the descendants of Jacob
and David my servant and will not choose one of his sons to rule
over the descendants of Abraham, Isaac and Jacob. For I will restore their fortunes[c] and have compassion on them.' "

[a] 16 Or *he* [b] 24 Or *families* [c] 26 Or *will bring them back from captivity*

(33:15–22) Your promise to multiply ministering generations has not failed, O God. Your Son Jesus, the King of kings and the Lord of lords, will Himself return to our world to sit on David's throne of rule forever. And He will not be alone! For Christ's blood, shed on the cross, has purchased us. From every tribe and language and people and nation, we are the promised priesthood that is destined to rule with Him forever—an innumerable multitude bearing witness to Your everlasting covenant.

The Lord will come and not be slow;
His footsteps cannot err;
Before Him righteousness shall go,
His royal harbinger.
To those who name His name in fear,
Salvation is at hand!
And soon His glory shall appear
And dwell within our land.

Then all the lands which You have made
Shall come and bend the knee
And, bowing low before their Lord,
Confess Your sovereignty.
For greatness, Lord, is Yours alone,
And, by Your mighty hand,
The rule established by Your throne
Forevermore shall stand.

"The Lord Will Come and Not Be Slow"
John Milton (1608-1674)

(34:8–17) Righteous Judge, You commanded Your people to release their brothers and sisters from slavery. When they refused to obey You, You delivered them into the hands of their enemies. In the same way, You commanded us to release one another from the bondage of past offenses, from the slavery of unpardoned wrongdoing. When we refuse to forgive others as You have forgiven us, You are gravely offended. Teach us, Father, to forgive not only in word, but also in deed and truth, lest we be subjected to the physical, emotional and spiritual torment that You allow us to suffer because of our unforgiving attitudes. Forgive us our debts, Father, as we forgive our debtors. (Mt 6:12; 18:21–35)

He that demands mercy, and shows none, ruins the bridge over which he himself is to pass.

Thomas Adams (1612-1653)

Warning to Zedekiah

34 While Nebuchadnezzar king of Babylon and all his army
and all the kingdoms and peoples in the empire he ruled
were fighting against Jerusalem and all its surrounding towns, this
word came to Jeremiah from the LORD: 2 "This is what the LORD,
the God of Israel, says: Go to Zedekiah king of Judah and tell him,
'This is what the LORD says: I am about to hand this city over to the
king of Babylon, and he will burn it down. 3 You will not escape
from his grasp but will surely be captured and handed over to
him. You will see the king of Babylon with your own eyes, and he
will speak with you face to face. And you will go to Babylon.
4 " 'Yet hear the promise of the LORD, O Zedekiah king of Judah.
This is what the LORD says concerning you: You will not die by the
sword; 5 you will die peacefully. As people made a funeral fire in
honor of your fathers, the former kings who preceded you, so
they will make a fire in your honor and lament, "Alas, O master!"
I myself make this promise, declares the LORD.' "
6 Then Jeremiah the prophet told all this to Zedekiah king of
Judah, in Jerusalem, 7 while the army of the king of Babylon was
fighting against Jerusalem and the other cities of Judah that were
still holding out—Lachish and Azekah. These were the only fortified cities left in Judah.

Freedom for Slaves

8 The word came to Jeremiah from the LORD after King Zedekiah had made a covenant with all the people in Jerusalem to proclaim freedom for the slaves. 9 Everyone was to free his Hebrew
slaves, both male and female; no one was to hold a fellow Jew in
bondage. 10 So all the officials and people who entered into this
covenant agreed that they would free their male and female slaves
and no longer hold them in bondage. They agreed, and set them
free. 11 But afterward they changed their minds and took back the
slaves they had freed and enslaved them again.
12 Then the word of the LORD came to Jeremiah: 13 "This is what
the LORD, the God of Israel, says: I made a covenant with your
forefathers when I brought them out of Egypt, out of the land of
slavery. I said, 14 'Every seventh year each of you must free any
fellow Hebrew who has sold himself to you. After he has served
you six years, you must let him go free.'[a] Your fathers, however,
did not listen to me or pay attention to me. 15 Recently you repented and did what is right in my sight: Each of you proclaimed
freedom to his countrymen. You even made a covenant before me
in the house that bears my Name. 16 But now you have turned
around and profaned my name; each of you has taken back the
male and female slaves you had set free to go where they wished.
You have forced them to become your slaves again.
17 "Therefore, this is what the LORD says: You have not obeyed
me; you have not proclaimed freedom for your fellow countrymen. So I now proclaim 'freedom' for you, declares the LORD—
'freedom' to fall by the sword, plague and famine. I will make
you abhorrent to all the kingdoms of the earth. 18 The men who
have violated my covenant and have not fulfilled the terms of the
covenant they made before me, I will treat like the calf they cut
in two and then walked between its pieces. 19 The leaders of
Judah and Jerusalem, the court officials, the priests and all the

[a] *14* Deut. 15:12

people of the land who walked between the pieces of the calf, [20]I
will hand over to their enemies who seek their lives. Their dead
bodies will become food for the birds of the air and the beasts of
the earth.
[21]"I will hand Zedekiah king of Judah and his officials over to
their enemies who seek their lives, to the army of the king of Babylon, which has withdrawn from you. [22]I am going to give the
order, declares the LORD, and I will bring them back to this city.
They will fight against it, take it and burn it down. And I will lay
waste the towns of Judah so no one can live there."

The Recabites

35 This is the word that came to Jeremiah from the LORD during the reign of Jehoiakim son of Josiah king of Judah:
[2]"Go to the Recabite family and invite them to come to one of the
side rooms of the house of the LORD and give them wine to drink."
[3]So I went to get Jaazaniah son of Jeremiah, the son of Habaz-
ziniah, and his brothers and all his sons—the whole family of the
Recabites. [4]I brought them into the house of the LORD, into the
room of the sons of Hanan son of Igdaliah the man of God. It was
next to the room of the officials, which was over that of Maaseiah
son of Shallum the doorkeeper. [5]Then I set bowls full of wine and
some cups before the men of the Recabite family and said to
them, "Drink some wine."
[6]But they replied, "We do not drink wine, because our forefather Jonadab son of Recab gave us this command: 'Neither you
nor your descendants must ever drink wine. [7]Also you must never
build houses, sow seed or plant vineyards; you must never have
any of these things, but must always live in tents. Then you will
live a long time in the land where you are nomads.' [8]We have
obeyed everything our forefather Jonadab son of Recab commanded us. Neither we nor our wives nor our sons and daughters
have ever drunk wine [9]or built houses to live in or had vineyards,
fields or crops. [10]We have lived in tents and have fully obeyed
everything our forefather Jonadab commanded us. [11]But when
Nebuchadnezzar king of Babylon invaded this land, we said,
'Come, we must go to Jerusalem to escape the Babylonian[a] and
Aramean armies.' So we have remained in Jerusalem."
[12]Then the word of the LORD came to Jeremiah, saying: [13]"This
is what the LORD Almighty, the God of Israel, says: Go and tell the
men of Judah and the people of Jerusalem, 'Will you not learn a
lesson and obey my words?' declares the LORD. [14]'Jonadab son of
Recab ordered his sons not to drink wine and this command has
been kept. To this day they do not drink wine, because they obey
their forefather's command. But I have spoken to you again and
again, yet you have not obeyed me. [15]Again and again I sent all my
servants the prophets to you. They said, "Each of you must turn
from your wicked ways and reform your actions; do not follow
other gods to serve them. Then you will live in the land I have
given to you and your fathers." But you have not paid attention or
listened to me. [16]The descendants of Jonadab son of Recab have
carried out the command their forefather gave them, but these
people have not obeyed me.'
[17]"Therefore, this is what the LORD God Almighty, the God of Israel, says: 'Listen! I am going to bring on Judah and on everyone

[a] 11 Or *Chaldean*

(35:8–16) Holy God, You do not want worship that is just "made up only of rules taught by men." For that which goes into a man's mouth does not make him unclean; rather, that which comes out of his mouth makes him unclean. What good will it do if I worship You with my lips while my heart is far from You? Help me to worship You in spirit and in truth, with a clean heart and clean lips and clean hands. Help me to flee from evil and to faithfully obey Your Word, for obedience is more important to You than sacrifice. Help me, Lord, to be righteous, not just religious. (1Sa 15:22; Isa 29:13; Mt 15:8–11; Jn 4:21–24)

If You call for sacrifices
I will bring them.
If You ask for songs of praise
Then I will sing them.
But what Your heart desires
Is what Your love requires:
A broken, contrite heart
You will receive.

Create in me a heart for You,
A heart to do Your will.
Make it a palace fit for a king;
Make it to praise You
And free it to sing.
You are the potter,
Make me like new;
Create in me a heart for You.

"A Heart For You"
Walt Harrah (©1986)

(36:2–3) The writing down of Your Word, O Lord, ensured unmistakable clarity concerning the consequences of sin and Your call to repentance. The Scriptures are God-breathed and useful for teaching, rebuking, correcting, training and equipping us for good works. Your Word is living and active. It leaves us with no question as to the reality of our sin, the righteousness of Your judgment, and the power of Your salvation. Thank You, Lord, for Your written Word. (2Ti 3:16–17; Heb 4:12)

It is not possible ever to exhaust the mind of the Scriptures. It is a well that has no bottom.

Saint John Chrysostom (c.347-407)

Holy Bible, book divine,
Precious treasure, Thou art mine;
Mine to tell me whence I came;
Mine to teach me what I am.

"Holy Bible, Book Divine"
John Burton (1803)

living in Jerusalem every disaster I pronounced against them. I
spoke to them, but they did not listen; I called to them, but they
did not answer.' "
[18]Then Jeremiah said to the family of the Recabites, "This is
what the LORD Almighty, the God of Israel, says: 'You have
obeyed the command of your forefather Jonadab and have followed all his instructions and have done everything he ordered.'
[19]Therefore, this is what the LORD Almighty, the God of Israel,
says: 'Jonadab son of Recab will never fail to have a man to
serve me.' "

Jehoiakim Burns Jeremiah's Scroll

36 In the fourth year of Jehoiakim son of Josiah king of
Judah, this word came to Jeremiah from the LORD: [2]"Take
a scroll and write on it all the words I have spoken to you concerning Israel, Judah and all the other nations from the time I
began speaking to you in the reign of Josiah till now. [3]Perhaps
when the people of Judah hear about every disaster I plan to inflict on them, each of them will turn from his wicked way; then I
will forgive their wickedness and their sin."
[4]So Jeremiah called Baruch son of Neriah, and while Jeremiah
dictated all the words the LORD had spoken to him, Baruch wrote
them on the scroll. [5]Then Jeremiah told Baruch, "I am restricted;
I cannot go to the LORD's temple. [6]So you go to the house of the
LORD on a day of fasting and read to the people from the scroll the
words of the LORD that you wrote as I dictated. Read them to all
the people of Judah who come in from their towns. [7]Perhaps they
will bring their petition before the LORD, and each will turn from
his wicked ways, for the anger and wrath pronounced against this
people by the LORD are great."
[8]Baruch son of Neriah did everything Jeremiah the prophet
told him to do; at the LORD's temple he read the words of the
LORD from the scroll. [9]In the ninth month of the fifth year of Jehoiakim son of Josiah king of Judah, a time of fasting before the
LORD was proclaimed for all the people in Jerusalem and those
who had come from the towns of Judah. [10]From the room of
Gemariah son of Shaphan the secretary, which was in the upper
courtyard at the entrance of the New Gate of the temple, Baruch
read to all the people at the LORD's temple the words of Jeremiah from the scroll.
[11]When Micaiah son of Gemariah, the son of Shaphan, heard
all the words of the LORD from the scroll, [12]he went down to the
secretary's room in the royal palace, where all the officials were
sitting: Elishama the secretary, Delaiah son of Shemaiah, Elnathan
son of Acbor, Gemariah son of Shaphan, Zedekiah son of Hananiah, and all the other officials. [13]After Micaiah told them everything he had heard Baruch read to the people from the scroll,
[14]all the officials sent Jehudi son of Nethaniah, the son of Shelemiah, the son of Cushi, to say to Baruch, "Bring the scroll from
which you have read to the people and come." So Baruch son of
Neriah went to them with the scroll in his hand. [15]They said to
him, "Sit down, please, and read it to us."
So Baruch read it to them. [16]When they heard all these words,
they looked at each other in fear and said to Baruch, "We must
report all these words to the king." [17]Then they asked Baruch,
"Tell us, how did you come to write all this? Did Jeremiah dictate it?"

18"Yes," Baruch replied, "he dictated all these words to me,
and I wrote them in ink on the scroll."
19Then the officials said to Baruch, "You and Jeremiah, go and
hide. Don't let anyone know where you are."
20After they put the scroll in the room of Elishama the secretary, they went to the king in the courtyard and reported everything to him. 21The king sent Jehudi to get the scroll, and Jehudi
brought it from the room of Elishama the secretary and read it to
the king and all the officials standing beside him. 22It was the
ninth month and the king was sitting in the winter apartment, with
a fire burning in the firepot in front of him. 23Whenever Jehudi
had read three or four columns of the scroll, the king cut them
off with a scribe's knife and threw them into the firepot, until the
entire scroll was burned in the fire. 24The king and all his attendants who heard all these words showed no fear, nor did they tear
their clothes. 25Even though Elnathan, Delaiah and Gemariah
urged the king not to burn the scroll, he would not listen to them.
26Instead, the king commanded Jerahmeel, a son of the king, Seraiah son of Azriel and Shelemiah son of Abdeel to arrest Baruch
the scribe and Jeremiah the prophet. But the LORD had hidden
them.
27After the king burned the scroll containing the words that
Baruch had written at Jeremiah's dictation, the word of the LORD
came to Jeremiah: 28"Take another scroll and write on it all the
words that were on the first scroll, which Jehoiakim king of Judah
burned up. 29Also tell Jehoiakim king of Judah, 'This is what the
LORD says: You burned that scroll and said, "Why did you write on
it that the king of Babylon would certainly come and destroy this
land and cut off both men and animals from it?" 30Therefore, this
is what the LORD says about Jehoiakim king of Judah: He will have
no one to sit on the throne of David; his body will be thrown out
and exposed to the heat by day and the frost by night. 31I will
punish him and his children and his attendants for their wickedness; I will bring on them and those living in Jerusalem and the
people of Judah every disaster I pronounced against them, because they have not listened.' "
32So Jeremiah took another scroll and gave it to the scribe
Baruch son of Neriah, and as Jeremiah dictated, Baruch wrote on
it all the words of the scroll that Jehoiakim king of Judah had
burned in the fire. And many similar words were added to them.

Jeremiah in Prison

37 Zedekiah son of Josiah was made king of Judah by Nebuchadnezzar king of Babylon; he reigned in place of Jehoiachin[a] son of Jehoiakim. 2Neither he nor his attendants nor
the people of the land paid any attention to the words the LORD
had spoken through Jeremiah the prophet.
3King Zedekiah, however, sent Jehucal son of Shelemiah with
the priest Zephaniah son of Maaseiah to Jeremiah the prophet
with this message: "Please pray to the LORD our God for us."
4Now Jeremiah was free to come and go among the people,
for he had not yet been put in prison. 5Pharaoh's army had
marched out of Egypt, and when the Babylonians[b] who were besieging Jerusalem heard the report about them, they withdrew
from Jerusalem.

[a] *1* Hebrew *Coniah,* a variant of *Jehoiachin* [b] *5* Or *Chaldeans*; also in verses 8, 9, 13 and 14

Obedience means marching right on whether we feel like it or not. Many times we go against our feelings. Faith is one thing, feeling is another.

Dwight Lyman Moody (1837-1899)

(36:23–24) O Lord, forgive me for the times when I refuse to hear Your direct, uncompromising words. Too often I long for comfort, not correction. I close my ears to Your persistent message, which has the power to transform my spirit. Forgive my complacency and stubbornness, Lord. Give me the courage I need to receive Your correction. Only in obedience will I find Your love, Your peace and my ultimate restoration.

6Then the word of the LORD came to Jeremiah the prophet:
7"This is what the LORD, the God of Israel, says: Tell the king of
Judah, who sent you to inquire of me, 'Pharaoh's army, which has
marched out to support you, will go back to its own land, to
Egypt. 8Then the Babylonians will return and attack this city; they
will capture it and burn it down.'
9"This is what the LORD says: Do not deceive yourselves, thinking, 'The Babylonians will surely leave us.' They will not! 10Even
if you were to defeat the entire Babylonian[a] army that is attacking
you and only wounded men were left in their tents, they would
come out and burn this city down."
11After the Babylonian army had withdrawn from Jerusalem
because of Pharaoh's army, 12Jeremiah started to leave the city to
go to the territory of Benjamin to get his share of the property
among the people there. 13But when he reached the Benjamin
Gate, the captain of the guard, whose name was Irijah son of
Shelemiah, the son of Hananiah, arrested him and said, "You are
deserting to the Babylonians!"
14"That's not true!" Jeremiah said. "I am not deserting to the
Babylonians." But Irijah would not listen to him; instead, he arrested Jeremiah and brought him to the officials. 15They were
angry with Jeremiah and had him beaten and imprisoned in the
house of Jonathan the secretary, which they had made into a
prison.
16Jeremiah was put into a vaulted cell in a dungeon, where he
remained a long time. 17Then King Zedekiah sent for him and
had him brought to the palace, where he asked him privately, "Is
there any word from the LORD?"
"Yes," Jeremiah replied, "you will be handed over to the king
of Babylon."
18Then Jeremiah said to King Zedekiah, "What crime have I
committed against you or your officials or this people, that you
have put me in prison? 19Where are your prophets who prophesied to you, 'The king of Babylon will not attack you or this land'?
20But now, my lord the king, please listen. Let me bring my petition before you: Do not send me back to the house of Jonathan
the secretary, or I will die there."
21King Zedekiah then gave orders for Jeremiah to be placed in
the courtyard of the guard and given bread from the street of the
bakers each day until all the bread in the city was gone. So Jeremiah remained in the courtyard of the guard.

Jeremiah Thrown Into a Cistern

38 Shephatiah son of Mattan, Gedaliah son of Pashhur, Jehucal[b] son of Shelemiah, and Pashhur son of Malkijah
heard what Jeremiah was telling all the people when he said,
2"This is what the LORD says: 'Whoever stays in this city will die by
the sword, famine or plague, but whoever goes over to the Babylonians[c] will live. He will escape with his life; he will live.' 3And
this is what the LORD says: 'This city will certainly be handed over
to the army of the king of Babylon, who will capture it.' "
4Then the officials said to the king, "This man should be put to
death. He is discouraging the soldiers who are left in this city, as
well as all the people, by the things he is saying to them. This man
is not seeking the good of these people but their ruin."

[a] *10* Or *Chaldean*; also in verse 11 [b] *1* Hebrew *Jucal*, a variant of *Jehucal* [c] *2* Or *Chaldeans*; also in verses 18, 19 and 23

(37:13–15) God of our fathers, Jeremiah suffered for the privilege of speaking Your truth. Yet his greatest passion was to speak that truth. Should I ever be called upon to suffer for the truth, grant that I may be like Jeremiah, Job, Joseph, Daniel, Stephen, Peter, Paul, and countless others of Your people. May my consolation, my joy in unrelenting pain be, as was theirs, that I would not deny the words of the Holy One. (Job 6:10; Jer 20:9)

And when the sorrow dims the light
Along our way,
Help us to see each time of darkness
Through eyes of faith;
A time for hope, a time for courage
Knowing You will lead us through,
And we'll march with hearts
courageous after You.

We're marching on with hearts
courageous;
We'll follow anywhere You want us
to.
And should You lead us where the
battle rages,
Let us march with hearts
courageous after You.

"Hearts Courageous"
Jamie Owens-Collins (©1984)

5"He is in your hands," King Zedekiah answered. "The king
can do nothing to oppose you."
6So they took Jeremiah and put him into the cistern of Malkijah, the king's son, which was in the courtyard of the guard. They lowered Jeremiah by ropes into the cistern; it had no water in it, only mud, and Jeremiah sank down into the mud.
7But Ebed-Melech, a Cushite,[a] an official[b] in the royal palace,
heard that they had put Jeremiah into the cistern. While the king
was sitting in the Benjamin Gate, 8Ebed-Melech went out of the
palace and said to him, 9"My lord the king, these men have acted wickedly in all they have done to Jeremiah the prophet. They have thrown him into a cistern, where he will starve to death when there is no longer any bread in the city."
10Then the king commanded Ebed-Melech the Cushite, "Take thirty men from here with you and lift Jeremiah the prophet out of the cistern before he dies."
11So Ebed-Melech took the men with him and went to a room under the treasury in the palace. He took some old rags and worn-out clothes from there and let them down with ropes to Jeremiah in the cistern. 12Ebed-Melech the Cushite said to Jeremiah,
"Put these old rags and worn-out clothes under your arms to pad
the ropes." Jeremiah did so, 13and they pulled him up with the
ropes and lifted him out of the cistern. And Jeremiah remained in the courtyard of the guard.

Zedekiah Questions Jeremiah Again

14Then King Zedekiah sent for Jeremiah the prophet and had him brought to the third entrance to the temple of the LORD. "I am going to ask you something," the king said to Jeremiah. "Do not hide anything from me."
15Jeremiah said to Zedekiah, "If I give you an answer, will you not kill me? Even if I did give you counsel, you would not listen to me."
16But King Zedekiah swore this oath secretly to Jeremiah: "As surely as the LORD lives, who has given us breath, I will neither kill you nor hand you over to those who are seeking your life."
17Then Jeremiah said to Zedekiah, "This is what the LORD God Almighty, the God of Israel, says: 'If you surrender to the officers of the king of Babylon, your life will be spared and this city will
not be burned down; you and your family will live. 18But if you
will not surrender to the officers of the king of Babylon, this city will be handed over to the Babylonians and they will burn it down; you yourself will not escape from their hands.' "
19King Zedekiah said to Jeremiah, "I am afraid of the Jews who have gone over to the Babylonians, for the Babylonians may hand me over to them and they will mistreat me."
20"They will not hand you over," Jeremiah replied. "Obey the LORD by doing what I tell you. Then it will go well with you, and
your life will be spared. 21But if you refuse to surrender, this is
what the LORD has revealed to me: 22All the women left in the
palace of the king of Judah will be brought out to the officials of the king of Babylon. Those women will say to you:

" 'They misled you and overcame you—
those trusted friends of yours.

[a] 7 Probably from the upper Nile region [b] 7 Or *a eunuch*

(38:6–13) Jeremiah was Your chosen man of destiny, O Lord, called to prophesy to the nations. You filled his mouth with the authoritative counsel of Your Word. Here in the mud was the one that You set apart for Yourself even before his birth. Now he was sinking in a cistern of suffering, a failure and a fool in the eyes of the world. But thank You, Lord, that You were faithful to fulfill the promise that You had made to him when You first called him to serve You: "Do not be afraid of them, for I am with you and will rescue you." (Jer 1:4–10)

With our hands upon the plow,
How could we ever look back now?
Forgetting all that's past we look to
days ahead.
Since we long to win the prize,
Lord, let us never compromise;
Keep us safe until the day we hear
You say:

"I have known the seeds you've sown;
You've persevered and faithfully
endured.

"Well done, thou good and faithful
servant,
My son, come take of your reward.
In every trial that's come and gone,
I have stood and cheered you on.
Thou good and faithful servant, well
done!"

"Good and Faithful Servant"
Walt Harrah (©1994)

(39:11–12) Thank You, Lord, for the triumph of Your mercy. You know how to take care of Your own. After bloody beatings, starvation in a muddy cistern and the humiliation of endless ridicule, You remembered Your servant Jeremiah and marked him for special blessing. Among the thousands who were killed or captured in the chaos of defeat, You singled out Your servant and personally cared for him. Thank You that You never lose sight of Your own and that Your grip on us is eternally strong.

When you pass through the waters,
I will be with you.
When you pass through the rivers,
They will not sweep over you.
When you walk through the fire,
You will not be burned.
The flames will not set you ablaze,
The flames will not set you ablaze.
For I am the Lord your God,
The Holy One of Israel;
I am the Lord your God, your
Savior.

"I Am the Lord Your God"
Walt Harrah (©1994)

Lord Jesus,
You were in prison, found guilty when you were innocent; You were executed
as traitor when in fact you were Savior. To you who died to set all free we pray for:
All makers of the laws of the land,
that they do so with reason and compassion.
All interpreters of the law—judges, lawyers—
that they be fair, honest and impartial.
All administrators of the law—prison guards and superintendents—
that they be merciful in their firmness.
All prisoners—
that they may know that you are in prison with them, in their homes with their loved ones. And that in you is their hope. Though bound, may they be perfectly free in you and in your service.

John B. Coburn (1914-)

Your feet are sunk in the mud;
your friends have deserted you.'

23"All your wives and children will be brought out to the Babylonians. You yourself will not escape from their hands but will be captured by the king of Babylon; and this city will[a] be burned down."
24Then Zedekiah said to Jeremiah, "Do not let anyone know about this conversation, or you may die. 25If the officials hear that I talked with you, and they come to you and say, 'Tell us what you said to the king and what the king said to you; do not hide it from us or we will kill you,' 26then tell them, 'I was pleading with the king not to send me back to Jonathan's house to die there.' "
27All the officials did come to Jeremiah and question him, and he told them everything the king had ordered him to say. So they said no more to him, for no one had heard his conversation with the king.
28And Jeremiah remained in the courtyard of the guard until the day Jerusalem was captured.

The Fall of Jerusalem

39 This is how Jerusalem was taken: 1In the ninth year of
Zedekiah king of Judah, in the tenth month, Nebuchadnezzar king of Babylon marched against Jerusalem with his whole army and laid siege to it. 2And on the ninth day of the fourth month of Zedekiah's eleventh year, the city wall was broken
through. 3Then all the officials of the king of Babylon came and took seats in the Middle Gate: Nergal-Sharezer of Samgar, Nebo-Sarsekim[b] a chief officer, Nergal-Sharezer a high official and all the other officials of the king of Babylon. 4When Zedekiah king of
Judah and all the soldiers saw them, they fled; they left the city at night by way of the king's garden, through the gate between the two walls, and headed toward the Arabah.[c]
5But the Babylonian[d] army pursued them and overtook Zedekiah in the plains of Jericho. They captured him and took him to Nebuchadnezzar king of Babylon at Riblah in the land of Hamath, where he pronounced sentence on him. 6There at Riblah the king
of Babylon slaughtered the sons of Zedekiah before his eyes and also killed all the nobles of Judah. 7Then he put out Zedekiah's
eyes and bound him with bronze shackles to take him to Babylon.
8The Babylonians[e] set fire to the royal palace and the houses of
the people and broke down the walls of Jerusalem. 9Nebuzaradan
commander of the imperial guard carried into exile to Babylon the people who remained in the city, along with those who had gone over to him, and the rest of the people. 10But Nebuzaradan
the commander of the guard left behind in the land of Judah some of the poor people, who owned nothing; and at that time he gave them vineyards and fields.
11Now Nebuchadnezzar king of Babylon had given these orders about Jeremiah through Nebuzaradan commander of the imperial guard: 12"Take him and look after him; don't harm him but do
for him whatever he asks." 13So Nebuzaradan the commander of
the guard, Nebushazban a chief officer, Nergal-Sharezer a high official and all the other officers of the king of Babylon 14sent and
had Jeremiah taken out of the courtyard of the guard. They turned

[a] 23 Or *and you will cause this city to*   [b] 3 Or *Nergal-Sharezer, Samgar-Nebo, Sarsekim*   [c] 4 Or *the Jordan Valley*   [d] 5 Or *Chaldean*   [e] 8 Or *Chaldeans*

him over to Gedaliah son of Ahikam, the son of Shaphan, to take
him back to his home. So he remained among his own people.
15While Jeremiah had been confined in the courtyard of the
guard, the word of the LORD came to him: 16"Go and tell Ebed-
Melech the Cushite, 'This is what the LORD Almighty, the God of Israel, says: I am about to fulfill my words against this city through
disaster, not prosperity. At that time they will be fulfilled before
your eyes. 17But I will rescue you on that day, declares the LORD;
you will not be handed over to those you fear. 18I will save you;
you will not fall by the sword but will escape with your life, because you trust in me, declares the LORD.'"

Jeremiah Freed

40 The word came to Jeremiah from the LORD after Nebuzaradan commander of the imperial guard had released
him at Ramah. He had found Jeremiah bound in chains among all
the captives from Jerusalem and Judah who were being carried
into exile to Babylon. 2When the commander of the guard found
Jeremiah, he said to him, "The LORD your God decreed this disaster for this place. 3And now the LORD has brought it about; he
has done just as he said he would. All this happened because you
people sinned against the LORD and did not obey him. 4But today
I am freeing you from the chains on your wrists. Come with me to
Babylon, if you like, and I will look after you; but if you do not
want to, then don't come. Look, the whole country lies before
you; go wherever you please." 5However, before Jeremiah turned
to go,[a] Nebuzaradan added, "Go back to Gedaliah son of Ahikam,
the son of Shaphan, whom the king of Babylon has appointed
over the towns of Judah, and live with him among the people, or
go anywhere else you please."
Then the commander gave him provisions and a present and
let him go. 6So Jeremiah went to Gedaliah son of Ahikam at Mizpah and stayed with him among the people who were left behind
in the land.

Gedaliah Assassinated

7When all the army officers and their men who were still in the
open country heard that the king of Babylon had appointed Gedaliah son of Ahikam as governor over the land and had put him in
charge of the men, women and children who were the poorest in
the land and who had not been carried into exile to Babylon,
8they came to Gedaliah at Mizpah—Ishmael son of Nethaniah,
Johanan and Jonathan the sons of Kareah, Seraiah son of Tanhumeth, the sons of Ephai the Netophathite, and Jaazaniah[b] the
son of the Maacathite, and their men. 9Gedaliah son of Ahikam,
the son of Shaphan, took an oath to reassure them and their men.
"Do not be afraid to serve the Babylonians,[c]" he said. "Settle
down in the land and serve the king of Babylon, and it will go
well with you. 10I myself will stay at Mizpah to represent you before the Babylonians who come to us, but you are to harvest the
wine, summer fruit and oil, and put them in your storage jars,
and live in the towns you have taken over."
11When all the Jews in Moab, Ammon, Edom and all the other
countries heard that the king of Babylon had left a remnant in
Judah and had appointed Gedaliah son of Ahikam, the son of

[a] 5 Or *Jeremiah answered* [b] 8 Hebrew *Jezaniah*, a variant of *Jaazaniah* [c] 9 Or *Chaldeans*; also in verse 10

(40:5) Almighty God, Your ability to use even one who does not know You to fulfill Your purposes is a tribute to Your sovereignty and authority. You used Nebuzaradan, the commander of the Babylonian imperial guard, as both an instrument of judgment and an instrument of protection. You, great God, control what we cannot control. Nothing is beyond the jurisdiction of Your sovereign will. Indeed, "Our God is in heaven; he does whatever pleases him." (Ps 115:3)

God governs the world, and we have only to do our duty wisely and leave the issue to him.

John Jay Chapman (1862-1933)

Only those who see themselves as utterly destitute can fully appreciate the grace of God.

Erwin W. Lutzer (1941-)

(41:1–7) Come save Your people, Lord. Save us from pride. Save us from jealousy. Save us from hatred. Save us from our rebellion against You and our treachery against one another. Without You, there is no end to the atrocities of which we are capable. O God, save us!

Shaphan, as governor over them, 12they all came back to the
land of Judah, to Gedaliah at Mizpah, from all the countries
where they had been scattered. And they harvested an abundance
of wine and summer fruit.
13Johanan son of Kareah and all the army officers still in the
open country came to Gedaliah at Mizpah 14and said to him,
"Don't you know that Baalis king of the Ammonites has sent Ishmael son of Nethaniah to take your life?" But Gedaliah son of Ahikam did not believe them.
15Then Johanan son of Kareah said privately to Gedaliah in
Mizpah, "Let me go and kill Ishmael son of Nethaniah, and no
one will know it. Why should he take your life and cause all the
Jews who are gathered around you to be scattered and the remnant of Judah to perish?"
16But Gedaliah son of Ahikam said to Johanan son of Kareah,
"Don't do such a thing! What you are saying about Ishmael is not
true."

41 In the seventh month Ishmael son of Nethaniah, the son of
Elishama, who was of royal blood and had been one of the
king's officers, came with ten men to Gedaliah son of Ahikam at
Mizpah. While they were eating together there, 2Ishmael son of
Nethaniah and the ten men who were with him got up and struck
down Gedaliah son of Ahikam, the son of Shaphan, with the
sword, killing the one whom the king of Babylon had appointed
as governor over the land. 3Ishmael also killed all the Jews who
were with Gedaliah at Mizpah, as well as the Babylonian[a] soldiers
who were there.
4The day after Gedaliah's assassination, before anyone knew
about it, 5eighty men who had shaved off their beards, torn their
clothes and cut themselves came from Shechem, Shiloh and
Samaria, bringing grain offerings and incense with them to the
house of the LORD. 6Ishmael son of Nethaniah went out from Mizpah to meet them, weeping as he went. When he met them, he
said, "Come to Gedaliah son of Ahikam." 7When they went into
the city, Ishmael son of Nethaniah and the men who were with
him slaughtered them and threw them into a cistern. 8But ten of
them said to Ishmael, "Don't kill us! We have wheat and barley,
oil and honey, hidden in a field." So he let them alone and did not
kill them with the others. 9Now the cistern where he threw all the
bodies of the men he had killed along with Gedaliah was the one
King Asa had made as part of his defense against Baasha king of
Israel. Ishmael son of Nethaniah filled it with the dead.
10Ishmael made captives of all the rest of the people who were
in Mizpah—the king's daughters along with all the others who
were left there, over whom Nebuzaradan commander of the imperial guard had appointed Gedaliah son of Ahikam. Ishmael son
of Nethaniah took them captive and set out to cross over to the
Ammonites.
11When Johanan son of Kareah and all the army officers who
were with him heard about all the crimes Ishmael son of Nethaniah had committed, 12they took all their men and went to fight
Ishmael son of Nethaniah. They caught up with him near the
great pool in Gibeon. 13When all the people Ishmael had with
him saw Johanan son of Kareah and the army officers who were
with him, they were glad. 14All the people Ishmael had taken

[a] 3 Or *Chaldean*

captive at Mizpah turned and went over to Johanan son of Kareah. 15 But Ishmael son of Nethaniah and eight of his men escaped
from Johanan and fled to the Ammonites.

Flight to Egypt

16 Then Johanan son of Kareah and all the army officers who
were with him led away all the survivors from Mizpah whom he
had recovered from Ishmael son of Nethaniah after he had assassinated Gedaliah son of Ahikam: the soldiers, women, children
and court officials he had brought from Gibeon. 17 And they went
on, stopping at Geruth Kimham near Bethlehem on their way to
Egypt 18 to escape the Babylonians.[a] They were afraid of them because Ishmael son of Nethaniah had killed Gedaliah son of Ahikam, whom the king of Babylon had appointed as governor over
the land.

42 Then all the army officers, including Johanan son of Kareah and Jezaniah[b] son of Hoshaiah, and all the people
from the least to the greatest approached 2 Jeremiah the prophet
and said to him, "Please hear our petition and pray to the LORD
your God for this entire remnant. For as you now see, though we
were once many, now only a few are left. 3 Pray that the LORD your
God will tell us where we should go and what we should do."

4 "I have heard you," replied Jeremiah the prophet. "I will certainly pray to the LORD your God as you have requested; I will tell
you everything the LORD says and will keep nothing back from
you."

5 Then they said to Jeremiah, "May the LORD be a true and
faithful witness against us if we do not act in accordance with
everything the LORD your God sends you to tell us. 6 Whether it is
favorable or unfavorable, we will obey the LORD our God, to
whom we are sending you, so that it will go well with us, for we
will obey the LORD our God."

7 Ten days later the word of the LORD came to Jeremiah. 8 So he
called together Johanan son of Kareah and all the army officers
who were with him and all the people from the least to the greatest. 9 He said to them, "This is what the LORD, the God of Israel, to
whom you sent me to present your petition, says: 10 'If you stay in
this land, I will build you up and not tear you down; I will plant
you and not uproot you, for I am grieved over the disaster I have
inflicted on you. 11 Do not be afraid of the king of Babylon, whom
you now fear. Do not be afraid of him, declares the LORD, for I am
with you and will save you and deliver you from his hands. 12 I will
show you compassion so that he will have compassion on you and
restore you to your land.'

13 "However, if you say, 'We will not stay in this land,' and so
disobey the LORD your God, 14 and if you say, 'No, we will go and
live in Egypt, where we will not see war or hear the trumpet or be
hungry for bread,' 15 then hear the word of the LORD, O remnant
of Judah. This is what the LORD Almighty, the God of Israel, says:
'If you are determined to go to Egypt and you do go to settle there,
16 then the sword you fear will overtake you there, and the famine
you dread will follow you into Egypt, and there you will die. 17 Indeed, all who are determined to go to Egypt to settle there will die
by the sword, famine and plague; not one of them will survive or
escape the disaster I will bring on them.' 18 This is what the LORD

[a] 18 Or *Chaldeans* [b] 1 Hebrew; Septuagint (see also 43:2) *Azariah*

Create in me a new heart, Lord,
That gladly I obey Your Word.
Let what You will be my desire,
And with new life my soul inspire.

"Renew Me, O Eternal Light"
Johann F. Ruopp (1672–1708)
Trans. August Crull (1846–1923)

(42:13–16) Lord God, Your judgments are righteous and pure. Yet, like Your people of old, we sometimes treat Your commands as if they were options. Forgive us, Lord, for our defiance. Teach us to submit to You soberly and with great reverence. The consequences of rebellion can be deadly, while obedience is the pathway to life.

Almighty, the God of Israel, says: 'As my anger and wrath have been poured out on those who lived in Jerusalem, so will my wrath be poured out on you when you go to Egypt. You will be an object of cursing and horror, of condemnation and reproach; you will never see this place again.'

19"O remnant of Judah, the LORD has told you, 'Do not go to Egypt.' Be sure of this: I warn you today 20that you made a fatal mistake[a] when you sent me to the LORD your God and said, 'Pray to the LORD our God for us; tell us everything he says and we will do it.' 21I have told you today, but you still have not obeyed the LORD your God in all he sent me to tell you. 22So now, be sure of this: You will die by the sword, famine and plague in the place where you want to go to settle."

43 When Jeremiah finished telling the people all the words of the LORD their God—everything the LORD had sent him to tell them— 2Azariah son of Hoshaiah and Johanan son of Kareah and all the arrogant men said to Jeremiah, "You are lying! The LORD our God has not sent you to say, 'You must not go to Egypt to settle there.' 3But Baruch son of Neriah is inciting you against us to hand us over to the Babylonians,[b] so they may kill us or carry us into exile to Babylon."

4So Johanan son of Kareah and all the army officers and all the people disobeyed the LORD's command to stay in the land of Judah. 5Instead, Johanan son of Kareah and all the army officers led away all the remnant of Judah who had come back to live in the land of Judah from all the nations where they had been scattered. 6They also led away all the men, women and children and the king's daughters whom Nebuzaradan commander of the imperial guard had left with Gedaliah son of Ahikam, the son of Shaphan, and Jeremiah the prophet and Baruch son of Neriah. 7So they entered Egypt in disobedience to the LORD and went as far as Tahpanhes.

8In Tahpanhes the word of the LORD came to Jeremiah: 9"While the Jews are watching, take some large stones with you and bury them in clay in the brick pavement at the entrance to Pharaoh's palace in Tahpanhes. 10Then say to them, 'This is what the LORD Almighty, the God of Israel, says: I will send for my servant Nebuchadnezzar king of Babylon, and I will set his throne over these stones I have buried here; he will spread his royal canopy above them. 11He will come and attack Egypt, bringing death to those destined for death, captivity to those destined for captivity, and the sword to those destined for the sword. 12He[c] will set fire to the temples of the gods of Egypt; he will burn their temples and take their gods captive. As a shepherd wraps his garment around him, so will he wrap Egypt around himself and depart from there unscathed. 13There in the temple of the sun[d] in Egypt he will demolish the sacred pillars and will burn down the temples of the gods of Egypt.' "

Disaster Because of Idolatry

44 This word came to Jeremiah concerning all the Jews living in Lower Egypt—in Migdol, Tahpanhes and Memphis[e]—and in Upper Egypt[f]: 2"This is what the LORD Almighty, the God of Israel, says: You saw the great disaster I brought on Jerusalem and on all the towns of Judah. Today they lie deserted

(42:19–21) Lord, You have promised to give me wisdom if I ask You for it. You give wisdom generously to all of us, without finding fault. But when I ask, help me to believe in Your Word and not to doubt. You have warned me that the one who seeks Your words and then doubts shouldn't expect to receive anything from You. Spare me from being double-minded, Lord, and protect me from the instability that inevitably accompanies faithlessness. (Jas 1:5–8)

Understanding is the reward of faith. Therefore seek not to understand that you may believe, but believe that you may understand.

Saint Augustine of Hippo (354-430)

[a] *20* Or *you erred in your hearts* [b] *3* Or *Chaldeans* [c] *12* Or *I* [d] *13* Or *in Heliopolis* [e] *1* Hebrew *Noph* [f] *1* Hebrew *in Pathros*

and in ruins [3]because of the evil they have done. They provoked
me to anger by burning incense and by worshiping other gods
that neither they nor you nor your fathers ever knew. [4]Again and
again I sent my servants the prophets, who said, 'Do not do this
detestable thing that I hate!' [5]But they did not listen or pay attention; they did not turn from their wickedness or stop burning incense to other gods. [6]Therefore, my fierce anger was poured out;
it raged against the towns of Judah and the streets of Jerusalem
and made them the desolate ruins they are today.

[7]"Now this is what the LORD God Almighty, the God of Israel,
says: Why bring such great disaster on yourselves by cutting off
from Judah the men and women, the children and infants, and so
leave yourselves without a remnant? [8]Why provoke me to anger
with what your hands have made, burning incense to other gods
in Egypt, where you have come to live? You will destroy yourselves
and make yourselves an object of cursing and reproach among
all the nations on earth. [9]Have you forgotten the wickedness committed by your fathers and by the kings and queens of Judah and
the wickedness committed by you and your wives in the land of
Judah and the streets of Jerusalem? [10]To this day they have not
humbled themselves or shown reverence, nor have they followed
my law and the decrees I set before you and your fathers.

[11]"Therefore, this is what the LORD Almighty, the God of Israel,
says: I am determined to bring disaster on you and to destroy all
Judah. [12]I will take away the remnant of Judah who were determined to go to Egypt to settle there. They will all perish in Egypt;
they will fall by the sword or die from famine. From the least to
the greatest, they will die by sword or famine. They will become
an object of cursing and horror, of condemnation and reproach.
[13]I will punish those who live in Egypt with the sword, famine and
plague, as I punished Jerusalem. [14]None of the remnant of Judah
who have gone to live in Egypt will escape or survive to return to
the land of Judah, to which they long to return and live; none will
return except a few fugitives."

[15]Then all the men who knew that their wives were burning incense to other gods, along with all the women who were present—a large assembly—and all the people living in Lower and
Upper Egypt,[a] said to Jeremiah, [16]"We will not listen to the message you have spoken to us in the name of the LORD! [17]We will
certainly do everything we said we would: We will burn incense to
the Queen of Heaven and will pour out drink offerings to her just
as we and our fathers, our kings and our officials did in the towns
of Judah and in the streets of Jerusalem. At that time we had plenty of food and were well off and suffered no harm. [18]But ever
since we stopped burning incense to the Queen of Heaven and
pouring out drink offerings to her, we have had nothing and have
been perishing by sword and famine."

[19]The women added, "When we burned incense to the Queen
of Heaven and poured out drink offerings to her, did not our husbands know that we were making cakes like her image and pouring out drink offerings to her?"

[20]Then Jeremiah said to all the people, both men and women,
who were answering him, [21]"Did not the LORD remember and
think about the incense burned in the towns of Judah and the
streets of Jerusalem by you and your fathers, your kings and your

[a] 15 Hebrew *in Egypt and Pathros*

The Bible is a letter from God with our personal address on it.
Søren Aabye Kierkegaard (1813-1855)

(44:9) Lord, in Your mercy You are always prompting us to remember the blessings of Your past goodness and the consequences of our past disobedience. The written Scriptures are full of Your timeless admonitions. "These things happened to them as examples and were written down as warnings for us, on whom the fulfillment of the ages has come." Our spiritual memories can be very poor. So we thank You, Lord, for Your many gracious reminders. (1Co 10:11)

God of our weary years,
God of our silent tears,
Thou who hast brought us
Thus far on the way;
Thou who hast by Thy might
Led us into the light:
Keep us forever in the path, we
pray.
Lest our feet stray from the places,
Our God, where we met Thee;
Lest, our hearts drunk
With the wine of the world,
We forget Thee;
Shadowed beneath Thy hand
May we forever stand,
True to our God,
True to our native land.

"Lift Every Voice and Sing"
James W. Johnson (1871-1938)

officials and the people of the land? [22]When the LORD could no
longer endure your wicked actions and the detestable things you
did, your land became an object of cursing and a desolate waste
without inhabitants, as it is today. [23]Because you have burned incense and have sinned against the LORD and have not obeyed him
or followed his law or his decrees or his stipulations, this disaster has come upon you, as you now see."
[24]Then Jeremiah said to all the people, including the women,
"Hear the word of the LORD, all you people of Judah in Egypt.
[25]This is what the LORD Almighty, the God of Israel, says: You and
your wives have shown by your actions what you promised when
you said, 'We will certainly carry out the vows we made to burn
incense and pour out drink offerings to the Queen of Heaven.'
"Go ahead then, do what you promised! Keep your vows! [26]But
hear the word of the LORD, all Jews living in Egypt: 'I swear by my
great name,' says the LORD, 'that no one from Judah living anywhere in Egypt will ever again invoke my name or swear, "As
surely as the Sovereign LORD lives." [27]For I am watching over
them for harm, not for good; the Jews in Egypt will perish by
sword and famine until they are all destroyed. [28]Those who escape the sword and return to the land of Judah from Egypt will be
very few. Then the whole remnant of Judah who came to live in
Egypt will know whose word will stand—mine or theirs.
[29]" 'This will be the sign to you that I will punish you in this
place,' declares the LORD, 'so that you will know that my threats of
harm against you will surely stand.' [30]This is what the LORD says:
'I am going to hand Pharaoh Hophra king of Egypt over to his enemies who seek his life, just as I handed Zedekiah king of Judah
over to Nebuchadnezzar king of Babylon, the enemy who was
seeking his life.' "

A Message to Baruch

45 This is what Jeremiah the prophet told Baruch son of Neriah in the fourth year of Jehoiakim son of Josiah king of
Judah, after Baruch had written on a scroll the words Jeremiah
was then dictating: [2]"This is what the LORD, the God of Israel, says
to you, Baruch: [3]You said, 'Woe to me! The LORD has added sorrow to my pain; I am worn out with groaning and find no rest.' "
[4]⌞The LORD said,⌟ "Say this to him: 'This is what the LORD says:
I will overthrow what I have built and uproot what I have planted,
throughout the land. [5]Should you then seek great things for yourself? Seek them not. For I will bring disaster on all people, declares the LORD, but wherever you go I will let you escape with
your life.' "

A Message About Egypt

46 This is the word of the LORD that came to Jeremiah the
prophet concerning the nations:

[2]Concerning Egypt:

This is the message against the army of Pharaoh Neco king of
Egypt, which was defeated at Carchemish on the Euphrates River
by Nebuchadnezzar king of Babylon in the fourth year of Jehoiakim son of Josiah king of Judah:

[3]"Prepare your shields, both large and small,
and march out for battle!

(45:4–5) Baruch had the honor of declaring the Word of the Lord. Yet because he was Your messenger, he thought himself exempt from the message. He did not realize that the suffering of Your servants for the sake of Your gospel is an honor in Your sight. Lord, if I am ever called upon to suffer for declaring Your truth, may I not respond to You with complaint, but may I count it a privilege to be considered worthy of suffering for Your name. (Ac 5:41)

Pearls are the product of pain . . . a precious, tiny jewel conceived through irritation, born of adversity, nursed by adjustments. Some oysters are never wounded . . . and those who seek for gems toss them aside, fit only for stew.

Charles R. Swindoll (1934-)

Should Thy mercy send me
Sorrow, toil, and woe,
Or should pain attend me
On my path below,
Grant that I may never
Fail Thy hand to see;
Grant that I may ever
Cast my care on Thee.

"In the Hour of Trial"
James Montgomery (1771-1854)

4 Harness the horses,
mount the steeds!
Take your positions
with helmets on!
Polish your spears,
put on your armor!
5 What do I see?
They are terrified,
they are retreating,
their warriors are defeated.
They flee in haste
without looking back,
and there is terror on every side,"
declares the LORD.
6 "The swift cannot flee
nor the strong escape.
In the north by the River Euphrates
they stumble and fall.

7 "Who is this that rises like the Nile,
like rivers of surging waters?
8 Egypt rises like the Nile,
like rivers of surging waters.
She says, 'I will rise and cover the earth;
I will destroy cities and their people.'
9 Charge, O horses!
Drive furiously, O charioteers!
March on, O warriors—
men of Cush[a] and Put who carry shields,
men of Lydia who draw the bow.
10 But that day belongs to the Lord, the LORD Almighty—
a day of vengeance, for vengeance on his foes.
The sword will devour till it is satisfied,
till it has quenched its thirst with blood.
For the Lord, the LORD Almighty, will offer sacrifice
in the land of the north by the River Euphrates.

11 "Go up to Gilead and get balm,
O Virgin Daughter of Egypt.
But you multiply remedies in vain;
there is no healing for you.
12 The nations will hear of your shame;
your cries will fill the earth.
One warrior will stumble over another;
both will fall down together."

13 This is the message the LORD spoke to Jeremiah the prophet about the coming of Nebuchadnezzar king of Babylon to attack Egypt:

14 "Announce this in Egypt, and proclaim it in Migdol;
proclaim it also in Memphis[b] and Tahpanhes:
'Take your positions and get ready,
for the sword devours those around you.'
15 Why will your warriors be laid low?
They cannot stand, for the LORD will push them
down.

[a] 9 That is, the upper Nile region [b] 14 Hebrew *Noph*; also in verse 19

(46:10) The times are in Your hands, O Lord. Justice and vengeance are Yours to mete out as You will and when You will. You would not allow Your enemies to go unpunished; You required their blood as a sacrifice for their sins against Your people. So "let not the strong man boast of his strength." When You come to take revenge, even Your strongest enemies flee in shame and confusion. (Jer 9:23)

Batter my heart, three-personed God; for, you
As yet but knock, breathe, shine, and seek to mend;
That I may rise, and stand, o'erthrow me, and bend
Your force, to break, blow, burn and make me new.
John Donne (1572–1631)

(46:27–28) I praise You, loving Lord, that even in Your chastisement there is always the hope of mercy. You have promised to save me and to be with me always. So help me not to run from You when I do wrong. Help me to submit to Your discipline so that You can restore me to peace and security.

O God of light,
Your Word, a lamp unfailing,
Shall pierce the darkness
Of our earthbound way
And show Your grace,
Your plan for us unveiling,
And guide our footsteps
To the perfect day.

Undimmed by time,
Those words are still revealing
To sinful hearts
Your justice and Your grace;
And questing spirits,
Longing for Your healing,
See Your compassion
In the Savior's face.

"O God of Light"
Sarah E. Taylor (1883–1954)

16 They will stumble repeatedly;
they will fall over each other.
They will say, 'Get up, let us go back
to our own people and our native lands,
away from the sword of the oppressor.'
17 There they will exclaim,
'Pharaoh king of Egypt is only a loud noise;
he has missed his opportunity.'

18 "As surely as I live," declares the King,
whose name is the LORD Almighty,
"one will come who is like Tabor among the mountains,
like Carmel by the sea.
19 Pack your belongings for exile,
you who live in Egypt,
for Memphis will be laid waste
and lie in ruins without inhabitant.

20 "Egypt is a beautiful heifer,
but a gadfly is coming
against her from the north.
21 The mercenaries in her ranks
are like fattened calves.
They too will turn and flee together,
they will not stand their ground,
for the day of disaster is coming upon them,
the time for them to be punished.
22 Egypt will hiss like a fleeing serpent
as the enemy advances in force;
they will come against her with axes,
like men who cut down trees.
23 They will chop down her forest,"
declares the LORD,
"dense though it be.
They are more numerous than locusts,
they cannot be counted.
24 The Daughter of Egypt will be put to shame,
handed over to the people of the north."

25 The LORD Almighty, the God of Israel, says: "I am about to
bring punishment on Amon god of Thebes,[a] on Pharaoh, on
Egypt and her gods and her kings, and on those who rely on Pharaoh. 26 I will hand them over to those who seek their lives, to Nebuchadnezzar king of Babylon and his officers. Later, however,
Egypt will be inhabited as in times past," declares the LORD.

27 "Do not fear, O Jacob my servant;
do not be dismayed, O Israel.
I will surely save you out of a distant place,
your descendants from the land of their exile.
Jacob will again have peace and security,
and no one will make him afraid.
28 Do not fear, O Jacob my servant,
for I am with you," declares the LORD.
"Though I completely destroy all the nations
among which I scatter you,
I will not completely destroy you.

[a] 25 Hebrew *No*

I will discipline you but only with justice;
I will not let you go entirely unpunished."

A Message About the Philistines

47 This is the word of the LORD that came to Jeremiah the prophet concerning the Philistines before Pharaoh attacked Gaza:

2 This is what the LORD says:

"See how the waters are rising in the north;
they will become an overflowing torrent.
They will overflow the land and everything in it,
the towns and those who live in them.
The people will cry out;
all who dwell in the land will wail
3 at the sound of the hoofs of galloping steeds,
at the noise of enemy chariots
and the rumble of their wheels.
Fathers will not turn to help their children;
their hands will hang limp.
4 For the day has come
to destroy all the Philistines
and to cut off all survivors
who could help Tyre and Sidon.
The LORD is about to destroy the Philistines,
the remnant from the coasts of Caphtor.[a]
5 Gaza will shave her head in mourning;
Ashkelon will be silenced.
O remnant on the plain,
how long will you cut yourselves?

6 " 'Ah, sword of the LORD,' ⌊you cry,⌋
'how long till you rest?
Return to your scabbard;
cease and be still.'
7 But how can it rest
when the LORD has commanded it,
when he has ordered it
to attack Ashkelon and the coast?"

A Message About Moab

48 Concerning Moab:

This is what the LORD Almighty, the God of Israel, says:
"Woe to Nebo, for it will be ruined.
Kiriathaim will be disgraced and captured;
the stronghold[b] will be disgraced and shattered.
2 Moab will be praised no more;
in Heshbon[c] men will plot her downfall:
'Come, let us put an end to that nation.'
You too, O Madmen,[d] will be silenced;
the sword will pursue you.
3 Listen to the cries from Horonaim,
cries of great havoc and destruction.

[a] 4 That is, Crete [b] 1 Or / *Misgab* [c] 2 The Hebrew for *Heshbon* sounds like the Hebrew for *plot.* [d] 2 The name of the Moabite town Madmen sounds like the Hebrew for *be silenced.*

(47:6–7) Your words of vengeance to Your enemies were words of hope to Your people. You would not allow the Philistines to escape Your wrath. They had delivered Your people into slavery; You would soon deliver the Philistines to the sword of war. And like the sword of Your Word that does not return to You until it accomplishes that for which it is sent, so Your sword of war would not return to its scabbard until it had accomplished its mission of vengeance. I praise You Lord, that You zealously defend Your people. (Isa 55:11)

O God of earth and altar,
Bow down and hear our cry,
Our earthly rulers falter,
Our people drift and die;
The walls of gold entomb us,
The swords of scorn divide;
Take not thy thunder from us,
But take away our pride.
G. K. Chesterton (1874-1936)

(48:7–11) Your warnings, O God, are always clear and consistent. Pride inevitably leads to captivity. The Moabites were complacent and self-sufficient. They trusted in their riches and their accomplishments. Eventually, their pride brought their fall. If You would not tolerate this in the lives of those who did not know You, how much less will You tolerate it in my life. By Your grace, give me humility so that I may live in Your favor. If I have centered my security on material possessions, forgive me. I repent of my devotion to anything and everything that has taken Your place in my life.

Thou, who still a sword delivers
Rather than a placid peace:
With Thy sharpened Word disturb
us,
From complacency release!
Save us now from satisfaction
When we privately are free,
Yet are undisturbed in spirit
By our neighbor's misery.
"Christ, Whose Purpose Is to Kindle"
D. Elton Trueblood (1900-1994)

4 Moab will be broken;
her little ones will cry out.[a]
5 They go up the way to Luhith,
weeping bitterly as they go;
on the road down to Horonaim
anguished cries over the destruction are heard.
6 Flee! Run for your lives;
become like a bush[b] in the desert.
7 Since you trust in your deeds and riches,
you too will be taken captive,
and Chemosh will go into exile,
together with his priests and officials.
8 The destroyer will come against every town,
and not a town will escape.
The valley will be ruined
and the plateau destroyed,
because the LORD has spoken.
9 Put salt on Moab,
for she will be laid waste[c];
her towns will become desolate,
with no one to live in them.

10 "A curse on him who is lax in doing the LORD's work!
A curse on him who keeps his sword from
bloodshed!

11 "Moab has been at rest from youth,
like wine left on its dregs,
not poured from one jar to another—
she has not gone into exile.
So she tastes as she did,
and her aroma is unchanged.
12 But days are coming,"
declares the LORD,
"when I will send men who pour from jars,
and they will pour her out;
they will empty her jars
and smash her jugs.
13 Then Moab will be ashamed of Chemosh,
as the house of Israel was ashamed
when they trusted in Bethel.

14 "How can you say, 'We are warriors,
men valiant in battle'?
15 Moab will be destroyed and her towns invaded;
her finest young men will go down in the slaughter,"
declares the King, whose name is the LORD Almighty.
16 "The fall of Moab is at hand;
her calamity will come quickly.
17 Mourn for her, all who live around her,
all who know her fame;
say, 'How broken is the mighty scepter,
how broken the glorious staff!'

18 "Come down from your glory
and sit on the parched ground,
O inhabitants of the Daughter of Dibon,

[a] 4 Hebrew; Septuagint */ proclaim it to Zoar* [b] 6 Or *like Aroer* [c] 9 Or *Give wings to Moab, / for she will fly away*

for he who destroys Moab
will come up against you
and ruin your fortified cities.
19 Stand by the road and watch,
you who live in Aroer.
Ask the man fleeing and the woman escaping,
ask them, 'What has happened?'
20 Moab is disgraced, for she is shattered.
Wail and cry out!
Announce by the Arnon
that Moab is destroyed.
21 Judgment has come to the plateau—
to Holon, Jahzah and Mephaath,
22 to Dibon, Nebo and Beth Diblathaim,
23 to Kiriathaim, Beth Gamul and Beth Meon,
24 to Kerioth and Bozrah—
to all the towns of Moab, far and near.
25 Moab's horn[a] is cut off;
her arm is broken,"
declares the LORD.

26 "Make her drunk,
for she has defied the LORD.
Let Moab wallow in her vomit;
let her be an object of ridicule.
27 Was not Israel the object of your ridicule?
Was she caught among thieves,
that you shake your head in scorn
whenever you speak of her?
28 Abandon your towns and dwell among the rocks,
you who live in Moab.
Be like a dove that makes its nest
at the mouth of a cave.

29 "We have heard of Moab's pride—
her overweening pride and conceit,
her pride and arrogance
and the haughtiness of her heart.
30 I know her insolence but it is futile,"
declares the LORD,
"and her boasts accomplish nothing.
31 Therefore I wail over Moab,
for all Moab I cry out,
I moan for the men of Kir Hareseth.
32 I weep for you, as Jazer weeps,
O vines of Sibmah.
Your branches spread as far as the sea;
they reached as far as the sea of Jazer.
The destroyer has fallen
on your ripened fruit and grapes.
33 Joy and gladness are gone
from the orchards and fields of Moab.
I have stopped the flow of wine from the presses;
no one treads them with shouts of joy.
Although there are shouts,
they are not shouts of joy.

[a] 25 *Horn* here symbolizes strength.

(48:29–31) Merciful God, the ruin of sinners gives You no pleasure. The Moabites brought about their own destruction by their own sin. In spite of Your warnings, they continued in their pride and arrogance. Those who sat in the midst of wealth and power would soon sit in ruins. That which brought them joy would be taken away, and they would be left with nothing to comfort them. Let no one be puffed up in pride or put their confidence in their strength or beauty, for You are not impressed with these things. Temporal riches will be driven off like leaves before the wind. But those who put their trust in You will find everlasting joy and comfort in Your presence.

34 "The sound of their cry rises
from Heshbon to Elealeh and Jahaz,
from Zoar as far as Horonaim and Eglath Shelishiyah,
for even the waters of Nimrim are dried up.
35 In Moab I will put an end
to those who make offerings on the high places
and burn incense to their gods,"
declares the LORD.
36 "So my heart laments for Moab like a flute;
it laments like a flute for the men of Kir Hareseth.
The wealth they acquired is gone.
37 Every head is shaved
and every beard cut off;
every hand is slashed
and every waist is covered with sackcloth.
38 On all the roofs in Moab
and in the public squares
there is nothing but mourning,
for I have broken Moab
like a jar that no one wants,"
declares the LORD.
39 "How shattered she is! How they wail!
How Moab turns her back in shame!
Moab has become an object of ridicule,
an object of horror to all those around her."

40 This is what the LORD says:

"Look! An eagle is swooping down,
spreading its wings over Moab.
41 Kerioth[a] will be captured
and the strongholds taken.
In that day the hearts of Moab's warriors
will be like the heart of a woman in labor.
42 Moab will be destroyed as a nation
because she defied the LORD.
43 Terror and pit and snare await you,
O people of Moab,"
declares the LORD.
44 "Whoever flees from the terror
will fall into a pit,
whoever climbs out of the pit
will be caught in a snare;
for I will bring upon Moab
the year of her punishment,"
declares the LORD.

45 "In the shadow of Heshbon
the fugitives stand helpless,
for a fire has gone out from Heshbon,
a blaze from the midst of Sihon;
it burns the foreheads of Moab,
the skulls of the noisy boasters.
46 Woe to you, O Moab!
The people of Chemosh are destroyed;
your sons are taken into exile
and your daughters into captivity.

[a] 41 Or *The cities*

Nobody can judge men but God, and we can hardly obtain a higher or more reverent view of God than that which represents him to us as judging men with perfect knowledge, unperplexed certainty, and undisturbed compassion.

Frederick William Faber (1814–1863)

(48:35–36) Even in judgment Your heart aches for those whom You afflict. You lament the lost and weep over the wanderer. Thank You, Father, for Your stunning love and saving grace. (La 3:33)

Come, ye sinners, poor and needy,
Weak and wounded, sick and sore;
Jesus ready stands to save you,
Full of pity, love and power.

"Come, Ye Sinners, Poor and Needy"
Joseph Hart (1759)

47 "Yet I will restore the fortunes of Moab
in days to come,"
declares the LORD.

Here ends the judgment on Moab.

A Message About Ammon

49 Concerning the Ammonites:

This is what the LORD says:

"Has Israel no sons?
Has she no heirs?
Why then has Molech[a] taken possession of Gad?
Why do his people live in its towns?
2 But the days are coming,"
declares the LORD,
"when I will sound the battle cry
against Rabbah of the Ammonites;
it will become a mound of ruins,
and its surrounding villages will be set on fire.
Then Israel will drive out
those who drove her out,"
says the LORD.
3 "Wail, O Heshbon, for Ai is destroyed!
Cry out, O inhabitants of Rabbah!
Put on sackcloth and mourn;
rush here and there inside the walls,
for Molech will go into exile,
together with his priests and officials.
4 Why do you boast of your valleys,
boast of your valleys so fruitful?
O unfaithful daughter,
you trust in your riches and say,
'Who will attack me?'
5 I will bring terror on you
from all those around you,"
declares the Lord, the LORD Almighty.
"Every one of you will be driven away,
and no one will gather the fugitives.

6 "Yet afterward, I will restore the fortunes of the
Ammonites,"
declares the LORD.

A Message About Edom

7 Concerning Edom:

This is what the LORD Almighty says:

"Is there no longer wisdom in Teman?
Has counsel perished from the prudent?
Has their wisdom decayed?
8 Turn and flee, hide in deep caves,
you who live in Dedan,
for I will bring disaster on Esau
at the time I punish him.
9 If grape pickers came to you,

[a] *1* Or *their king*; Hebrew *malcam*; also in verse 3

(49:4) Forgive us, Lord, for trusting in the temporal. You have warned us that if riches increase, we are not to set our hearts on them. Neither are we to be seduced by the false security they offer. Instead, we are to trust in You at all times. We are to pour our hearts out to You, for in You alone we find true refuge. (Ps 62:10b)

God is the being . . . that may properly only be addressed, not expressed.
Martin Buber (1878-1965)

(49:19) Lord of heaven, who is like You—majestic in holiness, awesome in glory, working wonders? Truly, You are incomparable! No one is like You. So we take great confidence in Who You are. You will drive out Your enemies. And in Your unfailing love You will lead the people You have redeemed. In Your strength You will guide us to Your holy dwelling. (Ex 15:11–13)

There is nobody else so worthy of
praise,
No one so wonderful in so many
ways.
You are the one who can claim the
highest place,
Up in heaven and in our hearts too.
There is nobody else, Oh Lord,
Nobody like You.

"Nobody Like You"
Bill Batstone (©1988)

would they not leave a few grapes?
If thieves came during the night,
would they not steal only as much as they wanted?
10 But I will strip Esau bare;
I will uncover his hiding places,
so that he cannot conceal himself.
His children, relatives and neighbors will perish,
and he will be no more.
11 Leave your orphans; I will protect their lives.
Your widows too can trust in me."

12 This is what the LORD says: "If those who do not deserve to
drink the cup must drink it, why should you go unpunished? You
will not go unpunished, but must drink it. 13 I swear by myself,"
declares the LORD, "that Bozrah will become a ruin and an object
of horror, of reproach and of cursing; and all its towns will be in
ruins forever."

14 I have heard a message from the LORD:
An envoy was sent to the nations to say,
"Assemble yourselves to attack it!
Rise up for battle!"

15 "Now I will make you small among the nations,
despised among men.
16 The terror you inspire
and the pride of your heart have deceived you,
you who live in the clefts of the rocks,
who occupy the heights of the hill.
Though you build your nest as high as the eagle's,
from there I will bring you down,"
declares the LORD.
17 "Edom will become an object of horror;
all who pass by will be appalled and will scoff
because of all its wounds.
18 As Sodom and Gomorrah were overthrown,
along with their neighboring towns,"
says the LORD,
"so no one will live there;
no man will dwell in it.

19 "Like a lion coming up from Jordan's thickets
to a rich pastureland,
I will chase Edom from its land in an instant.
Who is the chosen one I will appoint for this?
Who is like me and who can challenge me?
And what shepherd can stand against me?"
20 Therefore, hear what the LORD has planned against
Edom,
what he has purposed against those who live in
Teman:
The young of the flock will be dragged away;
he will completely destroy their pasture because of
them.
21 At the sound of their fall the earth will tremble;
their cry will resound to the Red Sea.[a]
22 Look! An eagle will soar and swoop down,

[a] 21 Hebrew *Yam Suph*; that is, Sea of Reeds

spreading its wings over Bozrah.
In that day the hearts of Edom's warriors
will be like the heart of a woman in labor.

A Message About Damascus

23 Concerning Damascus:

"Hamath and Arpad are dismayed,
for they have heard bad news.
They are disheartened,
troubled like[a] the restless sea.
24 Damascus has become feeble,
she has turned to flee
and panic has gripped her;
anguish and pain have seized her,
pain like that of a woman in labor.
25 Why has the city of renown not been abandoned,
the town in which I delight?
26 Surely, her young men will fall in the streets;
all her soldiers will be silenced in that day,"
declares the LORD Almighty.
27 "I will set fire to the walls of Damascus;
it will consume the fortresses of Ben-Hadad."

A Message About Kedar and Hazor

28 Concerning Kedar and the kingdoms of Hazor, which Nebuchadnezzar king of Babylon attacked:

This is what the LORD says:

"Arise, and attack Kedar
and destroy the people of the East.
29 Their tents and their flocks will be taken;
their shelters will be carried off
with all their goods and camels.
Men will shout to them,
'Terror on every side!'

30 "Flee quickly away!
Stay in deep caves, you who live in Hazor,"
declares the LORD.
"Nebuchadnezzar king of Babylon has plotted
against you;
he has devised a plan against you.

31 "Arise and attack a nation at ease,
which lives in confidence,"
declares the LORD,
"a nation that has neither gates nor bars;
its people live alone.
32 Their camels will become plunder,
and their large herds will be booty.
I will scatter to the winds those who are in distant
places[b]
and will bring disaster on them from every side,"
declares the LORD.
33 "Hazor will become a haunt of jackals,
a desolate place forever.

[a] 23 Hebrew *on* or *by* [b] 32 Or *who clip the hair by their foreheads*

(49:27) I tremble to consider the all-consuming fire of Your judgment, O God. Your anger is a direct expression of Your holiness. It is a deliberate response to the evil that plagues our world. Without it there would be no justice, either now or eternally. Your fiery judgment burns down the walls of wickedness and consumes the fortresses of fear. Your anger is always intentional, never out of control. In righteousness, it rages against all that ruins us and replaces You. So I worship You in godly fear and holy awe.

No one will live there;
no man will dwell in it."

A Message About Elam

34 This is the word of the LORD that came to Jeremiah the prophet concerning Elam, early in the reign of Zedekiah king of Judah:

35 This is what the LORD Almighty says:

"See, I will break the bow of Elam,
the mainstay of their might.
36 I will bring against Elam the four winds
from the four quarters of the heavens;
I will scatter them to the four winds,
and there will not be a nation
where Elam's exiles do not go.
37 I will shatter Elam before their foes,
before those who seek their lives;
I will bring disaster upon them,
even my fierce anger,"
declares the LORD.
"I will pursue them with the sword
until I have made an end of them.
38 I will set my throne in Elam
and destroy her king and officials,"
declares the LORD.
39 "Yet I will restore the fortunes of Elam
in days to come,"
declares the LORD.

A Message About Babylon

50 This is the word the LORD spoke through Jeremiah the prophet concerning Babylon and the land of the Babylonians[a]:

2 "Announce and proclaim among the nations,
lift up a banner and proclaim it;
keep nothing back, but say,
'Babylon will be captured;
Bel will be put to shame,
Marduk filled with terror.
Her images will be put to shame
and her idols filled with terror.'
3 A nation from the north will attack her
and lay waste her land.
No one will live in it;
both men and animals will flee away.
4 "In those days, at that time,"
declares the LORD,
"the people of Israel and the people of Judah
together
will go in tears to seek the LORD their God.
5 They will ask the way to Zion
and turn their faces toward it.
They will come and bind themselves to the LORD

(50:4–5) Thank You, Lord, for the day that You set my heart free. My captivity created in me a new hunger for You. This was Your plan. I began seeking You with tears of desperation and desire. My yearning for You helped me to start asking the right questions. I turned my face toward You, trying to find my way back to Your presence again. When I found it I bound myself to You with an eager heart, confident that You would still remember Your covenant with me. Now I praise You with freedom's new song: "The LORD has done great things for me, and I am filled with joy." (Ps 126:3)

[a] 1 Or *Chaldeans*; also in verses 8, 25, 35 and 45

in an everlasting covenant
that will not be forgotten.

6 "My people have been lost sheep;
their shepherds have led them astray
and caused them to roam on the mountains.
They wandered over mountain and hill
and forgot their own resting place.
7 Whoever found them devoured them;
their enemies said, 'We are not guilty,
for they sinned against the LORD, their true pasture,
the LORD, the hope of their fathers.'

8 "Flee out of Babylon;
leave the land of the Babylonians,
and be like the goats that lead the flock.
9 For I will stir up and bring against Babylon
an alliance of great nations from the land of the north.
They will take up their positions against her,
and from the north she will be captured.
Their arrows will be like skilled warriors
who do not return empty-handed.
10 So Babylonia[a] will be plundered;
all who plunder her will have their fill,"
declares the LORD.

11 "Because you rejoice and are glad,
you who pillage my inheritance,
because you frolic like a heifer threshing grain
and neigh like stallions,
12 your mother will be greatly ashamed;
she who gave you birth will be disgraced.
She will be the least of the nations—
a wilderness, a dry land, a desert.
13 Because of the LORD's anger she will not be inhabited
but will be completely desolate.
All who pass Babylon will be horrified and scoff
because of all her wounds.
14 "Take up your positions around Babylon,
all you who draw the bow.
Shoot at her! Spare no arrows,
for she has sinned against the LORD.
15 Shout against her on every side!
She surrenders, her towers fall,
her walls are torn down.
Since this is the vengeance of the LORD,
take vengeance on her;
do to her as she has done to others.
16 Cut off from Babylon the sower,
and the reaper with his sickle at harvest.
Because of the sword of the oppressor
let everyone return to his own people,
let everyone flee to his own land.
17 "Israel is a scattered flock
that lions have chased away.

[a] 10 Or *Chaldea*

(50:6–7) Great Shepherd, even when I have willfully wandered, You have looked upon me with compassion. You have sought me, Lord, leaving behind ninety-nine other sheep in search of one lost soul. You have understood that I not only roamed away from You, but that I was led astray. Now, at last, You have found me again, Lord. I pray that You will bring me back to Your fold, heal me, forgive me, and deal with those who have preyed on me in my weakness. (Mt 18:12–14)

Satan watches for those vessels that sail without a convoy.

George Swinnock (1627–1673)

(50:20) You, Lord, will not always accuse, nor will You harbor Your anger forever; You do not treat us as our sins deserve or repay us according to our iniquities. For as high as the heavens are above the earth, so great is Your love for those who fear You; as far as the east is from the west, so far have You removed our transgressions from us. Thank You, Lord, for full forgiveness. Indeed, "Blessed is he whose transgressions are forgiven, whose sins are covered." (Ps 32:1; 103:9–12)

Great things He hath taught us,
Great things He hath done,
And great our rejoicing
Through Jesus the Son;
But purer, and higher,
And greater will be
Our wonder, our transport,
When Jesus we see.

"To God Be the Glory"
Fanny J. Crosby (1875)

The first to devour him
was the king of Assyria;
the last to crush his bones
was Nebuchadnezzar king of Babylon."

18 Therefore this is what the LORD Almighty, the God of Israel, says:

"I will punish the king of Babylon and his land
as I punished the king of Assyria.
19 But I will bring Israel back to his own pasture
and he will graze on Carmel and Bashan;
his appetite will be satisfied
on the hills of Ephraim and Gilead.
20 In those days, at that time,"
declares the LORD,
"search will be made for Israel's guilt,
but there will be none,
and for the sins of Judah,
but none will be found,
for I will forgive the remnant I spare.

21 "Attack the land of Merathaim
and those who live in Pekod.
Pursue, kill and completely destroy[a] them,"
declares the LORD.
"Do everything I have commanded you.
22 The noise of battle is in the land,
the noise of great destruction!
23 How broken and shattered
is the hammer of the whole earth!
How desolate is Babylon
among the nations!
24 I set a trap for you, O Babylon,
and you were caught before you knew it;
you were found and captured
because you opposed the LORD.
25 The LORD has opened his arsenal
and brought out the weapons of his wrath,
for the Sovereign LORD Almighty has work to do
in the land of the Babylonians.
26 Come against her from afar.
Break open her granaries;
pile her up like heaps of grain.
Completely destroy her
and leave her no remnant.
27 Kill all her young bulls;
let them go down to the slaughter!
Woe to them! For their day has come,
the time for them to be punished.
28 Listen to the fugitives and refugees from Babylon
declaring in Zion
how the LORD our God has taken vengeance,
vengeance for his temple.

29 "Summon archers against Babylon,
all those who draw the bow.

[a] *21* The Hebrew term refers to the irrevocable giving over of things or persons to the LORD, often by totally destroying them; also in verse 26.

Encamp all around her;
let no one escape.
Repay her for her deeds;
do to her as she has done.
For she has defied the LORD,
the Holy One of Israel.
30 Therefore, her young men will fall in the streets;
all her soldiers will be silenced in that day,"
declares the LORD.
31 "See, I am against you, O arrogant one,"
declares the Lord, the LORD Almighty,
"for your day has come,
the time for you to be punished.
32 The arrogant one will stumble and fall
and no one will help her up;
I will kindle a fire in her towns
that will consume all who are around her."

33 This is what the LORD Almighty says:

"The people of Israel are oppressed,
and the people of Judah as well.
All their captors hold them fast,
refusing to let them go.
34 Yet their Redeemer is strong;
the LORD Almighty is his name.
He will vigorously defend their cause
so that he may bring rest to their land,
but unrest to those who live in Babylon.

35 "A sword against the Babylonians!"
declares the LORD—
"against those who live in Babylon
and against her officials and wise men!
36 A sword against her false prophets!
They will become fools.
A sword against her warriors!
They will be filled with terror.
37 A sword against her horses and chariots
and all the foreigners in her ranks!
They will become women.
A sword against her treasures!
They will be plundered.
38 A drought on[a] her waters!
They will dry up.
For it is a land of idols,
idols that will go mad with terror.

39 "So desert creatures and hyenas will live there,
and there the owl will dwell.
It will never again be inhabited
or lived in from generation to generation.
40 As God overthrew Sodom and Gomorrah
along with their neighboring towns,"
declares the LORD,
"so no one will live there;
no man will dwell in it.

[a] 38 Or *A sword against*

Just as Christian came up with the cross, his burden loosed from off his shoulders and fell from off his back and began to tumble, and so continued to do till it came to the mouth of the sepulcher, where it fell in, and I saw it no more.

John Bunyan (1628-1688)

(50:33–34) My Redeemer is strong; the Lord Almighty is His name. I praise You, Redeemer King, for Your rescuing strength and Your all-powerful name. Like Israel, I too was oppressed by sins and circumstances designed to defeat me. They held me fast, not wanting to let me go. But You were stronger, Lord Jesus! You triumphed once and for all over Satan's power. You set me free. I thank You that, having disarmed the powers and authorities, You made a public spectacle of them, triumphing over them by the cross. (Col 2:15)

Long my imprisoned spirit lay
Fast bound in sin and nature's night;
Thine eye diffused a quickening ray,
I woke, the dungeon flamed with light;
My chains fell off, my heart was free;
I rose, went forth and followed Thee.

"And Can It Be That I Should Gain?"
Charles Wesley (1738)

(51:5) In spite of my faithlessness, O Lord, You have always remained faithful. You have not forsaken me, even though ugly guilt has marred the landscape of my life. Even in the midst of judgment, gracious God, I am not consumed, for Your compassions never fail. They are new every morning; great is Your faithfulness. (La 3:22–23)

Hope of the world,
Thou Christ of great compassion,
Speak to our fearful hearts
By conflict rent.
Save us, Thy people,
From consuming passion,
Who by our own false hopes
And aims are spent.

"Hope of the World"
Georgia E. Harkness (©1954, 1982)

41 "Look! An army is coming from the north;
a great nation and many kings
are being stirred up from the ends of the earth.
42 They are armed with bows and spears;
they are cruel and without mercy.
They sound like the roaring sea
as they ride on their horses;
they come like men in battle formation
to attack you, O Daughter of Babylon.
43 The king of Babylon has heard reports about them,
and his hands hang limp.
Anguish has gripped him,
pain like that of a woman in labor.
44 Like a lion coming up from Jordan's thickets
to a rich pastureland,
I will chase Babylon from its land in an instant.
Who is the chosen one I will appoint for this?
Who is like me and who can challenge me?
And what shepherd can stand against me?"
45 Therefore, hear what the LORD has planned against Babylon,
what he has purposed against the land of the Babylonians:
The young of the flock will be dragged away;
he will completely destroy their pasture because of them.
46 At the sound of Babylon's capture the earth will tremble;
its cry will resound among the nations.

51

This is what the LORD says:

"See, I will stir up the spirit of a destroyer
against Babylon and the people of Leb Kamai.[a]
2 I will send foreigners to Babylon
to winnow her and to devastate her land;
they will oppose her on every side
in the day of her disaster.
3 Let not the archer string his bow,
nor let him put on his armor.
Do not spare her young men;
completely destroy[b] her army.
4 They will fall down slain in Babylon,[c]
fatally wounded in her streets.
5 For Israel and Judah have not been forsaken
by their God, the LORD Almighty,
though their land[d] is full of guilt
before the Holy One of Israel.

6 "Flee from Babylon!
Run for your lives!
Do not be destroyed because of her sins.
It is time for the LORD's vengeance;
he will pay her what she deserves.

[a] 1 *Leb Kamai* is a cryptogram for Chaldea, that is, Babylonia. [b] 3 The Hebrew term refers to the irrevocable giving over of things or persons to the LORD, often by totally destroying them. [c] 4 Or *Chaldea* [d] 5 Or / *and the land* ⌞*of the Babylonians*⌟

7 Babylon was a gold cup in the LORD's hand;
she made the whole earth drunk.
The nations drank her wine;
therefore they have now gone mad.
8 Babylon will suddenly fall and be broken.
Wail over her!
Get balm for her pain;
perhaps she can be healed.

9 " 'We would have healed Babylon,
but she cannot be healed;
let us leave her and each go to his own land,
for her judgment reaches to the skies,
it rises as high as the clouds.'

10 " 'The LORD has vindicated us;
come, let us tell in Zion
what the LORD our God has done.'

11 "Sharpen the arrows,
take up the shields!
The LORD has stirred up the kings of the Medes,
because his purpose is to destroy Babylon.
The LORD will take vengeance,
vengeance for his temple.
12 Lift up a banner against the walls of Babylon!
Reinforce the guard,
station the watchmen,
prepare an ambush!
The LORD will carry out his purpose,
his decree against the people of Babylon.
13 You who live by many waters
and are rich in treasures,
your end has come,
the time for you to be cut off.
14 The LORD Almighty has sworn by himself:
I will surely fill you with men, as with a swarm of locusts,
and they will shout in triumph over you.

15 "He made the earth by his power;
he founded the world by his wisdom
and stretched out the heavens by his understanding.
16 When he thunders, the waters in the heavens roar;
he makes clouds rise from the ends of the earth.
He sends lightning with the rain
and brings out the wind from his storehouses.

17 "Every man is senseless and without knowledge;
every goldsmith is shamed by his idols.
His images are a fraud;
they have no breath in them.
18 They are worthless, the objects of mockery;
when their judgment comes, they will perish.
19 He who is the Portion of Jacob is not like these,
for he is the Maker of all things,
including the tribe of his inheritance—
the LORD Almighty is his name.

20 "You are my war club,

(51:10) Thank You, Lord, for Your vindication and Your validation. You have forgiven, freed and filled me. Your works are wonderful, well beyond what I deserve. I praise You for Your great power, Your endless love and Your patience with me. For You have rescued me from the dominion of darkness and brought me into the kingdom of Jesus, the Son Whom You love, in Whom I have redemption, the forgiveness of sins. (Col 1:13–14)

(51:15) We praise You, Lord, that by Your great power, wisdom and understanding You created all things and You sustain all things. And by the same power, wisdom and understanding You accomplish Your will in us. Now to You Who are able to do immeasurably more than all we ask or imagine, to You be glory in the church and in Christ Jesus throughout all generations, for ever and ever! Amen. (Eph 3:20)

Do we want to contemplate his power? We see it in the immensity of the creation. Do we want to contemplate his wisdom? We see it in the unchangeable order by which the incomprehensible whole is governed. Do we want to contemplate his munificence? We see it in the abundance with which he fills the earth. Do we want to contemplate his mercy? We see it in his not withholding that abundance even from the unthankful.

Thomas Paine (1737-1809)

(51:29–37) Forgiving God, not only do You remove our sins as far as the east is from the west, but after You have disciplined us, You break the rod of punishment over Your knee. You have even eliminated our shame, and taken away our reproach. We praise and thank You for Your work of complete redemption, and for restoring our innocence.

Whoever defends himself will have himself for his defense, and he will have no other. But let him come defenseless before the Lord and he will have for his defender no less than God himself.

A.W. Tozer (1897-1963)

Lord, enthroned in heavenly
splendor,
First begotten from the dead,
You alone, our strong defender,
Lifting up Your people's head.
Alleluia! Alleluia! Alleluia!
Jesus, true and living bread!
Jesus, true and living bread!

"Lord, Enthroned in Heavenly Splendor"
George Hugh Bourne (1874)

my weapon for battle—
with you I shatter nations,
with you I destroy kingdoms,
21 with you I shatter horse and rider,
with you I shatter chariot and driver,
22 with you I shatter man and woman,
with you I shatter old man and youth,
with you I shatter young man and maiden,
23 with you I shatter shepherd and flock,
with you I shatter farmer and oxen,
with you I shatter governors and officials.

24 "Before your eyes I will repay Babylon and all who live in
Babylonia[a] for all the wrong they have done in Zion," declares
the LORD.

25 "I am against you, O destroying mountain,
you who destroy the whole earth,"
declares the LORD.
"I will stretch out my hand against you,
roll you off the cliffs,
and make you a burned-out mountain.
26 No rock will be taken from you for a cornerstone,
nor any stone for a foundation,
for you will be desolate forever,"
declares the LORD.

27 "Lift up a banner in the land!
Blow the trumpet among the nations!
Prepare the nations for battle against her;
summon against her these kingdoms:
Ararat, Minni and Ashkenaz.
Appoint a commander against her;
send up horses like a swarm of locusts.
28 Prepare the nations for battle against her—
the kings of the Medes,
their governors and all their officials,
and all the countries they rule.
29 The land trembles and writhes,
for the LORD's purposes against Babylon stand—
to lay waste the land of Babylon
so that no one will live there.
30 Babylon's warriors have stopped fighting;
they remain in their strongholds.
Their strength is exhausted;
they have become like women.
Her dwellings are set on fire;
the bars of her gates are broken.
31 One courier follows another
and messenger follows messenger
to announce to the king of Babylon
that his entire city is captured,
32 the river crossings seized,
the marshes set on fire,
and the soldiers terrified."

33 This is what the LORD Almighty, the God of Israel, says:

[a] *24* Or *Chaldea*; also in verse 35

"The Daughter of Babylon is like a threshing floor
at the time it is trampled;
the time to harvest her will soon come."

34 "Nebuchadnezzar king of Babylon has devoured us,
he has thrown us into confusion,
he has made us an empty jar.
Like a serpent he has swallowed us
and filled his stomach with our delicacies,
and then has spewed us out.

35 May the violence done to our flesh[a] be upon
Babylon,"
say the inhabitants of Zion.
"May our blood be on those who live in Babylonia,"
says Jerusalem.

36 Therefore, this is what the LORD says:

"See, I will defend your cause
and avenge you;
I will dry up her sea
and make her springs dry.

37 Babylon will be a heap of ruins,
a haunt of jackals,
an object of horror and scorn,
a place where no one lives.

38 Her people all roar like young lions,
they growl like lion cubs.

39 But while they are aroused,
I will set out a feast for them
and make them drunk,
so that they shout with laughter—
then sleep forever and not awake,"
declares the LORD.

40 "I will bring them down
like lambs to the slaughter,
like rams and goats.

41 "How Sheshach[b] will be captured,
the boast of the whole earth seized!
What a horror Babylon will be
among the nations!

42 The sea will rise over Babylon;
its roaring waves will cover her.

43 Her towns will be desolate,
a dry and desert land,
a land where no one lives,
through which no man travels.

44 I will punish Bel in Babylon
and make him spew out what he has swallowed.
The nations will no longer stream to him.
And the wall of Babylon will fall.

45 "Come out of her, my people!
Run for your lives!
Run from the fierce anger of the LORD.

46 Do not lose heart or be afraid
when rumors are heard in the land;

[a] 35 Or *done to us and to our children* [b] 41 *Sheshach* is a cryptogram for Babylon.

(51:45) Thank You, dear Father, for the clear and uncompromising call to "come out" from the spiritual pollutants that poison our hearts and draw us away from You. Let us never forget that You want us for Yourself, and that You will share us with no other. So we come out from among them and separate ourselves to You, O Lord, so that You might be a Father to us, receiving us as Your own sons and daughters. In You, and in no other, is life, blessing and well-being. (2Co 6:17–18)

Lord, I offer up my body as a living
sacrifice,
Holy and pleasing to You.
Lord, I offer up my body as a living
sacrifice,
Holy and pleasing to You.

The pattern of this world, I will deny
it.
The pattern of this world, I will deny
it.
Lord, renew my mind that I can find
That good and perfect will.

"Holy and Pleasing"
Walt Harrah (©1992)

Measure not God's love and favor by your own feeling. The sun shines as clearly in the darkest day as it does in the brightest. The difference is not in the sun, but in some clouds.

Richard Sibbs (1577-1635)

(51:50) "Remember the LORD in a distant land." When everything else is stripped away from us, when loss overwhelms us and failure disables us, You are waiting. The moment we remember You, You reach out to us with helping, healing hands. In You is hope, forgiveness and restoration—all that we need to begin again. Thank You for Your constancy, O Lord. Whenever we feel farthest away from You, You are never more than a prayer away from us.

I call to You from out of the deep,
O Lord, most high,
Aware of my sin and the distance I
keep
From the light, O Lord;
But there is forgiveness with Thee
And in wonder I fall on my knees.

My soul waits for the Lord
In the hope of His promise,
In the hope of His promise
Deliverance will come.
My souls waits for the Lord
Through the night till the morning,
Like a night watchman waiting
For the coming of the dawn.

"My Soul Waits"
(Psalm 130)
Bill Batstone (©1986)

one rumor comes this year, another the next,
rumors of violence in the land
and of ruler against ruler.
47 For the time will surely come
when I will punish the idols of Babylon;
her whole land will be disgraced
and her slain will all lie fallen within her.
48 Then heaven and earth and all that is in them
will shout for joy over Babylon,
for out of the north
destroyers will attack her,"
declares the LORD.

49 "Babylon must fall because of Israel's slain,
just as the slain in all the earth
have fallen because of Babylon.
50 You who have escaped the sword,
leave and do not linger!
Remember the LORD in a distant land,
and think on Jerusalem."

51 "We are disgraced,
for we have been insulted
and shame covers our faces,
because foreigners have entered
the holy places of the LORD's house."

52 "But days are coming," declares the LORD,
"when I will punish her idols,
and throughout her land
the wounded will groan.
53 Even if Babylon reaches the sky
and fortifies her lofty stronghold,
I will send destroyers against her,"
declares the LORD.

54 "The sound of a cry comes from Babylon,
the sound of great destruction
from the land of the Babylonians.[a]
55 The LORD will destroy Babylon;
he will silence her noisy din.
Waves ⌊of enemies⌋ will rage like great waters;
the roar of their voices will resound.
56 A destroyer will come against Babylon;
her warriors will be captured,
and their bows will be broken.
For the LORD is a God of retribution;
he will repay in full.
57 I will make her officials and wise men drunk,
her governors, officers and warriors as well;
they will sleep forever and not awake,"
declares the King, whose name is the LORD
Almighty.

58 This is what the LORD Almighty says:

"Babylon's thick wall will be leveled
and her high gates set on fire;

[a] 54 Or *Chaldeans*

the peoples exhaust themselves for nothing,
the nations' labor is only fuel for the flames."

59This is the message Jeremiah gave to the staff officer Seraiah
son of Neriah, the son of Mahseiah, when he went to Babylon with
Zedekiah king of Judah in the fourth year of his reign. 60Jeremi-
ah had written on a scroll about all the disasters that would come
upon Babylon—all that had been recorded concerning Babylon.
61He said to Seraiah, "When you get to Babylon, see that you read
all these words aloud. 62Then say, 'O LORD, you have said you will
destroy this place, so that neither man nor animal will live in it; it
will be desolate forever.' 63When you finish reading this scroll, tie
a stone to it and throw it into the Euphrates. 64Then say, 'So will
Babylon sink to rise no more because of the disaster I will bring
upon her. And her people will fall.' "

The words of Jeremiah end here.

The Fall of Jerusalem

52 Zedekiah was twenty-one years old when he became king,
and he reigned in Jerusalem eleven years. His mother's
name was Hamutal daughter of Jeremiah; she was from Libnah.
2He did evil in the eyes of the LORD, just as Jehoiakim had done.
3It was because of the LORD's anger that all this happened to Jerusalem and Judah, and in the end he thrust them from his presence.

Now Zedekiah rebelled against the king of Babylon.

4So in the ninth year of Zedekiah's reign, on the tenth day of
the tenth month, Nebuchadnezzar king of Babylon marched
against Jerusalem with his whole army. They camped outside the
city and built siege works all around it. 5The city was kept under
siege until the eleventh year of King Zedekiah.

6By the ninth day of the fourth month the famine in the city had
become so severe that there was no food for the people to eat.
7Then the city wall was broken through, and the whole army fled.
They left the city at night through the gate between the two walls
near the king's garden, though the Babylonians[a] were surrounding the city. They fled toward the Arabah,[b] 8but the Babylonian[c]
army pursued King Zedekiah and overtook him in the plains of
Jericho. All his soldiers were separated from him and scattered,
9and he was captured.

He was taken to the king of Babylon at Riblah in the land of Hamath, where he pronounced sentence on him. 10There at Riblah
the king of Babylon slaughtered the sons of Zedekiah before his
eyes; he also killed all the officials of Judah. 11Then he put out
Zedekiah's eyes, bound him with bronze shackles and took him
to Babylon, where he put him in prison till the day of his death.

12On the tenth day of the fifth month, in the nineteenth year of
Nebuchadnezzar king of Babylon, Nebuzaradan commander of
the imperial guard, who served the king of Babylon, came to Jerusalem. 13He set fire to the temple of the LORD, the royal palace
and all the houses of Jerusalem. Every important building he
burned down. 14The whole Babylonian army under the commander of the imperial guard broke down all the walls around Jerusalem. 15Nebuzaradan the commander of the guard carried
into exile some of the poorest people and those who remained in

[a] 7 Or *Chaldeans*; also in verse 17 [b] 7 Or *the Jordan Valley* [c] 8 Or *Chaldean*; also in verse 14

(52:13) Lord, You warned Your people of impending danger. You spoke of dire consequences. You cautioned them not to trifle with Your anger. Yet over and over they ignored Your warnings and did not repent, thinking there would be no judgment. They replaced Your words of warning with wishful thinking. And because they would not faithfully tend the fire of the altar, You allowed the enemy to set fire to the temple. If You could not have their relationship, then You would not have their religion. Help us, Lord, to learn from their tragic impudence. Teach us to listen, to believe, to realize that Your words of judgment are never idle nor empty, and that they can only be turned aside by our wholehearted repentance. (Jer 21:10)

The love of God, with arms extended on a cross, bars the way to hell. But if that love is ignored, rejected, and finally refused, there comes a time when love can only weep while man pushes past into the self-chosen alienation which Christ went to the cross to avert.

Michael Green (1930-)

the city, along with the rest of the craftsmen[a] and those who had
gone over to the king of Babylon. 16But Nebuzaradan left behind
the rest of the poorest people of the land to work the vineyards
and fields.

17The Babylonians broke up the bronze pillars, the movable
stands and the bronze Sea that were at the temple of the LORD and
they carried all the bronze to Babylon. 18They also took away the
pots, shovels, wick trimmers, sprinkling bowls, dishes and all the
bronze articles used in the temple service. 19The commander of
the imperial guard took away the basins, censers, sprinkling
bowls, pots, lampstands, dishes and bowls used for drink offerings—all that were made of pure gold or silver.

20The bronze from the two pillars, the Sea and the twelve
bronze bulls under it, and the movable stands, which King Solomon had made for the temple of the LORD, was more than could
be weighed. 21Each of the pillars was eighteen cubits high and
twelve cubits in circumference[b]; each was four fingers thick, and
hollow. 22The bronze capital on top of the one pillar was five cubits[c] high and was decorated with a network and pomegranates
of bronze all around. The other pillar, with its pomegranates, was
similar. 23There were ninety-six pomegranates on the sides; the
total number of pomegranates above the surrounding network
was a hundred.

24The commander of the guard took as prisoners Seraiah the
chief priest, Zephaniah the priest next in rank and the three doorkeepers. 25Of those still in the city, he took the officer in charge
of the fighting men, and seven royal advisers. He also took the
secretary who was chief officer in charge of conscripting the people of the land and sixty of his men who were found in the city.
26Nebuzaradan the commander took them all and brought them
to the king of Babylon at Riblah. 27There at Riblah, in the land of
Hamath, the king had them executed.

So Judah went into captivity, away from her land. 28This is the
number of the people Nebuchadnezzar carried into exile:

in the seventh year, 3,023 Jews;
29in Nebuchadnezzar's eighteenth year,
832 people from Jerusalem;
30in his twenty-third year,
745 Jews taken into exile by Nebuzaradan the commander of the imperial guard.
There were 4,600 people in all.

Jehoiachin Released

31In the thirty-seventh year of the exile of Jehoiachin king of
Judah, in the year Evil-Merodach[d] became king of Babylon, he
released Jehoiachin king of Judah and freed him from prison on
the twenty-fifth day of the twelfth month. 32He spoke kindly to
him and gave him a seat of honor higher than those of the other
kings who were with him in Babylon. 33So Jehoiachin put aside
his prison clothes and for the rest of his life ate regularly at the
king's table. 34Day by day the king of Babylon gave Jehoiachin a
regular allowance as long as he lived, till the day of his death.

[a] 15 Or *populace* [b] 21 That is, about 27 feet (about 8.1 meters) high and 18 feet (about 5.4 meters) in circumference [c] 22 That is, about 7 1/2 feet (about 2.3 meters) [d] 31 Also called *Amel-Marduk*

(52:17–23) The Babylonians were allowed to dismantle Your temple, O God, because Your people had found security in Your house without giving You their hearts. How we thank You that You are now building up a new Temple, a true house of praise made of living, human stones, with Your Son Jesus Christ as both the cornerstone and the capstone. In Him, You are building us together to become a dwelling in which You live by Your Spirit. How we praise You for Your promise: "I will build my church, and the gates of Hades will not overcome it." (Mt 16:18; Eph 2:22; 1Pe 2:4–8)

O Christ the great foundation
On which Your people stand
To preach Your true salvation
In every age and land:
Pour out Your Holy Spirit
To make us strong and pure,
To keep the faith unbroken
As long as worlds endure.

Where tyrants' hold is tightened,
Where strong devour the weak,
Where innocents are frightened,
The righteous fear to speak,
There let Your church awaking
Attack the powers of sin
And, all their ramparts breaking,
With You the victory win.

"O Christ the Great Foundation"
Timothy T'ing Fang Lew (©1977)

The LAMENTATIONS *of Jeremiah*

This book is well-named: It contains the sorrowful expressions of a writer and a nation as they grieve the destruction of Jerusalem by Babylon in 586 B.C. Though the text does not identify its author, tradition has attributed Lamentations to the prophet Jeremiah. This attribution cannot be proven, but undeniably the writer of these laments shares both Jeremiah's theological vision and the gut-wrenching experience of Judah's devastation.

According to Lamentations, the fall of Jerusalem was not merely a matter of human conquest: "The LORD has brought her grief because of her many sins" (1:5). God, Who is righteous and faithful in fulfilling His word, has finally punished His chosen people for their repeated rejection of Him and His law. With Jerusalem in flames, the temple destroyed, and the survivors led away into Babylonian exile, God's judgment is strict and painful.

Lamentations contains bold complaints against God as well as cries for mercy. Though God's righteousness is never questioned, the writer freely pours out his grief and discouragement. His example spurs us on to greater boldness in our prayers. When we fall into despair, when we wonder whether God has abandoned us, we can lay our hearts before the Lord without constraint or censorship.

Lamentations includes one of the most beloved of all Biblical passages: "Because of the LORD's great love we are not consumed, for his compassions never fail. They are new every morning; great is your faithfulness" (3:22–23). How different these verses sound when they are read in context: "[The LORD] has broken my teeth with gravel; he has trampled me in the dust . . . I remember my affliction and my wandering, the bitterness and the gall . . . Yet this I call to mind and therefore I have hope: Because of the LORD's great love we are not consumed, for his compassions never fail" (3:16,19,21–22). This moving confession of God's love comes not in the pleasure of prosperity but in the agony of adversity. God seeks from us not nice words, but intimate relationship, even and especially when that relationship is being refined in the fire of adversity.

God seeks from us not nice words, but intimate relationship, even and especially when that relationship is being refined in the fire of adversity.

Lamentations ends with a confession of God's sovereignty and a plea for restoration: "You, O LORD, reign forever; your throne endures from generation to generation. Why do you always forget us? Why do you forsake us so long? Restore us to yourself, O LORD, that we may return; renew our days as of old unless you have utterly rejected us and are angry with us beyond measure" (5:19–22). When our lives are shattered, nothing matters more than to be reconciled to God, Who alone can restore our broken relationship with Himself. The great news of the gospel is that God not only allows such restoration but that He seeks us when we are lost (Lk 15:4–7).

Lamentations

1[a] How deserted lies the city,
once so full of people!
How like a widow is she,
who once was great among the nations!
She who was queen among the provinces
has now become a slave.

2 Bitterly she weeps at night,
tears are upon her cheeks.
Among all her lovers
there is none to comfort her.
All her friends have betrayed her;
they have become her enemies.

3 After affliction and harsh labor,
Judah has gone into exile.
She dwells among the nations;
she finds no resting place.
All who pursue her have overtaken her
in the midst of her distress.

4 The roads to Zion mourn,
for no one comes to her appointed feasts.
All her gateways are desolate,
her priests groan,
her maidens grieve,
and she is in bitter anguish.

5 Her foes have become her masters;
her enemies are at ease.
The LORD has brought her grief
because of her many sins.
Her children have gone into exile,
captive before the foe.

6 All the splendor has departed
from the Daughter of Zion.
Her princes are like deer
that find no pasture;
in weakness they have fled
before the pursuer.

7 In the days of her affliction and wandering
Jerusalem remembers all the treasures
that were hers in days of old.
When her people fell into enemy hands,
there was no one to help her.
Her enemies looked at her
and laughed at her destruction.

8 Jerusalem has sinned greatly
and so has become unclean.
All who honored her despise her,
for they have seen her nakedness;
she herself groans
and turns away.

9 Her filthiness clung to her skirts;
she did not consider her future.

[a] This chapter is an acrostic poem, the verses of which begin with the successive letters of the Hebrew alphabet.

(1:1) The city, Lord—not just any city: Your city, the city You built, the city You love most of all, the city of which glorious things are spoken, the very city of God. How can it be that You let the city You have made—indeed, even Your whole perfect creation—groan with weeping and affliction? Even when Your heart yearns to comfort Your people under the safety of Your wings, yet in Your merciful and mysterious wisdom we are allowed to suffer. O the depth of Your riches, wisdom and knowledge! How unsearchable are Your judgments and unfathomable Your ways! (Ps 87:1–3; Mt 23:37; Ro 8:22; 11:33)

God seeks from us not nice words, but intimate relationship, even and especially when that relationship is being refined in the fire of adversity.

Show us Your Spirit, brooding o'er each city
As You once wept above Jerusalem,
Seeking to gather all in love and pity,
And healing those who touch Your garment's hem.

"O Jesus Christ, May Grateful Hymns Be Rising"
Bradford G. Webster (©1954)

Her fall was astounding;
 there was none to comfort her.
"Look, O LORD, on my affliction,
 for the enemy has triumphed."

10 The enemy laid hands
 on all her treasures;
she saw pagan nations
 enter her sanctuary—
those you had forbidden
 to enter your assembly.

11 All her people groan
 as they search for bread;
they barter their treasures for food
 to keep themselves alive.
"Look, O LORD, and consider,
 for I am despised."

12 "Is it nothing to you, all you who pass by?
 Look around and see.
Is any suffering like my suffering
 that was inflicted on me,
that the LORD brought on me
 in the day of his fierce anger?

13 "From on high he sent fire,
 sent it down into my bones.
He spread a net for my feet
 and turned me back.
He made me desolate,
 faint all the day long.

14 "My sins have been bound into a yoke[a];
 by his hands they were woven together.
They have come upon my neck
 and the Lord has sapped my strength.
He has handed me over
 to those I cannot withstand.

15 "The Lord has rejected
 all the warriors in my midst;
he has summoned an army against me
 to[b] crush my young men.
In his winepress the Lord has trampled
 the Virgin Daughter of Judah.

16 "This is why I weep
 and my eyes overflow with tears.
No one is near to comfort me,
 no one to restore my spirit.
My children are destitute
 because the enemy has prevailed."

17 Zion stretches out her hands,
 but there is no one to comfort her.
The LORD has decreed for Jacob
 that his neighbors become his foes;

[a] *14* Most Hebrew manuscripts; Septuagint *He kept watch over my sins* [b] *15* Or *has set a time for me / when he will*

(1:12) In times of suffering, Lord, no one seems to understand. I feel so heavy, so hopeless, so completely alone. Yet You have come as One Who was despised and rejected, a "man of sorrows, familiar with suffering." Surely You know my grief and have carried my sorrows all the way to the cross. Surely You do understand. You know what I feel. You have not passed by, leaving me alone. I do believe this, but still I wonder sometimes if You have forsaken me. In my suffering I cry, "Why are you so far from saving me, so far from the words of my groaning?" (Ps 22:1; Isa 53:3–4)

God is a specialist when the anguish is deep. His ability to heal the soul is profound . . . but only those who rely on his wounded Son will experience relief.

Charles R. Swindoll (1934-)

(1:14) My rebellions against You drag me down. From this yoke I cannot escape, nor find relief. But You, O God, bear me up each day. Through Christ You offer to take away the tiresome burden of my sin and to replace it with the easy yoke of grace-filled obedience. I receive Your invitation with joy: "Come to me, all you who are weary and burdened, and I will give You rest." (Ps 68:19; Mt 11:28–30).

Man is born with his face turned away from God. When he truly repents, he is turned right round toward God; he leaves his old life.

Dwight Lyman Moody (1837-1899)

(1:18) Whatever would cause me to admit my rebellion? Blinded by sin, mired in its muck, sinking ever deeper . . . how can I even see my sin—let alone humbly confess it to You—unless You help me? Indeed, Your kindness leads me to repentance. Your Spirit graciously makes me aware of my sin. The sorrow that You give, O Savior, leads to repentance and salvation. All praise be to You because You have come to call not the righteous, but sinners like me, to repentance. (Lk 5:32; Jn 16:7–11; Ro 2:4; 2Co 7:10)

Once we had not received
Your tender mercies;
Once we were not a people.
Once we deserved Your curse,
But You pursued us first;
You came to seek and save.

With cords of kindness,
You drew us to Your side,
Spoke tenderly to us
And loved us as Your bride.
With cords of kindness,
You drew us to the cross
And lifted from our eyes
The veil of blindness.
You drew us with
Your cords of kindness.

"Cords of Kindness"
Mark Altrogge (©1994)

Jerusalem has become
an unclean thing among them.

18 "The LORD is righteous,
yet I rebelled against his command.
Listen, all you peoples;
look upon my suffering.
My young men and maidens
have gone into exile.

19 "I called to my allies
but they betrayed me.
My priests and my elders
perished in the city
while they searched for food
to keep themselves alive.

20 "See, O LORD, how distressed I am!
I am in torment within,
and in my heart I am disturbed,
for I have been most rebellious.
Outside, the sword bereaves;
inside, there is only death.

21 "People have heard my groaning,
but there is no one to comfort me.
All my enemies have heard of my distress;
they rejoice at what you have done.
May you bring the day you have announced
so they may become like me.

22 "Let all their wickedness come before you;
deal with them
as you have dealt with me
because of all my sins.
My groans are many
and my heart is faint."

2[a] How the Lord has covered the Daughter of Zion
with the cloud of his anger[b]!
He has hurled down the splendor of Israel
from heaven to earth;
he has not remembered his footstool
in the day of his anger.

2 Without pity the Lord has swallowed up
all the dwellings of Jacob;
in his wrath he has torn down
the strongholds of the Daughter of Judah.
He has brought her kingdom and its princes
down to the ground in dishonor.

3 In fierce anger he has cut off
every horn[c] of Israel.
He has withdrawn his right hand
at the approach of the enemy.

[a] This chapter is an acrostic poem, the verses of which begin with the successive letters of the Hebrew alphabet. [b] *1* Or *How the Lord in his anger / has treated the Daughter of Zion with contempt* [c] *3* Or */ all the strength*; or *every king*; *horn* here symbolizes strength.

He has burned in Jacob like a flaming fire
that consumes everything around it.

4 Like an enemy he has strung his bow;
his right hand is ready.
Like a foe he has slain
all who were pleasing to the eye;
he has poured out his wrath like fire
on the tent of the Daughter of Zion.

5 The Lord is like an enemy;
he has swallowed up Israel.
He has swallowed up all her palaces
and destroyed her strongholds.
He has multiplied mourning and lamentation
for the Daughter of Judah.

6 He has laid waste his dwelling like a garden;
he has destroyed his place of meeting.
The LORD has made Zion forget
her appointed feasts and her Sabbaths;
in his fierce anger he has spurned
both king and priest.

7 The Lord has rejected his altar
and abandoned his sanctuary.
He has handed over to the enemy
the walls of her palaces;
they have raised a shout in the house of the LORD
as on the day of an appointed feast.

8 The LORD determined to tear down
the wall around the Daughter of Zion.
He stretched out a measuring line
and did not withhold his hand from destroying.
He made ramparts and walls lament;
together they wasted away.

9 Her gates have sunk into the ground;
their bars he has broken and destroyed.
Her king and her princes are exiled among the nations,
the law is no more,
and her prophets no longer find
visions from the LORD.

10 The elders of the Daughter of Zion
sit on the ground in silence;
they have sprinkled dust on their heads
and put on sackcloth.
The young women of Jerusalem
have bowed their heads to the ground.

11 My eyes fail from weeping,
I am in torment within,
my heart is poured out on the ground
because my people are destroyed,
because children and infants faint
in the streets of the city.

12 They say to their mothers,
"Where is bread and wine?"

(2:5) O God, You once promised to fight on my side. Now at times You seem like my enemy. Have I turned You against me by loving this world more than You? Indeed, my friendship with the world is enmity with You. Yet here I marvel at the mystery and magnitude of Your grace. While we were enemies, in the midst of my betrayal and rebellion, You reconciled me to Yourself through the death of Your only Son. No longer enemies, in Christ we have become friends. (Ex 14:14; Ro 5:10; Jas 4:4)

(2:6–7) It seems that it would be so easy for You, all-powerful God, to punish us in a way that was safe for You. You could simply throw thunderbolts from a distant heaven while hiding behind a cloud. But You have destroyed Your own dwelling, Your sanctuary, the altar for Your offerings. You have determined to share in the penalty that we alone deserve. You have allowed even Your own name and house to be dishonored. Centuries before You sent Your Son, You revealed Yourself as a God Who is neither safe, nor hidden in Your own safety. So You are today. (Jer 44:1–6; 52:13)

The judgment of God is the reaping that comes from sowing and is evidence of the love of God, not proof of his wrath. The penalty of an evil harvest is not God's punishment; it is the consequence of defying the moral order which in love he maintains as the only environment in which maturity of fellowship and communion can be achieved.

Kirby Page (1890-1957)

(2:13) Our wound is so deep, our agony so grating, and the pain is made worse by the thought that it comes from You, the Healer of our Souls. If Your arrows have pierced us because of our sin, where is our hope? How will we be made whole? "Come, let us return to the LORD. He has torn us to pieces but he will heal us; he has injured us but he will bind up our wounds." You, O Lord, can heal the incurable. You have been pierced for our transgressions, crushed for our iniquities. By Your wounds we are healed; our broken hearts are restored. "How good it is to sing praises to our God, how pleasant and fitting to praise him!" (Ps 38:1–8; 147:1–3; Isa 53:5; Jer 30:15–17; Hos 6:1)

(2:15) "Great is the LORD, and most worthy of praise, in the city of our God, his holy mountain." Now in this city, Lord, Your greatness is diminished. Your holy mountain is overrun with vileness. "Beautiful in its loftiness"—now ugly and debased. "The joy of the whole earth"—now scorned by all who pass by. With Your suffering people ages ago, we too long for the new Jerusalem yet to come. Then You will dwell with us forever, and we will be Your people. You will wipe every tear from our eyes; death and mourning will pass away. You will make everything new! (Ps 48:1–2; Rev 21:1–5)

as they faint like wounded men
in the streets of the city,
as their lives ebb away
in their mothers' arms.

13 What can I say for you?
With what can I compare you,
O Daughter of Jerusalem?
To what can I liken you,
that I may comfort you,
O Virgin Daughter of Zion?
Your wound is as deep as the sea.
Who can heal you?

14 The visions of your prophets
were false and worthless;
they did not expose your sin
to ward off your captivity.
The oracles they gave you
were false and misleading.

15 All who pass your way
clap their hands at you;
they scoff and shake their heads
at the Daughter of Jerusalem:
"Is this the city that was called
the perfection of beauty,
the joy of the whole earth?"

16 All your enemies open their mouths
wide against you;
they scoff and gnash their teeth
and say, "We have swallowed her up.
This is the day we have waited for;
we have lived to see it."

17 The LORD has done what he planned;
he has fulfilled his word,
which he decreed long ago.
He has overthrown you without pity,
he has let the enemy gloat over you,
he has exalted the horn[a] of your foes.

18 The hearts of the people
cry out to the Lord.
O wall of the Daughter of Zion,
let your tears flow like a river
day and night;
give yourself no relief,
your eyes no rest.

19 Arise, cry out in the night,
as the watches of the night begin;
pour out your heart like water
in the presence of the Lord.
Lift up your hands to him
for the lives of your children,
who faint from hunger
at the head of every street.

[a] 17 *Horn* here symbolizes strength.

20 "Look, O LORD, and consider:
Whom have you ever treated like this?
Should women eat their offspring,
the children they have cared for?
Should priest and prophet be killed
in the sanctuary of the Lord?

21 "Young and old lie together
in the dust of the streets;
my young men and maidens
have fallen by the sword.
You have slain them in the day of your anger;
you have slaughtered them without pity.

22 "As you summon to a feast day,
so you summoned against me terrors on every side.
In the day of the LORD's anger
no one escaped or survived;
those I cared for and reared,
my enemy has destroyed."

3[a] I am the man who has seen affliction
by the rod of his wrath.
2 He has driven me away and made me walk
in darkness rather than light;
3 indeed, he has turned his hand against me
again and again, all day long.

4 He has made my skin and my flesh grow old
and has broken my bones.
5 He has besieged me and surrounded me
with bitterness and hardship.
6 He has made me dwell in darkness
like those long dead.

7 He has walled me in so I cannot escape;
he has weighed me down with chains.
8 Even when I call out or cry for help,
he shuts out my prayer.
9 He has barred my way with blocks of stone;
he has made my paths crooked.

10 Like a bear lying in wait,
like a lion in hiding,
11 he dragged me from the path and mangled me
and left me without help.
12 He drew his bow
and made me the target for his arrows.

13 He pierced my heart
with arrows from his quiver.
14 I became the laughingstock of all my people;
they mock me in song all day long.
15 He has filled me with bitter herbs
and sated me with gall.

16 He has broken my teeth with gravel;
he has trampled me in the dust.

[a] This chapter is an acrostic poem; the verses of each stanza begin with the successive letters of the Hebrew alphabet, and the verses within each stanza begin with the same letter.

(3:2) Apart from You, Light of the World, I walked in darkness. I lived in gloom. Like the rest of humanity, I loved the darkness instead of Your light because my deeds were evil. In desperation, I looked to earthly flames and demonic fires for enlightenment, but they were soon snuffed out. Then I heard Your call: "Let him who walks in the dark, who has no light, trust in the name of the LORD and rely on his God." I saw Your blazing light dawning in Christ, Who is the Light of the World. Now I know that whoever follows You will never walk in darkness, but will have the light of life. (Isa 9:1–2; 50:10; Jn 3:19; 8:12)

(3:22–23) In my pit of disabling despair, in my moment of dreadful doubt, when hope has departed and deliverance is delayed, then Your Spirit whispers to my soul, reminding me of Who You really are. Though I may not feel it now, still I believe that Your steadfast love never ceases. You will never forget me. You will never forsake me. Nothing in all creation can separate me from Your eternal love. Even in my dark valley of death, You are always there. Praise be to You, O God with us, Immanuel! (Ro 8:38–39)

(3:31–33) O Heavenly Father, when we sin against You, You do not abandon us. Rather, You train us to be more like You. You did not create us to torment us, but to treasure us. Your chastisement flows from the depth of Your charity. So great is Your love for us that You have taken our sin upon Yourself in Your Son, so that we might live forever as Your beloved children. (2Co 5:21; Heb 12:5–11)

(3:38–42) You decreed long ago, O Lord, that if we walked in Your way we would be blessed, but if we departed from Your path we would be cursed. Is it any wonder that my sin has led to devastation? Yet even my suffering is a gift from You, a generous reminder of how much I need You. How could I not return to You, leaving the defilement of my sin to dwell in the purity of Your grace? For the promise You give to those who return to You is not only to receive us home in the embrace of Your merciful love, but also to crown our heads with everlasting joy. (Dt 4:23–31; Isa 51:11)

17 I have been deprived of peace;
I have forgotten what prosperity is.
18 So I say, "My splendor is gone
and all that I had hoped from the LORD."

19 I remember my affliction and my wandering,
the bitterness and the gall.
20 I well remember them,
and my soul is downcast within me.
21 Yet this I call to mind
and therefore I have hope:

22 Because of the LORD's great love we are not consumed,
for his compassions never fail.
23 They are new every morning;
great is your faithfulness.
24 I say to myself, "The LORD is my portion;
therefore I will wait for him."

25 The LORD is good to those whose hope is in him,
to the one who seeks him;
26 it is good to wait quietly
for the salvation of the LORD.
27 It is good for a man to bear the yoke
while he is young.

28 Let him sit alone in silence,
for the LORD has laid it on him.
29 Let him bury his face in the dust—
there may yet be hope.
30 Let him offer his cheek to one who would strike him,
and let him be filled with disgrace.

31 For men are not cast off
by the Lord forever.
32 Though he brings grief, he will show compassion,
so great is his unfailing love.
33 For he does not willingly bring affliction
or grief to the children of men.

34 To crush underfoot
all prisoners in the land,
35 to deny a man his rights
before the Most High,
36 to deprive a man of justice—
would not the Lord see such things?

37 Who can speak and have it happen
if the Lord has not decreed it?
38 Is it not from the mouth of the Most High
that both calamities and good things come?
39 Why should any living man complain
when punished for his sins?

40 Let us examine our ways and test them,
and let us return to the LORD.
41 Let us lift up our hearts and our hands
to God in heaven, and say:

MY BELOVED

I know it is hard sometimes to be patient. I hear your voice crying out in the morning hours and late at night. I make note of each request. Remember that I am not constrained by your time schedules or limited to your solutions. But be assured of this, I will deliver . . . in My time . . . in My way. Learn to wait in anticipation.

And when you wonder whether I will take care of you, think of this: Since I sacrificed My own Son for your salvation, will I not also, along with Him, graciously give you all things? You can count on it!

You see, there is no other God beside Me, Who acts on behalf of those who wait for Him. Not one. For I am a Father Who longs to be gracious to you. I freely show you My compassion.

I am a good God, a God of justice. And I will bless you when you confidently wait for Me. So be still and know that I am God. Be still before Me and wait patiently for Me to act. Wait for Me, My child, and put your hope in My Word.

Ps 5:3; 33:20; 37:7; 46:10; 130:5; Isa 25:9; 30:18; 64:4; La 3:26; Ro 8:32

42 "We have sinned and rebelled
and you have not forgiven.

43 "You have covered yourself with anger and
pursued us;
you have slain without pity.
44 You have covered yourself with a cloud
so that no prayer can get through.
45 You have made us scum and refuse
among the nations.

46 "All our enemies have opened their mouths
wide against us.
47 We have suffered terror and pitfalls,
ruin and destruction."
48 Streams of tears flow from my eyes
because my people are destroyed.

49 My eyes will flow unceasingly,
without relief,
50 until the LORD looks down
from heaven and sees.
51 What I see brings grief to my soul
because of all the women of my city.

52 Those who were my enemies without cause
hunted me like a bird.
53 They tried to end my life in a pit
and threw stones at me;
54 the waters closed over my head,
and I thought I was about to be cut off.

55 I called on your name, O LORD,
from the depths of the pit.
56 You heard my plea: "Do not close your ears
to my cry for relief."
57 You came near when I called you,
and you said, "Do not fear."

58 O Lord, you took up my case;
you redeemed my life.
59 You have seen, O LORD, the wrong done
to me.
Uphold my cause!
60 You have seen the depth of their vengeance,
all their plots against me.

61 O LORD, you have heard their insults,
all their plots against me—
62 what my enemies whisper and mutter
against me all day long.
63 Look at them! Sitting or standing,
they mock me in their songs.

64 Pay them back what they deserve, O LORD,
for what their hands have done.
65 Put a veil over their hearts,
and may your curse be on them!
66 Pursue them in anger and destroy them
from under the heavens of the LORD.

Surely it is God who saves me;
I shall trust and have no fear,
For the Lord defends and shields me
And His saving help is near.
So rejoice as you draw water
From salvation's living spring;
In the day of your deliverance
Thank the Lord, His mercies sing.

"Surely, It Is God Who Saves Me"
Carl P. Daw, Jr. (©1982)

(3:58) O Lord, You took up my case. And what a sad case it was: I was caught red-handed, my fingerprints all over the evidence: guilty as charged! Yet even as the sentence of death was pronounced upon me, You took not only my case, but also my place. The sinless Son of God became sin, so that I might become the righteousness of God. So I am justified freely by grace through the redemption that comes by Christ alone. O God my Judge, my Defender, my Savior, You have redeemed my life from the pit. You have crowned me with love and compassion. "Praise the LORD, O my soul; all my inmost being, praise his holy name!" (Ps 103:1–4; Ro 3:24; 2Co 5:21)

(4:11) How much easier to pretend that You are not a God Who would pour out His fierce anger! How much more palatable to ignore Your wrath! Are You not the God of love, the God of mercy? Then why are You breaking out in "fierce anger?" Lord, how readily I trivialize Your hatred of sin. How tragic when I ignore the fire of Your judgment. Teach me to know You, not according to my self-made images, but according to Your holy Word. Melt my idols so that I might know You in truth. O Refiner's Fire, refine and purify me so that I might be pure as gold. (Mal 3:2–3)

My life is like a broken bowl,
A broken bowl that cannot hold
One drop of water for my soul
Or cordial in the searching cold;
Cast in the fire the perished thing,
Melt and remold it, till it be
A royal cup for him, my King:
Jesus, drink of me.
Christina Rossetti (1830-1894)

4[a] How the gold has lost its luster,
the fine gold become dull!
The sacred gems are scattered
at the head of every street.

2 How the precious sons of Zion,
once worth their weight in gold,
are now considered as pots of clay,
the work of a potter's hands!

3 Even jackals offer their breasts
to nurse their young,
but my people have become heartless
like ostriches in the desert.

4 Because of thirst the infant's tongue
sticks to the roof of its mouth;
the children beg for bread,
but no one gives it to them.

5 Those who once ate delicacies
are destitute in the streets.
Those nurtured in purple
now lie on ash heaps.

6 The punishment of my people
is greater than that of Sodom,
which was overthrown in a moment
without a hand turned to help her.

7 Their princes were brighter than snow
and whiter than milk,
their bodies more ruddy than rubies,
their appearance like sapphires.[b]

8 But now they are blacker than soot;
they are not recognized in the streets.
Their skin has shriveled on their bones;
it has become as dry as a stick.

9 Those killed by the sword are better off
than those who die of famine;
racked with hunger, they waste away
for lack of food from the field.

10 With their own hands compassionate women
have cooked their own children,
who became their food
when my people were destroyed.

11 The LORD has given full vent to his wrath;
he has poured out his fierce anger.
He kindled a fire in Zion
that consumed her foundations.

12 The kings of the earth did not believe,
nor did any of the world's people,
that enemies and foes could enter
the gates of Jerusalem.

13 But it happened because of the sins of her prophets

[a] This chapter is an acrostic poem, the verses of which begin with the successive letters of the Hebrew alphabet. [b] 7 Or *lapis lazuli*

and the iniquities of her priests,
who shed within her
the blood of the righteous.

14 Now they grope through the streets
like men who are blind.
They are so defiled with blood
that no one dares to touch their garments.

15 "Go away! You are unclean!" men cry to them.
"Away! Away! Don't touch us!"
When they flee and wander about,
people among the nations say,
"They can stay here no longer."

16 The LORD himself has scattered them;
he no longer watches over them.
The priests are shown no honor,
the elders no favor.

17 Moreover, our eyes failed,
looking in vain for help;
from our towers we watched
for a nation that could not save us.

18 Men stalked us at every step,
so we could not walk in our streets.
Our end was near, our days were numbered,
for our end had come.

19 Our pursuers were swifter
than eagles in the sky;
they chased us over the mountains
and lay in wait for us in the desert.

20 The LORD's anointed, our very life breath,
was caught in their traps.
We thought that under his shadow
we would live among the nations.

21 Rejoice and be glad, O Daughter of Edom,
you who live in the land of Uz.
But to you also the cup will be passed;
you will be drunk and stripped naked.

22 O Daughter of Zion, your punishment will end;
he will not prolong your exile.
But, O Daughter of Edom, he will punish your sin
and expose your wickedness.

5 Remember, O LORD, what has happened to us;
look, and see our disgrace.
2 Our inheritance has been turned over to aliens,
our homes to foreigners.
3 We have become orphans and fatherless,
our mothers like widows.
4 We must buy the water we drink;
our wood can be had only at a price.
5 Those who pursue us are at our heels;
we are weary and find no rest.
6 We submitted to Egypt and Assyria
to get enough bread.

(4:20) O Lord, You allowed Your anointed, yes, even Your king, to be caught in the traps of his enemies. The hope of the nation was defeated; the kingdom destroyed; the king was taken into captivity. Centuries later another Anointed One fell once more into the hands of the Gentiles: the true Breath of Life, snuffed out on a Roman cross. But in the mystery of Your grace, by His capture we are set free; by His suffocation we receive the breath of eternal life. We find refuge under the shadow of Your Anointed, Your Messiah, Your Christ, "Because you are my help, I sing in the shadow of your wings." (Ps 36:7; 63:7)

(5:3) When we wander far from You, Heavenly Father, when we abandon the safety of Your care, suddenly the consequences of our choices strike home. We are like orphans—fatherless, helpless, vulnerable. Yet You are the Lord Who sustains the fatherless, Who sets the lonely in families. When we return to You, You rush to embrace us with Your forgiving love. Through Your only Son You become a Father to us, and by Your Spirit You invite us to call You "Abba"—"Dear Father." (Ps 68:5; Lk 15:20–24; Jn 14:18; Ro 8:15)

The resurrection of Jesus Christ is our hope today. It is our assurance that we have a living Savior to help us live as we should now, and that when, in the end, we set forth on that last great journey, we shall not travel an uncharted course, but rather we shall go on a planned voyage–life to death to eternal living.

Raymond MacKendree

(5:19) In times of bounty, Lord, You reign. In times of famine, still You reign. When I know Your plan and walk in Your ways, You reign. When I am confused, stuck in doubt, wandering about lost, still You reign. From everlasting to everlasting You alone are God. How I yearn for the final revealing of Your glory, when "the kingdom of this world [will] become the kingdom of our Lord and of his Christ, and he will reign for ever and ever." Then I will join the universal multitude in bowing before You as we proclaim that "Jesus Christ is Lord, to the glory of God the Father." "Now to the King eternal, immortal, invisible, the only God, be honor and glory for ever and ever. Amen." (Ps 90:1–2; Php 2:10–11; 1Ti 1:17; Rev 11:15)

(5:21) How easy it is to long for better days, Lord, to remember seasons of blessing and to yearn to live in them once again. How tempting to pray: "Restore the bounty, Lord! Make my life better again!" But what I need infinitely more is to be restored to You, to live once again in the intimacy of Your fold. In my lostness, Lord, find me. In my sinning, cleanse me. In my wandering, lead me home to You.

Defeat may serve as well as victory
To shake the soul and let the glory out.
When the great oak is straining in the wind
The boughs drink in new beauty, and the trunk
Sends down a deeper root on the windward side.
Only the soul that knows the mighty grief
Can know the mighty rapture. Sorrows come
To stretch out spaces in the heart for joy.
Edwin Markham (1852-1940)

7 Our fathers sinned and are no more,
and we bear their punishment.
8 Slaves rule over us,
and there is none to free us from their hands.
9 We get our bread at the risk of our lives
because of the sword in the desert.
10 Our skin is hot as an oven,
feverish from hunger.
11 Women have been ravished in Zion,
and virgins in the towns of Judah.
12 Princes have been hung up by their hands;
elders are shown no respect.
13 Young men toil at the millstones;
boys stagger under loads of wood.
14 The elders are gone from the city gate;
the young men have stopped their music.
15 Joy is gone from our hearts;
our dancing has turned to mourning.
16 The crown has fallen from our head.
Woe to us, for we have sinned!
17 Because of this our hearts are faint,
because of these things our eyes grow dim
18 for Mount Zion, which lies desolate,
with jackals prowling over it.

19 You, O LORD, reign forever;
your throne endures from generation to generation.
20 Why do you always forget us?
Why do you forsake us so long?
21 Restore us to yourself, O LORD, that we may return;
renew our days as of old
22 unless you have utterly rejected us
and are angry with us beyond measure.

The Book of the Prophet

EZEKIEL

While the people of Judah languish dejectedly during their exile in Babylon, God is not invisible. He reveals Himself to Ezekiel, an exiled priest who sees "visions of God" (1:1). In response to his vision of a radiant, burning, reigning, glorious God, Ezekiel falls facedown (1:28), a posture he frequently assumes throughout his prophetic career. As we read, we realize that our encounter with God in the book of Ezekiel will not leave us comfortably unfazed. We too must fall down in worship before our holy, majestic, mysterious God.

The first major section of Ezekiel (chs. 1—24) focuses on God's imminent judgment of Jerusalem. The sin of God's people is so great that He will destroy even His beloved city and His own temple. Yet God is sovereign over all peoples and judges all by His holy standards (chs. 25—32). Ezekiel calls us to obey our righteous God—and to repent when we fail to measure up to God's absolute mandates.

After the fall of Jerusalem (ch. 33) Ezekiel's prophecies move in a surprising new direction. They look ahead to the time when God will redeem His exiled people. Then the Lord will give new life to dead, dry bones (ch. 37). He will be the Good Shepherd of His sheep: " 'I myself will search for my sheep and look after them . . . I will rescue them from all the places where they were scattered . . . I myself will tend my sheep and have them lie down . . . I will search for the lost and bring back the strays.' " (see 34:11–16). The holy God of justice and judgment is also the loving Shepherd who seeks the lost. As people who have been found by God through Jesus Christ, the Good Shepherd, our worship centers in gratitude for God's merciful efforts to seek and to save us.

Our encounter with God in the book of Ezekiel will not leave us comfortably unfazed. We too must fall down in worship before our holy, majestic, mysterious God.

The final chapters of Ezekiel (chs. 40—48) contain a vision of a new Jerusalem and a new temple. Ezekiel looks forward to a time when God's presence will never depart from His people. Then Jerusalem will receive a new name: "THE LORD IS THERE" (48:35). How blessed we are to live after God's incarnation in Jesus, the One Who is "Immanuel," "God with us" (Mt 1:23). In this age, moreover, God continues to be with us through the Holy Spirit Who dwells in us. Though we share with Ezekiel a hope for the future revelation of God (Rev 21), through Jesus Christ and by His Spirit we have begun to live in that future now, however incompletely. Thus we worship a God Who lives not only in transcendent glory but also in our hearts and in our churches.

Ezekiel's vision of God keeps us from getting too chummy with our holy King. Yet Ezekiel's hope, realized in Jesus, invites us to share intimate fellowship with our Lord Who is always there for us.

Behold Him whom you cannot behold! Lift up your eyes to heaven, and see Him who stretched the heavens like a tent to dwell in and then did weave into their tapestry, with golden needle, stars that glitter in the darkness. Mark Him who spread the earth and created man upon it. He is all-sufficient, eternal, self-existent, unchangeable! Will you not reverence Him? He is good; He is loving; He is kind; He is gracious! See the bounties of His providence; behold the plentitude of His grace!

Charles Haddon Spurgeon (1834–1892)

(1:4–24) King of kings and Lord of lords, how majestic and mysterious You are. Ezekiel's first glimpse of You confirms that our ideas, imaginations and impressions of You are pathetically earthbound, rooted in human limitations. In fact, You are greater than any image humankind could ever conceive. You are the culmination of all energy, light, goodness, beauty and power. Even the angels that attend Your throne are beyond our wildest imagination. How amazing, then, that You should concern Yourself with our ordinary lives. How we praise You for considering us at all, much less loving us as Your own beloved children.

King of majesty,
Lord of royalty,
Angels bow before
Your holy throne.
Offering up their praise;
Hallelujahs raise.
Incense burning sweetly unto Thee.
Pure and Holy One,
Lord, we humbly come
In adoration, wanting more of You.

"Precious Lord"
Jean Munsey (©1996)

The Living Creatures and the Glory of the LORD

1 In the[a] thirtieth year, in the fourth month on the fifth day,
while I was among the exiles by the Kebar River, the heavens
were opened and I saw visions of God.
2 On the fifth of the month—it was the fifth year of the exile of
King Jehoiachin— 3 the word of the LORD came to Ezekiel the
priest, the son of Buzi,[b] by the Kebar River in the land of the
Babylonians.[c] There the hand of the LORD was upon him.
4 I looked, and I saw a windstorm coming out of the north—an
immense cloud with flashing lightning and surrounded by brilliant
light. The center of the fire looked like glowing metal, 5 and in the
fire was what looked like four living creatures. In appearance
their form was that of a man, 6 but each of them had four faces and
four wings. 7 Their legs were straight; their feet were like those of
a calf and gleamed like burnished bronze. 8 Under their wings on
their four sides they had the hands of a man. All four of them had
faces and wings, 9 and their wings touched one another. Each one
went straight ahead; they did not turn as they moved.
10 Their faces looked like this: Each of the four had the face of
a man, and on the right side each had the face of a lion, and on
the left the face of an ox; each also had the face of an eagle.
11 Such were their faces. Their wings were spread out upward;
each had two wings, one touching the wing of another creature
on either side, and two wings covering its body. 12 Each one went
straight ahead. Wherever the spirit would go, they would go, without turning as they went. 13 The appearance of the living creatures
was like burning coals of fire or like torches. Fire moved back
and forth among the creatures; it was bright, and lightning
flashed out of it. 14 The creatures sped back and forth like flashes
of lightning.
15 As I looked at the living creatures, I saw a wheel on the
ground beside each creature with its four faces. 16 This was the
appearance and structure of the wheels: They sparkled like chrysolite, and all four looked alike. Each appeared to be made like a
wheel intersecting a wheel. 17 As they moved, they would go in any
one of the four directions the creatures faced; the wheels did not
turn about[d] as the creatures went. 18 Their rims were high and
awesome, and all four rims were full of eyes all around.
19 When the living creatures moved, the wheels beside them
moved; and when the living creatures rose from the ground, the
wheels also rose. 20 Wherever the spirit would go, they would go,
and the wheels would rise along with them, because the spirit of
the living creatures was in the wheels. 21 When the creatures
moved, they also moved; when the creatures stood still, they also
stood still; and when the creatures rose from the ground, the
wheels rose along with them, because the spirit of the living creatures was in the wheels.
22 Spread out above the heads of the living creatures was what
looked like an expanse, sparkling like ice, and awesome.
23 Under the expanse their wings were stretched out one toward
the other, and each had two wings covering its body. 24 When the
creatures moved, I heard the sound of their wings, like the roar
of rushing waters, like the voice of the Almighty,[e] like the tumult
of an army. When they stood still, they lowered their wings.

[a] *1* Or ⌊*my*⌋ [b] *3* Or *Ezekiel son of Buzi the priest* [c] *3* Or *Chaldeans* [d] *17* Or *aside* [e] *24* Hebrew *Shaddai*

25Then there came a voice from above the expanse over their
heads as they stood with lowered wings. 26Above the expanse
over their heads was what looked like a throne of sapphire,[a] and
high above on the throne was a figure like that of a man. 27I saw
that from what appeared to be his waist up he looked like glowing metal, as if full of fire, and that from there down he looked
like fire; and brilliant light surrounded him. 28Like the appearance of a rainbow in the clouds on a rainy day, so was the radiance around him.

This was the appearance of the likeness of the glory of the
LORD. When I saw it, I fell facedown, and I heard the voice of one
speaking.

Ezekiel's Call

2 He said to me, "Son of man, stand up on your feet and I will
speak to you." 2As he spoke, the Spirit came into me and
raised me to my feet, and I heard him speaking to me.

3He said: "Son of man, I am sending you to the Israelites, to a
rebellious nation that has rebelled against me; they and their fathers have been in revolt against me to this very day. 4The people
to whom I am sending you are obstinate and stubborn. Say to
them, 'This is what the Sovereign LORD says.' 5And whether they
listen or fail to listen—for they are a rebellious house—they will
know that a prophet has been among them. 6And you, son of
man, do not be afraid of them or their words. Do not be afraid,
though briers and thorns are all around you and you live among
scorpions. Do not be afraid of what they say or terrified by them,
though they are a rebellious house. 7You must speak my words to
them, whether they listen or fail to listen, for they are rebellious.
8But you, son of man, listen to what I say to you. Do not rebel like
that rebellious house; open your mouth and eat what I give you."

9Then I looked, and I saw a hand stretched out to me. In it was
a scroll, 10which he unrolled before me. On both sides of it were
written words of lament and mourning and woe.

3 And he said to me, "Son of man, eat what is before you, eat
this scroll; then go and speak to the house of Israel." 2So I
opened my mouth, and he gave me the scroll to eat.

3Then he said to me, "Son of man, eat this scroll I am giving
you and fill your stomach with it." So I ate it, and it tasted as sweet
as honey in my mouth.

4He then said to me: "Son of man, go now to the house of Israel and speak my words to them. 5You are not being sent to a
people of obscure speech and difficult language, but to the house
of Israel— 6not to many peoples of obscure speech and difficult
language, whose words you cannot understand. Surely if I had
sent you to them, they would have listened to you. 7But the house
of Israel is not willing to listen to you because they are not willing to listen to me, for the whole house of Israel is hardened and
obstinate. 8But I will make you as unyielding and hardened as
they are. 9I will make your forehead like the hardest stone, harder than flint. Do not be afraid of them or terrified by them, though
they are a rebellious house."

10And he said to me, "Son of man, listen carefully and take to
heart all the words I speak to you. 11Go now to your countrymen

[a] 26 Or *lapis lazuli*

(2:8—3:4) Lord, as I approach Your holy Word, may I never take it lightly. You have taken such great care to preserve it through the ages. May I take equal care to cherish it this day. Help me to come to Your Word as I would to a fine meal—not just to taste it, but to savor it, to take it in and absorb it into the very fabric of my being. And then, out of the abundance of my heart may my mouth speak the truth of God. (Mt 12:34–37)

Your attention is no longer on outward things or on the surface thoughts of your mind; instead, sweetly and silently, your mind becomes occupied with what you have read and by that touch of his presence.

Oh, it is not that you will think about what you have read, but you will feed upon what you have read. Out of a love for the Lord you exert your will to hold your mind quiet before him. When you have come to this state, you must allow your mind to rest.

In this very peaceful state, swallow what you have tasted . . . take in what is there as nourishment.

Madame Jeanne Marie De La Mothe Guyon (1648–1717)

(3:16–19) Sovereign Lord, You have called Your people to be watchmen for the world. According to Your will, we are to stand on the wall of our communities and faithfully proclaim Your ways and Your warnings. Forgive us, God, when we choose compromise over confrontation. Teach us to speak Your truth boldly to all who will listen. Spare us the sorrow of having failed to offer Your salvation to others. Do not let anyone perish because of our disobedience. (1Ti 4:16; Jas 5:20)

We alone, who know Christ and are living yet upon this earth, can be messengers and witnesses to His Gospel and saving grace. What a solemn responsibility! And also what a holy privilege! Oh, how can we fail to hear the call of the lost that rises from the hearts of the living and dead, and to do all that in us is to get the message of Christ to those who may still be snatched as brands out of the fire?

George Christian Weiss (1910-)

We've a story to tell to the nations
That shall turn their hearts to the
right,
A story of truth and mercy,
A story of peace and light,
A story of peace and light.

For the darkness shall turn to
dawning,
And the dawning to noon-day
bright,
And Christ's great kingdom shall
come to earth,
The kingdom of love and light.

"We've a Story to Tell to the Nations"
H. Ernest Nichol (1896)

in exile and speak to them. Say to them, 'This is what the Sovereign LORD says,' whether they listen or fail to listen."
12Then the Spirit lifted me up, and I heard behind me a loud
rumbling sound—May the glory of the LORD be praised in his
dwelling place!— 13the sound of the wings of the living creatures
brushing against each other and the sound of the wheels beside
them, a loud rumbling sound. 14The Spirit then lifted me up and
took me away, and I went in bitterness and in the anger of my
spirit, with the strong hand of the LORD upon me. 15I came to the
exiles who lived at Tel Abib near the Kebar River. And there,
where they were living, I sat among them for seven days—overwhelmed.

Warning to Israel

16At the end of seven days the word of the LORD came to me:
17"Son of man, I have made you a watchman for the house of Israel; so hear the word I speak and give them warning from me.
18When I say to a wicked man, 'You will surely die,' and you do
not warn him or speak out to dissuade him from his evil ways in
order to save his life, that wicked man will die for[a] his sin, and I
will hold you accountable for his blood. 19But if you do warn the
wicked man and he does not turn from his wickedness or from his
evil ways, he will die for his sin; but you will have saved yourself.
20"Again, when a righteous man turns from his righteousness
and does evil, and I put a stumbling block before him, he will
die. Since you did not warn him, he will die for his sin. The righteous things he did will not be remembered, and I will hold you
accountable for his blood. 21But if you do warn the righteous
man not to sin and he does not sin, he will surely live because he
took warning, and you will have saved yourself."
22The hand of the LORD was upon me there, and he said to me,
"Get up and go out to the plain, and there I will speak to you."
23So I got up and went out to the plain. And the glory of the LORD
was standing there, like the glory I had seen by the Kebar River,
and I fell facedown.
24Then the Spirit came into me and raised me to my feet. He
spoke to me and said: "Go, shut yourself inside your house.
25And you, son of man, they will tie with ropes; you will be bound
so that you cannot go out among the people. 26I will make your
tongue stick to the roof of your mouth so that you will be silent
and unable to rebuke them, though they are a rebellious house.
27But when I speak to you, I will open your mouth and you shall
say to them, 'This is what the Sovereign LORD says.' Whoever will
listen let him listen, and whoever will refuse let him refuse; for
they are a rebellious house.

Siege of Jerusalem Symbolized

4 "Now, son of man, take a clay tablet, put it in front of you and
draw the city of Jerusalem on it. 2Then lay siege to it: Erect
siege works against it, build a ramp up to it, set up camps against
it and put battering rams around it. 3Then take an iron pan, place
it as an iron wall between you and the city and turn your face toward it. It will be under siege, and you shall besiege it. This will
be a sign to the house of Israel.
4"Then lie on your left side and put the sin of the house of Is-

[a] *18* Or *in*; also in verses 19 and 20

rael upon yourself.[a] You are to bear their sin for the number of
days you lie on your side. 5I have assigned you the same number
of days as the years of their sin. So for 390 days you will bear the
sin of the house of Israel.
6"After you have finished this, lie down again, this time on your
right side, and bear the sin of the house of Judah. I have assigned
you 40 days, a day for each year. 7Turn your face toward the siege
of Jerusalem and with bared arm prophesy against her. 8I will tie
you up with ropes so that you cannot turn from one side to the
other until you have finished the days of your siege.
9"Take wheat and barley, beans and lentils, millet and spelt;
put them in a storage jar and use them to make bread for yourself.
You are to eat it during the 390 days you lie on your side.
10Weigh out twenty shekels[b] of food to eat each day and eat it at
set times. 11Also measure out a sixth of a hin[c] of water and drink
it at set times. 12Eat the food as you would a barley cake; bake it
in the sight of the people, using human excrement for fuel."
13The LORD said, "In this way the people of Israel will eat defiled
food among the nations where I will drive them."
14Then I said, "Not so, Sovereign LORD! I have never defiled
myself. From my youth until now I have never eaten anything
found dead or torn by wild animals. No unclean meat has ever entered
my mouth."
15"Very well," he said, "I will let you bake your bread over cow
manure instead of human excrement."
16He then said to me: "Son of man, I will cut off the supply of
food in Jerusalem. The people will eat rationed food in anxiety
and drink rationed water in despair, 17for food and water will be
scarce. They will be appalled at the sight of each other and will
waste away because of[d] their sin.
5 "Now, son of man, take a sharp sword and use it as a barber's
razor to shave your head and your beard. Then take a
set of scales and divide up the hair. 2When the days of your siege
come to an end, burn a third of the hair with fire inside the city.
Take a third and strike it with the sword all around the city. And
scatter a third to the wind. For I will pursue them with drawn
sword. 3But take a few strands of hair and tuck them away in the
folds of your garment. 4Again, take a few of these and throw them
into the fire and burn them up. A fire will spread from there to the
whole house of Israel.
5"This is what the Sovereign LORD says: This is Jerusalem,
which I have set in the center of the nations, with countries all
around her. 6Yet in her wickedness she has rebelled against my
laws and decrees more than the nations and countries around
her. She has rejected my laws and has not followed my decrees.
7"Therefore this is what the Sovereign LORD says: You have
been more unruly than the nations around you and have not followed
my decrees or kept my laws. You have not even[e] conformed
to the standards of the nations around you.
8"Therefore this is what the Sovereign LORD says: I myself am
against you, Jerusalem, and I will inflict punishment on you in the
sight of the nations. 9Because of all your detestable idols, I will do
to you what I have never done before and will never do again.
10Therefore in your midst fathers will eat their children, and chil-

[a] 4 Or *your side* [b] 10 That is, about 8 ounces (about 0.2 kilogram) [c] 11 That is, about 2/3 quart (about 0.6 liter) [d] 17 Or *away in* [e] 7 Most Hebrew manuscripts; some Hebrew manuscripts and Syriac *You have*

(4:1—5:4) The ancient cities, the surrounding scenery and Ezekiel's symbolic actions are somewhat obscured by the mist of centuries. But Lord, Your message resounds with pristine clarity. Then, as now, You faithfully and continuously warned Your people that their rebellion would lead to disaster. Even now Your loving heart reaches out toward those who refuse to obey You. Most of all, You use every means available to communicate impending danger to those who have turned away from You and followed other gods. In whatever way You choose to speak to us, Lord, open our ears to hear Your voice.

It is clear that we are usually surrounded by so much outer noise that it is hard to truly hear our God when he is speaking to us. We have often become deaf, unable to know when God calls us and unable to understand in which direction he calls us.

Thus our lives have become absurd. In the word absurd we find the Latin word surdus, which means "deaf." . . . When, however, we learn to listen, our lives become obedient lives. The word obedient comes from the Latin word audire, which means "listening."

Henri Nouwen (1932–1996)

Those that profane God's dwelling-place as they had done can expect no other than that He should abandon theirs.

Matthew Henry (1662-1714)

(5:11—6:7) Sovereign Lord, You are slow to anger, abundantly merciful, full of love and grace. But You are also a jealous God. What horror, then, to think that Your people could be so stubborn as to exhaust the resource of Your patience and drive You to anger. Your mercy that had so long been abused was now silent. It had surrendered its cause to the hand of judgment. The sword that had been drawn for Your people's defense would now be drawn for their punishment. Those who forgot You in their prosperity would remember You in their captivity. If You are against us, O God, who can stand for us? (Joel 2:13)

(6:8–10) Judgment is ever Your "strange work" and Your "alien task." Though Your hand may stretch out in anger, Your eye looks toward reconciliation. In wrath You remember mercy. Though You may punish us and hide Your face in anger, even then You will hear our prayer, O God. As we have broken Your heart, so break our stubborn wills. Heal us, guide us, restore us to Your comforting side. Bring purity to our penitent hearts and create praise on our penitent lips. (Isa 28:21; 57:17–19; Hab 3:2)

You, O Lord, are a holy God,
Your ways are perfect and just.
Slow to anger and abounding in love,
You have shown us Your Father's heart.

But we, Your people, have turned from You,
Resisted Your power and grace.
Taking our lives into our hands,
We have stumbled and lost our way.

So we humble ourselves before You,
And confess our unfaithfulness toward You.
Forgive our sin, remove our shame,
Restore the church that bears Your name,
That revival may come to this land
Once again.

"We Humble Ourselves"
Malcolm duPlessis, Paul Baloche and Rita Baloche (©1997)

dren will eat their fathers. I will inflict punishment on you and will
scatter all your survivors to the winds. 11Therefore as surely as I
live, declares the Sovereign LORD, because you have defiled my
sanctuary with all your vile images and detestable practices, I myself will withdraw my favor; I will not look on you with pity or spare
you. 12A third of your people will die of the plague or perish by
famine inside you; a third will fall by the sword outside your walls;
and a third I will scatter to the winds and pursue with drawn sword.
13"Then my anger will cease and my wrath against them will
subside, and I will be avenged. And when I have spent my wrath
upon them, they will know that I the LORD have spoken in my zeal.
14"I will make you a ruin and a reproach among the nations
around you, in the sight of all who pass by. 15You will be a reproach and a taunt, a warning and an object of horror to the nations around you when I inflict punishment on you in anger and in
wrath and with stinging rebuke. I the LORD have spoken. 16When I
shoot at you with my deadly and destructive arrows of famine, I
will shoot to destroy you. I will bring more and more famine upon
you and cut off your supply of food. 17I will send famine and wild
beasts against you, and they will leave you childless. Plague and
bloodshed will sweep through you, and I will bring the sword
against you. I the LORD have spoken."

A Prophecy Against the Mountains of Israel

6 The word of the LORD came to me: 2"Son of man, set your
face against the mountains of Israel; prophesy against them
3and say: 'O mountains of Israel, hear the word of the Sovereign
LORD. This is what the Sovereign LORD says to the mountains and
hills, to the ravines and valleys: I am about to bring a sword
against you, and I will destroy your high places. 4Your altars will
be demolished and your incense altars will be smashed; and I will
slay your people in front of your idols. 5I will lay the dead bodies
of the Israelites in front of their idols, and I will scatter your
bones around your altars. 6Wherever you live, the towns will be
laid waste and the high places demolished, so that your altars will
be laid waste and devastated, your idols smashed and ruined,
your incense altars broken down, and what you have made wiped
out. 7Your people will fall slain among you, and you will know
that I am the LORD.
8" 'But I will spare some, for some of you will escape the
sword when you are scattered among the lands and nations.
9Then in the nations where they have been carried captive, those
who escape will remember me—how I have been grieved by
their adulterous hearts, which have turned away from me, and by
their eyes, which have lusted after their idols. They will loathe
themselves for the evil they have done and for all their detestable
practices. 10And they will know that I am the LORD; I did not
threaten in vain to bring this calamity on them.
11" 'This is what the Sovereign LORD says: Strike your hands together and stamp your feet and cry out "Alas!" because of all the
wicked and detestable practices of the house of Israel, for they will
fall by the sword, famine and plague. 12He that is far away will die
of the plague, and he that is near will fall by the sword, and he that
survives and is spared will die of famine. So will I spend my wrath
upon them. 13And they will know that I am the LORD, when their
people lie slain among their idols around their altars, on every high
hill and on all the mountaintops, under every spreading tree and

every leafy oak—places where they offered fragrant incense to all
their idols. 14And I will stretch out my hand against them and make
the land a desolate waste from the desert to Diblah[a]—wherever
they live. Then they will know that I am the LORD.' "

The End Has Come

7 The word of the LORD came to me: 2"Son of man, this is what
the Sovereign LORD says to the land of Israel: The end! The
end has come upon the four corners of the land. 3The end is now
upon you and I will unleash my anger against you. I will judge you
according to your conduct and repay you for all your detestable
practices. 4I will not look on you with pity or spare you; I will
surely repay you for your conduct and the detestable practices
among you. Then you will know that I am the LORD.

5"This is what the Sovereign LORD says: Disaster! An unheard-
of[b] disaster is coming. 6The end has come! The end has come! It
has roused itself against you. It has come! 7Doom has come upon
you—you who dwell in the land. The time has come, the day is
near; there is panic, not joy, upon the mountains. 8I am about to
pour out my wrath on you and spend my anger against you; I will
judge you according to your conduct and repay you for all your
detestable practices. 9I will not look on you with pity or spare
you; I will repay you in accordance with your conduct and the
detestable practices among you. Then you will know that it is I the
LORD who strikes the blow.

10"The day is here! It has come! Doom has burst forth, the rod
has budded, arrogance has blossomed! 11Violence has grown
into[c] a rod to punish wickedness; none of the people will be left,
none of that crowd—no wealth, nothing of value. 12The time has
come, the day has arrived. Let not the buyer rejoice nor the seller grieve, for wrath is upon the whole crowd. 13The seller will not
recover the land he has sold as long as both of them live, for the
vision concerning the whole crowd will not be reversed. Because
of their sins, not one of them will preserve his life. 14Though they
blow the trumpet and get everything ready, no one will go into
battle, for my wrath is upon the whole crowd.

15"Outside is the sword, inside are plague and famine; those in
the country will die by the sword, and those in the city will be devoured by famine and plague. 16All who survive and escape will
be in the mountains, moaning like doves of the valleys, each because of his sins. 17Every hand will go limp, and every knee will
become as weak as water. 18They will put on sackcloth and be
clothed with terror. Their faces will be covered with shame and
their heads will be shaved. 19They will throw their silver into the
streets, and their gold will be an unclean thing. Their silver and
gold will not be able to save them in the day of the LORD's wrath.
They will not satisfy their hunger or fill their stomachs with it, for
it has made them stumble into sin. 20They were proud of their
beautiful jewelry and used it to make their detestable idols and
vile images. Therefore I will turn these into an unclean thing for
them. 21I will hand it all over as plunder to foreigners and as loot
to the wicked of the earth, and they will defile it. 22I will turn my
face away from them, and they will desecrate my treasured place;
robbers will enter it and desecrate it.

[a] 14 Most Hebrew manuscripts; a few Hebrew manuscripts *Riblah* [b] 5 Most Hebrew manuscripts; some Hebrew manuscripts and Syriac *Disaster after one has become* [c] 11 Or *The violent one has become*

(7:5–14) You will have the last word, O Lord. Once again You will say, "The time has come, the day is here!" Yet, just as in Ezekiel's time, the impending disaster You have foretold seems unprecedented, unheard of. Oblivious to the coming judgment, people bustle about, doing business, building fortunes, pursuing pleasures. Meanwhile You are patiently watching, biding Your time, unwilling that any should perish. How much longer will You wait, Sovereign Lord, to release Your wrath? God forbid that we, Your people, should fail to warn those around us that the Day of the Lord is coming! (2Pe 3:9)

If sinners will be damned, at least let them leap to hell over our bodies. And if they will perish, let them perish with our arms about their knees, imploring them to stay. If hell must be filled, at least let it be filled in the teeth of our exertions, and let no one go there unwarned and unprayed for.

Charles Haddon Spurgeon (1834–1892)

O awesome Love, which finds no room
In life where sin denies you,
And, doomed to death, shall bring to doom
The pow'r which crucifies You,
Till not a stone was left on stone,
And then the nations' pride, o'er thrown,
Will nevermore defy You!

New advent of the love of Christ,
Will we again refuse You,
Till in the night of hate and war
We perish as we lose You?
From ancient doubts our minds release
To seek the kingdom of Your peace,
By which alone we choose You.

"Lord Christ, When First You Came to Earth"

W. Russell Bowie (1882–1969)

(8:3–18) Lord in heaven, You revealed Yourself to Your prophet Ezekiel as a jealous God. And although our glamorous, seductive idols seem more like playthings than false gods, when we are toying with them we rarely think of You at all. How Your loving heart rages at the sight of our unfaithfulness. How detestable are idols in Your holy sight. Forgive us, Lord! Teach us to recognize, by faith, Your immense devotion to us. Perhaps then we can understand better the depth and intensity of Your jealousy.

The one commandment suffices to blow away in a moment all the excuses which we could make for having reservations from God: "Thou shalt love the Lord thy God with all thy heart, with all thy soul, with all thy mind, and with all they strength." See how the terms were joined together by the Holy Spirit, to prevent all the reservations which a person could wish to make to the prejudice of this jealous and dominant love.

François Fénelon (1651-1715)

Earth, hear your Maker's voice;
Your great Redeemer own;
Believe, obey, rejoice,
And worship Him alone.
Cast down your pride,
Your sin deplore,
And bow before the Crucified.

"Before You, Lord, We Bow"
Francis S. Key (1779-1843)

23 "Prepare chains, because the land is full of bloodshed and
the city is full of violence. 24 I will bring the most wicked of the
nations to take possession of their houses; I will put an end to the
pride of the mighty, and their sanctuaries will be desecrated.
25 When terror comes, they will seek peace, but there will be
none. 26 Calamity upon calamity will come, and rumor upon
rumor. They will try to get a vision from the prophet; the teaching
of the law by the priest will be lost, as will the counsel of the elders. 27 The king will mourn, the prince will be clothed with despair, and the hands of the people of the land will tremble. I will
deal with them according to their conduct, and by their own standards I will judge them. Then they will know that I am the LORD."

Idolatry in the Temple

8 In the sixth year, in the sixth month on the fifth day, while I
was sitting in my house and the elders of Judah were sitting
before me, the hand of the Sovereign LORD came upon me there.
2 I looked, and I saw a figure like that of a man.[a] From what appeared to be his waist down he was like fire, and from there up
his appearance was as bright as glowing metal. 3 He stretched out
what looked like a hand and took me by the hair of my head. The
Spirit lifted me up between earth and heaven and in visions of
God he took me to Jerusalem, to the entrance to the north gate of
the inner court, where the idol that provokes to jealousy stood.
4 And there before me was the glory of the God of Israel, as in the
vision I had seen in the plain.
5 Then he said to me, "Son of man, look toward the north." So
I looked, and in the entrance north of the gate of the altar I saw
this idol of jealousy.
6 And he said to me, "Son of man, do you see what they are
doing—the utterly detestable things the house of Israel is doing
here, things that will drive me far from my sanctuary? But you will
see things that are even more detestable."
7 Then he brought me to the entrance to the court. I looked,
and I saw a hole in the wall. 8 He said to me, "Son of man, now dig
into the wall." So I dug into the wall and saw a doorway there.
9 And he said to me, "Go in and see the wicked and detestable
things they are doing here." 10 So I went in and looked, and I saw
portrayed all over the walls all kinds of crawling things and detestable animals and all the idols of the house of Israel. 11 In front
of them stood seventy elders of the house of Israel, and Jaazaniah son of Shaphan was standing among them. Each had a censer
in his hand, and a fragrant cloud of incense was rising.
12 He said to me, "Son of man, have you seen what the elders of
the house of Israel are doing in the darkness, each at the shrine
of his own idol? They say, 'The LORD does not see us; the LORD has
forsaken the land.'" 13 Again, he said, "You will see them doing
things that are even more detestable."
14 Then he brought me to the entrance to the north gate of the
house of the LORD, and I saw women sitting there, mourning for
Tammuz. 15 He said to me, "Do you see this, son of man? You will
see things that are even more detestable than this."
16 He then brought me into the inner court of the house of the
LORD, and there at the entrance to the temple, between the portico and the altar, were about twenty-five men. With their backs to-

[a] 2 Or *saw a fiery figure*

ward the temple of the LORD and their faces toward the east, they
were bowing down to the sun in the east.
17He said to me, "Have you seen this, son of man? Is it a trivial
matter for the house of Judah to do the detestable things they are
doing here? Must they also fill the land with violence and continually provoke me to anger? Look at them putting the branch to
their nose! 18Therefore I will deal with them in anger; I will not
look on them with pity or spare them. Although they shout in my
ears, I will not listen to them."

Idolaters Killed

9 Then I heard him call out in a loud voice, "Bring the guards
of the city here, each with a weapon in his hand." 2And I saw
six men coming from the direction of the upper gate, which faces
north, each with a deadly weapon in his hand. With them was a
man clothed in linen who had a writing kit at his side. They came
in and stood beside the bronze altar.
3Now the glory of the God of Israel went up from above the
cherubim, where it had been, and moved to the threshold of the
temple. Then the LORD called to the man clothed in linen who had
the writing kit at his side 4and said to him, "Go throughout the city
of Jerusalem and put a mark on the foreheads of those who grieve
and lament over all the detestable things that are done in it."
5As I listened, he said to the others, "Follow him through the
city and kill, without showing pity or compassion. 6Slaughter old
men, young men and maidens, women and children, but do not
touch anyone who has the mark. Begin at my sanctuary." So they
began with the elders who were in front of the temple.
7Then he said to them, "Defile the temple and fill the courts
with the slain. Go!" So they went out and began killing throughout the city. 8While they were killing and I was left alone, I fell
facedown, crying out, "Ah, Sovereign LORD! Are you going to destroy the entire remnant of Israel in this outpouring of your wrath
on Jerusalem?"
9He answered me, "The sin of the house of Israel and Judah is
exceedingly great; the land is full of bloodshed and the city is full
of injustice. They say, 'The LORD has forsaken the land; the LORD
does not see.' 10So I will not look on them with pity or spare
them, but I will bring down on their own heads what they have
done."
11Then the man in linen with the writing kit at his side brought
back word, saying, "I have done as you commanded."

The Glory Departs From the Temple

10 I looked, and I saw the likeness of a throne of sapphire[a]
above the expanse that was over the heads of the cherubim. 2The LORD said to the man clothed in linen, "Go in among
the wheels beneath the cherubim. Fill your hands with burning
coals from among the cherubim and scatter them over the city."
And as I watched, he went in.
3Now the cherubim were standing on the south side of the temple when the man went in, and a cloud filled the inner court.
4Then the glory of the LORD rose from above the cherubim and
moved to the threshold of the temple. The cloud filled the temple,
and the court was full of the radiance of the glory of the LORD.

[a] 1 Or *lapis lazuli*

(9:1–6) Sovereign Lord, Your eyes range throughout the earth to strengthen those whose hearts are fully committed to You. You have always provided a means of protection for those who love You when Your judgment finally falls—an ark, a mark on the forehead, the blood of the Passover Lamb. How we thank You, Father, that today the blood of Your only begotten Son not only protects us from Your judgment but also purifies us from our sins. (2Ch 16:9, 1Jn 1:7)

Jesus, Thy blood and righteousness
My beauty are, my glorious dress;
'Midst flaming worlds, in these
arrayed,
With joy shall I lift up my head.

Bold shall I stand in that great day,
For who aught to my charge shall
lay?
Fully absolved through these I am,
From sin and fear, from guilt and
shame.

"Jesus, Thy Blood and Righteousness"
Nicolaus L. von Zinzendorf (1739)
Trans. John Wesley (1703-1791)

Worship is our innermost being responding with praise for all that God is, through our attitudes, actions, thoughts, and words, based on the truth of God as He has revealed himself. Another way to say it is that worship is glorifying God. To be wholly obsessed with the glory of God is the consuming passion of the true worshiper, who lives to exalt God.

John MacArthur, Jr. (1939-)

(10:9–22) Lord, You have established Your throne in heaven, and Your kingdom rules over all. There, around Your throne, Your angels praise You, the mighty ones who do Your bidding, who obey Your commands and do Your will. All Your heavenly hosts praise You. All Your works everywhere in Your dominion praise You, Father in Heaven. And as we worship You, here and now, we join our voices with the vast choir of saints and angels singing praises to our God. (Ps 103:19–22)

Worship, honor, glory, blessing,
Lord we offer unto Thee;
Young and old, Thy praise
expressing,
In glad homage bend the knee.
All the saints in heav'n adore Thee;
We would bow before Thy throne:
As Thine angels serve before Thee,
So on earth Thy will be done.
"Praise the Lord! Ye Heaven's Adore Him"
Edward Osler (1798-1863)

5The sound of the wings of the cherubim could be heard as far
away as the outer court, like the voice of God Almighty[a] when he
speaks.
6When the LORD commanded the man in linen, "Take fire from
among the wheels, from among the cherubim," the man went in
and stood beside a wheel. 7Then one of the cherubim reached
out his hand to the fire that was among them. He took up some of
it and put it into the hands of the man in linen, who took it and
went out. 8(Under the wings of the cherubim could be seen what
looked like the hands of a man.)
9I looked, and I saw beside the cherubim four wheels, one beside each of the cherubim; the wheels sparkled like chrysolite.
10As for their appearance, the four of them looked alike; each
was like a wheel intersecting a wheel. 11As they moved, they
would go in any one of the four directions the cherubim faced;
the wheels did not turn about[b] as the cherubim went. The cherubim went in whatever direction the head faced, without turning as
they went. 12Their entire bodies, including their backs, their
hands and their wings, were completely full of eyes, as were their
four wheels. 13I heard the wheels being called "the whirling
wheels." 14Each of the cherubim had four faces: One face was
that of a cherub, the second the face of a man, the third the face
of a lion, and the fourth the face of an eagle.
15Then the cherubim rose upward. These were the living creatures I had seen by the Kebar River. 16When the cherubim moved,
the wheels beside them moved; and when the cherubim spread
their wings to rise from the ground, the wheels did not leave their
side. 17When the cherubim stood still, they also stood still; and
when the cherubim rose, they rose with them, because the spirit
of the living creatures was in them.
18Then the glory of the LORD departed from over the threshold
of the temple and stopped above the cherubim. 19While I
watched, the cherubim spread their wings and rose from the
ground, and as they went, the wheels went with them. They
stopped at the entrance to the east gate of the LORD's house, and
the glory of the God of Israel was above them.
20These were the living creatures I had seen beneath the God
of Israel by the Kebar River, and I realized that they were cherubim. 21Each had four faces and four wings, and under their wings
was what looked like the hands of a man. 22Their faces had the
same appearance as those I had seen by the Kebar River. Each
one went straight ahead.

Judgment on Israel's Leaders

11 Then the Spirit lifted me up and brought me to the gate of
the house of the LORD that faces east. There at the entrance
to the gate were twenty-five men, and I saw among them Jaazaniah son of Azzur and Pelatiah son of Benaiah, leaders of the people. 2The LORD said to me, "Son of man, these are the men who
are plotting evil and giving wicked advice in this city. 3They say,
'Will it not soon be time to build houses?[c] This city is a cooking
pot, and we are the meat.' 4Therefore prophesy against them;
prophesy, son of man."
5Then the Spirit of the LORD came upon me, and he told me to
say: "This is what the LORD says: That is what you are saying,

[a] 5 Hebrew *El-Shaddai* [b] 11 Or *aside* [c] 3 Or *This is not the time to build houses.*

O house of Israel, but I know what is going through your mind.
6You have killed many people in this city and filled its streets with
the dead.
7"Therefore this is what the Sovereign LORD says: The bodies
you have thrown there are the meat and this city is the pot, but I
will drive you out of it. 8You fear the sword, and the sword is what
I will bring against you, declares the Sovereign LORD. 9I will drive
you out of the city and hand you over to foreigners and inflict
punishment on you. 10You will fall by the sword, and I will execute judgment on you at the borders of Israel. Then you will know
that I am the LORD. 11This city will not be a pot for you, nor will
you be the meat in it; I will execute judgment on you at the borders of Israel. 12And you will know that I am the LORD, for you
have not followed my decrees or kept my laws but have conformed to the standards of the nations around you."
13Now as I was prophesying, Pelatiah son of Benaiah died.
Then I fell facedown and cried out in a loud voice, "Ah, Sovereign
LORD! Will you completely destroy the remnant of Israel?"
14The word of the LORD came to me: 15"Son of man, your
brothers—your brothers who are your blood relatives[a] and the
whole house of Israel—are those of whom the people of Jerusalem have said, 'They are[b] far away from the LORD; this land was
given to us as our possession.'

Promised Return of Israel

16"Therefore say: 'This is what the Sovereign LORD says: Although I sent them far away among the nations and scattered
them among the countries, yet for a little while I have been a
sanctuary for them in the countries where they have gone.'
17"Therefore say: 'This is what the Sovereign LORD says: I will
gather you from the nations and bring you back from the countries where you have been scattered, and I will give you back the
land of Israel again.'
18"They will return to it and remove all its vile images and detestable idols. 19I will give them an undivided heart and put a new
spirit in them; I will remove from them their heart of stone and
give them a heart of flesh. 20Then they will follow my decrees and
be careful to keep my laws. They will be my people, and I will be
their God. 21But as for those whose hearts are devoted to their
vile images and detestable idols, I will bring down on their own
heads what they have done, declares the Sovereign LORD."
22Then the cherubim, with the wheels beside them, spread
their wings, and the glory of the God of Israel was above them.
23The glory of the LORD went up from within the city and stopped
above the mountain east of it. 24The Spirit lifted me up and
brought me to the exiles in Babylonia[c] in the vision given by the
Spirit of God.

Then the vision I had seen went up from me, 25and I told the
exiles everything the LORD had shown me.

The Exile Symbolized

12 The word of the LORD came to me: 2"Son of man, you are
living among a rebellious people. They have eyes to see but
do not see and ears to hear but do not hear, for they are a rebellious people.

[a] 15 Or *are in exile with you* (see Septuagint and Syriac) [b] 15 Or *those to whom the people of Jerusalem have said, 'Stay* [c] 24 Or *Chaldea*

(11:19–20) O God, nothing is impossible for You. You change foolish people into sages, weak people into strong warriors, lifeless people into lively, spiritual beings. Would You change me, too? Years of pain and fear and disappointment have hardened my heart into stone. With Your tender, transforming touch, would You soften my heart, Lord? Please help me to love You, and to look after those who need to see Your love in me. (Mk 10:27; 1Co 1:27)

O Lord, you who are all merciful, take away my sins from me, and enkindle within me the fire of your Holy Spirit. Take away this heart of stone from me, and give me a heart of flesh and blood, a heart to love and adore you, a heart which may delight in you, love you and please you, for Christ's sake.

Saint Ambrose (339-397)

Create in me a clean heart, O God,
That I might serve You.
Create in me a clean heart, O God,
That I might be renewed.
So fill me, and heal me, and bring me
back to You.
Create in me a clean heart, O God,
That I might serve You.

"Create in Me"
Mary Rice Hopkins (©1989)

3"Therefore, son of man, pack your belongings for exile and in
the daytime, as they watch, set out and go from where you are to
another place. Perhaps they will understand, though they are a
rebellious house. 4During the daytime, while they watch, bring
out your belongings packed for exile. Then in the evening, while
they are watching, go out like those who go into exile. 5While they
watch, dig through the wall and take your belongings out through
it. 6Put them on your shoulder as they are watching and carry
them out at dusk. Cover your face so that you cannot see the land,
for I have made you a sign to the house of Israel."

7So I did as I was commanded. During the day I brought out
my things packed for exile. Then in the evening I dug through the
wall with my hands. I took my belongings out at dusk, carrying
them on my shoulders while they watched.

8In the morning the word of the LORD came to me: 9"Son of
man, did not that rebellious house of Israel ask you, 'What are
you doing?'

10"Say to them, 'This is what the Sovereign LORD says: This oracle concerns the prince in Jerusalem and the whole house of Israel who are there.' 11Say to them, 'I am a sign to you.'

"As I have done, so it will be done to them. They will go into
exile as captives.

12"The prince among them will put his things on his shoulder
at dusk and leave, and a hole will be dug in the wall for him to go
through. He will cover his face so that he cannot see the land. 13I
will spread my net for him, and he will be caught in my snare; I
will bring him to Babylonia, the land of the Chaldeans, but he will
not see it, and there he will die. 14I will scatter to the winds all
those around him—his staff and all his troops—and I will pursue them with drawn sword.

15"They will know that I am the LORD, when I disperse them
among the nations and scatter them through the countries. 16But
I will spare a few of them from the sword, famine and plague, so
that in the nations where they go they may acknowledge all their
detestable practices. Then they will know that I am the LORD."

17The word of the LORD came to me: 18"Son of man, tremble as
you eat your food, and shudder in fear as you drink your water.
19Say to the people of the land: 'This is what the Sovereign LORD
says about those living in Jerusalem and in the land of Israel: They
will eat their food in anxiety and drink their water in despair, for
their land will be stripped of everything in it because of the violence of all who live there. 20The inhabited towns will be laid
waste and the land will be desolate. Then you will know that I am
the LORD.' "

21The word of the LORD came to me: 22"Son of man, what is
this proverb you have in the land of Israel: 'The days go by and
every vision comes to nothing'? 23Say to them, 'This is what the
Sovereign LORD says: I am going to put an end to this proverb,
and they will no longer quote it in Israel.' Say to them, 'The days
are near when every vision will be fulfilled. 24For there will be no
more false visions or flattering divinations among the people of
Israel. 25But I the LORD will speak what I will, and it shall be fulfilled without delay. For in your days, you rebellious house, I will
fulfill whatever I say, declares the Sovereign LORD.' "

26The word of the LORD came to me: 27"Son of man, the house
of Israel is saying, 'The vision he sees is for many years from now,
and he prophesies about the distant future.'

(12:21–25) Lord, Your promises of blessing are rarely fulfilled as quickly as we would like. Despite our impatience, we thank You for the lessons we have to learn before we receive all that You have for us. Likewise, the disasters You foretell are also delayed, so that no one will be denied the opportunity to repent. Whatever You promise, Lord—joys or judgments—will be fulfilled in Your perfect timing. Help us to believe and to proclaim the reality of Your Word: "For the revelation awaits an appointed time; it speaks of the end and will not prove false. Though it linger, wait for it; it will certainly come and will not delay." (Hab 2:3; 2Pe 3:9)

God is going to test me with delays; and with the delays will come suffering, but through it all stands God's pledge: His new covenant with me in Christ, and His inviolable promise of every lesser blessing that I need. The delay and the suffering are part of the promised blessing; let me praise Him for them today; and let me wait on the Lord and be of good courage and He will strengthen my heart.

Charles G. Trumbull (1872-1941)

28“Therefore say to them, ‘This is what the Sovereign LORD
says: None of my words will be delayed any longer; whatever I say
will be fulfilled, declares the Sovereign LORD.’ ”

False Prophets Condemned

13 The word of the LORD came to me: 2“Son of man, prophesy against the prophets of Israel who are now prophesying.
Say to those who prophesy out of their own imagination: ‘Hear the
word of the LORD! 3This is what the Sovereign LORD says: Woe to
the foolish[a] prophets who follow their own spirit and have seen
nothing! 4Your prophets, O Israel, are like jackals among ruins.
5You have not gone up to the breaks in the wall to repair it for the
house of Israel so that it will stand firm in the battle on the day of
the LORD. 6Their visions are false and their divinations a lie. They
say, “The LORD declares,” when the LORD has not sent them; yet
they expect their words to be fulfilled. 7Have you not seen false visions and uttered lying divinations when you say, “The LORD declares,” though I have not spoken?

8“ ‘Therefore this is what the Sovereign LORD says: Because of
your false words and lying visions, I am against you, declares the
Sovereign LORD. 9My hand will be against the prophets who see
false visions and utter lying divinations. They will not belong to
the council of my people or be listed in the records of the house
of Israel, nor will they enter the land of Israel. Then you will
know that I am the Sovereign LORD.

10“ ‘Because they lead my people astray, saying, “Peace,” when
there is no peace, and because, when a flimsy wall is built, they
cover it with whitewash, 11therefore tell those who cover it with
whitewash that it is going to fall. Rain will come in torrents, and
I will send hailstones hurtling down, and violent winds will burst
forth. 12When the wall collapses, will people not ask you, “Where
is the whitewash you covered it with?”

13“ ‘Therefore this is what the Sovereign LORD says: In my
wrath I will unleash a violent wind, and in my anger hailstones
and torrents of rain will fall with destructive fury. 14I will tear
down the wall you have covered with whitewash and will level it
to the ground so that its foundation will be laid bare. When it[b]
falls, you will be destroyed in it; and you will know that I am the
LORD. 15So I will spend my wrath against the wall and against
those who covered it with whitewash. I will say to you, “The wall
is gone and so are those who whitewashed it, 16those prophets of
Israel who prophesied to Jerusalem and saw visions of peace for
her when there was no peace, declares the Sovereign LORD.” ’

17“Now, son of man, set your face against the daughters of your
people who prophesy out of their own imagination. Prophesy
against them 18and say, ‘This is what the Sovereign LORD says: Woe
to the women who sew magic charms on all their wrists and make
veils of various lengths for their heads in order to ensnare people. Will you ensnare the lives of my people but preserve your
own? 19You have profaned me among my people for a few handfuls of barley and scraps of bread. By lying to my people, who listen to lies, you have killed those who should not have died and
have spared those who should not live.

20“ ‘Therefore this is what the Sovereign LORD says: I am against
your magic charms with which you ensnare people like birds and

[a] 3 Or *wicked* [b] 14 Or *the city*

(13:8–12) You, O Lord, are the God of Truth. You despise false prophets and lying visions. You demand that Your people listen only to You and to those who truly speak for You. You always speak truth, and You always keep Your promises. Spare us the consequences of refusing to hear and obey Your Word. Your Spirit is the Spirit of truth, Lord God. Fill us with Your Spirit. (Jn 14:16–17)

(14:2–5) Recapture our hearts, Sovereign Lord. Too easily we have been seduced by the idols of our generation. Like Your people of old we have set them up in our hearts, and they have become stumbling blocks for us. Meet us in the midst of our quest for pleasure, for power, for profit, and turn our hearts and our faces back to You. You are the One true God, and we can have no peace until we worship You with all our hearts.

Strengthen for service, Lord, the hands
That holy things have taken;
And let the ears that heard your Word
To falsehood never waken.

The tongues that sang your holy name
Now purge of all deception;
Keep bright the eyes that saw your love
And sharpen their perception.

And may the feet that walked your courts
Be never lured to wander;
But lead the faithful nourished here
To journey on in splendor.

"Strengthen for Service, Lord"
The English Hymnal (1906)

God, how desperately I need your wisdom and how grateful I am that you are the only wise God. Thank you that you liberally share your truth. I ask you for your wisdom and expect that I will have precisely the insight and information I need to do your will. Thank you for forgiving me my sins so that I can receive your wisdom by faith and grace. I have made many mistakes, but I hope to make far fewer as I learn more about you and apply your wisdom to my daily tasks.

Charles Stanley (1932-)

I will tear them from your arms; I will set free the people that you
ensnare like birds. 21I will tear off your veils and save my people
from your hands, and they will no longer fall prey to your power.
Then you will know that I am the LORD. 22Because you disheartened the righteous with your lies, when I had brought them no
grief, and because you encouraged the wicked not to turn from
their evil ways and so save their lives, 23therefore you will no
longer see false visions or practice divination. I will save my people from your hands. And then you will know that I am the LORD.' "

Idolaters Condemned

14 Some of the elders of Israel came to me and sat down in
front of me. 2Then the word of the LORD came to me: 3"Son
of man, these men have set up idols in their hearts and put
wicked stumbling blocks before their faces. Should I let them inquire of me at all? 4Therefore speak to them and tell them, 'This
is what the Sovereign LORD says: When any Israelite sets up idols
in his heart and puts a wicked stumbling block before his face
and then goes to a prophet, I the LORD will answer him myself in
keeping with his great idolatry. 5I will do this to recapture the
hearts of the people of Israel, who have all deserted me for their
idols.'

6"Therefore say to the house of Israel, 'This is what the Sovereign LORD says: Repent! Turn from your idols and renounce all
your detestable practices!

7" 'When any Israelite or any alien living in Israel separates
himself from me and sets up idols in his heart and puts a wicked
stumbling block before his face and then goes to a prophet to inquire of me, I the LORD will answer him myself. 8I will set my face
against that man and make him an example and a byword. I will
cut him off from my people. Then you will know that I am the
LORD.

9" 'And if the prophet is enticed to utter a prophecy, I the LORD
have enticed that prophet, and I will stretch out my hand against
him and destroy him from among my people Israel. 10They will
bear their guilt—the prophet will be as guilty as the one who
consults him. 11Then the people of Israel will no longer stray
from me, nor will they defile themselves anymore with all their
sins. They will be my people, and I will be their God, declares the
Sovereign LORD.' "

Judgment Inescapable

12The word of the LORD came to me: 13"Son of man, if a country sins against me by being unfaithful and I stretch out my hand
against it to cut off its food supply and send famine upon it and
kill its men and their animals, 14even if these three men—Noah,
Daniel[a] and Job—were in it, they could save only themselves by
their righteousness, declares the Sovereign LORD.

15"Or if I send wild beasts through that country and they leave
it childless and it becomes desolate so that no one can pass
through it because of the beasts, 16as surely as I live, declares the
Sovereign LORD, even if these three men were in it, they could not
save their own sons or daughters. They alone would be saved, but
the land would be desolate.

17"Or if I bring a sword against that country and say, 'Let the

[a] *14* Or *Danel;* the Hebrew spelling may suggest a person other than the prophet Daniel; also in verse 20.

sword pass throughout the land,' and I kill its men and their animals, 18as surely as I live, declares the Sovereign LORD, even if
these three men were in it, they could not save their own sons or
daughters. They alone would be saved.
19"Or if I send a plague into that land and pour out my wrath
upon it through bloodshed, killing its men and their animals, 20as
surely as I live, declares the Sovereign LORD, even if Noah, Daniel
and Job were in it, they could save neither son nor daughter. They
would save only themselves by their righteousness.
21"For this is what the Sovereign LORD says: How much worse
will it be when I send against Jerusalem my four dreadful judgments—sword and famine and wild beasts and plague—to kill
its men and their animals! 22Yet there will be some survivors—
sons and daughters who will be brought out of it. They will come
to you, and when you see their conduct and their actions, you will
be consoled regarding the disaster I have brought upon Jerusalem—every disaster I have brought upon it. 23You will be consoled when you see their conduct and their actions, for you will
know that I have done nothing in it without cause, declares the
Sovereign LORD."

Jerusalem, A Useless Vine

15 The word of the LORD came to me: 2"Son of man, how is
the wood of a vine better than that of a branch on any of
the trees in the forest? 3Is wood ever taken from it to make anything useful? Do they make pegs from it to hang things on? 4And
after it is thrown on the fire as fuel and the fire burns both ends
and chars the middle, is it then useful for anything? 5If it was not
useful for anything when it was whole, how much less can it be
made into something useful when the fire has burned it and it is
charred?
6"Therefore this is what the Sovereign LORD says: As I have
given the wood of the vine among the trees of the forest as fuel for
the fire, so will I treat the people living in Jerusalem. 7I will set my
face against them. Although they have come out of the fire, the fire
will yet consume them. And when I set my face against them, you
will know that I am the LORD. 8I will make the land desolate because they have been unfaithful, declares the Sovereign LORD."

An Allegory of Unfaithful Jerusalem

16 The word of the LORD came to me: 2"Son of man, confront
Jerusalem with her detestable practices 3and say, 'This is
what the Sovereign LORD says to Jerusalem: Your ancestry and
birth were in the land of the Canaanites; your father was an Amorite and your mother a Hittite. 4On the day you were born your
cord was not cut, nor were you washed with water to make you
clean, nor were you rubbed with salt or wrapped in cloths. 5No
one looked on you with pity or had compassion enough to do any
of these things for you. Rather, you were thrown out into the open
field, for on the day you were born you were despised.
6" 'Then I passed by and saw you kicking about in your blood,
and as you lay there in your blood I said to you, "Live!"[a] 7I made
you grow like a plant of the field. You grew up and developed and
became the most beautiful of jewels.[b] Your breasts were formed
and your hair grew, you who were naked and bare.

[a] 6 A few Hebrew manuscripts, Septuagint and Syriac; most Hebrew manuscripts *"Live!" And as you lay there in your blood I said to you, "Live!"* [b] 7 Or *became mature*

(14:22–23) God, thank You that today, just as in Ezekiel's time, Your heart is motivated by love and mercy. Even as You discipline us You long to comfort us, to teach us, to help us see that You have just cause for Your actions. And when the test is over and the lesson has been learned, we see that You were justified in Your decision and should be glorified for the results. You bring us out of our troubles, as You brought out the remnant, to be monuments of Your mercy.

There is no loss in being a Christian and making God the first object. But, if you make anything else your goal, with all your running, should you run ever so well, you will fall short of the mark; or if you gain it, you will fall uncrowned, unhonored to the earth. "My soul, wait thou only upon God" (Ps. 62:5).

Charles Haddon Spurgeon (1834–1892)

Savior, when in dust to you
Low we bow in homage due;
When, repentant, to the skies
Scarce we lift our weeping eyes;
Oh, by all your pains and woe
Suffered once for us below,
Bending from your throne on high,
Hear our penitential cry!

"Savior, When in Dust to You"
Robert Grant (1779–1838)

We worship you, we confess to you, we praise you, we bless you, we sing to you, and we give thanks to you: Maker, Nourisher, Guardian, Healer, Lord, and Father of all.

You are the Fountain of Life, the Treasure of everlasting goods to whom the heavens sing praise—all the angels and heavenly powers, crying out to one another—while we, the weak and unworthy join with them singing:

"Holy, holy, holy, Lord God of Hosts, the whole earth is full of the majesty of your glory."

Lancelot Andrews (1555-1626)

(16:7–14) Sovereign Lord, You have always cared for Your chosen ones as a parent cherishes a child, as a husband adores a beloved wife. Your tender compassion toward us is revealed in rich gifts, in abundant provision, in blessings of beauty and favor. O God, spare us the errors of Your people of old, who betrayed Your trust and spurned Your love. Keep us faithful, grateful and holy. Everything we have comes from You, Father in Heaven. Do not allow us to forget You or to take lightly Your overwhelming generosity to us.

You rescued me and picked me up,
A living hope of grace revealed,
A life transformed in righteousness;
Oh Lord, You have rescued me.
Forgiving me, You healed my heart
And set me free from sin and death.
You bought me life,
You've made me whole;
Oh Lord, You have rescued me.

And You loved me
Before I knew You;
And You knew me for all time.
I've been created
In Your image, Oh Lord,
And You brought me,
And You sought me,
Your blood poured out for me,
A new creation
In Your image, Oh Lord.
You rescued me.

"You Rescued Me"
Geoff Bullock (©1993)

8" 'Later I passed by, and when I looked at you and saw that
you were old enough for love, I spread the corner of my garment
over you and covered your nakedness. I gave you my solemn oath
and entered into a covenant with you, declares the Sovereign
LORD, and you became mine.
9" 'I bathed[a] you with water and washed the blood from you
and put ointments on you. 10I clothed you with an embroidered
dress and put leather sandals on you. I dressed you in fine linen
and covered you with costly garments. 11I adorned you with jewelry: I put bracelets on your arms and a necklace around your
neck, 12and I put a ring on your nose, earrings on your ears and
a beautiful crown on your head. 13So you were adorned with gold
and silver; your clothes were of fine linen and costly fabric and
embroidered cloth. Your food was fine flour, honey and olive oil.
You became very beautiful and rose to be a queen. 14And your
fame spread among the nations on account of your beauty, because the splendor I had given you made your beauty perfect, declares the Sovereign LORD.
15" 'But you trusted in your beauty and used your fame to become a prostitute. You lavished your favors on anyone who
passed by and your beauty became his.[b] 16You took some of your
garments to make gaudy high places, where you carried on your
prostitution. Such things should not happen, nor should they ever
occur. 17You also took the fine jewelry I gave you, the jewelry
made of my gold and silver, and you made for yourself male idols
and engaged in prostitution with them. 18And you took your embroidered clothes to put on them, and you offered my oil and incense before them. 19Also the food I provided for you—the fine
flour, olive oil and honey I gave you to eat—you offered as fragrant incense before them. That is what happened, declares the
Sovereign LORD.
20" 'And you took your sons and daughters whom you bore to
me and sacrificed them as food to the idols. Was your prostitution
not enough? 21You slaughtered my children and sacrificed them[c]
to the idols. 22In all your detestable practices and your prostitution you did not remember the days of your youth, when you were
naked and bare, kicking about in your blood.
23" 'Woe! Woe to you, declares the Sovereign LORD. In addition
to all your other wickedness, 24you built a mound for yourself
and made a lofty shrine in every public square. 25At the head of
every street you built your lofty shrines and degraded your beauty, offering your body with increasing promiscuity to anyone who
passed by. 26You engaged in prostitution with the Egyptians, your
lustful neighbors, and provoked me to anger with your increasing
promiscuity. 27So I stretched out my hand against you and reduced your territory; I gave you over to the greed of your enemies, the daughters of the Philistines, who were shocked by your
lewd conduct. 28You engaged in prostitution with the Assyrians
too, because you were insatiable; and even after that, you still
were not satisfied. 29Then you increased your promiscuity to include Babylonia,[d] a land of merchants, but even with this you
were not satisfied.
30" 'How weak-willed you are, declares the Sovereign LORD,
when you do all these things, acting like a brazen prostitute!

[a] 9 Or *I had bathed* [b] 15 Most Hebrew manuscripts; one Hebrew manuscript (see some Septuagint manuscripts) *by. Such a thing should not happen* [c] 21 Or *and made them pass through ⌞the fire⌟* [d] 29 Or *Chaldea*

31When you built your mounds at the head of every street and
made your lofty shrines in every public square, you were unlike a
prostitute, because you scorned payment.
32" 'You adulterous wife! You prefer strangers to your own
husband! 33Every prostitute receives a fee, but you give gifts to all
your lovers, bribing them to come to you from everywhere for
your illicit favors. 34So in your prostitution you are the opposite
of others; no one runs after you for your favors. You are the very
opposite, for you give payment and none is given to you.
35" 'Therefore, you prostitute, hear the word of the LORD!
36This is what the Sovereign LORD says: Because you poured out
your wealth[a] and exposed your nakedness in your promiscuity
with your lovers, and because of all your detestable idols, and because you gave them your children's blood, 37therefore I am
going to gather all your lovers, with whom you found pleasure,
those you loved as well as those you hated. I will gather them
against you from all around and will strip you in front of them,
and they will see all your nakedness. 38I will sentence you to the
punishment of women who commit adultery and who shed blood;
I will bring upon you the blood vengeance of my wrath and jealous anger. 39Then I will hand you over to your lovers, and they
will tear down your mounds and destroy your lofty shrines. They
will strip you of your clothes and take your fine jewelry and leave
you naked and bare. 40They will bring a mob against you, who
will stone you and hack you to pieces with their swords. 41They
will burn down your houses and inflict punishment on you in the
sight of many women. I will put a stop to your prostitution, and
you will no longer pay your lovers. 42Then my wrath against you
will subside and my jealous anger will turn away from you; I will
be calm and no longer angry.
43" 'Because you did not remember the days of your youth but
enraged me with all these things, I will surely bring down on your
head what you have done, declares the Sovereign LORD. Did you
not add lewdness to all your other detestable practices?
44" 'Everyone who quotes proverbs will quote this proverb
about you: "Like mother, like daughter." 45You are a true daughter of your mother, who despised her husband and her children;
and you are a true sister of your sisters, who despised their husbands and their children. Your mother was a Hittite and your father an Amorite. 46Your older sister was Samaria, who lived to the
north of you with her daughters; and your younger sister, who
lived to the south of you with her daughters, was Sodom. 47You
not only walked in their ways and copied their detestable practices, but in all your ways you soon became more depraved than
they. 48As surely as I live, declares the Sovereign LORD, your sister
Sodom and her daughters never did what you and your daughters
have done.
49" 'Now this was the sin of your sister Sodom: She and her
daughters were arrogant, overfed and unconcerned; they did not
help the poor and needy. 50They were haughty and did detestable
things before me. Therefore I did away with them as you have
seen. 51Samaria did not commit half the sins you did. You have
done more detestable things than they, and have made your sisters seem righteous by all these things you have done. 52Bear
your disgrace, for you have furnished some justification for your

[a] 36 Or *lust*

(16:32–42) God, Your heart is impassioned for Your people, and Your jealousy is ignited by our unfaithfulness. How little we understand the love You have for us—a love that finds idolatry detestable and intolerable, a love intent on utterly destroying our false gods. And yet, in all Your rage against our sin, You never cease to cherish us and to look forward to a time of repentance and reconciliation. Help us to love You deeply, just as You have first loved us.

sisters. Because your sins were more vile than theirs, they appear more righteous than you. So then, be ashamed and bear your disgrace, for you have made your sisters appear righteous.

53“ ‘However, I will restore the fortunes of Sodom and her daughters and of Samaria and her daughters, and your fortunes along with them, 54so that you may bear your disgrace and be ashamed of all you have done in giving them comfort. 55And your sisters, Sodom with her daughters and Samaria with her daughters, will return to what they were before; and you and your daughters will return to what you were before. 56You would not even mention your sister Sodom in the day of your pride, 57before your wickedness was uncovered. Even so, you are now scorned by the daughters of Edom[a] and all her neighbors and the daughters of the Philistines—all those around you who despise you. 58You will bear the consequences of your lewdness and your detestable practices, declares the LORD.

59“ ‘This is what the Sovereign LORD says: I will deal with you as you deserve, because you have despised my oath by breaking the covenant. 60Yet I will remember the covenant I made with you in the days of your youth, and I will establish an everlasting covenant with you. 61Then you will remember your ways and be ashamed when you receive your sisters, both those who are older than you and those who are younger. I will give them to you as daughters, but not on the basis of my covenant with you. 62So I will establish my covenant with you, and you will know that I am the LORD. 63Then, when I make atonement for you for all you have done, you will remember and be ashamed and never again open your mouth because of your humiliation, declares the Sovereign LORD.’ ”

Two Eagles and a Vine

17 The word of the LORD came to me: 2“Son of man, set forth an allegory and tell the house of Israel a parable. 3Say to them, ‘This is what the Sovereign LORD says: A great eagle with powerful wings, long feathers and full plumage of varied colors came to Lebanon. Taking hold of the top of a cedar, 4he broke off its topmost shoot and carried it away to a land of merchants, where he planted it in a city of traders.

5“ ‘He took some of the seed of your land and put it in fertile soil. He planted it like a willow by abundant water, 6and it sprouted and became a low, spreading vine. Its branches turned toward him, but its roots remained under it. So it became a vine and produced branches and put out leafy boughs.

7“ ‘But there was another great eagle with powerful wings and full plumage. The vine now sent out its roots toward him from the plot where it was planted and stretched out its branches to him for water. 8It had been planted in good soil by abundant water so that it would produce branches, bear fruit and become a splendid vine.’

9“Say to them, ‘This is what the Sovereign LORD says: Will it thrive? Will it not be uprooted and stripped of its fruit so that it withers? All its new growth will wither. It will not take a strong arm or many people to pull it up by the roots. 10Even if it is transplanted, will it thrive? Will it not wither completely when the east wind strikes it—wither away in the plot where it grew?’ ”

[a] 57 Many Hebrew manuscripts and Syriac; most Hebrew manuscripts, Septuagint and Vulgate *Aram*

(16:59–63) Sovereign Lord, in Ezekiel's time You promised to establish an everlasting covenant with Your people. Today, Your everlasting covenant with us is sealed with the blood of Your only begotten Son. Not only have You remembered Your covenant with us, but You have also atoned for our sin through Jesus' death on the cross. We worship, praise and thank You for the amazing love that caused Him to die so that we can live with You forever.

In His death Christ supremely revealed the holiness and righteousness of God as well as the love of God which prompted the sacrifice. In a similar way the infinite wisdom of God is revealed as no human mind would ever have devised such a way of salvation, and only an infinite God would be willing to sacrifice His Son.

John F. Walvoord (1910-)

My hope is built on nothing less
Than Jesus' blood and righteousness;
I dare not trust the sweetest frame,
But wholly lean on Jesus' name.

On Christ the solid Rock, I stand;
All other ground is sinking sand,
All other ground is sinking sand.

His oath, His covenant, His blood,
Support me in the whelming flood;
When all around my soul gives way,
He then is all my hope and stay.

"The Solid Rock"
Edward Mote (1797-1874)

11 Then the word of the LORD came to me: 12 "Say to this rebellious house, 'Do you not know what these things mean?' Say to
them: 'The king of Babylon went to Jerusalem and carried off her
king and her nobles, bringing them back with him to Babylon.
13 Then he took a member of the royal family and made a treaty
with him, putting him under oath. He also carried away the leading men of the land, 14 so that the kingdom would be brought low,
unable to rise again, surviving only by keeping his treaty. 15 But
the king rebelled against him by sending his envoys to Egypt to get
horses and a large army. Will he succeed? Will he who does such
things escape? Will he break the treaty and yet escape?

16 " 'As surely as I live, declares the Sovereign LORD, he shall
die in Babylon, in the land of the king who put him on the throne,
whose oath he despised and whose treaty he broke. 17 Pharaoh
with his mighty army and great horde will be of no help to him in
war, when ramps are built and siege works erected to destroy
many lives. 18 He despised the oath by breaking the covenant. Because he had given his hand in pledge and yet did all these things,
he shall not escape.

19 " 'Therefore this is what the Sovereign LORD says: As surely as
I live, I will bring down on his head my oath that he despised and
my covenant that he broke. 20 I will spread my net for him, and he
will be caught in my snare. I will bring him to Babylon and execute judgment upon him there because he was unfaithful to me.
21 All his fleeing troops will fall by the sword, and the survivors
will be scattered to the winds. Then you will know that I the LORD
have spoken.

22 " 'This is what the Sovereign LORD says: I myself will take a
shoot from the very top of a cedar and plant it; I will break off a
tender sprig from its topmost shoots and plant it on a high and
lofty mountain. 23 On the mountain heights of Israel I will plant it;
it will produce branches and bear fruit and become a splendid
cedar. Birds of every kind will nest in it; they will find shelter in
the shade of its branches. 24 All the trees of the field will know that
I the LORD bring down the tall tree and make the low tree grow
tall. I dry up the green tree and make the dry tree flourish.

" 'I the LORD have spoken, and I will do it.' "

The Soul Who Sins Will Die

18 The word of the LORD came to me: 2 "What do you people
mean by quoting this proverb about the land of Israel:

" 'The fathers eat sour grapes,
and the children's teeth are set on edge'?

3 "As surely as I live, declares the Sovereign LORD, you will no
longer quote this proverb in Israel. 4 For every living soul belongs
to me, the father as well as the son—both alike belong to me. The
soul who sins is the one who will die.

5 "Suppose there is a righteous man
who does what is just and right.
6 He does not eat at the mountain shrines
or look to the idols of the house of Israel.
He does not defile his neighbor's wife
or lie with a woman during her period.
7 He does not oppress anyone,
but returns what he took in pledge for a
loan.

(17:24) You stand forever, Lord, against human pride and willfulness. Since ancient times You have humbled the mighty and raised up the humble. We are grateful to You, our God and Father, because we have been transformed by Your sovereign ways. We are foolish, but You make us wise. We struggle with weakness, but You provide strength. We deserve death, but You have given us eternal life.

Deep humility is a strong bulwark, and as we enter into it, we find safety and true exaltation. The foolishness of God is wiser than man, and the weakness of God is stronger than man. Being unclothed of our own wisdom and knowing the abasement of the creature, therein we find that power to arise which gives health and vigor to us.

John Woolman (1720-1772)

He does not commit robbery
but gives his food to the hungry
and provides clothing for the naked.
8 He does not lend at usury
or take excessive interest.[a]
He withholds his hand from doing wrong
and judges fairly between man and man.
9 He follows my decrees
and faithfully keeps my laws.
That man is righteous;
he will surely live,
declares the Sovereign LORD.

10 "Suppose he has a violent son, who sheds blood or does any
of these other things[b] 11 (though the father has done none of
them):

"He eats at the mountain shrines.
He defiles his neighbor's wife.
12 He oppresses the poor and needy.
He commits robbery.
He does not return what he took in pledge.
He looks to the idols.
He does detestable things.
13 He lends at usury and takes excessive interest.

Will such a man live? He will not! Because he has done all these detestable things, he will surely be put to death and his blood will be on his own head.

14 "But suppose this son has a son who sees all the sins his father commits, and though he sees them, he does not do such things:

15 "He does not eat at the mountain shrines
or look to the idols of the house of Israel.
He does not defile his neighbor's wife.
16 He does not oppress anyone
or require a pledge for a loan.
He does not commit robbery
but gives his food to the hungry
and provides clothing for the naked.
17 He withholds his hand from sin[c]
and takes no usury or excessive interest.
He keeps my laws and follows my decrees.

He will not die for his father's sin; he will surely live. 18 But his father will die for his own sin, because he practiced extortion,
robbed his brother and did what was wrong among his people.
19 "Yet you ask, 'Why does the son not share the guilt of his father?' Since the son has done what is just and right and has been
careful to keep all my decrees, he will surely live. 20 The soul who
sins is the one who will die. The son will not share the guilt of the father, nor will the father share the guilt of the son. The righteousness of the righteous man will be credited to him, and the wickedness of the wicked will be charged against him.
21 "But if a wicked man turns away from all the sins he has
committed and keeps all my decrees and does what is just and

[a] 8 Or *take interest*; similarly in verses 13 and 17 [b] 10 Or *things to a brother*
[c] 17 Septuagint (see also verse 8); Hebrew *from the poor*

(18:14–20) Father, we praise You for Your grace and mercy to us and to our children. You have extended great love to us as a family, yet You have always led us one by one as unique individuals. You have understood our personalities, encouraged our strengths and forgiven our sins, fathering us as if each of us were Your only child.

God is the Perfect Parent. He always disciplines in love. He is faithful, generous, kind, and just, and He longs to spend time with you. Your Father wants you to receive His love and to know that you are special and unique in His eyes.
Floyd McClung, Jr. (1945-)

right, he will surely live; he will not die. 22 None of the offenses he
has committed will be remembered against him. Because of the
righteous things he has done, he will live. 23 Do I take any pleasure in the death of the wicked? declares the Sovereign LORD.
Rather, am I not pleased when they turn from their ways and live?
24 "But if a righteous man turns from his righteousness and
commits sin and does the same detestable things the wicked man
does, will he live? None of the righteous things he has done will
be remembered. Because of the unfaithfulness he is guilty of and
because of the sins he has committed, he will die.
25 "Yet you say, 'The way of the Lord is not just.' Hear, O house
of Israel: Is my way unjust? Is it not your ways that are unjust?
26 If a righteous man turns from his righteousness and commits
sin, he will die for it; because of the sin he has committed he will
die. 27 But if a wicked man turns away from the wickedness he has
committed and does what is just and right, he will save his life.
28 Because he considers all the offenses he has committed and
turns away from them, he will surely live; he will not die. 29 Yet the
house of Israel says, 'The way of the Lord is not just.' Are my ways
unjust, O house of Israel? Is it not your ways that are unjust?
30 "Therefore, O house of Israel, I will judge you, each one according to his ways, declares the Sovereign LORD. Repent! Turn
away from all your offenses; then sin will not be your downfall.
31 Rid yourselves of all the offenses you have committed, and get
a new heart and a new spirit. Why will you die, O house of Israel?
32 For I take no pleasure in the death of anyone, declares the Sovereign LORD. Repent and live!

A Lament for Israel's Princes

19 "Take up a lament concerning the princes of Israel 2 and
say:

" 'What a lioness was your mother
among the lions!
She lay down among the young lions
and reared her cubs.
3 She brought up one of her cubs,
and he became a strong lion.
He learned to tear the prey
and he devoured men.
4 The nations heard about him,
and he was trapped in their pit.
They led him with hooks
to the land of Egypt.
5 " 'When she saw her hope unfulfilled,
her expectation gone,
she took another of her cubs
and made him a strong lion.
6 He prowled among the lions,
for he was now a strong lion.
He learned to tear the prey
and he devoured men.
7 He broke down[a] their strongholds
and devastated their towns.
The land and all who were in it

[a] 7 Targum (see Septuagint); Hebrew *He knew*

(18:25–29) Our God, You are the Father of Righteousness. Your ways are the standard of justice. Rather than striving against Your judgments, teach us to submit to them. And teach us, Lord, to please You in all that we do: to act justly, to love mercy and to walk humbly with You, our God. (Mic 6:8)

Holy One, Most Holy One,
Your ways are higher than mine.
Holy One, Most Holy One,
May Your ways be mine.

Your ways are higher than the
mountains.
Your love is deeper than the sea.
Your mercy, flowing like a fountain,
Has touched my heart and made me
free.

"Most Holy One"
Kelly Willard and Paul Baloche (©1990)

God of our fathers and our God, give us the faith to believe in the ultimate triumph of righteousness . . . We pray for bifocals of faith that see the despair and the need of the hour but also see, further on, the patience of our God working out His plan in the world He has made . . . Through Jesus our Lord. Amen.

Peter Marshall (1902-1949)

(19:1–14) Lord, like Ezekiel, we lament the sin that causes You deep grief, sin that causes You to take action against Your people. Ezekiel's words are Your lament, O Lord—the cry of a brokenhearted God. You love us so deeply, yet we turn from You again and again. We forget Your immense generosity and Your abundant blessings. Help us to learn from Your people of old, who grieved You with their rebellion. Teach us to return to You, to respond to You, to cling to You with all our hearts. (Ps 103:2–14)

Why is it that some of God's children live victorious lives while others are in a state of constant defeat? The difference is not accounted for by the presence or absence of the Spirit (for He dwells in the heart of every child of God) but by this, that some recognize His indwelling and others do not. True revelation of the fact of the Spirit's indwelling will revolutionize the life of any Christian.

Watchman Nee (1903–1972)

were terrified by his roaring.
8 Then the nations came against him,
those from regions round about.
They spread their net for him,
and he was trapped in their pit.
9 With hooks they pulled him into a cage
and brought him to the king of Babylon.
They put him in prison,
so his roar was heard no longer
on the mountains of Israel.

10 " 'Your mother was like a vine in your vineyard[a]
planted by the water;
it was fruitful and full of branches
because of abundant water.
11 Its branches were strong,
fit for a ruler's scepter.
It towered high
above the thick foliage,
conspicuous for its height
and for its many branches.
12 But it was uprooted in fury
and thrown to the ground.
The east wind made it shrivel,
it was stripped of its fruit;
its strong branches withered
and fire consumed them.
13 Now it is planted in the desert,
in a dry and thirsty land.
14 Fire spread from one of its main[b] branches
and consumed its fruit.
No strong branch is left on it
fit for a ruler's scepter.'

This is a lament and is to be used as a lament."

Rebellious Israel

20 In the seventh year, in the fifth month on the tenth day,
some of the elders of Israel came to inquire of the LORD,
and they sat down in front of me.
2 Then the word of the LORD came to me: 3 "Son of man, speak
to the elders of Israel and say to them, 'This is what the Sovereign
LORD says: Have you come to inquire of me? As surely as I live, I
will not let you inquire of me, declares the Sovereign LORD.'
4 "Will you judge them? Will you judge them, son of man? Then
confront them with the detestable practices of their fathers 5 and
say to them: 'This is what the Sovereign LORD says: On the day I
chose Israel, I swore with uplifted hand to the descendants of the
house of Jacob and revealed myself to them in Egypt. With uplifted hand I said to them, "I am the LORD your God." 6 On that day I
swore to them that I would bring them out of Egypt into a land I
had searched out for them, a land flowing with milk and honey,
the most beautiful of all lands. 7 And I said to them, "Each of you,
get rid of the vile images you have set your eyes on, and do not
defile yourselves with the idols of Egypt. I am the LORD your God."
8 " 'But they rebelled against me and would not listen to me;

[a] 10 Two Hebrew manuscripts; most Hebrew manuscripts *your blood* [b] 14 Or *from under its*

they did not get rid of the vile images they had set their eyes on,
nor did they forsake the idols of Egypt. So I said I would pour out
my wrath on them and spend my anger against them in Egypt.
9But for the sake of my name I did what would keep it from being
profaned in the eyes of the nations they lived among and in whose
sight I had revealed myself to the Israelites by bringing them out
of Egypt. 10Therefore I led them out of Egypt and brought them
into the desert. 11I gave them my decrees and made known to
them my laws, for the man who obeys them will live by them.
12Also I gave them my Sabbaths as a sign between us, so they
would know that I the LORD made them holy.

13" 'Yet the people of Israel rebelled against me in the desert.
They did not follow my decrees but rejected my laws—although
the man who obeys them will live by them—and they utterly desecrated my Sabbaths. So I said I would pour out my wrath on
them and destroy them in the desert. 14But for the sake of my
name I did what would keep it from being profaned in the eyes of
the nations in whose sight I had brought them out. 15Also with
uplifted hand I swore to them in the desert that I would not bring
them into the land I had given them—a land flowing with milk
and honey, most beautiful of all lands— 16because they rejected
my laws and did not follow my decrees and desecrated my Sabbaths. For their hearts were devoted to their idols. 17Yet I looked
on them with pity and did not destroy them or put an end to them
in the desert. 18I said to their children in the desert, "Do not follow the statutes of your fathers or keep their laws or defile yourselves with their idols. 19I am the LORD your God; follow my
decrees and be careful to keep my laws. 20Keep my Sabbaths holy,
that they may be a sign between us. Then you will know that I am
the LORD your God."

21" 'But the children rebelled against me: They did not follow
my decrees, they were not careful to keep my laws—although the
man who obeys them will live by them—and they desecrated my
Sabbaths. So I said I would pour out my wrath on them and spend
my anger against them in the desert. 22But I withheld my hand,
and for the sake of my name I did what would keep it from being
profaned in the eyes of the nations in whose sight I had brought
them out. 23Also with uplifted hand I swore to them in the desert
that I would disperse them among the nations and scatter them
through the countries, 24because they had not obeyed my laws
but had rejected my decrees and desecrated my Sabbaths, and
their eyes ⌊lusted⌋ after their fathers' idols. 25I also gave them
over to statutes that were not good and laws they could not live
by; 26I let them become defiled through their gifts—the sacrifice
of every firstborn[a]—that I might fill them with horror so they
would know that I am the LORD.'

27"Therefore, son of man, speak to the people of Israel and say
to them, 'This is what the Sovereign LORD says: In this also your fathers blasphemed me by forsaking me: 28When I brought them
into the land I had sworn to give them and they saw any high hill
or any leafy tree, there they offered their sacrifices, made offerings that provoked me to anger, presented their fragrant incense
and poured out their drink offerings. 29Then I said to them: What
is this high place you go to?' " (It is called Bamah[b] to this day.)

[a] 26 Or —*making every firstborn pass through ⌊the fire⌋* [b] 29 *Bamah* means *high place.*

Without the conviction of the Holy Spirit and the repentance that must follow, there is no way out of our [sinful] predicament. We have the capacity to change anything about our lives–jobs, homes, cars, even spouses–but we cannot change our own sinful nature.

Charles Colson (1931-)

(20:13–20) If only I hated sin as much as You do, Father! You have repeatedly demonstrated that disobedience is repugnant to You, idolatry is detestable and rebellion is abhorrent. I, however, am more often intrigued by sin than offended by it. Forgive me for toying with temptation and flirting with seduction. Change my heart, O God. Make me pure, as You are pure.

By His grace I am redeemed,
By His blood I am made clean,
And I now can know Him face to face.
By His power I have been raised,
Hidden now in Christ by faith,
I will praise the glory of His grace.

"By His Grace"
Steve Fry (©1996)

Judgment and Restoration

30"Therefore say to the house of Israel: 'This is what the Sovereign LORD says: Will you defile yourselves the way your fathers
did and lust after their vile images? 31When you offer your gifts—
the sacrifice of your sons in[a] the fire—you continue to defile
yourselves with all your idols to this day. Am I to let you inquire
of me, O house of Israel? As surely as I live, declares the Sovereign LORD, I will not let you inquire of me.
32" 'You say, "We want to be like the nations, like the peoples
of the world, who serve wood and stone." But what you have in
mind will never happen. 33As surely as I live, declares the Sovereign LORD, I will rule over you with a mighty hand and an outstretched arm and with outpoured wrath. 34I will bring you from
the nations and gather you from the countries where you have
been scattered—with a mighty hand and an outstretched arm and
with outpoured wrath. 35I will bring you into the desert of the nations and there, face to face, I will execute judgment upon you.
36As I judged your fathers in the desert of the land of Egypt, so I
will judge you, declares the Sovereign LORD. 37I will take note of
you as you pass under my rod, and I will bring you into the bond
of the covenant. 38I will purge you of those who revolt and rebel
against me. Although I will bring them out of the land where they
are living, yet they will not enter the land of Israel. Then you will
know that I am the LORD.
39" 'As for you, O house of Israel, this is what the Sovereign
LORD says: Go and serve your idols, every one of you! But afterward you will surely listen to me and no longer profane my holy
name with your gifts and idols. 40For on my holy mountain, the
high mountain of Israel, declares the Sovereign LORD, there in the
land the entire house of Israel will serve me, and there I will accept them. There I will require your offerings and your choice
gifts,[b] along with all your holy sacrifices. 41I will accept you as
fragrant incense when I bring you out from the nations and gather you from the countries where you have been scattered, and I
will show myself holy among you in the sight of the nations.
42Then you will know that I am the LORD, when I bring you into
the land of Israel, the land I had sworn with uplifted hand to give
to your fathers. 43There you will remember your conduct and all
the actions by which you have defiled yourselves, and you will
loathe yourselves for all the evil you have done. 44You will know
that I am the LORD, when I deal with you for my name's sake and
not according to your evil ways and your corrupt practices,
O house of Israel, declares the Sovereign LORD.' "

Prophecy Against the South

45The word of the LORD came to me: 46"Son of man, set your
face toward the south; preach against the south and prophesy
against the forest of the southland. 47Say to the southern forest:
'Hear the word of the LORD. This is what the Sovereign LORD says:
I am about to set fire to you, and it will consume all your trees,
both green and dry. The blazing flame will not be quenched, and
every face from south to north will be scorched by it. 48Everyone
will see that I the LORD have kindled it; it will not be quenched.' "

[a] 31 Or *—making your sons pass through* [b] 40 Or *and the gifts of your firstfruits*

(20:39–44) How You long to be in fellowship with Your people, Sovereign Lord. Even in the midst of Your wrath You spoke words of peace to Your servant Ezekiel, words of regathering and repentance. Your heart yearns to bless us, but at times we still turn away in pursuit of other gods. Teach us faithfulness, Father, and continue to be patient with us while we learn.

He is all love, and those who trust Him need never know anything but that love. He is just, indeed, and He will not condone sin; but through the blood of the everlasting covenant He is able to act toward us exactly as if we had never sinned. Toward the trusting sons of men His mercy will always triumph over justice.

A.W. Tozer (1897-1963)

Beautiful Savior, sent from above;
Joy of the Father, gift of His love.
Suffering Servant, acquainted with
grief;
Risen Redeemer, Prince of Peace.

Bread of Heaven has come from
above,
Son of the Father, given in love.
Rejected and wounded, He carried
our sin,
King of all glory, our Savior and
Friend.

Father, we extol the name of Jesus,
Giving Him the glory due His name;
For in Him Your mercies have
redeemed us,
And in Him we'll never be the same.
We give praises to Your name.

"We Extol The Name of Jesus"
Harlan Rogers (©1999)

49Then I said, "Ah, Sovereign LORD! They are saying of me,
'Isn't he just telling parables?' "

Babylon, God's Sword of Judgment

21 The word of the LORD came to me: 2"Son of man, set your
face against Jerusalem and preach against the sanctuary.
Prophesy against the land of Israel 3and say to her: 'This is what
the LORD says: I am against you. I will draw my sword from its
scabbard and cut off from you both the righteous and the wicked.
4Because I am going to cut off the righteous and the wicked, my
sword will be unsheathed against everyone from south to north.
5Then all people will know that I the LORD have drawn my sword
from its scabbard; it will not return again.'
6"Therefore groan, son of man! Groan before them with broken heart and bitter grief. 7And when they ask you, 'Why are you
groaning?' you shall say, 'Because of the news that is coming.
Every heart will melt and every hand go limp; every spirit will become faint and every knee become as weak as water.' It is coming! It will surely take place, declares the Sovereign LORD."
8The word of the LORD came to me: 9"Son of man, prophesy
and say, 'This is what the Lord says:

" 'A sword, a sword,
sharpened and polished—
10sharpened for the slaughter,
polished to flash like lightning!

" 'Shall we rejoice in the scepter of my son ⌞Judah⌟? The sword
despises every such stick.

11" 'The sword is appointed to be polished,
to be grasped with the hand;
it is sharpened and polished,
made ready for the hand of the slayer.
12Cry out and wail, son of man,
for it is against my people;
it is against all the princes of Israel.
They are thrown to the sword
along with my people.
Therefore beat your breast.

13" 'Testing will surely come. And what if the scepter ⌞of Ju-
dah⌟, which the sword despises, does not continue? declares the
Sovereign LORD.'

14"So then, son of man, prophesy
and strike your hands together.
Let the sword strike twice,
even three times.
It is a sword for slaughter—
a sword for great slaughter,
closing in on them from every side.
15So that hearts may melt
and the fallen be many,
I have stationed the sword for slaughter[a]
at all their gates.
Oh! It is made to flash like lightning,
it is grasped for slaughter.

[a] 15 Septuagint; the meaning of the Hebrew for this word is uncertain.

(21:6–10) O Father, as Ezekiel cried out to Jerusalem, so his words cry out to us today. Your final judgment against human sin and rebellion is yet to come. It is reserved for those who have rejected the redeeming sacrifice of Your Son, for those who have refused to accept Him as Savior and Lord. As believers in Jesus, we rejoice in our deliverance from that judgment. But we also have reason to grieve, Lord, over the fate of those who do not yet trust Him. Stir us up, Lord; with broken hearts and bitter grief send us out, equipped with Your Spirit, to tell all who will listen about Your coming wrath and about the hope of salvation.

(21:25–27) Jesus, You are the One to Whom all things rightfully belong. Your Father has delivered all dominion, power and authority into Your hand. It is because of Your sacrifice that God's wrath has been turned aside. It is through You that all creation will be restored. In You the lowly are indeed exalted, for You have adopted sinful humans into Your family, justified them and destined them to rule with You as daughters and sons of the Most High God.

In attempting to write of His adorable Person and His incomprehensible achievements–which achievements when completed will have perfected redemption, exercised to infinite satisfaction the divine attribute of grace, manifested the invisible God to His creatures, and subdued a rebellious universe in which sin had been permitted to demonstrate its exceeding sinfulness–the limitations of a finite mind which is weakened by a faulty perception are all too apparent.

Lewis S. Chafer (1871-1952)

16 O sword, slash to the right,
then to the left,
wherever your blade is turned.
17 I too will strike my hands together,
and my wrath will subside.
I the LORD have spoken."

18 The word of the LORD came to me: 19 "Son of man, mark out
two roads for the sword of the king of Babylon to take, both
starting from the same country. Make a signpost where the road
branches off to the city. 20 Mark out one road for the sword to
come against Rabbah of the Ammonites and another against
Judah and fortified Jerusalem. 21 For the king of Babylon will
stop at the fork in the road, at the junction of the two roads, to
seek an omen: He will cast lots with arrows, he will consult his
idols, he will examine the liver. 22 Into his right hand will come
the lot for Jerusalem, where he is to set up battering rams, to
give the command to slaughter, to sound the battle cry, to set battering rams against the gates, to build a ramp and to erect siege
works. 23 It will seem like a false omen to those who have sworn
allegiance to him, but he will remind them of their guilt and take
them captive.

24 "Therefore this is what the Sovereign LORD says: 'Because you
people have brought to mind your guilt by your open rebellion,
revealing your sins in all that you do—because you have done
this, you will be taken captive.

25 " 'O profane and wicked prince of Israel, whose day has
come, whose time of punishment has reached its climax, 26 this is
what the Sovereign LORD says: Take off the turban, remove the
crown. It will not be as it was: The lowly will be exalted and the
exalted will be brought low. 27 A ruin! A ruin! I will make it a ruin!
It will not be restored until he comes to whom it rightfully belongs; to him I will give it.'

28 "And you, son of man, prophesy and say, 'This is what the
Sovereign LORD says about the Ammonites and their insults:

" 'A sword, a sword,
drawn for the slaughter,
polished to consume
and to flash like lightning!
29 Despite false visions concerning you
and lying divinations about you,
it will be laid on the necks
of the wicked who are to be slain,
whose day has come,
whose time of punishment has reached its climax.
30 Return the sword to its scabbard.
In the place where you were created,
in the land of your ancestry,
I will judge you.
31 I will pour out my wrath upon you
and breathe out my fiery anger against you;
I will hand you over to brutal men,
men skilled in destruction.
32 You will be fuel for the fire,
your blood will be shed in your land,
you will be remembered no more;
for I the LORD have spoken.' "

Jerusalem's Sins

22 The word of the LORD came to me: 2“Son of man, will you
judge her? Will you judge this city of bloodshed? Then
confront her with all her detestable practices 3and say: ‘This is
what the Sovereign LORD says: O city that brings on herself doom
by shedding blood in her midst and defiles herself by making
idols, 4you have become guilty because of the blood you have
shed and have become defiled by the idols you have made. You
have brought your days to a close, and the end of your years has
come. Therefore I will make you an object of scorn to the nations
and a laughingstock to all the countries. 5Those who are near
and those who are far away will mock you, O infamous city, full of
turmoil.

6“ ‘See how each of the princes of Israel who are in you uses
his power to shed blood. 7In you they have treated father and
mother with contempt; in you they have oppressed the alien and
mistreated the fatherless and the widow. 8You have despised my
holy things and desecrated my Sabbaths. 9In you are slanderous
men bent on shedding blood; in you are those who eat at the
mountain shrines and commit lewd acts. 10In you are those who
dishonor their fathers' bed; in you are those who violate women
during their period, when they are ceremonially unclean. 11In
you one man commits a detestable offense with his neighbor's
wife, another shamefully defiles his daughter-in-law, and another
violates his sister, his own father's daughter. 12In you men accept
bribes to shed blood; you take usury and excessive interest[a] and
make unjust gain from your neighbors by extortion. And you have
forgotten me, declares the Sovereign LORD.

13“ ‘I will surely strike my hands together at the unjust gain
you have made and at the blood you have shed in your midst.
14Will your courage endure or your hands be strong in the day I
deal with you? I the LORD have spoken, and I will do it. 15I will disperse you among the nations and scatter you through the countries; and I will put an end to your uncleanness. 16When you have
been defiled[b] in the eyes of the nations, you will know that I am
the LORD.’ ”

17Then the word of the LORD came to me: 18“Son of man, the
house of Israel has become dross to me; all of them are the copper, tin, iron and lead left inside a furnace. They are but the dross
of silver. 19Therefore this is what the Sovereign LORD says: ‘Because you have all become dross, I will gather you into Jerusalem.
20As men gather silver, copper, iron, lead and tin into a furnace
to melt it with a fiery blast, so will I gather you in my anger and
my wrath and put you inside the city and melt you. 21I will gather you and I will blow on you with my fiery wrath, and you will be
melted inside her. 22As silver is melted in a furnace, so you will
be melted inside her, and you will know that I the LORD have
poured out my wrath upon you.’ ”

23Again the word of the LORD came to me: 24“Son of man, say
to the land, ‘You are a land that has had no rain or showers[c] in
the day of wrath.’ 25There is a conspiracy of her princes[d] within
her like a roaring lion tearing its prey; they devour people, take
treasures and precious things and make many widows within her.
26Her priests do violence to my law and profane my holy things;

[a] 12 Or *usury and interest* [b] 16 Or *When I have allotted you your inheritance*
[c] 24 Septuagint; Hebrew *has not been cleansed or rained on* [d] 25 Septuagint; Hebrew *prophets*

(22:17–22) Sovereign Lord, like Your people of old we are polluted by sin and corrupted by evil. Yet, in spite of our continual failures, we long to be holy. Purge away our dross and remove all our impurities. With the fire of Your Holy Spirit, refine us until we are the finest silver, pure enough to reflect Your image, beautiful enough for You to be glorified in us. (Isa 1:25)

Purify my heart,
Let me be as gold and precious silver.
Purify my heart,
Let me be as gold, pure gold.

Refiner's Fire –
My heart's one desire
Is to be holy,
Set apart for You, Lord.
I choose to be holy,
Set apart for You my Master,
Ready to do Your will.

"Refiner's Fire"
Brian Doerksen (©1990)

they do not distinguish between the holy and the common; they
teach that there is no difference between the unclean and the
clean; and they shut their eyes to the keeping of my Sabbaths, so
that I am profaned among them. 27Her officials within her are
like wolves tearing their prey; they shed blood and kill people to
make unjust gain. 28Her prophets whitewash these deeds for
them by false visions and lying divinations. They say, 'This is what
the Sovereign LORD says'—when the LORD has not spoken. 29The
people of the land practice extortion and commit robbery; they
oppress the poor and needy and mistreat the alien, denying them
justice.

30"I looked for a man among them who would build up the
wall and stand before me in the gap on behalf of the land so I
would not have to destroy it, but I found none. 31So I will pour
out my wrath on them and consume them with my fiery anger,
bringing down on their own heads all they have done, declares
the Sovereign LORD."

Two Adulterous Sisters

23 The word of the LORD came to me: 2"Son of man, there
were two women, daughters of the same mother. 3They
became prostitutes in Egypt, engaging in prostitution from their
youth. In that land their breasts were fondled and their virgin bosoms caressed. 4The older was named Oholah, and her sister was
Oholibah. They were mine and gave birth to sons and daughters.
Oholah is Samaria, and Oholibah is Jerusalem.

5"Oholah engaged in prostitution while she was still mine; and
she lusted after her lovers, the Assyrians—warriors 6clothed in
blue, governors and commanders, all of them handsome young
men, and mounted horsemen. 7She gave herself as a prostitute to
all the elite of the Assyrians and defiled herself with all the idols
of everyone she lusted after. 8She did not give up the prostitution
she began in Egypt, when during her youth men slept with her, caressed her virgin bosom and poured out their lust upon her.

9"Therefore I handed her over to her lovers, the Assyrians, for
whom she lusted. 10They stripped her naked, took away her sons
and daughters and killed her with the sword. She became a byword among women, and punishment was inflicted on her.

11"Her sister Oholibah saw this, yet in her lust and prostitution
she was more depraved than her sister. 12She too lusted after the
Assyrians—governors and commanders, warriors in full dress,
mounted horsemen, all handsome young men. 13I saw that she
too defiled herself; both of them went the same way.

14"But she carried her prostitution still further. She saw men
portrayed on a wall, figures of Chaldeans[a] portrayed in red,
15with belts around their waists and flowing turbans on their
heads; all of them looked like Babylonian chariot officers, natives
of Chaldea.[b] 16As soon as she saw them, she lusted after them
and sent messengers to them in Chaldea. 17Then the Babylonians
came to her, to the bed of love, and in their lust they defiled her.
After she had been defiled by them, she turned away from them in
disgust. 18When she carried on her prostitution openly and exposed her nakedness, I turned away from her in disgust, just as I
had turned away from her sister. 19Yet she became more and
more promiscuous as she recalled the days of her youth, when

[a] 14 Or *Babylonians* [b] 15 Or *Babylonia*; also in verse 16

(22:30–31) Lord, throughout Scripture we read of the power of intercessory prayer: Your servants Moses, Samuel, Daniel and Nehemiah pleaded with You on behalf of Your people; Job prayed for his friends; Jesus prayed for us and ever lives to make intercession for us. Just as they stood in the gap, help me to intercede for those who are in my life—those who are disobedient to You, those who face Your wrath. Far be it from me that I should sin against You by failing to pray for others. (Ex 32:9–14; 1Sa 12:23; Job 42:7–10; Da 9:3–19; Jn 17:6–25; Heb 7:25)

Genuine love sees faces, not a mass: the Good Shepherd "calleth his own sheep by name." Intercession is more than specific: it is pondered: it requires us to bear on our heart the burden of those for whom we pray.

George A. Buttrick (1892-1980)

In fellowship, alone,
To God with faith draw near;
Approach His courts, besiege His
throne
With all the pow'rs of prayer.
Your guides and brethren bear
Forever on your mind;
Extend the arms of mighty prayer
In grasping all mankind.

"Soldiers of Christ, Arise"
Charles Wesley (1749)

she was a prostitute in Egypt. 20There she lusted after her lovers,
whose genitals were like those of donkeys and whose emission
was like that of horses. 21So you longed for the lewdness of your
youth, when in Egypt your bosom was caressed and your young
breasts fondled.[a]
22"Therefore, Oholibah, this is what the Sovereign LORD says: I
will stir up your lovers against you, those you turned away from
in disgust, and I will bring them against you from every side—
23the Babylonians and all the Chaldeans, the men of Pekod and
Shoa and Koa, and all the Assyrians with them, handsome young
men, all of them governors and commanders, chariot officers and
men of high rank, all mounted on horses. 24They will come
against you with weapons,[b] chariots and wagons and with a
throng of people; they will take up positions against you on every
side with large and small shields and with helmets. I will turn you
over to them for punishment, and they will punish you according
to their standards. 25I will direct my jealous anger against you,
and they will deal with you in fury. They will cut off your noses
and your ears, and those of you who are left will fall by the sword.
They will take away your sons and daughters, and those of you
who are left will be consumed by fire. 26They will also strip you
of your clothes and take your fine jewelry. 27So I will put a stop
to the lewdness and prostitution you began in Egypt. You will not
look on these things with longing or remember Egypt anymore.
28"For this is what the Sovereign LORD says: I am about to hand
you over to those you hate, to those you turned away from in disgust. 29They will deal with you in hatred and take away everything
you have worked for. They will leave you naked and bare, and the
shame of your prostitution will be exposed. Your lewdness and
promiscuity 30have brought this upon you, because you lusted
after the nations and defiled yourself with their idols. 31You have
gone the way of your sister; so I will put her cup into your hand.
32"This is what the Sovereign LORD says:

"You will drink your sister's cup,
a cup large and deep;
it will bring scorn and derision,
for it holds so much.
33You will be filled with drunkenness and sorrow,
the cup of ruin and desolation,
the cup of your sister Samaria.
34You will drink it and drain it dry;
you will dash it to pieces
and tear your breasts.

I have spoken, declares the Sovereign LORD.

35"Therefore this is what the Sovereign LORD says: Since you
have forgotten me and thrust me behind your back, you must
bear the consequences of your lewdness and prostitution."
36The LORD said to me: "Son of man, will you judge Oholah and
Oholibah? Then confront them with their detestable practices,
37for they have committed adultery and blood is on their hands.
They committed adultery with their idols; they even sacrificed
their children, whom they bore to me,[c] as food for them. 38They

[a] 21 Syriac (see also verse 3); Hebrew *caressed because of your young breasts*
[b] 24 The meaning of the Hebrew for this word is uncertain. [c] 37 Or *even made the children they bore to me pass through ⌊the fire⌋*

(23:22–31) Lord God, our sins leave us naked and ashamed and bring grave consequences upon us. When we reject Your ways and choose to forge our own path, we make ourselves vulnerable to all kinds of trouble. Teach us to follow the way of holiness, Lord. We want to avoid the terrible consequences of sin; but much more, we do not wish to break Your heart with our ungodly actions.

Thank God for the mercy that will not let us rest in our self-complacency and sin. Happy for us that we have a Father who loves us well enough to hurt us and drive us home to His loving breast.

Albert Benjamin Simpson (1843–1919)

have also done this to me: At that same time they defiled my sanctuary and desecrated my Sabbaths. 39On the very day they sacrificed their children to their idols, they entered my sanctuary and
desecrated it. That is what they did in my house.
40"They even sent messengers for men who came from far
away, and when they arrived you bathed yourself for them, painted your eyes and put on your jewelry. 41You sat on an elegant
couch, with a table spread before it on which you had placed the
incense and oil that belonged to me.
42"The noise of a carefree crowd was around her; Sabeans[a]
were brought from the desert along with men from the rabble,
and they put bracelets on the arms of the woman and her sister
and beautiful crowns on their heads. 43Then I said about the one
worn out by adultery, 'Now let them use her as a prostitute, for
that is all she is.' 44And they slept with her. As men sleep with a
prostitute, so they slept with those lewd women, Oholah and
Oholibah. 45But righteous men will sentence them to the punishment of women who commit adultery and shed blood, because
they are adulterous and blood is on their hands.
46"This is what the Sovereign LORD says: Bring a mob against
them and give them over to terror and plunder. 47The mob will
stone them and cut them down with their swords; they will kill
their sons and daughters and burn down their houses.
48"So I will put an end to lewdness in the land, that all women
may take warning and not imitate you. 49You will suffer the penalty for your lewdness and bear the consequences of your sins of
idolatry. Then you will know that I am the Sovereign LORD."

The Cooking Pot

24 In the ninth year, in the tenth month on the tenth day, the
word of the LORD came to me: 2"Son of man, record this
date, this very date, because the king of Babylon has laid siege to
Jerusalem this very day. 3Tell this rebellious house a parable and
say to them: 'This is what the Sovereign LORD says:

" 'Put on the cooking pot; put it on
and pour water into it.
4Put into it the pieces of meat,
all the choice pieces—the leg and the shoulder.
Fill it with the best of these bones;
5 take the pick of the flock.
Pile wood beneath it for the bones;
bring it to a boil
and cook the bones in it.

6" 'For this is what the Sovereign LORD says:

" 'Woe to the city of bloodshed,
to the pot now encrusted,
whose deposit will not go away!
Empty it piece by piece
without casting lots for them.

7" 'For the blood she shed is in her midst:
She poured it on the bare rock;
she did not pour it on the ground,
where the dust would cover it.

[a] 42 Or *drunkards*

(23:39–41) Father, we recoil when we read about ancient pagan sacrifices in which children were offered to idols. We are shocked to hear that sacred items from Your temple, such as oil and incense, were used for evil purposes. But are we really so different today? Unborn children are sacrificed because of lust, financial considerations or convenience. And promises of prayer and healing are exchanged for money. Forgive us, Lord! Purify Your people, and use us to call our communities, churches and nations to repentance.

Give me a holy life,
Spotless and free,
Cleansed by the crystal flow
Coming from Thee.
Purge the dark halls of thought;
Here let Thy work be wrought,
Each wish and feeling brought
Captive to Thee.

"Give Me a Holy Life"
Leslie Taylor-Hunt (1924)

8 To stir up wrath and take revenge
I put her blood on the bare rock,
so that it would not be covered.

9 " 'Therefore this is what the Sovereign LORD says:

" 'Woe to the city of bloodshed!
I, too, will pile the wood high.
10 So heap on the wood
and kindle the fire.
Cook the meat well,
mixing in the spices;
and let the bones be charred.
11 Then set the empty pot on the coals
till it becomes hot and its copper glows
so its impurities may be melted
and its deposit burned away.
12 It has frustrated all efforts;
its heavy deposit has not been removed,
not even by fire.

13 " 'Now your impurity is lewdness. Because I tried to cleanse
you but you would not be cleansed from your impurity, you will
not be clean again until my wrath against you has subsided.

14 " 'I the LORD have spoken. The time has come for me to act.
I will not hold back; I will not have pity, nor will I relent. You will
be judged according to your conduct and your actions, declares
the Sovereign LORD.' "

Ezekiel's Wife Dies

15 The word of the LORD came to me: 16 "Son of man, with one
blow I am about to take away from you the delight of your eyes.
Yet do not lament or weep or shed any tears. 17 Groan quietly; do
not mourn for the dead. Keep your turban fastened and your sandals on your feet; do not cover the lower part of your face or eat
the customary food ⌞of mourners⌟."

18 So I spoke to the people in the morning, and in the evening
my wife died. The next morning I did as I had been commanded.

19 Then the people asked me, "Won't you tell us what these
things have to do with us?"

20 So I said to them, "The word of the LORD came to me: 21 Say
to the house of Israel, 'This is what the Sovereign LORD says: I am
about to desecrate my sanctuary—the stronghold in which you
take pride, the delight of your eyes, the object of your affection.
The sons and daughters you left behind will fall by the sword.
22 And you will do as I have done. You will not cover the lower
part of your face or eat the customary food ⌞of mourners⌟. 23 You
will keep your turbans on your heads and your sandals on your
feet. You will not mourn or weep but will waste away because of[a]
your sins and groan among yourselves. 24 Ezekiel will be a sign to
you; you will do just as he has done. When this happens, you will
know that I am the Sovereign LORD.'

25 "And you, son of man, on the day I take away their stronghold, their joy and glory, the delight of their eyes, their heart's
desire, and their sons and daughters as well— 26 on that day a
fugitive will come to tell you the news. 27 At that time your mouth

[a] 23 Or *away in*

If the warning admonitions of God's ministers fill the conscience with terror, what must it be to face the Lord himself? If one bolt of judgment brings a man into a cold sweat, what will it be to stand before an angry God in the last great day?

Charles Haddon Spurgeon (1834-1892)

(24:15–24) God, we do not always understand Your dealings with Your prophets. But we learn from their example that You speak to Your people in myriad ways. You use every means available to get our attention, to teach us Your ways and to turn our eyes in the right direction. Make us alert to Your message, Lord. Help us to listen, take warning and obey.

will be opened; you will speak with him and will no longer be silent. So you will be a sign to them, and they will know that I am the LORD."

A Prophecy Against Ammon

25 The word of the LORD came to me: 2"Son of man, set your face against the Ammonites and prophesy against them. 3Say to them, 'Hear the word of the Sovereign LORD. This is what the Sovereign LORD says: Because you said "Aha!" over my sanctuary when it was desecrated and over the land of Israel when it was laid waste and over the people of Judah when they went into exile, 4therefore I am going to give you to the people of the East as a possession. They will set up their camps and pitch their tents among you; they will eat your fruit and drink your milk. 5I will turn Rabbah into a pasture for camels and Ammon into a resting place for sheep. Then you will know that I am the LORD. 6For this is what the Sovereign LORD says: Because you have clapped your hands and stamped your feet, rejoicing with all the malice of your heart against the land of Israel, 7therefore I will stretch out my hand against you and give you as plunder to the nations. I will cut you off from the nations and exterminate you from the countries. I will destroy you, and you will know that I am the LORD.' "

A Prophecy Against Moab

8"This is what the Sovereign LORD says: 'Because Moab and Seir said, "Look, the house of Judah has become like all the other nations," 9therefore I will expose the flank of Moab, beginning at its frontier towns—Beth Jeshimoth, Baal Meon and Kiriathaim—the glory of that land. 10I will give Moab along with the Ammonites to the people of the East as a possession, so that the Ammonites will not be remembered among the nations; 11and I will inflict punishment on Moab. Then they will know that I am the LORD.' "

A Prophecy Against Edom

12"This is what the Sovereign LORD says: 'Because Edom took revenge on the house of Judah and became very guilty by doing so, 13therefore this is what the Sovereign LORD says: I will stretch out my hand against Edom and kill its men and their animals. I will lay it waste, and from Teman to Dedan they will fall by the sword. 14I will take vengeance on Edom by the hand of my people Israel, and they will deal with Edom in accordance with my anger and my wrath; they will know my vengeance, declares the Sovereign LORD.' "

A Prophecy Against Philistia

15"This is what the Sovereign LORD says: 'Because the Philistines acted in vengeance and took revenge with malice in their hearts, and with ancient hostility sought to destroy Judah, 16therefore this is what the Sovereign LORD says: I am about to stretch out my hand against the Philistines, and I will cut off the Kerethites and destroy those remaining along the coast. 17I will carry out great vengeance on them and punish them in my wrath. Then they will know that I am the LORD, when I take vengeance on them.' "

(25:1–17) At times, Lord, when we see people pay a hard price for their sins, we feel smug or even secretly pleased. Rather than grieving with You over their losses and disgrace, we somehow use their downfall to elevate ourselves in our own eyes. Remind us, Lord, that love does not delight in evil and that You have never been pleased with those who rejoice in Your people's distress, even when You are the One who has brought it about. (1Co 13:6)

With infinite love and compassion our Lord understood the human predicament. He had deep empathy with people; he saw their needs, their weaknesses, their desires, and their hurts. He understood and was concerned for people. Every word he spoke was uttered because he saw a need for that word in some human life. His concern was always to uplift and never to tear down, to heal and never hurt, to save and not condemn.

Charles L. Allen (1913-)

A Prophecy Against Tyre

26 In the eleventh year, on the first day of the month, the
word of the LORD came to me: 2“Son of man, because Tyre
has said of Jerusalem, ‘Aha! The gate to the nations is broken,
and its doors have swung open to me; now that she lies in ruins I
will prosper,’ 3therefore this is what the Sovereign LORD says: I am
against you, O Tyre, and I will bring many nations against you,
like the sea casting up its waves. 4They will destroy the walls of
Tyre and pull down her towers; I will scrape away her rubble and
make her a bare rock. 5Out in the sea she will become a place to
spread fishnets, for I have spoken, declares the Sovereign LORD.
She will become plunder for the nations, 6and her settlements on
the mainland will be ravaged by the sword. Then they will know
that I am the LORD.

7“For this is what the Sovereign LORD says: From the north I am
going to bring against Tyre Nebuchadnezzar[a] king of Babylon,
king of kings, with horses and chariots, with horsemen and a
great army. 8He will ravage your settlements on the mainland with
the sword; he will set up siege works against you, build a ramp up
to your walls and raise his shields against you. 9He will direct the
blows of his battering rams against your walls and demolish your
towers with his weapons. 10His horses will be so many that they
will cover you with dust. Your walls will tremble at the noise of
the war horses, wagons and chariots when he enters your gates as
men enter a city whose walls have been broken through. 11The
hoofs of his horses will trample all your streets; he will kill your
people with the sword, and your strong pillars will fall to the
ground. 12They will plunder your wealth and loot your merchandise; they will break down your walls and demolish your fine
houses and throw your stones, timber and rubble into the sea.
13I will put an end to your noisy songs, and the music of your
harps will be heard no more. 14I will make you a bare rock, and
you will become a place to spread fishnets. You will never be rebuilt, for I the LORD have spoken, declares the Sovereign LORD.

15“This is what the Sovereign LORD says to Tyre: Will not the
coastlands tremble at the sound of your fall, when the wounded
groan and the slaughter takes place in you? 16Then all the princes
of the coast will step down from their thrones and lay aside their
robes and take off their embroidered garments. Clothed with terror, they will sit on the ground, trembling every moment, appalled
at you. 17Then they will take up a lament concerning you and say
to you:

“ ‘How you are destroyed, O city of renown,
peopled by men of the sea!
You were a power on the seas,
you and your citizens;
you put your terror
on all who lived there.
18Now the coastlands tremble
on the day of your fall;
the islands in the sea
are terrified at your collapse.’

19“This is what the Sovereign LORD says: When I make you a

[a] 7 Hebrew *Nebuchadrezzar,* of which *Nebuchadnezzar* is a variant; here and often in Ezekiel and Jeremiah

O Lord, the house of my soul is narrow;
Enlarge it, that You may enter in.
It is ruinous, O repair it!
It displeases Your sight;
I confess it, I know.
But who shall cleanse it, to whom shall I
cry out but to You?
Cleanse me from my secret faults, O Lord,
And spare Your servant from strange sins.
Saint Augustine of Hippo (354-430)

(26:1–17) Israel’s punishment was Your doing. But You defended Your people jealously and zealously against those who were taking advantage of their despair. Even today You will humble the proud; Your judgments will fall, and they are just. There are no excuses for the wicked. Just as it was true so long ago, so it is true today: “For it is time for judgment to begin with the family of God; and if it begins with us, what will the outcome be for those who do not obey the gospel of God?” (Isa 10:12; 1Pe 4:17)

desolate city, like cities no longer inhabited, and when I bring the
ocean depths over you and its vast waters cover you, 20 then I will
bring you down with those who go down to the pit, to the people
of long ago. I will make you dwell in the earth below, as in ancient
ruins, with those who go down to the pit, and you will not return
or take your place[a] in the land of the living. 21 I will bring you to
a horrible end and you will be no more. You will be sought, but
you will never again be found, declares the Sovereign LORD."

A Lament for Tyre

27 The word of the LORD came to me: 2 "Son of man, take up
a lament concerning Tyre. 3 Say to Tyre, situated at the
gateway to the sea, merchant of peoples on many coasts, 'This is
what the Sovereign LORD says:

"'You say, O Tyre,
"I am perfect in beauty."
4 Your domain was on the high seas;
your builders brought your beauty to perfection.
5 They made all your timbers
of pine trees from Senir[b];
they took a cedar from Lebanon
to make a mast for you.
6 Of oaks from Bashan
they made your oars;
of cypress wood[c] from the coasts of Cyprus[d]
they made your deck, inlaid with ivory.
7 Fine embroidered linen from Egypt was your sail
and served as your banner;
your awnings were of blue and purple
from the coasts of Elishah.
8 Men of Sidon and Arvad were your oarsmen;
your skilled men, O Tyre, were aboard as your
seamen.
9 Veteran craftsmen of Gebal[e] were on board
as shipwrights to caulk your seams.
All the ships of the sea and their sailors
came alongside to trade for your wares.
10 "'Men of Persia, Lydia and Put
served as soldiers in your army.
They hung their shields and helmets on your walls,
bringing you splendor.
11 Men of Arvad and Helech
manned your walls on every side;
men of Gammad
were in your towers.
They hung their shields around your walls;
they brought your beauty to perfection.

12 "'Tarshish did business with you because of your great
wealth of goods; they exchanged silver, iron, tin and lead for your
merchandise.
13 "'Greece, Tubal and Meshech traded with you; they exchanged slaves and articles of bronze for your wares.

[a] *20* Septuagint; Hebrew *return, and I will give glory* [b] *5* That is, Hermon
[c] *6* Targum; the Masoretic Text has a different division of the consonants. [d] *6* Hebrew *Kittim* [e] *9* That is, Byblos

(27:3–11) Father, we are so attracted by elegance, prestige and affluence. We look for security and self-worth in beautiful people, places and things. And yet, apart from Your protection, all these earthly things are transient and vulnerable to destruction and theft. Teach us, Lord, to set our hearts and minds on things above and to store up our treasures in heaven. (Mt 6:20–21; Col 3:1–2)

Be an example to all of denying yourself and taking up your cross daily. Let others see that you are not interested in any pleasure that does not bring you nearer to God, nor regard any pain which does. Let them see that you simply aim at pleasing God in everything.

John Wesley (1703-1791)

Cure the people's warring madness;
Bend our pride to Thy control.
Shame our wanton, selfish gladness–
Rich in things and poor in soul.
Grant us wisdom, grant us courage,
Lest we miss Thy kingdom's goal,
Lest we miss Thy kingdom's goal.

"God of Grace and God of Glory"
Harry Emerson Fosdick (1930)

14“ ‘Men of Beth Togarmah exchanged work horses, war horses and mules for your merchandise.

15“ ‘The men of Rhodes[a] traded with you, and many coastlands were your customers; they paid you with ivory tusks and ebony.

16“ ‘Aram[b] did business with you because of your many products; they exchanged turquoise, purple fabric, embroidered work, fine linen, coral and rubies for your merchandise.

17“ ‘Judah and Israel traded with you; they exchanged wheat from Minnith and confections,[c] honey, oil and balm for your wares.

18“ ‘Damascus, because of your many products and great wealth of goods, did business with you in wine from Helbon and wool from Zahar.

19“ ‘Danites and Greeks from Uzal bought your merchandise; they exchanged wrought iron, cassia and calamus for your wares.

20“ ‘Dedan traded in saddle blankets with you.

21“ ‘Arabia and all the princes of Kedar were your customers; they did business with you in lambs, rams and goats.

22“ ‘The merchants of Sheba and Raamah traded with you; for your merchandise they exchanged the finest of all kinds of spices and precious stones, and gold.

23“ ‘Haran, Canneh and Eden and merchants of Sheba, Asshur
and Kilmad traded with you. 24In your marketplace they traded
with you beautiful garments, blue fabric, embroidered work and multicolored rugs with cords twisted and tightly knotted.

25“ ‘The ships of Tarshish serve
as carriers for your wares.
You are filled with heavy cargo
in the heart of the sea.
26Your oarsmen take you
out to the high seas.
But the east wind will break you to pieces
in the heart of the sea.
27Your wealth, merchandise and wares,
your mariners, seamen and shipwrights,
your merchants and all your soldiers,
and everyone else on board
will sink into the heart of the sea
on the day of your shipwreck.
28The shorelands will quake
when your seamen cry out.
29All who handle the oars
will abandon their ships;
the mariners and all the seamen
will stand on the shore.
30They will raise their voice
and cry bitterly over you;
they will sprinkle dust on their heads
and roll in ashes.
31They will shave their heads because of you
and will put on sackcloth.
They will weep over you with anguish of soul

[a] *15* Septuagint; Hebrew *Dedan* [b] *16* Most Hebrew manuscripts; some Hebrew manuscripts and Syriac *Edom* [c] *17* The meaning of the Hebrew for this word is uncertain.

We are so preciously loved by God that we cannot even comprehend it. No created being can ever know how much and how sweetly and tenderly God loves them. It is only with the help of his grace that we are able to persevere in spiritual contemplation with endless wonder at this high, surpassing, immeasurable love which our Lord in his goodness has for us.

Julian of Norwich (1343-1413)

(27:25–31) Lord Jesus, as I look back across the centuries at the fate of those who rebelled against God's authority, I can only thank You for saving me from the shipwreck my own sin would have brought about. You saw me in danger and reached out to me with concern and compassion. In Your great love You lifted me out of sin's treacherous waters and planted my feet on solid ground. Thank You, Lord, for sparing me the fate of others who have stubbornly refused Your lifesaving help.

Jesus, Savior, pilot me
Over life's tempestuous sea;
Unknown waves before me roll,
Hiding rock and treach'rous shoal;
Chart and compass come from thee.
Jesus, Savior, pilot me.

As a mother stills her child,
Thou canst hush the ocean wild;
Boist'rous waves obey thy will
When thou say'st to them: "Be still."
Wondrous sov'reign of the sea,
Jesus, Savior, pilot me.

"Jesus, Savior, Pilot Me"
Edward Hopper (1818-1888)

(28:2–5) Lord God, ever since the Garden of Eden the evil promise "You will be like God" has teased and tempted humanity. In Ezekiel's day the king of Tyre was seduced by that false promise. And we too are sometimes deceived by our successes. Reveling in our pride, we grasp for more power, more control and more financial gain. Forgive us, Lord! Our gradual descent into idolatry begins when we fail to thank You for all that we have. You are indeed the Sovereign Lord, and all good things come to us from Your almighty hand. (Ge 3:5)

and with bitter mourning.
32 As they wail and mourn over you,
they will take up a lament concerning you:
"Who was ever silenced like Tyre,
surrounded by the sea?"
33 When your merchandise went out on the seas,
you satisfied many nations;
with your great wealth and your wares
you enriched the kings of the earth.
34 Now you are shattered by the sea
in the depths of the waters;
your wares and all your company
have gone down with you.
35 All who live in the coastlands
are appalled at you;
their kings shudder with horror
and their faces are distorted with fear.
36 The merchants among the nations hiss at you;
you have come to a horrible end
and will be no more.' "

A Prophecy Against the King of Tyre

28 The word of the LORD came to me: 2 "Son of man, say to the ruler of Tyre, 'This is what the Sovereign LORD says:

" 'In the pride of your heart
you say, "I am a god;
I sit on the throne of a god
in the heart of the seas."
But you are a man and not a god,
though you think you are as wise as a god.
3 Are you wiser than Daniel[a]?
Is no secret hidden from you?
4 By your wisdom and understanding
you have gained wealth for yourself
and amassed gold and silver
in your treasuries.
5 By your great skill in trading
you have increased your wealth,
and because of your wealth
your heart has grown proud.

6 " 'Therefore this is what the Sovereign LORD says:

" 'Because you think you are wise,
as wise as a god,
7 I am going to bring foreigners against you,
the most ruthless of nations;
they will draw their swords against your beauty and wisdom
and pierce your shining splendor.
8 They will bring you down to the pit,
and you will die a violent death
in the heart of the seas.
9 Will you then say, "I am a god,"
in the presence of those who kill you?
You will be but a man, not a god,

[a] 3 Or *Danel*; the Hebrew spelling may suggest a person other than the prophet Daniel.

in the hands of those who slay you.
10 You will die the death of the uncircumcised
at the hands of foreigners.

I have spoken, declares the Sovereign LORD.' "

11 The word of the LORD came to me: 12 "Son of man, take up a
lament concerning the king of Tyre and say to him: 'This is what
the Sovereign LORD says:

" 'You were the model of perfection,
full of wisdom and perfect in beauty.
13 You were in Eden,
the garden of God;
every precious stone adorned you:
ruby, topaz and emerald,
chrysolite, onyx and jasper,
sapphire,[a] turquoise and beryl.[b]
Your settings and mountings[c] were made of gold;
on the day you were created they were prepared.
14 You were anointed as a guardian cherub,
for so I ordained you.
You were on the holy mount of God;
you walked among the fiery stones.
15 You were blameless in your ways
from the day you were created
till wickedness was found in you.
16 Through your widespread trade
you were filled with violence,
and you sinned.
So I drove you in disgrace from the mount of God,
and I expelled you, O guardian cherub,
from among the fiery stones.
17 Your heart became proud
on account of your beauty,
and you corrupted your wisdom
because of your splendor.
So I threw you to the earth;
I made a spectacle of you before kings.
18 By your many sins and dishonest trade
you have desecrated your sanctuaries.
So I made a fire come out from you,
and it consumed you,
and I reduced you to ashes on the ground
in the sight of all who were watching.
19 All the nations who knew you
are appalled at you;
you have come to a horrible end
and will be no more.' "

A Prophecy Against Sidon

20 The word of the LORD came to me: 21 "Son of man, set your
face against Sidon; prophesy against her 22 and say: 'This is what
the Sovereign LORD says:

" 'I am against you, O Sidon,
and I will gain glory within you.

[a] 13 Or *lapis lazuli* [b] 13 The precise identification of some of these precious stones is uncertain. [c] 13 The meaning of the Hebrew for this phrase is uncertain.

(28:12–19) "Pride goes before destruction, a haughty spirit before a fall." Your Word is true for mortals and angels, O God. When You cast Satan from heaven, from the ranks of the holy angels into the depths of the universe, he became the first of many proud and beautiful beings—angelic and human—who fell from glory into disgrace. The King of Tyre was another one, and throughout history, there have been thousands of others. Puffed up with pride, blinded by their own splendor and often filled with violence, they have fallen headlong into destruction. Father, keep us from pride, that subtle and seductive destroyer of men and women, families and friendships, churches and nations. Keep us humble, Lord. Sustain us in Your grace and crown us with salvation. (Ps 18:27; 147:6; 149:4; Pr 16:18; Isa 13:11)

The holiest men, the most free from impurity, have always felt it most. He whose garments are the whitest will best perceive the spots upon them, He whose crown shines the brightest will know when he has lost a jewel. He who gives the most light to the world will always be able to discover his own darkness. The angels of heaven veil their faces, and the angels of God on earth, His chosen people, must always veil their faces with humility when they think of what they were.

Charles Haddon Spurgeon (1834-1892)

They will know that I am the LORD,
when I inflict punishment on her
and show myself holy within her.
23 I will send a plague upon her
and make blood flow in her streets.
The slain will fall within her,
with the sword against her on every side.
Then they will know that I am the LORD.

24" 'No longer will the people of Israel have malicious neighbors who are painful briers and sharp thorns. Then they will
know that I am the Sovereign LORD.
25" 'This is what the Sovereign LORD says: When I gather the
people of Israel from the nations where they have been scattered,
I will show myself holy among them in the sight of the nations.
Then they will live in their own land, which I gave to my servant
Jacob. 26They will live there in safety and will build houses and
plant vineyards; they will live in safety when I inflict punishment
on all their neighbors who maligned them. Then they will know
that I am the LORD their God.' "

(28:25–26) Despite Your judgment against Your people, Lord God, You continued to vindicate them from the taunts of their neighbors. And in spite of Your decision to scatter them into other nations, You looked forward to the time when they would be brought back to their own land, where they would live safely, build houses and plant vineyards. Your heart is always set on restoration, rebuilding and redemption, Lord. How You love Your people, and how You long to bless us, no matter how little we deserve it.

A Prophecy Against Egypt

29 In the tenth year, in the tenth month on the twelfth day, the
word of the LORD came to me: 2"Son of man, set your face
against Pharaoh king of Egypt and prophesy against him and
against all Egypt. 3Speak to him and say: 'This is what the Sovereign LORD says:

" 'I am against you, Pharaoh king of Egypt,
you great monster lying among your streams.
You say, "The Nile is mine;
I made it for myself."
4 But I will put hooks in your jaws
and make the fish of your streams stick to your scales.
I will pull you out from among your streams,
with all the fish sticking to your scales.
5 I will leave you in the desert,
you and all the fish of your streams.
You will fall on the open field
and not be gathered or picked up.
I will give you as food
to the beasts of the earth and the birds of the air.

6Then all who live in Egypt will know that I am the LORD.

" 'You have been a staff of reed for the house of Israel. 7When
they grasped you with their hands, you splintered and you tore
open their shoulders; when they leaned on you, you broke and
their backs were wrenched.[a]
8" 'Therefore this is what the Sovereign LORD says: I will bring
a sword against you and kill your men and their animals. 9Egypt
will become a desolate wasteland. Then they will know that I am
the LORD.
" 'Because you said, "The Nile is mine; I made it," 10therefore
I am against you and against your streams, and I will make the
land of Egypt a ruin and a desolate waste from Migdol to Aswan,
as far as the border of Cush.[b] 11No foot of man or animal will

[a] 7 Syriac (see also Septuagint and Vulgate); Hebrew *and you caused their backs to stand*
[b] 10 That is, the upper Nile region

pass through it; no one will live there for forty years. 12I will
make the land of Egypt desolate among devastated lands, and her
cities will lie desolate forty years among ruined cities. And I will
disperse the Egyptians among the nations and scatter them
through the countries.
13" 'Yet this is what the Sovereign LORD says: At the end of forty
years I will gather the Egyptians from the nations where they were
scattered. 14I will bring them back from captivity and return them
to Upper Egypt,[a] the land of their ancestry. There they will be a
lowly kingdom. 15It will be the lowliest of kingdoms and will
never again exalt itself above the other nations. I will make it so
weak that it will never again rule over the nations. 16Egypt will no
longer be a source of confidence for the people of Israel but will
be a reminder of their sin in turning to her for help. Then they
will know that I am the Sovereign LORD.' "

17In the twenty-seventh year, in the first month on the first day,
the word of the LORD came to me: 18"Son of man, Nebuchadnezzar
king of Babylon drove his army in a hard campaign against Tyre;
every head was rubbed bare and every shoulder made raw. Yet he
and his army got no reward from the campaign he led against
Tyre. 19Therefore this is what the Sovereign LORD says: I am going
to give Egypt to Nebuchadnezzar king of Babylon, and he will carry
off its wealth. He will loot and plunder the land as pay for his army.
20I have given him Egypt as a reward for his efforts because he and
his army did it for me, declares the Sovereign LORD.
21"On that day I will make a horn[b] grow for the house of Israel, and I will open your mouth among them. Then they will know
that I am the LORD."

A Lament for Egypt

30 The word of the LORD came to me: 2"Son of man, prophesy and say: 'This is what the Sovereign LORD says:

" 'Wail and say,
"Alas for that day!"
3For the day is near,
the day of the LORD is near—
a day of clouds,
a time of doom for the nations.
4A sword will come against Egypt,
and anguish will come upon Cush.[c]
When the slain fall in Egypt,
her wealth will be carried away
and her foundations torn down.

5Cush and Put, Lydia and all Arabia, Libya[d] and the people of the
covenant land will fall by the sword along with Egypt.
6" 'This is what the LORD says:

" 'The allies of Egypt will fall
and her proud strength will fail.
From Migdol to Aswan
they will fall by the sword within her,
declares the Sovereign LORD.
7" 'They will be desolate
among desolate lands,

[a] 14 Hebrew *to Pathros* [b] 21 *Horn* here symbolizes strength. [c] 4 That is, the upper Nile region; also in verses 5 and 9 [d] 5 Hebrew *Cub*

(29:13–16) Father, Your dealings with Egypt were stern but compassionate. Even though the Egyptians were a people who did not honor You, they were restored, to some degree, by Your benevolent hand. But they were never the same after having faced Your judgment—they were weakened and were no longer a source of help for Israel. Your heart of love reaches out to all the world, Lord, even to those who have never known You. How much more will You care for us who have received Your salvation, for us who have turned to You for help in our time of need?

(30:13–19) O God, how often You have spoken out against idolatry! From the dawn of history, and throughout the pages of Your Word, You have warned Your people and threatened the nations around them, to destroy their idols—otherwise You would do it for them. Would You say anything less to us today? Our world is crowded with demigods of every kind—gods of passion, gods of pleasure, gods of fear and gods of power. Break our idols, God! Do not allow us to have any other gods before You.

Holy Spirit, all divine,
Dwell within this heart of mine.
Cast down every idol throne;
Reign supreme, and reign alone.
"Holy Spirit, Light Divine"
Andrew Reed (1787-1862)

and their cities will lie
among ruined cities.
8 Then they will know that I am the LORD,
when I set fire to Egypt
and all her helpers are crushed.

9 " 'On that day messengers will go out from me in ships to frighten Cush out of her complacency. Anguish will take hold of them on the day of Egypt's doom, for it is sure to come.

10 " 'This is what the Sovereign LORD says:

" 'I will put an end to the hordes of Egypt
by the hand of Nebuchadnezzar king of Babylon.
11 He and his army—the most ruthless of nations—
will be brought in to destroy the land.
They will draw their swords against Egypt
and fill the land with the slain.
12 I will dry up the streams of the Nile
and sell the land to evil men;
by the hand of foreigners
I will lay waste the land and everything in it.
I the LORD have spoken.

13 " 'This is what the Sovereign LORD says:

" 'I will destroy the idols
and put an end to the images in Memphis.[a]
No longer will there be a prince in Egypt,
and I will spread fear throughout the land.
14 I will lay waste Upper Egypt,[b]
set fire to Zoan
and inflict punishment on Thebes.[c]
15 I will pour out my wrath on Pelusium,[d]
the stronghold of Egypt,
and cut off the hordes of Thebes.
16 I will set fire to Egypt;
Pelusium will writhe in agony.
Thebes will be taken by storm;
Memphis will be in constant distress.
17 The young men of Heliopolis[e] and Bubastis[f]
will fall by the sword,
and the cities themselves will go into captivity.
18 Dark will be the day at Tahpanhes
when I break the yoke of Egypt;
there her proud strength will come to an end.
She will be covered with clouds,
and her villages will go into captivity.
19 So I will inflict punishment on Egypt,
and they will know that I am the LORD.' "

20 In the eleventh year, in the first month on the seventh day, the
word of the LORD came to me: 21 "Son of man, I have broken the
arm of Pharaoh king of Egypt. It has not been bound up for healing or put in a splint so as to become strong enough to hold a
sword. 22 Therefore this is what the Sovereign LORD says: I am

[a] *13* Hebrew *Noph*; also in verse 16 [b] *14* Hebrew *waste Pathros* [c] *14* Hebrew *No*; also in verses 15 and 16 [d] *15* Hebrew *Sin*; also in verse 16 [e] *17* Hebrew *Awen* (or *On*) [f] *17* Hebrew *Pi Beseth*

against Pharaoh king of Egypt. I will break both his arms, the good arm as well as the broken one, and make the sword fall from his hand.
23 I will disperse the Egyptians among the nations and scatter them through the countries.
24 I will strengthen the arms of the king of Babylon and put my sword in his hand, but I will break the arms of Pharaoh, and he will groan before him like a mortally wounded man.
25 I will strengthen the arms of the king of Babylon, but the arms of Pharaoh will fall limp. Then they will know that I am the LORD, when I put my sword into the hand of the king of Babylon and he brandishes it against Egypt.
26 I will disperse the Egyptians among the nations and scatter them through the countries. Then they will know that I am the LORD."

A Cedar in Lebanon

31 In the eleventh year, in the third month on the first day, the word of the LORD came to me:
2 "Son of man, say to Pharaoh king of Egypt and to his hordes:

" 'Who can be compared with you in majesty?
3 Consider Assyria, once a cedar in Lebanon,
with beautiful branches overshadowing the forest;
it towered on high,
its top above the thick foliage.
4 The waters nourished it,
deep springs made it grow tall;
their streams flowed
all around its base
and sent their channels
to all the trees of the field.
5 So it towered higher
than all the trees of the field;
its boughs increased
and its branches grew long,
spreading because of abundant waters.
6 All the birds of the air
nested in its boughs,
all the beasts of the field
gave birth under its branches;
all the great nations
lived in its shade.
7 It was majestic in beauty,
with its spreading boughs,
for its roots went down
to abundant waters.
8 The cedars in the garden of God
could not rival it,
nor could the pine trees
equal its boughs,
nor could the plane trees
compare with its branches—
no tree in the garden of God
could match its beauty.
9 I made it beautiful
with abundant branches,
the envy of all the trees of Eden
in the garden of God.

10 " 'Therefore this is what the Sovereign LORD says: Because it

(31:2–10) O God, rulers come and go, nations rise and fall, but Your Word is eternal. As You told the Egyptians to consider the lost glory of Assyria, even so teach us in this day to consider the lessons of history and to heed Your clear warning. Help us to take to heart the fundamental principles of national blessing. Those who trust in their own strength will be destroyed. But those who put their trust in You will be blessed.

towered on high, lifting its top above the thick foliage, and because
it was proud of its height, 11 I handed it over to the ruler of the nations, for him to deal with according to its wickedness. I cast it
aside, 12 and the most ruthless of foreign nations cut it down and
left it. Its boughs fell on the mountains and in all the valleys; its
branches lay broken in all the ravines of the land. All the nations
of the earth came out from under its shade and left it. 13 All the
birds of the air settled on the fallen tree, and all the beasts of the
field were among its branches. 14 Therefore no other trees by
the waters are ever to tower proudly on high, lifting their tops
above the thick foliage. No other trees so well-watered are ever to
reach such a height; they are all destined for death, for the earth
below, among mortal men, with those who go down to the pit.

15 " 'This is what the Sovereign LORD says: On the day it was
brought down to the grave[a] I covered the deep springs with
mourning for it; I held back its streams, and its abundant waters
were restrained. Because of it I clothed Lebanon with gloom, and
all the trees of the field withered away. 16 I made the nations tremble at the sound of its fall when I brought it down to the grave
with those who go down to the pit. Then all the trees of Eden, the
choicest and best of Lebanon, all the trees that were well-watered,
were consoled in the earth below. 17 Those who lived in its shade,
its allies among the nations, had also gone down to the grave with
it, joining those killed by the sword.

18 " 'Which of the trees of Eden can be compared with you in
splendor and majesty? Yet you, too, will be brought down with the
trees of Eden to the earth below; you will lie among the uncircumcised, with those killed by the sword.

" 'This is Pharaoh and all his hordes, declares the Sovereign
LORD.' "

A Lament for Pharaoh

32 In the twelfth year, in the twelfth month on the first day,
the word of the LORD came to me: 2 "Son of man, take up
a lament concerning Pharaoh king of Egypt and say to him:

" 'You are like a lion among the nations;
you are like a monster in the seas
thrashing about in your streams,
churning the water with your feet
and muddying the streams.

3 " 'This is what the Sovereign LORD says:

" 'With a great throng of people
I will cast my net over you,
and they will haul you up in my net.
4 I will throw you on the land
and hurl you on the open field.
I will let all the birds of the air settle on you
and all the beasts of the earth gorge themselves on you.
5 I will spread your flesh on the mountains
and fill the valleys with your remains.
6 I will drench the land with your flowing blood
all the way to the mountains,
and the ravines will be filled with your flesh.

(32:2) O merciful God, we know that You do not take pleasure in the death of anyone. You gave to Ezekiel a song of lament over Egypt, not a song of joy. You would not allow the nations to gloat over the downfall of Israel, and You will not allow us to gloat over Your judgment of the ungodly. (Eze 18:32)

The reward of the merciful is, that by their mercy they are rendered capable of receiving the mercy of God—yea, God himself, who is Mercy.

George MacDonald (1824-1905)

[a] *15* Hebrew *Sheol*; also in verses 16 and 17

7 When I snuff you out, I will cover the heavens
and darken their stars;
I will cover the sun with a cloud,
and the moon will not give its light.
8 All the shining lights in the heavens
I will darken over you;
I will bring darkness over your land,
declares the Sovereign LORD.
9 I will trouble the hearts of many peoples
when I bring about your destruction among the nations,
among[a] lands you have not known.
10 I will cause many peoples to be appalled at you,
and their kings will shudder with horror because of you
when I brandish my sword before them.
On the day of your downfall
each of them will tremble
every moment for his life.

11 " 'For this is what the Sovereign LORD says:

" 'The sword of the king of Babylon
will come against you.
12 I will cause your hordes to fall
by the swords of mighty men—
the most ruthless of all nations.
They will shatter the pride of Egypt,
and all her hordes will be overthrown.
13 I will destroy all her cattle
from beside abundant waters
no longer to be stirred by the foot of man
or muddied by the hoofs of cattle.
14 Then I will let her waters settle
and make her streams flow like oil,
declares the Sovereign LORD.
15 When I make Egypt desolate
and strip the land of everything in it,
when I strike down all who live there,
then they will know that I am the LORD.'

16 "This is the lament they will chant for her. The daughters of
the nations will chant it; for Egypt and all her hordes they will
chant it, declares the Sovereign LORD."

17 In the twelfth year, on the fifteenth day of the month, the
word of the LORD came to me: 18 "Son of man, wail for the hordes
of Egypt and consign to the earth below both her and the daughters of mighty nations, with those who go down to the pit. 19 Say to
them, 'Are you more favored than others? Go down and be laid
among the uncircumcised.' 20 They will fall among those killed by
the sword. The sword is drawn; let her be dragged off with all her
hordes. 21 From within the grave[b] the mighty leaders will say of
Egypt and her allies, 'They have come down and they lie with the
uncircumcised, with those killed by the sword.'
22 "Assyria is there with her whole army; she is surrounded by
the graves of all her slain, all who have fallen by the sword.

[a] 9 Hebrew; Septuagint *bring you into captivity among the nations, / to* [b] 21 Hebrew *Sheol*; also in verse 27

(32:15) Almighty God, Ruler of the nations, if we will not fall to our knees in worship we will be brought to our knees by Your judgment. For "[Your] mouth has uttered in all integrity a word that will not be revoked: Before [You] every knee will bow; by [You] every tongue will swear. They will say of [You], 'In the LORD alone are righteousness and strength.' All who have raged against [You] will come to [You] and be put to shame." (Isa 45:23–24)

With the word of his greatness has he assembled all that exists, and with a word he is able to overturn it again; for who can say to him, what have you done? Or who shall withstand the power of his might? He will act at all times as, and when, he chooses; and not one of his decrees shall fail. The entire universe lies open before him; and there is nothing that is hidden from his counsel.

Clement of Rome (30-100)

I cannot tell when he will rule the nations,
How He will claim His loved ones as His own;
And who can tell the holy jubilation
When all His children gather round His throne.
But this I know: all flesh will see His glory,
And skies will burst as all creation sings.
The Son will rise on one eternal morning
When Christ, the Savior of the world, is Lord and King!

"I Cannot Tell"
Ken Bible (©1996)

(33:1–6) O Lord, You have called me, like Ezekiel, to be a watchman on the wall to warn others of impending danger. Give me boldness to proclaim the risks, the threats, the consequences of sin and spiritual rebellion. Your Word has promised that "whoever turns a sinner from the error of his way will save him from death and cover over a multitude of sins." Let me be an alert and courageous watchman, Lord, offering eternal life and, by Your grace, helping to eliminate sin. (Jas 5:19–20)

If you cannot be the watchman
Standing high on Zion's wall,
Pointing out the path to heaven,
Off'ring life and peace to all,
If you cannot speak like angels,
If you cannot preach like Paul,
You can tell the love of Jesus,
You can say, "He died for all."

Let none hear you idly saying,
"There is nothing I can do,"
While the souls of men are dying,
And the Master calls for you:
Take the task He gives you gladly;
Let His work your pleasure be;
Answer quickly when He calleth,
"Here am I; send me, send me."

"Hark, the Voice of Jesus Calling"
Daniel March (1868)

23 Their graves are in the depths of the pit and her army lies
around her grave. All who had spread terror in the land of the living are slain, fallen by the sword.
24 "Elam is there, with all her hordes around her grave. All of
them are slain, fallen by the sword. All who had spread terror in
the land of the living went down uncircumcised to the earth
below. They bear their shame with those who go down to the pit.
25 A bed is made for her among the slain, with all her hordes
around her grave. All of them are uncircumcised, killed by the
sword. Because their terror had spread in the land of the living,
they bear their shame with those who go down to the pit; they are
laid among the slain.
26 "Meshech and Tubal are there, with all their hordes around
their graves. All of them are uncircumcised, killed by the sword
because they spread their terror in the land of the living. 27 Do
they not lie with the other uncircumcised warriors who have fall-
en, who went down to the grave with their weapons of war, whose
swords were placed under their heads? The punishment for their
sins rested on their bones, though the terror of these warriors
had stalked through the land of the living.
28 "You too, O Pharaoh, will be broken and will lie among the
uncircumcised, with those killed by the sword.
29 "Edom is there, her kings and all her princes; despite their
power, they are laid with those killed by the sword. They lie with
the uncircumcised, with those who go down to the pit.
30 "All the princes of the north and all the Sidonians are there;
they went down with the slain in disgrace despite the terror
caused by their power. They lie uncircumcised with those killed
by the sword and bear their shame with those who go down to the
pit.
31 "Pharaoh—he and all his army—will see them and he will
be consoled for all his hordes that were killed by the sword, declares the Sovereign LORD. 32 Although I had him spread terror in
the land of the living, Pharaoh and all his hordes will be laid
among the uncircumcised, with those killed by the sword, declares the Sovereign LORD."

Ezekiel a Watchman

33 The word of the LORD came to me: 2 "Son of man, speak to
your countrymen and say to them: 'When I bring the
sword against a land, and the people of the land choose one of
their men and make him their watchman, 3 and he sees the sword
coming against the land and blows the trumpet to warn the people, 4 then if anyone hears the trumpet but does not take warning
and the sword comes and takes his life, his blood will be on his
own head. 5 Since he heard the sound of the trumpet but did not
take warning, his blood will be on his own head. If he had taken
warning, he would have saved himself. 6 But if the watchman sees
the sword coming and does not blow the trumpet to warn the
people and the sword comes and takes the life of one of them,
that man will be taken away because of his sin, but I will hold the
watchman accountable for his blood.'
7 "Son of man, I have made you a watchman for the house of Israel; so hear the word I speak and give them warning from me.
8 When I say to the wicked, 'O wicked man, you will surely die,'
and you do not speak out to dissuade him from his ways, that

wicked man will die for[a] his sin, and I will hold you accountable
for his blood. 9But if you do warn the wicked man to turn from
his ways and he does not do so, he will die for his sin, but you will
have saved yourself.
10"Son of man, say to the house of Israel, 'This is what you are
saying: "Our offenses and sins weigh us down, and we are wasting away because of[b] them. How then can we live?"' 11Say to
them, 'As surely as I live, declares the Sovereign LORD, I take no
pleasure in the death of the wicked, but rather that they turn from
their ways and live. Turn! Turn from your evil ways! Why will you
die, O house of Israel?'
12"Therefore, son of man, say to your countrymen, 'The righteousness of the righteous man will not save him when he disobeys, and the wickedness of the wicked man will not cause him
to fall when he turns from it. The righteous man, if he sins, will
not be allowed to live because of his former righteousness.' 13If
I tell the righteous man that he will surely live, but then he trusts
in his righteousness and does evil, none of the righteous things he
has done will be remembered; he will die for the evil he has
done. 14And if I say to the wicked man, 'You will surely die,' but
he then turns away from his sin and does what is just and right—
15if he gives back what he took in pledge for a loan, returns what
he has stolen, follows the decrees that give life, and does no evil,
he will surely live; he will not die. 16None of the sins he has committed will be remembered against him. He has done what is just
and right; he will surely live.
17"Yet your countrymen say, 'The way of the Lord is not just.'
But it is their way that is not just. 18If a righteous man turns from
his righteousness and does evil, he will die for it. 19And if a
wicked man turns away from his wickedness and does what is
just and right, he will live by doing so. 20Yet, O house of Israel,
you say, 'The way of the Lord is not just.' But I will judge each of
you according to his own ways."

Jerusalem's Fall Explained

21In the twelfth year of our exile, in the tenth month on the
fifth day, a man who had escaped from Jerusalem came to me and
said, "The city has fallen!" 22Now the evening before the man arrived, the hand of the LORD was upon me, and he opened my
mouth before the man came to me in the morning. So my mouth
was opened and I was no longer silent.
23Then the word of the LORD came to me: 24"Son of man, the
people living in those ruins in the land of Israel are saying, 'Abraham was only one man, yet he possessed the land. But we are
many; surely the land has been given to us as our possession.'
25Therefore say to them, 'This is what the Sovereign LORD says:
Since you eat meat with the blood still in it and look to your idols
and shed blood, should you then possess the land? 26You rely on
your sword, you do detestable things, and each of you defiles his
neighbor's wife. Should you then possess the land?'
27"Say this to them: 'This is what the Sovereign LORD says: As
surely as I live, those who are left in the ruins will fall by the
sword, those out in the country I will give to the wild animals to
be devoured, and those in strongholds and caves will die of a
plague. 28I will make the land a desolate waste, and her proud

[a] *8* Or *in*; also in verse 9 [b] *10* Or *away in*

Come, O sinners, one and all,
Come, accept His invitation;
Come, obey His gracious call,
Come and take His free salvation!
Firmly in these words believe:
Jesus sinners will receive.

"Jesus Sinners Will Receive"
Erdmann Neumeister (1671–1756)
Trans. The Lutheran Hymnal (©1941)

(33:12–20) What more could You do for Your people than to offer them forgiveness for their sins? And what more can You do for us? Teach us the lesson of heartfelt repentance, Lord—genuine repentance that cannot wait to make right the wrongs that we have done. Change our hearts as well as our actions, and do not allow us to murmur against You. We know very well that Your way is just, and that we have much to learn about living justly.

Good and gracious Lord, as you give me grace to acknowledge my sins, so give me grace in both word and heart to repent them and utterly forsake them. And forgive me those sins which my pride blinds me from discerning.

Thomas More (1478–1535)

(34:11–15) You, O Lord, are my Shepherd; I shall not be in want. You make me lie down in green pastures, You lead me beside quiet waters, You restore my soul. You guide me in paths of righteousness for Your name's sake. Even though I walk through the valley of the shadow of death, I will fear no evil, for You are with me; Your rod and Your staff, they comfort me. You prepare a table before me in the presence of my enemies. You anoint my head with oil; my cup overflows. Surely goodness and love will follow me all the days of my life, and I will dwell in Your house, O Lord, forever. (Ps 23)

Who is it that is your Shepherd? The LORD*! Oh, my friends, what a wonderful announcement! The Lord God of heaven and earth, and Almighty Creator of all things, He who holds the universe in His hand as though it were a very little thing. He is your shepherd, and has charged himself with the care and keeping of you, as a shepherd is charged with the care and keeping of his sheep. If your hearts could really take in this thought you would never have a fear or a care again; for with such a Shepherd how could it be possible for you ever to want any good thing?*

Hannah Whitall Smith (1832–1911)

Savior, like a Shepherd lead us,
Much we need Thy tender care;
In Thy pleasant pastures feed us;
For our use Thy folds prepare.
Blessed Jesus, blessed Jesus,
Thou hast bought us, Thine we are;
Blessed Jesus, blessed Jesus,
Thou hast bought us, Thine we are.

We are Thine, do Thou befriend us;
Be the guardian of our way;
Keep Thy flock; from sin defend us;
Seek us when we go astray.
Blessed Jesus, blessed Jesus,
Hear, O hear us when we pray;
Blessed Jesus, blessed Jesus,
Hear, O hear us when we pray.

"Savior, Like a Shepherd Lead Us"
Dorothy A. Thrupp (1836)

strength will come to an end, and the mountains of Israel will become desolate so that no one will cross them. 29Then they will
know that I am the LORD, when I have made the land a desolate
waste because of all the detestable things they have done.'
30"As for you, son of man, your countrymen are talking together about you by the walls and at the doors of the houses, saying to each other, 'Come and hear the message that has come
from the LORD.' 31My people come to you, as they usually do, and
sit before you to listen to your words, but they do not put them
into practice. With their mouths they express devotion, but their
hearts are greedy for unjust gain. 32Indeed, to them you are nothing more than one who sings love songs with a beautiful voice
and plays an instrument well, for they hear your words but do not
put them into practice.
33"When all this comes true—and it surely will—then they
will know that a prophet has been among them."

Shepherds and Sheep

34 The word of the LORD came to me: 2"Son of man, prophesy against the shepherds of Israel; prophesy and say to
them: 'This is what the Sovereign LORD says: Woe to the shepherds
of Israel who only take care of themselves! Should not shepherds
take care of the flock? 3You eat the curds, clothe yourselves with
the wool and slaughter the choice animals, but you do not take
care of the flock. 4You have not strengthened the weak or healed
the sick or bound up the injured. You have not brought back the
strays or searched for the lost. You have ruled them harshly and
brutally. 5So they were scattered because there was no shepherd,
and when they were scattered they became food for all the wild
animals. 6My sheep wandered over all the mountains and on
every high hill. They were scattered over the whole earth, and no
one searched or looked for them.
7" 'Therefore, you shepherds, hear the word of the LORD: 8As
surely as I live, declares the Sovereign LORD, because my flock
lacks a shepherd and so has been plundered and has become
food for all the wild animals, and because my shepherds did not
search for my flock but cared for themselves rather than for my
flock, 9therefore, O shepherds, hear the word of the LORD: 10This
is what the Sovereign LORD says: I am against the shepherds and
will hold them accountable for my flock. I will remove them from
tending the flock so that the shepherds can no longer feed themselves. I will rescue my flock from their mouths, and it will no
longer be food for them.
11" 'For this is what the Sovereign LORD says: I myself will
search for my sheep and look after them. 12As a shepherd looks
after his scattered flock when he is with them, so will I look after
my sheep. I will rescue them from all the places where they were
scattered on a day of clouds and darkness. 13I will bring them out
from the nations and gather them from the countries, and I will
bring them into their own land. I will pasture them on the mountains of Israel, in the ravines and in all the settlements in the land.
14I will tend them in a good pasture, and the mountain heights of
Israel will be their grazing land. There they will lie down in good
grazing land, and there they will feed in a rich pasture on the
mountains of Israel. 15I myself will tend my sheep and have them
lie down, declares the Sovereign LORD. 16I will search for the lost
and bring back the strays. I will bind up the injured and strength-

en the weak, but the sleek and the strong I will destroy. I will
shepherd the flock with justice.
17" 'As for you, my flock, this is what the Sovereign LORD says:
I will judge between one sheep and another, and between rams
and goats. 18Is it not enough for you to feed on the good pasture?
Must you also trample the rest of your pasture with your feet? Is
it not enough for you to drink clear water? Must you also muddy
the rest with your feet? 19Must my flock feed on what you have
trampled and drink what you have muddied with your feet?
20" 'Therefore this is what the Sovereign LORD says to them: See,
I myself will judge between the fat sheep and the lean sheep. 21Be-
cause you shove with flank and shoulder, butting all the weak
sheep with your horns until you have driven them away, 22I will
save my flock, and they will no longer be plundered. I will judge
between one sheep and another. 23I will place over them one
shepherd, my servant David, and he will tend them; he will tend
them and be their shepherd. 24I the LORD will be their God, and my
servant David will be prince among them. I the LORD have spoken.
25" 'I will make a covenant of peace with them and rid the land
of wild beasts so that they may live in the desert and sleep in the
forests in safety. 26I will bless them and the places surrounding
my hill.[a] I will send down showers in season; there will be showers of blessing. 27The trees of the field will yield their fruit and the
ground will yield its crops; the people will be secure in their land.
They will know that I am the LORD, when I break the bars of their
yoke and rescue them from the hands of those who enslaved
them. 28They will no longer be plundered by the nations, nor will
wild animals devour them. They will live in safety, and no one will
make them afraid. 29I will provide for them a land renowned for
its crops, and they will no longer be victims of famine in the land
or bear the scorn of the nations. 30Then they will know that I, the
LORD their God, am with them and that they, the house of Israel,
are my people, declares the Sovereign LORD. 31You my sheep, the
sheep of my pasture, are people, and I am your God, declares the
Sovereign LORD.' "

A Prophecy Against Edom

35 The word of the LORD came to me: 2"Son of man, set your
face against Mount Seir; prophesy against it 3and say:
'This is what the Sovereign LORD says: I am against you, Mount
Seir, and I will stretch out my hand against you and make you a
desolate waste. 4I will turn your towns into ruins and you will be
desolate. Then you will know that I am the LORD.
5" 'Because you harbored an ancient hostility and delivered
the Israelites over to the sword at the time of their calamity, the
time their punishment reached its climax, 6therefore as surely as
I live, declares the Sovereign LORD, I will give you over to bloodshed and it will pursue you. Since you did not hate bloodshed,
bloodshed will pursue you. 7I will make Mount Seir a desolate
waste and cut off from it all who come and go. 8I will fill your
mountains with the slain; those killed by the sword will fall on
your hills and in your valleys and in all your ravines. 9I will make
you desolate forever; your towns will not be inhabited. Then you
will know that I am the LORD.
10" 'Because you have said, "These two nations and countries

[a] 26 Or *I will make them and the places surrounding my hill a blessing*

Come, let us worship and bow down,
Let us kneel before the Lord,
Our God, our Maker.
Come, let us worship and bow down,
Let us kneel before the Lord,
Our God, our Maker.

For He is our God,
And we are the people of His
pasture,
And the sheep of His hand,
Just the sheep of His hand.
"Come, Let Us Worship And Bow Down"
Dave Doherty (©1980)

(34:25–31) Father in heaven, just as You promised to do so long ago, You established a new covenant of peace with us when Your only Son gave His life. Through Him You have generously provided us with protection, blessings and fruitfulness. You have released us from our slavery to sin. You have brought forth the fruit of the Holy Spirit in our lives and have called us Your own, Your family, Your adopted children. How can we thank You for Your never-ending faithfulness?

Our dignity is that we are children of God, capable of communion with God, the object of the love of God—displayed to us on the Cross—and destined for eternal fellowship with God. Our true value is not what we are worth in ourselves, but what we are worth to God, and that worth is bestowed upon us by the utterly gratuitous love of God.

William Temple (1881-1944)

(36:8–12) I praise You, heavenly Father, that You delight in restoration—in restored lives, restored relationships, restored nations. Your restorative nature is also reflected in the second birth Jesus offers. When we are reborn in Your Spirit, we are indeed restored in our relationship with You, with ourselves and with one another. Only in the completed work of Your Son can humankind be fully restored; only through faith in Him can we become whole and fruitful.

Out of the same love that caused you to create us, you have now sent your only Son to save us. He is your perfect image and likeness, and so through him we can be restored to your image and likeness.

Saint Catherine of Siena (1347–1380)

will be ours and we will take possession of them," even though I
the LORD was there, 11therefore as surely as I live, declares the
Sovereign LORD, I will treat you in accordance with the anger and
jealousy you showed in your hatred of them and I will make myself known among them when I judge you. 12Then you will know
that I the LORD have heard all the contemptible things you have
said against the mountains of Israel. You said, "They have been
laid waste and have been given over to us to devour." 13You
boasted against me and spoke against me without restraint, and I
heard it. 14This is what the Sovereign LORD says: While the whole
earth rejoices, I will make you desolate. 15Because you rejoiced
when the inheritance of the house of Israel became desolate, that
is how I will treat you. You will be desolate, O Mount Seir, you and
all of Edom. Then they will know that I am the LORD.' "

A Prophecy to the Mountains of Israel

36 "Son of man, prophesy to the mountains of Israel and say,
'O mountains of Israel, hear the word of the LORD. 2This
is what the Sovereign LORD says: The enemy said of you, "Aha! The
ancient heights have become our possession." ' 3Therefore
prophesy and say, 'This is what the Sovereign LORD says: Because
they ravaged and hounded you from every side so that you became the possession of the rest of the nations and the object of
people's malicious talk and slander, 4therefore, O mountains of
Israel, hear the word of the Sovereign LORD: This is what the Sovereign LORD says to the mountains and hills, to the ravines and
valleys, to the desolate ruins and the deserted towns that have
been plundered and ridiculed by the rest of the nations around
you— 5this is what the Sovereign LORD says: In my burning zeal I
have spoken against the rest of the nations, and against all Edom,
for with glee and with malice in their hearts they made my land
their own possession so that they might plunder its pastureland.'
6Therefore prophesy concerning the land of Israel and say to the
mountains and hills, to the ravines and valleys: 'This is what the
Sovereign LORD says: I speak in my jealous wrath because you
have suffered the scorn of the nations. 7Therefore this is what the
Sovereign LORD says: I swear with uplifted hand that the nations
around you will also suffer scorn.

8" 'But you, O mountains of Israel, will produce branches and
fruit for my people Israel, for they will soon come home. 9I am
concerned for you and will look on you with favor; you will be
plowed and sown, 10and I will multiply the number of people
upon you, even the whole house of Israel. The towns will be inhabited and the ruins rebuilt. 11I will increase the number of men
and animals upon you, and they will be fruitful and become numerous. I will settle people on you as in the past and will make
you prosper more than before. Then you will know that I am the
LORD. 12I will cause people, my people Israel, to walk upon you.
They will possess you, and you will be their inheritance; you will
never again deprive them of their children.

13" 'This is what the Sovereign LORD says: Because people say
to you, "You devour men and deprive your nation of its children,"
14therefore you will no longer devour men or make your nation
childless, declares the Sovereign LORD. 15No longer will I make
you hear the taunts of the nations, and no longer will you suffer
the scorn of the peoples or cause your nation to fall, declares the
Sovereign LORD.' "

MY BELOVED

Have you noticed that sometimes you feel awkward coming before Me? During those times, remember this: I do not need anything from you. But I want your trust. Remember that I am the Good Shepherd. I made you, and you are Mine; You are My people, the sheep of My pasture.

I care for you. I watch over you. And when you wander I come looking for you. I even call you by name. At times, you have heard Me whisper your name. I diligently protect you from those who might want to harm you. Many times you are not even aware of the danger from which you are rescued.

To follow Me, you must listen to My voice. I will lead you to good places; places where you will be refreshed and where you will find rest. But remember that to get there you must follow Me. And to follow Me you must trust Me. As long as you are with Me you will never want for anything. I will care for you.

As you think about how simple our relationship is meant to be, I encourage you to lay down your anxiety about how to prove yourself to Me. Let Me be your Good Shepherd. Let Me be the One to watch over you. Allow yourself to be cared for, and trust the One Who will never fail you. Trust Me.

Ps 23:1-6; 37:3; 59:1; 100:3; Eze 34:12,31; Lk 15:4-6; Jn 10:3-4,11

16Again the word of the LORD came to me: 17"Son of man, when
the people of Israel were living in their own land, they defiled it
by their conduct and their actions. Their conduct was like a
woman's monthly uncleanness in my sight. 18So I poured out my
wrath on them because they had shed blood in the land and because they had defiled it with their idols. 19I dispersed them
among the nations, and they were scattered through the countries; I judged them according to their conduct and their actions.
20And wherever they went among the nations they profaned my
holy name, for it was said of them, 'These are the LORD's people,
and yet they had to leave his land.' 21I had concern for my holy
name, which the house of Israel profaned among the nations
where they had gone.

22"Therefore say to the house of Israel, 'This is what the Sovereign LORD says: It is not for your sake, O house of Israel, that I
am going to do these things, but for the sake of my holy name,
which you have profaned among the nations where you have
gone. 23I will show the holiness of my great name, which has
been profaned among the nations, the name you have profaned
among them. Then the nations will know that I am the LORD, declares the Sovereign LORD, when I show myself holy through you
before their eyes.

24" 'For I will take you out of the nations; I will gather you
from all the countries and bring you back into your own land. 25I
will sprinkle clean water on you, and you will be clean; I will
cleanse you from all your impurities and from all your idols. 26I
will give you a new heart and put a new spirit in you; I will remove
from you your heart of stone and give you a heart of flesh. 27And
I will put my Spirit in you and move you to follow my decrees and
be careful to keep my laws. 28You will live in the land I gave your
forefathers; you will be my people, and I will be your God. 29I will
save you from all your uncleanness. I will call for the grain and
make it plentiful and will not bring famine upon you. 30I will increase the fruit of the trees and the crops of the field, so that you
will no longer suffer disgrace among the nations because of
famine. 31Then you will remember your evil ways and wicked
deeds, and you will loathe yourselves for your sins and detestable
practices. 32I want you to know that I am not doing this for your
sake, declares the Sovereign LORD. Be ashamed and disgraced for
your conduct, O house of Israel!

33" 'This is what the Sovereign LORD says: On the day I cleanse
you from all your sins, I will resettle your towns, and the ruins
will be rebuilt. 34The desolate land will be cultivated instead of
lying desolate in the sight of all who pass through it. 35They will
say, "This land that was laid waste has become like the garden of
Eden; the cities that were lying in ruins, desolate and destroyed,
are now fortified and inhabited." 36Then the nations around you
that remain will know that I the LORD have rebuilt what was destroyed and have replanted what was desolate. I the LORD have
spoken, and I will do it.'

37"This is what the Sovereign LORD says: Once again I will yield
to the plea of the house of Israel and do this for them: I will make
their people as numerous as sheep, 38as numerous as the flocks
for offerings at Jerusalem during her appointed feasts. So will the
ruined cities be filled with flocks of people. Then they will know
that I am the LORD."

If, then, you sometimes fall, do not lose heart. Even more, do not cease striving to make progress from it, for even out of your fall God will bring some good.

Saint Teresa of Avila (1515-1582)

(36:24–32) O Lord, I yearn for purity of heart and for spiritual renewal. Please give me a new heart and spirit—the heart and Spirit of Jesus—so that I may live a holy life. I pray that the sins of my past will become appalling to me and that I will recoil from ever committing them again. Most of all, I pray that You will remove any disgrace I have brought upon Your name. Forgive me, Lord, and make me new. And may Your holiness be made known to the world through Your great acts of mercy to me.

Spirit of God, descend upon my heart;
Wean it from earth, through all its pulses move;
Stoop to my weakness, mighty as Thou art,
And make me love Thee as I ought to love.

"Spirit of God, Descend Upon My Heart"
George Croly (1867)

The Valley of Dry Bones

37 The hand of the LORD was upon me, and he brought me
out by the Spirit of the LORD and set me in the middle of a
valley; it was full of bones. 2He led me back and forth among
them, and I saw a great many bones on the floor of the valley,
bones that were very dry. 3He asked me, "Son of man, can these
bones live?"
I said, "O Sovereign LORD, you alone know."
4Then he said to me, "Prophesy to these bones and say to
them, 'Dry bones, hear the word of the LORD! 5This is what the
Sovereign LORD says to these bones: I will make breath[a] enter you,
and you will come to life. 6I will attach tendons to you and make
flesh come upon you and cover you with skin; I will put breath in
you, and you will come to life. Then you will know that I am the
LORD.' "
7So I prophesied as I was commanded. And as I was prophesying, there was a noise, a rattling sound, and the bones came together, bone to bone. 8I looked, and tendons and flesh appeared
on them and skin covered them, but there was no breath in them.
9Then he said to me, "Prophesy to the breath; prophesy, son of
man, and say to it, 'This is what the Sovereign LORD says: Come
from the four winds, O breath, and breathe into these slain, that
they may live.' " 10So I prophesied as he commanded me, and
breath entered them; they came to life and stood up on their
feet—a vast army.
11Then he said to me: "Son of man, these bones are the whole
house of Israel. They say, 'Our bones are dried up and our hope
is gone; we are cut off.' 12Therefore prophesy and say to them:
'This is what the Sovereign LORD says: O my people, I am going to
open your graves and bring you up from them; I will bring you
back to the land of Israel. 13Then you, my people, will know that
I am the LORD, when I open your graves and bring you up from
them. 14I will put my Spirit in you and you will live, and I will settle you in your own land. Then you will know that I the LORD have
spoken, and I have done it, declares the LORD.' "

One Nation Under One King

15The word of the LORD came to me: 16"Son of man, take a
stick of wood and write on it, 'Belonging to Judah and the Israelites associated with him.' Then take another stick of wood, and
write on it, 'Ephraim's stick, belonging to Joseph and all the
house of Israel associated with him.' 17Join them together into
one stick so that they will become one in your hand.
18"When your countrymen ask you, 'Won't you tell us what you
mean by this?' 19say to them, 'This is what the Sovereign LORD
says: I am going to take the stick of Joseph—which is in Ephraim's hand—and of the Israelite tribes associated with him, and
join it to Judah's stick, making them a single stick of wood, and
they will become one in my hand.' 20Hold before their eyes the
sticks you have written on 21and say to them, 'This is what the
Sovereign LORD says: I will take the Israelites out of the nations
where they have gone. I will gather them from all around and
bring them back into their own land. 22I will make them one nation in the land, on the mountains of Israel. There will be one
king over all of them and they will never again be two nations or

[a] 5 The Hebrew for this word can also mean *wind* or *spirit* (see verses 6–14).

(37:1–14) You have called us, Lord, to speak words of truth to the spiritually dead. You have put Your message in our mouths and have given us Your authority. But unless You breathe life into our labor it will not succeed. Unless You impart the power of the resurrection to our work it will never be worthwhile. You are the author and the giver of life, Sovereign Lord. Apart from Your life-giving Spirit, our best efforts are vain.

Without Him we can do nothing (John 15:5), but by His almighty energy the most extraordinary results can be produced. Everything depends upon His manifesting or concealing His power. Do we always look up to Him, both for our inner life and our outward service, with respectful dependence which is fitting?
Charles Haddon Spurgeon (1834–1892)

All we can do is done in vain
Unless God blesses the deed;
Vainly we hope for the harvest tide
Till God gives life to the seed:
Yet nearer and nearer draws the
time,
The time that shall surely be,
When the earth shall be filled
With the glory of God
As the waters cover the sea.
"God Is Working His Purpose Out"
Arthur C. Ainger (1894)

be divided into two kingdoms. 23They will no longer defile themselves with their idols and vile images or with any of their offenses, for I will save them from all their sinful backsliding,[a] and
I will cleanse them. They will be my people, and I will be their
God.

24" 'My servant David will be king over them, and they will all
have one shepherd. They will follow my laws and be careful to
keep my decrees. 25They will live in the land I gave to my servant
Jacob, the land where your fathers lived. They and their children
and their children's children will live there forever, and David my
servant will be their prince forever. 26I will make a covenant of
peace with them; it will be an everlasting covenant. I will establish
them and increase their numbers, and I will put my sanctuary
among them forever. 27My dwelling place will be with them; I will
be their God, and they will be my people. 28Then the nations will
know that I the LORD make Israel holy, when my sanctuary is
among them forever.' "

A Prophecy Against Gog

38 The word of the LORD came to me: 2"Son of man, set your
face against Gog, of the land of Magog, the chief prince
of[b] Meshech and Tubal; prophesy against him 3and say: 'This is
what the Sovereign LORD says: I am against you, O Gog, chief
prince of[c] Meshech and Tubal. 4I will turn you around, put hooks
in your jaws and bring you out with your whole army—your
horses, your horsemen fully armed, and a great horde with large
and small shields, all of them brandishing their swords. 5Persia,
Cush[d] and Put will be with them, all with shields and helmets,
6also Gomer with all its troops, and Beth Togarmah from the far
north with all its troops—the many nations with you.

7" 'Get ready; be prepared, you and all the hordes gathered
about you, and take command of them. 8After many days you will
be called to arms. In future years you will invade a land that has
recovered from war, whose people were gathered from many nations to the mountains of Israel, which had long been desolate.
They had been brought out from the nations, and now all of them
live in safety. 9You and all your troops and the many nations with
you will go up, advancing like a storm; you will be like a cloud
covering the land.

10" 'This is what the Sovereign LORD says: On that day thoughts
will come into your mind and you will devise an evil scheme.
11You will say, "I will invade a land of unwalled villages; I will attack a peaceful and unsuspecting people—all of them living without walls and without gates and bars. 12I will plunder and loot
and turn my hand against the resettled ruins and the people gathered from the nations, rich in livestock and goods, living at the
center of the land." 13Sheba and Dedan and the merchants of
Tarshish and all her villages[e] will say to you, "Have you come to
plunder? Have you gathered your hordes to loot, to carry off silver and gold, to take away livestock and goods and to seize much
plunder?" '

14"Therefore, son of man, prophesy and say to Gog: 'This is
what the Sovereign LORD says: In that day, when my people Israel
are living in safety, will you not take notice of it? 15You will come

[a] 23 Many Hebrew manuscripts (see also Septuagint); most Hebrew manuscripts *all their dwelling places where they sinned* [b] 2 Or *the prince of Rosh,* [c] 3 Or *Gog, prince of Rosh,* [d] 5 That is, the upper Nile region [e] 13 Or *her strong lions*

God, doubtless, is pursuing some design and carrying on some scheme in the various changes and revolutions which from age to age come to pass in the world. It is most reasonable to suppose that all revolutions, from the beginning of the world to the end of it, are but the various parts of the same scheme, all conspiring to bring to pass that great event which the Great Creator and Governor of the World has ultimately in view.

David Manning White (1917-1993)

(38:1–6) As we look back across centuries of history, Lord, and as we look forward to prophecies yet to be fulfilled, we see that Your invisible hand is always at work in the affairs of humankind. For Your own purposes You use the lusts and cravings of nations and kingdoms to draw them into war, and thus accomplish Your will through them. You rule, God; and at the end of time Your peace, Your justice and Your mercy will prevail. You truly are the King of kings and Lord of lords. (Rev 20:7–8)

from your place in the far north, you and many nations with you,
all of them riding on horses, a great horde, a mighty army. 16You
will advance against my people Israel like a cloud that covers the
land. In days to come, O Gog, I will bring you against my land, so
that the nations may know me when I show myself holy through
you before their eyes.
17" 'This is what the Sovereign LORD says: Are you not the one
I spoke of in former days by my servants the prophets of Israel?
At that time they prophesied for years that I would bring you
against them. 18This is what will happen in that day: When Gog attacks the land of Israel, my hot anger will be aroused, declares
the Sovereign LORD. 19In my zeal and fiery wrath I declare that at
that time there shall be a great earthquake in the land of Israel.
20The fish of the sea, the birds of the air, the beasts of the field,
every creature that moves along the ground, and all the people on
the face of the earth will tremble at my presence. The mountains
will be overturned, the cliffs will crumble and every wall will fall
to the ground. 21I will summon a sword against Gog on all my
mountains, declares the Sovereign LORD. Every man's sword will
be against his brother. 22I will execute judgment upon him with
plague and bloodshed; I will pour down torrents of rain, hailstones and burning sulfur on him and on his troops and on the
many nations with him. 23And so I will show my greatness and my
holiness, and I will make myself known in the sight of many nations. Then they will know that I am the LORD.'

39 "Son of man, prophesy against Gog and say: 'This is what
the Sovereign LORD says: I am against you, O Gog, chief
prince of[a] Meshech and Tubal. 2I will turn you around and drag
you along. I will bring you from the far north and send you
against the mountains of Israel. 3Then I will strike your bow from
your left hand and make your arrows drop from your right hand.
4On the mountains of Israel you will fall, you and all your troops
and the nations with you. I will give you as food to all kinds of
carrion birds and to the wild animals. 5You will fall in the open
field, for I have spoken, declares the Sovereign LORD. 6I will send
fire on Magog and on those who live in safety in the coastlands,
and they will know that I am the LORD.
7" 'I will make known my holy name among my people Israel.
I will no longer let my holy name be profaned, and the nations
will know that I the LORD am the Holy One in Israel. 8It is coming!
It will surely take place, declares the Sovereign LORD. This is the
day I have spoken of.
9" 'Then those who live in the towns of Israel will go out and
use the weapons for fuel and burn them up—the small and large
shields, the bows and arrows, the war clubs and spears. For seven
years they will use them for fuel. 10They will not need to gather
wood from the fields or cut it from the forests, because they will
use the weapons for fuel. And they will plunder those who plundered them and loot those who looted them, declares the Sovereign LORD.
11" 'On that day I will give Gog a burial place in Israel, in the
valley of those who travel east toward[b] the Sea.[c] It will block the
way of travelers, because Gog and all his hordes will be buried
there. So it will be called the Valley of Hamon Gog.[d]
12" 'For seven months the house of Israel will be burying them

He first makes us to know his holy name, and so keeps us from polluting it and engages us to honour it. The heathen, those that never knew it, or would not own it, shall know that "I am the Lord, the Holy One in Israel."

Matthew Henry (1662–1714)

(39:1–10) You have promised, Lord, to utterly destroy those who profane Your name. How we long for the day when You bring to a final conclusion the violent, brutal reign of ungodly nations. We grieve over Your persecuted children who suffer for their faith. We are saddened by the restrictions and injustices imposed by despots and dictators, often targeting Your sons and daughters. We plead for the afflicted and downtrodden, that in the near future You will deliver them to safety. We pray that, through the deliverance of Your people, their abusers will know that You are the Lord.

This is my Father's world,
O let me ne'er forget
That though the wrong
Seems oft so strong,
God is the Ruler yet.
This is my Father's world,
The battle is not done;
Jesus, who died,
Shall be satisfied,
And earth and heav'n be one.

"This Is My Father's World"
Maltbie D. Babcock (1901)

[a] 1 Or *Gog, prince of Rosh,* [b] 11 Or *of* [c] 11 That is, the Dead Sea [d] 11 *Hamon Gog* means *hordes of Gog.*

in order to cleanse the land. 13All the people of the land will bury
them, and the day I am glorified will be a memorable day for
them, declares the Sovereign LORD.
14" 'Men will be regularly employed to cleanse the land. Some
will go throughout the land and, in addition to them, others will
bury those that remain on the ground. At the end of the seven
months they will begin their search. 15As they go through the land
and one of them sees a human bone, he will set up a marker beside it until the gravediggers have buried it in the Valley of Hamon
Gog. 16(Also a town called Hamonah[a] will be there.) And so they
will cleanse the land.'
17"Son of man, this is what the Sovereign LORD says: Call out to
every kind of bird and all the wild animals: 'Assemble and come
together from all around to the sacrifice I am preparing for you,
the great sacrifice on the mountains of Israel. There you will eat
flesh and drink blood. 18You will eat the flesh of mighty men and
drink the blood of the princes of the earth as if they were rams
and lambs, goats and bulls—all of them fattened animals from
Bashan. 19At the sacrifice I am preparing for you, you will eat fat
till you are glutted and drink blood till you are drunk. 20At my
table you will eat your fill of horses and riders, mighty men and
soldiers of every kind,' declares the Sovereign LORD.
21"I will display my glory among the nations, and all the nations will see the punishment I inflict and the hand I lay upon
them. 22From that day forward the house of Israel will know that
I am the LORD their God. 23And the nations will know that the people of Israel went into exile for their sin, because they were unfaithful to me. So I hid my face from them and handed them over
to their enemies, and they all fell by the sword. 24I dealt with
them according to their uncleanness and their offenses, and I hid
my face from them.
25"Therefore this is what the Sovereign LORD says: I will now
bring Jacob back from captivity[b] and will have compassion on all
the people of Israel, and I will be zealous for my holy name.
26They will forget their shame and all the unfaithfulness they
showed toward me when they lived in safety in their land with no
one to make them afraid. 27When I have brought them back from
the nations and have gathered them from the countries of their
enemies, I will show myself holy through them in the sight of
many nations. 28Then they will know that I am the LORD their God,
for though I sent them into exile among the nations, I will gather
them to their own land, not leaving any behind. 29I will no longer
hide my face from them, for I will pour out my Spirit on the house
of Israel, declares the Sovereign LORD."

The New Temple Area

40 In the twenty-fifth year of our exile, at the beginning of
the year, on the tenth of the month, in the fourteenth year
after the fall of the city—on that very day the hand of the LORD was
upon me and he took me there. 2In visions of God he took me to
the land of Israel and set me on a very high mountain, on whose
south side were some buildings that looked like a city. 3He took
me there, and I saw a man whose appearance was like bronze; he
was standing in the gateway with a linen cord and a measuring
rod in his hand. 4The man said to me, "Son of man, look with

[a] 16 *Hamonah* means *horde.* [b] 25 Or *now restore the fortunes of Jacob*

(39:25–29) O God, just as the Israelites were blessed when You regathered them into their land, how blessed we are when You allow us to return to You after we have sinned. You do not always accuse us, nor do You harbor Your anger forever; You do not treat us as our sins deserve or repay us according to our iniquities. For as high as the heavens are above the earth, so great is Your love for those who fear You; as far as the east is from the west, so far have You removed our transgressions from us. As a father has compassion on his children, so You have compassion on those who fear You. (Ps 103:9–13)

Think about His love,
Think about His goodness,
Think about His grace
That's brought us through.
For as high as the heavens above,
So great is the measure of our
Father's love;
Great is the measure of our Father's
love.

"Think About His Love"
Walt Harrah (©1987)

your eyes and hear with your ears and pay attention to everything
I am going to show you, for that is why you have been brought
here. Tell the house of Israel everything you see."

The East Gate to the Outer Court

5 I saw a wall completely surrounding the temple area. The
length of the measuring rod in the man's hand was six long cubits, each of which was a cubit[a] and a handbreadth.[b] He measured the wall; it was one measuring rod thick and one rod high.
6 Then he went to the gate facing east. He climbed its steps and
measured the threshold of the gate; it was one rod deep.[c] 7 The alcoves for the guards were one rod long and one rod wide, and the
projecting walls between the alcoves were five cubits thick. And
the threshold of the gate next to the portico facing the temple was
one rod deep.
8 Then he measured the portico of the gateway; 9 it[d] was eight
cubits deep and its jambs were two cubits thick. The portico of
the gateway faced the temple.
10 Inside the east gate were three alcoves on each side; the
three had the same measurements, and the faces of the projecting walls on each side had the same measurements. 11 Then he
measured the width of the entrance to the gateway; it was ten cubits and its length was thirteen cubits. 12 In front of each alcove
was a wall one cubit high, and the alcoves were six cubits square.
13 Then he measured the gateway from the top of the rear wall of
one alcove to the top of the opposite one; the distance was twenty-five cubits from one parapet opening to the opposite one. 14 He
measured along the faces of the projecting walls all around the
inside of the gateway—sixty cubits. The measurement was up to
the portico[e] facing the courtyard.[f] 15 The distance from the entrance of the gateway to the far end of its portico was fifty cubits.
16 The alcoves and the projecting walls inside the gateway were
surmounted by narrow parapet openings all around, as was the
portico; the openings all around faced inward. The faces of the
projecting walls were decorated with palm trees.

The Outer Court

17 Then he brought me into the outer court. There I saw some
rooms and a pavement that had been constructed all around the
court; there were thirty rooms along the pavement. 18 It abutted
the sides of the gateways and was as wide as they were long; this
was the lower pavement. 19 Then he measured the distance from
the inside of the lower gateway to the outside of the inner court;
it was a hundred cubits on the east side as well as on the north.

The North Gate

20 Then he measured the length and width of the gate facing
north, leading into the outer court. 21 Its alcoves—three on each
side—its projecting walls and its portico had the same measurements as those of the first gateway. It was fifty cubits long and
twenty-five cubits wide. 22 Its openings, its portico and its palm
tree decorations had the same measurements as those of the gate

[a] *5* The common cubit was about 1 1/2 feet (about 0.5 meter). [b] *5* That is, about 3 inches (about 8 centimeters) [c] *6* Septuagint; Hebrew *deep, the first threshold, one rod deep* [d] *8,9* Many Hebrew manuscripts, Septuagint, Vulgate and Syriac; most Hebrew manuscripts *gateway facing the temple; it was one rod deep. 9Then he measured the portico of the gateway; it* [e] *14* Septuagint; Hebrew *projecting wall* [f] *14* The meaning of the Hebrew for this verse is uncertain.

(40:4) "The Lord confides in those who fear him." O God, I long to be a person of faith and faithfulness like Ezekiel, a person with whom You can entrust Your message. You knew You could trust him to "tell the house of Israel everything you see." Lord, please give me eyes to see, ears to hear and a heart to understand Your message of hope to those in turmoil in my day. And give me boldness to speak the truth in Jesus' name and for His sake. (Ps 25:14; Mk 4:11)

By faith, continually put off your self-life and put on the life of Christ (Galatians 3:27; Romans 13:14). Repeat this act until it becomes the attitude of your whole being. If you do this day after day, you will find that His life will be revealed in your mortal body . . . You will learn the full meaning of salvation and will have your eyes opened to secrets of the Lord that you had never dreamed of.

Catherine Jackson

facing east. Seven steps led up to it, with its portico opposite
them. 23There was a gate to the inner court facing the north gate,
just as there was on the east. He measured from one gate to the
opposite one; it was a hundred cubits.

The South Gate

24Then he led me to the south side and I saw a gate facing
south. He measured its jambs and its portico, and they had the
same measurements as the others. 25The gateway and its portico
had narrow openings all around, like the openings of the others.
It was fifty cubits long and twenty-five cubits wide. 26Seven steps
led up to it, with its portico opposite them; it had palm tree decorations on the faces of the projecting walls on each side. 27The
inner court also had a gate facing south, and he measured from
this gate to the outer gate on the south side; it was a hundred cubits.

Gates to the Inner Court

28Then he brought me into the inner court through the south
gate, and he measured the south gate; it had the same measurements as the others. 29Its alcoves, its projecting walls and its portico had the same measurements as the others. The gateway and
its portico had openings all around. It was fifty cubits long and
twenty-five cubits wide. 30(The porticoes of the gateways around
the inner court were twenty-five cubits wide and five cubits deep.)
31Its portico faced the outer court; palm trees decorated its
jambs, and eight steps led up to it.
32Then he brought me to the inner court on the east side, and
he measured the gateway; it had the same measurements as the
others. 33Its alcoves, its projecting walls and its portico had the
same measurements as the others. The gateway and its portico
had openings all around. It was fifty cubits long and twenty-five
cubits wide. 34Its portico faced the outer court; palm trees decorated the jambs on either side, and eight steps led up to it.
35Then he brought me to the north gate and measured it. It
had the same measurements as the others, 36as did its alcoves, its
projecting walls and its portico, and it had openings all around.
It was fifty cubits long and twenty-five cubits wide. 37Its portico[a]
faced the outer court; palm trees decorated the jambs on either
side, and eight steps led up to it.

The Rooms for Preparing Sacrifices

38A room with a doorway was by the portico in each of the
inner gateways, where the burnt offerings were washed. 39In the
portico of the gateway were two tables on each side, on which
the burnt offerings, sin offerings and guilt offerings were slaughtered. 40By the outside wall of the portico of the gateway, near
the steps at the entrance to the north gateway were two tables,
and on the other side of the steps were two tables. 41So there
were four tables on one side of the gateway and four on the
other—eight tables in all—on which the sacrifices were slaughtered. 42There were also four tables of dressed stone for the
burnt offerings, each a cubit and a half long, a cubit and a half
wide and a cubit high. On them were placed the utensils for
slaughtering the burnt offerings and the other sacrifices. 43And

[a] 37 Septuagint (see also verses 31 and 34); Hebrew *jambs*

(40:22–42) Father in heaven, we praise You for being the God of hope. In the midst of his captivity You gave Ezekiel a vision of a future more glorious than the past. Though we do not know the meaning of all of this splendor, and though we cannot clearly see or understand the future, we are certain that You know every detail of our lives just as surely as You knew every detail of this temple. And we are fully persuaded that the former things will pass away and that You will make all things new. As we await the fulfillment of this vision, O God of hope, fill us with all joy and peace as we trust in You, so that we may overflow with hope by the power of the Holy Spirit. (Isa 65:17; Ro 15:13; Rev 21:5)

double-pronged hooks, each a handbreadth long, were attached
to the wall all around. The tables were for the flesh of the offerings.

Rooms for the Priests

44Outside the inner gate, within the inner court, were two
rooms, one[a] at the side of the north gate and facing south, and
another at the side of the south[b] gate and facing north. 45He said
to me, "The room facing south is for the priests who have charge
of the temple, 46and the room facing north is for the priests who
have charge of the altar. These are the sons of Zadok, who are the
only Levites who may draw near to the LORD to minister before
him."
47Then he measured the court: It was square—a hundred cubits long and a hundred cubits wide. And the altar was in front of
the temple.

The Temple

48He brought me to the portico of the temple and measured
the jambs of the portico; they were five cubits wide on either side.
The width of the entrance was fourteen cubits and its projecting
walls were[c] three cubits wide on either side. 49The portico was
twenty cubits wide, and twelve[d] cubits from front to back. It was
reached by a flight of stairs,[e] and there were pillars on each side
of the jambs.

41 Then the man brought me to the outer sanctuary and measured the jambs; the width of the jambs was six cubits[f] on
each side.[g] 2The entrance was ten cubits wide, and the projecting
walls on each side of it were five cubits wide. He also measured
the outer sanctuary; it was forty cubits long and twenty cubits
wide.
3Then he went into the inner sanctuary and measured the
jambs of the entrance; each was two cubits wide. The entrance
was six cubits wide, and the projecting walls on each side of it
were seven cubits wide. 4And he measured the length of the inner
sanctuary; it was twenty cubits, and its width was twenty cubits
across the end of the outer sanctuary. He said to me, "This is the
Most Holy Place."
5Then he measured the wall of the temple; it was six cubits
thick, and each side room around the temple was four cubits
wide. 6The side rooms were on three levels, one above another,
thirty on each level. There were ledges all around the wall of the
temple to serve as supports for the side rooms, so that the supports were not inserted into the wall of the temple. 7The side
rooms all around the temple were wider at each successive level.
The structure surrounding the temple was built in ascending
stages, so that the rooms widened as one went upward. A stairway
went up from the lowest floor to the top floor through the middle
floor.
8I saw that the temple had a raised base all around it, forming
the foundation of the side rooms. It was the length of the rod, six
long cubits. 9The outer wall of the side rooms was five cubits
thick. The open area between the side rooms of the temple 10and

[a] 44 Septuagint; Hebrew *were rooms for singers, which were* [b] 44 Septuagint; Hebrew *east* [c] 48 Septuagint; Hebrew *entrance was* [d] 49 Septuagint; Hebrew *eleven* [e] 49 Hebrew; Septuagint *Ten steps led up to it* [f] 1 The common cubit was about 1 1/2 feet (about 0.5 meter). [g] 1 One Hebrew manuscript and Septuagint; most Hebrew manuscripts *side, the width of the tent*

(40:48—41:5) We thank You, Lord God, that there will always be a holy place of worship, constructed under Your direction and built according to Your design, whose glory is the very presence of the Living God. Whether it was Moses' tabernacle in the desert, or Solomon's temple in Jerusalem, or a glorious new temple in a city yet to come, or simply the temple of our hearts—our past, present and future with You are centered on worship. And You have ensured us that there will always be a community of worshipers who will worship You in spirit and in truth. You will forever be our God, and we will forever be Your people. (Jn 4:20–24; 1Co 3:16–17; 6:19; 2Co 6:16)

Every believer is a living, breathing temple in which God dwells. That means believers can worship anywhere, at any time–God goes with them in an abiding presence. A Christian can worship Him at the beach, in the mountains, driving down the road, sitting under a tree, walking in the woods, running in the country, sitting in the living room, in a church building, or anywhere under any kind of circumstance or condition. The sphere of worship is unlimited.

John MacArthur, Jr. (1939-)

the ⌊priests'⌋ rooms was twenty cubits wide all around the temple.
11There were entrances to the side rooms from the open area,
one on the north and another on the south; and the base adjoining the open area was five cubits wide all around.
12The building facing the temple courtyard on the west side
was seventy cubits wide. The wall of the building was five cubits
thick all around, and its length was ninety cubits.
13Then he measured the temple; it was a hundred cubits long,
and the temple courtyard and the building with its walls were also
a hundred cubits long. 14The width of the temple courtyard on
the east, including the front of the temple, was a hundred cubits.
15Then he measured the length of the building facing the
courtyard at the rear of the temple, including its galleries on each
side; it was a hundred cubits.

The outer sanctuary, the inner sanctuary and the portico facing
the court, 16as well as the thresholds and the narrow windows
and galleries around the three of them—everything beyond and
including the threshold was covered with wood. The floor, the
wall up to the windows, and the windows were covered. 17In the
space above the outside of the entrance to the inner sanctuary
and on the walls at regular intervals all around the inner and
outer sanctuary 18were carved cherubim and palm trees. Palm
trees alternated with cherubim. Each cherub had two faces: 19the
face of a man toward the palm tree on one side and the face of a
lion toward the palm tree on the other. They were carved all
around the whole temple. 20From the floor to the area above the
entrance, cherubim and palm trees were carved on the wall of
the outer sanctuary.
21The outer sanctuary had a rectangular doorframe, and the
one at the front of the Most Holy Place was similar. 22There was
a wooden altar three cubits high and two cubits square[a]; its corners, its base[b] and its sides were of wood. The man said to me,
"This is the table that is before the LORD." 23Both the outer sanctuary and the Most Holy Place had double doors. 24Each door
had two leaves—two hinged leaves for each door. 25And on the
doors of the outer sanctuary were carved cherubim and palm
trees like those carved on the walls, and there was a wooden
overhang on the front of the portico. 26On the sidewalls of the
portico were narrow windows with palm trees carved on each
side. The side rooms of the temple also had overhangs.

Rooms for the Priests

42 Then the man led me northward into the outer court and
brought me to the rooms opposite the temple courtyard
and opposite the outer wall on the north side. 2The building
whose door faced north was a hundred cubits[c] long and fifty cubits wide. 3Both in the section twenty cubits from the inner court
and in the section opposite the pavement of the outer court,
gallery faced gallery at the three levels. 4In front of the rooms was
an inner passageway ten cubits wide and a hundred cubits[d] long.
Their doors were on the north. 5Now the upper rooms were nar-
rower, for the galleries took more space from them than from the
rooms on the lower and middle floors of the building. 6The
rooms on the third floor had no pillars, as the courts had; so they

(41:18–22) Lord Jesus, we read of the temple Ezekiel envisioned, of the places of sacrifice, of the carvings of cherubim and palm trees. And as we come to the Most Holy Place and to "the table that is before the LORD," we remember You. When You died for us, the veil to the Most Holy Place was torn apart and the table "before the LORD" was set for everyone. Even now, holy bread and wine await us there, prepared for all who wish to partake of Your body and blood. We praise You, Jesus, for being the bread of life and for shedding Your blood so that we can freely come into the presence of God. (Mt 27:51; Jn 6:35; 1Co 11:23–26)

[a] *22* Septuagint; Hebrew *long* [b] *22* Septuagint; Hebrew *length* [c] *2* The common cubit was about 1 1/2 feet (about 0.5 meter). [d] *4* Septuagint and Syriac; Hebrew *and one cubit*

(43:1–5) Your glory, Sovereign Lord, is beyond our imagination. We long for the day when we will hear the sound of rushing waters that is Your voice; we long to see the radiance of Your Presence. Our greatest longing, though, is that Your glory be seen in us. You have come to live in our hearts, in the bodily temple of Your Holy Spirit. We pray that our voices will speak Your words and that our eyes will be alight with Your love. Shine on us and through us, Lord. Glorify Yourself in us. (1Co 6:19)

Oh, the glory of Your presence,
We, Your temple, give You
rev'rence.
Come and rise to Your rest
And be blest by our praise
As we glory in Your embrace;
As Your presence now fills this place
"Oh, The Glory of Your Presence"
Steve Fry (©1983)

were smaller in floor space than those on the lower and middle
floors. 7There was an outer wall parallel to the rooms and the
outer court; it extended in front of the rooms for fifty cubits.
8While the row of rooms on the side next to the outer court was
fifty cubits long, the row on the side nearest the sanctuary was a
hundred cubits long. 9The lower rooms had an entrance on the
east side as one enters them from the outer court.
10On the south side[a] along the length of the wall of the outer
court, adjoining the temple courtyard and opposite the outer
wall, were rooms 11with a passageway in front of them. These
were like the rooms on the north; they had the same length and
width, with similar exits and dimensions. Similar to the doorways
on the north 12were the doorways of the rooms on the south.
There was a doorway at the beginning of the passageway that was
parallel to the corresponding wall extending eastward, by which
one enters the rooms.
13Then he said to me, "The north and south rooms facing the
temple courtyard are the priests' rooms, where the priests who
approach the LORD will eat the most holy offerings. There they will
put the most holy offerings—the grain offerings, the sin offerings
and the guilt offerings—for the place is holy. 14Once the priests
enter the holy precincts, they are not to go into the outer court
until they leave behind the garments in which they minister, for
these are holy. They are to put on other clothes before they go
near the places that are for the people."
15When he had finished measuring what was inside the temple
area, he led me out by the east gate and measured the area all
around: 16He measured the east side with the measuring rod; it
was five hundred cubits.[b] 17He measured the north side; it was
five hundred cubits[c] by the measuring rod. 18He measured the
south side; it was five hundred cubits by the measuring rod.
19Then he turned to the west side and measured; it was five hundred cubits by the measuring rod. 20So he measured the area on
all four sides. It had a wall around it, five hundred cubits long
and five hundred cubits wide, to separate the holy from the common.

The Glory Returns to the Temple

43 Then the man brought me to the gate facing east, 2and I
saw the glory of the God of Israel coming from the east.
His voice was like the roar of rushing waters, and the land was radiant with his glory. 3The vision I saw was like the vision I had
seen when he[d] came to destroy the city and like the visions I had
seen by the Kebar River, and I fell facedown. 4The glory of the
LORD entered the temple through the gate facing east. 5Then the
Spirit lifted me up and brought me into the inner court, and
the glory of the LORD filled the temple.
6While the man was standing beside me, I heard someone
speaking to me from inside the temple. 7He said: "Son of man,
this is the place of my throne and the place for the soles of my feet.
This is where I will live among the Israelites forever. The house of
Israel will never again defile my holy name—neither they nor
their kings—by their prostitution[e] and the lifeless idols[f] of their

[a] *10* Septuagint; Hebrew *Eastward* [b] *16* See Septuagint of verse 17; Hebrew *rods*; also in verses 18 and 19. [c] *17* Septuagint; Hebrew *rods* [d] *3* Some Hebrew manuscripts and Vulgate; most Hebrew manuscripts *I* [e] *7* Or *their spiritual adultery*; also in verse 9 [f] *7* Or *the corpses*; also in verse 9

kings at their high places. 8When they placed their threshold next
to my threshold and their doorposts beside my doorposts, with
only a wall between me and them, they defiled my holy name by
their detestable practices. So I destroyed them in my anger. 9Now
let them put away from me their prostitution and the lifeless idols
of their kings, and I will live among them forever.

10"Son of man, describe the temple to the people of Israel, that
they may be ashamed of their sins. Let them consider the plan,
11and if they are ashamed of all they have done, make known to
them the design of the temple—its arrangement, its exits and entrances—its whole design and all its regulations[a] and laws. Write
these down before them so that they may be faithful to its design
and follow all its regulations.

12"This is the law of the temple: All the surrounding area on top
of the mountain will be most holy. Such is the law of the temple.

The Altar

13"These are the measurements of the altar in long cubits, that
cubit being a cubit[b] and a handbreadth[c]: Its gutter is a cubit deep
and a cubit wide, with a rim of one span[d] around the edge. And
this is the height of the altar: 14From the gutter on the ground up
to the lower ledge it is two cubits high and a cubit wide, and from
the smaller ledge up to the larger ledge it is four cubits high and
a cubit wide. 15The altar hearth is four cubits high, and four
horns project upward from the hearth. 16The altar hearth is
square, twelve cubits long and twelve cubits wide. 17The upper
ledge also is square, fourteen cubits long and fourteen cubits
wide, with a rim of half a cubit and a gutter of a cubit all around.
The steps of the altar face east."

18Then he said to me, "Son of man, this is what the Sovereign
LORD says: These will be the regulations for sacrificing burnt offerings and sprinkling blood upon the altar when it is built: 19You
are to give a young bull as a sin offering to the priests, who are
Levites, of the family of Zadok, who come near to minister before
me, declares the Sovereign LORD. 20You are to take some of its
blood and put it on the four horns of the altar and on the four
corners of the upper ledge and all around the rim, and so purify
the altar and make atonement for it. 21You are to take the bull for
the sin offering and burn it in the designated part of the temple
area outside the sanctuary.

22"On the second day you are to offer a male goat without defect
for a sin offering, and the altar is to be purified as it was purified
with the bull. 23When you have finished purifying it, you are to offer
a young bull and a ram from the flock, both without defect. 24You
are to offer them before the LORD, and the priests are to sprinkle
salt on them and sacrifice them as a burnt offering to the LORD.

25"For seven days you are to provide a male goat daily for a sin
offering; you are also to provide a young bull and a ram from the
flock, both without defect. 26For seven days they are to make
atonement for the altar and cleanse it; thus they will dedicate it.
27At the end of these days, from the eighth day on, the priests are
to present your burnt offerings and fellowship offerings[e] on the
altar. Then I will accept you, declares the Sovereign LORD."

[a] *11* Some Hebrew manuscripts and Septuagint; most Hebrew manuscripts *regulations and its whole design* [b] *13* The common cubit was about 1 1/2 feet (about 0.5 meter). [c] *13* That is, about 3 inches (about 8 centimeters) [d] *13* That is, about 9 inches (about 22 centimeters) [e] *27* Traditionally *peace offerings*

(43:13–27) When I consider the number of sacrifices that were made in Your ancient temple, Father, it seems like an exhausting, endless cycle of bloodshed, day after day, year after year. And so it had to be. My daily sins alone could never be fully accounted for—even I cannot keep track of them all—much less the sins of an entire nation. How grateful I am for Jesus' terrible, agonizing death for the sins of all people. He became the complete sacrifice, made once and for all; and because of Him, I and all who put their trust in Him have been made perfect in Your sight.

My Lord, what love is this that
pays so dearly;
That I, the guilty one, may go free?

Amazing love, O what sacrifice,
The Son of God giv'n for me;
My debt He pays and my death He
dies,
That I might live, that I might live.

And so they watched Him die,
despised, rejected;
But, O the blood He shed flowed for
me.

And now this love of Christ shall
flow like rivers;
Come wash your guilt away, live
again.

"Amazing Love"
Graham Kendrick (©1989)

(44:1–19) Jesus, Your Word makes it clear that the office of priest is a great honor, which also carries great responsibilities. Just as You are our high priest, so we are called to serve as priests on Your behalf. You have made us worthy to do so, and we pray that we will be earnest in our role and reverent in our service. Dress us in robes of righteousness, Lord, so Your work will be done with dignity. Fill us with compassion, so Your work will be done in love. (Heb 4:14; Rev 1:6)

The Prince, the Levites, the Priests

44 Then the man brought me back to the outer gate of the
sanctuary, the one facing east, and it was shut. 2 The LORD
said to me, "This gate is to remain shut. It must not be opened; no
one may enter through it. It is to remain shut because the LORD,
the God of Israel, has entered through it. 3 The prince himself is
the only one who may sit inside the gateway to eat in the presence
of the LORD. He is to enter by way of the portico of the gateway and
go out the same way."

4 Then the man brought me by way of the north gate to the front
of the temple. I looked and saw the glory of the LORD filling the
temple of the LORD, and I fell facedown.

5 The LORD said to me, "Son of man, look carefully, listen closely and give attention to everything I tell you concerning all the
regulations regarding the temple of the LORD. Give attention to the
entrance of the temple and all the exits of the sanctuary. 6 Say to
the rebellious house of Israel, 'This is what the Sovereign LORD
says: Enough of your detestable practices, O house of Israel! 7 In
addition to all your other detestable practices, you brought foreigners uncircumcised in heart and flesh into my sanctuary, desecrating my temple while you offered me food, fat and blood, and
you broke my covenant. 8 Instead of carrying out your duty in regard to my holy things, you put others in charge of my sanctuary.
9 This is what the Sovereign LORD says: No foreigner uncircumcised in heart and flesh is to enter my sanctuary, not even the foreigners who live among the Israelites.

10 " 'The Levites who went far from me when Israel went astray
and who wandered from me after their idols must bear the consequences of their sin. 11 They may serve in my sanctuary, having
charge of the gates of the temple and serving in it; they may
slaughter the burnt offerings and sacrifices for the people and
stand before the people and serve them. 12 But because they
served them in the presence of their idols and made the house of
Israel fall into sin, therefore I have sworn with uplifted hand that
they must bear the consequences of their sin, declares the Sovereign LORD. 13 They are not to come near to serve me as priests or
come near any of my holy things or my most holy offerings; they
must bear the shame of their detestable practices. 14 Yet I will put
them in charge of the duties of the temple and all the work that is
to be done in it.

15 " 'But the priests, who are Levites and descendants of Zadok
and who faithfully carried out the duties of my sanctuary when the
Israelites went astray from me, are to come near to minister before me; they are to stand before me to offer sacrifices of fat and
blood, declares the Sovereign LORD. 16 They alone are to enter my
sanctuary; they alone are to come near my table to minister before me and perform my service.

17 " 'When they enter the gates of the inner court, they are to
wear linen clothes; they must not wear any woolen garment while
ministering at the gates of the inner court or inside the temple.
18 They are to wear linen turbans on their heads and linen undergarments around their waists. They must not wear anything that
makes them perspire. 19 When they go out into the outer court
where the people are, they are to take off the clothes they have
been ministering in and are to leave them in the sacred rooms,
and put on other clothes, so that they do not consecrate the people by means of their garments.

20“ ‘They must not shave their heads or let their hair grow
long, but they are to keep the hair of their heads trimmed. 21No
priest is to drink wine when he enters the inner court. 22They
must not marry widows or divorced women; they may marry only
virgins of Israelite descent or widows of priests. 23They are to
teach my people the difference between the holy and the common and show them how to distinguish between the unclean and
the clean.

24“ ‘In any dispute, the priests are to serve as judges and decide it according to my ordinances. They are to keep my laws and
my decrees for all my appointed feasts, and they are to keep my
Sabbaths holy.

25“ ‘A priest must not defile himself by going near a dead person; however, if the dead person was his father or mother, son or
daughter, brother or unmarried sister, then he may defile himself.
26After he is cleansed, he must wait seven days. 27On the day he
goes into the inner court of the sanctuary to minister in the sanctuary, he is to offer a sin offering for himself, declares the Sovereign LORD.

28“ ‘I am to be the only inheritance the priests have. You are to
give them no possession in Israel; I will be their possession.
29They will eat the grain offerings, the sin offerings and the guilt
offerings; and everything in Israel devoted[a] to the LORD will belong to them. 30The best of all the firstfruits and of all your special gifts will belong to the priests. You are to give them the first
portion of your ground meal so that a blessing may rest on your
household. 31The priests must not eat anything, bird or animal,
found dead or torn by wild animals.

Division of the Land

45 “ ‘When you allot the land as an inheritance, you are to
present to the LORD a portion of the land as a sacred district, 25,000 cubits long and 20,000[b] cubits wide; the entire area
will be holy. 2Of this, a section 500 cubits square is to be for the
sanctuary, with 50 cubits around it for open land. 3In the sacred
district, measure off a section 25,000 cubits[c] long and 10,000
cubits[d] wide. In it will be the sanctuary, the Most Holy Place. 4It
will be the sacred portion of the land for the priests, who minister in the sanctuary and who draw near to minister before the
LORD. It will be a place for their houses as well as a holy place for
the sanctuary. 5An area 25,000 cubits long and 10,000 cubits
wide will belong to the Levites, who serve in the temple, as their
possession for towns to live in.[e]

6“ ‘You are to give the city as its property an area 5,000 cubits
wide and 25,000 cubits long, adjoining the sacred portion; it will
belong to the whole house of Israel.

7“ ‘The prince will have the land bordering each side of the
area formed by the sacred district and the property of the city. It
will extend westward from the west side and eastward from the
east side, running lengthwise from the western to the eastern
border parallel to one of the tribal portions. 8This land will be his
possession in Israel. And my princes will no longer oppress my

[a] *29* The Hebrew term refers to the irrevocable giving over of things or persons to the LORD.
[b] *1* Septuagint (see also verses 3 and 5 and 48:9); Hebrew *10,000* [c] *3* That is, about 7 miles (about 12 kilometers) [d] *3* That is, about 3 miles (about 5 kilometers)
[e] *5* Septuagint; Hebrew *temple; they will have as their possession 20 rooms*

(45:1–12) Sovereign Lord, Your character emanates from us only when You are at the center of our lives. Just as You once allotted a sacred place for Your temple in the midst of Your people, so now You have made our hearts the center of Your dwelling. We pray that You will use us—our presence in the world—to bring relief from the oppression and violence that surround us. Fill us with Your Spirit, Lord, so that we can impart peace, justice and mercy to all with whom we come in contact.

people but will allow the house of Israel to possess the land according to their tribes.
9“ ‘This is what the Sovereign LORD says: You have gone far
enough, O princes of Israel! Give up your violence and oppression and do what is just and right. Stop dispossessing my people,
declares the Sovereign LORD. 10You are to use accurate scales, an
accurate ephah[a] and an accurate bath.[b] 11The ephah and the
bath are to be the same size, the bath containing a tenth of a
homer[c] and the ephah a tenth of a homer; the homer is to be the
standard measure for both. 12The shekel[d] is to consist of twenty
gerahs. Twenty shekels plus twenty-five shekels plus fifteen
shekels equal one mina.[e]

Offerings and Holy Days

13“ ‘This is the special gift you are to offer: a sixth of an ephah
from each homer of wheat and a sixth of an ephah from each
homer of barley. 14The prescribed portion of oil, measured by
the bath, is a tenth of a bath from each cor (which consists of ten
baths or one homer, for ten baths are equivalent to a homer).
15Also one sheep is to be taken from every flock of two hundred
from the well-watered pastures of Israel. These will be used for
the grain offerings, burnt offerings and fellowship offerings[f] to
make atonement for the people, declares the Sovereign LORD.
16All the people of the land will participate in this special gift for
the use of the prince in Israel. 17It will be the duty of the prince
to provide the burnt offerings, grain offerings and drink offerings
at the festivals, the New Moons and the Sabbaths—at all the appointed feasts of the house of Israel. He will provide the sin offerings, grain offerings, burnt offerings and fellowship offerings
to make atonement for the house of Israel.
18“ ‘This is what the Sovereign LORD says: In the first month on
the first day you are to take a young bull without defect and purify the sanctuary. 19The priest is to take some of the blood of the
sin offering and put it on the doorposts of the temple, on the four
corners of the upper ledge of the altar and on the gateposts of the
inner court. 20You are to do the same on the seventh day of the
month for anyone who sins unintentionally or through ignorance;
so you are to make atonement for the temple.
21“ ‘In the first month on the fourteenth day you are to observe the Passover, a feast lasting seven days, during which you
shall eat bread made without yeast. 22On that day the prince is to
provide a bull as a sin offering for himself and for all the people
of the land. 23Every day during the seven days of the Feast he is
to provide seven bulls and seven rams without defect as a burnt
offering to the LORD, and a male goat for a sin offering. 24He is to
provide as a grain offering an ephah for each bull and an ephah
for each ram, along with a hin[g] of oil for each ephah.
25“ ‘During the seven days of the Feast, which begins in the
seventh month on the fifteenth day, he is to make the same provision for sin offerings, burnt offerings, grain offerings and oil.
46 “ ‘This is what the Sovereign LORD says: The gate of the
inner court facing east is to be shut on the six working
days, but on the Sabbath day and on the day of the New Moon it

(45:13–25) In the days of Ezekiel You established feasts to remind the people of Your work among them and to ordain special sacrifices for sins that might otherwise have been overlooked. We, too, have holy days of commemoration. But rather than remembering You in all the festivities, we are inclined to forget both You and the meaning of the occasion. And to make matters worse, some of us sin more than ever during those most sacred holidays! Forgive us, Lord, for our foolishness, and teach us to remember Your birth, death and resurrection with reverence, awe and holy gratitude.

[a] *10* An ephah was a dry measure. [b] *10* A bath was a liquid measure. [c] *11* A homer was a dry measure. [d] *12* A shekel weighed about 2/5 ounce (about 11.5 grams). [e] *12* That is, 60 shekels; the common mina was 50 shekels. [f] *15* Traditionally *peace offerings*; also in verse 17 [g] *24* That is, probably about 4 quarts (about 4 liters)

is to be opened. [2]The prince is to enter from the outside through
the portico of the gateway and stand by the gatepost. The priests
are to sacrifice his burnt offering and his fellowship offerings.[a]
He is to worship at the threshold of the gateway and then go out,
but the gate will not be shut until evening. [3]On the Sabbaths and
New Moons the people of the land are to worship in the presence
of the LORD at the entrance to that gateway. [4]The burnt offering the
prince brings to the LORD on the Sabbath day is to be six male
lambs and a ram, all without defect. [5]The grain offering given
with the ram is to be an ephah,[b] and the grain offering with the
lambs is to be as much as he pleases, along with a hin[c] of oil for
each ephah. [6]On the day of the New Moon he is to offer a young
bull, six lambs and a ram, all without defect. [7]He is to provide as
a grain offering one ephah with the bull, one ephah with the ram,
and with the lambs as much as he wants to give, along with a hin
of oil with each ephah. [8]When the prince enters, he is to go in
through the portico of the gateway, and he is to come out the
same way.

[9]" 'When the people of the land come before the LORD at the
appointed feasts, whoever enters by the north gate to worship is
to go out the south gate; and whoever enters by the south gate is
to go out the north gate. No one is to return through the gate by
which he entered, but each is to go out the opposite gate. [10]The
prince is to be among them, going in when they go in and going
out when they go out.

[11]" 'At the festivals and the appointed feasts, the grain offering
is to be an ephah with a bull, an ephah with a ram, and with the
lambs as much as one pleases, along with a hin of oil for each
ephah. [12]When the prince provides a freewill offering to the
LORD—whether a burnt offering or fellowship offerings—the gate
facing east is to be opened for him. He shall offer his burnt offering or his fellowship offerings as he does on the Sabbath day.
Then he shall go out, and after he has gone out, the gate will be
shut.

[13]" 'Every day you are to provide a year-old lamb without defect for a burnt offering to the LORD; morning by morning you
shall provide it. [14]You are also to provide with it morning by
morning a grain offering, consisting of a sixth of an ephah with a
third of a hin of oil to moisten the flour. The presenting of this
grain offering to the LORD is a lasting ordinance. [15]So the lamb
and the grain offering and the oil shall be provided morning by
morning for a regular burnt offering.

[16]" 'This is what the Sovereign LORD says: If the prince makes
a gift from his inheritance to one of his sons, it will also belong to
his descendants; it is to be their property by inheritance. [17]If,
however, he makes a gift from his inheritance to one of his servants, the servant may keep it until the year of freedom; then it
will revert to the prince. His inheritance belongs to his sons only;
it is theirs. [18]The prince must not take any of the inheritance of
the people, driving them off their property. He is to give his sons
their inheritance out of his own property, so that none of my people will be separated from his property.' "

[19]Then the man brought me through the entrance at the side of
the gate to the sacred rooms facing north, which belonged to the
priests, and showed me a place at the western end. [20]He said to

[a]2 Traditionally *peace offerings*; also in verse 12 [b]5 That is, probably about 3/5 bushel (about 22 liters) [c]5 That is, probably about 4 quarts (about 4 liters)

(46:1–16) Holy, holy, holy God, You appointed times, seasons, offerings and orders for the acceptable worship of Your people. Help us today, in the joy and freedom of our worship in Christ, to come before You with reverence and deep respect. Help us to remember that it is because of Your choice and by Your grace that we can come at all. And though the methods may be different, the timing is still the same—every day, morning by morning, You call us to present ourselves to You as living sacrifices, for this is our spiritual act of worship. (Ro 12:1)

The greatest privilege God gives to you is the freedom to approach Him at any time. You are not only authorized to speak to Him; you are invited. You are not only permitted; you are expected. God waits for you to communicate with Him. You have instant, direct access to God. God loves mankind so much, and in a very special sense His children, that He has made Himself available to you at all times.

Wesley L. Duewel (1916-)

It is good to praise the Lord.
It is good to gaze upon His majesty;
To proclaim His love in the morning,
And His faithfulness at night.
Oh, it is good to worship
And praise the Lord.

"It Is Good To Praise The Lord"
Lenny LeBlanc (©1989)

(47:1–12) Jesus, the river of living water that flows from Your heart courses through each of us in purifying streams. It removes the pollution from our lives. It flows into others with spiritual sustenance. It makes the soil of our hearts fertile and causes us to bear fruit that fills the hungry and heals the hurting. If anyone is thirsty, let him come to You and drink. And whoever believes in You, as the Scripture has said, streams of living water will flow from within him, too. (Jn 7:37–38)

We stand in awe of Your presence
And we seek Your holiness.
For Your love, it is eternal;
The living waters flow from You.

Father in heaven,
We've come to worship You.
Holy Spirit,
Teaching us to walk in You.
Jesus, sweet Savior
We want to glorify You,
Glorify You.

"Glorify You"
Lenny LeBlanc (©1989)

me, "This is the place where the priests will cook the guilt offering and the sin offering and bake the grain offering, to avoid
bringing them into the outer court and consecrating the people."
21He then brought me to the outer court and led me around to
its four corners, and I saw in each corner another court. 22In the
four corners of the outer court were enclosed[a] courts, forty cubits long and thirty cubits wide; each of the courts in the four corners was the same size. 23Around the inside of each of the four
courts was a ledge of stone, with places for fire built all around
under the ledge. 24He said to me, "These are the kitchens where
those who minister at the temple will cook the sacrifices of the
people."

The River From the Temple

47 The man brought me back to the entrance of the temple,
and I saw water coming out from under the threshold of
the temple toward the east (for the temple faced east). The water
was coming down from under the south side of the temple, south
of the altar. 2He then brought me out through the north gate and
led me around the outside to the outer gate facing east, and the
water was flowing from the south side.
3As the man went eastward with a measuring line in his hand,
he measured off a thousand cubits[b] and then led me through
water that was ankle-deep. 4He measured off another thousand
cubits and led me through water that was knee-deep. He measured off another thousand and led me through water that was up
to the waist. 5He measured off another thousand, but now it was
a river that I could not cross, because the water had risen and
was deep enough to swim in—a river that no one could cross.
6He asked me, "Son of man, do you see this?"
Then he led me back to the bank of the river. 7When I arrived
there, I saw a great number of trees on each side of the river. 8He
said to me, "This water flows toward the eastern region and goes
down into the Arabah,[c] where it enters the Sea.[d] When it empties
into the Sea,[d] the water there becomes fresh. 9Swarms of living
creatures will live wherever the river flows. There will be large
numbers of fish, because this water flows there and makes the
salt water fresh; so where the river flows everything will live.
10Fishermen will stand along the shore; from En Gedi to En Eglaim there will be places for spreading nets. The fish will be of
many kinds—like the fish of the Great Sea.[e] 11But the swamps
and marshes will not become fresh; they will be left for salt.
12Fruit trees of all kinds will grow on both banks of the river.
Their leaves will not wither, nor will their fruit fail. Every month
they will bear, because the water from the sanctuary flows to
them. Their fruit will serve for food and their leaves for healing."

The Boundaries of the Land

13This is what the Sovereign LORD says: "These are the boundaries by which you are to divide the land for an inheritance
among the twelve tribes of Israel, with two portions for Joseph.
14You are to divide it equally among them. Because I swore with
uplifted hand to give it to your forefathers, this land will become
your inheritance.

[a] *22* The meaning of the Hebrew for this word is uncertain. [b] *3* That is, about 1,500 feet (about 450 meters) [c] *8* Or *the Jordan Valley* [d] *8* That is, the Dead Sea [e] *10* That is, the Mediterranean; also in verses 15, 19 and 20

15"This is to be the boundary of the land:

"On the north side it will run from the Great Sea by the Heth-
lon road past Lebo[a] Hamath to Zedad, 16Berothah[b] and
Sibraim (which lies on the border between Damascus and
Hamath), as far as Hazer Hatticon, which is on the border
of Hauran. 17The boundary will extend from the sea to
Hazar Enan,[c] along the northern border of Damascus, with
the border of Hamath to the north. This will be the north
boundary.

18"On the east side the boundary will run between Hauran and
Damascus, along the Jordan between Gilead and the land of
Israel, to the eastern sea and as far as Tamar.[d] This will be
the east boundary.

19"On the south side it will run from Tamar as far as the waters
of Meribah Kadesh, then along the Wadi ⌊of Egypt⌋ to the
Great Sea. This will be the south boundary.

20"On the west side, the Great Sea will be the boundary to a point
opposite Lebo[e] Hamath. This will be the west boundary.

21"You are to distribute this land among yourselves according
to the tribes of Israel. 22You are to allot it as an inheritance for
yourselves and for the aliens who have settled among you and
who have children. You are to consider them as native-born Israelites; along with you they are to be allotted an inheritance among
the tribes of Israel. 23In whatever tribe the alien settles, there you
are to give him his inheritance," declares the Sovereign LORD.

The Division of the Land

48 "These are the tribes, listed by name: At the northern
frontier, Dan will have one portion; it will follow the Heth-
lon road to Lebo[f] Hamath; Hazar Enan and the northern border
of Damascus next to Hamath will be part of its border from the
east side to the west side.
2"Asher will have one portion; it will border the territory of
Dan from east to west.
3"Naphtali will have one portion; it will border the territory of
Asher from east to west.
4"Manasseh will have one portion; it will border the territory
of Naphtali from east to west.
5"Ephraim will have one portion; it will border the territory of
Manasseh from east to west.
6"Reuben will have one portion; it will border the territory of
Ephraim from east to west.
7"Judah will have one portion; it will border the territory of
Reuben from east to west.
8"Bordering the territory of Judah from east to west will be the
portion you are to present as a special gift. It will be 25,000 cubits[g] wide, and its length from east to west will equal one of the
tribal portions; the sanctuary will be in the center of it.
9"The special portion you are to offer to the LORD will be
25,000 cubits long and 10,000 cubits[h] wide. 10This will be the
sacred portion for the priests. It will be 25,000 cubits long on
the north side, 10,000 cubits wide on the west side, 10,000 cubits

[a] *15* Or *past the entrance to* [b] *15,16* See Septuagint and Ezekiel 48:1; Hebrew *road to go into Zedad, 16Hamath, Berothah* [c] *17* Hebrew *Enon,* a variant of *Enan*
[d] *18* Septuagint and Syriac; Hebrew *Israel. You will measure to the eastern sea*
[e] *20* Or *opposite the entrance to* [f] *1* Or *to the entrance to* [g] *8* That is, about 7 miles (about 12 kilometers) [h] *9* That is, about 3 miles (about 5 kilometers)

(47:21–23) Throughout history, You have admonished Your people to show kindness and justice to "aliens," to those who do not belong to the household of faith. Teach us, Lord, to demonstrate Your love toward those who do not know You, to reach out in grace and mercy toward those who are not yet part of Your family. Keep us from removing ourselves from those who seem "alien" to us. Your grace to us confirms that You do not want anyone to perish, but everyone to come to repentance. (Lev 19:34; 2Pe 3:9)

O sweetest Love, your grace on us
bestow;
Set our hearts with sacred fire
aglow,
That with hearts united we love
each other,
Ev'ry stranger, sister, and brother.
Lord, have mercy!

Shine in our hearts, O Spirit,
precious light;
Teach us Jesus Christ to know
aright,
That we may abide in the Lord who
bought us,
Till to our true home he has brought
us.
Lord, have mercy!

"To God the Holy Spirit Let Us Pray"
Martin Luther (1483–1546)
Trans. Worship Supplement (©1969)

wide on the east side and 25,000 cubits long on the south side. In
the center of it will be the sanctuary of the LORD. 11This will be for
the consecrated priests, the Zadokites, who were faithful in serving me and did not go astray as the Levites did when the Israelites
went astray. 12It will be a special gift to them from the sacred portion of the land, a most holy portion, bordering the territory of
the Levites.
13"Alongside the territory of the priests, the Levites will have
an allotment 25,000 cubits long and 10,000 cubits wide. Its total
length will be 25,000 cubits and its width 10,000 cubits. 14They
must not sell or exchange any of it. This is the best of the land
and must not pass into other hands, because it is holy to the
LORD.
15"The remaining area, 5,000 cubits wide and 25,000 cubits
long, will be for the common use of the city, for houses and for
pastureland. The city will be in the center of it 16and will have
these measurements: the north side 4,500 cubits, the south side
4,500 cubits, the east side 4,500 cubits, and the west side 4,500
cubits. 17The pastureland for the city will be 250 cubits on the
north, 250 cubits on the south, 250 cubits on the east, and 250
cubits on the west. 18What remains of the area, bordering on the
sacred portion and running the length of it, will be 10,000 cubits
on the east side and 10,000 cubits on the west side. Its produce
will supply food for the workers of the city. 19The workers from
the city who farm it will come from all the tribes of Israel. 20The
entire portion will be a square, 25,000 cubits on each side. As a
special gift you will set aside the sacred portion, along with the
property of the city.
21"What remains on both sides of the area formed by the sacred portion and the city property will belong to the prince. It
will extend eastward from the 25,000 cubits of the sacred portion
to the eastern border, and westward from the 25,000 cubits to
the western border. Both these areas running the length of the
tribal portions will belong to the prince, and the sacred portion
with the temple sanctuary will be in the center of them. 22So the
property of the Levites and the property of the city will lie in the
center of the area that belongs to the prince. The area belonging
to the prince will lie between the border of Judah and the border
of Benjamin.
23"As for the rest of the tribes: Benjamin will have one portion; it will extend from the east side to the west side.
24"Simeon will have one portion; it will border the territory of
Benjamin from east to west.
25"Issachar will have one portion; it will border the territory of
Simeon from east to west.
26"Zebulun will have one portion; it will border the territory of
Issachar from east to west.
27"Gad will have one portion; it will border the territory of
Zebulun from east to west.
28"The southern boundary of Gad will run south from Tamar to
the waters of Meribah Kadesh, then along the Wadi ⌞of Egypt⌟ to
the Great Sea.[a]
29"This is the land you are to allot as an inheritance to the
tribes of Israel, and these will be their portions," declares the
Sovereign LORD.

[a] 28 That is, the Mediterranean

(48:1–29) Just as You allotted a portion of the land to each tribe, so You have provided each of us with a particular place in the world, according to our calling and area of service. "You have assigned me my portion and my cup," Father, and "You have made my lot secure." When I look around, I am grateful: "The boundary lines have fallen for me in pleasant places"; and I really do have a delightful inheritance. Thank You, Father. (Ps 16:5–6)

The Lord has promised good to me;
His word my hope secures.
He will my shield and portion be
As long as life endures.

"Amazing Grace"
John Newton (1725-1807)

The Gates of the City

30"These will be the exits of the city: Beginning on the north
side, which is 4,500 cubits long, 31the gates of the city will be
named after the tribes of Israel. The three gates on the north side
will be the gate of Reuben, the gate of Judah and the gate of Levi.
32"On the east side, which is 4,500 cubits long, will be three
gates: the gate of Joseph, the gate of Benjamin and the gate of
Dan.
33"On the south side, which measures 4,500 cubits, will be
three gates: the gate of Simeon, the gate of Issachar and the gate
of Zebulun.
34"On the west side, which is 4,500 cubits long, will be three
gates: the gate of Gad, the gate of Asher and the gate of Naphtali.
35"The distance all around will be 18,000 cubits.
"And the name of the city from that time on will be:

THE LORD IS THERE."

(48:30–35) Sovereign Lord, in Your wisdom You revealed to Ezekiel a great city on a high mountain, reflecting Your glory for all the world to see. Like mirrors of that splendid place, You have called each of us to shine like a city on a hill. We pray that our lives will radiate Your love and light wherever we go. And we ask that all who come to know us, all who spend time with us, all who look into our eyes will recognize Your Presence in us and will say: "The Lord is there." (Mt. 5:14)

Lord Jesus,
speak into my life today, I pray.
Speak creative thoughts.
Beget creative events.
Flow creative life.
Let words of your invention flow through me to heal people.
Let ideas or your origin course through me to serve others.
Let newness of life in you influence hope wherever I go,
that a world of people
who are by-and-large without it
might look up . . .
and see You.

Dick Eastman (1944-) and
Jack Hayford (1934-)

Daniel

The Book of the Prophet

DANIEL

Children love the book of Daniel for its dramatic stories of God's miraculous deliverance—of Daniel from the lions' den (ch. 6) and of Shadrach, Meshach and Abednego from the fiery furnace (ch. 3). Adults love Daniel for its intriguing visions of the future (chs. 2; 7–12). Yet by these thrilling adventures and fantastic dreams the book of Daniel calls us to worship God humbly, faithfully, hopefully and in a Christian manner.

Through Daniel God reveals His sovereignty over all earthly powers: "Praise be to the name of God for ever and ever; wisdom and power are his. He changes times and seasons; he sets up kings and deposes them" (2:20–21). Even the haughty King Nebuchadnezzar, marveling at God's power, confesses God's preeminence as "God of gods and the Lord of kings" and "the Most High God" (2:46; 3:26).Before such an awesome, unrivaled God, we too bow down in humble worship.

Yet, unlike Nebuchadnezzar, we who know God truly will worship faithfully, continually and without compromise. When Shadrach, Meshach and Abednego refuse to bow before the golden idol, they profess confidence in God's power to save them. But even if He does not, they boldly declare to the king, "We want you to know, O king, that we will not serve your gods or worship the image of gold you have set up" (3:18). Similarly, when Daniel's worship of God might lead to his becoming lion food, he continues to pray openly (ch. 6). The example of Daniel and his friends reminds us that God deserves regular, unhesitating worship—no matter what the cost.

The example of Daniel and his friends reminds us that God deserves regular, unhesitating worship—no matter what the cost.

The end-time visions of Daniel serve not only as grist for apocalyptic conjectures but also as inspiration for worship. They reveal God's sovereignty over all of time. God is indeed the "Ancient of Days" (7:9,13,22) who controls both past and future. Even before history has played out its divinely dealt hand, we worship God with hopefulness because we know that He has all things under control. For every minute we spend figuring out the timetable for the future, may we spend two praising the God Who holds the future!

In Daniel's vision of the Ancient of Days, "one like a son of man" comes before the divine throne. He receives an eternal kingdom, and "all peoples, nations and men of every language [worship] him" (7:13–14). This mysterious figure foreshadows Jesus, Who claims to be the "Son of Man" (Mt 12:32) Who will reign in the glorious kingdom of God. Even as the "one like a son of man" in Daniel receives worldwide worship, so we worship Jesus the Son alongside God the Father. Jesus enables us to approach God's throne with boldness and shares in divine worship as the second member of the Trinity. As Biblical Christians, we worship God as Father, Son and Holy Spirit.

Daniel's Training in Babylon

1 In the third year of the reign of Jehoiakim king of Judah, Nebuchadnezzar king of Babylon came to Jerusalem and besieged
it. 2And the Lord delivered Jehoiakim king of Judah into his hand,
along with some of the articles from the temple of God. These he
carried off to the temple of his god in Babylonia[a] and put in the
treasure house of his god.
3Then the king ordered Ashpenaz, chief of his court officials,
to bring in some of the Israelites from the royal family and the
nobility— 4young men without any physical defect, handsome,
showing aptitude for every kind of learning, well informed, quick
to understand, and qualified to serve in the king's palace. He was
to teach them the language and literature of the Babylonians.[b]
5The king assigned them a daily amount of food and wine from
the king's table. They were to be trained for three years, and after
that they were to enter the king's service.
6Among these were some from Judah: Daniel, Hananiah, Mishael and Azariah. 7The chief official gave them new names: to Daniel, the name Belteshazzar; to Hananiah, Shadrach; to Mishael,
Meshach; and to Azariah, Abednego.
8But Daniel resolved not to defile himself with the royal food
and wine, and he asked the chief official for permission not to defile himself this way. 9Now God had caused the official to show
favor and sympathy to Daniel, 10but the official told Daniel, "I am
afraid of my lord the king, who has assigned your[c] food and drink.
Why should he see you looking worse than the other young men
your age? The king would then have my head because of you."
11Daniel then said to the guard whom the chief official had appointed over Daniel, Hananiah, Mishael and Azariah, 12"Please
test your servants for ten days: Give us nothing but vegetables to
eat and water to drink. 13Then compare our appearance with that
of the young men who eat the royal food, and treat your servants
in accordance with what you see." 14So he agreed to this and tested them for ten days.
15At the end of the ten days they looked healthier and better
nourished than any of the young men who ate the royal food. 16So
the guard took away their choice food and the wine they were to
drink and gave them vegetables instead.
17To these four young men God gave knowledge and understanding of all kinds of literature and learning. And Daniel could
understand visions and dreams of all kinds.
18At the end of the time set by the king to bring them in, the
chief official presented them to Nebuchadnezzar. 19The king
talked with them, and he found none equal to Daniel, Hananiah,
Mishael and Azariah; so they entered the king's service. 20In every
matter of wisdom and understanding about which the king questioned them, he found them ten times better than all the magicians and enchanters in his whole kingdom.
21And Daniel remained there until the first year of King Cyrus.

Nebuchadnezzar's Dream

2 In the second year of his reign, Nebuchadnezzar had
dreams; his mind was troubled and he could not sleep. 2So
the king summoned the magicians, enchanters, sorcerers and

[a] 2 Hebrew *Shinar* [b] 4 Or *Chaldeans* [c] 10 The Hebrew for *your* and *you* in this verse is plural.

For each of us the time is surely coming when we shall have nothing but God. Health and wealth and friends and hiding places will all be swept away, and we shall have only God. To the man of pseudo faith that is a terrifying thought, but to real faith it is one of the most comforting thoughts the heart can entertain.

A.W. Tozer (1897-1963)

(1:8–16) Lord God, You are the sun in our darkness, a shield in our weakness. You bestow favor and honor on us not because we are worthy, but because we are Your children. When we walk in a right relationship with You, Your blessings are extravagant and amazing. Daniel was a slave in the court of a king, yet You gave him favor in the sight of his superiors. I believe You will do the same for us when our hearts are right before You. When we humble ourselves before You, You will lift us up. What an awesome God You are! (Ps 84:11; 1Pe 5:6)

(1:17–20) Thank You, Lord, that You are able to give us spiritual freedom even when the world constructs its "prisons" around us. When our hands are tied, when we seem to be trapped by life's small frustrations or enormous tragedies, Your wisdom protects us and infuses us with an inner strength that moves us beyond the confines of our circumstances. You lead us in the midst of a world that has veered off course. You empower us to live out Your plan among people who refuse to call You God. (Ps 111:10; Pr 2:6)

(2:11) Father God, apart from You, surely we can do nothing. But with You all things are possible! When all around us faithless people see only roadblocks, You make a way for the faithful. Nothing is too difficult for You! Your plan for us is carried along by Your gift of faith. Our faith in You puts the strength in our spirits. Lord, we do believe. Help us overcome our unbelief! (Mt 19:26; Mk 9:24)

Faith is the possibility which belongs to men in God, in God himself, and only in God, when all human possibilities have been exhausted.

Karl Barth (1886-1968)

(2:17–18) Lord, thank You for the wonderful companions You have given me on this journey of faith—my sisters and brothers in Christ who have prayed for me in times of difficulty and sorrow. Thank You that I have also been given the privilege of praying for others. Forgive me when I forget to pray. Remind me today, Father, right this minute, of someone I need to lift up to You. Show me how to pray, and bring about Your perfect answer to my prayer. (Php 1:4; 2Th 1:11–12; Jas 5:16)

astrologers[a] to tell him what he had dreamed. When they came
in and stood before the king, 3he said to them, "I have had a
dream that troubles me and I want to know what it means.[b]"
4Then the astrologers answered the king in Aramaic,[c] "O king,
live forever! Tell your servants the dream, and we will interpret it."
5The king replied to the astrologers, "This is what I have firmly decided: If you do not tell me what my dream was and interpret
it, I will have you cut into pieces and your houses turned into
piles of rubble. 6But if you tell me the dream and explain it, you
will receive from me gifts and rewards and great honor. So tell me
the dream and interpret it for me."
7Once more they replied, "Let the king tell his servants the
dream, and we will interpret it."
8Then the king answered, "I am certain that you are trying to
gain time, because you realize that this is what I have firmly decided: 9If you do not tell me the dream, there is just one penalty
for you. You have conspired to tell me misleading and wicked
things, hoping the situation will change. So then, tell me the
dream, and I will know that you can interpret it for me."
10The astrologers answered the king, "There is not a man on
earth who can do what the king asks! No king, however great and
mighty, has ever asked such a thing of any magician or enchanter
or astrologer. 11What the king asks is too difficult. No one can reveal it to the king except the gods, and they do not live among
men."
12This made the king so angry and furious that he ordered the
execution of all the wise men of Babylon. 13So the decree was issued to put the wise men to death, and men were sent to look for
Daniel and his friends to put them to death.
14When Arioch, the commander of the king's guard, had gone
out to put to death the wise men of Babylon, Daniel spoke to him
with wisdom and tact. 15He asked the king's officer, "Why did the
king issue such a harsh decree?" Arioch then explained the matter to Daniel. 16At this, Daniel went in to the king and asked for
time, so that he might interpret the dream for him.
17Then Daniel returned to his house and explained the matter
to his friends Hananiah, Mishael and Azariah. 18He urged them to
plead for mercy from the God of heaven concerning this mystery,
so that he and his friends might not be executed with the rest of
the wise men of Babylon. 19During the night the mystery was revealed to Daniel in a vision. Then Daniel praised the God of heaven 20and said:

"Praise be to the name of God for ever and ever;
wisdom and power are his.
21He changes times and seasons;
he sets up kings and deposes them.
He gives wisdom to the wise
and knowledge to the discerning.
22He reveals deep and hidden things;
he knows what lies in darkness,
and light dwells with him.

[a] 2 Or *Chaldeans*; also in verses 4, 5 and 10 [b] 3 Or *was* [c] 4 The text from here through chapter 7 is in Aramaic.

23 I thank and praise you, O God of my fathers:
You have given me wisdom and power,
you have made known to me what we asked of you,
you have made known to us the dream of the
king."

Daniel Interprets the Dream

24 Then Daniel went to Arioch, whom the king had appointed to
execute the wise men of Babylon, and said to him, "Do not execute the wise men of Babylon. Take me to the king, and I will interpret his dream for him."
25 Arioch took Daniel to the king at once and said, "I have
found a man among the exiles from Judah who can tell the king
what his dream means."
26 The king asked Daniel (also called Belteshazzar), "Are you
able to tell me what I saw in my dream and interpret it?"
27 Daniel replied, "No wise man, enchanter, magician or divin-
er can explain to the king the mystery he has asked about, 28 but
there is a God in heaven who reveals mysteries. He has shown
King Nebuchadnezzar what will happen in days to come. Your
dream and the visions that passed through your mind as you lay
on your bed are these:
29 "As you were lying there, O king, your mind turned to things
to come, and the revealer of mysteries showed you what is going
to happen. 30 As for me, this mystery has been revealed to me, not
because I have greater wisdom than other living men, but so that
you, O king, may know the interpretation and that you may understand what went through your mind.
31 "You looked, O king, and there before you stood a large statue—an enormous, dazzling statue, awesome in appearance.
32 The head of the statue was made of pure gold, its chest and
arms of silver, its belly and thighs of bronze, 33 its legs of iron, its
feet partly of iron and partly of baked clay. 34 While you were
watching, a rock was cut out, but not by human hands. It struck
the statue on its feet of iron and clay and smashed them. 35 Then
the iron, the clay, the bronze, the silver and the gold were broken
to pieces at the same time and became like chaff on a threshing
floor in the summer. The wind swept them away without leaving a
trace. But the rock that struck the statue became a huge mountain
and filled the whole earth.
36 "This was the dream, and now we will interpret it to the king.
37 You, O king, are the king of kings. The God of heaven has given
you dominion and power and might and glory; 38 in your hands he
has placed mankind and the beasts of the field and the birds of
the air. Wherever they live, he has made you ruler over them all.
You are that head of gold.
39 "After you, another kingdom will rise, inferior to yours.
Next, a third kingdom, one of bronze, will rule over the whole
earth. 40 Finally, there will be a fourth kingdom, strong as iron—
for iron breaks and smashes everything—and as iron breaks
things to pieces, so it will crush and break all the others. 41 Just
as you saw that the feet and toes were partly of baked clay and
partly of iron, so this will be a divided kingdom; yet it will have
some of the strength of iron in it, even as you saw iron mixed
with clay. 42 As the toes were partly iron and partly clay, so this
kingdom will be partly strong and partly brittle. 43 And just as
you saw the iron mixed with baked clay, so the people will be a

(2:23–30) Our God and King, You understand the mysteries of the universe. You know our inmost thoughts as well. You give wisdom to the wise and knowledge to the discerning. But who is truly wise or discerning but the one who fears You and humbly acknowledges that You are God? Indeed, "The LORD confides in those who fear him." Lord, teach me to fear You so that I might hear You. (Ps 25:14)

You we call the true fount of wisdom and
the noble origin of all things.
Be pleased to shed on the darkness of mind
in which I was born,
the twofold beam of your light and
warmth to dispel my ignorance and sin.
You make eloquent the tongues of children.
Then instruct my speech and touch my lips
with graciousness.
Make me keen to understand, quick to
learn, able to remember;
make me delicate to interpret and ready to
speak.

Saint Thomas Aquinas (1225-1274)

mixture and will not remain united, any more than iron mixes
with clay.
44"In the time of those kings, the God of heaven will set up a
kingdom that will never be destroyed, nor will it be left to another people. It will crush all those kingdoms and bring them to an
end, but it will itself endure forever. 45This is the meaning of the
vision of the rock cut out of a mountain, but not by human
hands—a rock that broke the iron, the bronze, the clay, the silver and the gold to pieces.
"The great God has shown the king what will take place in
the future. The dream is true and the interpretation is trustworthy."

(2:44–45) Lord Jesus, how difficult it is at times to live in this shaky and uncertain world. Thank You for setting Your unshakable kingdom in our hearts. Thank You, too, that someday we will see it with our eyes. Lord, how we long for that time when there will be no more death or mourning or pain, when You will wipe every tear from our eyes. How we yearn for that place where there will be no more night, the place where we will join the praise of saints and angels who bow before You and continually sing, "Holy, holy, holy is the Lord God Almighty!" O Lord, let Your kingdom come! (Lk 17:20–21; Jn 18:36; Heb 12:27–28; Rev 4:8; 21:4)

46Then King Nebuchadnezzar fell prostrate before Daniel and
paid him honor and ordered that an offering and incense be presented to him. 47The king said to Daniel, "Surely your God is the
God of gods and the Lord of kings and a revealer of mysteries, for
you were able to reveal this mystery."
48Then the king placed Daniel in a high position and lavished
many gifts on him. He made him ruler over the entire province of
Babylon and placed him in charge of all its wise men. 49More-
over, at Daniel's request the king appointed Shadrach, Meshach
and Abednego administrators over the province of Babylon, while
Daniel himself remained at the royal court.

(2:48–49) Sovereign Lord, we pray that You will plant Your people in places of influence in our government. Raise up men and women with godly vision and values, who understand the times from Your perspective, who are "blameless and pure, children of God without fault in a crooked and depraved generation, in which [they] shine like stars in the universe as [they] hold out the word of life." Help each of us to hear Your call to serve the kingdom of God by serving the community and country in which we live. (1Ch 12:32; Php 2:15–16)

The Image of Gold and the Fiery Furnace

3 King Nebuchadnezzar made an image of gold, ninety feet
high and nine feet[a] wide, and set it up on the plain of Dura
in the province of Babylon. 2He then summoned the satraps, prefects, governors, advisers, treasurers, judges, magistrates and all
the other provincial officials to come to the dedication of the
image he had set up. 3So the satraps, prefects, governors, advisers, treasurers, judges, magistrates and all the other provincial
officials assembled for the dedication of the image that King Nebuchadnezzar had set up, and they stood before it.
4Then the herald loudly proclaimed, "This is what you are
commanded to do, O peoples, nations and men of every language: 5As soon as you hear the sound of the horn, flute, zither,
lyre, harp, pipes and all kinds of music, you must fall down and
worship the image of gold that King Nebuchadnezzar has set up.
6Whoever does not fall down and worship will immediately be
thrown into a blazing furnace."
7Therefore, as soon as they heard the sound of the horn, flute,
zither, lyre, harp and all kinds of music, all the peoples, nations
and men of every language fell down and worshiped the image of
gold that King Nebuchadnezzar had set up.
8At this time some astrologers[b] came forward and denounced
the Jews. 9They said to King Nebuchadnezzar, "O king, live forever! 10You have issued a decree, O king, that everyone who hears
the sound of the horn, flute, zither, lyre, harp, pipes and all kinds
of music must fall down and worship the image of gold, 11and
that whoever does not fall down and worship will be thrown into
a blazing furnace. 12But there are some Jews whom you have set
over the affairs of the province of Babylon—Shadrach, Meshach
and Abednego—who pay no attention to you, O king. They nei-

[a] *1* Aramaic *sixty cubits high and six cubits wide* (about 27 meters high and 2.7 meters wide) [b] *8* Or *Chaldeans*

ther serve your gods nor worship the image of gold you have
set up."
13 Furious with rage, Nebuchadnezzar summoned Shadrach,
Meshach and Abednego. So these men were brought before the
king, 14 and Nebuchadnezzar said to them, "Is it true, Shadrach,
Meshach and Abednego, that you do not serve my gods or worship the image of gold I have set up? 15 Now when you hear the
sound of the horn, flute, zither, lyre, harp, pipes and all kinds of
music, if you are ready to fall down and worship the image I
made, very good. But if you do not worship it, you will be thrown
immediately into a blazing furnace. Then what god will be able to
rescue you from my hand?"
16 Shadrach, Meshach and Abednego replied to the king,
"O Nebuchadnezzar, we do not need to defend ourselves before
you in this matter. 17 If we are thrown into the blazing furnace, the
God we serve is able to save us from it, and he will rescue us from
your hand, O king. 18 But even if he does not, we want you to
know, O king, that we will not serve your gods or worship the
image of gold you have set up."
19 Then Nebuchadnezzar was furious with Shadrach, Meshach
and Abednego, and his attitude toward them changed. He ordered
the furnace heated seven times hotter than usual 20 and commanded some of the strongest soldiers in his army to tie up Shadrach, Meshach and Abednego and throw them into the blazing
furnace. 21 So these men, wearing their robes, trousers, turbans
and other clothes, were bound and thrown into the blazing furnace. 22 The king's command was so urgent and the furnace so
hot that the flames of the fire killed the soldiers who took up Shadrach, Meshach and Abednego, 23 and these three men, firmly
tied, fell into the blazing furnace.
24 Then King Nebuchadnezzar leaped to his feet in amazement
and asked his advisers, "Weren't there three men that we tied up
and threw into the fire?"
They replied, "Certainly, O king."
25 He said, "Look! I see four men walking around in the fire,
unbound and unharmed, and the fourth looks like a son of the
gods."
26 Nebuchadnezzar then approached the opening of the blazing
furnace and shouted, "Shadrach, Meshach and Abednego, servants of the Most High God, come out! Come here!"
So Shadrach, Meshach and Abednego came out of the fire,
27 and the satraps, prefects, governors and royal advisers crowded around them. They saw that the fire had not harmed their bodies, nor was a hair of their heads singed; their robes were not
scorched, and there was no smell of fire on them.
28 Then Nebuchadnezzar said, "Praise be to the God of Shadrach, Meshach and Abednego, who has sent his angel and rescued his servants! They trusted in him and defied the king's
command and were willing to give up their lives rather than
serve or worship any god except their own God. 29 Therefore I
decree that the people of any nation or language who say anything against the God of Shadrach, Meshach and Abednego be
cut into pieces and their houses be turned into piles of rubble,
for no other god can save in this way."
30 Then the king promoted Shadrach, Meshach and Abednego
in the province of Babylon.

(3:16–28) Saving God, You never abandon those who fear You. Through faith I am shielded by Your power, even though I may suffer grief in all kinds of trials. But these trials come so that my faith, which is "of greater worth than gold, which perishes even though refined by fire," may be proved genuine and may result in praise, glory and honor when Jesus Christ is revealed. Even though I have not seen You, I love You. I believe in You, and I invite You to work Your perfect will in my life. Bring me through my fiery trials, I pray, so that Jesus Christ may be revealed in me. (1Pe 1:5–9)

Fear not, Christian; Jesus is with thee. In all thy fiery trials, His presence is both thy comfort and safety. He will never leave one whom He has chosen for His own. "Fear not, for I am with thee," is His sure word of promise to His chosen ones in "the furnace of affliction."

Charles Haddon Spurgeon (1834-1892)

When through fiery trials
Thy pathway shall lie,
My grace, all sufficient,
Shall be thy supply:
The flame shall not hurt thee;
I only design
Thy dross to consume,
And thy gold to refine.

Fear not, I am with thee,
O be not dismayed,
For I am thy God,
And will still give thee aid;
I'll strengthen thee, help thee,
And cause thee to stand,
Upheld by My righteous,
omnipotent hand.

"How Firm a Foundation"
Rippon's Selection of Hymns (1787)

Nebuchadnezzar's Dream of a Tree

4 King Nebuchadnezzar,

To the peoples, nations and men of every language, who
live in all the world:

May you prosper greatly!

2 It is my pleasure to tell you about the miraculous signs
and wonders that the Most High God has performed for me.

3 How great are his signs,
how mighty his wonders!
His kingdom is an eternal kingdom;
his dominion endures from generation to
generation.

4 I, Nebuchadnezzar, was at home in my palace, contented
and prosperous. 5 I had a dream that made me afraid. As I
was lying in my bed, the images and visions that passed
through my mind terrified me. 6 So I commanded that all the
wise men of Babylon be brought before me to interpret the
dream for me. 7 When the magicians, enchanters, astrologers[a] and diviners came, I told them the dream, but
they could not interpret it for me. 8 Finally, Daniel came into
my presence and I told him the dream. (He is called Belteshazzar, after the name of my god, and the spirit of the holy
gods is in him.)

9 I said, "Belteshazzar, chief of the magicians, I know that
the spirit of the holy gods is in you, and no mystery is too difficult for you. Here is my dream; interpret it for me. 10 These
are the visions I saw while lying in my bed: I looked, and
there before me stood a tree in the middle of the land. Its
height was enormous. 11 The tree grew large and strong and
its top touched the sky; it was visible to the ends of the earth.
12 Its leaves were beautiful, its fruit abundant, and on it was
food for all. Under it the beasts of the field found shelter,
and the birds of the air lived in its branches; from it every
creature was fed.

13 "In the visions I saw while lying in my bed, I looked,
and there before me was a messenger,[b] a holy one, coming
down from heaven. 14 He called in a loud voice: 'Cut down
the tree and trim off its branches; strip off its leaves and
scatter its fruit. Let the animals flee from under it and the
birds from its branches. 15 But let the stump and its roots,
bound with iron and bronze, remain in the ground, in the
grass of the field.

" 'Let him be drenched with the dew of heaven, and let
him live with the animals among the plants of the earth. 16 Let
his mind be changed from that of a man and let him be given
the mind of an animal, till seven times[c] pass by for him.

17 " 'The decision is announced by messengers, the holy
ones declare the verdict, so that the living may know that the
Most High is sovereign over the kingdoms of men and gives
them to anyone he wishes and sets over them the lowliest of
men.'

[a] 7 Or *Chaldeans* [b] 13 Or *watchman*; also in verses 17 and 23 [c] 16 Or *years*; also in verses 23, 25 and 32

Before there was an earth at all, or sun, or stars in the splashed heavens, before matter came into being, for endless eternities before, as Genesis puts it in four initial words, "In the beginning God," he has seen kingdoms and civilizations and earths and solar systems rise and wane. He, and he alone, knows the secret of history, the meaning of the mystery called time. Shall he not know the hearts of men and women?

Bernard Iddings Bell (1886-1958)

(4:1–17) Almighty God, the kingdoms of this world are neither above, nor below, nor beyond Your control. You are the sovereign Ruler of the universe, the jealous Lover of humankind, the omnipotent Controller of the destinies of the nations. Kings and emperors, presidents and prime ministers—all are Your servants. Time is in Your hands; our days are at Your disposal. You alone are worthy of our worship. One day, all creation will declare Your praise. (Isa 2:17)

18"This is the dream that I, King Nebuchadnezzar, had.
Now, Belteshazzar, tell me what it means, for none of the
wise men in my kingdom can interpret it for me. But you
can, because the spirit of the holy gods is in you."

Daniel Interprets the Dream

19Then Daniel (also called Belteshazzar) was greatly perplexed for a time, and his thoughts terrified him. So the king
said, "Belteshazzar, do not let the dream or its meaning
alarm you."

Belteshazzar answered, "My lord, if only the dream applied to your enemies and its meaning to your adversaries!
20The tree you saw, which grew large and strong, with its
top touching the sky, visible to the whole earth, 21with beautiful leaves and abundant fruit, providing food for all, giving
shelter to the beasts of the field, and having nesting places in
its branches for the birds of the air— 22you, O king, are
that tree! You have become great and strong; your greatness
has grown until it reaches the sky, and your dominion extends to distant parts of the earth.

23"You, O king, saw a messenger, a holy one, coming
down from heaven and saying, 'Cut down the tree and destroy it, but leave the stump, bound with iron and bronze, in
the grass of the field, while its roots remain in the ground.
Let him be drenched with the dew of heaven; let him live like
the wild animals, until seven times pass by for him.'

24"This is the interpretation, O king, and this is the decree the Most High has issued against my lord the king:
25You will be driven away from people and will live with
the wild animals; you will eat grass like cattle and be
drenched with the dew of heaven. Seven times will pass by
for you until you acknowledge that the Most High is sovereign over the kingdoms of men and gives them to anyone
he wishes. 26The command to leave the stump of the tree
with its roots means that your kingdom will be restored to
you when you acknowledge that Heaven rules. 27There-
fore, O king, be pleased to accept my advice: Renounce
your sins by doing what is right, and your wickedness by
being kind to the oppressed. It may be that then your prosperity will continue."

The Dream Is Fulfilled

28All this happened to King Nebuchadnezzar. 29Twelve
months later, as the king was walking on the roof of the
royal palace of Babylon, 30he said, "Is not this the great
Babylon I have built as the royal residence, by my mighty
power and for the glory of my majesty?"

31The words were still on his lips when a voice came
from heaven, "This is what is decreed for you, King Nebuchadnezzar: Your royal authority has been taken from you.
32You will be driven away from people and will live with the
wild animals; you will eat grass like cattle. Seven times will
pass by for you until you acknowledge that the Most High is
sovereign over the kingdoms of men and gives them to anyone he wishes."

33Immediately what had been said about Nebuchadnezzar was fulfilled. He was driven away from people and ate

It is so impossible for the world to exist without God that if God should forget it, it would immediately cease to be.

Søren Aabye Kierkegaard (1813-1855)

(4:24–26) I praise You, Lord, that You are the God of all mankind. Your great mercy extends even to the ungodly. In Your hand is the life of every creature and the breath of all humanity. If You withdrew Your Spirit and breath, all of us would perish together and return to the dust. But You do not take away life; instead, You devise ways to draw banished persons back to You. (2Sa 14:14; Job 12:10; 34:14–15; Jer 32:27)

God moves in a mysterious way
His wonders to perform;
He plants His footsteps in the sea,
And rides upon the storm.

Blind unbelief is sure to err
And scan His work in vain:
God is His own interpreter,
And He will make it plain.

"God Moves in a Mysterious Way"
William Cowper (1774)

(4:34–37) Heaven is Your throne, O God, and the earth is Your footstool. You are not impressed with our prosperity or power. Rather, the one You esteem is the one who is humble and contrite in spirit. When I look to myself, I see only myself. But when I look to You, I see everything more clearly. True honor, splendor, prosperity and contentment come from You. They are gifts of Your grace; and Your grace is given only to the humble. "You save the humble, but your eyes are on the haughty to bring them low." So I choose to humble myself before You so that You may lift me up. (2Sa 22:28; Isa 66:1–2; Jas 4:10)

Praise, my soul, the King of heaven,
To His feet your tribute bring;
Ransomed, healed, restored, forgiven,
Evermore His praises sing.
Alleluia! Alleluia!
Praise the everlasting King!

"Praise, My Soul, the King of Heaven"
Henry F. Lyte (1834)

grass like cattle. His body was drenched with the dew of
heaven until his hair grew like the feathers of an eagle and
his nails like the claws of a bird.

34 At the end of that time, I, Nebuchadnezzar, raised my
eyes toward heaven, and my sanity was restored. Then I
praised the Most High; I honored and glorified him who
lives forever.

His dominion is an eternal dominion;
his kingdom endures from generation to
generation.
35 All the peoples of the earth
are regarded as nothing.
He does as he pleases
with the powers of heaven
and the peoples of the earth.
No one can hold back his hand
or say to him: "What have you done?"

36 At the same time that my sanity was restored, my honor
and splendor were returned to me for the glory of my kingdom. My advisers and nobles sought me out, and I was restored to my throne and became even greater than before.
37 Now I, Nebuchadnezzar, praise and exalt and glorify the
King of heaven, because everything he does is right and all
his ways are just. And those who walk in pride he is able to
humble.

The Writing on the Wall

5 King Belshazzar gave a great banquet for a thousand of his
nobles and drank wine with them. 2 While Belshazzar was
drinking his wine, he gave orders to bring in the gold and silver
goblets that Nebuchadnezzar his father[a] had taken from the temple in Jerusalem, so that the king and his nobles, his wives and
his concubines might drink from them. 3 So they brought in the
gold goblets that had been taken from the temple of God in Jerusalem, and the king and his nobles, his wives and his concubines
drank from them. 4 As they drank the wine, they praised the gods
of gold and silver, of bronze, iron, wood and stone.
5 Suddenly the fingers of a human hand appeared and wrote on
the plaster of the wall, near the lampstand in the royal palace.
The king watched the hand as it wrote. 6 His face turned pale and
he was so frightened that his knees knocked together and his legs
gave way.
7 The king called out for the enchanters, astrologers[b] and diviners to be brought and said to these wise men of Babylon,
"Whoever reads this writing and tells me what it means will be
clothed in purple and have a gold chain placed around his neck,
and he will be made the third highest ruler in the kingdom."
8 Then all the king's wise men came in, but they could not read
the writing or tell the king what it meant. 9 So King Belshazzar became even more terrified and his face grew more pale. His nobles
were baffled.
10 The queen,[c] hearing the voices of the king and his nobles,
came into the banquet hall. "O king, live forever!" she said.

[a] *2* Or *ancestor*; or *predecessor*; also in verses 11, 13 and 18 [b] *7* Or *Chaldeans*; also in verse 11 [c] *10* Or *queen mother*

"Don't be alarmed! Don't look so pale! 11There is a man in your
kingdom who has the spirit of the holy gods in him. In the time
of your father he was found to have insight and intelligence and
wisdom like that of the gods. King Nebuchadnezzar your father—your father the king, I say—appointed him chief of the
magicians, enchanters, astrologers and diviners. 12This man
Daniel, whom the king called Belteshazzar, was found to have a
keen mind and knowledge and understanding, and also the ability to interpret dreams, explain riddles and solve difficult problems. Call for Daniel, and he will tell you what the writing
means."

13So Daniel was brought before the king, and the king said to
him, "Are you Daniel, one of the exiles my father the king brought
from Judah? 14I have heard that the spirit of the gods is in you and
that you have insight, intelligence and outstanding wisdom. 15The
wise men and enchanters were brought before me to read this
writing and tell me what it means, but they could not explain it.
16Now I have heard that you are able to give interpretations and
to solve difficult problems. If you can read this writing and tell me
what it means, you will be clothed in purple and have a gold chain
placed around your neck, and you will be made the third highest
ruler in the kingdom."

17Then Daniel answered the king, "You may keep your gifts for
yourself and give your rewards to someone else. Nevertheless, I
will read the writing for the king and tell him what it means.

18"O king, the Most High God gave your father Nebuchadnezzar sovereignty and greatness and glory and splendor. 19Because
of the high position he gave him, all the peoples and nations and
men of every language dreaded and feared him. Those the king
wanted to put to death, he put to death; those he wanted to spare,
he spared; those he wanted to promote, he promoted; and those
he wanted to humble, he humbled. 20But when his heart became
arrogant and hardened with pride, he was deposed from his royal
throne and stripped of his glory. 21He was driven away from people and given the mind of an animal; he lived with the wild donkeys and ate grass like cattle; and his body was drenched with
the dew of heaven, until he acknowledged that the Most High God
is sovereign over the kingdoms of men and sets over them anyone
he wishes.

22"But you his son,[a] O Belshazzar, have not humbled yourself,
though you knew all this. 23Instead, you have set yourself up
against the Lord of heaven. You had the goblets from his temple
brought to you, and you and your nobles, your wives and your
concubines drank wine from them. You praised the gods of silver
and gold, of bronze, iron, wood and stone, which cannot see or
hear or understand. But you did not honor the God who holds in
his hand your life and all your ways. 24Therefore he sent the hand
that wrote the inscription.

25"This is the inscription that was written:

MENE, MENE, TEKEL, PARSIN[b]

26"This is what these words mean:

Mene[c]: God has numbered the days of your reign and
brought it to an end.

[a] 22 Or *descendant*; or *successor* [b] 25 Aramaic *UPARSIN* (that is, *AND PARSIN*)
[c] 26 *Mene* can mean *numbered* or *mina* (a unit of money).

(5:17) O Lord, build in me the kind of character that values integrity over comfort. Give me boldness to speak truth without regard for my own welfare and without fearing the power of others. May I be like Daniel—one who is upright and honorable in my dealings, one who cannot be bought with money or position. You are worthy of my trust, Lord. I pray that I can be worthy of Yours. (Da 6:4)

Jesus, make a man of me
With Your integrity,
A man of the Spirit,
A man of the Word.
A servant of the Lord,
An offering outpoured
A man of the Spirit,
A man of the Word.

A man of mercy, fire and light,
A man who loves the truth.
Who runs to win the crown of life
And lives to honor You.

"Man of the Spirit, Man of the Word"
Bill Batstone (©1993)

(6:10) O God, would I be able to stand if I were persecuted for my faith in You? Daniel knew that praying put him in terrible danger, and yet three times a day he was on his knees. Forgive me for the days when I rush off without spending any time with You. Help me to never be lacking in zeal, but to keep my spiritual fervor in service to you, Lord. Help me to be like Daniel: joyful in hope, patient in affliction, and faithful in prayer. (Ps 102:17; Ro 12:11–12; 1Ti 4:7)

Don't pray when you feel like it. Have an appointment with the Lord and keep it. A man is powerful on his knees.

Corrie ten Boom (1892-1983)

Give ear to my words, O Lord,
Consider my meditation.
Hearken unto the voice of my cry,
My King, and my God:
For unto Thee will I pray,
My voice shalt Thou hear in the
morning.
O Lord, in the morning
Will I direct my prayer
Unto Thee, and will look up.

"Psalm 5"
Bill Sprouse, Jr. (©1975)

27 *Tekel*[a]: You have been weighed on the scales and found wanting.
28 *Peres*[b]: Your kingdom is divided and given to the Medes and Persians."

29 Then at Belshazzar's command, Daniel was clothed in purple, a gold chain was placed around his neck, and he was proclaimed the third highest ruler in the kingdom.

30 That very night Belshazzar, king of the Babylonians,[c] was slain, 31 and Darius the Mede took over the kingdom, at the age of sixty-two.

Daniel in the Den of Lions

6 It pleased Darius to appoint 120 satraps to rule throughout the kingdom, 2 with three administrators over them, one of whom was Daniel. The satraps were made accountable to them so that the king might not suffer loss. 3 Now Daniel so distinguished himself among the administrators and the satraps by his exceptional qualities that the king planned to set him over the whole kingdom. 4 At this, the administrators and the satraps tried to find grounds for charges against Daniel in his conduct of government affairs, but they were unable to do so. They could find no corruption in him, because he was trustworthy and neither corrupt nor negligent. 5 Finally these men said, "We will never find any basis for charges against this man Daniel unless it has something to do with the law of his God."

6 So the administrators and the satraps went as a group to the king and said: "O King Darius, live forever! 7 The royal administrators, prefects, satraps, advisers and governors have all agreed that the king should issue an edict and enforce the decree that anyone who prays to any god or man during the next thirty days, except to you, O king, shall be thrown into the lions' den. 8 Now, O king, issue the decree and put it in writing so that it cannot be altered—in accordance with the laws of the Medes and Persians, which cannot be repealed." 9 So King Darius put the decree in writing.

10 Now when Daniel learned that the decree had been published, he went home to his upstairs room where the windows opened toward Jerusalem. Three times a day he got down on his knees and prayed, giving thanks to his God, just as he had done before. 11 Then these men went as a group and found Daniel praying and asking God for help. 12 So they went to the king and spoke to him about his royal decree: "Did you not publish a decree that during the next thirty days anyone who prays to any god or man except to you, O king, would be thrown into the lions' den?"

The king answered, "The decree stands—in accordance with the laws of the Medes and Persians, which cannot be repealed."

13 Then they said to the king, "Daniel, who is one of the exiles from Judah, pays no attention to you, O king, or to the decree you put in writing. He still prays three times a day." 14 When the king heard this, he was greatly distressed; he was determined to rescue Daniel and made every effort until sundown to save him.

15 Then the men went as a group to the king and said to him, "Remember, O king, that according to the law of the Medes and Persians no decree or edict that the king issues can be changed."

[a] 27 *Tekel* can mean *weighed* or *shekel.* [b] 28 *Peres* (the singular of *Parsin*) can mean *divided* or *Persia* or *a half mina* or *a half shekel.* [c] 30 Or *Chaldeans*

16 So the king gave the order, and they brought Daniel and
threw him into the lions' den. The king said to Daniel, "May your
God, whom you serve continually, rescue you!"
17 A stone was brought and placed over the mouth of the den,
and the king sealed it with his own signet ring and with the rings
of his nobles, so that Daniel's situation might not be changed.
18 Then the king returned to his palace and spent the night without eating and without any entertainment being brought to him.
And he could not sleep.
19 At the first light of dawn, the king got up and hurried to the
lions' den. 20 When he came near the den, he called to Daniel in
an anguished voice, "Daniel, servant of the living God, has your
God, whom you serve continually, been able to rescue you from
the lions?"
21 Daniel answered, "O king, live forever! 22 My God sent his
angel, and he shut the mouths of the lions. They have not hurt
me, because I was found innocent in his sight. Nor have I ever
done any wrong before you, O king."
23 The king was overjoyed and gave orders to lift Daniel out of
the den. And when Daniel was lifted from the den, no wound was
found on him, because he had trusted in his God.
24 At the king's command, the men who had falsely accused
Daniel were brought in and thrown into the lions' den, along with
their wives and children. And before they reached the floor of the
den, the lions overpowered them and crushed all their bones.
25 Then King Darius wrote to all the peoples, nations and men
of every language throughout the land:

"May you prosper greatly!

26 "I issue a decree that in every part of my kingdom people must fear and reverence the God of Daniel.

"For he is the living God
and he endures forever;
his kingdom will not be destroyed,
his dominion will never end.
27 He rescues and he saves;
he performs signs and wonders
in the heavens and on the earth.
He has rescued Daniel
from the power of the lions."

28 So Daniel prospered during the reign of Darius and the reign
of Cyrus[a] the Persian.

Daniel's Dream of Four Beasts

7 In the first year of Belshazzar king of Babylon, Daniel had a
dream, and visions passed through his mind as he was lying
on his bed. He wrote down the substance of his dream.
2 Daniel said: "In my vision at night I looked, and there before
me were the four winds of heaven churning up the great sea. 3 Four
great beasts, each different from the others, came up out of the sea.
4 "The first was like a lion, and it had the wings of an eagle. I
watched until its wings were torn off and it was lifted from the
ground so that it stood on two feet like a man, and the heart of a
man was given to it.

[a] 28 Or *Darius, that is, the reign of Cyrus*

(6:17–21) Father, as I read about the stone being placed over the mouth of the lions' den, I am reminded of another stone that sealed another place of death. As the lifeless body of Your Son was sealed in a tomb, His followers mourned. But You brought Him out of that tomb, alive and victorious! Just as You shut the ravenous mouths of lions for Daniel, so You also opened the very jaws of death and released our Savior into the light of resurrection life. O Father, I believe that Your life of overcoming victory is for all of us who believe in Jesus and trust in You. Roll the stone of my captivity from the door of my tomb and release me into the fullness of everything You have for me. (Lk 23:33—24:9; Jn 11:25–27)

The same power that brought Christ back from the dead is operative within those who are Christ's. The Resurrection is an ongoing thing.

Leon Morris (1914-)

The Lord is my light and my
salvation,
The Lord is the strength of my life.
The Lord is my light and my
salvation,
The Lord is the strength of my life.
So I will not be afraid,
No, I will not be afraid;
Because the Lord is my light,
The Lord is my light,
The Lord is my light.

In the day of trouble
He will hide me;
He will keep me safe,
He will guide me through.

In the darkest hour
He will keep me;
Evil has no power
When He shelters me.

"The Lord is My Light"
Walt Harrah (©1987)

The fight for our planet, physical and spiritual, a fight of cosmic proportions, is not a vague matter of the future; it has already started. The forces of evil have begun their decisive offensive. You can feel their pressure, yet your screens and publications are full of prescribed smiles and raised glasses. What is the joy about?
Alexander Isayevich Solzenitsyn (1918-)

(7:13–18) I praise You, Living God, for the magnificent vision You gave to Daniel in his captivity—a vision of Jesus Christ. Daniel caught a glimpse of the reality that gives us hope. For You have exalted Jesus Christ to the highest place and have given Him a name that is above every name, that "at the name of Jesus every knee should bow, in heaven and on earth and under the earth, and every tongue confess that Jesus Christ is Lord, to the glory of God the Father." The kingdom of the world will become the kingdom of our Lord and of His Christ, and He will reign forever and ever! (Php 2:9–12; Rev 11:15)

Jesus, God's righteousness revealed,
The Son of man, the Son of God,
His Kingdom comes.
Jesus, redemption's sacrifice,
Now glorified, now justified,
His Kingdom comes.

And this kingdom will know no end,
And it's glory shall know no bounds,
For the majesty and power
Of this kingdom's King has come;
And this kingdom's reign
And this kingdom's rule
And this kingdom's power and
authority:
Jesus, God's righteousness revealed.
"This Kingdom"
Geoff Bullock (©1995)

5"And there before me was a second beast, which looked like
a bear. It was raised up on one of its sides, and it had three ribs
in its mouth between its teeth. It was told, 'Get up and eat your fill
of flesh!'
6"After that, I looked, and there before me was another beast,
one that looked like a leopard. And on its back it had four wings
like those of a bird. This beast had four heads, and it was given
authority to rule.
7"After that, in my vision at night I looked, and there before me
was a fourth beast—terrifying and frightening and very powerful.
It had large iron teeth; it crushed and devoured its victims and
trampled underfoot whatever was left. It was different from all the
former beasts, and it had ten horns.
8"While I was thinking about the horns, there before me was
another horn, a little one, which came up among them; and three
of the first horns were uprooted before it. This horn had eyes like
the eyes of a man and a mouth that spoke boastfully.
9"As I looked,

"thrones were set in place,
and the Ancient of Days took his seat.
His clothing was as white as snow;
the hair of his head was white like wool.
His throne was flaming with fire,
and its wheels were all ablaze.
10 A river of fire was flowing,
coming out from before him.
Thousands upon thousands attended him;
ten thousand times ten thousand stood before him.
The court was seated,
and the books were opened.

11"Then I continued to watch because of the boastful words
the horn was speaking. I kept looking until the beast was slain
and its body destroyed and thrown into the blazing fire. 12(The
other beasts had been stripped of their authority, but were allowed to live for a period of time.)
13"In my vision at night I looked, and there before me was one
like a son of man, coming with the clouds of heaven. He approached the Ancient of Days and was led into his presence. 14He
was given authority, glory and sovereign power; all peoples, nations and men of every language worshiped him. His dominion is
an everlasting dominion that will not pass away, and his kingdom
is one that will never be destroyed.

The Interpretation of the Dream

15"I, Daniel, was troubled in spirit, and the visions that passed
through my mind disturbed me. 16I approached one of those
standing there and asked him the true meaning of all this.
"So he told me and gave me the interpretation of these things:
17'The four great beasts are four kingdoms that will rise from the
earth. 18But the saints of the Most High will receive the kingdom
and will possess it forever—yes, for ever and ever.'
19"Then I wanted to know the true meaning of the fourth beast,
which was different from all the others and most terrifying, with its
iron teeth and bronze claws—the beast that crushed and devoured
its victims and trampled underfoot whatever was left. 20I also wanted to know about the ten horns on its head and about the other

horn that came up, before which three of them fell—the horn that
looked more imposing than the others and that had eyes and a
mouth that spoke boastfully. 21As I watched, this horn was waging
war against the saints and defeating them, 22until the Ancient of
Days came and pronounced judgment in favor of the saints of the
Most High, and the time came when they possessed the kingdom.

23"He gave me this explanation: 'The fourth beast is a fourth
kingdom that will appear on earth. It will be different from all the
other kingdoms and will devour the whole earth, trampling it
down and crushing it. 24The ten horns are ten kings who will
come from this kingdom. After them another king will arise, different from the earlier ones; he will subdue three kings. 25He will
speak against the Most High and oppress his saints and try to
change the set times and the laws. The saints will be handed over
to him for a time, times and half a time.[a]

26" 'But the court will sit, and his power will be taken away
and completely destroyed forever. 27Then the sovereignty, power
and greatness of the kingdoms under the whole heaven will be
handed over to the saints, the people of the Most High. His kingdom will be an everlasting kingdom, and all rulers will worship
and obey him.'

28"This is the end of the matter. I, Daniel, was deeply troubled
by my thoughts, and my face turned pale, but I kept the matter to
myself."

Daniel's Vision of a Ram and a Goat

8 In the third year of King Belshazzar's reign, I, Daniel, had a
vision, after the one that had already appeared to me. 2In my
vision I saw myself in the citadel of Susa in the province of Elam;
in the vision I was beside the Ulai Canal. 3I looked up, and there
before me was a ram with two horns, standing beside the canal,
and the horns were long. One of the horns was longer than the
other but grew up later. 4I watched the ram as he charged toward
the west and the north and the south. No animal could stand
against him, and none could rescue from his power. He did as he
pleased and became great.

5As I was thinking about this, suddenly a goat with a prominent
horn between his eyes came from the west, crossing the whole
earth without touching the ground. 6He came toward the two-
horned ram I had seen standing beside the canal and charged at
him in great rage. 7I saw him attack the ram furiously, striking the
ram and shattering his two horns. The ram was powerless to
stand against him; the goat knocked him to the ground and trampled on him, and none could rescue the ram from his power.
8The goat became very great, but at the height of his power his
large horn was broken off, and in its place four prominent horns
grew up toward the four winds of heaven.

9Out of one of them came another horn, which started small
but grew in power to the south and to the east and toward the
Beautiful Land. 10It grew until it reached the host of the heavens,
and it threw some of the starry host down to the earth and trampled on them. 11It set itself up to be as great as the Prince of the
host; it took away the daily sacrifice from him, and the place of
his sanctuary was brought low. 12Because of rebellion, the host
⌊of the saints⌋[b] and the daily sacrifice were given over to it. It

[a] 25 Or *for a year, two years and half a year* [b] 12 Or *rebellion, the armies*

(7:21–27) As we await the return of our Lord Jesus Christ, help Your church to be steadfast in our struggle against evil. Give us courage to faithfully contend for the cause of Christ in spite of setbacks and sufferings. Give us confidence to stand our ground in this great contest so that when we have done Your will, we will receive what You have promised. "For in just a very little while, 'He who is coming will come and will not delay. But my righteous one will live by faith. And if he shrinks back, I will not be pleased with him.' But we are not of those who shrink back and are destroyed, but of those who believe and are saved." (Hab 2:3–4; Heb 10:32–39)

(7:27) Lord God, we yearn for the day when You will reign—when there will be peace and justice for everyone, and the people of the Most High will live in unhindered fellowship with You. Now we live in a time when country is turned against country, race against race, and generation against generation. We are caught in the crossfire of a war-torn world. But we are not alone. You are with us, beside us, above us, beneath us and within us. We trust You to see us through to the other side of this troubled time. Stir up Your Holy Spirit in us so that we can be peacemakers in the midst of conflict, and sow a harvest of righteousness. (Mt 5:9; Jas 3:18)

Come, Thou Almighty King,
Help us Thy name to sing,
Help us to praise:
Father all glorious,
O'er all victorious,
Come, and reign over us,
Ancient of Days.

"Come, Thou Almighty King"
Italian Hymn (c.1757)

(8:25) God of all grace, You called us to Your eternal glory in Christ. Restore us and make us strong, firm and steadfast. Let us not be lulled into a false sense of security by our enemy, the deceiver. Awaken us, Lord, to be alert and self-controlled so that we will not be among those who are destroyed. Strengthen us with Your mighty power. "For our struggle is not against flesh and blood, but against the rulers, against the authorities, against the powers of this dark world and against the spiritual forces of evil in the heavenly realms." Clothe us in Your full armor, O God, so that when the day of evil comes we will be able to take our stand against the devil's schemes. (Eph 6:10–18; 1Pe 5:8–10)

The weapons of our warfare
Are not made with human hands;
And the enemy we face
Is not the flesh and blood of man;
But we serve a mighty captain
With a wondrous battle plan;
He's already won the victory,
Yet He calls us now to stand.

Hear the battle cry,
Put your armor on,
We must occupy the land
Until the kingdom comes.

"Hear the Battle Cry"
Jamie Owens-Collins (©1991)

prospered in everything it did, and truth was thrown to the
ground.
13 Then I heard a holy one speaking, and another holy one said
to him, "How long will it take for the vision to be fulfilled—the vision concerning the daily sacrifice, the rebellion that causes desolation, and the surrender of the sanctuary and of the host that
will be trampled underfoot?"
14 He said to me, "It will take 2,300 evenings and mornings;
then the sanctuary will be reconsecrated."

The Interpretation of the Vision

15 While I, Daniel, was watching the vision and trying to understand it, there before me stood one who looked like a man. 16 And
I heard a man's voice from the Ulai calling, "Gabriel, tell this man
the meaning of the vision."
17 As he came near the place where I was standing, I was terrified and fell prostrate. "Son of man," he said to me, "understand
that the vision concerns the time of the end."
18 While he was speaking to me, I was in a deep sleep, with my
face to the ground. Then he touched me and raised me to my feet.
19 He said: "I am going to tell you what will happen later in the
time of wrath, because the vision concerns the appointed time of
the end.[a] 20 The two-horned ram that you saw represents the
kings of Media and Persia. 21 The shaggy goat is the king of
Greece, and the large horn between his eyes is the first king.
22 The four horns that replaced the one that was broken off represent four kingdoms that will emerge from his nation but will not
have the same power.
23 "In the latter part of their reign, when rebels have become
completely wicked, a stern-faced king, a master of intrigue, will
arise. 24 He will become very strong, but not by his own power. He
will cause astounding devastation and will succeed in whatever he
does. He will destroy the mighty men and the holy people. 25 He
will cause deceit to prosper, and he will consider himself superi-
or. When they feel secure, he will destroy many and take his stand
against the Prince of princes. Yet he will be destroyed, but not by
human power.
26 "The vision of the evenings and mornings that has been given
you is true, but seal up the vision, for it concerns the distant
future."
27 I, Daniel, was exhausted and lay ill for several days. Then I
got up and went about the king's business. I was appalled by the
vision; it was beyond understanding.

Daniel's Prayer

9 In the first year of Darius son of Xerxes[b] (a Mede by descent), who was made ruler over the Babylonian[c] kingdom— 2 in the first year of his reign, I, Daniel, understood from
the Scriptures, according to the word of the LORD given to Jeremiah the prophet, that the desolation of Jerusalem would last seventy years. 3 So I turned to the Lord God and pleaded with him in
prayer and petition, in fasting, and in sackcloth and ashes.
4 I prayed to the LORD my God and confessed:

"O Lord, the great and awesome God, who keeps his cov-

[a] 19 Or *because the end will be at the appointed time* [b] 1 Hebrew *Abasuerus*
[c] 1 Or *Chaldean*

enant of love with all who love him and obey his commands,
5we have sinned and done wrong. We have been wicked and
have rebelled; we have turned away from your commands
and laws. 6We have not listened to your servants the prophets, who spoke in your name to our kings, our princes and
our fathers, and to all the people of the land.
7"Lord, you are righteous, but this day we are covered
with shame—the men of Judah and people of Jerusalem and
all Israel, both near and far, in all the countries where you
have scattered us because of our unfaithfulness to you.
8O LORD, we and our kings, our princes and our fathers are
covered with shame because we have sinned against you.
9The Lord our God is merciful and forgiving, even though
we have rebelled against him; 10we have not obeyed the
LORD our God or kept the laws he gave us through his servants the prophets. 11All Israel has transgressed your law
and turned away, refusing to obey you.

"Therefore the curses and sworn judgments written in the
Law of Moses, the servant of God, have been poured out on
us, because we have sinned against you. 12You have fulfilled
the words spoken against us and against our rulers by bringing upon us great disaster. Under the whole heaven nothing
has ever been done like what has been done to Jerusalem.
13Just as it is written in the Law of Moses, all this disaster
has come upon us, yet we have not sought the favor of the
LORD our God by turning from our sins and giving attention
to your truth. 14The LORD did not hesitate to bring the disaster upon us, for the LORD our God is righteous in everything
he does; yet we have not obeyed him.
15"Now, O Lord our God, who brought your people out of
Egypt with a mighty hand and who made for yourself a name
that endures to this day, we have sinned, we have done
wrong. 16O Lord, in keeping with all your righteous acts,
turn away your anger and your wrath from Jerusalem, your
city, your holy hill. Our sins and the iniquities of our fathers
have made Jerusalem and your people an object of scorn to
all those around us.
17"Now, our God, hear the prayers and petitions of your
servant. For your sake, O Lord, look with favor on your desolate sanctuary. 18Give ear, O God, and hear; open your
eyes and see the desolation of the city that bears your Name.
We do not make requests of you because we are righteous,
but because of your great mercy. 19O Lord, listen! O Lord,
forgive! O Lord, hear and act! For your sake, O my God, do
not delay, because your city and your people bear your
Name."

The Seventy "Sevens"

20While I was speaking and praying, confessing my sin and the
sin of my people Israel and making my request to the LORD my
God for his holy hill— 21while I was still in prayer, Gabriel, the
man I had seen in the earlier vision, came to me in swift flight
about the time of the evening sacrifice. 22He instructed me and
said to me, "Daniel, I have now come to give you insight and understanding. 23As soon as you began to pray, an answer was
given, which I have come to tell you, for you are highly esteemed.
Therefore, consider the message and understand the vision:

An intercessor means one who is in such vital contact with God and with his fellowmen that he is like a live wire closing the gap between the saving power of God and the sinful men who have been cut off from that power.

Hannah Hurnard (1905-1990)

(9:4–16) Lord, give me the compassionate heart of an intercessor. I pray for a heart like Daniel, who confessed the sins of others as though they were his own. I pray for a heart like Nehemiah, who wept as he confessed the sins of his people. I pray for a heart like Moses, who prayed, "please forgive their sin—but if not, then blot me out of the book you have written." Finally, Father, give me a heart like Jesus, the righteous One, who speaks to You in our defense when we sin. (Ex 32:32; Ne 1:4–7; 1Jn 2:1)

O Lord, hear,
O Lord, forgive us.
We have lost the awe of You.
Have mercy, have mercy.
O Lord, cleanse
Our hearts which are divided.
Stir the faith that we once knew.
We're thirsty, we're thirsty.

O Lord, restore
The church that bears Your name.
O Spirit, send
A revival to this nation.
Breathe on us again,
Breathe on us again.

"Breathe On Us Again"
Steve Fry (©1997)

(9:17–19) Gracious Father, we praise You for Your eagerness to answer prayer. You do so not because we are righteous, but because You are merciful. And in Your great mercy You hear, You see, You forgive, and You act mightily. It is for Your own sake that You answer the prayers of Your people. Thank You, Father, for Your saving love and compassion. (Tit 3:5)

(10:12) Almighty God, when I seek You in humility, You respond in majesty. So let this be the pattern of my prayer: that I will first seek to understand You, then seek to be understood by You; that I will first seek to know Your concerns, then seek to make my concerns known to You. I pray, Lord, that You will always find in me a listening ear—that I will be one in whom You can entrust the secret of Your kingdom. (Da 9:1–3; Mt 6:33; Mk 4:11)

Lord, teach us how to pray aright
With reverence and with fear;
Though weak and sinful in Your sight,
We may, we must draw near.

Patience to watch and weep and wait,
Whatever You may send;
Courage that will not hesitate
To trust You to the end.

Give these, and then Your will be done;
Thus, strengthened with all might,
We through Your Spirit and Your Son
Shall pray, and pray aright.

"Lord, Teach Us How to Pray Aright"
James Montgomery (1823)

24 "Seventy 'sevens'[a] are decreed for your people and your holy
city to finish[b] transgression, to put an end to sin, to atone for
wickedness, to bring in everlasting righteousness, to seal up vision and prophecy and to anoint the most holy.[c]
25 "Know and understand this: From the issuing of the decree[d]
to restore and rebuild Jerusalem until the Anointed One,[e] the
ruler, comes, there will be seven 'sevens,' and sixty-two 'sevens.'
It will be rebuilt with streets and a trench, but in times of trouble.
26 After the sixty-two 'sevens,' the Anointed One will be cut off and
will have nothing.[f] The people of the ruler who will come will destroy the city and the sanctuary. The end will come like a flood:
War will continue until the end, and desolations have been decreed. 27 He will confirm a covenant with many for one 'seven.'[g]
In the middle of the 'seven'[g] he will put an end to sacrifice and offering. And on a wing ⌊of the temple⌋ he will set up an abomination that causes desolation, until the end that is decreed is poured
out on him.[h]"[i]

Daniel's Vision of a Man

10 In the third year of Cyrus king of Persia, a revelation was
given to Daniel (who was called Belteshazzar). Its message
was true and it concerned a great war.[j] The understanding of the
message came to him in a vision.
2 At that time I, Daniel, mourned for three weeks. 3 I ate no
choice food; no meat or wine touched my lips; and I used no lotions at all until the three weeks were over.
4 On the twenty-fourth day of the first month, as I was standing
on the bank of the great river, the Tigris, 5 I looked up and there
before me was a man dressed in linen, with a belt of the finest
gold around his waist. 6 His body was like chrysolite, his face like
lightning, his eyes like flaming torches, his arms and legs like the
gleam of burnished bronze, and his voice like the sound of a multitude.
7 I, Daniel, was the only one who saw the vision; the men with
me did not see it, but such terror overwhelmed them that they
fled and hid themselves. 8 So I was left alone, gazing at this great
vision; I had no strength left, my face turned deathly pale and I
was helpless. 9 Then I heard him speaking, and as I listened to
him, I fell into a deep sleep, my face to the ground.
10 A hand touched me and set me trembling on my hands and
knees. 11 He said, "Daniel, you who are highly esteemed, consider carefully the words I am about to speak to you, and stand up,
for I have now been sent to you." And when he said this to me, I
stood up trembling.
12 Then he continued, "Do not be afraid, Daniel. Since the first
day that you set your mind to gain understanding and to humble
yourself before your God, your words were heard, and I have
come in response to them. 13 But the prince of the Persian kingdom resisted me twenty-one days. Then Michael, one of the chief
princes, came to help me, because I was detained there with the
king of Persia. 14 Now I have come to explain to you what will

[a] 24 Or *'weeks'*; also in verses 25 and 26 [b] 24 Or *restrain* [c] 24 Or *Most Holy Place*; or *most holy One* [d] 25 Or *word* [e] 25 Or *an anointed one*; also in verse 26 [f] 26 Or *off and will have no one*; or *off, but not for himself* [g] 27 Or *'week'* [h] 27 Or *it* [i] 27 Or *And one who causes desolation will come upon the pinnacle of the abominable ⌊temple⌋, until the end that is decreed is poured out on the desolated ⌊city⌋* [j] 1 Or *true and burdensome*

happen to your people in the future, for the vision concerns a
time yet to come."
15While he was saying this to me, I bowed with my face toward
the ground and was speechless. 16Then one who looked like a
man[a] touched my lips, and I opened my mouth and began to
speak. I said to the one standing before me, "I am overcome with
anguish because of the vision, my lord, and I am helpless. 17How
can I, your servant, talk with you, my lord? My strength is gone
and I can hardly breathe."
18Again the one who looked like a man touched me and gave
me strength. 19"Do not be afraid, O man highly esteemed," he
said. "Peace! Be strong now; be strong."
When he spoke to me, I was strengthened and said, "Speak, my
lord, since you have given me strength."
20So he said, "Do you know why I have come to you? Soon I
will return to fight against the prince of Persia, and when I go, the
prince of Greece will come; 21but first I will tell you what is written in the Book of Truth. (No one supports me against them
11 except Michael, your prince. 1And in the first year of Darius the Mede, I took my stand to support and protect him.)

The Kings of the South and the North

2"Now then, I tell you the truth: Three more kings will appear
in Persia, and then a fourth, who will be far richer than all the
others. When he has gained power by his wealth, he will stir up
everyone against the kingdom of Greece. 3Then a mighty king will
appear, who will rule with great power and do as he pleases.
4After he has appeared, his empire will be broken up and
parceled out toward the four winds of heaven. It will not go to his
descendants, nor will it have the power he exercised, because his
empire will be uprooted and given to others.
5"The king of the South will become strong, but one of his
commanders will become even stronger than he and will rule his
own kingdom with great power. 6After some years, they will become allies. The daughter of the king of the South will go to the
king of the North to make an alliance, but she will not retain her
power, and he and his power[b] will not last. In those days she will
be handed over, together with her royal escort and her father[c]
and the one who supported her.
7"One from her family line will arise to take her place. He will
attack the forces of the king of the North and enter his fortress; he
will fight against them and be victorious. 8He will also seize their
gods, their metal images and their valuable articles of silver and
gold and carry them off to Egypt. For some years he will leave the
king of the North alone. 9Then the king of the North will invade
the realm of the king of the South but will retreat to his own country. 10His sons will prepare for war and assemble a great army,
which will sweep on like an irresistible flood and carry the battle
as far as his fortress.
11"Then the king of the South will march out in a rage and fight
against the king of the North, who will raise a large army, but it
will be defeated. 12When the army is carried off, the king of the
South will be filled with pride and will slaughter many thousands,
yet he will not remain triumphant. 13For the king of the North will

(10:21—11:12) Sovereign Lord, You now how all things started and You know how all things will end. The future is already written in Your Book of Truth. You see the schemes of the ungodly. You are aware of the distress we suffer at their hands. Though nation may rage against nation, though empires may rise and fall, You care for the welfare of Your people. Ultimately, You are the Savior Who will come on the clouds of the sky with power and great glory to save us. (Mt 24:6–31)

[a] *16* Most manuscripts of the Masoretic Text; one manuscript of the Masoretic Text, Dead Sea Scrolls and Septuagint *Then something that looked like a man's hand* [b] *6* Or *offspring* [c] *6* Or *child* (see Vulgate and Syriac)

(11:32) Lord, I want to know You. While others may surrender their consciences to convenience, I want to be among those who resist the ways of the world and the flattery of the devil. I want to be among those who keep Your covenant—those whom You call Your treasured possession. I want to have the kind of faith and faithfulness that marks those who are known as Your friends. (Ex 19:5; Heb 10:36–38; Jas 2:23)

Let it be said of us
That the Lord was our passion,
That with gladness we bore
Ev'ry cross we were given;
That we fought the good fight,
That we finished the course,
Knowing within us
The pow'r of the risen Lord.

Let the cross be our glory
And the Lord be our song,
By mercy made holy,
By the Spirit made strong.
Let the cross be our glory
And the Lord be our song,
'Til the likeness of Jesus
Be through us made known.
Let the cross be our glory
And the Lord be our song.

"Let It Be Said of Us"
Steve Fry (©1996)

muster another army, larger than the first; and after several years,
he will advance with a huge army fully equipped.
14"In those times many will rise against the king of the South.
The violent men among your own people will rebel in fulfillment
of the vision, but without success. 15Then the king of the North
will come and build up siege ramps and will capture a fortified
city. The forces of the South will be powerless to resist; even their
best troops will not have the strength to stand. 16The invader will
do as he pleases; no one will be able to stand against him. He will
establish himself in the Beautiful Land and will have the power to
destroy it. 17He will determine to come with the might of his entire kingdom and will make an alliance with the king of the South.
And he will give him a daughter in marriage in order to overthrow
the kingdom, but his plans[a] will not succeed or help him. 18Then
he will turn his attention to the coastlands and will take many of
them, but a commander will put an end to his insolence and will
turn his insolence back upon him. 19After this, he will turn back
toward the fortresses of his own country but will stumble and fall,
to be seen no more.
20"His successor will send out a tax collector to maintain the
royal splendor. In a few years, however, he will be destroyed, yet
not in anger or in battle.
21"He will be succeeded by a contemptible person who has not
been given the honor of royalty. He will invade the kingdom when
its people feel secure, and he will seize it through intrigue.
22Then an overwhelming army will be swept away before him;
both it and a prince of the covenant will be destroyed. 23After
coming to an agreement with him, he will act deceitfully, and with
only a few people he will rise to power. 24When the richest
provinces feel secure, he will invade them and will achieve what
neither his fathers nor his forefathers did. He will distribute plunder, loot and wealth among his followers. He will plot the overthrow of fortresses—but only for a time.
25"With a large army he will stir up his strength and courage
against the king of the South. The king of the South will wage war
with a large and very powerful army, but he will not be able to
stand because of the plots devised against him. 26Those who eat
from the king's provisions will try to destroy him; his army will be
swept away, and many will fall in battle. 27The two kings, with their
hearts bent on evil, will sit at the same table and lie to each other,
but to no avail, because an end will still come at the appointed
time. 28The king of the North will return to his own country with
great wealth, but his heart will be set against the holy covenant. He
will take action against it and then return to his own country.
29"At the appointed time he will invade the South again, but
this time the outcome will be different from what it was before.
30Ships of the western coastlands[b] will oppose him, and he will
lose heart. Then he will turn back and vent his fury against the
holy covenant. He will return and show favor to those who forsake the holy covenant.
31"His armed forces will rise up to desecrate the temple
fortress and will abolish the daily sacrifice. Then they will set up
the abomination that causes desolation. 32With flattery he will
corrupt those who have violated the covenant, but the people who
know their God will firmly resist him.

[a] *17* Or *but she* [b] *30* Hebrew *of Kittim*

33"Those who are wise will instruct many, though for a time
they will fall by the sword or be burned or captured or plundered. 34When they fall, they will receive a little help, and many
who are not sincere will join them. 35Some of the wise will stumble, so that they may be refined, purified and made spotless until
the time of the end, for it will still come at the appointed time.

The King Who Exalts Himself

36"The king will do as he pleases. He will exalt and magnify
himself above every god and will say unheard-of things against
the God of gods. He will be successful until the time of wrath is
completed, for what has been determined must take place. 37He
will show no regard for the gods of his fathers or for the one desired by women, nor will he regard any god, but will exalt himself
above them all. 38Instead of them, he will honor a god of fortresses; a god unknown to his fathers he will honor with gold and
silver, with precious stones and costly gifts. 39He will attack the
mightiest fortresses with the help of a foreign god and will greatly honor those who acknowledge him. He will make them rulers
over many people and will distribute the land at a price.[a]

40"At the time of the end the king of the South will engage him
in battle, and the king of the North will storm out against him with
chariots and cavalry and a great fleet of ships. He will invade
many countries and sweep through them like a flood. 41He will
also invade the Beautiful Land. Many countries will fall, but
Edom, Moab and the leaders of Ammon will be delivered from his
hand. 42He will extend his power over many countries; Egypt will
not escape. 43He will gain control of the treasures of gold and
silver and all the riches of Egypt, with the Libyans and Nubians in
submission. 44But reports from the east and the north will alarm
him, and he will set out in a great rage to destroy and annihilate
many. 45He will pitch his royal tents between the seas at[b] the
beautiful holy mountain. Yet he will come to his end, and no one
will help him.

The End Times

12 "At that time Michael, the great prince who protects your
people, will arise. There will be a time of distress such as
has not happened from the beginning of nations until then. But at
that time your people—everyone whose name is found written in
the book—will be delivered. 2Multitudes who sleep in the dust of
the earth will awake: some to everlasting life, others to shame and
everlasting contempt. 3Those who are wise[c] will shine like the
brightness of the heavens, and those who lead many to righteousness, like the stars for ever and ever. 4But you, Daniel, close
up and seal the words of the scroll until the time of the end. Many
will go here and there to increase knowledge."

5Then I, Daniel, looked, and there before me stood two others,
one on this bank of the river and one on the opposite bank. 6One
of them said to the man clothed in linen, who was above the waters of the river, "How long will it be before these astonishing
things are fulfilled?"

7The man clothed in linen, who was above the waters of the
river, lifted his right hand and his left hand toward heaven, and I

[a] 39 Or *land for a reward* [b] 45 Or *the sea and* [c] 3 Or *who impart wisdom*

(12:1–4) Lord, in Your great wisdom You have chosen to hide the future as in a scroll, unfolding it in Your perfect time. Though I do not know what tomorrow may bring, this one thing I do know: "I know that my Redeemer lives, and that in the end he will stand upon the earth. And after my skin has been destroyed, yet in my flesh I will see God; I myself will see him with my own eyes—I, and not another. How my heart yearns within me!" (Job 19:25–27)

Soon and very soon,
We are going to see the King!
Soon and very soon,
We are going to see the King!
Soon and very soon,
We are going to see the King!
Hallelujah! Hallelujah!
We're going to see the King!

"Soon and Very Soon"
Andraé Crouch (©1976)

heard him swear by him who lives forever, saying, "It will be for
a time, times and half a time.[a] When the power of the holy people has been finally broken, all these things will be completed."
8I heard, but I did not understand. So I asked, "My lord, what
will the outcome of all this be?"
9He replied, "Go your way, Daniel, because the words are
closed up and sealed until the time of the end. 10Many will be purified, made spotless and refined, but the wicked will continue to
be wicked. None of the wicked will understand, but those who
are wise will understand.
11"From the time that the daily sacrifice is abolished and the
abomination that causes desolation is set up, there will be 1,290
days. 12Blessed is the one who waits for and reaches the end of
the 1,335 days.
13"As for you, go your way till the end. You will rest, and then
at the end of the days you will rise to receive your allotted inheritance."

(12:13) Lord Jesus, as I seek to know You more, expand my awareness of Who You are. By Your Holy Spirit, teach me all that You would have me understand. I trust You to hold my future in Your hands. Thank You for Your beautiful promise that when I see You, I will be like You. For now I see but a poor reflection as in a mirror, but someday I will see You face-to-face. Now I know in part, but then I will know fully, even as I am fully known by You. That is why I can be at peace with my limited vision. I can rest in the knowledge that at the end my inheritance will be eternal life with You. (Jn 3:16; 1Co 13:12; 1Jn 3:2)

Bring us, O Lord God, at our last awakening in the house and gate of heaven, to enter into that gate and dwell in that house, where there shall be no darkness nor dazzling, but one equal light; no noise nor silence, but one equal music; no fears nor hopes, but one equal possession; no ends nor beginnings, but one equal eternity; in the habitations of your glory and dominion, world without end.

John Donne (1572-1631)

[a] 7 Or *a year, two years and half a year*

The Book of HOSEA

In the eighth century B.C., as the northern kingdom of Israel continues to chase after pagan gods, the Lord raises up the prophet Hosea to call the people to repentance. God chooses to use not only Hosea's powerful and poetic words, but also his marriage, as a picture of Israel's sin and God's redeeming love. Astonishingly, God commands Hosea to marry a prostitute, whose physical adultery illustrates Israel's spiritual unfaithfulness to God (1:2). Even when Gomer repeatedly commits adultery against Hosea, God tells His prophet to love her again and to redeem her from her immorality (3:1). In this act of costly love Hosea mirrors the faithful, forgiving, restoring love of God for adulterous Israel.

For those of us who have wandered away from the Lord at times or who have failed to love God with the uncompromising love He deserves, the book of Hosea offers challenge, reassurance and hope. Although we are not tempted to worship the Canaanite baals, we are drawn by our culture to "worship" the idols of relativism, narcissism and materialism, the gods of success, security and emotional fulfillment. Even our worship can be so culturally "relevant" that it loses Biblical authenticity. But, although we might forget God and His standards, He has not forgotten us. God's compassion for His people—including us—turns His anger away (11:8–10). In His time He will heal us and restore us to relationship with Himself.

But we are called, not simply to wait for God's redemption but also to return to the Lord and to faithful relationship with Him (6:1–3). We respond to God's forgiving love by repenting, by turning to God in confession and by a genuine desire to live rightly with Him. Our repentance is not a matter of external religiosity, for, as God says: "I desire mercy, not sacrifice, and acknowledgment of God rather than burnt offerings" (6:6). The Hebrew term translated here as "mercy" signifies much more than the English word *mercy*. It describes a life of faithfulness within God's covenant, including both heartfelt worship and humble obedience.

As Hosea makes clear repeatedly, knowing God entails intimate relationship, not just intellectual assent. God wants us to know Him personally, actively and deeply.

The "acknowledgment of God" also comprises more than mere recognition of God's sovereign greatness. As Hosea makes clear repeatedly, knowing God entails intimate relationship, not just intellectual assent. God wants us to know Him personally, actively and deeply. When we worship "in spirit and in truth," we do much more than go through the motions (Jn 4:23–24). We enter into passionate fellowship with God. We respond with love to our Lord, Who has loved us first through Jesus Christ. Our knowledge of God must always be grounded in truth, in God's Biblical self-revelation. But merely knowing about God is not yet the "acknowledgement of God." This requires our worshipful, holistic, personal commitment. This *NIV Worship Bible* is meant to help us to move beyond mere knowledge about God and to enter into a Scripture-based relationship of worship with our living, loving, holy God.

(1:1) Your Word is precious, Lord. You spoke through Your prophets to Your people in a time and place far removed from my own. Yet this word was spoken for my life too. Unchanging God, reveal Your heart and mind to me. Give me ears to hear what You would say today through these living, prophetic words. Show me the things of Christ. Take them from this text and write them on the tablet of my heart. (Pr 7:2–3)

(1:11) Merciful God, Your faithful love is boundless. Only You can bring blessing from brokenness. Only You can bring triumph from tragedy. Only You can take the scattered remains of judgment and turn them into the miraculous seeds of a glorious future. All that You do is great, for it all flows from Your perfect love. Even judgment becomes Your work of transforming grace. Thank You for Your hand of discipline. Thank You for Your heart of mercy and love.

(2:6) Wall me in, Lord! Wide is the way that leads to destruction and narrow is the way that leads to life. You know my heart. You see my wandering ways. You know the dangers that lurk on every side. Before I stray too far, block my path. Keep me in the way of life. Let me feel the healing sting of Your correction, Lord, that I might not feel the cold and devastating outcome of my own folly. Then may I look up and see Your loving eyes and hear Your voice saying, "This is the way; walk in it." (Isa 30:21; Mt 7:13–14)

1 The word of the LORD that came to Hosea son of Beeri during
the reigns of Uzziah, Jotham, Ahaz and Hezekiah, kings of
Judah, and during the reign of Jeroboam son of Jehoash[a] king of
Israel:

Hosea's Wife and Children

2 When the LORD began to speak through Hosea, the LORD said
to him, "Go, take to yourself an adulterous wife and children of
unfaithfulness, because the land is guilty of the vilest adultery in
departing from the LORD." 3 So he married Gomer daughter of
Diblaim, and she conceived and bore him a son.
4 Then the LORD said to Hosea, "Call him Jezreel, because I will
soon punish the house of Jehu for the massacre at Jezreel, and I
will put an end to the kingdom of Israel. 5 In that day I will break
Israel's bow in the Valley of Jezreel."
6 Gomer conceived again and gave birth to a daughter. Then the
LORD said to Hosea, "Call her Lo-Ruhamah,[b] for I will no longer
show love to the house of Israel, that I should at all forgive them.
7 Yet I will show love to the house of Judah; and I will save them—
not by bow, sword or battle, or by horses and horsemen, but by
the LORD their God."
8 After she had weaned Lo-Ruhamah, Gomer had another son.
9 Then the LORD said, "Call him Lo-Ammi,[c] for you are not my people, and I am not your God.
10 "Yet the Israelites will be like the sand on the seashore,
which cannot be measured or counted. In the place where it was
said to them, 'You are not my people,' they will be called 'sons of
the living God.' 11 The people of Judah and the people of Israel
will be reunited, and they will appoint one leader and will come
up out of the land, for great will be the day of Jezreel.

2 "Say of your brothers, 'My people,' and of your sisters, 'My
loved one.'

Israel Punished and Restored

2 "Rebuke your mother, rebuke her,
for she is not my wife,
and I am not her husband.
Let her remove the adulterous look from her face
and the unfaithfulness from between her breasts.
3 Otherwise I will strip her naked
and make her as bare as on the day she was born;
I will make her like a desert,
turn her into a parched land,
and slay her with thirst.
4 I will not show my love to her children,
because they are the children of adultery.
5 Their mother has been unfaithful
and has conceived them in disgrace.
She said, 'I will go after my lovers,
who give me my food and my water,
my wool and my linen, my oil and my drink.'
6 Therefore I will block her path with thornbushes;
I will wall her in so that she cannot find her way.
7 She will chase after her lovers but not catch them;

[a] *1* Hebrew *Joash,* a variant of *Jehoash* [b] *6* *Lo-Ruhamah* means *not loved.*
[c] *9* *Lo-Ammi* means *not my people.*

she will look for them but not find them.
Then she will say,
'I will go back to my husband as at first,
for then I was better off than now.'
8 She has not acknowledged that I was the one
who gave her the grain, the new wine and oil,
who lavished on her the silver and gold—
which they used for Baal.
9 "Therefore I will take away my grain when it ripens,
and my new wine when it is ready.
I will take back my wool and my linen,
intended to cover her nakedness.
10 So now I will expose her lewdness
before the eyes of her lovers;
no one will take her out of my hands.
11 I will stop all her celebrations:
her yearly festivals, her New Moons,
her Sabbath days—all her appointed feasts.
12 I will ruin her vines and her fig trees,
which she said were her pay from her lovers;
I will make them a thicket,
and wild animals will devour them.
13 I will punish her for the days
she burned incense to the Baals;
she decked herself with rings and jewelry,
and went after her lovers,
but me she forgot,"
declares the LORD.

14 "Therefore I am now going to allure her;
I will lead her into the desert
and speak tenderly to her.
15 There I will give her back her vineyards,
and will make the Valley of Achor[a] a door of hope.
There she will sing[b] as in the days of her youth,
as in the day she came up out of Egypt.

16 "In that day," declares the LORD,
"you will call me 'my husband';
you will no longer call me 'my master.[c]'
17 I will remove the names of the Baals from her lips;
no longer will their names be invoked.
18 In that day I will make a covenant for them
with the beasts of the field and the birds of the air
and the creatures that move along the ground.
Bow and sword and battle
I will abolish from the land,
so that all may lie down in safety.
19 I will betroth you to me forever;
I will betroth you in[d] righteousness and justice,
in[e] love and compassion.
20 I will betroth you in faithfulness,
and you will acknowledge the LORD.

[a] *15 Achor* means *trouble.* [b] *15* Or *respond* [c] *16* Hebrew *baal* [d] *19* Or *with*; also in verse 20 [e] *19* Or *with*

(2:8) Here I am, Lord. I present my life, my gifts, my body to You. May they become instruments of Your righteousness. All that I have was first the gift of Your grace. Forgive me for taking Your good gifts and squandering them on myself. In the name of freedom I have used my hands and skills on pursuits that dishonor You. I have become fruitless and empty in the end. Receive me once again, Lord. By the power of Your Spirit, use my life and gifts in Your service and for Your glory. (Ro 6:21)

Yet dearly I loved you, and would be loved fain,
But am betrothed unto your enemy:
Divorce me, untie, or break that knot again,
Take me to you, imprison me, for I
Except you enthrall me, never shall be free,
Nor ever chaste, except you ravish me.
John Donne (1572–1631)

(2:14) Lord, I confess that I have been the wandering, unfaithful one. My heart has been enticed by so many glittering illusions. But Your amazing love will not let me go! Instead, You lead me to the wilderness. One by one You take away the illusions and reveal them to me for what they are. The empty world that I have created falls down around me. Lead me once again to the place where I may hear the tender call of Your love. By Your grace, renew my heart to sing Your praise with all the zeal of my first love!

Hitherto Thy love has blest me;
Thou hast bro't me to this place;
And I know Thy hand will bring me
Safely home by Thy good grace.
Jesus sought me when a stranger,
Wandering from the fold of God;
He, to rescue me from danger,
Bought me with His precious blood.
"Come Thou Fount of Every Blessing"
Robert Robinson (1758)

(2:23—3:1) Your love is relentless, Lord God. Time and again we have shown ourselves unworthy of our calling as Your special people. But Your love is triumphant, stronger than all our sin. You love us with forgiveness. You love us with grace. You love us with passion, with patience and with kindness. You love us without condition. It is as though You cannot help Yourself—love is not simply Your choice; it is Your nature.

Lord of love,
You have won my heart;
Your love forever will endure.

Every moment, every hour,
You remain a Faithful Tower;
In Your arms I rest secure.

"Lord of Love"
Bob W. Miller (©1989)

(4:1–6) Open our hearts and minds to know You more deeply, Lord. You are the source of everything good, lasting and helpful. Apart from You we drift in a world without love or faithfulness, without values or restraint. Glorious Father, give us the Spirit of wisdom and revelation, so that we may know You better. Open our eyes to Your goodness, Your glory and Your power. Then we will open our lips in true praise to Your holy name. (Eph 1:17–19)

21 "In that day I will respond,"
declares the LORD—
"I will respond to the skies,
and they will respond to the earth;
22 and the earth will respond to the grain,
the new wine and oil,
and they will respond to Jezreel.[a]
23 I will plant her for myself in the land;
I will show my love to the one I called 'Not my loved one.[b]'
I will say to those called 'Not my people,[c]' 'You are my people';
and they will say, 'You are my God.' "

Hosea's Reconciliation With His Wife

3 The LORD said to me, "Go, show your love to your wife again, though she is loved by another and is an adulteress. Love her as the LORD loves the Israelites, though they turn to other gods and love the sacred raisin cakes."

2 So I bought her for fifteen shekels[d] of silver and about a
homer and a lethek[e] of barley. 3 Then I told her, "You are to live
with[f] me many days; you must not be a prostitute or be intimate with any man, and I will live with[f] you."

4 For the Israelites will live many days without king or prince,
without sacrifice or sacred stones, without ephod or idol. 5 After-
ward the Israelites will return and seek the LORD their God and David their king. They will come trembling to the LORD and to his blessings in the last days.

The Charge Against Israel

4 Hear the word of the LORD, you Israelites,
because the LORD has a charge to bring
against you who live in the land:
"There is no faithfulness, no love,
no acknowledgment of God in the land.
2 There is only cursing,[g] lying and murder,
stealing and adultery;
they break all bounds,
and bloodshed follows bloodshed.
3 Because of this the land mourns,[h]
and all who live in it waste away;
the beasts of the field and the birds of the air
and the fish of the sea are dying.

4 "But let no man bring a charge,
let no man accuse another,
for your people are like those
who bring charges against a priest.
5 You stumble day and night,
and the prophets stumble with you.
So I will destroy your mother—
6 my people are destroyed from lack of knowledge.

"Because you have rejected knowledge,

[a] 22 *Jezreel* means *God plants.* [b] 23 Hebrew *Lo-Ruhamah* [c] 23 Hebrew *Lo-Ammi*
[d] 2 That is, about 6 ounces (about 170 grams) [e] 2 That is, probably about 10 bushels (about 330 liters) [f] 3 Or *wait for* [g] 2 That is, to pronounce a curse upon
[h] 3 Or *dries up*

I also reject you as my priests;
because you have ignored the law of your God,
I also will ignore your children.
7 The more the priests increased,
the more they sinned against me;
they exchanged[a] their[b] Glory for something
disgraceful.
8 They feed on the sins of my people
and relish their wickedness.
9 And it will be: Like people, like priests.
I will punish both of them for their ways
and repay them for their deeds.

10 "They will eat but not have enough;
they will engage in prostitution but not increase,
because they have deserted the LORD
to give themselves 11 to prostitution,
to old wine and new,
which take away the understanding 12 of my people.
They consult a wooden idol
and are answered by a stick of wood.
A spirit of prostitution leads them astray;
they are unfaithful to their God.
13 They sacrifice on the mountaintops
and burn offerings on the hills,
under oak, poplar and terebinth,
where the shade is pleasant.
Therefore your daughters turn to prostitution
and your daughters-in-law to adultery.

14 "I will not punish your daughters
when they turn to prostitution,
nor your daughters-in-law
when they commit adultery,
because the men themselves consort with harlots
and sacrifice with shrine prostitutes—
a people without understanding will come to ruin!

15 "Though you commit adultery, O Israel,
let not Judah become guilty.

"Do not go to Gilgal;
do not go up to Beth Aven.[c]
And do not swear, 'As surely as the LORD lives!'
16 The Israelites are stubborn,
like a stubborn heifer.
How then can the LORD pasture them
like lambs in a meadow?
17 Ephraim is joined to idols;
leave him alone!
18 Even when their drinks are gone,
they continue their prostitution;
their rulers dearly love shameful ways.
19 A whirlwind will sweep them away,
and their sacrifices will bring them shame.

[a] 7 Syriac and an ancient Hebrew scribal tradition; Masoretic Text *I will exchange*
[b] 7 Masoretic Text; an ancient Hebrew scribal tradition *my*
[c] 15 *Beth Aven* means *house of wickedness* (a name for Bethel, which means *house of God*).

(4:16) Stubbornness comes too naturally to me—the old me, the old self. But now, by Your grace, Lord, I am no longer bound in rebellion. The gospel promise is the promise of a new heart. Not a heart of stone, but a soft heart of flesh that has been touched by Your Spirit. Today, by faith, I will walk with You in newness of life. I will listen for Your voice and follow Your ways with a willing heart. (Eze 36:26)

Shepherd of my soul,
I give You full control,
Wherever You may lead
I will follow.
I have made the choice
To listen to Your voice,
Wherever You may lead
I will go.

"Shepherd of My Soul"
Martin Nystrom (©1988)

(5:5) Teach me the way of humility, Lord, for truly You resist the proud but give grace to the humble. To be filled with pride is the most dangerous sin of all. The greater my pride, the less I see my need of You. What arrogance that I would go about my day without first seeking and submitting to Your perfect will! When I choose my own path I stumble and fall in my sinful choices, blind to my foolishness. Forgive me, Lord. Teach me to walk in humility, with each step submitted to You and empowered by Your grace. (Jas 4:6)

Pride is the ground in which all the other sins grow, and the parent from which all the other sins come.

William Barclay (1907-1978)

(5:10) O Lord, we pray for the pastors, the shepherds, the leaders of the church. Strengthen them this day to stand firm in the Word that You have revealed. Grant them boldness in resisting the constant pressure to compromise the truth. Help them speak with clarity and conviction as they declare to us the nature of God, the gospel of Christ, and the guidelines for living that You have ordained.

Judgment Against Israel

5 "Hear this, you priests!
Pay attention, you Israelites!
Listen, O royal house!
This judgment is against you:
You have been a snare at Mizpah,
a net spread out on Tabor.
2 The rebels are deep in slaughter.
I will discipline all of them.
3 I know all about Ephraim;
Israel is not hidden from me.
Ephraim, you have now turned to prostitution;
Israel is corrupt.

4 "Their deeds do not permit them
to return to their God.
A spirit of prostitution is in their heart;
they do not acknowledge the LORD.
5 Israel's arrogance testifies against them;
the Israelites, even Ephraim, stumble in their sin;
Judah also stumbles with them.
6 When they go with their flocks and herds
to seek the LORD,
they will not find him;
he has withdrawn himself from them.
7 They are unfaithful to the LORD;
they give birth to illegitimate children.
Now their New Moon festivals
will devour them and their fields.

8 "Sound the trumpet in Gibeah,
the horn in Ramah.
Raise the battle cry in Beth Aven[a];
lead on, O Benjamin.
9 Ephraim will be laid waste
on the day of reckoning.
Among the tribes of Israel
I proclaim what is certain.
10 Judah's leaders are like those
who move boundary stones.
I will pour out my wrath on them
like a flood of water.
11 Ephraim is oppressed,
trampled in judgment,
intent on pursuing idols.[b]
12 I am like a moth to Ephraim,
like rot to the people of Judah.

13 "When Ephraim saw his sickness,
and Judah his sores,
then Ephraim turned to Assyria,
and sent to the great king for help.
But he is not able to cure you,
not able to heal your sores.
14 For I will be like a lion to Ephraim,
like a great lion to Judah.

[a] *8 Beth Aven* means *house of wickedness* (a name for Bethel, which means *house of God*). [b] *11* The meaning of the Hebrew for this word is uncertain.

I will tear them to pieces and go away;
I will carry them off, with no one to rescue them.
15 Then I will go back to my place
until they admit their guilt.
And they will seek my face;
in their misery they will earnestly seek me."

Israel Unrepentant

6 "Come, let us return to the LORD.
He has torn us to pieces
but he will heal us;
he has injured us
but he will bind up our wounds.
2 After two days he will revive us;
on the third day he will restore us,
that we may live in his presence.
3 Let us acknowledge the LORD;
let us press on to acknowledge him.
As surely as the sun rises,
he will appear;
he will come to us like the winter rains,
like the spring rains that water the earth."

4 "What can I do with you, Ephraim?
What can I do with you, Judah?
Your love is like the morning mist,
like the early dew that disappears.
5 Therefore I cut you in pieces with my prophets,
I killed you with the words of my mouth;
my judgments flashed like lightning upon you.
6 For I desire mercy, not sacrifice,
and acknowledgment of God rather than burnt offerings.
7 Like Adam,[a] they have broken the covenant—
they were unfaithful to me there.
8 Gilead is a city of wicked men,
stained with footprints of blood.
9 As marauders lie in ambush for a man,
so do bands of priests;
they murder on the road to Shechem,
committing shameful crimes.
10 I have seen a horrible thing
in the house of Israel.
There Ephraim is given to prostitution
and Israel is defiled.

11 "Also for you, Judah,
a harvest is appointed.

"Whenever I would restore the fortunes of my people,
7 1 whenever I would heal Israel,
the sins of Ephraim are exposed
and the crimes of Samaria revealed.
They practice deceit,
thieves break into houses,
bandits rob in the streets;

[a] 7 Or *As at Adam*; or *Like men*

(6:1) Lord, You have been with me with each step I have taken, even when I have walked away from You in self-will and pride. In Your faithful love You have allowed me to know the painful consequences of my rebellion. Your hand of discipline has been the hand of love all along. And now I am turning my heart fully back to you. Heal me, Lord, even as I turn. Bind up my broken heart. Put my fractured life back together again. My hope rests on Your gracious love and Your gentle faithfulness.

Broken by all the times I've failed,
And the days I've hung my head in shame.
Time and again I'm driven to my knees,
And I find Your great compassion there for me.

I'm amazed at all You've done for me;
Who am I, that You'd bless me so.
I stand in awe of all Your wondrous deeds;
You've dealt with me so graciously.

I'm Amazed
Rory Noland (©1991)

(6:6) Make my heart Your sanctuary, O God. Light a fire of holy passion in my soul. Move me beyond a spiritual life of empty rituals and religious observances. You are worthy of so much more, and You have called me to so much more. Let this love we share become the driving force in my life. Let it move me to love and compassion for all those You have loved and have given Your Son to save.

(7:13–16) Lord, how You long for us to reach out to You—to cry out for Your company. Instead, we cry out only for the things that You can give to us. Cause us to hunger and thirst for fellowship with You. May we never forget that You are the source of every good thing in life. (Jas 1:17)

Jesus, draw me close,
Closer, Lord, to You.
Let the world around me fade away.
Jesus, draw me close,
Closer, Lord, to You.
For I desire to worship and obey.

"Jesus, Draw Me Close"
Rick Founds (©1990)

2 but they do not realize
that I remember all their evil deeds.
Their sins engulf them;
they are always before me.

3 "They delight the king with their wickedness,
the princes with their lies.
4 They are all adulterers,
burning like an oven
whose fire the baker need not stir
from the kneading of the dough till it rises.
5 On the day of the festival of our king
the princes become inflamed with wine,
and he joins hands with the mockers.
6 Their hearts are like an oven;
they approach him with intrigue.
Their passion smolders all night;
in the morning it blazes like a flaming fire.
7 All of them are hot as an oven;
they devour their rulers.
All their kings fall,
and none of them calls on me.

8 "Ephraim mixes with the nations;
Ephraim is a flat cake not turned over.
9 Foreigners sap his strength,
but he does not realize it.
His hair is sprinkled with gray,
but he does not notice.
10 Israel's arrogance testifies against him,
but despite all this
he does not return to the LORD his God
or search for him.

11 "Ephraim is like a dove,
easily deceived and senseless—
now calling to Egypt,
now turning to Assyria.
12 When they go, I will throw my net over them;
I will pull them down like birds of the air.
When I hear them flocking together,
I will catch them.
13 Woe to them,
because they have strayed from me!
Destruction to them,
because they have rebelled against me!
I long to redeem them
but they speak lies against me.
14 They do not cry out to me from their hearts
but wail upon their beds.
They gather together[a] for grain and new wine
but turn away from me.
15 I trained them and strengthened them,
but they plot evil against me.
16 They do not turn to the Most High;
they are like a faulty bow.

[a] 14 Most Hebrew manuscripts; some Hebrew manuscripts and Septuagint *They slash themselves*

Their leaders will fall by the sword
because of their insolent words.
For this they will be ridiculed
in the land of Egypt.

Israel to Reap the Whirlwind

8 "Put the trumpet to your lips!
An eagle is over the house of the LORD
because the people have broken my covenant
and rebelled against my law.
2 Israel cries out to me,
'O our God, we acknowledge you!'
3 But Israel has rejected what is good;
an enemy will pursue him.
4 They set up kings without my consent;
they choose princes without my approval.
With their silver and gold
they make idols for themselves
to their own destruction.
5 Throw out your calf-idol, O Samaria!
My anger burns against them.
How long will they be incapable of purity?
6 They are from Israel!
This calf—a craftsman has made it;
it is not God.
It will be broken in pieces,
that calf of Samaria.

7 "They sow the wind
and reap the whirlwind.
The stalk has no head;
it will produce no flour.
Were it to yield grain,
foreigners would swallow it up.
8 Israel is swallowed up;
now she is among the nations
like a worthless thing.
9 For they have gone up to Assyria
like a wild donkey wandering alone.
Ephraim has sold herself to lovers.
10 Although they have sold themselves among the nations,
I will now gather them together.
They will begin to waste away
under the oppression of the mighty king.

11 "Though Ephraim built many altars for sin offerings,
these have become altars for sinning.
12 I wrote for them the many things of my law,
but they regarded them as something alien.
13 They offer sacrifices given to me
and they eat the meat,
but the LORD is not pleased with them.
Now he will remember their wickedness
and punish their sins:
They will return to Egypt.
14 Israel has forgotten his Maker
and built palaces;
Judah has fortified many towns.

Just as a planet rushing through space is only a comet on its way to destruction until it is caught by some central sun and begins to revolve around that sun as its center and its life; so my life is an aimless comet burning itself out in its own self-will, till it finds the pull and attractive of Christ's love, halts its deadly way, and forever revolves around him, its central sun and life.

E. Stanley Jones (1884–1973)

(8:1–14) Like Your people of old, I too have been guilty of these same sins of the heart. I have relied on my own strength, my own resourcefulness, my own cleverness, rather than surrendering to Your will. I have worshiped the work of my hands and have entered into unholy alliances with the world. The further I have pushed You from the center of my heart and mind, the greater the emptiness that has grown within me. Lord, forgive me. Now, in humility, I turn and submit myself to You. Rescue me from the hand of my enemy and send Your holy fire to burn away everything that displeases You.

(9:10) Who could have a greater hope for their children than You, Lord? You know the fullness of joy that awaits me, if only I will keep my eyes focused upon You! What pain it must bring You when I turn my eyes to worthless things and forfeit the blessing that You have reserved for me. As Your eyes are always on me, help me to keep my eyes always on you. (2Ki 17:15; Jnh 2:8)

Ah! For a vision of God!
For a mighty grasp of the real,
Feet firm based on granite in place of crumbling sand!

Roden Noel (1834–1894)

But I will send fire upon their cities
that will consume their fortresses."

Punishment for Israel

9 Do not rejoice, O Israel;
do not be jubilant like the other nations.
For you have been unfaithful to your God;
you love the wages of a prostitute
at every threshing floor.
2 Threshing floors and winepresses will not feed the people;
the new wine will fail them.
3 They will not remain in the LORD's land;
Ephraim will return to Egypt
and eat unclean[a] food in Assyria.
4 They will not pour out wine offerings to the LORD,
nor will their sacrifices please him.
Such sacrifices will be to them like the bread of mourners;
all who eat them will be unclean.
This food will be for themselves;
it will not come into the temple of the LORD.

5 What will you do on the day of your appointed feasts,
on the festival days of the LORD?
6 Even if they escape from destruction,
Egypt will gather them,
and Memphis will bury them.
Their treasures of silver will be taken over by briers,
and thorns will overrun their tents.
7 The days of punishment are coming,
the days of reckoning are at hand.
Let Israel know this.
Because your sins are so many
and your hostility so great,
the prophet is considered a fool,
the inspired man a maniac.
8 The prophet, along with my God,
is the watchman over Ephraim,[b]
yet snares await him on all his paths,
and hostility in the house of his God.
9 They have sunk deep into corruption,
as in the days of Gibeah.
God will remember their wickedness
and punish them for their sins.

10 "When I found Israel,
it was like finding grapes in the desert;
when I saw your fathers,
it was like seeing the early fruit on the fig tree.
But when they came to Baal Peor,
they consecrated themselves to that shameful idol
and became as vile as the thing they loved.
11 Ephraim's glory will fly away like a bird—
no birth, no pregnancy, no conception.

[a] 3 That is, ceremonially unclean [b] 8 Or *The prophet is the watchman over Ephraim, / the people of my God*

12 Even if they rear children,
 I will bereave them of every one.
Woe to them
 when I turn away from them!
13 I have seen Ephraim, like Tyre,
 planted in a pleasant place.
But Ephraim will bring out
 their children to the slayer."

14 Give them, O LORD—
 what will you give them?
Give them wombs that miscarry
 and breasts that are dry.

15 "Because of all their wickedness in Gilgal,
 I hated them there.
Because of their sinful deeds,
 I will drive them out of my house.
I will no longer love them;
 all their leaders are rebellious.
16 Ephraim is blighted,
 their root is withered,
 they yield no fruit.
Even if they bear children,
 I will slay their cherished offspring."

17 My God will reject them
 because they have not obeyed him;
 they will be wanderers among the nations.

10 Israel was a spreading vine;
 he brought forth fruit for himself.
As his fruit increased,
 he built more altars;
as his land prospered,
 he adorned his sacred stones.
2 Their heart is deceitful,
 and now they must bear their guilt.
The LORD will demolish their altars
 and destroy their sacred stones.

3 Then they will say, "We have no king
 because we did not revere the LORD.
But even if we had a king,
 what could he do for us?"
4 They make many promises,
 take false oaths
 and make agreements;
therefore lawsuits spring up
 like poisonous weeds in a plowed field.
5 The people who live in Samaria fear
 for the calf-idol of Beth Aven.[a]
Its people will mourn over it,
 and so will its idolatrous priests,
those who had rejoiced over its splendor,
 because it is taken from them into exile.
6 It will be carried to Assyria

[a] 5 *Beth Aven* means *house of wickedness* (a name for Bethel, which means *house of God*).

(9:13) Heal me, Lord. Free me from my sinful ways. My sin has caused me so much pain. Even worse, my sin has brought pain to those I dearly love. I have put my own family at risk through my sinful choices. Heal me, Lord! Do a cleansing work within my life. Let it overflow to bless my family. Let my life become the tool that leads these precious lives to You.

Son of God, eternal Savior,
Source of life and truth and grace,
Word made flesh, whose birth
 among us
Hallows all our human race,
You our head, who, throned in glory,
For Your own will ever plead:
Fill us with Your love and pity,
Heal our wrongs, and help our need.

"Son of God, Eternal Savior"
Somerset C. Lowry (1855–1932)

as tribute for the great king.
Ephraim will be disgraced;
Israel will be ashamed of its wooden idols.[a]
7 Samaria and its king will float away
like a twig on the surface of the waters.
8 The high places of wickedness[b] will be destroyed—
it is the sin of Israel.
Thorns and thistles will grow up
and cover their altars.
Then they will say to the mountains, "Cover us!"
and to the hills, "Fall on us!"

9 "Since the days of Gibeah, you have sinned, O Israel,
and there you have remained.[c]
Did not war overtake
the evildoers in Gibeah?
10 When I please, I will punish them;
nations will be gathered against them
to put them in bonds for their double sin.
11 Ephraim is a trained heifer
that loves to thresh;
so I will put a yoke
on her fair neck.
I will drive Ephraim,
Judah must plow,
and Jacob must break up the ground.
12 Sow for yourselves righteousness,
reap the fruit of unfailing love,
and break up your unplowed ground;
for it is time to seek the LORD,
until he comes
and showers righteousness on you.
13 But you have planted wickedness,
you have reaped evil,
you have eaten the fruit of deception.
Because you have depended on your own strength
and on your many warriors,
14 the roar of battle will rise against your people,
so that all your fortresses will be devastated—
as Shalman devastated Beth Arbel on the day of battle,
when mothers were dashed to the ground with their children.
15 Thus will it happen to you, O Bethel,
because your wickedness is great.
When that day dawns,
the king of Israel will be completely destroyed.

God's Love for Israel

11 "When Israel was a child, I loved him,
and out of Egypt I called my son.
2 But the more I[d] called Israel,
the further they went from me.[e]
They sacrificed to the Baals
and they burned incense to images.

[a] 6 Or *its counsel* [b] 8 Hebrew *aven,* a reference to Beth Aven (a derogatory name for Bethel) [c] 9 Or *there a stand was taken* [d] 2 Some Septuagint manuscripts; Hebrew *they* [e] 2 Septuagint; Hebrew *them*

(10:12) How great and wonderful is Your unfailing love, O God. Your love is poured out not according to my capacity to receive, but according to Your ability to give. In spite of what I do and because of Who You are, by Your grace You continue to love me. Teach me to soften my heart, Lord, to break up the unplowed ground, so that You can plant Your seeds of grace deep within my heart. And may Your seed bring forth the fruit of Your spirit in my life, manifest through an abundant harvest of acts of "love, joy, peace, patience, kindness, goodness, faithfulness, gentleness and self-control." (Gal 5:22–23)

Plow up the trodden way,
And clear the stone away;
Tear out the weed, and sow the seed.
Prepare our hearts Your Word to heed,
That we good soil may be.
Begin, O Lord, with me!
"When Seed Falls on Good Soil"
Norman P. Olsen (©1976)

3 It was I who taught Ephraim to walk,
taking them by the arms;
but they did not realize
it was I who healed them.
4 I led them with cords of human kindness,
with ties of love;
I lifted the yoke from their neck
and bent down to feed them.

5 "Will they not return to Egypt
and will not Assyria rule over them
because they refuse to repent?
6 Swords will flash in their cities,
will destroy the bars of their gates
and put an end to their plans.
7 My people are determined to turn from me.
Even if they call to the Most High,
he will by no means exalt them.

8 "How can I give you up, Ephraim?
How can I hand you over, Israel?
How can I treat you like Admah?
How can I make you like Zeboiim?
My heart is changed within me;
all my compassion is aroused.
9 I will not carry out my fierce anger,
nor will I turn and devastate Ephraim.
For I am God, and not man—
the Holy One among you.
I will not come in wrath.[a]
10 They will follow the LORD;
he will roar like a lion.
When he roars,
his children will come trembling from the west.
11 They will come trembling
like birds from Egypt,
like doves from Assyria.
I will settle them in their homes,"
declares the LORD.

Israel's Sin

12 Ephraim has surrounded me with lies,
the house of Israel with deceit.
And Judah is unruly against God,
even against the faithful Holy One.

12 1 Ephraim feeds on the wind;
he pursues the east wind all day
and multiplies lies and violence.
He makes a treaty with Assyria
and sends olive oil to Egypt.
2 The LORD has a charge to bring against Judah;
he will punish Jacob[b] according to his ways
and repay him according to his deeds.
3 In the womb he grasped his brother's heel;
as a man he struggled with God.
4 He struggled with the angel and overcame him;

Father, let me hold thy hand and like a child walk with thee down all my days, secure in thy love and strength.
Thomas à Kempis (c.1380–1471)

(11:1–9) You are our Healer, our Deliverer, and our Provider. Because You do all things so well and so bountifully, it is easy for us to overlook Your goodness or take it for granted. You woo us to Yourself with kindness. If we reject Your invitation, if we resist Your call, You will not give up on us. In Your great compassion You will drive us to Yourself through adversity. We praise You, O God, that even in Your discipline You do not deal with us out of cruelty, but out of love. (Heb 12:6–10)

O faithful God, You never fail me;
Your cov'nant surely will abide.
Let not eternal death assail me
Should I transgress it on my side!
Have mercy when I come defiled;
Forgive, lift up, restore Your child.
"Baptized Into Your Name Most Holy"
Johann J. Rambach (1693–1735)
Trans. Catherine Winkworth (1829–1878)

[a] 9 Or *come against any city* [b] 2 *Jacob* means *he grasps the heel* (figuratively, *he deceives*).

Though the Bible urges us on to perfection, it gives no encouragement to suppose that perfection is achieved. A man who thinks he is righteous is not righteous . . . for the reason, primarily, that he is full of spiritual pride, the most deadly form that sin can take.

D. Elton Trueblood (1900–1944)

(12:8) Spiritual blindness is the companion of pride. Am I blind, Lord? Have I confused prosperity with spirituality? What good will it do for me to gain the whole world if I lose my very self in the process? What can I give in exchange for my soul? My life does not consist in the abundance of possessions, nor can my status blind the eyes of Your justice. Open my eyes to see my life as You see it. Cleanse me from sin. Clothe me in the garments of Your righteousness and teach me to lay up treasures in heaven. (Mk 8:36–37; Lk 12:15–21; Rev 3:17–18)

All depends on our possessing
God's free grace and constant
blessing,
Though all earthly wealth depart.
They who trust with faith unshaken
By their God are not forsaken
And will keep a dauntless heart.

"All Depends on Our Possessing"
Anonymous German Hymn (1676)
Trans. Catherine Winkworth (1829–1878)

he wept and begged for his favor.
He found him at Bethel
and talked with him there—
5 the LORD God Almighty,
the LORD is his name of renown!
6 But you must return to your God;
maintain love and justice,
and wait for your God always.

7 The merchant uses dishonest scales;
he loves to defraud.
8 Ephraim boasts,
"I am very rich; I have become wealthy.
With all my wealth they will not find in me
any iniquity or sin."

9 "I am the LORD your God,
⌞who brought you⌟ out of[a] Egypt;
I will make you live in tents again,
as in the days of your appointed feasts.
10 I spoke to the prophets,
gave them many visions
and told parables through them."

11 Is Gilead wicked?
Its people are worthless!
Do they sacrifice bulls in Gilgal?
Their altars will be like piles of stones
on a plowed field.
12 Jacob fled to the country of Aram[b];
Israel served to get a wife,
and to pay for her he tended sheep.
13 The LORD used a prophet to bring Israel up from Egypt,
by a prophet he cared for him.
14 But Ephraim has bitterly provoked him to anger;
his Lord will leave upon him the guilt of his
bloodshed
and will repay him for his contempt.

The LORD's Anger Against Israel

13 When Ephraim spoke, men trembled;
he was exalted in Israel.
But he became guilty of Baal worship and died.
2 Now they sin more and more;
they make idols for themselves from their silver,
cleverly fashioned images,
all of them the work of craftsmen.
It is said of these people,
"They offer human sacrifice
and kiss[c] the calf-idols."
3 Therefore they will be like the morning mist,
like the early dew that disappears,
like chaff swirling from a threshing floor,
like smoke escaping through a window.

4 "But I am the LORD your God,
⌞who brought you⌟ out of[a] Egypt.

[a] 9,4 Or *God / ever since you were in* [b] 12 That is, Northwest Mesopotamia [c] 2 Or *"Men who sacrifice / kiss*

You shall acknowledge no God but me,
no Savior except me.
5 I cared for you in the desert,
in the land of burning heat.
6 When I fed them, they were satisfied;
when they were satisfied, they became proud;
then they forgot me.
7 So I will come upon them like a lion,
like a leopard I will lurk by the path.
8 Like a bear robbed of her cubs,
I will attack them and rip them open.
Like a lion I will devour them;
a wild animal will tear them apart.

9 "You are destroyed, O Israel,
because you are against me, against your helper.
10 Where is your king, that he may save you?
Where are your rulers in all your towns,
of whom you said,
'Give me a king and princes'?
11 So in my anger I gave you a king,
and in my wrath I took him away.
12 The guilt of Ephraim is stored up,
his sins are kept on record.
13 Pains as of a woman in childbirth come to him,
but he is a child without wisdom;
when the time arrives,
he does not come to the opening of the womb.

14 "I will ransom them from the power of the grave[a];
I will redeem them from death.
Where, O death, are your plagues?
Where, O grave,[a] is your destruction?

"I will have no compassion,
15 even though he thrives among his brothers.
An east wind from the LORD will come,
blowing in from the desert;
his spring will fail
and his well dry up.
His storehouse will be plundered
of all its treasures.
16 The people of Samaria must bear their guilt,
because they have rebelled against their God.
They will fall by the sword;
their little ones will be dashed to the ground,
their pregnant women ripped open."

Repentance to Bring Blessing

14 Return, O Israel, to the LORD your God.
Your sins have been your downfall!
2 Take words with you
and return to the LORD.
Say to him:
"Forgive all our sins
and receive us graciously,
that we may offer the fruit of our lips.[b]

[a] 14 Hebrew *Sheol* [b] 2 Or *offer our lips as sacrifices of bulls*

(13:14) This promise finds its fulfillment in You, Lord Jesus Christ, our Savior. Risen Lord, how great is Your victory! You have vanquished every foe. Death itself is the final enemy. The terror of the grave once overwhelmed us, enslaving our hearts with fear. But Your victory is complete, Lord Jesus, for You have triumphed over the grave. We praise You, Lord, for You have given us new birth, into a living hope, through Your glorious resurrection. (1Co 15:26, 55–57; Heb 2:15; 1Pe 1:3).

Oh God, most high,
Almighty King,
The champion of heaven,
Lord of everything,
You've fought, You've won,
Death's lost its sting,
And standing in Your victory
We sing.

You have broken the chains
That held our captive souls.
You have broken the chains
And used them on Your foes.
All Your enemies are bound,
They tremble at the sound of
Your name.
Jesus, You have broken the chains.

"You Have Broken the Chains"
Jamie Owens-Collins (©1991)

Confession, which means to agree with God regarding our sin, restores our fellowship. It is a form of discipline which God requires.

Erwin W. Lutzer (1941-)

(14:2–4) Thank you, merciful Father, for hearing us when we call. You receive us and restore us when we come to You in repentance. You freely give Your love to us, pouring it out on us without measure and without price. All of us may come, rich and poor alike, for all that You require of us are words—something every one of us can afford—heartfelt words of confession and repentance. You ask for words because You are a God Who hears. So receive my prayer, Lord. Hear me when I call out to You. I forsake all others, and I look to You alone for salvation. Cleanse my heart, Lord, and let the fruit of my lips bring You honor and not disgrace. (1Co 13:5; Heb 13:15; 1Jn 1:9)

(14:5) You see everything so clearly, Lord. You see what we are. You see what we may become by Your grace. You speak with words that tell us what grace can do. You called Israel a blossoming lily, a cedar of Lebanon. You call Your church a holy temple, Your people saints. It is more than wishful thinking—it is a pronouncement that shapes reality; a new creation You form by Your grace, power and presence. Come now, Lord, and be like the dew of heaven to our thirsty souls. Let us see what grace can do.

O to grace how great a debtor
Daily I'm constrained to be!
Let Thy goodness, like a fetter,
Bind my wandering heart to Thee:
Prone to wander, Lord, I feel it,
Prone to leave the God I love;
Here's my heart, O take and seal it;
Seal it for Thy courts above.

"Come Thou Fount of Every Blessing"
Robert Robinson (1758)

3 Assyria cannot save us;
we will not mount war-horses.
We will never again say 'Our gods'
to what our own hands have made,
for in you the fatherless find compassion."

4 "I will heal their waywardness
and love them freely,
for my anger has turned away from them.
5 I will be like the dew to Israel;
he will blossom like a lily.
Like a cedar of Lebanon
he will send down his roots;
6 his young shoots will grow.
His splendor will be like an olive tree,
his fragrance like a cedar of Lebanon.
7 Men will dwell again in his shade.
He will flourish like the grain.
He will blossom like a vine,
and his fame will be like the wine from Lebanon.
8 O Ephraim, what more have I[a] to do with idols?
I will answer him and care for him.
I am like a green pine tree;
your fruitfulness comes from me."

9 Who is wise? He will realize these things.
Who is discerning? He will understand them.
The ways of the LORD are right;
the righteous walk in them,
but the rebellious stumble in them.

[a] 8 Or *What more has Ephraim*

MY BELOVED

Others are watching you, wondering if your heart really belongs to Me. Do you know how they determine if you are My child? They look for evidence of our relationship. This evidence is love, joy, peace, patience, kindness, goodness, gentleness and self-control. They are also watching for your faithfulness.

But these qualities of character do not simply appear, nor do they grow through the force of your will. They are like fruit, and they grow into your life as a result of your being related to Me. You cannot bear this kind of fruit unless you are connected to Me. So do not leave Me.

When love, joy, peace, patience, kindness, goodness, faithfulness, gentleness and self-control are evident in your life, I am glorified. And I want everyone to know that you belong to Me. I am proud of you.

Jesus, My Son, summed up the key to developing these qualities. His commandment to you is this: Love others as I have loved you. If you heed His teaching, He will help you develop the qualities of character that prove to the world that you are Mine.

Hos 14:8; Jn 15:4-1; Gal 5:22; 1Jn 4:12

The Book of JOEL

The book of Joel begins with the horrible devastation of a locust plague (ch. 1). Yet this natural disaster turns out to be a "great army" sent by the Lord to bring judgment upon His rebellious people (2:25). Moreover, the invading locusts prefigure an even more insidious invasion as a powerful nation prepares to overthrow Israel. These signs point to the imminence of "the day of the LORD"—a day of "destruction from the Almighty" (1:15).

Joel introduces God as the Lord of creation who commands all of nature, including armies of locusts (2:23). God's awesome power, when coupled with His righteous judgment, brings all who sin to their knees in repentance: " 'Even now,' declares the LORD, 'return to me with all your heart, with fasting and weeping and mourning.' Rend your heart and not your garments. Return to the LORD your God, for he is gracious and compassionate, slow to anger and abounding in love" (2:12–13). Our repentance is a response, not only to God's painful judgment but also to His gracious love. We who know God through Jesus Christ abandon our sins and turn to Him, not because we fear His punishment but because we are overwhelmed by what Christ has done on the cross.

Joel calls us to genuine repentance—not to external displays that lack internal authenticity. However, Joel reminds us that public worship is essential to a complete response to God: "Blow the trumpet in Zion, declare a holy fast, call a sacred assembly. Gather the people, consecrate the assembly" (2:15–16). Lest we turn repentance into a comfortably individualistic activity, Joel urges us to keep private and public worship in balance. As we strive for ardent repentance, we are often encouraged by corporate expressions of sorrow over sin.

> **Public worship is essential to a complete response to God . . . Joel urges us to keep private and public worship in balance.**

Through Joel, God promises a new season of spiritual blessing: "And afterward, I will pour out my Spirit on all people. Your sons and daughters will prophesy . . . And everyone who calls on the name of the LORD will be saved" (2:28,32). This promise is fulfilled on the day of Pentecost, when the Holy Spirit is poured out upon the first followers of Jesus (Ac 2). The Good News for Christians is that, through faith in Jesus, we can receive the outpouring of the Spirit of God, the Spirit who helps us to worship "in spirit and in truth" (Jn 4:23–24; Ro 8:9–11).

God promises salvation to "everyone who calls on the name of the LORD" (2:32). The phrase "to call on the name of the LORD" connotes more than crying out to God in prayer. It is used in Scripture to describe divine worship (Ps 116:17; Zep 3:9–10). Salvation will be granted to "everyone," both Jew and Gentile, who calls upon God's name in genuine worship. As Christians, our worship celebrates God's salvation even as it draws us ever more deeply into the daily experience of saving grace.

1 The word of the LORD that came to Joel son of Pethuel.

An Invasion of Locusts

2 Hear this, you elders;
listen, all who live in the land.
Has anything like this ever happened in your days
or in the days of your forefathers?
3 Tell it to your children,
and let your children tell it to their children,
and their children to the next generation.
4 What the locust swarm has left
the great locusts have eaten;
what the great locusts have left
the young locusts have eaten;
what the young locusts have left
other locusts[a] have eaten.

5 Wake up, you drunkards, and weep!
Wail, all you drinkers of wine;
wail because of the new wine,
for it has been snatched from your lips.
6 A nation has invaded my land,
powerful and without number;
it has the teeth of a lion,
the fangs of a lioness.
7 It has laid waste my vines
and ruined my fig trees.
It has stripped off their bark
and thrown it away,
leaving their branches white.

8 Mourn like a virgin[b] in sackcloth
grieving for the husband[c] of her youth.
9 Grain offerings and drink offerings
are cut off from the house of the LORD.
The priests are in mourning,
those who minister before the LORD.
10 The fields are ruined,
the ground is dried up[d];
the grain is destroyed,
the new wine is dried up,
the oil fails.
11 Despair, you farmers,
wail, you vine growers;
grieve for the wheat and the barley,
because the harvest of the field is destroyed.
12 The vine is dried up
and the fig tree is withered;
the pomegranate, the palm and the apple tree—
all the trees of the field—are dried up.
Surely the joy of mankind
is withered away.

A Call to Repentance

13 Put on sackcloth, O priests, and mourn;
wail, you who minister before the altar.

[a] 4 The precise meaning of the four Hebrew words used here for locusts is uncertain.
[b] 8 Or *young woman* [c] 8 Or *betrothed* [d] 10 Or *ground mourns*

(1:1–12) Merciful Father, I see on these pages the dire consequences of sin. Yet I hear in the words of this prophet the sighs of a broken-hearted God. How it grieves You to see us in distress! You have such bountiful goodness in store for us, yet we turn our backs on You. When we turn from Your face, we also turn from Your hand. When we rebel against our provider, we also rebel against our protector. What peace we forfeit! What pain we bear! What loss we suffer! Yet You seem to mourn the loss even more than we do, because You know how things could be, indeed, how they *should* be, if only we would cling to You. I thank You, Father, that even in Your discipline Your love is evident. You always do what is best, even when it brings You sorrow. Hold me close to You, so that Your tears will not be wasted on an unrepentant heart.

The kingdom of God is challenge and
choice;
Believe the good news, repent and
rejoice!
His love for us sinners brought
Christ to His cross,
Our crisis of judgment for gain or
for loss.
"The Kingdom of God Is Justice and Joy"
Bryn Austin Rees (©1973)

Come, spend the night in sackcloth,
you who minister before my God;
for the grain offerings and drink offerings
are withheld from the house of your God.
14 Declare a holy fast;
call a sacred assembly.
Summon the elders
and all who live in the land
to the house of the LORD your God,
and cry out to the LORD.

15 Alas for that day!
For the day of the LORD is near;
it will come like destruction from the Almighty.[a]

16 Has not the food been cut off
before our very eyes—
joy and gladness
from the house of our God?
17 The seeds are shriveled
beneath the clods.[b]
The storehouses are in ruins,
the granaries have been broken down,
for the grain has dried up.
18 How the cattle moan!
The herds mill about
because they have no pasture;
even the flocks of sheep are suffering.

19 To you, O LORD, I call,
for fire has devoured the open pastures
and flames have burned up all the trees of the field.
20 Even the wild animals pant for you;
the streams of water have dried up
and fire has devoured the open pastures.

An Army of Locusts

2 Blow the trumpet in Zion;
sound the alarm on my holy hill.
Let all who live in the land tremble,
for the day of the LORD is coming.
It is close at hand—
2 a day of darkness and gloom,
a day of clouds and blackness.
Like dawn spreading across the mountains
a large and mighty army comes,
such as never was of old
nor ever will be in ages to come.

3 Before them fire devours,
behind them a flame blazes.
Before them the land is like the garden of Eden,
behind them, a desert waste—
nothing escapes them.
4 They have the appearance of horses;
they gallop along like cavalry.
5 With a noise like that of chariots

[a] 15 Hebrew *Shaddai* [b] 17 The meaning of the Hebrew for this word is uncertain.

Speak to him, thou, for he hears, and
Spirit with spirit can meet–
Closer is he than breathing, and nearer than hands and feet.
Alfred, Lord Tennyson (1809–1892)

(1:13–20) Gracious Father, how You long to give us life. But our sin has stripped us of our sensitivity and our sensibility. The seed of the Word has shriveled in the hard ground of our hearts; the fruit of our lips has died on the vine. How foolish we have been to turn away from You. Help us to feel Your sorrow over our loss of intimacy with You—to mourn the loss like a death. Call to us, woo us, draw us back to Your dwelling place—the place of fellowship and fruitfulness, of joy and gladness. Restore us to a right relationship with You, so that we may bring You the sacrifice of praise, the offering of contrition and the prayer of repentance. (Heb 13:15)

(2:1–5) Truly You are the Lord of hosts—for You marshal the hosts of heaven and the hosts of nature to do Your work and serve Your purposes. You are great and awesome, holy and all-powerful. Yet You are gracious and righteous, full of love and compassion. We praise You for Your great mercy. Your judgments could come without warning, but You warn us because You do not want to wound us. You do not delight in judgment, nor do You take joy in vengeance. You want all of us to be saved and to come to the knowledge of the truth.

(2:12–17) Thank You for loving us enough to call us to repentance. Thank You for the marvelous gift of forgiveness. Make us open and vulnerable before Your throne of grace. Teach us to bare our hearts in Your presence and to come to You in true humility and brokenness. Cleanse us as only You can. We are incredibly blessed to have a heavenly Father Who is filled with such compassion toward us. We praise Your holy name.

To the barren house He comes
To make of it a home;
Praise to the Lord,
Praise His name.

To the empty heart He calls,
Saying, "Come and be My own;"
Praise to the Lord,
Praise His name.

Praise to the One who is High,
Above every nation;
Who has raised us from the dust
To reign with Him.
Praise to the One who is Lord,
Above all creation;
Praise to the Lord,
Praise His name.

"Praise to the Lord"
Morris Chapman and
Claire Cloninger (©1986)

they leap over the mountaintops,
like a crackling fire consuming stubble,
like a mighty army drawn up for battle.

6 At the sight of them, nations are in anguish;
every face turns pale.
7 They charge like warriors;
they scale walls like soldiers.
They all march in line,
not swerving from their course.
8 They do not jostle each other;
each marches straight ahead.
They plunge through defenses
without breaking ranks.
9 They rush upon the city;
they run along the wall.
They climb into the houses;
like thieves they enter through the windows.

10 Before them the earth shakes,
the sky trembles,
the sun and moon are darkened,
and the stars no longer shine.
11 The LORD thunders
at the head of his army;
his forces are beyond number,
and mighty are those who obey his command.
The day of the LORD is great;
it is dreadful.
Who can endure it?

Rend Your Heart

12 "Even now," declares the LORD,
"return to me with all your heart,
with fasting and weeping and mourning."

13 Rend your heart
and not your garments.
Return to the LORD your God,
for he is gracious and compassionate,
slow to anger and abounding in love,
and he relents from sending calamity.
14 Who knows? He may turn and have pity
and leave behind a blessing—
grain offerings and drink offerings
for the LORD your God.

15 Blow the trumpet in Zion,
declare a holy fast,
call a sacred assembly.
16 Gather the people,
consecrate the assembly;
bring together the elders,
gather the children,
those nursing at the breast.
Let the bridegroom leave his room
and the bride her chamber.
17 Let the priests, who minister before the LORD,
weep between the temple porch and the altar.

Let them say, "Spare your people, O LORD.
Do not make your inheritance an object of scorn,
a byword among the nations.
Why should they say among the peoples,
'Where is their God?' "

The LORD's Answer

18 Then the LORD will be jealous for his land
and take pity on his people.

19 The LORD will reply[a] to them:

"I am sending you grain, new wine and oil,
enough to satisfy you fully;
never again will I make you
an object of scorn to the nations.

20 "I will drive the northern army far from you,
pushing it into a parched and barren land,
with its front columns going into the eastern sea[b]
and those in the rear into the western sea.[c]
And its stench will go up;
its smell will rise."

Surely he has done great things.[d]
21 Be not afraid, O land;
be glad and rejoice.
Surely the LORD has done great things.
22 Be not afraid, O wild animals,
for the open pastures are becoming green.
The trees are bearing their fruit;
the fig tree and the vine yield their riches.
23 Be glad, O people of Zion,
rejoice in the LORD your God,
for he has given you
the autumn rains in righteousness.[e]
He sends you abundant showers,
both autumn and spring rains, as before.
24 The threshing floors will be filled with grain;
the vats will overflow with new wine and oil.

25 "I will repay you for the years the locusts have eaten—
the great locust and the young locust,
the other locusts and the locust swarm[f]—
my great army that I sent among you.
26 You will have plenty to eat, until you are full,
and you will praise the name of the LORD your God,
who has worked wonders for you;
never again will my people be shamed.
27 Then you will know that I am in Israel,
that I am the LORD your God,
and that there is no other;
never again will my people be shamed.

[a] *18,19* Or *LORD was jealous . . . / and took pity . . . / 19The LORD replied* [b] *20* That is, the Dead Sea [c] *20* That is, the Mediterranean [d] *20* Or *rise. / Surely it has done great things."* [e] *23* Or / *the teacher for righteousness:* [f] *25* The precise meaning of the four Hebrew words used here for locusts is uncertain.

(2:18–27) What an honor it is to worship a jealous God. You alone are worthy of praise. You anticipate our repentance and extend Your loving arms to us. With eagerness You long for the day when You will restore to us all that has been withheld for the sake of our correction. Our praises rise up to You, the One and only Lord God Almighty.

Great is Thy faithfulness,
O God my Father,
There is no shadow of turning with Thee;
Thou changest not,
Thy compassions they fail not;
As Thou hast been Thou forever wilt be.

Great is Thy faithfulness!
Great is Thy faithfulness!
Morning by morning new mercies I see
All I have needed Thy hand hath provided
Great is Thy faithfulness
Lord unto me!

"Great is Thy Faithfulness"
Thomas Obadiah Chisholm (©1923, 1951)

The great King, immortal, invisible, the divine person called the Holy Ghost, the Holy Spirit: it is he that quickens the soul, or else it would lie dead forever; it is he that makes it tender, or else it would never feel; it is he that imparts efficacy to the Word preached, or else it could never reach farther than the ear; it is he who breaks the heart; it is he who makes it whole.
Charles Haddon Spurgeon (1834-1892)

(2:28–29) Holy Spirit, God of comfort and counsel, fall afresh on me. Give me the mind of Christ so that I may know Your thoughts and dream Your dreams. Grant me vision to see things the way You see them. Fill my mouth with the Word of truth so that I may declare Your greatness to the world.

O Breath of Life, come sweeping
through us,
Revive your church with life and
power;
O Breath of Life, come, cleanse,
renew us,
And fit your church to meet this
hour.

O Breath of Love, come breathe
within us,
Renewing thought and will and
heart;
Come, Love of Christ, afresh to win
us,
Revive your church in every part!
"O Breath of Life"
Elizabeth Ann P. Head (c.1914)

The Day of the LORD

28 "And afterward,
I will pour out my Spirit on all people.
Your sons and daughters will prophesy,
your old men will dream dreams,
your young men will see visions.
29 Even on my servants, both men and women,
I will pour out my Spirit in those days.
30 I will show wonders in the heavens
and on the earth,
blood and fire and billows of smoke.
31 The sun will be turned to darkness
and the moon to blood
before the coming of the great and dreadful day of
the LORD.
32 And everyone who calls
on the name of the LORD will be saved;
for on Mount Zion and in Jerusalem
there will be deliverance,
as the LORD has said,
among the survivors
whom the LORD calls.

The Nations Judged

3 "In those days and at that time,
when I restore the fortunes of Judah and Jerusalem,
2 I will gather all nations
and bring them down to the Valley of Jehoshaphat.[a]
There I will enter into judgment against them
concerning my inheritance, my people Israel,
for they scattered my people among the nations
and divided up my land.
3 They cast lots for my people
and traded boys for prostitutes;
they sold girls for wine
that they might drink.

4 "Now what have you against me, O Tyre and Sidon and all you
regions of Philistia? Are you repaying me for something I have
done? If you are paying me back, I will swiftly and speedily return
on your own heads what you have done. 5 For you took my silver
and my gold and carried off my finest treasures to your temples.
6 You sold the people of Judah and Jerusalem to the Greeks, that
you might send them far from their homeland.

7 "See, I am going to rouse them out of the places to which you
sold them, and I will return on your own heads what you have
done. 8 I will sell your sons and daughters to the people of Judah,
and they will sell them to the Sabeans, a nation far away." The
LORD has spoken.

9 Proclaim this among the nations:
Prepare for war!
Rouse the warriors!
Let all the fighting men draw near and attack.
10 Beat your plowshares into swords
and your pruning hooks into spears.

[a] 2 *Jehoshaphat* means *the LORD judges*; also in verse 12.

Let the weakling say,
"I am strong!"
11 Come quickly, all you nations from every side,
and assemble there.

Bring down your warriors, O LORD!

12 "Let the nations be roused;
let them advance into the Valley of Jehoshaphat,
for there I will sit
to judge all the nations on every side.
13 Swing the sickle,
for the harvest is ripe.
Come, trample the grapes,
for the winepress is full
and the vats overflow—
so great is their wickedness!"

14 Multitudes, multitudes
in the valley of decision!
For the day of the LORD is near
in the valley of decision.
15 The sun and moon will be darkened,
and the stars no longer shine.
16 The LORD will roar from Zion
and thunder from Jerusalem;
the earth and the sky will tremble.
But the LORD will be a refuge for his people,
a stronghold for the people of Israel.

Blessings for God's People

17 "Then you will know that I, the LORD your God,
dwell in Zion, my holy hill.
Jerusalem will be holy;
never again will foreigners invade her.

18 "In that day the mountains will drip new wine,
and the hills will flow with milk;
all the ravines of Judah will run with water.
A fountain will flow out of the LORD's house
and will water the valley of acacias.[a]
19 But Egypt will be desolate,
Edom a desert waste,
because of violence done to the people of Judah,
in whose land they shed innocent blood.
20 Judah will be inhabited forever
and Jerusalem through all generations.
21 Their bloodguilt, which I have not pardoned,
I will pardon."

The LORD dwells in Zion!

[a] 18 Or *Valley of Shittim*

(3:14–16) You are my hiding place, Lord. Thank You that in the day of judgment I need not fear; but rather, I rest secure in Christ. Even though I live for a time in a world that is dark and lost, You shelter me with Your love and light my way with Your Word of truth.

Lord, You are my refuge,
You are my hiding place.
Oh Lord, You are my refuge,
And I will rest in Your saving grace.

You're the Rock of my Salvation,
You're the One who calms the storm;
Lord, You set my feet on higher ground.
I will worship and adore You,
I will lift my voice on high,
For only in Your presence will I find . . .

Lord, You are my refuge,
You are my hiding place.
Oh Lord, You are my refuge,
And I will rest in Your saving grace.

"You Are My Refuge"
Lenny LeBlanc and Greg Gulley (©1990)

(3:18) Lord, out of Your house flows an endless supply of grace, a fountain of living water that springs up before us, turning our barrenness into fruitfulness. O merciful and loving God, thank You for Your patience and for Your great faithfulness to us. Thank You for abundant grace and abundant life in Christ. Keep us ever thankful for the many blessings that You provide. (Jn 7:37–38)

The Book of AMOS

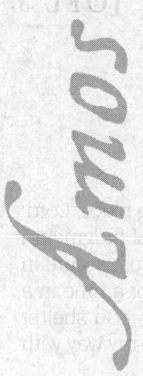

"The LORD roars from Zion and thunders from Jerusalem" (1:2). With this unsettling image, the book of Amos introduces the God who speaks and acts with the awesome power of a ferocious lion. Our encounter with God through Amos shakes us loose from any presumption that He lives tamely within our control like some domesticated kitty. Indeed, the Lion of Judah deserves and demands our rapt attention and reverential fear.

The book of Amos begins with God's judgment on Israel's neighbors (ch. 1). No limited national deity, the King of kings has the authority to execute justice upon all peoples. Yet by beginning with condemnation of Gentiles, God does not thereby excuse His covenant people. Judah will experience God's wrath for failing to keep the law and for serving false gods (2:4–5). Israel will be crushed for the sins of social injustice, sexual immorality and spiritual idolatry (2:6–16). Sadly, the people have rejected every divine effort to provoke repentance (4:1–13). No matter what God has done, His people have not returned to Him (4:6 8,9,10,11).

Yet the Lord continues to cry out through Amos, saying: "Seek me and live" (5:4). To seek Him is to turn away from sin and to return to covenant faithfulness. Seeking God, central to the heart of worship, must also be expressed through obedient actions. Thus Amos can add to God's intimate invitation: "Seek good, not evil, that you may live. Then the LORD God Almighty will be with you, just as you say he is" (5:14). We cannot pursue a relationship with a righteous, commanding God while ignoring His righteous commandments. Even as we strive to worship God with all of our heart, we must remember that genuine, heartfelt worship will be expressed in tangible acts of obedience.

Even as we strive to worship God with all of our heart, we must remember that genuine, heartfelt worship will be expressed in tangible acts of obedience.

In particular, the Lord challenges us through Amos to serve Him by acting justly in this world. As God declares, "I hate, I despise your religious feasts; I cannot stand your assemblies. Even though you bring me burnt offerings and grain offerings, I will not accept them. Though you bring choice fellowship offerings, I will have no regard for them. Away with the noise of your songs! I will not listen to the music of your harps. But let justice roll on like a river, righteousness like a never-failing stream!" (5:21–24). God hates worship that lacks heartfelt authenticity and is divorced from tangible acts of justice and righteousness. If we "oppress the poor and crush the needy" (4:1) we will fail to honor God, no matter how noble our expressions of worship. Conversely, when we care for the downtrodden in the name of Christ, we serve Christ Himself (Mt 25:31:46). Through Amos, God calls us to worship Him with active obedience and a commitment to seeking justice for all, especially for those whom society ignores or marginalizes. Fully Biblical worship flows from the heart, up to God's throne of grace, and out into the world He loves.

1 The words of Amos, one of the shepherds of Tekoa—what he saw concerning Israel two years before the earthquake, when Uzziah was king of Judah and Jeroboam son of Jehoash[a] was king of Israel.

2 He said:

"The LORD roars from Zion
and thunders from Jerusalem;
the pastures of the shepherds dry up,[b]
and the top of Carmel withers."

Judgment on Israel's Neighbors

3 This is what the LORD says:

"For three sins of Damascus,
even for four, I will not turn back ⌞my wrath⌟.
Because she threshed Gilead
with sledges having iron teeth,
4 I will send fire upon the house of Hazael
that will consume the fortresses of Ben-Hadad.
5 I will break down the gate of Damascus;
I will destroy the king who is in[c] the Valley of Aven[d]
and the one who holds the scepter in Beth Eden.
The people of Aram will go into exile to Kir,"
says the LORD.

6 This is what the LORD says:

"For three sins of Gaza,
even for four, I will not turn back ⌞my wrath⌟.
Because she took captive whole communities
and sold them to Edom,
7 I will send fire upon the walls of Gaza
that will consume her fortresses.
8 I will destroy the king[e] of Ashdod
and the one who holds the scepter in Ashkelon.
I will turn my hand against Ekron,
till the last of the Philistines is dead,"
says the Sovereign LORD.

9 This is what the LORD says:

"For three sins of Tyre,
even for four, I will not turn back ⌞my wrath⌟.
Because she sold whole communities of captives to Edom,
disregarding a treaty of brotherhood,
10 I will send fire upon the walls of Tyre
that will consume her fortresses."

11 This is what the LORD says:

"For three sins of Edom,
even for four, I will not turn back ⌞my wrath⌟.
Because he pursued his brother with a sword,
stifling all compassion,[f]
because his anger raged continually
and his fury flamed unchecked,

[a] 1 Hebrew *Joash*, a variant of *Jehoash* [b] 2 Or *shepherds mourn* [c] 5 Or *the inhabitants of* [d] 5 *Aven* means *wickedness.* [e] 8 Or *inhabitants* [f] 11 Or *sword / and destroyed his allies*

(1:2) Your word, O Lord, roars with the awesomeness of a lion. Your voice thunders with the fury of a storm. Your revelation calls us to listen, to tremble, to obey, to bow in reverence before Your majesty. "Ascribe to the LORD, O mighty ones, ascribe to the LORD glory and strength. Ascribe to the LORD the glory due his name; worship the LORD in the splendor of his holiness. The voice of the LORD is over the waters; the God of glory thunders, the LORD thunders over the mighty waters. The voice of the LORD is powerful; the voice of the LORD is majestic." With all who hear Your voice, we worship You, crying: "Glory! Glory! Glory be to our mighty God!" (Ps 29:1–10)

God the Omnipotent! King who ordainest
Thunder Thy clarion, the lightning Thy sword;
Show forth Thy pity on high where Thou reignest;
Give to us peace in our time, O Lord.

God the All-merciful! Earth hath forsaken
Meekness and mercy, and slighted Thy Word;
Let not Thy wrath in its terrors awaken;
Give to us peace in our time, O Lord.

"God the Omnipotent"
Henry F. Chorley and John Ellerton (1842)

(1:12–2:8) "The Lord reigns, let the nations tremble"! In Your righteousness, O God, You pronounce judgment upon all nations for their sins. Your censure falls even upon Your chosen people, those whom You love as Your children. No matter who we are, all of us "have sinned and fall short of the glory of God." Yet in Your matchless mercy, You have been both just and justifying, both the righteous Judge and the One who receives the punishment. You have made Your sinless Son to be sin, so that in Him we might become Your righteousness! Even as we tremble before Your sovereignty, so we also exalt You and worship at Your footstool, for You are holy. (Ps 99:1–5; Ro 3:23; 2Co 5:21)

Will you begin to look at sin as an offense against a holy God, instead of as a personal defeat only? . . .

This is where holiness begins—not with ourselves, but with God. It is only as we see His holiness, His absolute purity and moral hatred of sin, that we will be gripped by the awfulness of sin against the Holy God. To be gripped by that fact is the first step in our pursuit of holiness.

Jerry Bridges (1929-)

12 I will send fire upon Teman
that will consume the fortresses of Bozrah."

13 This is what the LORD says:

"For three sins of Ammon,
even for four, I will not turn back ⌊my wrath⌋.
Because he ripped open the pregnant women of Gilead
in order to extend his borders,
14 I will set fire to the walls of Rabbah
that will consume her fortresses
amid war cries on the day of battle,
amid violent winds on a stormy day.
15 Her king[a] will go into exile,
he and his officials together,"
says the LORD.

2 This is what the LORD says:

"For three sins of Moab,
even for four, I will not turn back ⌊my wrath⌋.
Because he burned, as if to lime,
the bones of Edom's king,
2 I will send fire upon Moab
that will consume the fortresses of Kerioth.[b]
Moab will go down in great tumult
amid war cries and the blast of the trumpet.
3 I will destroy her ruler
and kill all her officials with him,"
says the LORD.

4 This is what the LORD says:

"For three sins of Judah,
even for four, I will not turn back ⌊my wrath⌋.
Because they have rejected the law of the LORD
and have not kept his decrees,
because they have been led astray by false gods,[c]
the gods[d] their ancestors followed,
5 I will send fire upon Judah
that will consume the fortresses of Jerusalem."

Judgment on Israel

6 This is what the LORD says:

"For three sins of Israel,
even for four, I will not turn back ⌊my wrath⌋.
They sell the righteous for silver,
and the needy for a pair of sandals.
7 They trample on the heads of the poor
as upon the dust of the ground
and deny justice to the oppressed.
Father and son use the same girl
and so profane my holy name.
8 They lie down beside every altar
on garments taken in pledge.

[a] 15 Or / *Molech*; Hebrew *malcam* [b] 2 Or *of her cities* [c] 4 Or *by lies*
[d] 4 Or *lies*

In the house of their god
they drink wine taken as fines.

9 "I destroyed the Amorite before them,
though he was tall as the cedars
and strong as the oaks.
I destroyed his fruit above
and his roots below.

10 "I brought you up out of Egypt,
and I led you forty years in the desert
to give you the land of the Amorites.
11 I also raised up prophets from among your sons
and Nazirites from among your young men.
Is this not true, people of Israel?"
declares the LORD.

12 "But you made the Nazirites drink wine
and commanded the prophets not to prophesy.

13 "Now then, I will crush you
as a cart crushes when loaded with grain.
14 The swift will not escape,
the strong will not muster their strength,
and the warrior will not save his life.
15 The archer will not stand his ground,
the fleet-footed soldier will not get away,
and the horseman will not save his life.
16 Even the bravest warriors
will flee naked on that day,"
declares the LORD.

Witnesses Summoned Against Israel

3 Hear this word the LORD has spoken against you, O people of Israel—against the whole family I brought up out of Egypt:

2 "You only have I chosen
of all the families of the earth;
therefore I will punish you
for all your sins."

3 Do two walk together
unless they have agreed to do so?
4 Does a lion roar in the thicket
when he has no prey?
Does he growl in his den
when he has caught nothing?
5 Does a bird fall into a trap on the ground
where no snare has been set?
Does a trap spring up from the earth
when there is nothing to catch?
6 When a trumpet sounds in a city,
do not the people tremble?
When disaster comes to a city,
has not the LORD caused it?

7 Surely the Sovereign LORD does nothing
without revealing his plan
to his servants the prophets.

8 The lion has roared—
who will not fear?

(3:1–9) Even in Your wrath, Lord, You graciously warn us to turn away from our sin. Time and again You caution us, counsel us, cajole us. You never punish without first giving us every opportunity to repent. O God, help us to listen to you! Draw us away from the distractions and diversions that keep us from responding to Your voice. Open our ears to Your words of warning, so that we might respond in repentance and obedience. Thank You, dear Lord, for Your merciful efforts to keep us walking in Your righteous paths.

(3:11–4:3) O God, like Your people in Israel, we can become complacent and self-satisfied. And like the Christians in Laodicea, we sometimes go through the motions of religiosity, while deep in our hearts we congratulate ourselves, saying, "I am rich; I have acquired wealth and do not need a thing." Gracious Lord, when we glory in our attainments, give us eyes to see that we too are "wretched, pitiful, poor, blind and naked." Give us a portion of Your gold, Lord—gold of the Spirit, refined in Your fire. Dress us in Your robes of righteousness to cover our nakedness. Put Your salve upon our eyes. Grant that we might see ourselves in our great need of You, so that we might also see You as the great God Who meets our deepest needs. (Rev 3:14–18)

Apathy, selfishness and complacency blossom everywhere in the world except at the cross. There these noxious weeds shrivel and die. They are seen for the tatty, poisonous things they are. For if there was no way by which the righteous God could righteously forgive our unrighteousness, except that he should bear it himself in Christ, it must be serious indeed. It is only when we see this that, stripped of our self-righteousness and self-satisfaction, we are ready to put our trust in Jesus Christ as the Saviour we urgently need.

John R. W. Stott (1921-)

The Sovereign LORD has spoken—
who can but prophesy?

9 Proclaim to the fortresses of Ashdod
and to the fortresses of Egypt:
"Assemble yourselves on the mountains of Samaria;
see the great unrest within her
and the oppression among her people."

10 "They do not know how to do right," declares the LORD,
"who hoard plunder and loot in their fortresses."

11 Therefore this is what the Sovereign LORD says:

"An enemy will overrun the land;
he will pull down your strongholds
and plunder your fortresses."

12 This is what the LORD says:

"As a shepherd saves from the lion's mouth
only two leg bones or a piece of an ear,
so will the Israelites be saved,
those who sit in Samaria
on the edge of their beds
and in Damascus on their couches.[a]"

13 "Hear this and testify against the house of Jacob," declares the Lord, the LORD God Almighty.

14 "On the day I punish Israel for her sins,
I will destroy the altars of Bethel;
the horns of the altar will be cut off
and fall to the ground.
15 I will tear down the winter house
along with the summer house;
the houses adorned with ivory will be destroyed
and the mansions will be demolished,"
declares the LORD.

Israel Has Not Returned to God

4 Hear this word, you cows of Bashan on Mount Samaria,
you women who oppress the poor and crush the needy
and say to your husbands, "Bring us some drinks!"
2 The Sovereign LORD has sworn by his holiness:
"The time will surely come
when you will be taken away with hooks,
the last of you with fishhooks.
3 You will each go straight out
through breaks in the wall,
and you will be cast out toward Harmon,[b]"
declares the LORD.

4 "Go to Bethel and sin;
go to Gilgal and sin yet more.
Bring your sacrifices every morning,
your tithes every three years.[c]

[a] *12* The meaning of the Hebrew for this line is uncertain. [b] *3* Masoretic Text; with a different word division of the Hebrew (see Septuagint) *out, O mountain of oppression*
[c] *4* Or *tithes on the third day*

5 Burn leavened bread as a thank offering
and brag about your freewill offerings—
boast about them, you Israelites,
for this is what you love to do,"
declares the Sovereign LORD.

6 "I gave you empty stomachs[a] in every city
and lack of bread in every town,
yet you have not returned to me,"
declares the LORD.

7 "I also withheld rain from you
when the harvest was still three months away.
I sent rain on one town,
but withheld it from another.
One field had rain;
another had none and dried up.
8 People staggered from town to town for water
but did not get enough to drink,
yet you have not returned to me,"
declares the LORD.

9 "Many times I struck your gardens and vineyards,
I struck them with blight and mildew.
Locusts devoured your fig and olive trees,
yet you have not returned to me,"
declares the LORD.

10 "I sent plagues among you
as I did to Egypt.
I killed your young men with the sword,
along with your captured horses.
I filled your nostrils with the stench of your camps,
yet you have not returned to me,"
declares the LORD.

11 "I overthrew some of you
as I[b] overthrew Sodom and Gomorrah.
You were like a burning stick snatched from the fire,
yet you have not returned to me,"
declares the LORD.

12 "Therefore this is what I will do to you, Israel,
and because I will do this to you,
prepare to meet your God, O Israel."

13 He who forms the mountains,
creates the wind,
and reveals his thoughts to man,
he who turns dawn to darkness,
and treads the high places of the earth—
the LORD God Almighty is his name.

A Lament and Call to Repentance

5 Hear this word, O house of Israel, this lament I take up concerning you:

2 "Fallen is Virgin Israel,
never to rise again,

[a] 6 Hebrew *you cleanness of teeth* [b] 11 Hebrew *God*

(4:6–11) O God, as a father disciplines those whom he loves, so You discipline Your people. Time and again You brought hardships upon the Israelites—not merely to punish them, but so that they would return to You. We confess that this is not something we welcome in our lives. Like Your ancient people, we too can misinterpret our struggles as evidence of Your absence from us, rather than as a sign of Your merciful presence. Thank You, gracious Father, for caring so much about us that You will not let us forever go astray. Thank You even for times of painful discipline. We praise You for growing in us "a harvest of righteousness and peace," so that we might walk forever in Your blessing. (Heb 12:5–11)

The correction that God gives is actually a remarkable sign of his great love for us. Jesus said, "Those whom I love I rebuke and discipline" (Rev. 3:19) . . . His reproofs are always loving, just, and perfect. He never rebukes us in anger, never seeks to harm us or belittle us. His correction is for our welfare, for our success, for our enlightenment. Because he knows all things, he knows that our unwise actions or thoughts will lead to our eventual destruction; and in his mercy and grace, he intervenes with his kind but firm reproof.

Charles Stanley (1932-)

Take Thou my heart,
I would be Thine alone;
Take Thou my heart
And make it all Thine own;
Purge me from sin,
O Lord, I now implore,
Wash me and keep me
Thine forevermore.

More Like the Master
Charles H. Gabriel (1906)

deserted in her own land,
with no one to lift her up."

3 This is what the Sovereign LORD says:

"The city that marches out a thousand strong for Israel
will have only a hundred left;
the town that marches out a hundred strong
will have only ten left."

4 This is what the LORD says to the house of Israel:

"Seek me and live;
5 do not seek Bethel,
do not go to Gilgal,
do not journey to Beersheba.
For Gilgal will surely go into exile,
and Bethel will be reduced to nothing.[a]"
6 Seek the LORD and live,
or he will sweep through the house of Joseph like a fire;
it will devour,
and Bethel will have no one to quench it.

7 You who turn justice into bitterness
and cast righteousness to the ground
8 (he who made the Pleiades and Orion,
who turns blackness into dawn
and darkens day into night,
who calls for the waters of the sea
and pours them out over the face of the land—
the LORD is his name—
9 he flashes destruction on the stronghold
and brings the fortified city to ruin),
10 you hate the one who reproves in court
and despise him who tells the truth.

11 You trample on the poor
and force him to give you grain.
Therefore, though you have built stone mansions,
you will not live in them;
though you have planted lush vineyards,
you will not drink their wine.
12 For I know how many are your offenses
and how great your sins.

You oppress the righteous and take bribes
and you deprive the poor of justice in the courts.
13 Therefore the prudent man keeps quiet in such times,
for the times are evil.

14 Seek good, not evil,
that you may live.
Then the LORD God Almighty will be with you,
just as you say he is.
15 Hate evil, love good;
maintain justice in the courts.

[a] 5 Or *grief*; or *wickedness*; Hebrew *aven*, a reference to Beth Aven (a derogatory name for Bethel)

O hope of every contrite heart,
O joy of all the meek,
To those who ask, how kind Thou art,
How good to those who seek!

"Jesus, the Very Thought of Thee"
Latin Hymn (12th c.)
Trans. Edward Caswall (1814-1878)

(5:4–6) Merciful God, even when Your people persist in their sin, You continue to reach out to them. "Seek me and live," You say, offering the possibility of repentance, forgiveness and renewal through relationship with Yourself. Thank You for giving me the offer of eternal life in Christ. Thank You for allowing me to seek You—and to find You. I praise You that You are a God Who goes so far beyond being merely available to those who seek You. Indeed, You are the Good Shepherd Who seeks and finds every one who is lost. How I love You, dear Lord, because You have found me. (Jer 29:13; Eze 34:11–16; Mt 7:7; Lk 15:3–7)

The overflowing love of Jesus is exquisite in its method of reclamation . . . Love seeks the lost. It goes out into the night and over the path and the by-paths of the day's grazing. It looks for the place of fascination and temptation, and for the precipice over which the sheep may have stumbled. It examines in the dim light twigs and brush, looks underneath willows and rushes for some trace of the wayward feet. It is all eyes and ears. Like a hound it scents the air; like the eagle it penetrates the lowest deeps. But it persists until at length, far removed among the underbrush and in the mire, the stray sheep is found. That is the gospel, as it comes sweeping direct from the heart of God.

Calvin Weiss Laufer (1874-1938)

Perhaps the LORD God Almighty will have mercy
on the remnant of Joseph.

16 Therefore this is what the Lord, the LORD God Almighty, says:

"There will be wailing in all the streets
and cries of anguish in every public square.
The farmers will be summoned to weep
and the mourners to wail.
17 There will be wailing in all the vineyards,
for I will pass through your midst,"
says the LORD.

The Day of the LORD

18 Woe to you who long
for the day of the LORD!
Why do you long for the day of the LORD?
That day will be darkness, not light.
19 It will be as though a man fled from a lion
only to meet a bear,
as though he entered his house
and rested his hand on the wall
only to have a snake bite him.
20 Will not the day of the LORD be darkness, not light—
pitch-dark, without a ray of brightness?

21 "I hate, I despise your religious feasts;
I cannot stand your assemblies.
22 Even though you bring me burnt offerings and grain
offerings,
I will not accept them.
Though you bring choice fellowship offerings,[a]
I will have no regard for them.
23 Away with the noise of your songs!
I will not listen to the music of your harps.
24 But let justice roll on like a river,
righteousness like a never-failing stream!

25 "Did you bring me sacrifices and offerings
forty years in the desert, O house of Israel?
26 You have lifted up the shrine of your king,
the pedestal of your idols,
the star of your god[b]—
which you made for yourselves.
27 Therefore I will send you into exile beyond
Damascus,"
says the LORD, whose name is God Almighty.

Woe to the Complacent

6 Woe to you who are complacent in Zion,
and to you who feel secure on Mount Samaria,
you notable men of the foremost nation,
to whom the people of Israel come!
2 Go to Calneh and look at it;
go from there to great Hamath,
and then go down to Gath in Philistia.

[a] 22 Traditionally *peace offerings* [b] 26 Or *lifted up Sakkuth your king / and Kaiwan your idols, / your star-gods*; Septuagint *lifted up the shrine of Molech / and the star of your god Rephan, / their idols*

(5:21–24) Your word through Amos is not easy or comfortable, Lord. It is a double-edged sword that cuts to the center of our own hearts. When we gather for joyful fellowship, when we lift up songs of praise, how do You feel, O holy God? If our worship of You is not completed in acts of righteousness, are You pleased with us? We confess how easy it us for us to worship You without allowing that experience to transform our lives. We admit that we can profess our love for You, yet fail to love our own brothers and sisters. Help us, God of Justice, to worship You in every way that You deserve—in joyful praise and in acts of charity, by proclaiming Your sovereignty and by serving the needy as though we were serving You. In our lives and in our churches, may Your justice roll on like a river, Your righteousness like a never-failing stream. (Isa 30:18; Mt 25:31–46; Heb 4:12; 1Jn 4:11–20)

Stretch out Your hand
And heal this nation,
Stretch out Your hand
And bring restoration.
Let Your mercy overflow us
Like a never failing stream,
By the blood of Jesus, cleanse us,
Oh Lord, it's You we seek.
Cause Your face to shine
Upon us again.

"Stretch Out Your Hand"
Scott V. Smith and
Malcolm duPlessis (©1995)

It is easier to fill the head than to prepare the heart. But heart drew the Son of God from heaven, and heart will draw people to heaven. The world desperately needs men and women of heart to sympathize with its woe, to kiss away its sorrows, to show compassion in its misery, to alleviate its pain. Christ was eminently the man of sorrows because he was pre-eminently the man of heart.

"Give me thine heart," is God's requisition of men (Proverbs 23:26 KJV). "Give me thine heart" is also humanity's demand of us.

E. M. Bounds (1835-1913)

(6:4–7) Like Your children in the time of Amos, many of us live in comfort and pleasure, Lord. We sleep in luxurious beds. We fill our lives with music and entertainment, enjoying the good things of Your creation. Yet elsewhere in the world—and sometimes in our own churches—Your people are not so well off as we. They wander hungry and homeless. They suffer brutal persecution for their faithfulness to You. Wake us from our self-centered slumber, that we might seek first Your kingdom and Your justice. Give us a heart for the poor, the persecuted, the lonely, the lost. Stir us to action, so that our worship might be "pure and faultless" as we care for all who need Your protection and deliverance. (Mt 6:33; 2Co 9:8–11; Jas 1:27)

Forgive us for our sin,
Cleanse us from within,
Purify our hearts,
Conform us to Your likeness.
In all of our ways,
Through each and every day,
May we be Your hands
Reaching out to save the world.

"Baptize Us With Your Love"
Kelly Willard (©1999)

Are they better off than your two kingdoms?
Is their land larger than yours?
3 You put off the evil day
and bring near a reign of terror.
4 You lie on beds inlaid with ivory
and lounge on your couches.
You dine on choice lambs
and fattened calves.
5 You strum away on your harps like David
and improvise on musical instruments.
6 You drink wine by the bowlful
and use the finest lotions,
but you do not grieve over the ruin of Joseph.
7 Therefore you will be among the first to go into exile;
your feasting and lounging will end.

The LORD Abhors the Pride of Israel

8 The Sovereign LORD has sworn by himself—the LORD God
Almighty declares:

"I abhor the pride of Jacob
and detest his fortresses;
I will deliver up the city
and everything in it."

9 If ten men are left in one house, they too will die. 10 And if a
relative who is to burn the bodies comes to carry them out of the
house and asks anyone still hiding there, "Is anyone with you?"
and he says, "No," then he will say, "Hush! We must not mention
the name of the LORD."

11 For the LORD has given the command,
and he will smash the great house into pieces
and the small house into bits.

12 Do horses run on the rocky crags?
Does one plow there with oxen?
But you have turned justice into poison
and the fruit of righteousness into bitterness—
13 you who rejoice in the conquest of Lo Debar[a]
and say, "Did we not take Karnaim[b] by our own strength?"

14 For the LORD God Almighty declares,
"I will stir up a nation against you, O house of Israel,
that will oppress you all the way
from Lebo[c] Hamath to the valley of the Arabah."

Locusts, Fire and a Plumb Line

7 This is what the Sovereign LORD showed me: He was preparing swarms of locusts after the king's share had been harvested and just as the second crop was coming up. 2 When they
had stripped the land clean, I cried out, "Sovereign LORD, forgive!
How can Jacob survive? He is so small!"
3 So the LORD relented.
"This will not happen," the LORD said.

[a] 13 *Lo Debar* means *nothing.* [b] 13 *Karnaim* means *horns*; *horn* here symbolizes strength. [c] 14 Or *from the entrance to*

4This is what the Sovereign LORD showed me: The Sovereign
LORD was calling for judgment by fire; it dried up the great deep
and devoured the land. 5Then I cried out, "Sovereign LORD, I beg
you, stop! How can Jacob survive? He is so small!"
6So the LORD relented.
"This will not happen either," the Sovereign LORD said.

7This is what he showed me: The Lord was standing by a wall
that had been built true to plumb, with a plumb line in his hand.
8And the LORD asked me, "What do you see, Amos?"
"A plumb line," I replied.
Then the Lord said, "Look, I am setting a plumb line among my
people Israel; I will spare them no longer.

9 "The high places of Isaac will be destroyed
 and the sanctuaries of Israel will be ruined;
 with my sword I will rise against the house of
 Jeroboam."

Amos and Amaziah

10Then Amaziah the priest of Bethel sent a message to Jeroboam king of Israel: "Amos is raising a conspiracy against you in the
very heart of Israel. The land cannot bear all his words. 11For this
is what Amos is saying:

" 'Jeroboam will die by the sword,
 and Israel will surely go into exile,
 away from their native land.' "

12Then Amaziah said to Amos, "Get out, you seer! Go back to
the land of Judah. Earn your bread there and do your prophesying there. 13Don't prophesy anymore at Bethel, because this is
the king's sanctuary and the temple of the kingdom."
14Amos answered Amaziah, "I was neither a prophet nor a
prophet's son, but I was a shepherd, and I also took care of sycamore-fig trees. 15But the LORD took me from tending the flock
and said to me, 'Go, prophesy to my people Israel.' 16Now then,
hear the word of the LORD. You say,

" 'Do not prophesy against Israel,
 and stop preaching against the house of Isaac.'

17"Therefore this is what the LORD says:

" 'Your wife will become a prostitute in the city,
 and your sons and daughters will fall by the sword.
Your land will be measured and divided up,
 and you yourself will die in a pagan[a] country.
And Israel will certainly go into exile,
 away from their native land.' "

A Basket of Ripe Fruit

8 This is what the Sovereign LORD showed me: a basket of ripe
fruit. 2"What do you see, Amos?" he asked.
"A basket of ripe fruit," I answered.
Then the LORD said to me, "The time is ripe for my people Israel; I will spare them no longer.
3"In that day," declares the Sovereign LORD, "the songs in the

[a] 17 Hebrew *an unclean*

(7:7–9) You are the Plumb Line, O Lord. You are the Standard by which all things are measured. You are the Absolute by which all relativities are judged. You are the Justice that guides all right judgments. You are the Goodness that teaches us to value all good things. You are true Beauty, Whose radiance shines in all that is lovely. You are "love divine, all loves excelling." You are "the Alpha and the Omega, the First and the Last, the Beginning and the End." All praise be to You, God of gods, King of kings, Lord of lords! (Rev 22:13)

(7:14–15) Thank You, Lord, for using ordinary people to do Your extraordinary work. Frequently those of us who are sent forth as Your messengers are much like Amos: We never intended to speak for You. Yet You dispatch Your chosen ambassadors unexpectedly. When we are minding other business, You call us and send us out with Your Word. When, like Amos, we heed Your call, but without obvious blessing, please comfort us with the knowledge that we have honored You in our obedience. Grant us the humility to leave the results of our service in Your sovereign care.

The Lord Jesus Christ claims the use of your body, your whole being, your complete personality, so that as you give yourself to Him through the eternal Spirit, He may give Himself to you through the eternal Spirit, that all your activity as a human being on earth may be His activity in and through you; that every step you take, every word you speak, everything you do, everything you are, may be an expression of Christ, in you as man.

Major W. Ian Thomas (1914-)

(8:11–12) O God, what worse famine could there be than to be deprived of Your Word? What thirst could be more horrible than to be denied Your living water? Apart from Your nourishment, we stagger about, famished and depleted. But, by Your grace, You offer us life-giving food; You give us water from a spring that will never be dried up. Dear Jesus, Bread of life, when we come to You, we will never be hungry! O Spring of living water, when we believe in You, we will never be thirsty again! (Jn 4:10–14; 6:35; 7:37)

You who are thirsty,
Come to the well and drink
From the waters flowing.
You who are hungry,
Come to the bread and eat
Of His holiness.
You who are tired, find rest.
You who are weak, find strength.
You who are thirsty,
Come to the well and drink.

He will freely feed,
All of them who are weak.
He will quench the righteous thirst
Of all who humbly seek.

"You Who Are Thirsty"
Barbara Ross (©1992)

When we come to the Bread of Life, Jesus Himself, we continue to be fed by "every word that proceedeth out of the mouth of the LORD" (Deuteronomy 8:3 KJV) in His written Word . . . It has been prepared. Long ago? Yes, but fresh every day . . .

The result of this kind of eating is a delight—and, wonder of wonders, it is to be had without money and without price. Why? Because the price has already been paid for this fantastic supply of fresh bread daily, as well as for the offer to come to Him Who is the Bread of Life.

Edith Schaeffer (1914-)

temple will turn to wailing.[a] Many, many bodies—flung everywhere! Silence!"

4 Hear this, you who trample the needy
and do away with the poor of the land,

5 saying,

"When will the New Moon be over
that we may sell grain,
and the Sabbath be ended
that we may market wheat?"—
skimping the measure,
boosting the price
and cheating with dishonest scales,
6 buying the poor with silver
and the needy for a pair of sandals,
selling even the sweepings with the wheat.

7 The LORD has sworn by the Pride of Jacob: "I will never forget anything they have done.

8 "Will not the land tremble for this,
and all who live in it mourn?
The whole land will rise like the Nile;
it will be stirred up and then sink
like the river of Egypt.

9 "In that day," declares the Sovereign LORD,

"I will make the sun go down at noon
and darken the earth in broad daylight.
10 I will turn your religious feasts into mourning
and all your singing into weeping.
I will make all of you wear sackcloth
and shave your heads.
I will make that time like mourning for an only son
and the end of it like a bitter day.

11 "The days are coming," declares the Sovereign LORD,
"when I will send a famine through the land—
not a famine of food or a thirst for water,
but a famine of hearing the words of the LORD.
12 Men will stagger from sea to sea
and wander from north to east,
searching for the word of the LORD,
but they will not find it.

13 "In that day

"the lovely young women and strong young men
will faint because of thirst.
14 They who swear by the shame[b] of Samaria,
or say, 'As surely as your god lives, O Dan,'
or, 'As surely as the god[c] of Beersheba lives'—
they will fall,
never to rise again."

[a] 3 Or *"the temple singers will wail* [b] 14 Or *by Ashima*; or *by the idol*
[c] 14 Or *power*

Israel to Be Destroyed

9 I saw the Lord standing by the altar, and he said:

"Strike the tops of the pillars
so that the thresholds shake.
Bring them down on the heads of all the people;
those who are left I will kill with the sword.
Not one will get away,
none will escape.
2 Though they dig down to the depths of the grave,[a]
from there my hand will take them.
Though they climb up to the heavens,
from there I will bring them down.
3 Though they hide themselves on the top of Carmel,
there I will hunt them down and seize them.
Though they hide from me at the bottom of the sea,
there I will command the serpent to bite them.
4 Though they are driven into exile by their enemies,
there I will command the sword to slay them.
I will fix my eyes upon them
for evil and not for good."

5 The Lord, the LORD Almighty,
he who touches the earth and it melts,
and all who live in it mourn—
the whole land rises like the Nile,
then sinks like the river of Egypt—
6 he who builds his lofty palace[b] in the heavens
and sets its foundation[c] on the earth,
who calls for the waters of the sea
and pours them out over the face of the
land—
the LORD is his name.

7 "Are not you Israelites
the same to me as the Cushites[d]?"
declares the LORD.
"Did I not bring Israel up from Egypt,
the Philistines from Caphtor[e]
and the Arameans from Kir?

8 "Surely the eyes of the Sovereign LORD
are on the sinful kingdom.
I will destroy it
from the face of the earth—
yet I will not totally destroy
the house of Jacob,"
declares the LORD.
9 "For I will give the command,
and I will shake the house of Israel
among all the nations
as grain is shaken in a sieve,
and not a pebble will reach the ground.
10 All the sinners among my people
will die by the sword,

[a] 2 Hebrew *to Sheol* [b] 6 The meaning of the Hebrew for this phrase is uncertain.
[c] 6 The meaning of the Hebrew for this word is uncertain. [d] 7 That is, people from the upper Nile region [e] 7 That is, Crete

(9:1–4) Lord God, those who stand under Your judgment cannot escape. They must face the terrifying fact that they cannot hide from You. But when those of us who trust You rest in Your grace, we are comforted by this same fact: We cannot ever hide from You! For if we go up to the heavens, You are there; if we make our bed in the depths, You are there. If we rise on the wings of the dawn, if we settle on the far side of the sea, even there Your hand will guide us, and Your right hand will hold us fast. We praise You, all-knowing and ever-present God, for Your faithful and trustworthy care! (Ps 139:7–12)

God the All righteous One! Man
hath defied Thee;
Yet to eternity standeth Thy
Word;
Falsehood and wrong shall not tarry
beside Thee;
Give to us peace in our time,
O Lord.

So shall Thy people, with thankful
devotion,
Praise Him who saved them from
peril and sword,
Singing in chorus from ocean to
ocean,
Peace to the nations, and praise to
the Lord.

"God the Omnipotent"
Henry F. Chorley and John Ellerton (1842)

(9:11–15) Gracious heavenly Father, that which You promised through Amos, You brought to fulfillment in the life and death of Your Son. He brought the new wine of Your kingdom, offering Your Spirit to all who are thirsty. Through His death, Jesus drank from the cup of Your wrath so that He could give us the cup of the new covenant, the wine of forgiveness. As we drink from this cup of salvation, You bring us back from our exile and restore us to fellowship with You. You rebuild our ruined lives and plant us forever in Your heavenly garden. We thank You, O Father, for Your grace, poured out through Your Son. As we drink deeply of Your new wine, we offer ourselves to You in love and gratitude. (Mt 26:27–29; Mk 2:22; Jn 7:37)

Jesus has wine that no vineyard on earth could ever yield . . . I would prefer one mouthful of Christ's love and one sip of His fellowship than a whole world of carnal delights . . . There is not a spring which yields such sweet water as the well of God which was pierced with the soldier's spear . . . For nourishment, comfort, exhilaration, and refreshment, no wine can rival the love of Jesus. Drink deeply.

Charles Haddon Spurgeon (1834-1892)

Father, our God and Father,
You are the Author of Life.
And Father, You freely offer
Your healing water of life.
You welcome all the thirsty
Whose wells have run dry,
To love and tender mercy
Like a river from on high.
Father, the ones who love You
Drink deeply of You
And never die.

"Father of Life"
Phil Kristianson and Bill Batstone (©1998)

all those who say,
'Disaster will not overtake or meet us.'

Israel's Restoration

11 "In that day I will restore
David's fallen tent.
I will repair its broken places,
restore its ruins,
and build it as it used to be,
12 so that they may possess the remnant of Edom
and all the nations that bear my name,[a]"
declares the LORD, who will do these things.

13 "The days are coming," declares the LORD,

"when the reaper will be overtaken by the plowman
and the planter by the one treading grapes.
New wine will drip from the mountains
and flow from all the hills.
14 I will bring back my exiled[b] people Israel;
they will rebuild the ruined cities and live in them.
They will plant vineyards and drink their wine;
they will make gardens and eat their fruit.
15 I will plant Israel in their own land,
never again to be uprooted
from the land I have given them,"
says the LORD your God.

[a] 12 Hebrew; Septuagint *so that the remnant of men / and all the nations that bear my name may seek ⌊the Lord⌋* [b] 14 Or *will restore the fortunes of my*

The Book of OBADIAH

Obadiah

Through the prophet Obadiah, whose name means "servant of the LORD," God announces His judgment on the Edomites, the descendants of Esau. They have opposed and attacked Judah, even assisting foreign invaders in the destruction of Jerusalem. But God is loyal to His people and will avenge them. Verses 1–16 contain God's word of judgment against Edom. Verses 17–21 include God's word concerning the restoration of Israel.

In Obadiah we meet Yahweh, the divine warrior. God will defeat the nations who oppose and oppress His people. God declares to Edom through the prophet: "I will make you small among the nations; you will be utterly despised" (v. 2). Because God is the ruler of heaven and earth, He has the right to hold all nations accountable for their actions.

God is also the restorer of His people. He will make things right on behalf of His chosen nation. God will give Judah the land of the Edomites and bring peace to the land.

The book of Obadiah ends with an affirmation that is brimming with significance: "And the kingdom will be the LORD's" (v. 21). In the immediate context this refers to God's rule over all of the promised land, including Edom. But it points further to the day when God's kingdom will be limitless. We are reminded of an earlier prophecy given through Isaiah, in which a child to be born will reign on David's throne: "Of the increase of his government and peace," Isaiah proclaims, "there will be no end" (Isa 9:7). As this prophecy is fulfilled through Jesus Christ, all nations stand not only under God's righteous judgment, but also under His gracious provision. Even people like the Edomites—or like us!—can receive divine salvation and participate in God's reign.

In worship we celebrate God's sovereignty . . . We come boldly, but also humbly, remembering that we have the privilege of an audience with the King of kings.

As Christians we have come under the rule of God through Jesus Christ. We have begun to live in the kingdom that will someday encompass all of creation. In worship we celebrate God's sovereignty. We draw near to His throne of grace (Heb 4:16). We come boldly, but also humbly, remembering that we have the privilege of an audience with the King of kings. We look forward with joyful expectation to the day when we will sing: "The kingdom of the world has become the kingdom of our Lord and of his Christ, and he will reign for ever and ever" (Rev 11:15). In that day God's final justice will be executed. His matchless glory will be revealed. His amazing grace will be lavished upon us. In light of what is and what is to come, we heed the musical invitation of Robert Grant: "O worship the King, all glorious above! And gratefully sing his power and his love; Our shield and defender, the Ancient of Days, Pavilioned in splendor and girded with praise."*

*"O Worship the King," Robert Grant (c.1833).

(1–13) Lord, may I be as Obadiah—a servant who worships the Lord and a worshiper who serves Your purposes in my generation. Give me eyes to see things from Your perspective and a heart to feel the jealous love You have for Your people. Grant me power to do my part in bringing Your comfort to the afflicted and Your warning to the arrogant. Cleanse my own heart from jealousy, resentment, envy and bitterness, that I will not join with those who rejoice in the failure of another. Heal my broken relationships and let me walk in the righteousness of Christ, so that those who are fallen will see in me the hope of Your deliverance.

Make me what thou wouldst have me; I bargain for nothing; I make no terms; I seek for no previous information whither thou art taking me; I will be what thou wilt make me, and all that thou wilt make me. I say not, I will follow thee whithersoever thou goest, for I am weak; but I give myself to thee to lead me anywhere.
Cardinal John Henry Newman (1801-1890)

I'll tell to all that God is love;
For the world has never known
The great compassion of His heart
For the wayward and the lone.

Eternal glory is the goal
That awaits the sons of light;
Eternal darkness, black as death,
For the children of the night.
"I'll Tell to All that God is Love"
Alfred H. Ackley (1923)

1 The vision of Obadiah.

This is what the Sovereign LORD says about Edom—

We have heard a message from the LORD:
An envoy was sent to the nations to say,
"Rise, and let us go against her for battle"—

2 "See, I will make you small among the nations;
you will be utterly despised.
3 The pride of your heart has deceived you,
you who live in the clefts of the rocks[a]
and make your home on the heights,
you who say to yourself,
'Who can bring me down to the ground?'
4 Though you soar like the eagle
and make your nest among the stars,
from there I will bring you down,"
declares the LORD.
5 "If thieves came to you,
if robbers in the night—
Oh, what a disaster awaits you—
would they not steal only as much as they wanted?
If grape pickers came to you,
would they not leave a few grapes?
6 But how Esau will be ransacked,
his hidden treasures pillaged!
7 All your allies will force you to the border;
your friends will deceive and overpower you;
those who eat your bread will set a trap for you,[b]
but you will not detect it.

8 "In that day," declares the LORD,
"will I not destroy the wise men of Edom,
men of understanding in the mountains of Esau?
9 Your warriors, O Teman, will be terrified,
and everyone in Esau's mountains
will be cut down in the slaughter.
10 Because of the violence against your brother Jacob,
you will be covered with shame;
you will be destroyed forever.
11 On the day you stood aloof
while strangers carried off his wealth
and foreigners entered his gates
and cast lots for Jerusalem,
you were like one of them.
12 You should not look down on your brother
in the day of his misfortune,
nor rejoice over the people of Judah
in the day of their destruction,
nor boast so much
in the day of their trouble.
13 You should not march through the gates of my people
in the day of their disaster,
nor look down on them in their calamity
in the day of their disaster,

[a] 3 Or *of Sela* [b] 7 The meaning of the Hebrew for this clause is uncertain.

nor seize their wealth
in the day of their disaster.
14 You should not wait at the crossroads
to cut down their fugitives,
nor hand over their survivors
in the day of their trouble.

15 "The day of the LORD is near
for all nations.
As you have done, it will be done to you;
your deeds will return upon your own head.
16 Just as you drank on my holy hill,
so all the nations will drink continually;
they will drink and drink
and be as if they had never been.
17 But on Mount Zion will be deliverance;
it will be holy,
and the house of Jacob
will possess its inheritance.
18 The house of Jacob will be a fire
and the house of Joseph a flame;
the house of Esau will be stubble,
and they will set it on fire and consume it.
There will be no survivors
from the house of Esau."
The LORD has spoken.

19 People from the Negev will occupy
the mountains of Esau,
and people from the foothills will possess
the land of the Philistines.
They will occupy the fields of Ephraim and Samaria,
and Benjamin will possess Gilead.
20 This company of Israelite exiles who are in Canaan
will possess ⌞the land⌟ as far as Zarephath;
the exiles from Jerusalem who are in Sepharad
will possess the towns of the Negev.
21 Deliverers will go up on[a] Mount Zion
to govern the mountains of Esau.
And the kingdom will be the LORD's.

[a] 21 Or *from*

(17–21) O Lord my God, when I am overcome with the unfaithfulness of others, help me to remember Your great faithfulness. When I feel hopeless amidst the endless sorrows of earth, help me to remember Your promise of deliverance and the boundless joys of heaven. When I am betrayed by friend and bound by foe, help me to recall Your unfailing love and amazing grace. Let me hear the songs of freedom that the saints sing in glory. Let me recount to my own soul the wonder of redemption's story. Let me rise again from the worst of all circumstances to give You the best of all things—my heart singing Your praise, and my life proclaiming Your glory. (Ps 30:4–5)

Do not look forward to the changes and chances of this life in fear; rather look to them with full hope that, as they arise, God, whose you are, will deliver you out of them. He is your Keeper. He has kept you hitherto. Hold fast to his dear hand, and he will lead you safely through all things; and, when you cannot stand, he will bear you in his arms. Do not look forward to what may happen tomorrow. Our Father will either shield you from suffering, or he will give you strength to bear it.

Saint Francis of Sales (1567-1622)

Praise the Lord in joyful numbers,
Your Protector never slumbers;
At the will of your Defender
Ev'ry foeman must surrender.

Though He giveth or He taketh,
God His children ne'er forsaketh;
His the loving purpose solely
To preserve them pure and holy.

"Children of the Heavenly Father"
Carolina Sandell Berg (1858)
Trans. Ernest W. Olson (1925)

The Book of
JONAH

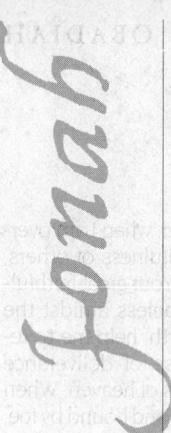

Every child—and every child at heart—loves the story of Jonah and the whale. But this is much more than a fish tale! The book of Jonah is about a reluctant prophet and a God Whose mercy exceeds our narrow expectations.

This book can be divided into two sections. In the first section (chs. 1—2) God saves Jonah, who is attempting to run away from his assignment to preach to the Assyrian capital of Nineveh. In the second section (chs. 3—4), God uses Jonah to save the citizens of Nineveh. Sadly, the prophet is not too happy about being an instrument of God's grace to such a people.

The God we meet in Jonah is persistently gracious. He does not give up on Jonah, even though the prophet attempts to run far away from God and His call. Neither does God abandon the Assyrians, probably the cruelest people of their day. Instead, He gives them an opportunity to repent and turn to Him.

Along with the prophet, we encounter the breadth of God's mercy in this book. His love and compassion are not reserved for Israel alone. Though He is the God of Israel, He is not their possession, nor is His grace limited by their prejudices. He is truly "the Lord, the God of all mankind" (Jer 32:27), who offers his salvation to all nations, even to Israel's most feared eenemies. Thus the book of Jonah prefigures the teaching and work of Jesus, who calls us to love our enemies and who dies on the cross so that all sinners might receive God's salvation.

In the midst of a desperate situation, Jonah nevertheless offers praise to God. His affirmations are shaped more by what he knows to be true of God than by his present condition.

In chapter 2, Jonah celebrates God's salvation, even while in the belly of the fish. "From inside the fish Jonah prayed to the LORD his God. He said: 'In my distress I called to the LORD, and he answered me. From the depths of the grave I called for help, and you listened to my cry . . . The engulfing waters threatened me, the deep surrounded me; seaweed was wrapped around my head. To the roots of the mountains I sank down; the earth beneath barred me in forever. But you brought my life up from the pit, O LORD my God . . . Those who cling to worthless idols forfeit the grace that could be theirs. But I, with a song of thanksgiving, will sacrifice to you. What I have vowed I will make good. Salvation comes from the LORD' " (2:1–2,5–6,8–9). In the midst of a desperate situation, Jonah nevertheless offers praise to God. His affirmations are shaped more by what he knows to be true of God than by his present condition.

Thus Jonah teaches us how to worship when we are in the midst of a crisis. In worship we proclaim the truth of who God is and what God has done, even when we feel as though we have been swallowed into the depths of despair. We do not thereby deny our feelings, but rather we anchor our worship in the certainty of God's Biblical revelation rather than the inconsistency of our emotions.

Jonah Flees From the LORD

1 The word of the LORD came to Jonah son of Amittai: 2“Go to the great city of Nineveh and preach against it, because its wickedness has come up before me.”

3But Jonah ran away from the LORD and headed for Tarshish. He went down to Joppa, where he found a ship bound for that port. After paying the fare, he went aboard and sailed for Tarshish to flee from the LORD.

4Then the LORD sent a great wind on the sea, and such a violent storm arose that the ship threatened to break up. 5All the sailors were afraid and each cried out to his own god. And they threw the cargo into the sea to lighten the ship.

But Jonah had gone below deck, where he lay down and fell into a deep sleep. 6The captain went to him and said, “How can you sleep? Get up and call on your god! Maybe he will take notice of us, and we will not perish.”

7Then the sailors said to each other, “Come, let us cast lots to find out who is responsible for this calamity.” They cast lots and the lot fell on Jonah.

8So they asked him, “Tell us, who is responsible for making all this trouble for us? What do you do? Where do you come from? What is your country? From what people are you?”

9He answered, “I am a Hebrew and I worship the LORD, the God of heaven, who made the sea and the land.”

10This terrified them and they asked, “What have you done?” (They knew he was running away from the LORD, because he had already told them so.)

11The sea was getting rougher and rougher. So they asked him, “What should we do to you to make the sea calm down for us?”

12“Pick me up and throw me into the sea,” he replied, “and it will become calm. I know that it is my fault that this great storm has come upon you.”

13Instead, the men did their best to row back to land. But they could not, for the sea grew even wilder than before. 14Then they cried to the LORD, “O LORD, please do not let us die for taking this man’s life. Do not hold us accountable for killing an innocent man, for you, O LORD, have done as you pleased.” 15Then they took Jonah and threw him overboard, and the raging sea grew calm. 16At this the men greatly feared the LORD, and they offered a sacrifice to the LORD and made vows to him.

17But the LORD provided a great fish to swallow Jonah, and Jonah was inside the fish three days and three nights.

Jonah’s Prayer

2 From inside the fish Jonah prayed to the LORD his God. 2He said:

“In my distress I called to the LORD,
  and he answered me.
From the depths of the grave[a] I called for help,
  and you listened to my cry.
3You hurled me into the deep,
  into the very heart of the seas,
  and the currents swirled about me;
all your waves and breakers
  swept over me.

[a] 2 Hebrew *Sheol*

Obedience is an unprepared defense before God. Obedience is the sepulcher of the will.

Saint John Climacus (570-649)

(1:2) Thank You, Lord, for Your great mercy. You long to reveal Yourself to those who do not ask for You, to be found by those who do not seek You or call on Your name. You take no pleasure in the death of the wicked, but rather that they turn from their ways and live. The Assyrians were brutal, godless enemies of Your people. They were headed for certain destruction. Yet in Your love and kindness, You sent them a word of warning, hoping they would repent. Truly, You are the God of all humankind; nothing is too hard for You. (Isa 65:1; Jer 32:27; Eze 33:11)

God perseveres in speaking to us in his own language. God speaks to us in this language that we do not know and do not want to learn, he speaks to us of acceptance, of sacrifice, of renunciation, of his plan, so vast in scale, so unimaginably bold, so improbably generous, the plan by which he wills to save us, us and the world.

Louis Evely (1910-)

(2:1–9) Lord, every circumstance is an unwritten song of worship. Whether my suffering is the result of my rebellion or a trial of my faith, let my tongue be the pen of a skillful writer, and my heart the quiet chamber where faith turns adversity into praise. Make my voice clear in proclaiming Your great faithfulness and love. As I turn my heart from worthless idols to Your matchless grace, please lift me from death to life, that I may joyfully serve You and glorify Your holy name. (Ps 45:1)

Jesus calls us o'er the tumult
Of our life's wild, restless sea;
Day by day His sweet voice
soundeth,
Saying, "Christian, follow Me."

Jesus calls us from the worship
Of the vain world's golden store,
From each idol that would keep us,
Saying, "Christian, love Me more."
"Jesus Calls Us O'er the Tumult"
Cecil F. Alexander (1852)

(3:1–2) Thank You, Father, for Your patience and determination. It is impossible to run from You. You could have let Jonah die and simply found a more willing servant, but You did not give up on him. You had mercy on him in spite of his rebellion, just as You would have mercy on the Ninevites in spite of theirs. Who am I to judge sinful people who do not even know You, when I who *do* know You willfully disobey You? Cleanse my heart, O God, and fill me with compassion for the lost.

Lord, make me a light to the nations,
A light so bright
That the whole world can see.
Your light is here to put out the
darkness;
O Lord, may the whole world
See Your light in me.
"Light To The Nations"
John Barbour (©1996)

He is Thy best servant who looks not so much to hear that from Thee which is conformable to his own will as rather to conform his will to what he heareth from Thee.

Saint Augustine of Hippo (354-430)

4 I said, 'I have been banished
from your sight;
yet I will look again
toward your holy temple.'
5 The engulfing waters threatened me,[a]
the deep surrounded me;
seaweed was wrapped around my head.
6 To the roots of the mountains I sank down;
the earth beneath barred me in forever.
But you brought my life up from the pit,
O LORD my God.

7 "When my life was ebbing away,
I remembered you, LORD,
and my prayer rose to you,
to your holy temple.

8 "Those who cling to worthless idols
forfeit the grace that could be theirs.
9 But I, with a song of thanksgiving,
will sacrifice to you.
What I have vowed I will make good.
Salvation comes from the LORD."

10 And the LORD commanded the fish, and it vomited Jonah onto
dry land.

Jonah Goes to Nineveh

3 Then the word of the LORD came to Jonah a second time:
2 "Go to the great city of Nineveh and proclaim to it the message I give you."

3 Jonah obeyed the word of the LORD and went to Nineveh. Now
Nineveh was a very important city—a visit required three days.
4 On the first day, Jonah started into the city. He proclaimed:
"Forty more days and Nineveh will be overturned." 5 The Ninevites believed God. They declared a fast, and all of them, from the
greatest to the least, put on sackcloth.
6 When the news reached the king of Nineveh, he rose from his
throne, took off his royal robes, covered himself with sackcloth and
sat down in the dust. 7 Then he issued a proclamation in Nineveh:

"By the decree of the king and his nobles:

Do not let any man or beast, herd or flock, taste anything;
do not let them eat or drink. 8 But let man and beast be covered with sackcloth. Let everyone call urgently on God. Let
them give up their evil ways and their violence. 9 Who
knows? God may yet relent and with compassion turn from
his fierce anger so that we will not perish."

10 When God saw what they did and how they turned from their
evil ways, he had compassion and did not bring upon them the
destruction he had threatened.

Jonah's Anger at the LORD's Compassion

4 But Jonah was greatly displeased and became angry. 2 He
prayed to the LORD, "O LORD, is this not what I said when I
was still at home? That is why I was so quick to flee to Tarshish. I

[a] 5 Or *waters were at my throat*

knew that you are a gracious and compassionate God, slow to
anger and abounding in love, a God who relents from sending
calamity. 3Now, O LORD, take away my life, for it is better for me
to die than to live."
4But the LORD replied, "Have you any right to be angry?"
5Jonah went out and sat down at a place east of the city. There
he made himself a shelter, sat in its shade and waited to see what
would happen to the city. 6Then the LORD God provided a vine and
made it grow up over Jonah to give shade for his head to ease his
discomfort, and Jonah was very happy about the vine. 7But at
dawn the next day God provided a worm, which chewed the vine
so that it withered. 8When the sun rose, God provided a scorching east wind, and the sun blazed on Jonah's head so that he grew
faint. He wanted to die, and said, "It would be better for me to die
than to live."
9But God said to Jonah, "Do you have a right to be angry about
the vine?"
"I do," he said. "I am angry enough to die."
10But the LORD said, "You have been concerned about this vine,
though you did not tend it or make it grow. It sprang up overnight
and died overnight. 11But Nineveh has more than a hundred and
twenty thousand people who cannot tell their right hand from
their left, and many cattle as well. Should I not be concerned
about that great city?"

Do not let it be imagined that one must remain silent about one's feelings of rebellion in order to enter into dialogue with God. Quite the opposite is the truth: it is precisely when one expresses them that a dialogue of truth begins.

Paul Tournier (1898-1986)

(4:1–4) Compassionate Lord, You are slow to anger. I, like Jonah, can be quick to judge. You are not willing that anyone should be lost. I am not always willing that certain people might be saved. You do not hate the world. You so loved the world that You gave Your Son to save it. Now please save it from my hateful prejudice. Who am I to decide who should stand or who should fall before You? Father, forgive me for my judgmental self-righteousness. Remove from me my heart of stone and give me a heart of flesh. Help me to extend the hand of mercy so that I might receive mercy. Help me to speak words of forgiveness so that I might be forgiven. Help me to rejoice with the angels over one sinner who repents. (Eze 36:26; Lk 6:37; 15:10; Jn 3:16; 1Ti 2:3–4)

Go ye therefore to every nation,
Preach the Gospel in every land.
To every language and every people,
In My name reach out your hand.

Tell the world the message,
Take it everywhere
To every tribe and nation
We are called to share.

"Tell the World"
Marsha Skidmore (©1994)

The Book of MICAH

Toward the end of the eighth century B.C., God raises up the prophet Micah to judge His chosen people. The awesome, judging Lord is coming to pronounce a guilty verdict upon both Israel and Judah because of their failure to live according to God's covenant. The people are so selfishly unjust that the Lord says: "I am planning disaster against this people, from which you cannot save yourselves" (2:3).

The sin of God's people is their failure to live faithfully in a covenant relationship with God. As the Lord brings His legal case against His people, the people respond: "With what shall I come before the LORD and bow down before the exalted God? Shall I come before him with burnt offerings, with calves a year old? . . . He has showed you, O man, what is good. And what does the LORD require of you? To act justly and to love mercy and to walk humbly with your God" (6:6–8). The word translated here as "mercy" refers to living in faithful, obedient relationship with God. Gestures of worship, however important and Biblically decreed, are empty apart from a right relationship with God and His people. Through Micah we recognize once again that God seeks our worship, not only in the expressions of our hearts and lips, but also through the actions of our daily lives.

Therefore, we respond to God's judgment in Micah, on the one hand, by humbly confessing our delinquency in being just and merciful. The prophetic conviction of God, even if originally intended for others, brings us to our knees in repentance. On the other hand, God's judgment also gets us up on our feet as we walk worthy of the Lord so that we may please Him in every way, bearing fruit in every good work (Col 1:10).

Through Micah we recognize once again that God seeks our worship, not only in the expressions of our hearts and lips, but also through the actions of our daily lives.

Though Micah does not hesitate to deliver his message of doom, he carefully intersperses words of hope within his predictions of ruin (2:12–13; 4:1–8,13; 5:1–9; 7:7–20). This book, so full of heaviness, ends with an encouraging climax: "Who is a God like you, who pardons sin and forgives the transgression of the remnant of his inheritance? You do not stay angry forever but delight to show mercy. You will again have compassion on us; you will tread our sins underfoot and hurl all our iniquities into the depths of the sea" (7:18–19). Micah offers hope to Israel, a remnant of whom God will gather after their dispersion (2:12; 4:6–7). Moreover, even the Gentiles can find hope in Micah, who foresees a day when many nations will walk in God's paths (4:1–3). Someday a ruler will be born in Bethlehem whose "greatness will reach to the ends of the earth" (5:2–5). Jesus is this ruler, through Whom we all can enter into a new covenant relationship with God, so that we might love God with all of our heart, soul, mind and strength (Mk 12:30).

1 The word of the LORD that came to Micah of Moresheth during the reigns of Jotham, Ahaz and Hezekiah, kings of Judah—the vision he saw concerning Samaria and Jerusalem.

2 Hear, O peoples, all of you,
listen, O earth and all who are in it,
that the Sovereign LORD may witness against you,
the Lord from his holy temple.

Judgment Against Samaria and Jerusalem

3 Look! The LORD is coming from his dwelling place;
he comes down and treads the high places of the earth.
4 The mountains melt beneath him
and the valleys split apart,
like wax before the fire,
like water rushing down a slope.
5 All this is because of Jacob's transgression,
because of the sins of the house of Israel.
What is Jacob's transgression?
Is it not Samaria?
What is Judah's high place?
Is it not Jerusalem?

6 "Therefore I will make Samaria a heap of rubble,
a place for planting vineyards.
I will pour her stones into the valley
and lay bare her foundations.
7 All her idols will be broken to pieces;
all her temple gifts will be burned with fire;
I will destroy all her images.
Since she gathered her gifts from the wages of prostitutes,
as the wages of prostitutes they will again be used."

Weeping and Mourning

8 Because of this I will weep and wail;
I will go about barefoot and naked.
I will howl like a jackal
and moan like an owl.
9 For her wound is incurable;
it has come to Judah.
It[a] has reached the very gate of my people,
even to Jerusalem itself.
10 Tell it not in Gath[b];
weep not at all.[c]
In Beth Ophrah[d]
roll in the dust.
11 Pass on in nakedness and shame,
you who live in Shaphir.[e]
Those who live in Zaanan[f]
will not come out.
Beth Ezel is in mourning;
its protection is taken from you.

[a] 9 Or *He* [b] 10 *Gath* sounds like the Hebrew for *tell.* [c] 10 Hebrew; Septuagint may suggest *not in Acco.* The Hebrew for *in Acco* sounds like the Hebrew for *weep.* [d] 10 *Beth Ophrah* means *house of dust.* [e] 11 *Shaphir* means *pleasant.* [f] 11 *Zaanan* sounds like the Hebrew for *come out.*

(1:1–2) O Sovereign Lord, at times Your Word comes to us in judgment. It witnesses against us and calls us to repent. Indeed, Your Word is living and active, sharper than any double-edged sword as it penetrates deep within us, judging the thoughts and attitudes of our hearts. That hurts, Lord! Yet there are times when You must wound us in order to heal us, when You must destroy our sinful nature so that we might be saved. Help us, Lord! Give us ears to hear Your word of grace that also judges, Your word of love that hates our sin. Help us, Lord, to return to You that we might be healed. (Hos 6:1; 1Co 5:5; Heb 4:12–13)

Better in bitterest agony to lie,
Before thy throne,
Than through much increase to be lifted up on high,
And stand alone.
Yet best—the need that broke me at thy feet,
In voiceless prayer,
And cast my chastened heart, a sacrifice complete,
Upon thy care.

John Oxenham (1861-1941)

(2:3) O Righteous Judge, when I consider the depth of my sin I am forced to see that, as it was for Your people so many centuries ago, so it is for me: I cannot save myself from Your just condemnation, or from the disaster that rightly should fall upon me. So who can help me? How can I be saved? I can only save myself by giving myself to You in humility and repentance. As it is written, "Repent and be baptized, every one of you, in the name of Jesus Christ for the forgiveness of your sins." "Salvation is found in no one else, for there is no other name under heaven given to men by which we must be saved." (Ac 2:38–40; 4:12; Ro 7:24–25)

We trust in You, O Captain of
salvation
In Your dear name, all other names
above:
Jesus, our righteousness, our sure
foundation,
Our Prince of glory and our King of
love.

"We Trust in You, Our Shield"
Edith G. Cherry (19th c.)

To say that God justifies the ungodly means quite simply that God in his amazing love treats the sinner as if he was a good man. Again, to put it very simply, God loves us, not for anything that we are, but for what he is.

William Barclay (1907-1978)

12 Those who live in Maroth[a] writhe in pain,
waiting for relief,
because disaster has come from the LORD,
even to the gate of Jerusalem.
13 You who live in Lachish,[b]
harness the team to the chariot.
You were the beginning of sin
to the Daughter of Zion,
for the transgressions of Israel
were found in you.
14 Therefore you will give parting gifts
to Moresheth Gath.
The town of Aczib[c] will prove deceptive
to the kings of Israel.
15 I will bring a conqueror against you
who live in Mareshah.[d]
He who is the glory of Israel
will come to Adullam.
16 Shave your heads in mourning
for the children in whom you delight;
make yourselves as bald as the vulture,
for they will go from you into exile.

Man's Plans and God's

2 Woe to those who plan iniquity,
to those who plot evil on their beds!
At morning's light they carry it out
because it is in their power to do it.
2 They covet fields and seize them,
and houses, and take them.
They defraud a man of his home,
a fellowman of his inheritance.

3 Therefore, the LORD says:

"I am planning disaster against this people,
from which you cannot save yourselves.
You will no longer walk proudly,
for it will be a time of calamity.
4 In that day men will ridicule you;
they will taunt you with this mournful song:
'We are utterly ruined;
my people's possession is divided up.
He takes it from me!
He assigns our fields to traitors.'"

5 Therefore you will have no one in the assembly of the LORD
to divide the land by lot.

False Prophets

6 "Do not prophesy," their prophets say.
"Do not prophesy about these things;
disgrace will not overtake us."
7 Should it be said, O house of Jacob:

[a] 12 *Maroth* sounds like the Hebrew for *bitter.* [b] 13 *Lachish* sounds like the Hebrew for *team.* [c] 14 *Aczib* means *deception.* [d] 15 *Mareshah* sounds like the Hebrew for *conqueror.*

"Is the Spirit of the LORD angry?
Does he do such things?"

"Do not my words do good
to him whose ways are upright?
8 Lately my people have risen up
like an enemy.
You strip off the rich robe
from those who pass by without a care,
like men returning from battle.
9 You drive the women of my people
from their pleasant homes.
You take away my blessing
from their children forever.
10 Get up, go away!
For this is not your resting place,
because it is defiled,
it is ruined, beyond all remedy.
11 If a liar and deceiver comes and says,
'I will prophesy for you plenty of wine and beer,'
he would be just the prophet for this people!

Deliverance Promised

12 "I will surely gather all of you, O Jacob;
I will surely bring together the remnant of Israel.
I will bring them together like sheep in a pen,
like a flock in its pasture;
the place will throng with people.
13 One who breaks open the way will go up before them;
they will break through the gate and go out.
Their king will pass through before them,
the LORD at their head."

Leaders and Prophets Rebuked

3 Then I said,

"Listen, you leaders of Jacob,
you rulers of the house of Israel.
Should you not know justice,
2 you who hate good and love evil;
who tear the skin from my people
and the flesh from their bones;
3 who eat my people's flesh,
strip off their skin
and break their bones in pieces;
who chop them up like meat for the pan,
like flesh for the pot?"

4 Then they will cry out to the LORD,
but he will not answer them.
At that time he will hide his face from them
because of the evil they have done.

5 This is what the LORD says:

"As for the prophets
who lead my people astray,
if one feeds them,
they proclaim 'peace';

(2:11) Your Word is life, Living Lord. Your Word alone gives hope that lasts and comfort that satisfies. Yet I must confess how much I want Your Word always to be pleasing to my ears and soothing to my soul. I want to hear that which is easy, that which affirms. How quickly I turn from hard words that name my sin and force me to confront my guilt. How readily I soothe my conscience with balm that never heals. Help me, Gracious God, to hear all that You would say to me. Help me to receive Your restoring Word even when it pierces my stony heart and cuts away the cancer of my sin. (2Ti 4:3–5)

Once you and I are face to face with the Word of God . . . we can only accept or reject it. Jesus becomes the two-edged sword that cuts right down the middle, dividing us into believers and nonbelievers.

John Powell (1927-)

(4:1–3) How I long for the day, exalted Lord, when Your glory will be seen in all its grandeur. Then all peoples will flock to Your presence. Your Word will go forth unhindered. Your justice will humble the nations. Your peace will reign upon the whole earth. Your magnificent majesty will be revealed. Every knee will bow before You and every tongue will confess that Jesus Christ is Lord. "Who will not fear you, O Lord, and bring glory to your name? For you alone are holy. All nations will come and worship before you, for your righteous acts have been revealed." (Php 2:9–11; Rev 15:4)

Our great High Priest is in glory, exalted above all created angels. But he is the same Jesus we knew in the days of his flesh. He is the same Jesus in heaven as he was on earth, as he was before the world began. The face shining above the brightness of the sun is the face that drew sinners to his feet. The hand that holds the seven stars is the hand that laid in blessing upon little children. The breast girt about with a golden girdle is the breast upon which the beloved disciple laid his head at the last supper.

A. D. Foreman, Jr.

O Lord God Almighty,
O Lord most holy;
You are King of kings
And Lord of lords,
The Father of us all.
And we bow down before You,
Every creature shall adore You.
You are mighty God, the Messiah,
The Savior of the world!

You alone are holy,
You alone, oh Lord!
You alone are worthy,
Lamb of God!

We behold Your splendor
Seated on the throne,
Robed and crowned with glory
Evermore, evermore, mighty Lord!
"You Alone are Holy"
Jim Cowan (©1986)

if he does not,
they prepare to wage war against him.
6 Therefore night will come over you, without visions,
and darkness, without divination.
The sun will set for the prophets,
and the day will go dark for them.
7 The seers will be ashamed
and the diviners disgraced.
They will all cover their faces
because there is no answer from God."

8 But as for me, I am filled with power,
with the Spirit of the LORD,
and with justice and might,
to declare to Jacob his transgression,
to Israel his sin.
9 Hear this, you leaders of the house of Jacob,
you rulers of the house of Israel,
who despise justice
and distort all that is right;
10 who build Zion with bloodshed,
and Jerusalem with wickedness.
11 Her leaders judge for a bribe,
her priests teach for a price,
and her prophets tell fortunes for money.
Yet they lean upon the LORD and say,
"Is not the LORD among us?
No disaster will come upon us."
12 Therefore because of you,
Zion will be plowed like a field,
Jerusalem will become a heap of rubble,
the temple hill a mound overgrown with thickets.

The Mountain of the LORD

4 In the last days

the mountain of the LORD's temple will be established
as chief among the mountains;
it will be raised above the hills,
and peoples will stream to it.

2 Many nations will come and say,

"Come, let us go up to the mountain of the LORD,
to the house of the God of Jacob.
He will teach us his ways,
so that we may walk in his paths."
The law will go out from Zion,
the word of the LORD from Jerusalem.
3 He will judge between many peoples
and will settle disputes for strong nations far and wide.
They will beat their swords into plowshares
and their spears into pruning hooks.
Nation will not take up sword against nation,
nor will they train for war anymore.
4 Every man will sit under his own vine
and under his own fig tree,
and no one will make them afraid,

MY BELOVED

My Word is eternal; it stands firm in the heavens. My faithfulness continues through all generations. My Word is a lamp to your feet and a light for your path.

I am your Refuge and your Shield because you have put your hope in My Word. But do not merely listen to My Word. Sermons, in themselves, will not save you. If you listen to My Word but do not do what it says, you will be like a man who looks at his face in the mirror and, after looking at himself, goes away and immediately forgets what he looks like.

On the other hand, if you hear these words of Mine and put them into practice you will be like a wise man who built his house on the rock. The rain came down, the streams rose, the winds blew and beat against that house; yet it did not fall, because it had its foundation on the rock—and that Rock is Me.

So fill your heart with My Word and I will direct your footsteps so that no sin may rule over you. Look intently into My perfect law that gives freedom, and continue to do this, not forgetting what you have heard, but doing it—and you will be blessed in what you do.

Great peace have they who love My law, and nothing can make them stumble.

Ps 119:11,89-91,105,114,133,165; Mt 7:24-25; Lk 11:28; Jn 8:31-32; 1Co 10:4; Jas 1:22-25

for the LORD Almighty has spoken.
5 All the nations may walk
in the name of their gods;
we will walk in the name of the LORD
our God for ever and ever.

The LORD's Plan

6 "In that day," declares the LORD,

"I will gather the lame;
I will assemble the exiles
and those I have brought to grief.
7 I will make the lame a remnant,
those driven away a strong nation.
The LORD will rule over them in Mount Zion
from that day and forever.
8 As for you, O watchtower of the flock,
O stronghold[a] of the Daughter of Zion,
the former dominion will be restored to you;
kingship will come to the Daughter of Jerusalem."

9 Why do you now cry aloud—
have you no king?
Has your counselor perished,
that pain seizes you like that of a woman in labor?
10 Writhe in agony, O Daughter of Zion,
like a woman in labor,
for now you must leave the city
to camp in the open field.
You will go to Babylon;
there you will be rescued.
There the LORD will redeem you
out of the hand of your enemies.

11 But now many nations
are gathered against you.
They say, "Let her be defiled,
let our eyes gloat over Zion!"
12 But they do not know
the thoughts of the LORD;
they do not understand his plan,
he who gathers them like sheaves to the threshing floor.
13 "Rise and thresh, O Daughter of Zion,
for I will give you horns of iron;
I will give you hoofs of bronze
and you will break to pieces many nations."

You will devote their ill-gotten gains to the LORD,
their wealth to the Lord of all the earth.

A Promised Ruler From Bethlehem

5 Marshal your troops, O city of troops,[b]
for a siege is laid against us.
They will strike Israel's ruler
on the cheek with a rod.

[a] 8 Or *hill* [b] 1 Or *Strengthen your walls, O walled city*

(4:9–10) O Loving Father, Your discipline hurts. Under Your just, strong hand we cry out. We writhe in agony. We wonder where You are and sometimes question Your goodness. Yet You discipline us because You love us as a father loves his children. Your judgment is, indeed, for our good, that we might share in Your holiness. All-knowing God, You see beyond the moment of chastisement to the future of mercy. Even as You sent Your people to Babylon, You knew that You would rescue them. When You turned them over to the consequences of their sin, You knew that You would redeem them. Help us, Gracious God, to accept Your discipline without losing heart. May we submit to You even through hardships, that we might be made pure, and that we might live forever in Your righteousness and peace. (Ps 94:12; Pr 3:12; Heb 12:4–12)

"The dark night of the soul" is not something bad or destructive. On the contrary it is an experience to be welcomed as a sick person might welcome a surgery that promises health and well-being. The purpose of the darkness is not to punish or afflict us. It is to set us free.

Richard J. Foster (1942-)

(5:2–5) O Jesus, Son of God, You are the One promised in the prophets. You are the One born in little Bethlehem, the Ruler of Israel from an ancient lineage. You are the Good Shepherd who guards Your flock with divine strength. Under Your care we live securely, never needing to doubt our safety. You bear the very name of God, ruling in matchless majesty. Your greatness exceeds and encompasses the whole earth. Through Your death on the cross, Your peace has begun to heal the wound of creation, mending the breaches torn open by sin. You alone are worthy, O Lamb of God, "to receive power and wealth and wisdom and strength and honor and glory and praise!" Hallelujah! (Jn 10:11; Eph 2:14; Rev 5:12)

Come and see the glory of the Lord,
Come, behold the Lamb.
Come and know the mercy of the King,
Bowing down before Him.

Come and give thanks unto the Lord.
Come, behold the Lamb.
Come and sing the praises of the King,
Bowing down before Him.

For He is Lord above the heavens,
Lord in all the earth.
Lord of all the angels,
Worthy to be served.
Alleluia, alleluia, Lord.

"Come and See"
Lenny LeBlanc (©1989)

Every passage in the history of our Lord and Savior is of unfathomable depth and affords inexhaustible matter for contemplation. All that concerns him is infinite, and what we first discern is but the surface of that which begins and ends in eternity.

Cardinal John Henry Newman (1801-1890)

2 "But you, Bethlehem Ephrathah,
though you are small among the clans[a] of Judah,
out of you will come for me
one who will be ruler over Israel,
whose origins[b] are from of old,
from ancient times.[c]"

3 Therefore Israel will be abandoned
until the time when she who is in labor gives birth
and the rest of his brothers return
to join the Israelites.

4 He will stand and shepherd his flock
in the strength of the LORD,
in the majesty of the name of the LORD his God.
And they will live securely, for then his greatness
will reach to the ends of the earth.
5 And he will be their peace.

Deliverance and Destruction

When the Assyrian invades our land
and marches through our fortresses,
we will raise against him seven shepherds,
even eight leaders of men.
6 They will rule[d] the land of Assyria with the sword,
the land of Nimrod with drawn sword.[e]
He will deliver us from the Assyrian
when he invades our land
and marches into our borders.

7 The remnant of Jacob will be
in the midst of many peoples
like dew from the LORD,
like showers on the grass,
which do not wait for man
or linger for mankind.
8 The remnant of Jacob will be among the nations,
in the midst of many peoples,
like a lion among the beasts of the forest,
like a young lion among flocks of sheep,
which mauls and mangles as it goes,
and no one can rescue.
9 Your hand will be lifted up in triumph over your enemies,
and all your foes will be destroyed.

10 "In that day," declares the LORD,

"I will destroy your horses from among you
and demolish your chariots.
11 I will destroy the cities of your land
and tear down all your strongholds.
12 I will destroy your witchcraft
and you will no longer cast spells.
13 I will destroy your carved images
and your sacred stones from among you;
you will no longer bow down

[a] 2 Or *rulers* [b] 2 Hebrew *goings out* [c] 2 Or *from days of eternity* [d] 6 Or *crush*
[e] 6 Or *Nimrod in its gates*

to the work of your hands.
14 I will uproot from among you your Asherah poles[a]
and demolish your cities.
15 I will take vengeance in anger and wrath
upon the nations that have not obeyed me."

The LORD's Case Against Israel

6 Listen to what the LORD says:

"Stand up, plead your case before the mountains;
let the hills hear what you have to say.
2 Hear, O mountains, the LORD's accusation;
listen, you everlasting foundations of the earth.
For the LORD has a case against his people;
he is lodging a charge against Israel.

3 "My people, what have I done to you?
How have I burdened you? Answer me.
4 I brought you up out of Egypt
and redeemed you from the land of slavery.
I sent Moses to lead you,
also Aaron and Miriam.
5 My people, remember
what Balak king of Moab counseled
and what Balaam son of Beor answered.
Remember ⌊your journey⌋ from Shittim to Gilgal,
that you may know the righteous acts of the LORD."

6 With what shall I come before the LORD
and bow down before the exalted God?
Shall I come before him with burnt offerings,
with calves a year old?
7 Will the LORD be pleased with thousands of rams,
with ten thousand rivers of oil?
Shall I offer my firstborn for my transgression,
the fruit of my body for the sin of my soul?
8 He has showed you, O man, what is good.
And what does the LORD require of you?
To act justly and to love mercy
and to walk humbly with your God.

Israel's Guilt and Punishment

9 Listen! The LORD is calling to the city—
and to fear your name is wisdom—
"Heed the rod and the One who appointed it.[b]
10 Am I still to forget, O wicked house,
your ill-gotten treasures
and the short ephah,[c] which is accursed?
11 Shall I acquit a man with dishonest scales,
with a bag of false weights?
12 Her rich men are violent;
her people are liars
and their tongues speak deceitfully.
13 Therefore, I have begun to destroy you,
to ruin you because of your sins.
14 You will eat but not be satisfied;

True spirituality manifests itself in:
The desire to be holy rather than happy.
The desire to see the honor of God advanced through his life.
The desire to carry his cross.
The desire to see everything from God's viewpoint.
The desire to die right rather than live wrong.
The desire to see others advance at his expense.
The desire to make eternity-judgments instead of time-judgments.
A.W. Tozer (1897-1963)

(6:6–8) With what shall I come before You in worship, O Lord? How shall I offer myself to You? Shall I come with songs of praise, with hymns of glory? Will You be pleased with shouts of thanksgiving, with prayers of confession? Shall I offer the tithe of my labor and gifts of gratitude? You have shown me what is good and what You require—not merely to do that which I call "worship," but to live my life in service to You, to present my body as a living sacrifice, holy and acceptable to You. This, indeed, is worship that pleases You. Awesome God, be glorified in my prayers and praises. Delight in my songs and hymns. Receive my tithe and my gifts. But help me, by Your indwelling Spirit, to worship You with all that I am, in each and every moment of each and every day. May my worship, once begun, never end! (Ro 12:1–2)

[a] *14* That is, symbols of the goddess Asherah [b] *9* The meaning of the Hebrew for this line is uncertain. [c] *10* An ephah was a dry measure.

(7:1–7) Faithful God, at times I place confidence elsewhere—in the skilled hands of doctors or the compassion of counselors, in the protection of laws or the visions of leaders, in the comfort of friends or the caring of family. But even these cannot help but let me down. You alone deserve my full confidence. You alone are my hope, a hope that will not fail. How much better to trust in You than to trust in people—even the best of Your people. Though others look for human solutions, as for me, I watch in hope for You. I wait for You, O God my Savior, like the night watchman waits for the morning. You will hear me. You will save me. With You is unfailing love; with You is full redemption. (Ps 118:8–9; 130:6–7; Isa 26:3–4)

Jesus! What a Friend for sinners!
Jesus! Lover of my soul;
Friends may fail me, foes assail me,
He, my Savior, makes me whole.

Hallelujah! What a Savior!
Hallelujah! What a Friend!
Saving, helping, keeping, loving,
He is with me to the end.

"Jesus! What a Friend for Sinners"
J. Wilbur Chapman (1910)

your stomach will still be empty.[a]
You will store up but save nothing,
because what you save I will give to the sword.
15 You will plant but not harvest;
you will press olives but not use the oil on yourselves,
you will crush grapes but not drink the wine.
16 You have observed the statutes of Omri
and all the practices of Ahab's house,
and you have followed their traditions.
Therefore I will give you over to ruin
and your people to derision;
you will bear the scorn of the nations.[b]"

Israel's Misery

7 What misery is mine!
I am like one who gathers summer fruit
at the gleaning of the vineyard;
there is no cluster of grapes to eat,
none of the early figs that I crave.
2 The godly have been swept from the land;
not one upright man remains.
All men lie in wait to shed blood;
each hunts his brother with a net.
3 Both hands are skilled in doing evil;
the ruler demands gifts,
the judge accepts bribes,
the powerful dictate what they desire—
they all conspire together.
4 The best of them is like a brier,
the most upright worse than a thorn hedge.
The day of your watchmen has come,
the day God visits you.
Now is the time of their confusion.
5 Do not trust a neighbor;
put no confidence in a friend.
Even with her who lies in your embrace
be careful of your words.
6 For a son dishonors his father,
a daughter rises up against her mother,
a daughter-in-law against her mother-in-law—
a man's enemies are the members of his own household.
7 But as for me, I watch in hope for the LORD,
I wait for God my Savior;
my God will hear me.

Israel Will Rise

8 Do not gloat over me, my enemy!
Though I have fallen, I will rise.
Though I sit in darkness,
the LORD will be my light.
9 Because I have sinned against him,
I will bear the LORD's wrath,

[a] 14 The meaning of the Hebrew for this word is uncertain. [b] 16 Septuagint; Hebrew *scorn due my people*

until he pleads my case
and establishes my right.
He will bring me out into the light;
I will see his righteousness.
10 Then my enemy will see it
and will be covered with shame,
she who said to me,
"Where is the LORD your God?"
My eyes will see her downfall;
even now she will be trampled underfoot
like mire in the streets.

11 The day for building your walls will come,
the day for extending your boundaries.
12 In that day people will come to you
from Assyria and the cities of Egypt,
even from Egypt to the Euphrates
and from sea to sea
and from mountain to mountain.
13 The earth will become desolate because of its inhabitants,
as the result of their deeds.

Prayer and Praise

14 Shepherd your people with your staff,
the flock of your inheritance,
which lives by itself in a forest,
in fertile pasturelands.[a]
Let them feed in Bashan and Gilead
as in days long ago.

15 "As in the days when you came out of Egypt,
I will show them my wonders."
16 Nations will see and be ashamed,
deprived of all their power.
They will lay their hands on their mouths
and their ears will become deaf.
17 They will lick dust like a snake,
like creatures that crawl on the ground.
They will come trembling out of their dens;
they will turn in fear to the LORD our God
and will be afraid of you.
18 Who is a God like you,
who pardons sin and forgives the transgression
of the remnant of his inheritance?
You do not stay angry forever
but delight to show mercy.
19 You will again have compassion on us;
you will tread our sins underfoot
and hurl all our iniquities into the depths of the sea.
20 You will be true to Jacob,
and show mercy to Abraham,
as you pledged on oath to our fathers
in days long ago.

[a] 14 Or *in the middle of Carmel*

(7:18–20) There is always hope with You, Father, for love "always hopes, always perseveres." Judgment is never Your final word against us. You warn us so that You might not have to wound us; You wound us so that You might heal us. You are compassionate and gracious, slow to anger, abounding in love. You will not always accuse, nor will You harbor Your anger forever. You do not treat us as our sins deserve; rather, You "tread our sins underfoot." You do not repay us according to our iniquities; rather, You "hurl all our iniquities into the depths of the sea." When we repent, You forgive our wickedness; our sins and our lawless acts You remember no more, for "love keeps no record of wrongs." Truly, You delight to show mercy. I praise Your holy name. (Ps 103:8–10; Jer 31:34; La 3:31–34; 1Co 13:5–7; Heb 10:17)

For who is like the Lord, my God?
Compassionate and full of mercy.
Who compares to Your great love?
There's none in all the earth.
I will sing of Your love and grace
That covers all my guilt and shame.
In all the earth
Who is like the Lord?

"Who Is Like the Lord?"
Holland Davis (©1998)

The love of God a perfect plan
Is planning now for thee,
It holds "a future and a hope,"
Which yet thou canst not see.

Freda Hanbury Allen

Nahum

The Book of

NAHUM

The prophet Nahum introduces God in terms rarely heard these days: "The LORD is a jealous and avenging God; the LORD takes vengeance and is filled with wrath" (1:2). How can the loving, gracious Father of Jesus be this same God? If we are to worship God "in spirit and *in truth*," (italics added), then we must worship Him as He has revealed Himself in the whole of inspired Scripture—even in Nahum.

How do we worship a jealous, wrath-filled God? Certainly not by taking this God lightly or by worshiping only at our convenience! The jealous God Who did not permit His people to worship idols still demands and deserves our full commitment and uncompromising worship. A wrathful God does not dismiss our sin but executes His judgment upon it. Therefore, we fall to our knees in repentance, and we raise our voices in thanksgiving for God's gracious decision to pour out His wrath—not upon us sinners, but upon His own sinless Son Who suffered and died in our place.

In Nahum God's wrath is turned, not against His people, but against those who have tormented them with endless cruelty (3:19). God is jealous for His people and avenges the injustices committed against them. Nahum reminds us that God is on our side, even if our present sufferings obscure this good news. When we suffer scorn for our faith, when we are persecuted for the name of Christ—as are thousands of believers each day throughout the world—we draw encouragement from the fact that God is with us. Someday He will settle the score with those who have opposed Him and His people.

> If we are to worship God "in spirit and *in truth*," then we must worship Him as He has revealed Himself in the whole of inspired Scripture.

In this way Nahum prefigures God's ultimate victory, not over human foes but over Satan. Though we may not face flesh-and-blood enemies, we all struggle "against the rulers, against the authorities, against the powers of this dark world and against the spiritual forces of evil in the heavenly realms" (Eph 6:12). Yet we press on in hope, knowing that God will ultimately defeat the powers of darkness. Thus, the prophecy of Nahum urges us to worship God in the classic words of Martin Luther: "And though this world, with devils filled, should threaten to undo us, we will not fear, for God hath willed His truth to triumph through us. The Prince of Darkness grim, we tremble not for him; his rage we can endure, for lo, his doom is sure; one little word shall fell him."* That "little" Word is Jesus, for it is at His name that "every knee shall bow in heaven and on earth and under the earth, and every tongue shall confess that Jesus Christ is Lord, to the glory of God the Father (Php 2:10–11).

*"A Mighty Fortess Is Our God," Martin Luther (1483–1546)

1 An oracle concerning Nineveh. The book of the vision of Nahum the Elkoshite.

The LORD's Anger Against Nineveh

2 The LORD is a jealous and avenging God;
the LORD takes vengeance and is filled with wrath.
The LORD takes vengeance on his foes
and maintains his wrath against his enemies.
3 The LORD is slow to anger and great in power;
the LORD will not leave the guilty unpunished.
His way is in the whirlwind and the storm,
and clouds are the dust of his feet.
4 He rebukes the sea and dries it up;
he makes all the rivers run dry.
Bashan and Carmel wither
and the blossoms of Lebanon fade.
5 The mountains quake before him
and the hills melt away.
The earth trembles at his presence,
the world and all who live in it.
6 Who can withstand his indignation?
Who can endure his fierce anger?
His wrath is poured out like fire;
the rocks are shattered before him.

7 The LORD is good,
a refuge in times of trouble.
He cares for those who trust in him,
8 but with an overwhelming flood
he will make an end of ⌞Nineveh⌟;
he will pursue his foes into darkness.

9 Whatever they plot against the LORD
he[a] will bring to an end;
trouble will not come a second time.
10 They will be entangled among thorns
and drunk from their wine;
they will be consumed like dry stubble.[b]
11 From you, ⌞O Nineveh,⌟ has one come forth
who plots evil against the LORD
and counsels wickedness.

12 This is what the LORD says:

"Although they have allies and are numerous,
they will be cut off and pass away.
Although I have afflicted you, ⌞O Judah,⌟
I will afflict you no more.
13 Now I will break their yoke from your neck
and tear your shackles away."

14 The LORD has given a command concerning you,
⌞Nineveh⌟:
"You will have no descendants to bear your
name.
I will destroy the carved images and cast idols
that are in the temple of your gods.

[a] 9 Or *What do you foes plot against the LORD? / He* [b] 10 The meaning of the Hebrew for this verse is uncertain.

(1:2–8) O Sovereign, jealous God, once You used the nation of Assyria as "the rod of [Your] anger" to execute judgment against Your chosen people for their idolatry. But You are the Judge, not only of Your people but of all nations. Not even prideful and powerful Assyria could stand in Your presence—You would take vengeance on their brutality. Yet for those who trust in You, after moments of discipline come seasons of blessing. For Your people, You will be a refuge once more, jealous for their wellbeing. O jealous, avenging, awesome God, with all the earth I bow humbly before You. O good, caring, protecting God, with Your people through the ages I hide myself in You. (2Ki 17:7–23; Isa 10:5–7)

We dare not think that God is absent or daydreaming. The do-nothing God. He's not tucked away in some far corner of the universe, uncaring, unfeeling, unthinking . . . uninvolved. Count on it–God intrudes in glorious and myriad ways.

Joni Eareckson Tada (1949-)

(2:2) I praise You, gracious God, for not abandoning us in our sin and brokenness. Just as You promised to restore Your people of old, so You promise us today in Christ. "For [You have] rescued us from the dominion of darkness and brought us into the kingdom of the Son [You love], in whom we have redemption, the forgiveness of sins." You mend broken lives and give hope to those who are oppressed. You set captives free and put an end to the tyranny of our enemy. I thank You for the restoration You have promised us in Christ: a restored relationship, restored holiness, restored purpose and fruitfulness. (Ezr 9:9; Col 1:13–14)

Holy Lord, most Holy Lord,
You alone are worthy of my praise;
O Holy Lord, most Holy Lord,
With all of my heart I sing.

Great are You, Lord.
Worthy of praise,
Holy and true,
Great are You, Lord,
Most Holy Lord.

"Great Are You, Lord"
Steve Cook and Vikki Cook (©1984)

I will prepare your grave,
for you are vile."

15 Look, there on the mountains,
the feet of one who brings good news,
who proclaims peace!
Celebrate your festivals, O Judah,
and fulfill your vows.
No more will the wicked invade you;
they will be completely destroyed.

Nineveh to Fall

2 An attacker advances against you, ⌊Nineveh⌋.
Guard the fortress,
watch the road,
brace yourselves,
marshal all your strength!

2 The LORD will restore the splendor of Jacob
like the splendor of Israel,
though destroyers have laid them waste
and have ruined their vines.

3 The shields of his soldiers are red;
the warriors are clad in scarlet.
The metal on the chariots flashes
on the day they are made ready;
the spears of pine are brandished.[a]
4 The chariots storm through the streets,
rushing back and forth through the squares.
They look like flaming torches;
they dart about like lightning.

5 He summons his picked troops,
yet they stumble on their way.
They dash to the city wall;
the protective shield is put in place.
6 The river gates are thrown open
and the palace collapses.
7 It is decreed[b] that ⌊the city⌋
be exiled and carried away.
Its slave girls moan like doves
and beat upon their breasts.
8 Nineveh is like a pool,
and its water is draining away.
"Stop! Stop!" they cry,
but no one turns back.
9 Plunder the silver!
Plunder the gold!
The supply is endless,
the wealth from all its treasures!
10 She is pillaged, plundered, stripped!
Hearts melt, knees give way,
bodies tremble, every face grows pale.

11 Where now is the lions' den,
the place where they fed their young,

[a] 3 Hebrew; Septuagint and Syriac / *the horsemen rush to and fro* [b] 7 The meaning of the Hebrew for this word is uncertain.

where the lion and lioness went,
and the cubs, with nothing to fear?
12 The lion killed enough for his cubs
and strangled the prey for his mate,
filling his lairs with the kill
and his dens with the prey.

13 "I am against you,"
declares the LORD Almighty.
"I will burn up your chariots in smoke,
and the sword will devour your young lions.
I will leave you no prey on the earth.
The voices of your messengers
will no longer be heard."

Woe to Nineveh

3 Woe to the city of blood,
full of lies,
full of plunder,
never without victims!
2 The crack of whips,
the clatter of wheels,
galloping horses
and jolting chariots!
3 Charging cavalry,
flashing swords
and glittering spears!
Many casualties,
piles of dead,
bodies without number,
people stumbling over the corpses—
4 all because of the wanton lust of a harlot,
alluring, the mistress of sorceries,
who enslaved nations by her prostitution
and peoples by her witchcraft.

5 "I am against you," declares the LORD Almighty.
"I will lift your skirts over your face.
I will show the nations your nakedness
and the kingdoms your shame.
6 I will pelt you with filth,
I will treat you with contempt
and make you a spectacle.
7 All who see you will flee from you and say,
'Nineveh is in ruins—who will mourn for her?'
Where can I find anyone to comfort you?"

8 Are you better than Thebes,[a]
situated on the Nile,
with water around her?
The river was her defense,
the waters her wall.
9 Cush[b] and Egypt were her boundless strength;
Put and Libya were among her allies.
10 Yet she was taken captive
and went into exile.
Her infants were dashed to pieces

[a] 8 Hebrew *No Amon* [b] 9 That is, the upper Nile region

(3:5–7) Lord, I confess that, because of my own imperfection, I sometimes struggle with the harshness of Your judgment against the ungodly. So often I try to soften the sting of Your wrath. How can the God of unlimited love and mercy also be the God of lethal justice? A part of me would like to claim one God as my own while leaving the other behind. But Your Scripture precludes this distortion. You are indeed the God of justice and love, the God of judgment and mercy. Help me to worship You in the fullness of Your truth. Only when I accept the gravity of Your condemnation can I appreciate the graciousness of Your condescension in Christ. Help me to worship You, Lord Almighty, as You are!

The wrath of God is as pure as the holiness of God. When God is angry he is perfectly angry. When he is displeased there is every reason he should be.

We tend to think of anger as sin; but sometimes it is sinful not to be angry. It is unthinkable that God would not be purely and perfectly angry with sin.

Stuart Briscoe (1930-)

(3:19) Righteous God, Your judgment upon the king of Assyria was final. Nothing could heal the wound of the one who opposed You, even though he had once been used as an instrument of Your will. Yet we know that behind this human opponent stood one who continues to rebel against You: the prince of this world. Through the death of Christ he has received a fatal wound. The time of his ultimate defeat draws near. We long for the day when the evil one and all of his kingdom will be crushed. We praise You, Almighty God! We exalt Your holy name! And we thank You, gracious Father, because through our Lord Jesus Christ You share Your eternal victory with us! (Isa 45:22–25; Jn 16:11; Ro 16:20; 1Co 15:57; Eph 6:12)

Come, let us worship Jesus,
King of nations, Lord of all;
Magnificent and glorious,
Just and merciful.

Fear God and give Him glory,
For His hour of judgment comes;
Creator, Lord Almighty,
Worship Him alone.

"King of the Nations"
Graham Kendrick (©1992)

at the head of every street.
Lots were cast for her nobles,
and all her great men were put in chains.
11 You too will become drunk;
you will go into hiding
and seek refuge from the enemy.

12 All your fortresses are like fig trees
with their first ripe fruit;
when they are shaken,
the figs fall into the mouth of the eater.
13 Look at your troops—
they are all women!
The gates of your land
are wide open to your enemies;
fire has consumed their bars.

14 Draw water for the siege,
strengthen your defenses!
Work the clay,
tread the mortar,
repair the brickwork!
15 There the fire will devour you;
the sword will cut you down
and, like grasshoppers, consume you.
Multiply like grasshoppers,
multiply like locusts!
16 You have increased the number of your merchants
till they are more than the stars of the sky,
but like locusts they strip the land
and then fly away.
17 Your guards are like locusts,
your officials like swarms of locusts
that settle in the walls on a cold day—
but when the sun appears they fly away,
and no one knows where.

18 O king of Assyria, your shepherds[a] slumber;
your nobles lie down to rest.
Your people are scattered on the mountains
with no one to gather them.
19 Nothing can heal your wound;
your injury is fatal.
Everyone who hears the news about you
claps his hands at your fall,
for who has not felt
your endless cruelty?

[a] 18 Or *rulers*

The Book of

HABAKKUK

The book of Habakkuk opens with a series of probing questions: "How long, O LORD, must I call for help, but you do not listen? Or cry out to you, 'Violence!' but you do not save? Why do you make me look at injustice? Why do you tolerate wrong?" (1:2–3). As the specter of the Babylonian invasion begins to loom over Judah, the prophet Habakkuk cries out to a God Who seems very far away. Though our circumstances differ from those of the prophet, we can feel the passion of his questions. Whether watching endless reports of violence on the news or standing at the bedside of a loved one who is dying from disease, we too have cried out to God: "Where are You?"

Habakkuk joins other Old Testament writers by exemplifying a blunt openness before the Lord. The prophet certainly recognizes God's majesty, yet he feels free nevertheless to lay himself and his doubts openly before God. He does not hold back or pretend, nor does he fill his prayers with pretty, empty words meant to charm the Lord.

God does not strike down Habakkuk for his boldness. Yet He does not answer Habakkuk's questions directly. In fact, God asserts His mysterious sovereignty by showing the prophet even greater sufferings yet to come (1:5–6). Only later will the day come when "the earth will be filled with the knowledge of the glory of the LORD" (2:14).

Habakkuk encourages us to be completely honest in our communication with God. Honesty and wordiness are not the same thing. Before an awesome God there is also a time for quiet: "The LORD is in his holy temple; let all the earth be silent before him" (2:20). Since God is real, unlike the Babylonian idols who cannot emerge from their slumber, there is no need to wake Him up with noisy worship. Though there is a time for loud rejoicing before God (Ne 12:43), Habakkuk reminds us that there is also a time for worship in reverential, humbled, awestruck silence.

Honesty and wordiness are not the same thing. Before an awesome God there is also a time for quiet.

The prophet invites us to trust God even in painful situations. As he condemns Babylonian unrighteousness, Habakkuk adds, "but the righteous will live by his faith" (2:4). This affirmation, which would later have a profound impact on the apostle Paul and his theological heirs, was originally meant to strengthen the trust of God's people as they suffered. Habakkuk urges us to remain faithful to God even when times are hard—and not only faithful, but also worshipful. "Though the fig tree does not bud and there are no grapes on the vines, though the olive crop fails and the fields produce no food, though there are no sheep in the pen and no cattle in the stalls, yet I will rejoice in the LORD, I will be joyful in God my Savior." (3:17–18). May God give to each of us the ability to worship Him with such faith and joy, even in seasons of distress and despair!

Habakkuk

God loves you dearly. He is willing to discipline you in order that you may share in his holiness and enjoy the blessings he has in store for the obedient Christian . . . The rod of God keeps you in his safe pasture and protects you from the consequences of foolish decisions.

Charles Stanley (1932-)

(1:2–6) O holy God, You are right in all Your judgments. You are patient and merciful to us, but You will not tolerate sin. You gave Your people the words of the Law, but they disobeyed them; You gave Your people the warnings of the prophets, but they disregarded them. Having shrugged away Your grace, they would now be swept away by Your anger. Since they would not be brought to repentance by Your lovingkindness, they would be brought to repentance by Your rod of discipline. O God, let us learn from their example to fear You and flee from evil.

1 The oracle that Habakkuk the prophet received.

Habakkuk's Complaint

2 How long, O LORD, must I call for help,
but you do not listen?
Or cry out to you, "Violence!"
but you do not save?
3 Why do you make me look at injustice?
Why do you tolerate wrong?
Destruction and violence are before me;
there is strife, and conflict abounds.
4 Therefore the law is paralyzed,
and justice never prevails.
The wicked hem in the righteous,
so that justice is perverted.

The LORD's Answer

5 "Look at the nations and watch—
and be utterly amazed.
For I am going to do something in your days
that you would not believe,
even if you were told.
6 I am raising up the Babylonians,[a]
that ruthless and impetuous people,
who sweep across the whole earth
to seize dwelling places not their own.
7 They are a feared and dreaded people;
they are a law to themselves
and promote their own honor.
8 Their horses are swifter than leopards,
fiercer than wolves at dusk.
Their cavalry gallops headlong;
their horsemen come from afar.
They fly like a vulture swooping to devour;
9 they all come bent on violence.
Their hordes[b] advance like a desert wind
and gather prisoners like sand.
10 They deride kings
and scoff at rulers.
They laugh at all fortified cities;
they build earthen ramps and capture them.
11 Then they sweep past like the wind and go on—
guilty men, whose own strength is their god."

Habakkuk's Second Complaint

12 O LORD, are you not from everlasting?
My God, my Holy One, we will not die.
O LORD, you have appointed them to execute judgment;
O Rock, you have ordained them to punish.
13 Your eyes are too pure to look on evil;
you cannot tolerate wrong.
Why then do you tolerate the treacherous?
Why are you silent while the wicked
swallow up those more righteous than themselves?
14 You have made men like fish in the sea,

[a] 6 Or *Chaldeans* [b] 9 The meaning of the Hebrew for this word is uncertain.

like sea creatures that have no ruler.
15 The wicked foe pulls all of them up with hooks,
he catches them in his net,
he gathers them up in his dragnet;
and so he rejoices and is glad.
16 Therefore he sacrifices to his net
and burns incense to his dragnet,
for by his net he lives in luxury
and enjoys the choicest food.
17 Is he to keep on emptying his net,
destroying nations without mercy?

2 I will stand at my watch
and station myself on the ramparts;
I will look to see what he will say to me,
and what answer I am to give to this complaint.[a]

The LORD's Answer

2 Then the LORD replied:

"Write down the revelation
and make it plain on tablets
so that a herald[b] may run with it.
3 For the revelation awaits an appointed time;
it speaks of the end
and will not prove false.
Though it linger, wait for it;
it[c] will certainly come and will not delay.

4 "See, he is puffed up;
his desires are not upright—
but the righteous will live by his faith[d]—
5 indeed, wine betrays him;
he is arrogant and never at rest.
Because he is as greedy as the grave[e]
and like death is never satisfied,
he gathers to himself all the nations
and takes captive all the peoples.

6 "Will not all of them taunt him with ridicule and scorn, saying,

" 'Woe to him who piles up stolen goods
and makes himself wealthy by extortion!
How long must this go on?'
7 Will not your debtors[f] suddenly arise?
Will they not wake up and make you tremble?
Then you will become their victim.
8 Because you have plundered many nations,
the peoples who are left will plunder you.
For you have shed man's blood;
you have destroyed lands and cities and everyone in them.

9 "Woe to him who builds his realm by unjust gain
to set his nest on high,
to escape the clutches of ruin!

[a] 1 Or *and what to answer when I am rebuked* [b] 2 Or *so that whoever reads it* [c] 3 Or *Though he linger, wait for him; / he* [d] 4 Or *faithfulness* [e] 5 Hebrew *Sheol* [f] 7 Or *creditors*

(1:12—2:9) O God, is it possible that You would use wicked people to punish those who were more righteous than themselves? Yes, in Your wisdom and divine justice You sometimes do use evil to punish evil. However, Your punishment is never for our destruction but always for our correction. And in the end, after You wash out the dish You will throw out the dish water; after You purify the gold You will put out the fire; after You discipline us with Your rod You will break that rod over Your knee. We praise You, O God, for Your promise of hope: " 'In a surge of anger I hid my face from you for a moment, but with everlasting kindness I will have compassion on you,' says the LORD your Redeemer." (2Ki 21:13; Ps 89:32–33; Isa 54:8; 1Pe 1:7)

(2:4) O Lord, thank You for this great promise of hope, this fundamental truth of our salvation: "The righteous will live by his faith." O God, strengthen both my faith and my faithfulness, my dependence and my dependability. May I truly find fullness of life through persistence in faith. (Ro 1:17; 2Co 5:7; Gal 3:11; Eph 2:8; Heb 10:38)

(2:10–17) O Lord, You are sovereign over all the earth. You are the Creator and Sustainer of all living things. Our Savior and our King, we long for You to come and put an end to oppression and violence. Come, O Lord; reveal your glory and deliver us from evil.

This is my Father's world,
O let me ne'er forget
That though the wrong
Seems oft so strong,
God is the Ruler yet.
This is my Father's world,
The battle is not done;
Jesus, who died,
Shall be satisfied,
And earth and heav'n be one.

"This Is My Father's World"
Maltbie Davenport Babcock (1901)

10 You have plotted the ruin of many peoples,
shaming your own house and forfeiting your life.
11 The stones of the wall will cry out,
and the beams of the woodwork will echo it.

12 "Woe to him who builds a city with bloodshed
and establishes a town by crime!
13 Has not the LORD Almighty determined
that the people's labor is only fuel for the fire,
that the nations exhaust themselves for nothing?
14 For the earth will be filled with the knowledge of the glory of the LORD,
as the waters cover the sea.

15 "Woe to him who gives drink to his neighbors,
pouring it from the wineskin till they are drunk,
so that he can gaze on their naked bodies.
16 You will be filled with shame instead of glory.
Now it is your turn! Drink and be exposed[a]!
The cup from the LORD's right hand is coming around to you,
and disgrace will cover your glory.
17 The violence you have done to Lebanon will overwhelm you,
and your destruction of animals will terrify you.
For you have shed man's blood;
you have destroyed lands and cities and everyone in them.

18 "Of what value is an idol, since a man has carved it?
Or an image that teaches lies?
For he who makes it trusts in his own creation;
he makes idols that cannot speak.
19 Woe to him who says to wood, 'Come to life!'
Or to lifeless stone, 'Wake up!'
Can it give guidance?
It is covered with gold and silver;
there is no breath in it.
20 But the LORD is in his holy temple;
let all the earth be silent before him."

Habakkuk's Prayer

3 A prayer of Habakkuk the prophet. On *shigionoth*.[b]

2 LORD, I have heard of your fame;
I stand in awe of your deeds, O LORD.
Renew them in our day,
in our time make them known;
in wrath remember mercy.

3 God came from Teman,
the Holy One from Mount Paran. *Selah*[c]
His glory covered the heavens
and his praise filled the earth.
4 His splendor was like the sunrise;
rays flashed from his hand,

[a] *16* Masoretic Text; Dead Sea Scrolls, Aquila, Vulgate and Syriac (see also Septuagint) *and stagger* [b] *1* Probably a literary or musical term [c] *3* A word of uncertain meaning; possibly a musical term; also in verses 9 and 13

where his power was hidden.
5 Plague went before him;
pestilence followed his steps.
6 He stood, and shook the earth;
he looked, and made the nations tremble.
The ancient mountains crumbled
and the age-old hills collapsed.
His ways are eternal.
7 I saw the tents of Cushan in distress,
the dwellings of Midian in anguish.
8 Were you angry with the rivers, O LORD?
Was your wrath against the streams?
Did you rage against the sea
when you rode with your horses
and your victorious chariots?
9 You uncovered your bow,
you called for many arrows. *Selah*
You split the earth with rivers;
10 the mountains saw you and writhed.
Torrents of water swept by;
the deep roared
and lifted its waves on high.

11 Sun and moon stood still in the heavens
at the glint of your flying arrows,
at the lightning of your flashing spear.
12 In wrath you strode through the earth
and in anger you threshed the nations.
13 You came out to deliver your people,
to save your anointed one.
You crushed the leader of the land of wickedness,
you stripped him from head to foot. *Selah*
14 With his own spear you pierced his head
when his warriors stormed out to scatter us,
gloating as though about to devour
the wretched who were in hiding.
15 You trampled the sea with your horses,
churning the great waters.

16 I heard and my heart pounded,
my lips quivered at the sound;
decay crept into my bones,
and my legs trembled.
Yet I will wait patiently for the day of calamity
to come on the nation invading us.
17 Though the fig tree does not bud
and there are no grapes on the vines,
though the olive crop fails
and the fields produce no food,
though there are no sheep in the pen
and no cattle in the stalls,
18 yet I will rejoice in the LORD,
I will be joyful in God my Savior.

19 The Sovereign LORD is my strength;
he makes my feet like the feet of a deer,
he enables me to go on the heights.

For the director of music. On my stringed instruments.

(3:17–19) O God, grant me faith like the faith of Habakkuk, this righteous man who lived by his faith. Help me to trust You regardless of circumstances. Raise my sights above the troubles of today, lift my heart above the sorrows of the season and help me to cling to You in the midst of the storm. Even in the face of suffering and loss, I will look to You for salvation. Your joy, O Lord, will be my strength. (Ne 8:10; Ps 28:7; Da 3:17–18)

I will not doubt, though all my ships at sea
Come drifting home with broken masts and sails;
I shall believe the hand which never fails,
From seeming evil worketh good to me.
And, though I weep because those sails are battered,
Still will I cry, while my best hopes lie shattered,
"I trust in thee."

Ella Wheeler Wilcox (1850-1919)

We expect a bright tomorrow,
All will be well.
Faith can sing through days of sorrow,
All will be well;
On our Father's love relying,
Jesus every need supplying,
In our living, in our dying,
All will be well.

"Through the Love of God Our Savior"
Mary Peters (1847)

The Book of ZEPHANIAH

In the final decades of the seventh century B.C., as Judah continues to skid down the precipice of covenant unfaithfulness, God raises up the prophet Zephaniah to shake up His lackadaisical people: "The great day of the LORD is near—near and coming quickly. Listen! The cry on the day of the LORD will be bitter, the shouting of the warrior there. That day will be a day of wrath, a day of distress and anguish" (1:14–15). The day of the Lord will bring judgment on God's people and their pagan neighbors.

How should the people of Israel respond to such a dire prediction? On the one hand, they must stop chattering and be quiet: "Be silent before the Sovereign LORD, for the day of the LORD is near" (1:7). On the other hand they must turn to God in obedience: "Seek the LORD, all you humble of the land, you who do what he commands. Seek righteousness, seek humility, perhaps you will be sheltered on the day of the LORD's anger" (2:3). As we reflect upon God's self-revelation through Zephaniah, we too are humbled before the majesty and holiness of the Lord. As we kneel before our mighty Judge and King, we worship in silence and seek after God.

Although the day of the Lord brings judgment, Zephaniah shows that it also ushers in a new season of worship. A faithful remnant of God's people will sing joyfully to the Lord (3:13–14). Moreover, after this remnant executes judgment upon the Gentile nations, even those peoples will bow before God: "The LORD will be awesome to them when he destroys all the gods of the land. The nations on every shore will worship him, every one in its own land" (2:11). The time will come when God will be hailed by all the earth: "Then will I purify the lips of the peoples, that all of them may call on the name of the LORD and serve him shoulder to shoulder. From beyond the rivers of Cush my worshipers, my scattered people, will bring me offerings" (3:9–10). With these promises Zephaniah foreshadows the extension of God's grace through Jesus Christ and the universal worship of the One before whom every knee shall bow and every tongue confess that "Jesus Christ is Lord" (Php 2:10–11).

We too are humbled before the majesty and holiness of the Lord. As we kneel before our mighty Judge and King, we worship in silence and seek after God.

Perhaps the most surprising and poignant passage of Zephaniah comes near the end of the book: "Sing, O Daughter of Zion; shout aloud, O Israel! Be glad and rejoice with all your heart, O Daughter of Jerusalem! . . . The LORD your God is with you, he is mighty to save. He will take great delight in you, he will quiet you with his love, he will rejoice over you with singing" (3:14,17). What an astounding picture of God's love for His people! How exuberant and fervent our worship will be when we remember that God delights in us, even with joyful singing!

The word of the LORD that came to Zephaniah son of Cushi, the son of Gedaliah, the son of Amariah, the son of Hezekiah, during the reign of Josiah son of Amon king of Judah:

Warning of Coming Destruction

"I will sweep away everything
from the face of the earth," declares the LORD.
"I will sweep away both men and animals;
I will sweep away the birds of the air
... heaps of rubble
... from the face of the earth," declares the LORD.

Against Judah

4 "I will stretch out my hand against Judah
and against all who live in Jerusalem.
I will cut off from this place every remnant of Baal,
the names of the pagan and the idolatrous priests—
5 those who bow down on the roofs
to worship the starry host,
those who bow down and swear by the LORD
and who also swear by Molech,[b]
6 those who turn back from following the LORD
and neither seek the LORD nor inquire of him.

7 Be silent before the Sovereign LORD,
for the day of the LORD is near.
The LORD has prepared a sacrifice;
he has consecrated those he has invited.
8 On the day of the LORD's sacrifice
I will punish the princes
and the king's sons
and all those clad
in foreign clothes.
9 On that day I will punish
all who avoid stepping on the threshold,[c]
who fill the temple of their gods
with violence and deceit.

10 "On that day," declares the LORD,
"a cry will go up from the Fish Gate,
wailing from the New Quarter,
and a loud crash from the hills.
11 Wail, you who live in the market district[d];
all your merchants will be wiped out,
all who trade with[e] silver will be ruined.
12 At that time I will search Jerusalem with lamps
and punish those who are complacent,
who are like wine left on its dregs,
who think, 'The LORD will do nothing,
either good or bad.'
13 Their wealth will be plundered,
their houses demolished.
They will build houses

[a] 3 The meaning of the Hebrew for this line is uncertain. [b] 5 Hebrew *Malcam*, that is, Milcom [c] 9 See 1 Samuel 5:5. [d] 11 Or *the Mortar* [e] 11 Or *in*

From first to last, [the prophet's] design was, not to drive the people to despair, but to drive them to God and to their duty—not to frighten them out of their wits, but to frighten them out of their sins.
Matthew Henry (1662–1714)

(1:1–13) Most holy and righteous Father, who cannot stand in judgment of these who mixed Your worship with idolatry. Instead, I need to ruthlessly examine the idols I have set up in my own heart. I declare that You and You alone are the One true God. I commit my life and love to You. I choose to humble myself under Your hand. Forgive me for my idolatry. Forgive me for my complacency. Forgive me for my presumption and disrespect. Although You are my Father, You are also the almighty, sovereign God of the universe. Though You are to be loved, You are also to be feared. May I always address You with deep reverence in worship. (Eze 14:7–8)

Christ, whose purpose is to kindle:
Now ignite us with Thy fire;
While the earth awaits Thy burning,
With Thy passion us inspire.
Overcome our sinful calmness,
Rouse us with redemptive shame;
Baptize with Thy fiery Spirit,
Crown our lives with tongues of
flame.

Thou, who still a sword delivers
Rather than a placid peace:
With Thy sharpened Word disturb
us,
From complacency release!
Save us now from satisfaction
When we privately are free,
Yet are undisturbed in spirit
By our neighbors misery.
"Christ, Whose Purpose Is to Kindle"
D. Elton Trueblood (1900-1994)

The great causes of God and Humanity are not defeated by the hot assaults of the Devil, but by the slow, crushing, glacierlike masses of thousands and thousands of indifferent nobodies. God's causes are never destroyed by being blown up, but by being sat upon.
George Adam Smith (1856-1942)

Pride is the cold mountain peak, sterile and bleak; humility is the quiet valley fertile and abounding in life, and peace lives there.

Anne Austin (1921-)

(2:1–3) Thank You, merciful God, that You do not wa
warn us because
wound us. Just as a day of judgmer
coming for the ancient world, so a
judgment is coming for our world.
face of such imminent danger You c
not to scatter and hide but to gather
pray. In Your kindness You lead us t
pentance. You will humble those
will not humble themselves. But th
who humble themselves and pray a
seek Your face and turn from their wick
ways—those who call on Your nam
Lord—will be saved. "Have mercy on m
O God, have mercy on me, for in you m
soul takes refuge. I will take refuge in th
shadow of your wings until the disaste
has passed." (2Ch 7:14; Ps 57:1; Joel 2:32; Zep 3:12; Ro 2:4)

Depth of mercy! Can there be
Mercy still reserved for me?
Can my God His wrath forbear,
Me, the chief of sinners, spare?

Lord, incline me to repent;
Let me now my sins lament;
Now my foul revolt deplore,
Weep, believe, and sin no more.

Still for me the Savior stands,
Holding forth His wounded hands;
God is love! I know, I feel,
Jesus weeps and loves me still.

"Depth of Mercy! Can There Be"
Charles Wesley (1740)

but not live in them;
they will plant vineyards
but not drink the wine.

The Great Day of the LORD

14 "The great day of the LORD is near—
near and coming quickly.
Listen! The cry on the day of
the shouting of the warrior
15 That day will be a day
a day of distress and anguish,
a day of trouble and
a day of darkness
a day of clouds
16 a day of trumpet and battle cry
against the fortified cities
and against the corner towers.
17 I will bring distress on the people
and they will walk like blind men,
because they have sinned against the LORD.
Their blood will be poured out like dust
and their entrails like filth.
18 Neither their silver nor their gold
will be able to save them
on the day of the LORD's wrath.
In the fire of his jealousy
the whole world will be consumed,
for he will make a sudden end
of all who live in the earth."

2 Gather together, gather together,
O shameful nation,
2 before the appointed time arrives
and that day sweeps on like chaff,
before the fierce anger of the LORD comes upon you,
before the day of the LORD's wrath comes upon you.
3 Seek the LORD, all you humble of the land,
you who do what he commands.
Seek righteousness, seek humility;
perhaps you will be sheltered
on the day of the LORD's anger.

Against Philistia

4 Gaza will be abandoned
and Ashkelon left in ruins.
At midday Ashdod will be emptied
and Ekron uprooted.
5 Woe to you who live by the sea,
O Kerethite people;
the word of the LORD is against you,
O Canaan, land of the Philistines.
"I will destroy you,
and none will be left."

6 The land by the sea, where the Kerethites[a]
dwell,

[a] 6 The meaning of the Hebrew for this word is uncertain.

Pride is the cold mountain peak, sterile and bleak; humility is the quiet valley fertile and abounding in life, and peace lives there.

Anne Austin (1921-)

(2:1–3) Thank You, merciful God, that You warn us because You do not want to wound us. Just as a day of judgment was coming for the ancient world, so a day of judgment is coming for our world. In the face of such imminent danger You call us not to scatter and hide but to gather and pray. In Your kindness You lead us to repentance. You will humble those who will not humble themselves. But those who humble themselves and pray and seek Your face and turn from their wicked ways—those who call on Your name, Lord—will be saved. "Have mercy on me, O God, have mercy on me, for in you my soul takes refuge. I will take refuge in the shadow of your wings until the disaster has passed." (2Ch 7:14; Ps 57:1; Joel 2:32; Zep 3:12; Ro 2:4)

Depth of mercy! Can there be
Mercy still reserved for me?
Can my God His wrath forbear,
Me, the chief of sinners, spare?

Lord, incline me to repent;
Let me now my sins lament;
Now my foul revolt deplore,
Weep, believe, and sin no more.

Still for me the Savior stands,
Holding forth His wounded hands;
God is love! I know, I feel,
Jesus weeps and loves me still.

"Depth of Mercy! Can There Be"
Charles Wesley (1740)

but not live in them;
they will plant vineyards
but not drink the wine.

The Great Day of the LORD

14 "The great day of the LORD is near—
near and coming quickly.
Listen! The cry on the day of the LORD will be bitter,
the shouting of the warrior there.
15 That day will be a day of wrath,
a day of distress and anguish,
a day of trouble and ruin,
a day of darkness and gloom,
a day of clouds and blackness,
16 a day of trumpet and battle cry
against the fortified cities
and against the corner towers.
17 I will bring distress on the people
and they will walk like blind men,
because they have sinned against the LORD.
Their blood will be poured out like dust
and their entrails like filth.
18 Neither their silver nor their gold
will be able to save them
on the day of the LORD's wrath.
In the fire of his jealousy
the whole world will be consumed,
for he will make a sudden end
of all who live in the earth."

2 Gather together, gather together,
O shameful nation,
2 before the appointed time arrives
and that day sweeps on like chaff,
before the fierce anger of the LORD comes upon you,
before the day of the LORD's wrath comes upon you.
3 Seek the LORD, all you humble of the land,
you who do what he commands.
Seek righteousness, seek humility;
perhaps you will be sheltered
on the day of the LORD's anger.

Against Philistia

4 Gaza will be abandoned
and Ashkelon left in ruins.
At midday Ashdod will be emptied
and Ekron uprooted.
5 Woe to you who live by the sea,
O Kerethite people;
the word of the LORD is against you,
O Canaan, land of the Philistines.

"I will destroy you,
and none will be left."

6 The land by the sea, where the Kerethites[a]
dwell,

[a] 6 The meaning of the Hebrew for this word is uncertain.

1 The word of the LORD that came to Zephaniah son of Cushi, the son of Gedaliah, the son of Amariah, the son of Hezekiah, during the reign of Josiah son of Amon king of Judah:

Warning of Coming Destruction

2 "I will sweep away everything
from the face of the earth,"
declares the LORD.
3 "I will sweep away both men and animals;
I will sweep away the birds of the air
and the fish of the sea.
The wicked will have only heaps of rubble[a]
when I cut off man from the face of the earth,"
declares the LORD.

Against Judah

4 "I will stretch out my hand against Judah
and against all who live in Jerusalem.
I will cut off from this place every remnant of Baal,
the names of the pagan and the idolatrous priests—
5 those who bow down on the roofs
to worship the starry host,
those who bow down and swear by the LORD
and who also swear by Molech,[b]
6 those who turn back from following the LORD
and neither seek the LORD nor inquire of him.
7 Be silent before the Sovereign LORD,
for the day of the LORD is near.
The LORD has prepared a sacrifice;
he has consecrated those he has invited.
8 On the day of the LORD's sacrifice
I will punish the princes
and the king's sons
and all those clad
in foreign clothes.
9 On that day I will punish
all who avoid stepping on the threshold,[c]
who fill the temple of their gods
with violence and deceit.

10 "On that day," declares the LORD,
"a cry will go up from the Fish Gate,
wailing from the New Quarter,
and a loud crash from the hills.
11 Wail, you who live in the market district[d];
all your merchants will be wiped out,
all who trade with[e] silver will be ruined.
12 At that time I will search Jerusalem with lamps
and punish those who are complacent,
who are like wine left on its dregs,
who think, 'The LORD will do nothing,
either good or bad.'
13 Their wealth will be plundered,
their houses demolished.
They will build houses

[a] *3* The meaning of the Hebrew for this line is uncertain. [b] *5* Hebrew *Malcam,* that is, Milcom [c] *9* See 1 Samuel 5:5. [d] *11* Or *the Mortar* [e] *11* Or *in*

From first to last, [the prophet's] design was, not to drive the people to despair, but to drive them to God and to their duty—not to frighten them out of their wits, but to frighten them out of their sins.
Matthew Henry (1662-1714)

(1:1–13) Most holy and righteous Father, I cannot stand in judgment of these who mixed Your worship with idolatry. Instead, I need to ruthlessly examine the idols I have set up in my own heart. I declare that You and You alone are the One true God. I commit my life and love to You. I choose to humble myself under Your hand. Forgive me for my idolatry. Forgive me for my complacency. Forgive me for my presumption and disrespect. Although You are my Father, You are also the almighty, sovereign God of the universe. Though You are to be loved, You are also to be feared. May I always address You with deep reverence in worship. (Eze 14:7–8)

Christ, whose purpose is to kindle:
Now ignite us with Thy fire;
While the earth awaits Thy burning,
With Thy passion us inspire.
Overcome our sinful calmness,
Rouse us with redemptive shame;
Baptize with Thy fiery Spirit,
Crown our lives with tongues of
flame.

Thou, who still a sword delivers
Rather than a placid peace:
With Thy sharpened Word disturb
us,
From complacency release!
Save us now from satisfaction
When we privately are free,
Yet are undisturbed in spirit
By our neighbor's misery.
"Christ, Whose Purpose Is to Kindle"
D. Elton Trueblood (1900-1994)

The great causes of God and Humanity are not defeated by the hot assaults of the Devil, but by the slow, crushing, glacierlike masses of thousands and thousands of indifferent nobodies. God's causes are never destroyed by being blown up, but by being sat upon.
George Adam Smith (1856-1942)

will be a place for shepherds and sheep pens.
7 It will belong to the remnant of the house of Judah;
there they will find pasture.
In the evening they will lie down
in the houses of Ashkelon.
The LORD their God will care for them;
he will restore their fortunes.[a]

Against Moab and Ammon

8 "I have heard the insults of Moab
and the taunts of the Ammonites,
who insulted my people
and made threats against their land.
9 Therefore, as surely as I live,"
declares the LORD Almighty, the God of Israel,
"surely Moab will become like Sodom,
the Ammonites like Gomorrah—
a place of weeds and salt pits,
a wasteland forever.
The remnant of my people will plunder them;
the survivors of my nation will inherit their
land."
10 This is what they will get in return for their pride,
for insulting and mocking the people of the LORD
Almighty.
11 The LORD will be awesome to them
when he destroys all the gods of the land.
The nations on every shore will worship him,
every one in its own land.

Against Cush

12 "You too, O Cushites,[b]
will be slain by my sword."

Against Assyria

13 He will stretch out his hand against the north
and destroy Assyria,
leaving Nineveh utterly desolate
and dry as the desert.
14 Flocks and herds will lie down there,
creatures of every kind.
The desert owl and the screech owl
will roost on her columns.
Their calls will echo through the windows,
rubble will be in the doorways,
the beams of cedar will be exposed.
15 This is the carefree city
that lived in safety.
She said to herself,
"I am, and there is none besides me."
What a ruin she has become,
a lair for wild beasts!
All who pass by her scoff
and shake their fists.

(2:11) From the North to the South, from the East to the West, Your name will be greatly exalted. Your ultimate purpose for judgment is that all the world will worship You as the One true God. When You delivered Israel from Egypt You brought judgment on all the gods of that nation. Against Moab and Ammon You also promised to destroy all the gods of the land so that the nations would worship You. And another day is yet coming when the idols of our time will be broken, when every knee shall bow and every tongue shall confess that Jesus Christ is Lord, to the glory of God the Father! (Ex 12:12; Php 2:9–11)

Let every kindred, every tribe,
On this terrestrial ball,
To Him all majesty ascribe,
And crown Him Lord of all!
To Him all majesty ascribe,
And crown Him Lord of all!

"All Hail the Power of Jesus' Name"
Edward Perronet (1779)

[a] 7 Or *will bring back their captives* [b] 12 That is, people from the upper Nile region

(3:9–12) In Your great wisdom, O God, You have chosen the meek and humble—those who are poor in the eyes of the world—to be rich in faith and to inherit the kingdom You promised to those who love You. Lord, let me be among those whom You favor. Purge me of my sinful pride. Purify my heart so that I might love You unreservedly. Purify my lips so that I might praise Your name, for it is in Your name that I put my trust. (Jas 2:5)

If you should ask me what are the ways of God, I would tell you that the first is humility, the second is humility, and the third is humility. Not that there are no other precepts to give, but if humility does not precede all that we do, our efforts are fruitless.

Saint Augustine of Hippo (354-430)

O for a heart to praise my God,
A heart from sin set free,
A heart that always feels Thy blood
So freely shed for me!

A humble, lowly, contrite heart,
Believing, true and clean;
Which neither life nor death can part
From Him that dwells within.

A heart in every thought renewed,
And full of love divine;
Perfect and right and pure and good,
A copy, Lord, of Thine!

"O for a Heart to Praise My God"
Charles Wesley (1742)

The Future of Jerusalem

3 Woe to the city of oppressors,
rebellious and defiled!
2 She obeys no one,
she accepts no correction.
She does not trust in the LORD,
she does not draw near to her God.
3 Her officials are roaring lions,
her rulers are evening wolves,
who leave nothing for the morning.
4 Her prophets are arrogant;
they are treacherous men.
Her priests profane the sanctuary
and do violence to the law.
5 The LORD within her is righteous;
he does no wrong.
Morning by morning he dispenses his justice,
and every new day he does not fail,
yet the unrighteous know no shame.

6 "I have cut off nations;
their strongholds are demolished.
I have left their streets deserted,
with no one passing through.
Their cities are destroyed;
no one will be left—no one at all.
7 I said to the city,
'Surely you will fear me
and accept correction!'
Then her dwelling would not be cut off,
nor all my punishments come upon her.
But they were still eager
to act corruptly in all they did.
8 Therefore wait for me," declares the LORD,
"for the day I will stand up to testify.[a]
I have decided to assemble the nations,
to gather the kingdoms
and to pour out my wrath on them—
all my fierce anger.
The whole world will be consumed
by the fire of my jealous anger.

9 "Then will I purify the lips of the peoples,
that all of them may call on the name of the LORD
and serve him shoulder to shoulder.
10 From beyond the rivers of Cush[b]
my worshipers, my scattered people,
will bring me offerings.
11 On that day you will not be put to shame
for all the wrongs you have done to me,
because I will remove from this city
those who rejoice in their pride.
Never again will you be haughty
on my holy hill.
12 But I will leave within you

[a] *8* Septuagint and Syriac; Hebrew *will rise up to plunder* [b] *10* That is, the upper Nile region

the meek and humble,
who trust in the name of the LORD.
13 The remnant of Israel will do no wrong;
they will speak no lies,
nor will deceit be found in their mouths.
They will eat and lie down
and no one will make them afraid."

14 Sing, O Daughter of Zion;
shout aloud, O Israel!
Be glad and rejoice with all your heart,
O Daughter of Jerusalem!
15 The LORD has taken away your punishment,
he has turned back your enemy.
The LORD, the King of Israel, is with you;
never again will you fear any harm.
16 On that day they will say to Jerusalem,
"Do not fear, O Zion;
do not let your hands hang limp.
17 The LORD your God is with you,
he is mighty to save.
He will take great delight in you,
he will quiet you with his love,
he will rejoice over you with singing."
18 "The sorrows for the appointed feasts
I will remove from you;
they are a burden and a reproach to you.[a]
19 At that time I will deal
with all who oppressed you;
I will rescue the lame
and gather those who have been scattered.
I will give them praise and honor
in every land where they were put to shame.
20 At that time I will gather you;
at that time I will bring you home.
I will give you honor and praise
among all the peoples of the earth
when I restore your fortunes[b]
before your very eyes,"
says the LORD.

[a] 18 Or *"I will gather you who mourn for the appointed feasts; / your reproach is a burden to you* [b] 20 Or *I bring back your captives*

(3:17) Such hope! Such mercy! Such everlasting love! You do not punish us to harm us but to correct us. It may appear that Your hand is set on our destruction, yet Your eye is focused on our restoration. We praise You, O God, that even though You may speak to us with words of judgment You will yet sing over us with words of comfort. For Your anger lasts only a moment, but Your love lasts a lifetime. "You are my hiding place; you will protect me from trouble and surround me with songs of deliverance." (Ps 30:5; 32:7)

There's a wideness in God's mercy
Like the wideness of the sea;
There's a kindness in His justice
Which is more than liberty.

There is welcome for the sinner
And more graces for the good;
There is mercy with the Savior;
There is healing in His blood.

For the love of God is broader
Than the measure of man's mind;
And the heart of the Eternal
Is most wonderfully kind.

"There's a Wideness in God's Mercy"
Frederick W. Faber (1862)

Lord, what a change within us one short hour
Spent in thy presence will avail to make!
What heavy burdens from our bosoms take!
What parched grounds refresh as with a shower!
We kneel, and all around us seems to lower;
We rise, and all, the distant and the near,
Stands forth in sunny outline brave and clear;
We kneel, how weak! We rise, how full of power!
Why, therefore, should we do ourselves this wrong
Or others, that we are not always strong,
That we should ever weak or heartless be,
Anxious or troubled, when with us is prayer,
And joy and strength and courage are with thee!

Archbishop Richard Chenevix Trench (1807-1886)

The Book of

HAGGAI

Haggai

In 539 B.C. the Persians overthrow the Babylonians, establishing a new empire that includes Judea among its territories. Cyrus, the Persian king, allows the Jews to return from exile in Babylon and to rebuild the temple in Jerusalem. But initial enthusiasm for the project wanes, and 18 years later the temple is still not finished. God sends the prophet Haggai (along with Zechariah) to spur the Jews on to finish rebuilding the temple.

The fact that the people have ignored the temple, while building fashionable houses for themselves (1:4), reveals their skewed priorities. They have placed their own comfort and enjoyment above the worship of God. By calling them to rebuild the temple, God challenges His people to establish right priorities for their lives—with worship as the highest priority of all. Haggai confronts us with the question of what comes first in our lives. Do we truly believe that we exist for the praise of God's glory (Eph 1:12)? Do we actually live as though our chief purpose is "to glorify God and to enjoy him forever"*

Sometimes, like the Jews who heed Haggai's prophecy, we need the Word of God to rearrange our priorities and to motivate us to give worship its proper place. As we study and meditate upon the Scriptures, we find it increasingly difficult to deny God the honor He deserves from us. Haggai informs us that displacing God and His worship can in fact compromise divine blessing in our lives (ch. 1). Though we should not worship out of a selfish desire to win God's favor, we do believe that right worship brings our lives into alignment with the flow of God's grace and blessing (2:18-19). When we give God proper place and glory, the rest of our life falls into proper order under God's reign. As Jesus taught us, when we "seek first his kingdom and his righteousness . . . all these things will be given to you as well" (Mt 6:33)

Haggai confronts us with the question of what comes first in our lives. Do we truly believe that we exist for the praise of God's glory?

Chapter 2 associates the temple with the coming of God's glory (2:7–9). Haggai looks through the window of his present day into the future when God will shake all nations and fill the temple with His full radiance. Zerubbabel, the one who oversees the rebuilding of the temple, will be God's "signet ring," thus prefiguring the Messiah yet to come (2:20–23). Though using images from the present day situation of Judah, Haggai's prophecy points ahead to the time when, through Jesus Christ, God's glory will be fully revealed. Jesus, Who claims to be greater even than the temple (Mt 12:6), is truly Immanuel, "God with us" (Mt 1:23). Thus we worship, not facing toward the Jerusalem temple as the Jews once did (1Ki 8:29–48; Da 6:10), but with our hearts focused on Jesus the Messiah, Who radiates the very glory of God (Jn 1:14).

*(*Westminster Shorter Catechism*, Question and Answer 1)

A Call to Build the House of the LORD

1 In the second year of King Darius, on the first day of the sixth
month, the word of the LORD came through the prophet Haggai to Zerubbabel son of Shealtiel, governor of Judah, and to
Joshua[a] son of Jehozadak, the high priest:
2This is what the LORD Almighty says: "These people say, 'The
time has not yet come for the LORD's house to be built.' "
3Then the word of the LORD came through the prophet Haggai:
4"Is it a time for you yourselves to be living in your paneled
houses, while this house remains a ruin?"
5Now this is what the LORD Almighty says: "Give careful thought
to your ways. 6You have planted much, but have harvested little.
You eat, but never have enough. You drink, but never have your
fill. You put on clothes, but are not warm. You earn wages, only
to put them in a purse with holes in it."
7This is what the LORD Almighty says: "Give careful thought to
your ways. 8Go up into the mountains and bring down timber and
build the house, so that I may take pleasure in it and be honored," says the LORD. 9"You expected much, but see, it turned out
to be little. What you brought home, I blew away. Why?" declares
the LORD Almighty. "Because of my house, which remains a ruin,
while each of you is busy with his own house. 10Therefore, because of you the heavens have withheld their dew and the earth its
crops. 11I called for a drought on the fields and the mountains,
on the grain, the new wine, the oil and whatever the ground produces, on men and cattle, and on the labor of your hands."

12Then Zerubbabel son of Shealtiel, Joshua son of Jehozadak,
the high priest, and the whole remnant of the people obeyed the
voice of the LORD their God and the message of the prophet Haggai, because the LORD their God had sent him. And the people
feared the LORD.
13Then Haggai, the LORD's messenger, gave this message of the
LORD to the people: "I am with you," declares the LORD. 14So the
LORD stirred up the spirit of Zerubbabel son of Shealtiel, governor
of Judah, and the spirit of Joshua son of Jehozadak, the high
priest, and the spirit of the whole remnant of the people. They
came and began to work on the house of the LORD Almighty, their
God, 15on the twenty-fourth day of the sixth month in the second
year of King Darius.

The Promised Glory of the New House

2 On the twenty-first day of the seventh month, the word of the
LORD came through the prophet Haggai: 2"Speak to Zerubbabel son of Shealtiel, governor of Judah, to Joshua son of Jehozadak, the high priest, and to the remnant of the people. Ask
them, 3'Who of you is left who saw this house in its former glory?
How does it look to you now? Does it not seem to you like nothing? 4But now be strong, O Zerubbabel,' declares the LORD. 'Be
strong, O Joshua son of Jehozadak, the high priest. Be strong, all
you people of the land,' declares the LORD, 'and work. For I am
with you,' declares the LORD Almighty. 5'This is what I covenanted
with you when you came out of Egypt. And my Spirit remains
among you. Do not fear.'
6"This is what the LORD Almighty says: 'In a little while I will

[a] *1* A variant of *Jeshua*; here and elsewhere in Haggai

(1:3–11) O Lord, our God, I praise You for fulfilling Your promise to return Your people from exile. Yet how quickly their priorities changed. And isn't it the same with me today? I fret and run after earthly needs and temporal wealth, and neglect that which is important to You—the heavenly task to which You have appointed me. Lord, teach me to be faithful in my care for Your temple. Straighten out my priorities so that I will seek first Your kingdom and Your righteousness. Then, as You have promised, all these other things will be given to me as well. Father in heaven, I dedicate all that I am and all that I have to Your kingdom purposes, and I trust You to take care of my needs. (Hag 2:18–19; Mt 6:25–33)

Dear Father, I want you to establish your truth in my innermost being. I am sometimes so easily distracted and disturbed by outward circumstances that I neglect to cultivate a genuine devotion to you. Work through your Spirit to remove any false way and teach me to guard my heart through your indwelling presence. Control my thoughts and motivations and bring me into conformity with your will.

Charles Stanley (1932-)

once more shake the heavens and the earth, the sea and the dry
land. 7I will shake all nations, and the desired of all nations will
come, and I will fill this house with glory,' says the LORD Almighty.
8'The silver is mine and the gold is mine,' declares the LORD
Almighty. 9'The glory of this present house will be greater than the
glory of the former house,' says the LORD Almighty. 'And in this
place I will grant peace,' declares the LORD Almighty."

Blessings for a Defiled People

10On the twenty-fourth day of the ninth month, in the second
year of Darius, the word of the LORD came to the prophet Haggai:
11"This is what the LORD Almighty says: 'Ask the priests what the
law says: 12If a person carries consecrated meat in the fold of his
garment, and that fold touches some bread or stew, some wine,
oil or other food, does it become consecrated?' "

The priests answered, "No."

13Then Haggai said, "If a person defiled by contact with a dead
body touches one of these things, does it become defiled?"

"Yes," the priests replied, "it becomes defiled."

14Then Haggai said, " 'So it is with this people and this nation
in my sight,' declares the LORD. 'Whatever they do and whatever
they offer there is defiled.

15" 'Now give careful thought to this from this day on[a]—consider how things were before one stone was laid on another in the
LORD's temple. 16When anyone came to a heap of twenty measures, there were only ten. When anyone went to a wine vat to
draw fifty measures, there were only twenty. 17I struck all the
work of your hands with blight, mildew and hail, yet you did not
turn to me,' declares the LORD. 18'From this day on, from this
twenty-fourth day of the ninth month, give careful thought to the
day when the foundation of the LORD's temple was laid. Give careful thought: 19Is there yet any seed left in the barn? Until now, the
vine and the fig tree, the pomegranate and the olive tree have not
borne fruit.

" 'From this day on I will bless you.' "

Zerubbabel the LORD's Signet Ring

20The word of the LORD came to Haggai a second time on the
twenty-fourth day of the month: 21"Tell Zerubbabel governor of
Judah that I will shake the heavens and the earth. 22I will overturn
royal thrones and shatter the power of the foreign kingdoms. I
will overthrow chariots and their drivers; horses and their riders
will fall, each by the sword of his brother.

23" 'On that day,' declares the LORD Almighty, 'I will take you,
my servant Zerubbabel son of Shealtiel,' declares the LORD, 'and I
will make you like my signet ring, for I have chosen you,' declares
the LORD Almighty."

(2:6–9) What a glorious promise You gave to Your people. But we see the promise of an even greater and more glorious temple, a temple made without hands, that is built out of living stones upon the foundation of Jesus Christ, Who is indeed the One "desired of all nations." We, Your people, are the temple of the Lord, more glorious than any building made with human hands, for we have been fashioned by Your own hands, purchased with Your own blood, and set apart to be Your residence on the earth. Come, Prince of Peace, and fill this temple with Your glory! (Ac 7:48; 17:24; 1Co 6:19,20; 1Pe 2:5)

Jesus, be not a guest
That tarrieth but a day;
Come to my longing breast,
Come, and forever stay.

R.F. Pechey

[a] 15 Or *to the days past*

The Book of ZECHARIAH

God uses the prophet Zechariah to inspire the remnant of His people to finish rebuilding the temple in Jerusalem (Ezr 6:14). The prophet's concern for the temple shows up in the book by his name, but there it plays a relatively small role in the drama (1:16; 4:9; 6:15). Zechariah's stage is the whole world, not simply Jerusalem. His play tells the story, not merely of temple-rebuilding, but of the vast future of cosmic history.

Zechariah is not any easy book to understand, partly because it is an example of apocalyptic literature. This genre includes fantastic visions, grand schemes and mysterious interpretations. Often history is "telescoped," with past, present and future described as happening at the same time. Above all, Jewish and Christian apocalyptic writings demonstrate God's ultimate sovereignty over everything. God is the cosmic playwright and authoritative director of the drama of history. We worship this God with awe, humble obedience and confidence in His rule over all that is and is to come.

Given the scope of the apocalyptic drama, God deserves to be worshiped, not only by His chosen people but by citizens of all nations: " 'Shout and be glad, O Daughter of Zion. For I am coming, and I will live among you,' declares the LORD. 'Many nations will be joined with the LORD in that day and will become my people' " (2:10–11). As living water flows from Jerusalem to the whole earth, so people from all nations will go up to Jerusalem "to worship the King, the LORD Almighty" (14:8,16). We live in partial fulfillment of Zechariah's prophecy, even as we anticipate the day when every knee shall bow before Christ and every tongue confess that He is Lord (Php 2:10–11). This vision enlivens our worship while filling us with hope.

Christian worship remembers God's faithfulness in the past while looking ahead to His victory in the future.

Zechariah helps to focus this hope upon the Lord's Messiah. He will be the promised Branch (3:8; 6:12), the cornerstone and tent peg (10:4). In a passage familiar to Christians, Zechariah prophesies: "Rejoice greatly, O Daughter of Zion! Shout, Daughter of Jerusalem! See, your king comes to you, righteous and having salvation, gentle and riding on a donkey, on a colt, the foal of a donkey" (9:9). Some five centuries after Zechariah a crowd of Jews gathered along the streets of Jerusalem to welcome the One Who fulfilled the prophet's vision of the humble Messianic King (Mt 21:1–9).

We now realize that Jesus came as Israel's Messiah, not to defeat the earthly power of Rome but rather to defeat the spiritual power of sin and death. In worship we celebrate what God has done through Christ, yet at the same time we yearn for the time when God will dwell fully with us, wiping every tear from our eyes and making all things new (Rev 21:3–5). Christian worship remembers God's faithfulness in the past while looking ahead to His victory in the future.

A Call to Return to the LORD

1 In the eighth month of the second year of Darius, the word of
the LORD came to the prophet Zechariah son of Berekiah, the
son of Iddo:
2"The LORD was very angry with your forefathers. 3Therefore
tell the people: This is what the LORD Almighty says: 'Return to
me,' declares the LORD Almighty, 'and I will return to you,' says
the LORD Almighty. 4Do not be like your forefathers, to whom the
earlier prophets proclaimed: This is what the LORD Almighty says:
'Turn from your evil ways and your evil practices.' But they would
not listen or pay attention to me, declares the LORD. 5Where are
your forefathers now? And the prophets, do they live forever? 6But
did not my words and my decrees, which I commanded my servants the prophets, overtake your forefathers?
"Then they repented and said, 'The LORD Almighty has done to
us what our ways and practices deserve, just as he determined
to do.' "

The Man Among the Myrtle Trees

7On the twenty-fourth day of the eleventh month, the month of
Shebat, in the second year of Darius, the word of the LORD came
to the prophet Zechariah son of Berekiah, the son of Iddo.
8During the night I had a vision—and there before me was a
man riding a red horse! He was standing among the myrtle trees
in a ravine. Behind him were red, brown and white horses.
9I asked, "What are these, my lord?"
The angel who was talking with me answered, "I will show you
what they are."
10Then the man standing among the myrtle trees explained,
"They are the ones the LORD has sent to go throughout the earth."
11And they reported to the angel of the LORD, who was standing
among the myrtle trees, "We have gone throughout the earth and
found the whole world at rest and in peace."
12Then the angel of the LORD said, "LORD Almighty, how long
will you withhold mercy from Jerusalem and from the towns of
Judah, which you have been angry with these seventy years?" 13So
the LORD spoke kind and comforting words to the angel who
talked with me.
14Then the angel who was speaking to me said, "Proclaim
this word: This is what the LORD Almighty says: 'I am very jealous
for Jerusalem and Zion, 15but I am very angry with the nations
that feel secure. I was only a little angry, but they added to the
calamity.'
16"Therefore, this is what the LORD says: 'I will return to Jerusalem with mercy, and there my house will be rebuilt. And the
measuring line will be stretched out over Jerusalem,' declares the
LORD Almighty.
17"Proclaim further: This is what the LORD Almighty says: 'My
towns will again overflow with prosperity, and the LORD will again
comfort Zion and choose Jerusalem.' "

Four Horns and Four Craftsmen

18Then I looked up—and there before me were four horns!
19I asked the angel who was speaking to me, "What are these?"
He answered me, "These are the horns that scattered Judah, Israel and Jerusalem."

(1:8–13) Lord, in the night seasons when moral darkness seems to close in about me, open my eyes to see what You are doing. Stir my imagination with vision. Capture my heart with divine mysteries. Flood my soul with the knowledge of Your unfailing love. Teach me in a faithless day to observe Your faithfulness in all things and at all times. You are neither quick to act nor slow to answer, but are always faithful to those who love You. O Lord, You are the God of all comfort. (2Co 1:3)

Christian worship remembers God's faithfulness in the past while looking ahead to His victory in the future.

Praise Him for His grace and favor
To our fathers in distress;
Praise Him, still the same as ever,
Slow to chide and swift to bless.
Alleluia! Alleluia!
Glorious in His faithfulness!

"Praise, My Soul, the King of Heaven"
Henry F. Lyte (1834)

20Then the LORD showed me four craftsmen. 21I asked, "What
are these coming to do?"
He answered, "These are the horns that scattered Judah so
that no one could raise his head, but the craftsmen have come
to terrify them and throw down these horns of the nations who
lifted up their horns against the land of Judah to scatter its
people."

A Man With a Measuring Line

2 Then I looked up—and there before me was a man with a
measuring line in his hand! 2I asked, "Where are you going?"
He answered me, "To measure Jerusalem, to find out how wide
and how long it is."
3Then the angel who was speaking to me left, and another
angel came to meet him 4and said to him: "Run, tell that young
man, 'Jerusalem will be a city without walls because of the great
number of men and livestock in it. 5And I myself will be a wall
of fire around it,' declares the LORD, 'and I will be its glory
within.'
6"Come! Come! Flee from the land of the north," declares the
LORD, "for I have scattered you to the four winds of heaven," declares the LORD.
7"Come, O Zion! Escape, you who live in the Daughter of Babylon!" 8For this is what the LORD Almighty says: "After he has honored me and has sent me against the nations that have plundered
you—for whoever touches you touches the apple of his eye— 9I
will surely raise my hand against them so that their slaves will
plunder them.[a] Then you will know that the LORD Almighty has
sent me.
10"Shout and be glad, O Daughter of Zion. For I am coming,
and I will live among you," declares the LORD. 11"Many nations
will be joined with the LORD in that day and will become my people. I will live among you and you will know that the LORD
Almighty has sent me to you. 12The LORD will inherit Judah as his
portion in the holy land and will again choose Jerusalem. 13Be
still before the LORD, all mankind, because he has roused himself
from his holy dwelling."

Clean Garments for the High Priest

3 Then he showed me Joshua[b] the high priest standing before
the angel of the LORD, and Satan[c] standing at his right side to
accuse him. 2The LORD said to Satan, "The LORD rebuke you,
Satan! The LORD, who has chosen Jerusalem, rebuke you! Is not
this man a burning stick snatched from the fire?"
3Now Joshua was dressed in filthy clothes as he stood before
the angel. 4The angel said to those who were standing before him,
"Take off his filthy clothes."
Then he said to Joshua, "See, I have taken away your sin, and
I will put rich garments on you."
5Then I said, "Put a clean turban on his head." So they put a
clean turban on his head and clothed him, while the angel of the
LORD stood by.
6The angel of the LORD gave this charge to Joshua: 7"This is
what the LORD Almighty says: 'If you will walk in my ways and keep
my requirements, then you will govern my house and have charge

[a] 8,9 Or *says after . . . eye: 9"I . . . plunder them."* [b] 1 A variant of *Jeshua*; here and elsewhere in Zechariah [c] 1 *Satan* means *accuser.*

(2:3–5) O God, You long to bless Your people beyond our small borders! The walls that we erect to protect us only serve to confine us from the fullness of Your immeasurable blessings. How shall we remain content within boundaries that human pride has built and the human mind can measure? You, O Lord, shall be our wall—a wall of fire. Cause Your glory to rest upon us as You accomplish Your work within us.

Within thy circling power I stand;
On every side I find thy hand;
Awake, asleep, at home, abroad,
I am surrounded still with God.

Isaac Watts (1674-1748)

God ruleth on high, almighty to save.
And still He is nigh; His presence we have.
The great congregation His triumph shall sing,
Ascribing salvation to Jesus our King.

"Ye Servants of God"
Charles Wesley (1744)

(2:10—3:5) We will shout and be glad! We will break forth and run for joy! You, O Lord God Almighty, have roused Yourself from Your holy dwelling that You might come and dwell with us. You have looked upon us in compassion and delivered us with Your mighty hand. You have rebuked our accuser and removed our shame. You have clothed us in Your righteousness and crowned us with everlasting joy.

Lord, what we know not, teach us.
Lord, what we have not, give us.
Lord, what we are not, make us.
Saint Augustine of Hippo (354–430)

(4:6) As I face the challenge of rebuilding my life from the ravages of sin and failure, it is reassuring to know that it is not my power that must do this job. You, Lord, take charge of the things that concern me. No fear in my heart, no fainting in my soul, no frustration in my thoughts, no feebleness in my hands will ever cause Your work to fail. Though at times the progress seems slow, Your Spirit's work in my life is advancing. The great mountains of opposition are crumbling, a glorious habitation for You is rising, and I sing for joy at Your amazing grace! (Php 1:6)

Holy Ghost, with light divine,
Shine upon this heart of mine;
Chase the shades of night away,
Turn my darkness into day.

Holy Ghost, with pow'r divine,
Cleanse this guilty heart of mine;
Long hath sin without control
Held dominion o'er my soul.

Holy Spirit, all divine,
Dwell within this heart of mine;
Cast down ev'ry idol throne,
Reign supreme and reign alone.
"Holy Ghost, with Light Divine"
Andrew Reed (1787–1862)

of my courts, and I will give you a place among these standing here.
8" 'Listen, O high priest Joshua and your associates seated before you, who are men symbolic of things to come: I am going to bring my servant, the Branch. 9See, the stone I have set in front of Joshua! There are seven eyes[a] on that one stone, and I will engrave an inscription on it,' says the LORD Almighty, 'and I will remove the sin of this land in a single day.
10" 'In that day each of you will invite his neighbor to sit under his vine and fig tree,' declares the LORD Almighty."

The Gold Lampstand and the Two Olive Trees

4 Then the angel who talked with me returned and wakened me, as a man is wakened from his sleep. 2He asked me, "What do you see?"
I answered, "I see a solid gold lampstand with a bowl at the top and seven lights on it, with seven channels to the lights. 3Also there are two olive trees by it, one on the right of the bowl and the other on its left."
4I asked the angel who talked with me, "What are these, my lord?"
5He answered, "Do you not know what these are?"
"No, my lord," I replied.
6So he said to me, "This is the word of the LORD to Zerubbabel: 'Not by might nor by power, but by my Spirit,' says the LORD Almighty.
7"What[b] are you, O mighty mountain? Before Zerubbabel you will become level ground. Then he will bring out the capstone to shouts of 'God bless it! God bless it!' "
8Then the word of the LORD came to me: 9"The hands of Zerubbabel have laid the foundation of this temple; his hands will also complete it. Then you will know that the LORD Almighty has sent me to you.
10"Who despises the day of small things? Men will rejoice when they see the plumb line in the hand of Zerubbabel.
"(These seven are the eyes of the LORD, which range throughout the earth.)"
11Then I asked the angel, "What are these two olive trees on the right and the left of the lampstand?"
12Again I asked him, "What are these two olive branches beside the two gold pipes that pour out golden oil?"
13He replied, "Do you not know what these are?"
"No, my lord," I said.
14So he said, "These are the two who are anointed to[c] serve the Lord of all the earth."

The Flying Scroll

5 I looked again—and there before me was a flying scroll!
2He asked me, "What do you see?"
I answered, "I see a flying scroll, thirty feet long and fifteen feet wide.[d]"
3And he said to me, "This is the curse that is going out over the whole land; for according to what it says on one side, every thief will be banished, and according to what it says on the other, everyone who swears falsely will be banished. 4The LORD Almighty

[a] 9 Or *facets* [b] 7 Or *Who* [c] 14 Or *two who bring oil and* [d] 2 Hebrew *twenty cubits long and ten cubits wide* (about 9 meters long and 4.5 meters wide)

declares, 'I will send it out, and it will enter the house of the thief
and the house of him who swears falsely by my name. It will remain in his house and destroy it, both its timbers and its
stones.' "

The Woman in a Basket

5Then the angel who was speaking to me came forward and
said to me, "Look up and see what this is that is appearing."
6I asked, "What is it?"
He replied, "It is a measuring basket.[a]" And he added, "This is
the iniquity[b] of the people throughout the land."
7Then the cover of lead was raised, and there in the basket sat
a woman! **8**He said, "This is wickedness," and he pushed her
back into the basket and pushed the lead cover down over its
mouth.
9Then I looked up—and there before me were two women,
with the wind in their wings! They had wings like those of a stork,
and they lifted up the basket between heaven and earth.
10"Where are they taking the basket?" I asked the angel who
was speaking to me.
11He replied, "To the country of Babylonia[c] to build a house
for it. When it is ready, the basket will be set there in its place."

Four Chariots

6 I looked up again—and there before me were four chariots
coming out from between two mountains—mountains of
bronze! **2**The first chariot had red horses, the second black, **3**the
third white, and the fourth dappled—all of them powerful. **4**I
asked the angel who was speaking to me, "What are these, my
lord?"
5The angel answered me, "These are the four spirits[d] of heav-
en, going out from standing in the presence of the Lord of the
whole world. **6**The one with the black horses is going toward the
north country, the one with the white horses toward the west,[e]
and the one with the dappled horses toward the south."
7When the powerful horses went out, they were straining to go
throughout the earth. And he said, "Go throughout the earth!" So
they went throughout the earth.
8Then he called to me, "Look, those going toward the north
country have given my Spirit[f] rest in the land of the north."

A Crown for Joshua

9The word of the LORD came to me: **10**"Take ⌊silver and gold⌋
from the exiles Heldai, Tobijah and Jedaiah, who have arrived
from Babylon. Go the same day to the house of Josiah son of
Zephaniah. **11**Take the silver and gold and make a crown, and set
it on the head of the high priest, Joshua son of Jehozadak. **12**Tell
him this is what the LORD Almighty says: 'Here is the man whose
name is the Branch, and he will branch out from his place and
build the temple of the LORD. **13**It is he who will build the temple
of the LORD, and he will be clothed with majesty and will sit and
rule on his throne. And he will be a priest on his throne. And
there will be harmony between the two.' **14**The crown will be
given to Heldai,[g] Tobijah, Jedaiah and Hen[h] son of Zephaniah as

[a] 6 Hebrew *an ephah*; also in verses 7–11 [b] 6 Or *appearance* [c] 11 Hebrew *Shinar*
[d] 5 Or *winds* [e] 6 Or *horses after them* [f] 8 Or *spirit* [g] 14 Syriac; Hebrew *Helem*
[h] 14 Or *and the gracious one, the*

(5:8–11) Lord God, how I long for the day when You will deliver me from the seduction of sin, when You will shut up the tempter's power and send it far away. Lord, let me never make peace with sin or settle for its presence in my life. Let me never relinquish any ground to its advances. Purify my heart, Lord, and let sin be carried away captive back to the place from which it came.

(6:12–13) O Christ, my Redeemer, who but You can be both high priest and eternal king? As my great Priest You have built the temple of the Lord, a temple built without hands, a habitation for my God. You have made the sacrifice that covers all my sin and makes me acceptable in God's holy presence. As my glorious King You have conquered the power of sin and death, and You reign victoriously in righteousness. Truth is Your law. Mercy is Your scepter. My Priest and my King, I worship You in reverence and awe.

(7:5–6) Lord, I confess that at times I equate saying the right words and doing the right things. I live in the midst of a people who honor speech above deeds. Forgive me, Lord, and lead me to a higher place of service, a deeper place of devotion. May my singing be an act of genuine worship. May my work be motivated by a genuine desire to serve You. May my religious actions be pleasing to you. Father, take me past the superficial gestures of religion, and bring me into the depths of a living faith born out of relationship with You.

A Christian should always remember that the value of his good works is not based on their number and excellence, but on the love of God which prompts him to do these things.

Saint John of the Cross (1542–1591)

If You asked me for an offering I'd
give it,
If You wanted sacrifice I would obey.
But my life is all I have and I will live
it,
Dedicated to the honor of Your
name.

Here I am, and I long to do Your
will.
Here I am, I'll follow Your command.
Here I am, until my calling is fulfilled.
Here I am, here I am.

"Here I Am"
Bill Batstone (©1996)

a memorial in the temple of the LORD. 15Those who are far away
will come and help to build the temple of the LORD, and you will
know that the LORD Almighty has sent me to you. This will happen
if you diligently obey the LORD your God."

Justice and Mercy, Not Fasting

7 In the fourth year of King Darius, the word of the LORD came
to Zechariah on the fourth day of the ninth month, the month
of Kislev. 2The people of Bethel had sent Sharezer and Regem-
Melech, together with their men, to entreat the LORD 3by asking
the priests of the house of the LORD Almighty and the prophets,
"Should I mourn and fast in the fifth month, as I have done for so
many years?"

4Then the word of the LORD Almighty came to me: 5"Ask all the
people of the land and the priests, 'When you fasted and
mourned in the fifth and seventh months for the past seventy
years, was it really for me that you fasted? 6And when you were
eating and drinking, were you not just feasting for yourselves?
7Are these not the words the LORD proclaimed through the earlier prophets when Jerusalem and its surrounding towns were at
rest and prosperous, and the Negev and the western foothills
were settled?' "

8And the word of the LORD came again to Zechariah: 9"This is
what the LORD Almighty says: 'Administer true justice; show mercy
and compassion to one another. 10Do not oppress the widow or
the fatherless, the alien or the poor. In your hearts do not think
evil of each other.'

11"But they refused to pay attention; stubbornly they turned
their backs and stopped up their ears. 12They made their hearts
as hard as flint and would not listen to the law or to the words
that the LORD Almighty had sent by his Spirit through the earlier
prophets. So the LORD Almighty was very angry.

13" 'When I called, they did not listen; so when they called, I
would not listen,' says the LORD Almighty. 14'I scattered them with
a whirlwind among all the nations, where they were strangers.
The land was left so desolate behind them that no one could
come or go. This is how they made the pleasant land desolate.' "

The LORD Promises to Bless Jerusalem

8 Again the word of the LORD Almighty came to me. 2This is
what the LORD Almighty says: "I am very jealous for Zion; I
am burning with jealousy for her."

3This is what the LORD says: "I will return to Zion and dwell in
Jerusalem. Then Jerusalem will be called the City of Truth, and
the mountain of the LORD Almighty will be called the Holy Mountain."

4This is what the LORD Almighty says: "Once again men and
women of ripe old age will sit in the streets of Jerusalem, each
with cane in hand because of his age. 5The city streets will be
filled with boys and girls playing there."

6This is what the LORD Almighty says: "It may seem marvelous
to the remnant of this people at that time, but will it seem marvelous to me?" declares the LORD Almighty.

7This is what the LORD Almighty says: "I will save my people
from the countries of the east and the west. 8I will bring them
back to live in Jerusalem; they will be my people, and I will be
faithful and righteous to them as their God."

9This is what the LORD Almighty says: "You who now hear these
words spoken by the prophets who were there when the foundation was laid for the house of the LORD Almighty, let your hands be
strong so that the temple may be built. 10Before that time there
were no wages for man or beast. No one could go about his business safely because of his enemy, for I had turned every man
against his neighbor. 11But now I will not deal with the remnant
of this people as I did in the past," declares the LORD Almighty.

12"The seed will grow well, the vine will yield its fruit, the
ground will produce its crops, and the heavens will drop their
dew. I will give all these things as an inheritance to the remnant
of this people. 13As you have been an object of cursing among the
nations, O Judah and Israel, so will I save you, and you will be a
blessing. Do not be afraid, but let your hands be strong."

14This is what the LORD Almighty says: "Just as I had determined to bring disaster upon you and showed no pity when your
fathers angered me," says the LORD Almighty, 15"so now I have
determined to do good again to Jerusalem and Judah. Do not be
afraid. 16These are the things you are to do: Speak the truth to
each other, and render true and sound judgment in your courts;
17do not plot evil against your neighbor, and do not love to swear
falsely. I hate all this," declares the LORD.

18Again the word of the LORD Almighty came to me. 19This is
what the LORD Almighty says: "The fasts of the fourth, fifth, seventh
and tenth months will become joyful and glad occasions and
happy festivals for Judah. Therefore love truth and peace."

20This is what the LORD Almighty says: "Many peoples and the
inhabitants of many cities will yet come, 21and the inhabitants of
one city will go to another and say, 'Let us go at once to entreat
the LORD and seek the LORD Almighty. I myself am going.' 22And
many peoples and powerful nations will come to Jerusalem to
seek the LORD Almighty and to entreat him."

23This is what the LORD Almighty says: "In those days ten men
from all languages and nations will take firm hold of one Jew by
the hem of his robe and say, 'Let us go with you, because we have
heard that God is with you.' "

Judgment on Israel's Enemies

An Oracle

9 The word of the LORD is against the land of Hadrach
and will rest upon Damascus—
for the eyes of men and all the tribes of Israel
are on the LORD—[a]
2and upon Hamath too, which borders on it,
and upon Tyre and Sidon, though they are very skillful.
3Tyre has built herself a stronghold;
she has heaped up silver like dust,
and gold like the dirt of the streets.
4But the Lord will take away her possessions
and destroy her power on the sea,
and she will be consumed by fire.
5Ashkelon will see it and fear;
Gaza will writhe in agony,

[a] 1 Or *Damascus. / For the eye of the LORD is on all mankind, / as well as on the tribes of Israel,*

(8:12) Under the curse of sin I have labored and brought forth nothing. The sweat of my brow has yielded little to me but thorns. O how fruitless is life apart from You. But in Christ, O hallelujah, how the seed does grow! The vines yield fruit, the ground produces crops, and the heavens drop their dew. Father, You are pleased to bless those whom You have saved, and in that salvation You make them a blessing to others. May the same be true of me today!

(8:18–23) Thank You, Father, for Your restoring mercies. You give us truth to rule our thoughts and peace to rule our hearts. You turn our fasting into feasting, and our mourning into great rejoicing. By these blessings and more, may the world see that You are with us, and come seeking Your salvation. (Ps 86:9; Isa 66:10)

and Ekron too, for her hope will wither.
Gaza will lose her king
and Ashkelon will be deserted.
6 Foreigners will occupy Ashdod,
and I will cut off the pride of the Philistines.
7 I will take the blood from their mouths,
the forbidden food from between their teeth.
Those who are left will belong to our God
and become leaders in Judah,
and Ekron will be like the Jebusites.
8 But I will defend my house
against marauding forces.
Never again will an oppressor overrun my people,
for now I am keeping watch.

The Coming of Zion's King

9 Rejoice greatly, O Daughter of Zion!
Shout, Daughter of Jerusalem!
See, your king[a] comes to you,
righteous and having salvation,
gentle and riding on a donkey,
on a colt, the foal of a donkey.
10 I will take away the chariots from Ephraim
and the war-horses from Jerusalem,
and the battle bow will be broken.
He will proclaim peace to the nations.
His rule will extend from sea to sea
and from the River[b] to the ends of the earth.[c]
11 As for you, because of the blood of my covenant with you,
I will free your prisoners from the waterless pit.
12 Return to your fortress, O prisoners of hope;
even now I announce that I will restore twice as much to you.
13 I will bend Judah as I bend my bow
and fill it with Ephraim.
I will rouse your sons, O Zion,
against your sons, O Greece,
and make you like a warrior's sword.

The LORD Will Appear

14 Then the LORD will appear over them;
his arrow will flash like lightning.
The Sovereign LORD will sound the trumpet;
he will march in the storms of the south,
15 and the LORD Almighty will shield them.
They will destroy
and overcome with slingstones.
They will drink and roar as with wine;
they will be full like a bowl
used for sprinkling[d] the corners of the altar.
16 The LORD their God will save them on that day
as the flock of his people.
They will sparkle in his land
like jewels in a crown.

[a] 9 Or *King* [b] 10 That is, the Euphrates [c] 10 Or *the end of the land*
[d] 15 Or *bowl, / like*

(9:9–11) Lord Jesus, You are our twice-coming eternal King. First You came in gentle righteousness, bringing salvation from heaven above. By Your blood of the new covenant You freed us from the prison of sin and filled us with hope of a glorious new world to come. At Your second coming, You will appear in majestic power to lift us from this world's desolation into the abundance of Your kingdom. While we await Your return, Lord Jesus, come and establish Your rule of peace in our hearts. (Mt 21:1–11)

O come, Desire of nations, bind
In one the hearts of all mankind;
Bid Thou our sad divisions cease,
And be Thyself our King of Peace.
"O Come, O Come, Emmanuel"
Latin Hymn (12th c.)
Trans. Henry S. Coffin (1916)

17 How attractive and beautiful they will be!
Grain will make the young men thrive,
and new wine the young women.

The LORD Will Care for Judah

10 Ask the LORD for rain in the springtime;
it is the LORD who makes the storm clouds.
He gives showers of rain to men,
and plants of the field to everyone.
2 The idols speak deceit,
diviners see visions that lie;
they tell dreams that are false,
they give comfort in vain.
Therefore the people wander like sheep
oppressed for lack of a shepherd.

3 "My anger burns against the shepherds,
and I will punish the leaders;
for the LORD Almighty will care
for his flock, the house of Judah,
and make them like a proud horse in
battle.
4 From Judah will come the cornerstone,
from him the tent peg,
from him the battle bow,
from him every ruler.
5 Together they[a] will be like mighty men
trampling the muddy streets in battle.
Because the LORD is with them,
they will fight and overthrow the horsemen.

6 "I will strengthen the house of Judah
and save the house of Joseph.
I will restore them
because I have compassion on them.
They will be as though
I had not rejected them,
for I am the LORD their God
and I will answer them.
7 The Ephraimites will become like mighty men,
and their hearts will be glad as with wine.
Their children will see it and be joyful;
their hearts will rejoice in the LORD.
8 I will signal for them
and gather them in.
Surely I will redeem them;
they will be as numerous as before.
9 Though I scatter them among the peoples,
yet in distant lands they will remember me.
They and their children will survive,
and they will return.
10 I will bring them back from Egypt
and gather them from Assyria.
I will bring them to Gilead and Lebanon,
and there will not be room enough for
them.

[a] 4,5 Or *ruler, all of them together.* / [5] *They*

(10:1–6) Just as You send rain to quench the thirst of the parched ground, so You send living water to quench the thirst of my soul. You are my only source of life and sustenance. Lead me like a shepherd into the green pastures of Your Word. Restore me, O God. In Your great compassion, grant to me Your strength and salvation. Then my way will be prosperous and my life will be secure.

As the deer panteth for the water,
So my soul longeth after Thee.
You alone are my heart's desire,
And I long to worship Thee.

You alone are my strength, my
shield;
To You alone may my spirit yield.
You alone are my heart's desire,
And I long to worship Thee.

"As the Deer"
Martin Nystrom (©1984)

11 They will pass through the sea of trouble;
the surging sea will be subdued
and all the depths of the Nile will dry up.
Assyria's pride will be brought down
and Egypt's scepter will pass away.
12 I will strengthen them in the LORD
and in his name they will walk,"
declares the LORD.

11 Open your doors, O Lebanon,
so that fire may devour your cedars!
2 Wail, O pine tree, for the cedar has fallen;
the stately trees are ruined!
Wail, oaks of Bashan;
the dense forest has been cut down!
3 Listen to the wail of the shepherds;
their rich pastures are destroyed!
Listen to the roar of the lions;
the lush thicket of the Jordan is ruined!

Two Shepherds

4 This is what the LORD my God says: "Pasture the flock marked
for slaughter. 5 Their buyers slaughter them and go unpunished.
Those who sell them say, 'Praise the LORD, I am rich!' Their own
shepherds do not spare them. 6 For I will no longer have pity on
the people of the land," declares the LORD. "I will hand everyone
over to his neighbor and his king. They will oppress the land, and
I will not rescue them from their hands."
7 So I pastured the flock marked for slaughter, particularly the
oppressed of the flock. Then I took two staffs and called one
Favor and the other Union, and I pastured the flock. 8 In one
month I got rid of the three shepherds.
The flock detested me, and I grew weary of them 9 and said, "I
will not be your shepherd. Let the dying die, and the perishing
perish. Let those who are left eat one another's flesh."
10 Then I took my staff called Favor and broke it, revoking the
covenant I had made with all the nations. 11 It was revoked on
that day, and so the afflicted of the flock who were watching me
knew it was the word of the LORD.
12 I told them, "If you think it best, give me my pay; but if not,
keep it." So they paid me thirty pieces of silver.
13 And the LORD said to me, "Throw it to the potter"—the
handsome price at which they priced me! So I took the thirty
pieces of silver and threw them into the house of the LORD to the
potter.
14 Then I broke my second staff called Union, breaking the
brotherhood between Judah and Israel.
15 Then the LORD said to me, "Take again the equipment of a
foolish shepherd. 16 For I am going to raise up a shepherd over
the land who will not care for the lost, or seek the young, or heal
the injured, or feed the healthy, but will eat the meat of the choice
sheep, tearing off their hoofs.

17 "Woe to the worthless shepherd,
who deserts the flock!
May the sword strike his arm and his right eye!
May his arm be completely withered,
his right eye totally blinded!"

(11:17) Lord Jesus, Great Shepherd of the sheep, I pray for those whom You have called to serve Your purposes by shepherding Your flock. Strengthen them with grace and bless them with success in doing Your will. Teach them to seek the lost, care for the young, heal the injured, and feed the hungry. (Ac 20:28–31; Heb 13:20; 1Pe 5:2)

Go, labor on; spend and be spent–
Thy joy to do the Father's will;
It is the way the Master went;
Should not the servant tread it still?
Horatius Bonar (1808-1889)

Jerusalem's Enemies to Be Destroyed

An Oracle

12 This is the word of the LORD concerning Israel. The LORD,
who stretches out the heavens, who lays the foundation of
the earth, and who forms the spirit of man within him, declares:
2"I am going to make Jerusalem a cup that sends all the surrounding peoples reeling. Judah will be besieged as well as Jerusalem. 3On that day, when all the nations of the earth are gathered
against her, I will make Jerusalem an immovable rock for all the
nations. All who try to move it will injure themselves. 4On that
day I will strike every horse with panic and its rider with madness," declares the LORD. "I will keep a watchful eye over the
house of Judah, but I will blind all the horses of the nations.
5Then the leaders of Judah will say in their hearts, 'The people of
Jerusalem are strong, because the LORD Almighty is their God.'
6"On that day I will make the leaders of Judah like a firepot in
a woodpile, like a flaming torch among sheaves. They will consume right and left all the surrounding peoples, but Jerusalem
will remain intact in her place.
7"The LORD will save the dwellings of Judah first, so that the
honor of the house of David and of Jerusalem's inhabitants may
not be greater than that of Judah. 8On that day the LORD will shield
those who live in Jerusalem, so that the feeblest among them will
be like David, and the house of David will be like God, like the
Angel of the LORD going before them. 9On that day I will set out to
destroy all the nations that attack Jerusalem.

Mourning for the One They Pierced

10"And I will pour out on the house of David and the inhabitants of Jerusalem a spirit[a] of grace and supplication. They will
look on[b] me, the one they have pierced, and they will mourn for
him as one mourns for an only child, and grieve bitterly for him
as one grieves for a firstborn son. 11On that day the weeping in
Jerusalem will be great, like the weeping of Hadad Rimmon in
the plain of Megiddo. 12The land will mourn, each clan by itself,
with their wives by themselves: the clan of the house of David and
their wives, the clan of the house of Nathan and their wives, 13the
clan of the house of Levi and their wives, the clan of Shimei and
their wives, 14and all the rest of the clans and their wives.

Cleansing From Sin

13 "On that day a fountain will be opened to the house of
David and the inhabitants of Jerusalem, to cleanse them
from sin and impurity.
2"On that day, I will banish the names of the idols from the
land, and they will be remembered no more," declares the LORD
Almighty. "I will remove both the prophets and the spirit of impurity from the land. 3And if anyone still prophesies, his father
and mother, to whom he was born, will say to him, 'You must die,
because you have told lies in the LORD's name.' When he prophesies, his own parents will stab him.
4"On that day every prophet will be ashamed of his prophetic
vision. He will not put on a prophet's garment of hair in order to
deceive. 5He will say, 'I am not a prophet. I am a farmer; the land
has been my livelihood since my youth.[c]' 6If someone asks him,

[a] *10* Or *the Spirit* [b] *10* Or *to* [c] *5* Or *farmer; a man sold me in my youth*

(12:10) My sins nailed You to the cross; my iniquities pierced Your hands and feet; my transgressions drove the spear into Your side. For me You prayed, "Father, forgive!" I grieve for the pain I have caused You. But You, merciful Lord, have turned my tears of sorrow at so great a death into tears of joy at so great a Savior! (Isa 53:5; Jn 19:34–37)

We should all like life to be free from suffering, and our love to be free from pain. But there is no true love without suffering. So the highest love of all, the love of Christ for men, showed unforgettably how deeply he must suffer in order to bring men to himself.

J. B. Phillips (1906–1982)

(13:1,7–9) Father, it was You Who struck the Great Shepherd, this One Who was so close to You, indeed, Your very own Son. From His side flowed a fountain of blood and water to cleanse us from our sins. He submitted to this death voluntarily so that He might purchase the flock with His own blood. Now, having bought us with such a price, He has made us to be Your people. Thank You, Father, for giving up Your Son. And thank You, Jesus, for giving up Your life for us. (Isa 53:4,10; Ac 20:28)

God proved his love on the cross. When Christ hung, and bled, and died it was God saying to the world–I love you.
Billy Graham (1918-)

There is a fountain filled with blood
Drawn from Immanuel's veins,
And sinners, plunged beneath that
flood,
Lose all their guilty stains.
"There Is A Fountain"
William Cowper (1731-1800)

(14:9) King Jesus, You descended to the depths of sorrow and in death; now God has exalted You to the highest place and has given You the name that is above every other name. At Your name every knee shall bow in heaven and on earth and under the earth, and every tongue shall confess that You are Lord, to the glory of God the Father. Yours is the only name that opens heaven's doors and God's heart, that breaks the power of sin and sets the captive free. No other name is worthy of such praise or deserving of such allegiance. Jesus, You are peerless in exaltation, incomparable in grace, invincible in power, unassisted in Your work as Redeemer, matchless in mercy, adored in glory and worshiped in the beauty of holiness. (Php 2:9–11)

'What are these wounds on your body[a]?' he will answer, 'The wounds I was given at the house of my friends.'

The Shepherd Struck, the Sheep Scattered

7 "Awake, O sword, against my shepherd,
against the man who is close to me!"
declares the LORD Almighty.
"Strike the shepherd,
and the sheep will be scattered,
and I will turn my hand against the little ones.
8 In the whole land," declares the LORD,
"two-thirds will be struck down and perish;
yet one-third will be left in it.
9 This third I will bring into the fire;
I will refine them like silver
and test them like gold.
They will call on my name
and I will answer them;
I will say, 'They are my people,'
and they will say, 'The LORD is our God.' "

The LORD Comes and Reigns

14 A day of the LORD is coming when your plunder will be divided among you.
2 I will gather all the nations to Jerusalem to fight against it; the city will be captured, the houses ransacked, and the women raped. Half of the city will go into exile, but the rest of the people will not be taken from the city.

3 Then the LORD will go out and fight against those nations, as he fights in the day of battle. 4 On that day his feet will stand on the Mount of Olives, east of Jerusalem, and the Mount of Olives will be split in two from east to west, forming a great valley, with half of the mountain moving north and half moving south. 5 You will flee by my mountain valley, for it will extend to Azel. You will flee as you fled from the earthquake[b] in the days of Uzziah king of Judah. Then the LORD my God will come, and all the holy ones with him.

6 On that day there will be no light, no cold or frost. 7 It will be a unique day, without daytime or nighttime—a day known to the LORD. When evening comes, there will be light.

8 On that day living water will flow out from Jerusalem, half to the eastern sea[c] and half to the western sea,[d] in summer and in winter.

9 The LORD will be king over the whole earth. On that day there will be one LORD, and his name the only name.

10 The whole land, from Geba to Rimmon, south of Jerusalem, will become like the Arabah. But Jerusalem will be raised up and remain in its place, from the Benjamin Gate to the site of the First Gate, to the Corner Gate, and from the Tower of Hananel to the royal winepresses. 11 It will be inhabited; never again will it be destroyed. Jerusalem will be secure.

12 This is the plague with which the LORD will strike all the nations that fought against Jerusalem: Their flesh will rot while they are still standing on their feet, their eyes will rot in their sockets,

[a] 6 Or *wounds between your hands* [b] 5 Or [5]*My mountain valley will be blocked and will extend to Azel. It will be blocked as it was blocked because of the earthquake*
[c] 8 That is, the Dead Sea [d] 8 That is, the Mediterranean

and their tongues will rot in their mouths. 13On that day men will
be stricken by the LORD with great panic. Each man will seize the
hand of another, and they will attack each other. 14Judah too will
fight at Jerusalem. The wealth of all the surrounding nations will
be collected—great quantities of gold and silver and clothing.
15A similar plague will strike the horses and mules, the camels
and donkeys, and all the animals in those camps.

16Then the survivors from all the nations that have attacked Jerusalem will go up year after year to worship the King, the LORD
Almighty, and to celebrate the Feast of Tabernacles. 17If any of the
peoples of the earth do not go up to Jerusalem to worship the
King, the LORD Almighty, they will have no rain. 18If the Egyptian
people do not go up and take part, they will have no rain. The
LORD[a] will bring on them the plague he inflicts on the nations that
do not go up to celebrate the Feast of Tabernacles. 19This will be
the punishment of Egypt and the punishment of all the nations
that do not go up to celebrate the Feast of Tabernacles.

20On that day HOLY TO THE LORD will be inscribed on the bells of
the horses, and the cooking pots in the LORD's house will be like
the sacred bowls in front of the altar. 21Every pot in Jerusalem
and Judah will be holy to the LORD Almighty, and all who come to
sacrifice will take some of the pots and cook in them. And on that
day there will no longer be a Canaanite[b] in the house of the LORD
Almighty.

(14:20–21) O Lord, how we long for the day when You will absorb all of the kingdoms of the earth into Your holy kingdom, when You will reign forever and ever. You will come and make holiness so pervasive that it will be common among us. You will inscribe holiness like a signature on all that is Yours. As we wait for Your return, Lord Jesus, come and reign over our forgiven hearts—hearts that You have cleansed as our Priest by Your death, hearts that You have won as our King by Your resurrection. Amen.

Holy, holy, holy! Lord God Almighty!
All Thy works shall praise Thy name,
In earth, and sky, and sea;
Holy, holy, holy! Merciful and
mighty!
God in three persons, blessed
Trinity!
"Holy, Holy, Holy! Lord God Almighty"
Reginald Heber (1783-1826)

[a] 18 Or *part, then the LORD* [b] 21 Or *merchant*

The Book of

MALACHI

As the Jews return from exile in Babylon, their expectations soar. But the reality of postexilic life hardly matches their hopes. Life under Persian rule is not unbearable, but it falls short of God's promises for a universal kingdom ruled by a Davidic king. As times passes the people become mired in discouragement. They begin to question God's love and justice (1:2; 2:17). Their worship becomes lazy, cheap and formalistic. They offer blemished sacrifices (1:8,13–14) and incomplete tithes (3:8–9).

If we have ever been stuck in the spiritual doldrums, and especially if we have experienced deep disappointment with God, then we can understand the predicament of God's people. Why keep on worshiping God when it seems so empty, so fruitless?

God sends a prophet known as Malachi to jolt His people into renewed faithfulness in worship. The Lord reminds them of His love (1:1–2), greatness (1:5,11), fearsomeness (1:14), awesomeness (2:5), justice (3:1–5) and sovereign control over the future (3:1–2; 4:1–2). He condemns their practice of giving cheap offerings and insists that they stop robbing Him (3:8–9). If, by contrast, they worship God faithfully, then He will bless them abundantly in the present (3:10) and in the coming day of the Lord (4:1–2).

The book of Malachi motivates us to worship God with excellence because God commands it and because we will be blessed if we do so. But, more profoundly, Malachi renews our worship with a vision of God's unsurpassed greatness: " 'My name will be great among the nations, from the rising to the setting of the sun. In every place incense and pure offerings will be brought to my name, because my name will be great among the nations,' says the LORD Almighty" (1:11). We worship, not only out of obedience, but also because God is awesome, majestic and worthy of our unrestrained honor (1:5–8). When we are discouraged, when we question God's goodness, we must focus not upon our feelings but upon God's glorious nature as revealed through His Word.

Malachi renews our worship with a vision of God's unsurpassed greatness.

Malachi looks beyond the near horizon of Jewish experience to the future, in which God will completely fulfill His prophetic promises. When the Lord Almighty appears, "he will sit as a refiner and purifier of silver; he will purify the Levites and refine them like gold and silver. Then the LORD will have men who will bring offerings in righteousness" (3:3). When God comes He will refine His people so that they will bring right offerings. After God has fully restored His creation, we who know Him will worship truly, purely and righteously.

The last book of the Old Testament points ahead to the coming of Jesus Christ, Who fulfills God's promises by fashioning a people who exist for the praise of God's glory (Eph 1:12). As new covenant people through Christ, we have no higher purpose than to worship God with our very best, until that day when we join all creation in bowing before the throne of God.

1 An oracle: The word of the LORD to Israel through Malachi.[a]

Jacob Loved, Esau Hated

2 “I have loved you,” says the LORD.
“But you ask, ‘How have you loved us?’
“Was not Esau Jacob’s brother?” the LORD says. “Yet I have
loved Jacob, 3 but Esau I have hated, and I have turned his mountains into a wasteland and left his inheritance to the desert jackals.”
4 Edom may say, “Though we have been crushed, we will rebuild the ruins.”
But this is what the LORD Almighty says: “They may build, but I
will demolish. They will be called the Wicked Land, a people always under the wrath of the LORD. 5 You will see it with your own
eyes and say, ‘Great is the LORD—even beyond the borders of Israel!’

(1:2) As we approach You, Sovereign Lord, we want to do so with the kind of childlikeness that simply accepts Your love for what it is—Your unmerited gift of grace. We do not deserve Your love, neither can we earn it. Though we may sometimes question Your love for us, still Your love never ends and it never fails. Like strong cords, Your love constantly draws us closer to You and reminds us that we are Yours. (Jer 31:3)

Blemished Sacrifices

6 “A son honors his father, and a servant his master. If I am a father, where is the honor due me? If I am a master, where is the respect due me?” says the LORD Almighty. “It is you, O priests, who
show contempt for my name.
“But you ask, ‘How have we shown contempt for your name?’
7 “You place defiled food on my altar.
“But you ask, ‘How have we defiled you?’
“By saying that the LORD’s table is contemptible. 8 When you
bring blind animals for sacrifice, is that not wrong? When you
sacrifice crippled or diseased animals, is that not wrong? Try offering them to your governor! Would he be pleased with you?
Would he accept you?” says the LORD Almighty.
9 “Now implore God to be gracious to us. With such offerings
from your hands, will he accept you?”—says the LORD Almighty.
10 “Oh, that one of you would shut the temple doors, so that
you would not light useless fires on my altar! I am not pleased
with you,” says the LORD Almighty, “and I will accept no offering
from your hands. 11 My name will be great among the nations,
from the rising to the setting of the sun. In every place incense
and pure offerings will be brought to my name, because my name
will be great among the nations,” says the LORD Almighty.
12 “But you profane it by saying of the Lord’s table, ‘It is defiled,’ and of its food, ‘It is contemptible.’ 13 And you say, ‘What a
burden!’ and you sniff at it contemptuously,” says the LORD
Almighty.
“When you bring injured, crippled or diseased animals and
offer them as sacrifices, should I accept them from your hands?”
says the LORD. 14 “Cursed is the cheat who has an acceptable male
in his flock and vows to give it, but then sacrifices a blemished
animal to the Lord. For I am a great king,” says the LORD Almighty,
“and my name is to be feared among the nations.

(1:6–11) Holy God, my desire is to truly honor You. Your worth is immeasurable. Yet my worship so often falls short of showing You the adoration and respect that You deserve. Forgive me for not fearing You, for hurriedly throwing at You the leftovers and extras of my life. Take the place of honor in my worship again. I will give You my best—the best of my heart and my praise, the best of my money and my time, the best of my energy and my life. No one is more worthy than You. With all of my life may I shape a sanctuary of praise to You. With all of my heart I ascribe to You, O Lord of all, the glory due Your name, and I worship You in the splendor of Your holiness. (Ps 29:2)

(1:11) From the rising of the sun to the place where it goes down, Your name, O Lord, is to be praised. You alone rule over the nations, exalted in glory and enthroned on high. Where could I find another to compare with You? Who else would stoop so low as to lift me from despairing need and loss to sit with You in ruling places? You alone, O Lord Almighty, are such a God. From every nation and people may Your praise be lifted as an offering of holy worship. Let everything that has breath give You praise! (Ps 113:3–8; 150:6; Eph 2:6)

Admonition for the Priests

2 “And now this admonition is for you, O priests. 2 If you do not
listen, and if you do not set your heart to honor my name,”
says the LORD Almighty, “I will send a curse upon you, and I will

[a] 1 *Malachi* means *my messenger.*

curse your blessings. Yes, I have already cursed them, because
you have not set your heart to honor me.
3"Because of you I will rebuke[a] your descendants[b]; I will
spread on your faces the offal from your festival sacrifices, and
you will be carried off with it. 4And you will know that I have sent
you this admonition so that my covenant with Levi may continue,"
says the LORD Almighty. 5"My covenant was with him, a covenant
of life and peace, and I gave them to him; this called for reverence and he revered me and stood in awe of my name. 6True instruction was in his mouth and nothing false was found on his
lips. He walked with me in peace and uprightness, and turned
many from sin.
7"For the lips of a priest ought to preserve knowledge, and
from his mouth men should seek instruction—because he is the
messenger of the LORD Almighty. 8But you have turned from the
way and by your teaching have caused many to stumble; you have
violated the covenant with Levi," says the LORD Almighty. 9"So I
have caused you to be despised and humiliated before all the people, because you have not followed my ways but have shown partiality in matters of the law."

Judah Unfaithful

10Have we not all one Father[c]? Did not one God create us? Why
do we profane the covenant of our fathers by breaking faith with
one another?
11Judah has broken faith. A detestable thing has been committed in Israel and in Jerusalem: Judah has desecrated the sanctuary the LORD loves, by marrying the daughter of a foreign god.
12As for the man who does this, whoever he may be, may the LORD
cut him off from the tents of Jacob[d]—even though he brings offerings to the LORD Almighty.
13Another thing you do: You flood the LORD's altar with tears.
You weep and wail because he no longer pays attention to your
offerings or accepts them with pleasure from your hands. 14You
ask, "Why?" It is because the LORD is acting as the witness between you and the wife of your youth, because you have broken
faith with her, though she is your partner, the wife of your marriage covenant.
15Has not ⌊the LORD⌋ made them one? In flesh and spirit they
are his. And why one? Because he was seeking godly offspring.[e]
So guard yourself in your spirit, and do not break faith with the
wife of your youth.
16"I hate divorce," says the LORD God of Israel, "and I hate a
man's covering himself[f] with violence as well as with his garment," says the LORD Almighty.
So guard yourself in your spirit, and do not break faith.

The Day of Judgment

17You have wearied the LORD with your words.
"How have we wearied him?" you ask.
By saying, "All who do evil are good in the eyes of the LORD, and
he is pleased with them" or "Where is the God of justice?"

(2:13–16) O Lord, give us Your passion for holiness in our marriages. Divorce grieves Your Spirit, but the oil of Your anointing and presence is poured out when Your people walk in faithfulness to one another. Even the vitality of our prayer life is affected by the way we honor and serve our spouses. How can we truly keep our covenant with You if we will not keep our covenant with one another? If we cannot be faithful to those whom we have seen, how can we be faithful to You Whom we have not seen? Lord, make us faithful as You are faithful. (Eph 5:21–33; 1Pe 3:7; 1Jn 4:20–21)

[a] *3* Or *cut off* (see Septuagint) [b] *3* Or *will blight your grain* [c] *10* Or *father*
[d] *12* Or [12]*May the LORD cut off from the tents of Jacob anyone who gives testimony in behalf of the man who does this* [e] *15* Or [15]*But the one ⌊who is our father⌋ did not do this, not as long as life remained in him. And what was he seeking? An offspring from God* [f] *16* Or *his wife*

3 "See, I will send my messenger, who will prepare the way before me. Then suddenly the Lord you are seeking will come
to his temple; the messenger of the covenant, whom you desire,
will come," says the LORD Almighty.
2But who can endure the day of his coming? Who can stand
when he appears? For he will be like a refiner's fire or a laun-
derer's soap. 3He will sit as a refiner and purifier of silver; he will
purify the Levites and refine them like gold and silver. Then the
LORD will have men who will bring offerings in righteousness,
4and the offerings of Judah and Jerusalem will be acceptable to
the LORD, as in days gone by, as in former years.
5"So I will come near to you for judgment. I will be quick to
testify against sorcerers, adulterers and perjurers, against those
who defraud laborers of their wages, who oppress the widows
and the fatherless, and deprive aliens of justice, but do not fear
me," says the LORD Almighty.

Robbing God

6"I the LORD do not change. So you, O descendants of Jacob,
are not destroyed. 7Ever since the time of your forefathers you
have turned away from my decrees and have not kept them. Return to me, and I will return to you," says the LORD Almighty.
"But you ask, 'How are we to return?'
8"Will a man rob God? Yet you rob me.
"But you ask, 'How do we rob you?'
"In tithes and offerings. 9You are under a curse—the whole nation of you—because you are robbing me. 10Bring the whole tithe
into the storehouse, that there may be food in my house. Test me in
this," says the LORD Almighty, "and see if I will not throw open the
floodgates of heaven and pour out so much blessing that you will
not have room enough for it. 11I will prevent pests from devouring
your crops, and the vines in your fields will not cast their fruit,"
says the LORD Almighty. 12"Then all the nations will call you blessed,
for yours will be a delightful land," says the LORD Almighty.
13"You have said harsh things against me," says the LORD.
"Yet you ask, 'What have we said against you?'
14"You have said, 'It is futile to serve God. What did we gain by
carrying out his requirements and going about like mourners before the LORD Almighty? 15But now we call the arrogant blessed.
Certainly the evildoers prosper, and even those who challenge
God escape.' "
16Then those who feared the LORD talked with each other, and
the LORD listened and heard. A scroll of remembrance was written in his presence concerning those who feared the LORD and
honored his name.
17"They will be mine," says the LORD Almighty, "in the day when
I make up my treasured possession.[a] I will spare them, just as in
compassion a man spares his son who serves him. 18And you will
again see the distinction between the righteous and the wicked,
between those who serve God and those who do not.

The Day of the LORD

4 "Surely the day is coming; it will burn like a furnace. All the
arrogant and every evildoer will be stubble, and that day that
is coming will set them on fire," says the LORD Almighty. "Not a

(3:1–4) We long to see You, O Lord, but are we really ready to face You? As Your people we seek You, but would we be able to stand the fire of Your holy presence if it were truly revealed? We may want Your blessings, but You want our purity. You would refine us until, like pure gold, our lives reflect Your glory. O Holy God, consuming fire, purify my heart so that my worship may be acceptable to You. (Zec 13:9; Heb 12:29; 1Pe 1:6–7)

Our Father, who seeks to perfect His saints in holiness, knows the value of the refiner's fire. It is with the most precious metals that the assayer takes the most pains, and subjects them to the hot fire, because such fires melt the metal, and only the molten mass releases its alloy or takes perfectly its new form in the mould. The old refiner never leaves his crucible, but sits down by it, lest there should be one excessive degree of heat to mar the metal. But as soon as he skims from the surface the last of the dross, and sees his own face reflected, he puts out the fire.

Arthur T. Pierson (1837–1911)

(3:8–12) You, Almighty God, are my source and my hope. From Your gracious hand come life and blessings, wealth and honor. Indeed, "Everything comes from you, and we have given you only what comes from your hand." Teach me to be a channel of Your provision—to not live in fear but in the joy of giving. Open the windows of heaven. Turn back the devouring powers. May I be found a trustworthy steward as I worship You with my giving. (1Ch 29:10–16)

We give Thee but Thine own,
What e'er the gift may be.
All that we have is Thine alone
A trust, O Lord, from Thee.

May we Thy bounties thus
As stewards true receive,
And gladly as Thou blessest us,
To Thee our first fruits give.

"We Give Thee But Thine Own"
William W. How (1823–1897)

[a] 17 Or *Almighty, "my treasured possession, in the day when I act*

root or a branch will be left to them. 2But for you who revere my
name, the sun of righteousness will rise with healing in its wings.
And you will go out and leap like calves released from the stall.
3Then you will trample down the wicked; they will be ashes under
the soles of your feet on the day when I do these things," says the
LORD Almighty.

4"Remember the law of my servant Moses, the decrees and
laws I gave him at Horeb for all Israel.

5"See, I will send you the prophet Elijah before that great and
dreadful day of the LORD comes. 6He will turn the hearts of the fathers to their children, and the hearts of the children to their fathers; or else I will come and strike the land with a curse."

(4:2) Sun of righteousness, rise in me with healing and life. Lift me on Your wings of grace and freedom. You, Lord Jesus, are the promised rising Sun, the glorious and righteous One. You were wounded for my healing, delivered over to death for my sins and raised to life for my justification. Your name is above every name, high and lifted up, exalted over every human authority or spiritual power. You are the First and the Last, the living One who holds the keys of death and hell. O Light of the world, rise to light my way with healing and joy. Keep alive in me heaven's song of hope and praise—"Hallelujah, for our Lord God Almighty reigns!" (Jn 8:12; Ac 10:38; Ro 4:25; Rev 1:17–18; 19:6)

Christ, whose glory fills the skies,
Christ, the true, the only light,
Sun of righteousness, arise,
Triumph over shades of night:
Dayspring from on high, be near,
Daystar, in my heart appear!

Visit then this soul of mine;
Pierce the gloom of sin and grief;
Fill me, radiancy divine;
Scatter all my unbelief;
More and more Thyself display,
Shining to the perfect day.

"Christ, Whose Glory Fills the Skies"
Charles Wesley (1740)

Thou, who art the true Sun of the world, evermore rising, and never going down; who, by Thy most wholesome appearing and sight dost nourish, and make joyful all things as well that are in heaven, as also that are on earth; we beseech Thee mercifully and favorably to shine into our hearts, that the night and darkness of sin, and the mists of error on every side, being driven away, Thou brightly shining within our hearts, we may all our life long go without any stumbling or offence, and may walk as in the day-time, being pure and clean from the works of darkness, and abounding in all good works which Thou hast prepared for us to walk in.

Desiderius Erasmus (c. 1466–1536)

The
New Testament

The Gospel according to

MATTHEW

The first verse of the New Testament bonds the New with the Old (1:1). Jesus is the "Christ," the Jewish Messiah promised by the Hebrew prophets. He is the "son of David" whose righteous rule over Judah will have no end (Isa 9:7). He is the "son of Abraham" in whom God fulfills His covenant vows to the patriarch and his descendants (Ge 12:1–3).

Like the New Testament itself, Christian worship rests solidly upon the foundation of the Old Testament. Apart from this footing, we can neither understand Jesus the Messiah nor worship God according to His self-revelation. Our God is consistent, faithful to fulfill all that He has spoken, and therefore worthy of our unrelenting trust and undivided praise.

Matthew emphasizes that Jesus is not only the Son of David but also the Son of God. Many voices use this exalted title for Jesus (2:15; 4:3; 8:29; 26:63). Perhaps most significantly, God identifies Jesus as "my Son" (3:17, 17:5). In a Jewish context, the title "Son of God" was used of a human being to signify his special relationship with God, but not his divinity (Ps 2:7; 72:1). In Matthew, however, Jesus' intimacy with God the Father is truly extraordinary (11:27). He is the "Son of God," not only as God's royal representative on earth, but also as the One Who is "Immanuel"—God with us! (1:23).

Because of His unique identity as God's divine Son, Jesus is worthy of worship. Although Jesus Himself states that God alone should be worshiped (4:10), the fact that He often receives worship reveals His own deity. Shortly after His birth the magi come to worship Jesus (2:2,11). In Matthew's account of Jesus' walking on the water, we find a detail not recorded in the other Gospels: "Then those who were in the boat worshiped him, saying, 'Truly you are the Son of God' " (14:33). As Jesus manifests the power of God over nature, His followers realize His deity and worship Him as the Son of God. His resurrection inspires a similar reaction (28:9,17).

Like the New Testament itself, Christian worship rests solidly upon the foundation of the Old Testament. Apart from this footing, we can neither understand Jesus the Messiah nor worship God according to His self-revelation.

How extraordinary it must have been for the disciples of Jesus to offer worship to a man—even a man they knew to be the Son of God! Jews have always insisted that God alone deserves worship. Yet Jesus was so uniquely Immanuel, "God with us," that many of His Jewish followers could not keep from worshiping Him as God.

As Christians we continue to affirm the startling truth that Jesus is fully human and fully divine. We too offer worship to the One Who is Son of David and Son of God. Our confession of Jesus' singular identity and the worship that follows from this confession set us apart from those who would laud Jesus solely as an exemplary human being. We worship God alone, including Jesus, Who is God the Son. Hence, the first book of the New Testament both anchors our worship in the Old Testament and draws us into an astounding new dimension of divine worship. Like the disciples marveling at Jesus' power over the seas, we worship our Lord, proclaiming "Truly you are the Son of God!"

(1:1–17) Lord Jesus, what a wonder it is that You entered the human race as You did. You chose to incarnate Yourself through a genealogy of mixed tribes and races, bluebloods and bullies, heroes and harlots, saints and sinners. Thank You for representing each person on earth, for identifying with every one of us. Thank You, Lord, for reaching out to me here and now, right where I am. Amen.

God became man; the divine Son became a Jew; the Almighty appeared on earth as a helpless human baby, unable to do more than lie and stare and wriggle and make noises, needing to be fed and changed and taught to talk like any other child. And there was no illusion or deception in this: the babyhood of the Son of God was a reality. The more you think about it, the more staggering it gets. Nothing in fiction is so fantastic as is this truth of the Incarnation.

J. I. Packer (1926-)

Angels sing over fields of light,
There is born tonight
A Son, a Savior.
Joyful tidings are on the wing:
A newborn King,
A Son, a Savior.

Find this Child and share the joy
Of Mary's boy,
A Son, a Savior.
There's redemption within His hand
For every man;
A Son, a Savior.

Glory to God in the highest;
Peace and goodwill to the earth have
come!
Heaven has sent us a Savior;
The Father has given a Son.

"A Son, A Savior"
Bill Batstone (©1988)

The Genealogy of Jesus

1 A record of the genealogy of Jesus Christ the son of David, the son of Abraham:

2 Abraham was the father of Isaac,
Isaac the father of Jacob,
Jacob the father of Judah and his brothers,
3 Judah the father of Perez and Zerah, whose mother was Tamar,
Perez the father of Hezron,
Hezron the father of Ram,
4 Ram the father of Amminadab,
Amminadab the father of Nahshon,
Nahshon the father of Salmon,
5 Salmon the father of Boaz, whose mother was Rahab,
Boaz the father of Obed, whose mother was Ruth,
Obed the father of Jesse,
6 and Jesse the father of King David.

David was the father of Solomon, whose mother had been Uriah's wife,
7 Solomon the father of Rehoboam,
Rehoboam the father of Abijah,
Abijah the father of Asa,
8 Asa the father of Jehoshaphat,
Jehoshaphat the father of Jehoram,
Jehoram the father of Uzziah,
9 Uzziah the father of Jotham,
Jotham the father of Ahaz,
Ahaz the father of Hezekiah,
10 Hezekiah the father of Manasseh,
Manasseh the father of Amon,
Amon the father of Josiah,
11 and Josiah the father of Jeconiah[a] and his brothers at the time of the exile to Babylon.

12 After the exile to Babylon:
Jeconiah was the father of Shealtiel,
Shealtiel the father of Zerubbabel,
13 Zerubbabel the father of Abiud,
Abiud the father of Eliakim,
Eliakim the father of Azor,
14 Azor the father of Zadok,
Zadok the father of Akim,
Akim the father of Eliud,
15 Eliud the father of Eleazar,
Eleazar the father of Matthan,
Matthan the father of Jacob,
16 and Jacob the father of Joseph, the husband of Mary, of whom was born Jesus, who is called Christ.

17 Thus there were fourteen generations in all from Abraham to David, fourteen from David to the exile to Babylon, and fourteen from the exile to the Christ.[b]

[a] *11* That is, Jehoiachin; also in verse 12 [b] *17* Or *Messiah.* "The Christ" (Greek) and "the Messiah" (Hebrew) both mean "the Anointed One."

The Birth of Jesus Christ

18 This is how the birth of Jesus Christ came about: His mother
Mary was pledged to be married to Joseph, but before they came
together, she was found to be with child through the Holy Spirit.
19 Because Joseph her husband was a righteous man and did not
want to expose her to public disgrace, he had in mind to divorce
her quietly.
20 But after he had considered this, an angel of the Lord appeared to him in a dream and said, "Joseph son of David, do not
be afraid to take Mary home as your wife, because what is conceived in her is from the Holy Spirit.
21 She will give birth to a
son, and you are to give him the name Jesus,[a] because he will
save his people from their sins."
22 All this took place to fulfill what the Lord had said through
the prophet:
23 "The virgin will be with child and will give birth to
a son, and they will call him Immanuel"[b]—which means, "God
with us."
24 When Joseph woke up, he did what the angel of the Lord had
commanded him and took Mary home as his wife.
25 But he had
no union with her until she gave birth to a son. And he gave him
the name Jesus.

The Visit of the Magi

2 After Jesus was born in Bethlehem in Judea, during the time
of King Herod, Magi[c] from the east came to Jerusalem
2 and
asked, "Where is the one who has been born king of the Jews? We
saw his star in the east[d] and have come to worship him."
3 When King Herod heard this he was disturbed, and all Jerusalem with him.
4 When he had called together all the people's chief
priests and teachers of the law, he asked them where the Christ[e]
was to be born.
5 "In Bethlehem in Judea," they replied, "for this
is what the prophet has written:

6 " 'But you, Bethlehem, in the land of Judah,
are by no means least among the rulers of Judah;
for out of you will come a ruler
who will be the shepherd of my people Israel.'[f]"

7 Then Herod called the Magi secretly and found out from them
the exact time the star had appeared.
8 He sent them to Bethlehem
and said, "Go and make a careful search for the child. As soon as
you find him, report to me, so that I too may go and worship
him."
9 After they had heard the king, they went on their way, and the
star they had seen in the east[g] went ahead of them until it stopped
over the place where the child was.
10 When they saw the star, they
were overjoyed.
11 On coming to the house, they saw the child
with his mother Mary, and they bowed down and worshiped him.
Then they opened their treasures and presented him with gifts of
gold and of incense and of myrrh.
12 And having been warned in
a dream not to go back to Herod, they returned to their country
by another route.

[a] *21 Jesus* is the Greek form of *Joshua*, which means *the LORD saves.* [b] *23* Isaiah 7:14
[c] *1* Traditionally *Wise Men* [d] *2* Or *star when it rose* [e] *4* Or *Messiah* [f] *6* Micah 5:2
[g] *9* Or *seen when it rose*

(1:23) Jesus, You amaze us—You were present when the earth was spun into orbit and the stars were ordered in the night sky. You designed the awesome workings of our planet and all that live here on it. You shared with Your Father in the joy and wonder of creating everything that now exists. And yet when we were lost and fallen, You were willing to take on the frailty of our human nature and become one of us so that we might be saved. We praise and worship You, Immanuel. You are indeed "God with us"! (Jn 1:1–4)

Watch and wonder and do not fear;
Your Lord is near,
A son, a Savior.
God above with us to dwell,
Immanuel.
A Son, a Savior.

Glory to God in the highest;
Peace and goodwill to the earth have
come!
Heaven has sent us a Savior;
The Father has given a Son.

"A Son, A Savior"
Bill Batstone (©1988)

It becomes very evident that Jesus Christ is beyond our noblest thought of him. Our intellectual gauge of him neither comprehends nor exceeds him. The best and frankest estimate does him scant justice. One may sit down and, in a moment of adoration, pour out his love in song to his character, put into it all the idealism and nobility the heart can command or the brain conceive, or weave into his thought of him threads of gold, figures of light, and symbols of beauty; but when all is done and the delineation is complete, the incomparableness of his personality towers in glorious effulgence above what has been thought and wrought. Before his transcendent character the soul stands confused and ashamed. Its most finished thought of him fails of adequate expression, and its most silvery notes are but echoes of the symphony he is.

Calvin Weiss Laufer (1874–1938)

(3:1–3) I praise You, Father, that You speak to us in ways and through means that can be clearly understood. John was a voice—not a disembodied voice, but a voice in human flesh. Jesus is the Word—not a disembodied word, but the Word in human flesh. The gospel of the kingdom of heaven was the message—not a disembodied kingdom, but the kingdom established and expressed and expanded in our human flesh. The gospel of the kingdom is not simply an abstract theory or a lofty ideal; it is instead a spiritual reality to be experienced and lived in right here, right now, by anyone who will confess and repent and receive Jesus as Savior and Lord. For this I give You praise. And I pray for the privilege, Lord, that my voice may be used to declare Your Word and to prepare the way for Your kingdom to come into the lives of others. (Jn 1:1–14)

For the herald's voice is calling
In the desert far and near,
Bidding us to make repentance
Since the kingdom now is here.
O that warning cry obey!
Now prepare for God a way;
Let the valleys rise in meeting
And the hills bow down in greeting.

"Comfort, Comfort You My People"
Johannes Olearius (1671)
Trans. Catherine Winkworth (1827-1878)

My soul, hearken to the voice of your God. He is always ready to speak with you when you are prepared to hear. If there is any slowness to commune, it is not on His part but altogether on your own, for He stands at the door and knocks, and if His people will but open, He rejoices to enter.

Charles Haddon Spurgeon (1834-1892)

The Escape to Egypt

13 When they had gone, an angel of the Lord appeared to Joseph in a dream. "Get up," he said, "take the child and his mother and escape to Egypt. Stay there until I tell you, for Herod is
going to search for the child to kill him."
14 So he got up, took the child and his mother during the night
and left for Egypt, 15 where he stayed until the death of Herod.
And so was fulfilled what the Lord had said through the prophet:
"Out of Egypt I called my son."[a]
16 When Herod realized that he had been outwitted by the Magi,
he was furious, and he gave orders to kill all the boys in Bethlehem and its vicinity who were two years old and under, in accordance with the time he had learned from the Magi. 17 Then what
was said through the prophet Jeremiah was fulfilled:

18 "A voice is heard in Ramah,
weeping and great mourning,
Rachel weeping for her children
and refusing to be comforted,
because they are no more."[b]

The Return to Nazareth

19 After Herod died, an angel of the Lord appeared in a dream
to Joseph in Egypt 20 and said, "Get up, take the child and his
mother and go to the land of Israel, for those who were trying to
take the child's life are dead."
21 So he got up, took the child and his mother and went to the
land of Israel. 22 But when he heard that Archelaus was reigning
in Judea in place of his father Herod, he was afraid to go there.
Having been warned in a dream, he withdrew to the district of
Galilee, 23 and he went and lived in a town called Nazareth. So
was fulfilled what was said through the prophets: "He will be
called a Nazarene."

John the Baptist Prepares the Way

3 In those days John the Baptist came, preaching in the Desert
of Judea 2 and saying, "Repent, for the kingdom of heaven is
near." 3 This is he who was spoken of through the prophet Isaiah:

"A voice of one calling in the desert,
'Prepare the way for the Lord,
make straight paths for him.'"[c]

4 John's clothes were made of camel's hair, and he had a
leather belt around his waist. His food was locusts and wild
honey. 5 People went out to him from Jerusalem and all Judea and
the whole region of the Jordan. 6 Confessing their sins, they were
baptized by him in the Jordan River.
7 But when he saw many of the Pharisees and Sadducees coming to where he was baptizing, he said to them: "You brood of
vipers! Who warned you to flee from the coming wrath? 8 Produce fruit in keeping with repentance. 9 And do not think you can
say to yourselves, 'We have Abraham as our father.' I tell you that
out of these stones God can raise up children for Abraham.
10 The ax is already at the root of the trees, and every tree that
does not produce good fruit will be cut down and thrown into
the fire.

[a] *15* Hosea 11:1 [b] *18* Jer. 31:15 [c] *3* Isaiah 40:3

11“I baptize you with[a] water for repentance. But after me will
come one who is more powerful than I, whose sandals I am not
fit to carry. He will baptize you with the Holy Spirit and with fire.
12His winnowing fork is in his hand, and he will clear his threshing floor, gathering his wheat into the barn and burning up the
chaff with unquenchable fire.”

The Baptism of Jesus

13Then Jesus came from Galilee to the Jordan to be baptized by
John. 14But John tried to deter him, saying, “I need to be baptized
by you, and do you come to me?”
15Jesus replied, “Let it be so now; it is proper for us to do this
to fulfill all righteousness.” Then John consented.
16As soon as Jesus was baptized, he went up out of the water.
At that moment heaven was opened, and he saw the Spirit of God
descending like a dove and lighting on him. 17And a voice from
heaven said, “This is my Son, whom I love; with him I am well
pleased.”

The Temptation of Jesus

4 Then Jesus was led by the Spirit into the desert to be tempted by the devil. 2After fasting forty days and forty nights, he
was hungry. 3The tempter came to him and said, “If you are the
Son of God, tell these stones to become bread.”
4Jesus answered, “It is written: ‘Man does not live on bread
alone, but on every word that comes from the mouth of God.’[b]”
5Then the devil took him to the holy city and had him stand on
the highest point of the temple. 6“If you are the Son of God,” he
said, “throw yourself down. For it is written:

“ ‘He will command his angels concerning you,
and they will lift you up in their hands,
so that you will not strike your foot against a stone.’[c]”

7Jesus answered him, “It is also written: ‘Do not put the Lord
your God to the test.’[d]”
8Again, the devil took him to a very high mountain and showed
him all the kingdoms of the world and their splendor. 9“All this I
will give you,” he said, “if you will bow down and worship me.”
10Jesus said to him, “Away from me, Satan! For it is written:
‘Worship the Lord your God, and serve him only.’[e]”
11Then the devil left him, and angels came and attended him.

Jesus Begins to Preach

12When Jesus heard that John had been put in prison, he returned to Galilee. 13Leaving Nazareth, he went and lived in Capernaum, which was by the lake in the area of Zebulun and
Naphtali— 14to fulfill what was said through the prophet Isaiah:
15“Land of Zebulun and land of Naphtali,
the way to the sea, along the Jordan,
Galilee of the Gentiles—
16the people living in darkness
have seen a great light;
on those living in the land of the shadow of death
a light has dawned.”[f]

[a] *11* Or *in* [b] *4* Deut. 8:3 [c] *6* Psalm 91:11,12 [d] *7* Deut. 6:16 [e] *10* Deut. 6:13
[f] *16* Isaiah 9:1,2

From morning to night keep Jesus in your heart, long for nothing, desire nothing, hope for nothing, but to have all that is within you changed into the spirit and temper of the Holy Jesus.

William Law (1686-1761)

(3:13–17) Lord Jesus, I thank You that even though You had no sin, You humbly submitted to the baptism of sinners. And to this simple yet profound act of obedience the Father responded with love and favor: “This is my Son, whom I love; with him I am well pleased.” I thank You, Lord, that as I follow You into the waters of baptism I too will find the Father's love and favor. Please teach me to walk in the spirit of my baptism. Help me to live a lifestyle of repentance, in the delight of my heavenly Father. (Ro 6:4; 2Co 5:21; Col 2:12)

We bless the name of Christ the
Lord,
We bless Him for His holy Word,
Who loved to do His Father's will,
And all His righteousness fulfill.

We follow Him with pure delight
To sanctify His sacred rite,
And thus our faith with water seal,
To prove obedience that we feel.

“We Bless the Name of Christ the Lord”
Samuel F. Coffman (1926)

17From that time on Jesus began to preach, "Repent, for the
kingdom of heaven is near."

The Calling of the First Disciples

18As Jesus was walking beside the Sea of Galilee, he saw two
brothers, Simon called Peter and his brother Andrew. They were
casting a net into the lake, for they were fishermen. 19"Come, follow me," Jesus said, "and I will make you fishers of men." 20At
once they left their nets and followed him.

21Going on from there, he saw two other brothers, James son
of Zebedee and his brother John. They were in a boat with their
father Zebedee, preparing their nets. Jesus called them, 22and
immediately they left the boat and their father and followed him.

Jesus Heals the Sick

23Jesus went throughout Galilee, teaching in their synagogues,
preaching the good news of the kingdom, and healing every disease and sickness among the people. 24News about him spread
all over Syria, and people brought to him all who were ill with
various diseases, those suffering severe pain, the demon-possessed, those having seizures, and the paralyzed, and he healed
them. 25Large crowds from Galilee, the Decapolis,[a] Jerusalem,
Judea and the region across the Jordan followed him.

The Beatitudes

5 Now when he saw the crowds, he went up on a mountainside
and sat down. His disciples came to him, 2and he began to
teach them, saying:

3"Blessed are the poor in spirit,
for theirs is the kingdom of heaven.
4Blessed are those who mourn,
for they will be comforted.
5Blessed are the meek,
for they will inherit the earth.
6Blessed are those who hunger and thirst for
righteousness,
for they will be filled.
7Blessed are the merciful,
for they will be shown mercy.
8Blessed are the pure in heart,
for they will see God.
9Blessed are the peacemakers,
for they will be called sons of God.
10Blessed are those who are persecuted because of
righteousness,
for theirs is the kingdom of heaven.

11"Blessed are you when people insult you, persecute you and
falsely say all kinds of evil against you because of me. 12Rejoice
and be glad, because great is your reward in heaven, for in the
same way they persecuted the prophets who were before you.

Salt and Light

13"You are the salt of the earth. But if the salt loses its saltiness,
how can it be made salty again? It is no longer good for anything,
except to be thrown out and trampled by men.

[a] *25* That is, the Ten Cities

(4:17—5:12) "Repent, for the kingdom of heaven is near." The king has come; the kingdom at last is here. "Blessed are the poor in spirit . . . those who mourn . . . the meek . . . those who hunger and thirst for righteousness . . . the merciful . . . the pure in heart . . . the peacemakers . . . those who are persecuted because of righteousness . . ." With a new ruler there comes a new set of rules: a new economy, new hope, new destiny, new values, new justice, new vision, new identity, new responsibilities, new privileges, new rewards and a new day. Lord Jesus, as I worship You as my King, help me to live in the new way of Your kingdom.

Christ turned the world's accepted standards upside down. It was the poor, not the rich, who were blessed; the weak, not the strong, who were to be esteemed; the pure in heart, not the sophisticated and the worldly, who understood what life was about. Righteousness, not power or money or sensual pleasure, should be man's pursuit.

Malcolm Muggeridge (1903-1990)

Just as I am, poor, wretched, blind,
Sight, riches, healing of the mind,
Yea, all I need in Thee I find,
O Lamb of God, I come, I come.

"Just As I Am"
Charlotte Elliott (1834)

14 “You are the light of the world. A city on a hill cannot be hidden. 15 Neither do people light a lamp and put it under a bowl. Instead they put it on its stand, and it gives light to everyone in the
house. 16 In the same way, let your light shine before men, that
they may see your good deeds and praise your Father in heaven.

The Fulfillment of the Law

17 “Do not think that I have come to abolish the Law or the
Prophets; I have not come to abolish them but to fulfill them. 18 I
tell you the truth, until heaven and earth disappear, not the smallest letter, not the least stroke of a pen, will by any means disappear from the Law until everything is accomplished. 19 Anyone
who breaks one of the least of these commandments and teaches
others to do the same will be called least in the kingdom of heav-
en, but whoever practices and teaches these commands will be
called great in the kingdom of heaven. 20 For I tell you that unless
your righteousness surpasses that of the Pharisees and the teachers of the law, you will certainly not enter the kingdom of heaven.

Murder

21 “You have heard that it was said to the people long ago, ‘Do
not murder,[a] and anyone who murders will be subject to judgment.’ 22 But I tell you that anyone who is angry with his brother[b]
will be subject to judgment. Again, anyone who says to his brother, ‘Raca,[c]’ is answerable to the Sanhedrin. But anyone who says,
‘You fool!’ will be in danger of the fire of hell.

23 “Therefore, if you are offering your gift at the altar and there
remember that your brother has something against you, 24 leave
your gift there in front of the altar. First go and be reconciled to
your brother; then come and offer your gift.

25 “Settle matters quickly with your adversary who is taking
you to court. Do it while you are still with him on the way, or he
may hand you over to the judge, and the judge may hand you
over to the officer, and you may be thrown into prison. 26 I tell
you the truth, you will not get out until you have paid the last
penny.[d]

Adultery

27 “You have heard that it was said, ‘Do not commit adultery.’[e]
28 But I tell you that anyone who looks at a woman lustfully has already committed adultery with her in his heart. 29 If your right eye
causes you to sin, gouge it out and throw it away. It is better for
you to lose one part of your body than for your whole body to be
thrown into hell. 30 And if your right hand causes you to sin, cut it
off and throw it away. It is better for you to lose one part of your
body than for your whole body to go into hell.

Divorce

31 “It has been said, ‘Anyone who divorces his wife must give
her a certificate of divorce.’[f] 32 But I tell you that anyone who divorces his wife, except for marital unfaithfulness, causes her to
become an adulteress, and anyone who marries the divorced
woman commits adultery.

[a] *21* Exodus 20:13 [b] *22* Some manuscripts *brother without cause*
[c] *22* An Aramaic term of contempt [d] *26* Greek *kodrantes* [e] *27* Exodus 20:14
[f] *31* Deut. 24:1

(5:14–16) Lord Jesus, how can You call me a light? In my own strength, by my own power, I can't light up anything. I am only the candle, not the flame. But when You touch me with Your holy fire my faith ignites into a holy flame, and I am able to illumine the lives of others with Your love. So touch me, Lord, and light my life for You. Use me to bring Your hope and truth, Your joy and healing to others. Lord, shine through me!

Come, brokenhearted, take good cheer;
Come, crushed in spirit, do not fear.
The Lord who reigns in blinding light
Dwells with the lowly and contrite.

Now let us set the world aflame;
Proclaim the glory of His name!
His light be everywhere adored,
And every creature own Him Lord!

"Let There Be Light!"
John Piper (©1990)

(5:21–26) God, I confess that there are broken relationships impeding my progress in my walk with You. Forgive me for the times I have hurt others. Forgive me for allowing wounds to fester and for holding hatred and vindictiveness in my heart. According to Your Son if I hate my brother in my heart I might as well be a murderer. Strengthen me to go—today—to make peace with those I have wronged. Then bring me back, renewed and rejoicing, to worship You without hindrance. (1Jn 4:20)

The best tests of my Christian growth occur in the mainstream of life, not in the quietness of my study.

Charles R. Swindoll (1934-)

Oaths

33"Again, you have heard that it was said to the people long
ago, 'Do not break your oath, but keep the oaths you have made
to the Lord.' 34But I tell you, Do not swear at all: either by heav-
en, for it is God's throne; 35or by the earth, for it is his footstool;
or by Jerusalem, for it is the city of the Great King. 36And do not
swear by your head, for you cannot make even one hair white or
black. 37Simply let your 'Yes' be 'Yes,' and your 'No,' 'No'; anything beyond this comes from the evil one.

An Eye for an Eye

38"You have heard that it was said, 'Eye for eye, and tooth for
tooth.'[a] 39But I tell you, Do not resist an evil person. If someone
strikes you on the right cheek, turn to him the other also. 40And
if someone wants to sue you and take your tunic, let him have
your cloak as well. 41If someone forces you to go one mile, go
with him two miles. 42Give to the one who asks you, and do not
turn away from the one who wants to borrow from you.

Love for Enemies

43"You have heard that it was said, 'Love your neighbor[b] and
hate your enemy.' 44But I tell you: Love your enemies[c] and pray
for those who persecute you, 45that you may be sons of your Father in heaven. He causes his sun to rise on the evil and the good,
and sends rain on the righteous and the unrighteous. 46If you
love those who love you, what reward will you get? Are not even
the tax collectors doing that? 47And if you greet only your brothers, what are you doing more than others? Do not even pagans do
that? 48Be perfect, therefore, as your heavenly Father is perfect.

Giving to the Needy

6 "Be careful not to do your 'acts of righteousness' before
men, to be seen by them. If you do, you will have no reward
from your Father in heaven.

2"So when you give to the needy, do not announce it with trumpets, as the hypocrites do in the synagogues and on the streets, to
be honored by men. I tell you the truth, they have received their
reward in full. 3But when you give to the needy, do not let your
left hand know what your right hand is doing, 4so that your giving may be in secret. Then your Father, who sees what is done in
secret, will reward you.

Prayer

5"And when you pray, do not be like the hypocrites, for they
love to pray standing in the synagogues and on the street corners
to be seen by men. I tell you the truth, they have received their reward in full. 6But when you pray, go into your room, close the
door and pray to your Father, who is unseen. Then your Father,
who sees what is done in secret, will reward you. 7And when you
pray, do not keep on babbling like pagans, for they think they will
be heard because of their many words. 8Do not be like them, for
your Father knows what you need before you ask him.

9"This, then, is how you should pray:

" 'Our Father in heaven,

[a] 38 Exodus 21:24; Lev. 24:20; Deut. 19:21 [b] 43 Lev. 19:18 [c] 44 Some late manuscripts *enemies, bless those who curse you, do good to those who hate you*

(5:43–48) Like Father, like Son. Like Father, like sons. Father, teach me to live like Your Son. Jesus said that He did only what He saw His Father doing—and what did He do? He loved sinners while they were sinning against Him. He prayed for sinners while they were sinning against Him. He gave His life for sinners while they were sinning against Him. This was the way of His Father. This is the way of my Father. O Father, let this be my way too. (Lk 23:34; Jn 5:19; Ro 5:8)

Let each live a life of labour and self-denial as his master doth, and make himself a servant of all; let him stoop, and let him toil, and do all the good he can, and then he will be a complete disciple.

Matthew Henry (1662-1714)

MY BELOVED

Have you ever doubted My heart for you? Is that why you find it hard to ask for My help when you are in such great need? Have faith in your heavenly Father. Know that My promises to you are true.

If you ask of Me, you will receive. Not on your terms, but on Mine. If you seek Me you will find Me; I will come to you. If you knock, I will open the door for you. I have spoken; I have promised; I have invited you to come to Me. Now I am awaiting your response.

I long to spend time alone with you, My beloved. Sometimes it is hard for you to be transparent with Me when others are around. So get away somewhere private, in your room or in a quiet garden. And when you come to Me in secret, I will demonstrate My goodness to you before many. They will know of My love for you.

If you wonder whether I desire to bless you, think about this: Even evil people know how to give good gifts to their children. So just imagine how much more I not only want to do, but also can do for you, if you will just ask Me. For I am your heavenly Father, the Lord Who delights in those who put their hope in My unfailing love.

Ps 147:11; Mt 6:6; 7:7-11; Jn 16:23-24; 1Jn 5:14-15

hallowed be your name,
[10]your kingdom come,
your will be done
on earth as it is in heaven.
[11]Give us today our daily bread.
[12]Forgive us our debts,
as we also have forgiven our debtors.
[13]And lead us not into temptation,
but deliver us from the evil one.[a]'

[14]For if you forgive men when they sin against you, your heavenly Father will also forgive you. [15]But if you do not forgive men
their sins, your Father will not forgive your sins.

Fasting

[16]"When you fast, do not look somber as the hypocrites do,
for they disfigure their faces to show men they are fasting. I tell
you the truth, they have received their reward in full. [17]But when
you fast, put oil on your head and wash your face, [18]so that it will
not be obvious to men that you are fasting, but only to your Father, who is unseen; and your Father, who sees what is done in secret, will reward you.

Treasures in Heaven

[19]"Do not store up for yourselves treasures on earth, where
moth and rust destroy, and where thieves break in and steal.
[20]But store up for yourselves treasures in heaven, where moth
and rust do not destroy, and where thieves do not break in and
steal. [21]For where your treasure is, there your heart will be also.
[22]"The eye is the lamp of the body. If your eyes are good, your
whole body will be full of light. [23]But if your eyes are bad, your
whole body will be full of darkness. If then the light within you is
darkness, how great is that darkness!
[24]"No one can serve two masters. Either he will hate the one
and love the other, or he will be devoted to the one and despise
the other. You cannot serve both God and Money.

Do Not Worry

[25]"Therefore I tell you, do not worry about your life, what you
will eat or drink; or about your body, what you will wear. Is not
life more important than food, and the body more important than
clothes? [26]Look at the birds of the air; they do not sow or reap or
store away in barns, and yet your heavenly Father feeds them. Are
you not much more valuable than they? [27]Who of you by worrying
can add a single hour to his life[b]?
[28]"And why do you worry about clothes? See how the lilies of
the field grow. They do not labor or spin. [29]Yet I tell you that not
even Solomon in all his splendor was dressed like one of these.
[30]If that is how God clothes the grass of the field, which is here
today and tomorrow is thrown into the fire, will he not much more
clothe you, O you of little faith? [31]So do not worry, saying, 'What
shall we eat?' or 'What shall we drink?' or 'What shall we wear?'
[32]For the pagans run after all these things, and your heavenly Father knows that you need them. [33]But seek first his kingdom and
his righteousness, and all these things will be given to you as well.

[a] 13 Or *from evil*; some late manuscripts *one, / for yours is the kingdom and the power and the glory forever. Amen.* [b] 27 Or *single cubit to his height*

(6:5–15) Father in heaven, You are Lord of all. Your will is perfect, and You provide generously for all of Your creatures. You cleanse us from all our sins. You lead us in paths that are safe and right. Your kingdom is to be desired above all else; Your power is the greatest force in the universe; Your glory radiates from every corner of Creation. We praise and adore You, Heavenly Father, for all that You are and for the amazing grace and forgiveness You have extended to us.

(6:25–33) Father, in Your hand are the untold riches of heaven and earth. In Your hand are the life of every creature and the breath of all mankind. In Your hand are strength and power to exalt and give strength to all. In Your hand are my life, my times and all my ways. All blessing, all provision, all protection, all comfort, all joy, all peace, all righteousness are in Your hand. O let me stay hidden in Your hand, Father, and I will lack nothing. (1Ch 29:12; Job 12:10; Ps 31:5; Da 5:23)

Seek ye first the kingdom of God
And His righteousness,
And all these things
Shall be added unto you
Allelu, alleluia!

"Seek Ye First"
Karen Lafferty (©1972)

(6:34) Father God, it's so hard for me to rest in the present—to trust You for this one day. I want to go back to yesterday and say, "Oh if only I'd done this or that." I want to jump ahead to tomorrow and ask, "But what about this or that terrible thing that could happen?" Help me, Lord, to learn the lesson of living in the present moment. Strengthen my faith as I release to You both yesterday and tomorrow. And meet me today in the here and now, in this precious, never-to-be-repeated time, in which I can simply trust You to meet my needs. (Jas 4:13–15)

Enough for today is all we can enjoy. We cannot eat or drink or wear more than today's supply of food and clothing. The surplus gives us the care of storing it and the anxiety that someone might steal it. One staff aids a traveler; a bunch of staves is a heavy burden. Enough is as good as a feast and more than gluttony can enjoy. Enough is all we should expect, but a craving for more is ungratefulness. When our Father does not give you more, be content with your daily allowance.

Charles Haddon Spurgeon (1834-1892)

(7:7–12) Lord, You have instructed us to keep asking for all that we need and want. You have taught us to keep seeking those things we cannot grasp. And You have told us to keep knocking on unopened doors. This affirms that we are utterly reliant upon You. You are our sole Provider. You are the One who understands and explains all mysteries. You alone have the power to unlock the doors into the future. Apart from You, Lord, we can do nothing. But with You all things are possible. (Mt 19:26; Jn 15:5)

34Therefore do not worry about tomorrow, for tomorrow will
worry about itself. Each day has enough trouble of its own.

Judging Others

7 "Do not judge, or you too will be judged. 2For in the same
way you judge others, you will be judged, and with the measure you use, it will be measured to you.
3"Why do you look at the speck of sawdust in your brother's
eye and pay no attention to the plank in your own eye? 4How can
you say to your brother, 'Let me take the speck out of your eye,'
when all the time there is a plank in your own eye? 5You hypocrite, first take the plank out of your own eye, and then you will
see clearly to remove the speck from your brother's eye.
6"Do not give dogs what is sacred; do not throw your pearls to
pigs. If you do, they may trample them under their feet, and then
turn and tear you to pieces.

Ask, Seek, Knock

7"Ask and it will be given to you; seek and you will find; knock
and the door will be opened to you. 8For everyone who asks receives; he who seeks finds; and to him who knocks, the door will
be opened.
9"Which of you, if his son asks for bread, will give him a stone?
10Or if he asks for a fish, will give him a snake? 11If you, then,
though you are evil, know how to give good gifts to your children,
how much more will your Father in heaven give good gifts to
those who ask him! 12So in everything, do to others what you
would have them do to you, for this sums up the Law and the
Prophets.

The Narrow and Wide Gates

13"Enter through the narrow gate. For wide is the gate and
broad is the road that leads to destruction, and many enter
through it. 14But small is the gate and narrow the road that leads
to life, and only a few find it.

A Tree and Its Fruit

15"Watch out for false prophets. They come to you in sheep's
clothing, but inwardly they are ferocious wolves. 16By their fruit
you will recognize them. Do people pick grapes from thornbushes, or figs from thistles? 17Likewise every good tree bears
good fruit, but a bad tree bears bad fruit. 18A good tree cannot
bear bad fruit, and a bad tree cannot bear good fruit. 19Every tree
that does not bear good fruit is cut down and thrown into the fire.
20Thus, by their fruit you will recognize them.
21"Not everyone who says to me, 'Lord, Lord,' will enter the
kingdom of heaven, but only he who does the will of my Father
who is in heaven. 22Many will say to me on that day, 'Lord, Lord,
did we not prophesy in your name, and in your name drive out
demons and perform many miracles?' 23Then I will tell them
plainly, 'I never knew you. Away from me, you evildoers!'

The Wise and Foolish Builders

24"Therefore everyone who hears these words of mine and
puts them into practice is like a wise man who built his house on
the rock. 25The rain came down, the streams rose, and the winds
blew and beat against that house; yet it did not fall, because it had

its foundation on the rock. 26 But everyone who hears these words
of mine and does not put them into practice is like a foolish man
who built his house on sand. 27 The rain came down, the streams
rose, and the winds blew and beat against that house, and it fell
with a great crash."

28 When Jesus had finished saying these things, the crowds
were amazed at his teaching, 29 because he taught as one who had
authority, and not as their teachers of the law.

The Man With Leprosy

8 When he came down from the mountainside, large crowds
followed him. 2 A man with leprosy[a] came and knelt before
him and said, "Lord, if you are willing, you can make me clean."
3 Jesus reached out his hand and touched the man. "I am willing," he said. "Be clean!" Immediately he was cured[b] of his leprosy. 4 Then Jesus said to him, "See that you don't tell anyone. But
go, show yourself to the priest and offer the gift Moses commanded, as a testimony to them."

The Faith of the Centurion

5 When Jesus had entered Capernaum, a centurion came to
him, asking for help. 6 "Lord," he said, "my servant lies at home
paralyzed and in terrible suffering."
7 Jesus said to him, "I will go and heal him."
8 The centurion replied, "Lord, I do not deserve to have you
come under my roof. But just say the word, and my servant will be
healed. 9 For I myself am a man under authority, with soldiers
under me. I tell this one, 'Go,' and he goes; and that one, 'Come,'
and he comes. I say to my servant, 'Do this,' and he does it."
10 When Jesus heard this, he was astonished and said to those
following him, "I tell you the truth, I have not found anyone in Israel with such great faith. 11 I say to you that many will come from
the east and the west, and will take their places at the feast with
Abraham, Isaac and Jacob in the kingdom of heaven. 12 But the
subjects of the kingdom will be thrown outside, into the darkness, where there will be weeping and gnashing of teeth."
13 Then Jesus said to the centurion, "Go! It will be done just as
you believed it would." And his servant was healed at that very
hour.

Jesus Heals Many

14 When Jesus came into Peter's house, he saw Peter's mother-
in-law lying in bed with a fever. 15 He touched her hand and the
fever left her, and she got up and began to wait on him.
16 When evening came, many who were demon-possessed were
brought to him, and he drove out the spirits with a word and
healed all the sick. 17 This was to fulfill what was spoken through
the prophet Isaiah:

> "He took up our infirmities
> and carried our diseases."[c]

The Cost of Following Jesus

18 When Jesus saw the crowd around him, he gave orders to
cross to the other side of the lake. 19 Then a teacher of the law

[a] 2 The Greek word was used for various diseases affecting the skin—not necessarily leprosy. [b] 3 Greek *made clean* [c] 17 Isaiah 53:4

(8:2–3) Lord Jesus, You are so willing to meet us, if only we will come to You—if only we will reach out to You and ask. But so often we continue to wrap ourselves in the filthy rags of our own sinfulness. We become comfortable with our misery. O Lord, I don't want to live without wholeness or holiness. Your healing is so near and so powerful. I know You are willing to touch me. I'm reaching out to You. Speak to me those powerful words, "Be clean." (Jn 6:35–45)

(8:23–27) Lord, if You are able to calm the storm at sea, surely You can calm the storms in my life. I find myself day by day in the middle of the swirling, raging storms of this world—the snarled traffic, the incessant noise, the political unrest, the wars, the fear and the violence. But Lord, I confess that there are other storms—storms inside of me, storms of my own making. I worry and allow myself to succumb to stress instead of trusting You. I get caught up in little spats and feuds with loved ones when You've called me to be a peacemaker. I now see so clearly what little faith I really have. Forgive me, Lord. Come and speak to the storms within and without. Come and be my Peace. (Isa 26:3,12)

Why are ye fearful? Doubt not but the ship will come safe to land; though Christ seem for the present to be asleep, the prayers of His disciples will awake Him, and He will rebuke the winds and the waves; though the bush burn, if God be in it, it shall not be consumed.

Matthew Henry (1662-1714)

When the days are like a battle with
no relief in sight,
I know that if I trust You, You will
come.
You will turn my grief to dancing,
and turn my tears to joy
And just beyond the night, I'll find
the sun.
I've seen You still a reckless sea and
hush a howling wind,
And I know Your love will rescue me
again.

"I Know Your Love Will Rescue Me Again"
Claire Cloninger (©1999)

came to him and said, "Teacher, I will follow you wherever you go."
20 Jesus replied, "Foxes have holes and birds of the air have
nests, but the Son of Man has no place to lay his head."
21 Another disciple said to him, "Lord, first let me go and bury
my father."
22 But Jesus told him, "Follow me, and let the dead bury their
own dead."

Jesus Calms the Storm

23 Then he got into the boat and his disciples followed him.
24 Without warning, a furious storm came up on the lake, so that
the waves swept over the boat. But Jesus was sleeping. 25 The disciples went and woke him, saying, "Lord, save us! We're going to
drown!"
26 He replied, "You of little faith, why are you so afraid?" Then
he got up and rebuked the winds and the waves, and it was completely calm.
27 The men were amazed and asked, "What kind of man is this?
Even the winds and the waves obey him!"

The Healing of Two Demon-possessed Men

28 When he arrived at the other side in the region of the Gadarenes,[a] two demon-possessed men coming from the tombs met
him. They were so violent that no one could pass that way.
29 "What do you want with us, Son of God?" they shouted. "Have
you come here to torture us before the appointed time?"
30 Some distance from them a large herd of pigs was feeding.
31 The demons begged Jesus, "If you drive us out, send us into
the herd of pigs."
32 He said to them, "Go!" So they came out and went into the
pigs, and the whole herd rushed down the steep bank into the
lake and died in the water. 33 Those tending the pigs ran off, went
into the town and reported all this, including what had happened
to the demon-possessed men. 34 Then the whole town went out to
meet Jesus. And when they saw him, they pleaded with him to
leave their region.

Jesus Heals a Paralytic

9 Jesus stepped into a boat, crossed over and came to his own
town. 2 Some men brought to him a paralytic, lying on a mat.
When Jesus saw their faith, he said to the paralytic, "Take heart,
son; your sins are forgiven."
3 At this, some of the teachers of the law said to themselves,
"This fellow is blaspheming!"
4 Knowing their thoughts, Jesus said, "Why do you entertain evil
thoughts in your hearts? 5 Which is easier: to say, 'Your sins are
forgiven,' or to say, 'Get up and walk'? 6 But so that you may know
that the Son of Man has authority on earth to forgive sins . . ."
Then he said to the paralytic, "Get up, take your mat and go
home." 7 And the man got up and went home. 8 When the crowd
saw this, they were filled with awe; and they praised God, who
had given such authority to men.

[a] 28 Some manuscripts *Gergesenes*; others *Gerasenes*

The Calling of Matthew

9As Jesus went on from there, he saw a man named Matthew
sitting at the tax collector's booth. "Follow me," he told him, and
Matthew got up and followed him.
10While Jesus was having dinner at Matthew's house, many tax
collectors and "sinners" came and ate with him and his disciples.
11When the Pharisees saw this, they asked his disciples, "Why
does your teacher eat with tax collectors and 'sinners'?"
12On hearing this, Jesus said, "It is not the healthy who need a
doctor, but the sick. 13But go and learn what this means: 'I desire
mercy, not sacrifice.'[a] For I have not come to call the righteous,
but sinners."

Jesus Questioned About Fasting

14Then John's disciples came and asked him, "How is it that
we and the Pharisees fast, but your disciples do not fast?"
15Jesus answered, "How can the guests of the bridegroom
mourn while he is with them? The time will come when the bridegroom will be taken from them; then they will fast.
16"No one sews a patch of unshrunk cloth on an old garment,
for the patch will pull away from the garment, making the tear
worse. 17Neither do men pour new wine into old wineskins. If
they do, the skins will burst, the wine will run out and the wineskins will be ruined. No, they pour new wine into new wineskins,
and both are preserved."

A Dead Girl and a Sick Woman

18While he was saying this, a ruler came and knelt before him
and said, "My daughter has just died. But come and put your
hand on her, and she will live." 19Jesus got up and went with him,
and so did his disciples.
20Just then a woman who had been subject to bleeding for
twelve years came up behind him and touched the edge of his
cloak. 21She said to herself, "If I only touch his cloak, I will be
healed."
22Jesus turned and saw her. "Take heart, daughter," he said,
"your faith has healed you." And the woman was healed from that
moment.
23When Jesus entered the ruler's house and saw the flute players and the noisy crowd, 24he said, "Go away. The girl is not dead
but asleep." But they laughed at him. 25After the crowd had been
put outside, he went in and took the girl by the hand, and she got
up. 26News of this spread through all that region.

Jesus Heals the Blind and Mute

27As Jesus went on from there, two blind men followed him,
calling out, "Have mercy on us, Son of David!"
28When he had gone indoors, the blind men came to him, and
he asked them, "Do you believe that I am able to do this?"
"Yes, Lord," they replied.
29Then he touched their eyes and said, "According to your
faith will it be done to you"; 30and their sight was restored. Jesus
warned them sternly, "See that no one knows about this." 31But
they went out and spread the news about him all over that region.
32While they were going out, a man who was demon-possessed

[a] *13* Hosea 6:6

(9:18–26) Lord, a ruler and an outcast woman both came to You for help. Both were facing death. You responded willingly to the ruler's request, which was clearly articulated and urgently expressed. The woman, in her shame and agony, didn't say a word. She simply followed You, caught the corner of Your robe in her hand and believed. The same power that raised the ruler's daughter from the dead healed the woman's deadly hemorrhaging. And the same power that raised You from the grave heals us all—no matter how important we are in the eyes of the world or how eloquently we pray. Thank You for the life You give to our mortal bodies through Your Spirit, Who lives within us. (Ro 8:11)

Heal us, Immanuel, hear our prayer;
We wait to feel your touch;
Deep wounded souls to You repair,
And, Savior, we are such.

She, too, who touched
You in the press,
And healing virtue stole,
Was answered,
"Daughter, go in peace:
Your faith has made you whole."

Like her, with hopes and fears
We come to touch You if we may;
O send us not despairing home,
Send none unhealed away.

"Heal Us, Immanuel, Hear Our Prayer"
William Cowper (1779)

All pow'r is giv'n in Jesus' name,
In earth and heav'n in Jesus' name;
And in Jesus' name I come to you
To share His power as He told me
to.

He said, "Freely, freely you have
received
Freely, freely give;
Go in My name and, because you
believe,
Others will know that I live."

"Freely, Freely"
Carol Owens (©1972)

(10:1–8) What a marvelous risk You have taken in sending out ordinary people—people like me—in Your name! Only in Your power can ordinary people accomplish extraordinary things for Your kingdom. Thank You for choosing me to be Your disciple, Lord Jesus. Please teach me and empower me to live a life that is worthy of Your calling. (Eph 4:1)

The church was not designed to be a reservoir, ever-receiving and retaining for itself God's spiritual blessings, but rather a conduit, conveying them on and out to others everywhere.

Robert Hall Glover (1871–1947)

(10:19–20) Thank You, Lord, for Your Holy Spirit. Thank You that He works and speaks through me and supplies me with wisdom that is not my own. O Lord, I choose to trust You. I choose to listen for Your still, small voice of guidance. Help me to hear You. Help me not to rely on my human effort but on Your Spirit's power working in my life. (Jer 1:9)

and could not talk was brought to Jesus. 33And when the demon
was driven out, the man who had been mute spoke. The crowd was
amazed and said, "Nothing like this has ever been seen in Israel."
34But the Pharisees said, "It is by the prince of demons that he
drives out demons."

The Workers Are Few

35Jesus went through all the towns and villages, teaching in
their synagogues, preaching the good news of the kingdom and
healing every disease and sickness. 36When he saw the crowds,
he had compassion on them, because they were harassed and
helpless, like sheep without a shepherd. 37Then he said to his
disciples, "The harvest is plentiful but the workers are few. 38Ask
the Lord of the harvest, therefore, to send out workers into his
harvest field."

Jesus Sends Out the Twelve

10 He called his twelve disciples to him and gave them authority to drive out evil[a] spirits and to heal every disease
and sickness.
2These are the names of the twelve apostles: first, Simon (who
is called Peter) and his brother Andrew; James son of Zebedee,
and his brother John; 3Philip and Bartholomew; Thomas and
Matthew the tax collector; James son of Alphaeus, and Thaddaeus; 4Simon the Zealot and Judas Iscariot, who betrayed him.
5These twelve Jesus sent out with the following instructions:
"Do not go among the Gentiles or enter any town of the Samaritans. 6Go rather to the lost sheep of Israel. 7As you go, preach
this message: 'The kingdom of heaven is near.' 8Heal the sick,
raise the dead, cleanse those who have leprosy,[b] drive out
demons. Freely you have received, freely give. 9Do not take along
any gold or silver or copper in your belts; 10take no bag for the
journey, or extra tunic, or sandals or a staff; for the worker is
worth his keep.
11"Whatever town or village you enter, search for some worthy
person there and stay at his house until you leave. 12As you enter
the home, give it your greeting. 13If the home is deserving, let
your peace rest on it; if it is not, let your peace return to you. 14If
anyone will not welcome you or listen to your words, shake the
dust off your feet when you leave that home or town. 15I tell you
the truth, it will be more bearable for Sodom and Gomorrah on
the day of judgment than for that town. 16I am sending you out
like sheep among wolves. Therefore be as shrewd as snakes and
as innocent as doves.
17"Be on your guard against men; they will hand you over to
the local councils and flog you in their synagogues. 18On my account you will be brought before governors and kings as witnesses to them and to the Gentiles. 19But when they arrest you, do
not worry about what to say or how to say it. At that time you will
be given what to say, 20for it will not be you speaking, but the
Spirit of your Father speaking through you.
21"Brother will betray brother to death, and a father his child;
children will rebel against their parents and have them put to
death. 22All men will hate you because of me, but he who stands
firm to the end will be saved. 23When you are persecuted in one

[a] 1 Greek *unclean* [b] 8 The Greek word was used for various diseases affecting the skin—not necessarily leprosy.

place, flee to another. I tell you the truth, you will not finish going
through the cities of Israel before the Son of Man comes.
24"A student is not above his teacher, nor a servant above his
master. 25It is enough for the student to be like his teacher, and
the servant like his master. If the head of the house has been
called Beelzebub,[a] how much more the members of his household!

26"So do not be afraid of them. There is nothing concealed that
will not be disclosed, or hidden that will not be made known.
27What I tell you in the dark, speak in the daylight; what is whispered in your ear, proclaim from the roofs. 28Do not be afraid of
those who kill the body but cannot kill the soul. Rather, be afraid
of the One who can destroy both soul and body in hell. 29Are not
two sparrows sold for a penny[b]? Yet not one of them will fall to
the ground apart from the will of your Father. 30And even the very
hairs of your head are all numbered. 31So don't be afraid; you are
worth more than many sparrows.

32"Whoever acknowledges me before men, I will also acknowledge him before my Father in heaven. 33But whoever disowns me
before men, I will disown him before my Father in heaven.

34"Do not suppose that I have come to bring peace to the
earth. I did not come to bring peace, but a sword. 35For I have
come to turn

" 'a man against his father,
a daughter against her mother,
a daughter-in-law against her mother-in-law—
36 a man's enemies will be the members of his own
household.'[c]

37"Anyone who loves his father or mother more than me is not
worthy of me; anyone who loves his son or daughter more than
me is not worthy of me; 38and anyone who does not take his
cross and follow me is not worthy of me. 39Whoever finds his life
will lose it, and whoever loses his life for my sake will find it.

40"He who receives you receives me, and he who receives me
receives the one who sent me. 41Anyone who receives a prophet
because he is a prophet will receive a prophet's reward, and anyone who receives a righteous man because he is a righteous man
will receive a righteous man's reward. 42And if anyone gives even
a cup of cold water to one of these little ones because he is my
disciple, I tell you the truth, he will certainly not lose his reward."

Jesus and John the Baptist

11 After Jesus had finished instructing his twelve disciples, he went on from there to teach and preach in the towns of Galilee.[d]

2When John heard in prison what Christ was doing, he sent his
disciples 3to ask him, "Are you the one who was to come, or
should we expect someone else?"

4Jesus replied, "Go back and report to John what you hear and
see: 5The blind receive sight, the lame walk, those who have leprosy[e] are cured, the deaf hear, the dead are raised, and the good
news is preached to the poor. 6Blessed is the man who does not
fall away on account of me."

[a] 25 Greek *Beezeboul* or *Beelzeboul* [b] 29 Greek *an assarion* [c] 36 Micah 7:6
[d] 1 Greek *in their towns* [e] 5 The Greek word was used for various diseases affecting the skin—not necessarily leprosy.

(10:28–42) Lord, please give me strength to follow You with all of my heart. Help me to believe that You value me far more than a sparrow, that You care for me enough to number the hairs of my head. Give me courage to speak Your name boldly. Give me strength to bear the loss of loved ones and friends who might reject me because of You. Give me love enough to lay down my life for You, and hope enough to receive my life back again. Give me faith to believe that those who sow in tears will reap in joy, and reassure me that when I go out weeping I will surely return again rejoicing. (Ps 126:5–6)

"Let not your heart be troubled,"
His tender word I hear,
And resting on His goodness
I lose my doubt and fears;
Tho' by the path He leadeth
But one step I may see:
His eye is on the sparrow,
And I know He watches me;
His eye is on the sparrow,
And I know He watches me.

"His Eye Is On the Sparrow"
Civilla D. Martin (1905)

The most effective workers I know are those who don't allow themselves a moment's anxiety about their work. They commit it all to Jesus, asking Him to guide them step by step and trusting Him implicitly to provide the wisdom and strength they need for each day's work. To see them, you might almost think that they are too free from care, where such important matters are at stake. But when you have learned God's secret of trusting, you will see that a life yielded up to His working is one of rest as well as power.

Catherine Jackson

Relinquishment of burdens and fears begins where adoration and worship of God become the occupation of the soul.
Frances J. Roberts

(11:25–30) Lord God, how is it that You reveal Yourself to the simple and not to the wise? In my ignorance, be my wisdom. In my blindness, be my vision. In my weakness, be my strength. In my constant agitation, be my peace. Lift my burden, Lord. Teach me Your humility and humbleness of heart, and give rest to my soul.

When he says to your disturbed, distracted, restless soul or mind, "Come unto me," he is saying, come out of the strife and doubt and struggle of what is at the moment where you stand, into that which was and is and is to be—the eternal, the essential, the absolute.
Phillips Brooks (1835-1893)

Come, ye sinners, poor and needy,
Weak and wounded, sick and sore;
Jesus ready stands to save you,
Full of pity, love and power.

Come, ye weary, heavy laden,
Lost and ruined by the Fall;
If you tarry till you're better,
You will never come at all.
"Come, Ye Sinners, Poor and Needy"
Joseph Hart (1759)

7 As John's disciples were leaving, Jesus began to speak to the
crowd about John: "What did you go out into the desert to see? A
reed swayed by the wind? 8 If not, what did you go out to see? A
man dressed in fine clothes? No, those who wear fine clothes are
in kings' palaces. 9 Then what did you go out to see? A prophet?
Yes, I tell you, and more than a prophet. 10 This is the one about
whom it is written:

" 'I will send my messenger ahead of you,
who will prepare your way before you.'[a]

11 I tell you the truth: Among those born of women there has not
risen anyone greater than John the Baptist; yet he who is least in
the kingdom of heaven is greater than he. 12 From the days of
John the Baptist until now, the kingdom of heaven has been forcefully advancing, and forceful men lay hold of it. 13 For all the
Prophets and the Law prophesied until John. 14 And if you are
willing to accept it, he is the Elijah who was to come. 15 He who
has ears, let him hear.

16 "To what can I compare this generation? They are like children sitting in the marketplaces and calling out to others:

17 " 'We played the flute for you,
and you did not dance;
we sang a dirge,
and you did not mourn.'

18 For John came neither eating nor drinking, and they say, 'He
has a demon.' 19 The Son of Man came eating and drinking, and
they say, 'Here is a glutton and a drunkard, a friend of tax collectors and "sinners." ' But wisdom is proved right by her actions."

Woe on Unrepentant Cities

20 Then Jesus began to denounce the cities in which most of his
miracles had been performed, because they did not repent.
21 "Woe to you, Korazin! Woe to you, Bethsaida! If the miracles
that were performed in you had been performed in Tyre and
Sidon, they would have repented long ago in sackcloth and ashes.
22 But I tell you, it will be more bearable for Tyre and Sidon on the
day of judgment than for you. 23 And you, Capernaum, will you be
lifted up to the skies? No, you will go down to the depths.[b] If the
miracles that were performed in you had been performed in
Sodom, it would have remained to this day. 24 But I tell you that it
will be more bearable for Sodom on the day of judgment than for
you."

Rest for the Weary

25 At that time Jesus said, "I praise you, Father, Lord of heaven
and earth, because you have hidden these things from the wise
and learned, and revealed them to little children. 26 Yes, Father,
for this was your good pleasure.

27 "All things have been committed to me by my Father. No one
knows the Son except the Father, and no one knows the Father
except the Son and those to whom the Son chooses to reveal
him.

28 "Come to me, all you who are weary and burdened, and I
will give you rest. 29 Take my yoke upon you and learn from me,

[a] *10* Mal. 3:1 [b] *23* Greek *Hades*

for I am gentle and humble in heart, and you will find rest for your souls. 30For my yoke is easy and my burden is light."

Lord of the Sabbath

12 At that time Jesus went through the grainfields on the Sabbath. His disciples were hungry and began to pick some heads of grain and eat them. 2When the Pharisees saw this, they said to him, "Look! Your disciples are doing what is unlawful on the Sabbath."

3He answered, "Haven't you read what David did when he and his companions were hungry? 4He entered the house of God, and he and his companions ate the consecrated bread—which was not lawful for them to do, but only for the priests. 5Or haven't you read in the Law that on the Sabbath the priests in the temple desecrate the day and yet are innocent? 6I tell you that one[a] greater than the temple is here. 7If you had known what these words mean, 'I desire mercy, not sacrifice,'[b] you would not have condemned the innocent. 8For the Son of Man is Lord of the Sabbath."

9Going on from that place, he went into their synagogue, 10and a man with a shriveled hand was there. Looking for a reason to accuse Jesus, they asked him, "Is it lawful to heal on the Sabbath?"

11He said to them, "If any of you has a sheep and it falls into a pit on the Sabbath, will you not take hold of it and lift it out? 12How much more valuable is a man than a sheep! Therefore it is lawful to do good on the Sabbath."

13Then he said to the man, "Stretch out your hand." So he stretched it out and it was completely restored, just as sound as the other. 14But the Pharisees went out and plotted how they might kill Jesus.

God's Chosen Servant

15Aware of this, Jesus withdrew from that place. Many followed him, and he healed all their sick, 16warning them not to tell who he was. 17This was to fulfill what was spoken through the prophet Isaiah:

18"Here is my servant whom I have chosen,
the one I love, in whom I delight;
I will put my Spirit on him,
and he will proclaim justice to the nations.
19He will not quarrel or cry out;
no one will hear his voice in the streets.
20A bruised reed he will not break,
and a smoldering wick he will not snuff out,
till he leads justice to victory.
21 In his name the nations will put their
hope."[c]

Jesus and Beelzebub

22Then they brought him a demon-possessed man who was blind and mute, and Jesus healed him, so that he could both talk and see. 23All the people were astonished and said, "Could this be the Son of David?"

24But when the Pharisees heard this, they said, "It is only by

[a] 6 Or *something*; also in verses 41 and 42 [b] 7 Hosea 6:6 [c] 21 Isaiah 42:1–4

(12:9–14) Jesus, You spent the day of rest restoring life. The Pharisees spent the day of rest plotting murder. You saved this "sheep" from the pit of despair, while they made plans to kill the Shepherd. Lord, You clearly demonstrated that people are more important than protocol and that love is more important than legalism. Free me, then, from cold rules and empty traditions that inhibit the work of Your Spirit. May I never be satisfied to let anyone leave Your house without having received Your blessing. Please teach me to embrace the freedom and spontaneity of Your abundant life.

As we give the gifts of compassion and humility, our lives become demonstrations of the truth of God's Word. We create an atmosphere of grace, and build a highway of love between our hearts and the hearts of other people. Our willingness to be used as God's vessels can make His tender Father-heart a reality to our hurting world.

Floyd McClung, Jr. (1945-)

Jesus' hands were kind hands,
Doing good to all,
Healing pain and sickness,
Blessing children small,
Washing tired feet
And saving those who fall;
Jesus' hands were kind hands,
Doing good to all.

Take my hands, Lord Jesus,
Let them work for You;
Make them strong and gentle,
Kind in all I do;
Let me watch You, Jesus,
Till I'm gentle too,
Till my hands are kind hands,
Quick to work for You.

"Jesus' Hands Were Kind Hands"
Margaret Cropper (©1926)

(12:33–37) My heart is a fountain and my words its streams. You listen to my speech, Lord, so it must be important to You. Please help me to store up Your Word of life in my heart, so that words of life will flow out of my mouth. As Elisha threw salt into the spring to purify the water, so I ask You to season my heart and my speech with the salt of grace. (2Ki 2:19–22; Col 4:6)

I must admit, Lord, I have great trouble controlling my tongue. In fact, I can't. Unless you work in my heart to transform my thinking, my words will reveal the ugliness of sin. Cleanse me from my unrighteousness. Show me how to reduce my volume of words while you cleanse me and implant your wisdom in my heart. I want to bless others with my tongue, not hurt them. Make my mouth an instrument of righteousness through the power of the Holy Spirit, who resides at the fountainhead of my speech—my heart.

Charles Stanley (1932-)

Beelzebub,[a] the prince of demons, that this fellow drives out
demons."
25 Jesus knew their thoughts and said to them, "Every kingdom
divided against itself will be ruined, and every city or household
divided against itself will not stand. 26 If Satan drives out Satan, he
is divided against himself. How then can his kingdom stand?
27 And if I drive out demons by Beelzebub, by whom do your people drive them out? So then, they will be your judges. 28 But if I
drive out demons by the Spirit of God, then the kingdom of God
has come upon you.
29 "Or again, how can anyone enter a strong man's house and
carry off his possessions unless he first ties up the strong man?
Then he can rob his house.
30 "He who is not with me is against me, and he who does not
gather with me scatters. 31 And so I tell you, every sin and blasphemy will be forgiven men, but the blasphemy against the Spirit
will not be forgiven. 32 Anyone who speaks a word against the Son
of Man will be forgiven, but anyone who speaks against the Holy
Spirit will not be forgiven, either in this age or in the age to come.
33 "Make a tree good and its fruit will be good, or make a tree
bad and its fruit will be bad, for a tree is recognized by its fruit.
34 You brood of vipers, how can you who are evil say anything
good? For out of the overflow of the heart the mouth speaks.
35 The good man brings good things out of the good stored up in
him, and the evil man brings evil things out of the evil stored up
in him. 36 But I tell you that men will have to give account on the
day of judgment for every careless word they have spoken. 37 For
by your words you will be acquitted, and by your words you will
be condemned."

The Sign of Jonah

38 Then some of the Pharisees and teachers of the law said to
him, "Teacher, we want to see a miraculous sign from you."
39 He answered, "A wicked and adulterous generation asks for
a miraculous sign! But none will be given it except the sign of the
prophet Jonah. 40 For as Jonah was three days and three nights in
the belly of a huge fish, so the Son of Man will be three days and
three nights in the heart of the earth. 41 The men of Nineveh will
stand up at the judgment with this generation and condemn it;
for they repented at the preaching of Jonah, and now one[b]
greater than Jonah is here. 42 The Queen of the South will rise at
the judgment with this generation and condemn it; for she came
from the ends of the earth to listen to Solomon's wisdom, and
now one greater than Solomon is here.
43 "When an evil[c] spirit comes out of a man, it goes through
arid places seeking rest and does not find it. 44 Then it says, 'I
will return to the house I left.' When it arrives, it finds the house
unoccupied, swept clean and put in order. 45 Then it goes and
takes with it seven other spirits more wicked than itself, and they
go in and live there. And the final condition of that man is worse
than the first. That is how it will be with this wicked generation."

Jesus' Mother and Brothers

46 While Jesus was still talking to the crowd, his mother and
brothers stood outside, wanting to speak to him. 47 Someone told

[a] 24 Greek *Beezeboul* or *Beelzeboul*; also in verse 27 [b] 41 Or *something*; also in verse 42 [c] 43 Greek *unclean*

him, "Your mother and brothers are standing outside, wanting to
speak to you."[a]
48He replied to him, "Who is my mother, and who are my
brothers?" 49Pointing to his disciples, he said, "Here are my
mother and my brothers. 50For whoever does the will of my Father in heaven is my brother and sister and mother."

The Parable of the Sower

13 That same day Jesus went out of the house and sat by the
lake. 2Such large crowds gathered around him that he got
into a boat and sat in it, while all the people stood on the shore.
3Then he told them many things in parables, saying: "A farmer
went out to sow his seed. 4As he was scattering the seed, some fell
along the path, and the birds came and ate it up. 5Some fell on
rocky places, where it did not have much soil. It sprang up quickly, because the soil was shallow. 6But when the sun came up, the
plants were scorched, and they withered because they had no
root. 7Other seed fell among thorns, which grew up and choked
the plants. 8Still other seed fell on good soil, where it produced
a crop—a hundred, sixty or thirty times what was sown. 9He who
has ears, let him hear."
10The disciples came to him and asked, "Why do you speak to
the people in parables?"
11He replied, "The knowledge of the secrets of the kingdom of
heaven has been given to you, but not to them. 12Whoever has
will be given more, and he will have an abundance. Whoever does
not have, even what he has will be taken from him. 13This is why
I speak to them in parables:

"Though seeing, they do not see;
though hearing, they do not hear or understand.

14In them is fulfilled the prophecy of Isaiah:

" 'You will be ever hearing but never understanding;
you will be ever seeing but never perceiving.
15For this people's heart has become calloused;
they hardly hear with their ears,
and they have closed their eyes.
Otherwise they might see with their eyes,
hear with their ears,
understand with their hearts
and turn, and I would heal them.'[b]

16But blessed are your eyes because they see, and your ears because they hear. 17For I tell you the truth, many prophets and
righteous men longed to see what you see but did not see it, and
to hear what you hear but did not hear it.
18"Listen then to what the parable of the sower means: 19When
anyone hears the message about the kingdom and does not understand it, the evil one comes and snatches away what was sown
in his heart. This is the seed sown along the path. 20The one who
received the seed that fell on rocky places is the man who hears
the word and at once receives it with joy. 21But since he has no
root, he lasts only a short time. When trouble or persecution
comes because of the word, he quickly falls away. 22The one who
received the seed that fell among the thorns is the man who hears

[a] 47 Some manuscripts do not have verse 47. [b] 15 Isaiah 6:9,10

(13:1–23) Lord Jesus, I praise and thank You for choosing to plant Your Word in my life. I yearn to be fertile ground for Your truth. I long to bear good fruit for You. Remove the rocks, chase away the birds and rebuke the evil One who would hinder my growth. Lord, in Your mercy hear my prayer. May I listen and understand and live according to Your Word today, and in so doing bring a bountiful harvest to You, the Wise and Eternal Gardener.

Now that which distinguished this good ground from the rest, was, in one word, fruitfulness. He does not say that this good ground has no stones in it, or no thorns; but there were none that prevailed to hinder its fruitfulness. Saints, in this world, are not perfectly free from the remains of sin; but happily freed from the reign of it.

Matthew Henry (1662-1714)

the word, but the worries of this life and the deceitfulness of
wealth choke it, making it unfruitful. 23But the one who received
the seed that fell on good soil is the man who hears the word and
understands it. He produces a crop, yielding a hundred, sixty or
thirty times what was sown."

The Parable of the Weeds

24Jesus told them another parable: "The kingdom of heaven is
like a man who sowed good seed in his field. 25But while everyone was sleeping, his enemy came and sowed weeds among the
wheat, and went away. 26When the wheat sprouted and formed
heads, then the weeds also appeared.

27"The owner's servants came to him and said, 'Sir, didn't you
sow good seed in your field? Where then did the weeds come
from?'

28" 'An enemy did this,' he replied.

"The servants asked him, 'Do you want us to go and pull
them up?'

29" 'No,' he answered, 'because while you are pulling the
weeds, you may root up the wheat with them. 30Let both grow together until the harvest. At that time I will tell the harvesters: First
collect the weeds and tie them in bundles to be burned; then
gather the wheat and bring it into my barn.' "

The Parables of the Mustard Seed and the Yeast

31He told them another parable: "The kingdom of heaven is
like a mustard seed, which a man took and planted in his field.
32Though it is the smallest of all your seeds, yet when it grows, it
is the largest of garden plants and becomes a tree, so that the
birds of the air come and perch in its branches."

33He told them still another parable: "The kingdom of heaven
is like yeast that a woman took and mixed into a large amount[a] of
flour until it worked all through the dough."

34Jesus spoke all these things to the crowd in parables; he did
not say anything to them without using a parable. 35So was fulfilled what was spoken through the prophet:

"I will open my mouth in parables,
I will utter things hidden since the creation of the
world."[b]

The Parable of the Weeds Explained

36Then he left the crowd and went into the house. His disciples
came to him and said, "Explain to us the parable of the weeds in
the field."

37He answered, "The one who sowed the good seed is the Son
of Man. 38The field is the world, and the good seed stands for the
sons of the kingdom. The weeds are the sons of the evil one,
39and the enemy who sows them is the devil. The harvest is the
end of the age, and the harvesters are angels.

40"As the weeds are pulled up and burned in the fire, so it will
be at the end of the age. 41The Son of Man will send out his angels, and they will weed out of his kingdom everything that causes
sin and all who do evil. 42They will throw them into the fiery furnace, where there will be weeping and gnashing of teeth. 43Then

[a] 33 Greek *three satas* (probably about 1/2 bushel or 22 liters) [b] 35 Psalm 78:2

(13:22) O Lord, sometimes my faith feels as though it's choking in the million weeds of worry that crop up all around me on a daily basis. So much competes with the serenity, the tranquility, the life of prayer I long to nurture. Was my life really meant to be this chaotic and stressed? Most of the things I worry about are not essential. When I stop to think about it, only one thing really matters, and that is You. Please weed the garden of my life today. Pull up the unnecessary commitments, preoccupations, distractions and complications. Help me to seek Your kingdom first and set the focus of my heart where it belongs—on my relationship with You. (Lk 10:38–42)

For the Lord our God shall come
And shall take His harvest home,
From His field shall in that day
All offenses purge away,
Give His angels charge at last
In the fire the tares to cast,
But the fruitful ears to store
In His garner evermore.

Even so, Lord, quickly come
To Your final harvest home,
Gather all Your people in,
Free from sorrow, free from sin,
There, forever purified,
In Your presence to abide.
Come, with all Your angels,
Come, raise the glorious harvest
home.

"Come, Ye Thankful People, Come"
Henry Alford (1844)

the righteous will shine like the sun in the kingdom of their Father. He who has ears, let him hear.

The Parables of the Hidden Treasure and the Pearl

44"The kingdom of heaven is like treasure hidden in a field.
When a man found it, he hid it again, and then in his joy went and
sold all he had and bought that field.
45"Again, the kingdom of heaven is like a merchant looking
for fine pearls. 46When he found one of great value, he went away
and sold everything he had and bought it.

The Parable of the Net

47"Once again, the kingdom of heaven is like a net that was let
down into the lake and caught all kinds of fish. 48When it was full,
the fishermen pulled it up on the shore. Then they sat down and
collected the good fish in baskets, but threw the bad away. 49This
is how it will be at the end of the age. The angels will come and
separate the wicked from the righteous 50and throw them into the
fiery furnace, where there will be weeping and gnashing of teeth.
51"Have you understood all these things?" Jesus asked.
"Yes," they replied.
52He said to them, "Therefore every teacher of the law who has
been instructed about the kingdom of heaven is like the owner of
a house who brings out of his storeroom new treasures as well as
old."

A Prophet Without Honor

53When Jesus had finished these parables, he moved on from
there. 54Coming to his hometown, he began teaching the people
in their synagogue, and they were amazed. "Where did this man
get this wisdom and these miraculous powers?" they asked.
55"Isn't this the carpenter's son? Isn't his mother's name Mary,
and aren't his brothers James, Joseph, Simon and Judas? 56Aren't
all his sisters with us? Where then did this man get all these
things?" 57And they took offense at him.
But Jesus said to them, "Only in his hometown and in his own
house is a prophet without honor."
58And he did not do many miracles there because of their lack
of faith.

John the Baptist Beheaded

14 At that time Herod the tetrarch heard the reports about
Jesus, 2and he said to his attendants, "This is John the
Baptist; he has risen from the dead! That is why miraculous powers are at work in him."
3Now Herod had arrested John and bound him and put him in
prison because of Herodias, his brother Philip's wife, 4for John
had been saying to him: "It is not lawful for you to have her."
5Herod wanted to kill John, but he was afraid of the people, because they considered him a prophet.
6On Herod's birthday the daughter of Herodias danced for
them and pleased Herod so much 7that he promised with an oath
to give her whatever she asked. 8Prompted by her mother, she
said, "Give me here on a platter the head of John the Baptist."
9The king was distressed, but because of his oaths and his dinner
guests, he ordered that her request be granted 10and had John
beheaded in the prison. 11His head was brought in on a platter

(13:44–46) Lord Jesus, help us to love You the way You love us. For we are more precious to You than anything else in all of creation. In Your eyes we are a treasure of incomparable value. We are humbled that , though You were rich, for our sakes You became poor, so that we through Your poverty might become rich. We are astonished that, though in Your very nature You are God, still You laid aside every divine privilege and, for the joy set before You, endured the cross and shed Your own blood to purchase us. Help us in return to be willing to lay aside every earthly treasure and, for the joy that awaits us, carry our cross and, if necessary, shed our own blood for the sake of Your kingdom. (2Co 8:9; Php 2:6–8; Heb 12:2)

You are my life
Oh, precious Christ,
You are to me
The pearl of greatest price.
My love for You
Will never die,
Jesus, You are my life.

I come to You,
I run to You,
There's no greater joy
Than knowing You.

"Jesus, You are my Life"
Steve Fry (©1996)

(14:1–12) It sometimes costs everything to speak the truth. Refusal to count the cost, or recant, or remain silent, has made martyrs of many. But when their shed blood rains on the parched world, souls spring forth, rooted in the faith by the living sacrifices that confirm the reality of the gospel. After all, men do not willingly die for nothing. But the gospel is worth dying for—and worth living for. God, give Your church that commitment and passionate love for You that, in our living or our dying, confirms our worship and authenticates our faith to the world. (Ro 12:1)

and given to the girl, who carried it to her mother. 12John's disciples came and took his body and buried it. Then they went and told Jesus.

Jesus Feeds the Five Thousand

13When Jesus heard what had happened, he withdrew by boat privately to a solitary place. Hearing of this, the crowds followed him on foot from the towns. 14When Jesus landed and saw a large crowd, he had compassion on them and healed their sick.

15As evening approached, the disciples came to him and said, "This is a remote place, and it's already getting late. Send the crowds away, so they can go to the villages and buy themselves some food."

16Jesus replied, "They do not need to go away. You give them something to eat."

17"We have here only five loaves of bread and two fish," they answered.

18"Bring them here to me," he said. 19And he directed the people to sit down on the grass. Taking the five loaves and the two fish and looking up to heaven, he gave thanks and broke the loaves. Then he gave them to the disciples, and the disciples gave them to the people. 20They all ate and were satisfied, and the disciples picked up twelve basketfuls of broken pieces that were left over. 21The number of those who ate was about five thousand men, besides women and children.

Jesus Walks on the Water

22Immediately Jesus made the disciples get into the boat and go on ahead of him to the other side, while he dismissed the crowd. 23After he had dismissed them, he went up on a mountainside by himself to pray. When evening came, he was there alone, 24but the boat was already a considerable distance[a] from land, buffeted by the waves because the wind was against it.

25During the fourth watch of the night Jesus went out to them, walking on the lake. 26When the disciples saw him walking on the lake, they were terrified. "It's a ghost," they said, and cried out in fear.

27But Jesus immediately said to them: "Take courage! It is I. Don't be afraid."

28"Lord, if it's you," Peter replied, "tell me to come to you on the water."

29"Come," he said.

Then Peter got down out of the boat, walked on the water and came toward Jesus. 30But when he saw the wind, he was afraid and, beginning to sink, cried out, "Lord, save me!"

31Immediately Jesus reached out his hand and caught him. "You of little faith," he said, "why did you doubt?"

32And when they climbed into the boat, the wind died down. 33Then those who were in the boat worshiped him, saying, "Truly you are the Son of God."

34When they had crossed over, they landed at Gennesaret. 35And when the men of that place recognized Jesus, they sent word to all the surrounding country. People brought all their sick to him 36and begged him to let the sick just touch the edge of his cloak, and all who touched him were healed.

[a] 24 Greek *many stadia*

(14:22–32) O Lord, when obedience to Your command leads me into the path of the storm and I find myself bailing water to save my life, give me courage to step out of the boat and walk with You on the raging seas. Help me not to fear or be distracted by my surroundings; rather, help me to keep my eyes of faith—the gaze of my soul—focused on You. Come to me when I am desperate, catch me when I fall, and bring me safely through the tempest to the other side of my troubles.

I heard the Master calling
Across the stormy sea:
"There is life for anyone who'll take it.
Not a path of safety
Or false security;
Put your trust in me and you will make it."

Leave the boat behind
And step into the angry tide,
Walking on, walking on the water.
Come and follow me
Down a road you cannot see,
Walking on, walking on the water.

"Walking on the Water"
Bill Batstone (©1991)

He is with us on our journeys. He is there when we are home. He sits with us at our table. He knows about funerals and weddings and commencements and hospitals and jails and unemployment and labor and laughter and rest and tears. He knows because He is with us–He comes to us again and again–until we can say, "It's You! It's You!"

Bob Benson (1930–1986)

Clean and Unclean

15 Then some Pharisees and teachers of the law came to Jesus
from Jerusalem and asked, 2"Why do your disciples break
the tradition of the elders? They don't wash their hands before
they eat!"
3Jesus replied, "And why do you break the command of God
for the sake of your tradition? 4For God said, 'Honor your father
and mother'[a] and 'Anyone who curses his father or mother must
be put to death.'[b] 5But you say that if a man says to his father or
mother, 'Whatever help you might otherwise have received from
me is a gift devoted to God,' 6he is not to 'honor his father[c]' with
it. Thus you nullify the word of God for the sake of your tradition. 7You hypocrites! Isaiah was right when he prophesied
about you:

8" 'These people honor me with their lips,
but their hearts are far from me.
9They worship me in vain;
their teachings are but rules taught by men.'[d]"

10Jesus called the crowd to him and said, "Listen and understand. 11What goes into a man's mouth does not make him 'unclean,' but what comes out of his mouth, that is what makes him
'unclean.' "
12Then the disciples came to him and asked, "Do you know
that the Pharisees were offended when they heard this?"
13He replied, "Every plant that my heavenly Father has not
planted will be pulled up by the roots. 14Leave them; they are
blind guides.[e] If a blind man leads a blind man, both will fall into
a pit."
15Peter said, "Explain the parable to us."
16"Are you still so dull?" Jesus asked them. 17"Don't you see
that whatever enters the mouth goes into the stomach and then
out of the body? 18But the things that come out of the mouth
come from the heart, and these make a man 'unclean.' 19For out
of the heart come evil thoughts, murder, adultery, sexual immorality, theft, false testimony, slander. 20These are what make a
man 'unclean'; but eating with unwashed hands does not make
him 'unclean.' "

The Faith of the Canaanite Woman

21Leaving that place, Jesus withdrew to the region of Tyre and
Sidon. 22A Canaanite woman from that vicinity came to him, crying out, "Lord, Son of David, have mercy on me! My daughter is
suffering terribly from demon-possession."
23Jesus did not answer a word. So his disciples came to him
and urged him, "Send her away, for she keeps crying out
after us."
24He answered, "I was sent only to the lost sheep of Israel."
25The woman came and knelt before him. "Lord, help me!"
she said.
26He replied, "It is not right to take the children's bread and
toss it to their dogs."
27"Yes, Lord," she said, "but even the dogs eat the crumbs that
fall from their masters' table."

[a] 4 Exodus 20:12; Deut. 5:16 [b] 4 Exodus 21:17; Lev. 20:9 [c] 6 Some manuscripts *father or his mother* [d] 9 Isaiah 29:13 [e] 14 Some manuscripts *guides of the blind*

(15:1–20) We thank You, Father, for the great value You place on the purity of our hearts in worship. Great traditions are no substitute for a pure heart in worship. Great preaching is no substitute for a pure heart in worship. Great talent, or leadership ability, or pageantry, are no substitutes for a pure heart in worship. If our hearts are not pure before You, then our energies are wasted. We know, Lord, that You do not look at the outward appearance; You look at the heart. O Lord, purify my heart so that its overflow will be pure worship that is pleasing to You. (1Sa 16:7)

Oh, holy fire,
Love's purest light,
Burn all desires
Till You are my one delight.
My love for You will never die,
Jesus, You are my life.

I come to You,
I run to You,
There's no greater joy
Than knowing You.

"Jesus, You are my Life"
Steve Fry (©1996)

Worship demands purity. Over and over we have seen that the prerequisite to the privilege of entering God's presence is the recognition of personal sinfulness and a willingness to abandon that sinfulness. A consuming desire to be pure and clean is the normal result of being with God. The closer we draw to God, the more overwhelmed we become with our sinfulness . . . If the corporate worship in the church leaves people unchanged, the church is not really worshiping. If what goes on in the church service does not spur the saints to greater obedience, call it what you will, it isn't worship. Worship always results in a transformation, and the church is edified by it.

John MacArthur, Jr. (1939-)

[28]Then Jesus answered, "Woman, you have great faith! Your
request is granted." And her daughter was healed from that very
hour.

Jesus Feeds the Four Thousand

[29]Jesus left there and went along the Sea of Galilee. Then he
went up on a mountainside and sat down. [30]Great crowds came
to him, bringing the lame, the blind, the crippled, the mute and
many others, and laid them at his feet; and he healed them. [31]The
people were amazed when they saw the mute speaking, the crippled made well, the lame walking and the blind seeing. And they
praised the God of Israel.

[32]Jesus called his disciples to him and said, "I have compassion for these people; they have already been with me three days
and have nothing to eat. I do not want to send them away hungry,
or they may collapse on the way."

[33]His disciples answered, "Where could we get enough bread
in this remote place to feed such a crowd?"

[34]"How many loaves do you have?" Jesus asked.

"Seven," they replied, "and a few small fish."

[35]He told the crowd to sit down on the ground. [36]Then he took
the seven loaves and the fish, and when he had given thanks, he
broke them and gave them to the disciples, and they in turn to the
people. [37]They all ate and were satisfied. Afterward the disciples
picked up seven basketfuls of broken pieces that were left over.
[38]The number of those who ate was four thousand, besides
women and children. [39]After Jesus had sent the crowd away, he
got into the boat and went to the vicinity of Magadan.

(15:32–38) Lord Jesus, there are so many hungry people all around me—people who are hungry for bread to feed their bodies, for encouragement and love to feed their hungry hearts. When the need seems great and my resources seem small, it is easy to feel inadequate. Lord, help me not to worry about what I do not have but to thankfully offer what I do have, knowing that You will do the rest. Thank You for giving me gifts and then multiplying them to feed Your hungry family. Thank You that it is in sharing what I have that I myself am healed and nourished. (Isa 58:7–8)

The Demand for a Sign

16 The Pharisees and Sadducees came to Jesus and tested
him by asking him to show them a sign from heaven.

[2]He replied,[a] "When evening comes, you say, 'It will be fair
weather, for the sky is red,' [3]and in the morning, 'Today it will be
stormy, for the sky is red and overcast.' You know how to interpret the appearance of the sky, but you cannot interpret the signs
of the times. [4]A wicked and adulterous generation looks for a
miraculous sign, but none will be given it except the sign of
Jonah." Jesus then left them and went away.

The Yeast of the Pharisees and Sadducees

[5]When they went across the lake, the disciples forgot to take
bread. [6]"Be careful," Jesus said to them. "Be on your guard
against the yeast of the Pharisees and Sadducees."

[7]They discussed this among themselves and said, "It is because
we didn't bring any bread."

[8]Aware of their discussion, Jesus asked, "You of little faith, why
are you talking among yourselves about having no bread? [9]Do
you still not understand? Don't you remember the five loaves for
the five thousand, and how many basketfuls you gathered? [10]Or
the seven loaves for the four thousand, and how many basketfuls
you gathered? [11]How is it you don't understand that I was not
talking to you about bread? But be on your guard against the yeast
of the Pharisees and Sadducees." [12]Then they understood that he

[a] 2 Some early manuscripts do not have the rest of verse 2 and all of verse 3.

was not telling them to guard against the yeast used in bread, but against the teaching of the Pharisees and Sadducees.

Peter's Confession of Christ

13When Jesus came to the region of Caesarea Philippi, he asked his disciples, "Who do people say the Son of Man is?"

14They replied, "Some say John the Baptist; others say Elijah; and still others, Jeremiah or one of the prophets."

15"But what about you?" he asked. "Who do you say I am?"

16Simon Peter answered, "You are the Christ,[a] the Son of the living God."

17Jesus replied, "Blessed are you, Simon son of Jonah, for this
was not revealed to you by man, but by my Father in heaven.
18And I tell you that you are Peter,[b] and on this rock I will build
my church, and the gates of Hades[c] will not overcome it.[d] 19I will
give you the keys of the kingdom of heaven; whatever you bind on
earth will be[e] bound in heaven, and whatever you loose on earth
will be[e] loosed in heaven." 20Then he warned his disciples not to
tell anyone that he was the Christ.

Jesus Predicts His Death

21From that time on Jesus began to explain to his disciples that he must go to Jerusalem and suffer many things at the hands of the elders, chief priests and teachers of the law, and that he must be killed and on the third day be raised to life.

22Peter took him aside and began to rebuke him. "Never, Lord!" he said. "This shall never happen to you!"

23Jesus turned and said to Peter, "Get behind me, Satan! You are a stumbling block to me; you do not have in mind the things of God, but the things of men."

24Then Jesus said to his disciples, "If anyone would come after
me, he must deny himself and take up his cross and follow me.
25For whoever wants to save his life[f] will lose it, but whoever
loses his life for me will find it. 26What good will it be for a man
if he gains the whole world, yet forfeits his soul? Or what can a
man give in exchange for his soul? 27For the Son of Man is going
to come in his Father's glory with his angels, and then he will reward each person according to what he has done. 28I tell you the
truth, some who are standing here will not taste death before they
see the Son of Man coming in his kingdom."

The Transfiguration

17 After six days Jesus took with him Peter, James and John
the brother of James, and led them up a high mountain by
themselves. 2There he was transfigured before them. His face
shone like the sun, and his clothes became as white as the light.
3Just then there appeared before them Moses and Elijah, talking
with Jesus.

4Peter said to Jesus, "Lord, it is good for us to be here. If you wish, I will put up three shelters—one for you, one for Moses and one for Elijah."

5While he was still speaking, a bright cloud enveloped them, and a voice from the cloud said, "This is my Son, whom I love; with him I am well pleased. Listen to him!"

(16:15–17) Lord Jesus, this question You asked Your disciples is the question that all of us have to answer, regardless of what any one else has to say: "Who do You say that I am?" With Peter, and with Your Father in heaven, I affirm that You are the Christ, the anointed One, the Son of the living God, the Son whom the Father loves. May Your name be praised forever, Lord Jesus Christ. (Mt 3:17; 17:5)

[a] 16 Or *Messiah*; also in verse 20 [b] 18 *Peter* means *rock*. [c] 18 Or *hell* [d] 18 Or *not prove stronger than it* [e] 19 Or *have been* [f] 25 The Greek word means either *life* or *soul*; also in verse 26.

6When the disciples heard this, they fell facedown to the ground, terrified. 7But Jesus came and touched them. "Get up," he said. "Don't be afraid." 8When they looked up, they saw no one except Jesus.

9As they were coming down the mountain, Jesus instructed them, "Don't tell anyone what you have seen, until the Son of Man has been raised from the dead."

10The disciples asked him, "Why then do the teachers of the law say that Elijah must come first?"

11Jesus replied, "To be sure, Elijah comes and will restore all things. 12But I tell you, Elijah has already come, and they did not recognize him, but have done to him everything they wished. In the same way the Son of Man is going to suffer at their hands." 13Then the disciples understood that he was talking to them about John the Baptist.

The Healing of a Boy With a Demon

14When they came to the crowd, a man approached Jesus and knelt before him. 15"Lord, have mercy on my son," he said. "He has seizures and is suffering greatly. He often falls into the fire or into the water. 16I brought him to your disciples, but they could not heal him."

17"O unbelieving and perverse generation," Jesus replied, "how long shall I stay with you? How long shall I put up with you? Bring the boy here to me." 18Jesus rebuked the demon, and it came out of the boy, and he was healed from that moment.

19Then the disciples came to Jesus in private and asked, "Why couldn't we drive it out?"

20He replied, "Because you have so little faith. I tell you the truth, if you have faith as small as a mustard seed, you can say to this mountain, 'Move from here to there' and it will move. Nothing will be impossible for you.[a]"

22When they came together in Galilee, he said to them, "The Son of Man is going to be betrayed into the hands of men. 23They will kill him, and on the third day he will be raised to life." And the disciples were filled with grief.

The Temple Tax

24After Jesus and his disciples arrived in Capernaum, the collectors of the two-drachma tax came to Peter and asked, "Doesn't your teacher pay the temple tax[b]?"

25"Yes, he does," he replied.

When Peter came into the house, Jesus was the first to speak. "What do you think, Simon?" he asked. "From whom do the kings of the earth collect duty and taxes—from their own sons or from others?"

26"From others," Peter answered.

"Then the sons are exempt," Jesus said to him. 27"But so that we may not offend them, go to the lake and throw out your line. Take the first fish you catch; open its mouth and you will find a four-drachma coin. Take it and give it to them for my tax and yours."

[a] *20* Some manuscripts *you. 21But this kind does not go out except by prayer and fasting.* [b] *24* Greek *the two drachmas*

(17:14–23) I thank You, Lord, that in Your mercy You do not require faith the size of a mountain in order to move a mustard seed. All that You require is faith the size of a mustard seed in order to move the mountain. Lord, if You can do so much with so little, what greater things could be accomplished for Your kingdom if I would only believe Your promises? As I come to Your Word—the green-house of faith—please increase my faith to be like Abraham, who "believed, and so became . . ." and who "did not waver through unbelief regarding the promise of God, but was strengthened in his faith and gave glory to God, being fully persuaded that God had power to do what he had promised." Lord, I do believe that You have the power to do what You have promised—in my life and in the lives of those You send my way. (Ro 4:18–21; 10:17)

The Christian's faith is strengthened as he keeps the promises of God before him and considers, not the difficulties in the way of the things promised, but the character and resources of God Who has made the promise.

Paul Little (1928-)

Heal us, Immanuel, hear our prayer;
We wait to feel your touch;
Deep wounded souls to You repair,
And, Savior, we are such.

Our faith is feeble, we confess;
We faintly trust Your word;
But will You pity us the less?
Be that far from You, Lord!

"Heal Us, Immanuel, Hear Our Prayer"
William Cowper (1779)

The Greatest in the Kingdom of Heaven

18 At that time the disciples came to Jesus and asked, "Who is
the greatest in the kingdom of heaven?"
2He called a little child and had him stand among them. 3And
he said: "I tell you the truth, unless you change and become like
little children, you will never enter the kingdom of heaven.
4Therefore, whoever humbles himself like this child is the greatest in the kingdom of heaven.
5"And whoever welcomes a little child like this in my name
welcomes me. 6But if anyone causes one of these little ones who
believe in me to sin, it would be better for him to have a large
millstone hung around his neck and to be drowned in the depths
of the sea.
7"Woe to the world because of the things that cause people to
sin! Such things must come, but woe to the man through whom
they come! 8If your hand or your foot causes you to sin, cut it off
and throw it away. It is better for you to enter life maimed or crippled than to have two hands or two feet and be thrown into eternal fire. 9And if your eye causes you to sin, gouge it out and throw
it away. It is better for you to enter life with one eye than to have
two eyes and be thrown into the fire of hell.

The Parable of the Lost Sheep

10"See that you do not look down on one of these little ones.
For I tell you that their angels in heaven always see the face of my
Father in heaven.[a]
12"What do you think? If a man owns a hundred sheep, and
one of them wanders away, will he not leave the ninety-nine on
the hills and go to look for the one that wandered off? 13And if he
finds it, I tell you the truth, he is happier about that one sheep
than about the ninety-nine that did not wander off. 14In the same
way your Father in heaven is not willing that any of these little
ones should be lost.

A Brother Who Sins Against You

15"If your brother sins against you,[b] go and show him his fault,
just between the two of you. If he listens to you, you have won
your brother over. 16But if he will not listen, take one or two others along, so that 'every matter may be established by the testimony of two or three witnesses.'[c] 17If he refuses to listen to them,
tell it to the church; and if he refuses to listen even to the church,
treat him as you would a pagan or a tax collector.
18"I tell you the truth, whatever you bind on earth will be[d]
bound in heaven, and whatever you loose on earth will be[d] loosed
in heaven.
19"Again, I tell you that if two of you on earth agree about anything you ask for, it will be done for you by my Father in heaven.
20For where two or three come together in my name, there am I
with them."

The Parable of the Unmerciful Servant

21Then Peter came to Jesus and asked, "Lord, how many times
shall I forgive my brother when he sins against me? Up to seven
times?"

[a] 10 Some manuscripts *heaven.* *11The Son of Man came to save what was lost.*
[b] 15 Some manuscripts do not have *against you.* [c] 16 Deut. 19:15
[d] 18 Or *have been*

(18:1–9) Lord God, grant me the heart of a child to receive Your truth and to do Your will. And grant me the wisdom to look after children in a godly way. In a world where boys and girls are becoming not only victims but vicious themselves, grant me—grant all of Your people—the wisdom necessary to protect them and to provide the godly guidance they need to live holy lives. Keep us from doing anything that might cause Your little ones to sin. Help us to bring them up to know You, to fear You and to love You.

(18:21–35) Father, we are assured in Your Word that "judgment without mercy will be shown to anyone who has not been merciful." But if we forgive others when they sin against us, then You will forgive us as well. For in the same way we judge others, we will be judged, and with the measure we use, it will be measured to us. So, Father, right now I release into Your hands those who have done me wrong. I open the door of the debtors' prison I have held them in, and I set them free. And I ask, in Jesus' name, that You will set me free from the torment of bitterness and unforgiveness. O God, help me to walk away in freedom and to never look back. (Jer 34:8–22; Mt 6:12,14; 7:2; Jas 2:13)

Of him that hopes to be forgiven, it is indispensably required that he forgive. It is therefore superfluous to urge any other motive. On this great duty eternity is suspended; and to him that refuses to practice it, the throne of mercy is inaccessible, and the Saviour of the world has been born in vain.

Samuel Johnson (1709-1784)

I then shall live
As one who's been forgiven;
I'll walk with joy
To know my debts are paid.
I know my name
Is clear before my Father;
I am His child,
And I am not afraid.
So greatly pardoned,
I'll forgive another;
The law of love
I gladly will obey.

"I Then Shall Live"
Gloria Gaither (©1981)

22 Jesus answered, "I tell you, not seven times, but seventy-
seven times.[a]
23 "Therefore, the kingdom of heaven is like a king who wanted to settle accounts with his servants. 24 As he began the settlement, a man who owed him ten thousand talents[b] was brought to
him. 25 Since he was not able to pay, the master ordered that he
and his wife and his children and all that he had be sold to repay
the debt.
26 "The servant fell on his knees before him. 'Be patient with
me,' he begged, 'and I will pay back everything.' 27 The servant's
master took pity on him, canceled the debt and let him go.
28 "But when that servant went out, he found one of his fellow
servants who owed him a hundred denarii.[c] He grabbed him and
began to choke him. 'Pay back what you owe me!' he demanded.
29 "His fellow servant fell to his knees and begged him, 'Be patient with me, and I will pay you back.'
30 "But he refused. Instead, he went off and had the man
thrown into prison until he could pay the debt. 31 When the other
servants saw what had happened, they were greatly distressed and
went and told their master everything that had happened.
32 "Then the master called the servant in. 'You wicked servant,'
he said, 'I canceled all that debt of yours because you begged me
to. 33 Shouldn't you have had mercy on your fellow servant just as
I had on you?' 34 In anger his master turned him over to the jail-
ers to be tortured, until he should pay back all he owed.
35 "This is how my heavenly Father will treat each of you unless
you forgive your brother from your heart."

Divorce

19 When Jesus had finished saying these things, he left Galilee
and went into the region of Judea to the other side of the
Jordan. 2 Large crowds followed him, and he healed them there.
3 Some Pharisees came to him to test him. They asked, "Is it
lawful for a man to divorce his wife for any and every reason?"
4 "Haven't you read," he replied, "that at the beginning the Creator 'made them male and female,'[d] 5 and said, 'For this reason a
man will leave his father and mother and be united to his wife,
and the two will become one flesh'[e]? 6 So they are no longer two,
but one. Therefore what God has joined together, let man not separate."
7 "Why then," they asked, "did Moses command that a man give
his wife a certificate of divorce and send her away?"
8 Jesus replied, "Moses permitted you to divorce your wives because your hearts were hard. But it was not this way from the beginning. 9 I tell you that anyone who divorces his wife, except for
marital unfaithfulness, and marries another woman commits
adultery."
10 The disciples said to him, "If this is the situation between a
husband and wife, it is better not to marry."
11 Jesus replied, "Not everyone can accept this word, but only
those to whom it has been given. 12 For some are eunuchs because they were born that way; others were made that way by
men; and others have renounced marriage[f] because of the

[a] 22 Or *seventy times seven* [b] 24 That is, millions of dollars [c] 28 That is, a few dollars [d] 4 Gen. 1:27 [e] 5 Gen. 2:24 [f] 12 Or *have made themselves eunuchs*

kingdom of heaven. The one who can accept this should accept it."

The Little Children and Jesus

13Then little children were brought to Jesus for him to place
his hands on them and pray for them. But the disciples rebuked
those who brought them.
14Jesus said, "Let the little children come to me, and do not
hinder them, for the kingdom of heaven belongs to such as
these." 15When he had placed his hands on them, he went on
from there.

The Rich Young Man

16Now a man came up to Jesus and asked, "Teacher, what good
thing must I do to get eternal life?"
17"Why do you ask me about what is good?" Jesus replied.
"There is only One who is good. If you want to enter life, obey the
commandments."
18"Which ones?" the man inquired.
Jesus replied, " 'Do not murder, do not commit adultery, do
not steal, do not give false testimony, 19honor your father and
mother,'[a] and 'love your neighbor as yourself.'[b]"
20"All these I have kept," the young man said. "What do I still
lack?"
21Jesus answered, "If you want to be perfect, go, sell your possessions and give to the poor, and you will have treasure in heav-
en. Then come, follow me."
22When the young man heard this, he went away sad, because
he had great wealth.
23Then Jesus said to his disciples, "I tell you the truth, it is
hard for a rich man to enter the kingdom of heaven. 24Again I tell
you, it is easier for a camel to go through the eye of a needle than
for a rich man to enter the kingdom of God."
25When the disciples heard this, they were greatly astonished
and asked, "Who then can be saved?"
26Jesus looked at them and said, "With man this is impossible,
but with God all things are possible."
27Peter answered him, "We have left everything to follow you!
What then will there be for us?"
28Jesus said to them, "I tell you the truth, at the renewal of all
things, when the Son of Man sits on his glorious throne, you who
have followed me will also sit on twelve thrones, judging the
twelve tribes of Israel. 29And everyone who has left houses or
brothers or sisters or father or mother[c] or children or fields for
my sake will receive a hundred times as much and will inherit
eternal life. 30But many who are first will be last, and many who
are last will be first.

The Parable of the Workers in the Vineyard

20 "For the kingdom of heaven is like a landowner who went
out early in the morning to hire men to work in his vineyard. 2He agreed to pay them a denarius for the day and sent
them into his vineyard.
3"About the third hour he went out and saw others standing in
the marketplace doing nothing. 4He told them, 'You also go and

[a] 19 Exodus 20:12–16; Deut. 5:16–20 [b] 19 Lev. 19:18 [c] 29 Some manuscripts *mother or wife*

He is no fool who gives what he cannot keep to gain what he cannot lose.

Jim Elliot (1927-1956)

(19:16–28) Lord, Your invitation to drop everything and follow You is wonderful, but oh so difficult. Deliver me from the cares of this world and from trying to be "properly" religious without the motivation of serving You from a heart of love and thankfulness. May I not be guilty of selective obedience. Instead, take everything that I am, everything that I treasure and everything that I dream about and set it all aside. In its place, simply make me willing to be used for Your purposes without profit or recognition. Teach me to consider all my gains as losses compared to the surpassing greatness of knowing and following You. (Php 3:7–8)

work in my vineyard, and I will pay you whatever is right.' 5So
they went.
"He went out again about the sixth hour and the ninth hour
and did the same thing. 6About the eleventh hour he went out and
found still others standing around. He asked them, 'Why have you
been standing here all day long doing nothing?'
7" 'Because no one has hired us,' they answered.
"He said to them, 'You also go and work in my vineyard.'
8"When evening came, the owner of the vineyard said to his
foreman, 'Call the workers and pay them their wages, beginning
with the last ones hired and going on to the first.'
9"The workers who were hired about the eleventh hour came
and each received a denarius. 10So when those came who were
hired first, they expected to receive more. But each one of them also
received a denarius. 11When they received it, they began to grumble
against the landowner. 12'These men who were hired last worked
only one hour,' they said, 'and you have made them equal to us who
have borne the burden of the work and the heat of the day.'
13"But he answered one of them, 'Friend, I am not being unfair to you. Didn't you agree to work for a denarius? 14Take your
pay and go. I want to give the man who was hired last the same
as I gave you. 15Don't I have the right to do what I want with my
own money? Or are you envious because I am generous?'
16"So the last will be first, and the first will be last."

Jesus Again Predicts His Death

17Now as Jesus was going up to Jerusalem, he took the twelve
disciples aside and said to them, 18"We are going up to Jerusalem, and the Son of Man will be betrayed to the chief priests and
the teachers of the law. They will condemn him to death 19and
will turn him over to the Gentiles to be mocked and flogged and
crucified. On the third day he will be raised to life!"

A Mother's Request

20Then the mother of Zebedee's sons came to Jesus with her
sons and, kneeling down, asked a favor of him.
21"What is it you want?" he asked.
She said, "Grant that one of these two sons of mine may sit at
your right and the other at your left in your kingdom."
22"You don't know what you are asking," Jesus said to them.
"Can you drink the cup I am going to drink?"
"We can," they answered.
23Jesus said to them, "You will indeed drink from my cup, but
to sit at my right or left is not for me to grant. These places belong
to those for whom they have been prepared by my Father."
24When the ten heard about this, they were indignant with the
two brothers. 25Jesus called them together and said, "You know
that the rulers of the Gentiles lord it over them, and their high officials exercise authority over them. 26Not so with you. Instead,
whoever wants to become great among you must be your servant, 27and whoever wants to be first must be your slave— 28just
as the Son of Man did not come to be served, but to serve, and
to give his life as a ransom for many."

Two Blind Men Receive Sight

29As Jesus and his disciples were leaving Jericho, a large
crowd followed him. 30Two blind men were sitting by the road-

(20:20–28) Lord Jesus, please teach me the ways of Your kingdom. Your kingdom is so very different from the kingdoms of this world. Grant me the grace to place myself last in a society where everyone scrambles to be first. I desire a servant's heart like the one I see in You, Lord. I surrender to You all position, power and wealth for the sake of becoming more like You. Please grant me a heart to care, ears to listen, and hands to serve and help and heal.

Make me a servant, humble and
meek.
Lord, let me lift up those who are
weak.
And may the prayer of my heart
always be:
Make me a servant, make me a
servant,
Make me a servant today.

"Make Me a Servant"
Kelly Willard (©1982)

What is the kingdom of Christ? A rule of love, of truth—a rule of service. The king is the chief servant in it. "The kings of the earth have dominion: it shall not be so among you." "My Father works now, and I work." The great Workman is the great King, laboring for his own. So he that would be greatest among them, and come nearest to the King himself, must be the servant of all. It is like king, like subject, in the kingdom of heaven. No rule of force, as of one kind over another kind. It is the rule of kind, of nature, of deepest nature—of God. If, then, to enter into this kingdom we must become children, the spirit of children must be its pervading spirit throughout, from lowly subject to lowliest king.

George MacDonald (1824-1905)

side, and when they heard that Jesus was going by, they shouted,
"Lord, Son of David, have mercy on us!"
31The crowd rebuked them and told them to be quiet, but
they shouted all the louder, "Lord, Son of David, have mercy
on us!"
32Jesus stopped and called them. "What do you want me to do
for you?" he asked.
33"Lord," they answered, "we want our sight."
34Jesus had compassion on them and touched their eyes. Immediately they received their sight and followed him.

The Triumphal Entry

21 As they approached Jerusalem and came to Bethphage on
the Mount of Olives, Jesus sent two disciples, 2saying to
them, "Go to the village ahead of you, and at once you will find a
donkey tied there, with her colt by her. Untie them and bring
them to me. 3If anyone says anything to you, tell him that the Lord
needs them, and he will send them right away."
4This took place to fulfill what was spoken through the
prophet:

5"Say to the Daughter of Zion,
'See, your king comes to you,
gentle and riding on a donkey,
on a colt, the foal of a donkey.' "[a]

6The disciples went and did as Jesus had instructed them.
7They brought the donkey and the colt, placed their cloaks on
them, and Jesus sat on them. 8A very large crowd spread their
cloaks on the road, while others cut branches from the trees and
spread them on the road. 9The crowds that went ahead of him
and those that followed shouted,

"Hosanna[b] to the Son of David!"

"Blessed is he who comes in the name of the Lord!"[c]

"Hosanna[b] in the highest!"

10When Jesus entered Jerusalem, the whole city was stirred
and asked, "Who is this?"
11The crowds answered, "This is Jesus, the prophet from Nazareth in Galilee."

Jesus at the Temple

12Jesus entered the temple area and drove out all who were
buying and selling there. He overturned the tables of the money
changers and the benches of those selling doves. 13"It is written,"
he said to them, " 'My house will be called a house of prayer,'[d]
but you are making it a 'den of robbers.'[e]"
14The blind and the lame came to him at the temple, and he
healed them. 15But when the chief priests and the teachers of the
law saw the wonderful things he did and the children shouting in
the temple area, "Hosanna to the Son of David," they were indignant.

[a] 5 Zech. 9:9 [b] 9 A Hebrew expression meaning "Save!" which became an exclamation of praise; also in verse 15 [c] 9 Psalm 118:26 [d] 13 Isaiah 56:7 [e] 13 Jer. 7:11

(21:12–13) Lord Jesus, You came to Your people as a king, but not the kind of king they were expecting. They thought You would do things their way, but You came to do things Your way. They thought You would bring judgment on their enemies; but judgment had to begin with the family of God. You did not come to save them from other sinners but to save them from their own sins. You did not come to expel the Romans but to expose the hypocrites. You did not come to root out a garrison of soldiers from David's city but to drive out the garrison of thieves from Your Father's house. The submission of earthly kingdoms and authorities would come in due time. But that was not Your purpose on this day. (1Pe 4:17)

O God, whose dearly beloved Son was greeted by the crowd on Olivet with hallelujahs, but who in that same week was mocked as he went lonely to the Cross, forbid that our welcome to him should be in words alone. Help us, we beg you, to keep the road open for him into our hearts; and let him find there not another crucifixion, but love and loyalty in which his kingdom may be established evermore. Amen.

Walter Russell Bowie (1882–1969)

(21:23–27) Lord Jesus, Your authority emanates from the great Trinity: Father, Son and Holy Ghost. You are begotten, not made, the human incarnation of God Himself. You existed before anything else, and in You all things are held together. In You are hidden all the treasures of wisdom and knowledge, and in You all the fullness of the Deity lives in bodily form. I bow to Your authority, Lord, and I humble myself before You. I seek Your will above my own and honor You above all else. (Col 1:17; 2:3,9)

He is more than mere man and filled with the fullness of God. Though we were made in the image of God and can apprehend the divine, here is one that rises above us. There are depths and heights in his nature which elude the compass of human knowledge. He embodies in himself what humanity needs to know of God, but there are deeps no mental plummet has sounded yet. He incarnates a humanity that pulsates with the throbbing motion of the Eternal; but that sovereign movement no stethoscope has registered or recorded.

Calvin Weiss Laufer (1874-1938)

16"Do you hear what these children are saying?" they asked
him.
"Yes," replied Jesus, "have you never read,

" 'From the lips of children and infants
you have ordained praise'[a]?"

17And he left them and went out of the city to Bethany, where
he spent the night.

The Fig Tree Withers

18Early in the morning, as he was on his way back to the city,
he was hungry. 19Seeing a fig tree by the road, he went up to it but
found nothing on it except leaves. Then he said to it, "May you
never bear fruit again!" Immediately the tree withered.
20When the disciples saw this, they were amazed. "How did the
fig tree wither so quickly?" they asked.
21Jesus replied, "I tell you the truth, if you have faith and do
not doubt, not only can you do what was done to the fig tree, but
also you can say to this mountain, 'Go, throw yourself into the
sea,' and it will be done. 22If you believe, you will receive whatever you ask for in prayer."

The Authority of Jesus Questioned

23Jesus entered the temple courts, and, while he was teaching,
the chief priests and the elders of the people came to him. "By
what authority are you doing these things?" they asked. "And who
gave you this authority?"
24Jesus replied, "I will also ask you one question. If you answer me, I will tell you by what authority I am doing these things.
25John's baptism—where did it come from? Was it from heaven,
or from men?"
They discussed it among themselves and said, "If we say, 'From
heaven,' he will ask, 'Then why didn't you believe him?' 26But if
we say, 'From men'—we are afraid of the people, for they all hold
that John was a prophet."
27So they answered Jesus, "We don't know."
Then he said, "Neither will I tell you by what authority I am
doing these things.

The Parable of the Two Sons

28"What do you think? There was a man who had two sons. He
went to the first and said, 'Son, go and work today in the vineyard.'
29" 'I will not,' he answered, but later he changed his mind
and went.
30"Then the father went to the other son and said the same
thing. He answered, 'I will, sir,' but he did not go.
31"Which of the two did what his father wanted?"
"The first," they answered.
Jesus said to them, "I tell you the truth, the tax collectors and
the prostitutes are entering the kingdom of God ahead of you.
32For John came to you to show you the way of righteousness,
and you did not believe him, but the tax collectors and the prostitutes did. And even after you saw this, you did not repent and
believe him.

[a] *16* Psalm 8:2

The Parable of the Tenants

33"Listen to another parable: There was a landowner who
planted a vineyard. He put a wall around it, dug a winepress in it
and built a watchtower. Then he rented the vineyard to some
farmers and went away on a journey. 34When the harvest time approached, he sent his servants to the tenants to collect his fruit.
35"The tenants seized his servants; they beat one, killed another, and stoned a third. 36Then he sent other servants to them,
more than the first time, and the tenants treated them the same
way. 37Last of all, he sent his son to them. 'They will respect my
son,' he said.
38"But when the tenants saw the son, they said to each other,
'This is the heir. Come, let's kill him and take his inheritance.'
39So they took him and threw him out of the vineyard and killed
him.
40"Therefore, when the owner of the vineyard comes, what will
he do to those tenants?"
41"He will bring those wretches to a wretched end," they
replied, "and he will rent the vineyard to other tenants, who will
give him his share of the crop at harvest time."
42Jesus said to them, "Have you never read in the Scriptures:

" 'The stone the builders rejected
has become the capstone[a];
the Lord has done this,
and it is marvelous in our eyes'[b]?

43"Therefore I tell you that the kingdom of God will be taken
away from you and given to a people who will produce its fruit.
44He who falls on this stone will be broken to pieces, but he on
whom it falls will be crushed."[c]
45When the chief priests and the Pharisees heard Jesus' parables, they knew he was talking about them. 46They looked for a
way to arrest him, but they were afraid of the crowd because the
people held that he was a prophet.

The Parable of the Wedding Banquet

22 Jesus spoke to them again in parables, saying: 2"The kingdom of heaven is like a king who prepared a wedding
banquet for his son. 3He sent his servants to those who had been
invited to the banquet to tell them to come, but they refused to
come.
4"Then he sent some more servants and said, 'Tell those who
have been invited that I have prepared my dinner: My oxen and
fattened cattle have been butchered, and everything is ready.
Come to the wedding banquet.'
5"But they paid no attention and went off—one to his field, another to his business. 6The rest seized his servants, mistreated
them and killed them. 7The king was enraged. He sent his army
and destroyed those murderers and burned their city.
8"Then he said to his servants, 'The wedding banquet is ready,
but those I invited did not deserve to come. 9Go to the street corners and invite to the banquet anyone you find.' 10So the servants
went out into the streets and gathered all the people they could

[a] 42 Or *cornerstone* [b] 42 Psalm 118:22,23 [c] 44 Some manuscripts do not have verse 44.

(21:33–46) Father, I thank You for protecting me with the wall of Your grace. Thank You for guarding me with the watchtower of Your Word. Thank You for proving me in the winepress of Your discipline. Now help me to tend well the vineyard of my soul. Give me hearing ears, a receptive heart and open arms to welcome the servants You send my way, those who carry with them the words of life. May I bear a bountiful harvest for You, full of the good fruit of the Spirit.

Victory has to do with my happiness alone; fruitfulness means happiness for others and is only possible through seeming defeat. The corn of wheat must fall into the ground and die, else it abideth alone, but if it die it beareth much fruit. It is in the fruit, Jesus says, that the Father is glorified. The Saviour's ultimate for His followers is much fruit—not safety, not social security, not ease, not pleasure, not prosperity.

Frederick Julius Huegel (1889–1971)

(22:15–22) Lord, You have called us to live responsibly in this world, and therefore we will not shirk our responsibilities to our neighbors or to our nation. But our primary allegiance is to You. You are the mighty God, the King of kings and Lord of lords. While some may challenge You and resist Your kingdom, we bow before You and submit to Your authority. Rule over us, Lord, with justice and mercy, and empower us to be Your ambassadors of reconciliation upon the earth. (2Co 5:20)

There is not a spider hanging on the king's wall that does not have its errand; there is not a nettle that grows in the corner of the churchyard that does not have its purpose; there is not a single insect fluttering in the breeze that does not accomplish some divine decree; and I will never have it that God created any man, especially any Christian man, to be a blank and to be a nothing. He made you for an end. Find out what that end is. Find out your niche and fill it. If it is ever so little, if it is only to be a chopper of wood and a drawer of water, do something in this great battle for God and truth.

Charles Haddon Spurgeon (1834-1892)

find, both good and bad, and the wedding hall was filled with
guests.
11 "But when the king came in to see the guests, he noticed a
man there who was not wearing wedding clothes. 12 'Friend,' he
asked, 'how did you get in here without wedding clothes?' The
man was speechless.
13 "Then the king told the attendants, 'Tie him hand and foot,
and throw him outside, into the darkness, where there will be
weeping and gnashing of teeth.'
14 "For many are invited, but few are chosen."

Paying Taxes to Caesar

15 Then the Pharisees went out and laid plans to trap him in his
words. 16 They sent their disciples to him along with the Herodians. "Teacher," they said, "we know you are a man of integrity
and that you teach the way of God in accordance with the truth.
You aren't swayed by men, because you pay no attention to who
they are. 17 Tell us then, what is your opinion? Is it right to pay
taxes to Caesar or not?"
18 But Jesus, knowing their evil intent, said, "You hypocrites,
why are you trying to trap me? 19 Show me the coin used for paying the tax." They brought him a denarius, 20 and he asked them,
"Whose portrait is this? And whose inscription?"
21 "Caesar's," they replied.
Then he said to them, "Give to Caesar what is Caesar's, and to
God what is God's."
22 When they heard this, they were amazed. So they left him and
went away.

Marriage at the Resurrection

23 That same day the Sadducees, who say there is no resurrection, came to him with a question. 24 "Teacher," they said, "Moses
told us that if a man dies without having children, his brother
must marry the widow and have children for him. 25 Now there
were seven brothers among us. The first one married and died,
and since he had no children, he left his wife to his brother.
26 The same thing happened to the second and third brother, right
on down to the seventh. 27 Finally, the woman died. 28 Now then,
at the resurrection, whose wife will she be of the seven, since all
of them were married to her?"
29 Jesus replied, "You are in error because you do not know
the Scriptures or the power of God. 30 At the resurrection people
will neither marry nor be given in marriage; they will be like the
angels in heaven. 31 But about the resurrection of the dead—have
you not read what God said to you, 32 'I am the God of Abraham,
the God of Isaac, and the God of Jacob'[a]? He is not the God of the
dead but of the living."
33 When the crowds heard this, they were astonished at his
teaching.

The Greatest Commandment

34 Hearing that Jesus had silenced the Sadducees, the Pharisees
got together. 35 One of them, an expert in the law, tested him with
this question: 36 "Teacher, which is the greatest commandment in
the Law?"

[a] 32 Exodus 3:6

37Jesus replied: " 'Love the Lord your God with all your heart
and with all your soul and with all your mind.'[a] 38This is the first
and greatest commandment. 39And the second is like it: 'Love
your neighbor as yourself.'[b] 40All the Law and the Prophets hang
on these two commandments."

Whose Son Is the Christ?

41While the Pharisees were gathered together, Jesus asked
them, 42"What do you think about the Christ[c]? Whose son is he?"
"The son of David," they replied.
43He said to them, "How is it then that David, speaking by the
Spirit, calls him 'Lord'? For he says,

44" 'The Lord said to my Lord:
"Sit at my right hand
until I put your enemies
under your feet." '[d]

45If then David calls him 'Lord,' how can he be his son?" 46No
one could say a word in reply, and from that day on no one dared
to ask him any more questions.

Seven Woes

23 Then Jesus said to the crowds and to his disciples: 2"The
teachers of the law and the Pharisees sit in Moses' seat.
3So you must obey them and do everything they tell you. But do
not do what they do, for they do not practice what they preach.
4They tie up heavy loads and put them on men's shoulders, but
they themselves are not willing to lift a finger to move them.
5"Everything they do is done for men to see: They make their
phylacteries[e] wide and the tassels on their garments long; 6they
love the place of honor at banquets and the most important seats
in the synagogues; 7they love to be greeted in the marketplaces
and to have men call them 'Rabbi.'
8"But you are not to be called 'Rabbi,' for you have only one
Master and you are all brothers. 9And do not call anyone on earth
'father,' for you have one Father, and he is in heaven. 10Nor are
you to be called 'teacher,' for you have one Teacher, the Christ.[c]
11The greatest among you will be your servant. 12For whoever exalts himself will be humbled, and whoever humbles himself will
be exalted.
13"Woe to you, teachers of the law and Pharisees, you hypocrites! You shut the kingdom of heaven in men's faces. You yourselves do not enter, nor will you let those enter who are trying
to.[f]
15"Woe to you, teachers of the law and Pharisees, you hypocrites! You travel over land and sea to win a single convert, and
when he becomes one, you make him twice as much a son of hell
as you are.
16"Woe to you, blind guides! You say, 'If anyone swears by the
temple, it means nothing; but if anyone swears by the gold of the
temple, he is bound by his oath.' 17You blind fools! Which is
greater: the gold, or the temple that makes the gold sacred? 18You
also say, 'If anyone swears by the altar, it means nothing; but if

[a] *37* Deut. 6:5 [b] *39* Lev. 19:18 [c] *42,10* Or *Messiah* [d] *44* Psalm 110:1 [e] *5* That is, boxes containing Scripture verses, worn on forehead and arm [f] *13* Some manuscripts *to. 14Woe to you, teachers of the law and Pharisees, you hypocrites! You devour widows' houses and for a show make lengthy prayers. Therefore you will be punished more severely.*

(22:37–40) O God, I am so thankful that Your greatest desire for us is intimacy with Yourself. So teach me to love You sincerely, wholeheartedly and intimately. And then, as one of Your chosen people, holy and dearly loved, clothe me with compassion, kindness, humility, gentleness and patience. Teach me to bear with others and to forgive whatever grievances I may have against them. Help me to forgive others as You have forgiven me. And over all these virtues clothe me with love, for love is the fulfillment of the law. (Ro 13:10; Col 3:12–14)

Teach us to love, with strength of
heart and mind,
Each and all, humankind;
Break down old walls of prejudice
and hate,
Leave us not to our fate.
As You have loved and given Your
life
To end hostility and strife,
O share Your grace from heaven
above,
Teach us, Lord, how to love.

"Renew Your Church, Her Ministries Restore"

Kenneth L. Cober (©1966, 1985)

Once we have felt the power of God's love—the way he accepts us as his children, trusts us with the most precious message in the world, and heals us of the ugly effects of sin—we will never be the same. We will want to pass it on to others by responding to them in a way that will draw them closer to that love.

Floyd McClung, Jr. (1945-)

(23:23–28) Lord Jesus, I pray for the leaders of Your church today, and for those of us who follow them. Lord, keep us from mere religious activity. Correct us when we try to fool ourselves into thinking that our good deeds outweigh our "indiscretions" or somehow exempt us from Your requirement of inner holiness. Forgive us for "[taking] pride in what is seen rather than in what is in the heart." As the Psalmist wrote: "Who may ascend the hill of the Lord? Who may stand in his holy place? He who has clean hands and a pure heart, who does not lift up his soul to an idol or swear by what is false. He will receive blessing from the LORD and vindication from God his Savior." (Ps 24:3–5; 2Co 5:12)

anyone swears by the gift on it, he is bound by his oath.' 19You
blind men! Which is greater: the gift, or the altar that makes the
gift sacred? 20Therefore, he who swears by the altar swears by it
and by everything on it. 21And he who swears by the temple
swears by it and by the one who dwells in it. 22And he who swears
by heaven swears by God's throne and by the one who sits on it.

23"Woe to you, teachers of the law and Pharisees, you hypocrites! You give a tenth of your spices—mint, dill and cummin.
But you have neglected the more important matters of the law—
justice, mercy and faithfulness. You should have practiced the latter, without neglecting the former. 24You blind guides! You strain
out a gnat but swallow a camel.

25"Woe to you, teachers of the law and Pharisees, you hypocrites! You clean the outside of the cup and dish, but inside they
are full of greed and self-indulgence. 26Blind Pharisee! First clean
the inside of the cup and dish, and then the outside also will be
clean.

27"Woe to you, teachers of the law and Pharisees, you hypocrites! You are like whitewashed tombs, which look beautiful on
the outside but on the inside are full of dead men's bones and
everything unclean. 28In the same way, on the outside you appear
to people as righteous but on the inside you are full of hypocrisy
and wickedness.

29"Woe to you, teachers of the law and Pharisees, you hypocrites! You build tombs for the prophets and decorate the graves
of the righteous. 30And you say, 'If we had lived in the days of our
forefathers, we would not have taken part with them in shedding
the blood of the prophets.' 31So you testify against yourselves that
you are the descendants of those who murdered the prophets.
32Fill up, then, the measure of the sin of your forefathers!

33"You snakes! You brood of vipers! How will you escape being
condemned to hell? 34Therefore I am sending you prophets and
wise men and teachers. Some of them you will kill and crucify;
others you will flog in your synagogues and pursue from town to
town. 35And so upon you will come all the righteous blood that
has been shed on earth, from the blood of righteous Abel to the
blood of Zechariah son of Berekiah, whom you murdered between the temple and the altar. 36I tell you the truth, all this will
come upon this generation.

37"O Jerusalem, Jerusalem, you who kill the prophets and
stone those sent to you, how often I have longed to gather your
children together, as a hen gathers her chicks under her wings,
but you were not willing. 38Look, your house is left to you desolate. 39For I tell you, you will not see me again until you say,
'Blessed is he who comes in the name of the Lord.'[a]"

Signs of the End of the Age

24 Jesus left the temple and was walking away when his disciples came up to him to call his attention to its buildings.
2"Do you see all these things?" he asked. "I tell you the truth, not
one stone here will be left on another; every one will be thrown
down."

3As Jesus was sitting on the Mount of Olives, the disciples came
to him privately. "Tell us," they said, "when will this happen, and
what will be the sign of your coming and of the end of the age?"

[a] 39 Psalm 118:26

4 Jesus answered: "Watch out that no one deceives you. 5 For
many will come in my name, claiming, 'I am the Christ,[a]' and will
deceive many. 6 You will hear of wars and rumors of wars, but see
to it that you are not alarmed. Such things must happen, but the
end is still to come. 7 Nation will rise against nation, and kingdom
against kingdom. There will be famines and earthquakes in various places. 8 All these are the beginning of birth pains.
9 "Then you will be handed over to be persecuted and put to
death, and you will be hated by all nations because of me. 10 At
that time many will turn away from the faith and will betray and
hate each other, 11 and many false prophets will appear and deceive many people. 12 Because of the increase of wickedness, the
love of most will grow cold, 13 but he who stands firm to the end
will be saved. 14 And this gospel of the kingdom will be preached
in the whole world as a testimony to all nations, and then the end
will come.
15 "So when you see standing in the holy place 'the abomination that causes desolation,'[b] spoken of through the prophet Daniel—let the reader understand— 16 then let those who are in
Judea flee to the mountains. 17 Let no one on the roof of his house
go down to take anything out of the house. 18 Let no one in the
field go back to get his cloak. 19 How dreadful it will be in those
days for pregnant women and nursing mothers! 20 Pray that your
flight will not take place in winter or on the Sabbath. 21 For then
there will be great distress, unequaled from the beginning of the
world until now—and never to be equaled again. 22 If those days
had not been cut short, no one would survive, but for the sake of
the elect those days will be shortened. 23 At that time if anyone
says to you, 'Look, here is the Christ!' or, 'There he is!' do not believe it. 24 For false Christs and false prophets will appear and perform great signs and miracles to deceive even the elect—if that
were possible. 25 See, I have told you ahead of time.
26 "So if anyone tells you, 'There he is, out in the desert,' do not
go out; or, 'Here he is, in the inner rooms,' do not believe it.
27 For as lightning that comes from the east is visible even in the
west, so will be the coming of the Son of Man. 28 Wherever there
is a carcass, there the vultures will gather.
29 "Immediately after the distress of those days

" 'the sun will be darkened,
  and the moon will not give its light;
the stars will fall from the sky,
  and the heavenly bodies will be shaken.'[c]

30 "At that time the sign of the Son of Man will appear in the sky,
and all the nations of the earth will mourn. They will see the Son
of Man coming on the clouds of the sky, with power and great
glory. 31 And he will send his angels with a loud trumpet call, and
they will gather his elect from the four winds, from one end of the
heavens to the other.
32 "Now learn this lesson from the fig tree: As soon as its twigs
get tender and its leaves come out, you know that summer is near.
33 Even so, when you see all these things, you know that it[d] is
near, right at the door. 34 I tell you the truth, this generation[e] will
certainly not pass away until all these things have happened.

[a] 5 Or *Messiah*; also in verse 23 [b] 15 Daniel 9:27; 11:31; 12:11 [c] 29 Isaiah 13:10; 34:4 [d] 33 Or *he* [e] 34 Or *race*

Truly, those who follow Jesus have great reason to be glad . . . If you are today a child of God, desiring above all else to belong to the Lord, you may be sure that your name is written in heaven.

J. N. Kildahl (1857-1920)

(24:3–34) Lord Jesus, some days it seems that we are surely living in the end times. The volatile changes in weather, the violent wars and rumors of wars sound so like the end-time warnings given in Your Word. But help us, Lord, not to get so caught up in tracking the signs that we take our eyes off You. For our hope lies not in determining when You will write earth's final chapter or in plotting how to save ourselves from end-time calamities. Our hope lies in loving and trusting You minute by minute. Help us, Lord, to live each day in the same joyful wonder that we felt on the first day of our salvation, and in the hopeful expectation of heaven. (Lk 21:9–11)

One day the trumpet will sound for
His coming,
One day the skies with His glory will
shine;
Wonderful day, my beloved ones
bringing;
Glorious Savior, this Jesus is mine!

Living, He loved me;
Dying, He saved me;
Buried, He carried my sins far away;
Rising, He justified freely forever;
One day He's coming
O glorious day!

"One Day"
J. Wilbur Chapman (1910)

35Heaven and earth will pass away, but my words will never pass
away.

The Day and Hour Unknown

36"No one knows about that day or hour, not even the angels in
heaven, nor the Son,[a] but only the Father. 37As it was in the days
of Noah, so it will be at the coming of the Son of Man. 38For in the
days before the flood, people were eating and drinking, marrying
and giving in marriage, up to the day Noah entered the ark; 39and
they knew nothing about what would happen until the flood came
and took them all away. That is how it will be at the coming of the
Son of Man. 40Two men will be in the field; one will be taken and
the other left. 41Two women will be grinding with a hand mill;
one will be taken and the other left.

42"Therefore keep watch, because you do not know on what
day your Lord will come. 43But understand this: If the owner of
the house had known at what time of night the thief was coming,
he would have kept watch and would not have let his house be
broken into. 44So you also must be ready, because the Son of Man
will come at an hour when you do not expect him.

45"Who then is the faithful and wise servant, whom the master
has put in charge of the servants in his household to give them
their food at the proper time? 46It will be good for that servant
whose master finds him doing so when he returns. 47I tell you
the truth, he will put him in charge of all his possessions. 48But
suppose that servant is wicked and says to himself, 'My master is
staying away a long time,' 49and he then begins to beat his fellow
servants and to eat and drink with drunkards. 50The master of
that servant will come on a day when he does not expect him and
at an hour he is not aware of. 51He will cut him to pieces and assign him a place with the hypocrites, where there will be weeping and gnashing of teeth.

The Parable of the Ten Virgins

25 "At that time the kingdom of heaven will be like ten virgins
who took their lamps and went out to meet the bridegroom. 2Five of them were foolish and five were wise. 3The foolish ones took their lamps but did not take any oil with them. 4The
wise, however, took oil in jars along with their lamps. 5The bridegroom was a long time in coming, and they all became drowsy
and fell asleep.

6"At midnight the cry rang out: 'Here's the bridegroom! Come
out to meet him!'

7"Then all the virgins woke up and trimmed their lamps. 8The
foolish ones said to the wise, 'Give us some of your oil; our lamps
are going out.'

9" 'No,' they replied, 'there may not be enough for both us and
you. Instead, go to those who sell oil and buy some for yourselves.'

10"But while they were on their way to buy the oil, the bridegroom arrived. The virgins who were ready went in with him to
the wedding banquet. And the door was shut.

11"Later the others also came. 'Sir! Sir!' they said. 'Open the
door for us!'

12"But he replied, 'I tell you the truth, I don't know you.'

[a] 36 Some manuscripts do not have *nor the Son.*

(24:36–44) Lord, I long for the day of Your return; but much more, I desire to live in constant communion with You even now. I do not seek to know the day or the hour of Your coming; only let me know the glory and warmth of Your presence in my life today. And when You come in triumph, may I then be found in You and You in me. When I finally look into Your face, then I will know You even as You know me. (1Co 13:12)

When we see Him
We'll see our Blessed Hope.
On that long awaited day
There will be no more hate or pain.
On that white horse He'll ride;
He'll split the eastern sky.

And we'll proclaim, proclaim
Jesus Christ is Lord.

When We See Him
Tommy Walker (©1995)

13 "Therefore keep watch, because you do not know the day or
the hour.

The Parable of the Talents

14 "Again, it will be like a man going on a journey, who called
his servants and entrusted his property to them. 15 To one he gave
five talents[a] of money, to another two talents, and to another one
talent, each according to his ability. Then he went on his journey.
16 The man who had received the five talents went at once and put
his money to work and gained five more. 17 So also, the one with
the two talents gained two more. 18 But the man who had received
the one talent went off, dug a hole in the ground and hid his master's money.
19 "After a long time the master of those servants returned and
settled accounts with them. 20 The man who had received the five
talents brought the other five. 'Master,' he said, 'you entrusted me
with five talents. See, I have gained five more.'
21 "His master replied, 'Well done, good and faithful servant!
You have been faithful with a few things; I will put you in charge
of many things. Come and share your master's happiness!'
22 "The man with the two talents also came. 'Master,' he said,
'you entrusted me with two talents; see, I have gained two more.'
23 "His master replied, 'Well done, good and faithful servant!
You have been faithful with a few things; I will put you in charge
of many things. Come and share your master's happiness!'
24 "Then the man who had received the one talent came. 'Master,' he said, 'I knew that you are a hard man, harvesting where
you have not sown and gathering where you have not scattered
seed. 25 So I was afraid and went out and hid your talent in the
ground. See, here is what belongs to you.'
26 "His master replied, 'You wicked, lazy servant! So you knew
that I harvest where I have not sown and gather where I have not
scattered seed? 27 Well then, you should have put my money on
deposit with the bankers, so that when I returned I would have
received it back with interest.
28 " 'Take the talent from him and give it to the one who has the
ten talents. 29 For everyone who has will be given more, and he
will have an abundance. Whoever does not have, even what he
has will be taken from him. 30 And throw that worthless servant
outside, into the darkness, where there will be weeping and
gnashing of teeth.'

The Sheep and the Goats

31 "When the Son of Man comes in his glory, and all the angels
with him, he will sit on his throne in heavenly glory. 32 All the nations will be gathered before him, and he will separate the people one from another as a shepherd separates the sheep from the
goats. 33 He will put the sheep on his right and the goats on his
left.
34 "Then the King will say to those on his right, 'Come, you who
are blessed by my Father; take your inheritance, the kingdom
prepared for you since the creation of the world. 35 For I was hungry and you gave me something to eat, I was thirsty and you gave
me something to drink, I was a stranger and you invited me in,

[a] 15 A talent was worth more than a thousand dollars.

(25:14–30) My Lord and Master, I want to please You by using the talents and gifts You have given me for Your glory and for Your pleasure. Let me not take them lightly or bury them under rationalization or procrastination. Help me to make the most of what I have been given and to faithfully discharge my duties as Your humble servant.

The kind of religion that God requires, and will accept, does not consist in weak, dull, and lifeless "wouldings"—those weak inclinations that lack convictions—that raise us but a little above indifference. God, in his word, greatly insists that we be in good earnest, fervent in spirit, and that our hearts be engaged vigorously in our religion: "Be fervent in spirit, serving the Lord" (Ro 12:11).

Jonathan Edwards (1703-1758)

Faithful and true would He find us here,
If He should come today?
Watching in gladness and not in fear,
If He should come today?
Signs of His coming multiply,
Morning light breaks in eastern sky;
Watch, for the time is drawing nigh:
What if it were today?

"What If It Were Today?"
Leila N. Morris (1912)

(26:6–12) Precious Savior, You gave Yourself so generously, so completely for me. You suffered and bled and finally died for me. I have so little to offer in the face of Your total sacrifice. And yet there is a yearning in my heart to love You totally, purely, extravagantly. I long to break the alabaster vessel of my heart and pour out my love. Yet I hold back. I fear that my offering will be unacceptable. So let me hear You speak to me the words You spoke to the woman in Bethany when You told her that her sacrifice was a beautiful thing. And I in turn will come to You and pour out my life in worship. (1Sa 15:22; SS 2:10)

Your love and devotion are Jesus' reward for all He has done for you, and they are unspeakably sweet to Him. Don't be afraid to give yourself wholeheartedly and without reservation to your Lord. Others may not approve, but He will—and that is enough.

Catherine Jackson

36 I needed clothes and you clothed me, I was sick and you
looked after me, I was in prison and you came to visit me.'
37 "Then the righteous will answer him, 'Lord, when did we see
you hungry and feed you, or thirsty and give you something to
drink? 38 When did we see you a stranger and invite you in, or
needing clothes and clothe you? 39 When did we see you sick or in
prison and go to visit you?'
40 "The King will reply, 'I tell you the truth, whatever you did for
one of the least of these brothers of mine, you did for me.'
41 "Then he will say to those on his left, 'Depart from me, you
who are cursed, into the eternal fire prepared for the devil and
his angels. 42 For I was hungry and you gave me nothing to eat, I
was thirsty and you gave me nothing to drink, 43 I was a stranger
and you did not invite me in, I needed clothes and you did not
clothe me, I was sick and in prison and you did not look
after me.'
44 "They also will answer, 'Lord, when did we see you hungry or
thirsty or a stranger or needing clothes or sick or in prison, and
did not help you?'
45 "He will reply, 'I tell you the truth, whatever you did not do
for one of the least of these, you did not do for me.'
46 "Then they will go away to eternal punishment, but the righteous to eternal life."

The Plot Against Jesus

26 When Jesus had finished saying all these things, he said to
his disciples, 2 "As you know, the Passover is two days
away—and the Son of Man will be handed over to be crucified."
3 Then the chief priests and the elders of the people assembled
in the palace of the high priest, whose name was Caiaphas, 4 and
they plotted to arrest Jesus in some sly way and kill him. 5 "But
not during the Feast," they said, "or there may be a riot among
the people."

Jesus Anointed at Bethany

6 While Jesus was in Bethany in the home of a man known as
Simon the Leper, 7 a woman came to him with an alabaster jar of
very expensive perfume, which she poured on his head as he was
reclining at the table.
8 When the disciples saw this, they were indignant. "Why this
waste?" they asked. 9 "This perfume could have been sold at a
high price and the money given to the poor."
10 Aware of this, Jesus said to them, "Why are you bothering
this woman? She has done a beautiful thing to me. 11 The poor
you will always have with you, but you will not always have me.
12 When she poured this perfume on my body, she did it to prepare me for burial. 13 I tell you the truth, wherever this gospel is
preached throughout the world, what she has done will also be
told, in memory of her."

Judas Agrees to Betray Jesus

14 Then one of the Twelve—the one called Judas Iscariot—
went to the chief priests 15 and asked, "What are you willing to
give me if I hand him over to you?" So they counted out for him
thirty silver coins. 16 From then on Judas watched for an opportunity to hand him over.

The Lord's Supper

17 On the first day of the Feast of Unleavened Bread, the disciples came to Jesus and asked, "Where do you want us to make
preparations for you to eat the Passover?"
18 He replied, "Go into the city to a certain man and tell him,
'The Teacher says: My appointed time is near. I am going to celebrate the Passover with my disciples at your house.' " 19 So the
disciples did as Jesus had directed them and prepared the
Passover.
20 When evening came, Jesus was reclining at the table with the
Twelve. 21 And while they were eating, he said, "I tell you the truth,
one of you will betray me."
22 They were very sad and began to say to him one after the
other, "Surely not I, Lord?"
23 Jesus replied, "The one who has dipped his hand into the
bowl with me will betray me. 24 The Son of Man will go just as it
is written about him. But woe to that man who betrays the Son of
Man! It would be better for him if he had not been born."
25 Then Judas, the one who would betray him, said, "Surely not
I, Rabbi?"

Jesus answered, "Yes, it is you."[a]
26 While they were eating, Jesus took bread, gave thanks and
broke it, and gave it to his disciples, saying, "Take and eat; this is
my body."
27 Then he took the cup, gave thanks and offered it to them,
saying, "Drink from it, all of you. 28 This is my blood of the[b] covenant, which is poured out for many for the forgiveness of sins.
29 I tell you, I will not drink of this fruit of the vine from now on
until that day when I drink it anew with you in my Father's kingdom."
30 When they had sung a hymn, they went out to the Mount of
Olives.

Jesus Predicts Peter's Denial

31 Then Jesus told them, "This very night you will all fall away
on account of me, for it is written:

" 'I will strike the shepherd,
and the sheep of the flock will be scattered.'[c]

32 But after I have risen, I will go ahead of you into Galilee."
33 Peter replied, "Even if all fall away on account of you, I never
will."
34 "I tell you the truth," Jesus answered, "this very night, before
the rooster crows, you will disown me three times."
35 But Peter declared, "Even if I have to die with you, I will
never disown you." And all the other disciples said the same.

Gethsemane

36 Then Jesus went with his disciples to a place called Gethsemane, and he said to them, "Sit here while I go over there and
pray." 37 He took Peter and the two sons of Zebedee along with
him, and he began to be sorrowful and troubled. 38 Then he said
to them, "My soul is overwhelmed with sorrow to the point of
death. Stay here and keep watch with me."

[a] 25 Or *"You yourself have said it"* [b] 28 Some manuscripts *the new*
[c] 31 Zech. 13:7

(26:26–28) Lord Jesus, we praise You for giving us Your body and Your blood—for calling us to gather together as Your family to remember what You did for us, what You gave and what it cost You. Thank You for feeding us the bread of life and satisfying our thirst with the cup we pass from friend to friend. Thank You for these visible, tangible symbols that make Your love for us more vivid. But we praise You most of all that this ceremony that we share with one another is not the sad remembrance of Your defeat but the joyful celebration of Your victory over sin. Alleluia! (Jn 6:35)

There is a table set for a feast.
All will come gather,
From the greatest to least.
The Groom has been waiting;
The bride is complete;
She enters to dine at His crucified
feet.
Robed in white linen, clean and
bright;
Spotless before Him, purest light.
All is forgiven, sins left behind;
We've been invited to join Him and
dine.
We will rejoice, and give Him the
glory.
All the redeemed ones of Abraham.
We will exalt Him, the Son of the
Highest,
Feasting forever, the bride and the
Lamb.
Here at this table, we celebrate;
With bread and with wine,
We anticipate a day on that
mountain,
The table all set, when there'll be a
feast
We will never forget.
All of the chosen, bought with a
price,
Will sing to the Lamb, our great
sacrifice.

"The Feast"
Walt Harrah (©1986)

Do you think, Christian, that you can measure the love of Christ? Think of what His love has brought you—justification, adoption, sanctification, eternal life! The riches of His goodness are unsearchable! Oh, the breadth of the love of Christ! Will such a love as this have half our hearts? Will Jesus' marvelous lovingkindness and tender care meet with but faint response and tardy acknowledgment? Oh my soul, tune your heart to a glad song of thanksgiving! Go through the day rejoicing, for you are no desolate wanderer but a beloved child, watched over, cared for, supplied, and defended by your Lord.

Charles Haddon Spurgeon (1834–1892)

(26:47–56) When I think of the pain and sorrow You suffered, Lord Jesus, my heart aches with both sadness and gratitude. What a wonderful Savior You are to suffer so much for me. Even in Your darkest hours You were faithful to Your Father and true to Your nature. You spoke of love and peace in the midst of betrayal and violence. Make me an instrument of Your peace, Lord. Help me to love others unreservedly and to obey You faithfully, even in my darkest hours.

39 Going a little farther, he fell with his face to the ground and
prayed, "My Father, if it is possible, may this cup be taken from
me. Yet not as I will, but as you will."
40 Then he returned to his disciples and found them sleeping.
"Could you men not keep watch with me for one hour?" he asked
Peter. 41 "Watch and pray so that you will not fall into temptation.
The spirit is willing, but the body is weak."
42 He went away a second time and prayed, "My Father, if it is
not possible for this cup to be taken away unless I drink it, may
your will be done."
43 When he came back, he again found them sleeping, because
their eyes were heavy. 44 So he left them and went away once more
and prayed the third time, saying the same thing.
45 Then he returned to the disciples and said to them, "Are you
still sleeping and resting? Look, the hour is near, and the Son of
Man is betrayed into the hands of sinners. 46 Rise, let us go! Here
comes my betrayer!"

Jesus Arrested

47 While he was still speaking, Judas, one of the Twelve, arrived.
With him was a large crowd armed with swords and clubs, sent
from the chief priests and the elders of the people. 48 Now the betrayer had arranged a signal with them: "The one I kiss is the
man; arrest him." 49 Going at once to Jesus, Judas said, "Greetings, Rabbi!" and kissed him.
50 Jesus replied, "Friend, do what you came for."[a]
Then the men stepped forward, seized Jesus and arrested him.
51 With that, one of Jesus' companions reached for his sword,
drew it out and struck the servant of the high priest, cutting off his
ear.
52 "Put your sword back in its place," Jesus said to him, "for all
who draw the sword will die by the sword. 53 Do you think I cannot call on my Father, and he will at once put at my disposal more
than twelve legions of angels? 54 But how then would the Scriptures be fulfilled that say it must happen in this way?"
55 At that time Jesus said to the crowd, "Am I leading a rebellion, that you have come out with swords and clubs to capture
me? Every day I sat in the temple courts teaching, and you did not
arrest me. 56 But this has all taken place that the writings of the
prophets might be fulfilled." Then all the disciples deserted him
and fled.

Before the Sanhedrin

57 Those who had arrested Jesus took him to Caiaphas, the high
priest, where the teachers of the law and the elders had assembled. 58 But Peter followed him at a distance, right up to the courtyard of the high priest. He entered and sat down with the guards
to see the outcome.
59 The chief priests and the whole Sanhedrin were looking for
false evidence against Jesus so that they could put him to death.
60 But they did not find any, though many false witnesses came
forward.
Finally two came forward 61 and declared, "This fellow said, 'I
am able to destroy the temple of God and rebuild it in three
days.' "

[a] 50 Or *"Friend, why have you come?"*

62Then the high priest stood up and said to Jesus, "Are you not
going to answer? What is this testimony that these men are bringing against you?" 63But Jesus remained silent.
The high priest said to him, "I charge you under oath by the
living God: Tell us if you are the Christ,[a] the Son of God."
64"Yes, it is as you say," Jesus replied. "But I say to all of you:
In the future you will see the Son of Man sitting at the right hand
of the Mighty One and coming on the clouds of heaven."
65Then the high priest tore his clothes and said, "He has spoken blasphemy! Why do we need any more witnesses? Look, now
you have heard the blasphemy. 66What do you think?"
"He is worthy of death," they answered.
67Then they spit in his face and struck him with their fists. Others slapped him 68and said, "Prophesy to us, Christ. Who hit
you?"

Peter Disowns Jesus

69Now Peter was sitting out in the courtyard, and a servant girl
came to him. "You also were with Jesus of Galilee," she said.
70But he denied it before them all. "I don't know what you're
talking about," he said.
71Then he went out to the gateway, where another girl saw him
and said to the people there, "This fellow was with Jesus of Nazareth."
72He denied it again, with an oath: "I don't know the man!"
73After a little while, those standing there went up to Peter and
said, "Surely you are one of them, for your accent gives you
away."
74Then he began to call down curses on himself and he swore
to them, "I don't know the man!"
Immediately a rooster crowed. 75Then Peter remembered the
word Jesus had spoken: "Before the rooster crows, you will disown me three times." And he went outside and wept bitterly.

Judas Hangs Himself

27 Early in the morning, all the chief priests and the elders of
the people came to the decision to put Jesus to death.
2They bound him, led him away and handed him over to Pilate,
the governor.
3When Judas, who had betrayed him, saw that Jesus was condemned, he was seized with remorse and returned the thirty silver coins to the chief priests and the elders. 4"I have sinned," he
said, "for I have betrayed innocent blood."
"What is that to us?" they replied. "That's your responsibility."
5So Judas threw the money into the temple and left. Then he
went away and hanged himself.
6The chief priests picked up the coins and said, "It is against
the law to put this into the treasury, since it is blood money." 7So
they decided to use the money to buy the potter's field as a burial
place for foreigners. 8That is why it has been called the Field of
Blood to this day. 9Then what was spoken by Jeremiah the prophet was fulfilled: "They took the thirty silver coins, the price set on
him by the people of Israel, 10and they used them to buy the potter's field, as the Lord commanded me."[b]

[a] 63 Or *Messiah*; also in verse 68 [b] 10 See Zech. 11:12,13; Jer. 19:1–13; 32:6–9.

(26:69–75) Lord Jesus, I have betrayed You in thought, word and deed. I have denied You in guilty silence. I have chosen to please others rather than You. I have behaved in ways that are not fit for Your kingdom. Gracious Savior, forgive my weakness and restore me to wholeness. Make me less like Peter and more like You.

Jesus Before Pilate

11 Meanwhile Jesus stood before the governor, and the governor asked him, "Are you the king of the Jews?"

"Yes, it is as you say," Jesus replied.

12 When he was accused by the chief priests and the elders, he gave no answer. 13 Then Pilate asked him, "Don't you hear the testimony they are bringing against you?" 14 But Jesus made no reply, not even to a single charge—to the great amazement of the governor.

15 Now it was the governor's custom at the Feast to release a prisoner chosen by the crowd. 16 At that time they had a notorious prisoner, called Barabbas. 17 So when the crowd had gathered, Pilate asked them, "Which one do you want me to release to you: Barabbas, or Jesus who is called Christ?" 18 For he knew it was out of envy that they had handed Jesus over to him.

19 While Pilate was sitting on the judge's seat, his wife sent him this message: "Don't have anything to do with that innocent man, for I have suffered a great deal today in a dream because of him."

20 But the chief priests and the elders persuaded the crowd to ask for Barabbas and to have Jesus executed.

21 "Which of the two do you want me to release to you?" asked the governor.

"Barabbas," they answered.

22 "What shall I do, then, with Jesus who is called Christ?" Pilate asked.

They all answered, "Crucify him!"

23 "Why? What crime has he committed?" asked Pilate.

But they shouted all the louder, "Crucify him!"

24 When Pilate saw that he was getting nowhere, but that instead an uproar was starting, he took water and washed his hands in front of the crowd. "I am innocent of this man's blood," he said. "It is your responsibility!"

25 All the people answered, "Let his blood be on us and on our children!"

26 Then he released Barabbas to them. But he had Jesus flogged, and handed him over to be crucified.

The Soldiers Mock Jesus

27 Then the governor's soldiers took Jesus into the Praetorium and gathered the whole company of soldiers around him. 28 They stripped him and put a scarlet robe on him, 29 and then twisted together a crown of thorns and set it on his head. They put a staff in his right hand and knelt in front of him and mocked him. "Hail, king of the Jews!" they said. 30 They spit on him, and took the staff and struck him on the head again and again. 31 After they had mocked him, they took off the robe and put his own clothes on him. Then they led him away to crucify him.

The Crucifixion

32 As they were going out, they met a man from Cyrene, named Simon, and they forced him to carry the cross. 33 They came to a place called Golgotha (which means The Place of the Skull). 34 There they offered Jesus wine to drink, mixed with gall; but after tasting it, he refused to drink it. 35 When they had crucified

(27:25) "Let his blood be on us and on our children!" And so it was meant to be—Your blood will be upon all of us, either in guilt or in pardon, to condemn us or to save us. Lord Jesus, I confess the guilt of my sin that caused You to die. I pray that Your blood will cover me in mercy and atonement rather than be upon me in judgment. I worship You, Jesus, as my Savior and my God. (Ps 32:5)

Jesus, Thy blood and righteousness
My beauty are, my glorious dress;
'Midst flaming worlds, in these arrayed,
With joy shall I lift up my head.

"Jesus, Thy Blood and Righteousness"
Nicolaus L. von Zinzendorf (1700–1760)
Trans. John Wesley (1703–1791)

him, they divided up his clothes by casting lots.[a] 36And sitting
down, they kept watch over him there. 37Above his head they
placed the written charge against him: THIS IS JESUS, THE KING OF THE
JEWS. 38Two robbers were crucified with him, one on his right and
one on his left. 39Those who passed by hurled insults at him,
shaking their heads 40and saying, "You who are going to destroy
the temple and build it in three days, save yourself! Come down
from the cross, if you are the Son of God!"
41In the same way the chief priests, the teachers of the law and
the elders mocked him. 42"He saved others," they said, "but he
can't save himself! He's the King of Israel! Let him come down
now from the cross, and we will believe in him. 43He trusts in
God. Let God rescue him now if he wants him, for he said, 'I am
the Son of God.' " 44In the same way the robbers who were crucified with him also heaped insults on him.

The Death of Jesus

45From the sixth hour until the ninth hour darkness came over
all the land. 46About the ninth hour Jesus cried out in a loud
voice, *"Eloi, Eloi,*[b] *lama sabachthani?"*—which means, "My
God, my God, why have you forsaken me?"[c]
47When some of those standing there heard this, they said,
"He's calling Elijah."
48Immediately one of them ran and got a sponge. He filled it
with wine vinegar, put it on a stick, and offered it to Jesus to
drink. 49The rest said, "Now leave him alone. Let's see if Elijah
comes to save him."
50And when Jesus had cried out again in a loud voice, he gave
up his spirit.
51At that moment the curtain of the temple was torn in two
from top to bottom. The earth shook and the rocks split. 52The
tombs broke open and the bodies of many holy people who had
died were raised to life. 53They came out of the tombs, and after
Jesus' resurrection they went into the holy city and appeared to
many people.
54When the centurion and those with him who were guarding
Jesus saw the earthquake and all that had happened, they were
terrified, and exclaimed, "Surely he was the Son[d] of God!"
55Many women were there, watching from a distance. They had
followed Jesus from Galilee to care for his needs. 56Among them
were Mary Magdalene, Mary the mother of James and Joses, and
the mother of Zebedee's sons.

The Burial of Jesus

57As evening approached, there came a rich man from Arimathea, named Joseph, who had himself become a disciple of Jesus.
58Going to Pilate, he asked for Jesus' body, and Pilate ordered
that it be given to him. 59Joseph took the body, wrapped it in a
clean linen cloth, 60and placed it in his own new tomb that he
had cut out of the rock. He rolled a big stone in front of the entrance to the tomb and went away. 61Mary Magdalene and the
other Mary were sitting there opposite the tomb.

[a] *35* A few late manuscripts *lots that the word spoken by the prophet might be fulfilled: "They divided my garments among themselves and cast lots for my clothing"* (Psalm 22:18) [b] *46* Some manuscripts *Eli, Eli* [c] *46* Psalm 22:1
[d] *54* Or *a son*

(27:45–50) For several dark hours all of creation held its breath and the sun withheld its light. But, You, Lord, did not hold back Your love and grace. As Your blood spilled forth, my life was purchased. As You exhaled Your spirit in death, my own spirit breathed new life. Man of Sorrows, Your humiliation was my triumph. You were pierced for my transgressions, You were crushed for my iniquities; the punishment that brought my peace was upon You, and by Your wounds I am healed. (Isa 53:3–6)

Willingly He laid His glory down,
Traded wealth to wear a piercing
crown
'Til the Father's one demand He met
at Calvary.
Alone, stripped of His majesty
He cried, "Thou has forsaken Me."

Instead of me,
He took the blame, the misery.
Instead of me
He suffered silent agony.
And in that final breath
He died alone the sinner's death
Instead of me.

"Instead of Me"
Walt Harrah (©1986)

Savior, who in human flesh conquered tears by crying, pain by suffering, death by dying, we, your servants, gather before the Cross to commemorate your Passion and to contemplate anew the wonder of your compassionate love. As we listen to your gracious words, uttered with dying lips, illumine our souls that we may know the truth, melt our hearts that we may hate our sins, nerve our wills that we may do your bidding; to the glory of your name and our own eternal gain.

Charles Henry Brent (1862–1929)

(28:18–20) You are true to Your name, Immanuel, God with us. This name proclaimed at Your birth was also hailed at Your ascension. You are with us always—with us, not against us; with us, not absent from us; with us, not oblivious to us. You are indeed "our refuge and strength, an ever-present help in trouble." And if You are with us, who can stand against us? As the Father commissioned Moses to bring His people into freedom with the words, "I AM," so You, Lord Jesus, have commissioned us with the same words, "I am," to bring those who are slaves to sin into the promised freedom of new life in Christ. And so we go forth in Your authority to raise up a spiritual army, to build up Your glorious church and to lift up Your magnificent name among the nations. (Ex 3:1–14; Ps 46:1; Mt 1:23; Ro 8:31)

The Lord Jesus is in the midst of His church. He walks among the golden candlesticks (Rev 2:13). His promise, "Lo, I am with you always," is as effectual now as it was the morning He prepared breakfast for His disciples at the lake (Jn 21:9) . . .

If we know that Jesus is with us, every power will be developed and every grace will be strengthened. We will throw ourselves into the Lord's service with heart, soul, and strength.

Charles Haddon Spurgeon (1834–1892)

All authority and power,
Every status and domain,
Now belongs to one who suffered
Our redemption to obtain;
Angels, demons, kings and rulers,
Over all shall Jesus reign!

All the nations owe Him worship,
Every tongue shall call Him Lord;
How are they to call upon Him
If His name they have not heard?
Therefore go and make disciples,
Preach His gospel, spread His Word.

"All Authority and Power"
Christopher Idle (©1973)

Without Christ, not one step; with him, anywhere!

David Livingstone (1813–1873)

The Guard at the Tomb

62 The next day, the one after Preparation Day, the chief priests
and the Pharisees went to Pilate. 63 "Sir," they said, "we remember that while he was still alive that deceiver said, 'After three days
I will rise again.' 64 So give the order for the tomb to be made secure until the third day. Otherwise, his disciples may come and
steal the body and tell the people that he has been raised from the
dead. This last deception will be worse than the first."
65 "Take a guard," Pilate answered. "Go, make the tomb as secure as you know how." 66 So they went and made the tomb secure by putting a seal on the stone and posting the guard.

The Resurrection

28 After the Sabbath, at dawn on the first day of the week,
Mary Magdalene and the other Mary went to look at the
tomb.
2 There was a violent earthquake, for an angel of the Lord came
down from heaven and, going to the tomb, rolled back the stone
and sat on it. 3 His appearance was like lightning, and his clothes
were white as snow. 4 The guards were so afraid of him that they
shook and became like dead men.
5 The angel said to the women, "Do not be afraid, for I know
that you are looking for Jesus, who was crucified. 6 He is not here;
he has risen, just as he said. Come and see the place where he lay.
7 Then go quickly and tell his disciples: 'He has risen from the
dead and is going ahead of you into Galilee. There you will see
him.' Now I have told you."
8 So the women hurried away from the tomb, afraid yet filled
with joy, and ran to tell his disciples. 9 Suddenly Jesus met them.
"Greetings," he said. They came to him, clasped his feet and worshiped him. 10 Then Jesus said to them, "Do not be afraid. Go and
tell my brothers to go to Galilee; there they will see me."

The Guards' Report

11 While the women were on their way, some of the guards went
into the city and reported to the chief priests everything that had
happened. 12 When the chief priests had met with the elders and
devised a plan, they gave the soldiers a large sum of money,
13 telling them, "You are to say, 'His disciples came during the
night and stole him away while we were asleep.' 14 If this report
gets to the governor, we will satisfy him and keep you out of trouble." 15 So the soldiers took the money and did as they were instructed. And this story has been widely circulated among the
Jews to this very day.

The Great Commission

16 Then the eleven disciples went to Galilee, to the mountain
where Jesus had told them to go. 17 When they saw him, they worshiped him; but some doubted. 18 Then Jesus came to them and
said, "All authority in heaven and on earth has been given to me.
19 Therefore go and make disciples of all nations, baptizing them
in[a] the name of the Father and of the Son and of the Holy Spirit,
20 and teaching them to obey everything I have commanded you.
And surely I am with you always, to the very end of the age."

[a] *19* Or *into*; see Acts 8:16; 19:5; Romans 6:3; 1 Cor. 1:13; 10:2 and Gal. 3:27.

The Gospel according to

MARK

As the Gospel of Mark begins, Jesus proclaims challenging Good News: " 'The time has come . . . The kingdom of God is near. Repent and believe the good news!' " (1:15). God's reign on earth, proclaimed by the prophets and hoped for by the Jews, has begun in the ministry of Jesus.

The proclamation of Jesus demands a comprehensive response. We respond, in part, by "believing the good news," accepting that what Jesus says is true and committing our lives to this truth. But Jesus calls for repentance, not just belief. To repent is to change one's mind completely, to embrace a new way of life. As we accept the Good News of God's reign, we put ourselves under His sovereignty. We worship, not merely through verbal communication with God, but by offering ourselves to Him in obedience to His Word.

The verses immediately succeeding Mark's summary of Jesus' preaching provide an example of repentance. As Jesus walks beside the Sea of Galilee, He calls to two fishermen: " 'Come, follow me . . . and I will make you fishers of men' " (1:17). How do they respond? Not with praise for Jesus but with life-changing obedience: "At once they left their nets and followed him" (1:18).

As the story of Mark unfolds we discover that following Jesus costs more than we might have thought. Immediately after Peter confesses Jesus as the Messiah (8:29), Jesus predicts His own imminent death (8:31). Yet it is not He alone who must sacrifice: "If anyone would come after me, he must deny himself and take up his cross and follow me. For whoever wants to save his life will lose it, but whoever loses his life for me and for the gospel will save it" (8:34–35).

Although the first followers of Jesus expect to join Him in God's political victory, they must confront an unforeseen call to sacrificial servanthood: " 'Whoever wants to become great among you must be your servant, and whoever wants to be first must be slave of all. For even the Son of Man did not come to be served, but to serve, and to give his life as a ransom for many' " (10:43–45). The ultimate victory of Jesus, the Son of Man, comes not through vanquishing the Romans but through dying upon the Roman cross. We who follow Jesus Christ must worship God, not merely by offering our gifts of praise, but by surrendering ourselves as living sacrifices to the will of God (Ro 12:1–2).

We who follow Jesus Christ must worship God, not merely by offering our gifts of praise, but by surrendering ourselves as living sacrifices to the will of God.

Thus, in this Gospel exemplary worship takes unexpected forms. A poor widow who puts a pittance into the temple treasury has contributed, in Jesus' view, more than rich donors who have given fortunes, because she "put in everything—all she had to live on" (12:44). When a woman anoints Jesus with exorbitantly expensive perfume and the bystanders criticize her failure to devote the perfume to a better use, Jesus defends the woman for doing "a beautiful thing" (14:6). How costly it will be to worship God in the person of Jesus! We too must give everything, sparing no cost, as we give ourselves to glorify and adore God.

Jesus, draw me close,
Closer, Lord, to You.
Let the world around me fade away.
Jesus, draw me close,
Closer, Lord, to You.
For I desire to worship and obey.
"Jesus, Draw Me Close"
Rick Founds (©1990)

(1:1) O holy God, Your Word proclaims two "beginnings," marking the most momentous epochs in history. The first heralded the creation of the human race—a people beautiful, pure, powerful, as You had intended them to be. Yet, O God, how soon we became disfigured, defiled and diminished, sinful and lost. But then began the second great epoch, "the beginning of the gospel about Jesus Christ, the Son of God." Redemption, restoration, the fresh start, the new birth! Grace! I thank You, Lord, from my worshiping heart. (Ge 1:1,26–27)

(1:10–13) How often after the blessing comes the trial. First the empowerment, then the test: The flesh is scourged, circumstances threaten and Satan tempts. Yet You, Father, see from heaven and send angels to attend. They are there in our midst; You do care; Your love will deliver. Help me to remember this, Lord, and to praise in the dark places, to rejoice always, and to cast myself upon You with abandon.

John the Baptist Prepares the Way

1 The beginning of the gospel about Jesus Christ, the Son of God.[a]

2It is written in Isaiah the prophet:

> "I will send my messenger ahead of you,
> who will prepare your way"[b]—
> **3**"a voice of one calling in the desert,
> 'Prepare the way for the Lord,
> make straight paths for him.' "[c]

4And so John came, baptizing in the desert region and preaching
a baptism of repentance for the forgiveness of sins. **5**The whole
Judean countryside and all the people of Jerusalem went out to
him. Confessing their sins, they were baptized by him in the Jordan River. **6**John wore clothing made of camel's hair, with a
leather belt around his waist, and he ate locusts and wild honey.
7And this was his message: "After me will come one more powerful than I, the thongs of whose sandals I am not worthy to stoop
down and untie. **8**I baptize you with[d] water, but he will baptize
you with the Holy Spirit."

The Baptism and Temptation of Jesus

9At that time Jesus came from Nazareth in Galilee and was baptized by John in the Jordan. **10**As Jesus was coming up out of the
water, he saw heaven being torn open and the Spirit descending
on him like a dove. **11**And a voice came from heaven: "You are my
Son, whom I love; with you I am well pleased."
12At once the Spirit sent him out into the desert, **13**and he was
in the desert forty days, being tempted by Satan. He was with the
wild animals, and angels attended him.

The Calling of the First Disciples

14After John was put in prison, Jesus went into Galilee, proclaiming the good news of God. **15**"The time has come," he said.
"The kingdom of God is near. Repent and believe the good news!"
16As Jesus walked beside the Sea of Galilee, he saw Simon and
his brother Andrew casting a net into the lake, for they were fishermen. **17**"Come, follow me," Jesus said, "and I will make you
fishers of men." **18**At once they left their nets and followed him.
19When he had gone a little farther, he saw James son of Zebedee and his brother John in a boat, preparing their nets. **20**Without delay he called them, and they left their father Zebedee in the
boat with the hired men and followed him.

Jesus Drives Out an Evil Spirit

21They went to Capernaum, and when the Sabbath came, Jesus
went into the synagogue and began to teach. **22**The people were
amazed at his teaching, because he taught them as one who had
authority, not as the teachers of the law. **23**Just then a man in their
synagogue who was possessed by an evil[e] spirit cried out,
24"What do you want with us, Jesus of Nazareth? Have you come
to destroy us? I know who you are—the Holy One of God!"

[a] *1* Some manuscripts do not have *the Son of God.* [b] *2* Mal. 3:1 [c] *3* Isaiah 40:3
[d] *8* Or *in* [e] *23* Greek *unclean*; also in verses 26 and 27

25"Be quiet!" said Jesus sternly. "Come out of him!" 26The evil
spirit shook the man violently and came out of him with a shriek.
27The people were all so amazed that they asked each other,
"What is this? A new teaching—and with authority! He even gives
orders to evil spirits and they obey him." 28News about him
spread quickly over the whole region of Galilee.

Jesus Heals Many

29As soon as they left the synagogue, they went with James and
John to the home of Simon and Andrew. 30Simon's mother-in-law
was in bed with a fever, and they told Jesus about her. 31So he
went to her, took her hand and helped her up. The fever left her
and she began to wait on them.

32That evening after sunset the people brought to Jesus all the
sick and demon-possessed. 33The whole town gathered at the
door, 34and Jesus healed many who had various diseases. He also
drove out many demons, but he would not let the demons speak
because they knew who he was.

Jesus Prays in a Solitary Place

35Very early in the morning, while it was still dark, Jesus got
up, left the house and went off to a solitary place, where he
prayed. 36Simon and his companions went to look for him, 37and
when they found him, they exclaimed: "Everyone is looking for
you!"
38Jesus replied, "Let us go somewhere else—to the nearby villages—so I can preach there also. That is why I have come." 39So
he traveled throughout Galilee, preaching in their synagogues and
driving out demons.

A Man With Leprosy

40A man with leprosy[a] came to him and begged him on his
knees, "If you are willing, you can make me clean."
41Filled with compassion, Jesus reached out his hand and
touched the man. "I am willing," he said. "Be clean!" 42Immedi-
ately the leprosy left him and he was cured.
43Jesus sent him away at once with a strong warning: 44"See
that you don't tell this to anyone. But go, show yourself to the
priest and offer the sacrifices that Moses commanded for your
cleansing, as a testimony to them." 45Instead he went out and
began to talk freely, spreading the news. As a result, Jesus could
no longer enter a town openly but stayed outside in lonely places.
Yet the people still came to him from everywhere.

Jesus Heals a Paralytic

2 A few days later, when Jesus again entered Capernaum, the
people heard that he had come home. 2So many gathered
that there was no room left, not even outside the door, and he
preached the word to them. 3Some men came, bringing to him a
paralytic, carried by four of them. 4Since they could not get him
to Jesus because of the crowd, they made an opening in the roof
above Jesus and, after digging through it, lowered the mat the
paralyzed man was lying on. 5When Jesus saw their faith, he said
to the paralytic, "Son, your sins are forgiven."
6Now some teachers of the law were sitting there, thinking to

[a] *40* The Greek word was used for various diseases affecting the skin—not necessarily leprosy.

(1:35) Early in the morning You prayed, Lord. Sometimes You prayed all night long. You, the Son of God Who worked miracles and banished devils, prayed and prayed and prayed. You knew the power source and returned repeatedly to it for strength. You knew the voice and came for instruction. Your ways are our path to the Father. O Lord, put the hunger in my heart to follow those footsteps that daily lead me to the holy resources of Home.

What was our Lord thinking about as he walked along the roads of Galilee, so often alone? What were his thoughts in times of repose, during the journeys by boat that he liked making with his disciples after a day's exhausting preaching? What occupied his mind among the hills where he liked to go alone, without even the disciples? The answer, we may think, is easy: he was thinking of men, of sinners and their salvation, and what he had to do to effect that salvation. But, surprising as it may seem to us, it wasn't with us that Jesus was concerned. The constant object of his meditation, the natural orientation of his heart and mind and soul, the food that constantly nourished him, was his Father.

Louis Evely (1910-)

(2:1–5) O God, make me an intercessor who opens the way for the needy to come to You. Give me faith that stands in the gap for those too weak to reach out for themselves. I want to care enough to pray them through the obstacles that separate them from You. I want to love enough to climb or dig or do whatever it takes to bring them into Your manifest presence. Father, fill me with this passion and holy desperation, for I am surrounded by the lost.

(2:5–12) Jesus, You look for our faith, longing to say to us as You said to the paralyzed man, "Son, daughter, your sins are forgiven." The scandalized religious leaders saw only a blasphemer and charlatan and walked away in their sins. The paralytic saw a healer and redeemer and walked away forgiven. I, too, declare that You are my Redeemer, Lord Jesus! Let my faith make me whole and keep me holy. (Eph 2:8)

(2:15–17) Lord Jesus, thank You that when we were yet sinners You came to us and died for us. Help us to be like You—to scandalize the Pharisees and teachers of the law by associating with "the wrong people" who need to come to You . . . through us.

Jesus comes not for the super-spiritual but for the wobbly and the weak-kneed who know they don't have it all together, and who are not too proud to accept the handout of amazing grace.

Brennan Manning (1934-)

themselves, 7"Why does this fellow talk like that? He's blaspheming! Who can forgive sins but God alone?"
8Immediately Jesus knew in his spirit that this was what they
were thinking in their hearts, and he said to them, "Why are you
thinking these things? 9Which is easier: to say to the paralytic,
'Your sins are forgiven,' or to say, 'Get up, take your mat and
walk'? 10But that you may know that the Son of Man has authority on earth to forgive sins . . ." He said to the paralytic, 11"I tell
you, get up, take your mat and go home." 12He got up, took his
mat and walked out in full view of them all. This amazed everyone
and they praised God, saying, "We have never seen anything like
this!"

The Calling of Levi

13Once again Jesus went out beside the lake. A large crowd
came to him, and he began to teach them. 14As he walked along,
he saw Levi son of Alphaeus sitting at the tax collector's booth.
"Follow me," Jesus told him, and Levi got up and followed him.
15While Jesus was having dinner at Levi's house, many tax collectors and "sinners" were eating with him and his disciples, for
there were many who followed him. 16When the teachers of the
law who were Pharisees saw him eating with the "sinners" and tax
collectors, they asked his disciples: "Why does he eat with tax
collectors and 'sinners'?"
17On hearing this, Jesus said to them, "It is not the healthy who
need a doctor, but the sick. I have not come to call the righteous,
but sinners."

Jesus Questioned About Fasting

18Now John's disciples and the Pharisees were fasting. Some
people came and asked Jesus, "How is it that John's disciples
and the disciples of the Pharisees are fasting, but yours are
not?"
19Jesus answered, "How can the guests of the bridegroom fast
while he is with them? They cannot, so long as they have him with
them. 20But the time will come when the bridegroom will be
taken from them, and on that day they will fast.
21"No one sews a patch of unshrunk cloth on an old garment.
If he does, the new piece will pull away from the old, making the
tear worse. 22And no one pours new wine into old wineskins. If
he does, the wine will burst the skins, and both the wine and the
wineskins will be ruined. No, he pours new wine into new wineskins."

Lord of the Sabbath

23One Sabbath Jesus was going through the grainfields, and as
his disciples walked along, they began to pick some heads of
grain. 24The Pharisees said to him, "Look, why are they doing
what is unlawful on the Sabbath?"
25He answered, "Have you never read what David did when he
and his companions were hungry and in need? 26In the days of
Abiathar the high priest, he entered the house of God and ate the
consecrated bread, which is lawful only for priests to eat. And he
also gave some to his companions."
27Then he said to them, "The Sabbath was made for man, not
man for the Sabbath. 28So the Son of Man is Lord even of the Sabbath."

3 Another time he went into the synagogue, and a man with a shriveled hand was there. 2Some of them were looking for a reason to accuse Jesus, so they watched him closely to see if he would heal him on the Sabbath. 3Jesus said to the man with the shriveled hand, "Stand up in front of everyone."

4Then Jesus asked them, "Which is lawful on the Sabbath: to do good or to do evil, to save life or to kill?" But they remained silent.

5He looked around at them in anger and, deeply distressed at their stubborn hearts, said to the man, "Stretch out your hand." He stretched it out, and his hand was completely restored. 6Then the Pharisees went out and began to plot with the Herodians how they might kill Jesus.

Crowds Follow Jesus

7Jesus withdrew with his disciples to the lake, and a large crowd from Galilee followed. 8When they heard all he was doing, many people came to him from Judea, Jerusalem, Idumea, and the regions across the Jordan and around Tyre and Sidon. 9Because of the crowd he told his disciples to have a small boat ready for him, to keep the people from crowding him. 10For he had healed many, so that those with diseases were pushing forward to touch him. 11Whenever the evil[a] spirits saw him, they fell down before him and cried out, "You are the Son of God." 12But he gave them strict orders not to tell who he was.

The Appointing of the Twelve Apostles

13Jesus went up on a mountainside and called to him those he wanted, and they came to him. 14He appointed twelve—designating them apostles[b]—that they might be with him and that he might send them out to preach 15and to have authority to drive out demons. 16These are the twelve he appointed: Simon (to whom he gave the name Peter); 17James son of Zebedee and his brother John (to them he gave the name Boanerges, which means Sons of Thunder); 18Andrew, Philip, Bartholomew, Matthew, Thomas, James son of Alphaeus, Thaddaeus, Simon the Zealot 19and Judas Iscariot, who betrayed him.

Jesus and Beelzebub

20Then Jesus entered a house, and again a crowd gathered, so that he and his disciples were not even able to eat. 21When his family heard about this, they went to take charge of him, for they said, "He is out of his mind."

22And the teachers of the law who came down from Jerusalem said, "He is possessed by Beelzebub[c]! By the prince of demons he is driving out demons."

23So Jesus called them and spoke to them in parables: "How can Satan drive out Satan? 24If a kingdom is divided against itself, that kingdom cannot stand. 25If a house is divided against itself, that house cannot stand. 26And if Satan opposes himself and is divided, he cannot stand; his end has come. 27In fact, no one can enter a strong man's house and carry off his possessions unless he first ties up the strong man. Then he can rob his house. 28I tell you the truth, all the sins and blasphemies of men will be forgiv-

[a] *11* Greek *unclean*; also in verse 30 [b] *14* Some manuscripts do not have *designating them apostles.* [c] *22* Greek *Beezeboul* or *Beelzeboul*

The way to be humble is not to stoop until you are smaller than yourself but to stand at your real height against some higher nature that will show you how small your greatness is.

Phillips Brooks (1835-1893)

(3:1–6) Lord, help me to be ever aware of how little I know. Keep me from being, like the Pharisees, busy with rules and rituals while You are busy being the sovereign God, doing things Your way, crying "I AM" when I take exception to Your timing or Your methods. Your Word is a lamp to my feet, but You Yourself are the Way—living and dynamic, straight and true. I never want to resist You through arrogance or unbelief. I come now with utmost humility and pray, Lord, let Your will be done in whatever way You choose. (Ex 3:14; Ps 119:105; Jn 14:6)

(3:21) Lord, You know by experience how hard it is when those we love best understand us least. Yet when even our fathers and mothers reject us, You take us up and declare that we are Yours and You are ours. You will never leave us nor forsake us. We praise You for a new birth and an everlasting heritage. (Ps 27:10; Mt 28:20; Heb 13:5)

(4:13–20) Here is my heart, Father. Protect the living Word that resides within it. You are my defense from the enemy, my shelter from the heat of the battle. Plant my roots so deep in You that we become inextricably entwined, so that no trouble, no heartache, no temptation, no persecution can uproot what You have sown within me. (Ro 8:35)

Being a Christian is more than just an instantaneous conversion—it is a daily process whereby you grow to be more and more like Christ.

Billy Graham (1918-)

en them. 29But whoever blasphemes against the Holy Spirit will
never be forgiven; he is guilty of an eternal sin."
30He said this because they were saying, "He has an evil spirit."

Jesus' Mother and Brothers

31Then Jesus' mother and brothers arrived. Standing outside,
they sent someone in to call him. 32A crowd was sitting around
him, and they told him, "Your mother and brothers are outside
looking for you."
33"Who are my mother and my brothers?" he asked.
34Then he looked at those seated in a circle around him and
said, "Here are my mother and my brothers! 35Whoever does
God's will is my brother and sister and mother."

The Parable of the Sower

4 Again Jesus began to teach by the lake. The crowd that gathered around him was so large that he got into a boat and sat
in it out on the lake, while all the people were along the shore at
the water's edge. 2He taught them many things by parables, and in
his teaching said: 3"Listen! A farmer went out to sow his seed.
4As he was scattering the seed, some fell along the path, and the
birds came and ate it up. 5Some fell on rocky places, where it did
not have much soil. It sprang up quickly, because the soil was
shallow. 6But when the sun came up, the plants were scorched,
and they withered because they had no root. 7Other seed fell
among thorns, which grew up and choked the plants, so that they
did not bear grain. 8Still other seed fell on good soil. It came up,
grew and produced a crop, multiplying thirty, sixty, or even a hundred times."
9Then Jesus said, "He who has ears to hear, let him hear."
10When he was alone, the Twelve and the others around him
asked him about the parables. 11He told them, "The secret of the
kingdom of God has been given to you. But to those on the outside everything is said in parables 12so that,

" 'they may be ever seeing but never perceiving,
and ever hearing but never understanding;
otherwise they might turn and be forgiven!'[a]"

13Then Jesus said to them, "Don't you understand this parable?
How then will you understand any parable? 14The farmer sows
the word. 15Some people are like seed along the path, where the
word is sown. As soon as they hear it, Satan comes and takes away
the word that was sown in them. 16Others, like seed sown on
rocky places, hear the word and at once receive it with joy. 17But
since they have no root, they last only a short time. When trouble
or persecution comes because of the word, they quickly fall away.
18Still others, like seed sown among thorns, hear the word; 19but
the worries of this life, the deceitfulness of wealth and the desires
for other things come in and choke the word, making it unfruitful. 20Others, like seed sown on good soil, hear the word, accept
it, and produce a crop—thirty, sixty or even a hundred times
what was sown."

A Lamp on a Stand

21He said to them, "Do you bring in a lamp to put it under a
bowl or a bed? Instead, don't you put it on its stand? 22For what-

[a] *12* Isaiah 6:9,10

ever is hidden is meant to be disclosed, and whatever is concealed is meant to be brought out into the open. 23If anyone has
ears to hear, let him hear."
24"Consider carefully what you hear," he continued. "With the
measure you use, it will be measured to you—and even more.
25Whoever has will be given more; whoever does not have, even
what he has will be taken from him."

The Parable of the Growing Seed

26He also said, "This is what the kingdom of God is like. A man
scatters seed on the ground. 27Night and day, whether he sleeps
or gets up, the seed sprouts and grows, though he does not know
how. 28All by itself the soil produces grain—first the stalk, then
the head, then the full kernel in the head. 29As soon as the grain
is ripe, he puts the sickle to it, because the harvest has come."

The Parable of the Mustard Seed

30Again he said, "What shall we say the kingdom of God is like,
or what parable shall we use to describe it? 31It is like a mustard
seed, which is the smallest seed you plant in the ground. 32Yet
when planted, it grows and becomes the largest of all garden
plants, with such big branches that the birds of the air can perch
in its shade."
33With many similar parables Jesus spoke the word to them, as
much as they could understand. 34He did not say anything to
them without using a parable. But when he was alone with his
own disciples, he explained everything.

Jesus Calms the Storm

35That day when evening came, he said to his disciples, "Let us
go over to the other side." 36Leaving the crowd behind, they took
him along, just as he was, in the boat. There were also other
boats with him. 37A furious squall came up, and the waves broke
over the boat, so that it was nearly swamped. 38Jesus was in the
stern, sleeping on a cushion. The disciples woke him and said to
him, "Teacher, don't you care if we drown?"
39He got up, rebuked the wind and said to the waves, "Quiet!
Be still!" Then the wind died down and it was completely calm.
40He said to his disciples, "Why are you so afraid? Do you still
have no faith?"
41They were terrified and asked each other, "Who is this? Even
the wind and the waves obey him!"

The Healing of a Demon-possessed Man

5 They went across the lake to the region of the Gerasenes.[a]
2When Jesus got out of the boat, a man with an evil[b] spirit
came from the tombs to meet him. 3This man lived in the tombs,
and no one could bind him any more, not even with a chain. 4For
he had often been chained hand and foot, but he tore the chains
apart and broke the irons on his feet. No one was strong enough
to subdue him. 5Night and day among the tombs and in the hills
he would cry out and cut himself with stones.
6When he saw Jesus from a distance, he ran and fell on his
knees in front of him. 7He shouted at the top of his voice, "What
do you want with me, Jesus, Son of the Most High God? Swear to

[a] *1* Some manuscripts *Gadarenes*; other manuscripts *Gergesenes* [b] *2* Greek *unclean*; also in verses 8 and 13

If the vessel of our soul is still battered by winds or by storm, let us call on our Lord who rests therein. He will soon calm the sea.

Brother Lawrence of the Resurrection (c.1605–1691)

(4:35–41) "Quiet! Be still!" You commanded the rioting winds and waves. It seems they recognized Your voice. The same Voice had spoken them into being out of the primeval chaos at the dawning of the world. This time You spoke into the chaos of the fallen creation. And, like unruly children responding to the rebuke of their father, they obeyed and subsided into peace. Even so, Jesus, You are Lord over my fallen creation. In the midst of my chaotic world, I pray You will speak peace today. (Ge 1; Jn 1:1–3; 14:27)

Be still, my soul! Thy God doth
undertake
To guide the future as He has the
past.
Thy hope, thy confidence let nothing
shake;
All now mysterious shall be bright at
last.
Be still, my soul! The waves and
winds still know
His voice who ruled them while He
dwelt below.

"Be Still My Soul"
Katharina von Schlegel (1752)
Trans. Jane L. Borthwick (1813–1897)

God that you won't torture me!" 8For Jesus had said to him,
"Come out of this man, you evil spirit!"
9Then Jesus asked him, "What is your name?"
"My name is Legion," he replied, "for we are many." 10And he
begged Jesus again and again not to send them out of the area.
11A large herd of pigs was feeding on the nearby hillside. 12The
demons begged Jesus, "Send us among the pigs; allow us to go
into them." 13He gave them permission, and the evil spirits came
out and went into the pigs. The herd, about two thousand in
number, rushed down the steep bank into the lake and were
drowned.
14Those tending the pigs ran off and reported this in the town
and countryside, and the people went out to see what had happened. 15When they came to Jesus, they saw the man who had
been possessed by the legion of demons, sitting there, dressed
and in his right mind; and they were afraid. 16Those who had
seen it told the people what had happened to the demon-possessed man—and told about the pigs as well. 17Then the people
began to plead with Jesus to leave their region.
18As Jesus was getting into the boat, the man who had been
demon-possessed begged to go with him. 19Jesus did not let him,
but said, "Go home to your family and tell them how much the
Lord has done for you, and how he has had mercy on you." 20So
the man went away and began to tell in the Decapolis[a] how much
Jesus had done for him. And all the people were amazed.

A Dead Girl and a Sick Woman

21When Jesus had again crossed over by boat to the other side
of the lake, a large crowd gathered around him while he was by
the lake. 22Then one of the synagogue rulers, named Jairus, came
there. Seeing Jesus, he fell at his feet 23and pleaded earnestly with
him, "My little daughter is dying. Please come and put your hands
on her so that she will be healed and live." 24So Jesus went with
him.
A large crowd followed and pressed around him. 25And a
woman was there who had been subject to bleeding for twelve
years. 26She had suffered a great deal under the care of many
doctors and had spent all she had, yet instead of getting better
she grew worse. 27When she heard about Jesus, she came up behind him in the crowd and touched his cloak, 28because she
thought, "If I just touch his clothes, I will be healed." 29Immedi-
ately her bleeding stopped and she felt in her body that she was
freed from her suffering.
30At once Jesus realized that power had gone out from him.
He turned around in the crowd and asked, "Who touched my
clothes?"
31"You see the people crowding against you," his disciples answered, "and yet you can ask, 'Who touched me?' "
32But Jesus kept looking around to see who had done it.
33Then the woman, knowing what had happened to her, came
and fell at his feet and, trembling with fear, told him the whole
truth. 34He said to her, "Daughter, your faith has healed you. Go
in peace and be freed from your suffering."
35While Jesus was still speaking, some men came from the

(5:15–20) Thank You, Lord, that there are no hopeless cases with You. The rejects of society—the mad, the diseased, the demon possessed—were recipients of Your power and deliverance while You walked this earth. It was deliverance so complete, so life-transforming that they rushed away on fire with thanksgiving and love to tell the world the Good News. O Lord, give all Your liberated children that heart. Please, Lord, give it to me.

I'm amazed at all You've done for me;
Who am I, that You'd bless me so.
I stand in awe of all Your wondrous
deeds;
You've dealt with me so graciously.

"I'm Amazed"
Rory Noland (©1991)

(5:25–34) Often I feel too unclean to come to You, Lord, as though I am soiled beyond cleansing. Under the law this woman was unclean. Moreover, anyone who touched her would have become unclean also. She dared not ask You to take the chance but, in a desperate leap of faith, she initiated a covert test of Your power. Unnoticed, she reached out and touched Your robe. Like lightning from heaven, Your virtue leaped to meet her faith and sent her forth whole and in peace. Lord Jesus, loose my faith so that I too may reach out to touch You. (Lev 15:25–27)

a20 That is, the Ten Cities

MY BELOVED

I have something important for you to understand. Our relationship is based on My faithfulness. Your faith may wax and wane, but My faithfulness endures forever. I will never let you go. So put your trust in Me. In every situation, remember these words: Don't be afraid; just believe.

I know the plans I have for you; plans to prosper you, not to harm you; plans to give you hope and a future. But this will only happen if you put your hope in Me and live according to My Word.

Don't be afraid; just believe. That is your responsibility in our relationship: Believe that My love for you is unfailing; believe and trust in My goodness. And when you get discouraged, quickly turn to Me; call out to Me for help and I will deliver you from trouble. My faithfulness will be your shield and your fortress. I will fill you with joy and peace as you trust in Me, so that you may overflow with hope by the power of My Spirit.

Don't be afraid; just believe. Be strong and courageous, for I am with you. I will not fail you nor forsake you. I will never betray My faithfulness. I am the Lord; when you hope in Me you will not be disappointed.

Don't be afraid; just believe.

1Ch 28:20; Ps 33:21-22; 42:5; 89:33; 91:4; 130:5,7; Isa 49:23; Jer 29:11; Mk 5:36; Ro 3:3-4; 15:13

house of Jairus, the synagogue ruler. "Your daughter is dead,"
they said. "Why bother the teacher any more?"
36Ignoring what they said, Jesus told the synagogue ruler,
"Don't be afraid; just believe."
37He did not let anyone follow him except Peter, James and
John the brother of James. 38When they came to the home of the
synagogue ruler, Jesus saw a commotion, with people crying and
wailing loudly. 39He went in and said to them, "Why all this commotion and wailing? The child is not dead but asleep." 40But they
laughed at him.
After he put them all out, he took the child's father and mother and the disciples who were with him, and went in where the
child was. 41He took her by the hand and said to her, *"Talitha
koum!"* (which means, "Little girl, I say to you, get up!"). 42Im-
mediately the girl stood up and walked around (she was twelve
years old). At this they were completely astonished. 43He gave
strict orders not to let anyone know about this, and told them to
give her something to eat.

A Prophet Without Honor

6 Jesus left there and went to his hometown, accompanied by
his disciples. 2When the Sabbath came, he began to teach in
the synagogue, and many who heard him were amazed.
"Where did this man get these things?" they asked. "What's this
wisdom that has been given him, that he even does miracles!
3Isn't this the carpenter? Isn't this Mary's son and the brother of
James, Joseph,[a] Judas and Simon? Aren't his sisters here with
us?" And they took offense at him.
4Jesus said to them, "Only in his hometown, among his relatives and in his own house is a prophet without honor." 5He could
not do any miracles there, except lay his hands on a few sick people and heal them. 6And he was amazed at their lack of faith.

Jesus Sends Out the Twelve

Then Jesus went around teaching from village to village. 7Call-
ing the Twelve to him, he sent them out two by two and gave them
authority over evil[b] spirits.
8These were his instructions: "Take nothing for the journey except a staff—no bread, no bag, no money in your belts. 9Wear
sandals but not an extra tunic. 10Whenever you enter a house,
stay there until you leave that town. 11And if any place will not
welcome you or listen to you, shake the dust off your feet when
you leave, as a testimony against them."
12They went out and preached that people should repent.
13They drove out many demons and anointed many sick people
with oil and healed them.

John the Baptist Beheaded

14King Herod heard about this, for Jesus' name had become
well known. Some were saying,[c] "John the Baptist has been
raised from the dead, and that is why miraculous powers are at
work in him."
15Others said, "He is Elijah."
And still others claimed, "He is a prophet, like one of the
prophets of long ago."

[a] *3* Greek *Joses,* a variant of *Joseph* [b] *7* Greek *unclean* [c] *14* Some early manuscripts *He was saying*

(6:1–4) Too often we, like Jesus' neighbors, judge by our world-tainted wisdom rather than by Your Spirit. We think, "How could one less educated than I, one less experienced, one so young, so old, so poor, my neighbor, my own brother—or the carpenter's son—show me anything about God's ways? How could he be a bearer of the anointing?" The answer is that You have chosen the humble to know You best and to confound the proud. Help me God, to live in humility, so that I will never miss Your messenger or Your message. (Ro 1:21–22; Jas 4:6; 1Pe 5:5)

(6:4–5) In the place where You were without honor, Lord Jesus, You could not work many miracles. It was not that You were unwilling; Your Word says that You were unable. Because You could do only the things You saw the Father doing, is it possible that the Father withheld His permission because the people treated You with doubt and disrespect? Lord, deliver me from a doubting spirit. I want to honor You with my whole heart so that You can minister Your life freely to me. (Jn 5:19,30)

Regardless of how we define Christ's separation from the world, one fact is clear: he did not separate himself from human beings and their needs. Nor did he limit his concern to the spiritual part of man's personality.

Erwin W. Lutzer (1941-)

(6:30–44) Father, give us Jesus' wisdom, Jesus' heart, Jesus' determination to minister to all the needs of hungry humanity. Jesus could simply have preached and then sent the masses away to the nearby villages to have their physical needs met by the world. But He had compassion on the hungry and instructed His disciples to feed them. Again today, Lord, minister to our famished world through Your church with bread for both body and soul. May we never send the hungry away to be fed by the world. Rather, may compassion and generosity accompany our confession of the gospel of Christ and result in thanksgiving to You. (2Co 9:10–15)

You worked your miracles
On hills beneath the desert sun.
Kind of like the place that I come from;
And if I close my eyes
I can see you work one more.

There were five thousand fed
From a single meal there in your hand.
Now you fill my hunger just like then,
But the feast is so much better than
before.

In your hands
A little broken bread can satisfy
This heart of mine;
By your might
My empty cup now overflows with
holy wine.

"A Little Broken Bread"
Bill Batstone (©1987)

16But when Herod heard this, he said, "John, the man I beheaded, has been raised from the dead!"
17For Herod himself had given orders to have John arrested,
and he had him bound and put in prison. He did this because of
Herodias, his brother Philip's wife, whom he had married. 18For
John had been saying to Herod, "It is not lawful for you to have
your brother's wife." 19So Herodias nursed a grudge against John
and wanted to kill him. But she was not able to, 20because Herod
feared John and protected him, knowing him to be a righteous
and holy man. When Herod heard John, he was greatly puzzled[a];
yet he liked to listen to him.
21Finally the opportune time came. On his birthday Herod gave
a banquet for his high officials and military commanders and the
leading men of Galilee. 22When the daughter of Herodias came in
and danced, she pleased Herod and his dinner guests.
The king said to the girl, "Ask me for anything you want, and
I'll give it to you." 23And he promised her with an oath, "Whatever you ask I will give you, up to half my kingdom."
24She went out and said to her mother, "What shall I ask for?"
"The head of John the Baptist," she answered.
25At once the girl hurried in to the king with the request: "I
want you to give me right now the head of John the Baptist on a
platter."
26The king was greatly distressed, but because of his oaths and
his dinner guests, he did not want to refuse her. 27So he immediately sent an executioner with orders to bring John's head. The
man went, beheaded John in the prison, 28and brought back his
head on a platter. He presented it to the girl, and she gave it to her
mother. 29On hearing of this, John's disciples came and took his
body and laid it in a tomb.

Jesus Feeds the Five Thousand

30The apostles gathered around Jesus and reported to him all
they had done and taught. 31Then, because so many people were
coming and going that they did not even have a chance to eat, he
said to them, "Come with me by yourselves to a quiet place and
get some rest."
32So they went away by themselves in a boat to a solitary place.
33But many who saw them leaving recognized them and ran on
foot from all the towns and got there ahead of them. 34When
Jesus landed and saw a large crowd, he had compassion on them,
because they were like sheep without a shepherd. So he began
teaching them many things.
35By this time it was late in the day, so his disciples came to
him. "This is a remote place," they said, "and it's already very
late. 36Send the people away so they can go to the surrounding
countryside and villages and buy themselves something to eat."
37But he answered, "You give them something to eat."
They said to him, "That would take eight months of a man's
wages[b]! Are we to go and spend that much on bread and give it to
them to eat?"
38"How many loaves do you have?" he asked. "Go and see."
When they found out, they said, "Five—and two fish."
39Then Jesus directed them to have all the people sit down in
groups on the green grass. 40So they sat down in groups of hun-

[a] 20 Some early manuscripts *he did many things* [b] 37 Greek *take two hundred denarii*

dreds and fifties. 41Taking the five loaves and the two fish and
looking up to heaven, he gave thanks and broke the loaves. Then
he gave them to his disciples to set before the people. He also divided the two fish among them all. 42They all ate and were satisfied, 43and the disciples picked up twelve basketfuls of broken
pieces of bread and fish. 44The number of the men who had eaten
was five thousand.

Jesus Walks on the Water

45Immediately Jesus made his disciples get into the boat and
go on ahead of him to Bethsaida, while he dismissed the crowd.
46After leaving them, he went up on a mountainside to pray.

47When evening came, the boat was in the middle of the lake,
and he was alone on land. 48He saw the disciples straining at the
oars, because the wind was against them. About the fourth watch
of the night he went out to them, walking on the lake. He was
about to pass by them, 49but when they saw him walking on the
lake, they thought he was a ghost. They cried out, 50because they
all saw him and were terrified.

Immediately he spoke to them and said, "Take courage! It is I.
Don't be afraid." 51Then he climbed into the boat with them, and
the wind died down. They were completely amazed, 52for they
had not understood about the loaves; their hearts were hardened.

53When they had crossed over, they landed at Gennesaret and
anchored there. 54As soon as they got out of the boat, people
recognized Jesus. 55They ran throughout that whole region and
carried the sick on mats to wherever they heard he was. 56And
wherever he went—into villages, towns or countryside—they
placed the sick in the marketplaces. They begged him to let them
touch even the edge of his cloak, and all who touched him were
healed.

Clean and Unclean

7 The Pharisees and some of the teachers of the law who had
come from Jerusalem gathered around Jesus and 2saw some
of his disciples eating food with hands that were "unclean," that
is, unwashed. 3(The Pharisees and all the Jews do not eat unless
they give their hands a ceremonial washing, holding to the tradition of the elders. 4When they come from the marketplace they do
not eat unless they wash. And they observe many other traditions,
such as the washing of cups, pitchers and kettles.[a])

5So the Pharisees and teachers of the law asked Jesus, "Why
don't your disciples live according to the tradition of the elders
instead of eating their food with 'unclean' hands?"

6He replied, "Isaiah was right when he prophesied about you
hypocrites; as it is written:

> " 'These people honor me with their lips,
> but their hearts are far from me.
> 7They worship me in vain;
> their teachings are but rules taught by men.'[b]

8You have let go of the commands of God and are holding on to
the traditions of men."

9And he said to them: "You have a fine way of setting aside the
commands of God in order to observe[c] your own traditions!

[a] 4 Some early manuscripts *pitchers, kettles and dining couches* [b] 6,7 Isaiah 29:13
[c] 9 Some manuscripts *set up*

(6:45–52) Lord, You sometimes set us out to sea at night in the storm and allow us to strain at the oars. Then You appear upon the waves waiting for us to invite You into our boat so that You can solve our predicament. But too often we are afraid to trust You or too proud to acknowledge our need of divine assistance, so we just keep rowing. If we would only remember to give ceaseless thanks for Your former provision, our faith would remain vital. Then we would watch for You and eagerly pull You into our boat—and see our storms abate. Help us, Lord, to continually offer heartfelt thanks that will increase the level and quality of our faith.

(7:9–13) It is easy to confuse zealously taught tradition with Your Word, O God, to confuse man-made codes with true righteousness. Father, give me an insatiable hunger for Your Word, and let it anchor me to Your will. I want no person, nor my own wayward heart, to deceive me. Help me never to rationalize behavior that is contrary to Your expressed will; help me never to be shackled by the chains of human tradition. And most of all, Lord, help me to be true to Your Word and faithful to Your ways. (Mk 7:1–6)

May the mind of Christ my Savior
Live in me from day to day,
By His love and power controlling
All I do and say.

May the Word of God dwell richly
In my heart from hour to hour,
So that all may see I triumph
Only through His power.

"May the Mind of Christ My Savior"
Kate B. Wilkinson (1925)

(7:25–35) O God, help me not to judge! I believe that You still extend redeeming grace to people who, like this woman, are not part of the religious establishment. And You still touch people, as You touched this deaf man, through methods that cause some of us, who know how things "should" be done, to recoil. Deliver me from being so proper that You can no longer use me to do the "improper," the outrageous—the divine.

10For Moses said, 'Honor your father and your mother,'[a] and,
'Anyone who curses his father or mother must be put to death.'[b]
11But you say that if a man says to his father or mother: 'Whatever help you might otherwise have received from me is Corban' (that is, a gift devoted to God),
12then you no longer let him do anything for his father or mother.
13Thus you nullify the word of God by your tradition that you have handed down. And you do many things like that."

14Again Jesus called the crowd to him and said, "Listen to me, everyone, and understand this.
15Nothing outside a man can make him 'unclean' by going into him. Rather, it is what comes out of a man that makes him 'unclean.'[c]"

17After he had left the crowd and entered the house, his disciples asked him about this parable.
18"Are you so dull?" he asked. "Don't you see that nothing that enters a man from the outside can make him 'unclean'?
19For it doesn't go into his heart but into his stomach, and then out of his body." (In saying this, Jesus declared all foods "clean.")

20He went on: "What comes out of a man is what makes him 'unclean.'
21For from within, out of men's hearts, come evil thoughts, sexual immorality, theft, murder, adultery,
22greed, malice, deceit, lewdness, envy, slander, arrogance and folly.
23All these evils come from inside and make a man 'unclean.' "

The Faith of a Syrophoenician Woman

24Jesus left that place and went to the vicinity of Tyre.[d] He entered a house and did not want anyone to know it; yet he could not keep his presence secret.
25In fact, as soon as she heard about him, a woman whose little daughter was possessed by an evil[e] spirit came and fell at his feet.
26The woman was a Greek, born in Syrian Phoenicia. She begged Jesus to drive the demon out of her daughter.

27"First let the children eat all they want," he told her, "for it is not right to take the children's bread and toss it to their dogs."
28"Yes, Lord," she replied, "but even the dogs under the table eat the children's crumbs."
29Then he told her, "For such a reply, you may go; the demon has left your daughter."
30She went home and found her child lying on the bed, and the demon gone.

The Healing of a Deaf and Mute Man

31Then Jesus left the vicinity of Tyre and went through Sidon, down to the Sea of Galilee and into the region of the Decapolis.[f]
32There some people brought to him a man who was deaf and could hardly talk, and they begged him to place his hand on the man.
33After he took him aside, away from the crowd, Jesus put his fingers into the man's ears. Then he spit and touched the man's tongue.
34He looked up to heaven and with a deep sigh said to him, *"Ephphatha!"* (which means, "Be opened!").
35At this, the man's ears were opened, his tongue was loosened and he began to speak plainly.
36Jesus commanded them not to tell anyone. But the more he

[a] *10* Exodus 20:12; Deut. 5:16 [b] *10* Exodus 21:17; Lev. 20:9 [c] *15* Some early manuscripts *'unclean.' 16If anyone has ears to hear, let him hear.* [d] *24* Many early manuscripts *Tyre and Sidon* [e] *25* Greek *unclean* [f] *31* That is, the Ten Cities

did so, the more they kept talking about it. 37People were overwhelmed with amazement. "He has done everything well," they
said. "He even makes the deaf hear and the mute speak."

Jesus Feeds the Four Thousand

8 During those days another large crowd gathered. Since they
had nothing to eat, Jesus called his disciples to him and said,
2"I have compassion for these people; they have already been
with me three days and have nothing to eat. 3If I send them home
hungry, they will collapse on the way, because some of them have
come a long distance."
4His disciples answered, "But where in this remote place can
anyone get enough bread to feed them?"
5"How many loaves do you have?" Jesus asked.
"Seven," they replied.
6He told the crowd to sit down on the ground. When he had
taken the seven loaves and given thanks, he broke them and gave
them to his disciples to set before the people, and they did so.
7They had a few small fish as well; he gave thanks for them also
and told the disciples to distribute them. 8The people ate and
were satisfied. Afterward the disciples picked up seven basketfuls
of broken pieces that were left over. 9About four thousand men
were present. And having sent them away, 10he got into the boat
with his disciples and went to the region of Dalmanutha.
11The Pharisees came and began to question Jesus. To test
him, they asked him for a sign from heaven. 12He sighed deeply
and said, "Why does this generation ask for a miraculous sign? I
tell you the truth, no sign will be given to it." 13Then he left them,
got back into the boat and crossed to the other side.

The Yeast of the Pharisees and Herod

14The disciples had forgotten to bring bread, except for one
loaf they had with them in the boat. 15"Be careful," Jesus warned
them. "Watch out for the yeast of the Pharisees and that of
Herod."
16They discussed this with one another and said, "It is because
we have no bread."
17Aware of their discussion, Jesus asked them: "Why are you
talking about having no bread? Do you still not see or understand?
Are your hearts hardened? 18Do you have eyes but fail to see, and
ears but fail to hear? And don't you remember? 19When I broke
the five loaves for the five thousand, how many basketfuls of
pieces did you pick up?"
"Twelve," they replied.
20"And when I broke the seven loaves for the four thousand,
how many basketfuls of pieces did you pick up?"
They answered, "Seven."
21He said to them, "Do you still not understand?"

The Healing of a Blind Man at Bethsaida

22They came to Bethsaida, and some people brought a blind
man and begged Jesus to touch him. 23He took the blind man by
the hand and led him outside the village. When he had spit on the
man's eyes and put his hands on him, Jesus asked, "Do you see
anything?"
24He looked up and said, "I see people; they look like trees
walking around."

(8:1–10) Lord, You ask us for everything we have. Then You take all our loaves and fishes and leave us standing empty-handed. But once we have handed everything over to you, the miracle begins. You multiply our meager offering and feed not only the multitude but ourselves as well. You are faithful, Lord, always and forever. I offer You all I have, knowing that You are my Provider. (Ge 22:14; Mk 10:29–30)

The presence of Christ brings us his power and ability to use our limited resources in his limitless ways.

Rebecca Manley Pippert (1948-)

(8:15) Help us, too, Lord, to beware of the yeast of the Pharisees. Keep Your church from the legalism, self-righteousness, spiritual arrogance, bigotry and elitism that will make us judgmental and unholy. By Your Spirit, fill us with the unfeigned love and humility that will attract Your grace and captivate the lost. (Jas 4:6)

25Once more Jesus put his hands on the man's eyes. Then his
eyes were opened, his sight was restored, and he saw everything
clearly. 26Jesus sent him home, saying, "Don't go into the village.[a]"

Peter's Confession of Christ

27Jesus and his disciples went on to the villages around Caesarea Philippi. On the way he asked them, "Who do people say
I am?"
28They replied, "Some say John the Baptist; others say Elijah;
and still others, one of the prophets."
29"But what about you?" he asked. "Who do you say I am?"
Peter answered, "You are the Christ.[b]"
30Jesus warned them not to tell anyone about him.

Jesus Predicts His Death

31He then began to teach them that the Son of Man must suffer
many things and be rejected by the elders, chief priests and
teachers of the law, and that he must be killed and after three
days rise again. 32He spoke plainly about this, and Peter took him
aside and began to rebuke him.
33But when Jesus turned and looked at his disciples, he rebuked Peter. "Get behind me, Satan!" he said. "You do not have
in mind the things of God, but the things of men."
34Then he called the crowd to him along with his disciples and
said: "If anyone would come after me, he must deny himself and
take up his cross and follow me. 35For whoever wants to save his
life[c] will lose it, but whoever loses his life for me and for the
gospel will save it. 36What good is it for a man to gain the whole
world, yet forfeit his soul? 37Or what can a man give in exchange
for his soul? 38If anyone is ashamed of me and my words in this
adulterous and sinful generation, the Son of Man will be ashamed
of him when he comes in his Father's glory with the holy angels."
9 And he said to them, "I tell you the truth, some who are
standing here will not taste death before they see the kingdom of God come with power."

The Transfiguration

2After six days Jesus took Peter, James and John with him and
led them up a high mountain, where they were all alone. There he
was transfigured before them. 3His clothes became dazzling
white, whiter than anyone in the world could bleach them. 4And
there appeared before them Elijah and Moses, who were talking
with Jesus.
5Peter said to Jesus, "Rabbi, it is good for us to be here. Let us
put up three shelters—one for you, one for Moses and one for
Elijah." 6(He did not know what to say, they were so frightened.)
7Then a cloud appeared and enveloped them, and a voice
came from the cloud: "This is my Son, whom I love. Listen to
him!"
8Suddenly, when they looked around, they no longer saw anyone with them except Jesus.
9As they were coming down the mountain, Jesus gave them orders not to tell anyone what they had seen until the Son of Man

[a] *26* Some manuscripts *Don't go and tell anyone in the village* [b] *29* Or *Messiah.* "The Christ" (Greek) and "the Messiah" (Hebrew) both mean "the Anointed One." [c] *35* The Greek word means either *life* or *soul*; also in verse 36.

(8:29) The revelation came from the Father in Heaven, but its declaration came from a man: "You are the Christ!" With that simple statement the world was changed forever. From then until now, that proclamation has secured the blessing and transforming power of God on those who believe it in their hearts and confess it with their lips. Lord, it is my confession, too: "You are the Christ." As I speak it out with faith and joy, may it pierce other hearts with its power and transform multitudes with its truth. (Mt 16:15–19; Ro 10:9–10)

(8:31–35) How hard it is to understand why bad things happen to good people. But You, Lord Jesus, the very best of all, were about to suffer the worst of all. The cross lay ahead for You. And so it does for me, because I am Your follower. This crucifixion begins with my self-life, my lusts and ambitions; my hesitation to suffer for the One Who so willingly suffered for me. Lord, by faith I truly count myself dead unto sin and alive unto God. Make this confession a reality in my life. (Mt 16:24; Ro 6:11)

(9:2–7) The revelations given through the law and the prophets came together on the mountain. Moses, your servant the lawgiver, and Elijah, your servant the prophet, witnessed with their own eyes the glorious confirmation of Jesus Christ as Your only Son, the Messiah, the Savior of the world. When the cloud lifted, the only one left was Jesus. We praise You, O God, that in Jesus both the law and the prophets are fulfilled. (Mt 5:17; Jn 1:45)

had risen from the dead. 10They kept the matter to themselves,
discussing what "rising from the dead" meant.
11And they asked him, "Why do the teachers of the law say that
Elijah must come first?"
12Jesus replied, "To be sure, Elijah does come first, and restores all things. Why then is it written that the Son of Man must
suffer much and be rejected? 13But I tell you, Elijah has come,
and they have done to him everything they wished, just as it is
written about him."

The Healing of a Boy With an Evil Spirit

14When they came to the other disciples, they saw a large
crowd around them and the teachers of the law arguing with
them. 15As soon as all the people saw Jesus, they were overwhelmed with wonder and ran to greet him.
16"What are you arguing with them about?" he asked.
17A man in the crowd answered, "Teacher, I brought you my
son, who is possessed by a spirit that has robbed him of speech.
18Whenever it seizes him, it throws him to the ground. He foams
at the mouth, gnashes his teeth and becomes rigid. I asked your
disciples to drive out the spirit, but they could not."
19"O unbelieving generation," Jesus replied, "how long shall I
stay with you? How long shall I put up with you? Bring the boy
to me."
20So they brought him. When the spirit saw Jesus, it immediately threw the boy into a convulsion. He fell to the ground and
rolled around, foaming at the mouth.
21Jesus asked the boy's father, "How long has he been like
this?"
"From childhood," he answered. 22"It has often thrown him
into fire or water to kill him. But if you can do anything, take pity
on us and help us."
23" 'If you can'?" said Jesus. "Everything is possible for him
who believes."
24Immediately the boy's father exclaimed, "I do believe; help
me overcome my unbelief!"
25When Jesus saw that a crowd was running to the scene, he
rebuked the evil[a] spirit. "You deaf and mute spirit," he said, "I
command you, come out of him and never enter him again."
26The spirit shrieked, convulsed him violently and came out.
The boy looked so much like a corpse that many said, "He's
dead." 27But Jesus took him by the hand and lifted him to his
feet, and he stood up.
28After Jesus had gone indoors, his disciples asked him privately, "Why couldn't we drive it out?"
29He replied, "This kind can come out only by prayer.[b]"
30They left that place and passed through Galilee. Jesus did not
want anyone to know where they were, 31because he was teaching his disciples. He said to them, "The Son of Man is going to be
betrayed into the hands of men. They will kill him, and after three
days he will rise." 32But they did not understand what he meant
and were afraid to ask him about it.

Who Is the Greatest?

33They came to Capernaum. When he was in the house, he
asked them, "What were you arguing about on the road?" 34But

[a] 25 Greek *unclean* [b] 29 Some manuscripts *prayer and fasting*

(9:23–24) O God, help us to overcome our unbelief. Let the Holy Spirit fill us with the faith and power that rescue the prisoners enchained by the enemy. Make us deliverers. Make us people who pray. Make us people who believe. Make us like Jesus.

Here, Master, in this quiet place,
Where anyone may kneel,
I also come to ask for grace,
Believing You can heal.

Of all my prayers, may this be chief:
Till faith is fully grown,
Lord, disbelieve my unbelief,
And claim me as Your own.

"Here, Master, in This Quiet Place"
Fred Pratt Green (©1974)

(9:35) Lord, this is such a hard lesson to remember. Everything in our society, and much in the church, contradicts it. A servant is the last thing most of us really want to be. Our insecure hearts long for recognition, position, fame. But humility, real humility, is as powerful as it is rare. It is the surest path to blessing and to Your overflowing, enabling grace. Please, Lord, in Jesus' name, give me a servant's heart. (Jas 4:6; 1Pe 5:5)

(9:42–48) Lord, even if I severed my hands and feet to keep from sinning, what would I do about my wayward heart? I would run to the cross. There You took all of me, heart and soul, into death with You. And yet I live; and by the power of the Spirit You live and work in me as I, by faith, make a place for You in my heart. This is the cleansing of the new covenant. In this I rest. O God, thank You! I will worship You forever and ever. (Php 2:13)

I come to the cross
Seeking mercy and grace,
I come to the cross
Where You died in my place,
Out of my weakness
And into Your strength,
Humbly, I come to the cross.

Your arms are open,
You call me by name.
You welcome this child
That was lost.
You paid the price
For my guilt and shame.
Jesus, I come, Jesus, I come,
Jesus, I come to the cross.

"I Come to the Cross"
Bob Somma and Bill Batstone (©1996)

they kept quiet because on the way they had argued about who
was the greatest.
35 Sitting down, Jesus called the Twelve and said, "If anyone
wants to be first, he must be the very last, and the servant of all."
36 He took a little child and had him stand among them. Taking
him in his arms, he said to them,
37 "Whoever welcomes one of
these little children in my name welcomes me; and whoever welcomes me does not welcome me but the one who sent me."

Whoever Is Not Against Us Is for Us

38 "Teacher," said John, "we saw a man driving out demons in
your name and we told him to stop, because he was not one
of us."
39 "Do not stop him," Jesus said. "No one who does a miracle
in my name can in the next moment say anything bad about me,
40 for whoever is not against us is for us.
41 I tell you the truth,
anyone who gives you a cup of water in my name because you belong to Christ will certainly not lose his reward.

Causing to Sin

42 "And if anyone causes one of these little ones who believe in
me to sin, it would be better for him to be thrown into the sea
with a large millstone tied around his neck.
43 If your hand causes
you to sin, cut it off. It is better for you to enter life maimed than
with two hands to go into hell, where the fire never goes out.[a]
45 And if your foot causes you to sin, cut it off. It is better for you
to enter life crippled than to have two feet and be thrown into
hell.[b]
47 And if your eye causes you to sin, pluck it out. It is better
for you to enter the kingdom of God with one eye than to have two
eyes and be thrown into hell,
48 where

" 'their worm does not die,
and the fire is not quenched.'[c]

49 Everyone will be salted with fire.
50 "Salt is good, but if it loses its saltiness, how can you make it
salty again? Have salt in yourselves, and be at peace with each
other."

Divorce

10 Jesus then left that place and went into the region of Judea
and across the Jordan. Again crowds of people came to
him, and as was his custom, he taught them.
2 Some Pharisees came and tested him by asking, "Is it lawful
for a man to divorce his wife?"
3 "What did Moses command you?" he replied.
4 They said, "Moses permitted a man to write a certificate of divorce and send her away."
5 "It was because your hearts were hard that Moses wrote you
this law," Jesus replied.
6 "But at the beginning of creation God
'made them male and female.'[d]
7 'For this reason a man will leave
his father and mother and be united to his wife,[e]
8 and the two will
become one flesh.'[f] So they are no longer two, but one.
9 Therefore what God has joined together, let man not separate."

[a] 43 Some manuscripts *out,* [44]*where /* " *'their worm does not die, / and the fire is not quenched.'* [b] 45 Some manuscripts *hell,* [46]*where /* " *'their worm does not die, / and the fire is not quenched.'* [c] 48 Isaiah 66:24 [d] 6 Gen. 1:27 [e] 7 Some early manuscripts do not have *and be united to his wife.* [f] 8 Gen. 2:24

10When they were in the house again, the disciples asked Jesus
about this. 11He answered, "Anyone who divorces his wife and
marries another woman commits adultery against her. 12And if
she divorces her husband and marries another man, she commits adultery."

The Little Children and Jesus

13People were bringing little children to Jesus to have him
touch them, but the disciples rebuked them. 14When Jesus saw
this, he was indignant. He said to them, "Let the little children
come to me, and do not hinder them, for the kingdom of God belongs to such as these. 15I tell you the truth, anyone who will not
receive the kingdom of God like a little child will never enter it."
16And he took the children in his arms, put his hands on them
and blessed them.

The Rich Young Man

17As Jesus started on his way, a man ran up to him and fell on
his knees before him. "Good teacher," he asked, "what must I do
to inherit eternal life?"
18"Why do you call me good?" Jesus answered. "No one is
good—except God alone. 19You know the commandments: 'Do
not murder, do not commit adultery, do not steal, do not give false
testimony, do not defraud, honor your father and mother.'[a]"
20"Teacher," he declared, "all these I have kept since I was a
boy."
21Jesus looked at him and loved him. "One thing you lack," he
said. "Go, sell everything you have and give to the poor, and you
will have treasure in heaven. Then come, follow me."
22At this the man's face fell. He went away sad, because he had
great wealth.
23Jesus looked around and said to his disciples, "How hard it
is for the rich to enter the kingdom of God!"
24The disciples were amazed at his words. But Jesus said
again, "Children, how hard it is[b] to enter the kingdom of God!
25It is easier for a camel to go through the eye of a needle than
for a rich man to enter the kingdom of God."
26The disciples were even more amazed, and said to each
other, "Who then can be saved?"
27Jesus looked at them and said, "With man this is impossible,
but not with God; all things are possible with God."
28Peter said to him, "We have left everything to follow you!"
29"I tell you the truth," Jesus replied, "no one who has left
home or brothers or sisters or mother or father or children or
fields for me and the gospel 30will fail to receive a hundred times
as much in this present age (homes, brothers, sisters, mothers,
children and fields—and with them, persecutions) and in the age
to come, eternal life. 31But many who are first will be last, and the
last first."

Jesus Again Predicts His Death

32They were on their way up to Jerusalem, with Jesus leading
the way, and the disciples were astonished, while those who followed were afraid. Again he took the Twelve aside and told them
what was going to happen to him. 33"We are going up to Jerusa-

[a] *19* Exodus 20:12–16; Deut. 5:16–20 [b] *24* Some manuscripts *is for those who trust in riches*

(10:28) Lord, I honor Your faithful messengers who offered themselves as living sacrifices to You. They abandoned dignity, renounced comfort and relinquished possessions to go forth and cry redemption to the lost. Give me that heart, Lord. I come to the cross and by faith declare myself crucified with Christ and alive unto God, ready to worship and serve You with my life. (Ro 6:6; 1Co 4:10; Gal 2:20)

World Christians are tramps for the Lord who have left their hiding places to roam the Gap with the Savior. They are heaven's expatriates, camping where the kingdom is best served. They are earth's dispossessed, who have journeyed forth to give a dying world not only the gospel but their own souls as well. They are members of God's global dispersion down through history and out through the nations, reaching the unreached and blessing the families of earth.

Corrie ten Boom (1892–1983)

(10:29–30) Nothing is ever lost when it is given to You, Lord. You can provide an abundance of houses, lands and goods when they are needed, just as easily as You can multiply fish and bread. Open my grip on what little I have so that I might receive from Your boundless wealth. Make me in turn Your hand of blessing to a needy world. Use me, Lord, extravagantly, redemptively, for Your glory.

All to Jesus I surrender,
All to Him I freely give;
I will ever love and trust Him,
In His presence daily live.

I surrender all,
I surrender all,
All to Thee, my blessed Savior,
I surrender all.

"I Surrender All"
Judson W. Van deVenter (1896)

lem," he said, "and the Son of Man will be betrayed to the chief priests and teachers of the law. They will condemn him to death and will hand him over to the Gentiles, 34who will mock him and spit on him, flog him and kill him. Three days later he will rise."

The Request of James and John

35Then James and John, the sons of Zebedee, came to him. "Teacher," they said, "we want you to do for us whatever we ask."

36"What do you want me to do for you?" he asked.

37They replied, "Let one of us sit at your right and the other at your left in your glory."

38"You don't know what you are asking," Jesus said. "Can you drink the cup I drink or be baptized with the baptism I am baptized with?"

39"We can," they answered.

Jesus said to them, "You will drink the cup I drink and be baptized with the baptism I am baptized with, 40but to sit at my right or left is not for me to grant. These places belong to those for whom they have been prepared."

41When the ten heard about this, they became indignant with James and John. 42Jesus called them together and said, "You know that those who are regarded as rulers of the Gentiles lord it over them, and their high officials exercise authority over them. 43Not so with you. Instead, whoever wants to become great among you must be your servant, 44and whoever wants to be first must be slave of all. 45For even the Son of Man did not come to be served, but to serve, and to give his life as a ransom for many."

Blind Bartimaeus Receives His Sight

46Then they came to Jericho. As Jesus and his disciples, together with a large crowd, were leaving the city, a blind man, Bartimaeus (that is, the Son of Timaeus), was sitting by the roadside begging. 47When he heard that it was Jesus of Nazareth, he began to shout, "Jesus, Son of David, have mercy on me!"

48Many rebuked him and told him to be quiet, but he shouted all the more, "Son of David, have mercy on me!"

49Jesus stopped and said, "Call him."

So they called to the blind man, "Cheer up! On your feet! He's calling you." 50Throwing his cloak aside, he jumped to his feet and came to Jesus.

51"What do you want me to do for you?" Jesus asked him.

The blind man said, "Rabbi, I want to see."

52"Go," said Jesus, "your faith has healed you." Immediately he received his sight and followed Jesus along the road.

The Triumphal Entry

11 As they approached Jerusalem and came to Bethphage and Bethany at the Mount of Olives, Jesus sent two of his disciples, 2saying to them, "Go to the village ahead of you, and just as you enter it, you will find a colt tied there, which no one has ever ridden. Untie it and bring it here. 3If anyone asks you, 'Why are you doing this?' tell him, 'The Lord needs it and will send it back here shortly.'"

4They went and found a colt outside in the street, tied at a doorway. As they untied it, 5some people standing there asked, "What are you doing, untying that colt?" 6They answered as Jesus had told them to, and the people let them go. 7When they brought

(10:33–34) Jesus, You saw it coming: degradation and death. Love would take You through the pain, and love alone would hold You on the cross. Crucifixion, looming heavy in Your heart, was Your chosen destiny, Your supreme act of adoration for the Father, Your ultimate act of passion for mankind. Lord Jesus, I want to thank You from the depths of my soul for Your obedience. I know You could have refused, but because You submitted You ransomed us lost ones. You were our only hope, and You came through for us. (Mk 14:35–36)

(10:43–44) Why are Your principles so hard for me to comprehend? Why must I be reminded so often? Perhaps because the ways of Your kingdom oppose the ways of my fallen human heart. Again and again You call me to serve everyone, to love even my enemies, to give myself away. But I cannot always seem to do it, Lord. So I repent and ask once more for pardon and for a fresh, full infusion of Your living Holy Spirit Who is able to make me a servant like You. (Mt 5:3–12,42–48)

the colt to Jesus and threw their cloaks over it, he sat on it. 8Many
people spread their cloaks on the road, while others spread
branches they had cut in the fields. 9Those who went ahead and
those who followed shouted,

"Hosanna![a]"

"Blessed is he who comes in the name of the Lord!"[b]

10 "Blessed is the coming kingdom of our father David!"

"Hosanna in the highest!"

11Jesus entered Jerusalem and went to the temple. He looked
around at everything, but since it was already late, he went out to
Bethany with the Twelve.

Jesus Clears the Temple

12The next day as they were leaving Bethany, Jesus was hungry.
13Seeing in the distance a fig tree in leaf, he went to find out if it
had any fruit. When he reached it, he found nothing but leaves,
because it was not the season for figs. 14Then he said to the tree,
"May no one ever eat fruit from you again." And his disciples
heard him say it.
15On reaching Jerusalem, Jesus entered the temple area and
began driving out those who were buying and selling there. He
overturned the tables of the money changers and the benches of
those selling doves, 16and would not allow anyone to carry merchandise through the temple courts. 17And as he taught them, he
said, "Is it not written:

" 'My house will be called
a house of prayer for all nations'[c]?

But you have made it 'a den of robbers.'[d]"
18The chief priests and the teachers of the law heard this and
began looking for a way to kill him, for they feared him, because
the whole crowd was amazed at his teaching.
19When evening came, they[e] went out of the city.

The Withered Fig Tree

20In the morning, as they went along, they saw the fig tree withered from the roots. 21Peter remembered and said to Jesus,
"Rabbi, look! The fig tree you cursed has withered!"
22"Have[f] faith in God," Jesus answered. 23"I tell you the truth,
if anyone says to this mountain, 'Go, throw yourself into the sea,'
and does not doubt in his heart but believes that what he says will
happen, it will be done for him. 24Therefore I tell you, whatever
you ask for in prayer, believe that you have received it, and it will
be yours. 25And when you stand praying, if you hold anything
against anyone, forgive him, so that your Father in heaven may
forgive you your sins.[g]"

The Authority of Jesus Questioned

27They arrived again in Jerusalem, and while Jesus was walking in the temple courts, the chief priests, the teachers of the law

[a] *9* A Hebrew expression meaning "Save!" which became an exclamation of praise; also in verse 10 [b] *9* Psalm 118:25,26 [c] *17* Isaiah 56:7 [d] *17* Jer. 7:11 [e] *19* Some early manuscripts *he* [f] *22* Some early manuscripts *If you have* [g] *25* Some manuscripts *sins. 26But if you do not forgive, neither will your Father who is in heaven forgive your sins.*

(11:7–8) No pomp, high-flying banners or red carpet for You, my King. Your retinue were peasants; Your banners were palm branches; Your welcoming carpet was coats strewn on a dusty road. So You entered Jerusalem: God on a donkey. Here is humility that will imprint itself on my heart forever. Here is the character of God. Lord, remove every trace of arrogance from my soul. Make me like You.

Ride on! Ride on in majesty!
In lowly pomp ride on to die:
O Christ, Thy triumphs now begin
O'er captive death and conquered sin.

"Ride On! Ride On in Majesty!"
Henry Hart Milman (1827)

(11:25) Lord, I relinquish all my hurts for You to heal. As an act of obedience and worship, I leave all bitterness and resentment at Your altar. By the help of Your Spirit I will pour forgiveness on everyone who has deceived, defrauded or defamed me. Why should I allow the past to hurt me further by creating a rift between my spirit and Yours? What will these things matter when I am ready to come Home? Freely I release my antagonists; and I release myself into Your forgiveness.

Only one petition in the Lord's Prayer has any condition attached to it. It is the petition for forgiveness.

Sir William Temple (1628-1699)

(12:10) You, Lord Jesus, are the capstone, the cornerstone, the very foundation of my life and the foundation of Your church. Without You all we have constructed would crumble. We will build everything upon You; our mortal present and our immortal future. You are the bedrock of our being, our high tower, our fortress and our eternal home.

and the elders came to him. 28"By what authority are you doing
these things?" they asked. "And who gave you authority to do
this?"
29Jesus replied, "I will ask you one question. Answer me, and
I will tell you by what authority I am doing these things. 30John's
baptism—was it from heaven, or from men? Tell me!"
31They discussed it among themselves and said, "If we say,
'From heaven,' he will ask, 'Then why didn't you believe him?'
32But if we say, 'From men' . . ." (They feared the people, for
everyone held that John really was a prophet.)
33So they answered Jesus, "We don't know."
Jesus said, "Neither will I tell you by what authority I am doing
these things."

The Parable of the Tenants

12 He then began to speak to them in parables: "A man planted a vineyard. He put a wall around it, dug a pit for the
winepress and built a watchtower. Then he rented the vineyard to
some farmers and went away on a journey. 2At harvest time he
sent a servant to the tenants to collect from them some of the fruit
of the vineyard. 3But they seized him, beat him and sent him away
empty-handed. 4Then he sent another servant to them; they
struck this man on the head and treated him shamefully. 5He sent
still another, and that one they killed. He sent many others; some
of them they beat, others they killed.
6"He had one left to send, a son, whom he loved. He sent him
last of all, saying, 'They will respect my son.'
7"But the tenants said to one another, 'This is the heir. Come,
let's kill him, and the inheritance will be ours.' 8So they took him
and killed him, and threw him out of the vineyard.
9"What then will the owner of the vineyard do? He will come
and kill those tenants and give the vineyard to others. 10Haven't
you read this scripture:

" 'The stone the builders rejected
has become the capstone[a];
11the Lord has done this,
and it is marvelous in our eyes'[b]?"

12Then they looked for a way to arrest him because they knew
he had spoken the parable against them. But they were afraid of
the crowd; so they left him and went away.

Paying Taxes to Caesar

13Later they sent some of the Pharisees and Herodians to Jesus
to catch him in his words. 14They came to him and said,
"Teacher, we know you are a man of integrity. You aren't swayed
by men, because you pay no attention to who they are; but you
teach the way of God in accordance with the truth. Is it right to
pay taxes to Caesar or not? 15Should we pay or shouldn't we?"
But Jesus knew their hypocrisy. "Why are you trying to trap
me?" he asked. "Bring me a denarius and let me look at it."
16They brought the coin, and he asked them, "Whose portrait is
this? And whose inscription?"
"Caesar's," they replied.

[a] 10 Or *cornerstone* [b] 11 Psalm 118:22,23

17Then Jesus said to them, "Give to Caesar what is Caesar's and
to God what is God's."
And they were amazed at him.

Marriage at the Resurrection

18Then the Sadducees, who say there is no resurrection, came
to him with a question. 19"Teacher," they said, "Moses wrote for
us that if a man's brother dies and leaves a wife but no children,
the man must marry the widow and have children for his brother. 20Now there were seven brothers. The first one married and
died without leaving any children. 21The second one married the
widow, but he also died, leaving no child. It was the same with
the third. 22In fact, none of the seven left any children. Last of
all, the woman died too. 23At the resurrection[a] whose wife will
she be, since the seven were married to her?"

24Jesus replied, "Are you not in error because you do not
know the Scriptures or the power of God? 25When the dead rise,
they will neither marry nor be given in marriage; they will be like
the angels in heaven. 26Now about the dead rising—have you not
read in the book of Moses, in the account of the bush, how God
said to him, 'I am the God of Abraham, the God of Isaac, and the
God of Jacob'[b]? 27He is not the God of the dead, but of the living.
You are badly mistaken!"

The Greatest Commandment

28One of the teachers of the law came and heard them debat-
ing. Noticing that Jesus had given them a good answer, he asked
him, "Of all the commandments, which is the most important?"

29"The most important one," answered Jesus, "is this: 'Hear,
O Israel, the Lord our God, the Lord is one.[c] 30Love the Lord your
God with all your heart and with all your soul and with all your
mind and with all your strength.'[d] 31The second is this: 'Love
your neighbor as yourself.'[e] There is no commandment greater
than these."

32"Well said, teacher," the man replied. "You are right in saying that God is one and there is no other but him. 33To love him
with all your heart, with all your understanding and with all your
strength, and to love your neighbor as yourself is more important
than all burnt offerings and sacrifices."

34When Jesus saw that he had answered wisely, he said to him,
"You are not far from the kingdom of God." And from then on no
one dared ask him any more questions.

Whose Son Is the Christ?

35While Jesus was teaching in the temple courts, he asked,
"How is it that the teachers of the law say that the Christ[f] is the son
of David? 36David himself, speaking by the Holy Spirit, declared:

" 'The Lord said to my Lord:
"Sit at my right hand
until I put your enemies
under your feet." '[g]

37David himself calls him 'Lord.' How then can he be his son?"
The large crowd listened to him with delight.

[a] *23* Some manuscripts *resurrection, when men rise from the dead,* [b] *26* Exodus 3:6 [c] *29* Or *the Lord our God is one Lord* [d] *30* Deut. 6:4,5 [e] *31* Lev. 19:18 [f] *35* Or *Messiah* [g] *36* Psalm 110:1

(12:26–27) You are the God of the living: of Abraham, Isaac, Jacob and every other saint who has ever lived. They all live, now and forever. And so will I and all who know and love You. You are the Life-giver, our Hope and Source and Provider. With the saints and angels gathered around Your throne I will bless Your name today, tomorrow and forever.

(12:29–31) Here is the key to the diagnosis of my true spiritual condition: Your first commandment. I know it, Lord: all my good works, all my prayers, all my righteous words can mask a barren love relationship with You. Nothing brings me face-to-face with my true heart-condition as these words do: "Love the Lord your God with all your heart and with all your soul and with all your mind and with all your strength." Help me, Lord, to love You with all that is within me. And then, out of my love for You, help me to love others too.

O Lord, our God, grant us grace to desire thee with our whole heart; that so desiring, we may seek, and seeking, find thee; and so finding thee, may love thee; and loving thee, may hate those sins from which thou hast redeemed us. Amen.

Saint Anselm (1033-1109)

38As he taught, Jesus said, "Watch out for the teachers of the
law. They like to walk around in flowing robes and be greeted in
the marketplaces, 39and have the most important seats in the synagogues and the places of honor at banquets. 40They devour widows' houses and for a show make lengthy prayers. Such men will
be punished most severely."

The Widow's Offering

41Jesus sat down opposite the place where the offerings were
put and watched the crowd putting their money into the temple
treasury. Many rich people threw in large amounts. 42But a poor
widow came and put in two very small copper coins,[a] worth only
a fraction of a penny.[b]

43Calling his disciples to him, Jesus said, "I tell you the truth,
this poor widow has put more into the treasury than all the others. 44They all gave out of their wealth; but she, out of her poverty, put in everything—all she had to live on."

Signs of the End of the Age

13 As he was leaving the temple, one of his disciples said to
him, "Look, Teacher! What massive stones! What magnificent buildings!"

2"Do you see all these great buildings?" replied Jesus. "Not one
stone here will be left on another; every one will be thrown
down."

3As Jesus was sitting on the Mount of Olives opposite the temple, Peter, James, John and Andrew asked him privately, 4"Tell
us, when will these things happen? And what will be the sign that
they are all about to be fulfilled?"

5Jesus said to them: "Watch out that no one deceives you.
6Many will come in my name, claiming, 'I am he,' and will deceive many. 7When you hear of wars and rumors of wars, do not
be alarmed. Such things must happen, but the end is still to come.
8Nation will rise against nation, and kingdom against kingdom.
There will be earthquakes in various places, and famines. These
are the beginning of birth pains.

9"You must be on your guard. You will be handed over to the
local councils and flogged in the synagogues. On account of me
you will stand before governors and kings as witnesses to them.
10And the gospel must first be preached to all nations. 11When-
ever you are arrested and brought to trial, do not worry beforehand about what to say. Just say whatever is given you at the time,
for it is not you speaking, but the Holy Spirit.

12"Brother will betray brother to death, and a father his child.
Children will rebel against their parents and have them put to
death. 13All men will hate you because of me, but he who stands
firm to the end will be saved.

14"When you see 'the abomination that causes desolation'[c]
standing where it[d] does not belong—let the reader understand—then let those who are in Judea flee to the mountains.
15Let no one on the roof of his house go down or enter the house
to take anything out. 16Let no one in the field go back to get his
cloak. 17How dreadful it will be in those days for pregnant
women and nursing mothers! 18Pray that this will not take place
in winter, 19because those will be days of distress unequaled from

[a] 42 Greek *two lepta* [b] 42 Greek *kodrantes* [c] 14 Daniel 9:27; 11:31; 12:11
[d] 14 Or *he*; also in verse 29

(12:38–40) O God, deliver me from my self-righteousness and hypocrisy. Let humility and goodness, compassion and generosity be the hallmarks of my character. Fill my heart with love, my mouth with truth and my life with holiness.

(12:41–44) Lord, I bring everything I have to Your treasury. I know You want all I have, all I am and all I do to be at Your disposal, an offering of joyful faith and love, an ongoing act of deepest spiritual worship. Take all of it, Lord, and multiply it to feed and serve and save a lost world. (Ro 12:1)

"Give out of love" Your Word
 commands;
We are Your head, Your heart,
 Your hands.
Your Word You underscore with
 deeds
By using us to answer needs.

"All Things Are Yours"
Bryan Jeffery Leech (©1989)

the beginning, when God created the world, until now—and
never to be equaled again. 20If the Lord had not cut short those
days, no one would survive. But for the sake of the elect, whom he
has chosen, he has shortened them. 21At that time if anyone says
to you, 'Look, here is the Christ[a]!' or, 'Look, there he is!' do not
believe it. 22For false Christs and false prophets will appear and
perform signs and miracles to deceive the elect—if that were
possible. 23So be on your guard; I have told you everything ahead
of time.

24"But in those days, following that distress,

" 'the sun will be darkened,
and the moon will not give its light;
25the stars will fall from the sky,
and the heavenly bodies will be shaken.'[b]

26"At that time men will see the Son of Man coming in clouds
with great power and glory. 27And he will send his angels and
gather his elect from the four winds, from the ends of the earth to
the ends of the heavens.

28"Now learn this lesson from the fig tree: As soon as its twigs
get tender and its leaves come out, you know that summer is near.
29Even so, when you see these things happening, you know that it
is near, right at the door. 30I tell you the truth, this generation[c]
will certainly not pass away until all these things have happened.
31Heaven and earth will pass away, but my words will never pass
away.

The Day and Hour Unknown

32"No one knows about that day or hour, not even the angels in
heaven, nor the Son, but only the Father. 33Be on guard! Be
alert[d]! You do not know when that time will come. 34It's like a
man going away: He leaves his house and puts his servants in
charge, each with his assigned task, and tells the one at the door
to keep watch.

35"Therefore keep watch because you do not know when the
owner of the house will come back—whether in the evening, or
at midnight, or when the rooster crows, or at dawn. 36If he comes
suddenly, do not let him find you sleeping. 37What I say to you, I
say to everyone: 'Watch!' "

Jesus Anointed at Bethany

14 Now the Passover and the Feast of Unleavened Bread were
only two days away, and the chief priests and the teachers
of the law were looking for some sly way to arrest Jesus and kill
him. 2"But not during the Feast," they said, "or the people may
riot."

3While he was in Bethany, reclining at the table in the home of
a man known as Simon the Leper, a woman came with an alabaster jar of very expensive perfume, made of pure nard. She
broke the jar and poured the perfume on his head.

4Some of those present were saying indignantly to one another, "Why this waste of perfume? 5It could have been sold for more
than a year's wages[e] and the money given to the poor." And they
rebuked her harshly.

6"Leave her alone," said Jesus. "Why are you bothering her?

(13:26–37) How I long for the day of Your coming! As I watch and wait, help me to keep short accounts with You, to be sensitive to my sins or failures, to be immediate in confession and wholehearted in repentance, to receive Your cleansing and restoration with a joyful and worshiping heart. Let me not be ashamed, but rather rejoice at Your appearing. Come soon, Lord Jesus! (Rev 22:20)

[a] 21 Or *Messiah* [b] 25 Isaiah 13:10; 34:4 [c] 30 Or *race* [d] 33 Some manuscripts *alert and pray* [e] 5 Greek *than three hundred denarii*

(14:3–9) This woman took a risk in order to touch You, Jesus. She interrupted a dinner party to perform a public act of lavish, extravagant adoration that You will remember forever. O Lord, help me to worship like that—not for others' approval, but from the deepest springs of my heart, with acts and expressions of overwhelming devotion and awe. By Your Spirit, Lord, teach me how. (Mk 5:25–34)

Down at Your feet, oh Lord,
Is the most high place.
In Your presence, Lord,
I seek Your face,
I seek Your face.

There is no higher calling,
No greater honor
Than to bow and kneel
Before Your throne.
I'm amazed at Your glory,
Embraced by Your mercy,
Oh Lord, I live to worship You.

"No Higher Calling"
Lenny LeBlanc and Greg Gulley (©1989)

(14:18–31) Lord, You know my heart. You know my fears. You know my weaknesses and my sinful ways. You know that I am prone to wander and capable of betrayal. And the truth is, I know it too. Yet You love me and offer me the broken bread of Your body and the poured-out wine of Your blood. Lord, help me to be loyal to Your covenant. Please look past my faults and into the deepest part of my spirit where I love You with all of my being.

She has done a beautiful thing to me. 7The poor you will always
have with you, and you can help them any time you want. But you
will not always have me. 8She did what she could. She poured
perfume on my body beforehand to prepare for my burial. 9I tell
you the truth, wherever the gospel is preached throughout the
world, what she has done will also be told, in memory of her."
10Then Judas Iscariot, one of the Twelve, went to the chief
priests to betray Jesus to them. 11They were delighted to hear this
and promised to give him money. So he watched for an opportunity to hand him over.

The Lord's Supper

12On the first day of the Feast of Unleavened Bread, when it
was customary to sacrifice the Passover lamb, Jesus' disciples
asked him, "Where do you want us to go and make preparations
for you to eat the Passover?"
13So he sent two of his disciples, telling them, "Go into the city,
and a man carrying a jar of water will meet you. Follow him.
14Say to the owner of the house he enters, 'The Teacher asks:
Where is my guest room, where I may eat the Passover with my
disciples?' 15He will show you a large upper room, furnished and
ready. Make preparations for us there."
16The disciples left, went into the city and found things just as
Jesus had told them. So they prepared the Passover.
17When evening came, Jesus arrived with the Twelve. 18While
they were reclining at the table eating, he said, "I tell you the
truth, one of you will betray me—one who is eating with me."
19They were saddened, and one by one they said to him, "Surely not I?"
20"It is one of the Twelve," he replied, "one who dips bread
into the bowl with me. 21The Son of Man will go just as it is written about him. But woe to that man who betrays the Son of Man!
It would be better for him if he had not been born."
22While they were eating, Jesus took bread, gave thanks and
broke it, and gave it to his disciples, saying, "Take it; this is my
body."
23Then he took the cup, gave thanks and offered it to them,
and they all drank from it.
24"This is my blood of the[a] covenant, which is poured out for
many," he said to them. 25"I tell you the truth, I will not drink
again of the fruit of the vine until that day when I drink it anew in
the kingdom of God."
26When they had sung a hymn, they went out to the Mount of
Olives.

Jesus Predicts Peter's Denial

27"You will all fall away," Jesus told them, "for it is written:

" 'I will strike the shepherd,
and the sheep will be scattered.'[b]

28But after I have risen, I will go ahead of you into Galilee."
29Peter declared, "Even if all fall away, I will not."
30"I tell you the truth," Jesus answered, "today—yes,
tonight—before the rooster crows twice[c] you yourself will disown me three times."

[a] 24 Some manuscripts *the new* [b] 27 Zech. 13:7 [c] 30 Some early manuscripts do not have *twice.*

31But Peter insisted emphatically, "Even if I have to die with
you, I will never disown you." And all the others said the same.

Gethsemane

32They went to a place called Gethsemane, and Jesus said to
his disciples, "Sit here while I pray." 33He took Peter, James and
John along with him, and he began to be deeply distressed and
troubled. 34"My soul is overwhelmed with sorrow to the point of
death," he said to them. "Stay here and keep watch."
35Going a little farther, he fell to the ground and prayed that if
possible the hour might pass from him. 36"*Abba*,[a] Father," he
said, "everything is possible for you. Take this cup from me. Yet
not what I will, but what you will."
37Then he returned to his disciples and found them sleeping.
"Simon," he said to Peter, "are you asleep? Could you not keep
watch for one hour? 38Watch and pray so that you will not fall
into temptation. The spirit is willing, but the body is weak."
39Once more he went away and prayed the same thing. 40When
he came back, he again found them sleeping, because their eyes
were heavy. They did not know what to say to him.
41Returning the third time, he said to them, "Are you still
sleeping and resting? Enough! The hour has come. Look, the Son
of Man is betrayed into the hands of sinners. 42Rise! Let us go!
Here comes my betrayer!"

Jesus Arrested

43Just as he was speaking, Judas, one of the Twelve, appeared.
With him was a crowd armed with swords and clubs, sent from
the chief priests, the teachers of the law, and the elders.
44Now the betrayer had arranged a signal with them: "The one
I kiss is the man; arrest him and lead him away under guard."
45Going at once to Jesus, Judas said, "Rabbi!" and kissed him.
46The men seized Jesus and arrested him. 47Then one of those
standing near drew his sword and struck the servant of the high
priest, cutting off his ear.
48"Am I leading a rebellion," said Jesus, "that you have come
out with swords and clubs to capture me? 49Every day I was with
you, teaching in the temple courts, and you did not arrest me.
But the Scriptures must be fulfilled." 50Then everyone deserted
him and fled.
51A young man, wearing nothing but a linen garment, was following Jesus. When they seized him, 52he fled naked, leaving his
garment behind.

Before the Sanhedrin

53They took Jesus to the high priest, and all the chief priests,
elders and teachers of the law came together. 54Peter followed
him at a distance, right into the courtyard of the high priest.
There he sat with the guards and warmed himself at the fire.
55The chief priests and the whole Sanhedrin were looking for
evidence against Jesus so that they could put him to death, but
they did not find any. 56Many testified falsely against him, but
their statements did not agree.
57Then some stood up and gave this false testimony against
him: 58"We heard him say, 'I will destroy this man-made temple

[a] 36 Aramaic for *Father*

(14:32–38) How can I repay the debt I owe to You, my Lord? How can I thank You for suffering for me? Here in the garden was the beginning of Your final sorrow. You had always and only done what You saw the Father doing. Now You saw what He was about to do—and You agonized over it. Though You had never sinned, the Father was about to place the sins of all humankind squarely on Your shoulders. You saw the wrath of God toward sin and the hatred of the people toward You, the sinless One. Yet You persevered. You trusted. You obeyed. Out of love for the Father and for me, You once again did what You saw Your Father doing. While Your friends slept and Your enemies schemed, You submitted to the will of the Father and knowingly, deliberately surrendered Yourself to death. Though I will live forever, I will never be able to thank You enough. (Jn 5:19; 2Co 5:21; Php 2:8)

From heav'n You came, helpless Babe,
Entered our world, Your glory
veiled;
Not to be served, but to serve,
And give Your life that we might
live.

There in the garden of tears,
My heavy load He chose to bear;
His heart with sorrow was torn,
"Yet not My will, but Yours," He
said.

Come, see His hands and His feet,
The scars that speak of sacrifice;
Hands that flung stars into space,
To cruel nails surrendered.

This is our God, the Servant King,
He calls us now to follow Him
To bring our lives as a daily offering
Of worship to the Servant King.

"The Servant King"
Graham Kendrick (©1983)

and in three days will build another, not made by man.' " 59Yet even then their testimony did not agree.

60Then the high priest stood up before them and asked Jesus, "Are you not going to answer? What is this testimony that these men are bringing against you?" 61But Jesus remained silent and gave no answer.

Again the high priest asked him, "Are you the Christ,[a] the Son of the Blessed One?"

62"I am," said Jesus. "And you will see the Son of Man sitting at the right hand of the Mighty One and coming on the clouds of heaven."

63The high priest tore his clothes. "Why do we need any more witnesses?" he asked. 64"You have heard the blasphemy. What do you think?"

They all condemned him as worthy of death. 65Then some began to spit at him; they blindfolded him, struck him with their fists, and said, "Prophesy!" And the guards took him and beat him.

Peter Disowns Jesus

66While Peter was below in the courtyard, one of the servant girls of the high priest came by. 67When she saw Peter warming himself, she looked closely at him.

"You also were with that Nazarene, Jesus," she said.

68But he denied it. "I don't know or understand what you're talking about," he said, and went out into the entryway.[b]

69When the servant girl saw him there, she said again to those standing around, "This fellow is one of them." 70Again he denied it.

After a little while, those standing near said to Peter, "Surely you are one of them, for you are a Galilean."

71He began to call down curses on himself, and he swore to them, "I don't know this man you're talking about."

72Immediately the rooster crowed the second time.[c] Then Peter remembered the word Jesus had spoken to him: "Before the rooster crows twice[d] you will disown me three times." And he broke down and wept.

Jesus Before Pilate

15 Very early in the morning, the chief priests, with the elders, the teachers of the law and the whole Sanhedrin, reached a decision. They bound Jesus, led him away and handed him over to Pilate.

2"Are you the king of the Jews?" asked Pilate.

"Yes, it is as you say," Jesus replied.

3The chief priests accused him of many things. 4So again Pilate asked him, "Aren't you going to answer? See how many things they are accusing you of."

5But Jesus still made no reply, and Pilate was amazed.

6Now it was the custom at the Feast to release a prisoner whom the people requested. 7A man called Barabbas was in prison with the insurrectionists who had committed murder in the uprising. 8The crowd came up and asked Pilate to do for them what he usually did.

[a] *61* Or *Messiah* [b] *68* Some early manuscripts *entryway and the rooster crowed*
[c] *72* Some early manuscripts do not have *the second time.* [d] *72* Some early manuscripts do not have *twice.*

(15:2–5) "He was oppressed and afflicted, yet he did not open his mouth; he was led like a lamb to the slaughter, and as a sheep before her shearers is silent, so he did not open his mouth." To fulfill this prophecy, to obey the Father, to save the lost, You practiced what You had preached on the mountain and never answered Your accusers. When You were called on to defend Yourself, You gave only Your name and rank, as it were, and said no more. Lord, if I suffer for doing good, give me the courage to live by Your example—to not retaliate, to make no threats, but to entrust myself to the One Who judges fairly. (Isa 53:7; Mt 5:11–12; 1Pe 2:20–23)

O Jesus Christ, the mirror of all gentleness of mind, the example of highest obedience and patience, grant us your servants with true devotion to consider how you, innocent and undefiled Lamb, were bound, taken, and hailed away to death for our sins; how well content you were to suffer such things, not opening your mouth in impatience, but willingly offering yourself unto death. O gracious God, how vilely were you mishandled for our sakes!

Miles Coverdale (c.1488–1569)

[9]"Do you want me to release to you the king of the Jews?" asked Pilate, [10]knowing it was out of envy that the chief priests had handed Jesus over to him. [11]But the chief priests stirred up the crowd to have Pilate release Barabbas instead.

[12]"What shall I do, then, with the one you call the king of the Jews?" Pilate asked them.

[13]"Crucify him!" they shouted.

[14]"Why? What crime has he committed?" asked Pilate.

But they shouted all the louder, "Crucify him!"

[15]Wanting to satisfy the crowd, Pilate released Barabbas to them. He had Jesus flogged, and handed him over to be crucified.

The Soldiers Mock Jesus

[16]The soldiers led Jesus away into the palace (that is, the Praetorium) and called together the whole company of soldiers. [17]They put a purple robe on him, then twisted together a crown of thorns and set it on him. [18]And they began to call out to him, "Hail, king of the Jews!" [19]Again and again they struck him on the head with a staff and spit on him. Falling on their knees, they paid homage to him. [20]And when they had mocked him, they took off the purple robe and put his own clothes on him. Then they led him out to crucify him.

The Crucifixion

[21]A certain man from Cyrene, Simon, the father of Alexander and Rufus, was passing by on his way in from the country, and they forced him to carry the cross. [22]They brought Jesus to the place called Golgotha (which means The Place of the Skull). [23]Then they offered him wine mixed with myrrh, but he did not take it. [24]And they crucified him. Dividing up his clothes, they cast lots to see what each would get.

[25]It was the third hour when they crucified him. [26]The written notice of the charge against him read: THE KING OF THE JEWS. [27]They crucified two robbers with him, one on his right and one on his left.[a] [29]Those who passed by hurled insults at him, shaking their heads and saying, "So! You who are going to destroy the temple and build it in three days, [30]come down from the cross and save yourself!"

[31]In the same way the chief priests and the teachers of the law mocked him among themselves. "He saved others," they said, "but he can't save himself! [32]Let this Christ,[b] this King of Israel, come down now from the cross, that we may see and believe." Those crucified with him also heaped insults on him.

The Death of Jesus

[33]At the sixth hour darkness came over the whole land until the ninth hour. [34]And at the ninth hour Jesus cried out in a loud voice, *"Eloi, Eloi, lama sabachthani?"*—which means, "My God, my God, why have you forsaken me?"[c]

[35]When some of those standing near heard this, they said, "Listen, he's calling Elijah."

[36]One man ran, filled a sponge with wine vinegar, put it on a stick, and offered it to Jesus to drink. "Now leave him alone. Let's see if Elijah comes to take him down," he said.

[37]With a loud cry, Jesus breathed his last.

[a] *27* Some manuscripts *left,* [28]*and the scripture was fulfilled which says, "He was counted with the lawless ones"* (Isaiah 53:12) [b] *32* Or *Messiah* [c] *34* Psalm 22:1

(15:16–20) Lord Jesus, I see Your horror of the cross—the spittle, the lash, the thorns, the spikes and the spear. And much more: the sicknesses and the unspeakable sins of a polluted world heaped upon You bodily—a foul, enveloping blackness. Most unbearable of all, rejection by the Father. I know that You could have walked away and left us all in our sins. But You did not. Courageous, obedient Son, wonderful Lord, I give You eternal thanksgiving, everlasting honor and undying allegiance. (Ps 22:1,6–8,12–18; Isa 53; Mk 14:36)

(15:25–37) Finally, Your blood flowed. The heavens watched it and mourned. The earth received it and convulsed with its power. Surely this was, and is, the blood of the Son of God. That same blood has shaken my world, too. Jesus, Your darkness and death have released me from my own. And because of what followed, I know with certainty that after tribulation comes glory, after darkness comes eternal light and after death comes everlasting life. O Jesus, my Lord and Savior, I will give You my love and praise forever, in this world and the next. (Am 8:9; Mt 27:51–52; Lk 23:44)

Well might the sun in darkness hide
And shut his glories in,
When Christ, the great Redeemer, died
For man the creature's sin.

Thus might I hide my blushing face
While His dear cross appears,
Dissolve my heart in thankfulness,
And melt mine eyes to tears.

Alas! and Did My Savior Bleed
Isaac Watts (1707)

38 The curtain of the temple was torn in two from top to bottom. 39 And when the centurion, who stood there in front of Jesus,
heard his cry and[a] saw how he died, he said, "Surely this man
was the Son[b] of God!"

40 Some women were watching from a distance. Among them
were Mary Magdalene, Mary the mother of James the younger and
of Joses, and Salome. 41 In Galilee these women had followed him
and cared for his needs. Many other women who had come up
with him to Jerusalem were also there.

The Burial of Jesus

42 It was Preparation Day (that is, the day before the Sabbath).
So as evening approached, 43 Joseph of Arimathea, a prominent
member of the Council, who was himself waiting for the kingdom
of God, went boldly to Pilate and asked for Jesus' body. 44 Pilate
was surprised to hear that he was already dead. Summoning the
centurion, he asked him if Jesus had already died. 45 When he
learned from the centurion that it was so, he gave the body to Joseph. 46 So Joseph bought some linen cloth, took down the body,
wrapped it in the linen, and placed it in a tomb cut out of rock.
Then he rolled a stone against the entrance of the tomb. 47 Mary
Magdalene and Mary the mother of Joses saw where he was laid.

The Resurrection

16 When the Sabbath was over, Mary Magdalene, Mary the
mother of James, and Salome bought spices so that they
might go to anoint Jesus' body. 2 Very early on the first day of the
week, just after sunrise, they were on their way to the tomb 3 and
they asked each other, "Who will roll the stone away from the entrance of the tomb?"

4 But when they looked up, they saw that the stone, which was
very large, had been rolled away. 5 As they entered the tomb, they
saw a young man dressed in a white robe sitting on the right side,
and they were alarmed.

6 "Don't be alarmed," he said. "You are looking for Jesus the
Nazarene, who was crucified. He has risen! He is not here. See the
place where they laid him. 7 But go, tell his disciples and Peter,
'He is going ahead of you into Galilee. There you will see him, just
as he told you.' "

8 Trembling and bewildered, the women went out and fled from
the tomb. They said nothing to anyone, because they were afraid.

[The earliest manuscripts and some other ancient witnesses
do not have Mark 16:9–20.]

9 When Jesus rose early on the first day of the week, he appeared first to Mary Magdalene, out of whom he had driven seven
demons. 10 She went and told those who had been with him and
who were mourning and weeping. 11 When they heard that Jesus
was alive and that she had seen him, they did not believe it.

12 Afterward Jesus appeared in a different form to two of them
while they were walking in the country. 13 These returned and reported it to the rest; but they did not believe them either.

[a] 39 Some manuscripts do not have *heard his cry and* [b] 39 Or *a son*

(15:38) Jesus, I praise You for Your work of suffering, for I see what You accomplished. At the moment of Your death the temple veil that once kept me from the presence of Your Father was ripped apart. The veil was ripped not from the bottom to the top—not by human hands trying to break in to His presence—but ripped from top to bottom by the hands of God. He Himself opened the Holy of Holies, the heart of His heart, to every human being who will ever desire a relationship with Him. Through You, Lord Jesus, we can now "approach the throne of grace with confidence, so that we may receive mercy and find grace to help us in our time of need." (Ex 26:31–33; Heb 4:16)

(16:1–10) Resurrection! The other side of the cross. The most astounding event in the history of the universe. It changed everything forever. It became the crossroads of life and death for us all, our place of eternal decision. Because You rose from the dead, Jesus, and because You live now, I know that the promise of redemption and of eternal life is true. You are the Son of God. You are Messiah, Redeemer, King—and my Lord forever.

Lord, I lift Your name on high;
Lord, I love to sing Your praises.
I'm so glad You're in my life;
I'm so glad You came to save us.

You came from heaven to earth
To show the way,
From the earth to the cross
My debt to pay;
From the cross to the grave,
From the grave to the sky;
Lord, I lift Your name on high.

"Lord, I Lift Your Name on High"
Rick Founds (©1989)

14Later Jesus appeared to the Eleven as they were eating; he rebuked them for their lack of faith and their stubborn refusal to
believe those who had seen him after he had risen.
15He said to them, "Go into all the world and preach the good
news to all creation. 16Whoever believes and is baptized will be
saved, but whoever does not believe will be condemned. 17And
these signs will accompany those who believe: In my name they
will drive out demons; they will speak in new tongues; 18they will
pick up snakes with their hands; and when they drink deadly poison, it will not hurt them at all; they will place their hands on sick
people, and they will get well."
19After the Lord Jesus had spoken to them, he was taken up
into heaven and he sat at the right hand of God. 20Then the disciples went out and preached everywhere, and the Lord worked
with them and confirmed his word by the signs that accompanied it.

Jesus departed from our sight that he might return to our heart. He departed, and behold, he is here.

Saint Augustine of Hippo (354-430)

(16:15–20) O Lord! Fill us again to the brim! Let Your Spirit manifest Your life and gifts freely through Your people. May the world see Your light and power alive and moving in us. Fill our mouths with truth and praise. Use us, Lord God, to preach the Good News to all creation, to bless the earth with the blessing we have received from You. Amen.

Go ye therefore to every nation,
Preach the Gospel in every land.
To every language and every people,
In My name reach out your hand.

Tell the world the message,
Take it everywhere
To every tribe and nation
We are called to share.

Go ye therefore to every neighbor,
Share My love with every man.
The world will know that you are
Mine
If in My name you reach out your
hand.

"Tell the World"
Marsha Skidmore (©1994)

The Gospel according to LUKE

The Gospel of Luke overflows with the worship of God. From the spontaneous praise of Mary and Zechariah in the first chapter to the final words of the Gospel ("praising God," 24:53), Luke inspires us to join our voices with the worshipers who have gone before us. Like them, we glorify God because of His saving work in history, and especially through His Son, Jesus Christ. Thus, we echo Mary in her song of joy: "My soul glorifies the Lord and my spirit rejoices in God my Savior . . . His mercy extends to those who fear him" (1:46, 50). We blend our voices with Zechariah's as he proclaims: "Praise be to the Lord, the God of Israel, because he has come and has redeemed his people" (1:68). And we join the chorus of angels as they sing: "Glory to God in the highest, and on earth peace to men on whom his favor rests" (2:14).

More than any other Gospel, Luke shows how God's gracious work motivates us to praise God. We are like the shepherds who, after having seen the baby Jesus, "returned, glorifying and praising God for all the things they had heard and seen" (2:20). We empathize with the paralyzed man who, after having received healing at the word of Jesus, went home "praising God" (5:25). We stand in awe with the centurion who, having witnessed the death of Jesus, "praised God" (23:47).

Although worship is our response to God, it is not merely a human activity. The Spirit of God empowers us to worship.

Although Luke certainly understands Jesus to be the Son of God and therefore worthy of worship, he records the worship of Jesus in only one verse (24:52, after the ascension). Luke focuses our attention instead upon the worship of God the Father. Even Jesus exemplifies such devotion: "At that time Jesus, full of joy through the Holy Spirit, said, 'I praise you, Father, Lord of heaven and earth, because you have hidden these things from the wise and learned, and revealed them to little children' " (10:21).

This example highlights two other major emphases in the Gospel of Luke. Jesus praises His Father when He is "full of joy through the Holy Spirit." Luke portrays worship as joyful. Besides Jesus, Mary "rejoices" in God her Savior (1:47), the crowds begin "joyfully to praise God in loud voices" as Jesus enters Jerusalem on Palm Sunday (19:37), and the disciples celebrate the ascension of Jesus "with great joy" (24:52). Christians rejoice in worship because we have received God's salvation in Jesus. Gladness is the appropriate reaction to the angelic gospel: "I bring you good news of great joy that will be for all the people" (2:10). Luke impels us to worship with joyful exuberance.

The example of Jesus also connects worship with the Holy Spirit. Jesus joins others in Luke who praise God as they are moved by the Spirit (1:67–68; 2:27–28). Although worship is our response to God, it is not merely a human activity. The Spirit of God empowers us to worship, reminding us of God's saving work, pouring out God's amazing grace upon us and filling our hearts with praise and adoration.

Introduction

1 Many have undertaken to draw up an account of the things
that have been fulfilled[a] among us, **2**just as they were handed
down to us by those who from the first were eyewitnesses and
servants of the word. **3**Therefore, since I myself have carefully investigated everything from the beginning, it seemed good also to
me to write an orderly account for you, most excellent Theophilus, **4**so that you may know the certainty of the things you have
been taught.

The Birth of John the Baptist Foretold

5In the time of Herod king of Judea there was a priest named
Zechariah, who belonged to the priestly division of Abijah; his
wife Elizabeth was also a descendant of Aaron. **6**Both of them
were upright in the sight of God, observing all the Lord's commandments and regulations blamelessly. **7**But they had no children, because Elizabeth was barren; and they were both well
along in years.

8Once when Zechariah's division was on duty and he was serving as priest before God, **9**he was chosen by lot, according to the
custom of the priesthood, to go into the temple of the Lord and
burn incense. **10**And when the time for the burning of incense
came, all the assembled worshipers were praying outside.

11Then an angel of the Lord appeared to him, standing at the
right side of the altar of incense. **12**When Zechariah saw him, he
was startled and was gripped with fear. **13**But the angel said to
him: "Do not be afraid, Zechariah; your prayer has been heard.
Your wife Elizabeth will bear you a son, and you are to give him
the name John. **14**He will be a joy and delight to you, and many
will rejoice because of his birth, **15**for he will be great in the sight
of the Lord. He is never to take wine or other fermented drink,
and he will be filled with the Holy Spirit even from birth.[b] **16**Many
of the people of Israel will he bring back to the Lord their God.
17And he will go on before the Lord, in the spirit and power of
Elijah, to turn the hearts of the fathers to their children and the
disobedient to the wisdom of the righteous—to make ready a
people prepared for the Lord."

18Zechariah asked the angel, "How can I be sure of this? I am
an old man and my wife is well along in years."

19The angel answered, "I am Gabriel. I stand in the presence
of God, and I have been sent to speak to you and to tell you this
good news. **20**And now you will be silent and not able to speak
until the day this happens, because you did not believe my words,
which will come true at their proper time."

21Meanwhile, the people were waiting for Zechariah and wondering why he stayed so long in the temple. **22**When he came out,
he could not speak to them. They realized he had seen a vision in
the temple, for he kept making signs to them but remained unable to speak.

23When his time of service was completed, he returned home.
24After this his wife Elizabeth became pregnant and for five
months remained in seclusion. **25**"The Lord has done this for
me," she said. "In these days he has shown his favor and taken
away my disgrace among the people."

[a] 1 Or *been surely believed* [b] 15 Or *from his mother's womb*

It is good to praise the Lord.
It is good to gaze upon His majesty;
To proclaim His love in the morning,
And His faithfulness at night.
Oh, it is good to worship
And praise the Lord.

"It Is Good To Praise The Lord"
Lenny LeBlanc (©1989)

(1:11–13) Thank You, Father, for Your faithfulness to hear and answer my prayers. Even when my life seems fruitless and my case seems hopeless, Your ear is tuned to my cry. In Your time, Sovereign Lord, You will act according to Your good pleasure. Help me to wait, to trust and to receive with faith and thanksgiving Your words of assurance: "Your prayer has been heard."

The Birth of Jesus Foretold

26 In the sixth month, God sent the angel Gabriel to Nazareth, a
town in Galilee, 27 to a virgin pledged to be married to a man
named Joseph, a descendant of David. The virgin's name was
Mary. 28 The angel went to her and said, "Greetings, you who are
highly favored! The Lord is with you."
29 Mary was greatly troubled at his words and wondered what
kind of greeting this might be. 30 But the angel said to her, "Do
not be afraid, Mary, you have found favor with God. 31 You will be
with child and give birth to a son, and you are to give him the
name Jesus. 32 He will be great and will be called the Son of the
Most High. The Lord God will give him the throne of his father
David, 33 and he will reign over the house of Jacob forever; his
kingdom will never end."
34 "How will this be," Mary asked the angel, "since I am a virgin?"
35 The angel answered, "The Holy Spirit will come upon you,
and the power of the Most High will overshadow you. So the holy
one to be born will be called[a] the Son of God. 36 Even Elizabeth
your relative is going to have a child in her old age, and she who
was said to be barren is in her sixth month. 37 For nothing is impossible with God."
38 "I am the Lord's servant," Mary answered. "May it be to me
as you have said." Then the angel left her.

(1:38) Your plan of redemption was advanced when one simple peasant girl said yes to You—a yes that would change the world. There was no complicated ritual, nor advanced theological training involved. Just the trusting words, "I am the Lord's servant. May it be to me as you have said." Lord, may it be the same in my life. Help me to cooperate with Your plan for the world by saying yes to You. Even now, I say yes to You, Holy Spirit. Come upon me so that the life of Christ may be manifested through me to the needy world around me.

Mary Visits Elizabeth

39 At that time Mary got ready and hurried to a town in the hill
country of Judea, 40 where she entered Zechariah's home and
greeted Elizabeth. 41 When Elizabeth heard Mary's greeting, the
baby leaped in her womb, and Elizabeth was filled with the Holy
Spirit. 42 In a loud voice she exclaimed: "Blessed are you among
women, and blessed is the child you will bear! 43 But why am I so
favored, that the mother of my Lord should come to me? 44 As
soon as the sound of your greeting reached my ears, the baby in
my womb leaped for joy. 45 Blessed is she who has believed that
what the Lord has said to her will be accomplished!"

Mary's Song

46 And Mary said:

"My soul glorifies the Lord
47 and my spirit rejoices in God my Savior,
48 for he has been mindful
of the humble state of his servant.
From now on all generations will call me blessed,
49 for the Mighty One has done great things for me—
holy is his name.
50 His mercy extends to those who fear him,
from generation to generation.
51 He has performed mighty deeds with his arm;
he has scattered those who are proud in their
inmost thoughts.
52 He has brought down rulers from their thrones
but has lifted up the humble.
53 He has filled the hungry with good things
but has sent the rich away empty.

Christ, by highest heaven adored,
Christ, the everlasting Lord!
Late in time behold Him come,
Offspring of the virgin's womb.
Veiled in flesh the God-head see;
Hail the incarnate Deity,
Pleased as man with men to dwell,
Jesus, our Emmanuel.
Hark! The herald angels sing,
"Glory to the newborn King!"
"Hark! The Herald Angels Sing"
Charles Wesley (1739)

[a] 35 Or *So the child to be born will be called holy,*

54 He has helped his servant Israel,
remembering to be merciful
55 to Abraham and his descendants forever,
even as he said to our fathers."

56 Mary stayed with Elizabeth for about three months and then
returned home.

The Birth of John the Baptist

57 When it was time for Elizabeth to have her baby, she gave
birth to a son. 58 Her neighbors and relatives heard that the Lord
had shown her great mercy, and they shared her joy.
59 On the eighth day they came to circumcise the child, and
they were going to name him after his father Zechariah, 60 but his
mother spoke up and said, "No! He is to be called John."
61 They said to her, "There is no one among your relatives who
has that name."
62 Then they made signs to his father, to find out what he would
like to name the child. 63 He asked for a writing tablet, and to
everyone's astonishment he wrote, "His name is John." 64 Immediately his mouth was opened and his tongue was loosed, and he
began to speak, praising God. 65 The neighbors were all filled with
awe, and throughout the hill country of Judea people were talking about all these things. 66 Everyone who heard this wondered
about it, asking, "What then is this child going to be?" For the
Lord's hand was with him.

Zechariah's Song

67 His father Zechariah was filled with the Holy Spirit and
prophesied:

68 "Praise be to the Lord, the God of Israel,
because he has come and has redeemed his
people.
69 He has raised up a horn[a] of salvation for us
in the house of his servant David
70 (as he said through his holy prophets of long ago),
71 salvation from our enemies
and from the hand of all who hate us—
72 to show mercy to our fathers
and to remember his holy covenant,
73 the oath he swore to our father Abraham:
74 to rescue us from the hand of our enemies,
and to enable us to serve him without fear
75 in holiness and righteousness before him all our
days.

76 And you, my child, will be called a prophet of the
Most High;
for you will go on before the Lord to prepare the
way for him,
77 to give his people the knowledge of salvation
through the forgiveness of their sins,
78 because of the tender mercy of our God,
by which the rising sun will come to us from
heaven

[a] 69 *Horn* here symbolizes strength.

(1:68–79) We praise You, O God, that You sent Your Son Jesus to save us. You do not deliver us into the hands of the enemy when we sin; rather, You make a way to restore us into relationship with Yourself. You do not abandon us even though we stray from You; instead, You rescue us, redeem us, forgive us and guide our feet into the path of peace. (2Sa 14:14; Lk 15:20; Jn 3:17)

Join all the glorious names
Of wisdom, love, and power,
That ever mortals knew,
That angels ever bore:
All are too poor to speak His worth,
Too poor to set my Savior forth.

"Join All the Glorious Names"
Isaac Watts (1707)

(2:6–20) Lord, I cannot comprehend that You, the Creator of the universe, took on flesh and were born of a peasant girl. You, the One who spoke galaxies into existence, became a speechless newborn baby. You, the One who gave the stars their light, veiled Your own glory and slipped unnoticed into the human race. You, the One who clothed all of nature in its boundless beauty and order, came to us wrapped in rags and lying in a feeding trough. The miracle of Your incarnation is all too unexpected, too mysterious, too holy for me to understand. I can only follow the shepherds to the manger and bow in astonishment and thanksgiving, glorifying and praising You for all that I have heard and seen. (Jn 1:14)

Let all mortal flesh keep silence,
And with fear and trembling stand;
Ponder nothing worldly minded,
For with blessing in His hand
Christ our God to earth descendeth,
Our full homage to demand.

King of kings, yet born of Mary,
As of old on earth He stood,
Lord of lords in human vesture,
In the body and the blood,
He will give to all the faithful
His own self for heavenly food.

"Let All Mortal Flesh Keep Silence"
Liturgy of St. James (4th c.)
Trans. Gerard Moultrie (1829-1885)

We want our Father to step out of the impersonal picture and meet us as a person. The human heart is personal and wants a personal response . . .

"Why do we need a personal God?" someone asks. Well, suppose you go to a child crying for its mother and say, "Don't cry, little child: I'm giving to you the principle of motherhood." Would the tears dry and the face light up? Hardly. The child would brush aside your principle of motherhood and cry for its mother. We all want, not a principle nor a picture, but a person.

The Father has stepped out of the picture. The Word has become flesh. That is the meaning of Christmas. Jesus is Immanuel—God with us.

E. Stanley Jones (1884-1973)

79 to shine on those living in darkness
and in the shadow of death,
to guide our feet into the path of peace."

80 And the child grew and became strong in spirit; and he lived in the desert until he appeared publicly to Israel.

The Birth of Jesus

2 In those days Caesar Augustus issued a decree that a census
should be taken of the entire Roman world. 2 (This was the
first census that took place while Quirinius was governor of
Syria.) 3 And everyone went to his own town to register.
4 So Joseph also went up from the town of Nazareth in Galilee
to Judea, to Bethlehem the town of David, because he belonged to
the house and line of David. 5 He went there to register with Mary,
who was pledged to be married to him and was expecting a child.
6 While they were there, the time came for the baby to be born,
7 and she gave birth to her firstborn, a son. She wrapped him in
cloths and placed him in a manger, because there was no room
for them in the inn.

The Shepherds and the Angels

8 And there were shepherds living out in the fields nearby,
keeping watch over their flocks at night. 9 An angel of the Lord appeared to them, and the glory of the Lord shone around them,
and they were terrified. 10 But the angel said to them, "Do not be
afraid. I bring you good news of great joy that will be for all the
people. 11 Today in the town of David a Savior has been born to
you; he is Christ[a] the Lord. 12 This will be a sign to you: You will
find a baby wrapped in cloths and lying in a manger."
13 Suddenly a great company of the heavenly host appeared
with the angel, praising God and saying,

14 "Glory to God in the highest,
and on earth peace to men on whom his favor
rests."

15 When the angels had left them and gone into heaven, the
shepherds said to one another, "Let's go to Bethlehem and see
this thing that has happened, which the Lord has told us about."
16 So they hurried off and found Mary and Joseph, and the baby,
who was lying in the manger. 17 When they had seen him, they
spread the word concerning what had been told them about this
child, 18 and all who heard it were amazed at what the shepherds
said to them. 19 But Mary treasured up all these things and pondered them in her heart. 20 The shepherds returned, glorifying
and praising God for all the things they had heard and seen,
which were just as they had been told.

Jesus Presented in the Temple

21 On the eighth day, when it was time to circumcise him, he
was named Jesus, the name the angel had given him before he
had been conceived.
22 When the time of their purification according to the Law of
Moses had been completed, Joseph and Mary took him to Jerusalem to present him to the Lord 23 (as it is written in the Law of the

[a] *11* Or *Messiah.* "The Christ" (Greek) and "the Messiah" (Hebrew) both mean "the Anointed One"; also in verse 26.

Lord, "Every firstborn male is to be consecrated to the Lord"[a]),
24and to offer a sacrifice in keeping with what is said in the Law
of the Lord: "a pair of doves or two young pigeons."[b]
25Now there was a man in Jerusalem called Simeon, who was
righteous and devout. He was waiting for the consolation of Israel, and the Holy Spirit was upon him. 26It had been revealed to
him by the Holy Spirit that he would not die before he had seen
the Lord's Christ. 27Moved by the Spirit, he went into the temple
courts. When the parents brought in the child Jesus to do for him
what the custom of the Law required, 28Simeon took him in his
arms and praised God, saying:

29"Sovereign Lord, as you have promised,
you now dismiss[c] your servant in peace.
30For my eyes have seen your salvation,
31 which you have prepared in the sight of all people,
32a light for revelation to the Gentiles
and for glory to your people Israel."

33The child's father and mother marveled at what was said
about him. 34Then Simeon blessed them and said to Mary, his
mother: "This child is destined to cause the falling and rising of
many in Israel, and to be a sign that will be spoken against, 35so
that the thoughts of many hearts will be revealed. And a sword
will pierce your own soul too."
36There was also a prophetess, Anna, the daughter of Phanuel,
of the tribe of Asher. She was very old; she had lived with her husband seven years after her marriage, 37and then was a widow
until she was eighty-four.[d] She never left the temple but worshiped night and day, fasting and praying. 38Coming up to them at
that very moment, she gave thanks to God and spoke about the
child to all who were looking forward to the redemption of Jerusalem.
39When Joseph and Mary had done everything required by the
Law of the Lord, they returned to Galilee to their own town of Nazareth. 40And the child grew and became strong; he was filled with
wisdom, and the grace of God was upon him.

The Boy Jesus at the Temple

41Every year his parents went to Jerusalem for the Feast of the
Passover. 42When he was twelve years old, they went up to the
Feast, according to the custom. 43After the Feast was over, while
his parents were returning home, the boy Jesus stayed behind in
Jerusalem, but they were unaware of it. 44Thinking he was in
their company, they traveled on for a day. Then they began looking for him among their relatives and friends. 45When they did
not find him, they went back to Jerusalem to look for him. 46After
three days they found him in the temple courts, sitting among the
teachers, listening to them and asking them questions. 47Every-
one who heard him was amazed at his understanding and his answers. 48When his parents saw him, they were astonished. His
mother said to him, "Son, why have you treated us like this? Your
father and I have been anxiously searching for you."
49"Why were you searching for me?" he asked. "Didn't you
know I had to be in my Father's house?" 50But they did not understand what he was saying to them.

[a]23 Exodus 13:2,12 [b]24 Lev. 12:8 [c]29 Or *promised, / now dismiss*
[d]37 Or *widow for eighty-four years*

(2:25–32) Thank You for fulfilling the desire of Simeon's heart—not only did he see You, but he held You in his arms. And I thank You, Lord, that what Simeon waited a lifetime to see has been revealed for all who will open their eyes. You are the light of the world. You are the hope of salvation for all who believe. (Jn 8:12; Ac 13:47)

Men overlooked a baby's birth
When love unnoticed came to earth;
And later, seeking in the skies,
Passed by a man in workman's guise.
Only children paused to stare
While God Incarnate made a chair.
Mary Tatlow

Come, Thou long expected Jesus,
Born to set Thy people free;
From our fears and sins release us;
Let us find our rest in Thee.

Israel's strength and consolation,
Hope of all the earth Thou art;
Dear Desire of every nation,
Joy of every longing heart.
"Come, Thou Long Expected Jesus"
Charles Wesley (1744)

(3:3–18) Thank You, Lord, for the ministry of John the Baptist. His message still lifts the downtrodden, humbles the proud and convicts the sinful. Today, as I hear his words again, may they prepare the way for Your presence in my life. Come, Lord Jesus. Find a home in my heart. Give me spiritual integrity so that the fruit of my life will match the words of my mouth. Help me to follow You in the way You have prepared for those who love You. And I pray, Lord, that You will use me, as You used John, to prepare the way for You in the hearts of others. (Ps 25:21; Pr 11:3; Jer 32:39; 1Co 2:9; Tit 2:7)

Prepare ye the way for the Lord,
Make a highway straight for our God.
Prepare ye the way for the Lord,
Every valley raised up
And mountain made low,
Let's all make a way for the Lord.

And His glory will shine,
It will be shown to all mankind.
And we shall behold
Our Savior come with His reward.
Prepare ye the way,
Make a way for the Lord.

"Prepare Ye the Way"
Tommy Walker (©1997)

51Then he went down to Nazareth with them and was obedient
to them. But his mother treasured all these things in her heart.
52And Jesus grew in wisdom and stature, and in favor with God
and men.

John the Baptist Prepares the Way

3 In the fifteenth year of the reign of Tiberius Caesar—when
Pontius Pilate was governor of Judea, Herod tetrarch of Galilee, his brother Philip tetrarch of Iturea and Traconitis, and Lysanias tetrarch of Abilene— 2during the high priesthood of
Annas and Caiaphas, the word of God came to John son of
Zechariah in the desert. 3He went into all the country around the
Jordan, preaching a baptism of repentance for the forgiveness
of sins. 4As is written in the book of the words of Isaiah the
prophet:

"A voice of one calling in the desert,
'Prepare the way for the Lord,
make straight paths for him.
5Every valley shall be filled in,
every mountain and hill made low.
The crooked roads shall become straight,
the rough ways smooth.
6And all mankind will see God's salvation.' "[a]

7John said to the crowds coming out to be baptized by him,
"You brood of vipers! Who warned you to flee from the coming
wrath? 8Produce fruit in keeping with repentance. And do not
begin to say to yourselves, 'We have Abraham as our father.' For
I tell you that out of these stones God can raise up children for
Abraham. 9The ax is already at the root of the trees, and every
tree that does not produce good fruit will be cut down and
thrown into the fire."

10"What should we do then?" the crowd asked.

11John answered, "The man with two tunics should share with
him who has none, and the one who has food should do the
same."

12Tax collectors also came to be baptized. "Teacher," they
asked, "what should we do?"

13"Don't collect any more than you are required to," he told
them.

14Then some soldiers asked him, "And what should we do?"
He replied, "Don't extort money and don't accuse people falsely—be content with your pay."

15The people were waiting expectantly and were all wondering in their hearts if John might possibly be the Christ.[b] 16John
answered them all, "I baptize you with[c] water. But one more
powerful than I will come, the thongs of whose sandals I am not
worthy to untie. He will baptize you with the Holy Spirit and with
fire. 17His winnowing fork is in his hand to clear his threshing
floor and to gather the wheat into his barn, but he will burn up
the chaff with unquenchable fire." 18And with many other words
John exhorted the people and preached the good news to them.
19But when John rebuked Herod the tetrarch because of Herodias, his brother's wife, and all the other evil things he had done,
20Herod added this to them all: He locked John up in prison.

[a] *6* Isaiah 40:3–5 [b] *15* Or *Messiah* [c] *16* Or *in*

The Baptism and Genealogy of Jesus

21When all the people were being baptized, Jesus was baptized
too. And as he was praying, heaven was opened 22and the Holy
Spirit descended on him in bodily form like a dove. And a voice
came from heaven: "You are my Son, whom I love; with you I am
well pleased."

23Now Jesus himself was about thirty years old when he began
his ministry. He was the son, so it was thought, of Joseph,

the son of Heli, 24the son of Matthat,
the son of Levi, the son of Melki,
the son of Jannai, the son of Joseph,
25 the son of Mattathias, the son of Amos,
the son of Nahum, the son of Esli,
the son of Naggai, 26the son of Maath,
the son of Mattathias, the son of Semein,
the son of Josech, the son of Joda,
27 the son of Joanan, the son of Rhesa,
the son of Zerubbabel, the son of Shealtiel,
the son of Neri, 28the son of Melki,
the son of Addi, the son of Cosam,
the son of Elmadam, the son of Er,
29 the son of Joshua, the son of Eliezer,
the son of Jorim, the son of Matthat,
the son of Levi, 30the son of Simeon,
the son of Judah, the son of Joseph,
the son of Jonam, the son of Eliakim,
31 the son of Melea, the son of Menna,
the son of Mattatha, the son of Nathan,
the son of David, 32the son of Jesse,
the son of Obed, the son of Boaz,
the son of Salmon,[a] the son of Nahshon,
33 the son of Amminadab, the son of Ram,[b]
the son of Hezron, the son of Perez,
the son of Judah, 34the son of Jacob,
the son of Isaac, the son of Abraham,
the son of Terah, the son of Nahor,
35 the son of Serug, the son of Reu,
the son of Peleg, the son of Eber,
the son of Shelah, 36the son of Cainan,
the son of Arphaxad, the son of Shem,
the son of Noah, the son of Lamech,
37 the son of Methuselah, the son of Enoch,
the son of Jared, the son of Mahalalel,
the son of Kenan, 38the son of Enosh,
the son of Seth, the son of Adam,
the son of God.

The Temptation of Jesus

4 Jesus, full of the Holy Spirit, returned from the Jordan and
was led by the Spirit in the desert, 2where for forty days he
was tempted by the devil. He ate nothing during those days, and
at the end of them he was hungry.

3The devil said to him, "If you are the Son of God, tell this
stone to become bread."

[a] 32 Some early manuscripts *Sala* [b] 33 Some manuscripts *Amminadab, the son of Admin, the son of Arni*; other manuscripts vary widely.

(3:21–22) Heavenly Father, thank You for first identifying Jesus as Your Son, not as Your servant. There were as yet no grand accomplishments in His life, just simple obedience. May the foundation of my own relationship with You—the very essence of my identity—be as Your child. As I follow Jesus into the waters of baptism, may I hear You say these words to me: "You are My child. I love you and I am proud of you." Then, out of my love for You as my Father, may I live a life of service for You as my Master.

(3:23–37) Lord, we are all the products of the many generations that have lived before us. You have promised to bless the children of the faithful. Let me so live that unborn generations will be blessed by my faithfulness. (Dt 5:10)

[4]Jesus answered, "It is written: 'Man does not live on bread
alone.'[a]"
[5]The devil led him up to a high place and showed him in an instant all the kingdoms of the world. [6]And he said to him, "I will
give you all their authority and splendor, for it has been given to
me, and I can give it to anyone I want to. [7]So if you worship me,
it will all be yours."
[8]Jesus answered, "It is written: 'Worship the Lord your God
and serve him only.'[b]"
[9]The devil led him to Jerusalem and had him stand on the
highest point of the temple. "If you are the Son of God," he said,
"throw yourself down from here. [10]For it is written:

" 'He will command his angels concerning you
to guard you carefully;
[11] they will lift you up in their hands,
so that you will not strike your foot against a
stone.'[c]"

[12]Jesus answered, "It says: 'Do not put the Lord your God to
the test.'[d]"
[13]When the devil had finished all this tempting, he left him
until an opportune time.

Jesus Rejected at Nazareth

[14]Jesus returned to Galilee in the power of the Spirit, and news
about him spread through the whole countryside. [15]He taught in
their synagogues, and everyone praised him.
[16]He went to Nazareth, where he had been brought up, and on
the Sabbath day he went into the synagogue, as was his custom.
And he stood up to read. [17]The scroll of the prophet Isaiah was
handed to him. Unrolling it, he found the place where it is written:

[18] "The Spirit of the Lord is on me,
because he has anointed me
to preach good news to the poor.
He has sent me to proclaim freedom for the
prisoners
and recovery of sight for the blind,
to release the oppressed,
[19] to proclaim the year of the Lord's favor."[e]

[20]Then he rolled up the scroll, gave it back to the attendant
and sat down. The eyes of everyone in the synagogue were fastened on him, [21]and he began by saying to them, "Today this
scripture is fulfilled in your hearing."
[22]All spoke well of him and were amazed at the gracious words
that came from his lips. "Isn't this Joseph's son?" they asked.
[23]Jesus said to them, "Surely you will quote this proverb to me:
'Physician, heal yourself! Do here in your hometown what we
have heard that you did in Capernaum.' "
[24]"I tell you the truth," he continued, "no prophet is accepted
in his hometown. [25]I assure you that there were many widows in
Israel in Elijah's time, when the sky was shut for three and a half
years and there was a severe famine throughout the land. [26]Yet
Elijah was not sent to any of them, but to a widow in Zarephath in

No matter how many pleasures Satan offers you, his ultimate intention is to ruin you. Your destruction is his highest priority.

Erwin W. Lutzer (1941-)

(4:1–13) O my Lord, how often I hear these words: "Take care of yourself; sell yourself; prove yourself." How often I face these same temptations: the lust of the flesh, the lust of the eyes, the pride of life. My faith and faithfulness are constantly under siege. So I call on Your powerful name, Lord Jesus Christ. Please fill me with the Holy Spirit and give me strength to overcome the temptation to satisfy my fleshly desires, my craving for power and my unquenchable need to prove my self-worth. (1Jn 2:16)

Lord, who throughout these forty days
For us did fast and pray,
Teach us with You to mourn our sins,
And close by You to stay.

As You with Satan did contend,
And did the victory win,
O give us strength in You to fight,
In You to conquer sin.

As You did hunger and did thirst,
So teach us, gracious Lord,
To die to self, and so to live
By Your most holy Word.

"Lord, Who Throughout"
Claudia F. Hernaman (1873)

[a] *4* Deut. 8:3 [b] *8* Deut. 6:13 [c] *11* Psalm 91:11,12 [d] *12* Deut. 6:16
[e] *19* Isaiah 61:1,2

the region of Sidon. 27And there were many in Israel with leprosy[a] in the time of Elisha the prophet, yet not one of them was
cleansed—only Naaman the Syrian."
28All the people in the synagogue were furious when they
heard this. 29They got up, drove him out of the town, and took
him to the brow of the hill on which the town was built, in order
to throw him down the cliff. 30But he walked right through the
crowd and went on his way.

Jesus Drives Out an Evil Spirit

31Then he went down to Capernaum, a town in Galilee, and on
the Sabbath began to teach the people. 32They were amazed at his
teaching, because his message had authority.
33In the synagogue there was a man possessed by a demon, an
evil[b] spirit. He cried out at the top of his voice, 34"Ha! What do
you want with us, Jesus of Nazareth? Have you come to destroy us?
I know who you are—the Holy One of God!"
35"Be quiet!" Jesus said sternly. "Come out of him!" Then the
demon threw the man down before them all and came out without injuring him.
36All the people were amazed and said to each other, "What is
this teaching? With authority and power he gives orders to evil
spirits and they come out!" 37And the news about him spread
throughout the surrounding area.

Jesus Heals Many

38Jesus left the synagogue and went to the home of Simon. Now
Simon's mother-in-law was suffering from a high fever, and they
asked Jesus to help her. 39So he bent over her and rebuked the
fever, and it left her. She got up at once and began to wait on them.
40When the sun was setting, the people brought to Jesus all
who had various kinds of sickness, and laying his hands on each
one, he healed them. 41Moreover, demons came out of many people, shouting, "You are the Son of God!" But he rebuked them
and would not allow them to speak, because they knew he was
the Christ.[c]
42At daybreak Jesus went out to a solitary place. The people
were looking for him and when they came to where he was, they
tried to keep him from leaving them. 43But he said, "I must
preach the good news of the kingdom of God to the other towns
also, because that is why I was sent." 44And he kept on preaching
in the synagogues of Judea.[d]

The Calling of the First Disciples

5 One day as Jesus was standing by the Lake of Gennesaret,[e]
with the people crowding around him and listening to the
word of God, 2he saw at the water's edge two boats, left there by
the fishermen, who were washing their nets. 3He got into one of
the boats, the one belonging to Simon, and asked him to put out
a little from shore. Then he sat down and taught the people from
the boat.
4When he had finished speaking, he said to Simon, "Put out
into deep water, and let down[f] the nets for a catch."

[a] 27 The Greek word was used for various diseases affecting the skin—not necessarily leprosy. [b] 33 Greek *unclean*; also in verse 36 [c] 41 Or *Messiah* [d] 44 Or *the land of the Jews*; some manuscripts *Galilee* [e] 1 That is, Sea of Galilee [f] 4 The Greek verb is plural.

(4:36–37) Jesus, let my service to You be marked by the authority of Your Spirit. Let me so live that Your power in and through me can heal, help and liberate others.

Thanks to God whose Word
Incarnate
Heights and depths of life did share;
Deeds and words and death and
rising,
Grace in human form declare.
God has spoken:
Praise to God for His open Word.

"Thanks to God Whose Word Was Spoken"
R.T. Brooks (©1954, 1982)

(5:1–11) Lord, don't let me miss Your call. I know there must be so much more to life than the daily grind. Isn't there something I can do for You? Surely there are still lives to be gathered in Your net of salvation. Take me out to the deep waters, Lord, and teach me to fish for souls.

(5:15–16) God, I see throughout the Gospels that Your beloved Son needed time alone to communicate with You. He resisted the demands of the crowds and the pressure to perform, choosing instead to seek Your face. How much more do I need to be with You! Help me to commit the times of my days to Your Lordship, seeking the strength and wisdom that I can only receive in Your presence.

Remember who your ruler is. Don't forget his daily briefing.

Carl F. H. Henry (1913-)

(5:20) Jesus, You healed a man not because of his faith but because of the faith of his friends. May my own faith be so strong that my friends and all those within the circle of my concern will be blessed through my prayers. (Ge 19:29)

5Simon answered, "Master, we've worked hard all night and
haven't caught anything. But because you say so, I will let down
the nets."
6When they had done so, they caught such a large number of
fish that their nets began to break. 7So they signaled their partners in the other boat to come and help them, and they came and
filled both boats so full that they began to sink.
8When Simon Peter saw this, he fell at Jesus' knees and said,
"Go away from me, Lord; I am a sinful man!" 9For he and all his
companions were astonished at the catch of fish they had taken,
10and so were James and John, the sons of Zebedee, Simon's
partners.

Then Jesus said to Simon, "Don't be afraid; from now on you
will catch men." 11So they pulled their boats up on shore, left
everything and followed him.

The Man With Leprosy

12While Jesus was in one of the towns, a man came along who
was covered with leprosy.[a] When he saw Jesus, he fell with his
face to the ground and begged him, "Lord, if you are willing, you
can make me clean."
13Jesus reached out his hand and touched the man. "I am
willing," he said. "Be clean!" And immediately the leprosy left
him.
14Then Jesus ordered him, "Don't tell anyone, but go, show
yourself to the priest and offer the sacrifices that Moses commanded for your cleansing, as a testimony to them."
15Yet the news about him spread all the more, so that crowds
of people came to hear him and to be healed of their sicknesses.
16But Jesus often withdrew to lonely places and prayed.

Jesus Heals a Paralytic

17One day as he was teaching, Pharisees and teachers of the
law, who had come from every village of Galilee and from Judea
and Jerusalem, were sitting there. And the power of the Lord was
present for him to heal the sick. 18Some men came carrying a
paralytic on a mat and tried to take him into the house to lay him
before Jesus. 19When they could not find a way to do this because
of the crowd, they went up on the roof and lowered him on his
mat through the tiles into the middle of the crowd, right in front
of Jesus.
20When Jesus saw their faith, he said, "Friend, your sins are
forgiven."
21The Pharisees and the teachers of the law began thinking to
themselves, "Who is this fellow who speaks blasphemy? Who can
forgive sins but God alone?"
22Jesus knew what they were thinking and asked, "Why are
you thinking these things in your hearts? 23Which is easier: to
say, 'Your sins are forgiven,' or to say, 'Get up and walk'? 24But
that you may know that the Son of Man has authority on earth to
forgive sins . . ." He said to the paralyzed man, "I tell you, get up,
take your mat and go home." 25Immediately he stood up in front
of them, took what he had been lying on and went home praising God. 26Everyone was amazed and gave praise to God. They

[a] *12* The Greek word was used for various diseases affecting the skin—not necessarily leprosy.

were filled with awe and said, "We have seen remarkable things
today."

The Calling of Levi

27After this, Jesus went out and saw a tax collector by the name
of Levi sitting at his tax booth. "Follow me," Jesus said to him,
28and Levi got up, left everything and followed him.
29Then Levi held a great banquet for Jesus at his house, and a
large crowd of tax collectors and others were eating with them.
30But the Pharisees and the teachers of the law who belonged to
their sect complained to his disciples, "Why do you eat and drink
with tax collectors and 'sinners'?"
31Jesus answered them, "It is not the healthy who need a doctor, but the sick. 32I have not come to call the righteous, but sinners to repentance."

Jesus Questioned About Fasting

33They said to him, "John's disciples often fast and pray, and so
do the disciples of the Pharisees, but yours go on eating and
drinking."
34Jesus answered, "Can you make the guests of the bridegroom fast while he is with them? 35But the time will come when
the bridegroom will be taken from them; in those days they will
fast."
36He told them this parable: "No one tears a patch from a new
garment and sews it on an old one. If he does, he will have torn
the new garment, and the patch from the new will not match the
old. 37And no one pours new wine into old wineskins. If he does,
the new wine will burst the skins, the wine will run out and the
wineskins will be ruined. 38No, new wine must be poured into
new wineskins. 39And no one after drinking old wine wants the
new, for he says, 'The old is better.'"

Lord of the Sabbath

6 One Sabbath Jesus was going through the grainfields, and
his disciples began to pick some heads of grain, rub them in
their hands and eat the kernels. 2Some of the Pharisees asked,
"Why are you doing what is unlawful on the Sabbath?"
3Jesus answered them, "Have you never read what David did
when he and his companions were hungry? 4He entered the
house of God, and taking the consecrated bread, he ate what is
lawful only for priests to eat. And he also gave some to his companions." 5Then Jesus said to them, "The Son of Man is Lord of
the Sabbath."
6On another Sabbath he went into the synagogue and was
teaching, and a man was there whose right hand was shriveled.
7The Pharisees and the teachers of the law were looking for a
reason to accuse Jesus, so they watched him closely to see if he
would heal on the Sabbath. 8But Jesus knew what they were
thinking and said to the man with the shriveled hand, "Get up and
stand in front of everyone." So he got up and stood there.
9Then Jesus said to them, "I ask you, which is lawful on the
Sabbath: to do good or to do evil, to save life or to destroy it?"
10He looked around at them all, and then said to the man,
"Stretch out your hand." He did so, and his hand was completely
restored. 11But they were furious and began to discuss with one
another what they might do to Jesus.

I stand amazed in the presence
Of Jesus the Nazarene,
And wonder how He could love me,
A sinner, condemned, unclean.

How marvelous, how wonderful!
And my song shall ever be:
How marvelous, how wonderful
Is my Savior's love for me!

"My Savior's Love"
Charles H. Gabriel (1905)

(5:30) O Lord, You were so often accused of associating with the wrong people. Help me to understand that there are no "wrong" people. Everyone I meet matters to You and therefore must be treated with love and respect. This is the wonder of Your grace: that You reach out to those with the worst reputations—those who need You the most—and call them to follow You. Place Your compassion in my heart for all who cross my path, so that I may see them through Your eyes and speak Your words of grace to them.

(6:20–26) Lord Jesus, when we are poor and hungry, when we weep and are hated by others, help us to see that we have not been abandoned by You; rather, You are preparing us to receive eternal blessings. Help us not to overlook the spiritual when we are overwhelmed by the physical. Teach us to follow in Your footsteps—footsteps that lead us to the Father—knowing that as we walk in Your ways the Father is perfecting us, tending and nurturing our faith, and working out all things for His good purposes. (Ro 8:28; Heb 12:7–12)

Come unto Me if you are heavy laden.
My yoke is easy and my burden is light.
If you follow Me, you will not be forsaken.
I'll never leave you alone in the night.

Blessed are the poor in spirit,
Theirs is My kingdom.
Blessed are the meek,
For they shall rule all the earth.
And blessed are the merciful
For they shall know My mercy;
And blessed are the pure in heart,
For they shall see the Lord.

Blessed Are They
Lenny LeBlanc (©1990)

To the poor in spirit the Kingdom of Heaven is assigned as a present recompense, for theirs is the Kingdom of Heaven.

Alphonsus Liguori (1696-1787)

The Twelve Apostles

12 One of those days Jesus went out to a mountainside to pray,
and spent the night praying to God. 13 When morning came, he
called his disciples to him and chose twelve of them, whom he
also designated apostles: 14 Simon (whom he named Peter), his
brother Andrew, James, John, Philip, Bartholomew, 15 Matthew,
Thomas, James son of Alphaeus, Simon who was called the
Zealot, 16 Judas son of James, and Judas Iscariot, who became a
traitor.

Blessings and Woes

17 He went down with them and stood on a level place. A large
crowd of his disciples was there and a great number of people
from all over Judea, from Jerusalem, and from the coast of Tyre
and Sidon, 18 who had come to hear him and to be healed of their
diseases. Those troubled by evil[a] spirits were cured, 19 and the
people all tried to touch him, because power was coming from
him and healing them all.
20 Looking at his disciples, he said:

"Blessed are you who are poor,
for yours is the kingdom of God.
21 Blessed are you who hunger now,
for you will be satisfied.
Blessed are you who weep now,
for you will laugh.
22 Blessed are you when men hate you,
when they exclude you and insult you
and reject your name as evil,
because of the Son of Man.

23 "Rejoice in that day and leap for joy, because great is your
reward in heaven. For that is how their fathers treated the
prophets.

24 "But woe to you who are rich,
for you have already received your comfort.
25 Woe to you who are well fed now,
for you will go hungry.
Woe to you who laugh now,
for you will mourn and weep.
26 Woe to you when all men speak well of you,
for that is how their fathers treated the false
prophets.

Love for Enemies

27 "But I tell you who hear me: Love your enemies, do good to
those who hate you, 28 bless those who curse you, pray for those
who mistreat you. 29 If someone strikes you on one cheek, turn
to him the other also. If someone takes your cloak, do not stop
him from taking your tunic. 30 Give to everyone who asks you,
and if anyone takes what belongs to you, do not demand it back.
31 Do to others as you would have them do to you.
32 "If you love those who love you, what credit is that to you?
Even 'sinners' love those who love them. 33 And if you do good to
those who are good to you, what credit is that to you? Even 'sinners' do that. 34 And if you lend to those from whom you expect

[a] 18 Greek *unclean*

MY BELOVED

I love a cheerful giver. So give generously to your brother who is in need, and do so without a grudging heart. Then because of this I will abundantly bless you in all your work and in everything you put your hand to.

When you give freely you show My heart to others. When you give freely, it means you are better able to handle all that I want to give you. So know that I see everything that you give.

Why do I care so much about whether you are a cheerful giver? Because it shows Me what you love the most. You have seen people who do not know how to give but instead try to hold on to everything. They are always left wanting. If they would learn to give, they would discover a life of plenty. For a generous person will prosper; I will refresh the one who refreshes others.

But when you give, do not give in anticipation of something in return or because you want to impress others. Instead, give with a cheerful attitude, and when possible, do it in secret. When you give freely, you will discover the joy-filled life of a cheerful giver. Remember that I am the One who makes it possible for you to be generous; so when you give it is only right that your generosity will cause others to give thanks to Me. I am a giver; you be a giver too.

Dt 15:7-11; Ps 37:21; Pr 11:24-25; Mt 6:2-4; Lk 6:38; 12:33-34; 2Co 9:6-8,10-11

repayment, what credit is that to you? Even 'sinners' lend to 'sinners,' expecting to be repaid in full. 35But love your enemies, do good to them, and lend to them without expecting to get anything back. Then your reward will be great, and you will be sons of the Most High, because he is kind to the ungrateful and wicked. 36Be merciful, just as your Father is merciful.

Judging Others

37"Do not judge, and you will not be judged. Do not condemn, and you will not be condemned. Forgive, and you will be forgiven. 38Give, and it will be given to you. A good measure, pressed down, shaken together and running over, will be poured into your lap. For with the measure you use, it will be measured to you."

39He also told them this parable: "Can a blind man lead a blind man? Will they not both fall into a pit? 40A student is not above his teacher, but everyone who is fully trained will be like his teacher.

41"Why do you look at the speck of sawdust in your brother's eye and pay no attention to the plank in your own eye? 42How can you say to your brother, 'Brother, let me take the speck out of your eye,' when you yourself fail to see the plank in your own eye? You hypocrite, first take the plank out of your eye, and then you will see clearly to remove the speck from your brother's eye.

A Tree and Its Fruit

43"No good tree bears bad fruit, nor does a bad tree bear good fruit. 44Each tree is recognized by its own fruit. People do not pick figs from thornbushes, or grapes from briers. 45The good man brings good things out of the good stored up in his heart, and the evil man brings evil things out of the evil stored up in his heart. For out of the overflow of his heart his mouth speaks.

The Wise and Foolish Builders

46"Why do you call me, 'Lord, Lord,' and do not do what I say? 47I will show you what he is like who comes to me and hears my words and puts them into practice. 48He is like a man building a house, who dug down deep and laid the foundation on rock. When a flood came, the torrent struck that house but could not shake it, because it was well built. 49But the one who hears my words and does not put them into practice is like a man who built a house on the ground without a foundation. The moment the torrent struck that house, it collapsed and its destruction was complete."

The Faith of the Centurion

7 When Jesus had finished saying all this in the hearing of the people, he entered Capernaum. 2There a centurion's servant, whom his master valued highly, was sick and about to die. 3The centurion heard of Jesus and sent some elders of the Jews to him, asking him to come and heal his servant. 4When they came to Jesus, they pleaded earnestly with him, "This man deserves to have you do this, 5because he loves our nation and has built our synagogue." 6So Jesus went with them.

He was not far from the house when the centurion sent friends

Love ever gives,
Forgives, outlives,
And ever stands
With open hands.
And while it lives,
It gives.
For this is love's prerogative–
O give, and give, and give.

John Oxenham (1861-1941)

(6:35–36) This is Your love, O God. You are merciful and kind to all people. You provide even for those who are ungrateful. And it is to this kind of love that You have called me. But I cannot love this way without Your help. I can do this only because I have received mercy and forgiveness from You. By the power of Your Spirit, extend Your grace through me so that I can offer Your mercy and forgiveness to others.

(6:41–42) Father God, I confess that I am quick to see the faults in my brother and slow to recognize, let alone admit, my own weaknesses. I judge others by their worst actions while judging myself by my best intentions. Help me to see myself as You see me, and help me to see other people through Your eyes.

(7:13–15) Gracious Lord, into the most hopeless situations You bring hope and healing. You are indeed the God of life. You see my despair, Your heart is moved and You come to me with comfort and help. You turn my sadness into joy and my mourning into dancing. But Lord, what about the times when children die, when prayers seem to go unanswered, when hope is snuffed out by pain? Sometimes I just do not understand how or why things happen. I can only ask, Lord, that You bring me reassurance of Your care. Give me strength to cling to You. Give me faith to believe that You love me. Give me grace to carry on, trusting that You are at work even in the darkest hour of my life. (Ps 30:11)

Does Jesus care when my heart is
pained
Too deeply for mirth and song;
As the burdens press and the cares
distress,
And the way grows weary and long?

O yes, He cares; I know He cares,
His heart is touched with my grief;
When the days are weary,
The long nights dreary,
I know my Savior cares.

"Does Jesus Care?"
Frank E. Graeff (1901)

If you should temporarily lose your sense of well-being, don't be too quick to despair. With humility and patience, wait for God who is able to give you back even more comfort. There is nothing novel about this to those who are familiar with God's ways. The great saints and ancient prophets frequently experienced the alternation of up and down, joy and sorrow.

Thomas à Kempis (c.1380–1471)

to say to him: "Lord, don't trouble yourself, for I do not deserve
to have you come under my roof.
7 That is why I did not even
consider myself worthy to come to you. But say the word, and my
servant will be healed.
8 For I myself am a man under authority,
with soldiers under me. I tell this one, 'Go,' and he goes; and
that one, 'Come,' and he comes. I say to my servant, 'Do this,'
and he does it."

9 When Jesus heard this, he was amazed at him, and turning to
the crowd following him, he said, "I tell you, I have not found
such great faith even in Israel."
10 Then the men who had been
sent returned to the house and found the servant well.

Jesus Raises a Widow's Son

11 Soon afterward, Jesus went to a town called Nain, and his
disciples and a large crowd went along with him.
12 As he approached the town gate, a dead person was being carried out—
the only son of his mother, and she was a widow. And a large
crowd from the town was with her.
13 When the Lord saw her, his
heart went out to her and he said, "Don't cry."

14 Then he went up and touched the coffin, and those carrying
it stood still. He said, "Young man, I say to you, get up!"
15 The
dead man sat up and began to talk, and Jesus gave him back to
his mother.

16 They were all filled with awe and praised God. "A great
prophet has appeared among us," they said. "God has come to
help his people."
17 This news about Jesus spread throughout
Judea[a] and the surrounding country.

Jesus and John the Baptist

18 John's disciples told him about all these things. Calling two of
them,
19 he sent them to the Lord to ask, "Are you the one who
was to come, or should we expect someone else?"

20 When the men came to Jesus, they said, "John the Baptist
sent us to you to ask, 'Are you the one who was to come, or
should we expect someone else?' "

21 At that very time Jesus cured many who had diseases, sicknesses and evil spirits, and gave sight to many who were blind.
22 So he replied to the messengers, "Go back and report to John
what you have seen and heard: The blind receive sight, the lame
walk, those who have leprosy[b] are cured, the deaf hear, the dead
are raised, and the good news is preached to the poor.
23 Blessed
is the man who does not fall away on account of me."

24 After John's messengers left, Jesus began to speak to the
crowd about John: "What did you go out into the desert to see? A
reed swayed by the wind?
25 If not, what did you go out to see? A
man dressed in fine clothes? No, those who wear expensive
clothes and indulge in luxury are in palaces.
26 But what did you
go out to see? A prophet? Yes, I tell you, and more than a prophet.
27 This is the one about whom it is written:

" 'I will send my messenger ahead of you,
who will prepare your way before you.'[c]

28 I tell you, among those born of women there is no one greater
than John; yet the one who is least in the kingdom of God is
greater than he."

[a] 17 Or *the land of the Jews* [b] 22 The Greek word was used for various diseases affecting the skin—not necessarily leprosy. [c] 27 Mal. 3:1

29(All the people, even the tax collectors, when they heard
Jesus' words, acknowledged that God's way was right, because
they had been baptized by John. 30But the Pharisees and experts
in the law rejected God's purpose for themselves, because they
had not been baptized by John.)

31"To what, then, can I compare the people of this generation?
What are they like? 32They are like children sitting in the marketplace and calling out to each other:

" 'We played the flute for you,
and you did not dance;
we sang a dirge,
and you did not cry.'

33For John the Baptist came neither eating bread nor drinking
wine, and you say, 'He has a demon.' 34The Son of Man came eating and drinking, and you say, 'Here is a glutton and a drunkard,
a friend of tax collectors and "sinners." ' 35But wisdom is proved
right by all her children."

Jesus Anointed by a Sinful Woman

36Now one of the Pharisees invited Jesus to have dinner with
him, so he went to the Pharisee's house and reclined at the
table. 37When a woman who had lived a sinful life in that town
learned that Jesus was eating at the Pharisee's house, she
brought an alabaster jar of perfume, 38and as she stood behind
him at his feet weeping, she began to wet his feet with her tears.
Then she wiped them with her hair, kissed them and poured
perfume on them.

39When the Pharisee who had invited him saw this, he said to
himself, "If this man were a prophet, he would know who is
touching him and what kind of woman she is—that she is a sinner."

40Jesus answered him, "Simon, I have something to tell you."

"Tell me, teacher," he said.

41"Two men owed money to a certain moneylender. One owed
him five hundred denarii,[a] and the other fifty. 42Neither of them
had the money to pay him back, so he canceled the debts of both.
Now which of them will love him more?"

43Simon replied, "I suppose the one who had the bigger debt
canceled."

"You have judged correctly," Jesus said.

44Then he turned toward the woman and said to Simon, "Do
you see this woman? I came into your house. You did not give me
any water for my feet, but she wet my feet with her tears and
wiped them with her hair. 45You did not give me a kiss, but this
woman, from the time I entered, has not stopped kissing my feet.
46You did not put oil on my head, but she has poured perfume on
my feet. 47Therefore, I tell you, her many sins have been forgiv-
en—for she loved much. But he who has been forgiven little loves
little."

48Then Jesus said to her, "Your sins are forgiven."

49The other guests began to say among themselves, "Who is
this who even forgives sins?"

50Jesus said to the woman, "Your faith has saved you; go in
peace."

[a] *41* A denarius was a coin worth about a day's wages.

(7:44–47) Lord Jesus, You did not come for people who insist they are good but for people who know they are not. Deliver me from self-righteousness. Forgive me for being too stubborn to repent, too proud to fall at Your feet. Help me to remember the depths from which You saved me. Help me to remember that I am not worthy of Your grace. May I never be a stumbling block for anyone who is reaching out for You. And God forbid that I should ever chase off the ones You came to save.

Wonderful grace of Jesus,
Reaching the most defiled,
By its transforming power
Making me God's dear child,
Purchasing peace and heaven
For all eternity
And the wonderful grace of Jesus
Reaches me.

"Wonderful Grace of Jesus"
Haldor Lillenas (1918)

The Parable of the Sower

8 After this, Jesus traveled about from one town and village to
another, proclaiming the good news of the kingdom of God.
The Twelve were with him, 2and also some women who had been
cured of evil spirits and diseases: Mary (called Magdalene) from
whom seven demons had come out; 3Joanna the wife of Cuza,
the manager of Herod's household; Susanna; and many others.
These women were helping to support them out of their own
means.

4While a large crowd was gathering and people were coming
to Jesus from town after town, he told this parable: 5"A farmer
went out to sow his seed. As he was scattering the seed, some fell
along the path; it was trampled on, and the birds of the air ate it
up. 6Some fell on rock, and when it came up, the plants withered
because they had no moisture. 7Other seed fell among thorns,
which grew up with it and choked the plants. 8Still other seed fell
on good soil. It came up and yielded a crop, a hundred times
more than was sown."

When he said this, he called out, "He who has ears to hear, let
him hear."

9His disciples asked him what this parable meant. 10He said,
"The knowledge of the secrets of the kingdom of God has been
given to you, but to others I speak in parables, so that,

" 'though seeing, they may not see;
though hearing, they may not understand.'[a]

11"This is the meaning of the parable: The seed is the word of
God. 12Those along the path are the ones who hear, and then
the devil comes and takes away the word from their hearts, so
that they may not believe and be saved. 13Those on the rock are
the ones who receive the word with joy when they hear it, but
they have no root. They believe for a while, but in the time of
testing they fall away. 14The seed that fell among thorns stands
for those who hear, but as they go on their way they are choked
by life's worries, riches and pleasures, and they do not mature.
15But the seed on good soil stands for those with a noble and
good heart, who hear the word, retain it, and by persevering
produce a crop.

A Lamp on a Stand

16"No one lights a lamp and hides it in a jar or puts it under a
bed. Instead, he puts it on a stand, so that those who come in can
see the light. 17For there is nothing hidden that will not be disclosed, and nothing concealed that will not be known or brought
out into the open. 18Therefore consider carefully how you listen.
Whoever has will be given more; whoever does not have, even
what he thinks he has will be taken from him."

Jesus' Mother and Brothers

19Now Jesus' mother and brothers came to see him, but they
were not able to get near him because of the crowd. 20Someone
told him, "Your mother and brothers are standing outside, wanting to see you."
21He replied, "My mother and brothers are those who hear
God's word and put it into practice."

[a] *10* Isaiah 6:9

(8:11–15) What is the condition of my heart today, Lord? Am I too busy to slow down long enough to listen? Is my heart hardened toward You? Are there weeds of worry or worldliness that are choking out Your Word of life? Plow the soil of my heart, Lord. Break up the worn, hard places. Root out the weeds that compete with the seed of Your Word. May I be fertile ground that bears a rich harvest for Your kingdom. (Eze 33:31–32; Jas 1:22–25)

He's the Lord of every season,
He's the master of all time.
And He's come to sow His seeds in
This field of humankind.
The eternal Word of heaven
Is among us in this place.
And if you have ears to listen,
You can hear Him call your name.

He's calling out your name,
He's calling out your name.
If you have ears to listen,
He's calling out your name.

"He's Calling Out Your Name"
Bob Somma, Phil Kristianson and
Bill Batstone (©1996)

(8:16–18) Thank You, Father, for the dazzling presence of Your Son, Whose life is the light of the world. As He lives in me, let His glory shine through my eyes, His love through my face, His grace through the works of my hands. Dispel my inner darkness and make me a beacon for the lost, illuminating their way to You. Ignite me with His fire, Lord, and keep my lamp burning ever brighter until He comes again. (Jn 1:4)

Jesus Calms the Storm

22One day Jesus said to his disciples, "Let's go over to the other
side of the lake." So they got into a boat and set out. 23As they
sailed, he fell asleep. A squall came down on the lake, so that the
boat was being swamped, and they were in great danger.
24The disciples went and woke him, saying, "Master, Master,
we're going to drown!"
He got up and rebuked the wind and the raging waters; the
storm subsided, and all was calm. 25"Where is your faith?" he
asked his disciples.
In fear and amazement they asked one another, "Who is this?
He commands even the winds and the water, and they obey him."

The Healing of a Demon-possessed Man

26They sailed to the region of the Gerasenes,[a] which is across
the lake from Galilee. 27When Jesus stepped ashore, he was met
by a demon-possessed man from the town. For a long time this
man had not worn clothes or lived in a house, but had lived in the
tombs. 28When he saw Jesus, he cried out and fell at his feet,
shouting at the top of his voice, "What do you want with me,
Jesus, Son of the Most High God? I beg you, don't torture me!"
29For Jesus had commanded the evil[b] spirit to come out of the
man. Many times it had seized him, and though he was chained
hand and foot and kept under guard, he had broken his chains
and had been driven by the demon into solitary places.
30Jesus asked him, "What is your name?"
"Legion," he replied, because many demons had gone into
him. 31And they begged him repeatedly not to order them to go
into the Abyss.
32A large herd of pigs was feeding there on the hillside. The
demons begged Jesus to let them go into them, and he gave them
permission. 33When the demons came out of the man, they went
into the pigs, and the herd rushed down the steep bank into the
lake and was drowned.
34When those tending the pigs saw what had happened, they
ran off and reported this in the town and countryside, 35and the
people went out to see what had happened. When they came to
Jesus, they found the man from whom the demons had gone out,
sitting at Jesus' feet, dressed and in his right mind; and they were
afraid. 36Those who had seen it told the people how the demon-
possessed man had been cured. 37Then all the people of the region of the Gerasenes asked Jesus to leave them, because they
were overcome with fear. So he got into the boat and left.
38The man from whom the demons had gone out begged to go
with him, but Jesus sent him away, saying, 39"Return home and
tell how much God has done for you." So the man went away and
told all over town how much Jesus had done for him.

A Dead Girl and a Sick Woman

40Now when Jesus returned, a crowd welcomed him, for they
were all expecting him. 41Then a man named Jairus, a ruler of the
synagogue, came and fell at Jesus' feet, pleading with him to
come to his house 42because his only daughter, a girl of about
twelve, was dying.

[a] 26 Some manuscripts *Gadarenes*; other manuscripts *Gergesenes*; also in verse 37
[b] 29 Greek *unclean*

(8:22–25) Jesus, we have all been battered by the wind and waves on the sea of life. Hard things can indeed happen to good people—even to those in ministry—even when they are obeying You—even when You are present. Your disciples were not protected from the storms of life and neither are we. But we are grateful to know that You are in the boat with us, that no situation is hopeless and that You are ever in command.

Jesus, Savior, pilot me
Over life's tempestuous sea;
Unknown waves before me roll,
Hiding rock and treach'rous shoal;
Chart and compass came from Thee:
Jesus, Savior, pilot me.

"Jesus, Savior, Pilot Me"
Edward Hopper (1871)

(8:35–38) Thank You, Lord, for this miracle of redemption and health and sanity. The same Voice that calmed the storm at sea now calmed the storm in this poor man's soul. He was under Your authority now. He had been set free in his spirit and transformed by the renewing of his mind. Thank You for the redemption You bring to each of our lives. Like this man may I be found sitting at Your feet, healed and clothed in Your righteousness, longing to tell everyone I meet how good You have been to me. (Isa 61:10)

(8:43–46) Lord, I know this woman. I too have felt the heartache of facing a hopeless situation and wondered what I had done to deserve it. I too have thought, "If I can somehow reach out and touch You, everything will be fine." But my shame has kept me from approaching You face-to-face. Still, You always know I am there. You feel my desperate reach of faith, and Your virtue flows to meet me. Thank You, Lord, for not allowing the frenzy of the world to crowd out my need for You. Thank You for caring enough to stop and turn and call me out from the crowd, and for affirming my faith in spite of my fears.

(9:1–2) Lord, help me to live with the same holy boldness that You gave to Your first 12 disciples. Your power and authority to heal and liberate others and to preach the Good News is as available to me as it was to them; so as You once commissioned them I now ask You to commission me. Fill me with Your Spirit so that I can do Your works and bring new disciples into Your kingdom.

As Jesus was on his way, the crowds almost crushed him. [43]And
a woman was there who had been subject to bleeding for twelve
years,[a] but no one could heal her. [44]She came up behind him
and touched the edge of his cloak, and immediately her bleeding
stopped.

[45]"Who touched me?" Jesus asked.

When they all denied it, Peter said, "Master, the people are
crowding and pressing against you."

[46]But Jesus said, "Someone touched me; I know that power
has gone out from me."

[47]Then the woman, seeing that she could not go unnoticed,
came trembling and fell at his feet. In the presence of all the people, she told why she had touched him and how she had been instantly healed. [48]Then he said to her, "Daughter, your faith has
healed you. Go in peace."

[49]While Jesus was still speaking, someone came from the
house of Jairus, the synagogue ruler. "Your daughter is dead," he
said. "Don't bother the teacher any more."

[50]Hearing this, Jesus said to Jairus, "Don't be afraid; just believe, and she will be healed."

[51]When he arrived at the house of Jairus, he did not let anyone
go in with him except Peter, John and James, and the child's father and mother. [52]Meanwhile, all the people were wailing and
mourning for her. "Stop wailing," Jesus said. "She is not dead but
asleep."

[53]They laughed at him, knowing that she was dead. [54]But he
took her by the hand and said, "My child, get up!" [55]Her spirit returned, and at once she stood up. Then Jesus told them to give
her something to eat. [56]Her parents were astonished, but he ordered them not to tell anyone what had happened.

Jesus Sends Out the Twelve

9 When Jesus had called the Twelve together, he gave them
power and authority to drive out all demons and to cure diseases, [2]and he sent them out to preach the kingdom of God and
to heal the sick. [3]He told them: "Take nothing for the journey—
no staff, no bag, no bread, no money, no extra tunic. [4]Whatever
house you enter, stay there until you leave that town. [5]If people do
not welcome you, shake the dust off your feet when you leave
their town, as a testimony against them." [6]So they set out and
went from village to village, preaching the gospel and healing
people everywhere.

[7]Now Herod the tetrarch heard about all that was going on.
And he was perplexed, because some were saying that John had
been raised from the dead, [8]others that Elijah had appeared, and
still others that one of the prophets of long ago had come back to
life. [9]But Herod said, "I beheaded John. Who, then, is this I hear
such things about?" And he tried to see him.

Jesus Feeds the Five Thousand

[10]When the apostles returned, they reported to Jesus what they
had done. Then he took them with him and they withdrew by
themselves to a town called Bethsaida, [11]but the crowds learned
about it and followed him. He welcomed them and spoke to them
about the kingdom of God, and healed those who needed healing.

[a] 43 Many manuscripts *years, and she had spent all she had on doctors*

12Late in the afternoon the Twelve came to him and said, "Send
the crowd away so they can go to the surrounding villages and
countryside and find food and lodging, because we are in a remote place here."
13He replied, "You give them something to eat."
They answered, "We have only five loaves of bread and two
fish—unless we go and buy food for all this crowd." 14(About
five thousand men were there.)
But he said to his disciples, "Have them sit down in groups of
about fifty each." 15The disciples did so, and everybody sat down.
16Taking the five loaves and the two fish and looking up to heav-
en, he gave thanks and broke them. Then he gave them to the disciples to set before the people. 17They all ate and were satisfied,
and the disciples picked up twelve basketfuls of broken pieces
that were left over.

Peter's Confession of Christ

18Once when Jesus was praying in private and his disciples
were with him, he asked them, "Who do the crowds say I am?"
19They replied, "Some say John the Baptist; others say Elijah;
and still others, that one of the prophets of long ago has come
back to life."
20"But what about you?" he asked. "Who do you say I am?"
Peter answered, "The Christ[a] of God."
21Jesus strictly warned them not to tell this to anyone. 22And he
said, "The Son of Man must suffer many things and be rejected by
the elders, chief priests and teachers of the law, and he must be
killed and on the third day be raised to life."
23Then he said to them all: "If anyone would come after me, he
must deny himself and take up his cross daily and follow me.
24For whoever wants to save his life will lose it, but whoever loses
his life for me will save it. 25What good is it for a man to gain the
whole world, and yet lose or forfeit his very self? 26If anyone is
ashamed of me and my words, the Son of Man will be ashamed of
him when he comes in his glory and in the glory of the Father and
of the holy angels. 27I tell you the truth, some who are standing
here will not taste death before they see the kingdom of God."

The Transfiguration

28About eight days after Jesus said this, he took Peter, John and
James with him and went up onto a mountain to pray. 29As he was
praying, the appearance of his face changed, and his clothes became as bright as a flash of lightning. 30Two men, Moses and Elijah, 31appeared in glorious splendor, talking with Jesus. They
spoke about his departure, which he was about to bring to fulfillment at Jerusalem. 32Peter and his companions were very sleepy,
but when they became fully awake, they saw his glory and the two
men standing with him. 33As the men were leaving Jesus, Peter
said to him, "Master, it is good for us to be here. Let us put up
three shelters—one for you, one for Moses and one for Elijah."
(He did not know what he was saying.)
34While he was speaking, a cloud appeared and enveloped
them, and they were afraid as they entered the cloud. 35A voice
came from the cloud, saying, "This is my Son, whom I have chosen; listen to him." 36When the voice had spoken, they found that

[a] 20 Or *Messiah*

(9:12–17) Jesus, I am so prone to suggest other resources when someone comes to me in need: "See your local pastor; talk to a counselor; visit some social agency." But then I hear Your words again: "*You* give them something to eat." Lord, give me the faith to respond with obedience to Your command. Take all that I have to offer, break it and multiply it for Your glory.

(9:20) Lord Jesus, I proclaim that You are the Christ, the Messiah, the Anointed One, the Son of the Living God. This confession is the cornerstone of my faith, the foundation of my being. I will build my life upon this rock, and the gates of hell will not defeat me.

(9:46–48) Lord, Your ways are so much greater than our ways, and Your thoughts are so much wiser than ours. True spiritual growth is downward, not upward. In Your kingdom, pride is reduced to humility, human wisdom is reduced to foolishness, and Your strength is perfected in our weakness. As we grow in our faith, make us more dependent and more childlike, full of wonder and awe and gratitude for Your limitless power, which is always at work in our lives (Isa 55:8; 1Co 1:27–29; 2Co 12:9–10)

(9:57–58) Jesus, how much we want easy discipleship. We gladly serve You as long as we are comfortable and secure. Yet in Your earthly ministry You had neither comfort nor security. Draw us out of our recliners, our hammocks and our well-upholstered church pews, Lord, and launch us into the matchless adventure of spiritual pilgrimage. Teach us that our journey can only begin when we are willing to abandon everything and wholeheartedly follow You. (Ps 84)

I have been before God; and have given myself, all that I am and have to God, so that I am not in any respect my own. I can claim no right in myself, no right in this understanding, this will, these affections that are in me; neither have I any right to this body or any of its members; no right to this tongue, these hands nor feet; no right to these senses, these ears, this smell or taste. I have given myself clear away . . . This I have done. And I pray God, for the sake of Christ, to look upon it as a self-dedication; and to receive me now as entirely His own, and deal with me in all respects as such; whether he afflicts me or prospers me, or whatever He pleases to do with me, who am His.

Jonathan Edwards (1703-1758)

Jesus was alone. The disciples kept this to themselves, and told no one at that time what they had seen.

The Healing of a Boy With an Evil Spirit

37 The next day, when they came down from the mountain, a
large crowd met him. 38 A man in the crowd called out, "Teacher,
I beg you to look at my son, for he is my only child. 39 A spirit
seizes him and he suddenly screams; it throws him into convulsions so that he foams at the mouth. It scarcely ever leaves him
and is destroying him. 40 I begged your disciples to drive it out,
but they could not."

41 "O unbelieving and perverse generation," Jesus replied, "how long shall I stay with you and put up with you? Bring your son here."

42 Even while the boy was coming, the demon threw him to the
ground in a convulsion. But Jesus rebuked the evil[a] spirit, healed
the boy and gave him back to his father. 43 And they were all
amazed at the greatness of God.

While everyone was marveling at all that Jesus did, he said to
his disciples, 44 "Listen carefully to what I am about to tell you:
The Son of Man is going to be betrayed into the hands of men."
45 But they did not understand what this meant. It was hidden
from them, so that they did not grasp it, and they were afraid to ask him about it.

Who Will Be the Greatest?

46 An argument started among the disciples as to which of them
would be the greatest. 47 Jesus, knowing their thoughts, took a little child and had him stand beside him. 48 Then he said to them,
"Whoever welcomes this little child in my name welcomes me; and whoever welcomes me welcomes the one who sent me. For he who is least among you all—he is the greatest."

49 "Master," said John, "we saw a man driving out demons in your name and we tried to stop him, because he is not one of us."

50 "Do not stop him," Jesus said, "for whoever is not against you is for you."

Samaritan Opposition

51 As the time approached for him to be taken up to heaven,
Jesus resolutely set out for Jerusalem. 52 And he sent messengers
on ahead, who went into a Samaritan village to get things ready
for him; 53 but the people there did not welcome him, because he
was heading for Jerusalem. 54 When the disciples James and John
saw this, they asked, "Lord, do you want us to call fire down from
heaven to destroy them[b]?" 55 But Jesus turned and rebuked them,
56 and[c] they went to another village.

The Cost of Following Jesus

57 As they were walking along the road, a man said to him, "I will follow you wherever you go."

58 Jesus replied, "Foxes have holes and birds of the air have nests, but the Son of Man has no place to lay his head."

59 He said to another man, "Follow me."

But the man replied, "Lord, first let me go and bury my father."

[a] 42 Greek *unclean* [b] 54 Some manuscripts *them, even as Elijah did* [c] 55,56 Some manuscripts *them. And he said, "You do not know what kind of spirit you are of, for the Son of Man did not come to destroy men's lives, but to save them."* 56 *And*

60 Jesus said to him, "Let the dead bury their own dead, but you
go and proclaim the kingdom of God."
61 Still another said, "I will follow you, Lord; but first let me go
back and say good-by to my family."
62 Jesus replied, "No one who puts his hand to the plow and
looks back is fit for service in the kingdom of God."

Jesus Sends Out the Seventy-two

10 After this the Lord appointed seventy-two[a] others and sent
them two by two ahead of him to every town and place
where he was about to go. 2 He told them, "The harvest is plentiful, but the workers are few. Ask the Lord of the harvest, therefore,
to send out workers into his harvest field. 3 Go! I am sending you
out like lambs among wolves. 4 Do not take a purse or bag or sandals; and do not greet anyone on the road.
5 "When you enter a house, first say, 'Peace to this house.' 6 If a
man of peace is there, your peace will rest on him; if not, it will
return to you. 7 Stay in that house, eating and drinking whatever
they give you, for the worker deserves his wages. Do not move
around from house to house.
8 "When you enter a town and are welcomed, eat what is set before you. 9 Heal the sick who are there and tell them, 'The kingdom of God is near you.' 10 But when you enter a town and are not
welcomed, go into its streets and say, 11 'Even the dust of your
town that sticks to our feet we wipe off against you. Yet be sure of
this: The kingdom of God is near.' 12 I tell you, it will be more
bearable on that day for Sodom than for that town.
13 "Woe to you, Korazin! Woe to you, Bethsaida! For if the miracles that were performed in you had been performed in Tyre and
Sidon, they would have repented long ago, sitting in sackcloth
and ashes. 14 But it will be more bearable for Tyre and Sidon at
the judgment than for you. 15 And you, Capernaum, will you be
lifted up to the skies? No, you will go down to the depths.[b]
16 "He who listens to you listens to me; he who rejects you rejects me; but he who rejects me rejects him who sent me."
17 The seventy-two returned with joy and said, "Lord, even the
demons submit to us in your name."
18 He replied, "I saw Satan fall like lightning from heaven. 19 I
have given you authority to trample on snakes and scorpions and
to overcome all the power of the enemy; nothing will harm you.
20 However, do not rejoice that the spirits submit to you, but rejoice that your names are written in heaven."
21 At that time Jesus, full of joy through the Holy Spirit, said, "I
praise you, Father, Lord of heaven and earth, because you have
hidden these things from the wise and learned, and revealed them
to little children. Yes, Father, for this was your good pleasure.
22 "All things have been committed to me by my Father. No one
knows who the Son is except the Father, and no one knows who
the Father is except the Son and those to whom the Son chooses
to reveal him."
23 Then he turned to his disciples and said privately, "Blessed
are the eyes that see what you see. 24 For I tell you that many
prophets and kings wanted to see what you see but did not see it,
and to hear what you hear but did not hear it."

[a] 1 Some manuscripts *seventy*; also in verse 17 [b] 15 Greek *Hades*

(10:16–17) Christ Jesus, we are humbled by the fact that You have chosen to speak and act through us. By the power of Your Holy Spirit we carry on the ministry that You began so long ago. Increase our faith, Lord, so we can act on Your behalf. Make us sensitive to Your will, so we can participate in the Father's purposes. Just as You did only what You saw the Father doing, even so, apart from You, we can do nothing. (Jn 5:19; 14:12; 15:5)

(10:27–37) God, how often we seek answers, as this man did, when we already know what the answers are. We try to justify ourselves through complicated theologies, when Your demands are so clear and so simple. Help us to love You with all our heart, soul, strength and mind and to begin to love our neighbors, despite our differences, just as we love ourselves.

Beloved, let us love one another,
For love is of God,
And everyone that loveth is born of
God,
And knoweth God.
He that loveth not, knoweth not
God,
For God is love.
Beloved, let us love one another.

"Beloved" (1 John 4:7-8)
Dennis Ryder (©1974)

(10:41–42) I thank You that You are not a harsh task master. You did not save me to make me Your slave; nor must I try somehow to "work off" my debt to You. You want me to serve You from the motivation of love rather than the obligation of duty. And love requires time alone together. Lord, help me to heed Your call to come away from the activities of the day and to sit quietly in Your presence and commune with You.

The Parable of the Good Samaritan

25 On one occasion an expert in the law stood up to test Jesus.
"Teacher," he asked, "what must I do to inherit eternal life?"
26 "What is written in the Law?" he replied. "How do you
read it?"
27 He answered: " 'Love the Lord your God with all your heart
and with all your soul and with all your strength and with all your
mind'[a]; and, 'Love your neighbor as yourself.'[b]"
28 "You have answered correctly," Jesus replied. "Do this and
you will live."
29 But he wanted to justify himself, so he asked Jesus, "And who
is my neighbor?"
30 In reply Jesus said: "A man was going down from Jerusalem
to Jericho, when he fell into the hands of robbers. They stripped
him of his clothes, beat him and went away, leaving him half dead.
31 A priest happened to be going down the same road, and when
he saw the man, he passed by on the other side. 32 So too, a Levite, when he came to the place and saw him, passed by on the
other side. 33 But a Samaritan, as he traveled, came where the
man was; and when he saw him, he took pity on him. 34 He went
to him and bandaged his wounds, pouring on oil and wine. Then
he put the man on his own donkey, took him to an inn and took
care of him. 35 The next day he took out two silver coins[c] and
gave them to the innkeeper. 'Look after him,' he said, 'and when
I return, I will reimburse you for any extra expense you may
have.'
36 "Which of these three do you think was a neighbor to the
man who fell into the hands of robbers?"
37 The expert in the law replied, "The one who had mercy on
him."
Jesus told him, "Go and do likewise."

At the Home of Martha and Mary

38 As Jesus and his disciples were on their way, he came to a village where a woman named Martha opened her home to him.
39 She had a sister called Mary, who sat at the Lord's feet listening
to what he said. 40 But Martha was distracted by all the preparations that had to be made. She came to him and asked, "Lord,
don't you care that my sister has left me to do the work by myself?
Tell her to help me!"
41 "Martha, Martha," the Lord answered, "you are worried and
upset about many things, 42 but only one thing is needed.[d] Mary
has chosen what is better, and it will not be taken away from her."

Jesus' Teaching on Prayer

11 One day Jesus was praying in a certain place. When he finished, one of his disciples said to him, "Lord, teach us to
pray, just as John taught his disciples."
2 He said to them, "When you pray, say:

" 'Father,[e]
hallowed be your name,
your kingdom come.[f]

[a] 27 Deut. 6:5 [b] 27 Lev. 19:18 [c] 35 Greek *two denarii* [d] 42 Some manuscripts *but few things are needed—or only one* [e] 2 Some manuscripts *Our Father in heaven* [f] 2 Some manuscripts *come. May your will be done on earth as it is in heaven.*

3 Give us each day our daily bread.
4 Forgive us our sins,
for we also forgive everyone who sins
against us.[a]
And lead us not into temptation.[b]' "

5 Then he said to them, "Suppose one of you has a friend, and
he goes to him at midnight and says, 'Friend, lend me three loaves
of bread, 6 because a friend of mine on a journey has come to
me, and I have nothing to set before him.'
7 "Then the one inside answers, 'Don't bother me. The door is
already locked, and my children are with me in bed. I can't get
up and give you anything.' 8 I tell you, though he will not get up
and give him the bread because he is his friend, yet because of
the man's boldness[c] he will get up and give him as much as he
needs.
9 "So I say to you: Ask and it will be given to you; seek and you
will find; knock and the door will be opened to you. 10 For everyone who asks receives; he who seeks finds; and to him who
knocks, the door will be opened.
11 "Which of you fathers, if your son asks for[d] a fish, will give
him a snake instead? 12 Or if he asks for an egg, will give him a
scorpion? 13 If you then, though you are evil, know how to give
good gifts to your children, how much more will your Father in
heaven give the Holy Spirit to those who ask him!"

Jesus and Beelzebub

14 Jesus was driving out a demon that was mute. When the
demon left, the man who had been mute spoke, and the crowd
was amazed. 15 But some of them said, "By Beelzebub,[e] the prince
of demons, he is driving out demons." 16 Others tested him by
asking for a sign from heaven.
17 Jesus knew their thoughts and said to them: "Any kingdom
divided against itself will be ruined, and a house divided against
itself will fall. 18 If Satan is divided against himself, how can his
kingdom stand? I say this because you claim that I drive out
demons by Beelzebub. 19 Now if I drive out demons by Beelzebub,
by whom do your followers drive them out? So then, they will be
your judges. 20 But if I drive out demons by the finger of God, then
the kingdom of God has come to you.
21 "When a strong man, fully armed, guards his own house, his
possessions are safe. 22 But when someone stronger attacks and
overpowers him, he takes away the armor in which the man trusted and divides up the spoils.
23 "He who is not with me is against me, and he who does not
gather with me, scatters.
24 "When an evil[f] spirit comes out of a man, it goes through
arid places seeking rest and does not find it. Then it says, 'I will
return to the house I left.' 25 When it arrives, it finds the house
swept clean and put in order. 26 Then it goes and takes seven
other spirits more wicked than itself, and they go in and live
there. And the final condition of that man is worse than the first."
27 As Jesus was saying these things, a woman in the crowd

[a] 4 Greek *everyone who is indebted to us* [b] 4 Some manuscripts *temptation but deliver us from the evil one* [c] 8 Or *persistence* [d] 11 Some manuscripts *for bread, will give him a stone; or if he asks for* [e] 15 Greek *Beezeboul* or *Beelzeboul*; also in verses 18 and 19 [f] 24 Greek *unclean*

(11:9–10) As the Sovereign God, You have the right to do whatever You want, with no regard whatsoever for our concerns or desires. But love is Your sovereign choice. You are not bothered by us; You are delighted with us. You invite us to come, to speak, to ask, to seek—and You take joy in answering our prayers. (Ps 149:4; Zep 3:17)

If man is man and God is God, to live without prayer is not merely an awful thing; it is an infinitely foolish thing.
Phillips Brooks (1835-1893)

Sweet hour of prayer,
Sweet hour of prayer,
That calls me from a world of care,
And bids me at my Father's throne
Make all my wants and wishes
known;
In seasons of distress and grief,
My soul has often found relief,
And oft escaped the tempter's snare,
By thy return, sweet hour of prayer.
"Sweet Hour of Prayer"
William W. Walford (1845)

(11:46–52) Bring purity to Your church today, Lord. Deliver us from the hypocrisy of the Pharisees. They preached a hard line; they lived a soft life. Their rules were unbearable; their lives were deplorable. They were hard-hearted, selfish and deceptive. Examine our hearts, Lord, and cleanse us from willful sins that we hide beneath the cloak of religious zeal. Break our hearts so that You can inhabit them; open our hands so that You can fill them; cleanse our lives so that You can use them.

called out, "Blessed is the mother who gave you birth and nursed you."

28He replied, "Blessed rather are those who hear the word of God and obey it."

The Sign of Jonah

29As the crowds increased, Jesus said, "This is a wicked generation. It asks for a miraculous sign, but none will be given it except the sign of Jonah.
30For as Jonah was a sign to the Ninevites,
so also will the Son of Man be to this generation. 31The Queen of
the South will rise at the judgment with the men of this generation and condemn them; for she came from the ends of the earth to listen to Solomon's wisdom, and now one[a] greater than Solomon
is here. 32The men of Nineveh will stand up at the judgment with
this generation and condemn it; for they repented at the preaching of Jonah, and now one greater than Jonah is here.

The Lamp of the Body

33"No one lights a lamp and puts it in a place where it will be hidden, or under a bowl. Instead he puts it on its stand, so that
those who come in may see the light. 34Your eye is the lamp of
your body. When your eyes are good, your whole body also is full of light. But when they are bad, your body also is full of darkness.
35See to it, then, that the light within you is not darkness.
36Therefore, if your whole body is full of light, and no part of it dark, it will be completely lighted, as when the light of a lamp shines on you."

Six Woes

37When Jesus had finished speaking, a Pharisee invited him to eat with him; so he went in and reclined at the table.
38But the Pharisee, noticing that Jesus did not first wash before the meal, was surprised.

39Then the Lord said to him, "Now then, you Pharisees clean the outside of the cup and dish, but inside you are full of greed and wickedness.
40You foolish people! Did not the one who made the outside make the inside also?
41But give what is inside ⌞the dish⌟[b] to the poor, and everything will be clean for you.

42"Woe to you Pharisees, because you give God a tenth of your mint, rue and all other kinds of garden herbs, but you neglect justice and the love of God. You should have practiced the latter without leaving the former undone.

43"Woe to you Pharisees, because you love the most important seats in the synagogues and greetings in the marketplaces.

44"Woe to you, because you are like unmarked graves, which men walk over without knowing it."

45One of the experts in the law answered him, "Teacher, when you say these things, you insult us also."

46Jesus replied, "And you experts in the law, woe to you, because you load people down with burdens they can hardly carry, and you yourselves will not lift one finger to help them.

47"Woe to you, because you build tombs for the prophets, and it was your forefathers who killed them.
48So you testify that you approve of what your forefathers did; they killed the prophets, and you build their tombs.
49Because of this, God in his wisdom

[a] 31 Or *something*; also in verse 32 [b] 41 Or *what you have*

said, 'I will send them prophets and apostles, some of whom they
will kill and others they will persecute.' 50Therefore this generation will be held responsible for the blood of all the prophets that
has been shed since the beginning of the world, 51from the blood
of Abel to the blood of Zechariah, who was killed between the
altar and the sanctuary. Yes, I tell you, this generation will be held
responsible for it all.
52"Woe to you experts in the law, because you have taken away
the key to knowledge. You yourselves have not entered, and you
have hindered those who were entering."
53When Jesus left there, the Pharisees and the teachers of the
law began to oppose him fiercely and to besiege him with questions, 54waiting to catch him in something he might say.

Warnings and Encouragements

12 Meanwhile, when a crowd of many thousands had gathered, so that they were trampling on one another, Jesus
began to speak first to his disciples, saying: "Be on your guard
against the yeast of the Pharisees, which is hypocrisy. 2There is
nothing concealed that will not be disclosed, or hidden that will
not be made known. 3What you have said in the dark will be
heard in the daylight, and what you have whispered in the ear in
the inner rooms will be proclaimed from the roofs.
4"I tell you, my friends, do not be afraid of those who kill the
body and after that can do no more. 5But I will show you whom
you should fear: Fear him who, after the killing of the body, has
power to throw you into hell. Yes, I tell you, fear him. 6Are not
five sparrows sold for two pennies[a]? Yet not one of them is forgotten by God. 7Indeed, the very hairs of your head are all numbered. Don't be afraid; you are worth more than many sparrows.
8"I tell you, whoever acknowledges me before men, the Son of
Man will also acknowledge him before the angels of God. 9But he
who disowns me before men will be disowned before the angels
of God. 10And everyone who speaks a word against the Son of
Man will be forgiven, but anyone who blasphemes against the
Holy Spirit will not be forgiven.
11"When you are brought before synagogues, rulers and authorities, do not worry about how you will defend yourselves or
what you will say, 12for the Holy Spirit will teach you at that time
what you should say."

The Parable of the Rich Fool

13Someone in the crowd said to him, "Teacher, tell my brother to divide the inheritance with me."
14Jesus replied, "Man, who appointed me a judge or an arbiter
between you?" 15Then he said to them, "Watch out! Be on your
guard against all kinds of greed; a man's life does not consist in
the abundance of his possessions."
16And he told them this parable: "The ground of a certain rich
man produced a good crop. 17He thought to himself, 'What shall
I do? I have no place to store my crops.'
18"Then he said, 'This is what I'll do. I will tear down my barns
and build bigger ones, and there I will store all my grain and my
goods. 19And I'll say to myself, "You have plenty of good things
laid up for many years. Take life easy; eat, drink and be merry." '

[a] 6 Greek *two assaria*

If we are correct and right in our Christian life at every point, but refuse to stand for the truth at a particular point where the battle rages—then we are traitors to Christ.

Martin Luther (1483-1546)

(12:8–12) Jesus, You know how weak I am and how much I seek the good opinion of others. I pray that I will always be loyal to You. Let me be bold to proclaim Your name as Lord of Creation, Giver of Salvation and my personal friend and Savior. And as I learn boldness, Lord, teach me also to rely on Your Spirit. When I am asked to give a reason for my faith, give me the right words to say and the proper attitude with which to say them. (1Pe 3:15–16)

Come Holy Spirit,
Fall afresh on me.
Fill me with Your power,
Satisfy my needs.
Only You can make me whole,
Give me strength to make me grow.
Come Holy Spirit,
Fall afresh on me.

"Come Holy Spirit"
Malcolm Fletcher (©1986, 1994)

20“But God said to him, ‘You fool! This very night your life will
be demanded from you. Then who will get what you have prepared for yourself?’
21“This is how it will be with anyone who stores up things for
himself but is not rich toward God.”

Do Not Worry

22Then Jesus said to his disciples: “Therefore I tell you, do not
worry about your life, what you will eat; or about your body, what
you will wear. 23Life is more than food, and the body more than
clothes. 24Consider the ravens: They do not sow or reap, they
have no storeroom or barn; yet God feeds them. And how much
more valuable you are than birds! 25Who of you by worrying can
add a single hour to his life[a]? 26Since you cannot do this very little thing, why do you worry about the rest?
27“Consider how the lilies grow. They do not labor or spin. Yet
I tell you, not even Solomon in all his splendor was dressed like
one of these. 28If that is how God clothes the grass of the field,
which is here today, and tomorrow is thrown into the fire, how
much more will he clothe you, O you of little faith! 29And do not
set your heart on what you will eat or drink; do not worry about
it. 30For the pagan world runs after all such things, and your Father knows that you need them. 31But seek his kingdom, and
these things will be given to you as well.
32“Do not be afraid, little flock, for your Father has been
pleased to give you the kingdom. 33Sell your possessions and give
to the poor. Provide purses for yourselves that will not wear out,
a treasure in heaven that will not be exhausted, where no thief
comes near and no moth destroys. 34For where your treasure is,
there your heart will be also.

Watchfulness

35“Be dressed ready for service and keep your lamps burning,
36like men waiting for their master to return from a wedding banquet, so that when he comes and knocks they can immediately
open the door for him. 37It will be good for those servants whose
master finds them watching when he comes. I tell you the truth,
he will dress himself to serve, will have them recline at the table
and will come and wait on them. 38It will be good for those servants whose master finds them ready, even if he comes in the second or third watch of the night. 39But understand this: If the
owner of the house had known at what hour the thief was coming,
he would not have let his house be broken into. 40You also must
be ready, because the Son of Man will come at an hour when you
do not expect him.”
41Peter asked, “Lord, are you telling this parable to us, or to
everyone?”
42The Lord answered, “Who then is the faithful and wise manager, whom the master puts in charge of his servants to give them
their food allowance at the proper time? 43It will be good for that
servant whom the master finds doing so when he returns. 44I tell
you the truth, he will put him in charge of all his possessions.
45But suppose the servant says to himself, ‘My master is taking a
long time in coming,’ and he then begins to beat the menservants
and maidservants and to eat and drink and get drunk. 46The mas-

[a]25 Or *single cubit to his height*

(12:22–34) How wonderful it is to know that my Father is the God of all creation. My Father is the Provider Who feeds and clothes all of nature. My Father rules over an unshakeable kingdom that I am inheriting, and the riches of heaven have been set aside for me. O *Abba*, my dear Father, You are my greatest treasure. You are an endless supply of all that I need for life and godliness. (2Pe 1:3)

Let us, with a gladsome mind,
Praise the Lord for He is kind:
For His mercies shall endure,
Ever faithful, ever sure.

All things living He doth feed;
His full hand supplies their need:
For His mercies shall endure,
Ever faithful, ever sure.

“Let Us, With a Gladsome Mind”
John Milton (1623)

ter of that servant will come on a day when he does not expect
him and at an hour he is not aware of. He will cut him to pieces
and assign him a place with the unbelievers.
47“That servant who knows his master’s will and does not get
ready or does not do what his master wants will be beaten with
many blows. 48But the one who does not know and does things
deserving punishment will be beaten with few blows. From everyone who has been given much, much will be demanded; and from
the one who has been entrusted with much, much more will be
asked.

Not Peace but Division

49“I have come to bring fire on the earth, and how I wish it
were already kindled! 50But I have a baptism to undergo, and
how distressed I am until it is completed! 51Do you think I came
to bring peace on earth? No, I tell you, but division. 52From now
on there will be five in one family divided against each other,
three against two and two against three. 53They will be divided,
father against son and son against father, mother against daughter and daughter against mother, mother-in-law against daughter-
in-law and daughter-in-law against mother-in-law.”

Interpreting the Times

54He said to the crowd: “When you see a cloud rising in the
west, immediately you say, ‘It’s going to rain,’ and it does. 55And
when the south wind blows, you say, ‘It’s going to be hot,’ and it
is. 56Hypocrites! You know how to interpret the appearance of
the earth and the sky. How is it that you don’t know how to interpret this present time?
57“Why don’t you judge for yourselves what is right? 58As you
are going with your adversary to the magistrate, try hard to be
reconciled to him on the way, or he may drag you off to the judge,
and the judge turn you over to the officer, and the officer throw
you into prison. 59I tell you, you will not get out until you have
paid the last penny.[a]”

Repent or Perish

13 Now there were some present at that time who told Jesus
about the Galileans whose blood Pilate had mixed with
their sacrifices. 2Jesus answered, “Do you think that these Galileans were worse sinners than all the other Galileans because they
suffered this way? 3I tell you, no! But unless you repent, you too
will all perish. 4Or those eighteen who died when the tower in Siloam fell on them—do you think they were more guilty than all
the others living in Jerusalem? 5I tell you, no! But unless you repent, you too will all perish.”
6Then he told this parable: “A man had a fig tree, planted in
his vineyard, and he went to look for fruit on it, but did not find
any. 7So he said to the man who took care of the vineyard, ‘For
three years now I’ve been coming to look for fruit on this fig tree
and haven’t found any. Cut it down! Why should it use up the
soil?’
8“ ‘Sir,’ the man replied, ‘leave it alone for one more year, and
I’ll dig around it and fertilize it. 9If it bears fruit next year, fine! If
not, then cut it down.’ ”

[a] 59 Greek *lepton*

(12:49–53) Lord Jesus, I have been baptized into Your death. Now baptize me in Your fire. Kindle the flame of holiness in my heart. Burn up everything that displeases You, and purify me. Fill me with Your Holy Spirit and give me boldness to stand for my convictions even if I encounter resistance from acquaintances, friends or loved ones. (Lk 3:16–17; Ro 6:3)

Christ made it clear that his coming, far from meaning peace, meant war. His message was a fire that would set society ablaze with division and strife.

Billy Graham (1918-)

Christ, whose purpose is to kindle:
Now ignite us with Thy fire;
While the earth awaits Thy burning,
With Thy passion us inspire.
Overcome our sinful calmness,
Rouse us with redemptive shame;
Baptize with Thy fiery Spirit,
Crown our lives with tongues of
flame.

Thou, who still a sword delivers
Rather than a placid peace:
With Thy sharpened Word disturb
us,
From complacency release!
Save us now from satisfaction
When we privately are free,
Yet are undisturbed in spirit
By our neighbor's misery.

"Christ, Whose Purpose Is to Kindle"
D. Elton Trueblood (1900-1994)

(13:18–21) Lord, I praise You for Your wise and mysterious ways. I would expect You to invade my life with one cataclysmic or cathartic transformation. Instead, like Your birth in Bethlehem Your kingdom comes without pomp and circumstance or great showmanship. Your kingdom comes quietly and grows steadily like a seed that must be nurtured and fed, or like yeast that slowly spreads its influence throughout the entire loaf. Your rule does not begin on the outside and work its way to the center; it begins on the inside and steadily works its way out to the unexplored frontiers of my life. Lord, thank You for the small victories that let me know You are at work in me. Please give me patience in the process.

(13:28–30) Jesus, we may all be in for a surprise when we enter heaven and find any number of people there whom we did not expect to see. And we may be just as surprised about those who are absent. I thank You that judgment is in Your hands, not mine. Keep me from attempting in this life to sort out the sheep from the goats. I know that no one who trusts in You will be denied the eternal life You have promised. (Mt 25:31–46)

If I ever reach heaven, I expect to find three wonders there: first, to meet some I had not thought to see there; second, to miss some I had expected to see there; and third, the greatest wonder of all, to find myself there.

John Newton (1725–1807)

A Crippled Woman Healed on the Sabbath

10 On a Sabbath Jesus was teaching in one of the synagogues,
11 and a woman was there who had been crippled by a spirit for
eighteen years. She was bent over and could not straighten up at
all. 12 When Jesus saw her, he called her forward and said to her,
"Woman, you are set free from your infirmity." 13 Then he put his
hands on her, and immediately she straightened up and praised
God.

14 Indignant because Jesus had healed on the Sabbath, the synagogue ruler said to the people, "There are six days for work. So come and be healed on those days, not on the Sabbath."

15 The Lord answered him, "You hypocrites! Doesn't each of
you on the Sabbath untie his ox or donkey from the stall and lead
it out to give it water? 16 Then should not this woman, a daughter
of Abraham, whom Satan has kept bound for eighteen long years,
be set free on the Sabbath day from what bound her?"

17 When he said this, all his opponents were humiliated, but the people were delighted with all the wonderful things he was doing.

The Parables of the Mustard Seed and the Yeast

18 Then Jesus asked, "What is the kingdom of God like? What
shall I compare it to? 19 It is like a mustard seed, which a man
took and planted in his garden. It grew and became a tree, and
the birds of the air perched in its branches."

20 Again he asked, "What shall I compare the kingdom of God
to? 21 It is like yeast that a woman took and mixed into a large
amount[a] of flour until it worked all through the dough."

The Narrow Door

22 Then Jesus went through the towns and villages, teaching as
he made his way to Jerusalem. 23 Someone asked him, "Lord, are
only a few people going to be saved?"

He said to them, 24 "Make every effort to enter through the narrow door, because many, I tell you, will try to enter and will not
be able to. 25 Once the owner of the house gets up and closes the
door, you will stand outside knocking and pleading, 'Sir, open the door for us.'

"But he will answer, 'I don't know you or where you come from.'

26 "Then you will say, 'We ate and drank with you, and you taught in our streets.'

27 "But he will reply, 'I don't know you or where you come from. Away from me, all you evildoers!'

28 "There will be weeping there, and gnashing of teeth, when
you see Abraham, Isaac and Jacob and all the prophets in the
kingdom of God, but you yourselves thrown out. 29 People will
come from east and west and north and south, and will take their
places at the feast in the kingdom of God. 30 Indeed there are
those who are last who will be first, and first who will be last."

Jesus' Sorrow for Jerusalem

31 At that time some Pharisees came to Jesus and said to him, "Leave this place and go somewhere else. Herod wants to kill you."

[a] 21 Greek *three satas* (probably about 1/2 bushel or 22 liters)

32He replied, "Go tell that fox, 'I will drive out demons and heal
people today and tomorrow, and on the third day I will reach my
goal.' 33In any case, I must keep going today and tomorrow and
the next day—for surely no prophet can die outside Jerusalem!

34"O Jerusalem, Jerusalem, you who kill the prophets and
stone those sent to you, how often I have longed to gather your
children together, as a hen gathers her chicks under her wings,
but you were not willing! 35Look, your house is left to you desolate. I tell you, you will not see me again until you say, 'Blessed is
he who comes in the name of the Lord.'[a]"

Jesus at a Pharisee's House

14 One Sabbath, when Jesus went to eat in the house of a
prominent Pharisee, he was being carefully watched.
2There in front of him was a man suffering from dropsy. 3Jesus
asked the Pharisees and experts in the law, "Is it lawful to heal on
the Sabbath or not?" 4But they remained silent. So taking hold of
the man, he healed him and sent him away.

5Then he asked them, "If one of you has a son[b] or an ox that
falls into a well on the Sabbath day, will you not immediately pull
him out?" 6And they had nothing to say.

7When he noticed how the guests picked the places of honor at
the table, he told them this parable: 8"When someone invites you
to a wedding feast, do not take the place of honor, for a person
more distinguished than you may have been invited. 9If so, the
host who invited both of you will come and say to you, 'Give this
man your seat.' Then, humiliated, you will have to take the least
important place. 10But when you are invited, take the lowest
place, so that when your host comes, he will say to you, 'Friend,
move up to a better place.' Then you will be honored in the presence of all your fellow guests. 11For everyone who exalts himself
will be humbled, and he who humbles himself will be exalted."

12Then Jesus said to his host, "When you give a luncheon or
dinner, do not invite your friends, your brothers or relatives, or
your rich neighbors; if you do, they may invite you back and so
you will be repaid. 13But when you give a banquet, invite the
poor, the crippled, the lame, the blind, 14and you will be blessed.
Although they cannot repay you, you will be repaid at the resurrection of the righteous."

The Parable of the Great Banquet

15When one of those at the table with him heard this, he said
to Jesus, "Blessed is the man who will eat at the feast in the kingdom of God."

16Jesus replied: "A certain man was preparing a great banquet
and invited many guests. 17At the time of the banquet he sent his
servant to tell those who had been invited, 'Come, for everything
is now ready.'

18"But they all alike began to make excuses. The first said, 'I
have just bought a field, and I must go and see it. Please excuse me.'

19"Another said, 'I have just bought five yoke of oxen, and I'm
on my way to try them out. Please excuse me.'

20"Still another said, 'I just got married, so I can't come.'

21"The servant came back and reported this to his master.

[a] 35 Psalm 118:26 [b] 5 Some manuscripts *donkey*

(14:1–4) Help me, O Jesus, to create an environment where mercy takes precedence over rules and regulations. Let me be a part of Your answer to the cries of hurting people wherever I go, and do not let me be drawn into rigid forms of religion that leave no room for the unplanned or the unexpected.

(14:12–14) Lord, I am so inclined to entertain or do favors for people who I know will reciprocate. Help me today to give generously of my time or effort or money to someone who will have no means of repaying me. It will give me great pleasure to do so, for I know that when I offer my love and service to someone else I am really offering it to You. (Mt 25:40)

(15:3–10) I praise You, Lord, for the incredible value You place on sinners! You do not passively wait for us to come to You. You actively, passionately seek us out of our wanderings and hiding places. Your pursuit is relentless. Nine out of ten is not good enough for You. 99 out of 100 is still unacceptable. You are not willing that *any* should perish. You want all people to repent and be saved and to come to a knowledge of the truth. When You find us You carry us on Your shoulders into the safety of the fold. You rejoice over us with saints and angels. Thank You, Lord, for Your limitless, bountiful, passionate, merciful, fervent, unshakeable love! (Dt:33:12; Mt 18:14; 1Ti 2:4; 2Pe 3:9)

Show me, O Lord, your mercy, and delight my heart with it . . . I am the sheep who wandered into the wilderness–seek after me, and bring me home again to your fold. Do with me what you will, that I may stay by you all the days of my life, and praise you with all those who are with you in heaven for all eternity.

Saint Jerome (c.347–420)

I was lost but Jesus found me,
Found the sheep that went astray,
Threw His loving arms around me,
Drew me back into His way.

"I Will Sing the Wondrous Story"
Francis H. Rowley (1886)

Then the owner of the house became angry and ordered his servant, 'Go out quickly into the streets and alleys of the town and bring in the poor, the crippled, the blind and the lame.'
22" 'Sir,' the servant said, 'what you ordered has been done, but there is still room.'
23"Then the master told his servant, 'Go out to the roads and country lanes and make them come in, so that my house will be full.
24I tell you, not one of those men who were invited will get a taste of my banquet.' "

The Cost of Being a Disciple

25Large crowds were traveling with Jesus, and turning to them he said:
26"If anyone comes to me and does not hate his father and mother, his wife and children, his brothers and sisters—yes, even his own life—he cannot be my disciple.
27And anyone who does not carry his cross and follow me cannot be my disciple.
28"Suppose one of you wants to build a tower. Will he not first sit down and estimate the cost to see if he has enough money to complete it?
29For if he lays the foundation and is not able to finish it, everyone who sees it will ridicule him,
30saying, 'This fellow began to build and was not able to finish.'
31"Or suppose a king is about to go to war against another king. Will he not first sit down and consider whether he is able with ten thousand men to oppose the one coming against him with twenty thousand?
32If he is not able, he will send a delegation while the other is still a long way off and will ask for terms of peace.
33In the same way, any of you who does not give up everything he has cannot be my disciple.
34"Salt is good, but if it loses its saltiness, how can it be made salty again?
35It is fit neither for the soil nor for the manure pile; it is thrown out.
"He who has ears to hear, let him hear."

The Parable of the Lost Sheep

15 Now the tax collectors and "sinners" were all gathering around to hear him.
2But the Pharisees and the teachers of the law muttered, "This man welcomes sinners and eats with them."
3Then Jesus told them this parable:
4"Suppose one of you has a hundred sheep and loses one of them. Does he not leave the ninety-nine in the open country and go after the lost sheep until he finds it?
5And when he finds it, he joyfully puts it on his shoulders
6and goes home. Then he calls his friends and neighbors together and says, 'Rejoice with me; I have found my lost sheep.'
7I tell you that in the same way there will be more rejoicing in heaven over one sinner who repents than over ninety-nine righteous persons who do not need to repent.

The Parable of the Lost Coin

8"Or suppose a woman has ten silver coins[a] and loses one. Does she not light a lamp, sweep the house and search carefully until she finds it?
9And when she finds it, she calls her friends and neighbors together and says, 'Rejoice with me; I have found my lost coin.'
10In the same way, I tell you, there is rejoicing in the presence of the angels of God over one sinner who repents."

[a] 8 Greek *ten drachmas,* each worth about a day's wages

The Parable of the Lost Son

11Jesus continued: "There was a man who had two sons. 12The
younger one said to his father, 'Father, give me my share of the estate.' So he divided his property between them.

13"Not long after that, the younger son got together all he had,
set off for a distant country and there squandered his wealth in
wild living. 14After he had spent everything, there was a severe
famine in that whole country, and he began to be in need. 15So
he went and hired himself out to a citizen of that country, who
sent him to his fields to feed pigs. 16He longed to fill his stomach
with the pods that the pigs were eating, but no one gave him anything.

17"When he came to his senses, he said, 'How many of my father's hired men have food to spare, and here I am starving to
death! 18I will set out and go back to my father and say to him: Father, I have sinned against heaven and against you. 19I am no
longer worthy to be called your son; make me like one of your
hired men.' 20So he got up and went to his father.

"But while he was still a long way off, his father saw him and
was filled with compassion for him; he ran to his son, threw his
arms around him and kissed him.

21"The son said to him, 'Father, I have sinned against heaven
and against you. I am no longer worthy to be called your son.[a]'

22"But the father said to his servants, 'Quick! Bring the best
robe and put it on him. Put a ring on his finger and sandals on his
feet. 23Bring the fattened calf and kill it. Let's have a feast and celebrate. 24For this son of mine was dead and is alive again; he was
lost and is found.' So they began to celebrate.

25"Meanwhile, the older son was in the field. When he came
near the house, he heard music and dancing. 26So he called one
of the servants and asked him what was going on. 27'Your brother has come,' he replied, 'and your father has killed the fattened
calf because he has him back safe and sound.'

28"The older brother became angry and refused to go in. So
his father went out and pleaded with him. 29But he answered his
father, 'Look! All these years I've been slaving for you and never
disobeyed your orders. Yet you never gave me even a young goat
so I could celebrate with my friends. 30But when this son of yours
who has squandered your property with prostitutes comes home,
you kill the fattened calf for him!'

31" 'My son,' the father said, 'you are always with me, and
everything I have is yours. 32But we had to celebrate and be glad,
because this brother of yours was dead and is alive again; he was
lost and is found.' "

The Parable of the Shrewd Manager

16 Jesus told his disciples: "There was a rich man whose
manager was accused of wasting his possessions. 2So he
called him in and asked him, 'What is this I hear about you? Give
an account of your management, because you cannot be manager any longer.'

3"The manager said to himself, 'What shall I do now? My master is taking away my job. I'm not strong enough to dig, and I'm
ashamed to beg— 4I know what I'll do so that, when I lose my
job here, people will welcome me into their houses.'

[a] *21* Some early manuscripts *son. Make me like one of your hired men.*

(15:17–30) Father God, help me to see how impoverished my life is without You and all that You offer. Coming home to You is not a religious decision; it is a matter of common sense. Without You I am starving for nourishment, and I have nothing. With You I have all that I need and more.

Though here I stand
Unworthy before You,
I still am washed in Your holiness.
And I feel the warmth
Of Your heavenly smile,
So glad I have come home.

What a glorious wonder my Lord is.
What a glorious wonder my Lord is.
My light and salvation,
My strength and shield.
What a glorious wonder my Lord is.

"Glorious Wonder"
Rob Mathes (©1996)

(15:28–32) Lord, deliver me from the self-righteousness of the elder brother who thought he was entitled to his father's love while his erring brother was not. Thank You for extending Your grace so that all people everywhere are invited to receive from Your generous, forgiving heart.

(16:13) Lord Jesus, help me to keep my life free from the love of money and to be content with what I have. Help me to value the treasures of Your kingdom above the pleasures of the world. For when I seek first Your kingdom, You take care of my needs. But if I seek first to meet my own needs, I will not be able to serve Your kingdom. (Mt 6:33; Heb 13:5)

There's no greater love than Jesus,
There's no greater love than He gives.
There's no greater love that frees us
So deep within.

All the world's empty pleasures
Will soon pass away,
But His love will last forever,
In my heart it shall remain.

"No Greater Love"
Tommy Walker (©1996)

5"So he called in each one of his master's debtors. He asked
the first, 'How much do you owe my master?'
6" 'Eight hundred gallons[a] of olive oil,' he replied.
"The manager told him, 'Take your bill, sit down quickly, and
make it four hundred.'
7"Then he asked the second, 'And how much do you owe?'
" 'A thousand bushels[b] of wheat,' he replied.
"He told him, 'Take your bill and make it eight hundred.'
8"The master commended the dishonest manager because he
had acted shrewdly. For the people of this world are more
shrewd in dealing with their own kind than are the people of the
light. 9I tell you, use worldly wealth to gain friends for yourselves, so that when it is gone, you will be welcomed into eternal
dwellings.
10"Whoever can be trusted with very little can also be trusted
with much, and whoever is dishonest with very little will also be
dishonest with much. 11So if you have not been trustworthy in
handling worldly wealth, who will trust you with true riches?
12And if you have not been trustworthy with someone else's property, who will give you property of your own?
13"No servant can serve two masters. Either he will hate the
one and love the other, or he will be devoted to the one and despise the other. You cannot serve both God and Money."
14The Pharisees, who loved money, heard all this and were
sneering at Jesus. 15He said to them, "You are the ones who justify yourselves in the eyes of men, but God knows your hearts.
What is highly valued among men is detestable in God's sight.

Additional Teachings

16"The Law and the Prophets were proclaimed until John.
Since that time, the good news of the kingdom of God is being
preached, and everyone is forcing his way into it. 17It is easier for
heaven and earth to disappear than for the least stroke of a pen
to drop out of the Law.
18"Anyone who divorces his wife and marries another woman
commits adultery, and the man who marries a divorced woman
commits adultery.

The Rich Man and Lazarus

19"There was a rich man who was dressed in purple and fine
linen and lived in luxury every day. 20At his gate was laid a beggar
named Lazarus, covered with sores 21and longing to eat what fell
from the rich man's table. Even the dogs came and licked his
sores.
22"The time came when the beggar died and the angels carried
him to Abraham's side. The rich man also died and was buried.
23In hell,[c] where he was in torment, he looked up and saw Abraham far away, with Lazarus by his side. 24So he called to him, 'Father Abraham, have pity on me and send Lazarus to dip the tip of
his finger in water and cool my tongue, because I am in agony in
this fire.'
25"But Abraham replied, 'Son, remember that in your lifetime
you received your good things, while Lazarus received bad things,
but now he is comforted here and you are in agony. 26And besides all this, between us and you a great chasm has been fixed,

[a] 6 Greek *one hundred batous* (probably about 3 kiloliters) [b] 7 Greek *one hundred korous* (probably about 35 kiloliters) [c] 23 Greek *Hades*

so that those who want to go from here to you cannot, nor can
anyone cross over from there to us.'
27"He answered, 'Then I beg you, father, send Lazarus to my father's house, 28for I have five brothers. Let him warn them, so
that they will not also come to this place of torment.'
29"Abraham replied, 'They have Moses and the Prophets; let
them listen to them.'
30" 'No, father Abraham,' he said, 'but if someone from the
dead goes to them, they will repent.'
31"He said to him, 'If they do not listen to Moses and the
Prophets, they will not be convinced even if someone rises from
the dead.' "

Sin, Faith, Duty

17 Jesus said to his disciples: "Things that cause people to sin
are bound to come, but woe to that person through whom
they come. 2It would be better for him to be thrown into the sea
with a millstone tied around his neck than for him to cause one
of these little ones to sin. 3So watch yourselves.
"If your brother sins, rebuke him, and if he repents, forgive
him. 4If he sins against you seven times in a day, and seven times
comes back to you and says, 'I repent,' forgive him."
5The apostles said to the Lord, "Increase our faith!"
6He replied, "If you have faith as small as a mustard seed, you
can say to this mulberry tree, 'Be uprooted and planted in the
sea,' and it will obey you.
7"Suppose one of you had a servant plowing or looking after
the sheep. Would he say to the servant when he comes in from the
field, 'Come along now and sit down to eat'? 8Would he not rather
say, 'Prepare my supper, get yourself ready and wait on me while
I eat and drink; after that you may eat and drink'? 9Would he
thank the servant because he did what he was told to do? 10So you
also, when you have done everything you were told to do, should
say, 'We are unworthy servants; we have only done our duty.' "

Ten Healed of Leprosy

11Now on his way to Jerusalem, Jesus traveled along the border
between Samaria and Galilee. 12As he was going into a village, ten
men who had leprosy[a] met him. They stood at a distance 13and
called out in a loud voice, "Jesus, Master, have pity on us!"
14When he saw them, he said, "Go, show yourselves to the
priests." And as they went, they were cleansed.
15One of them, when he saw he was healed, came back, praising God in a loud voice. 16He threw himself at Jesus' feet and
thanked him—and he was a Samaritan.
17Jesus asked, "Were not all ten cleansed? Where are the other
nine? 18Was no one found to return and give praise to God except
this foreigner?" 19Then he said to him, "Rise and go; your faith
has made you well."

The Coming of the Kingdom of God

20Once, having been asked by the Pharisees when the kingdom
of God would come, Jesus replied, "The kingdom of God does
not come with your careful observation, 21nor will people say,

[a] 12 The Greek word was used for various diseases affecting the skin—not necessarily leprosy.

(17:4) Merciful God, thank You for Your inexhaustible forgiveness. When I offend You, You are always willing to pardon. Help me to extend that same forgiveness to others when they sin against me—not my own kind of forgiveness, but Your forgiveness through me. I cannot forgive of my own accord, for although I try to forgive, I cannot forget unless You renew my mind with the love of Christ. So fill me with Your love—the love that "keeps no record of wrongs." (1Co 13:5)

(17:6) Thank You, Father, for the magnificent "economy" of faith! I do not have to have a great faith to be a great person of faith. Just a seed of faith will do.

(17:17–18) As a Samaritan, this cleansed leper would have been the last to expect the compassion of Jesus, a Jew; yet he was the most grateful. Lord, deliver me from the sin of ingratitude. Help me always to remember to "be thankful, and so worship God acceptably." (Heb 12:28)

(17:21) Lord Jesus, when You came You ushered in the kingdom of God; and now, because of Your finished work, eternal life has already begun. How I thank You that I need to look no further for the kingdom than to see the King's work in my own life—the kingdom at work within me. And, beyond myself, how wonderful it is to know that Your kingdom is flourishing all around the world wherever two or three are gathered together in Your name. (Mt 18:20)

(17:33) Jesus, everything in me wants to save and preserve—my life, my resources, my comfortable circumstances. Show me ways today that I can lose my life for You. Keep me from holding back my time, my money, my reputation. Let me invest my life in Your causes rather than in my own.

(18:1–8) "Answer me, O LORD, out of the goodness of your love; in your great mercy turn to me. Do not hide your face from your servant; answer me quickly, for I am in trouble." Gracious God, You are not like the unjust judge. You do not answer me to get rid of me; You invite me to "approach the throne of grace with confidence," so that I may receive mercy and find grace to help me in my time of need. You are full of righteousness and compassion, always willing to listen to my prayers. I place my confidence not in the justice of my cause but in the justice of my righteous Judge. (Ps 69:16–17; Isa 11:2–5; Heb 4:16)

'Here it is,' or 'There it is,' because the kingdom of God is within[a] you."

22Then he said to his disciples, "The time is coming when you will long to see one of the days of the Son of Man, but you will not see it. 23Men will tell you, 'There he is!' or 'Here he is!' Do not go running off after them. 24For the Son of Man in his day[b] will be like the lightning, which flashes and lights up the sky from one end to the other. 25But first he must suffer many things and be rejected by this generation.

26"Just as it was in the days of Noah, so also will it be in the days of the Son of Man. 27People were eating, drinking, marrying and being given in marriage up to the day Noah entered the ark. Then the flood came and destroyed them all.

28"It was the same in the days of Lot. People were eating and drinking, buying and selling, planting and building. 29But the day Lot left Sodom, fire and sulfur rained down from heaven and destroyed them all.

30"It will be just like this on the day the Son of Man is revealed. 31On that day no one who is on the roof of his house, with his goods inside, should go down to get them. Likewise, no one in the field should go back for anything. 32Remember Lot's wife! 33Whoever tries to keep his life will lose it, and whoever loses his life will preserve it. 34I tell you, on that night two people will be in one bed; one will be taken and the other left. 35Two women will be grinding grain together; one will be taken and the other left.[c]"

37"Where, Lord?" they asked.

He replied, "Where there is a dead body, there the vultures will gather."

The Parable of the Persistent Widow

18 Then Jesus told his disciples a parable to show them that they should always pray and not give up. 2He said: "In a certain town there was a judge who neither feared God nor cared about men. 3And there was a widow in that town who kept coming to him with the plea, 'Grant me justice against my adversary.'

4"For some time he refused. But finally he said to himself, 'Even though I don't fear God or care about men, 5yet because this widow keeps bothering me, I will see that she gets justice, so that she won't eventually wear me out with her coming!' "

6And the Lord said, "Listen to what the unjust judge says. 7And will not God bring about justice for his chosen ones, who cry out to him day and night? Will he keep putting them off? 8I tell you, he will see that they get justice, and quickly. However, when the Son of Man comes, will he find faith on the earth?"

The Parable of the Pharisee and the Tax Collector

9To some who were confident of their own righteousness and looked down on everybody else, Jesus told this parable: 10"Two men went up to the temple to pray, one a Pharisee and the other a tax collector. 11The Pharisee stood up and prayed about[d] himself: 'God, I thank you that I am not like other men—robbers, evildoers, adulterers—or even like this tax collector. 12I fast twice a week and give a tenth of all I get.'

[a] *21* Or *among* [b] *24* Some manuscripts do not have *in his day.* [c] *35* Some manuscripts *left.* [36]*Two men will be in the field; one will be taken and the other left.* [d] *11* Or *to*

13"But the tax collector stood at a distance. He would not even look up to heaven, but beat his breast and said, 'God, have mercy on me, a sinner.'

14"I tell you that this man, rather than the other, went home justified before God. For everyone who exalts himself will be humbled, and he who humbles himself will be exalted."

The Little Children and Jesus

15People were also bringing babies to Jesus to have him touch
them. When the disciples saw this, they rebuked them. 16But
Jesus called the children to him and said, "Let the little children come to me, and do not hinder them, for the kingdom of God belongs to such as these. 17I tell you the truth, anyone who will not
receive the kingdom of God like a little child will never enter it."

The Rich Ruler

18A certain ruler asked him, "Good teacher, what must I do to inherit eternal life?"

19"Why do you call me good?" Jesus answered. "No one is
good—except God alone. 20You know the commandments: 'Do not commit adultery, do not murder, do not steal, do not give false testimony, honor your father and mother.'[a]"

21"All these I have kept since I was a boy," he said.

22When Jesus heard this, he said to him, "You still lack one thing. Sell everything you have and give to the poor, and you will have treasure in heaven. Then come, follow me."

23When he heard this, he became very sad, because he was a
man of great wealth. 24Jesus looked at him and said, "How hard
it is for the rich to enter the kingdom of God! 25Indeed, it is easier for a camel to go through the eye of a needle than for a rich man to enter the kingdom of God."

26Those who heard this asked, "Who then can be saved?"

27Jesus replied, "What is impossible with men is possible with God."

28Peter said to him, "We have left all we had to follow you!"

29"I tell you the truth," Jesus said to them, "no one who has left home or wife or brothers or parents or children for the sake
of the kingdom of God 30will fail to receive many times as much in this age and, in the age to come, eternal life."

Jesus Again Predicts His Death

31Jesus took the Twelve aside and told them, "We are going up to Jerusalem, and everything that is written by the prophets about
the Son of Man will be fulfilled. 32He will be handed over to the
Gentiles. They will mock him, insult him, spit on him, flog him
and kill him. 33On the third day he will rise again."

34The disciples did not understand any of this. Its meaning was hidden from them, and they did not know what he was talking about.

A Blind Beggar Receives His Sight

35As Jesus approached Jericho, a blind man was sitting by the
roadside begging. 36When he heard the crowd going by, he asked
what was happening. 37They told him, "Jesus of Nazareth is passing by."

[a] 20 Exodus 20:12–16; Deut. 5:16–20

(18:15–17) No magic formulas, no grand accomplishments, no religious pedigrees, no merit of my own. Just the heart of a child, faith as small as a mustard seed, the simple "yes" of a peasant girl, the helplessness of a lost sheep, the innocence of a dove. Father, give me the gift of childlikeness. Fill me with wonder and awe. You have so much to give; help me to receive it all with the trusting heart of a child. (Mt 10:16; Lk 1:38; 15:4–7; 17:6)

(18:22–30) Dear Lord, we can never outgive You. Your love and generosity are overwhelming! When we offer You what little we have in commitment, service and even sacrifice, we receive so much more. You have given us not only eternal life but all that we need in this life as well, pressed down, shaken together and running over. (Lk 6:38)

All you are unable to give possesses you.
André Gide (1869-1951)

Jesus, I my cross have taken,
All to leave and follow Thee;
Destitute, despised, forsaken,
Thou from hence my all shalt be:
Perish every fond ambition,
All I've sought, and hoped, and known;
Yet how rich is my condition,
God and heav'n are still my own!
"Jesus, I My Cross Have Taken"
Henry F. Lyte (1824)

(18:38–43) Lord, make me a person of persistent faith. You have promised that my requests will be heard and answered according to Your will. Yet too often I grow discouraged when I do not receive immediate results. Help me to be patient, Lord, and to remember that You are not only interested in solving my problems but are even more concerned about increasing my faith and teaching me Your ways. Give me wisdom, faith and tenacity to keep asking until You have answered. (1Jn 5:14–15)

All comes at the proper time to him who knows how to wait.

Saint Vincent de Paul (1581-1660)

(19:8–9) Father in heaven, teach me to weigh my spiritual concerns against my view of worldly goods. Am I honest in my financial transactions? Am I generous with those who are in need? As You change my heart through Your love and forgiveness, also change my perspective about wealth. Like Zacchaeus, help me to set my heart on eternal values instead of on earthly possessions. Help me to give freely to others as You have given so freely to me.

38He called out, "Jesus, Son of David, have mercy on me!"
39Those who led the way rebuked him and told him to be
quiet, but he shouted all the more, "Son of David, have mercy
on me!"
40Jesus stopped and ordered the man to be brought to him.
When he came near, Jesus asked him, **41**"What do you want me to
do for you?"
"Lord, I want to see," he replied.
42Jesus said to him, "Receive your sight; your faith has healed
you." **43**Immediately he received his sight and followed Jesus,
praising God. When all the people saw it, they also praised God.

Zacchaeus the Tax Collector

19 Jesus entered Jericho and was passing through. **2**A man
was there by the name of Zacchaeus; he was a chief tax
collector and was wealthy. **3**He wanted to see who Jesus was, but
being a short man he could not, because of the crowd. **4**So he ran
ahead and climbed a sycamore-fig tree to see him, since Jesus
was coming that way.
5When Jesus reached the spot, he looked up and said to him,
"Zacchaeus, come down immediately. I must stay at your house
today." **6**So he came down at once and welcomed him gladly.
7All the people saw this and began to mutter, "He has gone to
be the guest of a 'sinner.' "
8But Zacchaeus stood up and said to the Lord, "Look, Lord!
Here and now I give half of my possessions to the poor, and if I
have cheated anybody out of anything, I will pay back four times
the amount."
9Jesus said to him, "Today salvation has come to this house,
because this man, too, is a son of Abraham. **10**For the Son of Man
came to seek and to save what was lost."

The Parable of the Ten Minas

11While they were listening to this, he went on to tell them a
parable, because he was near Jerusalem and the people thought
that the kingdom of God was going to appear at once. **12**He said:
"A man of noble birth went to a distant country to have himself
appointed king and then to return. **13**So he called ten of his servants and gave them ten minas.[a] 'Put this money to work,' he
said, 'until I come back.'
14"But his subjects hated him and sent a delegation after him
to say, 'We don't want this man to be our king.'
15"He was made king, however, and returned home. Then he
sent for the servants to whom he had given the money, in order to
find out what they had gained with it.
16"The first one came and said, 'Sir, your mina has earned ten
more.'
17" 'Well done, my good servant!' his master replied. 'Because
you have been trustworthy in a very small matter, take charge of
ten cities.'
18"The second came and said, 'Sir, your mina has earned five
more.'
19"His master answered, 'You take charge of five cities.'
20"Then another servant came and said, 'Sir, here is your
mina; I have kept it laid away in a piece of cloth. **21**I was afraid of

[a] *13* A mina was about three months' wages.

you, because you are a hard man. You take out what you did not
put in and reap what you did not sow.'
22"His master replied, 'I will judge you by your own words,
you wicked servant! You knew, did you, that I am a hard man,
taking out what I did not put in, and reaping what I did not sow?
23Why then didn't you put my money on deposit, so that when I
came back, I could have collected it with interest?'
24"Then he said to those standing by, 'Take his mina away from
him and give it to the one who has ten minas.'
25" 'Sir,' they said, 'he already has ten!'
26"He replied, 'I tell you that to everyone who has, more will
be given, but as for the one who has nothing, even what he has
will be taken away. 27But those enemies of mine who did not want
me to be king over them—bring them here and kill them in front
of me.' "

The Triumphal Entry

28After Jesus had said this, he went on ahead, going up to Jerusalem. 29As he approached Bethphage and Bethany at the hill
called the Mount of Olives, he sent two of his disciples, saying to
them, 30"Go to the village ahead of you, and as you enter it, you
will find a colt tied there, which no one has ever ridden. Untie it
and bring it here. 31If anyone asks you, 'Why are you untying it?'
tell him, 'The Lord needs it.' "
32Those who were sent ahead went and found it just as he had
told them. 33As they were untying the colt, its owners asked them,
"Why are you untying the colt?"
34They replied, "The Lord needs it."
35They brought it to Jesus, threw their cloaks on the colt and
put Jesus on it. 36As he went along, people spread their cloaks on
the road.
37When he came near the place where the road goes down the
Mount of Olives, the whole crowd of disciples began joyfully to
praise God in loud voices for all the miracles they had seen:

38"Blessed is the king who comes in the name of the
Lord!"[a]
"Peace in heaven and glory in the highest!"

39Some of the Pharisees in the crowd said to Jesus, "Teacher,
rebuke your disciples!"
40"I tell you," he replied, "if they keep quiet, the stones will cry
out."
41As he approached Jerusalem and saw the city, he wept over
it 42and said, "If you, even you, had only known on this day
what would bring you peace—but now it is hidden from your
eyes. 43The days will come upon you when your enemies will
build an embankment against you and encircle you and hem
you in on every side. 44They will dash you to the ground, you
and the children within your walls. They will not leave one stone
on another, because you did not recognize the time of God's
coming to you."

Jesus at the Temple

45Then he entered the temple area and began driving out
those who were selling. 46"It is written," he said to them, " 'My

[a]38 Psalm 118:26

(19:38–44) This city that rang out with cries of "Hosanna!" ("Lord save us!") would soon resound with shouts of "Crucify him!" Little did the people realize that the one could not be accomplished without the other. Lord Jesus, although You knew full well that you would be killed, still Your heart ached with compassion for those who would put You to death. Thank You, Lord, for Your passion, for Your courage, for seeing the way and walking in it. (Mt 21:9; Lk 23:21)

All glory, laud, and honor
To Thee, Redeemer, King!
To whom the lips of children
Made sweet hosannas ring.

Thou art the King of Israel,
Thou David's royal Son,
Who in the Lord's name comest,
The King and blessed One!

"All Glory, Laud and Honor"
Theodulph of Orleans (c. 820)
Trans. John M. Neale (1818-1866)

(19:38) "Peace on earth," the angels cried when they announced Your birth. "Peace in heaven," the people cried when they announced Your triumphal entry into Jerusalem. When You hung on the cross, You satisfied the desire of heaven and fulfilled the longing of earth. In Your death and resurrection You met all of the requirements to bring peace between the two. Truly, Lord Jesus, You are the Prince of Peace. (Isa 9:6; Lk 2:14)

(20:9–19) Father, help me to tend well the vineyard of my soul. Give me hearing ears, a receptive heart and open arms to welcome the servants You send my way who carry with them the words of life. May I bear a bountiful harvest for You, full of the good fruit of the Spirit.

If I'm to be whom You desire
All throughout my life,
A vessel unto honor, Lord, to Thee,
And before Your throne
To hear You say
That I have done my part,
Lord, I need an undivided heart.

That I might know You,
That I might serve You,
That I might worship You as King,
To see the Morning Star,
To know how great You are,
Lord, I need an undivided heart.

"Undivided Heart"
Dan Marks (©1996)

house will be a house of prayer'[a]; but you have made it 'a den of
robbers.'[b]"
47Every day he was teaching at the temple. But the chief priests,
the teachers of the law and the leaders among the people were
trying to kill him. 48Yet they could not find any way to do it, because all the people hung on his words.

The Authority of Jesus Questioned

20 One day as he was teaching the people in the temple
courts and preaching the gospel, the chief priests and the
teachers of the law, together with the elders, came up to him.
2"Tell us by what authority you are doing these things," they said.
"Who gave you this authority?"
3He replied, "I will also ask you a question. Tell me, 4John's
baptism—was it from heaven, or from men?"
5They discussed it among themselves and said, "If we say,
'From heaven,' he will ask, 'Why didn't you believe him?' 6But if
we say, 'From men,' all the people will stone us, because they are
persuaded that John was a prophet."
7So they answered, "We don't know where it was from."
8Jesus said, "Neither will I tell you by what authority I am doing
these things."

The Parable of the Tenants

9He went on to tell the people this parable: "A man planted a
vineyard, rented it to some farmers and went away for a long
time. 10At harvest time he sent a servant to the tenants so they
would give him some of the fruit of the vineyard. But the tenants
beat him and sent him away empty-handed. 11He sent another
servant, but that one also they beat and treated shamefully and
sent away empty-handed. 12He sent still a third, and they wounded him and threw him out.
13"Then the owner of the vineyard said, 'What shall I do? I will
send my son, whom I love; perhaps they will respect him.'
14"But when the tenants saw him, they talked the matter over.
'This is the heir,' they said. 'Let's kill him, and the inheritance
will be ours.' 15So they threw him out of the vineyard and killed
him.
"What then will the owner of the vineyard do to them? 16He
will come and kill those tenants and give the vineyard to others."
When the people heard this, they said, "May this never be!"
17Jesus looked directly at them and asked, "Then what is the
meaning of that which is written:

" 'The stone the builders rejected
has become the capstone[c]'[d]?

18Everyone who falls on that stone will be broken to pieces, but
he on whom it falls will be crushed."
19The teachers of the law and the chief priests looked for a
way to arrest him immediately, because they knew he had spoken
this parable against them. But they were afraid of the people.

Paying Taxes to Caesar

20Keeping a close watch on him, they sent spies, who pretended to be honest. They hoped to catch Jesus in something he said

[a] 46 Isaiah 56:7 [b] 46 Jer. 7:11 [c] 17 Or *cornerstone* [d] 17 Psalm 118:22

so that they might hand him over to the power and authority of the
governor. 21So the spies questioned him: "Teacher, we know that
you speak and teach what is right, and that you do not show partiality but teach the way of God in accordance with the truth. 22Is
it right for us to pay taxes to Caesar or not?"
23He saw through their duplicity and said to them, 24"Show
me a denarius. Whose portrait and inscription are on it?"
25"Caesar's," they replied.

He said to them, "Then give to Caesar what is Caesar's, and to God what is God's."

26They were unable to trap him in what he had said there in
public. And astonished by his answer, they became silent.

The Resurrection and Marriage

27Some of the Sadducees, who say there is no resurrection,
came to Jesus with a question. 28"Teacher," they said, "Moses
wrote for us that if a man's brother dies and leaves a wife but no
children, the man must marry the widow and have children for
his brother. 29Now there were seven brothers. The first one married a woman and died childless. 30The second 31and then the
third married her, and in the same way the seven died, leaving no
children. 32Finally, the woman died too. 33Now then, at the resurrection whose wife will she be, since the seven were married to
her?"

34Jesus replied, "The people of this age marry and are given in
marriage. 35But those who are considered worthy of taking part
in that age and in the resurrection from the dead will neither
marry nor be given in marriage, 36and they can no longer die; for
they are like the angels. They are God's children, since they are
children of the resurrection. 37But in the account of the bush,
even Moses showed that the dead rise, for he calls the Lord 'the
God of Abraham, and the God of Isaac, and the God of Jacob.'[a]
38He is not the God of the dead, but of the living, for to him all are
alive."

39Some of the teachers of the law responded, "Well said,
teacher!" 40And no one dared to ask him any more questions.

Whose Son Is the Christ?

41Then Jesus said to them, "How is it that they say the Christ[b]
is the Son of David? 42David himself declares in the Book of
Psalms:

" 'The Lord said to my Lord:
"Sit at my right hand
43until I make your enemies
a footstool for your feet." '[c]

44David calls him 'Lord.' How then can he be his son?"

45While all the people were listening, Jesus said to his disciples, 46"Beware of the teachers of the law. They like to walk
around in flowing robes and love to be greeted in the marketplaces and have the most important seats in the synagogues and
the places of honor at banquets. 47They devour widows' houses
and for a show make lengthy prayers. Such men will be punished
most severely."

[a] 37 Exodus 3:6 [b] 41 Or *Messiah* [c] 43 Psalm 110:1

(20:21–26) Caesar's name and likeness are inscribed on my money. I guess that makes it his. Your name and likeness are inscribed on my heart. I guess that makes it Yours. Please receive it, all of it, as my loving tribute to You, my Lord and King.

The Widow's Offering

21 As he looked up, Jesus saw the rich putting their gifts into
the temple treasury. 2He also saw a poor widow put in two
very small copper coins.[a] 3"I tell you the truth," he said, "this
poor widow has put in more than all the others. 4All these people
gave their gifts out of their wealth; but she out of her poverty put
in all she had to live on."

Signs of the End of the Age

5Some of his disciples were remarking about how the temple
was adorned with beautiful stones and with gifts dedicated to
God. But Jesus said, 6"As for what you see here, the time will
come when not one stone will be left on another; every one of
them will be thrown down."

7"Teacher," they asked, "when will these things happen? And
what will be the sign that they are about to take place?"

8He replied: "Watch out that you are not deceived. For many
will come in my name, claiming, 'I am he,' and, 'The time is near.'
Do not follow them. 9When you hear of wars and revolutions, do
not be frightened. These things must happen first, but the end will
not come right away."

10Then he said to them: "Nation will rise against nation, and
kingdom against kingdom. 11There will be great earthquakes,
famines and pestilences in various places, and fearful events and
great signs from heaven.

12"But before all this, they will lay hands on you and persecute
you. They will deliver you to synagogues and prisons, and you will
be brought before kings and governors, and all on account of my
name. 13This will result in your being witnesses to them. 14But
make up your mind not to worry beforehand how you will defend
yourselves. 15For I will give you words and wisdom that none of
your adversaries will be able to resist or contradict. 16You will be
betrayed even by parents, brothers, relatives and friends, and they
will put some of you to death. 17All men will hate you because of
me. 18But not a hair of your head will perish. 19By standing firm
you will gain life.

20"When you see Jerusalem being surrounded by armies, you
will know that its desolation is near. 21Then let those who are in
Judea flee to the mountains, let those in the city get out, and let
those in the country not enter the city. 22For this is the time of
punishment in fulfillment of all that has been written. 23How
dreadful it will be in those days for pregnant women and nursing
mothers! There will be great distress in the land and wrath
against this people. 24They will fall by the sword and will be taken
as prisoners to all the nations. Jerusalem will be trampled on by
the Gentiles until the times of the Gentiles are fulfilled.

25"There will be signs in the sun, moon and stars. On the
earth, nations will be in anguish and perplexity at the roaring and
tossing of the sea. 26Men will faint from terror, apprehensive of
what is coming on the world, for the heavenly bodies will be
shaken. 27At that time they will see the Son of Man coming in a
cloud with power and great glory. 28When these things begin to
take place, stand up and lift up your heads, because your redemption is drawing near."

29He told them this parable: "Look at the fig tree and all the

(21:1–4) "Where your treasure is, there your heart will be also." Lord, let nothing come between us. You held nothing back when You gave Yourself for me. Forgive me for holding anything back from You. You have offered me the riches of heaven, but I have hoarded the trinkets of earth. Lord, I don't want to be held captive by the cares of this world or the deceitfulness of riches. Free me from financial fears. Forgive me for giving only when I think I can afford to. I want to trust You with my whole heart, but if my heart is where I keep my treasures, then I must learn to trust You with my wealth, as much or as little as that may be. Help me to remember that all I have comes from Your hand and that I can only give to You what You have already given to me. (1Ch 29:10–20; Mt 6:21)

Take my lips and let them be
Filled with messages for Thee;
Take my silver and my gold,
Not a mite would I withhold,
Not a mite would I withhold.

"Take My Life, and Let It Be"
Frances Ridley Havergal (1874)

[a] 2 Greek *two lepta*

trees. 30When they sprout leaves, you can see for yourselves and
know that summer is near. 31Even so, when you see these things
happening, you know that the kingdom of God is near.
32"I tell you the truth, this generation[a] will certainly not pass
away until all these things have happened. 33Heaven and earth
will pass away, but my words will never pass away.
34"Be careful, or your hearts will be weighed down with dissipation, drunkenness and the anxieties of life, and that day will
close on you unexpectedly like a trap. 35For it will come upon all
those who live on the face of the whole earth. 36Be always on the
watch, and pray that you may be able to escape all that is about to
happen, and that you may be able to stand before the Son of Man."
37Each day Jesus was teaching at the temple, and each evening
he went out to spend the night on the hill called the Mount of Olives, 38and all the people came early in the morning to hear him
at the temple.

Judas Agrees to Betray Jesus

22 Now the Feast of Unleavened Bread, called the Passover,
was approaching, 2and the chief priests and the teachers
of the law were looking for some way to get rid of Jesus, for they
were afraid of the people. 3Then Satan entered Judas, called Iscariot, one of the Twelve. 4And Judas went to the chief priests and
the officers of the temple guard and discussed with them how he
might betray Jesus. 5They were delighted and agreed to give him
money. 6He consented, and watched for an opportunity to hand
Jesus over to them when no crowd was present.

The Last Supper

7Then came the day of Unleavened Bread on which the
Passover lamb had to be sacrificed. 8Jesus sent Peter and John,
saying, "Go and make preparations for us to eat the Passover."
9"Where do you want us to prepare for it?" they asked.
10He replied, "As you enter the city, a man carrying a jar of
water will meet you. Follow him to the house that he enters, 11and
say to the owner of the house, 'The Teacher asks: Where is the
guest room, where I may eat the Passover with my disciples?'
12He will show you a large upper room, all furnished. Make
preparations there."
13They left and found things just as Jesus had told them. So
they prepared the Passover.
14When the hour came, Jesus and his apostles reclined at the
table. 15And he said to them, "I have eagerly desired to eat this
Passover with you before I suffer. 16For I tell you, I will not eat it
again until it finds fulfillment in the kingdom of God."
17After taking the cup, he gave thanks and said, "Take this and
divide it among you. 18For I tell you I will not drink again of the
fruit of the vine until the kingdom of God comes."
19And he took bread, gave thanks and broke it, and gave it to
them, saying, "This is my body given for you; do this in remembrance of me."
20In the same way, after the supper he took the cup, saying,
"This cup is the new covenant in my blood, which is poured out
for you. 21But the hand of him who is going to betray me is with
mine on the table. 22The Son of Man will go as it has been de-

[a] 32 Or *race*

(22:19) How profound, Lord, that Your ultimate gift to us—Your body and blood—is symbolized in a simple piece of bread and a cup of wine. As I eat and drink at the communion table, those elements become a part of me. They identify me with You and with Your body, the church. They become my declaration that Christ is in me and I am in Christ. O Lord, may I be a person through whom You speak and act and love and care in this broken world.

Come to the table of mercy,
Prepared with the wine and the
bread;
All who are hungry and thirsty,
Come and your souls will be fed.
Come at the Lord's invitation;
Receive from His nail-scarred hand.
Eat of the bread of salvation;
Drink of the blood of the Lamb.

"Come to the Table"
Claire Cloninger (©1991)

creed, but woe to that man who betrays him." 23They began to
question among themselves which of them it might be who would
do this.
24Also a dispute arose among them as to which of them was
considered to be greatest. 25Jesus said to them, "The kings of the
Gentiles lord it over them; and those who exercise authority over
them call themselves Benefactors. 26But you are not to be like
that. Instead, the greatest among you should be like the youngest,
and the one who rules like the one who serves. 27For who is
greater, the one who is at the table or the one who serves? Is it not
the one who is at the table? But I am among you as one who
serves. 28You are those who have stood by me in my trials. 29And
I confer on you a kingdom, just as my Father conferred one on
me, 30so that you may eat and drink at my table in my kingdom
and sit on thrones, judging the twelve tribes of Israel.
31"Simon, Simon, Satan has asked to sift you[a] as wheat. 32But
I have prayed for you, Simon, that your faith may not fail. And
when you have turned back, strengthen your brothers."
33But he replied, "Lord, I am ready to go with you to prison
and to death."
34Jesus answered, "I tell you, Peter, before the rooster crows
today, you will deny three times that you know me."
35Then Jesus asked them, "When I sent you without purse, bag
or sandals, did you lack anything?"
"Nothing," they answered.
36He said to them, "But now if you have a purse, take it, and
also a bag; and if you don't have a sword, sell your cloak and buy
one. 37It is written: 'And he was numbered with the transgressors'[b]; and I tell you that this must be fulfilled in me. Yes, what is
written about me is reaching its fulfillment."
38The disciples said, "See, Lord, here are two swords."
"That is enough," he replied.

Jesus Prays on the Mount of Olives

39Jesus went out as usual to the Mount of Olives, and his disciples followed him. 40On reaching the place, he said to them,
"Pray that you will not fall into temptation." 41He withdrew about
a stone's throw beyond them, knelt down and prayed, 42"Father,
if you are willing, take this cup from me; yet not my will, but yours
be done." 43An angel from heaven appeared to him and strengthened him. 44And being in anguish, he prayed more earnestly, and
his sweat was like drops of blood falling to the ground.[c]
45When he rose from prayer and went back to the disciples, he
found them asleep, exhausted from sorrow. 46"Why are you
sleeping?" he asked them. "Get up and pray so that you will not
fall into temptation."

Jesus Arrested

47While he was still speaking a crowd came up, and the man
who was called Judas, one of the Twelve, was leading them. He
approached Jesus to kiss him, 48but Jesus asked him, "Judas, are
you betraying the Son of Man with a kiss?"
49When Jesus' followers saw what was going to happen, they
said, "Lord, should we strike with our swords?" 50And one of
them struck the servant of the high priest, cutting off his right ear.

[a] *31* The Greek is plural. [b] *37* Isaiah 53:12 [c] *44* Some early manuscripts do not have verses 43 and 44.

Humility is a divine veil that covers our good deeds and hides them from our eyes.
Saint John Climacus (570-649)

(22:24–26) Gracious Master, when I am tempted to compare myself to others in terms of commitment and service, help me to remember these words of Yours. Give me the heart of a servant, willing to live without recognition or reward. Let me put myself under the authority of those who have walked with You longer than I, so that I can learn Your ways from them and honor them for their faithfulness. May humility rule over my spirit, and may my longing be for Your glory and not for my own. (1Co 11:1–2; 2Co 10:12; Heb 13:7)

My Lord, You wore no royal crown;
You did not wield the powers of
state,
Nor did You need a scholar's gown
Or priestly robe, to make You
great.

You came unequaled, undeserved,
To be what we were meant to be;
To serve, instead of being served,
A light for all the world to see.
"My Lord, You Wore No Royal Crown"
Christopher Idle (©1982)

(22:34–35) Dear Jesus, like Peter I mean well but I often fail. Many times I promise more than I can deliver. I thank You that Your love for me is not based on my courage or integrity or performance. Thank You that in my failures You do not abandon me. Thank You that in my foolishness You always offer another chance.

51But Jesus answered, "No more of this!" And he touched the
man's ear and healed him.
52Then Jesus said to the chief priests, the officers of the temple
guard, and the elders, who had come for him, "Am I leading a rebellion, that you have come with swords and clubs? 53Every day I
was with you in the temple courts, and you did not lay a hand on
me. But this is your hour—when darkness reigns."

Peter Disowns Jesus

54Then seizing him, they led him away and took him into the
house of the high priest. Peter followed at a distance. 55But when
they had kindled a fire in the middle of the courtyard and had sat
down together, Peter sat down with them. 56A servant girl saw him
seated there in the firelight. She looked closely at him and said,
"This man was with him."
57But he denied it. "Woman, I don't know him," he said.
58A little later someone else saw him and said, "You also are
one of them."
"Man, I am not!" Peter replied.
59About an hour later another asserted, "Certainly this fellow
was with him, for he is a Galilean."
60Peter replied, "Man, I don't know what you're talking
about!" Just as he was speaking, the rooster crowed. 61The Lord
turned and looked straight at Peter. Then Peter remembered the
word the Lord had spoken to him: "Before the rooster crows
today, you will disown me three times." 62And he went outside
and wept bitterly.

The Guards Mock Jesus

63The men who were guarding Jesus began mocking and beating him. 64They blindfolded him and demanded, "Prophesy! Who
hit you?" 65And they said many other insulting things to him.

Jesus Before Pilate and Herod

66At daybreak the council of the elders of the people, both the
chief priests and teachers of the law, met together, and Jesus was
led before them. 67"If you are the Christ,[a]" they said, "tell us."
Jesus answered, "If I tell you, you will not believe me, 68and if
I asked you, you would not answer. 69But from now on, the Son
of Man will be seated at the right hand of the mighty God."
70They all asked, "Are you then the Son of God?"
He replied, "You are right in saying I am."
71Then they said, "Why do we need any more testimony? We
have heard it from his own lips."

23 Then the whole assembly rose and led him off to Pilate.
2And they began to accuse him, saying, "We have found
this man subverting our nation. He opposes payment of taxes to
Caesar and claims to be Christ,[b] a king."
3So Pilate asked Jesus, "Are you the king of the Jews?"
"Yes, it is as you say," Jesus replied.
4Then Pilate announced to the chief priests and the crowd, "I
find no basis for a charge against this man."
5But they insisted, "He stirs up the people all over Judea[c] by
his teaching. He started in Galilee and has come all the way
here."

[a] 67 Or *Messiah* [b] 2 Or *Messiah*; also in verses 35 and 39 [c] 5 Or *over the land of the Jews*

Only he who can say, "The Lord is the strength of my life," can say, "Of whom shall I be afraid?"

Alexander Maclaren (1826-1910)

(22:56–60) Lord, in my heart I love You more than anyone or anything in the world. Yet how often total strangers can make me feel cowardly, and I find myself denying You by words or by silence. Forgive me for my weakness and my fear. Help me to stand firm in my love for You.

Ah, holy Jesus,
How have You offended,
That mortal judgment
Has on You descended?
By foes derided,
By Your own rejected,
O most afflicted!

Who was the guilty?
Who brought this upon You?
It is my treason, Lord,
That has undone You.
'Twas I, Lord Jesus,
I it was denied You;
I crucified You.

"Ah, Holy Jesus"
Johann Heermann (1630)
Trans. Robert Bridges (1844-1930)

(22:70) O Jesus, You are truly the Son of God. You alone are the center of our faith and life and worship. As You bore witness to Yourself, help us also to bear witness to You. Thank You for coming to live among us to be our Redeemer and Savior and Friend.

(23:14–25) Lord Jesus, You did not die because of the will of a fickle crowd or the cowardice of a wicked ruler. You died because the Father chose to reconcile all sinners to Himself. In Your death He provided one perfect sacrifice for all our sins. You died because You were obedient to both His justice and His mercy. You, Jesus, are the holy Lamb of God. I worship You in sorrow, in thankfulness and in repentance.

(23:34) Lord, thank You for teaching us by Your own example the power of forgiveness. You came to forgive even the worst of sinners. Help me to forgive all those who have sinned against me. Unless I do, I am a prisoner of hatred and resentment. Thank You, Lord, for Your forgiveness.

6 On hearing this, Pilate asked if the man was a Galilean. 7 When
he learned that Jesus was under Herod's jurisdiction, he sent him
to Herod, who was also in Jerusalem at that time.
8 When Herod saw Jesus, he was greatly pleased, because for
a long time he had been wanting to see him. From what he had
heard about him, he hoped to see him perform some miracle.
9 He plied him with many questions, but Jesus gave him no answer. 10 The chief priests and the teachers of the law were standing there, vehemently accusing him. 11 Then Herod and his
soldiers ridiculed and mocked him. Dressing him in an elegant
robe, they sent him back to Pilate. 12 That day Herod and Pilate
became friends—before this they had been enemies.
13 Pilate called together the chief priests, the rulers and the
people, 14 and said to them, "You brought me this man as one
who was inciting the people to rebellion. I have examined him in
your presence and have found no basis for your charges against
him. 15 Neither has Herod, for he sent him back to us; as you can
see, he has done nothing to deserve death. 16 Therefore, I will
punish him and then release him.[a]"
18 With one voice they cried out, "Away with this man! Release
Barabbas to us!" 19 (Barabbas had been thrown into prison for an
insurrection in the city, and for murder.)
20 Wanting to release Jesus, Pilate appealed to them again.
21 But they kept shouting, "Crucify him! Crucify him!"
22 For the third time he spoke to them: "Why? What crime has
this man committed? I have found in him no grounds for the
death penalty. Therefore I will have him punished and then release him."
23 But with loud shouts they insistently demanded that he be
crucified, and their shouts prevailed. 24 So Pilate decided to grant
their demand. 25 He released the man who had been thrown into
prison for insurrection and murder, the one they asked for, and
surrendered Jesus to their will.

The Crucifixion

26 As they led him away, they seized Simon from Cyrene, who
was on his way in from the country, and put the cross on him and
made him carry it behind Jesus. 27 A large number of people followed him, including women who mourned and wailed for him.
28 Jesus turned and said to them, "Daughters of Jerusalem, do not
weep for me; weep for yourselves and for your children. 29 For
the time will come when you will say, 'Blessed are the barren
women, the wombs that never bore and the breasts that never
nursed!' 30 Then

"'they will say to the mountains, "Fall on us!"
and to the hills, "Cover us!"'[b]

31 For if men do these things when the tree is green, what will
happen when it is dry?"
32 Two other men, both criminals, were also led out with him to
be executed. 33 When they came to the place called the Skull,
there they crucified him, along with the criminals—one on his
right, the other on his left. 34 Jesus said, "Father, forgive them, for
they do not know what they are doing."[c] And they divided up his
clothes by casting lots.

[a] *16* Some manuscripts *him."* [17] *Now he was obliged to release one man to them at the Feast.* [b] *30* Hosea 10:8 [c] *34* Some early manuscripts do not have this sentence.

[35]The people stood watching, and the rulers even sneered at him. They said, "He saved others; let him save himself if he is the Christ of God, the Chosen One."

[36]The soldiers also came up and mocked him. They offered him wine vinegar [37]and said, "If you are the king of the Jews, save yourself."

[38]There was a written notice above him, which read: THIS IS THE KING OF THE JEWS.

[39]One of the criminals who hung there hurled insults at him: "Aren't you the Christ? Save yourself and us!"

[40]But the other criminal rebuked him. "Don't you fear God," he said, "since you are under the same sentence? [41]We are punished justly, for we are getting what our deeds deserve. But this man has done nothing wrong."

[42]Then he said, "Jesus, remember me when you come into your kingdom.[a]"

[43]Jesus answered him, "I tell you the truth, today you will be with me in paradise."

Jesus' Death

[44]It was now about the sixth hour, and darkness came over the whole land until the ninth hour, [45]for the sun stopped shining. And the curtain of the temple was torn in two. [46]Jesus called out with a loud voice, "Father, into your hands I commit my spirit." When he had said this, he breathed his last.

[47]The centurion, seeing what had happened, praised God and said, "Surely this was a righteous man." [48]When all the people who had gathered to witness this sight saw what took place, they beat their breasts and went away. [49]But all those who knew him, including the women who had followed him from Galilee, stood at a distance, watching these things.

Jesus' Burial

[50]Now there was a man named Joseph, a member of the Council, a good and upright man, [51]who had not consented to their decision and action. He came from the Judean town of Arimathea and he was waiting for the kingdom of God. [52]Going to Pilate, he asked for Jesus' body. [53]Then he took it down, wrapped it in linen cloth and placed it in a tomb cut in the rock, one in which no one had yet been laid. [54]It was Preparation Day, and the Sabbath was about to begin.

[55]The women who had come with Jesus from Galilee followed Joseph and saw the tomb and how his body was laid in it. [56]Then they went home and prepared spices and perfumes. But they rested on the Sabbath in obedience to the commandment.

The Resurrection

24 On the first day of the week, very early in the morning, the women took the spices they had prepared and went to the tomb. [2]They found the stone rolled away from the tomb, [3]but when they entered, they did not find the body of the Lord Jesus. [4]While they were wondering about this, suddenly two men in clothes that gleamed like lightning stood beside them. [5]In their fright the women bowed down with their faces to the ground, but the men said to them, "Why do you look for the living among the

[a] 42 Some manuscripts *come with your kingly power*

(23:42–43) Is it possible, O Jesus, that salvation is as simple as believing in Your grace and asking for it? Here a man with no opportunity to do good or change his behavior is offered the ultimate gift of salvation and eternal life. He accepts Your grace and mercy and is forever with You in heaven. Truly, You are the one door through Whom we gain entrance into God's eternal presence.

(23:44–46) O, Lord Jesus, Lamb of God, friend of sinners, both priest and sacrifice, how can I ever thank You for dying for me? What words can express my sorrow and shame? What plea can protect me from the wrath of God, now that His Son has been killed because of my sin? Only the plea from Your very own lips: "Father, forgive them, for they do not know what they are doing." Take me to Your cross with You, my Savior, and let it do its deadly work in me. Hide me in Your grace. In faith I join my voice with Yours, O Christ, and plead for God's mercy: "Father, into Your hands I commit my spirit." (Gal 2:20; Col 3:3)

Alas! and did my Savior bleed,
And did my sovereign die?
Would He devote that sacred Head
For such a worm as I?

Was it for sins that I have done
He suffered on the tree?
Amazing pity! Grace unknown!
And love beyond degree!

"Alas! and Did My Savior Bleed"
Isaac Watts (1707)

There is nothing we can truly call our own but our sins and our graves . . . When we go to the grave, we go to our own place; but our Lord Jesus, who had no sin of His own, had no grave of His own; dying under imputed sin, it was fit that he should be buried in a borrowed grave.

Matthew Henry (1662-1714)

(24:1–12) All praise to You, Jesus Christ, risen Savior! You triumphed over death and hell. You are the King of kings and the Lord of lords. Forgiveness and salvation are Yours. You have redeemed us and made us holy in the sight of God. Grace and peace flow from You. In You and through You we find strength and blessing and abundant life. Let all of heaven and earth declare Your praise as the risen Son of God, the Savior of the world!

Swallowed into earth's dark womb
Death has triumphed,
That's what they say.
But try to hold Him in the tomb
The Son of life
Rose on the third day!

It is finished,
He has done it.
Life conquered death.
Jesus Christ has won it!

"The Victor"
Jamie Owens-Collins (©1975)

(24:13–32) How often do I fail to recognize Your presence? Open the eyes of my heart, Lord. Give me the simplicity and faith to see You as my companion on all the highways and byways of life. May I hear Your voice each day as You open the Scriptures to me. May I sense Your presence at the table when I break bread with friends. Cause my heart to burn within me whenever You are near.

There is no moment at which God does not present Himself under the guise of some suffering, some consolation, or some duty. All that occurs within us, around us, and by our means covers and hides His divine action. His action is there, most really and certainly present, but in an invisible manner, the result of which is that we are always being taken by surprise and that we only recognize His action after it has passed away. Could we pierce the veil, and were we vigilant and attentive, God would reveal Himself continuously to us. At every occurrence we should say: Dominus est—it is the Lord; and in all circumstances we should find a gift from God . . . God's constant care leads Him to give us each instant what is suited to us.

J. P. de Caussade (1675-1751)

dead? 6He is not here; he has risen! Remember how he told you,
while he was still with you in Galilee: 7'The Son of Man must be
delivered into the hands of sinful men, be crucified and on the
third day be raised again.' " 8Then they remembered his words.
9When they came back from the tomb, they told all these things
to the Eleven and to all the others. 10It was Mary Magdalene, Jo-
anna, Mary the mother of James, and the others with them who
told this to the apostles. 11But they did not believe the women, because their words seemed to them like nonsense. 12Peter, however, got up and ran to the tomb. Bending over, he saw the strips
of linen lying by themselves, and he went away, wondering to himself what had happened.

On the Road to Emmaus

13Now that same day two of them were going to a village called
Emmaus, about seven miles[a] from Jerusalem. 14They were talking with each other about everything that had happened. 15As they
talked and discussed these things with each other, Jesus himself
came up and walked along with them; 16but they were kept from
recognizing him.
17He asked them, "What are you discussing together as you
walk along?"
They stood still, their faces downcast. 18One of them, named
Cleopas, asked him, "Are you only a visitor to Jerusalem and do
not know the things that have happened there in these days?"
19"What things?" he asked.
"About Jesus of Nazareth," they replied. "He was a prophet,
powerful in word and deed before God and all the people. 20The
chief priests and our rulers handed him over to be sentenced to
death, and they crucified him; 21but we had hoped that he was the
one who was going to redeem Israel. And what is more, it is the
third day since all this took place. 22In addition, some of our
women amazed us. They went to the tomb early this morning
23but didn't find his body. They came and told us that they had
seen a vision of angels, who said he was alive. 24Then some of
our companions went to the tomb and found it just as the women
had said, but him they did not see."
25He said to them, "How foolish you are, and how slow of
heart to believe all that the prophets have spoken! 26Did not the
Christ[b] have to suffer these things and then enter his glory?"
27And beginning with Moses and all the Prophets, he explained to
them what was said in all the Scriptures concerning himself.
28As they approached the village to which they were going,
Jesus acted as if he were going farther. 29But they urged him
strongly, "Stay with us, for it is nearly evening; the day is almost
over." So he went in to stay with them.
30When he was at the table with them, he took bread, gave
thanks, broke it and began to give it to them. 31Then their eyes
were opened and they recognized him, and he disappeared from
their sight. 32They asked each other, "Were not our hearts burning within us while he talked with us on the road and opened the
Scriptures to us?"
33They got up and returned at once to Jerusalem. There they
found the Eleven and those with them, assembled together 34and
saying, "It is true! The Lord has risen and has appeared to

[a] *13* Greek *sixty stadia* (about 11 kilometers) [b] *26* Or *Messiah*; also in verse 46

Simon." 35Then the two told what had happened on the way, and
how Jesus was recognized by them when he broke the bread.

Jesus Appears to the Disciples

36While they were still talking about this, Jesus himself stood
among them and said to them, "Peace be with you."
37They were startled and frightened, thinking they saw a ghost.
38He said to them, "Why are you troubled, and why do doubts
rise in your minds? 39Look at my hands and my feet. It is I myself!
Touch me and see; a ghost does not have flesh and bones, as you
see I have."
40When he had said this, he showed them his hands and feet.
41And while they still did not believe it because of joy and amazement, he asked them, "Do you have anything here to eat?" 42They
gave him a piece of broiled fish, 43and he took it and ate it in
their presence.
44He said to them, "This is what I told you while I was still with
you: Everything must be fulfilled that is written about me in the
Law of Moses, the Prophets and the Psalms."
45Then he opened their minds so they could understand the
Scriptures. 46He told them, "This is what is written: The Christ
will suffer and rise from the dead on the third day, 47and repentance and forgiveness of sins will be preached in his name to all
nations, beginning at Jerusalem. 48You are witnesses of these
things. 49I am going to send you what my Father has promised;
but stay in the city until you have been clothed with power from
on high."

The Ascension

50When he had led them out to the vicinity of Bethany, he lifted up his hands and blessed them. 51While he was blessing them,
he left them and was taken up into heaven. 52Then they worshiped him and returned to Jerusalem with great joy. 53And they
stayed continually at the temple, praising God.

Open our eyes, Lord
We want to see Jesus,
To reach out and touch Him
And say that we love Him.
Open our ears, Lord
Help us to listen.
Open our eyes, Lord
We want to see Jesus.

"Open Our Eyes"
Bob Cull (©1976)

(24:36–49) Lord, move afresh in the midst of Your church today. Come in Your peace; remove all our doubt. Open our minds so that we may understand the Scriptures. Fill us with the power of the Holy Spirit so that we may be witnesses of Your resurrection, preachers of repentance and messengers of forgiveness.

The world has yet to see what God can do with and for and through and in a man who is fully and wholly consecrated to Christ.

Henry Varley (1835-1912)

Now let the heav'ns be joyful!
Let earth her song begin!
The world resound in triumph,
And all that is therein;
Let all things seen and unseen
Their notes of gladness blend;
For Christ the Lord hath risen,
Our joy that hath no end.

"The Day of Resurrection"
John of Damascus (8th c.)
Trans. John M. Neale (1818-1866)

The Gospel according to JOHN

The Gospel of John includes a watershed Biblical passage on worship. When a Samaritan woman mentions the proper location for worship, Jesus responds: " 'Believe me, woman, a time is coming when you will worship the Father neither on this mountain nor in Jerusalem . . . A time is coming and has now come when the true worshipers will worship the Father in spirit and truth, for they are the kind of worshipers the Father seeks" (4:21,23). How incredible that God actually seeks people to worship Him! Reading this, our hearts burn to be found among those who worship God "in spirit and in truth."

To worship "in truth" means that we worship God as He has revealed Himself. We must not create and worship an image of God fashioned according to our preferences. Genuine worship responds to God's truthful revelation in His Word. John shows that this Word is embodied not only in Scripture but also in the living person of Jesus, the incarnate Word of God, "full of grace and truth" (1:14). He is "the way and the truth and the life," through Whom we come to God (14:6). We know and worship God, therefore, only through Jesus Christ. He reveals God's nature and glory to us, drawing us into the eternal life of God.

Though our worship surely involves love for God, we worship God also through loving each other with the love given to us in Christ.

Aside from chapter 4, John's Gospel does not often refer to actions we associate with worship: praise, adoration, thanksgiving, etc. Rather, John urges us to respond to God's activity in Jesus by "believing in" Jesus (3:16). We do this when we accept that He is "the Christ, the Son of God" (20:31) and when we entrust ourselves fully to Him.

The relationship we have with God the Father and with Jesus the Son begins with God's love for us: "For God so loved the world . . . " (3:16). Though John's Gospel mentions our love for Jesus (14:21–34), it does not call us to respond to God's love by loving Him in return. Rather, we remain in divine love by loving each other as Jesus has loved us (15:11). Though our worship surely involves love for God (Mk 12:30), John helps us to understand that we worship God also through loving each other with the love given to us in Christ.

To worship "in spirit" means that we worship God through intimate fellowship with Him. Because "God is spirit" (4:24) and because the Spirit of God lives in us (14:17), we worship God not from a distance but by sharing in the life and love of the triune God. When we love Jesus by obeying His command to love each other, He and the Father love us and dwell within us (14:23). Correspondingly, we dwell in the love of Jesus, a love like that of the Father for His Son (15:9). Thus the Gospel of John helps us to worship, not as if God lived in some distant corner of the universe, but by entering into vital, loving communion with God, Who is Father, Son and Holy Spirit.

The Word Became Flesh

1 In the beginning was the Word, and the Word was with God,
and the Word was God. 2He was with God in the beginning.
3Through him all things were made; without him nothing was
made that has been made. 4In him was life, and that life was the
light of men. 5The light shines in the darkness, but the darkness
has not understood[a] it.
6There came a man who was sent from God; his name was
John. 7He came as a witness to testify concerning that light, so
that through him all men might believe. 8He himself was not the
light; he came only as a witness to the light. 9The true light that
gives light to every man was coming into the world.[b]
10He was in the world, and though the world was made
through him, the world did not recognize him. 11He came to that
which was his own, but his own did not receive him. 12Yet to all
who received him, to those who believed in his name, he gave the
right to become children of God— 13children born not of natural descent,[c] nor of human decision or a husband's will, but born
of God.
14The Word became flesh and made his dwelling among us.
We have seen his glory, the glory of the One and Only,[d] who came
from the Father, full of grace and truth.
15John testifies concerning him. He cries out, saying, "This was
he of whom I said, 'He who comes after me has surpassed me because he was before me.' " 16From the fullness of his grace we
have all received one blessing after another. 17For the law was
given through Moses; grace and truth came through Jesus Christ.
18No one has ever seen God, but God the One and Only,[d,e] who is
at the Father's side, has made him known.

John the Baptist Denies Being the Christ

19Now this was John's testimony when the Jews of Jerusalem
sent priests and Levites to ask him who he was. 20He did not fail
to confess, but confessed freely, "I am not the Christ.[f]"
21They asked him, "Then who are you? Are you Elijah?"
He said, "I am not."
"Are you the Prophet?"
He answered, "No."
22Finally they said, "Who are you? Give us an answer to take
back to those who sent us. What do you say about yourself?"
23John replied in the words of Isaiah the prophet, "I am the
voice of one calling in the desert, 'Make straight the way for the
Lord.' "[g]
24Now some Pharisees who had been sent 25questioned him,
"Why then do you baptize if you are not the Christ, nor Elijah, nor
the Prophet?"
26"I baptize with[h] water," John replied, "but among you stands
one you do not know. 27He is the one who comes after me, the
thongs of whose sandals I am not worthy to untie."
28This all happened at Bethany on the other side of the Jordan,
where John was baptizing.

[a]5 Or *darkness, and the darkness has not overcome* [b]9 Or *This was the true light that gives light to every man who comes into the world* [c]13 Greek *of bloods* [d]14,18 Or *the Only Begotten* [e]18 Some manuscripts *but the only* (or *only begotten*) *Son* [f]20 Or *Messiah.* "The Christ" (Greek) and "the Messiah" (Hebrew) both mean "the Anointed One"; also in verse 25. [g]23 Isaiah 40:3 [h]26 Or *in;* also in verses 31 and 33

(1:1–18) How glorious You are, O Jesus, Word of God! My finite mind can only begin to comprehend Your infinite wonders. My words can never aptly reflect Who You are as the divine Word. You are before all things. Through You all things are created. By Your light all things are seen. Your fellowship with the Father surpasses all other intimacies. Indeed You are God! Yet You have become human. You have become like me. The incomprehensible has become known. The eternal has taken on temporality. The creator has joined the creation. The light has entered the darkness. And You have done all of this so that mortals might see Your glory, the very glory of God, so that we might know the Father, so that we might receive grace and truth. What a wonder! What a mystery! How glorious You are, O Word of God!

Jesus, Son of David, Send Your holy
light;
Let me feel the warmth of Heaven
deep inside.
May a vision of Your glory
Flood my point of view
As in faith I bow in prayer
And look to You.

How I long to see You, even now.
May my eyes be open, even now.

"Even Now"
Rick Founds and Bill Batstone (©1990)

And [I believe] in one Lord, Jesus Christ,
The only-begotten Son of God,
Begotten of the Father before all worlds;
God of God, Light of Light,
Very God of very God,
Begotten, not made,
Being of one substance with the Father;
By whom all things were made;
Who, for us men and for our salvation,
Came down from heaven,
And was incarnate by the Holy Spirit of
the Virgin Mary,
And was made man.

The Nicene Creed (325)

God became man, took upon Him a birth from the fallen nature. But why was this done? Or wherein lies the adorable depth of this mystery? How does all this manifest the infinity of the divine love towards man? It is because nothing less than this mysterious incarnation (which astonishes angels) could open a way, or begin a possibility, for fallen man to be born again from above, and made again a partaker of the divine nature.

William Law (1686-1761)

(1:29) O Jesus, Word of God Incarnate Who shines with the very glory of God, are You also the Lamb of God? Will You bear the sin of the world upon Your sinless shoulders? Will You, the Author of life, die in the place of sinful humanity? O Lord Jesus, You have come in the flesh not only to reveal the Father but also to pay for the sins of humanity. What a wonder! What a sacrifice! Lamb of God, Who takes away the sin of the world, have mercy on me, a sinner!

O Lamb of God most holy!
Who on the cross did suffer,
And patient still and lowly,
Yourself to scorn did offer;
Our sins by You were taken,
Or hope had us forsaken:
Have mercy on us, Jesus!

"O Lamb of God Most Holy!"
Nikolaus Decius (1541)
Trans. Arthur Tozer Russell (1806-1874)

Jesus the Lamb of God

29 The next day John saw Jesus coming toward him and said,
"Look, the Lamb of God, who takes away the sin of the world!
30 This is the one I meant when I said, 'A man who comes after me
has surpassed me because he was before me.' 31 I myself did not
know him, but the reason I came baptizing with water was that he
might be revealed to Israel."
32 Then John gave this testimony: "I saw the Spirit come down
from heaven as a dove and remain on him. 33 I would not have
known him, except that the one who sent me to baptize with water
told me, 'The man on whom you see the Spirit come down and remain is he who will baptize with the Holy Spirit.' 34 I have seen
and I testify that this is the Son of God."

Jesus' First Disciples

35 The next day John was there again with two of his disciples.
36 When he saw Jesus passing by, he said, "Look, the Lamb of
God!"
37 When the two disciples heard him say this, they followed
Jesus. 38 Turning around, Jesus saw them following and asked,
"What do you want?"

They said, "Rabbi" (which means Teacher), "where are you staying?"
39 "Come," he replied, "and you will see."

So they went and saw where he was staying, and spent that day with him. It was about the tenth hour.
40 Andrew, Simon Peter's brother, was one of the two who
heard what John had said and who had followed Jesus. 41 The first
thing Andrew did was to find his brother Simon and tell him, "We
have found the Messiah" (that is, the Christ). 42 And he brought
him to Jesus.

Jesus looked at him and said, "You are Simon son of John. You will be called Cephas" (which, when translated, is Peter[a]).

Jesus Calls Philip and Nathanael

43 The next day Jesus decided to leave for Galilee. Finding Philip, he said to him, "Follow me."
44 Philip, like Andrew and Peter, was from the town of Bethsa-
ida. 45 Philip found Nathanael and told him, "We have found the
one Moses wrote about in the Law, and about whom the prophets also wrote—Jesus of Nazareth, the son of Joseph."
46 "Nazareth! Can anything good come from there?" Nathanael asked.

"Come and see," said Philip.
47 When Jesus saw Nathanael approaching, he said of him, "Here is a true Israelite, in whom there is nothing false."
48 "How do you know me?" Nathanael asked.

Jesus answered, "I saw you while you were still under the fig tree before Philip called you."
49 Then Nathanael declared, "Rabbi, you are the Son of God; you are the King of Israel."
50 Jesus said, "You believe[b] because I told you I saw you
under the fig tree. You shall see greater things than that." 51 He
then added, "I tell you[c] the truth, you[c] shall see heaven open,

[a] 42 Both *Cephas* (Aramaic) and *Peter* (Greek) mean *rock*. [b] 50 Or *Do you believe . . . ?* [c] 51 The Greek is plural.

MY BELOVED

Never forget the sacrifice My Son made so that you could know Me. His blood provided the basis for the new covenant. By My will and through My grace, you have been made holy through the sacrifice of the body of Jesus Christ once for all.

What I require from you is that you believe and trust in My Son, through whom you know Me. For whoever believes in Him shall not perish, but will have eternal life. Salvation is found in no one else, for there is no other name under heaven given to men by which you must be saved. He has become My guarantee to this new and better covenant.

When you received My Son Jesus as your Savior and believed on His name, you became My child. At that moment, I gave you a new heart and put My own Spirit in you to compel you to follow My Word and walk in My ways.

My beloved, you are now My child, and what you will be I have not yet made known. But when Jesus appears, you shall be like Him, for you shall see Him as He is. In light of this hope, walk in purity before Me.

Eze 36:26-27; Jn 1:12; 3:16; 6:28-29; Ac 4:12; Heb 7:22; 10:9-10; 1Jn 3:2-3

and the angels of God ascending and descending on the Son of
Man."

Jesus Changes Water to Wine

2 On the third day a wedding took place at Cana in Galilee.
Jesus' mother was there, 2and Jesus and his disciples had
also been invited to the wedding. 3When the wine was gone,
Jesus' mother said to him, "They have no more wine."
4"Dear woman, why do you involve me?" Jesus replied. "My
time has not yet come."
5His mother said to the servants, "Do whatever he tells you."
6Nearby stood six stone water jars, the kind used by the Jews
for ceremonial washing, each holding from twenty to thirty gallons.[a]
7Jesus said to the servants, "Fill the jars with water"; so they
filled them to the brim.
8Then he told them, "Now draw some out and take it to the
master of the banquet."
They did so, 9and the master of the banquet tasted the water
that had been turned into wine. He did not realize where it had
come from, though the servants who had drawn the water knew.
Then he called the bridegroom aside 10and said, "Everyone
brings out the choice wine first and then the cheaper wine after
the guests have had too much to drink; but you have saved the
best till now."
11This, the first of his miraculous signs, Jesus performed at
Cana in Galilee. He thus revealed his glory, and his disciples put
their faith in him.

Jesus Clears the Temple

12After this he went down to Capernaum with his mother and
brothers and his disciples. There they stayed for a few days.
13When it was almost time for the Jewish Passover, Jesus went
up to Jerusalem. 14In the temple courts he found men selling cattle, sheep and doves, and others sitting at tables exchanging
money. 15So he made a whip out of cords, and drove all from the
temple area, both sheep and cattle; he scattered the coins of the
money changers and overturned their tables. 16To those who sold
doves he said, "Get these out of here! How dare you turn my Father's house into a market!"
17His disciples remembered that it is written: "Zeal for your
house will consume me."[b]
18Then the Jews demanded of him, "What miraculous sign can
you show us to prove your authority to do all this?"
19Jesus answered them, "Destroy this temple, and I will raise it
again in three days."
20The Jews replied, "It has taken forty-six years to build this
temple, and you are going to raise it in three days?" 21But the
temple he had spoken of was his body. 22After he was raised from
the dead, his disciples recalled what he had said. Then they believed the Scripture and the words that Jesus had spoken.
23Now while he was in Jerusalem at the Passover Feast, many
people saw the miraculous signs he was doing and believed in his
name.[c] 24But Jesus would not entrust himself to them, for he

[a] 6 Greek *two to three metretes* (probably about 75 to 115 liters) [b] 17 Psalm 69:9
[c] 23 Or *and believed in him*

God passes through the thicket of the world, and wherever his glance falls he turns all things to beauty.

Saint John of the Cross (1542–1591)

(2:1–11) With Your disciples of long ago, O Lord, I trust in You, because I too have caught a glimpse of Your glory. I marvel at Your creative power as You change water into wine. Even today, even in my life, You transform the ceremonial water of the law into the wine of grace and truth. Your wine, O Jesus, is the very best. You pour it not drop by drop, but from Your fullness You generously pour out gallon upon gallon, grace upon grace. I drink deeply of Your wine! With gladness I join in celebration of Your glory! (Jn 1:1–17)

(3:16) Heavenly Father, great is Your love for the world, far beyond all comprehension. Great is Your love, even for us, those who have sinned against You, who have lived as Your enemies. Great is Your love, so great that You sent Your beloved Son to die so that we who believe in Him might live forever with You. So great is Your love, lavished upon us, that we may be called Your children. So great is Your love that nothing in all creation can take it away from us. "Amazing love! How can it be that Thou, my God, shouldst die for me?" (Ro 5:8, 8:38–39; 1Jn 3:1)

It took more love for God to give his Son to die than it would to die himself. You would a thousand times sooner die yourself in your son's place than have him taken away. If the executioner was about to take your son to the gallows, you would say, "Let me die in his stead; let my son be spared." Oh, think of the love God must have had for this world that he gave his only begotten Son to die for it.

Dwight L. Moody (1837-1899)

Could we with ink the ocean fill,
And were the skies of parchment made,
Were every stalk on earth a quill,
And every man a scribe by trade,
To write the love of God above
Would drain the ocean dry.
Nor could the scroll contain the whole,
Though stretched from sky to sky.

O love of God, how rich and pure!
How measureless and strong!
It shall forevermore endure
The saints' and angels' song.

"The Love of God"
F.M. Lehman (1917)

knew all men. 25He did not need man's testimony about man, for he knew what was in a man.

Jesus Teaches Nicodemus

3 Now there was a man of the Pharisees named Nicodemus, a member of the Jewish ruling council. 2He came to Jesus at night and said, "Rabbi, we know you are a teacher who has come from God. For no one could perform the miraculous signs you are doing if God were not with him."

3In reply Jesus declared, "I tell you the truth, no one can see the kingdom of God unless he is born again.[a]"

4"How can a man be born when he is old?" Nicodemus asked. "Surely he cannot enter a second time into his mother's womb to be born!"

5Jesus answered, "I tell you the truth, no one can enter the kingdom of God unless he is born of water and the Spirit. 6Flesh gives birth to flesh, but the Spirit[b] gives birth to spirit. 7You should not be surprised at my saying, 'You[c] must be born again.' 8The wind blows wherever it pleases. You hear its sound, but you cannot tell where it comes from or where it is going. So it is with everyone born of the Spirit."

9"How can this be?" Nicodemus asked.

10"You are Israel's teacher," said Jesus, "and do you not understand these things? 11I tell you the truth, we speak of what we know, and we testify to what we have seen, but still you people do not accept our testimony. 12I have spoken to you of earthly things and you do not believe; how then will you believe if I speak of heavenly things? 13No one has ever gone into heaven except the one who came from heaven—the Son of Man.[d] 14Just as Moses lifted up the snake in the desert, so the Son of Man must be lifted up, 15that everyone who believes in him may have eternal life.[e]

16"For God so loved the world that he gave his one and only Son,[f] that whoever believes in him shall not perish but have eternal life. 17For God did not send his Son into the world to condemn the world, but to save the world through him. 18Whoever believes in him is not condemned, but whoever does not believe stands condemned already because he has not believed in the name of God's one and only Son.[g] 19This is the verdict: Light has come into the world, but men loved darkness instead of light because their deeds were evil. 20Everyone who does evil hates the light, and will not come into the light for fear that his deeds will be exposed. 21But whoever lives by the truth comes into the light, so that it may be seen plainly that what he has done has been done through God."[h]

John the Baptist's Testimony About Jesus

22After this, Jesus and his disciples went out into the Judean countryside, where he spent some time with them, and baptized. 23Now John also was baptizing at Aenon near Salim, because there was plenty of water, and people were constantly coming to be baptized. 24(This was before John was put in prison.) 25An argument developed between some of John's disciples and a certain Jew[i] over the matter of ceremonial washing. 26They came to

[a] 3 Or *born from above*; also in verse 7 [b] 6 Or *but spirit* [c] 7 The Greek is plural.
[d] 13 Some manuscripts *Man, who is in heaven* [e] 15 Or *believes may have eternal life in him* [f] 16 Or *his only begotten Son* [g] 18 Or *God's only begotten Son*
[h] 21 Some interpreters end the quotation after verse 15. [i] 25 Some manuscripts *and certain Jews*

John and said to him, "Rabbi, that man who was with you on the
other side of the Jordan—the one you testified about—well, he
is baptizing, and everyone is going to him."

27To this John replied, "A man can receive only what is given
him from heaven. 28You yourselves can testify that I said, 'I am
not the Christ[a] but am sent ahead of him.' 29The bride belongs to
the bridegroom. The friend who attends the bridegroom waits
and listens for him, and is full of joy when he hears the bridegroom's voice. That joy is mine, and it is now complete. 30He
must become greater; I must become less.

31"The one who comes from above is above all; the one who is
from the earth belongs to the earth, and speaks as one from the
earth. The one who comes from heaven is above all. 32He testifies
to what he has seen and heard, but no one accepts his testimony.
33The man who has accepted it has certified that God is truthful.
34For the one whom God has sent speaks the words of God, for
God[b] gives the Spirit without limit. 35The Father loves the Son and
has placed everything in his hands. 36Whoever believes in the Son
has eternal life, but whoever rejects the Son will not see life, for
God's wrath remains on him."[c]

Jesus Talks With a Samaritan Woman

4 The Pharisees heard that Jesus was gaining and baptizing
more disciples than John, 2although in fact it was not Jesus
who baptized, but his disciples. 3When the Lord learned of this,
he left Judea and went back once more to Galilee.

4Now he had to go through Samaria. 5So he came to a town in
Samaria called Sychar, near the plot of ground Jacob had given to
his son Joseph. 6Jacob's well was there, and Jesus, tired as he
was from the journey, sat down by the well. It was about the sixth
hour.

7When a Samaritan woman came to draw water, Jesus said to
her, "Will you give me a drink?" 8(His disciples had gone into the
town to buy food.)

9The Samaritan woman said to him, "You are a Jew and I am a
Samaritan woman. How can you ask me for a drink?" (For Jews
do not associate with Samaritans.[d])

10Jesus answered her, "If you knew the gift of God and who it
is that asks you for a drink, you would have asked him and he
would have given you living water."

11"Sir," the woman said, "you have nothing to draw with and
the well is deep. Where can you get this living water? 12Are you
greater than our father Jacob, who gave us the well and drank
from it himself, as did also his sons and his flocks and herds?"

13Jesus answered, "Everyone who drinks this water will be
thirsty again, 14but whoever drinks the water I give him will never
thirst. Indeed, the water I give him will become in him a spring of
water welling up to eternal life."

15The woman said to him, "Sir, give me this water so that I
won't get thirsty and have to keep coming here to draw water."

16He told her, "Go, call your husband and come back."

17"I have no husband," she replied.

Jesus said to her, "You are right when you say you have no husband. 18The fact is, you have had five husbands, and the man you

[a] 28 Or *Messiah* [b] 34 Greek *he* [c] 36 Some interpreters end the quotation after verse 30. [d] 9 Or *do not use dishes Samaritans have used*

The heart is as insatiable as the grave till Jesus enters it, and then it is a cup full to overflowing.
Charles Haddon Spurgeon (1834–1892)

(4:4–18) A Samaritan. An outcast. A nobody. Living in shame. Living with failure. She was not looking for You on this day. But You were waiting for her. Thank You, Lord, for the surprise of grace. Thank You for reaching out to the "wrong" people—people who know they are sinners, people who have given up hope, people like me. In Your mercy You penetrate beneath my carefully polished veneer to touch my heart, to expose my sin, to heal my pain. You offer healing and forgiveness far beyond what I would dare to seek. You quench the thirst of my soul. All praise be to You, my gracious, saving Lord. (Mk 2:17; Heb 4:13)

Lord, look upon my need.
I need You, I need You.
Lord, have mercy now on me.
Forgive me, O Lord forgive me
And I will be clean.
O Lord, You are familiar with my ways;
There is nothing hid from You.
O Lord, You know the number of my days.
I want to live my life for You.

"I Need You"
Rick Founds (©1989)

(4:23–24) What an astounding revelation, Heavenly Father, that You are seeking people to worship You in spirit and in truth. You are complete, Lord. No one can add to Your perfection. Yet You seek worshipers, not to augment Your glory, but because it is right for You to be glorified. We who have been created to worship You are more complete when we fulfill this deepest purpose of our lives. When we worship You in the power of Your Spirit and in light of Your revealed truth, we find our rightful place in life. O God, I want to be just what You are looking for—someone who worships You in spirit and in truth!

The Father is looking for worshipers. So if you are looking for God and you just can't seem to find him, then stop what you are doing and worship Him—and He will come and find you.

Joseph Garlington (1939-)

Come and see the glory of the Lord,
Come, behold the Lamb.
Come and see the mercy of the
  King,
Bowing down before Him.

For He is Lord above the heavens,
Lord in all the earth.
Lord of all the angels,
Worthy to be served.
Alleluia, alleluia, Lord.

Come and give thanks unto the
  Lord.
Come, behold the Lamb.
Come and sing the praises of the
  King,
Bowing down before Him.

"Come and See"
Lenny LeBlanc (©1989)

now have is not your husband. What you have just said is quite true."

19"Sir," the woman said, "I can see that you are a prophet.
20Our fathers worshiped on this mountain, but you Jews claim that the place where we must worship is in Jerusalem."

21Jesus declared, "Believe me, woman, a time is coming when you will worship the Father neither on this mountain nor in Jerusalem.
22You Samaritans worship what you do not know; we worship what we do know, for salvation is from the Jews.
23Yet a time is coming and has now come when the true worshipers will worship the Father in spirit and truth, for they are the kind of worshipers the Father seeks.
24God is spirit, and his worshipers must worship in spirit and in truth."

25The woman said, "I know that Messiah" (called Christ) "is coming. When he comes, he will explain everything to us."

26Then Jesus declared, "I who speak to you am he."

The Disciples Rejoin Jesus

27Just then his disciples returned and were surprised to find him talking with a woman. But no one asked, "What do you want?" or "Why are you talking with her?"

28Then, leaving her water jar, the woman went back to the town and said to the people,
29"Come, see a man who told me everything I ever did. Could this be the Christ[a]?"
30They came out of the town and made their way toward him.

31Meanwhile his disciples urged him, "Rabbi, eat something."
32But he said to them, "I have food to eat that you know nothing about."

33Then his disciples said to each other, "Could someone have brought him food?"

34"My food," said Jesus, "is to do the will of him who sent me and to finish his work.
35Do you not say, 'Four months more and then the harvest'? I tell you, open your eyes and look at the fields! They are ripe for harvest.
36Even now the reaper draws his wages, even now he harvests the crop for eternal life, so that the sower and the reaper may be glad together.
37Thus the saying 'One sows and another reaps' is true.
38I sent you to reap what you have not worked for. Others have done the hard work, and you have reaped the benefits of their labor."

Many Samaritans Believe

39Many of the Samaritans from that town believed in him because of the woman's testimony, "He told me everything I ever did."
40So when the Samaritans came to him, they urged him to stay with them, and he stayed two days.
41And because of his words many more became believers.

42They said to the woman, "We no longer believe just because of what you said; now we have heard for ourselves, and we know that this man really is the Savior of the world."

Jesus Heals the Official's Son

43After the two days he left for Galilee.
44(Now Jesus himself had pointed out that a prophet has no honor in his own country.)
45When he arrived in Galilee, the Galileans welcomed him. They had seen all that he had done in Jerusalem at the Passover Feast, for they also had been there.

[a] 29 Or *Messiah*

[46]Once more he visited Cana in Galilee, where he had turned
the water into wine. And there was a certain royal official whose
son lay sick at Capernaum. [47]When this man heard that Jesus had
arrived in Galilee from Judea, he went to him and begged him to
come and heal his son, who was close to death.
[48]"Unless you people see miraculous signs and wonders,"
Jesus told him, "you will never believe."
[49]The royal official said, "Sir, come down before my child
dies."
[50]Jesus replied, "You may go. Your son will live."
The man took Jesus at his word and departed. [51]While he was
still on the way, his servants met him with the news that his boy
was living. [52]When he inquired as to the time when his son got
better, they said to him, "The fever left him yesterday at the seventh hour."
[53]Then the father realized that this was the exact time at which
Jesus had said to him, "Your son will live." So he and all his
household believed.
[54]This was the second miraculous sign that Jesus performed,
having come from Judea to Galilee.

The Healing at the Pool

5 Some time later, Jesus went up to Jerusalem for a feast of the
Jews. [2]Now there is in Jerusalem near the Sheep Gate a pool,
which in Aramaic is called Bethesda[a] and which is surrounded
by five covered colonnades. [3]Here a great number of disabled
people used to lie—the blind, the lame, the paralyzed.[b] [5]One
who was there had been an invalid for thirty-eight years. [6]When
Jesus saw him lying there and learned that he had been in this
condition for a long time, he asked him, "Do you want to get
well?"
[7]"Sir," the invalid replied, "I have no one to help me into the
pool when the water is stirred. While I am trying to get in, someone else goes down ahead of me."
[8]Then Jesus said to him, "Get up! Pick up your mat and walk."
[9]At once the man was cured; he picked up his mat and walked.
The day on which this took place was a Sabbath, [10]and so the
Jews said to the man who had been healed, "It is the Sabbath; the
law forbids you to carry your mat."
[11]But he replied, "The man who made me well said to me,
'Pick up your mat and walk.'"
[12]So they asked him, "Who is this fellow who told you to pick
it up and walk?"
[13]The man who was healed had no idea who it was, for Jesus
had slipped away into the crowd that was there.
[14]Later Jesus found him at the temple and said to him, "See,
you are well again. Stop sinning or something worse may happen
to you." [15]The man went away and told the Jews that it was Jesus
who had made him well.

Life Through the Son

[16]So, because Jesus was doing these things on the Sabbath, the
Jews persecuted him. [17]Jesus said to them, "My Father is always

[a] 2 Some manuscripts *Bethzatha*; other manuscripts *Bethsaida* [b] 3 Some less important manuscripts *paralyzed—and they waited for the moving of the waters. [4]From time to time an angel of the Lord would come down and stir up the waters. The first one into the pool after each such disturbance would be cured of whatever disease he had.*

By a Carpenter mankind was made, and only by that Carpenter can mankind be remade.

Desiderius Erasmus (c.1466–1536)

(5:6) How gracious You are, healing Lord! You ask me if I want to get well—not just a little better, but whole and healthy. You come to remove not only my symptoms but also the underlying disease that is the root cause of those symptoms. You transform not just my behavior but also my heart. Your love forces me to confront myself as I am. Your Word pierces my soul. Before You I am naked, without the cover of pretense. Thank You, dear Jesus, for risking my rejection in order that I might receive the fullness of Your salvation. I praise You for the completeness of Your healing, for the penetrating power of Your love!

(5:22–27) How worthy You are, Jesus, Son of God! As Son of Man, You are the supreme Judge of all things. As incarnate Word, You are the expression of the very glory of God. By dying on the cross You have received glory and honor. Worthy are You, O Lamb Who was slain, "to receive power and wealth and wisdom and strength and honor and glory and praise!" To You God has given the name above all names. All creation bows before Your majesty. Hallelujah! (Jn 1:14; Php 2:9–11; Heb 2:9; Rev 5:12)

Fairest Lord Jesus,
Ruler of all nature,
O Thou of God and man the Son,
Thee will I cherish,
Thee will I honor,
Thou, my soul's glory, joy and crown!

"Fairest Lord Jesus"
Anonymous German Hymn (1677)
Trans. Anonymous (1850)

Jesus knew where he had come from, why he was here, and what he was supposed to accomplish. He came down from heaven, not to do his own will, but the will of the Father. That determination controlled every decision he made.

As a result, he was not distracted with trivia. He was never in a hurry, for he knew his Father would not give a task without the time to do it. Christ was not driven by crises, feeling he must heal everyone in Israel. He could say, "It is finished," even when many people were still bound by demons and twisted by disease. What mattered ultimately was not the number of people healed or fed, but whether the Father's will was being done. His clearly defined goals simplified his decisions.

Erwin W. Lutzer (1941-)

at his work to this very day, and I, too, am working." 18For this
reason the Jews tried all the harder to kill him; not only was he
breaking the Sabbath, but he was even calling God his own Father,
making himself equal with God.

19Jesus gave them this answer: "I tell you the truth, the Son can
do nothing by himself; he can do only what he sees his Father
doing, because whatever the Father does the Son also does. 20For
the Father loves the Son and shows him all he does. Yes, to your
amazement he will show him even greater things than these. 21For
just as the Father raises the dead and gives them life, even so the
Son gives life to whom he is pleased to give it. 22Moreover, the Father judges no one, but has entrusted all judgment to the Son,
23that all may honor the Son just as they honor the Father. He who
does not honor the Son does not honor the Father, who sent him.

24"I tell you the truth, whoever hears my word and believes
him who sent me has eternal life and will not be condemned; he
has crossed over from death to life. 25I tell you the truth, a time
is coming and has now come when the dead will hear the voice of
the Son of God and those who hear will live. 26For as the Father
has life in himself, so he has granted the Son to have life in himself. 27And he has given him authority to judge because he is the
Son of Man.

28"Do not be amazed at this, for a time is coming when all who
are in their graves will hear his voice 29and come out—those
who have done good will rise to live, and those who have done
evil will rise to be condemned. 30By myself I can do nothing; I
judge only as I hear, and my judgment is just, for I seek not to
please myself but him who sent me.

Testimonies About Jesus

31"If I testify about myself, my testimony is not valid. 32There
is another who testifies in my favor, and I know that his testimony about me is valid.

33"You have sent to John and he has testified to the truth. 34Not
that I accept human testimony; but I mention it that you may be
saved. 35John was a lamp that burned and gave light, and you
chose for a time to enjoy his light.

36"I have testimony weightier than that of John. For the very
work that the Father has given me to finish, and which I am
doing, testifies that the Father has sent me. 37And the Father who
sent me has himself testified concerning me. You have never
heard his voice nor seen his form, 38nor does his word dwell in
you, for you do not believe the one he sent. 39You diligently
study[a] the Scriptures because you think that by them you possess
eternal life. These are the Scriptures that testify about me, 40yet
you refuse to come to me to have life.

41"I do not accept praise from men, 42but I know you. I know
that you do not have the love of God in your hearts. 43I have come
in my Father's name, and you do not accept me; but if someone
else comes in his own name, you will accept him. 44How can you
believe if you accept praise from one another, yet make no effort
to obtain the praise that comes from the only God[b]?

45"But do not think I will accuse you before the Father. Your
accuser is Moses, on whom your hopes are set. 46If you believed
Moses, you would believe me, for he wrote about me. 47But since

[a] 39 Or *Study diligently* (the imperative) [b] 44 Some early manuscripts *the Only One*

you do not believe what he wrote, how are you going to believe
what I say?"

Jesus Feeds the Five Thousand

6 Some time after this, Jesus crossed to the far shore of the
Sea of Galilee (that is, the Sea of Tiberias), 2and a great
crowd of people followed him because they saw the miraculous
signs he had performed on the sick. 3Then Jesus went up on a
mountainside and sat down with his disciples. 4The Jewish Passover Feast was near.

5When Jesus looked up and saw a great crowd coming toward
him, he said to Philip, "Where shall we buy bread for these people to eat?" 6He asked this only to test him, for he already had in
mind what he was going to do.

7Philip answered him, "Eight months' wages[a] would not buy
enough bread for each one to have a bite!"

8Another of his disciples, Andrew, Simon Peter's brother,
spoke up, 9"Here is a boy with five small barley loaves and two
small fish, but how far will they go among so many?"

10Jesus said, "Have the people sit down." There was plenty of
grass in that place, and the men sat down, about five thousand of
them. 11Jesus then took the loaves, gave thanks, and distributed
to those who were seated as much as they wanted. He did the
same with the fish.

12When they had all had enough to eat, he said to his disciples,
"Gather the pieces that are left over. Let nothing be wasted." 13So
they gathered them and filled twelve baskets with the pieces of
the five barley loaves left over by those who had eaten.

14After the people saw the miraculous sign that Jesus did, they
began to say, "Surely this is the Prophet who is to come into the
world." 15Jesus, knowing that they intended to come and make
him king by force, withdrew again to a mountain by himself.

Jesus Walks on the Water

16When evening came, his disciples went down to the lake,
17where they got into a boat and set off across the lake for Capernaum. By now it was dark, and Jesus had not yet joined them.
18A strong wind was blowing and the waters grew rough. 19When
they had rowed three or three and a half miles,[b] they saw Jesus
approaching the boat, walking on the water; and they were terrified. 20But he said to them, "It is I; don't be afraid." 21Then they
were willing to take him into the boat, and immediately the boat
reached the shore where they were heading.

22The next day the crowd that had stayed on the opposite shore
of the lake realized that only one boat had been there, and that
Jesus had not entered it with his disciples, but that they had gone
away alone. 23Then some boats from Tiberias landed near the
place where the people had eaten the bread after the Lord had
given thanks. 24Once the crowd realized that neither Jesus nor
his disciples were there, they got into the boats and went to Capernaum in search of Jesus.

Jesus the Bread of Life

25When they found him on the other side of the lake, they
asked him, "Rabbi, when did you get here?"

[a] 7 Greek *two hundred denarii* [b] 19 Greek *rowed twenty-five or thirty stadia* (about 5 or 6 kilometers)

He clothed himself with our lowliness in order to invest us with his grandeur.

Richardson Wright (1885-)

(6:15) How often, Lord Jesus, have I tried to force You into my mold, to shrink You down to the size of my expectations! Delighted to know You as my Friend, I forget Your holy grandeur. So glad to receive You as Savior, I hesitate to proclaim You as Lord. Eager to enjoy the fruits of Your grace, I neglect Your call to costly discipleship. Forgive me for my impertinent attempts to diminish You. Cleanse my presumptuous heart. O Lord, do not withdraw from me, but reveal Who You are that I might know You accurately, follow You faithfully and worship You humbly. (Jn 15:15)

(6:31–55) Praise be to You, Jesus, Bread of Life. You have come from heaven to feed us with divine vitality. Your sustenance alone nourishes eternal life in us. When we are fed by You, the living bread, we will never die. You are the bread that has been broken for us, so that we might live in divine wholeness. O Jesus, Bread of Life, feed me. (Mt 26:26)

You are the food that satisfies all hunger.
Saint Catherine of Siena (1347-1380)

Jesus, Thou joy of loving hearts;
Thou fount of life, Thou light of men,
From the best bliss that earth imparts
We turn, unfilled, to Thee again.

We taste Thee, O Thou living bread,
And long to feast upon Thee still;
We drink of Thee, the fountainhead,
And thirst our souls from Thee to fill.

"Jesus, Thou Joy of Loving Hearts"
Bernard of Clairvaux (1150)
Trans. Ray Palmer (1808-1887)

26Jesus answered, "I tell you the truth, you are looking for me,
not because you saw miraculous signs but because you ate the
loaves and had your fill. 27Do not work for food that spoils, but
for food that endures to eternal life, which the Son of Man will
give you. On him God the Father has placed his seal of approval."
28Then they asked him, "What must we do to do the works God
requires?"
29Jesus answered, "The work of God is this: to believe in the
one he has sent."
30So they asked him, "What miraculous sign then will you give
that we may see it and believe you? What will you do? 31Our forefathers ate the manna in the desert; as it is written: 'He gave them
bread from heaven to eat.'[a]"
32Jesus said to them, "I tell you the truth, it is not Moses who
has given you the bread from heaven, but it is my Father who gives
you the true bread from heaven. 33For the bread of God is he who
comes down from heaven and gives life to the world."
34"Sir," they said, "from now on give us this bread."
35Then Jesus declared, "I am the bread of life. He who comes
to me will never go hungry, and he who believes in me will never
be thirsty. 36But as I told you, you have seen me and still you do
not believe. 37All that the Father gives me will come to me, and
whoever comes to me I will never drive away. 38For I have come
down from heaven not to do my will but to do the will of him who
sent me. 39And this is the will of him who sent me, that I shall lose
none of all that he has given me, but raise them up at the last day.
40For my Father's will is that everyone who looks to the Son and
believes in him shall have eternal life, and I will raise him up at
the last day."
41At this the Jews began to grumble about him because he said,
"I am the bread that came down from heaven." 42They said, "Is
this not Jesus, the son of Joseph, whose father and mother we
know? How can he now say, 'I came down from heaven'?"
43"Stop grumbling among yourselves," Jesus answered. 44"No
one can come to me unless the Father who sent me draws him,
and I will raise him up at the last day. 45It is written in the Prophets: 'They will all be taught by God.'[b] Everyone who listens to the
Father and learns from him comes to me. 46No one has seen the
Father except the one who is from God; only he has seen the Father. 47I tell you the truth, he who believes has everlasting life. 48I
am the bread of life. 49Your forefathers ate the manna in the
desert, yet they died. 50But here is the bread that comes down
from heaven, which a man may eat and not die. 51I am the living
bread that came down from heaven. If anyone eats of this bread,
he will live forever. This bread is my flesh, which I will give for the
life of the world."
52Then the Jews began to argue sharply among themselves,
"How can this man give us his flesh to eat?"
53Jesus said to them, "I tell you the truth, unless you eat the
flesh of the Son of Man and drink his blood, you have no life in
you. 54Whoever eats my flesh and drinks my blood has eternal
life, and I will raise him up at the last day. 55For my flesh is real
food and my blood is real drink. 56Whoever eats my flesh and
drinks my blood remains in me, and I in him. 57Just as the living
Father sent me and I live because of the Father, so the one who

[a] *31* Exodus 16:4; Neh. 9:15; Psalm 78:24,25 [b] *45* Isaiah 54:13

feeds on me will live because of me. 58This is the bread that came
down from heaven. Your forefathers ate manna and died, but he
who feeds on this bread will live forever." 59He said this while
teaching in the synagogue in Capernaum.

Many Disciples Desert Jesus

60On hearing it, many of his disciples said, "This is a hard
teaching. Who can accept it?"

61Aware that his disciples were grumbling about this, Jesus
said to them, "Does this offend you? 62What if you see the Son of
Man ascend to where he was before! 63The Spirit gives life; the
flesh counts for nothing. The words I have spoken to you are spirit[a] and they are life. 64Yet there are some of you who do not believe." For Jesus had known from the beginning which of them
did not believe and who would betray him. 65He went on to say,
"This is why I told you that no one can come to me unless the Father has enabled him."

66From this time many of his disciples turned back and no
longer followed him.

67"You do not want to leave too, do you?" Jesus asked the
Twelve.

68Simon Peter answered him, "Lord, to whom shall we go? You
have the words of eternal life. 69We believe and know that you are
the Holy One of God."

70Then Jesus replied, "Have I not chosen you, the Twelve? Yet
one of you is a devil!" 71(He meant Judas, the son of Simon Iscariot, who, though one of the Twelve, was later to betray him.)

Jesus Goes to the Feast of Tabernacles

7 After this, Jesus went around in Galilee, purposely staying
away from Judea because the Jews there were waiting to take
his life. 2But when the Jewish Feast of Tabernacles was near,
3Jesus' brothers said to him, "You ought to leave here and go to
Judea, so that your disciples may see the miracles you do. 4No
one who wants to become a public figure acts in secret. Since you
are doing these things, show yourself to the world." 5For even his
own brothers did not believe in him.

6Therefore Jesus told them, "The right time for me has not yet
come; for you any time is right. 7The world cannot hate you, but it
hates me because I testify that what it does is evil. 8You go to the
Feast. I am not yet[b] going up to this Feast, because for me the right
time has not yet come." 9Having said this, he stayed in Galilee.

10However, after his brothers had left for the Feast, he went
also, not publicly, but in secret. 11Now at the Feast the Jews were
watching for him and asking, "Where is that man?"

12Among the crowds there was widespread whispering about
him. Some said, "He is a good man."

Others replied, "No, he deceives the people." 13But no one
would say anything publicly about him for fear of the Jews.

Jesus Teaches at the Feast

14Not until halfway through the Feast did Jesus go up to the
temple courts and begin to teach. 15The Jews were amazed and
asked, "How did this man get such learning without having studied?"

[a] 63 Or *Spirit* [b] 8 Some early manuscripts do not have *yet*.

(6:66–69) Jesus, Holy One of God, to whom shall I go but to You? Where else can I find the words of eternal life? Where else can I receive grace upon grace? Who besides You has suffered for my sins? Who besides You offers living water and heavenly bread? Precious Jesus, to You alone I turn for salvation from my sins, for deliverance from my bondage. In You alone I find life as it was meant to be. No one else but You, O Lord, will satisfy the longing of my soul.

I no longer want just to hear about you, beloved Lord, through messengers. I no longer want to hear doctrines about you, nor to have my emotions stirred by people speaking of you. I yearn for your presence.

Saint John of the Cross (1542–1591)

Other refuge have I none;
Hangs my helpless soul on Thee;
Leave, O leave me not alone,
Still support and comfort me.
All my trust on Thee is stayed,
All my help from Thee I bring;
Cover my defenseless head
With the shadow of Thy wing.

"Jesus, Lover of My Soul"
Charles Wesley (1738)

16Jesus answered, "My teaching is not my own. It comes from
him who sent me. 17If anyone chooses to do God's will, he will
find out whether my teaching comes from God or whether I speak
on my own. 18He who speaks on his own does so to gain honor
for himself, but he who works for the honor of the one who sent
him is a man of truth; there is nothing false about him. 19Has not
Moses given you the law? Yet not one of you keeps the law. Why
are you trying to kill me?"
20"You are demon-possessed," the crowd answered. "Who is
trying to kill you?"
21Jesus said to them, "I did one miracle, and you are all astonished. 22Yet, because Moses gave you circumcision (though
actually it did not come from Moses, but from the patriarchs),
you circumcise a child on the Sabbath. 23Now if a child can be
circumcised on the Sabbath so that the law of Moses may not be
broken, why are you angry with me for healing the whole man on
the Sabbath? 24Stop judging by mere appearances, and make a
right judgment."

Is Jesus the Christ?

25At that point some of the people of Jerusalem began to ask,
"Isn't this the man they are trying to kill? 26Here he is, speaking
publicly, and they are not saying a word to him. Have the authorities really concluded that he is the Christ[a]? 27But we know where
this man is from; when the Christ comes, no one will know where
he is from."
28Then Jesus, still teaching in the temple courts, cried out,
"Yes, you know me, and you know where I am from. I am not
here on my own, but he who sent me is true. You do not know
him, 29but I know him because I am from him and he sent me."
30At this they tried to seize him, but no one laid a hand on him,
because his time had not yet come. 31Still, many in the crowd put
their faith in him. They said, "When the Christ comes, will he do
more miraculous signs than this man?"
32The Pharisees heard the crowd whispering such things about
him. Then the chief priests and the Pharisees sent temple guards
to arrest him.
33Jesus said, "I am with you for only a short time, and then I go
to the one who sent me. 34You will look for me, but you will not
find me; and where I am, you cannot come."
35The Jews said to one another, "Where does this man intend
to go that we cannot find him? Will he go where our people live
scattered among the Greeks, and teach the Greeks? 36What did he
mean when he said, 'You will look for me, but you will not find
me,' and 'Where I am, you cannot come'?"
37On the last and greatest day of the Feast, Jesus stood and said
in a loud voice, "If anyone is thirsty, let him come to me and
drink. 38Whoever believes in me, as[b] the Scripture has said,
streams of living water will flow from within him." 39By this he
meant the Spirit, whom those who believed in him were later to
receive. Up to that time the Spirit had not been given, since Jesus
had not yet been glorified.
40On hearing his words, some of the people said, "Surely this
man is the Prophet."
41Others said, "He is the Christ."

[a] 26 Or *Messiah*; also in verses 27, 31, 41 and 42 [b] *37,38* Or / *If anyone is thirsty, let him come to me. / And let him drink, 38who believes in me. / As*

(7:37–39) "As the deer pants for streams of water, so my soul pants for you, O God. My soul thirsts for God, for the living God." I thirst for You, Jesus, Son of God. I yearn for Your living water. My spirit is parched until You fill me with the water of Your Spirit. My vitality ebbs away until Your stream of water flows within me, never to run dry. Nothing but Your water of life will satisfy my deepest thirst. Come and fill my thirsty heart, O Christ. Let my cup overflow with You! (Ps 42:1–2; Jn 4:13–15)

Come just as you are,
Hear the Spirit call.
Come just as you are.
Come and see, come receive.
Come and live forever.

Life everlasting,
And strength for today;
Taste the Living Water,
And never thirst again.

"Come Just As You Are"
Joseph Sabolick (©1994)

Have we come to the fountain of life? Are we drinking of its fullness? Are we living in His love? This is the life of our spirit; the health of our body; the secret of our joy!

May we seek this overflowing life, and become "channels only," with "all His wondrous power flowing through us" so that He can use us every day and every hour!

Evan Henry Hopkins (1837-1918)

Still others asked, "How can the Christ come from Galilee?
42 Does not the Scripture say that the Christ will come from
David's family[a] and from Bethlehem, the town where David
lived?" 43 Thus the people were divided because of Jesus. 44 Some
wanted to seize him, but no one laid a hand on him.

Unbelief of the Jewish Leaders

45 Finally the temple guards went back to the chief priests and
Pharisees, who asked them, "Why didn't you bring him in?"
46 "No one ever spoke the way this man does," the guards declared.

47 "You mean he has deceived you also?" the Pharisees retort-
ed. 48 "Has any of the rulers or of the Pharisees believed in him?
49 No! But this mob that knows nothing of the law—there is a
curse on them."

50 Nicodemus, who had gone to Jesus earlier and who was one
of their own number, asked, 51 "Does our law condemn anyone
without first hearing him to find out what he is doing?"

52 They replied, "Are you from Galilee, too? Look into it, and
you will find that a prophet[b] does not come out of Galilee."

[The earliest manuscripts and many other ancient witnesses
do not have John 7:53–8:11.]

53 Then each went to his own home.

8 But Jesus went to the Mount of Olives. 2 At dawn he appeared
again in the temple courts, where all the people gathered
around him, and he sat down to teach them. 3 The teachers of the
law and the Pharisees brought in a woman caught in adultery.
They made her stand before the group 4 and said to Jesus,
"Teacher, this woman was caught in the act of adultery. 5 In the
Law Moses commanded us to stone such women. Now what do
you say?" 6 They were using this question as a trap, in order to
have a basis for accusing him.

But Jesus bent down and started to write on the ground with
his finger. 7 When they kept on questioning him, he straightened
up and said to them, "If any one of you is without sin, let him be
the first to throw a stone at her." 8 Again he stooped down and
wrote on the ground.

9 At this, those who heard began to go away one at a time, the
older ones first, until only Jesus was left, with the woman still
standing there. 10 Jesus straightened up and asked her, "Woman,
where are they? Has no one condemned you?"

11 "No one, sir," she said.

"Then neither do I condemn you," Jesus declared. "Go now
and leave your life of sin."

The Validity of Jesus' Testimony

12 When Jesus spoke again to the people, he said, "I am the
light of the world. Whoever follows me will never walk in darkness, but will have the light of life."

[a] 42 Greek *seed* [b] 52 Two early manuscripts *the Prophet*

(8:1–11) I can feel the shame of this woman, Lord: mired in sin, caught red-handed, without excuse or escape. How often have I stood in her shoes, drawn into Your holy presence, convicted of my sin! I too deserve the sentence of death. You have every reason to condemn me. Yet You do not. As the Lamb of God You take my sentence of "Guilty" upon Yourself. As Judge You pronounce me "Not Guilty." You give me a life sentence—not life in prison, but life eternal, life abundant, life free from the penalty of sin. Oh, how I praise You for Your infinite mercy! I owe my very life to You!

(8:12) O Jesus, You are the light of the world! God is light and You are the image of the invisible God, the radiance of His glory, the exact representation of His being. In You there is no darkness at all. You are the light for all people, the Sun of righteousness who alone illuminates the way to the Father. You reveal the truth of God to us, penetrating the fog of our confusion, burning off the morning mist of doubt. How radiant You are, O light of the world! (Da 2:22; Mal 4:2; Lk 2:32; Jn 1:4–5,9; 3:19–21; Col 1:15; Heb 1:3; 1Jn 1:5)

Thou heavenly brightness!
Light divine!
O deep within my heart now shine,
And make Thee there an altar!
Fill me with joy and strength
To be Thy member,
Ever joined to Thee in love
That cannot falter!
Toward Thee longing
Doth possess me;
Turn and bless me;
Here in sadness
Eye and heart long for Thy gladness!
"O Morning Star, How Fair and Bright"
Philipp Nicolai (1597)
Trans. Catherine Winkworth (1827-1878)

13The Pharisees challenged him, "Here you are, appearing as your own witness; your testimony is not valid."

14Jesus answered, "Even if I testify on my own behalf, my testimony is valid, for I know where I came from and where I am going. But you have no idea where I come from or where I am going. 15You judge by human standards; I pass judgment on no one. 16But if I do judge, my decisions are right, because I am not alone. I stand with the Father, who sent me. 17In your own Law it is written that the testimony of two men is valid. 18I am one who testifies for myself; my other witness is the Father, who sent me."

19Then they asked him, "Where is your father?"

"You do not know me or my Father," Jesus replied. "If you knew me, you would know my Father also." 20He spoke these words while teaching in the temple area near the place where the offerings were put. Yet no one seized him, because his time had not yet come.

21Once more Jesus said to them, "I am going away, and you will look for me, and you will die in your sin. Where I go, you cannot come."

22This made the Jews ask, "Will he kill himself? Is that why he says, 'Where I go, you cannot come'?"

23But he continued, "You are from below; I am from above. You are of this world; I am not of this world. 24I told you that you would die in your sins; if you do not believe that I am ⌊the one I claim to be⌋,[a] you will indeed die in your sins."

25"Who are you?" they asked.

"Just what I have been claiming all along," Jesus replied. 26"I have much to say in judgment of you. But he who sent me is reliable, and what I have heard from him I tell the world."

27They did not understand that he was telling them about his Father. 28So Jesus said, "When you have lifted up the Son of Man, then you will know that I am ⌊the one I claim to be⌋ and that I do nothing on my own but speak just what the Father has taught me. 29The one who sent me is with me; he has not left me alone, for I always do what pleases him." 30Even as he spoke, many put their faith in him.

The Children of Abraham

31To the Jews who had believed him, Jesus said, "If you hold to my teaching, you are really my disciples. 32Then you will know the truth, and the truth will set you free."

33They answered him, "We are Abraham's descendants[b] and have never been slaves of anyone. How can you say that we shall be set free?"

34Jesus replied, "I tell you the truth, everyone who sins is a slave to sin. 35Now a slave has no permanent place in the family, but a son belongs to it forever. 36So if the Son sets you free, you will be free indeed. 37I know you are Abraham's descendants. Yet you are ready to kill me, because you have no room for my word. 38I am telling you what I have seen in the Father's presence, and you do what you have heard from your father.[c]"

39"Abraham is our father," they answered.

"If you were Abraham's children," said Jesus, "then you

[a] *24* Or *I am he*; also in verse 28 [b] *33* Greek *seed*; also in verse 37 [c] *38* Or *presence. Therefore do what you have heard from the Father.*

would[a] do the things Abraham did. 40As it is, you are determined to kill me, a man who has told you the truth that I heard from God. Abraham did not do such things. 41You are doing the things your own father does."

"We are not illegitimate children," they protested. "The only Father we have is God himself."

The Children of the Devil

42Jesus said to them, "If God were your Father, you would love me, for I came from God and now am here. I have not come on my own; but he sent me. 43Why is my language not clear to you? Because you are unable to hear what I say. 44You belong to your father, the devil, and you want to carry out your father's desire. He was a murderer from the beginning, not holding to the truth, for there is no truth in him. When he lies, he speaks his native language, for he is a liar and the father of lies. 45Yet because I tell the truth, you do not believe me! 46Can any of you prove me guilty of sin? If I am telling the truth, why don't you believe me? 47He who belongs to God hears what God says. The reason you do not hear is that you do not belong to God."

The Claims of Jesus About Himself

48The Jews answered him, "Aren't we right in saying that you are a Samaritan and demon-possessed?"

49"I am not possessed by a demon," said Jesus, "but I honor my Father and you dishonor me. 50I am not seeking glory for myself; but there is one who seeks it, and he is the judge. 51I tell you the truth, if anyone keeps my word, he will never see death."

52At this the Jews exclaimed, "Now we know that you are demon-possessed! Abraham died and so did the prophets, yet you say that if anyone keeps your word, he will never taste death. 53Are you greater than our father Abraham? He died, and so did the prophets. Who do you think you are?"

54Jesus replied, "If I glorify myself, my glory means nothing. My Father, whom you claim as your God, is the one who glorifies me. 55Though you do not know him, I know him. If I said I did not, I would be a liar like you, but I do know him and keep his word. 56Your father Abraham rejoiced at the thought of seeing my day; he saw it and was glad."

57"You are not yet fifty years old," the Jews said to him, "and you have seen Abraham!"

58"I tell you the truth," Jesus answered, "before Abraham was born, I am!" 59At this, they picked up stones to stone him, but Jesus hid himself, slipping away from the temple grounds.

Jesus Heals a Man Born Blind

9 As he went along, he saw a man blind from birth. 2His disciples asked him, "Rabbi, who sinned, this man or his parents, that he was born blind?"

3"Neither this man nor his parents sinned," said Jesus, "but this happened so that the work of God might be displayed in his life. 4As long as it is day, we must do the work of him who sent me. Night is coming, when no one can work. 5While I am in the world, I am the light of the world."

[a] 39 Some early manuscripts *"If you are Abraham's children," said Jesus, "then*

(8:58) What a mystery! Before Abraham took his first breath, You existed, O Christ. Even at the dawn of creation, You were there. Before time came into being, You were—You are! Who else can claim such a thing, except God in the flesh? Who else can truly bear the name "I AM," the very name of God? Who else cradles the vast expanse of history in his hands? Yet into that history You have come, the transcendent made immanent, the Creator becoming part of the creation, the eternal Word of God made flesh. All praise be to You, Jesus Christ, my Living Lord and my Eternal God! (Ex 3:14)

You only are the Holy One,
Who came for our salvation,
And only You are God's true Son,
Who was before creation.
You only, Christ, as Lord we own,
And with the Spirit, You alone
Share in the Father's glory.

"All Glory Be to God on High"
Nikolaus Decius (1522)
Trans. F. Bland Tucker (©1977)

(9:25) Your grace touches us, Lord, long before we know Who You are. In Your mercy, You do not require theological correctness from those You choose to heal. Indeed, it is only as You restore our spiritual sight that we are able to see You in the light of truth. How blind I was before You gave me sight! How confused I was before You healed the eyes of my soul! Yet even now I do not pretend to have fully understood the mystery of Your manifold, infinite, amazing grace. There is so much I still cannot comprehend about You. But one thing I do know: "I was blind but now I see!" (1Co 13:12)

Amazing grace! How sweet the sound
That saved a wretch like me!
I once was lost but now am found,
Was blind, but now I see.

"Amazing Grace"
John Newton (1779)

Oh, the blindness of men who, not having yet understood that they were created only for God, dare to think it strange that we should always think of God, and that we have no more familiar object than God.

François Malaval (1627-1719)

6 Having said this, he spit on the ground, made some mud with
the saliva, and put it on the man's eyes. 7 "Go," he told him, "wash
in the Pool of Siloam" (this word means Sent). So the man went
and washed, and came home seeing.
8 His neighbors and those who had formerly seen him begging
asked, "Isn't this the same man who used to sit and beg?" 9 Some
claimed that he was.
Others said, "No, he only looks like him."
But he himself insisted, "I am the man."
10 "How then were your eyes opened?" they demanded.
11 He replied, "The man they call Jesus made some mud and
put it on my eyes. He told me to go to Siloam and wash. So I went
and washed, and then I could see."
12 "Where is this man?" they asked him.
"I don't know," he said.

The Pharisees Investigate the Healing

13 They brought to the Pharisees the man who had been blind.
14 Now the day on which Jesus had made the mud and opened the
man's eyes was a Sabbath. 15 Therefore the Pharisees also asked
him how he had received his sight. "He put mud on my eyes," the
man replied, "and I washed, and now I see."
16 Some of the Pharisees said, "This man is not from God, for
he does not keep the Sabbath."
But others asked, "How can a sinner do such miraculous
signs?" So they were divided.
17 Finally they turned again to the blind man, "What have you to
say about him? It was your eyes he opened."
The man replied, "He is a prophet."
18 The Jews still did not believe that he had been blind and had
received his sight until they sent for the man's parents. 19 "Is this
your son?" they asked. "Is this the one you say was born blind?
How is it that now he can see?"
20 "We know he is our son," the parents answered, "and we
know he was born blind. 21 But how he can see now, or who
opened his eyes, we don't know. Ask him. He is of age; he will
speak for himself." 22 His parents said this because they were
afraid of the Jews, for already the Jews had decided that anyone
who acknowledged that Jesus was the Christ[a] would be put out of
the synagogue. 23 That was why his parents said, "He is of age;
ask him."
24 A second time they summoned the man who had been blind.
"Give glory to God,[b]" they said. "We know this man is a sinner."
25 He replied, "Whether he is a sinner or not, I don't know. One
thing I do know. I was blind but now I see!"
26 Then they asked him, "What did he do to you? How did he
open your eyes?"
27 He answered, "I have told you already and you did not listen.
Why do you want to hear it again? Do you want to become his disciples, too?"
28 Then they hurled insults at him and said, "You are this fellow's disciple! We are disciples of Moses! 29 We know that God
spoke to Moses, but as for this fellow, we don't even know where
he comes from."
30 The man answered, "Now that is remarkable! You don't

[a] 22 Or *Messiah* [b] 24 A solemn charge to tell the truth (see Joshua 7:19)

know where he comes from, yet he opened my eyes. 31We know
that God does not listen to sinners. He listens to the godly man
who does his will. 32Nobody has ever heard of opening the eyes
of a man born blind. 33If this man were not from God, he could
do nothing."
34To this they replied, "You were steeped in sin at birth; how
dare you lecture us!" And they threw him out.

Spiritual Blindness

35Jesus heard that they had thrown him out, and when he
found him, he said, "Do you believe in the Son of Man?"
36"Who is he, sir?" the man asked. "Tell me so that I may believe in him."
37Jesus said, "You have now seen him; in fact, he is the one
speaking with you."
38Then the man said, "Lord, I believe," and he worshiped him.
39Jesus said, "For judgment I have come into this world, so
that the blind will see and those who see will become blind."
40Some Pharisees who were with him heard him say this and
asked, "What? Are we blind too?"
41Jesus said, "If you were blind, you would not be guilty of sin;
but now that you claim you can see, your guilt remains.

The Shepherd and His Flock

10 "I tell you the truth, the man who does not enter the sheep
pen by the gate, but climbs in by some other way, is a thief
and a robber. 2The man who enters by the gate is the shepherd of
his sheep. 3The watchman opens the gate for him, and the sheep
listen to his voice. He calls his own sheep by name and leads
them out. 4When he has brought out all his own, he goes on
ahead of them, and his sheep follow him because they know his
voice. 5But they will never follow a stranger; in fact, they will run
away from him because they do not recognize a stranger's voice."
6Jesus used this figure of speech, but they did not understand
what he was telling them.
7Therefore Jesus said again, "I tell you the truth, I am the gate
for the sheep. 8All who ever came before me were thieves and
robbers, but the sheep did not listen to them. 9I am the gate; whoever enters through me will be saved.[a] He will come in and go
out, and find pasture. 10The thief comes only to steal and kill and
destroy; I have come that they may have life, and have it to the full.
11"I am the good shepherd. The good shepherd lays down his
life for the sheep. 12The hired hand is not the shepherd who owns
the sheep. So when he sees the wolf coming, he abandons the
sheep and runs away. Then the wolf attacks the flock and scatters
it. 13The man runs away because he is a hired hand and cares
nothing for the sheep.
14"I am the good shepherd; I know my sheep and my sheep
know me— 15just as the Father knows me and I know the Father—and I lay down my life for the sheep. 16I have other sheep
that are not of this sheep pen. I must bring them also. They too
will listen to my voice, and there shall be one flock and one
shepherd. 17The reason my Father loves me is that I lay down my
life—only to take it up again. 18No one takes it from me, but I
lay it down of my own accord. I have authority to lay it down and

[a]9 Or *kept safe*

(10:1–18) How tenderly You care for me, Jesus, my Shepherd! When I hear Your reassuring voice I know that I am secure. When I wander far away You search for me. And when You find me, You hoist me upon Your strong shoulders, rejoicing that I have been found. You are the gate that leads to the fold of salvation. You are the fold in which I find safety. When I am in danger, You lay down Your own life for me. You give me the gift of life, life to the full. Oh to know You, gracious Shepherd, and to be known by You—this is true life! (Dt 33:12; Ps 23; Lk 15:4–7; Jn 17:3)

I look to the Shepherd.
He meets all my needs;
Beside the still waters
He faithfully leads,
Bringing peace to my soul
As His love makes me whole.

Surely goodness and mercy shall
  follow me,
Follow me all the days of my life.
Surely goodness and mercy shall
  follow me,
All my life.

"I Look to the Shepherd"
Walt Harrah (©1987)

(10:30) Lord Jesus, my Savior and Friend, You are one with God the Father. You are the Word of God made flesh, the image of the invisible God revealed to us. In You dwells all the fullness of God. You are the radiance of God's own glory and the exact representation of His own being. Being equal to God, You are God in Your very nature. You have been exalted to the highest place and given God's own name. My Lord, and Lord of all creation, I bow before You. I lift up Your holy name and proclaim that You, my Savior and Friend, are indeed God! (Jn 1:1; Php 2:6–9; Col 1:15,19; Heb 1:3)

God has spoken by Christ Jesus,
Christ the everlasting Son,
Brightness of the Father's glory,
With the Father ever one;
Spoken by the Word incarnate,
God of God, ere time was born;
Light of Light, to earth descending,
Christ, as God in human form.

"God Has Spoken by His Prophets"
George W. Briggs (©1953)

authority to take it up again. This command I received from my
Father."
19At these words the Jews were again divided. 20Many of them
said, "He is demon-possessed and raving mad. Why listen to
him?"
21But others said, "These are not the sayings of a man possessed by a demon. Can a demon open the eyes of the blind?"

The Unbelief of the Jews

22Then came the Feast of Dedication[a] at Jerusalem. It was
winter, 23and Jesus was in the temple area walking in Solomon's
Colonnade. 24The Jews gathered around him, saying, "How long
will you keep us in suspense? If you are the Christ,[b] tell us
plainly."
25Jesus answered, "I did tell you, but you do not believe. The
miracles I do in my Father's name speak for me, 26but you do
not believe because you are not my sheep. 27My sheep listen to
my voice; I know them, and they follow me. 28I give them eternal
life, and they shall never perish; no one can snatch them out of
my hand. 29My Father, who has given them to me, is greater than
all[c]; no one can snatch them out of my Father's hand. 30I and the
Father are one."
31Again the Jews picked up stones to stone him, 32but Jesus
said to them, "I have shown you many great miracles from the Father. For which of these do you stone me?"
33"We are not stoning you for any of these," replied the Jews,
"but for blasphemy, because you, a mere man, claim to be God."
34Jesus answered them, "Is it not written in your Law, 'I have
said you are gods'[d]? 35If he called them 'gods,' to whom the word
of God came—and the Scripture cannot be broken— 36what
about the one whom the Father set apart as his very own and sent
into the world? Why then do you accuse me of blasphemy because
I said, 'I am God's Son'? 37Do not believe me unless I do what my
Father does. 38But if I do it, even though you do not believe me,
believe the miracles, that you may know and understand that the
Father is in me, and I in the Father." 39Again they tried to seize
him, but he escaped their grasp.
40Then Jesus went back across the Jordan to the place where
John had been baptizing in the early days. Here he stayed 41and
many people came to him. They said, "Though John never performed a miraculous sign, all that John said about this man was
true." 42And in that place many believed in Jesus.

The Death of Lazarus

11 Now a man named Lazarus was sick. He was from Bethany,
the village of Mary and her sister Martha. 2This Mary,
whose brother Lazarus now lay sick, was the same one who
poured perfume on the Lord and wiped his feet with her hair. 3So
the sisters sent word to Jesus, "Lord, the one you love is sick."
4When he heard this, Jesus said, "This sickness will not end in
death. No, it is for God's glory so that God's Son may be glorified
through it." 5Jesus loved Martha and her sister and Lazarus. 6Yet
when he heard that Lazarus was sick, he stayed where he was two
more days.
7Then he said to his disciples, "Let us go back to Judea."

[a] 22 That is, Hanukkah [b] 24 Or *Messiah* [c] 29 Many early manuscripts *What my Father has given me is greater than all* [d] 34 Psalm 82:6

MY BELOVED

I have made many promises to you, and My Word is true. What I have spoken will come to pass.

The evil one comes to you only to steal, kill and destroy. There is nothing good that can come from him. He will endeavor to trick you into believing differently, but be aware of his desire to see that you are destroyed.

Jesus has come that you may have life, and have it to the fullest! In fact, My beloved, every good and perfect gift is from Me. It originates with Me and passes to you through My Son.

I have given you very great and precious promises. Through these promises you may participate in My divine nature and escape the corruption in the world caused by evil desires. Everything you need for life and godliness is available to you through My Son. Through faith in Him, You will be able to have a life that represents My heart.

Be assured that I am faithful. I do not change My mind later regarding My promises. I do not say first "yes" and then later "no." I am faithful to you! What I have promised, I will provide.

So rejoice in My promises like one who finds great spoil. Believe My promises and sing praises to My name. You will see their fulfillment because, through faith in My Son Jesus, you believe them. My Word is true!

1Sa 15:29; Ps 106:12; 119:162; 145:13; Jn 10:10; 2Co 1:19-20; Gal 3:22; Jas 1:17; 2Pe 1:3-4

8“But Rabbi,” they said, “a short while ago the Jews tried to
stone you, and yet you are going back there?”
9Jesus answered, “Are there not twelve hours of daylight? A
man who walks by day will not stumble, for he sees by this world’s
light. 10It is when he walks by night that he stumbles, for he has
no light.”
11After he had said this, he went on to tell them, “Our friend
Lazarus has fallen asleep; but I am going there to wake him up.”
12His disciples replied, “Lord, if he sleeps, he will get better.”
13Jesus had been speaking of his death, but his disciples thought
he meant natural sleep.
14So then he told them plainly, “Lazarus is dead, 15and for
your sake I am glad I was not there, so that you may believe. But
let us go to him.”
16Then Thomas (called Didymus) said to the rest of the disciples, “Let us also go, that we may die with him.”

Jesus Comforts the Sisters

17On his arrival, Jesus found that Lazarus had already been in
the tomb for four days. 18Bethany was less than two miles[a] from
Jerusalem, 19and many Jews had come to Martha and Mary to
comfort them in the loss of their brother. 20When Martha heard
that Jesus was coming, she went out to meet him, but Mary stayed
at home.
21“Lord,” Martha said to Jesus, “if you had been here, my
brother would not have died. 22But I know that even now God
will give you whatever you ask.”
23Jesus said to her, “Your brother will rise again.”
24Martha answered, “I know he will rise again in the resurrection at the last day.”
25Jesus said to her, “I am the resurrection and the life. He who
believes in me will live, even though he dies; 26and whoever lives
and believes in me will never die. Do you believe this?”
27“Yes, Lord,” she told him, “I believe that you are the Christ,[b]
the Son of God, who was to come into the world.”
28And after she had said this, she went back and called her sister Mary aside. “The Teacher is here,” she said, “and is asking for
you.” 29When Mary heard this, she got up quickly and went to
him. 30Now Jesus had not yet entered the village, but was still at
the place where Martha had met him. 31When the Jews who had
been with Mary in the house, comforting her, noticed how quickly she got up and went out, they followed her, supposing she was
going to the tomb to mourn there.
32When Mary reached the place where Jesus was and saw him,
she fell at his feet and said, “Lord, if you had been here, my
brother would not have died.”
33When Jesus saw her weeping, and the Jews who had come
along with her also weeping, he was deeply moved in spirit and
troubled. 34“Where have you laid him?” he asked.
“Come and see, Lord,” they replied.
35Jesus wept.
36Then the Jews said, “See how he loved him!”
37But some of them said, “Could not he who opened the eyes
of the blind man have kept this man from dying?”

[a] *18* Greek *fifteen stadia* (about 3 kilometers) [b] *27* Or *Messiah*

(11:25–27) Yes, Lord Jesus, I believe. I believe that You are the resurrection, the One who has conquered death. I believe that You are the life, the One from Whom we receive divine abundance forever. I believe that You are the Christ, God’s Anointed One Who has come to save us. I believe that You are the Son of God, the King who reigns forever, the only Son Who reveals the Father to us. My mind affirms that all of this is true and my heart confirms with a resounding “Amen!” I place my full confidence in You, for You alone are worthy of my trust. Yes, Lord, I do believe! (Jn 1:18,49)

You are the Rock of my salvation,
You are the strength of my life.
You are my hope and my inspiration,
Lord, unto You will I cry.

I believe in You, believe in You,
For Your faithful love to me.
You have been my help in time of
need;
Lord, unto You will I cleave.

“Rock of My Salvation”
Teresa Muller (©1982)

Jesus Raises Lazarus From the Dead

38 Jesus, once more deeply moved, came to the tomb. It was a cave with a stone laid across the entrance. 39 "Take away the stone," he said.

"But, Lord," said Martha, the sister of the dead man, "by this time there is a bad odor, for he has been there four days."

40 Then Jesus said, "Did I not tell you that if you believed, you would see the glory of God?"

41 So they took away the stone. Then Jesus looked up and said, "Father, I thank you that you have heard me. 42 I knew that you always hear me, but I said this for the benefit of the people standing here, that they may believe that you sent me."

43 When he had said this, Jesus called in a loud voice, "Lazarus, come out!" 44 The dead man came out, his hands and feet wrapped with strips of linen, and a cloth around his face.

Jesus said to them, "Take off the grave clothes and let him go."

The Plot to Kill Jesus

45 Therefore many of the Jews who had come to visit Mary, and had seen what Jesus did, put their faith in him. 46 But some of them went to the Pharisees and told them what Jesus had done. 47 Then the chief priests and the Pharisees called a meeting of the Sanhedrin.

"What are we accomplishing?" they asked. "Here is this man performing many miraculous signs. 48 If we let him go on like this, everyone will believe in him, and then the Romans will come and take away both our place[a] and our nation."

49 Then one of them, named Caiaphas, who was high priest that year, spoke up, "You know nothing at all! 50 You do not realize that it is better for you that one man die for the people than that the whole nation perish."

51 He did not say this on his own, but as high priest that year he prophesied that Jesus would die for the Jewish nation, 52 and not only for that nation but also for the scattered children of God, to bring them together and make them one. 53 So from that day on they plotted to take his life.

54 Therefore Jesus no longer moved about publicly among the Jews. Instead he withdrew to a region near the desert, to a village called Ephraim, where he stayed with his disciples.

55 When it was almost time for the Jewish Passover, many went up from the country to Jerusalem for their ceremonial cleansing before the Passover. 56 They kept looking for Jesus, and as they stood in the temple area they asked one another, "What do you think? Isn't he coming to the Feast at all?" 57 But the chief priests and Pharisees had given orders that if anyone found out where Jesus was, he should report it so that they might arrest him.

Jesus Anointed at Bethany

12 Six days before the Passover, Jesus arrived at Bethany, where Lazarus lived, whom Jesus had raised from the dead. 2 Here a dinner was given in Jesus' honor. Martha served, while Lazarus was among those reclining at the table with him. 3 Then Mary took about a pint[b] of pure nard, an expensive perfume; she poured it on Jesus' feet and wiped his feet with her hair. And the house was filled with the fragrance of the perfume.

[a] 48 Or *temple* [b] 3 Greek *a litra* (probably about 0.5 liter)

(12:3) What extravagance, Lord!—a perfume so expensive that it took a year of labor to purchase one small pint. A luxury such as this not delicately daubed upon You, but lavishly poured out, dripping onto the floor, filling the house with its precious fragrance. O that my worship would be so unreserved! O that I would offer to You my very best without limit or hesitation! You are worth it, Lord; You are worth every drop.

Take my love; my Lord, I pour
At Thy feet its treasure store.
Take myself, and I will be
Ever, only, all for Thee,
Ever, only, all for Thee.

"Take My Life and Let It Be"
Frances Ridley Havergal (1874)

4 But one of his disciples, Judas Iscariot, who was later to betray him, objected, 5 "Why wasn't this perfume sold and the money given to the poor? It was worth a year's wages.[a]" 6 He did not say this because he cared about the poor but because he was a thief; as keeper of the money bag, he used to help himself to what was put into it.

7 "Leave her alone," Jesus replied. "⌊It was intended⌋ that she should save this perfume for the day of my burial. 8 You will always have the poor among you, but you will not always have me."

9 Meanwhile a large crowd of Jews found out that Jesus was there and came, not only because of him but also to see Lazarus, whom he had raised from the dead. 10 So the chief priests made plans to kill Lazarus as well, 11 for on account of him many of the Jews were going over to Jesus and putting their faith in him.

The Triumphal Entry

12 The next day the great crowd that had come for the Feast heard that Jesus was on his way to Jerusalem. 13 They took palm branches and went out to meet him, shouting,

"Hosanna![b]"

"Blessed is he who comes in the name of the Lord!"[c]

"Blessed is the King of Israel!"

14 Jesus found a young donkey and sat upon it, as it is written,

15 "Do not be afraid, O Daughter of Zion;
see, your king is coming,
seated on a donkey's colt."[d]

16 At first his disciples did not understand all this. Only after Jesus was glorified did they realize that these things had been written about him and that they had done these things to him.

17 Now the crowd that was with him when he called Lazarus from the tomb and raised him from the dead continued to spread the word. 18 Many people, because they had heard that he had given this miraculous sign, went out to meet him. 19 So the Pharisees said to one another, "See, this is getting us nowhere. Look how the whole world has gone after him!"

Jesus Predicts His Death

20 Now there were some Greeks among those who went up to worship at the Feast. 21 They came to Philip, who was from Bethsaida in Galilee, with a request. "Sir," they said, "we would like to see Jesus." 22 Philip went to tell Andrew; Andrew and Philip in turn told Jesus.

23 Jesus replied, "The hour has come for the Son of Man to be glorified. 24 I tell you the truth, unless a kernel of wheat falls to the ground and dies, it remains only a single seed. But if it dies, it produces many seeds. 25 The man who loves his life will lose it, while the man who hates his life in this world will keep it for eternal life. 26 Whoever serves me must follow me; and where I am, my servant also will be. My Father will honor the one who serves me.

27 "Now my heart is troubled, and what shall I say? 'Father, save

[a] 5 Greek *three hundred denarii* [b] 13 A Hebrew expression meaning "Save!" which became an exclamation of praise [c] 13 Psalm 118:25,26 [d] 15 Zech. 9:9

(12:12–13) "Hosanna! Save now!" Rescue us, Jesus! We need Your help! We need Your deliverance! "Hosanna! Save now!" That is precisely what You came to do, but in a way we did not expect. In order to save us You had to lay down Your life. Before You would wear the crown of glory You first had to wear the crown of thorns. You heard our cry for mercy. You answered our prayer for a Savior King. Today, we join our voices with the song of this crowd and with the song of the countless multitudes who are waving palm branches before the throne of the Lamb. And we cry out to You, our King: "Salvation belongs to our God, who sits on the throne, and to the Lamb." (Ps 118:25–26; Rev 7:9–10)

"Hosanna in the highest!"
That ancient song we sing,
For Christ is our Redeemer,
The Lord of heaven our King.
O may we ever praise Him
With heart and life and voice,
And in His holy presence
Eternally rejoice!

"Hosanna, Loud Hosanna"
Jennette Threlfall (1873)

(12:32–34) O Jesus, Son of Man, You are high and lifted up. You have been raised to glory, not by the power of human might, nor by the adulation of mortal praise, but by the weakness of the shameful cross. As You were lifted up to a humiliating death, so You have been lifted infinitely higher to the glorious throne of God. You have been given authority, glory and sovereign power so that all peoples will worship You. And now You draw people from all nations to Your everlasting kingdom. All praise and glory and honor be to You, Jesus, Son of Man and Son of God, to You Who have suffered and died, Who have been raised to new life and Who are now exalted on high! (Da 7:13–14; Jn 3:14–15)

The sovereignty of Christ from the cross is a new sovereignty. It has destroyed forever the formula that might is right. It has put to shame the self-assertion of false heroism. It has surrounded with imperishable dignity the completeness of sacrifice. It has made clear to the pure heart that the prerogative of authority is wider service. The divine King rules forever by dying.

Brooke Foss Westcott (1825–1901)

Jesus, we love You,
We worship and adore You;
Glorify Thy name in all the earth.
Glorify Thy name,
Glorify Thy name,
Glorify Thy name in all the earth.

"Glorify Thy Name"
Donna Adkins (©1976, 1981)

me from this hour'? No, it was for this very reason I came to this
hour. 28Father, glorify your name!"
Then a voice came from heaven, "I have glorified it, and will
glorify it again." 29The crowd that was there and heard it said it
had thundered; others said an angel had spoken to him.
30Jesus said, "This voice was for your benefit, not mine. 31Now
is the time for judgment on this world; now the prince of this
world will be driven out. 32But I, when I am lifted up from the
earth, will draw all men to myself." 33He said this to show the
kind of death he was going to die.
34The crowd spoke up, "We have heard from the Law that the
Christ[a] will remain forever, so how can you say, 'The Son of Man
must be lifted up'? Who is this 'Son of Man'?"
35Then Jesus told them, "You are going to have the light just a
little while longer. Walk while you have the light, before darkness
overtakes you. The man who walks in the dark does not know
where he is going. 36Put your trust in the light while you have it,
so that you may become sons of light." When he had finished
speaking, Jesus left and hid himself from them.

The Jews Continue in Their Unbelief

37Even after Jesus had done all these miraculous signs in their
presence, they still would not believe in him. 38This was to fulfill
the word of Isaiah the prophet:

"Lord, who has believed our message
and to whom has the arm of the Lord been
revealed?"[b]

39For this reason they could not believe, because, as Isaiah
says elsewhere:

40"He has blinded their eyes
and deadened their hearts,
so they can neither see with their eyes,
nor understand with their hearts,
nor turn—and I would heal them."[c]

41Isaiah said this because he saw Jesus' glory and spoke about
him.
42Yet at the same time many even among the leaders believed
in him. But because of the Pharisees they would not confess their
faith for fear they would be put out of the synagogue; 43for they
loved praise from men more than praise from God.
44Then Jesus cried out, "When a man believes in me, he does
not believe in me only, but in the one who sent me. 45When he
looks at me, he sees the one who sent me. 46I have come into the
world as a light, so that no one who believes in me should stay in
darkness.
47"As for the person who hears my words but does not keep
them, I do not judge him. For I did not come to judge the world,
but to save it. 48There is a judge for the one who rejects me and
does not accept my words; that very word which I spoke will condemn him at the last day. 49For I did not speak of my own accord,
but the Father who sent me commanded me what to say and how
to say it. 50I know that his command leads to eternal life. So whatever I say is just what the Father has told me to say."

[a] 34 Or *Messiah* [b] 38 Isaiah 53:1 [c] 40 Isaiah 6:10

Jesus Washes His Disciples' Feet

13 It was just before the Passover Feast. Jesus knew that the time had come for him to leave this world and go to the Father. Having loved his own who were in the world, he now showed them the full extent of his love.[a]

2The evening meal was being served, and the devil had already prompted Judas Iscariot, son of Simon, to betray Jesus. 3Jesus knew that the Father had put all things under his power, and that he had come from God and was returning to God; 4so he got up from the meal, took off his outer clothing, and wrapped a towel around his waist. 5After that, he poured water into a basin and began to wash his disciples' feet, drying them with the towel that was wrapped around him.

6He came to Simon Peter, who said to him, "Lord, are you going to wash my feet?"

7Jesus replied, "You do not realize now what I am doing, but later you will understand."

8"No," said Peter, "you shall never wash my feet."

Jesus answered, "Unless I wash you, you have no part with me."

9"Then, Lord," Simon Peter replied, "not just my feet but my hands and my head as well!"

10Jesus answered, "A person who has had a bath needs only to wash his feet; his whole body is clean. And you are clean, though not every one of you." 11For he knew who was going to betray him, and that was why he said not every one was clean.

12When he had finished washing their feet, he put on his clothes and returned to his place. "Do you understand what I have done for you?" he asked them. 13"You call me 'Teacher' and 'Lord,' and rightly so, for that is what I am. 14Now that I, your Lord and Teacher, have washed your feet, you also should wash one another's feet. 15I have set you an example that you should do as I have done for you. 16I tell you the truth, no servant is greater than his master, nor is a messenger greater than the one who sent him. 17Now that you know these things, you will be blessed if you do them.

Jesus Predicts His Betrayal

18"I am not referring to all of you; I know those I have chosen. But this is to fulfill the scripture: 'He who shares my bread has lifted up his heel against me.'[b]

19"I am telling you now before it happens, so that when it does happen you will believe that I am He. 20I tell you the truth, whoever accepts anyone I send accepts me; and whoever accepts me accepts the one who sent me."

21After he had said this, Jesus was troubled in spirit and testified, "I tell you the truth, one of you is going to betray me."

22His disciples stared at one another, at a loss to know which of them he meant. 23One of them, the disciple whom Jesus loved, was reclining next to him. 24Simon Peter motioned to this disciple and said, "Ask him which one he means."

25Leaning back against Jesus, he asked him, "Lord, who is it?"

26Jesus answered, "It is the one to whom I will give this piece of bread when I have dipped it in the dish." Then, dipping the piece of bread, he gave it to Judas Iscariot, son of Simon. 27As soon as Judas took the bread, Satan entered into him.

[a] *1* Or *he loved them to the last* [b] *18* Psalm 41:9

(13:1–17) Dear Jesus, my Lord and Teacher, as You humbly wash the feet of Your disciples I glimpse a portent of the greater humiliation to come, when You will be crucified for all humanity. Even though You possessed the very nature of God, You claimed nothing for Your own advantage but emptied Yourself, taking the form of a slave. As the Son of Man, destined for divine glory, You came to serve, not to be served, and to give Your life as a ransom for many. With Your disciples I hear Your call to imitate You in humble servanthood. O Master, teach me to serve You gratefully by washing the feet of my sisters and brothers. Help me to worship You by giving myself sacrificially to Your people. (Mk 10:45; Php 2:6–8)

Brother, let me be your servant,
Let me be as Christ to you.
Pray that I might have the grace
To let you be my servant too.

"The Servant Song"
Richard Gillard (©1977)

"What you are about to do, do quickly," Jesus told him, 28but
no one at the meal understood why Jesus said this to him. 29Since
Judas had charge of the money, some thought Jesus was telling
him to buy what was needed for the Feast, or to give something to
the poor. 30As soon as Judas had taken the bread, he went out.
And it was night.

Jesus Predicts Peter's Denial

31When he was gone, Jesus said, "Now is the Son of Man glorified and God is glorified in him. 32If God is glorified in him,[a]
God will glorify the Son in himself, and will glorify him at once.
33"My children, I will be with you only a little longer. You will
look for me, and just as I told the Jews, so I tell you now: Where
I am going, you cannot come.
34"A new command I give you: Love one another. As I have
loved you, so you must love one another. 35By this all men will
know that you are my disciples, if you love one another."
36Simon Peter asked him, "Lord, where are you going?"
Jesus replied, "Where I am going, you cannot follow now, but
you will follow later."
37Peter asked, "Lord, why can't I follow you now? I will lay
down my life for you."
38Then Jesus answered, "Will you really lay down your life for
me? I tell you the truth, before the rooster crows, you will disown
me three times!

Jesus Comforts His Disciples

14 "Do not let your hearts be troubled. Trust in God[b]; trust
also in me. 2In my Father's house are many rooms; if it
were not so, I would have told you. I am going there to prepare a
place for you. 3And if I go and prepare a place for you, I will
come back and take you to be with me that you also may be
where I am. 4You know the way to the place where I am going."

Jesus the Way to the Father

5Thomas said to him, "Lord, we don't know where you are
going, so how can we know the way?"
6Jesus answered, "I am the way and the truth and the life. No
one comes to the Father except through me. 7If you really knew
me, you would know[c] my Father as well. From now on, you do
know him and have seen him."
8Philip said, "Lord, show us the Father and that will be enough
for us."
9Jesus answered: "Don't you know me, Philip, even after I have
been among you such a long time? Anyone who has seen me has
seen the Father. How can you say, 'Show us the Father'? 10Don't
you believe that I am in the Father, and that the Father is in me?
The words I say to you are not just my own. Rather, it is the Father, living in me, who is doing his work. 11Believe me when I say
that I am in the Father and the Father is in me; or at least believe
on the evidence of the miracles themselves. 12I tell you the truth,
anyone who has faith in me will do what I have been doing. He
will do even greater things than these, because I am going to the
Father. 13And I will do whatever you ask in my name, so that the

[a] 32 Many early manuscripts do not have *If God is glorified in him.* [b] 1 Or *You trust in God* [c] 7 Some early manuscripts *If you really have known me, you will know*

I am the Way unchangeable; the Truth infallible; the Life everlasting.
Thomas à Kempis (c.1380-1471)

(14:6) The world around us denies it, Lord. "Surely," we are told, "there are many ways to God, many roads up the mountain. Surely no one has cornered the market on truth." But then we hear again Your simple statement: "I am the way and the truth and the life." How audacious! How gracious! How inviting! You alone are the Son of Man, lifted up upon the cross for our salvation. You alone have taken our sin upon Yourself so that we might live in right relationship with God. No other way leads to the throne of grace. No other truth speaks as the Word of God. No other life promises the fullness of divine blessing. In the midst of a world that cannot comprehend it, we joyfully proclaim Your uniqueness, Your amazing grace, Your reconciling sacrifice. (2Co 5:21)

Christ is not one of many ways to approach God, nor is he the best of several ways; he is the only way.
A.W. Tozer (1897-1963)

I believe You're the Lord of all,
The only righteous One;
You're the mighty Creator,
Great are the things You've done!
I believe that You died for me,
That You live, and death is
overcome.
You're the way to the Father;
You're the Truth, the Life, the Son.
"The Truth, The Life, The Son"
Bill Batstone and
Sven Gunnarsen (©1994)

Son may bring glory to the Father. 14You may ask me for anything
in my name, and I will do it.

Jesus Promises the Holy Spirit

15"If you love me, you will obey what I command. 16And I will
ask the Father, and he will give you another Counselor to be with
you forever— 17the Spirit of truth. The world cannot accept him,
because it neither sees him nor knows him. But you know him,
for he lives with you and will be[a] in you. 18I will not leave you as
orphans; I will come to you. 19Before long, the world will not see
me anymore, but you will see me. Because I live, you also will
live. 20On that day you will realize that I am in my Father, and you
are in me, and I am in you. 21Whoever has my commands and
obeys them, he is the one who loves me. He who loves me will be
loved by my Father, and I too will love him and show myself to
him."

22Then Judas (not Judas Iscariot) said, "But, Lord, why do you
intend to show yourself to us and not to the world?"

23Jesus replied, "If anyone loves me, he will obey my teaching.
My Father will love him, and we will come to him and make our
home with him. 24He who does not love me will not obey my
teaching. These words you hear are not my own; they belong to
the Father who sent me.

25"All this I have spoken while still with you. 26But the Counselor, the Holy Spirit, whom the Father will send in my name, will
teach you all things and will remind you of everything I have said
to you. 27Peace I leave with you; my peace I give you. I do not give
to you as the world gives. Do not let your hearts be troubled and
do not be afraid.

28"You heard me say, 'I am going away and I am coming back
to you.' If you loved me, you would be glad that I am going to the
Father, for the Father is greater than I. 29I have told you now before it happens, so that when it does happen you will believe. 30I
will not speak with you much longer, for the prince of this world
is coming. He has no hold on me, 31but the world must learn that
I love the Father and that I do exactly what my Father has commanded me.

"Come now; let us leave.

The Vine and the Branches

15 "I am the true vine, and my Father is the gardener. 2He cuts
off every branch in me that bears no fruit, while every
branch that does bear fruit he prunes[b] so that it will be even
more fruitful. 3You are already clean because of the word I have
spoken to you. 4Remain in me, and I will remain in you. No
branch can bear fruit by itself; it must remain in the vine. Neither
can you bear fruit unless you remain in me.

5"I am the vine; you are the branches. If a man remains in me
and I in him, he will bear much fruit; apart from me you can do
nothing. 6If anyone does not remain in me, he is like a branch
that is thrown away and withers; such branches are picked up,
thrown into the fire and burned. 7If you remain in me and my
words remain in you, ask whatever you wish, and it will be given
you. 8This is to my Father's glory, that you bear much fruit, showing yourselves to be my disciples.

[a] 17 Some early manuscripts *and is* [b] 2 The Greek for *prunes* also means *cleans.*

(15:1–8) Jesus, many other "vines" contend for my allegiance. But they promise what they cannot deliver: "Remain in me," says my job, "and you will be find true success." "Make us top priority," says my family, "and you will find unmatched love." "Stick with me," says my religious tradition, "and you will enjoy the deepest spiritual experiences." "Plug into status or riches or pleasure" says this world, "and you will find yourself." But all of these "vines," dear Lord, even those created for our good, cannot compete with You. You alone are the true vine. In You alone do I find my rightful place in the world. Through Your strength alone will my brief life count for eternity. So I choose, by Your grace, to remain in You, to make my home in You forever.

Let us all become a true and fruitful branch on the vine Jesus, by accepting Him in our lives as it pleases Him to come: as the Truth to be told; as the Life to be lived; as the Light to be lighted; as the Love to be loved; as the Way to be walked; as the Joy to be given; as the Peace to be spread; as the Sacrifice to be offered, in our families and within our neighborhood.

Mother Teresa of Calcutta (1910–1997)

Vine of heaven, Thy love supplies
This blest cup of sacrifice
'Tis Thy wounds our healing give;
To Thy cross we look and live:
Thou our life! O let us be
Rooted, grafted, built on Thee.

"Bread of Heaven, On Thee We Feed"
Josiah Conder (1824)

[9]"As the Father has loved me, so have I loved you. Now remain in my love. [10]If you obey my commands, you will remain in my love, just as I have obeyed my Father's commands and remain in his love. [11]I have told you this so that my joy may be in you and that your joy may be complete. [12]My command is this: Love each other as I have loved you. [13]Greater love has no one than this, that he lay down his life for his friends. [14]You are my friends if you do what I command. [15]I no longer call you servants, because a servant does not know his master's business. Instead, I have called you friends, for everything that I learned from my Father I have made known to you. [16]You did not choose me, but I chose you and appointed you to go and bear fruit—fruit that will last. Then the Father will give you whatever you ask in my name. [17]This is my command: Love each other.

The World Hates the Disciples

[18]"If the world hates you, keep in mind that it hated me first. [19]If you belonged to the world, it would love you as its own. As it is, you do not belong to the world, but I have chosen you out of the world. That is why the world hates you. [20]Remember the words I spoke to you: 'No servant is greater than his master.'[a] If they persecuted me, they will persecute you also. If they obeyed my teaching, they will obey yours also. [21]They will treat you this way because of my name, for they do not know the One who sent me. [22]If I had not come and spoken to them, they would not be guilty of sin. Now, however, they have no excuse for their sin. [23]He who hates me hates my Father as well. [24]If I had not done among them what no one else did, they would not be guilty of sin. But now they have seen these miracles, and yet they have hated both me and my Father. [25]But this is to fulfill what is written in their Law: 'They hated me without reason.'[b]

[26]"When the Counselor comes, whom I will send to you from the Father, the Spirit of truth who goes out from the Father, he will testify about me. [27]And you also must testify, for you have been with me from the beginning.

16 "All this I have told you so that you will not go astray. [2]They will put you out of the synagogue; in fact, a time is coming when anyone who kills you will think he is offering a service to God. [3]They will do such things because they have not known the Father or me. [4]I have told you this, so that when the time comes you will remember that I warned you. I did not tell you this at first because I was with you.

The Work of the Holy Spirit

[5]"Now I am going to him who sent me, yet none of you asks me, 'Where are you going?' [6]Because I have said these things, you are filled with grief. [7]But I tell you the truth: It is for your good that I am going away. Unless I go away, the Counselor will not come to you; but if I go, I will send him to you. [8]When he comes, he will convict the world of guilt[c] in regard to sin and righteousness and judgment: [9]in regard to sin, because men do not believe in me; [10]in regard to righteousness, because I am going to the Father, where you can see me no longer; [11]and in regard to judgment, because the prince of this world now stands condemned.

[a] 20 John 13:16 [b] 25 Psalms 35:19; 69:4 [c] 8 Or *will expose the guilt of the world*

(15:13–15) O Jesus, I have no other friend like You. In times of trial You are always there. You always hear the unspoken longings of my heart. You have hidden nothing of Your Father's truth. Everything I need to know You have revealed. You have loved me with an unsurpassable love. You have given Your life for me, choosing by grace to call me Your friend. Help me, dearest Friend, to love as You have loved and to live as You have lived. Help me to trust You enough to do all that You command.

You took my burden shamelessly,
Paid my debt for eternity.
Wondering of Your love for me
Has become life's greatest mystery.

Greater love has no man than this:
That he lay down his life for his
friends.
Greater love has no man than this:
That he lay down his life for his
friends.

"Greater Love"
John Barbour and Anne Barbour (©1993)

12"I have much more to say to you, more than you can now
bear. 13But when he, the Spirit of truth, comes, he will guide you
into all truth. He will not speak on his own; he will speak only
what he hears, and he will tell you what is yet to come. 14He will
bring glory to me by taking from what is mine and making it
known to you. 15All that belongs to the Father is mine. That is
why I said the Spirit will take from what is mine and make it
known to you.

16"In a little while you will see me no more, and then after a
little while you will see me."

The Disciples' Grief Will Turn to Joy

17Some of his disciples said to one another, "What does he
mean by saying, 'In a little while you will see me no more, and
then after a little while you will see me,' and 'Because I am going
to the Father'?" 18They kept asking, "What does he mean by 'a little while'? We don't understand what he is saying."

19Jesus saw that they wanted to ask him about this, so he said
to them, "Are you asking one another what I meant when I said,
'In a little while you will see me no more, and then after a little
while you will see me'? 20I tell you the truth, you will weep and
mourn while the world rejoices. You will grieve, but your grief
will turn to joy. 21A woman giving birth to a child has pain because her time has come; but when her baby is born she forgets
the anguish because of her joy that a child is born into the world.
22So with you: Now is your time of grief, but I will see you again
and you will rejoice, and no one will take away your joy. 23In that
day you will no longer ask me anything. I tell you the truth, my Father will give you whatever you ask in my name. 24Until now you
have not asked for anything in my name. Ask and you will receive,
and your joy will be complete.

25"Though I have been speaking figuratively, a time is coming
when I will no longer use this kind of language but will tell you
plainly about my Father. 26In that day you will ask in my name. I
am not saying that I will ask the Father on your behalf. 27No, the
Father himself loves you because you have loved me and have believed that I came from God. 28I came from the Father and entered the world; now I am leaving the world and going back to the
Father."

29Then Jesus' disciples said, "Now you are speaking clearly
and without figures of speech. 30Now we can see that you know
all things and that you do not even need to have anyone ask you
questions. This makes us believe that you came from God."

31"You believe at last!"[a] Jesus answered. 32"But a time is coming, and has come, when you will be scattered, each to his own
home. You will leave me all alone. Yet I am not alone, for my Father is with me.

33"I have told you these things, so that in me you may have
peace. In this world you will have trouble. But take heart! I have
overcome the world."

Jesus Prays for Himself

17 After Jesus said this, he looked toward heaven and prayed:

"Father, the time has come. Glorify your Son, that your
Son may glorify you. 2For you granted him authority over all

[a]31 Or *"Do you now believe?"*

We believe in the Holy Spirit, the Lord and Giver of Life, who proceeds from the Father and the Son, who with the Father and the Son together is worshiped and glorified, who spoke by the prophets.

The Nicene Creed (325)

(16:13–15) O Holy Spirit, You are worthy to be worshiped along with the Father and the Son. Spirit of truth, You speak throughout the Scripture and help us to grasp its truth. Indeed, You teach us everything we need to know. You bear witness to the Son, Whom You glorify in all Your works. You are the Counselor Whom the Father has sent in the name of Jesus to dwell in us. You breathe upon us the very life of God. O Spirit of truth, teach me! Help me to know and to glorify the Son! Breathe on me, breath of God! (Jn 14:16–17,26)

Come, Holy Comforter,
Thy sacred witness bear
In this glad hour:
Thou who almighty art,
Now rule in every heart,
And ne'er from us depart,
Spirit of power.

"Come, Thou Almighty King"
Italian Hymn (c.1757)

people that he might give eternal life to all those you have
given him. 3Now this is eternal life: that they may know you,
the only true God, and Jesus Christ, whom you have sent. 4I
have brought you glory on earth by completing the work
you gave me to do. 5And now, Father, glorify me in your
presence with the glory I had with you before the world
began.

Jesus Prays for His Disciples

6"I have revealed you[a] to those whom you gave me out of
the world. They were yours; you gave them to me and they
have obeyed your word. 7Now they know that everything you
have given me comes from you. 8For I gave them the words
you gave me and they accepted them. They knew with certainty that I came from you, and they believed that you sent
me. 9I pray for them. I am not praying for the world, but for
those you have given me, for they are yours. 10All I have is
yours, and all you have is mine. And glory has come to me
through them. 11I will remain in the world no longer, but
they are still in the world, and I am coming to you. Holy Father, protect them by the power of your name—the name
you gave me—so that they may be one as we are one.
12While I was with them, I protected them and kept them
safe by that name you gave me. None has been lost except
the one doomed to destruction so that Scripture would be
fulfilled.

13"I am coming to you now, but I say these things while I
am still in the world, so that they may have the full measure
of my joy within them. 14I have given them your word and
the world has hated them, for they are not of the world any
more than I am of the world. 15My prayer is not that you
take them out of the world but that you protect them from
the evil one. 16They are not of the world, even as I am not of
it. 17Sanctify[b] them by the truth; your word is truth. 18As you
sent me into the world, I have sent them into the world.
19For them I sanctify myself, that they too may be truly sanctified.

Jesus Prays for All Believers

20"My prayer is not for them alone. I pray also for those
who will believe in me through their message, 21that all of
them may be one, Father, just as you are in me and I am in
you. May they also be in us so that the world may believe
that you have sent me. 22I have given them the glory that you
gave me, that they may be one as we are one: 23I in them and
you in me. May they be brought to complete unity to let the
world know that you sent me and have loved them even as
you have loved me.

24"Father, I want those you have given me to be with me
where I am, and to see my glory, the glory you have given me
because you loved me before the creation of the world.

25"Righteous Father, though the world does not know
you, I know you, and they know that you have sent me. 26I
have made you known to them, and will continue to make

[a] 6 Greek *your name*; also in verse 26 [b] 17 Greek *hagiazo (set apart for sacred use or make holy)*; also in verse 19

(17:20–23) O Lord Jesus, may I be an answer to Your prayer! May I be one with my brothers and sisters in Christ, even as You are one with the Father. What a wonder! What a high calling! But Lord, You know how often I discount the unity of Your people. I confess my penchant for emphasizing that which sets me apart from my brothers and sisters rather than that which unites us. Tragically, I can even make worship a point of division, preferring my own "style" to that of others. Forgive me, Lord, for my narrowness, for my failure to live in the unity You have bequeathed to Your church. Renew in me a passion for the unity of Your people, that we might all be one in You, even as You are one with the Father.

The best proof that Christ has risen is that he is still alive. And for the immense majority of our contemporaries, the only way of seeing him alive is for us Christians to love one another.

Louis Evely (1910-)

Oh, let us be the generation
Of reconciliation and peace,
And let us be a holy nation
Where pride and prejudice shall
cease.
Let us speak the truth in love
To the lost and least of these,
Let us serve the Lord in unity
So others will believe.
Let us be a generation
Of reconciliation and peace.

Have we not one Father?
Have we not one faith?
Have we not one calling
To become one holy race?

"The Reconciliation Song"
Morris Chapman, Buddy Owens and
Claire Cloninger (©1995)

you known in order that the love you have for me may be in them and that I myself may be in them."

Jesus Arrested

18 When he had finished praying, Jesus left with his disciples and crossed the Kidron Valley. On the other side there was an olive grove, and he and his disciples went into it.

2Now Judas, who betrayed him, knew the place, because Jesus had often met there with his disciples. 3So Judas came to the grove, guiding a detachment of soldiers and some officials from the chief priests and Pharisees. They were carrying torches, lanterns and weapons.

4Jesus, knowing all that was going to happen to him, went out and asked them, "Who is it you want?"

5"Jesus of Nazareth," they replied.

"I am he," Jesus said. (And Judas the traitor was standing there with them.) 6When Jesus said, "I am he," they drew back and fell to the ground.

7Again he asked them, "Who is it you want?"

And they said, "Jesus of Nazareth."

8"I told you that I am he," Jesus answered. "If you are looking for me, then let these men go." 9This happened so that the words he had spoken would be fulfilled: "I have not lost one of those you gave me."[a]

10Then Simon Peter, who had a sword, drew it and struck the high priest's servant, cutting off his right ear. (The servant's name was Malchus.)

11Jesus commanded Peter, "Put your sword away! Shall I not drink the cup the Father has given me?"

Jesus Taken to Annas

12Then the detachment of soldiers with its commander and the Jewish officials arrested Jesus. They bound him 13and brought him first to Annas, who was the father-in-law of Caiaphas, the high priest that year. 14Caiaphas was the one who had advised the Jews that it would be good if one man died for the people.

Peter's First Denial

15Simon Peter and another disciple were following Jesus. Because this disciple was known to the high priest, he went with Jesus into the high priest's courtyard, 16but Peter had to wait outside at the door. The other disciple, who was known to the high priest, came back, spoke to the girl on duty there and brought Peter in.

17"You are not one of his disciples, are you?" the girl at the door asked Peter.

He replied, "I am not."

18It was cold, and the servants and officials stood around a fire they had made to keep warm. Peter also was standing with them, warming himself.

The High Priest Questions Jesus

19Meanwhile, the high priest questioned Jesus about his disciples and his teaching.

[a] 9 John 6:39

I never made a sacrifice. We ought not to talk of sacrifice when we remember the great sacrifice that he made who left his Father's throne on high to give himself for us.

David Livingstone (1813-1873)

(18:4) None of it took You by surprise, Lord—neither betrayal by one friend nor denial by another, neither the mock trial nor the guilty verdict, neither the taunting of Your accusers nor the trauma of the cross. You knew all that was going to happen to You. Yet You chose to go through with it. You chose to endure that which You did not deserve. You chose condemnation and death so that I might receive vindication and life. O gracious Lord, thank You for knowingly embracing Your sacrifice for me. Thank You for willingly embracing me through Your saving death.

He left His Father's throne above,
So free, so infinite His grace;
Emptied Himself of all but love,
And bled for Adam's helpless race;
'Tis mercy all, immense and free;
For, O my God, it found out me.

Amazing love! how can it be,
That Thou, my God, shouldst die for me.

"And Can It Be That I Should Gain?"
Charles Wesley (1738)

(18:25–27) I too have denied You, Lord. Like Peter, I have been afraid of people's scorn. I have wanted to be accepted in the company of those who reject You. Usually I am not so blunt as Peter. I often deny You so subtly and craftily that I can easily rationalize what I have done. But, in truth, I have disowned You. Forgive me, Lord, for my unfaithfulness and cowardice. Give me boldness, even eagerness, to name You as my Lord, my Savior, my God—no matter what the risk, no matter what the cost.

When in his mercy God leads a soul in the higher path of sanctification, he begins by stripping it of all self-confidence, and to this end he allows our own schemes to fail, our judgment to mislead us. We grope and totter and make countless mistakes until we learn wholly to mistrust ourselves and to put all our confidence in him.

Jean Nicolas Grou (1731-1803)

20"I have spoken openly to the world," Jesus replied. "I always
taught in synagogues or at the temple, where all the Jews come
together. I said nothing in secret. 21Why question me? Ask those
who heard me. Surely they know what I said."

22When Jesus said this, one of the officials nearby struck him
in the face. "Is this the way you answer the high priest?" he demanded.

23"If I said something wrong," Jesus replied, "testify as to
what is wrong. But if I spoke the truth, why did you strike me?"
24Then Annas sent him, still bound, to Caiaphas the high priest.[a]

Peter's Second and Third Denials

25As Simon Peter stood warming himself, he was asked, "You are not one of his disciples, are you?"

He denied it, saying, "I am not."

26One of the high priest's servants, a relative of the man whose
ear Peter had cut off, challenged him, "Didn't I see you with him
in the olive grove?" 27Again Peter denied it, and at that moment a
rooster began to crow.

Jesus Before Pilate

28Then the Jews led Jesus from Caiaphas to the palace of the
Roman governor. By now it was early morning, and to avoid ceremonial uncleanness the Jews did not enter the palace; they
wanted to be able to eat the Passover. 29So Pilate came out to
them and asked, "What charges are you bringing against this man?"

30"If he were not a criminal," they replied, "we would not have handed him over to you."

31Pilate said, "Take him yourselves and judge him by your own law."

"But we have no right to execute anyone," the Jews objected.
32This happened so that the words Jesus had spoken indicating the kind of death he was going to die would be fulfilled.

33Pilate then went back inside the palace, summoned Jesus and asked him, "Are you the king of the Jews?"

34"Is that your own idea," Jesus asked, "or did others talk to you about me?"

35"Am I a Jew?" Pilate replied. "It was your people and your chief priests who handed you over to me. What is it you have done?"

36Jesus said, "My kingdom is not of this world. If it were, my servants would fight to prevent my arrest by the Jews. But now my kingdom is from another place."

37"You are a king, then!" said Pilate.

Jesus answered, "You are right in saying I am a king. In fact, for this reason I was born, and for this I came into the world, to testify to the truth. Everyone on the side of truth listens to me."

38"What is truth?" Pilate asked. With this he went out again to
the Jews and said, "I find no basis for a charge against him.
39But it is your custom for me to release to you one prisoner at
the time of the Passover. Do you want me to release 'the king of the Jews'?"

40They shouted back, "No, not him! Give us Barabbas!" Now Barabbas had taken part in a rebellion.

[a] 24 Or *(Now Annas had sent him, still bound, to Caiaphas the high priest.)*

Jesus Sentenced to Be Crucified

19 Then Pilate took Jesus and had him flogged. 2The soldiers
twisted together a crown of thorns and put it on his head.
They clothed him in a purple robe 3and went up to him again and
again, saying, "Hail, king of the Jews!" And they struck him in the
face.
4Once more Pilate came out and said to the Jews, "Look, I am
bringing him out to you to let you know that I find no basis for a
charge against him." 5When Jesus came out wearing the crown of
thorns and the purple robe, Pilate said to them, "Here is the
man!"
6As soon as the chief priests and their officials saw him, they
shouted, "Crucify! Crucify!"
But Pilate answered, "You take him and crucify him. As for me,
I find no basis for a charge against him."
7The Jews insisted, "We have a law, and according to that law
he must die, because he claimed to be the Son of God."
8When Pilate heard this, he was even more afraid, 9and he
went back inside the palace. "Where do you come from?" he
asked Jesus, but Jesus gave him no answer. 10"Do you refuse to
speak to me?" Pilate said. "Don't you realize I have power either
to free you or to crucify you?"
11Jesus answered, "You would have no power over me if it
were not given to you from above. Therefore the one who handed me over to you is guilty of a greater sin."
12From then on, Pilate tried to set Jesus free, but the Jews kept
shouting, "If you let this man go, you are no friend of Caesar. Anyone who claims to be a king opposes Caesar."
13When Pilate heard this, he brought Jesus out and sat down
on the judge's seat at a place known as the Stone Pavement
(which in Aramaic is Gabbatha). 14It was the day of Preparation
of Passover Week, about the sixth hour.
"Here is your king," Pilate said to the Jews.
15But they shouted, "Take him away! Take him away! Crucify
him!"
"Shall I crucify your king?" Pilate asked.
"We have no king but Caesar," the chief priests answered.
16Finally Pilate handed him over to them to be crucified.

The Crucifixion

So the soldiers took charge of Jesus. 17Carrying his own cross,
he went out to the place of the Skull (which in Aramaic is called
Golgotha). 18Here they crucified him, and with him two others—
one on each side and Jesus in the middle.
19Pilate had a notice prepared and fastened to the cross. It
read: JESUS OF NAZARETH, THE KING OF THE JEWS. 20Many of the Jews
read this sign, for the place where Jesus was crucified was near
the city, and the sign was written in Aramaic, Latin and Greek.
21The chief priests of the Jews protested to Pilate, "Do not write
'The King of the Jews,' but that this man claimed to be king of the
Jews."
22Pilate answered, "What I have written, I have written."
23When the soldiers crucified Jesus, they took his clothes, dividing them into four shares, one for each of them, with the un-
dergarment remaining. This garment was seamless, woven in one
piece from top to bottom.

(19:17–18) How quickly my eye passes over this familiar line: "They crucified him." O Lord, expand my mind! Renew my sense of horror—and my wonder! Awaken my soul! For they crucified You: the Author of life now dying on the place of the Skull; the Lord of all now a slave to death; the blessed One of God now a curse; the sinless One now made to be sin; the only Son of God now forsaken by Your Father. O dear Jesus, they crucified You, my true Savior. They crucified You, my heart's desire. They crucified You, my only hope. They crucified You, in my place, on my cross, for my sin. O Lord, I crucified You!

What Thou, my Lord, hast suffered
Was all for sinners' gain:
Mine, mine was the transgression,
But Thine the deadly pain.
Lo, here I fall, my Savior!
'Tis I deserve Thy place;
Look on me with Thy favor,
Vouchsafe to me Thy grace.

What language shall I borrow
To thank Thee, dearest Friend,
For this Thy dying sorrow,
Thy pity without end?
O make me Thine forever;
And should I fainting be,
Lord, let me never, never
Outlive my love to Thee.

"O Sacred Head, Now Wounded"
Bernard of Clairvaux (1091-1153)
Trans. James W. Alexander (1804-1859)

The Crucifixion, however else we may interpret it, accuses human nature, accuses all of us in the very things that we think are our righteousness . . . Our attitude to the Crucifixion must be that of self-identification with the rest of human nature—we must say, "We did it"; and the inability to adopt something of the same attitude in the case of twentieth-century events has caused our phenomenal failure to deal with the problem of evil.

Herbert Butterfield (1900-1979)

That law which is perfect because it takes away all imperfections is charity, and you will find it written with a strange beauty when you gaze at Jesus your Savior stretched out like a sheet of parchment on the Cross, inscribed with wounds, illustrated in his own loving blood. Where else, I ask you, my dearest, is there a comparable book of love to read from?

Jordan of Saxony (d. 1237)

(19:30) You finished Your work, my Jesus. You did all that Your Father directed. You drank the cup of suffering that He gave to You. You completed that which had been planned from before the foundation of the world. You came as the Word of God made flesh, revealing the Father's love, becoming for us the Way to God. You freely chose the way of suffering: Your path to glory, the shameful cross, Your exaltation, being lifted high on the tree of death. You finished it all, my Savior, dying, so that we—so that I—might enter into eternal life. All praise, glory and honor be to You, my Rock and my Redeemer! (Jn 4:34; 5:36; 18:11)

The Holy Heart was broken,
Sent from the Father's side.
The Son of God forsaken,
The holy sacrifice.

For me He was forsaken,
For me He died alone.
My sins forever taken
That I might be His own.

The Holy Lamb was stricken,
Abandoned and alone.
He bore the world's affliction,
He bore it as His own.

"The Holy Heart"
Anne Barbour and
Marsha Skidmore (©1993)

24"Let's not tear it," they said to one another. "Let's decide by
lot who will get it."
This happened that the scripture might be fulfilled which said,

"They divided my garments among them
and cast lots for my clothing."[a]

So this is what the soldiers did.
25Near the cross of Jesus stood his mother, his mother's sister,
Mary the wife of Clopas, and Mary Magdalene. 26When Jesus saw
his mother there, and the disciple whom he loved standing nearby, he said to his mother, "Dear woman, here is your son," 27and
to the disciple, "Here is your mother." From that time on, this
disciple took her into his home.

The Death of Jesus

28Later, knowing that all was now completed, and so that the
Scripture would be fulfilled, Jesus said, "I am thirsty." 29A jar of
wine vinegar was there, so they soaked a sponge in it, put the
sponge on a stalk of the hyssop plant, and lifted it to Jesus' lips.
30When he had received the drink, Jesus said, "It is finished."
With that, he bowed his head and gave up his spirit.
31Now it was the day of Preparation, and the next day was to
be a special Sabbath. Because the Jews did not want the bodies
left on the crosses during the Sabbath, they asked Pilate to have
the legs broken and the bodies taken down. 32The soldiers
therefore came and broke the legs of the first man who had been
crucified with Jesus, and then those of the other. 33But when they
came to Jesus and found that he was already dead, they did not
break his legs. 34Instead, one of the soldiers pierced Jesus' side
with a spear, bringing a sudden flow of blood and water. 35The
man who saw it has given testimony, and his testimony is true. He
knows that he tells the truth, and he testifies so that you also may
believe. 36These things happened so that the scripture would be
fulfilled: "Not one of his bones will be broken,"[b] 37and, as another scripture says, "They will look on the one they have
pierced."[c]

The Burial of Jesus

38Later, Joseph of Arimathea asked Pilate for the body of Jesus.
Now Joseph was a disciple of Jesus, but secretly because he
feared the Jews. With Pilate's permission, he came and took the
body away. 39He was accompanied by Nicodemus, the man who
earlier had visited Jesus at night. Nicodemus brought a mixture of
myrrh and aloes, about seventy-five pounds.[d] 40Taking Jesus'
body, the two of them wrapped it, with the spices, in strips of
linen. This was in accordance with Jewish burial customs. 41At
the place where Jesus was crucified, there was a garden, and in
the garden a new tomb, in which no one had ever been laid.
42Because it was the Jewish day of Preparation and since the
tomb was nearby, they laid Jesus there.

The Empty Tomb

20 Early on the first day of the week, while it was still dark,
Mary Magdalene went to the tomb and saw that the stone
had been removed from the entrance. 2So she came running to

[a] 24 Psalm 22:18 [b] 36 Exodus 12:46; Num. 9:12; Psalm 34:20 [c] 37 Zech. 12:10
[d] 39 Greek *a hundred litrai* (about 34 kilograms)

Simon Peter and the other disciple, the one Jesus loved, and said,
"They have taken the Lord out of the tomb, and we don't know
where they have put him!"
3So Peter and the other disciple started for the tomb. 4Both
were running, but the other disciple outran Peter and reached
the tomb first. 5He bent over and looked in at the strips of linen
lying there but did not go in. 6Then Simon Peter, who was behind
him, arrived and went into the tomb. He saw the strips of linen
lying there, 7as well as the burial cloth that had been around
Jesus' head. The cloth was folded up by itself, separate from the
linen. 8Finally the other disciple, who had reached the tomb first,
also went inside. He saw and believed. 9(They still did not understand from Scripture that Jesus had to rise from the dead.)

Jesus Appears to Mary Magdalene

10Then the disciples went back to their homes, 11but Mary
stood outside the tomb crying. As she wept, she bent over to look
into the tomb 12and saw two angels in white, seated where Jesus'
body had been, one at the head and the other at the foot.
13They asked her, "Woman, why are you crying?"
"They have taken my Lord away," she said, "and I don't know
where they have put him." 14At this, she turned around and saw
Jesus standing there, but she did not realize that it was Jesus.
15"Woman," he said, "why are you crying? Who is it you are
looking for?"

Thinking he was the gardener, she said, "Sir, if you have carried him away, tell me where you have put him, and I will get him."

16Jesus said to her, "Mary."

She turned toward him and cried out in Aramaic, "Rabboni!" (which means Teacher).

17Jesus said, "Do not hold on to me, for I have not yet returned to the Father. Go instead to my brothers and tell them, 'I am returning to my Father and your Father, to my God and your God.' "

18Mary Magdalene went to the disciples with the news: "I have seen the Lord!" And she told them that he had said these things to her.

Jesus Appears to His Disciples

19On the evening of that first day of the week, when the disciples were together, with the doors locked for fear of the Jews,
Jesus came and stood among them and said, "Peace be with you!"
20After he said this, he showed them his hands and side. The disciples were overjoyed when they saw the Lord.
21Again Jesus said, "Peace be with you! As the Father has sent
me, I am sending you." 22And with that he breathed on them
and said, "Receive the Holy Spirit. 23If you forgive anyone his
sins, they are forgiven; if you do not forgive them, they are not
forgiven."

Jesus Appears to Thomas

24Now Thomas (called Didymus), one of the Twelve, was not
with the disciples when Jesus came. 25So the other disciples told
him, "We have seen the Lord!"

But he said to them, "Unless I see the nail marks in his hands and put my finger where the nails were, and put my hand into his side, I will not believe it."

(20:16) Risen Christ, through Your death, sin has been vanquished and death itself has been defeated. Reigning King, You have been exalted to the highest place and have been given the name above all names. Every soul in all creation shall bow before You. Yet You are not only the Savior of the world, You are also my personal Savior. You call my name. You know me through and through. Nothing about me is hidden from You. What a privilege to acknowledge You as God Almighty and to walk with You as my Friend! (Php 2:9)

I'm so glad I learned to trust Thee,
Precious Jesus, Savior, Friend,
And I know that Thou art with me,
Wilt be with me to the end.

Jesus, Jesus, how I trust Him!
How I've proved Him o'er and o'er!
Jesus, Jesus, precious Jesus!
O for grace to trust Him more!

"Tis So Sweet to Trust in Jesus"
Louisa M.R. Stead (1882)

26A week later his disciples were in the house again, and
Thomas was with them. Though the doors were locked, Jesus
came and stood among them and said, "Peace be with you!"
27Then he said to Thomas, "Put your finger here; see my hands.
Reach out your hand and put it into my side. Stop doubting and
believe."
28Thomas said to him, "My Lord and my God!"
29Then Jesus told him, "Because you have seen me, you have
believed; blessed are those who have not seen and yet have believed."
30Jesus did many other miraculous signs in the presence of his
disciples, which are not recorded in this book. 31But these are
written that you may[a] believe that Jesus is the Christ, the Son of
God, and that by believing you may have life in his name.

(20:28) O Jesus, You are the Word of God; God the One and only; the Lamb of God Who takes away the sin of the world; Messiah and Christ; Rabbi; Son of God; King of Israel; Son of Man; Savior of the world; Bread of life and living Bread; holy One of God; Light of the world; "I AM"; the Gate into salvation; Good Shepherd; the Resurrection and the Life; the One who comes in the name of the Lord; the Way, the Truth, and the Life; true Vine; Friend. O Jesus, You are "my Lord and my God!" (Jn 1:1,18,29,41,49; 3:13; 4:42; 6:35,51,69; 8:12, 58; 10:9,11; 11:25; 12:13; 14:6; 15:1,14–15)

Jesus and the Miraculous Catch of Fish

21 Afterward Jesus appeared again to his disciples, by the Sea
of Tiberias.[b] It happened this way: 2Simon Peter, Thomas
(called Didymus), Nathanael from Cana in Galilee, the sons of
Zebedee, and two other disciples were together. 3"I'm going out
to fish," Simon Peter told them, and they said, "We'll go with
you." So they went out and got into the boat, but that night they
caught nothing.
4Early in the morning, Jesus stood on the shore, but the disciples did not realize that it was Jesus.
5He called out to them, "Friends, haven't you any fish?"
"No," they answered.
6He said, "Throw your net on the right side of the boat and you
will find some." When they did, they were unable to haul the net
in because of the large number of fish.
7Then the disciple whom Jesus loved said to Peter, "It is the
Lord!" As soon as Simon Peter heard him say, "It is the Lord," he
wrapped his outer garment around him (for he had taken it off)
and jumped into the water. 8The other disciples followed in the
boat, towing the net full of fish, for they were not far from shore,
about a hundred yards.[c] 9When they landed, they saw a fire of
burning coals there with fish on it, and some bread.
10Jesus said to them, "Bring some of the fish you have just
caught."
11Simon Peter climbed aboard and dragged the net ashore. It
was full of large fish, 153, but even with so many the net was not
torn. 12Jesus said to them, "Come and have breakfast." None of
the disciples dared ask him, "Who are you?" They knew it was the
Lord. 13Jesus came, took the bread and gave it to them, and did
the same with the fish. 14This was now the third time Jesus appeared to his disciples after he was raised from the dead.

O For a thousand tongues to sing
My great Redeemer's praise,
The glories of my God and King,
The triumphs of His grace.

My gracious Master and my God,
Assist me to proclaim,
To spread through all the earth
abroad
The honors of Thy name.
"O For A Thousand Tongues To Sing"
Charles Wesley (1739)

Jesus Reinstates Peter

15When they had finished eating, Jesus said to Simon Peter,
"Simon son of John, do you truly love me more than these?"
"Yes, Lord," he said, "you know that I love you."
Jesus said, "Feed my lambs."
16Again Jesus said, "Simon son of John, do you truly love me?"
He answered, "Yes, Lord, you know that I love you."
Jesus said, "Take care of my sheep."

[a] *31* Some manuscripts *may continue to* [b] *1* That is, Sea of Galilee [c] *8* Greek *about two hundred cubits* (about 90 meters)

17The third time he said to him, "Simon son of John, do you love me?"

Peter was hurt because Jesus asked him the third time, "Do you love me?" He said, "Lord, you know all things; you know that I love you."

Jesus said, "Feed my sheep. 18I tell you the truth, when you were younger you dressed yourself and went where you wanted; but when you are old you will stretch out your hands, and someone else will dress you and lead you where you do not want to go." 19Jesus said this to indicate the kind of death by which Peter would glorify God. Then he said to him, "Follow me!"

20Peter turned and saw that the disciple whom Jesus loved was following them. (This was the one who had leaned back against Jesus at the supper and had said, "Lord, who is going to betray you?") 21When Peter saw him, he asked, "Lord, what about him?"

22Jesus answered, "If I want him to remain alive until I return, what is that to you? You must follow me." 23Because of this, the rumor spread among the brothers that this disciple would not die. But Jesus did not say that he would not die; he only said, "If I want him to remain alive until I return, what is that to you?"

24This is the disciple who testifies to these things and who wrote them down. We know that his testimony is true.

25Jesus did many other things as well. If every one of them were written down, I suppose that even the whole world would not have room for the books that would be written.

The work that Jesus called Peter to do was the work of shepherding the flock of God . . . There could only be one motivation. Love. Not a love for the open fields. Not a love for shepherding. Not even a love for the sheep. It had to be more than that. It had to be a love for the Shepherd Himself. Everything had to come from there. Every sermon. Every prayer for the sick. Every search for someone who was lost . . . All of the work, even the lowliest part of it, had to come from there.

Ken Gire (1950-)

(21:15–17) Your encounter with Peter reminds me, Lord, that my worship of You ought to flow into service to others. I do love You and delight to communicate this love in prayer and song. But You have said that if I love You, I will obey Your commandments. And what have You commanded? That I love my sisters and brothers. So, as I worship You with all my heart, soul, mind and strength, may I also love those whom You love. Let my love for You spill over into service to Your people! (Jn 14:15; 1Th 1:3; 1Jn 4:20)

God forgave my sin in Jesus' name.
I've been born again in Jesus' name,
And in Jesus' name I come to you
To share His love as He told me to.

He said: "Freely, freely, you have
received;
Freely, freely give.
Go in my name; and because you
believe,
Others will know that I live."

"Freely, Freely"
Carol Owens (©1972)

Acts

The ACTS *of the Apostles*

The prophet Joel envisioned a day when God's Spirit would be poured out upon all people (Joel 2:28–29). Other Old Testament prophets looked forward to the time when God's salvation would reach to the ends of the earth (Isa 42:6; Zec 9:9–10). Following the ascension of Jesus these prophetic hopes began to be fulfilled. The book of Acts depicts the outpouring of the Holy Spirit, that which empowers God's people to bring the Good News of salvation to all the earth. Through this book we are reminded of God's worldwide mission. Yet this global God is also immanent, dwelling within us by the Holy Spirit. In worship our hearts and minds are stretched as we praise our great God, allowing His Spirit to inspire our adoration.

Luke, the author of the third Gospel, wrote Acts. In his first volume he describes what Jesus "began to do and to teach" (1:1) In Acts, his second volume, Luke continues to tell the story of Jesus' activity. Though He has fulfilled His calling to suffer (Lk 9:22; 24:26), the resurrected Jesus keeps on working—now through the Christian believers.

Yet the followers of Jesus will not work in their own strength. Jesus promises to baptize them with the same Spirit that empowered His own ministry (Lk 3:16; 4:1,14; Ac 1:5). When they receive the Holy Spirit, Jesus' followers will be witnesses "in Jerusalem, and in all Judea and Samaria, and to the ends of the earth" (1:8). On the day of Pentecost Jesus fulfills His promise to baptize His followers with the Spirit. When God's own power fills them, they speak in other languages, "declaring the wonders of God" (2:11).

The book of Acts urges us to worship God both in Spirit-empowered praise and in Spirit-empowered evangelism.

The book of Acts urges us to worship God both in Spirit-empowered praise and in Spirit-empowered evangelism. Looking back upon the dramatic expansion of the early church, we praise God for His limitless mercy. We marvel at the gracious power of the Holy Spirit at work within the early Christian movement.

Yet we are not merely observers of the Spirit's work but also participants in it. Though we were not privileged to stand with the disciples as Jesus promised the gift of the Spirit, we are blessed to receive that same gift today (Gal 3:14). We too can be filled with the Holy Spirit and experience the power and joy of the Lord (Ro 15:13). The story of Jesus' ongoing ministry in the church encourages us to live in this same reality. We yearn to "be filled with the Spirit" in all aspects of our lives, so that we might live and worship in God's own strength (Eph 5:18). As we worship in the Spirit, our zeal for God's grace and glory will spill over into witness. The fullness of the Holy Spirit thus unites and empowers worship and witness, as we live for the praise of God's glory (Eph 1:12).

Jesus Taken Up Into Heaven

1 In my former book, Theophilus, I wrote about all that Jesus
began to do and to teach 2until the day he was taken up to
heaven, after giving instructions through the Holy Spirit to the
apostles he had chosen. 3After his suffering, he showed himself to
these men and gave many convincing proofs that he was alive. He
appeared to them over a period of forty days and spoke about the
kingdom of God. 4On one occasion, while he was eating with
them, he gave them this command: "Do not leave Jerusalem, but
wait for the gift my Father promised, which you have heard me
speak about. 5For John baptized with[a] water, but in a few days
you will be baptized with the Holy Spirit."
6So when they met together, they asked him, "Lord, are you at
this time going to restore the kingdom to Israel?"
7He said to them: "It is not for you to know the times or dates
the Father has set by his own authority. 8But you will receive
power when the Holy Spirit comes on you; and you will be my
witnesses in Jerusalem, and in all Judea and Samaria, and to the
ends of the earth."
9After he said this, he was taken up before their very eyes, and
a cloud hid him from their sight.
10They were looking intently up into the sky as he was going,
when suddenly two men dressed in white stood beside them.
11"Men of Galilee," they said, "why do you stand here looking
into the sky? This same Jesus, who has been taken from you into
heaven, will come back in the same way you have seen him go
into heaven."

Matthias Chosen to Replace Judas

12Then they returned to Jerusalem from the hill called the
Mount of Olives, a Sabbath day's walk[b] from the city. 13When they
arrived, they went upstairs to the room where they were staying.
Those present were Peter, John, James and Andrew; Philip and
Thomas, Bartholomew and Matthew; James son of Alphaeus and
Simon the Zealot, and Judas son of James. 14They all joined together constantly in prayer, along with the women and Mary the
mother of Jesus, and with his brothers.
15In those days Peter stood up among the believers[c] (a group
numbering about a hundred and twenty) 16and said, "Brothers,
the Scripture had to be fulfilled which the Holy Spirit spoke long
ago through the mouth of David concerning Judas, who served as
guide for those who arrested Jesus— 17he was one of our number and shared in this ministry."
18(With the reward he got for his wickedness, Judas bought a
field; there he fell headlong, his body burst open and all his intestines spilled out. 19Everyone in Jerusalem heard about this, so
they called that field in their language Akeldama, that is, Field of
Blood.)
20"For," said Peter, "it is written in the book of Psalms,

" 'May his place be deserted;
let there be no one to dwell in it,'[d]

and,

" 'May another take his place of leadership.'[e]

[a] 5 Or *in* [b] 12 That is, about 3/4 mile (about 1,100 meters) [c] 15 Greek *brothers*
[d] 20 Psalm 69:25 [e] 20 Psalm 109:8

(1:4–8) Father, as You promised, You sent the Spirit of Truth, the Comforter, to testify about Jesus Christ and to give power to all who believe in him. I stand before You believing in His name, having been sealed with Your Holy Spirit. When You empower me, I am set free to please You and to live as Your child. Enable me today to keep in step with You and to be Your witness wherever I go. (Jn 15:26, Ro 8:2,16; Gal 5:25; Eph 1:13)

The people of God are not merely to mark time, waiting for God to step in and set right all that is wrong. Rather, they are to model the new heaven and new earth, and by so doing awaken longings for what God will someday bring to pass.
Philip Yancey (1949-)

(1:11) Lord Jesus, as surely as You rose from the dead and ascended into heaven, so You will return at an hour that only the Father knows. Help me to live each day as one who is ready to welcome Your return, as one who has been faithful with that which You have entrusted to me. (Mt 24:36–44; 25:21–23)

Hail the day that sees Him rise,
To His throne above the skies;
Christ, the Lamb for sinners given,
Enters now the highest heaven.

See! The heaven its Lord receives,
Yet He loves the earth He leaves,
Though returning to His throne,
Still He calls the world His own.
"Hail the Day That Sees Him Rise"
Charles Wesley (1739)

All honour, all glory, all power to
You.
Holy Father, we worship You,
Precious Jesus, our Saviour.
Holy Spirit, we wait on You,
For fire.

"All Honour"
Chris Falson (©1990)

(2:2–11) We praise You, Lord, that the gospel is not just for an elite few but for whoever will believe: "Everyone who calls on the name of the Lord will be saved." At the birth of Your church, the gospel was made clear to everyone who could hear, in the language they could understand. Lord, fill us anew today with the power of Your Holy Spirit. Enable us to declare Your wonders wherever we are sent, whether it be to a nation across the sea or the family next door. Empower us to be Your witnesses to the ends of the earth. (Jn 3:16; Ac 1:8; Ro 10:13–17)

21Therefore it is necessary to choose one of the men who have
been with us the whole time the Lord Jesus went in and out
among us, 22beginning from John's baptism to the time when
Jesus was taken up from us. For one of these must become a witness with us of his resurrection."
23So they proposed two men: Joseph called Barsabbas (also
known as Justus) and Matthias. 24Then they prayed, "Lord, you
know everyone's heart. Show us which of these two you have chosen 25to take over this apostolic ministry, which Judas left to go
where he belongs." 26Then they cast lots, and the lot fell to Matthias; so he was added to the eleven apostles.

The Holy Spirit Comes at Pentecost

2 When the day of Pentecost came, they were all together in
one place. 2Suddenly a sound like the blowing of a violent
wind came from heaven and filled the whole house where they
were sitting. 3They saw what seemed to be tongues of fire that
separated and came to rest on each of them. 4All of them were
filled with the Holy Spirit and began to speak in other tongues[a] as
the Spirit enabled them.
5Now there were staying in Jerusalem God-fearing Jews from
every nation under heaven. 6When they heard this sound, a
crowd came together in bewilderment, because each one heard
them speaking in his own language. 7Utterly amazed, they asked:
"Are not all these men who are speaking Galileans? 8Then how is
it that each of us hears them in his own native language? 9Parthi-
ans, Medes and Elamites; residents of Mesopotamia, Judea and
Cappadocia, Pontus and Asia, 10Phrygia and Pamphylia, Egypt
and the parts of Libya near Cyrene; visitors from Rome 11(both
Jews and converts to Judaism); Cretans and Arabs—we hear
them declaring the wonders of God in our own tongues!"
12Amazed and perplexed, they asked one another, "What does
this mean?"
13Some, however, made fun of them and said, "They have had
too much wine.[b]"

Peter Addresses the Crowd

14Then Peter stood up with the Eleven, raised his voice and addressed the crowd: "Fellow Jews and all of you who live in Jerusalem, let me explain this to you; listen carefully to what I say.
15These men are not drunk, as you suppose. It's only nine in the
morning! 16No, this is what was spoken by the prophet Joel:

17" 'In the last days, God says,
I will pour out my Spirit on all people.
Your sons and daughters will prophesy,
your young men will see visions,
your old men will dream dreams.
18Even on my servants, both men and women,
I will pour out my Spirit in those days,
and they will prophesy.
19I will show wonders in the heaven above
and signs on the earth below,
blood and fire and billows of smoke.
20The sun will be turned to darkness
and the moon to blood

[a] 4 Or *languages*; also in verse 11 [b] 13 Or *sweet wine*

before the coming of the great and glorious day of
the Lord.
21 And everyone who calls
on the name of the Lord will be saved.'[a]

22 "Men of Israel, listen to this: Jesus of Nazareth was a man accredited by God to you by miracles, wonders and signs, which
God did among you through him, as you yourselves know. 23 This
man was handed over to you by God's set purpose and foreknowledge; and you, with the help of wicked men,[b] put him to
death by nailing him to the cross. 24 But God raised him from the
dead, freeing him from the agony of death, because it was impossible for death to keep its hold on him. 25 David said about
him:

" 'I saw the Lord always before me.
Because he is at my right hand,
I will not be shaken.
26 Therefore my heart is glad and my tongue rejoices;
my body also will live in hope,
27 because you will not abandon me to the grave,
nor will you let your Holy One see decay.
28 You have made known to me the paths of life;
you will fill me with joy in your presence.'[c]

29 "Brothers, I can tell you confidently that the patriarch David
died and was buried, and his tomb is here to this day. 30 But he
was a prophet and knew that God had promised him on oath that
he would place one of his descendants on his throne. 31 Seeing
what was ahead, he spoke of the resurrection of the Christ,[d] that
he was not abandoned to the grave, nor did his body see decay.
32 God has raised this Jesus to life, and we are all witnesses of the
fact. 33 Exalted to the right hand of God, he has received from the
Father the promised Holy Spirit and has poured out what you now
see and hear. 34 For David did not ascend to heaven, and yet he
said,

" 'The Lord said to my Lord:
"Sit at my right hand
35 until I make your enemies
a footstool for your feet." '[e]

36 "Therefore let all Israel be assured of this: God has made
this Jesus, whom you crucified, both Lord and Christ."
37 When the people heard this, they were cut to the heart and
said to Peter and the other apostles, "Brothers, what shall
we do?"
38 Peter replied, "Repent and be baptized, every one of you, in
the name of Jesus Christ for the forgiveness of your sins. And you
will receive the gift of the Holy Spirit. 39 The promise is for you
and your children and for all who are far off—for all whom the
Lord our God will call."
40 With many other words he warned them; and he pleaded
with them, "Save yourselves from this corrupt generation."
41 Those who accepted his message were baptized, and about
three thousand were added to their number that day.

[a] *21* Joel 2:28–32 [b] *23* Or *of those not having the law* (that is, Gentiles)
[c] *28* Psalm 16:8–11 [d] *31* Or *Messiah.* "The Christ" (Greek) and "the Messiah" (Hebrew) both mean "the Anointed One"; also in verse 36. [e] *35* Psalm 110:1

The Spirit-filled life is not a special, deluxe edition of Christianity. It is part and parcel of the total plan of God for his people.
A.W. Tozer (1897-1963)

(2:20–41) Lord, I praise You for the glorious birth of Your church. This was not merely the beginning of an institution. This was the fulfillment of a plan You had set in motion at the foundation of the world. The resurrected Christ reconciled us to You, and through Him You continue to pour out Your Holy Spirit on all who believe. Lord, I believe. Fill me afresh today until I overflow with the power of Your Spirit. (Col 1:22)

The Fellowship of the Believers

42They devoted themselves to the apostles' teaching and to the
fellowship, to the breaking of bread and to prayer. 43Everyone
was filled with awe, and many wonders and miraculous signs
were done by the apostles. 44All the believers were together and
had everything in common. 45Selling their possessions and
goods, they gave to anyone as he had need. 46Every day they continued to meet together in the temple courts. They broke bread in
their homes and ate together with glad and sincere hearts,
47praising God and enjoying the favor of all the people. And the
Lord added to their number daily those who were being saved.

Peter Heals the Crippled Beggar

3 One day Peter and John were going up to the temple at the
time of prayer—at three in the afternoon. 2Now a man crippled from birth was being carried to the temple gate called Beautiful, where he was put every day to beg from those going into the
temple courts. 3When he saw Peter and John about to enter, he
asked them for money. 4Peter looked straight at him, as did John.
Then Peter said, "Look at us!" 5So the man gave them his attention, expecting to get something from them.

6Then Peter said, "Silver or gold I do not have, but what I have
I give you. In the name of Jesus Christ of Nazareth, walk." 7Tak-
ing him by the right hand, he helped him up, and instantly the
man's feet and ankles became strong. 8He jumped to his feet and
began to walk. Then he went with them into the temple courts,
walking and jumping, and praising God. 9When all the people
saw him walking and praising God, 10they recognized him as the
same man who used to sit begging at the temple gate called Beautiful, and they were filled with wonder and amazement at what
had happened to him.

Peter Speaks to the Onlookers

11While the beggar held on to Peter and John, all the people
were astonished and came running to them in the place called
Solomon's Colonnade. 12When Peter saw this, he said to them:
"Men of Israel, why does this surprise you? Why do you stare at us
as if by our own power or godliness we had made this man walk?
13The God of Abraham, Isaac and Jacob, the God of our fathers,
has glorified his servant Jesus. You handed him over to be killed,
and you disowned him before Pilate, though he had decided to let
him go. 14You disowned the Holy and Righteous One and asked
that a murderer be released to you. 15You killed the author of
life, but God raised him from the dead. We are witnesses of this.
16By faith in the name of Jesus, this man whom you see and know
was made strong. It is Jesus' name and the faith that comes
through him that has given this complete healing to him, as you
can all see.

17"Now, brothers, I know that you acted in ignorance, as did
your leaders. 18But this is how God fulfilled what he had foretold
through all the prophets, saying that his Christ[a] would suffer.
19Repent, then, and turn to God, so that your sins may be wiped
out, that times of refreshing may come from the Lord, 20and that
he may send the Christ, who has been appointed for you—even
Jesus. 21He must remain in heaven until the time comes for God

[a] 18 Or *Messiah*; also in verse 20

(3:6) Lord, You have given me all that I have. You offer me so many invisible but real gifts—gifts with eternal value. The gift of Your Spirit in my life empowers me far beyond my own capacities. The gift of Your forgiveness enables me to forgive. The gifts of Your mercy and grace enable me to extend the same kindness to others. You have made me to be a storehouse of Your blessings, Lord. Please work through me to impart those blessings to others. (Jas 1:16–18)

(3:19–21) Sovereign God, this day I repent. I turn away from sin and self and turn to You. Wipe away my sins, refresh my heart with Your holiness and prepare me for the coming of Christ. I wait for Your promised new heaven and new earth—"the home of righteousness." I long to be restored and to see Your creation receive its anticipated glory. You have always kept Your word. Surely You will be faithful in Your own timing to fulfill everything You have promised. (Isa 65:17; Ro 8:18–21; 2Pe 3:13; Rev 21:1)

to restore everything, as he promised long ago through his holy
prophets. 22For Moses said, 'The Lord your God will raise up for
you a prophet like me from among your own people; you must
listen to everything he tells you. 23Anyone who does not listen to
him will be completely cut off from among his people.'[a]
24"Indeed, all the prophets from Samuel on, as many as have
spoken, have foretold these days. 25And you are heirs of the
prophets and of the covenant God made with your fathers. He said
to Abraham, 'Through your offspring all peoples on earth will be
blessed.'[b] 26When God raised up his servant, he sent him first to
you to bless you by turning each of you from your wicked ways."

Peter and John Before the Sanhedrin

4 The priests and the captain of the temple guard and the Sadducees came up to Peter and John while they were speaking
to the people. 2They were greatly disturbed because the apostles
were teaching the people and proclaiming in Jesus the resurrection of the dead. 3They seized Peter and John, and because it was
evening, they put them in jail until the next day. 4But many who
heard the message believed, and the number of men grew to
about five thousand.
5The next day the rulers, elders and teachers of the law met in
Jerusalem. 6Annas the high priest was there, and so were Caiaphas, John, Alexander and the other men of the high priest's family. 7They had Peter and John brought before them and began to
question them: "By what power or what name did you do this?"
8Then Peter, filled with the Holy Spirit, said to them: "Rulers
and elders of the people! 9If we are being called to account today
for an act of kindness shown to a cripple and are asked how he
was healed, 10then know this, you and all the people of Israel: It
is by the name of Jesus Christ of Nazareth, whom you crucified
but whom God raised from the dead, that this man stands before
you healed. 11He is

" 'the stone you builders rejected,
which has become the capstone.[c]'[d]

12Salvation is found in no one else, for there is no other name
under heaven given to men by which we must be saved."
13When they saw the courage of Peter and John and realized
that they were unschooled, ordinary men, they were astonished
and they took note that these men had been with Jesus. 14But
since they could see the man who had been healed standing there
with them, there was nothing they could say. 15So they ordered
them to withdraw from the Sanhedrin and then conferred together. 16"What are we going to do with these men?" they asked.
"Everybody living in Jerusalem knows they have done an outstanding miracle, and we cannot deny it. 17But to stop this thing
from spreading any further among the people, we must warn
these men to speak no longer to anyone in this name."
18Then they called them in again and commanded them not to
speak or teach at all in the name of Jesus. 19But Peter and John
replied, "Judge for yourselves whether it is right in God's sight to
obey you rather than God. 20For we cannot help speaking about
what we have seen and heard."
21After further threats they let them go. They could not decide

[a] 23 Deut. 18:15,18,19 [b] 25 Gen. 22:18; 26:4 [c] 11 Or *cornerstone*
[d] 11 Psalm 118:22

(4:12–13) I am Your witness, Lord, that You are God, and apart from You there is no Savior. Help me to declare the truth with boldness. May the words of my mouth and the testimony of my life make it clear to all that I have been with You. (Isa 43:11)

(4:19–20) "Fear of man will prove to be a snare, but whoever trusts in the LORD is kept safe." Spirit of God, imprint the Word on my heart so profoundly that I cannot help but speak about what I have seen and heard. May the declaration of my heart be that of the prophet Jeremiah: "His word is in my heart like a fire, a fire shut up in my bones. I am weary of holding it in; indeed, I cannot." (Pr 29:25; Jer 20:9)

how to punish them, because all the people were praising God for
what had happened. 22For the man who was miraculously healed
was over forty years old.

The Believers' Prayer

23On their release, Peter and John went back to their own people and reported all that the chief priests and elders had said to
them. 24When they heard this, they raised their voices together in
prayer to God. "Sovereign Lord," they said, "you made the heaven
and the earth and the sea, and everything in them. 25You spoke by
the Holy Spirit through the mouth of your servant, our father David:

" 'Why do the nations rage
  and the peoples plot in vain?
26The kings of the earth take their stand
  and the rulers gather together
against the Lord
  and against his Anointed One.[a] [b]

27Indeed Herod and Pontius Pilate met together with the Gentiles
and the people[c] of Israel in this city to conspire against your holy
servant Jesus, whom you anointed. 28They did what your power
and will had decided beforehand should happen. 29Now, Lord,
consider their threats and enable your servants to speak your
word with great boldness. 30Stretch out your hand to heal and
perform miraculous signs and wonders through the name of your
holy servant Jesus."

31After they prayed, the place where they were meeting was
shaken. And they were all filled with the Holy Spirit and spoke
the word of God boldly.

The Believers Share Their Possessions

32All the believers were one in heart and mind. No one claimed
that any of his possessions was his own, but they shared everything they had. 33With great power the apostles continued to testify to the resurrection of the Lord Jesus, and much grace was
upon them all. 34There were no needy persons among them. For
from time to time those who owned lands or houses sold them,
brought the money from the sales 35and put it at the apostles'
feet, and it was distributed to anyone as he had need.

36Joseph, a Levite from Cyprus, whom the apostles called Barnabas (which means Son of Encouragement), 37sold a field he
owned and brought the money and put it at the apostles' feet.

Ananias and Sapphira

5 Now a man named Ananias, together with his wife Sapphira,
also sold a piece of property. 2With his wife's full knowledge
he kept back part of the money for himself, but brought the rest
and put it at the apostles' feet.

3Then Peter said, "Ananias, how is it that Satan has so filled
your heart that you have lied to the Holy Spirit and have kept for
yourself some of the money you received for the land? 4Didn't it
belong to you before it was sold? And after it was sold, wasn't the
money at your disposal? What made you think of doing such a
thing? You have not lied to men but to God."

5When Ananias heard this, he fell down and died. And great

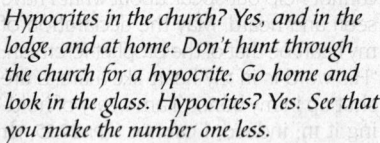

(5:2–9) O Lord our Provider, everything comes from You, and we can give You only what has first come from Your hand. You test our hearts and are pleased with integrity, but You are displeased with those who pretend to own a spiritual beauty that simply is not theirs. Keep my heart humble, Lord, and help me to serve You with wholehearted devotion, a willing mind and open hands. (1Ch 28:9; 29:14–17)

Hypocrites in the church? Yes, and in the lodge, and at home. Don't hunt through the church for a hypocrite. Go home and look in the glass. Hypocrites? Yes. See that you make the number one less.

Billy Sunday (1862-1935)

[a] 26 That is, Christ or Messiah [b] 26 Psalm 2:1,2 [c] 27 The Greek is plural.

fear seized all who heard what had happened. [6]Then the young men came forward, wrapped up his body, and carried him out and buried him.

[7]About three hours later his wife came in, not knowing what had happened. [8]Peter asked her, "Tell me, is this the price you and Ananias got for the land?"

"Yes," she said, "that is the price."

[9]Peter said to her, "How could you agree to test the Spirit of the Lord? Look! The feet of the men who buried your husband are at the door, and they will carry you out also."

[10]At that moment she fell down at his feet and died. Then the young men came in and, finding her dead, carried her out and buried her beside her husband. [11]Great fear seized the whole church and all who heard about these events.

The Apostles Heal Many

[12]The apostles performed many miraculous signs and wonders among the people. And all the believers used to meet together in Solomon's Colonnade. [13]No one else dared join them, even though they were highly regarded by the people. [14]Nevertheless, more and more men and women believed in the Lord and were added to their number. [15]As a result, people brought the sick into the streets and laid them on beds and mats so that at least Peter's shadow might fall on some of them as he passed by. [16]Crowds gathered also from the towns around Jerusalem, bringing their sick and those tormented by evil[a] spirits, and all of them were healed.

The Apostles Persecuted

[17]Then the high priest and all his associates, who were members of the party of the Sadducees, were filled with jealousy. [18]They arrested the apostles and put them in the public jail. [19]But during the night an angel of the Lord opened the doors of the jail and brought them out. [20]"Go, stand in the temple courts," he said, "and tell the people the full message of this new life."

[21]At daybreak they entered the temple courts, as they had been told, and began to teach the people.

When the high priest and his associates arrived, they called together the Sanhedrin—the full assembly of the elders of Israel—and sent to the jail for the apostles. [22]But on arriving at the jail, the officers did not find them there. So they went back and reported, [23]"We found the jail securely locked, with the guards standing at the doors; but when we opened them, we found no one inside." [24]On hearing this report, the captain of the temple guard and the chief priests were puzzled, wondering what would come of this.

[25]Then someone came and said, "Look! The men you put in jail are standing in the temple courts teaching the people." [26]At that, the captain went with his officers and brought the apostles. They did not use force, because they feared that the people would stone them.

[27]Having brought the apostles, they made them appear before the Sanhedrin to be questioned by the high priest. [28]"We gave you strict orders not to teach in this name," he said. "Yet you have filled Jerusalem with your teaching and are determined to make us guilty of this man's blood."

[a] *16* Greek *unclean*

(5:20) Father, You are the Author of the message of life. You chose us from before the foundation of the world to receive through Jesus Christ every spiritual blessing. Through Him we are made holy and blameless in Your sight. Through Him we are adopted into Your family. Through Him our sins are forgiven and our lives are redeemed. And in the fullness of time You will bring all things in heaven and earth together under Him. (Eph 1:3–10)

(5:41–42) Lord God, surely You bless those who rejoice in their persecutions for Your name's sake. Those believers who are faithful to You even unto death await a special reward in Your kingdom. Help Your people to be courageous and faithful today even in the face of persecution, for You have promised that those who suffer with You will also reign with You. (Ps 116:15; Mt 5:10; 2Ti 2:11–12; 1Pe 4:16)

Nothing is more to be feared than too long a peace. You are deceived if you think that a Christian can live without persecution . . . A storm puts a man on his guard and obliges him to exert his utmost efforts to avoid shipwreck.

St. Jerome (c.347-420)

I believe in God, the Father,
Maker of heaven and earth;
And in Jesus, His only Son,
Born of a virgin birth.
On a cross He was crucified;
He descended into hell.
But the third day Jesus rose again,
He's alive and all is well.

This is what I believe,
It is written on my heart.
This is what I believe;
Every promise, every part.
This is what I believe.

"This Is What I Believe"
John A. Schreiner and
Walt Harrah (©1992)

29 Peter and the other apostles replied: "We must obey God
rather than men! 30 The God of our fathers raised Jesus from the
dead—whom you had killed by hanging him on a tree. 31 God exalted him to his own right hand as Prince and Savior that he might
give repentance and forgiveness of sins to Israel. 32 We are witnesses of these things, and so is the Holy Spirit, whom God has
given to those who obey him."
33 When they heard this, they were furious and wanted to put
them to death. 34 But a Pharisee named Gamaliel, a teacher of the
law, who was honored by all the people, stood up in the Sanhedrin and ordered that the men be put outside for a little while.
35 Then he addressed them: "Men of Israel, consider carefully
what you intend to do to these men. 36 Some time ago Theudas appeared, claiming to be somebody, and about four hundred men
rallied to him. He was killed, all his followers were dispersed,
and it all came to nothing. 37 After him, Judas the Galilean appeared in the days of the census and led a band of people in revolt. He too was killed, and all his followers were scattered.
38 Therefore, in the present case I advise you: Leave these men
alone! Let them go! For if their purpose or activity is of human
origin, it will fail. 39 But if it is from God, you will not be able to
stop these men; you will only find yourselves fighting against
God."
40 His speech persuaded them. They called the apostles in and
had them flogged. Then they ordered them not to speak in the
name of Jesus, and let them go.
41 The apostles left the Sanhedrin, rejoicing because they had
been counted worthy of suffering disgrace for the Name. 42 Day
after day, in the temple courts and from house to house, they
never stopped teaching and proclaiming the good news that Jesus
is the Christ.[a]

The Choosing of the Seven

6 In those days when the number of disciples was increasing,
the Grecian Jews among them complained against the He-
braic Jews because their widows were being overlooked in the
daily distribution of food. 2 So the Twelve gathered all the disciples together and said, "It would not be right for us to neglect the
ministry of the word of God in order to wait on tables. 3 Brothers,
choose seven men from among you who are known to be full of
the Spirit and wisdom. We will turn this responsibility over to
them 4 and will give our attention to prayer and the ministry of
the word."
5 This proposal pleased the whole group. They chose Stephen,
a man full of faith and of the Holy Spirit; also Philip, Procorus, Ni-
canor, Timon, Parmenas, and Nicolas from Antioch, a convert to
Judaism. 6 They presented these men to the apostles, who prayed
and laid their hands on them.
7 So the word of God spread. The number of disciples in Jerusalem increased rapidly, and a large number of priests became
obedient to the faith.

Stephen Seized

8 Now Stephen, a man full of God's grace and power, did great
wonders and miraculous signs among the people. 9 Opposition

[a] 42 Or *Messiah*

arose, however, from members of the Synagogue of the Freedmen
(as it was called)—Jews of Cyrene and Alexandria as well as the
provinces of Cilicia and Asia. These men began to argue with Stephen, 10but they could not stand up against his wisdom or the
Spirit by whom he spoke.
11Then they secretly persuaded some men to say, "We have
heard Stephen speak words of blasphemy against Moses and
against God."
12So they stirred up the people and the elders and the teachers
of the law. They seized Stephen and brought him before the Sanhedrin. 13They produced false witnesses, who testified, "This fellow never stops speaking against this holy place and against the
law. 14For we have heard him say that this Jesus of Nazareth will
destroy this place and change the customs Moses handed down
to us."
15All who were sitting in the Sanhedrin looked intently at Stephen, and they saw that his face was like the face of an angel.

Stephen's Speech to the Sanhedrin

7 Then the high priest asked him, "Are these charges true?"
2To this he replied: "Brothers and fathers, listen to me! The
God of glory appeared to our father Abraham while he was still in
Mesopotamia, before he lived in Haran. 3'Leave your country and
your people,' God said, 'and go to the land I will show you.'[a]
4"So he left the land of the Chaldeans and settled in Haran.
After the death of his father, God sent him to this land where you
are now living. 5He gave him no inheritance here, not even a foot
of ground. But God promised him that he and his descendants
after him would possess the land, even though at that time Abraham had no child. 6God spoke to him in this way: 'Your descendants will be strangers in a country not their own, and they will be
enslaved and mistreated four hundred years. 7But I will punish
the nation they serve as slaves,' God said, 'and afterward they will
come out of that country and worship me in this place.'[b] 8Then
he gave Abraham the covenant of circumcision. And Abraham became the father of Isaac and circumcised him eight days after his
birth. Later Isaac became the father of Jacob, and Jacob became
the father of the twelve patriarchs.
9"Because the patriarchs were jealous of Joseph, they sold him
as a slave into Egypt. But God was with him 10and rescued him
from all his troubles. He gave Joseph wisdom and enabled him to
gain the goodwill of Pharaoh king of Egypt; so he made him ruler
over Egypt and all his palace.
11"Then a famine struck all Egypt and Canaan, bringing great
suffering, and our fathers could not find food. 12When Jacob
heard that there was grain in Egypt, he sent our fathers on their
first visit. 13On their second visit, Joseph told his brothers who he
was, and Pharaoh learned about Joseph's family. 14After this, Joseph sent for his father Jacob and his whole family, seventy-five in
all. 15Then Jacob went down to Egypt, where he and our fathers
died. 16Their bodies were brought back to Shechem and placed
in the tomb that Abraham had bought from the sons of Hamor at
Shechem for a certain sum of money.
17"As the time drew near for God to fulfill his promise to Abraham, the number of our people in Egypt greatly increased.

[a] *3* Gen. 12:1 [b] *7* Gen. 15:13,14

(6:9–15) Thank You, Lord, for all of the men and women throughout the ages who, like Stephen, have given their lives for the sake of the gospel. Like kernels of wheat that fall to the ground and die, their deaths have not been in vain. Their testimonies have produced a harvest of new believers to take their places in the great mission of spreading the gospel throughout the earth. (Jn 12:24–25; Php 1:14)

For the truth-teller and truth-seeker, indeed, the whole world has very little liking. He is always unpopular, and not infrequently his unpopularity is so excessive that it endangers his life. Run your eye back over the list of martyrs, lay and clerical; nine-tenths of them stood accused of nothing worse than honest efforts to find out and announce the truth.

H. L. Mencken (1880–1956)

18Then another king, who knew nothing about Joseph, became ruler of Egypt. **19**He dealt treacherously with our people and oppressed our forefathers by forcing them to throw out their newborn babies so that they would die.

20"At that time Moses was born, and he was no ordinary child.[a] For three months he was cared for in his father's house. **21**When he was placed outside, Pharaoh's daughter took him and brought him up as her own son. **22**Moses was educated in all the wisdom of the Egyptians and was powerful in speech and action.

23"When Moses was forty years old, he decided to visit his fellow Israelites. **24**He saw one of them being mistreated by an Egyptian, so he went to his defense and avenged him by killing the Egyptian. **25**Moses thought that his own people would realize that God was using him to rescue them, but they did not. **26**The next day Moses came upon two Israelites who were fighting. He tried to reconcile them by saying, 'Men, you are brothers; why do you want to hurt each other?'

27"But the man who was mistreating the other pushed Moses aside and said, 'Who made you ruler and judge over us? **28**Do you want to kill me as you killed the Egyptian yesterday?'[b] **29**When Moses heard this, he fled to Midian, where he settled as a foreigner and had two sons.

30"After forty years had passed, an angel appeared to Moses in the flames of a burning bush in the desert near Mount Sinai. **31**When he saw this, he was amazed at the sight. As he went over to look more closely, he heard the Lord's voice: **32**'I am the God of your fathers, the God of Abraham, Isaac and Jacob.'[c] Moses trembled with fear and did not dare to look.

33"Then the Lord said to him, 'Take off your sandals; the place where you are standing is holy ground. **34**I have indeed seen the oppression of my people in Egypt. I have heard their groaning and have come down to set them free. Now come, I will send you back to Egypt.'[d]

35"This is the same Moses whom they had rejected with the words, 'Who made you ruler and judge?' He was sent to be their ruler and deliverer by God himself, through the angel who appeared to him in the bush. **36**He led them out of Egypt and did wonders and miraculous signs in Egypt, at the Red Sea[e] and for forty years in the desert.

37"This is that Moses who told the Israelites, 'God will send you a prophet like me from your own people.'[f] **38**He was in the assembly in the desert, with the angel who spoke to him on Mount Sinai, and with our fathers; and he received living words to pass on to us.

39"But our fathers refused to obey him. Instead, they rejected him and in their hearts turned back to Egypt. **40**They told Aaron, 'Make us gods who will go before us. As for this fellow Moses who led us out of Egypt—we don't know what has happened to him!'[g] **41**That was the time they made an idol in the form of a calf. They brought sacrifices to it and held a celebration in honor of what their hands had made. **42**But God turned away and gave them over to the worship of the heavenly bodies. This agrees with what is written in the book of the prophets:

[a] *20* Or *was fair in the sight of God* [b] *28* Exodus 2:14 [c] *32* Exodus 3:6
[d] *34* Exodus 3:5,7,8,10 [e] *36* That is, Sea of Reeds [f] *37* Deut. 18:15
[g] *40* Exodus 32:1

(7:17–38) Lord, if I am ever persecuted on Your behalf, give to me the single-minded commitment of Stephen, who did not speak in his own defense but spoke only in Yours. Give me his courage, Lord, for he knew that he belonged to You in life and in death. Help me to remember Your words of instruction: "When you are brought before synagogues, rulers and authorities, do not worry about how you will defend yourselves or what you will say, for the Holy Spirit will teach you at that time what you should say." (Da 3:16–18; Lk 12:11–12)

For myself, I never heard the sound of his voice, but I know that he dwells within me all the time, guiding me and inspiring me whenever I do or say anything. A light, of which I'd caught no glimmer before, comes to me at the very moment when it's needed.

Therese de Lisieux (1873-1897)

True apostles, faithful prophets,
Saints who set their world ablaze,
Martyrs, once unknown, unheeded,
Join one growing song of praise,
While Your church on earth
Confesses one majestic Trinity:
Father, Son, and Holy Spirit,
God, our hope eternally.

"God, We Praise You!"
Christopher Idle (©1982)

" 'Did you bring me sacrifices and offerings
forty years in the desert, O house of Israel?
43 You have lifted up the shrine of Molech
and the star of your god Rephan,
the idols you made to worship.
Therefore I will send you into exile'[a] beyond Babylon.

44 "Our forefathers had the tabernacle of the Testimony with
them in the desert. It had been made as God directed Moses, according to the pattern he had seen. 45 Having received the tabernacle, our fathers under Joshua brought it with them when they
took the land from the nations God drove out before them. It remained in the land until the time of David, 46 who enjoyed God's
favor and asked that he might provide a dwelling place for the
God of Jacob.[b] 47 But it was Solomon who built the house for him.
48 "However, the Most High does not live in houses made by
men. As the prophet says:

49 " 'Heaven is my throne,
and the earth is my footstool.
What kind of house will you build for me?
says the Lord.
Or where will my resting place be?
50 Has not my hand made all these things?'[c]

51 "You stiff-necked people, with uncircumcised hearts and
ears! You are just like your fathers: You always resist the Holy
Spirit! 52 Was there ever a prophet your fathers did not persecute?
They even killed those who predicted the coming of the Righteous
One. And now you have betrayed and murdered him— 53 you
who have received the law that was put into effect through angels
but have not obeyed it."

The Stoning of Stephen

54 When they heard this, they were furious and gnashed their
teeth at him. 55 But Stephen, full of the Holy Spirit, looked up to
heaven and saw the glory of God, and Jesus standing at the right
hand of God. 56 "Look," he said, "I see heaven open and the Son
of Man standing at the right hand of God."
57 At this they covered their ears and, yelling at the top of their
voices, they all rushed at him, 58 dragged him out of the city and
began to stone him. Meanwhile, the witnesses laid their clothes at
the feet of a young man named Saul.
59 While they were stoning him, Stephen prayed, "Lord Jesus,
receive my spirit." 60 Then he fell on his knees and cried out,
"Lord, do not hold this sin against them." When he had said this,
he fell asleep.

8 And Saul was there, giving approval to his death.

The Church Persecuted and Scattered

On that day a great persecution broke out against the church at
Jerusalem, and all except the apostles were scattered throughout
Judea and Samaria. 2 Godly men buried Stephen and mourned
deeply for him. 3 But Saul began to destroy the church. Going
from house to house, he dragged off men and women and put
them in prison.

[a] 43 Amos 5:25–27 [b] 46 Some early manuscripts *the house of Jacob*
[c] 50 Isaiah 66:1,2

(8:1–8) Like seeds scattered by the wind of persecution and taking root in new soil, Your believers carried the Good News of Jesus Christ throughout the ancient world. I pray for Your church today. Deepen our faith and our resolve to represent You in our modern world. May we too find the courage to uproot ourselves if necessary for the sake of the gospel. (Mt. 5:10–12)

Go ye therefore to every nation,
Preach the Gospel in every land.
To every language and every people,
In My name reach out your hand.

Tell the world the message,
Take it everywhere
To every tribe and nation
We are called to share.

"Tell the World"
Marsha Skidmore (©1994)

God considers not the action, but the spirit of the action.

Peter Abelard (1079–1142)

(8:21–23) Lord, Your gifts cannot be bought; Your power cannot be sold; Your grace cannot be bartered or traded away. Your Spirit is freely available to anyone whose heart is right before You. Lord, purify my heart and my hands so that I can be a channel of Your life to a needy world. Free me from the greed and bitterness that block the flow of Your gifts. Let my motivation be pure and selfless so that I can minister in the power of Your Holy Spirit.

Father, grant Your Holy Spirit
In our hearts may rule today,
Grieved not, quenched not,
But unhindered,
Work in us His sovereign way.
Fill us with Your holy fullness,
God the Father, Spirit, Son;
In us, through us, then, forever
Shall Your perfect will be done.

"For Your Gift of God the Spirit"
Margaret Clarkson (©1960, 1976, 1988)

Philip in Samaria

[4]Those who had been scattered preached the word wherever
they went. [5]Philip went down to a city in Samaria and proclaimed
the Christ[a] there. [6]When the crowds heard Philip and saw the
miraculous signs he did, they all paid close attention to what he
said. [7]With shrieks, evil[b] spirits came out of many, and many par-
alytics and cripples were healed. [8]So there was great joy in that
city.

Simon the Sorcerer

[9]Now for some time a man named Simon had practiced sorcery in the city and amazed all the people of Samaria. He boasted
that he was someone great, [10]and all the people, both high and
low, gave him their attention and exclaimed, "This man is the divine power known as the Great Power." [11]They followed him because he had amazed them for a long time with his magic. [12]But
when they believed Philip as he preached the good news of the
kingdom of God and the name of Jesus Christ, they were baptized,
both men and women. [13]Simon himself believed and was baptized. And he followed Philip everywhere, astonished by the great
signs and miracles he saw.

[14]When the apostles in Jerusalem heard that Samaria had accepted the word of God, they sent Peter and John to them.
[15]When they arrived, they prayed for them that they might receive
the Holy Spirit, [16]because the Holy Spirit had not yet come upon
any of them; they had simply been baptized into[c] the name of the
Lord Jesus. [17]Then Peter and John placed their hands on them,
and they received the Holy Spirit.

[18]When Simon saw that the Spirit was given at the laying on of
the apostles' hands, he offered them money [19]and said, "Give me
also this ability so that everyone on whom I lay my hands may receive the Holy Spirit."

[20]Peter answered: "May your money perish with you, because
you thought you could buy the gift of God with money! [21]You have
no part or share in this ministry, because your heart is not right
before God. [22]Repent of this wickedness and pray to the Lord.
Perhaps he will forgive you for having such a thought in your
heart. [23]For I see that you are full of bitterness and captive to
sin."

[24]Then Simon answered, "Pray to the Lord for me so that nothing you have said may happen to me."

[25]When they had testified and proclaimed the word of the
Lord, Peter and John returned to Jerusalem, preaching the gospel
in many Samaritan villages.

Philip and the Ethiopian

[26]Now an angel of the Lord said to Philip, "Go south to the
road—the desert road—that goes down from Jerusalem to
Gaza." [27]So he started out, and on his way he met an Ethiopian[d]
eunuch, an important official in charge of all the treasury of Can-
dace, queen of the Ethiopians. This man had gone to Jerusalem to
worship, [28]and on his way home was sitting in his chariot reading the book of Isaiah the prophet. [29]The Spirit told Philip, "Go
to that chariot and stay near it."

[a] 5 Or *Messiah* [b] 7 Greek *unclean* [c] 16 Or *in* [d] 27 That is, from the upper Nile region

30 Then Philip ran up to the chariot and heard the man reading
Isaiah the prophet. "Do you understand what you are reading?"
Philip asked.
31 "How can I," he said, "unless someone explains it to me?"
So he invited Philip to come up and sit with him.
32 The eunuch was reading this passage of Scripture:

"He was led like a sheep to the slaughter,
and as a lamb before the shearer is silent,
so he did not open his mouth.
33 In his humiliation he was deprived of justice.
Who can speak of his descendants?
For his life was taken from the earth."[a]

34 The eunuch asked Philip, "Tell me, please, who is the prophet talking about, himself or someone else?" 35 Then Philip began
with that very passage of Scripture and told him the good news
about Jesus.
36 As they traveled along the road, they came to some water and
the eunuch said, "Look, here is water. Why shouldn't I be baptized?"[b] 38 And he gave orders to stop the chariot. Then both Philip and the eunuch went down into the water and Philip baptized
him. 39 When they came up out of the water, the Spirit of the Lord
suddenly took Philip away, and the eunuch did not see him again,
but went on his way rejoicing. 40 Philip, however, appeared at
Azotus and traveled about, preaching the gospel in all the towns
until he reached Caesarea.

Saul's Conversion

9 Meanwhile, Saul was still breathing out murderous threats
against the Lord's disciples. He went to the high priest 2 and
asked him for letters to the synagogues in Damascus, so that if he
found any there who belonged to the Way, whether men or
women, he might take them as prisoners to Jerusalem. 3 As he
neared Damascus on his journey, suddenly a light from heaven
flashed around him. 4 He fell to the ground and heard a voice say
to him, "Saul, Saul, why do you persecute me?"
5 "Who are you, Lord?" Saul asked.
"I am Jesus, whom you are persecuting," he replied. 6 "Now
get up and go into the city, and you will be told what you
must do."
7 The men traveling with Saul stood there speechless; they
heard the sound but did not see anyone. 8 Saul got up from the
ground, but when he opened his eyes he could see nothing. So
they led him by the hand into Damascus. 9 For three days he was
blind, and did not eat or drink anything.
10 In Damascus there was a disciple named Ananias. The Lord
called to him in a vision, "Ananias!"
"Yes, Lord," he answered.
11 The Lord told him, "Go to the house of Judas on Straight
Street and ask for a man from Tarsus named Saul, for he is praying. 12 In a vision he has seen a man named Ananias come and
place his hands on him to restore his sight."
13 "Lord," Ananias answered, "I have heard many reports
about this man and all the harm he has done to your saints in Je-

[a] *33* Isaiah 53:7,8 [b] *36* Some late manuscripts *baptized?" 37Philip said, "If you believe with all your heart, you may." The eunuch answered, "I believe that Jesus Christ is the Son of God."*

(8:26–39) Lord, give me a heart like Philip's, willing to step out in faith wherever You want me to go. Sow Your Word into my life and make me ready for the day that You call upon me to deliver the right answer to the right question at the right time.

There is no situation so chaotic that God cannot from that situation create something that is surpassingly good. He did it at creation. He did it at the cross. He is doing it today.
Bishop Handley Carr Glyn Moule (1841-1920)

(9:1–9) Saul's conversion tells us much about Your power to change lives. You turned his mission of death into an encounter with Your resurrection. You blinded his physical sight so that You could open his spiritual eyes. You transformed this enemy of Your church into a father of the faith. You could have destroyed him, but instead You chose to employ him. We praise You, Lord, for the saving power of Your love.

Lord, the light of Your love is
shining,
In the midst of the darkness shining;
Jesus, Light of the world, shine upon
us;
Set us free by the truth You now
bring us,
Shine on me, shine on me.
"Shine, Jesus Shine"
Graham Kendrick (©1987)

If Christ lives in us, controlling our personalities, we will leave glorious marks on the lives we touch. Not because of us but because of Him.

Eugenia Price (1916-)

(9:20–28) I may not have had the radical, face-to-face encounter with You that Saul experienced on the Damascus road, but I have encountered Your truth, Your love, Your forgiveness and Your free gift of salvation. Just as You transformed Saul into Your instrument, so too make me Your instrument, perfectly tuned to Your voice and resonant with Your message.

Lord, I was blind; I could not see
In Your marred visage any grace:
But now the beauty of Your face
In radiant vision dawns on me.

Lord, I was deaf; I could not hear
The thrilling music of Your voice:
But now I hear You and rejoice,
And all Your spoken words are dear.

Lord, I was mute; I could not speak
The grace and glory of Your name:
But now, as touched with living
 flame,
My lips will speak for Jesus' sake.

Lord, I was dead; I could not move
My lifeless soul from sin's dark
 grave:
But now the power of life You gave
Has raised me up to know Your love.

"Lord, I Was Blind"
William T. Matson (©1982)

rusalem. [14]And he has come here with authority from the chief
priests to arrest all who call on your name."
[15]But the Lord said to Ananias, "Go! This man is my chosen instrument to carry my name before the Gentiles and their kings
and before the people of Israel. [16]I will show him how much he
must suffer for my name."
[17]Then Ananias went to the house and entered it. Placing his
hands on Saul, he said, "Brother Saul, the Lord—Jesus, who appeared to you on the road as you were coming here—has sent
me so that you may see again and be filled with the Holy Spirit."
[18]Immediately, something like scales fell from Saul's eyes, and he
could see again. He got up and was baptized, [19]and after taking
some food, he regained his strength.

Saul in Damascus and Jerusalem

Saul spent several days with the disciples in Damascus. [20]At
once he began to preach in the synagogues that Jesus is the Son
of God. [21]All those who heard him were astonished and asked,
"Isn't he the man who raised havoc in Jerusalem among those
who call on this name? And hasn't he come here to take them as
prisoners to the chief priests?" [22]Yet Saul grew more and more
powerful and baffled the Jews living in Damascus by proving that
Jesus is the Christ.[a]
[23]After many days had gone by, the Jews conspired to kill him,
[24]but Saul learned of their plan. Day and night they kept close
watch on the city gates in order to kill him. [25]But his followers
took him by night and lowered him in a basket through an opening in the wall.
[26]When he came to Jerusalem, he tried to join the disciples,
but they were all afraid of him, not believing that he really was a
disciple. [27]But Barnabas took him and brought him to the apostles. He told them how Saul on his journey had seen the Lord and
that the Lord had spoken to him, and how in Damascus he had
preached fearlessly in the name of Jesus. [28]So Saul stayed with
them and moved about freely in Jerusalem, speaking boldly in the
name of the Lord. [29]He talked and debated with the Grecian Jews,
but they tried to kill him. [30]When the brothers learned of this,
they took him down to Caesarea and sent him off to Tarsus.
[31]Then the church throughout Judea, Galilee and Samaria enjoyed a time of peace. It was strengthened; and encouraged by the
Holy Spirit, it grew in numbers, living in the fear of the Lord.

Aeneas and Dorcas

[32]As Peter traveled about the country, he went to visit the saints
in Lydda. [33]There he found a man named Aeneas, a paralytic who
had been bedridden for eight years. [34]"Aeneas," Peter said to
him, "Jesus Christ heals you. Get up and take care of your mat."
Immediately Aeneas got up. [35]All those who lived in Lydda and
Sharon saw him and turned to the Lord.
[36]In Joppa there was a disciple named Tabitha (which, when
translated, is Dorcas[b]), who was always doing good and helping
the poor. [37]About that time she became sick and died, and her
body was washed and placed in an upstairs room. [38]Lydda was
near Joppa; so when the disciples heard that Peter was in Lydda,
they sent two men to him and urged him, "Please come at once!"

[a] 22 Or *Messiah* [b] 36 Both *Tabitha* (Aramaic) and *Dorcas* (Greek) mean *gazelle*.

39 Peter went with them, and when he arrived he was taken upstairs to the room. All the widows stood around him, crying and
showing him the robes and other clothing that Dorcas had made
while she was still with them.
40 Peter sent them all out of the room; then he got down on his
knees and prayed. Turning toward the dead woman, he said,
"Tabitha, get up." She opened her eyes, and seeing Peter she sat
up. 41 He took her by the hand and helped her to her feet. Then
he called the believers and the widows and presented her to them
alive. 42 This became known all over Joppa, and many people believed in the Lord. 43 Peter stayed in Joppa for some time with a
tanner named Simon.

Cornelius Calls for Peter

10 At Caesarea there was a man named Cornelius, a centurion
in what was known as the Italian Regiment. 2 He and all his
family were devout and God-fearing; he gave generously to those
in need and prayed to God regularly. 3 One day at about three in
the afternoon he had a vision. He distinctly saw an angel of God,
who came to him and said, "Cornelius!"
4 Cornelius stared at him in fear. "What is it, Lord?" he asked.
The angel answered, "Your prayers and gifts to the poor have
come up as a memorial offering before God. 5 Now send men to
Joppa to bring back a man named Simon who is called Peter. 6 He
is staying with Simon the tanner, whose house is by the sea."
7 When the angel who spoke to him had gone, Cornelius called
two of his servants and a devout soldier who was one of his attendants. 8 He told them everything that had happened and sent
them to Joppa.

Peter's Vision

9 About noon the following day as they were on their journey
and approaching the city, Peter went up on the roof to pray. 10 He
became hungry and wanted something to eat, and while the meal
was being prepared, he fell into a trance. 11 He saw heaven
opened and something like a large sheet being let down to earth
by its four corners. 12 It contained all kinds of four-footed animals, as well as reptiles of the earth and birds of the air. 13 Then
a voice told him, "Get up, Peter. Kill and eat."
14 "Surely not, Lord!" Peter replied. "I have never eaten anything impure or unclean."
15 The voice spoke to him a second time, "Do not call anything
impure that God has made clean."
16 This happened three times, and immediately the sheet was
taken back to heaven.
17 While Peter was wondering about the meaning of the vision,
the men sent by Cornelius found out where Simon's house was
and stopped at the gate. 18 They called out, asking if Simon who
was known as Peter was staying there.
19 While Peter was still thinking about the vision, the Spirit said
to him, "Simon, three[a] men are looking for you. 20 So get up and
go downstairs. Do not hesitate to go with them, for I have sent
them."
21 Peter went down and said to the men, "I'm the one you're
looking for. Why have you come?"

[a] *19* One early manuscript *two*; other manuscripts do not have the number.

(10:1–23) Lord, thank You for looking upon our hearts and not upon our outward appearances. You used this righteous man to deal with Peter's self-righteousness. Cornelius was a Roman, a centurion and a Gentile. Yet the law of love was written on his heart. He prayed to You, and You called to him by name. He hungered for You, and You fed him with the bread of life. He gave to the poor, and You received his gifts as offerings of genuine worship. Thank You for Your mercy, Lord. Thank You for the embrace of Your grace. Help me never to assume that anyone is beyond or beneath Your reach, for You accept people from every nation who fear You and do what is right. (Ac 10:34–35)

O Christian, haste, your mission
high fulfilling,
To tell to all the world that God is
Light;
That He who made all nations is not
willing
One soul should perish, lost in shades
of night.

Proclaim to every people, tongue and
nation
That God, in whom they live and
move, is love:
Tell how He stooped to save His lost
creation,
And died on earth that man might
live above.

"O Christian, Haste, Your Mission High"
Mary Thomson (1868)

(10:33–48) Father, there are still millions of people, just like Cornelius, who are looking for you. Use me to reach them. Cleanse me from any prejudice or preconceptions that I might use as an excuse for my silence. Help me to see beyond cultural divisions and ethnic distinctions. Give me your vision and compassion for the lost. Lead me to those who have ears to hear, and give me a voice to speak the message of hope and salvation in Jesus Christ. Let me never withhold your blessing when it is within my power to give it.

When the church fails to break the [cultural] barrier, both sides lose. Those who need the gospel message of hope and the reality of love, don't get it, and the isolated church keeps evangelizing the same people over and over until its only mission finally is to entertain itself . . . When the church transcends culture, it can transform culture.

Charles Colson (1931-)

One by one we're drawn together,
One by one to Jesus' side.
One in Him, we'll live forever,
Strangers He has reconciled.

In His love no walls between us,
In His love a common ground.
Kneeling at the cross of Jesus,
All our pride comes tumbling down.

Let the walls fall down.
Let the walls fall down.
Let the walls fall down.
By His love let the walls fall down.

"Let the Walls Fall Down"
Bill Batstone, Anne Barbour and
John Barbour (©1993)

22 The men replied, "We have come from Cornelius the centurion. He is a righteous and God-fearing man, who is respected by
all the Jewish people. A holy angel told him to have you come to
his house so that he could hear what you have to say." 23 Then
Peter invited the men into the house to be his guests.

Peter at Cornelius's House

The next day Peter started out with them, and some of the
brothers from Joppa went along. 24 The following day he arrived in
Caesarea. Cornelius was expecting them and had called together
his relatives and close friends. 25 As Peter entered the house, Cornelius met him and fell at his feet in reverence. 26 But Peter made
him get up. "Stand up," he said, "I am only a man myself."

27 Talking with him, Peter went inside and found a large gathering of people. 28 He said to them: "You are well aware that it is
against our law for a Jew to associate with a Gentile or visit him.
But God has shown me that I should not call any man impure or
unclean. 29 So when I was sent for, I came without raising any ob-
jection. May I ask why you sent for me?"

30 Cornelius answered: "Four days ago I was in my house praying at this hour, at three in the afternoon. Suddenly a man in shining clothes stood before me 31 and said, 'Cornelius, God has
heard your prayer and remembered your gifts to the poor. 32 Send
to Joppa for Simon who is called Peter. He is a guest in the home
of Simon the tanner, who lives by the sea.' 33 So I sent for you immediately, and it was good of you to come. Now we are all here in
the presence of God to listen to everything the Lord has commanded you to tell us."

34 Then Peter began to speak: "I now realize how true it is that
God does not show favoritism 35 but accepts men from every nation who fear him and do what is right. 36 You know the message
God sent to the people of Israel, telling the good news of peace
through Jesus Christ, who is Lord of all. 37 You know what has
happened throughout Judea, beginning in Galilee after the baptism that John preached— 38 how God anointed Jesus of Nazareth with the Holy Spirit and power, and how he went around
doing good and healing all who were under the power of the
devil, because God was with him.

39 "We are witnesses of everything he did in the country of the
Jews and in Jerusalem. They killed him by hanging him on a tree,
40 but God raised him from the dead on the third day and caused
him to be seen. 41 He was not seen by all the people, but by witnesses whom God had already chosen—by us who ate and drank
with him after he rose from the dead. 42 He commanded us to
preach to the people and to testify that he is the one whom God
appointed as judge of the living and the dead. 43 All the prophets
testify about him that everyone who believes in him receives forgiveness of sins through his name."

44 While Peter was still speaking these words, the Holy Spirit
came on all who heard the message. 45 The circumcised believers
who had come with Peter were astonished that the gift of the Holy
Spirit had been poured out even on the Gentiles. 46 For they heard
them speaking in tongues[a] and praising God.

Then Peter said, 47 "Can anyone keep these people from being
baptized with water? They have received the Holy Spirit just as we

[a] 46 Or *other languages*

have." **48**So he ordered that they be baptized in the name of Jesus
Christ. Then they asked Peter to stay with them for a few days.

Peter Explains His Actions

11 The apostles and the brothers throughout Judea heard that
the Gentiles also had received the word of God. **2**So when
Peter went up to Jerusalem, the circumcised believers criticized
him **3**and said, "You went into the house of uncircumcised men
and ate with them."

4Peter began and explained everything to them precisely as it
had happened: **5**"I was in the city of Joppa praying, and in a
trance I saw a vision. I saw something like a large sheet being let
down from heaven by its four corners, and it came down to where
I was. **6**I looked into it and saw four-footed animals of the earth,
wild beasts, reptiles, and birds of the air. **7**Then I heard a voice
telling me, 'Get up, Peter. Kill and eat.'

8"I replied, 'Surely not, Lord! Nothing impure or unclean has
ever entered my mouth.'

9"The voice spoke from heaven a second time, 'Do not call
anything impure that God has made clean.' **10**This happened
three times, and then it was all pulled up to heaven again.

11"Right then three men who had been sent to me from Caesarea stopped at the house where I was staying. **12**The Spirit told
me to have no hesitation about going with them. These six brothers also went with me, and we entered the man's house. **13**He told
us how he had seen an angel appear in his house and say, 'Send
to Joppa for Simon who is called Peter. **14**He will bring you a message through which you and all your household will be saved.'

15"As I began to speak, the Holy Spirit came on them as he had
come on us at the beginning. **16**Then I remembered what the Lord
had said: 'John baptized with[a] water, but you will be baptized with
the Holy Spirit.' **17**So if God gave them the same gift as he gave us,
who believed in the Lord Jesus Christ, who was I to think that I
could oppose God?"

18When they heard this, they had no further objections and
praised God, saying, "So then, God has granted even the Gentiles
repentance unto life."

The Church in Antioch

19Now those who had been scattered by the persecution in
connection with Stephen traveled as far as Phoenicia, Cyprus and
Antioch, telling the message only to Jews. **20**Some of them, however, men from Cyprus and Cyrene, went to Antioch and began to
speak to Greeks also, telling them the good news about the Lord
Jesus. **21**The Lord's hand was with them, and a great number of
people believed and turned to the Lord.

22News of this reached the ears of the church at Jerusalem,
and they sent Barnabas to Antioch. **23**When he arrived and saw
the evidence of the grace of God, he was glad and encouraged
them all to remain true to the Lord with all their hearts. **24**He was
a good man, full of the Holy Spirit and faith, and a great number
of people were brought to the Lord.

25Then Barnabas went to Tarsus to look for Saul, **26**and when
he found him, he brought him to Antioch. So for a whole year
Barnabas and Saul met with the church and taught great numbers
of people. The disciples were called Christians first at Antioch.

[a] 16 Or *in*

(11:15–18) Lord, I worship You as the God of all mankind. You do not limit Your love to a small group of insiders; rather, You pour out Your Spirit on all who believe in the Lord Jesus Christ. When You welcome "whoever believes" into Your kingdom, who can question Your judgment? Lord, I praise You and thank You that faith and grace and repentance are gifts from Your generous hand, freely given to all who will receive. (Jer 32:27; Jn 3:16–18; Rev 22:17)

Jesus, I believe;
Jesus, I believe.
You're my Maker, my God and
Savior.
Your Spirit I receive,
O, Jesus, I believe.

Jesus, live in me;
Jesus, live in me.
The new creation of Your salvation,
Your dwelling place I'll be.
Jesus, live in me;
Jesus, I believe.

I believe in Your great love,
A love that led You to die.
A faithful Son of the Father above,
Lord of all, come and be
The Lord within my life.

"Jesus, I Believe"
Bill Batstone (©1994)

27During this time some prophets came down from Jerusalem
to Antioch. 28One of them, named Agabus, stood up and through
the Spirit predicted that a severe famine would spread over the
entire Roman world. (This happened during the reign of Claudius.) 29The disciples, each according to his ability, decided to
provide help for the brothers living in Judea. 30This they did,
sending their gift to the elders by Barnabas and Saul.

Peter's Miraculous Escape From Prison

12 It was about this time that King Herod arrested some who
belonged to the church, intending to persecute them. 2He
had James, the brother of John, put to death with the sword.
3When he saw that this pleased the Jews, he proceeded to seize
Peter also. This happened during the Feast of Unleavened Bread.
4After arresting him, he put him in prison, handing him over to
be guarded by four squads of four soldiers each. Herod intended
to bring him out for public trial after the Passover.

5So Peter was kept in prison, but the church was earnestly
praying to God for him.

6The night before Herod was to bring him to trial, Peter was
sleeping between two soldiers, bound with two chains, and sen-
tries stood guard at the entrance. 7Suddenly an angel of the Lord
appeared and a light shone in the cell. He struck Peter on the
side and woke him up. "Quick, get up!" he said, and the chains
fell off Peter's wrists.

8Then the angel said to him, "Put on your clothes and sandals." And Peter did so. "Wrap your cloak around you and follow
me," the angel told him. 9Peter followed him out of the prison,
but he had no idea that what the angel was doing was really happening; he thought he was seeing a vision. 10They passed the first
and second guards and came to the iron gate leading to the city.
It opened for them by itself, and they went through it. When they
had walked the length of one street, suddenly the angel left him.

11Then Peter came to himself and said, "Now I know without a
doubt that the Lord sent his angel and rescued me from Herod's
clutches and from everything the Jewish people were anticipating."

12When this had dawned on him, he went to the house of Mary
the mother of John, also called Mark, where many people had
gathered and were praying. 13Peter knocked at the outer entrance, and a servant girl named Rhoda came to answer the door.
14When she recognized Peter's voice, she was so overjoyed she
ran back without opening it and exclaimed, "Peter is at the door!"

15"You're out of your mind," they told her. When she kept in-
sisting that it was so, they said, "It must be his angel."

16But Peter kept on knocking, and when they opened the door
and saw him, they were astonished. 17Peter motioned with his
hand for them to be quiet and described how the Lord had
brought him out of prison. "Tell James and the brothers about
this," he said, and then he left for another place.

18In the morning, there was no small commotion among the
soldiers as to what had become of Peter. 19After Herod had a
thorough search made for him and did not find him, he cross-ex-
amined the guards and ordered that they be executed.

Herod's Death

Then Herod went from Judea to Caesarea and stayed there a
while. 20He had been quarreling with the people of Tyre and

(12:5–19) "Peter was kept in prison." He was truly kept there—kept safe, kept secure, kept in Your hand, kept for Your glorious purpose. He was locked up by Herod, but You held the key to freedom. I praise You, Lord, for turning adversity into victory when Your people prevail in prayer.

We like to be always "on the go"; the Lord would sometimes prefer to have us in prison. We think in terms of apostolic journeys; God dares to put his greatest ambassadors in chains.

Watchman Nee (1903-1972)

Sidon; they now joined together and sought an audience with
him. Having secured the support of Blastus, a trusted personal
servant of the king, they asked for peace, because they depended
on the king's country for their food supply.
21 On the appointed day Herod, wearing his royal robes, sat on
his throne and delivered a public address to the people. 22 They
shouted, "This is the voice of a god, not of a man." 23 Immediately, because Herod did not give praise to God, an angel of the Lord
struck him down, and he was eaten by worms and died.
24 But the word of God continued to increase and spread.
25 When Barnabas and Saul had finished their mission, they returned from[a] Jerusalem, taking with them John, also called Mark.

Barnabas and Saul Sent Off

13 In the church at Antioch there were prophets and teachers:
Barnabas, Simeon called Niger, Lucius of Cyrene, Manaen
(who had been brought up with Herod the tetrarch) and Saul.
2 While they were worshiping the Lord and fasting, the Holy Spirit said, "Set apart for me Barnabas and Saul for the work to which
I have called them." 3 So after they had fasted and prayed, they
placed their hands on them and sent them off.

On Cyprus

4 The two of them, sent on their way by the Holy Spirit, went
down to Seleucia and sailed from there to Cyprus. 5 When they arrived at Salamis, they proclaimed the word of God in the Jewish
synagogues. John was with them as their helper.
6 They traveled through the whole island until they came to Paphos. There they met a Jewish sorcerer and false prophet named
Bar-Jesus, 7 who was an attendant of the proconsul, Sergius Pau-
lus. The proconsul, an intelligent man, sent for Barnabas and
Saul because he wanted to hear the word of God. 8 But Elymas the
sorcerer (for that is what his name means) opposed them and
tried to turn the proconsul from the faith. 9 Then Saul, who was
also called Paul, filled with the Holy Spirit, looked straight at Elymas and said, 10 "You are a child of the devil and an enemy of
everything that is right! You are full of all kinds of deceit and
trickery. Will you never stop perverting the right ways of the Lord?
11 Now the hand of the Lord is against you. You are going to be
blind, and for a time you will be unable to see the light of the
sun."

Immediately mist and darkness came over him, and he groped
about, seeking someone to lead him by the hand. 12 When the
proconsul saw what had happened, he believed, for he was
amazed at the teaching about the Lord.

In Pisidian Antioch

13 From Paphos, Paul and his companions sailed to Perga in
Pamphylia, where John left them to return to Jerusalem. 14 From
Perga they went on to Pisidian Antioch. On the Sabbath they entered the synagogue and sat down. 15 After the reading from the
Law and the Prophets, the synagogue rulers sent word to them,
saying, "Brothers, if you have a message of encouragement for
the people, please speak."
16 Standing up, Paul motioned with his hand and said: "Men of

(12:23–24) Lord, who can challenge or deny Your sovereignty? Kings and rulers have tried, only to face their Creator without excuse. I thank You that through Your gift of grace I have been spared from the same judgment. Teach me to continuously praise You and to mingle holy praise with holy service. You alone are worthy of worship.

[a] 25 Some manuscripts *to*

(13:16–40) Father, what a message of encouragement! For those who gathered in worship Paul unrolled the scroll and revealed Your great plan of salvation. What better news could there be for them or for us? In accordance with ancient prophecies, Your Son Jesus came to live among us. He laid down His life, He was raised from the dead, He forgave our sins and made us clean in Your eyes. How we thank You for Your love, for Your provision and for the great record of Your grace that continues to write itself in our lives, right here, right now. (2Co 3:3)

Come, every soul by sin oppressed,
There's mercy with the Lord;
And He will surely give you rest
By trusting in His Word.

For Jesus shed His precious blood
Rich blessings to bestow;
Plunge now into the crimson flood
That washes white as snow.

Come, then, and join this holy band,
And on to glory go,
To dwell in that celestial land,
Where joys immortal flow.

"Only Trust Him"
John H. Stockton (1874)

Israel and you Gentiles who worship God, listen to me! 17 The God
of the people of Israel chose our fathers; he made the people
prosper during their stay in Egypt, with mighty power he led them
out of that country, 18 he endured their conduct[a] for about forty
years in the desert, 19 he overthrew seven nations in Canaan and
gave their land to his people as their inheritance. 20 All this took
about 450 years.

"After this, God gave them judges until the time of Samuel the
prophet. 21 Then the people asked for a king, and he gave them
Saul son of Kish, of the tribe of Benjamin, who ruled forty years.
22 After removing Saul, he made David their king. He testified concerning him: 'I have found David son of Jesse a man after my own
heart; he will do everything I want him to do.'

23 "From this man's descendants God has brought to Israel the
Savior Jesus, as he promised. 24 Before the coming of Jesus, John
preached repentance and baptism to all the people of Israel. 25 As
John was completing his work, he said: 'Who do you think I am?
I am not that one. No, but he is coming after me, whose sandals
I am not worthy to untie.'

26 "Brothers, children of Abraham, and you God-fearing Gentiles, it is to us that this message of salvation has been sent. 27 The
people of Jerusalem and their rulers did not recognize Jesus, yet
in condemning him they fulfilled the words of the prophets that
are read every Sabbath. 28 Though they found no proper ground
for a death sentence, they asked Pilate to have him executed.
29 When they had carried out all that was written about him, they
took him down from the tree and laid him in a tomb. 30 But God
raised him from the dead, 31 and for many days he was seen by
those who had traveled with him from Galilee to Jerusalem. They
are now his witnesses to our people.

32 "We tell you the good news: What God promised our fathers
33 he has fulfilled for us, their children, by raising up Jesus. As it
is written in the second Psalm:

"'You are my Son;
today I have become your Father.'[b][c]

34 The fact that God raised him from the dead, never to decay, is
stated in these words:

"'I will give you the holy and sure blessings promised
to David.'[d]

35 So it is stated elsewhere:

"'You will not let your Holy One see decay.'[e]

36 "For when David had served God's purpose in his own generation, he fell asleep; he was buried with his fathers and his body
decayed. 37 But the one whom God raised from the dead did not
see decay.

38 "Therefore, my brothers, I want you to know that through
Jesus the forgiveness of sins is proclaimed to you. 39 Through him
everyone who believes is justified from everything you could not
be justified from by the law of Moses. 40 Take care that what the
prophets have said does not happen to you:

41 "'Look, you scoffers,

[a] 18 Some manuscripts *and cared for them* [b] 33 Or *have begotten you*
[c] 33 Psalm 2:7 [d] 34 Isaiah 55:3 [e] 35 Psalm 16:10

wonder and perish,
for I am going to do something in your days
that you would never believe,
even if someone told you.'[a]"

42As Paul and Barnabas were leaving the synagogue, the people invited them to speak further about these things on the next Sabbath. 43When the congregation was dismissed, many of the Jews and devout converts to Judaism followed Paul and Barnabas, who talked with them and urged them to continue in the grace of God.

44On the next Sabbath almost the whole city gathered to hear the word of the Lord. 45When the Jews saw the crowds, they were filled with jealousy and talked abusively against what Paul was saying.

46Then Paul and Barnabas answered them boldly: "We had to speak the word of God to you first. Since you reject it and do not consider yourselves worthy of eternal life, we now turn to the Gentiles. 47For this is what the Lord has commanded us:

" 'I have made you[b] a light for the Gentiles,
that you[b] may bring salvation to the ends of the earth.'[c]"

48When the Gentiles heard this, they were glad and honored the word of the Lord; and all who were appointed for eternal life believed.

49The word of the Lord spread through the whole region. 50But the Jews incited the God-fearing women of high standing and the leading men of the city. They stirred up persecution against Paul and Barnabas, and expelled them from their region. 51So they shook the dust from their feet in protest against them and went to Iconium. 52And the disciples were filled with joy and with the Holy Spirit.

In Iconium

14 At Iconium Paul and Barnabas went as usual into the Jewish synagogue. There they spoke so effectively that a great number of Jews and Gentiles believed. 2But the Jews who refused to believe stirred up the Gentiles and poisoned their minds against the brothers. 3So Paul and Barnabas spent considerable time there, speaking boldly for the Lord, who confirmed the message of his grace by enabling them to do miraculous signs and wonders. 4The people of the city were divided; some sided with the Jews, others with the apostles. 5There was a plot afoot among the Gentiles and Jews, together with their leaders, to mistreat them and stone them. 6But they found out about it and fled to the Lycaonian cities of Lystra and Derbe and to the surrounding country, 7where they continued to preach the good news.

In Lystra and Derbe

8In Lystra there sat a man crippled in his feet, who was lame from birth and had never walked. 9He listened to Paul as he was speaking. Paul looked directly at him, saw that he had faith to be healed 10and called out, "Stand up on your feet!" At that, the man jumped up and began to walk.

[a] 41 Hab. 1:5 [b] 47 The Greek is singular. [c] 47 Isaiah 49:6

(13:48–52) In Your great wisdom You allow all people to choose for or against You. Some listen to the truth about You and believe it, while others listen to that same truth and reject it. Lord Jesus, just as You sent out the 12 disciples with this understanding, empower me also to deliver Your message, trusting in You alone to work in the hearts of those who hear. (Mt 10:14)

11When the crowd saw what Paul had done, they shouted in
the Lycaonian language, "The gods have come down to us in
human form!" 12Barnabas they called Zeus, and Paul they called
Hermes because he was the chief speaker. 13The priest of Zeus,
whose temple was just outside the city, brought bulls and wreaths
to the city gates because he and the crowd wanted to offer sacrifices to them.
14But when the apostles Barnabas and Paul heard of this, they
tore their clothes and rushed out into the crowd, shouting:
15"Men, why are you doing this? We too are only men, human
like you. We are bringing you good news, telling you to turn from
these worthless things to the living God, who made heaven and
earth and sea and everything in them. 16In the past, he let all nations go their own way. 17Yet he has not left himself without testimony: He has shown kindness by giving you rain from heaven and
crops in their seasons; he provides you with plenty of food and
fills your hearts with joy." 18Even with these words, they had difficulty keeping the crowd from sacrificing to them.
19Then some Jews came from Antioch and Iconium and won
the crowd over. They stoned Paul and dragged him outside the
city, thinking he was dead. 20But after the disciples had gathered
around him, he got up and went back into the city. The next day
he and Barnabas left for Derbe.

The Return to Antioch in Syria

21They preached the good news in that city and won a large
number of disciples. Then they returned to Lystra, Iconium and
Antioch, 22strengthening the disciples and encouraging them to
remain true to the faith. "We must go through many hardships to
enter the kingdom of God," they said. 23Paul and Barnabas appointed elders[a] for them in each church and, with prayer and
fasting, committed them to the Lord, in whom they had put their
trust. 24After going through Pisidia, they came into Pamphylia,
25and when they had preached the word in Perga, they went down
to Attalia.
26From Attalia they sailed back to Antioch, where they had
been committed to the grace of God for the work they had now
completed. 27On arriving there, they gathered the church together and reported all that God had done through them and how he
had opened the door of faith to the Gentiles. 28And they stayed
there a long time with the disciples.

The Council at Jerusalem

15 Some men came down from Judea to Antioch and were
teaching the brothers: "Unless you are circumcised, according to the custom taught by Moses, you cannot be saved."
2This brought Paul and Barnabas into sharp dispute and debate
with them. So Paul and Barnabas were appointed, along with
some other believers, to go up to Jerusalem to see the apostles
and elders about this question. 3The church sent them on their
way, and as they traveled through Phoenicia and Samaria, they
told how the Gentiles had been converted. This news made all the
brothers very glad. 4When they came to Jerusalem, they were welcomed by the church and the apostles and elders, to whom they
reported everything God had done through them.

[a] 23 Or *Barnabas ordained elders*; or *Barnabas had elders elected*

(14:11–20) Lord, You know that the greatest goal to which I can aspire is to be used by You. But deep in my heart of hearts, do I really want You to use me, or do I just want to use You? Who gets the credit when You move through my life? When I speak healing words to someone, or when I reach out to the needy, do they glorify You or me? Am I willing to be unknown, unappreciated, unrecognized? Is my need for human approval greater than my desire to see You praised? Lord, have mercy on me. Don't let me squander the eternal rewards of heaven on the fleeting accolades of men. May all that I do be for the praise and honor of Your name. (Mt 6:1–6)

It is no great thing to be humble when you are brought low; but to be humble when you are praised is a great and rare attainment.

Bernard of Clairvaux (1090-1153)

5 Then some of the believers who belonged to the party of the
Pharisees stood up and said, "The Gentiles must be circumcised
and required to obey the law of Moses."
6 The apostles and elders met to consider this question. 7 After
much discussion, Peter got up and addressed them: "Brothers,
you know that some time ago God made a choice among you
that the Gentiles might hear from my lips the message of the
gospel and believe. 8 God, who knows the heart, showed that he
accepted them by giving the Holy Spirit to them, just as he did to
us. 9 He made no distinction between us and them, for he purified their hearts by faith. 10 Now then, why do you try to test God
by putting on the necks of the disciples a yoke that neither we
nor our fathers have been able to bear? 11 No! We believe it is
through the grace of our Lord Jesus that we are saved, just as
they are."
12 The whole assembly became silent as they listened to Barnabas and Paul telling about the miraculous signs and wonders God
had done among the Gentiles through them. 13 When they finished, James spoke up: "Brothers, listen to me. 14 Simon[a] has described to us how God at first showed his concern by taking from
the Gentiles a people for himself. 15 The words of the prophets
are in agreement with this, as it is written:

16 " 'After this I will return
and rebuild David's fallen tent.
Its ruins I will rebuild,
and I will restore it,
17 that the remnant of men may seek the Lord,
and all the Gentiles who bear my name,
says the Lord, who does these things'[b]
18 that have been known for ages.[c]

19 "It is my judgment, therefore, that we should not make it difficult for the Gentiles who are turning to God. 20 Instead we
should write to them, telling them to abstain from food polluted
by idols, from sexual immorality, from the meat of strangled animals and from blood. 21 For Moses has been preached in every
city from the earliest times and is read in the synagogues on every
Sabbath."

The Council's Letter to Gentile Believers

22 Then the apostles and elders, with the whole church, decided to choose some of their own men and send them to Antioch
with Paul and Barnabas. They chose Judas (called Barsabbas)
and Silas, two men who were leaders among the brothers. 23 With
them they sent the following letter:

The apostles and elders, your brothers,

To the Gentile believers in Antioch, Syria and Cilicia:

Greetings.

24 We have heard that some went out from us without our
authorization and disturbed you, troubling your minds by
what they said. 25 So we all agreed to choose some men and
send them to you with our dear friends Barnabas and

[a] *14* Greek *Simeon,* a variant of *Simon;* that is, Peter [b] *17* Amos 9:11,12
[c] *17,18* Some manuscripts *things'— / [18] known to the Lord for ages is his work*

(15:5–19) Thank You, Lord, for Your easy yoke and Your light burden. Thank You for reaching out to us, for offering us Your hand, for revealing Yourself even to those who do not seek You. Help me never to interpose myself between You and the ones You are calling. Help me to clear the path of stumbling blocks and obstacles, to flatten out the mountains and fill in the valleys, and to prepare the way for You in the lives of others. (Ge 3:8–9; Isa 40:3–5; 65:1; Mt 11:30)

Did you ever stop to ask what a yoke is really for? Is it to be a burden to the animal which wears it? It is just the opposite. It is to make its burden light. Attached to the oxen in any other way than by a yoke the plough would be intolerable. Worked by means of a yoke it is light. A yoke is not an instrument of torture; it is an instrument of mercy. It is not a malicious contrivance for making work hard; it is a gentle device to make hard labor light. It is not meant to give pain, but to save pain. And yet men speak of the yoke of Christ as if it were a slavery and look upon those who wear it as objects of compassion.

Henry Drummond (1851-1897)

Paul— 26men who have risked their lives for the name of our Lord Jesus Christ. 27Therefore we are sending Judas and Silas to confirm by word of mouth what we are writing. 28It seemed good to the Holy Spirit and to us not to burden you with anything beyond the following requirements: 29You are to abstain from food sacrificed to idols, from blood, from the meat of strangled animals and from sexual immorality. You will do well to avoid these things.

Farewell.

30The men were sent off and went down to Antioch, where they gathered the church together and delivered the letter. 31The people read it and were glad for its encouraging message. 32Judas and Silas, who themselves were prophets, said much to encourage and strengthen the brothers. 33After spending some time there, they were sent off by the brothers with the blessing of peace to return to those who had sent them.[a] 35But Paul and Barnabas remained in Antioch, where they and many others taught and preached the word of the Lord.

Disagreement Between Paul and Barnabas

36Some time later Paul said to Barnabas, "Let us go back and visit the brothers in all the towns where we preached the word of the Lord and see how they are doing." 37Barnabas wanted to take John, also called Mark, with them, 38but Paul did not think it wise to take him, because he had deserted them in Pamphylia and had not continued with them in the work. 39They had such a sharp disagreement that they parted company. Barnabas took Mark and sailed for Cyprus, 40but Paul chose Silas and left, commended by the brothers to the grace of the Lord. 41He went through Syria and Cilicia, strengthening the churches.

Timothy Joins Paul and Silas

16 He came to Derbe and then to Lystra, where a disciple named Timothy lived, whose mother was a Jewess and a believer, but whose father was a Greek. 2The brothers at Lystra and Iconium spoke well of him. 3Paul wanted to take him along on the journey, so he circumcised him because of the Jews who lived in that area, for they all knew that his father was a Greek. 4As they traveled from town to town, they delivered the decisions reached by the apostles and elders in Jerusalem for the people to obey. 5So the churches were strengthened in the faith and grew daily in numbers.

Paul's Vision of the Man of Macedonia

6Paul and his companions traveled throughout the region of Phrygia and Galatia, having been kept by the Holy Spirit from preaching the word in the province of Asia. 7When they came to the border of Mysia, they tried to enter Bithynia, but the Spirit of Jesus would not allow them to. 8So they passed by Mysia and went down to Troas. 9During the night Paul had a vision of a man of Macedonia standing and begging him, "Come over to Macedonia and help us." 10After Paul had seen the vision, we got ready at once to leave for Macedonia, concluding that God had called us to preach the gospel to them.

[a] 33 Some manuscripts *them, 34but Silas decided to remain there*

A retrospect of my whole life, from the earliest period of my recollection down to the present hour, leaves me with this impression, that I have been, and am being, guided by a gracious and a mighty Hand, which has made, and is making, that possible to me which otherwise to me had been impossible. Oh that I had at all times unhesitatingly trusted and yielded myself to its guidance!

Richard Rothe (1799–1867)

(16:7) Spirit of Jesus, my life is not my own; it is not for me to direct my own steps. Therefore, I ask You to "direct my footsteps according to your word; let no sin rule over me." Guide me, Holy Spirit, into the Father's love and Christ's perseverance. (Ps 119:133; Jer 10:23; 2Th 3:5)

Lydia's Conversion in Philippi

11 From Troas we put out to sea and sailed straight for Samo-
thrace, and the next day on to Neapolis. 12 From there we traveled
to Philippi, a Roman colony and the leading city of that district of
Macedonia. And we stayed there several days.
13 On the Sabbath we went outside the city gate to the river,
where we expected to find a place of prayer. We sat down and
began to speak to the women who had gathered there. 14 One of
those listening was a woman named Lydia, a dealer in purple
cloth from the city of Thyatira, who was a worshiper of God. The
Lord opened her heart to respond to Paul's message. 15 When she
and the members of her household were baptized, she invited us
to her home. "If you consider me a believer in the Lord," she
said, "come and stay at my house." And she persuaded us.

Paul and Silas in Prison

16 Once when we were going to the place of prayer, we were
met by a slave girl who had a spirit by which she predicted the future. She earned a great deal of money for her owners by fortune-
telling. 17 This girl followed Paul and the rest of us, shouting,
"These men are servants of the Most High God, who are telling
you the way to be saved." 18 She kept this up for many days. Finally Paul became so troubled that he turned around and said to
the spirit, "In the name of Jesus Christ I command you to come
out of her!" At that moment the spirit left her.
19 When the owners of the slave girl realized that their hope of
making money was gone, they seized Paul and Silas and dragged
them into the marketplace to face the authorities. 20 They brought
them before the magistrates and said, "These men are Jews, and
are throwing our city into an uproar 21 by advocating customs unlawful for us Romans to accept or practice."
22 The crowd joined in the attack against Paul and Silas, and
the magistrates ordered them to be stripped and beaten. 23 After
they had been severely flogged, they were thrown into prison, and
the jailer was commanded to guard them carefully. 24 Upon receiving such orders, he put them in the inner cell and fastened
their feet in the stocks.
25 About midnight Paul and Silas were praying and singing
hymns to God, and the other prisoners were listening to them.
26 Suddenly there was such a violent earthquake that the foundations of the prison were shaken. At once all the prison doors flew
open, and everybody's chains came loose. 27 The jailer woke up,
and when he saw the prison doors open, he drew his sword and
was about to kill himself because he thought the prisoners had
escaped. 28 But Paul shouted, "Don't harm yourself! We are all
here!"
29 The jailer called for lights, rushed in and fell trembling before Paul and Silas. 30 He then brought them out and asked, "Sirs,
what must I do to be saved?"
31 They replied, "Believe in the Lord Jesus, and you will be
saved—you and your household." 32 Then they spoke the word of
the Lord to him and to all the others in his house. 33 At that hour
of the night the jailer took them and washed their wounds; then
immediately he and all his family were baptized. 34 The jailer
brought them into his house and set a meal before them; he was
filled with joy because he had come to believe in God—he and
his whole family.

(16:25–27) How real You were to Paul and Silas. Day after day they saw Your power and love displayed all around them. Nothing could diminish their delight in You or their faith in Your ability to save them. O God, make Yourself as real to me as You were to those faithful servants. Help me to see my tests and trials as opportunities to grow deeper in You. And teach me, like Paul and Silas, to sing for joy in the darkness as I await my deliverance. (Ro 5:3–5)

Every joy or testing
Comes from God above,
Given to His children
As an act of love;
We may trust Him fully
All for us to do;
Those who trust Him wholly
Find Him wholly true.

"Like a River Glorious"
Frances Ridley Havergal (1874)

35When it was daylight, the magistrates sent their officers to
the jailer with the order: "Release those men." 36The jailer told
Paul, "The magistrates have ordered that you and Silas be released. Now you can leave. Go in peace."
37But Paul said to the officers: "They beat us publicly without
a trial, even though we are Roman citizens, and threw us into
prison. And now do they want to get rid of us quietly? No! Let them
come themselves and escort us out."
38The officers reported this to the magistrates, and when they
heard that Paul and Silas were Roman citizens, they were
alarmed. 39They came to appease them and escorted them from
the prison, requesting them to leave the city. 40After Paul and
Silas came out of the prison, they went to Lydia's house, where
they met with the brothers and encouraged them. Then they left.

In Thessalonica

17 When they had passed through Amphipolis and Apollonia,
they came to Thessalonica, where there was a Jewish synagogue. 2As his custom was, Paul went into the synagogue, and on
three Sabbath days he reasoned with them from the Scriptures,
3explaining and proving that the Christ[a] had to suffer and rise
from the dead. "This Jesus I am proclaiming to you is the
Christ,[a]" he said. 4Some of the Jews were persuaded and joined
Paul and Silas, as did a large number of God-fearing Greeks and
not a few prominent women.
5But the Jews were jealous; so they rounded up some bad
characters from the marketplace, formed a mob and started a
riot in the city. They rushed to Jason's house in search of Paul
and Silas in order to bring them out to the crowd.[b] 6But when
they did not find them, they dragged Jason and some other brothers before the city officials, shouting: "These men who have
caused trouble all over the world have now come here, 7and
Jason has welcomed them into his house. They are all defying
Caesar's decrees, saying that there is another king, one called
Jesus." 8When they heard this, the crowd and the city officials
were thrown into turmoil. 9Then they made Jason and the others
post bond and let them go.

In Berea

10As soon as it was night, the brothers sent Paul and Silas away
to Berea. On arriving there, they went to the Jewish synagogue.
11Now the Bereans were of more noble character than the Thessalonians, for they received the message with great eagerness and
examined the Scriptures every day to see if what Paul said was
true. 12Many of the Jews believed, as did also a number of prominent Greek women and many Greek men.
13When the Jews in Thessalonica learned that Paul was preaching the word of God at Berea, they went there too, agitating the
crowds and stirring them up. 14The brothers immediately sent
Paul to the coast, but Silas and Timothy stayed at Berea. 15The
men who escorted Paul brought him to Athens and then left with
instructions for Silas and Timothy to join him as soon as possible.

In Athens

16While Paul was waiting for them in Athens, he was greatly
distressed to see that the city was full of idols. 17So he reasoned

[a] 3 Or *Messiah*   [b] 5 Or *the assembly of the people*

God alone knows all the facts, sets all the goals, and determines morality. Nowhere in Scripture are his principles to be replaced in favor of human calculation. He allows us to play the game; he does not allow us to make the rules.

Erwin W. Lutzer (1941–)

(17:11) O Lord, we live in a culture without a moral compass, lost in a desert of relativistic notions. Your eyes look to and fro across our land, searching for those noble ones who eagerly seek truth and test it against Your unchanging Word. For Your Word, Lord, is the measure of all truth. May we, Your people, become courageous defenders of Your Word in our generation. (2Ch 16:9)

How sure the Scriptures are!
God's vital, urgent word,
As true as steel,
And far more sharp than any sword:
So deep and fine,
At His control they pierce
Where soul and spirit join.

They test each human thought,
Refining like a fire;
They measure what we
Ought to do and to desire:
For God knows all
Exposed it lies before His eyes
To whom we call.

"How Sure the Scriptures Are!"
Christopher Idle (©1982)

MY BELOVED

Salvation is a household word. My Son gave His life for you and your entire family. So I urge you to make requests, prayers, intercession, and thanksgiving for them. This is good, and it pleases Me, for I want them to be saved and to come to a knowledge of the truth. It is not My desire that they should perish, but that they would come to repentance.

The evil one has blinded those in your family who are unsaved, so that they cannot see the light of the gospel of the glory of Christ. Therefore, pray that the eyes of their heart may be enlightened so that they may know the hope to which I have called them.

When their eyes are opened they will turn from darkness to light, and from the power of Satan to Me, so that they may receive forgiveness of their sins and a place among those who are sanctified by faith in Christ.

My will is that everyone who looks to My Son and believes in Him shall have eternal life, and I will raise him up at the last day. If anyone turns to Me in repentance and faith, I will rescue him from the dominion of darkness and bring him into the kingdom of My Son, in Whom he will have redemption, and the forgiveness of sins.

So pray and keep on praying for your family. Let it be your regular custom.

Job 1:5; Jn 6:40; Ac 16:31; 28:18; 2Co 4:4; Eph 1:18; Col 1:13-14; 1Ti 2:1,3-4; Jas 5:16; 2Pe 3:9

in the synagogue with the Jews and the God-fearing Greeks, as
well as in the marketplace day by day with those who happened to
be there. 18A group of Epicurean and Stoic philosophers began to
dispute with him. Some of them asked, "What is this babbler trying to say?" Others remarked, "He seems to be advocating foreign
gods." They said this because Paul was preaching the good news
about Jesus and the resurrection. 19Then they took him and
brought him to a meeting of the Areopagus, where they said to
him, "May we know what this new teaching is that you are presenting? 20You are bringing some strange ideas to our ears, and
we want to know what they mean." 21 (All the Athenians and the
foreigners who lived there spent their time doing nothing but
talking about and listening to the latest ideas.)

22Paul then stood up in the meeting of the Areopagus and said:
"Men of Athens! I see that in every way you are very religious.
23For as I walked around and looked carefully at your objects of
worship, I even found an altar with this inscription: TO AN UNKNOWN
GOD. Now what you worship as something unknown I am going to
proclaim to you.

24"The God who made the world and everything in it is the
Lord of heaven and earth and does not live in temples built by
hands. 25And he is not served by human hands, as if he needed
anything, because he himself gives all men life and breath and
everything else. 26From one man he made every nation of men,
that they should inhabit the whole earth; and he determined the
times set for them and the exact places where they should live.
27God did this so that men would seek him and perhaps reach
out for him and find him, though he is not far from each one of
us. 28'For in him we live and move and have our being.' As some
of your own poets have said, 'We are his offspring.'

29"Therefore since we are God's offspring, we should not think
that the divine being is like gold or silver or stone—an image
made by man's design and skill. 30In the past God overlooked
such ignorance, but now he commands all people everywhere to
repent. 31For he has set a day when he will judge the world with
justice by the man he has appointed. He has given proof of this to
all men by raising him from the dead."

32When they heard about the resurrection of the dead, some of
them sneered, but others said, "We want to hear you again on
this subject." 33At that, Paul left the Council. 34A few men became
followers of Paul and believed. Among them was Dionysius, a
member of the Areopagus, also a woman named Damaris, and a
number of others.

In Corinth

18 After this, Paul left Athens and went to Corinth. 2There he
met a Jew named Aquila, a native of Pontus, who had recently come from Italy with his wife Priscilla, because Claudius
had ordered all the Jews to leave Rome. Paul went to see them,
3and because he was a tentmaker as they were, he stayed and
worked with them. 4Every Sabbath he reasoned in the synagogue,
trying to persuade Jews and Greeks.

5When Silas and Timothy came from Macedonia, Paul devoted
himself exclusively to preaching, testifying to the Jews that Jesus
was the Christ.[a] 6But when the Jews opposed Paul and became

[a] 5 Or *Messiah;* also in verse 28

(17:23–27) Our great, loving and merciful God, I praise You for making Yourself known to us. Yet even in Your disclosure You remain a mystery. You cannot be contained, yet You dwell in my heart. You cannot be restrained, yet You wait for me to follow. You cannot be defined, yet You delight in my words of worship. You are more powerful than all the forces of nature combined, yet You choose to be moved by the prayer of a child. You make all the rules, yet You choose to love me without condition. You are more than life itself. You are what all of nature is trying to describe. O wonderful, awesome God, though now I see only a shadow of Your glory, I know that one day I will see You face-to-face. (Ro 1:19–20)

We know God but as men born blind know the fire; they know that there is such a thing as fire, for they feel it warm them, but what it is they know not. So, that there is a God we know, but what he is we know little, and indeed we can never search him out to perfection; a finite creature can never fully comprehend that which is infinite.

Thomas Manton (1620-1677)

abusive, he shook out his clothes in protest and said to them,
"Your blood be on your own heads! I am clear of my responsibility. From now on I will go to the Gentiles."
7 Then Paul left the synagogue and went next door to the
house of Titius Justus, a worshiper of God. 8 Crispus, the synagogue ruler, and his entire household believed in the Lord; and
many of the Corinthians who heard him believed and were baptized.
9 One night the Lord spoke to Paul in a vision: "Do not be
afraid; keep on speaking, do not be silent. 10 For I am with you,
and no one is going to attack and harm you, because I have many
people in this city." 11 So Paul stayed for a year and a half, teaching them the word of God.
12 While Gallio was proconsul of Achaia, the Jews made a united attack on Paul and brought him into court. 13 "This man," they
charged, "is persuading the people to worship God in ways contrary to the law."
14 Just as Paul was about to speak, Gallio said to the Jews, "If
you Jews were making a complaint about some misdemeanor or
serious crime, it would be reasonable for me to listen to you.
15 But since it involves questions about words and names and
your own law—settle the matter yourselves. I will not be a judge
of such things." 16 So he had them ejected from the court.
17 Then they all turned on Sosthenes the synagogue ruler and
beat him in front of the court. But Gallio showed no concern
whatever.

Priscilla, Aquila and Apollos

18 Paul stayed on in Corinth for some time. Then he left the
brothers and sailed for Syria, accompanied by Priscilla and Aquila. Before he sailed, he had his hair cut off at Cenchrea because
of a vow he had taken. 19 They arrived at Ephesus, where Paul left
Priscilla and Aquila. He himself went into the synagogue and reasoned with the Jews. 20 When they asked him to spend more time
with them, he declined. 21 But as he left, he promised, "I will
come back if it is God's will." Then he set sail from Ephesus.
22 When he landed at Caesarea, he went up and greeted the
church and then went down to Antioch.
23 After spending some time in Antioch, Paul set out from there
and traveled from place to place throughout the region of Galatia
and Phrygia, strengthening all the disciples.
24 Meanwhile a Jew named Apollos, a native of Alexandria,
came to Ephesus. He was a learned man, with a thorough knowledge of the Scriptures. 25 He had been instructed in the way of the
Lord, and he spoke with great fervor[a] and taught about Jesus accurately, though he knew only the baptism of John. 26 He began to
speak boldly in the synagogue. When Priscilla and Aquila heard
him, they invited him to their home and explained to him the way
of God more adequately.
27 When Apollos wanted to go to Achaia, the brothers encouraged him and wrote to the disciples there to welcome him. On arriving, he was a great help to those who by grace had believed.
28 For he vigorously refuted the Jews in public debate, proving
from the Scriptures that Jesus was the Christ.

[a] 25 Or *with fervor in the Spirit*

(18:9–10) Almighty God, You protect Your people with Your presence. When You are with us there is nothing to fear. You strengthen us with Your might and hold us with Your righteous right hand. You send us help from among Your people, and You place us in the care of Your angels. Thank You for the promise of Your protection, Lord, which allows us to be bold in the proclamation of Your Word. (Ps 20; 91:11–12; Isa 41:10; 51:7–8)

Lord, I'm in Your hands,
Lord, I'm in Your heart.
In Your thoughts, in Your plans,
Never on my own.

And when the darkness closes in
And fear begins to rise,
Help me to remember
You're always by my side.

Lord, I'm in Your hands,
Lord, I'm in Your heart.
In Your thoughts, in Your plans,
Never left alone.

"Lord, I'm in Your Hands"
Tim Weeks (©1994)

Paul in Ephesus

19 While Apollos was at Corinth, Paul took the road through the interior and arrived at Ephesus. There he found some disciples 2and asked them, "Did you receive the Holy Spirit when[a] you believed?"

They answered, "No, we have not even heard that there is a Holy Spirit."

3So Paul asked, "Then what baptism did you receive?"

"John's baptism," they replied.

4Paul said, "John's baptism was a baptism of repentance. He told the people to believe in the one coming after him, that is, in Jesus." 5On hearing this, they were baptized into[b] the name of the Lord Jesus. 6When Paul placed his hands on them, the Holy Spirit came on them, and they spoke in tongues[c] and prophesied. 7There were about twelve men in all.

8Paul entered the synagogue and spoke boldly there for three months, arguing persuasively about the kingdom of God. 9But some of them became obstinate; they refused to believe and publicly maligned the Way. So Paul left them. He took the disciples with him and had discussions daily in the lecture hall of Tyrannus. 10This went on for two years, so that all the Jews and Greeks who lived in the province of Asia heard the word of the Lord.

11God did extraordinary miracles through Paul, 12so that even handkerchiefs and aprons that had touched him were taken to the sick, and their illnesses were cured and the evil spirits left them.

13Some Jews who went around driving out evil spirits tried to invoke the name of the Lord Jesus over those who were demon-possessed. They would say, "In the name of Jesus, whom Paul preaches, I command you to come out." 14Seven sons of Sceva, a Jewish chief priest, were doing this. 15⌊One day⌋ the evil spirit answered them, "Jesus I know, and I know about Paul, but who are you?" 16Then the man who had the evil spirit jumped on them and overpowered them all. He gave them such a beating that they ran out of the house naked and bleeding.

17When this became known to the Jews and Greeks living in Ephesus, they were all seized with fear, and the name of the Lord Jesus was held in high honor. 18Many of those who believed now came and openly confessed their evil deeds. 19A number who had practiced sorcery brought their scrolls together and burned them publicly. When they calculated the value of the scrolls, the total came to fifty thousand drachmas.[d] 20In this way the word of the Lord spread widely and grew in power.

21After all this had happened, Paul decided to go to Jerusalem, passing through Macedonia and Achaia. "After I have been there," he said, "I must visit Rome also." 22He sent two of his helpers, Timothy and Erastus, to Macedonia, while he stayed in the province of Asia a little longer.

The Riot in Ephesus

23About that time there arose a great disturbance about the Way. 24A silversmith named Demetrius, who made silver shrines of Artemis, brought in no little business for the craftsmen. 25He called them together, along with the workmen in related trades,

[a]2 Or *after* [b]5 Or *in* [c]6 Or *other languages* [d]19 A drachma was a silver coin worth about a day's wages.

I am the vase of God, he fills me to the brim;
He is the ocean deep, contained I am in him.

Angelus Silesius (1624-1677)

(19:2) Like these disciples in Ephesus, I hunger for You, Lord. I want everything that You have to offer. I long to be so full of Your Spirit that I overflow with Your presence and power. Live through me, Lord. Touch through me. Speak through me. Love through me. Help me to be faithful to what I believe. And help me never to be satisfied with anything less than Your fullness.

Gracious Father,
Send Your Spirit
Like a rushing mighty wind;
Fan the fire
Of my desire
For Your holiness within.

Breath of heaven,
Breath of heaven,
Breathe on me.

"Breath Of Heaven"
Buddy Owens and
Morris Chapman (©1999)

(19:26–41) Father, we declare that there are no other gods but You. All other gods are simply the work of mortal hands, but we are the work of Your hands. We did not make You; You made us. Help us not to fear the anger and hatred and confusion that come against the preaching of the gospel. Let us not shrink back, but boldly proclaim the Lordship of Jesus Christ. Use us, Lord, to "convince and lead astray large numbers of people" from their false worship, and to expose man-made gods for what they are—no gods at all. As You protected the young church at Ephesus, so protect Your church today as we proclaim the truth of the gospel of Christ. (Ps 100:3)

Go ye therefore to every neighbor,
Share My love with every man.
The world will know that you are
Mine
If in My name you reach out your
hand.

Tell the world the message,
Take it everywhere
To every tribe and nation
We are called to share.

"Tell the World"
Marsha Skidmore (©1994)

and said: "Men, you know we receive a good income from this
business. 26And you see and hear how this fellow Paul has convinced and led astray large numbers of people here in Ephesus
and in practically the whole province of Asia. He says that man-
made gods are no gods at all. 27There is danger not only that our
trade will lose its good name, but also that the temple of the great
goddess Artemis will be discredited, and the goddess herself, who
is worshiped throughout the province of Asia and the world, will
be robbed of her divine majesty."

28When they heard this, they were furious and began shouting:
"Great is Artemis of the Ephesians!" 29Soon the whole city was in
an uproar. The people seized Gaius and Aristarchus, Paul's traveling companions from Macedonia, and rushed as one man into
the theater. 30Paul wanted to appear before the crowd, but the
disciples would not let him. 31Even some of the officials of the
province, friends of Paul, sent him a message begging him not to
venture into the theater.

32The assembly was in confusion: Some were shouting one
thing, some another. Most of the people did not even know why
they were there. 33The Jews pushed Alexander to the front, and
some of the crowd shouted instructions to him. He motioned for
silence in order to make a defense before the people. 34But when
they realized he was a Jew, they all shouted in unison for about
two hours: "Great is Artemis of the Ephesians!"

35The city clerk quieted the crowd and said: "Men of Ephesus,
doesn't all the world know that the city of Ephesus is the guardian
of the temple of the great Artemis and of her image, which fell
from heaven? 36Therefore, since these facts are undeniable, you
ought to be quiet and not do anything rash. 37You have brought
these men here, though they have neither robbed temples nor
blasphemed our goddess. 38If, then, Demetrius and his fellow
craftsmen have a grievance against anybody, the courts are open
and there are proconsuls. They can press charges. 39If there is
anything further you want to bring up, it must be settled in a legal
assembly. 40As it is, we are in danger of being charged with rioting because of today's events. In that case we would not be able
to account for this commotion, since there is no reason for it."
41After he had said this, he dismissed the assembly.

Through Macedonia and Greece

20 When the uproar had ended, Paul sent for the disciples
and, after encouraging them, said good-by and set out for
Macedonia. 2He traveled through that area, speaking many words
of encouragement to the people, and finally arrived in Greece,
3where he stayed three months. Because the Jews made a plot
against him just as he was about to sail for Syria, he decided to go
back through Macedonia. 4He was accompanied by Sopater son
of Pyrrhus from Berea, Aristarchus and Secundus from Thessalonica, Gaius from Derbe, Timothy also, and Tychicus and Trophimus from the province of Asia. 5These men went on ahead and
waited for us at Troas. 6But we sailed from Philippi after the Feast
of Unleavened Bread, and five days later joined the others at
Troas, where we stayed seven days.

Eutychus Raised From the Dead at Troas

7On the first day of the week we came together to break bread.
Paul spoke to the people and, because he intended to leave the

next day, kept on talking until midnight. [8]There were many lamps
in the upstairs room where we were meeting. [9]Seated in a window was a young man named Eutychus, who was sinking into a
deep sleep as Paul talked on and on. When he was sound asleep,
he fell to the ground from the third story and was picked up dead.
[10]Paul went down, threw himself on the young man and put his
arms around him. "Don't be alarmed," he said. "He's alive!"
[11]Then he went upstairs again and broke bread and ate. After
talking until daylight, he left. [12]The people took the young man
home alive and were greatly comforted.

Paul's Farewell to the Ephesian Elders

[13]We went on ahead to the ship and sailed for Assos, where we
were going to take Paul aboard. He had made this arrangement
because he was going there on foot. [14]When he met us at Assos,
we took him aboard and went on to Mitylene. [15]The next day we
set sail from there and arrived off Kios. The day after that we
crossed over to Samos, and on the following day arrived at Miletus. [16]Paul had decided to sail past Ephesus to avoid spending
time in the province of Asia, for he was in a hurry to reach Jerusalem, if possible, by the day of Pentecost.

[17]From Miletus, Paul sent to Ephesus for the elders of the
church. [18]When they arrived, he said to them: "You know how I
lived the whole time I was with you, from the first day I came into
the province of Asia. [19]I served the Lord with great humility and
with tears, although I was severely tested by the plots of the Jews.
[20]You know that I have not hesitated to preach anything that would
be helpful to you but have taught you publicly and from house to
house. [21]I have declared to both Jews and Greeks that they must
turn to God in repentance and have faith in our Lord Jesus.

[22]"And now, compelled by the Spirit, I am going to Jerusalem,
not knowing what will happen to me there. [23]I only know that in
every city the Holy Spirit warns me that prison and hardships are
facing me. [24]However, I consider my life worth nothing to me, if
only I may finish the race and complete the task the Lord Jesus
has given me—the task of testifying to the gospel of God's grace.

[25]"Now I know that none of you among whom I have gone
about preaching the kingdom will ever see me again. [26]There-
fore, I declare to you today that I am innocent of the blood of all
men. [27]For I have not hesitated to proclaim to you the whole will
of God. [28]Keep watch over yourselves and all the flock of which
the Holy Spirit has made you overseers.[a] Be shepherds of the
church of God,[b] which he bought with his own blood. [29]I know
that after I leave, savage wolves will come in among you and will
not spare the flock. [30]Even from your own number men will arise
and distort the truth in order to draw away disciples after them.
[31]So be on your guard! Remember that for three years I never
stopped warning each of you night and day with tears.

[32]"Now I commit you to God and to the word of his grace,
which can build you up and give you an inheritance among all
those who are sanctified. [33]I have not coveted anyone's silver or
gold or clothing. [34]You yourselves know that these hands of mine
have supplied my own needs and the needs of my companions.
[35]In everything I did, I showed you that by this kind of hard work
we must help the weak, remembering the words the Lord Jesus
himself said: 'It is more blessed to give than to receive.' "

[a] 28 Traditionally *bishops* [b] 28 Many manuscripts *of the Lord*

(20:22–24) In faithful obedience to You Abraham set out not knowing where he was going. In faithful obedience to You Paul set out with only a partial vision of what lay ahead. Father, I pray that You will find in me this kind of unquestioning eagerness to obey, this unhesitating readiness to follow. In response to Your great mercy I present myself to You as a living sacrifice, fully surrendered to Your will. (Ro 12:1; Heb 11:8)

Obedience leads to faith. Live faithfully by the little bit of light you now have, and you will be given more.

Louis Cassels (1922–1974)

(20:28) Father, You have always cared for Your people as a shepherd oversees his flock, warding away predators and protecting them from thieves. And You have entrusted the role of earthly shepherd to servants who walk with You and who possess Your Spirit. Lord, raise up faithful shepherds in our day. Empower them to keep watch over themselves and over the flock You have placed in their care. By Your grace, help them to lead us into the safe, green pastures of Your Word. (Eze 34:11–16; Mk 6:34; 1Pe 5:1–4)

Am I a soldier of the cross,
A follower of the Lamb?
And shall I fear to own His cause,
Or blush to speak His name?

Sure I must fight if I would reign;
Increase my courage, Lord;
I'll bear the toil, endure the pain,
Supported by Thy word.

"Am I a Soldier of the Cross?"
Isaac Watts (c.1724)

(21:12–14) Father, help me to place my calling above my comfort. So often You have a higher purpose than I realize. Although I try to shield myself or others from trouble, the path of obedience sometimes leads directly into harm's way. Even if You choose to lead me through the valley of the shadow of death, help me to follow without fear. Because of the resurrection, death is now only a shadow of its former self. (Ps 23:4; 1Co 15:55)

May Your kingdom come,
May Your will be done,
Father in heaven, lift my eyes to the sky.
One day I will see heaven's Royalty,
'Til the day the trumpet rings in my ear.
Bid me to come and I will follow.

I will follow You where You want me to.
I will follow You.

"I Will Follow"
John Barbour and Anne Barbour (©1991)

36 When he had said this, he knelt down with all of them and prayed. 37 They all wept as they embraced him and kissed him. 38 What grieved them most was his statement that they would never see his face again. Then they accompanied him to the ship.

On to Jerusalem

21 1 After we had torn ourselves away from them, we put out to sea and sailed straight to Cos. The next day we went to Rhodes and from there to Patara. 2 We found a ship crossing over to Phoenicia, went on board and set sail. 3 After sighting Cyprus and passing to the south of it, we sailed on to Syria. We landed at Tyre, where our ship was to unload its cargo. 4 Finding the disciples there, we stayed with them seven days. Through the Spirit they urged Paul not to go on to Jerusalem. 5 But when our time was up, we left and continued on our way. All the disciples and their wives and children accompanied us out of the city, and there on the beach we knelt to pray. 6 After saying good-by to each other, we went aboard the ship, and they returned home.

7 We continued our voyage from Tyre and landed at Ptolemais, where we greeted the brothers and stayed with them for a day. 8 Leaving the next day, we reached Caesarea and stayed at the house of Philip the evangelist, one of the Seven. 9 He had four unmarried daughters who prophesied.

10 After we had been there a number of days, a prophet named Agabus came down from Judea. 11 Coming over to us, he took Paul's belt, tied his own hands and feet with it and said, "The Holy Spirit says, 'In this way the Jews of Jerusalem will bind the owner of this belt and will hand him over to the Gentiles.' "

12 When we heard this, we and the people there pleaded with Paul not to go up to Jerusalem. 13 Then Paul answered, "Why are you weeping and breaking my heart? I am ready not only to be bound, but also to die in Jerusalem for the name of the Lord Jesus." 14 When he would not be dissuaded, we gave up and said, "The Lord's will be done."

15 After this, we got ready and went up to Jerusalem. 16 Some of the disciples from Caesarea accompanied us and brought us to the home of Mnason, where we were to stay. He was a man from Cyprus and one of the early disciples.

Paul's Arrival at Jerusalem

17 When we arrived at Jerusalem, the brothers received us warmly. 18 The next day Paul and the rest of us went to see James, and all the elders were present. 19 Paul greeted them and reported in detail what God had done among the Gentiles through his ministry.

20 When they heard this, they praised God. Then they said to Paul: "You see, brother, how many thousands of Jews have believed, and all of them are zealous for the law. 21 They have been informed that you teach all the Jews who live among the Gentiles to turn away from Moses, telling them not to circumcise their children or live according to our customs. 22 What shall we do? They will certainly hear that you have come, 23 so do what we tell you. There are four men with us who have made a vow. 24 Take these men, join in their purification rites and pay their expenses, so that they can have their heads shaved. Then everybody will know there is no truth in these reports about you, but that you yourself are living in obedience to the law. 25 As for the Gentile believers, we have written to them our decision that they should

abstain from food sacrificed to idols, from blood, from the meat
of strangled animals and from sexual immorality."
26 The next day Paul took the men and purified himself along
with them. Then he went to the temple to give notice of the date
when the days of purification would end and the offering would
be made for each of them.

Paul Arrested

27 When the seven days were nearly over, some Jews from the
province of Asia saw Paul at the temple. They stirred up the whole
crowd and seized him, 28 shouting, "Men of Israel, help us! This
is the man who teaches all men everywhere against our people
and our law and this place. And besides, he has brought Greeks
into the temple area and defiled this holy place." 29 (They had
previously seen Trophimus the Ephesian in the city with Paul and
assumed that Paul had brought him into the temple area.)
30 The whole city was aroused, and the people came running
from all directions. Seizing Paul, they dragged him from the temple, and immediately the gates were shut. 31 While they were trying to kill him, news reached the commander of the Roman
troops that the whole city of Jerusalem was in an uproar. 32 He at
once took some officers and soldiers and ran down to the crowd.
When the rioters saw the commander and his soldiers, they
stopped beating Paul.
33 The commander came up and arrested him and ordered him
to be bound with two chains. Then he asked who he was and what
he had done. 34 Some in the crowd shouted one thing and some
another, and since the commander could not get at the truth because of the uproar, he ordered that Paul be taken into the barracks. 35 When Paul reached the steps, the violence of the mob
was so great he had to be carried by the soldiers. 36 The crowd
that followed kept shouting, "Away with him!"

Paul Speaks to the Crowd

37 As the soldiers were about to take Paul into the barracks, he
asked the commander, "May I say something to you?"
"Do you speak Greek?" he replied. 38 "Aren't you the Egyptian
who started a revolt and led four thousand terrorists out into the
desert some time ago?"
39 Paul answered, "I am a Jew, from Tarsus in Cilicia, a citizen
of no ordinary city. Please let me speak to the people."
40 Having received the commander's permission, Paul stood on
the steps and motioned to the crowd. When they were all silent,
22 he said to them in Aramaic[a]: 1 "Brothers and fathers, listen now to my defense."
2 When they heard him speak to them in Aramaic, they became
very quiet.
Then Paul said: 3 "I am a Jew, born in Tarsus of Cilicia, but
brought up in this city. Under Gamaliel I was thoroughly trained
in the law of our fathers and was just as zealous for God as any of
you are today. 4 I persecuted the followers of this Way to their
death, arresting both men and women and throwing them into
prison, 5 as also the high priest and all the Council can testify. I
even obtained letters from them to their brothers in Damascus,
and went there to bring these people as prisoners to Jerusalem to
be punished.

[a] 40 Or possibly *Hebrew*; also in 22:2

(21:27–36) Lord Jesus, You never promised an easy life for those who serve You. At the time You called Paul to be Your servant You warned him that he would suffer greatly for Your Name's sake. Indeed, Your Word tells us that "everyone who wants to live a godly life in Christ Jesus will be persecuted." O Lord, when I am pressured, perplexed or persecuted, help me not to despair. When I am cursed, teach me to bless; when I am oppressed, teach me to endure it; when I am slandered, teach me to answer kindly. And even if I should be given over to death for Your sake, may Your resurrection life be revealed in my mortal body. (Ac 9:16; 1Co 4:12–13; 2Co 4:8–11; 2Ti 3:12)

O God, early in the morning I cry to you.
Help me to pray
And to concentrate my thoughts on you:
I cannot do this alone.
In me there is darkness,
But with you there is light;
I am lonely, but you do not leave me;
I am feeble in heart, but with you there is help;
I am restless, but with you there is peace.
In me there is bitterness, but with you there is patience;
I do not understand your ways,
But you know the way for me . . .
Restore me to liberty,
And enable me so to live now
That I may answer before you and before me.
Lord, whatever this day may bring
Your name be praised.

Dietrich Bonhoeffer (1906-1945)
while awaiting execution

(22:6–21) Thank You, Father, that even when I suffer for what is right I am blessed. For in my heart, where no mortal can rob me, I have set apart Christ as Lord. Help me, like Paul, to always be prepared to give an answer to everyone who asks me to give the reason for the hope that I have. And help me to do this with gentleness and respect, keeping a clear conscience, so that those who speak maliciously against my good behavior in Christ may be ashamed of their slander. (1Pe 3:15–16)

6"About noon as I came near Damascus, suddenly a bright
light from heaven flashed around me. 7I fell to the ground and
heard a voice say to me, 'Saul! Saul! Why do you persecute me?'
8" 'Who are you, Lord?' I asked.
" 'I am Jesus of Nazareth, whom you are persecuting,' he
replied. 9My companions saw the light, but they did not understand the voice of him who was speaking to me.
10" 'What shall I do, Lord?' I asked.
" 'Get up,' the Lord said, 'and go into Damascus. There you will be told all that you have been assigned to do.' 11My companions led me by the hand into Damascus, because the brilliance of the light had blinded me.
12"A man named Ananias came to see me. He was a devout observer of the law and highly respected by all the Jews living there.
13He stood beside me and said, 'Brother Saul, receive your sight!' And at that very moment I was able to see him.
14"Then he said: 'The God of our fathers has chosen you to know his will and to see the Righteous One and to hear words
from his mouth. 15You will be his witness to all men of what you
have seen and heard. 16And now what are you waiting for? Get up, be baptized and wash your sins away, calling on his name.'
17"When I returned to Jerusalem and was praying at the tem-
ple, I fell into a trance 18and saw the Lord speaking. 'Quick!' he said to me. 'Leave Jerusalem immediately, because they will not accept your testimony about me.'
19" 'Lord,' I replied, 'these men know that I went from one synagogue to another to imprison and beat those who believe in
you. 20And when the blood of your martyr[a] Stephen was shed, I stood there giving my approval and guarding the clothes of those who were killing him.'
21"Then the Lord said to me, 'Go; I will send you far away to the Gentiles.' "

Paul the Roman Citizen

22The crowd listened to Paul until he said this. Then they raised their voices and shouted, "Rid the earth of him! He's not fit to live!"
23As they were shouting and throwing off their cloaks and flinging dust into the air, 24the commander ordered Paul to be taken into the barracks. He directed that he be flogged and questioned in order to find out why the people were shouting at him
like this. 25As they stretched him out to flog him, Paul said to the centurion standing there, "Is it legal for you to flog a Roman citizen who hasn't even been found guilty?"
26When the centurion heard this, he went to the commander and reported it. "What are you going to do?" he asked. "This man is a Roman citizen."
27The commander went to Paul and asked, "Tell me, are you a Roman citizen?"
"Yes, I am," he answered.
28Then the commander said, "I had to pay a big price for my citizenship."
"But I was born a citizen," Paul replied.
29Those who were about to question him withdrew immedi-
ately. The commander himself was alarmed when he realized that he had put Paul, a Roman citizen, in chains.

[a] 20 Or *witness*

Before the Sanhedrin

30The next day, since the commander wanted to find out exactly why Paul was being accused by the Jews, he released him and ordered the chief priests and all the Sanhedrin to assemble. Then he brought Paul and had him stand before them.

23 Paul looked straight at the Sanhedrin and said, "My brothers, I have fulfilled my duty to God in all good conscience
to this day." 2At this the high priest Ananias ordered those stand-
ing near Paul to strike him on the mouth. 3Then Paul said to him,
"God will strike you, you whitewashed wall! You sit there to judge me according to the law, yet you yourself violate the law by commanding that I be struck!"

4Those who were standing near Paul said, "You dare to insult God's high priest?"

5Paul replied, "Brothers, I did not realize that he was the high priest; for it is written: 'Do not speak evil about the ruler of your people.'[a]"

6Then Paul, knowing that some of them were Sadducees and the others Pharisees, called out in the Sanhedrin, "My brothers, I am a Pharisee, the son of a Pharisee. I stand on trial because of
my hope in the resurrection of the dead." 7When he said this, a
dispute broke out between the Pharisees and the Sadducees, and
the assembly was divided. 8(The Sadducees say that there is no
resurrection, and that there are neither angels nor spirits, but the Pharisees acknowledge them all.)

9There was a great uproar, and some of the teachers of the law who were Pharisees stood up and argued vigorously. "We find nothing wrong with this man," they said. "What if a spirit or an
angel has spoken to him?" 10The dispute became so violent that
the commander was afraid Paul would be torn to pieces by them. He ordered the troops to go down and take him away from them by force and bring him into the barracks.

11The following night the Lord stood near Paul and said, "Take courage! As you have testified about me in Jerusalem, so you must also testify in Rome."

The Plot to Kill Paul

12The next morning the Jews formed a conspiracy and bound themselves with an oath not to eat or drink until they had killed
Paul. 13More than forty men were involved in this plot. 14They
went to the chief priests and elders and said, "We have taken a solemn oath not to eat anything until we have killed Paul. 15Now
then, you and the Sanhedrin petition the commander to bring him before you on the pretext of wanting more accurate information about his case. We are ready to kill him before he gets here."

16But when the son of Paul's sister heard of this plot, he went into the barracks and told Paul.

17Then Paul called one of the centurions and said, "Take this young man to the commander; he has something to tell him."
18So he took him to the commander.

The centurion said, "Paul, the prisoner, sent for me and asked me to bring this young man to you because he has something to tell you."

19The commander took the young man by the hand, drew him aside and asked, "What is it you want to tell me?"

[a]5 Exodus 22:28

(23:1–10) Lord, Your church was born with so much pain—persecutions and hardships on every hand, hatred and violence from every quarter. Thank You for the strength of the Holy Spirit that enabled Paul to persevere. Thank You for Your gift of grace that enabled him to hold true to the testimony of Christ. Father, if I ever experience this kind of pain, help me to see with spiritual eyes the new life that is being birthed through my suffering. Help me to hold out and hold on to the testimony of Christ.

God had one Son on earth without sin, but never one without suffering.
Saint Augustine of Hippo (354-430)

20He said: "The Jews have agreed to ask you to bring Paul before the Sanhedrin tomorrow on the pretext of wanting more accurate information about him. 21Don't give in to them, because
more than forty of them are waiting in ambush for him. They have
taken an oath not to eat or drink until they have killed him. They
are ready now, waiting for your consent to their request."
22The commander dismissed the young man and cautioned
him, "Don't tell anyone that you have reported this to me."

Paul Transferred to Caesarea

23Then he called two of his centurions and ordered them, "Get
ready a detachment of two hundred soldiers, seventy horsemen
and two hundred spearmen[a] to go to Caesarea at nine tonight.
24Provide mounts for Paul so that he may be taken safely to Governor Felix."
25He wrote a letter as follows:

26Claudius Lysias,

To His Excellency, Governor Felix:

Greetings.

27This man was seized by the Jews and they were about to
kill him, but I came with my troops and rescued him, for I
had learned that he is a Roman citizen. 28I wanted to know
why they were accusing him, so I brought him to their Sanhedrin. 29I found that the accusation had to do with questions about their law, but there was no charge against him
that deserved death or imprisonment. 30When I was informed of a plot to be carried out against the man, I sent
him to you at once. I also ordered his accusers to present to
you their case against him.

31So the soldiers, carrying out their orders, took Paul with
them during the night and brought him as far as Antipatris. 32The
next day they let the cavalry go on with him, while they returned
to the barracks. 33When the cavalry arrived in Caesarea, they delivered the letter to the governor and handed Paul over to him.
34The governor read the letter and asked what province he was
from. Learning that he was from Cilicia, 35he said, "I will hear
your case when your accusers get here." Then he ordered that
Paul be kept under guard in Herod's palace.

The Trial Before Felix

24 Five days later the high priest Ananias went down to Caesarea with some of the elders and a lawyer named Tertullus,
and they brought their charges against Paul before the governor.
2When Paul was called in, Tertullus presented his case before
Felix: "We have enjoyed a long period of peace under you, and
your foresight has brought about reforms in this nation. 3Every-
where and in every way, most excellent Felix, we acknowledge this
with profound gratitude. 4But in order not to weary you further, I
would request that you be kind enough to hear us briefly.
5"We have found this man to be a troublemaker, stirring up
riots among the Jews all over the world. He is a ringleader of the
Nazarene sect 6and even tried to desecrate the temple; so we

[a] 23 The meaning of the Greek for this word is uncertain.

(23:18–31) I praise You, Almighty God, that no prison can contain the spread of the gospel; indeed, Roman imprisonment became the means of the gospel's safe passage to Rome. When I find myself "imprisoned," hemmed in on every side, remind me of Your faithfulness to Paul and Your ability to exploit even the best laid plans of Your enemies.

The Bible—banned, burned, beloved. More widely read, more frequently attacked than any other book in history. Generations of intellectuals have attempted to discredit it; dictators of every age have outlawed it and executed those who read it. Yet soldiers carry it into battle believing it more powerful than their weapons. Fragments of it smuggled into solitary prison cells have transformed ruthless killers into gentle saints.

Charles Colson (1931-)

The battle is the Lord's!
Stand still, my soul, and see
The great salvation
God has wrought
Revealed for thee.
Then, resting in His might,
Lift high His triumph song,
For power, dominion,
Kingdom, strength
To Christ belong!

"The Battle is the Lord's!"
Margaret Clarkson (©1960)

seized him. 8By[a] examining him yourself you will be able to learn
the truth about all these charges we are bringing against him."
9The Jews joined in the accusation, asserting that these things
were true.
10When the governor motioned for him to speak, Paul replied:
"I know that for a number of years you have been a judge over
this nation; so I gladly make my defense. 11You can easily verify
that no more than twelve days ago I went up to Jerusalem to worship. 12My accusers did not find me arguing with anyone at the
temple, or stirring up a crowd in the synagogues or anywhere else
in the city. 13And they cannot prove to you the charges they are
now making against me. 14However, I admit that I worship the
God of our fathers as a follower of the Way, which they call a sect.
I believe everything that agrees with the Law and that is written in
the Prophets, 15and I have the same hope in God as these men,
that there will be a resurrection of both the righteous and the
wicked. 16So I strive always to keep my conscience clear before
God and man.
17"After an absence of several years, I came to Jerusalem to
bring my people gifts for the poor and to present offerings. 18I
was ceremonially clean when they found me in the temple courts
doing this. There was no crowd with me, nor was I involved in any
disturbance. 19But there are some Jews from the province of Asia,
who ought to be here before you and bring charges if they have
anything against me. 20Or these who are here should state what
crime they found in me when I stood before the Sanhedrin—
21unless it was this one thing I shouted as I stood in their presence: 'It is concerning the resurrection of the dead that I am on
trial before you today.' "
22Then Felix, who was well acquainted with the Way, adjourned
the proceedings. "When Lysias the commander comes," he said,
"I will decide your case." 23He ordered the centurion to keep
Paul under guard but to give him some freedom and permit his
friends to take care of his needs.
24Several days later Felix came with his wife Drusilla, who was
a Jewess. He sent for Paul and listened to him as he spoke about
faith in Christ Jesus. 25As Paul discoursed on righteousness, self-
control and the judgment to come, Felix was afraid and said,
"That's enough for now! You may leave. When I find it convenient,
I will send for you." 26At the same time he was hoping that Paul
would offer him a bribe, so he sent for him frequently and talked
with him.
27When two years had passed, Felix was succeeded by Porcius
Festus, but because Felix wanted to grant a favor to the Jews, he
left Paul in prison.

The Trial Before Festus

25 Three days after arriving in the province, Festus went up
from Caesarea to Jerusalem, 2where the chief priests and
Jewish leaders appeared before him and presented the charges
against Paul. 3They urgently requested Festus, as a favor to them,
to have Paul transferred to Jerusalem, for they were preparing an
ambush to kill him along the way. 4Festus answered, "Paul is
being held at Caesarea, and I myself am going there soon. 5Let

[a] 6–8 Some manuscripts *him and wanted to judge him according to our law. 7But the commander, Lysias, came and with the use of much force snatched him from our hands 8and ordered his accusers to come before you. By*

(24:24–26) Paul resisted the temptation to bribe his way out of prison. Instead, he made the most of every opportunity to speak about faith in Christ Jesus. Lord, should I ever be called upon to suffer for Your sake, help me to remember how deeply You suffered for mine. Let me not take the easy way out when the gospel is at stake. May I never sell myself out to my adversary or try to buy my way out of persecution. Give me the integrity to place my convictions before my convenience.

I pray God may open Your eyes and let you see what hidden treasures he bestows on us in the trials from which the world thinks only to flee.

John of Avila (1499-1569)

Lord, You are my refuge,
My life is in Your hand.
I know that I can trust You,
And with Your help I'll stand.
I will not be shaken
If Your favor I can see.
I'll stand strong like a mountain
If You just shine Your light on me,
Shine Your light on me.

I will not be shaken, I'll not be
shaken,
I will not be shaken now.

"I Will Not Be Shaken"
Rick Founds (©1995)

(25:10–12) Father, just as You set the earth in motion and the planets in their courses, so You set the gospel in motion as well. From the beginning of time, all Your dealings with us have pointed the way to our coming Christ. I praise You that there is no prison strong enough and no grave deep enough to impede the spread of the gospel. For Your Word does not return to You empty, O God, but accomplishes the purposes for which it is sent. May we, Your servants, be faithful to this great, ongoing missionary journey. Send forth Your Word through us to the uttermost parts of the earth. Whether we face certain death or the uncertainties of life, let us carry the Good News with courage to every tribe, tongue and nation. In living or in dying, in freedom or in chains, let all we do bring glory to You, as we bring the Good News to the lost. (Isa 55:10–11; Ac 1:8)

Talk about the question of the day! There is but one question and that is the gospel. It can and will correct everything needing correction. All men at the head of great movements are Christian men. During the many years I was in the cabinet I was brought into association with sixty master minds, and all but five of them were Christians. My only hope for the world is in bringing the human mind into contact with divine revelation.

William Ewart Gladstone (1809-1898)

some of your leaders come with me and press charges against the man there, if he has done anything wrong."

[6]After spending eight or ten days with them, he went down to Caesarea, and the next day he convened the court and ordered that Paul be brought before him. [7]When Paul appeared, the Jews who had come down from Jerusalem stood around him, bringing many serious charges against him, which they could not prove.

[8]Then Paul made his defense: "I have done nothing wrong against the law of the Jews or against the temple or against Caesar."

[9]Festus, wishing to do the Jews a favor, said to Paul, "Are you willing to go up to Jerusalem and stand trial before me there on these charges?"

[10]Paul answered: "I am now standing before Caesar's court, where I ought to be tried. I have not done any wrong to the Jews, as you yourself know very well. [11]If, however, I am guilty of doing anything deserving death, I do not refuse to die. But if the charges brought against me by these Jews are not true, no one has the right to hand me over to them. I appeal to Caesar!"

[12]After Festus had conferred with his council, he declared: "You have appealed to Caesar. To Caesar you will go!"

Festus Consults King Agrippa

[13]A few days later King Agrippa and Bernice arrived at Caesarea to pay their respects to Festus. [14]Since they were spending many days there, Festus discussed Paul's case with the king. He said: "There is a man here whom Felix left as a prisoner. [15]When I went to Jerusalem, the chief priests and elders of the Jews brought charges against him and asked that he be condemned.

[16]"I told them that it is not the Roman custom to hand over any man before he has faced his accusers and has had an opportunity to defend himself against their charges. [17]When they came here with me, I did not delay the case, but convened the court the next day and ordered the man to be brought in. [18]When his accusers got up to speak, they did not charge him with any of the crimes I had expected. [19]Instead, they had some points of dispute with him about their own religion and about a dead man named Jesus who Paul claimed was alive. [20]I was at a loss how to investigate such matters; so I asked if he would be willing to go to Jerusalem and stand trial there on these charges. [21]When Paul made his appeal to be held over for the Emperor's decision, I ordered him held until I could send him to Caesar."

[22]Then Agrippa said to Festus, "I would like to hear this man myself."

He replied, "Tomorrow you will hear him."

Paul Before Agrippa

[23]The next day Agrippa and Bernice came with great pomp and entered the audience room with the high ranking officers and the leading men of the city. At the command of Festus, Paul was brought in. [24]Festus said: "King Agrippa, and all who are present with us, you see this man! The whole Jewish community has petitioned me about him in Jerusalem and here in Caesarea, shouting that he ought not to live any longer. [25]I found he had done nothing deserving of death, but because he made his appeal to the Emperor I decided to send him to Rome. [26]But I have nothing definite to write to His Majesty about him. Therefore I have

brought him before all of you, and especially before you, King
Agrippa, so that as a result of this investigation I may have something to write. 27For I think it is unreasonable to send on a prisoner without specifying the charges against him."

26 Then Agrippa said to Paul, "You have permission to speak
for yourself."
So Paul motioned with his hand and began his defense: 2"King
Agrippa, I consider myself fortunate to stand before you today as
I make my defense against all the accusations of the Jews, 3and
especially so because you are well acquainted with all the Jewish
customs and controversies. Therefore, I beg you to listen to me
patiently.

4"The Jews all know the way I have lived ever since I was a
child, from the beginning of my life in my own country, and also
in Jerusalem. 5They have known me for a long time and can testify, if they are willing, that according to the strictest sect of our
religion, I lived as a Pharisee. 6And now it is because of my hope
in what God has promised our fathers that I am on trial today.
7This is the promise our twelve tribes are hoping to see fulfilled
as they earnestly serve God day and night. O king, it is because of
this hope that the Jews are accusing me. 8Why should any of you
consider it incredible that God raises the dead?

9"I too was convinced that I ought to do all that was possible
to oppose the name of Jesus of Nazareth. 10And that is just what I
did in Jerusalem. On the authority of the chief priests I put many
of the saints in prison, and when they were put to death, I cast my
vote against them. 11Many a time I went from one synagogue to
another to have them punished, and I tried to force them to blaspheme. In my obsession against them, I even went to foreign cities to persecute them.

12"On one of these journeys I was going to Damascus with the
authority and commission of the chief priests. 13About noon,
O king, as I was on the road, I saw a light from heaven, brighter
than the sun, blazing around me and my companions. 14We all
fell to the ground, and I heard a voice saying to me in Aramaic,[a]
'Saul, Saul, why do you persecute me? It is hard for you to kick
against the goads.'

15"Then I asked, 'Who are you, Lord?'

" 'I am Jesus, whom you are persecuting,' the Lord replied.
16'Now get up and stand on your feet. I have appeared to you to
appoint you as a servant and as a witness of what you have seen
of me and what I will show you. 17I will rescue you from your
own people and from the Gentiles. I am sending you to them 18to
open their eyes and turn them from darkness to light, and from
the power of Satan to God, so that they may receive forgiveness of
sins and a place among those who are sanctified by faith in me.'

19"So then, King Agrippa, I was not disobedient to the vision
from heaven. 20First to those in Damascus, then to those in Jerusalem and in all Judea, and to the Gentiles also, I preached that
they should repent and turn to God and prove their repentance by
their deeds. 21That is why the Jews seized me in the temple courts
and tried to kill me. 22But I have had God's help to this very day,
and so I stand here and testify to small and great alike. I am saying nothing beyond what the prophets and Moses said would happen— 23that the Christ[b] would suffer and, as the first to rise from

[a] *14* Or *Hebrew* [b] *23* Or *Messiah*

(26:1–23) Thank You, Father, for the inspiration of Paul's total commitment to his testimony. He spoke directly, fearlessly and powerfully. His listeners could have argued with his doctrine, but they could not argue with his changed life. Let me learn from Paul not to be argumentative or self-defensive. Rather, let me learn simply to be a witness to what I have seen and heard and to tell faithfully of Your saving, life-changing grace.

the dead, would proclaim light to his own people and to the Gentiles."
24 At this point Festus interrupted Paul's defense. "You are out
of your mind, Paul!" he shouted. "Your great learning is driving
you insane."
25 "I am not insane, most excellent Festus," Paul replied. "What
I am saying is true and reasonable. 26 The king is familiar with
these things, and I can speak freely to him. I am convinced that
none of this has escaped his notice, because it was not done in a
corner. 27 King Agrippa, do you believe the prophets? I know
you do."
28 Then Agrippa said to Paul, "Do you think that in such a short
time you can persuade me to be a Christian?"
29 Paul replied, "Short time or long—I pray God that not only
you but all who are listening to me today may become what I am,
except for these chains."
30 The king rose, and with him the governor and Bernice and
those sitting with them. 31 They left the room, and while talking
with one another, they said, "This man is not doing anything that
deserves death or imprisonment."
32 Agrippa said to Festus, "This man could have been set free if
he had not appealed to Caesar."

(26:25–32) Paul's tenacity convicts me, Lord. For him, there was no turning back. How courageous, how selfless, how committed he was to the message of Your salvation. If my life were on the line for the gospel, would I be able to forget my circumstances and reach out in concern toward those who were judging me? Would I have the strength to carry on in my mission? O God, help me to learn as Paul learned that Your "power is made perfect in weakness." Help me to "delight in weaknesses, in insults, in hardships, in persecutions, in difficulties" for Christ' s sake. "For when I am weak, then I am strong." (2Co 12:9–10)

Paul Sails for Rome

27 When it was decided that we would sail for Italy, Paul and
some other prisoners were handed over to a centurion
named Julius, who belonged to the Imperial Regiment. 2 We
boarded a ship from Adramyttium about to sail for ports along the
coast of the province of Asia, and we put out to sea. Aristarchus,
a Macedonian from Thessalonica, was with us.
3 The next day we landed at Sidon; and Julius, in kindness to
Paul, allowed him to go to his friends so they might provide for
his needs. 4 From there we put out to sea again and passed to the
lee of Cyprus because the winds were against us. 5 When we had
sailed across the open sea off the coast of Cilicia and Pamphylia,
we landed at Myra in Lycia. 6 There the centurion found an
Alexandrian ship sailing for Italy and put us on board. 7 We made
slow headway for many days and had difficulty arriving off Cnidus.
When the wind did not allow us to hold our course, we sailed to
the lee of Crete, opposite Salmone. 8 We moved along the coast
with difficulty and came to a place called Fair Havens, near the
town of Lasea.
9 Much time had been lost, and sailing had already become
dangerous because by now it was after the Fast.[a] So Paul warned
them, 10 "Men, I can see that our voyage is going to be disastrous
and bring great loss to ship and cargo, and to our own lives also."
11 But the centurion, instead of listening to what Paul said, followed the advice of the pilot and of the owner of the ship. 12 Since
the harbor was unsuitable to winter in, the majority decided that
we should sail on, hoping to reach Phoenix and winter there. This
was a harbor in Crete, facing both southwest and northwest.

The Storm

13 When a gentle south wind began to blow, they thought they
had obtained what they wanted; so they weighed anchor and

[a] 9 That is, the Day of Atonement (Yom Kippur)

sailed along the shore of Crete. 14Before very long, a wind of hur-
ricane force, called the "northeaster," swept down from the island. 15The ship was caught by the storm and could not head into
the wind; so we gave way to it and were driven along. 16As we
passed to the lee of a small island called Cauda, we were hardly
able to make the lifeboat secure. 17When the men had hoisted it
aboard, they passed ropes under the ship itself to hold it together. Fearing that they would run aground on the sandbars of Syr-
tis, they lowered the sea anchor and let the ship be driven along.
18We took such a violent battering from the storm that the next
day they began to throw the cargo overboard. 19On the third day,
they threw the ship's tackle overboard with their own hands.
20When neither sun nor stars appeared for many days and the
storm continued raging, we finally gave up all hope of being
saved.
21After the men had gone a long time without food, Paul stood
up before them and said: "Men, you should have taken my advice
not to sail from Crete; then you would have spared yourselves this
damage and loss. 22But now I urge you to keep up your courage,
because not one of you will be lost; only the ship will be destroyed. 23Last night an angel of the God whose I am and whom I
serve stood beside me 24and said, 'Do not be afraid, Paul. You
must stand trial before Caesar; and God has graciously given you
the lives of all who sail with you.' 25So keep up your courage,
men, for I have faith in God that it will happen just as he told me.
26Nevertheless, we must run aground on some island."

The Shipwreck

27On the fourteenth night we were still being driven across the
Adriatic[a] Sea, when about midnight the sailors sensed they were
approaching land. 28They took soundings and found that the
water was a hundred and twenty feet[b] deep. A short time later
they took soundings again and found it was ninety feet[c] deep.
29Fearing that we would be dashed against the rocks, they
dropped four anchors from the stern and prayed for daylight.
30In an attempt to escape from the ship, the sailors let the lifeboat
down into the sea, pretending they were going to lower some anchors from the bow. 31Then Paul said to the centurion and the
soldiers, "Unless these men stay with the ship, you cannot be
saved." 32So the soldiers cut the ropes that held the lifeboat and
let it fall away.
33Just before dawn Paul urged them all to eat. "For the last
fourteen days," he said, "you have been in constant suspense and
have gone without food—you haven't eaten anything. 34Now I
urge you to take some food. You need it to survive. Not one of you
will lose a single hair from his head." 35After he said this, he took
some bread and gave thanks to God in front of them all. Then he
broke it and began to eat. 36They were all encouraged and ate
some food themselves. 37Altogether there were 276 of us on
board. 38When they had eaten as much as they wanted, they light-
ened the ship by throwing the grain into the sea.
39When daylight came, they did not recognize the land, but
they saw a bay with a sandy beach, where they decided to run the
ship aground if they could. 40Cutting loose the anchors, they left

[a] 27 In ancient times the name referred to an area extending well south of Italy.
[b] 28 Greek *twenty orguias* (about 37 meters) [c] 28 Greek *fifteen orguias* (about 27 meters)

(27:23–36) Neither the raging crowds in Jerusalem nor the raging waves of the sea could shipwreck Paul's faith or thwart Your plan for him to preach the gospel in Rome. Even when he was lost in the storm, You knew where he was, and You sent him a message of hope. You renewed Paul's faith and courage, and he became the chaplain to his captors and their comforter in the storm. Lord, help me to see every storm of life as an opportunity to build the faith of others. When we are lost, You know where we can be found. While we wait for You to save us from our distress, send words of hope to save us from our despair.

What He has done, He not only may do again but will do, wherever He finds a truly humble heart in which to work and rest. If He stood by Paul saying, "Fear not," just as really and maybe as evidently will He stand by you. If He guided him in his work, restraining him from preaching here, and calling him to service there, He will give you also leadings just as certain and maybe as distinct.

J. Rendel Harris (1892-)

Like the sun that rises every day,
You are so faithful,
Lord, You are faithful.
Like the rain that You send
And every breath that I breathe,
You are so faithful, Lord.

And in the midst of a storm,
Through the wind and the waves,
You'll still be faithful,
You'll still be faithful.
When the stars refuse to shine
And time is no more,
You'll still be faithful,
You'll still be faithful, Lord.

"You Are So Faithful"
Lenny LeBlanc and Greg Gulley (©1989)

them in the sea and at the same time untied the ropes that held
the rudders. Then they hoisted the foresail to the wind and made
for the beach. 41But the ship struck a sandbar and ran aground.
The bow stuck fast and would not move, and the stern was broken to pieces by the pounding of the surf.
42The soldiers planned to kill the prisoners to prevent any of
them from swimming away and escaping. 43But the centurion
wanted to spare Paul's life and kept them from carrying out their
plan. He ordered those who could swim to jump overboard first
and get to land. 44The rest were to get there on planks or on
pieces of the ship. In this way everyone reached land in safety.

Ashore on Malta

28 Once safely on shore, we found out that the island was
called Malta. 2The islanders showed us unusual kindness.
They built a fire and welcomed us all because it was raining and
cold. 3Paul gathered a pile of brushwood and, as he put it on the
fire, a viper, driven out by the heat, fastened itself on his hand.
4When the islanders saw the snake hanging from his hand, they
said to each other, "This man must be a murderer; for though he
escaped from the sea, Justice has not allowed him to live." 5But
Paul shook the snake off into the fire and suffered no ill effects.
6The people expected him to swell up or suddenly fall dead, but
after waiting a long time and seeing nothing unusual happen to
him, they changed their minds and said he was a god.
7There was an estate nearby that belonged to Publius, the chief
official of the island. He welcomed us to his home and for three
days entertained us hospitably. 8His father was sick in bed, suffering from fever and dysentery. Paul went in to see him and, after
prayer, placed his hands on him and healed him. 9When this had
happened, the rest of the sick on the island came and were cured.
10They honored us in many ways and when we were ready to sail,
they furnished us with the supplies we needed.

Arrival at Rome

11After three months we put out to sea in a ship that had win-
tered in the island. It was an Alexandrian ship with the figurehead
of the twin gods Castor and Pollux. 12We put in at Syracuse and
stayed there three days. 13From there we set sail and arrived at
Rhegium. The next day the south wind came up, and on the following day we reached Puteoli. 14There we found some brothers
who invited us to spend a week with them. And so we came to
Rome. 15The brothers there had heard that we were coming, and
they traveled as far as the Forum of Appius and the Three Taverns
to meet us. At the sight of these men Paul thanked God and was
encouraged. 16When we got to Rome, Paul was allowed to live by
himself, with a soldier to guard him.

Paul Preaches at Rome Under Guard

17Three days later he called together the leaders of the Jews.
When they had assembled, Paul said to them: "My brothers, although I have done nothing against our people or against the customs of our ancestors, I was arrested in Jerusalem and handed
over to the Romans. 18They examined me and wanted to release
me, because I was not guilty of any crime deserving death. 19But
when the Jews objected, I was compelled to appeal to Caesar—
not that I had any charge to bring against my own people. 20For

(28:1–10) Paul had a mission in mind—to preach the gospel in Rome. He knew only the ultimate destination. But You, Lord, held the road map. You knew the detours. You knew what lay ahead on the journey. So often I, too, have a goal in mind, a vision of ministry to fulfill. But You, O God, are Sovereign. I am employed for Your service; and You maintain the right to alter my plans in whatever way You wish. Keep me alert to Your leading and attuned to Your purposes. Help me to be prepared in season and out of season, ready to do the good works which You have prepared in advance for me to do. (Eph 2:10; 2Ti 4:2)

Give us ears to hear that still, small voice;
And give us lips forever willing to rejoice.
And may our eyes be lit with wisdom,
May we know the path that's true;
And we'll march with hearts
Courageous after You.

We're marching on with hearts courageous;
We'll follow anywhere You want us to.
And should You lead us where the battle rages,
Let us march with hearts
courageous after You.

"Hearts Courageous"
Jamie Owens-Collins (©1984)

this reason I have asked to see you and talk with you. It is because of the hope of Israel that I am bound with this chain."

21 They replied, "We have not received any letters from Judea concerning you, and none of the brothers who have come from
there has reported or said anything bad about you. 22 But we want
to hear what your views are, for we know that people everywhere are talking against this sect."

23 They arranged to meet Paul on a certain day, and came in even larger numbers to the place where he was staying. From morning till evening he explained and declared to them the kingdom of God and tried to convince them about Jesus from the Law
of Moses and from the Prophets. 24 Some were convinced by what
he said, but others would not believe. 25 They disagreed among
themselves and began to leave after Paul had made this final statement: "The Holy Spirit spoke the truth to your forefathers when he said through Isaiah the prophet:

26 " 'Go to this people and say,
"You will be ever hearing but never understanding;
you will be ever seeing but never perceiving."
27 For this people's heart has become calloused;
they hardly hear with their ears,
and they have closed their eyes.
Otherwise they might see with their eyes,
hear with their ears,
understand with their hearts
and turn, and I would heal them.'[a]

28 "Therefore I want you to know that God's salvation has been sent to the Gentiles, and they will listen!"[b]

30 For two whole years Paul stayed there in his own rented
house and welcomed all who came to see him. 31 Boldly and without hindrance he preached the kingdom of God and taught about the Lord Jesus Christ.

God fully expects the church of Jesus Christ to prove itself a miraculous group in the very midst of a hostile world. Christians of necessity must be in contact with the world but in being and spirit ought to be separated from the world—and as such, we should be the most amazing people in the world.

A.W. Tozer (1897-1963)

(28:31) Revive us today, Lord, that we may accomplish mighty acts of faith. As You did at Pentecost, breathe the breath of life into Your church. Let us see Your power at work among us and through us, accompanying the preaching of the Gospel. Give us a strong, living, active faith. Put fire in our tongues when we declare Your wonders. Plant joy in our hearts when we suffer persecution. May it be said of us as it was said of the first believers: "Then the disciples went out and preached everywhere, and the Lord worked with them and confirmed his word by the signs that accompanied it." (Mk 16:20; Ac 1:8; 2:1–11; 1Pe 4:13)

Holy Spirit,
Send Your anointing,
Stir the gift You've placed inside;
From this hour
Release Your power;
Through my life be glorified.

Breath of heaven,
Breath of heaven,
Breathe on me.

"Breath Of Heaven"
Buddy Owens, Morris Chapman (©1999)

[a] 27 Isaiah 6:9,10 [b] 28 Some manuscripts *listen!" 29 After he said this, the Jews left, arguing vigorously among themselves.*

Romans

The Epistle of Paul the Apostle to the ROMANS

How do we respond to a God who loves us so much that He saves us from our desperate, fatal condition—even at great cost to Himself? Paul's letter to the Romans helps us to answer this question.

This majestic epistle focuses upon the gospel: the Good News of what God has done for us through Jesus Christ (1:1–4). This gospel is "the power of God for the salvation of everyone who believes: first for the Jew, then for the Gentile" (1:16). Initially, we receive the account of God's work in Christ through faith. We believe that Christ has taken our sin upon Himself, and we trust Him for our salvation. When this happens, we are brought into a right relationship with the God Who loves us even before we are reconciled to Him (5:1–10). Our original response of faith flows spontaneously into thanksgiving and joy, as we "rejoice in God through our Lord Jesus Christ, through whom we have now received reconciliation" (5:11).

Romans does not, however, look at the world through rose-colored glasses. It begins with a frank appraisal of our sinful condition, that which deserves eternal death (3:23; 6:23). We have rejected God in favor of worshiping idols and indulging in "every kind of wickedness" (1:29). The One true God does not look the other way, but righteously condemns our sin and reveals His holy wrath (1:18; 2:5). Yet this same God overflows with grace and mercy (5:15–17; 11:30–32). He is both "just and the one who justifies," bringing us into a right relationship with Himself through Christ (3:26).

The Good News impels us to offer our bodies, not in death, but in living each day for God as the Spirit empowers us.

In chapter 11, as Paul concludes his exposition of the gospel, he cannot help but break forth into worshipful astonishment: "Oh, the depth of the riches of the wisdom and knowledge of God! How unsearchable his judgments, and his paths beyond tracing out! . . . For from him and through him and to him are all things. To him be the glory forever! Amen." (11:33,36). Such praise flows effervescently from a recognition of God's majestic and mysterious mercy. As we reflect upon the magnitude of this mercy—and the fact that it has embraced us personally—we cannot help but join in Paul's exclamation of praise!

But immediately after glorifying God with such uplifting words, Paul calls us to respond to God's mercy by offering our bodies to Him: "Therefore, I urge you . . . to offer your bodies as living sacrifices, holy and pleasing to God—this is your spiritual act of worship" (12:1). The Good News impels us to offer our bodies, not in death, but in living each day for God as the Spirit empowers us (8:1–27; 14:17). Chapters 12—16 of Romans spell out in detail how we are to do this: by mental renewal (12:2), by exercising spiritual gifts (12:4–8), by living a life of active love (12:9–21), etc. Devotion to God involves not only our lips and hearts but also our whole selves as we live worshipfully in the church and in the world.

1 Paul, a servant of Christ Jesus, called to be an apostle and set
apart for the gospel of God— 2the gospel he promised beforehand through his prophets in the Holy Scriptures 3regard-
ing his Son, who as to his human nature was a descendant of
David, 4and who through the Spirit[a] of holiness was declared
with power to be the Son of God[b] by his resurrection from the
dead: Jesus Christ our Lord. 5Through him and for his name's
sake, we received grace and apostleship to call people from
among all the Gentiles to the obedience that comes from faith.
6And you also are among those who are called to belong to
Jesus Christ.

7To all in Rome who are loved by God and called to be saints:

Grace and peace to you from God our Father and from the
Lord Jesus Christ.

Paul's Longing to Visit Rome

8First, I thank my God through Jesus Christ for all of you, because your faith is being reported all over the world. 9God, whom
I serve with my whole heart in preaching the gospel of his Son, is
my witness how constantly I remember you 10in my prayers at all
times; and I pray that now at last by God's will the way may be
opened for me to come to you.
11I long to see you so that I may impart to you some spiritual
gift to make you strong— 12that is, that you and I may be mutu-
ally encouraged by each other's faith. 13I do not want you to be
unaware, brothers, that I planned many times to come to you (but
have been prevented from doing so until now) in order that I
might have a harvest among you, just as I have had among the
other Gentiles.
14I am obligated both to Greeks and non-Greeks, both to the
wise and the foolish. 15That is why I am so eager to preach the
gospel also to you who are at Rome.
16I am not ashamed of the gospel, because it is the power of
God for the salvation of everyone who believes: first for the Jew,
then for the Gentile. 17For in the gospel a righteousness from God
is revealed, a righteousness that is by faith from first to last,[c] just
as it is written: "The righteous will live by faith."[d]

God's Wrath Against Mankind

18The wrath of God is being revealed from heaven against all
the godlessness and wickedness of men who suppress the truth
by their wickedness, 19since what may be known about God is
plain to them, because God has made it plain to them. 20For since
the creation of the world God's invisible qualities—his eternal
power and divine nature—have been clearly seen, being understood from what has been made, so that men are without excuse.
21For although they knew God, they neither glorified him as
God nor gave thanks to him, but their thinking became futile and
their foolish hearts were darkened. 22Although they claimed to be
wise, they became fools 23and exchanged the glory of the immortal God for images made to look like mortal man and birds
and animals and reptiles.
24Therefore God gave them over in the sinful desires of their
hearts to sexual impurity for the degrading of their bodies with

[a] 4 Or *who as to his spirit* [b] 4 Or *was appointed to be the Son of God with power*
[c] 17 Or *is from faith to faith* [d] 17 Hab. 2:4

(1:16–17) Lord, I believe! This faith from first to last is a faith in the One Who is the Beginning and the End. Your gospel is indeed the best news in the world. It is the headline imprinted on every saved heart. Knowing, seeing, believing what You have done for us—that You have purchased us from a sure death with Your own life—how can we keep silent? O Lord, open our mouths and create praise on our lips. Empower us to tell the world the Good News of Your mercy. (Isa 57:19; Ac 1:8; Rev 22:13)

The power of speech which you have bestowed on me can give me no greater pleasure than to serve you by preaching your gospel.

Hilary of Poitiers (c.315-368)

(1:18–24) O Lord my Creator, the whole earth is full of Your glory. I choose this day to glorify You and to give You thanks. I will worship and serve You as my God. I will look to You, rather than to my own mind, for wisdom. I will hold on to Your Word of truth and resist anything that raises itself up against the gospel. I will flee anarchy and its degradation: a darkened heart, shameful lusts, a depraved mind, the suppression of truth and the worship of lies. I will stop making excuses and instead seek Your face, O God.

O Lord my God!
When I in awesome wonder
Consider all the worlds
Thy hands have made,
I see the stars,
I hear the rolling thunder,
Thy power throughout
The universe displayed.

Then sings my soul,
My Savior God, to Thee;
How great Thou art,
How great Thou art!

"How Great Thou Art"
Stuart K. Hine (©1953, 1981)

one another. 25They exchanged the truth of God for a lie, and worshiped and served created things rather than the Creator—who is forever praised. Amen.

26Because of this, God gave them over to shameful lusts. Even their women exchanged natural relations for unnatural ones. 27In the same way the men also abandoned natural relations with women and were inflamed with lust for one another. Men committed indecent acts with other men, and received in themselves the due penalty for their perversion.

28Furthermore, since they did not think it worthwhile to retain the knowledge of God, he gave them over to a depraved mind, to do what ought not to be done. 29They have become filled with every kind of wickedness, evil, greed and depravity. They are full of envy, murder, strife, deceit and malice. They are gossips, 30slanderers, God-haters, insolent, arrogant and boastful; they invent ways of doing evil; they disobey their parents; 31they are senseless, faithless, heartless, ruthless. 32Although they know God's righteous decree that those who do such things deserve death, they not only continue to do these very things but also approve of those who practice them.

God's Righteous Judgment

2 You, therefore, have no excuse, you who pass judgment on someone else, for at whatever point you judge the other, you are condemning yourself, because you who pass judgment do the same things. 2Now we know that God's judgment against those who do such things is based on truth. 3So when you, a mere man, pass judgment on them and yet do the same things, do you think you will escape God's judgment? 4Or do you show contempt for the riches of his kindness, tolerance and patience, not realizing that God's kindness leads you toward repentance?

5But because of your stubbornness and your unrepentant heart, you are storing up wrath against yourself for the day of God's wrath, when his righteous judgment will be revealed. 6God "will give to each person according to what he has done."[a] 7To those who by persistence in doing good seek glory, honor and immortality, he will give eternal life. 8But for those who are self-seeking and who reject the truth and follow evil, there will be wrath and anger. 9There will be trouble and distress for every human being who does evil: first for the Jew, then for the Gentile; 10but glory, honor and peace for everyone who does good: first for the Jew, then for the Gentile. 11For God does not show favoritism.

12All who sin apart from the law will also perish apart from the law, and all who sin under the law will be judged by the law. 13For it is not those who hear the law who are righteous in God's sight, but it is those who obey the law who will be declared righteous. 14(Indeed, when Gentiles, who do not have the law, do by nature things required by the law, they are a law for themselves, even though they do not have the law, 15since they show that the requirements of the law are written on their hearts, their consciences also bearing witness, and their thoughts now accusing, now even defending them.) 16This will take place on the day when God will judge men's secrets through Jesus Christ, as my gospel declares.

[a]6 Psalm 62:12; Prov. 24:12

(2:4) I praise You, Lord, for Your merciful kindness and love. More frightening than the thought of letting go of You is the thought of Your letting go of me, of relinquishing me to the consequences of my sin. You could have abandoned me. You could have destroyed me. But instead You led me to repentance. O God, may I never take Your kindness for granted.

Waiting for angry words to sear my soul,
Knowing I don't deserve another chance,
Then suddenly the kindest words
I've ever heard
Come flooding through my heart:

It's Your kindness that leads us
To repentance, O Lord.
Knowing that You love us
No matter what we do,
Makes us want to love You, too.

"Your Kindness"
Leslie Phillips (©1985)

The Jews and the Law

17Now you, if you call yourself a Jew; if you rely on the law and
brag about your relationship to God; 18if you know his will and
approve of what is superior because you are instructed by the
law; 19if you are convinced that you are a guide for the blind, a
light for those who are in the dark, 20an instructor of the foolish,
a teacher of infants, because you have in the law the embodiment
of knowledge and truth— 21you, then, who teach others, do you
not teach yourself? You who preach against stealing, do you steal?
22You who say that people should not commit adultery, do you
commit adultery? You who abhor idols, do you rob temples?
23You who brag about the law, do you dishonor God by breaking
the law? 24As it is written: "God's name is blasphemed among the
Gentiles because of you."[a]

25Circumcision has value if you observe the law, but if you
break the law, you have become as though you had not been circumcised. 26If those who are not circumcised keep the law's
requirements, will they not be regarded as though they were circumcised? 27The one who is not circumcised physically and yet
obeys the law will condemn you who, even though you have the[b]
written code and circumcision, are a lawbreaker.

28A man is not a Jew if he is only one outwardly, nor is circumcision merely outward and physical. 29No, a man is a Jew if
he is one inwardly; and circumcision is circumcision of the heart,
by the Spirit, not by the written code. Such a man's praise is not
from men, but from God.

God's Faithfulness

3 What advantage, then, is there in being a Jew, or what value
is there in circumcision? 2Much in every way! First of all, they
have been entrusted with the very words of God.

3What if some did not have faith? Will their lack of faith nullify
God's faithfulness? 4Not at all! Let God be true, and every man a
liar. As it is written:

"So that you may be proved right when you speak
and prevail when you judge."[c]

5But if our unrighteousness brings out God's righteousness
more clearly, what shall we say? That God is unjust in bringing his
wrath on us? (I am using a human argument.) 6Certainly not! If
that were so, how could God judge the world? 7Someone might
argue, "If my falsehood enhances God's truthfulness and so increases his glory, why am I still condemned as a sinner?" 8Why
not say—as we are being slanderously reported as saying and as
some claim that we say—"Let us do evil that good may result"?
Their condemnation is deserved.

No One Is Righteous

9What shall we conclude then? Are we any better[d]? Not at all!
We have already made the charge that Jews and Gentiles alike are
all under sin. 10As it is written:

"There is no one righteous, not even one;
11 there is no one who understands,
no one who seeks God.

[a] 24 Isaiah 52:5; Ezek. 36:22 [b] 27 Or *who, by means of a* [c] 4 Psalm 51:4
[d] 9 Or *worse*

(2:29) Lord, put Your mark on my heart—the sign that You have staked Your claim to my life. Cut away everything that keeps me from following You. You cannot be fooled by the outward signs of religion, for You do not look at the outward appearance, You look at the heart. As circumcision was the physical sign of Your covenant with Abraham, so let the circumcision of my heart be the sign of Your covenant with me. (Ge 17:11; Dt 30:6; 1Sa 16:7; Col 2:1–12)

Spiritual surgery is more painful than physical surgery. God doesn't use an anesthetic; he doesn't do his work while we are asleep. God can take any brokenhearted believer and make him or her a radiant, loving person. But when he performs such "heart operations," his children are wide awake.

Erwin W. Lutzer (1941-)

Create in me a heart for You,
A heart to do Your will.
Make it a palace fit for a king;
Make it to praise You
And free it to sing.
You are the potter,
Make me like new;
Create in me a heart for You.

"A Heart For You"
Walt Harrah, (©1986)

(3:10–18) O Lord, we try so hard to follow You, but the compass of the human heart is faulty, and we so easily veer off course. Our words are condemning and merciless, our actions are harmful, and the cruel tendencies hidden within us—the jealousy, bitterness and ingratitude—eat at us like poison. There is only one condition at the heart of our problem, and that is sin. There is only one Person Who is capable of our rescue, and that is You. Come, Lord Jesus, and save us from ourselves. (Isa 53:6)

(3:22–25) You, O Lord, are holy, righteous, perfect in every way. We, on our own, are none of these things. You cannot accept anything less than perfection, and we cannot achieve anything greater than imperfection. None of us can live up to Your standard, and each of us knows it. There are no excuses, but—O Hallelujah!—there is a pardon. By Your grace, through faith in the blood of Jesus, we have been saved and made alive with Christ. Thank You, Father, for Your love and mercy. (Eph 2:4–9)

O perfect redemption,
The purchase of blood!
To every believer
The promise of God;
The vilest offender
Who truly believes,
That moment from Jesus
A pardon receives.

"To God Be The Glory"
Fanny J. Crosby (1875)

12 All have turned away,
they have together become worthless;
there is no one who does good,
not even one."[a]
13 "Their throats are open graves;
their tongues practice deceit."[b]
"The poison of vipers is on their lips."[c]
14 "Their mouths are full of cursing and bitterness."[d]
15 "Their feet are swift to shed blood;
16 ruin and misery mark their ways,
17 and the way of peace they do not know."[e]
18 "There is no fear of God before their eyes."[f]

19 Now we know that whatever the law says, it says to those who
are under the law, so that every mouth may be silenced and the
whole world held accountable to God. 20 Therefore no one will be
declared righteous in his sight by observing the law; rather,
through the law we become conscious of sin.

Righteousness Through Faith

21 But now a righteousness from God, apart from law, has been
made known, to which the Law and the Prophets testify. 22 This
righteousness from God comes through faith in Jesus Christ to all
who believe. There is no difference, 23 for all have sinned and fall
short of the glory of God, 24 and are justified freely by his grace
through the redemption that came by Christ Jesus. 25 God presented him as a sacrifice of atonement,[g] through faith in his
blood. He did this to demonstrate his justice, because in his for-
bearance he had left the sins committed beforehand unpunished— 26 he did it to demonstrate his justice at the present time,
so as to be just and the one who justifies those who have faith in
Jesus.

27 Where, then, is boasting? It is excluded. On what principle?
On that of observing the law? No, but on that of faith. 28 For we
maintain that a man is justified by faith apart from observing the
law. 29 Is God the God of Jews only? Is he not the God of Gentiles
too? Yes, of Gentiles too, 30 since there is only one God, who will
justify the circumcised by faith and the uncircumcised through
that same faith. 31 Do we, then, nullify the law by this faith? Not at
all! Rather, we uphold the law.

Abraham Justified by Faith

4 What then shall we say that Abraham, our forefather, discovered in this matter? 2 If, in fact, Abraham was justified by
works, he had something to boast about—but not before God.
3 What does the Scripture say? "Abraham believed God, and it was
credited to him as righteousness."[h]

4 Now when a man works, his wages are not credited to him as
a gift, but as an obligation. 5 However, to the man who does not
work but trusts God who justifies the wicked, his faith is credited
as righteousness. 6 David says the same thing when he speaks of
the blessedness of the man to whom God credits righteousness
apart from works:

7 "Blessed are they

[a] *12* Psalms 14:1–3; 53:1–3; Eccles. 7:20 [b] *13* Psalm 5:9 [c] *13* Psalm 140:3
[d] *14* Psalm 10:7 [e] *17* Isaiah 59:7,8 [f] *18* Psalm 36:1 [g] *25* Or *as the one who would turn aside his wrath, taking away sin* [h] *3* Gen. 15:6; also in verse 22

whose transgressions are forgiven,
whose sins are covered.
8 Blessed is the man
whose sin the Lord will never count against
him."[a]

9 Is this blessedness only for the circumcised, or also for the
uncircumcised? We have been saying that Abraham's faith was
credited to him as righteousness. 10 Under what circumstances
was it credited? Was it after he was circumcised, or before? It was
not after, but before! 11 And he received the sign of circumcision,
a seal of the righteousness that he had by faith while he was still
uncircumcised. So then, he is the father of all who believe but
have not been circumcised, in order that righteousness might be
credited to them. 12 And he is also the father of the circumcised
who not only are circumcised but who also walk in the footsteps
of the faith that our father Abraham had before he was circumcised.

13 It was not through law that Abraham and his offspring received the promise that he would be heir of the world, but
through the righteousness that comes by faith. 14 For if those who
live by law are heirs, faith has no value and the promise is worthless, 15 because law brings wrath. And where there is no law there
is no transgression.

16 Therefore, the promise comes by faith, so that it may be by
grace and may be guaranteed to all Abraham's offspring—not
only to those who are of the law but also to those who are of the
faith of Abraham. He is the father of us all. 17 As it is written: "I
have made you a father of many nations."[b] He is our father in the
sight of God, in whom he believed—the God who gives life to the
dead and calls things that are not as though they were.

18 Against all hope, Abraham in hope believed and so became
the father of many nations, just as it had been said to him, "So
shall your offspring be."[c] 19 Without weakening in his faith, he
faced the fact that his body was as good as dead—since he was
about a hundred years old—and that Sarah's womb was also
dead. 20 Yet he did not waver through unbelief regarding the
promise of God, but was strengthened in his faith and gave glory
to God, 21 being fully persuaded that God had power to do what he
had promised. 22 This is why "it was credited to him as righteousness." 23 The words "it was credited to him" were written
not for him alone, 24 but also for us, to whom God will credit righteousness—for us who believe in him who raised Jesus our Lord
from the dead. 25 He was delivered over to death for our sins and
was raised to life for our justification.

Peace and Joy

5 Therefore, since we have been justified through faith, we[d]
have peace with God through our Lord Jesus Christ, 2 through
whom we have gained access by faith into this grace in which we
now stand. And we[d] rejoice in the hope of the glory of God. 3 Not
only so, but we[d] also rejoice in our sufferings, because we know
that suffering produces perseverance; 4 perseverance, character;
and character, hope. 5 And hope does not disappoint us, because
God has poured out his love into our hearts by the Holy Spirit,
whom he has given us.

[a] *8* Psalm 32:1,2 [b] *17* Gen. 17:5 [c] *18* Gen. 15:5 [d] *1,2,3* Or *let us*

Eternal life does not begin with death; it begins with faith.

Samuel M. Shoemaker (1893-1963)

(4:7—5:1) Out of the hopelessness of death You bring new life. Out of the prison of sin You bring redemption. Out of the weakness of human flesh You bring victory. All by grace. All by faith. And that is all You are looking for from us—faith. Not great accomplishments, not self-righteousness, not pedigree but simple faith—faith that brings You glory, faith that perseveres in spite of adversity, faith no larger than a mustard seed. For faith is the seed that grows into the tree of righteousness, and the fruit of righteousness is peace with You. Strengthen my faith, Lord, so that I may move deeper into the cycle of life in Christ: from faith to faith, from strength to strength, and from glory to glory. (Ps 84:7; Isa 32:17; Mt 17:20; Ro 1:17; 2Co 3:18; Gal 3:22)

Be still, my soul! The Lord is on thy
side;
Bear patiently the cross of grief or
pain;
Leave to thy God to order and
provide;
In every change He faithful will
remain.
Be still, my soul! Thy best, thy
heavenly Friend
Through thorny ways leads to a
joyful end.

"Be Still My Soul"
Katharina von Schlegel (1752)
Trans. Jane L. Borthwick (1813-1897)

(5:1–5) Peace with God! The war is won! Victory is Yours, O God, through Jesus Christ. I am the reward of Your victory. I am the spoil of war! I am now reconciled to You and holy in Your sight, "without blemish and free from accusation." What grace is mine in Christ, through His blood and resurrection! Hallelujah! (Col 1:22)

(5:6–8) I thank You, merciful Lord Jesus, that You did not wait for us to repent. You did not wait for us to change our ways or clean up our act. You saved us while we were still sinners. And we are all sinners: sinners by birth, sinners by nature, sinners by choice, sinners by default—sinners for whom You died. There is no sin that Your blood cannot cover, no stain that Your blood cannot cleanse. There is no one so lost that You cannot find him, no prodigal so distant that You cannot hear her prayer. There is no person too sinful to be saved—just too stubborn to accept Your gift of salvation.

Justification by grace through faith is the theologian's learned phrase for what Chesterton once called "the furious love of God." He is not moody or capricious; he knows no seasons of change. He has a single relentless stance toward us; he loves us. He is the only God man has ever heard of who loves sinners.

Brennan Manning (1934-)

You rescued me and picked me up,
A living hope of grace revealed,
A life transformed in righteousness;
Oh Lord, You have rescued me.
Forgiving me, You healed my heart
And set me free from sin and death.
You bought me life,
You've made me whole;
Oh Lord, You have rescued me.

And You loved me
Before I knew You.
And You knew me for all time.
I've been created
In Your image, Oh Lord,
And You brought me,
And You sought me.
Your blood poured out for me,
A new creation
In Your image, Oh Lord.
You rescued me.

"You Rescued Me"
Geoff Bullock (©1993)

6You see, at just the right time, when we were still powerless,
Christ died for the ungodly. 7Very rarely will anyone die for a righteous man, though for a good man someone might possibly dare
to die. 8But God demonstrates his own love for us in this: While
we were still sinners, Christ died for us.
9Since we have now been justified by his blood, how much
more shall we be saved from God's wrath through him! 10For if,
when we were God's enemies, we were reconciled to him through
the death of his Son, how much more, having been reconciled,
shall we be saved through his life! 11Not only is this so, but we
also rejoice in God through our Lord Jesus Christ, through whom
we have now received reconciliation.

Death Through Adam, Life Through Christ

12Therefore, just as sin entered the world through one man,
and death through sin, and in this way death came to all men, because all sinned— 13for before the law was given, sin was in the
world. But sin is not taken into account when there is no law.
14Nevertheless, death reigned from the time of Adam to the time
of Moses, even over those who did not sin by breaking a command, as did Adam, who was a pattern of the one to come.
15But the gift is not like the trespass. For if the many died by
the trespass of the one man, how much more did God's grace and
the gift that came by the grace of the one man, Jesus Christ, overflow to the many! 16Again, the gift of God is not like the result of
the one man's sin: The judgment followed one sin and brought
condemnation, but the gift followed many trespasses and brought
justification. 17For if, by the trespass of the one man, death
reigned through that one man, how much more will those who
receive God's abundant provision of grace and of the gift of righteousness reign in life through the one man, Jesus Christ.
18Consequently, just as the result of one trespass was condemnation for all men, so also the result of one act of righteousness
was justification that brings life for all men. 19For just as through
the disobedience of the one man the many were made sinners, so
also through the obedience of the one man the many will be made
righteous.
20The law was added so that the trespass might increase. But
where sin increased, grace increased all the more, 21so that, just
as sin reigned in death, so also grace might reign through righteousness to bring eternal life through Jesus Christ our Lord.

Dead to Sin, Alive in Christ

6 What shall we say, then? Shall we go on sinning so that grace
may increase? 2By no means! We died to sin; how can we
live in it any longer? 3Or don't you know that all of us who were
baptized into Christ Jesus were baptized into his death? 4We were
therefore buried with him through baptism into death in order
that, just as Christ was raised from the dead through the glory of
the Father, we too may live a new life.
5If we have been united with him like this in his death, we will
certainly also be united with him in his resurrection. 6For we
know that our old self was crucified with him so that the body of
sin might be done away with,[a] that we should no longer be slaves
to sin— 7because anyone who has died has been freed from sin.

[a] 6 Or *be rendered powerless*

MY BELOVED

Who would you die for? Would you die for a stranger or for a wicked person? Would you die for someone who has hurt others? It is hard to think of someone dying for a righteous person, let alone for a sinner, as you once were. But that is what Jesus did.

This is how I showed My love for you. While you were still a sinner, My Son Jesus died for you. I sent My one and only Son into the world that you might live through Him. This is love. I did not wait for you to love Me. I loved you first and sent My Son as an atoning sacrifice for your sins.

Jesus Christ redeemed you from the curse of the law by becoming a curse for you. I made Him who had no sin to be sin for you, so that in Him you might become the righteousness of God.

He Himself bore your sins in His body on the tree, so that you might die to sin and live for righteousness. Your healing is a result of His wounds.

So in Him you have redemption through His blood and the forgiveness of your sins, in accordance with the riches of My grace that I lavished on you.

Never forget what My Son did for you. He defines love. Because of Him, you are My child.

Ro 5:6-8; 2Co 5:21; Gal 3:13; Eph 1:7-8; 1Pe 2:24; 1Jn 4:9-10

8Now if we died with Christ, we believe that we will also live
with him. 9For we know that since Christ was raised from the
dead, he cannot die again; death no longer has mastery over him.
10The death he died, he died to sin once for all; but the life he
lives, he lives to God.

11In the same way, count yourselves dead to sin but alive to
God in Christ Jesus. 12Therefore do not let sin reign in your mortal body so that you obey its evil desires. 13Do not offer the parts
of your body to sin, as instruments of wickedness, but rather offer
yourselves to God, as those who have been brought from death to
life; and offer the parts of your body to him as instruments of
righteousness. 14For sin shall not be your master, because you
are not under law, but under grace.

Slaves to Righteousness

15What then? Shall we sin because we are not under law but
under grace? By no means! 16Don't you know that when you offer
yourselves to someone to obey him as slaves, you are slaves to the
one whom you obey—whether you are slaves to sin, which leads
to death, or to obedience, which leads to righteousness? 17But
thanks be to God that, though you used to be slaves to sin, you
wholeheartedly obeyed the form of teaching to which you were
entrusted. 18You have been set free from sin and have become
slaves to righteousness.

19I put this in human terms because you are weak in your natural selves. Just as you used to offer the parts of your body in slavery to impurity and to ever-increasing wickedness, so now offer
them in slavery to righteousness leading to holiness. 20When you
were slaves to sin, you were free from the control of righteousness. 21What benefit did you reap at that time from the things you
are now ashamed of? Those things result in death! 22But now that
you have been set free from sin and have become slaves to God,
the benefit you reap leads to holiness, and the result is eternal
life. 23For the wages of sin is death, but the gift of God is eternal
life in[a] Christ Jesus our Lord.

An Illustration From Marriage

7 Do you not know, brothers—for I am speaking to men who
know the law—that the law has authority over a man only as
long as he lives? 2For example, by law a married woman is
bound to her husband as long as he is alive, but if her husband
dies, she is released from the law of marriage. 3So then, if she
marries another man while her husband is still alive, she is
called an adulteress. But if her husband dies, she is released
from that law and is not an adulteress, even though she marries
another man.

4So, my brothers, you also died to the law through the body of
Christ, that you might belong to another, to him who was raised
from the dead, in order that we might bear fruit to God. 5For
when we were controlled by the sinful nature,[b] the sinful passions aroused by the law were at work in our bodies, so that we
bore fruit for death. 6But now, by dying to what once bound us,
we have been released from the law so that we serve in the new
way of the Spirit, and not in the old way of the written code.

[a]23 Or *through* [b]5 Or *the flesh*; also in verse 25

(6:8—7:6) "I have been crucified with Christ and I no longer live, but Christ lives in me. The life I live in the body, I live by faith in the Son of God, who loved me and gave himself for me." Lord, teach me the right way to live in freedom—not freedom to live in whatever manner I choose but freedom to live the way You have always wanted me to live. You have set me free from sin; now teach me to flee from sin. Teach me to walk in the new way of the Spirit. May I never bring shame or disgrace to the name of Jesus; rather, may I point the way for others to meet You and receive Your gift of grace as well. (Gal 2:20)

Praise the Lord, for He is gracious;
Never shall His promise fail;
God has made His saints victorious;
Sin and death shall not prevail.
Praise the God of our salvation;
Hosts on high, His power proclaim;
Heaven and earth, and all creation,
Laud and magnify His name.

"Praise the Lord! O Heavens, Adore Him"
The Foundling Hospital Collection,
London (1796)

(7:14—8:2) O Lord our Maker, You know our condition better than we know it ourselves. There is no one exempt from sin, no mortal so holy that he doesn't fail, no person so mature that she doesn't behave foolishly. Even Paul, Your servant, wrestled with sin just as I do. We all need You, Lord. And we thank You that now, through Christ Jesus, we no longer live under the pall of sin's darkness; we no longer face the penalty of death. You have pardoned us and set us free. You have commuted our sentence from death to eternal life through Jesus Christ, our Lord.

Now are we free—there's no
condemnation,
Jesus provides a perfect salvation;
"Come unto Me," O hear His sweet
call,
Come, and He saves us once for all.

Children of God, O glorious calling,
Surely His grace will keep us from
falling;
Passing from death to life at His call,
Blessed salvation once for all.

"Free from the Law"
Philip P. Bliss (1873)

Struggling With Sin

7What shall we say, then? Is the law sin? Certainly not! Indeed I
would not have known what sin was except through the law. For
I would not have known what coveting really was if the law had
not said, "Do not covet."[a] 8But sin, seizing the opportunity afforded by the commandment, produced in me every kind of cov-
etous desire. For apart from law, sin is dead. 9Once I was alive
apart from law; but when the commandment came, sin sprang to
life and I died. 10I found that the very commandment that was intended to bring life actually brought death. 11For sin, seizing the
opportunity afforded by the commandment, deceived me, and
through the commandment put me to death. 12So then, the law is
holy, and the commandment is holy, righteous and good.

13Did that which is good, then, become death to me? By no
means! But in order that sin might be recognized as sin, it produced death in me through what was good, so that through the
commandment sin might become utterly sinful.

14We know that the law is spiritual; but I am unspiritual, sold
as a slave to sin. 15I do not understand what I do. For what I want
to do I do not do, but what I hate I do. 16And if I do what I do not
want to do, I agree that the law is good. 17As it is, it is no longer
I myself who do it, but it is sin living in me. 18I know that nothing
good lives in me, that is, in my sinful nature.[b] For I have the desire to do what is good, but I cannot carry it out. 19For what I do
is not the good I want to do; no, the evil I do not want to do—this
I keep on doing. 20Now if I do what I do not want to do, it is no
longer I who do it, but it is sin living in me that does it.

21So I find this law at work: When I want to do good, evil is
right there with me. 22For in my inner being I delight in God's
law; 23but I see another law at work in the members of my body,
waging war against the law of my mind and making me a prisoner of the law of sin at work within my members. 24What a
wretched man I am! Who will rescue me from this body of death?
25Thanks be to God—through Jesus Christ our Lord!

So then, I myself in my mind am a slave to God's law, but in the
sinful nature a slave to the law of sin.

Life Through the Spirit

8 Therefore, there is now no condemnation for those who are
in Christ Jesus,[c] 2because through Christ Jesus the law of
the Spirit of life set me free from the law of sin and death. 3For
what the law was powerless to do in that it was weakened by the
sinful nature,[d] God did by sending his own Son in the likeness of
sinful man to be a sin offering.[e] And so he condemned sin in sinful man,[f] 4in order that the righteous requirements of the law
might be fully met in us, who do not live according to the sinful
nature but according to the Spirit.

5Those who live according to the sinful nature have their
minds set on what that nature desires; but those who live in accordance with the Spirit have their minds set on what the Spirit
desires. 6The mind of sinful man[g] is death, but the mind controlled by the Spirit is life and peace; 7the sinful mind[h] is hostile

[a] 7 Exodus 20:17; Deut. 5:21 [b] 18 Or *my flesh* [c] 1 Some later manuscripts *Jesus, who do not live according to the sinful nature but according to the Spirit,* [d] 3 Or *the flesh*; also in verses 4, 5, 8, 9, 12 and 13 [e] 3 Or *man, for sin* [f] 3 Or *in the flesh* [g] 6 Or *mind set on the flesh* [h] 7 Or *the mind set on the flesh*

to God. It does not submit to God's law, nor can it do so. 8Those
controlled by the sinful nature cannot please God.
9You, however, are controlled not by the sinful nature but by
the Spirit, if the Spirit of God lives in you. And if anyone does not
have the Spirit of Christ, he does not belong to Christ. 10But if
Christ is in you, your body is dead because of sin, yet your spirit
is alive because of righteousness. 11And if the Spirit of him who
raised Jesus from the dead is living in you, he who raised Christ
from the dead will also give life to your mortal bodies through his
Spirit, who lives in you.
12Therefore, brothers, we have an obligation—but it is not to
the sinful nature, to live according to it. 13For if you live according to the sinful nature, you will die; but if by the Spirit you put to
death the misdeeds of the body, you will live, 14because those
who are led by the Spirit of God are sons of God. 15For you did
not receive a spirit that makes you a slave again to fear, but you
received the Spirit of sonship.[a] And by him we cry, *"Abba,*[b] Father." 16The Spirit himself testifies with our spirit that we are
God's children. 17Now if we are children, then we are heirs—
heirs of God and co-heirs with Christ, if indeed we share in his
sufferings in order that we may also share in his glory.

Future Glory

18I consider that our present sufferings are not worth comparing with the glory that will be revealed in us. 19The creation
waits in eager expectation for the sons of God to be revealed.
20For the creation was subjected to frustration, not by its own
choice, but by the will of the one who subjected it, in hope 21that[c]
the creation itself will be liberated from its bondage to decay and
brought into the glorious freedom of the children of God.
22We know that the whole creation has been groaning as in the
pains of childbirth right up to the present time. 23Not only so, but
we ourselves, who have the firstfruits of the Spirit, groan inwardly as we wait eagerly for our adoption as sons, the redemption of
our bodies. 24For in this hope we were saved. But hope that is
seen is no hope at all. Who hopes for what he already has? 25But
if we hope for what we do not yet have, we wait for it patiently.
26In the same way, the Spirit helps us in our weakness. We do
not know what we ought to pray for, but the Spirit himself intercedes for us with groans that words cannot express. 27And he
who searches our hearts knows the mind of the Spirit, because
the Spirit intercedes for the saints in accordance with God's will.

More Than Conquerors

28And we know that in all things God works for the good of those
who love him,[d] who[e] have been called according to his purpose.
29For those God foreknew he also predestined to be conformed to
the likeness of his Son, that he might be the firstborn among many
brothers. 30And those he predestined, he also called; those he
called, he also justified; those he justified, he also glorified.
31What, then, shall we say in response to this? If God is for us,
who can be against us? 32He who did not spare his own Son, but
gave him up for us all—how will he not also, along with him,

[a] 15 Or *adoption* [b] 15 Aramaic for *Father* [c] 20,21 Or *subjected it in hope.* 21*For*
[d] 28 Some manuscripts *And we know that all things work together for good to those who love God* [e] 28 Or *works together with those who love him to bring about what is good—with those who*

(8:12–17) "How great is the love the Father has lavished on us, that we should be called children of God!" O Father, I praise You and thank You for Your mercy and love. I was once Your enemy; now I am Your heir. You saved me from the slavery of sin and gave me a new life in Christ. I pray, Father, lead me by Your Spirit and teach me to live a life that You can be proud of. Give me faith to surrender to You and to pray as Jesus prayed, "*Abba*, Father . . . not what I will, but what you will." (Mk 14:36; Gal 4:1–7; 1Jn 3:1)

Behold, what manner of love
The Father has given unto us,
Behold, what manner of love
The Father has given unto us;
That we should be called the sons of God,
That we should be called the sons of God.

"Behold What Manner of Love"
Patricia Van Tine (©1978)

This blessed name of Father . . . must underlie every other name by which he has ever been known. Has he been called a judge? Yes, but he is a father judge, one who judges as a loving father would. Is he a king? Yes, but he is a king who is at the same time the father of his subjects, and who rules them with a father's tenderness. Is he a lawgiver? Yes, but he is a lawgiver who gives laws as a father would, remembering the weakness and ignorance of his helpless children . . .

Never, never must we think of God in any other way than as "our Father." All other attributes with which we endow him in our conceptions must be based upon and limited by this one of "our Father."

Hannah Whitall Smith (1832-1911)

graciously give us all things? 33 Who will bring any charge against those whom God has chosen? It is God who justifies. 34 Who is he that condemns? Christ Jesus, who died—more than that, who was raised to life—is at the right hand of God and is also interceding for us. 35 Who shall separate us from the love of Christ? Shall trouble or hardship or persecution or famine or nakedness or danger or sword? 36 As it is written:

"For your sake we face death all day long;
we are considered as sheep to be slaughtered."[a]

37 No, in all these things we are more than conquerors through him who loved us. 38 For I am convinced that neither death nor life, neither angels nor demons,[b] neither the present nor the future, nor any powers, 39 neither height nor depth, nor anything else in all creation, will be able to separate us from the love of God that is in Christ Jesus our Lord.

(8:35–39) O Father, what greater words of comfort can there be than these? Nothing will ever separate me from Your love because I am in Christ—not merely with Christ, or beside Christ, or near Christ, but *in* Christ. In Christ, Who is seated at Your right hand and Who lives forever to intercede for us; in Christ, Who is the exact representation of Your being; in Christ, Who sustains all things by His powerful word; in Christ, Who is risen and exalted above all powers and dominions; in Christ, Who is the embodiment of Your love and compassion; in Christ, Who alone is able to keep me from falling and to present me before Your glorious presence without fault and with great joy. I am Yours in Christ, and in Christ I will be Yours forever! (Eph 1:20–21; Php 2:9–10; Heb 1:3; 7:24–25; Jude 24)

O the deep, deep love of Jesus,
Vast, unmeasured, boundless, free
Rolling as a mighty ocean
In its fullness over me.
Underneath me, all around me,
Is the current of Thy love;
Leading onward, leading homeward
To my glorious rest above.

O the deep, deep love of Jesus,
Spread His praise from shore to
shore!
How He loveth, ever loveth,
Changeth never, never more;
How He watches o'er His loved ones,
Died to call them all His own;
How for them He intercedeth,
Watcheth o'er them from the
throne.

"O the Deep, Deep Love of Jesus"
S. Trevor Francis (1890)

God's Sovereign Choice

9 I speak the truth in Christ—I am not lying, my conscience confirms it in the Holy Spirit— 2 I have great sorrow and unceasing anguish in my heart. 3 For I could wish that I myself were cursed and cut off from Christ for the sake of my brothers, those of my own race, 4 the people of Israel. Theirs is the adoption as sons; theirs the divine glory, the covenants, the receiving of the law, the temple worship and the promises. 5 Theirs are the patriarchs, and from them is traced the human ancestry of Christ, who is God over all, forever praised![c] Amen.

6 It is not as though God's word had failed. For not all who are descended from Israel are Israel. 7 Nor because they are his descendants are they all Abraham's children. On the contrary, "It is through Isaac that your offspring will be reckoned."[d] 8 In other words, it is not the natural children who are God's children, but it is the children of the promise who are regarded as Abraham's offspring. 9 For this was how the promise was stated: "At the appointed time I will return, and Sarah will have a son."[e]

10 Not only that, but Rebekah's children had one and the same father, our father Isaac. 11 Yet, before the twins were born or had done anything good or bad—in order that God's purpose in election might stand: 12 not by works but by him who calls—she was told, "The older will serve the younger."[f] 13 Just as it is written: "Jacob I loved, but Esau I hated."[g]

14 What then shall we say? Is God unjust? Not at all! 15 For he says to Moses,

"I will have mercy on whom I have mercy,
and I will have compassion on whom I have
compassion."[h]

16 It does not, therefore, depend on man's desire or effort, but on God's mercy. 17 For the Scripture says to Pharaoh: "I raised you up for this very purpose, that I might display my power in you and that my name might be proclaimed in all the earth."[i] 18 Therefore God has mercy on whom he wants to have mercy, and he hardens whom he wants to harden.

[a] *36* Psalm 44:22 [b] *38* Or *nor heavenly rulers* [c] *5* Or *Christ, who is over all. God be forever praised!* Or *Christ. God who is over all be forever praised!* [d] *7* Gen. 21:12 [e] *9* Gen. 18:10,14 [f] *12* Gen. 25:23 [g] *13* Mal. 1:2,3 [h] *15* Exodus 33:19 [i] *17* Exodus 9:16

19 One of you will say to me: "Then why does God still blame
us? For who resists his will?" 20 But who are you, O man, to talk
back to God? "Shall what is formed say to him who formed it,
'Why did you make me like this?' "[a] 21 Does not the potter have
the right to make out of the same lump of clay some pottery for
noble purposes and some for common use?
22 What if God, choosing to show his wrath and make his power
known, bore with great patience the objects of his wrath—prepared for destruction? 23 What if he did this to make the riches of
his glory known to the objects of his mercy, whom he prepared in
advance for glory— 24 even us, whom he also called, not only
from the Jews but also from the Gentiles? 25 As he says in Hosea:

"I will call them 'my people' who are not my people;
and I will call her 'my loved one' who is not my
loved one,"[b]

26 and,

"It will happen that in the very place where it was said
to them,
'You are not my people,'
they will be called 'sons of the living God.' "[c]

27 Isaiah cries out concerning Israel:

"Though the number of the Israelites be like the sand
by the sea,
only the remnant will be saved.
28 For the Lord will carry out
his sentence on earth with speed and finality."[d]

29 It is just as Isaiah said previously:

"Unless the Lord Almighty
had left us descendants,
we would have become like Sodom,
we would have been like Gomorrah."[e]

Israel's Unbelief

30 What then shall we say? That the Gentiles, who did not pursue righteousness, have obtained it, a righteousness that is by
faith; 31 but Israel, who pursued a law of righteousness, has not
attained it. 32 Why not? Because they pursued it not by faith but as
if it were by works. They stumbled over the "stumbling stone."
33 As it is written:

"See, I lay in Zion a stone that causes men to stumble
and a rock that makes them fall,
and the one who trusts in him will never be put to
shame."[f]

10 Brothers, my heart's desire and prayer to God for the Israelites is that they may be saved. 2 For I can testify about
them that they are zealous for God, but their zeal is not based on
knowledge. 3 Since they did not know the righteousness that
comes from God and sought to establish their own, they did not
submit to God's righteousness. 4 Christ is the end of the law so
that there may be righteousness for everyone who believes.

[a] 20 Isaiah 29:16; 45:9 [b] 25 Hosea 2:23 [c] 26 Hosea 1:10 [d] 28 Isaiah 10:22,23
[e] 29 Isaiah 1:9 [f] 33 Isaiah 8:14; 28:16

(9:20–26) You, O God, are sovereign. And You, O God, are free to act in whatever way You choose—with regard to my life and to all of humanity. All authority in heaven and on earth belongs to You. Justice and mercy are Yours. You have made Your salvation known and revealed Your righteousness to the nations. "May all who seek you rejoice and be glad in you; may those who love your salvation always say, 'The LORD be exalted!' " (Ps 40:16; 98:2)

Have Thine own way, Lord!
Have Thine own way!
Thou art the potter,
I am the clay!
Mold me and make me
After Thy will,
While I am waiting,
Yielded and still.

"Have Thine Own Way, Lord!"
Adelaide A. Pollard (1902)

[I] prayed for faith and thought that some day faith would come down and strike me like lightning. But faith did not seem to come. One day I read in the tenth chapter of Romans, "Faith cometh by hearing, and hearing by the Word of God." I had up to this time closed my Bible and prayed for faith. I now opened my Bible and began to study, and faith has been growing ever since.

Dwight Lyman Moody (1837-1899)

(10:8–17) Lord Jesus, I confess that I believe! You are the author of life, the author of our faith and the author of our salvation. Come, Author, and write Your Word on the tablet of my heart. Fill my heart with faith. Purify my lips. Give me boldness to declare the gospel. You are not ashamed to call us Your brothers and sisters; let me never be ashamed to call You my Lord. May the prayer of Isaiah be my prayer as well: "Here am I. Send me!" (Isa 6:7–8; Ac 3:15; Heb 2:10–11; 12:2)

Let me sow the seeds of life
To a parched and dying land,
Watering with Your words of love
So that they will understand
That the love that God has shed
upon us
Is a love that will never fade away.
Let me share it with the world.
I'll go, I'll be the one to go.

Here am I, send me.
Here am I, send me,
Until every nation knows
The power of Your love.
Give me a hunger to know
Where it is You want me to go.
Father, I'm saying
Here am I, send me.

"Send Me"
Denise Graves (©1995)

5Moses describes in this way the righteousness that is by the
law: "The man who does these things will live by them."[a] 6But the
righteousness that is by faith says: "Do not say in your heart, 'Who
will ascend into heaven?'[b]" (that is, to bring Christ down) 7"or
'Who will descend into the deep?'[c]" (that is, to bring Christ up
from the dead). 8But what does it say? "The word is near you; it
is in your mouth and in your heart,"[d] that is, the word of faith we
are proclaiming: 9That if you confess with your mouth, "Jesus is
Lord," and believe in your heart that God raised him from the
dead, you will be saved. 10For it is with your heart that you believe
and are justified, and it is with your mouth that you confess and
are saved. 11As the Scripture says, "Anyone who trusts in him will
never be put to shame."[e] 12For there is no difference between
Jew and Gentile—the same Lord is Lord of all and richly blesses
all who call on him, 13for, "Everyone who calls on the name of the
Lord will be saved."[f]

14How, then, can they call on the one they have not believed in?
And how can they believe in the one of whom they have not heard?
And how can they hear without someone preaching to them? 15And
how can they preach unless they are sent? As it is written, "How
beautiful are the feet of those who bring good news!"[g]

16But not all the Israelites accepted the good news. For Isaiah
says, "Lord, who has believed our message?"[h] 17Consequently,
faith comes from hearing the message, and the message is heard
through the word of Christ. 18But I ask: Did they not hear? Of
course they did:

"Their voice has gone out into all the earth,
their words to the ends of the world."[i]

19Again I ask: Did Israel not understand? First, Moses says,

"I will make you envious by those who are not a
nation;
I will make you angry by a nation that has no
understanding."[j]

20And Isaiah boldly says,

"I was found by those who did not seek me;
I revealed myself to those who did not ask
for me."[k]

21But concerning Israel he says,

"All day long I have held out my hands
to a disobedient and obstinate people."[l]

The Remnant of Israel

11 I ask then: Did God reject his people? By no means! I am an
Israelite myself, a descendant of Abraham, from the tribe of
Benjamin. 2God did not reject his people, whom he foreknew.
Don't you know what the Scripture says in the passage about Elijah—how he appealed to God against Israel: 3"Lord, they have
killed your prophets and torn down your altars; I am the only one
left, and they are trying to kill me"[m]? 4And what was God's answer to him? "I have reserved for myself seven thousand who have

[a] 5 Lev. 18:5 [b] 6 Deut. 30:12 [c] 7 Deut. 30:13 [d] 8 Deut. 30:14
[e] 11 Isaiah 28:16 [f] 13 Joel 2:32 [g] 15 Isaiah 52:7 [h] 16 Isaiah 53:1
[i] 18 Psalm 19:4 [j] 19 Deut. 32:21 [k] 20 Isaiah 65:1 [l] 21 Isaiah 65:2
[m] 3 1 Kings 19:10,14

not bowed the knee to Baal."[a] 5So too, at the present time there
is a remnant chosen by grace. 6And if by grace, then it is no
longer by works; if it were, grace would no longer be grace.[b]
7What then? What Israel sought so earnestly it did not obtain,
but the elect did. The others were hardened, 8as it is written:

"God gave them a spirit of stupor,
 eyes so that they could not see
 and ears so that they could not hear,
to this very day."[c]

9And David says:

"May their table become a snare and a trap,
 a stumbling block and a retribution for them.
10May their eyes be darkened so they cannot see,
 and their backs be bent forever."[d]

Ingrafted Branches

11Again I ask: Did they stumble so as to fall beyond recovery?
Not at all! Rather, because of their transgression, salvation has
come to the Gentiles to make Israel envious. 12But if their transgression means riches for the world, and their loss means riches
for the Gentiles, how much greater riches will their fullness bring!
13I am talking to you Gentiles. Inasmuch as I am the apostle to
the Gentiles, I make much of my ministry 14in the hope that I may
somehow arouse my own people to envy and save some of them.
15For if their rejection is the reconciliation of the world, what will
their acceptance be but life from the dead? 16If the part of the
dough offered as firstfruits is holy, then the whole batch is holy; if
the root is holy, so are the branches.
17If some of the branches have been broken off, and you,
though a wild olive shoot, have been grafted in among the others
and now share in the nourishing sap from the olive root, 18do
not boast over those branches. If you do, consider this: You do
not support the root, but the root supports you. 19You will say
then, "Branches were broken off so that I could be grafted in."
20Granted. But they were broken off because of unbelief, and you
stand by faith. Do not be arrogant, but be afraid. 21For if God did
not spare the natural branches, he will not spare you either.
22Consider therefore the kindness and sternness of God:
sternness to those who fell, but kindness to you, provided that
you continue in his kindness. Otherwise, you also will be cut off.
23And if they do not persist in unbelief, they will be grafted in, for
God is able to graft them in again. 24After all, if you were cut out
of an olive tree that is wild by nature, and contrary to nature
were grafted into a cultivated olive tree, how much more readily
will these, the natural branches, be grafted into their own olive
tree!

All Israel Will Be Saved

25I do not want you to be ignorant of this mystery, brothers, so
that you may not be conceited: Israel has experienced a hardening in part until the full number of the Gentiles has come in.
26And so all Israel will be saved, as it is written:

[a] 4 1 Kings 19:18 [b] 6 Some manuscripts *by grace. But if by works, then it is no longer grace; if it were, work would no longer be work.* [c] 8 Deut. 29:4; Isaiah 29:10
[d] 10 Psalm 69:22,23

(11:17–25) Father in heaven, thank You for grafting me into the tree of life in Christ—for making me a part of Your church, Your people. Father, I look forward with You to the day when all of Your people will be fully reconciled to You. I praise You for Your kindness that leads us to repentance and for Your sternness with which You discipline Your children whom You love. Lord, please keep me humble so that I may live in the joy of salvation.

(12:1–2) In light of Your kind mercy to me, dear Father, I offer to You my whole self without reservation, holding nothing back. My body is now Your temple. I am no longer my own; I was bought at a price. Therefore, I will honor You with my body. I will live as one who has been crucified with Christ, and who lives again in Him, through Him and for His glory. I bring every thought captive to obedience to Christ. I make a covenant with my eyes to keep them pure. I offer You my hands and feet for the service of Your ministry. Come and fill me with Your Spirit, Lord, and teach me to live a life that is worthy of Your calling and that conforms with Your good, pleasing and perfect will. (Job 31:1; Ro 6:1–8; 1Co 6:19–20; 2Co 10:5; Eph 2:10; 4:1)

If You asked me for an offering I'd give it,
If You wanted sacrifice I would obey.
But my life is all I have and I will live it,
Dedicated to the honor of Your name.
Gladly will I bow down as Your servant;
Gladly will I wait for Your command.
I commit my trust to You,
For You deserve it;
I delight within the guidance of Your hand.

Here I am, and I long to do Your will.
Here I am, I'll follow Your command.
Here I am, until my calling is fulfilled.
Here I am, here I am.

"Here I Am"
Bill Batstone (©1996)

Lord Jesus, all power is given to you in heaven and earth: transform our understandings and our wills; cleanse our hearts; send your Holy Spirit into our souls; subdue us to yourself, so that our flesh may be brought into subjection to the Spirit, and our affections made obedient to your pure and holy law, to the praise and glory of your sovereign grace.

Juan Luis Vives (1492-1540)

"The deliverer will come from Zion;
he will turn godlessness away from Jacob.
27 And this is[a] my covenant with them
when I take away their sins."[b]

28 As far as the gospel is concerned, they are enemies on your
account; but as far as election is concerned, they are loved on
account of the patriarchs, 29 for God's gifts and his call are irrevocable. 30 Just as you who were at one time disobedient to God
have now received mercy as a result of their disobedience, 31 so
they too have now become disobedient in order that they too may
now[c] receive mercy as a result of God's mercy to you. 32 For God
has bound all men over to disobedience so that he may have
mercy on them all.

Doxology

33 Oh, the depth of the riches of the wisdom and[d]
knowledge of God!
How unsearchable his judgments,
and his paths beyond tracing out!
34 "Who has known the mind of the Lord?
Or who has been his counselor?"[e]
35 "Who has ever given to God,
that God should repay him?"[f]
36 For from him and through him and to him are all
things.
To him be the glory forever! Amen.

Living Sacrifices

12 Therefore, I urge you, brothers, in view of God's mercy,
to offer your bodies as living sacrifices, holy and pleasing to God—this is your spiritual[g] act of worship. 2 Do not
conform any longer to the pattern of this world, but be transformed by the renewing of your mind. Then you will be able to
test and approve what God's will is—his good, pleasing and
perfect will.

3 For by the grace given me I say to every one of you: Do not
think of yourself more highly than you ought, but rather think of
yourself with sober judgment, in accordance with the measure of
faith God has given you. 4 Just as each of us has one body with
many members, and these members do not all have the same
function, 5 so in Christ we who are many form one body, and each
member belongs to all the others. 6 We have different gifts, according to the grace given us. If a man's gift is prophesying, let
him use it in proportion to his[h] faith. 7 If it is serving, let him
serve; if it is teaching, let him teach; 8 if it is encouraging, let him
encourage; if it is contributing to the needs of others, let him give
generously; if it is leadership, let him govern diligently; if it is
showing mercy, let him do it cheerfully.

Love

9 Love must be sincere. Hate what is evil; cling to what is good.
10 Be devoted to one another in brotherly love. Honor one another above yourselves. 11 Never be lacking in zeal, but keep your

[a] 27 Or *will be* [b] 27 Isaiah 59:20,21; 27:9; Jer. 31:33,34 [c] 31 Some manuscripts do not have *now.* [d] 33 Or *riches and the wisdom and the* [e] 34 Isaiah 40:13 [f] 35 Job 41:11 [g] 1 Or *reasonable* [h] 6 Or *in agreement with the*

spiritual fervor, serving the Lord. 12Be joyful in hope, patient in
affliction, faithful in prayer. 13Share with God's people who are in
need. Practice hospitality.

14Bless those who persecute you; bless and do not curse.
15Rejoice with those who rejoice; mourn with those who mourn.
16Live in harmony with one another. Do not be proud, but be
willing to associate with people of low position.[a] Do not be conceited.

17Do not repay anyone evil for evil. Be careful to do what is
right in the eyes of everybody. 18If it is possible, as far as it depends on you, live at peace with everyone. 19Do not take revenge, my friends, but leave room for God's wrath, for it is
written: "It is mine to avenge; I will repay,"[b] says the Lord. 20On
the contrary:

> "If your enemy is hungry, feed him;
> if he is thirsty, give him something to drink.
> In doing this, you will heap burning coals on his
> head."[c]

21Do not be overcome by evil, but overcome evil with good.

Submission to the Authorities

13 Everyone must submit himself to the governing authorities,
for there is no authority except that which God has established. The authorities that exist have been established by God.
2Consequently, he who rebels against the authority is rebelling
against what God has instituted, and those who do so will bring
judgment on themselves. 3For rulers hold no terror for those who
do right, but for those who do wrong. Do you want to be free
from fear of the one in authority? Then do what is right and he
will commend you. 4For he is God's servant to do you good. But
if you do wrong, be afraid, for he does not bear the sword for
nothing. He is God's servant, an agent of wrath to bring punishment on the wrongdoer. 5Therefore, it is necessary to submit to
the authorities, not only because of possible punishment but also
because of conscience.

6This is also why you pay taxes, for the authorities are God's
servants, who give their full time to governing. 7Give everyone
what you owe him: If you owe taxes, pay taxes; if revenue, then
revenue; if respect, then respect; if honor, then honor.

Love, for the Day Is Near

8Let no debt remain outstanding, except the continuing debt to
love one another, for he who loves his fellowman has fulfilled the
law. 9The commandments, "Do not commit adultery," "Do not
murder," "Do not steal," "Do not covet,"[d] and whatever other
commandment there may be, are summed up in this one rule:
"Love your neighbor as yourself."[e] 10Love does no harm to its
neighbor. Therefore love is the fulfillment of the law.

11And do this, understanding the present time. The hour has
come for you to wake up from your slumber, because our salvation is nearer now than when we first believed. 12The night is
nearly over; the day is almost here. So let us put aside the deeds
of darkness and put on the armor of light. 13Let us behave decently, as in the daytime, not in orgies and drunkenness, not

[a] *16* Or *willing to do menial work* [b] *19* Deut. 32:35 [c] *20* Prov. 25:21,22
[d] *9* Exodus 20:13–15,17; Deut. 5:17–19,21 [e] *9* Lev. 19:18

(12:12–21) Now that I am alive in Christ, help me to live like Christ. May the presence of Your Holy Spirit be manifested through my life to those around me. May I abound in the fruit of the Spirit—love, joy, peace, patience, kindness, goodness, faithfulness, gentleness and self-control. And let everything I do be done for Your glory, O God, and bring praise to Your holy name. (Gal 5:22–26; 1Pe 3:8–9)

Lord,
make me an instrument of your peace.
Where there is hatred, let me sow love;
where there is injury, pardon;
where there is doubt, faith;
where there is despair, hope;
where there is darkness, light; and
where there is sadness, joy.
O divine Master,
grant that I may not so much seek
to be consoled as to console;
to be understood as to understand;
to be loved as to love.
For it is in giving that we receive;
it is in pardoning that we are pardoned;
and it is in dying that we are born to eternal life.

Saint Francis of Assisi (1181–1226)

in sexual immorality and debauchery, not in dissension and jealousy. 14Rather, clothe yourselves with the Lord Jesus Christ, and do not think about how to gratify the desires of the sinful nature.[a]

The Weak and the Strong

14 Accept him whose faith is weak, without passing judgment on disputable matters. 2One man's faith allows him to eat everything, but another man, whose faith is weak, eats only vegetables. 3The man who eats everything must not look down on him who does not, and the man who does not eat everything must not condemn the man who does, for God has accepted him. 4Who are you to judge someone else's servant? To his own master he stands or falls. And he will stand, for the Lord is able to make him stand.

5One man considers one day more sacred than another; another man considers every day alike. Each one should be fully convinced in his own mind. 6He who regards one day as special, does so to the Lord. He who eats meat, eats to the Lord, for he gives thanks to God; and he who abstains, does so to the Lord and gives thanks to God. 7For none of us lives to himself alone and none of us dies to himself alone. 8If we live, we live to the Lord; and if we die, we die to the Lord. So, whether we live or die, we belong to the Lord.

9For this very reason, Christ died and returned to life so that he might be the Lord of both the dead and the living. 10You, then, why do you judge your brother? Or why do you look down on your brother? For we will all stand before God's judgment seat. 11It is written:

" 'As surely as I live,' says the Lord,
'every knee will bow before me;
every tongue will confess to God.' "[b]

12So then, each of us will give an account of himself to God.

13Therefore let us stop passing judgment on one another. Instead, make up your mind not to put any stumbling block or obstacle in your brother's way. 14As one who is in the Lord Jesus, I am fully convinced that no food[c] is unclean in itself. But if anyone regards something as unclean, then for him it is unclean. 15If your brother is distressed because of what you eat, you are no longer acting in love. Do not by your eating destroy your brother for whom Christ died. 16Do not allow what you consider good to be spoken of as evil. 17For the kingdom of God is not a matter of eating and drinking, but of righteousness, peace and joy in the Holy Spirit, 18because anyone who serves Christ in this way is pleasing to God and approved by men.

19Let us therefore make every effort to do what leads to peace and to mutual edification. 20Do not destroy the work of God for the sake of food. All food is clean, but it is wrong for a man to eat anything that causes someone else to stumble. 21It is better not to eat meat or drink wine or to do anything else that will cause your brother to fall.

22So whatever you believe about these things keep between yourself and God. Blessed is the man who does not condemn himself by what he approves. 23But the man who has doubts is

[a] 14 Or *the flesh* [b] 11 Isaiah 45:23 [c] 14 Or *that nothing*

(14:1–2) Thank You, Father, for the gift of people. Thank You for teaching us how to live with one another. Now please help us to put Your teaching into practice, so that we might live a life worthy of the calling we have received. Help us to serve one another in love, for "the entire law is summed up in a single command: 'Love your neighbor as yourself.' " Teach us to love one another as Christ loved the church and gave His life for our sakes. (Gal 5:13–14; Eph 4:1–6)

You learn to speak by speaking, to study by studying, to run by running, to work by working; and just so you learn to love God and man by loving. Begin as a mere apprentice, and the very power of love will lead you on to become a master of the art.
Saint Francis of Sales (1567-1622)

Oh, let us be the generation
Of reconciliation and peace,
And let us pray for restoration
And seek the Lord
Together on our knees,
Let us keep our hearts from evil
And cling to what is good.
Let us honor one another
And love the brotherhood.
Let us be the generation
Of reconciliation and peace.
"The Reconciliation Song"
Morris Chapman, Buddy Owens and Claire Cloninger (©1995)

condemned if he eats, because his eating is not from faith; and
everything that does not come from faith is sin.

15 We who are strong ought to bear with the failings of the
weak and not to please ourselves. 2Each of us should
please his neighbor for his good, to build him up. 3For even
Christ did not please himself but, as it is written: "The insults of
those who insult you have fallen on me."[a] 4For everything that
was written in the past was written to teach us, so that through endurance and the encouragement of the Scriptures we might have
hope.

5May the God who gives endurance and encouragement give
you a spirit of unity among yourselves as you follow Christ Jesus,
6so that with one heart and mouth you may glorify the God and
Father of our Lord Jesus Christ.

7Accept one another, then, just as Christ accepted you, in order
to bring praise to God. 8For I tell you that Christ has become a
servant of the Jews[b] on behalf of God's truth, to confirm the
promises made to the patriarchs 9so that the Gentiles may glorify God for his mercy, as it is written:

> "Therefore I will praise you among the Gentiles;
> I will sing hymns to your name."[c]

10Again, it says,

> "Rejoice, O Gentiles, with his people."[d]

11And again,

> "Praise the Lord, all you Gentiles,
> and sing praises to him, all you peoples."[e]

12And again, Isaiah says,

> "The Root of Jesse will spring up,
> one who will arise to rule over the nations;
> the Gentiles will hope in him."[f]

13May the God of hope fill you with all joy and peace as you
trust in him, so that you may overflow with hope by the power of
the Holy Spirit.

Paul the Minister to the Gentiles

14I myself am convinced, my brothers, that you yourselves are
full of goodness, complete in knowledge and competent to instruct one another. 15I have written you quite boldly on some
points, as if to remind you of them again, because of the grace
God gave me 16to be a minister of Christ Jesus to the Gentiles with
the priestly duty of proclaiming the gospel of God, so that the
Gentiles might become an offering acceptable to God, sanctified
by the Holy Spirit.

17Therefore I glory in Christ Jesus in my service to God. 18I
will not venture to speak of anything except what Christ has accomplished through me in leading the Gentiles to obey God by
what I have said and done— 19by the power of signs and miracles, through the power of the Spirit. So from Jerusalem all the
way around to Illyricum, I have fully proclaimed the gospel of
Christ. 20It has always been my ambition to preach the gospel

[a] *3* Psalm 69:9 [b] *8* Greek *circumcision* [c] *9* 2 Samuel 22:50; Psalm 18:49
[d] *10* Deut. 32:43 [e] *11* Psalm 117:1 [f] *12* Isaiah 11:10

(15:1–13) Lord Jesus, Suffering Servant, teach us to model ourselves after You. Fill our hearts with joy and thanksgiving as we share Your life and love with one another. By the power of Your Holy Spirit help us to protect and build up those who are weak. Bring all Your people together in unity, Lord—weak and strong, rich and poor, young and old—so that with one heart and one mind we might glorify our Father in heaven and bring praise to Your wonderful name.

Baptize us with Your love,
Enfold us with Your peace,
Uplift us with Your joy,
Unite us by Your Spirit.
Lord, we long to please You,
To glorify and bless You;
So we humbly say,
Father, have Your perfect way.

Forgive us for our sin,
Cleanse us from within,
Purify our hearts,
Conform us to Your likeness.
In all of our ways,
Through each and every day,
May we be Your hands
Reaching out to save the world.

"Baptize Us With Your Love"
Kelly Willard (©1999)

(15:30) Thank You, Father, for the fellowship of the Spirit in the body of Christ. Thank You that when we come to You in prayer we are joined to one another. How comforting it is to know that, even when I am separated physically from my brothers and sisters in Christ, I am never alone as long as I am in their prayers.

where Christ was not known, so that I would not be building on
someone else's foundation. 21 Rather, as it is written:

> "Those who were not told about him will see,
> and those who have not heard will understand."[a]

22 This is why I have often been hindered from coming to you.

Paul's Plan to Visit Rome

23 But now that there is no more place for me to work in these
regions, and since I have been longing for many years to see you,
24 I plan to do so when I go to Spain. I hope to visit you while
passing through and to have you assist me on my journey there,
after I have enjoyed your company for a while. 25 Now, however, I
am on my way to Jerusalem in the service of the saints there.
26 For Macedonia and Achaia were pleased to make a contribution for the poor among the saints in Jerusalem. 27 They were
pleased to do it, and indeed they owe it to them. For if the Gentiles have shared in the Jews' spiritual blessings, they owe it to the
Jews to share with them their material blessings. 28 So after I have
completed this task and have made sure that they have received
this fruit, I will go to Spain and visit you on the way. 29 I know that
when I come to you, I will come in the full measure of the blessing of Christ.

30 I urge you, brothers, by our Lord Jesus Christ and by the love
of the Spirit, to join me in my struggle by praying to God for me.
31 Pray that I may be rescued from the unbelievers in Judea and
that my service in Jerusalem may be acceptable to the saints
there, 32 so that by God's will I may come to you with joy and together with you be refreshed. 33 The God of peace be with you all.
Amen.

Personal Greetings

16 I commend to you our sister Phoebe, a servant[b] of the
church in Cenchrea. 2 I ask you to receive her in the Lord
in a way worthy of the saints and to give her any help she may
need from you, for she has been a great help to many people, including me.

3 Greet Priscilla[c] and Aquila, my fellow workers in Christ Jesus.
4 They risked their lives for me. Not only I but all the churches of the Gentiles are grateful to them.
5 Greet also the church that meets at their house.
Greet my dear friend Epenetus, who was the first convert to Christ in the province of Asia.
6 Greet Mary, who worked very hard for you.
7 Greet Andronicus and Junias, my relatives who have been in prison with me. They are outstanding among the apostles, and they were in Christ before I was.
8 Greet Ampliatus, whom I love in the Lord.
9 Greet Urbanus, our fellow worker in Christ, and my dear friend Stachys.
10 Greet Apelles, tested and approved in Christ.
Greet those who belong to the household of Aristobulus.
11 Greet Herodion, my relative.
Greet those in the household of Narcissus who are in the Lord.

[a] *21* Isaiah 52:15 [b] *1* Or *deaconess* [c] *3* Greek *Prisca*, a variant of *Priscilla*

12 Greet Tryphena and Tryphosa, those women who work hard in the Lord.
Greet my dear friend Persis, another woman who has worked very hard in the Lord.
13 Greet Rufus, chosen in the Lord, and his mother, who has been a mother to me, too.
14 Greet Asyncritus, Phlegon, Hermes, Patrobas, Hermas and the brothers with them.
15 Greet Philologus, Julia, Nereus and his sister, and Olympas and all the saints with them.
16 Greet one another with a holy kiss.
All the churches of Christ send greetings.

17 I urge you, brothers, to watch out for those who cause divisions and put obstacles in your way that are contrary to the teaching you have learned. Keep away from them. 18 For such people
are not serving our Lord Christ, but their own appetites. By
smooth talk and flattery they deceive the minds of naive people.
19 Everyone has heard about your obedience, so I am full of joy
over you; but I want you to be wise about what is good, and innocent about what is evil.
20 The God of peace will soon crush Satan under your feet.
The grace of our Lord Jesus be with you.
21 Timothy, my fellow worker, sends his greetings to you, as do
Lucius, Jason and Sosipater, my relatives.
22 I, Tertius, who wrote down this letter, greet you in the Lord.
23 Gaius, whose hospitality I and the whole church here enjoy,
sends you his greetings.
Erastus, who is the city's director of public works, and our
brother Quartus send you their greetings.[a]
25 Now to him who is able to establish you by my gospel and the
proclamation of Jesus Christ, according to the revelation of the
mystery hidden for long ages past, 26 but now revealed and made
known through the prophetic writings by the command of the
eternal God, so that all nations might believe and obey him—
27 to the only wise God be glory forever through Jesus Christ!
Amen.

[a] 23 Some manuscripts *their greetings. 24 May the grace of our Lord Jesus Christ be with all of you. Amen.*

(16:12–20) As I read through Paul's list of names, Father, I am stirred to know that Your temple—made from the living stones of saints and rising on the foundation of Christ—is both my home and my heritage. These names are my family members, limbs from which I branch. Teach me to honor my contemporary family members too, to love and pray for my brothers and sisters in Christ. I pledge to protect Your church from divisiveness and corruption and to serve side by side with my fellow workers in Your kingdom as we wait for the day of Christ's return. (1Co 3:11; Eph 2:19–22; 1Pe 2:4–6)

(16:25–27) O Lord, by Your Word You have revealed the mystery hidden for ages—that Jesus came to live and die and live again, not only in heaven but also in our hearts! By Your Word You are calling us to bear witness to that fact so that all people in all nations might believe in Him and obey Him. Use our lives, Lord. Fulfill in us Your call—to live the gospel humbly in our lives and to speak it boldly with our mouths, until every heart has heard the Good News of Jesus Christ. (Col 1:24–27)

Let the heavens be glad today,
Let the people of the earth rejoice.
Sing together in joyful praise
In the hope that we all share.
The Lord is on His way,
He will come to restore all things.
He will judge in righteousness,
Shout the message everywhere!

Our God reigns,
He reigns in righteousness;
A reign of righteousness
That will never end.
Our Lord comes
And every eye shall see
The Lord of majesty
When He comes again.

"Let The Heavens Be Glad"
Rick Founds (©1989)

The First Epistle of Paul the Apostle to the

CORINTHIANS

Corinthians

When we worship we utilize the forms of our particular culture. We cannot praise God in words unless we use human language. We cannot live in this world as Christians except by interacting with its values and institutions. How, then, can we be a holy people—set apart for God—if we cannot escape our own culture? How can we honor God in worship, using our cultural forms, yet without compromising God's holiness—and our own?

Paul wrestles with these challenges in 1 Corinthians. He writes "to the church of God in Corinth, to those sanctified in Christ Jesus and called to be holy" (1:2). Yet what motivates his letter is the absence of holiness among the Corinthian believers. As immature Christians, they have clung to the profane values of their culture, prizing religious experience, self-centered individualism, social privilege and personal freedom. Paul calls them to a new life, shaped not so much by their culture as by the gospel of the crucified Christ (1:17–18). Such Christ-centered living esteems revealed truth over spiritual experience (chs. 1—2), corporate growth over individual gain (ch. 14), counter-cultural concern over social privilege (chs. 8—11), self-giving love over self-expressive freedom (chs. 8—10,13). When we allow the gospel of Christ and the revealed Word of God to mold our lives, then we will live and worship as holy people.

How can we honor God in worship, using our cultural forms, yet without compromising God's holiness—and our own?

Although Paul alludes to his extensive private worship (14:18–19), his focus in this letter is upon corporate gatherings. He calls the Corinthians away from their self-absorption to a loving concern for one another and for the edification of the whole church (chs. 11—14). It is no accident that the "love chapter" (ch. 13), comes right in the middle of Paul's discussion of Corinthian worship. We will serve God fully and truly only when we serve one anther with a Christlike love. Love guides and gives eternal value to our acts of worship (13:1–3; 14:1).

Paul's counsel speaks incisively to us as well. Like the Corinthians, we can weigh corporate worship solely in terms of "what I got out of it." If our emotions are not moved, we can easily disparage our experience of church. How easily we forget Paul's exhortation that we seek to build up one another and not just ourselves in corporate gatherings. In fact, even our times of individual worship have communal ramifications, since they strengthen us for ministry to our fellow Christians. According to 1 Corinthians, the church is God's sacred temple, indwelt by the Holy Spirit (3:16–17). Thus, God is honored when we cherish and build up His church.

The Corinthians must have been astounded by Paul's references to the temple. Not only is the church a temple for God—so is the Christian's physical body! "Do you not know that your body is a temple of the Holy Spirit, who is in you, whom you have received from God?" (6:19). Contrary to the widespread pagan assumption that the gods lived in sacred buildings, Paul affirms that God dwells within each of us. Therefore we worship, not by going to some hallowed place but by honoring the Lord in every aspect of our lives—including bodily activities that might seem spiritually irrelevant (6:20). God is glorified as much by our moral purity as by our spiritual songs.

1 Paul, called to be an apostle of Christ Jesus by the will of God,
and our brother Sosthenes,
2To the church of God in Corinth, to those sanctified in Christ
Jesus and called to be holy, together with all those everywhere
who call on the name of our Lord Jesus Christ—their Lord and
ours:
3Grace and peace to you from God our Father and the Lord
Jesus Christ.

Thanksgiving

4I always thank God for you because of his grace given you in
Christ Jesus. 5For in him you have been enriched in every way—
in all your speaking and in all your knowledge— 6because our
testimony about Christ was confirmed in you. 7Therefore you do
not lack any spiritual gift as you eagerly wait for our Lord Jesus
Christ to be revealed. 8He will keep you strong to the end, so that
you will be blameless on the day of our Lord Jesus Christ. 9God,
who has called you into fellowship with his Son Jesus Christ our
Lord, is faithful.

Divisions in the Church

10I appeal to you, brothers, in the name of our Lord Jesus
Christ, that all of you agree with one another so that there may be
no divisions among you and that you may be perfectly united in
mind and thought. 11My brothers, some from Chloe's household
have informed me that there are quarrels among you. 12What I
mean is this: One of you says, "I follow Paul"; another, "I follow
Apollos"; another, "I follow Cephas[a]"; still another, "I follow
Christ."
13Is Christ divided? Was Paul crucified for you? Were you baptized into[b] the name of Paul? 14I am thankful that I did not baptize any of you except Crispus and Gaius, 15so no one can say that
you were baptized into my name. 16(Yes, I also baptized the
household of Stephanas; beyond that, I don't remember if I baptized anyone else.) 17For Christ did not send me to baptize, but to
preach the gospel—not with words of human wisdom, lest the
cross of Christ be emptied of its power.

Christ the Wisdom and Power of God

18For the message of the cross is foolishness to those who are
perishing, but to us who are being saved it is the power of God.
19For it is written:

"I will destroy the wisdom of the wise;
the intelligence of the intelligent I will frustrate."[c]

20Where is the wise man? Where is the scholar? Where is the
philosopher of this age? Has not God made foolish the wisdom of
the world? 21For since in the wisdom of God the world through its
wisdom did not know him, God was pleased through the foolishness of what was preached to save those who believe. 22Jews demand miraculous signs and Greeks look for wisdom, 23but we
preach Christ crucified: a stumbling block to Jews and foolishness to Gentiles, 24but to those whom God has called, both Jews
and Greeks, Christ the power of God and the wisdom of God.

[a] *12* That is, Peter [b] *13* Or *in*; also in verse 15 [c] *19* Isaiah 29:14

(1:20–21) Lord, You hide Your message in simple words offered by ordinary people living unadorned lives. Their eyes see You so readily. Their ears tune easily to Your voice. Your wisdom is not wasted on the arrogant but lavished on the humble into whose hearts You pour vast oceans of grace and forgiveness. How it must make You smile when one searching soul hears Your voice for the first time, looks into Your eyes and believes!

God entrusted his reputation to ordinary people. Yet in some way invisible to us, those ordinary people filled with the Spirit are helping to restore the universe to its place under the reign of God. At our repentance, the angels rejoice. By our prayers, mountains are moved.

Philip Yancey (1949-)

Forbid it, Lord, that I should boast,
Save in the death of Christ, my God.
All the vain things that charm me most,
I sacrifice them to His blood.

Were the whole realm of nature mine,
That were a present far too small.
Love so amazing, so divine,
Demands my soul, my life, my all!

"When I Survey The Wondrous Cross"
Isaac Watts (1707)

25 For the foolishness of God is wiser than man's wisdom, and the
weakness of God is stronger than man's strength.
26 Brothers, think of what you were when you were called. Not
many of you were wise by human standards; not many were in-
fluential; not many were of noble birth. 27 But God chose the foolish things of the world to shame the wise; God chose the weak
things of the world to shame the strong. 28 He chose the lowly
things of this world and the despised things—and the things that
are not—to nullify the things that are, 29 so that no one may boast
before him. 30 It is because of him that you are in Christ Jesus,
who has become for us wisdom from God—that is, our righteousness, holiness and redemption. 31 Therefore, as it is written:
"Let him who boasts boast in the Lord."[a]

2 When I came to you, brothers, I did not come with eloquence
or superior wisdom as I proclaimed to you the testimony
about God.[b] 2 For I resolved to know nothing while I was with you
except Jesus Christ and him crucified. 3 I came to you in weakness
and fear, and with much trembling. 4 My message and my preaching were not with wise and persuasive words, but with a demonstration of the Spirit's power, 5 so that your faith might not rest on
men's wisdom, but on God's power.

Wisdom From the Spirit

6 We do, however, speak a message of wisdom among the mature, but not the wisdom of this age or of the rulers of this age,
who are coming to nothing. 7 No, we speak of God's secret wisdom, a wisdom that has been hidden and that God destined for
our glory before time began. 8 None of the rulers of this age understood it, for if they had, they would not have crucified the Lord
of glory. 9 However, as it is written:

"No eye has seen,
 no ear has heard,
no mind has conceived
 what God has prepared for those who love
  him"[c]—

10 but God has revealed it to us by his Spirit.
The Spirit searches all things, even the deep things of God.
11 For who among men knows the thoughts of a man except the
man's spirit within him? In the same way no one knows the
thoughts of God except the Spirit of God. 12 We have not received
the spirit of the world but the Spirit who is from God, that we may
understand what God has freely given us. 13 This is what we speak,
not in words taught us by human wisdom but in words taught by
the Spirit, expressing spiritual truths in spiritual words.[d] 14 The
man without the Spirit does not accept the things that come from
the Spirit of God, for they are foolishness to him, and he cannot
understand them, because they are spiritually discerned. 15 The
spiritual man makes judgments about all things, but he himself is
not subject to any man's judgment:

16 "For who has known the mind of the Lord
 that he may instruct him?"[e]

But we have the mind of Christ.

[a] 31 Jer. 9:24 [b] 1 Some manuscripts *as I proclaimed to you God's mystery*
[c] 9 Isaiah 64:4 [d] 13 Or *Spirit, interpreting spiritual truths to spiritual men*
[e] 16 Isaiah 40:13

(2:7–9) Father of light, Creator and Keeper of mysteries, we, Your children, sit in the back row of humanity's classroom, failing the test on the wisdom of this age. Yet even as honors are bestowed on those who bow to mortal knowledge, You reveal the wealth of heaven's secrets to those You have called Your own. The others don't see You standing outside, smiling, waiting for the bell. But we who do are eager to spill out of the school doors and run into Your waiting arms. (Ps 25:14)

(2:14) O magnificent Holy Spirit, God's heart in flight, You are Grace and Truth racing through a soul's dark house plugging in lights, turning on heat, opening doors long locked. And when those doors are thrown open the stale, unlit spaces freshly fill with Your sweet breath and radiant light. Only You can answer faith's faintest whisper with such swift understanding! You alone bring wisdom . . . the Spirit's housewarming gift.

On Divisions in the Church

3 Brothers, I could not address you as spiritual but as worldly—mere infants in Christ. 2I gave you milk, not solid food,
for you were not yet ready for it. Indeed, you are still not ready.
3You are still worldly. For since there is jealousy and quarreling
among you, are you not worldly? Are you not acting like mere
men? 4For when one says, "I follow Paul," and another, "I follow
Apollos," are you not mere men?
5What, after all, is Apollos? And what is Paul? Only servants,
through whom you came to believe—as the Lord has assigned to
each his task. 6I planted the seed, Apollos watered it, but God
made it grow. 7So neither he who plants nor he who waters is
anything, but only God, who makes things grow. 8The man who
plants and the man who waters have one purpose, and each will
be rewarded according to his own labor. 9For we are God's fellow
workers; you are God's field, God's building.
10By the grace God has given me, I laid a foundation as an expert builder, and someone else is building on it. But each one
should be careful how he builds. 11For no one can lay any foundation other than the one already laid, which is Jesus Christ. 12If
any man builds on this foundation using gold, silver, costly
stones, wood, hay or straw, 13his work will be shown for what it
is, because the Day will bring it to light. It will be revealed with
fire, and the fire will test the quality of each man's work. 14If what
he has built survives, he will receive his reward. 15If it is burned
up, he will suffer loss; he himself will be saved, but only as one
escaping through the flames.
16Don't you know that you yourselves are God's temple and
that God's Spirit lives in you? 17If anyone destroys God's temple,
God will destroy him; for God's temple is sacred, and you are that
temple.
18Do not deceive yourselves. If any one of you thinks he is wise
by the standards of this age, he should become a "fool" so that he
may become wise. 19For the wisdom of this world is foolishness
in God's sight. As it is written: "He catches the wise in their craftiness"[a]; 20and again, "The Lord knows that the thoughts of the
wise are futile."[b] 21So then, no more boasting about men! All
things are yours, 22whether Paul or Apollos or Cephas[c] or the
world or life or death or the present or the future—all are yours,
23and you are of Christ, and Christ is of God.

Apostles of Christ

4 So then, men ought to regard us as servants of Christ and as
those entrusted with the secret things of God. 2Now it is required that those who have been given a trust must prove faithful.
3I care very little if I am judged by you or by any human court; indeed, I do not even judge myself. 4My conscience is clear, but
that does not make me innocent. It is the Lord who judges me.
5Therefore judge nothing before the appointed time; wait till the
Lord comes. He will bring to light what is hidden in darkness and
will expose the motives of men's hearts. At that time each will receive his praise from God.
6Now, brothers, I have applied these things to myself and Apollos for your benefit, so that you may learn from us the meaning of
the saying, "Do not go beyond what is written." Then you will not

[a] *19* Job 5:13 [b] *20* Psalm 94:11 [c] *22* That is, Peter

(3:12–15) Lord Jesus, Lord of the Day, Your pledge of judgment at once terrifies and comforts me. I know Your fire may reduce much of my life's work to ashes. Yet in the end I will know You cherished me—not simply what I did or what I said; but *me.* There I will be, standing tall among the ashes—me, the person You love, the one for whom You died.

Before the judgment seat of Christ my service will not be judged by how much I have done . . . but by how much of me there is in it. No man gives at all until he has given all. No man gives anything acceptable to God until he has first given himself in love and sacrifice.

A.W. Tozer (1897-1963)

(4:20) Master, You are at once my intimate Friend and a total stranger, unfathomable in Your righteousness and power. How I yearn for Your promised power in my life. How I long to live in Your kingdom! Yet vainly I prattle on as though my words had weight and my notions glory. Silence my self-indulgent chatter and fill me with awe! Blow Your mighty wind and whisk away my words like leaves, that I might be left as bare branches silently awaiting the mysterious renewal that one word from You will bring.

(5:9–11) Lord Jesus, Friend of sinners, You scolded religious hypocrites whose hearts were cold and empty. Yet You loved pagans with bad reputations. I sometimes forget Your example and get these things all turned around. I so quickly condemn the unsaved for their sins, when they are just doing what sinners do; but I wink at the sin in my brother's life, as though somehow his good works will make up for his disobedience. Lord, forgive me for tolerating sin in my own heart and in the life of Your church. Give me a heart that warmly accepts those who have not yet heard Your voice and arms that fearlessly embrace those who need You most. You befriended me when I was lost in sin. So with Your help, and as an act of worship, I too will be a friend of sinners. (Mt 9:10–13; 11:19; 15:8; Jn 3:17)

take pride in one man over against another. 7For who makes you
different from anyone else? What do you have that you did not receive? And if you did receive it, why do you boast as though you
did not?
8Already you have all you want! Already you have become rich!
You have become kings—and that without us! How I wish that
you really had become kings so that we might be kings with you!
9For it seems to me that God has put us apostles on display at the
end of the procession, like men condemned to die in the arena.
We have been made a spectacle to the whole universe, to angels
as well as to men. 10We are fools for Christ, but you are so wise
in Christ! We are weak, but you are strong! You are honored, we
are dishonored! 11To this very hour we go hungry and thirsty, we
are in rags, we are brutally treated, we are homeless. 12We work
hard with our own hands. When we are cursed, we bless; when
we are persecuted, we endure it; 13when we are slandered, we
answer kindly. Up to this moment we have become the scum of
the earth, the refuse of the world.
14I am not writing this to shame you, but to warn you, as my
dear children. 15Even though you have ten thousand guardians in
Christ, you do not have many fathers, for in Christ Jesus I became
your father through the gospel. 16Therefore I urge you to imitate
me. 17For this reason I am sending to you Timothy, my son whom
I love, who is faithful in the Lord. He will remind you of my way
of life in Christ Jesus, which agrees with what I teach everywhere
in every church.
18Some of you have become arrogant, as if I were not coming
to you. 19But I will come to you very soon, if the Lord is willing,
and then I will find out not only how these arrogant people are
talking, but what power they have. 20For the kingdom of God is
not a matter of talk but of power. 21What do you prefer? Shall I
come to you with a whip, or in love and with a gentle spirit?

Expel the Immoral Brother!

5 It is actually reported that there is sexual immorality among
you, and of a kind that does not occur even among pagans: A
man has his father's wife. 2And you are proud! Shouldn't you
rather have been filled with grief and have put out of your fellowship the man who did this? 3Even though I am not physically present, I am with you in spirit. And I have already passed judgment
on the one who did this, just as if I were present. 4When you are
assembled in the name of our Lord Jesus and I am with you in
spirit, and the power of our Lord Jesus is present, 5hand this man
over to Satan, so that the sinful nature[a] may be destroyed and his
spirit saved on the day of the Lord.
6Your boasting is not good. Don't you know that a little yeast
works through the whole batch of dough? 7Get rid of the old yeast
that you may be a new batch without yeast—as you really are. For
Christ, our Passover lamb, has been sacrificed. 8Therefore let us
keep the Festival, not with the old yeast, the yeast of malice and
wickedness, but with bread without yeast, the bread of sincerity
and truth.
9I have written you in my letter not to associate with sexually
immoral people— 10not at all meaning the people of this world
who are immoral, or the greedy and swindlers, or idolaters. In

[a]5 Or *that his body*; or *that the flesh*

that case you would have to leave this world. 11But now I am writing you that you must not associate with anyone who calls himself a brother but is sexually immoral or greedy, an idolater or a slanderer, a drunkard or a swindler. With such a man do not even eat.

12What business is it of mine to judge those outside the church? Are you not to judge those inside? 13God will judge those outside. "Expel the wicked man from among you."[a]

Lawsuits Among Believers

6 If any of you has a dispute with another, dare he take it before the ungodly for judgment instead of before the saints? 2Do you not know that the saints will judge the world? And if you are to judge the world, are you not competent to judge trivial cases? 3Do you not know that we will judge angels? How much more the things of this life! 4Therefore, if you have disputes about such matters, appoint as judges even men of little account in the church![b] 5I say this to shame you. Is it possible that there is nobody among you wise enough to judge a dispute between believers? 6But instead, one brother goes to law against another—and this in front of unbelievers!

7The very fact that you have lawsuits among you means you have been completely defeated already. Why not rather be wronged? Why not rather be cheated? 8Instead, you yourselves cheat and do wrong, and you do this to your brothers.

9Do you not know that the wicked will not inherit the kingdom of God? Do not be deceived: Neither the sexually immoral nor idolaters nor adulterers nor male prostitutes nor homosexual offenders 10nor thieves nor the greedy nor drunkards nor slanderers nor swindlers will inherit the kingdom of God. 11And that is what some of you were. But you were washed, you were sanctified, you were justified in the name of the Lord Jesus Christ and by the Spirit of our God.

Sexual Immorality

12"Everything is permissible for me"—but not everything is beneficial. "Everything is permissible for me"—but I will not be mastered by anything. 13"Food for the stomach and the stomach for food"—but God will destroy them both. The body is not meant for sexual immorality, but for the Lord, and the Lord for the body. 14By his power God raised the Lord from the dead, and he will raise us also. 15Do you not know that your bodies are members of Christ himself? Shall I then take the members of Christ and unite them with a prostitute? Never! 16Do you not know that he who unites himself with a prostitute is one with her in body? For it is said, "The two will become one flesh."[c] 17But he who unites himself with the Lord is one with him in spirit.

18Flee from sexual immorality. All other sins a man commits are outside his body, but he who sins sexually sins against his own body. 19Do you not know that your body is a temple of the Holy Spirit, who is in you, whom you have received from God? You are not your own; 20you were bought at a price. Therefore honor God with your body.

[a] *13* Deut. 17:7; 19:19; 21:21; 22:21,24; 24:7 [b] *4* Or *matters, do you appoint as judges men of little account in the church?* [c] *16* Gen. 2:24

(6:11) Of the many wonders of Your world, Savior, these three words tell so much about You—*wash, sanctify* and *justify*. And I have experienced each of them firsthand! In Your giant, gentle hands this grimy sinner has been washed clean, acquitted of all crimes. Unstained! Unpolluted! And, as if that were not enough, made an heir. You freely gave me what I could not give myself: a bath, a robe, a name.

(6:19) Precious Jesus, forgive me for disparaging this temple's value. I have lived to please myself, often forgetting that this flesh, these bones are to be a living sacrifice. How it must hurt You when I diminish the worth of Your sacred residence, behaving as though only mind and spirit matter. After all, You gave Your body for me! The very least I can do is to honor You with mine. (Ro 12:1; 1Co 3:16)

He belongs to you, but more than that, he longs to be in you, living and ruling in you as the head lives and rules in the body. He wants his breath to be in your breath, his heart in your heart, and his soul in your soul, so that you may indeed "Glorify God and bear him in your body, that the life of Jesus may be made manifest in you."

Jean Eudes (1601–1680)

Marriage

7 Now for the matters you wrote about: It is good for a man not
to marry.[a] 2But since there is so much immorality, each man
should have his own wife, and each woman her own husband.
3The husband should fulfill his marital duty to his wife, and likewise the wife to her husband. 4The wife's body does not belong to
her alone but also to her husband. In the same way, the husband's
body does not belong to him alone but also to his wife. 5Do not
deprive each other except by mutual consent and for a time, so
that you may devote yourselves to prayer. Then come together
again so that Satan will not tempt you because of your lack of self-
control. 6I say this as a concession, not as a command. 7I wish
that all men were as I am. But each man has his own gift from
God; one has this gift, another has that.
8Now to the unmarried and the widows I say: It is good for
them to stay unmarried, as I am. 9But if they cannot control themselves, they should marry, for it is better to marry than to burn
with passion.
10To the married I give this command (not I, but the Lord): A
wife must not separate from her husband. 11But if she does, she
must remain unmarried or else be reconciled to her husband.
And a husband must not divorce his wife.
12To the rest I say this (I, not the Lord): If any brother has a
wife who is not a believer and she is willing to live with him, he
must not divorce her. 13And if a woman has a husband who is not
a believer and he is willing to live with her, she must not divorce
him. 14For the unbelieving husband has been sanctified through
his wife, and the unbelieving wife has been sanctified through her
believing husband. Otherwise your children would be unclean,
but as it is, they are holy.
15But if the unbeliever leaves, let him do so. A believing man or
woman is not bound in such circumstances; God has called us to
live in peace. 16How do you know, wife, whether you will save
your husband? Or, how do you know, husband, whether you will
save your wife?
17Nevertheless, each one should retain the place in life that the
Lord assigned to him and to which God has called him. This is the
rule I lay down in all the churches. 18Was a man already circumcised when he was called? He should not become uncircumcised.
Was a man uncircumcised when he was called? He should not be
circumcised. 19Circumcision is nothing and uncircumcision is
nothing. Keeping God's commands is what counts. 20Each one
should remain in the situation which he was in when God called
him. 21Were you a slave when you were called? Don't let it trouble you—although if you can gain your freedom, do so. 22For he
who was a slave when he was called by the Lord is the Lord's
freedman; similarly, he who was a free man when he was called
is Christ's slave. 23You were bought at a price; do not become
slaves of men. 24Brothers, each man, as responsible to God,
should remain in the situation God called him to.
25Now about virgins: I have no command from the Lord, but I
give a judgment as one who by the Lord's mercy is trustworthy.
26Because of the present crisis, I think that it is good for you to
remain as you are. 27Are you married? Do not seek a divorce. Are
you unmarried? Do not look for a wife. 28But if you do marry, you

[a] 1 Or *"It is good for a man not to have sexual relations with a woman."*

(7:3–4) God, You are the Great Architect of Life, Who gives each wedded couple Your set of blueprints for a cathedral called Marriage. You so graciously give us ways and means, tools and arts for fashioning its rooms. Help us trust Your flawless design! Live with us, as over the years we build each magnificent space and spire, every intimate chamber. Let our cathedral glorify You, Lord. May its beauty delight you.

have not sinned; and if a virgin marries, she has not sinned. But
those who marry will face many troubles in this life, and I want to
spare you this.
29 What I mean, brothers, is that the time is short. From now on
those who have wives should live as if they had none; 30 those who
mourn, as if they did not; those who are happy, as if they were
not; those who buy something, as if it were not theirs to keep;
31 those who use the things of the world, as if not engrossed in
them. For this world in its present form is passing away.
32 I would like you to be free from concern. An unmarried man
is concerned about the Lord's affairs—how he can please the
Lord. 33 But a married man is concerned about the affairs of this
world—how he can please his wife— 34 and his interests are divided. An unmarried woman or virgin is concerned about the
Lord's affairs: Her aim is to be devoted to the Lord in both body
and spirit. But a married woman is concerned about the affairs of
this world—how she can please her husband. 35 I am saying this
for your own good, not to restrict you, but that you may live in a
right way in undivided devotion to the Lord.
36 If anyone thinks he is acting improperly toward the virgin he
is engaged to, and if she is getting along in years and he feels he
ought to marry, he should do as he wants. He is not sinning. They
should get married. 37 But the man who has settled the matter in
his own mind, who is under no compulsion but has control over
his own will, and who has made up his mind not to marry the virgin—this man also does the right thing. 38 So then, he who marries the virgin does right, but he who does not marry her does
even better.[a]
39 A woman is bound to her husband as long as he lives. But if
her husband dies, she is free to marry anyone she wishes, but he
must belong to the Lord. 40 In my judgment, she is happier if she
stays as she is—and I think that I too have the Spirit of God.

Food Sacrificed to Idols

8 Now about food sacrificed to idols: We know that we all possess knowledge.[b] Knowledge puffs up, but love builds up.
2 The man who thinks he knows something does not yet know as
he ought to know. 3 But the man who loves God is known by God.
4 So then, about eating food sacrificed to idols: We know that
an idol is nothing at all in the world and that there is no God but
one. 5 For even if there are so-called gods, whether in heaven or
on earth (as indeed there are many "gods" and many "lords"),
6 yet for us there is but one God, the Father, from whom all things
came and for whom we live; and there is but one Lord, Jesus
Christ, through whom all things came and through whom we live.
7 But not everyone knows this. Some people are still so accustomed to idols that when they eat such food they think of it as
having been sacrificed to an idol, and since their conscience is
weak, it is defiled. 8 But food does not bring us near to God; we
are no worse if we do not eat, and no better if we do.
9 Be careful, however, that the exercise of your freedom does

[a] *36–38* Or 36 *If anyone thinks he is not treating his daughter properly, and if she is getting along in years, and he feels she ought to marry, he should do as he wants. He is not sinning. He should let her get married.* 37 *But the man who has settled the matter in his own mind, who is under no compulsion but has control over his own will, and who has made up his mind to keep the virgin unmarried—this man also does the right thing.* 38 *So then, he who gives his virgin in marriage does right, but he who does not give her in marriage does even better.* [b] *1* Or *"We all possess knowledge," as you say*

(8:3) I may think I know all about You, that I have You all figured out, that I know all the rules to keep and the steps to take to win Your approval. But the real issue is not what I know; the real issue is whom You know. You look for love, not laws. You look at my heart, not just my actions. The test boils down to one question: Do I love You? For if I love You, then You know me; but if I do not love You, then none of my religious activities or abstinences will count for anything. O God, I do love You. Help me to love You more.

Eternal light, shine in my heart;
Eternal hope, lift up my eyes;
Eternal power, be my support;
Eternal wisdom, make me wise.

Until by Your most costly grace,
Invited by Your holy Word,
At last I come before Your face
To know You, my eternal God.

"Eternal Light, Shine in My Heart"
Christopher Idle (©1982)

(8:13) Father, You are the Source of all pleasures, and You give them to Your children for their delight. Yet sometimes You ask me to set aside enjoyment to help save a soul. When I look at what You gave up to save mine, I see my sacrifice as insignificant. Please accept my simple offering, honor it and bless my friend.

Let it be said of us:
We were marked by forgiveness,
We were known by our love,
And delighted in meekness.
We were ruled by His peace,
Heeding unity's call;
Joined as one body
That Christ would be seen by all.

"Let It Be Said of Us"
Steve Fry (©1996)

(9:19) Jesus, You empower free men and women to become willing slaves to all, so that many might come to You. In the light of that truth, I confess that I have been a slave to few. Forgive me! Here are my hands; put Your chains around them. Here are my feet; lock them in Your shackles. Here is my life, Lord; my freedom freely given as a sacrifice for You to use as You please.

We do not have to give up our reason, our intelligence, our knowledge, our faculty to judge, nor our emotions, our likes, our desires, our instincts, our conscious and unconscious aspirations, but rather to place them all in God's hands, so that he may direct, stimulate, fertilize, develop, and use them.

Paul Tournier (1898–1986)

not become a stumbling block to the weak. 10For if anyone with
a weak conscience sees you who have this knowledge eating in
an idol's temple, won't he be emboldened to eat what has been
sacrificed to idols? 11So this weak brother, for whom Christ died,
is destroyed by your knowledge. 12When you sin against your
brothers in this way and wound their weak conscience, you sin
against Christ. 13Therefore, if what I eat causes my brother to
fall into sin, I will never eat meat again, so that I will not cause
him to fall.

The Rights of an Apostle

9 Am I not free? Am I not an apostle? Have I not seen Jesus our
Lord? Are you not the result of my work in the Lord? 2Even
though I may not be an apostle to others, surely I am to you! For
you are the seal of my apostleship in the Lord.

3This is my defense to those who sit in judgment on me. 4Don't
we have the right to food and drink? 5Don't we have the right to
take a believing wife along with us, as do the other apostles and
the Lord's brothers and Cephas[a]? 6Or is it only I and Barnabas
who must work for a living?

7Who serves as a soldier at his own expense? Who plants a
vineyard and does not eat of its grapes? Who tends a flock and
does not drink of the milk? 8Do I say this merely from a human
point of view? Doesn't the Law say the same thing? 9For it is written in the Law of Moses: "Do not muzzle an ox while it is treading
out the grain."[b] Is it about oxen that God is concerned? 10Surely
he says this for us, doesn't he? Yes, this was written for us, because when the plowman plows and the thresher threshes, they
ought to do so in the hope of sharing in the harvest. 11If we have
sown spiritual seed among you, is it too much if we reap a material harvest from you? 12If others have this right of support from
you, shouldn't we have it all the more?

But we did not use this right. On the contrary, we put up with
anything rather than hinder the gospel of Christ. 13Don't you
know that those who work in the temple get their food from the
temple, and those who serve at the altar share in what is offered
on the altar? 14In the same way, the Lord has commanded that
those who preach the gospel should receive their living from the
gospel.

15But I have not used any of these rights. And I am not writing
this in the hope that you will do such things for me. I would
rather die than have anyone deprive me of this boast. 16Yet when
I preach the gospel, I cannot boast, for I am compelled to preach.
Woe to me if I do not preach the gospel! 17If I preach voluntarily, I have a reward; if not voluntarily, I am simply discharging the
trust committed to me. 18What then is my reward? Just this: that
in preaching the gospel I may offer it free of charge, and so not
make use of my rights in preaching it.

19Though I am free and belong to no man, I make myself a
slave to everyone, to win as many as possible. 20To the Jews I became like a Jew, to win the Jews. To those under the law I became
like one under the law (though I myself am not under the law),
so as to win those under the law. 21To those not having the law I
became like one not having the law (though I am not free from
God's law but am under Christ's law), so as to win those not hav-

[a] 5 That is, Peter [b] 9 Deut. 25:4

ing the law. 22To the weak I became weak, to win the weak. I have
become all things to all men so that by all possible means I might
save some. 23I do all this for the sake of the gospel, that I may
share in its blessings.

24Do you not know that in a race all the runners run, but only
one gets the prize? Run in such a way as to get the prize. 25Every-
one who competes in the games goes into strict training. They do
it to get a crown that will not last; but we do it to get a crown that
will last forever. 26Therefore I do not run like a man running aim-
lessly; I do not fight like a man beating the air. 27No, I beat my
body and make it my slave so that after I have preached to others,
I myself will not be disqualified for the prize.

Warnings From Israel's History

10 For I do not want you to be ignorant of the fact, brothers,
that our forefathers were all under the cloud and that they
all passed through the sea. 2They were all baptized into Moses in
the cloud and in the sea. 3They all ate the same spiritual food
4and drank the same spiritual drink; for they drank from the spiritual rock that accompanied them, and that rock was Christ.
5Nevertheless, God was not pleased with most of them; their bodies were scattered over the desert.

6Now these things occurred as examples[a] to keep us from setting our hearts on evil things as they did. 7Do not be idolaters, as
some of them were; as it is written: "The people sat down to eat
and drink and got up to indulge in pagan revelry."[b] 8We should
not commit sexual immorality, as some of them did—and in one
day twenty-three thousand of them died. 9We should not test the
Lord, as some of them did—and were killed by snakes. 10And do
not grumble, as some of them did—and were killed by the destroying angel.

11These things happened to them as examples and were written down as warnings for us, on whom the fulfillment of the ages
has come. 12So, if you think you are standing firm, be careful that
you don't fall! 13No temptation has seized you except what is common to man. And God is faithful; he will not let you be tempted
beyond what you can bear. But when you are tempted, he will also
provide a way out so that you can stand up under it.

Idol Feasts and the Lord's Supper

14Therefore, my dear friends, flee from idolatry. 15I speak to
sensible people; judge for yourselves what I say. 16Is not the cup
of thanksgiving for which we give thanks a participation in the
blood of Christ? And is not the bread that we break a participation
in the body of Christ? 17Because there is one loaf, we, who are
many, are one body, for we all partake of the one loaf.

18Consider the people of Israel: Do not those who eat the sacrifices participate in the altar? 19Do I mean then that a sacrifice
offered to an idol is anything, or that an idol is anything? 20No,
but the sacrifices of pagans are offered to demons, not to God,
and I do not want you to be participants with demons. 21You cannot drink the cup of the Lord and the cup of demons too; you
cannot have a part in both the Lord's table and the table of
demons. 22Are we trying to arouse the Lord's jealousy? Are we
stronger than he?

[a] 6 Or *types*; also in verse 11 [b] 7 Exodus 32:6

(9:24) Jesus, with Your eyes fixed firmly on the Father You ran a race that led to Calvary. Near the finish line, when He turned His face away, You kept on running, completely alone, for me. And now I run my race for You! No detours, no distractions, no dropped batons. I run the race with my eyes on You, knowing that You will not turn away, knowing that You are the prize. (Mt 27:45–50; Lk 23:44–46; Heb 12:1–3)

Jesus, our only joy be Thou,
As Thou our prize wilt be;
In Thee be all our glory now,
And through eternity.

"Jesus, the Very Thought of Thee"
Latin Hymn (12th c.)
Trans. Edward Caswall (1814–1878)

(10:13) Jesus, You made it through Your wilderness of temptation. You survived the pinnacle of testing. But where do I go when my body and mind crave the forbidden, when my heart and flesh constantly cry, "Surrender to sin"? I know You promise escape, but that faintly lighted exit in the distance seems so far away. O sweet Savior, when I am too weak to resist, whisper Your faithfulness to me. When I turn away from all help, give me the strength to change direction and turn to You. (Mt 4:1–11)

(10:31) How great and gracious You are, my God, to give me ways to participate in Your glory. Your glory calls me when I stray from You and fills me when I look to You. You fill my life with choices—how will I glorify You today? What means will I choose tomorrow? You make it easy for me to offer my praise! To live for Your glory is pure joy.

It is not only prayer that gives God glory but work. Smiting on an anvil, sawing a beam, whitewashing a wall, driving horses, sweeping, scouring, everything gives God glory if being in his grace you do it as your duty. To go to Communion worthily gives God great glory, but to take food in thankfulness and temperance gives him glory too. To lift up the hands in prayer gives God glory, but a man with a dungfork in his hand, a woman with a slop pail, gives him glory too. He is so great that all things give him glory if you mean they should.

Gerard Manley Hopkins (1844–1889)

Gives me pure joy to sing to You,
And that joy becomes my strength.
Gives me pure joy to sing Your
name,
Jesus, Jesus.

Gives me pure joy to walk with You,
And that joy becomes my strength.
Gives me pure joy to be with You,
Jesus, Jesus.

There is no other life.
There is no other way.
There is no higher love.
There is no higher name.

"Pure Joy"
Chris Falson (©1995)

The Believer's Freedom

23“Everything is permissible”—but not everything is beneficial. “Everything is permissible”—but not everything is constructive. 24Nobody should seek his own good, but the good of
others.

25Eat anything sold in the meat market without raising questions of conscience, 26for, “The earth is the Lord's, and everything in it.”[a]

27If some unbeliever invites you to a meal and you want to go,
eat whatever is put before you without raising questions of conscience. 28But if anyone says to you, “This has been offered in
sacrifice,” then do not eat it, both for the sake of the man who
told you and for conscience' sake[b]— 29the other man's conscience, I mean, not yours. For why should my freedom be judged
by another's conscience? 30If I take part in the meal with thankfulness, why am I denounced because of something I thank God
for?

31So whether you eat or drink or whatever you do, do it all for
the glory of God. 32Do not cause anyone to stumble, whether
Jews, Greeks or the church of God— 33even as I try to please
everybody in every way. For I am not seeking my own good but the
11 good of many, so that they may be saved. 1Follow my example, as I follow the example of Christ.

Propriety in Worship

2I praise you for remembering me in everything and for holding to the teachings,[c] just as I passed them on to you.

3Now I want you to realize that the head of every man is Christ,
and the head of the woman is man, and the head of Christ is God.
4Every man who prays or prophesies with his head covered dishonors his head. 5And every woman who prays or prophesies
with her head uncovered dishonors her head—it is just as
though her head were shaved. 6If a woman does not cover her
head, she should have her hair cut off; and if it is a disgrace for a
woman to have her hair cut or shaved off, she should cover her
head. 7A man ought not to cover his head,[d] since he is the image
and glory of God; but the woman is the glory of man. 8For man
did not come from woman, but woman from man; 9neither was
man created for woman, but woman for man. 10For this reason,
and because of the angels, the woman ought to have a sign of authority on her head.

11In the Lord, however, woman is not independent of man,
nor is man independent of woman. 12For as woman came from
man, so also man is born of woman. But everything comes from
God. 13Judge for yourselves: Is it proper for a woman to pray to
God with her head uncovered? 14Does not the very nature of
things teach you that if a man has long hair, it is a disgrace to
him, 15but that if a woman has long hair, it is her glory? For long
hair is given to her as a covering. 16If anyone wants to be con-
tentious about this, we have no other practice—nor do the
churches of God.

[a] 26 Psalm 24:1 [b] 28 Some manuscripts *conscience' sake, for "the earth is the Lord's and everything in it"* [c] 2 Or *traditions* [d] 4–7 Or *4Every man who prays or prophesies with long hair dishonors his head. 5And every woman who prays or prophesies with no covering ⌊of hair⌋ on her head dishonors her head—she is just like one of the "shorn women." 6If a woman has no covering, let her be for now with short hair, but since it is a disgrace for a woman to have her hair shorn or shaved, she should grow it again. 7A man ought not to have long hair*

MY BELOVED

I know that you are often tempted. I know the thing with which you struggle the most. What you are experiencing is not unique. So do not let the evil one make you feel isolated in your battle against temptation.

When you are tempted, do not say, "God is tempting me," for I cannot be tempted by evil, nor do I tempt anyone. Don't be deceived, My child. Every good and perfect gift comes from Me.

This is what you must grasp: I am faithful. I will not let you be tempted beyond what you can bear. But when you are tempted, I will always provide a way out so that you can stand up under it. I will rescue you.

Remember that My Son Jesus was made like you in every way, in order that He might become a merciful and faithful high priest in service to Me, and that He might make atonement for your sins. Because He Himself suffered when He was tempted, He is able to help you when you are being tempted.

For you have a high priest who is able to sympathize with your weaknesses, one who has been tempted in every way, just as you are—yet was without sin. Therefore, approach My throne of grace with confidence, so that you may receive mercy and find grace to help you in your time of need.

1Co 10:13; Heb 2:17-18; 4:15-16; Jas 1:13,16-17

The Lord's Supper

17In the following directives I have no praise for you, for your
meetings do more harm than good. 18In the first place, I hear
that when you come together as a church, there are divisions
among you, and to some extent I believe it. 19No doubt there have
to be differences among you to show which of you have God's approval. 20When you come together, it is not the Lord's Supper you
eat, 21for as you eat, each of you goes ahead without waiting for
anybody else. One remains hungry, another gets drunk. 22Don't
you have homes to eat and drink in? Or do you despise the church
of God and humiliate those who have nothing? What shall I say to
you? Shall I praise you for this? Certainly not!
23For I received from the Lord what I also passed on to you:
The Lord Jesus, on the night he was betrayed, took bread, 24and
when he had given thanks, he broke it and said, "This is my body,
which is for you; do this in remembrance of me." 25In the same
way, after supper he took the cup, saying, "This cup is the new
covenant in my blood; do this, whenever you drink it, in remembrance of me." 26For whenever you eat this bread and drink this
cup, you proclaim the Lord's death until he comes.
27Therefore, whoever eats the bread or drinks the cup of the
Lord in an unworthy manner will be guilty of sinning against the
body and blood of the Lord. 28A man ought to examine himself
before he eats of the bread and drinks of the cup. 29For anyone
who eats and drinks without recognizing the body of the Lord eats
and drinks judgment on himself. 30That is why many among you
are weak and sick, and a number of you have fallen asleep. 31But
if we judged ourselves, we would not come under judgment.
32When we are judged by the Lord, we are being disciplined so
that we will not be condemned with the world.
33So then, my brothers, when you come together to eat, wait
for each other. 34If anyone is hungry, he should eat at home, so
that when you meet together it may not result in judgment.
And when I come I will give further directions.

Spiritual Gifts

12 Now about spiritual gifts, brothers, I do not want you to be
ignorant. 2You know that when you were pagans, somehow
or other you were influenced and led astray to mute idols.
3Therefore I tell you that no one who is speaking by the Spirit of
God says, "Jesus be cursed," and no one can say, "Jesus is Lord,"
except by the Holy Spirit.
4There are different kinds of gifts, but the same Spirit. 5There are
different kinds of service, but the same Lord. 6There are different
kinds of working, but the same God works all of them in all men.
7Now to each one the manifestation of the Spirit is given for the
common good. 8To one there is given through the Spirit the message of wisdom, to another the message of knowledge by means
of the same Spirit, 9to another faith by the same Spirit, to another gifts of healing by that one Spirit, 10to another miraculous
powers, to another prophecy, to another distinguishing between
spirits, to another speaking in different kinds of tongues,[a] and to
still another the interpretation of tongues.[a] 11All these are the
work of one and the same Spirit, and he gives them to each one,
just as he determines.

[a] *10* Or *languages*; also in verse 28

(11:25–26) Lamb of Glory, I am humbled that You ask me to remember You—in spite of my wandering heart and habitual need for pardon. But gratefully I take Your cup of mercy in the company of others. Together we worship, beckoned by grace to Your side, where we eat, drink and remember Your sacrifice. (Ro 12:5; 1Co 10:16–17)

We remember You, we remember You.
By Your sacrifice of love all glory now is due.
At this table here, mercy hovers near,
Thanks is offered up, in this bread and cup,
We remember You.

Precious risen Lamb, Jesus who was slain,
Now enthroned in glory, forever You will reign,
Gladly we embrace both these signs of grace.
Thanks is offered up, in this bread and cup,
We remember You.

"We Remember You"
Walt Harrah (©1996)

(12:3) The mystery of Your power is seen in everything, but never so decidedly as in this: The music of Your Name can only be sung by those who know the composer. I sing of Your lordship, Jesus!

One Body, Many Parts

12The body is a unit, though it is made up of many parts; and
though all its parts are many, they form one body. So it is with
Christ. **13**For we were all baptized by[a] one Spirit into one body—
whether Jews or Greeks, slave or free—and we were all given the
one Spirit to drink.
14Now the body is not made up of one part but of many. **15**If the
foot should say, "Because I am not a hand, I do not belong to the
body," it would not for that reason cease to be part of the body.
16And if the ear should say, "Because I am not an eye, I do not belong to the body," it would not for that reason cease to be part of
the body. **17**If the whole body were an eye, where would the sense
of hearing be? If the whole body were an ear, where would the
sense of smell be? **18**But in fact God has arranged the parts in the
body, every one of them, just as he wanted them to be. **19**If they
were all one part, where would the body be? **20**As it is, there are
many parts, but one body.
21The eye cannot say to the hand, "I don't need you!" And the
head cannot say to the feet, "I don't need you!" **22**On the contrary, those parts of the body that seem to be weaker are indispensable, **23**and the parts that we think are less honorable we
treat with special honor. And the parts that are unpresentable are
treated with special modesty, **24**while our presentable parts need
no special treatment. But God has combined the members of the
body and has given greater honor to the parts that lacked it, **25**so
that there should be no division in the body, but that its parts
should have equal concern for each other. **26**If one part suffers,
every part suffers with it; if one part is honored, every part rejoices with it.
27Now you are the body of Christ, and each one of you is a
part of it. **28**And in the church God has appointed first of all
apostles, second prophets, third teachers, then workers of
miracles, also those having gifts of healing, those able to help
others, those with gifts of administration, and those speaking in
different kinds of tongues. **29**Are all apostles? Are all prophets?
Are all teachers? Do all work miracles? **30**Do all have gifts of
healing? Do all speak in tongues[b]? Do all interpret? **31**But
eagerly desire[c] the greater gifts.

Love

And now I will show you the most excellent way.

13 If I speak in the tongues[d] of men and of angels, but have
not love, I am only a resounding gong or a clanging cymbal. **2**If I have the gift of prophecy and can fathom all mysteries
and all knowledge, and if I have a faith that can move mountains,
but have not love, I am nothing. **3**If I give all I possess to the poor
and surrender my body to the flames,[e] but have not love, I gain
nothing.
4Love is patient, love is kind. It does not envy, it does not boast,
it is not proud. **5**It is not rude, it is not self-seeking, it is not easily angered, it keeps no record of wrongs. **6**Love does not delight
in evil but rejoices with the truth. **7**It always protects, always
trusts, always hopes, always perseveres.
8Love never fails. But where there are prophecies, they will

[a] *13* Or *with*; or *in* [b] *30* Or *other languages* [c] *31* Or *But you are eagerly desiring*
[d] *1* Or *languages* [e] *3* Some early manuscripts *body that I may boast*

(13:1) Lord Jesus, Your transforming love is beyond my understanding. I know it was Your deep, infinite, compelling love that motivated Your heart to save me, yet I cannot really comprehend this reality. Maybe if I could see the lives and hear the cries of all Earth's people, my heart would break as Yours did for the love of each of them. Perhaps if I let the weight of the cross burrow its imprint on my back I would begin to understand what a lost world meant to You, and why You consented to Calvary out of love for me.

This, this is the God we adore,
Our faithful, unchangeable friend,
Whose love is as great as his power,
And neither knows measure nor end.

Joseph Hart (1712–1768)

(13:4–7) God, Your love for me is fierce, soaring above sentiment. It is the mightiest force in the universe, whispering, roaring, creating, redeeming . . . and taking delight in me. Thank You for Your Word that offers me this simple measure of Godly love: If I am impatient, if I am unkind, if I do not protect, if I delight in another's trouble, then I am not loving with Your love. But thank You for empowering me to love by Your standard—my will washed in submission, ever rejoicing in heaven's best for the sake of others.

If I have not charity
If love does not flow from me
I am nothing
Jesus, reduce me to love.

"Charity"
Kenn Gulliksen (©1971)

cease; where there are tongues, they will be stilled; where there
is knowledge, it will pass away. 9For we know in part and we
prophesy in part, 10but when perfection comes, the imperfect
disappears. 11When I was a child, I talked like a child, I thought
like a child, I reasoned like a child. When I became a man, I put
childish ways behind me. 12Now we see but a poor reflection as
in a mirror; then we shall see face to face. Now I know in part;
then I shall know fully, even as I am fully known.

13And now these three remain: faith, hope and love. But the
greatest of these is love.

Gifts of Prophecy and Tongues

14 Follow the way of love and eagerly desire spiritual gifts, especially the gift of prophecy. 2For anyone who speaks in a
tongue[a] does not speak to men but to God. Indeed, no one understands him; he utters mysteries with his spirit.[b] 3But everyone
who prophesies speaks to men for their strengthening, encouragement and comfort. 4He who speaks in a tongue edifies himself, but he who prophesies edifies the church. 5I would like
every one of you to speak in tongues,[c] but I would rather have
you prophesy. He who prophesies is greater than one who speaks
in tongues,[c] unless he interprets, so that the church may be edified.

6Now, brothers, if I come to you and speak in tongues, what
good will I be to you, unless I bring you some revelation or
knowledge or prophecy or word of instruction? 7Even in the case
of lifeless things that make sounds, such as the flute or harp, how
will anyone know what tune is being played unless there is a distinction in the notes? 8Again, if the trumpet does not sound a
clear call, who will get ready for battle? 9So it is with you. Unless
you speak intelligible words with your tongue, how will anyone
know what you are saying? You will just be speaking into the air.
10Undoubtedly there are all sorts of languages in the world, yet
none of them is without meaning. 11If then I do not grasp the
meaning of what someone is saying, I am a foreigner to the
speaker, and he is a foreigner to me. 12So it is with you. Since you
are eager to have spiritual gifts, try to excel in gifts that build up
the church.

13For this reason anyone who speaks in a tongue should pray
that he may interpret what he says. 14For if I pray in a tongue, my
spirit prays, but my mind is unfruitful. 15So what shall I do? I will
pray with my spirit, but I will also pray with my mind; I will sing
with my spirit, but I will also sing with my mind. 16If you are
praising God with your spirit, how can one who finds himself
among those who do not understand[d] say "Amen" to your thanksgiving, since he does not know what you are saying? 17You may be
giving thanks well enough, but the other man is not edified.

18I thank God that I speak in tongues more than all of you.
19But in the church I would rather speak five intelligible words to
instruct others than ten thousand words in a tongue.

20Brothers, stop thinking like children. In regard to evil be infants, but in your thinking be adults. 21In the Law it is written:

"Through men of strange tongues

[a] 2 Or *another language*; also in verses 4, 13, 14, 19, 26 and 27 [b] 2 Or *by the Spirit*
[c] 5 Or *other languages*; also in verses 6, 18, 22, 23 and 39 [d] 16 Or *among the inquirers*

(14:12) By Your hands, Father, we are sustained with gifts fashioned for our nurture. You place these treasures within us so that we can share in bringing life to one another. I thank You, Lord, for ministering to me through the hearts and hands of Your church. I am eager to participate in blessing others, hopeful that I may help build them up, and delighted to be banqueting at Your family table. Be generous through me, Lord, so that I will not be empty-handed when I come into Your house.

(14:26) How sweet is Your presence when Your church worships according to Your Word! Put Your praise on our lips, O Lord! Put Your truth in our mouths and cause us to rejoice in Your company. May the teaching and revelation You impart through us bring strength to Your body and glory to Your name. (Pr 27:17)

Lord, we have come to this house
Where we love to sing Your praises;
We lift our hearts and our hands
To the King of all the ages.
Hear us, Lord, we pray.
Come, Jesus, come,
Come fill this place.

Meet us here,
Meet us here, Lord
We are few but we are strong
When You surround us.
Meet us here,
Meet us here, Lord
As we gather in Your name,
Meet us here.

"Meet Us Here"
Dan Marks (©1987)

and through the lips of foreigners
I will speak to this people,
but even then they will not listen to me,"[a]
says the Lord.

22Tongues, then, are a sign, not for believers but for unbelievers; prophecy, however, is for believers, not for unbelievers. 23So if the whole church comes together and everyone speaks in tongues, and some who do not understand[b] or some unbelievers come in, will they not say that you are out of your mind? 24But if an unbeliever or someone who does not understand[c] comes in while everybody is prophesying, he will be convinced by all that he is a sinner and will be judged by all, 25and the secrets of his heart will be laid bare. So he will fall down and worship God, exclaiming, "God is really among you!"

Orderly Worship

26What then shall we say, brothers? When you come together, everyone has a hymn, or a word of instruction, a revelation, a tongue or an interpretation. All of these must be done for the strengthening of the church. 27If anyone speaks in a tongue, two—or at the most three—should speak, one at a time, and someone must interpret. 28If there is no interpreter, the speaker should keep quiet in the church and speak to himself and God.

29Two or three prophets should speak, and the others should weigh carefully what is said. 30And if a revelation comes to someone who is sitting down, the first speaker should stop. 31For you can all prophesy in turn so that everyone may be instructed and encouraged. 32The spirits of prophets are subject to the control of prophets. 33For God is not a God of disorder but of peace.

As in all the congregations of the saints, 34women should remain silent in the churches. They are not allowed to speak, but must be in submission, as the Law says. 35If they want to inquire about something, they should ask their own husbands at home; for it is disgraceful for a woman to speak in the church.

36Did the word of God originate with you? Or are you the only people it has reached? 37If anybody thinks he is a prophet or spiritually gifted, let him acknowledge that what I am writing to you is the Lord's command. 38If he ignores this, he himself will be ignored.[d]

39Therefore, my brothers, be eager to prophesy, and do not forbid speaking in tongues. 40But everything should be done in a fitting and orderly way.

The Resurrection of Christ

15 Now, brothers, I want to remind you of the gospel I preached to you, which you received and on which you have taken your stand. 2By this gospel you are saved, if you hold firmly to the word I preached to you. Otherwise, you have believed in vain.

3For what I received I passed on to you as of first importance[e]: that Christ died for our sins according to the Scriptures, 4that he was buried, that he was raised on the third day according to the Scriptures, 5and that he appeared to Peter,[f] and then to the

[a] *21* Isaiah 28:11,12 [b] *23* Or *some inquirers* [c] *24* Or *or some inquirer*
[d] *38* Some manuscripts *If he is ignorant of this, let him be ignorant* [e] *3* Or *you at the first* [f] *5* Greek *Cephas*

Twelve. 6After that, he appeared to more than five hundred of the
brothers at the same time, most of whom are still living, though
some have fallen asleep. 7Then he appeared to James, then to all
the apostles, 8and last of all he appeared to me also, as to one ab-
normally born.
9For I am the least of the apostles and do not even deserve to be
called an apostle, because I persecuted the church of God. 10But
by the grace of God I am what I am, and his grace to me was not
without effect. No, I worked harder than all of them—yet not I,
but the grace of God that was with me. 11Whether, then, it was I or
they, this is what we preach, and this is what you believed.

The Resurrection of the Dead

12But if it is preached that Christ has been raised from the
dead, how can some of you say that there is no resurrection of the
dead? 13If there is no resurrection of the dead, then not even
Christ has been raised. 14And if Christ has not been raised, our
preaching is useless and so is your faith. 15More than that, we
are then found to be false witnesses about God, for we have testified about God that he raised Christ from the dead. But he did not
raise him if in fact the dead are not raised. 16For if the dead are
not raised, then Christ has not been raised either. 17And if Christ
has not been raised, your faith is futile; you are still in your sins.
18Then those also who have fallen asleep in Christ are lost. 19If
only for this life we have hope in Christ, we are to be pitied more
than all men.
20But Christ has indeed been raised from the dead, the firstfruits of those who have fallen asleep. 21For since death came
through a man, the resurrection of the dead comes also through
a man. 22For as in Adam all die, so in Christ all will be made alive.
23But each in his own turn: Christ, the firstfruits; then, when he
comes, those who belong to him. 24Then the end will come, when
he hands over the kingdom to God the Father after he has destroyed all dominion, authority and power. 25For he must reign
until he has put all his enemies under his feet. 26The last enemy
to be destroyed is death. 27For he "has put everything under his
feet."[a] Now when it says that "everything" has been put under
him, it is clear that this does not include God himself, who put
everything under Christ. 28When he has done this, then the Son
himself will be made subject to him who put everything under
him, so that God may be all in all.
29Now if there is no resurrection, what will those do who are
baptized for the dead? If the dead are not raised at all, why are
people baptized for them? 30And as for us, why do we endanger
ourselves every hour? 31I die every day—I mean that, brothers—
just as surely as I glory over you in Christ Jesus our Lord. 32If I
fought wild beasts in Ephesus for merely human reasons, what
have I gained? If the dead are not raised,

> "Let us eat and drink,
> for tomorrow we die."[b]

33Do not be misled: "Bad company corrupts good character."
34Come back to your senses as you ought, and stop sinning; for
there are some who are ignorant of God—I say this to your
shame.

[a] *27* Psalm 8:6 [b] *32* Isaiah 22:13

(15:22–23) O Father, the seed of sin that was planted in the Garden of Eden has spread its roots relentlessly through the soil of every human heart. The harvest was grim; death was the fruit. But then another seed was planted. Our Lord Jesus, Your beloved Son, the holy Seed of righteousness, gave up His life like "a kernel of wheat [that] falls to the ground and dies." His blood washed and watered the ground of our hearts. And then He came forth from death's planting, again in a garden, the firstfruit of an eternal harvest. Our hearts cry, "Alleluia!" (Jn 12:24; 19:41; Ro 5:12–21)

By His grace I am redeemed,
By His blood I am made clean,
And I now can know Him face to
Face.
By His power I have been raised,
Hidden now in Christ by faith,
I will praise the glory of His grace.

"By His Grace"
Steve Fry (©1996)

(15:52–57) Eternal Christ, Giver of Life, how this truth deepens as my life lengthens. Grief's forced but temporary goodbyes increase in number, yet with each one I move closer to Your trumpet's resounding signal. With every dark diagnosis I cling more tenaciously to Your promise that we who believe shall live again in a place more whole, more shining and substantial than anything this Earth could ever boast. The faint taste of victory I now savor is only a foretaste of Your everlasting Wedding Feast!

Jesus lives and so shall I.
Death! Thy sting is gone forever.
He, who deigned for me to die,
Lives the bands of death to sever.
He shall raise me with the just;
Jesus is my Hope and Trust.

"Jesus Lives and So Shall I"
Christian F. Gellert (1757)
Trans. J.D. Lang (1826)

The Resurrection Body

35But someone may ask, "How are the dead raised? With what
kind of body will they come?" 36How foolish! What you sow does
not come to life unless it dies. 37When you sow, you do not plant
the body that will be, but just a seed, perhaps of wheat or of
something else. 38But God gives it a body as he has determined,
and to each kind of seed he gives its own body. 39All flesh is not
the same: Men have one kind of flesh, animals have another, birds
another and fish another. 40There are also heavenly bodies and
there are earthly bodies; but the splendor of the heavenly bodies
is one kind, and the splendor of the earthly bodies is another.
41The sun has one kind of splendor, the moon another and the
stars another; and star differs from star in splendor.

42So will it be with the resurrection of the dead. The body that
is sown is perishable, it is raised imperishable; 43it is sown in
dishonor, it is raised in glory; it is sown in weakness, it is raised
in power; 44it is sown a natural body, it is raised a spiritual body.

If there is a natural body, there is also a spiritual body. 45So it
is written: "The first man Adam became a living being"[a]; the last
Adam, a life-giving spirit. 46The spiritual did not come first, but
the natural, and after that the spiritual. 47The first man was of the
dust of the earth, the second man from heaven. 48As was the
earthly man, so are those who are of the earth; and as is the man
from heaven, so also are those who are of heaven. 49And just as
we have borne the likeness of the earthly man, so shall we[b] bear
the likeness of the man from heaven.

50I declare to you, brothers, that flesh and blood cannot inherit the kingdom of God, nor does the perishable inherit the imperishable. 51Listen, I tell you a mystery: We will not all sleep,
but we will all be changed— 52in a flash, in the twinkling of an
eye, at the last trumpet. For the trumpet will sound, the dead will
be raised imperishable, and we will be changed. 53For the perishable must clothe itself with the imperishable, and the mortal
with immortality. 54When the perishable has been clothed with
the imperishable, and the mortal with immortality, then the saying
that is written will come true: "Death has been swallowed up in
victory."[c]

55"Where, O death, is your victory?
Where, O death, is your sting?"[d]

56The sting of death is sin, and the power of sin is the law. 57But
thanks be to God! He gives us the victory through our Lord Jesus
Christ.

58Therefore, my dear brothers, stand firm. Let nothing move
you. Always give yourselves fully to the work of the Lord, because
you know that your labor in the Lord is not in vain.

The Collection for God's People

16 Now about the collection for God's people: Do what I told
the Galatian churches to do. 2On the first day of every
week, each one of you should set aside a sum of money in keeping with his income, saving it up, so that when I come no collec-
tions will have to be made. 3Then, when I arrive, I will give letters
of introduction to the men you approve and send them with your

[a] 45 Gen. 2:7 [b] 49 Some early manuscripts *so let us* [c] 54 Isaiah 25:8
[d] 55 Hosea 13:14

gift to Jerusalem. 4If it seems advisable for me to go also, they will
accompany me.

Personal Requests

5After I go through Macedonia, I will come to you—for I will
be going through Macedonia. 6Perhaps I will stay with you
awhile, or even spend the winter, so that you can help me on my
journey, wherever I go. 7I do not want to see you now and make
only a passing visit; I hope to spend some time with you, if the
Lord permits. 8But I will stay on at Ephesus until Pentecost, 9be-
cause a great door for effective work has opened to me, and there
are many who oppose me.
10If Timothy comes, see to it that he has nothing to fear while
he is with you, for he is carrying on the work of the Lord, just as
I am. 11No one, then, should refuse to accept him. Send him on
his way in peace so that he may return to me. I am expecting him
along with the brothers.
12Now about our brother Apollos: I strongly urged him to go to
you with the brothers. He was quite unwilling to go now, but he
will go when he has the opportunity.
13Be on your guard; stand firm in the faith; be men of courage;
be strong. 14Do everything in love.
15You know that the household of Stephanas were the first converts in Achaia, and they have devoted themselves to the service of
the saints. I urge you, brothers, 16to submit to such as these and
to everyone who joins in the work, and labors at it. 17I was glad
when Stephanas, Fortunatus and Achaicus arrived, because they
have supplied what was lacking from you. 18For they refreshed
my spirit and yours also. Such men deserve recognition.

Final Greetings

19The churches in the province of Asia send you greetings. Aquila and Priscilla[a] greet you warmly in the Lord, and so does the
church that meets at their house. 20All the brothers here send
you greetings. Greet one another with a holy kiss.
21I, Paul, write this greeting in my own hand.
22If anyone does not love the Lord—a curse be on him. Come,
O Lord[b]!
23The grace of the Lord Jesus be with you.
24My love to all of you in Christ Jesus. Amen.[c]

[a] 19 Greek *Prisca*, a variant of *Priscilla* [b] 22 In Aramaic the expression *Come, O Lord* is *Marana tha.* [c] 24 Some manuscripts do not have *Amen.*

(16:13–14) Loving Lord, You give me all I need to fulfill these commands. I bless Your name for spiritual eyes to see the battle. I thank You for the gift of faith and for the armor of God. For the courage and strength You give, I praise You. And now I bow before You, Sovereign Lord, asking You to constantly tend Your fire of love in me so that I may do none of these things from a cold and empty heart. (Eph 6:11–18; 2 Pet 1:3)

Come, Holy Spirit, heavenly Dove,
With all Thy quickening powers;
Kindle a flame of sacred love
In these cold hearts of ours.

Awake our souls to joyful songs;
Let pure devotion rise,
Till praise employs our thankful
tongues,
And doubt forever dies.

Come, Holy Spirit, heavenly Dove,
With all Thy quickening powers;
Come, shed abroad a Savior's love,
And that shall kindle ours.

"Come, Holy Spirit, Heavenly Dove"
Isaac Watts (1707)

2 Corinthians

The Second Epistle of Paul the Apostle to the

CORINTHIANS

Occasionally we encounter Christians who boast of living without pain or weakness. Their bravado implies that those of us who continue to struggle with human frailty must be second-class disciples. An encounter with such "super-Christians" rarely leads us to a deeper experience of God. Often it increases our discouragement and doubt.

"Super-Christianity" of this sort is nothing new. Shortly after Paul wrote his first letter to Corinth, a band of "super-apostles" invaded the church there (ch. 11). They were people of power and eloquence who deceived the Corinthian believers into seeking an unreal utopia rather than a real, Christ-like existence. Paul wrote 2 Corinthians to reestablish the Corinthian church on the solid foundation of Christ, the One Whose death reconciles us to God (5:21).

Undeniably, when we become Christians we begin to participate in the "new Creation"—"the old has gone, the new has come" (5:17). But this newness, however real and pervasive, does not completely obliterate our human weaknesses (chs. 11–12). We still groan in our flesh, "longing to be clothed with our heavenly dwelling" (5:2). Yet, paradoxically, we experience the power of Christ in the midst of our frailty (12:9–10). Within our fleshly "jars of clay," God gives us "the light of the knowledge of the glory of God in the face of Christ" (4:7).

We worship God, not because He insulates us from struggles but because He is a compassionate, consoling Father Who meets us in the midst of our suffering.

In the first paragraphs of 2 Corinthians Paul openly shares his recent hardships as well as God's comfort and deliverance (1:3–11). Yet he begins his account of suffering with praise: "Praise be to the God and Father of our Lord Jesus Christ, the Father of compassion and the God of all comfort, who comforts us in all our troubles" (1:3–4). We worship God, not because He insulates us from struggles but because He is a compassionate, consoling Father Who meets us in the midst of our suffering. The apostle Paul, by his testimony and example, shows us that our difficulties can provide occasions to worship God.

But this is not the whole story. In an astounding passage Paul explains that we, "who with unveiled faces all reflect the Lord's glory, are being transformed into his likeness with ever-increasing glory, which comes from the Lord, who is the Spirit" (3:18). Not only do we glimpse God's glory now, but His Spirit is in the process of transforming us more and more into the glorious likeness of God.

Surprisingly, the Spirit uses suffering to prepare us for the "eternal glory" we shall one day receive (4:17). Thus, we can endure troubles by looking to the resplendent future God has prepared for us: "So we fix our eyes not on what is seen, but on what is unseen" (4:18). What a marvelous verse to guide our worship! When we worship, we take our eyes off ourselves and our struggles. We fix our eyes upon the Father Who has compassion upon us, the Son Who has reconciled us to God, and the Spirit Who is in the process of transforming us into the glory of God.

1 Paul, an apostle of Christ Jesus by the will of God, and Timothy our brother,

To the church of God in Corinth, together with all the saints
throughout Achaia:

2Grace and peace to you from God our Father and the Lord
Jesus Christ.

The God of All Comfort

3Praise be to the God and Father of our Lord Jesus Christ, the
Father of compassion and the God of all comfort, 4who comforts
us in all our troubles, so that we can comfort those in any trouble with the comfort we ourselves have received from God. 5For
just as the sufferings of Christ flow over into our lives, so also
through Christ our comfort overflows. 6If we are distressed, it is
for your comfort and salvation; if we are comforted, it is for your
comfort, which produces in you patient endurance of the same
sufferings we suffer. 7And our hope for you is firm, because we
know that just as you share in our sufferings, so also you share in
our comfort.

8We do not want you to be uninformed, brothers, about the
hardships we suffered in the province of Asia. We were under
great pressure, far beyond our ability to endure, so that we despaired even of life. 9Indeed, in our hearts we felt the sentence of
death. But this happened that we might not rely on ourselves but
on God, who raises the dead. 10He has delivered us from such a
deadly peril, and he will deliver us. On him we have set our hope
that he will continue to deliver us, 11as you help us by your
prayers. Then many will give thanks on our[a] behalf for the gracious favor granted us in answer to the prayers of many.

Paul's Change of Plans

12Now this is our boast: Our conscience testifies that we have
conducted ourselves in the world, and especially in our relations
with you, in the holiness and sincerity that are from God. We have
done so not according to worldly wisdom but according to God's
grace. 13For we do not write you anything you cannot read or understand. And I hope that, 14as you have understood us in part,
you will come to understand fully that you can boast of us just as
we will boast of you in the day of the Lord Jesus.

15Because I was confident of this, I planned to visit you first so
that you might benefit twice. 16I planned to visit you on my way to
Macedonia and to come back to you from Macedonia, and then to
have you send me on my way to Judea. 17When I planned this, did
I do it lightly? Or do I make my plans in a worldly manner so that
in the same breath I say, "Yes, yes" and "No, no"?

18But as surely as God is faithful, our message to you is not
"Yes" and "No." 19For the Son of God, Jesus Christ, who was
preached among you by me and Silas[b] and Timothy, was not "Yes"
and "No," but in him it has always been "Yes." 20For no matter
how many promises God has made, they are "Yes" in Christ. And
so through him the "Amen" is spoken by us to the glory of God.
21Now it is God who makes both us and you stand firm in Christ.
He anointed us, 22set his seal of ownership on us, and put his Spirit in our hearts as a deposit, guaranteeing what is to come.

[a] *11* Many manuscripts *your* [b] *19* Greek *Silvanus*, a variant of *Silas*

(1:3–5) Thank You, Father, for the comfort You give to us. And thank You for the comfort You give through us to those in need around us. Lord, through the power of Your Holy Spirit please make me a minister of comfort to those who are suffering. May I give as freely and generously as I have received from You. And when I suffer, help me to graciously receive Your comfort from my brothers and sisters in Christ whom You send my way.

God does not leave us comfortless, but we have to be in dire need of comfort to know the truth of his promise. It is in time of calamity . . . in days and nights of sorrow and trouble that the presence, the sufficiency, and the sympathy of God grow very sure and very wonderful. Then we find out that the grace of God is sufficient for all our needs, for every problem and for every difficulty, for every broken heart, and for every human sorrow.

Peter Marshall (1902–1949)

(1:21–22) Holy Spirit, God's Essence, You animate our faith, communicate beyond words and reveal the mysteries of God to us. You are the indwelling presence of God in our lives. And if Your presence is merely the deposit of things to come, what vast, astounding realities must God be preparing for us? If this is just the preview, what unfathomable glories await us when we arrive at our Lord's feet to claim our prize?

23I call God as my witness that it was in order to spare you that
I did not return to Corinth. 24Not that we lord it over your faith,
but we work with you for your joy, because it is by faith you stand
firm. 2 1So I made up my mind that I would not make another
painful visit to you. 2For if I grieve you, who is left to make
me glad but you whom I have grieved? 3I wrote as I did so that
when I came I should not be distressed by those who ought to
make me rejoice. I had confidence in all of you, that you would
all share my joy. 4For I wrote you out of great distress and anguish of heart and with many tears, not to grieve you but to let you
know the depth of my love for you.

Forgiveness for the Sinner

5If anyone has caused grief, he has not so much grieved me
as he has grieved all of you, to some extent—not to put it too
severely. 6The punishment inflicted on him by the majority is
sufficient for him. 7Now instead, you ought to forgive and comfort him, so that he will not be overwhelmed by excessive sorrow. 8I urge you, therefore, to reaffirm your love for him. 9The
reason I wrote you was to see if you would stand the test and be
obedient in everything. 10If you forgive anyone, I also forgive
him. And what I have forgiven—if there was anything to forgive—I have forgiven in the sight of Christ for your sake, 11in
order that Satan might not outwit us. For we are not unaware of
his schemes.

Ministers of the New Covenant

12Now when I went to Troas to preach the gospel of Christ and
found that the Lord had opened a door for me, 13I still had no
peace of mind, because I did not find my brother Titus there. So
I said good-by to them and went on to Macedonia.

14But thanks be to God, who always leads us in triumphal procession in Christ and through us spreads everywhere the fragrance of the knowledge of him. 15For we are to God the aroma
of Christ among those who are being saved and those who are
perishing. 16To the one we are the smell of death; to the other, the
fragrance of life. And who is equal to such a task? 17Unlike so
many, we do not peddle the word of God for profit. On the contrary, in Christ we speak before God with sincerity, like men sent
from God.

3 Are we beginning to commend ourselves again? Or do we
need, like some people, letters of recommendation to you or
from you? 2You yourselves are our letter, written on our hearts,
known and read by everybody. 3You show that you are a letter
from Christ, the result of our ministry, written not with ink but
with the Spirit of the living God, not on tablets of stone but on
tablets of human hearts.

4Such confidence as this is ours through Christ before God.
5Not that we are competent in ourselves to claim anything for
ourselves, but our competence comes from God. 6He has made
us competent as ministers of a new covenant—not of the letter
but of the Spirit; for the letter kills, but the Spirit gives life.

The Glory of the New Covenant

7Now if the ministry that brought death, which was engraved in
letters on stone, came with glory, so that the Israelites could not
look steadily at the face of Moses because of its glory, fading

(3:2–3) Lord Jesus, may Your pure and perfect message be inscribed across my life moment by moment, letter by holy letter. Let Your work in me become my only story, read by many, and may it bring You glory.

The books the Holy Spirit is writing are living, and every soul a volume in which the divine author makes a true revelation of His Word, explaining it to every heart, unfolding it in every moment.

Jean-Pierre de Caussade (1675–1751)

May this life that I live make You glad,
Help me praise You with all that I have.
May the thoughts of my heart bring a smile to Your face,
I will worship You, Lord, all my days.

Ev'ry day is a gift from Your hand,
You're the Author of all that I am.
Let my story be told in this heart-spoken phrase:
I will worship You, Lord, all my days.

"All My Days"
Bill Batstone and Bob Somma (©1990)

MY BELOVED

Delight yourself in the Me and I will give you the desires of your heart. Commit your way to Me; trust in Me and I will do this: I will make your righteousness shine like the dawn, the justice of your cause like the noonday sun. All who see you will acknowledge that you are My very own child whom I have richly blessed.

For I am your heavenly Father, your Father of compassion and the God of all comfort. I will turn your mourning into gladness; I will give you comfort and joy instead of sorrow. I will comfort you in all your troubles, so that you can comfort those who are in trouble with the comfort you have received from Me.

I will also heal your broken heart and bind up your wounds. I will bestow on you a crown of beauty instead of ashes, the oil of gladness instead of mourning, and a garment of praise instead of a spirit of despair.

All this I will do because I delight to be gracious to you, My child. So commit your ways to Me, for I love you dearly.

Ps 37:4-6; 147:3; Isa 30:18; 61:3,9; 66:13; Jer 31:13; 2Co 1:3-4

though it was, 8will not the ministry of the Spirit be even more
glorious? 9If the ministry that condemns men is glorious, how
much more glorious is the ministry that brings righteousness!
10For what was glorious has no glory now in comparison with the
surpassing glory. 11And if what was fading away came with glory,
how much greater is the glory of that which lasts!
12Therefore, since we have such a hope, we are very bold.
13We are not like Moses, who would put a veil over his face to
keep the Israelites from gazing at it while the radiance was fading
away. 14But their minds were made dull, for to this day the same
veil remains when the old covenant is read. It has not been removed, because only in Christ is it taken away. 15Even to this day
when Moses is read, a veil covers their hearts. 16But whenever
anyone turns to the Lord, the veil is taken away. 17Now the Lord
is the Spirit, and where the Spirit of the Lord is, there is freedom.
18And we, who with unveiled faces all reflect[a] the Lord's glory,
are being transformed into his likeness with ever-increasing glory,
which comes from the Lord, who is the Spirit.

Treasures in Jars of Clay

4 Therefore, since through God's mercy we have this ministry,
we do not lose heart. 2Rather, we have renounced secret and
shameful ways; we do not use deception, nor do we distort the
word of God. On the contrary, by setting forth the truth plainly we
commend ourselves to every man's conscience in the sight of
God. 3And even if our gospel is veiled, it is veiled to those who are
perishing. 4The god of this age has blinded the minds of unbelievers, so that they cannot see the light of the gospel of the glory
of Christ, who is the image of God. 5For we do not preach ourselves, but Jesus Christ as Lord, and ourselves as your servants for
Jesus' sake. 6For God, who said, "Let light shine out of darkness,"[b] made his light shine in our hearts to give us the light of
the knowledge of the glory of God in the face of Christ.
7But we have this treasure in jars of clay to show that this all-
surpassing power is from God and not from us. 8We are hard
pressed on every side, but not crushed; perplexed, but not in despair; 9persecuted, but not abandoned; struck down, but not destroyed. 10We always carry around in our body the death of Jesus,
so that the life of Jesus may also be revealed in our body. 11For we
who are alive are always being given over to death for Jesus' sake,
so that his life may be revealed in our mortal body. 12So then,
death is at work in us, but life is at work in you.
13It is written: "I believed; therefore I have spoken."[c] With that
same spirit of faith we also believe and therefore speak, 14be-
cause we know that the one who raised the Lord Jesus from the
dead will also raise us with Jesus and present us with you in his
presence. 15All this is for your benefit, so that the grace that is
reaching more and more people may cause thanksgiving to overflow to the glory of God.
16Therefore we do not lose heart. Though outwardly we are
wasting away, yet inwardly we are being renewed day by day.
17For our light and momentary troubles are achieving for us an
eternal glory that far outweighs them all. 18So we fix our eyes not
on what is seen, but on what is unseen. For what is seen is temporary, but what is unseen is eternal.

[a] 18 Or *contemplate* [b] 6 Gen. 1:3 [c] 13 Psalm 116:10

(3:12–18) Father, I praise You. Through Jesus You have removed the veil of doubt from my mind so that I might understand Your Word more clearly. You have removed the veil of bondage from my heart so that I might live in freedom before You. You have removed the veil of darkness from my face so that I might reflect Your light to others. Help me to live boldly for You, realizing that You have placed me here to fill the world with the hope and glory of Christ.

Dear Jesus,
Help us to spread your fragrance everywhere we go.
Flood our souls with your spirit and life.
Penetrate and possess our whole being so utterly
that our lives may only be a radiance of yours . . .
Let us thus praise you in the way you love best
By shining on those around us.
Let us preach you without preaching,
not by words, but by our example,
by the catching force,
the sympathetic influence of what we do,
the evident fullness of the love our hearts bear to you.
Amen.

Mother Teresa of Calcutta (1910-1997)

Faith is the daring of the soul to go farther than it can see.
William Newton Clarke (1841–1912)

(5:7) "Faith is being sure of what we hope for and certain of what we do not see." Lord, we know that we do not see things as they really are. True spiritual sight is reserved for the day when we will see as we are seen. Faith is for this world; sight is for the next. You bless those who believe without seeing. O Lord, give us strength to walk by faith until that great Day when we will truly walk by sight. (1Co 13:12; Heb 11:1)

And Lord, haste the day
When my faith shall be sight,
The clouds be rolled back as a scroll,
The trump shall resound
And the Lord shall descend,
"Even so," it is well with my soul.
"It Is Well With My Soul"
Horatio G. Spafford (1873)

(5:18–21) Lord Jesus Christ, Mender of the broken, Healer of the wounded, Restorer of the withered, here among the tissues, limbs and organs of Your Body is the need for Your powerful touch. For You are Love's ligature, binding flesh to wounded flesh, mending muscle split by sin's swift blade. O perfect, pure and righteous One, Your sacrifice for us has won this prize. May we wear healing's holy scars as medals for the world to see—emblems of Your victory.

Our Heavenly Dwelling

5 Now we know that if the earthly tent we live in is destroyed,
we have a building from God, an eternal house in heaven,
not built by human hands. 2Meanwhile we groan, longing to be
clothed with our heavenly dwelling, 3because when we are
clothed, we will not be found naked. 4For while we are in this
tent, we groan and are burdened, because we do not wish to be
unclothed but to be clothed with our heavenly dwelling, so that
what is mortal may be swallowed up by life. 5Now it is God who
has made us for this very purpose and has given us the Spirit as a
deposit, guaranteeing what is to come.

6Therefore we are always confident and know that as long as
we are at home in the body we are away from the Lord. 7We live
by faith, not by sight. 8We are confident, I say, and would prefer
to be away from the body and at home with the Lord. 9So we
make it our goal to please him, whether we are at home in the
body or away from it. 10For we must all appear before the judgment seat of Christ, that each one may receive what is due him for
the things done while in the body, whether good or bad.

The Ministry of Reconciliation

11Since, then, we know what it is to fear the Lord, we try to
persuade men. What we are is plain to God, and I hope it is also
plain to your conscience. 12We are not trying to commend ourselves to you again, but are giving you an opportunity to take
pride in us, so that you can answer those who take pride in what
is seen rather than in what is in the heart. 13If we are out of our
mind, it is for the sake of God; if we are in our right mind, it is for
you. 14For Christ's love compels us, because we are convinced
that one died for all, and therefore all died. 15And he died for all,
that those who live should no longer live for themselves but for
him who died for them and was raised again.

16So from now on we regard no one from a worldly point of
view. Though we once regarded Christ in this way, we do so no
longer. 17Therefore, if anyone is in Christ, he is a new creation;
the old has gone, the new has come! 18All this is from God, who
reconciled us to himself through Christ and gave us the ministry
of reconciliation: 19that God was reconciling the world to himself
in Christ, not counting men's sins against them. And he has committed to us the message of reconciliation. 20We are therefore
Christ's ambassadors, as though God were making his appeal
through us. We implore you on Christ's behalf: Be reconciled to
God. 21God made him who had no sin to be sin[a] for us, so that in
him we might become the righteousness of God.

6 As God's fellow workers we urge you not to receive God's
grace in vain. 2For he says,

> "In the time of my favor I heard you,
> and in the day of salvation I helped you."[b]

I tell you, now is the time of God's favor, now is the day of salvation.

Paul's Hardships

3We put no stumbling block in anyone's path, so that our ministry will not be discredited. 4Rather, as servants of God we com-

[a] 21 Or *be a sin offering* [b] 2 Isaiah 49:8

mend ourselves in every way: in great endurance; in troubles,
hardships and distresses; 5in beatings, imprisonments and riots;
in hard work, sleepless nights and hunger; 6in purity, understanding, patience and kindness; in the Holy Spirit and in sincere
love; 7in truthful speech and in the power of God; with weapons
of righteousness in the right hand and in the left; 8through glory
and dishonor, bad report and good report; genuine, yet regarded
as impostors; 9known, yet regarded as unknown; dying, and yet
we live on; beaten, and yet not killed; 10sorrowful, yet always rejoicing; poor, yet making many rich; having nothing, and yet possessing everything.
11We have spoken freely to you, Corinthians, and opened wide
our hearts to you. 12We are not withholding our affection from
you, but you are withholding yours from us. 13As a fair exchange—I speak as to my children—open wide your hearts
also.

Do Not Be Yoked With Unbelievers

14Do not be yoked together with unbelievers. For what do righteousness and wickedness have in common? Or what fellowship
can light have with darkness? 15What harmony is there between
Christ and Belial[a]? What does a believer have in common with an
unbeliever? 16What agreement is there between the temple of God
and idols? For we are the temple of the living God. As God has
said: "I will live with them and walk among them, and I will be
their God, and they will be my people."[b]

17 "Therefore come out from them
and be separate,
says the Lord.
Touch no unclean thing,
and I will receive you."[c]
18 "I will be a Father to you,
and you will be my sons and daughters,
says the Lord Almighty."[d]

7 Since we have these promises, dear friends, let us purify ourselves from everything that contaminates body and spirit,
perfecting holiness out of reverence for God.

Paul's Joy

2Make room for us in your hearts. We have wronged no one,
we have corrupted no one, we have exploited no one. 3I do not
say this to condemn you; I have said before that you have such a
place in our hearts that we would live or die with you. 4I have
great confidence in you; I take great pride in you. I am greatly encouraged; in all our troubles my joy knows no bounds.
5For when we came into Macedonia, this body of ours had no
rest, but we were harassed at every turn—conflicts on the outside, fears within. 6But God, who comforts the downcast, comforted us by the coming of Titus, 7and not only by his coming but
also by the comfort you had given him. He told us about your
longing for me, your deep sorrow, your ardent concern for me,
so that my joy was greater than ever.
8Even if I caused you sorrow by my letter, I do not regret it.
Though I did regret it—I see that my letter hurt you, but only for

[a] *15* Greek *Beliar*, a variant of *Belial* [b] *16* Lev. 26:12; Jer. 32:38; Ezek. 37:27
[c] *17* Isaiah 52:11; Ezek. 20:34,41 [d] *18* 2 Samuel 7:14; 7:8

(6:16) O Lord, how quickly the unholy cravings return when I take my eyes off you. A glance here, a step there, and soon I am waltzing with the world once again. "Who will rescue me from this body of death?" Draw me to Yourself, Lord, when I do not want to be drawn. Hold me close, Lord, when I resist Your embrace. Remind me that You are here in power, and reawaken my desire for holiness. Possess me, Lord, and make of me a temple of worship. (Ro 7:24)

We are His people, His holy nation,
Called out of darkness to light.
We are His building, His holy
temple,
We're living by faith, not by sight.

Be ye holy, holy,
For the Lord God Almighty is holy,
Be ye holy, holy,
For holy, holy is the Lord.

"Be Ye Holy"
Walt Harrah (©1985)

Everything that God brings into our life is directed to one purpose: that we might be conformed to the image of Christ.
Erwin W. Lutzer (1941-)

(7:10–11) Holy Spirit, as I repent You gently reveal to me how I got here and what needs to be removed from my heart. You bring me to my knees under the weight of Your conviction, and You raise me up again with the power of Your forgiveness. I know You are at work in me, because Your holy sorrow reaches deep; and when Your work is done I feel relief and peace. Thank You, Lord, for not leaving me in my sin. Thank You for the blessing of conviction without condemnation. Thank You for the gift of godly sorrow. And most of all, thank You for Your forgiveness.

Purify my heart,
Touch me with Your cleansing fire.
Take me to the cross,
Your holiness is my desire.

Breathe Your life in me,
Kindle a love that
Flows from Your throne.
Oh, purify my heart,
Purify my heart.

"Purify My Heart"
Jeff Nelson (©1992)

a little while— 9 yet now I am happy, not because you were made
sorry, but because your sorrow led you to repentance. For you
became sorrowful as God intended and so were not harmed in
any way by us. 10 Godly sorrow brings repentance that leads to
salvation and leaves no regret, but worldly sorrow brings death.
11 See what this godly sorrow has produced in you: what earnestness, what eagerness to clear yourselves, what indignation, what
alarm, what longing, what concern, what readiness to see justice
done. At every point you have proved yourselves to be innocent in
this matter. 12 So even though I wrote to you, it was not on account of the one who did the wrong or of the injured party, but
rather that before God you could see for yourselves how devoted
to us you are. 13 By all this we are encouraged.

In addition to our own encouragement, we were especially delighted to see how happy Titus was, because his spirit has been
refreshed by all of you. 14 I had boasted to him about you, and
you have not embarrassed me. But just as everything we said to
you was true, so our boasting about you to Titus has proved to be
true as well. 15 And his affection for you is all the greater when he
remembers that you were all obedient, receiving him with fear
and trembling. 16 I am glad I can have complete confidence in
you.

Generosity Encouraged

8 And now, brothers, we want you to know about the grace that
God has given the Macedonian churches. 2 Out of the most
severe trial, their overflowing joy and their extreme poverty
welled up in rich generosity. 3 For I testify that they gave as much
as they were able, and even beyond their ability. Entirely on their
own, 4 they urgently pleaded with us for the privilege of sharing in
this service to the saints. 5 And they did not do as we expected, but
they gave themselves first to the Lord and then to us in keeping
with God's will. 6 So we urged Titus, since he had earlier made a
beginning, to bring also to completion this act of grace on your
part. 7 But just as you excel in everything—in faith, in speech, in
knowledge, in complete earnestness and in your love for us[a]—
see that you also excel in this grace of giving.

8 I am not commanding you, but I want to test the sincerity of
your love by comparing it with the earnestness of others. 9 For
you know the grace of our Lord Jesus Christ, that though he was
rich, yet for your sakes he became poor, so that you through his
poverty might become rich.

10 And here is my advice about what is best for you in this matter: Last year you were the first not only to give but also to have
the desire to do so. 11 Now finish the work, so that your eager
willingness to do it may be matched by your completion of it, according to your means. 12 For if the willingness is there, the gift is
acceptable according to what one has, not according to what he
does not have.

13 Our desire is not that others might be relieved while you are
hard pressed, but that there might be equality. 14 At the present
time your plenty will supply what they need, so that in turn their
plenty will supply what you need. Then there will be equality, 15 as
it is written: "He who gathered much did not have too much, and
he who gathered little did not have too little."[b]

[a] 7 Some manuscripts *in our love for you* [b] 15 Exodus 16:18

Titus Sent to Corinth

16I thank God, who put into the heart of Titus the same concern I have for you. 17For Titus not only welcomed our appeal,
but he is coming to you with much enthusiasm and on his own
initiative. 18And we are sending along with him the brother who
is praised by all the churches for his service to the gospel. 19What
is more, he was chosen by the churches to accompany us as we
carry the offering, which we administer in order to honor the
Lord himself and to show our eagerness to help. 20We want to
avoid any criticism of the way we administer this liberal gift. 21For
we are taking pains to do what is right, not only in the eyes of the
Lord but also in the eyes of men.
22In addition, we are sending with them our brother who has
often proved to us in many ways that he is zealous, and now even
more so because of his great confidence in you. 23As for Titus, he
is my partner and fellow worker among you; as for our brothers,
they are representatives of the churches and an honor to Christ.
24Therefore show these men the proof of your love and the reason for our pride in you, so that the churches can see it.
9 There is no need for me to write to you about this service to
the saints. 2For I know your eagerness to help, and I have
been boasting about it to the Macedonians, telling them that since
last year you in Achaia were ready to give; and your enthusiasm
has stirred most of them to action. 3But I am sending the brothers in order that our boasting about you in this matter should not
prove hollow, but that you may be ready, as I said you would be.
4For if any Macedonians come with me and find you unprepared,
we—not to say anything about you—would be ashamed of having been so confident. 5So I thought it necessary to urge the
brothers to visit you in advance and finish the arrangements for
the generous gift you had promised. Then it will be ready as a
generous gift, not as one grudgingly given.

Sowing Generously

6Remember this: Whoever sows sparingly will also reap sparingly, and whoever sows generously will also reap generously.
7Each man should give what he has decided in his heart to give,
not reluctantly or under compulsion, for God loves a cheerful
giver. 8And God is able to make all grace abound to you, so that
in all things at all times, having all that you need, you will abound
in every good work. 9As it is written:

> "He has scattered abroad his gifts to the poor;
> his righteousness endures forever."[a]

10Now he who supplies seed to the sower and bread for food will
also supply and increase your store of seed and will enlarge the
harvest of your righteousness. 11You will be made rich in every
way so that you can be generous on every occasion, and through
us your generosity will result in thanksgiving to God.
12This service that you perform is not only supplying the needs
of God's people but is also overflowing in many expressions of
thanks to God. 13Because of the service by which you have proved
yourselves, men will praise God for the obedience that accompanies your confession of the gospel of Christ, and for your generosity in sharing with them and with everyone else. 14And in

Christians are often accused of being morbid when they talk of the joy of sacrificing. I think it is one of the deepest truths of the Christian religion. Far from being a source of sadness, sacrifice is a great joy and source of illumination–perhaps the greatest of all.

Malcolm Muggeridge (1903-1990)

(9:6) Lord, I confess that sometimes I am too casual, too cavalier about giving to You. From now on, according to Your Word, I want to give deliberately and generously, from a heart of faith and with open hands as an act of worship to You. So I ask for Your help—whether my gift will involve money, time, attention, service or prayer, I want to give liberally, with passion and purpose, never squandering an opportunity to sacrifice for You.

a9 Psalm 112:9

their prayers for you their hearts will go out to you, because of the surpassing grace God has given you. 15 Thanks be to God for his indescribable gift!

Paul's Defense of His Ministry

10 By the meekness and gentleness of Christ, I appeal to you—I, Paul, who am "timid" when face to face with you, but "bold" when away! 2 I beg you that when I come I may not have to be as bold as I expect to be toward some people who think that we live by the standards of this world. 3 For though we live in the world, we do not wage war as the world does. 4 The weapons we fight with are not the weapons of the world. On the contrary, they have divine power to demolish strongholds. 5 We demolish arguments and every pretension that sets itself up against the knowledge of God, and we take captive every thought to make it obedient to Christ. 6 And we will be ready to punish every act of disobedience, once your obedience is complete.

7 You are looking only on the surface of things.[a] If anyone is confident that he belongs to Christ, he should consider again that we belong to Christ just as much as he. 8 For even if I boast somewhat freely about the authority the Lord gave us for building you up rather than pulling you down, I will not be ashamed of it. 9 I do not want to seem to be trying to frighten you with my letters. 10 For some say, "His letters are weighty and forceful, but in person he is unimpressive and his speaking amounts to nothing." 11 Such people should realize that what we are in our letters when we are absent, we will be in our actions when we are present.

12 We do not dare to classify or compare ourselves with some who commend themselves. When they measure themselves by themselves and compare themselves with themselves, they are not wise. 13 We, however, will not boast beyond proper limits, but will confine our boasting to the field God has assigned to us, a field that reaches even to you. 14 We are not going too far in our boasting, as would be the case if we had not come to you, for we did get as far as you with the gospel of Christ. 15 Neither do we go beyond our limits by boasting of work done by others.[b] Our hope is that, as your faith continues to grow, our area of activity among you will greatly expand, 16 so that we can preach the gospel in the regions beyond you. For we do not want to boast about work already done in another man's territory. 17 But, "Let him who boasts boast in the Lord."[c] 18 For it is not the one who commends himself who is approved, but the one whom the Lord commends.

Paul and the False Apostles

11 I hope you will put up with a little of my foolishness; but you are already doing that. 2 I am jealous for you with a godly jealousy. I promised you to one husband, to Christ, so that I might present you as a pure virgin to him. 3 But I am afraid that just as Eve was deceived by the serpent's cunning, your minds may somehow be led astray from your sincere and pure devotion to Christ. 4 For if someone comes to you and preaches a Jesus other than the Jesus we preached, or if you receive a different spirit from the one you received, or a different gospel from the

[a] 7 Or *Look at the obvious facts* [b] *13–15* Or *13We, however, will not boast about things that cannot be measured, but we will boast according to the standard of measurement that the God of measure has assigned us—a measurement that relates even to you. 14 . . . 15Neither do we boast about things that cannot be measured in regard to the work done by others.* [c] *17* Jer. 9:24

(10:3–4) Almighty God, strong to save, we worship You! For we are not helpless against the enemy of our souls; no, You have armed us with the weapons of the Spirit. We praise You! For by Your power we fight and win. In Your strength, we accomplish feats of righteousness. Victory is ours through the power of the name and the blood of our Lord Jesus Christ! (Eph 6:10–18)

Jesus, mighty God,
Our Rock, our Fortress, our defense.
Your conq'ring arm
Will be our strength,
O God of pow'r and righteousness,
And ev'ry foe will
Tremble at Your name.

"Jesus, Mighty God"
Rick Founds (©1989)

one you accepted, you put up with it easily enough. 5But I do not
think I am in the least inferior to those "super-apostles." 6I may
not be a trained speaker, but I do have knowledge. We have made
this perfectly clear to you in every way.
7Was it a sin for me to lower myself in order to elevate you by
preaching the gospel of God to you free of charge? 8I robbed
other churches by receiving support from them so as to serve
you. 9And when I was with you and needed something, I was not
a burden to anyone, for the brothers who came from Macedonia
supplied what I needed. I have kept myself from being a burden
to you in any way, and will continue to do so. 10As surely as the
truth of Christ is in me, nobody in the regions of Achaia will stop
this boasting of mine. 11Why? Because I do not love you? God
knows I do! 12And I will keep on doing what I am doing in order
to cut the ground from under those who want an opportunity to
be considered equal with us in the things they boast about.
13For such men are false apostles, deceitful workmen, masquerading as apostles of Christ. 14And no wonder, for Satan himself masquerades as an angel of light. 15It is not surprising, then,
if his servants masquerade as servants of righteousness. Their end
will be what their actions deserve.

Paul Boasts About His Sufferings

16I repeat: Let no one take me for a fool. But if you do, then receive me just as you would a fool, so that I may do a little boasting. 17In this self-confident boasting I am not talking as the Lord
would, but as a fool. 18Since many are boasting in the way the
world does, I too will boast. 19You gladly put up with fools since
you are so wise! 20In fact, you even put up with anyone who en-
slaves you or exploits you or takes advantage of you or pushes
himself forward or slaps you in the face. 21To my shame I admit
that we were too weak for that!
What anyone else dares to boast about—I am speaking as a
fool—I also dare to boast about. 22Are they Hebrews? So am I.
Are they Israelites? So am I. Are they Abraham's descendants? So
am I. 23Are they servants of Christ? (I am out of my mind to talk
like this.) I am more. I have worked much harder, been in prison
more frequently, been flogged more severely, and been exposed
to death again and again. 24Five times I received from the Jews
the forty lashes minus one. 25Three times I was beaten with rods,
once I was stoned, three times I was shipwrecked, I spent a night
and a day in the open sea, 26I have been constantly on the move.
I have been in danger from rivers, in danger from bandits, in danger from my own countrymen, in danger from Gentiles; in danger
in the city, in danger in the country, in danger at sea; and in danger from false brothers. 27I have labored and toiled and have
often gone without sleep; I have known hunger and thirst and
have often gone without food; I have been cold and naked. 28Be-
sides everything else, I face daily the pressure of my concern for
all the churches. 29Who is weak, and I do not feel weak? Who is
led into sin, and I do not inwardly burn?
30If I must boast, I will boast of the things that show my weakness. 31The God and Father of the Lord Jesus, who is to be
praised forever, knows that I am not lying. 32In Damascus the
governor under King Aretas had the city of the Damascenes
guarded in order to arrest me. 33But I was lowered in a basket
from a window in the wall and slipped through his hands.

When the mind floats on the sea of the majesty of God and his incomprehensibility, it is amazed and lost in wonder at the serene majesty of God. And forthwith the soul becomes humble, so that if it were possible, when the effulgence of God's majesty envelops it, it would take its place below the whole creation because of its awe and wondering amazement at the majesty of God, ineffable, incomprehensible as it is, beyond the penetration of his servants.

John of Lycopolis (d. 394)

(11:30) "Therefore, as it is written, 'Let him who boasts, boast in the Lord.' " Lord God, there are not enough words, there is not enough breath, there are not enough ways to describe Your greatness. I am nothing, but You are everything. And I can only begin to lift up Your name and tell of Your goodness. The Psalmist's words are my prayer, that "my mouth will tell of your righteousness, of your salvation all day long, though I know not its measure." (Ps 71:15; 1Co 1:31)

Lift your voice, let your praises ring.
Let every tongue glorify our King.
Let's become the generation
Who will passionately praise Him.
Boasting in the greatness of our God.

Sing to the Lord with all of your heart.
Sing to Him a new song,
Sing to Him a new song.

"Sing to the Lord"
Rita Baloche and Paul Baloche (©1992)

Paul's Vision and His Thorn

12 I must go on boasting. Although there is nothing to be
gained, I will go on to visions and revelations from the
Lord. 2I know a man in Christ who fourteen years ago was caught
up to the third heaven. Whether it was in the body or out of the
body I do not know—God knows. 3And I know that this man—
whether in the body or apart from the body I do not know, but
God knows— 4was caught up to paradise. He heard inexpressible things, things that man is not permitted to tell. 5I will boast
about a man like that, but I will not boast about myself, except
about my weaknesses. 6Even if I should choose to boast, I would
not be a fool, because I would be speaking the truth. But I refrain, so no one will think more of me than is warranted by what
I do or say.
7To keep me from becoming conceited because of these surpassingly great revelations, there was given me a thorn in my
flesh, a messenger of Satan, to torment me. 8Three times I pleaded with the Lord to take it away from me. 9But he said to me, "My
grace is sufficient for you, for my power is made perfect in weakness." Therefore I will boast all the more gladly about my weaknesses, so that Christ's power may rest on me. 10That is why, for
Christ's sake, I delight in weaknesses, in insults, in hardships, in
persecutions, in difficulties. For when I am weak, then I am
strong.

Paul's Concern for the Corinthians

11I have made a fool of myself, but you drove me to it. I ought
to have been commended by you, for I am not in the least inferi-
or to the "super-apostles," even though I am nothing. 12The
things that mark an apostle—signs, wonders and miracles—
were done among you with great perseverance. 13How were you
inferior to the other churches, except that I was never a burden
to you? Forgive me this wrong!
14Now I am ready to visit you for the third time, and I will not
be a burden to you, because what I want is not your possessions
but you. After all, children should not have to save up for their
parents, but parents for their children. 15So I will very gladly
spend for you everything I have and expend myself as well. If I
love you more, will you love me less? 16Be that as it may, I have
not been a burden to you. Yet, crafty fellow that I am, I caught you
by trickery! 17Did I exploit you through any of the men I sent you?
18I urged Titus to go to you and I sent our brother with him. Titus
did not exploit you, did he? Did we not act in the same spirit and
follow the same course?
19Have you been thinking all along that we have been defending ourselves to you? We have been speaking in the sight of God
as those in Christ; and everything we do, dear friends, is for your
strengthening. 20For I am afraid that when I come I may not find
you as I want you to be, and you may not find me as you want me
to be. I fear that there may be quarreling, jealousy, outbursts of
anger, factions, slander, gossip, arrogance and disorder. 21I am
afraid that when I come again my God will humble me before you,
and I will be grieved over many who have sinned earlier and have
not repented of the impurity, sexual sin and debauchery in which
they have indulged.

(12:7–10) Great Healer, we are the wounded lambs You hold. We know that You hear our cries for help and healing. We trust You with our sufferings. Help us to understand Your great compassion, even when You choose to let us remain broken. Teach us through our weaknesses to lean on Your strength. Give us grace as You keep us humble, so that Christ's power may rest on us. (Jas 4:6)

My God, I have never thanked thee for my thorn. I have thanked thee a thousand times for my roses, but not once for my thorn. I have been looking forward to a world where I shall get compensation for my cross, but I have never thought of my cross as itself a present glory. Thou divine Love, whose human path has been perfected through sufferings, teach me the glory of my cross, teach me the value of my thorn.

George Matheson (1842–1906)

Hold me close,
Let Your love surround me;
Bring me near,
Draw me to Your side.
And as I wait,
I'll rise up like the eagle,
And I will soar with You,
Your Spirit leads me on
In the power of Your love.

"The Power Of Your Love"
Geoff Bullock (©1992)

Final Warnings

13 This will be my third visit to you. "Every matter must be established by the testimony of two or three witnesses."[a] 2I
already gave you a warning when I was with you the second time.
I now repeat it while absent: On my return I will not spare those
who sinned earlier or any of the others, 3since you are demanding proof that Christ is speaking through me. He is not weak in
dealing with you, but is powerful among you. 4For to be sure, he
was crucified in weakness, yet he lives by God's power. Likewise,
we are weak in him, yet by God's power we will live with him to
serve you.
5Examine yourselves to see whether you are in the faith; test
yourselves. Do you not realize that Christ Jesus is in you—unless,
of course, you fail the test? 6And I trust that you will discover that
we have not failed the test. 7Now we pray to God that you will not
do anything wrong. Not that people will see that we have stood the
test but that you will do what is right even though we may seem to
have failed. 8For we cannot do anything against the truth, but only
for the truth. 9We are glad whenever we are weak but you are
strong; and our prayer is for your perfection. 10This is why I write
these things when I am absent, that when I come I may not have
to be harsh in my use of authority—the authority the Lord gave
me for building you up, not for tearing you down.

Final Greetings

11Finally, brothers, good-by. Aim for perfection, listen to my
appeal, be of one mind, live in peace. And the God of love and
peace will be with you.
12Greet one another with a holy kiss. 13All the saints send their
greetings.
14May the grace of the Lord Jesus Christ, and the love of God,
and the fellowship of the Holy Spirit be with you all.

[a] 1 Deut. 19:15

(13:11–14) Lord Jesus, in this world where condemnation pursues every one of us, You bring us grace. Father, in this world where hate devours hearts, You bestow love. Holy Spirit, in this world where fear isolates us, You unite us in the fellowship of the church. O God of love and peace, may we live in the grace, love and fellowship into which You have called us. May we experience Your presence daily, deeply. And may our lives bear witness to Your greatness, now and forever. Amen.

To thee, great One in Three,
Eternal praises be
Hence, evermore!
Thy sovereign majesty
May we in glory see,
And to eternity love and adore.

"Come, Thou Almighty King"
Italian Hymn (c.1757)

galatians

The Epistle of Paul the Apostle to the

GALATIANS

What motivates us to worship God? A sense of gratitude or a sense of guilt? A desire to respond to God's grace or a desire to earn it? Sometimes we treat worship as a religious obligation, a means by which we attempt to secure God's favor. That which God intends as a joyful exercise of freedom becomes a dreary experience of legalism.

Issues like these perplexed Christians in Galatia. Though they had begun to walk with God by believing the gospel, outsiders who claimed to have a better religious experience shook their confidence in their faith. These "Judaizers" were Gentiles who kept the Jewish ceremonial laws, especially those concerning religious rituals and circumcision (4:10; 6:12). They put their faith not in the gospel but in their observance of the law—and they urged the Galatians to join them. According to the way of the Judaizers, the Christian life becomes a matter of earning God's grace by religious observance.

Paul writes his letter to the Galatians because they are abandoning their authentic faith in Christ under the influence of the Judaizers. Having begun with the "grace of Christ," they are now "turning to a different gospel" (1:6). Having started with the Spirit, they are living by "human effort" (3:3). Such legalistic behavior contradicts the basic message of the gospel: that God, by grace, sent His Son to redeem us (2:20–21; 3:26; 4:4–5). We receive the benefits of His redemption not by works but by faith in Christ. Our faith brings us into right relationship with God and also enables us to receive the Holy Spirit (3:14). As Christians we continue to live by faith, in the freedom of the Spirit Who helps us to live as Christ lived (ch. 5).

Genuine faith involves a comprehensive investment of oneself in Christ.

True faith is not "easy believism"—a superficial acknowledgment that the gospel is true without any personal commitment. Paul writes: "I have been crucified with Christ and I no longer live, but Christ lives in me. The life I live in the body, I live by faith in the Son of God, who loved me and gave himself for me" (2:20). Genuine faith involves a comprehensive investment of oneself in Christ.

The Christian life flows from the gospel of grace as it is received through faith. Legalistic efforts to earn God's favor are, therefore, fundamentally inconsistent with true Christianity. Like Paul, we live—and worship—by faith in the One Who loved us and gave Himself for us. We are welcomed into God's holy presence, not because of anything we do, but because of what Jesus Christ has already done for us. Thus, our worship will always be a faithful, committed, joyful and free response to God's grace given in Christ. He "gave himself for our sins to rescue us from the present evil age, according to the will of our God and Father, to whom be glory for ever and ever" (1:4–5).

1 Paul, an apostle—sent not from men nor by man, but by Jesus
Christ and God the Father, who raised him from the dead—
2and all the brothers with me,

To the churches in Galatia:

3Grace and peace to you from God our Father and the Lord
Jesus Christ, 4who gave himself for our sins to rescue us from the
present evil age, according to the will of our God and Father, 5to
whom be glory for ever and ever. Amen.

No Other Gospel

6I am astonished that you are so quickly deserting the one who
called you by the grace of Christ and are turning to a different
gospel— 7which is really no gospel at all. Evidently some people
are throwing you into confusion and are trying to pervert the
gospel of Christ. 8But even if we or an angel from heaven should
preach a gospel other than the one we preached to you, let him
be eternally condemned! 9As we have already said, so now I say
again: If anybody is preaching to you a gospel other than what
you accepted, let him be eternally condemned!

10Am I now trying to win the approval of men, or of God? Or
am I trying to please men? If I were still trying to please men, I
would not be a servant of Christ.

Paul Called by God

11I want you to know, brothers, that the gospel I preached is
not something that man made up. 12I did not receive it from any
man, nor was I taught it; rather, I received it by revelation from
Jesus Christ.

13For you have heard of my previous way of life in Judaism,
how intensely I persecuted the church of God and tried to destroy
it. 14I was advancing in Judaism beyond many Jews of my own
age and was extremely zealous for the traditions of my fathers.
15But when God, who set me apart from birth[a] and called me by
his grace, was pleased 16to reveal his Son in me so that I might
preach him among the Gentiles, I did not consult any man, 17nor
did I go up to Jerusalem to see those who were apostles before I
was, but I went immediately into Arabia and later returned to Damascus.

18Then after three years, I went up to Jerusalem to get acquainted with Peter[b] and stayed with him fifteen days. 19I saw
none of the other apostles—only James, the Lord's brother. 20I
assure you before God that what I am writing you is no lie. 21Later
I went to Syria and Cilicia. 22I was personally unknown to the
churches of Judea that are in Christ. 23They only heard the report: "The man who formerly persecuted us is now preaching the
faith he once tried to destroy." 24And they praised God because
of me.

Paul Accepted by the Apostles

2 Fourteen years later I went up again to Jerusalem, this time
with Barnabas. I took Titus along also. 2I went in response to
a revelation and set before them the gospel that I preach among
the Gentiles. But I did this privately to those who seemed to be
leaders, for fear that I was running or had run my race in vain.

[a] 15 Or *from my mother's womb* [b] 18 Greek *Cephas*

(1:3–4) O Father, I live in a world that worships wealth and power and success. But when You saw that I needed to be saved from the seductive idols in my heart, You sent a Savior. And when You saw that I needed deliverance from my own sin, You sent a Deliverer. The One You sent was Your Son, and my deliverance cost Him His life. Still You did it for me. This was Your will, Your delight. I worship You with all my heart. (Eze 14:3; 36:25; Jn 3:16)

Life passes, riches fly away, popularity is fickle, the senses decay, the world changes. One alone is true to us; one alone can be all things to us; one alone can supply our need.

Cardinal John Henry Newman (1801–1890)

Jesus! I do now receive Him,
More than all in Him I find,
He has granted me forgiveness,
I am His, and He is mine.

Hallelujah! What a Savior!
Hallelujah! What a Friend!
Saving, helping, keeping, loving,
He is with me to the end.

"Jesus, What a Friend for Sinners"
J. Wilbur Chapman (1910)

(1:6–9) O Lord God, I hereby confess that salvation is by grace alone, through faith alone, in Jesus Christ alone. "Christ plus anything else" is blasphemy. "Christ alone" is the essence of the true gospel. He alone is the Way, the Truth, the Life. His blood is my ransom note. His name is my banner. Whoever tries to supplement or sully the message of "Christ alone" has missed the point. Thank You for Jesus. He is more than enough. (Jn 14:6; Ac 2:38, 3:16; Heb 10:19)

(2:6) You, Lord, do not look at the things that we look at, nor are you impressed with the things that impress the world. We look at the outward appearance, but You look at the heart. Forgive me when I am more concerned with the face I show to the world than with the heart I present to You. Tear down my façade, Father, so that I can share my real self with You. (1Sa 16:7)

God is not asking you to make a promise that you cannot keep–He is asking you to receive a promise that only He can keep.

James Ryle (1950–

(2:20) Lord, I choose to follow You and to die to myself. Crucify my sinful nature with its passions and desires. Come and breathe the life of Christ into these dry bones. Come and fill this hollow shell with the presence of Your Holy Spirit. Unlock for me the incredible mystery of it all—that in this new life Jesus Christ will be the breath in my lungs, the music in my soul, my peace, my joy, my only hope of glory. (Eze 37:5–6; Gal 5:24–25; Col. 1:27)

3Yet not even Titus, who was with me, was compelled to be circumcised, even though he was a Greek. 4⌊This matter arose⌋ because some false brothers had infiltrated our ranks to spy on the
freedom we have in Christ Jesus and to make us slaves. 5We did
not give in to them for a moment, so that the truth of the gospel
might remain with you.
6As for those who seemed to be important—whatever they
were makes no difference to me; God does not judge by external
appearance—those men added nothing to my message. 7On the
contrary, they saw that I had been entrusted with the task of
preaching the gospel to the Gentiles,[a] just as Peter had been to
the Jews.[b] 8For God, who was at work in the ministry of Peter as
an apostle to the Jews, was also at work in my ministry as an
apostle to the Gentiles. 9James, Peter[c] and John, those reputed to
be pillars, gave me and Barnabas the right hand of fellowship
when they recognized the grace given to me. They agreed that we
should go to the Gentiles, and they to the Jews. 10All they asked
was that we should continue to remember the poor, the very thing
I was eager to do.

Paul Opposes Peter

11When Peter came to Antioch, I opposed him to his face, because he was clearly in the wrong. 12Before certain men came
from James, he used to eat with the Gentiles. But when they
arrived, he began to draw back and separate himself from the
Gentiles because he was afraid of those who belonged to the circumcision group. 13The other Jews joined him in his hypocrisy,
so that by their hypocrisy even Barnabas was led astray.
14When I saw that they were not acting in line with the truth of
the gospel, I said to Peter in front of them all, "You are a Jew, yet
you live like a Gentile and not like a Jew. How is it, then, that you
force Gentiles to follow Jewish customs?
15"We who are Jews by birth and not 'Gentile sinners' 16know
that a man is not justified by observing the law, but by faith in
Jesus Christ. So we, too, have put our faith in Christ Jesus that we
may be justified by faith in Christ and not by observing the law, because by observing the law no one will be justified.
17"If, while we seek to be justified in Christ, it becomes evident
that we ourselves are sinners, does that mean that Christ promotes sin? Absolutely not! 18If I rebuild what I destroyed, I prove
that I am a lawbreaker. 19For through the law I died to the law so
that I might live for God. 20I have been crucified with Christ and
I no longer live, but Christ lives in me. The life I live in the body,
I live by faith in the Son of God, who loved me and gave himself
for me. 21I do not set aside the grace of God, for if righteousness
could be gained through the law, Christ died for nothing!"[d]

Faith or Observance of the Law

3 You foolish Galatians! Who has bewitched you? Before your
very eyes Jesus Christ was clearly portrayed as crucified. 2I
would like to learn just one thing from you: Did you receive the
Spirit by observing the law, or by believing what you heard? 3Are
you so foolish? After beginning with the Spirit, are you now trying
to attain your goal by human effort? 4Have you suffered so much

[a] 7 Greek *uncircumcised* [b] 7 Greek *circumcised*; also in verses 8 and 9
[c] 9 Greek *Cephas*; also in verses 11 and 14 [d] 21 Some interpreters end the quotation after verse 14.

for nothing—if it really was for nothing? 5Does God give you his
Spirit and work miracles among you because you observe the law,
or because you believe what you heard?
6Consider Abraham: "He believed God, and it was credited to
him as righteousness."[a] 7Understand, then, that those who believe are children of Abraham. 8The Scripture foresaw that God
would justify the Gentiles by faith, and announced the gospel in
advance to Abraham: "All nations will be blessed through you."[b]
9So those who have faith are blessed along with Abraham, the
man of faith.
10All who rely on observing the law are under a curse, for it is
written: "Cursed is everyone who does not continue to do everything written in the Book of the Law."[c] 11Clearly no one is justified before God by the law, because, "The righteous will live by
faith."[d] 12The law is not based on faith; on the contrary, "The
man who does these things will live by them."[e] 13Christ redeemed
us from the curse of the law by becoming a curse for us, for it is
written: "Cursed is everyone who is hung on a tree."[f] 14He redeemed us in order that the blessing given to Abraham might
come to the Gentiles through Christ Jesus, so that by faith we
might receive the promise of the Spirit.

The Law and the Promise

15Brothers, let me take an example from everyday life. Just as
no one can set aside or add to a human covenant that has been
duly established, so it is in this case. 16The promises were spoken
to Abraham and to his seed. The Scripture does not say "and to
seeds," meaning many people, but "and to your seed,"[g] meaning
one person, who is Christ. 17What I mean is this: The law, introduced 430 years later, does not set aside the covenant previously
established by God and thus do away with the promise. 18For if
the inheritance depends on the law, then it no longer depends on
a promise; but God in his grace gave it to Abraham through a
promise.
19What, then, was the purpose of the law? It was added because of transgressions until the Seed to whom the promise referred had come. The law was put into effect through angels by a
mediator. 20A mediator, however, does not represent just one
party; but God is one.
21Is the law, therefore, opposed to the promises of God? Absolutely not! For if a law had been given that could impart life,
then righteousness would certainly have come by the law. 22But
the Scripture declares that the whole world is a prisoner of sin, so
that what was promised, being given through faith in Jesus Christ,
might be given to those who believe.
23Before this faith came, we were held prisoners by the law,
locked up until faith should be revealed. 24So the law was put in
charge to lead us to Christ[h] that we might be justified by faith.
25Now that faith has come, we are no longer under the supervision of the law.

Sons of God

26You are all sons of God through faith in Christ Jesus, 27for all
of you who were baptized into Christ have clothed yourselves with

[a] *6* Gen. 15:6 [b] *8* Gen. 12:3; 18:18; 22:18 [c] *10* Deut. 27:26 [d] *11* Hab. 2:4
[e] *12* Lev. 18:5 [f] *13* Deut. 21:23 [g] *16* Gen. 12:7; 13:15; 24:7 [h] *24* Or *charge until Christ came*

(3:10–14;24–25) Righteous Judge, I look into the stark light of Your law as one looks into a mirror. The cumulative weight of the law leads me to just one conclusion—I am a sinner, desperately in need of a Savior! Apart from You I can do nothing. In Your mercy and grace, Lord, save me and make me holy. And then, by the power of Your Spirit, help me to live a life that is pleasing to You. (Jn 15:5; Jas 1:23)

The Christian life isn't difficult—it is impossible. If we don't know that, we will try to do things ourselves. Faith is not necessary when we think we can do it ourselves. Faith comes along when we realize that we cannot do it on our own.

Joseph Garlington (1939-)

Christ. 28There is neither Jew nor Greek, slave nor free, male nor
female, for you are all one in Christ Jesus. 29If you belong to
Christ, then you are Abraham's seed, and heirs according to the
promise.

4 What I am saying is that as long as the heir is a child, he is no
different from a slave, although he owns the whole estate.
2He is subject to guardians and trustees until the time set by his
father. 3So also, when we were children, we were in slavery under
the basic principles of the world. 4But when the time had fully
come, God sent his Son, born of a woman, born under law, 5to
redeem those under law, that we might receive the full rights of
sons. 6Because you are sons, God sent the Spirit of his Son into
our hearts, the Spirit who calls out, *"Abba,*[a] Father." 7So you are
no longer a slave, but a son; and since you are a son, God has
made you also an heir.

Paul's Concern for the Galatians

8Formerly, when you did not know God, you were slaves to
those who by nature are not gods. 9But now that you know God—
or rather are known by God—how is it that you are turning back
to those weak and miserable principles? Do you wish to be enslaved by them all over again? 10You are observing special days
and months and seasons and years! 11I fear for you, that somehow I have wasted my efforts on you.

12I plead with you, brothers, become like me, for I became
like you. You have done me no wrong. 13As you know, it was because of an illness that I first preached the gospel to you. 14Even
though my illness was a trial to you, you did not treat me with
contempt or scorn. Instead, you welcomed me as if I were an
angel of God, as if I were Christ Jesus himself. 15What has happened to all your joy? I can testify that, if you could have done so,
you would have torn out your eyes and given them to me. 16Have
I now become your enemy by telling you the truth?

17Those people are zealous to win you over, but for no good.
What they want is to alienate you ⌞from us⌟, so that you may be
zealous for them. 18It is fine to be zealous, provided the purpose
is good, and to be so always and not just when I am with you.
19My dear children, for whom I am again in the pains of childbirth until Christ is formed in you, 20how I wish I could be with
you now and change my tone, because I am perplexed about you!

Hagar and Sarah

21Tell me, you who want to be under the law, are you not aware
of what the law says? 22For it is written that Abraham had two
sons, one by the slave woman and the other by the free woman.
23His son by the slave woman was born in the ordinary way; but
his son by the free woman was born as the result of a promise.

24These things may be taken figuratively, for the women represent two covenants. One covenant is from Mount Sinai and bears
children who are to be slaves: This is Hagar. 25Now Hagar stands
for Mount Sinai in Arabia and corresponds to the present city of
Jerusalem, because she is in slavery with her children. 26But the
Jerusalem that is above is free, and she is our mother. 27For it is
written:

"Be glad, O barren woman,

[a] 6 Aramaic for *Father*

(4:1–7) Father God, You were not content for me to dwell in Your household as a slave, but yearned instead to love me as Your child. So You sent Jesus from the heights of heaven down to the depths of earth. You allowed Him to lower Himself to the position of a slave so that I might be lifted to the position of a child. You removed from me the yoke of slavery and filled me instead with the Spirit of adoption, by which I may cry out to You "Abba, Father!" just as Jesus did. O Father, how good You are to me! (Mk 14:36; Ro 8:15; Gal 5:1; Php 2:5–8)

Abba Father we approach Thee
In our Savior's precious name;
We, the children of Your mercy
Bow before your throne today.
Free from guilt, his blood has washed
us,
Now through Him our souls draw
nigh
By Your Spirit, You inspire us.
"Abba, Father," is our cry.

"Abba, Father, We Approach Thee"
James Deck (1807–1884)
Adapted by Bill Batstone (©1988)

(4:8–9) Lord, I remember the days before I knew You. I was bound by chains of loneliness and fear. But You broke those chains and released me into the joy of Your freedom. So what insanity would cause me to turn back to the days of slavery? Why would I scoop up the broken chains and try to shackle myself again? Forgive me, Lord, when I find myself looking back. Help me to forget what lies behind and to press on toward the incredible prize of knowing You and living with You forever. (Nu 11:4–6; Pr 26:11; Php 3:12–14)

who bears no children;
break forth and cry aloud,
you who have no labor pains;
because more are the children of the desolate woman
than of her who has a husband."[a]

28Now you, brothers, like Isaac, are children of promise. 29At
that time the son born in the ordinary way persecuted the son
born by the power of the Spirit. It is the same now. 30But what
does the Scripture say? "Get rid of the slave woman and her son,
for the slave woman's son will never share in the inheritance with
the free woman's son."[b] 31Therefore, brothers, we are not children of the slave woman, but of the free woman.

Freedom in Christ

5 It is for freedom that Christ has set us free. Stand firm, then,
and do not let yourselves be burdened again by a yoke of
slavery.

2Mark my words! I, Paul, tell you that if you let yourselves be
circumcised, Christ will be of no value to you at all. 3Again I declare to every man who lets himself be circumcised that he is obligated to obey the whole law. 4You who are trying to be justified
by law have been alienated from Christ; you have fallen away from
grace. 5But by faith we eagerly await through the Spirit the righteousness for which we hope. 6For in Christ Jesus neither circumcision nor uncircumcision has any value. The only thing that
counts is faith expressing itself through love.

7You were running a good race. Who cut in on you and kept
you from obeying the truth? 8That kind of persuasion does not
come from the one who calls you. 9"A little yeast works through
the whole batch of dough." 10I am confident in the Lord that you
will take no other view. The one who is throwing you into confusion will pay the penalty, whoever he may be. 11Brothers, if I am
still preaching circumcision, why am I still being persecuted? In
that case the offense of the cross has been abolished. 12As for
those agitators, I wish they would go the whole way and emascu-
late themselves!

13You, my brothers, were called to be free. But do not use your
freedom to indulge the sinful nature[c]; rather, serve one another
in love. 14The entire law is summed up in a single command:
"Love your neighbor as yourself."[d] 15If you keep on biting and
devouring each other, watch out or you will be destroyed by each
other.

Life by the Spirit

16So I say, live by the Spirit, and you will not gratify the desires
of the sinful nature. 17For the sinful nature desires what is contrary to the Spirit, and the Spirit what is contrary to the sinful nature. They are in conflict with each other, so that you do not do
what you want. 18But if you are led by the Spirit, you are not
under law.

19The acts of the sinful nature are obvious: sexual immorality,
impurity and debauchery; 20idolatry and witchcraft; hatred, discord, jealousy, fits of rage, selfish ambition, dissensions, factions
21and envy; drunkenness, orgies, and the like. I warn you, as I

(5:13–14) Lord, open my eyes and help me to recognize my neighbors. Open my heart so I can feel their suffering and understand their needs. Help me to see that my freedom in You is actually a yoke of service to the "others" You have placed in my life. Help me to honor You by honoring them. Seal this assignment in the center of my soul, Lord, so that every day I may love my neighbor more, and in doing so, I may love You more as well. (Mt 25:34–45; Lk 10:29–37)

[a] *27* Isaiah 54:1 [b] *30* Gen. 21:10 [c] *13* Or *the flesh*; also in verses 16, 17, 19 and 24
[d] *14* Lev. 19:18

did before, that those who live like this will not inherit the kingdom of God.

22But the fruit of the Spirit is love, joy, peace, patience, kindness, goodness, faithfulness, 23gentleness and self-control. Against such things there is no law. 24Those who belong to Christ Jesus have crucified the sinful nature with its passions and desires. 25Since we live by the Spirit, let us keep in step with the Spirit. 26Let us not become conceited, provoking and envying each other.

Doing Good to All

6 Brothers, if someone is caught in a sin, you who are spiritual should restore him gently. But watch yourself, or you also may be tempted. 2Carry each other's burdens, and in this way you will fulfill the law of Christ. 3If anyone thinks he is something when he is nothing, he deceives himself. 4Each one should test his own actions. Then he can take pride in himself, without comparing himself to somebody else, 5for each one should carry his own load.

6Anyone who receives instruction in the word must share all good things with his instructor.

7Do not be deceived: God cannot be mocked. A man reaps what he sows. 8The one who sows to please his sinful nature, from that nature[a] will reap destruction; the one who sows to please the Spirit, from the Spirit will reap eternal life. 9Let us not become weary in doing good, for at the proper time we will reap a harvest if we do not give up. 10Therefore, as we have opportunity, let us do good to all people, especially to those who belong to the family of believers.

Not Circumcision but a New Creation

11See what large letters I use as I write to you with my own hand!

12Those who want to make a good impression outwardly are trying to compel you to be circumcised. The only reason they do this is to avoid being persecuted for the cross of Christ. 13Not even those who are circumcised obey the law, yet they want you to be circumcised that they may boast about your flesh. 14May I never boast except in the cross of our Lord Jesus Christ, through which[b] the world has been crucified to me, and I to the world. 15Neither circumcision nor uncircumcision means anything; what counts is a new creation. 16Peace and mercy to all who follow this rule, even to the Israel of God.

17Finally, let no one cause me trouble, for I bear on my body the marks of Jesus.

18The grace of our Lord Jesus Christ be with your spirit, brothers. Amen.

[a] 8 Or *his flesh, from the flesh* [b] 14 Or *whom*

(5:22–23; 6:7–9) O Father, Your natural world follows absolute laws. Apple trees bear apples; lemon trees bear lemons. Human nature, too, follows Your laws. If I sow seeds of my sinful nature, I will reap a life of selfishness and depravity. If I sow seeds of the Spirit, I will reap the spiritual fruit of love, joy, peace, patience, kindness, goodness, faithfulness, gentleness and self-control. I choose to sow to the Spirit, Lord. Bring forth in me a harvest that will honor You. (Pr 11:18; 22:8–9)

(6:13–15) All praise and glory are Yours, O Lord. Salvation comes from Your hand alone. I cannot boast about any sacrifice or suffering of my own—I can only boast in the nails in Your hands and feet, the thorns on Your brow, the wooden cross on which You died. I cannot boast about any spiritual gift or competency, for everything is a gift from You. My righteousness is not my own—it comes from my faith in You. And I cannot even boast in my faith, for faith itself is a gift of Your grace. You, O Lord, are the Giver of every good and perfect gift. May I live my life as a new creation, fully devoted to Your service. (Eph. 2:8–9; Php 3:7–8; Jas 1:17)

In the cross is health, in the cross is life, in the cross is protection from enemies, in the cross is heavenly sweetness, in the cross strength of mind, in the cross joy of the Spirit, in the cross the height of virtue, in the cross perfection of holiness. There is no health of the soul, no hope of eternal life, save in the cross.

Thomas à Kempis (c.1380-1471)

So I'll cherish the old rugged cross,
'Til my trophies at last I lay down;
I will cling to the old rugged cross,
And exchange it some day for a
crown.

"The Old Rugged Cross"
George Bennard (1873-1958)

The Epistle of Paul the Apostle to the

EPHESIANS

Why do we worship God? . . . because we get so much out of it? . . . because the Bible says we should? . . . because we love God? All of these answers may be true, and we could probably suggest many other valid reasons. Yet, apart from the first chapter of Ephesians we might never come up with an answer so stunning as what Paul offers there.

The apostle begins by praising God, who has: blessed us in every way (1:3); chosen us before creation (1:4); predestined us in love to be His children (1:5,11); redeemed us (1:7); forgiven our sins (1:7); lavished His grace upon us (1:8); and made known to us His plan for creation (1:9–10). Why has God done all these marvelous things? "In order that we . . . might *be* for the praise of his glory" (1:12). Our very being as God's people is defined in terms of worship. We exist to praise our glorious God!

We worship because that's why we are here on earth. We worship because God determined, even before creation, that this would be our chief purpose. We worship because nothing else is more important. How different our lives would be if we were to begin each day by saying: "I exist for the primary purpose of praising God. That's why I'm alive today!"

We live for God's glory by regularly worshiping Him through praise, thanksgiving and other obviously worshipful actions. But true worship happens not only in words but also in the whole scope of our lives. "For you were once darkness, but now you are light in the Lord. Live as children of light . . . and find out what pleases the Lord" (5:8, 10). We will please God when we live each moment consistently with our new identity in Christ.

How different our lives would be if we were to begin each day by saying: "I exist for the primary purpose of praising God. That's why I'm alive today!"

Yet Ephesians specifically encourages us to do that which we typically identify as worship: "Be filled with the Spirit. Speak to one another with psalms, hymns and spiritual songs. Sing and make music in your heart to the Lord, always giving thanks to God . . . Submit to one another out of reverence for Christ" (5:18–21).

This passage also underscores the corporate dimension of worship. We sing to the Lord in the presence of our Christian family (5:19). Moreover, we submit to one another as a logical extension of our worship. (The original Greek of 5:18–21 makes singing, thanking and submitting inseparable. All follow from being filled with the Spirit.) Together with our brothers and sisters in Christ, we are being built into a holy temple for God – a dwelling for the Holy Spirit and a locus of worship (2:21–22). Consequently, the church exists to glorify God: "To him be glory *in the church*" and in Christ Jesus throughout all generations, for ever and ever!" (3:21). No matter how faithfully we worship when alone, we must also join with God's people in order to live completely for the praise of His glory.

Ephesians

(1:4–8) Lord God, You have sought us in Your love, You have pursued us with Your grace, You have captured us by Your mercy in Jesus. Your intention from the dawn of creation was to be in relationship with us. Why would You choose us? We hide. You seek. We hold back. You pour Yourself out on our behalf. We are weak, broken and unresponsive. Yet You are relentless in Your pursuit of us. You are determined to make us holy and blameless in Your sight. We will never fully comprehend the depth of Your love or the riches of Your grace in Christ Jesus. All praise be to You, our loving Lord! (Ge 3:8–9; Lev 20:8)

Lord, in Your faithfulness
You have pursued me;
Gently and tenderly,
Lord, You have wooed me.
Who could imagine I would find
All of the riches that are mine?

So great a salvation,
So costly the gift,
So great a redemption,
So the dying might live,
So great a salvation,
So high the price,
So kind a Redeemer,
Supreme sacrifice,
Great is Your love,
Great is Your love.

"So Great a Salvation"
David Durham and Becky Durham (©1998)

(1:17–23) We praise You, glorious Father, for Your great power and wisdom. We, Your church—this immense collection of frail humanity—we are the body of Christ on earth. The Spirit that raised Jesus Christ from the dead now inhabits each of us with that same resurrection power. I am a part of Your living body, Lord Jesus. Fill me afresh with Your Spirit and open my eyes of faith so that I might understand not just in theory, but in day-to-day living, what it means to be a part of Your body. Teach me to think Your thoughts, to see with Your eyes, to hear with Your ears—to live and move and have my very existence in You. (Acts 17:28; Ro 12:5; 1Co 2:16)

1 Paul, an apostle of Christ Jesus by the will of God,

To the saints in Ephesus,[a] the faithful[b] in Christ Jesus:

2Grace and peace to you from God our Father and the Lord
Jesus Christ.

Spiritual Blessings in Christ

3Praise be to the God and Father of our Lord Jesus Christ, who
has blessed us in the heavenly realms with every spiritual blessing
in Christ. 4For he chose us in him before the creation of the world
to be holy and blameless in his sight. In love 5he[c] predestined us
to be adopted as his sons through Jesus Christ, in accordance
with his pleasure and will— 6to the praise of his glorious grace,
which he has freely given us in the One he loves. 7In him we have
redemption through his blood, the forgiveness of sins, in accordance with the riches of God's grace 8that he lavished on us with
all wisdom and understanding. 9And he[d] made known to us the
mystery of his will according to his good pleasure, which he purposed in Christ, 10to be put into effect when the times will have
reached their fulfillment—to bring all things in heaven and on
earth together under one head, even Christ.

11In him we were also chosen,[e] having been predestined according to the plan of him who works out everything in conformity with the purpose of his will, 12in order that we, who were
the first to hope in Christ, might be for the praise of his glory.
13And you also were included in Christ when you heard the word
of truth, the gospel of your salvation. Having believed, you were
marked in him with a seal, the promised Holy Spirit, 14who is a
deposit guaranteeing our inheritance until the redemption of
those who are God's possession—to the praise of his glory.

Thanksgiving and Prayer

15For this reason, ever since I heard about your faith in the
Lord Jesus and your love for all the saints, 16I have not stopped
giving thanks for you, remembering you in my prayers. 17I keep
asking that the God of our Lord Jesus Christ, the glorious Father,
may give you the Spirit[f] of wisdom and revelation, so that you may
know him better. 18I pray also that the eyes of your heart may be
enlightened in order that you may know the hope to which he has
called you, the riches of his glorious inheritance in the saints,
19and his incomparably great power for us who believe. That
power is like the working of his mighty strength, 20which he ex-
erted in Christ when he raised him from the dead and seated him
at his right hand in the heavenly realms, 21far above all rule and
authority, power and dominion, and every title that can be given,
not only in the present age but also in the one to come. 22And God
placed all things under his feet and appointed him to be head over
everything for the church, 23which is his body, the fullness of him
who fills everything in every way.

Made Alive in Christ

2 As for you, you were dead in your transgressions and sins,
2in which you used to live when you followed the ways of
this world and of the ruler of the kingdom of the air, the spirit

[a] *1* Some early manuscripts do not have *in Ephesus.* [b] *1* Or *believers who are*
[c] *4,5* Or *sight in love.* [5]*He* [d] *8,9* Or *us. With all wisdom and understanding,* [9]*he*
[e] *11* Or *were made heirs* [f] *17* Or *a spirit*

MY BELOVED

Because of My great love for you, and in the richness of My mercy, I made you alive with Christ even when you were dead in sin. I saved you and called you to live a holy life. I did this, not because of anything you have done but because of My own purpose and grace. For it is by grace you have been saved, through faith. This is not from yourself or by your works, it is simply My gift to you. You could never buy or earn this gift. Jesus paid the full price; by His blood you are now justified.

Never think that your observance of My laws will save you. As you keep them, they will have their own measure of reward, but they will not save you. It is only My grace that makes you whole.

No amount of good works will save you; rather, you have been created in Christ Jesus to do good works, which I prepared in advance for you to do. The fact is that you have been crucified with Christ and you no longer live, but Christ lives in you. The life you live in the body, you must live by faith in My Son, who loved you and gave Himself for you.

Therefore, count yourself dead to sin but alive in Christ Jesus, and live a life worthy of the calling you have received.

Ps 19:9-11; Jn 1:16-17; Ro 3:20-22,24; 5:9; 6:11; Gal 2:16,20-21; Eph 2:4-5,8-10; 4:1; 2Ti 1:9

who is now at work in those who are disobedient. 3All of us also
lived among them at one time, gratifying the cravings of our sinful nature[a] and following its desires and thoughts. Like the rest,
we were by nature objects of wrath. 4But because of his great
love for us, God, who is rich in mercy, 5made us alive with Christ
even when we were dead in transgressions—it is by grace you
have been saved. 6And God raised us up with Christ and seated
us with him in the heavenly realms in Christ Jesus, 7in order that
in the coming ages he might show the incomparable riches of his
grace, expressed in his kindness to us in Christ Jesus. 8For it is
by grace you have been saved, through faith—and this not from
yourselves, it is the gift of God— 9not by works, so that no one
can boast. 10For we are God's workmanship, created in Christ
Jesus to do good works, which God prepared in advance for us
to do.

One in Christ

11Therefore, remember that formerly you who are Gentiles by
birth and called "uncircumcised" by those who call themselves
"the circumcision" (that done in the body by the hands of
men)— 12remember that at that time you were separate from
Christ, excluded from citizenship in Israel and foreigners to the
covenants of the promise, without hope and without God in the
world. 13But now in Christ Jesus you who once were far away
have been brought near through the blood of Christ.
14For he himself is our peace, who has made the two one and
has destroyed the barrier, the dividing wall of hostility, 15by abol-
ishing in his flesh the law with its commandments and regulations. His purpose was to create in himself one new man out of
the two, thus making peace, 16and in this one body to reconcile
both of them to God through the cross, by which he put to death
their hostility. 17He came and preached peace to you who were
far away and peace to those who were near. 18For through him
we both have access to the Father by one Spirit.
19Consequently, you are no longer foreigners and aliens, but
fellow citizens with God's people and members of God's household, 20built on the foundation of the apostles and prophets, with
Christ Jesus himself as the chief cornerstone. 21In him the whole
building is joined together and rises to become a holy temple in
the Lord. 22And in him you too are being built together to become a dwelling in which God lives by his Spirit.

Paul the Preacher to the Gentiles

3 For this reason I, Paul, the prisoner of Christ Jesus for the
sake of you Gentiles—
2Surely you have heard about the administration of God's
grace that was given to me for you, 3that is, the mystery made
known to me by revelation, as I have already written briefly. 4In
reading this, then, you will be able to understand my insight into
the mystery of Christ, 5which was not made known to men in
other generations as it has now been revealed by the Spirit to
God's holy apostles and prophets. 6This mystery is that through
the gospel the Gentiles are heirs together with Israel, members
together of one body, and sharers together in the promise in
Christ Jesus.

[a] 3 Or *our flesh*

Hitherto Thy love has blest me;
Thou hast bro't me to this place;
And I know Thy hand will bring me
Safely home by Thy good grace.
Jesus sought me when a stranger,
Wandering from the fold of God;
He, to rescue me from danger,
Bought me with His precious blood.
"Come, Thou Fount of Every Blessing"
Robert Robinson (1758)

(2:1–10) While I was a sinner, lost and hopeless, without purpose or value, You saved me. I did nothing to earn this salvation. It was only by Your power and for Your pleasure that You saved me. You crafted me into a new creation full of divine purpose and value. I have been transformed from death to life, from hopelessness to purposefulness, from ashes to beauty, and all by the power and prerogative of Your grace. What can I do in response but to thank You for living in me and to seek with all my heart to live in You? (Ro 5:8)

For grace is given not because we have done good works, but in order that we may be able to do them.

Saint Augustine of Hippo (354-430)

7I became a servant of this gospel by the gift of God's grace
given me through the working of his power. 8Although I am less
than the least of all God's people, this grace was given me: to
preach to the Gentiles the unsearchable riches of Christ, 9and to
make plain to everyone the administration of this mystery, which
for ages past was kept hidden in God, who created all things.
10His intent was that now, through the church, the manifold wisdom of God should be made known to the rulers and authorities
in the heavenly realms, 11according to his eternal purpose which
he accomplished in Christ Jesus our Lord. 12In him and through
faith in him we may approach God with freedom and confidence.
13I ask you, therefore, not to be discouraged because of my sufferings for you, which are your glory.

A Prayer for the Ephesians

14For this reason I kneel before the Father, 15from whom his
whole family[a] in heaven and on earth derives its name. 16I pray
that out of his glorious riches he may strengthen you with power
through his Spirit in your inner being, 17so that Christ may dwell
in your hearts through faith. And I pray that you, being rooted
and established in love, 18may have power, together with all the
saints, to grasp how wide and long and high and deep is the love
of Christ, 19and to know this love that surpasses knowledge—
that you may be filled to the measure of all the fullness of God.
20Now to him who is able to do immeasurably more than all we
ask or imagine, according to his power that is at work within us,
21to him be glory in the church and in Christ Jesus throughout all
generations, for ever and ever! Amen.

Unity in the Body of Christ

4 As a prisoner for the Lord, then, I urge you to live a life worthy of the calling you have received. 2Be completely humble
and gentle; be patient, bearing with one another in love. 3Make
every effort to keep the unity of the Spirit through the bond of
peace. 4There is one body and one Spirit— just as you were
called to one hope when you were called— 5one Lord, one faith,
one baptism; 6one God and Father of all, who is over all and
through all and in all.
7But to each one of us grace has been given as Christ apportioned it. 8This is why it[b] says:

"When he ascended on high,
he led captives in his train
and gave gifts to men."[c]

9(What does "he ascended" mean except that he also descended to the lower, earthly regions[d]? 10He who descended is the
very one who ascended higher than all the heavens, in order to
fill the whole universe.) 11It was he who gave some to be apostles, some to be prophets, some to be evangelists, and some to
be pastors and teachers, 12to prepare God's people for works of
service, so that the body of Christ may be built up 13until we all
reach unity in the faith and in the knowledge of the Son of God
and become mature, attaining to the whole measure of the fullness of Christ.
14Then we will no longer be infants, tossed back and forth by

(3:16–19) How can we understand that which is beyond imagination? How can we know that which surpasses knowledge? After all the evil we have done to You, Lord Jesus, who of us would even dare to ask for Your love? It would be unthinkable. Yet we are contained within its boundaries. We will never find the outermost limits of Your love for us. Your love is immeasurable, inexhaustible, inescapable, irrepressible, insatiable, irrational. O Lord, my deepest desire is to know Your love through personal experience and, in my limited capacity, to be filled from Your unlimited resources until I am fully occupied by You.

Higher than the highest heavens,
Deeper than the deepest sea,
Wider than I can ever imagine,
Is Your great love for me,
Your great love for me.

"Higher Than the Highest Heavens"
Morris Chapman (©1997)

a 15 Or *whom all fatherhood of the earth* *b* 8 Or *God* *c* 8 Psalm 68:18 *d* 9 Or *the depths of the earth*

the waves, and blown here and there by every wind of teaching and by the cunning and craftiness of men in their deceitful scheming. 15 Instead, speaking the truth in love, we will in all things grow up into him who is the Head, that is, Christ. 16 From him the whole body, joined and held together by every supporting ligament, grows and builds itself up in love, as each part does its work.

Living as Children of Light

17 So I tell you this, and insist on it in the Lord, that you must no longer live as the Gentiles do, in the futility of their thinking. 18 They are darkened in their understanding and separated from the life of God because of the ignorance that is in them due to the hardening of their hearts. 19 Having lost all sensitivity, they have given themselves over to sensuality so as to indulge in every kind of impurity, with a continual lust for more.

20 You, however, did not come to know Christ that way. 21 Surely you heard of him and were taught in him in accordance with the truth that is in Jesus. 22 You were taught, with regard to your former way of life, to put off your old self, which is being corrupted by its deceitful desires; 23 to be made new in the attitude of your minds; 24 and to put on the new self, created to be like God in true righteousness and holiness.

25 Therefore each of you must put off falsehood and speak truthfully to his neighbor, for we are all members of one body. 26 "In your anger do not sin"[a]: Do not let the sun go down while you are still angry, 27 and do not give the devil a foothold. 28 He who has been stealing must steal no longer, but must work, doing something useful with his own hands, that he may have something to share with those in need.

29 Do not let any unwholesome talk come out of your mouths, but only what is helpful for building others up according to their needs, that it may benefit those who listen. 30 And do not grieve the Holy Spirit of God, with whom you were sealed for the day of redemption. 31 Get rid of all bitterness, rage and anger, brawling and slander, along with every form of malice. 32 Be kind and compassionate to one another, forgiving each other, just as in Christ God forgave you.

5 Be imitators of God, therefore, as dearly loved children 2 and live a life of love, just as Christ loved us and gave himself up for us as a fragrant offering and sacrifice to God.

3 But among you there must not be even a hint of sexual immorality, or of any kind of impurity, or of greed, because these are improper for God's holy people. 4 Nor should there be obscenity, foolish talk or coarse joking, which are out of place, but rather thanksgiving. 5 For of this you can be sure: No immoral, impure or greedy person—such a man is an idolater—has any inheritance in the kingdom of Christ and of God.[b] 6 Let no one deceive you with empty words, for because of such things God's wrath comes on those who are disobedient. 7 Therefore do not be partners with them.

8 For you were once darkness, but now you are light in the Lord. Live as children of light 9 (for the fruit of the light consists in all goodness, righteousness and truth) 10 and find out what pleases the Lord. 11 Have nothing to do with the fruitless deeds of

[a] 26 Psalm 4:4 [b] 5 Or *kingdom of the Christ and God*

(5:1) Heavenly Father, I thank You for the words of Your Son, Jesus: "The Son can do nothing by himself; he can do only what he sees his Father doing." And again: "The words I say to you are not just my own. Rather, it is the Father, living in me, who is doing his work . . . Anyone who has faith in me will do what I have been doing." And now, Father, through faith in Jesus, I am also Your child. Please teach me how to live up to Your family name. Open my eyes to see what You are doing, and then please come and do Your work through me. Show me how to live like Christ, so that it might also be said of me: "Anyone who has seen me has seen the Father." (Jn 5:19; 14:9–12; 2Co 3:18)

Give me a heart like Your heart,
Beating for the lost.
Give me a love like Your love
No matter what the cost.
Give me a road to travel,
A race that I can run.
Give me a heart like Your heart,
To stand until You come.

"Give Me A Heart"
Greg Fadness and Pamela Fadness (©1999)

darkness, but rather expose them. 12For it is shameful even to
mention what the disobedient do in secret. 13But everything exposed by the light becomes visible, 14for it is light that makes
everything visible. This is why it is said:

"Wake up, O sleeper,
rise from the dead,
and Christ will shine on you."

15Be very careful, then, how you live—not as unwise but as
wise, 16making the most of every opportunity, because the days
are evil. 17Therefore do not be foolish, but understand what the
Lord's will is. 18Do not get drunk on wine, which leads to debauchery. Instead, be filled with the Spirit. 19Speak to one another with psalms, hymns and spiritual songs. Sing and make music
in your heart to the Lord, 20always giving thanks to God the Father
for everything, in the name of our Lord Jesus Christ.
21Submit to one another out of reverence for Christ.

Wives and Husbands

22Wives, submit to your husbands as to the Lord. 23For the
husband is the head of the wife as Christ is the head of the
church, his body, of which he is the Savior. 24Now as the church
submits to Christ, so also wives should submit to their husbands
in everything.
25Husbands, love your wives, just as Christ loved the church
and gave himself up for her 26to make her holy, cleansing[a] her by
the washing with water through the word, 27and to present her to
himself as a radiant church, without stain or wrinkle or any other
blemish, but holy and blameless. 28In this same way, husbands
ought to love their wives as their own bodies. He who loves his
wife loves himself. 29After all, no one ever hated his own body,
but he feeds and cares for it, just as Christ does the church—
30for we are members of his body. 31"For this reason a man will
leave his father and mother and be united to his wife, and the two
will become one flesh."[b] 32This is a profound mystery—but I am
talking about Christ and the church. 33However, each one of you
also must love his wife as he loves himself, and the wife must respect her husband.

Children and Parents

6 Children, obey your parents in the Lord, for this is right.
2"Honor your father and mother"—which is the first commandment with a promise— 3"that it may go well with you and
that you may enjoy long life on the earth."[c]
4Fathers, do not exasperate your children; instead, bring them
up in the training and instruction of the Lord.

Slaves and Masters

5Slaves, obey your earthly masters with respect and fear, and
with sincerity of heart, just as you would obey Christ. 6Obey them
not only to win their favor when their eye is on you, but like slaves
of Christ, doing the will of God from your heart. 7Serve wholeheartedly, as if you were serving the Lord, not men, 8because you
know that the Lord will reward everyone for whatever good he
does, whether he is slave or free.

[a] 26 Or *having cleansed* [b] 31 Gen. 2:24 [c] 3 Deut. 5:16

(6:5–9) Lord, You have called us both to serve and to be served. So let us serve with humility and joy, and allow ourselves to be served with a spirit of gentleness and gratitude. Bring wholeness and dignity to all who live in our society. When we are called on to serve, give us a vision that it is You we serve; and when we are called on to receive, grant us an awareness that through Your servants, You, Lord Jesus Christ, are serving us.

So let us learn how to serve,
And in our life enthrone Him;
Each other's needs to prefer,
For it is Christ we're serving.

This is our God, the Servant King,
He calls us now to follow Him;
To bring our lives as a daily offering
Of worship to the Servant King.

"The Servant King"
Graham Kendrick (©1983)

9And masters, treat your slaves in the same way. Do not threat-
en them, since you know that he who is both their Master and
yours is in heaven, and there is no favoritism with him.

The Armor of God

10Finally, be strong in the Lord and in his mighty power. 11Put
on the full armor of God so that you can take your stand against
the devil's schemes. 12For our struggle is not against flesh and
blood, but against the rulers, against the authorities, against the
powers of this dark world and against the spiritual forces of evil
in the heavenly realms. 13Therefore put on the full armor of God,
so that when the day of evil comes, you may be able to stand your
ground, and after you have done everything, to stand. 14Stand
firm then, with the belt of truth buckled around your waist, with
the breastplate of righteousness in place, 15and with your feet fitted with the readiness that comes from the gospel of peace. 16In
addition to all this, take up the shield of faith, with which you can
extinguish all the flaming arrows of the evil one. 17Take the helmet of salvation and the sword of the Spirit, which is the word of
God. 18And pray in the Spirit on all occasions with all kinds of
prayers and requests. With this in mind, be alert and always keep
on praying for all the saints.
19Pray also for me, that whenever I open my mouth, words may
be given me so that I will fearlessly make known the mystery of
the gospel, 20for which I am an ambassador in chains. Pray that
I may declare it fearlessly, as I should.

Final Greetings

21Tychicus, the dear brother and faithful servant in the Lord,
will tell you everything, so that you also may know how I am and
what I am doing. 22I am sending him to you for this very purpose,
that you may know how we are, and that he may encourage you.
23Peace to the brothers, and love with faith from God the Father and the Lord Jesus Christ. 24Grace to all who love our Lord
Jesus Christ with an undying love.

(6:10–20) We thank You, Father, that You have not left Your church defenseless. Rather, You have called us to the battleground of prayer and have fully equipped us for the task. Now strengthen us each day to carry forward the gospel of Christ as we wage war against the evil one. Teach us to preach, to pray and to persevere; and as the dust settles after each victory, may we be found standing our ground, prepared for the next foray into battle.

Do not pray for easy lives,
Pray to be stronger men.
Do not pray for tasks equal to your powers,
Pray for powers equal to your task.
Phillips Brooks (1835-1893)

In heavenly armor we'll enter the land,
The battle belongs to the Lord.
No weapon that's fashioned against us will stand,
The battle belongs to the Lord.

We sing glory, honor,
Power and strength to the Lord.
We sing glory, honor,
Power and strength to the Lord.
"The Battle Belongs to the Lord"
Jamie Owens-Collins (©1984)

The Epistle of Paul the Apostle to the PHILIPPIANS

How often do the circumstances of life determine the quality of our worship? When things are going well, we find it easy to offer thanks to God. But when times are difficult, worship can be a struggle. We wonder: "How can I worship God when my life is so hard?"

The apostle Paul in his letter to the Philippians helps to us to answer this question. His physical situation could not be much worse. He is locked in chains because of his testimony to Christ (1:12–13). Yet Paul fills his letter with worship, even with rejoicing (1:4; 2:17; 4:10). How is this possible? How can one who is suffering nevertheless "rejoice in the Lord"?

In part, Paul rejoices because of his "partnership in the gospel" with the Philippian church. This congregation not only responded to Paul's preaching with faith but also joined in his evangelistic enterprise (1:3–5; 4:15). Furthermore, Paul exults because he knows that God will complete the "good work" He has begun among the Philippians (1:6). On the day when Christ returns, they will be "filled with the fruit of righteousness that comes through Jesus Christ—to the glory and praise of God" (1:11). Accordingly, Paul is able to rejoice in suffering because he looks ahead to the glorious day of Christ. We too can worship with gladness when we lift our eyes above our momentary afflictions and focus on the innumerable blessings of eternity.

Paul's vision of the future features the universal worship of Jesus. In Philippians 2:5–11 Paul incorporates an ancient Christian hymn just as a modern preacher might quote familiar lyrics. This early hymn celebrates the condescension of Christ, Who gave up the privileges of divinity by becoming human. He freely humbled Himself, even to the point of dying on a cross. For this reason "God exalted him to the highest place and gave him the name that is above every name, that at the name of Jesus every knee should bow . . . and every tongue confess that Jesus Christ is Lord, to the glory of God the Father" (2:9–11). When we suffer, the vision of Christ's ultimate victory and glory sustains us and fills us with gladness.

We too can worship with gladness when we lift our eyes above our momentary afflictions and focus on the innumerable blessings of eternity.

After urging the Philippians to rejoice in the Lord (4:3), Paul invites them to think in new ways: "Finally, brothers, whatever is true, whatever is noble, whatever is right, whatever is pure, whatever is lovely, whatever is admirable—if anything is excellent or praiseworthy—think about such things" (4:8). Though Paul would not advise us to deny the reality of our pain, neither would he support undue fixation upon earthly struggles. Instead, we should turn our attention to things that are true, noble, right, etc. In other words, we should occupy our minds with God and His good gifts. We are enabled to worship, no matter what our circumstances, when we remember all that God has given to us. Moreover, the very act of worship, in which we consider God's glorious nature, fills our hearts with joy.

1 Paul and Timothy, servants of Christ Jesus,

To all the saints in Christ Jesus at Philippi, together with the
overseers[a] and deacons:

2 Grace and peace to you from God our Father and the Lord
Jesus Christ.

Thanksgiving and Prayer

3 I thank my God every time I remember you. 4 In all my prayers
for all of you, I always pray with joy 5 because of your partnership
in the gospel from the first day until now, 6 being confident of this,
that he who began a good work in you will carry it on to completion until the day of Christ Jesus.

7 It is right for me to feel this way about all of you, since I have
you in my heart; for whether I am in chains or defending and con-
firming the gospel, all of you share in God's grace with me. 8 God
can testify how I long for all of you with the affection of Christ
Jesus.

9 And this is my prayer: that your love may abound more and
more in knowledge and depth of insight, 10 so that you may be
able to discern what is best and may be pure and blameless
until the day of Christ, 11 filled with the fruit of righteousness
that comes through Jesus Christ—to the glory and praise of
God.

Paul's Chains Advance the Gospel

12 Now I want you to know, brothers, that what has happened to
me has really served to advance the gospel. 13 As a result, it has
become clear throughout the whole palace guard[b] and to everyone else that I am in chains for Christ. 14 Because of my chains,
most of the brothers in the Lord have been encouraged to speak
the word of God more courageously and fearlessly.

15 It is true that some preach Christ out of envy and rivalry, but
others out of goodwill. 16 The latter do so in love, knowing that I
am put here for the defense of the gospel. 17 The former preach
Christ out of selfish ambition, not sincerely, supposing that they
can stir up trouble for me while I am in chains.[c] 18 But what does
it matter? The important thing is that in every way, whether from
false motives or true, Christ is preached. And because of this I rejoice.

Yes, and I will continue to rejoice, 19 for I know that through
your prayers and the help given by the Spirit of Jesus Christ, what
has happened to me will turn out for my deliverance.[d] 20 I eagerly expect and hope that I will in no way be ashamed, but will have
sufficient courage so that now as always Christ will be exalted in
my body, whether by life or by death. 21 For to me, to live is Christ
and to die is gain. 22 If I am to go on living in the body, this will
mean fruitful labor for me. Yet what shall I choose? I do not
know! 23 I am torn between the two: I desire to depart and be with
Christ, which is better by far; 24 but it is more necessary for you
that I remain in the body. 25 Convinced of this, I know that I will
remain, and I will continue with all of you for your progress and
joy in the faith, 26 so that through my being with you again your
joy in Christ Jesus will overflow on account of me.

[a] 1 Traditionally *bishops* [b] 13 Or *whole palace* [c] 16,17 Some late manuscripts have verses 16 and 17 in reverse order. [d] 19 Or *salvation*

(1:6) Almighty God, I praise You for Your great faithfulness. You continue to this day to carry forward the mission of Your church throughout the earth. And You continue to this day to carry forward Your plan for my life, bringing to complete fruition that which You began at the moment of my conversion. I am saved! I am being saved! I will be saved! I am Your child! I am being transformed into the likeness of Your Son. I will be like Him when He appears! You will finish what You have started! Hallelujah! (Ac 2:21; 1Co 1:18; 2Co 3:18; Eph 2:4–10; 1Jn 3:1–2)

He who began a good work in you,
He who began a good work in you
Will be faithful to complete it,
He'll be faithful to complete it;
He who started the work
Will be faithful to complete it in you.

"He Who Began a Good Work in You"
Jon Mohr (©1987)

(1:21–26) What a sobering thought, Lord—the primary reason for me to remain on this earth is to aid in the spiritual progress of others. You created me for "good works," and You desire that I bear much fruit while I am yet on earth. So work through me, Lord! Once again I bow my knee and humble my heart to meet Your objectives: not my peace but their progress, not my comfort but their conversion, not my satisfaction but their sanctification. Lord, give me more time and more opportunities to reach more people for You before You call me home. (Jn 15:8; Eph 2:10)

(2:3–8) Heavenly Father, I confess my hidden motives of selfish ambition and vain conceit. I admit that my heart still seeks its own. Forgive me, Lord! Replace my selfishness with the selflessness of Christ, Who laid down His life for me. Replace my ambitions with the attitude of Christ, Who purposefully took on the very nature of a servant. Teach me to love and to live as Jesus did. As Christ was made in human likeness, so also may I be transformed into the likeness of Christ.

(2:9–11) I exalt the glorious name of Jesus Christ the Lord. He alone has defeated the enemy. He alone has paid the full price for my sins. Now He has been exalted to the highest place, and His is the name that is above every name. One day every knee will bow before Him in worship and every tongue will confess that He is Lord, to Your glory, Father. Even now I bow at His feet, confess His name and plead with You to transform me into His image.

Jesus, Your name is power,
Jesus, Your name is might.
Jesus, Your name
Will break every stronghold;
Jesus, Your name is life.

Jesus, Your name is holy,
Jesus, Your name brings light.
Jesus, Your name
Above every other,
Jesus, Your name is life.

"Jesus, Your Name"
Morris Chapman and
Claire Cloninger (©1990)

(2:15) Your standard is far beyond me, Lord! Without Your grace, it is impossible to attain. You call me to become blameless and pure, even without fault. But, O Father, in my own strength I cannot meet Your standard for my life. I humbly confess that I am not blameless, I am not pure, I am not without fault. By Your grace, Father, cleanse my heart, cleanse my conduct, cleanse my character, cleanse my motives! O Spirit of the Lord, purify me until I am clean in Your sight. Transform my soul until I stand spotless before Your holy fire. Just as I am now "in Christ," so make me holy "as Christ"!

27 Whatever happens, conduct yourselves in a manner worthy
of the gospel of Christ. Then, whether I come and see you or only
hear about you in my absence, I will know that you stand firm in
one spirit, contending as one man for the faith of the gospel
28 without being frightened in any way by those who oppose you.
This is a sign to them that they will be destroyed, but that you will
be saved—and that by God. 29 For it has been granted to you on
behalf of Christ not only to believe on him, but also to suffer for
him, 30 since you are going through the same struggle you saw I
had, and now hear that I still have.

Imitating Christ's Humility

2 If you have any encouragement from being united with Christ,
if any comfort from his love, if any fellowship with the Spirit,
if any tenderness and compassion, 2 then make my joy complete
by being like-minded, having the same love, being one in spirit
and purpose. 3 Do nothing out of selfish ambition or vain conceit,
but in humility consider others better than yourselves. 4 Each of
you should look not only to your own interests, but also to the interests of others.

5 Your attitude should be the same as that of Christ Jesus:

6 Who, being in very nature[a] God,
did not consider equality with God something to be grasped,
7 but made himself nothing,
taking the very nature[b] of a servant,
being made in human likeness.
8 And being found in appearance as a man,
he humbled himself
and became obedient to death—
even death on a cross!
9 Therefore God exalted him to the highest place
and gave him the name that is above every name,
10 that at the name of Jesus every knee should bow,
in heaven and on earth and under the earth,
11 and every tongue confess that Jesus Christ is Lord,
to the glory of God the Father.

Shining as Stars

12 Therefore, my dear friends, as you have always obeyed—not
only in my presence, but now much more in my absence—continue to work out your salvation with fear and trembling, 13 for it
is God who works in you to will and to act according to his good
purpose.

14 Do everything without complaining or arguing, 15 so that you
may become blameless and pure, children of God without fault in
a crooked and depraved generation, in which you shine like stars
in the universe 16 as you hold out[c] the word of life—in order that
I may boast on the day of Christ that I did not run or labor for
nothing. 17 But even if I am being poured out like a drink offering
on the sacrifice and service coming from your faith, I am glad
and rejoice with all of you. 18 So you too should be glad and rejoice with me.

[a]6 Or *in the form of* [b]7 Or *the form* [c]16 Or *hold on to*

Timothy and Epaphroditus

19 I hope in the Lord Jesus to send Timothy to you soon, that I
also may be cheered when I receive news about you. 20 I have no
one else like him, who takes a genuine interest in your welfare.
21 For everyone looks out for his own interests, not those of Jesus
Christ. 22 But you know that Timothy has proved himself, because
as a son with his father he has served with me in the work of the
gospel. 23 I hope, therefore, to send him as soon as I see how
things go with me. 24 And I am confident in the Lord that I myself
will come soon.
25 But I think it is necessary to send back to you Epaphroditus,
my brother, fellow worker and fellow soldier, who is also your
messenger, whom you sent to take care of my needs. 26 For he
longs for all of you and is distressed because you heard he was ill.
27 Indeed he was ill, and almost died. But God had mercy on him,
and not on him only but also on me, to spare me sorrow upon
sorrow. 28 Therefore I am all the more eager to send him, so that
when you see him again you may be glad and I may have less anxiety. 29 Welcome him in the Lord with great joy, and honor men
like him, 30 because he almost died for the work of Christ, risking
his life to make up for the help you could not give me.

No Confidence in the Flesh

3 Finally, my brothers, rejoice in the Lord! It is no trouble for
me to write the same things to you again, and it is a safeguard for you.
2 Watch out for those dogs, those men who do evil, those muti-
lators of the flesh. 3 For it is we who are the circumcision, we who
worship by the Spirit of God, who glory in Christ Jesus, and who
put no confidence in the flesh— 4 though I myself have reasons
for such confidence.
If anyone else thinks he has reasons to put confidence in the
flesh, I have more: 5 circumcised on the eighth day, of the people
of Israel, of the tribe of Benjamin, a Hebrew of Hebrews; in regard to the law, a Pharisee; 6 as for zeal, persecuting the church;
as for legalistic righteousness, faultless.
7 But whatever was to my profit I now consider loss for the sake
of Christ. 8 What is more, I consider everything a loss compared
to the surpassing greatness of knowing Christ Jesus my Lord, for
whose sake I have lost all things. I consider them rubbish, that I
may gain Christ 9 and be found in him, not having a righteousness
of my own that comes from the law, but that which is through faith
in Christ—the righteousness that comes from God and is by faith.
10 I want to know Christ and the power of his resurrection and the
fellowship of sharing in his sufferings, becoming like him in his
death, 11 and so, somehow, to attain to the resurrection from the
dead.

Pressing on Toward the Goal

12 Not that I have already obtained all this, or have already been
made perfect, but I press on to take hold of that for which Christ
Jesus took hold of me. 13 Brothers, I do not consider myself yet to
have taken hold of it. But one thing I do: Forgetting what is behind and straining toward what is ahead, 14 I press on toward the
goal to win the prize for which God has called me heavenward in
Christ Jesus.
15 All of us who are mature should take such a view of things.

(3:7–11) There is an immeasurable exchange at work in Your gospel. The more I give up for You, Lord Jesus, the more I receive from You. Only as I lay down the things that I've held on to am I free to embrace You. I long to give up everything for You. O Lord, search in the hidden recesses of my life for that which remains "untraded." Show me what still has a hold on my heart and, by Your grace, it too will be laid at Your feet.

I regard myself as the most wretched of all men, stinking and covered with sores, and as one who has committed all sorts of crimes against his King. Overcome by remorse, I confess all my wickedness to Him, ask His pardon and abandon myself entirely to Him to do with as He will. But this King, filled with goodness and mercy, far from chastising me, lovingly embraces me, makes me eat at His table, serves me with His own hands, gives me the keys of His treasures and treats me as His favorite. He talks with me and is delighted with me in a thousand and one ways; He forgives me and relieves me of my principal bad habits without talking about them; I beg Him to make me according to His heart and always the more weak and despicable I see myself to be, the more beloved I am of God.

Brother Lawrence of the Resurrection (c.1605–1691)

Riches I heed not,
Nor man's empty praise,
Thou mine inheritance,
Now and always:
Thou and Thou only,
First in my heart,
High King of heaven,
My Treasure Thou art.

"Be Thou My Vision"
Ancient Irish Poem (8th c.)
Trans. Mary E. Byrne (1880–1931)
Versified by Eleanor H. Hull (1860–1935)

(3:13–14) The longer I live, the more I respect Your servant Paul. He narrowed his focus to encompass only that which was eternal. Lord, teach me to live with a heavenly perspective and a heavenward goal. Even now, my desire is to say with Paul, "This one thing I do . . ." Teach me to leave behind peripheral distractions and to fix my eyes on the goal as I seek to run the race You have set before me. (Isa 43:18–19)

(4:6–8) Lord, thank You for providing prayer as an antidote to fretfulness. When my heart is full of anxiety I can see only my limitations; I cannot find Your peace. But when my heart is full of thanksgiving I can see Your every provision; Your peace is unavoidable. So in response to Your generous invitation, I bring my thoughts, one by one, into captivity to the obedience of Your Son. I focus my heart and mind on the virtue of Jesus Christ. I cast all my cares upon You; I receive in return Your incomparable gift of peace. (Ps 55:22; 2Co 10:5; 1Pe 5:7)

I cast all my cares upon You,
I lay all of my burdens
Down at Your feet.
And anytime that I don't know
What to do,
I will cast all my cares upon You.

"Cares Chorus"
Kelly Willard (©1978)

Begin at once; before you venture away from this quiet moment, ask your King to take you wholly into his service, and place all the hours of this day quite simply at his disposal, and ask him to make and keep you ready to do just exactly what he appoints. Never mind about tomorrow; one day at a time is enough. Try it today, and see if it is not a day of strange, almost curious peace, so sweet that you will be only too thankful when tomorrow comes to ask him to take it also.

Francis Ridley Havergal (1836–1879)

And if on some point you think differently, that too God will make
clear to you. 16Only let us live up to what we have already attained.
17Join with others in following my example, brothers, and take
note of those who live according to the pattern we gave you.
18For, as I have often told you before and now say again even with
tears, many live as enemies of the cross of Christ. 19Their destiny
is destruction, their god is their stomach, and their glory is in
their shame. Their mind is on earthly things. 20But our citizenship is in heaven. And we eagerly await a Savior from there, the
Lord Jesus Christ, 21who, by the power that enables him to bring
everything under his control, will transform our lowly bodies so
that they will be like his glorious body.

4 Therefore, my brothers, you whom I love and long for, my
joy and crown, that is how you should stand firm in the Lord,
dear friends!

Exhortations

2I plead with Euodia and I plead with Syntyche to agree with
each other in the Lord. 3Yes, and I ask you, loyal yokefellow,[a]
help these women who have contended at my side in the cause of
the gospel, along with Clement and the rest of my fellow workers,
whose names are in the book of life.
4Rejoice in the Lord always. I will say it again: Rejoice! 5Let
your gentleness be evident to all. The Lord is near. 6Do not be
anxious about anything, but in everything, by prayer and petition,
with thanksgiving, present your requests to God. 7And the peace
of God, which transcends all understanding, will guard your
hearts and your minds in Christ Jesus.
8Finally, brothers, whatever is true, whatever is noble, whatever is right, whatever is pure, whatever is lovely, whatever is admirable—if anything is excellent or praiseworthy—think about
such things. 9Whatever you have learned or received or heard
from me, or seen in me—put it into practice. And the God of
peace will be with you.

Thanks for Their Gifts

10I rejoice greatly in the Lord that at last you have renewed
your concern for me. Indeed, you have been concerned, but you
had no opportunity to show it. 11I am not saying this because I
am in need, for I have learned to be content whatever the circumstances. 12I know what it is to be in need, and I know what it
is to have plenty. I have learned the secret of being content in any
and every situation, whether well fed or hungry, whether living in
plenty or in want. 13I can do everything through him who gives
me strength.
14Yet it was good of you to share in my troubles. 15Moreover,
as you Philippians know, in the early days of your acquaintance
with the gospel, when I set out from Macedonia, not one church
shared with me in the matter of giving and receiving, except you
only; 16for even when I was in Thessalonica, you sent me aid
again and again when I was in need. 17Not that I am looking for
a gift, but I am looking for what may be credited to your account.
18I have received full payment and even more; I am amply supplied, now that I have received from Epaphroditus the gifts you

[a] 3 Or *loyal Syzygus*

MY BELOVED

I will meet all your needs according to My glorious riches in Christ Jesus. So do not worry about your life, what you will eat or drink; or about your body, what you will wear. Is not life more important than food, and the body more important than clothes? Look at the birds of the air. They do not sow or reap or store away in barns. I feed them. Are you not much more valuable than they?

Will worrying add a single hour to your life? Or will worrying provide you with shelter and clothing? See how the lilies of the field grow. They do not labor or spin. Yet not even King Solomon in all his splendor was dressed like one of these.

If that is how I clothe the grass in the field, which is here today and tomorrow is thrown into the fire, will I not much more clothe you, My beloved?

So do not worry, saying, "What shall I eat?" or "What shall I drink?" or "What shall I wear?" Most people spend their entire lives pursuing these things, but I already know that you need them. Instead, seek first My kingdom and My righteousness, and all these things will be given to you as well.

Therefore do not worry about tomorrow, for tomorrow will worry about itself. Each day has enough trouble of its own.

Ps 34:9; Mt 6:25-34; Php 4:19

sent. They are a fragrant offering, an acceptable sacrifice, pleasing to God. 19And my God will meet all your needs according to
his glorious riches in Christ Jesus.
20To our God and Father be glory for ever and ever. Amen.

Final Greetings

21Greet all the saints in Christ Jesus. The brothers who are with
me send greetings. 22All the saints send you greetings, especially
those who belong to Caesar's household.
23The grace of the Lord Jesus Christ be with your spirit.
Amen.[a]

[a] 23 Some manuscripts do not have *Amen*.

God hath given unto you Christ Jesus, the greatest gift He had; and since your heart is laid out for Him, He will with Him give you all things that are good for you in their season.

William Guthrie of Fenwick (1620-1665)

(4:19) Lord, You are so generous. You have not only promised to meet my needs, but You have also vowed to give me the desires of my heart if I will simply delight myself in You. How marvelous that my needs are met not according to what I deserve but according to Your inexhaustible, limitless riches. You are able to do immeasurably more than all I could ask or even imagine. To You, my God and Father, be glory forever and ever. Amen. (Ps 37:4; Eph 3:20)

In the Lord, the Lord alone
Are life and health and peace;
His mercies and His loving kindness
Never cease.
In the Lord, the Lord alone
Are life and health and peace;
In the Lord, in the Lord alone.

In the Lord, the Lord alone
Is everything I need;
The Son of Man now reigning high
Will intercede.
In the Lord, the Lord alone
Is everything I need;
In the Lord, in the Lord alone.

"In the Lord Alone"
Walt Harrah (©1989)

The Epistle of Paul the Apostle to the COLOSSIANS

Colossians

Seductive philosophy, dietary restrictions, fascination with angels, new religious practices created from tidbits of other traditions, worship shaped to suit individual preferences . . . all of these tempted the first-century Colossian believers to wander away from authentic Christianity (2:8–23). Sounds familiar, doesn't it? Almost two millennia later we encounter similar temptations as we try to live out our faith in Christ. Thus, like the original recipients, we have much to gain from Paul's letter to the Colossian Christians.

The apostle writes to strengthen those who are struggling with a "hollow and deceptive philosophy" that "depends on human tradition . . . rather than on Christ" (2:8). Paul explains that, contrary to this philosophy, we have no need to relate to God through legalistic rituals or the worship of angels, because God has come fully in Jesus Christ (2:9,16–22). When we first believed in Him we entered into a complete relationship with God (2:10). Every sin that once separated us from God was crucified with Christ (2:13–14). Therefore, to grow closer to God we do not need to adopt new religious rituals, but to live in relationship with Jesus Christ and to be strengthened in that relationship (2:6–7,19).

Paul makes it clear that Christ is not one spiritual guide among many religious gurus. In fact, He is "the image of the invisible God, the firstborn over all creation. For by him all things were created . . . He is before all things, and in him all things hold together. And he is the head of the body, the church; he is the beginning and the firstborn from among the dead, so that in everything he might have the supremacy" (1:15–18). Therefore we grow to spiritual maturity, not by adding extraneous elements onto faith in Christ but by remaining in that faith, confident that Christ is all-sufficient. He alone will lead us to experience God more deeply, even to sharing in divine glory (1:27–28; 2:23; 3:4).

> **To grow closer to God we do not need to adopt new religious rituals, but to live in relationship with Jesus Christ and to be strengthened in that relationship.**

We worship as Christians by living as God's special people: "Therefore, as God's chosen people, holy and dearly loved, clothe yourselves with compassion, kindness, humility, gentleness and patience. Bear with each other and forgive . . . Put on love . . . Let the peace of Christ rule in your hearts . . . Be thankful . . . Let the word of Christ dwell in you richly as you teach and admonish one another . . . and as you sing psalms, hymns and spiritual songs with gratitude in your hearts to God" (Col 3:12–16). Such familiar acts of worship as thanksgiving and singing are essential to holy living. But everything we do can glorify God when we do it in the name of Christ, guided by His word and full of thanksgiving.

1 Paul, an apostle of Christ Jesus by the will of God, and Timothy our brother,

2 To the holy and faithful[a] brothers in Christ at Colosse:

Grace and peace to you from God our Father.[b]

Thanksgiving and Prayer

3 We always thank God, the Father of our Lord Jesus Christ,
when we pray for you, 4 because we have heard of your faith in
Christ Jesus and of the love you have for all the saints— 5 the faith
and love that spring from the hope that is stored up for you in
heaven and that you have already heard about in the word of
truth, the gospel 6 that has come to you. All over the world this
gospel is bearing fruit and growing, just as it has been doing
among you since the day you heard it and understood God's grace
in all its truth. 7 You learned it from Epaphras, our dear fellow
servant, who is a faithful minister of Christ on our[c] behalf, 8 and
who also told us of your love in the Spirit.

9 For this reason, since the day we heard about you, we have
not stopped praying for you and asking God to fill you with the
knowledge of his will through all spiritual wisdom and understanding. 10 And we pray this in order that you may live a life worthy of the Lord and may please him in every way: bearing fruit in
every good work, growing in the knowledge of God, 11 being
strengthened with all power according to his glorious might so
that you may have great endurance and patience, and joyfully
12 giving thanks to the Father, who has qualified you[d] to share in
the inheritance of the saints in the kingdom of light. 13 For he has
rescued us from the dominion of darkness and brought us into
the kingdom of the Son he loves, 14 in whom we have redemption,[e] the forgiveness of sins.

The Supremacy of Christ

15 He is the image of the invisible God, the firstborn over all
creation. 16 For by him all things were created: things in heaven
and on earth, visible and invisible, whether thrones or powers or
rulers or authorities; all things were created by him and for him.
17 He is before all things, and in him all things hold together.
18 And he is the head of the body, the church; he is the beginning
and the firstborn from among the dead, so that in everything he
might have the supremacy. 19 For God was pleased to have all his
fullness dwell in him, 20 and through him to reconcile to himself
all things, whether things on earth or things in heaven, by making
peace through his blood, shed on the cross.

21 Once you were alienated from God and were enemies in
your minds because of[f] your evil behavior. 22 But now he has
reconciled you by Christ's physical body through death to present you holy in his sight, without blemish and free from accusation— 23 if you continue in your faith, established and firm,
not moved from the hope held out in the gospel. This is the
gospel that you heard and that has been proclaimed to every
creature under heaven, and of which I, Paul, have become a
servant.

[a] 2 Or *believing* [b] 2 Some manuscripts *Father and the Lord Jesus Christ* [c] 7 Some manuscripts *your* [d] 12 Some manuscripts *us* [e] 14 A few late manuscripts *redemption through his blood* [f] 21 Or *minds, as shown by*

Christ is the aperture through which the immensity and magnificence of God can be seen.

J. B. Phillips (1906-1982)

(1:15–23) Lord Jesus Christ, I worship You as my God and Savior. You are the invisible God made visible, the container for that which cannot be contained, the exact image of that which is beyond imagination. You are at once the means and the end of creation. You are the gateway to the will of God and the pathway to eternal life. In this life You are the source of peace and forgiveness, joy and fruitfulness, faith and holiness, and You are the hope of heaven to come. (Jn 1:3; Ro 11:36; Heb 1:3)

Sovereign Creator
Who holds the worlds in place,
By You and for You creation was made.
There is none beside You,
For You rule all things alone,
And Yours is the everlasting throne.

Jesus, You reign over all.
Heaven and earth together proclaim
Jesus, You reign over all.
We bow down in awe
And worship Your name,
For You reign.

"Jesus, You Reign Over All"
Steve Cook and Vikki Cook (©1991)

Paul's Labor for the Church

24Now I rejoice in what was suffered for you, and I fill up in my
flesh what is still lacking in regard to Christ's afflictions, for the
sake of his body, which is the church. 25I have become its servant
by the commission God gave me to present to you the word of
God in its fullness— 26the mystery that has been kept hidden for
ages and generations, but is now disclosed to the saints. 27To
them God has chosen to make known among the Gentiles the glorious riches of this mystery, which is Christ in you, the hope of
glory.
28We proclaim him, admonishing and teaching everyone with
all wisdom, so that we may present everyone perfect in Christ.
29To this end I labor, struggling with all his energy, which so powerfully works in me.

2 I want you to know how much I am struggling for you and for
those at Laodicea, and for all who have not met me personally. 2My purpose is that they may be encouraged in heart and
united in love, so that they may have the full riches of complete
understanding, in order that they may know the mystery of God,
namely, Christ, 3in whom are hidden all the treasures of wisdom
and knowledge. 4I tell you this so that no one may deceive you by
fine-sounding arguments. 5For though I am absent from you in
body, I am present with you in spirit and delight to see how orderly you are and how firm your faith in Christ is.

Freedom From Human Regulations Through Life With Christ

6So then, just as you received Christ Jesus as Lord, continue to
live in him, 7rooted and built up in him, strengthened in the faith
as you were taught, and overflowing with thankfulness.
8See to it that no one takes you captive through hollow and deceptive philosophy, which depends on human tradition and the
basic principles of this world rather than on Christ.
9For in Christ all the fullness of the Deity lives in bodily form,
10and you have been given fullness in Christ, who is the head over
every power and authority. 11In him you were also circumcised,
in the putting off of the sinful nature,[a] not with a circumcision
done by the hands of men but with the circumcision done by
Christ, 12having been buried with him in baptism and raised with
him through your faith in the power of God, who raised him from
the dead.
13When you were dead in your sins and in the uncircumcision
of your sinful nature,[b] God made you[c] alive with Christ. He forgave us all our sins, 14having canceled the written code, with its
regulations, that was against us and that stood opposed to us; he
took it away, nailing it to the cross. 15And having disarmed the
powers and authorities, he made a public spectacle of them, triumphing over them by the cross.[d]
16Therefore do not let anyone judge you by what you eat or
drink, or with regard to a religious festival, a New Moon celebration or a Sabbath day. 17These are a shadow of the things that
were to come; the reality, however, is found in Christ. 18Do not let
anyone who delights in false humility and the worship of angels
disqualify you for the prize. Such a person goes into great detail

[a] 11 Or *the flesh* [b] 13 Or *your flesh* [c] 13 Some manuscripts *us* [d] 15 Or *them in him*

God carries your picture in his wallet.
Tony Campolo (1935-)

(2:2–3,9–10) I am made complete in the One Who is completely God. I am possessed and embraced by the One in Whose nature is fullness of life and hope and peace. In You, Christ Jesus, Holy One, I am now holy. In You, Christ Jesus, Peace Maker, I am now reconciled to God. In You, Christ Jesus, Mystery of God, I am now hidden. Only in You is found this truth beyond imagination, this love beyond reason, this grace beyond measure: God is not ashamed of me! What rest, what joy, what unspeakable wonder is mine to know that because I am in You, Lord Jesus, God is proud to call Himself my Father. (Heb 2:11; 11:16)

In the Lord, the Lord alone
Are righteousness and strength:
The height and breadth and length
Of love is found in Him.
In the Lord, the Lord alone
Are righteousness and strength;
In the Lord, in the Lord alone.
"In the Lord Alone"
Walt Harrah (©1989)

about what he has seen, and his unspiritual mind puffs him up
with idle notions. **19**He has lost connection with the Head, from
whom the whole body, supported and held together by its liga-
ments and sinews, grows as God causes it to grow.
20Since you died with Christ to the basic principles of this
world, why, as though you still belonged to it, do you submit to its
rules: **21**"Do not handle! Do not taste! Do not touch!"? **22**These
are all destined to perish with use, because they are based on
human commands and teachings. **23**Such regulations indeed have
an appearance of wisdom, with their self-imposed worship, their
false humility and their harsh treatment of the body, but they lack
any value in restraining sensual indulgence.

Rules for Holy Living

3 Since, then, you have been raised with Christ, set your hearts
on things above, where Christ is seated at the right hand of
God. **2**Set your minds on things above, not on earthly things. **3**For
you died, and your life is now hidden with Christ in God. **4**When
Christ, who is your[a] life, appears, then you also will appear with
him in glory.
5Put to death, therefore, whatever belongs to your earthly nature: sexual immorality, impurity, lust, evil desires and greed,
which is idolatry. **6**Because of these, the wrath of God is coming.[b]
7You used to walk in these ways, in the life you once lived. **8**But
now you must rid yourselves of all such things as these: anger,
rage, malice, slander, and filthy language from your lips. **9**Do not
lie to each other, since you have taken off your old self with its
practices **10**and have put on the new self, which is being renewed
in knowledge in the image of its Creator. **11**Here there is no Greek
or Jew, circumcised or uncircumcised, barbarian, Scythian, slave
or free, but Christ is all, and is in all.
12Therefore, as God's chosen people, holy and dearly loved,
clothe yourselves with compassion, kindness, humility, gentleness
and patience. **13**Bear with each other and forgive whatever grievances you may have against one another. Forgive as the Lord forgave you. **14**And over all these virtues put on love, which binds
them all together in perfect unity.
15Let the peace of Christ rule in your hearts, since as members
of one body you were called to peace. And be thankful. **16**Let the
word of Christ dwell in you richly as you teach and admonish one
another with all wisdom, and as you sing psalms, hymns and spiritual songs with gratitude in your hearts to God. **17**And whatever
you do, whether in word or deed, do it all in the name of the Lord
Jesus, giving thanks to God the Father through him.

Rules for Christian Households

18Wives, submit to your husbands, as is fitting in the Lord.
19Husbands, love your wives and do not be harsh with them.
20Children, obey your parents in everything, for this pleases
the Lord.
21Fathers, do not embitter your children, or they will become
discouraged.
22Slaves, obey your earthly masters in everything; and do it, not
only when their eye is on you and to win their favor, but with sincerity of heart and reverence for the Lord. **23**Whatever you do,

[a] *4* Some manuscripts *our*
[b] *6* Some early manuscripts *coming on those who are disobedient*

God has a program of character development for each one of us. He wants others to look at our lives and say, "He walks with God, for he lives like Christ."

Erwin W. Lutzer (1941-)

(3:1–17) Lord Jesus, my Savior, I have been crucified with You. Teach me now to live my new life with You. Help me to take every thought captive to make it obedient to You, to cast aside everything that hinders and the sin that so easily entangles me. Even that which has been to my profit on this earth I now consider a loss compared to the surpassing greatness of knowing You. Take my life and make it new. Let my heart be the realm of Your peace and the residence of Your Word. Help me to become what I already am in Your eyes: clean, holy, beautiful—a reflection of Your glory and grace. (2Co 3:18; 10:5; Php 2:7–8; Col 3:16; Heb 12:1;)

Oh, conquering King
Conquer my heart,
And make of me
A pleasing gift to God.
My love for You
Will never die,
Jesus, You are my life.

I come to You,
I run to You,
There's no greater joy
Than knowing You.

"Jesus, You Are My Life"
Steve Fry (©1996)

work at it with all your heart, as working for the Lord, not for
men, 24since you know that you will receive an inheritance from
the Lord as a reward. It is the Lord Christ you are serving. 25Any-
one who does wrong will be repaid for his wrong, and there is no
favoritism.

4 Masters, provide your slaves with what is right and fair, because you know that you also have a Master in heaven.

Further Instructions

2Devote yourselves to prayer, being watchful and thankful.
3And pray for us, too, that God may open a door for our message,
so that we may proclaim the mystery of Christ, for which I am in
chains. 4Pray that I may proclaim it clearly, as I should. 5Be wise
in the way you act toward outsiders; make the most of every opportunity. 6Let your conversation be always full of grace, seasoned with salt, so that you may know how to answer everyone.

Final Greetings

7Tychicus will tell you all the news about me. He is a dear
brother, a faithful minister and fellow servant in the Lord. 8I am
sending him to you for the express purpose that you may know
about our[a] circumstances and that he may encourage your
hearts. 9He is coming with Onesimus, our faithful and dear brother, who is one of you. They will tell you everything that is happening here.

10My fellow prisoner Aristarchus sends you his greetings, as
does Mark, the cousin of Barnabas. (You have received instructions about him; if he comes to you, welcome him.) 11Jesus, who
is called Justus, also sends greetings. These are the only Jews
among my fellow workers for the kingdom of God, and they have
proved a comfort to me. 12Epaphras, who is one of you and a servant of Christ Jesus, sends greetings. He is always wrestling in
prayer for you, that you may stand firm in all the will of God, mature and fully assured. 13I vouch for him that he is working hard
for you and for those at Laodicea and Hierapolis. 14Our dear
friend Luke, the doctor, and Demas send greetings. 15Give my
greetings to the brothers at Laodicea, and to Nympha and the
church in her house.

16After this letter has been read to you, see that it is also read
in the church of the Laodiceans and that you in turn read the letter from Laodicea.

17Tell Archippus: "See to it that you complete the work you
have received in the Lord."

18I, Paul, write this greeting in my own hand. Remember my
chains. Grace be with you.

(4:5–6) "Out of the overflow of the heart the mouth speaks." O Lord, may my heart overflow with worship. May my conversation be a feast of life: May Christ be the bread and Your Spirit the wine, may praise be the fruit and grace the salt, may love be the table and wisdom the candle. May I always be prepared to feed anyone who hungers for the hope that I have in Christ. (Mt 12:34; Heb 13:15; 1Pe 3:15)

[a] 8 Some manuscripts *that he may know about your*

The First & Second Epistles of Paul the Apostle to the THESSALONIANS

What difference should the second coming of Christ make in our lives? Some Christians spend countless hours speculating about the timetable for His return. Others seem to ignore it altogether. Should the hope of Jesus' return impact our daily lives, even our worship?

For first-century Christians in Thessalonica, the second coming provokes anxiety. They grieve over friends who have died, believing that they have missed out on Jesus' return (1Th 4:13–18). The Thessalonians become alarmed when told that the day of the Lord has already come (2Th 2:1–2). Paul writes two letters to these new believers to encourage them in their faith and, in particular, to reassure them concerning the second coming. Christ's return provides reasons, not to worry, but to live and to worship with joyful confidence.

As Christians, we "serve the living and true God" and "wait for his Son from heaven" (1Th 1:9–10). When Jesus comes again He will execute judgment upon unbelievers (2Th 1:6–9). But if we know Christ, He will save us from the coming wrath (1Th 1:10). Thus we do not need to fear His coming but can anticipate it with hope. In fact, God is already at work in us, making us like Himself, so that when Christ returns we will be blameless and holy before Him (1Th 3:13; 5:23–24). This magnificent thought fills us with joy, even as it strengthens us to stand firm in the midst of trials (2Th 2:15).

Christ will come again, not only to judge sin and to finish His good work in us, but also "to be glorified in his holy people and to be marveled at among all those who have believed" (2Th 1:10). Christ will return to receive worship from those of us who have been set apart for this purpose. In the meantime, the vision of all Christians glorifying Christ inspires our present-day worship: "Holy, holy, holy! All the saints adore Thee, casting down their golden crowns around the glassy sea."*

The Lord's return helps us to encourage one another, and it motivates us to "be joyful always; pray continually; [and] give thanks in all circumstances."

As we live in expectation of Christ's return, we seek "to live lives worthy of God, who calls [us] into his kingdom and glory" (1Th 2:12). God is bidding us to live right now under His sovereign reign and to reflect His glory. When Christ returns, we will share in His divine glory (2Th 2:14). For the time being, He is glorified as God's work in us is fulfilled (2Th 1:12).

Hence, the second coming of Christ encourages us in our daily discipleship even as it inspires our worship. Moreover, it gives us confidence concerning the fate of fellow Christians who have died. They will not be excluded from Christ's victorious return but will actually precede the living as the Lord gathers His saints together (1Th 4:13–17). Therefore hope permeates our lives, even in times of grief. The Lord's return helps us to encourage one another, and it motivates us to "be joyful always; pray continually; [and] give thanks in all circumstances" (1Th 5:16).

*"Holy, Holy, Holy! Lord God Almighty." Text: Reginald Heber (1783-1826)

1 & 2 Thessalonians

(1:3) Jesus, draw me close. Apart from You I can do nothing. But if I live in You and You live in me, then I will bear much fruit. So fill me with faith that overflows into good works. Fill me with love that overflows into service to others. And fill me with hope that overflows into courage to do Your will. (Jn 15:5)

By faith we are led, not against reason but beyond reason, to the knowledge of God in himself and therefore of ourselves. By hope we are kept young of heart; for it teaches us to trust in God, to work with all our energy but to leave the future to him; it gives us poverty of spirit and so saves us from solicitude. And by love we are not told about God, we are brought to him.

Gerald Vann (1906-1963)

I have one deep, supreme desire,
That I may be like Jesus.
To this I fervently aspire,
That I may be like Jesus.
I want my heart His throne to be,
So that a watching world may see
His likeness shining forth in me.
I want to be like Jesus.

"I Want to Be Like Jesus"
Thomas O. Chisholm (©1945, 1973)

(1:5–6) Thank You, Lord, for the gospel. It is so much more than words. It is "the power of God for the salvation of everyone who believes." It is an open door to Your counsel room, a map for holy living. It is both a mirror that reflects the flaws in me that You wish to correct and a picture of what You are making me to be. It is the grace and peace of God, come in the flesh to save us from our sins. It is the promise of fullness of life in this world and of eternal life to come. (Ro 1:16)

1 Paul, Silas[a] and Timothy,

To the church of the Thessalonians in God the Father and the Lord Jesus Christ:

Grace and peace to you.[b]

Thanksgiving for the Thessalonians' Faith

2We always thank God for all of you, mentioning you in our prayers. 3We continually remember before our God and Father your work produced by faith, your labor prompted by love, and your endurance inspired by hope in our Lord Jesus Christ.

4For we know, brothers loved by God, that he has chosen you, 5because our gospel came to you not simply with words, but also with power, with the Holy Spirit and with deep conviction. You know how we lived among you for your sake. 6You became imitators of us and of the Lord; in spite of severe suffering, you welcomed the message with the joy given by the Holy Spirit. 7And so you became a model to all the believers in Macedonia and Achaia. 8The Lord's message rang out from you not only in Macedonia and Achaia—your faith in God has become known everywhere. Therefore we do not need to say anything about it, 9for they themselves report what kind of reception you gave us. They tell how you turned to God from idols to serve the living and true God, 10and to wait for his Son from heaven, whom he raised from the dead—Jesus, who rescues us from the coming wrath.

Paul's Ministry in Thessalonica

2 You know, brothers, that our visit to you was not a failure. 2We had previously suffered and been insulted in Philippi, as you know, but with the help of our God we dared to tell you his gospel in spite of strong opposition. 3For the appeal we make does not spring from error or impure motives, nor are we trying to trick you. 4On the contrary, we speak as men approved by God to be entrusted with the gospel. We are not trying to please men but God, who tests our hearts. 5You know we never used flattery, nor did we put on a mask to cover up greed—God is our witness. 6We were not looking for praise from men, not from you or anyone else.

As apostles of Christ we could have been a burden to you, 7but we were gentle among you, like a mother caring for her little children. 8We loved you so much that we were delighted to share with you not only the gospel of God but our lives as well, because you had become so dear to us. 9Surely you remember, brothers, our toil and hardship; we worked night and day in order not to be a burden to anyone while we preached the gospel of God to you.

10You are witnesses, and so is God, of how holy, righteous and blameless we were among you who believed. 11For you know that we dealt with each of you as a father deals with his own children, 12encouraging, comforting and urging you to live lives worthy of God, who calls you into his kingdom and glory.

13And we also thank God continually because, when you received the word of God, which you heard from us, you accepted it not as the word of men, but as it actually is, the word of God, which is at work in you who believe. 14For you, brothers, became imita-

[a] *1* Greek *Silvanus*, a variant of *Silas* [b] *1* Some early manuscripts *you from God our Father and the Lord Jesus Christ*

tors of God's churches in Judea, which are in Christ Jesus: You suffered from your own countrymen the same things those churches suffered from the Jews, 15who killed the Lord Jesus and the prophets and also drove us out. They displease God and are hostile to all men 16in their effort to keep us from speaking to the Gentiles so that they may be saved. In this way they always heap up their sins to the limit. The wrath of God has come upon them at last.[a]

Paul's Longing to See the Thessalonians

17But, brothers, when we were torn away from you for a short time (in person, not in thought), out of our intense longing we made every effort to see you. 18For we wanted to come to you—certainly I, Paul, did, again and again—but Satan stopped us. 19For what is our hope, our joy, or the crown in which we will glory in the presence of our Lord Jesus when he comes? Is it not you? 20Indeed, you are our glory and joy.

3 So when we could stand it no longer, we thought it best to be left by ourselves in Athens. 2We sent Timothy, who is our brother and God's fellow worker[b] in spreading the gospel of Christ, to strengthen and encourage you in your faith, 3so that no one would be unsettled by these trials. You know quite well that we were destined for them. 4In fact, when we were with you, we kept telling you that we would be persecuted. And it turned out that way, as you well know. 5For this reason, when I could stand it no longer, I sent to find out about your faith. I was afraid that in some way the tempter might have tempted you and our efforts might have been useless.

Timothy's Encouraging Report

6But Timothy has just now come to us from you and has brought good news about your faith and love. He has told us that you always have pleasant memories of us and that you long to see us, just as we also long to see you. 7Therefore, brothers, in all our distress and persecution we were encouraged about you because of your faith. 8For now we really live, since you are standing firm in the Lord. 9How can we thank God enough for you in return for all the joy we have in the presence of our God because of you? 10Night and day we pray most earnestly that we may see you again and supply what is lacking in your faith.

11Now may our God and Father himself and our Lord Jesus clear the way for us to come to you. 12May the Lord make your love increase and overflow for each other and for everyone else, just as ours does for you. 13May he strengthen your hearts so that you will be blameless and holy in the presence of our God and Father when our Lord Jesus comes with all his holy ones.

Living to Please God

4 Finally, brothers, we instructed you how to live in order to please God, as in fact you are living. Now we ask you and urge you in the Lord Jesus to do this more and more. 2For you know what instructions we gave you by the authority of the Lord Jesus.

3It is God's will that you should be sanctified: that you should avoid sexual immorality; 4that each of you should learn to control his own body[c] in a way that is holy and honorable, 5not in pas-

[a] 16 Or *them fully* [b] 2 Some manuscripts *brother and fellow worker*; other manuscripts *brother and God's servant* [c] 4 Or *learn to live with his own wife*; or *learn to acquire a wife*

(2:19–20) Father, I love the whole body of Christ. But I thank You especially for those brothers and sisters You have brought into my life, those for whom I carry a burden, those whom You have led me to pray for and encourage and support. Love them through me, Lord. Let me impart to them Your hope, Your grace, Your holy vision for their lives; and when You come again, may they be the crown I place at Your feet. (Isa 62:3; Col 1:27)

(3:2–4) Father, why am I surprised by trials and persecutions? Did I really expect to follow the "man of sorrows" without having sorrows of my own? When troubles come to me, Father, let me hear my Savior's words: "In this world you will have trouble." And then as I take up my cross to follow Him, may I hear His words of comfort, "I have overcome the world." (Isa 53:3; Mt 10:38; Jn 16:33; 1Pe 1:6–7)

No matter how great a sorrow may be,
God has already suffered it.
Meister Eckhart (c.1260–c.1327)

sionate lust like the heathen, who do not know God; 6and that in
this matter no one should wrong his brother or take advantage of
him. The Lord will punish men for all such sins, as we have already told you and warned you. 7For God did not call us to be
impure, but to live a holy life. 8Therefore, he who rejects this instruction does not reject man but God, who gives you his Holy
Spirit.

9Now about brotherly love we do not need to write to you, for
you yourselves have been taught by God to love each other. 10And
in fact, you do love all the brothers throughout Macedonia. Yet we
urge you, brothers, to do so more and more.

11Make it your ambition to lead a quiet life, to mind your own
business and to work with your hands, just as we told you, 12so
that your daily life may win the respect of outsiders and so that
you will not be dependent on anybody.

The Coming of the Lord

13Brothers, we do not want you to be ignorant about those who
fall asleep, or to grieve like the rest of men, who have no hope.
14We believe that Jesus died and rose again and so we believe that
God will bring with Jesus those who have fallen asleep in him.
15According to the Lord's own word, we tell you that we who are
still alive, who are left till the coming of the Lord, will certainly
not precede those who have fallen asleep. 16For the Lord himself
will come down from heaven, with a loud command, with the
voice of the archangel and with the trumpet call of God, and the
dead in Christ will rise first. 17After that, we who are still alive and
are left will be caught up together with them in the clouds to meet
the Lord in the air. And so we will be with the Lord forever.
18Therefore encourage each other with these words.

5 Now, brothers, about times and dates we do not need to write
to you, 2for you know very well that the day of the Lord will
come like a thief in the night. 3While people are saying, "Peace
and safety," destruction will come on them suddenly, as labor
pains on a pregnant woman, and they will not escape.

4But you, brothers, are not in darkness so that this day should
surprise you like a thief. 5You are all sons of the light and sons of
the day. We do not belong to the night or to the darkness. 6So
then, let us not be like others, who are asleep, but let us be alert
and self-controlled. 7For those who sleep, sleep at night, and
those who get drunk, get drunk at night. 8But since we belong to
the day, let us be self-controlled, putting on faith and love as a
breastplate, and the hope of salvation as a helmet. 9For God did
not appoint us to suffer wrath but to receive salvation through
our Lord Jesus Christ. 10He died for us so that, whether we are
awake or asleep, we may live together with him. 11Therefore encourage one another and build each other up, just as in fact you
are doing.

Final Instructions

12Now we ask you, brothers, to respect those who work hard
among you, who are over you in the Lord and who admonish you.
13Hold them in the highest regard in love because of their work.
Live in peace with each other. 14And we urge you, brothers, warn
those who are idle, encourage the timid, help the weak, be patient
with everyone. 15Make sure that nobody pays back wrong for

(4:13) Thank You, Father, for the hope You give me in my times of grief. You continually remind me that this world is only a stopping place on the way to a better home where I will be with You forever. So I can face even tragedy without despair. I can weep and feel the pain of earthly loss and still keep my eyes on heaven. Thank You, Father, for holding me when I'm hurting and for comforting me with the hope of a different time and place: a time when You will wipe every tear from my eyes and a place where there will be no more death or mourning or crying or pain. (Rev 21:4)

Our valleys may be filled with foes and tears; but we can lift our eyes to the hills to see God and the angels, heaven's spectators, who support us according to God's infinite wisdom as they prepare our welcome home.

Billy Graham (1918-)

Be still, my soul! The hour is
hastening on
When we shall be forever with the
Lord,
When disappointment, grief and fear
are gone,
Sorrow forgot, love's purest joys
restored.
Be still, my soul! When change and
tears are past,
All safe and blessed we shall meet at
last.

Be Still My Soul
Katharina von Schlegel (1752)
Trans. Jane L. Borthwick (1813-1897)

wrong, but always try to be kind to each other and to everyone else.

16Be joyful always; 17pray continually; 18give thanks in all circumstances, for this is God's will for you in Christ Jesus.

19Do not put out the Spirit's fire; 20do not treat prophecies with contempt. 21Test everything. Hold on to the good. 22Avoid every kind of evil.

23May God himself, the God of peace, sanctify you through and through. May your whole spirit, soul and body be kept blameless at the coming of our Lord Jesus Christ. 24The one who calls you is faithful and he will do it.

25Brothers, pray for us. 26Greet all the brothers with a holy kiss. 27I charge you before the Lord to have this letter read to all the brothers.

28The grace of our Lord Jesus Christ be with you.

God evermore gives power answerable to what He requires of us.

Bishop Thomas Wilson (1663-1735)

(5:12–24) I thank You, Father, for these closing words from our brother Paul. They are instructions for life, conceived in Your heart and passed on to us through his pen. You have told us these things so that we might know how to live out the holiness that You are working in us. May these actions be the fruit of godliness in our lives, evidences of Your grace working in us and through us. You have begun this good work in us. We know You will be faithful to complete it, for You give to us all that You require of us. Truly our sufficiency is wrapped up in Your grace, and Your grace is all-sufficient. (2Co 9:8; 12:9; Php 1:6; Col 1:10)

1 Paul, Silas[a] and Timothy,

To the church of the Thessalonians in God our Father and the
Lord Jesus Christ:

2Grace and peace to you from God the Father and the Lord
Jesus Christ.

Thanksgiving and Prayer

3We ought always to thank God for you, brothers, and rightly
so, because your faith is growing more and more, and the love
every one of you has for each other is increasing. 4Therefore,
among God's churches we boast about your perseverance and
faith in all the persecutions and trials you are enduring.
5All this is evidence that God's judgment is right, and as a result you will be counted worthy of the kingdom of God, for which
you are suffering. 6God is just: He will pay back trouble to those
who trouble you 7and give relief to you who are troubled, and to
us as well. This will happen when the Lord Jesus is revealed from
heaven in blazing fire with his powerful angels. 8He will punish
those who do not know God and do not obey the gospel of our
Lord Jesus. 9They will be punished with everlasting destruction
and shut out from the presence of the Lord and from the majesty
of his power 10on the day he comes to be glorified in his holy
people and to be marveled at among all those who have believed.
This includes you, because you believed our testimony to you.
11With this in mind, we constantly pray for you, that our God
may count you worthy of his calling, and that by his power he may
fulfill every good purpose of yours and every act prompted by
your faith. 12We pray this so that the name of our Lord Jesus may
be glorified in you, and you in him, according to the grace of our
God and the Lord Jesus Christ.[b]

The Man of Lawlessness

2 Concerning the coming of our Lord Jesus Christ and our
being gathered to him, we ask you, brothers, 2not to become
easily unsettled or alarmed by some prophecy, report or letter
supposed to have come from us, saying that the day of the Lord
has already come. 3Don't let anyone deceive you in any way, for
⌊that day will not come⌋ until the rebellion occurs and the man of
lawlessness[c] is revealed, the man doomed to destruction. 4He
will oppose and will exalt himself over everything that is called
God or is worshiped, so that he sets himself up in God's temple,
proclaiming himself to be God.
5Don't you remember that when I was with you I used to tell
you these things? 6And now you know what is holding him back,
so that he may be revealed at the proper time. 7For the secret
power of lawlessness is already at work; but the one who now
holds it back will continue to do so till he is taken out of the way.
8And then the lawless one will be revealed, whom the Lord Jesus
will overthrow with the breath of his mouth and destroy by the
splendor of his coming. 9The coming of the lawless one will be in
accordance with the work of Satan displayed in all kinds of counterfeit miracles, signs and wonders, 10and in every sort of evil
that deceives those who are perishing. They perish because they

[a] *1* Greek *Silvanus*, a variant of *Silas* [b] *12* Or *God and Lord, Jesus Christ*
[c] *3* Some manuscripts *sin*

(1:11) Father, I want to live a life that pleases You. I want to walk through each day depending on Your power, looking for Your hand, listening for the still, small voice of Your guidance. Use me for Your kingdom's purposes. Nudge me into greater acts of faith. Call me to a deeper level of trust. Soften my heart, O Lord, so that I may live worthy of Your calling and fulfill Your highest purpose for my life.
(Isa 30:21; Eph 4:1; Col 1:9–12; Heb 4:7)

Bad will be the day for every man when he becomes absolutely content with the life that he is living, with the thoughts that he is thinking, with the deeds that he is doing, when there is not forever beating at the doors of his soul some great desire to do something larger, which he knows that he was meant and made to do because he is still, in spite of all, the child of God.
Phillips Brooks (1835-1893)

Christ in us be glorified.
Christ in us be lifted high.
Let His love be shown
And His praises be known.
Let Christ be glorified.

In every song we sing,
In the praises that we bring,
Let Christ be glorified.
In the service that we give,
And the lives that we live,
Let Christ be glorified.
"Christ In Us Be Glorified"
Morris Chapman (©1995)

refused to love the truth and so be saved. 11For this reason God
sends them a powerful delusion so that they will believe the lie
12and so that all will be condemned who have not believed the
truth but have delighted in wickedness.

Stand Firm

13But we ought always to thank God for you, brothers loved by
the Lord, because from the beginning God chose you[a] to be saved
through the sanctifying work of the Spirit and through belief in
the truth. 14He called you to this through our gospel, that you
might share in the glory of our Lord Jesus Christ. 15So then,
brothers, stand firm and hold to the teachings[b] we passed on to
you, whether by word of mouth or by letter.
16May our Lord Jesus Christ himself and God our Father, who
loved us and by his grace gave us eternal encouragement and
good hope, 17encourage your hearts and strengthen you in every
good deed and word.

Request for Prayer

3 Finally, brothers, pray for us that the message of the Lord
may spread rapidly and be honored, just as it was with you.
2And pray that we may be delivered from wicked and evil men,
for not everyone has faith. 3But the Lord is faithful, and he will
strengthen and protect you from the evil one. 4We have confidence in the Lord that you are doing and will continue to do the
things we command. 5May the Lord direct your hearts into God's
love and Christ's perseverance.

Warning Against Idleness

6In the name of the Lord Jesus Christ, we command you, brothers, to keep away from every brother who is idle and does not live
according to the teaching[c] you received from us. 7For you yourselves know how you ought to follow our example. We were not
idle when we were with you, 8nor did we eat anyone's food without paying for it. On the contrary, we worked night and day, laboring and toiling so that we would not be a burden to any of
you. 9We did this, not because we do not have the right to such
help, but in order to make ourselves a model for you to follow.
10For even when we were with you, we gave you this rule: "If a
man will not work, he shall not eat."
11We hear that some among you are idle. They are not busy;
they are busybodies. 12Such people we command and urge in the
Lord Jesus Christ to settle down and earn the bread they eat.
13And as for you, brothers, never tire of doing what is right.
14If anyone does not obey our instruction in this letter, take
special note of him. Do not associate with him, in order that he
may feel ashamed. 15Yet do not regard him as an enemy, but warn
him as a brother.

Final Greetings

16Now may the Lord of peace himself give you peace at all
times and in every way. The Lord be with all of you.
17I, Paul, write this greeting in my own hand, which is the distinguishing mark in all my letters. This is how I write.
18The grace of our Lord Jesus Christ be with you all.

[a] *13* Some manuscripts *because God chose you as his firstfruits* [b] *15* Or *traditions*
[c] *6* Or *tradition*

For most men the world is centered in self, which is misery; to have one's world centered in God is peace.

Donald Hankey (1874-1917)

(3:16) O Lord of peace, in Your presence is peace in its perfection—peace beyond imagination: peace with God, peace with others, peace with ourselves, peace in the storm, peace in our fears, peace in this world and peace in the world to come. Your peace is the guardian of our hearts and minds. It is our calling, our path and our destination. Peace flowed from Your veins at Calvary. Peace is Your message, and Your emissary. Peace is Your gift, Your promise, and the constant companion of Your grace. At all times and in all our ways, teach us, dear Lord, to avail ourselves of the peace that awaits us in Your presence. (Lk 1:79; Ro 1:7; Ro 5:1; Ro 12:18; 1Co 1:3; 2Co 1:2; Eph 2:14–18; Php 4:7; Col 1:20; Col 3:15; 2Th 1:2)

He is our peace
Who has broken down every wall,
He is our peace,
He is our peace.
Cast all your cares on Him,
For He cares for you,
He is our peace,
He is our peace.

"He Is Our Peace"
Kandela Groves (©1975)

The Pastoral Epistles of Paul the Apostle to

TIMOTHY & TITUS

Timothy & Titus

In the religion section of our local bookstores we will find many volumes authored by writers who claim to be Christian but whose writings contradict basic Christian truth. False teaching by purported believers is nothing new, however. It was a major problem in the latter years of Paul's ministry and has continued to plague the church for generations.

Paul writes letters to Timothy and Titus to encourage his protégés as they confront the problem of false teaching in the church. Scholars often refer to these letters as the "Pastoral Epistles" because of the pastoral concern expressed for church leaders and the congregations they shepherd. These three letters demonstrate Paul's many concerns, especially for right doctrine and godly leadership.

The activity of heretical teachers in the church comes as no surprise, according to Paul, because "the Spirit clearly says that in later times some will abandon the faith and follow deceiving spirits" (1Ti 4:1). By teaching their deceptions, these people "promote controversies" and "godless chatter" as they turn believers away from genuine Christian faith (1Ti 1:4; 6:20).

Paul urges Timothy and Titus to oppose such false teachers with the revealed truth of God (1Ti 1:3; Tit 1:10–14). Timothy should hold on to what he has learned from Paul, keeping it "as the pattern of sound teaching" (2Ti 1:13). Titus must "teach what is in accord with sound doctrine" (Tit 2:1).

The Bible shows us more of God's nature, freeing us from redundant worship that comes when our vision of God is limited by our own experience.

But how are we to know what is consistent with sound doctrine? Paul advises that theology must be measured by its conformity to the Bible, since "all Scripture is God-breathed and is useful for teaching, rebuking, correcting and training in righteousness" (2Ti 3:16). God's written Word is able "to make [us] wise for salvation through faith in Christ Jesus" and also to help us become "thoroughly equipped for every good work" (2Ti 3:15,17).

It follows, therefore, that the Bible prepares us for the good work of worship. In particular, it supplies the content of our praise so that we will worship "in truth" (Jn 4:23–24). Scriptural guidance ensures that our worship, in addition to our teaching, will be in accord with sound doctrine. The Bible helps us to focus upon aspects of God that inspire our adoration. Moreover, it shows us more of God's nature, freeing us from redundant worship that comes when our vision of God is limited by our own experience.

Paul models theologically sound and expansive worship that flows from God's revealed truth. Twice in writing to Timothy he breaks into praise, probably using early Christian worship language. Thus he provides an example for us as we seek to worship God truthfully and majestically: "Now to the King eternal, immortal, invisible, the only God, be honor and glory for ever and ever. Amen" (1Ti 1:17). "God, the blessed and only Ruler, the King of kings and Lord of lords, who alone is immortal and who lives in unapproachable light, whom no one has seen or can see. To him be honor and might forever. Amen" (1Ti 6:15–16).

1 Paul, an apostle of Christ Jesus by the command of God our
Savior and of Christ Jesus our hope,

2To Timothy my true son in the faith:

Grace, mercy and peace from God the Father and Christ Jesus
our Lord.

Warning Against False Teachers of the Law

3As I urged you when I went into Macedonia, stay there in Ephesus so that you may command certain men not to teach false
doctrines any longer 4nor to devote themselves to myths and endless genealogies. These promote controversies rather than God's
work—which is by faith. 5The goal of this command is love,
which comes from a pure heart and a good conscience and a sincere faith. 6Some have wandered away from these and turned to
meaningless talk. 7They want to be teachers of the law, but they
do not know what they are talking about or what they so confidently affirm.

8We know that the law is good if one uses it properly. 9We also
know that law[a] is made not for the righteous but for lawbreakers
and rebels, the ungodly and sinful, the unholy and irreligious; for
those who kill their fathers or mothers, for murderers, 10for
adulterers and perverts, for slave traders and liars and perjurers—and for whatever else is contrary to the sound doctrine
11that conforms to the glorious gospel of the blessed God, which
he entrusted to me.

The Lord's Grace to Paul

12I thank Christ Jesus our Lord, who has given me strength,
that he considered me faithful, appointing me to his service.
13Even though I was once a blasphemer and a persecutor and a
violent man, I was shown mercy because I acted in ignorance and
unbelief. 14The grace of our Lord was poured out on me abundantly, along with the faith and love that are in Christ Jesus.

15Here is a trustworthy saying that deserves full acceptance:
Christ Jesus came into the world to save sinners—of whom I am
the worst. 16But for that very reason I was shown mercy so that in
me, the worst of sinners, Christ Jesus might display his unlimited
patience as an example for those who would believe on him and
receive eternal life. 17Now to the King eternal, immortal, invisible,
the only God, be honor and glory for ever and ever. Amen.

18Timothy, my son, I give you this instruction in keeping with
the prophecies once made about you, so that by following them
you may fight the good fight, 19holding on to faith and a good
conscience. Some have rejected these and so have shipwrecked
their faith. 20Among them are Hymenaeus and Alexander, whom
I have handed over to Satan to be taught not to blaspheme.

Instructions on Worship

2 I urge, then, first of all, that requests, prayers, intercession
and thanksgiving be made for everyone— 2for kings and all
those in authority, that we may live peaceful and quiet lives in all
godliness and holiness. 3This is good, and pleases God our Savior, 4who wants all men to be saved and to come to a knowledge
of the truth. 5For there is one God and one mediator between God

[a] 9 Or *that the law*

(1:2) Gracious Father, tender Lord Jesus, how I love to sit refreshed beneath the cascading waterfall of Your provision. Every day You pour forth anew on me the grace of forgiveness, the mercy of compassion and the peace that transcends my finite understanding. Your steadfast love will never come to an end. Great is Your faithfulness. (La 3:22–23; Php 4:7)

(2:1–5) Father, I cannot begin to fathom the mystery of intercession. You spoke a word and a universe was created. You will speak a second time and a new heaven and earth will be ushered in. Nothing happens apart from Your decree. You are dependent upon no one and nothing. Yet the prayers of Your people matter to You. Though nothing in all of creation is hidden from Your sight, You invite each of us to bring our concerns and requests to Your attention. When we ask, we receive. When we seek, we find. When we knock, You open doors. So, gracious Lord, hear our prayer today: Lord, save; Lord, heal; Lord, reign. Bring Your kingdom and Your righteousness to bear in our land and in our lives. And may the fruit of righteousness be peace, quietness and confidence forever. (Isa 32:17; Mt 7:7; Heb 4:13)

Stretch out Your hand
And heal this nation,
Stretch out Your hand
And bring restoration.
Let Your mercy overflow us
Like a never failing stream,
By the blood of Jesus, cleanse us,
Oh Lord, it's You we seek.
Cause Your face to shine
Upon us again.

"Stretch Out Your Hand"
Scott V. Smith and
Malcolm duPlessis (©1995)

Behold, bless ye the Lord,
All ye servants of the Lord.
Lift up your hands in the sanctuary
And bless, bless ye the Lord.

"Behold, Bless Ye The Lord"
Bob Probert (©1979)

(2:8) Father, we lift up our hands to You in prayer—hands that You have made holy. May they reveal hearts that are committed to forgiveness and reconciliation with each other. It is an awesome witness when we, Your people, lead lives of humility and gentleness before a watching world, when the music of our worship is not just heard in Your holy sanctuary but reverberates through all our relationships.

O Lord, give us more charity, more self-denial, more likeness to you. Teach us to sacrifice our comforts to others, and our likings for the sake of doing good. Make us kindly in thought, gentle in word, generous in deed. Teach us that it is better to give than to receive; better to forget ourselves than put ourselves forward; better to minister than be ministered to. And to you, the God of love, be glory and praise for ever. Amen.

Henry Alford (1810–1871)

(3:16) The mystery of godliness is beyond comprehension. What we know of You has only been revealed by Your mercy. And if we do not fully understand what we have seen, how much greater is the mystery of that which we have not seen? It is only fitting that You Who are beyond comprehension would grant us gifts that are infinitely beyond our wildest imaginings: hope that surpasses all doubt, love that overrules all conditions, strength that exceeds all challenges and peace that transcends understanding. Let us not try to explain You but simply worship You with reverence and awe. (Eph 3:20; Heb 12:28)

and men, the man Christ Jesus, 6 who gave himself as a ransom
for all men—the testimony given in its proper time. 7 And for this
purpose I was appointed a herald and an apostle—I am telling
the truth, I am not lying—and a teacher of the true faith to the
Gentiles.
8 I want men everywhere to lift up holy hands in prayer, without
anger or disputing.
9 I also want women to dress modestly, with decency and propriety, not with braided hair or gold or pearls or expensive
clothes, 10 but with good deeds, appropriate for women who profess to worship God.
11 A woman should learn in quietness and full submission. 12 I do
not permit a woman to teach or to have authority over a man; she
must be silent. 13 For Adam was formed first, then Eve. 14 And Adam
was not the one deceived; it was the woman who was deceived and
became a sinner. 15 But women[a] will be saved[b] through childbearing—if they continue in faith, love and holiness with propriety.

Overseers and Deacons

3 Here is a trustworthy saying: If anyone sets his heart on being
an overseer,[c] he desires a noble task. 2 Now the overseer
must be above reproach, the husband of but one wife, temperate,
self-controlled, respectable, hospitable, able to teach, 3 not given
to drunkenness, not violent but gentle, not quarrelsome, not a
lover of money. 4 He must manage his own family well and see
that his children obey him with proper respect. 5 (If anyone does
not know how to manage his own family, how can he take care of
God's church?) 6 He must not be a recent convert, or he may become conceited and fall under the same judgment as the devil.
7 He must also have a good reputation with outsiders, so that he
will not fall into disgrace and into the devil's trap.
8 Deacons, likewise, are to be men worthy of respect, sincere,
not indulging in much wine, and not pursuing dishonest gain.
9 They must keep hold of the deep truths of the faith with a clear
conscience. 10 They must first be tested; and then if there is nothing against them, let them serve as deacons.
11 In the same way, their wives[d] are to be women worthy of respect, not malicious talkers but temperate and trustworthy in
everything.
12 A deacon must be the husband of but one wife and must
manage his children and his household well. 13 Those who have
served well gain an excellent standing and great assurance in
their faith in Christ Jesus.
14 Although I hope to come to you soon, I am writing you these
instructions so that, 15 if I am delayed, you will know how people
ought to conduct themselves in God's household, which is the
church of the living God, the pillar and foundation of the truth.
16 Beyond all question, the mystery of godliness is great:

He[e] appeared in a body,[f]
  was vindicated by the Spirit,
was seen by angels,
  was preached among the nations,
was believed on in the world,
  was taken up in glory.

[a] 15 Greek *she* [b] 15 Or *restored* [c] 1 Traditionally *bishop*; also in verse 2
[d] 11 Or *way, deaconesses* [e] 16 Some manuscripts *God* [f] 16 Or *in the flesh*

Instructions to Timothy

4 The Spirit clearly says that in later times some will abandon
the faith and follow deceiving spirits and things taught by
demons. 2Such teachings come through hypocritical liars, whose
consciences have been seared as with a hot iron. 3They forbid
people to marry and order them to abstain from certain foods,
which God created to be received with thanksgiving by those who
believe and who know the truth. 4For everything God created is
good, and nothing is to be rejected if it is received with thanksgiving, 5because it is consecrated by the word of God and prayer.
6If you point these things out to the brothers, you will be a
good minister of Christ Jesus, brought up in the truths of the faith
and of the good teaching that you have followed. 7Have nothing to
do with godless myths and old wives' tales; rather, train yourself
to be godly. 8For physical training is of some value, but godliness
has value for all things, holding promise for both the present life
and the life to come.
9This is a trustworthy saying that deserves full acceptance
10(and for this we labor and strive), that we have put our hope in
the living God, who is the Savior of all men, and especially of
those who believe.
11Command and teach these things. 12Don't let anyone look
down on you because you are young, but set an example for the
believers in speech, in life, in love, in faith and in purity. 13Until I
come, devote yourself to the public reading of Scripture, to
preaching and to teaching. 14Do not neglect your gift, which was
given you through a prophetic message when the body of elders
laid their hands on you.
15Be diligent in these matters; give yourself wholly to them, so
that everyone may see your progress. 16Watch your life and doctrine closely. Persevere in them, because if you do, you will save
both yourself and your hearers.

Advice About Widows, Elders and Slaves

5 Do not rebuke an older man harshly, but exhort him as if he
were your father. Treat younger men as brothers, 2older
women as mothers, and younger women as sisters, with absolute
purity.
3Give proper recognition to those widows who are really in
need. 4But if a widow has children or grandchildren, these
should learn first of all to put their religion into practice by caring for their own family and so repaying their parents and grand-
parents, for this is pleasing to God. 5The widow who is really in
need and left all alone puts her hope in God and continues night
and day to pray and to ask God for help. 6But the widow who lives
for pleasure is dead even while she lives. 7Give the people these
instructions, too, so that no one may be open to blame. 8If anyone does not provide for his relatives, and especially for his
immediate family, he has denied the faith and is worse than an
unbeliever.
9No widow may be put on the list of widows unless she is over
sixty, has been faithful to her husband,[a] 10and is well known for
her good deeds, such as bringing up children, showing hospitality, washing the feet of the saints, helping those in trouble and devoting herself to all kinds of good deeds.

[a] 9 Or *has had but one husband*

(4:4) We give You thanks, our great and gracious God, for all the good things You have created. These innumerable blessings are daily showered upon us by Your good will, and You delight in sharing them with us. (Rev 4:11)

Give thanks with a grateful heart,
Give thanks to the Holy One,
Give thanks because He's given Jesus
Christ, His Son.

And now let the weak say, "I am
strong,"
Let the poor say, "I am rich
Because of what the Lord has done
for us!"
Give thanks.

"Give Thanks"
Henry Smith (©1978)

(4:7–16) Gracious Father, help me to practice daily and diligently the imitation of Christ. Help me to walk faithfully in the disciplines of godliness, so that they may produce in me a harvest of righteousness and peace. Strengthen my feeble arms and weak knees, and grant me singleness of heart and action so that I may live, love, believe and behave in a manner that brings honor to the Family name. (Jer 32:39; Eph 5:1; Heb 12:11–12)

11As for younger widows, do not put them on such a list. For
when their sensual desires overcome their dedication to Christ,
they want to marry. 12Thus they bring judgment on themselves,
because they have broken their first pledge. 13Besides, they get
into the habit of being idle and going about from house to house.
And not only do they become idlers, but also gossips and busybodies, saying things they ought not to. 14So I counsel younger
widows to marry, to have children, to manage their homes and to
give the enemy no opportunity for slander. 15Some have in fact already turned away to follow Satan.
16If any woman who is a believer has widows in her family, she
should help them and not let the church be burdened with them,
so that the church can help those widows who are really in need.
17The elders who direct the affairs of the church well are worthy of double honor, especially those whose work is preaching
and teaching. 18For the Scripture says, "Do not muzzle the ox
while it is treading out the grain,"[a] and "The worker deserves his
wages."[b] 19Do not entertain an accusation against an elder unless
it is brought by two or three witnesses. 20Those who sin are to be
rebuked publicly, so that the others may take warning.
21I charge you, in the sight of God and Christ Jesus and the
elect angels, to keep these instructions without partiality, and to
do nothing out of favoritism.
22Do not be hasty in the laying on of hands, and do not share
in the sins of others. Keep yourself pure.
23Stop drinking only water, and use a little wine because of
your stomach and your frequent illnesses.
24The sins of some men are obvious, reaching the place of
judgment ahead of them; the sins of others trail behind them.
25In the same way, good deeds are obvious, and even those that
are not cannot be hidden.

6 All who are under the yoke of slavery should consider their
masters worthy of full respect, so that God's name and our
teaching may not be slandered. 2Those who have believing masters are not to show less respect for them because they are brothers. Instead, they are to serve them even better, because those
who benefit from their service are believers, and dear to them.
These are the things you are to teach and urge on them.

Love of Money

3If anyone teaches false doctrines and does not agree to the
sound instruction of our Lord Jesus Christ and to godly teaching,
4he is conceited and understands nothing. He has an unhealthy
interest in controversies and quarrels about words that result in
envy, strife, malicious talk, evil suspicions 5and constant friction
between men of corrupt mind, who have been robbed of the truth
and who think that godliness is a means to financial gain.
6But godliness with contentment is great gain. 7For we brought
nothing into the world, and we can take nothing out of it. 8But if
we have food and clothing, we will be content with that. 9People
who want to get rich fall into temptation and a trap and into many
foolish and harmful desires that plunge men into ruin and destruction. 10For the love of money is a root of all kinds of evil.
Some people, eager for money, have wandered from the faith and
pierced themselves with many griefs.

[a] 18 Deut. 25:4 [b] 18 Luke 10:7

(6:6–7) Thank You, Lord, for Your great faithfulness. You know what is best for me. All of my sufficiency is in You. You are my source and my sustenance. You supply bread for my daily needs, forgiveness for my daily sins and strength for my daily burdens. Help me in every circumstance to be fully content with that which issues from Your gracious hand. "Better the little that the righteous have than the wealth of many wicked; for the power of the wicked will be broken, but the LORD upholds the righteous." (Ps 37:16–17; Php 4:11)

The children of Israel did not find in the manna all the sweetness and strength they might have found in it; not because the manna did not contain them, but because they longed for other meat.
Saint John of the Cross (1542–1591)

Paul's Charge to Timothy

11But you, man of God, flee from all this, and pursue righteousness, godliness, faith, love, endurance and gentleness. 12Fight the good fight of the faith. Take hold of the eternal life to which you were called when you made your good confession in the presence of many witnesses. 13In the sight of God, who gives life to everything, and of Christ Jesus, who while testifying before Pontius Pilate made the good confession, I charge you 14to keep this command without spot or blame until the appearing of our Lord Jesus Christ, 15which God will bring about in his own time—God, the blessed and only Ruler, the King of kings and Lord of lords, 16who alone is immortal and who lives in unapproachable light, whom no one has seen or can see. To him be honor and might forever. Amen.

17Command those who are rich in this present world not to be arrogant nor to put their hope in wealth, which is so uncertain, but to put their hope in God, who richly provides us with everything for our enjoyment. 18Command them to do good, to be rich in good deeds, and to be generous and willing to share. 19In this way they will lay up treasure for themselves as a firm foundation for the coming age, so that they may take hold of the life that is truly life.

20Timothy, guard what has been entrusted to your care. Turn away from godless chatter and the opposing ideas of what is falsely called knowledge, 21which some have professed and in so doing have wandered from the faith.

Grace be with you.

(6:11–12) Your calling is always accompanied by Your provision. To take hold of eternal life is simply to drink from the fountain of living water that is always available, to eat the manna so faithfully provided in the Lord Jesus, to turn from that which is not life to that which is life indeed.

Rise up, O men of God!
Have done with lesser things;
Give heart and soul
And mind and strength
To serve the King of kings.

Rise up, the Lord is calling!
Rise up, this is the day;
Rise up, and seize the moment,
Rise up, O men of faith!

"Rise Up, O Men of God"
William P. Merrill and
William Walter (c.1911) and
New Words by Bill Batstone and
Buddy Owens (©1994)

(6:17) When I am tempted to feel more secure because of an increase in income, more at peace when my financial portfolio looks impressive, more in control because my debts are decreasing . . . then bring me back to my senses, dear God. There is nothing and no one but You that can give lasting peace. I will enjoy the things You provide; but I will hope only in You.

(1:6–7) Almighty God, send the wind of Your Spirit to blow across the embers of my heart. Stir up the fire of faith and re-ignite my passion for holiness. Kindle within me a desire to use the spiritual gifts You have given me for the good of Your kingdom. May Your Spirit shine forth in power, may that power be governed by self-discipline, and may all that I do be done in the love of God.

More love, more power,
More of You in my life.
More love, more power,
More of You in my life.

And I will worship You
With all of my heart.
And I will worship You
With all of my mind.
And I will worship You
With all of my strength,
For You are my Lord,
You are my Lord.

"More Love, More Power"
Jude Del Hierro (©1987)

(1:12–14) Father, into Your hands I have entrusted my spirit. Into my hands You have entrusted the message of the gospel. I know You will be faithful in guarding what I have entrusted to You. By the power of the Holy Spirit, help me to be faithful in guarding what You have entrusted to me.

He who is faithful over a few things is a lord of cities. It does not matter whether you preach in Westminster Abbey, or teach a ragged class, so you be faithful. The faithfulness is all.

George MacDonald (1824-1905)

1 Paul, an apostle of Christ Jesus by the will of God, according
to the promise of life that is in Christ Jesus,
2To Timothy, my dear son:
Grace, mercy and peace from God the Father and Christ Jesus
our Lord.

Encouragement to Be Faithful

3I thank God, whom I serve, as my forefathers did, with a clear
conscience, as night and day I constantly remember you in my
prayers. 4Recalling your tears, I long to see you, so that I may be
filled with joy. 5I have been reminded of your sincere faith, which
first lived in your grandmother Lois and in your mother Eunice
and, I am persuaded, now lives in you also. 6For this reason I remind you to fan into flame the gift of God, which is in you through
the laying on of my hands. 7For God did not give us a spirit of
timidity, but a spirit of power, of love and of self-discipline.
8So do not be ashamed to testify about our Lord, or ashamed
of me his prisoner. But join with me in suffering for the gospel, by
the power of God, 9who has saved us and called us to a holy
life—not because of anything we have done but because of his
own purpose and grace. This grace was given us in Christ Jesus
before the beginning of time, 10but it has now been revealed
through the appearing of our Savior, Christ Jesus, who has destroyed death and has brought life and immortality to light
through the gospel. 11And of this gospel I was appointed a herald
and an apostle and a teacher. 12That is why I am suffering as I am.
Yet I am not ashamed, because I know whom I have believed, and
am convinced that he is able to guard what I have entrusted to
him for that day.
13What you heard from me, keep as the pattern of sound
teaching, with faith and love in Christ Jesus. 14Guard the good deposit that was entrusted to you—guard it with the help of the Holy
Spirit who lives in us.
15You know that everyone in the province of Asia has deserted
me, including Phygelus and Hermogenes.
16May the Lord show mercy to the household of Onesiphorus,
because he often refreshed me and was not ashamed of my
chains. 17On the contrary, when he was in Rome, he searched
hard for me until he found me. 18May the Lord grant that he will
find mercy from the Lord on that day! You know very well in how
many ways he helped me in Ephesus.

2 You then, my son, be strong in the grace that is in Christ
Jesus. 2And the things you have heard me say in the presence
of many witnesses entrust to reliable men who will also be qualified to teach others. 3Endure hardship with us like a good soldier
of Christ Jesus. 4No one serving as a soldier gets involved in civilian affairs—he wants to please his commanding officer. 5Simi-
larly, if anyone competes as an athlete, he does not receive the
victor's crown unless he competes according to the rules. 6The
hardworking farmer should be the first to receive a share of
the crops. 7Reflect on what I am saying, for the Lord will give you
insight into all this.
8Remember Jesus Christ, raised from the dead, descended
from David. This is my gospel, 9for which I am suffering even to
the point of being chained like a criminal. But God's word is not
chained. 10Therefore I endure everything for the sake of the elect,

that they too may obtain the salvation that is in Christ Jesus, with eternal glory.

11 Here is a trustworthy saying:

If we died with him,
we will also live with him;
12 if we endure,
we will also reign with him.
If we disown him,
he will also disown us;
13 if we are faithless,
he will remain faithful,
for he cannot disown himself.

A Workman Approved by God

14 Keep reminding them of these things. Warn them before God
against quarreling about words; it is of no value, and only ruins
those who listen. 15 Do your best to present yourself to God as
one approved, a workman who does not need to be ashamed and
who correctly handles the word of truth. 16 Avoid godless chatter,
because those who indulge in it will become more and more ungodly. 17 Their teaching will spread like gangrene. Among them
are Hymenaeus and Philetus, 18 who have wandered away from
the truth. They say that the resurrection has already taken place,
and they destroy the faith of some. 19 Nevertheless, God's solid
foundation stands firm, sealed with this inscription: "The Lord
knows those who are his,"[a] and, "Everyone who confesses the
name of the Lord must turn away from wickedness."

20 In a large house there are articles not only of gold and silver,
but also of wood and clay; some are for noble purposes and some
for ignoble. 21 If a man cleanses himself from the latter, he will be
an instrument for noble purposes, made holy, useful to the Master and prepared to do any good work.

22 Flee the evil desires of youth, and pursue righteousness,
faith, love and peace, along with those who call on the Lord out
of a pure heart. 23 Don't have anything to do with foolish and stupid arguments, because you know they produce quarrels. 24 And
the Lord's servant must not quarrel; instead, he must be kind to
everyone, able to teach, not resentful. 25 Those who oppose him
he must gently instruct, in the hope that God will grant them repentance leading them to a knowledge of the truth, 26 and that
they will come to their senses and escape from the trap of the
devil, who has taken them captive to do his will.

Godlessness in the Last Days

3 But mark this: There will be terrible times in the last days.
2 People will be lovers of themselves, lovers of money, boastful, proud, abusive, disobedient to their parents, ungrateful, unholy, 3 without love, unforgiving, slanderous, without self-control,
brutal, not lovers of the good, 4 treacherous, rash, conceited,
lovers of pleasure rather than lovers of God— 5 having a form of
godliness but denying its power. Have nothing to do with them.

6 They are the kind who worm their way into homes and gain
control over weak-willed women, who are loaded down with sins
and are swayed by all kinds of evil desires, 7 always learning but
never able to acknowledge the truth. 8 Just as Jannes and Jambres

[a] 19 Num. 16:5 (see Septuagint)

I desire only Him and to be wholly His.
Brother Lawrence of the Resurrection
(c.1605-1691)

(2:19–21) Almighty God, You possess all power, all authority, all knowledge. Nothing is impossible for You; and yet You choose to work through Your people. What greater honor could there be in life than to be used by You for Your good pleasure? Lord, set me apart for Your noble purposes. Help me to live in a way that is pleasing to You, to always be ready for service. You have made me holy, so help me not to defile myself and miss out on what You have in store for me. (Lev 20:7–8)

Breathe on me, Breath of God,
Until my heart is pure,
Until with Thee I will one will,
To do and to endure.

Breathe on me, Breath of God,
Till I am wholly Thine,
Until this earthly part of me
Glows with Thy fire divine.
"Breathe on Me, Breath of God"
Edwin Hatch (1886)

(3:1–5) Lord Jesus, purify us as Your people. May Your holy love so burn in our hearts that everything that competes for our attention and allegiance may be exposed as an unworthy suitor. May the power of Your love call forth in us a renewed zeal for the beauty of holiness.

(3:15–17) Holy Spirit, breath of God, breathe through the words on these pages once more. May they become life and health and peace for my soul. May I find in their wisdom all that I need to be fully equipped for a life of service to God. Intensify my hunger for the Scriptures, clarify their meaning and quicken my heart to a swifter obedience.

Approach our Bible with the idea that it is not only a book which was once spoken, but a book which is now speaking . . . God's speaking is in the continuous present . . . a word of God once spoken continues to be spoken, as a child once born continues to be alive, or a world once created continues to exist. And those are but imperfect illustrations, for children die and worlds burn out, but the word of our God endureth forever.

A.W. Tozer (1897-1963)

God is speaking by His Spirit,
Speaking to our hearts again;
In the ageless Word expounding
God's own message, now as then.
Through the rise and fall of nations
One sure faith yet standing fast:
God abides, His Word unchanging,
God the first, and God the last.

"God Has Spoken by His Prophets"
George W. Briggs (©1953)

(4:8) Holy and righteous Father, I want my life and not merely my lips to offer the worship of which You alone are worthy. In view of Your mercy, I offer my body, my whole being, as a living sacrifice. Consume me with Your grace; compel me with Your love. In my living and in my dying may You alone be glorified. (Ro 12:1)

opposed Moses, so also these men oppose the truth—men of depraved minds, who, as far as the faith is concerned, are rejected.
9But they will not get very far because, as in the case of those
men, their folly will be clear to everyone.

Paul's Charge to Timothy

10You, however, know all about my teaching, my way of life, my
purpose, faith, patience, love, endurance, 11persecutions, sufferings—what kinds of things happened to me in Antioch, Iconium
and Lystra, the persecutions I endured. Yet the Lord rescued me
from all of them. 12In fact, everyone who wants to live a godly life
in Christ Jesus will be persecuted, 13while evil men and impostors
will go from bad to worse, deceiving and being deceived. 14But as
for you, continue in what you have learned and have become convinced of, because you know those from whom you learned it,
15and how from infancy you have known the holy Scriptures,
which are able to make you wise for salvation through faith in
Christ Jesus. 16All Scripture is God-breathed and is useful for
teaching, rebuking, correcting and training in righteousness,
17so that the man of God may be thoroughly equipped for every
good work.

4 In the presence of God and of Christ Jesus, who will judge
the living and the dead, and in view of his appearing and his
kingdom, I give you this charge: 2Preach the Word; be prepared
in season and out of season; correct, rebuke and encourage—
with great patience and careful instruction. 3For the time will
come when men will not put up with sound doctrine. Instead, to
suit their own desires, they will gather around them a great
number of teachers to say what their itching ears want to hear.
4They will turn their ears away from the truth and turn aside to
myths. 5But you, keep your head in all situations, endure hardship, do the work of an evangelist, discharge all the duties of
your ministry.

6For I am already being poured out like a drink offering, and
the time has come for my departure. 7I have fought the good
fight, I have finished the race, I have kept the faith. 8Now there is
in store for me the crown of righteousness, which the Lord, the
righteous Judge, will award to me on that day—and not only to
me, but also to all who have longed for his appearing.

Personal Remarks

9Do your best to come to me quickly, 10for Demas, because he
loved this world, has deserted me and has gone to Thessalonica.
Crescens has gone to Galatia, and Titus to Dalmatia. 11Only Luke
is with me. Get Mark and bring him with you, because he is helpful to me in my ministry. 12I sent Tychicus to Ephesus. 13When
you come, bring the cloak that I left with Carpus at Troas, and my
scrolls, especially the parchments.

14Alexander the metalworker did me a great deal of harm. The
Lord will repay him for what he has done. 15You too should be on
your guard against him, because he strongly opposed our message.

16At my first defense, no one came to my support, but everyone
deserted me. May it not be held against them. 17But the Lord
stood at my side and gave me strength, so that through me the
message might be fully proclaimed and all the Gentiles might hear
it. And I was delivered from the lion's mouth. 18The Lord will res-

cue me from every evil attack and will bring me safely to his heavenly kingdom. To him be glory for ever and ever. Amen.

Final Greetings

19Greet Priscilla[a] and Aquila and the household of Onesiphorus. 20Erastus stayed in Corinth, and I left Trophimus sick in Miletus. 21Do your best to get here before winter. Eubulus greets
you, and so do Pudens, Linus, Claudia and all the brothers.
22The Lord be with your spirit. Grace be with you.

[a] *19* Greek *Prisca,* a variant of *Priscilla*

(4:22) God of all comfort, Your first and last word to me is *grace.* I praise You that no problem or challenge will come into my life for which Your grace will not be sufficient. There is no pain or need that will ever be greater than the provision of Your loving and sustaining heart.

Every promise we can make,
Every prayer and step of faith,
Every difference we can make,
Is only by His grace.
Every mountain we will climb,
Every ray of hope we shine,
Every blessing left behind,
Is only by His grace.

Grace alone
Which God supplies,
Strength unknown
He will provide,
Christ in us
Our Cornerstone,
We will go forth in grace alone.

"Grace Alone"
Scott Wesley Brown and
Jeff Nelson (©1998)

(1:6–9) Thank You for giving us elders who show us how to follow Your Word and how to live godly lives. May our elders reflect the character of Jesus Christ and demonstrate His love and grace through the integrity of their words and actions. Give to them a faith worth imitating and a godly heritage to pass on. Help us to follow their example as they follow the example of Christ. (1Co 11:1; Heb 13:7; 2Pe 1:3)

If we work upon marble, it will perish. If we work upon brass, time will efface it. If we rear temples, they will crumble to dust. But if we work upon men's immortal minds, if we imbue them with high principles, with the just fear of God and love of their fellowmen, we engrave on those tablets something which no time can efface and which will brighten to all eternity.

Daniel Webster (1782-1852)

(1:15–16) Purify my heart, Lord, and make my motives pleasing to You. Purify my mind, so that I can view the world with childlike innocence, without suspicion or cynicism. Purify my conscience, Lord, and remove every trace of perversion or prejudice. According to Your grace and mercy, grant me singleness of heart and action so that with everything that is in me I can serve You better and love You more. (Jer 32:39)

Lord, I want to live my life to please
You,
I bring my heart before You to
remold;
Make of me a vessel fit for honor
That I might shine for You as
sparkling gold.

Lord, I lift my heart in full
surrender,
All that I hold dear I give to You;
Purify my heart and make me holy
So that I might walk the way that's
pleasing You.

"To Be Pleasing You"
Teresa Muller (©1984)

1 Paul, a servant of God and an apostle of Jesus Christ for the
faith of God's elect and the knowledge of the truth that leads
to godliness— 2a faith and knowledge resting on the hope of
eternal life, which God, who does not lie, promised before the
beginning of time, 3and at his appointed season he brought his
word to light through the preaching entrusted to me by the command of God our Savior,

4To Titus, my true son in our common faith:

Grace and peace from God the Father and Christ Jesus our Savior.

Titus's Task on Crete

5The reason I left you in Crete was that you might straighten
out what was left unfinished and appoint[a] elders in every town, as
I directed you. 6An elder must be blameless, the husband of but
one wife, a man whose children believe and are not open to the
charge of being wild and disobedient. 7Since an overseer[b] is entrusted with God's work, he must be blameless—not overbear-
ing, not quick-tempered, not given to drunkenness, not violent,
not pursuing dishonest gain. 8Rather he must be hospitable, one
who loves what is good, who is self-controlled, upright, holy and
disciplined. 9He must hold firmly to the trustworthy message as it
has been taught, so that he can encourage others by sound doctrine and refute those who oppose it.

10For there are many rebellious people, mere talkers and deceivers, especially those of the circumcision group. 11They must
be silenced, because they are ruining whole households by teaching things they ought not to teach—and that for the sake of dishonest gain. 12Even one of their own prophets has said, "Cretans
are always liars, evil brutes, lazy gluttons." 13This testimony is
true. Therefore, rebuke them sharply, so that they will be sound
in the faith 14and will pay no attention to Jewish myths or to the
commands of those who reject the truth. 15To the pure, all things
are pure, but to those who are corrupted and do not believe,
nothing is pure. In fact, both their minds and consciences are
corrupted. 16They claim to know God, but by their actions they
deny him. They are detestable, disobedient and unfit for doing
anything good.

What Must Be Taught to Various Groups

2 You must teach what is in accord with sound doctrine.
2Teach the older men to be temperate, worthy of respect,
self-controlled, and sound in faith, in love and in endurance.

3Likewise, teach the older women to be reverent in the way
they live, not to be slanderers or addicted to much wine, but to
teach what is good. 4Then they can train the younger women to
love their husbands and children, 5to be self-controlled and pure,
to be busy at home, to be kind, and to be subject to their husbands, so that no one will malign the word of God.

6Similarly, encourage the young men to be self-controlled. 7In
everything set them an example by doing what is good. In your
teaching show integrity, seriousness 8and soundness of speech
that cannot be condemned, so that those who oppose you may be
ashamed because they have nothing bad to say about us.

[a]5 Or *ordain* [b]7 Traditionally *bishop*

9Teach slaves to be subject to their masters in everything, to try
to please them, not to talk back to them, 10and not to steal from
them, but to show that they can be fully trusted, so that in every
way they will make the teaching about God our Savior attractive.
11For the grace of God that brings salvation has appeared to all
men. 12It teaches us to say "No" to ungodliness and worldly passions, and to live self-controlled, upright and godly lives in this
present age, 13while we wait for the blessed hope—the glorious
appearing of our great God and Savior, Jesus Christ, 14who gave
himself for us to redeem us from all wickedness and to purify for
himself a people that are his very own, eager to do what is good.
15These, then, are the things you should teach. Encourage and
rebuke with all authority. Do not let anyone despise you.

Doing What Is Good

3 Remind the people to be subject to rulers and authorities, to
be obedient, to be ready to do whatever is good, 2to slander
no one, to be peaceable and considerate, and to show true humility toward all men.
3At one time we too were foolish, disobedient, deceived and
enslaved by all kinds of passions and pleasures. We lived in malice and envy, being hated and hating one another. 4But when the
kindness and love of God our Savior appeared, 5he saved us, not
because of righteous things we had done, but because of his
mercy. He saved us through the washing of rebirth and renewal by
the Holy Spirit, 6whom he poured out on us generously through
Jesus Christ our Savior, 7so that, having been justified by his
grace, we might become heirs having the hope of eternal life.
8This is a trustworthy saying. And I want you to stress these
things, so that those who have trusted in God may be careful to
devote themselves to doing what is good. These things are excellent and profitable for everyone.
9But avoid foolish controversies and genealogies and arguments and quarrels about the law, because these are unprofitable
and useless. 10Warn a divisive person once, and then warn him a
second time. After that, have nothing to do with him. 11You may
be sure that such a man is warped and sinful; he is self-con-
demned.

Final Remarks

12As soon as I send Artemas or Tychicus to you, do your best
to come to me at Nicopolis, because I have decided to winter
there. 13Do everything you can to help Zenas the lawyer and Apollos on their way and see that they have everything they need.
14Our people must learn to devote themselves to doing what is
good, in order that they may provide for daily necessities and not
live unproductive lives.
15Everyone with me sends you greetings. Greet those who love
us in the faith.
Grace be with you all.

(2:11–14) You chose us and set us apart as Your church to be Your bride. Now help us to keep ourselves pure as we await the day of Your second coming. Save us, Lord, from our tendency to sin. By Your grace, teach us to be holy and faithful to You. We love You, Lord Jesus, and we long to please You in all that we do. (Isa 62:5; Rev 21:2)

(3:4–5) Like a brilliant shaft of sunlight piercing the dark clouds of a stormy day . . . like an unexpected visit from a dear friend at a moment of pained loneliness . . . like the surprise of winning when loss had already been conceded . . . so the appearing of Your love and kindness, Jesus, has astonished me and set my heart at rest. Thank You for loving me, Lord—not because of my goodness but because of Your grace.

You did not wait for me
To draw near to You,
But You clothed Yourself
With frail humanity.
You did not wait for me
To cry out to You,
But You let me hear Your voice
Calling me.

And I'm forever grateful to You.
I'm forever grateful for the cross.
I'm forever grateful to You
That You came
To seek and save the lost.

"I'm Forever Grateful"
Mark Altrogge (©1986)

The Epistle of Paul to PHILEMON

The letter of Paul to Philemon deals with a particular problem in Philemon's personal affairs. One of his slaves, Onesimus, is returning from Paul to his master. The letter advises Philemon to welcome his slave with open arms, even as he would welcome Paul (v. 17).

Paul, it appears, previously led Philemon to faith in Christ (v. 19). Some time later, Onesimus ran away to be with Paul without Philemon's consent. Perhaps this slave believed that Paul could help him gain his freedom. What Onesimus did obtain from Paul, however, greatly exceeded his hopes: He received faith in Jesus Christ (vv. 10,15–16). For a short period of time thereafter, Onesimus remained with Paul as his assistant (v. 13).

Paul writes because, though he would like to keep Onesimus as his helper, he wants to encourage Philemon's sense of responsibility in Christ and to follow the laws that require a slave to be returned to his master. Yet Paul is also eager to ensure that Onesimus will be well-treated by Philemon, who would have every legal right to punish Onesimus harshly—even with death. Moreover, Paul seems to hope that Philemon will allow his slave to return to Paul's service (vv. 11–14).

At first glance the letter to Philemon seems to have little direct relevance to Christian worship. It is a short, personal letter that deals with a particular problem long since past. It includes little in the way of obvious worship, other than a brief thanksgiving (vv. 4–5).

The more we genuinely encounter God in worship, the more every other part of life, including our relationships, will be transformed by His presence and grace.

But this little letter illustrates something wonderful about God. In writing to the Galatians, Paul proclaims that "there is neither Jew nor Greek, slave nor free, male nor female, for you are all one in Christ Jesus" (Gal 3:28). God loves, justifies and adopts people in Christ regardless of social circumstances. Though we might live at the bottom of the socioeconomic ladder, that makes no difference to God. His Son died for us so that, no matter what our external conditions, we might each be adopted into His family as one of His beloved children. What a wonderful reason to praise God! The case of Onesimus reminds us of the unmerited, free and marvelous grace of God, thus giving us every reason to lift up God's name with joyful exuberance.

This letter also reminds us that true worship transforms our human relationships. If Philemon praises God as his heavenly Father, how can he not accept Onesimus as his brother in Christ, no matter what their social relationship? We cannot worship God in a vacuum, as though we could separate our relationship with Him from all other relationships. In fact, Jesus teaches that at times we should seek to reconcile broken human relationships even before we begin to worship God (Mt 5:23–24). What an astounding priority! The letter of Philemon helps us to understand that, the more we genuinely encounter God in worship, the more every other part of life, including our relationships, will be transformed by His presence and grace.

[1]Paul, a prisoner of Christ Jesus, and Timothy our brother,

To Philemon our dear friend and fellow worker, [2]to Apphia our sister, to Archippus our fellow soldier and to the church that meets in your home:

[3]Grace to you and peace from God our Father and the Lord Jesus Christ.

Thanksgiving and Prayer

[4]I always thank my God as I remember you in my prayers, [5]because I hear about your faith in the Lord Jesus and your love for all the saints. [6]I pray that you may be active in sharing your faith, so that you will have a full understanding of every good thing we have in Christ. [7]Your love has given me great joy and encouragement, because you, brother, have refreshed the hearts of the saints.

Paul's Plea for Onesimus

[8]Therefore, although in Christ I could be bold and order you to do what you ought to do, [9]yet I appeal to you on the basis of love. I then, as Paul—an old man and now also a prisoner of Christ Jesus— [10]I appeal to you for my son Onesimus,[a] who became my son while I was in chains. [11]Formerly he was useless to you, but now he has become useful both to you and to me.

[12]I am sending him—who is my very heart—back to you. [13]I would have liked to keep him with me so that he could take your place in helping me while I am in chains for the gospel. [14]But I did not want to do anything without your consent, so that any favor you do will be spontaneous and not forced. [15]Perhaps the reason he was separated from you for a little while was that you might have him back for good— [16]no longer as a slave, but better than a slave, as a dear brother. He is very dear to me but even dearer to you, both as a man and as a brother in the Lord.

[17]So if you consider me a partner, welcome him as you would welcome me. [18]If he has done you any wrong or owes you anything, charge it to me. [19]I, Paul, am writing this with my own hand. I will pay it back—not to mention that you owe me your very self. [20]I do wish, brother, that I may have some benefit from you in the Lord; refresh my heart in Christ. [21]Confident of your obedience, I write to you, knowing that you will do even more than I ask.

[22]And one thing more: Prepare a guest room for me, because I hope to be restored to you in answer to your prayers.

[23]Epaphras, my fellow prisoner in Christ Jesus, sends you greetings. [24]And so do Mark, Aristarchus, Demas and Luke, my fellow workers.

[25]The grace of the Lord Jesus Christ be with your spirit.

[a] 10 *Onesimus* means *useful.*

(vv. 1–25) Heavenly Father, like Onesimus I was once a fugitive. I ran from You. I hid from You. I deserved death. But I found life in Jesus Christ, Who interceded on my behalf. He paid the price for my sins and made it possible for me to return to You. I praise You for the love of Jesus that reaches toward me, dwells within me and lives through me as an extension of Your gracious, forgiving heart. Because He has reconciled me to You, I can now carry the message of reconciliation. (2Co 5:1–19)

(vv. 1–25) Gracious Redeemer, I am also like Philemon. You have forgiven me so great a debt; help me also to forgive my debtors, knowing that when I do it for my brothers, I do it for You. Help me to look beyond my temporal rights to the higher value of heavenly investment. Help me to follow Paul's appeal to live on the basis of love rather than law, so that ultimately through my life mercy may triumph over judgment. (Mt 18:23–35; 25:40; Jas 2:13)

Mercy comes down from heaven to earth so that man by practicing it may resemble God.

Giambattista Giraldi (1504–1573)

The Epistle to the

HEBREWS

As Christians, our worship is based on God's revelation to the Jews. We praise God with Jewish psalms. We are inspired by Jewish prophets. But because of what God has done in Jesus, the Jewish Messiah and Savior of the world, our worship also differs significantly from ancient Jewish practice.

Hebrews teaches that the ministry of Jesus resembles the activity of the Jewish high priest but that it is superior in all respects. Whereas human priests served only until death, Jesus has a "permanent priesthood" (7:23).Whereas the high priest entered a physical Holy Place, Jesus entered into the very presence of God (9:24). Unlike the priest, who continually presented animal sacrifices, Jesus offered Himself "once for all" (7:27; 9:26). Under the old covenant with its human priesthood, sins were never fully removed (10:4). But Jesus, as mediator of a new, superior covenant, has provided the permanent remedy for sin (8:6; 9:15).

As a result of Jesus' priestly work, we receive atonement for our sins (2:17). We are saved completely by Christ, Who continues to intercede for us (7:25). We have been redeemed forever from our bondage to sin (9:12). Our sins are not merely ignored, but are taken away so that we might have clear consciences (9:14,28).

The good news of Hebrews inspires our worship, filling us with gratitude. The letter actually spells out several specific implications for worship.

Even the awareness of our sin will not keep us from God but will draw us to His gracious throne. We never worship to earn God's favor, but in response to it.

First, we enter into God's holy presence with confidence, knowing that Christ has opened for us the way to God (10:19-23). Thus, even the awareness of our sin will not keep us from God but will draw us to His gracious throne (4:16). We never worship to earn God's favor, but in response to it.

Second, we have been cleansed "so that we may serve the living God!" (9:14). We who have received the benefits of Christ's high priestly work become priests ourselves. In place of animal sacrifices, we "continually offer to God a sacrifice of praise" and good works (13:15-16).

Third, as Christians we worship God through Jesus (9:14; 13:15). Hebrews reveals Jesus' unique nature as Son of God (4:14). He shines with the radiance of divine glory and exactly represents God's being (1:3). Even God, speaking through the writer of Psalm 45, refers to Jesus as "God" Whose throne lasts forever (1:8; Ps 45:6). Therefore Jesus is "crowned with glory and honor" (2:9).

Fourth, as we "fix our eyes on Jesus, the author and perfecter of our faith," we worship through living "by faith," by trusting the living God at all times (ch. 11). Like Abel, we offer our spiritual sacrifices to God "by faith" (11:4). Like Abraham, we honor God as we obey Him "by faith" (11:8). Even when we go through difficult times, we "run with perseverance the race marked out for us," encouraged in our effort by the "great cloud of witnesses" surrounding us—men and women exemplary in their faith and faithfulness (12:1). As we imitate their example by trusting God in all things, He "works in us what is pleasing to him, through Jesus Christ, to whom be glory for ever and ever. Amen" (13:21).

The Son Superior to Angels

1 In the past God spoke to our forefathers through the prophets
at many times and in various ways, 2but in these last days he
has spoken to us by his Son, whom he appointed heir of all
things, and through whom he made the universe. 3The Son is the
radiance of God's glory and the exact representation of his being,
sustaining all things by his powerful word. After he had provided
purification for sins, he sat down at the right hand of the Majesty
in heaven. 4So he became as much superior to the angels as the
name he has inherited is superior to theirs.

5For to which of the angels did God ever say,

"You are my Son;
today I have become your Father"[a][b]?

Or again,

"I will be his Father,
and he will be my Son"[c]?

6And again, when God brings his firstborn into the world, he says,

"Let all God's angels worship him."[d]

7In speaking of the angels he says,

"He makes his angels winds,
his servants flames of fire."[e]

8But about the Son he says,

"Your throne, O God, will last for ever and ever,
and righteousness will be the scepter of your
kingdom.
9You have loved righteousness and hated
wickedness;
therefore God, your God, has set you above your
companions
by anointing you with the oil of joy."[f]

10He also says,

"In the beginning, O Lord, you laid the foundations of
the earth,
and the heavens are the work of your hands.
11They will perish, but you remain;
they will all wear out like a garment.
12You will roll them up like a robe;
like a garment they will be changed.
But you remain the same,
and your years will never end."[g]

13To which of the angels did God ever say,

"Sit at my right hand
until I make your enemies
a footstool for your feet"[h]?

14Are not all angels ministering spirits sent to serve those who
will inherit salvation?

[a] 5 Or *have begotten you* [b] 5 Psalm 2:7 [c] 5 2 Samuel 7:14; 1 Chron. 17:13
[d] 6 Deut. 32:43 (see Dead Sea Scrolls and Septuagint) [e] 7 Psalm 104:4
[f] 9 Psalm 45:6,7 [g] 12 Psalm 102:25–27 [h] 13 Psalm 110:1

(1:1–4) Son of God, before Whom angels bow, I kneel humbly at Your feet. Word of God, through Whom all things were created and by Whom God has spoken, I am silent and awestruck before You. Light of Light, Who outshines the radiance of heaven, I glorify You. Even so, O Lord, how can my worship begin to be worthy of You? However extravagant my praise, You are greater still!

O Light whose splendor thrills and
gladdens,
With radiance brighter than the
sun,
Pure gleam of God's unending glory,
O Jesus, blest anointed One.

In all life's brilliant, timeless
moments,
Let faithful voices sing Your praise,
O Son of God, our life bestower,
Whose glory lightens endless days.

"O Light Whose Splendor Thrills"
Phos Hilaron (3rd c.)
Paraphrase by Carl P. Daw, Jr. (©1989)

Warning to Pay Attention

2 We must pay more careful attention, therefore, to what we
have heard, so that we do not drift away. 2 For if the message
spoken by angels was binding, and every violation and disobedience received its just punishment, 3 how shall we escape if we
ignore such a great salvation? This salvation, which was first announced by the Lord, was confirmed to us by those who heard
him. 4 God also testified to it by signs, wonders and various miracles, and gifts of the Holy Spirit distributed according to his
will.

Jesus Made Like His Brothers

5 It is not to angels that he has subjected the world to come,
about which we are speaking. 6 But there is a place where someone has testified:

> "What is man that you are mindful of him,
> the son of man that you care for him?
> 7 You made him a little[a] lower than the angels;
> you crowned him with glory and honor
> 8 and put everything under his feet."[b]

In putting everything under him, God left nothing that is not subject to him. Yet at present we do not see everything subject to
him. 9 But we see Jesus, who was made a little lower than the angels, now crowned with glory and honor because he suffered
death, so that by the grace of God he might taste death for everyone.

10 In bringing many sons to glory, it was fitting that God, for
whom and through whom everything exists, should make the author of their salvation perfect through suffering. 11 Both the one
who makes men holy and those who are made holy are of the
same family. So Jesus is not ashamed to call them brothers. 12 He
says,

> "I will declare your name to my brothers;
> in the presence of the congregation I will sing your
> praises."[c]

13 And again,

> "I will put my trust in him."[d]

And again he says,

> "Here am I, and the children God has given me."[e]

14 Since the children have flesh and blood, he too shared in
their humanity so that by his death he might destroy him who
holds the power of death—that is, the devil— 15 and free those
who all their lives were held in slavery by their fear of death.
16 For surely it is not angels he helps, but Abraham's descendants.
17 For this reason he had to be made like his brothers in every
way, in order that he might become a merciful and faithful high
priest in service to God, and that he might make atonement for[f]
the sins of the people. 18 Because he himself suffered when he
was tempted, he is able to help those who are being tempted.

[a] 7 Or *him for a little while*; also in verse 9 [b] 8 Psalm 8:4–6 [c] 12 Psalm 22:22
[d] 13 Isaiah 8:17 [e] 13 Isaiah 8:18 [f] 17 Or *and that he might turn aside God's wrath, taking away*

God, who had fashioned time and space in a clockwork of billions of suns and stars and moons, in the form of his beloved Son became a human being like ourselves. On the microscopic midge of planet he remained for thirty-three years. He became a real man, and the only perfect one. While continuing to be the true God, he was born in a stable and lived as a workingman and died on a cross. He came to show us how to live, not for a few years but eternally.

Fulton Oursler (1949-)

(2:9) I see You, Jesus . . . not with the eyes of flesh but with the eyes of faith. I see You in Your humiliation, becoming human, taking the form of a servant, accepting a degrading death on the cross. I see You in Your exaltation, even now crowned with glory and honor because of Your faithful suffering. I see You as one day You will be, King of kings, Lord of lords, exalted by all creation. (Php 2:5–11)

The head that once was crowned
with thorns
Is crowned with glory now;
A royal diadem adorns
The mighty Victor's brow.

The highest place that heaven
affords
Is his, is his by right,
The King of kings and Lord of lords,
And heaven's eternal light.

"The Head That Once Was Crowned"
Thomas Kelly (1820)

Jesus Greater Than Moses

3 Therefore, holy brothers, who share in the heavenly calling,
fix your thoughts on Jesus, the apostle and high priest whom
we confess. 2He was faithful to the one who appointed him, just
as Moses was faithful in all God's house. 3Jesus has been found
worthy of greater honor than Moses, just as the builder of a house
has greater honor than the house itself. 4For every house is built
by someone, but God is the builder of everything. 5Moses was
faithful as a servant in all God's house, testifying to what would be
said in the future. 6But Christ is faithful as a son over God's
house. And we are his house, if we hold on to our courage and
the hope of which we boast.

Warning Against Unbelief

7So, as the Holy Spirit says:

"Today, if you hear his voice,
8 do not harden your hearts
as you did in the rebellion,
during the time of testing in the desert,
9 where your fathers tested and tried me
and for forty years saw what I did.
10 That is why I was angry with that generation,
and I said, 'Their hearts are always going astray,
and they have not known my ways.'
11 So I declared on oath in my anger,
'They shall never enter my rest.' "[a]

12See to it, brothers, that none of you has a sinful, unbelieving
heart that turns away from the living God. 13But encourage one
another daily, as long as it is called Today, so that none of you may
be hardened by sin's deceitfulness. 14We have come to share in
Christ if we hold firmly till the end the confidence we had at first.
15As has just been said:

"Today, if you hear his voice,
do not harden your hearts
as you did in the rebellion."[b]

16Who were they who heard and rebelled? Were they not all
those Moses led out of Egypt? 17And with whom was he angry for
forty years? Was it not with those who sinned, whose bodies fell in
the desert? 18And to whom did God swear that they would never
enter his rest if not to those who disobeyed[c]? 19So we see that
they were not able to enter, because of their unbelief.

A Sabbath-Rest for the People of God

4 Therefore, since the promise of entering his rest still stands,
let us be careful that none of you be found to have fallen
short of it. 2For we also have had the gospel preached to us, just
as they did; but the message they heard was of no value to them,
because those who heard did not combine it with faith.[d] 3Now we
who have believed enter that rest, just as God has said,

"So I declared on oath in my anger,
'They shall never enter my rest.' "[e]

[a] 11 Psalm 95:7–11 [b] 15 Psalm 95:7,8 [c] 18 Or *disbelieved* [d] 2 Many manuscripts *because they did not share in the faith of those who obeyed*
[e] 3 Psalm 95:11; also in verse 5

(3:12–13) How easily my heart grows hard to You, Lord. How readily I presume upon Your grace. How willingly I barricade myself behind the deceitfulness of sin, growing ever more calloused to Your tender mercy. "Create in me a pure heart, O God, and renew a steadfast spirit within me." Remove my heart of stone. Resurrect my heart of flesh. Rekindle my gratitude for Your grace. Revive my aversion to sin. "Restore to me the joy of your salvation." (Ps 51:10–12; Eze 36:26)

O grant that nothing in my soul
May dwell, but Thy pure love alone;
O may Thy love possess me whole,
My joy, my treasure, and my crown!
All coldness from my heart remove;
May every act, word, thought be
love.

"Jesus, Thy Boundless Love to Me"
Paul Gerhardt (1653)
Trans. John Wesley (1703–1791)

(4:12–16) Lord Jesus Christ, You are the vital Word of God. Your judgment pierces every façade. Nothing about me is hidden from You—neither thought nor action, neither fear nor fantasy. Before You I am completely exposed, and to You I must account for my life. But, O Son of God, You are also a great high priest Who understands every one of my weaknesses. You have been tempted even as I am tempted. You know the lure of sin, even though You did not succumb to its power. Therefore I come before Your throne, the throne of judgment now transformed to be the throne of grace. Where once I would justly have received condemnation, now I receive forgiveness. So I draw near to You, no longer cowering, but with confidence that I will receive mercy and find grace to help me in my time of need. (Ps 9:4–7)

Since God has prepared himself a lamb, a sacrifice, a priest, a throne of grace, and has bid thee come to him, come to him as there sitting–come, come boldly, as he bids thee. What better warrant canst thou have to come, than to be bid to come of God?
John Bunyan (1628-1688)

No condemnation now I dread;
Jesus and all in Him, is mine!
Alive in Him, my living Head;
And clothed in righteousness divine,
Bold I approach th'eternal throne,
And claim the crown, through
Christ, my own.
Amazing love! How can it be,
That Thou, my God, shouldst die for
me?
"And Can It Be That I Should Gain?"
Charles Wesley (1738)

And yet his work has been finished since the creation of the
world. 4For somewhere he has spoken about the seventh day in
these words: "And on the seventh day God rested from all his
work."[a] 5And again in the passage above he says, "They shall
never enter my rest."
6It still remains that some will enter that rest, and those who
formerly had the gospel preached to them did not go in, because
of their disobedience. 7Therefore God again set a certain day,
calling it Today, when a long time later he spoke through David,
as was said before:

"Today, if you hear his voice,
do not harden your hearts."[b]

8For if Joshua had given them rest, God would not have spoken
later about another day. 9There remains, then, a Sabbath-rest for
the people of God; 10for anyone who enters God's rest also rests
from his own work, just as God did from his. 11Let us, therefore,
make every effort to enter that rest, so that no one will fall by following their example of disobedience.
12For the word of God is living and active. Sharper than any
double-edged sword, it penetrates even to dividing soul and spirit, joints and marrow; it judges the thoughts and attitudes of the
heart. 13Nothing in all creation is hidden from God's sight. Everything is uncovered and laid bare before the eyes of him to whom
we must give account.

Jesus the Great High Priest

14Therefore, since we have a great high priest who has gone
through the heavens,[c] Jesus the Son of God, let us hold firmly to
the faith we profess. 15For we do not have a high priest who is unable to sympathize with our weaknesses, but we have one who
has been tempted in every way, just as we are—yet was without
sin. 16Let us then approach the throne of grace with confidence,
so that we may receive mercy and find grace to help us in our
time of need.

5 Every high priest is selected from among men and is appointed to represent them in matters related to God, to offer
gifts and sacrifices for sins. 2He is able to deal gently with those
who are ignorant and are going astray, since he himself is subject
to weakness. 3This is why he has to offer sacrifices for his own
sins, as well as for the sins of the people.
4No one takes this honor upon himself; he must be called by
God, just as Aaron was. 5So Christ also did not take upon himself
the glory of becoming a high priest. But God said to him,

"You are my Son;
today I have become your Father.[d]"[e]

6And he says in another place,

"You are a priest forever,
in the order of Melchizedek."[f]

7During the days of Jesus' life on earth, he offered up prayers
and petitions with loud cries and tears to the one who could save
him from death, and he was heard because of his reverent submission. 8Although he was a son, he learned obedience from

[a] 4 Gen. 2:2 [b] 7 Psalm 95:7,8 [c] 14 Or *gone into heaven* [d] 5 Or *have begotten you* [e] 5 Psalm 2:7 [f] 6 Psalm 110:4

MY BELOVED

Come to Me when you are weary and burdened, and I will give you rest. Come to Me when you are thirsty, come to the waters and drink. Come to Me, you who have no money, come buy and eat! Come, buy wine and milk without money and without cost.

Listen, listen to Me, and eat what is good, and your soul will delight in the richest of fare. Give ear and come to Me; hear Me, that your soul may live. Seek Me while I may be found; call on Me while I am near. Turn away from your wicked ways and your evil thoughts. Come to Me and I will have mercy on you; turn to Me and I will freely pardon you.

Come to My throne of grace. Come to Me with freedom and confidence. By the blood of Jesus, enter the Most Holy Place. Draw near to Me with a sincere heart in full assurance of faith, cleansed from a guilty conscience and washed with pure water.

Come before Me with thanksgiving and praise, with music and joyful songs. Rejoice in My name all day long. Tell others of My righteousness.

Come to Me, My beloved, for in My presence is fullness of joy, and eternal pleasures are in My right hand.

Ps 89:16; 100:4; Isa 55:1-7; Mt 11:28; Jn 7:37; Ac 2:28; Eph 3:12; Heb 4:16; 10:19-22

what he suffered **9**and, once made perfect, he became the source
of eternal salvation for all who obey him **10**and was designated by
God to be high priest in the order of Melchizedek.

Warning Against Falling Away

11We have much to say about this, but it is hard to explain because you are slow to learn. **12**In fact, though by this time you
ought to be teachers, you need someone to teach you the elementary truths of God's word all over again. You need milk, not
solid food! **13**Anyone who lives on milk, being still an infant, is not
acquainted with the teaching about righteousness. **14**But solid
food is for the mature, who by constant use have trained themselves to distinguish good from evil.

6 Therefore let us leave the elementary teachings about Christ
and go on to maturity, not laying again the foundation of
repentance from acts that lead to death,[a] and of faith in God, **2**instruction about baptisms, the laying on of hands, the resurrection of the dead, and eternal judgment. **3**And God permitting, we
will do so.

4It is impossible for those who have once been enlightened,
who have tasted the heavenly gift, who have shared in the Holy
Spirit, **5**who have tasted the goodness of the word of God and the
powers of the coming age, **6**if they fall away, to be brought back
to repentance, because[b] to their loss they are crucifying the Son
of God all over again and subjecting him to public disgrace.

7Land that drinks in the rain often falling on it and that produces a crop useful to those for whom it is farmed receives the
blessing of God. **8**But land that produces thorns and thistles is
worthless and is in danger of being cursed. In the end it will be
burned.

9Even though we speak like this, dear friends, we are confident
of better things in your case—things that accompany salvation.
10God is not unjust; he will not forget your work and the love you
have shown him as you have helped his people and continue to
help them. **11**We want each of you to show this same diligence to
the very end, in order to make your hope sure. **12**We do not want
you to become lazy, but to imitate those who through faith and patience inherit what has been promised.

The Certainty of God's Promise

13When God made his promise to Abraham, since there was no
one greater for him to swear by, he swore by himself, **14**saying, "I
will surely bless you and give you many descendants."[c] **15**And so
after waiting patiently, Abraham received what was promised.

16Men swear by someone greater than themselves, and the
oath confirms what is said and puts an end to all argument. **17**Because God wanted to make the unchanging nature of his purpose
very clear to the heirs of what was promised, he confirmed it with
an oath. **18**God did this so that, by two unchangeable things in
which it is impossible for God to lie, we who have fled to take
hold of the hope offered to us may be greatly encouraged. **19**We
have this hope as an anchor for the soul, firm and secure. It enters the inner sanctuary behind the curtain, **20**where Jesus, who
went before us, has entered on our behalf. He has become a high
priest forever, in the order of Melchizedek.

[a] *1* Or *from useless rituals* [b] *6* Or *repentance while* [c] *14* Gen. 22:17

(6:19–20) Only in You, dear Jesus, is my hope secure. Wherever else I place my hope I will someday be disappointed—whether in hard work or a strong economy, in skilled doctors or faithful friends, in government programs or a loving family. But in You alone my hope is firm and secure, because through You I am anchored, not to transient opportunities or human frailties, but to the one, true, living, changeless God. On our behalf—indeed, on my behalf—You have opened the veil into the holiest presence of God. In You alone I place my hope! You alone are my refuge, my rock and my Redeemer! (Ps 62:5–8)

My hope is built on nothing less
Than Jesus' blood and righteousness;
I dare not trust the sweetest frame,
But wholly lean on Jesus' name.

On Christ, the solid Rock, I stand;
All other ground is sinking sand,
All other ground is sinking sand.

When darkness veils His lovely face,
I rest on His unchanging grace;
In every high and stormy gale,
My anchor holds within the veil.

The Solid Rock
Edward Mote (1834)

Melchizedek the Priest

7 This Melchizedek was king of Salem and priest of God Most
High. He met Abraham returning from the defeat of the kings
and blessed him, 2and Abraham gave him a tenth of everything.
First, his name means "king of righteousness"; then also, "king of
Salem" means "king of peace." 3Without father or mother, without genealogy, without beginning of days or end of life, like the
Son of God he remains a priest forever.
4Just think how great he was: Even the patriarch Abraham gave
him a tenth of the plunder! 5Now the law requires the descendants
of Levi who become priests to collect a tenth from the people—
that is, their brothers—even though their brothers are descended
from Abraham. 6This man, however, did not trace his descent
from Levi, yet he collected a tenth from Abraham and blessed him
who had the promises. 7And without doubt the lesser person is
blessed by the greater. 8In the one case, the tenth is collected by
men who die; but in the other case, by him who is declared to be
living. 9One might even say that Levi, who collects the tenth, paid
the tenth through Abraham, 10because when Melchizedek met
Abraham, Levi was still in the body of his ancestor.

Jesus Like Melchizedek

11If perfection could have been attained through the Levitical
priesthood (for on the basis of it the law was given to the people),
why was there still need for another priest to come—one in the
order of Melchizedek, not in the order of Aaron? 12For when
there is a change of the priesthood, there must also be a change
of the law. 13He of whom these things are said belonged to a different tribe, and no one from that tribe has ever served at the
altar. 14For it is clear that our Lord descended from Judah, and in
regard to that tribe Moses said nothing about priests. 15And what
we have said is even more clear if another priest like Melchizedek
appears, 16one who has become a priest not on the basis of a
regulation as to his ancestry but on the basis of the power of an
indestructible life. 17For it is declared:

> "You are a priest forever,
> in the order of Melchizedek."[a]

18The former regulation is set aside because it was weak and
useless 19(for the law made nothing perfect), and a better hope
is introduced, by which we draw near to God.
20And it was not without an oath! Others became priests without any oath, 21but he became a priest with an oath when God
said to him:

> "The Lord has sworn
> and will not change his mind:
> 'You are a priest forever.' "[a]

22Because of this oath, Jesus has become the guarantee of a better covenant.
23Now there have been many of those priests, since death prevented them from continuing in office; 24but because Jesus lives
forever, he has a permanent priesthood. 25Therefore he is able to
save completely[b] those who come to God through him, because
he always lives to intercede for them.

[a] *17,21* Psalm 110:4 [b] *25* Or *forever*

(7:24–25) Thank You, Jesus, my eternal priest. You save me, not partially, but completely. From sickness You save me. From despair You save me. From loneliness You save me. From meaninglessness You save me. From myself You save me. From the Evil One You save me. From sin You save me. From death You save me. Into life abundant You save me. For eternal friendship You save me. Thank You, Jesus, my precious Savior!

It is not your hold of Christ that saves you, but his hold of you!
Charles Haddon Spurgeon (1834-1892)

He ever lives above,
For me to intercede;
His all redeeming love,
His precious blood to plead;
His blood atoned for all our race,
His blood atoned for all our race,
And sprinkles now the throne of
grace.

The Father hears him pray,
His dear anointed One;
He cannot turn away
The presence of his Son.
His Spirit answers to the blood,
His Spirit answers to the blood,
And tells me I am born of God.

"Arise, My Soul, Arise"
Charles Wesley (1742)

26Such a high priest meets our need—one who is holy, blameless, pure, set apart from sinners, exalted above the heavens.
27Unlike the other high priests, he does not need to offer sacrifices day after day, first for his own sins, and then for the sins of
the people. He sacrificed for their sins once for all when he offered himself. 28For the law appoints as high priests men who are
weak; but the oath, which came after the law, appointed the Son,
who has been made perfect forever.

The High Priest of a New Covenant

8 The point of what we are saying is this: We do have such a
high priest, who sat down at the right hand of the throne of
the Majesty in heaven, 2and who serves in the sanctuary, the true
tabernacle set up by the Lord, not by man.

3Every high priest is appointed to offer both gifts and sacrifices, and so it was necessary for this one also to have something
to offer. 4If he were on earth, he would not be a priest, for there
are already men who offer the gifts prescribed by the law. 5They
serve at a sanctuary that is a copy and shadow of what is in heav-
en. This is why Moses was warned when he was about to build the
tabernacle: "See to it that you make everything according to the
pattern shown you on the mountain."[a] 6But the ministry Jesus has
received is as superior to theirs as the covenant of which he is
mediator is superior to the old one, and it is founded on better
promises.

7For if there had been nothing wrong with that first covenant,
no place would have been sought for another. 8But God found
fault with the people and said[b]:

"The time is coming, declares the Lord,
when I will make a new covenant
with the house of Israel
and with the house of Judah.
9It will not be like the covenant
I made with their forefathers
when I took them by the hand
to lead them out of Egypt,
because they did not remain faithful to my covenant,
and I turned away from them,
declares the Lord.
10This is the covenant I will make with the house of
Israel
after that time, declares the Lord.
I will put my laws in their minds
and write them on their hearts.
I will be their God,
and they will be my people.
11No longer will a man teach his neighbor,
or a man his brother, saying, 'Know the Lord,'
because they will all know me,
from the least of them to the greatest.
12For I will forgive their wickedness
and will remember their sins no more."[c]

13By calling this covenant "new," he has made the first one obsolete; and what is obsolete and aging will soon disappear.

[a] *5* Exodus 25:40 [b] *8* Some manuscripts may be translated *fault and said to the people.* [c] *12* Jer. 31:31–34

(7:26–28) O Lord Jesus, the Holy One of God, there is none like You. Blameless, pure, untainted by sin, You are the one great high priest. And Yours is the one perfect sacrifice given once for all—for all time, for all sins, for all people—even for me. How unworthy I am of such a gift, yet You have made me worthy by Your grace alone! Blessed Jesus, Holy One of God, receive my praise and gratitude, my love and my life! I owe it all to You.

Accept, O Lord God, our Father, the sacrifices of our thanksgiving; this, of praise, for your great mercies already afforded to us; and this, of prayer, for the continuance and enlargement of them; this, of penitence, for such only recompense as our sinful nature can endeavor; and this, of the love of our hearts, as the only gift you ask or desire, and all these, through the all-holy and atoning sacrifice of Jesus Christ your Son our Savior.

John Donne (1572–1631)

Holy Lord, most Holy Lord,
You alone are worthy of my praise;
O Holy Lord, most Holy Lord,
With all of my heart I sing.

Great are You, Lord.
Worthy of praise,
Holy and true,
Great are You, Lord,
Most Holy Lord.

"Great Are You, Lord"
Steve Cook and Vikki Cook (©1984)

Worship in the Earthly Tabernacle

9 Now the first covenant had regulations for worship and also
an earthly sanctuary. 2A tabernacle was set up. In its first
room were the lampstand, the table and the consecrated bread;
this was called the Holy Place. 3Behind the second curtain was a
room called the Most Holy Place, 4which had the golden altar of
incense and the gold-covered ark of the covenant. This ark contained the gold jar of manna, Aaron's staff that had budded, and
the stone tablets of the covenant. 5Above the ark were the cherubim of the Glory, overshadowing the atonement cover.[a] But we
cannot discuss these things in detail now.
6When everything had been arranged like this, the priests entered regularly into the outer room to carry on their ministry.
7But only the high priest entered the inner room, and that only
once a year, and never without blood, which he offered for himself and for the sins the people had committed in ignorance.
8The Holy Spirit was showing by this that the way into the Most
Holy Place had not yet been disclosed as long as the first tabernacle was still standing. 9This is an illustration for the present
time, indicating that the gifts and sacrifices being offered were
not able to clear the conscience of the worshiper. 10They are
only a matter of food and drink and various ceremonial wash-
ings—external regulations applying until the time of the new
order.

The Blood of Christ

11When Christ came as high priest of the good things that are
already here,[b] he went through the greater and more perfect
tabernacle that is not man-made, that is to say, not a part of this
creation. 12He did not enter by means of the blood of goats and
calves; but he entered the Most Holy Place once for all by his own
blood, having obtained eternal redemption. 13The blood of goats
and bulls and the ashes of a heifer sprinkled on those who are
ceremonially unclean sanctify them so that they are outwardly
clean. 14How much more, then, will the blood of Christ, who
through the eternal Spirit offered himself unblemished to God,
cleanse our consciences from acts that lead to death,[c] so that we
may serve the living God!
15For this reason Christ is the mediator of a new covenant, that
those who are called may receive the promised eternal inheritance—now that he has died as a ransom to set them free from
the sins committed under the first covenant.
16In the case of a will,[d] it is necessary to prove the death of
the one who made it, 17because a will is in force only when
somebody has died; it never takes effect while the one who
made it is living. 18This is why even the first covenant was not
put into effect without blood. 19When Moses had proclaimed
every commandment of the law to all the people, he took the
blood of calves, together with water, scarlet wool and branches
of hyssop, and sprinkled the scroll and all the people. 20He
said, "This is the blood of the covenant, which God has commanded you to keep."[e] 21In the same way, he sprinkled with the
blood both the tabernacle and everything used in its ceremo-
nies. 22In fact, the law requires that nearly everything be

[a] 5 Traditionally *the mercy seat* [b] 11 Some early manuscripts *are to come*
[c] 14 Or *from useless rituals* [d] 16 Same Greek word as *covenant*; also in verse 17
[e] 20 Exodus 24:8

(9:14) Lamb of God, Who takes away the sin of the world, have mercy on me! Cleanse my conscience, so that I might serve You not in guilt but in grace. Purify my mind, so that I might know You not in falsehood, but in truth. Sanctify my will, so that I might approach You not in fear but in freedom. Transform my life, so that I might worship You not in part but in whole, always offering all that I am to You as a living sacrifice. Lamb of God, Whose blood washes away all sin, have mercy on me!

Create in me, a clean heart, O God,
That I might serve You.
Create in me, a clean heart, O God,
That I might be renewed.
So fill me, and heal me, and bring me
back to You.
Create in me, a clean heart, O God,
That I might serve You.

Create In Me
Mary Rice Hopkins (©1989)

cleansed with blood, and without the shedding of blood there is
no forgiveness.
23 It was necessary, then, for the copies of the heavenly things
to be purified with these sacrifices, but the heavenly things themselves with better sacrifices than these. 24 For Christ did not enter
a man-made sanctuary that was only a copy of the true one; he entered heaven itself, now to appear for us in God's presence. 25 Nor
did he enter heaven to offer himself again and again, the way the
high priest enters the Most Holy Place every year with blood that
is not his own. 26 Then Christ would have had to suffer many times
since the creation of the world. But now he has appeared once
for all at the end of the ages to do away with sin by the sacrifice
of himself. 27 Just as man is destined to die once, and after that to
face judgment, 28 so Christ was sacrificed once to take away the
sins of many people; and he will appear a second time, not to
bear sin, but to bring salvation to those who are waiting for him.

Christ's Sacrifice Once for All

10 The law is only a shadow of the good things that are coming—not the realities themselves. For this reason it can
never, by the same sacrifices repeated endlessly year after year,
make perfect those who draw near to worship. 2 If it could, would
they not have stopped being offered? For the worshipers would
have been cleansed once for all, and would no longer have felt
guilty for their sins. 3 But those sacrifices are an annual reminder
of sins, 4 because it is impossible for the blood of bulls and goats
to take away sins.
5 Therefore, when Christ came into the world, he said:

"Sacrifice and offering you did not desire,
but a body you prepared for me;
6 with burnt offerings and sin offerings
you were not pleased.
7 Then I said, 'Here I am—it is written about me in the
scroll—
I have come to do your will, O God.' "[a]

8 First he said, "Sacrifices and offerings, burnt offerings and sin
offerings you did not desire, nor were you pleased with them"
(although the law required them to be made). 9 Then he said,
"Here I am, I have come to do your will." He sets aside the first
to establish the second. 10 And by that will, we have been made
holy through the sacrifice of the body of Jesus Christ once for all.
11 Day after day every priest stands and performs his religious
duties; again and again he offers the same sacrifices, which can
never take away sins. 12 But when this priest had offered for all
time one sacrifice for sins, he sat down at the right hand of God.
13 Since that time he waits for his enemies to be made his footstool, 14 because by one sacrifice he has made perfect forever
those who are being made holy.
15 The Holy Spirit also testifies to us about this. First he says:

16 "This is the covenant I will make with them
after that time, says the Lord.
I will put my laws in their hearts,
and I will write them on their minds."[b]

[a] 7 Psalm 40:6–8 (see Septuagint) [b] 16 Jer. 31:33

God creates out of nothing—wonderful, you say; yes, to be sure, but he does what is still more wonderful. He makes saints out of sinners.

Søren Aabye Kierkegaard (1813-1855)

(10:10–14) O Lord, here is a mystery indeed. By Your holy sacrifice I have been made holy—set apart for You, purified from sin, ready for Your service. By Your perfect sacrifice I have been made perfect. But how can that be, Lord, when my imperfections are still so conspicuous? Could it be that You can see me, not only as I am today, but also as I will be: pure, holy, even *perfect*? Do You know me as a new creation in Christ? Do You see me dressed, not in my rags of self-righteousness, but in the gleaming robes of Your righteousness? What a mystery! What a wonder! What a joy! (Isa 61:10)

Finish, then, Thy new creation;
Pure and spotless let us be;
Let us see Thy great salvation
Perfectly restored in Thee;
Changed from glory into glory,
Till in heaven we take our place,
Till we cast our crowns before Thee,
Lost in wonder, love, and praise.

"Love Divine, All Loves Excelling"
Charles Wesley (1747)

As no darkness can be seen by anyone surrounded by light, so no trivialities can capture the attention of anyone who has his eyes on Christ.

Gregory of Nyssa (c.335–c.394)

(10:19–23) I am so thankful, Lord Jesus, that in You and through faith in You I may approach God the Father with freedom and confidence. You provided the way where there was no way. You opened the curtain and invited me into the Most Holy Place to enjoy fellowship with God Himself. Because I am hidden in You I am safe in the very presence of God. And I can come to Him with permission to speak freely, as a child speaks to her father. Lord, let me never take this privilege for granted or make light of the price that You and Your Father had to pay to make this possible. (Lev 16:2; Jn 14:6; Eph 3:12; Heb 9:7–8,11–14)

Lord, I lay my heart before Your
  throne;
Lord, I bow my knee to You alone.
And though I know I'm guilty,
You forgive my sin;
Cleanse me with Your blood,
So I may enter in.
In Your presence,
That's where I want to be;
In Your presence for all eternity.
And though I know I'm guilty,
You forgive my sin;
Cleanse me with Your blood,
So I may enter in
To Your presence,
To Your presence.

"In Your Presence"
Debbie Cissna (©1998)

17 Then he adds:

"Their sins and lawless acts
  I will remember no more."[a]

18 And where these have been forgiven, there is no longer any sacrifice for sin.

A Call to Persevere

19 Therefore, brothers, since we have confidence to enter the
Most Holy Place by the blood of Jesus, 20 by a new and living way
opened for us through the curtain, that is, his body, 21 and since
we have a great priest over the house of God, 22 let us draw near
to God with a sincere heart in full assurance of faith, having our
hearts sprinkled to cleanse us from a guilty conscience and having our bodies washed with pure water. 23 Let us hold unswervingly to the hope we profess, for he who promised is faithful.
24 And let us consider how we may spur one another on toward
love and good deeds. 25 Let us not give up meeting together, as
some are in the habit of doing, but let us encourage one another—and all the more as you see the Day approaching.

26 If we deliberately keep on sinning after we have received the
knowledge of the truth, no sacrifice for sins is left, 27 but only a
fearful expectation of judgment and of raging fire that will consume the enemies of God. 28 Anyone who rejected the law of
Moses died without mercy on the testimony of two or three witnesses. 29 How much more severely do you think a man deserves
to be punished who has trampled the Son of God under foot, who
has treated as an unholy thing the blood of the covenant that
sanctified him, and who has insulted the Spirit of grace? 30 For we
know him who said, "It is mine to avenge; I will repay,"[b] and
again, "The Lord will judge his people."[c] 31 It is a dreadful thing
to fall into the hands of the living God.

32 Remember those earlier days after you had received the
light, when you stood your ground in a great contest in the face of
suffering. 33 Sometimes you were publicly exposed to insult and
persecution; at other times you stood side by side with those who
were so treated. 34 You sympathized with those in prison and joyfully accepted the confiscation of your property, because you
knew that you yourselves had better and lasting possessions.

35 So do not throw away your confidence; it will be richly rewarded. 36 You need to persevere so that when you have done the
will of God, you will receive what he has promised. 37 For in just
a very little while,

"He who is coming will come and will not delay.
38 But my righteous one[d] will live by faith.
And if he shrinks back,
  I will not be pleased with him."[e]

39 But we are not of those who shrink back and are destroyed,
but of those who believe and are saved.

By Faith

11 Now faith is being sure of what we hope for and certain of
what we do not see. 2 This is what the ancients were commended for.

[a] *17* Jer. 31:34 [b] *30* Deut. 32:35 [c] *30* Deut. 32:36; Psalm 135:14 [d] *38* One early manuscript *But the righteous* [e] *38* Hab. 2:3,4

[3]By faith we understand that the universe was formed at God's
command, so that what is seen was not made out of what was visible.

[4]By faith Abel offered God a better sacrifice than Cain did. By
faith he was commended as a righteous man, when God spoke
well of his offerings. And by faith he still speaks, even though he
is dead.

[5]By faith Enoch was taken from this life, so that he did not experience death; he could not be found, because God had taken
him away. For before he was taken, he was commended as one
who pleased God. [6]And without faith it is impossible to please
God, because anyone who comes to him must believe that he exists and that he rewards those who earnestly seek him.

[7]By faith Noah, when warned about things not yet seen, in
holy fear built an ark to save his family. By his faith he condemned the world and became heir of the righteousness that
comes by faith.

[8]By faith Abraham, when called to go to a place he would later
receive as his inheritance, obeyed and went, even though he did
not know where he was going. [9]By faith he made his home in the
promised land like a stranger in a foreign country; he lived in
tents, as did Isaac and Jacob, who were heirs with him of the
same promise. [10]For he was looking forward to the city with
foundations, whose architect and builder is God.

[11]By faith Abraham, even though he was past age—and Sarah
herself was barren—was enabled to become a father because
he[a] considered him faithful who had made the promise. [12]And so
from this one man, and he as good as dead, came descendants as
numerous as the stars in the sky and as countless as the sand on
the seashore.

[13]All these people were still living by faith when they died.
They did not receive the things promised; they only saw them
and welcomed them from a distance. And they admitted that
they were aliens and strangers on earth. [14]People who say such
things show that they are looking for a country of their own. [15]If
they had been thinking of the country they had left, they would
have had opportunity to return. [16]Instead, they were longing for
a better country—a heavenly one. Therefore God is not
ashamed to be called their God, for he has prepared a city for
them.

[17]By faith Abraham, when God tested him, offered Isaac as a
sacrifice. He who had received the promises was about to sacrifice his one and only son, [18]even though God had said to him, "It
is through Isaac that your offspring[b] will be reckoned."[c] [19]Abra-
ham reasoned that God could raise the dead, and figuratively
speaking, he did receive Isaac back from death.

[20]By faith Isaac blessed Jacob and Esau in regard to their future.

[21]By faith Jacob, when he was dying, blessed each of Joseph's
sons, and worshiped as he leaned on the top of his staff.

[22]By faith Joseph, when his end was near, spoke about the exodus of the Israelites from Egypt and gave instructions about his
bones.

[23]By faith Moses' parents hid him for three months after he

[a] *11* Or *By faith even Sarah, who was past age, was enabled to bear children because she* [b] *18* Greek *seed* [c] *18* Gen. 21:12

(11:1–22) By faith, O God, I worship You. Though my eyes cannot see You my heart believes. Though my hands cannot touch You my spirit receives Your embrace. In exalting Your name I confess that You are the one true God. In offering myself to You I trust in Your unfailing love. When I cannot fathom Your ways, nevertheless I have confidence in You. Even in times of suffering, when "the fig tree does not bud and there are no grapes on the vines, . . . yet I will rejoice in the LORD, I will be joyful in God my Savior." (Hab 3:17–18)

Day by day and with each passing
moment,
Strength I find to meet my trials
here;
Trusting in my Father's wise
bestowment,
I've no cause for worry or for fear.
He whose heart is kind beyond all
measure
Gives unto each day what He deems
best
Lovingly, its part of pain and
pleasure,
Mingling toil with peace and rest.

Help me then in every tribulation
So to trust Thy promises, O Lord,
That I lose not faith's sweet
consolation
Offered me within Thy holy Word.
Help me, Lord, when toil and trouble
meeting,
E'er to take, as from a father's hand,
One by one, the days, the moments
fleeting,
Till I reach the promised land.

"Day By Day and With Each Passing Moment"

Carolina Sandell Berg (1865)

Trans. Andrew L. Skoog (1856-1934)

Turn your eyes upon Jesus,
Look full in His wonderful face;
And the things of earth
Will grow strangely dim
In the light of His glory and grace.

"Turn Your Eyes Upon Jesus"
Helen H. Lemmel (1922)

(12:2–3) As I run my race for the crown of life, Lord Jesus, I fix the eyes of my heart upon You. I see You as the author of my faith, Whose atoning death and glorious resurrection I trust for my salvation. I see You as the Lamb of God, Whose perfect sacrifice atones for my sin. I see You as the risen Lord, Whose victory over death confirms to me the promise of eternal life. I see You enthroned in heaven, rejoicing in the praise of Your jubilant saints. As I see You, Lord Jesus, I worship You, not with apathy but with zeal, with all that I am—heart, soul, mind and strength. All praise be to You, Lord Jesus Christ! (1Co 9:24–25; Jas 1:12)

Let it be said of us
That the Lord was our passion,
That with gladness we bore
Ev'ry cross we were given;
That we fought the good fight,
That we finished the course
Knowing within us
The pow'r of the risen Lord.

Let the cross be our glory
And the Lord be our song,
By mercy made holy,
By the Spirit made strong.
Let the cross be our glory
And the Lord be our song
'Til the likeness of Jesus
Be through us made known.
Let the cross be our glory
And the Lord be our song.

"Let It Be Said of Us"
Steve Fry (©1996)

was born, because they saw he was no ordinary child, and they
were not afraid of the king's edict.
24By faith Moses, when he had grown up, refused to be known
as the son of Pharaoh's daughter. 25He chose to be mistreated
along with the people of God rather than to enjoy the pleasures of
sin for a short time. 26He regarded disgrace for the sake of Christ
as of greater value than the treasures of Egypt, because he was
looking ahead to his reward. 27By faith he left Egypt, not fearing
the king's anger; he persevered because he saw him who is invisible. 28By faith he kept the Passover and the sprinkling of blood,
so that the destroyer of the firstborn would not touch the firstborn
of Israel.
29By faith the people passed through the Red Sea[a] as on dry
land; but when the Egyptians tried to do so, they were drowned.
30By faith the walls of Jericho fell, after the people had
marched around them for seven days.
31By faith the prostitute Rahab, because she welcomed the
spies, was not killed with those who were disobedient.[b]
32And what more shall I say? I do not have time to tell about
Gideon, Barak, Samson, Jephthah, David, Samuel and the prophets, 33who through faith conquered kingdoms, administered justice, and gained what was promised; who shut the mouths of
lions, 34quenched the fury of the flames, and escaped the edge of
the sword; whose weakness was turned to strength; and who became powerful in battle and routed foreign armies. 35Women received back their dead, raised to life again. Others were tortured
and refused to be released, so that they might gain a better resurrection. 36Some faced jeers and flogging, while still others
were chained and put in prison. 37They were stoned[c]; they were
sawed in two; they were put to death by the sword. They went
about in sheepskins and goatskins, destitute, persecuted and
mistreated— 38the world was not worthy of them. They wandered in deserts and mountains, and in caves and holes in the
ground.
39These were all commended for their faith, yet none of them
received what had been promised. 40God had planned something
better for us so that only together with us would they be made
perfect.

God Disciplines His Sons

12 Therefore, since we are surrounded by such a great cloud
of witnesses, let us throw off everything that hinders and
the sin that so easily entangles, and let us run with perseverance
the race marked out for us. 2Let us fix our eyes on Jesus, the author and perfecter of our faith, who for the joy set before him endured the cross, scorning its shame, and sat down at the right
hand of the throne of God. 3Consider him who endured such opposition from sinful men, so that you will not grow weary and lose
heart.
4In your struggle against sin, you have not yet resisted to the
point of shedding your blood. 5And you have forgotten that word
of encouragement that addresses you as sons:

"My son, do not make light of the Lord's discipline,
and do not lose heart when he rebukes you,

[a] 29 That is, Sea of Reeds [b] 31 Or *unbelieving* [c] 37 Some early manuscripts *stoned; they were put to the test;*

6 because the Lord disciplines those he loves,
and he punishes everyone he accepts as a
son."[a]

7 Endure hardship as discipline; God is treating you as sons.
For what son is not disciplined by his father? 8 If you are not disciplined (and everyone undergoes discipline), then you are illegitimate children and not true sons. 9 Moreover, we have all had
human fathers who disciplined us and we respected them for it.
How much more should we submit to the Father of our spirits
and live! 10 Our fathers disciplined us for a little while as they
thought best; but God disciplines us for our good, that we may
share in his holiness. 11 No discipline seems pleasant at the time,
but painful. Later on, however, it produces a harvest of righteousness and peace for those who have been trained by it.
12 Therefore, strengthen your feeble arms and weak knees.
13 "Make level paths for your feet,"[b] so that the lame may not be
disabled, but rather healed.

Warning Against Refusing God

14 Make every effort to live in peace with all men and to be
holy; without holiness no one will see the Lord. 15 See to it that
no one misses the grace of God and that no bitter root grows up
to cause trouble and defile many. 16 See that no one is sexually
immoral, or is godless like Esau, who for a single meal sold his
inheritance rights as the oldest son. 17 Afterward, as you know,
when he wanted to inherit this blessing, he was rejected. He
could bring about no change of mind, though he sought the
blessing with tears.
18 You have not come to a mountain that can be touched and
that is burning with fire; to darkness, gloom and storm; 19 to a
trumpet blast or to such a voice speaking words that those who
heard it begged that no further word be spoken to them, 20 because they could not bear what was commanded: "If even an animal touches the mountain, it must be stoned."[c] 21 The sight was
so terrifying that Moses said, "I am trembling with fear."[d]
22 But you have come to Mount Zion, to the heavenly Jerusalem, the city of the living God. You have come to thousands
upon thousands of angels in joyful assembly, 23 to the church of
the firstborn, whose names are written in heaven. You have
come to God, the judge of all men, to the spirits of righteous
men made perfect, 24 to Jesus the mediator of a new covenant,
and to the sprinkled blood that speaks a better word than the
blood of Abel.
25 See to it that you do not refuse him who speaks. If they did
not escape when they refused him who warned them on earth,
how much less will we, if we turn away from him who warns us
from heaven? 26 At that time his voice shook the earth, but now he
has promised, "Once more I will shake not only the earth but also
the heavens."[e] 27 The words "once more" indicate the removing
of what can be shaken—that is, created things—so that what
cannot be shaken may remain.
28 Therefore, since we are receiving a kingdom that cannot be
shaken, let us be thankful, and so worship God acceptably with
reverence and awe, 29 for our "God is a consuming fire."[f]

[a] *6* Prov. 3:11,12 [b] *13* Prov. 4:26 [c] *20* Exodus 19:12,13 [d] *21* Deut. 9:19
[e] *26* Haggai 2:6 [f] *29* Deut. 4:24

(12:28–29) Gracious God, You invite me to draw near to You, to approach Your throne of grace with confidence. Yet in the safety of Your presence I sometimes forget Who You are—a holy God in Whom there is no hint of evil, a righteous God Who tolerates no sin, a consuming fire Who destroys sin forever. Forgive me for reducing You to something that fits comfortably within my self-centered little world. Teach me to worship You acceptably, with reverence and intimacy, with gratitude and boldness. (Heb 4:16; 10:22).

I come by Faith
Into the holy place,
Where saints and seraphim
Behold Your holy Face.
And there in wonder and in awe
I lift my voice in praise.
Holy, holy,
My Lord, my God.

"I Come By Faith"
Jimmy Owens (©1989)

Concluding Exhortations

13 Keep on loving each other as brothers. 2Do not forget to
entertain strangers, for by so doing some people have entertained angels without knowing it. 3Remember those in prison
as if you were their fellow prisoners, and those who are mistreated as if you yourselves were suffering.
4Marriage should be honored by all, and the marriage bed
kept pure, for God will judge the adulterer and all the sexually
immoral. 5Keep your lives free from the love of money and be
content with what you have, because God has said,

> "Never will I leave you;
> never will I forsake you."[a]

6So we say with confidence,

> "The Lord is my helper; I will not be afraid.
> What can man do to me?"[b]

7Remember your leaders, who spoke the word of God to you.
Consider the outcome of their way of life and imitate their faith.
8Jesus Christ is the same yesterday and today and forever.
9Do not be carried away by all kinds of strange teachings. It is
good for our hearts to be strengthened by grace, not by ceremonial foods, which are of no value to those who eat them. 10We
have an altar from which those who minister at the tabernacle
have no right to eat.
11The high priest carries the blood of animals into the Most Holy
Place as a sin offering, but the bodies are burned outside the camp.
12And so Jesus also suffered outside the city gate to make the people holy through his own blood. 13Let us, then, go to him outside
the camp, bearing the disgrace he bore. 14For here we do not have
an enduring city, but we are looking for the city that is to come.
15Through Jesus, therefore, let us continually offer to God a
sacrifice of praise—the fruit of lips that confess his name. 16And
do not forget to do good and to share with others, for with such
sacrifices God is pleased.
17Obey your leaders and submit to their authority. They keep
watch over you as men who must give an account. Obey them so
that their work will be a joy, not a burden, for that would be of no
advantage to you.
18Pray for us. We are sure that we have a clear conscience and
desire to live honorably in every way. 19I particularly urge you to
pray so that I may be restored to you soon.
20May the God of peace, who through the blood of the eternal
covenant brought back from the dead our Lord Jesus, that great
Shepherd of the sheep, 21equip you with everything good for
doing his will, and may he work in us what is pleasing to him,
through Jesus Christ, to whom be glory for ever and ever. Amen.

22Brothers, I urge you to bear with my word of exhortation, for
I have written you only a short letter.
23I want you to know that our brother Timothy has been released. If he arrives soon, I will come with him to see you.
24Greet all your leaders and all God's people. Those from Italy
send you their greetings.
25Grace be with you all.

[a] 5 Deut. 31:6 [b] 6 Psalm 118:6,7

The Lord is in His holy temple,
The Lord is on His heavenly throne,
We bring our praises unto Jesus
For all the love that He has shown.

We sense the beauty of His
presence,
We hear the great triumphant
shout!
The lamb for sinners slain is worthy,
How can we keep from crying out?

Singing alleluia, alleluia, alleluia!
Singing alleluia, alleluia, alleluia!

"We Sing Alleluia"
Walt Harrah (©1988)

(13:15) We bring our sacrifices through You, Lord Jesus Christ, our great high priest. You offered the perfect sacrifice of Your own blood, once for all, thus opening to us forever the way to the Father. Through You, O Christ, we know that our sacrifices, imperfect as they may be, are nevertheless acceptable to God. Awesome, triune God—Father, Son, and Holy Spirit—receive our praise. To You be glory for ever and ever. Amen. (Heb 13:21; 1Pt 2:5)

The General Epistle of JAMES

One of the most frequent criticisms applied to Christians is that we are "hypocrites." Many times this is simply a cheap shot. But, sadly, sometimes we deserve this label. We can easily believe one thing, yet do another. Or we might sweetly praise God's name in a worship service, only to yell mercilessly at the driver who cuts in front of us on the way home from church.

The issue of hypocrisy is as old as Christianity itself. Just a few years after the church was born, James wrote a letter addressing the problem of Christians who fail to live out their faith. In his letter he offers practical advice for how our lives as Christians can reflect well upon our faith, and, indeed, upon God.

Perhaps the most familiar section of James is the discussion of faith and works in chapter 2. On a superficial level, James appears to contradict Paul's teaching on justification by faith when he says that "a person is justified by what he does and not by faith alone" (2:24; compare Gal 2:16). But a more careful reading of James (and Paul) corrects this misunderstanding. For Paul, genuine faith in Christ will always be expressed in good works (Eph 2:8–10). Similarly, James claims that faith without works is dead (2:17).

Why does James emphasize the negative side of the discussion? He is probably responding to a group of Christians who distorted Paul's original teaching. These individuals claimed that it was sufficient merely to affirm the truth of the gospel. Faith, for them, required no active response or life transformation. In fact, their theology provided a solid foundation for a life of blatant Christian hypocrisy. James writes to correct their confusion. Both he and Paul would agree that true faith will transform one's life and be demonstrated in good works.

True faith will transform one's life and be demonstrated in good works . . . If our worship is genuine the experience of offering praise to God should transform the way we speak and relate to others.

Not surprisingly, James's comments on worship emphasize its active, daily-life implications: "If anyone considers himself religious and yet does not keep a tight rein on his tongue, he deceives himself and his religion is worthless" (1:26). What a tragedy that the same mouth can praise God and curse people created in God's image (3:9-10)! To frame the matter more positively, if our worship is genuine the experience of offering praise to God should transform the way we speak and relate to others.

Furthermore, our worship must be expressed not only in praise to God, but also in tangible care for people: "Religion that God our Father accepts as pure and faultless is this: to look after orphans and widows in their distress" (1:27). Since God, Who is full of compassion and mercy, gives generously to us (1:5, 17; 5:11), we should do likewise to others. This passage reminds us of what Jesus says in Matthew 25:31–46. When we care for "the least" in Jesus' family, we are caring for Him. So, when we show love to orphans, widows and others in need, God receives our actions as offerings of love to Him.

(1:2–12) I look to You, Lord, to bring me through every trial I face today. Sometimes it is hard to remember that trials are part of a spiritual process designed to produce maturity, character and integrity in my life. I confess that at times I wish You had some other way for me to grow. But I praise You, Lord, that along with the problems I face You graciously provide me with wisdom and strength to carry on. Have Your way in my life, Father. Make me a child You can be proud of.

Have we trials and temptations?
Is there trouble anywhere?
We should never be discouraged,
Take it to the Lord in prayer!
Can we find a friend so faithful
Who will all our sorrows share?
Jesus knows our every weakness,
Take it to the Lord in prayer!

"What a Friend We Have in Jesus"
Joseph Scriven (c.1855)

(1:22–25) Lord, I want my faith to be authentic. I want to be a doer of the Word, not just a hearer. Teach me, Lord, to break up the unplowed ground in my hard heart so that it might be fertile soil for the seed of Your Word. Plant that Word deep within my soul that it may bear much fruit to Your glory.

Make it the first morning business of your life to understand some part of the Bible clearly, and make it your daily business to obey it in all that you do understand.

John Ruskin (1819-1900)

1 James, a servant of God and of the Lord Jesus Christ,

To the twelve tribes scattered among the nations:
Greetings.

Trials and Temptations

2Consider it pure joy, my brothers, whenever you face trials of
many kinds, 3because you know that the testing of your faith develops perseverance. 4Perseverance must finish its work so that
you may be mature and complete, not lacking anything. 5If any of
you lacks wisdom, he should ask God, who gives generously to all
without finding fault, and it will be given to him. 6But when he
asks, he must believe and not doubt, because he who doubts is
like a wave of the sea, blown and tossed by the wind. 7That man
should not think he will receive anything from the Lord; 8he is a
double-minded man, unstable in all he does.
9The brother in humble circumstances ought to take pride in
his high position. 10But the one who is rich should take pride in
his low position, because he will pass away like a wild flower.
11For the sun rises with scorching heat and withers the plant; its
blossom falls and its beauty is destroyed. In the same way, the
rich man will fade away even while he goes about his business.
12Blessed is the man who perseveres under trial, because
when he has stood the test, he will receive the crown of life that
God has promised to those who love him.
13When tempted, no one should say, "God is tempting me." For
God cannot be tempted by evil, nor does he tempt anyone; 14but
each one is tempted when, by his own evil desire, he is dragged
away and enticed. 15Then, after desire has conceived, it gives
birth to sin; and sin, when it is full-grown, gives birth to death.
16Don't be deceived, my dear brothers. 17Every good and perfect gift is from above, coming down from the Father of the heavenly lights, who does not change like shifting shadows. 18He
chose to give us birth through the word of truth, that we might be
a kind of firstfruits of all he created.

Listening and Doing

19My dear brothers, take note of this: Everyone should be
quick to listen, slow to speak and slow to become angry, 20for
man's anger does not bring about the righteous life that God desires. 21Therefore, get rid of all moral filth and the evil that is so
prevalent and humbly accept the word planted in you, which can
save you.
22Do not merely listen to the word, and so deceive yourselves.
Do what it says. 23Anyone who listens to the word but does not do
what it says is like a man who looks at his face in a mirror 24and,
after looking at himself, goes away and immediately forgets what
he looks like. 25But the man who looks intently into the perfect
law that gives freedom, and continues to do this, not forgetting
what he has heard, but doing it—he will be blessed in what he
does.
26If anyone considers himself religious and yet does not keep
a tight rein on his tongue, he deceives himself and his religion is
worthless. 27Religion that God our Father accepts as pure and
faultless is this: to look after orphans and widows in their distress and to keep oneself from being polluted by the world.

MY BELOVED

Life is not without difficult seasons. But consider it pure joy whenever you face trials of many kinds, because the testing of your faith develops perseverance; perseverance produces character; and character produces hope. In order for you to become mature and complete in Me, perseverance must finish its work in you.

Though now for a little while you may have to suffer grief in all kinds of trials, remember that trials come so that your faith—of greater worth than gold, which perishes even though refined by fire—may be proved genuine and may result in praise, glory and honor when Jesus Christ is revealed.

Just think of My prophets of old who spoke in My name only to face suffering. In the end they were blessed because they persevered. You too will be blessed when you persevere under trials, because when you have stood the test, you will receive the crown of life that I have promised to those who love Me.

You have heard of Job's perseverance and have seen what I finally brought about for him. I made him prosperous again and gave him twice as much as he had before. I blessed the latter part of his life more than the first.

So take heart and do not throw away your confidence in Me. You need to persevere so that when you have done My will, you will receive all that I have promised. Hold on tight!

Job 42:10,12; Ro 5:3-4; Heb 10:35-36; Jas 1:2-4, 12; 5:10-11; 1Pe 1:6-7

Favoritism Forbidden

2 My brothers, as believers in our glorious Lord Jesus Christ,
don't show favoritism. 2Suppose a man comes into your
meeting wearing a gold ring and fine clothes, and a poor man in
shabby clothes also comes in. 3If you show special attention to
the man wearing fine clothes and say, "Here's a good seat for
you," but say to the poor man, "You stand there" or "Sit on the
floor by my feet," 4have you not discriminated among yourselves
and become judges with evil thoughts?

5Listen, my dear brothers: Has not God chosen those who are
poor in the eyes of the world to be rich in faith and to inherit the
kingdom he promised those who love him? 6But you have insulted the poor. Is it not the rich who are exploiting you? Are they
not the ones who are dragging you into court? 7Are they not the
ones who are slandering the noble name of him to whom you
belong?

8If you really keep the royal law found in Scripture, "Love your
neighbor as yourself,"[a] you are doing right. 9But if you show favoritism, you sin and are convicted by the law as lawbreakers.
10For whoever keeps the whole law and yet stumbles at just one
point is guilty of breaking all of it. 11For he who said, "Do not
commit adultery,"[b] also said, "Do not murder."[c] If you do not
commit adultery but do commit murder, you have become a lawbreaker.

12Speak and act as those who are going to be judged by the law
that gives freedom, 13because judgment without mercy will be
shown to anyone who has not been merciful. Mercy triumphs
over judgment!

Faith and Deeds

14What good is it, my brothers, if a man claims to have faith but
has no deeds? Can such faith save him? 15Suppose a brother or
sister is without clothes and daily food. 16If one of you says to
him, "Go, I wish you well; keep warm and well fed," but does
nothing about his physical needs, what good is it? 17In the same
way, faith by itself, if it is not accompanied by action, is dead.

18But someone will say, "You have faith; I have deeds."

Show me your faith without deeds, and I will show you my faith
by what I do. 19You believe that there is one God. Good! Even the
demons believe that—and shudder.

20You foolish man, do you want evidence that faith without
deeds is useless[d]? 21Was not our ancestor Abraham considered
righteous for what he did when he offered his son Isaac on the
altar? 22You see that his faith and his actions were working together, and his faith was made complete by what he did. 23And
the scripture was fulfilled that says, "Abraham believed God, and
it was credited to him as righteousness,"[e] and he was called
God's friend. 24You see that a person is justified by what he does
and not by faith alone.

25In the same way, was not even Rahab the prostitute considered righteous for what she did when she gave lodging to the
spies and sent them off in a different direction? 26As the body
without the spirit is dead, so faith without deeds is dead.

[a] *8* Lev. 19:18 [b] *11* Exodus 20:14; Deut. 5:18 [c] *11* Exodus 20:13; Deut. 5:17
[d] *20* Some early manuscripts *dead* [e] *23* Gen. 15:6

Preach the Gospel. If necessary, use words.
Saint Francis of Assisi (c.1181–1226)

(2:14–26) Lord, I want my faith to be authentic. I want to be a doer of the Word, not just a talker. I want to be a living testimony of faith in Jesus Christ—a testimony that is seen, not just heard, of a faith that is proven, not just theory. Because of his active faith, You called Abraham Your friend. Lord, I want to be Your friend too.

You do right when you offer faith to God; you do right when you offer works. But if you separate the two, then you do wrong. For faith without works is dead; and lack of charity in action murders faith, just as Cain murdered Abel, so that God cannot respect your offering.
Bernard of Clairvaux (1090–1153)

(3:2–12) Lord, I cry out with Your servant, Isaiah: "Woe to me! . . . I am ruined! For I am a man of unclean lips, and I live among a people of unclean lips, and my eyes have seen the King, the LORD Almighty." Lord, touch my lips with holy fire. Purify my heart, and so purify my mouth; for out of the overflow of the heart the mouth speaks. (Isa 6:5–7; Mt 12:34)

The criminal we are dealing with is pronounced by an inspired writer, 'an unruly evil, full of deadly poison' . . . Against this Goliath therefore we go forth to battle, though armed only with a sling and a stone, 'in the name of the LORD of hosts, the God of the armies of Israel, whom it hath defied,' leaving the success of the attempt to him that made man's mouth, and is alone able to make it new, as he certainly does, wherever he gives a new heart.

Matthew Henry (1662-1714)

(4:1–10) Forgive me, O Lord, for I have been unfaithful to You. I have chased after the pleasures of the flesh and the ways of the world. My self-centeredness has caused conflicts in my relationships with others and has compromised my relationship with You. The evidence is in my ineffective, selfish prayers. Forgive me, O God. Right now, I humble myself as best as I know how, so that You will not have to humble me Yourself. At Your invitation I approach Your throne of grace so that I may receive mercy and find grace to help me in my time of need. (Heb 4:16)

What we seek or shun in prayer we should equally pursue or avoid in our daily walk. Earnestly avoid temptation. Walk so guarded in the path of obedience that you will never tempt the devil to tempt you.

Charles Haddon Spurgeon (1834-1892)

Taming the Tongue

3 Not many of you should presume to be teachers, my brothers, because you know that we who teach will be judged
more strictly. 2We all stumble in many ways. If anyone is never at
fault in what he says, he is a perfect man, able to keep his whole
body in check.
3When we put bits into the mouths of horses to make them
obey us, we can turn the whole animal. 4Or take ships as an example. Although they are so large and are driven by strong winds,
they are steered by a very small rudder wherever the pilot wants
to go. 5Likewise the tongue is a small part of the body, but it
makes great boasts. Consider what a great forest is set on fire by
a small spark. 6The tongue also is a fire, a world of evil among
the parts of the body. It corrupts the whole person, sets the whole
course of his life on fire, and is itself set on fire by hell.
7All kinds of animals, birds, reptiles and creatures of the sea
are being tamed and have been tamed by man, 8but no man can
tame the tongue. It is a restless evil, full of deadly poison.
9With the tongue we praise our Lord and Father, and with it we
curse men, who have been made in God's likeness. 10Out of the
same mouth come praise and cursing. My brothers, this should
not be. 11Can both fresh water and salt[a] water flow from the
same spring? 12My brothers, can a fig tree bear olives, or a
grapevine bear figs? Neither can a salt spring produce fresh
water.

Two Kinds of Wisdom

13Who is wise and understanding among you? Let him show it
by his good life, by deeds done in the humility that comes from
wisdom. 14But if you harbor bitter envy and selfish ambition in
your hearts, do not boast about it or deny the truth. 15Such "wisdom" does not come down from heaven but is earthly, unspiritual, of the devil. 16For where you have envy and selfish ambition,
there you find disorder and every evil practice.
17But the wisdom that comes from heaven is first of all pure;
then peace-loving, considerate, submissive, full of mercy and
good fruit, impartial and sincere. 18Peacemakers who sow in
peace raise a harvest of righteousness.

Submit Yourselves to God

4 What causes fights and quarrels among you? Don't they come from your desires that battle within you? 2You want something but don't get it. You kill and covet, but you cannot have what
you want. You quarrel and fight. You do not have, because you do
not ask God. 3When you ask, you do not receive, because you ask
with wrong motives, that you may spend what you get on your
pleasures.
4You adulterous people, don't you know that friendship with
the world is hatred toward God? Anyone who chooses to be a
friend of the world becomes an enemy of God. 5Or do you think
Scripture says without reason that the spirit he caused to live in us
envies intensely?[b] 6But he gives us more grace. That is why Scripture says:

[a] 11 Greek *bitter* (see also verse 14) [b] 5 Or *that God jealously longs for the spirit that he made to live in us*; or *that the Spirit he caused to live in us longs jealously*

"God opposes the proud
but gives grace to the humble."[a]

7Submit yourselves, then, to God. Resist the devil, and he will
flee from you. 8Come near to God and he will come near to you.
Wash your hands, you sinners, and purify your hearts, you double-minded. 9Grieve, mourn and wail. Change your laughter to
mourning and your joy to gloom. 10Humble yourselves before the
Lord, and he will lift you up.

11Brothers, do not slander one another. Anyone who speaks
against his brother or judges him speaks against the law and
judges it. When you judge the law, you are not keeping it, but sitting in judgment on it. 12There is only one Lawgiver and Judge,
the one who is able to save and destroy. But you—who are you to
judge your neighbor?

Boasting About Tomorrow

13Now listen, you who say, "Today or tomorrow we will go to
this or that city, spend a year there, carry on business and make
money." 14Why, you do not even know what will happen tomorrow. What is your life? You are a mist that appears for a little while
and then vanishes. 15Instead, you ought to say, "If it is the Lord's
will, we will live and do this or that." 16As it is, you boast and
brag. All such boasting is evil. 17Anyone, then, who knows the
good he ought to do and doesn't do it, sins.

Warning to Rich Oppressors

5 Now listen, you rich people, weep and wail because of the
misery that is coming upon you. 2Your wealth has rotted, and
moths have eaten your clothes. 3Your gold and silver are corrod-
ed. Their corrosion will testify against you and eat your flesh like
fire. You have hoarded wealth in the last days. 4Look! The wages
you failed to pay the workmen who mowed your fields are crying
out against you. The cries of the harvesters have reached the ears
of the Lord Almighty. 5You have lived on earth in luxury and self-
indulgence. You have fattened yourselves in the day of slaughter.[b]
6You have condemned and murdered innocent men, who were
not opposing you.

Patience in Suffering

7Be patient, then, brothers, until the Lord's coming. See how
the farmer waits for the land to yield its valuable crop and how
patient he is for the autumn and spring rains. 8You too, be patient
and stand firm, because the Lord's coming is near. 9Don't grumble against each other, brothers, or you will be judged. The Judge
is standing at the door!

10Brothers, as an example of patience in the face of suffering, take the prophets who spoke in the name of the Lord. 11As
you know, we consider blessed those who have persevered. You
have heard of Job's perseverance and have seen what the Lord
finally brought about. The Lord is full of compassion and
mercy.

12Above all, my brothers, do not swear—not by heaven or by
earth or by anything else. Let your "Yes" be yes, and your "No,"
no, or you will be condemned.

[a]6 Prov. 3:34 [b]5 Or *yourselves as in a day of feasting*

(4:6–8) Thank You, dear Father, for this gracious invitation to come to You. When we come in humility, You do not move away, You come closer. Like the father of the lost son, You see us coming from afar and run to embrace us. You come to us bearing gifts of grace—grace upon grace to meet our every need: salvation when we are lost, wisdom when we are confused, strength when we are weak, healing when we are broken. Thank You, dear Father, for Your kindness that leads us to repentance. (Lk 15:11–24; Ro 2:4)

To this place You call me,
I will come,
To Your sanctuary I will run.
I'll leave it all behind,
My selfishness, my pride,
I'll lay it all aside,
For this is my heart's cry.

Oh, how I long
To come into Your holy place
To behold the Lamb, and bow
Before Your throne of grace.
Oh, how I long,
Oh, how I long
To see You face to face.

"Oh, How I Long"
Jane Billington (©1997)

The Prayer of Faith

13Is any one of you in trouble? He should pray. Is anyone
happy? Let him sing songs of praise. 14Is any one of you sick? He
should call the elders of the church to pray over him and anoint
him with oil in the name of the Lord. 15And the prayer offered in
faith will make the sick person well; the Lord will raise him up. If
he has sinned, he will be forgiven. 16Therefore confess your sins
to each other and pray for each other so that you may be healed.
The prayer of a righteous man is powerful and effective.

17Elijah was a man just like us. He prayed earnestly that it
would not rain, and it did not rain on the land for three and a half
years. 18Again he prayed, and the heavens gave rain, and the
earth produced its crops.

19My brothers, if one of you should wander from the truth and
someone should bring him back, 20remember this: Whoever
turns a sinner from the error of his way will save him from death
and cover over a multitude of sins.

(5:13–19) Thank You, Lord, for Your church—the fellowship of saints, the community of faith, the body of Christ, the family of God. Help us all to learn well the purpose of our service to one another. Teach us the blessed ministry of intercession—to be like Jesus Christ Who ever lives, not for His own pleasure or comfort, but to intercede for us. Teach us to pray like He does. Teach us to listen like He does. Teach us to care, to give, to serve, knowing that the lives and eternal destinies of others are at stake. May we each live as mediators—presenting the needs and requests of others to You and in turn extending Your hand of grace, forgiveness, healing and provision to those who need Your help. Amen.

Our prayers lay the track down by which God's power can come. Like a mighty locomotive, his power is irresistible, but it cannot reach us without rails.

Watchman Nee (1903-1972)

Every soul we long to reach,
Every heart we hope to teach,
Everywhere we share His peace,
Is only by His grace.

Every loving word we say,
Every tear we wipe away,
Every sorrow turned to praise,
Is only by His grace.

Grace alone
Which God supplies,
Strength unknown
He will provide,
Christ in us
Our Cornerstone,
We will go forth in grace alone.

"Grace Alone"
Scott Wesley Brown and
Jeff Nelson (©1998)

The First & Second Epistles General of PETER

1&2 Peter

How can we endure difficult times? How can we worship God, and even grow in our faith, in the midst of earthly struggles? The apostle Peter seeks to answer these questions by writing two letters in which he encourages Christians to stand firm in Christ. In his first letter he writes to those who are suffering because of their faith in Christ (1Pe 4:16). In the second he addresses believers who are being harassed by false teachers (2Pe 2:1).

Peter begins by emphasizing what we have received in Christ and who we are as His people. In His "great mercy" God has "given us new birth into a living hope through the resurrection of Jesus Christ from the dead" (1Pe 1:3). Moreover, though once we "were not a people," now we are "a chosen people, a royal priesthood, a holy nation, a people belonging to God" (1Pe 2:9–10).

God has set us apart to be His special people so that we "may declare the praises of him who called [us] out of darkness into his wonderful light" (1Pe 2:9). We "are being built into a spiritual house to be a holy priesthood, offering spiritual sacrifices acceptable to God through Jesus Christ" (1Pe 2:5). Worship stands at the center of our purpose as God's people. We are His temple and His priests. Knowledge of our identity in Christ and our calling to worship helps us to keep on praising God even in difficult times.

> **Worship stands at the center of our purpose as God's people. We are His temple and His priests.**

Hope for the future also sustains and motivates our worship of God. The recipients of 1 Peter, though suffering "grief in all kinds of trials," are nevertheless able to rejoice greatly because of their hope in the "salvation that is ready to be revealed in the last time" and the inheritance kept in heaven for them (1Pe 1:4–6). We too are able to rejoice even in the midst of pain because we look ahead to that glorious day. In our struggles, we must "set [our] hope fully on the grace to be given [us] when Jesus Christ is revealed" (1Pe 1:13).

Of course it would be hard to draw strength and hope from the second coming of Christ if people around us were to deny that He will return. In his second letter Peter explains that "scoffers" will come who reject the coming of Christ (2Pe 3:3–4). Although the day of the Lord may appear to be delayed, Peter reassures us that it will come "like a thief" (2Pe 3:10). One day we will be citizens in "a new heaven and a new earth" (2Pe 3:13). Therefore, we "ought to live holy and godly lives as [we] look forward to the day of God" (2Pe 3:11–12). Our confidence in Christ's second coming will motivate us to "grow in the grace and knowledge of our Lord and Savior Jesus Christ. To him be glory both now and forever! Amen" (2Pe 3:18).

1

Peter, an apostle of Jesus Christ,

To God's elect, strangers in the world, scattered throughout
Pontus, Galatia, Cappadocia, Asia and Bithynia, 2 who have been
chosen according to the foreknowledge of God the Father,
through the sanctifying work of the Spirit, for obedience to Jesus
Christ and sprinkling by his blood:

Grace and peace be yours in abundance.

Praise to God for a Living Hope

3 Praise be to the God and Father of our Lord Jesus Christ! In
his great mercy he has given us new birth into a living hope
through the resurrection of Jesus Christ from the dead, 4 and into
an inheritance that can never perish, spoil or fade—kept in heav-
en for you, 5 who through faith are shielded by God's power until
the coming of the salvation that is ready to be revealed in the last
time. 6 In this you greatly rejoice, though now for a little while
you may have had to suffer grief in all kinds of trials. 7 These have
come so that your faith—of greater worth than gold, which perishes even though refined by fire—may be proved genuine and
may result in praise, glory and honor when Jesus Christ is revealed. 8 Though you have not seen him, you love him; and even
though you do not see him now, you believe in him and are filled
with an inexpressible and glorious joy, 9 for you are receiving the
goal of your faith, the salvation of your souls.

10 Concerning this salvation, the prophets, who spoke of the
grace that was to come to you, searched intently and with the
greatest care, 11 trying to find out the time and circumstances to
which the Spirit of Christ in them was pointing when he predicted the sufferings of Christ and the glories that would follow. 12 It
was revealed to them that they were not serving themselves but
you, when they spoke of the things that have now been told you by
those who have preached the gospel to you by the Holy Spirit sent
from heaven. Even angels long to look into these things.

Be Holy

13 Therefore, prepare your minds for action; be self-controlled;
set your hope fully on the grace to be given you when Jesus Christ
is revealed. 14 As obedient children, do not conform to the evil
desires you had when you lived in ignorance. 15 But just as he who
called you is holy, so be holy in all you do; 16 for it is written: "Be
holy, because I am holy."[a]

17 Since you call on a Father who judges each man's work impartially, live your lives as strangers here in reverent fear. 18 For
you know that it was not with perishable things such as silver or
gold that you were redeemed from the empty way of life handed
down to you from your forefathers, 19 but with the precious blood
of Christ, a lamb without blemish or defect. 20 He was chosen before the creation of the world, but was revealed in these last times
for your sake. 21 Through him you believe in God, who raised him
from the dead and glorified him, and so your faith and hope are
in God.

22 Now that you have purified yourselves by obeying the truth so
that you have sincere love for your brothers, love one another
deeply, from the heart.[b] 23 For you have been born again, not of

[a] *16* Lev. 11:44,45; 19:2; 20:7 [b] *22* Some early manuscripts *from a pure heart*

(1:1–9) I am chosen and cherished by God, but a stranger in this world. Lord Jesus, by Your blood You cleanse me, by Your mercy You save me, by Your resurrection You give me hope. By Your faithfulness and power You protect me in a fallen and polluted world. By Your wisdom You sustain me through the fiery trials that must refine my life. By all of these You bring out the very best of everything You have placed within me. How can I help but live to give You praise! Though I do not see You, I love You more than words can say. Oh, what then shall it be when I see You fully on that Day! (2Ti 1:12; 1Jn 3:2)

(1:13–16) Holy God, how can I be holy in all I do unless You first, by Your grace, make me holy in all that I am? For there is no real holiness apart from Your grace—only self-righteousness. So I set my hope fully on Your grace and ask that You make me holy. And then help me to cultivate that which You have planted in my life, so that I may bear the fruit of holiness for Your glory. (Lev 20:8; Php 2:12; Heb 2:11)

More like You,
Jesus, more like You,
Fill my heart with Your desire
To make me more like You.
More like You,
Jesus, more like You,
Touch my lips with holy fire
And make me more like You.

"More Like You"
Scott Wesley Brown (©1997)

perishable seed, but of imperishable, through the living and enduring word of God. 24For,

> "All men are like grass,
> and all their glory is like the flowers of the field;
> the grass withers and the flowers fall,
> 25 but the word of the Lord stands forever."[a]

And this is the word that was preached to you.

2 Therefore, rid yourselves of all malice and all deceit, hypocrisy, envy, and slander of every kind. 2Like newborn babies,
crave pure spiritual milk, so that by it you may grow up in your
salvation, 3now that you have tasted that the Lord is good.

The Living Stone and a Chosen People

4As you come to him, the living Stone—rejected by men but
chosen by God and precious to him— 5you also, like living
stones, are being built into a spiritual house to be a holy priesthood, offering spiritual sacrifices acceptable to God through
Jesus Christ. 6For in Scripture it says:

> "See, I lay a stone in Zion,
> a chosen and precious cornerstone,
> and the one who trusts in him
> will never be put to shame."[b]

7Now to you who believe, this stone is precious. But to those who
do not believe,

> "The stone the builders rejected
> has become the capstone,[c]"[d]

8and,

> "A stone that causes men to stumble
> and a rock that makes them fall."[e]

They stumble because they disobey the message—which is also
what they were destined for.

9But you are a chosen people, a royal priesthood, a holy nation, a people belonging to God, that you may declare the praises
of him who called you out of darkness into his wonderful light.
10Once you were not a people, but now you are the people of
God; once you had not received mercy, but now you have received
mercy.

11Dear friends, I urge you, as aliens and strangers in the
world, to abstain from sinful desires, which war against your
soul. 12Live such good lives among the pagans that, though they
accuse you of doing wrong, they may see your good deeds and
glorify God on the day he visits us.

Submission to Rulers and Masters

13Submit yourselves for the Lord's sake to every authority instituted among men: whether to the king, as the supreme authority, 14or to governors, who are sent by him to punish those who
do wrong and to commend those who do right. 15For it is God's
will that by doing good you should silence the ignorant talk of
foolish men. 16Live as free men, but do not use your freedom as
a cover-up for evil; live as servants of God. 17Show proper respect

[a] 25 Isaiah 40:6–8 [b] 6 Isaiah 28:16 [c] 7 Or *cornerstone* [d] 7 Psalm 118:22
[e] 8 Isaiah 8:14

(1:23–25) Eternal God and Father, by the power of Your eternal gospel I have been born again to eternal life. Your enduring Word is an eternal seed, and now I, as the fruit of that seed, will live forever. (Ro 1:16)

(2:9–10) We did not choose You; You chose us. We are humbled by Your mercy which You have lavished upon us. It was not enough for You to forgive us; it was not enough for You to rescue us—You had so much more in mind. You have done immeasurably more than we could possibly have asked or imagined. We are amazed at Your boundless love: What honor to be Your priesthood; what security to be Your cherished possession; what grace to be made holy; what joy to be rescued from the dominion of darkness; what privilege to be granted a share in the inheritance of the saints in the kingdom of light! For You have made us to be like the lights in the vast expanse of the sky to reflect the light of Your life on the earth. (Ge 15:5; Mt 5:14–16; Jn 15:16; Gal 3:29; Eph 3:20; Col 1:12–14)

(2:12) O God, by Your Spirit set Your hand upon me that I might prosper in my quest to show forth Your praise in the world. Do not allow the darkness around me, nor the dark desires within me, to gain any advantage against my soul. Strengthen me with Your Word, secure me in Your mercy and fill me with Your Spirit. Let the goodness of Your work within me give rise to Your worship around me.

(2:20–21) I cannot escape Your call; help me not to resist it. You have set Your love upon me and summoned me from above, calling me out of darkness into light. Now therefore, here in the midst of suffering I will sing! Though I am reproached, I will rejoice! When threatened with chaos I will answer with a chorus that declares Your great glory and spreads Your praise to others yet outside Your loving embrace. (1Pe 2:9; 3:9)

My Good Shepherd, who have shown Your very gentle mercy to us unworthy sinners in various physical pains and sufferings, give grace and strength to me, Your little lamb, that in no tribulation or anguish or pain may I turn away from you.

Saint Francis of Assisi (c.1181-1226)

(2:23–25) Shepherd of Love, You alone give justice to the oppressed, compassion to the afflicted, help to the helpless, strength to the weak and courage to the faint of heart. I am content, therefore, to trust in You when I suffer for doing what is right. Whether You lead me beside quiet waters or through the valley of the shadow of death, help me to follow You down the paths of righteousness, my Shepherd, and to gain wisdom from the experience. As Your wounds became my healing, so let my wounds be to Your glory. (Ps 23:2–4)

Shepherd of my soul,
I give You full control,
Wherever You may lead
I will follow.
I have made the choice
To listen to Your voice,
Wherever You may lead
I will go.

Be it in a quiet pasture
Or by a gentle stream,
The Shepherd of my soul
Is by my side.
Should I face a mighty mountain
Or a valley dark and deep
The Shepherd of my soul
Will be my guide.

"Shepherd of My Soul"
Martin Nystrom (©1988)

to everyone: Love the brotherhood of believers, fear God, honor
the king.
18Slaves, submit yourselves to your masters with all respect,
not only to those who are good and considerate, but also to those
who are harsh. 19For it is commendable if a man bears up under
the pain of unjust suffering because he is conscious of God. 20But
how is it to your credit if you receive a beating for doing wrong
and endure it? But if you suffer for doing good and you endure it,
this is commendable before God. 21To this you were called, because Christ suffered for you, leaving you an example, that you
should follow in his steps.

22"He committed no sin,
and no deceit was found in his mouth."[a]

23When they hurled their insults at him, he did not retaliate; when
he suffered, he made no threats. Instead, he entrusted himself to
him who judges justly. 24He himself bore our sins in his body on
the tree, so that we might die to sins and live for righteousness; by
his wounds you have been healed. 25For you were like sheep
going astray, but now you have returned to the Shepherd and
Overseer of your souls.

Wives and Husbands

3 Wives, in the same way be submissive to your husbands so
that, if any of them do not believe the word, they may be won
over without words by the behavior of their wives, 2when they see
the purity and reverence of your lives. 3Your beauty should not
come from outward adornment, such as braided hair and the
wearing of gold jewelry and fine clothes. 4Instead, it should be
that of your inner self, the unfading beauty of a gentle and quiet
spirit, which is of great worth in God's sight. 5For this is the way
the holy women of the past who put their hope in God used to
make themselves beautiful. They were submissive to their own
husbands, 6like Sarah, who obeyed Abraham and called him her
master. You are her daughters if you do what is right and do not
give way to fear.
7Husbands, in the same way be considerate as you live with
your wives, and treat them with respect as the weaker partner and
as heirs with you of the gracious gift of life, so that nothing will
hinder your prayers.

Suffering for Doing Good

8Finally, all of you, live in harmony with one another; be sympathetic, love as brothers, be compassionate and humble. 9Do
not repay evil with evil or insult with insult, but with blessing, because to this you were called so that you may inherit a blessing.
10For,

"Whoever would love life
and see good days
must keep his tongue from evil
and his lips from deceitful speech.
11He must turn from evil and do good;
he must seek peace and pursue it.
12For the eyes of the Lord are on the righteous
and his ears are attentive to their prayer,

[a] 22 Isaiah 53:9

but the face of the Lord is against those who do
evil."[a]

13Who is going to harm you if you are eager to do good? 14But
even if you should suffer for what is right, you are blessed. "Do
not fear what they fear[b]; do not be frightened."[c] 15But in your
hearts set apart Christ as Lord. Always be prepared to give an answer to everyone who asks you to give the reason for the hope
that you have. But do this with gentleness and respect, 16keeping
a clear conscience, so that those who speak maliciously against
your good behavior in Christ may be ashamed of their slander.
17It is better, if it is God's will, to suffer for doing good than for
doing evil. 18For Christ died for sins once for all, the righteous for
the unrighteous, to bring you to God. He was put to death in the
body but made alive by the Spirit, 19through whom[d] also he went
and preached to the spirits in prison 20who disobeyed long ago
when God waited patiently in the days of Noah while the ark was
being built. In it only a few people, eight in all, were saved
through water, 21and this water symbolizes baptism that now
saves you also—not the removal of dirt from the body but the
pledge[e] of a good conscience toward God. It saves you by the resurrection of Jesus Christ, 22who has gone into heaven and is at
God's right hand—with angels, authorities and powers in submission to him.

Living for God

4 Therefore, since Christ suffered in his body, arm yourselves
also with the same attitude, because he who has suffered in
his body is done with sin. 2As a result, he does not live the rest of
his earthly life for evil human desires, but rather for the will of
God. 3For you have spent enough time in the past doing what pagans choose to do—living in debauchery, lust, drunkenness, orgies, carousing and detestable idolatry. 4They think it strange that
you do not plunge with them into the same flood of dissipation,
and they heap abuse on you. 5But they will have to give account
to him who is ready to judge the living and the dead. 6For this is
the reason the gospel was preached even to those who are now
dead, so that they might be judged according to men in regard to
the body, but live according to God in regard to the spirit.
7The end of all things is near. Therefore be clear minded and
self-controlled so that you can pray. 8Above all, love each other
deeply, because love covers over a multitude of sins. 9Offer hospitality to one another without grumbling. 10Each one should use
whatever gift he has received to serve others, faithfully administering God's grace in its various forms. 11If anyone speaks, he
should do it as one speaking the very words of God. If anyone
serves, he should do it with the strength God provides, so that in
all things God may be praised through Jesus Christ. To him be the
glory and the power for ever and ever. Amen.

Suffering for Being a Christian

12Dear friends, do not be surprised at the painful trial you are
suffering, as though something strange were happening to you.
13But rejoice that you participate in the sufferings of Christ, so
that you may be overjoyed when his glory is revealed. 14If you are

[a] *12* Psalm 34:12–16 [b] *14* Or *not fear their threats* [c] *14* Isaiah 8:12 [d] *18,19* Or *alive in the spirit, 19through which* [e] *21* Or *response*

(4:1) As the world around me becomes increasingly hopeless, does Your work within me cause me to grow unceasingly hopeful? Does my face reflect Your peace? Do my thoughts express Your purposes, my deeds exemplify Your power and my lips proclaim Your praise? Am I a merchant of hope in a hopeless world? Does my light shine brighter as the room grows darker? Lord, use me that those who have no hope may find their hope in You.

Shine through me,
Shine through me,
Lord, make my life
A stream of light
For everyone to see.
A flowing, reaching, loving light
Is what I need to be;
So take control,
Ignite my soul,
And shine through me.

"Shine Through Me"
Gary Chapman (©1979)

As long as matters are really hopeful, hope is a mere flattery or platitude; it is only when everything is hopeless that hope begins to be a strength. Like all the Christian virtues, it is as unreasonable as it is indispensable.

G.K. Chesterton (1874-1936)

(4:14–16) If I were to say that I will not mention You or speak anymore in Your name, Your Word would be in my heart like a flame, a fire shut up in my bones. I would waste away from holding it in; indeed, I could not. So I will rejoice in being counted worthy of suffering disgrace for the Name, knowing that if I die with You I will live with You, and if I endure with You I will also reign with You. (Jer 20:9; Ac 5:41; 2Ti 2:11–12)

Jesus did not come to explain away suffering or remove it. He came to fill it with his presence.

Paul Claudel (1868-1955)

(5:5–6) How can I be humble without Your grace? I cannot. For humility without grace is just pride in disguise. In Your grace, O Lord, grant me the gift of humility. And in return accept all of my anxieties into Your caring hands.

Who is the man to whom
The Lord will have regard?
He who is broken
And has a humble heart.
God is not impressed
With the loftiness of man,
For everything was made for Him,
And comes from His own hand.

Humble yourself before your Lord
and King,
Give Him your heart, offer your
everything.
There's no limit on the love He has
for you,
So humble yourself and see what
God will do.

"Humble Yourself"
Kelly Willard (©1985)

insulted because of the name of Christ, you are blessed, for the
Spirit of glory and of God rests on you. 15If you suffer, it should
not be as a murderer or thief or any other kind of criminal, or
even as a meddler. 16However, if you suffer as a Christian, do not
be ashamed, but praise God that you bear that name. 17For it is
time for judgment to begin with the family of God; and if it begins
with us, what will the outcome be for those who do not obey the
gospel of God? 18And,

"If it is hard for the righteous to be saved,
what will become of the ungodly and the sinner?"[a]

19So then, those who suffer according to God's will should
commit themselves to their faithful Creator and continue to do
good.

To Elders and Young Men

5 To the elders among you, I appeal as a fellow elder, a witness
of Christ's sufferings and one who also will share in the glory
to be revealed: 2Be shepherds of God's flock that is under your
care, serving as overseers—not because you must, but because
you are willing, as God wants you to be; not greedy for money, but
eager to serve; 3not lording it over those entrusted to you, but
being examples to the flock. 4And when the Chief Shepherd appears, you will receive the crown of glory that will never fade
away.

5Young men, in the same way be submissive to those who are
older. All of you, clothe yourselves with humility toward one another, because,

"God opposes the proud
but gives grace to the humble."[b]

6Humble yourselves, therefore, under God's mighty hand, that he
may lift you up in due time. 7Cast all your anxiety on him because
he cares for you.
8Be self-controlled and alert. Your enemy the devil prowls
around like a roaring lion looking for someone to devour. 9Resist
him, standing firm in the faith, because you know that your brothers throughout the world are undergoing the same kind of sufferings.
10And the God of all grace, who called you to his eternal glory
in Christ, after you have suffered a little while, will himself restore
you and make you strong, firm and steadfast. 11To him be the
power for ever and ever. Amen.

Final Greetings

12With the help of Silas,[c] whom I regard as a faithful brother,
I have written to you briefly, encouraging you and testifying that
this is the true grace of God. Stand fast in it.
13She who is in Babylon, chosen together with you, sends you
her greetings, and so does my son Mark. 14Greet one another
with a kiss of love.

Peace to all of you who are in Christ.

[a] 18 Prov. 11:31 [b] 5 Prov. 3:34 [c] 12 Greek *Silvanus*, a variant of *Silas*

1

Simon Peter, a servant and apostle of Jesus Christ,

To those who through the righteousness of our God and Savior
Jesus Christ have received a faith as precious as ours:

2 Grace and peace be yours in abundance through the knowledge of God and of Jesus our Lord.

Making One's Calling and Election Sure

3 His divine power has given us everything we need for life and
godliness through our knowledge of him who called us by his
own glory and goodness. 4 Through these he has given us his very
great and precious promises, so that through them you may participate in the divine nature and escape the corruption in the
world caused by evil desires.

5 For this very reason, make every effort to add to your faith
goodness; and to goodness, knowledge; 6 and to knowledge, self-
control; and to self-control, perseverance; and to perseverance,
godliness; 7 and to godliness, brotherly kindness; and to brotherly kindness, love. 8 For if you possess these qualities in increasing measure, they will keep you from being ineffective and
unproductive in your knowledge of our Lord Jesus Christ. 9 But if
anyone does not have them, he is nearsighted and blind, and has
forgotten that he has been cleansed from his past sins.

10 Therefore, my brothers, be all the more eager to make your
calling and election sure. For if you do these things, you will
never fall, 11 and you will receive a rich welcome into the eternal
kingdom of our Lord and Savior Jesus Christ.

Prophecy of Scripture

12 So I will always remind you of these things, even though you
know them and are firmly established in the truth you now have.
13 I think it is right to refresh your memory as long as I live in the
tent of this body, 14 because I know that I will soon put it aside, as
our Lord Jesus Christ has made clear to me. 15 And I will make
every effort to see that after my departure you will always be able
to remember these things.

16 We did not follow cleverly invented stories when we told you
about the power and coming of our Lord Jesus Christ, but we
were eyewitnesses of his majesty. 17 For he received honor and
glory from God the Father when the voice came to him from the
Majestic Glory, saying, "This is my Son, whom I love; with him I
am well pleased."[a] 18 We ourselves heard this voice that came
from heaven when we were with him on the sacred mountain.

19 And we have the word of the prophets made more certain,
and you will do well to pay attention to it, as to a light shining in
a dark place, until the day dawns and the morning star rises in
your hearts. 20 Above all, you must understand that no prophecy
of Scripture came about by the prophet's own interpretation.
21 For prophecy never had its origin in the will of man, but men
spoke from God as they were carried along by the Holy Spirit.

False Teachers and Their Destruction

2

But there were also false prophets among the people, just as
there will be false teachers among you. They will secretly introduce destructive heresies, even denying the sovereign Lord

[a] *17* Matt. 17:5; Mark 9:7; Luke 9:35

(1:1–8) Your glory and goodness have called me; Your grace and peace have filled me. Knowing You is my soul's delight. You gave me this most precious faith and continually strengthen it with Your unfailing power. You cleanse me from this world's corruption and empower my life with the great promises in Your Word. By Your grace, Lord, I will make every effort to grow in every way—in goodness, knowledge, patience, hope and brotherly love. I will press on along the upward way, keeping my eyes fixed upon You. (Php 3:12–14)

Jesus did not say, "Come to me and get it over with." He said, "If any man would come after me, let him take up his cross daily and follow me." Daily is the key word. Our commitment to Christ, however genuine and whole-hearted it may be today, must be renewed tomorrow . . . and the day after that . . . and the day after that . . . until the path comes at last to the river.

Louis Cassels (1922–1974)

Living for Jesus a life that is true,
Striving to please Him in all that I do,
Yielding allegiance gladhearted and free,
This is the pathway of blessing for me.

O Jesus, Lord and Savior,
I give myself to Thee;
For Thou, in Thy atonement,
Didst give Thyself for me.
I own no other master;
My heart shall be Thy throne.
My life I give, henceforth to live,
O Christ, for Thee alone.

"Living for Jesus"
Thomas O. Chisholm (1917)

who bought them—bringing swift destruction on themselves.
2Many will follow their shameful ways and will bring the way of
truth into disrepute. 3In their greed these teachers will exploit
you with stories they have made up. Their condemnation has long
been hanging over them, and their destruction has not been
sleeping.
4For if God did not spare angels when they sinned, but sent
them to hell,[a] putting them into gloomy dungeons[b] to be held for
judgment; 5if he did not spare the ancient world when he brought
the flood on its ungodly people, but protected Noah, a preacher
of righteousness, and seven others; 6if he condemned the cities of
Sodom and Gomorrah by burning them to ashes, and made them
an example of what is going to happen to the ungodly; 7and if he
rescued Lot, a righteous man, who was distressed by the filthy
lives of lawless men 8(for that righteous man, living among them
day after day, was tormented in his righteous soul by the lawless
deeds he saw and heard)— 9if this is so, then the Lord knows
how to rescue godly men from trials and to hold the unrighteous
for the day of judgment, while continuing their punishment.[c]
10This is especially true of those who follow the corrupt desire of
the sinful nature[d] and despise authority.

Bold and arrogant, these men are not afraid to slander celestial beings;
11yet even angels, although they are stronger and
more powerful, do not bring slanderous accusations against such
beings in the presence of the Lord. 12But these men blaspheme in
matters they do not understand. They are like brute beasts, creatures of instinct, born only to be caught and destroyed, and like beasts they too will perish.

13They will be paid back with harm for the harm they have
done. Their idea of pleasure is to carouse in broad daylight. They
are blots and blemishes, reveling in their pleasures while they
feast with you.[e] 14With eyes full of adultery, they never stop sinning; they seduce the unstable; they are experts in greed—an accursed brood!
15They have left the straight way and wandered off
to follow the way of Balaam son of Beor, who loved the wages of
wickedness. 16But he was rebuked for his wrongdoing by a donkey—a beast without speech—who spoke with a man's voice and restrained the prophet's madness.
17These men are springs without water and mists driven by a
storm. Blackest darkness is reserved for them. 18For they mouth
empty, boastful words and, by appealing to the lustful desires of
sinful human nature, they entice people who are just escaping
from those who live in error. 19They promise them freedom,
while they themselves are slaves of depravity—for a man is a
slave to whatever has mastered him. 20If they have escaped the
corruption of the world by knowing our Lord and Savior Jesus
Christ and are again entangled in it and overcome, they are worse
off at the end than they were at the beginning. 21It would have
been better for them not to have known the way of righteousness,
than to have known it and then to turn their backs on the sacred
command that was passed on to them. 22Of them the proverbs
are true: "A dog returns to its vomit,"[f] and, "A sow that is washed
goes back to her wallowing in the mud."

[a] 4 Greek *Tartarus* [b] 4 Some manuscripts *into chains of darkness* [c] 9 Or *unrighteous for punishment until the day of judgment* [d] 10 Or *the flesh*
[e] 13 Some manuscripts *in their love feasts* [f] 22 Prov. 26:11

(2:9) Mighty angels have fallen from heaven, famous cities have been destroyed by fire, and the entire world was once covered with a flood in judgment. Who am I to think I can overcome sin when so many others have failed so miserably? How I thank You, Almighty God! By the power of Your Spirit You will deliver me from temptation and the torment of sin, and I in turn will show forth Your praise. (Ro 7:24–25)

Eternal and most glorious God, you have stamped the soul of humanity with your Image, received it into your revenue, and made it part of your treasure; do not allow us so to undervalue ourselves, so to impoverish you, as to give away these souls for nothing, and all the world is nothing if the soul must be given for it. Do this, O God, for his sake who knows our natural infirmities, for he had them, and knows the weight of our sins, for he paid a dear price for them; your Son, our Savior Jesus Christ.

John Donne (1572–1631)

(2:17) During periods of drought a cloud represents a promise of rain. During times of thirst a spring is a promise of refreshment. Am I keeping my promises? I come to You, Lord, that out of my innermost being may flow rivers of living water to refresh the weary and sustain those who thirst for You. (Jn 7:38)

A charge to keep I have,
A God to glorify,
Who gave His Son my soul to save,
And fit it for the sky.

Help me to watch and pray,
And still on Thee rely,
O let me not my trust betray,
But press to realms on high.

"A Charge to Keep I Have"
Charles Wesley (1762)

MY BELOVED

Are you experiencing many trials? Do not be afraid any longer. You belong to Me. I called you by name and you are Mine. So when you pass through threatening waters, I will be with you. Even rushing rivers will not sweep over you.

When you walk through fire, you will not be burned. Those flames that you feel will not set you ablaze. For I am the Lord, your God, your Savior. I take hold of your right hand and say to you, "Do not be afraid." I will help you.

I will make rivers flow on your barren heights and springs within the valleys. I will turn the desert into pools of water and the parched ground into springs. People will see and know that I have done this with My own hand, that the Holy One of Israel has created it. So cry out for Me when you are surrounded by trouble and be confident that I will deliver you.

Remember that My eyes are upon you and My ears hear your voice every time you cry out. My promise to you is that I will deliver you from all your troubles. You see, I am close to the brokenhearted and I save those who are crushed in spirit. Though you may have many troubles, I will deliver you out of them all! For you are Mine.

Ps 34:15,17-19; 50:15; Isa 41:10,13,18-20; 43:1-3; 2Pe 2:9

The Day of the Lord

3 Dear friends, this is now my second letter to you. I have written both of them as reminders to stimulate you to wholesome
thinking. 2I want you to recall the words spoken in the past by the
holy prophets and the command given by our Lord and Savior
through your apostles.
3First of all, you must understand that in the last days scoffers
will come, scoffing and following their own evil desires. 4They
will say, "Where is this 'coming' he promised? Ever since our fathers died, everything goes on as it has since the beginning of creation." 5But they deliberately forget that long ago by God's word
the heavens existed and the earth was formed out of water and by
water. 6By these waters also the world of that time was deluged
and destroyed. 7By the same word the present heavens and earth
are reserved for fire, being kept for the day of judgment and destruction of ungodly men.
8But do not forget this one thing, dear friends: With the Lord a
day is like a thousand years, and a thousand years are like a day.
9The Lord is not slow in keeping his promise, as some understand slowness. He is patient with you, not wanting anyone to perish, but everyone to come to repentance.
10But the day of the Lord will come like a thief. The heavens
will disappear with a roar; the elements will be destroyed by fire,
and the earth and everything in it will be laid bare.[a]
11Since everything will be destroyed in this way, what kind of
people ought you to be? You ought to live holy and godly lives
12as you look forward to the day of God and speed its coming.[b]
That day will bring about the destruction of the heavens by fire,
and the elements will melt in the heat. 13But in keeping with his
promise we are looking forward to a new heaven and a new
earth, the home of righteousness.
14So then, dear friends, since you are looking forward to this,
make every effort to be found spotless, blameless and at peace
with him. 15Bear in mind that our Lord's patience means salvation, just as our dear brother Paul also wrote you with the
wisdom that God gave him. 16He writes the same way in all his
letters, speaking in them of these matters. His letters contain
some things that are hard to understand, which ignorant and
unstable people distort, as they do the other Scriptures, to their
own destruction.
17Therefore, dear friends, since you already know this, be on
your guard so that you may not be carried away by the error of
lawless men and fall from your secure position. 18But grow in the
grace and knowledge of our Lord and Savior Jesus Christ. To him
be glory both now and forever! Amen.

[a] *10* Some manuscripts *be burned up* [b] *12* Or *as you wait eagerly for the day of God to come*

(3:9) Lord, fill my heart with Your love for the lost, for You take no pleasure in the death of the wicked. Teach me to be patient and passionate in helping others come to know and love You, even as You know and love them. May Your presence in my life inspire others to put their faith in Christ alone. (Eze 33:11)

Heaven is filled with converted sinners of all kinds and there is room for more.

Joseph Cafasso (1811–1860)

(3:14) If ever there was a need for beauty and grace it is now. The land is dark with evil and the people of God are divided into rival camps. O God, let the trumpet of praise be heard on the earth before the great trumpet of judgment rips open the sky! Empower us with an extraordinary anointing to lift our voices and instruments in harmony to call Your scattered people together in unity. One day we shall sing the song of the Lamb around Your throne in heaven. Lead us in a dress rehearsal while we yet live on the earth! (Rev 15:3)

1, 2 & 3 John

The Epistles General of JOHN

Sometimes we picture worship as a long-distance phone call to a God who hears us from a far off heaven. We communicate with Him, but more impersonally than intimately. The letters of John, on the contrary, invite us into close fellowship with God that forever transforms our experience of worship.

The three letters usually attributed to John are actually anonymous, although many similarities between them and the Gospel of John have led to the traditional conclusion that they were written by the man who penned the fourth Gospel and the book of Revelation. John writes primarily to encourage Christians who are grappling with false teachers. The lure of these "deceivers" is especially tempting because they were once a part of the community to which John writes (1Jn 2:19; 2Jn 1:7). So he urges his spiritual children to remain in the truth they have believed from the beginning and to express their faith by loving one another (1Jn 2:24; 3:23).

John envisions the Christian life as an intimate relationship between us, our triune God, and our Christian family. He writes so that his letters' recipients "may have fellowship with us. And our fellowship is with the Father and with his Son, Jesus Christ" (1Jn 1:3–4). Life in Christ is sharing in God, through Whom we also share with one another (1Jn 1:7). In worship, therefore, we do not stand back at a distance, but rather enter into close fellowship with God and with those who join us in worship.

Genuine fellowship with God will always include fellowship with God's people. True love for God must spill over onto others.

John uses a favorite Greek verb to explain the depth of our relationship with God. This verb, *meno*, means "to live, to remain, to continue, to abide." When we first believe in Jesus, we begin to live in God (1Jn 4:15). We remain in both the Son and the Father (1Jn 2:24). We know this because of the Holy Spirit Who has been given to us (1Jn 3:24). Through the Spirit, God lives in us (1Jn 4:15).

By his use of the verb *meno* to characterize our relationship with God, John erases the picture of a distant deity dwelling on a far away cloud. When we believe in Jesus, we live in God and God lives in us. Therefore, worship is not long-distance communication; it is intimate communion. We share in the very life of God. We love God because we are surrounded and filled with His love, the unparalleled love given through Jesus Christ (1Jn 4:9–10).

Yet we must express this love, not only for God but also for God's people. As John urges, "Dear friends, since God so loved us, we also ought to love one another" (1Jn 4:11). Moreover, "If anyone says, 'I love God,' yet hates his brother, he is a liar. For anyone who does not love his brother, whom he has seen, cannot love God, whom he has not seen" (1Jn 4:20). Genuine fellowship with God will always include fellowship with God's people. True love for God must spill over onto others.

The Word of Life

1 That which was from the beginning, which we have heard,
which we have seen with our eyes, which we have looked at
and our hands have touched—this we proclaim concerning the
Word of life. 2The life appeared; we have seen it and testify to it,
and we proclaim to you the eternal life, which was with the Father and has appeared to us. 3We proclaim to you what we have
seen and heard, so that you also may have fellowship with us.
And our fellowship is with the Father and with his Son, Jesus
Christ. 4We write this to make our[a] joy complete.

Walking in the Light

5This is the message we have heard from him and declare to
you: God is light; in him there is no darkness at all. 6If we claim
to have fellowship with him yet walk in the darkness, we lie and
do not live by the truth. 7But if we walk in the light, as he is in the
light, we have fellowship with one another, and the blood of Jesus,
his Son, purifies us from all[b] sin.
8If we claim to be without sin, we deceive ourselves and the
truth is not in us. 9If we confess our sins, he is faithful and just
and will forgive us our sins and purify us from all unrighteousness. 10If we claim we have not sinned, we make him out to be a
liar and his word has no place in our lives.

2 My dear children, I write this to you so that you will not sin.
But if anybody does sin, we have one who speaks to the Father in our defense—Jesus Christ, the Righteous One. 2He is the
atoning sacrifice for our sins, and not only for ours but also for[c]
the sins of the whole world.
3We know that we have come to know him if we obey his commands. 4The man who says, "I know him," but does not do what
he commands is a liar, and the truth is not in him. 5But if anyone
obeys his word, God's love[d] is truly made complete in him. This
is how we know we are in him: 6Whoever claims to live in him
must walk as Jesus did.
7Dear friends, I am not writing you a new command but an old
one, which you have had since the beginning. This old command
is the message you have heard. 8Yet I am writing you a new command; its truth is seen in him and you, because the darkness is
passing and the true light is already shining.
9Anyone who claims to be in the light but hates his brother is
still in the darkness. 10Whoever loves his brother lives in the
light, and there is nothing in him[e] to make him stumble. 11But
whoever hates his brother is in the darkness and walks around in
the darkness; he does not know where he is going, because the
darkness has blinded him.

12I write to you, dear children,
because your sins have been forgiven on account of
his name.
13I write to you, fathers,
because you have known him who is from the
beginning.
I write to you, young men,
because you have overcome the evil one.

[a] 4 Some manuscripts *your* [b] 7 Or *every* [c] 2 Or *He is the one who turns aside God's wrath, taking away our sins, and not only ours but also* [d] 5 Or *word, love for God* [e] 10 Or *it*

It is only because we follow Jesus that we can be genuinely truthful, for then He reveals to us our sin upon the cross. The cross is God's truth about us, and therefore it is the only power which can make us truthful. When we know the cross we are no longer afraid of the truth.

Dietrich Bonhoeffer (1906-1945)

(1:8–9) An honest confession is all You ask. No hoops to jump through, no self-flagellation, and certainly no pay-offs or imprisonment. Just an acknowledgement of the truth—truth that You already know, truth that I have to admit. There is nothing I can do to earn Your forgiveness. I can only surrender to it. Christ died for sinners while we were sinners. The price has already been paid. Here I am, Lord, a sinner in need of a Savior. Purify me with the blood of Jesus. In Your faithfulness and justice, please forgive me and make me clean. (Ro 5:8; 1Ti 1:15)

Hide me, Lord, in Your holiness,
Ev'ry sin I now confess.
Praise to You, forgiving Lord,
Hide me in Your holiness
Hide me in Your holiness.

"Hide Me In Your Holiness"
Steve Ragsdale (©1986)

I write to you, dear children,
because you have known the Father.
14 I write to you, fathers,
because you have known him who is from the beginning.
I write to you, young men,
because you are strong,
and the word of God lives in you,
and you have overcome the evil one.

(2:15–17) Lord, we are pilgrims and sojourners in this world, moving toward the eternal future You have planned for us. Yet we are easily distracted from our destination by all the activity that swirls around us—the sights and sounds, the pride and passion, the lusts and longings that spring from human nature. Give us greater vision, Lord! Grant us a glimpse of eternity, and keep our eyes fixed on You and on the everlasting life You have prepared for us. (1Co 2:9)

Do Not Love the World

15 Do not love the world or anything in the world. If anyone
loves the world, the love of the Father is not in him. 16 For everything in the world—the cravings of sinful man, the lust of his eyes
and the boasting of what he has and does—comes not from the
Father but from the world. 17 The world and its desires pass away,
but the man who does the will of God lives forever.

As we begin to focus upon God, the things of the Spirit will take shape before our inner eyes.

A.W. Tozer (1897-1963)

Warning Against Antichrists

18 Dear children, this is the last hour; and as you have heard
that the antichrist is coming, even now many antichrists have
come. This is how we know it is the last hour. 19 They went out
from us, but they did not really belong to us. For if they had belonged to us, they would have remained with us; but their going
showed that none of them belonged to us.
20 But you have an anointing from the Holy One, and all of you
know the truth.[a] 21 I do not write to you because you do not know
the truth, but because you do know it and because no lie comes
from the truth. 22 Who is the liar? It is the man who denies that
Jesus is the Christ. Such a man is the antichrist—he denies the
Father and the Son. 23 No one who denies the Son has the Father;
whoever acknowledges the Son has the Father also.
24 See that what you have heard from the beginning remains in
you. If it does, you also will remain in the Son and in the Father.
25 And this is what he promised us—even eternal life.
26 I am writing these things to you about those who are trying
to lead you astray. 27 As for you, the anointing you received from
him remains in you, and you do not need anyone to teach you.
But as his anointing teaches you about all things and as that
anointing is real, not counterfeit—just as it has taught you, remain in him.

Be Thou my vision,
O Lord of my heart;
Nought be all else to me,
Save that Thou art.
Thou my best thought,
By day or by night,
Waking or sleeping,
Thy presence my light.

"Be Thou My Vision"
Ancient Irish Poem (8th c.)
Trans. Mary E. Byrne (1880-1931)
Versified Eleanor H. Hull (1860-1935)

Children of God

28 And now, dear children, continue in him, so that when he
appears we may be confident and unashamed before him at his
coming.
29 If you know that he is righteous, you know that everyone who
does what is right has been born of him.

(3:1–3) How can we thank You, Father, for adopting us as Your sons and daughters? And how can we even begin to grasp what that adoption really means? For reasons we will never understand, You have chosen us to be heirs of a heavenly legacy, and even more remarkably to be joint-heirs with Your only begotten Son. We are so grateful, Lord; and in our gratitude we long to be like Jesus. Transform us into His likeness, so that in this life, as well as in the life to come, we will come to bear a family resemblance to Him. (Ro 8:17; 2Co 3:18)

3 How great is the love the Father has lavished on us, that we
should be called children of God! And that is what we are!
The reason the world does not know us is that it did not know
him. 2 Dear friends, now we are children of God, and what we will
be has not yet been made known. But we know that when he appears,[b] we shall be like him, for we shall see him as he is. 3 Everyone who has this hope in him purifies himself, just as he is pure.

[a] 20 Some manuscripts *and you know all things* [b] 2 Or *when it is made known*

4Everyone who sins breaks the law; in fact, sin is lawlessness.
5But you know that he appeared so that he might take away our
sins. And in him is no sin. 6No one who lives in him keeps on sinning. No one who continues to sin has either seen him or known
him.
7Dear children, do not let anyone lead you astray. He who does
what is right is righteous, just as he is righteous. 8He who does
what is sinful is of the devil, because the devil has been sinning
from the beginning. The reason the Son of God appeared was to
destroy the devil's work. 9No one who is born of God will continue to sin, because God's seed remains in him; he cannot go on
sinning, because he has been born of God. 10This is how we
know who the children of God are and who the children of the
devil are: Anyone who does not do what is right is not a child of
God; nor is anyone who does not love his brother.

Love One Another

11This is the message you heard from the beginning: We
should love one another. 12Do not be like Cain, who belonged to
the evil one and murdered his brother. And why did he murder
him? Because his own actions were evil and his brother's were
righteous. 13Do not be surprised, my brothers, if the world hates
you. 14We know that we have passed from death to life, because
we love our brothers. Anyone who does not love remains in
death. 15Anyone who hates his brother is a murderer, and you
know that no murderer has eternal life in him.
16This is how we know what love is: Jesus Christ laid down his
life for us. And we ought to lay down our lives for our brothers.
17If anyone has material possessions and sees his brother in need
but has no pity on him, how can the love of God be in him?
18Dear children, let us not love with words or tongue but with
actions and in truth. 19This then is how we know that we belong
to the truth, and how we set our hearts at rest in his presence
20whenever our hearts condemn us. For God is greater than our
hearts, and he knows everything.
21Dear friends, if our hearts do not condemn us, we have confidence before God 22and receive from him anything we ask, because we obey his commands and do what pleases him. 23And
this is his command: to believe in the name of his Son, Jesus
Christ, and to love one another as he commanded us. 24Those
who obey his commands live in him, and he in them. And this is
how we know that he lives in us: We know it by the Spirit he
gave us.

Test the Spirits

4 Dear friends, do not believe every spirit, but test the spirits to
see whether they are from God, because many false prophets
have gone out into the world. 2This is how you can recognize the
Spirit of God: Every spirit that acknowledges that Jesus Christ has
come in the flesh is from God, 3but every spirit that does not acknowledge Jesus is not from God. This is the spirit of the antichrist, which you have heard is coming and even now is already
in the world.
4You, dear children, are from God and have overcome them,
because the one who is in you is greater than the one who is in
the world. 5They are from the world and therefore speak from the
viewpoint of the world, and the world listens to them. 6We are

(3:11–20) Jesus, teach us to love as You love, and teach us the meaning of love as Your Word defines it. Help us practice patience and kindness. Remove from us envy and pride, rudeness and selfishness, and the holding of grudges. Teach us to protect one another from harm, to trust each other without cynicism, to hope for one another's best and to persevere even when we feel like walking away. You have taught us to overcome evil with good; teach us also to overcome hatred and indifference with Your holy, heavenly love. (Ro 12:21; 1Co 13:4–7)

Give us love, sweetest of all gifts, which knows no enemy. Give us in our hearts pure love, born of your love to us, that we may love others as you love us. O most loving Father of Jesus Christ, from whom flows all love, let our hearts, frozen in sin, cold to you and cold to others, be warmed by this divine fire. So help and bless us in your Son. Amen.

St. Anselm (1033-1109)

Unshakable, immovable,
Faithful and true;
Full of wisdom, strength and beauty:
These things are true of You.
Fearless, courageous,
Righteousness shines
Through in all You do;
Yet You're so humble,
You laid down Your life:
These things are true of You.

And as I turn my face to You,
Oh Lord, I ask and pray,
By the power of Your love and
grace,
Make these things true of me, too,
Make these things true of me, too.

"These Things are True of You"
Tommy Walker (©1996)

(4:7–12) Lord, You have provided a simple but sobering test of Christian spirituality—our love for You can be measured by our love for others. And we have all, without exception, failed Your test. Every time we refuse to lend a helping hand, to listen to a hurting friend, to curb a critical tongue, we refuse to love You or to obey Your commandments. Strip away our selfishness, Lord, and help us learn to love our neighbors as ourselves, and in doing so to love You wholeheartedly. (Mt 22:34–40; 25:34–45)

Once you say the yes of faith to Jesus and accept his blueprint for the fullness of life, the whole world can no longer revolve around you, your needs, your gratifications; you'll have to revolve around the world, seeking to bandage its wounds, loving dead men into life, finding the lost, wanting the unwanted, and leaving far behind all the selfish, parasitical concerns which drain our time and energies.

John Powell (1927-)

Patient, compassionate,
Love flows through You;
You never give up on the hopeless
ones:
These things are true of You.
Holy and blameless,
You stand up for justice and truth;
Yet You love mercy and forgiveness:
These things are true of You.

And as I turn my face to You,
Oh Lord, I ask and pray,
By the power of Your love and
grace,
Make these things true of me, too.
Make these things true of me, too.

"These Things Are True Of You"
Tommy Walker (©1996)

from God, and whoever knows God listens to us; but whoever is
not from God does not listen to us. This is how we recognize the
Spirit[a] of truth and the spirit of falsehood.

God's Love and Ours

7Dear friends, let us love one another, for love comes from
God. Everyone who loves has been born of God and knows God.
8Whoever does not love does not know God, because God is love.
9This is how God showed his love among us: He sent his one and
only Son[b] into the world that we might live through him. 10This is
love: not that we loved God, but that he loved us and sent his Son
as an atoning sacrifice for[c] our sins. 11Dear friends, since God so
loved us, we also ought to love one another. 12No one has ever
seen God; but if we love one another, God lives in us and his love
is made complete in us.

13We know that we live in him and he in us, because he has
given us of his Spirit. 14And we have seen and testify that the Father has sent his Son to be the Savior of the world. 15If anyone acknowledges that Jesus is the Son of God, God lives in him and he
in God. 16And so we know and rely on the love God has for us.

God is love. Whoever lives in love lives in God, and God in him.
17In this way, love is made complete among us so that we will
have confidence on the day of judgment, because in this world we
are like him. 18There is no fear in love. But perfect love drives out
fear, because fear has to do with punishment. The one who fears
is not made perfect in love.

19We love because he first loved us. 20If anyone says, "I love
God," yet hates his brother, he is a liar. For anyone who does not
love his brother, whom he has seen, cannot love God, whom he
has not seen. 21And he has given us this command: Whoever loves
God must also love his brother.

Faith in the Son of God

5 Everyone who believes that Jesus is the Christ is born of God,
and everyone who loves the father loves his child as well.
2This is how we know that we love the children of God: by loving
God and carrying out his commands. 3This is love for God: to
obey his commands. And his commands are not burdensome,
4for everyone born of God overcomes the world. This is the victory that has overcome the world, even our faith. 5Who is it that
overcomes the world? Only he who believes that Jesus is the Son
of God.

6This is the one who came by water and blood—Jesus Christ.
He did not come by water only, but by water and blood. And it is
the Spirit who testifies, because the Spirit is the truth. 7For there
are three that testify: 8the[d] Spirit, the water and the blood; and
the three are in agreement. 9We accept man's testimony, but
God's testimony is greater because it is the testimony of God,
which he has given about his Son. 10Anyone who believes in the
Son of God has this testimony in his heart. Anyone who does not
believe God has made him out to be a liar, because he has not
believed the testimony God has given about his Son. 11And this is
the testimony: God has given us eternal life, and this life is in his

[a] *6* Or *spirit* [b] *9* Or *his only begotten Son* [c] *10* Or *as the one who would turn aside his wrath, taking away* [d] *7,8* Late manuscripts of the Vulgate *testify in heaven: the Father, the Word and the Holy Spirit, and these three are one. 8And there are three that testify on earth: the* (not found in any Greek manuscript before the sixteenth century)

Son. 12He who has the Son has life; he who does not have the
Son of God does not have life.

Concluding Remarks

13I write these things to you who believe in the name of the
Son of God so that you may know that you have eternal life. 14This
is the confidence we have in approaching God: that if we ask anything according to his will, he hears us. 15And if we know that he
hears us—whatever we ask—we know that we have what we
asked of him.
16If anyone sees his brother commit a sin that does not lead to
death, he should pray and God will give him life. I refer to those
whose sin does not lead to death. There is a sin that leads to
death. I am not saying that he should pray about that. 17All
wrongdoing is sin, and there is sin that does not lead to death.
18We know that anyone born of God does not continue to sin;
the one who was born of God keeps him safe, and the evil one
cannot harm him. 19We know that we are children of God, and
that the whole world is under the control of the evil one. 20We
know also that the Son of God has come and has given us understanding, so that we may know him who is true. And we are in
him who is true—even in his Son Jesus Christ. He is the true God
and eternal life.
21Dear children, keep yourselves from idols.

(5:13–15) Thank You for the privilege of prayer, Father. Throughout Your Word You challenge us to pray, to ask, to seek, to call upon You, expressing both our needs and our desires. Again and again You have promised to answer us, responding to our requests as a kindhearted Father responds to a little child. As we grow in our faith, teach us to want what You want, Lord, so that our prayers will be more fruitful. And eventually, may our most heartfelt prayer echo the words of Jesus: "Not my will, but yours be done." (Lk 22:42)

The one thing God wants most from you in prayer is YOU.

Robert Bakke (1950-)

Who are the people
That the Lord will bless?
Those who love and fear Him
And seek His righteousness.
Nothing else in all the world
Can satisfy your soul;
But the One who made the universe,
He longs to make you whole.

Humble yourself and let Him have
His way,
Love His Word, and His will obey.
For His eyes are on the one whose
heart is true.
So humble yourself and see what
God will do.

"Humble Yourself"
Kelly Willard (©1985)

(vv. 1–13) Heavenly Father, Your Gospel is deep and rich and powerful, but it is also astonishingly simple: In love You sent Your only Son to reconcile the world to Yourself, and You require those who come to You through Him to love one another. Give us discernment, Lord, so that we are not distracted from Your intentions. Give us transformed minds so we are able to overcome our innate selfishness. And give us perseverance, so we can continue in Your will—receiving love from You, passing it on to others and thus fulfilling the Gospel. (Jn 3:16; 1Jn 4:11–12)

What does love look like? It has hands to help others. It has feet to hasten to the poor and needy. It has eyes to see misery and want. It has ears to hear the sighs and sorrows of men. That is what love looks like.

Saint Augustine of Hippo (354-430)

Walk in the light!
And you shall know
That fellowship of love
His Spirit only can bestow
Who reigns in light above.

Walk in the light!
And you shall find
Your heart made truly His,
Who dwells in cloudless light
enshrined,
In whom no darkness is.

Walk in the light!
And you shall share
Your path, though thorny, bright;
For God in grace walks with you
there,
And God Himself is light.

"Walk in the Light"
Bernard Barton (1826)

1 The elder,

To the chosen lady and her children, whom I love in the
truth—and not I only, but also all who know the truth— 2 because of the truth, which lives in us and will be with us forever:

3 Grace, mercy and peace from God the Father and from Jesus
Christ, the Father's Son, will be with us in truth and love.

4 It has given me great joy to find some of your children walking in the truth, just as the Father commanded us. 5 And now, dear
lady, I am not writing you a new command but one we have had
from the beginning. I ask that we love one another. 6 And this is
love: that we walk in obedience to his commands. As you have
heard from the beginning, his command is that you walk in love.

7 Many deceivers, who do not acknowledge Jesus Christ as
coming in the flesh, have gone out into the world. Any such person is the deceiver and the antichrist. 8 Watch out that you do not
lose what you have worked for, but that you may be rewarded
fully. 9 Anyone who runs ahead and does not continue in the
teaching of Christ does not have God; whoever continues in the
teaching has both the Father and the Son. 10 If anyone comes to
you and does not bring this teaching, do not take him into your
house or welcome him. 11 Anyone who welcomes him shares in
his wicked work.

12 I have much to write to you, but I do not want to use paper
and ink. Instead, I hope to visit you and talk with you face to face,
so that our joy may be complete.

13 The children of your chosen sister send their greetings.

1The elder,

To my dear friend Gaius, whom I love in the truth.

2Dear friend, I pray that you may enjoy good health and that all
may go well with you, even as your soul is getting along well. 3It
gave me great joy to have some brothers come and tell about your
faithfulness to the truth and how you continue to walk in the
truth. 4I have no greater joy than to hear that my children are
walking in the truth.
5Dear friend, you are faithful in what you are doing for the
brothers, even though they are strangers to you. 6They have told
the church about your love. You will do well to send them on
their way in a manner worthy of God. 7It was for the sake of the
Name that they went out, receiving no help from the pagans. 8We
ought therefore to show hospitality to such men so that we may
work together for the truth.
9I wrote to the church, but Diotrephes, who loves to be first,
will have nothing to do with us. 10So if I come, I will call attention
to what he is doing, gossiping maliciously about us. Not satisfied
with that, he refuses to welcome the brothers. He also stops those
who want to do so and puts them out of the church.
11Dear friend, do not imitate what is evil but what is good. Anyone who does what is good is from God. Anyone who does what
is evil has not seen God. 12Demetrius is well spoken of by everyone—and even by the truth itself. We also speak well of him, and
you know that our testimony is true.
13I have much to write you, but I do not want to do so with pen
and ink. 14I hope to see you soon, and we will talk face to face.

Peace to you. The friends here send their greetings. Greet the
friends there by name.

Faith, like light, should always be simple and unbending; while love, like warmth, should beam forth on every side and bend to every necessity of our brethren.

Martin Luther (1483-1546)

(vv. 1–14) The eternal battle between good and evil, Lord, is acted out in everyday relationships between ordinary people. Good triumphs through generosity, hospitality and courtesy. Evil makes inroads through pride, gossip and divisiveness. As John reminds us, our daily behavior reflects the condition of our souls. Help us, Lord, to act in loving ways even when we don't feel like loving; and continue to change our hearts until we do. Amen.

More like the Master I would ever be,
More of His meekness, more humility;
More zeal to labor, more courage to be true,
More consecration for work He bids me do.

More like the Master is my daily prayer
More strength to carry crosses I must bear;
More earnest effort to bring His kingdom in,
More of His Spirit, the wanderer to win.

"More Like the Master"
Charles H. Gabriel (1906)

Jude

The General Epistle of JUDE

The author of this letter identifies himself simply as "Jude, a servant of Jesus Christ and a brother of James" (v. 1). Traditionally, he has been identified as Judas, one of the brothers of James, who was also the brother of Jesus of Nazareth. This Jude was not a follower of Jesus during Christ's earthly ministry but became a Christian and church leader sometime after Jesus' ascension.

The short letter from Jude confronts the problem of false teachers in the church. Certain people secretly slipped into a Christian community, where they taught their heresies while living immorally (v. 4). Jude urges the recipients of his letter to "contend for the faith that was once for all entrusted to the saints" (v. 3). Christian truth is not something to be taken for granted or valued lightly. When it is threatened by false teaching, we must vigorously fight for the truth. To illustrate his point, Jude draws broadly from Jewish tradition, using Biblical and extra-biblical examples, much as a preacher today might use illustrations from a wide variety of sources.

If we worship God "in spirit and truth" (Jn 4:23), we will not sit idly by when God's truth is threatened. Rather, we will contend for the truth as a way of honoring God. In a day when the very concept of truth is itself widely discredited, we find ourselves in a position of claiming, first, that there is absolute truth, and, second, that such truth is to be found only in God as revealed in Jesus. Neither our absolutism ("Truth exists") nor our exclusivism ("Truth is found in God and is revealed in His Son, Jesus Christ") will win any popularity contests. But the very act of "contending for the faith that was once for all entrusted to the saints" is, when done out of love for God, an indispensable way to worship Him.

Praising God refreshes our hearts so that we might be strengthened to contend for His truth.

Jude concludes his brief letter with a doxology that has inspired Christian worship throughout the ages: "To him who is able to keep you from falling and to present you before his glorious presence without fault and with great joy—to the only God our Savior be glory, majesty, power and authority, through Jesus Christ our Lord, before all ages, now and forevermore! Amen" (vv. 24–25).

This exclamation of praise begins by celebrating God's faithfulness in keeping us from falling away from Him. When we stand before His glorious throne, we will be faultless and full of joy. Therefore, even when we struggle with advocates of heresy and immorality, we can be certain of God's ultimate victory and our participation in it. For this reason we praise "the only God our Savior"—there is no other! We acknowledge His glory, majesty, power and eternal authority. When we defend God's truth with integrity, we end up glorifying Him. Rightly undertaken, theology and apologetics flow into worship. Moreover, praising God refreshes our hearts so that we might be strengthened to contend for His truth.

1Jude, a servant of Jesus Christ and a brother of James,

To those who have been called, who are loved by God the Father and kept by[a] Jesus Christ:

2Mercy, peace and love be yours in abundance.

The Sin and Doom of Godless Men

3Dear friends, although I was very eager to write to you about
the salvation we share, I felt I had to write and urge you to contend for the faith that was once for all entrusted to the saints. 4For
certain men whose condemnation was written about[b] long ago
have secretly slipped in among you. They are godless men, who
change the grace of our God into a license for immorality and
deny Jesus Christ our only Sovereign and Lord.

5Though you already know all this, I want to remind you that
the Lord[c] delivered his people out of Egypt, but later destroyed
those who did not believe. 6And the angels who did not keep their
positions of authority but abandoned their own home—these he
has kept in darkness, bound with everlasting chains for judgment
on the great Day. 7In a similar way, Sodom and Gomorrah and the
surrounding towns gave themselves up to sexual immorality and
perversion. They serve as an example of those who suffer the punishment of eternal fire.

8In the very same way, these dreamers pollute their own bodies, reject authority and slander celestial beings. 9But even the
archangel Michael, when he was disputing with the devil about
the body of Moses, did not dare to bring a slanderous accusation
against him, but said, "The Lord rebuke you!" 10Yet these men
speak abusively against whatever they do not understand; and
what things they do understand by instinct, like unreasoning animals—these are the very things that destroy them.

11Woe to them! They have taken the way of Cain; they have
rushed for profit into Balaam's error; they have been destroyed in
Korah's rebellion.

12These men are blemishes at your love feasts, eating with you
without the slightest qualm—shepherds who feed only themselves. They are clouds without rain, blown along by the wind;
autumn trees, without fruit and uprooted—twice dead. 13They
are wild waves of the sea, foaming up their shame; wandering
stars, for whom blackest darkness has been reserved forever.

14Enoch, the seventh from Adam, prophesied about these men:
"See, the Lord is coming with thousands upon thousands of his
holy ones 15to judge everyone, and to convict all the ungodly of
all the ungodly acts they have done in the ungodly way, and of all
the harsh words ungodly sinners have spoken against him."
16These men are grumblers and faultfinders; they follow their
own evil desires; they boast about themselves and flatter others
for their own advantage.

A Call to Persevere

17But, dear friends, remember what the apostles of our Lord
Jesus Christ foretold. 18They said to you, "In the last times there
will be scoffers who will follow their own ungodly desires."
19These are the men who divide you, who follow mere natural instincts and do not have the Spirit.

[a] *1* Or *for*; or *in* [b] *4* Or *men who were marked out for condemnation* [c] *5* Some early manuscripts *Jesus*

(v. 3) Our gracious God and Father, as You have so faithfully contended for us, so may we faithfully contend for the faith. You have taken such great care to reveal the truth to us. Help us to be diligent in defending that truth. Protect us from the slow, corrosive effects of sin. May we never presume upon Your grace and forgiveness. Make us aware of the subtle erosion of our zeal. Teach us to fight the good fight, to lay hold of the deep truths of the faith, to watch our lives and our doctrine closely, to persevere in following in Your ways and to guard what You have entrusted to our care. May we not stray from the path of life, relax our moral standards, loosen our armor or water down the fire of truth. Rather, in the love of Jesus Christ and in the power of the Holy Spirit, may we protect and defend the priceless treasure that is our faith. (1Ti 1:18; 3:9; 4:16; 6:20)

My Lord, I am ready on the threshold of this new day to go forth armed with thy power, seeking adventure on the high road, to right wrong, to overcome evil, to suffer wounds and endure pain if need be, but in all things to serve thee bravely, faithfully, joyfully, that at the end of the day's labor, kneeling for thy blessing, thou mayst find no blot upon my shield.

Knight's Prayer–Inscribed in Chester Cathedral

We human beings instinctively regard the seen world as the "real" world and the unseen world as the "unreal" world, but the Bible calls for almost the opposite. Through faith, the unseen world increasingly takes shape as the real world and sets the course for how we live in the seen world.

Philip Yancey (1949-)

(vv. 24–25) "But as for me, my feet had almost slipped; I had nearly lost my foothold . . . Yet I am always with you; you hold me by my right hand. You guide me with your counsel, and afterward you will take me into glory. Whom have I in heaven but you? And earth has nothing I desire besides you. My flesh and my heart may fail, but God is the strength of my heart and my portion forever." O Jesus my Savior, if I were left to my own devices I would surely fail. Only You are able to save me. Not only are You able, but You are willing. Not only are You willing, but You are active in my salvation. I praise You, my Savior, that You bring Your saving power to bear on my behalf. You alone keep me from falling. You alone present me faultless before God, right now, this very day, and forevermore. (Ps 73:2,23–26)

The work which his goodness began
The arm of his strength will
complete;
His promise is 'Yes' and 'Amen',
And never was forfeited yet:
Things future, nor things that are
now,
Nor all things below or above,
Can make him his purpose forego,
Or sever my soul from his love.

Eternity will not erase
My name from the palms of his
hands;
In marks of indelible grace
Impressed on his heart it remains:
Yes, I to the end shall endure,
As sure as the promise is given;
More happy, but not more secure
The glorified spirits in heaven.

"A Debtor to Mercy Alone"
A. Toplady (1740-1778)

20But you, dear friends, build yourselves up in your most holy faith and pray in the Holy Spirit. 21Keep yourselves in God's love as you wait for the mercy of our Lord Jesus Christ to bring you to eternal life.

22Be merciful to those who doubt; 23snatch others from the fire and save them; to others show mercy, mixed with fear—hating even the clothing stained by corrupted flesh.

Doxology

24To him who is able to keep you from falling and to present you before his glorious presence without fault and with great joy— 25to the only God our Savior be glory, majesty, power and authority, through Jesus Christ our Lord, before all ages, now and forevermore! Amen.

The REVELATION *of St. John the Divine*

Revelation

Given its popular use, we might think of Revelation as a mysterious or even bizarre guide to the future. But when we actually read the text, we may be surprised to discover how much it can inspire our worship today.

Though we usually refer to this book as "The Revelation of John," verse 1 points to a higher source: "The revelation of Jesus Christ, which God gave him to show his servants what must soon take place. He made it known by sending an angel to his servant John" (1:1).

This book is the revelation of Jesus in several senses. First, it belongs to Him since God gave it to Him. Second, it comes from Him since He revealed it to John. Third, it is about Him. More than any other Biblical volume, Revelation shows us a vision of the exalted, reigning Jesus—the Son of Man Whose "eyes were like blazing fire" and Whose "face was like the sun shining in all of its brilliance" (1:14,16). When John falls at the feet of the glorious Son of Man, Jesus reassures him and calls him to write down what he sees (1:18–19).

These visions frequently reveal scenes of heavenly worship. For example, chapters 4 and 5 depict the awesome throne of God, before which humans, angels and other heavenly beings proclaim God's holiness and supreme worthiness (4:8,11). Standing in the center of the throne is a Lamb, Jesus Christ Who was slain (5:6,12). So closely identified is He with God that He receives worship alongside the Almighty: "To him who sits on the throne and to the Lamb be praise and honor and glory and power, for ever and ever!" (5:13). As Christians we worship God the Father and Jesus Christ. In the mystery of the Trinity, however, we are not worshiping a man in addition to God, or two Gods, but one God in three persons: Father, Son and Holy Spirit.

When we worship, we join the future heavenly chorus. Though continuing to live in this world with its suffering, we step momentarily into the glorious future of God.

The book of Revelation looks ahead to the final victory of God over Satan. With sensational imagery God's final plans are played out. For centuries Christians have puzzled over the precise interpretation of this imagery, trying to predict future human events. Yet, regardless of which interpretive scenario proves to be correct, the ultimate end is not in doubt: God will win! Jesus Christ will reign forever as Son of Man! In that glorious day, we will live in a new heaven and a new earth (21:1). God will dwell with us and "wipe every tear from [our] eyes" as He makes "everything new" (21:4–5).

When we worship, we join the future heavenly chorus. Though continuing to live in this world with its suffering, we step momentarily into the glorious future of God. With hopeful joy, we sing: "The kingdom of the world has become the kingdom of our Lord and of his Christ, and he will reign for ever and ever . . . KING OF KINGS AND LORD OF LORDS . . . Hallelujah!" (11:15; 19:16,3)

(1:1–18) Lord Jesus, You are the faithful Witness—our witness to God and God's witness to us. As Son of God and Son of Man You have redeemed us from our sins and reconciled us with the Father so that we can come before Him in peace and confidence. As sovereign Lord, You have made us kings and priests to serve with You. As Alpha and Omega, You have begun a good work of salvation in our hearts, and You will complete it. As the Living One Who has died and returned to life, You continue to dwell in our midst as our Sustainer, our Protector and our Friend. (Eph 2:12–19; Php 1:6)

Majesty, worship His majesty.
Unto Jesus be all glory,
Honor, and praise.
Majesty, kingdom authority
Flows from His throne unto His
own;
His anthem raise.

So exalt, lift up on high
The name of Jesus.
Magnify, come glorify
Christ Jesus, the King.
Majesty, worship His majesty
Jesus, who died, now glorified,
King of all kings.

"Majesty"
Jack W. Hayford (©1981)

He is every way higher and deeper and broader than the shallow and ebb hand-breadth of my short and dim light can take up; and therefore I would that my heart could be silent and sit down in the learnedly-ignorant wondering at the Lord whom men and angels cannot comprehend. I know that the noon-day light of the highest angels, who see Him face to face, seeth not the borders of His infiniteness. They apprehend God near at hand; but they cannot comprehend Him.

Samuel Rutherford (1600-1661)

Prologue

1 The revelation of Jesus Christ, which God gave him to show his
servants what must soon take place. He made it known by
sending his angel to his servant John, 2who testifies to everything
he saw—that is, the word of God and the testimony of Jesus
Christ. 3Blessed is the one who reads the words of this prophecy,
and blessed are those who hear it and take to heart what is written in it, because the time is near.

Greetings and Doxology

4John,

To the seven churches in the province of Asia:

Grace and peace to you from him who is, and who was, and
who is to come, and from the seven spirits[a] before his throne,
5and from Jesus Christ, who is the faithful witness, the firstborn
from the dead, and the ruler of the kings of the earth.

To him who loves us and has freed us from our sins by his
blood, 6and has made us to be a kingdom and priests to serve his
God and Father—to him be glory and power for ever and ever!
Amen.

7Look, he is coming with the clouds,
and every eye will see him,
even those who pierced him;
and all the peoples of the earth will mourn because
of him.
So shall it be! Amen.

8"I am the Alpha and the Omega," says the Lord God, "who is,
and who was, and who is to come, the Almighty."

One Like a Son of Man

9I, John, your brother and companion in the suffering and kingdom and patient endurance that are ours in Jesus, was on the island of Patmos because of the word of God and the testimony of
Jesus. 10On the Lord's Day I was in the Spirit, and I heard behind
me a loud voice like a trumpet, 11which said: "Write on a scroll
what you see and send it to the seven churches: to Ephesus, Smyrna, Pergamum, Thyatira, Sardis, Philadelphia and Laodicea."
12I turned around to see the voice that was speaking to me.
And when I turned I saw seven golden lampstands, 13and among
the lampstands was someone "like a son of man,"[b] dressed in a
robe reaching down to his feet and with a golden sash around his
chest. 14His head and hair were white like wool, as white as snow,
and his eyes were like blazing fire. 15His feet were like bronze
glowing in a furnace, and his voice was like the sound of rushing
waters. 16In his right hand he held seven stars, and out of his
mouth came a sharp double-edged sword. His face was like the
sun shining in all its brilliance.
17When I saw him, I fell at his feet as though dead. Then he
placed his right hand on me and said: "Do not be afraid. I am the
First and the Last. 18I am the Living One; I was dead, and behold
I am alive for ever and ever! And I hold the keys of death and
Hades.

[a] *4* Or *the sevenfold Spirit* [b] *13* Daniel 7:13

19 “Write, therefore, what you have seen, what is now and what
will take place later. 20 The mystery of the seven stars that you saw
in my right hand and of the seven golden lampstands is this: The
seven stars are the angels[a] of the seven churches, and the seven
lampstands are the seven churches.

To the Church in Ephesus

2 “To the angel[b] of the church in Ephesus write:

These are the words of him who holds the seven stars in
his right hand and walks among the seven golden lampstands: 2 I know your deeds, your hard work and your perseverance. I know that you cannot tolerate wicked men, that
you have tested those who claim to be apostles but are not,
and have found them false. 3 You have persevered and have
endured hardships for my name, and have not grown weary.
4 Yet I hold this against you: You have forsaken your first
love. 5 Remember the height from which you have fallen! Repent and do the things you did at first. If you do not repent,
I will come to you and remove your lampstand from its
place. 6 But you have this in your favor: You hate the practices of the Nicolaitans, which I also hate.
7 He who has an ear, let him hear what the Spirit says to
the churches. To him who overcomes, I will give the right to
eat from the tree of life, which is in the paradise of God.

To the Church in Smyrna

8 “To the angel of the church in Smyrna write:

These are the words of him who is the First and the Last,
who died and came to life again. 9 I know your afflictions
and your poverty—yet you are rich! I know the slander of
those who say they are Jews and are not, but are a synagogue
of Satan. 10 Do not be afraid of what you are about to suffer.
I tell you, the devil will put some of you in prison to test you,
and you will suffer persecution for ten days. Be faithful, even
to the point of death, and I will give you the crown of life.
11 He who has an ear, let him hear what the Spirit says to
the churches. He who overcomes will not be hurt at all by
the second death.

To the Church in Pergamum

12 “To the angel of the church in Pergamum write:

These are the words of him who has the sharp, double-
edged sword. 13 I know where you live—where Satan has
his throne. Yet you remain true to my name. You did not renounce your faith in me, even in the days of Antipas, my
faithful witness, who was put to death in your city—where
Satan lives.
14 Nevertheless, I have a few things against you: You have
people there who hold to the teaching of Balaam, who
taught Balak to entice the Israelites to sin by eating food
sacrificed to idols and by committing sexual immorality.
15 Likewise you also have those who hold to the teaching of
the Nicolaitans. 16 Repent therefore! Otherwise, I will soon

[a] 20 Or *messengers* [b] 1 Or *messenger*; also in verses 8, 12 and 18

(2:8–11) From here to eternity, Lord Jesus, You know all things. You see the pain Your people suffer; You hear the slander which is spoken against us. And because You have suffered shame and rejection You are able to encourage us. Even in the face of grave threats and intense struggles, You remind us not to be weary in our efforts to do well, for You have prepared an eternal reward for us—the crown of life. Strengthen us, Lord, and make us faithful to You, just as You are faithful to us. (Gal 6:9)

What we need very badly these days is a company of Christians who are prepared to trust God as completely now as they know they must do at the last day. For each of us the time is coming when we shall have nothing but God. Health and wealth and friends and hiding places will be swept away, and we shall have only God. To the man of pseudo faith that is a terrifying thought, but to real faith it is one of the most comforting thoughts the heart can entertain.

A.W. Tozer (1897–1963)

Beautiful Savior, sent from above;
Joy of the Father, gift of His love.
Suffering Servant, acquainted with grief;
Risen Redeemer, Prince of Peace.

Father, we extol the name of Jesus,
Giving Him the glory due His name;
For in Him Your mercies have redeemed us,
And in Him we'll never be the same.
We give praises to Your name.

“We Extol The Name of Jesus”
Harlan Rogers (©1999)

(2:16–29) You call Your people to repentance, Jesus, so that we can receive the immeasurable riches of grace. If, by Your grace, we remain faithful to You in the midst of adversity, You offer us Yourself as food and sustenance. If, through Your strength, we finish the course You have set before us, You give us the white stone of victory. If, by Your Spirit, we continue in You, we receive a new name—Your name—and with it, Your character and Your righteousness. You, Lord Jesus, are our sustenance; You are our innocence; You are our victory and our reward. (Mt 26:26–28; Jn 6:48–58; 2Ti 4:7)

O God, the true and only life, in whom and from whom and by whom are all good things that are good indeed; from whom to be turned is to fall, to whom to turn is to rise again; in whom to abide is to dwell for ever, from whom to depart is to die; to whom to come again is to revive, and in whom to lodge is to live: take away from me whatever you will as long as you give me only yourself.

Thomas Dekker (c.1570–1632)

come to you and will fight against them with the sword of
my mouth.
17 He who has an ear, let him hear what the Spirit says to
the churches. To him who overcomes, I will give some of
the hidden manna. I will also give him a white stone with a
new name written on it, known only to him who receives it.

To the Church in Thyatira

18 "To the angel of the church in Thyatira write:

These are the words of the Son of God, whose eyes are
like blazing fire and whose feet are like burnished bronze.
19 I know your deeds, your love and faith, your service and
perseverance, and that you are now doing more than you
did at first.
20 Nevertheless, I have this against you: You tolerate that
woman Jezebel, who calls herself a prophetess. By her
teaching she misleads my servants into sexual immorality
and the eating of food sacrificed to idols. 21 I have given her
time to repent of her immorality, but she is unwilling. 22 So I
will cast her on a bed of suffering, and I will make those
who commit adultery with her suffer intensely, unless they
repent of her ways. 23 I will strike her children dead. Then
all the churches will know that I am he who searches hearts
and minds, and I will repay each of you according to your
deeds. 24 Now I say to the rest of you in Thyatira, to you who
do not hold to her teaching and have not learned Satan's so-
called deep secrets (I will not impose any other burden on
you): 25 Only hold on to what you have until I come.
26 To him who overcomes and does my will to the end, I
will give authority over the nations—
27 'He will rule them with an iron scepter;
he will dash them to pieces like pottery'[a]—
just as I have received authority from my Father. 28 I will also
give him the morning star. 29 He who has an ear, let him hear
what the Spirit says to the churches.

To the Church in Sardis

3 "To the angel[b] of the church in Sardis write:

These are the words of him who holds the seven spirits[c]
of God and the seven stars. I know your deeds; you have a
reputation of being alive, but you are dead. 2 Wake up!
Strengthen what remains and is about to die, for I have not
found your deeds complete in the sight of my God. 3 Remember, therefore, what you have received and heard; obey
it, and repent. But if you do not wake up, I will come like a
thief, and you will not know at what time I will come to you.
4 Yet you have a few people in Sardis who have not soiled
their clothes. They will walk with me, dressed in white, for
they are worthy. 5 He who overcomes will, like them, be
dressed in white. I will never blot out his name from the
book of life, but will acknowledge his name before my Fa-

[a] 27 Psalm 2:9 [b] 1 Or *messenger*; also in verses 7 and 14 [c] 1 Or *the sevenfold Spirit*

ther and his angels. 6He who has an ear, let him hear what
the Spirit says to the churches.

To the Church in Philadelphia

7"To the angel of the church in Philadelphia write:

These are the words of him who is holy and true, who
holds the key of David. What he opens no one can shut, and
what he shuts no one can open. 8I know your deeds. See, I
have placed before you an open door that no one can shut.
I know that you have little strength, yet you have kept my
word and have not denied my name. 9I will make those who
are of the synagogue of Satan, who claim to be Jews though
they are not, but are liars—I will make them come and fall
down at your feet and acknowledge that I have loved you.
10Since you have kept my command to endure patiently, I
will also keep you from the hour of trial that is going to
come upon the whole world to test those who live on the
earth.

11I am coming soon. Hold on to what you have, so that no
one will take your crown. 12Him who overcomes I will make
a pillar in the temple of my God. Never again will he leave it.
I will write on him the name of my God and the name of the
city of my God, the new Jerusalem, which is coming down
out of heaven from my God; and I will also write on him my
new name. 13He who has an ear, let him hear what the Spirit says to the churches.

To the Church in Laodicea

14"To the angel of the church in Laodicea write:

These are the words of the Amen, the faithful and true witness, the ruler of God's creation. 15I know your deeds, that
you are neither cold nor hot. I wish you were either one or
the other! 16So, because you are lukewarm—neither hot
nor cold—I am about to spit you out of my mouth. 17You
say, 'I am rich; I have acquired wealth and do not need a
thing.' But you do not realize that you are wretched, pitiful,
poor, blind and naked. 18I counsel you to buy from me gold
refined in the fire, so you can become rich; and white
clothes to wear, so you can cover your shameful nakedness;
and salve to put on your eyes, so you can see.

19Those whom I love I rebuke and discipline. So be
earnest, and repent. 20Here I am! I stand at the door and
knock. If anyone hears my voice and opens the door, I will
come in and eat with him, and he with me.

21To him who overcomes, I will give the right to sit with
me on my throne, just as I overcame and sat down with my
Father on his throne. 22He who has an ear, let him hear what
the Spirit says to the churches."

The Throne in Heaven

4 After this I looked, and there before me was a door standing open in heaven. And the voice I had first heard speaking
to me like a trumpet said, "Come up here, and I will show you
what must take place after this." 2At once I was in the Spirit, and
there before me was a throne in heaven with someone sitting on
it. 3And the one who sat there had the appearance of jasper and

(3:11–12) O Lord, what joy there will be when all things become new in You! There will be a new heaven and a new earth, and upon each of us who remain faithful to You, You will write Your own name as an author signs his name to a finished work. Lord, You are aware of my struggles and see my limitations, but You know my potential. So strengthen my grip of faith. Renew my hope of eternal life. Grow me into the identity that yet awaits me; transform me into the person You always knew I would become. And help me to remember, in this present time, that all earthly titles, labels, degrees and honors are worth less than the dust of the earth compared to the glory that awaits Your people. (Isa 62:12; 2Co 3:18; 1Jn 3:2; Rev 21:1–5).

Thy nature, gracious Lord, impart;
Come quickly from above;
Write Thy new name upon my
heart,
Thy new best name of Love.

"O for a Heart to Praise My God"
Charles Wesley (1742)

In what strange quarries and stoneyards the stones for the celestial wall are being hewn! Out of the hillsides of humiliated pride; deep in the darkness of crushed despair; in the fretting and dusty atmosphere of little cares; in the hard cruel contacts that man has with man; wherever souls are being tried and ripened, in whatever commonplace and homely way, there God is hewing out the pillars for His temple.

Phillips Brooks (1835-1893)

carnelian. A rainbow, resembling an emerald, encircled the
throne. [4]Surrounding the throne were twenty-four other thrones,
and seated on them were twenty-four elders. They were dressed
in white and had crowns of gold on their heads. [5]From the
throne came flashes of lightning, rumblings and peals of thunder. Before the throne, seven lamps were blazing. These are the
seven spirits[a] of God. [6]Also before the throne there was what
looked like a sea of glass, clear as crystal.

In the center, around the throne, were four living creatures,
and they were covered with eyes, in front and in back. [7]The first
living creature was like a lion, the second was like an ox, the
third had a face like a man, the fourth was like a flying eagle.
[8]Each of the four living creatures had six wings and was covered
with eyes all around, even under his wings. Day and night they
never stop saying:

"Holy, holy, holy
is the Lord God Almighty,
who was, and is, and is to come."

[9]Whenever the living creatures give glory, honor and thanks to
him who sits on the throne and who lives for ever and ever, [10]the
twenty-four elders fall down before him who sits on the throne,
and worship him who lives for ever and ever. They lay their
crowns before the throne and say:

[11]"You are worthy, our Lord and God,
to receive glory and honor and power,
for you created all things,
and by your will they were created
and have their being."

The Scroll and the Lamb

5 Then I saw in the right hand of him who sat on the throne a
scroll with writing on both sides and sealed with seven seals.
[2]And I saw a mighty angel proclaiming in a loud voice, "Who is
worthy to break the seals and open the scroll?" [3]But no one in
heaven or on earth or under the earth could open the scroll or
even look inside it. [4]I wept and wept because no one was found
who was worthy to open the scroll or look inside. [5]Then one of
the elders said to me, "Do not weep! See, the Lion of the tribe of
Judah, the Root of David, has triumphed. He is able to open the
scroll and its seven seals."

[6]Then I saw a Lamb, looking as if it had been slain, standing in
the center of the throne, encircled by the four living creatures
and the elders. He had seven horns and seven eyes, which are the
seven spirits[a] of God sent out into all the earth. [7]He came and
took the scroll from the right hand of him who sat on the throne.
[8]And when he had taken it, the four living creatures and the twenty-four elders fell down before the Lamb. Each one had a harp
and they were holding golden bowls full of incense, which are the
prayers of the saints. [9]And they sang a new song:

"You are worthy to take the scroll
and to open its seals,
because you were slain,

[a]5,6 Or *the sevenfold Spirit*

O God, you who have prepared a place for my soul, prepare my soul for that place; prepare it with holiness; prepare it with desire; and even while it remains on earth, let it dwell in heaven with you; seeing the beauty of your face and the glory of your saints, now and forevermore.

Joseph Hall (1574-1656)

(4:8) "Holy, holy, holy" is the continual cry of those who dwell in Your presence. It is their response to Your magnificent glory, an eternal interplay of worship and revelation. Worship will never end, because Your glory is inexhaustible, O God, and eternity will be an endless discovery of who You are—the ultimate Source of all that is right and good. I join my voice today to this angelic song and cry "Holy, holy, holy," for You alone are holy. (Isa 6:3)

Holy, holy, holy!
All the saints adore Thee,
Casting down their golden crowns
Around the glassy sea;
Cherubim and seraphim
Falling down before Thee,
Who wert, and art,
And evermore shalt be.

"Holy! Holy! Holy! Lord God Almighty"
Reginald Heber (1783-1826)

(5:1–13) Lord Jesus, Anointed One, Lion of Judah, Lamb of God, You are the convergence of majesty and meekness. You embody the very essence of the Father's love for us. "Slain from the creation of the world," triumphant over death and hell, eternally enthroned in glory, You are the Savior of the world, the central figure of heaven, the flash point of the fire of true worship. All glory, honor and praise be to You, my Savior and my God. (Rev 13:8)

and with your blood you purchased men for God
from every tribe and language and people and
nation.
10 You have made them to be a kingdom and priests to
serve our God,
and they will reign on the earth."

11 Then I looked and heard the voice of many angels, numbering thousands upon thousands, and ten thousand times ten thousand. They encircled the throne and the living creatures and the
elders. 12 In a loud voice they sang:

"Worthy is the Lamb, who was slain,
to receive power and wealth and wisdom and strength
and honor and glory and praise!"

13 Then I heard every creature in heaven and on earth and
under the earth and on the sea, and all that is in them, singing:

"To him who sits on the throne and to the Lamb
be praise and honor and glory and power,
for ever and ever!"

14 The four living creatures said, "Amen," and the elders fell down
and worshiped.

The Seals

6 I watched as the Lamb opened the first of the seven seals.
Then I heard one of the four living creatures say in a voice
like thunder, "Come!" 2 I looked, and there before me was a white
horse! Its rider held a bow, and he was given a crown, and he
rode out as a conqueror bent on conquest.
3 When the Lamb opened the second seal, I heard the second
living creature say, "Come!" 4 Then another horse came out, a
fiery red one. Its rider was given power to take peace from the
earth and to make men slay each other. To him was given a large
sword.
5 When the Lamb opened the third seal, I heard the third living
creature say, "Come!" I looked, and there before me was a black
horse! Its rider was holding a pair of scales in his hand. 6 Then I
heard what sounded like a voice among the four living creatures,
saying, "A quart[a] of wheat for a day's wages,[b] and three quarts of
barley for a day's wages,[b] and do not damage the oil and the
wine!"
7 When the Lamb opened the fourth seal, I heard the voice of
the fourth living creature say, "Come!" 8 I looked, and there before me was a pale horse! Its rider was named Death, and Hades
was following close behind him. They were given power over a
fourth of the earth to kill by sword, famine and plague, and by the
wild beasts of the earth.
9 When he opened the fifth seal, I saw under the altar the souls
of those who had been slain because of the word of God and the
testimony they had maintained. 10 They called out in a loud voice,
"How long, Sovereign Lord, holy and true, until you judge the inhabitants of the earth and avenge our blood?" 11 Then each of
them was given a white robe, and they were told to wait a little
longer, until the number of their fellow servants and brothers
who were to be killed as they had been was completed.

[a] 6 Greek *a choinix* (probably about a liter) [b] 6 Greek *a denarius*

Blessing, honour, glory to the Lamb.
Holy, righteous, worthy is the Lamb.
Death could not hold Him down,
For He is risen!
Seated upon the throne,
He is the Lamb of God!

"Blessing, Honour and Glory"
Geoff Bullock and David Reidy (©1990)

(6:1–8) The powerful image of the four horsemen has haunted humankind for centuries. The mysterious vision of judgment and the eerie finality of the riders' mission sobers and silences us. We read the unfolding of Your plans in awesome fear—afraid of the avenging judgment You will surely bring upon Your enemies and awestruck by Your grace to those who cry out to You for help. Have mercy on us, Lord, and grant us faith that we may be found worthy to stand among Your saints on the last day.

The cross for the first time revealed God in terms of weakness and lowliness and suffering; even, humanly speaking, of absurdity. He was seen thenceforth in the image of the most timid, most gentle, and most vulnerable of all living creatures—a lamb. Agnus Dei!
Malcolm Muggeridge (1903–1990)

(7:9–17) Great Lamb of God, Your blood purifies us, protects us from eternal death and grants us entrance into the presence of Your Father. Just as the Passover Lamb fed Your people long ago, giving them strength for their journey, so You, our Paschal Lamb, sustain us and enable us to follow You wherever You lead. We bow before You, Jesus, for You have clothed us in righteousness, You have put palm branches of victory in our hands and have placed words of praise and worship on our lips. (Ex 12; Isa 57:1–19; Mt 26:26–28; Heb 10:19)

O that with yonder sacred throng
We at His feet may fall!
We'll join the everlasting song,
And crown Him Lord of all!
We'll join the everlasting song,
And crown Him Lord of all!
"All Hail the Power of Jesus' Name"
Edward Perronet (1779)

12I watched as he opened the sixth seal. There was a great
earthquake. The sun turned black like sackcloth made of goat
hair, the whole moon turned blood red, 13and the stars in the sky
fell to earth, as late figs drop from a fig tree when shaken by a
strong wind. 14The sky receded like a scroll, rolling up, and every
mountain and island was removed from its place.
15Then the kings of the earth, the princes, the generals, the
rich, the mighty, and every slave and every free man hid in caves
and among the rocks of the mountains. 16They called to the
mountains and the rocks, "Fall on us and hide us from the face of
him who sits on the throne and from the wrath of the Lamb! 17For
the great day of their wrath has come, and who can stand?"

144,000 Sealed

7 After this I saw four angels standing at the four corners of
the earth, holding back the four winds of the earth to prevent
any wind from blowing on the land or on the sea or on any tree.
2Then I saw another angel coming up from the east, having the
seal of the living God. He called out in a loud voice to the four angels who had been given power to harm the land and the sea:
3"Do not harm the land or the sea or the trees until we put a seal
on the foreheads of the servants of our God." 4Then I heard the
number of those who were sealed: 144,000 from all the tribes of
Israel.

5From the tribe of Judah 12,000 were sealed,
from the tribe of Reuben 12,000,
from the tribe of Gad 12,000,
6from the tribe of Asher 12,000,
from the tribe of Naphtali 12,000,
from the tribe of Manasseh 12,000,
7from the tribe of Simeon 12,000,
from the tribe of Levi 12,000,
from the tribe of Issachar 12,000,
8from the tribe of Zebulun 12,000,
from the tribe of Joseph 12,000,
from the tribe of Benjamin 12,000.

The Great Multitude in White Robes

9After this I looked and there before me was a great multitude
that no one could count, from every nation, tribe, people and language, standing before the throne and in front of the Lamb. They
were wearing white robes and were holding palm branches in
their hands. 10And they cried out in a loud voice:

"Salvation belongs to our God,
who sits on the throne,
and to the Lamb."

11All the angels were standing around the throne and around the
elders and the four living creatures. They fell down on their faces
before the throne and worshiped God, 12saying:

"Amen!
Praise and glory
and wisdom and thanks and honor
and power and strength
be to our God for ever and ever.
Amen!"

[13]Then one of the elders asked me, "These in white robes—who are they, and where did they come from?"

[14]I answered, "Sir, you know."

And he said, "These are they who have come out of the great tribulation; they have washed their robes and made them white in the blood of the Lamb. [15]Therefore,

"they are before the throne of God
and serve him day and night in his temple;
and he who sits on the throne will spread his tent over them.
[16]Never again will they hunger;
never again will they thirst.
The sun will not beat upon them,
nor any scorching heat.
[17]For the Lamb at the center of the throne will be their shepherd;
he will lead them to springs of living water.
And God will wipe away every tear from their eyes."

The Seventh Seal and the Golden Censer

8 When he opened the seventh seal, there was silence in heaven for about half an hour.

[2]And I saw the seven angels who stand before God, and to them were given seven trumpets.

[3]Another angel, who had a golden censer, came and stood at the altar. He was given much incense to offer, with the prayers of all the saints, on the golden altar before the throne. [4]The smoke of the incense, together with the prayers of the saints, went up before God from the angel's hand. [5]Then the angel took the censer, filled it with fire from the altar, and hurled it on the earth; and there came peals of thunder, rumblings, flashes of lightning and an earthquake.

The Trumpets

[6]Then the seven angels who had the seven trumpets prepared to sound them.

[7]The first angel sounded his trumpet, and there came hail and fire mixed with blood, and it was hurled down upon the earth. A third of the earth was burned up, a third of the trees were burned up, and all the green grass was burned up.

[8]The second angel sounded his trumpet, and something like a huge mountain, all ablaze, was thrown into the sea. A third of the sea turned into blood, [9]a third of the living creatures in the sea died, and a third of the ships were destroyed.

[10]The third angel sounded his trumpet, and a great star, blazing like a torch, fell from the sky on a third of the rivers and on the springs of water— [11]the name of the star is Wormwood.[a] A third of the waters turned bitter, and many people died from the waters that had become bitter.

[12]The fourth angel sounded his trumpet, and a third of the sun was struck, a third of the moon, and a third of the stars, so that a third of them turned dark. A third of the day was without light, and also a third of the night.

[13]As I watched, I heard an eagle that was flying in midair call out in a loud voice: "Woe! Woe! Woe to the inhabitants of the

[a] *11* That is, Bitterness

(7:14–17) Your compassion toward Your people, Lord Jesus, is touching and beautiful. Your desire for us, Your longing for our love, is written across every page of Your Word. And here we catch a glimpse of that longing fulfilled: We look with wonder upon this gathering of saints who, at last, are united with You forever. As they stand in Your presence, You joyfully extend to them eternal protection, provision and comfort, for they have paid the ultimate price for their faith. What tenderness You have for them, Lord, and for all of us who have sought in You a refuge from life's tribulations.

Be still, my soul: the Lord is on thy side;
Bear patiently the cross of grief or pain;
Leave to thy God to order and provide;
In every change he faithful will remain.
Be still, my soul; thy best, thy heavenly Friend
Through thorny ways leads to a joyful end.

Katharina von Schlegel (b. 1697)

We will be together
To worship You forever
Crying, "Holy is the Lord."
In the light of heaven,
Thankful and forgiven
Crying, "Holy is the Lord."

You laid Your glory down,
Suffered and died alone;
To see the lost ones found,
Gathered around Your throne.

Surrounded by Your grace,
Warm in Your holy light;
There we will see Your face;
There we will never die.

"Holy Is The Lord"
Bill Batstone and Phil Kristianson (©1994)

earth, because of the trumpet blasts about to be sounded by the
other three angels!"

9 The fifth angel sounded his trumpet, and I saw a star that had
fallen from the sky to the earth. The star was given the key to
the shaft of the Abyss. 2When he opened the Abyss, smoke rose
from it like the smoke from a gigantic furnace. The sun and sky
were darkened by the smoke from the Abyss. 3And out of the
smoke locusts came down upon the earth and were given power
like that of scorpions of the earth. 4They were told not to harm
the grass of the earth or any plant or tree, but only those people
who did not have the seal of God on their foreheads. 5They were
not given power to kill them, but only to torture them for five
months. And the agony they suffered was like that of the sting of
a scorpion when it strikes a man. 6During those days men will
seek death, but will not find it; they will long to die, but death will
elude them.

7The locusts looked like horses prepared for battle. On their
heads they wore something like crowns of gold, and their faces
resembled human faces. 8Their hair was like women's hair, and
their teeth were like lions' teeth. 9They had breastplates like
breastplates of iron, and the sound of their wings was like the
thundering of many horses and chariots rushing into battle.
10They had tails and stings like scorpions, and in their tails they
had power to torment people for five months. 11They had as king
over them the angel of the Abyss, whose name in Hebrew is Abaddon, and in Greek, Apollyon.[a]

12The first woe is past; two other woes are yet to come.

13The sixth angel sounded his trumpet, and I heard a voice
coming from the horns[b] of the golden altar that is before God.
14It said to the sixth angel who had the trumpet, "Release the four
angels who are bound at the great river Euphrates." 15And the
four angels who had been kept ready for this very hour and day
and month and year were released to kill a third of mankind.
16The number of the mounted troops was two hundred million. I
heard their number.

17The horses and riders I saw in my vision looked like this:
Their breastplates were fiery red, dark blue, and yellow as sulfur.
The heads of the horses resembled the heads of lions, and out of
their mouths came fire, smoke and sulfur. 18A third of mankind
was killed by the three plagues of fire, smoke and sulfur that
came out of their mouths. 19The power of the horses was in their
mouths and in their tails; for their tails were like snakes, having
heads with which they inflict injury.

20The rest of mankind that were not killed by these plagues
still did not repent of the work of their hands; they did not stop
worshiping demons, and idols of gold, silver, bronze, stone and
wood—idols that cannot see or hear or walk. 21Nor did they repent of their murders, their magic arts, their sexual immorality or
their thefts.

The Angel and the Little Scroll

10 Then I saw another mighty angel coming down from heaven.
He was robed in a cloud, with a rainbow above his head; his
face was like the sun, and his legs were like fiery pillars. 2He was
holding a little scroll, which lay open in his hand. He planted his

(9:2–4) We thank You and praise You, Righteous Judge, that You protect Your own in the day of Your vengeance. You rescued Noah and his family from the flood. You set apart the Israelites while Egypt was tormented by plagues. And in the last days of Your judgment, as the torrent of Your anger is released upon the earth, we will be kept safe, as in an ark, by the grace of our Lord Jesus Christ. (Ge 6–7; Ex 8–11; 2Pe 2:5–9)

At the heart of the cyclone tearing the sky
And flinging the clouds and the towers by,
Is a place of central calm;
So here in the roar of mortal things,
I have a place where my spirit sings,
In the hollow of God's palm.

Edwin Markham (1852-1940)

[a] *11 Abaddon* and *Apollyon* mean *Destroyer.* [b] *13* That is, projections

right foot on the sea and his left foot on the land, 3and he gave a
loud shout like the roar of a lion. When he shouted, the voices of
the seven thunders spoke. 4And when the seven thunders spoke, I
was about to write; but I heard a voice from heaven say, "Seal up
what the seven thunders have said and do not write it down."
5Then the angel I had seen standing on the sea and on the land
raised his right hand to heaven. 6And he swore by him who lives for
ever and ever, who created the heavens and all that is in them, the
earth and all that is in it, and the sea and all that is in it, and said,
"There will be no more delay! 7But in the days when the seventh
angel is about to sound his trumpet, the mystery of God will be accomplished, just as he announced to his servants the prophets."
8Then the voice that I had heard from heaven spoke to me
once more: "Go, take the scroll that lies open in the hand of the
angel who is standing on the sea and on the land."
9So I went to the angel and asked him to give me the little
scroll. He said to me, "Take it and eat it. It will turn your stomach
sour, but in your mouth it will be as sweet as honey." 10I took the
little scroll from the angel's hand and ate it. It tasted as sweet as
honey in my mouth, but when I had eaten it, my stomach turned
sour. 11Then I was told, "You must prophesy again about many
peoples, nations, languages and kings."

The Two Witnesses

11 I was given a reed like a measuring rod and was told, "Go
and measure the temple of God and the altar, and count the
worshipers there. 2But exclude the outer court; do not measure
it, because it has been given to the Gentiles. They will trample on
the holy city for 42 months. 3And I will give power to my two witnesses, and they will prophesy for 1,260 days, clothed in sackcloth." 4These are the two olive trees and the two lampstands that
stand before the Lord of the earth. 5If anyone tries to harm them,
fire comes from their mouths and devours their enemies. This is
how anyone who wants to harm them must die. 6These men have
power to shut up the sky so that it will not rain during the time
they are prophesying; and they have power to turn the waters into
blood and to strike the earth with every kind of plague as often as
they want.
7Now when they have finished their testimony, the beast that
comes up from the Abyss will attack them, and overpower and
kill them. 8Their bodies will lie in the street of the great city,
which is figuratively called Sodom and Egypt, where also their
Lord was crucified. 9For three and a half days men from every
people, tribe, language and nation will gaze on their bodies and
refuse them burial. 10The inhabitants of the earth will gloat over
them and will celebrate by sending each other gifts, because these
two prophets had tormented those who live on the earth.
11But after the three and a half days a breath of life from God
entered them, and they stood on their feet, and terror struck
those who saw them. 12Then they heard a loud voice from heav-
en saying to them, "Come up here." And they went up to heaven
in a cloud, while their enemies looked on.
13At that very hour there was a severe earthquake and a tenth
of the city collapsed. Seven thousand people were killed in the
earthquake, and the survivors were terrified and gave glory to the
God of heaven.
14The second woe has passed; the third woe is coming soon.

(10:6–7) We praise You, almighty, eternal Lord Jesus, for You are Lord over all creation. You have orchestrated the end of things, the grand finale of history. You live forever—You have no beginning or end. Because You encompass all of time, therefore, You are Lord of time itself—time is truly in Your hands. You are greater than the mightiest angel. You are to be feared more than the worst of these judgments. You, Lord Jesus, are the key to God's mystery; You are the means and the end of God's purposes. We bow our hearts before You and worship You in reverence and awe. (Col 2:2–3)

We declare Your majesty,
We proclaim that Your name is
exalted!
For You reign magnificently,
Rule victoriously
And Your power is shown
Throughout the earth.

And we exclaim:
"Our God is mighty!"
Lift up Your name,
For You are holy!
Sing it again,
All honor and glory!
In adoration we bow
Before Your throne!

"We Declare Your Majesty"
Malcolm duPlessis (©1985)

(12:7–11) Like the archangels, each of us has been called into the great war against evil. Just as we see Michael fighting valiantly against the dragon, so we are reminded that our own battles—large and small—are not against flesh and blood but against the spiritual enemies of Christ. But thanks be to You, O God! You give us the victory through our Lord Jesus Christ; and You will soon crush Satan under our feet. Make us courageous, Lord, in a battle that will ultimately end in Your victory. Keep us from growing passive, because whether or not we feel like fighting, the enemy will never relent in his assaults against Your people until You and Your best warriors have conquered him in the last day. (Ro 16:20; 1Co 15:57; Eph 6:10–18)

Glory be to God, we know the end of the war. The great dragon shall be cast out and forever destroyed, while Jesus and they who are with Him shall receive the crown. Let us sharpen our swords tonight, and pray the Holy Spirit to nerve our arms for the conflict. Never battle so important, never crown so glorious. Every man to his post, ye warriors of the cross, and may the Lord tread Satan under Your feet shortly!

Charles Haddon Spurgeon (1834–1892)

Rejoice, the Lord is King!
Your Lord and King adore!
Rejoice, give thanks, and sing,
And triumph evermore:
Lift up your heart, lift up your voice!
Rejoice, again I say, rejoice!

"Rejoice, the Lord is King!"
Charles Wesley (1746)

The Seventh Trumpet

15 The seventh angel sounded his trumpet, and there were loud voices in heaven, which said:

"The kingdom of the world has become the kingdom
of our Lord and of his Christ,
and he will reign for ever and ever."

16 And the twenty-four elders, who were seated on their thrones before God, fell on their faces and worshiped God, 17 saying:

"We give thanks to you, Lord God Almighty,
the One who is and who was,
because you have taken your great power
and have begun to reign.
18 The nations were angry;
and your wrath has come.
The time has come for judging the dead,
and for rewarding your servants the prophets
and your saints and those who reverence your name,
both small and great—
and for destroying those who destroy the earth."

19 Then God's temple in heaven was opened, and within his temple was seen the ark of his covenant. And there came flashes of lightning, rumblings, peals of thunder, an earthquake and a great hailstorm.

The Woman and the Dragon

12 A great and wondrous sign appeared in heaven: a woman
clothed with the sun, with the moon under her feet and a
crown of twelve stars on her head. 2 She was pregnant and cried
out in pain as she was about to give birth. 3 Then another sign appeared in heaven: an enormous red dragon with seven heads and
ten horns and seven crowns on his heads. 4 His tail swept a third
of the stars out of the sky and flung them to the earth. The dragon stood in front of the woman who was about to give birth, so
that he might devour her child the moment it was born. 5 She gave
birth to a son, a male child, who will rule all the nations with an
iron scepter. And her child was snatched up to God and to his
throne. 6 The woman fled into the desert to a place prepared for
her by God, where she might be taken care of for 1,260 days.
7 And there was war in heaven. Michael and his angels fought
against the dragon, and the dragon and his angels fought back.
8 But he was not strong enough, and they lost their place in heav-
en. 9 The great dragon was hurled down—that ancient serpent
called the devil, or Satan, who leads the whole world astray. He
was hurled to the earth, and his angels with him.
10 Then I heard a loud voice in heaven say:

"Now have come the salvation and the power and the
kingdom of our God,
and the authority of his Christ.
For the accuser of our brothers,
who accuses them before our God day and night,
has been hurled down.
11 They overcame him
by the blood of the Lamb

and by the word of their testimony;
they did not love their lives so much
as to shrink from death.
12 Therefore rejoice, you heavens
and you who dwell in them!
But woe to the earth and the sea,
because the devil has gone down to you!
He is filled with fury,
because he knows that his time is short."

13 When the dragon saw that he had been hurled to the earth,
he pursued the woman who had given birth to the male child.
14 The woman was given the two wings of a great eagle, so that
she might fly to the place prepared for her in the desert, where
she would be taken care of for a time, times and half a time, out
of the serpent's reach. 15 Then from his mouth the serpent
spewed water like a river, to overtake the woman and sweep her
away with the torrent. 16 But the earth helped the woman by
opening its mouth and swallowing the river that the dragon had
spewed out of his mouth. 17 Then the dragon was enraged at the
woman and went off to make war against the rest of her offspring—those who obey God's commandments and hold to the
13 testimony of Jesus. 1 And the dragon[a] stood on the shore of
the sea.

The Beast out of the Sea

And I saw a beast coming out of the sea. He had ten horns and
seven heads, with ten crowns on his horns, and on each head a
blasphemous name. 2 The beast I saw resembled a leopard, but
had feet like those of a bear and a mouth like that of a lion. The
dragon gave the beast his power and his throne and great authority. 3 One of the heads of the beast seemed to have had a fatal
wound, but the fatal wound had been healed. The whole world
was astonished and followed the beast. 4 Men worshiped the dragon because he had given authority to the beast, and they also worshiped the beast and asked, "Who is like the beast? Who can
make war against him?"
5 The beast was given a mouth to utter proud words and blasphemies and to exercise his authority for forty-two months. 6 He
opened his mouth to blaspheme God, and to slander his name
and his dwelling place and those who live in heaven. 7 He was
given power to make war against the saints and to conquer them.
And he was given authority over every tribe, people, language and
nation. 8 All inhabitants of the earth will worship the beast—all
whose names have not been written in the book of life belonging
to the Lamb that was slain from the creation of the world.[b]
9 He who has an ear, let him hear.

10 If anyone is to go into captivity,
into captivity he will go.
If anyone is to be killed[c] with the sword,
with the sword he will be killed.

This calls for patient endurance and faithfulness on the part of the
saints.

[a] *1* Some late manuscripts *And I* [b] *8* Or *written from the creation of the world in the book of life belonging to the Lamb that was slain* [c] *10* Some manuscripts *anyone kills*

(13:1–10) Lord Jesus, however the events in prophecy play out across the world's stage, keep the eyes of our spirits fixed upon You. Whatever we may encounter as the final days unfold, we ask You to provide us with patience, loyalty and discernment to remain faithful to You and You alone, until the final Amen is spoken. (Heb 12:2–3)

Today I am one day nearer home than ever before. One day nearer the dawning when the fog will lift, mysteries clear, and all question marks straighten up into exclamation points! I shall see the King!

Vance Havner (1901-)

(14:1) It is You, Lord Jesus, Who are the Lamb. You dwell eternally in the midst of Your people, those whom You have purchased as gifts for Your Father. You are the focal point of John's vision, the heart of the heavenly realm he describes, the centerpiece of the eternal gospel. Without You there is no glorious light, no eternal life, no celestial worship, no song of the saints, no cosmic victory. You, O Lamb of God, have gone to prepare a place for us, and You will eventually call us to be with You in our everlasting home. (Mt 28:20; Jn 14:2–3)

Crown Him with many crowns,
The Lamb upon His throne;
Hark! how the heavenly anthem
  drowns
All music but its own!
Awake, my soul, and sing
Of Him who died for thee,
And hail Him as thy matchless King
Through all eternity.

"Crown Him with Many Crowns"
Matthew Bridges (1851)

Bring us, O Lord God, at our last awakening into the house and gate of heaven, to enter into that gate and dwell in that house, where there shall be no darkness nor dazzling, but one equal light; no noise nor silence, but one equal music; no fears nor hopes, but one equal possession; no ends nor beginnings, but one equal eternity; in the habitations of your glory and dominion, world without end.

John Donne (1572-1631)

The Beast out of the Earth

11Then I saw another beast, coming out of the earth. He had
two horns like a lamb, but he spoke like a dragon. 12He exercised all the authority of the first beast on his behalf, and made
the earth and its inhabitants worship the first beast, whose fatal
wound had been healed. 13And he performed great and miraculous signs, even causing fire to come down from heaven to earth
in full view of men. 14Because of the signs he was given power to
do on behalf of the first beast, he deceived the inhabitants of the
earth. He ordered them to set up an image in honor of the beast
who was wounded by the sword and yet lived. 15He was given
power to give breath to the image of the first beast, so that it could
speak and cause all who refused to worship the image to be
killed. 16He also forced everyone, small and great, rich and poor,
free and slave, to receive a mark on his right hand or on his forehead, 17so that no one could buy or sell unless he had the mark,
which is the name of the beast or the number of his name.
18This calls for wisdom. If anyone has insight, let him calculate
the number of the beast, for it is man's number. His number is
666.

The Lamb and the 144,000

14 Then I looked, and there before me was the Lamb, standing on Mount Zion, and with him 144,000 who had his
name and his Father's name written on their foreheads. 2And I
heard a sound from heaven like the roar of rushing waters and
like a loud peal of thunder. The sound I heard was like that of
harpists playing their harps. 3And they sang a new song before the
throne and before the four living creatures and the elders. No one
could learn the song except the 144,000 who had been redeemed
from the earth. 4These are those who did not defile themselves
with women, for they kept themselves pure. They follow the Lamb
wherever he goes. They were purchased from among men and
offered as firstfruits to God and the Lamb. 5No lie was found in
their mouths; they are blameless.

The Three Angels

6Then I saw another angel flying in midair, and he had the eternal gospel to proclaim to those who live on the earth—to every
nation, tribe, language and people. 7He said in a loud voice,
"Fear God and give him glory, because the hour of his judgment
has come. Worship him who made the heavens, the earth, the sea
and the springs of water."
8A second angel followed and said, "Fallen! Fallen is Babylon
the Great, which made all the nations drink the maddening wine
of her adulteries."
9A third angel followed them and said in a loud voice: "If anyone worships the beast and his image and receives his mark on
the forehead or on the hand, 10he, too, will drink of the wine of
God's fury, which has been poured full strength into the cup of his
wrath. He will be tormented with burning sulfur in the presence
of the holy angels and of the Lamb. 11And the smoke of their torment rises for ever and ever. There is no rest day or night for
those who worship the beast and his image, or for anyone who
receives the mark of his name." 12This calls for patient endurance on the part of the saints who obey God's commandments
and remain faithful to Jesus.

13Then I heard a voice from heaven say, "Write: Blessed are the
dead who die in the Lord from now on."
"Yes," says the Spirit, "they will rest from their labor, for their
deeds will follow them."

The Harvest of the Earth

14I looked, and there before me was a white cloud, and seated
on the cloud was one "like a son of man"[a] with a crown of gold
on his head and a sharp sickle in his hand. 15Then another angel
came out of the temple and called in a loud voice to him who was
sitting on the cloud, "Take your sickle and reap, because the time
to reap has come, for the harvest of the earth is ripe." 16So he
who was seated on the cloud swung his sickle over the earth, and
the earth was harvested.
17Another angel came out of the temple in heaven, and he too
had a sharp sickle. 18Still another angel, who had charge of the
fire, came from the altar and called in a loud voice to him who
had the sharp sickle, "Take your sharp sickle and gather the clusters of grapes from the earth's vine, because its grapes are ripe."
19The angel swung his sickle on the earth, gathered its grapes
and threw them into the great winepress of God's wrath. 20They
were trampled in the winepress outside the city, and blood flowed
out of the press, rising as high as the horses' bridles for a distance of 1,600 stadia.[b]

Seven Angels With Seven Plagues

15 I saw in heaven another great and marvelous sign: seven
angels with the seven last plagues—last, because with
them God's wrath is completed. 2And I saw what looked like a sea
of glass mixed with fire and, standing beside the sea, those who
had been victorious over the beast and his image and over the
number of his name. They held harps given them by God 3and
sang the song of Moses the servant of God and the song of the
Lamb:

"Great and marvelous are your deeds,
 Lord God Almighty.
Just and true are your ways,
 King of the ages.
4Who will not fear you, O Lord,
 and bring glory to your name?
For you alone are holy.
All nations will come
 and worship before you,
for your righteous acts have been revealed."

5After this I looked and in heaven the temple, that is, the tabernacle of the Testimony, was opened. 6Out of the temple came the
seven angels with the seven plagues. They were dressed in clean,
shining linen and wore golden sashes around their chests. 7Then
one of the four living creatures gave to the seven angels seven
golden bowls filled with the wrath of God, who lives for ever and
ever. 8And the temple was filled with smoke from the glory of God
and from his power, and no one could enter the temple until the
seven plagues of the seven angels were completed.

[a] 14 Daniel 7:13 [b] 20 That is, about 180 miles (about 300 kilometers)

(15:3–4) The song of Moses is Your song, Lamb of God, for You have fulfilled the prophetic essence of the Father's mighty deeds among His covenant people of old. We join the saints of all ages and sing joyfully of Your mighty acts, Your holiness and Your salvation. We long for the day when the nations of the world will bow their knees and worship You, acknowledging what we already know—that You are King of all kings, Lord of all lords, and You alone are holy. (Php 2:9–11; 1Ti 6:15)

To the reigning King of heaven,
Alleluia, alleluia.
To the One whose life was given,
Glory to Your Name.
To the One whose blood redeemed
 us,
Alleluia, alleluia.
To the Holy One called Jesus,
Glory to Your name.
Alleluia, glory to the Lamb
Alleluia.

"Glory To The Lamb"
Bill Batstone (©1993)

(16:1) You, Lord, are not slow in keeping Your promise, as some understand slowness. In Your mercy You are patient with us, not wanting anyone to perish, but everyone to come to repentance, for You do not take pleasure in the death of anyone. Why, why, why do we choose death rather than life? We cannot run from Your hand, so let us run to Your side and seek Your mercy while there is still time. For we know that Your day of vengeance will come like a thief—that day when You will cry out from Your temple, "Enough!" The heavens will disappear with a roar, the elements will be destroyed by fire, and the earth and everything in it will be laid bare. In keeping with Your promise we are looking forward to a new heaven and a new earth, the home of righteousness. As we wait, help us to live holy and godly lives, to make every effort to be found spotless, blameless and at peace with You, and to grow in the grace and knowledge of You, our Lord and Savior Jesus Christ. To You be glory both now and forever! Amen. (Eze 33:11; Mt 24:42–44; 2Pe 3:8–18)

When Christ shall come with shout
of acclamation
And take me home, what joy shall fill
my heart!
Then I shall bow in humble adoration,
And there proclaim, my God, how
great Thou art.

"How Great Thou Art"
Stuart K. Hine (©1953, 1981)

The Seven Bowls of God's Wrath

16 Then I heard a loud voice from the temple saying to the
seven angels, "Go, pour out the seven bowls of God's wrath
on the earth."
2The first angel went and poured out his bowl on the land, and
ugly and painful sores broke out on the people who had the mark
of the beast and worshiped his image.
3The second angel poured out his bowl on the sea, and it
turned into blood like that of a dead man, and every living thing
in the sea died.
4The third angel poured out his bowl on the rivers and springs
of water, and they became blood. 5Then I heard the angel in
charge of the waters say:

"You are just in these judgments,
you who are and who were, the Holy One,
because you have so judged;
6for they have shed the blood of your saints and
prophets,
and you have given them blood to drink as they
deserve."

7And I heard the altar respond:

"Yes, Lord God Almighty,
true and just are your judgments."

8The fourth angel poured out his bowl on the sun, and the sun
was given power to scorch people with fire. 9They were seared by
the intense heat and they cursed the name of God, who had control over these plagues, but they refused to repent and glorify
him.
10The fifth angel poured out his bowl on the throne of the
beast, and his kingdom was plunged into darkness. Men gnawed
their tongues in agony 11and cursed the God of heaven because of
their pains and their sores, but they refused to repent of what they
had done.
12The sixth angel poured out his bowl on the great river Euphrates, and its water was dried up to prepare the way for the
kings from the East. 13Then I saw three evil[a] spirits that looked
like frogs; they came out of the mouth of the dragon, out of the
mouth of the beast and out of the mouth of the false prophet.
14They are spirits of demons performing miraculous signs, and
they go out to the kings of the whole world, to gather them for the
battle on the great day of God Almighty.
15"Behold, I come like a thief! Blessed is he who stays awake
and keeps his clothes with him, so that he may not go naked and
be shamefully exposed."
16Then they gathered the kings together to the place that in Hebrew is called Armageddon.
17The seventh angel poured out his bowl into the air, and out
of the temple came a loud voice from the throne, saying, "It is
done!" 18Then there came flashes of lightning, rumblings, peals
of thunder and a severe earthquake. No earthquake like it has
ever occurred since man has been on earth, so tremendous was
the quake. 19The great city split into three parts, and the cities of
the nations collapsed. God remembered Babylon the Great and

[a] 13 Greek *unclean*

gave her the cup filled with the wine of the fury of his wrath.
[20]Every island fled away and the mountains could not be found.
[21]From the sky huge hailstones of about a hundred pounds each
fell upon men. And they cursed God on account of the plague of
hail, because the plague was so terrible.

The Woman on the Beast

17 One of the seven angels who had the seven bowls came and
said to me, "Come, I will show you the punishment of the
great prostitute, who sits on many waters. [2]With her the kings of
the earth committed adultery and the inhabitants of the earth
were intoxicated with the wine of her adulteries."
[3]Then the angel carried me away in the Spirit into a desert.
There I saw a woman sitting on a scarlet beast that was covered
with blasphemous names and had seven heads and ten horns.
[4]The woman was dressed in purple and scarlet, and was glittering with gold, precious stones and pearls. She held a golden cup
in her hand, filled with abominable things and the filth of her
adulteries. [5]This title was written on her forehead:

MYSTERY
BABYLON THE GREAT
THE MOTHER OF PROSTITUTES
AND OF THE ABOMINATIONS OF THE EARTH.

[6]I saw that the woman was drunk with the blood of the saints, the
blood of those who bore testimony to Jesus.
When I saw her, I was greatly astonished. [7]Then the angel said
to me: "Why are you astonished? I will explain to you the mystery
of the woman and of the beast she rides, which has the seven
heads and ten horns. [8]The beast, which you saw, once was, now
is not, and will come up out of the Abyss and go to his destruction. The inhabitants of the earth whose names have not been
written in the book of life from the creation of the world will be
astonished when they see the beast, because he once was, now is
not, and yet will come.
[9]"This calls for a mind with wisdom. The seven heads are
seven hills on which the woman sits. [10]They are also seven kings.
Five have fallen, one is, the other has not yet come; but when he
does come, he must remain for a little while. [11]The beast who
once was, and now is not, is an eighth king. He belongs to the
seven and is going to his destruction.
[12]"The ten horns you saw are ten kings who have not yet received a kingdom, but who for one hour will receive authority as
kings along with the beast. [13]They have one purpose and will give
their power and authority to the beast. [14]They will make war
against the Lamb, but the Lamb will overcome them because he is
Lord of lords and King of kings—and with him will be his called,
chosen and faithful followers."
[15]Then the angel said to me, "The waters you saw, where the
prostitute sits, are peoples, multitudes, nations and languages.
[16]The beast and the ten horns you saw will hate the prostitute.
They will bring her to ruin and leave her naked; they will eat her
flesh and burn her with fire. [17]For God has put it into their hearts
to accomplish his purpose by agreeing to give the beast their
power to rule, until God's words are fulfilled. [18]The woman you
saw is the great city that rules over the kings of the earth."

(17:6) Lord Jesus Christ, Your message of salvation was written first in Your own blood and then copied in the blood of martyrs. You could have split the skies the moment You walked out of the tomb, and announced Your victory to all humankind. You chose instead to conquer the nations slowly, laboriously, counting on a few witnesses passing on a gospel that often cost them their lives. What process could have been more unlikely or seemed less efficient? And yet for two millennia, generation after generation has been transformed by the testimony of Your martyred saints. Until the day of Your appearing Your ongoing defeat of evil forces will be accomplished through the weakest of instruments in the most impossible of circumstances—Your children singing songs of Life beneath the dark shadow of death.

Pliny: I will banish thee.
Christian: Thou canst not, for the whole world is my Father's house.
Pliny: I will slay thee.
Christian: Thou canst not, for my life is hid with Christ in God.
Pliny: I will take away thy treasures.
Christian: Thou canst not, for my treasure is in heaven.
Pliny: I will drive thee away from men, and thou wilt have no friends.
Christian: Thou canst not, for I have a Friend from whom thou canst never separate me.

Pliny the Elder (23-79)

(18:4–5) O Lord, in these days as we await Your final judgment, help us to heed this warning: "Come out of her, my people, so that You will not share in her sins." For if we do not repent of our sins, we will surely lament our ruin. O Lord, save us from the worries of this life and the deceitfulness of wealth. Teach us to flee from evil. While we are in the world, may we not be of the world. "For what do righteousness and wickedness have in common? Or what fellowship can light have with darkness? What harmony is there between Christ and Belial? What does a believer have in common with an unbeliever? What agreement is there between the temple of God and idols? For we are the temple of the living God." As You have said, " 'I will live with them and walk among them, and I will be their God, and they will be my people.' " (Mk 4:19; Jn 15:19; 17:14–16; 2Co 6:14–16; 1Ti 6:11; 2Ti 2:22)

The Fall of Babylon

18 After this I saw another angel coming down from heaven. He had great authority, and the earth was illuminated by his splendor. 2With a mighty voice he shouted:

"Fallen! Fallen is Babylon the Great!
She has become a home for demons
and a haunt for every evil[a] spirit,
a haunt for every unclean and detestable bird.
3For all the nations have drunk
the maddening wine of her adulteries.
The kings of the earth committed adultery with her,
and the merchants of the earth grew rich from her
excessive luxuries."

4Then I heard another voice from heaven say:

"Come out of her, my people,
so that you will not share in her sins,
so that you will not receive any of her plagues;
5for her sins are piled up to heaven,
and God has remembered her crimes.
6Give back to her as she has given;
pay her back double for what she has done.
Mix her a double portion from her own cup.
7Give her as much torture and grief
as the glory and luxury she gave herself.
In her heart she boasts,
'I sit as queen; I am not a widow,
and I will never mourn.'
8Therefore in one day her plagues will overtake her:
death, mourning and famine.
She will be consumed by fire,
for mighty is the Lord God who judges her.

9"When the kings of the earth who committed adultery with
her and shared her luxury see the smoke of her burning, they will
weep and mourn over her. 10Terrified at her torment, they will
stand far off and cry:

" 'Woe! Woe, O great city,
O Babylon, city of power!
In one hour your doom has come!'

11"The merchants of the earth will weep and mourn over her
because no one buys their cargoes any more— 12cargoes of
gold, silver, precious stones and pearls; fine linen, purple, silk
and scarlet cloth; every sort of citron wood, and articles of every
kind made of ivory, costly wood, bronze, iron and marble; 13cargoes of cinnamon and spice, of incense, myrrh and frankincense,
of wine and olive oil, of fine flour and wheat; cattle and sheep;
horses and carriages; and bodies and souls of men.

14"They will say, 'The fruit you longed for is gone from you. All
your riches and splendor have vanished, never to be recovered.'
15The merchants who sold these things and gained their wealth
from her will stand far off, terrified at her torment. They will weep
and mourn 16and cry out:

[a] 2 Greek *unclean*

" 'Woe! Woe, O great city,
dressed in fine linen, purple and scarlet,
and glittering with gold, precious stones and pearls!
17 In one hour such great wealth has been brought to ruin!'

"Every sea captain, and all who travel by ship, the sailors, and
all who earn their living from the sea, will stand far off. 18 When
they see the smoke of her burning, they will exclaim, 'Was there
ever a city like this great city?' 19 They will throw dust on their
heads, and with weeping and mourning cry out:

" 'Woe! Woe, O great city,
where all who had ships on the sea
became rich through her wealth!
In one hour she has been brought to ruin!
20 Rejoice over her, O heaven!
Rejoice, saints and apostles and prophets!
God has judged her for the way she treated you.' "

21 Then a mighty angel picked up a boulder the size of a large
millstone and threw it into the sea, and said:

"With such violence
the great city of Babylon will be thrown down,
never to be found again.
22 The music of harpists and musicians, flute players and trumpeters,
will never be heard in you again.
No workman of any trade
will ever be found in you again.
The sound of a millstone
will never be heard in you again.
23 The light of a lamp
will never shine in you again.
The voice of bridegroom and bride
will never be heard in you again.
Your merchants were the world's great men.
By your magic spell all the nations were led astray.
24 In her was found the blood of prophets and of the saints,
and of all who have been killed on the earth."

Hallelujah!

19 After this I heard what sounded like the roar of a great multitude in heaven shouting:

"Hallelujah!
Salvation and glory and power belong to our God,
2 for true and just are his judgments.
He has condemned the great prostitute
who corrupted the earth by her adulteries.
He has avenged on her the blood of his servants."

3 And again they shouted:

"Hallelujah!
The smoke from her goes up for ever and ever."

4 The twenty-four elders and the four living creatures fell down

(18:20—19:2) We praise You and thank You, our sovereign Lord Jesus, that You are a jealous and avenging God Who will not leave the guilty unpunished. You wear righteousness as Your breastplate, and the helmet of salvation crowns Your head; You are clothed in garments of vengeance, and You have wrapped Yourself in the cloak of zeal. Come strengthen our feeble hands and steady our weak knees. Make us strong and courageous in the midst of evil. We look to You alone to deliver us, for You, our God and Savior, will come with vengeance and divine retribution; You will repay! (Isa 35:3–4; Na 1:2–3; Heb 10:30)

Rejoice in glorious hope!
Our Lord the Judge shall come
And take His servants up
To their eternal home.
Lift up your heart,
Lift up your voice,
Rejoice, again I say rejoice!

"Rejoice, The Lord Is King"
Charles Wesley (1746)

The best way to understand the doctrine of the wrath of God is to consider the alternatives. The alternative is not love; since rightly considered love and wrath are only the obverse and reverse of the same thing . . . the alternative to wrath is neutrality—neutrality in the conflict of the world . . . to live in such a world would be a nightmare. It is only the doctrine of the wrath of God, of his irreconcilable hostility to all evil, which makes human life tolerable in such a world as ours.

Stephen Neill (1900-1984)

and worshiped God, who was seated on the throne. And they
cried:

"Amen, Hallelujah!"

5 Then a voice came from the throne, saying:

"Praise our God,
all you his servants,
you who fear him,
both small and great!"

6 Then I heard what sounded like a great multitude, like the
roar of rushing waters and like loud peals of thunder, shouting:

"Hallelujah!
For our Lord God Almighty reigns.
7 Let us rejoice and be glad
and give him glory!
For the wedding of the Lamb has come,
and his bride has made herself ready.
8 Fine linen, bright and clean,
was given her to wear."

(Fine linen stands for the righteous acts of the saints.)

9 Then the angel said to me, "Write: 'Blessed are those who are
invited to the wedding supper of the Lamb!' " And he added,
"These are the true words of God."
10 At this I fell at his feet to worship him. But he said to me, "Do
not do it! I am a fellow servant with you and with your brothers
who hold to the testimony of Jesus. Worship God! For the testimony of Jesus is the spirit of prophecy."

The Rider on the White Horse

11 I saw heaven standing open and there before me was a white
horse, whose rider is called Faithful and True. With justice he
judges and makes war. 12 His eyes are like blazing fire, and on
his head are many crowns. He has a name written on him that no
one knows but he himself. 13 He is dressed in a robe dipped in
blood, and his name is the Word of God. 14 The armies of heav-
en were following him, riding on white horses and dressed in
fine linen, white and clean. 15 Out of his mouth comes a sharp
sword with which to strike down the nations. "He will rule them
with an iron scepter."[a] He treads the winepress of the fury of the
wrath of God Almighty. 16 On his robe and on his thigh he has this
name written:

KING OF KINGS AND LORD OF LORDS.

17 And I saw an angel standing in the sun, who cried in a loud
voice to all the birds flying in midair, "Come, gather together for
the great supper of God, 18 so that you may eat the flesh of kings,
generals, and mighty men, of horses and their riders, and the
flesh of all people, free and slave, small and great."
19 Then I saw the beast and the kings of the earth and their armies gathered together to make war against the rider on the
horse and his army. 20 But the beast was captured, and with him
the false prophet who had performed the miraculous signs on his
behalf. With these signs he had deluded those who had received

[a] 15 Psalm 2:9

(19:11–16) What joy it will be to see You at last, my Lord and my God! You, King Jesus, Word of God, are the very expression of the heart and mind of the Father. The fullness of Your character, like the fullness of Your name, is beyond human comprehension. You are the commander of the armies of heaven. You are supremely sovereign over the nations of the earth. You are the one being over all the universe Who is worthy of my unquestioning loyalty; the one mighty hero over all the world Who is worthy of my wholehearted admiration; the one righteous Savior over all creation Who is worthy of my absolute worship. (Heb 1:3)

When we see Him
We shall be like Him.
When we see Him
There will be only tears of joy.
When we see Him in the clouds
Every nation will bow.
And we'll proclaim, proclaim
Jesus Christ is Lord.

When we see Him
We'll see our Blessed Hope.
On that long awaited day
There will be no more hate or pain.
On that white horse He'll ride;
He'll split the eastern sky.
And we'll proclaim, proclaim
Jesus Christ is Lord.

"When We See Him"
Tommy Walker (©1995)

the mark of the beast and worshiped his image. The two of them
were thrown alive into the fiery lake of burning sulfur. 21 The rest
of them were killed with the sword that came out of the mouth of
the rider on the horse, and all the birds gorged themselves on
their flesh.

The Thousand Years

20 And I saw an angel coming down out of heaven, having
the key to the Abyss and holding in his hand a great chain.
2 He seized the dragon, that ancient serpent, who is the devil, or
Satan, and bound him for a thousand years. 3 He threw him into
the Abyss, and locked and sealed it over him, to keep him from
deceiving the nations anymore until the thousand years were
ended. After that, he must be set free for a short time.
4 I saw thrones on which were seated those who had been given
authority to judge. And I saw the souls of those who had been beheaded because of their testimony for Jesus and because of the
word of God. They had not worshiped the beast or his image and
had not received his mark on their foreheads or their hands. They
came to life and reigned with Christ a thousand years. 5 (The rest
of the dead did not come to life until the thousand years were
ended.) This is the first resurrection. 6 Blessed and holy are those
who have part in the first resurrection. The second death has no
power over them, but they will be priests of God and of Christ and
will reign with him for a thousand years.

Satan's Doom

7 When the thousand years are over, Satan will be released from
his prison 8 and will go out to deceive the nations in the four corners of the earth—Gog and Magog—to gather them for battle. In
number they are like the sand on the seashore. 9 They marched
across the breadth of the earth and surrounded the camp of
God's people, the city he loves. But fire came down from heaven
and devoured them. 10 And the devil, who deceived them, was
thrown into the lake of burning sulfur, where the beast and the
false prophet had been thrown. They will be tormented day and
night for ever and ever.

The Dead Are Judged

11 Then I saw a great white throne and him who was seated on
it. Earth and sky fled from his presence, and there was no place
for them. 12 And I saw the dead, great and small, standing before
the throne, and books were opened. Another book was opened,
which is the book of life. The dead were judged according to what
they had done as recorded in the books. 13 The sea gave up the
dead that were in it, and death and Hades gave up the dead that
were in them, and each person was judged according to what he
had done. 14 Then death and Hades were thrown into the lake of
fire. The lake of fire is the second death. 15 If anyone's name was
not found written in the book of life, he was thrown into the lake
of fire.

The New Jerusalem

21 Then I saw a new heaven and a new earth, for the first
heaven and the first earth had passed away, and there was
no longer any sea. 2 I saw the Holy City, the new Jerusalem, coming down out of heaven from God, prepared as a bride beauti-

(20:7–15) We praise You, Lord Jesus, our great conquering King! All Your ways are righteous and true. You have supreme authority over all principalities and powers in heaven and on earth. The Father has entrusted all judgment to You. You are the Savior of Your people, the Author of the Lamb's book of life and the destroyer of death and hell. "Righteousness and justice are the foundation of your throne; love and faithfulness go before you. Blessed are those who have learned to acclaim you, who walk in the light of your presence, O LORD. They rejoice in your name all day long; they exult in your righteousness." (Ps 89:14–16; Jn 5:22)

His Kingdom cannot fail,
He rules o'er earth and heav'n.
The keys of death and hell
Are to our Jesus giv'n.
Lift up your heart,
Lift up your voice,
Rejoice, again I say rejoice!

"Rejoice, The Lord Is King"
Charles Wesley (1746)

fully dressed for her husband. 3And I heard a loud voice from
the throne saying, "Now the dwelling of God is with men, and he
will live with them. They will be his people, and God himself will
be with them and be their God. 4He will wipe every tear from
their eyes. There will be no more death or mourning or crying or
pain, for the old order of things has passed away."
5He who was seated on the throne said, "I am making everything new!" Then he said, "Write this down, for these words are
trustworthy and true."
6He said to me: "It is done. I am the Alpha and the Omega, the
Beginning and the End. To him who is thirsty I will give to drink
without cost from the spring of the water of life. 7He who overcomes will inherit all this, and I will be his God and he will be my
son. 8But the cowardly, the unbelieving, the vile, the murderers,
the sexually immoral, those who practice magic arts, the idolaters
and all liars—their place will be in the fiery lake of burning sulfur. This is the second death."
9One of the seven angels who had the seven bowls full of the
seven last plagues came and said to me, "Come, I will show you
the bride, the wife of the Lamb." 10And he carried me away in the
Spirit to a mountain great and high, and showed me the Holy City,
Jerusalem, coming down out of heaven from God. 11It shone with
the glory of God, and its brilliance was like that of a very precious
jewel, like a jasper, clear as crystal. 12It had a great, high wall
with twelve gates, and with twelve angels at the gates. On the gates
were written the names of the twelve tribes of Israel. 13There
were three gates on the east, three on the north, three on the
south and three on the west. 14The wall of the city had twelve
foundations, and on them were the names of the twelve apostles
of the Lamb.
15The angel who talked with me had a measuring rod of gold
to measure the city, its gates and its walls. 16The city was laid out
like a square, as long as it was wide. He measured the city with
the rod and found it to be 12,000 stadia[a] in length, and as wide
and high as it is long. 17He measured its wall and it was 144 cubits[b] thick,[c] by man's measurement, which the angel was using.
18The wall was made of jasper, and the city of pure gold, as pure
as glass. 19The foundations of the city walls were decorated with
every kind of precious stone. The first foundation was jasper,
the second sapphire, the third chalcedony, the fourth emerald,
20the fifth sardonyx, the sixth carnelian, the seventh chrysolite,
the eighth beryl, the ninth topaz, the tenth chrysoprase, the
eleventh jacinth, and the twelfth amethyst.[d] 21The twelve gates
were twelve pearls, each gate made of a single pearl. The great
street of the city was of pure gold, like transparent glass.
22I did not see a temple in the city, because the Lord God
Almighty and the Lamb are its temple. 23The city does not need
the sun or the moon to shine on it, for the glory of God gives it
light, and the Lamb is its lamp. 24The nations will walk by its light,
and the kings of the earth will bring their splendor into it. 25On
no day will its gates ever be shut, for there will be no night there.
26The glory and honor of the nations will be brought into it.
27Nothing impure will ever enter it, nor will anyone who does

[a] *16* That is, about 1,400 miles (about 2,200 kilometers) [b] *17* That is, about 200 feet (about 65 meters) [c] *17* Or *high* [d] *20* The precise identification of some of these precious stones is uncertain.

(21:23) You, Lamb of God, are the Light of lights, the Sun of righteousness. Compared to You the sun is but a flickering candle in broad daylight. Yours is the light of joy, the light of revelation, the light of truth and the light of purity. Guide us, O Lord, with the light of Your beautiful presence, both now and forever. (Mal 4:2; Jn 8:12)

In heaven above, in heaven above,
What glory deep and bright!
The splendor of the noonday sun
Grows pale before its light;
That mighty Sun that ne'er goes
down,
Before whose face clouds never
frown,
Is God the Lord of hosts!

"In Heaven Above"
Laurentius Laurentii Laurinus (1622)
Trans. William Maccall (1812-1888)

Jesus whom I look at shrouded here below,
I beseech you send me what I thirst for so,
Some day to gaze on you face to face in light
And be blest forever with your glory's sight.

Latin (13th c.)
Translated by Gerard Manley Hopkins (1844-1889)

MY BELOVED

I know that many doubt My return and act as if I do not even exist. There are those who scoff at your hope saying, "Where is this 'coming' He promised? Much time has passed and yet everything goes on as it has since the beginning of creation."

But do not forget this, My beloved: With Me a day is like a thousand years, and a thousand years are like a day. I am not bound by your time constraints.

And do not think I am slow in keeping My promise to return, as some might say. Instead, I am patient. I want as many as possible to repent of their sins and join our family. I want a big reunion.

When I do return, I will come for all true believers—those who have already died and those who are yet alive. It will be a spectacular day! With a loud command, with the voice of the archangel and with the trumpet call of God, all of you who are Mine will be brought up together to live with Me forever.

Look forward to that day. I do. And be encouraged, My beloved. I am coming soon! Maranatha!

1Th 4:15-18; 2Pe 3:3-4,8-9; Rev 22:12,20

what is shameful or deceitful, but only those whose names are
written in the Lamb's book of life.

The River of Life

22 Then the angel showed me the river of the water of life, as
clear as crystal, flowing from the throne of God and of
the Lamb 2down the middle of the great street of the city. On
each side of the river stood the tree of life, bearing twelve crops
of fruit, yielding its fruit every month. And the leaves of the tree
are for the healing of the nations. 3No longer will there be any
curse. The throne of God and of the Lamb will be in the city, and
his servants will serve him. 4They will see his face, and his name
will be on their foreheads. 5There will be no more night. They
will not need the light of a lamp or the light of the sun, for the
Lord God will give them light. And they will reign for ever and
ever.
6The angel said to me, "These words are trustworthy and true.
The Lord, the God of the spirits of the prophets, sent his angel to
show his servants the things that must soon take place."

Jesus Is Coming

7"Behold, I am coming soon! Blessed is he who keeps the
words of the prophecy in this book."

8I, John, am the one who heard and saw these things. And
when I had heard and seen them, I fell down to worship at the
feet of the angel who had been showing them to me. 9But he said
to me, "Do not do it! I am a fellow servant with you and with your
brothers the prophets and of all who keep the words of this book.
Worship God!"
10Then he told me, "Do not seal up the words of the prophecy
of this book, because the time is near. 11Let him who does wrong
continue to do wrong; let him who is vile continue to be vile; let
him who does right continue to do right; and let him who is holy
continue to be holy."

12"Behold, I am coming soon! My reward is with me, and I will
give to everyone according to what he has done. 13I am the Alpha
and the Omega, the First and the Last, the Beginning and the End.
14"Blessed are those who wash their robes, that they may have
the right to the tree of life and may go through the gates into the
city. 15Outside are the dogs, those who practice magic arts, the
sexually immoral, the murderers, the idolaters and everyone who
loves and practices falsehood.
16"I, Jesus, have sent my angel to give you[a] this testimony for
the churches. I am the Root and the Offspring of David, and the
bright Morning Star."

17The Spirit and the bride say, "Come!" And let him who hears
say, "Come!" Whoever is thirsty, let him come; and whoever
wishes, let him take the free gift of the water of life.

18I warn everyone who hears the words of the prophecy of this
book: If anyone adds anything to them, God will add to him the
plagues described in this book. 19And if anyone takes words away
from this book of prophecy, God will take away from him his

[a] *16* The Greek is plural.

Fountain of life, and all-abounding grace,
Our source, our center, and our dwelling place!

Madame Jeanne Marie de La Mothe Guyon (1648–1717)

(22:12–17) Looking to the end, we remember our beginning. You have been there all along. You are Alpha and Omega, the Beginning and the End, the starting point and the destination of life. We long for the day of Your return, Lord Jesus. Come to us. Abide with us. Feed us and heal us. Cleanse us and possess us. Refresh us and sustain us. Live in us and reign through us. We give You praise, our glorious Lord and Savior, as we wait restlessly for Your return.

You are my dwelling place,
My tower of strength,
And at Your throne of grace
I humbly bow.
My affections I pour out,
My eyes release their tears
As I behold the beauty of You, Lord.

How I long to see Your face,
Yes, I long to see Your face.
You are my dwelling place,
With You my heart will stay.

"You Are My Dwelling Place"
John Sellers (©1985)

share in the tree of life and in the holy city, which are described
in this book.
20He who testifies to these things says, "Yes, I am coming
soon."

Amen. Come, Lord Jesus.

21The grace of the Lord Jesus be with God's people. Amen.

Eternity will not be long enough to learn all he is, or to praise him for all he has done, but then, that matters not; for we shall be always with him, and we desire nothing more.

Frederick William Faber (1814-1863)

(22:20) Across the centuries, throughout all recorded history, You have called out to us in Your gracious love. You have offered Yourself to us, and pleaded with us to come to You. You have invited us to come when we are thirsty; come when we are wounded; come when we are lost in sin; come when we are poor, alone and without hope. And we have come, Lord, in faith, in humility and in gratitude. Now we join our voices with John's, and we invite You to come to us. Return to us, Lord Jesus, and make Your dwelling place among us. We pray that You will come soon and come quickly, for above all else we long to see Your face. Come, Lord Jesus. Maranatha! (Isa 27:5; 55:1–3; Mt 11:28; Jn 7:37–38; Rev 22:17)

Jesus comes with clouds descending
See the Lamb for sinners slain!
Thousand thousand saints attending
Join to sing the glad refrain:
Alleluia! Alleluia! Alleluia!
God appears on earth to reign;
God appears on earth to reign.

Yes, Amen! Let all adore you
High on your eternal throne;
Crowns and empires fall before you
Claim the kingdom for your own.
Come, Lord Jesus,
Come, Lord Jesus,
Come, Lord Jesus,
Everlasting God, come down;
Everlasting God, come down!

"Jesus Comes with Clouds Descending"
Charles Wesley (1758)

Study Helps

WEIGHTS AND MEASURES

INDEX OF QUOTATIONS

BIBLIOGRAPHY OF QUOTATIONS

INDEX OF LYRICS

DIRECTORY OF SONG PUBLISHERS

CONCORDANCE

WEIGHTS AND MEASURES

		BIBLICAL UNIT	APPROXIMATE AMERICAN EQUIVALENT	APPROXIMATE METRIC EQUIVALENT
WEIGHTS	talent	(60 minas)	75 pounds	34 kilograms
	mina	(50 shekels)	1 1/4 pounds	0.6 kilogram
	shekel	(2 bekas)	2/5 ounce	11.5 grams
	pim	(2/3 shekel)	1/3 ounce	7.6 grams
	beka	(10 gerahs)	1/5 ounce	5.5 grams
	gerah		1/50 ounce	0.6 gram
LENGTH	cubit		18 inches	0.5 meter
	span		9 inches	23 centimeters
	handbreadth		3 inches	8 centimeters
CAPACITY				
Dry Measure	cor [homer]	(10 ephahs)	6 bushels	220 liters
	lethek	(5 ephahs)	3 bushels	110 liters
	ephah	(10 omers)	3/5 bushel	22 liters
	seah	(1/3 ephah)	7 quarts	7.3 liters
	omer	(1/10 ephah)	2 quarts	2 liters
	cab	(1/18 ephah)	1 quart	1 liter
Liquid Measure	bath	(1 ephah)	6 gallons	22 liters
	hin	(1/6 bath)	4 quarts	4 liters
	log	(1/72 bath)	1/3 quart	0.3 liter

The figures of the table are calculated on the basis of a shekel equaling 11.5 grams, a cubit equaling 18 inches and an ephah equaling 22 liters. The quart referred to is either a dry quart (slightly larger than a liter) or a liquid quart (slightly smaller than a liter), whichever is applicable. The ton referred to in the footnotes is the American ton of 2,000 pounds.

This table is based upon the best available information, but it is not intended to be mathematically precise; like the measurement equivalents in the footnotes, it merely gives approximate amounts and distances. Weights and measures differed somewhat at various times and places in the ancient world. There is uncertainty particularly about the ephah and the bath; further discoveries may shed more light on these units of capacity.

Index of Quotations

Bibliography of Quotations

Auch, Ron, pp. 408, 559, 588. From *Taught by the Spirit: an In-Depth Look at Spiritual Warfare*, ©1991, New Leaf Press, Green Forest, AR.

Austin, Anne, p. 1264. From *Draper's Book of Quotations from the Christian World*, Edited by Edythe Draper, ©1992, Tyndale House Publishers, Inc., Wheaton, IL.

Barclay, William, pp. 1200, 1242. From *Draper's Book of Quotations from the Christian World*, Edited by Edythe Draper, ©1992, Tyndale House Publishers, Inc., Wheaton, IL.

Barker, William P., p. 839. From *A Savior for All Seasons*, ©1986 by William P. Barker, Fleming H. Revell, a division of Baker Book House, Grand Rapids, MI.

Barth, Karl, p. 1176. From *Draper's Book of Quotations from the Christian World*, Edited by Edythe Draper, ©1992, Tyndale House Publishers, Inc., Wheaton, IL.

Benson, Bob, pp. 378, 842, 1314. From *In Quest of the Shared Life*, ©1986, Generoux Publishers, 3900 Plantation Drive, Hermitage, TN, 37076.

Brand, Paul and Philip Yancey, p. 181. From *In His Image*, ©1984 by Paul Brand and Philip Yancey, Zondervan Publishing House, Grand Rapids, MI.

Bridges, Jerry, pp. 306, 366, 440, 834, 1222. From *The Pursuit of Holiness*, ©1978, NavPress Publishing Group, Colorado Springs, CO.

Bridges, Jerry, p. 176. From *Transforming Grace*, ©1991 by Jerry Bridges, NavPress Publishing Group, Colorado Springs, CO.

Briscoe, Jill, p. 868. From *The One Year Book of Quiet Times with God*, ©1997, Tyndale House Publishers, Inc., Wheaton, IL.

Briscoe, Stuart, p. 1255. From *Draper's Book of Quotations from the Christian World*, Edited by Edythe Draper, ©1992, Tyndale House Publishers, Inc., Wheaton, IL.

Bubeck, Mark I., p. 870. From *The Adversary*, © 1975, Moody Press, Chicago, IL.

Buber, Martin, p. 1078. From *Draper's Book of Quotations from the Christian World*, Edited by Edythe Draper, ©1992, Tyndale House Publishers, Inc., Wheaton, IL.

Buechner, Frederick, p. 684. From *Draper's Book of Quotations from the Christian World*, Edited by Edythe Draper, ©1992, Tyndale House Publishers, Inc., Wheaton, IL.

Buttrick, George A., pp. 321,436, 1132. From *Prayer*, ©1942, Whitmore & Stone; Copyright renewed 1969 by George A. Buttrick, Abingdon Press, Nashville, TN.

Carmichael, Amy, pp. 276, 888. From *Draper's Book of Quotations from the Christian World*, Edited by Edythe Draper, ©1992, Tyndale House Publishers, Inc., Wheaton, IL.

Carmichael, Amy, pp. 572, 865. From *Candles in the Dark*, Amy Carmichael, ©1981, Christian Literature Crusade, Fort Washington, PA.

Cassels, Louis, pp. 114, 261, 273, 286, 1493, 1643. From *Draper's Book of Quotations from the Christian World*, Edited by Edythe Draper, ©1992, Tyndale House Publishers, Inc., Wheaton, IL.

Colson, Charles, pp. 86, 1476, 1498. From *Draper's Book of Quotations from the Christian World*, Edited by Edythe Draper, ©1992, Tyndale House Publishers, Inc., Wheaton, IL.

Colson, Charles, pp. 328, 1127. From *Loving God*, Charles W. Colson, © 1983, 1987, Zondervan Publishing House, Grand Rapids, MI.

Couchman, Judith, p. 397. From *His Gentle Voice*, ©1998 by Judith Couchman, Multnomah Publishers, Inc., Portland, OR.

Cowman, Lettie B., pp. 376, 451, 614. From *Streams in the Desert*, ©1925, Zondervan Publishing House, Grand Rapids, MI.

Cowman, Lettie B., pp. 938, 957. From *Springs in the Valley* ©1939, Cowman Publications, Inc., Los Angeles, CA.

Duewel, Wesley L., pp. 381, 836, 1169. From *Touch the World through Prayer*, ©1986, Francis Asbury Press of Zondervan Publishing House, Grand Rapids, MI.

Eastman, Dick and Jack Hayford, pp. 183, 371, 428, 601, 849, 1173. From *Living & Praying in Jesus' Name*, ©1988, Tyndale House Publishers, Inc., Wheaton, IL.

Edman, Victor Raymond, pp. 185, 568, 835. From *The Disciplines of Life*, ©1948, Scripture Press Foundation, Colorado Springs, CO.

Evely, Louis, pp. 667, 1237, 1341, 1452. From *Draper's Book of Quotations from the Christian World*, Edited by Edythe Draper, ©1992, Tyndale House Publishers, Inc., Wheaton, IL.

Foster, Richard J., pp. 8, 670, 1247. From *Draper's Book of Quotations from the Christian World*, Edited by Edythe Draper, ©1992, Tyndale House Publishers, Inc., Wheaton, IL.

Gire, Ken, p. 1459. From *Reflections on the Word*, ©1998, Chariot Victor Publishing Company, Colorado Springs, CO.

Gordon, Samuel Dickey (S. D.), pp. 209, 308, 407, 579, 856, 955, 959. From *Quiet Talks on Service*.

Graham, Billy, pp. 87, 133, 283, 546, 905, 1042, 1282, 1344, 1399, 1594. From *Draper's Book of Quotations from the Christian World*, Edited by Edythe Draper, ©1992, Tyndale House Publishers, Inc., Wheaton, IL.

Graham, Billy, p. 869. From *The Holy Spirit*, ©1978, Published by Warner Books, P.O. Box 690, New York, NY 10019.

Graham, Ruth Bell, p. 647. From *Draper's Book of Quotations from the Christian World*, Edited by Edythe Draper, ©1992, Tyndale House Publishers, Inc., Wheaton, IL.

Grubb, Norman, p. 640. From *Touching the Invisible*, ©1940, 1987, Christian Literature Crusade, Fort Washington, PA.

Halverson, Richard C., p. 299. From *Draper's Book of Quotations from the Christian World*, Edited by Edythe Draper, ©1992, Tyndale House Publishers, Inc., Wheaton, IL.

Hansel, Tim, p. 907. From *Draper's Book of Quotations from the Christian World*, Edited by Edythe Draper, ©1992, Tyndale House Publishers, Inc., Wheaton, IL.

Harkness, Georgia, p. 98. From *Draper's Book of Quotations from the Christian World*, Edited by Edythe Draper, ©1992, Tyndale House Publishers, Inc., Wheaton, IL.

Harris, Sydney J., p. 118. From *Draper's Book of Quotations from the Christian World*, Edited by Edythe Draper, ©1992, Tyndale House Publishers, Inc., Wheaton, IL.

Hatch, Clarence W., pp. 179, 387, 430. From *Stewardship Enriches Life*, ©1951 by Clarence Hatch, revised edition copyright 1962 by Mildred Hatch, published by The Warner Press, Anderson, IN.

Havner, Vance, pp. 95, 1671. From *Draper's Book of Quotations from the Christian World*, Edited by Edythe Draper, ©1992, Tyndale House Publishers, Inc., Wheaton, IL.

Henry, Carl F. H., p. 1380. From *Draper's Book of Quotations from the Christian World*, Edited by Edythe Draper, ©1992, Tyndale House Publishers, Inc., Wheaton, IL.

Henry, Matthew, pp. 6, 13, 141, 275, 303, 332, 342, 359, 392, 401, 417, 423, 442, 459, 484, 504, 555, 609, 617, 671, 840, 863, 1028, 1110, 1158, 1263, 1304, 1311, 1417, 1634. From *A Commentary on the Whole Bible, Vols. 1-6*, First published in 1712.

Henry, Matthew, p. 1298. From *The Secret of Communion with God*, Matthew Henry, First published in 1712

Huegel, Frederick Julius, pp. 305. 380, 1325. From *Forever Triumphant: The Secret of Victory in the Christian Life*, ©1955, Zondervan Publishing House, Grand Rapids, MI.

Jackson, Catherine, pp. 191, 341, 373, 626, 853, 1160, 1307, 1332. From *The Christian's Secret of a Happy Life for Today: A Paraphrase of Hannah Whitall Smith's Classic*, Catherine Jackson. ©1979. Published by Fleming H. Revell, a division of Baker Book House, Grand Rapids, MI.

Jones, E. Stanley, pp. 549, 941, 1203. From *Draper's Book of Quotations from the Christian World*, Edited by Edythe Draper, ©1992, Tyndale House Publishers, Inc., Wheaton, IL.

Jones, E. Stanley, p. 1374. From *Abundant Living*, ©1942, Whitmore & Stone, Published by Abingdon Press, Nashville, TN.

Jones, E. Stanley, p. 855. From *The Way to Power and Poise*, ©1949, Pierce & Smith, Published by Abingdon Press, Nashville, TN.

Jones, Rufus Matthew, p. 127. From *Draper's Book of Quotations from the Christian World*, Edited by Edythe Draper, ©1992, Tyndale House Publishers, Inc., Wheaton, IL.

Keller, Helen Adams, p. 50. From *Draper's Book of Quotations from the Christian World*, Edited by Edythe Draper, ©1992, Tyndale House Publishers, Inc., Wheaton, IL.

Kildahl, J.N., pp. 327, 394, 564, 1329. From *Concerning Sin and Grace*, Translated by Bernhard H. J. Habel, ©1954, Augsburg Publishing House, Minneapolis, MN.

King, Jr. Martin Luther, pp. 79, 333, 630. by arrangement with The Heirs to the Estate of Martin Luther King, Jr. c/o Writers House, Inc. as agent for the proprietor.

Kreeft, Peter, p. vi. From *Reading and Praying the New Testament.*

Laubach, Frank, pp. 355, 433. From *Letters by a Modern Mystic*, ©1955, 1990, New Reader's Press, Publishing Division of Laubach Literacy International, Syracuse, NY.

Laufer, Calvin Weiss, pp. 861, 1226, 1293, 1324. From *The Incomparable Christ.*

Lawrence of the Resurrection, Brother, pp. 341, 364, 592, 1345, 1581, 1605. From *The Practice of the Presence of God.*

Lewis, C. S., pp., 257, 513. From *Draper's Book of Quotations from the Christian World*, Edited by Edythe Draper, ©1992, Tyndale House Publishers, Inc., Wheaton, IL.

Little, Paul, p. 1318. From *How to Give Away Your Faith*, ©1988, Marie Little, Revised edition. InterVarsity Press, P. O. Box 1400, Downers Grove, IL, 60515.

Lucado, Max, p. 24. From *Draper's Book of Quotations from the Christian World*, Edited by Edythe Draper, ©1992, Tyndale House Publishers, Inc., Wheaton, IL.

Lutzer, Erwin W., pp. 81, 140, 239, 455, 501, 665, 878, 939, 1005, 1066, 1210, 1350, 1378, 1430, 1486, 1509, 1556, 1589. From *Draper's Book of Quotations from the Christian World*, Edited by Edythe Draper, ©1992, Tyndale House Publishers, Inc., Wheaton, IL.

MacArthur, Jr. John., pp. 217, 315, 419, 429, 600, 632, 1114, 1162, 1315. From *The Ultimate Priority*, ©1983, Moody Press, Chicago, IL.

Malik, Charles Habib, p. 940. From *Draper's Book of Quotations from the Christian World*, Edited by Edythe Draper, ©1992, Tyndale House Publishers, Inc., Wheaton, IL.

Manning, Brennan, pp. 288, 1342, 1512. From *The Ragamuffin Gospel*, ©1990, Multnomah Press, Portland, OR.

Markham, Edwin, pp. 1104, 1668. From *Draper's Book of Quotations from the Christian World*, Edited by Edythe Draper, ©1992, Tyndale House Publishers, Inc., Wheaton, IL.

Marshall, Peter, pp. 216, 361, 409, 427 599, 850, 1125. From *Mr. Jones, Meet the Master: Sermons and Prayers of Peter Marshall*, ©1949 & 1950, Fleming H. Revell, a division of Baker Book House, Grand Rapids, MI.

Marshall, Peter, p. 457. From *The Prayers of Peter Marshall*, Catherine Marshall, ed. ©1982 by Catherine Marshall. Published by Chosen Books, a division of Baker Book House, Grand Rapids, MI.

Marshall, Peter, p. 1549. From *Draper's Book of Quotations from the Christian World*, Edited by Edythe Draper, ©1992, Tyndale House Publishers, Inc., Wheaton, IL.

Maxwell, L. E., p. 406. From *Born Crucified*, ©1945, renewal 1973, Moody Press, Chicago IL.

McClung, Jr. Floyd, pp. 320, 372, 1309, 1327. From *Father, Make Us One* Copyright 1987 by Floyd McClung, Jr.

McClung, Jr. Floyd, pp. 426, 616, 1124. From *The Father Heart of God* Copyright 1985 by Floyd McClung, Jr. Published by Harvest House Publishers, Eugene, OR.

Miller, Calvin, p. 606. From *The Taste of Joy*, ©1983.

Miller, Calvin, p. 867. From *A Hunger for Meaning*, ©1984.

Morgan, G. Campbell, pp. 16, 942. From *Draper's Book of Quotations from the Christian World*, Edited by Edythe Draper, ©1992, Tyndale House Publishers, Inc., Wheaton, IL.

Morgan, G. Campbell, pp. 85, 307, 590. From *Searchlights from the Word*, ©1977, Fleming H. Revell, a division of Baker Book House, Grand Rapids, MI.

Muggeridge, Malcolm, pp. 35, 873, 1296, 1557, 1666. From *Draper's Book of Quotations from the Christian World*, Edited by Edythe Draper, ©1992, Tyndale House Publishers, Inc., Wheaton, IL.

Murray, Andrew, p. 201. From *Abide in Christ*, ©1995, Christian Literature Crusade, Fort Washington, PA.

Murray, Andrew, p. 434. From *Absolute Surrender and Other Addresses*, ©1987, Moody Press, Chicago, IL.

Murray, Andrew, p. 448. From *Freedom from a Self-Centered Life: Dying to Self. Selections from the Writings of William Law with commentary*, Andrew Murray, editor, ©1977, Bethany House Publishers, Minneapolis, MN.

Nee, Watchman, pp. 594, 1126, 1478. From *The Normal Christian Life*, Watchman Nee, ©1957 by Angus I. Kinnear. Published by Tyndale House Publishers, Inc., Wheaton, IL.

Nee, Watchman, p. 1636. From *Draper's Book of Quotations from the Christian World*, Edited by Edythe Draper, ©1992, Tyndale House Publishers, Inc., Wheaton, IL.

Nouwen, Henri, p. 515. From *In the Name of Jesus*, ©1989, Crossroad Publishing Company, New York, NY.

Nouwen, Henri, pp. 673, 1018. From *Draper's Book of Quotations from the Christian World*, Edited by Edythe Draper, ©1992, Tyndale House Publishers, Inc., Wheaton, IL.

Nouwen, Henri, p. 1109. From *Making All Things New: An Invitation to the Spiritual Life*, ©1981, Henri J.M. Nouwen.

Ortlund, Raymund C., p. 124. From *Draper's Book of Quotations from the Christian World*, Edited by Edythe Draper, ©1992, Tyndale House Publishers, Inc., Wheaton, IL.

Oursler, Fulton, p. 1614. From *Draper's Book of Quotations from the Christian World*, Edited by Edythe Draper, ©1992, Tyndale House Publishers, Inc., Wheaton, IL.

Oxenham, John, pp. 89, 1241, 1385. From *Draper's Book of Quotations from the Christian World*, Edited by Edythe Draper, ©1992, Tyndale House Publishers, Inc., Wheaton, IL.

Packer, J. I., p. 860. From *Knowing God*, ©1973, Published by InterVarsity Press, Downers Grove, IL, with permission of Hodder and Stoughton Limited, London.

Packer, J. I., p. 1292. From *Draper's Book of Quotations from the Christian World*, Edited by Edythe Draper, ©1992, Tyndale House Publishers, Inc., Wheaton, IL.

Paxson, Ruth, p. 348. From *Called Unto Holiness*, Moody Press, Chicago, IL.

Pippert, Rebecca Manley, pp. 99, 1353. From *Draper's Book of Quotations from the Christian World*, Edited by Edythe Draper, ©1992, Tyndale House Publishers, Inc., Wheaton, IL.

Powell, John, pp. 1243, 1652. From *Draper's Book of Quotations from the Christian World*, Edited by Edythe Draper, ©1992, Tyndale House Publishers, Inc., Wheaton, IL.

Quoist, Michel, pp. 231, 535. From *Draper's Book of Quotations from the Christian World*, Edited by Edythe Draper, ©1992, Tyndale House Publishers, Inc., Wheaton, IL.

Schaeffer, Edith, p. 1230. From *A Way of Seeing*, ©1977, Fleming H. Revell, a division of Baker Book House, Grand Rapids, MI.

Stanley, Charles, pp. 345, 367, 388, 421, 567, 596, 604, 627, 841, 854, 1118, 1225, 1258, 1269, 1310. From *A Touch of His Wisdom*, ©1992, Zondervan Publishing House, Grand Rapids, MI.

Stott, John R., pp. 68, 862, 1224. From *The Cross of Christ*, ©1986, InterVarsity Press, Downers Grove, IL 60515.

Swindoll, Charles R., pp. 138, 362, 1015, 1070, 1093, 1297. From *Draper's Book of Quotations from the Christian World*, Edited by Edythe Draper, ©1992, Tyndale House Publishers, Inc., Wheaton, IL.

Tada, Joni Eareckson, pp. 75, 690, 988, 1254. From *Draper's Book of Quotations from the Christian World*, Edited by Edythe Draper, ©1992, Tyndale House Publishers, Inc., Wheaton, IL.

ten Boom, Corrie, pp. 30, 291, 310, 920, 1055, 1184, 1357. From *Draper's Book of Quotations from the Christian World*, Edited by Edythe Draper, ©1992, Tyndale House Publishers, Inc., Wheaton, IL.

ten Boom, Corrie, p. 866. From *Plenty for Everyone*, ©1967, Fleming H. Revell, a division of Baker Book House, Grand Rapids, MI.

Thomas, W. Ian, Major, p. 1229. From *The Saving Life of Christ*, ©1961, 1978, Zondervan Publishing House, Grand Rapids, MI.

Tozer, A.W., p. 648. From *The Pursuit of Man*, ©1950, 1978, Lowell Tozer. Published by Christian Publications, Camp Hill, PA.

Tozer, A.W., p. 1463. From *How to Be Filled with the Holy Spirit*, Christian Publications, Camp Hill, PA.

Tozer, A.W., p. 1505. From *I Call It Heresy!* ©1991, Christian Publications, Camp Hill, PA.

Tozer, A.W., pp. 2, 198, 256, 982, 1086, 1606, 1650. From *The Pursuit of God*, ©1948, 1982, Christian Publications, Camp Hill, PA.

Tozer, A.W., pp. 446, 1128, 1175, 1661. From *The Root of Righteousness*, ©1955, 1986, Lowell Tozer, Published by Christian Publications, Camp Hill, PA.

Tozer, A.W., pp. 874, 996, 1249, 1448, 1531. From *That Incredible Christian*, ©1964, Christian Publications, Camp Hill, PA.

Trobisch, Ingrid, p. 844. From *The Confident Woman*, ©1993, HarperCollins Publishers, Inc, New York, NY.

Weiss , G. Christian, p. 172. From *The Perfect Will of God*, ©1950, Back to the Bible Publishers, Lincoln, NE.

White, Jerry, p. 847. From *Choosing Plan A in a Plan B World*, ©1987.
White, David Manning, p. 1157. From *The Search for God*, ©1983, Macmillan Publishing Company, New York, NY.
Wood, George O., pp. 316, 587, 597, 622, 829. From *A Psalm in Your Heart. Vol. 1*, ©1997, Gospel Publishing House, Springfield, MO.

INDEX OF LYRICS

Directory of Song Publishers

Acuff-Rose Music Publishing, Inc., 65 Music Square West, Nashville, TN 37203
Anderson, Fred, Madison Avenue Presbyterian Church, 921 Madison Avenue, New York, NY 10021
Batstone, Bill, 2387 Westminster, Costa Mesa, CA 92627
Big Steps 4 U, see Music Services
BMG Songs, 1 Music Circle North, Nashville, TN 37203
Brentwood/Benson Music Publishing, 741 Cool Springs Blvd., Brentwood, TN 37067
Bridge, Basil, Rev., 124 Linacre Avenue, Sprowston, Norwich, NR7, 8JS England
Broadman Press, see Genevox Music Group
C. A. Music, see Music Services
Cassell PLC, Wellington House, 125 Strand, London, WC2R, 0BB England
Celebration, see The Copyright Company
Christian Conference of Asia, 57 Peking Road 5/F, Kowloon, Hong Kong
Christian Publications, 3825 Hartzdale Street, Camphill, PA 17011
Church Pension Fund, see Church Publishing Inc.
Church Publishing, Inc., 445 5th Avenue, New York, NY 10022
Concordia Publishing House, 3558 South Jefferson Avenue, St. Louis, MO 63118-3968
Dayspring Music, see Acuff-Rose Music Publishing, Inc.
Deep Fryed Music, see Music Services
Doulos Publishing, see The Copyright Company
EMI Christian Music Group, P.O. Box 5010, 101 Winners Circle, Brentwood, TN 37024-5010
Emurian, Ernest K., 5000 Fairbanks Ave., Alexandria, VA 22311
Fairhill Music, Inc., P.O. Box 4467, Oceanside, CA 92052
Farnsworth Music, a div. of Hummingbird, P.O. Box 120753, Nashville, TN 37212
Gaither Music Co., see Gaither Copyright Management
Gaither Copyright Management, P.O. Box 737, Alexandria, IN 46001
Genevox Music Group, 127 Ninth Avenue North, Nashville, TN 37234
Heartservice, see Music Services
Hope Publishing, 308 South Main Street, Carol Stream, IL 60187
House Of Mercy Music, see The Copyright Company
Integrity Music, Inc., 1000 Cody Road, Mobile, AL 36609
Integrity's Hosanna! Music, see Integrity Music, Inc.
Jimmy and Carol Music, see The Copyright Company
John W. Peterson Music Co., 13610 North Scottsdale Road, Scottsdale, AZ 85254
Judson Press, P.O. Box 851, Valley Forge, PA 19482-0851
Kenwood Music, see The Copyright Company
K. L. Cober, see Judson Press
Lillenas Publishing Co., see The Copyright Company
Make Way Music, see Integrity Music, Inc.
Manna Music, Inc., P.O. Box 218, Pacific City, OR 97135
Maranatha! Music, see The Copyright Company
Maranatha Praise Inc., see The Copyright Company
Meadowgreen Music Co., see EMI Christian Music Group
Mercy/Vineyard, see Music Services
Music Services, 209 Chapelwood Drive, Franklin, TN 37064
Olsen, Norman P., RR 3, Box 154, Starbuck, MN 56381
Ortlund, Anne, Renewal Ministries, 4500 Campus Drive, Suite 662, Newport Beach, CA 92660
Palm Branch Music, see Acuff-Rose Music Publishing, Inc.
Paragon Music Co., see Brentwood/Benson Music Publishing
People Of Destiny, see Acuff-Rose Music Publishing, Inc.
Rees, M. E., Estate of, 19 London Road , Neath, W. Glamorgan Wales
Roberts, Mark, 5081 Chateau, Irvine, CA 92604
Rocksmith, see Trust Music Management
Scripture In Song, see Integrity Music, Inc.
Seedsower Music, 87 West Yale Loop, Irvine, CA 92714; www.waltharrah.com
Singspiration, see Brentwood/Benson Music Publishing
Stainer & Bell, see Hope Publishing
Straightway Music, see EMI Christian Music Group
The Copyright Company, 40 Music Square East, Nashville, TN 37203
The Hymn Society, see Hope Publishing
The Rodeheaver Company, see Acuff-Rose Music Publishing, Inc.
Trust Music Management, P.O. Box 22274, Carmel, CA 93922-0274
Willing Heart Music, see The Copyright Company
Word Music, see Acuff-Rose Music Publishing, Inc.

INTRODUCTION
to the NIV Concordance

The NIV Concordance, created by Edward W. Goodrick and John R. Kohlenberger III, has been developed specifically for use with the New International Version. Like all concordances, it is a special index which contains an alphabetical listing of words used in the Bible text. By looking up key words, readers can find verses and passages for which they remember a word or two but not their location.

This concordance contains 2,000 word entries, with some 13,000 Scripture references. Each word entry is followed by the Scripture references in which that particular word is found, as well as by a brief excerpt from the surrounding context. The first letter of the entry word is italicized to conserve space and to allow for a longer context excerpt. Variant spellings due to number and tense and compound forms follow the entry in parentheses and direct the reader to check other forms of that word in locating a passage.

This concordance contains a number of "block entries," which highlight some of the key events and characteristics in the lives of certain Bible figures. The descriptive phrases replace the brief context surrounding each occurrence of the name. In those instances where more than one Bible character has the same name, that name is placed under one block entry, and each person is given a number (1), (2), etc. Insignificant names are not included.

Word or block entries marked with an asterisk (*) list every verse in the Bible in which the word appears.

This concordance is a valuable tool for Bible study. While one of its key purposes is to help the reader find forgotten references to verses, it can also be used to do word studies and to locate and trace biblical themes. Be sure to use this concordance as more than just a verse finder. Whenever you look up a verse, aim to discover the intended meaning of the verse in context. Give special attention to the flow of thought from the beginning of the passage to the end.

CONCORDANCE ABBREVIATIONS FOR THE BOOKS OF THE BIBLE

Genesis	Ge	Isaiah	Isa	Romans	Ro
Exodus	Ex	Jeremiah	Jer	1 Corinthians	1Co
Leviticus	Lev	Lamentations	La	2 Corinthians	2Co
Numbers	Nu	Ezekiel	Eze	Galations	Gal
Deuteronomy	Dt	Daniel	Da	Ephesians	Eph
Joshua	Jos	Hosea	Hos	Philippians	Php
Judges	Jdg	Joel	Joel	Colossians	Col
Ruth	Ru	Amos	Am	1 Thessalonians	1Th
1 Samuel	1Sa	Obadiah	Ob	2 Thessalonians	2Th
2 Samuel	2Sa	Jonah	Jnh	1 Timothy	1Ti
1 Kings	1Ki	Micah	Mic	2 Timothy	2Ti
2 Kings	2Ki	Nahum	Na	Titus	Tit
1 Chronicles	1Ch	Habakkuk	Hab	Philemon	Phm
2 Chronicles	2Ch	Zephaniah	Zep	Hebrews	Heb
Ezra	Ezr	Haggai	Hag	James	Jas
Nehemiah	Ne	Zechariah	Zec	1 Peter	1Pe
Esther	Est	Malachi	Mal	2 Peter	2Pe
Job	Job	Matthew	Mt	1 John	1Jn
Psalm	Ps	Mark	Mk	2 John	2Jn
Proverbs	Pr	Luke	Lk	3 John	3Jn
Ecclesiastes	Ecc	John	Jn	Jude	Jude
Song of Solomon	SS	Acts	Ac	Revelation	Rev

CONCORDANCE

AARON

Priesthood of (Ex 28:1; Nu 17; Heb 5:1-4; 7), garments (Ex 28; 39), consecration (Ex 29), ordination (Lev 8).

Spokesman for Moses (Ex 4:14-16, 27-31; 7:1-2). Supported Moses' hands in battle (Ex 17:8-13). Built golden calf (Ex 32; Dt 9:20). Talked against Moses (Nu 12). Priesthood opposed (Nu 16); staff budded (Nu 17). Forbidden to enter land (Nu 20:1-12). Death (Nu 20:22-29; 33:38-39).

ABANDON

Dt 4:31 he will not *a* or destroy you
1Ti 4: 1 in later times some will *a* the faith

ABBA

Ro 8:15 And by him we cry, "*A*, Father."
Gal 4: 6 the Spirit who calls out, "*A*, Father

ABEL

Second son of Adam (Ge 4:2). Offered proper sacrifice (Ge 4:4; Heb 11:4). Murdered by Cain (Ge 4:8; Mt 23:35; Lk 11:51; 1Jn 3:12).

ABHORS

Pr 11: 1 The LORD *a* dishonest scales,

ABIGAIL

Wife of Nabal (1Sa 25:30); pled for his life with David (1Sa 25:14-35). Became David's wife (1Sa 25:36-42).

ABIJAH

Son of Rehoboam; king of Judah (1Ki 14:31-15:8; 2Ch 12:16-14:1).

ABILITY (ABLE)

Ezr 2:69 According to their *a* they gave
2Co 1: 8 far beyond our *a* to endure,
8: 3 were able, and even beyond their *a*.

ABIMELECH

1. King of Gerar who took Abraham's wife Sarah, believing her to be his sister (Ge 20). Later made a covenant with Abraham (Ge 21:22-33).

2. King of Gerar who took Isaac's wife Rebekah, believing her to be his sister (Ge 26:1-11). Later made a covenant with Isaac (Ge 26:12-31).

ABLE (ABILITY ENABLE ENABLED ENABLES)

Eze 7:19 and gold will not be *a* to save them
Da 3:17 the God we serve is *a* to save us
Ro 8:39 will be *a* to separate us
14: 4 for the Lord is *a* to make him stand
16:25 to him who is *a* to establish you
2Co 9: 8 God is *a* to make all grace abound
Eph 3:20 him who is *a* to do immeasurably
2Ti 1:12 and am convinced that he is *a*
3:15 which are *a* to make you wise
Heb 7:25 he is *a* to save completely
Jude :24 To him who is *a* to keep you
Rev 5: 5 He is *a* to open the scroll

ABOLISH

Mt 5:17 that I have come to *a* the Law

ABOMINATION

Da 11:31 set up the *a* that causes desolation.

ABOUND (ABOUNDING)

2Co 9: 8 able to make all grace *a* to you,
Php 1: 9 that your love may *a* more

ABOUNDING (ABOUND)

Ex 34: 6 slow to anger, *a* in love
Ps 86: 5 *a* in love to all who call to you.

ABRAHAM

Covenant relation with the LORD (Ge 12:1-3; 13:14-17; 15; 17; 22:15-18; Ex 2:24; Ne 9:8; Ps 105; Mic 7:20; Lk 1:68-75; Ro 4; Heb 6:13-15).

Called from Ur, via Haran, to Canaan (Ge 12:1; Ac 7:2-4; Heb 11:8-10). Moved to Egypt, nearly lost Sarah to Pharoah (Ge 12:10-20). Divided the land with Lot (Ge 13). Saved Lot from four kings (Ge 14:1-16); blessed by Melchizedek (Ge 14:17-20; Heb 7:1-20). Declared righteous by faith (Ge 15:6; Ro 4:3; Gal 3:6-9). Fathered Ishmael by Hagar (Ge 16).

Name changed from Abram (Ge 17:5; Ne 9:7). Circumcised (Ge 17; Ro 4:9-12). Entertained three visitors (Ge 18); promised a son by Sarah (Ge 18:9-15; 17:16). Moved to Gerar; nearly lost Sarah to Abimelech (Ge 20). Fathered Isaac by Sarah (Ge 21:1-7; Ac 7:8; Heb 11:11-12); sent away Hagar and Ishmael (Ge 21:8-21; Gal 4:22-30). Tested by offering Isaac (Ge 22; Heb 11:17-19; Jas 2:21-24). Sarah died; bought field of Ephron for burial (Ge 23). Secured wife for Isaac (Ge 24). Death (Ge 25:7-11).

ABSALOM

Son of David by Maacah (2Sa 3:3; 1Ch 3:2). Killed Amnon for rape of his sister Tamar; banished by David (2Sa 13). Returned to Jerusalem; received by David (2Sa 14). Rebelled against David; seized kingdom (2Sa 15-17). Killed (2Sa 18).

ABSTAIN (ABSTAINS)

1Pe 2:11 to *a* from sinful desires,

ABSTAINS* (ABSTAIN)

Ro 14: 6 thanks to God; and he who *a*,

ABUNDANCE (ABUNDANT)

Lk 12:15 consist in the *a* of his possessions."
Jude : 2 peace and love be yours in *a*.

ABUNDANT (ABUNDANCE)

Dt 28:11 will grant you *a* prosperity—
Ps 145: 7 will celebrate your *a* goodness
Pr 28:19 works his land will have *a* food,
Ro 5:17 who receive God's *a* provision

ACCEPT (ACCEPTED ACCEPTS)

Ex 23: 8 "Do not *a* a bribe,
Pr 10: 8 The wise in heart *a* commands,
19:20 Listen to advice and *a* instruction,
Ro 15: 7 *A* one another, then, just
Jas 1:21 humbly *a* the word planted in you,

ACCEPTED (ACCEPT)

Lk 4:24 "no prophet is *a* in his hometown.

ACCEPTS (ACCEPT)

Ps 6: 9 the LORD *a* my prayer.
Jn 13:20 whoever *a* anyone I send *a* me;

ACCOMPANY

Mk 16:17 these signs will *a* those who believe
Heb 6: 9 your case—things that *a* salvation.

ACCOMPLISH

Isa 55:11 but will *a* what I desire

ACCORD

Nu 24:13 not do anything of my own *a*,
Jn 10:18 but I lay it down of my own *a*.
12:49 For I did not speak of my own *a*,

ACCOUNT (ACCOUNTABLE)

Mt 12:36 to give *a* on the day of judgment
Ro 14:12 each of us will give an *a* of himself
Heb 4:13 of him to whom we must give *a*.

ACCOUNTABLE (ACCOUNT)

Eze 33: 6 but I will hold the watchman *a*
Ro 3:19 and the whole world held *a* to God.

ACCUSATION (ACCUSE)

1Ti 5:19 Do not entertain an *a*

ACCUSATIONS (ACCUSE)

2Pe 2:11 do not bring slanderous *a*

ACCUSE (ACCUSATION ACCUSATIONS)

Pr 3:30 Do not *a* a man for no reason—
Lk 3:14 and don't *a* people falsely—

ACHAN*

Sin at Jericho caused defeat at Ai; stoned (Jos 7; 22:20; 1Ch 2:7).

ACHE*

Pr 14:13 Even in laughter the heart may *a*,

ACKNOWLEDGE

Mt 10:32 *a* him before my Father in heaven.
1Jn 4: 3 spirit that does not *a* Jesus is not

ACQUIT

Ex 23: 7 to death, for I will not *a* the guilty.

ACTION (ACTIONS ACTIVE ACTS)

Jas 2:17 if it is not accompanied by *a*,
1Pe 1:13 minds for *a*; be self-controlled;

ACTIONS (ACTION)

Mt 11:19 wisdom is proved right by her *a*."
Gal 6: 4 Each one should test his own *a*.
Tit 1:16 but by their *a* they deny him.

ACTIVE (ACTION)

Heb 4:12 For the word of God is living and *a*

ACTS (ACTION)

Ps 145:12 all men may know of your mighty *a*
150: 2 Praise him for his *a* of power;
Isa 64: 6 all our righteous *a* are like filthy
Mt 6: 1 not to do your '*a* of righteousness'

ADAM
First man (Ge 1:26-2:25; Ro 5:14; 1Ti 2:13). Sin of (Ge 3; Hos 6:7; Ro 5:12-21). Children of (Ge 4:1-5:5). Death of (Ge 5:5; Ro 5:12-21; 1Co 15:22).

ADD
Dt 12:32 do not *a* to it or take away from it.
Pr 30: 6 Do not *a* to his words,
Lk 12:25 by worrying can *a* a single hour
Rev 22:18 God will *a* to him the plagues

ADMIRABLE*
Php 4: 8 whatever is lovely, whatever is *a*—

ADMONISH
Col 3:16 and *a* one another with all wisdom,

ADOPTED (ADOPTION)
Eph 1: 5 In love he predestined us to be *a*

ADOPTION (ADOPTED)
Ro 8:23 as we wait eagerly for our *a* as sons,

ADORE*
SS 1: 4 How right they are to *a* you!

ADORNMENT* (ADORNS)
1Pe 3: 3 should not come from outward *a*,

ADORNS (ADORNMENT)
Ps 93: 5 holiness *a* your house

ADULTERY
Ex 20:14 "You shall not commit *a*.
Mt 5:27 that it was said, 'Do not commit *a*.'
5:28 lustfully has already committed *a*
5:32 the divorced woman commits *a*.
15:19 murder, *a*, sexual immorality, theft

ADULTS*
1Co 14:20 but in your thinking be *a*.

ADVANCED
Job 32: 7 *a* years should teach wisdom.'

ADVANTAGE
Ex 22:22 "Do not take *a* of a widow
Dt 24:14 Do not take *a* of a hired man who is
1Th 4: 6 should wrong his brother or take *a*

ADVERSITY
Pr 17:17 and a brother is born for *a*.

ADVICE
1Ki 12: 8 rejected the *a* the elders
12:14 he followed the *a* of the young men
Pr 12: 5 but the *a* of the wicked is deceitful.
12:15 but a wise man listens to *a*.
19:20 Listen to *a* and accept instruction,
20:18 Make plans by seeking *a*;

AFFLICTION
Ro 12:12 patient in *a*, faithful in prayer.

AFRAID (FEAR)
Ge 26:24 Do not be *a*, for I am with you;
Ex 3: 6 because he was *a* to look at God.
Ps 27: 1 of whom shall I be *a*?
56: 3 When I am *a*, / I will trust in you.
Pr 3:24 lie down, you will not be *a*;
Jer 1: 8 Do not be *a* of them, for I am
Mt 8:26 You of little faith, why are you so *a*
10:28 be *a* of the One who can destroy
10:31 So don't be *a*; you are worth more
Mk 5:36 "Don't be *a*; just believe."
Jn 14:27 hearts be troubled and do not be *a*.
Heb 13: 6 Lord is my helper; I will not be *a*.

AGED
Job 12:12 Is not wisdom found among the *a*?
Pr 17: 6 children are a crown to the *a*,

AGREE
Mt 18:19 on earth *a* about anything you ask
Ro 7:16 want to do, I *a* that the law is good.
Php 4: 2 with Syntyche to *a* with each other

AHAB
Son of Omri; king of Israel (1Ki 16:28-22:40), husband of Jezebel (1Ki 16:31). Promoted Baal worship (1Ki 16:31-33); opposed by Elijah (1Ki 17:1; 18; 21), a prophet (1Ki 20:35-43), Micaiah (1Ki 22:1-28). Defeated Ben-Hadad (1Ki 20). Killed for failing to kill Ben-Hadad and for murder of Naboth (1Ki 20:35-21:40).

AHAZ
Son of Jotham; king of Judah, (2Ki 16; 2Ch 28; Isa 7).

AHAZIAH
1. Son of Ahab; king of Israel (1Ki 22:51-2Ki 1:18; 2Ch 20:35-37).
2. Son of Jehoram; king of Judah (2Ki 8:25-29; 9:14-29), also called Jehoahaz (2Ch 21:17-22:9; 25:23).

AIM
1Co 7:34 Her *a* is to be devoted to the Lord
2Co 13:11 *A* for perfection, listen

AIR
Mt 8:20 and birds of the *a* have nests,
1Co 9:26 not fight like a man beating the *a*.
Eph 2: 2 of the ruler of the kingdom of the *a*,
1Th 4:17 clouds to meet the Lord in the *a*.

ALABASTER
Mt 26: 7 came to him with an *a* jar

ALERT
Jos 8: 4 All of you be on the *a*.
Mk 13:33 Be *a*! You do not know
Eph 6:18 be *a* and always keep on praying
1Th 5: 6 but let us be *a* and self-controlled.

ALIEN (ALIENATED)
Ex 22:21 "Do not mistreat an *a*

ALIENATED (ALIEN)
Gal 5: 4 by law have been *a* from Christ;

ALIVE (LIVE)
Ac 1: 3 convincing proofs that he was *a*.
Ro 6:11 but *a* to God in Christ Jesus.
1Co 15:22 so in Christ all will be made *a*.

ALMIGHTY (MIGHT)
Ge 17: 1 "I am God *A*; walk before me
Job 11: 7 Can you probe the limits of the *A*?
33: 4 the breath of the *A* gives me life.
Ps 91: 1 will rest in the shadow of the *A*.
Isa 6: 3 "Holy, holy, holy is the LORD *A*;

ALTAR
Ge 22: 9 his son Isaac and laid him on the *a*,
Ex 27: 1 "Build an *a* of acacia wood,
1Ki 18:30 and he repaired the *a* of the LORD
2Ch 4: 1 made a bronze *a* twenty cubits
4:19 the golden *a*; the tables

ALWAYS
Ps 16: 8 I have set the LORD *a* before me.
51: 3 and my sin is *a* before me.
Mt 26:11 The poor you will *a* have with you,
28:20 And surely I will be with you *a*,
1Co 13: 7 *a* protects, *a* trusts, *a* hopes, *a*
Php 4: 4 Rejoice in the Lord *a*.
1Pe 3:15 *A* be prepared to give an answer

AMAZIAH
Son of Joash; king of Judah (2Ki 14; 2Ch 25).

AMBASSADORS
2Co 5:20 We are therefore Christ's *a*,

AMBITION
Ro 15:20 It has always been my *a*
1Th 4:11 Make it your *a* to lead a quiet life,

AMON
Son of Manasseh; king of Judah (2Ki 21:18-26; 1Ch 3:14; 2Ch 33:21-25).

ANANIAS
1. Husband of Sapphira; died for lying to God (Ac 5:1-11).
2. Disciple who baptized Saul (Ac 9:10-19).
3. High priest at Paul's arrest (Ac 22:30-24:1).

ANCHOR
Heb 6:19 We have this hope as an *a*

ANCIENT
Da 7: 9 and the *A* of Days took his seat.

ANDREW*
Apostle; brother of Simon Peter (Mt 4:18; 10:2; Mk 1:16-18, 29; 3:18; 13:3; Lk 6:14; Jn 1:35-44; 6:8-9; 12:22; Ac 1:13).

ANGEL (ANGELS ARCHANGEL)
Ps 34: 7 The *a* of the LORD encamps
Ac 6:15 his face was like the face of an *a*.
2Co 11:14 Satan himself masquerades as an *a*
Gal 1: 8 or an *a* from heaven should preach

ANGELS (ANGEL)
Ps 91:11 command his *a* concerning you
Mt 18:10 For I tell you that their *a*
25:41 prepared for the devil and his *a*.
Lk 20:36 for they are like the *a*.
1Co 6: 3 you not know that we will judge *a*?
Heb 1: 4 as much superior to the *a*
1:14 Are not all *a* ministering spirits
2: 7 made him a little lower than the *a*;
13: 2 some people have entertained *a*
1Pe 1:12 Even *a* long to look
2Pe 2: 4 For if God did not spare *a*

ANGER (ANGERED ANGRY)
Ex 32:10 alone so that my *a* may burn
34: 6 slow to *a*, abounding in love
Dt 29:28 In furious *a* and in great wrath
2Ki 22:13 Great is the LORD's *a* that burns
Ps 30: 5 For his *a* lasts only a moment,
Pr 15: 1 but a harsh word stirs up *a*.
29:11 A fool gives full vent to his *a*,

ANGERED (ANGER)
Pr 22:24 do not associate with one easily *a*,
1Co 13: 5 it is not easily *a*, it keeps no record

ANGRY (ANGER)
Ps 2:12 Kiss the Son, lest he be *a*
Pr 29:22 An *a* man stirs up dissension,
Jas 1:19 slow to speak and slow to become *a*

ANGUISH
Ps 118: 5 In my *a* I cried to the LORD,

ANOINT
Ps 23: 5 You *a* my head with oil;
Jas 5:14 and *a* him with oil in the name

ANT*
Pr 6: 6 Go to the *a,* you sluggard;

ANTICHRIST
1Jn 2:18 have heard that the *a* is coming,
2Jn : 7 person is the deceiver and the *a.*

ANTIOCH
Ac 11:26 were called Christians first at *A.*

ANXIETY (ANXIOUS)
1Pe 5: 7 Cast all your *a* on him

ANXIOUS (ANXIETY)
Pr 12:25 An *a* heart weighs a man down,
Php 4: 6 Do not be *a* about anything,

APOLLOS*
Christian from Alexandria, learned in the Scriptures; instructed by Aquila and Priscilla (Ac 18:24-28). Ministered at Corinth (Ac 19:1; 1Co 1:12; 3; Tit 3:13).

APOSTLES
See also Andrew, Bartholomew, James, John, Judas, Matthew, Nathanael, Paul, Peter, Philip, Simon, Thaddaeus, Thomas.
Mk 3:14 twelve—designating them *a*—
Ac 1:26 so he was added to the eleven *a.*
2:43 signs were done by the *a.*
1Co 12:28 God has appointed first of all *a,*
15: 9 For I am the least of the *a*
2Co 11:13 masquerading as *a* of Christ.
Eph 2:20 built on the foundation of the *a*

APPEAR (APPEARANCE APPEARING)
Mk 13:22 false prophets will *a* and perform
2Co 5:10 we must all *a* before the judgment
Col 3: 4 also will *a* with him in glory.
Heb 9:24 now to *a* for us in God's presence.
9:28 and he will *a* a second time,

APPEARANCE (APPEAR)
1Sa 16: 7 Man looks at the outward *a,*
Gal 2: 6 God does not judge by external *a*—

APPEARING (APPEAR)
2Ti 4: 8 to all who have longed for his *a.*
Tit 2:13 the glorious *a* of our great God

APPLY
Pr 22:17 *a* your heart to what I teach,
23:12 *A* your heart to instruction

APPROACH
Eph 3:12 in him we may *a* God with freedom
Heb 4:16 Let us then *a* the throne of grace

APPROVED
2Ti 2:15 to present yourself to God as one *a,*

AQUILA*
Husband of Priscilla; co-worker with Paul, instructor of Apollos (Ac 18; Ro 16:3; 1Co 16:19; 2Ti 4:19).

ARARAT
Ge 8: 4 came to rest on the mountains of *A.*

ARCHANGEL* (ANGEL)
1Th 4:16 with the voice of the *a*
Jude : 9 *a* Michael, when he was disputing

ARCHITECT*
Heb 11:10 whose *a* and builder is God.

ARK
Ge 6:14 So make yourself an *a*
Dt 10: 5 put the tablets in the *a* I had made,
2Ch 35: 3 "Put the sacred *a* in the temple that
Heb 9: 4 This *a* contained the gold jar

ARM (ARMY)
Nu 11:23 "Is the LORD's *a* too short?
1Pe 4: 1 *a* yourselves also with the same

ARMAGEDDON*
Rev 16:16 that in Hebrew is called *A.*

ARMOR (ARMY)
1Ki 20:11 on his *a* should not boast like one
Eph 6:11 Put on the full *a* of God
6:13 Therefore put on the full *a* of God,

ARMS (ARMY)
Dt 33:27 underneath are the everlasting *a.*
Ps 18:32 It is God who *a* me with strength
Pr 31:20 She opens her *a* to the poor
Isa 40:11 He gathers the lambs in his *a*
Mk 10:16 And he took the children in his *a,*

ARMY (ARM ARMOR ARMS)
Ps 33:16 No king is saved by the size of his *a*
Rev 19:19 the rider on the horse and his *a.*

AROMA
2Co 2:15 For we are to God the *a* of Christ

ARRAYED*
Ps 110: 3 *A* in holy majesty,
Isa 61:10 and *a* me in a robe of righteousness

ARROGANT
Ro 11:20 Do not be *a,* but be afraid.

ARROWS
Eph 6:16 you can extinguish all the flaming *a*

ASA
King of Judah (1Ki 15:8-24; 1Ch 3:10; 2Ch 14-16).

ASCENDED
Eph 4: 8 "When he *a* on high,

ASCRIBE
1Ch 16:28 *a* to the LORD glory and strength,
Job 36: 3 I will *a* justice to my Maker.
Ps 29: 2 *A* to the LORD the glory due his

ASHAMED (SHAME)
Lk 9:26 If anyone is *a* of me and my words,
Ro 1:16 I am not *a* of the gospel,
2Ti 1: 8 So do not be *a* to testify about our
2:15 who does not need to be *a*

ASSIGNED
Mk 13:34 with his *a* task, and tells the one
1Co 3: 5 as the Lord has *a* to each his task.
7:17 place in life that the Lord *a* to him

ASSOCIATE
Pr 22:24 do not *a* with one easily angered,
Ro 12:16 but be willing to *a* with people
1Co 5:11 am writing you that you must not *a*
2Th 3:14 Do not *a* with him,

ASSURANCE
Heb 10:22 with a sincere heart in full *a* of faith

ASTRAY
Pr 10:17 ignores correction leads others *a.*
Isa 53: 6 We all, like sheep, have gone *a,*
Jer 50: 6 their shepherds have led them *a*
Jn 16: 1 you so that you will not go *a.*
1Pe 2:25 For you were like sheep going *a,*
1Jn 3: 7 do not let anyone lead you *a.*

ATHALIAH
Evil queen of Judah (2Ki 11; 2Ch 23).

ATHLETE*
2Ti 2: 5 if anyone competes as an *a,*

ATONEMENT
Ex 25:17 "Make an *a* cover of pure gold—
30:10 Once a year Aaron shall make *a*
Lev 17:11 it is the blood that makes *a*
23:27 this seventh month is the Day of *A.*
Nu 25:13 and made *a* for the Israelites."
Ro 3:25 presented him as a sacrifice of *a,*
Heb 2:17 that he might make *a* for the sins

ATTENTION
Pr 4: 1 pay *a* and gain understanding.
5: 1 My son, pay *a* to my wisdom,
22:17 Pay *a* and listen to the sayings
Tit 1:14 and will pay no *a* to Jewish myths

ATTITUDE (ATTITUDES)
Eph 4:23 new in the *a* of your minds;
Php 2: 5 Your *a* should be the same
1Pe 4: 1 yourselves also with the same *a,*

ATTITUDES (ATTITUDE)
Heb 4:12 it judges the thoughts and *a*

ATTRACTIVE
Tit 2:10 teaching about God our Savior *a.*

AUTHORITIES (AUTHORITY)
Ro 13: 5 it is necessary to submit to the *a,*
13: 6 for the *a* are God's servants,
Tit 3: 1 people to be subject to rulers and *a,*
1Pe 3:22 *a* and powers in submission to him.

AUTHORITY (AUTHORITIES)
Mt 7:29 because he taught as one who had *a*
9: 6 the Son of Man has *a* on earth
28:18 "All *a* in heaven and on earth has
Ro 13: 1 for there is no *a* except that which
13: 2 rebels against the *a* is rebelling
1Co 11:10 to have a sign of *a* on her head.
1Ti 2: 2 for kings and all those in *a,*
2:12 to teach or to have *a* over a man;
Heb 13:17 your leaders and submit to their *a.*

AVENGE (VENGEANCE)
Dt 32:35 It is mine to *a;* I will repay.

AVOID
Pr 20: 3 It is to a man's honor to *a* strife,
20:19 so *a* a man who talks too much.
1Th 4: 3 you should *a* sexual immorality;
5:22 *A* every kind of evil.
2Ti 2:16 *A* godless chatter, because those
Tit 3: 9 But *a* foolish controversies

AWAKE
Ps 17:15 when I *a,* I will be satisfied

AWE (AWESOME)
Job 25: 2 "Dominion and *a* belong to God;
Ps 119:120 I stand in *a* of your laws.
Ecc 5: 7 Therefore stand in *a* of God.
Isa 29:23 will stand in *a* of the God of Israel.
Jer 33: 9 they will be in *a* and will tremble
Hab 3: 2 I stand in *a* of your deeds,
Mal 2: 5 and stood in *a* of my name.
Mt 9: 8 they were filled with *a;*
Lk 7:16 They were all filled with *a*
Ac 2:43 Everyone was filled with *a,*
Heb 12:28 acceptably with reverence and *a,*

AWESOME (AWE)
Ge 28:17 and said, "How *a* is this place!
Ex 15:11 *a* in glory,
Dt 7:21 is among you, is a great and *a* God.
10:17 the great God, mighty and *a*,
28:58 revere this glorious and *a* name—
Jdg 13: 6 like an angel of God, very *a*.
Ne 1: 5 of heaven, the great and *a* God,
9:32 the great, mighty and *a* God,
Job 10:16 again display your *a* power
37:22 God comes in *a* majesty.
Ps 45: 4 let your right hand display *a* deeds.
47: 2 How *a* is the LORD Most High,
66: 5 how *a* his works in man's behalf!
68:35 You are *a*, O God,
89: 7 he is more *a* than all who surround
99: 3 praise your great and *a* name—
111: 9 holy and *a* is his name.
145: 6 of the power of your *a* works,
Da 9: 4 "O Lord, the great and *a* God,

BAAL
1Ki 18:25 Elijah said to the prophets of *B*,

BAASHA
King of Israel (1Ki 15:16-16:7; 2Ch 16:1-6).

BABIES (BABY)
Lk 18:15 also bringing *b* to Jesus
1Pe 2: 2 Like newborn *b*, crave pure

BABY (BABIES)
Isa 49:15 "Can a mother forget the *b*
Lk 1:44 the *b* in my womb leaped for joy.
2:12 You will find a *b* wrapped in strips
Jn 16:21 but when her *b* is born she forgets

BABYLON
Ps 137: 1 By the rivers of *B* we sat and wept

BACKSLIDING
Jer 3:22 I will cure you of *b*."
14: 7 For our *b* is great;
Eze 37:23 them from all their sinful *b*,

BALAAM
Prophet who attempted to curse Israel (Nu 22-24; Dt 23:4-5; 2Pe 2:15; Jude 11). Killed (Nu 31:8; Jos 13:22).

BALM
Jer 8:22 Is there no *b* in Gilead?

BANISH
Jer 25:10 I will *b* from them the sounds of joy

BANQUET
SS 2: 4 He has taken me to the *b* hall,
Lk 14:13 when you give a *b*, invite the poor,

BAPTIZE (BAPTIZED)
Mt 3:11 He will *b* you with the Holy Spirit
Mk 1: 8 he will *b* you with the Holy Spirit."
1Co 1:17 For Christ did not send me to *b*,

BAPTIZED (BAPTIZE)
Mt 3: 6 they were *b* by him in the Jordan
Mk 1: 9 and was *b* by John in the Jordan.
10:38 or be *b* with the baptism I am
16:16 believes and is *b* will be saved,
Jn 4: 2 in fact it was not Jesus who *b*,
Ac 1: 5 but in a few days you will be *b*

BARABBAS
Mt 27:26 Then he released *B* to them.

BARBS*
Nu 33:55 allow to remain will become *b*

BARE
Heb 4:13 and laid *b* before the eyes of him

BARNABAS*
Disciple, originally Joseph (Ac 4:36), prophet (Ac 13:1), apostle (Ac 14:14). Brought Paul to apostles (Ac 9:27), Antioch (Ac 11:22-29; Gal 2:1-13), on the first missionary journey (Ac 13-14). Together at Jerusalem Council, they separated over John Mark (Ac 15). Later co-workers (1Co 9:6; Col 4:10).

BARREN
Ps 113: 9 He settles the *b* woman

BARTHOLOMEW*
Apostle (Mt 10:3; Mk 3:18; Lk 6:14; Ac 1:13). Possibly also known as Nathanael (Jn 1:45-49; 21:2).

BATH
Jn 13:10 person who has had a *b* needs only

BATHSHEBA
Wife of Uriah who committed adultery with and became wife of David (2Sa 11), mother of Solomon (2Sa 12:24; 1Ki 1-2; 1Ch 3:5).

BATTLE
2Ch 20:15 For the *b* is not yours, but God's.
Ps 24: 8 the LORD mighty in *b*.
Ecc 9:11 or the *b* to the strong,

BEAR (BEARING BIRTH BIRTHRIGHT BORN FIRSTBORN NEWBORN)
Ge 4:13 punishment is more than I can *b*.
Ps 38: 4 like a burden too heavy to *b*.
Isa 53:11 and he will *b* their iniquities.
Da 7: 5 beast, which looked like a *b*.
Mt 7:18 A good tree cannot *b* bad fruit,
Jn 15: 2 branch that does *b* fruit he prunes
15:16 and appointed you to go and *b* fruit—
Ro 15: 1 ought to *b* with the failings
1Co 10:13 tempted beyond what you can *b*.
Col 3:13 *B* with each other and forgive

BEARING (BEAR)
Eph 4: 2 *b* with one another in love.
Col 1:10 *b* fruit in every good work,

BEAST
Rev 13:18 him calculate the number of the *b*,

BEAT (BEATING)
Isa 2: 4 They will *b* their swords
Joel 3:10 *B* your plowshares into swords
1Co 9:27 I *b* my body and make it my slave

BEATING (BEAT)
1Co 9:26 I do not fight like a man *b* the air.
1Pe 2:20 if you receive a *b* for doing wrong

BEAUTIFUL (BEAUTY)
Ge 6: 2 that the daughters of men were *b*,
12:11 "I know what a *b* woman you are.
12:14 saw that she was a very *b* woman.
24:16 The girl was very *b*, a virgin;
26: 7 of Rebekah, because she is *b*."
29:17 Rachel was lovely in form, and *b*.
Job 38:31 "Can you bind the *b* Pleiades?
Pr 11:22 is a *b* woman who shows no
Ecc 3:11 He has made everything *b*
Isa 4: 2 of the LORD will be *b*
52: 7 How *b* on the mountains
Eze 20: 6 and honey, the most *b* of all lands.
Zec 9:17 How attractive and *b* they will be!
Mt 23:27 which look *b* on the outside
26:10 She has done a *b* thing to me.

Ro 10:15 "How *b* are the feet
1Pe 3: 5 in God used to make themselves *b*.

BEAUTY (BEAUTIFUL)
Ps 27: 4 to gaze upon the *b* of the LORD
45:11 The king is enthralled by your *b*;
Pr 31:30 is deceptive, and *b* is fleeting;
Isa 33:17 Your eyes will see the king in his *b*
53: 2 He had no *b* or majesty
61: 3 to bestow on them a crown of *b*
Eze 28:12 full of wisdom and perfect in *b*.
1Pe 3: 4 the unfading *b* of a gentle

BED
Heb 13: 4 and the marriage *b* kept pure,

BEELZEBUB
Lk 11:15 "By *B*, the prince of demons,

BEER
Pr 20: 1 Wine is a mocker and *b* a brawler;

BEERSHEBA
Jdg 20: 1 all the Israelites from Dan to *B*

BEGINNING
Ge 1: 1 In the *b* God created the heavens
Ps 102:25 In the *b* you laid the foundations
111:10 of the LORD is the *b* of wisdom;
Pr 1: 7 of the LORD is the *b* of knowledge
Jn 1: 1 In the *b* was the Word,
1Jn 1: 1 That which was from the *b*,
Rev 21: 6 and the Omega, the *B* and the End.

BEHAVE
Ro 13:13 Let us *b* decently, as in the daytime

BELIEVE (BELIEVED BELIEVER BELIEVERS BELIEVES BELIEVING)
Mt 18: 6 one of these little ones who *b* in me
21:22 If you *b*, you will receive whatever
Mk 1:15 Repent and *b* the good news!"
9:24 "I do *b*; help me overcome my
16:17 signs will accompany those who *b*:
Lk 8:50 just *b*, and she will be healed."
24:25 to *b* all that the prophets have
Jn 1: 7 that through him all men might *b*.
3:18 does not *b* stands condemned
6:29 to *b* in the one he has sent."
10:38 you do not *b* me, *b* the miracles,
11:27 "I *b* that you are the Christ,
14:11 *B* me when I say that I am
16:30 This makes us *b* that you came
16:31 "You *b* at last!" Jesus answered.
17:21 that the world may *b* that you have
20:27 Stop doubting and *b*."
20:31 written that you may *b* that Jesus is
Ac 16:31 They replied, "*B* in the Lord Jesus,
24:14 I *b* everything that agrees
Ro 3:22 faith in Jesus Christ to all who *b*.
4:11 he is the father of all who *b*
10: 9 *b* in your heart that God raised him
10:14 And how can they *b* in the one
16:26 so that all nations might *b*
1Th 4:14 We *b* that Jesus died and rose again
2Th 2:11 delusion so that they will *b* the lie
1Ti 4:10 and especially of those who *b*.
Tit 1: 6 a man whose children *b*
Heb 11: 6 comes to him must *b* that he exists
Jas 2:19 Even the demons *b* that—
1Jn 4: 1 Dear friends, do not *b* every spirit,

BELIEVED (BELIEVE)
Ge 15: 6 Abram *b* the LORD, and he
Jnh 3: 5 The Ninevites *b* God.
Jn 1:12 to those who *b* in his name,
2:22 Then they *b* the Scripture
3:18 because he has not *b* in the name

Jn 20: 8 He saw and *b.*
20:29 who have not seen and yet have *b."*
Ac 13:48 were appointed for eternal life *b.*
Ro 4: 3 Scripture say? "Abraham *b* God,
10:14 call on the one they have not *b* in?
1Co 15: 2 Otherwise, you have *b* in vain.
Gal 3: 6 Consider Abraham: "He *b* God,
2Ti 1:12 because I know whom I have *b,*
Jas 2:23 that says, "Abraham *b* God,

BELIEVER (BELIEVE)
1Co 7:12 brother has a wife who is not a *b*
2Co 6:15 What does a *b* have in common

BELIEVERS (BELIEVE)
Ac 4:32 All the *b* were one in heart
5:12 And all the *b* used to meet together
1Co 6: 5 to judge a dispute between *b?*
1Ti 4:12 set an example for the *b* in speech,
1Pe 2:17 Love the brotherhood of *b,*

BELIEVES (BELIEVE)
Pr 14:15 A simple man *b* anything,
Mk 9:23 is possible for him who *b."*
11:23 *b* that what he says will happen,
16:16 Whoever *b* and is baptized will be
Jn 3:16 that whoever *b* in him shall not
3:36 Whoever *b* in the Son has eternal
5:24 *b* him who sent me has eternal life
6:35 and he who *b* in me will never be
6:40 and *b* in him shall have eternal life,
6:47 he who *b* has everlasting life.
7:38 Whoever *b* in me, as the Scripture
11:26 and *b* in me will never die.
Ro 1:16 for the salvation of everyone who *b*
10: 4 righteousness for everyone who *b.*
1Jn 5: 1 Everyone who *b* that Jesus is
5: 5 Only he who *b* that Jesus is the Son

BELIEVING (BELIEVE)
Jn 20:31 and that by *b* you may have life

BELONG (BELONGS)
Dt 29:29 The secret things *b*
Job 25: 2 "Dominion and awe *b* to God;
Ps 47: 9 for the kings of the earth *b* to God;
95: 4 and the mountain peaks *b* to him.
Jn 8:44 You *b* to your father, the devil,
15:19 As it is, you do not *b* to the world,
Ro 1: 6 called to *b* to Jesus Christ.
7: 4 that you might *b* to another,
14: 8 we live or die, we *b* to the Lord.
Gal 5:24 Those who *b* to Christ Jesus have
1Th 5: 8 But since we *b* to the day, let us be

BELONGS (BELONG)
Job 41:11 Everything under heaven *b* to me.
Ps 111:10 To him *b* eternal praise.
Eze 18: 4 For every living soul *b* to me,
Jn 8:47 He who *b* to God hears what God
Ro 12: 5 each member *b* to all the others.

BELOVED (LOVE)
Dt 33:12 "Let the *b* of the LORD rest secure

BELT
Isa 11: 5 Righteousness will be his *b*
Eph 6:14 with the *b* of truth buckled

BENEFIT (BENEFITS)
Ro 6:22 the *b* you reap leads to holiness,
2Co 4:15 All this is for your *b,*

BENEFITS (BENEFIT)
Ps 103: 2 and forget not all his *b.*
Jn 4:38 you have reaped the *b* of their labor

BENJAMIN
Twelfth son of Jacob by Rachel (Ge 35:16-24; 46:19-21; 1Ch 2:2). Jacob refused to send him to Egypt, but relented (Ge 42-45).

BEREANS*
Ac 17:11 the *B* were of more noble character

BESTOWS
Ps 84:11 the LORD *b* favor and honor;

BETHLEHEM
Mt 2: 1 After Jesus was born in *B* in Judea,

BETRAY
Pr 25: 9 do not *b* another man's confidence,

BIND (BINDS)
Dt 6: 8 and *b* them on your foreheads.
Pr 6:21 *B* them upon your heart forever;
Isa 61: 1 me to *b* up the brokenhearted,
Mt 16:19 whatever you *b* on earth will be

BINDS (BIND)
Ps 147: 3 and *b* up their wounds.
Isa 30:26 when the LORD *b* up the bruises

BIRDS
Mt 8:20 and *b* of the air have nests,

BIRTH (BEAR)
Ps 58: 3 Even from *b* the wicked go astray;
Mt 1:18 This is how the *b* of Jesus Christ
1Pe 1: 3 great mercy he has given us new *b*

BIRTHRIGHT (BEAR)
Ge 25:34 So Esau despised his *b.*

BLAMELESS
Ge 17: 1 walk before me and be *b.*
Job 1: 1 This man was *b* and upright;
Ps 84:11 from those whose walk is *b.*
119: 1 Blessed are they whose ways are *b,*
Pr 19: 1 Better a poor man whose walk is *b*
1Co 1: 8 so that you will be *b* on the day
Eph 5:27 any other blemish, but holy and *b.*
Php 2:15 so that you may become *b* and pure
1Th 3:13 hearts so that you will be *b*
5:23 and body be kept *b* at the coming
Tit 1: 6 An elder must be *b,* the husband of
Heb 7:26 *b,* pure, set apart from sinners,
2Pe 3:14 effort to be found spotless, *b*

BLASPHEMES
Mk 3:29 whoever *b* against the Holy Spirit

BLEMISH
1Pe 1:19 a lamb without *b* or defect.

BLESS (BLESSED BLESSING BLESSINGS)
Ge 12: 3 I will *b* those who *b* you,
Ro 12:14 Bless those who persecute you; *b*

BLESSED (BLESS)
Ge 1:22 God *b* them and said, "Be fruitful
2: 3 And God *b* the seventh day
22:18 nations on earth will be *b,*
Ps 1: 1 *B* is the man
2:12 *B* are all who take refuge in him.
33:12 *B* is the nation whose God is
41: 1 *B* is he who has regard for the weak
84: 5 *B* are those whose strength is
106: 3 *B* are they who maintain justice,
112: 1 *B* is the man who fears the LORD,
118:26 *B* is he who comes in the name
Pr 29:18 but *b* is he who keeps the law.
31:28 Her children arise and call her *b;*
Mt 5: 3 saying: "*B* are the poor in spirit,
5: 4 *B* are those who mourn,
5: 5 *B* are the meek,
5: 6 *B* are those who hunger
5: 7 *B* are the merciful,
5: 8 *B* are the pure in heart,
5: 9 *B* are the peacemakers,
5:10 *B* are those who are persecuted
5:11 "*B* are you when people insult you,
Lk 1:48 on all generations will call me *b,*
Jn 12:13 "*B* is he who comes in the name
Ac 20:35 'It is more *b* to give than to receive
Tit 2:13 while we wait for the *b* hope—
Jas 1:12 *B* is the man who perseveres
Rev 1: 3 *B* is the one who reads the words
22:14 "*B* are those who wash their robes,

BLESSING (BLESS)
Eze 34:26 there will be showers of *b.*

BLESSINGS (BLESS)
Pr 10: 6 *B* crown the head of the righteous,

BLIND
Mt 15:14 a *b* man leads a *b* man, both will fall
23:16 "Woe to you, *b* guides! You say,
Jn 9:25 I was *b* but now I see!"

BLOOD
Ge 9: 6 "Whoever sheds the *b* of man,
Ex 12:13 and when I see the *b,* I will pass
24: 8 "This is the *b* of the covenant that
Lev 17:11 For the life of a creature is in the *b,*
Ps 72:14 for precious is their *b* in his sight.
Pr 6:17 hands that shed innocent *b,*
Mt 26:28 This is my *b* of the covenant,
Ro 3:25 of atonement, through faith in his *b*
5: 9 have now been justified by his *b,*
1Co 11:25 cup is the new covenant in my *b;*
Eph 1: 7 we have redemption through his *b,*
2:13 near through the *b* of Christ.
Col 1:20 by making peace through his *b,*
Heb 9:12 once for all by his own *b,*
9:22 of *b* there is no forgiveness.
1Pe 1:19 but with the precious *b* of Christ,
1Jn 1: 7 and the *b* of Jesus, his Son,
Rev 1: 5 has freed us from our sins by his *b,*
5: 9 with your *b* you purchased men
7:14 white in the *b* of the Lamb.
12:11 him by the *b* of the Lamb

BLOT (BLOTS)
Ex 32:32 then *b* me out of the book you have
Ps 51: 1 *b* out my transgressions.
Rev 3: 5 I will never *b* out his name

BLOTS (BLOT)
Isa 43:25 "I, even I, am he who *b* out

BLOWN
Eph 4:14 and *b* here and there by every wind
Jas 1: 6 doubts is like a wave of the sea, *b*

BOAST
1Ki 20:11 armor should not *b* like one who
Ps 34: 2 My soul will *b* in the LORD;
44: 8 In God we make our *b* all day long,
Pr 27: 1 Do not *b* about tomorrow,
1Co 1:31 Let him who boasts *b* in the Lord."
Gal 6:14 May I never *b* except in the cross
Eph 2: 9 not by works, so that no one can *b.*

BOAZ
Wealthy Bethlehemite who showed favor to Ruth (Ru 2), married her (Ru 4). Ancestor of David (Ru 4:18-22; 1Ch 2:12-15), Jesus (Mt 1:5-16; Lk 3:23-32).

BODIES (BODY)
Ro 12: 1 to offer your *b* as living sacrifices,
1Co 6:15 not know that your *b* are members
Eph 5:28 to love their wives as their own *b*.

BODY (BODIES)
Zec 13: 6 What are these wounds on your *b?*'
Mt 10:28 afraid of those who kill the *b*
26:26 saying, "Take and eat; this is my *b*
26:41 spirit is willing, but the *b* is weak."
Jn 13:10 wash his feet; his whole *b* is clean.
Ro 6:13 Do not offer the parts of your *b*
12: 4 us has one *b* with many members,
1Co 6:19 not know that your *b* is a temple
11:24 "This is my *b*, which is for you;
12:12 The *b* is a unit, though it is made up
Eph 5:30 for we are members of his *b*.

BOLD (BOLDNESS)
Ps 138: 3 you made me *b* and stouthearted.
Pr 21:29 A wicked man puts up a *b* front,
28: 1 but the righteous are as *b* as a lion.

BOLDNESS* (BOLD)
Ac 4:29 to speak your word with great *b*.

BONDAGE
Ezr 9: 9 God has not deserted us in our *b*.

BOOK (BOOKS)
Jos 1: 8 Do not let this *B* of the Law depart
Ne 8: 8 They read from the *B* of the Law
Jn 20:30 which are not recorded in this *b*.
Php 4: 3 whose names are in the *b* of life.
Rev 21:27 written in the Lamb's *b* of life.

BOOKS (BOOK)
Ecc 12:12 Of making many *b* there is no end,

BORN (BEAR)
Isa 9: 6 For to us a child is *b*,
Jn 3: 7 at my saying, 'You must be *b* again
1Pe 1:23 For you have been *b* again,
1Jn 4: 7 Everyone who loves has been *b*
5: 1 believes that Jesus is the Christ is *b*

BORROWER
Pr 22: 7 and the *b* is servant to the lender.

BOUGHT
Ac 20:28 which he *b* with his own blood.
1Co 6:20 You are not your own; you were *b*
7:23 You were *b* at a price; do not
2Pe 2: 1 the sovereign Lord who *b* them—

BOW
Ps 95: 6 Come, let us *b* down in worship,
Isa 45:23 Before me every knee will *b*;
Ro 14:11 'every knee will *b* before me;
Php 2:10 name of Jesus every knee should *b*,

BRANCH (BRANCHES)
Isa 4: 2 In that day the *B* of the LORD will
Jer 33:15 I will make a righteous *B* sprout

BRANCHES (BRANCH)
Jn 15: 5 "I am the vine; you are the *b*.

BRAVE
2Sa 2: 7 Now then, be strong and *b*,

BREAD
Dt 8: 3 that man does not live on *b* alone
Pr 30: 8 but give me only my daily *b*.
Ecc 11: 1 Cast your *b* upon the waters,
Isa 55: 2 Why spend money on what is not *b*
Mt 4: 4 'Man does not live on *b* alone,
6:11 Give us today our daily *b*.
Jn 6:35 Jesus declared, "I am the *b* of life.
21:13 took the *b* and gave it to them,
1Co 11:23 took *b*, and when he had given

BREAK (BREAKING BROKEN)
Nu 30: 2 he must not *b* his word
Jdg 2: 1 'I will never *b* my covenant
Isa 42: 3 A bruised reed he will not *b*,
Mt 12:20 A bruised reed he will not *b*,

BREAKING (BREAK)
Jas 2:10 at just one point is guilty of *b* all

BREASTPIECE (BREASTPLATE)
Ex 28:15 Fashion a *b* for making decisions—

BREASTPLATE* (BREASTPIECE)
Isa 59:17 He put on righteousness as his *b*,
Eph 6:14 with the *b* of righteousness in place
1Th 5: 8 putting on faith and love as a *b*,

BREATHED (GOD-BREATHED)
Ge 2: 7 *b* into his nostrils the breath of life,
Jn 20:22 And with that he *b* on them

BREEDS*
Pr 13:10 Pride only *b* quarrels,

BRIBE
Ex 23: 8 "Do not accept a *b*,
Pr 6:35 will refuse the *b*, however great it

BRIDE
Rev 19: 7 and his *b* has made herself ready,

BRIGHTER (BRIGHTNESS)
Pr 4:18 shining ever *b* till the full light

BRIGHTNESS (BRIGHTER)
2Sa 22:13 Out of the *b* of his presence
Da 12: 3 who are wise will shine like the *b*

BROAD
Mt 7:13 and *b* is the road that leads

BROKEN (BREAK)
Ps 51:17 The sacrifices of God are a *b* spirit;
Ecc 4:12 of three strands is not quickly *b*.
Jn 10:35 and the Scripture cannot be *b*—

BROKENHEARTED* (HEART)
Ps 34:18 The LORD is close to the *b*
109:16 and the needy and the *b*.
147: 3 He heals the *b*
Isa 61: 1 He has sent me to bind up the *b*,

BROTHER (BROTHER'S BROTHERS)
Pr 17:17 and a *b* is born for adversity.
18:24 a friend who sticks closer than a *b*.
27:10 neighbor nearby than a *b* far away.
Mt 5:24 and be reconciled to your *b*;
18:15 "If your *b* sins against you,
Mk 3:35 Whoever does God's will is my *b*
Lk 17: 3 "If your *b* sins, rebuke him,
1Co 8:13 if what I eat causes my *b* to fall
1Jn 2:10 Whoever loves his *b* lives
4:21 loves God must also love his *b*.

BROTHER'S (BROTHER)
Ge 4: 9 "Am I my *b* keeper?" The LORD

BROTHERS (BROTHER)
Ps 133: 1 is when *b* live together in unity!
Pr 6:19 who stirs up dissension among *b*.
Mt 25:40 one of the least of these *b* of mine,
Mk 10:29 or *b* or sisters or mother or father
Heb 13: 1 Keep on loving each other as *b*.
1Pe 3: 8 be sympathetic, love as *b*,
1Jn 3:14 death to life, because we love our *b*.

BUILD (BUILDING BUILDS BUILT)
Mt 16:18 and on this rock I will *b* my church,
Ac 20:32 which can *b* you up and give you
1Co 14:12 excel in gifts that *b* up the church.
1Th 5:11 one another and *b* each other up,

BUILDING (BUILD)
1Co 3: 9 you are God's field, God's *b*.
2Co 10: 8 us for *b* you up rather
Eph 4:29 helpful for *b* others up according

BUILDS (BUILD)
Ps 127: 1 Unless the LORD *b* the house,
1Co 3:10 one should be careful how he *b*.
8: 1 Knowledge puffs up, but love *b* up.

BUILT (BUILD)
Mt 7:24 is like a wise man who *b* his house
Eph 2:20 *b* on the foundation of the apostles
4:12 the body of Christ may be *b* up

BURDEN (BURDENED BURDENS)
Ps 38: 4 like a *b* too heavy to bear.
Mt 11:30 my yoke is easy and my *b* is light."

BURDENED (BURDEN)
Gal 5: 1 do not let yourselves be *b* again

BURDENS (BURDEN)
Ps 68:19 who daily bears our *b*.
Gal 6: 2 Carry each other's *b*,

BURIED
Ro 6: 4 *b* with him through baptism
1Co 15: 4 that he was *b*, that he was raised

BURNING
Lev 6: 9 the fire must be kept *b* on the altar.
Ro 12:20 you will heap *b* coals on his head."

BUSINESS
Da 8:27 and went about the king's *b*.
1Th 4:11 to mind your own *b* and to work

BUSY
1Ki 20:40 While your servant was *b* here
2Th 3:11 They are not *b*; they are
Tit 2: 5 to be *b* at home, to be kind,

CAESAR
Mt 22:21 "Give to *C* what is Caesar's,

CAIN
Firstborn of Adam (Ge 4:1), murdered brother Abel (Ge 4:1-16; 1Jn 3:12).

CALEB
Judahite who spied out Canaan (Nu 13:6); allowed to enter land because of faith (Nu 13:30-14:38; Dt 1:36). Possessed Hebron (Jos 14:6-15:19).

CALF
Ex 32: 4 into an idol cast in the shape of a *c*,
Lk 15:23 Bring the fattened *c* and kill it.

CALL (CALLED CALLING CALLS)
Ps 105: 1 to the LORD, *c* on his name;
145:18 near to all who *c* on him,
Pr 31:28 children arise and *c* her blessed;
Isa 5:20 Woe to those who *c* evil good
55: 6 *c* on him while he is near.
65:24 Before they *c* I will answer;
Jer 33: 3 '*C* to me and I will answer you
Mt 9:13 come to *c* the righteous,
Ro 10:12 and richly blesses all who *c* on him,

Ro 11:29 gifts and his *c* are irrevocable.
1Th 4: 7 For God did not *c* us to be impure,

CALLED (CALL)
1Sa 3: 5 and said, "Here I am; you *c* me."
2Ch 7:14 if my people, who are *c*
Ps 34: 6 This poor man *c*, and the LORD
Mt 21:13 " 'My house will be *c* a house
Ro 8:30 And those he predestined, he also *c*
1Co 7:15 God has *c* us to live in peace.
Gal 5:13 You, my brothers, were *c* to be free
1Pe 2: 9 of him who *c* you out of darkness

CALLING (CALL)
Jn 1:23 I am the voice of one *c* in the desert
Ac 22:16 wash your sins away, *c* on his name
Eph 4: 1 worthy of the *c* you have received.
2Pe 1:10 all the more eager to make your *c*

CALLS (CALL)
Joel 2:32 And everyone who *c*
Jn 10: 3 He *c* his own sheep by name
Ro 10:13 "Everyone who *c* on the name

CAMEL
Mt 19:24 it is easier for a *c* to go
23:24 strain out a gnat but swallow a *c*.

CANAAN
1Ch 16:18 "To you I will give the land of *C*

CANCELED
Lk 7:42 so he *c* the debts of both.
Col 2:14 having *c* the written code,

CAPITAL
Dt 21:22 guilty of a *c* offense is put to death

CAPSTONE (STONE)
Ps 118:22 has become the *c*;
1Pe 2: 7 has become the *c*,"

CARE (CAREFUL CARES CARING)
Ps 8: 4 the son of man that you *c* for him?
Pr 29: 7 The righteous *c* about justice
Lk 10:34 him to an inn and took *c* of him.
Jn 21:16 Jesus said, "Take *c* of my sheep."
Heb 2: 6 the son of man that you *c* for him?
1Pe 5: 2 of God's flock that is under your *c*,

CAREFUL (CARE)
Ex 23:13 "Be *c* to do everything I have said
Dt 6: 3 be *c* to obey so that it may go well
Jos 23: 6 be *c* to obey all that is written
23:11 be very *c* to love the LORD your
Pr 13:24 he who loves him is *c*
Mt 6: 1 "Be *c* not to do your 'acts
Ro 12:17 Be *c* to do what is right in the eyes
1Co 3:10 each one should be *c* how he builds
8: 9 Be *c*, however, that the exercise
Eph 5:15 Be very *c*, then, how you live—

CARELESS
Mt 12:36 for every *c* word they have spoken.

CARES (CARE)
Ps 55:22 Cast your *c* on the LORD
Na 1: 7 He *c* for those who trust in him,
Eph 5:29 but he feeds and *c* for it, just
1Pe 5: 7 on him because he *c* for you.

CARING* (CARE)
1Th 2: 7 like a mother *c* for her little
1Ti 5: 4 practice by *c* for their own family

CARRIED (CARRY)
Ex 19: 4 and how I *c* you on eagles' wings
Isa 53: 4 and *c* our sorrows,
Heb 13: 9 Do not be *c* away by all kinds
2Pe 1:21 as they were *c* along by the Holy

CARRIES (CARRY)
Dt 32:11 and *c* them on its pinions.
Isa 40:11 and *c* them close to his heart;

CARRY (CARRIED CARRIES)
Lk 14:27 anyone who does not *c* his cross
Gal 6: 2 *C* each other's burdens,
6: 5 for each one should *c* his own load.

CAST
Ps 22:18 and *c* lots for my clothing.
55:22 *C* your cares on the LORD
Ecc 11: 1 *C* your bread upon the waters,
Jn 19:24 and *c* lots for my clothing."
1Pe 5: 7 *C* all your anxiety on him

CATCH (CAUGHT)
Lk 5:10 from now on you will *c* men."

CATTLE
Ps 50:10 and the *c* on a thousand hills.

CAUGHT (CATCH)
1Th 4:17 and are left will be *c* up together

CAUSE (CAUSES)
Pr 24:28 against your neighbor without *c*,
Ecc 8: 3 Do not stand up for a bad *c*,
Mt 18: 7 of the things that *c* people to sin!
Ro 14:21 else that will *c* your brother
1Co 10:32 Do not *c* anyone to stumble,

CAUSES (CAUSE)
Isa 8:14 a stone that *c* men to stumble
Mt 18: 6 if anyone *c* one of these little ones

CAUTIOUS*
Pr 12:26 A righteous man is *c* in friendship,

CEASE
Ps 46: 9 He makes wars *c* to the ends

CENSER
Lev 16:12 is to take a *c* full of burning coals

CENTURION
Mt 8: 5 had entered Capernaum, a *c* came

CERTAIN (CERTAINTY)
2Pe 1:19 word of the prophets made more *c*,

CERTAINTY* (CERTAIN)
Lk 1: 4 so that you may know the *c*
Jn 17: 8 They knew with *c* that I came

CHAFF
Ps 1: 4 They are like *c*

CHAINED
2Ti 2: 9 But God's word is not *c*.

CHAMPION
Ps 19: 5 like a *c* rejoicing to run his course.

CHANGE (CHANGED)
1Sa 15:29 of Israel does not lie or *c* his mind;
Ps 110: 4 and will not *c* his mind:
Jer 7: 5 If you really *c* your ways
Mal 3: 6 "I the LORD do not *c*.
Mt 18: 3 unless you *c* and become like little
Heb 7:21 and will not *c* his mind:
Jas 1:17 who does not *c* like shifting

CHANGED (CHANGE)
1Co 15:51 but we will all be *c*— in a flash,

CHARACTER
Ru 3:11 that you are a woman of noble *c*.
Pr 31:10 A wife of noble *c* who can find?
Ro 5: 4 perseverance, *c*; and *c*, hope.
1Co 15:33 "Bad company corrupts good *c*."

CHARGE
Ro 8:33 Who will bring any *c*
2Co 11: 7 the gospel of God to you free of *c*?
2Ti 4: 1 I give you this *c*: Preach the Word;

CHARIOTS
2Ki 6:17 and *c* of fire all around Elisha.
Ps 20: 7 Some trust in *c* and some in horses,

CHARM
Pr 31:30 *C* is deceptive, and beauty is

CHASES
Pr 12:11 he who *c* fantasies lacks judgment.

CHATTER* (CHATTERING)
1Ti 6:20 Turn away from godless *c*
2Ti 2:16 Avoid godless *c*, because those

CHATTERING* (CHATTER)
Pr 10: 8 but a *c* fool comes to ruin.
10:10 and a *c* fool comes to ruin.

CHEAT* (CHEATED)
Mal 1:14 "Cursed is the *c* who has
1Co 6: 8 you yourselves *c* and do wrong,

CHEATED (CHEAT)
Lk 19: 8 if I have *c* anybody out of anything,
1Co 6: 7 Why not rather be *c*? Instead,

CHEEK
Mt 5:39 someone strikes you on the right *c*,

CHEERFUL* (CHEERS)
Pr 15:13 A happy heart makes the face *c*,
15:15 but the *c* heart has a continual feast
15:30 A *c* look brings joy to the heart,
17:22 A *c* heart is good medicine,
2Co 9: 7 for God loves a *c* giver.

CHEERS (CHEERFUL)
Pr 12:25 but a kind word *c* him up.

CHILD (CHILDISH CHILDREN)
Pr 20:11 Even a *c* is known by his actions,
22: 6 Train a *c* in the way he should go,
22:15 Folly is bound up in the heart of a *c*
23:13 not withhold discipline from a *c*;
29:15 *c* left to himself disgraces his mother.
Isa 7:14 The virgin will be with *c*
9: 6 For to us a *c* is born,
11: 6 and a little *c* will lead them.
66:13 As a mother comforts her *c*,
Mt 1:23 "The virgin will be with *c*
18: 2 He called a little *c* and had him
Lk 1:42 and blessed is the *c* you will bear!
1:80 And the *c* grew and became strong
1Co 13:11 When I was a *c*, I talked like a *c*,
1Jn 5: 1 who loves the father loves his *c*

CHILDISH* (CHILD)
1Co 13:11 When I became a man, I put *c* ways

CHILDREN (CHILD)
Dt 4: 9 Teach them to your *c*
11:19 them to your *c*, talking about them
Ps 8: 2 From the lips of *c* and infants
Pr 17: 6 Children's *c* are a crown
31:28 Her *c* arise and call her blessed;
Mt 7:11 how to give good gifts to your *c*,
11:25 and revealed them to little *c*.

Mt 18: 3 you change and become like little *c*
19:14 "Let the little *c* come to me,
21:16 " 'From the lips of *c* and infants
Mk 9:37 one of these little *c* in my name
10:14 "Let the little *c* come to me,
10:16 And he took the *c* in his arms,
13:12 *C* will rebel against their parents
Lk 10:21 and revealed them to little *c.*
18:16 "Let the little *c* come to me,
Ro 8:16 with our spirit that we are God's *c.*
2Co 12:14 parents, but parents for their *c.*
Eph 6: 1 *C,* obey your parents in the Lord,
6: 4 do not exasperate your *c;* instead,
Col 3:20 *C,* obey your parents in everything,
3:21 Fathers, do not embitter your *c,*
1Ti 3: 4 and see that his *c* obey him
3:12 and must manage his *c* and his
5:10 bringing up *c,* showing hospitality,
1Jn 3: 1 that we should be called *c* of God!

CHOOSE (CHOOSES CHOSE CHOSEN)
Dt 30:19 Now *c* life, so that you
Jos 24:15 then *c* for yourselves this day
Pr 8:10 *C* my instruction instead of silver,
16:16 to *c* understanding rather
Jn 15:16 You did not *c* me, but I chose you

CHOOSES (CHOOSE)
Jn 7:17 If anyone *c* to do God's will,

CHOSE (CHOOSE)
Ge 13:11 So Lot *c* for himself the whole plain
Ps 33:12 the people he *c* for his inheritance.
Jn 15:16 but I *c* you and appointed you to go
1Co 1:27 But God *c* the foolish things
Eph 1: 4 he *c* us in him before the creation
2Th 2:13 from the beginning God *c* you

CHOSEN (CHOOSE)
Isa 41: 8 Jacob, whom I have *c,*
Mt 22:14 For many are invited, but few are *c*
Lk 10:42 Mary has *c* what is better,
23:35 the Christ of God, the *C* One."
Jn 15:19 but I have *c* you out of the world.
1Pe 1:20 He was *c* before the creation
2: 9 But you are a *c* people, a royal

CHRIST (CHRIST'S CHRISTIAN CHRISTS)
Mt 1:16 was born Jesus, who is called *C.*
16:16 Peter answered, "You are the *C,*
22:42 "What do you think about the *C?*
Jn 1:41 found the Messiah" (that is, the *C*).
20:31 you may believe that Jesus is the *C,*
Ac 2:36 you crucified, both Lord and *C.*"
5:42 the good news that Jesus is the *C.*
9:22 by proving that Jesus is the *C.*
17: 3 proving that the *C* had to suffer
18:28 the Scriptures that Jesus was the *C.*
26:23 that the *C* would suffer and,
Ro 3:22 comes through faith in Jesus *C*
5: 6 we were still powerless, *C* died
5: 8 While we were still sinners, *C* died
5:17 life through the one man, Jesus *C.*
6: 4 as *C* was raised from the dead
8: 1 for those who are in *C* Jesus,
8: 9 Spirit of *C,* he does not belong to *C.*
8:35 us from the love of *C?*
10: 4 *C* is the end of the law
14: 9 *C* died and returned to life
15: 3 For even *C* did not please himself
1Co 1:23 but we preach *C* crucified:
2: 2 except Jesus *C* and him crucified.
3:11 one already laid, which is Jesus *C.*
5: 7 For *C,* our Passover lamb,
8: 6 and there is but one Lord, Jesus *C,*
10: 4 them, and that rock was *C.*
11: 1 as I follow the example of *C.*
11: 3 the head of every man is *C,*
1Co 12:27 Now you are the body of *C,*
15: 3 that *C* died for our sins according
15:14 And if *C* has not been raised,
15:22 so in *C* all will be made alive.
15:57 victory through our Lord Jesus *C.*
2Co 3: 3 show that you are a letter from *C,*
4: 5 not preach ourselves, but Jesus *C*
5:10 before the judgment seat of *C,*
5:17 Therefore, if anyone is in *C,*
11: 2 you to one husband, to *C,*
Gal 2:20 I have been crucified with *C*
3:13 *C* redeemed us from the curse
6:14 in the cross of our Lord Jesus *C,*
Eph 1: 3 with every spiritual blessing in *C.*
3: 8 the unsearchable riches of *C,*
4:13 measure of the fullness of *C.*
5: 2 as *C* loved us and gave himself up
5:23 as *C* is the head of the church,
5:25 just as *C* loved the church
Php 1:21 to live is *C* and to die is gain.
1:27 worthy of the gospel of *C.*
4:19 to his glorious riches in *C* Jesus.
Col 1:27 which is *C* in you, the hope of glory
1:28 may present everyone perfect in *C.*
2: 6 as you received *C* Jesus as Lord,
2:17 the reality, however, is found in *C.*
3:15 Let the peace of *C* rule
2Th 2: 1 the coming of our Lord Jesus *C*
1Ti 1:15 *C* Jesus came into the world
2: 5 the man *C* Jesus, who gave himself
2Ti 2: 3 us like a good soldier of *C* Jesus.
3:15 salvation through faith in *C* Jesus.
Tit 2:13 our great God and Savior, Jesus *C,*
Heb 3:14 to share in *C* if we hold firmly
9:14 more, then, will the blood of *C,*
9:15 For this reason *C* is the mediator
9:28 so *C* was sacrificed once
10:10 of the body of Jesus *C* once for all.
13: 8 Jesus *C* is the same yesterday
1Pe 1:19 but with the precious blood of *C,*
2:21 because *C* suffered for you,
3:18 For *C* died for sins once for all,
4:14 insulted because of the name of *C,*
1Jn 2:22 man who denies that Jesus is the *C.*
3:16 Jesus *C* laid down his life for us.
5: 1 believes that Jesus is the *C* is born
Rev 20: 4 reigned with *C* a thousand years.

CHRIST'S (CHRIST)
2Co 5:14 For *C* love compels us,
5:20 We are therefore *C* ambassadors,
12: 9 so that *C* power may rest on me.

CHRISTIAN (CHRIST)
1Pe 4:16 as a *C,* do not be ashamed,

CHRISTS (CHRIST)
Mt 24:24 For false *C* and false prophets will

CHURCH
Mt 16:18 and on this rock I will build my *c,*
18:17 if he refuses to listen even to the *c,*
Ac 20:28 Be shepherds of the *c* of God,
1Co 5:12 of mine to judge those outside the *c*
14: 4 but he who prophesies edifies the *c.*
14:12 to excel in gifts that build up the *c.*
14:26 done for the strengthening of the *c.*
Eph 5:23 as Christ is the head of the *c,*
Col 1:24 the sake of his body, which is the *c.*

CIRCUMCISED
Ge 17:10 Every male among you shall be *c.*

CIRCUMSTANCES
Php 4:11 to be content whatever the *c.*
1Th 5:18 continually; give thanks in all *c,*

CITIZENS (CITIZENSHIP)
Eph 2:19 but fellow *c* with God's people

CITIZENSHIP (CITIZENS)
Php 3:20 But our *c* is in heaven.

CITY
Mt 5:14 A *c* on a hill cannot be hidden.
Heb 13:14 here we do not have an enduring *c,*

CIVILIAN*
2Ti 2: 4 a soldier gets involved in *c* affairs—

CLAIM (CLAIMS)
Pr 25: 6 do not *c* a place among great men;
1Jn 1: 6 If we *c* to have fellowship
1: 8 If we *c* to be without sin, we
1:10 If we *c* we have not sinned,

CLAIMS (CLAIM)
Jas 2:14 if a man *c* to have faith
1Jn 2: 6 Whoever *c* to live in him must walk
2: 9 Anyone who *c* to be in the light

CLAP
Ps 47: 1 *C* your hands, all you nations;
Isa 55:12 will *c* their hands.

CLAY
Isa 45: 9 Does the *c* say to the potter,
64: 8 We are the *c,* you are the potter;
Jer 18: 6 "Like *c* in the hand of the potter,
La 4: 2 are now considered as pots of *c,*
Da 2:33 partly of iron and partly of baked *c.*
Ro 9:21 of the same lump of *c* some pottery
2Co 4: 7 we have this treasure in jars of *c*
2Ti 2:20 and *c;* some are for noble purposes

CLEAN
Lev 16:30 you will be *c* from all your sins.
Ps 24: 4 He who has *c* hands and a pure
Mt 12:44 the house unoccupied, swept *c*
23:25 You *c* the outside of the cup
Mk 7:19 Jesus declared all foods "*c.*")
Jn 13:10 to wash his feet; his whole body is *c*
15: 3 are already *c* because of the word
Ac 10:15 impure that God has made *c.*"
Ro 14:20 All food is *c,* but it is wrong

CLING (CLINGS)
Ro 12: 9 Hate what is evil; *c* to what is good.

CLINGS (CLING)
Ps 63: 8 My soul *c* to you;

CLOAK
2Ki 4:29 "Tuck your *c* into your belt,

CLOSE (CLOSER)
Ps 34:18 LORD is *c* to the brokenhearted
Isa 40:11 and carries them *c* to his heart;
Jer 30:21 himself to be *c* to me?'

CLOSER (CLOSE)
Ex 3: 5 "Do not come any *c,*" God said.
Pr 18:24 there is a friend who sticks *c*

CLOTHE (CLOTHED CLOTHES CLOTHING)
Ps 45: 3 *c* yourself with splendor
Isa 52: 1 *c* yourself with strength.
Ro 13:14 *c* yourselves with the Lord Jesus
Col 3:12 *c* yourselves with compassion,
1Pe 5: 5 *c* yourselves with humility

CLOTHED (CLOTHE)
Ps 30:11 removed my sackcloth and *c* me
Pr 31:25 She is *c* with strength and dignity;
Lk 24:49 until you have been *c* with power

CLOTHES (CLOTHE)
Mt 6:25 the body more important than *c?*
6:28 "And why do you worry about *c?*
Jn 11:44 Take off the grave *c* and let him go

CLOTHING (CLOTHE)
Dt 22: 5 A woman must not wear men's *c,*
Mt 7:15 They come to you in sheep's *c,*

CLOUD (CLOUDS)
Ex 13:21 them in a pillar of *c* to guide them
Isa 19: 1 See, the LORD rides on a swift *c*
Lk 21:27 of Man coming in a *c* with power
Heb 12: 1 by such a great *c* of witnesses,

CLOUDS (CLOUD)
Ps 104: 3 He makes the *c* his chariot
Da 7:13 coming with the *c* of heaven.
Mk 13:26 coming in *c* with great power
1Th 4:17 with them in the *c* to meet the Lord

CO-HEIRS* (INHERIT)
Ro 8:17 heirs of God and *c* with Christ,

COALS
Pr 25:22 you will heap burning *c* on his head
Ro 12:20 you will heap burning *c* on his head

COLD
Pr 25:25 Like *c* water to a weary soul
Mt 10:42 if anyone gives even a cup of *c* water
24:12 the love of most will grow *c,*

COMFORT (COMFORTED COMFORTS)
Ps 23: 4 rod and your staff, they *c* me.
119:52 and I find *c* in them.
119:76 May your unfailing love be my *c,*
Zec 1:17 and the LORD will again *c* Zion
1Co 14: 3 encouragement and *c.*
2Co 1: 4 so that we can *c* those
2: 7 you ought to forgive and *c* him,

COMFORTED (COMFORT)
Mt 5: 4 for they will be *c.*

COMFORTS* (COMFORT)
Job 29:25 I was like one who *c* mourners.
Isa 49:13 For the LORD *c* his people
51:12 "I, even I, am he who *c* you.
66:13 As a mother *c* her child,
2Co 1: 4 who *c* us in all our troubles,
7: 6 But God, who *c* the downcast,

COMMAND (COMMANDED COMMANDING COMMANDMENT COMMANDMENTS COMMANDS)
Ex 7: 2 You are to say everything I *c* you,
Nu 24:13 to go beyond the *c* of the LORD—
Dt 4: 2 Do not add to what I *c* you
30:16 For I *c* you today to love
32:46 so that you may *c* your children
Ps 91:11 For he will *c* his angels concerning
Pr 13:13 but he who respects a *c* is rewarded
Ecc 8: 2 Obey the king's *c,* I say,
Joel 2:11 mighty are those who obey his *c.*
Jn 14:15 love me, you will obey what I *c.*
15:12 My *c* is this: Love each other
1Co 14:37 writing to you is the Lord's *c.*
Gal 5:14 law is summed up in a single *c:*
1Ti 1: 5 goal of this *c* is love, which comes
Heb 11: 3 universe was formed at God's *c,*
1Jn 3:23 this is his *c:* to believe in the name
2Jn : 6 his *c* is that you walk in love.

COMMANDED (COMMAND)
Ps 33: 9 he *c,* and it stood firm.
148: 5 for he *c* and they were created.
Mt 28:20 to obey everything I have *c* you.
1Co 9:14 Lord has *c* that those who preach
1Jn 3:23 and to love one another as he *c* us.

COMMANDING (COMMAND)
2Ti 2: 4 he wants to please his *c* officer.

COMMANDMENT (COMMAND)
Jos 22: 5 But be very careful to keep the *c*
Mt 22:38 This is the first and greatest *c.*
Jn 13:34 "A new *c* I give you: Love one
Ro 7:12 and the *c* is holy, righteous
Eph 6: 2 which is the first *c* with a promise

COMMANDMENTS (COMMAND)
Ex 20: 6 who love me and keep my *c.*
34:28 of the covenant—the Ten *C.*
Ecc 12:13 Fear God and keep his *c,*
Mt 5:19 one of the least of these *c*
22:40 the Prophets hang on these two *c."*

COMMANDS (COMMAND)
Dt 7: 9 those who love him and keep his *c.*
11:27 the blessing if you obey the *c*
Ps 112: 1 who finds great delight in his *c.*
119:47 for I delight in your *c*
119:86 All your *c* are trustworthy;
119:98 Your *c* make me wiser
119:127 Because I love your *c*
119:143 but your *c* are my delight.
119:172 for all your *c* are righteous.
Pr 3: 1 but keep my *c* in your heart,
6:23 For these *c* are a lamp,
10: 8 The wise in heart accept *c,*
Da 9: 4 all who love him and obey his *c,*
Mt 5:19 teaches these *c* will be called great
Jn 14:21 Whoever has my *c* and obeys them,
Ac 17:30 but now he *c* all people everywhere
1Co 7:19 Keeping God's *c* is what counts.
1Jn 5: 3 And his *c* are not burdensome,
5: 3 This is love for God: to obey his *c.*

COMMEND (COMMENDED COMMENDS)
Ecc 8:15 So I *c* the enjoyment of life,
Ro 13: 3 do what is right and he will *c* you.
1Pe 2:14 and to *c* those who do right.

COMMENDED (COMMEND)
Heb 11:39 These were all *c* for their faith,

COMMENDS (COMMEND)
2Co 10:18 not the one who *c* himself who is

COMMIT (COMMITS COMMITTED)
Ex 20:14 "You shall not *c* adultery.
Ps 37: 5 *C* your way to the LORD;
Mt 5:27 that it was said, 'Do not *c* adultery.'
Lk 23:46 into your hands I *c* my spirit."
Ac 20:32 I *c* you to God and to the word
1Co 10: 8 We should not *c* sexual immorality,
1Pe 4:19 to God's will should *c* themselves

COMMITS (COMMIT)
Pr 6:32 man who *c* adultery lacks
29:22 a hot-tempered one *c* many sins.
Mt 19: 9 marries another woman *c* adultery

COMMITTED (COMMIT)
Nu 5: 7 and must confess the sin he has *c.*
1Ki 8:61 But your hearts must be fully *c*
2Ch 16: 9 those whose hearts are fully *c*
Mt 5:28 lustfully has already *c* adultery
2Co 5:19 And he has *c* to us the message
1Pe 2:22 "He *c* no sin,

COMMON
Pr 22: 2 Rich and poor have this in *c:*
1Co 10:13 has seized you except what is *c*
2Co 6:14 and wickedness have in *c?*

COMPANION (COMPANIONS)
Pr 13:20 but a *c* of fools suffers harm.
28: 7 a *c* of gluttons disgraces his father.
29: 3 *c* of prostitutes squanders his

COMPANIONS (COMPANION)
Pr 18:24 A man of many *c* may come to ruin

COMPANY
Pr 24: 1 do not desire their *c;*
Jer 15:17 I never sat in the *c* of revelers,
1Co 15:33 "Bad *c* corrupts good character."

COMPARED (COMPARING)
Eze 31: 2 Who can be *c* with you in majesty?
Php 3: 8 I consider everything a loss *c*

COMPARING* (COMPARED)
Ro 8:18 present sufferings are not worth *c*
2Co 8: 8 the sincerity of your love by *c* it
Gal 6: 4 without *c* himself to somebody else

COMPASSION (COMPASSIONATE COMPASSIONS)
Ex 33:19 I will have *c* on whom I will have *c.*
Ne 9:19 of your great *c* you did not
9:28 in your *c* you delivered them time
Ps 51: 1 according to your great *c*
103: 4 and crowns you with love and *c.*
103:13 As a father has *c* on his children,
145: 9 he has *c* on all he has made.
Isa 49:13 and will have *c* on his afflicted ones
49:15 and have no *c* on the child she has
Hos 2:19 in love and *c.*
11: 8 all my *c* is aroused.
Jnh 3: 9 with *c* turn from his fierce anger
Mt 9:36 When he saw the crowds, he had *c*
Mk 8: 2 "I have *c* for these people;
Ro 9:15 and I will have *c* on whom I have *c*
Col 3:12 clothe yourselves with *c,* kindness,
Jas 5:11 The Lord is full of *c* and mercy.

COMPASSIONATE (COMPASSION)
Ne 9:17 gracious and *c,* slow to anger
Ps 103: 8 The LORD is *c* and gracious,
112: 4 the gracious and *c* and righteous
Eph 4:32 Be kind and *c* to one another,
1Pe 3: 8 love as brothers, be *c* and humble.

COMPASSIONS* (COMPASSION)
La 3:22 for his *c* never fail.

COMPELLED (COMPELS)
Ac 20:22 "And now, *c* by the Spirit,
1Co 9:16 I cannot boast, for I am *c* to preach.

COMPELS (COMPELLED)
2Co 5:14 For Christ's love *c* us, because we

COMPETENCE* (COMPETENT)
2Co 3: 5 but our *c* comes from God.

COMPETENT* (COMPETENCE)
Ro 15:14 and *c* to instruct one another.
1Co 6: 2 are you not *c* to judge trivial cases?
2Co 3: 5 Not that we are *c* in ourselves
3: 6 He has made us *c* as ministers

COMPETES*
1Co 9:25 Everyone who *c* in the games goes
2Ti 2: 5 Similarly, if anyone *c* as an athlete,
2: 5 unless he *c* according to the rules.

COMPLACENT
Am 6: 1 Woe to you who are *c* in Zion,

COMPLAINING*
Php 2:14 Do everything without *c* or arguing

COMPLETE
Jn 15:11 and that your joy may be *c.*
16:24 will receive, and your joy will be *c.*
17:23 May they be brought to *c* unity
Ac 20:24 *c* the task the Lord Jesus has given
Php 2: 2 then make my joy *c*
Col 4:17 to it that you *c* the work you have
Jas 1: 4 so that you may be mature and *c,*
2:22 his faith was made *c* by what he did

CONCEAL (CONCEALED CONCEALS)
Ps 40:10 I do not *c* your love and your truth
Pr 25: 2 It is the glory of God to *c* a matter;

CONCEALED (CONCEAL)
Jer 16:17 nor is their sin *c* from my eyes.
Mt 10:26 There is nothing *c* that will not be
Mk 4:22 and whatever is *c* is meant

CONCEALS (CONCEAL)
Pr 28:13 He who *c* his sins does not prosper,

CONCEITED
Ro 12:16 Do not be *c.*
Gal 5:26 Let us not become *c,* provoking
1Ti 6: 4 he is *c* and understands nothing.

CONCEIVED
Mt 1:20 what is *c* in her is from the Holy
1Co 2: 9 no mind has *c*

CONCERN (CONCERNED)
Eze 36:21 I had *c* for my holy name, which
1Co 7:32 I would like you to be free from *c.*
12:25 that its parts should have equal *c*
2Co 11:28 of my *c* for all the churches.

CONCERNED (CONCERN)
Jnh 4:10 "You have been *c* about this vine,
1Co 7:32 An unmarried man is *c* about

CONDEMN (CONDEMNATION CONDEMNED CONDEMNING CONDEMNS)
Job 40: 8 Would you *c* me to justify yourself?
Isa 50: 9 Who is he that will *c* me?
Lk 6:37 Do not *c,* and you will not be
Jn 3:17 Son into the world to *c* the world,
12:48 very word which I spoke will *c* him
Ro 2:27 yet obeys the law will *c* you who,
1Jn 3:20 presence whenever our hearts *c* us.

CONDEMNATION (CONDEMN)
Ro 5:18 of one trespass was *c* for all men,
8: 1 there is now no *c* for those who are

CONDEMNED (CONDEMN)
Ps 34:22 no one will be *c* who takes refuge
Mt 12:37 and by your words you will be *c."*
23:33 How will you escape being *c* to hell
Jn 3:18 Whoever believes in him is not *c,*
5:24 has eternal life and will not be *c;*
16:11 prince of this world now stands *c.*
Ro 14:23 But the man who has doubts is *c*
1Co 11:32 disciplined so that we will not be *c*
Heb 11: 7 By his faith he *c* the world

CONDEMNING (CONDEMN)
Pr 17:15 the guilty and *c* the innocent—
Ro 2: 1 judge the other, you are *c* yourself,

CONDEMNS (CONDEMN)
Ro 8:34 Who is he that *c?* Christ Jesus,
2Co 3: 9 the ministry that *c* men is glorious,

CONDUCT
Pr 10:23 A fool finds pleasure in evil *c,*
20:11 by whether his *c* is pure and right.
21: 8 but the *c* of the innocent is upright.
Ecc 6: 8 how to *c* himself before others?
Jer 4:18 "Your own *c* and actions
17:10 to reward a man according to his *c,*
Eze 7: 3 I will judge you according to your *c*
Php 1:27 *c* yourselves in a manner worthy
1Ti 3:15 to *c* themselves in God's household

CONFESS (CONFESSION)
Lev 16:21 and *c* over it all the wickedness
26:40 " 'But if they will *c* their sins
Nu 5: 7 must *c* the sin he has committed.
Ps 38:18 I *c* my iniquity;
Ro 10: 9 That if you *c* with your mouth,
Php 2:11 every tongue *c* that Jesus Christ is
Jas 5:16 Therefore *c* your sins to each other
1Jn 1: 9 If we *c* our sins, he is faithful

CONFESSION (CONFESS)
Ezr 10:11 Now make *c* to the LORD,
2Co 9:13 obedience that accompanies your *c*

CONFIDENCE
Ps 71: 5 my *c* since my youth.
Pr 3:26 for the LORD will be your *c*
11:13 A gossip betrays a *c,*
25: 9 do not betray another man's *c,*
31:11 Her husband has full *c* in her
Isa 32:17 will be quietness and *c* forever.
Jer 17: 7 whose *c* is in him.
Php 3: 3 and who put no *c* in the flesh—
Heb 3:14 till the end the *c* we had at first.
4:16 the throne of grace with *c,*
10:19 since we have *c* to enter the Most
10:35 So do not throw away your *c;*
1Jn 5:14 This is the *c* we have

CONFORM* (CONFORMED)
Ro 12: 2 Do not *c* any longer to the pattern
1Pe 1:14 do not *c* to the evil desires you had

CONFORMED (CONFORM)
Ro 8:29 predestined to be *c* to the likeness

CONQUERORS
Ro 8:37 than *c* through him who loved us.

CONSCIENCE (CONSCIENCES)
Ro 13: 5 punishment but also because of *c.*
1Co 8: 7 since their *c* is weak, it is defiled.
8:12 in this way and wound their weak *c*
10:25 without raising questions of *c,*
10:29 freedom be judged by another's *c?*
Heb 10:22 to cleanse us from a guilty *c*
1Pe 3:16 and respect, keeping a clear *c,*

CONSCIENCES* (CONSCIENCE)
Ro 2:15 their *c* also bearing witness,
1Ti 4: 2 whose *c* have been seared
Tit 1:15 their minds and *c* are corrupted.
Heb 9:14 cleanse our *c* from acts that lead

CONSCIOUS*
Ro 3:20 through the law we become *c* of sin
1Pe 2:19 of unjust suffering because he is *c*

CONSECRATE (CONSECRATED)
Ex 13: 2 "*C* to me every firstborn male.
Lev 20: 7 " '*C* yourselves and be holy,

CONSECRATED (CONSECRATE)
Ex 29:43 and the place will be *c* by my glory.
1Ti 4: 5 because it is *c* by the word of God

CONSIDER (CONSIDERATE CONSIDERED CONSIDERS)
1Sa 12:24 *c* what great things he has done
Job 37:14 stop and *c* God's wonders.
Ps 8: 3 When I *c* your heavens,
Ps 107:43 and *c* the great love of the LORD.
143: 5 and *c* what your hands have done.
Lk 12:24 *C* the ravens: They do not sow
12:27 about the rest? "*C* how the lilies
Php 2: 3 but in humility *c* others better
3: 8 I *c* everything a loss compared
Heb 10:24 And let us *c* how we may spur one
Jas 1: 2 *C* it pure joy, my brothers,

CONSIDERATE* (CONSIDER)
Tit 3: 2 to be peaceable and *c,*
Jas 3:17 then peace-loving, *c,* submissive,
1Pe 2:18 only to those who are good and *c,*
3: 7 in the same way be *c* as you live

CONSIDERED (CONSIDER)
Job 1: 8 "Have you *c* my servant Job?
2: 3 "Have you *c* my servant Job?
Ps 44:22 we are *c* as sheep to be slaughtered.
Isa 53: 4 yet we *c* him stricken by God,
Ro 8:36 we are *c* as sheep to be slaughtered

CONSIDERS (CONSIDER)
Pr 31:16 She *c* a field and buys it;
Ro 14: 5 One man *c* one day more sacred
Jas 1:26 If anyone *c* himself religious

CONSIST
Lk 12:15 a man's life does not *c*

CONSOLATION
Ps 94:19 your *c* brought joy to my soul.

CONSTRUCTIVE*
1Co 10:23 but not everything is *c.*

CONSUME (CONSUMING)
Jn 2:17 "Zeal for your house will *c* me."

CONSUMING (CONSUME)
Dt 4:24 For the LORD your God is a *c* fire,
Heb 12:29 and awe, for our "God is a *c* fire."

CONTAIN
1Ki 8:27 the highest heaven, cannot *c* you.
2Pe 3:16 His letters *c* some things that are

CONTAMINATES*
2Co 7: 1 from everything that *c* body

CONTEMPT
Pr 14:31 He who oppresses the poor shows *c*
17: 5 He who mocks the poor shows *c*
18: 3 When wickedness comes, so does *c*
Da 12: 2 others to shame and everlasting *c.*
Ro 2: 4 Or do you show *c* for the riches
Gal 4:14 you did not treat me with *c*
1Th 5:20 do not treat prophecies with *c.*

CONTEND (CONTENDING)
Jude : 3 you to *c* for the faith that was once

CONTENDING* (CONTEND)
Php 1:27 *c* as one man for the faith

CONTENT (CONTENTMENT)
Pr 13:25 The righteous eat to their hearts' *c,*
Php 4:11 to be *c* whatever the circumstances
4:12 I have learned the secret of being *c*
1Ti 6: 8 and clothing, we will be *c* with that.
Heb 13: 5 and be *c* with what you have,

CONTENTMENT (CONTENT)
1Ti 6: 6 But godliness with *c* is great gain.

CONTINUAL (CONTINUE)
Pr 15:15 but the cheerful heart has a *c* feast.

CONTINUE (CONTINUAL)
Php 2:12 *c* to work out your salvation
2Ti 3:14 *c* in what you have learned
1Jn 5:18 born of God does not *c* to sin;
Rev 22:11 and let him who is holy *c* to be holy
22:11 let him who does right *c* to do right;

CONTRITE*
Ps 51:17 a broken and *c* heart,
Isa 57:15 also with him who is *c* and lowly
57:15 and to revive the heart of the *c*.
66: 2 he who is humble and *c* in spirit,

CONTROL (CONTROLLED SELF-CONTROL SELF-CONTROLLED)
Pr 29:11 a wise man keeps himself under *c*.
1Co 7: 9 But if they cannot *c* themselves,
7:37 but has *c* over his own will,
1Th 4: 4 you should learn to *c* his own body

CONTROLLED (CONTROL)
Ps 32: 9 but must be *c* by bit and bridle
Ro 8: 6 but the mind *c* by the Spirit is life
8: 8 Those *c* by the sinful nature cannot

CONTROVERSIES
Tit 3: 9 But avoid foolish *c* and genealogies

CONVERSATION
Col 4: 6 Let your *c* be always full of grace,

CONVERT
1Ti 3: 6 He must not be a recent *c*,

CONVICT
Jn 16: 8 he will *c* the world of guilt in regard

CONVINCED (CONVINCING)
Ro 8:38 For I am *c* that neither death
2Ti 1:12 and am *c* that he is able
3:14 have learned and have become *c*

CONVINCING* (CONVINCED)
Ac 1: 3 and gave many *c* proofs that he was

CORNELIUS*
Roman to whom Peter preached; first Gentile Christian (Ac 10).

CORNERSTONE (STONE)
Isa 28:16 a precious *c* for a sure foundation;
Eph 2:20 Christ Jesus himself as the chief *c*.
1Pe 2: 6 a chosen and precious *c*,

CORRECT (CORRECTING CORRECTION CORRECTS)
2Ti 4: 2 *c*, rebuke and encourage—

CORRECTING* (CORRECT)
2Ti 3:16 *c* and training in righteousness,

CORRECTION (CORRECT)
Pr 10:17 whoever ignores *c* leads others
12: 1 but he who hates *c* is stupid.
15: 5 whoever heeds *c* shows prudence.
15:10 he who hates *c* will die.
29:15 The rod of *c* imparts wisdom,

CORRECTS* (CORRECT)
Job 5:17 "Blessed is the man whom God *c*;
Pr 9: 7 Whoever *c* a mocker invites insult;

CORRUPT (CORRUPTS)
Ge 6:11 Now the earth was *c* in God's sight

CORRUPTS* (CORRUPT)
Ecc 7: 7 and a bribe *c* the heart.
1Co 15:33 "Bad company *c* good character."
Jas 3: 6 It *c* the whole person, sets

COST
Pr 4: 7 Though it *c* all you have, get
Isa 55: 1 milk without money and without *c*.
Rev 21: 6 to drink without *c* from the spring

COUNSEL (COUNSELOR)
1Ki 22: 5 "First seek the *c* of the LORD."
Pr 15:22 Plans fail for lack of *c*,
Rev 3:18 I *c* you to buy from me gold refined

COUNSELOR (COUNSEL)
Isa 9: 6 Wonderful *C*, Mighty God,
Jn 14:16 he will give you another *C* to be
14:26 But the *C*, the Holy Spirit,

COUNT (COUNTING COUNTS)
Ro 4: 8 whose sin the Lord will never *c*
6:11 *c* yourselves dead to sin

COUNTING (COUNT)
2Co 5:19 not *c* men's sins against them.

COUNTRY
Jn 4:44 prophet has no honor in his own *c*.)

COUNTS (COUNT)
Jn 6:63 The Spirit gives life; the flesh *c*
1Co 7:19 God's commands is what *c*.
Gal 5: 6 only thing that *c* is faith expressing

COURAGE (COURAGEOUS)
Ac 23:11 "Take *c*! As you have testified
1Co 16:13 stand firm in the faith; be men of *c*;

COURAGEOUS (COURAGE)
Dt 31: 6 Be strong and *c*.
Jos 1: 6 and *c*, because you will lead these

COURSE
Ps 19: 5 a champion rejoicing to run his *c*.
Pr 15:21 of understanding keeps a straight *c*.

COURTS
Ps 84:10 Better is one day in your *c*
100: 4 and his *c* with praise;

COVENANT (COVENANTS)
Ge 9: 9 "I now establish my *c* with you
Ex 19: 5 if you obey me fully and keep my *c*,
1Ch 16:15 He remembers his *c* forever,
Job 31: 1 "I made a *c* with my eyes
Jer 31:31 "when I will make a new *c*
1Co 11:25 "This cup is the new *c* in my blood;
Gal 4:24 One *c* is from Mount Sinai
Heb 9:15 Christ is the mediator of a new *c*,

COVENANTS (COVENANT)
Ro 9: 4 theirs the divine glory, the *c*,
Gal 4:24 for the women represent two *c*.

COVER (COVER-UP COVERED COVERS)
Ps 91: 4 He will *c* you with his feathers,
Jas 5:20 and *c* over a multitude of sins.

COVER-UP (COVER)
1Pe 2:16 but do not use your freedom as a *c*

COVERED (COVER)
Ps 32: 1 whose sins are *c*.
Isa 6: 2 With two wings they *c* their faces,
Ro 4: 7 whose sins are *c*.
1Co 11: 4 with his head *c* dishonors his head.

COVERS (COVER)
Pr 10:12 but love *c* over all wrongs.
1Pe 4: 8 love *c* over a multitude of sins.

COVET
Ex 20:17 You shall not *c* your neighbor's
Ro 13: 9 "Do not steal," "Do not *c*,"

COWARDLY*
Rev 21: 8 But the *c*, the unbelieving, the vile,

CRAFTINESS (CRAFTY)
1Co 3:19 "He catches the wise in their *c*";

CRAFTY (CRAFTINESS)
Ge 3: 1 the serpent was more *c* than any
2Co 12:16 *c* fellow that I am, I caught you

CRAVE
Pr 23: 3 Do not *c* his delicacies,
1Pe 2: 2 newborn babies, *c* pure spiritual

CREATE (CREATED CREATION CREATOR)
Ps 51:10 *C* in me a pure heart, O God,
Isa 45:18 he did not *c* it to be empty,

CREATED (CREATE)
Ge 1: 1 In the beginning God *c* the heavens
1:21 God *c* the great creatures of the sea
1:27 So God *c* man in his own image,
Ps 148: 5 for he commanded and they were *c*
Isa 42: 5 he who *c* the heavens and stretched
Ro 1:25 and served *c* things rather
1Co 11: 9 neither was man *c* for woman,
Col 1:16 For by him all things were *c*:
1Ti 4: 4 For everything God *c* is good,
Rev 10: 6 who *c* the heavens and all that is

CREATION (CREATE)
Mk 16:15 and preach the good news to all *c*.
Jn 17:24 me before the *c* of the world.
Ro 8:19 The *c* waits in eager expectation
8:39 depth, nor anything else in all *c*,
2Co 5:17 he is a new *c*; the old has gone,
Col 1:15 God, the firstborn over all *c*.
1Pe 1:20 chosen before the *c* of the world,
Rev 13: 8 slain from the *c* of the world.

CREATOR (CREATE)
Ge 14:22 God Most High, *C* of heaven
Ro 1:25 created things rather than the *C*—

CREATURE (CREATURES)
Lev 17:11 For the life of a *c* is in the blood,

CREATURES (CREATURE)
Ge 6:19 bring into the ark two of all living *c*,
Ps 104:24 the earth is full of your *c*.

CREDIT (CREDITED)
Ro 4:24 to whom God will *c* righteousness
1Pe 2:20 it to your *c* if you receive a beating

CREDITED (CREDIT)
Ge 15: 6 and he *c* it to him as righteousness.
Ro 4: 5 his faith is *c* as righteousness.
Gal 3: 6 and it was *c* to him as righteousness
Jas 2:23 and it was *c* to him as righteousness

CRIED (CRY)
Ps 18: 6 I *c* to my God for help.

CRIMSON
Isa 1:18 though they are red as *c*,

CRIPPLED
Mk 9:45 better for you to enter life *c*

CRITICISM
2Co 8:20 We want to avoid any *c*

CROOKED
Pr 10: 9 he who takes *c* paths will be found
Php 2:15 children of God without fault in a *c*

CROSS
Mt 10:38 and anyone who does not take his *c*
Lk 9:23 take up his *c* daily and follow me.
Ac 2:23 to death by nailing him to the *c.*
1Co 1:17 lest the *c* of Christ be emptied
Gal 6:14 in the *c* of our Lord Jesus Christ,
Php 2: 8 even death on a *c!*
Col 1:20 through his blood, shed on the *c.*
2:14 he took it away, nailing it to the *c.*
2:15 triumphing over them by the *c.*
Heb 12: 2 set before him endured the *c,*

CROWD
Ex 23: 2 Do not follow the *c* in doing wrong.

CROWN (CROWNED CROWNS)
Pr 4: 9 present you with a *c* of splendor."
10: 6 Blessings *c* the head
12: 4 noble character is her husband's *c,*
17: 6 Children's children are a *c*
Isa 61: 3 to bestow on them a *c* of beauty
Zec 9:16 like jewels in a *c.*
Mt 27:29 then twisted together a *c* of thorns
1Co 9:25 it to get a *c* that will last forever.
2Ti 4: 8 store for me the *c* of righteousness,
Rev 2:10 and I will give you the *c* of life.

CROWNED (CROWN)
Ps 8: 5 and *c* him with glory and honor.
Pr 14:18 the prudent are *c* with knowledge.
Heb 2: 7 you *c* him with glory and honor

CROWNS (CROWN)
Rev 4:10 They lay their *c* before the throne
19:12 and on his head are many *c.*

CRUCIFIED (CRUCIFY)
Mt 20:19 to be mocked and flogged and *c.*
27:38 Two robbers were *c* with him,
Lk 24: 7 be *c* and on the third day be raised
Jn 19:18 Here they *c* him, and with him two
Ac 2:36 whom you *c,* both Lord and Christ
Ro 6: 6 For we know that our old self was *c*
1Co 1:23 but we preach Christ *c:* a stumbling
2: 2 except Jesus Christ and him *c.*
Gal 2:20 I have been *c* with Christ
5:24 Christ Jesus have *c* the sinful

CRUCIFY (CRUCIFIED CRUCIFYING)
Mt 27:22 They all answered, *"C* him!" "Why
27:31 Then they led him away to *c* him.

CRUCIFYING* (CRUCIFY)
Heb 6: 6 to their loss they are *c* the Son

CRUSH (CRUSHED)
Ge 3:15 he will *c* your head,
Isa 53:10 it was the LORD's will to *c* him
Ro 16:20 The God of peace will soon *c* Satan

CRUSHED (CRUSH)
Ps 34:18 and saves those who are *c* in spirit.
Isa 53: 5 he was *c* for our iniquities;
2Co 4: 8 not *c;* perplexed, but not in despair;

CRY (CRIED)
Ps 34:15 and his ears are attentive to their *c;*
40: 1 he turned to me and heard my *c.*
130: 1 Out of the depths I *c* to you,

CUP
Ps 23: 5 my *c* overflows.
Mt 10:42 if anyone gives even a *c* of cold water
23:25 You clean the outside of the *c*
26:39 may this *c* be taken from me.
1Co 11:25 after supper he took the *c,* saying,

CURSE (CURSED)
Dt 11:26 before you today a blessing and a *c*
21:23 hung on a tree is under God's *c.*
Lk 6:28 bless those who *c* you, pray
Gal 3:13 of the law by becoming a *c* for us,
Rev 22: 3 No longer will there be any *c.*

CURSED (CURSE)
Ge 3:17 *"C* is the ground because of you;
Dt 27:15 *"C* is the man who carves an image
27:16 *"C* is the man who dishonors his
27:17 *"C* is the man who moves his
27:18 *"C* is the man who leads the blind
27:19 *C* is the man who withholds justice
27:20 *"C* is the man who sleeps
27:21 *"C* is the man who has sexual
27:22 *"C* is the man who sleeps
27:23 *"C* is the man who sleeps
27:24 *"C* is the man who kills his
27:25 *"C* is the man who accepts a bribe
27:26 *"C* is the man who does not uphold
Ro 9: 3 I could wish that I myself were *c*
Gal 3:10 *"C* is everyone who does not

CURTAIN
Ex 26:33 The *c* will separate the Holy Place
Lk 23:45 the *c* of the temple was torn in two.
Heb 10:20 opened for us through the *c,*

CYMBAL*
1Co 13: 1 a resounding gong or a clanging *c.*

DANCE (DANCING)
Ecc 3: 4 a time to mourn and a time to *d,*
Mt 11:17 and you did not *d;*

DANCING (DANCE)
Ps 30:11 You turned my wailing into *d;*
149: 3 Let them praise his name with *d*

DANGER
Pr 27:12 The prudent see *d* and take refuge,
Ro 8:35 famine or nakedness or *d* or sword?

DANIEL

Hebrew exile to Babylon, name changed to Belteshazzar (Da 1:6-7). Refused to eat unclean food (Da 1:8-21). Interpreted Nebuchadnezzar's dreams (Da 2; 4), writing on the wall (Da 5). Thrown into lion's den (Da 6). Visions of (Da 7-12).

DARK (DARKNESS)
Job 34:22 There is no *d* place, no deep
Pr 31:15 She gets up while it is still *d;*
Ro 2:19 a light for those who are in the *d,*
2Pe 1:19 as to a light shining in a *d* place,

DARKNESS (DARK)
Ge 1: 4 he separated the light from the *d.*
2Sa 22:29 the LORD turns my *d* into light.
Jn 3:19 but men loved *d* instead of light
2Co 6:14 fellowship can light have with *d?*
Eph 5: 8 For you were once *d,* but now you
1Pe 2: 9 out of *d* into his wonderful light.
1Jn 1: 5 in him there is no *d* at all.
2: 9 but hates his brother is still in the *d.*

DAUGHTERS
Joel 2:28 sons and *d* will prophesy,

DAVID

Son of Jesse (Ru 4:17-22; 1Ch 2:13-15), ancestor of Jesus (Mt 1:1-17; Lk 3:31).

Anointed king by Samuel (1Sa 16:1-13). Musician to Saul (1Sa 16:14-23; 18:10). Killed Goliath (1Sa 17). Relation with Jonathan (1Sa 18:1-4; 19-20; 23:16-18; 2Sa 1). Disfavor of Saul (1Sa 18:6-23:29). Spared Saul's life (1Sa 24; 26). Among Philistines (1Sa 21:10-14; 27-30). Lament for Saul and Jonathan (2Sa 1).

Anointed king of Judah (2Sa 2:1-11); of Israel (2Sa 5:1-4; 1Ch 11:1-3). Promised eternal dynasty (2Sa 7; 1Ch 17; Ps 132). Adultery with Bathsheba (2Sa 11-12). Absalom's revolt (2Sa 14-18). Last words (2Sa 23:1-7). Death (1Ki 2:10-12; 1Ch 29:28).

DAWN
Ps 37: 6 your righteousness shine like the *d,*
Pr 4:18 is like the first gleam of *d,*

DAY (DAYS)
Ge 1: 5 God called the light *"d,"*
Ex 20: 8 "Remember the Sabbath *d*
Lev 23:28 because it is the *D* of Atonement,
Nu 14:14 before them in a pillar of cloud by *d*
Jos 1: 8 meditate on it *d* and night,
Ps 84:10 Better is one *d* in your courts
96: 2 proclaim his salvation *d* after *d.*
118:24 This is the *d* the LORD has made;
Pr 27: 1 not know what a *d* may bring forth.
Joel 2:31 and dreadful *d* of the LORD.
Ob :15 The *d* of the LORD is near
Lk 11: 3 Give us each *d* our daily bread.
Ac 17:11 examined the Scriptures every *d*
2Co 4:16 we are being renewed *d* by *d.*
1Th 5: 2 for you know very well that the *d*
2Pe 3: 8 With the Lord a *d* is like

DAYS (DAY)
Dt 17:19 he is to read it all the *d,* of his life
Ps 23: 6 all the *d* of my life,
90:10 The length of our *d* is seventy years
Ecc 12: 1 Creator in the *d* of your youth,
Joel 2:29 I will pour out my Spirit in those *d.*
Mic 4: 1 In the last *d*
Heb 1: 2 in these last *d* he has spoken to us
2Pe 3: 3 that in the last *d* scoffers will come,

DEACONS
1Ti 3: 8 *D,* likewise, are to be men worthy

DEAD (DIE)
Dt 18:11 or spiritist or who consults the *d.*
Mt 28: 7 'He has risen from the *d*
Ro 6:11 count yourselves *d* to sin
Eph 2: 1 you were *d* in your transgressions
1Th 4:16 and the *d* in Christ will rise first.
Jas 2:17 is not accompanied by action, is *d.*
2:26 so faith without deeds is *d.*

DEATH (DIE)
Nu 35:16 the murderer shall be put to *d.*
Ps 23: 4 the valley of the shadow of *d,*
116:15 is the *d* of his saints.
Pr 8:36 all who hate me love *d."*
14:12 but in the end it leads to *d.*
Ecc 7: 2 for *d* is the destiny of every man;
Isa 25: 8 he will swallow up *d* forever.
53:12 he poured out his life unto *d,*
Jn 5:24 he has crossed over from *d* to life.
Ro 5:12 and in this way *d* came to all men,
6:23 For the wages of sin is *d,*
8:13 put to *d* the misdeeds of the body,
1Co 15:21 For since *d* came through a man,
15:55 Where, O *d,* is your sting?"
Rev 1:18 And I hold the keys of *d* and Hades
20: 6 The second *d* has no power
20:14 The lake of fire is the second *d.*
21: 4 There will be no more *d*

DEBAUCHERY
Ro 13:13 not in sexual immorality and *d,*
Eph 5:18 drunk on wine, which leads to *d.*

DEBORAH
Prophetess who led Israel to victory over Canaanites (Jdg 4-5).

DEBT (DEBTORS DEBTS)
Ro 13: 8 Let no *d* remain outstanding,
13: 8 continuing *d* to love one another,

DEBTORS (DEBT)
Mt 6:12 as we also have forgiven our *d.*

DEBTS (DEBT)
Dt 15: 1 seven years you must cancel *d.*
Mt 6:12 Forgive us our *d,*

DECAY
Ps 16:10 will you let your Holy One see *d.*
Ac 2:27 will you let your Holy One see *d.*

DECEIT (DECEIVE)
Mk 7:22 greed, malice, *d,* lewdness, envy,
1Pe 2: 1 yourselves of all malice and all *d,*
2:22 and no *d* was found in his mouth."

DECEITFUL (DECEIVE)
Jer 17: 9 The heart is *d* above all things
2Co 11:13 men are false apostles, *d* workmen,

DECEITFULNESS (DECEIVE)
Mk 4:19 the *d* of wealth and the desires
Heb 3:13 of you may be hardened by sin's *d.*

DECEIVE (DECEIT DECEITFUL DECEITFULNESS DECEIVED DECEIVES DECEPTIVE)
Lev 19:11 " 'Do not *d* one another.
Pr 14: 5 A truthful witness does not *d,*
Mt 24: 5 'I am the Christ,' and will *d* many.
Ro 16:18 and flattery they *d* the minds
1Co 3:18 Do not *d* yourselves.
Eph 5: 6 Let no one *d* you with empty words
Jas 1:22 to the word, and so *d* yourselves.
1Jn 1: 8 we *d* ourselves and the truth is not

DECEIVED (DECEIVE)
Ge 3:13 "The serpent *d* me, and I ate."
Gal 6: 7 Do not be *d:* God cannot be
1Ti 2:14 And Adam was not the one *d;*
2Ti 3:13 to worse, deceiving and being *d.*
Jas 1:16 Don't be *d,* my dear brothers.

DECEIVES (DECEIVE)
Gal 6: 3 when he is nothing, he *d* himself.
Jas 1:26 he *d* himself and his religion is

DECENCY*
1Ti 2: 9 women to dress modestly, with *d*

DECEPTIVE (DECEIVE)
Pr 31:30 Charm is *d,* and beauty is fleeting;
Col 2: 8 through hollow and *d* philosophy,

DECLARE (DECLARED DECLARING)
1Ch 16:24 *D* his glory among the nations,
Ps 19: 1 The heavens *d* the glory of God;
96: 3 *D* his glory among the nations,
Isa 42: 9 and new things I *d;*

DECLARED (DECLARE)
Mk 7:19 Jesus *d* all foods "clean.")
Ro 2:13 the law who will be *d* righteous.
3:20 no one will be *d* righteous

DECLARING (DECLARE)
Ps 71: 8 *d* your splendor all day long.
Ac 2:11 we hear them *d* the wonders

DECREED (DECREES)
La 3:37 happen if the Lord has not *d* it?
Lk 22:22 Son of Man will go as it has been *d,*

DECREES (DECREED)
Lev 10:11 Israelites all the *d* the LORD has
Ps 119:112 My heart is set on keeping your *d*

DEDICATE (DEDICATION)
Nu 6:12 He must *d* himself to the LORD
Pr 20:25 for a man to *d* something rashly

DEDICATION (DEDICATE)
1Ti 5:11 sensual desires overcome their *d*

DEED (DEEDS)
Col 3:17 you do, whether in word or *d,*

DEEDS (DEED)
1Sa 2: 3 and by him *d* are weighed.
Ps 65: 5 with awesome *d* of righteousness,
66: 3 "How awesome are your *d!*
78: 4 the praiseworthy *d* of the LORD,
86:10 you are great and do marvelous *d;*
92: 4 For you make me glad by your *d,*
111: 3 Glorious and majestic are his *d,*
Hab 3: 2 I stand in awe of your *d,* O LORD.
Mt 5:16 that they may see your good *d*
Ac 26:20 prove their repentance by their *d.*
Jas 2:14 claims to have faith but has no *d?*
2:20 faith without *d* is useless?
1Pe 2:12 they may see your good *d*

DEEP (DEPTH)
1Co 2:10 all things, even the *d* things
1Ti 3: 9 hold of the *d* truths of the faith

DEER
Ps 42: 1 As the *d* pants for streams of water,

DEFEND (DEFENSE)
Ps 74:22 Rise up, O God, and *d* your cause;
Pr 31: 9 *d* the rights of the poor and needy
Jer 50:34 He will vigorously *d* their cause

DEFENSE (DEFEND)
Ps 35:23 Awake, and rise to my *d!*
Php 1:16 here for the *d* of the gospel.
1Jn 2: 1 speaks to the Father in our *d*—

DEFERRED*
Pr 13:12 Hope *d* makes the heart sick,

DEFILE (DEFILED)
Da 1: 8 Daniel resolved not to *d* himself

DEFILED (DEFILE)
Isa 24: 5 The earth is *d* by its people;

DEFRAUD
Lev 19:13 Do not *d* your neighbor or rob him.

DEITY*
Col 2: 9 of the *D* lives in bodily form,

DELIGHT (DELIGHTS)
1Sa 15:22 "Does the LORD *d*
Ps 1: 2 But his *d* is in the law of the LORD
16: 3 in whom is all my *d.*
35: 9 and *d* in his salvation.
37: 4 *D* yourself in the LORD
43: 4 to God, my joy and my *d.*
51:16 You do not *d* in sacrifice,
119:77 for your law is my *d.*
Pr 29:17 he will bring *d* to your soul.
Isa 42: 1 my chosen one in whom I *d;*
55: 2 and your soul will *d* in the richest
61:10 I *d* greatly in the LORD;
Jer 9:24 for in these I *d,"*
15:16 they were my joy and my heart's *d,*
Mic 7:18 but *d* to show mercy.
Zep 3:17 He will take great *d* in you,
Mt 12:18 the one I love, in whom I *d;*
1Co 13: 6 Love does not *d* in evil
2Co 12:10 for Christ's sake, I *d* in weaknesses,

DELIGHTS (DELIGHT)
Ps 22: 8 since he *d* in him."
35:27 who *d* in the well-being
36: 8 from your river of *d.*
37:23 if the LORD *d* in a man's way,
Pr 3:12 as a father the son he *d* in.
12:22 but he *d* in men who are truthful.
23:24 he who has a wise son *d* in him.

DELILAH*
Woman who betrayed Samson (Jdg 16:4-22).

DELIVER (DELIVERANCE DELIVERED DELIVERER DELIVERS)
Ps 72:12 For he will *d* the needy who cry out
79: 9 *d* us and forgive our sins
Mt 6:13 but *d* us from the evil one.'
2Co 1:10 hope that he will continue to *d* us,

DELIVERANCE (DELIVER)
Ps 3: 8 From the LORD comes *d.*
32: 7 and surround me with songs of *d.*
33:17 A horse is a vain hope for *d;*

DELIVERED (DELIVER)
Ps 34: 4 he *d* me from all my fears.
Ro 4:25 He was *d* over to death for our sins

DELIVERER (DELIVER)
Ps 18: 2 is my rock, my fortress and my *d;*
40:17 You are my help and my *d;*
140: 7 O Sovereign LORD, my strong *d,*
144: 2 my stronghold and my *d,*

DELIVERS (DELIVER)
Ps 34:17 he *d* them from all their troubles.
34:19 but the LORD *d* him from them all
37:40 The LORD helps them and *d* them
37:40 he *d* them from the wicked

DEMANDED
Lk 12:20 This very night your life will be *d*
12:48 been given much, much will be *d;*

DEMONS
Mt 12:27 And if I drive out *d* by Beelzebub,
Mk 5:15 possessed by the legion of *d,*
Ro 8:38 neither angels nor *d,* neither
Jas 2:19 Good! Even the *d* believe that—

DEMONSTRATE (DEMONSTRATES)
Ro 3:26 he did it to *d* his justice

DEMONSTRATES* (DEMONSTRATE)
Ro 5: 8 God *d* his own love for us in this:

DEN
Da 6:16 and threw him into the lions' *d.*
Mt 21:13 you are making it a '*d* of robbers.' "

DENARIUS
Mk 12:15 Bring me a *d* and let me look at it."

DENIED (DENY)
1Ti 5: 8 he has *d* the faith and is worse

DENIES (DENY)
1Jn 2:23 No one who *d* the Son has

DENY (DENIED DENIES DENYING)
Ex 23: 6 "Do not *d* justice to your poor
Job 27: 5 till I die, I will not *d* my integrity.
La 3:35 to *d* a man his rights
Lk 9:23 he must *d* himself and take up his
Tit 1:16 but by their actions they *d* him.

DENYING* (DENY)
Eze 22:29 mistreat the alien, *d* them justice.
2Ti 3: 5 a form of godliness but *d* its power.
2Pe 2: 1 *d* the sovereign Lord who bought

DEPART (DEPARTED)
Ge 49:10 The scepter will not *d* from Judah,
Job 1:21 and naked I will *d.*
Mt 25:41 '*D* from me, you who are cursed,
Php 1:23 I desire to *d* and be with Christ,

DEPARTED (DEPART)
1Sa 4:21 "The glory has *d* from Israel"—
Ps 119:102 I have not *d* from your laws,

DEPOSIT
2Co 1:22 put his Spirit in our hearts as a *d,*
5: 5 and has given us the Spirit as a *d,*
Eph 1:14 who is a *d* guaranteeing our
2Ti 1:14 Guard the good *d* that was

DEPRAVED (DEPRAVITY)
Ro 1:28 he gave them over to a *d* mind,
Php 2:15 fault in a crooked and *d* generation,

DEPRAVITY (DEPRAVED)
Ro 1:29 of wickedness, evil, greed and *d.*

DEPRIVE
Dt 24:17 Do not *d* the alien or the fatherless
Pr 18: 5 or to *d* the innocent of justice.
Isa 10: 2 to *d* the poor of their rights
29:21 with false testimony *d* the innocent
1Co 7: 5 Do not *d* each other

DEPTH (DEEP)
Ro 8:39 any powers, neither height nor *d,*
11:33 the *d* of the riches of the wisdom

DESERT
Nu 32:13 wander in the *d* forty years,
Ne 9:19 you did not abandon them in the *d.*
Ps 78:19 "Can God spread a table in the *d?*
78:52 led them like sheep through the *d.*
Mk 1:13 and he was in the *d* forty days,

DESERTED (DESERTS)
Ezr 9: 9 our God has not *d* us
Mt 26:56 all the disciples *d* him and fled.
2Ti 1:15 in the province of Asia has *d* me,

DESERTING (DESERTS)
Gal 1: 6 are so quickly *d* the one who called

DESERTS (DESERTED DESERTING)
Zec 11:17 who *d* the flock!

DESERVE (DESERVES)
Ps 103:10 he does not treat us as our sins *d*
Jer 21:14 I will punish you as your deeds *d,*
Mt 22: 8 those I invited did not *d* to come.
Ro 1:32 those who do such things *d* death,

DESERVES (DESERVE)
2Sa 12: 5 the man who did this *d* to die!
Lk 10: 7 for the worker *d* his wages.
1Ti 5:18 and "The worker *d* his wages."

DESIRABLE (DESIRE)
Pr 22: 1 A good name is more *d*

DESIRE (DESIRABLE DESIRES)
Ge 3:16 Your *d* will be for your husband,
Dt 5:21 You shall not set your *d*
1Ch 29:18 keep this *d* in the hearts
Ps 40: 6 Sacrifice and offering you did not *d*
40: 8 I *d* to do your will, O my God;
73:25 earth has nothing I *d* besides you
Pr 3:15 nothing you *d* can compare
10:24 what the righteous *d* will be
11:23 The *d* of the righteous ends only
Isa 26: 8 are the *d* of our hearts.
53: 2 appearance that we should *d* him.
55:11 but will accomplish what I *d*
Hos 6: 6 For I *d* mercy, not sacrifice,
Mt 9:13 learn what this means: 'I *d* mercy,
Ro 7:18 For I have the *d* to do what is good,
1Co 12:31 But eagerly *d* the greater gifts.
14: 1 and eagerly *d* spiritual gifts,
Php 1:23 I *d* to depart and be with Christ,
Heb 13:18 *d* to live honorably in every way.
Jas 1:15 Then, after *d* has conceived,

DESIRES (DESIRE)
Ge 4: 7 at your door; it *d* to have you,
Ps 34:12 and *d* to see many good days,
37: 4 he will give you the *d* of your heart.
103: 5 satisfies your *d* with good things,
145:19 He fulfills the *d* of those who fear
Pr 11: 6 the unfaithful are trapped by evil *d.*
19:22 What a man *d* is unfailing love;
Mk 4:19 and the *d* for other things come in
Ro 8: 5 set on what that nature *d;*
13:14 to gratify the *d* of the sinful nature.
Gal 5:16 and you will not gratify the *d*
5:17 the sinful nature *d* what is contrary
1Ti 3: 1 an overseer, he *d* a noble task.
6: 9 and harmful *d* that plunge men
2Ti 2:22 Flee the evil *d* of youth,
Jas 1:20 about the righteous life that God *d.*
4: 1 from your *d* that battle within you?
1Pe 2:11 to abstain from sinful *d,* which war
1Jn 2:17 The world and its *d* pass away,

DESOLATE
Isa 54: 1 are the children of the *d* woman

DESPAIR
Isa 61: 3 instead of a spirit of *d.*
2Co 4: 8 perplexed, but not in *d;* persecuted,

DESPISE (DESPISED DESPISES)
Job 42: 6 Therefore I *d* myself
Pr 1: 7 but fools *d* wisdom and discipline.
3:11 do not *d* the LORD's discipline
23:22 do not *d* your mother
Lk 16:13 devoted to the one and *d* the other.
Tit 2:15 Do not let anyone *d* you.

DESPISED (DESPISE)
Ge 25:34 So Esau *d* his birthright.
Isa 53: 3 He was *d* and rejected by men,
1Co 1:28 of this world and the *d* things—

DESPISES (DESPISE)
Pr 14:21 He who *d* his neighbor sins,
15:20 but a foolish man *d* his mother.
15:32 who ignores discipline *d* himself,
Zec 4:10 "Who *d* the day of small things?

DESTINED (DESTINY)
Lk 2:34 "This child is *d* to cause the falling

DESTINY (DESTINED PREDESTINED)
Ps 73:17 then I understood their final *d.*
Ecc 7: 2 for death is the *d* of every man;

DESTITUTE
Pr 31: 8 for the rights of all who are *d.*

Heb 11:37 *d,* persecuted and mistreated—

DESTROY (DESTROYED DESTROYS DESTRUCTION)
Pr 1:32 complacency of fools will *d* them;
Mt 10:28 of the One who can *d* both soul

DESTROYED (DESTROY)
Job 19:26 And after my skin has been *d,*
Isa 55:13 which will not be *d."*
1Co 8:11 for whom Christ died, is *d*
15:26 The last enemy to be *d* is death.
2Co 5: 1 if the earthly tent we live in is *d,*
Heb 10:39 of those who shrink back and are *d,*
2Pe 3:10 the elements will be *d* by fire,

DESTROYS (DESTROY)
Pr 6:32 whoever does so *d* himself.
11: 9 mouth the godless *d* his neighbor,
18: 9 is brother to one who *d.*
28:24 he is partner to him who *d.*
Ecc 9:18 but one sinner *d* much good.
1Co 3:17 If anyone *d* God's temple,

DESTRUCTION (DESTROY)
Pr 16:18 Pride goes before *d,*
Hos 13:14 Where, O grave, is your *d?*
Mt 7:13 broad is the road that leads to *d,*
Gal 6: 8 from that nature will reap *d;*
2Th 1: 9 punished with everlasting *d*
1Ti 6: 9 that plunge men into ruin and *d.*
2Pe 2: 1 bringing swift *d* on themselves.
3:16 other Scriptures, to their own *d.*

DETERMINED (DETERMINES)
Job 14: 5 Man's days are *d;*
Isa 14:26 This is the plan *d* for the whole
Da 11:36 for what has been *d* must take place
Ac 17:26 and he *d* the times set for them

DETERMINES* (DETERMINED)
Ps 147: 4 He *d* the number of the stars
Pr 16: 9 but the LORD *d* his steps.
1Co 12:11 them to each one, just as he *d.*

DETESTABLE (DETESTS)
Pr 21:27 The sacrifice of the wicked is *d*—
28: 9 even his prayers are *d.*
Isa 1:13 Your incense is *d* to me.
Lk 16:15 among men is *d* in God's sight.
Tit 1:16 They are *d,* disobedient

DETESTS (DETESTABLE)
Dt 22: 5 LORD your God *d* anyone who
23:18 the LORD your God *d* them both.
25:16 LORD your God *d* anyone who
Pr 12:22 The LORD *d* lying lips,
15: 8 The LORD *d* the sacrifice
15: 9 The LORD *d* the way
15:26 The LORD *d* the thoughts
16: 5 The LORD *d* all the proud of heart
17:15 the LORD *d* them both.
20:23 The LORD *d* differing weights,

DEVIL (DEVIL'S)
Mt 13:39 the enemy who sows them is the *d.*
25:41 the eternal fire prepared for the *d*
Lk 4: 2 forty days he was tempted by the *d.*
8:12 then the *d* comes and takes away
Eph 4:27 and do not give the *d* a foothold.
2Ti 2:26 and escape from the trap of the *d,*
Jas 4: 7 Resist the *d,* and he will flee
1Pe 5: 8 Your enemy the *d* prowls
1Jn 3: 8 who does what is sinful is of the *d,*
Rev 12: 9 that ancient serpent called the *d*

DEVIL'S* (DEVIL)
Eph 6:11 stand against the *d* schemes.

1Ti 3: 7 into disgrace and into the *d* trap.
1Jn 3: 8 was to destroy the *d* work.

DEVOTE (DEVOTED DEVOTING DEVOTION DEVOUT)
Job 11:13 "Yet if you *d* your heart to him
Jer 30:21 for who is he who will *d* himself
Col 4: 2 *D* yourselves to prayer, being
1Ti 4:13 *d* yourself to the public reading
Tit 3: 8 may be careful to *d* themselves

DEVOTED (DEVOTE)
Ezr 7:10 For Ezra had *d* himself to the study
Ac 2:42 They *d* themselves
Ro 12:10 Be *d* to one another
1Co 7:34 Her aim is to be *d* to the Lord

DEVOTING (DEVOTE)
1Ti 5:10 *d* herself to all kinds of good deeds.

DEVOTION (DEVOTE)
1Ch 28: 9 and serve him with wholehearted *d*
Eze 33:31 With their mouths they express *d*,
1Co 7:35 way in undivided *d* to the Lord.
2Co 11: 3 from your sincere and pure *d*

DEVOUR
2Sa 2:26 "Must the sword *d* forever?
Mk 12:40 They *d* widows' houses
1Pe 5: 8 lion looking for someone to *d*.

DEVOUT (DEVOTE)
Lk 2:25 Simeon, who was righteous and *d*.

DIE (DEAD DEATH DIED DIES)
Ge 2:17 when you eat of it you will surely *d*
Ex 11: 5 Every firstborn son in Egypt will *d*,
Ru 1:17 Where you *d* I will *d*, and there I
2Ki 14: 6 each is to *d* for his own sins."
Pr 5:23 He will *d* for lack of discipline,
10:21 but fools *d* for lack of judgment.
15:10 he who hates correction will *d*.
23:13 with the rod, he will not *d*.
Ecc 3: 2 a time to be born and a time to *d*,
Isa 66:24 their worm will not *d*, nor will their
Eze 3:18 that wicked man will *d* for his sin,
18: 4 soul who sins is the one who will *d*.
33: 8 'O wicked man, you will surely *d*,'
Mt 26:52 "for all who draw the sword will *d*
Jn 11:26 and believes in me will never *d*.
Ro 5: 7 Very rarely will anyone *d*
14: 8 and if we *d*, we *d* to the Lord.
1Co 15:22 in Adam all *d*, so in Christ all will
15:31 I *d* every day—I mean that,
Php 1:21 to live is Christ and to *d* is gain.
Heb 9:27 Just as man is destined to *d* once,
Rev 14:13 Blessed are the dead who *d*

DIED (DIE)
Ro 5: 6 we were still powerless, Christ *d*
6: 2 By no means! We *d* to sin;
6: 8 if we *d* with Christ, we believe that
14:15 brother for whom Christ *d*.
1Co 8:11 for whom Christ *d*, is destroyed
15: 3 that Christ *d* for our sins according
2Co 5:14 *d* for all, and therefore all *d*.
Col 3: 3 For you *d*, and your life is now
1Th 5:10 He *d* for us so that, whether we are
2Ti 2:11 If we *d* with him,
Heb 9:15 now that he has *d* as a ransom
1Pe 3:18 For Christ *d* for sins once for all,
Rev 2: 8 who *d* and came to life again.

DIES (DIE)
Job 14:14 If a man *d*, will he live again?
Pr 11: 7 a wicked man *d*, his hope perishes;
Jn 11:25 in me will live, even though he *d*;
1Co 15:36 does not come to life unless it *d*.

DIFFERENCE (DIFFERENT)
Ro 10:12 For there is no *d* between Jew

DIFFERENT (DIFFERENCE)
1Co 12: 4 There are *d* kinds of gifts,
2Co 11: 4 or a *d* gospel from the one you

DIGNITY
Pr 31:25 She is clothed with strength and *d*;

DIGS
Pr 26:27 If a man *d* a pit, he will fall into it;

DILIGENCE (DILIGENT)
Heb 6:11 to show this same *d* to the very end

DILIGENT (DILIGENCE)
Pr 21: 5 The plans of the *d* lead to profit
1Ti 4:15 Be *d* in these matters; give yourself

DIRECT (DIRECTS)
Ps 119:35 *D* me in the path of your
119:133 *D* my footsteps according
Jer 10:23 it is not for man to *d* his steps.
2Th 3: 5 May the Lord *d* your hearts

DIRECTS (DIRECT)
Ps 42: 8 By day the LORD *d* his love,
Isa 48:17 who *d* you in the way you should

DIRGE
Mt 11:17 we sang a *d*,

DISAPPEAR
Mt 5:18 will by any means *d* from the Law
Lk 16:17 earth to *d* than for the least stroke

DISAPPOINT* (DISAPPOINTED)
Ro 5: 5 And hope does not *d* us,

DISAPPOINTED (DISAPPOINT)
Ps 22: 5 in you they trusted and were not *d*.

DISASTER
Ps 57: 1 wings until the *d* has passed.
Pr 3:25 Have no fear of sudden *d*
17: 5 over *d* will not go unpunished.
Isa 45: 7 I bring prosperity and create *d*;
Eze 7: 5 An unheard-of *d* is coming.

DISCERN (DISCERNING DISCERNMENT)
Ps 19:12 Who can *d* his errors?
139: 3 You *d* my going out and my lying
Php 1:10 you may be able to *d* what is best

DISCERNING (DISCERN)
Pr 14: 6 knowledge comes easily to the *d*.
15:14 The *d* heart seeks knowledge,
17:24 A *d* man keeps wisdom in view,
17:28 and *d* if he holds his tongue.
19:25 rebuke a *d* man, and he will gain

DISCERNMENT (DISCERN)
Pr 17:10 A rebuke impresses a man of *d*
28:11 a poor man who has *d* sees

DISCIPLE (DISCIPLES)
Mt 10:42 these little ones because he is my *d*,
Lk 14:27 and follow me cannot be my *d*.

DISCIPLES (DISCIPLE)
Mt 28:19 Therefore go and make *d*
Jn 8:31 to my teaching, you are really my *d*
13:35 men will know that you are my *d*
Ac 11:26 The *d* were called Christians first

DISCIPLINE (DISCIPLINED DISCIPLINES)
Ps 38: 1 or *d* me in your wrath.
39:11 You rebuke and *d* men for their sin;
94:12 Blessed is the man you *d*, O LORD
Pr 1: 7 but fools despise wisdom and *d*.
3:11 do not despise the LORD's *d*
5:12 You will say, "How I hated *d*!
5:23 He will die for lack of *d*,
6:23 and the corrections of *d*
10:17 He who heeds *d* shows the way
12: 1 Whoever loves *d* loves knowledge,
13:18 He who ignores *d* comes to poverty
13:24 who loves him is careful to *d* him.
15: 5 A fool spurns his father's *d*,
15:32 He who ignores *d* despises himself,
19:18 *D* your son, for in that there is hope
22:15 the rod of *d* will drive it far
23:13 Do not withhold *d* from a child;
29:17 *D* your son, and he will give you
Heb 12: 5 do not make light of the Lord's *d*,
12: 7 as *d*; God is treating you
12:11 No *d* seems pleasant at the time,
Rev 3:19 Those whom I love I rebuke and *d*.

DISCIPLINED (DISCIPLINE)
Pr 1: 3 for acquiring a *d* and prudent life,
Jer 31:18 'You *d* me like an unruly calf,
1Co 11:32 we are being *d* so that we will not
Tit 1: 8 upright, holy and *d*.
Heb 12: 7 For what son is not *d* by his father?

DISCIPLINES (DISCIPLINE)
Dt 8: 5 your heart that as a man *d* his son,
Pr 3:12 the LORD *d* those he loves,
Heb 12: 6 because the Lord *d* those he loves,
12:10 but God *d* us for our good,

DISCLOSED
Lk 8:17 is nothing hidden that will not be *d*,

DISCOURAGED
Jos 1: 9 Do not be terrified; do not be *d*,
10:25 "Do not be afraid; do not be *d*.
1Ch 28:20 or *d*, for the LORD God,
Isa 42: 4 he will not falter or be *d*
Col 3:21 children, or they will become *d*.

DISCREDITED
2Co 6: 3 so that our ministry will not be *d*.

DISCRETION*
1Ch 22:12 May the LORD give you *d*
Pr 1: 4 knowledge and *d* to the young—
2:11 *D* will protect you,
5: 2 that you may maintain *d*
8:12 I possess knowledge and *d*.
11:22 a beautiful woman who shows no *d*.

DISCRIMINATED*
Jas 2: 4 have you not *d* among yourselves

DISFIGURED
Isa 52:14 his appearance was so *d*

DISGRACE (DISGRACEFUL DISGRACES)
Pr 11: 2 When pride comes, then comes *d*,
14:34 but sin is a *d* to any people.
19:26 is a son who brings shame and *d*.
Ac 5:41 of suffering *d* for the Name.
Heb 13:13 the camp, bearing the *d* he bore.

DISGRACEFUL (DISGRACE)
Pr 10: 5 during harvest is a *d* son.
17: 2 wise servant will rule over a *d* son,

DISGRACES (DISGRACE)
Pr 28: 7 of gluttons *d* his father.
29:15 but a child left to itself *d* his mother

DISHONEST
Pr 11: 1 The LORD abhors *d* scales,
29:27 The righteous detest the *d;*
Lk 16:10 whoever is *d* with very little will
1Ti 3: 8 wine, and not pursuing *d* gain.

DISHONOR (DISHONORS)
Lev 18: 7 " 'Do not *d* your father
Pr 30: 9 and so *d* the name of my God.
1Co 15:43 it is sown in *d,* it is raised in glory;

DISHONORS (DISHONOR)
Dt 27:16 Cursed is the man who *d* his father

DISMAYED
Isa 28:16 the one who trusts will never be *d.*
41:10 do not be *d,* for I am your God.

DISOBEDIENCE (DISOBEY)
Ro 5:19 as through the *d* of the one man
11:32 to *d* so that he may have mercy
Heb 2: 2 and *d* received its just punishment,
4: 6 go in, because of their *d.*
4:11 fall by following their example of *d.*

DISOBEDIENT (DISOBEY)
2Ti 3: 2 proud, abusive, *d* to their parents,
Tit 1: 6 to the charge of being wild and *d.*
1:16 *d* and unfit for doing anything

DISOBEY (DISOBEDIENCE DISOBEDIENT)
Dt 11:28 the curse if you *d* the commands
2Ch 24:20 'Why do you *d* the LORD's
Ro 1:30 they *d* their parents; they are

DISORDER
1Co 14:33 For God is not a God of *d*
2Co 12:20 slander, gossip, arrogance and *d.*
Jas 3:16 there you find *d* and every evil

DISOWN
Pr 30: 9 I may have too much and *d* you
Mt 10:33 I will *d* him before my Father
26:35 to die with you, I will never *d* you."
2Ti 2:12 If we *d* him,

DISPLAY (DISPLAYS)
Eze 39:21 I will *d* my glory among the nations
1Ti 1:16 Christ Jesus might *d* his unlimited

DISPLAYS (DISPLAY)
Isa 44:23 he *d* his glory in Israel.

DISPUTE (DISPUTES)
Pr 17:14 before a *d* breaks out.
1Co 6: 1 If any of you has a *d* with another,

DISPUTES (DISPUTE)
Pr 18:18 Casting the lot settles *d*

DISQUALIFIED
1Co 9:27 I myself will not be *d* for the prize.

DISREPUTE*
2Pe 2: 2 will bring the way of truth into *d.*

DISSENSION*
Pr 6:14 he always stirs up *d.*
6:19 and a man who stirs up *d*
10:12 Hatred stirs up *d,*
15:18 A hot-tempered man stirs up *d,*
16:28 A perverse man stirs up *d,*
28:25 A greedy man stirs up *d,*
29:22 An angry man stirs up *d,*
Ro 13:13 debauchery, not in *d* and jealousy.

DISSIPATION*
Lk 21:34 will be weighed down with *d,*

1Pe 4: 4 with them into the same flood of *d,*

DISTINGUISH
1Ki 3: 9 and to *d* between right and wrong.
Heb 5:14 themselves to *d* good from evil.

DISTORT
2Co 4: 2 nor do we *d* the word of God.
2Pe 3:16 ignorant and unstable people *d,*

DISTRESS (DISTRESSED)
Ps 18: 6 In my *d* I called to the LORD;
Jnh 2: 2 "In my *d* I called to the LORD,
Jas 1:27 after orphans and widows in their *d*

DISTRESSED (DISTRESS)
Ro 14:15 If your brother is *d*

DIVIDED (DIVISION)
Mt 12:25 household *d* against itself will not
Lk 23:34 they *d* up his clothes by casting lots
1Co 1:13 Is Christ *d?* Was Paul crucified

DIVINATION
Lev 19:26 " 'Do not practice *d* or sorcery.

DIVINE
Ro 1:20 his eternal power and *d* nature—
2Co 10: 4 they have *d* power
2Pe 1: 4 you may participate in the *d* nature

DIVISION (DIVIDED DIVISIONS DIVISIVE)
Lk 12:51 on earth? No, I tell you, but *d.*
1Co 12:25 so that there should be no *d*

DIVISIONS (DIVISION)
Ro 16:17 to watch out for those who cause *d*
1Co 1:10 another so that there may be no *d*
11:18 there are *d* among you,

DIVISIVE* (DIVISION)
Tit 3:10 Warn a *d* person once,

DIVORCE
Mal 2:16 "I hate *d,*" says the LORD God
Mt 19: 3 for a man to *d* his wife for any
1Co 7:11 And a husband must not *d* his wife.
7:27 Are you married? Do not seek a *d.*

DOCTOR
Mt 9:12 "It is not the healthy who need a *d,*

DOCTRINE
1Ti 4:16 Watch your life and *d* closely.
Tit 2: 1 is in accord with sound *d.*

DOMINION
Ps 22:28 for *d* belongs to the LORD

DOOR
Ps 141: 3 keep watch over the *d* of my lips.
Mt 6: 6 close the *d* and pray to your Father
7: 7 and the *d* will be opened to you.
Rev 3:20 I stand at the *d* and knock.

DOORKEEPER
Ps 84:10 I would rather be a *d* in the house

DOUBLE-EDGED
Heb 4:12 Sharper than any *d* sword,
Rev 1:16 of his mouth came a sharp *d* sword.
2:12 of him who has the sharp, *d* sword.

DOUBLE-MINDED (MIND)
Ps 119:113 I hate *d* men,
Jas 1: 8 he is a *d* man, unstable

DOUBT
Mt 14:31 he said, "why did you *d?*"
21:21 if you have faith and do not *d,*
Mk 11:23 and does not *d* in his heart
Jas 1: 6 he must believe and not *d,*
Jude :22 Be merciful to those who *d;*

DOWNCAST
Ps 42: 5 Why are you *d,* O my soul?
2Co 7: 6 But God, who comforts the *d,*

DRAW (DRAWING DRAWS)
Mt 26:52 "for all who *d* the sword will die
Jn 12:32 up from the earth, will *d* all men
Heb 10:22 let us *d* near to God

DRAWING (DRAW)
Lk 21:28 because your redemption is *d* near

DRAWS (DRAW)
Jn 6:44 the Father who sent me *d* him,

DREADFUL
Heb 10:31 It is a *d* thing to fall into the hands

DRESS
1Ti 2: 9 I also want women to *d* modestly,

DRINK (DRUNK DRUNKARDS DRUNKENNESS)
Pr 5:15 *D* water from your own cistern,
Lk 12:19 Take life easy; eat, *d* and be merry
Jn 7:37 let him come to me and *d.*
1Co 12:13 were all given the one Spirit to *d.*
Rev 21: 6 to *d* without cost from the spring

DRIVES
1Jn 4:18 But perfect love *d* out fear,

DROP
Pr 17:14 so *d* the matter before a dispute
Isa 40:15 Surely the nations are like a *d*

DRUNK (DRINK)
Eph 5:18 Do not get *d* on wine, which leads

DRUNKARDS (DRINK)
Pr 23:21 for *d* and gluttons become poor,
1Co 6:10 nor the greedy nor *d* nor slanderers

DRUNKENNESS (DRINK)
Lk 21:34 weighed down with dissipation, *d*
Ro 13:13 and *d,* not in sexual immorality
Gal 5:21 factions and envy; *d,* orgies,
1Pe 4: 3 living in debauchery, lust, *d,* orgies,

DRY
Isa 53: 2 and like a root out of *d* ground.
Eze 37: 4 '*D* bones, hear the word

DUST
Ge 2: 7 man from the *d* of the ground
Ps 103:14 he remembers that we are *d.*
Ecc 3:20 all come from *d,* and to *d* all return.

DUTY
Ecc 12:13 for this is the whole *d* of man.
Ac 23: 1 I have fulfilled my *d* to God
1Co 7: 3 husband should fulfill his marital *d*

DWELL (DWELLING)
1Ki 8:27 "But will God really *d* on earth?
Ps 23: 6 I will *d* in the house of the LORD
Isa 43:18 do not *d* on the past.
Eph 3:17 so that Christ may *d* in your hearts
Col 1:19 to have all his fullness *d* in him,
3:16 the word of Christ *d* in you richly

DWELLING (DWELL)
Eph 2:22 to become a *d* in which God lives

EAGER
Pr 31:13 and works with *e* hands.
1Pe 5: 2 greedy for money, but *e* to serve;

EAGLE'S (EAGLES)
Ps 103: 5 your youth is renewed like the *e.*

EAGLES (EAGLE'S)
Isa 40:31 They will soar on wings like *e;*

EAR (EARS)
1Co 2: 9 no *e* has heard,
12:16 if the *e* should say, "Because I am

EARNED
Pr 31:31 Give her the reward she has *e,*

EARS (EAR)
Job 42: 5 My *e* had heard of you
Ps 34:15 and his *e* are attentive to their cry;
Pr 21:13 If a man shuts his *e* to the cry
2Ti 4: 3 to say what their itching *e* want

EARTH (EARTHLY)
Ge 1: 1 God created the heavens and the *e.*
Ps 24: 1 *e* is the LORD'S, and everything
108: 5 and let your glory be over all the *e.*
Isa 6: 3 the whole *e* is full of his glory."
51: 6 the *e* will wear out like a garment
55: 9 the heavens are higher than the *e,*
66: 1 and the *e* is my footstool.
Jer 23:24 "Do not I fill heaven and *e?"*
Hab 2:20 let all the *e* be silent before him."
Mt 6:10 done on *e* as it is in heaven.
16:19 bind on *e* will be bound
24:35 Heaven and *e* will pass away,
28:18 and on *e* has been given to me.
Lk 2:14 on *e* peace to men
1Co 10:26 The *e* is the Lord's, and everything
Php 2:10 in heaven and on *e* and under the *e,*
2Pe 3:13 to a new heaven and a new *e,*

EARTHLY (EARTH)
Php 3:19 Their mind is on *e* things.
Col 3: 2 on things above, not on *e* things.

EAST
Ps 103:12 as far as the *e* is from the west,

EASY
Mt 11:30 For my yoke is *e* and my burden is

EAT (EATING)
Ge 2:17 but you must not *e* from the tree
Isa 55: 1 come, buy and *e!*
65:25 and the lion will *e* straw like the ox,
Mt 26:26 "Take and *e;* this is my body."
Ro 14: 2 faith allows him to *e* everything,
1Co 8:13 if what I *e* causes my brother to fall
10:31 So whether you *e* or drink
2Th 3:10 man will not work, he shall not *e."*

EATING (EAT)
Ro 14:17 kingdom of God is not a matter of *e*

EDICT
Heb 11:23 they were not afraid of the king's *e.*

EDIFIES
1Co 14: 4 but he who prophesies *e* the church

EFFECT
Isa 32:17 *e* of righteousness will be quietness
Heb 9:18 put into *e* without blood.

EFFORT
Lk 13:24 "Make every *e* to enter
Ro 9:16 depend on man's desire or *e,*
14:19 make every *e* to do what leads
Eph 4: 3 Make every *e* to keep the unity
Heb 4:11 make every *e* to enter that rest,
12:14 Make every *e* to live in peace
2Pe 1: 5 make every *e* to add
3:14 make every *e* to be found spotless,

ELAH
Son of Baasha; king of Israel (1Ki 16:6-14).

ELDERLY* (ELDERS)
Lev 19:32 show respect for the *e*

ELDERS (ELDERLY)
1Ti 5:17 The *e* who direct the affairs

ELECTION
Ro 9:11 God's purpose in *e* might stand:
2Pe 1:10 to make your calling and *e* sure.

ELI
High priest in youth of Samuel (1Sa 1-4). Blessed Hannah (1Sa 1:12-18); raised Samuel (1Sa 2:11-26).

ELIJAH
Prophet; predicted famine in Israel (1Ki 17:1; Jas 5:17). Fed by ravens (1Ki 17:2-6). Raised Sidonian widow's son (1Ki 17:7-24). Defeated prophets of Baal at Carmel (1Ki 18:16-46). Ran from Jezebel (1Ki 19:1-9). Prophesied death of Azariah (2Ki 1). Succeeded by Elishah (1Ki 19:19-21; 2Ki 2:1-18). Taken to heaven in whirlwind (2Ki 2:11-12).
Return prophesied (Mal 4:5-6); equated with John the Baptist (Mt 17:9-13; Mk 9:9-13; Lk 1:17). Appeared with Moses in transfiguration of Jesus (Mt 17:1-8; Mk 9:1-8).

ELISHA
Prophet; successor of Elijah (1Ki 19:16-21); inherited his cloak (2Ki 2:1-18). Miracles of (2Ki 2-6).

ELIZABETH*
Mother of John the Baptist, relative of Mary (Lk 1:5-58).

EMBITTER*
Col 3:21 Fathers, do not *e* your children,

EMPTY
Eph 5: 6 no one deceive you with *e* words,
1Pe 1:18 from the *e* way of life handed

ENABLE (ABLE)
Lk 1:74 to *e* us to serve him without fear
Ac 4:29 *e* your servants to speak your word

ENABLED (ABLE)
Lev 26:13 *e* you to walk with heads held high.
Jn 6:65 unless the Father has *e* him."

ENABLES (ABLE)
Php 3:21 by the power that *e* him

ENCAMPS*
Ps 34: 7 The angel of the LORD *e*

ENCOURAGE (ENCOURAGEMENT)
Ps 10:17 you *e* them, and you listen
Isa 1:17 *e* the oppressed.
Ac 15:32 to *e* and strengthen the brothers.
Ro 12: 8 if it is encouraging, let him *e;*
1Th 4:18 Therefore *e* each other
2Ti 4: 2 rebuke and *e*— with great patience
Tit 2: 6 *e* the young men to be
Heb 3:13 But *e* one another daily, as long
10:25 but let us *e* one another—

ENCOURAGEMENT (ENCOURAGE)
Ac 4:36 Barnabas (which means Son of *E),*
Ro 15: 4 *e* of the Scriptures we might have
15: 5 and *e* give you a spirit of unity
1Co 14: 3 to men for their strengthening, *e*
Heb 12: 5 word of *e* that addresses you

END
Ps 119:33 then I will keep them to the *e.*
Pr 14:12 but in the *e* it leads to death.
19:20 and in the *e* you will be wise.
23:32 In the *e* it bites like a snake
Ecc 12:12 making many books there is no *e,*
Mt 10:22 firm to the *e* will be saved.
Lk 21: 9 but the *e* will not come right away
Ro 10: 4 Christ is the *e* of the law
1Co 15:24 the *e* will come, when he hands

ENDURANCE (ENDURE)
Ro 15: 4 through *e* and the encouragement
15: 5 May the God who gives *e*
2Co 1: 6 which produces in you patient *e*
Col 1:11 might so that you may have great *e*
1Ti 6:11 faith, love, *e* and gentleness.
Tit 2: 2 and sound in faith, in love and in *e.*

ENDURE (ENDURANCE ENDURES)
Ps 72:17 May his name *e* forever;
Pr 12:19 Truthful lips *e* forever,
27:24 for riches do not *e* forever,
Ecc 3:14 everything God does will *e* forever;
Mal 3: 2 who can *e* the day of his coming?
2Ti 2: 3 *E* hardship with us like a good
2:12 if we *e,* / we will also reign
Heb 12: 7 *E* hardship as discipline; God is
Rev 3:10 kept my command to *e* patiently,

ENDURES (ENDURE)
Ps 112: 9 his righteousness *e* forever;
136: 1 *His love e forever.*
Da 9:15 made for yourself a name that *e*

ENEMIES (ENEMY)
Ps 23: 5 in the presence of my *e.*
Mic 7: 6 a man's *e* are the members
Mt 5:44 Love your *e* and pray
Lk 20:43 hand until I make your *e*

ENEMY (ENEMIES ENMITY)
Pr 24:17 Do not gloat when your *e* falls;
25:21 If your *e* is hungry, give him food
27: 6 but an *e* multiplies kisses.
1Co 15:26 The last *e* to be destroyed is death.
1Ti 5:14 and to give the *e* no opportunity

ENJOY (JOY)
Dt 6: 2 and so that you may *e* long life.
Eph 6: 3 and that you may *e* long life
Heb 11:25 rather than to *e* the pleasures of sin

ENJOYMENT (JOY)
Ecc 4: 8 and why am I depriving myself of *e*
1Ti 6:17 us with everything for our *e.*

ENLIGHTENED* (LIGHT)
Eph 1:18 that the eyes of your heart may be *e*
Heb 6: 4 for those who have once been *e,*

ENMITY* (ENEMY)
Ge 3:15 And I will put *e*

ENOCH
Walked with God and taken by him (Ge 5:18-24; Heb 11:5). Prophet (Jude 14).

ENTANGLED (ENTANGLES)
2Pe 2:20 and are again *e* in it and overcome,

ENTANGLES* (ENTANGLED)
Heb 12: 1 and the sin that so easily *e,*

ENTER (ENTERED ENTERS ENTRANCE)
Ps 100: 4 *E* his gates with thanksgiving
Mt 5:20 will certainly not *e* the kingdom
7:13 "*E* through the narrow gate.
18: 8 It is better for you to *e* life maimed
Mk 10:15 like a little child will never *e* it."
10:23 is for the rich to *e* the kingdom

ENTERED (ENTER)
Ro 5:12 as sin *e* the world through one man,
Heb 9:12 but he *e* the Most Holy Place once

ENTERS (ENTER)
Mk 7:18 you see that nothing that *e* a man
Jn 10: 2 The man who *e* by the gate is

ENTERTAIN
1Ti 5:19 Do not *e* an accusation
Heb 13: 2 Do not forget to *e* strangers,

ENTHRALLED*
Ps 45:11 The king is *e* by your beauty;

ENTHRONED (THRONE)
1Sa 4: 4 who is *e* between the cherubim.
Ps 2: 4 The One *e* in heaven laughs;
102:12 But you, O LORD, sit *e* forever;
Isa 40:22 He sits *e* above the circle

ENTICE
Pr 1:10 My son, if sinners *e* you,
2Pe 2:18 they *e* people who are just escaping

ENTIRE
Gal 5:14 The *e* law is summed up

ENTRUSTED (TRUST)
1Ti 6:20 guard what has been *e* to your care.
2Ti 1:12 able to guard what I have *e* to him
1:14 Guard the good deposit that was *e*
Jude : 3 once for all *e* to the saints.

ENVY
Pr 3:31 Do not *e* a violent man
14:30 but *e* rots the bones.
1Co 13: 4 It does not *e,* it does not boast,

EPHRAIM
1. Second son of Joseph (Ge 41:52; 46:20). Blessed as firstborn by Jacob (Ge 48).
2. Synonymous with Northern Kingdom (Isa 7:17; Hos 5).

EQUAL
Isa 40:25 who is my *e?"* says the Holy One.
Jn 5:18 making himself *e* with God.
1Co 12:25 that its parts should have *e* concern

EQUIP* (EQUIPPED)
Heb 13:21 *e* you with everything good

EQUIPPED (EQUIP)
2Ti 3:17 man of God may be thoroughly *e*

ERROR
Jas 5:20 Whoever turns a sinner from the *e*

ESAU
Firstborn of Isaac, twin of Jacob (Ge 25:21-26). Also called Edom (Ge 25:30). Sold Jacob his birthright (Ge 25:29-34); lost blessing (Ge 27). Reconciled to Jacob (Gen 33).

ESCAPE (ESCAPING)
Ro 2: 3 think you will *e* God's judgment?
Heb 2: 3 how shall we *e* if we ignore such

ESCAPING (ESCAPE)
1Co 3:15 only as one *e* through the flames.

ESTABLISH
Ge 6:18 But I will *e* my covenant with you,
1Ch 28: 7 I will *e* his kingdom forever
Ro 10: 3 God and sought to *e* their own,

ESTEEMED
Pr 22: 1 to be *e* is better than silver or gold.
Isa 53: 3 he was despised, and we *e* him not.

ESTHER
Jewess who lived in Persia; cousin of Mordecai (Est 2:7). Chosen queen of Xerxes (Est 2:8-18). Foiled Haman's plan to exterminate the Jews (Est 3-4; 7-9).

ETERNAL (ETERNALLY ETERNITY)
Ps 16:11 with *e* pleasures at your right hand.
111:10 To him belongs *e* praise.
119:89 Your word, O LORD, is *e;*
Isa 26: 4 LORD, the LORD, is the Rock *e.*
Mt 19:16 good thing must I do to get *e* life?"
25:41 into the *e* fire prepared for the devil
25:46 they will go away to *e* punishment,
Jn 3:15 believes in him may have *e* life.
3:16 him shall not perish but have *e* life.
3:36 believes in the Son has *e* life,
4:14 spring of water welling up to *e* life."
5:24 believes him who sent me has *e* life
6:68 You have the words of *e* life.
10:28 I give them *e* life, and they shall
17: 3 this is *e* life: that they may know
Ro 1:20 his *e* power and divine nature—
6:23 but the gift of God is *e* life
2Co 4:17 for us an *e* glory that far outweighs
4:18 temporary, but what is unseen is *e.*
1Ti 1:16 believe on him and receive *e* life.
1:17 Now to the King *e,* immortal,
Heb 9:12 having obtained *e* redemption.
1Jn 5:11 God has given us *e* life,
5:13 you may know that you have *e* life.

ETERNALLY (ETERNAL)
Gal 1: 8 let him be *e* condemned! As we

ETERNITY (ETERNAL)
Ps 93: 2 you are from all *e.*
Ecc 3:11 also set *e* in the hearts of men;

ETHIOPIAN
Jer 13:23 Can the *E* change his skin

EUNUCHS
Mt 19:12 For some are *e* because they were

EVANGELIST (EVANGELISTS)
2Ti 4: 5 hardship, do the work of an *e,*

EVANGELISTS* (EVANGELIST)
Eph 4:11 some to be prophets, some to be *e,*

EVE
2Co 11: 3 as *E* was deceived by the serpent's
1Ti 2:13 For Adam was formed first, then *E*

EVEN-TEMPERED*
Pr 17:27 and a man of understanding is *e.*

EVER (EVERLASTING FOREVER)
Ex 15:18 LORD will reign for *e* and *e."*
Dt 8:19 If you *e* forget the LORD your
Ps 5:11 let them *e* sing for joy.
10:16 The LORD is King for *e* and *e;*
25: 3 will *e* be put to shame,
26: 3 for your love is *e* before me,
45: 6 O God, will last for *e* and *e;*
52: 8 God's unfailing love for *e* and *e.*
89:33 nor will I *e* betray my faithfulness.
145: 1 I will praise your name for *e* and *e.*
Pr 4:18 shining *e* brighter till the full light
5:19 may you *e* be captivated
Isa 66: 8 Who has *e* heard of such a thing?
Jer 31:36 the descendants of Israel *e* cease
Da 7:18 it forever—yes, for *e* and *e.'*
12: 3 like the stars for *e* and *e.*
Mk 4:12 *e* hearing but never understanding;
Jn 1:18 No one has *e* seen God,
Rev 1:18 and behold I am alive for *e* and *e!*
22: 5 And they will reign for *e* and *e.*

EVER-INCREASING* (INCREASE)
Ro 6:19 to impurity and to *e* wickedness,
2Co 3:18 into his likeness with *e* glory,

EVERLASTING (EVER)
Dt 33:27 and underneath are the *e* arms.
Ne 9: 5 your God, who is from *e* to *e."*
Ps 90: 2 from *e* to *e* you are God.
139:24 and lead me in the way *e.*
Isa 9: 6 *E* Father, Prince of Peace.
33:14 Who of us can dwell with *e* burning
35:10 *e* joy will crown their heads.
45:17 the LORD with an *e* salvation;
54: 8 but with *e* kindness
55: 3 I will make an *e* covenant with you,
63:12 to gain for himself *e* renown,
Jer 31: 3 "I have loved you with an *e* love;
Da 9:24 to bring in *e* righteousness,
12: 2 some to *e* life, others to shame
Jn 6:47 the truth, he who believes has *e* life.
2Th 1: 9 punished with *e* destruction
Jude : 6 bound with *e* chains for judgment

EVER-PRESENT*
Ps 46: 1 an *e* help in trouble

EVIDENCE (EVIDENT)
Jn 14:11 on the *e* of the miracles themselves.

EVIDENT (EVIDENCE)
Php 4: 5 Let your gentleness be *e* to all.

EVIL
Ge 2: 9 of the knowledge of good and *e.*
Job 1: 1 he feared God and shunned *e.*
1: 8 a man who fears God and shuns *e."*
34:10 Far be it from God to do *e,*
Ps 23: 4 I will fear no *e,*
34:14 Turn from *e* and do good;
51: 4 and done what is *e* in your sight,
97:10 those who love the LORD hate *e,*
101: 4 I will have nothing to do with *e.*
Pr 8:13 To fear the LORD is to hate *e;*
10:23 A fool finds pleasure in *e* conduct,
11:27 *e* comes to him who searches for it.
24:19 Do not fret because of *e* men
24:20 for the *e* man has no future hope,
Isa 5:20 Woe to those who call *e* good
13:11 I will punish the world for its *e,*
55: 7 and the *e* man his thoughts.
Hab 1:13 Your eyes are too pure to look on *e;*
Mt 5:45 He causes his sun to rise on the *e*
6:13 but deliver us from the *e* one.'

Mt 7:11 If you, then, though you are *e,*
12:35 and the *e* man brings *e* things out
Jn 17:15 you protect them from the *e* one.
Ro 2: 9 for every human being who does *e:*
12: 9 Hate what is *e;* cling
12:17 Do not repay anyone *e* for *e.*
16:19 and innocent about what is *e.*
1Co 13: 6 Love does not delight in *e*
14:20 In regard to *e* be infants,
Eph 6:16 all the flaming arrows of the *e* one.
1Th 5:22 Avoid every kind of *e.*
1Ti 6:10 of money is a root of all kinds of *e.*
2Ti 2:22 Flee the *e* desires of youth,
Jas 1:13 For God cannot be tempted by *e,*
1Pe 2:16 your freedom as a cover-up for *e;*
3: 9 Do not repay *e* with *e* or insult

EXACT
Heb 1: 3 the *e* representation of his being,

EXALT (EXALTED EXALTS)
Ps 30: 1 I will *e* you, O LORD,
34: 3 let us *e* his name together.
118:28 you are my God, and I will *e* you.
Isa 24:15 *e* the name of the LORD, the God

EXALTED (EXALT)
2Sa 22:47 *E* be God, the Rock, my Savior!
1Ch 29:11 you are *e* as head over all.
Ne 9: 5 and may it be *e* above all blessing
Ps 21:13 Be *e,* O LORD, in your strength;
46:10 I will be *e* among the nations,
57: 5 Be *e,* O God, above the heavens;
97: 9 you are *e* far above all gods.
99: 2 he is *e* over all the nations.
108: 5 Be *e,* O God, above the heavens,
148:13 for his name alone is *e;*
Isa 6: 1 *e,* and the train of his robe filled
12: 4 and proclaim that his name is *e.*
33: 5 The LORD is *e,* for he dwells
Eze 21:26 The lowly will be *e* and the *e* will be
Mt 23:12 whoever humbles himself will be *e.*
Php 1:20 always Christ will be *e* in my body,
2: 9 Therefore God *e* him

EXALTS (EXALT)
Ps 75: 7 He brings one down, he *e* another.
Pr 14:34 Righteousness *e* a nation,
Mt 23:12 For whoever *e* himself will be

EXAMINE (EXAMINED)
Ps 26: 2 *e* my heart and my mind;
Jer 17:10 and *e* the mind,
La 3:40 Let us *e* our ways and test them,
1Co 11:28 A man ought to *e* himself
2Co 13: 5 *E* yourselves to see whether you

EXAMINED (EXAMINE)
Ac 17:11 *e* the Scriptures every day to see

EXAMPLE (EXAMPLES)
Jn 13:15 have set you an *e* that you should
1Co 11: 1 Follow my *e,* as I follow
1Ti 4:12 set an *e* for the believers in speech,
Tit 2: 7 In everything set them an *e*
1Pe 2:21 leaving you an *e,* that you should

EXAMPLES* (EXAMPLE)
1Co 10: 6 Now these things occurred as *e*
10:11 as *e* and were written down
1Pe 5: 3 to you, but being *e* to the flock.

EXASPERATE*
Eph 6: 4 Fathers, do not *e* your children;

EXCEL (EXCELLENT)
1Co 14:12 to *e* in gifts that build up the church
2Co 8: 7 But just as you *e* in everything—

EXCELLENT (EXCEL)
1Co 12:31 now I will show you the most *e* way
Php 4: 8 if anything is *e* or praiseworthy—
1Ti 3:13 have served well gain an *e* standing
Tit 3: 8 These things are *e* and profitable

EXCHANGED
Ro 1:23 *e* the glory of the immortal God
1:25 They *e* the truth of God for a lie,

EXCUSE (EXCUSES)
Jn 15:22 they have no *e* for their sin.
Ro 1:20 so that men are without *e.*

EXCUSES* (EXCUSE)
Lk 14:18 "But they all alike began to make *e.*

EXISTS
Heb 2:10 and through whom everything *e,*
11: 6 to him must believe that he *e*

EXPECT (EXPECTATION)
Mt 24:44 at an hour when you do not *e* him.

EXPECTATION (EXPECT)
Ro 8:19 waits in eager *e* for the sons
Heb 10:27 but only a fearful *e* of judgment

EXPEL*
1Co 5:13 *E* the wicked man from among you

EXPENSIVE
1Ti 2: 9 or gold or pearls or *e* clothes,

EXPLOIT
Pr 22:22 Do not *e* the poor because they are
2Co 12:17 Did I *e* you through any

EXPOSE
1Co 4: 5 will *e* the motives of men's hearts.
Eph 5:11 of darkness, but rather *e* them.

EXTENDS
Pr 31:20 and *e* her hands to the needy.
Lk 1:50 His mercy *e* to those who fear him,

EXTINGUISHED
2Sa 21:17 the lamp of Israel will not be *e."*

EXTOL*
Job 36:24 Remember to *e* his work,
Ps 34: 1 I will *e* the LORD at all times;
68: 4 *e* him who rides on the clouds—
95: 2 and *e* him with music and song.
109:30 mouth I will greatly *e* the LORD;
111: 1 I will *e* the LORD with all my heart
115:18 it is we who *e* the LORD,
117: 1 *e* him, all you peoples.
145: 2 and *e* your name for ever and ever.
145:10 your saints will *e* you.
147:12 *E* the LORD, O Jerusalem;

EXTORT*
Lk 3:14 "Don't *e* money and don't accuse

EYE (EYES)
Ex 21:24 you are to take life for life, *e* for *e,*
Ps 94: 9 Does he who formed the *e* not see?
Mt 5:29 If your right *e* causes you to sin,
5:38 '*E* for *e,* and tooth for tooth.'
7: 3 of sawdust in your brother's *e*
1Co 2: 9 "No *e* has seen,
Col 3:22 not only when their *e* is on you
Rev 1: 7 and every *e* will see him,

EYES (EYE)
Nu 33:55 remain will become barbs in your *e*
Jos 23:13 on your backs and thorns in your *e,*
2Ch 16: 9 For the *e* of the LORD range
Job 31: 1 "I made a covenant with my *e*
36: 7 He does not take his *e*
Ps 119:18 Open my *e* that I may see
121: 1 I lift up my *e* to the hills—
141: 8 But my *e* are fixed on you,
Pr 3: 7 Do not be wise in your own *e;*
4:25 Let your *e* look straight ahead,
15: 3 The *e* of the LORD are everywhere
Isa 6: 5 and my *e* have seen the King,
Hab 1:13 Your *e* are too pure to look on evil;
Jn 4:35 open your *e* and look at the fields!
2Co 4:18 So we fix our *e* not on what is seen,
Heb 12: 2 Let us fix our *e* on Jesus, the author
Jas 2: 5 poor in the *e* of the world to be rich
1Pe 3:12 For the *e* of the Lord are
Rev 7:17 wipe away every tear from their *e."*
21: 4 He will wipe every tear from their *e*

EZEKIEL
Priest called to be prophet to the exiles (Eze 1-3).

EZRA
Priest and teacher of the Law who led a return of exiles to Israel to reestablish temple and worship (Ezr 7-8). Corrected intermarriage of priests (Ezr 9-10). Read Law at celebration of Feast of Tabernacles (Neh 8).

FACE (FACES)
Ge 32:30 "It is because I saw God *f* to *f,*
Ex 34:29 was not aware that his *f* was radiant
Nu 6:25 the LORD make his *f* shine
1Ch 16:11 seek his *f* always.
2Ch 7:14 and seek my *f* and turn
Ps 4: 6 Let the light of your *f* shine upon us
27: 8 Your *f,* LORD, I will seek.
31:16 Let your *f* shine on your servant;
105: 4 seek his *f* always.
119:135 Make your *f* shine
Isa 50: 7 Therefore have I set my *f* like flint,
Mt 17: 2 His *f* shone like the sun,
1Co 13:12 mirror; then we shall see *f* to *f.*
2Co 4: 6 the glory of God in the *f* of Christ.
1Pe 3:12 but the *f* of the Lord is
Rev 1:16 His *f* was like the sun shining

FACES (FACE)
2Co 3:18 who with unveiled *f* all reflect

FACTIONS
Gal 5:20 selfish ambition, dissensions, *f*

FADE
1Pe 5: 4 of glory that will never *f* away.

FAIL (FAILING FAILINGS FAILS)
1Ch 28:20 He will not *f* you or forsake you
2Ch 34:33 they did not *f* to follow the LORD,
Ps 89:28 my covenant with him will never *f.*
Pr 15:22 Plans *f* for lack of counsel,
Isa 51: 6 my righteousness will never *f.*
La 3:22 for his compassions never *f.*
2Co 13: 5 unless, of course, you *f* the test?

FAILING (FAIL)
1Sa 12:23 sin against the LORD by *f* to pray

FAILINGS (FAIL)
Ro 15: 1 ought to bear with the *f* of the weak

FAILS (FAIL)
1Co 13: 8 Love never *f.*

FAINT
Isa 40:31 they will walk and not be *f.*

FAIR
Pr 1: 3 doing what is right and just and *f*;
Col 4: 1 slaves with what is right and *f*,

FAITH (FAITHFUL FAITHFULLY FAITHFULNESS FAITHLESS)
2Ch 20:20 Have *f* in the LORD your God
Hab 2: 4 but the righteous will live by his *f*—
Mt 9:29 According to your *f* will it be done
17:20 if you have *f* as small as a mustard
24:10 many will turn away from the *f*
Mk 11:22 "Have *f* in God," Jesus answered.
Lk 7: 9 I have not found such great *f*
12:28 will he clothe you, O you of little *f*!
17: 5 "Increase our *f*!" He replied,
18: 8 will he find *f* on the earth?"
Ac 14: 9 saw that he had *f* to be healed
14:27 the door of *f* to the Gentiles.
Ro 1:12 encouraged by each other's *f*.
1:17 is by *f* from first to last,
1:17 "The righteous will live by *f*."
3: 3 What if some did not have *f*?
3:22 comes through *f* in Jesus Christ
3:25 a sacrifice of atonement, through *f*
4: 5 his *f* is credited as righteousness.
5: 1 we have been justified through *f*,
10:17 *f* comes from hearing the message,
14: 1 Accept him whose *f* is weak,
14:23 that does not come from *f* is sin.
1Co 13: 2 and if I have a *f* that can move
13:13 And now these three remain: *f*,
16:13 stand firm in the *f*; be men
2Co 5: 7 We live by *f*, not by sight.
13: 5 to see whether you are in the *f*;
Gal 2:16 Jesus that we may be justified by *f*
2:20 I live by *f* in the Son of God,
3:11 "The righteous will live by *f*."
3:24 that we might be justified by *f*.
Eph 2: 8 through *f*— and this not
4: 5 one Lord, one *f*, one baptism;
6:16 to all this, take up the shield of *f*,
Col 1:23 continue in your *f*, established
1Th 5: 8 on *f* and love as a breastplate,
1Ti 2:15 if they continue in *f*, love
4: 1 later times some will abandon the *f*
5: 8 he has denied the *f* and is worse
6:12 Fight the good fight of the *f*.
2Ti 3:15 wise for salvation through *f*
4: 7 finished the race, I have kept the *f*.
Phm : 6 may be active in sharing your *f*,
Heb 10:38 But my righteous one will live by *f*.
11: 1 *f* is being sure of what we hope for
11: 3 By *f* we understand that
11: 5 By *f* Enoch was taken from this life
11: 6 And without *f* it is impossible
11: 7 By *f* Noah, when warned about
11: 8 By *f* Abraham, when called to go
11:17 By *f* Abraham, when God tested
11:20 By *f* Isaac blessed Jacob
11:21 By *f* Jacob, when he was dying,
11:22 By *f* Joseph, when his end was near
11:24 By *f* Moses, when he had grown up
11:31 By *f* the prostitute Rahab,
12: 2 the author and perfecter of our *f*,
Jas 2:14 if a man claims to have *f*
2:17 In the same way, *f* by itself,
2:26 so *f* without deeds is dead.
2Pe 1: 5 effort to add to your *f* goodness;
1Jn 5: 4 overcome the world, even our *f*.
Jude : 3 to contend for the *f* that was once

FAITHFUL (FAITH)
Nu 12: 7 he is *f* in all my house.
Dt 7: 9 your God is God; he is the *f* God,
32: 4 A *f* God who does no wrong,
2Sa 22:26 "To the *f* you show yourself *f*,
Ps 25:10 of the LORD are loving and *f*
31:23 The LORD preserves the *f*,
Ps 33: 4 he is *f* in all he does.
37:28 and will not forsake his *f* ones.
97:10 for he guards the lives of his *f* ones
145:13 The LORD is *f* to all his promises
146: 6 the LORD, who remains *f* forever.
Pr 31:26 and *f* instruction is on her tongue.
Mt 25:21 'Well done, good and *f* servant!
Ro 12:12 patient in affliction, *f* in prayer.
1Co 4: 2 been given a trust must prove *f*.
10:13 And God is *f*; he will not let you be
1Th 5:24 The one who calls you is *f*
2Ti 2:13 he will remain *f*,
Heb 3: 6 But Christ is *f* as a son
10:23 for he who promised is *f*.
1Pe 4:19 themselves to their *f* Creator
1Jn 1: 9 he is *f* and just and will forgive us
Rev 1: 5 who is the *f* witness, the firstborn
2:10 Be *f*, even to the point of death,
19:11 whose rider is called *F* and True.

FAITHFULLY (FAITH)
Dt 11:13 if you *f* obey the commands I am
1Sa 12:24 and serve him *f* with all your heart;
1Ki 2: 4 and if they walk *f* before me
1Pe 4:10 *f* administering God's grace

FAITHFULNESS (FAITH)
Ps 57:10 your *f* reaches to the skies.
85:10 Love and *f* meet together;
86:15 to anger, abounding in love and *f*.
89: 1 mouth I will make your *f* known
89:14 love and *f* go before you.
91: 4 his *f* will be your shield
117: 2 the *f* of the LORD endures forever.
119:75 and in *f* you have afflicted me.
Pr 3: 3 Let love and *f* never leave you;
Isa 11: 5 and *f* the sash around his waist.
La 3:23 great is your *f*.
Ro 3: 3 lack of faith nullify God's *f*?
Gal 5:22 patience, kindness, goodness, *f*,

FAITHLESS (FAITH)
Ps 119:158 I look on the *f* with loathing,
Jer 3:22 "Return, *f* people;
Ro 1:31 they are senseless, *f*, heartless,
2Ti 2:13 if we are *f*,

FALL (FALLEN FALLING FALLS)
Ps 37:24 though he stumble, he will not *f*,
55:22 he will never let the righteous *f*.
69: 9 of those who insult you *f* on me.
Pr 11:28 Whoever trusts in his riches will *f*,
Lk 11:17 a house divided against itself will *f*.
Ro 3:23 and *f* short of the glory of God,
Heb 6: 6 if they *f* away, to be brought back

FALLEN (FALL)
2Sa 1:19 How the mighty have *f*!
Isa 14:12 How you have *f* from heaven,
1Co 15:20 of those who have *f* asleep.
Gal 5: 4 you have *f* away from grace.
1Th 4:15 precede those who have *f* asleep.

FALLING (FALL)
Jude :24 able to keep you from *f*

FALLS (FALL)
Pr 24:17 Do not gloat when your enemy *f*;
Jn 12:24 a kernel of wheat *f* to the ground
Ro 14: 4 To his own master he stands or *f*.

FALSE (FALSEHOOD FALSELY)
Ex 20:16 "You shall not give *f* testimony
23: 1 "Do not spread *f* reports.
Pr 13: 5 The righteous hate what is *f*,
19: 5 A *f* witness will not go unpunished,
Mt 7:15 "Watch out for *f* prophets.
19:18 not steal, do not give *f* testimony,
Mt 24:11 and many *f* prophets will appear
Php 1:18 whether from *f* motives or true,
1Ti 1: 3 not to teach *f* doctrines any longer
2Pe 2: 1 there will be *f* teachers among you.

FALSEHOOD (FALSE)
Ps 119:163 I hate and abhor *f*
Pr 30: 8 Keep *f* and lies far from me;
Eph 4:25 each of you must put off *f*

FALSELY (FALSE)
Lev 19:12 " 'Do not swear *f* by my name
Lk 3:14 and don't accuse people *f*—
1Ti 6:20 ideas of what is *f* called knowledge,

FALTER*
Pr 24:10 If you *f* in times of trouble,
Isa 42: 4 he will not *f* or be discouraged

FAMILIES (FAMILY)
Ps 68: 6 God sets the lonely in *f*,

FAMILY (FAMILIES)
Pr 15:27 greedy man brings trouble to his *f*,
31:15 she provides food for her *f*
Lk 9:61 go back and say good-by to my *f*."
12:52 in one *f* divided against each other,
1Ti 3: 4 He must manage his own *f* well
3: 5 how to manage his own *f*,
5: 4 practice by caring for their own *f*
5: 8 and especially for his immediate *f*,

FAMINE
Ge 41:30 seven years of *f* will follow them.
Am 8:11 but a *f* of hearing the words
Ro 8:35 or persecution or *f* or nakedness

FAN*
2Ti 1: 6 you to *f* into flame the gift of God,

FAST
Dt 13: 4 serve him and hold *f* to him.
Jos 22: 5 to hold *f* to him and to serve him
23: 8 to hold *f* to the LORD your God,
Ps 119:31 I hold *f* to your statutes, O LORD;
139:10 your right hand will hold me *f*.
Mt 6:16 "When you *f*, do not look somber
1Pe 5:12 Stand *f* in it.

FATHER (FATHER'S FATHERLESS FATHERS FOREFATHERS)
Ge 2:24 this reason a man will leave his *f*
17: 4 You will be the *f* of many nations.
Ex 20:12 "Honor your *f* and your mother,
21:15 "Anyone who attacks his *f*
21:17 "Anyone who curses his *f*
Lev 18: 7 " 'Do not dishonor your *f*
19: 3 you must respect his mother and *f*,
Dt 5:16 "Honor your *f* and your mother,
21:18 son who does not obey his *f*
Ps 27:10 Though my *f* and mother forsake
68: 5 A *f* to the fatherless, a defender
Pr 10: 1 A wise son brings joy to his *f*,
17:21 there is no joy for the *f* of a fool.
23:22 Listen to your *f*, who gave you life,
23:24 *f* of a righteous man has great joy;
28: 7 of gluttons disgraces his *f*.
29: 3 loves wisdom brings joy to his *f*,
Isa 9: 6 Everlasting *F*, Prince of Peace.
Mt 6: 9 " 'Our *F* in heaven,
10:37 "Anyone who loves his *f*
15: 4 'Honor your *f* and mother'
19: 5 this reason a man will leave his *f*
Lk 12:53 *f* against son and son against *f*,
23:34 Jesus said, "*F*, forgive them,
Jn 6:44 the *F* who sent me draws him,
6:46 No one has seen the *F*
8:44 You belong to your *f*, the devil,

Jn 10:30 I and the *F* are one."
14: 6 No one comes to the *F*
14: 9 who has seen me has seen the *F*.
Ro 4:11 he is the *f* of all who believe
2Co 6:18 "I will be a *F* to you,
Eph 6: 2 "Honor your *f* and mother"—
Heb 12: 7 what son is not disciplined by his *f*?

FATHER'S (FATHER)
Pr 13: 1 A wise son heeds his *f* instruction,
15: 5 A fool spurns his *f* discipline,
19:13 A foolish son is his *f* ruin,
Lk 2:49 had to be in my *F* house?"
Jn 2:16 How dare you turn my *F* house
10:29 can snatch them out of my *F* hand.
14: 2 In my *F* house are many rooms;

FATHERLESS (FATHER)
Dt 10:18 He defends the cause of the *f*
24:17 Do not deprive the alien or the *f*
24:19 Leave it for the alien, the *f*
Ps 68: 5 A father to the *f*, a defender
Pr 23:10 or encroach on the fields of the *f*,

FATHERS (FATHER)
Ex 20: 5 for the sin of the *f* to the third
Lk 11:11 "Which of you *f*, if your son asks
Eph 6: 4 *F*, do not exasperate your children;
Col 3:21 *F*, do not embitter your children,

FATHOM*
Job 11: 7 "Can you *f* the mysteries of God?
Ps 145: 3 his greatness no one can *f*.
Ecc 3:11 yet they cannot *f* what God has
Isa 40:28 and his understanding no one can *f*.
1Co 13: 2 and can *f* all mysteries and all

FAULT (FAULTS)
Mt 18:15 and show him his *f*, just
Php 2:15 of God without *f* in a crooked
Jas 1: 5 generously to all without finding *f*,
Jude :24 his glorious presence without *f*

FAULTFINDERS*
Jude :16 These men are grumblers and *f*;

FAULTS (FAULT)
Ps 19:12 Forgive my hidden *f*.

FAVORITISM*
Ex 23: 3 and do not show *f* to a poor man
Lev 19:15 to the poor or *f* to the great,
Ac 10:34 true it is that God does not show *f*
Ro 2:11 For God does not show *f*.
Eph 6: 9 and there is no *f* with him.
Col 3:25 for his wrong, and there is no *f*.
1Ti 5:21 and to do nothing out of *f*.
Jas 2: 1 Lord Jesus Christ, don't show *f*.
2: 9 But if you show *f*, you sin

FEAR (AFRAID FEARS)
Dt 6:13 *F* the LORD your God, serve him
10:12 but to *f* the LORD your God,
31:12 and learn to *f* the LORD your God
Ps 19: 9 The *f* of the LORD is pure,
23: 4 I will *f* no evil,
27: 1 whom shall I *f*?
91: 5 You will not *f* the terror of night,
111:10 *f* of the LORD is the beginning
Pr 8:13 To *f* the LORD is to hate evil;
9:10 *f* of the LORD is the beginning
10:27 The *f* of the LORD adds length
14:27 The *f* of the LORD is a fountain
15:33 *f* of the LORD teaches a man
16: 6 through the *f* of the LORD a man
19:23 The *f* of the LORD leads to life:
29:25 *F* of man will prove to be a snare,
Isa 11: 3 delight in the *f* of the LORD.
41:10 So do not *f*, for I am with you;
Lk 12: 5 I will show you whom you should *f*:
Php 2:12 to work out your salvation with *f*
1Jn 4:18 But perfect love drives out *f*,

FEARS (FEAR)
Job 1: 8 a man who *f* God and shuns evil."
Ps 34: 4 he delivered me from all my *f*.
Pr 31:30 a woman who *f* the LORD is
1Jn 4:18 The one who *f* is not made perfect

FEED
Jn 21:15 Jesus said, "*F* my lambs."
21:17 Jesus said, "*F* my sheep.
Ro 12:20 "If your enemy is hungry, *f* him;
Jude :12 shepherds who *f* only themselves.

FEET (FOOT)
Ps 8: 6 you put everything under his *f*:
22:16 have pierced my hands and my *f*.
40: 2 he set my *f* on a rock
110: 1 a footstool for your *f*."
119:105 Your word is a lamp to my *f*
Ro 10:15 "How beautiful are the *f*
1Co 12:21 And the head cannot say to the *f*,
15:25 has put all his enemies under his *f*.
Heb 12:13 "Make level paths for your *f*,"

FELLOWSHIP
2Co 6:14 what *f* can light have with darkness
13:14 and the *f* of the Holy Spirit be
Php 3:10 the *f* of sharing in his sufferings,
1Jn 1: 6 claim to have *f* with him yet walk
1: 7 we have *f* with one another,

FEMALE
Ge 1:27 male and *f* he created them.
Gal 3:28 *f*, for you are all one in Christ Jesus

FERVOR
Ro 12:11 but keep your spiritual *f*, serving

FIELD (FIELDS)
Mt 6:28 See how the lilies of the *f* grow.
13:38 *f* is the world, and the good seed
1Co 3: 9 you are God's *f*, God's building.

FIELDS (FIELD)
Lk 2: 8 were shepherds living out in the *f*
Jn 4:35 open your eyes and look at the *f*!

FIG (FIGS)
Ge 3: 7 so they sewed *f* leaves together

FIGHT (FOUGHT)
Ex 14:14 The LORD will *f* for you; you need
Dt 1:30 going before you, will *f* for you,
3:22 the LORD your God himself will *f*
Ne 4:20 Our God will *f* for us!"
Ps 35: 1 *f* against those who *f* against me.
Jn 18:36 my servants would *f*
1Co 9:26 I do not *f* like a man beating the air.
2Co 10: 4 The weapons we *f*
1Ti 1:18 them you may *f* the good *f*,
6:12 Fight the good *f* of the faith.
2Ti 4: 7 fought the good *f*, I have finished

FIGS (FIG)
Lk 6:44 People do not pick *f*

FILL (FILLED FILLS FULL FULLNESS FULLY)
Ge 1:28 and increase in number; *f* the earth
Ps 16:11 you will *f* me with joy
81:10 wide your mouth and I will *f* it.
Pr 28:19 who chases fantasies will have his *f*
Hag 2: 7 and I will *f* this house with glory,'
Jn 6:26 you ate the loaves and had your *f*.
Ac 2:28 you will *f* me with joy
Ro 15:13 the God of hope *f* you with all joy

FILLED (FILL)
Ps 72:19 may the whole earth be *f*
119:64 The earth is *f* with your love,
Eze 43: 5 the glory of the LORD *f* the temple
Hab 2:14 For the earth will be *f*
Lk 1:15 and he will be *f* with the Holy Spirit
1:41 and Elizabeth was *f* with the Holy
Jn 12: 3 the house was *f* with the fragrance
Ac 2: 4 All of them were *f*
4: 8 Then Peter, *f* with the Holy Spirit,
9:17 and be *f* with the Holy Spirit."
13: 9 called Paul, *f* with the Holy Spirit,
Eph 5:18 Instead, be *f* with the Spirit.
Php 1:11 *f* with the fruit of righteousness

FILLS (FILL)
Nu 14:21 of the LORD *f* the whole earth,
Ps 107: 9 and *f* the hungry with good things.
Eph 1:23 fullness of him who *f* everything

FILTHY
Isa 64: 6 all our righteous acts are like *f* rags;
Col 3: 8 and *f* language from your lips.
2Pe 2: 7 by the *f* lives of lawless men

FIND (FINDS FOUND)
Nu 32:23 be sure that your sin will *f* you out.
Dt 4:29 you will *f* him if you look for him
1Sa 23:16 and helped him *f* strength in God.
Ps 36: 7 *f* refuge in the shadow
91: 4 under his wings you will *f* refuge;
Pr 14:22 those who plan what is good *f* love
31:10 A wife of noble character who can *f*
Jer 6:16 and you will *f* rest for your souls.
Mt 7: 7 seek and you will *f*; knock
11:29 and you will *f* rest for your souls.
16:25 loses his life for me will *f* it.
Lk 18: 8 will he *f* faith on the earth?"
Jn 10: 9 come in and go out, and *f* pasture.

FINDS (FIND)
Ps 62: 1 My soul *f* rest in God alone;
112: 1 who *f* great delight
119:162 like one who *f* great spoil.
Pr 18:22 He who *f* a wife *f* what is good
Mt 7: 8 he who seeks *f*; and to him who
10:39 Whoever *f* his life will lose it,
Lk 12:37 whose master *f* them watching
15: 4 go after the lost sheep until he *f* it?

FINISH (FINISHED)
Jn 4:34 him who sent me and to *f* his work.
5:36 that the Father has given me to *f*,
Ac 20:24 if only I may *f* the race
2Co 8:11 Now *f* the work, so that your eager
Jas 1: 4 Perseverance must *f* its work

FINISHED (FINISH)
Ge 2: 2 seventh day God had *f* the work he
Jn 19:30 the drink, Jesus said, "It is *f*."
2Ti 4: 7 I have *f* the race, I have kept

FIRE
Ex 13:21 in a pillar of *f* to give them light,
Lev 6:12 *f* on the altar must be kept burning;
Isa 30:27 and his tongue is a consuming *f*.
Jer 23:29 my word like *f*," declares
Mt 3:11 you with the Holy Spirit and with *f*.
5:22 will be in danger of the *f* of hell.
25:41 into the eternal *f* prepared
Mk 9:43 where the *f* never goes out.
Ac 2: 3 to be tongues of *f* that separated
1Co 3:13 It will be revealed with *f*,
1Th 5:19 Do not put out the Spirit's *f*;
Heb 12:29 for our "God is a consuming *f*."
Jas 3: 5 set on *f* by a small spark.

FOREFATHERS (FATHER)
Heb 1: 1 spoke to our f through the prophets

FOREKNEW* (KNOW)
Ro 8:29 For those God f he
11: 2 not reject his people, whom he f.

FOREVER (EVER)
1Ch 16:15 He remembers his covenant f,
16:34 his love endures f.
Ps 9: 7 The LORD reigns f;
23: 6 dwell in the house of the LORD f.
33:11 the plans of the LORD stand firm f
86:12 I will glorify your name f.
92: 8 But you, O LORD, are exalted f.
110: 4 "You are a priest f,
119:111 Your statutes are my heritage f;
Jn 6:51 eats of this bread, he will live f.
14:16 Counselor to be with you f—
1Co 9:25 it to get a crown that will last f.
1Th 4:17 And so we will be with the Lord f.
Heb 13: 8 same yesterday and today and f.
1Pe 1:25 but the word of the Lord stands f."
1Jn 2:17 who does the will of God lives f.

FORFEIT
Lk 9:25 and yet lose or f his very self?

FORGAVE (FORGIVE)
Ps 32: 5 and you f
Eph 4:32 just as in Christ God f you.
Col 2:13 He f us all our sins, having
3:13 Forgive as the Lord f you.

FORGET (FORGETS FORGETTING)
Dt 6:12 that you do not f the LORD,
Ps 103: 2 and f not all his benefits.
137: 5 may my right hand f ⌊its skill⌋.
Isa 49:15 "Can a mother f the baby
Heb 6:10 he will not f your work

FORGETS (FORGET)
Jn 16:21 her baby is born she f the anguish
Jas 1:24 immediately f what he looks like.

FORGETTING (FORGET)
Php 3:13 F what is behind and straining

FORGIVE (FORGAVE FORGIVENESS FORGIVING)
2Ch 7:14 will f their sin and will heal their
Ps 19:12 F my hidden faults.
Mt 6:12 F us our debts,
6:14 For if you f men when they sin
18:21 many times shall I f my brother
Mk 11:25 in heaven may f you your sins."
Lk 11: 4 F us our sins,
23:34 Jesus said, "Father, f them,
Col 3:13 F as the Lord forgave you.
1Jn 1: 9 and just and will f us our sins

FORGIVENESS (FORGIVE)
Ps 130: 4 But with you there is f;
Ac 10:43 believes in him receives f of sins
Eph 1: 7 through his blood, the f of sins,
Col 1:14 in whom we have redemption, the f
Heb 9:22 the shedding of blood there is no f.

FORGIVING (FORGIVE)
Ne 9:17 But you are a f God, gracious
Eph 4:32 to one another, f each other,

FORMED
Ge 2: 7 And the LORD God f man
Ps 103:14 for he knows how we are f,
Isa 45:18 but f it to be inhabited—
Ro 9:20 "Shall what is f say to him who f it,
1Ti 2:13 For Adam was f first, then Eve.
Heb 11: 3 understand that the universe was f

FORSAKE (FORSAKEN)
Jos 1: 5 I will never leave you nor f you.
24:16 "Far be it from us to f the LORD
2Ch 15: 2 but if you f him, he will f you.
Ps 27:10 Though my father and mother f me
Isa 55: 7 Let the wicked f his way
Heb 13: 5 never will I f you."

FORSAKEN (FORSAKE)
Ps 22: 1 my God, why have you f me?
37:25 I have never seen the righteous f
Mt 27:46 my God, why have you f me?"
Rev 2: 4 You have f your first love.

FORTRESS
Ps 18: 2 The LORD is my rock, my f
71: 3 for you are my rock and my f.

FOUGHT (FIGHT)
2Ti 4: 7 I have f the good fight, I have

FOUND (FIND)
1Ch 28: 9 If you seek him, he will be f by you;
Isa 55: 6 Seek the LORD while he may be f;
Da 5:27 on the scales and f wanting.
Lk 15: 6 with me; I have f my lost sheep.'
15: 9 with me; I have f my lost coin.'
Ac 4:12 Salvation is f in no one else,

FOUNDATION
Isa 28:16 a precious cornerstone for a sure f;
1Co 3:11 For no one can lay any f other
Eph 2:20 built on the f of the apostles
2Ti 2:19 God's solid f stands firm,

FOXES
Mt 8:20 "F have holes and birds

FRAGRANCE
2Co 2:16 of death; to the other, the f of life.

FREE (FREED FREEDOM FREELY)
Ps 146: 7 The LORD sets prisoners f,
Jn 8:32 and the truth will set you f."
Ro 6:18 You have been set f from sin
Gal 3:28 slave nor f, male nor female,
1Pe 2:16 f men, but do not use your freedom

FREED (FREE)
Rev 1: 5 has f us from our sins by his blood,

FREEDOM (FREE)
Ro 8:21 into the glorious f of the children
2Co 3:17 the Spirit of the Lord is, there is f.
Gal 5:13 But do not use your f to indulge
1Pe 2:16 but do not use your f as a cover-up

FREELY (FREE)
Isa 55: 7 and to our God, for he will f pardon
Mt 10: 8 Freely you have received, f give.
Ro 3:24 and are justified f by his grace
Eph 1: 6 which he has f given us

FRIEND (FRIENDS)
Ex 33:11 as a man speaks with his f.
Pr 17:17 A f loves at all times,
18:24 there is a f who sticks closer
27: 6 Wounds from a f can be trusted,
27:10 Do not forsake your f and the f
Jas 4: 4 Anyone who chooses to be a f

FRIENDS (FRIEND)
Pr 16:28 and a gossip separates close f.
Zec 13: 6 given at the house of my f.'
Jn 15:13 that he lay down his life for his f.

FRUIT (FRUITFUL)
Ps 1: 3 which yields its f in season
Pr 11:30 The f of the righteous is a tree
Mt 7:16 By their f you will recognize them.
Jn 15: 2 branch in me that bears no f,
Gal 5:22 But the f of the Spirit is love, joy,
Rev 22: 2 of f, yielding its f every month.

FRUITFUL (FRUIT)
Ge 1:22 "Be f and increase in number
Ps 128: 3 Your wife will be like a f vine
Jn 15: 2 prunes so that it will be even more f.

FULFILL (FULFILLED FULFILLMENT)
Ps 116:14 I will f my vows to the LORD
Mt 5:17 come to abolish them but to f them.
1Co 7: 3 husband should f his marital duty

FULFILLED (FULFILL)
Pr 13:19 A longing f is sweet to the soul,
Mk 14:49 But the Scriptures must be f."
Ro 13: 8 loves his fellowman has f the law.

FULFILLMENT (FULFILL)
Ro 13:10 Therefore love is the f of the law.

FULL (FILL)
Ps 127: 5 whose quiver is f of them.
Pr 31:11 Her husband has f confidence
Isa 6: 3 the whole earth is f of his glory."
11: 9 for the earth will be f
Jn 10:10 may have life, and have it to the f.
Ac 6: 3 known to be f of the Spirit

FULLNESS (FILL)
Col 1:19 to have all his f dwell in him,
2: 9 in Christ all the f of the Deity lives

FULLY (FILL)
1Ki 8:61 your hearts must be f committed
2Ch 16: 9 whose hearts are f committed
Ps 119: 4 that are to be f obeyed.
119:138 they are f trustworthy.
1Co 15:58 Always give yourselves f

FUTURE
Ps 37:37 there is a f for the man of peace.
Pr 23:18 There is surely a f hope for you,
Ro 8:38 neither the present nor the f,

GABRIEL*

Angel who interpreted Daniel's visions (Da 8:16-26; 9:20-27); announced births of John (Lk 1:11-20), Jesus (Lk 1:26-38).

GAIN (GAINED)
Ps 60:12 With God we will g the victory,
Mk 8:36 it for a man to g the whole world,
1Co 13: 3 but have not love, I g nothing.
Php 1:21 to live is Christ and to die is g.
3: 8 that I may g Christ and be found
1Ti 6: 6 with contentment is great g.

GAINED (GAIN)
Ro 5: 2 through whom we have g access

GALILEE
Isa 9: 1 but in the future he will honor G

GALL
Mt 27:34 mixed with g; but after tasting it,

GAP
Eze 22:30 stand before me in the g on behalf

GARDENER
Jn 15: 1 true vine, and my Father is the g.

GARMENT (GARMENTS)
Ps 102:26 they will all wear out like a g.

Mt 9:16 of unshrunk cloth on an old g,
Jn 19:23 This g was seamless, woven

GARMENTS (GARMENT)
Ge 3:21 The LORD God made g of skin
Isa 61:10 me with g of salvation
63: 1 with his g stained crimson?
Jn 19:24 "They divided my g among them

GATE (GATES)
Mt 7:13 For wide is the g and broad is
Jn 10: 9 I am the g; whoever enters

GATES (GATE)
Ps 100: 4 Enter his g with thanksgiving
Mt 16:18 the g of Hades will not overcome it

GATHER (GATHERS)
Zec 14: 2 I will g all the nations to Jerusalem
Mt 12:30 he who does not g with me scatters
23:37 longed to g your children together,

GATHERS (GATHER)
Isa 40:11 He g the lambs in his arms
Mt 23:37 a hen g her chicks under her wings,

GAVE (GIVE)
Ezr 2:69 According to their ability they g
Job 1:21 LORD g and the LORD has taken
Jn 3:16 so loved the world that he g his one
2Co 8: 5 they g themselves first to the Lord
Gal 2:20 who loved me and g himself for me
1Ti 2: 6 who g himself as a ransom

GAZE
Ps 27: 4 to g upon the beauty of the LORD
Pr 4:25 fix your g directly before you.

GENEALOGIES
1Ti 1: 4 themselves to myths and endless g.

GENERATIONS
Ps 22:30 future g will be told about the Lord
102:12 your renown endures through all g.
145:13 dominion endures through all g.
Lk 1:48 now on all g will call me blessed,
Eph 3: 5 not made known to men in other g

GENEROUS
Ps 112: 5 Good will come to him who is g
Pr 22: 9 A g man will himself be blessed,
2Co 9: 5 Then it will be ready as a g gift,
1Ti 6:18 and to be g and willing to share.

GENTILE (GENTILES)
Ro 1:16 first for the Jew, then for the G.
10:12 difference between Jew and G—

GENTILES (GENTILE)
Isa 42: 6 and a light for the G,
Ro 3: 9 and G alike are all under sin.
11:13 as I am the apostle to the G,
1Co 1:23 block to Jews and foolishness to G,

GENTLE (GENTLENESS)
Pr 15: 1 A g answer turns away wrath,
Zec 9: 9 g and riding on a donkey,
Mt 11:29 for I am g and humble in heart,
21: 5 g and riding on a donkey,
1Co 4:21 or in love and with a g spirit?
1Pe 3: 4 the unfading beauty of a g

GENTLENESS* (GENTLE)
2Co 10: 1 By the meekness and g of Christ,
Gal 5:23 faithfulness, g and self-control.
Php 4: 5 Let your g be evident to all.
Col 3:12 kindness, humility, g and patience.
1Ti 6:11 faith, love, endurance and g.
1Pe 3:15 But do this with g and respect,

GETHSEMANE
Mt 26:36 disciples to a place called G,

GIDEON*
Judge, also called Jerub-Baal; freed Israel from Midianites (Jdg 6-8; Heb 11:32). Given sign of fleece (Jdg 8:36-40).

GIFT (GIFTS)
Pr 21:14 A g given in secret soothes anger,
Mt 5:23 if you are offering your g
Ac 2:38 And you will receive the g
Ro 6:23 but the g of God is eternal life
1Co 7: 7 each man has his own g from God;
2Co 8:12 the g is acceptable according
9:15 be to God for his indescribable g!
Eph 2: 8 it is the g of God—not by works,
1Ti 4:14 not neglect your g, which was
2Ti 1: 6 you to fan into flame the g of God,
Jas 1:17 and perfect g is from above,
1Pe 4:10 should use whatever g he has

GIFTS (GIFT)
Ro 11:29 for God's g and his call are
12: 6 We have different g, according
1Co 12: 4 There are different kinds of g,
12:31 But eagerly desire the greater g.
14: 1 and eagerly desire spiritual g,
14:12 excel in g that build up the church.

GILEAD
Jer 8:22 Is there no balm in G?

GIVE (GAVE GIVEN GIVER GIVES GIVING)
Nu 6:26 and g you peace." '
1Sa 1:11 then I will g him to the LORD
2Ch 15: 7 be strong and do not g up,
Pr 21:26 but the righteous g without sparing
23:26 My son, g me your heart
30: 8 but g me only my daily bread.
31:31 G her the reward she has earned,
Isa 42: 8 I will not g my glory to another
Eze 36:26 I will g you a new heart
Mt 6:11 G us today our daily bread.
10: 8 Freely you have received, freely g.
22:21 "G to Caesar what is Caesar's,
Mk 8:37 Or what can a man g in exchange
Lk 6:38 G, and it will be given to you.
11:13 Father in heaven g the Holy Spirit
Jn 10:28 I g them eternal life, and they shall
13:34 "A new commandment I g you:
Ac 20:35 blessed to g than to receive.' "
Ro 12: 8 let him g generously;
13: 7 G everyone what you owe him:
14:12 each of us will g an account
2Co 9: 7 Each man should g what he has
Rev 14: 7 "Fear God and g him glory,

GIVEN (GIVE)
Nu 8:16 are to be g wholly to me.
Ps 115:16 but the earth he has g to man.
Isa 9: 6 to us a son is g,
Mt 6:33 and all these things will be g to you
7: 7 "Ask and it will be g to you;
Lk 22:19 saying, "This is my body g for you;
Jn 3:27 man can receive only what is g him
Ro 5: 5 the Holy Spirit, whom he has g us.
1Co 4: 2 those who have been g a trust must
12:13 we were all g the one Spirit to drink
Eph 4: 7 to each one of us grace has been g

GIVER* (GIVE)
Pr 18:16 A gift opens the way for the g
2Co 9: 7 for God loves a cheerful g.

GIVES (GIVE)
Ps 119:130 The unfolding of your words g light;
Pr 14:30 A heart at peace g life to the body,
15:30 good news g health to the bones.
28:27 He who g to the poor will lack
Isa 40:29 He g strength to the weary
Mt 10:42 if anyone g even a cup of cold water
Jn 6:63 The Spirit g life; the flesh counts
1Co 15:57 He g us the victory
2Co 3: 6 the letter kills, but the Spirit g life.

GIVING (GIVE)
Ne 8: 8 g the meaning so that the people
Ps 19: 8 g joy to the heart.
Mt 6: 4 so that your g may be in secret.
2Co 8: 7 also excel in this grace of g.

GLAD (GLADNESS)
Ps 31: 7 I will be g and rejoice in your love,
46: 4 whose streams make g the city
97: 1 LORD reigns, let the earth be g;
118:24 let us rejoice and be g in it.
Pr 23:25 May your father and mother be g;
Zec 2:10 and be g, O Daughter of Zion.
Mt 5:12 be g, because great is your reward

GLADNESS (GLAD)
Ps 45:15 They are led in with joy and g;
51: 8 Let me hear joy and g;
100: 2 Serve the LORD with g;
Jer 31:13 I will turn their mourning into g;

GLORIFIED (GLORY)
Jn 13:31 Son of Man g and God is g in him.
Ro 8:30 those he justified, he also g.
2Th 1:10 comes to be g in his holy people

GLORIFY (GLORY)
Ps 34: 3 G the LORD with me;
86:12 I will g your name forever.
Jn 13:32 God will g the Son in himself,
17: 1 G your Son, that your Son may

GLORIOUS (GLORY)
Ps 45:13 All g is the princess
111: 3 G and majestic are his deeds,
145: 5 of the g splendor of your majesty,
Isa 4: 2 the LORD will be beautiful and g,
12: 5 for he has done g things;
42:21 to make his law great and g.
63:15 from your lofty throne, holy and g.
Mt 19:28 the Son of Man sits on his g throne,
Lk 9:31 appeared in g splendor, talking
Ac 2:20 of the great and g day of the Lord.
2Co 3: 8 of the Spirit be even more g?
Php 3:21 so that they will be like his g body.
4:19 to his g riches in Christ Jesus.
Tit 2:13 the g appearing of our great God
Jude :24 before his g presence without fault

GLORY (GLORIFIED GLORIFY GLORIOUS)
Ex 15:11 awesome in g,
33:18 Moses said, "Now show me your g
1Sa 4:21 "The g has departed from Israel"—
1Ch 16:24 Declare his g among the nations,
16:28 ascribe to the LORD g
29:11 and the g and the majesty
Ps 8: 5 and crowned him with g and honor
19: 1 The heavens declare the g of God;
24: 7 that the King of g may come in.
29: 1 ascribe to the LORD g
72:19 the whole earth be filled with his g.
96: 3 Declare his g among the nations,
Pr 19:11 it is to his g to overlook an offense.
25: 2 It is the g of God to conceal
Isa 6: 3 the whole earth is full of his g."
48:11 I will not yield my g to another.
Eze 43: 2 and the land was radiant with his g.

Mt 24:30 of the sky, with power and great *g*.
25:31 the Son of Man comes in his *g*,
Mk 8:38 in his Father's *g* with the holy
13:26 in clouds with great power and *g*.
Lk 2: 9 and the *g* of the Lord shone
2:14 saying, "*G* to God in the highest,
Jn 1:14 We have seen his *g*, the *g* of the One
17: 5 presence with the *g* I had with you
17:24 to see my *g*, the *g* you have given
Ac 7: 2 The God of *g* appeared
Ro 1:23 exchanged the *g* of the immortal
3:23 and fall short of the *g* of God,
8:18 with the *g* that will be revealed
9: 4 theirs the divine *g*, the covenants,
1Co 10:31 whatever you do, do it all for the *g*
11: 7 but the woman is the *g* of man.
15:43 it is raised in *g*; it is sown
2Co 3:10 comparison with the surpassing *g*.
3:18 faces all reflect the Lord's *g*,
4:17 us an eternal *g* that far outweighs
Col 1:27 Christ in you, the hope of *g*.
3: 4 also will appear with him in *g*.
1Ti 3:16 was taken up in *g*.
Heb 1: 3 The Son is the radiance of God's *g*
2: 7 you crowned him with *g* and honor
1Pe 1:24 and all their *g* is like the flowers
Rev 4:11 to receive *g* and honor and power,
21:23 for the *g* of God gives it light,

GLUTTONS
Tit 1:12 always liars, evil brutes, lazy *g*."

GNASHING
Mt 8:12 where there will be weeping and *g*

GNAT*
Mt 23:24 You strain out a *g* but swallow

GOAL
2Co 5: 9 So we make it our *g* to please him,
Gal 3: 3 to attain your *g* by human effort?
Php 3:14 on toward the *g* to win the prize

GOAT (GOATS SCAPEGOAT)
Isa 11: 6 the leopard will lie down with the *g*

GOATS (GOAT)
Nu 7:17 five male *g* and five male lambs

GOD (GOD'S GODLINESS GODLY GODS)
Ge 1: 1 In the beginning *G* created
1: 2 and the Spirit of *G* was hovering
1:26 Then *G* said, "Let us make man
1:27 So *G* created man in his own image
1:31 *G* saw all that he had made,
2: 3 And *G* blessed the seventh day
2:22 Then the LORD *G* made a woman
3:21 The LORD *G* made garments
3:23 So the LORD *G* banished him
5:22 Enoch walked with *G* 300 years
6: 2 sons of *G* saw that the daughters
9:16 everlasting covenant between *G*
17: 1 "I am *G* Almighty; walk before me
21:33 name of the LORD, the Eternal *G*.
22: 8 "*G* himself will provide the lamb
28:12 and the angels of *G* were ascending
32:28 because you have struggled with *G*
32:30 "It is because I saw *G* face to face,
35:10 *G* said to him, "Your name is Jacob
41:51 *G* has made me forget all my
50:20 but *G* intended it for good
Ex 2:24 *G* heard their groaning
3: 6 because he was afraid to look at *G*.
6: 7 own people, and I will be your *G*.
8:10 is no one like the LORD our *G*.
13:18 So *G* led the people
15: 2 He is my *G*, and I will praise him,
17: 9 with the staff of *G* in my hands."
Ex 19: 3 Then Moses went up to *G*,
20: 2 the LORD your *G*, who brought
20: 5 the LORD your *G*, am a jealous *G*,
20:19 But do not have *G* speak to us
22:28 "Do not blaspheme *G*
31:18 inscribed by the finger of *G*.
34: 6 the compassionate and gracious *G*,
34:14 name is Jealous, is a jealous *G*.
Lev 18:21 not profane the name of your *G*.
19: 2 the LORD your *G*, am holy.
26:12 walk among you and be your *G*,
Nu 22:38 I must speak only what *G* puts
23:19 *G* is not a man, that he should lie,
Dt 1:17 for judgment belongs to *G*.
3:22 LORD your *G* himself will fight
3:24 For what *g* is there in heaven
4:24 is a consuming fire, a jealous *G*.
4:31 the LORD your *G* is a merciful *G*;
4:39 heart this day that the LORD is *G*
5:11 the name of the LORD your *G*,
5:14 a Sabbath to the LORD your *G*.
5:26 of the living *G* speaking out of fire,
6: 4 LORD our *G*, the LORD is one.
6: 5 Love the LORD your *G*
6:13 the LORD your *G*, serve him only
6:16 Do not test the LORD your *G*
7: 9 your *G* is *G*; he is the faithful *G*,
7:12 the LORD your *G* will keep his
7:21 is a great and awesome *G*.
8: 5 the LORD your *G* disciplines you.
10:12 but to fear the LORD your *G*,
10:14 the LORD your *G* belong
10:17 For the LORD your *G* is *G* of gods
11:13 to love the LORD your *G*
13: 3 The LORD your *G* is testing you
13: 4 the LORD your *G* you must
15: 6 the LORD your *G* will bless you
19: 9 to love the LORD your *G*
25:16 the LORD your *G* detests anyone
29:29 belong to the LORD our *G*,
30: 2 return to the LORD your *G*
30:16 today to love the LORD your *G*,
30:20 you may love the LORD your *G*,
31: 6 for the LORD your *G* goes
32: 3 Oh, praise the greatness of our *G*!
32: 4 A faithful *G* who does no wrong,
33:27 The eternal *G* is your refuge,
Jos 1: 9 for the LORD your *G* will be
14: 8 the LORD my *G* wholeheartedly.
22: 5 to love the LORD your *G*,
22:34 Between Us that the LORD is *G*.
23:11 careful to love the LORD your *G*.
23:14 the LORD your *G* gave you has
Jdg 16:28 O *G*, please strengthen me just
Ru 1:16 be my people and your *G* my *G*.
1Sa 2: 2 there is no Rock like our *G*.
2: 3 for the LORD is a *G* who knows,
2:25 another man, *G* may mediate
10:26 men whose hearts *G* had touched.
12:12 the LORD your *G* was your king.
17:26 defy the armies of the living *G*?"
17:46 world will know that there is a *G*
30: 6 strength in the LORD his *G*.
2Sa 14:14 But *G* does not take away life;
22: 3 my *G* is my rock, in whom I take
22:31 "As for *G*, his way is perfect;
1Ki 4:29 *G* gave Solomon wisdom
8:23 there is no *G* like you in heaven
8:27 "But will *G* really dwell on earth?
8:61 committed to the LORD our *G*,
18:21 If the LORD is *G*, follow him;
18:37 are *G*, and that you are turning
20:28 a *g* of the hills and not a *g*
2Ki 19:15 *G* of Israel, enthroned
1Ch 16:35 Cry out, "Save us, O *G* our Savior;
28: 2 for the footstool of our *G*,
28: 9 acknowledge the *G* of your father,
29:10 *G* of our father Israel,
1Ch 29:17 my *G*, that you test the heart
2Ch 2: 4 for the Name of the LORD my *G*
5:14 of the LORD filled the temple of *G*
6:18 "But will *G* really dwell on earth
18:13 I can tell him only what my *G* says
20: 6 are you not the *G* who is in heaven?
25: 8 for *G* has the power to help
30: 9 for the LORD your *G* is gracious
33:12 the favor of the LORD his *G*
Ezr 8:22 "The good hand of our *G* is
9: 6 "O my *G*, I am too ashamed
9:13 our *G*, you have punished us less
Ne 1: 5 the great and awesome *G*,
8: 8 from the Book of the Law of *G*,
9:17 But you are a forgiving *G*,
9:32 the great, mighty and awesome *G*,
Job 1: 1 he feared *G* and shunned evil.
2:10 Shall we accept good from *G*,
4:17 a mortal be more righteous than *G*?
5:17 is the man whom *G* corrects;
11: 7 Can you fathom the mysteries of *G*
19:26 yet in my flesh I will see *G*;
22:13 Yet you say, 'What does *G* know?
25: 4 can a man be righteous before *G*?
33:14 For *G* does speak—now one way,
34:12 is unthinkable that *G* would do
36:26 is *G*— beyond our understanding!
37:22 *G* comes in awesome majesty.
Ps 18: 2 my *G* is my rock, in whom I take
18:28 my *G* turns my darkness into light.
19: 1 The heavens declare the glory of *G*;
22: 1 *G*, my *G*, why have you forsaken
29: 3 the *G* of glory thunders,
31:14 I say, "You are my *G*."
40: 3 a hymn of praise to our *G*.
40: 8 I desire to do your will, O my *G*;
42: 2 thirsts for *G*, for the living *G*.
42:11 Put your hope in *G*,
45: 6 O *G*, will last for ever and ever;
46: 1 *G* is our refuge and strength,
46:10 "Be still, and know that I am *G*;
47: 7 For *G* is the King of all the earth;
50: 3 Our *G* comes and will not be silent;
51: 1 Have mercy on me, O *G*,
51:10 Create in me a pure heart, O *G*,
51:17 O *G*, you will not despise.
62: 7 my honor depend on *G*;
65: 5 O *G* our Savior,
66: 1 Shout with joy to *G*, all the earth!
66:16 listen, all you who fear *G*;
68: 6 *G* sets the lonely in families,
71:17 my youth, O *G*, you have taught
71:19 reaches to the skies, O *G*,
71:22 harp for your faithfulness, O my *G*;
73:26 but *G* is the strength of my heart
77:13 What *g* is so great as our God?
78:19 Can *G* spread a table in the desert?
81: 1 Sing for joy to *G* our strength;
84: 2 out for the living *G*.
84:10 a doorkeeper in the house of my *G*
86:12 O Lord my *G*, with all my heart;
89: 7 of the holy ones *G* is greatly feared;
90: 2 to everlasting you are *G*.
91: 2 my *G*, in whom I trust."
95: 7 for he is our *G*
100: 3 Know that the LORD is *G*.
108: 1 My heart is steadfast, O *G*;
113: 5 Who is like the LORD our *G*,
139:23 Search me, O *G*, and know my
Pr 3: 4 in the sight of *G* and man.
25: 2 of *G* to conceal a matter;
30: 5 "Every word of *G* is flawless;
Ecc 3:11 cannot fathom what *G* has done
11: 5 cannot understand the work of *G*,
12:13 Fear *G* and keep his
Isa 9: 6 Wonderful Counselor, Mighty *G*,
37:16 you alone are *G* over all
40: 3 a highway for our *G*.

1Ti 6:18 them to do *g,* to be rich in *g* deeds,
2Ti 3:17 equipped for every *g* work.
4: 7 I have fought the *g* fight, I have
Heb 12:10 but God disciplines us for our *g,*
1Pe 2: 3 you have tasted that the Lord is *g.*
2:12 Live such *g* lives among the pagans

GOSPEL
Ro 1:16 I am not ashamed of the *g,*
15:16 duty of proclaiming the *g* of God,
1Co 1:17 to preach the *g*— not with words
9:16 Woe to me if I do not preach the *g!*
15: 1 you of the *g* I preached to you,
Gal 1: 7 a different *g*— which is really no *g*
Php 1:27 in a manner worthy of the *g*

GOSSIP
Pr 11:13 A *g* betrays a confidence,
16:28 and a *g* separates close friends.
18: 8 of a *g* are like choice morsels;
26:20 without *g* a quarrel dies down.
2Co 12:20 slander, *g,* arrogance and disorder.

GRACE (GRACIOUS)
Ps 45: 2 lips have been anointed with *g,*
Jn 1:17 *g* and truth came through Jesus
Ac 20:32 to God and to the word of his *g,*
Ro 3:24 and are justified freely by his *g*
5:15 came by the *g* of the one man,
5:17 God's abundant provision of *g*
5:20 where sin increased, *g* increased all
6:14 you are not under law, but under *g.*
11: 6 if by *g,* then it is no longer by works
2Co 6: 1 not to receive God's *g* in vain.
8: 9 For you know the *g*
9: 8 able to make all *g* abound to you,
12: 9 "My *g* is sufficient for you,
Gal 2:21 I do not set aside the *g* of God,
5: 4 you have fallen away from *g.*
Eph 1: 7 riches of God's *g* that he lavished
2: 5 it is by *g* you have been saved.
2: 7 the incomparable riches of his *g,*
2: 8 For it is by *g* you have been saved,
Php 1: 7 all of you share in God's *g* with me.
Col 4: 6 conversation be always full of *g,*
2Th 2:16 and by his *g* gave us eternal
2Ti 2: 1 be strong in the *g* that is
Tit 2:11 For the *g* of God that brings
3: 7 having been justified by his *g,*
Heb 2: 9 that by the *g* of God he might taste
4:16 find *g* to help us in our time of need
4:16 the throne of *g* with confidence,
Jas 4: 6 but gives *g* to the humble."
2Pe 3:18 But grow in the *g* and knowledge

GRACIOUS (GRACE)
Nu 6:25 and be *g* to you;
Pr 22:11 a pure heart and whose speech is *g*
Isa 30:18 Yet the LORD longs to be *g* to you

GRAIN
1Co 9: 9 ox while it is treading out the *g."*

GRANTED
Php 1:29 For it has been *g* to you on behalf

GRASS
Ps 103:15 As for man, his days are like *g,*
1Pe 1:24 "All men are like *g,*

GRAVE (GRAVES)
Pr 7:27 Her house is a highway to the *g,*
Hos 13:14 Where, O *g,* is your destruction?

GRAVES (GRAVE)
Jn 5:28 are in their *g* will hear his voice
Ro 3:13 "Their throats are open *g;*

GREAT (GREATER GREATEST GREATNESS)
Ge 12: 2 "I will make you into a *g* nation
Dt 10:17 the *g* God, mighty and awesome,
2Sa 22:36 you stoop down to make me *g.*
Ps 19:11 in keeping them there is *g* reward.
89: 1 of the LORD's *g* love forever;
103:11 so *g* is his love for those who fear
107:43 consider the *g* love of the LORD.
108: 4 For *g* is your love, higher
119:165 *G* peace have they who love your
145: 3 *G* is the LORD and most worthy
Pr 23:24 of a righteous man has *g* joy;
Isa 42:21 to make his law *g* and glorious.
La 3:23 *g* is your faithfulness.
Mk 10:43 whoever wants to become *g*
Lk 21:27 in a cloud with power and *g* glory.
1Ti 6: 6 with contentment is *g* gain.
Tit 2:13 glorious appearing of our *g* God
Heb 2: 3 if we ignore such a *g* salvation?
1Jn 3: 1 How *g* is the love the Father has

GREATER (GREAT)
Mk 12:31 There is no commandment *g*
Jn 1:50 You shall see *g* things than that."
15:13 *G* love has no one than this,
1Co 12:31 But eagerly desire the *g* gifts.
Heb 11:26 as of *g* value than the treasures
1Jn 3:20 For God is *g* than our hearts,
4: 4 is in you is *g* than the one who is

GREATEST (GREAT)
Mt 22:38 is the first and *g* commandment.
Lk 9:48 least among you all—he is the *g."*
1Co 13:13 But the *g* of these is love.

GREATNESS (GREAT)
Ps 145: 3 his *g* no one can fathom.
150: 2 praise him for his surpassing *g.*
Isa 63: 1 forward in the *g* of his strength?
Php 3: 8 compared to the surpassing *g*

GREED (GREEDY)
Lk 12:15 on your guard against all kinds of *g*
Ro 1:29 kind of wickedness, evil, *g*
Eph 5: 3 or of any kind of impurity, or of *g,*
Col 3: 5 evil desires and *g,* which is idolatry
2Pe 2:14 experts in *g*— an accursed brood!

GREEDY (GREED)
Pr 15:27 A *g* man brings trouble
1Co 6:10 nor thieves nor the *g* nor drunkards
Eph 5: 5 No immoral, impure or *g* person—
1Pe 5: 2 not *g* for money, but eager to serve;

GREEN
Ps 23: 2 makes me lie down in *g* pastures,

GREW (GROW)
Lk 2:52 And Jesus *g* in wisdom and stature,
Ac 16: 5 in the faith and *g* daily in numbers.

GRIEF (GRIEVE)
Ps 10:14 O God, do see trouble and *g;*
Pr 14:13 and joy may end in *g.*
La 3:32 Though he brings *g,* he will show
Jn 16:20 but your *g* will turn to joy.
1Pe 1: 6 had to suffer *g* in all kinds of trials.

GRIEVE (GRIEF)
Eph 4:30 do not *g* the Holy Spirit of God,
1Th 4:13 or to *g* like the rest of men,

GROUND
Ge 3:17 "Cursed is the *g* because of you;
Ex 3: 5 where you are standing is holy *g."*
Eph 6:13 you may be able to stand your *g,*

GROW (GREW)
Pr 13:11 by little makes it *g.*
1Co 3: 6 watered it, but God made it *g.*
2Pe 3:18 But *g* in the grace and knowledge

GRUMBLE (GRUMBLING)
1Co 10:10 And do not *g,* as some of them did
Jas 5: 9 Don't *g* against each other,

GRUMBLING (GRUMBLE)
Jn 6:43 "Stop *g* among yourselves,"
1Pe 4: 9 to one another without *g.*

GUARANTEE (GUARANTEEING)
Heb 7:22 Jesus has become the *g*

GUARANTEEING (GUARANTEE)
2Co 1:22 as a deposit, *g* what is to come.
Eph 1:14 who is a deposit *g* our inheritance

GUARD (GUARDS)
Ps 141: 3 Set a *g* over my mouth, O LORD;
Pr 4:23 Above all else, *g* your heart,
Isa 52:12 the God of Israel will be your rear *g*
Mk 13:33 Be on *g!* Be alert! You do not know
1Co 16:13 Be on your *g;* stand firm in the faith
Php 4: 7 will *g* your hearts and your minds
1Ti 6:20 *g* what has been entrusted

GUARDS (GUARD)
Pr 13: 3 He who *g* his lips *g* his life,
19:16 who obeys instructions *g* his life,
21:23 He who *g* his mouth and his tongue
22: 5 he who *g* his soul stays far

GUIDE
Ex 13:21 of cloud to *g* them on their way
15:13 In your strength you will *g* them
Ne 9:19 cease to *g* them on their path,
Ps 25: 5 *g* me in your truth and teach me,
43: 3 let them *g* me;
48:14 he will be our *g* even to the end.
67: 4 and *g* the nations of the earth.
73:24 You *g* me with your counsel,
139:10 even there your hand will *g* me,
Pr 4:11 I *g* you in the way of wisdom
6:22 When you walk, they will *g* you;
Isa 58:11 The LORD will *g* you always;
Jn 16:13 comes, he will *g* you into all truth.

GUILTY
Ex 34: 7 does not leave the *g* unpunished;
Jn 8:46 Can any of you prove me *g* of sin?
Heb 10:22 to cleanse us from a *g* conscience
Jas 2:10 at just one point is *g* of breaking all

HADES
Mt 16:18 the gates of *H* will not overcome it.

HAGAR
Servant of Sarah, wife of Abraham, mother of Ishmael (Ge 16:1-6; 25:12). Driven away by Sarah while pregnant (Ge 16:5-16); after birth of Isaac (Ge 21:9-21; Gal 4:21-31).

HAGGAI*
Post-exilic prophet who encouraged rebuilding of the temple (Ezr 5:1; 6:14; Hag 1-2).

HAIR (HAIRS)
Lk 21:18 But not a *h* of your head will perish
1Co 11: 6 for a woman to have her *h* cut

HAIRS (HAIR)
Mt 10:30 even the very *h* of your head are all

HALLELUJAH*
Rev 19: 1, 3, 4, 6

HALLOWED (HOLY)
Mt 6: 9 *h* be your name,

HAND (HANDS)
Ps 16: 8 Because he is at my right *h,*
37:24 the LORD upholds him with his *h.*
139:10 even there your *h* will guide me,
Ecc 9:10 Whatever your *h* finds to do,
Mt 6: 3 know what your right *h* is doing,
Jn 10:28 one can snatch them out of my *h.*
1Co 12:15 I am not a *h,* I do not belong

HANDS (HAND)
Ps 22:16 they have pierced my *h*
24: 4 He who has clean *h* and a pure
31: 5 Into your *h* I commit my spirit;
31:15 My times are in your *h;*
Pr 10: 4 Lazy *h* make a man poor,
31:20 and extends her *h* to the needy.
Isa 55:12 will clap their *h.*
65: 2 All day long I have held out my *h*
Lk 23:46 into your *h* I commit my spirit."
1Th 4:11 and to work with your *h,*
1Ti 2: 8 to lift up holy *h* in prayer,
5:22 hasty in the laying on of *h,*

HANNAH*
Wife of Elkanah, mother of Samuel (1Sa 1). Prayer at dedication of Samuel (1Sa 2:1-10). Blessed (1Sa 2:18-21).

HAPPY
Ps 68: 3 may they be *h* and joyful.
Pr 15:13 A *h* heart makes the face cheerful,
Ecc 3:12 better for men than to be *h*
Jas 5:13 Is anyone *h?* Let him sing songs

HARD (HARDEN HARDSHIP)
Ge 18:14 Is anything too *h* for the LORD?
Mt 19:23 it is *h* for a rich man
1Co 4:12 We work *h* with our own hands.
1Th 5:12 to respect those who work *h*

HARDEN (HARD)
Ro 9:18 he hardens whom he wants to *h.*
Heb 3: 8 do not *h* your hearts

HARDHEARTED* (HEART)
Dt 15: 7 do not be *h* or tightfisted

HARDSHIP (HARD)
Ro 8:35 Shall trouble or *h* or persecution
2Ti 2: 3 Endure *h* with us like a good
4: 5 endure *h,* do the work
Heb 12: 7 Endure *h* as discipline; God is

HARM
Ps 121: 6 the sun will not *h* you by day,
Pr 3:29 not plot *h* against your neighbor,
31:12 She brings him good, not *h,*
Ro 13:10 Love does no *h* to its neighbor.
1Jn 5:18 and the evil one cannot *h* him.

HARMONY
Ro 12:16 Live in *h* with one another.
2Co 6:15 What *h* is there between Christ
1Pe 3: 8 live in *h* with one another;

HARVEST
Mt 9:37 *h* is plentiful but the workers are
Jn 4:35 at the fields! They are ripe for *h.*
Gal 6: 9 at the proper time we will reap a *h*
Heb 12:11 it produces a *h* of righteousness

HASTE (HASTY)
Pr 21: 5 as surely as *h* leads to poverty.
29:20 Do you see a man who speaks in *h?*

HASTY* (HASTE)
Pr 19: 2 nor to be *h* and miss the way.
Ecc 5: 2 do not be *h* in your heart
1Ti 5:22 Do not be *h* in the laying

HATE (HATED HATES HATRED)
Lev 19:17 " 'Do not *h* your brother
Ps 5: 5 you *h* all who do wrong.
45: 7 righteousness and *h* wickedness;
97:10 those who love the LORD *h* evil,
139:21 Do I not *h* those who *h* you,
Pr 8:13 To fear the LORD is to *h* evil;
Am 5:15 *H* evil, love good;
Mal 2:16 "I *h* divorce," says the LORD God
Mt 5:43 your neighbor and *h* your enemy.'
10:22 All men will *h* you because of me,
Lk 6:27 do good to those who *h* you,
Ro 12: 9 *H* what is evil; cling to what is good

HATED (HATE)
Ro 9:13 "Jacob I loved, but Esau I *h."*
Eph 5:29 no one ever *h* his own body,
Heb 1: 9 righteousness and *h* wickedness;

HATES (HATE)
Pr 6:16 There are six things the LORD *h,*
13:24 He who spares the rod *h* his son,
Jn 3:20 Everyone who does evil *h* the light,
1Jn 2: 9 *h* his brother is still in the darkness.

HATRED (HATE)
Pr 10:12 *H* stirs up dissension,
Jas 4: 4 with the world is *h* toward God?

HAUGHTY
Pr 16:18 a *h* spirit before a fall.

HAY
1Co 3:12 costly stones, wood, *h* or straw,

HEAD (HEADS HOTHEADED)
Ge 3:15 he will crush your *h,*
Ps 23: 5 You anoint my *h* with oil;
Pr 25:22 will heap burning coals on his *h,*
Isa 59:17 and the helmet of salvation on his *h*
Mt 8:20 of Man has no place to lay his *h."*
Ro 12:20 will heap burning coals on his *h."*
1Co 11: 3 and the *h* of Christ is God.
12:21 And the *h* cannot say to the feet,
Eph 5:23 For the husband is the *h* of the wife
2Ti 4: 5 keep your *h* in all situations,
Rev 19:12 and on his *h* are many crowns.

HEADS (HEAD)
Lev 26:13 you to walk with *h* held high.
Isa 35:10 everlasting joy will crown their *h.*

HEAL (HEALED HEALING HEALS)
2Ch 7:14 their sin and will *h* their land.
Ps 41: 4 *h* me, for I have sinned against you
Mt 10: 8 *H* the sick, raise the dead,
Lk 4:23 to me: 'Physician, *h* yourself!
5:17 present for him to *h* the sick.

HEALED (HEAL)
Isa 53: 5 and by his wounds we are *h.*
Mt 9:22 he said, "your faith has *h* you."
14:36 and all who touched him were *h.*
Ac 4:10 this man stands before you *h.*
14: 9 saw that he had faith to be *h*
Jas 5:16 for each other so that you may be *h*
1Pe 2:24 by his wounds you have been *h.*

HEALING (HEAL)
Eze 47:12 for food and their leaves for *h."*
Mal 4: 2 rise with *h* in its wings.
1Co 12: 9 to another gifts of *h*
12:30 Do all have gifts of *h?* Do all speak

Rev 22: 2 are for the *h* of the nations.

HEALS (HEAL)
Ex 15:26 for I am the LORD, who *h* you."
Ps 103: 3 and *h* all your diseases;
147: 3 He *h* the brokenhearted

HEALTH (HEALTHY)
Pr 3: 8 This will bring *h* to your body
15:30 and good news gives *h* to the bones

HEALTHY (HEALTH)
Mk 2:17 "It is not the *h* who need a doctor,

HEAR (HEARD HEARING HEARS)
Dt 6: 4 *H,* O Israel: The LORD our God,
31:13 must *h* it and learn
2Ch 7:14 then will I *h* from heaven
Ps 94: 9 he who implanted the ear not *h?*
Isa 29:18 that day the deaf will *h* the words
65:24 while they are still speaking I will *h*
Mt 11:15 He who has ears, let him *h.*
Jn 8:47 reason you do not *h* is that you do
2Ti 4: 3 what their itching ears want to *h.*

HEARD (HEAR)
Job 42: 5 My ears had *h* of you
Isa 66: 8 Who has ever *h* of such a thing?
Mt 5:21 "You have *h* that it was said
5:27 "You have *h* that it was said,
5:33 you have *h* that it was said
5:38 "You have *h* that it was said,
5:43 "You have *h* that it was said,
1Co 2: 9 no ear has *h,*
1Th 2:13 word of God, which you *h* from us,
2Ti 1:13 What you *h* from me, keep
Jas 1:25 not forgetting what he has *h,*

HEARING (HEAR)
Ro 10:17 faith comes from *h* the message,

HEARS (HEAR)
Jn 5:24 whoever *h* my word and believes
1Jn 5:14 according to his will, he *h* us.
Rev 3:20 If anyone *h* my voice and opens

HEART (BROKENHEARTED HARDHEARTED HEARTS WHOLEHEARTEDLY)
Ex 25: 2 each man whose *h* prompts him
Lev 19:17 Do not hate your brother in your *h.*
Dt 4:29 if you look for him with all your *h*
6: 5 LORD your God with all your *h*
10:12 LORD your God with all your *h*
15:10 and do so without a grudging *h;*
30: 6 you may love him with all your *h*
30:10 LORD your God with all your *h*
Jos 22: 5 and to serve him with all your *h*
1Sa 13:14 sought out a man after his own *h*
16: 7 but the LORD looks at the *h."*
2Ki 23: 3 with all his *h* and all his soul,
1Ch 28: 9 for the LORD searches every *h*
2Ch 7:16 and my *h* will always be there.
Job 22:22 and lay up his words in your *h.*
37: 1 "At this my *h* pounds
Ps 14: 1 The fool says in his *h,*
19:14 and the meditation of my *h*
37: 4 will give you the desires of your *h.*
45: 1 My *h* is stirred by a noble theme
51:10 Create in me a pure *h,* O God,
51:17 a broken and contrite *h,*
66:18 If I had cherished sin in my *h,*
86:11 give me an undivided *h,*
119:11 I have hidden your word in my *h*
119:32 for you have set my *h* free.
139:23 Search me, O God, and know my *h*
Pr 3: 5 Trust in the LORD with all your *h*
4:21 keep them within your *h;*
4:23 Above all else, guard your *h,*

Pr 7: 3 write them on the tablet of your *h.*
13:12 Hope deferred makes the *h* sick,
14:13 Even in laughter the *h* may ache,
15:30 A cheerful look brings joy to the *h,*
17:22 A cheerful *h* is good medicine,
24:17 stumbles, do not let your *h* rejoice,
27:19 so a man's *h* reflects the man.
Ecc 8: 5 wise *h* will know the proper time
SS 4: 9 You have stolen my *h,* my sister,
Isa 40:11 and carries them close to his *h;*
57:15 and to revive the *h* of the contrite.
Jer 17: 9 The *h* is deceitful above all things
29:13 when you seek me with all your *h.*
Eze 36:26 I will give you a new *h*
Mt 5: 8 Blessed are the pure in *h,*
6:21 treasure is, there your *h* will be
12:34 of the *h* the mouth speaks.
22:37 the Lord your God with all your *h*
Lk 6:45 overflow of his *h* his mouth speaks.
Ro 2:29 is circumcision of the *h,*
10:10 is with your *h* that you believe
1Co 14:25 the secrets of his *h* will be laid bare.
Eph 5:19 make music in your *h* to the Lord,
6: 6 doing the will of God from your *h.*
Col 3:23 work at it with all your *h,*
1Pe 1:22 one another deeply, from the *h.*

HEARTS (HEART)
Dt 11:18 Fix these words of mine in your *h*
1Ki 8:39 for you alone know the *h* of all men
8:61 your *h* must be fully committed
Ps 62: 8 pour out your *h* to him,
Ecc 3:11 also set eternity in the *h* of men;
Jer 31:33 and write it on their *h.*
Lk 16:15 of men, but God knows your *h.*
24:32 "Were not our *h* burning within us
Jn 14: 1 "Do not let your *h* be troubled.
Ac 15: 9 for he purified their *h* by faith.
Ro 2:15 of the law are written on their *h,*
2Co 3: 2 written on our *h,* known
3: 3 but on tablets of human *h.*
4: 6 shine in our *h* to give us the light
Eph 3:17 dwell in your *h* through faith.
Col 3: 1 set your *h* on things above,
Heb 3: 8 do not harden your *h*
10:16 I will put my laws in their *h,*
1Jn 3:20 For God is greater than our *h,*

HEAT
2Pe 3:12 and the elements will melt in the *h.*

HEAVEN (HEAVENLY HEAVENS)
Ge 14:19 Creator of *h* and earth.
1Ki 8:27 the highest *h,* cannot contain you.
2Ki 2: 1 up to *h* in a whirlwind,
2Ch 7:14 then will I hear from *h*
Isa 14:12 How you have fallen from *h,*
66: 1 "*H* is my throne,
Da 7:13 coming with the clouds of *h.*
Mt 6: 9 " 'Our Father in *h,*
6:20 up for yourselves treasures in *h,*
16:19 bind on earth will be bound in *h,*
19:23 man to enter the kingdom of *h.*
24:35 *H* and earth will pass away,
26:64 and coming on the clouds of *h."*
28:18 "All authority in *h*
Mk 16:19 he was taken up into *h*
Lk 15: 7 in *h* over one sinner who repents
18:22 and you will have treasure in *h.*
Ro 10: 6 'Who will ascend into *h?'* " (that is,
2Co 5: 1 an eternal house in *h,* not built
12: 2 ago was caught up to the third *h.*
Php 2:10 *h* and on earth and under the earth,
3:20 But our citizenship is in *h.*
1Th 1:10 and to wait for his Son from *h,*
Heb 8: 5 and shadow of what is in *h.*
9:24 he entered *h* itself, now to appear
2Pe 3:13 we are looking forward to a new *h*
Rev 21: 1 Then I saw a new *h* and a new earth

HEAVENLY (HEAVEN)
Ps 8: 5 him a little lower than the *h* beings
2Co 5: 2 to be clothed with our *h* dwelling,
Eph 1: 3 in the *h* realms with every spiritual
1:20 at his right hand in the *h* realms,
2Ti 4:18 bring me safely to his *h* kingdom.
Heb 12:22 to the *h* Jerusalem, the city

HEAVENS (HEAVEN)
Ge 1: 1 In the beginning God created the *h*
1Ki 8:27 The *h,* even the highest heaven,
2Ch 2: 6 since the *h,* even the highest
Ps 8: 3 When I consider your *h,*
19: 1 The *h* declare the glory of God;
102:25 the *h* are the work of your hands.
108: 4 is your love, higher than the *h;*
119:89 it stands firm in the *h.*
139: 8 If I go up to the *h,* you are there;
Isa 51: 6 Lift up your eyes to the *h,*
55: 9 "As the *h* are higher than the earth,
65:17 new *h* and a new earth.
Joel 2:30 I will show wonders in the *h*
Eph 4:10 who ascended higher than all the *h,*
2Pe 3:10 The *h* will disappear with a roar;

HEBREW
Ge 14:13 and reported this to Abram the *H.*

HEEDS
Pr 13: 1 wise son *h* his father's instruction,
13:18 whoever *h* correction is honored.
15: 5 whoever *h* correction shows
15:32 whoever *h* correction gains

HEEL
Ge 3:15 and you will strike his *h."*

HEIRS (INHERIT)
Ro 8:17 then we are *h*—*h* of God
Gal 3:29 and *h* according to the promise.
Eph 3: 6 gospel the Gentiles are *h* together
1Pe 3: 7 as *h* with you of the gracious gift

HELL
Mt 5:22 will be in danger of the fire of *h.*
Lk 16:23 In *h,* where he was in torment,
2Pe 2: 4 but sent them to *h,* putting them

HELMET
Isa 59:17 and the *h* of salvation on his head;
Eph 6:17 Take the *h* of salvation
1Th 5: 8 and the hope of salvation as a *h.*

HELP (HELPED HELPER HELPING HELPS)
Ps 18: 6 I cried to my God for *h.*
30: 2 my God, I called to you for *h*
46: 1 an ever-present *h* in trouble.
79: 9 *H* us, O God our Savior,
121: 1 where does my *h* come from?
Isa 41:10 I will strengthen you and *h* you;
Jnh 2: 2 depths of the grave I called for *h,*
Mk 9:24 *h* me overcome my unbelief!"
Ac 16: 9 Come over to Macedonia and *h* us
1Co 12:28 those able to *h* others, those

HELPED (HELP)
1Sa 7:12 "Thus far has the LORD *h* us."

HELPER (HELP)
Ge 2:18 I will make a *h* suitable for him."
Ps 10:14 you are the *h* of the fatherless.
Heb 13: 6 Lord is my *h;* I will not be afraid.

HELPING (HELP)
Ac 9:36 always doing good and *h* the poor.
1Ti 5:10 *h* those in trouble and devoting

HELPS (HELP)
Ro 8:26 the Spirit *h* us in our weakness.

HEN
Mt 23:37 as a *h* gathers her chicks

HERITAGE (INHERIT)
Ps 127: 3 Sons are a *h* from the LORD,

HEROD

1. King of Judea who tried to kill Jesus (Mt 2; Lk 1:5).

2. Son of 1. Tetrarch of Galilee who arrested and beheaded John the Baptist (Mt 14:1-12; Mk 6:14-29; Lk 3:1, 19-20; 9:7-9); tried Jesus (Lk 23:6-15).

3. Grandson of 1. King of Judea who killed James (Ac 12:2); arrested Peter (Ac 12:3-19). Death (Ac 12:19-23).

HERODIAS

Wife of Herod the Tetrarch who persuaded her daughter to ask for John the Baptist's head (Mt 14:1-12; Mk 6:14-29).

HEZEKIAH

King of Judah. Restored the temple and worship (2Ch 29-31). Sought the LORD for help against Assyria (2Ki 18-19; 2Ch 32:1-23; Isa 36-37). Illness healed (2Ki 20:1-11; 2Ch 32:24-26; Isa 38). Judged for showing Babylonians his treasures (2Ki 20:12-21; 2Ch 32:31; Isa 39).

HID (HIDE)
Ge 3: 8 and they *h* from the LORD God
Ex 2: 2 she *h* him for three months.
Jos 6:17 because she *h* the spies we sent.
Heb 11:23 By faith Moses' parents *h* him

HIDDEN (HIDE)
Ps 19:12 Forgive my *h* faults.
119:11 I have *h* your word in my heart
Pr 2: 4 and search for it as for *h* treasure,
Isa 59: 2 your sins have *h* his face from you,
Mt 5:14 A city on a hill cannot be *h.*
13:44 of heaven is like treasure *h*
Col 1:26 the mystery that has been kept *h*
2: 3 in whom are *h* all the treasures
3: 3 and your life is now *h* with Christ

HIDE (HID HIDDEN)
Ps 17: 8 *h* me in the shadow of your wings
143: 9 for I *h* myself in you.

HILL (HILLS)
Mt 5:14 A city on a *h* cannot be hidden.

HILLS (HILL)
Ps 50:10 and the cattle on a thousand *h.*
121: 1 I lift up my eyes to the *h*—

HINDER (HINDERS)
1Sa 14: 6 Nothing can *h* the LORD
Mt 19:14 come to me, and do not *h* them,
1Co 9:12 anything rather than *h* the gospel
1Pe 3: 7 so that nothing will *h* your prayers.

HINDERS (HINDER)
Heb 12: 1 let us throw off everything that *h*

HINT*
Eph 5: 3 even a *h* of sexual immorality,

HOLD
Ex 20: 7 LORD will not *h* anyone guiltless
Lev 19:13 " 'Do not *h* back the wages
Jos 22: 5 to *h* fast to him and to serve him
Ps 73:23 you *h* me by my right hand.

Pr 4: 4 "Lay *h* of my words
Isa 54: 2 do not *h* back;
Mk 11:25 if you *h* anything against anyone,
Php 2:16 as you *h* out the word of life—
3:12 but I press on to take *h* of that
Col 1:17 and in him all things *h* together.
1Th 5:21 *H* on to the good.
1Ti 6:12 Take *h* of the eternal life
Heb 10:23 Let us *h* unswervingly

HOLINESS (HOLY)
Ex 15:11 majestic in *h,*
Ps 29: 2 in the splendor of his *h.*
96: 9 in the splendor of his *h;*
Ro 6:19 to righteousness leading to *h.*
2Co 7: 1 perfecting *h* out of reverence
Eph 4:24 God in true righteousness and *h.*
Heb 12:10 that we may share in his *h.*
12:14 without *h* no one will see the Lord.

HOLY (HALLOWED HOLINESS)
Ex 19: 6 kingdom of priests and a *h* nation.'
20: 8 the Sabbath day by keeping it *h.*
Lev 11:44 and be *h,* because I am *h.*
20: 7 " 'Consecrate yourselves and be *h,*
20:26 You are to be *h* to me because I,
21: 8 Consider them *h,* because I
22:32 Do not profane my *h* name.
Ps 16:10 will you let your *H* One see decay.
24: 3 Who may stand in his *h* place?
77:13 Your ways, O God, are *h.*
99: 3 he is *h.*
99: 5 he is *h.*
99: 9 for the LORD our God is *h.*
111: 9 *h* and awesome is his name.
Isa 5:16 the *h* God will show himself *h*
6: 3 *H, h, h* is the LORD Almighty;
40:25 who is my equal?" says the *H* One.
57:15 who lives forever, whose name is *h:*
Eze 28:25 I will show myself *h* among them
Da 9:24 prophecy and to anoint the most *h.*
Hab 2:20 But the LORD is in his *h* temple;
Ac 2:27 will you let your *H* One see decay.
Ro 7:12 and the commandment is *h,*
12: 1 as living sacrifices, *h* and pleasing
Eph 5: 3 improper for God's *h* people.
2Th 1:10 to be glorified in his *h* people
2Ti 1: 9 saved us and called us to a *h* life—
3:15 you have known the *h* Scriptures,
Tit 1: 8 upright, *h* and disciplined.
1Pe 1:15 But just as he who called you is *h,*
1:16 is written: "Be *h,* because I am *h."*
2: 9 a royal priesthood, a *h* nation,
2Pe 3:11 You ought to live *h* and godly lives
Rev 4: 8 *"H, h, h* is the Lord God

HOME (HOMES)
Dt 6: 7 Talk about them when you sit at *h*
Ps 84: 3 Even the sparrow has found a *h,*
Pr 3:33 but he blesses the *h* of the righteous
Mk 10:29 "no one who has left *h* or brothers
Jn 14:23 to him and make our *h* with him.
Tit 2: 5 to be busy at *h,* to be kind,

HOMES (HOME)
Ne 4:14 daughters, your wives and your *h."*
1Ti 5:14 to manage their *h* and to give

HOMOSEXUAL*
1Co 6: 9 male prostitutes nor *h* offenders

HONEST
Lev 19:36 Use *h* scales and *h* weights,
Dt 25:15 and *h* weights and measures,
Job 31: 6 let God weigh me in *h* scales
Pr 12:17 truthful witness gives *h* testimony,

HONEY
Ex 3: 8 a land flowing with milk and *h*—
Ps 19:10 than *h* from the comb.
119:103 sweeter than *h* to my mouth!

HONOR (HONORABLE HONORABLY HONORED HONORS)
Ex 20:12 *"H* your father and your mother,
Nu 25:13 he was zealous for the *h* of his God
Dt 5:16 *"H* your father and your mother,
1Sa 2:30 Those who *h* me I will *h,*
Ps 8: 5 and crowned him with glory and *h.*
Pr 3: 9 *H* the LORD with your wealth,
15:33 and humility comes before *h.*
20: 3 It is to a man's *h* to avoid strife,
Mt 15: 4 *'H* your father and mother'
Ro 12:10 *H* one another above yourselves.
1Co 6:20 Therefore *h* God with your body.
Eph 6: 2 *"H* your father and mother"—
1Ti 5:17 well are worthy of double *h,*
Heb 2: 7 you crowned him with glory and *h*
Rev 4: 9 *h* and thanks to him who sits

HONORABLE (HONOR)
1Th 4: 4 body in a way that is holy and *h,*

HONORABLY (HONOR)
Heb 13:18 and desire to live *h* in every way.

HONORED (HONOR)
Ps 12: 8 when what is vile is *h* among men.
Pr 13:18 but whoever heeds correction is *h.*
1Co 12:26 if one part is *h,* every part rejoices
Heb 13: 4 Marriage should be *h* by all,

HONORS (HONOR)
Ps 15: 4 but *h* those who fear the LORD,
Pr 14:31 to the needy *h* God.

HOOKS
Isa 2: 4 and their spears into pruning *h.*
Joel 3:10 and your pruning *h* into spears.

HOPE (HOPES)
Job 13:15 Though he slay me, yet will I *h*
Ps 42: 5 Put your *h* in God,
62: 5 my *h* comes from him.
119:74 for I have put my *h* in your word.
130: 7 O Israel, put your *h* in the LORD,
147:11 who put their *h* in his unfailing love
Pr 13:12 *H* deferred makes the heart sick,
Isa 40:31 but those who *h* in the LORD
Ro 5: 4 character; and character, *h.*
8:24 But *h* that is seen is no *h* at all.
12:12 Be joyful in *h,* patient in affliction,
15: 4 of the Scriptures we might have *h.*
1Co 13:13 now these three remain: faith, *h*
15:19 for this life we have *h* in Christ,
Col 1:27 Christ in you, the *h* of glory.
1Th 5: 8 and the *h* of salvation as a helmet.
1Ti 6:17 but to put their *h* in God,
Tit 2:13 while we wait for the blessed *h*—
Heb 6:19 We have this *h* as an anchor
11: 1 faith is being sure of what we *h* for
1Jn 3: 3 Everyone who has this *h*

HOPES (HOPE)
1Co 13: 7 always *h,* always perseveres.

HORSE
Ps 147:10 not in the strength of the *h,*
Pr 26: 3 A whip for the *h,* a halter
Zec 1: 8 before me was a man riding a red *h*
Rev 6: 2 and there before me was a white *h!*
6: 4 Come!" Then another *h* came out,
6: 5 and there before me was a black *h!*
6: 8 and there before me was a pale *h!*
19:11 and there before me was a white *h,*

HOSANNA
Mt 21: 9 *"H* in the highest!"

HOSHEA
Last king of Israel (2Ki 15:30; 17:1-6).

HOSPITABLE* (HOSPITALITY)
1Ti 3: 2 self-controlled, respectable, *h,*
Tit 1: 8 Rather he must be *h,* one who loves

HOSPITALITY (HOSPITABLE)
Ro 12:13 Practice *h.*
1Ti 5:10 as bringing up children, showing *h,*
1Pe 4: 9 Offer *h* to one another

HOSTILE
Ro 8: 7 the sinful mind is *h* to God.

HOT
1Ti 4: 2 have been seared as with a *h* iron.
Rev 3:15 that you are neither cold nor *h.*

HOT-TEMPERED
Pr 15:18 A *h* man stirs up dissension,
19:19 A *h* man must pay the penalty;
22:24 Do not make friends with a *h* man,
29:22 and a *h* one commits many sins.

HOTHEADED (HEAD)
Pr 14:16 but a fool is *h* and reckless.

HOUR
Ecc 9:12 knows when his *h* will come:
Mt 6:27 you by worrying can add a single *h*
Lk 12:40 the Son of Man will come at an *h*
Jn 12:23 The *h* has come for the Son of Man
12:27 for this very reason I came to this *h*

HOUSE (HOUSEHOLD STOREHOUSE)
Ex 20:17 shall not covet your neighbor's *h.*
Ps 23: 6 I will dwell in the *h* of the LORD
84:10 a doorkeeper in the *h* of my God
122: 1 "Let us go to the *h* of the LORD."
127: 1 Unless the LORD builds the *h,*
Pr 7:27 Her *h* is a highway to the grave,
21: 9 than share a *h* with a quarrelsome
Isa 56: 7 a *h* of prayer for all nations."
Zec 13: 6 given at the *h* of my friends.'
Mt 7:24 is like a wise man who built his *h*
12:29 can anyone enter a strong man's *h*
21:13 My *h* will be called a *h* of prayer,'
Mk 3:25 If a *h* is divided against itself,
Lk 11:17 a *h* divided against itself will fall.
Jn 2:16 How dare you turn my Father's *h*
12: 3 the *h* was filled with the fragrance
14: 2 In my Father's *h* are many rooms;
Heb 3: 3 the builder of a *h* has greater honor

HOUSEHOLD (HOUSE)
Jos 24:15 my *h,* we will serve the LORD."
Mic 7: 6 are the members of his own *h.*
Mt 10:36 will be the members of his own *h.'*
12:25 or *h* divided against itself will not
1Ti 3:12 manage his children and his *h* well.
3:15 to conduct themselves in God's *h,*

HUMAN (HUMANITY)
Gal 3: 3 to attain your goal by *h* effort?

HUMANITY* (HUMAN)
Heb 2:14 he too shared in their *h* so that

HUMBLE (HUMBLED HUMBLES HUMILIATE HUMILITY)
2Ch 7:14 will *h* themselves and pray
Ps 25: 9 He guides the *h* in what is right
Pr 3:34 but gives grace to the *h.*
Isa 66: 2 he who is *h* and contrite in spirit,

Mt 11:29 for I am gentle and *h* in heart,
Eph 4: 2 Be completely *h* and gentle;
Jas 4:10 *H* yourselves before the Lord,
1Pe 5: 6 *H* yourselves,

HUMBLED (HUMBLE)
Mt 23:12 whoever exalts himself will be *h*,
Php 2: 8 he *h* himself

HUMBLES (HUMBLE)
Mt 18: 4 whoever *h* himself like this child is
23:12 whoever *h* himself will be exalted.

HUMILIATE* (HUMBLE)
Pr 25: 7 than for him to *h* you
1Co 11:22 and *h* those who have nothing?

HUMILITY (HUMBLE)
Pr 11: 2 but with *h* comes wisdom.
15:33 and *h* comes before honor.
Php 2: 3 but in *h* consider others better
Tit 3: 2 and to show true *h* toward all men.
1Pe 5: 5 clothe yourselves with *h*

HUNGRY
Ps 107: 9 and fills the *h* with good things.
146: 7 and gives food to the *h*.
Pr 25:21 If your enemy is *h*, give him food
Eze 18: 7 but gives his food to the *h*
Mt 25:35 For I was *h* and you gave me
Lk 1:53 He has filled the *h* with good things
Jn 6:35 comes to me will never go *h*,
Ro 12:20 "If your enemy is *h*, feed him;

HURT (HURTS)
Ecc 8: 9 it over others to his own *h*.
Mk 16:18 deadly poison, it will not *h* them
Rev 2:11 He who overcomes will not be *h*

HURTS* (HURT)
Ps 15: 4 even when it *h*,
Pr 26:28 A lying tongue hates those it *h*,

HUSBAND (HUSBAND'S HUSBANDS)
1Co 7: 3 The *h* should fulfill his marital duty
7:10 wife must not separate from her *h*.
7:11 And a *h* must not divorce his wife.
7:13 And if a woman has a *h* who is not
7:39 A woman is bound to her *h* as long
2Co 11: 2 I promised you to one *h*, to Christ,
Eph 5:23 For the *h* is the head of the wife
5:33 and the wife must respect her *h*.
1Ti 3: 2 the *h* of but one wife, temperate,

HUSBAND'S (HUSBAND)
Pr 12: 4 of noble character is her *h* crown,
1Co 7: 4 the *h* body does not belong

HUSBANDS (HUSBAND)
Eph 5:22 submit to your *h* as to the Lord.
5:25 *H*, love your wives, just
Tit 2: 4 the younger women to love their *h*
1Pe 3: 1 same way be submissive to your *h*
3: 7 *H*, in the same way be considerate

HYMN
1Co 14:26 everyone has a *h*, or a word

HYPOCRISY (HYPOCRITE HYPOCRITES)
Mt 23:28 but on the inside you are full of *h*
1Pe 2: 1 *h*, envy, and slander of every kind.

HYPOCRITE (HYPOCRISY)
Mt 7: 5 You *h*, first take the plank out

HYPOCRITES (HYPOCRISY)
Ps 26: 4 nor do I consort with *h*;
Mt 6: 5 when you pray, do not be like the *h*

HYSSOP
Ps 51: 7 with *h*, and I will be clean;

IDLE (IDLENESS)
1Th 5:14 those who are *i*, encourage
2Th 3: 6 away from every brother who is *i*
1Ti 5:13 they get into the habit of being *i*

IDLENESS* (IDLE)
Pr 31:27 and does not eat the bread of *i*.

IDOL (IDOLATRY IDOLS)
Isa 44:17 From the rest he makes a god, his *i*;
1Co 8: 4 We know that an *i* is nothing at all

IDOLATRY (IDOL)
Col 3: 5 evil desires and greed, which is *i*.

IDOLS (IDOL)
1Co 8: 1 Now about food sacrificed to *i*:

IGNORANT (IGNORE)
1Co 15:34 for there are some who are *i* of God
Heb 5: 2 to deal gently with those who are *i*
1Pe 2:15 good you should silence the *i* talk
2Pe 3:16 which *i* and unstable people distort

IGNORE (IGNORANT IGNORES)
Dt 22: 1 do not *i* it but be sure
Ps 9:12 he does not *i* the cry of the afflicted
Heb 2: 3 if we *i* such a great salvation?

IGNORES (IGNORE)
Pr 10:17 whoever *i* correction leads others
15:32 He who *i* discipline despises

ILLUMINATED*
Rev 18: 1 and the earth was *i* by his splendor.

IMAGE
Ge 1:26 "Let us make man in our *i*,
1:27 So God created man in his own *i*,
1Co 11: 7 since he is the *i* and glory of God;
Col 1:15 He is the *i* of the invisible God,
3:10 in knowledge in the *i* of its Creator.

IMAGINE
Eph 3:20 more than all we ask or *i*,

IMITATE (IMITATORS)
1Co 4:16 Therefore I urge you to *i* me.
Heb 6:12 but to *i* those who through faith
13: 7 of their way of life and *i* their faith.
3Jn :11 do not *i* what is evil but what is

IMITATORS* (IMITATE)
Eph 5: 1 Be *i* of God, therefore,
1Th 1: 6 You became *i* of us and of the Lord
2:14 became *i* of God's churches

IMMANUEL
Isa 7:14 birth to a son, and will call him *I*.
Mt 1:23 and they will call him *I*"—

IMMORAL* (IMMORALITY)
Pr 6:24 keeping you from the *i* woman,
1Co 5: 9 to associate with sexually *i* people
5:10 the people of this world who are *i*,
5:11 but is sexually *i* or greedy,
6: 9 Neither the sexually *i* nor idolaters
Eph 5: 5 No *i*, impure or greedy person—
Heb 12:16 See that no one is sexually *i*,
13: 4 the adulterer and all the sexually *i*.
Rev 21: 8 the murderers, the sexually *i*,
22:15 the sexually *i*, the murderers,

IMMORALITY (IMMORAL)
1Co 6:13 The body is not meant for sexual *i*,
6:18 Flee from sexual *i*.
10: 8 We should not commit sexual *i*,
Gal 5:19 sexual *i*, impurity and debauchery;
Eph 5: 3 must not be even a hint of sexual *i*,
1Th 4: 3 that you should avoid sexual *i*;
Jude : 4 grace of our God into a license for *i*

IMMORTAL* (IMMORTALITY)
Ro 1:23 glory of the *i* God for images made
1Ti 1:17 Now to the King eternal, *i*,
6:16 who alone is *i* and who lives

IMMORTALITY (IMMORTAL)
Ro 2: 7 honor and *i*, he will give eternal life
1Co 15:53 and the mortal with *i*.
2Ti 1:10 and *i* to light through the gospel.

IMPERISHABLE
1Pe 1:23 not of perishable seed, but of *i*,

IMPORTANCE* (IMPORTANT)
1Co 15: 3 passed on to you as of first *i*:

IMPORTANT (IMPORTANCE)
Mt 6:25 Is not life more *i* than food,
23:23 have neglected the more *i* matters
Mk 12:29 "The most *i* one," answered Jesus,
12:33 as yourself is more *i* than all burnt
Php 1:18 The *i* thing is that in every way,

IMPOSSIBLE
Mt 17:20 Nothing will be *i* for you."
Lk 1:37 For nothing is *i* with God."
18:27 "What is *i* with men is possible
Heb 6:18 things in which it is *i* for God to lie,
11: 6 without faith it is *i* to please God,

IMPROPER*
Eph 5: 3 these are *i* for God's holy people.

IMPURE (IMPURITY)
Ac 10:15 not call anything *i* that God has
Eph 5: 5 No immoral, *i* or greedy person—
1Th 4: 7 For God did not call us to be *i*,
Rev 21:27 Nothing *i* will ever enter it,

IMPURITY (IMPURE)
Ro 1:24 hearts to sexual *i* for the degrading
Eph 5: 3 or of any kind of *i*, or of greed,

INCENSE
Ex 40: 5 Place the gold altar of *i* in front
Ps 141: 2 my prayer be set before you like *i*;
Mt 2:11 him with gifts of gold and of *i*

INCOME
Ecc 5:10 wealth is never satisfied with his *i*.
1Co 16: 2 sum of money in keeping with his *i*,

INCOMPARABLE*
Eph 2: 7 ages he might show the *i* riches

INCREASE (EVER-INCREASING INCREASED INCREASES INCREASING)
Ge 1:22 "Be fruitful and *i* in number
Ps 62:10 though your riches *i*,
Isa 9: 7 Of the *i* of his government
Lk 17: 5 said to the Lord, "*I* our faith!"
1Th 3:12 May the Lord make your love *i*

INCREASED (INCREASE)
Ac 6: 7 of disciples in Jerusalem *i* rapidly,
Ro 5:20 But where sin *i*, grace *i* all the more

INCREASES (INCREASE)
Pr 24: 5 and a man of knowledge *i* strength;

INCREASING (INCREASE)
Ac 6: 1 when the number of disciples was *i,*
2Th 1: 3 one of you has for each other is *i.*
2Pe 1: 8 these qualities in *i* measure,

INDEPENDENT*
1Co 11:11 however, woman is not *i* of man,
11:11 of man, nor is man *i* of woman.

INDESCRIBABLE*
2Co 9:15 Thanks be to God for his *i* gift!

INDISPENSABLE*
1Co 12:22 seem to be weaker are *i,*

INEFFECTIVE*
2Pe 1: 8 they will keep you from being *i*

INEXPRESSIBLE*
2Co 12: 4 He heard *i* things, things that man
1Pe 1: 8 are filled with an *i* and glorious joy,

INFANTS
Mt 21:16 " 'From the lips of children and *i*
1Co 14:20 In regard to evil be *i,*

INFIRMITIES
Isa 53: 4 Surely he took up our *i*

INHERIT (CO-HEIRS HEIRS HERITAGE INHERITANCE)
Ps 37:11 But the meek will *i* the land
37:29 the righteous will *i* the land
Mt 5: 5 for they will *i* the earth.
Mk 10:17 "what must I do to *i* eternal life?"
1Co 15:50 blood cannot *i* the kingdom of God

INHERITANCE (INHERIT)
Dt 4:20 to be the people of his *i,*
Pr 13:22 A good man leaves an *i*
Eph 1:14 who is a deposit guaranteeing our *i*
5: 5 has any *i* in the kingdom of Christ
Heb 9:15 receive the promised eternal *i*—
1Pe 1: 4 and into an *i* that can never perish,

INIQUITIES (INIQUITY)
Ps 78:38 he forgave their *i*
103:10 or repay us according to our *i.*
Isa 59: 2 But your *i* have separated
Mic 7:19 and hurl all our *i* into the depths

INIQUITY (INIQUITIES)
Ps 51: 2 Wash away all my *i*
Isa 53: 6 the *i* of us all.

INJUSTICE
2Ch 19: 7 the LORD our God there is no *i*

INNOCENT
Pr 17:26 It is not good to punish an *i* man,
Mt 10:16 shrewd as snakes and as *i* as doves.
27: 4 "for I have betrayed *i* blood."
1Co 4: 4 but that does not make me *i.*

INSCRIPTION
Mt 22:20 And whose *i?"* "Caesar's,"

INSOLENT
Ro 1:30 God-haters, *i,* arrogant

INSTITUTED
Ro 13: 2 rebelling against what God has *i,*
1Pe 2:13 to every authority *i* among men:

INSTRUCT (INSTRUCTION)
Ps 32: 8 I will *i* you and teach you
Pr 9: 9 *I* a wise man and he will be wiser
Ro 15:14 and competent to *i* one another.
2Ti 2:25 who oppose him he must gently *i,*

INSTRUCTION (INSTRUCT)
Pr 1: 8 Listen, my son, to your father's *i*
4: 1 Listen, my sons, to a father's *i;*
4:13 Hold on to *i,* do not let it go;
8:10 Choose my *i* instead of silver,
8:33 Listen to my *i* and be wise;
13: 1 A wise son heeds his father's *i,*
13:13 He who scorns *i* will pay for it,
16:20 Whoever gives heed to *i* prospers,
16:21 and pleasant words promote *i.*
19:20 Listen to advice and accept *i,*
23:12 Apply your heart to *i*
1Co 14: 6 or prophecy or word of *i?*
14:26 or a word of *i,* a revelation,
Eph 6: 4 up in the training and *i* of the Lord.
1Th 4: 8 he who rejects this *i* does not reject
2Th 3:14 If anyone does not obey our *i*
1Ti 1:18 I give you this *i* in keeping
6: 3 to the sound *i* of our Lord Jesus
2Ti 4: 2 with great patience and careful *i.*

INSULT
Pr 9: 7 corrects a mocker invites *i;*
12:16 but a prudent man overlooks an *i.*
Mt 5:11 Blessed are you when people *i* you,
Lk 6:22 when they exclude you and *i* you
1Pe 3: 9 evil with evil or *i* with *i,*

INTEGRITY
1Ki 9: 4 if you walk before me in *i* of heart
Job 2: 3 And he still maintains his *i,*
27: 5 till I die, I will not deny my *i.*
Pr 10: 9 The man of *i* walks securely,
11: 3 The *i* of the upright guides them,
29:10 Bloodthirsty men hate a man of *i*
Tit 2: 7 your teaching show *i,* seriousness

INTELLIGENCE
Isa 29:14 the *i* of the intelligent will vanish."
1Co 1:19 *i* of the intelligent I will frustrate."

INTELLIGIBLE
1Co 14:19 I would rather speak five *i* words

INTERCEDE (INTERCEDES INTERCESSION)
Heb 7:25 he always lives to *i* for them.

INTERCEDES (INTERCEDE)
Ro 8:26 but the Spirit himself *i* for us

INTERCESSION* (INTERCEDE)
Isa 53:12 and made *i* for the transgressors.
1Ti 2: 1 *i* and thanksgiving be made

INTERESTS
1Co 7:34 his wife—and his *i* are divided.
Php 2: 4 only to your own *i,* but also to the *i*
2:21 everyone looks out for his own *i,*

INTERMARRY (MARRY)
Dt 7: 3 Do not *i* with them.

INVENTED*
2Pe 1:16 We did not follow cleverly *i* stories

INVESTIGATED
Lk 1: 3 I myself have carefully *i* everything

INVISIBLE
Ro 1:20 of the world God's *i* qualities—
Col 1:15 He is the image of the *i* God,
1Ti 1:17 immortal, *i,* the only God,

INVITE (INVITED INVITES)
Lk 14:13 you give a banquet, *i* the poor,

INVITED (INVITE)
Mt 22:14 For many are *i,* but few are chosen
25:35 I was a stranger and you *i* me in,

INVITES (INVITE)
1Co 10:27 If some unbeliever *i* you to a meal

INVOLVED
2Ti 2: 4 a soldier gets *i* in civilian affairs—

IRON
1Ti 4: 2 have been seared as with a hot *i.*
Rev 2:27 He will rule them with an *i* scepter;

IRREVOCABLE*
Ro 11:29 for God's gifts and his call are *i.*

ISAAC
Son of Abraham by Sarah (Ge 17:19; 21:1-7; 1Ch 1:28). Offered up by Abraham (Ge 22; Heb 11:17-19). Rebekah taken as wife (Ge 24). Fathered Esau and Jacob (Ge 25:19-26; 1Ch 1:34). Tricked into blessing Jacob (Ge 27). Father of Israel (Ex 3:6; Dt 29:13; Ro 9:10).

ISAIAH
Prophet to Judah (Isa 1:1). Called by the LORD (Isa 6).

ISHMAEL
Son of Abraham by Hagar (Ge 16; 1Ch 1:28). Blessed, but not son of covenant (Ge 17:18-21; Gal 4:21-31). Sent away by Sarah (Ge 21:8-21).

ISRAEL (ISRAELITES)
1. Name given to Jacob (see JACOB).
2. Corporate name of Jacob's descendants; often specifically Northern Kingdom.
Dt 6: 4 Hear, O *I:* The LORD our God,
1Sa 4:21 "The glory has departed from *I"*—
Isa 27: 6 *I* will bud and blossom
Jer 31:10 'He who scattered *I* will gather
Eze 39:23 of *I* went into exile for their sin,
Mk 12:29 'Hear, O *I,* the Lord our God,
Lk 22:30 judging the twelve tribes of *I.*
Ro 9: 6 all who are descended from *I* are *I.*
11:26 And so all *I* will be saved,
Eph 3: 6 Gentiles are heirs together with *I,*

ISRAELITES (ISRAEL)
Ex 14:22 and the *I* went through the sea
16:35 The *I* ate manna forty years,
Hos 1:10 "Yet the *I* will be like the sand
Ro 9:27 the number of the *I* be like the sand

ITCHING*
2Ti 4: 3 to say what their *i* ears want to hear

JACOB
Second son of Isaac, twin of Esau (Ge 26:21-26; 1Ch 1:34). Bought Esau's birthright (Ge 26:29-34); tricked Isaac into blessing him (Ge 27:1-37). Abrahamic covenant perpetuated through (Ge 28:13-15; Mal 1:2). Vision at Bethel (Ge 28:10-22). Wives and children (Ge 29:1-30:24; 35:16-26; 1Ch 2-9). Wrestled with God; name changed to Israel (Ge 32:22-32). Sent sons to Egypt during famine (Ge 42-43). Settled in Egypt (Ge 46). Blessed Ephraim and Manasseh (Ge 48). Blessed sons (Ge 49:1-28; Heb 11:21). Death (Ge 49:29-33). Burial (Ge 50:1-14).

JAMES
1. Apostle; brother of John (Mt 4:21-22; 10:2; Mk 3:17; Lk 5:1-10). At transfiguration (Mt 17:1-13; Mk 9:1-13; Lk 9:28-36). Killed by Herod (Ac 12:2).

2. Apostle; son of Alphaeus (Mt 10:3; Mk 3:18; Lk 6:15).

3. Brother of Jesus (Mt 13:55; Mk 6:3; Lk 24:10; Gal 1:19) and Judas (Jude 1). With believers before Pentecost (Ac 1:13). Leader of church at Jerusalem (Ac 12:17; 15; 21:18; Gal 2:9, 12). Author of epistle (Jas 1:1).

JAPHETH

Son of Noah (Ge 5:32; 1Ch 1:4-5). Blessed (Ge 9:18-28).

JARS

2Co 4: 7 we have this treasure in *j* of clay

JEALOUS (JEALOUSY)

Ex 20: 5 the LORD your God, am a *j* God,
34:14 whose name is Jealous, is a *j* God.
Dt 4:24 God is a consuming fire, a *j* God.
Joel 2:18 the LORD will be *j* for his land
Zec 1:14 I am very *j* for Jerusalem and Zion,
2Co 11: 2 I am *j* for you with a godly jealousy

JEALOUSY (JEALOUS)

1Co 3: 3 For since there is *j* and quarreling
2Co 11: 2 I am jealous for you with a godly *j*.
Gal 5:20 hatred, discord, *j*, fits of rage,

JEHOAHAZ

1. Son of Jehu; king of Israel (2Ki 13:1-9).

2. Son of Josiah; king of Judah (2Ki 23:31-34; 2Ch 36:1-4).

JEHOASH

Son of Jehoahaz; king of Israel (2Ki 13-14; 2Ch 25).

JEHOIACHIN

Son of Jehoiakim; king of Judah exiled by Nebuchadnezzar (2Ki 24:8-17; 2Ch 36:8-10; Jer 22:24-30; 24:1). Raised from prisoner status (2Ki 25:27-30; Jer 52:31-34).

JEHOIAKIM

Son of Josiah; king of Judah (2Ki 23:34-24:6; 2Ch 36:4-8; Jer 22:18-23; 36).

JEHORAM

Son of Jehoshaphat; king of Judah (2Ki 8:16-24).

JEHOSHAPHAT

Son of Asa; king of Judah (1Ki 22:41-50; 2Ki 3; 2Ch 17-20).

JEHU

King of Israel (1Ki 19:16-19; 2Ki 9-10).

JEPHTHAH

Judge from Gilead who delivered Israel from Ammon (Jdg 10:6-12:7). Made rash vow concerning his daughter (Jdg 11:30-40).

JEREMIAH

Prophet to Judah (Jer 1:1-3). Called by the LORD (Jer 1). Put in stocks (Jer 20:1-3). Threatened for prophesying (Jer 11:18-23; 26). Opposed by Hananiah (Jer 28). Scroll burned (Jer 36). Imprisoned (Jer 37). Thrown into cistern (Jer 38). Forced to Egypt with those fleeing Babylonians (Jer 43).

JEROBOAM

1. Official of Solomon; rebelled to become first king of Israel (1Ki 11:26-40; 12:1-20; 2Ch 10). Idolatry (1Ki 12:25-33); judgment for (1Ki 13-14; 2Ch 13).

2. Son of Jehoash; king of Israel (1Ki 14:23-29).

JERUSALEM

2Ki 23:27 and I will reject *J*, the city I chose,
2Ch 6: 6 now I have chosen *J* for my Name
Ne 2:17 Come, let us rebuild the wall of *J*,
Ps 122: 6 Pray for the peace of *J*:
125: 2 As the mountains surround *J*,
137: 5 If I forget you, O *J*,
Isa 40: 9 You who bring good tidings to *J*,
65:18 for I will create *J* to be a delight
Joel 3:17 *J* will be holy;
Zep 3:16 On that day they will say to *J*,
Zec 2: 4 '*J* will be a city without walls
8: 8 I will bring them back to live in *J*;
14: 8 living water will flow out from *J*,
Mt 23:37 "O *J*, *J*, you who kill the prophets
Lk 13:34 die outside *J*! "O *J*, *J*,
21:24 *J* will be trampled
Jn 4:20 where we must worship is in *J*."
Ac 1: 8 and you will be my witnesses in *J*,
Gal 4:25 corresponds to the present city of *J*
Rev 21: 2 I saw the Holy City, the new *J*,

JESUS

LIFE: Genealogy (Mt 1:1-17; Lk 3:21-37). Birth announced (Mt 1:18-25; Lk 1:26-45). Birth (Mt 2:1-12; Lk 2:1-40). Escape to Egypt (Mt 2:13-23). As a boy in the temple (Lk 2:41-52). Baptism (Mt 3:13-17; Mk 1:9-11; Lk 3:21-22; Jn 1:32-34). Temptation (Mt 4:1-11; Mk 1:12-13; Lk 4:1-13). Ministry in Galilee (Mt 4:12-18:35; Mk 1:14-9:50; Lk 4:14-13:9; Jn 1:35-2:11; 4; 6), Transfiguration (Mt 17:1-8; Mk 9:2-8; Lk 9:28-36), on the way to Jerusalem (Mt 19-20; Mk 10; Lk 13:10-19:27), in Jerusalem (Mt 21-25; Mk 11-13; Lk 19:28-21:38; Jn 2:12-3:36; 5; 7-12). Last supper (Mt 26:17-35; Mk 14:12-31; Lk 22:1-38; Jn 13-17). Arrest and trial (Mt 26:36-27:31; Mk 14:43-15:20; Lk 22:39-23:25; Jn 18:1-19:16). Crucifixion (Mt 27:32-66; Mk 15:21-47; Lk 23:26-55; Jn 19:28-42). Resurrection and appearances (Mt 28; Mk 16; Lk 24; Jn 20-21; Ac 1:1-11; 7:56; 9:3-6; 1Co 15:1-8; Rev 1:1-20).

MIRACLES. Healings: official's son (Jn 4:43-54), demoniac in Capernaum (Mk 1:23-26; Lk 4:33-35), Peter's mother-in-law (Mt 8:14-17; Mk 1:29-31; Lk 4:38-39), leper (Mt 8:2-4; Mk 1:40-45; Lk 5:12-16), paralytic (Mt 9:1-8; Mk 2:1-12; Lk 5:17-26), cripple (Jn 5:1-9), shriveled hand (Mt 12:10-13; Mk 3:1-5; Lk 6:6-11), centurion's servant (Mt 8:5-13; Lk 7:1-10), widow's son raised (Lk 7:11-17), demoniac (Mt 12:22-23; Lk 11:14), Gadarene demoniacs (Mt 8:28-34; Mk 5:1-20; Lk 8:26-39), woman's bleeding and Jairus' daughter (Mt 9:18-26; Mk 5:21-43; Lk 8:40-56), blind man (Mt 9:27-31), mute man (Mt 9:32-33), Canaanite woman's daughter (Mt 15:21-28; Mk 7:24-30), deaf man (Mk 7:31-37), blind man (Mk 8:22-26), demoniac boy (Mt 17:14-18; Mk 9:14-29; Lk 9:37-43), ten lepers (Lk 17:11-19), man born blind (Jn 9:1-7), Lazarus raised (Jn 11), crippled woman (Lk 13:11-17), man with dropsy (Lk 14:1-6), two blind men (Mt 20:29-34; Mk 10:46-52; Lk 18:35-43), Malchus' ear (Lk 22:50-51). Other Miracles: water to wine (Jn 2:1-11), catch of fish (Lk 5:1-11), storm stilled (Mt 8:23-27; Mk 4:37-41; Lk 8:22-25), 5,000 fed (Mt 14:15-21; Mk 6:35-44; Lk 9:10-17; Jn 6:1-14), walking on water (Mt 14:25-33; Mk 6:48-52; Jn 6:15-21), 4,000 fed (Mt 15:32-39; Mk 8:1-9), money from fish (Mt 17:24-27), fig tree cursed (Mt 21:18-22; Mk 11:12-14), catch of fish (Jn 21:1-14).

MAJOR TEACHING: Sermon on the Mount (Mt 5-7; Lk 6:17-49), to Nicodemus (Jn 3), to Samaritan woman (Jn 4), Bread of Life (Jn 6:22-59), at Feast of Tabernacles (Jn 7-8); woes to Pharisees (Mt 23; Lk 11:37-54), Good Shepherd (Jn 10:1-18), Olivet Discourse (Mt 24-25; Mk 13; Lk 21:5-36), Upper Room Discourse (Jn 13-16).

PARABLES: Sower (Mt 13:3-23; Mk 4:3-25; Lk 8:5-18), seed's growth (Mk 4:26-29), wheat and weeds (Mt 13:24-30, 36-43), mustard seed (Mt 13:31-32; Mk 4:30-32), yeast (Mt 13:33; Lk 13:20-21), hidden treasure (Mt 13:44), valuable pearl (Mt 13:45-46), net (Mt 13:47-51), house owner (Mt 13:52), good Samaritan (Lk 10:25-37), unmerciful servant (Mt 18:15-35), lost sheep (Mt 18:10-14; Lk 15:4-7), lost coin (Lk 15:8-10), prodigal son (Lk 15:11-32), dishonest manager (Lk 16:1-13), rich man and Lazarus (Lk 16:19-31), persistent widow (Lk 18:1-8), Pharisee and tax collector (Lk 18:9-14), payment of workers (Mt 20:1-16), tenants and the vineyard (Mt 21:28-46; Mk 12:1-12; Lk 20:9-19), wedding banquet (Mt 22:1-14), faithful servant (Mt 24:45-51), ten virgins (Mt 25:1-13), talents (Mt 25:1-30; Lk 19:12-27).

DISCIPLES see APOSTLES. Call of (Jn 1:35-51; Mt 4:18-22; 9:9; Mk 1:16-20; 2:13-14; Lk 5:1-11, 27-28). Named Apostles (Mk 3:13-19; Lk 6:12-16). Twelve sent out (Mt 10; Mk 6:7-11; Lk 9:1-5). Seventy sent out (Lk 10:1-24). Defection of (Jn 6:60-71; Mt 26:56; Mk 14:50-52). Final commission (Mt 28:16-20; Jn 21:15-23; Ac 1:3-8).

Ac 2:32 God has raised this *J* to life,
9: 5 "I am *J*, whom you are persecuting
15:11 of our Lord *J* that we are saved,
16:31 "Believe in the Lord *J*,
Ro 3:24 redemption that came by Christ *J*.
5:17 life through the one man, *J* Christ.
8: 1 for those who are in Christ *J*,
1Co 2: 2 except *J* Christ and him crucified.
8: 6 and there is but one Lord, *J* Christ,
12: 3 and no one can say, "*J* is Lord,"
2Co 4: 5 not preach ourselves, but *J* Christ
Gal 2:16 but by faith in *J* Christ.
3:28 for you are all one in Christ *J*.
5: 6 in Christ *J* neither circumcision
Eph 2:10 created in Christ *J*
2:20 with Christ *J* himself as the chief
Php 1: 6 until the day of Christ *J*.
2: 5 be the same as that of Christ *J*:
2:10 name of *J* every knee should bow,
Col 3:17 do it all in the name of the Lord *J*,
2Th 2: 1 the coming of our Lord *J* Christ
1Ti 1:15 Christ *J* came into the world
2Ti 3:12 life in Christ *J* will be persecuted,
Tit 2:13 our great God and Savior, *J* Christ,
Heb 2: 9 But we see *J*, who was made a little
3: 1 fix your thoughts on *J*, the apostle
4:14 through the heavens, *J* the Son
7:22 *J* has become the guarantee
7:24 but because *J* lives forever,
12: 2 Let us fix our eyes on *J*, the author
2Pe 1:16 and coming of our Lord *J* Christ,
1Jn 1: 7 and the blood of *J*, his Son,
2: 1 *J* Christ, the Righteous One.
2: 6 to live in him must walk as *J* did.
4:15 anyone acknowledges that *J* is
Rev 22:20 Come, Lord *J*.

JEW (JEWS JUDAISM)

Zec 8:23 of one *J* by the edge of his robe
Ro 1:16 first for the *J*, then for the Gentile.
10:12 there is no difference between *J*
1Co 9:20 To the Jews I became like a *J*,
Gal 3:28 There is neither *J* nor Greek,

JEWELRY (JEWELS)

1Pe 3: 3 wearing of gold *j* and fine clothes.

JEWELS (JEWELRY)

Isa 61:10 as a bride adorns herself with her *j*.

Zec 9:16 like *j* in a crown.

JEWS (JEW)
Mt 2: 2 who has been born king of the *J*?
27:11 "Are you the king of the *J*?" "Yes,
Jn 4:22 for salvation is from the *J*.
Ro 3:29 Is God the God of *J* only?
1Co 1:22 *J* demand miraculous signs
9:20 To the *J* I became like a Jew,
12:13 whether *J* or Greeks, slave or free
Gal 2: 8 of Peter as an apostle to the *J*,
Rev 3: 9 claim to be *J* though they are not,

JEZEBEL
Sidonian wife of Ahab (1Ki 16:31). Promoted Baal worship (1Ki 16:32-33). Killed prophets of the LORD (1Ki 18:4, 13). Opposed Elijah (1Ki 19:1-2). Had Naboth killed (1Ki 21). Death prophesied (1Ki 21:17-24). Killed by Jehu (2Ki 9:30-37).

JOASH
Son of Ahaziah; king of Judah. Sheltered from Athaliah by Jehoiada (2Ki 11; 2Ch 22:10-23:21). Repaired temple (2Ki 12; 2Ch 24).

JOB
Wealthy man from Uz; feared God (Job 1:1-5). Righteousness tested by disaster (Job 1:6-22), personal affliction (Job 2). Maintained innocence in debate with three friends (Job 3-31), Elihu (Job 32-37). Rebuked by the LORD (Job 38-41). Vindicated and restored to greater stature by the LORD (Job 42). Example of righteousness (Eze 14:14, 20).

JOHN
1. Son of Zechariah and Elizabeth (Lk 1). Called the Baptist (Mt 3:1-12; Mk 1:2-8). Witness to Jesus (Mt 3:11-12; Mk 1:7-8; Lk 3:15-18; Jn 1:6-35; 3:27-30; 5:33-36). Doubts about Jesus (Mt 11:2-6; Lk 7:18-23). Arrest (Mt 4:12; Mk 1:14). Execution (Mt 14:1-12; Mk 6:14-29; Lk 9:7-9). Ministry compared to Elijah (Mt 11:7-19; Mk 9:11-13; Lk 7:24-35).

2. Apostle; brother of James (Mt 4:21-22; 10:2; Mk 3:17; Lk 5:1-10). At transfiguration (Mt 17:1-13; Mk 9:1-13; Lk 9:28-36). Desire to be greatest (Mk 10:35-45). Leader of church at Jerusalem (Ac 4:1-3; Gal 2:9). Elder who wrote epistles (2Jn 1; 3Jn 1). Prophet who wrote Revelation (Rev 1:1; 22:8).

3. Cousin of Barnabas, co-worker with Paul, (Ac 12:12-13:13; 15:37), see MARK.

JOIN (JOINED)
Pr 23:20 Do not *j* those who drink too much
24:21 and do not *j* with the rebellious,
Ro 15:30 to *j* me in my struggle by praying
2Ti 1: 8 *j* with me in suffering for the gospel

JOINED (JOIN)
Mt 19: 6 Therefore what God has *j* together,
Mk 10: 9 Therefore what God has *j* together,
Eph 2:21 him the whole building is *j* together
4:16 *j* and held together

JOINTS
Heb 4:12 even to dividing soul and spirit, *j*

JOKING
Eph 5: 4 or coarse *j*, which are out of place,

JONAH
Prophet in days of Jeroboam II (2Ki 14:25). Called to Nineveh; fled to Tarshish (Jnh 1:1-3). Cause of storm; thrown into sea (Jnh 1:4-16). Swallowed by fish (Jnh 1:17). Prayer (Jnh 2). Preached to Nineveh (Jnh 3). Attitude reproved by the LORD (Jnh 4). Sign of (Mt 12:39-41; Lk 11:29-32).

JONATHAN
Son of Saul (1Sa 13:16; 1Ch 8:33). Valiant warrior (1Sa 13-14). Relation to David (1Sa 18:1-4; 19-20; 23:16-18). Killed at Gilboa (1Sa 31). Mourned by David (2Sa 1).

JORAM
1. Son of Ahab; king of Israel (2Ki 3; 8-9; 2Ch 22).

JORDAN
Nu 34:12 boundary will go down along the *J*
Jos 4:22 Israel crossed the *J* on dry ground.'
Mt 3: 6 baptized by him in the *J* River.

JOSEPH
1. Son of Jacob by Rachel (Ge 30:24; 1Ch 2:2). Favored by Jacob, hated by brothers (Ge 37:3-4). Dreams (Ge 37:5-11). Sold by brothers (Ge 37:12-36). Served Potiphar; imprisoned by false accusation (Ge 39). Interpreted dreams of Pharaoh's servants (Ge 40), of Pharaoh (Ge 41:4-40). Made greatest in Egypt (Ge 41:41-57). Sold grain to brothers (Ge 42-45). Brought Jacob and sons to Egypt (Ge 46-47). Sons Ephraim and Manasseh blessed (Ge 48). Blessed (Ge 49:22-26; Dt 33:13-17). Death (Ge 50:22-26; Ex 13:19; Heb 11:22). 12,000 from (Rev 7:8).

2. Husband of Mary, mother of Jesus (Mt 1:16-24; 2:13-19; Lk 1:27; 2; Jn 1:45).

3. Disciple from Arimathea, who gave his tomb for Jesus' burial (Mt 27:57-61; Mk 15:43-47; Lk 24:50-52).

4. Original name of Barnabas (Ac 4:36).

JOSHUA
1. Son of Nun; name changed from Hoshea (Nu 13:8, 16; 1Ch 7:27). Fought Amalekites under Moses (Ex 17:9-14). Servant of Moses on Sinai (Ex 24:13; 32:17). Spied Canaan (Nu 13). With Caleb, allowed to enter land (Nu 14:6, 30). Succeeded Moses (Dt 1:38; 31:1-8; 34:9).

Charged Israel to conquer Canaan (Jos 1). Crossed Jordan (Jos 3-4). Circumcised sons of wilderness wanderings (Jos 5). Conquered Jericho (Jos 6), Ai (Jos 7-8), five kings at Gibeon (Jos 10:1-28), southern Canaan (Jos 10:29-43), northern Canaan (Jos 11-12). Defeated at Ai (Jos 7). Deceived by Gibeonites (Jos 9). Renewed covenant (Jos 8:30-35; 24:1-27). Divided land among tribes (Jos 13-22). Last words (Jos 23). Death (Jos 24:28-31).

2. High priest during rebuilding of temple (Hag 1-2; Zec 3:1-9; 6:11).

JOSIAH
Son of Amon; king of Judah (2Ki 22-23; 2Ch 34-35).

JOTHAM
Son of Azariah (Uzziah); king of Judah (2Ki 15:32-38; 2Ch 26:21-27:9).

JOY (ENJOY ENJOYMENT JOYFUL OVERJOYED REJOICE REJOICES REJOICING)
Dt 16:15 and your *j* will be complete.
1Ch 16:27 strength and *j* in his dwelling place.
Ne 8:10 for the *j* of the LORD is your
Est 9:22 their sorrow was turned into *j*
Job 38: 7 and all the angels shouted for *j*?
Ps 4: 7 have filled my heart with greater *j*
21: 6 with the *j* of your presence.
30:11 sackcloth and clothed me with *j*,
43: 4 to God, my *j* and my delight.
Ps 51:12 to me the *j* of your salvation
66: 1 Shout with *j* to God, all the earth!
96:12 the trees of the forest will sing for *j*;
107:22 and tell of his works with songs of *j*
119:111 they are the *j* of my heart.
Pr 10: 1 A wise son brings *j* to his father,
10:28 The prospect of the righteous is *j*,
12:20 but *j* for those who promote peace.
Isa 35:10 everlasting *j* will crown their heads
51:11 Gladness and *j* will overtake them,
55:12 You will go out in *j*
Lk 1:44 the baby in my womb leaped for *j*.
2:10 news of great *j* that will be
Jn 15:11 and that your *j* may be complete.
16:20 but your grief will turn to *j*.
2Co 8: 2 their overflowing *j* and their
Php 2: 2 then make my *j* complete
4: 1 and long for, my *j* and crown,
1Th 2:19 For what is our hope, our *j*,
Phm : 7 Your love has given me great *j*
Heb 12: 2 for the *j* set before him endured
Jas 1: 2 Consider it pure *j*, my brothers,
1Pe 1: 8 with an inexpressible and glorious *j*
2Jn : 4 It has given me great *j* to find some
3Jn : 4 I have no greater *j*

JOYFUL (JOY)
Ps 100: 2 come before him with *j* songs.
Hab 3:18 I will be *j* in God my Savior.
1Th 5:16 Be *j* always; pray continually;

JUDAH
1. Son of Jacob by Leah (Ge 29:35; 35:23; 1Ch 2:1). Tribe of blessed as ruling tribe (Ge 49:8-12; Dt 33:7).

2. Name used for people and land of Southern Kingdom.
Jer 13:19 All *J* will be carried into exile,
Zec 10: 4 From *J* will come the cornerstone,
Heb 7:14 that our Lord descended from *J*,

JUDAISM (JEW)
Gal 1:13 of my previous way of life in *J*,

JUDAS
1. Apostle (Lk 6:16; Jn 14:22; Ac 1:13). Probably also called Thaddaeus (Mt 10:3; Mk 3:18).

2. Brother of James and Jesus (Mt 13:55; Mk 6:3), also called Jude (Jude 1).

3. Apostle, also called Iscariot, who betrayed Jesus (Mt 10:4; 26:14-56; Mk 3:19; 14:10-50; Lk 6:16; 22:3-53; Jn 6:71; 12:4; 13:2-30; 18:2-11). Suicide of (Mt 27:3-5; Ac 1:16-25).

JUDGE (JUDGED JUDGES JUDGING JUDGMENT)
Ge 18:25 Will not the *J* of all the earth do
1Ch 16:33 for he comes to *j* the earth.
Ps 9: 8 He will *j* the world in righteousness
Joel 3:12 sit to *j* all the nations on every side.
Mt 7: 1 Do not *j*, or you too will be judged.
Jn 12:47 For I did not come to *j* the world,
Ac 17:31 a day when he will *j* the world
Ro 2:16 day when God will *j* men's secrets
1Co 4: 3 indeed, I do not even *j* myself.
6: 2 that the saints will *j* the world?
Gal 2: 6 not *j* by external appearance—
2Ti 4: 1 who will *j* the living and the dead,
4: 8 which the Lord, the righteous *J*,
Jas 4:12 There is only one Lawgiver and *J*,
4:12 who are you to *j* your neighbor?
Rev 20: 4 who had been given authority to *j*.

JUDGED (JUDGE)
Mt 7: 1 "Do not judge, or you too will be *j*.
1Co 11:31 But if we *j* ourselves, we would not
Jas 3: 1 who teach will be *j* more strictly.
Rev 20:12 The dead were *j* according

JUDGES (JUDGE)
Jdg 2:16 Then the LORD raised up *j*,
Ps 58:11 there is a God who *j* the earth."
Heb 4:12 it *j* the thoughts and attitudes
Rev 19:11 With justice he *j* and makes war.

JUDGING (JUDGE)
Mt 19:28 *j* the twelve tribes of Israel.
Jn 7:24 Stop *j* by mere appearances,

JUDGMENT (JUDGE)
Dt 1:17 of any man, for *j* belongs to God.
Ps 1: 5 the wicked will not stand in the *j*,
119:66 Teach me knowledge and good *j*,
Pr 6:32 man who commits adultery lacks *j*;
12:11 but he who chases fantasies lacks *j*.
Ecc 12:14 God will bring every deed into *j*,
Isa 66:16 the LORD will execute *j*
Mt 5:21 who murders will be subject to *j*.'
10:15 on the day of *j* than for that town.
12:36 have to give account on the day of *j*
Jn 5:22 but has entrusted all *j* to the Son,
7:24 appearances, and make a right *j*."
16: 8 to sin and righteousness and *j*:
Ro 14:10 stand before God's *j* seat.
14:13 Therefore let us stop passing *j*
1Co 11:29 body of the Lord eats and drinks *j*
2Co 5:10 appear before the *j* seat of Christ,
Heb 9:27 to die once, and after that to face *j*,
10:27 but only a fearful expectation of *j*
1Pe 4:17 For it is time for *j* to begin
Jude : 6 bound with everlasting chains for *j*

JUST (JUSTICE JUSTIFICATION JUSTIFIED JUSTIFY JUSTLY)
Dt 32: 4 and all his ways are *j*.
Ps 37:28 For the LORD loves the *j*
111: 7 of his hands are faithful and *j*;
Pr 1: 3 doing what is right and *j* and fair;
2: 8 for he guards the course of the *j*
Da 4:37 does is right and all his ways are *j*.
Ro 3:26 as to be *j* and the one who justifies
Heb 2: 2 received its *j* punishment,
1Jn 1: 9 and *j* and will forgive us our sins
Rev 16: 7 true and *j* are your judgments."

JUSTICE (JUST)
Ex 23: 2 do not pervert *j* by siding
23: 6 "Do not deny *j* to your poor people
Job 37:23 in his *j* and great righteousness,
Ps 9: 8 he will govern the peoples with *j*.
9:16 The LORD is known by his *j*;
11: 7 he loves *j*;
45: 6 a scepter of *j* will be the scepter
101: 1 I will sing of your love and *j*;
106: 3 Blessed are they who maintain *j*,
Pr 21:15 When *j* is done, it brings joy
28: 5 Evil men do not understand *j*,
29: 4 By *j* a king gives a country stability
29:26 from the LORD that man gets *j*.
Isa 9: 7 it with *j* and righteousness
28:17 I will make *j* the measuring line
30:18 For the LORD is a God of *j*.
42: 1 and he will bring *j* to the nations.
42: 4 till he establishes *j* on earth.
56: 1 "Maintain *j*
61: 8 "For I, the LORD, love *j*;
Jer 30:11 I will discipline you but only with *j*;
Eze 34:16 I will shepherd the flock with *j*.
Am 5:15 maintain *j* in the courts.
5:24 But let *j* roll on like a river,
Zec 7: 9 'Administer true *j*; show mercy
Lk 11:42 you neglect *j* and the love of God.
Ro 3:25 He did this to demonstrate his *j*,

JUSTIFICATION (JUST)
Ro 4:25 and was raised to life for our *j*.
5:18 of righteousness was *j* that brings

JUSTIFIED (JUST)
Ac 13:39 him everyone who believes is *j*
Ro 3:24 and are *j* freely by his grace
3:28 For we maintain that a man is *j*
5: 1 since we have been *j* through faith,
5: 9 Since we have now been *j*
8:30 those he called, he also *j*; those he *j*,
1Co 6:11 you were *j* in the name
Gal 2:16 observing the law no one will be *j*.
3:11 Clearly no one is *j* before God
3:24 to Christ that we might be *j* by faith
Jas 2:24 You see that a person is *j*

JUSTIFY (JUST)
Gal 3: 8 that God would *j* the Gentiles

JUSTLY (JUST)
Mic 6: 8 To act *j* and to love mercy

KEEP (KEEPER KEEPING KEEPS KEPT)
Ge 31:49 "May the LORD *k* watch
Ex 20: 6 and *k* my commandments.
Nu 6:24 and *k* you;
Ps 18:28 You, O LORD, *k* my lamp burning
19:13 *K* your servant also from willful
119: 9 can a young man *k* his way pure?
121: 7 The LORD will *k* you
141: 3 *k* watch over the door of my lips.
Pr 4:24 *k* corrupt talk far from your lips.
Isa 26: 3 You will *k* in perfect peace
Mt 10:10 for the worker is worth his *k*.
Lk 12:35 and *k* your lamps burning,
Gal 5:25 let us *k* in step with the Spirit.
Eph 4: 3 Make every effort to *k* the unity
1Ti 5:22 *K* yourself pure.
2Ti 4: 5 *k* your head in all situations,
Heb 13: 5 *K* your lives free from the love
Jas 1:26 and yet does not *k* a tight rein
2: 8 If you really *k* the royal law found
Jude :24 able to *k* you from falling

KEEPER (KEEP)
Ge 4: 9 I my brother's *k*?" The LORD

KEEPING (KEEP)
Ex 20: 8 the Sabbath day by *k* it holy.
Ps 19:11 in *k* them there is great reward.
Mt 3: 8 Produce fruit in *k* with repentance.
Lk 2: 8 *k* watch over their flocks at night.
1Co 7:19 *K* God's commands is what counts.
2Pe 3: 9 Lord is not slow in *k* his promise,

KEEPS (KEEP)
Pr 17:28 a fool is thought wise if he *k* silent,
Am 5:13 Therefore the prudent man *k* quiet
1Co 13: 5 is not easily angered, it *k* no record
Jas 2:10 For whoever *k* the whole law

KEPT (KEEP)
Ps 130: 3 If you, O LORD, *k* a record of sins,
2Ti 4: 7 finished the race, I have *k* the faith.
1Pe 1: 4 spoil or fade—*k* in heaven for you,

KEYS
Mt 16:19 I will give you the *k* of the kingdom

KILL (KILLS)
Mt 17:23 They will *k* him, and on the third

KILLS (KILL)
Lev 24:21 but whoever *k* a man must be put
2Co 3: 6 for the letter *k*, but the Spirit gives

KIND (KINDNESS KINDS)
Ge 1:24 animals, each according to its *k*."
2Ch 10: 7 "If you will be *k* to these people
Pr 11:17 A *k* man benefits himself,
12:25 but a *k* word cheers him up.
14:21 blessed is he who is *k* to the needy.
14:31 whoever is *k* to the needy honors
19:17 He who is *k* to the poor lends
Da 4:27 by being *k* to the oppressed.
Lk 6:35 because he is *k* to the ungrateful
1Co 13: 4 Love is patient, love is *k*.
15:35 With what *k* of body will they
Eph 4:32 Be *k* and compassionate
1Th 5:15 but always try to be *k* to each other
2Ti 2:24 instead, he must be *k* to everyone,
Tit 2: 5 to be busy at home, to be *k*,

KINDNESS (KIND)
Ac 14:17 He has shown *k* by giving you rain
Ro 11:22 Consider therefore the *k*
Gal 5:22 peace, patience, *k*, goodness,
Eph 2: 7 expressed in his *k* to us
2Pe 1: 7 brotherly *k*; and to brotherly *k*,

KINDS (KIND)
1Co 12: 4 There are different *k* of gifts,
1Ti 6:10 of money is a root of all *k* of evil.

KING (KINGDOM KINGS)
1. Kings of Judah and Israel: see Saul, David, Solomon.
2. Kings of Judah: see Rehoboam, Abijah, Asa, Jehoshaphat, Jehoram, Ahaziah, Athaliah (Queen), Joash, Amaziah, Uzziah, Jotham, Ahaz, Hezekiah, Manasseh, Amon, Josiah, Jehoahaz, Jehoiakim, Jehoiachin, Zedekiah.
3. Kings of Israel: see Jeroboam I, Nadab, Baasha, Elah, Zimri, Tibni, Omri, Ahab, Ahaziah, Joram, Jehu, Jehoahaz, Jehoash, Jeroboam II, Zechariah, Shallum, Menahem, Pekah, Pekahiah, Hoshea.
Jdg 17: 6 In those days Israel had no *k*;
1Sa 12:12 the LORD your God was your *k*.
Ps 24: 7 that the *K* of glory may come in.
Isa 32: 1 See, a *k* will reign in righteousness
Zec 9: 9 See, your *k* comes to you,
1Ti 6:15 the *K* of kings and Lord of lords,
1Pe 2:17 of believers, fear God, honor the *k*.
Rev 19:16 *K* OF KINGS AND LORD

KINGDOM (KING)
Ex 19: 6 you will be for me a *k* of priests
1Ch 29:11 Yours, O LORD, is the *k*;
Ps 45: 6 justice will be the scepter of your *k*.
Da 4: 3 His *k* is an eternal *k*;
Mt 3: 2 Repent, for the *k* of heaven is near
5: 3 for theirs is the *k* of heaven.
6:10 your *k* come,
6:33 But seek first his *k* and his
7:21 Lord,' will enter the *k* of heaven,
11:11 least in the *k* of heaven is greater
13:24 "The *k* of heaven is like a man who
13:31 *k* of heaven is like a mustard seed,
13:33 "The *k* of heaven is like yeast that
13:44 *k* of heaven is like treasure hidden
13:45 the *k* of heaven is like a merchant
13:47 *k* of heaven is like a net that was let
16:19 the keys of the *k* of heaven;
18:23 the *k* of heaven is like a king who
19:24 for a rich man to enter the *k* of God
24: 7 rise against nation, and *k* against *k*.
24:14 gospel of the *k* will be preached
25:34 the *k* prepared for you
Mk 9:47 better for you to enter the *k* of God
10:14 for the *k* of God belongs to such
10:23 for the rich to enter the *k* of God!"
Lk 10: 9 'The *k* of God is near you.'
12:31 seek his *k*, and these things will be
17:21 because the *k* of God is within you
Jn 3: 5 no one can enter the *k* of God
18:36 "My *k* is not of this world.
1Co 6: 9 the wicked will not inherit the *k*
15:24 hands over the *k* to God the Father

LASTS (LAST)
Ps 30: 5 For his anger *l* only a moment,
2Co 3:11 greater is the glory of that which *l!*

LATTER (LAST)
Job 42:12 The LORD blessed the *l* part

LAUGH (LAUGHS)
Ecc 3: 4 a time to weep and a time to *l,*

LAUGHS (LAUGH)
Ps 2: 4 The One enthroned in heaven *l;*
37:13 but the Lord *l* at the wicked,

LAVISHED
Eph 1: 8 of God's grace that he *l* on us
1Jn 3: 1 great is the love the Father has *l*

LAW (LAWS)
Dt 31:11 you shall read this *l* before them
31:26 "Take this Book of the *L*
Jos 1: 8 of the *L* depart from your mouth;
Ne 8: 8 from the Book of the *L* of God,
Ps 1: 2 and on his *l* he meditates day
19: 7 The *l* of the LORD is perfect,
119:18 wonderful things in your *l.*
119:72 *l* from your mouth is more precious
119:97 Oh, how I love your *l!*
119:165 peace have they who love your *l,*
Isa 8:20 To the *l* and to the testimony!
Jer 31:33 "I will put my *l* in their minds
Mt 5:17 that I have come to abolish the *L*
7:12 sums up the *L* and the Prophets.
22:40 All the *L* and the Prophets hang
Lk 16:17 stroke of a pen to drop out of the *L.*
Jn 1:17 For the *l* was given through Moses;
Ro 2:12 All who sin apart from the *l* will
2:15 of the *l* are written on their hearts,
5:13 for before the *l* was given,
5:20 *l* was added so that the trespass
6:14 because you are not under *l,*
7: 6 released from the *l* so that we serve
7:12 *l* is holy, and the commandment is
8: 3 For what the *l* was powerless to do
10: 4 Christ is the end of the *l*
13:10 love is the fulfillment of the *l.*
Gal 3:13 curse of the *l* by becoming a curse
3:24 So the *l* was put in charge to lead us
5: 3 obligated to obey the whole *l.*
5: 4 justified by *l* have been alienated
5:14 The entire *l* is summed up
Heb 7:19 (for the *l* made nothing perfect),
10: 1 The *l* is only a shadow
Jas 1:25 intently into the perfect *l* that gives
2:10 For whoever keeps the whole *l*

LAWLESSNESS*
2Th 2: 3 and the man of *l* is revealed,
2: 7 power of *l* is already at work;
1Jn 3: 4 sins breaks the law; in fact, sin is *l.*

LAWS (LAW)
Lev 25:18 and be careful to obey my *l,*
Ps 119:30 I have set my heart on your *l.*
119:120 I stand in awe of your *l.*
Heb 8:10 I will put my *l* in their minds
10:16 I will put my *l* in their hearts,

LAY (LAID LAYING)
Job 22:22 and *l* up his words in your heart.
Isa 28:16 "See, I *l* a stone in Zion,
Mt 8:20 of Man has no place to *l* his head."
Jn 10:15 and I *l* down my life for the sheep.
15:13 that he *l* down his life
1Co 3:11 no one can *l* any foundation other
1Jn 3:16 And we ought to *l* down our lives
Rev 4:10 They *l* their crowns

LAYING (LAY)
1Ti 5:22 Do not be hasty in the *l* on of hands
Heb 6: 1 not *l* again the foundation

LAZARUS
1. Poor man in Jesus' parable (Lk 16:19-31).
2. Brother of Mary and Martha whom Jesus raised from the dead (Jn 11:1-12:19).

LAZY
Pr 10: 4 *L* hands make a man poor,
Heb 6:12 We do not want you to become *l,*

LEAD (LEADERS LEADERSHIP LEADS LED)
Ex 15:13 "In your unfailing love you will *l*
Ps 27:11 *l* me in a straight path
61: 2 *l* me to the rock that is higher
139:24 and *l* me in the way everlasting.
143:10 *l* me on level ground.
Ecc 5: 6 Do not let your mouth *l* you
Isa 11: 6 and a little child will *l* them.
Da 12: 3 those who *l* many to righteousness,
Mt 6:13 And *l* us not into temptation,
1Jn 3: 7 do not let anyone *l* you astray.

LEADERS (LEAD)
Heb 13: 7 Remember your *l,* who spoke
13:17 Obey your *l* and submit

LEADERSHIP (LEAD)
Ro 12: 8 if it is *l,* let him govern diligently;

LEADS (LEAD)
Ps 23: 2 he *l* me beside quiet waters,
Pr 19:23 The fear of the LORD *l* to life:
Isa 40:11 he gently *l* those that have young.
Mt 7:13 and broad is the road that *l*
15:14 If a blind man *l* a blind man,
Jn 10: 3 sheep by name and *l* them out.
Ro 14:19 effort to do what *l* to peace
2Co 2:14 always *l* us in triumphal procession

LEAH
Wife of Jacob (Ge 29:16-30); bore six sons and one daughter (Ge 29:31-30:21; 34:1; 35:23).

LEAN
Pr 3: 5 *l* not on your own understanding;

LEARN (LEARNED LEARNING)
Isa 1:17 *l* to do right!
Mt 11:29 yoke upon you and *l* from me,

LEARNED (LEARN)
Php 4:11 for I have *l* to be content whatever
2Ti 3:14 continue in what you have *l*

LEARNING (LEARN)
Pr 1: 5 let the wise listen and add to their *l,*
2Ti 3: 7 always *l* but never able

LED (LEAD)
Ps 68:18 you *l* captives in your train;
Isa 53: 7 he was *l* like a lamb to the slaughter
Am 2:10 and I *l* you forty years in the desert
Ro 8:14 those who are *l* by the Spirit
Eph 4: 8 he *l* captives in his train

LEFT
Jos 1: 7 turn from it to the right or to the *l,*
Pr 4:27 Do not swerve to the right or the *l;*
Mt 6: 3 do not let your *l* hand know what
25:33 on his right and the goats on his *l.*

LEGION
Mk 5: 9 "My name is *L,*" he replied,

LEND (LENDS)
Dt 15: 8 freely *l* him whatever he needs.
Ps 37:26 are always generous and *l* freely;
Lk 6:34 if you *l* to those from whom you

LENDS (LEND)
Pr 19:17 to the poor *l* to the LORD,

LENGTH (LONG)
Ps 90:10 The *l* of our days is seventy years—
Pr 10:27 The fear of the LORD adds *l* to life

LEPROSY
2Ki 7: 3 men with *l* at the entrance

LETTER (LETTERS)
Mt 5:18 not the smallest *l,* not the least
2Co 3: 2 You yourselves are our *l,* written
3: 6 for the *l* kills, but the Spirit gives
2Th 3:14 not obey our instruction in this *l,*

LETTERS (LETTER)
2Co 3: 7 which was engraved in *l* on stone,
10:10 "His *l* are weighty and forceful,
2Pe 3:16 His *l* contain some things that are

LEVEL
Ps 143:10 lead me on *l* ground.
Pr 4:26 Make *l* paths for your feet
Isa 26: 7 The path of the righteous is *l;*
Heb 12:13 "Make *l* paths for your feet,"

LEVI (LEVITES)
1. Son of Jacob by Leah (Ge 29:34; 46:11; 1Ch 2:1). Tribe of blessed (Ge 49:5-7; Dt 33:8-11), chosen as priests (Nu 3-4), numbered (Nu 3:39; 26:62), allotted cities, but not land (Nu 18; 35; Dt 10:9; Jos 13:14; 21), land (Eze 48:8-22), 12,000 from (Rev 7:7).
2. See MATTHEW.

LEVITES (LEVI)
Nu 1:53 The *L* are to be responsible
8: 6 "Take the *L* from among the other
18:21 I give to the *L* all the tithes in Israel

LEWDNESS
Mk 7:22 malice, deceit, *l,* envy, slander,

LIAR (LIE)
Pr 19:22 better to be poor than a *l.*
Jn 8:44 for he is a *l* and the father of lies.
Ro 3: 4 Let God be true, and every man a *l.*

LIBERATED*
Ro 8:21 that the creation itself will be *l*

LIE (LIAR LIED LIES LYING)
Lev 19:11 " 'Do not *l.*
Nu 23:19 God is not a man, that he should *l,*
Dt 6: 7 when you *l* down and when you get
Ps 23: 2 me *l* down in green pastures,
Isa 11: 6 leopard will *l* down with the goat,
Eze 34:14 they will *l* down in good grazing
Ro 1:25 exchanged the truth of God for a *l,*
Col 3: 9 Do not *l* to each other,
Heb 6:18 which it is impossible for God to *l,*

LIED (LIE)
Ac 5: 4 You have not *l* to men but to God."

LIES (LIE)
Ps 34:13 and your lips from speaking *l.*
Jn 8:44 for he is a liar and the father of *l.*

LIFE (LIVE)
Ge 2: 7 into his nostrils the breath of *l,*
2: 9 of the garden were the tree of *l*

Ge 9:11 Never again will all *l* be cut
Ex 21:23 you are to take *l* for *l,* eye for eye,
Lev 17:14 the *l* of every creature is its blood.
24:18 must make restitution—*l* for *l.*
Dt 30:19 Now choose *l,* so that you
Ps 16:11 known to me the path of *l;*
23: 6 all the days of my *l,*
34:12 Whoever of you loves *l*
39: 4 let me know how fleeting is my *l.*
49: 7 No man can redeem the *l*
104:33 I will sing to the LORD all my *l;*
Pr 1: 3 a disciplined and prudent *l,*
6:23 are the way to *l,*
7:23 little knowing it will cost him his *l.*
8:35 For whoever finds me finds *l*
11:30 of the righteous is a tree of *l,*
21:21 finds *l,* prosperity and honor.
Jer 10:23 that a man's *l* is not his own;
Eze 37: 5 enter you, and you will come to *l.*
Da 12: 2 some to everlasting *l,* others
Mt 6:25 Is not *l* more important than food,
7:14 and narrow the road that leads to *l,*
10:39 Whoever finds his *l* will lose it,
16:25 wants to save his *l* will lose it,
20:28 to give his *l* as a ransom for many."
Mk 10:45 to give his *l* as a ransom for many."
Lk 12:15 a man's *l* does not consist
12:22 do not worry about your *l,*
14:26 even his own *l*— he cannot be my
Jn 1: 4 In him was *l,* and that *l* was
3:15 believes in him may have eternal *l.*
3:36 believes in the Son has eternal *l,*
4:14 of water welling up to eternal *l."*
5:24 him who sent me has eternal *l*
6:35 Jesus declared, "I am the bread of *l*
6:47 he who believes has everlasting *l.*
6:68 You have the words of eternal *l.*
10:10 I have come that they may have *l,*
10:15 and I lay down my *l* for the sheep.
10:28 I give them eternal *l,* and they shall
11:25 "I am the resurrection and the *l.*
14: 6 am the way and the truth and the *l.*
15:13 lay down his *l* for his friends.
20:31 that by believing you may have *l*
Ac 13:48 appointed for eternal *l* believed.
Ro 4:25 was raised to *l* for our justification.
6:13 have been brought from death to *l;*
6:23 but the gift of God is eternal *l*
8:38 convinced that neither death nor *l,*
1Co 15:19 If only for this *l* we have hope
2Co 3: 6 letter kills, but the Spirit gives *l.*
Gal 2:20 The *l* I live in the body, I live
Eph 4: 1 I urge you to live a *l* worthy
Php 2:16 as you hold out the word of *l*—
Col 1:10 order that you may live a *l* worthy
1Th 4:12 so that your daily *l* may win
1Ti 4: 8 for both the present *l* and the *l*
4:16 Watch your *l* and doctrine closely.
6:19 hold of the *l* that is truly *l.*
2Ti 3:12 to live a godly *l* in Christ Jesus will
Jas 1:12 crown of *l* that God has promised
3:13 Let him show it by his good *l,*
1Pe 3:10 "Whoever would love *l*
2Pe 1: 3 given us everything we need for *l*
1Jn 3:14 we have passed from death to *l,*
5:11 has given us eternal *l,* and this *l* is
Rev 13: 8 written in the book of *l* belonging
20:12 was opened, which is the book of *l.*
21:27 written in the Lamb's book of *l.*
22: 2 side of the river stood the tree of *l,*

LIFT (LIFTED)
Ps 121: 1 I *l* up my eyes to the hills—
134: 2 *L* up your hands in the sanctuary
La 3:41 Let us *l* up our hearts and our
1Ti 2: 8 everywhere to *l* up holy hands

LIFTED (LIFT)
Ps 40: 2 He *l* me out of the slimy pit,
Jn 3:14 Moses *l* up the snake in the desert,
12:32 when I am *l* up from the earth,

LIGHT (ENLIGHTENED)
Ge 1: 3 "Let there be *l,"* and there was *l.*
2Sa 22:29 LORD turns my darkness into *l.*
Job 38:19 "What is the way to the abode of *l?*
Ps 4: 6 Let the *l* of your face shine upon us
19: 8 giving *l* to the eyes.
27: 1 LORD is my *l* and my salvation—
56:13 God in the *l* of life.
76: 4 You are resplendent with *l,*
104: 2 He wraps himself in *l*
119:105 and a *l* for my path.
119:130 The unfolding of your words gives *l;*
Isa 2: 5 let us walk in the *l* of the LORD.
9: 2 have seen a great *l;*
49: 6 also make you a *l* for the Gentiles,
Mt 4:16 have seen a great *l;*
5:16 let your *l* shine before men,
11:30 yoke is easy and my burden is *l."*
Jn 3:19 but men loved darkness instead of *l*
8:12 he said, "I am the *l* of the world.
2Co 4: 6 made his *l* shine in our hearts
6:14 Or what fellowship can *l* have
11:14 masquerades as an angel of *l.*
1Ti 6:16 and who lives in unapproachable *l,*
1Pe 2: 9 of darkness into his wonderful *l.*
1Jn 1: 5 God is *l;* in him there is no
1: 7 But if we walk in the *l,*
Rev 21:23 for the glory of God gives it *l,*

LIGHTNING
Da 10: 6 his face like *l,* his eyes like flaming
Mt 24:27 For as the *l* that comes from the east
28: 3 His appearance was like *l,*

LIKENESS
Ge 1:26 man in our image, in our *l,*
Ps 17:15 I will be satisfied with seeing your *l*
Isa 52:14 his form marred beyond human *l*—
Ro 8: 3 Son in the *l* of sinful man
8:29 to be conformed to the *l* of his Son,
2Co 3:18 his *l* with ever-increasing glory,
Php 2: 7 being made in human *l.*
Jas 3: 9 who have been made in God's *l.*

LILIES
Lk 12:27 "Consider how the *l* grow.

LION
Isa 11: 7 and the *l* will eat straw like the ox.
1Pe 5: 8 around like a roaring *l* looking
Rev 5: 5 See, the *L* of the tribe of Judah,

LIPS
Ps 8: 2 From the *l* of children and infants
34: 1 his praise will always be on my *l.*
119:171 May my *l* overflow with praise,
Pr 13: 3 He who guards his *l* guards his life,
27: 2 someone else, and not your own *l.*
Isa 6: 5 For I am a man of unclean *l,*
Mt 21:16 " 'From the *l* of children
Col 3: 8 and filthy language from your *l.*

LISTEN (LISTENING LISTENS)
Dt 30:20 *l* to his voice, and hold fast to him.
Pr 1: 5 let the wise *l* and add
Jn 10:27 My sheep *l* to my voice; I know
Jas 1:19 Everyone should be quick to *l,*
1:22 Do not merely *l* to the word,

LISTENING (LISTEN)
1Sa 3: 9 Speak, LORD, for your servant is *l*
Pr 18:13 He who answers before *l*—

LISTENS (LISTEN)
Pr 12:15 but a wise man *l* to advice.

LIVE (ALIVE LIFE LIVES LIVING)
Ex 20:12 so that you may *l* long
33:20 for no one may see me and *l."*
Dt 8: 3 to teach you that man does not *l*
Job 14:14 If a man dies, will he *l* again?
Ps 119:175 Let me *l* that I may praise you,
Isa 55: 3 hear me, that your soul may *l.*
Eze 37: 3 can these bones *l?"* I said,
Hab 2: 4 but the righteous will *l* by his faith
Mt 4: 4 'Man does not *l* on bread alone,
Ac 17:24 does not *l* in temples built by hands
17:28 'For in him we *l* and move
Ro 1:17 "The righteous will *l* by faith."
2Co 5: 7 We *l* by faith, not by sight.
Gal 2:20 The life I *l* in the body, I *l* by faith
5:25 Since we *l* by the Spirit, let us keep
Php 1:21 to *l* is Christ and to die is gain.
1Th 5:13 *L* in peace with each other.
2Ti 3:12 who wants to *l* a godly life
Heb 12:14 Make every effort to *l* in peace
1Pe 1:17 *l* your lives as strangers here

LIVES (LIVE)
Job 19:25 I know that my Redeemer *l,*
Isa 57:15 he who *l* forever, whose name is
Da 3:28 to give up their *l* rather than serve
Jn 14:17 for he *l* with you and will be in you.
Ro 7:18 I know that nothing good *l* in me,
14: 7 For none of us *l* to himself alone
1Co 3:16 and that God's Spirit *l* in you?
Gal 2:20 I no longer live, but Christ *l* in me.
Heb 13: 5 Keep your *l* free from the love
2Pe 3:11 You ought to live holy and godly *l*
1Jn 3:16 to lay down our *l* for our brothers.
4:16 Whoever *l* in love *l* in God,

LIVING (LIVE)
Ge 2: 7 and man became a *l* being.
Jer 2:13 the spring of *l* water,
Mt 22:32 the God of the dead but of the *l."*
Jn 7:38 streams of *l* water will flow
Ro 12: 1 to offer your bodies as *l* sacrifices,
Heb 4:12 For the word of God is *l* and active.
10:31 to fall into the hands of the *l* God.
Rev 1:18 I am the *L* One; I was dead,

LOAD
Gal 6: 5 for each one should carry his own *l.*

LOCUSTS
Mt 3: 4 His food was *l* and wild honey.

LOFTY
Ps 139: 6 too *l* for me to attain.
Isa 57:15 is what the high and *l* One says—

LONELY
Ps 68: 6 God sets the *l* in families,

LONG (LENGTH LONGED LONGING LONGS)
1Ki 18:21 "How *l* will you waver
Jn 9: 4 As *l* as it is day, we must do
Eph 3:18 to grasp how wide and *l* and high
1Pe 1:12 Even angels *l* to look

LONGED (LONG)
Mt 13:17 righteous men *l* to see what you see
23:37 how often I have *l*
2Ti 4: 8 to all who have *l* for his appearing.

LONGING (LONG)
Pr 13:19 A *l* fulfilled is sweet to the soul,
2Co 5: 2 *l* to be clothed with our heavenly

LONGS (LONG)
Isa 30:18 Yet the LORD *l* to be gracious

LOOK (LOOKING LOOKS)
Dt 4:29 you will find him if you *l* for him
Job 31: 1 not to *l* lustfully at a girl.
Ps 34: 5 Those who *l* to him are radiant;
Pr 4:25 Let your eyes *l* straight ahead,
Isa 60: 5 Then you will *l* and be radiant,
Hab 1:13 Your eyes are too pure to *l* on evil;
Zec 12:10 They will *l* on me, the one they
Mk 13:21 '*L*, here is the Christ!' or, '*L*,
Lk 24:39 *L* at my hands and my feet.
Jn 1:36 he said, "*L*, the Lamb of God!"
4:35 open your eyes and *l* at the fields!
19:37 "They will *l* on the one they have
Jas 1:27 to *l* after orphans and widows
1Pe 1:12 long to *l* into these things.

LOOKING (LOOK)
2Co 10: 7 You are *l* only on the surface
Rev 5: 6 I saw a Lamb, *l* as if it had been

LOOKS (LOOK)
1Sa 16: 7 Man *l* at the outward appearance,
Lk 9:62 and *l* back is fit for service
Php 2:21 For everyone *l* out

LORD† (LORD'S† LORDING)
Ne 4:14 Remember the *L*, who is great
Job 28:28 'The fear of the *L*— that is wisdom,
Ps 54: 4 the *L* is the one who sustains me.
62:12 and that you, O *L*, are loving.
86: 5 You are forgiving and good, O *L*,
110: 1 The LORD says to my *L*:
147: 5 Great is our *L* and mighty in power
Isa 6: 1 I saw the *L* seated on a throne,
Da 9: 4 "O *L*, the great and awesome God,
Mt 3: 3 'Prepare the way for the *L*,
4: 7 'Do not put the *L* your God
7:21 "Not everyone who says to me, '*L*,
22:37 " 'Love the *L* your God
22:44 For he says, " 'The *L* said to my *L*:
Mk 12:11 the *L* has done this,
12:29 the *L* our God, the *L* is one.
Lk 2: 9 glory of the *L* shone around them,
6:46 "Why do you call me, '*L*, *L*,'
10:27 " 'Love the *L* your God
Ac 2:21 on the name of the *L* will be saved.'
16:31 replied, "Believe in the *L* Jesus,
Ro 10: 9 with your mouth, "Jesus is *L*,"
10:13 on the name of the *L* will be saved
12:11 your spiritual fervor, serving the *L*.
14: 8 we live to the *L*; and if we die,
1Co 1:31 Let him who boasts boast in the *L*."
3: 5 the *L* has assigned to each his task.
7:34 to be devoted to the *L* in both body
10: 9 We should not test the *L*,
11:23 For I received from the *L* what I
12: 3 "Jesus is *L*," except by the Holy
15:57 victory through our *L* Jesus Christ.
16:22 If anyone does not love the *L*—
2Co 3:17 Now the *L* is the Spirit,
8: 5 they gave themselves first to the *L*
10:17 Let him who boasts boast in the *L*."
Gal 6:14 in the cross of our *L* Jesus Christ,
Eph 4: 5 one *L*, one faith, one baptism;
5:10 and find out what pleases the *L*.
5:19 make music in your heart to the *L*,
Php 2:11 confess that Jesus Christ is *L*,
3: 1 my brothers, rejoice in the *L*!
4: 4 Rejoice in the *L* always.
Col 2: 6 as you received Christ Jesus as *L*,
3:17 do it all in the name of the *L* Jesus,
3:23 as working for the *L*, not for men,
4:17 work you have received in the *L*."
1Th 3:12 May the *L* make your love increase
5: 2 day of the *L* will come like a thief
1Th 5:23 at the coming of our *L* Jesus Christ.
2Th 2: 1 the coming of our *L* Jesus Christ
2Ti 2:19 "The *L* knows those who are his,"
Heb 12:14 holiness no one will see the *L*.
13: 6 *L* is my helper; I will not be afraid.
Jas 4:10 Humble yourselves before the *L*,
1Pe 1:25 the word of the *L* stands forever."
2: 3 you have tasted that the *L* is good.
3:15 in your hearts set apart Christ as *L*.
2Pe 1:16 and coming of our *L* Jesus Christ,
2: 1 the sovereign *L* who bought
3: 9 The *L* is not slow in keeping his
Jude :14 the *L* is coming with thousands
Rev 4: 8 holy, holy is the *L* God Almighty,
4:11 "You are worthy, our *L* and God,
17:14 he is *L* of lords and King of kings—
22:20 Come, *L* Jesus.

LORD'S† (LORD†)
Ac 21:14 and said, "The *L* will be done."
1Co 10:26 "The earth is the *L*, and everything
11:26 you proclaim the *L* death
2Co 3:18 faces all reflect the *L* glory,
2Ti 2:24 And the *L* servant must not quarrel
Jas 4:15 you ought to say, "If it is the *L* will,

LORDING* (LORD†)
1Pe 5: 3 not *l* it over those entrusted to you,

LORD‡ (LORD'S‡)
Ge 2: 4 When the *L* God made the earth
2: 7 the *L* God formed the man
3:21 The *L* God made garments of skin
7:16 Then the *L* shut him in.
15: 6 Abram believed the *L*,
18:14 Is anything too hard for the *L*?
31:49 "May the *L* keep watch
Ex 3: 2 the angel of the *L* appeared to him
9:12 the *L* hardened Pharaoh's heart
14:30 That day the *L* saved Israel
20: 2 "I am the *L* your God, who
33:11 The *L* would speak to Moses face
40:34 glory of the *L* filled the tabernacle.
Lev 19: 2 'Be holy because I, the *L* your God,
Nu 8: 5 *L* said to Moses: "Take the Levites
14:21 glory of the *L* fills the whole earth,
Dt 2: 7 forty years the *L* your God has
5: 9 the *L* your God, am a jealous God,
6: 4 The *L* our God, the *L* is one.
6: 5 Love the *L* your God
6:16 Do not test the *L* your God
10:14 To the *L* your God belong
10:17 For the *L* your God is God of gods
11: 1 Love the *L* your God and keep his
28: 1 If you fully obey the *L* your God
30:16 today to love the *L* your God,
30:20 For the *L* is your life, and he will
31: 6 for the *L* your God goes with you;
Jos 22: 5 to love the *L* your God, to walk
24:15 my household, we will serve the *L*
1Sa 1:28 So now I give him to the *L*.
2: 2 "There is no one holy like the *L*;
7:12 "Thus far has the *L* helped us."
12:22 his great name the *L* will not reject
15:22 "Does the *L* delight
2Sa 22: 2 "The *L* is my rock, my fortress
1Ki 2: 3 and observe what the *L* your God
8:11 the glory of the *L* filled his temple.
8:61 fully committed to the *L* our God,
18:21 If the *L* is God, follow him;
2Ki 13:23 But the *L* was gracious to them
1Ch 16: 8 Give thanks to the *L*, call
16:23 Sing to the *L*, all the earth;
28: 9 for the *L* searches every heart
29:11 O *L*, is the greatness and the power
2Ch 5:14 the glory of the *L* filled the temple
16: 9 of the *L* range throughout the earth
19: 6 judging for man but for the *L*,
2Ch 30: 9 for the *L* your God is gracious
Ne 1: 5 Then I said: "O *L*, God of heaven,
Job 1:21 *L* gave and the *L* has taken away;
38: 1 the *L* answered Job out
42: 9 and the *L* accepted Job's prayer.
Ps 1: 2 But his delight is in the law of the *L*
9: 9 The *L* is a refuge for the oppressed,
12: 6 And the words of the *L* are flawless
16: 8 I have set the *L* always before me.
18:30 the word of the *L* is flawless.
19: 7 The law of the *L* is perfect,
19:14 O *L*, my Rock and my Redeemer.
23: 1 The *L* is my shepherd, I shall not be
23: 6 I will dwell in the house of the *L*
27: 1 The *L* is my light and my salvation
27: 4 to gaze upon the beauty of the *L*
29: 1 Ascribe to the *L*, O mighty ones,
32: 2 whose sin the *L* does not count
33:12 is the nation whose God is the *L*,
33:18 But the eyes of the *L* are
34: 3 Glorify the *L* with me;
34: 7 The angel of the *L* encamps
34: 8 Taste and see that the *L* is good;
34:18 The *L* is close to the brokenhearted
37: 4 Delight yourself in the *L*
40: 1 I waited patiently for the *L*;
47: 2 How awesome is the *L* Most High,
48: 1 Great is the *L*, and most worthy
55:22 Cast your cares on the *L*
75: 8 In the hand of the *L* is a cup
84:11 For the *L* God is a sun and shield;
86:11 Teach me your way, O *L*,
89: 5 heavens praise your wonders, O *L*,
91: 2 I will say of the *L*, "He is my refuge
95: 1 Come, let us sing for joy to the *L*;
96: 1 Sing to the *L* a new song;
98: 4 Shout for joy to the *L*, all the earth,
100: 1 Shout for joy to the *L*, all the earth.
103: 1 Praise the *L*, O my soul;
103: 8 The *L* is compassionate
104: 1 O *L* my God, you are very great;
107: 8 to the *L* for his unfailing love
110: 1 The *L* says to my Lord:
113: 4 *L* is exalted over all the nations,
115: 1 Not to us, O *L*, not to us
116:15 Precious in the sight of the *L*
118: 1 Give thanks to the *L*, for he is good
118:24 This is the day the *L* has made;
121: 2 My help comes from the *L*,
121: 5 The *L* watches over you—
125: 2 so the *L* surrounds his people
127: 1 Unless the *L* builds the house,
127: 3 Sons are a heritage from the *L*,
130: 3 If you, O *L*, kept a record of sins,
135: 6 The *L* does whatever pleases him,
136: 1 Give thanks to the *L*, for he is good
139: 1 O *L*, you have searched me
144: 3 O *L*, what is man that you care
145: 3 Great is the *L* and most worthy
145:18 The *L* is near to all who call on him
Pr 1: 7 The fear of the *L* is the beginning
3: 5 Trust in the *L* with all your heart
3: 9 Honor the *L* with your wealth,
3:12 the *L* disciplines those he loves,
3:19 By wisdom the *L* laid the earth's
5:21 are in full view of the *L*,
6:16 There are six things the *L* hates,
10:27 The fear of the *L* adds length to life
11: 1 The *L* abhors dishonest scales,
12:22 The *L* detests lying lips,
14:26 He who fears the *L* has a secure
15: 3 The eyes of the *L* are everywhere,
16: 2 but motives are weighed by the *L*.
16: 4 The *L* works out everything
16: 9 but the *L* determines his steps.
16:33 but its every decision is from the *L*.
18:10 The name of the *L* is a strong tower
18:22 and receives favor from the *L*.

Pr 19:14 but a prudent wife is from the *L.*
19:17 to the poor lends to the *L,*
21: 3 to the *L* than sacrifice.
21:30 that can succeed against the *L.*
21:31 but victory rests with the *L.*
22: 2 The *L* is the Maker of them all.
24:18 or the *L* will see and disapprove
31:30 a woman who fears the *L* is
Isa 6: 3 holy, holy is the *L* Almighty;
11: 2 The Spirit of the *L* will rest on him
11: 9 full of the knowledge of the *L*
12: 2 The *L,* the *L,* is my strength
24: 1 the *L* is going to lay waste the earth
25: 8 The Sovereign *L* will wipe away
29:15 to hide their plans from the *L,*
33: 6 the fear of the *L* is the key
35:10 the ransomed of the *L* will return.
40: 5 the glory of the *L* will be revealed,
40: 7 the breath of the *L* blows on them.
40:10 the Sovereign *L* comes with power,
40:28 The *L* is the everlasting God,
40:31 but those who hope in the *L*
42: 8 "I am the *L;* that is my name!
43:11 I, even I, am the *L,*
44:24 I am the *L,*
45: 5 I am the *L,* and there is no other;
45:21 Was it not I, the *L?*
51:11 The ransomed of the *L* will return.
53: 6 and the *L* has laid on him
53:10 and the will of the *L* will prosper
55: 6 Seek the *L* while he may be found;
58: 8 of the *L* will be your rear guard.
58:11 The *L* will guide you always;
59: 1 the arm of the *L* is not too short
61: 3 a planting of the *L*
61:10 I delight greatly in the *L;*
Jer 1: 9 Then the *L* reached out his hand
9:24 I am the *L,* who exercises kindness,
16:19 O *L,* my strength and my fortress,
17: 7 is the man who trusts in the *L,*
La 3:40 and let us return to the *L.*
Eze 1:28 of the likeness of the glory of the *L.*
Hos 1: 7 horsemen, but by the *L* their God."
3: 5 They will come trembling to the *L*
6: 1 "Come, let us return to the *L.*
Joel 2: 1 for the day of the *L* is coming.
2:11 The day of the *L* is great;
3:14 For the day of the *L* is near
Am 5:18 long for the day of the *L?*
Jnh 1: 3 But Jonah ran away from the *L*
Mic 4: 2 up to the mountain of the *L,*
6: 8 And what does the *L* require of you
Na 1: 2 The *L* takes vengeance on his foes
1: 3 The *L* is slow to anger
Hab 2:14 knowledge of the glory of the *L,*
2:20 But the *L* is in his holy temple;
Zep 3:17 The *L* your God is with you,
Zec 1:17 and the *L* will again comfort Zion
9:16 The *L* their God will save them
14: 5 Then the *L* my God will come,
14: 9 The *L* will be king
Mal 4: 5 and dreadful day of the *L* comes.

LORD'S‡ (LORD‡)
Ex 34:34 he entered the *L* presence
Nu 14:41 you disobeying the *L* command?
Dt 6:18 is right and good in the *L* sight,
32: 9 For the *L* portion is his people,
Jos 21:45 Not one of all the *L* good promises
Ps 24: 1 The earth is the *L,* and everything
32:10 but the *L* unfailing love
89: 1 of the *L* great love forever;
103:17 *L* love is with those who fear him,
Pr 3:11 do not despise the *L* discipline
Isa 24:14 west they acclaim the *L* majesty.
62: 3 of splendor in the *L* hand,
Jer 48:10 lax in doing the *L* work!
La 3:22 of the *L* great love we are not

Mic 4: 1 of the *L* temple will be established

LOSE (LOSES LOSS LOST)
1Sa 17:32 "Let no one *l* heart on account
Mt 10:39 Whoever finds his life will *l* it,
Lk 9:25 and yet *l* or forfeit his very self?
Jn 6:39 that I shall *l* none of all that he has
Heb 12: 3 will not grow weary and *l* heart.
12: 5 do not *l* heart when he rebukes you

LOSES (LOSE)
Mt 5:13 But if the salt *l* its saltiness,
Lk 15: 4 you has a hundred sheep and *l* one
15: 8 has ten silver coins and *l* one.

LOSS (LOSE)
Ro 11:12 and their *l* means riches
1Co 3:15 he will suffer *l;* he himself will be
Php 3: 8 I consider everything a *l* compared

LOST (LOSE)
Ps 73: 2 I had nearly *l* my foothold.
Jer 50: 6 "My people have been *l* sheep;
Eze 34: 4 the strays or searched for the *l.*
34:16 for the *l* and bring back the strays.
Mt 18:14 any of these little ones should be *l.*
Lk 15: 4 go after the *l* sheep until he finds it?
15: 6 with me; I have found my *l* sheep.'
15: 9 with me; I have found my *l* coin.'
15:24 is alive again; he was *l* and is found
19:10 to seek and to save what was *l.*"
Php 3: 8 for whose sake I have *l* all things.

LOT (LOTS)

Nephew of Abraham (Ge 11:27; 12:5). Chose to live in Sodom (Ge 13). Rescued from four kings (Ge 14). Rescued from Sodom (Ge 19:1-29; 2Pe 2:7). Fathered Moab and Ammon by his daughters (Ge 19:30-38).

Est 3: 7 the *l)* in the presence of Haman
9:24 the *l)* for their ruin and destruction.
Pr 16:33 The *l* is cast into the lap,
18:18 Casting the *l* settles disputes
Ecc 3:22 his work, because that is his *l.*
Ac 1:26 Then they drew lots, and the *l* fell

LOTS (LOT)
Ps 22:18 and cast *l* for my clothing.
Mt 27:35 divided up his clothes by casting *l.*

LOVE (BELOVED LOVED LOVELY LOVER LOVERS LOVES LOVING)
Ge 22: 2 your only son, Isaac, whom you *l,*
Ex 15:13 "In your unfailing *l* you will lead
20: 6 showing *l* to a thousand generations
20: 6 of those who *l* me
34: 6 abounding in *l* and faithfulness,
Lev 19:18 but *l* your neighbor as yourself.
19:34 *L* him as yourself,
Nu 14:18 abounding in *l* and forgiving sin
Dt 5:10 showing *l* to a thousand generations
5:10 of those who *l* me
6: 5 *L* the LORD your God
7:13 He will *l* you and bless you
10:12 to walk in all his ways, to *l* him,
11:13 to *l* the LORD your God
13: 6 wife you *l,* or your closest friend
30: 6 so that you may *l* him
Jos 22: 5 to *l* the LORD your God, to walk
1Ki 3: 3 Solomon showed his *l*
8:23 you who keep your covenant of *l*
2Ch 5:13 his *l* endures forever."
Ne 1: 5 covenant of *l* with those who *l* him
Ps 18: 1 I *l* you, O LORD, my strength.
23: 6 Surely goodness and *l* will follow
25: 6 O LORD, your great mercy and *l,*
31:16 save me in your unfailing *l.*
32:10 but the LORD's unfailing *l*

Ps 33: 5 the earth is full of his unfailing *l.*
33:18 whose hope is in his unfailing *l,*
36: 5 Your *l,* O LORD, reaches
36: 7 How priceless is your unfailing *l!*
45: 7 You *l* righteousness and hate
51: 1 according to your unfailing *l;*
57:10 For great is your *l,* reaching
63: 3 Because your *l* is better than life,
66:20 or withheld his *l* from me!
70: 4 may those who *l* your salvation
77: 8 Has his unfailing *l* vanished forever
85: 7 Show us your unfailing *l,* O LORD
85:10 *L* and faithfulness meet together;
86:13 For great is your *l* toward me;
89: 1 of the LORD's great *l* forever;
89:33 but I will not take my *l* from him,
92: 2 to proclaim your *l* in the morning
94:18 your *l,* O LORD, supported me.
100: 5 is good and his *l* endures forever;
101: 1 I will sing of your *l* and justice;
103: 4 crowns you with *l* and compassion.
103: 8 slow to anger, abounding in *l.*
103:11 so great is his *l* for those who fear
107: 8 to the LORD for his unfailing *l*
108: 4 For great is your *l,* higher
116: 1 I *l* the LORD, for he heard my
118: 1 his *l* endures forever.
119:47 because I *l* them.
119:64 The earth is filled with your *l,*
119:76 May your unfailing *l* be my
119:97 Oh, how I *l* your law!
119:119 therefore I *l* your statutes.
119:124 your servant according to your *l*
119:132 to those who *l* your name.
119:159 O LORD, according to your *l.*
119:163 but I *l* your law.
119:165 peace have they who *l* your law,
122: 6 "May those who *l* you be secure.
130: 7 for with the LORD is unfailing *l*
136: 1 *His l endures forever.*
143: 8 of your unfailing *l,*
145: 8 slow to anger and rich in *l.*
145:20 over all who *l* him,
147:11 who put their hope in his unfailing *l*
Pr 3: 3 Let *l* and faithfulness never leave
4: 6 *l* her, and she will watch over you.
5:19 you ever be captivated by her *l.*
8:17 I *l* those who *l* me,
9: 8 rebuke a wise man and he will *l* you
10:12 but *l* covers over all wrongs.
14:22 those who plan what is good find *l*
15:17 of vegetables where there is *l*
17: 9 over an offense promotes *l,*
19:22 What a man desires is unfailing *l;*
20: 6 claims to have unfailing *l,*
20:13 Do not *l* sleep or you will grow
20:28 through *l* his throne is made secure
21:21 who pursues righteousness and *l*
27: 5 rebuke than hidden *l.*
Ecc 9: 6 Their *l,* their hate
9: 9 life with your wife, whom you *l,*
SS 2: 4 and his banner over me is *l.*
8: 6 for *l* is as strong as death,
8: 7 Many waters cannot quench *l;*
8: 7 all the wealth of his house for *l,*
Isa 5: 1 I will sing for the one I *l*
16: 5 In *l* a throne will be established;
38:17 In your *l* you kept me
54:10 yet my unfailing *l* for you will not
55: 3 my faithful *l* promised to David.
61: 8 "For I, the LORD, *l* justice;
63: 9 In his *l* and mercy he redeemed
Jer 5:31 and my people *l* it this way.
31: 3 you with an everlasting *l;*
32:18 You show *l* to thousands
33:11 his *l* endures forever."
La 3:22 of the LORD's great *l* we are not
3:32 so great is his unfailing *l.*

Eze 33:32 more than one who sings *l* songs
Da 9: 4 covenant of *l* with all who *l* him
Hos 2:19 in *l* and compassion.
3: 1 Go, show your *l* to your wife again,
11: 4 with ties of *l*;
12: 6 maintain *l* and justice,
Joel 2:13 slow to anger and abounding in *l*,
Am 5:15 Hate evil, *l* good;
Mic 3: 2 you who hate good and *l* evil;
6: 8 To act justly and to *l* mercy
Zep 3:17 he will quiet you with his *l*,
Zec 8:19 Therefore *l* truth and peace."
Mt 3:17 "This is my Son, whom I *l*;
5:44 *L* your enemies and pray
6:24 he will hate the one and *l* the other,
17: 5 "This is my Son, whom I *l*;
19:19 and '*l* your neighbor as yourself.' "
22:37 " '*L* the Lord your God
Lk 6:32 Even 'sinners' *l* those who *l* them.
7:42 which of them will *l* him more?"
20:13 whom I *l*; perhaps they will respect
Jn 13:34 I give you: *L* one another.
13:35 disciples, if you *l* one another."
14:15 "If you *l* me, you will obey what I
15:13 Greater *l* has no one than this,
15:17 This is my command: *L* each other.
21:15 do you truly *l* me more than these
Ro 5: 5 because God has poured out his *l*
5: 8 God demonstrates his own *l* for us
8:28 for the good of those who *l* him,
8:35 us from the *l* of Christ?
8:39 us from the *l* of God that is
12: 9 *L* must be sincere.
12:10 to one another in brotherly *l*.
13: 8 continuing debt to *l* one another,
13: 9 "*L* your neighbor as yourself."
13:10 Therefore *l* is the fulfillment
13:10 *L* does no harm to its neighbor.
1Co 2: 9 prepared for those who *l* him"—
8: 1 Knowledge puffs up, but *l* builds up
13: 1 have not *l*, I am only a resounding
13: 2 but have not *l*, I am nothing.
13: 3 but have not *l*, I gain nothing.
13: 4 Love is patient, *l* is kind.
13: 4 *L* is patient, love is kind.
13: 6 *L* does not delight in evil
13: 8 *L* never fails.
13:13 But the greatest of these is *l*.
13:13 three remain: faith, hope and *l*.
14: 1 way of *l* and eagerly desire spiritual
16:14 Do everything in *l*.
2Co 5:14 For Christ's *l* compels us,
8: 8 sincerity of your *l* by comparing it
8:24 show these men the proof of your *l*
Gal 5: 6 is faith expressing itself through *l*.
5:13 rather, serve one another in *l*.
5:22 But the fruit of the Spirit is *l*, joy,
Eph 1: 4 In *l* he predestined us
2: 4 But because of his great *l* for us,
3:17 being rooted and established in *l*,
3:18 and high and deep is the *l* of Christ,
3:19 and to know this *l* that surpasses
4: 2 bearing with one another in *l*.
4:15 Instead, speaking the truth in *l*,
5: 2 loved children and live a life of *l*,
5:25 *l* your wives, just as Christ loved
5:28 husbands ought to *l* their wives
5:33 each one of you also must *l* his wife
Php 1: 9 that your *l* may abound more
2: 2 having the same *l*, being one
Col 1: 5 *l* that spring from the hope that is
2: 2 in heart and united in *l*,
3:14 And over all these virtues put on *l*,
3:19 *l* your wives and do not be harsh
1Th 1: 3 your labor prompted by *l*,
4: 9 taught by God to *l* each other.
5: 8 on faith and *l* as a breastplate,
2Th 3: 5 direct your hearts into God's *l*
1Ti 1: 5 The goal of this command is *l*,
2:15 *l* and holiness with propriety.
4:12 in life, in *l*, in faith and in purity.
6:10 For the *l* of money is a root
6:11 faith, *l*, endurance and gentleness.
2Ti 1: 7 of power, of *l* and of self-discipline.
2:22 and pursue righteousness, faith, *l*
3:10 faith, patience, *l*, endurance,
Tit 2: 4 women to *l* their husbands
Phm : 9 yet I appeal to you on the basis of *l*.
Heb 6:10 and the *l* you have shown him
10:24 may spur one another on toward *l*
13: 5 free from the *l* of money
Jas 1:12 promised to those who *l* him.
2: 5 he promised those who *l* him?
2: 8 "*L* your neighbor as yourself,"
1Pe 1:22 the truth so that you have sincere *l*
1:22 *l* one another deeply,
2:17 *L* the brotherhood of believers,
3: 8 be sympathetic, *l* as brothers,
3:10 "Whoever would *l* life
4: 8 Above all, *l* each other deeply,
4: 8 *l* covers over a multitude of sins.
5:14 Greet one another with a kiss of *l*.
2Pe 1: 7 and to brotherly kindness, *l*.
1:17 "This is my Son, whom I *l*;
1Jn 2: 5 God's *l* is truly made complete
2:15 Do not *l* the world or anything
3: 1 How great is the *l* the Father has
3:10 anyone who does not *l* his brother.
3:11 We should *l* one another.
3:14 Anyone who does not *l* remains
3:16 This is how we know what *l* is:
3:18 let us not *l* with words or tongue
3:23 to *l* one another as he commanded
4: 7 Dear friends, let us *l* one another,
4: 7 for *l* comes from God.
4: 8 Whoever does not *l* does not know
4: 9 This is how God showed his *l*
4:10 This is *l*: not that we loved God,
4:11 we also ought to *l* one another.
4:12 and his *l* is made complete in us.
4:16 God is *l*.
4:16 Whoever lives in *l* lives in God,
4:17 *l* is made complete among us
4:18 But perfect *l* drives out fear,
4:19 We *l* because he first loved us.
4:20 If anyone says, "I *l* God,"
4:21 loves God must also *l* his brother.
5: 2 we know that we *l* the children
5: 3 This is *l* for God: to obey his
2Jn : 5 I ask that we *l* one another.
: 6 his command is that you walk in *l*.
: 6 this is *l*: that we walk in obedience
Jude :12 men are blemishes at your *l* feasts,
:21 Keep yourselves in God's *l*
Rev 2: 4 You have forsaken your first *l*.
3:19 Those whom I *l* I rebuke
12:11 they did not *l* their lives so much

LOVED (LOVE)
Ge 24:67 she became his wife, and he *l* her;
29:30 and he *l* Rachel more than Leah.
37: 3 Now Israel *l* Joseph more than any
Dt 7: 8 But it was because the LORD *l* you
1Sa 1: 5 a double portion because he *l* her,
20:17 because he *l* him as he *l* himself.
Ps 44: 3 light of your face, for you *l* them.
Jer 2: 2 how as a bride you *l* me
31: 3 "I have *l* you with an everlasting
Hos 2:23 to the one I called 'Not my *l* one.'
3: 1 though she is *l* by another
9:10 became as vile as the thing they *l*.
11: 1 "When Israel was a child, I *l* him,
Mal 1: 2 "But you ask, 'How have you *l* us?'
Mk 12: 6 left to send, a son, whom he *l*.
Jn 3:16 so *l* the world that he gave his one
3:19 but men *l* darkness instead of light
11: 5 Jesus *l* Martha and her sister
12:43 for they *l* praise from men more
13: 1 Having *l* his own who were
13:23 the disciple whom Jesus *l*,
13:34 As I have *l* you, so you must love
14:21 He who loves me will be *l*
15: 9 the Father has *l* me, so have I *l* you.
15:12 Love each other as I have *l* you.
19:26 the disciple whom he *l* standing
Ro 8:37 conquerors through him who *l* us.
9:13 "Jacob I *l*, but Esau I hated."
9:25 her 'my *l* one' who is not my *l* one,"
11:28 they are *l* on account
Gal 2:20 who *l* me and gave himself for me.
Eph 5: 2 as Christ *l* us and gave himself up
5:25 just as Christ *l* the church
2Th 2:16 who *l* us and by his grace gave us
2Ti 4:10 for Demas, because he *l* this world,
Heb 1: 9 You have *l* righteousness
1Jn 4:10 This is love: not that we *l* God,
4:11 Dear friends, since God so *l* us,
4:19 We love because he first *l* us.

LOVELY (LOVE)
Ps 84: 1 How *l* is your dwelling place,
SS 2:14 and your face is *l*.
5:16 he is altogether *l*.
Php 4: 8 whatever is *l*, whatever is

LOVER (LOVE)
SS 2:16 *Beloved* My *l* is mine and I am his;
7:10 I belong to my *l*,
1Ti 3: 3 not quarrelsome, not a *l* of money.

LOVERS (LOVE)
2Ti 3: 2 People will be *l* of themselves,
3: 3 without self-control, brutal, not *l*
3: 4 *l* of pleasure rather than *l* of God—

LOVES (LOVE)
Ps 11: 7 he *l* justice;
33: 5 The LORD *l* righteousness
34:12 Whoever of you *l* life
91:14 Because he *l* me," says the LORD,
127: 2 for he grants sleep to those he *l*.
Pr 3:12 the LORD disciplines those he *l*,
12: 1 Whoever *l* discipline *l* knowledge,
13:24 he who *l* him is careful
17:17 A friend *l* at all times,
17:19 He who *l* a quarrel *l* sin;
22:11 He who *l* a pure heart and whose
Ecc 5:10 whoever *l* wealth is never satisfied
Mt 10:37 anyone who *l* his son or daughter
Lk 7:47 has been forgiven little *l* little."
Jn 3:35 Father *l* the Son and has placed
10:17 reason my Father *l* me is that I lay
12:25 The man who *l* his life will lose it,
14:21 obeys them, he is the one who *l* me.
14:23 Jesus replied, "If anyone *l* me,
Ro 13: 8 for he who *l* his fellowman has
2Co 9: 7 for God *l* a cheerful giver.
Eph 5:28 He who *l* his wife *l* himself.
5:33 must love his wife as he *l* himself,
Heb 12: 6 the Lord disciplines those he *l*,
1Jn 2:10 Whoever *l* his brother lives
2:15 If anyone *l* the world, the love
4: 7 Everyone who *l* has been born
4:21 Whoever *l* God must also love his
5: 1 who *l* the father *l* his child
3Jn : 9 but Diotrephes, who *l* to be first,
Rev 1: 5 To him who *l* us and has freed us

LOVING (LOVE)
Ps 25:10 All the ways of the LORD are *l*
62:12 and that you, O Lord, are *l*.
145:17 and *l* toward all he has made.
Heb 13: 1 Keep on *l* each other as brothers.
1Jn 5: 2 by *l* God and carrying out his

LOWLY
Job 5:11 The *l* he sets on high,
Pr 29:23 but a man of *l* spirit gains honor.
Isa 57:15 also with him who is contrite and *l*
Eze 21:26 *l* will be exalted and the exalted
1Co 1:28 He chose the *l* things of this world

LUKE*
Co-worker with Paul (Col 4:14; 2Ti 4:11; Phm 24).

LUKEWARM*
Rev 3:16 So, because you are *l*— neither hot

LUST
Pr 6:25 Do not *l* in your heart
Col 3: 5 sexual immorality, impurity, *l*,
1Th 4: 5 not in passionate *l* like the heathen,
1Jn 2:16 the *l* of his eyes and the boasting

LYING (LIE)
Pr 6:17 a *l* tongue,
26:28 A *l* tongue hates those it hurts,

MACEDONIA
Ac 16: 9 "Come over to *M* and help us."

MADE (MAKE)
Ge 1:16 He also *m* the stars.
1:25 God *m* the wild animals according
2:22 Then the LORD God *m* a woman
2Ki 19:15 You have *m* heaven and earth.
Ps 95: 5 The sea is his, for he *m* it,
100: 3 It is he who *m* us, and we are his;
118:24 This is the day the LORD has *m*;
139:14 I am fearfully and wonderfully *m*;
Ecc 3:11 He has *m* everything beautiful
Mk 2:27 "The Sabbath was *m* for man,
Jn 1: 3 Through him all things were *m*;
Ac 17:24 "The God who *m* the world
Heb 1: 2 through whom he *m* the universe.
Rev 14: 7 Worship him who *m* the heavens,

MAGI
Mt 2: 1 *M* from the east came to Jerusalem

MAGOG
Eze 38: 2 of the land of *M*, the chief prince
39: 6 I will send fire on *M*
Rev 20: 8 and *M*— to gather them for battle.

MAIDEN
Pr 30:19 and the way of a man with a *m*.
Isa 62: 5 As a young man marries a *m*,
Jer 2:32 Does a *m* forget her jewelry,

MAIMED
Mt 18: 8 It is better for you to enter life *m*

MAJESTIC (MAJESTY)
Ex 15: 6 was *m* in power.
15:11 *m* in holiness,
Ps 8: 1 how *m* is your name in all the earth
29: 4 the voice of the LORD is *m*.
111: 3 Glorious and *m* are his deeds,
SS 6:10 *m* as the stars in procession?
2Pe 1:17 came to him from the *M* Glory,

MAJESTY (MAJESTIC)
Ex 15: 7 In the greatness of your *m*
Dt 33:26 and on the clouds in his *m*.
1Ch 16:27 Splendor and *m* are before him;
Est 1: 4 the splendor and glory of his *m*.
Job 37:22 God comes in awesome *m*.
40:10 and clothe yourself in honor and *m*
Ps 45: 4 In your *m* ride forth victoriously
93: 1 The LORD reigns, he is robed in *m*
110: 3 Arrayed in holy *m*,
145: 5 of the glorious splendor of your *m*,
Isa 53: 2 or *m* to attract us to him,
Eze 31: 2 can be compared with you in *m*?
2Pe 1:16 but we were eyewitnesses of his *m*.
Jude :25 only God our Savior be glory, *m*,

MAKE (MADE MAKER MAKES MAKING)
Ge 1:26 "Let us *m* man in our image,
2:18 I will *m* a helper suitable for him."
12: 2 "I will *m* you into a great nation
Ex 22: 3 thief must certainly *m* restitution,
Nu 6:25 the LORD *m* his face shine
Ps 108: 1 *m* music with all my soul.
Isa 14:14 I will *m* myself like the Most High
29:16 "He did not *m* me"?
Jer 31:31 "when I will *m* a new covenant
Mt 3: 3 *m* straight paths for him.' "
28:19 and *m* disciples of all nations,
Mk 1:17 "and I will *m* you fishers of men."
Lk 13:24 "*M* every effort to enter
14:23 country lanes and *m* them come in,
Ro 14:19 *m* every effort to do what leads
2Co 5: 9 So we *m* it our goal to please him,
Eph 4: 3 *M* every effort to keep the unity
Col 4: 5 *m* the most of every opportunity.
1Th 4:11 *M* it your ambition
Heb 4:11 *m* every effort to enter that rest,
12:14 *M* every effort to live in peace
2Pe 1: 5 *m* every effort to add
3:14 *m* every effort to be found spotless,

MAKER (MAKE)
Job 4:17 Can a man be more pure than his *M*
36: 3 I will ascribe justice to my *M*.
Ps 95: 6 kneel before the LORD our *M*;
Pr 22: 2 The LORD is the *M* of them all.
Isa 45: 9 to him who quarrels with his *M*,
54: 5 For your *M* is your husband—
Jer 10:16 for he is the *M* of all things,

MAKES (MAKE)
1Co 3: 7 but only God, who *m* things grow.

MAKING (MAKE)
Ps 19: 7 *m* wise the simple.
Ecc 12:12 Of *m* many books there is no end,
Jn 5:18 *m* himself equal with God.
Eph 5:16 *m* the most of every opportunity,

MALE
Ge 1:27 *m* and female he created them.
Gal 3:28 slave nor free, *m* nor female,

MALICE (MALICIOUS)
Ro 1:29 murder, strife, deceit and *m*.
Col 3: 8 *m*, slander, and filthy language
1Pe 2: 1 rid yourselves of all *m*

MALICIOUS (MALICE)
Pr 26:24 A *m* man disguises himself
1Ti 3:11 not *m* talkers but temperate
6: 4 *m* talk, evil suspicions

MAN (MEN WOMAN WOMEN)
Ge 1:26 "Let us make *m* in our image,
2: 7 God formed the *m* from the dust
2:18 for the *m* to be alone
2:23 she was taken out of *m*.
9: 6 Whoever sheds the blood of *m*,
Dt 8: 3 *m* does not live on bread
1Sa 13:14 a *m* after his own heart
15:29 he is not a *m* that he
Job 14: 1 *M* born of woman is of few
14:14 If a *m* dies, will he live
Ps 1: 1 Blessed is the *m* who does
8: 4 what is *m* that you are
119: 9 can a young *m* keep his
127: 5 Blessed is the *m* whose quiver
Pr 14:12 that seems right to a *m*,
30:19 way of a *m* with a maiden.
Isa 53: 3 a *m* of sorrows,
Mt 19: 5 a *m* will leave his father
Mk 8:36 What good is it for a *m*
Lk 4: 4 '*M* does not live on bread
Ro 5:12 entered the world through one *m*
1Co 7: 2 each *m* should have his own
11: 3 head of every *m* is Christ,
11: 3 head of woman is *m*
13:11 When I became a *m*,
Php 2: 8 found in appearance as a *m*,
1Ti 2: 5 the *m* Christ Jesus,
2:11 have authority over a *m*;
Heb 9:27 as *m* is destined to die

MANAGE
Jer 12: 5 how will you *m* in the thickets
1Ti 3: 4 He must *m* his own family well
3:12 one wife and must *m* his children
5:14 to *m* their homes and to give

MANASSEH
1. Firstborn of Joseph (Ge 41:51; 46:20). Blessed (Ge 48).
2. Son of Hezekiah; king of Judah (2Ki 21:1-18; 2Ch 33:1-20).

MANGER
Lk 2:12 in strips of cloth and lying in a *m*."

MANNA
Ex 16:31 people of Israel called the bread *m*.
Dt 8:16 He gave you *m* to eat in the desert,
Jn 6:49 Your forefathers ate the *m*
Rev 2:17 I will give some of the hidden *m*.

MANNER
1Co 11:27 in an unworthy *m* will be guilty
Php 1:27 conduct yourselves in a *m* worthy

MARITAL* (MARRY)
Ex 21:10 of her food, clothing and *m* rights.
Mt 5:32 except for *m* unfaithfulness,
19: 9 except for *m* unfaithfulness,
1Co 7: 3 husband should fulfill his *m* duty

MARK (MARKS)
Cousin of Barnabas (Col 4:10; 2Ti 4:11; Phm 24; 1Pe 5:13), see JOHN.
Ge 4:15 Then the LORD put a *m* on Cain
Rev 13:16 to receive a *m* on his right hand

MARKS (MARK)
Jn 20:25 Unless I see the nail *m* in his hands
Gal 6:17 bear on my body the *m* of Jesus.

MARRED
Isa 52:14 his form *m* beyond human likeness

MARRIAGE (MARRY)
Mt 22:30 neither marry nor be given in *m*;
24:38 marrying and giving in *m*,
Ro 7: 2 she is released from the law of *m*.
Heb 13: 4 by all, and the *m* bed kept pure,

MARRIED (MARRY)
Ro 7: 2 by law a *m* woman is bound
1Co 7:27 Are you *m*? Do not seek a divorce.
7:33 But a *m* man is concerned about
7:36 They should get *m*.

MARRIES (MARRY)
Mt 5:32 and anyone who *m* the divorced
19: 9 and *m* another woman commits
Lk 16:18 the man who *m* a divorced woman

MARRY (INTERMARRY MARITAL MARRIAGE MARRIED MARRIES)
Mt 22:30 resurrection people will neither *m*
1Co 7: 1 It is good for a man not to *m.*
7: 9 control themselves, they should *m,*
1Ti 5:14 So I counsel younger widows to *m,*

MARTHA*
Sister of Mary and Lazarus (Lk 10:38-42; Jn 11; 12:2).

MARVELED
Lk 2:33 mother *m* at what was said about

MARY
1. Mother of Jesus (Mt 1:16-25; Lk 1:27-56; 2:1-40). With Jesus at temple (Lk 2:41-52), at the wedding in Cana (Jn 2:1-5), questioning his sanity (Mk 3:21), at the cross (Jn 19:25-27). Among disciples after Ascension (Ac 1:14).
2. Magdalene; former demoniac (Lk 8:2). Helped support Jesus' ministry (Lk 8:1-3). At the cross (Mt 27:56; Mk 15:40; Jn 19:25), burial (Mt 27:61; Mk 15:47). Saw angel after resurrection (Mt 28:1-10; Mk 16:1-9; Lk 24:1-12); also Jesus (Jn 20:1-18).
3. Sister of Martha and Lazarus (Jn 11). Washed Jesus' feet (Jn 12:1-8).

MASQUERADES*
2Co 11:14 for Satan himself *m* as an angel

MASTER (MASTERED MASTERS)
Mt 10:24 nor a servant above his *m.*
23: 8 for you have only one *M*
24:46 that servant whose *m* finds him
25:21 "His *m* replied, 'Well done,
Ro 6:14 For sin shall not be your *m,*
14: 4 To his own *m* he stands or falls.
2Ti 2:21 useful to the *M* and prepared

MASTERED* (MASTER)
1Co 6:12 but I will not be *m* by anything.
2Pe 2:19 a slave to whatever has *m* him.

MASTERS (MASTER)
Mt 6:24 "No one can serve two *m.*
Eph 6: 5 obey your earthly *m* with respect
6: 9 And *m,* treat your slaves
Tit 2: 9 subject to their *m* in everything,

MATTHEW*
Apostle; former tax collector (Mt 9:9-13; 10:3; Mk 3:18; Lk 6:15; Ac 1:13). Also called Levi (Mk 2:14-17; Lk 5:27-32).

MATURE (MATURITY)
Eph 4:13 of the Son of God and become *m,*
Php 3:15 of us who are *m* should take such
Heb 5:14 But solid food is for the *m,*
Jas 1: 4 work so that you may be *m*

MATURITY* (MATURE)
Heb 6: 1 about Christ and go on to *m,*

MEAL
Pr 15:17 Better a *m* of vegetables where
1Co 10:27 some unbeliever invites you to a *m*
Heb 12:16 for a single *m* sold his inheritance

MEANING
Ne 8: 8 and giving the *m* so that the people

MEANS
1Co 9:22 by all possible *m* I might save some

MEAT
Ro 14: 6 He who eats *m,* eats to the Lord,
14:21 It is better not to eat *m*

MEDIATOR
1Ti 2: 5 and one *m* between God and men,
Heb 8: 6 of which he is *m* is superior
9:15 For this reason Christ is the *m*
12:24 to Jesus the *m* of a new covenant,

MEDICINE*
Pr 17:22 A cheerful heart is good *m,*

MEDITATE (MEDITATES MEDITATION)
Jos 1: 8 from your mouth; *m* on it day
Ps 119:15 I *m* on your precepts
119:78 but I will *m* on your precepts.
119:97 I *m* on it all day long.
145: 5 I will *m* on your wonderful works.

MEDITATES* (MEDITATE)
Ps 1: 2 and on his law he *m* day and night.

MEDITATION* (MEDITATE)
Ps 19:14 of my mouth and the *m* of my heart
104:34 May my *m* be pleasing to him,

MEDIUM
Lev 20:27 " 'A man or woman who is a *m*

MEEK (MEEKNESS)
Ps 37:11 But the *m* will inherit the land
Mt 5: 5 Blessed are the *m,*

MEEKNESS* (MEEK)
2Co 10: 1 By the *m* and gentleness of Christ,

MEET (MEETING)
Ps 85:10 Love and faithfulness *m* together;
Am 4:12 prepare to *m* your God, O Israel."
1Th 4:17 them in the clouds to *m* the Lord

MEETING (MEET)
Heb 10:25 Let us not give up *m* together,

MELCHIZEDEK
Ge 14:18 *M* king of Salem brought out bread
Ps 110: 4 in the order of *M.*"
Heb 7:11 in the order of *M,* not in the order

MELT
2Pe 3:12 and the elements will *m* in the heat.

MEMBERS
Mic 7: 6 a man's enemies are the *m*
Ro 7:23 law at work in the *m* of my body,
12: 4 of us has one body with many *m,*
1Co 6:15 not know that your bodies are *m*
12:24 But God has combined the *m*
Eph 4:25 for we are all *m* of one body.
Col 3:15 as *m* of one body you were called

MEN (MAN)
Mt 4:19 will make you fishers of *m*
5:16 your light shine before *m*
12:36 *m* will have to give account
Jn 12:32 will draw all *m* to myself
Ac 5:29 obey God rather than *m!*
Ro 1:27 indecent acts with other *m,*
5:12 death came to all *m,*
1Co 9:22 all things to all *m*
2Co 5:11 we try to persuade *m.*
1Ti 2: 4 wants all *m* to be saved
2Ti 2: 2 entrust to reliable *m*
2Pe 1:21 but *m* spoke from God

MENAHEM
King of Israel (2Ki 15:17-22).

MERCIFUL (MERCY)
Dt 4:31 the LORD your God is a *m* God;
Ne 9:31 for you are a gracious and *m* God.
Mt 5: 7 Blessed are the *m,*
Lk 6:36 Be *m,* just as your Father is *m.*
Heb 2:17 in order that he might become a *m*
Jude :22 Be *m* to those who doubt; snatch

MERCY (MERCIFUL)
Ex 33:19 *m* on whom I will have *m,*
Ps 25: 6 O LORD, your great *m* and love,
Isa 63: 9 and *m* he redeemed them;
Hos 6: 6 For I desire *m,* not sacrifice,
Mic 6: 8 To act justly and to love *m*
Hab 3: 2 in wrath remember *m.*
Mt 12: 7 'I desire *m,* not sacrifice,' you
23:23 justice, *m* and faithfulness.
Ro 9:15 "I will have *m* on whom I have *m,*
Eph 2: 4 who is rich in *m,* made us alive
Jas 2:13 *M* triumphs over judgment!
1Pe 1: 3 In his great *m* he has given us new

MESSAGE
Isa 53: 1 Who has believed our *m*
Jn 12:38 "Lord, who has believed our *m*
Ro 10:17 faith comes from hearing the *m,*
1Co 1:18 For the *m* of the cross is
2Co 5:19 to us the *m* of reconciliation.

MESSIAH*
Jn 1:41 "We have found the *M*" (that is,
4:25 "I know that *M*" (called Christ) "is

METHUSELAH
Ge 5:27 Altogether, *M* lived 969 years,

MICHAEL
Archangel (Jude 9); warrior in angelic realm, protector of Israel (Da 10:13, 21; 12:1; Rev 12:7).

MIDWIVES
Ex 1:17 The *m,* however, feared God

MIGHT (ALMIGHTY MIGHTY)
Jdg 16:30 Then he pushed with all his *m,*
2Sa 6:14 before the LORD with all his *m,*
Ps 21:13 we will sing and praise your *m.*
Zec 4: 6 'Not by *m* nor by power,
1Ti 6:16 To him be honor and *m* forever.

MIGHTY (MIGHT)
Ex 6: 1 of my *m* hand he will drive them
Dt 7: 8 he brought you out with a *m* hand
2Sa 1:19 How the *m* have fallen!
23: 8 the names of David's *m* men:
Ps 24: 8 The LORD strong and *m,*
50: 1 The *M* One, God, the LORD,
89: 8 You are *m,* O LORD,
136:12 with a *m* hand and outstretched
147: 5 Great is our Lord and *m* in power;
Isa 9: 6 Wonderful Counselor, *M* God,
Zep 3:17 he is *m* to save.
Eph 6:10 in the Lord and in his *m* power.

MILE*
Mt 5:41 If someone forces you to go one *m,*

MILK
Ex 3: 8 a land flowing with *m* and honey—
Isa 55: 1 Come, buy wine and *m*
1Co 3: 2 I gave you *m,* not solid food,
Heb 5:12 You need *m,* not solid food!
1Pe 2: 2 babies, crave pure spiritual *m,*

MILLSTONE (STONE)
Lk 17: 2 sea with a *m* tied around his neck

MIND (DOUBLE-MINDED MINDFUL MINDS)
1Sa 15:29 Israel does not lie or change his *m;*
1Ch 28: 9 devotion and with a willing *m,*
Ps 26: 2 examine my heart and my *m;*
Isa 26: 3 him whose *m* is steadfast,
Mt 22:37 all your soul and with all your *m.'*
Ac 4:32 believers were one in heart and *m.*
Ro 7:25 I myself in my *m* am a slave
8: 7 the sinful *m* is hostile to God.
12: 2 by the renewing of your *m.*
1Co 2: 9 no *m* has conceived
14:14 spirit prays, but my *m* is unfruitful.
2Co 13:11 be of one *m,* live in peace.
Php 3:19 Their *m* is on earthly things.
1Th 4:11 to *m* your own business
Heb 7:21 and will not change his *m:*

MINDFUL* (MIND)
Ps 8: 4 what is man that you are *m* of him,
Lk 1:48 God my Savior, for he has been *m*
Heb 2: 6 What is man that you are *m* of him,

MINDS (MIND)
Ps 7: 9 who searches *m* and hearts,
Jer 31:33 "I will put my law in their *m*
Eph 4:23 new in the attitude of your *m;*
Col 3: 2 Set your *m* on things above,
Heb 8:10 I will put my laws in their *m*
Rev 2:23 I am he who searches hearts and *m,*

MINISTERING (MINISTRY)
Heb 1:14 Are not all angels *m* spirits sent

MINISTRY (MINISTERING)
Ac 6: 4 to prayer and the *m* of the word."
2Co 5:18 gave us the *m* of reconciliation:
2Ti 4: 5 discharge all the duties of your *m.*

MIRACLES (MIRACULOUS)
1Ch 16:12 his *m,* and the judgments he
Ps 77:14 You are the God who performs *m;*
Mt 11:20 most of his *m* had been performed,
11:21 If the *m* that were performed
24:24 and perform great signs and *m*
Mk 6: 2 does *m!* Isn't this the carpenter?
Jn 10:32 "I have shown you many great *m*
14:11 the evidence of the *m* themselves.
Ac 2:22 accredited by God to you by *m,*
19:11 God did extraordinary *m*
1Co 12:28 third teachers, then workers of *m,*
Heb 2: 4 it by signs, wonders and various *m,*

MIRACULOUS (MIRACLES)
Jn 3: 2 could perform the *m* signs you are
9:16 "How can a sinner do such *m* signs
20:30 Jesus did many other *m* signs
1Co 1:22 Jews demand *m* signs and Greeks

MIRE
Ps 40: 2 out of the mud and *m;*
Isa 57:20 whose waves cast up *m* and mud.

MIRIAM
Sister of Moses and Aaron (Nu 26:59). Led dancing at Red Sea (Ex 15:20-21). Struck with leprosy for criticizing Moses (Nu 12). Death (Nu 20:1).

MIRROR
Jas 1:23 a man who looks at his face in a *m*

MISERY
Ex 3: 7 "I have indeed seen the *m*
Jdg 10:16 he could bear Israel's *m* no longer.
Hos 5:15 in their *m* they will earnestly seek
Ro 3:16 ruin and *m* mark their ways,
Jas 5: 1 of the *m* that is coming upon you.

MISLED
1Co 15:33 Do not be *m:* "Bad company

MISS
Pr 19: 2 nor to be hasty and *m* the way.

MIST
Hos 6: 4 Your love is like the morning *m,*
Jas 4:14 You are a *m* that appears for a little

MISUSE*
Ex 20: 7 "You shall not *m* the name
Dt 5:11 "You shall not *m* the name
Ps 139:20 your adversaries *m* your name.

MOCK (MOCKED MOCKER MOCKERS MOCKING)
Ps 22: 7 All who see me *m* me;
Pr 14: 9 Fools *m* at making amends for sin,
Mk 10:34 who will *m* him and spit on him,

MOCKED (MOCK)
Mt 27:29 knelt in front of him and *m* him.
27:41 of the law and the elders *m* him.
Gal 6: 7 not be deceived: God cannot be *m.*

MOCKER (MOCK)
Pr 9: 7 corrects a *m* invites insult;
9:12 if you are a *m,* you alone will suffer
20: 1 Wine is a *m* and beer a brawler;
22:10 Drive out the *m,* and out goes strife

MOCKERS (MOCK)
Ps 1: 1 or sit in the seat of *m.*

MOCKING (MOCK)
Isa 50: 6 face from *m* and spitting.

MODEL*
Eze 28:12 " 'You were the *m* of perfection,
1Th 1: 7 And so you became a *m*
2Th 3: 9 to make ourselves a *m* for you

MOMENT
Job 20: 5 the joy of the godless lasts but a *m.*
Ps 30: 5 For his anger lasts only a *m,*
Isa 66: 8 or a nation be brought forth in a *m?*
Gal 2: 5 We did not give in to them for a *m,*

MONEY
Ecc 5:10 Whoever loves *m* never has *m*
Isa 55: 1 and you who have no *m,*
Mt 6:24 You cannot serve both God and *M.*
Lk 9: 3 no bread, no *m,* no extra tunic.
1Co 16: 2 set aside a sum of *m* in keeping
1Ti 3: 3 not quarrelsome, not a lover of *m.*
6:10 For the love of *m* is a root
2Ti 3: 2 lovers of *m,* boastful, proud,
Heb 13: 5 free from the love of *m*
1Pe 5: 2 not greedy for *m,* but eager to serve

MOON
Ps 121: 6 nor the *m* by night.
Joel 2:31 and the *m* to blood
1Co 15:41 *m* another and the stars another;

MORNING
Ge 1: 5 and there was *m*— the first day.
Dt 28:67 In the *m* you will say, "If only it
Ps 5: 3 In the *m,* O LORD,
2Pe 1:19 and the *m* star rises in your hearts.
Rev 22:16 of David, and the bright *M* Star."

MORTAL
1Co 15:53 and the *m* with immortality.

MOSES
Levite; brother of Aaron (Ex 6:20; 1Ch 6:3). Put in basket into Nile; discovered and raised by Pharaoh's daughter (Ex 2:1-10). Fled to Midian after killing Egyptian (Ex 2:11-15). Married to Zipporah, fathered Gershom (Ex 2:16-22).

Called by the LORD to deliver Israel (Ex 3-4). Pharaoh's resistance (Ex 5). Ten plagues (Ex 7-11). Passover and Exodus (Ex 12-13). Led Israel through Red Sea (Ex 14). Song of deliverance (Ex 15:1-21). Brought water from rock (Ex 17:1-7). Raised hands to defeat Amalekites (Ex 17:8-16). Delegated judges (Ex 18; Dt 1:9-18).

Received Law at Sinai (Ex 19-23; 25-31; Jn 1:17). Announced Law to Israel (Ex 19:7-8; 24; 35). Broke tablets because of golden calf (Ex 32; Dt 9). Saw glory of the LORD (Ex 33-34). Supervised building of tabernacle (Ex 36-40). Set apart Aaron and priests (Lev 8-9). Numbered tribes (Nu 1-4; 26). Opposed by Aaron and Miriam (Nu 12). Sent spies into Canaan (Nu 13). Announced forty years of wandering for failure to enter land (Nu 14). Opposed by Korah (Nu 16). Forbidden to enter land for striking rock (Nu 20:1-13; Dt 1:37). Lifted bronze snake for healing (Nu 21:4-9; Jn 3:14). Final address to Israel (Dt 1-33). Succeeded by Joshua (Nu 27:12-23; Dt 34). Death (Dt 34:5-12).

"Law of Moses" (1Ki 2:3; Ezr 3:2; Mk 12:26; Lk 24:44). "Book of Moses" (2Ch 25:12; Ne 13:1). "Song of Moses" (Ex 15:1-21; Rev 15:3). "Prayer of Moses" (Ps 90).

MOTH
Mt 6:19 where *m* and rust destroy,

MOTHER (MOTHER'S)
Ge 2:24 and *m* and be united to his wife,
3:20 because she would become the *m*
Ex 20:12 "Honor your father and your *m,*
Lev 20: 9 " 'If anyone curses his father or *m,*
Dt 5:16 "Honor your father and your *m,*
21:18 who does not obey his father and *m*
27:16 who dishonors his father or his *m."*
1Sa 2:19 Each year his *m* made him a little
Ps 113: 9 as a happy *m* of children.
Pr 23:25 May your father and *m* be glad;
29:15 child left to himself disgraces his *m.*
31: 1 an oracle his *m* taught him:
Isa 49:15 "Can a *m* forget the baby
66:13 As a *m* comforts her child,
Mt 10:37 or *m* more than me is not worthy
15: 4 'Honor your father and *m'*
19: 5 and *m* and be united to his wife,
Mk 7:10 'Honor your father and your *m,'*
10:19 honor your father and *m.' "*
Jn 19:27 to the disciple, "Here is your *m."*

MOTHER'S (MOTHER)
Job 1:21 "Naked I came from my *m* womb,
Pr 1: 8 and do not forsake your *m* teaching

MOTIVES*
Pr 16: 2 but *m* are weighed by the LORD.
1Co 4: 5 will expose the *m* of men's hearts.
Php 1:18 whether from false *m* or true,
1Th 2: 3 spring from error or impure *m,*
Jas 4: 3 because you ask with wrong *m,*

MOUNTAIN (MOUNTAINS)
Mic 4: 2 let us go up to the *m* of the LORD,
Mt 17:20 say to this *m,* 'Move from here

MOUNTAINS (MOUNTAIN)
Isa 52: 7 How beautiful on the *m*
55:12 the *m* and hills
1Co 13: 2 if I have a faith that can move *m,*

MOURN (MOURNING)
Ecc 3: 4 a time to *m* and a time to dance,

Isa 61: 2 to comfort all who *m,*
Mt 5: 4 Blessed are those who *m,*
Ro 12:15 *m* with those who *m.*

MOURNING (MOURN)
Jer 31:13 I will turn their *m* into gladness;
Rev 21: 4 There will be no more death or *m*

MOUTH
Jos 1: 8 of the Law depart from your *m;*
Ps 19:14 May the words of my *m*
40: 3 He put a new song in my *m,*
119:103 sweeter than honey to my *m!*
Pr 16:23 A wise man's heart guides his *m,*
27: 2 praise you, and not your own *m;*
Isa 51:16 I have put my words in your *m*
Mt 12:34 overflow of the heart the *m* speaks.
15:11 into a man's *m* does not make him
Ro 10: 9 That if you confess with your *m,*

MUD
Ps 40: 2 out of the *m* and mire;
Isa 57:20 whose waves cast up mire and *m.*
2Pe 2:22 back to her wallowing in the *m."*

MULTITUDE (MULTITUDES)
Isa 31: 1 who trust in the *m* of their chariots
1Pe 4: 8 love covers over a *m* of sins.
Rev 7: 9 me was a great *m* that no one could

MULTITUDES (MULTITUDE)
Joel 3:14 *M, m* in the valley of decision!

MURDER (MURDERER MURDERERS)
Ex 20:13 "You shall not *m.*
Mt 15:19 *m,* adultery, sexual immorality,
Ro 13: 9 "Do not *m,"* "Do not steal,"
Jas 2:11 adultery," also said, "Do not *m."*

MURDERER (MURDER)
Nu 35:16 he is a *m;* the *m* shall be put
Jn 8:44 He was a *m* from the beginning,
1Jn 3:15 who hates his brother is a *m,*

MURDERERS (MURDER)
1Ti 1: 9 for *m,* for adulterers and perverts,
Rev 21: 8 the *m,* the sexually immoral,

MUSIC
Jdg 5: 3 I will make *m* to the LORD,
Ps 27: 6 and make *m* to the LORD.
95: 2 and extol him with *m* and song.
98: 4 burst into jubilant song with *m;*
108: 1 make *m* with all my soul.
Eph 5:19 make *m* in your heart to the Lord,

MUSTARD
Mt 13:31 kingdom of heaven is like a *m* seed,
17:20 you have faith as small as a *m* seed,

MUZZLE
Dt 25: 4 Do not *m* an ox while it is treading
Ps 39: 1 I will put a *m* on my mouth
1Co 9: 9 "Do not *m* an ox while it is

MYRRH
Mt 2:11 of gold and of incense and of *m.*
Mk 15:23 offered him wine mixed with *m,*

MYSTERY
Ro 16:25 to the revelation of the *m* hidden
1Co 15:51 I tell you a *m:* We will not all sleep,
Eph 5:32 This is a profound *m*—
Col 1:26 the *m* that has been kept hidden
1Ti 3:16 the *m* of godliness is great:

MYTHS
1Ti 4: 7 Have nothing to do with godless *m*

NADAB
Son of Jeroboam I; king of Israel (1Ki 15:25-32).

NAIL* (NAILING)
Jn 20:25 "Unless I see the *n* marks

NAILING* (NAIL)
Ac 2:23 him to death by *n* him to the cross.
Col 2:14 he took it away, *n* it to the cross.

NAKED
Ge 2:25 The man and his wife were both *n,*
Job 1:21 *N* I came from my mother's womb,
Isa 58: 7 when you see the *n,* to clothe him,
2Co 5: 3 are clothed, we will not be found *n.*

NAME
Ex 3:15 This is my *n* forever, the *n*
20: 7 "You shall not misuse the *n*
Dt 5:11 "You shall not misuse the *n*
28:58 this glorious and awesome *n*—
1Ki 5: 5 will build the temple for my *N.'*
2Ch 7:14 my people, who are called by my *n,*
Ps 34: 3 let us exalt his *n* together.
103: 1 my inmost being, praise his holy *n.*
147: 4 and calls them each by *n.*
Pr 22: 1 A good *n* is more desirable
30: 4 What is his *n,* and the *n* of his son?
Isa 40:26 and calls them each by *n.*
57:15 who lives forever, whose *n* is holy:
Jer 14: 7 do something for the sake of your *n*
Da 12: 1 everyone whose *n* is found written
Joel 2:32 on the *n* of the LORD will be saved
Zec 14: 9 one LORD, and his *n* the only *n.*
Mt 1:21 and you are to give him the *n* Jesus,
6: 9 hallowed be your *n,*
18:20 or three come together in my *n,*
Jn 10: 3 He calls his own sheep by *n*
16:24 asked for anything in my *n.*
Ac 4:12 for there is no other *n*
Ro 10:13 "Everyone who calls on the *n*
Php 2: 9 him the *n* that is above every *n,*
Col 3:17 do it all in the *n* of the Lord Jesus,
Heb 1: 4 as the *n* he has inherited is superior
Rev 20:15 If anyone's *n* was not found written

NAOMI
Mother-in-law of Ruth (Ru 1). Advised Ruth to seek marriage with Boaz (Ru 2-4).

NARROW
Mt 7:13 "Enter through the *n* gate.

NATHANAEL
Apostle (Jn 1:45-49; 21:2). Probably also called Bartholomew (Mt 10:3).

NATION (NATIONS)
Ge 12: 2 "I will make you into a great *n*
Ps 33:12 Blessed is the *n* whose God is
Pr 14:34 Righteousness exalts a *n,*
Isa 65: 1 To a *n* that did not call on my name
1Pe 2: 9 a royal priesthood, a holy *n,*
Rev 7: 9 from every *n,* tribe, people

NATIONS (NATION)
Ge 17: 4 You will be the father of many *n.*
18:18 and all *n* on earth will be blessed
Ex 19: 5 of all *n* you will be my treasured
Ne 1: 8 I will scatter you among the *n,*
Ps 96: 3 Declare his glory among the *n,*
Isa 40:15 Surely the *n* are like a drop
Eze 36:23 *n* will know that I am the LORD,
Hag 2: 7 and the desired of all *n* will come,
Zec 8:23 *n* will take firm hold of one Jew
14: 2 I will gather all the *n* to Jerusalem
Mt 28:19 and make disciples of all *n,*

Rev 21:24 The *n* will walk by its light,

NATURAL (NATURE)
Ro 6:19 you are weak in your *n* selves.
1Co 15:44 If there is a *n* body, there is

NATURE (NATURAL)
Ro 8: 4 do not live according to the sinful *n*
8: 8 by the sinful *n* cannot please God.
Gal 5:19 The acts of the sinful *n* are obvious:
5:24 Jesus have crucified the sinful *n*
Php 2: 6 Who, being in very *n* God,

NAZARENE
Mt 2:23 prophets: "He will be called a *N."*

NAZIRITE
Jdg 13: 7 because the boy will be a *N* of God

NECESSARY
Ro 13: 5 it is *n* to submit to the authorities,

NEED (NEEDS NEEDY)
Ps 116: 6 when I was in great *n,* he saved me.
Mt 6: 8 for your Father knows what you *n*
Ro 12:13 with God's people who are in *n.*
1Co 12:21 say to the hand, "I don't *n* you!"
1Jn 3:17 sees his brother in *n* but has no pity

NEEDLE
Mt 19:24 go through the eye of a *n*

NEEDS (NEED)
Isa 58:11 he will satisfy your *n*
Php 4:19 God will meet all your *n* according

NEEDY (NEED)
Pr 14:21 blessed is he who is kind to the *n.*
14:31 to the *n* honors God.
31:20 and extends her hands to the *n.*
Mt 6: 2 "So when you give to the *n,*

NEGLECT (NEGLECTED)
Ne 10:39 We will not *n* the house of our God
Ps 119:16 I will not *n* your word.
Ac 6: 2 for us to *n* the ministry of the word
1Ti 4:14 Do not *n* your gift, which was

NEGLECTED (NEGLECT)
Mt 23:23 But you have *n* the more important

NEHEMIAH
Cupbearer of Artaxerxes (Ne 2:1); governor of Israel (Ne 8:9). Returned to Jerusalem to rebuild walls (Ne 2-6). With Ezra, reestablished worship (Ne 8). Prayer confessing nation's sin (Ne 9). Dedicated wall (Ne 12).

NEIGHBOR (NEIGHBOR'S)
Ex 20:16 give false testimony against your *n.*
Lev 19:13 Do not defraud your *n* or rob him.
19:18 but love your *n* as yourself.
Pr 27:10 better a *n* nearby than a brother far
Mt 19:19 and 'love your *n* as yourself.'"
Lk 10:29 who is my *n?"* In reply Jesus said:
Ro 13:10 Love does no harm to its *n.*

NEIGHBOR'S (NEIGHBOR)
Ex 20:17 You shall not covet your *n* wife,
Dt 5:21 not set your desire on your *n* house
19:14 not move your *n* boundary stone
Pr 25:17 Seldom set foot in your *n* house—

NEW
Ps 40: 3 He put a *n* song in my mouth,
Ecc 1: 9 there is nothing *n* under the sun.
Isa 65:17 *n* heavens and a *n* earth.
Jer 31:31 "when I will make a *n* covenant

Eze 36:26 give you a *n* heart and put a *n* spirit
Mt 9:17 Neither do men pour *n* wine
Lk 22:20 "This cup is the *n* covenant
2Co 5:17 he is a *n* creation; the old has gone,
Eph 4:24 and to put on the *n* self, created
2Pe 3:13 to a *n* heaven and a *n* earth,
1Jn 2: 8 Yet I am writing you a *n* command;

NEWBORN (BEAR)
1Pe 2: 2 Like *n* babies, crave pure spiritual

NEWS
Isa 52: 7 the feet of those who bring good *n*,
Mk 1:15 Repent and believe the good *n!"*
16:15 preach the good *n* to all creation.
Lk 2:10 I bring you good *n*
Ac 5:42 proclaiming the good *n* that Jesus
17:18 preaching the good *n* about Jesus
Ro 10:15 feet of those who bring good *n!"*

NICODEMUS*
Pharisee who visted Jesus at night (Jn 3). Argued fair treatment of Jesus (Jn 7:50-52). With Joseph, prepared Jesus for burial (Jn 19:38-42).

NIGHT
Job 35:10 who gives songs in the *n*,
Ps 1: 2 on his law he meditates day and *n*.
91: 5 You will not fear the terror of *n*,
Jn 3: 2 He came to Jesus at *n* and said,
1Th 5: 2 Lord will come like a thief in the *n*.
5: 5 We do not belong to the *n*
Rev 21:25 for there will be no *n* there.

NOAH
Righteous man (Eze 14:14, 20) called to build ark (Ge 6-8; Heb 11:7; 1Pe 3:20; 2Pe 2:5). God's covenant with (Ge 9:1-17). Drunkenness of (Ge 9:18-23). Blessed sons, cursed Canaan (Ge 9:24-27).

NOBLE
Ru 3:11 you are a woman of *n* character.
Ps 45: 1 My heart is stirred by a *n* theme
Pr 12: 4 of *n* character is her husband's
31:10 A wife of *n* character who can find?
31:29 "Many women do *n* things,
Isa 32: 8 But the *n* man makes *n* plans,
Lk 8:15 good soil stands for those with a *n*
Ro 9:21 of clay some pottery for *n* purposes
Php 4: 8 whatever is *n*, whatever is right,
2Ti 2:20 some are for *n* purposes

NOTHING
Ne 9:21 in the desert; they lacked *n*,
Jer 32:17 *N* is too hard for you
Jn 15: 5 apart from me you can do *n*.

NULLIFY
Ro 3:31 Do we, then, *n* the law by this faith

OATH
Dt 7: 8 and kept the *o* he swore

OBEDIENCE (OBEY)
2Ch 31:21 in *o* to the law and the commands,
Pr 30:17 that scorns *o* to a mother,
Ro 1: 5 to the *o* that comes from faith.
6:16 to *o*, which leads to righteousness?
2Jn : 6 that we walk in *o* to his commands.

OBEDIENT (OBEY)
Lk 2:51 with them and was *o* to them.
Php 2: 8 and became *o* to death—
1Pe 1:14 As *o* children, do not conform

OBEY (OBEDIENCE OBEDIENT OBEYED)
Ex 12:24 *"O* these instructions as a lasting
Dt 6: 3 careful to *o* so that it may go well
13: 4 Keep his commands and *o* him;
21:18 son who does not *o* his father
30: 2 and *o* him with all your heart
32:46 children to *o* carefully all the words
1Sa 15:22 To *o* is better than sacrifice,
Ps 119:34 and *o* it with all my heart.
Mt 28:20 to *o* everything I have commanded
Jn 14:23 loves me, he will *o* my teaching.
Ac 5:29 "We must *o* God rather than men!
Ro 6:16 slaves to the one whom you *o*—
Gal 5: 3 obligated to *o* the whole law.
Eph 6: 1 *o* your parents in the Lord,
6: 5 *o* your earthly masters with respect
Col 3:20 *o* your parents in everything,
1Ti 3: 4 and see that his children *o* him
Heb 13:17 *O* your leaders and submit
1Jn 5: 3 love for God: to *o* his commands.

OBEYED (OBEY)
Ps 119: 4 that are to be fully *o*.
Jnh 3: 3 Jonah *o* the word of the LORD
Jn 17: 6 and they have *o* your word.
Ro 6:17 you wholeheartedly *o* the form
Heb 11: 8 *o* and went, even though he did not
1Pe 3: 6 who *o* Abraham and called him her

OBLIGATED
Ro 1:14 I am *o* both to Greeks
Gal 5: 3 himself be circumcised that he is *o*

OBSCENITY
Eph 5: 4 Nor should there be *o*, foolish talk

OBSOLETE
Heb 8:13 he has made the first one *o;*

OBTAINED
Ro 9:30 not pursue righteousness, have *o* it,
Php 3:12 Not that I have already *o* all this,
Heb 9:12 having *o* eternal redemption.

OFFENDED (OFFENSE)
Pr 18:19 An *o* brother is more unyielding

OFFENSE (OFFENDED OFFENSIVE)
Pr 17: 9 over an *o* promotes love,
19:11 it is to his glory to overlook an *o*.

OFFENSIVE (OFFENSE)
Ps 139:24 See if there is any *o* way in me,

OFFER (OFFERED OFFERING OFFERINGS)
Ro 12: 1 to *o* your bodies as living sacrifices,
Heb 13:15 therefore, let us continually *o*

OFFERED (OFFER)
Heb 7:27 once for all when he *o* himself.
11: 4 By faith Abel *o* God a better

OFFERING (OFFER)
Ge 22: 8 provide the lamb for the burnt *o*,
Ps 40: 6 Sacrifice and *o* you did not desire,
Isa 53:10 the LORD makes his life a guilt *o*,
Mt 5:23 if you are *o* your gift at the altar
Eph 5: 2 as a fragrant *o* and sacrifice to God.
Heb 10: 5 "Sacrifice and *o* you did not desire,

OFFERINGS (OFFER)
Mal 3: 8 do we rob you?' "In tithes and *o*.
Mk 12:33 is more important than all burnt *o*

OFFICER
2Ti 2: 4 wants to please his commanding *o*.

OFFSPRING
Ge 3:15 and between your *o* and hers;
12: 7 "To your *o* I will give this land."

OIL
Ps 23: 5 You anoint my head with *o;*
Isa 61: 3 the *o* of gladness
Heb 1: 9 by anointing you with the *o* of joy."

OLIVE (OLIVES)
Zec 4: 3 Also there are two *o* trees by it,
Ro 11:17 and you, though a wild *o* shoot,
Rev 11: 4 These are the two *o* trees

OLIVES (OLIVE)
Jas 3:12 a fig tree bear *o*, or a grapevine bear

OMEGA
Rev 1: 8 "I am the Alpha and the *O,"*

OMRI
King of Israel (1Ki 16:21-26).

OPINIONS*
1Ki 18:21 will you waver between two *o?*
Pr 18: 2 but delights in airing his own *o*.

OPPORTUNITY
Ro 7:11 seizing the *o* afforded
Gal 6:10 as we have *o*, let us do good
Eph 5:16 making the most of every *o*,
Col 4: 5 make the most of every *o*.
1Ti 5:14 to give the enemy no *o* for slander.

OPPOSES
Jas 4: 6 "God *o* the proud
1Pe 5: 5 because, "God *o* the proud

OPPRESS (OPPRESSED)
Ex 22:21 "Do not mistreat an alien or *o* him,
Zec 7:10 Do not *o* the widow

OPPRESSED (OPPRESS)
Ps 9: 9 The LORD is a refuge for the *o*,
Isa 53: 7 He was *o* and afflicted,
Zec 10: 2 *o* for lack of a shepherd.

ORDAINED
Ps 8: 2 you have *o* praise

ORDERLY
1Co 14:40 done in a fitting and *o* way.
Col 2: 5 and delight to see how *o* you are

ORGIES*
Ro 13:13 not in *o* and drunkenness,
Gal 5:21 drunkenness, *o*, and the like.
1Pe 4: 3 *o*, carousing and detestable

ORIGIN
2Pe 1:21 For prophecy never had its *o*

ORPHANS
Jn 14:18 will not leave you as *o;* I will come
Jas 1:27 to look after *o* and widows

OUTCOME
Heb 13: 7 Consider the *o* of their way of life
1Pe 4:17 what will the *o* be for those who do

OUTSIDERS*
Col 4: 5 wise in the way you act toward *o;*
1Th 4:12 daily life may win the respect of *o*
1Ti 3: 7 also have a good reputation with *o*,

OUTSTANDING
SS 5:10 *o* among ten thousand.
Ro 13: 8 no debt remain *o*,

OUTSTRETCHED
Ex 6: 6 and will redeem you with an *o* arm
Jer 27: 5 and *o* arm I made the earth

Eze 20:33 an *o* arm and with outpoured wrath

OUTWEIGHS
2Co 4:17 an eternal glory that far *o* them all.

OVERCOME (OVERCOMES)
Mt 16:18 and the gates of Hades will not *o* it.
Mk 9:24 I do believe; help me *o* my unbelief
Jn 16:33 But take heart! I have *o* the world."
Ro 12:21 Do not be *o* by evil, but *o* evil
1Jn 5: 4 is the victory that has *o* the world,
Rev 17:14 but the Lamb will *o* them

OVERCOMES* (OVERCOME)
1Jn 5: 4 born of God *o* the world.
5: 5 Who is it that *o* the world?
Rev 2: 7 To him who *o,* I will give the right
2:11 He who *o* will not be hurt at all
2:17 To him who *o,* I will give some
2:26 To him who *o* and does my will
3: 5 He who *o* will, like them, be
3:12 Him who *o* I will make a pillar
3:21 To him who *o,* I will give the right
21: 7 He who *o* will inherit all this,

OVERFLOW (OVERFLOWS)
Ps 119:171 May my lips *o* with praise,
Lk 6:45 out of the *o* of his heart his mouth
Ro 15:13 so that you may *o* with hope
2Co 4:15 to *o* to the glory of God.
1Th 3:12 *o* for each other and for everyone

OVERFLOWS* (OVERFLOW)
Ps 23: 5 my cup *o.*
2Co 1: 5 also through Christ our comfort *o.*

OVERJOYED* (JOY)
Da 6:23 The king was *o* and gave orders
Mt 2:10 they saw the star, they were *o.*
Jn 20:20 The disciples were *o*
Ac 12:14 she was so *o* she ran back
1Pe 4:13 so that you may be *o*

OVERSEER (OVERSEERS)
1Ti 3: 1 anyone sets his heart on being an *o,*
3: 2 Now the *o* must be above reproach,
Tit 1: 7 Since an *o* is entrusted

OVERSEERS* (OVERSEER)
Ac 20:28 the Holy Spirit has made you *o.*
Php 1: 1 together with the *o* and deacons:
1Pe 5: 2 as *o*— not because you must,

OVERWHELMED
Ps 38: 4 My guilt has *o* me
65: 3 When we were *o* by sins,
Mt 26:38 "My soul is *o* with sorrow
Mk 7:37 People were *o* with amazement.

OWE
Ro 13: 7 If you *o* taxes, pay taxes; if revenue
Phm :19 to mention that you *o* me your very

OX
Dt 25: 4 Do not muzzle an *o*
Isa 11: 7 and the lion will eat straw like the *o.*
1Co 9: 9 "Do not muzzle an *o*

PAGANS
Mt 5:47 Do not even *p* do that? Be perfect,
1Pe 2:12 such good lives among the *p* that,

PAIN (PAINFUL)
Ge 3:16 with *p* you will give birth
Job 33:19 may be chastened on a bed of *p*
Jn 16:21 woman giving birth to a child has *p*

PAINFUL (PAIN)
Ge 3:17 through *p* toil you will eat of it
Heb 12:11 seems pleasant at the time, but *p.*
1Pe 4:12 at the *p* trial you are suffering,

PALMS
Isa 49:16 you on the *p* of my hands;

PANTS
Ps 42: 1 As the deer *p* for streams of water,

PARADISE*
Lk 23:43 today you will be with me in *p."*
2Co 12: 4 God knows—was caught up to *p.*
Rev 2: 7 of life, which is in the *p* of God.

PARALYTIC
Mk 2: 3 bringing to him a *p,* carried by four

PARDON (PARDONS)
Isa 55: 7 and to our God, for he will freely *p.*

PARDONS* (PARDON)
Mic 7:18 who *p* sin and forgives

PARENTS
Pr 17: 6 and *p* are the pride of their children
Lk 18:29 left home or wife or brothers or *p*
21:16 You will be betrayed even by *p,*
Ro 1:30 they disobey their *p;* they are
2Co 12:14 for their *p,* but *p* for their children.
Eph 6: 1 Children, obey your *p* in the Lord,
Col 3:20 obey your *p* in everything,
2Ti 3: 2 disobedient to their *p,* ungrateful,

PARTIALITY
Dt 10:17 who shows no *p* and accepts no
2Ch 19: 7 our God there is no injustice or *p*
Lk 20:21 and that you do not show *p*

PARTICIPATION
1Co 10:16 is not the bread that we break a *p*

PASS
Ex 12:13 and when I see the blood, I will *p*
La 1:12 to you, all you who *p* by?
Lk 21:33 Heaven and earth will *p* away,
1Co 13: 8 there is knowledge, it will *p* away.

PASSION (PASSIONS)
1Co 7: 9 better to marry than to burn with *p.*

PASSIONS (PASSION)
Gal 5:24 crucified the sinful nature with its *p*
Tit 2:12 to ungodliness and worldly *p,*

PASSOVER
Ex 12:11 Eat it in haste; it is the LORD's *P.*
Dt 16: 1 celebrate the *P* of the LORD your
1Co 5: 7 our *P* lamb, has been sacrificed.

PAST
Isa 43:18 do not dwell on the *p.*
Ro 15: 4 in the *p* was written to teach us,
Heb 1: 1 In the *p* God spoke

PASTORS*
Eph 4:11 and some to be *p* and teachers,

PASTURE (PASTURES)
Ps 37: 3 dwell in the land and enjoy safe *p.*
100: 3 we are his people, the sheep of his *p*
Jer 50: 7 against the LORD, their true *p,*
Eze 34:13 I will *p* them on the mountains
Jn 10: 9 come in and go out, and find *p.*

PASTURES (PASTURE)
Ps 23: 2 He makes me lie down in green *p,*

PATCH
Mt 9:16 No one sews a *p* of unshrunk cloth

PATH (PATHS)
Ps 27:11 lead me in a straight *p*
119:105 and a light for my *p.*
Pr 15:19 the *p* of the upright is a highway.
15:24 The *p* of life leads upward
Isa 26: 7 The *p* of the righteous is level;
Lk 1:79 to guide our feet into the *p* of peace
2Co 6: 3 no stumbling block in anyone's *p,*

PATHS (PATH)
Ps 23: 3 He guides me in *p* of righteousness
25: 4 teach me your *p;*
Pr 3: 6 and he will make your *p* straight.
Ro 11:33 and his *p* beyond tracing out!
Heb 12:13 "Make level *p* for your feet,"

PATIENCE (PATIENT)
Pr 19:11 A man's wisdom gives him *p;*
2Co 6: 6 understanding, *p* and kindness;
Gal 5:22 joy, peace, *p,* kindness, goodness,
Col 1:11 may have great endurance and *p,*
3:12 humility, gentleness and *p.*

PATIENT (PATIENCE PATIENTLY)
Pr 15:18 but a *p* man calms a quarrel.
Ro 12:12 Be joyful in hope, *p* in affliction,
1Co 13: 4 Love is *p,* love is kind.
Eph 4: 2 humble and gentle; be *p,*
1Th 5:14 help the weak, be *p* with everyone.

PATIENTLY (PATIENT)
Ps 40: 1 I waited *p* for the LORD;
Ro 8:25 we do not yet have, we wait for it *p.*

PATTERN
Ro 5:14 who was a *p* of the one to come.
12: 2 longer to the *p* of this world,
2Ti 1:13 keep as the *p* of sound teaching,

PAUL

Also called Saul (Ac 13:9). Pharisee from Tarsus (Ac 9:11; Php 3:5). Apostle (Gal 1). At stoning of Stephen (Ac 8:1). Persecuted Church (Ac 9:1-2; Gal 1:13). Vision of Jesus on road to Damascus (Ac 9:4-9; 26:12-18). In Arabia (Gal 1:17). Preached in Damascus; escaped death through the wall in a basket (Ac 9:19-25). In Jerusalem; sent back to Tarsus (Ac 9:26-30).

Brought to Antioch by Barnabas (Ac 11:22-26). First missionary journey to Cyprus and Galatia (Ac 13-14). Stoned at Lystra (Ac 14:19-20). At Jerusalem council (Ac 15). Split with Barnabas over Mark (Ac 15:36-41).

Second missionary journey with Silas (Ac 16-20). Called to Macedonia (Ac 16:6-10). Freed from prison in Philippi (Ac 16:16-40). In Thessalonica (Ac 17:1-9). Speech in Athens (Ac 17:16-33). In Corinth (Ac 18). In Ephesus (Ac 19). Return to Jerusalem (Ac 20). Farewell to Ephesian elders (Ac 20:13-38). Arrival in Jerusalem (Ac 21:1-26). Arrested (Ac 21:27-36). Addressed crowds (Ac 22), Sanhedrin (Ac 23:1-11). Transferred to Caesarea (Ac 23:12-35). Trial before Felix (Ac 24), Festus (Ac 25:1-12). Before Agrippa (Ac 25:13-26:32). Voyage to Rome; shipwreck (Ac 27). Arrival in Rome (Ac 28).

PAY (REPAID REPAY)
Lev 26:43 They will *p* for their sins
Pr 22:17 *P* attention and listen
Mt 22:17 Is it right to *p* taxes to Caesar
Ro 13: 6 This is also why you *p* taxes,
2Pe 1:19 you will do well to *p* attention to it,

PEACE (PEACEMAKERS)
Nu 6:26 and give you *p.*"'
Ps 34:14 seek *p* and pursue it.
85:10 righteousness and *p* kiss each other
119:165 Great *p* have they who love your
122: 6 Pray for the *p* of Jerusalem:
Pr 14:30 A heart at *p* gives life to the body,
17: 1 Better a dry crust with *p* and quiet
Isa 9: 6 Everlasting Father, Prince of *P.*
26: 3 You will keep in perfect *p*
48:22 "There is no *p,*" says the LORD,
Zec 9:10 He will proclaim *p* to the nations.
Mt 10:34 I did not come to bring *p,*
Lk 2:14 on earth *p* to men on whom his
Jn 14:27 *P* I leave with you; my *p*
16:33 so that in me you may have *p.*
Ro 5: 1 we have *p* with God
1Co 7:15 God has called us to live in *p.*
14:33 a God of disorder but of *p.*
Gal 5:22 joy, *p,* patience, kindness,
Eph 2:14 he himself is our *p,* who has made
Php 4: 7 the *p* of God, which transcends all
Col 1:20 by making *p* through his blood,
3:15 Let the *p* of Christ rule
1Th 5: 3 While people are saying, "*P*
2Th 3:16 the Lord of *p* himself give you *p*
2Ti 2:22 righteousness, faith, love and *p,*
1Pe 3:11 he must seek *p* and pursue it.
Rev 6: 4 power to take *p* from the earth

PEACEMAKERS* (PEACE)
Mt 5: 9 Blessed are the *p,*
Jas 3:18 *P* who sow in peace raise a harvest

PEARL* (PEARLS)
Rev 21:21 each gate made of a single *p.*

PEARLS (PEARL)
Mt 7: 6 do not throw your *p* to pigs.
13:45 like a merchant looking for fine *p.*
1Ti 2: 9 or gold or *p* or expensive clothes,
Rev 21:21 The twelve gates were twelve *p,*

PEKAH
King of Israel (2Ki 15:25-31; Isa 7:1).

PEKAHIAH*
Son of Menahem; king of Israel (2Ki 15:22-26).

PEN
Mt 5:18 letter, not the least stroke of a *p,*

PENTECOST
Ac 2: 1 of *P* came, they were all together

PEOPLE (PEOPLES)
Dt 32: 9 the LORD's portion is his *p,*
Ru 1:16 Your *p* will be my *p*
2Ch 7:14 if my *p,* who are called
Jer 24: 7 They will be my *p,*
Zec 2:11 and will become my *p.*
Lk 2:10 joy that will be for all the *p.*
Ac 15:14 from the Gentiles a *p.*
2Co 6:16 and they will be my *p.*"
Tit 2:14 a *p* that are his very own,
1Pe 2: 9 you are a chosen *p,*
Rev 21: 3 They will be his *p,*

PEOPLES (PEOPLE)
Da 7:14 all *p,* nations and men
Mic 4: 1 and *p* will stream to it.

PERCEIVING
Isa 6: 9 be ever seeing, but never *p.*'

PERFECT (PERFECTER PERFECTION)
SS 6: 9 but my dove, my *p* one, is unique,
Isa 26: 3 You will keep in *p* peace
Mt 5:48 as your heavenly Father is *p.*
Ro 12: 2 his good, pleasing and *p* will.
2Co 12: 9 for my power is made *p*
Col 1:28 so that we may present everyone *p*
3:14 binds them all together in *p* unity.
Heb 9:11 and more *p* tabernacle that is not
10:14 he has made *p* forever those who
Jas 1:17 Every good and *p* gift is from above
1:25 into the *p* law that gives freedom,
3: 2 he is a *p* man, able
1Jn 4:18 But *p* love drives out fear,

PERFECTER* (PERFECT)
Heb 12: 2 the author and *p* of our faith,

PERFECTION (PERFECT)
Ps 119:96 To all *p* I see a limit;
2Co 13:11 Aim for *p,* listen to my appeal,
Heb 7:11 If *p* could have been attained

PERFORMS
Ps 77:14 You are the God who *p* miracles;

PERISH (PERISHABLE)
Ps 1: 6 but the way of the wicked will *p.*
102:26 They will *p,* but you remain;
Lk 13: 3 unless you repent, you too will all *p*
Jn 10:28 eternal life, and they shall never *p;*
Col 2:22 These are all destined to *p* with use,
Heb 1:11 They will *p,* but you remain;
2Pe 3: 9 not wanting anyone to *p,*

PERISHABLE (PERISH)
1Co 15:42 The body that is sown is *p,*

PERJURERS
1Ti 1:10 for slave traders and liars and *p*—

PERMISSIBLE (PERMIT)
1Co 10:23 "Everything is *p*"— but not

PERMIT (PERMISSIBLE)
1Ti 2:12 I do not *p* a woman to teach

PERSECUTE (PERSECUTED PERSECUTION)
Mt 5:11 *p* you and falsely say all kinds
Jn 15:20 they persecuted me, they will *p* you
Ac 9: 4 why do you *p* me?" "Who are you,
Ro 12:14 Bless those who *p* you; bless

PERSECUTED (PERSECUTE)
1Co 4:12 when we are *p,* we endure it;
2Ti 3:12 life in Christ Jesus will be *p,*

PERSECUTION (PERSECUTE)
Ro 8:35 or hardship or *p* or famine

PERSEVERANCE (PERSEVERE)
Ro 5: 3 we know that suffering produces *p;*
5: 4 *p,* character; and character, hope.
Heb 12: 1 run with *p* the race marked out
Jas 1: 3 the testing of your faith develops *p.*
2Pe 1: 6 *p;* and to *p,* godliness;

PERSEVERE* (PERSEVERANCE PERSEVERED PERSEVERES)
1Ti 4:16 *P* in them, because if you do,
Heb 10:36 You need to *p* so that

PERSEVERED* (PERSEVERE)
Heb 11:27 he *p* because he saw him who is
Jas 5:11 consider blessed those who have *p.*
Rev 2: 3 You have *p* and have endured

PERSEVERES* (PERSEVERE)
1Co 13: 7 trusts, always hopes, always *p.*
Jas 1:12 Blessed is the man who *p*

PERSUADE
2Co 5:11 is to fear the Lord, we try to *p* men.

PERVERSION (PERVERT)
Lev 18:23 sexual relations with it; that is a *p.*
Jude : 7 up to sexual immorality and *p.*

PERVERT (PERVERSION PERVERTS)
Gal 1: 7 are trying to *p* the gospel of Christ.

PERVERTS* (PERVERT)
1Ti 1:10 for murderers, for adulterers and *p,*

PESTILENCE
Ps 91: 6 nor the *p* that stalks in the darkness

PETER
Apostle, brother of Andrew, also called Simon (Mt 10:2; Mk 3:16; Lk 6:14; Ac 1:13), and Cephas (Jn 1:42). Confession of Christ (Mt 16:13-20; Mk 8:27-30; Lk 9:18-27). At transfiguration (Mt 17:1-8; Mk 9:2-8; Lk 9:28-36; 2Pe 1:16-18). Caught fish with coin (Mt 17:24-27). Denial of Jesus predicted (Mt 26:31-35; Mk 14:27-31; Lk 22:31-34; Jn 13:31-38). Denied Jesus (Mt 26:69-75; Mk 14:66-72; Lk 22:54-62; Jn 18:15-27). Commissioned by Jesus to shepherd his flock (Jn 21:15-23).

Speech at Pentecost (Ac 2). Healed beggar (Ac 3:1-10). Speech at temple (Ac 3:11-26), before Sanhedrin (Ac 4:1-22). In Samaria (Ac 8:14-25). Sent by vision to Cornelius (Ac 10). Announced salvation of Gentiles in Jerusalem (Ac 11; 15). Freed from prison (Ac 12). Inconsistency at Antioch (Gal 2:11-21). At Jerusalem Council (Ac 15).

PHARISEES
Mt 5:20 surpasses that of the *P*

PHILIP
1. Apostle (Mt 10:3; Mk 3:18; Lk 6:14; Jn 1:43-48; 14:8; Ac 1:13).
2. Deacon (Ac 6:1-7); evangelist in Samaria (Ac 8:4-25), to Ethiopian (Ac 8:26-40).

PHILOSOPHY*
Col 2: 8 through hollow and deceptive *p,*

PHYLACTERIES*
Mt 23: 5 They make their *p* wide

PHYSICAL
1Ti 4: 8 For *p* training is of some value,
Jas 2:16 but does nothing about his *p* needs,

PIECES
Ge 15:17 and passed between the *p.*
Jer 34:18 and then walked between its *p.*

PIERCED
Ps 22:16 they have *p* my hands and my feet.
Isa 53: 5 But he was *p* for our transgressions,
Zec 12:10 look on me, the one they have *p,*
Jn 19:37 look on the one they have *p.*"

PIGS
Mt 7: 6 do not throw your pearls to *p.*

PILATE
Governor of Judea. Questioned Jesus (Mt 27:1-26; Mk 15:15; Lk 22:66-23:25; Jn 18:28-19:16); sent him to Herod (Lk 23:6-12); consented to his crucifixion when crowds chose Barabbas (Mt 27:15-26; Mk 15:6-15; Lk 23:13-25; Jn 19:1-10).

PILLAR
Ge 19:26 and she became a *p* of salt.
Ex 13:21 ahead of them in a *p* of cloud

2Co 8: 2 and their extreme *p* welled up
8: 9 through his *p* might become rich.

POWER (POWERFUL POWERS)
1Ch 29:11 LORD, is the greatness and the *p*
2Ch 32: 7 for there is a greater *p* with us
Job 36:22 "God is exalted in his *p*.
Ps 63: 2 and beheld your *p* and your glory.
68:34 Proclaim the *p* of God,
147: 5 Great is our Lord and mighty in *p*;
Pr 24: 5 A wise man has great *p*,
Isa 40:10 the Sovereign LORD comes with *p*
Zec 4: 6 nor by *p*, but by my Spirit,'
Mt 22:29 do not know the Scriptures or the *p*
24:30 on the clouds of the sky, with *p*
Ac 1: 8 you will receive *p* when the Holy
4:33 With great *p* the apostles
10:38 with the Holy Spirit and *p*,
Ro 1:16 it is the *p* of God for the salvation
1Co 1:18 to us who are being saved it is the *p*
15:56 of death is sin, and the *p*
2Co 12: 9 for my *p* is made perfect
Eph 1:19 and his incomparably great *p*
Php 3:10 and the *p* of his resurrection
Col 1:11 strengthened with all *p* according
2Ti 1: 7 but a spirit of *p*, of love
Heb 7:16 of the *p* of an indestructible life.
Rev 4:11 to receive glory and honor and *p*,
19: 1 and glory and *p* belong to our God,
20: 6 The second death has no *p*

POWERFUL (POWER)
Ps 29: 4 The voice of the LORD is *p*;
Lk 24:19 *p* in word and deed before God
2Th 1: 7 in blazing fire with his *p* angels.
Heb 1: 3 sustaining all things by his *p* word.
Jas 5:16 The prayer of a righteous man is *p*

POWERLESS
Ro 5: 6 when we were still *p*, Christ died
8: 3 For what the law was *p* to do

POWERS (POWER)
Ro 8:38 nor any *p*, neither height nor depth
1Co 12:10 to another miraculous *p*,
Col 1:16 whether thrones or *p* or rulers
2:15 And having disarmed the *p*

PRACTICE
Lev 19:26 " 'Do not *p* divination or sorcery.
Mt 23: 3 for they do not *p* what they preach.
Lk 8:21 hear God's word and put it into *p*."
Ro 12:13 *P* hospitality.
1Ti 5: 4 to put their religion into *p* by caring

PRAISE (PRAISED PRAISES PRAISING)
Ex 15: 2 He is my God, and I will *p* him,
Dt 32: 3 Oh, *p* the greatness of our God!
Ru 4:14 said to Naomi: "*P* be to the LORD,
2Sa 22:47 The LORD lives! *P* be to my Rock
1Ch 16:25 is the LORD and most worthy of *p*;
2Ch 20:21 and to *p* him for the splendor
Ps 8: 2 you have ordained *p*
33: 1 it is fitting for the upright to *p* him.
34: 1 his *p* will always be on my lips.
40: 3 a hymn of *p* to our God.
48: 1 the LORD, and most worthy of *p*,
68:19 *P* be to the Lord, to God our Savior
89: 5 The heavens *p* your wonders,
100: 4 and his courts with *p*;
105: 2 Sing to him, sing *p* to him;
106: 1 *P* the LORD.
119:175 Let me live that I may *p* you,
139:14 I *p* you because I am fearfully
145:21 Let every creature *p* his holy name
146: 1 *P* the LORD, O my soul.
150: 2 *p* him for his surpassing greatness.
150: 6 that has breath *p* the LORD.

Pr 27: 2 Let another *p* you, and not your
27:21 man is tested by the *p* he receives.
31:31 let her works bring her *p*
Mt 5:16 and *p* your Father in heaven.
21:16 you have ordained *p*'?"
Jn 12:43 for they loved *p* from men more
Eph 1: 6 to the *p* of his glorious grace,
1:12 might be for the *p* of his glory.
1:14 to the *p* of his glory.
Heb 13:15 offer to God a sacrifice of *p*—
Jas 5:13 happy? Let him sing songs of *p*.

PRAISED (PRAISE)
1Ch 29:10 David *p* the LORD in the presence
Ne 8: 6 Ezra *p* the LORD, the great God;
Da 2:19 Then Daniel *p* the God of heaven
Ro 9: 5 who is God over all, forever *p*!
1Pe 4:11 that in all things God may be *p*

PRAISES (PRAISE)
2Sa 22:50 I will sing *p* to your name.
Ps 47: 6 Sing *p* to God, sing *p*;
147: 1 How good it is to sing *p* to our God,
Pr 31:28 her husband also, and he *p* her:

PRAISING (PRAISE)
Ac 10:46 speaking in tongues and *p* God.
1Co 14:16 If you are *p* God with your spirit,

PRAY (PRAYED PRAYER PRAYERS PRAYING)
Dt 4: 7 is near us whenever we *p* to him?
1Sa 12:23 the LORD by failing to *p* for you.
2Ch 7:14 will humble themselves and *p*
Job 42: 8 My servant Job will *p* for you,
Ps 122: 6 *P* for the peace of Jerusalem:
Mt 5:44 and *p* for those who persecute you,
6: 5 "And when you *p*, do not be like
6: 9 "This, then, is how you should *p*:
26:36 Sit here while I go over there and *p*
Lk 6:28 *p* for those who mistreat you.
18: 1 them that they should always *p*
22:40 "*P* that you will not fall
Ro 8:26 do not know what we ought to *p*,
1Co 14:13 in a tongue should *p* that he may
1Th 5:17 Be joyful always; *p* continually;
Jas 5:13 one of you in trouble? He should *p*.
5:16 *p* for each other so that you may be

PRAYED (PRAY)
1Sa 1:27 I *p* for this child, and the LORD
Jnh 2: 1 From inside the fish Jonah *p*
Mk 14:35 *p* that if possible the hour might

PRAYER (PRAY)
2Ch 30:27 for their *p* reached heaven,
Ezr 8:23 about this, and he answered our *p*.
Ps 6: 9 the LORD accepts my *p*.
86: 6 Hear my *p*, O LORD;
Pr 15: 8 but the *p* of the upright pleases him
Isa 56: 7 a house of *p* for all nations."
Mt 21:13 house will be called a house of *p*,'
Mk 11:24 whatever you ask for in *p*,
Jn 17:15 My *p* is not that you take them out
Ac 6: 4 and will give our attention to *p*
Php 4: 6 but in everything, by *p* and petition
Jas 5:15 *p* offered in faith will make the sick
1Pe 3:12 and his ears are attentive to their *p*,

PRAYERS (PRAY)
1Ch 5:20 He answered their *p*, because they
Mk 12:40 and for a show make lengthy *p*.
1Pe 3: 7 so that nothing will hinder your *p*.
Rev 5: 8 which are the *p* of the saints.

PRAYING (PRAY)
Mk 11:25 And when you stand *p*,
Jn 17: 9 I am not *p* for the world,
Ac 16:25 and Silas were *p* and singing hymns

Eph 6:18 always keep on *p* for all the saints.

PREACH (PREACHED PREACHING)
Mt 23: 3 they do not practice what they *p*.
Mk 16:15 and *p* the good news to all creation.
Ac 9:20 At once he began to *p*
Ro 10:15 how can they *p* unless they are sent
15:20 to *p* the gospel where Christ was
1Co 1:17 to *p* the gospel—not with words
1:23 wisdom, but we *p* Christ crucified:
9:14 that those who *p* the gospel should
9:16 Woe to me if I do not *p* the gospel!
2Co 10:16 so that we can *p* the gospel
Gal 1: 8 from heaven should *p* a gospel
2Ti 4: 2 I give you this charge: *P* the Word;

PREACHED (PREACH)
Mk 13:10 And the gospel must first be *p*
Ac 8: 4 had been scattered *p* the word
1Co 9:27 so that after I have *p* to others,
15: 1 you of the gospel I *p* to you,
2Co 11: 4 other than the Jesus we *p*,
Gal 1: 8 other than the one we *p* to you,
Php 1:18 false motives or true, Christ is *p*.
1Ti 3:16 was *p* among the nations,

PREACHING (PREACH)
Ro 10:14 hear without someone *p* to them?
1Co 9:18 in *p* the gospel I may offer it free
1Ti 4:13 the public reading of Scripture, to *p*
5:17 especially those whose work is *p*

PRECEPTS
Ps 19: 8 The *p* of the LORD are right,
111: 7 all his *p* are trustworthy.
111:10 who follow his *p* have good
119:40 How I long for your *p*!
119:69 I keep your *p* with all my heart.
119:104 I gain understanding from your *p*;
119:159 See how I love your *p*;

PRECIOUS
Ps 19:10 They are more *p* than gold,
116:15 *P* in the sight of the LORD
Pr 8:11 for wisdom is more *p* than rubies,
Isa 28:16 a *p* cornerstone for a sure
1Pe 1:19 but with the *p* blood of Christ,
2: 6 a chosen and *p* cornerstone,
2Pe 1: 4 us his very great and *p* promises,

PREDESTINED* (DESTINY)
Ro 8:29 *p* to be conformed to the likeness
8:30 And those he *p*, he also called;
Eph 1: 5 In love he *p* us to be adopted
1:11 having been *p* according

PREDICTION*
Jer 28: 9 only if his *p* comes true."

PREPARE (PREPARED)
Ps 23: 5 You *p* a table before me
Am 4:12 *p* to meet your God, O Israel."
Jn 14: 2 there to *p* a place for you.
Eph 4:12 to *p* God's people for works

PREPARED (PREPARE)
Mt 25:34 the kingdom *p* for you
1Co 2: 9 what God has *p* for those who love
Eph 2:10 which God *p* in advance for us
2Ti 4: 2 be *p* in season and out of season;
1Pe 3:15 Always be *p* to give an answer

PRESENCE (PRESENT)
Ex 25:30 Put the bread of the *P* on this table
Ezr 9:15 one of us can stand in your *p*."
Ps 31:20 the shelter of your *p* you hide them
89:15 who walk in the light of your *p*,
90: 8 our secret sins in the light of your *p*

Ps 139: 7 Where can I flee from your *p?*
Jer 5:22 "Should you not tremble in my *p?*
Heb 9:24 now to appear for us in God's *p.*
Jude :24 before his glorious *p* without fault

PRESENT (PRESENCE)
2Co 11: 2 so that I might *p* you as a pure
Eph 5:27 and to *p* her to himself
2Ti 2:15 Do your best to *p* yourself to God

PRESERVES
Ps 1 19:50 Your promise *p* my life.

PRESS (PRESSED PRESSURE)
Php 3:14 I *p* on toward the goal

PRESSED (PRESS)
Lk 6:38 *p* down, shaken together

PRESSURE (PRESS)
2Co 1: 8 We were under great *p,* far
11:28 I face daily the *p* of my concern

PREVAILS
1Sa 2: 9 "It is not by strength that one *p;*

PRICE
Job 28:18 the *p* of wisdom is beyond rubies.
1Co 6:20 your own; you were bought at a *p.*
7:23 bought at a *p;* do not become slaves

PRIDE (PROUD)
Pr 8:13 I hate *p* and arrogance,
16:18 *P* goes before destruction,
Da 4:37 And those who walk in *p* he is able
Gal 6: 4 Then he can take *p* in himself,
Jas 1: 9 ought to take *p* in his high position.

PRIEST (PRIESTHOOD PRIESTS)
Heb 4:14 have a great high *p* who has gone
4:15 do not have a high *p* who is unable
7:26 Such a high *p* meets our need—
8: 1 We do have such a high *p,*

PRIESTHOOD (PRIEST)
Heb 7:24 lives forever, he has a permanent *p.*
1Pe 2: 5 into a spiritual house to be a holy *p,*
2: 9 you are a chosen people, a royal *p,*

PRIESTS (PRIEST)
Ex 19: 6 you will be for me a kingdom of *p*
Rev 5:10 to be a kingdom and *p*

PRINCE
Isa 9: 6 Everlasting Father, *P* of Peace.
Jn 12:31 now the *p* of this world will be
Ac 5:31 as *P* and Savior that he might give

PRISON (PRISONER)
Isa 42: 7 to free captives from *p*
Mt 25:36 I was in *p* and you came to visit me
1Pe 3:19 spirits in *p* who disobeyed long ago
Rev 20: 7 Satan will be released from his *p*

PRISONER (PRISON)
Ro 7:23 and making me a *p* of the law of sin
Gal 3:22 declares that the whole world is a *p*
Eph 3: 1 the *p* of Christ Jesus for the sake

PRIVILEGE*
2Co 8: 4 pleaded with us for the *p* of sharing

PRIZE
1Co 9:24 Run in such a way as to get the *p.*
Php 3:14 on toward the goal to win the *p*

PROCLAIM (PROCLAIMED PROCLAIMING)
1Ch 16:23 *p* his salvation day after day.
Ps 19: 1 the skies *p* the work of his hands.
50: 6 the heavens *p* his righteousness,
68:34 *P* the power of God,
118:17 will *p* what the LORD has done.
Zec 9:10 He will *p* peace to the nations.
Ac 20:27 hesitated to *p* to you the whole will
1Co 11:26 you *p* the Lord's death

PROCLAIMED (PROCLAIM)
Ro 15:19 I have fully *p* the gospel of Christ.
Col 1:23 that has been *p* to every creature

PROCLAIMING (PROCLAIM)
Ro 10: 8 the word of faith we are *p:*

PRODUCE (PRODUCES)
Mt 3: 8 *P* fruit in keeping with repentance.
3:10 tree that does not *p* good fruit will

PRODUCES (PRODUCE)
Pr 30:33 so stirring up anger *p* strife."
Ro 5: 3 that suffering *p* perseverance;
Heb 12:11 it *p* a harvest of righteousness

PROFANE
Lev 22:32 Do not *p* my holy name.

PROFESS*
1Ti 2:10 for women who *p* to worship God.
Heb 4:14 let us hold firmly to the faith we *p.*
10:23 unswervingly to the hope we *p,*

PROMISE (PROMISED PROMISES)
1Ki 8:20 The LORD has kept the *p* he made
Ac 2:39 The *p* is for you and your children
Gal 3:14 that by faith we might receive the *p*
1Ti 4: 8 holding *p* for both the present life
2Pe 3: 9 Lord is not slow in keeping his *p,*

PROMISED (PROMISE)
Ex 3:17 And I have *p* to bring you up out
Dt 26:18 his treasured possession as he *p,*
Ps 119:57 I have *p* to obey your words.
Ro 4:21 power to do what he had *p.*
Heb 10:23 for he who *p* is faithful.
2Pe 3: 4 "Where is this 'coming' he *p?*

PROMISES (PROMISE)
Jos 21:45 one of all the LORD's good *p*
Ro 9: 4 the temple worship and the *p.*
2Pe 1: 4 us his very great and precious *p,*

PROMPTED
1Th 1: 3 your labor *p* by love, and your
2Th 1:11 and every act *p* by your faith.

PROPHECIES (PROPHESY)
1Co 13: 8 where there are *p,* they will cease;
1Th 5:20 do not treat *p* with contempt.

PROPHECY (PROPHESY)
1Co 14: 1 gifts, especially the gift of *p.*
2Pe 1:20 you must understand that no *p*

PROPHESY (PROPHECIES PROPHECY PROPHESYING PROPHET PROPHETS)
Joel 2:28 Your sons and daughters will *p,*
Mt 7:22 Lord, did we not *p* in your name,
1Co 14:39 my brothers, be eager to *p,*

PROPHESYING (PROPHESY)
Ro 12: 6 If a man's gift is *p,* let him use it

PROPHET (PROPHESY)
Dt 18:18 up for them a *p* like you
Am 7:14 "I was neither a *p* nor a prophet's
Mt 10:41 Anyone who receives a *p*
Lk 4:24 "no *p* is accepted in his hometown.

PROPHETS (PROPHESY)
Ps 105:15 do my *p* no harm."
Mt 5:17 come to abolish the Law or the *P;*
7:12 for this sums up the Law and the *P.*
24:24 false Christs and false *p* will appear
Lk 24:25 believe all that the *p* have spoken!
Ac 10:43 All the *p* testify about him that
1Co 12:28 second *p,* third teachers, then
14:32 The spirits of *p* are subject
Eph 2:20 foundation of the apostles and *p,*
Heb 1: 1 through the *p* at many times
1Pe 1:10 Concerning this salvation, the *p,*
2Pe 1:19 word of the *p* made more certain,

PROSPER (PROSPERITY PROSPERS)
Pr 28:25 he who trusts in the LORD will *p.*

PROSPERITY (PROSPER)
Ps 73: 3 when I saw the *p* of the wicked.
Pr 13:21 but *p* is the reward of the righteous.

PROSPERS (PROSPER)
Ps 1: 3 Whatever he does *p.*

PROSTITUTE (PROSTITUTES)
1Co 6:15 of Christ and unite them with a *p?*

PROSTITUTES (PROSTITUTE)
Lk 15:30 property with *p* comes home,
1Co 6: 9 male *p* nor homosexual offenders

PROSTRATE
Dt 9:18 again I fell *p* before the LORD

PROTECT (PROTECTS)
Ps 32: 7 you will *p* me from trouble
Pr 2:11 Discretion will *p* you,
Jn 17:11 *p* them by the power of your name

PROTECTS (PROTECT)
1Co 13: 7 It always *p,* always trusts,

PROUD (PRIDE)
Pr 16: 5 The LORD detests all the *p*
Ro 12:16 Do not be *p,* but be willing
1Co 13: 4 it does not boast, it is not *p.*

PROVE
Ac 26:20 *p* their repentance by their deeds.
1Co 4: 2 been given a trust must *p* faithful.

PROVIDE (PROVIDED PROVIDES)
Ge 22: 8 "God himself will *p* the lamb
Isa 43:20 because I *p* water in the desert
1Ti 5: 8 If anyone does not *p*

PROVIDED (PROVIDE)
Jnh 1:17 But the LORD *p* a great fish
4: 6 Then the LORD God *p* a vine
4: 7 dawn the next day God *p* a worm,
4: 8 God *p* a scorching east wind,

PROVIDES (PROVIDE)
1Ti 6:17 who richly *p* us with everything
1Pe 4:11 it with the strength God *p,*

PROVOKED
Ecc 7: 9 Do not be quickly *p* in your spirit,

PRUDENT
Pr 14:15 a *p* man gives thought to his steps.
19:14 but a *p* wife is from the LORD.
Am 5:13 Therefore the *p* man keeps quiet

PRUNING
Isa 2: 4 and their spears into *p* hooks.
Joel 3:10 and your *p* hooks into spears.

PSALMS
Eph 5:19 Speak to one another with *p,*
Col 3:16 and as you sing *p,* hymns

PUBLICLY
Ac 20:20 have taught you *p* and from house
1Ti 5:20 Those who sin are to be rebuked *p,*

PUFFS
1Co 8: 1 Knowledge *p* up, but love builds up

PULLING
2Co 10: 8 building you up rather than *p* you

PUNISH (PUNISHED PUNISHES)
Ex 32:34 I will *p* them for their sin."
Pr 23:13 if you *p* him with the rod, he will
Isa 13:11 I will *p* the world for its evil,
1Pe 2:14 by him to *p* those who do wrong

PUNISHED (PUNISH)
La 3:39 complain when *p* for his sins?
2Th 1: 9 be *p* with everlasting destruction
Heb 10:29 to be *p* who has trampled the Son

PUNISHES (PUNISH)
Heb 12: 6 and he *p* everyone he accepts

PURE (PURIFIES PURIFY PURITY)
2Sa 22:27 to the *p* you show yourself *p,*
Ps 24: 4 who has clean hands and a *p* heart,
51:10 Create in me a *p* heart, O God,
119: 9 can a young man keep his way *p?*
Pr 20: 9 can say, "I have kept my heart *p;*
Isa 52:11 Come out from it and be *p,*
Hab 1:13 Your eyes are too *p* to look on evil;
Mt 5: 8 Blessed are the *p* in heart,
2Co 11: 2 I might present you as a *p* virgin
Php 4: 8 whatever is *p,* whatever is lovely,
1Ti 5:22 Keep yourself *p.*
Tit 1:15 To the *p,* all things are *p,*
2: 5 to be self-controlled and *p,*
Heb 13: 4 and the marriage bed kept *p,*
1Jn 3: 3 him purifies himself, just as he is *p.*

PURGE
Pr 20:30 and beatings *p* the inmost being.

PURIFIES* (PURE)
1Jn 1: 7 of Jesus, his Son, *p* us from all sin.
3: 3 who has this hope in him *p* himself,

PURIFY (PURE)
Tit 2:14 to *p* for himself a people that are
1Jn 1: 9 and *p* us from all unrighteousness.

PURITY (PURE)
2Co 6: 6 in *p,* understanding, patience
1Ti 4:12 in life, in love, in faith and in *p.*

PURPOSE
Pr 19:21 but it is the LORD's *p* that prevails
Isa 55:11 and achieve the *p* for which I sent it
Ro 8:28 have been called according to his *p.*
Php 2: 2 love, being one in spirit and *p.*

PURSES
Lk 12:33 Provide *p* for yourselves that will

PURSUE
Ps 34:14 seek peace and *p* it.
2Ti 2:22 and *p* righteousness, faith,
1Pe 3:11 he must seek peace and *p* it.

QUALITIES (QUALITY)
2Pe 1: 8 For if you possess these *q*

QUALITY (QUALITIES)
1Co 3:13 and the fire will test the *q*

QUARREL (QUARRELSOME)
Pr 15:18 but a patient man calms a *q.*
17:14 Starting a *q* is like breaching a dam;
17:19 He who loves a *q* loves sin;
2Ti 2:24 And the Lord's servant must not *q;*

QUARRELSOME (QUARREL)
Pr 19:13 a *q* wife is like a constant dripping.
1Ti 3: 3 not violent but gentle, not *q,*

QUICK-TEMPERED
Tit 1: 7 not *q,* not given to drunkenness,

QUIET (QUIETNESS)
Ps 23: 2 he leads me beside *q* waters,
Zep 3:17 he will *q* you with his love,
Lk 19:40 he replied, "if they keep *q,*
1Ti 2: 2 we may live peaceful and *q* lives
1Pe 3: 4 beauty of a gentle and *q* spirit,

QUIETNESS (QUIET)
Isa 30:15 in *q* and trust is your strength,
32:17 the effect of righteousness will be *q*
1Ti 2:11 A woman should learn in *q*

QUIVER
Ps 127: 5 whose *q* is full of them.

RACE
Ecc 9:11 The *r* is not to the swift
1Co 9:24 that in a *r* all the runners run,
2Ti 4: 7 I have finished the *r,* I have kept
Heb 12: 1 perseverance the *r* marked out

RACHEL
Daughter of Laban (Ge 29:16); wife of Jacob (Ge 29:28); bore two sons (Ge 30:22-24; 35:16-24; 46:19).

RADIANCE (RADIANT)
Heb 1: 3 The Son is the *r* of God's glory

RADIANT (RADIANCE)
Ex 34:29 he was not aware that his face was *r*
Ps 34: 5 Those who look to him are *r;*
SS 5:10 *Beloved* My lover is *r* and ruddy,
Isa 60: 5 Then you will look and be *r,*
Eph 5:27 her to himself as a *r* church,

RAIN (RAINBOW)
Mt 5:45 and sends *r* on the righteous

RAINBOW (RAIN)
Ge 9:13 I have set my *r* in the clouds,

RAISED (RISE)
Ro 4:25 was *r* to life for our justification.
10: 9 in your heart that God *r* him
1Co 15: 4 that he was *r* on the third day

RAN (RUN)
Jnh 1: 3 But Jonah *r* away from the LORD

RANSOM
Mt 20:28 and to give his life as a *r* for many."
Heb 9:15 as a *r* to set them free

RAVENS
1Ki 17: 6 The *r* brought him bread
Lk 12:24 Consider the *r:* They do not sow

READ (READS)
Jos 8:34 Joshua *r* all the words of the law—
Ne 8: 8 They *r* from the Book of the Law
2Co 3: 2 known and *r* by everybody.

READS (READ)
Rev 1: 3 Blessed is the one who *r* the words

REAL (REALITY)
Jn 6:55 is *r* food and my blood is *r* drink.

REALITY* (REAL)
Col 2:17 the *r,* however, is found in Christ.

REAP (REAPS)
Job 4: 8 and those who sow trouble *r* it.
2Co 9: 6 generously will also *r* generously.

REAPS (REAP)
Gal 6: 7 A man *r* what he sows.

REASON
Isa 1:18 "Come now, let us *r* together,"
1Pe 3:15 to give the *r* for the hope that you

REBEKAH
Sister of Laban, secured as bride for Isaac (Ge 24). Mother of Esau and Jacob (Ge 25:19-26). Taken by Abimelech as sister of Isaac; returned (Ge 26:1-11). Encouraged Jacob to trick Isaac out of blessing (Ge 27:1-17).

REBEL
Mt 10:21 children will *r* against their parents

REBUKE (REBUKED REBUKING)
Pr 9: 8 *r* a wise man and he will love you.
27: 5 Better is open *r*
Lk 17: 3 "If your brother sins, *r* him,
2Ti 4: 2 correct, *r* and encourage—
Rev 3:19 Those whom I love I *r*

REBUKED (REBUKE)
1Ti 5:20 Those who sin are to be *r* publicly,

REBUKING (REBUKE)
2Ti 3:16 *r,* correcting and training

RECEIVE (RECEIVED RECEIVES)
Ac 1: 8 you will *r* power when the Holy
20:35 'It is more blessed to give than to *r*
2Co 6:17 and I will *r* you."
Rev 4:11 to *r* glory and honor and power,

RECEIVED (RECEIVE)
Mt 6: 2 they have *r* their reward in full.
10: 8 Freely you have *r,* freely give.
1Co 11:23 For I *r* from the Lord what I
Col 2: 6 just as you *r* Christ Jesus as Lord,
1Pe 4:10 should use whatever gift he has *r*

RECEIVES (RECEIVE)
Mt 7: 8 everyone who asks *r;* he who seeks
10:40 he who *r* me *r* the one who sent me.
Ac 10:43 believes in him *r* forgiveness of sins

RECKONING
Isa 10: 3 What will you do on the day of *r,*

RECOGNIZE (RECOGNIZED)
Mt 7:16 By their fruit you will *r* them.

RECOGNIZED (RECOGNIZE)
Mt 12:33 for a tree is *r* by its fruit.
Ro 7:13 in order that sin might be *r* as sin,

RECOMPENSE
Isa 40:10 and his *r* accompanies him.

RECONCILE (RECONCILED RECONCILIATION)
Eph 2:16 in this one body to *r* both of them

RECONCILED (RECONCILE)
Mt 5:24 First go and be *r* to your brother;
Ro 5:10 we were *r* to him through the death
2Co 5:18 who *r* us to himself through Christ

RECONCILIATION* (RECONCILE)
Ro 5:11 whom we have now received *r.*
11:15 For if their rejection is the *r*
2Co 5:18 and gave us the ministry of *r:*
5:19 committed to us the message of *r.*

RECORD
Ps 130: 3 If you, O LORD, kept a *r* of sins,

RED
Isa 1:18 though they are *r* as crimson,

REDEEM (KINSMAN-REDEEMER REDEEMED REDEEMER REDEMPTION)
2Sa 7:23 on earth that God went out to *r*
Ps 49: 7 No man can *r* the life of another
Gal 4: 5 under law, to *r* those under law,

REDEEMED (REDEEM)
Gal 3:13 Christ *r* us from the curse
1Pe 1:18 or gold that you were *r*

REDEEMER (REDEEM)
Job 19:25 I know that my *R* lives,

REDEMPTION (REDEEM)
Ps 130: 7 and with him is full *r.*
Lk 21:28 because your *r* is drawing near."
Ro 8:23 as sons, the *r* of our bodies.
Eph 1: 7 In him we have *r* through his blood
Col 1:14 in whom we have *r,* the forgiveness
Heb 9:12 having obtained eternal *r.*

REFLECT
2Co 3:18 unveiled faces all *r* the Lord's

REFUGE
Nu 35:11 towns to be your cities of *r,*
Dt 33:27 The eternal God is your *r,*
Ru 2:12 wings you have come to take *r."*
Ps 46: 1 God is our *r* and strength,
91: 2 "He is my *r* and my fortress,

REHOBOAM
Son of Solomon (1Ki 11:43; 1Ch 3:10). Harsh treatment of subjects caused divided kingdom (1Ki 12:1-24; 14:21-31; 2Ch 10-12).

REIGN
Ex 15:18 The LORD will *r*
Ro 6:12 Therefore do not let sin *r*
1Co 15:25 For he must *r* until he has put all
2Ti 2:12 we will also *r* with him.
Rev 20: 6 will *r* with him for a thousand years

REJECTED (REJECTS)
Ps 118:22 The stone the builders *r*
Isa 53: 3 He was despised and *r* by men,
1Ti 4: 4 nothing is to be *r* if it is received
1Pe 2: 4 *r* by men but chosen by God
2: 7 "The stone the builders *r*

REJECTS (REJECTED)
Lk 10:16 but he who *r* me *r* him who sent me
Jn 3:36 whoever *r* the Son will not see life,

REJOICE (JOY)
Ps 2:11 and *r* with trembling.
66: 6 come, let us *r* in him.
118:24 let us *r* and be glad in it.
Pr 5:18 may you *r* in the wife of your youth
Lk 10:20 but *r* that your names are written
15: 6 '*R* with me; I have found my lost
Ro 12:15 Rejoice with those who *r;* mourn
Php 4: 4 *R* in the Lord always.

REJOICES (JOY)
Isa 61:10 my soul *r* in my God.
Lk 1:47 and my spirit *r* in God my Savior,
1Co 12:26 if one part is honored, every part *r*
13: 6 delight in evil but *r* with the truth.

REJOICING (JOY)
Ps 30: 5 but *r* comes in the morning.
Lk 15: 7 in the same way there will be more *r*
Ac 5:41 *r* because they had been counted

RELIABLE
2Ti 2: 2 witnesses entrust to *r* men who will

RELIGION
1Ti 5: 4 all to put their *r* into practice
Jas 1:27 *R* that God our Father accepts

REMAIN (REMAINS)
Nu 33:55 allow to *r* will become barbs
Jn 15: 7 If you *r* in me and my words
Ro 13: 8 Let no debt *r* outstanding,
1Co 13:13 And now these three *r:* faith,
2Ti 2:13 he will *r* faithful,

REMAINS (REMAIN)
Ps 146: 6 the LORD, who *r* faithful forever.
Heb 7: 3 Son of God he *r* a priest forever.

REMEMBER (REMEMBERS REMEMBRANCE)
Ex 20: 8 "*R* the Sabbath day
1Ch 16:12 *R* the wonders he has done,
Ecc 12: 1 *R* your Creator
Jer 31:34 and will *r* their sins no more."
Gal 2:10 we should continue to *r* the poor,
Php 1: 3 I thank my God every time I *r* you.
Heb 8:12 and will *r* their sins no more."

REMEMBERS (REMEMBER)
Ps 103:14 he *r* that we are dust.
111: 5 he *r* his covenant forever.
Isa 43:25 and *r* your sins no more.

REMEMBRANCE (REMEMBER)
1Co 11:24 which is for you; do this in *r* of me

REMIND
Jn 14:26 will *r* you of everything I have said

REMOVED
Ps 30:11 you *r* my sackcloth and clothed me
103:12 so far has he *r* our transgressions
Jn 20: 1 and saw that the stone had been *r*

RENEW (RENEWED RENEWING)
Ps 51:10 and *r* a steadfast spirit within me.
Isa 40:31 will *r* their strength.

RENEWED (RENEW)
Ps 103: 5 that your youth is *r* like the eagle's.
2Co 4:16 yet inwardly we are being *r* day

RENEWING (RENEW)
Ro 12: 2 transformed by the *r* of your mind.

RENOUNCE (RENOUNCES)
Da 4:27 *R* your sins by doing what is right,

RENOUNCES (RENOUNCE)
Pr 28:13 confesses and *r* them finds

RENOWN
Isa 63:12 to gain for himself everlasting *r,*
Jer 32:20 have gained the *r* that is still yours.

REPAID (PAY)
Lk 14:14 you will be *r* at the resurrection
Col 3:25 Anyone who does wrong will be *r*

REPAY (PAY)
Dt 32:35 It is mine to avenge; I will *r.*
Ru 2:12 May the LORD *r* you
Ps 116:12 How can I *r* the LORD
Ro 12:19 "It is mine to avenge; I will *r,"*
1Pe 3: 9 Do not *r* evil with evil

REPENT (REPENTANCE REPENTS)
Job 42: 6 and *r* in dust and ashes."
Jer 15:19 "If you *r,* I will restore you
Mt 4:17 "*R,* for the kingdom of heaven is
Lk 13: 3 unless you *r,* you too will all perish.
Ac 2:38 Peter replied, "*R* and be baptized,
17:30 all people everywhere to *r,*

REPENTANCE (REPENT)
Lk 3: 8 Produce fruit in keeping with *r.*
5:32 call the righteous, but sinners to *r."*
Ac 26:20 and prove their *r* by their deeds.
2Co 7:10 Godly sorrow brings *r* that leads

REPENTS (REPENT)
Lk 15:10 of God over one sinner who *r."*
17: 3 rebuke him, and if he *r,* forgive him

REPROACH
1Ti 3: 2 Now the overseer must be above *r,*

REPUTATION
1Ti 3: 7 also have a good *r* with outsiders,

REQUESTS
Ps 20: 5 May the LORD grant all your *r.*
Php 4: 6 with thanksgiving, present your *r*

REQUIRE
Mic 6: 8 And what does the LORD *r* of you

RESCUE (RESCUES)
Da 6:20 been able to *r* you from the lions?"
2Pe 2: 9 how to *r* godly men from trials

RESCUES (RESCUE)
1Th 1:10 who *r* us from the coming wrath.

RESIST
Jas 4: 7 *R* the devil, and he will flee
1Pe 5: 9 *R* him, standing firm in the faith,

RESOLVED
Ps 17: 3 I have *r* that my mouth will not sin.
Da 1: 8 But Daniel *r* not to defile himself
1Co 2: 2 For I *r* to know nothing while I was

RESPECT (RESPECTABLE)
Lev 19: 3 " 'Each of you must *r* his mother
19:32 show *r* for the elderly and revere
Pr 11:16 A kindhearted woman gains *r,*
Mal 1: 6 where is the *r* due me?" says
1Th 4:12 so that your daily life may win the *r*
5:12 to *r* those who work hard
1Ti 3: 4 children obey him with proper *r.*
1Pe 2:17 Show proper *r* to everyone:
3: 7 them with *r* as the weaker partner

RESPECTABLE* (RESPECT)
1Ti 3: 2 self-controlled, *r,* hospitable,

REST
Ex 31:15 the seventh day is a Sabbath of *r,*
Ps 91: 1 will *r* in the shadow
Jer 6:16 and you will find *r* for your souls.
Mt 11:28 and burdened, and I will give you *r.*

RESTITUTION
Ex 22: 3 "A thief must certainly make *r*,
Lev 6: 5 He must make *r* in full, add a fifth

RESTORE (RESTORES)
Ps 51:12 *R* to me the joy of your salvation
Gal 6: 1 are spiritual should *r* him gently.

RESTORES (RESTORE)
Ps 23: 3 he *r* my soul.

RESURRECTION
Mt 22:30 At the *r* people will neither marry
Lk 14:14 repaid at the *r* of the righteous."
Jn 11:25 Jesus said to her, "I am the *r*
Ro 1: 4 Son of God by his *r* from the dead:
1Co 15:12 some of you say that there is no *r*
Php 3:10 power of his *r* and the fellowship
Rev 20: 5 This is the first *r*.

RETRIBUTION
Jer 51:56 For the LORD is a God of *r*;

RETURN
2Ch 30: 9 If you *r* to the LORD, then your
Ne 1: 9 but if you *r* to me and obey my
Isa 55:11 It will not *r* to me empty,
Hos 6: 1 "Come, let us *r* to the LORD.
Joel 2:12 "*r* to me with all your heart,

REVEALED (REVELATION)
Dt 29:29 but the things *r* belong to us
Isa 40: 5 the glory of the LORD will be *r*,
Mt 11:25 and *r* them to little children.
Ro 1:17 a righteousness from God is *r*,
8:18 with the glory that will be *r* in us.

REVELATION (REVEALED)
Gal 1:12 I received it by *r* from Jesus Christ.
Rev 1: 1 *r* of Jesus Christ, which God gave

REVENGE (VENGEANCE)
Lev 19:18 " 'Do not seek *r* or bear a grudge
Ro 12:19 Do not take *r*, my friends,

REVERE (REVERENCE)
Ps 33: 8 let all the people of the world *r* him

REVERENCE (REVERE)
Lev 19:30 and have *r* for my sanctuary.
Ps 5: 7 in *r* will I bow down
Col 3:22 of heart and *r* for the Lord.
1Pe 3: 2 when they see the purity and *r*

REVIVE (REVIVING)
Ps 85: 6 Will you not *r* us again,
Isa 57:15 to *r* the spirit of the lowly

REVIVING (REVIVE)
Ps 19: 7 *r* the soul.

REWARD (REWARDED)
Ps 19:11 in keeping them there is great *r*.
127: 3 children a *r* from him.
Pr 19:17 he will *r* him for what he has done.
25:22 and the LORD will *r* you.
31:31 Give her the *r* she has earned,
Jer 17:10 to *r* a man according to his conduct
Mt 5:12 because great is your *r* in heaven,
6: 5 they have received their *r* in full.
16:27 and then he will *r* each person
1Co 3:14 built survives, he will receive his *r*.
Rev 22:12 I am coming soon! My *r* is with me

REWARDED (REWARD)
Ru 2:12 May you be richly *r* by the LORD,
Ps 18:24 The LORD has *r* me according
Pr 14:14 and the good man *r* for his.
1Co 3: 8 and each will be *r* according

RICH (RICHES)
Pr 23: 4 Do not wear yourself out to get *r*;
Jer 9:23 or the *r* man boast of his riches,
Mt 19:23 it is hard for a *r* man
2Co 6:10 yet making many *r*; having nothing
8: 9 he was *r*, yet for your sakes he
1Ti 6:17 Command those who are *r*

RICHES (RICH)
Ps 119:14 as one rejoices in great *r*.
Pr 30: 8 give me neither poverty nor *r*,
Isa 10: 3 Where will you leave your *r*?
Ro 9:23 to make the *r* of his glory known
11:33 the depth of the *r* of the wisdom
Eph 2: 7 he might show the incomparable *r*
3: 8 to the Gentiles the unsearchable *r*
Col 1:27 among the Gentiles the glorious *r*

RID
Ge 21:10 "Get *r* of that slave woman
1Co 5: 7 Get *r* of the old yeast that you may
Gal 4:30 "Get *r* of the slave woman

RIGHT (RIGHTS)
Ge 18:25 the Judge of all the earth do *r*?"
Ex 15:26 and do what is *r* in his eyes,
Dt 5:32 do not turn aside to the *r*
Ps 16: 8 Because he is at my *r* hand,
19: 8 The precepts of the LORD are *r*,
63: 8 your *r* hand upholds me.
110: 1 "Sit at my *r* hand
Pr 4:27 Do not swerve to the *r* or the left;
14:12 There is a way that seems *r*
Isa 1:17 learn to do *r*!
Jer 23: 5 and do what is just and *r* in the land
Hos 14: 9 The ways of the LORD are *r*;
Mt 6: 3 know what your *r* hand is doing,
Jn 1:12 he gave the *r* to become children
Ro 9:21 Does not the potter have the *r*
12:17 careful to do what is *r* in the eyes
Eph 1:20 and seated him at his *r* hand
Php 4: 8 whatever is *r*, whatever is pure,
2Th 3:13 never tire of doing what is *r*.

RIGHTEOUS (RIGHTEOUSNESS)
Ps 34:15 The eyes of the LORD are on the *r*
37:25 yet I have never seen the *r* forsaken
119:137 *R* are you, O LORD,
143: 2 for no one living is *r* before you.
Pr 3:33 but he blesses the home of the *r*.
11:30 The fruit of the *r* is a tree of life,
18:10 the *r* run to it and are safe.
Isa 64: 6 and all our *r* acts are like filthy rags
Hab 2: 4 but the *r* will live by his faith—
Mt 5:45 rain on the *r* and the unrighteous.
9:13 For I have not come to call the *r*,
13:49 and separate the wicked from the *r*
25:46 to eternal punishment, but the *r*
Ro 1:17 as it is written: "The *r* will live
3:10 "There is no one *r*, not even one;
1Ti 1: 9 that law is made not for the *r*
1Pe 3:18 the *r* for the unrighteous,
1Jn 3: 7 does what is right is *r*, just as he is *r*.
Rev 19: 8 stands for the *r* acts of the saints.)

RIGHTEOUSNESS (RIGHTEOUS)
Ge 15: 6 and he credited it to him as *r*.
1Sa 26:23 LORD rewards every man for his *r*
Ps 9: 8 He will judge the world in *r*;
23: 3 He guides me in paths of *r*
45: 7 You love *r* and hate wickedness;
85:10 *r* and peace kiss each other.
89:14 *R* and justice are the foundation
111: 3 and his *r* endures forever.
Pr 14:34 *R* exalts a nation,
21:21 He who pursues *r* and love
Isa 5:16 will show himself holy by his *r*.
59:17 He put on *r* as his breastplate,
Eze 18:20 The *r* of the righteous man will be
Da 9:24 to bring in everlasting *r*,
12: 3 and those who lead many to *r*,
Mal 4: 2 the sun of *r* will rise with healing
Mt 5: 6 those who hunger and thirst for *r*,
5:20 unless your *r* surpasses that
6:33 But seek first his kingdom and his *r*
Ro 4: 3 and it was credited to him as *r*."
4: 9 faith was credited to him as *r*.
6:13 body to him as instruments of *r*.
2Co 5:21 that in him we might become the *r*
Gal 2:21 for if *r* could be gained
3: 6 and it was credited to him as *r*."
Eph 6:14 with the breastplate of *r* in place,
Php 3: 9 not having a *r* of my own that
2Ti 3:16 correcting and training in *r*,
4: 8 is in store for me the crown of *r*,
Heb 11: 7 became heir of the *r* that comes
2Pe 2:21 not to have known the way of *r*,

RIGHTS (RIGHT)
La 3:35 to deny a man his *r*
Gal 4: 5 that we might receive the full *r*

RISE (RAISED)
Isa 26:19 their bodies will *r*.
Mt 27:63 'After three days I will *r* again.'
Jn 5:29 those who have done good will *r*
1Th 4:16 and the dead in Christ will *r* first.

ROAD
Mt 7:13 and broad is the *r* that leads

ROBBERS
Jer 7:11 become a den of *r* to you?
Mk 15:27 They crucified two *r* with him,
Lk 19:46 but you have made it 'a den of *r*.' "
Jn 10: 8 came before me were thieves and *r*,

ROCK
Ps 18: 2 The LORD is my *r*, my fortress
40: 2 he set my feet on a *r*
Mt 7:24 man who built his house on the *r*.
16:18 and on this *r* I will build my church
Ro 9:33 and a *r* that makes them fall,
1Co 10: 4 the spiritual *r* that accompanied

ROD
Ps 23: 4 your *r* and your staff,
Pr 13:24 He who spares the *r* hates his son,
23:13 if you punish him with the *r*,

ROOM (ROOMS)
Mt 6: 6 But when you pray, go into your *r*,
Lk 2: 7 there was no *r* for them in the inn.
Jn 21:25 the whole world would not have *r*

ROOMS (ROOM)
Jn 14: 2 In my Father's house are many *r*;

ROOT
Isa 53: 2 and like a *r* out of dry ground.
1Ti 6:10 of money is a *r* of all kinds of evil.

ROYAL
Jas 2: 8 If you really keep the *r* law found
1Pe 2: 9 a *r* priesthood, a holy nation,

RUBBISH*
Php 3: 8 I consider them *r*, that I may gain

RUDE*
1Co 13: 5 It is not *r*, it is not self-seeking,

RUIN (RUINS)
Pr 18:24 many companions may come to *r*,

1Ti 6: 9 desires that plunge men into *r*

RUINS (RUIN)
Pr 19: 3 A man's own folly *r* his life,
2Ti 2:14 and only *r* those who listen.

RULE (RULER RULERS RULES)
1Sa 12:12 'No, we want a king to *r* over us'—
Ps 2: 9 You will *r* them with an iron
119:133 let no sin *r* over me.
Zec 9:10 His *r* will extend from sea to sea
Col 3:15 the peace of Christ *r* in your hearts,
Rev 2:27 He will *r* them with an iron scepter;

RULER (RULE)
Ps 8: 6 You made him *r* over the works
Eph 2: 2 of the *r* of the kingdom of the air,
1Ti 6:15 God, the blessed and only *R*,

RULERS (RULE)
Ps 2: 2 and the *r* gather together
Col 1:16 or powers or *r* or authorities;

RULES (RULE)
Ps 103:19 and his kingdom *r* over all.
Lk 22:26 one who *r* like the one who serves.
2Ti 2: 5 he competes according to the *r*.

RUMORS
Mt 24: 6 You will hear of wars and *r* of wars,

RUN (RAN)
Isa 40:31 they will *r* and not grow weary,
1Co 9:24 *R* in such a way as to get the prize.
Heb 12: 1 let us *r* with perseverance the race

RUST
Mt 6:19 where moth and *r* destroy,

RUTH*
Moabitess; widow who went to Bethlehem with mother-in-law Naomi (Ru 1). Gleaned in field of Boaz; shown favor (Ru 2). Proposed marriage to Boaz (Ru 3). Married (Ru 4:1-12); bore Obed, ancestor of David (Ru 4:13-22), Jesus (Mt 1:5).

SABBATH
Ex 20: 8 "Remember the *S* day
Dt 5:12 "Observe the *S* day
Col 2:16 a New Moon celebration or a *S* day

SACKCLOTH
Mt 11:21 would have repented long ago in *s*

SACRED
Mt 7: 6 "Do not give dogs what is *s*;
1Co 3:17 for God's temple is *s*, and you are

SACRIFICE (SACRIFICED SACRIFICES)
Ge 22: 2 *S* him there as a burnt offering
Ex 12:27 'It is the Passover *s* to the LORD,
1Sa 15:22 To obey is better than *s*,
Hos 6: 6 For I desire mercy, not *s*,
Mt 9:13 this means: 'I desire mercy, not *s*.'
Heb 9:26 away with sin by the *s* of himself.
13:15 offer to God a *s* of praise—
1Jn 2: 2 He is the atoning *s* for our sins,

SACRIFICED (SACRIFICE)
1Co 5: 7 our Passover lamb, has been *s*.
8: 1 Now about food *s* to idols:
Heb 9:28 so Christ was *s* once

SACRIFICES (SACRIFICE)
Ps 51:17 The *s* of God are a broken spirit;
Ro 12: 1 to offer your bodies as living *s*,

SADDUCEES
Mk 12:18 *S*, who say there is no resurrection,

SAFE (SAVE)
Ps 37: 3 in the land and enjoy *s* pasture.
Pr 18:10 the righteous run to it and are *s*.

SAFETY (SAVE)
Ps 4: 8 make me dwell in *s*.
1Th 5: 3 people are saying, "Peace and *s*,"

SAINTS
Ps 116:15 is the death of his *s*.
Ro 8:27 intercedes for the *s* in accordance
Eph 1:18 of his glorious inheritance in the *s*,
6:18 always keep on praying for all the *s*
Rev 5: 8 which are the prayers of the *s*.
19: 8 for the righteous acts of the *s*.)

SAKE
Ps 44:22 Yet for your *s* we face death all day
Php 3: 7 loss for the *s* of Christ.
Heb 11:26 He regarded disgrace for the *s*

SALT
Ge 19:26 and she became a pillar of *s*.
Mt 5:13 "You are the *s* of the earth.

SALVATION (SAVE)
Ex 15: 2 he has become my *s*.
1Ch 16:23 proclaim his *s* day after day.
Ps 27: 1 The LORD is my light and my *s*—
51:12 Restore to me the joy of your *s*
62: 2 He alone is my rock and my *s*;
85: 9 Surely his *s* is near those who fear
96: 2 proclaim his *s* day after day.
Isa 25: 9 let us rejoice and be glad in his *s*."
45:17 the LORD with an everlasting *s*;
51: 6 But my *s* will last forever,
59:17 and the helmet of *s* on his head;
61:10 me with garments of *s*
Jnh 2: 9 *S* comes from the LORD."
Zec 9: 9 righteous and having *s*,
Lk 2:30 For my eyes have seen your *s*,
Jn 4:22 for *s* is from the Jews.
Ac 4:12 *S* is found in no one else,
13:47 that you may bring *s* to the ends
Ro 11:11 *s* has come to the Gentiles
2Co 7:10 brings repentance that leads to *s*
Eph 6:17 Take the helmet of *s* and the sword
Php 2:12 to work out your *s* with fear
1Th 5: 8 and the hope of *s* as a helmet.
2Ti 3:15 wise for *s* through faith
Heb 2: 3 escape if we ignore such a great *s*?
6: 9 case—things that accompany *s*.
1Pe 1:10 Concerning this *s*, the prophets,
2: 2 by it you may grow up in your *s*,

SAMARITAN
Lk 10:33 But a *S*, as he traveled, came where

SAMSON
Danite judge. Birth promised (Jdg 13). Married to Philistine (Jdg 14). Vengeance on Philistines (Jdg 15). Betrayed by Delilah (Jdg 16:1-22). Death (Jdg 16:23-31). Feats of strength: killed lion (Jdg 14:6), 30 Philistines (Jdg 14:19), 1,000 Philistines with jawbone (Jdg 15:13-17), carried off gates of Gaza (Jdg 16:3), pushed down temple of Dagon (Jdg 16:25-30).

SAMUEL
Ephraimite judge and prophet (Heb 11:32). Birth prayed for (1Sa 1:10-18). Dedicated to temple by Hannah (1Sa 1:21-28). Raised by Eli (1Sa 2:11, 18-26). Called as prophet (1Sa 3). Led Israel to victory over Philistines (1Sa 7). Asked by Israel for a king (1Sa 8). Anointed Saul as king (1Sa 9-10). Farewell speech (1Sa 12). Rebuked Saul for sacrifice (1Sa 13). Announced rejection of Saul (1Sa 15). Anointed David as king (1Sa 16). Protected David from Saul (1Sa 19:18-24). Death (1Sa 25:1). Returned from dead to condemn Saul (1Sa 28).

SANCTIFIED (SANCTIFY)
Ac 20:32 among all those who are *s*.
Ro 15:16 to God, *s* by the Holy Spirit.
1Co 6:11 But you were washed, you were *s*,
7:14 and the unbelieving wife has been *s*
Heb 10:29 blood of the covenant that *s* him,

SANCTIFY (SANCTIFIED SANCTIFYING)
1Th 5:23 *s* you through and through.

SANCTIFYING (SANCTIFY)
2Th 2:13 through the *s* work of the Spirit

SANCTUARY
Ex 25: 8 "Then have them make a *s* for me,

SAND
Ge 22:17 and as the *s* on the seashore.
Mt 7:26 man who built his house on *s*.

SANDALS
Ex 3: 5 off your *s*, for the place where you
Jos 5:15 off your *s*, for the place where you

SANG (SING)
Job 38: 7 while the morning stars *s* together
Rev 5: 9 And they *s* a new song:

SARAH
Wife of Abraham, originally named Sarai; barren (Ge 11:29-31; 1Pe 3:6). Taken by Pharaoh as Abraham's sister; returned (Ge 12:10-20). Gave Hagar to Abraham; sent her away in pregnancy (Ge 16). Name changed; Isaac promised (Ge 17:15-21; 18:10-15; Heb 11:11). Taken by Abimelech as Abraham's sister; returned (Ge 20). Isaac born; Hagar and Ishmael sent away (Ge 21:1-21; Gal 4:21-31). Death (Ge 23).

SATAN
Job 1: 6 and *S* also came with them.
Zec 3: 2 said to *S*, "The LORD rebuke you,
Mk 4:15 *S* comes and takes away the word
2Co 11:14 for *S* himself masquerades
12: 7 a messenger of *S*, to torment me.
Rev 12: 9 serpent called the devil, or *S*,
20: 2 or *S*, and bound him for a thousand
20: 7 *S* will be released from his prison

SATISFIED (SATISFY)
Isa 53:11 he will see the light ⌞of life⌟ and be *s*

SATISFIES (SATISFY)
Ps 103: 5 who *s* your desires with good things,

SATISFY (SATISFIED SATISFIES)
Isa 55: 2 and your labor on what does not *s*?

SAUL
1. Benjamite; anointed by Samuel as first king of Israel (1Sa 9-10). Defeated Ammonites (1Sa 11). Rebuked for offering sacrifice (1Sa 13:1-15). Defeated Philistines (1Sa 14). Rejected as king for failing to annihilate Amalekites (1Sa 15). Soothed from evil spirit by David (1Sa 16:14-23). Sent David against Goliath (1Sa 17). Jealousy and attempted murder of David (1Sa 18:1-11). Gave David Michal as wife (1Sa 18:12-30). Second attempt to kill David (1Sa 19). Anger at Jonathan (1Sa 20:26-34). Pursued David: killed priests at Nob (1Sa 22), went to Keilah and Ziph (1Sa 23),

life spared by David at En Gedi (1Sa 24) and in his tent (1Sa 26). Rebuked by Samuel's spirit for consulting witch at Endor (1Sa 28). Wounded by Philistines; took his own life (1Sa 31; 1Ch 10).
2. See PAUL

SAVE (SAFE SAFETY SALVATION SAVED SAVIOR)
Isa 63: 1 mighty to *s.*"
Da 3:17 the God we serve is able to *s* us
Zep 3:17 he is mighty to *s.*
Mt 1:21 he will *s* his people from their sins
16:25 wants to *s* his life will lose it,
Lk 19:10 to seek and to *s* what was lost."
Jn 3:17 but to *s* the world through him.
1Ti 1:15 came into the world to *s* sinners—
Jas 5:20 of his way will *s* him from death

SAVED (SAVE)
Ps 34: 6 he *s* him out of all his troubles.
Isa 45:22 "Turn to me and be *s,*
Joel 2:32 on the name of the LORD will be *s;*
Mk 13:13 firm to the end will be *s.*
16:16 believes and is baptized will be *s,*
Jn 10: 9 enters through me will be *s.*
Ac 4:12 to men by which we must be *s."*
16:30 do to be *s?*" They replied,
Ro 9:27 only the remnant will be *s.*
10: 9 him from the dead, you will be *s.*
1Co 3:15 will suffer loss; he himself will be *s,*
15: 2 By this gospel you are *s,*
Eph 2: 5 it is by grace you have been *s.*
2: 8 For it is by grace you have been *s,*
1Ti 2: 4 who wants all men to be *s*

SAVIOR (SAVE)
Ps 89:26 my God, the Rock my *S.*'
Isa 43:11 and apart from me there is no *s.*
Hos 13: 4 no *S* except me.
Lk 1:47 and my spirit rejoices in God my *S,*
2:11 of David a *S* has been born to you;
Jn 4:42 know that this man really is the *S*
Eph 5:23 his body, of which he is the *S.*
1Ti 4:10 who is the *S* of all men,
Tit 2:10 about God our *S* attractive.
2:13 appearing of our great God and *S,*
3: 4 and love of God our *S* appeared,
1Jn 4:14 Son to be the *S* of the world.
Jude :25 to the only God our *S* be glory,

SCALES
Lev 19:36 Use honest *s* and honest weights,
Da 5:27 You have been weighed on the *s*

SCAPEGOAT (GOAT)
Lev 16:10 by sending it into the desert as a *s.*

SCARLET
Isa 1:18 "Though your sins are like *s,*

SCATTERED
Jer 31:10 'He who *s* Israel will gather them
Ac 8: 4 who had been *s* preached the word

SCEPTER
Rev 19:15 "He will rule them with an iron *s."*

SCHEMES
2Co 2:11 For we are not unaware of his *s.*
Eph 6:11 stand against the devil's *s.*

SCOFFERS
2Pe 3: 3 that in the last days *s* will come,

SCORPION
Rev 9: 5 sting of a *s* when it strikes a man.

SCRIPTURE (SCRIPTURES)
Jn 10:35 and the *S* cannot be broken—
1Ti 4:13 yourself to the public reading of *S,*
2Ti 3:16 All *S* is God-breathed
2Pe 1:20 that no prophecy of *S* came about

SCRIPTURES (SCRIPTURE)
Lk 24:27 said in all the *S* concerning himself.
Jn 5:39 These are the *S* that testify about
Ac 17:11 examined the *S* every day to see

SCROLL
Eze 3: 1 eat what is before you, eat this *s;*

SEA
Ex 14:16 go through the *s* on dry ground.
Isa 57:20 the wicked are like the tossing *s,*
Mic 7:19 iniquities into the depths of the *s.*
Jas 1: 6 who doubts is like a wave of the *s,*
Rev 13: 1 I saw a beast coming out of the *s.*

SEAL (SEALS)
Jn 6:27 God the Father has placed his *s*
2Co 1:22 set his *s* of ownership on us,
Eph 1:13 you were marked in him with a *s,*

SEALS (SEAL)
Rev 5: 2 "Who is worthy to break the *s*
6: 1 opened the first of the seven *s.*

SEARCH (SEARCHED SEARCHES SEARCHING)
Ps 4: 4 *s* your hearts and be silent.
139:23 *S* me, O God, and know my heart;
Pr 2: 4 and *s* for it as for hidden treasure,
Jer 17:10 "I the LORD *s* the heart
Eze 34:16 I will *s* for the lost and bring back
Lk 15: 8 and *s* carefully until she finds it?

SEARCHED (SEARCH)
Ps 139: 1 O LORD, you have *s* me

SEARCHES (SEARCH)
Ro 8:27 And he who *s* our hearts knows
1Co 2:10 The Spirit *s* all things,

SEARCHING (SEARCH)
Am 8:12 *s* for the word of the LORD,

SEARED
1Ti 4: 2 whose consciences have been *s*

SEASON
2Ti 4: 2 be prepared in *s* and out of *s;*

SEAT (SEATED SEATS)
Ps 1: 1 or sit in the *s* of mockers.
Da 7: 9 and the Ancient of Days took his *s.*
2Co 5:10 before the judgment *s* of Christ,

SEATED (SEAT)
Ps 47: 8 God is *s* on his holy throne.
Isa 6: 1 I saw the Lord *s* on a throne,
Col 3: 1 where Christ is *s* at the right hand

SEATS (SEAT)
Lk 11:43 you love the most important *s*

SECRET (SECRETS)
Dt 29:29 The *s* things belong
Jdg 16: 6 Tell me the *s* of your great strength
Ps 90: 8 our *s* sins in the light
Pr 11:13 but a trustworthy man keeps a *s.*
Mt 6: 4 so that your giving may be in *s.*
2Co 4: 2 we have renounced *s* and shameful
Php 4:12 I have learned the *s*

SECRETS (SECRET)
Ps 44:21 since he knows the *s* of the heart?
1Co 14:25 the *s* of his heart will be laid bare.

SECURE (SECURITY)
Ps 112: 8 His heart is *s,* he will have no fear;
Heb 6:19 an anchor for the soul, firm and *s.*

SECURITY (SECURE)
Job 31:24 or said to pure gold, 'You are my *s,*'

SEED (SEEDS)
Lk 8:11 of the parable: The *s* is the word
1Co 3: 6 I planted the *s,* Apollos watered it,
2Co 9:10 he who supplies *s* to the sower
Gal 3:29 then you are Abraham's *s,*
1Pe 1:23 not of perishable *s,*

SEEDS (SEED)
Jn 12:24 But if it dies, it produces many *s.*
Gal 3:16 Scripture does not say "and to *s,"*

SEEK (SEEKS SELF-SEEKING)
Dt 4:29 if from there you *s* the LORD your
1Ch 28: 9 If you *s* him, he will be found
2Ch 7:14 themselves and pray and *s* my face
Ps 119:10 I *s* you with all my heart;
Isa 55: 6 *S* the LORD while he may be
65: 1 found by those who did not *s* me.
Mt 6:33 But *s* first his kingdom
Lk 19:10 For the Son of Man came to *s*
Ro 10:20 found by those who did not *s* me;
1Co 7:27 you married? Do not *s* a divorce.

SEEKS (SEEK)
Jn 4:23 the kind of worshipers the Father *s.*

SEER
1Sa 9: 9 of today used to be called a *s.)*

SELF-CONTROL (CONTROL)
1Co 7: 5 you because of your lack of *s.*
Gal 5:23 faithfulness, gentleness and *s.*
2Pe 1: 6 and to knowledge, *s;* and to *s,*

SELF-CONTROLLED* (CONTROL)
1Th 5: 6 are asleep, but let us be alert and *s.*
5: 8 let us be *s,* putting on faith and love
1Ti 3: 2 *s,* respectable, hospitable,
Tit 1: 8 who is *s,* upright, holy
2: 2 worthy of respect, *s,* and sound
2: 5 to be *s* and pure, to be busy at home
2: 6 encourage the young men to be *s.*
2:12 to live *s,* upright and godly lives
1Pe 1:13 prepare your minds for action; be *s;*
4: 7 and *s* so that you can pray.
5: 8 Be *s* and alert.

SELF-INDULGENCE
Mt 23:25 inside they are full of greed and *s.*

SELF-SEEKING (SEEK)
1Co 13: 5 it is not *s,* it is not easily angered,

SELFISH*
Ps 119:36 and not toward *s* gain.
Pr 18: 1 An unfriendly man pursues *s* ends;
Gal 5:20 fits of rage, *s* ambition, dissensions,
Php 1:17 preach Christ out of *s* ambition,
2: 3 Do nothing out of *s* ambition
Jas 3:14 and *s* ambition in your hearts,
3:16 you have envy and *s* ambition,

SEND (SENDING SENT)
Isa 6: 8 *S* me!" He said, "Go and tell this
Mt 9:38 to *s* out workers into his harvest
Jn 16: 7 but if I go, I will *s* him to you.

SENDING (SEND)
Jn 20:21 Father has sent me, I am *s* you."

SENSES*
Lk 15:17 "When he came to his *s,* he said,
1Co 15:34 Come back to your *s* as you ought,
2Ti 2:26 and that they will come to their *s*

SENSUAL
Col 2:23 value in restraining *s* indulgence.

SENT (SEND)
Isa 55:11 achieve the purpose for which I *s* it.
Mt 10:40 me receives the one who *s* me.
Jn 4:34 "is to do the will of him who *s* me
Ro 10:15 can they preach unless they are *s?*
1Jn 4:10 but that he loved us and *s* his Son

SEPARATE (SEPARATED SEPARATES)
Mt 19: 6 has joined together, let man not *s.*"
Ro 8:35 Who shall *s* us from the love
1Co 7:10 wife must not *s* from her husband.
2Co 6:17 and be *s,* says the Lord.

SEPARATED (SEPARATE)
Isa 59: 2 But your iniquities have *s*

SEPARATES (SEPARATE)
Pr 16:28 and a gossip *s* close friends.

SERPENT
Ge 3: 1 the *s* was more crafty than any
Rev 12: 9 that ancient *s* called the devil

SERVANT (SERVANTS)
1Sa 3:10 "Speak, for your *s* is listening."
Mt 20:26 great among you must be your *s,*
25:21 'Well done, good and faithful *s!*
Lk 16:13 "No *s* can serve two masters.
Php 2: 7 taking the very nature of a *s,*
2Ti 2:24 And the Lord's *s* must not quarrel;

SERVANTS (SERVANT)
Lk 17:10 should say, 'We are unworthy *s;*
Jn 15:15 longer call you *s,* because a servant

SERVE (SERVICE SERVING)
Dt 10:12 to *s* the LORD your God
Jos 22: 5 and to *s* him with all your heart
24:15 this day whom you will *s,*
Mt 4:10 Lord your God, and *s* him only.' "
6:24 "No one can *s* two masters.
20:28 but to *s,* and to give his life
Eph 6: 7 *S* wholeheartedly,

SERVICE (SERVE)
1Co 12: 5 There are different kinds of *s,*
Eph 4:12 God's people for works of *s,*

SERVING (SERVE)
Ro 12:11 your spiritual fervor, *s* the Lord.
Eph 6: 7 as if you were *s* the Lord, not men,
Col 3:24 It is the Lord Christ you are *s.*
2Ti 2: 4 No one *s* as a soldier gets involved

SEVEN (SEVENTH)
Ge 7: 2 Take with you *s* of every kind
Jos 6: 4 march around the city *s* times,
1Ki 19:18 Yet I reserve *s* thousand in Israel—
Pr 6:16 *s* that are detestable to him:
24:16 a righteous man falls *s* times,
Isa 4: 1 In that day *s* women
Da 9:25 comes, there will be *s* 'sevens,'
Mt 18:21 Up to *s* times?" Jesus answered,
Lk 11:26 takes *s* other spirits more wicked
Ro 11: 4 for myself *s* thousand who have not
Rev 1: 4 To the *s* churches in the province
6: 1 opened the first of the *s* seals.
8: 2 and to them were given *s* trumpets.
10: 4 And when the *s* thunders spoke,
15: 7 to the *s* angels *s* golden bowls filled

SEVENTH (SEVEN)
Ge 2: 2 By the *s* day God had finished
Ex 23:12 but on the *s* day do not work,

SEXUAL (SEXUALLY)
1Co 6:13 body is not meant for *s* immorality,
6:18 Flee from *s* immorality.
10: 8 should not commit *s* immorality,
Eph 5: 3 even a hint of *s* immorality,
1Th 4: 3 that you should avoid *s* immorality

SEXUALLY (SEXUAL)
1Co 5: 9 to associate with *s* immoral people
6:18 he who sins *s* sins against his own

SHADOW
Ps 23: 4 through the valley of the *s* of death,
36: 7 find refuge in the *s* of your wings.
Heb 10: 1 The law is only a *s*

SHALLUM
King of Israel (2Ki 15:10-16).

SHAME (ASHAMED)
Ps 34: 5 their faces are never covered with *s*
Pr 13:18 discipline comes to poverty and *s,*
Heb 12: 2 endured the cross, scorning its *s,*

SHARE (SHARED)
Ge 21:10 that slave woman's son will never *s*
Lk 3:11 "The man with two tunics should *s*
Gal 4:30 the slave woman's son will never *s*
6: 6 in the word must *s* all good things
Eph 4:28 something to *s* with those in need.
1Ti 6:18 and to be generous and willing to *s.*
Heb 12:10 that we may *s* in his holiness.
13:16 to do good and to *s* with others,

SHARED (SHARE)
Heb 2:14 he too *s* in their humanity so that

SHARON
SS 2: 1 I am a rose of *S,*

SHARPER*
Heb 4:12 *S* than any double-edged sword,

SHED (SHEDDING)
Ge 9: 6 by man shall his blood be *s;*
Col 1:20 through his blood, *s* on the cross.

SHEDDING (SHED)
Heb 9:22 without the *s* of blood there is no

SHEEP
Ps 100: 3 we are his people, the *s*
119:176 I have strayed like a lost *s.*
Isa 53: 6 We all, like *s,* have gone astray,
Jer 50: 6 "My people have been lost *s;*
Eze 34:11 I myself will search for my *s*
Mt 9:36 helpless, like *s* without a shepherd.
Jn 10: 3 He calls his own *s* by name
10:15 and I lay down my life for the *s.*
10:27 My *s* listen to my voice; I know
21:17 Jesus said, "Feed my *s.*
1Pe 2:25 For you were like *s* going astray,

SHELTER
Ps 61: 4 take refuge in the *s* of your wings.
91: 1 in the *s* of the Most High

SHEM
Son of Noah (Ge 5:32; 6:10). Blessed (Ge 9:26). Descendants (Ge 10:21-31; 11:10-32).

SHEPHERD (SHEPHERDS)
Ps 23: 1 LORD is my *s,* I shall not be in want.
Isa 40:11 He tends his flock like a *s:*
Jer 31:10 will watch over his flock like a *s.'*
Eze 34:12 As a *s* looks after his scattered
Zec 11:17 "Woe to the worthless *s,*
Mt 9:36 and helpless, like sheep without a *s.*
Jn 10:11 The good *s* lays down his life
10:16 there shall be one flock and one *s.*
1Pe 5: 4 And when the Chief *S* appears,

SHEPHERDS (SHEPHERD)
Jer 23: 1 "Woe to the *s* who are destroying
Lk 2: 8 there were *s* living out in the fields
Ac 20:28 Be *s* of the church of God,
1Pe 5: 2 Be *s* of God's flock that is

SHIELD
Ps 28: 7 LORD is my strength and my *s;*
Eph 6:16 to all this, take up the *s* of faith,

SHINE (SHONE)
Ps 4: 6 Let the light of your face *s* upon us,
80: 1 between the cherubim, *s* forth
Isa 60: 1 "Arise, *s,* for your light has come,
Da 12: 3 are wise will *s* like the brightness
Mt 5:16 let your light *s* before men,
13:43 the righteous will *s* like the sun
2Co 4: 6 made his light *s* in our hearts
Eph 5:14 and Christ will *s* on you."

SHIPWRECKED*
2Co 11:25 I was stoned, three times I was *s,*
1Ti 1:19 and so have *s* their faith.

SHONE (SHINE)
Mt 17: 2 His face *s* like the sun,
Lk 2: 9 glory of the Lord *s* around them,
Rev 21:11 It *s* with the glory of God,

SHORT
Isa 59: 1 of the LORD is not too *s* to save,
Ro 3:23 and fall *s* of the glory of God,

SHOULDERS
Isa 9: 6 and the government will be on his *s*
Lk 15: 5 he joyfully puts it on his *s*

SHOWED
1Jn 4: 9 This is how God *s* his love

SHREWD
Mt 10:16 Therefore be as *s* as snakes and

SHUN*
Job 28:28 and to *s* evil is understanding.' "
Pr 3: 7 fear the LORD and *s* evil.

SICK
Pr 13:12 Hope deferred makes the heart *s,*
Mt 9:12 who need a doctor, but the *s.*
25:36 I was *s* and you looked after me,
Jas 5:14 of you *s?* He should call the elders

SICKLE
Joel 3:13 Swing the *s,*

SIDE
Ps 91: 7 A thousand may fall at your *s,*
124: 1 If the LORD had not been on our *s*
2Ti 4:17 But the Lord stood at my *s*

SIGHT
Ps 90: 4 For a thousand years in your *s*
116:15 Precious in the *s* of the LORD
2Co 5: 7 We live by faith, not by *s.*
1Pe 3: 4 which is of great worth in God's *s.*

SIGN (SIGNS)
Isa 7:14 the Lord himself will give you a *s:*

SIGNS (SIGN)
Mk 16:17 these *s* will accompany those who
Jn 20:30 Jesus did many other miraculous *s*

SILENT
Pr 17:28 a fool is thought wise if he keeps *s,*
Isa 53: 7 as a sheep before her shearers is *s,*
Hab 2:20 let all the earth be *s* before him."
1Co 14:34 women should remain *s.*
1Ti 2:12 over a man; she must be *s.*

SILVER
Pr 25:11 is like apples of gold in settings of *s.*
Hag 2: 8 'The *s* is mine and the gold is mine,'
1Co 3:12 *s,* costly stones, wood, hay or straw

SIMON
1. See PETER.
2. Apostle, called the Zealot (Mt 10:4; Mk 3:18; Lk 6:15; Ac 1:13).
3. Samaritan sorcerer (Ac 8:9-24).

SIN (SINFUL SINNED SINNER SINNERS SINNING SINS)
Nu 5: 7 and must confess the *s* he has
32:23 be sure that your *s* will find you
Dt 24:16 each is to die for his own *s.*
1Ki 8:46 for there is no one who does not *s*
2Ch 7:14 and will forgive their *s* and will heal
Ps 4: 4 In your anger do not *s;*
32: 2 whose *s* the LORD does not count
32: 5 Then I acknowledged my *s* to you
51: 2 and cleanse me from my *s.*
66:18 If I had cherished *s* in my heart,
119:11 that I might not *s* against you.
119:133 let no *s* rule over me.
Isa 6: 7 is taken away and your *s* atoned
Mic 7:18 who pardons *s* and forgives
Mt 18: 6 little ones who believe in me to *s,*
Jn 1:29 who takes away the *s* of the world!
8:34 everyone who sins is a slave to *s.*
Ro 5:12 as *s* entered the world
5:20 where *s* increased, grace increased
6:11 count yourselves dead to *s*
6:23 For the wages of *s* is death,
14:23 that does not come from faith is *s.*
2Co 5:21 God made him who had no *s* to be *s*
Gal 6: 1 if someone is caught in a *s,*
Heb 9:26 to do away with *s* by the sacrifice
11:25 the pleasures of *s* for a short time.
12: 1 and the *s* that so easily entangles,
1Pe 2:22 "He committed no *s,*
1Jn 1: 8 If we claim to be without *s,*
3: 4 in fact, *s* is lawlessness.
3: 5 And in him is no *s.*
3: 9 born of God will continue to *s,*
5:18 born of God does not continue to *s;*

SINCERE
Ro 12: 9 Love must be *s.*
Heb 10:22 near to God with a *s* heart

SINFUL (SIN)
Ps 51: 5 Surely I was *s* at birth
51: 5 *s* from the time my mother
Ro 7: 5 we were controlled by the *s* nature,
8: 4 not live according to the *s* nature
8: 9 are controlled not by the *s* nature
Gal 5:19 The acts of the *s* nature are obvious
5:24 Jesus have crucified the *s* nature
1Pe 2:11 abstain from *s* desires, which war

SING (SANG SINGING SONG SONGS)
Ps 30: 4 *S* to the LORD, you saints of his;
47: 6 *S* praises to God, *s* praises;
59:16 But I will *s* of your strength,
89: 1 I will *s* of the LORD's great love
101: 1 I will *s* of your love and justice;
Eph 5:19 *S* and make music in your heart

SINGING (SING)
Ps 63: 5 with *s* lips my mouth will praise
Ac 16:25 Silas were praying and *s* hymns

SINNED (SIN)
2Sa 12:13 "I have *s* against the LORD."
Job 1: 5 "Perhaps my children have *s*
Ps 51: 4 Against you, you only, have I *s*
Da 9: 5 we have *s* and done wrong.
Mic 7: 9 Because I have *s* against him,
Lk 15:18 I have *s* against heaven
Ro 3:23 for all have *s* and fall short
1Jn 1:10 claim we have not *s,* we make him

SINNER (SIN)
Ecc 9:18 but one *s* destroys much good.
Lk 15: 7 in heaven over one *s* who repents
18:13 'God, have mercy on me, a *s.*'
1Co 14:24 convinced by all that he is a *s*
Jas 5:20 Whoever turns a *s* from the error
1Pe 4:18 become of the ungodly and the *s?*"

SINNERS (SIN)
Ps 1: 1 or stand in the way of *s*
Pr 23:17 Do not let your heart envy *s,*
Mt 9:13 come to call the righteous, but *s.*"
Ro 5: 8 While we were still *s,* Christ died
1Ti 1:15 came into the world to save *s*—

SINNING (SIN)
Ex 20:20 be with you to keep you from *s.*"
1Co 15:34 stop *s;* for there are some who are
Heb 10:26 If we deliberately keep on *s*
1Jn 3: 6 No one who lives in him keeps on *s*
3: 9 go on *s,* because he has been born

SINS (SIN)
2Ki 14: 6 each is to die for his own *s.*"
Ezr 9: 6 our *s* are higher than our heads
Ps 19:13 your servant also from willful *s;*
32: 1 whose *s* are covered.
103: 3 who forgives all your *s*
130: 3 O LORD, kept a record of *s,*
Pr 28:13 who conceals his *s* does not
Isa 1:18 "Though your *s* are like scarlet,
43:25 and remembers your *s* no more.
59: 2 your *s* have hidden his face
Eze 18: 4 soul who *s* is the one who will die.
Mt 1:21 he will save his people from their *s*
18:15 "If your brother *s* against you,
Lk 11: 4 Forgive us our *s,*
17: 3 "If your brother *s,* rebuke him,
Ac 22:16 be baptized and wash your *s* away,
1Co 15: 3 died for our *s* according
Eph 2: 1 dead in your transgressions and *s,*
Col 2:13 us all our *s,* having canceled
Heb 1: 3 he had provided purification for *s,*
7:27 He sacrificed for their *s* once for all
8:12 and will remember their *s* no more
10:12 for all time one sacrifice for *s,*
Jas 4:17 ought to do and doesn't do it, *s.*
5:16 Therefore confess your *s*
5:20 and cover over a multitude of *s.*
1Pe 2:24 He himself bore our *s* in his body
3:18 For Christ died for *s* once for all,
1Jn 1: 9 If we confess our *s,* he is faithful
Rev 1: 5 has freed us from our *s* by his blood

SITS
Ps 99: 1 *s* enthroned between the cherubim,
Isa 40:22 He *s* enthroned above the circle
Mt 19:28 of Man *s* on his glorious throne,
Rev 4: 9 thanks to him who *s* on the throne

SKIN
Job 19:20 with only the *s* of my teeth.
Job 19:26 And after my *s* has been destroyed,
Jer 13:23 Can the Ethiopian change his *s*

SLAIN (SLAY)
Rev 5:12 "Worthy is the Lamb, who was *s,*

SLANDER (SLANDERED SLANDERERS)
Lev 19:16 " 'Do not go about spreading *s*
1Ti 5:14 the enemy no opportunity for *s.*
Tit 3: 2 to *s* no one, to be peaceable

SLANDERED (SLANDER)
1Co 4:13 when we are *s,* we answer kindly.

SLANDERERS (SLANDER)
Ro 1:30 They are gossips, *s,* God-haters,
1Co 6:10 nor the greedy nor drunkards nor *s*
Tit 2: 3 not to be *s* or addicted

SLAUGHTER
Isa 53: 7 he was led like a lamb to the *s,*

SLAVE (SLAVERY SLAVES)
Ge 21:10 "Get rid of that *s* woman
Mt 20:27 wants to be first must be your *s*—
Jn 8:34 everyone who sins is a *s* to sin.
1Co 12:13 whether Jews or Greeks, *s* or free
Gal 3:28 *s* nor free, male nor female,
4:30 Get rid of the *s* woman and her son
2Pe 2:19 a man is a *s* to whatever has

SLAVERY (SLAVE)
Ro 6:19 parts of your body in *s* to impurity
Gal 4: 3 were in *s* under the basic principles

SLAVES (SLAVE)
Ro 6: 6 that we should no longer be *s* to sin
6:22 and have become *s* to God,

SLAY (SLAIN)
Job 13:15 Though he *s* me, yet will I hope

SLEEP (SLEEPING)
Ps 121: 4 will neither slumber nor *s.*
1Co 15:51 We will not all *s,* but we will all be

SLEEPING (SLEEP)
Mk 13:36 suddenly, do not let him find you *s.*

SLOW
Ex 34: 6 and gracious God, *s* to anger,
Jas 1:19 *s* to speak and *s* to become angry,
2Pe 3: 9 The Lord is not *s* in keeping his

SLUGGARD
Pr 6: 6 Go to the ant, you *s;*
20: 4 A *s* does not plow in season;

SLUMBER
Ps 121: 3 he who watches over you will not *s;*
Pr 6:10 A little sleep, a little *s,*
Ro 13:11 for you to wake up from your *s,*

SNAKE (SNAKES)
Nu 21: 8 "Make a *s* and put it up on a pole;
Pr 23:32 In the end it bites like a *s*
Jn 3:14 Moses lifted up the *s* in the desert,

SNAKES (SNAKE)
Mt 10:16 as shrewd as *s* and as innocent
Mk 16:18 they will pick up *s* with their hands;

SNATCH
Jn 10:28 no one can *s* them out of my hand.
Jude :23 *s* others from the fire and save

SNOW
Ps 51: 7 and I will be whiter than *s.*

SOAR
Isa 40:31 They will *s* on wings like eagles;

SODOM
Ge 19:24 rained down burning sulfur on *S*
Ro 9:29 we would have become like *S*,

SOIL
Ge 4: 2 kept flocks, and Cain worked the *s*.
Mt 13:23 on good *s* is the man who hears

SOLDIER
1Co 9: 7 as a *s* at his own expense?
2Ti 2: 3 with us like a good *s* of Christ Jesus

SOLE
Dt 28:65 place for the *s* of your foot.
Isa 1: 6 From the *s* of your foot to the top

SOLID
2Ti 2:19 God's *s* foundation stands firm,
Heb 5:12 You need milk, not *s* food!

SOLOMON
Son of David by Bathsheba; king of Judah (2Sa 12:24; 1Ch 3:5, 10). Appointed king by David (1Ki 1); adversaries Adonijah, Joab, Shimei killed by Benaiah (1Ki 2). Asked for wisdom (1Ki 3; 2Ch 1). Judged between two prostitutes (1Ki 3:16-28). Built temple (1Ki 5-7; 2Ch 2-5); prayer of dedication (1Ki 8; 2Ch 6). Visited by Queen of Sheba (1Ki 10; 2Ch 9). Wives turned his heart from God (1Ki 11:1-13). Jeroboam rebelled against (1Ki 11:26-40). Death (1Ki 11:41-43; 2Ch 9:29-31).
Proverbs of (1Ki 4:32; Pr 1:1; 10:1; 25:1); psalms of (Ps 72; 127); song of (SS 1:1).

SON (SONS)
Ge 22: 2 "Take your *s*, your only *s*, Isaac,
Ex 11: 5 Every firstborn *s* in Egypt will die,
Dt 21:18 rebellious *s* who does not obey his
Ps 2: 7 He said to me, "You are my *S*;
2:12 Kiss the *S*, lest he be angry
Pr 10: 1 A wise *s* brings joy to his father,
13:24 He who spares the rod hates his *s*,
29:17 Discipline your *s*, and he will give
Isa 7:14 with child and will give birth to a *s*,
Hos 11: 1 and out of Egypt I called my *s*.
Mt 2:15 "Out of Egypt I called my *s*."
3:17 "This is my *S*, whom I love;
11:27 one knows the *S* except the Father,
16:16 "You are the Christ, the *S*
17: 5 "This is my *S*, whom I love;
20:18 and the *S* of Man will be betrayed
24:30 They will see the *S* of Man coming
24:44 the *S* of Man will come at an hour
27:54 "Surely he was the *S* of God!"
28:19 and of the *S* and of the Holy Spirit,
Mk 10:45 even the *S* of Man did not come
14:62 you will see the *S* of Man sitting
Lk 9:58 but the *S* of Man has no place
18: 8 when the *S* of Man comes,
19:10 For the *S* of Man came to seek
Jn 3:14 so the *S* of Man must be lifted up,
3:16 that he gave his one and only *S*,
17: 1 Glorify your *S*, that your *S* may
Ro 8:29 conformed to the likeness of his *S*,
8:32 He who did not spare his own *S*,
1Co 15:28 then the *S* himself will be made
Gal 4:30 rid of the slave woman and her *s*,
1Th 1:10 and to wait for his *S* from heaven,
Heb 1: 2 days he has spoken to us by his *S*,
10:29 punished who has trampled the *S*
1Jn 1: 7 his *S*, purifies us from all sin.
4: 9 only *S* into the world that we might
5: 5 he who believes that Jesus is the *S*
5:11 eternal life, and this life is in his *S*.

SONG (SING)
Ps 40: 3 He put a new *s* in my mouth,
96: 1 Sing to the LORD a new *s*;
149: 1 Sing to the LORD a new *s*,
Isa 49:13 burst into *s*, O mountains!
55:12 will burst into *s* before you,
Rev 5: 9 And they sang a new *s*:
15: 3 and sang the *s* of Moses the servant

SONGS (SING)
Job 35:10 who gives *s* in the night,
Ps 100: 2 come before him with joyful *s*.
Eph 5:19 with psalms, hymns and spiritual *s*.
Jas 5:13 Is anyone happy? Let him sing *s*

SONS (SON)
Joel 2:28 Your *s* and daughters will prophesy
Jn 12:36 so that you may become *s* of light."
Ro 8:14 by the Spirit of God are *s* of God.
2Co 6:18 and you will be my *s* and daughters
Gal 4: 5 we might receive the full rights of *s*.
Heb 12: 7 discipline; God is treating you as *s*.

SORROW (SORROWS)
Jer 31:12 and they will *s* no more.
Ro 9: 2 I have great *s* and unceasing
2Co 7:10 Godly *s* brings repentance that

SORROWS (SORROW)
Isa 53: 3 a man of *s*, and familiar

SOUL (SOULS)
Dt 6: 5 with all your *s* and with all your
10:12 all your heart and with all your *s*,
Jos 22: 5 with all your heart and all your *s*."
Ps 23: 3 he restores my *s*.
42: 1 so my *s* pants for you, O God.
42:11 Why are you downcast, O my *s*?
103: 1 Praise the LORD, O my *s*;
Pr 13:19 A longing fulfilled is sweet to the *s*,
Isa 55: 2 your *s* will delight in the richest
Mt 10:28 kill the body but cannot kill the *s*.
16:26 yet forfeits his *s*? Or what can
22:37 with all your *s* and with all your
Heb 4:12 even to dividing *s* and spirit,

SOULS (SOUL)
Pr 11:30 and he who wins *s* is wise.
Jer 6:16 and you will find rest for your *s*.
Mt 11:29 and you will find rest for your *s*.

SOUND
1Co 14: 8 if the trumpet does not *s* a clear call
15:52 the trumpet will *s*, the dead will
2Ti 4: 3 men will not put up with *s* doctrine.

SOVEREIGN
Da 4:25 that the Most High is *s*

SOW (SOWS)
Job 4: 8 and those who *s* trouble reap it.
Mt 6:26 they do not *s* or reap or store away
2Pe 2:22 and, "A *s* that is washed goes back

SOWS (SOW)
Pr 11:18 he who *s* righteousness reaps a sure
22: 8 He who *s* wickedness reaps trouble
2Co 9: 6 Whoever *s* sparingly will
Gal 6: 7 A man reaps what he *s*.

SPARE (SPARES)
Ro 8:32 He who did not *s* his own Son,
11:21 natural branches, he will not *s* you

SPARES (SPARE)
Pr 13:24 He who *s* the rod hates his son,

SPEARS
Isa 2: 4 and their *s* into pruning hooks.
Joel 3:10 and your pruning hooks into *s*.
Mic 4: 3 and their *s* into pruning hooks.

SPECTACLE
1Co 4: 9 We have been made a *s*
Col 2:15 he made a public *s* of them,

SPIN
Mt 6:28 They do not labor or *s*.

SPIRIT (SPIRIT'S SPIRITS SPIRITUAL SPIRITUALLY)
Ge 1: 2 and the *S* of God was hovering
6: 3 "My *S* will not contend
2Ki 2: 9 inherit a double portion of your *s*,"
Job 33: 4 The *S* of God has made me;
Ps 31: 5 Into your hands I commit my *s*;
51:10 and renew a steadfast *s* within me.
51:11 or take your Holy *S* from me.
51:17 sacrifices of God are a broken *s*;
139: 7 Where can I go from your *S*?
Isa 57:15 him who is contrite and lowly in *s*,
63:10 and grieved his Holy *S*.
Eze 11:19 an undivided heart and put a new *s*
36:26 you a new heart and put a new *s*
Joel 2:28 I will pour out my *S* on all people.
Zec 4: 6 but by my *S*,' says the LORD
Mt 1:18 to be with child through the Holy *S*
3:11 will baptize you with the Holy *S*
3:16 he saw the *S* of God descending
4: 1 led by the *S* into the desert
5: 3 saying: "Blessed are the poor in *s*,
26:41 *s* is willing, but the body is weak."
28:19 and of the Son and of the Holy *S*,
Lk 1:80 child grew and became strong in *s*;
11:13 Father in heaven give the Holy *S*
Jn 4:24 God is *s*, and his worshipers must
7:39 Up to that time the *S* had not been
14:26 But the Counselor, the Holy *S*,
16:13 But when he, the *S* of truth, comes,
20:22 and said, "Receive the Holy *S*.
Ac 1: 5 will be baptized with the Holy *S*."
2: 4 of them were filled with the Holy *S*
2:38 will receive the gift of the Holy *S*.
6: 3 who are known to be full of the *S*
19: 2 "Did you receive the Holy *S*
Ro 8: 9 And if anyone does not have the *S*
8:26 the *S* helps us in our weakness.
1Co 2:10 God has revealed it to us by his *S*.
2:14 man without the *S* does not accept
6:19 body is a temple of the Holy *S*,
12:13 baptized by one *S* into one body—
2Co 3: 6 the letter kills, but the *S* gives life.
5: 5 and has given us the *S* as a deposit,
Gal 5:16 by the *S*, and you will not gratify
5:22 But the fruit of the *S* is love, joy,
5:25 let us keep in step with the *S*.
Eph 1:13 with a seal, the promised Holy *S*,
4:30 do not grieve the Holy *S* of God,
5:18 Instead, be filled with the *S*.
6:17 of salvation and the sword of the *S*,
2Th 2:13 the sanctifying work of the *S*
Heb 4:12 even to dividing soul and *s*,
1Pe 3: 4 beauty of a gentle and quiet *s*,
2Pe 1:21 carried along by the Holy *S*.
1Jn 4: 1 Dear friends, do not believe every *s*

SPIRIT'S (SPIRIT)
1Th 5:19 not put out the *S* fire; do not treat

SPIRITS (SPIRIT)
1Co 12:10 to another distinguishing between *s*,
14:32 The *s* of prophets are subject
1Jn 4: 1 test the *s* to see whether they are

SPIRITUAL (SPIRIT)
Ro 12: 1 this is your *s* act of worship.
12:11 but keep your *s* fervor, serving
1Co 2:13 expressing *s* truths in *s* words.
3: 1 I could not address you as *s* but
12: 1 Now about *s* gifts, brothers,
14: 1 of love and eagerly desire *s* gifts,
15:44 a natural body, it is raised a *s* body.
Gal 6: 1 you who are *s* should restore him
Eph 1: 3 with every *s* blessing in Christ.
5:19 with psalms, hymns and *s* songs.
6:12 and against the *s* forces of evil
1Pe 2: 2 newborn babies, crave pure *s* milk,
2: 5 are being built into a *s* house

SPIRITUALLY (SPIRIT)
1Co 2:14 because they are *s* discerned.

SPLENDOR
1Ch 16:29 the LORD in the *s* of his holiness.
29:11 the glory and the majesty and the *s*,
Job 37:22 of the north he comes in golden *s*;
Ps 29: 2 in the *s* of his holiness.
45: 3 clothe yourself with *s* and majesty.
96: 6 *S* and majesty are before him;
96: 9 in the *s* of his holiness;
104: 1 you are clothed with *s* and majesty.
145: 5 of the glorious *s* of your majesty,
Isa 61: 3 the LORD for the display of his *s*.
63: 1 Who is this, robed in *s*,
Lk 9:31 appeared in glorious *s*, talking
2Th 2: 8 and destroy by the *s* of his coming.

SPOIL
Ps 119:162 like one who finds great *s*.

SPOTLESS
2Pe 3:14 make every effort to be found *s*,

SPREAD (SPREADING)
Ac 12:24 of God continued to increase and *s*.
19:20 the word of the Lord *s* widely

SPREADING (SPREAD)
1Th 3: 2 God's fellow worker in *s* the gospel

SPRING
Jer 2:13 the *s* of living water,
Jn 4:14 in him a *s* of water welling up
Jas 3:12 can a salt *s* produce fresh water.

SPUR*
Heb 10:24 how we may *s* one another

SPURNS*
Pr 15: 5 A fool *s* his father's discipline,

STAFF
Ps 23: 4 your rod and your *s*,

STAKES
Isa 54: 2 strengthen your *s*.

STAND (STANDING STANDS)
Ex 14:13 *S* firm and you will see
2Ch 20:17 *s* firm and see the deliverance
Ps 1: 5 Therefore the wicked will not *s*
40: 2 and gave me a firm place to *s*.
119:120 I *s* in awe of your laws.
Eze 22:30 *s* before me in the gap on behalf
Zec 14: 4 On that day his feet will *s*
Mt 12:25 divided against itself will not *s*.
Ro 14:10 we will all *s* before God's judgment
1Co 10:13 out so that you can *s* up under it.
15:58 Therefore, my dear brothers, *s* firm
Eph 6:14 *S* firm then, with the belt
2Th 2:15 *s* firm and hold to the teachings we
Jas 5: 8 You too, be patient and *s* firm,
Rev 3:20 Here I am! I *s* at the door

STANDING (STAND)
Ex 3: 5 where you are *s* is holy ground."
Jos 5:15 the place where you are *s* is holy."
1Pe 5: 9 Resist him, *s* firm in the faith,

STANDS (STAND)
Ps 89: 2 that your love *s* firm forever,
119:89 it *s* firm in the heavens.
Mt 10:22 but he who *s* firm to the end will be
2Ti 2:19 God's solid foundation *s* firm,
1Pe 1:25 but the word of the Lord *s* forever

STAR (STARS)
Nu 24:17 A *s* will come out of Jacob;
Rev 22:16 and the bright Morning *S*."

STARS (STAR)
Da 12: 3 like the *s* for ever and ever.
Php 2:15 in which you shine like *s*

STATURE
Lk 2:52 And Jesus grew in wisdom and *s*,

STEADFAST
Ps 51:10 and renew a *s* spirit within me.
Isa 26: 3 him whose mind is *s*,
1Pe 5:10 and make you strong, firm and *s*.

STEAL
Ex 20:15 "You shall not *s*.
Mt 19:18 do not *s*, do not give false
Eph 4:28 has been stealing must *s* no longer,

STEP (STEPS)
Gal 5:25 let us keep in *s* with the Spirit.

STEPS (STEP)
Pr 16: 9 but the LORD determines his *s*.
Jer 10:23 it is not for man to direct his *s*.
1Pe 2:21 that you should follow in his *s*.

STICKS
Pr 18:24 there is a friend who *s* closer

STIFF-NECKED
Ex 34: 9 Although this is a *s* people,

STILL
Ps 46:10 "Be *s*, and know that I am God;
Zec 2:13 Be *s* before the LORD, all mankind

STIRS
Pr 6:19 and a man who *s* up dissension
10:12 Hatred *s* up dissension,
15: 1 but a harsh word *s* up anger.
15:18 hot-tempered man *s* up dissension,
16:28 A perverse man *s* up dissension,
28:25 A greedy man *s* up dissension,
29:22 An angry man *s* up dissension,

STONE (CAPSTONE CORNERSTONE MILLSTONE)
1Sa 17:50 the Philistine with a sling and a *s*;
Isa 8:14 a *s* that causes men to stumble
Eze 11:19 remove from them their heart of *s*
Mk 16: 3 "Who will roll the *s* away
Lk 4: 3 tell this *s* to become bread."
Jn 8: 7 the first to throw a *s* at her."
2Co 3: 3 not on tablets of *s* but on tablets

STOOP
2Sa 22:36 you *s* down to make me great.

STORE
Pr 10:14 Wise men *s* up knowledge,
Mt 6:19 not *s* up for yourselves treasures

STOREHOUSE (HOUSE)
Mal 3:10 Bring the whole tithe into the *s*,

STRAIGHT
Pr 3: 6 and he will make your paths *s*.
4:25 Let your eyes look *s* ahead,
15:21 of understanding keeps a *s* course.
Jn 1:23 'Make *s* the way for the Lord.' "

STRAIN
Mt 23:24 You *s* out a gnat but swallow

STRANGER (STRANGERS)
Mt 25:35 I was a *s* and you invited me in,
Jn 10: 5 But they will never follow a *s*;

STRANGERS (STRANGER)
1Pe 2:11 as aliens and *s* in the world,

STREAMS
Ps 1: 3 He is like a tree planted by *s*
46: 4 is a river whose *s* make glad
Ecc 1: 7 All *s* flow into the sea,
Jn 7:38 *s* of living water will flow

STRENGTH (STRONG)
Ex 15: 2 The LORD is my *s* and my song;
Dt 6: 5 all your soul and with all your *s*.
2Sa 22:33 It is God who arms me with *s*
Ne 8:10 for the joy of the LORD is your *s*."
Ps 28: 7 The LORD is my *s* and my shield;
46: 1 God is our refuge and *s*,
96: 7 ascribe to the LORD glory and *s*.
118:14 The LORD is my *s* and my song;
147:10 not in the *s* of the horse,
Isa 40:31 will renew their *s*.
Mk 12:30 all your mind and with all your *s*.'
1Co 1:25 of God is stronger than man's *s*.
Php 4:13 through him who gives me *s*.
1Pe 4:11 it with the *s* God provides,

STRENGTHEN (STRONG)
2Ch 16: 9 to *s* those whose hearts are fully
Ps 119:28 *s* me according to your word.
Isa 35: 3 *S* the feeble hands,
41:10 I will *s* you and help you;
Eph 3:16 of his glorious riches he may *s* you
2Th 2:17 and *s* you in every good deed
Heb 12:12 *s* your feeble arms and weak knees.

STRENGTHENING (STRONG)
1Co 14:26 done for the *s* of the church.

STRIFE
Pr 20: 3 It is to a man's honor to avoid *s*,
22:10 out the mocker, and out goes *s*;

STRIKE (STRIKES)
Ge 3:15 and you will *s* his heel."
Zec 13: 7 "*S* the shepherd,
Mt 26:31 " 'I will *s* the shepherd,

STRIKES (STRIKE)
Mt 5:39 If someone *s* you on the right

STRONG (STRENGTH STRENGTHEN STRENGTHENING)
Dt 31: 6 Be *s* and courageous.
1Ki 2: 2 "So be *s*, show yourself a man,
Pr 18:10 The name of the LORD is a *s* tower
31:17 her arms are *s* for her tasks.
SS 8: 6 for love is as *s* as death,
Lk 2:40 And the child grew and became *s*;
Ro 15: 1 We who are *s* ought to bear
1Co 1:27 things of the world to shame the *s*.
16:13 in the faith; be men of courage; be *s*
2Co 12:10 For when I am weak, then I am *s*.
Eph 6:10 be *s* in the Lord and in his mighty

STRUGGLE
Ro 15:30 me in my *s* by praying to God
Eph 6:12 For our *s* is not against flesh
Heb 12: 4 In your *s* against sin, you have not

STUDY
Ezr 7:10 Ezra had devoted himself to the *s*
Ecc 12:12 and much *s* wearies the body.
Jn 5:39 You diligently *s* the Scriptures

STUMBLE (STUMBLING)
Ps 37:24 though he *s,* he will not fall,
119:165 and nothing can make them *s.*
Isa 8:14 a stone that causes men to *s*
Jer 31: 9 a level path where they will not *s,*
Eze 7:19 for it has made them *s* into sin.
1Co 10:32 Do not cause anyone to *s,*
1Pe 2: 8 and, "A stone that causes men to *s*

STUMBLING (STUMBLE)
Ro 14:13 up your mind not to put any *s* block
1Co 8: 9 freedom does not become a *s* block
2Co 6: 3 We put no *s* block in anyone's path,

SUBDUE
Ge 1:28 in number; fill the earth and *s* it.

SUBJECT (SUBJECTED)
1Co 14:32 of prophets are *s* to the control
15:28 then the Son himself will be made *s*
Tit 2: 5 and to be *s* to their husbands,
2: 9 slaves to be *s* to their masters
3: 1 Remind the people to be *s* to rulers

SUBJECTED (SUBJECT)
Ro 8:20 For the creation was *s*

SUBMISSION (SUBMIT)
1Co 14:34 but must be in *s,* as the Law says.
1Ti 2:11 learn in quietness and full *s.*

SUBMISSIVE (SUBMIT)
Jas 3:17 then peace-loving, considerate, *s,*
1Pe 3: 1 in the same way be *s*
5: 5 in the same way be *s*

SUBMIT (SUBMISSION SUBMISSIVE SUBMITS)
Ro 13: 1 Everyone must *s* himself
13: 5 necessary to *s* to the authorities,
1Co 16:16 to *s* to such as these
Eph 5:21 *S* to one another out of reverence
Col 3:18 Wives, *s* to your husbands,
Heb 12: 9 How much more should we *s*
13:17 Obey your leaders and *s*
Jas 4: 7 *S* yourselves, then, to God.
1Pe 2:18 *s* yourselves to your masters

SUBMITS* (SUBMIT)
Eph 5:24 Now as the church *s* to Christ,

SUCCESSFUL
Jos 1: 7 that you may be *s* wherever you go.
2Ki 18: 7 he was *s* in whatever he undertook.
2Ch 20:20 in his prophets and you will be *s."*

SUFFER (SUFFERED SUFFERING SUFFERINGS SUFFERS)
Isa 53:10 to crush him and cause him to *s,*
Mk 8:31 the Son of Man must *s* many things
Lk 24:26 the Christ have to *s* these things
24:46 The Christ will *s* and rise
Php 1:29 to *s* for him, since you are going
1Pe 4:16 However, if you *s* as a Christian,

SUFFERED (SUFFER)
Heb 2: 9 and honor because he *s* death,
2:18 Because he himself *s*
1Pe 2:21 Christ *s* for you, leaving you

SUFFERING (SUFFER)
Isa 53: 3 of sorrows, and familiar with *s.*
Ac 5:41 worthy of *s* disgrace for the Name.
2Ti 1: 8 But join with me in *s* for the gospel,
Heb 2:10 of their salvation perfect through *s.*

SUFFERINGS (SUFFER)
Ro 8:17 share in his *s* in order that we may
8:18 that our present *s* are not worth
2Co 1: 5 as the *s* of Christ flow
Php 3:10 the fellowship of sharing in his *s,*

SUFFERS (SUFFER)
Pr 13:20 but a companion of fools *s* harm.
1Co 12:26 If one part *s,* every part *s* with it;

SUFFICIENT
2Co 12: 9 said to me, "My grace is *s* for you,

SUITABLE
Ge 2:18 I will make a helper *s* for him."

SUN
Ecc 1: 9 there is nothing new under the *s.*
Mal 4: 2 the *s* of righteousness will rise
Mt 5:45 He causes his *s* to rise on the evil
17: 2 His face shone like the *s,*
Rev 1:16 His face was like the *s* shining
21:23 The city does not need the *s*

SUPERIOR
Heb 1: 4 he became as much *s* to the angels
8: 6 ministry Jesus has received is as *s*

SUPERVISION
Gal 3:25 longer under the *s* of the law.

SUPREMACY* (SUPREME)
Col 1:18 in everything he might have the *s.*

SUPREME (SUPREMACY)
Pr 4: 7 Wisdom is *s;* therefore get wisdom.

SURE
Nu 32:23 you may be *s* that your sin will find
Dt 6:17 Be *s* to keep the commands
14:22 Be *s* to set aside a tenth
Isa 28:16 cornerstone for a *s* foundation;
Heb 11: 1 faith is being *s* of what we hope for
2Pe 1:10 to make your calling and election *s.*

SURPASS* (SURPASSES SURPASSING)
Pr 31:29 but you *s* them all."

SURPASSES (SURPASS)
Mt 5:20 unless your righteousness *s* that
Eph 3:19 to know this love that *s* knowledge

SURPASSING* (SURPASS)
Ps 150: 2 praise him for his *s* greatness.
2Co 3:10 in comparison with the *s* glory.
9:14 of the *s* grace God has given you.
Php 3: 8 the *s* greatness of knowing Christ

SURROUNDED
Heb 12: 1 since we are *s* by such a great cloud

SUSPENDS*
Job 26: 7 he *s* the earth over nothing.

SUSTAINING* (SUSTAINS)
Heb 1: 3 *s* all things by his powerful word.

SUSTAINS (SUSTAINING)
Ps 18:35 and your right hand *s* me;
146: 9 and *s* the fatherless and the widow,
147: 6 The LORD *s* the humble
Isa 50: 4 to know the word that *s* the weary.

SWALLOWED
1Co 15:54 "Death has been *s* up in victory."
2Co 5: 4 so that what is mortal may be *s* up

SWEAR
Mt 5:34 Do not *s* at all: either by heaven,

SWORD (SWORDS)
Ps 45: 3 Gird your *s* upon your side,
Pr 12:18 Reckless words pierce like a *s,*
Mt 10:34 come to bring peace, but a *s.*
26:52 all who draw the *s* will die by the *s.*
Lk 2:35 a *s* will pierce your own soul too."
Ro 13: 4 for he does not bear the *s*
Eph 6:17 of salvation and the *s* of the Spirit,
Heb 4:12 Sharper than any double-edged *s,*
Rev 1:16 came a sharp double-edged *s.*

SWORDS (SWORD)
Isa 2: 4 They will beat their *s*
Joel 3:10 Beat your plowshares into *s*

SYMPATHETIC*
1Pe 3: 8 in harmony with one another; be *s,*

SYNAGOGUE
Lk 4:16 the Sabbath day he went into the *s,*
Ac 17: 2 custom was, Paul went into the *s,*

TABERNACLE
Ex 40:34 the glory of the LORD filled the *t.*

TABLE (TABLES)
Ps 23: 5 You prepare a *t* before me

TABLES (TABLE)
Ac 6: 2 word of God in order to wait on *t.*

TABLET (TABLETS)
Pr 3: 3 write them on the *t* of your heart.
7: 3 write them on the *t* of your heart.

TABLETS (TABLET)
Ex 31:18 he gave him the two *t*
Dt 10: 5 and put the *t* in the ark I had made,
2Co 3: 3 not on *t* of stone but on *t*

TAKE (TAKEN TAKES TAKING TOOK)
Dt 12:32 do not add to it or *t* away from it.
31:26 *"T* this Book of the Law
Job 23:10 But he knows the way that I *t;*
Ps 49:17 for he will *t* nothing with him
51:11 or *t* your Holy Spirit from me.
Mt 10:38 anyone who does not *t* his cross
11:29 *T* my yoke upon you and learn
16:24 deny himself and *t* up his cross

TAKEN (TAKE)
Lev 6: 4 must return what he has stolen or *t*
Isa 6: 7 your guilt is *t* away and your sin
Mt 24:40 one will be *t* and the other left.
Mk 16:19 he was *t* up into heaven
1Ti 3:16 was *t* up in glory.

TAKES (TAKE)
1Ki 20:11 should not boast like one who *t* it
Ps 5: 4 You are not a God who *t* pleasure
Jn 1:29 who *t* away the sin of the world!
Rev 22:19 And if anyone *t* words away

TAKING (TAKE)
Ac 15:14 by *t* from the Gentiles a people
Php 2: 7 *t* the very nature of a servant,

TALENT
Mt 25:15 to another one *t,* each according

TAME*
Jas 3: 8 but no man can *t* the tongue.

TASK
Mk 13:34 each with his assigned *t,*
Ac 20:24 complete the *t* the Lord Jesus has
1Co 3: 5 the Lord has assigned to each his *t.*
2Co 2:16 And who is equal to such a *t?*

TASTE (TASTED)
Ps 34: 8 *T* and see that the LORD is good;
Col 2:21 Do not *t!* Do not touch!"?
Heb 2: 9 the grace of God he might *t* death

TASTED (TASTE)
1Pe 2: 3 now that you have *t* that the Lord

TAUGHT (TEACH)
Mt 7:29 he *t* as one who had authority,
1Co 2:13 but in words *t* by the Spirit,
Gal 1:12 nor was I *t* it; rather, I received it

TAXES
Mt 22:17 Is it right to pay *t* to Caesar or not
Ro 13: 7 If you owe *t,* pay *t;* if revenue,

TEACH (TAUGHT TEACHER TEACHERS TEACHES TEACHING)
Ex 33:13 *t* me your ways so I may know you
Dt 4: 9 *T* them to your children
8: 3 to *t* you that man does not live
11:19 *T* them to your children, talking
1Sa 12:23 I will *t* you the way that is good
Ps 32: 8 *t* you in the way you should go;
51:13 I will *t* transgressors your ways,
90:12 *T* us to number our days aright,
143:10 *T* me to do your will,
Jer 31:34 No longer will a man *t* his neighbor
Lk 11: 1 said to him, "Lord, *t* us to pray,
Jn 14:26 will *t* you all things and will remind
1Ti 2:12 I do not permit a woman to *t*
3: 2 respectable, hospitable, able to *t,*
Tit 2: 1 You must *t* what is in accord
Heb 8:11 No longer will a man *t* his neighbor
Jas 3: 1 know that we who *t* will be judged
1Jn 2:27 you do not need anyone to *t* you.

TEACHER (TEACH)
Mt 10:24 "A student is not above his *t,*
Jn 13:14 and *T,* have washed your feet,

TEACHERS (TEACH)
1Co 12:28 third *t,* then workers of miracles,
Eph 4:11 and some to be pastors and *t,*
Heb 5:12 by this time you ought to be *t,*

TEACHES (TEACH)
1Ti 6: 3 If anyone *t* false doctrines

TEACHING (TEACH)
Pr 1: 8 and do not forsake your mother's *t.*
Mt 28:20 *t* them to obey everything I have
Jn 7:17 whether my *t* comes from God or
14:23 loves me, he will obey my *t.*
1Ti 4:13 of Scripture, to preaching and to *t.*
2Ti 3:16 is God-breathed and is useful for *t,*
Tit 2: 7 In your *t* show integrity,

TEAR (TEARS)
Rev 7:17 God will wipe away every *t*

TEARS (TEAR)
Ps 126: 5 Those who sow in *t*
Php 3:18 and now say again even with *t,*

TEETH (TOOTH)
Mt 8:12 will be weeping and gnashing of *t."*

TEMPERATE*
1Ti 3: 2 *t,* self-controlled, respectable,
3:11 not malicious talkers but *t*
Tit 2: 2 Teach the older men to be *t,*

TEMPEST
Ps 55: 8 far from the *t* and storm."

TEMPLE (TEMPLES)
1Ki 8:27 How much less this *t* I have built!
Hab 2:20 But the LORD is in his holy *t;*
1Co 3:16 that you yourselves are God's *t*
6:19 you not know that your body is a *t*
2Co 6:16 For we are the *t* of the living God.

TEMPLES (TEMPLE)
Ac 17:24 does not live in *t* built by hands.

TEMPT (TEMPTATION TEMPTED)
1Co 7: 5 again so that Satan will not *t* you

TEMPTATION (TEMPT)
Mt 6:13 And lead us not into *t,*
26:41 pray so that you will not fall into *t.*
1Co 10:13 No *t* has seized you except what is

TEMPTED (TEMPT)
Mt 4: 1 into the desert to be *t* by the devil.
1Co 10:13 he will not let you be *t*
Heb 2:18 he himself suffered when he was *t,*
4:15 but we have one who has been *t*
Jas 1:13 For God cannot be *t* by evil,

TEN (TENTH TITHE TITHES)
Ex 34:28 covenant—the *T* Commandments.
Ps 91: 7 *t* thousand at your right hand,
Mt 25:28 it to the one who has the *t* talents.
Lk 15: 8 suppose a woman has *t* silver coins

TENTH (TEN)
Dt 14:22 Be sure to set aside a *t*

TERRIBLE (TERROR)
2Ti 3: 1 There will be *t* times

TERROR (TERRIBLE)
Ps 91: 5 You will not fear the *t* of night,
Lk 21:26 Men will faint from *t,* apprehensive
Ro 13: 3 For rulers hold no *t*

TEST (TESTED TESTS)
Dt 6:16 Do not *t* the LORD your God
Ps 139:23 *t* me and know my anxious
Ro 12: 2 Then you will be able to *t*
1Co 3:13 and the fire will *t* the quality
1Jn 4: 1 *t* the spirits to see whether they are

TESTED (TEST)
Ge 22: 1 Some time later God *t* Abraham.
Job 23:10 when he has *t* me, I will come forth
Pr 27:21 man is *t* by the praise he receives.
1Ti 3:10 They must first be *t;* and then

TESTIFY (TESTIMONY)
Jn 5:39 are the Scriptures that *t* about me,
2Ti 1: 8 ashamed to *t* about our Lord,

TESTIMONY (TESTIFY)
Isa 8:20 and to the *t!* If they do not speak
Lk 18:20 not give false *t,* honor your father

TESTS (TEST)
Pr 17: 3 but the LORD *t* the heart.
1Th 2: 4 but God, who *t* our hearts.

THADDAEUS
Apostle (Mt 10:3; Mk 3:18); probably also known as Judas son of James (Lk 6:16; Ac 1:13).

THANKFUL (THANKS)
Heb 12:28 let us be *t,* and so worship God

THANKS (THANKFUL THANKSGIVING)
1Ch 16: 8 Give *t* to the LORD, call
Ne 12:31 assigned two large choirs to give *t.*
Ps 100: 4 give *t* to him and praise his name.
1Co 15:57 *t* be to God! He gives us the victory
2Co 2:14 *t* be to God, who always leads us
9:15 *T* be to God for his indescribable
1Th 5:18 give *t* in all circumstances,

THANKSGIVING (THANKS)
Ps 95: 2 Let us come before him with *t*
100: 4 Enter his gates with *t*
Php 4: 6 by prayer and petition, with *t,*
1Ti 4: 3 created to be received with *t*

THIEF (THIEVES)
Ex 22: 3 A *t* must certainly make restitution
1Th 5: 2 day of the Lord will come like a *t*
Rev 16:15 I come like a *t!* Blessed is he who

THIEVES (THIEF)
1Co 6:10 nor homosexual offenders nor *t*

THINK (THOUGHT THOUGHTS)
Ro 12: 3 Do not *t* of yourself more highly
Php 4: 8 praiseworthy—*t* about such things

THIRST (THIRSTY)
Ps 69:21 and gave me vinegar for my *t.*
Mt 5: 6 Blessed are those who hunger and *t*
Jn 4:14 the water I give him will never *t.*

THIRSTY (THIRST)
Isa 55: 1 "Come, all you who are *t,*
Jn 7:37 "If anyone is *t,* let him come to me
Rev 22:17 Whoever is *t,* let him come;

THOMAS
Apostle (Mt 10:3; Mk 3:18; Lk 6:15; Jn 11:16; 14:5; 21:2; Ac 1:13). Doubted resurrection (Jn 20:24-28).

THONGS
Mk 1: 7 *t* of whose sandals I am not worthy

THORN (THORNS)
2Co 12: 7 there was given me a *t* in my flesh,

THORNS (THORN)
Nu 33:55 in your eyes and *t* in your sides.
Mt 27:29 then twisted together a crown of *t*
Heb 6: 8 But land that produces *t*

THOUGHT (THINK)
Pr 14:15 a prudent man gives *t* to his steps.
1Co 13:11 I talked like a child, I *t* like a child,

THOUGHTS (THINK)
Ps 94:11 The LORD knows the *t* of man;
139:23 test me and know my anxious *t.*
Isa 55: 8 "For my *t* are not your *t,*
Heb 4:12 it judges the *t* and attitudes

THREE
Ecc 4:12 of *t* strands is not quickly broken.
Mt 12:40 *t* nights in the belly of a huge fish,
18:20 or *t* come together in my name,
27:63 'After *t* days I will rise again.'
1Co 13:13 And now these *t* remain: faith,
14:27 or at the most *t*— should speak,
2Co 13: 1 testimony of two or *t* witnesses."

THRESHING
2Sa 24:18 an altar to the LORD on the *t* floor

THRONE (ENTHRONED)
2Sa 7:16 your *t* will be established forever
Ps 45: 6 Your *t,* O God, will last for ever
47: 8 God is seated on his holy *t.*
Isa 6: 1 I saw the Lord seated on a *t,*
66: 1 "Heaven is my *t*
Heb 4:16 Let us then approach the *t* of grace
12: 2 at the right hand of the *t* of God.
Rev 4:10 They lay their crowns before the *t*
20:11 Then I saw a great white *t*
22: 3 *t* of God and of the Lamb will be

THROW
Jn 8: 7 the first to *t* a stone at her."
Heb 10:35 So do not *t* away your confidence;
12: 1 let us *t* off everything that hinders

THWART*
Isa 14:27 has purposed, and who can *t* him?

TIBNI
King of Israel (1Ki 16:21-22).

TIME (TIMES)
Est 4:14 come to royal position for such a *t*
Da 7:25 to him for a *t,* times and half a *t.*
Hos 10:12 for it is *t* to seek the LORD,
Ro 9: 9 "At the appointed *t* I will return,
Heb 9:28 and he will appear a second *t,*
10:12 for all *t* one sacrifice for sins,
1Pe 4:17 For it is *t* for judgment to begin

TIMES (TIME)
Ps 9: 9 a stronghold in *t* of trouble.
31:15 My *t* are in your hands;
62: 8 Trust in him at all *t,* O people;
Pr 17:17 A friend loves at all *t,*
Am 5:13 for the *t* are evil.
Mt 18:21 how many *t* shall I forgive my
Ac 1: 7 "It is not for you to know the *t*
Rev 12:14 *t* and half a time, out

TIMIDITY*
2Ti 1: 7 For God did not give us a spirit of *t*

TIMOTHY
Believer from Lystra (Ac 16:1). Joined Paul on second missionary journey (Ac 16-20). Sent to settle problems at Corinth (1Co 4:17; 16:10). Led church at Ephesus (1Ti 1:3). Co-writer with Paul (1Th 1:1; 2Th 1:1; Phm 1).

TIRE (TIRED)
2Th 3:13 never *t* of doing what is right.

TIRED (TIRE)
Ex 17:12 When Moses' hands grew *t,*
Isa 40:28 He will not grow *t* or weary,

TITHE (TEN)
Lev 27:30 " 'A *t* of everything from the land,
Dt 12:17 eat in your own towns the *t*
Mal 3:10 the whole *t* into the storehouse,

TITHES (TEN)
Mal 3: 8 'How do we rob you?' "In *t*

TITUS
Gentile co-worker of Paul (Gal 2:1-3; 2Ti 4:10); sent to Corinth (2Co 2:13; 7-8; 12:18), Crete (Tit 1:4-5).

TODAY
Mt 6:11 Give us *t* our daily bread.
Lk 23:43 *t* you will be with me in paradise."
Heb 3:13 daily, as long as it is called *T,*
13: 8 Christ is the same yesterday and *t*

TOIL
Ge 3:17 through painful *t* you will eat of it

TOLERATE
Hab 1:13 you cannot *t* wrong.
Rev 2: 2 that you cannot *t* wicked men,

TOMB
Mt 27:65 make the *t* as secure as you know
Lk 24: 2 the stone rolled away from the *t,*

TOMORROW
Pr 27: 1 Do not boast about *t,*
Isa 22:13 "for *t* we die!"
Mt 6:34 Therefore do not worry about *t,*
Jas 4:13 "Today or *t* we will go to this

TONGUE (TONGUES)
Ps 39: 1 and keep my *t* from sin;
Pr 12:18 but the *t* of the wise brings healing.
1Co 14: 2 speaks in a *t* does not speak to men
14: 4 He who speaks in a *t* edifies himself
14:13 in a *t* should pray that he may
14:19 than ten thousand words in a *t.*
Php 2:11 every *t* confess that Jesus Christ is
Jas 1:26 does not keep a tight rein on his *t,*
3: 8 but no man can tame the *t.*

TONGUES (TONGUE)
Isa 28:11 with foreign lips and strange *t*
66:18 and gather all nations and *t,*
Mk 16:17 in new *t;* they will pick up snakes
Ac 2: 4 and began to speak in other *t*
10:46 For they heard them speaking in *t*
19: 6 and they spoke in *t* and prophesied
1Co 12:30 Do all speak in *t?* Do all interpret?
14:18 speak in *t* more than all of you.
14:39 and do not forbid speaking in *t.*

TOOK (TAKE)
1Co 11:23 the night he was betrayed, *t* bread,
Php 3:12 for which Christ Jesus *t* hold of me.

TOOTH (TEETH)
Ex 21:24 eye for eye, *t* for *t,* hand for hand,
Mt 5:38 'Eye for eye, and *t* for *t.*'

TORMENTED
Rev 20:10 They will be *t* day and night

TORN
Gal 4:15 you would have *t* out your eyes
Php 1:23 I do not know! I am *t*

TOUCH (TOUCHED)
Ps 105:15 "Do not *t* my anointed ones;
Lk 24:39 It is I myself! *T* me and see;
2Co 6:17 *T* no unclean thing,
Col 2:21 Do not taste! Do not *t!*"?

TOUCHED (TOUCH)
1Sa 10:26 men whose hearts God had *t.*
Mt 14:36 and all who *t* him were healed.

TOWER
Ge 11: 4 with a *t* that reaches to the heavens
Pr 18:10 of the LORD is a strong *t;*

TOWNS
Nu 35: 2 to give the Levites *t* to live
35:15 These six *t* will be a place of refuge

TRACING*
Ro 11:33 and his paths beyond *t* out!

TRADITION
Mt 15: 6 word of God for the sake of your *t.*
Col 2: 8 which depends on human *t*

TRAIN (TRAINING)
Pr 22: 6 *T* a child in the way he should go,
Eph 4: 8 he led captives in his *t*

TRAINING (TRAIN)
1Co 9:25 in the games goes into strict *t.*
2Ti 3:16 correcting and *t* in righteousness,

TRAMPLED
Lk 21:24 Jerusalem will be *t*
Heb 10:29 to be punished who has *t* the Son

TRANCE
Ac 10:10 was being prepared, he fell into a *t.*

TRANSCENDS*
Php 4: 7 which *t* all understanding,

TRANSFIGURED
Mt 17: 2 There he was *t* before them.

TRANSFORM* (TRANSFORMED)
Php 3:21 will *t* our lowly bodies

TRANSFORMED (TRANSFORM)
Ro 12: 2 be *t* by the renewing of your mind.
2Co 3:18 are being *t* into his likeness

TRANSGRESSION (TRANSGRESSIONS TRANSGRESSORS)
Isa 53: 8 for the *t* of my people he was
Ro 4:15 where there is no law there is no *t.*

TRANSGRESSIONS (TRANSGRESSION)
Ps 32: 1 whose *t* are forgiven,
51: 1 blot out my *t.*
103:12 so far has he removed our *t* from us
Isa 53: 5 But he was pierced for our *t,*
Eph 2: 1 you were dead in your *t* and sins,

TRANSGRESSORS (TRANSGRESSION)
Ps 51:13 Then I will teach *t* your ways,
Isa 53:12 and made intercession for the *t.*
53:12 and was numbered with the *t.*

TREADING
Dt 25: 4 an ox while it is *t* out the grain.
1Co 9: 9 an ox while it is *t* out the grain."

TREASURE (TREASURED TREASURES)
Isa 33: 6 of the LORD is the key to this *t.*
Mt 6:21 For where your *t* is, there your
2Co 4: 7 But we have this *t* in jars of clay

TREASURED (TREASURE)
Dt 7: 6 to be his people, his *t* possession.
Lk 2:19 But Mary *t* up all these things

TREASURES (TREASURE)
Mt 6:19 up for yourselves *t* on earth,
Col 2: 3 in whom are hidden all the *t*
Heb 11:26 of greater value than the *t* of Egypt,

TREAT
Lev 22: 2 sons to *t* with respect the sacred
1Ti 5: 1 *T* younger men as brothers,
1Pe 3: 7 and *t* them with respect

TREATY
Dt 7: 2 Make no *t* with them, and show

TREE
Ge 2: 9 and the *t* of the knowledge of good
2: 9 of the garden were the *t* of life
Dt 21:23 hung on a *t* is under God's curse.
Ps 1: 3 He is like a *t* planted by streams
Mt 3:10 every *t* that does not produce good
12:33 for a *t* is recognized by its fruit.

Gal 3:13 is everyone who is hung on a *t.*"
Rev 22:14 they may have the right to the *t*

TREMBLE (TREMBLING)
1Ch 16:30 *T* before him, all the earth!
Ps 114: 7 *T,* O earth, at the presence

TREMBLING (TREMBLE)
Ps 2:11 and rejoice with *t.*
Php 2:12 out your salvation with fear and *t,*

TRESPASS
Ro 5:17 For if, by the *t* of the one man,

TRIALS
1Th 3: 3 one would be unsettled by these *t.*
Jas 1: 2 whenever you face *t* of many kinds,
2Pe 2: 9 how to rescue godly men from *t*

TRIBES
Ge 49:28 All these are the twelve *t* of Israel,
Mt 19:28 judging the twelve *t* of Israel.

TRIBULATION*
Rev 7:14 who have come out of the great *t;*

TRIUMPHAL* (TRIUMPHING)
Isa 60:11 their kings led in *t* procession.
2Co 2:14 us in *t* procession in Christ

TRIUMPHING* (TRIUMPHAL)
Col 2:15 of them, *t* over them by the cross.

TROUBLE (TROUBLED TROUBLES)
Job 14: 1 is of few days and full of *t.*
Ps 46: 1 an ever-present help in *t.*
107:13 they cried to the LORD in their *t,*
Pr 11:29 He who brings *t* on his family will
24:10 If you falter in times of *t,*
Mt 6:34 Each day has enough *t* of its own.
Jn 16:33 In this world you will have *t.*
Ro 8:35 Shall *t* or hardship or persecution

TROUBLED (TROUBLE)
Jn 14: 1 "Do not let your hearts be *t.*
14:27 Do not let your hearts be *t*

TROUBLES (TROUBLE)
1Co 7:28 those who marry will face many *t*
2Co 1: 4 who comforts us in all our *t,*
4:17 and momentary *t* are achieving

TRUE (TRUTH)
Dt 18:22 does not take place or come *t,*
1Sa 9: 6 and everything he says comes *t.*
Ps 119:160 All your words are *t;*
Jn 17: 3 the only *t* God, and Jesus Christ,
Ro 3: 4 Let God be *t,* and every man a liar.
Php 4: 8 whatever is *t,* whatever is noble,
Rev 22: 6 These words are trustworthy and *t.*

TRUMPET
1Co 14: 8 if the *t* does not sound a clear call,
15:52 For the *t* will sound, the dead will

TRUST (ENTRUSTED TRUSTED TRUSTS TRUSTWORTHY)
Ps 20: 7 we *t* in the name of the LORD our
37: 3 *T* in the LORD and do good;
56: 4 in God I *t;* I will not be afraid.
119:42 for I *t* in your word.
Pr 3: 5 *T* in the LORD with all your heart
Isa 30:15 in quietness and *t* is your strength,
Jn 14: 1 *T* in God; *t* also in me.
1Co 4: 2 been given a *t* must prove faithful.

TRUSTED (TRUST)
Ps 26: 1 I have *t* in the LORD
Isa 25: 9 we *t* in him, and he saved us.
Da 3:28 They *t* in him and defied the king's
Lk 16:10 *t* with very little can also be *t*

TRUSTS (TRUST)
Ps 32:10 surrounds the man who *t* in him.
Pr 11:28 Whoever *t* in his riches will fall,
28:26 He who *t* in himself is a fool,
Ro 9:33 one who *t* in him will never be put

TRUSTWORTHY (TRUST)
Ps 119:138 they are fully *t.*
Pr 11:13 but a *t* man keeps a secret.
Rev 22: 6 "These words are *t* and true.

TRUTH (TRUE TRUTHFUL TRUTHS)
Ps 51: 6 Surely you desire *t*
Isa 45:19 I, the LORD, speak the *t;*
Zec 8:16 are to do: Speak the *t* to each other,
Jn 4:23 worship the Father in spirit and *t,*
8:32 Then you will know the *t,*
8:32 and the *t* will set you free."
14: 6 I am the way and the *t* and the life.
16:13 comes, he will guide you into all *t.*
18:38 "What is *t?"* Pilate asked.
Ro 1:25 They exchanged the *t* of God
1Co 13: 6 in evil but rejoices with the *t.*
2Co 13: 8 against the *t,* but only for the *t.*
Eph 4:15 Instead, speaking the *t* in love,
6:14 with the belt of *t* buckled
2Th 2:10 because they refused to love the *t*
1Ti 2: 4 to come to a knowledge of the *t.*
3:15 the pillar and foundation of the *t.*
2Ti 2:15 correctly handles the word of *t.*
3: 7 never able to acknowledge the *t.*
Heb 10:26 received the knowledge of the *t,*
1Pe 1:22 by obeying the *t* so that you have
2Pe 2: 2 the way of *t* into disrepute.
1Jn 1: 6 we lie and do not live by the *t.*
1: 8 deceive ourselves and the *t* is not

TRUTHFUL (TRUTH)
Pr 12:22 but he delights in men who are *t.*
Jn 3:33 it has certified that God is *t.*

TRUTHS (TRUTH)
1Co 2:13 expressing spiritual *t*
1Ti 3: 9 hold of the deep *t* of the faith
Heb 5:12 to teach you the elementary *t*

TRY (TRYING)
Ps 26: 2 Test me, O LORD, and *t* me,
Isa 7:13 enough to *t* the patience of men?
1Co 14:12 *t* to excel in gifts that build up
2Co 5:11 is to fear the Lord, we *t*
1Th 5:15 always *t* to be kind to each other

TRYING (TRY)
2Co 5:12 We are not *t* to commend ourselves
1Th 2: 4 We are not *t* to please men but God

TUNIC
Lk 6:29 do not stop him from taking your *t.*

TURN (TURNED TURNS)
Ex 32:12 *T* from your fierce anger; relent
Dt 5:32 do not *t* aside to the right
28:14 Do not *t* aside from any
Jos 1: 7 do not *t* from it to the right
2Ch 7:14 and *t* from their wicked ways,
30: 9 He will not *t* his face from you
Ps 78: 6 they in *t* would tell their children.
Pr 22: 6 when he is old he will not *t* from it.
Isa 29:16 You *t* things upside down,
30:21 Whether you *t* to the right
45:22 "*T* to me and be saved,
55: 7 Let him *t* to the LORD,
Eze 33:11 *T! T* from your evil ways!
Mal 4: 6 He will *t* the hearts of the fathers
Mt 5:39 you on the right cheek, *t*
10:35 For I have come to *t*
Jn 12:40 nor *t*— and I would heal them."
Ac 3:19 Repent, then, and *t* to God,
26:18 and *t* them from darkness to light,
1Ti 6:20 *T* away from godless chatter
1Pe 3:11 He must *t* from evil and do good;

TURNED (TURN)
Ps 30:11 You *t* my wailing into dancing;
40: 1 he *t* to me and heard my cry.
Isa 53: 6 each of us has *t* to his own way;
Hos 7: 8 Ephraim is a flat cake not *t* over.
Joel 2:31 The sun will be *t* to darkness
Ro 3:12 All have *t* away,

TURNS (TURN)
2Sa 22:29 the LORD *t* my darkness into light
Pr 15: 1 A gentle answer *t* away wrath,
Isa 44:25 and *t* it into nonsense,
Jas 5:20 Whoever *t* a sinner from the error

TWELVE
Ge 49:28 All these are the *t* tribes of Israel,
Mt 10: 1 He called his *t* disciples to him

TWINKLING*
1Co 15:52 in a flash, in the *t* of an eye,

UNAPPROACHABLE*
1Ti 6:16 immortal and who lives in *u* light,

UNBELIEF (UNBELIEVER UNBELIEVERS UNBELIEVING)
Mk 9:24 help me overcome my *u!"*
Ro 11:20 they were broken off because of *u,*
Heb 3:19 able to enter, because of their *u.*

UNBELIEVER* (UNBELIEF)
1Co 7:15 But if the *u* leaves, let him do so.
10:27 If some *u* invites you to a meal
14:24 if an *u* or someone who does not
2Co 6:15 have in common with an *u?*
1Ti 5: 8 the faith and is worse than an *u.*

UNBELIEVERS (UNBELIEF)
1Co 6: 6 another—and this in front of *u!*
2Co 6:14 Do not be yoked together with *u.*

UNBELIEVING (UNBELIEF)
1Co 7:14 For the *u* husband has been
Rev 21: 8 But the cowardly, the *u,* the vile,

UNCERTAIN*
1Ti 6:17 which is so *u,* but to put their hope

UNCHANGEABLE*
Heb 6:18 by two *u* things in which it is

UNCIRCUMCISED
1Sa 17:26 Who is this *u* Philistine that he
Col 3:11 circumcised or *u,* barbarian,

UNCIRCUMCISION
1Co 7:19 is nothing and *u* is nothing.
Gal 5: 6 neither circumcision nor *u* has any

UNCLEAN
Isa 6: 5 ruined! For I am a man of *u* lips,
Ro 14:14 fully convinced that no food is *u*
2Co 6:17 Touch no *u* thing,

UNCONCERNED*
Eze 16:49 were arrogant, overfed and *u;*

UNCOVERED
Heb 4:13 Everything is *u* and laid bare

UNDERSTAND (UNDERSTANDING UNDERSTANDS)
Job 42: 3 Surely I spoke of things I did not *u*,
Ps 73:16 When I tried to *u* all this,
119:125 that I may *u* your statutes.
Lk 24:45 so they could *u* the Scriptures.
Ac 8:30 "Do you *u* what you are reading?"
Ro 7:15 I do not *u* what I do.
1Co 2:14 and he cannot *u* them,
Eph 5:17 but *u* what the Lord's will is.
2Pe 3:16 some things that are hard to *u*,

UNDERSTANDING (UNDERSTAND)
Ps 119:104 I gain *u* from your precepts;
147: 5 his *u* has no limit.
Pr 3: 5 and lean not on your own *u;*
4: 7 Though it cost all you have, get *u*.
10:23 but a man of *u* delights in wisdom.
11:12 but a man of *u* holds his tongue.
15:21 a man of *u* keeps a straight course.
15:32 whoever heeds correction gains *u*.
23:23 get wisdom, discipline and *u*.
Isa 40:28 and his *u* no one can fathom.
Da 5:12 a keen mind and knowledge and *u*,
Mk 4:12 and ever hearing but never *u;*
12:33 with all your *u* and with all your
Php 4: 7 of God, which transcends all *u*,

UNDERSTANDS (UNDERSTAND)
1Ch 28: 9 and *u* every motive
1Ti 6: 4 he is conceited and *u* nothing.

UNDIVIDED*
1Ch 12:33 to help David with *u* loyalty—
Ps 86:11 give me an *u* heart,
Eze 11:19 I will give them an *u* heart
1Co 7:35 way in *u* devotion to the Lord.

UNDOING
Pr 18: 7 A fool's mouth is his *u*,

UNDYING*
Eph 6:24 Lord Jesus Christ with an *u* love.

UNFADING*
1Pe 3: 4 the *u* beauty of a gentle

UNFAILING
Ps 33: 5 the earth is full of his *u* love.
119:76 May your *u* love be my comfort,
143: 8 bring me word of your *u* love,
Pr 19:22 What a man desires is *u* love;
La 3:32 so great is his *u* love.

UNFAITHFUL (UNFAITHFULNESS)
Lev 6: 2 is *u* to the LORD by deceiving his
1Ch 10:13 because he was *u* to the LORD;
Pr 13:15 but the way of the *u* is hard.

UNFAITHFULNESS (UNFAITHFUL)
Mt 5:32 except for marital *u*, causes her
19: 9 for marital *u*, and marries another

UNFOLDING
Ps 119:130 the *u* of your words gives light;

UNGODLINESS
Tit 2:12 It teaches us to say "No" to *u*

UNIT
1Co 12:12 body is a *u*, though it is made up

UNITED (UNITY)
Ro 6: 5 If we have been *u* with him
Php 2: 1 from being *u* with Christ,
Col 2: 2 encouraged in heart and *u* in love,

UNITY (UNITED)
Ps 133: 1 is when brothers live together in *u!*
Ro 15: 5 a spirit of *u* among yourselves
Eph 4: 3 effort to keep the *u* of the Spirit
4:13 up until we all reach *u* in the faith
Col 3:14 them all together in perfect *u*.

UNIVERSE
Php 2:15 which you shine like stars in the *u*
Heb 1: 2 and through whom he made the *u*.

UNKNOWN
Ac 17:23 TO AN *U* GOD.

UNLEAVENED
Ex 12:17 "Celebrate the Feast of *U* Bread,

UNPROFITABLE
Tit 3: 9 because these are *u* and useless.

UNPUNISHED
Ex 34: 7 Yet he does not leave the guilty *u;*
Pr 19: 5 A false witness will not go *u*,

UNREPENTANT*
Ro 2: 5 stubbornness and your *u* heart,

UNRIGHTEOUS*
Zep 3: 5 yet the *u* know no shame.
Mt 5:45 rain on the righteous and the *u*.
1Pe 3:18 the righteous for the *u*, to bring you
2Pe 2: 9 and to hold the *u* for the day

UNSEARCHABLE
Ro 11:33 How *u* his judgments,
Eph 3: 8 preach to the Gentiles the *u* riches

UNSEEN
2Co 4:18 on what is seen, but on what is *u*.
4:18 temporary, but what is *u* is eternal.

UNSTABLE*
Jas 1: 8 he is a double-minded man, *u*
2Pe 2:14 they seduce the *u;* they are experts
3:16 ignorant and *u* people distort,

UNTHINKABLE*
Job 34:12 It is *u* that God would do wrong,

UNVEILED*
2Co 3:18 with *u* faces all reflect the Lord's

UNWORTHY
Job 40: 4 "I am *u*— how can I reply to you?
Lk 17:10 should say, 'We are *u* servants;

UPRIGHT
Job 1: 1 This man was blameless and *u;*
Pr 2: 7 He holds victory in store for the *u*,
15: 8 but the prayer of the *u* pleases him.
Tit 1: 8 who is self-controlled, *u*, holy
2:12 *u* and godly lives in this present

UPROOTED
Jude :12 without fruit and *u*— twice dead.

USEFUL
2Ti 2:21 *u* to the Master and prepared
3:16 Scripture is God-breathed and is *u*

USELESS
1Co 15:14 our preaching is *u*
Jas 2:20 faith without deeds is *u?*

USURY
Ne 5:10 But let the exacting of *u* stop!

UTTER
Ps 78: 2 I will *u* hidden things, things from of

UZZIAH
Son of Amaziah; king of Judah also known as Azariah (2Ki 15:1-7; 1Ch 6:24; 2Ch 26).

VAIN
Ps 33:17 A horse is a *v* hope for deliverance;
Isa 65:23 They will not toil in *v*
1Co 15: 2 Otherwise, you have believed in *v*.
15:58 labor in the Lord is not in *v*.
2Co 6: 1 not to receive God's grace in *v*.

VALLEY
Ps 23: 4 walk through the *v* of the shadow
Isa 40: 4 Every *v* shall be raised up,
Joel 3:14 multitudes in the *v* of decision!

VALUABLE (VALUE)
Lk 12:24 And how much more *v* you are

VALUE (VALUABLE)
Mt 13:46 When he found one of great *v*,
1Ti 4: 8 For physical training is of some *v*,
Heb 11:26 as of greater *v* than the treasures

VEIL
Ex 34:33 to them, he put a *v* over his face.
2Co 3:14 for to this day the same *v* remains

VENGEANCE (AVENGE REVENGE)
Isa 34: 8 For the LORD has a day of *v*,

VICTORIES (VICTORY)
Ps 18:50 He gives his king great *v;*
21: 1 great is his joy in the *v* you give!

VICTORIOUSLY* (VICTORY)
Ps 45: 4 In your majesty ride forth *v*

VICTORY (VICTORIES VICTORIOUSLY)
Ps 60:12 With God we will gain the *v*,
1Co 15:54 "Death has been swallowed up in *v*
15:57 He gives us the *v* through our Lord
1Jn 5: 4 This is the *v* that has overcome

VINDICATED
1Ti 3:16 was *v* by the Spirit,

VINE
Jn 15: 1 "I am the true *v*, and my Father is

VINEGAR
Mk 15:36 filled a sponge with wine *v*,

VIOLATION
Heb 2: 2 every *v* and disobedience received

VIOLENCE
Isa 60:18 No longer will *v* be heard
Eze 45: 9 Give up your *v* and oppression

VIPERS
Ro 3:13 "The poison of *v* is on their lips."

VIRGIN
Isa 7:14 The *v* will be with child
Mt 1:23 "The *v* will be with child
2Co 11: 2 that I might present you as a pure *v*

VIRTUES*
Col 3:14 And over all these *v* put on love,

VISION
Ac 26:19 disobedient to the *v* from heaven.

VOICE
Ps 95: 7 Today, if you hear his *v,*
Isa 30:21 your ears will hear a *v* behind you,
Jn 5:28 are in their graves will hear his *v*
10: 3 and the sheep listen to his *v.*
Heb 3: 7 "Today, if you hear his *v,*
Rev 3:20 If anyone hears my *v* and opens

VOMIT
Pr 26:11 As a dog returns to its *v,*
2Pe 2:22 "A dog returns to its *v,"* and,

VOW
Nu 30: 2 When a man makes a *v*

WAGES
Lk 10: 7 for the worker deserves his *w.*
Ro 4: 4 his *w* are not credited to him
6:23 For the *w* of sin is death,

WAILING
Ps 30:11 You turned my *w* into dancing;

WAIST
2Ki 1: 8 with a leather belt around his *w."*
Mt 3: 4 he had a leather belt around his *w.*

WAIT (WAITED WAITS)
Ps 27:14 *W* for the LORD;
130: 5 I *w* for the LORD, my soul waits,
Isa 30:18 Blessed are all who *w* for him!
Ac 1: 4 *w* for the gift my Father promised,
Ro 8:23 as we *w* eagerly for our adoption
1Th 1:10 and to *w* for his Son from heaven,
Tit 2:13 while we *w* for the blessed hope—

WAITED (WAIT)
Ps 40: 1 I *w* patiently for the LORD;

WAITS (WAIT)
Ro 8:19 creation *w* in eager expectation

WALK (WALKED WALKS)
Dt 11:19 and when you *w* along the road,
Ps 1: 1 who does not *w* in the counsel
23: 4 Even though I *w*
89:15 who *w* in the light of your presence
Isa 2: 5 let us *w* in the light of the LORD.
30:21 saying, "This is the way; *w* in it."
40:31 they will *w* and not be faint.
Jer 6:16 ask where the good way is, and *w*
Da 4:37 And those who *w* in pride he is able
Am 3: 3 Do two *w* together
Mic 6: 8 and to *w* humbly with your God.
Mk 2: 9 'Get up, take your mat and *w'?*
Jn 8:12 Whoever follows me will never *w*
1Jn 1: 7 But if we *w* in the light,
2Jn : 6 his command is that you *w* in love.

WALKED (WALK)
Ge 5:24 Enoch *w* with God; then he was no
Jos 14: 9 which your feet have *w* will be your
Mt 14:29 *w* on the water and came toward

WALKS (WALK)
Pr 13:20 He who *w* with the wise grows wise

WALL
Jos 6:20 *w* collapsed; so every man charged
Ne 2:17 let us rebuild the *w* of Jerusalem,
Rev 21:12 It had a great, high *w*

WALLOWING
2Pe 2:22 back to her *w* in the mud."

WANT (WANTED WANTING WANTS)
1Sa 8:19 "We *w* a king over us.
Ps 23: 1 is my shepherd, I shall not be in *w.*
Lk 19:14 'We don't *w* this man to be our king
Ro 7:15 For what I *w* to do I do not do,
Php 3:10 I *w* to know Christ and the power

WANTED (WANT)
1Co 12:18 of them, just as he *w* them to be.

WANTING (WANT)
Da 5:27 weighed on the scales and found *w.*
2Pe 3: 9 with you, not *w* anyone to perish,

WANTS (WANT)
Mt 20:26 whoever *w* to become great
Mk 8:35 For whoever *w* to save his life will
Ro 9:18 he hardens whom he *w* to harden.
1Ti 2: 4 who *w* all men to be saved

WAR (WARS)
Isa 2: 4 nor will they train for *w* anymore.
Da 9:26 *W* will continue until the end,
2Co 10: 3 we do not wage *w* as the world does
Rev 19:11 With justice he judges and makes *w*

WARN (WARNED WARNINGS)
Eze 3:19 But if you do *w* the wicked man
33: 9 if you do *w* the wicked man to turn

WARNED (WARN)
Ps 19:11 By them is your servant *w;*

WARNINGS (WARN)
1Co 10:11 and were written down as *w* for us,

WARS (WAR)
Ps 46: 9 He makes *w* cease to the ends
Mt 24: 6 You will hear of *w* and rumors of *w,*

WASH (WASHED WASHING)
Ps 51: 7 *w* me, and I will be whiter
Jn 13: 5 and began to *w* his disciples' feet,
Ac 22:16 be baptized and *w* your sins away,
Rev 22:14 Blessed are those who *w* their robes

WASHED (WASH)
1Co 6:11 you were *w,* you were sanctified,
Rev 7:14 they have *w* their robes

WASHING (WASH)
Eph 5:26 cleansing her by the *w* with water
Tit 3: 5 us through the *w* of rebirth

WATCH (WATCHES WATCHING WATCHMAN)
Ge 31:49 "May the LORD keep *w*
Jer 31:10 will *w* over his flock like a shepherd
Mt 24:42 "Therefore keep *w,* because you do
26:41 *W* and pray so that you will not fall
Lk 2: 8 keeping *w* over their flocks at night
1Ti 4:16 *W* your life and doctrine closely.

WATCHES (WATCH)
Ps 1: 6 For the LORD *w* over the way
121: 3 he who *w* over you will not slumber

WATCHING (WATCH)
Lk 12:37 whose master finds them *w*

WATCHMAN (WATCH)
Eze 3:17 I have made you a *w* for the house

WATER (WATERED WATERS)
Ps 1: 3 like a tree planted by streams of *w,*
22:14 I am poured out like *w,*
Pr 25:21 if he is thirsty, give him *w* to drink.
Isa 49:10 and lead them beside springs of *w.*
Jer 2:13 broken cisterns that cannot hold *w.*
Zec 14: 8 On that day living *w* will flow out
Mk 9:41 anyone who gives you a cup of *w*
Jn 4:10 he would have given you living *w."*
Jn 7:38 streams of living *w* will flow
Eph 5:26 washing with *w* through the word,
1Pe 3:21 this *w* symbolizes baptism that now
Rev 21: 6 cost from the spring of the *w* of life.

WATERED (WATER)
1Co 3: 6 I planted the seed, Apollos *w* it,

WATERS (WATER)
Ps 23: 2 he leads me beside quiet *w,*
Ecc 11: 1 Cast your bread upon the *w,*
Isa 58:11 like a spring whose *w* never fail.
1Co 3: 7 plants nor he who *w* is anything,

WAVE (WAVES)
Jas 1: 6 he who doubts is like a *w* of the sea,

WAVES (WAVE)
Isa 57:20 whose *w* cast up mire and mud.
Mt 8:27 Even the winds and the *w* obey him
Eph 4:14 tossed back and forth by the *w,*

WAY (WAYS)
Dt 1:33 to show you the *w* you should go.
2Sa 22:31 "As for God, his *w* is perfect;
Job 23:10 But he knows the *w* that I take;
Ps 1: 1 or stand in the *w* of sinners
37: 5 Commit your *w* to the LORD;
119: 9 can a young man keep his *w* pure?
139:24 See if there is any offensive *w* in me
Pr 14:12 There is a *w* that seems right
16:17 he who guards his *w* guards his life.
22: 6 Train a child in the *w* he should go,
Isa 30:21 saying, "This is the *w;* walk in it."
53: 6 each of us has turned to his own *w;*
55: 7 Let the wicked forsake his *w*
Mt 3: 3 'Prepare the *w* for the Lord,
Jn 14: 6 "I am the *w* and the truth
1Co 10:13 also provide a *w* out so that you can
12:31 will show you the most excellent *w.*
Heb 4:15 who has been tempted in every *w,*
9: 8 was showing by this that the *w*
10:20 and living *w* opened for us

WAYS (WAY)
Ex 33:13 teach me your *w* so I may know
Ps 25:10 All the *w* of the LORD are loving
51:13 I will teach transgressors your *w,*
Pr 3: 6 in all your *w* acknowledge him,
Isa 55: 8 neither are your *w* my *w,"*
Jas 3: 2 We all stumble in many *w.*

WEAK (WEAKER WEAKNESS)
Mt 26:41 spirit is willing, but the body is *w."*
Ro 14: 1 Accept him whose faith is *w,*
1Co 1:27 God chose the *w* things
8: 9 become a stumbling block to the *w.*
9:22 To the *w* I became *w,* to win the *w.*
2Co 12:10 For when I am *w,* then I am strong.
Heb 12:12 your feeble arms and *w* knees.

WEAKER (WEAK)
1Co 12:22 seem to be *w* are indispensable,
1Pe 3: 7 them with respect as the *w* partner

WEAKNESS (WEAK)
Ro 8:26 the Spirit helps us in our *w.*
1Co 1:25 and the *w* of God is stronger
2Co 12: 9 for my power is made perfect in *w*
Heb 5: 2 since he himself is subject to *w.*

WEALTH
Pr 3: 9 Honor the LORD with your *w,*
Mk 10:22 away sad, because he had great *w.*
Lk 15:13 and there squandered his *w*

WEAPONS
2Co 10: 4 The *w* we fight with are not

WEARIES (WEARY)
Ecc 12:12 and much study *w* the body.

WEARY (WEARIES)
Isa 40:31 they will run and not grow *w*,
Mt 11:28 all you who are *w* and burdened,
Gal 6: 9 Let us not become *w* in doing good,

WEDDING
Mt 22:11 who was not wearing *w* clothes.
Rev 19: 7 For the *w* of the Lamb has come,

WEEP (WEEPING WEPT)
Ecc 3: 4 a time to *w* and a time to laugh,
Lk 6:21 Blessed are you who *w* now,

WEEPING (WEEP)
Ps 30: 5 *w* may remain for a night,
126: 6 He who goes out *w*,
Mt 8:12 where there will be *w* and gnashing

WELCOMES
Mt 18: 5 whoever *w* a little child like this
2Jn :11 Anyone who *w* him shares

WELL
Lk 17:19 your faith has made you *w*."
Jas 5:15 in faith will make the sick person *w*

WEPT (WEEP)
Ps 137: 1 of Babylon we sat and *w*
Jn 11:35 Jesus *w*.

WEST
Ps 103:12 as far as the east is from the *w*,

WHIRLWIND (WIND)
2Ki 2: 1 to take Elijah up to heaven in a *w*,
Hos 8: 7 and reap the *w*.
Na 1: 3 His way is in the *w* and the storm,

WHITE (WHITER)
Isa 1:18 they shall be as *w* as snow;
Da 7: 9 His clothing was as *w* as snow;
Rev 1:14 hair were *w* like wool, as *w* as snow,
3: 4 dressed in *w*, for they are worthy.
20:11 Then I saw a great *w* throne

WHITER (WHITE)
Ps 51: 7 and I will be *w* than snow.

WHOLE
Mt 16:26 for a man if he gains the *w* world,
24:14 will be preached in the *w* world
Jn 13:10 to wash his feet; his *w* body is clean
21:25 the *w* world would not have room
Ac 20:27 proclaim to you the *w* will of God.
Ro 3:19 and the *w* world held accountable
8:22 know that the *w* creation has been
Gal 3:22 declares that the *w* world is
5: 3 obligated to obey the *w* law.
Eph 4:13 attaining to the *w* measure
Jas 2:10 For whoever keeps the *w* law
1Jn 2: 2 but also for the sins of the *w* world.

WHOLEHEARTEDLY (HEART)
Dt 1:36 because he followed the LORD *w*
Eph 6: 7 Serve *w*, as if you were serving

WICKED (WICKEDNESS)
Ps 1: 1 walk in the counsel of the *w*
1: 5 Therefore the *w* will not stand
73: 3 when I saw the prosperity of the *w*.
Pr 10:20 the heart of the *w* is of little value.
11:21 The *w* will not go unpunished,
Isa 53: 9 He was assigned a grave with the *w*
55: 7 Let the *w* forsake his way
57:20 But the *w* are like the tossing sea,
Eze 3:18 that *w* man will die for his sin,
18:23 pleasure in the death of the *w*?
33:14 to the *w* man, 'You will surely die,'

WICKEDNESS (WICKED)
Eze 28:15 created till *w* was found in you.

WIDE
Isa 54: 2 stretch your tent curtains *w*,
Mt 7:13 For *w* is the gate and broad is
Eph 3:18 to grasp how *w* and long and high

WIDOW (WIDOWS)
Dt 10:18 cause of the fatherless and the *w*,
Lk 21: 2 saw a poor *w* put in two very small

WIDOWS (WIDOW)
Jas 1:27 look after orphans and *w*

WIFE (WIVES)
Ge 2:24 and mother and be united to his *w*,
24:67 she became his *w*, and he loved her;
Ex 20:17 shall not covet your neighbor's *w*,
Dt 5:21 shall not covet your neighbor's *w*.
Pr 5:18 in the *w* of your youth.
12: 4 *w* of noble character is her
18:22 He who finds a *w* finds what is
19:13 quarrelsome *w* is like a constant
31:10 *w* of noble character who can find?
Mt 19: 3 for a man to divorce his *w* for any
1Co 7: 2 each man should have his own *w*,
7:33 how he can please his *w*—
Eph 5:23 the husband is the head of the *w*
5:33 must love his *w* as he loves himself,
1Ti 3: 2 husband of but one *w*, temperate,
Rev 21: 9 I will show you the bride, the *w*

WILD
Lk 15:13 squandered his wealth in *w* living.
Ro 11:17 and you, though a *w* olive shoot,

WILL (WILLING WILLINGNESS)
Ps 40: 8 I desire to do your *w*, O my God;
143:10 Teach me to do your *w*,
Isa 53:10 Yet it was the LORD's *w*
Mt 6:10 your *w* be done
26:39 Yet not as I *w*, but as you *w*."
Jn 7:17 If anyone chooses to do God's *w*,
Ac 20:27 to you the whole *w* of God.
Ro 12: 2 and approve what God's *w* is—
1Co 7:37 but has control over his own *w*,
Eph 5:17 understand what the Lord's *w* is.
Php 2:13 for it is God who works in you to *w*
1Th 4: 3 God's *w* that you should be
5:18 for this is God's *w* for you
Heb 9:16 In the case of a *w*, it is necessary
10: 7 I have come to do your *w*, O God
Jas 4:15 "If it is the Lord's *w*,
1Jn 5:14 we ask anything according to his *w*,
Rev 4:11 and by your *w* they were created

WILLING (WILL)
Ps 51:12 grant me a *w* spirit, to sustain me.
Da 3:28 were *w* to give up their lives rather
Mt 18:14 Father in heaven is not *w* that any
23:37 her wings, but you were not *w*.
26:41 The spirit is *w*, but the body is weak

WILLINGNESS (WILL)
2Co 8:12 For if the *w* is there, the gift is

WIN (WINS)
Php 3:14 on toward the goal to *w* the prize
1Th 4:12 your daily life may *w* the respect

WIND (WHIRLWIND)
Jas 1: 6 blown and tossed by the *w*.

WINE
Pr 20: 1 *W* is a mocker and beer a brawler;
Isa 55: 1 Come, buy *w* and milk
Mt 9:17 Neither do men pour new *w*
Lk 23:36 They offered him *w* vinegar
Ro 14:21 not to eat meat or drink *w*
Eph 5:18 on *w*, which leads to debauchery.

WINESKINS
Mt 9:17 do men pour new wine into old *w*.

WINGS
Ru 2:12 under whose *w* you have come
Ps 17: 8 hide me in the shadow of your *w*
Isa 40:31 They will soar on *w* like eagles;
Mal 4: 2 rise with healing in its *w*.
Lk 13:34 hen gathers her chicks under her *w*,

WINS (WIN)
Pr 11:30 and he who *w* souls is wise.

WIPE
Rev 7:17 God will *w* away every tear

WISDOM (WISE)
1Ki 4:29 God gave Solomon *w* and very
Ps 111:10 of the LORD is the beginning of *w*;
Pr 31:26 She speaks with *w*,
Jer 10:12 he founded the world by his *w*
Mt 11:19 But *w* is proved right by her actions
Lk 2:52 And Jesus grew in *w* and stature,
Ro 11:33 the depth of the riches of the *w*
Col 2: 3 are hidden all the treasures of *w*
Jas 1: 5 of you lacks *w*, he should ask God,

WISE (WISDOM WISER)
1Ki 3:12 give you a *w* and discerning heart,
Job 5:13 He catches the *w* in their craftiness
Ps 19: 7 making *w* the simple.
Pr 3: 7 Do not be *w* in your own eyes;
9: 8 rebuke a *w* man and he will love
10: 1 A *w* son brings joy to his father,
11:30 and he who wins souls is *w*.
13:20 He who walks with the *w* grows *w*,
17:28 Even a fool is thought *w*
Da 12: 3 Those who are *w* will shine like
Mt 11:25 hidden these things from the *w*
1Co 1:27 things of the world to shame the *w*;
2Ti 3:15 able to make you *w* for salvation

WISER (WISE)
1Co 1:25 of God is *w* than man's wisdom,

WITHER (WITHERS)
Ps 1: 3 and whose leaf does not *w*.

WITHERS (WITHER)
Isa 40: 7 The grass *w* and the flowers fall,
1Pe 1:24 the grass *w* and the flowers fall,

WITHHOLD
Ps 84:11 no good thing does he *w*
Pr 23:13 Do not *w* discipline from a child;

WITNESS (WITNESSES)
Jn 1: 8 he came only as a *w* to the light.

WITNESSES (WITNESS)
Dt 19:15 by the testimony of two or three *w*.
Ac 1: 8 and you will be my *w* in Jerusalem,

WIVES (WIFE)
Eph 5:22 *W*, submit to your husbands
5:25 love your *w*, just as Christ loved
1Pe 3: 1 words by the behavior of their *w*,

WOE
Isa 6: 5 "*W* to me!" I cried.

WOLF
Isa 65:25 *w* and the lamb will feed together,

WOMAN (MAN)
Ge 2:22 God made a *w* from
3:15 between you and the *w,*
Lev 20:13 as one lies with a *w,*
Dt 22: 5 *w* must not wear men's
Ru 3:11 a *w* of noble character
Pr 31:30 a *w* who fears the LORD
Mt 5:28 looks at a *w* lustfully
Jn 8: 3 a *w* caught in adultery.
Ro 7: 2 a married *w* is bound to
1Co 11: 3 the head of the *w* is man,
11:13 a *w* to pray to God with
1Ti 2:11 A *w* should learn in

WOMEN (MAN)
Lk 1:42 Blessed are you among *w,*
1Co 14:34 *w* should remain silent in
1Ti 2: 9 want *w* to dress modestly
Tit 2: 3 teach the older *w* to be
1Pe 3: 5 the holy *w* of the past

WOMB
Job 1:21 Naked I came from my mother's *w,*
Jer 1: 5 you in the *w* I knew you,
Lk 1:44 the baby in my *w* leaped for joy.

WONDER (WONDERFUL WONDERS)
Ps 17: 7 Show the *w* of your great love,

WONDERFUL (WONDER)
Job 42: 3 things too *w* for me to know.
Ps 31:21 for he showed his *w* love to me
119:18 *w* things in your law.
119:129 Your statutes are *w;*
139: 6 Such knowledge is too *w* for me,
Isa 9: 6 *W* Counselor, Mighty God,
1Pe 2: 9 out of darkness into his *w* light.

WONDERS (WONDER)
Job 37:14 stop and consider God's *w.*
Ps 119:27 then I will meditate on your *w.*
Joel 2:30 I will show *w* in the heavens
Ac 2:19 I will show *w* in the heaven above

WOOD
Isa 44:19 Shall I bow down to a block of *w?"*
1Co 3:12 costly stones, *w,* hay or straw,

WORD (WORDS)
Dt 8: 3 but on every *w* that comes
2Sa 22:31 the *w* of the LORD is flawless.
Ps 119: 9 By living according to your *w.*
119:11 I have hidden your *w* in my heart
119:105 Your *w* is a lamp to my feet
Pr 12:25 but a kind *w* cheers him up.
25:11 A *w* aptly spoken
30: 5 "Every *w* of God is flawless;
Isa 55:11 so is my *w* that goes out
Jn 1: 1 was the *W,* and the *W* was
1:14 The *W* became flesh and made his
2Co 2:17 we do not peddle the *w* of God
4: 2 nor do we distort the *w* of God.
Eph 6:17 of the Spirit, which is the *w* of God.
Php 2:16 as you hold out the *w* of life—
Col 3:16 Let the *w* of Christ dwell
2Ti 2:15 and who correctly handles the *w*
Heb 4:12 For the *w* of God is living
Jas 1:22 Do not merely listen to the *w,*
2Pe 1:19 And we have the *w* of the prophets

WORDS (WORD)
Dt 11:18 Fix these *w* of mine in your hearts
Ps 119:103 How sweet are your *w* to my taste
119:130 The unfolding of your *w* gives light;
119:160 All your *w* are true;
Pr 30: 6 Do not add to his *w,*
Jer 15:16 When your *w* came, I ate them;
Mt 24:35 but my *w* will never pass away.
Jn 6:68 You have the *w* of eternal life.
15: 7 in me and my *w* remain in you,
1Co 14:19 rather speak five intelligible *w*
Rev 22:19 And if anyone takes *w* away

WORK (WORKER WORKERS WORKING WORKMAN WORKMANSHIP WORKS)
Ex 23:12 "Six days do your *w,*
Nu 8:11 ready to do the *w* of the LORD.
Dt 5:14 On it you shall not do any *w,*
Ecc 5:19 his lot and be happy in his *w*—
Jer 48:10 lax in doing the LORD's *w!*
Jn 6:27 Do not *w* for food that spoils,
9: 4 we must do the *w* of him who sent
1Co 3:13 test the quality of each man's *w.*
Php 1: 6 that he who began a good *w*
2:12 continue to *w* out your salvation
Col 3:23 Whatever you do, *w* at it
1Th 5:12 to respect those who *w* hard
2Th 3:10 If a man will not *w,* he shall not eat
2Ti 3:17 equipped for every good *w.*
Heb 6:10 he will not forget your *w*

WORKER (WORK)
Lk 10: 7 for the *w* deserves his wages.
1Ti 5:18 and "The *w* deserves his wages."

WORKERS (WORK)
Mt 9:37 is plentiful but the *w* are few.
1Co 3: 9 For we are God's fellow *w;*

WORKING (WORK)
Col 3:23 as *w* for the Lord, not for men,

WORKMAN (WORK)
2Ti 2:15 a *w* who does not need

WORKMANSHIP* (WORK)
Eph 2:10 For we are God's *w,* created

WORKS (WORK)
Pr 31:31 let her *w* bring her praise
Ro 8:28 in all things God *w* for the good
Eph 2: 9 not by *w,* so that no one can boast.
4:12 to prepare God's people for *w*

WORLD (WORLDLY)
Ps 50:12 for the *w* is mine, and all that is in it
Isa 13:11 I will punish the *w* for its evil,
Mt 5:14 "You are the light of the *w.*
16:26 for a man if he gains the whole *w,*
Mk 16:15 into all the *w* and preach the good
Jn 1:29 who takes away the sin of the *w!*
3:16 so loved the *w* that he gave his one
8:12 he said, "I am the light of the *w.*
15:19 As it is, you do not belong to the *w,*
16:33 In this *w* you will have trouble.
18:36 "My kingdom is not of this *w.*
Ro 3:19 and the whole *w* held accountable
1Co 3:19 the wisdom of this *w* is foolishness
2Co 5:19 that God was reconciling the *w*
10: 3 For though we live in the *w,*
1Ti 6: 7 For we brought nothing into the *w,*
1Jn 2: 2 but also for the sins of the whole *w.*
2:15 not love the *w* or anything in the *w.*
Rev 13: 8 slain from the creation of the *w.*

WORLDLY (WORLD)
Tit 2:12 to ungodliness and *w* passions,

WORM
Mk 9:48 " 'their *w* does not die,

WORRY (WORRYING)
Mt 6:25 I tell you, do not *w* about your life,
10:19 do not *w* about what to say

WORRYING (WORRY)
Mt 6:27 of you by *w* can add a single hour

WORSHIP
1Ch 16:29 *w* the LORD in the splendor
Ps 95: 6 Come, let us bow down in *w,*
Mt 2: 2 and have come to *w* him."
Jn 4:24 and his worshipers must *w* in spirit
Ro 12: 1 this is your spiritual act of *w.*

WORTH (WORTHY)
Job 28:13 Man does not comprehend its *w;*
Pr 31:10 She is *w* far more than rubies.
Mt 10:31 are *w* more than many sparrows.
Ro 8:18 sufferings are not *w* comparing
1Pe 1: 7 of greater *w* than gold,
3: 4 which is of great *w* in God's sight.

WORTHLESS
Pr 11: 4 Wealth is *w* in the day of wrath,
Jas 1:26 himself and his religion is *w.*

WORTHY (WORTH)
1Ch 16:25 For great is the LORD and most *w*
Eph 4: 1 to live a life *w* of the calling you
Php 1:27 in a manner *w* of the gospel
3Jn : 6 on their way in a manner *w* of God.
Rev 5: 2 "Who is *w* to break the seals

WOUNDS
Pr 27: 6 *W* from a friend can be trusted,
Isa 53: 5 and by his *w* we are healed.
Zec 13: 6 'What are these *w* on your body?'
1Pe 2:24 by his *w* you have been healed.

WRATH
2Ch 36:16 scoffed at his prophets until the *w*
Ps 2: 5 and terrifies them in his *w,* saying,
76:10 Surely your *w* against men brings
Pr 15: 1 A gentle answer turns away *w,*
Jer 25:15 filled with the wine of my *w*
Ro 1:18 The *w* of God is being revealed
5: 9 saved from God's *w* through him!
1Th 5: 9 God did not appoint us to suffer *w*
Rev 6:16 and from the *w* of the Lamb!

WRESTLED
Ge 32:24 and a man *w* with him till daybreak

WRITE (WRITING WRITTEN)
Dt 6: 9 *W* them on the doorframes
Pr 7: 3 *w* them on the tablet of your heart.
Heb 8:10 and *w* them on their hearts.

WRITING (WRITE)
1Co 14:37 him acknowledge that what I am *w*

WRITTEN (WRITE)
Jos 1: 8 careful to do everything *w* in it.
Da 12: 1 everyone whose name is found *w*
Lk 10:20 but rejoice that your names are *w*
Jn 20:31 these are *w* that you may believe
1Co 4: 6 "Do not go beyond what is *w."*
2Co 3: 3 *w* not with ink but with the Spirit
Col 2:14 having canceled the *w* code,
Heb 12:23 whose names are *w* in heaven.

WRONG (WRONGDOING WRONGED WRONGS)
Ex 23: 2 Do not follow the crowd in doing *w*
Nu 5: 7 must make full restitution for his *w,*
Job 34:12 unthinkable that God would do *w,*
1Th 5:15 that nobody pays back *w* for *w,*

WRONGDOING (WRONG)
Job 1:22 sin by charging God with *w.*

WRONGED (WRONG)
1Co 6: 7 not rather be *w?* Why not rather

WRONGS (WRONG)
Pr 10:12 but love covers over all *w.*
1Co 13: 5 angered, it keeps no record of *w.*

YEARS
Ps 90: 4 For a thousand *y* in your sight
90:10 The length of our days is seventy *y*
2Pe 3: 8 the Lord a day is like a thousand *y,*
Rev 20: 2 and bound him for a thousand *y.*

YESTERDAY
Heb 13: 8 Jesus Christ is the same *y*

YOKE (YOKED)
Mt 11:29 Take my *y* upon you and learn

YOKED (YOKE)
2Co 6:14 Do not be *y* together

YOUNG (YOUTH)
Ps 119: 9 How can a *y* man keep his way
1Ti 4:12 down on you because you are *y,*

YOUTH (YOUNG)
Ps 103: 5 so that your *y* is renewed like
Ecc 12: 1 Creator in the days of your *y,*
2Ti 2:22 Flee the evil desires of *y,*

ZEAL
Pr 19: 2 to have *z* without knowledge,
Ro 12:11 Never be lacking in *z,*

ZECHARIAH

1. Son of Jeroboam II; king of Israel (2Ki 15:8-12).

2. Post-exilic prophet who encouraged rebuilding of temple (Ezr 5:1; 6:14; Zec 1:1).

3. Father of John the Baptist (Lk 1:13; 3:2).

ZEDEKIAH

Mattaniah, son of Josiah (1Ch 3:15), made king of Judah by Nebuchadnezzar (2Ki 24:17-25:7; 2Ch 36:10-14; Jer 37-39; 52:1-11).

ZERUBBABEL

Descendant of David (1Ch 3:19; Mt 1:3). Led return from exile (Ezr 2-3; Ne 7:7; Hag 1-2; Zec 4).

ZIMRI

King of Israel (1Ki 16:9-20).

ZION
Ps 137: 3 "Sing us one of the songs of *Z!"*
Jer 50: 5 They will ask the way to *Z*
Ro 9:33 I lay in *Z* a stone that causes men
11:26 "The deliverer will come from *Z;*

THE NIV WORSHIP BIBLE

Buddy Owens, Maranatha! Music, General Editor

[See Contributors page for a listing of authors and contributors]

Zondervan project management and editorial by Michael Vander Klipp

Editorial assistance by Donna Huisjen

Production management by Jean Entingh

Interior design by Cathy Camarillo and Russell Heistuman

Cover design by David Uttley Design, Sisters, OR

Interior proofreading by Peachtree Editorial and Proofreading Service,
Peachtree City, GA

Interior typesetting by Blue Heron Bookcraft, Battle Ground, WA

Printing and binding by R.R. Donnelley, Crawfordsville, IN

Guarantee

Zondervan Publishing House guarantees leather Bibles
unconditionally against manufacturing defects for a lifetime
and hardcover and softcover Bibles for four years.
This guarantee does not apply to normal wear.
Contact Zondervan Customer Service, 800-727-1309,
for replacement instructions.

Care

We suggest loosening the binding of your new Bible by gently
pressing on a small section of pages at a time from the center.
To ensure against breakage of the spine, it is best not to bend
the cover backward around the spine or to carry study notes,
church bulletins, pens, etc., inside the cover.
Because a felt-tipped marker will "bleed" through the pages,
we recommend use of a ball-point pen or pencil to underline favorite passages.
Your Bible should not be exposed to excessive heat, cold, or humidity.
Protecting the gold or silver edges of the paper from moisture
will avoid spotting, streaking, or fading.